CHAMBERS COLLEGE DICTIONARY

Edited by
A M MacDonald OBE BA(Oxon)

Chambers

PREFACE

This is a dictionary of the words essential to daily life. Its aim is to cover the vocabulary of people who speak and write effective English without using very literary terms (such as poetical or archaic words) or highly technical ones.

It reflects, as far as its scope allows, modern developments in words, meanings and outlook. The reader will find in it such terms as *ombudsman*, *digital computer*, *karate* and *clearway*. Additional words in current use are given on page 629.

Spelling

(1) Words such as *realise* and *realisation* are spelled *-ise* and *-isation* in this dictionary, but it is correct also to spell them *-ize*, *-ization* (*realize*, *realization*). The latter is the usual American spelling.

(2) Fewer hyphens are given in this dictionary than in some other English dictionaries. The use of hyphens is to a great extent a question of personal choice. It does not matter whether we write *doorkeeper* or *door-keeper*. Compounds that have been used for a long time tend to be written as one word; we always write *afternoon* and *afterthought*, but usually *after-care* and *after-effect*.

The main purpose of a hyphen is to make meaning absolutely clear.

Pronunciation

Accented syllables are shown by putting a stress mark after the accented syllable, thus:

ban'dit, dis-pel', dis-gust'ing.

The key words are as follows:

fär, fāte, câstle; mē, tėrm; mīne
mōte, förm; mūte; mo͞on; tûrn; THen
H as in loch; *ü* as in coiffure; *n*^{g} as in ensemble.

ABBREVIATIONS USED IN THE DICTIONARY

abbrev.	abbreviation	*fem.*	feminine	*perh.*	perhaps
adj(s).	adjective(s)	*fol.*	following	*pfx.*	prefix
adv(s).	adverb(s)	*i.e.*	(L. *id est*) that is	*pl.*	plural
and/or	'and' or 'or'—both or either	*imit.*	imitative	*pr.p.*	present participle
cap.	capital	*imper.*	imperative	*pr.t.*	present tense
cent.	century	*incl.*	including	*prep.*	preposition
coll.	colloquial(ly)	*interj.*	interjection	*prob.*	probably
comp.	comparative	*masc.*	masculine	*pron(s).*	pronoun(s)
conj.	conjunction	*mod.*	modern	*R.C.*	Roman Catholic
conn.	connected (with), connexion	*N.*	North	*S.*	South
contr.	contracted	*n(s).*	noun(s)	*sing.*	singular
dial.	dialect	*neut.*	neuter	*suffx.*	suffix
Dict.	dictionary	*n.pl.*	noun plural	*superl.*	superlative
dim.	diminutive (see word in Dict.)	*opp.*	opposed	*usu.*	usual(ly)
E.	East	*orig.*	origin, original(ly)	*v(s).i.*	verb(s) intransitive
e.g.	(L. *exempli gratia*) for example	*pa.p.*	past participle	*vb(s).*	verb(s)
esp.	especially	*pass.*	passive	*v(s).t.*	verb(s) transitive
		pa.t.	past tense	*vulg.*	vulgar(ly)
				W.	West

Abbreviations of Names of Languages (or of Regions)

Afr.	African	*Norw.*	Norwegian
Amer.	American	*N.Z.*	New Zealand
Austr.	Australian	*O.*	Old, as in
Dan.	Danish	*O.E.*	Old English
Du.	Dutch	*O.Fr.*	Old French
Engl.	English	*Pers.*	Persian
Fr.	French	*Port.*	Portuguese
Gael.	Gaelic	*Russ.*	Russian
Ger.	German	*S. Afr.*	South African
Gk.	Greek	*Scand.*	Scandinavian
Heb.	Hebrew	*Scot.*	Scottish
Ir.	Irish	*Sp.*	Spanish
It.	Italian	*Swed.*	Swedish
Jap.	Japanese	*Turk.*	Turkish
L.	Latin	*U.S.(A.)*	United States
M.	Middle, as in	*W.*	Welsh
M.E.	Middle English		

A

a, *ȧ*, *adj.* the indefinite article (used before words beginning with the sound of a consonant; e.g. *a dog, a year*): one: any.

A1, *ā'wun'*, classed as A1 in Lloyd's Register of ships: (*coll.*) very good.

aback, *ȧ-bak'*, *adv.* (of sails) pressed backward against the mast by the wind.
taken aback, taken by surprise and rather upset.

abacus, *ab'ȧ-kus*, *n.* counting-frame. [L.]

abaft, *ȧ-bäft'*, *adv.* and *prep.* on the stern part of a ship: behind.
[O.E. *bæftan*, behind.]

abandon, *ȧ-ban'don*, *v.t.* to give up: to desert: to yield (oneself) without restraint (to; e.g. *to abandon oneself to despair*).—*n.* careless freedom of action.
aban'doned, *adj.* completely deserted: very wicked.
aban'donment, *n.* act of abandoning.
[O.Fr. *à bandon*, at one's disposal.]

abase, *ȧ-bās'*, *v.t.* to humble.
abase'ment, *n.*
[Through O.Fr.—same L. root as **base.**]

abash, *ȧ-bash'*, *v.t.* to make ashamed or confused, disconcert.
[O.Fr. *esbahir*, to be amazed—*interj. bah!*]

abate, *ȧ-bāt'*, *v.t.* to make less: to deduct. —*v.i.* to grow less.
abate'ment, *n.* the act of abating: the sum or quantity abated.
[O.Fr. *abatre*, to beat down.]

abattoir, *a'bät-wär,-bät',-wär'*, *n.* a public slaughterhouse. [Fr.]

abbacy, *ab'ȧ-si*, *n.* the office of an abbot: an abbey.
abbé, *ab'ā*, *n.* orig. the French name for an abbot: a priest or clergyman.
abbess, *ab'es*. See **abbot.**
abbey, *ab'i*, *n.* a convent under an abbot or abbess: the church now or formerly attached to it:—*pl.* **abb'eys.**
abbot, *ab'ȯt*, *n.* the male head of an abbey:—*fem.* **abb'ess.**
[Late L. *abbātia*, abbey; L. *abbās*, abbot (from Palestine word for 'father').]

abbreviate, *ȧ-brē'vi-āt*, *v.t.* to shorten, to abridge.
abbreviā'tion, *n.* an act of shortening: a part of a word written or printed for the whole.
[L. *abbreviāre—brevis*, short.]

ABC, *ā-bē-sē*, *n.* the alphabet: a railway timetable.

abdicate, *ab'di-kāt*, *v.t.* and *v.i.* formally to give up (office or dignity).
abdicā'tion, *n.*
[L. *ab*, from, *dicāre*, to proclaim.]

abdomen, *ab-dō'men*, or *ab'*, *n.* the belly: the part of the body below the chest.
abdominal (*-dom'-*), *adj.* [L.]

abduct, *ab-dukt'*, *v.t.* to take away by fraud or violence: to kidnap.
abduc'tion, *n.*
[L. *ab*, from, *dūcere*, to draw, lead.]

abeam, *ȧ-bēm'*, *adv.* on the beam, or in a line at right angles to a vessel's length.

aberration, *ab-ėr-āsh'(ȯ)n*, *n.* act of wandering from the right path or from the normal way of behaving.
[L. *aberrāre—errāre*, to wander.]

abet, *ȧ-bet'*, *v.t.* to give encouragement or aid to (used chiefly in a bad sense): —*pr.p.* **abett'ing**; *pa.p.* **abett'ed.**
abett'or, *n.*
[O.Fr. *abeter*.]

abeyance, *ȧ-bā'ȧns*, *n.* used in the phrase 'in abeyance' (e.g. *The matter was left in abeyance*, i.e. 'left undecided'; *The office of president was in abeyance*, i.e. 'left unfilled for the time being').
[O.Fr. *abeance—beer, baer*, to gape.]

abhor, *ȧb-hör'*, *v.t.* to detest, loathe:—*pr.p.* **abhorr'ing**; *pa.p.* **abhorred'.**
abhorr'ence, *n.*
abhorr'ent, *adj.* hateful (e.g. *Deceit was abhorrent to him*).
[L. *ab*, from; same root as **horror.**]

abide, *ȧ-bīd'*, *v.t.* to endure, tolerate (e.g. *I cannot abide an unpunctual person*).
to abide by, to adhere to, act according to (e.g. *to abide by one's promise*; *to abide by the terms of the treaty*).
[O.E. *ābīdan—bīdan*, to wait.]

ability. See **able.**

abject, *ab′jekt, adj.* cowering, miserable.
ab′jectly, *adv.* **ab′jectness,** *n.*
[L. *abjectus*, cast away—*jacĕre*, to throw.]

abjure, *ȧb-jōōr′, v.t.* to swear to give up or to leave for ever.
[L. *ab*, from, *jurāre*, to swear.]

ablaze, *ȧ-blāz′, adv., adj.* (in predicate; not used before noun) burning strongly: very bright.

able, *ā′bl, adj.* having enough strength, power, or means (to do a thing): skilful, talented, clever.
a′bly, *adv.*
ability, *ȧ-bil′i-ti, n.* quality of being able: power (physical or mental): sufficient strength, skill, etc. (to do something):—*pl.* **abil′ities.**
a′ble-bod′ied, *adj.* having a strong body.
able seaman, able-bodied seaman (*abbrev.* **A.B.**), one able to perform all the duties of seamanship and having a higher rating than the ordinary sailor.
[O.Fr. *(h)able*—L. *habēre*, to have.]

ablution, *ȧ-blōō′sh(ȯ)n, n.* (often in *pl.*) act of washing, esp. the body.
[L. *ab*, away, *luĕre*, to wash.]

abnormal, *ab-nör′mȧl, adj.* not normal: very unusual.
abnormal′ity, *n.* **abnor′mally,** *adv.*
[Gk. *an-*, not, *nomalos*, even.]

aboard, *ȧ-bōrd′, -börd′, adv.* or *prep.* on board: in, or into (a ship, a train, etc.).

abode, *ȧ-bōd′, n.* a dwelling-place, house.
[O.E. *ābidan* (pa.t. *ābād*), to wait.]

abolish, *ȧ-bol′ish, v.t.* to put an end to, to do away with: to annul.
aboli′tion, *n.*
aboli′tionist, *n.* one who seeks to abolish anything, esp. slavery.
Fr. *abolir*; from L.]

A-bomb, *ā′bom, n.* atomic bomb.

abominate, *ȧ-bom′in-āt, v.t.* to loathe, detest extremely.
abom′inable, *adj.* hateful, detestable.
abom′inably, *adv.*
abominā′tion, *n.* loathing: anything disgusting or detestable.
[L. *abōminārī*, turn from as of bad omen.]

aborigines, *ab-ȯ-rij′in-ēz, n.pl.* the original or native inhabitants of a country (a *sing.* **aborig′inē**—*slang abbrev.* **abo**—is used).
aborig′inal, *adj.* earliest, primitive.—*n.* one of the aborigines.
[L. *ab origine*, from the beginning.]

abort, *ȧ-bört′, v.i.* to miscarry in birth: to cease to develop before development is complete: to come to nothing.
abor′tion, *n.*
abor′tive, *adj.* unsuccessful (e.g. *an abortive attempt*).
[L. *ab* (reversing meaning), *orīrī*, rise.]

abound, *ȧ-bownd′, v.i.* to be in great plenty: to be rich (in), well supplied (with). See also **abundance.**
[L. *abundāre*, to overflow—*unda*, a wave.]

about, *ȧ-bowt′, prep.* round on the outside of: all round: here and there in: on (one's person): near (place, time, size, etc.): concerning.—*adv.* around: near: nearly: here and there: on the opposite tack: in the opposite direction (e.g. *to face about*).
to be about to, to be on the point of.
to bring about, to cause to take place.
to come about, to happen.
put about, distressed: (also see **put**).
time, turn, about, alternately, in turn.
week (etc.) **about,** every second period of seven days (etc.).
[O.E. *on būtan.*]

above, *ȧ-buv′, prep.* on or to the upside of: higher than: more than: too proud or too good to descend to.—*adv.* overhead: in a higher position, order, or power: at an earlier point in a writing.
above′-board, *adj.* open, honourable.
[O.E. *ābūfan.*]

abrade, *ȧ-brād′, v.t.* to rub off (skin, etc.): to wear down by friction.
abrasion, *ȧ-brā′zh(ȯ)n, n.* the act of rubbing off: an injury due to scraping or rubbing.
abrā′sive (*-ziv, -siv*), *adj.* scraping.—*n.* something that abrades (as **emery**).
[L. *ab*, off, *rādĕre*, to scrape.]

abreast, *ȧ-brest′, adv.* with fronts in a line: side by side: up with (e.g. *abreast of the times*).

abridge, *ȧ-brij′, v.t.* to shorten.
abridg′ment (sometimes **abridge′-ment**), *n.*
[From O.Fr.; L. root as **abbreviate.**]

abroad, *ȧ-bröd′, adv.* over a wide area: out of doors: in or to another country.—Also *n.*, as in *from abroad.*
[O.E. *on*, on, and **broad.**]

abrogate, *ab′ro-gāt, v.t.* to set aside, to do away with (e.g. a law).
abrogā′tion, *n.*
[L. *ab*, away, *rogāre*, ask, propose a law.]

abrupt, *ȧ-brupt′, adj.* the opposite of gradual: steep: sudden, hasty: (of style) passing suddenly from one thought to another: (of manners) ungracious, rude.
abrupt′ly, *adv.* **abrupt′ness,** *n.*
[L. *ab*, off, *rumpĕre, ruptum*, to break.]

abscess, *ab′ses, n.* a collection of pus within a tissue of the body.
[L. *abs*, away, *cēdĕre, cessum*, to go.]

abscond, *ȧb-skond′, v.i.* to run away secretly, esp. in order to escape the law.
[L. *abs*, away, *condĕre*, to hide.]

absent, *ab′sėnt, adj.* away, not present: not existing: inattentive.—*v.t.* (*ab-sent′*) to keep (oneself) away (from e.g. a meeting).
ab′sently, *adv.*
ab′sence, *n.* the state of being away: want (of): inattention.
absentee′ (*-tē′*), *n.* one who is absent: one who makes a habit of being away from his estate, office or employment.—Also *adj.*
absentee′ism, *n.* the practice of being absent from duty.

ab'sent-mind'ed, *adj.* inattentive to what is happening round one.
[L. *ab*, away from, *esse*, to be.]

absinth(e), *ab'sinth, n.* wormwood: a liqueur containing (orig. at least) extract of wormwood.
[Fr. *absinthe*; from L.]

absolute, *ab'sol-ūt*, or *-ōōt, adj.* free from limits or restrictions: not limited by rules or laws (e.g. *an absolute monarch*): complete, certain (e.g. *absolute proof*).
ab'solutely, *adv.*
absolute alcohol, water-free alcohol.
absolute zero, approximately −273°C.
[L. *absolūtus*; same root as **absolve.**]

absolution. See **absolve.**

absolve, *ȧb-zolv'*, or *-solv', v.t.* to set free, release (from a promise or duty, or from blame): to pardon: to acquit.
absolution, *ab-sol-ū'sh(ȯ)n*, or *-ōō', n.* setting free from punishment: forgiveness, esp. forgiveness of sins formally declared by a priest.
[L. *ab*, from *solvěre, solūtum*, to free.]

absorb, *ȧb-sörb'*, or *-zörb', v.t.* to suck in: to take in: to take up the whole attention of (a person).
absor'bent, *adj.* and *n.* (something) able to absorb.
absorp'tion, *n.* the act of absorbing: entire occupation of mind.
[L. *ab*, from, *sorbēre*, to suck in.]

abstain, *ȧb-stān', v.i.* to keep oneself away (from), refrain (from).
abstain'er, *n.* (used esp. of one who does not take alcoholic drinks).
absten'tion, *n.* act of refraining (from).
abstinent, *ab'stin-ėnt, adj.* keeping oneself from indulgence (e.g. in strong drink).
ab'stinence, *n.*
[L. *abs*, from, *tenēre*, to hold.]

abstemious, *ȧb-stēm'i-ȧs, adj.* taking little food, drink, or enjoyment.
abstem'iously, *adv.*
abstem'iousness, *n.*
[L. *abs*, from, *tēmētum*, strong wine.]

abstention, abstinence, etc. See **abstain.**

abstract, *ȧb-strakt', v.t.* to draw away or out: to remove quietly: to summarise.—*adj.* (*ab'strakt*; of a noun) denoting a quality or condition (e.g. *Redness, courage, justice, poverty, are abstract nouns*).—*n.* a summary.
abstract'ed, *adj.* absent-minded.
abstract'edly, *adv.*
abstrac'tion, *n.* the act of abstracting: absence of mind.
in the abstract, in theory.
[L. *abs*, away, *trahěre*, to draw.]

abstruse, *ȧb-strōōs', adj.* difficult to understand (e.g. *an abstruse problem*).
abstruse'ness, *n.*
[L. *abs*, away from, *trūděre*, to thrust.]

absurd, *ȧb-sûrd', adj.* unreasonable: ridiculous.
absurd'ness, absurd'ity (*pl.* **-ies**), *ns.*
absurd'ly, *adv.*
[L. *surdus*, deaf, dull.]

abundance, *ȧ-bun'dȧns, n.* great plenty.
abund'ant, *adj.* plentiful: rich (in).
abund'antly, *adv.*.
[Same root as **abound.**]

abuse, *ȧ-būz', v.t.* to use wrongly: to betray (e.g. a confidence): to injure: to reproach, scold violently.—*n.* (*ȧb-ūs'*) ill use: unjust use: harsh, rude language: a bad custom.
abusive (*-ūs'-*), *adj.* rudely scolding or reproachful.
abus'ively, *adv.* **abus'iveness,** *n.*
[L. *ab*, away (from what is right), *ūti*, to use.]

abut, *ȧ-but', v.i.* to end or lean (on, upon, against): to border (on):—*pr.p.* **abutt'ing**; *pa.p.* **abutt'ed.**
[Fr. *à*, to, *bout*, end.]

abysmal, *ȧ-biz'mȧl, adj.* bottomless: very deep or great (e.g. *abysmal gloom*).
[L. *abyssimus*; same root as **abyss.**]

abyss, *ȧ-bis', n.* a bottomless depth, chasm.
[Gk. *abyssos*, bottomless.]

acacia, *ȧ-kā'sh(y)ȧ, n.* a thorny plant, a wattle.
[Gk. *akē*, a sharp point.]

academic. See **academy.**

academy, *ȧ-kad'ėm-i, n.* a higher school: a society for the encouragement of science or art:—*pl.* **-ies.**
academ'ic, *adj.* of an academy: scholarly: theoretical as opposed to practical.
academ'ical, *adj.* academic.—*n.* (in *pl.*) university cap and gown.
academ'ically, *adv.*
academician, *ȧ-kȧ-dė-mish'ȧn, n.* a member of an academy, e.g. of the Royal Academy in London (painting, etc.).
[Gk. *Akadēmia*, the name of the garden near Athens where Plato taught.]

acanthus, *ȧ-kan'thȧs, n.* a prickly-leaved plant: an ornament resembling its leaves used in architecture.
[L.—Gk. *akantha*, thorn.]

accede, *ak-sēd', v.i.* to come into office: to give consent (e.g. *I cannot accede to your request*).
See also **accession.**
[L. *ad*, to, *cēděre, cessum*, to go.]

accelerate, *ak-sel'ėr-āt, v.t.* to increase the speed of: to cause to happen sooner.—*v.i.* to move faster.
accelerā'tion, *n.* increase of speed: rate of change of velocity.
accel'erator, *n.* something that accelerates, e.g. an apparatus for regulating the speed of a machine: an apparatus for giving high energy to atomic particles.
[L. *ad*, to, *celer*, swift.]

accent, *ak'sėnt, n.* tone of the voice (*usu.* in *pl.*): stress on a syllable or word: a mark (') to show this stress: kind of speech characteristic of a region, a class, or a person.—*v.t.* (*ȧk-sent'*) to stress.

accent′uate, *v.t.* to emphasise: to make more obvious.
accentuā′tion, *n.*
[Fr.—L. *ad*, to, *cantus*, song.]

accept, *ȧk-sept′*, *v.t.* to take (something offered): to take upon oneself (e.g. responsibility): to acknowledge as true (e.g. *I accept your story of what happened*): to agree to: to undertake to pay (e.g. *to accept a bill of exchange*).
accept′ance, *n.* act of accepting: approval.
acceptable, *ȧk-sept′ȧ-bl*, or *ak′-*, *adj.* satisfactory (to someone): pleasing.
accept′ably, *adv.*
acceptā′tion, *n.* meaning, esp. the generally understood meaning.
accept′ed, *adj.* generally approved of or believed in.
[L. *ad*, to, *capĕre*, to take.]

access, *ak′ses*, *n.* means or right of approach: entrance: increase: attack (of illness): a fit (e.g. *an access of rage*).
access′ible, *adj.* able to be reached: open (to).
accessibil′ity, *n.*
accession, *ȧk-sesh′(ȯ)n*, *n.* a coming to (e.g. *Charles II's accession to the throne*): addition (e.g. *accessions to the library*).
[Same root as **accede.**]

accessory, *ȧk-ses′ȯr-i*, *adj.* additional: (*law*) taking part as a helper in a crime.—*n.* anything additional (*esp.* in *pl.*): one who aids a crime:—*pl.* **access′ories.**
[Same root as **accede.**]

accident, *ak′si-dėnt*, *n.* an unexpected event: chance: a mishap or disaster.
accident′al, *adj.* happening by chance.—*n.* (*music*) a sharp, flat, or natural not in the key signature.
accident′ally, *adv.*
chapter of accidents, a series of unfortunate happenings.
[L. *accidĕre*, to happen—*cadĕre*, to fall.]

acclaim, *ȧ-klām′*, *v.t.* to applaud: to hail as (e.g. *They acclaimed him winner*).—*n.* enthusiastic approval.
acclamā′tion, *n.* a shout of applause, or of agreement or approval.
[L. *clāmāre*, to shout.]

acclimatise, *ȧ-klīm′ȧ-tīz*, *v.t.* to accustom to a new climate or new surroundings.
acclimatisā′tion, *n.*
[Fr. *à*, to, *climat*, climate.]

accolade, *ak′ol-ād*, *-äd′*, *n.* the mark used in making a man a knight, nowadays a light touch on each shoulder with the flat of a sword: any recognition of merit.
[Fr.—L. *ad*, to, *collum*, neck.]

accommodate, *ȧ-kom′od-āt*, *v.t.* to make suitable: to adjust: to supply (with): to oblige: to provide with a place to stay: to find, or be, a place for (something).
accomm′odating, *adj.* obliging.
accommodā′tion, *n.* lodging: room, space (for).
[L. *commodus*, suitable.]

accompany, *ȧ-kum′pȧn-i*, *v.t.* to go with: to escort: to exist or occur along with: to perform a musical accompaniment to or for.
accom′paniment, *n.* something that accompanies: music played to support a soloist.
accom′panist, *n.* one who plays music for a soloist.
[Fr. *à*, to, *compagne*, companion.]

accomplice, *ȧ-kom′plis*, or *kum′-*, *n.* a helper, esp. in crime.
[Same root as **complicity.**]

accomplish, *ȧ-kom′plish*, or *-kum′-*, *v.t.* to finish: to fulfil.
accom′plished, *adj.* highly skilled.
accom′plishment, *n.* finishing, completion: achievement: a special skill.
[O.Fr. *acomplir*—L. *complēre*, to fill up.]

accord, *ȧ-körd′*, *v.i.* to agree (with), be in keeping (with).—*v.t.* to grant, give to (a person).—*n.* agreement.
accord′ance, *n.* agreement.
accord′ingly, *adv.* therefore.
according to, in agreement with (e.g. *He acted according to his promise*): as said or told by (e.g. *according to the witness*).
of one's own accord, without being prompted to do it by someone else.
[L. *ad*, to, *cor*, *cordis*, heart.]

accordion, *ȧ-kör′di-on*, *n.* a musical instrument with bellows, keyboard, and metal reeds.
accordion-pleating, *n.* pleating with very narrow folds.
[From **accord.**]

accost, *ȧ-kost′*, *v.t.* to go up to and speak to.
[L. *ad*, to, *costa*, a side.]

account, *ȧ-kownt′*, *v.i.* to give a reason (for): to be a reason (for): to deal with, get rid of (with *for*).—*n.* a counting: a statement of money due: story: sake (e.g. *on my account*, for my sake, because of me).
account′able, *adj.* able to be explained: responsible (*for* something, *to* someone).
account′ant, *n.* one who is trained to keep accounts.
account′ancy, *n.* the work of an accountant.
on account of, because of.
on no account, not for any reason.
to take into account, to consider as part of the problem (e.g. *When judging his ability you must take into account the difficulties he has had to face*).
to take (no) account of, (not) to take into consideration.
to turn to account, to turn to one's advantage.
[L. *ad*, to, *computāre*, to reckon.]

accoutrements, *ȧ-ko͞o′tėr-mėnts*, *n.pl.* dress: military equipment.
[Fr. *accoutrer*, to equip.]

accredit, *ȧ-kred′it*, *v.t.* to give authority to.
accred′ited, *adj.* having power to act on

behalf of some person or group of persons.
[L. *crēdĕre*, to believe, trust.]

accrue, *à-krōō'*, *v.i.* to come as a natural result (from): to fall naturally (to a person) as a right.
[Through O.Fr.—L. *crescĕre*, to grow.]

accumulate, *à-kūm'ūl-āt*, *v.t.* to pile up, to amass.—*v.i.* to increase greatly through time.
accumulā'tion, *n.* the act of piling up: a mass or pile.
accum'ulative, *adj.* heaping up.
accum'ulator, *n.* a thing or person that accumulates: an electric battery that can be recharged by sending a reverse current through it.
[From L. *cumulus*, a heap.]

accurate, *ak'ūr-it*, *adj.* exactly right: exact.
acc'uracy, *n.* **acc'urately,** *adv.*
[L. *accūrātus*—*cūra*, care.]

accursed, *à-kûrs'id*, *adj.* lying under a curse: doomed: extremely wicked.
[O.E. *cursian*, to curse.]

accuse, *à-kūz'*, *v.t.* to make, or bring, a charge against (e.g. *They accused him of stealing*).
accusā'tion, *n.* the charge brought against anyone.
accused, *à-kūzd'*, *n.* the person accused in a court of law.
[L. *accūsāre*—*ad*, to, *causa*, cause.]

accustom, *à-kus'tòm*, *v.t.* to make (a person) familiar with, or used (to; e.g. *We must accustom the child to the dark*).
accus'tomed, *adj.* usual: used (to).
[O.Fr. *acostumer*.]

ace, *ās*, *n.* the one in dice, cards, dominoes, etc.: a single point: a hair's-breadth (e.g. *within an ace of*): a crack airman, etc.
[Fr.—L. *as*, unity.]

acerbity, *à-sėr'bi-ti*, *n.* bitterness, sourness: harshness.
[L. *acerbus*, bitter.]

acetic, *à-sēt'ik*, or *-set'*, *adj.* of vinegar: sour.
[L. *acetum*, vinegar.]

acetylene, *à-set'i-lēn*, *n.* a gas used for welding, etc., made from water and calcium carbide.
[**acetic,** and Gk. *hylē*, matter.]

ache, *āk*, *n.* a continued pain.—*v.i.* to be in continued pain:—*pr.p.* **āch'ing**; *pa.p.* **āched.**
ach'ing, *n.* and *adj.*
[O.E. vb. *acan*, to ache.]

achieve, *à-chēv'*, *v.t.* to carry out, perform: to gain, win.
achieve'ment, *n.* performance: gaining: a deed to be admired.
[Fr. *achever*.]

acid, *as'id*, *adj.* sharp: sour.—*n.* a sour substance: (*chemistry*) a substance that turns blue litmus red, combines with a base to form a salt, etc.
acid'ity, ac'idness, *ns.*
acid'ify, *v.t.* to make acid.
acid'ulate, *v.t.* to make slightly acid.
acid test, a test for gold by acid: a searching test.
[L. *acidus*—*acēre*, to be sour.]

acknowledge, *àk-nol'ij*, *v.t.* to own as true: to confess: to announce receipt of (e.g. *to acknowledge a letter*).
acknowl'edg(e)ment, *n.* admission: confession: thanks: a receipt.
[O.E. *on*, on, and **knowledge.**]

acme, *ak'mē*, *-mi*, *n.* the top or highest point (e.g. *the acme of perfection*).
[Gk. *ackmē* (also *akē*), a point.]

acne, *ak'nē*, *-ni*, *n.* a pimple: a common skin disease with pimples.
[Origin uncertain.]

acolyte, *ak'o-līt*, *n.* a minor church officer: an attendant.
[Gk. *akolouthos*, an attendant.]

aconite, *ak'on-īt*, *n.* a plant of the buttercup family.
[L. *aconitum*.]

acorn, *ā'kŏrn*, *n.* the fruit of the oak.
[O.E. *æcern*.]

acoustic, *à-kōōs'tik*, or *-kows'-*, *adj.* having to do with hearing, or with sound: used in hearing: worked, set off, by sound (as *an acoustic mine*).
acous'tics, *n. pl.* properties (e.g. of a room or hall) which make hearing in it good or bad: the science of sound.
[Gk. *akouein*, to hear.]

acquaint, *à-kwānt'*, *v.t.* to make (oneself) familiar (with): to inform (a person) of (e.g. *Acquaint her with your plans*).
acquaint'ance, *n.* slight knowledge (also **acquaint'anceship**): a person known slightly.
[Through O.Fr.—L. *ad*, to, *cognitus*, known.]

acquiesce, *ak-wi-es'*, *v.i.* to agree: (with *in*) to accept (e.g. *to acquiesce in this plan*).
acquies'cence, *n.* **acquies'cent,** *adj.*
[L. *ad*, *quiēs*, quiet.]

acquire, *à-kwīr'*, *v.t.* to gain: to get.
acquire'ment, *n.* something learned or got by effort.
acquisition, *à-kwi-zi'sh(ò)n*, *n.* the act of acquiring: something acquired: a useful gain.
acquis'itive, *adj.* eager to get possessions.
acquis'itiveness, *n.*
[**L.** *ad*, to, *quaerĕre*, *quaesitum*, seek.]

acquit, *à-kwit'*, *v.t.* to declare innocent:—*pr.p.* **acquitt'ing**; *pa.p.* **acquitt'ed.**
acquitt'al, *n.* a freeing from an accusation.
to acquit oneself, to carry out one's task (e.g. *He acquitted himself well in the debate*).
[O.Fr. *aquiter*; same root as **quit.**]

acre, *ā'kėr*, *n.* a measure of land, 4840 sq. yards (0.405 hectare): (in *pl.*) lands, estates.
acreage, *ā'kėr-ij*, *n.* the number of acres in a piece of land.
[O. E. *æcer*.]

acrid, *ak'rid*, *adj.* bitter in taste: harsh.

acrid′ity, ac′ridness, *ns.*
[L. *ācer,* sharp.]

acrimony, *ak′ri-mȯn-i, n.* bitterness of feeling or speech.
acrimōn′ious, *adj.*
[L. *acrimonia* ; same root as **acrid.**]

acrobat, *ak′ro-bat, n.* one who performs gymnastic feats.
acrobat′ic, *adj.*
acrobat′ics, *n.pl.* acrobatic performances.
[Gk. *akrobatos,* walking on tiptoe.]

across, *ȧ-kros′, prep.* from side to side of : on, or to, the other side of.—Also *adv.*
[O.E. *on,* on, and **cross.**]

acrostic, *ȧ-kros′tik, n.* a poem or puzzle in which the first or last letters of each line, taken in order, spell a word or a sentence.
[Gk. *akros,* extreme, *stichos,* a line.]

act, *akt, v.i.* to do something : to produce an effect (on) : to behave (e.g. *If this happened, how would you act?*) : to perform (e.g. on the stage) : to pretend.—*v.t.* to perform : to imitate or play the part of.—*n.* a deed : the very process (of doing something) : a law : a section of a play.
act′or, *n.* :—*fem.* (*theatre*) **act′ress.**
act′ing, *n.* action : performing.—*adj.* carrying out the duties of, esp. for a time (e.g. *the acting president*).
action, *ak′sh(ȯ)n, n.* a deed : operation (e.g. *The machine is not in action*) : a battle : a gesture : a lawsuit : the events (of a play, etc.) : the mechanism (e.g. of a watch).
ac′tionable, *adj.* liable to be the subject of a lawsuit.
active, *ak′tiv, adj.* energetic : nimble : busy : causing action : in force.
ac′tively, *adv.* **ac′tiveness,** *n.*
activ′ity, *n.* activeness : action, motion : occupation (*pl.* **activ′ities).**
act′ivate, *v.t.* to make more active : to make radioactive.
action station, a post to be manned during, or in readiness for, battle or other operation.
[L. *agĕre, actum.*]

actual, *ak′tū-ȧl, adj.* real : existing in fact.
actual′ity, *n.* reality.
ac′tually, *adv.* really.
[L. *actuālis* ; same root as **act.**]

actuary, *ak′tū-ȧr-i, n.* one who makes the calculations in an insurance office.
actuarial, *ak-tū-ā′ri-ȧl, adj.*
[L. *actuārius* (*scriba*), a clerk.]

actuate, *ak′tū-āt, v.t.* to put in motion : to move (a person) to a particular action.
[Same root as **act.**]

acumen, *ȧ-kū′mėn,* or *ak′, n.* sharpness, quickness of understanding.
[L. *acūmen* ; same root as **acute.**]

acute, *ȧ-kūt′, adj.* sharp-pointed : keen : shrewd : very great (e.g. *acute disappointment*) : (of a disease) coming to a crisis.
acute′ly, *adv.* **acute′ness,** *n.*
acute accent, a mark (′) over a vowel.
acute angle, an angle less than a right angle.
[L. *acuĕre, acūtum,* to sharpen.]

ad, *ad, n.* Short for **advertisement.**

adage, *ad′ij, n.* an old saying, proverb.
[Fr.—L. *ad,* to, *aio,* I say.]

adamant, *ad′ȧ-mȧnt, n.* a very hard stone.—*adj.* like adamant : utterly refusing to yield.
[Gk. *a-,* not, *damaein,* to break, tame.]

Adam's-apple, *ad′amz-ap′l, n.* the hard projection in front of the throat.

adapt, *ȧ-dapt′, v.t.* to make suitable (*for,* e.g. a purpose ; *to,* e.g. circumstances) : to alter so as to suit.
adapt′able, *adj.* that may be adapted : (of a person) able and willing to fit in with different circumstances.
adaptabil′ity, *n.*
adaptā′tion, *n.* the act of adapting : something adapted.
adapt′er, adapt′or, *n.* an attachment enabling a piece of apparatus to be put to a new use, or to be fitted to something else when it is not otherwise the right size or shape.
[L. *ad,* to, *aptāre,* to fit.]

add, *ad, v.t.* to put (one thing) to (another) : to find the sum of : to say further (e.g. *He added that he was sorry this was all he could tell*).—Also *v.i.*
addi′tion, *n.* the act of adding : the thing added.
addi′tional, *adj.* that is added : extra.
add′itive, *n.* a substance to be added.
adden′dum, *n.* a thing to be added (to e.g. statement, book) :—*pl.* **adden′da.**
to add to, to increase.
[L. *ad,* to, *dăre,* to put, give.]

adder, *ad′ėr, n.* a viper.
[O.E. *nædre* ; *an adder* was orig. *a nadder.*]

addict, *ad′ikt, n.* a slave to a habit or vice, esp. drugs.
addict′ed, *adj.* given up (to).
addic′tion, *n.*
[L. *addīcĕre,* to consent, devote.]

addition, additive. See **add.**

addle, *ad′l, v.t.* to make rotten : to confuse.
add′led, add′le-headed, *adjs.* muddled : unsound in brain.
[O.E. *adela,* mud.]

address, *ȧ-dres′, v.t.* to speak or write to : to put a name and address on (an envelope, etc.).—*n.* a speech : manner, bearing : skill : the place to which a letter is directed : the place where one lives.
addressee′ (*ē′*), *n.* the person to whom a letter is addressed.
to address oneself to, to turn one's energies to : to address (a person).
[L. *ad,* to, *directum,* straight.]

adduce, *ȧ-dūs′, v.t.* to quote as example.
[L. *ad,* to, *ducĕre,* to bring.]

adenoids, *ad′ėn-oidz, n. pl.* swollen tissue at the back of the nose.
[Gk. *adēn,* a gland, *eidos,* form.]

adept, *ad'ept, ȧ-dept', adj.* completely skilled.—*n.* an expert.
[L. *adeptus*, pa.p. of *adipisci*, to attain.]

adequate, *ad'i-kwit, adj.* sufficient.
ad'equately, *adv.*
ad'equateness, ad'equacy, *ns.*
[L. *ad*, to, *aequus*, equal.]

adhere, *ȧd-hēr', v.i.* to stick (to): to remain loyal (to).
adher'ence, *n.* (usu.) steady loyalty.
adher'ent, *n.* a follower, supporter.
adhesion, *ȧd-hē'zh(ȯ)n, n.* (usu.) act of sticking: (also) steady attachment (to).
adhes'ive (*-hēs'* or *-hēz'*), *adj.* sticky.—*n.* a substance (e.g. gum, glue) used to make substances stick to each other.
[L. *ad*, to, *haerēre, haesum,* to stick.]

ad hoc, *ad hok, adj.* (of a committee or other body) set up for this very purpose.
[L., to this.]

adieu, *ȧ-dū', interj.* (I commend you) to God: farewell.—*n.* a farewell:—*pl.* **adieus** or **adieux** (*ȧ-dūz'*).
[Fr. *à Dieu*, to God.]

adipose, *ad'i-pōs, adj.* fatty.
[L. *adeps, adipis,* soft fat.]

adjacent, *ȧ-jās'ėnt, adj.* lying near (to).
adjac'ency, *n.*
[L. *ad*, to, *jacēre*, to lie.]

adjective, *aj'ek-tiv, n.* a word added to a noun to describe it (e.g. a *red* flower, an *upper* room; the air is *cool*).
adjectīv'al, *adj.*
[L. *adjicĕre*, add—*ad*, to, *jacĕre*, throw.]

adjoin, *ȧ-join', v.t.* to lie next to.—*v.i.* to lie side by side, in contact.
[L. *ad*, to, *jungĕre*, to join.]

adjourn, *ȧ-jûrn', v.t.* to discontinue (a meeting) in order to continue it at another time or place.—Also *v.i.*
adjourn'ment, *n.*
[Through O.Fr.—L. *diurnus*, daily.]

adjudge, *ȧ-juj', v.t.* to pronounce as a judge does (e.g. *They adjudged him the winner*): to award (something to someone).
adjudicate, *ȧ-jōō'di-kāt, v.t.* to give judgment on.—*v.i.* to pronounce judgment: to act as judge in a competition.
adjudicā'tion, *n.* **adju'dicator,** *n.*
[L. *adjudicāre*, to judge.]

adjunct, *a'jungkt, n.* a thing joined or added.
[L. *adjunctus*; same root as **adjoin.**]

adjure, *ȧ-jōōr', v.t.* to command solemnly, request earnestly.
[L. *jurāre*, to swear.]

adjust, *ȧ-just', v.t.* to arrange properly: to regulate the parts of (e.g. a mechanism): to settle (e.g. differences of opinion).
adjust'able, *adj.* **adjust'ment,** *n.*
[Late L. *adjuxtāre*, to put side by side.]

adjutant, *a'joo-tȧnt, n.* an officer who assists a commanding officer: a large Indian stork.
adjutancy, *a'joo-tȧn-si, n.* rank of an adjutant.
[L. *adjūtāre, adjuvāre,* to assist.]

ad-lib, *ad-lib', v.i.* to say something on the spur of the moment or without preparation, esp. to fill up time.—Also *v.t.*
[L. *ad libitum*, at pleasure.]

administer, *ȧd-min'is-tėr, v.t.* to govern: to manage: to give (e.g. medicine, a rebuke).
administrā'tion, *n.* management: (**the administration**) the government in its various branches.
admin'istrative (*-trȧ-*), *adj.*
admin'istrātor, *n.*
[L. *ad*, to, *ministrāre*, to minister.]

admiral, *ad'mir-ȧl, n.* a naval officer of the highest rank (see Appendices): a kind of butterfly.
Ad'miralty (Board), government body in charge of naval affairs, or the building in which it carries on business.
[Through Fr.—Arabic *amīr*, a lord.]

admire, *ȧd-mīr', v.t.* to approve of highly: to look up to.
admir'ing, *adj.* **admir'ingly,** *adv.*
admirā'tion (*-mir-*), *n.* **admīr'er,** *n.*
ad'mirable (*-mir-*), *adj.* worthy of approval: extremely good.
ad'mirably, *adv.* extremely well.
[L. *ad*, at, *mīrārī*, to wonder.]

admission. See **admit.**

admit, *ȧd-mit', v.t.* to allow to enter: to have room for: to acknowledge, confess: to allow (also **admit of**; e.g. *This action admits of another explanation*):—*pr.p.* **admitt'ing**; *pa.p.* **admitt'ed.**
admiss'ible, *adj.* allowable.
admitt'ance, *n.* the right to enter.
admiss'ion, *n.* admittance: anything acknowledged or admitted.
admitt'edly, *adv.* unquestionably.
[L. *ad*, to, *mittĕre, missum,* to send.]

admixture, *ȧd-miks'chŭr, n.* mixing: mixture.
[L. *ad*, to, and **mix.**]

admonish, *ȧd-mon'ish, v.t.* to warn: to reprove.
admoni'tion, *n.* reproof: warning.
admon'itory, *adj.*
[Through Fr.—L. *ad, monēre,* to warn.]

ado, *ȧ-dōō', n.* a to-do: bustle, fuss.
[*at do*=to do; Scand. form of infin.]

adobe, *ȧ-dō'bi, n.* a sun-dried brick: a house made of such bricks.
[Sp. *adobar*, to plaster.]

adolescent, *ad-o-les'ėnt, adj.* growing out of childhood, becoming adult.
adoles'cence, *n.* the period between childhood and maturity.
[L. *adolescĕre*, to grow up.]

adopt, *ȧ-dopt', v.t.* to take up (e.g. an opinion, a habit): to take as one's own (e.g. a child).
adop'tion, *n.*
adop'tive, *adj.* by adoption (e.g. *his adoptive father*).
[L. *adoptāre—optāre*, to choose.]

adore, *ȧ-dōr', -dör', v.t.* to love intensely.
ador'er, *n.*

ador′ing, *adj.* **ador′ingly,** *adv.*
ador′able, *adj.* worthy of being adored.
adorā′tion, *n.* worship: great love.
[L. *ad*, to, *ōrāre*, to pray.]

adorn, *ȧ-dörn′*, *v.t.* to deck, make beautiful.
adorn′ment, *n.* decoration: ornament.
[L. *ad*, to, *ornāre*, to furnish.]

adrift, *ȧ-drift′*, *adj.* and *adv.* drifting.

adroit, *ȧ-droit′*, *adj.* skilful.
adroit′ly, *adv.* **adroit′ness,** *n.*
[Fr. *à droit*, according to right.]

adulation, *ad-ū-lā′sh(ȯ)n*, *n.* flattery.
ad′ulatory, *adj.*
[L. *adūlārī*, *adūlātus*, to fawn upon.]

adult, *ad′ult*, *a-dult′*, *adj.* fully grown: mature.—*n.* a grown-up person.
[L. *adolescĕre*, *adultum*, to grow.]

adulterate, *ȧ-dul′tėr-āt*, *v.t* to make impure by mixing in something else.
adulterā′tion, *n.*
[L. *adulterāre*, to corrupt; same root as **adultery.**]

adultery, *ȧ-dul′tėr-i*, *n.* unfaithfulness to one's wife with another woman, or to one's husband with another man.
adul′terer, *n.*:—*fem.* **adul′teress.**
adul′terous, *adj.*
[From L.; prob.—*ad*, to, *alter*, another.]

advance, *ȧd-vâns′*, *v.t.* to put forward (e.g. a suggestion): to promote: to encourage the progress of: to supply or pay beforehand.—*v.i.* to go forward: to make progress.—*n.* progress: improvement: a loan: (often in *pl.*) an approach towards friendship, etc.—*adj.* made or given before due: (of e.g. military force) sent forward in front of main force.
advance′ment, *n.* progress: promotion.
in advance, beforehand: before due.
in advance of, before: farther forward than.
[O.Fr. *avancer*—L. *ab ante*, from before.]

advantage, *ȧd-vân′tij*, *n.* superiority over another: gain, benefit: (*lawn tennis*) first point gained after deuce.—*v.t.* to benefit ‘profit.
advanta′geous (*-tā′jùs*), *adj.*
advantā′geously, *adv.*
to advantage, in a way that shows the good qualities clearly: in a way that brings profit.
to take advantage of. See **take.**
[Fr. *avantage*; same root as **advance.**]

advent, *ad′vent*, *n.* coming, or arrival, esp. of Christ: (*cap.*) a period including four Sundays before Christmas.
[L. *ad*, to, *venīre*, to come.]

adventure, *ȧd-ven′chùr*, *n.* a strange or exciting experience.—*v.t.* to risk.
adven′turer, *n.* one who seeks adventure: one who seeks his fortune by discreditable means:—*fem.* **adven′turess.**
adven′turous, *adj.*
adven′turously, *adv.*
[L. *adventūrus*, about to happen.]

adverb, *ad′vėrb*, *n.* a word added to a verb, adjective, or other adverb to show time, manner, place, degree, etc. (e.g. *Yesterday* he looked *more carefully* in the drawer, and *there* he found the *very* small key).
adver′bial, *adj.* **adver′bially,** *adv.*
[L. *ad*, to, *verbum*, a word.]

adversary, *ad′vėr-sȧr-i*, *n.* an opponent: an enemy.
ad′verse, *adj.* acting against one (e.g. *adverse winds, circumstances*): expressing disapproval (e.g. *adverse criticism*).
ad′versely (or *-vers′*), *adv.*
adver′sity, *n.* misfortune:—*pl.* **-ies.**
[L. *ad*, to, *vertĕre*, *versum*, to turn.]

advert, *ȧd-vėrt′*, *v.i.* to refer (to).
[Same root as **adversary,** etc.]

advertise, *ad′vėr-tīz*, or *-tīz′*, *v.t.* to bring (something) to public notice, by an account of its good qualities: to notify, inform (of one's intentions).
advert′isement (*-iz-*, *-is-*), *n.*
advertis′er (*-tīz′*), *n.*
[Fr.; same root as **advert, adversary.**]

advice, *ȧd-vīs′*, *n.* recommendation to a person about what he should do: a formal notice.
advise, *ȧd-vīz′*, *v.t.* to give advice to: to recommend (e.g. *I advise buying the house*): to inform (usu. with *of*).
advīs′able, *adj.* (of action) wise.
advīsabil′ity, *n.*
advised′, *adj.* deliberate: considered (as *a well-advised*, or *ill-advised*, *action*): guided (e.g. *You would be ill-advised to sell your house*).
advis′edly (*-id-li*), *adv.* after careful consideration.
advis′er, *n.* one who advises.
[L. *ad vīsum*, according to what is seen.]

advocacy, *ad′vȯ-kȧ-si*, *n.* the work or part of an advocate: pleading for (e.g. *His advocacy of this action had a selfish motive*).
advocate, *ad′vȯ-kit*, *-kāt*, *n.* one who pleads the cause of another, esp. in a court of law in Scotland: a supporter (e.g. *an advocate of reform*): (*cap*) the Holy Spirit.—*v.t.* (*-kāt*) to plead in favour of, recommend.
[Through O.Fr.—L. *ad*, *vocāre*, call.]

adze, adz, *adz*, *n.* a carpenter's tool with a thin arched blade with its edge at right angles to the handle.
[O.E. *adesa.*]

aegis, *ē′jis*, *n.* protection: patronage.
[Gk. *aigis*, shield belonging to god Zeus or goddess Athena.]

aerate, *ā′ėr-āt*, *v.t.* to put air, or a gas, into.
[L. *āēr*, air.]

aerial, *ā′ėr-i-ȧl*, *ār′*, *n.* any exposed wire able to radiate or receive electromagnetic waves (e.g. a wireless or television aerial).
[L. *āēr*, air.]

aerie, *ā′ė-ri*, *ī′ri*, *n.* the nest of any bird of prey, esp. of an eagle.—Also **aery, eyrie, eyry.**
[O.Fr. *aire.*]

aero-, *ā-ėr-ō-*, (as part of a word) air.

aerobatics, *ā-ėr-ō-bat'iks, n.* stunts performed in an aircraft.
aerodrome, *ā'ėr-ō-drōm, n.* a landing and maintenance station for aircraft.
aerodynamics, *-dī-nam'iks, n.* the study of forces acting on bodies in motion in air.
aerodynam'ic, *adj.*
aerofoil, *ā'ėr-ō-foil, n.* an air-resisting surface—wing, plane, aileron, etc.
aeronaut, *ā'ėr-ō-nöt, n.* one who travels in a balloon or aircraft.
aeronaut'ics, *n.* the science or art of navigation in the air.
aeroplane, *-plān, n.* a flying machine, heavier than air, with planes or wings.
aerosol, *-sol, n.* a liquid, e.g. an insecticide, in a container under pressure: the container.
[Gk. *āēr*, air (**acrobatics**; *dromos*, running; *dynamis*, power; **foil**; *nautēs* sailor; **plane,** 1).]

aesthetics, *es-thet'iks,* or *ēs-*, *n.* the principles of the fine arts.
aesthete, *ēs'thēt,* or *es'-*, *n.* one who pretends that he has a great love of the arts and is not interested in practical affairs.
aesthet'ic (*-thet'*), **aesthet'ical,** *adjs.*
aesthet'ically, *adv.*
[Gk. *aisthētikos*, quick to perceive.]

afar, *ȧ-fär', adv.* from, at, or to, a distance—usu. **from afar, afar off.**

affable, *af'ȧ-bl, adj.* easy to speak to: courteous.
affabil'ity, *n.* **aff'ably,** *adv.*
[L. *affāri*, to speak to.]

affair, *ȧ-fār', n.* business (in *pl.*, business dealings in general): a love affair: a minor battle: (*vaguely*) a thing.
affair of honour, a duel.
[Fr. *à* (L. *ad*), *faire* (L. *facĕre*), to do.]

affect[1], *ȧ-fekt', v.t.* to act upon: to change: to move the feelings of.
affect'ed, *adj.* touched with feeling (e.g. *I was much affected by her death*): (see also **affect** (2)).
affect'ing, *adj.* having power to move the feelings: pathetic. [L. *ad*, to, *facĕre*, to do.]

affect[2], *ȧ-fekt', v.t.* to make a show or pretence of: to show a liking for.
affectā'tion, *n.* a striving after something not natural or real: pretence.
affect'ed, *adj.* not natural: sham.
[Same root as **affect** (1).]

affection, *ȧ-fek'sh(ȯ)n, n.* kindness or love, attachment (*for* or *towards*): a disease or diseased condition.
affec'tionate, *adj.* loving.
affec'tionately, *adv.*
[Same root as **affect** (1).]

affiance, *ȧ-fī'ȧns, v.t.* to betroth.
[O.Fr. (n.) *afiance*—L. *ad*, to, *fides*, faith.]

affidavit, *af-i-dā'vit, n.* a written declaration on oath.
[Late L. *affīdāvit*, he pledged his faith.]

affiliate, *ȧ-fil'i-āt, v.t.* to attach (to), connect (with), as a minor college to a university.
affiliā'tion, *n.*
[L. *affiliāre*—*ad*, to, *filius*, son.]

affinity, *ȧ-fin'i-ti, n.* relationship by marriage: nearness of kin: similarity, likeness: attraction, liking.
[L. *affinitās*—*ad*, at, *finis*, boundary.]

affirm, *ȧ-fėrm', v.t.* to state positively.
affirmā'tion, *n.*
affirm'ative, *adj.* affirming: saying yes: not negative.—Also *n.*
affirm'atively, *adv.*
[L. *ad*, to, *firmus*, firm.]

affix, *ȧ-fiks', v.t.* to attach (with *to, on, upon*): to add.
[L. *ad*, to, *fīgĕre*, *fixum*, to fix.]

afflict, *ȧ-flikt', v.t.* to give continued pain or distress to.
afflic'tion, *n.* state or cause of distress: an ailment.
[L. *ad*, *flīgĕre*, *flictum*, dash to ground.]

affluent, *af'lōō-ėnt, adj.* wealthy.—*n.* a stream flowing into a river or lake.
aff'luence, *n.* wealth.
[L. *ad*, to, *fluĕre*, to flow.]

afford, *ȧ-fōrd', -förd', v.t.* to yield, produce: (with *can*) to bear the expense of: to do, or omit to do, without loss (e.g. *We cannot afford to miss the chance*).
[O.E. (*ge*)*forthian*, to cause to come forth.]

afforest, *a-for'ist, v.t.* to turn into forest by planting young trees.
affores tā'tion, *n.*
[Same root as **forest.**]

affranchise, *ȧ-fran'chīz, v.t.* to free from slavery.
[Fr. *à*, to, *franchir*, to free.]

affray, *ȧ-frā', n.* a fight: a brawl.
[Late L. *exfridiāre*, to break king's peace—Germanic *fridu*, peace.]

affright, *ȧ-frīt', v.t.* to frighten.
[Same root as **fright.**]

affront, *ȧ-frunt', v.t.* to meet face to face: to insult openly.—*n.* an insult.
[L. *ad*, to, *frons*, *frontis*, forehead.]

afield, *ȧ-fēld', adv.* out, abroad: away from the beaten track.

aflame, *ȧ-flām', adv., adj.* (in predicate; not used before noun) flaming: glowing.

afloat, *ȧ-flōt', adv., adj.* (in predicate; not used before noun) floating: at sea: in circulation (e.g. *Rumours are afloat*).

afoot, *ȧ-foot', adv., adj.* (in predicate; not used before noun) on foot: astir: in progress.

aforesaid, *ȧ-fōr'sed,* or *-för',* **aforementioned,** *-men'sh(ȯ)nd, adjs.* said or named before.
[O.E. *on*, prep., and adv. *foran*, in front.]

afraid, *ȧ-frād', adj.* (in predicate; not used before noun) struck with fear: frightened (of): unwillingly inclined to think (that).
[Pa.p. of old vb. *affray*, to frighten.]

afresh, *ȧ-fresh', adv.* anew, again.
[O.E. *of*, of, off, from, **fresh.**]

Afrikaner, *af-ri-kän'ėr*, formerly **Afrikander,** *n.* one born in South Africa of white parents (esp. of Dutch descent).
Afrikaans, *af-ri-käns'*, *n.* one of the two official languages of S. Africa, developed from 17th cent. Dutch.
[Du. *Afrikaner.*]

Afro-Asian, *af'rō-azh'yȧn*, *adj.* of, consisting of, Africans and Asians: of Asian origin but African citizenship: of mixed Asian and African blood.

aft, *âft*, *adj.* and *adv.* behind: near or towards the stern of a vessel.
[O.E. *æftan.*]

after, *âf'tėr*, *prep.* and *adv.* behind in place: later, later than: following in search of: in imitation of: according to.—*adj.* behind in place: later in time: more toward the stern of a vessel.
af'ter-care, *n.* care given to someone after a period of treatment.
af'ter-effect, *n.* an effect that comes after an interval or when the first effect has passed.
af'termath (O.E. *mæth*, mowing), *n.* a second mowing of grass in the same season: later consequences (esp. if bad).
afternoon, *âf-tėr-nōōn'*, *n.* the time between noon and evening (*adj.*, *âf'*).
af'terthought, *n.* a later thought, or the action resulting from it.
af'terwards, *adv.* later.
[O.E. *æfter.*]

again, *ȧ-gen'*, *ȧ-gān'*, *adv.* once more: in addition: moreover: back.
against, *ȧ-genst'*, *ȧ-gānst'*, *prep.* in the opposite direction to: in opposition to: in contact or in collision with.
[O.E. *ongēan*, again, opposite.]

agate, *ag'ėt*, *n.* precious stone formed of layers of quartz of various tints.
[Gk. *achatēs.*]

agave, *ȧ-gā'vi*, *n.* an American aloe-like plant, a source of sisal.
[Gk. *Agauē*, a woman in Greek legend.]

age, *āj*, *n.* the time during which a person or thing has lived or existed: later years of life: a period of time: (*coll.*) a long time (often in *pl.*).—*v.i.* to grow old.—*v.t.* to make old:—*pr.p.* **aging** (*āj'ing*); *pa.p.* **aged** (*ājd*).
aged, *adj.* (*āj'id*) advanced in age: (*ājd*) of the age of.—*n. pl.* (*āj'id*) old people.
age'less, *adj.* never growing old.
of age, aged 18 or over.
[O.Fr. *aage*, *edage*—L. *aetas.*]

agency. See **agent.**

agenda, *ȧ-jen'da*, *n.* things to be done, esp. items of business to be considered.
[L.—*agĕre*, to do; same root as **act.**]

agent, *ā'jėnt*, *n.* a person or thing that acts or is the cause of something that happens (e.g. *Insects are the agent in the spread of some diseases*): one authorised to transact business for another.
a'gency, *n.* the office or business of an agent.
by, through, the agency of, by the action of.
[L. *agĕre*, to do; same root as **act.**]

agglomeration, *ȧ-glom-ėr-ā'sh(ȯ)n*, *n.* heap, mass.
[L. *glomus*, *glomeris*, a ball.]

aggrandise, *ȧ-gran'dīz*, or *ag'*, *v.t.* to make greater in power, rank, etc.
aggrandisement, *ȧ-gran'diz-ment*, *n.*
[L. *ad*, to, *grandis*, large.]

aggravate, *ag'rȧ-vāt*, *v.t.* to make worse: (*coll.*) to provoke, irritate.
aggravā'tion, *n.* **agg'ravāting,** *adj.*
[L. *ad*, to, *gravis*, heavy.]

aggregate, *ag'ri-gāt*, *v.t.* and *v.i.* to collect into a mass: to accumulate.—*v.i.* (*coll.*) to amount to.—*adj.* (*-it*, *-āt*) formed of parts collected in a mass.—*n.* the sum total: a mass consisting of rock fragments: any material added to cement to make concrete.
aggregā'tion, *n.*
in the aggregate, considered as a whole.
[L. *aggregāre*—*grex*, *gregis*, a flock.]

aggress, *ȧ-gres'*, *v.i.* to attack first.—*v.t.* to attack.
aggress'ive, *adj.* making the first attack: inclined to do so, quarrelsome.
aggress'ively, *adv.* **-iveness,** *n.*
aggression, *ȧ-gresh'(ȯ)n*, *n.* first act of hostility.
aggress'or, *n.*
[L. *aggredī*, *-gressus*—*ad*, *gradī*, to step.]

aggrieve, *ȧ-grēv'*, *v.t.* to pain or injure: to cause to feel unjustly treated.
[O.Fr. *agrever*—L. *ad*, to, *gravis*, heavy.]

aghast, *ȧ-gâst'*, *adj.* stunned with horror.
[For *agast*; O.E. *gæstan*, to terrify.]

agile, *aj'īl*, *aj'il*, *adj.* active, nimble.
agility, *ȧ-jil'i-ti*, *n.* nimbleness.
[Fr.—L. *agilis*—*agĕre*, to do or act.]

agitate, *aj'i-tāt*, *v.t.* to shake: to stir violently: to disturb, excite.—*v.i.* to make an agitation (for; e.g. *to agitate for reform of the law*).
ag'itated, *adj.* anxious, excited.
agitā'tion, *n.* disturbance: excitement: stirring up of public feeling.
ag'itator, *n.*
[L. *agitāre*—*agĕre*; same root as **act.**]

aglow, *ȧ-glō'*, *adv.*, *adj.* (in predicate; not used before noun) warm: red hot.

agnostic, *ag-nos'tik*, *n.* one who holds that we know (and can know) nothing of God, or of anything beyond the material world.
agnosticism, *ag-nos'ti-sizm*, *n.*
[Gk. *a-*, not, *gnōstikos*, good at knowing.]

ago, *ȧ-gō'*, *adv.* past: since.
[O.E. *āgān*, to pass away—*gan*, to go.]

agog, *ȧ-gog'*, *adv.*, *adj.* (in predicate; not used before noun) eager: astir.
[Origin uncertain.]

agoing, *ȧ-gō'ing*, *adv.* in motion.

agony, *ag'ȯ-ni*, *n.* extreme suffering.
ag'onise, *v.i.* to suffer agony: to struggle hard (to).

ag′onising (or **-iz′**), *adj.* extremely painful.
[Gk. *agōniā—agōn*, contest.]

agrarian, *ȧ-grā′ri-ȧn, adj.* relating to land, or its management.
[L. *ager*, a field.]

agree, *ȧ-grē′, v.i.* to get on with one another: to come to a decision that both or all accept: to think the same as (with *with*): to consent (to): to suit (with *with*; e.g. *Heat does not agree with him*):—*pr.p.* **agree′ing**; *pa.p.* **agreed′.**
agreed′, *adj.* agreed upon (e.g. *an agreed syllabus*).
agree′able, *adj.* pleasant: pleasing (to): in favour of (with *to*): willing.
agree′ableness, *n.* **agree′ably,** *adv.*
agree′ment, *n.* state of agreeing: a bargain or contract.
[L. *ad*, to, *grātus*, pleasing.]

agriculture, *ag′ri-kul-chůr, n.* the cultivation of land.
agricul′tural, *adj.*
agricul′tu■alist, *n.* one skilled in agriculture.
[L. *ager*, field, *cultūra*, cultivation.]

aground, *ȧ-grownd′, adv., adj.* (in predicate; not used before noun) on, on to, the sea, etc., bottom: stranded.

ague, *ā′gū, n.* a fever coming in fits: a fit of shivering.
[L. *acūta* (*febris*), acute (fever).]

ahead, *ȧ-hed′, adv.* farther on: in advance: on, onward.

ahoy, *ȧ-hoi′, interj.* a call used in hailing at sea.

aid, *ād, v.t.* to help, assist.—*n.* help: anything that helps: a helper.
[O.Fr. *aider*—L. *ad*, *juvāre*, to help.]

aide-de-camp, *ā′de-kon^g, n.* an officer attending a general, a king, or a governor, etc.:—*pl.* **aides′-de-camp** (pron. as *sing.*).
[Fr., assistant on the field.]

aigrette, *ā′gret, n.* a small white heron (also **egret**): a plume of feathers, or of gems, like a heron's crest. [Fr.]

ail, *āl, v.i.* to be ill.
ail′ment, *n.* trouble, illness.
What ails you? What is the matter?
[O.E. *eglan*, to pain.]

aileron, *ā′lėr-on, el′ėr-on^g, n.* a flap at the rear of aeroplane wings.
[L. *āla*, a wing.]

aim, *ām, v.i.* (with *at*) to try to hit: to try to (with *at*; e.g. *to aim at increasing the number of members*).—*v.t.* to point, throw, etc. (at).—*n.* act of, or skill in, aiming: point aimed at: intention.
aim′less, *adj.* without purpose.
aim′lessly, *adv.* **aim′lessness,** *n.*
[O.Fr. *esmer*—L. *aestimāre*, to estimate.]

ain't, *ānt*, (*coll.*) contracted form of *are not*, *am not* or *is not*: also *has not, have not.*

air, *ār, n.* the mixture of gases we breathe, the atmosphere: a light breeze: appearance, look (e.g. *The house had an air of neglect*): a melody: (in. *pl.*) affectation.—*v.t.* to expose to the air: to dry: to bring to public notice (e.g. *He loved to air his grievances*).
air′y, *adj.* open to passage of air: like air: light in appearance: light-hearted, flippant: imaginary:—*comp.* **air′ier**; *superl.* **air′iest.**
air′ily, *adv.* **air′iness,** *n.*
air′ing, *n.* exposure to air or heat: a short walk, etc., in the open air.
air′less, *adj.* still, windless: stuffy.
air arm, the branch of the fighting services that uses aircraft.
air′borne, *adj.* transported by air: in the air.
air bridge, a link by air transport between two points.
air′-condi′tioning. See **condition.**
air corridor, in an area where flying is restricted, a strip along which flying is allowed.
air′craft, *n.* any machine for flying in the air:—*pl.* **air′craft.**
aircraft carrier, *n.* a ship from which aircraft can take off and on which they may alight.
air cushion, an airtight cushion that can be inflated or blown up.
air force, a force organised for war in the air.
air′gun, *n.* a gun that discharges missiles by means of compressed air.
air hostess, a young woman who looks after the comfort of passengers in an aircraft.
air lift, a transport operation carried out by air.
air line, a route followed by aircraft: (a company that owns) a regular air transport service.
air′-lock, *n.* a small chamber in which pressure of air can be raised or lowered: a bubble in a pipe interfering with flow of liquid.
air mail, system of carrying mail by air: mail carried by air.
air′man, *n.* an aviator, flyer.
air′-mind′ed, *adj.* conscious of the importance of flying: favouring air transport.
air′plane, *n.* (*U.S.*) an aeroplane.
air pocket, a region of thinner air, in which aircraft drop.
air′port, *n.* an aerodrome where commercial aircraft arrive and depart.
air raid, a raid by enemy aircraft.
air′-screw, *n.* propeller of an aircraft.
air′-sea rescue, combined use of aircraft and high-speed launches in sea rescue.
air′ship, *n.* a lighter-than-air craft.
air′tight, *adj.* so tight as not to admit air.
air′-trap, *n.* a device to prevent the escape of bad air.
air′way, *n.* a passage for air: a regular route for air travel.

air'worthy, *adj.* in a condition for safe flying.

airy. See above.

in the air, vague (e.g. *The whole plan is rather in the air*): influencing the thought of many people (e.g. *Today the idea that we ought to improve our prisons is in the air*).

on the air, in the act of broadcasting: broadcasting, or being broadcast, regularly.

off the air, not broadcasting.

[L. *āēr*—Gk. *āēr*.]

aisle, *īl, n.* the wing or side of a church: a passage in a church.

[O.Fr.—L. *āla*, wing.]

aitchbone, *āch'bōn, n.* the bone of the rump: the cut of beef over this bone.

[Orig. *nache*-bone—L. *natis*, buttock.]

ajar, *à-jär', adv.* partly open.

[O.E. *on*, on, *cerr*, a turn.]

akimbo, *à-kim'bō, adv.* or *adj.* (in predicate; not used before noun) with hand on hip and elbow bent outward.

[Origin uncertain.]

akin, *à-kin', adj.* related by blood: similar in nature.

[O.E. prep. *of*, and **kin.**]

alabaster, *al'à-bâs-tėr,* or *-bâs'-, n.* a white semi-transparent material used for ornamental objects.

[Gk. *alabastros*.]

à la carte, *ä lä kärt, adv.* according to the bill of fare—each dish chosen and priced separately. [Fr.]

alacrity, *à-lak'ri-ti, n.* briskness, cheerful readiness.

[L. *alacer, alacris*, brisk.]

à la mode, *â-lä-mōd', adv.* and *adj.* according to the fashion. [Fr.]

alarm, *à-lärm', n.* warning of danger: sudden fear: a contrivance to rouse from sleep or to attract attention (e.g. *alarm clock, fire alarm*).—*v.t.* to fill with fear.

alarm'ing, *adj.* **alarm'ingly,** *adv.*

alarm'ist, *n.* one who is too much inclined to expect trouble.

[Orig. a call to arms—Fr. *alarme*—It. *all' arme*, to arms.]

alas, *à-lâs', interj.* exclamation of grief.

[O.Fr. *(h)a las*—L. *lassus*, wearied.]

alb, *alb, n.* in R.C. churches, a white linen vestment reaching to the feet.

[L. *albus*, white.]

albatross, *al'bà-tros, n.* a large, web-footed sea bird of the Southern Ocean.

[Sp. *alcatraz*, pelican, etc.]

albino, *al-bē'nō, n.* a person or animal whose skin and hair are white:—*pl.* **albi'nos.**

[L. *albus*, white.]

album, *al'bùm, n.* a blank book for photographs, autographs, etc.: a book-like container for gramophone records.

[L. *albus*, white.]

albumen, *al-bū'min, n.* white of egg.

albū'minous, *adj.*

[L. *albus*, white.]

alchemy, *al'ki-mi, n.* the early stage of chemistry, its chief aims being to change other metals into gold, and to discover the elixir (see this word) of life.

al'chemist, *n.* one who studies alchemy.

[Arabic *al-kīmiā*.]

alcohol, *al'kō-hol, n.* an intoxicating liquid made by the fermentation of sugar, etc.

alcohol'ic, *adj.* of, like, caused by, alcohol.—*n.* a person who has craving for alcohol and drinks too much.

al'coholism, *n.* poisoning by too much alcohol.

[Arabic *al-koh'l—koh'l*, powder of great fineness, used to stain eyelids.]

alcove, *al'kōv, n.* a recess.

[Sp. *alcoba*—Arabic *al*, the, *gobbah*, vault.]

alder, *öl'dėr, n.* a tree related to the birch, usu. growing in moist ground.

[O.E. *alor*; conn. with L. *alnus*.]

alderman, *öl'dėr-màn, n.* in English boroughs, an official next in rank to the mayor.

[O.E. *aldor, ealdor*, senior, chief.]

ale, *āl, n.* a drink made from malt by fermentation, name given to certain beers.

ale'house, *n.* a place where ale is sold.

[O.E. *alu, ealu*.]

alert, *à-lėrt', adj.* watchful: brisk.—*n.* a warning of danger.—*v.t.* to warn to be ready.

alert'ly, *adv.* **alert'ness,** *n.*

on the alert, on the watch (for).

[It. *erto*, erect, upright—L. *ērectus*.]

alfalfa, *al-fal'fa, n.* lucerne.

[Sp.—Arabic *alfaçfaçah*.]

alfresco, *al-fres'kō, adv.* and *adj.* in the fresh or cool air.

[It. *al fresco*.]

alga, *al'gà, n.* a seaweed or related plant:—*pl.* **algae** (*al'jē*).

[L. *alga*, seaweed.]

algebra, *al'ji-brà, n.* a method of calculation using letters to represent numbers.

algebrā'ic, -al, *adjs.*

[Arabic *al-jebr*.]

alias, *ā'li-as, n.* an assumed name:—*pl.* **a'liases.**

[L. *aliās*, otherwise—*alius*, other.]

alibi, *al'i-bī, n.* plea that a person charged with a crime was elsewhere when it was committed: (*coll.*) an excuse.

[L., elsewhere—*alius*, other, *ibi*, there.]

alien, *āl'yen,* or *ā'li-en, adj.* foreign: not in keeping with (e.g. *Unkindness was alien to his gentle nature*).—*n.* a foreigner: one of foreign birth who has not been naturalised.

alienate, *āl'yėn-āt, ā'li-en-āt, v.t.* to make (a person) feel unfriendly to one: to turn away (a person's affections).

alienā'tion, *n.*

[L. *aliēnus*—*alius*, other.]

alight[1], *à-līt', v.i.* to come down from a horse, out of a vehicle, etc.: to come accidentally (upon).

[O.E. *ālīhtan*, to come down, dismount.]

alight², *à-lit′*, *adv.*, *adj.* (in predicate; not used before noun) on fire.
[O.E. *on*, on, and **light** (1).]

align, *à-lin′*, *v.t.* to bring into line: (with *oneself*) to take a side in an argument, politics, etc. (e.g. *to align oneself with the rebels*).
align′ment, *n.*
[L. *ad*, to, *linea*, a line.]

alike, *à-lik′*, *adj.* (in predicate; not used before noun) like, having resemblance.—*adv.* in the same manner (e.g. *He treated all his children alike*).
[O.E. *gelic*—*lic*, like.]

aliment, *al′i-mėnt*, *n.* food.
alimen′tary, *adj.*
al′imony, *n.* an allowance for support made to a wife by her husband when they are legally separated.
alimentary canal, the passage for food in animals, including the gullet, stomach, intestines, etc.
[L. *alĕre*, to nourish.]

alive, *à-liv′*, *adj.* (in predicate; not used before noun) in life (e.g. *Victoria was still alive in 1900*): brisk: alert: full of activity.
alive to, conscious of (e.g. *He was alive to the dangers of the situation*).
[O.E. *on life*—*lif*, life.]

alkali, *al′kà-lī*, *n.* a soluble salt with basic (see **base,** 1) qualities:—*pl.* **al′kali(e)s.**
alkaline, *al′kà-līn*, or *-lin*, *adj.*
[Arabic *al-qaliy*, ashes; orig. applied to salts from ashes of plants.]

all, *öl*, *adj.* the whole of: every one of.—*adv.* wholly: completely (e.g. *all-powerful*): entirely.—*n.* the whole: everything.
all at once, suddenly.
all but, very nearly.
all in, everything included: (*coll.*) exhausted.
all right (note spelling), yes, agreed: safe and sound: good enough.
all-round. See page 14.
all up, the end, with no further hope.
all′-up′, *n.* (of loaded aircraft, etc.) the total weight.—Also *adj.*
at all, in the least degree.
for good and all, finally.
[O.E. *all*, *eall.*]

allay, *à-lā′*, *v.t.* to make less, relieve (e.g. *to allay one's fears*):—*pr.p.* **allay′ing**; *pa.p.* **allayed′.**
[O.E. *ālecgan*, to put down.]

allege, *à-lej′*, *v.t.* to assert without proof:—*pr.p.* **alleg′ing**; *pa.p.* **alleged′.**
allegation, *à-lė-gā′sh(ȯ)n*, *n.*
[Late L. *exlitigāre*, to clear at law.]

allegiance, *à-lē′jàns*, *n.* the duty of a subject to his sovereign: loyalty.
[L. *ad*, to, and **liege.**]

allegory, *al′ė-gòr-i*, *n.* a story with a second or hidden meaning.
allegor′ical, *adj.* **allegor′ically,** *adv.*
[Gk. *allos*, other, *agoreuein*, to speak.]

allegro, *a-lā′grō*, or *-le′-*, *adv.*, *adj.* (*music*) brisk(ly), rapid(ly).—Also *n.*
[It.—L. *alacer*, brisk.]

alleluia(h), *al-i-lōō′yä.* Same as **halleluiah.**

allergy, *al′ėr-ji*, *n.* abnormal sensitiveness of the body to substances usu. harmless: (*coll.*) dislike.
aller′gic, *adj.* (with *to*) affected in a bad way by (certain substances): (*coll.*) feeling dislike for (with *to*).
[Gk. *allos*, other, *ergon*, work.]

alleviate, *à-lē′vi-āt*, *v.t.* to make lighter, lessen (e.g. pain).
alleviā′tion, *n.*
[L. *alleviāre*—*levis*, light.]

alley, *al′i*, *n.* a walk in a garden between hedges: a narrow passage in a city: an enclosure for skittles, etc.—*pl.* **all′eys.**
[O.Fr. *allee*, passage—*aller*, to go.]

All Fools' Day, *öl fōōlz′ dā*, April 1.

All-hallow, *öl-hal′ō*, **All-hallows,** *öl-hal′ōz*, Same as **All Saints' Day.**

alliance, allied. See **ally.**

alligator, *al′i-gā-tòr*, *n.* a reptile of the crocodile group found mainly in America.
[Sp. *el lagarto*—L. *lacerta*, a lizard.]

alliteration, *à-lit-ėr-ā′sh(ȯ)n*, *n.* the repeating of the same *sound* (not necessarily the same *letter*) at the beginning of two or more words in close succession, as '*s*even *g*rave and *s*tately *c*edars'.
allit′erative, *adj.*
[L. *ad*, to *litera*, a letter.]

allocate, *al′o-kāt*, *v.t.* to give as a share (to): to set apart (for a purpose).
allocā′tion, *n.*
[L. *ad*, to, *locāre*, to place—*locus*, a place.]

allot, *à-lot′*, *v.t.* to distribute in portions: to give as one's share:—*pr.p.* **allott′ing**; *pa.p.* **allott′ed.**
allot′ment *n.* the act of allotting: share: a piece of ground let out for spare-time cultivation.
[O.Fr. *aloter*; same root as **lot.**]

allow, *à-low′*, *v.t.* to permit (e.g. *I do not allow smoking*): to admit (e.g. *I allow this action was foolish*): to give (a person a sum of money, esp. at regular intervals): to add or deduct in estimating.—*v.i.* to permit, admit (of; e.g. *His silence allows of only one explanation*).
allow′able, *adj.*
allow′ance, *n.* a fixed sum or quantity allowed.
to allow for, to make provision for: to take into consideration when judging or deciding (also **to make allowance for**).
[Through O.Fr.—L. *ad*, to, *locāre*, to place.]

alloy, *à-loi′*, *v.t.* to mix (one metal) with another: to make less perfect (e.g. *There is always something to alloy one's pleasure*):—*pa.p.* **alloyed** (*à-loid′*).—*n.* (usu. *al′oi*) a mixture of two or more metals: anything that makes quality poorer.
[O.Fr. *aleier*, combine—L. *alligāre*, bind.]

all-round, *öl′rownd′*, *adj.* (good) in all branches (e.g. *an all-round sportsman*).
All Saints' Day, *öl sānts′ dā*, November 1.
All Souls' Day, *öl sōlz′ dā*, November 2.
allspice, *öl′spis*, *n.* Jamaica pepper.
[**all, spice.**]
allude, *à-lūd′*, or *-lo͞od′*, *v.i.* to refer (to) indirectly or in passing: to have reference to (e.g *This remark in his letter alludes to something I told him*).
allū′sion, *n.* (an) indirect reference..
allū′sive (*-siv*), *adj.* containing an allusion: full of allusions.
[L. *ad*, to, *lūdĕre*, *lūsum*, to play.]
allure, *à-lūr′*, or *-lo͞or′*, *v.t.* to draw on by, or as if by, a lure (see this word).—*n.* ability to charm.
allure′ment, *n.* fascination, charm: act of alluring: something serving to tempt or encourage.
allur′ing, *adj.* **allur′ingly,** *adv.*
[O.Fr. *à*, to, *loerre*, lure.]
allusion, allusive. See **allude.**
alluvium, *à-lū′vi-ùm*, or *-lo͞o′*, *n.* earth, sand, gravel, etc., carried along by rivers and deposited on lower lands:—*pl.* **allū′via.**
allū′vial, *adj.*
[L. *ad*, to, *luĕre*, to wash.]
ally, *à-lī′*, *a′lī*, *v.t.* to join by marriage, friendship, treaty, etc:—*pr.p.* **ally′ing**; *pa.p.* **allied′.**—*n.* (usu. *a′lī*) a state, etc., united by treaty: a helper:—*pl.* **allies** (*-līz*).
alli′ance, *n.* union by treaty, etc.
allied, *al′*, or *à-līd′*, *adj.* joined by treaty: related.
[O.Fr. *alier*—L. *ad*, to, *ligāre*, to bind.]
Alma Mater, *al′ma mā′tėr*, *n.* one's university or school.
[L., kind mother.]
almanac, *öl′mà-nak*, *n.* a calendar with information about various events.
[Prob. Sp.—Arabic *al-manākh*.]
almighty, *öl-mī′ti*, *adj.* having all might or power.
the Almighty, God.
[O.E. *eall*, all, *mihtig*, mighty.]
almond, *ä′mònd*, *n.* the fruit, esp. the kernel, of the almond tree, related to the peach but with a dry husk instead of flesh.
[L. *amygdala*—Gk. *amygdalē*.]
almoner, almonry. See **alms.**
almost, *öl′mōst*, *adv.* nearly.
[**all** and **most** (adv.).]
alms, *ämz*, *n. sing.* or *pl.* money, etc., given to the poor: charity.
almoner, *al′mòn-ėr*, or *ä′mòn-*, *n.* one who distributes alms: a social worker attached to a hospital to help and advise patients.
al′monry (*al′* or *ä′*), *n.* a place where alms are distributed.
[Gk. *eleēmosynē*—*eleos*, compassion.]
aloe, *al′ō*, *n.* a plant of the lily family used in medicine:—*pl.* **aloes** (also used as *sing.* as the name of a drug obtained from aloe leaves). [Gk. *aloē*.]
aloft, *à-loft′*, *adv.* overhead: at a great height: above the deck, or at the masthead.
[Old Norse *ā lopt* (pron. *loft*), *ā lopti*.]
alone, *à-lōn′*, *adj.* (in predicate; not used before noun) by oneself, solitary.—*adv.* by oneself: only.
[**all** (adv.), and **one.**]
along, *à-long′*, *adv.* in the direction of the length: onward: (followed by *with*) in company of.—*prep.* by the side of: near.
along′side, *prep.* and *adv.* beside: side by side: close to a ship's side.
all along, all the time.
[O.E. pfx. *and-*, against, and *lang*, long.]
aloof, *à-lo͞of′*, *adv.* at a distance.—*adj.* showing aloofness.
aloof′ness, *n.* unwillingness to associate freely with others.
[Prob. conn. with **luff.**]
aloud, *à-lowd′*, *adv.* loudly: not in a whisper or merely in one's mind.
[O.E. *on*, on, and *hlūd*, noise.]
alp, *alp*, *n.* a high mountain.
al′pine, *adj.* of the high mountains (e.g. *alpine flowers*).
al′penstock, *n.* a long spiked stick used by climbers.
[L. *Alpēs*; perh. of Celtic origin.]
alpaca, *al-pak′a*, *n.* a kind of llama, with long silky wool: cloth made of its wool.
[Sp. *alpaca* or *al-paco*.]
alpenstock. See **alp.**
alpha, *al′fa*, *n.* the first letter of the Greek alphabet: the chief (e.g. the brightest star of a constellation).
alpha and omega, the beginning and the end: the chief purpose.
[Gk.—Heb. *aleph*, ox (name of first letter of Heb. alphabet).]
alphabet, *al′fà-bet*, *n.* the letters of a language arranged in order.
alphabet′ical, *adj.* **alphabet′ically,** *adv.*
[Gk. *alpha*, *beta*, first two Greek letters.]
alpine. See **alp.**
already, *öl-red′i*, *adv.* previously, or before the time being spoken of.
[**all** (adv.) and **ready.**]
Alsatian, *al-sā′sh(y)àn*, *adj.* of *Alsace*.—*n.* a large wolf-like dog.
also, *öl′sō*, *adv.* in addition, besides.
al′so-ran, *n.* a racehorse which has not been placed in the first three: an unsuccessful or unimportant person.
[**all** (*adv.*) and **so.**]
altar, *öl′tàr n.* a high place or structure on which sacrifices were once offered: in Christian churches, the table on which the eucharist is consecrated.
al′tarpiece, *n.* a work of art placed above and behind the altar. [L. *altus*, high.]
alter, *öl′tėr*, *v.t.* to make different: to change.—*v.i.* to become different.
al′terable, *adj.* **alterā′tion,** *n.*
[L. *alter*, the other.]

altercate, *ōl'tėr-kāt, v.i.* to dispute or wrangle.
altercā'tion, *n.*
[L. *altercārī, -catus—alter,* the other.]

alter ego, *al'ter eg'o, n.* second self: a bosom friend.
[L. *alter,* other, *ego,* I.]

alternate, *ōl'tėr-nāt,* or *-tėr', v.t.* to use, do, etc. by turns.—*v.i.* to happen by turns.—*adj.* (*ōl-tėr'nit*) coming, or following, by turns.
alter'nately, *adv.* **alternā'tion,** *n.*
alter'native, *adj.* offering a choice of two things.—*n.* a choice between two things: either of these.
alter'natively, *adv.*
alternating current, an electric current that at intervals reverses its direction.
[L. *alternāre*; same root as **alter.**]

although, *ōl-*THō', *conj.* admitting that: in spite of the fact that.
[**all** (adv.) and **though.**]

altimeter, *al-tim'ė-tėr, n.* instrument for measuring height above sea lev ', etc.
altitude, *al'ti-tūd, n.* height: high rank.
[L. *altus,* high; **meter.**]

alto, *âl'tō, n.* correctly, the highest male voice, but also used for the lowest female voice (contralto).
[It.—L. *altus,* high.]

altogether, *ōl-tȯ-ge*TH'*ėr, adv.* completely.
[**all, together.**]

altruism, *al'trōō-izm, n.* living or acting for the good of others.
altruis'tic, *adj.* **altruis'tically,** *adv.*
[L. *alter,* the other.]

alum, *al'ŭm, n.* a mineral salt containing aluminium, used in dyeing.
alumina, *ȧ-lū'min-a,* or *-lōō', n.* the oxide of aluminium.
aluminium, *a-lū-min'i-ŭm,* or *-lōō-, n.* a light metal resembling silver.—Also **alu'minum.**
[L. *alūmen.*]

alumnus, *ȧ-lum'nus, n.* a pupil, student, of school or university :—pl. **alum'nī.**
[L.—*alĕre,* to nourish.]

always, *ōl'wāz, adv.* at all times: continually: in any case.
[**all, way.**]

am. See **be.**

amalgam, *ȧ-mal'gȧm, n.* a mixture.
amal'gamate, *v.t.* to unite (e.g. business firms).—*v.i.* to unite: to blend.
amalgamā'tion, *n.*
[L.—Gk. *malagma,* something that softens.]

amass, *ȧ-mas', v.t.* and *v.i.* to gather in large quantity, accumulate.
[L. *ad,* to, *massa,* a mass.]

amateur, *am'ȧ-tėr, -tyŭr, n.* one who takes part in a study, game, etc. for the love of it, not for professional gain.
amateur'ish, *adj.* not very skilful.
[Same root as **amatory.**]

amatory, *am'ȧ-tȯr-i, adj.* of love.
[L. *amāre, amātum,* to love.]

amaze, *ȧ-māz', v.t.* to astonish greatly.
amaze'ment, *n.* great astonishment.
amaz'ing, *adj.* **amaz'ingly,** *adv.*
[O.E. *āmasod,* amazed.]

Amazon, *am'ȧ-zȯn, n.* one of a nation of female warriors in Greek story: a masculine or large, strong woman. [Gk.]

ambassador, *am-bas'ȧ-dȯr, n.* a minister of the highest rank representing a state in another country: a representative, messenger :—*fem.* **ambass'adress.**
[L. *ambactus,* a vassal.]

amber, *am'bėr, n.* a yellowish fossil resin, used for ornaments, etc.
[Fr. *ambre.*]

ambidextrous, *am-bi-deks'trus, adj.* able to use both hands equally well.
[L. *ambo,* both, *dexter,* right hand.]

ambiguous, *am-big'ū-ŭs, adj.* having more than one possible meaning.
ambigū'ity, *n.* uncertainty of meaning (also **ambig'uousness**): an ambiguous word or statement :—*pl.* **ambigū'ities.**
ambig'uously, *adv.*
[L. *ambi-,* about, *agĕre,* to go.]

ambition, *am-bish'(ȯ)n, n.* desire for power, honour, fame, excellence.
ambi'tious, *adj.* **ambi'tiously,** *adv.*
ambi'tiousness, *n.*
[L. *ambitiō,* canvassing for votes in ancient Rome—*ambi-,* about, *īre, itum,* to go.]

amble, *am'bl, v.i.* (of a horse, etc.) to move at an easy pace.—*n.* a pace of a horse between a trot and a walk.
[L. *ambulāre,* to walk about.]

ambrosia, *am-brō'z(h)i-a, n.* in Greek story the food of the gods.
ambrōs'ial, *adj.*
[Gk. *ambrotos,* immortal.]

ambulance, *am'bŭl-ȧns, n.* a vehicle for the sick and injured.
am'bulant, *n.* a sick or injured person who is able to walk.
[Same root as **amble.**]

ambuscade, *am'bŭs-kād, n.* ambush.
am'bush, *n.* concealment in order to make a surprise attack: people so hidden, or their place of concealment.—*v.t.* to attack from an ambush.
[Through O.Fr.—L. *in, boscus,* a bush.]

ameliorate, *ȧ-mēl'yȯr-āt, v.t.* and *v.i.* to make, or to become, better.
ameliorā'tion, *n.*
[L. *ad,* to, *melior,* better.]

amenable, *ȧ-mēn'ȧ-bl, adj.* easy to lead or persuade.
amenabil'ity, amen'ableness, *ns.*
[Late L. *mināre,* to lead, drive (e.g. cattle)—L. *minārī,* to threaten.]

amend, *ȧ-mend', v.t.* to correct, improve.
amend'ment, *n.* correction: improvement: an alteration proposed on a bill, motion, etc.
to make amends, to make good a loss, to make up (for).
[L. *ē* (*ex*), out of, *menda,* a fault.]

amenity, *ȧ-mēn'i-ti,* or *-men',* *n.* pleasantness of situation, etc.: (in. *pl.*) attractive features of locality (e.g. parks):—*pl.* **-ies.**
[L. *amoenus,* pleasant; *amāre,* love.]

American, *ȧ-mer'i-kȧn, adj.* of America, esp. of the United States.—*n.* a native of America.

amethyst, *am'i-thist, n.* a bluish quartz.
[Gk. *a-*, not, *methyein,* to be drunken; once used to make drinking cups, supposed to prevent drunkenness.]

amiable, *ām'yė-bl,* or *-i-ȧ-bl, adj.* likable: of sweet disposition: friendly.
amiabil'ity, am'iableness, *ns.*
am'iably, *adv.*
amicable, *am'i-kȧ-bl, adj.* friendly.
am'icableness, amicabil'ity, *ns.*
am'icably, *adv.*
amity, *am'i-ti, n.* friendship: goodwill.
[L. *amīcus,* a friend—*amāre,* to love.]

amice, *am'is, n.* a strip of fine linen worn by R.C. priests at mass.
[L. *amicēre,* to wrap about.]

amid, *ȧ-mid',* **amidst,** *ȧ-midst', prep.* in the middle of: among.—Also *adv.*
amid'ships, *adv.* halfway between the stem and the stern of a ship.
[O.E. *on,* on, and **mid.**]

amiss, *ȧ-mis', adj.* (in predicate; not used before noun) wrong: out of place, out of order.—*adv.* badly.
amiss'ing, *adj.* missing, lost.
to take amiss, to resent.
[O.E. *on,* on, and **miss,** failure.]

amity. See **amiable.**

ammeter, *am'i-tėr, n.* an instrument for measuring an electric current.
[*am*pere (see this word), and **meter.**]

ammonia, *ȧ-mō'ni-ȧ, n.* a sharp-smelling gas, very soluble in water: a solution of ammonia gas in water.
ammo'niated, *adj.* containing ammonia.
[From temple of *Ammon* in Libya, near which a salt of ammonia was found.]

ammunition, *am-ū-nish'(ȯ)n, n.* powder, shot, shells, bombs, etc.: material used against opponents in an argument.
[Same root as **munition.**]

amnesia, *am-nē'zh(y)ȧ,* or *-zi-ȧ, n.* loss of memory.
[Gk. *a-*, not, *mnaesthai,* to remember.]

amnesty, *am'nis-ti, n.* a general pardon given to people guilty of hostile acts against the government.
[Same root as **amnesia.**]

amoeba, *ȧ-mē'bȧ, n.* a very simple animal, of variable shape:—*pl.* **amoe'bae** (*-bē*).
[Gk. *amoibē,* change, alteration.]

amok, *ȧ-mok', adv.* with a furious impulse to attack all comers (esp. in phrase **to run amok**).—Also **amuck.**
[Malay *amoq,* frenzied.]

among, *ȧ-mung',* **amongst,** *ȧ-mungst', prep.* amidst: in the group of: to each of.
[O.E. *(ge)mengan,* to mingle.]

amoral, *a-mor'ȧl,* or *ā adj.* incapable of distinguishing between right and wrong.
[Gk. *a-*, without, and **moral.**]

amorous, *am'ȯr-ůs, adj.* inclined to love: showing love.
am'orously, *adv.* **am'orousness,** *n.*
[L. *amor,* love.]

amount, *ȧ-mownt', v.i.* to come in total (to): to be equal in effect (to; e.g. *This action amounts to rebellion*).—*n.* the whole sum: a quantity.
[Fr. *amonter,* to go up—L. *mons,* mountain.]

ampere, *am'per, n.* the unit by which an electric current is measured.
[From *Ampère,* a French physicist.]

ampersand, *am'pėr-sand, n.* a name for the character &, 'and'.
[*and per se and*—i.e. '& standing by itself means *and*'.]

amphibian, *am-fib'i-ȧn, n.* an animal that spends part of its life in water, part on land (e.g. a frog): an aeroplane able to take off from, or alight on, land or water: a vehicle for use on land or water.—Also *adj.*
amphib'ious, *adj.* adapted to life, or to use, on land and on or in water.
[Gk. *amphi,* on both sides, *bios,* life.]

amphitheatre, *am-fi-thē'ȧ-tėr, n.* an oval or circular building with rows of seats rising from an open space (the arena): anything like an amphitheatre in form.
[Gk. *amphi,* round, *theātron,* theatre.]

ample, *am'pl, adj.* large: enough: in generous quantity.
am'pleness, *n.* **am'ply,** *adv.*
am'plify, *v.t.* to make larger: to add details to (e.g. *He amplified his previous statement*):—*pr.p.* **am'plifying**; *pa.p.* **am'plified.**
amplificā'tion, *n.*
am'plifier (*-fi-ėr*), *n.* something that enlarges: a device for increasing the power-level of electric currents (e.g. so as to increase the volume of sound in a wireless set).
amplitude, *am'pli-tūd, n.* largeness: ampleness: extent of variation of a regularly varying quantity (e.g. the distance of the swing of a pendulum from rest to farthest point).
[L. *amplus* (*facĕre,* to make; *amplitūdō*).]

amputate, *am'pū-tāt, v.t.* to cut off (e.g. a limb).
amputā'tion, *n.*
[L. *amb-*, round about, *putāre,* to cut.]

amuck, *ȧ-muk'.* Same as **amok.**

amulet, *am'ū-lit, n.* an object worn as a charm against evil.
[L. *amulētum*; of unknown origin.]

amuse, *ȧ-mūz', v.t.* to entertain pleasantly: to arouse mirth in.
amuse'ment, *n.* something that entertains: enjoyment: mirth.
amus'ing, *adj.* **amus'ingly,** *adv.*
[Fr. *amuser.*]

an, *an, adj.* one: the indefinite article, used before words beginning with the sound of a vowel (e.g. *an ear, an honour*).
[O.E. *ān*, one.]

anachronism, *an-ak'ron-izm, n.* an instance of placing something in a time earlier or later than the period to which it belongs (e.g. describing an aircraft carrier at Trafalgar or chain armour in a recent battle).
[Gk. *ana*, backwards, *chronos*, time.]

anaconda, *an-à-kon'da, n.* a large South American water-snake.
[Origin uncertain.]

anaemia, *à-nē'mi-à, n.* bloodlessness.
anae'mic, *adj.* suffering from anaemia: feeble, without brightness or spirit.
[Gk. *an-*, not, *haima*, blood.]

anaesthetic, *an-is-thet'ik, -ēs-thet'ik, adj.* producing loss of consciousness or loss of feeling.—*n.* a substance that does this.
anaesthes'ia (*-thēz'yà*), *n.* loss of consciousness or of sensation.
anaes'thetise (*-ēs'*), *v.t.* to give an anaesthetic to.
anaes'thetist (*-ēs'*), *n.*
[Gk. *anaesthētos*, without feeling.]

anagram, *an'à-gram, n.* a word or sentence formed from the letters of another, e.g. 'live' for 'evil' or 'Flit on, cheering angel' for 'Florence Nightingale'.
[Gk. *ana*, again, *gramma*, letter.]

analgesia, *an-àl-jē'zi-a, n.* painlessness.
analge'sic (*-sik*), *n.* a remedy that lessens pain.—Also *adj.*
[Gk. *an-*, not, *algeein*, to feel pain.]

analogy, *àn-al'ò-ji, n.* resemblance in certain respects (e.g. *the analogy between the gills of a fish and the lungs of an animal*): reasoning from similar cases.
anal'ogous, *adj.* similar.
[Gk. *ana*, according to, *logos*, proportion.]

analysis, *à-nal'i-sis, n.* breaking up of (e.g. a sentence into clauses, or a chemical compound into its elements): psychoanalysis (see this word).
an'alyse (*-īz*), *v.t.* to break up (a whole) into its elements or parts: to examine the nature of (e.g. *to analyse her charm*).
an'alyst (*-ist*), *n.* one who analyses.
analyt'ical (*-lit'*), *adj.* analysing.
bowling analysis, (*cricket*) record of overs, runs, wickets taken, and average number of runs per wicket.
[Gk. *ana*, up, *lyein*, to loose.]

anara(c)k. Same as **anorak.**

anarchy, *an'àr-ki, n.* absence or failure of government: confusion.
anar'chical (*-ki-kàl*), *adj.*
an'archist, *n.* a person who tries to overturn government by violence, or to bring about disorder of any kind.
[Gk. *an-*, without, *archē*, government.]

anathema, *à-nath'ė-ma, n.* a solemn curse: a hated person or thing.
[Gk. *anathēma*, an offering in a temple.]

anatomy, *à-nat'ò-mi, n.* dissection or cutting up of a body: the structure of the body thus learned.
anatom'ical, *adj.* **anatom'ically,** *adv.*
anat'omist, *n.* a dissector of bodies.
[Gk. *ana*, up, *temnein*, to cut.]

ancestor, *an'ses-tòr*, or *an'sis-, n.* one from whom a person is descended, a forefather:—*fem.* **an'cestress.**
ances'tral (*-ses'*), *adj.*
an'cestry, *n.* a line of ancestors: lineage.
[L. *ante*, before, *cēdĕre*, to go.]

anchor, *ang'kòr, n.* something thrown overboard to hold a ship, etc. in position, esp. a device with barbs that stick into the bed of the sea, etc.: anything that gives steadiness.—*v.t.* to fix by an anchor.—Also *v.i.*
anch'orage, *n.* a place for anchoring.
at anchor, anchored.
to cast anchor, to let down the anchor.
to weigh anchor, to take up the anchor: to sail away.
[O.E. *ancor*—L. *ancora.*]

anchorite, *ang'kòr-īt, n.* a hermit:—*fem.* **anch'oress.**
[Gk. *ana*, apart, *chōreein*, to withdraw.]

anchovy, *an'chò-vi*, or *-chō', n.* a small Mediterranean fish of the herring family.
[Sp. and Port. *anchova.*]

ancient, *ān'shėnt, adj.* very old: belonging to times long past, esp. before the fall of the Roman Empire.—*n.* an aged man: one who lived in ancient times.
[(O.) Fr. *ancien*—L. *ante*, before.]

ancillary, *an-sil'àr-i, adj.* helping or related but of less importance.
[L. *ancilla*, female servant.]

and, *and, conj.* showing addition, repetition, or result. [O.E.]

andante, *ân-dân'tā, adv.* and *adj.* (*music*) moderately slow(ly), and even(ly.) [It.]

anecdote, *an'ek-dōt, n.* a brief account of an interesting incident.
[Gk. *an-*, not, *ekdotos*, published; orig, used of details of history.]

anemometer, *an-ė-mom'it-ėr, n.* an instrument for measuring wind velocity.
[Gk. *anemos*, wind, *metron*, measure.]

anemone, *à-nem'ò-ni, n.* a flower related to the buttercup, windflower: a sea anemone (see this term).
[Gk. *anemōnē*—*anemos*, wind.]

aneroid, *an'ė-roid, adj.* (of a barometer) in which pressure of air is measured without use of mercury or other fluid.
[Gk. *a-*, not, *nēros*, wet, *eidos*, form.]

anew, *à-nū', adj.* afresh: again.

angel, *ān'jėl, n.* a divine messenger: a guardian spirit.
angel'ic (*an-*), *adj.* **angel'ically,** *adv.*
[Gk. *angelos*, a messenger.]

angelus, *an'ji-lùs, n.* a short act of worship repeated at morning, noon, and night: a bell rung to announce the time of it.
[From its first word (in Latin).]

anger, *ang'gėr, n.* hot displeasure : wrath.—*v.t.* to make angry.
ang'ry, *adj.* excited with anger : inflamed : threatening (e.g. of the sky).
ang'rily, *adv.* **ang'riness,** *n.*
[Old Norse *angr* ; conn. with **anguish.**]

angina (pectoris), *an-jī'na (pek'tor-is),* a heart disease with attacks of intense pain.
[L. *ang(u)ĕre,* to strangle ; *pectoris,* of the chest.]

angle[1], *ang'gl, n.* a corner : space between two straight lines, or three surfaces, meeting in a point, or between two surfaces meeting in a line : point of view.—*v.t.* to give (an account, e.g. of news) in such a way as to suit a particular point of view.
ang'ular, *adj.* having an angle or angles : bony : stiff and awkward in manner.
angular'ity, *n.*
[L. *angulus.*]

angle[2], *ang'gl, v.i.* to fish with rod and line : to scheme (for).
ang'ler, *n.* **ang'ling,** *n.*
[O.E. *angul,* a hook.]

Angles, *ang'glz, n. pl.* a north German tribe who founded settlements in Britain and from whom England took its name.
Ang'lican (*-kȧn*), *adj.* of the Church of England.
ang'licise (*-sīz*), *v.t.* to make English or more like English (e.g. *to anglicise the pronunciation of a French word*).
Anglo-, *ang'glō-, pfx.* English.
Ang'lo-Sax'on, *n.* Old English, the earliest form of the English Language : a Germanic settler in England or southern Scotland.—Also *adj.* (applied also to English-speaking people generally).
[L. *Anglus,* pl. *Angli.*]

Anglo-. See **Angles.**
Ang'lophile (*-fīl*), *adj.* and *n.* (person) who likes or admires the English.
Anglophil'ia, (*-fil'*), *n.* liking for England and the English.
Ang'lophobe (*-fōb*), *adj.* and *n.* (person) having fear or dislike of the English.
Anglophob'ia, *n.* hatred of England and the English.
[See **phil(o)-,** and **phobia.**]

Angora, *ang-gō'rȧ, -gö', n.* a goat, cat, or rabbit, with long silky hair.
[*Angora,* now *Ankara,* in Turkey.]

angry. See **anger.**

anguish, *ang'gwish, n.* very great pain of body or mind, agony.
ang'uished, *adj.*
[O.Fr. *angoisse* ; same root as **angina.**]

angular, angularity. See **angle** (1).

aniline *an'i-lēn, -lin, n.* oily liquid from coal tar, used in dyeing, etc.
[Arabic *an-nīl,* the indigo plant.]

animadvert, *an-i-mad-vėrt', v.i.* (with *on*) to express criticism of (e.g. *He animadverted on the follies of this plan.*)
animadver'sion (*-vėr'sh(ȯ)n*), *n.*
[L. *animus,* mind, *ad,* to, *vertĕre,* to turn.]

animal, *an'i-mȧl, n.* a being having life, sensation, and motion at will, distinguished from a plant, which has life, but apparently not sensation or voluntary motion : one of the lower animals as opp. to man.—Also *adj.*
an'imate, *v.t.* to give life to : to make lively : to cause (someone to act) : to be the motive of (an action).—*adj.* (*-it*) living.
an'imated, *adj.* able to move as if alive (e.g. *an animated doll*) : lively (e.g. *an animated discussion*).
animā'tion, *n.*
[L. *anima,* air, breath, life.]

animosity, *an-i-mos'i-ti, n.* strong dislike: hostility.
[L. *animōsus,* full of spirit.]

aniseed, *an'i-sēd, n.* the seed of anise, a plant of Mediterranean regions.
[Gk. *anison,* anise.]

ankle, *angk'l, n.* the joint connecting the foot and leg.
ank'let, *n.* an ornament or covering for the ankle.
[O.E. *anclēow.*]

annals, *an'ȧlz, n. pl.* historical records.
[L. *annus,* a year.]

anneal, *ȧ-nēl', v.t.* to bring (glass or metals) to a proper condition by means of strong heat and gradual cooling.
[O.E. *an-,* on, *ǣlan,* to burn.]

annex, *ȧ-neks', v.t.* to add : to attach (e.g. a penalty) : to take possession of (e.g. another's territory).—*n.* (*an'eks*) an additional building (usu. spelled **annexe**).
annexā'tion, *n.*
[L. *ad,* to, *nectĕre, nexum,* to tie.]

annihilate, *ȧ-nī'hil-āt, v.t.* to destroy utterly : to crush by look or word.
annihilā'tion, *n.*
[L. *ad,* to, *nihil,* nothing.]

anniversary, *an-i-vėr'sȧr-i, n.* the day of the year on which an event (e.g. a birthday or wedding) occurred or is commemorated.—Also *adj.*
[L. *annus,* a year, *vertĕre,* to turn.]

annotate, *an'ō-tāt, v.t.* to make notes on.
annotā'tion, *n.*
[L. *ad,* to, *notāre, -ātum,* to mark.]

announce, *ȧ-nowns', v.t.* to make known publicly : to be evidence of (e.g. *A familiar smell announced the goat's return*).
announce'ment, *n.*
announc'er, *n.* one who announces, esp. who introduces items of a wireless or television programme.
[L. *ad,* to, *nuntiāre,* to deliver news.]

annoy, *ȧ-noi', v.t.* to anger slightly : to tease :—*pr.p.* **annoy'ing ;** *pa.p.* **annoyed'.**
annoy'ance, *n.* **annoy'ingly,** *adv.*
[O.Fr. *anoier.*]

annual, *an'ū-ȧl, adj.* yearly.—*n.* a plant that lives only one year : a book that is one of a series published yearly.
ann'ually, *adv.*

annuity, *ȧ-nū′i-ti, n.* a payment made each year during a given period (usu. the receiver's life).
annū′itant, *n.* one who receives an annuity.
[L. *annus*, year.]

annul, *ȧ-nul′, v.t.* to cancel, abolish: to declare not valid (see this word):—*pr.p.* **annull′ing**; *pa.p.* **annulled′**.
annul′ment, *n.*
[L. *ad*, to, *nullus*, none.]

annular, *an′ū-lȧr, adj.* ring-shaped.
[L. *ānulus*, later *annulus*, a ring.]

annunciation, *ȧ-nun-si-ā′sh(ȯ)n, n.* the Angel's salutation to the Virgin Mary (Luke i. 28): (*cap.*) the 25th of March, Lady Day.
[Same root as **announce.**]

anode, *an′ōd, n.* the conductor through which an electric current enters a battery, etc.: also that by which electrons leave an electron tube.
[Gk. *ana*, up, *hodos*, way.]

anoint, *ȧ-noint′, v.t.* to smear with ointment or oil: to consecrate with oil.
[Through Fr.—L. *in*, on, *ung(u)ĕre*, to smear.]

anomaly, *ȧ-nom′ȧ-li, n.* irregularity: a thing that is not according to rule.
anom′alous, *adj.* irregular: nor normal.
[Gk. *an-*, not, *homalos*, even—*homos*, same.]

anon[1], *ȧ-non′, adv.* immediately: soon.
[O.E. *on*, in, *ān*, one (i.e. one instant).]

anon[2], *ȧ-non′*, short for **anonymous.**

anonymous, *ȧ-non′i-mus, adj.* without the name of the author, contributor, etc.
anon′ymousness, anonym′ity, *ns.*
anon′ymously, *adv.*
[Gk. *an-*, without, *onoma*, name.]

anorak, *an′ȯ-rak, n.* a Greenlander's fur coat: a hooded waterproof jacket.
[Greenland word.]

another, *an-uTH′ėr, adj.* a different (thing or person): one more of the same kind.—Also *pron.*
one another, each other.
[Orig. **an other.**]

answer, *ân′sėr, n.* a reply: a reply in the form of an action (e.g. *His answer to this was to draw his sword*): the solution of a problem.—*v.t.* to reply or respond: to act in response to (e.g. *to answer the bell*): to satisfy (e.g. one's requirements).—*v.i.* to reply: to be responsible (for): to suffer (for e.g. a fault): to correspond (to e.g. a description).
an′swerable, *adj.* able to be answered: responsible (e.g. *I will be answerable to you for his good behaviour*): to be blamed (for).
[O.E. *andswarian*, to answer.]

ant, *ant, n.* a small insect, related to bees, wasps, etc., commonly thought of as very industrious.
ant′eater, *n.* an ant-eating S. American animal.
ant(s') eggs, pupae, not eggs, of ants.
ant hill, hillock built as nest by ants.
[Contr. of *emmet*—O.E. *ǣmete*.]

antagonist, *ȧn-tag′on-ist, n.* one who strives against another: an opponent.
antagonist′ic, *adj.* unfriendly: opposed (to).
antagonist′ically, *adv.*
antag′onise (*-īz*), *v.t.* to arouse opposition or hostile feelings in.
antag′onism, *n.* hostility: opposition.
[Gk. *anti*, against, *agōn*, a contest.]

Antarctic, *ant-ärk′tik, adj.* of south pole or south polar regions.
Antarctic Circle, imaginary circle round south pole at distance of about 23½ degrees.
[Gk. *anti*, opposite, and **Arctic.**]

ante-, *an-ti-, pfx.* before (place or time).
an′tedate, *v.t.* to date before the true time: to be of an earlier date than (something else).
antena′tal (*-nā′*), *adj.* before birth.
anteroom, *an′ti-rōōm, n.* a room leading into another.
[L. *ante*, before (L. *nātālis*, of birth).]

antecedent, *an-ti-sēd′ėnt, adj.* going before in time (often with *to*; e.g. *The decision not to invite Joe was antecedent to his illness*).—*n.* the noun to which a relative pronoun refers (e.g. *boy* in *Send a boy who can run fast*): (in *pl.*) previous conduct, history, etc.
[L. *ante*, before, *cēdĕre*, to go.]

antedate. See **ante-.**

antediluvian, *an-ti di-lōō′vi-ȧn*, or *-lū′*, *adj.* existing or happening before Noah's Flood: aged.
[L. *ante*, before, *dīluvium*, flood.]

antelope, *an′ti-lōp, n.* swift, graceful animal related to the goat:—*pl.* **an′telope**(s).
[Late L. *antalopus*.]

antenatal. See **ante-.**

antenna, *an-ten′a, n.* a feeler or horn in insects, etc.: a system of conductors used for sending out or receiving electromagnetic waves: sometimes used as meaning *aerial*:—*pl.* **antenn′ae** (*-ē*), (in *radio*) **antenn′as.**
[L. *antenna*, the yard of a sail.]

anterior, *an-tē′ri-ȯr, adj.* more to the front.
[L. *anterior*, comp. of *ante*, before.]

anteroom. See **ante-.**

anthem, *an′thėm, n.* a piece of music for a church choir, usu. set to words from Scripture: any song of praise or gladness.
[Gk. *anti*, in return, *phōnē*, the voice.]

anther, *an′thėr, n.* the part of the stamen in a flower that contains the pollen.
[Through L.—Gk. *anthos*, a flower.]

anthology, *an-thol′ȯ-ji, n.* a chosen collection of pieces of poetry or prose.
anthol′ogist, *n.* one who makes an anthology.
[Gk. *anthos*, a flower, *legein*, to gather.]

anthracite, *an'thrȧ-sīt, n.* a kind of coal that burns nearly without flame.
[Gk. *anthrax, anthrakos*, coal, carbuncle.]

anthrax, *an'thraks, n.* a deadly disease of sheep and cattle that may be given to man. [Same root as **anthracite.**]

anthrop(o)-, (as part of a word) man.
anthropoid, *an'thro-poid*, or *-thrō'-, adj.* man-like (applied esp. to the highest apes).—Also *n.*
anthropology, *an-thrō-pol'ȯ-ji, n.* the science of man.
anthropol'ogist, *n.* one who studies anthropology.
[Gk. *anthrōpos*, man (*eidos*, form; *logos*, discourse).]

anti-, *an-ti-, pfx.* (1) against, (2) the opposite of.
anti-aircraft (*-ār'krâft*), *adj.* used to fight against enemy aircraft.
anticli'max (*-klī'*), *n.* the opp. of a climax, a dull or disappointing ending after mounting excitement or interest.
an'ticlock'wise, *adj., adv.* in the opposite direction to that in which clock hands move.
anticyclone (*-sī'klōn*), *n.* the opp. of a cyclone, a spiral flow of air out from an area of high atmospheric pressure.
antimacassar (*-mȧ-kas'ȧr*), *n.* a covering to protect chair backs, etc. (orig. to protect from Macassar hair oil).
an'ti-personnel', *adj.* intended to destroy military personnel (see this word) or other people.
anti-semit'ic, *adj.* hating or opposing Semites (Jews).
anti-sem'itism *n.*
antisocial (*-sō'sh(ȧ)l*), *adj.* against the welfare of the community, etc. (e.g. *Vandalism is antisocial*): not showing fondness for the company of others.
an'ti-tank', *adj.* for use against tanks.
antitoxin (*-tok'sin*), *n.* a substance formed in the body that fights against poisons due to bacteria.
an'ti-trade', *n.* a wind that blows in the opposite direction to the trade wind.
[Gk. *anti*, against, instead of, etc.]

antibiotic, *an-ti-bī-ot'ik, adj.* and *n.* (a chemical compound, e.g. penicillin) used to stop the growth of bacteria that cause disease. [Gk. *anti*, against, *bios*, life.]

antibody, *an'ti-bod'i, n.* a substance produced in (e.g.) the human body to fight bacteria, etc. [Gk. *anti*, against, and **body.**]

antic, *an'tik, n.* a caper, an odd or unexpected action.—Also *adj.* and *v.i.*
[It. *antico*, ancient; same root as **antique.**]

anticipate, *an-tis'i-pāt, v.t.* to act before, forestall (another person or thing): to foresee: to expect.—*v.i.* to speak, act, before the appropriate time.
anticipā'tion, *n.* **anti'cipātory,** *adj.*
[L. *ante*, before, *capĕre*, to take.]

anticlimax, anticyclone. See **anti-.**

antidote, *an'ti-dōt, n.* something given to act against poison: anything that prevents evil (with *against, for, to*).
[Gk. *anti*, against, *didonai*, to give.]

antimacassar. See **anti-.**

antimony, *an'ti-mȯn-i, n.* a brittle, bluish-white metal.
[Late L. *antimonium.*]

antipathy, *an-tip'ȧth-i, n.* strong dislike (*to, against, between*):—*pl.* **-ies.**
antipathet'ic, *adj.*
[Gk. *anti*, against, *pathos*, feeling.]

anti-personnel. See **anti-.**

antipodes, *an-tip'ȯ-dēz, n. pl.* (also *sing.*) the other side of the globe: the exact opposite of a person or thing.
[Gk. *anti*, opposite to, *pous, podos*, foot.]

antiquary, *an'ti-kwȧr-i, n.* one who studies relics of the past:—*pl.* **-ies.**
antiquar'ian (*-kwār'*), *adj.* connected with the study of antiquities.—*n.* an antiquary.
antique, *an-tēk', adj.* old: old-fashioned.—*n.* anything very old: a piece of old furniture, etc., sought by collectors.
an'tiquated, *adj.* grown old or out of fashion.
antiquity, *an-tik'wi-ti, n.* ancient times, esp. those of the ancient Greeks and Rŏmans: great age: something remaining from ancient times:—*pl.* **-ies.**
[L. *antiquus*, old.]

antirrhinum, *an-ti-rī'nȯm, n.* snapdragon.
[Gk. *anti*, mimicking, *rhīs, rhīnos*, nose.]

anti-semitic, See **anti-.**

antiseptic, *an-ti-sep'tik, n.* a substance that destroys bacteria (e.g. in a wound) or prevents their growth.—Also *adj.*
antisep'sis, *n.* antiseptic treatment.
[Gk. *anti*, against, *septikos*, rotten.]

antisocial, anti-tank. See **anti-.**

antithesis, *an-tith'i-sis, n.* the direct opposite (of): sharp contrast.
[Gk. *anti*, against, *tithenai*, to place.]

antitoxin, anti-trade. See **anti-.**

antler, *ant'lėr, n.* a deer's horn or a branch of it.
[L. *ante*, before, *oculus*, eye.]

anus, *ān'us, n.* lower opening of the alimentary canal or digestive system.
[L. *ānus*, a ring.]

anvil, *an'vil, n.* an iron block on which metals are hammered into shape.
[O.E. *anfilte.*]

anxious, *angk'shus, adj.* agitated by hope and fear: causing fear and uneasiness: eager (e.g. *anxious to please, anxious for a change*).
anx'iously, *adv.* **anx'iousness,** *n.*
anxiety, *ang-zī'i-ti, n.* anxiousness: eagerness, concern: a cause of worry:—*pl.* **anx'ieties.**
[L. *anxius*; same root as **anguish.**]

any, *en'i, adj.* and *pron.* one, no matter which.—*adv.* at all.
an'ybody, *pron.* any person.
an'yhow, *adv.* in any way: in any case: in a careless way: in an untidy state.

an'yone, *pron.* any person.
an'ything, *pron.* a thing of any kind.
an'ywhere *adv.* in any place at all.
at any rate whatever may happen or have happened.
[O.E. *ǣnig—ān*, one.]

Anzac, *an'zak*, *n.* a soldier from Australia or New Zealand (orig. First World War).
[*A*ustralian-*N*ew *Z*ealand *A*rmy *C*orps.]

aorta, *ā-ör'ta*, *n.* the great artery that carries blood from the heart to different parts of the body.
[Gk. *aortē—aeirein*, to raise up.]

apace, *à-pās'*, *adv.* swiftly.
[O.E. *on*, on, and **pace.**]

apart, *à-pärt'*, *adv.* aside: in, into pieces.
apart from, except for.
[L. *a parte*, from the part or side.]

apartheid, *à-pärt'hīd*, *n.* keeping people of different races apart by making them live in different areas, etc. [Afrikaans.]

apartment, *à-pärt'mėnt*, *n.* a room in a house: (usu. in *pl.*) a set of rooms.
[Fr. *appartement*; from It.]

apathy, *ap'à-thi*, *n.* want of feeling or interest.
apathet'ic, *adj.* **apathet'ically,** *adv.*
[Gk. *a-*, not, *pathos*, feeling.]

ape, *āp*, *n.* a monkey, esp. a large one with little or no tail: one who copies another person.—*v.t.* to imitate.
[O.E. *apa.*]

aperient, *à-pē'ri-ėnt*, *n.* a laxative medicine.
[L. *aperiens*, pr.p. of *aperīre*, to open.]

apéritif, *ä-pār-i-tēf*, *n.* an appetiser, esp. alcoholic.
[Fr.—L. *aperīre*, to open.]

aperture, *ap'ėr-tyůr*, *-chůr*, *n.* an opening.
[L. *aperire*, *apertum*, to open.]

apex, *ā'peks*, *n.* the summit, top, tip:—*pl.* **ā'pexes, apices** (*āp'i-sēz*). [L.]

aphis, *af'is*, *ā'fis*, *n.* a greenfly:—*pl.* **aphides** (*af'i-dēz*, *ā'fi-dēz*).
[Origin unknown.]

apiary, *āp'i-àr-i*, *n.* a place where bees are kept.
ap'iarist, *n.* one who keeps bees.
ap'iculture, (*-cul-chůr*), *n.* bee-keeping.
[L. *apis*, a bee, *colĕre*, *cultum*, to keep.]

apiece, *à-pēs'*, *adv.* to or for each one.

aplomb, *a-plon^g'*, *à-plom'*, *n.* self-possession, coolness.
[Fr. *aplomb*, upright position—*plomb*, plummet.]

Apocalypse, *à-pok'à-lips*, *n.* the last book of the New Testament containing the 'revelation' granted to St. John.
[Gk., revelation—*apo*, from, *kalyptein*, cover.]

apocrypha, *à-pok'rif-a*, *n.* fourteen books left out of the Protestant Old Testament.
apoc'ryphal, *adj.* of the Apocrypha: told in story but perhaps untrue.
[Gk. 'things hidden'—*kryptein*, to hide.]

apologetic. See **apology.**

apology, *à-pol'ȯ-ji*, *n.* an expression of penitence.
apol'ogise, *v.i.* to express regret for a fault.
apologetic, -al, *à-pol-o-jet'ik*, *-àl*, *adjs.* saying one is sorry: penitently acknowledging one's fault.
apologet'ically, *adv.* **-icness,** *n.*
[Gk. *apologia—apo*, from, *logos*, speech.]

apoplexy, *ap'o-pleks-i*, *n.* loss of sensation and power of motion due to bursting or stoppage of a blood-vessel.
apoplep'tic, *adj.*
[Gk. *apoplēxia—plēssein*, to strike.]

apostasy, apostacy, *à-pos'tà-si*, *n.* abandonment of one's religion, principles, or party.
apos'tate, *n.* one guilty of apostasy.
[Gk. *apo*, from, *histanai*, to stand.]

apostle, *à-pos'l*, *n.* one sent to preach the gospel, esp. one of the twelve disciples of Christ: the principal champion of a new cause.
apostolic, *à-pos-tol'ik*, *adj.*
[Gk. *apo*, away, *stellein*, to send.]

apostrophe, *à-pos'tro-fi*, *n.* a mark (') showing the omission of a letter or letters in a word (e.g. *can't* for *cannot*): also a sign of the modern Eng. possessive case (e.g. *the boy's coat*).
[Gk. *apostrophos*, turned away.]

apothecary, *à-poth'ik-àr-i*, *n.* one who dispenses drugs and medicines.
[Gk. *apothēkē*, storehouse.]

appal, *à-pöl'*, *v.t.* to terrify, dismay:—*pr.p.* **appall'ing**; *pa.p.* **appalled'.**
appall'ing, *adj.* **appall'ingly,** *adv.*
[Perh. O.Fr. *apal(l)ir*, to make pale.]

apparatus, *ap-àr-ā'tus*, also *-a'tus*, *n.* set of tools or instruments: equipment.
[L.—*ad*, to, *parātus*, prepared.]

apparel, *à-par'ėl*, *n.* clothing.—*v.t.* to dress:—*pr.p.* **appar'elling**; *pa.p.* **appar'elled.**
[O.Fr. *apareiller* (vb.)—L. *pār*, equal.]

apparent, *à-par'ėnt*, or *-pār'*, *adj.* easy to see, evident: seeming but perhaps not real (e.g. *His apparent unwillingness would disappear if we paid him enough*).
appar'ently, *adv.*
[L. *apparens*, *-entis*; root as **appear.**]

apparition, *ap-àr-ish'(ȯ)n*, *n.* an appearance, esp. of a supernatural being: a ghost.
[L. *appāritiō*; same root as **appear.**]

appeal, *à-pēl'*, *v.i.* to call upon for help, sympathy, etc. (with *to*; e.g. *G. appealed to K. for support*): to take a case one has lost to a higher court: to be pleasing to (e.g. *She appeals to me*).—Also *n.*
appeal'ing, *adj.* imploring: arousing sympathy or liking.
appeal'ingly, *adv.*
[L. *appellāre*, to call by name, appeal to.]

appear, *à-pēr'*, *v.i.* to become visible: to come into view: to arrive: to present oneself: to be published: to seem (to be).
appear'ance, *n.* the act of appearing: form, aspect, outward look: outward show (e.g. *an appearance of truth*).

See also **apparition, apparent.**
[L. *ad*, to, *pārēre*, to come forth.]
appease, *ȧ-pēz'*, *v.t.* to pacify, esp. by granting demands: to satisfy (e.g. hunger, curiosity) :—*pr.p.* **appeas'ing.**
appease'ment, *n.*
[O.Fr. *apeser*—L. *pax*, *pācis*, peace.]
appellation, *ap-il-ā'sh(ȯ)n*, *n.* a name or title.
[Same L. root as **appeal.**]
append, *ȧ-pend'*, *v.t.* to add, attach.
append'age, *n.* something appended.
appendici'tis, *n.* inflammation of the appendix in the body.
append'ix, *n.* something added, as information at the end of a book or document: a narrow tube leading from the large intestine.—*pl.* **append'ixes, append'ices.**
[L. *ad*, to, *pendĕre*, to hang.]
appertain, *ap-ėr-tān'*, *v.t.* to belong (to).
See also **appurtenance.**
[L. *ad*, to, and root of **pertain.**]
appetite, *ap'it-īt*, *n.* natural desire: desire for food: hunger (with *for*).
appetise' (*-īz'*), *v.t.* to create or increase the appetite of.
appetis'er, *n.* **appetis'ing,** *adj.*
[L. *ad*, to, *petĕre*, to seek.]
applaud, *ȧ-plöd'*, *v.t.* to praise by clapping the hands: to praise loudly.
applause', *n.* praise loudly expressed, esp. by clapping.
[L. *ad*, to, *plaudĕre*, *plausum*, to clap.]
apple, *ap'l*, *n.* the fruit of the **apple tree,** tree related to the rose.
apple of the eye, the pupil of the eye: something especially dear.
apple-pie order, complete order.
[O.E. *æppel.*]
appliance, applicant, etc. See **apply.**
apply, *ȧ-plī'*, *v.t.* to put close (to): to use in dealing with (e.g. *to apply force to the jammed door*).—*v.i.* to ask formally (for, e.g. a job): to have a bearing, come into use (e.g. *The rule does not apply in this case*): to have reference to, affect (e.g. *The order does not apply to me*) :—*pr.p.* **apply'ing** ; *pa.p.* **applied'** (*-plīd*).
appli'ance, *n.* anything applied: means, apparatus, used.
app'licable, (or *-plik'*), *adj.* that may be applied (to; e.g. *The rule is applicable to this problem*).
applicabil'ity, applicableness, *ns.*
app'licant, *n.* one who applies.
applicā'tion, *n.* act of applying: a remedy applied to the body: diligent effort or attentive study: a request (for employment, etc.).
applied science, science put to use, generally industrial.
to apply oneself, to give one's full attention and energy (to a task, to doing something).
[L. *ad*, to, *plicāre* to fold.]
appoint, *ȧ-point'*, *v.t.* to fix (e.g. *to appoint a day for the meeting*): to choose (a person) for an office or employment.
appoint'ed, *adj.* fixed: furnished (e.g. *a well-appointed house*).
appoint'ment, *n.* settlement: engagement: employment: (in *pl.*) equipment, furnishing.
[L. *ad*, to, *punctum*, point.]
apportion, *ȧ-pōr'sh(ȯ)n*, or *-pör'*, *v.t.* to divide in shares.
[L. *ad-*, to, and **portion.**]
apposite, *ap'oz-it*, *adj.* suitable, appropriate (e.g. *an apposite remark*).
app'ositely, *adv.* **app'ositeness,** *n.*
[L. *ad*, to, *pōnĕre*, *positum*, to put.]
appraise, *ȧ-prāz'*, *v.t.* to set a price on: to judge, estimate, the quality of.
apprais'al, *n.*
[Orig. used in same sense as **praise.**]
appreciate, *ȧ-prē'shi-āt*, *v.t.* to know the value of: to understand: to value highly. —*v.i.* to rise in value.
apprē'ciable, *adj.* capable of being perceived or noticed.
apprē'ciably, *adv.* to an extent that can be noticed.
appreciā'tion, *n.* estimating the value (of something): understanding (of): realisation of the good qualities (of): a talk or article describing these: an increase in value.
apprē'ciative, *adj.* showing appreciation.
[L. *ad*, to, *pretium*, price.]
apprehend, *ap-ri-hend'*, *v.t.* to arrest: to understand: to fear.
apprehen'sion, *ap-ri-hen'sh(ȯ)n*, *n.*
apprehen'sive, *adj.* anxious, timid.
[L. *ad*, to, *prehendĕre*, to lay hold of.]
apprentice, *ȧ-pren'tis*, *n.* one bound to another to learn a trade or art.—*v.t.* to bind as an apprentice.
appren'ticeship, *n.* the state of an apprentice: the term for which he is bound.
[O.Fr. *aprentis*—*aprendre*, to learn.]
apprise, *ȧ-prīz'*, *v.t.* to inform.
[Fr. *appris*, pa.p. of *apprendre*, learn, teach.]
approach, *ȧ-prōch'*, *v.t.* to draw near to: to be nearly equal to: to speak to (a person) for the purpose of getting him to do something.—*v.i.* to come near.—*n.* a coming near: a way leading (to): advance, overture (often in *pl.*).
approach'able *adj.* that can be approached: ready to listen and be friendly.
[O.Fr. *aprochier*—L. *ad*, to, *prope*, near.]
approbation *ap-ro-bā'sh(ȯ)n*, *n.* approval.
[L. *approbāre*; same root as **approve.**]
appropriate *ȧ-prō'pri-āt*, *v.t.* to take as one's own, take possession of: to set apart for a purpose.—*adj.* (*-pri-it*) suitable: proper (e.g. *Make your complaint to the appropriate authority*).
apprō'priately, *adv.* suitably.
appro'priateness, *n.*

appropriā′tion, *n.* the act of appropriating: assignment (of money) to a purpose.
[L. *ad*, to, *proprius*, one's own.]

approve, *à-prōōv′, v.t.* to speak or think well of: to give permission for, sanction.—*v.i.* (with *of*) to be satisfied with, pleased with.
approv′al, *n.* **approv′ingly,** *adv.*
on approval, on trial.
See also **approbation.**
approved school, *n.* (till 1969) a state school for young people who have broken the law.
[L. *ad*, to, *probāre*, to test—*probus*, good.]

approximate, *à-proks′im-it, adj.* very nearly correct.—*v.i.* (*-im-āt*) to come very near, e.g. in value (to).
approx′imately, *adv.*
approximā′tion, *n.* a result not exact but near enough for the purpose.
[L. *ad*, *proximus*, nearest—*prope*, near.]

appurtenance, *à-pûr′tėn-àns, n.* something which belongs, as a part, or as a right or privilege: (in *pl.*) apparatus.
[Same root as **appertain.**]

apricot, *ā′*, or *a′pri-kot, n.* an orange-coloured fruit of the plum kind.
[L. *praecoquum*, or *praecox*, early ripe.]

April, *ā′pril, n.* fourth month of the year.
April fool, the victim of a hoax on the 1st of April, All Fools' Day.
[L. *Aprīlis*.]

apron, *ā′pròn, n.* a cloth or piece of leather worn to protect the front of the dress: a short cassock worn by a bishop, etc.: anything like an apron in shape, including things made from hard materials, e.g. a hard surface on an airfield.
[*an apron—a napron*—O.Fr. *naperon*—L. *mappa*, napkin.]

apropos, *a-pro-pō′, adv., adj.* appropriate(ly) (e.g. *His entrance came, was, apropos*).—*prep.* in reference to (e.g. *My remark about air travel is apropos, apropos of, your holiday*).
[Fr. *à*, to, *propos*, purpose.]

apse, *aps, n.* an arched recess, esp. at the east end of the choir of a church.
[Gk. *hapsis*, a connexion, an arch.]

apt, *apt, adj.* liable (to): suitable, appropriate (e.g. *an apt quotation*): clever (at).
apt′ly, *adv.* **apt′ness,** *n.*
ap′titude, *n.* fitness: a talent (for).
[L. *aptus*, fit.]

aqua vitae, *a′kwa vī′tē, n.* old name for alcohol: brandy, whisky, etc.
[L. *aqua*, water, *vitae*, of life.]

aqu(a)-, *a-kw(a)-*, (as part of a word) water.
aqualung, *a′kwa-lung, n.* a light-weight diving apparatus, with compressed-air supply carried on the back.
aquamarine, *ak-wà-mà-rēn′, n.* a bluish-green precious stone, or its colour.
a′quaplane, *n.* a board on which one stands and is towed behind a motor boat.
aquarium, *à-kwā′ri-ùm, n.* a tank or tanks for keeping water animals.
aquatic, *à-kwat′ik, adj.* living, growing, or taking place (e.g. sports), in water.
aquatint, *ak′wà-tint, n.* a method of etching on copper, using *aqua fortis* (L., 'strong water'), nitric acid.
aqueduct, *ak′wi-dukt, n.* a bridge carrying water, e.g. taking a canal across a valley.
aqueous, *ā′kwi-ùs, adj.* watery.
[L. *aqua*, water (L. *marina—mare*, sea; *tingĕre, tinctum*, to colour; *ducĕre, ductum*, to lead).]

aquiline, *ak′wil-in*, or *-īn, adj.* curved like an eagle's beak. [L. *aquila*, eagle.]

Arab, *ar′àb, n.* one of the inhabitants of Arabia, etc.: an Arabian horse.—Also *adj.*
Arabian, *à-rā′bi-àn, n., adj.* (a native) of Arabia.
Arabic, *ar′à-bik, n.* the language of Arabia.
Arabic numerals, 1, 2, 3, etc.
[L. *Arabs*—Gk. *Araps*.]

arable, *ar′à-bl, adj.* fit for growing crops.
[L. *arāre*, to plough.]

arbiter, *är′bit-ėr, n.* one chosen by parties in a dispute to decide between them: person having control over (with *of*; e.g. *Who are the arbiters of women's fashions?*).
ar′bitrate, *v.i.* to act as arbitrator.
arbitrā′tion, *n.*
ar′bitrator, *n.* one who decides between parties in a dispute, arbiter.
[L. *arbiter*, witness, judge.]

arbitrary, *är′bi-tràr-i, adj.* (of a decision, etc.) not bound by rules but depending on a person's will or judgment: (of a person) tyrannical, wilful.
ar′bitrarily, *adv.* **ar′bitrariness,** *n.*
[Same root as **arbiter.**]

arbitrate, etc. See **arbiter.**

arboreal, *är-bōr′i-àl, -bör′, adj.* living in trees: adapted for this.
arboriculture, *är′bò-ri-kul-chùr, n.* forestry, growing of trees.
[L. *arbor*, a tree.]

arbour, *är′bor, n.* a seat in a garden covered by branches of trees, etc.
[L. *herba*, grass.]

arc, *ärk, n.* a part of the circumference of a circle or other curve: a luminous discharge of electricity across a gap.
arc-lamp, arc-light, *ns.* a lamp in which the source of light is an electric arc.
[L. *arcus*, a bow.]

arcade, *är-kād′, n.* a walk arched over, esp. one with shops on both sides.
[L. *arcus*, a bow; same root as **arc.**]

arch[1], *ärch, n.* a curved stone (or other) structure in which parts support each other by pressing against each other, and which can bear a load.—*v.t.* to curve, raise in an arch.
arch′way, *n.* an arched passage.
[O.Fr.—same L. root as **arc.**]

arch[2], *ärch, adj.* mischievous, roguish.
arch′ly, *adv.* **arch′ness,** *n.*
[Pfx. **arch-,** as used in *arch-rogue*, etc.]

arch-, *ärch-* (*ärk-* in some words taken straight from Greek), *pfx.* chief (often in a bad sense, e.g. *arch-enemy*).
[Gk. *archi-*; *archein*, to be first, rule.]

archaeology, *är-ki-ol'ö-ji, n.* the study of relics of times before history.
archaeolog'ical, *adj.*
archaeol'ogist, *n.*
archaic, *är-kā'ik, adj.* (esp. of language) no longer in common use.
[Gk. *archē*, beginning (*logos*, discourse).]

archangel, *ärk-ān'jėl, n.* a chief angel.
[Pfx. **arch-**.]

archbishop, *ärch-bish'ȯp, n.* a chief bishop.
archbish'opric, *n.* the see, or office, of an archbishop. [Pfx. **arch-**.]

archdeacon, *ärch-dē'kȯn, n.* the chief deacon, the ecclesiastic next under the bishop. [Pfx. **arch-**.]

archduke, *ärch-dūk', n.* the title of the former ruling princes of Austria:—*fem.* **archduch'ess** (*-duch'*).
archduch'y, archduke'dom, *ns.*
[Pfx. **arch-**.]

archer, *är'chėr, n.* one who shoots with a bow and arrows.
ar'chery, *n.* shooting with the bow.
[L. *arcus*, bow; root as **arc, arch.**]

archipelago, *är-ki-pel'ȧ-gō, n.* a group of islands:—*pl.* **archipel'ago(e)s.**
[It.—Gk. *archi-*, chief, *pelagos*, sea; the Aegean, the 'chief sea' of the Greeks, has many islands.]

architect, *är'ki-tekt, n.* one who designs buildings: one who creates.
architecture, *är-ki-tek'chùr, n.* the art of building: a style of building (e.g. *modern architecture*).
architec'tural, *adj.*
[Gk. *archi-*, chief, *tecton*, builder.]

archives, *är'kīvz, n. pl.* a place in which government, or other, records, esp. documents, are kept: public records.
arch'ivist (*-iv-*), *n.* a keeper of archives.
[Gk. *archē*, beginning, power, government.]

Arctic, *ärk'tik, adj.* of the north pole or north polar regions: very cold.
Arctic Circle, imaginary circle round north pole at distance of about 23½ degrees.
[Gk. *arktos*, a bear.]

ardent, *är'dėnt, adj.* fiery, passionate.
ar'dently, *adv.*
ar'dour, ar'dency, ar'dentness, *ns.* warmth of passion or feeling: eagerness.
[L. *ardens*—*ardēre*, to burn.]

arduous, *är'dū-ùs, adj.* requiring much hard work, laborious.
ar'duously, *adv.* **ar'duousness,** *n.*
[L. *arduus*, high, steep.]

are[1], *är, n.* unit of French land measure.

are[2]. See **be.**

area, *ā'ri-ȧ, n.* a surface or an enclosed space: sunken space round the basement of a building: extent, range.
[L. *ārea.*]

arena, *ȧ-rē'nȧ, n.* a sanded space in an ancient amphitheatre where gladiators, etc., fought: a place of action.
[L. *arēna*, sand.]

argosy, *är'gȯ-si, n.* a large merchant vessel richly laden:—*pl.* **-ies.**
[Prob. *Ragusa* on the Adriatic.]

argot, *är'got, n.* slang, originally that of thieves and vagabonds. [Fr.]

argue, *är'gū, v.i., v.t.* to debate, dispute.—*v.t.* to prove, or try to prove, by reasoning (that): to be evidence of, imply: to persuade (*into, out of*; e.g. *Try to argue him out of his decision to go*):—*pr.p.* **ar'gūing**; *pa.p.* **argued** (*är'gūd*).
ar'guable, *adj.* capable of being argued (the context shows whether for or against; e.g. *It is arguable that he would have been better to go*; *the wisdom of this decision is arguable.*)
ar'gument, *n.* a discussion, dispute: reason, or reasoning, supporting (or against) an opinion, etc. (e.g. *an argument for, in favour of, communism*): an outline of the subject (of e.g. a book).
argumen'tative, *adj.* arguing: fond of arguing.
[L. *arguĕre*, to prove.]

aria, *ä'ri-ȧ, n.* an air, in a cantata, oratorio, or opera, for one voice.
[It.—L. root of **air.**]

arid, *ar'id, adj.* dry, parched: (of e.g. a discussion) fruitless, without result.
arid'ity, ar'idness, *ns.*
[L. *āridus.*]

aright, *ȧ-rīt', adv.* in a right way.

arise, *ȧ-rīz', v.i.* to rise up: to come into being (e.g. *if the need, question, etc; arises*): to spring (from):—*pa.t.* **arose'**; *pa.p.* **arisen** (*ȧ-riz'n*).
[O.E. *ārisan*; same root as **rise.**]

aristocracy, *ar-is-tok'rȧs-i, n.* government by the nobility: the upper classes generally: persons of great distinction.
aristocrat, *ar'is-to-krat*, or *ar-is'-, n.* a member of the aristocracy.
aristocrat'ic, *adj.* **-crat'ically,** *adv.*
[Gk. *aristos*, best, *kratos*, power.]

arithmetic, *ȧ-rith'met-ik, n.* the art of counting and reckoning by figures.
arithmet'ical, *adj.*
arithmet'ically, *adv.*
arithmetician (*-mė-tish'ȧn*), *n.* one skilled in arithmetic.
[Gk. *arithmos*, number.]

ark, *ärk, n.* (*Bible*) the sacred chest in which the Tables of the Law were kept (Exodus xxv. 10-16): the vessel in which Noah escaped the Flood (Genesis vi.-viii.)
[L. *arca*, a chest—*arcēre*, to guard.]

arm[1], *ärm, n.* the part of the body between the shoulder and the hand: anything like this (e.g. an inlet of the sea, a rail at the side of a chair): power (e.g. *the arm of the law*).
arm'chair, *n.* a chair with arms or rests at each side.—*adj.* with no practical

experience (e.g. *an armchair critic of football*).

arm'ful, *n.* as much as the arms can hold.

arm'let, *n.* a band round the arm.

arm'pit, *n.* the hollow under the arm at the shoulder.

with open arms, with hearty welcome.

[O.E.; conn, L. *armus*, shoulder-joint.]

arm², *ärm*, *n.* a weapon: a branch of a military service: (in *pl.*) weapons.—*v.t.* to supply with arms.—*v.i.* to take arms, make ready for war.

armament, *är'mȧ-mėnt*, *n.* equipment for war, esp. the guns of a ship, aeroplane, tank.

armed (*ärmd*), *adj.* carrying a gun: supplied with weapons.

armour, *är'mȯr*, *n.* (long ago) protective clothing of metal: defensive steel- or iron-plating: vehicles, esp. tanks, with armour and guns, and the forces that fight in them.

ar'moured, *adj.* protected by armour: fought by armoured vehicles (e.g. *an armoured battle*).

ar'mourer, *n.* a maker or repairer of, or one who has charge of, armour.

ar'moury, *n.* the place in which arms are made or kept.

army, *är'mi*, *n.* large body of men armed for war: a body of men banded together in a special cause (e.g. *Salvation Army*): a great number:—*pl.* **ar'mies.**

ar'mour-plat'ed, *adj.* strengthened with plates of specially hardened steel.

to lay down arms, to surrender.

up in arms, armed for battle: ready for hot argument, defiant.

[L. *arma*; conn. with **arm** (1).]

armada, *är-mä'dȧ, är-mā'dȧ*, *n.* a fleet of armed ships.

[Sp.—L. *armāre*, to arm.]

armadillo, *är-mȧ-dil'ō*, *n.* a small American animal armed with bony plates:—*pl.* **armadill'os.**

[Sp.—*armado*, armed.]

armament. See **arm** (2).

armistice, *är'mis-tis*, *n.* a ceasing of hostilities, a truce.

[L. *arma*, arms, *sistĕre*, to stop.]

armorial, *är-mōr'i-ȧl, -mör'*, *adj.* used in the phrase **armorial bearings,** the design in a coat of arms.

[O.Fr. *armoirie*, heraldry—L. *arma*, arms.]

armour, army, etc. See **arm** (2).

aroma, *ȧ-rō'mȧ*, *n.* sweet smell.

aromat'ic, *adj.* fragrant: spicy.

[Gk. *arōma*, spice.]

arose. See **arise.**

around, *ȧ-rownd'*, *prep.* on all sides of: (*U.S.*) round about: about.—*adv.* on every side: in a circle: (*U.S.*) somewhere near.

arouse, *ȧ-rowz'*, *v.t.* to rouse, waken into activity (e.g. *to arouse suspicion*).

[Same root as **rouse.**]

arpeggio, *är-pej'i-ō*, *n.* a chord of which the notes are given, not together, but in rapid succession.

[It. *arpeggiare*, to play upon the harp.]

arraign, *ȧ-rān'*, *v.t.* to put (a prisoner) on trial: to accuse publicly.

arraign'ment, *n.*

[L. *ad*, to, *ratiō, -ōnis*, reason.]

arrange, *ȧ-rānj'*, *v.t.* to put in order: to settle: (*music*) to adapt (a composition) for performance by instruments or voices different from those for which it was orig. written.—*v.i.* to come to an agreement (with a person).

arrange'ment, *n.* setting in order: settlement: plan: a piece of music arranged as described above.

[O.Fr. *rangier, rengier—rang*, rank.]

arrant, *ar'ȧnt*, *adj.* downright (e.g. *arrant nonsense*): notorious (e.g. *arrant thief*).

[Same root as **errant.**]

arras, *ar'ȧs*, *n.* tapestry hung round the walls of rooms.

[From *Arras* in Northern France.]

array, *ȧ-rā'*, *n.* order: dress.—*v.t.* to dress, adorn, or equip.

[O.Fr. *arei*; conn. with **ready.**]

arrear, *ȧ-rēr'*, *n.* something that remains unpaid or undone (usu. in *pl.*).

in arrears, not up to date (e.g. in payments).

[L. *ad*, *retro*, back, behind.]

arrest, *ȧ-rest'*, *v.t.* to stop: to seize by legal authority: to catch the attention of.—*n.* stoppage: seizure by warrant.

[L. *ad*, *restāre*, to stand still.]

arrive, *ȧ-rīv'*, *v.i.* to reach a destination: to come to (e.g. a conclusion; with *at*): (*coll.*) to obtain success.

arriv'al, *n.* act of arriving: person or thing that arrives.

[L. *ad*, to, *rīpa*, a bank.]

arrogance, *ar'ȯ-gȧns*, *n.* a great show of superiority or importance.

arr'ogant, *adj.* overbearing: haughty.

[L. *ad*, to, *rogāre*, to ask, to claim.]

arrow, *ar'ō*, *n.* a straight, pointed weapon, made to be shot from a bow: any arrow-shaped object.

[O.E. *arwe*; conn. L. *arcus*, bow.]

arrowroot, *ar'ō-rōōt*, *n.* a starchy food obtained from roots of certain tropical plants.

[From its use by S. American Indians as an antidote to arrow-poisoning.]

arsenal, *är'si-nȧl*, *n.* a government-owned place where weapons and ammunition are stored or manufactured.

[Arabic *dār aççinā'ah*, workshop.]

arsenic, *är's(e-)nik*, *n.* an element metallic grey in colour: a highly poisonous compound of this element and oxygen (also **white arsenic**).

[Gk. *arsenikon*, a sulphide of arsenic.]

arson, *är'sȯn*, *n.* the crime of wilfully setting on fire (e.g. a house).

[L. *ardēre*, *arsum*, to burn.]

art¹. See **be.**

art[2], *ärt, n* human skill (e.g. *produced by art and not by nature*): skill (e.g. *the art of making a little go a long way*): taste and skill (e.g. *the art of the painter in creating this effect*): painting, sculpture, etc.: rules, methods (e.g. *the art of war*): (in *pl.*) used of certain university subjects: craft, cunning.
art'ful, *adj.* cunning: showing art.
art'fully, *adv.* **art'fulness,** *n.*
art'less, *adj.* simple: without cunning.
art'lessly, *adv.* **art'lessness,** *n.*
artist, *är'tist, n.* one who practises an art, esp. painting, sculpture, etc.
artis'tic, *adj.* (of person) having gifts of an artist: showing good taste.
artis'tically, *adv.*
ar'tistry, *n.* artistic skill.
See also **artifice, artisan.**
[L. *ars, artis*, art.]

artery, *är'tėr-i, n.* a tube or vessel that carries blood away from the heart: any main route of communication (e.g. a long-distance road):—*pl.* **-ies.**
arterial, *är-tē'r'i-àl, adj.* of, or like, an artery.
[Gk. *artēria*, prob. orig. the windpipe.]

artesian, *är-tē'zhàn, -zi-àn, adj.* of a type of well in which water rises in a borehole by internal pressure.
[*Artois* (L. *Artesium*) in France.]

arthritis, *är-thri'tis, n.* inflammation of a joint.
arthritic (*-thrit'ik*), *adj.*
[Gk. *arthron*, a joint.]

artichoke, *är'ti-chōk, n.* a thistle-like plant with large scaly heads, parts of which can be eaten.
Jerusalem artichoke, a kind of sunflower having potato-like tubers (Jerusalem being for It. *girasole*, sunflower).
[Through It. from Arabic.]

article, *är'ti-kl, n.* a separate object: (in *pl.*) an agreement made up of clauses (e.g. *articles of apprenticeship*, etc.): a section of a document: a literary composition in a newspaper, etc., dealing with a particular subject: name given in grammar to *the* (**definite article**) and *a* or *an* (**indefinite article**).—*v.t.* to bind by articles.
[L. *articulus*, a little joint.]

articulate, *är-tik'ū-lāt, v.t.* to pronounce in distinct syllables: to joint.—*v.i.* to speak distinctly.—*adj.* (*-it*) able to express one's thoughts clearly.
artic'ulated, *adj.* jointed: in connected sections, as **articulated truck,** etc., a vehicle with detachable cab which, when attached, can move at an angle to the rest.
artic'ulately, *adv.* **artic'ulateness,** *n.*
articulā'tion, *n.* a joining of bones: (distinct) utterance.
[L. *articulāre*; same root as **article.**]

artifice, *är'ti-fis, n.* a device: a trick: skill: trickery.
artificer (*är-tif'is-ėr*), *n.* a workman: an inventor.
artificial, *är-ti-fish'àl, adj.* made by art: (of a person) not natural in manner.
artificial'ity, *n.* **artific'ially,** *adv.*
[L. *ars, artis*, art, *facĕre*, to make.]

artillery, *är-til'ėr-i, n.* big guns: the soldiers who manage them.
[O.Fr. *artillerie—artiller*, to arm.]

artisan, *är-ti-zan'*, or *är'-, n.* a skilled workman.
[L. *ars, artis*, art.]

artist, artistic, etc. See **art** (2).

artiste, *är-tēst', n.* a public performer. [Fr.]

arum lily, *ā'rùm lil'i, n.* a tall, white decorative house plant.
[Gk. *aron.*]

Aryan, *ā'ri-àn, är'yàn, adj.* of a large group of peoples of Europe and Asia (incl. Germans, British, French, Italians, many Indians, ancient Persians, etc.) whose languages can be shown to have developed from one parent language of very long ago: (as used in Hitler's Germany) non-Jewish.—Also *n.*
[L. *ariānus*, of Ariana (part of Persia).]

as, *az, adv.* and *conj.* (showing comparison or result) in phrases such as: *as good as new, as soon as I can, as much as to say, so good as to do* (the first *as* in each case being *adv.*, the second *conj.*).
[*all-so*—O.E. *all-swa*, wholly so.]

asbestos, *az-bes'tos, n.* a mineral that will not burn, fibrous and capable of being woven.
[Gk. *a-*, not, *sbestos—sbennunai*, to quench.]

ascend, *à-send', v.i.* to climb up: to rise.—*v.t.* to go up: to mount.
ascend'ancy, -ency, *n.* control (over).
ascend'ant, -ent, *adj.* rising.
ascension, *à-sen'sh(ö)n, n.* a rising up.
ascent', *n.* act, or way, of ascending: rise: slope, gradient.
Ascension day, festival held on Holy Thursday, ten days before Whitsunday, commemorating Christ's ascent to heaven.
in the ascendant, supreme, in a controlling position.
[L. *ad*, to, *scandĕre, scansum*, to climb.]

ascertain, *as-ėr-tān', v.t.* to find out: to make certain.
ascertain'able, *adj.* **ascertain'ment,** *n.*
[O.Fr. *acertener*; same root as **certain.**]

ascetic, *à-set'ik, n.* one who endures severe bodily hardships, or denies himself much, esp. as a religious discipline.—Also *adj.*
ascet'ically, *adv.* **ascet'icism,** *n.*
[Gk. *askeein*, to work, exercise.]

ascribe, *à-skrīb', v.i.* to attribute, consider as belonging (to; e.g. *The play was wrongly ascribed to Shakespeare*).
ascrib'able (*-skrīb'*), *adj.*
ascrip'tion (*-skrip'*), *n.* act of ascribing.
[L. *ad*, to, *scrībĕre*, to write.]

Asdic, *as'dik, n.* an apparatus for locating

submarines, etc., by means of ultrasonic waves echoed back from them.
[*A*llied *S*ubmarine *D*etection *I*nvestigation *C*ommittee.]

asepsis, *a-sep'sis, n.* freedom in surgery from bacteria that cause wounds to become septic, by the use of sterilised dressings and instruments.
asep'tic, *adj.* **asep'tically,** *adv.*
[Gk. *a-*, not, *sēpein*, to cause to decay.]

asexual, *a-seks'ū-ȧl, adj.* without sex: not depending on sex.
[Gk. *a-*, not, and **sexual.**]

ash[1], *ash, n.* a timber tree with silvery bark: its hard white wood.
[O.E. *æsc.*]

ash[2], *ash, n.* (often in *pl.*) the dust of anything burnt: (in *pl.*) the remains of the human body, esp. when burnt: a sign of repentance or sorrow.
ash'en, ashy, *adjs.*
Ash Wednesday, the first day of Lent.
the Ashes, the ashes of English cricket, which, according to a mock 'In Memoriam' notice in the *Sporting Times* in 1882, the victorious Australians carried home with them.
[O.E. *asce*—Old Norse *aska.*]

ashamed, *ȧ-shāmd', adj.* (in predicate; not used before noun) feeling shame.
[From old verb *ashame*; root of **shame.**]

ashore, *ȧ-shōr', -shör', adv.* on shore.

Asiatic, *ā-zhi-at'ik, āsh-i-at'ik, adj.* belonging to *Asia.*—*n.* a native of *Asia.*—Also **Asian** (*āzh'yȧn*, or *āsh'i-ȧn*).

aside, *ȧ-sid', adv.* on or to one side: privately.—*n.* words spoken by an actor which the other persons on the stage are supposed not to hear.

asinine, *as'in-īn, adj.* stupid.
asininity, *as-in-in'i-ti, n.*
[L. *asinus*, ass.]

ask, *âsk, v.t.* to request, beg: to put a question to: to inquire what is (e.g. *to ask the time, the way*): to invite.—*v.i.* to make request or inquiry (for, about).
[O.E. *āscian, ācsian.*].

askance, *ȧ-skans', adv.* sideways.
to eye, look at, or view, askance, to look at with suspicion. [Orig. uncertain.]

askew, *ȧ-skū', adv.* and *adj.* (in predicate; not used before noun) to one side.
[Prob. conn. with **skew.**]

aslant, *ȧ-slânt', adv.* and *adj.* (in predicate; not used before noun) slanting(ly).

asleep, *ȧ-slēp', adv.* and *adj.* (in predicate; not used before noun) sleeping: dead: (of limbs) numbed.

asp, *asp, n.* a small poisonous snake.
[Gk. *aspis.*]

asparagus, *as-par'ȧ-gȧs, n.* a plant of which the young shoots are a table delicacy.
[Gk. *asparagos.*]

aspect, *as'pekt, n.* look: appearance to the mind: view, point of view: direction of facing.
[L. *ad*, to, *specĕre*, to look.]

aspen, *as'pėn, n.* the trembling poplar.
[O.E. *æspe.*]

asperity, *as-per'i-ti, n.* harshness, sharpness (e.g. of manner): bitter coldness (of weather).
[L. *asper*, rough.]

aspersion, *as-pėr'sh(ȯ)n, n.* slander, damaging criticism (e.g. *to cast aspersions on someone*).
[L. *ad*, to, *spargĕre, sparsum*, to sprinkle.]

asphalt, *as'fölt, -falt, n.* a dark, hard substance, used for paving, road-making, roofing, etc.
[Gk. *asphaltos* (from an Eastern word).]

asphyxia, *as-fiks'i-ȧ, n.* suffocation: suspended animation due to lack of oxygen in the blood.
asphyx'iate, *v.t.* to suffocate.
asphyxiā'tion, *n.*
[Gk. *a-*, not, *sphyxis*, the pulse.]

aspic, *as'pik, n.* a savoury meat jelly containing fish, game, etc. [Fr.]

aspidistra, *as-pi-dis'trȧ, n.* a plant with large thick leaves, often grown in a pot.
[Perh. Gk. *aspis, aspidis*, a shield.]

aspirant. See **aspire.**

aspirate, *as'pir-it, n.* the sound of the letter *h.*—*v.t.* (*-āt*) to pronounce with an *h*, as in *house.*
[Same root as **aspire.**]

aspire, *ȧs-pīr', v.i.* (with *to* or *after*) to desire eagerly: to have high aims.
aspirant, *as-pīr'ȧnt, as'pir-ȧnt, n.* one who aspires, a candidate.
aspirā'tion, *n.* ambition: eager desire.
[L. *ad*, to, *spīrāre, -ātum*, to breathe.]

aspirin, *as'pir-in, n.* a sedative drug.
[Orig. a trademark.]

ass, *as, n.* a small horse-like animal, a donkey: a stupid person.
[O.E. *assa*—L. *asinus.*]

assagai. Same as **assegai.**

assail, *ȧ-sāl', v.t.* to attack suddenly, or again and again, with force, energy, arguments, etc.
assail'ant, *n.* one who attacks.
[L. *ad*, upon, *salīre*, to leap.]

assassin, *as-as'in, n.* (long ago) one of a military and religious order who carried out secret murders: one who assassinates.
assass'inate, *v.t.* to murder (esp. a politically important person) by violence.
assassinā'tion, *n.*
[Arabic *hashshāshīn*, 'hashish-eaters'; the assassins drugged themselves with hashish before committing their crimes.]

assault, *ȧ-sölt', n.* an attack, esp. a sudden one.—*v.t.* to make an assault on.
[L. *ad*, on, *saltus*, a leap; as **assail.**]

assay, *ȧ-sā', v.t.* to find the proportion of a metal in (an ore or alloy):—Also *n.*
[Fr. *assayer*; same root as **essay.**]

assegai, *as'ė-gi, n.* spear used by tribes of southern Africa.
[Arabic *azzaghāyah.*]

assemble, *ȧ-sem'bl, v.t.* to call together:

to collect: to put together the parts of (a machine).—*v.i.* to meet together.
assem′blage, *n.* a collection of persons or things.
assem′bly, *n.* the act of assembling: a gathering of persons for a particular purpose:—*pl.* **assem′blies.**
assembly line, the machines and workers necessary for the manufacture of an article, arranged in such a way that each article can follow the one before through all the necessary processes without a break.
[Fr. *assembler*—L. *ad*, to, *similis*, like.]

assent, *ȧ-sent′*, *v.i.* to agree (to).—*n.* saying 'yes', agreement.
[L. *ad*, to, *sentīre*, to think.]

assert, *ȧ-sėrt′*, *v.t.* to declare strongly: to defend (e.g. one's right; *He managed to assert his right to be present at the discussion*).
assertion, *ȧ-sėr′sh(ȯ)n*, *n.* act of asserting: a firm statement.
asser′tive, *adj.* inclined to make assertions, or to assert oneself.
to assert oneself, to refuse to have oneself or one's opinions ignored.
[L. *asserĕre*, to affirm, declare.]

assess, *ȧ-ses′*, *v.t.* to value for taxation: to estimate the value, power, etc., of (e.g. *to assess one's chances, one's opponent.*)
assess′ment, *n.*
assess′or, *n.* an assistant or adviser to a judge or magistrate: one who assesses taxes.
[L. *ad*, to, at, *sedēre*, *sessum*, to sit.]

assets, *as′ets*, *n. pl.* (orig. *sing.*) the property of a deceased person, or a debtor, or a merchant, etc.
asset (*false sing.*), an item of property: something advantageous (e.g. *His charming voice is an asset*).
[O.Fr. *asez*, enough—L. *ad*, *satis*, enough.]

asseverate, *ȧ-sev′ėr-āt*, *v.t.* to declare solemnly.
asseverā′tion, *n.*
[L. *ad*, to, *sevērus*, serious.]

assiduity, *as-i-dū′i-ti*, *n.* constant attention and effort.
assid′uous, *adj.* diligent: diligent (in).
assid′uously, *adv.* **assid′uousness,** *n.*
[L. *assiduitās*—*assiduus*, sitting close.]

assign, *ȧ-sīn′*, *v.t.* to allot, give (e.g. *I assign to you the task of making tea*; *I assign the armchair to Mary*): to fix, appoint (a place or time): to ascribe.
assignation, *ȧ-sig-nā′sh(ȯ)n*, *n.* an appointment to meet, esp. of lovers.
assignee, *as-in-ē′*, or *-sīn-*, *n.* one to whom a right or property is assigned.
assignment (*-sīn′*), *n.* act of assigning: (orig. *U.S.*) a task allotted.
[L. *ad*, to, *signum*, a mark or sign.]

assimilate, *ȧ-sim′il-āt*, *v.t.* to make similar (to): (of plants and animals) to digest (food): to take in (knowledge).
assimilā′tion, *n.*
[L. *ad*, to, *similis*, like.]

assist, *ȧ-sist′*, *v.t.* to help.—*v.i.* to be present (at a ceremony).
assis′tance, *n.*
assis′tant, *adj.* helping.—*n.* a helper, esp. one appointed to help.
[L. *ad*, to, *sedēre*, to sit.]

assize, *ȧ-sīz′*, *n.* (*Scot.*) a trial by jury: (in *pl.*) sittings of a court in English counties at which cases are tried by judges on circuit (i.e. travelling round) and a jury.
[O.Fr. *assise*; same root as **assist.**]

associate, *ȧ-sō′shi-āt*, *v.t.* to join in friendship or partnership: to connect in thought.—*v.i.* to keep company (with): to unite.—*adj.* allied or connected.—*n.* a companion, friend, partner, or ally.
associā′tion (*-si-* or *-shi-*), *n.* a society: union or combination: the game played under the rules of the Football Association, 'soccer'.
[L. *ad*, to, *socius*, a companion.]

assort, *ȧ-sört′*, *v.t.* to separate into classes or kinds.
assort′ed, *adj.* mixed in kind, miscellaneous.
assort′ment, *n.* a variety, mixture.
[L. *ad*, to, *sors*, *sortis*, a lot, fate.]

assuage, *ȧ-swāj′*, *v.t.* to soothe, ease (e.g. pain): to satisfy (e.g. hunger).
[L. *ad*, to, *suāvis*, mild.]

assume, *ȧ-sūm′*, *-sōōm′*, *v.t.* to put on (e.g. a disguise): to take upon oneself (e.g. responsibility): to take for granted, suppose to be a fact.
assum′ed, *adj.* pretended: taken for granted.
assum′ing, *adj.* taking too much upon oneself, forward, arrogant.
assumption, *ȧ-sum(p)′sh(ȯ)n*, *n.* act of assuming: something taken for granted.
Assumption of the Virgin, a church festival, 15th of August: the R.C. dogma that after death the soul and body of Mary were taken up to heaven.
[L. *ad*, to, *sumĕre*, *sumptum*, to take.]

assure, *ȧ-shōōr′*, *v.t.* to tell positively (that): to give (a person) confidence: to ensure.
assur′ance *n.* feeling of certainty: confidence: a solemn declaration or promise: insurance (in the case of *life assurance* only).
assured′, *adj.* certain: confident.
assur′edly (*-id-li*), *adv.* certainly.
[L. *ad*, to, *sēcūrus*, safe.]

aster, *as′tėr*, *n.* a perennial plant with flowers like stars, the Michaelmas daisy: also (*China aster*) a related summer annual.
as′teroid, *n.* one of a large number of small planets, most of which move in orbits between Mars and Jupiter.
as′terisk, *n.* a star-shaped mark, used in printing to point out a note, show the omission of words, etc., thus *.

See also **astro-**.
[Gk. *astēr*, a star.]
astern, *ȧ-stėrn′*, *adv.* towards the stern or hinder part of a ship.
asteroid. See **aster.**
asthma, *as(th)′mȧ*, *n.* a disorder of the organs of breathing, with painful gasping, coughing, etc.
asthmat′ic, *adj.* **asthmat′ically,** *adv.*
[Gk.; from *aazein*, to breathe hard.]
astigmatism, *ȧ-stig′mȧ-tizm*, *n.* a defect of the eye, in which rays of light coming from one point are not brought (as they should be) to focus at *one* point.
[Gk. *a-*, not, *stigma*, *-atos*, a point.]
astir, *ȧ-stėr′*, *adv.*, *adj.* on the move, stirring: out of bed.
astonish, *ȧ-ston′ish*, *v.t.* to strike with surprise or wonder, to amaze.
aston′ishing, *adj.* **aston′ishment,** *n.*
[L. *ex*, out, *tonāre*, to thunder.]
astound, *ȧ-stownd′*, *v.t.* to amaze, astonish, utterly.
[From same root as **astonish.**]
astrakhan, *as-trȧ-kan′*, *n.* lambskin with curled wool: fabric in imitation of it.
[From *Astrakhan* on the Caspian Sea.]
astray, *ȧ-strā′*, *adv.* or *adj.* (in predicate; not used before noun) out of the right way, straying.
astride, *ȧ-strīd′*, *prep.* with legs on each side of.—*adv.* with legs on each side: with legs apart.
[O.E. *on*, on, and **stride** (*n.*).]
astringent, *ȧ-strin′jėnt*, *adj.* drawing together body tissues—e.g. so as to stop bleeding: (of manner, etc.) stern, severe.
astrin′gency, *n.* **astrin′gently,** *adv.*
[L. *ad*, to, *stringĕre*, to bind.]
astro-, *as-tro-*, (as part of word) star.
astrology, *ȧs-trol′ȯ-ji*, *n.* the study of the stars and their supposed influence on the lives of human beings.
astrol′oger, *n.* **astrolog′ical,** *adj.*
astronomy, *ȧs-tron′ȯ-mi*, *n.* study of the stars and heavenly bodies (a later and more scientific study than astrology).
astron′omer, *n.*
astronom′ical, *adj.* of, concerned with, astronomy: (of numbers) very large.
astronom′ically, *adv.*
astronaut, *as′trō-nöt*, *n.* one who travels in space.
astronaut′ical, *adj.*
astronaut′ics, *n.* the science of travel in space.
[Gk. *astron* (also *astēr*), star (*logos*, discourse; *nomos*, law; *nautēs*, sailor).]
astute, *ȧs-tūt′*, *adj.* shrewd: cunning.
astute′ly, *adv.* **astute′ness,** *n.*
[L. *astūtus*—*astus*, craft.]
asunder, *ȧ-sun′dėr*, *adv.* into parts.
[O.E. *on*, on, and **sunder.**]
asylum, *ȧ-sīl′ŭm*, *n.* a place of refuge, esp. for fugitives: an institution for the care of the unfortunate, esp. the insane.
[Gk. *a-*, not, *sylē*, right of seizure.]
asymmetrical, *a-si-met′ri-kȧl*, *adj.* not symmetrical. [Gk. *a-*, not.]
at, *at*, *prep.* expressing exact position in space, time, etc.
[O.E. *æt*; conn. with L. *ad.*]
ate. See **eat.**
atheism, *ā′thi-izm*, *n.* disbelief in the existence of God.
a′theist, *n.* one who disbelieves in God.
atheist′ic(al), *adjs.* **atheist′ically,** *adv.*
[Gk. *a-*, not, *theos*, God.]
athlete, *ath′lēt*, *n.* a competitor in contests of speed, strength, agility, etc.
athlet′ic (*-let′*), *adj.* of athletics: strong, vigorous.
athlet′ics (*-let′*), *n. pl.* sports such as running, jumping, or others that show physical strength and skill.
athlete's foot, a contagious disease of the foot caused by a fungus.
[Gk. *athlos* (also *athlon*), a contest.]
athwart, *ȧ-thwört′*, *prep.* across.
[O.E. *on*, on, and **thwart.**]
Atlantic, *at-lan′tik*, *adj.* of the Atlantic Ocean.—*n.* the ocean between Europe, Africa, and America.
[Mt. *Atlas*, in N.W. Africa; named after giant (see **atlas**).]
atlas, *at′lȧs*, *n.* a book of maps.
[Gk. *Atlas*, the giant who bore heaven on his shoulders, whose figure used to be shown on atlases.]
atmosphere, *at′mos-fēr*, *n.* the gases that surround the earth or any of the heavenly bodies: any surrounding feeling or influence.
atmospher′ic (*-fer′*), *adj.*
atmospher′ics. *n. pl.* in wireless reception, disturbing signals caused by atmospheric conditions.
[Gk. *atmos*, air, *sphaira*, sphere.]
atoll, *a′tol*, *ȧ-tol′*, *n.* an island formed of a belt of coral enclosing a lagoon.
[Name in Maldive Islands.]
atom, *at′ȯm*, *n.* the smallest part of an element that can take part in a chemical change, once thought to be indivisible, but now known to be composed of still smaller particles (electrons, etc.): anything very small (e.g. *There is not an atom of truth in that story*).—Also *adj.*
atom′ic, *adj.* of an atom: driven by atomic power (e.g. *atomic submarine*).
atom(ic) bomb, a bomb in which the explosion is caused by the splitting of nuclei of atoms of certain elements, e.g. uranium.
atomic energy, nuclear energy (see **nucleus**).
atomic pile (see **pile**).
atomic power, power for making electricity, etc., obtained by splitting atomic nuclei.
[Gk. *atomos*—*a-*, not, *temnein*, to cut.]
atonal, *ȧ-tōn′ȧl*, *adj.* not in any key.
atonal′ity (*-ton-al′*), *n.*
[Gk. *a-*, not, *tonos*; same root as **tone.**]

atone, *ȧ-tōn'*, *v.i.* to make amends (for): to make up (for).
atone'ment, *n.* amends: reparation: reconciliation of God and man.
[**at, one** (as if to make at one).]

atrocious, *ȧ-trō'shus, adj.* extremely cruel or wicked.
atro'ciously, *adv.* **atro'ciousness,** *n.*
atroc'ity, *n.* an atrocious act: atrociousness:—*pl.* **atroc'ities.**
[L. *ātrox, ātrocis,* cruel—*āter,* black.]

atrophy, *at'rȯf-i, n.* wasting away of an organ of the body.—Also *v.t.* and *v.i.*
[Gk. *a-,* without, *trophē,* nourishment.]

attach, *ȧ-tach', v.t.* to fasten (to something): to join (oneself to; e.g. *He attached himself to our party*): to add (e.g. *to attach a condition to a promise*): to consider as having (importance; e.g. *I do not attach much importance to his opinion*).
attached', *adj.* fastened, joined, added (to): fond of (with *to*).
attach'ment, *n.* something attached, e.g. an extra part to enable a machine to do special work: a feeling or tie of affection: legal seizure (of goods).
[O.Fr. *atachier.*]

attaché, *ȧ-tash'ā, n.* a junior member of an ambassador's suite.
attaché-case, *n.* a rectangular leather hand case, e.g. for documents.
[Fr., attached.]

attack, *ȧ-tak', v.t.* to fall upon, assault: to speak or write against.—*n.* an assault: severe criticism: a fit (of illness).
[Fr. *attaquer*; conn. with **attach.**]

attain, *ȧ-tān', v.t.* to reach or gain by effort: to arrive at.—*v.i.* (with *to*) to come to or arrive at (aim, possession, state).
attain'able, *adj.*
attain'ment, *n.* act of attaining: the thing attained: an accomplishment in learning (e.g. *a man of great attainments*).
[Through Fr.—L. *ad,* to, *tangĕre,* touch.]

attainder, *ȧ-tān'dėr, n.* loss of civil rights because of treason.
[Same root as **attain.**]

attempt, *ȧ-tem(p)t', v.t.* to try.—*n.* an endeavour, effort: an attack (e.g. *an attempt on one's life*).
[L. *ad,* to, *temptāre, tentāre,* to try.]

attend, *ȧ-tend', v.t.* to wait on or accompany (an important person): to be present at: to wait for.—*v.i.* to give heed, listen.
atten'dance, *n.* act of attending: presence: the number of persons attending.
atten'dant, *adj.* accompanying (e.g. *attendant circumstances,* circumstances at the time of an action, event).—*n.* one who attends, a servant.
attention, *ȧ-ten'sh(ȯ)n, n.* notice, heed (as in *to attract, call, pay, give, attention*): steady application of the mind: care: erect position with hands by the sides and heels together.
atten'tive, *adj.* listening or observing: courteous.
atten'tively, *adv.* **atten'tiveness,** *n.*
[L. *ad,* to, *tendĕre,* to stretch.]

attest, *ȧ-test', v.t.* to testify or bear witness to, e.g. by signature.
attestā'tion, *n.*
[L. *ad,* to, *testis,* a witness.]

attic, *at'ik, n.* a room in the roof of a house.
[Gk. *Attikos,* of Athens.]

attire, *ȧ-tīr', v.t.* to dress.—*n.* clothing.
[O.Fr. *atirer,* put in order—*à tire,* in a row.]

attitude, *at'i-tūd, n.* posture: position: state of thought or feeling (e.g. *What is your attitude to jazz?*)
to strike an attitude, to assume a pose, esp. an affected one.
[Late L. *aptitūdō—aptus,* fit.]

attorney, *ȧ-tûr'ni, n.* one who has legal power to act for another:—*pl.* **attor'neys.**
Attorney General, the chief law officer of the state in England.
district attorney, *n.* (*U.S.*) a public prosecutor for a district.
[Late L. *atornāre,* to hand over business to another; same root as **turn.**]

attract, *ȧ-trakt', v.t.* to draw (to; e.g. *What attracts you to medicine as a career?*): to allure: to draw forth, obtain (e.g. *I could not attract her attention*).
attrac'tion, *n.*
attrac'tive, *adj.* pleasing, alluring.
attrac'tively, *adv.* **attrac'tiveness,** *n.*
[L. *ad,* to, *trahĕre,* to draw.]

attribute, *ȧ-trib'ūt, v.t.* to consider as belonging (to): to consider to be caused by (e.g. *I attribute his failure to lack of effort*).—*n.* (*at'ri-būt*) a quality, esp. one always thought of as belonging to a person or thing.
attrib'utable, *adj.*
attribū'tion, *n.* act of attributing.
[L. *ad,* to, *tribuĕre,* to give.]

attrition, *ȧ-tri'sh(ȯ)n, n.* wearing down by, or as if by, friction.
[L. *ad,* and *terĕre, trītum,* to rub.]

au revoir, *ō rė-vwär,* (goodbye) until we meet again. [Fr.]

auburn, *ö'bûrn, adj.* reddish brown.
[Old meaning was light yellow. Late L. *alburnus,* whitish—L. *albus,* white.]

auction, *ök'sh(ȯ)n,* a public sale in which articles are sold to the person who 'bids' or offers the highest price.—*v.t.* to sell thus.
auctioneer', *n.* one who is licensed to sell by auction.
[L. *augēre, auctum,* to increase.]

audacious, *ö-dā'shus, adj.* daring, bold: impudent.
audā'ciously, *adv.*
audā'ciousness, audac'ity (*-das'*), *ns.*
[L. *audax,* bold—*audēre,* to dare.]

audible, *öd'i-bl, adj.* able to be heard.

aud'ibleness, audibil'ity, *ns.*
aud'ibly, *adv.*
aud'ience, *n.* a ceremonial interview: an assembly of people who listen or watch.
aud'it, *n.* an examination of accounts by authorised person(s).—Also *v.t.*
audi'tion, *n.* a hearing to test a performer.
aud'itor, *n.* a hearer: one who audits accounts.
auditor'ium, *n.* space allotted to the audience in a public building.
aud'itory, *adj.* connected with hearing.
aud'io-engineer', *n.* one concerned with broadcasting sound.
audio-vis'ual (*viz'*) **aids,** films, recordings, etc. used in teaching.
[L. *audire, auditum,* to hear.]

auger, *ö'gėr, n.* a carpenter's tool for boring holes.
[M.E. (*a*) *nauger*; became *an auger.*]

aught, *öt, n.* a whit, ought, anything.
[O.E. *āwiht—ā,* ever, *wiht,* creature.]

augment, *ög-ment', v.t., v.i.* to increase.
augmentā'tion, *n.*
Augmented Roman Alphabet, a teaching alphabet of over 40 characters.
[L. *augmentum,* increase.]

augur, *ö'gėr, v.t.* to foretell.—*v.i.* (of things) to promise (well, ill).
augury, *ö'gūr-i, n.*
[L., a soothsayer.]

august, *ö-gust', adj.* inspiring reverence: dignified: majestic.
[L. *augēre,* to increase, honour.]

August, *ö'gůst, n.* the eighth month of the year, called after the first Roman emperor, *Augustus* Caesar.

auk, *ök, n.* a sea bird with short wings found in northern seas.
[Old Norse *alka.*]

auld lang syne, *öld lang sīn,* (*Scot.*) 'old long since', the dear distant past.

aunt, *änt, n.* a father's or a mother's sister: an uncle's wife.
[O.Fr. *ante*—L. *amita,* a father's sister.]

auricle, *ör'i-kl, n.* either of the two upper cavities (hollow divisions) of the heart.
[L. *auricula—auris,* the ear.]

aurora, *ö-rō'rȧ, -rö', n.* dawn: a display of coloured lights, caused by high speed particles thrown out from the sun.
aurora borealis (*bō-ri-āl'is,* or *bö-*) the northern aurora, or 'northern lights'.
aurora australis (*ös-trā'lis*), the 'southern lights', seen near the South Pole.
[L. *Aurora,* goddess of the dawn.]

auscultation, *ös-kul-tā'sh(ȯ)n, n.* listening to the lungs and heart with a stethoscope.
[L. *auscultāre,* to listen.]

auspice, *ös'pis, n.* (now used in *pl.*) formal encouragement, patronage (e.g. *a fête held under the auspices of the Tennis Club*): prospects (*under good auspices*).
auspicious, *ös-pi'shůs, adj.* having good omens of success: favourable, fortunate.
auspi'ciously, *adv.* **auspi'ciousness,** *n.*
[L. *auspex,* one who foretells the future from the behaviour of birds—*avis,* bird *specěre,* to observe.]

austere, *ös-tēr', adj.* stern: strictly upright: simple in a bare, severe way.
austere'ness, auster'ity (*-ter'*), *ns.*
austere'ly, *adv.*
[Gk. *austeros—auein,* to dry.]

authentic, *ö-then'tik, adj.* genuine: unquestionably true.
authen'tically, *adv.*
authen'ticate, *v.t.* to prove genuine: to make valid or legal.
authenticity (*-tis'*), *n.* genuineness.
[Gk. *authentēs,* one who does something with his own hand—same root as **auto-**.]

author, *ö'thȯr, n.* (*masc.* or *fem.*) the writer of a book, article, etc.: the creator or beginner (of anything):—*fem.* **auth'oress.**
auth'orship, *n.*
[L. *augēre, auctum,* to increase, produce.]

authorise, *ö'thȯr-iz, v.t.* to give permission for (e.g. *to authorise a holiday*): to give power, right to (e.g. *They authorised her to buy balls for the club*).
authorisā'tion, *n.*
Authorised Version, the 1611 translation of the Bible.
author'ity, *n.* legal power or right: personal power due to one's office or to one's character: a book or person quoted because regarded as very reliable or important: permission: a body or board in control: (in *pl.*) persons in power:—*pl.* **author'ities.**
author'itative, *adj.* coming from one who has authority or power, or who has knowledge.
author'itatively, *adv.*
[Same root as **author.**]

auto-, aut-, auth-, (as part of a word) for oneself: by oneself.
autobiography, *ö-to-bī-og'rȧf-i, n.* the life of a person written by himself or herself.
autobiog'rapher, *n.*
autobiograph'ic(al), *adjs.*
autocrat, *öt'o-krat, n.* a ruler or other person whose word is law.
autocracy, *ö-tok'rȧs-i, n.* government by one man, despotism.
autocrat'ic, *adj.* of, suited to, an autocrat (e.g. *an autocratic manner*): expecting to be obeyed.
autocrat'ically, *adv.*
autograph, *ö'to-grâf, n.* one's own handwriting: a signature.—*v.t.* to write one's signature in or on.
[Gk. *autos,* self (*bios,* life, *graphein,* to write; *kratos,* power).]

auto- (*continued*).
automatic, *ö-to-mat'ik, adj.* self-acting, working of itself: not conscious, without thinking (e.g. *His action was automatic, for his thoughts were on something else*).
automat'ically, *adv.*

automation, *ö-to-mā'sh(ȯ)n, n.* extensive use of machines, esp. of electronic devices for controlling other machines.
aut'omate, *v.t.* to convert to, or work by, automation.
autom'aton (*-ȧ-tȯn*), *n.* a human being who acts like a machine and without intelligence :—*pls.* **autom'atons, -ata.**
automobile, *ö'to-mō-bēl,* or *-bēl', n.* a motor car.
autonomy, *ö-ton'ȯ-mi,* self-government.
auton'omous, *adj.* having self-government.
autopsy, *ö'top-si,* or *-top', n.* examination of a body after death.
[Gk. *autŏs,* self (*automatos,* self-moving; **mobile**; Gk. *nomos,* law; *opsis,* sight).]

autumn, *ö'tụm, n.* the third season of the year, in northern regions from August or September to October or November.
autum'nal, *adj.*
[L. *autumnus.*]

auxiliary, *ög-zil'yȧr-i, adj.* helping, additional (e.g. *auxiliary forces*).—*n.* a helper: (*grammar*) a verb that forms tenses of other verbs (e.g. He *is* going; she *has* gone; I *shall* go): (esp. in *pl.*) a soldier serving with another nation :—*pl.* **-ies.**
[L. *auxilium,* help.]

avail, *ȧ-vāl', v.t.* to help, benefit.—*v.i.* to be of use, achieve the purpose (also *n.*).
avail'able, *adj.* that can be used: within reach.
avail'ableness, availabil'ity, *ns.*
of little, no, avail, of little, no, use in carrying out the purpose.
to avail oneself of, to take advantage of, use.
[L. *ad,* to, *valēre,* to be strong.]

avalanche, *av'ȧl-ânsh, n.* a mass of snow and ice sliding down from a mountain.
[L. *ad,* to, *vallis,* valley.]

avant-garde, *a-vänᵍ-gärd, n.* those who take a leading part in a new movement.—Also *adj.* [Fr.]

avarice, *av'ȧr-is, n.* eager desire for wealth.
avaricious, *av-ȧ-ri'shụs, adj.* extremely greedy.
avari'ciously, *adv.* **avari'ciousness,** *n.*
[L. *avārus,* greedy—*avēre,* to pant after.]

avast, *ȧ-väst', interj.* (*at sea*) stop!
[Du. *houd vast,* hold fast.]

avenge, *ȧ-venj', -venzh', v.t.* to take revenge for (an injury; e.g. *to avenge his brother's death*), or on behalf of (a person; e.g. *to avenge the murdered king*).
aveng'er, *n.*
[O.Fr. *avengier*—L. *vindicāre.*]

avenue, *av'in-ū, n.* a tree-bordered approach to a house in its grounds: a street: means, way of reaching (*an avenue of escape*; *avenues to success*).
[L. *ad.* to, *venīre.* to come.]

aver, *ȧ-vėr', v.t.* to declare, assert :—*pr.p.* **averr'ing**; *pa.p.* **averred'.**
[L. *ad,* and *vērus,* true.]

average, *av'ėr-ij, n.* the result obtained by dividing a sum of quantities by their number (e.g. *The average of the four numbers 1, 5, 8, and 10 is 24÷4=6*) :—*adj.* midway between extremes: ordinary.—*v.t.* to fix the average of.—*v.i.* to form an average of.
[Word appears about A.D. 1500 in connexion with Mediterranean sea trade.]

averse, *ȧ-vėrs', adj.* disinclined or opposed (with *to* or *from*).
averse'ness, *n.*
aver'sion, *n.* dislike: the object of dislike.
avert', *v.t.* to turn (e.g. eyes, thoughts) from or aside: to prevent, ward off.
[L. *avertĕre, aversum,* to turn from.]

aviary, *ā'vi-ȧr-i, n.* a place for keeping birds.
[L. *avis,* a bird.]

aviation, *ā-vi-ā'sh(ȯ)n, n.* the science of flying in aircraft.
a'viator, *n.*
[L. *avis,* bird; same root as **aviary.**]

avid, *av'id, adj.* greedy, eager.
avid'ity, *n.* **av'idly,** *adv.*
[L. *avidus,* greedy—root as **avarice.**]

avocation, *av-o-kā'sh(ȯ)n, n.* a distraction or hobby: calling, vocation.
[L. *ab,* away, *vocāre,* to call.]

avoid, *ȧ-void', v.t.* to escape, keep clear of: to shun.
avoid'able, *adj.* **avoid'ance,** *n.*
[Pfx. *a-* (L. *ex,* out) and **void.**]

avoirdupois, *av-ėr-dė-poiz',* or *av'-, adj.* or *n.* (according to) the system of weights in which the lb. equals 16 oz.
[O.Fr. *aveir de pes,* to have weight.]

avouch, *ȧ-vowch', v.t.* to say positively.
[Through O.Fr.—L. *ad,* to, *vocāre,* to call.]

avow, *ȧ-vow', v.t.* to declare openly: to confess.
avowed', *adj.* acknowledged, declared.
avow'al, *n.* a declaration: a frank confession.
[Same root as **avouch.**]

avuncular, *ȧ-vung'kūl-ȧr, adj.* of an uncle: like that of an uncle.
[L. *avunculus,* an uncle.]

await, *ȧ-wāt', v.t.* to wait or look for: to be in store for.
[Same root as **wait.**]

awake, *ȧ-wāk', v.t.* to rouse from sleep, or from inaction.—*v.i.* to cease sleeping :—*pa.t.* **awaked', awoke'**; *pa.p.* **awaked'.**—*adj.* not asleep: watchful, vigilant.
awak'en, *v.t.* and *v.i.* to awake: to rouse into interest or attention.
awak'ening, *n.*
awake to, fully aware of.
[Same root as **wake, watch.**]

award, *ȧ-wörd', v.t.* to grant, bestow: to give, assign, legally.—*n.* judgment: portion, payment, prize assigned.
[Same root as **ward, guard.**]

aware, *ȧ-wār', adj.* (in predicate; not

used before noun) informed: conscious (of).
aware′ness, *n.*
[Same root as **wary.**]

awash, *ȧ-wosh′*, *adv.* (of e.g. a deck) with waves washing over: covered with water: tossed by the waves.
[O.E. *on*, on, and **wash.**]

away, *ȧ-wā′*, *adv.* from a place: absent: continuously (e.g. *They blazed away at the enemy*): at once (*straight away*).
away with him, take him away.
to make away with, to steal and escape with: to squander: to destroy.
to do away with, to make an end of: to abolish.
[O.E. *aweg—on*, on, *weg*, way.]

awe, *ö*, *n.* reverence and wonder: dread.—*v.t.* to strike with fear.
awe′some, *adj.* weird, dreadful.
awe′struck, *adj.* struck with awe.
aw′ful, *adj.* terrible: inspiring respect: (*slang*) very great.
aw′fully, *adv.* **aw′fulness,** *n.*
[Old Norse *agi* (O.E. *ege*), fear.]

awhile, *ȧ-hwīl′*, *adv.* for a short time.
[O.E. *āne hwile*, a while.]

awkward, *ök′wȧrd*, *adj.* clumsy: not graceful: embarrassing: difficult to deal with.
awk′wardly, *adv.* **awk′wardness,** *n.*
[Prob. Old Norse *afug*,turned wrong way, and *-ward*, expressing direction.]

awl, *öl*, *n.* a pointed instrument for boring small holes in leather.
[O.E. *æl.*]

awning, *ön′ing*, *n.* a covering above or in front to give shelter from the sun.
[Origin uncertain.]

awoke. See **awake.**

awry, *ȧ-rī′*, *adj.* (in predicate; not used before noun) crooked.—*adv.* crookedly: not the way desired, wrong (e.g. *The whole scheme went awry*).
[O.E. *on*, on, and **wry.**]

axe, ax, *aks*, *n.* a tool for hewing or chopping:—*pl.* **ax′es.**—*v.t.* to cut down, reduce: to dismiss as not required.
an axe to grind, a purpose of one's own to serve.
[O.E. *æx.*]

axiom, *aks′i-ȯm*, *aks′yȯm*, *n.* a truth or statement that needs no proof: an accepted principle or rule.
axiomat′ic, *adj.*
[Gk. *axioein*, think worth, take for granted.]

axis, *aks′is*, *n.* the line, real or imaginary, about which a body rotates, or about which the parts of a figure, etc. are arranged: a fixed line adopted for reference: an alliance:—*pl.* **axes** (*aks′ēz*).
[L.]

axle, *aks′l*, **axle-tree,** *aks′l-trē*, *n.* the pin or rod on which a wheel turns.
[Old Norse *öxull.*]

ay, aye, *ī*, *adv.* yes: indeed.—*n.* **aye** (*ī*) a vote in favour: (in *pl.*) those who vote thus.
[Perh. a *dial.* form of *aye*, ever.]

ayah, *ī′ya*, *n.* an Indian children's nurse.
[Indian word *āyā*—Port. *aia*, nurse.]

aye, ay, *ā*, *adv.* ever: always.
[Old Norse *ei*, ever.]

azalea, *ȧ-zāl′ya*, *-i-a*, *n.* a shrubby plant like a rhododendron.
[Gk. *azaleos*, dry.]

azure, *azh′ůr*, *ā′zhůr*, *adj.* sky-coloured: clear, cloudless.
[O.Fr. *azur*—Pers. *lājward*, lapis lazuli.]

B

babble, *bab′l*, *v.i.* to talk indistinctly or continually: (of water) to make a murmuring sound: to tell a secret or secrets (to). [Imit.]

babe, *bāb*, **baby,** *bā′bi*, *ns.* an infant: (*slang*) a girl:—*pls.* **babes, ba′bies.**
bā′byish, *adj.*
bā′byhood, *n.* time of being a baby.
bā′by-sitter, *n.* one who remains in the house with a child while its mother or usual guardian goes out.
[Prob. conn. with **babble.**]

babel, *bā′bėl*, *n.* (see *Genesis xi*) a confused mixture (of sounds): a scene of noise and confusion.
[Heb. *Bābel*, Babylon.]

baboon, *bȧ-bōōn′*, *n.* a large monkey with long face, large canine teeth, short tail.
[Fr. *babouin.*]

baby. See **babe.**

bachelor, *bach′ė-lȯr*, *n.* an unmarried man.
Bachelor of Science, etc. one who has taken a university degree in science, etc.
[O.Fr. *bacheler*—Late L. *baccalārius*, small farmer.]

bacillus, *bȧ-sil′ůs*, *n.* a rod-shaped or (*loosely*) other bacterium causing disease.
[L. *baculus*, a rod.]

back, *bak*, *n.* the hind part of the body in man, and the upper part in animals: the part in the rear: the curved part of the outside of a book: (football, etc.) one of the players behind the forwards.—*adj.* lying at the back: due some time ago (e.g. *back pay*): out of date (e.g. *a back number of a magazine*).—*adv.* to the place from which the person or thing came: to a former time or condition: in return (e.g. *He gave back blow for blow*)—*v.t.* to move back: to give a back to: to help, support (a person, etc.; often **back up**): to bet on.—*v.i.* to move back: (of wind) to change in the direction opposite to that of the movement of the hands of a clock.

back′er, *n.* one who supports another in an undertaking, e.g. with money.

back′bite, *v.t.* to speak evil of (a person) behind his back.—Also *v.i.*

back′blocks, *n.pl.* (*Austr.*) thinly settled country, esp. far from seacoast or river.

back′bone, *n.* the spine: chief support: firmness.

back fire, *n.* ignition of gas in internal-combustion engine's cylinder at wrong time, or *within* gas-burner instead of at outlet.—Also *v.i.* (**back-fire′**).

back′ground, *n.* the space behind the principal figures of a picture: previous happenings that explain an event: one's origin, education, etc.

back′hand, *n.* a stroke made, shot played, with hand turned backwards: writing with the letters sloping backwards.

back′hand(ed), *adjs.* and *advs.*

back number, an out of date copy or issue, or person, or thing.

back-seat driver, a person with no responsibility who gives much advice.

back′side′, *n.* the rump, bottom.

backslide′, *v.i.* to fall back into sin or error.

back′stairs, *adj.* secret or underhand.

back′stroke, *n.* a backhand stroke: (*swimming*) a stroke made when on the back.

back′wash, *n.* a backward current, e.g. that of a receding wave.

back′water, *n.* a river pool not in the main stream: a place not affected by what is happening in the world outside.

back′woods, *n.pl.* forest or uncultivated country.

to back down, to give up one's opinion, claim, etc.

to back out, to move out backwards: to withdraw from a promise, etc.

to back water, to keep a boat steady or make it move backwards by reversing the action of the oars.

to break the back of, to burden too heavily: to complete the heaviest part of (a task).

to put one's back into, to do with might and main.

to put one's back up, to anger one.

to take a back seat, to take an unimportant position.

[O.E. *bæc.*]

backward, *bak′wȧrd, adv.* and *adj.* towards the back: on the back: towards the past: from a better to a worse state.—*adj.* late in developing or in becoming civilised: dull, stupid: shy, bashful.

back′wardness, *n.*

back′wards, *adv.* [**back.**]

bacon, *bā′kȯn, n.* back and sides of pig salted, dried, etc.

to save one's bacon, to come off unharmed, though with difficulty.

[O.Fr.; a Germanic word.]

bacteria, *bak-tē′ri-ȧ, n.pl.* organisms visible only under a microscope found in countless numbers in decomposing matter, in air, soil and its products, and in living bodies. Their activities are essential to plant and animal life, but some are the germs of disease:—*sing.* **bactē′rium.**

bacteriol′ogy, *n.* the study of bacteria.

bacteriol′ogist, *n.*

[Gk. *baktērion,* little stick.]

bad, *bad, adj.* not good: wicked: hurtful: rotten (e.g. *a bad egg*): faulty (e.g. *a bad guess*): worthless (e.g. *bad money*): painful: unwell: severe, serious:—*comp.* **worse** (*wûrs*); *superl.* **worst** (*wûrst*).

bad′ly, *adv.*:—*comp.* **worse**; *superl.* **worst.**

bad′ness, *n.*

bad blood, ill-feeling.

bad debt, debt that will never be paid.

to go to the bad, to go to moral ruin.

with (a) bad grace, ungraciously.

[M.E. *badde.*]

bade. See **bid.**

badge, *baj, n.* a mark, emblem, or ornament giving some information about the wearer.

[M.E. *bage.*]

badger, *baj′ėr, n.* a burrowing animal of the weasel family.—*v.t.* to pursue as dogs hunt the badger, to pester or worry.

[Prob. from **badge,** referring to white mark on badger's forehead.]

badinage, *bad-in-äzh, bad′in-ij, n.* light playful talk, banter. [Fr.]

badminton, *bad′min-tȯn, n.* a game played with shuttlecocks.

[*Badminton,* Duke of Beaufort's seat.]

baffle, *baf′l, v.t.* to check or make useless (*to baffle an attempt*): to bewilder, be too difficult for (a person):—*pa.p.* **baffled.**

baff′ling, *adj.*

baffle plate, a device for regulating flow of liquids, etc. [Orig. uncertain.]

bag, *bag, n.* a sack, pouch: a measure of quantity: the quantity of fish, game, etc., secured by a sportsman.—*v.t.* to put into a bag: to kill (game): to seize, secure, or steal.—*v.i.* to hang like an empty bag:—*pr.p.* **bagg′ing**; *pa.p.* **bagged.**

bagg′y, *adj.* loose like an empty bag.

bag and baggage, whole equipment.

to let the cat out of the bag, to let out the secret.

[M.E. *bagge.*]

bagatelle, *bag-ȧ-tel′, n.* a trifle: a game played on a board with balls and a cue.

[It. *bagatella,* a conjurer's trick, a trifle.]

baggage, *bag′ij, n.* the tents, provisions,

etc., of an army: traveller's luggage: a playful term for a woman.
[O.Fr. *baguer*, to bind up.]

bagpipe, *bag'pīp, n.* (often in *pl.*) a wind instrument, a bag fitted with pipes.
[**bag, pipe.**]

bail[1], *bāl, v.t.* to set (a person) free by giving security for his appearance in court when required (with *out*).—*n.* money given as security for this: the person who gives it.
to go bail, to act as bail (for person).
[O.Fr., control, jurisdiction.]

bail[2], *bāl, n.* one of the cross pieces laid on the top of the wicket in cricket.
[O.Fr. *baile*, a cross piece of wood.]

bail[3], *bāl, v.t.* to clear (a boat) of water with shallow buckets, etc.: to scoop (water out) from a boat.—Also **bale.**
to bale (bail) out, to escape from an aeroplane by parachute.
[Fr. *baille*, a bucket.]

Bailey bridge, *bā'li brij*, a prefabricated bridge quickly put up.
[Named from the inventor.]

bailie, *bāl'i, n.* in Scotland, the title of a magistrate who presides in a burgh or police court.
[O.Fr. *baillis*; same orig. as **bailiff.**]

bailiff, *bāl'if, n.* a sheriff's officer: one who manages an estate, or a farm, etc., for its owner.
[O.Fr. *baillif*; same root as **bail** (1).]

bairn, *bārn, bėrn, n.* a child.
[O.E. *beran*, to bear.]

bait, *bāt, n.* food put on a hook to make fish bite: anything intended to attract or allure.—*v.t.* to put food as a lure on (hook), in (trap): to set dogs on (a bear, badger, etc.): to tease unkindly, annoy.
[Scand. *beita*, to cause to bite.]

baize, *bāz, n.* a coarse woollen cloth.
[O.Fr. *baies*—L. *badius*, bay-coloured.]

bake, *bāk, v.t.* to dry, harden, or cook by the heat of the sun or of fire: to cook in an oven.—*v.i.* to become very hot or baked.
bak'er, *n.* one who bakes bread, etc.
bak'ery, *n.* a place where baking is done, or where bread, cakes, etc. are sold.
bak'ing, *n.*
baking powder, a powder containing a carbonate (such as *baking soda*) and an acid substance (such as *cream of tartar*) used to make cakes, etc. rise.
baking soda, a white powder, sodium bicarbonate.
[O.E. *bacan.*]

baksheesh, *bak'shēsh, n.* a present of money.
[Pers. *bakhshīsh.*]

balalaika, *bä-lä-lī'kä, n.* a musical instrument with a triangular body and a guitar neck. [Russ.]

balance, *bal'ȧns, n.* a weighing instrument with two dishes or scales hanging from a beam supported in the middle: steadiness: steadiness, calmness, of mind: the sum required to make the two sides of an account equal: the sum due on an account.—*v.t.* to make, or keep, steady: to weigh in one's mind (against something else): to make the debtor and creditor sides of (an account) agree.—*v.i.* to have equal weight or power, etc.: to hesitate or waver (between).
balance sheet, a paper showing a summary and balance of accounts.
balance wheel, a wheel in a watch regulating the beat.
[L. *bilanx*, having two scales.]

balcony, *bal'kȯn-i, n.* a platform projecting from the wall of a building: in theatres, etc., an upper floor or gallery:—*pl.* **-ies.**
[Perh. It. *balcone.*]

bald, *böld, adj.* without hair (or feathers, etc.) on the head (or top): bare, plain (e.g. *a bald statement*).
bald'ing, *adj.* going bald.
bald'ly, *adv.* **bald'ness,** *n.*
[M.E. *balled.*]

balderdash, *böl'dėr-dash, n.* nonsense.
[Origin unknown.]

bale[1], *bāl, n.* a, usu. large, tight bundle of goods.—*v.t.* to make into bales. [M.E.]

bale[2]. Same as **bail** (3).

baleful, *bāl'fl, adj.* having evil results (e.g. *a baleful influence*).
[O.E. *bealu*, evil, injury.]

balk, baulk, *bö(l)k, n.* an unploughed ridge.—*v.t.* to check, hinder: to baffle.—*v.i.* to pull up, stop (at an obstacle): to refuse to act in a particular way (e.g. *He agreed to the plan, but balked at telling such an unkind lie*).
[O.E. *balca*, ridge.]

ball[1], *böl, n.* anything roughly the shape of a sphere: a round or roundish object used in games: a bullet: a rounded part of the body (e.g. *the ball of the thumb*).
ball'-bearings, *n.pl.* in machinery, a device for lessening friction by making a revolving part turn on loose steel balls.
ball'cock, *n.* a valve in a cistern, shut or opened by the rise or fall of a floating ball.
ball'-point, *n.* and *adj.* (a pen) having a tiny ball as the writing point.
no ball (*cricket*), a ball bowled in a way judged to be contrary to rule.
to have the ball at one's feet, to have success within reach.
[M.E. *bal*—Scand. *böllr.*]

ball[2], *böl, n.* a formal gathering for dancing.
ball'room, *n.*
[O.Fr. *bal.*]

ballad, *bal'ȧd, n.* a simple poem in stanzas of two or four lines telling a story: a simple, often sentimental, song.
ball'admonger (*-mung-ger*), *n.* a dealer in, or composer of, ballads.
[O.Fr. *balade* (orig. a dancing song).]

ballast, *bal'ȧst, n.* heavy matter placed in a

ship to keep it steady when it has no cargo: anything that gives steadiness.—*v.t.* to make or keep steady.

in ballast, without cargo.

[Prob. Old Swed. *bar*, bare, *last*, load.]

ballerina, *bal-ė-rē'nȧ*, *n.* a female ballet dancer:—*pl.* **ballerin'as, -rine** (*-rē'nā*). [It.]

ballet, *bal'ā*, *n.* a theatrical performance of dancing with intricate steps and mime, often telling a story: the troupe that performs it.

balletomane, *bȧ-let'ō-mān*, *n.* a ballet enthusiast.

[Fr.; dim. of *bal*, a dance.]

ballistics, *bȧ-lis'tiks*, *n.* the science of projectiles.

ballis'tic, *adj.*

ballistic missile, a missile guided for part of its course but falling as an ordinary projectile.

[Gk. *ballein*, to throw.]

balloon, *bȧ-lo͞on'*, *n.* a large bag, made of light material and filled with a gas lighter than air—often with car attached: a toy of form similar to the bag.

[It. *ballone*—*balla*, ball.]

ballot, *bal'ȯt*, *n.* a ball or piece of paper put into a box for secret voting: this method of voting.—*v.i.* to vote by ballot: to draw lots (for):—*pr.p.* **ball'oting**; *pa.p.* **ball'oted.**

[It. *ballotta*, dim. of *balla*, ball.]

ballyhoo, *bal-i-ho͞o'* (or *bal'-*), *n.* (*U.S. slang*) noisy or sensational advertising: outcry.

balm, *bäm*, *n.* an oily, fragrant substance: ointment: anything that heals or soothes pain.

balm'y, *adj.* fragrant: soothing: (*slang*) mad, crazy:—*comp.* **balm'ier**; *superl.* **balm'iest.**

balm'iness, *n.*

[Same root as **balsam.**]

balmoral, *bal-mor'ȧl*, *n.* a flat Scottish bonnet.

[*Balmoral*, royal castle in Aberdeenshire.]

balsa, *bal'sȧ*, *böl'sȧ*, *n.* a tropical American tree with very light wood. [Sp.]

balsam, *böl'sȧm*, *n.* a fragrant liquid resin or resin-like substance obtained from certain trees: a garden annual.

[L. *balsamum*—Gk. *balsamon.*]

baluster, *bal'ŭs-tėr*, *n.* a small pillar supporting a stair rail, etc.

bal'ustrade, *n.* a row of balusters joined by a rail.

[Late L. *balaustium.*]

bamboo, *bam-bo͞o'*, *n.* a gigantic grass with hollow, jointed, woody stem.

[Malay *bambu.*]

bamboozle, *bam-bo͞o'zl*, *v.t.* to deceive: to confuse completely, mystify.

[Origin unknown.]

ban, *ban*, *n.* a prohibiting, forbidding.—*v.t.* to forbid: to disapprove of strongly.

[O.E. *bannan*, to summon.]

banal, *bȧ-näl'*, *bā'nȧl*, *adj.* commonplace, trivial (e.g. *The speaker made a few banal remarks and sat down*).

banal'ity, *n.* [Fr.]

banana, *bȧ-nä'nȧ*, *n.* a gigantic tropical tree: its yellow fruit.

[Sp. or Port.—native African name.]

band[1], *band*, *n.* (usu. in *pl.*) anything that binds or fetters—now usu. **bond**(**s**).

[M.E.; from Scand.]

band[2], *band*, *n.* a strip of cloth, etc. to put round anything: a stripe of different colour or material crossing a surface: (in *pl.*) two linen strips hanging in front from the collar of a clergyman or barrister: (*radio*, etc.) a group of frequencies or wavelengths.

bandage, *ban'dij*, *n.* a strip to bind up a wound or break.—Also *v.t.*

band'box, *n.* a box for millinery, etc.

[M.E. *bande*—O.Fr.; a Germanic word.]

band[3], *band*, *n.* a number of persons bound together for a purpose: a body of musicians (esp. wind, percussion).—*v.t.* and *v.i.* to associate, unite (e.g. *They banded themselves together to oppose him*).

band'master, *n.* conductor of a band of musicians.

bands'man, *n.* a member of a band of musicians.

band'stand, *n.* a platform for out-of-door musicians.

[Conn. with **band** (2).]

bandage. See **band** (2).

bandana, bandanna, *ban-dân'ȧ*, *n.* a silk or cotton coloured handkerchief.

[Hindustani *bāndhnū*, a method of dyeing.]

bandbox. See **band** (2).

bandicoot, *ban'di-ko͞ot*, *n.* a very large rat of India, etc.: a small pouched, insect-eating animal of Australia, etc.

[From an Indian word meaning pig-rat.]

bandied. See **bandy** (1).

bandit, *ban'dit*, *n.* an outlaw: a robber: a gangster:—*pl.* **ban'dits, banditti** (*-dit'ē*).

[It. *bandito.*]

bandoleer, bandolier, *ban-do-lēr'*, *n.* shoulder belt, esp. for holding cartridges.

[Through O.Fr.—It. *banda*, band.]

bandy[1], *ban'di*, *v.t.* to strike, throw, to and fro: to give and take (e.g. blows, words, reproaches):—*pr.p.* **ban'dying**; *pa.p.* **ban'died.** [Origin uncertain.]

bandy[2], *ban'di*, *adj.* (of legs) bent outward at the knee. [Origin uncertain.]

bane, *bān*, *n.* ruin, woe: source or cause of evil.

bane'ful, *adj.* hurtful, destructive.

bane'fully, *adv.* **bane'fulness,** *n.*

[O.E. *bana*, murderer.]

bang, *bang*, *n.* a heavy blow: a sudden loud noise.—*v.t.* to beat: to slam.

[Scand. *banga*, to hammer.]

bangle, *bang'gl*, *n.* ring worn on arm or leg.

[Hindustani *bangri.*]

banian. Same as **banyan.**

banish, *ban'ish, v.t.* to exile: to drive away.
ban'ishment, *n.*
[Same root as **ban.**]

banister, *ban'is-tėr, n.* Same as **baluster.**

banjo, *ban'jō,* or *-jō', n.* a musical instrument of the guitar kind.
[Negro form of Fr. *bandore*—Gk. *pandoura.*]

bank[1], *bangk, n.* a mound, ridge: the margin of a river, lake, etc.: rising ground in the sea.—*v.t.* (often with *up*) to enclose, strengthen, with a bank: to cover (a fire) so as to make it burn more slowly.—*v.t.* and *v.i.* (of aircraft) to tilt in turning.
[M.E. *banke*; of Scand. origin.]

bank[2], *bangk, n.* a place where money is deposited, lent, exchanged: a place for storing other valuable material (e.g. **blood bank,** where blood plasma is kept).—*v.t.* to put into a bank.
bank'er, *n.* one employed in banking: the stake-holder in certain gambling games.
bank'ing, *n.* and *adj.*
bank book, a book recording money deposited in, or withdrawn from, a bank.
bank note, a note issued by a bank, which passes as money.
bank rate, the rate at which the Bank of England is prepared to discount (see this word) bills of exchange.
to bank on, to rely, reckon, on.
to break the bank, to win from the casino management the sum fixed as the limit it is willing to lose on one day.
[Fr. *banque*; a Germanic word.]

bankrupt, *bangk'rupt, n.* one who fails in business.—*adj.* insolvent: having none left (with *of, in*).—*v.t.* to make bankrupt.
bank'ruptcy, *n.*:—*pl.* **-cies.**
[Fr. *banqueroute* (L. *ruptus,* broken).]

banner, *ban'ėr, n.* a military flag: a large strip of cloth bearing a slogan, etc.
banner headline, one right across a newspaper.
[O.Fr. *banere*; conn. with **band** (2).]

bannock, *ban'ȯk, n.* flat cake esp. plain one.
[O.E. *bannuc.*]

banns, *banz, n.pl.* a proclamation of intention to marry.
to forbid the banns, to object formally to a proposed marriage. [From **ban.**]

banquet, *bang'kwit, n.* a feast: a ceremonial dinner, with speeches.—*v.t.* and *v.i.* to give, or to share in, a feast:—*pr.p.* **ban'queting**; *pa.p.* **ban'queted.**
[Fr. *banc,* bench.]

banshee, *ban'shē, n.* a fairy who wails before a death in the family to which she is attached.
[Old Ir. *ben síde,* woman of the fairies.]

bantam, *ban'tȧm, n.* a small variety of domestic fowl, notable for courage.
ban'tamweight, *n.* a boxer not heavier than 8 st. 6 lb. (amateur 8 st. 7 lb.) or less than 8 st.
[Prob. *Bantam* in Java.]

banter, *ban'tėr, v.t.* to tease good-humouredly.—*n.* humorous ridicule: jesting. [Origin unknown.]

banyan, banian, *ban'yȧn, n.* an Indian fig tree with rooting branches.
[Port. *banian.*]

baptise, *bap-tīz', v.t.* to dip in, or sprinkle with, water as a religious ceremony: to give a name to, christen.
bap'tism (*-tizm*), *n.* **baptis'mal,** *adj.*
Baptist, *n.* one of a sect that approves of adult baptism only.
baptism of fire, an ordeal, as a soldier's first experience of battle.
[Gk. *baptizein*—*baptein,* to dip in water.]

bar, *bär, n.* a rod of a solid substance: a bolt: a hindrance: a bank of sand, gravel, at the mouth of a river, etc: a counter across which drinks are served: a counter at which articles of one kind are sold: a public house: the rail dividing off the judge's seat at which prisoners stand to be charged or sentenced: the lawyers who plead in court: a division in music.—*v.t.* to fasten with a bar: to shut out: to hinder (from):—*pr.p.* **barr'ing**; *pa.p.* **barred.**
bar'maid, -man, -tender, *ns.* attendants who serve at the bar of a public house or hotel.
barrister, *bar'is-tėr, n.* one qualified to plead at the bar in English or in Irish law courts.
called to the bar, admitted as barrister or advocate.
[O.Fr. *barre.*]

barb, *bärb, n.* the beard-like jag near the point of an arrow, fish-hook, etc.—*v.t.* to arm with barbs.
barbed, *adj.* having barb(s) (e.g. **barbed-wire,** wire with sharp points at intervals, used for fencing, etc.).
[L. *barba,* a beard.]

barbarous, *bär'bȧr-ŭs, adj.* uncivilised: brutal.
bar'barousness, *n.*
barbar'ity, *n.* barbarousness: a barbarous act:—*pl.* **-ities.**
barbār'ian, *adj.* and *n.* uncivilised (person): cruel, brutal (person).
barbar'ic (*-bar'*), *adj.* uncivilised: (of e.g. ornaments) primitive but rich and splendid.
bar'barism, *n.* state of being uncivilised.
[Gk. *barbaros,* foreign (orig. 'stammering', from strange sound of foreign speech).]

Barbary ape, *bär'bȧr-i āp, n.* a small tailless ape found in Africa and Gibraltar.
[*Barbary* in N. Africa, and **ape.**]

barbecue, *bär'bė-kū, n.* a framework for drying and smoking meat: an animal roasted whole: a large social or political entertainment in U.S.—*v.t.* to roast whole:—*pr.p.* **bar'becuing**; *pa.p.* **bar'becued.**
[Sp. *barbacoa.*]

barber, *bär'bėr, n.* one who shaves faces and cuts hair.
[L. *barba*, a beard.]

barberry, *bär'bėr-i, n.* a thorny shrub with yellow flowers and usu. red berries.
[Late L. *berberis*; not from *berry*.]

barcarole, *bär'kȧ-rōl, n.* a gondolier's boating song.
[It. *barcaròla—barca*, boat.]

bard, *bärd, n.* a poet and singer among the Celts: a poet.—**bard'ic,** *adj.*
[Gael. and Ir. *bàrd*.]

bare, *bār, adj.* uncovered, naked: empty: mere, only, without anything in addition (e.g. *his bare needs*).—*v.t.* to strip, uncover.
bare'ness, *n.*
bare'ly, *adv.* scantily, with little: scarcely, only just (e.g. *barely enough food*).
bare'backed, *adj.* without saddle.
bare'faced, *adj.* without beard, etc.: undisguised, impudent (e.g. *a barefaced lie*).
bare'foot(ed), *adjs.* **bare'head'ed,** *adj.*
[O.E. *bær*.]

bargain, *bär'gin, n.* an agreement: something bought cheaply.—*v.i.* to haggle about price, about the terms of an agreement, etc.—*v.t.* to make it a condition of an agreement (that something should be done).
into the bargain, in addition, besides.
to bargain for, to expect.
[O.Fr. *bargaigne*.]

barge, *bärj, n.* a flat-bottomed boat, used on rivers and canals.—*v.i.* to move clumsily: to bump (into).
bargee' (-*ē'*), *n.* a bargeman.
[Late L. *barga*.]

baritone, *bar'i-tōn, n.* (a singer with) a deep-toned male voice between bass and tenor.
[Gk. *barys*, heavy, deep, *tonos*, tone.]

barium, *bā'ri-ŭm, n.* a whitish metal.
[Gk. *barys*, heavy.]

bark[1], *bärk, n.* the short, explosive sound made by a dog, wolf, etc.—*v.i.* to yelp like a dog.
bark'er, *n.* a person who stands urging passers to enter e.g. a booth at a fair.
to bark up the wrong tree, to be on the wrong scent, esp. to try to lay the blame on the wrong person.
[O.E. *beorcan*.]

bark[2], barque, *bärk, n.* (*in poetry*) a boat.
[Late L. *barca*.]

bark[3], *bärk, n.* the corky and other material that can be peeled from a woody stem.
[Scand. *börkr*.]

barley, *bär'li, n.* a grain used for food and for making malt liquors and spirits.
barley sugar, sugar candied by melting and cooling to make a sweetmeat.
barley water, a drink for invalids made from pearl barley.
[O.E. *bærlic*, of barley.]

barm, *bärm, n.* froth of beer or other fermenting liquor.
barm'y, *adj.* frothy: (slang) crazy.
[O.E. *beorma*.]

barmaid, etc. See **bar.**

barn, *bärn, n.* a building in which grain, hay, etc. are stored.
barn dance, a dance held in a barn: a ballroom dance like a schottische.
barn owl, *n.* an owl, buff-coloured above, white below.
barn'stormer, *n.* a touring actor, esp. one who rants.
[O.E. *bere*, barley, *ern*, a house.]

barnacle, *bär'nȧ-kl, n.* a shellfish that sticks to rocks and ship bottoms: a companion who sticks closely.
[O.Fr. *bernacle*.]

bar(o)-, *bar(-ō)-*, (as part of word) weight.
barograph, *bar'ō-grâf, n.* a barometer that makes a record of changes in the pressure of the atmosphere.
barometer, *bȧ-rom'i-tėr, n.* an instrument by which the weight or pressure of the atmosphere is measured and changes of weather are indicated.
baromet'ric, *adj.*
[Gk. *baros*, weight (*graphein*, to write; *metron*, measure).]

baron, *bar'on, n.* a title of rank, lowest in the House of Lords: a foreign noble of similar grade: (in *pl.*) under the feudal system, the chief holders of land from the Crown, later the great lords generally: a powerful person (e.g. *a newspaper baron*).
bar'oness, *n.* a baron's wife, or a lady holding a baronial title in her own right.
barōn'ial, *adj.* of a baron: (*architecture*) of a style imitating that of old castles.
bar'ony, *n.* rank or land of a baron.
bar'onet, *n.* a holder of the lowest British title that can be passed on to an heir (see **sir**).
bar'onetcy, *n.* the rank of a baronet.
[O.Fr. *barun* (earlier sense 'strong man').]

barque. Same as **bark** (2).

barrack[1], *bar'ȧk, n.* a building for housing soldiers (generally in *pl.*).
[Fr. *baraque*—It. *baracca*, a tent.]

barrack[2], *bar'ȧk, v.i.* to shout in an unfriendly way, cheer mockingly.—Also *v.t.*
barr'acking, *n.* and *adj.*
[Australian *borak*.]

barrage, *bar'äzh, -azh', n.* an artificial bar across a river: a barrier formed by artillery fire, or by captive balloons: an overwhelming number at one time (e.g. *a barrage of questions*). [Fr.]

barrel, *bar'ėl, n.* a wooden container made of curved staves bound with hoops: the quantity it holds: anything long and hollow (e.g. the tube of a gun).
barr'elled, *adj.*
barrel organ, instrument for playing tunes by means of revolving cylinder set with pins which operate keys and thus admit air to a set of pipes.
[Fr. *baril*.]

barren, *bar'ėn, adj.* incapable of bearing offspring: unfruitful: (of land) bare, desolate: dull: unprofitable.
barr'enly, *adv.* **barr'enness,** *n.*
[O.Fr. *barhaine.*]

barricade, *bar'i-kād, n.* a barrier quickly put up to block e.g. a street.—*v.t.* to block (e.g. a street) thus: to shut (e.g. oneself) away behind a barrier.
[Fr. *barricade,* or Sp. *barricada.*]

barrier, *bar'i-ėr, n.* a defence against attack: any obstacle that keeps apart.
barrier cream, a skin cream that prevents dirt, etc. from entering the pores.
[Late L. *barrāria*; conn. with **bar.**]

barrister. See **bar.**

barrow[1], *bar'ō, n.* a small wheeled vehicle used to carry a load.
barrow boy, a fruit seller with a barrow.
[M.E. *barewe,* prob.—*beran,* to carry.]

barrow[2], *bar'ō, n.* a mound raised over a grave in former times.
[O.E. *beorg.*]

bartender. See **bar.**

barter, *bär'tėr, v.t.* to give (one thing) in exchange (for another): to give away for unworthy gain.—Also *v.i.* and *n.*
[Prob. from O.Fr. *barat,* deceit.]

basalt, *bas'ölt, bas-ölt', n.* name for certain dark-coloured rocks.
basalt'ic, *adj.*
[L. *basaltes*—an African word.]

base[1], *bās, n.* foundation, support: lowest part: the chief ingredient or substance in a mixture: a substance added for a purpose that is not the main purpose of the mixture (e.g. to give it bulk): a place from which a military or other action is carried on: the line (or surface) on which a plane (or solid) figure is regarded as standing: (*chemistry*) a substance that turns red litmus blue, reacts with an acid to form a salt, etc.: the number on which a system of numbers (e.g. of logarithms) is founded.—*v.t.* to found (on):—*pr.p.* **bas'ing**; *pa.p.* **based** (*bāst*).
bās'al, *adj.* of, or situated at, the base, esp. of the skull.
base'less, *adj.* without a base: groundless, without reason (e.g. *a baseless fear, claim*).
bas'ic, *adj.* of, forming, like, a base: fundamental, essential (e.g. *a basic principle*).
base'ment, *n.* the lowest storey of a building, below street level.
Basic English, an English vocabulary of a very few of the most useful words.
basic slag, a by-product in the manufacture of steel, used as manure.
[L. *basis.*]

base[2], *bās, adj.* low: mean, vile, worthless: (of money) counterfeit, imitation.
base'ly, *adv.* **base'ness,** *n.*
[Fr. *bas*—Late L. *bassus,* thick, fat.]

baseball, *bas'böl, n.* the American national game since 1865.
[**base** (1) and **ball.**]

baseless, basement. See **base** (1).

bash, *bash, v.t.* to beat or smash in.—*n.* a heavy blow: a dint. [Prob. Scand.]

bashful, *bash'fl, adj.* shy, lacking confidence.
bash'fulness, *n.* **bash'fully,** *adv.*
[*bash* for **abash,** and suffx. *-ful.*]

basic. See **base** (1).

basin, *bās'n, n.* a wide, open dish: any hollow place containing water, as a dock: the area drained by a river and its tributaries.
[O.Fr. *bacin.*]

basis, *bās'is, n.* same as **base** (1) esp. in the sense of a foundation for something not material (e.g. *Their friendship rested on the basis of trust*):—*pl.* **bas'es** (*-ēz*). [L.]

bask, *bâsk, v.i.* to lie (in warmth or sunshine): to enjoy (e.g. *He basked in the approval of his friends*).
[Old Norse *bathask,* to bathe oneself.]

basket, *bâs'kit, n.* a container of plaited twigs, rushes, or other materials.
bas'ketful, *n.*
basket ball, a game in which goals are scored by throwing a ball into a raised net (orig. a basket).
bas'ketwork, *n.* any material made of interlaced twigs, etc. [Origin unknown.]

Basque, *bâsk, n.* one of a people inhabiting the western Pyrenees in Spain and France, or their language.—Also *adj.* [Fr.]

bas-relief, *bas'-ri-lēf, bä', n.* sculpture in which the figures do not stand out far from the background. [Fr.]

bass[1], *bās, n.* (*music*) the lowest part sung or played: a bass singer.—Also *adj.*
[From **base** (2).]

bass[2], **basse,** *bas, n.* a fish related to the perch.
[O.E. *bærs*; conn. Ger. *bars,* perch.]

basset, *bas'it, n.* a hound like a dachshund, but bigger.
[Fr. *bas,* low.]

bassinet(te), *bas'i-net, n.* a hooded basket used as a cradle: a form of perambulator.
[Fr.; dim. of *bassin,* a basin.]

bassoon, *bå-sōōn', -zōōn', n.* a woodwind instrument of very low sound.
[It. *bassone*—*basso,* low.]

bast, *bâst, n.* the inner bark, esp. of the lime tree: fibre: matting.
[O.E. *bæst.*]

bastard, *bâs'tård, n.* a child born of parents not married to each other.—Also *adj.*
[O.Fr. *fils de bast,* son of the packsaddle.]

baste[1], *bāst, v.t.* to beat with a stick.
bast'ing, *n.*
[Prob. conn. with Old Norse *beysta.*]

baste[2], *bāst, v.t.* to drop fat or butter over (roasting meat, etc.). [Origin unknown.]

baste[3], *bāst, v.t.* to sew slightly or with long stitches, to tack.
[O.Fr. *bastir*; from a Germanic word.]

bastinado, *bas-ti-nā'dō, v.t.* to beat esp.

on the soles of the feet (an Eastern punishment) :—*pa.p.* **bastinā'doed.**
[Sp. *bastonada*; same root as **baton.**]

bastion, *bas'ti-ȯn, bas'tyȯn, n.* a part sticking out at the angle of a fortification: a defence (against).
[O.Fr. *bastir*, to build.]

bat[1], *bat, n.* a flat club for striking the ball in cricket: a club for baseball: a batsman.—*v.i.* to use a bat.—Also *v.t.* :—*pr.p.* **batt'ing**; *pa.p.* **batt'ed.**
batt'er, bats'man, *ns.*
batt'ing, *n.* the use of a bat: cotton, etc., fibre prepared in sheets.
Prob. Celt. *bat*, staff.]

bat[2], *bat, n.* a mouse-like flying animal with very long arm and hand bones, the finger bones supporting its 'wings' as the ribs do an umbrella.
batt'y, (*slang*) crazy.
[M.E. *bakke*; from Scand.]

bat[3], *bat, v.t.* to flutter, wink (an eyelid, eye) :—*pr.p.* **batt'ing**; *pa.p.* **batt'ed.**
[Perh. conn. with Fr. *battre*, beat.]

batch, *bach, n.* the quantity of bread baked, or of anything made or got ready, at one time.
[M.E. *bache*; same root as **bake.**]

bated breath. See **breath.**

bath, *bâth, n.* water into which to dip the body: a vessel (also **bath'tub**), artificial pool, or house, for bathing: exposing of body to sunlight, mud, etc.: liquid, sand, etc., into which something is put for heating, washing, etc. :—*pl.* **baths** (*bäTHz, baths*).—*v.t.* to wash in a bath.
bath'house, *n.* **bath'room,** *n.*
Order of the Bath, an order of knighthood.
See also **bathe.**
[O.E. *bæth*; conn. with Ger. *bad.*]

Bath, *bäth, n.* a city in Somerset with Roman *baths.*
Bath bun, a rich sweet bun.
Bath chair, an invalid's wheeled chair.

bathe, *bāTH, v.t.* to wash as in a bath: to moisten (with, in).—*v.i.* to take a bath or bathe.—*n.* a swim or dip.
bath'er, *n.* **bath'ing,** *n.*
[O.E. *bathian*; same root as **bath.**]

bathyscaphe, *bath'i-skāf,* **bathyscope,** *-skōp,* **bathysphere,** *-sfēr, ns.* observation chambers for natural history work under water.
[Gk. *bathys*, deep (*skaphē*, boat; *skopeein*, to look at; *sphaira*, sphere).]

batman, *bat'mȧn, n.* an officer's servant.
[Fr. *bât*, a packsaddle.]

baton, *bat'ȯn, n.* a staff or truncheon, esp. of a policeman: (*music*) a conductor's stick.
[Late L. *basto*, a stick.]

batsman. See **bat** (1).

battalion, *bȧ-tal'yȯn, n.* a large body of soldiers.
[Fr.; from root of **battle.**]

batten[1], *bat'n, v.i.* to feed gluttonously.
to batten on, to revel in (e.g. *to batten on horrors*): to live well at the expense of (e.g. *He did not mind battening on his aunt*).
[Old Norse *batna*, to grow better.]

batten[2], *bat'n, n.* sawn timber used for flooring: in ships, a strip of wood used to fasten down the hatches.—*v.t.* to fasten with battens.
[Same as **baton.**]

batter[1]. See **bat** (1).

batter[2], *bat'ėr, v.t.* to beat with blow after blow: to wear, spoil, with beating or by use.—*n.* (*cooking*) materials beaten with liquid into a paste.
batt'ery, *n.* a number of pieces of artillery: a unit group of artillery and the people manning it: a series of two or more electric cells arranged to produce, or store, a current: a similar arrangement of other apparatus: an arrangement of cages in which laying hens are kept: (*law*) assault by blow or touch :—*pl.* **-ies.**
battering ram, a large beam with a metal head, formerly used in war for battering down walls.
[O.Fr. *batre*—L. *bat(t)uĕre*, beat.]

batting. See **bat** (1) and (3).

battle, *bat'l, n.* a contest between opposing armies: a fight between persons or animals.—*v.i.* to fight: to struggle (*with, against,* or *for*).
batt'leax(e), *n.* an axe once used in battle.
battle cry, a shout in battle: a slogan.
batt'lefield, *n.* the place where a battle is fought.
battle royal, a fight of great fierceness, or one in which many take part.
batt'le-scarred, *adj.* bearing marks of damage in battle.
batt'leship, *n.* a heavily armed and armoured warship.
half the battle, anything that brings one well on the way to success.
to join, do, battle, to fight.
[O.Fr. *bataille*; same root as **batter.**]

battledore, *bat'l-dōr, -dör, n.* a light bat for striking a shuttlecock.
[Perh. Sp. *batidor*, a beater.]

battlement, *bat'l-mėnt, n.* a wall or parapet with openings for firing from.
[O.Fr. *batailles*, movable turrets.]

batty. See **bat** (2).

bauble, *bö'bl, n.* a trifling trinket: a toy: a court jester's stick bearing a head with ass's ears.
[O.Fr. *babel.*]

baulk. See **balk.**

bauxite, *bök'sīt, -zīt, n.* an aluminium ore, found at *Les Baux* (near Arles), etc.

bawbee, *bö-bē', n.* a halfpenny.
[Prob. from a 16th-century Scottish mint-master, the laird of *Sillebawby.*]

bawl, *böl, v.i.* to shout or cry out loudly.—*n.* a loud cry or shout.
[Perh. Late L. *baulāre*, to bark.]

bay[1], *bā, adj.* reddish brown.—*n.* a bay horse.
[L. *badius*, chestnut-coloured.]

bay[2], *bā*, *n.* a wide inlet of the sea, etc.
[Fr. *baie.*]

bay[3], *bā*, *n.* the space between two columns: a recess: a compartment in an aircraft.
bay window, window forming recess.
sick bay, ship's, etc., hospital.
[O.Fr. *baee*, opening.]

bay[4], *bā*, *n.* a laurel tree: (in *pl.*) a garland or crown of victory, orig. of laurel.
[O.Fr. *baie*, a berry.]

bay[5], *bā*, *n.* the deep cry of hounds when hunting.—*v.i.* (esp. of large dogs) to bark.
to hold, keep, at bay, to fight off, keep from overwhelming one.
to stand, be, at bay, to be forced to turn and face an enemy, a difficulty, etc.
[From O.Fr.]

bayonet, *bā'on-it*, *n.* a stabbing instrument of steel fixed to the muzzle of a rifle.—*v.t.* to stab with a bayonet.
[Fr. *baïonnette.*]

bay window. See **bay** (3).

bazaar, *bȧ-zär'*, *n.* an Eastern market place: a shop, etc., where miscellaneous goods are sold: a sale of work.
[Pers. *bāzār*, a market.]

bazooka, *bȧ-zōō'kȧ*, *n.* a weapon consisting of a long tube that launches a projectile with an explosive head.
[From the name of a musical instrument used for comic purposes.]

be, *bē*, *v.i.* to live: to exist: to occur.—Also used to form tenses of other verbs:—*pr.p.* **bē'ing**; *pa.p.* **been** (*bin*); *pr.t.* (*sing.*) *am, art, is*, (*pl.*) *are*; *pa.t.* (*sing.*) *was, wert, was*, (*pl.*) *were* (*wėr*).
being, *bē'ing*, *n.* existence: any person or thing existing.
[O.E. *beon*, conn. with Ger. *bin* (am), Gael. *bi*; *am* from O.E. *eom*, conn. with L. *sum*, Gk. *eimi*; *was, were* from O.E. *wesan*, to remain, be, conn. Ger. *war.*]

be-, *pfx.* (1) around, on all sides, thoroughly, etc. (e.g. *besmear*, to smear over): (2) used to form verbs from *adjs.* (e.g. *befoul*, to make foul): (3) to call or treat as (something; e.g. **befriend**—see this).
[O.E. *bi-.*]

beach, *bēch*, *n.* the shore of a sea or lake, esp. when sandy or pebbly.—*v.t.* to drive or haul (a boat) up on the beach.
beach'comber (*-kōm-ėr*), *n.* a long rolling wave: a drunken loafer in Pacific seaports: a settler on a Pacific island.
beach'head, *n.* an area on a seashore in enemy territory seized by an advance force and held to cover the main landing.
[Orig. a dial. English word for 'shingle'.]

beacon, *bē'kȯn*, *n.* a fire on a high place used as a sign of danger: anything that warns of danger, e.g. a sign or light marking rocks, shoals, etc.: a sign marking a street crossing: a wireless transmitter that sends out signals to guide shipping or aircraft.
[O.E. *bēacn.*]

bead, *bēd*, *n.* a little ball of glass, etc., strung with others in a rosary or a necklace: a drop of liquid: a bubble: the foresight of a gun.
bead'y, *adj.* (of eyes) small and bright:—*comp.* **bead'ier**; *superl.* **bead'iest.**
to tell, count, one's beads, to say prayers.
[O.E. (*ge*)*bed*, prayer; same root as **bid.**]

beadle, *bēd'l*, *n.* a mace-bearer: an officer with minor duties of a church, college, etc.: in Scotland, the 'church officer', attending on the minister, etc.
[O.E. *bydel*—*bēodan*, to proclaim, to bid.]

beady. See **bead.**

beagle, *bē'gl*, *n.* a small hound.
[Origin unknown.]

beak, *bēk*, *n.* the bill of a bird: anything pointed or projecting: the nose.
[O.Fr. *bec.*]

beaker, *bēk'ėr*, *n.* a large drinking-bowl or cup: deep glass vessel used in chemistry.
[Scand. *bikarr.*]

beam, *bēm*, *n.* a long straight piece of timber, etc. for building, etc.: one of the pieces of timber or metal placed from side to side in forming a ship's frame: the greatest width of a ship or boat: the part of a balance from which the scales hang: a shaft (of light, etc.): a radio signal sent out along a narrow course to guide aircraft.
on the beam, in the direction of ship's beams, at right angles to her course: on the course indicated by a radio beam.
on her beam ends, (of a ship) so much inclined to one side that the beams become nearly upright.
on one's beam ends, at the end of one's resources in money, etc.
[O.E. *bēam*, a tree, a ray of light.]

bean, *bēn*, *n.* name of several pod-bearing plants and their seeds: the bean-like seeds of other plants, e.g. coffee.
full of beans, in high spirits.
[O.E. *bēan*; conn. with Ger. *bohne.*]

bear[1], *bār*, *v.t.* to carry: to support: to heave, thrust (back): to endure: to behave or conduct (oneself): to bring forth or produce:—*pr.p.* **bear'ing**; *pa.t.* **bore** (*bōr, bör*); *pa.p.* **borne** (*bōrn, börn*), **born** (*börn*)—'born' referring to something brought forth, e.g. offspring, idea.
bear'able, *adj.* that can be endured.
bear'er, *n.* one who, or something that, bears: one who helps to carry a body to the grave: a carrier, messenger, or (India) body-servant.
bear'ing, *n.* manner, posture, etc.: direction, situation (of one object with regard to another): connexion with (e.g. *This has no bearing on the question*): (usu. in *pl.*) a part of a machine that bears friction, because another part turns or moves in it.
to bear a hand, to give help with something.

to bear down, to overthrow; to swoop (upon).
to bear fruit, to produce fruit: to have the desired result.
to bear hard, heavily, on one, to be difficult for one to endure.
to bear in mind. See **mind.**
to bear out, to support, confirm (e.g. *This bears out what you said*).
to bear up, to keep up one's courage.
to bear with, to be patient with.
to be borne in upon one, to be impressed on one's mind.
to bring to bear, to bring into operation (with *on, upon, against*; e.g. *to bring pressure to bear on him so as to get him to agree*).
to find, get, one's bearings, to find one's position with reference to e.g. a known landmark: to come to understand a new situation.
to lose one's bearings, to become uncertain of one's position.
[O.E. *beran*; conn. with L. *ferre.*]

bear[2], *bār*, *n.* a heavy animal with shaggy hair and hooked claws: *(cap.)* the name of two northern groups of stars, the Great and the Little Bear.
bear′-bait′ing, *n.* setting dogs to attack a tethered bear.
bear garden, enclosure where bears are kept: a rough, noisy place or scene.
bear′skin, *n.* the skin of a bear: high fur cap worn by the Guards in England.
[O.E. *bera*; conn. with Ger. *bär.*]

beard, *bērd*, *n.* hair that grows on the chin and cheeks: something that suggests this: prickles on ears of corn.—*v.t.* to take by the beard: to face deliberately, oppose boldly.
beard′ed, *adj.* **beard′less,** *adj.*
[O.E.; conn. Ger. *bart.*]

bearer, bearing. See **bear** (1).

beast, *bēst*, *n.* an animal, as opposed to man: a four-footed animal: a brutal person.
beast′ly, *adj.* like a beast in actions or behaviour: coarse: *(coll.)* disagreeable.
beast′liness, *n.*
See also **bestial.** [L. *bestia.*]

beat, *bēt*, *v.t.* to strike repeatedly: to strike (e.g. bushes) to rouse game: to overcome: to be too difficult for: to mark (time) with a baton, etc.—*v.i.* to move with regular strokes: to throb: (of waves) to dash (on, against):—*pr.p.* **beat′ing**; *pa.t.* **beat**; *pa.p.* **beat′en.**—*n.* a stroke, or its sound, as of a watch or the pulse: a round or course (e.g. *a policeman's beat*).
beat′en, *adj.* made smooth or hard by treading (e.g. *a beaten path*): shaped by hammering: overcome, defeated.
beat′er, *n.*
beat′ing, *n.* thrashing: throbbing: rousing of game.
to beat about the bush, to approach a subject in an indirect way.
to beat a retreat, to withdraw in a hurry.
to beat down, to reduce (the price) by haggling: to force (a person) to take a lower price.
to beat the bounds, to trace out the boundaries of a parish by going round them.
to beat one's brains, to make a great effort to think of, or to remember, something.
to beat up, to make way against wind or tide: to collect (e.g. recruits, helpers): *(slang)* to knock about severely.
dead beat, completely exhausted.
[O.E. *bēatan.*]

beatify, *bē-at′i-fī*, *v.t.* to make, or declare to be, blessed or happy:—*pa.p.* **-fied.**
beatif′ic, -al, *adjs.* making very happy: expressing happiness (e.g. *a beatific smile*).
beatificā′tion, *n.* (*R.C. Church*) declaration by the Pope that a person is blessed in heaven, the first step to canonisation.
beatitude, *bē-at′i-tūd*, *n.* heavenly happiness: (in *pl.*) sayings of Christ in Matthew v., declaring certain classes of persons to be blessed.
[L. *beātus*, blessed (*facĕre*, to make).]

beating. See **beat.**

beatnik, *bēt′nik*, *n.* (*orig.*) one of a group of writers in U.S.A. who disapproved of, and tried to cut themselves off from, the modern world and conventional people: (*usu.*) people who dress and behave in a deliberately unconventional way.
[Prob. **beat**; Russ. suffx. *-nik.*]

beau, *bō*, *n.* a dandy: a lover:—*pl.* **beaux** (*bōz*):—*fem.* **belle** (see this word).
beau ideal, *bō ī-dē′ȧl*, a person one considers of the highest excellence.
[Fr.—L. *bellus*, fine, gay.]

beauteous, beautiful, etc. See **beauty.**

beauty, *bū′ti*, *n.* quality very pleasing to eye, or ear, etc.: a woman or girl having such quality: an object, etc., attractive-looking or very good (sometimes meaning the opposite; e.g. *The black eye he got was a beauty*):—*pl.* **beau′ties.**
beauteous (*bū′tyůs, -ti-ůs*; chiefly in poetry), **beau′tiful,** *adjs.*
beau′tifully, *adv.*
beau′tify (*-fī*), *v.t.* to make beautiful: to adorn.
[O.Fr. *biaute, beaute*; same root as **beau.**]

beaver, *bēv′ėr*, *n.* a gnawing animal noted for skill in damming streams: its fur, or a hat made of it.
beav′er-board, *n.* a building board of wood fibre.
[O.E. *be(o)for*; conn. with names in Du., Ger., Gael., L.]

becalm, *bi-käm′*, *v.t.* to calm: to make motionless (esp. a ship).
becalmed′, *adj.* [Pfx. **be-** (2).]

became. See **become.**

because, *bi-koz′, bi-köz′, conj.* and *adv.* for the reason that: on account (of).
[Prep. *by*, and **cause.**]

beck[1], *bek, n.* a brook.
[Old Norse *bekkr.*]

beck[2], *bek, n.* a sign with the finger: a nod.
at one's beck and call, always ready to serve and obey one. [**beckon.**]

beckon, *bek′ȯn, v.t.* and *v.i.* to summon by nodding or making a sign (to).
[Same root as **beacon.**]

become, *bi-kum′, v.i.* to come to be: to be the fate (of; e.g. *What has become of it? What is to become of me?*).—*v.t.* to suit or befit:—*pa.t.* **becāme**; *pa.p.* **become′.**
becom′ing, *adj.* suitable (to): that adorns one attractively (e.g. *a becoming hat*).
becom′ingly, *adv.*
[O.E. pfx. *be-*, and *cuman*, to come.]

bed, *bed, n.* a place to sleep on: the channel of a river: a plot in a garden: a place in which anything rests: a layer.
bedd′ed, *adj.* in bed.
bedd′ing, *n.* mattress, bedclothes, etc.: litter for cattle.
bed′clothes, *n.pl.* sheets, blankets, etc.
bed′cover, *n.* upper cover for bed.
bed′fellow, *n.* a sharer of the same bed.
bed′ridden, *adj.* permanently in bed because of age or sickness.
bed′rock, *n.* the solid rock underneath soil or rock fragments: lowest layer: foundation, basis: hard essential facts.
bed′room, *n.* a room for sleeping in.
bed′spread, *n.* a cover put over a bed during the day.
bed′stead, *n.* frame for supporting a bed.
bed and board, food and lodging.
bed of down, or **roses,** any easy or comfortable place.
to lie in the bed one has made, to take the consequences of one's own acts.
[O.E. *bed(d)*; conn. with Ger. *bett.*]

bedaub, *bi-döb′, v.t.* to smear.
[Pfx. **be-** (1).]

bedevil, *bi-dev′l, v.t.* to torment: to bewitch: to muddle, spoil. [Pfx. **be-** (1).]

bedizen, *bi-dīz′n, -diz′, v.t.* to dress gaudily.
[Pfx. **be-**, and same root as **distaff.**]

bedlam, *bed′lȧm, n.* a place of uproar.
[From *Bethlehem* Royal Hospital for the insane, London.]

bedouin, *bed′o͞o-in, n.* a tent-dwelling Arab.
[Arabic *badāwin*, dwellers in the desert.]

bedraggled, *bi-drag′ld, adj.* soiled as by dragging in the wet or dirt. [Pfx. **be-** (1).]

bee, *bē, n.* a four-winged insect, related to wasps and ants, esp. (**honey-bee**) the insect that makes honey: (esp. *U.S.*) a social gathering for work or entertainment.
bee′hive, *n.* a box in which bees are kept, of straw-work, wood, etc.—*adj.* like a dome-shaped beehive.
bees′wax, *n.* the yellowish, solid substance produced by bees, and used by them in making their cells.
a bee in one's bonnet, crazy notions.
to make a bee-line for, to take the most direct road to.
[O.E. *bēo*; conn. with Ger. *biene.*]

beech, *bēch, n.* a forest tree with smooth silvery bark and small nuts.
beech mast, the nuts of the beech tree, which yield a valuable oil.
copper beech, a variety of beech with purplish-brown leaves.
[O.E. *bēce*; conn. with names in Ger., L., Gk.]

beef, *bēf, n.* (the flesh of) a bull, cow, etc.: muscle as opp. to brain.
beef′y, *adj.* like beef; fleshy, heavy:—*comp.* **beef′ier**; *superl.* **beef′iest.**
beef′iness, *n.*
beefeater, *bēf′ēt′ėr, n.* a yeoman of the sovereign's guard: also a warder of the Tower of London.
beef tea, the juice of chopped beef.
[O.Fr. *boef*—L. *bos.*]

beehive. See **bee.** **been.** See **be.**

beer, *bēr, n.* an alcoholic drink made by fermentation from malted barley, flavoured with hops.
beer′y, *adj.* **beer′iness,** *n.*
beer and skittles, idle enjoyment.
small beer, weak beer: trivial affairs: an unimportant person.
[O.E. *bēor*; conn. Ger. and Du. *bier.*]

beeswax. See **bee.**

beet, *bēt, n.* a plant with carrot-shaped root, one variety (**red beet**) used as food, another (**sugar beet**) as a source of sugar.
beet′root, *n.* the root of the beet.
[O.E. *bēte*—L. *bēta.*]

beetle[1], *bē′tl, n.* an insect with four wings, the front pair hard and horny and forming a cover for the hind pair.
[O.E. *bitula, bitela*—*bītan*, to bite.]

beetle[2], *bē′tl, n.* a heavy wooden mallet used for driving wedges, etc.: a pestle-shaped implement, e.g. for mashing potatoes.
[O.E. *bietel*—same root as **beat.**]

beetle[3], *bē′tl, v.i.* (of e.g. cliff) to jut, stick out, hang over.
[From next word.]

beetle-browed, *bē′tl-browd, adj.* with projecting, heavy eyebrows: scowling, sullen.
[Prob. meaning 'with eyebrows like a beetle's'—i.e. sticking out.]

befall, *bi-föl′, v.t.* to happen to (a person or thing).—*v.i.* to happen:—*pr.p.* **befall′ing**; *pa.t.* **befell′**; *pa.p.* **befall′en.**
[O.E. pfx. *be-*, and *feallan*, to fall.]

befit, *bi-fit′, v.t.* to be suitable to, fitting, right for:—*pr.p.* **befitt′ing**; *pa.p.* **befitt′ed.**
befitt′ing, *adj.* **befitt′ingly,** *adv.*
[Pfx. **be-** (1).]

befog, *bi-fog′, v.t.* to envelop in fog: to confuse (a person, etc.). [Pfx. **be-** (1).]

befool, *bi-fo͞ol′, v.t.* to call a fool: to make

a fool of or deceive. [Pfx. **be-** (1) or (3).]

before, *bi-fōr′, -fór′, prep.* in front of: earlier than: in preference to: better than.—*adv.* in front: earlier.—*conj.* earlier than the time when.

before′hand, *adv.* before the time, esp. as preparation.

[O.E. *beforan*; same root as **fore.**]

befoul. See **be-.**

befriend, *bi-frend′, v.t.* to act as a friend to: to help. [Pfx. **be-** (3).]

beg, *beg, v.i.* to ask alms or charity.—*v.t.* to ask earnestly:—*pr.p.* **begg′ing**; *pa.p.* **begged.**

beggar, *beg′ȧr, n.* one who lives by begging: a mean fellow: (*playfully*) rogue, rascal.—*v.t.* to make very poor.

begg′arly, *adj.* poor: mean.

begg′arliness, *n.*

begg′ary, *n.* extreme poverty.

to beggar description, to be greater than the speaker can find words to describe.

to beg off, to get (a person) excused from a punishment, a duty, etc.

to beg the question, to take for granted the very point that is required to be proved.

to go a-begging, to find no claimant or purchaser. [Origin uncertain.]

began. See **begin.**

beget, *bi-get′, v.t.* (of a male parent) to procreate: to cause (e.g. *to beget ill-feeling*):—*pr.p.* **begett′ing**; *pa.t.* **begot′**; *pa.p.* **begott′en.**

begett′er, *n.*

[O.E. pfx. *be-*, and same root as **get.**]

beggar, beggarly, etc. See **beg.**

begin, *bi-gin′, v.i.* to arise (from): to be the first to do something: to open, start, commence.—Also *v.t.*:—*pr.p.* **beginn′ing**; *pa.t.* **began′**; *pa.p.* **begun′.**

beginn′er, *n.* **beginn′ing,** *n.*

[O.E. *be-, ginnan*, to begin.]

begonia, *bi-gōn′ya, -i-a, n.* a greenhouse plant usually with pink flowers and often with coloured leaves.

[From a Frenchman Michel *Bégon.*]

begot, begotten. See **beget.**

begrime, *bi-grīm′, v.t.* to cover with grime. [Pfx. **be-** (1).]

begrudge, *bi-gruj′, v.t.* to grudge, envy (e.g. *to begrudge him his success*).

[Pfx. **be-** (1).]

beguile, *bi-gīl′, v.t.* to cheat (of, out of, something): to lead by deception (into; e.g. *He beguiled him into buying the faked antique*): to deceive: to take the attention from anything dull or painful, charm, amuse.

beguile′ment, *n.*

[Conn. with the noun **guile.**]

begum, *bē′gum, bā′, n.* in Pakistan and India, Moslem princess or lady of rank. [Fem. of *beg*, or **bey.**]

begun. See **begin.**

behalf, *bi-häf′, n.* sake, account, part (e.g. *acting in, on, my behalf*; *on behalf of the members of the club*).

[O.E. *be healfe*, by the side (see **half**).]

behave, *bi-hāv′, v.t.* to conduct (oneself) well (e.g. *If you come, you must behave yourself*).—*v.i.* to conduct oneself well: to conduct oneself (well, badly, etc.): (of persons, things) to act in response to something done or happening (e.g. *How did he behave when told the news?*).

behaved′, *pa.p.* used in phrases **well (ill, badly) behaved,** showing, esp. as a habit, good (bad) manners or conduct.

behaviour, *bi-hāv′yȯr, n.* conduct, manners: response to what is done or happens.

to be (up)on one's (good) behaviour, to be trying to conduct oneself well.

[Prob. *be-* and **have.**]

behead, *bi-hed′, v.t.* to cut off the head of.

behead′ing, *n.*

[O.E. *behēafdian—be-, hēafod*, head.]

beheld. See **behold.**

behest, *bi-hest′, n.* a command: bidding. [O.E. *behæs*, a promise.]

behind, *bi-hīnd′, prep.* at the back of: at the far side of: in support of, encouraging: in a direction backward from: later than: less good than.—*adv.* at the back, in the rear: backward: past.

behind′(hand), *adv.* or *adj.* late, in arrears (with e.g. work, payments).

[O.E. behindan.]

behold, *bi-hōld′, v.t.* to see, observe: to look at.—*v.i.* to look:—*pa.t.* and *pa.p.* **beheld′.**

behold′en, *adj.* obliged, indebted, grateful (to).

behold′er, *n.*

[O.E. pfx. *be-*, and *h(e)aldan*, to hold]

beholden. See **behold.**

behoof, *bi-hōōf′. n.* benefit, convenience.

beho(o)ve, *bi-hōv′, -hōōv′, v.t.* now only in phrase **it beho(o)ves,** it is right or necessary for (e.g. *It behoves you to show gratitude*).

[O.E. *behōfian*, to be fit.]

beige, *bāzh, n.* a fabric made of undyed wool: the colour of this: now, a pinkish buff colour. [Fr.]

being. See **be.**

belabour, *bi-lā′bȯr, v.t.* to beat soundly. [Pfx. **be-,** and **labour.**]

belated, *bi-lāt′id, adj.* happening late or too late.

[Pfx. **be-** and **late.**]

belay, *bi-lā′, v.t.* to fasten (a rope) by coiling it round a **belay′ing-pin** or short rod.

[O.E. *belecgan.*]

belch, *belch, belsh, v.t.* and *v.i.* to give out wind by the mouth: (of a gun, volcano, etc.) to throw out violently.

[O.E. *bealcian.*]

beleaguer, *bi-lēg′ėr, v.t.* to lay siege to. [Du. *belegeren*, to besiege—*leger*, a camp.]

belfry, *bel'fri, n.* the part of a steeple or tower in which bells are hung:—*pl.* **-ies.**
[Orig. a watchtower—O.Fr. *berfroi.*]

Belgian, *bel'jȧn, n.* and *adj.* (a native) of *Belgium.*

belie, *bi-lī', v.t.* to prove false: to fail to act up to (e.g. a promise): to give a false picture of:—*pr.p.* **bely'ing**; *pa.p.* **belied'.**
[Pfx. **be-,** and **lie** (1).]

belief. See **believe.**

believe, *bi-lēv', v.t.* to regard (something) as true: to trust (a person), accepting what he says as true: to think, suppose.—*v.i.* to have faith (in).
belief', *n.* faith: trust.
believ'able, *adj.* **believ'er,** *n.*
[M.E. *bileven.*]

belittle, *bi-lit'l, v.t.* to make to seem small: to speak slightingly of. [Pfx. **be-** (2).]

bell[1], *bel, n.* a hollow vessel of metal struck by a tongue or clapper: other device for giving a ringing sound: anything bell-shaped, as in *bell-tent,* etc.: the sound of a bell.
bell'-tower, *n.* a tower built to contain bells.
[O.E. *belle.*]

bell[2], *bel, v.i.* (esp. of stag) to bellow, roar.
[O.E. *bellan,* to roar.]

belladonna, *bel-ȧ-don'ȧ, n.* deadly nightshade, all parts of which are poisonous: the drug prepared from it.
[It. *bella donna,* fair lady; belladonna in the eyes makes the pupils larger.]

belle, *bel, n.* a beautiful girl: the fairest lady at a dance, etc.
See also **beau.**
[Fr.—L. *bellus,* (fem.) *bella,* fine, gay.]

bellicose, *bel'i-kōs, adj.* warlike, quarrelsome.
belligerent (*be-lij'*), *adj.* carrying on war: warlike (e.g. *a belligerent attitude*).—*n.* a nation or person waging war.
bellig'erency, *n.* **bellig'erently,** *adv.*
[L. *bellum,* war, *belligerāre,* to wage war.]

bellow, *bel'ō, v.i.* to roar like a bull: to make a loud outcry.—Also *v.t.*—*n.* the roar of a bull: any deep sound or cry.
[M.E. *belwen.*]

bellows, *bel'ōz, n.pl.* an instrument for making a current of air to be directed on to (e.g. a fire).
[Same as **belly.**]

belly, *bel'i, n.* the part of the body between the breast and the thighs: the interior of anything: the bulging part of anything:—*pl.* **bell'ies.**—*v.t., v.i.* to swell out:—*pr.p.* **bell'ying**; *pa.p.* **bell'ied.**
bell'yful, *n.* a quantity sufficient or more than sufficient.
[O.E. *bæl(i)g, bel(i)g,* bag.]

belong, *bi-long', v.i.* to go along (with): to be the property of (with *to*): to be a native, member, etc., of (with *to*).
belong'ings, *n.pl.* possessions.
[M.E. *bi-, be-longen.*]

belove, *bi-luv', v.t.* now used only in *pa.p.* **beloved** (*bi-luvd'*) meaning much loved (by, of).—*adj.* and *n.* (*bi-luv'id*) very dear (person). [Pfx. **be-** (1).]

below, *bi-lō', prep.* beneath: underneath: not worthy of.—*adv.* in a lower place: on earth.
[Pfx. **be-,** and **low,** *adj.*]

belt, *belt, n.* a girdle, zone, or band: a zone of country.—*v.t.* to surround with a belt: to thrash with a belt.
belt'ed, *adj.* (of knight, earl) wearing a ceremonial belt: (of an animal) marked with a belt of different colour.
belt'ing, *n.* material for belts: a thrashing. [O.E.]

bemoan, *bi-mōn', v.t.* to moan about, lament. [Pfx. **be-** (1).]

bemuse, *bi-mūz', v.t.* to stupefy.
bemused', *adj.* dazed: absorbed.
[Pfx. **be-** and **muse** (1).]

ben, *ben, n.* a mountain peak.
[Gael. *beann.*]

bench, *bench, -sh, n.* a long seat, form: a mechanic's work-table: a judge's seat.
[O.E. *benc*; conn. Ger. and Du. *bank.*]

bend, *bend, v.t.* to curve (e.g. a bow): to make crooked: to force to submit (e.g. *to bend a person to one's will*): to apply closely (e.g. *to bend one's energies to the job*): to turn, direct (e.g. steps, eyes): (on ship, boat) to tie, make fast.—*v.i.* to be crooked or curved: to stoop: to lean: to submit (with *to, before, towards*):—*pa.t.* and *pa.p.* usu. **bent** (but *on one's* **bend'ed** *knees*).—*n.* a curve.
bent'wood, *n.* wood artificially curved for chair-making, etc.
to be bent on, to be determined on (e.g. *bent on going, bent on reform*).
See also **bent** (2).
[O.E. *bendan,* to bind, to string (a bow).]

bene-, *ben-i-,* (as part of word) well. [L.]

beneath, *bi-nēth', prep.* under, below.—Also *adv.*
beneath contempt, not even worth despising.
beneath one, unworthy of one, not in keeping with one's dignity.
[O.E. *be-,* and *neothan,* under.]

benediction, *ben-i-dik'sh(ȯ)n, n.* prayer asking for the divine blessing: blessedness.
[L. *bene,*well, and *dīcĕre, dictum,* to say.]

benefaction, *ben-i-fak'sh(ȯ)n, n.* a good deed: a grant or gift.
ben'efactor (or *-fak'*), *n.* one who gives friendly help: one who makes a gift to a charity:—*fem.* **ben'efactress** (or *-fak'*).
See also **beneficence,** etc.
[L. *bene,* well, *facĕre,* to do.]

benefice, *ben'i-fis, n.* a church living such as that of a rector or vicar.
[Same root as **beneficence,** etc.]

beneficence, *bi-nef'i-sėns, n.* active kindness, charity.
benef'icent, *adj.*

beneficial, *ben-i-fish'àl, adj.* useful, advantageous, having good results.
benefic'ially, *adv.*
benefic'iary, *n.* one who receives a gift, legacy, advantage, etc:—*pl.* **-ies.**
benefit, *ben'i-fit, n.* something good to receive or have done to one: an advantage: a performance at a theatre, game, etc. at which proceeds go to one player: a right under an insurance scheme (e.g. *unemployment benefit*).—*v.t.* to do good to.—*v.i.* to gain advantage (from, by):—*pr.p.* **ben'efiting**; *pa.t.* and *pa.p.* **ben'efited.**
See also **benefaction,** etc.
[L. *bene,* well, *facĕre, factum,* to do.]

benevolence, *ben-ev'òl-èns, n.* will to do good: kindness: generosity.
benev'olent, *ad.* charitable, generous: feeling kindly, wishing well.
benev'olently, *adv.*
[L. *bene,* well, *volens, -entis,* wishing.]

benign, *bi-nīn', adj.* favourable—opp. to *malign*: gracious: kindly.
benign'ly, *adj.*
benignant, *bi-nig'nànt, adj.* kind: gracious.
benig'nity, *n.* goodness of disposition: kindness and graciousness.
[O.Fr. *benigne*—L. *benignus.*]

bent[1]. See **bend.**

bent[2], *bent, n.* leaning, tendency, inclination of the mind.
to the top of one's bent, as much as one likes. [From **bend.**]

bent[3], *bent, n.* any stiff or wiry grass.
[O.E. *beonet.*]

bentwood. See **bend.**

benumb, *bi-num', v.t.* to make numb or powerless: to deaden (feelings).
benumbed', *adj.* [Pfx. **be-** (2).]

benzene, *ben'zēn, n.* a liquid hydrocarbon obtained from coal tar.
benzine (*-zēn*), *n.* a mixture of hydrocarbons got from petroleum, used as solvent of grease, etc., and for motor fuel.
ben'zol(e), *n.* crude benzene, used as a motor spirit.
[From Arabic name of a fragrant gum.]

bequeath, *bi-kwēth', v.t.* to leave (personal estate) by will: to hand down.
bequest, *bi-kwest', n.* act of bequeathing: a legacy.
[O.E. pfx. *bi-, be-, cwethan,* to say.]

bereave, *bi-rēv', v.t.* to deprive (of), esp. by death:—*pa.p.* **bereaved'** or **bereft'.**
bereaved', *adj.* robbed by death.
bereave'ment, *n.*
[O.E. *be-, rēafian,* to rob.]

beret, *ber'ā, n.* a round, woollen cap.
[Fr. *béret.*]

berg, *bèrg, n.* a hill, mountain: an iceberg.
[Ger., Du., Swed.]

beriberi, *ber'i-ber'i, n.* an Eastern disease, due to lack of vitamin B.
[Sinhalese *beri,* weakness.]

berry, *ber'i, n.* a small juicy fruit: a coffee bean.
[O.E. *berie.*]

berth, *bèrth, n.* a ship's station in port: a sleeping-place in a ship, etc.: a job, place of employment.—*v.t.* to moor a ship.
to give a wide berth to, to keep well away from. [Origin uncertain.]

beryl, *ber'il, n.* a precious stone of which emerald and aquamarine are varieties.
beryllium, *n.* a light steely element.
[O.Fr.—Late L. *bēryllus.*]

beseech, *bi-sēch', v.t.* to beg, entreat: to beg for:—*pa.t.* and *pa.p.* **besought'.**
[Pfx. *be-* and M.E. *sechen,* to seek.]

beset, *bi-set', v.t.* to attack on all sides; to surround (e.g. *to beset with troubles*): to set, stud (*to beset with jewels*):—*pr.p.* **besett'ing**; *pa.t.* and *pa.p.* **beset'.**
besetting sin, the sin that most often tempts one.
[O.E. *besettan.*]

beside, *bi-sīd', prep.* by the side of, near: over and above, in addition to.—Also *adv.*
besides, *bi-sīdz', prep.* over and above, in addition to.—Also *adv.*
beside the mark, irrelevant, not to the point.
to be beside oneself, to be frantic with anxiety, fear, or anger.
[O.E. *be sīdan,* by the side.]

besiege, *bis-ēj', v.t.* to set armed forces round (e.g. a town) in order to force it to surrender: to throng round: to assail (with requests, questions).
besieg'er, *n.*
[M.E. pfx. *be-, segen*—L. *sedēre,* sit.]

besmear. See **be-** (1).

besmirch, *bi-smèrch', v.t.* to soil, dirty.
[Pfx. **be-** (1).]

besom, *bē'zòm, bez'òm, n.* a bunch of twigs for sweeping, a broom.
[O.E. *besema.*]

besot, *bi-sot', v.t.* to make stupid, like a sot: to infatuate (with):—*pr.p.* **besott'ing**; *pa.p.* **besott'ed.** [Pfx. **be-** (3).]

besought. See **beseech.**

bespatter, *bi-spat'èr, v.t.* to sprinkle with dirt or anything moist. [Pfx. **be-** (1).]

bespeak, *bi-spēk', v.t.* to engage beforehand: to show (e.g. *His action bespeaks great courage*):—*pa.t.* **bespōke'**; *pa.p.* **bespoke'** and **bespōk'en.**
bespoke(n), *bi-spōk'(n), adj.* ordered (as boots, clothes, etc.).
[O.E. pfx. *be-,* and *sprecan,* to speak.]

best, *best, adj.* (used as *superl.* of good) good in the highest degree.—*n.* one's utmost effort: the highest perfection: the best part.—*adv.* (*superl.* of well) in the highest degree: in the best manner.—*v.t.* to get the better of.
best man, the bridegroom's attendant at a wedding.
for the best, with the best intentions: with the best results all things considered.

I had best, it would be best for me to.
to put one's best foot foremost, to make one's best effort.
[O.E. *betst, betest*; same root as *better.*]

bestial, *best'yal, -i-ȧl, adj.* brutal: depraved.
bestial'ity, *n.* **best'ially,** *adv.*
[L. *bestiālis*; same root as **beast.**]

bestir, *bi-stėr', v.t.* to rouse to action (esp. oneself).
[O.E. *bestyrian.*]

bestow, *bi-stō', v.t.* to place, or store, put away: to give (with *on*).
bestow'al, *n.*
[M.E. *bistowen*; same root as **stow.**]

bestrew, *bi-strōō', v.t.* to scatter (with).—*pa.t.* **bestrewed'**; *pa.p.* **bestrewed', bestrown', bestrewn'.**
[O.E. *bestrēowian.*]

bestride, *bi-strīd', v.t.* to stride over: to sit or stand across:—*pa.t.* **bestrid', bestrode'**; *pa.p.* **bestrid', bestridd'en.**
[O.E. *bestrīdan.*]

bet, *bet, n.* a wager, money staked to be lost or won.—*v.t.* and *v.i.* to lay or stake:—*pr.p.* **bett'ing**; *pa.t., pa.p.* **bet** or **bett'ed.**
bett'er, *n.* **bett'ing,** *n.*
[Perh. shortened from **abet.**]

beta, *bē'ta, n.* the second letter of the Greek alphabet.

betake, *bi-tāk', v.t.* to take (oneself to; e.g. *He decided to betake himself to church*):—*pa.t.* **betook'**; *pa.p.* **betak'en.**
[Pfx. **be-** (1).]

betel, *bē'tl, n.* the leaf of the betel-pepper, which is chewed in the East along with certain nut-like seeds and lime.
[Through Port. from an Indian word.]

bethink, *bi-thingk', v.* (with *oneself*) to call to mind:—*pa.t.* and *pa.p.* **bethought** (*bi-thöt'*).
[O.E. *bithencan*; same root as **think.**]

betide, *bi-tīd', v.t.* to happen to (e.g. *Woe betide him*).—*v.i.* to happen, come to pass.
[M.E. *betīden.*]

betimes, *bi-tīmz', adv.* in good time.

betoken, *bi-tō'kn, v.t.* to be evidence of, show.
[M.E. bitacnian; same root as **token.**]

betook. See **betake.**

betray, *bi-trā', v.t.* to give up treacherously (e.g. friends, secrets): to deceive: to show signs of (e.g. *to betray anxiety*).
betray'al, *n.* **betray'er,** *n.*
[Pfx. *be-*, L. *trādĕre*, to deliver up.]

betroth, *bi-trōTH'* (or *-troth'*), *v.t.* to promise in marriage.
betrōth'al, *n.* **betrōthed',** *n.* and *adj.*
[M.E. *bitreuthien*—root of **truth.**]

better¹, etc. See **bet.**

better², *bet'ėr, adj.* (used as *comp.* of good) good in a greater degree: preferable: improved: stronger in health.—*adv.* (as *comp.* of well) well in a greater degree.—*n.* a superior (esp. in *pl.*).—*v.t.* to improve: to surpass.
bett'erment, *n.* improvement.
better off, richer: happier.
had better, would be wiser to.
to be better than one's word, to do more than one had promised.
to get the better of, to outwit: to overcome.
to think better of (it), to change one's mind about (it).
[O.E. *bet* (adv.), *betera* (adj.).]

between, *bi-twēn', prep.* and *adv.* in, to, through, or across an interval of space, time, etc.: to and from: connecting: by combined action of: part to (one), part to (the other).
between times, -whiles, *advs.* at intervals.
between you and me, between ourselves, in confidence.
[O.E. *be, twēgen* (see **two**).]

betwixt, *bi-twikst', prep., adv.* between.
betwixt and between, neither the one nor the other.
[O.E. *betweax*—root as **between.**]

bevel, *bev'l, n.* a slant on a surface: an instrument for measuring angles.—*v.t.* to form with a bevel or slant:—*pr.p.* **bev'elling**; *pa.p.* **bev'elled.**
[Fr. *biveau*, instrument for measuring.]

beverage, *bev'ėr-ij, n.* drink.
[O.Fr. *bevrage*—L. *bibĕre*, to drink.]

bevy, *bev'i, n.* a flock of birds, esp. of quails: a company, esp of ladies.
[M.E. *bevey.*]

bewail, *bi-wāl', v.t.* to wail, lament.
[Pfx. **be-** (1).]

beware, *bi-wār', v.i.* to be on one's guard (with *of, lest*, etc.: e.g. *Beware of the dog*).—Also *v.t.* (e.g. *Beware the hidden danger*). Used only in *imper.* and in *to beware, shall, should, must*, etc., *beware.*
[Same root as **wary.**]

bewilder, *bi-wil'dėr, v.t.* to perplex, puzzle.
bewil'derment, *n.* perplexity.
[O.E. *wildēoren*, wilderness.]

bewitch, *bi-wich', v.t.* to cast a spell on: to fascinate, charm.
bewitch'ing, *adj.* **bewitch'ingly,** *adv.*
[O.E. *wicca, wicce*, witch.]

bey, *bā, n.* a governor or ruler.
[Turk. *beg* (pronounced *bā*), a governor.]

beyond, *bi-yond', prep.* on the farther side of: farther on than: later than: out of reach, range, power, etc. of (e.g. *beyond help, understanding, one's strength*).—*adv.* farther away.—*n.* the unknown: the hereafter.
to be beyond caring, etc., to be too tired, esp. emotionally, to care, etc.
to be beyond one, to be too much for one to do, to understand, etc.
the back of beyond, a very remote place.
[O.E. *begeondan.*]

bhang, *bang, n.* the leaves and shoots of

hemp used to deaden feeling or to intoxicate.
[Indian word *bhāng*; Pers. *bang*.]

bi-, *bī-*, *pfx.* two: twice: in two parts.
[L. *bi-*, twice.]

biannual, *bi-an'ū-ȧl*, *adj.* half-yearly.
[L. *bi-*, twice, *annus*, a year.]

bias, *bī'as*, *n.* a greater weight on one side: a leaning to one side: prejudice.—*v.t.* to give a bias to: to prejudice:—*pr.p.* **bī'as(s)ing**; *pa.p.* **bī'as(s)ed.**—*adj.* (of material) cut on the cross.
[Fr. *biais*, slant.]

bib, *bib*, *n.* a cloth put under a child's chin: the top part of an apron.
bibb'er, *n.* one who drinks much (as in *wine-bibber*).
[Prob. same root as **bibulous.**]

Bible, *bī'bl*, *n.* the sacred writings of the Christian Church, consisting of the Old and New Testaments.
biblical, *bib'li-kl*, *adj.*
[Gk. *biblia*, books—*biblos*, papyrus.]

bibliography, *bib-li-og'rȧf-i*, *n.* a descriptive list of books of one author, or on one subject, etc.
bibliog'rapher, *n.*
bibliograph'ic(al), *adjs.*
bibliomā'nia, *n.* a mania for collecting rare books.
[Gk. *biblion*, book (see **Bible**) (*graphein*, to write; **mania**).]

bibulous, *bib'ū-lus*, *adj.* too fond of drink.
[L. *bibulus*—*bibĕre*, to drink.]

bicameral, *bī-kam'ėr-ȧl*, *adj.* (of a parliament) consisting of two houses.
[L. *bi-*, twice, *camera*, chamber.]

bicarbonate, *bi-kär'bon-it*, *n.* sodium bicarbonate (see this).
[Pfx. **bi**, and **carbonate.**]

bicentenary, *bī-sen-tēn'ȧr-i*, or *-ten'*, or *bī-sen'ten-ȧr-i*, *adj.* and *n.* (of) the two hundredth anniversary.
[L. *bi-*, twice, *centum*, a hundred.]

biceps, *bī'seps*, *n.* the muscle with two heads in front of the upper arm.
[L. *bis*, twice, *caput*, head.]

bicker, *bik'ėr*, *v.i.* to keep on quarrelling about small things: to quiver, as a flame: to gurgle, as running water.
[Perh. *bicker*=*picker*, to peck.]

bicuspid, *bī-kus'pid*, *n.* a premolar tooth.
[Pfx. **bi-** and L. *cuspis*, a point.]

bicycle, *bī'si-kl*, *n.* a vehicle, driven by pedals or a motor, with two wheels and a seat.—Also **bike** (*coll.*).—*v.i.* to ride a bicycle.
[L. *bi-*, *bis*, twice, Gk. *kyklos*, wheel.]

bid, *bid*. *v.t.* to tell to (do something): (*old-fashioned*) to invite (e.g. *to bid one to a feast*): to wish (e.g. *to bid one good morning*)—(in these senses, *pr.p.* **bidd'ing**: *pa.t.* **bade** (*bad*, *bād*), *pa.p.* **bidd'en**): to offer to pay at an auction: to call in a card game—(in these senses, *pr.p.* **bidd'ing**; *pa.t.* and *pa.p.* **bid**).—Also *v.i.*—*n.* an offer of a price: a call at cards: an attempt to obtain (e.g. *to make a bid for power*).
bidd'able, *adj.* obedient, docile.
bidd'er, *n.* **bidd'ing**, *n.*
to bid fair, to seem likely (to).
[O.E. *bēodan*, to offer, *biddan*, to ask.]

bide, *bīd*, *v.t.* to wait for; chiefly in **to bide one's time, to** wait for a good opportunity.
[O.E. *bīdan*.]

biennial, *bī-en'i-ȧl*, *-yȧl*, *adj.* lasting two years: happening once in two years.—*n.* a plant that flowers only in its second year, then dies.
bienn'ially, *adv.*
[L. *bi-*, twice, *annus*, a year.]

bier, *bēr*, *n.* a carriage or frame of wood for carrying the dead to the grave.
[From root of verb to **bear.**]

bifocal, *bī-fō'kȧl*, *adj.* (of spectacles for near and distant vision) having two focuses.
[Pfx. **bi-**, and **focal** (see **focus**).]

big, *big*, *adj.* large, great: important: pompous.
bigg'ish, *adj.* rather big.
big'wig, *n.* a person of importance.
big game, large animals that are hunted.
to talk big, to talk as if one were important. [Origin unknown.]

bigamy, *big'ȧm-i*, *n.* the crime of having two wives or two husbands at once.
big'amist, *n.* **big'amous**, *adj.*
[L. *bi-*, twice; Gk. *gamos*, marriage.]

bight, *bīt*, *n.* a wide bay: a coil of rope.
[O.E. *byht*.]

bigot, *big'ȯt*, *n.* one who blindly and obstinately supports a cause, party, etc.
big'oted, *adj.*
big'otry, *n.* bigoted attitude or conduct.
[O.Fr.]

bijou, *bē-zhōō*, *n.* a trinket.—*adj.* small and neat. [Fr.]

bike. See **bicycle.**

bilateral, *bī-lat'ėr-ȧl*, *adj.* having two sides: affecting two sides, countries, etc. (e.g. *a bilateral agreement*).
[Pfx. **bi-**, and **lateral.**]

bilberry, *bil'bėr-i*, *n.* a shrub with a dark blue berry. [Scand.]

bile, *bīl*, *n.* a thick bitter fluid in the liver: ill-humour.
bilious, *bil'yus*, *adj.* of, or affected by, bile.
bil'iousness, *n.*
[L. *bilis*.]

bilge, *bilj*, *n.* the bulging part of a cask: the broadest part of a ship's bottom: filth such as collects there.
[Most prob. conn. with **bulge.**]

bilingual, *bī-ling'gwȧl*, *adj.* written in two languages: speaking two languages (e.g. English and Welsh) equally well.
[L. *bi-*, twice, *lingua*, tongue, language.]

bilk, *bilk*, *v.t.* to avoid paying (debt, creditor): to avoid, slip away from.
[Perh. a form of **balk.**]

bill[1], *bil*, *n.* a kind of battleaxe: a tool with a long blade, used in cutting hedges.
bill'hook, *n.* a bill having a hooked point.
[O.E. *bil.*]

bill[2], *bil*, *n.* a bird's beak: a sharp promontory.—*v.i.* to join bills as doves do.
to bill and coo, to caress fondly.
[O.E. *bile*; prob. same word as **bill** (1).]

bill[3], *bil*, *n.* a draft of a proposed law: an account of money owed for goods, etc.: a bill of exchange (see below): (*U.S.*) a banknote: a placard or advertisement.—*v.t.* to announce by bill.
bill'sticker, bill'poster, *ns.* one who sticks up bills or placards.
bill of exchange, a written order from one person (*the drawer*) to another (*the drawee*) desiring the latter to pay to a named person a sum of money on a certain future date.
bill of fare, a menu.
bill of lading, a paper signed by the master of a ship which makes him responsible for the safe delivery of the goods listed in it.
[Late L. *billa*, a seal.]

billabong, *bil'ȧ-bong*, *n.* (*Austr.*) a branch of a river flowing out of the main stream: a waterhole, pond.
[Native words *billa*, river, *bung*, dead.]

billet, *bil'it*, *n.* a note: a lodging, esp. for a soldier: (*coll.*) a post, job.—*v.t.* to lodge (e.g. soldiers):—*pr.p.* **bill'eting**; *pa.p.* **bill'eted.** [Fr.]

billet-doux, *bil'ā-dōō'*, *n.* a love letter:—*pl.* **billets-doux** (*bil'ā-dōōz'*).
[Fr. *billet*, a letter, *doux*, sweet.]

billiards, *bil'yȧrdz*, *n.* a game played with a cue and balls on a table with pockets at the sides and corners.
bill'iard, *adj.*
[Fr. *billard.*]

billion, *bil'yon*, *n.* a million millions (1,000,000,000,000 or 10^{12}): in U.S.A. a thousand millions (1,000,000,000 or 10^9).
[L. *bi-*, twice, and **million.**]

billow, *bil'ō*, *n.* a great wave of the sea swelled by wind.—*v.i.* to roll as in waves.
bill'owy, *adj.* [Scand.]

billy, billie, *bil'i*, *n.* an Australian bushman's can for cooking or making tea (also **bill'ycan**):—*pl.* **bill'ies.**
bill'y-goat, *n.* a he-goat.
[Prob. *Bill*, for William.]

biltong, *bil'tong*, *n.* (*S. Africa*) sun-dried meat in tongue-shaped strips.
[Du. *bil*, buttock, *tong*, tongue.]

bimonthly, *bī-munth'li*, *adj.* and *adv.* once in two months: twice a month.
[Pfx. **bi-.**]

bin, *bin*, *n.* a receptacle for corn, wine, dust, etc.
[O.E. *binn*, a manger.]

binary, *bī'nȧr-i*, *adj.* consisting of two.
[L. *bīnī*, two by two.]

bind, *bīnd*, *v.t.* to tie with a band, bandage, or bond: to make fast (to): to sew a border on: to fasten together and put a cover on (a book): to make (a person) swear or promise (to do something): to oblige (a person to do something):—*pa.t.* and *pa.p.* **bound.**
bind'er, *n.* one who binds books: a reaping-machine that binds grain into sheaves as it cuts it.
bind'ing, *adj.* restraining: compelling.—*n.* the act of binding: anything that binds: the covering in which the leaves of a book are fixed.
bound to, obliged to: sure to.
to be bound up in, to give all one's interest and affection to.
to bind over, to subject to legal obligation (e.g. to appear in court, to behave well).
[O.E. *bindan.*]

bingo, *bing'gō*, *n.* game of chance using numbers.

binoculars, *bin-ok'ūl-ȧrz*, or *bīn-*, *n.pl.* field-glasses (see **field**).
[L. *bīnī*, two by two, *oculus*, eye.]

bi(o)-, *bī(-ō)-*, (as part of word) life: living thing(s). [Gk.]

biochemistry, *bī-ō-kem'is-tri*, *n.* the chemistry of living substances.
biochem'ical, *adj.* **biochem'ist,** *n.*
[Gk. *bios*, life, and **chemistry.**]

biography, *bī-og'rȧf-i*, *n.* a written account of a person's life.
biog'rapher, *n.* **biograph'ic, -al,** *adjs.*
[Gk. *bios*, life, *graphein*, to write.]

biology, *bī-ol'ȯ-ji*, *n.* the science of living things (animals and plants).
biolog'ical, *adj.* **biolog'ically,** *adv.*
biol'ogist, *n.*
[Gk. *bios*, life, *logos*, a discourse.]

bipartite, *bī-pärt'īt*, *adj.* affecting two parties (as a treaty or agreement).
[L. *bi-*, twice, *partīrī*, to divide.]

biped, *bī'ped*, *n.* animal with two feet.
[L. *bi-*, twice, *pēs, pedis*, foot.]

biplane, *bī'plān*, *n.* an aeroplane with two sets of wings, one above the other.
[L. *bi-*, twice, and **plane.**]

birch, *bėrch*, *n.* a valuable timber tree with smooth white bark: a rod for punishment, made of birch twigs.—*v.t.* to flog.
[O.E. *berc*, *bierce.*]

bird, *bėrd*, *n.* a general name for feathered animals.
bird'-fan'cier (see **fancy**).
bird'-lime, *n.* a sticky substance for catching birds.
bird's-eye view, a general view from above: a summary (of a subject).
[O.E. *brid.*]

birth, *bėrth*, *n.* coming into the world: lineage (e.g. *a man of noble birth*): beginning.
birth'day, *n.* (the anniversary of) the day on which one is born.
birth rate, ratio of births to population.
birth'right, *n.* the right one may claim by birth.
[Prob. Old Norse *byrthr.*]

biscuit, *bis'kit, n.* a crisp bread in small flat cakes: (*U.S.*) a soft round cake: pottery after first baking but not yet glazed.—*adj.* pale brown.
[L. *bis*, twice, *coquĕre*, *coctum*, to cook.]

bisect, *bī-sekt', v.t.* to cut into two equal parts.
bisec'tor, *n.* a line that bisects.
[L. *bi-*, twice, *secāre*, *sectum*, to cut.]

bishop, *bish'ȯp, n.* a clergyman in spiritual charge of a group of churches or diocese: one of the pieces in chess.
bish'opric, *n.* the office of a bishop: a diocese.
[Gk. *episkopos*, an overseer.]

bismuth, *biz'muth*, or *bis'-, n.* a brittle reddish-white element.
[Ger. (now *wismut*).]

bison, *bī'son, n.* a large wild ox; there are two species, the European, almost extinct, and the American, commonly called buffalo.
[L.—Gk. *bisōn*.]

bit[1], *bit, n.* a small piece: a coin, esp. small: a short time: a small tool for boring: the part of the bridle that the horse holds in his mouth.
bit by bit, gradually.
to do one's bit, to take one's share in a task.
to take the bit in one's teeth, to be beyond control.
two bits (*U.S.*), 25 cents.
[From **bite.**]

bit[2]. See **bite.**

bitch, *bich, n.* the female of the dog, wolf, and fox: (abusively) a woman.
[O.E. *bicce*.]

bite, *bīt, v.t.* and *v.i.* to seize or tear with the teeth: to pierce with the mouth parts, as an insect: to eat into with a chemical: (of an implement) to grip:—*pa.t.* **bit**; *pa.p.* **bitt'en.**—*n.* a grasp by the teeth: a puncture by an insect: a mouthful: a small meal.
bit'er, *n.*
bit'ing, *adj.* stinging (e.g. *a biting wind*): wounding (e.g. *a biting remark*).
[O.E. *bītan*.]

bitter, *bit'ėr, adj.* biting to the taste: painful: harsh.
bitt'erly, *adv.* **bitt'erness,** *n.*
bitt'ers, *n.pl.* a liquid prepared from bitter herbs or roots.
bitt'ersweet, *n.* a nightshade.
the bitter end, the very end, however painful.
[O.E. *biter*; conn. *bītan*, to bite.]

bittern, *bit'ėrn, n.* a bird like the heron.
[M.E. *bittour*, *botor*.]

bitumen, *bit'ū-min*, or *bi-tū', n.* an inflammable substance consisting mainly of hydrocarbons, as certain kinds of naphtha, petroleum, asphalt.
bitūm'inous, *adj.* containing bitumen, esp. much bitumen. [L.]

bivalve, *bī'valv, n.* and *adj.* (an animal) having a shell in two valves or parts, as an oyster has.
[L. *bi-*, twice, *valva*, leaf of a door.]

bivouac, *biv'ōō-ak, n.* resting at night in the open air (esp. by soldiers).—Also *v.i.*:—*pr.p.* **biv'ouacking**; *pa.p.* **biv'ouacked.**
[Fr.—Ger. *bei*, by, *wachen*, to watch.]

biweekly, *bī-wēk'li, adj.* occurring once in two weeks or twice a week.—*n.* a biweekly publication. [Pfx. **bi-.**]

bizarre, *bi-zär', adj.* odd, fantastic.
[Fr.; prob.—Sp. *bizarro*, gallant.]

blab, *blab, v.i.* to talk much: to tell tales.—*v.t.* to let out (a secret):—*pr.p.* **blabb'ing**; *pa.p.* **blabbed.**
[M.E. *blabbe*, a chatterer.]

black, *blak, adj.* of the darkest colour: without colour: dismal: sullen: horrible: foul: under trade union ban.—*n.* black colour: absence of colour: a Negro.—*v.t.* to make black.
black'en, *v.t., v.i.* to make, become, black.
black'ly, *adv.* **black'ness,** *n.*
black'ing, *n.* a substance used for black ing leather, etc.
black'amoor, *n.* a dark-skinned person.
black art, magic.
black'ball, *v.t.* to reject (someone) in voting (by putting a black ball into a ballot box, or otherwise).
black beetle, a cockroach (not a true beetle).
black'berry, *n.* a very dark-coloured fruit on a trailing prickly stem, usu. growing wild.—*v.i.* to gather blackberries.
black'bird, *n.* a dark-coloured bird of the thrush family.
black'board, *n.* a board painted black for writing on in chalk.
black box, an instrument for detecting earthquakes or underground explosions.
black bread, rye bread.
black'cock, *n.* the male of the **black grouse,** a grouse of N. England and Scotland.
black currant, a shrub related to the gooseberry, with small black fruit.
black-eye, discoloration round eye.
black'fellow, *n.* Australian aborigine.
black flag, a pirate's flag.
blackguard, *blag'ärd, n.* a scoundrel, a low, evil person.—*v.t.* to abuse, revile.
black'guardly, *adj.*
black'lead, *n.* a black mineral (graphite, not lead) used in making pencils, etc.
black'leg, *n.* a man willing to work during a strike.
black list, a list of people suspected, not approved of, etc. (*v.t.* **black'-list**).
black'mail, *v.t.* to extort money by threatening to reveal something the victim wants to keep secret: to force (into doing something) by threats.—Also *n.*
black'mailer, *n.*
black Maria, a prison van.
black market, illegal buying and selling

at high prices of goods that are scarce, rationed, etc.

black′-out, *n.* darkness produced by putting out all lights: unconsciousness: loss of memory.

black pudding, a sausage of suet, blood, etc.

black sheep, a disreputable member of a family or group.

black′smith, *n.* a smith working in iron.

black′thorn, *n.* a dark-coloured thorny shrub bearing sloes.

in black and white, in writing or print: in no colours but black and white.

to be black in the face, to have the face purple through anger, effort, etc.

to be in anyone's black books, to be out of favour with him or her.

[O.E. *blæc.*]

bladder, *blad′ėr, n.* a thin bag stretched by filling with liquid or air: the receptacle for the urine in the body.

[O.E. *blǣdre—blawan,* to blow.]

blade, *blād, n.* the flat part of a leaf or petal, esp. a leaf of grass or corn: the cutting part of a knife, sword, etc.: the flat part of an oar: dashing fellow.

[O.E. *blæd*; conn. with Ger. *blatt.*]

blaeberry, *blā′bėr-i, n.* a bilberry.

[*blae,* livid, blue; from Old Norse.]

blain, *blān, n.* a boil or blister.

[O.E. *blegen.*]

blame, *blām, v.t.* to criticise, express disapproval of: to consider the responsibility as belonging to (e.g. *I blame you, the wet road, for the skid*).—*n.* finding of fault: responsibility for something bad.

blame′less, *adj.* innocent.

blame′lessly, *adv.* **blame′lessness,** *n.*

blame′worthy, *adj.* worthy of blame.

blame′worthiness, *n.*

to be to blame (for), to be responsible (for an unfortunate happening).

[Fr. *blâmer*—Gk. *blasphēmeein,* speak ill.]

blanch, *blânch* or *-sh, v.t., v.i.* to make, or grow, white.

[Fr. *blanc,* white.]

blanc-mange, *blȧ-monzh′, n.* a jelly-like pudding prepared with milk.

[Fr. *blanc,* white, *manger,* food.]

bland, *bland, adj.* soothing: mild: polite.

bland′ly, *adv.* **bland′ness,** *n.*

bland′ish, *v.t.* to flatter, coax.

blandishment, *bland′ish-mėnt, n.* (usu. in *pl.*) flattering or coaxing action or speech: soft, agreeable words or caresses.

[L. *blandus*; *blandīrī,* to coax.]

blank, *blangk, adj.* (of paper) without writing or marks: empty: expressionless.—Also *n.*

blank′ly, *adv.* **blank′ness,** *n.*

blank cartridge, one without a bullet.

blank cheque, a cheque on which the sum to be paid has not been entered.

blank verse, unrhymed verse.

[Fr. *blanc,* white.]

blanket, *blang′kit, n.* a warm, usu. woollen, covering for a bed, or one used as a garment by American Indians, etc.: a covering generally.—*adj.* covering a group of things (e.g. *a blanket agreement*).—*v.t.* to cover with, or as with, a blanket.

[O.Fr. *blankete*; from *blanc,* white.]

blare, *blār, v.i.* (of e.g. a trumpet) to sound loudly.—Also *n.*

[M.E. *blaren.*]

blarney, *blär′ni, n.* pleasant talk or flattery.

[*Blarney* Castle, near Cork, where is a stone that is said to give skill in coaxing to those who kiss it.]

blasé, *blä′zā, adj.* bored with pleasures through having had too many. [Fr.]

blaspheme, *blas-fēm′, v.t.* and *v.i.* to speak irreverently of (God): (*v.i.*) to swear.

blasphem′er, *n.*

blasphemous, *blas′fėm-ŭs, adj.*

blas′phemy (*-fėm-i*), *n.*

[Gk. *blasphēmeein*; same root as **blame.**]

blast, *blâst, n.* a gust of wind: a forcible stream of air: the sound of a wind instrument: an explosion, or the strong wave of air spreading out from it.—*v.t.* to blight, wither: to ruin, destroy: to tear apart by an explosion.

blast′ed, *adj.* blighted: cursed.

blast′ing, *n.*

blast furnace, a smelting furnace into which hot air is blown.

blast′-off, *n.* the explosive start of the journey of a rocket-propelled missile or space capsule.

[O.E. *blæst*; conn. Ger. *blasen,* to sound.]

blatant, *blāt′ȧnt, adj.* glaring, obvious (e.g. *a blatant lie*): vulgarly showy.

[Prob. coined by the poet Spenser.]

blather. Same as **blether.**

blaze[1], *blāz, n.* a rush of light or flame: an outburst (e.g. of anger): a bright display.—*v.i.* to burn, shine brightly.

blaz′er, *n.* a light sports jacket, usu. of bright colour.

to blaze away, to go on without pause firing gun(s), or speaking angrily, or working energetically.

[O.E. *blæse,* a torch.]

blaze[2], *blāz, n.* a white mark on an animal's face: a guiding mark made on a tree.

to blaze a trail, to show a forest track by marking trees: to lead the way in any change or development.

[Perh. Du. *bles,* or Old Norse *blesi.*]

blaze[3], *blāz, v.t.* to proclaim, spread abroad.

[Conn. with Old Norse *blāsa,* to blow.]

blazon, *blā′zn, v.t.* to make public, publish: to display very obviously.

bla′zonry, *n.* brilliant display.

[Fr. *blason,* shield; confused with **blaze** (3).]

bleach, *blēch, v.t.* and *v.i.* to take out, or lose, colour, to whiten.

bleaching powder, powder for bleaching, esp. chloride of lime.

[O.E. *blǣcan*; same root as bleak.]

bleak, *blēk, adj.* dull and cheerless: cold, unsheltered.
bleak'ly, *adv.* **bleak'ness,** *n.*
[O.E. *blāc,* pale.]

bleary, *blēr'i, adj.* (of eyes) sore and red:—*comp.* **blear'ier**; *superl.* **blear'iest.**—Also **blear.** [Origin uncertain.]

bleat, *blēt, v.i.* to cry as a sheep.—Also *n.*
[O.E. *blǣtan.*]

bled. See **bleed.**

bleed, *blēd, v.i.* to lose blood: to die in battle: to lose sap:—*v.t.* to draw blood or sap from: to extort money from:—*pa.t.* and *pa.p.* **bled.**
bleed'er, *n.* a person whose blood does not clot quickly enough, and who therefore tends to bleed immoderately.
bleed'ing, *n.* and *adj.*
[O.E. *blēdan.*]

blemish, *blem'ish, n.* a stain or defect.—*v.t.* to spoil.
[O.Fr. *blesmir, blemir,* to stain.]

blench, *blench* or *-sh, v.i.* to shrink, flinch.
[O.E. *blencan.*]

blend, *blend, v.t.* to mix together, esp. with good result.—*v.i.* to go well together (as colours):—*pa.p.* **blend'ed.**—*n.* a mixture.
blend'er, *n.* **blend'ing,** *n.* and *adj.*
[M.E. *blenden.*]

bless, *bles, v.t.* to pronounce holy: to ask God to show favour to: to make happy:—*pa.p.* and *adj.* **blessed** (*blest*; *adj.* usu. *bles'id*) or **blest.**
bless'edly, *adv.* **bless'edness,** *n.*
bless'ing, *n.* a wish or prayer for happiness or success: any cause of happiness.
[O.E. *blēdsian, blētsian.*]

blest. See **bless.**

blether, *bleTH'ėr, v.i.* to chatter foolishly.
bleth'erskate, (*U.S.*) **blath'erskite,** *ns.* a talkative fool.
[M.E. *blather*; from Old Norse; *blether* is Scots form.]

blew. See **blow.**

blight, *blīt, n.* a disease in plants that withers them: anything that spoils.—*v.t.* to cause to wither: to bring to nothing (e.g. *to blight our hopes*).
blight'er, *n.* a scamp, wretch.
[Prob. of Scand. origin.]

blighty, *blī'ti, n.* home, Britain.
[Indian word *bilāyatī,* foreign, European.]

blind, *blīnd, adj.* without sight: not noticing: unable to understand or to foresee: concealed: without an opening.—*n.* something to mislead: a window-screen.—Also *v.t.*
blind'ing, *adj.* tending to make blind.
blind'ly, *adv.* **blind'ness,** *n.*
blind'fold, *adj.* with the eyes bandaged so as not to see.—Also *v.t.*
blind alley, a passage without an exit: a job with no prospects.
blind flying, flying by means of instruments alone.
blindman's buff, a game in which one person is blindfolded and tries to catch the others.
blind spot, the point on the retina of the eye on which no images are formed: any matter about which one always shows lack of understanding.
blind to, unable to see or appreciate.
[O.E.; conn. with Old Norse *blindr.*]

blink, *blingk, v.i.* to twinkle or wink rapidly: to look with half-shut eyes (at).—*v.t.* to refuse to look at (e.g. *to blink the fact that*).—*n.* a glimpse: a gleam.
blink'ers, *n.pl.* leather flaps on a bridle preventing a horse from seeing sideways.
[Prob. the same as **blench.**]

bliss, *blis, n.* the highest happiness.
bliss'ful, *adj.* **bliss'fully,** *adv.*
bliss'fulness, *n.*
[O.E. *blītho*; same root as **blithe.**]

blister, *blis'tėr, n.* a thin bubble on the skin, containing watery matter: a similar spot on any surface.—*v.t.* to raise a blister or blisters on.—Also *v.i.*
[Prob. O.Fr. *blestre.*]

blithe, *blīTH, adj.* gay, light-hearted.
blithe'ly, *adv.* **blithe'ness,** *n.*
[O.E. *blīthe,* joyful.]

blitz, *blits, n.* (for Ger. *blitzkrieg,* lightning war) any sudden, vigorous attack.

blizzard, *bliz'ȧrd, n.* a blinding storm of wind and snow. [Imit.]

bloat, *blōt, v.t.* to swell or puff out.
bloat'ed, *adj.*
bloat'er, *n.* a herring partly dried in smoke.
[Scand., as in Swed. *blöt,* soft.]

blob, *blob, n.* a drop of liquid: zero. [Imit.]

bloc, *blok, n.* a group, combination, of nations, or of parties, etc., who have an interest or purpose in common. [Fr.]

block, *blok, n.* a mass of wood or stone, etc., usu. flat-sided: wood on which a person is beheaded: a piece of wood used for chopping on, for printing (illustrations) or as a toy (for building): (*machinery*) a pulley with its framework, or the framework alone: a connected group of houses: an obstruction: a stolid, stupid, or unfeeling person.—*v.t.* to obstruct (e.g. *to block his path*): to hinder: to stop (a ball) with bat resting upright on the ground.
block capital, letter, a capital letter written in imitation of printing type (e.g. those in NAME).
block'head, *n.* a stupid fellow.
block'house, *n.* a small temporary fort.
block system, a system of signalling by which no train can enter a section of the railway till the previous train has left it.
[Same root as **bloc.**]

blockade, *blȯ-kād', n.* blocking every approach to a place by land or sea.—Also *v.t.*
blockade'-runn'er, *n.* a person or ship that passes through a blockading force.
[Same root as **block, bloc.**]

blond, (*fem.*) **blonde,** *blond, n.* a person of fair complexion and light-coloured hair. —*adj.* fair. [Fr.]

blood, *blud, n.* the red fluid in the arteries and veins: shedding of blood: royal or aristocratic descent: descent: relationship: a dandy: temper (e.g. *His blood was up*).
blood'ed, *adj.* having blood: having been in battle.
blood'less, *adj.* anaemic: without spirit: without the shedding of blood.
blood'y, *adj.* stained with blood: murderous, cruel: (*bad language*) annoying (sometimes used without meaning):—*comp.* **blood'ier**; *superl.* **blood'iest.**
blood'ily, *adv.* **blood'iness,** *n.*
blood bath, a massacre.
blood'curdling, *adj.* terrifying: horrible.
blood donor, one who gives blood for use in transfusion.
blood group, any one of the kinds into which human blood is classified.
blood heat, the temperature of the human blood (about 98° Fahrenheit).
blood'hound, *n.* a large, keen-scented hound, used for tracking: a detective.
blood'-poisoning, *n.* disease due to poisonous matter or bacteria in the blood.
blood'shed(ding), *ns.* shedding of blood slaughter.
blood'shot, *adj.* (of eyes) red, inflamed with blood.
blood'stained, *adj.* stained with blood: guilty of murder.
blood'stream, *n.* the blood flowing through the body: something thought of as like this (e.g. *tapping the country's bloodstream of skilled men*).
blood'thirsty, *adj.* eager, or seeming to show eagerness, to shed blood.
blood'thirstiness, *n.*
blood pressure, the pressure of the blood on the walls of the blood-vessels.
blood sports, those in which animals are killed.
blood transfusion. See **transfusion.**
blood'-vessel, *n.* any of the tubes in the body through which the blood flows.
in hot (or **cold**) **blood,** while under (or free from) excitement or passion.
[O.E. *blōd.*]

bloom, *blōōm, n.* a blossom, flower: state of flowering: freshness, perfection: rosy colour: powder on the rind of fresh fruits.—*v.i.* to flower.
bloom'ing, *adj.* flourishing.
[Old Norse *blōm*; conn. Ger. *blume.*]

blossom, *blos'ŏm, n.* a flower, esp. of a fruit tree.—*v.i.* to put forth flowers: to flourish, prosper.
[O.E. *blōstm(a)*; same root as **bloom.**]

blot, *blot, n.* a spot or stain.—*v.t.* to spot or stain: to dry with blotting paper:—*pr.p.* **blott'ing**; *pa.p.* **blott'ed.**
blott'er, *n.* pad or book of blotting paper.
blotting paper, soft, unglazed paper used for sucking up ink.
to blot out, to hide from sight, or conceal from memory: to destroy completely.
[Perh. Scand.]

blotch, *bloch, n.* a discoloration on skin.—Also *v.t.*
blotched, blotch'y, *adjs.* [Prob. **blot.**]

blouse, *blowz, n.* a loose outer garment usu. tucked in at the waist. [Fr.]

blow[1], *blō, n.* a stroke or knock: a sudden misfortune.
[Prob. from **blow** (2).]

blow[2], *blō, v.i.* (of current of air) to be in motion: to drive air (upon or into): to breathe hard: to spout, as a whale.—*v.t.* to drive by a current of air: to sound (a wind instrument): to drive air into: (of insects) to lay eggs on.—*pa.t.* **blew** (*blōō*); *pa.p.* **blown** (*blōn*).
blown, *adj.* out of breath.
blow'y, *adj.* windy. **blow'iness,** *n.*
blow'fly, *n.* a fly of the family to which the house fly and the bluebottle belong.
blow'hole, *n.* a breathing hole in ice for whales, etc.: a whale's nostril: a vent for the escape of gas.
blow'out, *n.* the bursting of a car tyre: a violent escape of gas, etc.
blow'pipe, *n.* a pipe through which air or gas is blown on a flame to increase its heat: a tube from which an arrow is blown.
to blow over, to pass over or away.
to blow up, to shatter, or be shattered, by explosion: to lose one's temper: to fill with air or a gas: to scold.
[O.E. *blāwan*; conn. with Ger. *blähen.*]

blowzy, *blowz'i, adj.* fat and red: dishevelled. [Orig. unknown.]

blubber, *blub'ėr, n.* the fat of whales and other sea animals.—*v.i.* to weep noisily.
[M.E. *blober, bluber.*]

bludgeon, *bluj'ŏn, n.* a short stick with a heavy end for striking.—Also *v.t.*
[First used 18th cent.; origin unknown.]

blue, *blōō, adj.* of the colour of the sky or the deep sea: dismal: depressed.—*n.* the sky: the sea: a blue colour or paint: a blue powder or liquid used in washing clothes: (a distinction given to) one who has represented his university in athletics, etc.
blu'ish, *adj.* slightly blue.
bluey, *blōō'i, n.* an Australian bushman's bundle.
blue'bell, *n.* the wood hyacinth: (often *-bel'*) in Scotland and N. England the harebell.
blue'-book, *n.* a parliamentary report (from its blue paper wrapper).
blue'bottle, *n.* the blue cornflower: a large fly with blue abdomen.
blue'jacket, *n.* a seaman in the navy.
blue pencil, a pencil for correcting or censoring.—*v.t.* (**blue'-pen'cil**) to mark

out with blue pencil:—*pr.p.* **blue′-pen′cilling**; *pa.p.* **blue′-pen′cilled.**
Blue Peter, a blue flag with white square in centre hoisted as sign that ship is about to sail.
blue′print, *n.* a white photographic print on a blue ground: a detailed plan of work to be carried out.
blue ribbon, the ribbon of Knights of the Garter: any great prize.
blue stocking, a learned lady.
from (or **out of**) **the blue,** without warning.
once in a blue moon, very seldom.
(the) blues, low spirits: a very slow dismal song, of American Negro origin.
[M.E. *blew*—O.Fr. *bleu*; Germanic.]

bluff[1], *bluf*, *adj.* rough, hearty, frank in manner.—*n.* a steep cliff, esp. along seashore or river.
bluff′ness, *n.* [Prob. Du.]

bluff[2], *bluf*, *v.t.* and *v.i.* to deceive, or try to deceive, by pretending to have something (e.g. good cards) that one does not have.—Also *n.* [Origin unknown.]

blunder, *blun′dėr*, *v.i.* to make a bad mistake: to stumble about.—Also *n.*
[M.E. *blondren*; origin uncertain.]

blunderbuss, *blun′dėr-bus*, *n.* a short handgun with a wide bore: a stupid person.
[Du. *donder*, thunder, *bus*, box.]

blunt, *blunt*, *adj.* having a dull edge or point, not sharp: rough, outspoken.—*v.t.* to make less sharp or painful.
blunt′ly, *adv.* **blunt′ness,** *n.*
[Prob. conn. Old Norse *blunda*, to doze.]

blur, *blûr*, *n.* a smudge, smear: a dimness.—*v.t.* to blot: to dim:—*pr.p.* **blurr′ing**; *pa.p.* **blurred.**
[Same root as **blear.**]

blurb, *blûrb*, *n.* a publisher's description of a book, usu. printed on the jacket.

blurt, *blûrt*, *v.t.* (with *out*) to say suddenly or without thinking of the effect or result. [From the sound.]

blush, *blush*, *n.* a red glow on the skin caused by shame, etc.—*v.i.* to show shame, joy, etc., by growing red in the face.
[M.E. *blusche*—O.E. *blyscan*, to blush.]

bluster, *blus′tėr*, *v.i.* to make a noise like a blast of wind: bully, swagger.—Also *n.*
blus′tering, *adj.* and *n.*
blus′teringly, *adv.*
[Prob. conn. with **blast.**]

boa, *bō′ȧ*, *n.* a kind of large snake (especially the **boa-constric′tor**) that kills by winding itself round its prey: a long wrap of fur or feathers for the neck.
[L. *bŏa*, a kind of snake.]

boar, *bōr*, *bör*, *n.* the male of swine.
[O.E. *bār.*]

board, *bōrd*, *börd*, *n.* a broad and thin strip of timber: a table for food: meals: an official group of persons (e.g. *a board of directors*): (in *pl.*) the stage: a sheet of stiff material, e.g. for binding books.—*v.t.* to cover with boards: to supply with meals (and lodging) at a fixed price: to enter (a ship, etc.), esp. by force.—*v.i.* to lodge and take meals.
board′er, *n.* **board′ing,** *n.* and *adj.*
boarding house, a house where boarders are kept.
boarding school, a school in which board as well as instruction is given.
above board, open(ly).
on board, on, or in, a ship, plane, etc.
to go by the board, to go over the ship's side: to be discarded, lost.
to sweep the board, to win every point in a game or contest.
[O.E. *bord*, board, side of ship.]

boast, *bōst*, *v.i.* to talk with too much pride: to brag (of, about).—*n.* a brag: a subject of pride.
boast′ing, *n.* **boast′ful,** *adj.*
boast′fully, *adv.* **boast′fulness,** *n.*
to boast (of), to possess, have.
[M.E. *bost*; origin uncertain.]

boat, *bōt*, *n.* a small open craft usu. moved by oars: a ship: a dish shaped like a boat.—*v.i.* to sail about in a boat.
boat′ing, *n.* and *adj.*
boat hook, a metal hook fixed to a pole, for pulling or pushing a boat.
boat′man, *n.* a man in charge of a boat:—*pl.* **boat′men.**
boat train, a train taking passengers to or from a ship in dock.
in the same boat, in the same difficulty.
[O.E. *bat*; conn. Du. *boot*, Fr. *bateau.*]

boatswain, *bō′sn*, *n.* an officer who looks after a ship's boats, rigging, etc.
[**boat** and **swain.**]

bob[1], *bob*, *v.i.* to move up and down: to curtsy.—*v.t.* to cut (hair) so that it does not fall beyond the neck:—*pr.p.* **bobb′ing**; *pa.p.* **bobbed.**—*n.* a short jerky movement: the weight on a pendulum, plumb line, etc.
bob′sled, bob′sleigh (*-slā*), *ns.* a short sledge: a sleigh made up of two of these, usu. with one common seat.
bob′tail, *n.* a short or cut tail.
[Origin unknown.]

bob[2], *bob*, *n.* (*slang*) a shilling:—*pl.* **bob.**
[Origin uncertain.]

bobbin, *bob′in*, *n.* a reel or spool for winding yarn, wire, etc.
[Fr. *bobine*; prob. Celt.]

bobby, *bob′i*, *n.* (*slang*) a policeman.
[Sir *Robert* Peel, who reorganised London police in 1829.]

bobsled, bobtail, etc. See **bob** (1).

bode, *bōd*, *v.t.* to be an omen of, foretell.—*v.i.* (of fact) to promise (well, ill).
[O.E. *bodian*, to announce.]

bodice, *bod′is*, *n.* a close-fitting part of a woman's dress covering the trunk.
[A form of *bodies*, pl. of **body.**]

bodkin, *bod′kin*, *n.* a small dagger: a large blunt needle.
[Perh. conn. with W. *bidog*, a dagger.]

body, *bod′i, n.* the whole frame of a man or animal: a corpse: the main part of anything: a mass: (*coll.*) a person: a group of persons considered as acting as one:—*pl.* **bod′ies.**
bod′ied, *adj.* having a body of a certain kind (e.g. *strong-bodied*).
bod′ily, *adj.* of the body.—*adv.* as one whole and completely (e.g. *to remove bodily*).
bod′yguard, *n.* a guard to protect (esp. an important person).
bod′y-servant, personal attendant, valet. [O.E. *bodig.*]

Boer, *bŏŏr, n.* a South African of Dutch descent.—Also *adj.* [Du., a farmer.]

boffin, *bof′in, n.* (*slang*) a scientist.

bog, *bog, n.* spongy ground, a marsh.—*v.i.* (often **bog down**) to sink, or be hindered in movement or progress, in, or as if in, a bog.—Also *v.t.*
bogg′y, *adj.* **bogg′iness,** *n.* [Ir. and Scot. Gael. *bogach*; *bog*, soft.]

bogey[1], *bō′gi, n.* (*golf*) the score, for a hole or for the full round, of an imaginary good player, Colonel *Bogey*.

bogey[2]. See **bogie.** **bogey**[3]. See **bogy.**

boggle, *bog′l, v.i.* to start back: to make difficulties (about—or with *at*). [Perh. from *bogle*, a bogy.]

bogie, bogey, *bō′gi, n.* a low truck: a four- or six-wheel truck supporting part of a long vehicle, e.g. a locomotive body, and making it able to run on a curved track. [Origin unknown.]

bogus, *bō′gus, adj.* sham, not genuine. [Orig. U.S.; origin unknown.]

bogy, bogey, *bō′gi, n.* a goblin: something specially dreaded: the devil. [Origin unknown.]

Bohemian, *bō-hē′mi-ȧn, n.* a Czech: (often without *cap.*) one who lives in a free and easy way, taking no notice of conventional rules of behaviour.—Also *adj.* [Fr. *bohémien*, a gipsy.]

boil[1], *boil, v.i.* to turn rapidly from liquid to vapour: to bubble up: to be hot: to be angry.—*v.t.* to cook by boiling.
boil′er, *n.* a vessel in which water is heated or steam is produced. [L. *bullīre*—*bulla*, a bubble.]

boil[2], *boil, n.* an inflamed swelling. [O.E. *bȳl.*]

boisterous, *bois′tėr-ŭs, adj.* wild, noisy, stormy.
bois′terously, *adv.* **bois′terousness,** *n.* [M.E. *boistous.*]

bolas, *bō′lȧs, n.* a thong, weighted with balls, thrown so as to curl round an animal's legs and hobble it. [Sp., balls.]

bold, *bōld, adj.* daring: impudent: spirited: striking, well-marked.
bold′ly, *adv.* **bold′ness,** *n.*
to make bold, to take the liberty (to). [O.E. *bald.*]

bole, *bōl, n.* the round stem of a tree. [Scand. *bolr*; conn. Ger. *bohle*, plank.]

boll, *bol, n.* a round seed-vessel as in cotton, flax, poppy, etc. [O.E. *bolla.*]

bollard, *bol′ȧrd, n.* a short post on a wharf or ship round which ropes are fastened. [Prob. **bole.**]

bolster, *bōl′stėr, n.* a long round pillow: a pad, prop.—*v.t.* to prop up: to aid.—Also **bolster up.** [O.E.]

bolt[1], *bōlt, n.* a bar to fasten a door, etc.: an arrow: a thunderbolt: a stout pin: a roll of cloth:—*v.t.* to fasten with a bolt: to swallow hastily.—*v.i.* to go away fast (like an arrow from a bow).
bolt′-up′right, *adv.* upright, and straight as an arrow. [O.E.]

bolt[2], *bōlt, v.t.* to sift (flour).—Also **boult.** [O.Fr. *bulter.*]

bomb, *bom, n.* a hollow case containing explosive or other harmful material, thrown or dropped.—*v.t.* to drop bombs on.
bomber, *bom′ėr, n.* an aeroplane built for bombing.
bomb′proof, *adj.* strong enough to resist bombs.
bomb′shell, *n.* formerly, a bomb: startling news. [L. *bombus*, a humming sound.]

bombard, *bom-bärd′, v.t.* to attack with artillery: to batter or pelt (with).
bombardier (*-bȧr-dēr′*), *n.* the bomb aimer in a bombing aeroplane: a corporal in the artillery.
bombard′ment, *n.* [**bomb.**]

bombast, *bom′bast, n.* pompous language.
bombas′tic, *adj.* **bombas′tically,** *adv.* [Orig. 'stuffing'—Late L. *bombax*, cotton.]

bona fide, *bō′na fīd′ā, adv., adj.* genuine(ly).
bona fides, *n.* genuineness. [L.]

bonbon, *bong′bong, n.* a sweetmeat. [Fr.—*bon*, good.]

bond, *bond, n.* something that binds: something that unites people: a written promise to pay a sum of money, usu. by a certain date: (in *pl.*) captivity.
bonded store or **warehouse,** a warehouse where goods are kept until customs or other duty on them is paid. [Same as **band** (1).]

bondage, *bon′dij, n.* slavery: state of being completely under the control of another person. [O.E. *bonda*, a peasant; from Old Norse.]

bone, *bōn, n.* a hard substance forming the skeleton of higher animals: (in *pl.*) the skeleton: (in *pl.*) any framework.—*v.t.* to take the bones out of (e.g. meat).
boned, *adj.* having bones: with bones removed.
bony, *bō′ni, adj.* full of, or like, bones: having large bones or little flesh:—*comp.* **bo′nier**; *superl.* **bo′niest.**
bon′iness, *n.*

bone china, china in making which ashes of burnt bones are used.
bone meal, ground bones.
bone dry, absolutely dry.
bone′-sett′er, *n.* one who, without the normal surgeon's training, treats broken or displaced bones.
a bone of contention, a cause of argument or quarrelling.
a bone to pick with, a grievance against (a person).
to make no bones about, to have no hesitation, scruple, about.
[O.E. *bān.*]

bonfire, *bon′fīr, n.* a fire in the open air.
[**bone, fire.**]

bonnet, *bon′it, n.* a headdress fastened by strings: (*Scot.*) a cap: the cover of a motor-car engine, etc.
[Late L. *bonnetum.*]

bonny, bonnie, *bon′i, adj.* pretty: healthy-looking: fine:—*comp.* **bonn′ier**; *superl.* **bonn′iest.**
[Perh. conn. with Fr. *bon*(*ne*), good.]

bonus, *bō′nus, n.* an addition to the sum due as interest, dividend, or wages.
[L. *bonus*, good.]

bony. See **bone.**

booby, *bōō′bi, n.* a stupid person: a kind of gannet.
booby prize, a prize for the lowest score.
boo′by-trap, *n.* something put above a door so as to fall on the person who opens the door: a bomb or mine made to look like something harmless.
[Perh. Sp. *bobo.*]

book, *book, n.* a number of sheets of paper (esp. printed) bound together: a literary composition: the words of a musical drama: a record of bets: (in *pl.*) records, e.g. of a business.—*v.t.* to note in a book: to engage in advance.—*v.i.* to buy a ticket (for).
book′ish, *adj.* fond of reading.
book′ie, *n.* (*coll.*), a bookmaker.
book′binding, *n.* putting the covers on books.
book′binder, *n.*
booking office, an office where tickets are sold.
book′keeping, *n.* keeping accounts.
book′keeper, *n.*
book′maker, *n.* a professional betting man who takes bets and pays winnings.
book′mark, *n.* something put in a book to mark a page.
book plate, a label pasted inside the cover of a book, with owner's name, etc.
book′stall, *n.* a stand where books, etc. are sold.
book′worm, *n.* a grub that eats holes in books: one who reads continually.
to be in another's good (or **bad**) **books,** to be approved of (or disapproved of) by him at the time.
to bring to book, to make (a person) explain, or suffer for, his conduct.
to take a leaf out of another's book, to follow his example.
[O.E. *bōc*, book, beech tree.]

boom[1], *bōōm, n.* a pole by which a sail is stretched: a chain or bar stretched across a harbour.
[Du. *boom*, beam, tree.]

boom[2], *bōōm, v.i.* to make a hollow sound, as of the sea.—Also *n.*
[Conn. with O.E. *bȳme*, a trumpet.]

boom[3], *bōōm, v.i.* to become suddenly prosperous.—*n.* a sudden increase in business, etc.
boom town, suddenly prosperous town.
[Prob. from **boom** (2).]

boomerang, *bōōm′e-rang, n.* a curved wooden missile used by natives of Australia, so balanced that, when thrown to a distance, it returns to the thrower.
[Austr.]

boon[1], *bōōn, n.* a blessing, thing to be thankful for.
[Old Norse *bōn*, prayer.]

boon[2], *bōōn, adj.* in the phrase **boon companion,** gay, pleasant to make merry with.
[Fr. *bon*, good—L. *bonus.*]

boor, *bōōr, n.* a peasant; a coarse, ill-mannered person.
boor′ish, *adj.*
[Du. *boer* (conn. Ger. *bauer*), farmer.]

boost, *bōōst, v.t.* to advertise: to push up.—*n.* a push up.
boost′er, *n.* person or thing that boosts: a device for increasing power, force, etc.: part of a system producing movement at high speed, e.g. first stage of a rocket that works by several stages.
[Orig. uncertain.]

boot[1], *bōōt, n.* a covering for the foot and lower part of the leg, usu. of leather: place for luggage in a motor car.—*v.t.* to put boots on: to kick.
boot′legger, one who smuggles alcoholic liquor (orig. in leg of long boot): an illegal dealer (also *v.t., v.i.* and *adj.* **boot′leg**).
boots, *n.* hotel servant who may clean boots.
to have one's heart in one's boots, to be in terror.
[O.Fr. *bote*; from Late Latin.]

boot[2], *boot, n.* (*old word*) advantage.
boot′less, *adj.* (of an action) useless.
to boot, in addition.
[O.E. *bōt.*]

bootee, *bōōt-ē′, n.* woollen boot for a baby.

booth, *bōōTH*, or *-th, n.* a tent at a fair: a covered stall: a polling place.
[Old Norse *būth.*]

bootleg, etc. See **boot** (1) or (2).

booty, *bōōt′i, n.* spoil, plunder: a prize.
[Old Norse *bȳti*, share.]

booze, *bōōz, v.i.* to drink deeply.—*n.* strong drink: a drinking bout.
[Prob. Middle Du. *būsen.*]

borax, *bō′raks, bö′, n.* a mineral compound,

found as a salty crust on shores of certain lakes, used as cleansing agent, etc.
bo′ric, boracic (*bò-ras′ik*), *adjs.*
[Through Fr., Late L.—Arabic *bûraq.*]

border, *bör′dėr, n.* the edge of anything: the boundary of a country: (*cap*; in *pl.*) the part of Scotland nearest to the boundary with England: a flower bed in a garden.—*v.i.* to come near, to lie on the border of (with *on, upon*).
bor′derer, *n.* one who lives on the border of a country.
bor′derland, *n.*
[O.Fr. *bordure*; from root of **board.**]

bore[1], *bōr, bör, v.t.* to pierce by a rotating tool so as to form a round hole: to make (a hole) thus: to thrust against (as one racehorse against another).—*n.* hole made by boring: size of hollow tube of a gun.
[O.E. *borian*, to bore.]

bore[2], *bōr, bör, v.t.* to weary, seem dull to.—*n.* a tiresome person or thing.
bore′dom, *n.* state of being bored.
[Origin uncertain.]

bore[3]. See **bear** (1).

bore[4], *bōr, bör, n.* a tidal flood which rushes up the estuaries of certain rivers.
[Old Norse *bāra*, a wave or swell.]

boric. See **borax.**

born, borne. See **bear** (1).

boron, *bō′ron, bö′, n.* element found in borax, etc.

borough, *bûr′ȯ, n.* a town with a corporation and special privileges granted by royal charter: a town that sends representatives to parliament.
county borough, a borough of 100,000 inhabitants or more.
See also **burgh.**
[O.E. *burg, burh*, a city.]

borrow, *bor′ō, v.t.* to take on loan: to adopt (words) from another language.
borr′ower, *n.* **borr′owing,** *n.*
[O.E. *borgian—borg, borh*, a pledge.]

borstal, *bör′stål, adj.* applied to a system of training delinquents while they are in custody.—Also *n.*
[*Borstal* in Kent.]

borzoi, *bör′zoi, n.* Russian hound bred orig. for hunting wolves.
[Russ. *borzoy*, swift.]

bosh, *bosh, n.* nonsense.—Also *interj.*
[Turk., worthless.]

bosom, *booz′-, bōōz′ȯm, n.* the breast.—*adj.* intimate (*bosom friend*).
[O.E. *bōsm.*]

boss[1], *bos, n.* a knob or stud.
[O.Fr. *boce*—Old Ger. *bōzan*, to beat.]

boss[2], *bos, n.* the master, manager.—*v.t.* to manage: to order about.
boss′y, *adj.* inclined to order others about:—*comp.* **boss′ier**; *superl.* **-iest.**
boss′iness, *n.*
[New York Dutch *baas*, master.]

botany, *bot′ȧn-i, n.* the science of plants.
botan′ic, -ical, *adjs.*
bot′anist, *n.* one skilled in botany.
botanic garden(s), a public park stocked with native and foreign plants.
[Gk. *botanē*, grass, plant.]

botch, *boch, n.* a clumsy patch: ill-finished work.—*v.t.* to mend clumsily: to do badly. [Orig. unknown.]

both, *bōth, adj.* and *pron.* the two: the one and the other.—*conj.* (or *adv.*) as well, equally.
[Old Norse *bāther*; conn. Ger. *beide.*]

bother, *boTH′ėr, v.t.* to annoy: to worry.
both′er, botherā′tion, *ns.*
both′ersome, *adj.*
[18th cent. by Irish-born writers.]

bothy, bothie, *both′i, n.* a hut, esp. one shared by farm servants.
[Conn. with Gael. *both*, a hut.]

bottle, *bot′l, n.* a hollow narrow-necked vessel for holding liquids: its contents.—*v.t.* to put into bottles.
bott′le-green, *adj.* dark green.
bott′lehead, bott′lenose, *ns.* toothed whale.
bott′leneck, *n.* a narrow part of a road apt to become very crowded with traffic: any stage of a process where progress is obstructed.
to bottle up, to keep in, repress (e.g. one's feelings).
[O.Fr. *bouteille*—Late L. *butis*, a vessel.]

bottom, *bot′ȯm, n.* the lowest part of anything: the sitting part of the body: the seat of a chair: the hull of a ship, hence the ship itself: the bed of the sea, etc.
bott′omless, *adj.* very deep.
at bottom, in reality.
to be at the bottom of, to be the real cause of.
to get to the bottom of, to discover the explanation of, or real facts of.
[O.E. *botm*; conn. Ger. *boden*, L. *fundus.*]

boudoir, *bōōd′wär, n.* a lady's private sittingroom.
[Fr.—*bouder*, to pout, to be sulky.]

bough, *bow, n.* a branch of a tree.
[O.E. *bōg, bōh*, an arm.]

bought. See **buy.**

boulder, *bōl′dėr, n.* a large stone, often one rounded by the action of water.
[Prob. Swed. *bullra*, Dan. *buldre*, to roar like thunder, as pebbles do on beach.]

boulevard, *bōōl′ė-vär(d), n.* a broad road lined with trees. [Fr.]

bounce, *bowns, v.i.* to spring suddenly: to rebound like a ball: to boast.—*v.t.* to make (e.g. a ball) rebound.—Also *n.*
bounc′ing, *adj.* strong and lively: big.
[Du. *bonzen*, to strike.]

bound[1]. See **bind.**

bound[2], *bownd, v.t.* to limit, restrain, or surround.—Also *n.*
boun′dary, *n.* the line by which an area is marked off.
bound′less, *adj.* having no limit: vast.
out of bounds, outside the area that the rules allow to be visited.
[Late L. *bodina.*]

bound[3], *bownd, v.i.* to spring or leap.—*n.* a spring or leap.
[Fr. *bondir* (orig. to resound).]

bound[4], *bownd, adj.* ready to go to, on the way to (usu. with *for*; e.g. *bound for the North.*)
[O. Norse *būinn*, pa.p. of *būa*, prepare.]

bounty, *bown'ti, n.* generosity in giving: gifts bestowed: a sum given to encourage e.g. the production of a commodity.
boun'teous (*-ti-ŭs*, or *-tyŭs*), **boun'tiful,** *adjs.* generous: plentiful.
[L. *bonitās—bonus*, good.]

bouquet, *bōōk'ā*, or *-ā'*, *n.* a bunch of flowers: the perfume of wine.
[Fr. *bosquet*, dim. of *bois*, a wood.]

bourgeois, *bōōr'zhwä, n.* one of the **bourgeoisie** (*bōōr'zhwä-zē* or *-zē'*), or middle class of citizens. [Fr.]

bout, *bowt, n.* a period, spell, fit (of): a contest.
[From root of **bow,** to bend.]

boutique, *bōō-tēk', n.* a small, exclusive, independent, esp. clothes, shop. [Fr.]

bovine, *bō'vīn, adj.* of cattle: dull.
[L. *bōs, bovis*, an ox or cow.]

bow[1], *bow, v.i.* to bend (e.g. *to bow before the storm*): to submit (*He bowed to his fate*): to bend the head in greeting a person, etc.—*v.t.* to bend: to weigh down, crush.—Also *n.*
[Old Norse *būgan*, to bend.]

bow[2], *bō, n.* anything in the shape of an arch, as the rainbow: a springy curved rod bent by a string, by which arrows are shot: the instrument by which the strings of a violin, etc. are sounded: a looped knot of ribbon, etc.
bow'man, *n.* an archer.
bow window, a curved window.
to have two strings to one's bow, to have more than one choice, plan, etc.
[O.E. *boga*; conn. with Ger. *bogen.*]

bow[3], *bow, n.* the fore part of a ship—often used in *pl.* [Prob. Scand.]

bowel, *bow'ėl, n.* (usu. in *pl.*) the entrails, intestines: (in *pl.*) the inside of anything.
[L. *botellus*, sausage, intestine.]

bower, *bow'ėr, n.* an arbour: a boudoir.
bower'-bird, *n.* Australian bird that makes a bower ornamented with feathers, shells, etc.
[O.E. *būr*, a dwelling.]

bowie-knife, *bō'i-nīf, n.* a long heavy sheathed knife, designed by Colonel *Bowie.*

bowl[1], *bōl, n.* a wooden ball used for rolling along the ground: (in *pl.*) a game played on a green with bowls having a bias.—*v.i.* to play at bowls: to speed smoothly (along): to deliver ball(s), in cricket.—*v.t.* to deliver (a ball) in cricket: to put (a batsman) out thus.
bowl'er, *n.* **bowl'ing,** *n.*
bowling alley, a long narrow covered rink for skittles.
bowling green, a smooth green for bowls.
to bowl over, to knock down: to overcome with emotion.
[Fr. *boule*—L. *bulla.*]

bowl[2], *bōl, n.* a basin for holding liquids: a round hollow part (e.g. of a tobacco pipe).
[O.E. *bolla.*]

bowler[1]. See **bowl** (1).

bowler[2], *bōl'ėr, n.* a hard, felt hat.
[Perh. name of a hatter.]

bowline, *bō'lin, n.* a rope to keep a sail close to the wind.
bowline (knot), a knot used to tie a bowline so that it will not slip or jam.
[M.E.]

bowsprit, *bō'sprit, n.* a strong spar projecting over the bows of a ship.
[Prob. Du. *boegspriet.*]

box[1], *boks, n.* an evergreen shrub: a small tree with hard wood: a case for holding something: a (Christmas) present: in a theatre, a group of enclosed seats.—*v.t.* to put into boxes: (usu. with *up*) to enclose, shut in uncomfortably.
Boxing day, the day after Christmas, when presents are given.
box office, a theatre booking office: receipts from a play, etc.: an attraction as judged by the money taken.
box pleat, a double fold of cloth.
to box the compass, to name the 32 points in order and backwards.
[O.E.—L. *buxus*, a box tree.]

box[2], *boks, n.* a blow on the ear with the hand.—*v.t.* to strike with the hand.—*v.i.* to fight with the fists.
box'er, *n.* **box'ing,** *n.*
box'ing-glove, *n.* a boxer's padded glove.
[M.E.; origin unknown.]

boxer[1]. See **box** (2).

boxer[2], *boks'ėr, n.* German police dog with smooth brown hair.

boy, *boi, n.* a male child: a servant.
boy'ish, *adj.*
boy'hood, *n.* time of being a boy.
Boys' Brigade, an organisation of boys to promote discipline, etc.
Boy Scout (now **Scout**), a member of an organisation of boys formed to develop alertness and strong character.
[M.E. *boi, boy.*]

boycott, *boi'kot, v.t.* to shut out from all social or business dealings.
[From Captain *Boycott*, treated thus by his Irish neighbours.]

brace, *brās, n.* anything that draws together and holds tightly: a pair, couple: (in *pl.*) straps for supporting the trousers: rope for turning a yard (see this word) of a ship.—*v.t.* to tighten: to strengthen (e.g. *He braced himself for the struggle*).
brac'ing, *adj.* strengthening: filling with energy.
[L. *brachium*, the arm.]

bracelet, *brās'lit, n.* an ornament for the wrist: (*coll.*) a handcuff.
[L. *brachium*, the arm.]

bracken, *brak'ėn,* **n.** a fern, esp. the commonest British fern. [Origin uncertain.]
bracket, *brak'it,* **n.** a support for a shelf, etc.: a small shelf: a number of people grouped according to income: (in *pl.*) in printing, the marks [ ] used to enclose one or more words.—*v.t.* to enclose by brackets: to group together (similar or equal things). [L. *brācae*, breeches.]
brackish, *brak'ish, adj.* (of water) saltish. [Du. *brak*, and suffx. *-ish*.]
bract, *brakt,* **n.** a leaf-like part at the base of a flower. [L. *bractea*, gold leaf.]
brad, *brad,* **n.** a small nail.
brad'awl, **n.** an awl to pierce holes.
[O. Norse *broddr*, pointed piece of iron.]
brae, *brā,* **n.** (*Scot.*) a hill slope.
[Old Norse *brā*.]
brag, *brag, v.i.* to boast:—*pr.p.* **bragg'ing**; *pa.p.* **bragged.**—Also **n.**
[Most prob. Celt.]
braggart, *brag'ȧrt,* **n.** a boaster.
[Fr. *bragard*, bragging.]
Brahman, -min, *brä'man, -min,* **n.** a Hindu of the highest or priestly caste.
Brah'manism, or **-min-,** **n.** the worship of the god **Brah'ma.**
braid, *brād, v.t.* to plait or entwine.—**n.** a narrow band made by plaiting.
[O.E. *bregdan*.]
braille, *brāl,* **n.** printing for the blind, using raised dots.
[From Louis *Braille*, the inventor.]
brain, *brān,* **n.** a greyish substance, the part of the nervous system within the skull: (in *pl.*) cleverness, intelligence.—*v.t.* to dash out the brains of.
brain'y, *adj.* clever. **brain'iness,** **n.**
brain'pan, **n.** the skull.
brain storm, a sudden mental disturbance: a brain wave.
brain'wash, *v.t.* to force a person to conform, confess, etc., by subjecting him to indoctrination or mental pressure.
brain wave, a sudden bright idea.
brains trust, **n.** a group of experts esp. one answering questions in public.
[O.E. *brægen*.]
braise, *brāz, v.t.* to stew in a closed dish.
[Fr. *braiser*.]
brake[1], *brāk,* **n.** a thicket.
[Origin uncertain.]
brake[2], *brāk,* **n.** a device to slow down the motion of a wheel or vehicle.
[From root of **break.**]
bramble, *bram'bl,* **n.** the blackberry bush: (*Scot.*) a blackberry. [O.E. *brēmel*.]
bran, *bran,* **n.** the inner husks of grain sifted from the flour. [O.Fr.]
branch, *brânch,* or *-sh,* **n.** a limb of a tree: any offshoot from a parent stem (e.g. of road, railway, family): a department of a business, etc.—*v.i.* to spread out as a branch or branches (with *out, off, from*).
branch officer, (*navy*) an officer holding a warrant.
[Late L. *branca*, a beast's paw.]
brand, *brand,* **n.** a piece of wood burning or partly burned: a mark stamped with a hot iron: a make, quality (of goods): a sword.—*v.t.* to mark with a hot iron: to fix a mark of disgrace upon.
bran(d)'-new, *adj.* very new.
[O.E. from root of **burn** (2).]
brandish, *brand'ish, v.t.* to wave (e.g. a weapon).
[From root of *brand*, a sword.]
brandy, *bran'di,* **n.** a strong spirit distilled from wine.
bran'dy-snap, **n.** a gingerbread biscuit orig. flavoured with brandy.
[Du. *brandewijn*, 'burnt wine', brandy.]
brass, *brâs,* **n.** an alloy of copper and zinc: (*slang*) money: (usu. in *pl.*) memorial tablets of brass: boldness, impudence.
brass'y, *adj,* like brass: impudent: harsh in tone:—*comp.* **brass'ier**; *superl.* **brass'iest.**
brass'ily, *adv.* **brass'iness,** **n.**
brass band, a band of players of (mainly) brass wind instruments.
brass hat, (*slang*) a staff officer.
brass plate, a nameplate on a door.
See also **brazen.**
[O.E. *bræs*.]
brassière, *bras'i-ėr,* **n.** a woman's undergarment supporting the breasts. [Fr.]
brat, *brat,* **n.** a scornful name for a child.
[O.E. *bratt*; of Celt. origin.]
bravado, *brav-ä'dō,* **n.** a show of bravery, bold pretence.
[Sp. *bravada*—*bravo*, brave.]
brave, *brāv, adj.* courageous: noble: finely dressed.—*v.t.* to meet boldly: to face (it out).—**n.** a Red Indian warrior.
brave'ly, *adv.* **brav'ery,** **n.**
[Fr. *brave*; perh. from Celt.]
bravo, *brä'vō', interj.* well done! [It.]
brawl, *bröl,* **n.** a noisy quarrel.—Also *v.i.*
[M.E. *bralle*.]
brawn, *brön,* **n.** muscle, esp. of the arm or leg: strength: potted meat from pig's flesh.
brawn'y, *adj.* **brawn'iness,** **n.**
[O.Fr. *braon*, flesh (for roasting).]
bray, *brā,* **n.** the cry of the ass.—Also *v.i.*
[Late L. *bragire*.]
brazen, *brā'zn, adj.* of brass: impudent.—*v.t.* to face (a situation) with impudent boldness (e.g. *to brazen it out*).
brazier[1], *brāz'yėr, brāzh'(y)ėr,* **n.** a worker in brass.
[O.E. *bræsian*—*bræs*, brass.]
brazier[2], *brāz'yėr, brāzh'(y)ėr,* **n.** a pan for hot coals.
[O.Fr. *braser*, to burn.]
Brazilian, *brȧ-zil'yėn, adj.* of Brazil.—**n.** a native of Brazil.
breach, *brēch,* **n.** a break or gap: a breaking (of law, promise, etc.): a quarrel.—*v.t.* to make an opening in.
a breach of the peace, a riot, disturbance.
[O.E. *bryce, brice*; conn. with **break.**]

bread, *bred, n.* food made of flour or meal baked: food: livelihood (also **bread and butter**).
bread'fruit tree, a tree of the South Sea Islands, whose starchy fruit is eaten baked or roasted.
bread'winner, *n.* one who earns a living for a family.
[O.E. *brēad.*]

breadth. See **broad.**

break, *brāk, v.t.* to divide into parts by force: to shatter: to tame, train (e.g. a horse; also **break in**): to check (e.g. a fall): to interrupt (e.g. silence): to cure (of a habit): to tell (news).—*v.i.* to fall in pieces: to dawn: to crack (as the voice): to change direction (as a cricket-ball):—*pa.t.* **brōke**; *pa.p.* **brōk'en** (see this word).—*n.* an opening: a pause: (*billiards*) a series of successful strokes: (*cricket*) change of direction of a ball: (*U.S. slang*) a stroke of luck (good or ill): also a chance or opportunity.
break'able, *adj.*—Also *n.* (in *pl.*).
break'age, *n.* the act of breaking, or its results.
break'er, *n.* person or thing that breaks: wave broken on rocks or beach.
break'down, *n.* collapse: an accidental stoppage.
breakdown gang, a squad of men to remove wreckage.
break'neck, *adj.* reckless.
break'through, *n.* a sudden solution of a problem leading to further advances, esp. in science: a sudden success after effort.
break'water, *n.* a barrier to break the force of the waves.
to break camp, to pack up tents, etc. so as to move on.
to break cover, to burst out of hiding.
to break down, to crush: to fail: to be overcome with emotion: to divide into parts.
to break in, (also **into**) to enter violently or unexpectedly: to interrupt someone speaking.
to break loose. See **loose.**
to break out, to appear suddenly: to escape: to become covered with (e.g. *to break out in a rash*).
to break the ice, to overcome the first shyness, etc.
to break up, to break in pieces: to go to pieces: to separate, depart (e.g. *The group, meeting, broke up*).
to break with, to quarrel with, or stop being connected with.
[O.E. *brecan.*]

breakfast, *brek'fȧst, n.* the first meal of the day.—*v.i.* to take this.
[**break** and **fast** (*n.*).]

breast, *brest, n.* the front of the human or animal body between the neck and belly: affections.—*v.t.* to oppose: to go up (e.g. *to breast a hill*).
breast'plate, *n.* armour for the breast.
to make a clean breast, to confess fully.
[O.E. *brēost*; conn. Ger. *brust.*]

breath, *breth, n.* the air drawn into and then sent out from the lungs: life: an act of breathing: a faint breeze.
breath'less, *adj.* out of breath: having difficulty in breathing: very eager or excited.
breath'lessly, *adv.* **breath'lessness,** *n.*
with bated breath, with breathing checked by awe or anxiety (*bate v.t.* same as *abate*).
breathe, *brēTH, v.i.* to draw in and let out from the lungs breath or air: to rest or pause: to live.—*v.t.* to draw in (e.g. air) or send out from the lungs: to whisper: to let (a horse) recover breath.
breath'er (-ēTH'), *n.* a spell of exercise: a rest to recover breath.
breath'ing, *n.* and *adj.*
[O.E. *brǣth,* breath.]

bred. See **breed.**

breech, *brēch, n.* the hinder part, esp. of a gun.
breeches, *brich'iz, n.pl.* trousers, esp. ones coming just below the knee.
breech'es-buoy, *n.* a life-saving apparatus in part like a pair of breeches.
[O.E. *brēc*; in all Germanic languages.]

breed, *brēd, v.t.* to produce (offspring): to train or bring up: to raise (e.g. *He breeds horses*): to cause.—*v.i.* to produce offspring: to be produced (e.g. *Trouble breeds there*):—*pa.t.* and *pa.p.* **bred.**—*n.* offspring: kind or race.
breed'ing, *n.* act of producing: education and training: good manners.
[O.E. *brēdan,* to cherish.]

breeze, *brēz, n.* a gentle wind: a quarrel.
breez'y, *adj.* windy: bright, lively.
breez'ily, *adv.* **breez'iness,** *n.*
[Old Sp. *briza,* It. *brezza.*]

brethren. See **brother.**

Breton, *bret'ȯn, n.* a native of Brittany (*Bretagne*), France.—*adj.* of Brittany.

breviary, *brēv'i-ȧr-i, brēv'yȧr-, n.* book containing the daily service of the R.C. Church.
[L. *breviārium—brevis,* short.]

brevity. See **brief.**

brew, *broo͞, v.t.* to make (beer, ale): to make (tea): to plot.—*v.i.* to brew beer, etc.: to be in preparation (e.g. *Mischief was brewing*).
brew'er, *n.*
brew'ery, *n.* place for brewing:—*pl.* **-ies.**
[O.E. *brēowan*; conn. with Ger. *brauen.*]

briar[1], brier, *brī'ėr, n.* a prickly shrub: a wild rose bush.
[Northern O.E. *brēr.*]

briar[2], brier, *brī'ėr, n.* the white heath, from whose root tobacco pipes are made: a pipe of this wood.
[Fr. *bruyère,* heath.]

bribe, *brīb, n.* a gift offered to persuade.

person to do something, usu. dishonest.—Also *v.t.*
brib′ery, *n.* giving or taking bribes.
[O.Fr., a lump of bread.]

bric-a-brac, *brik′à-brak, n.* treasured odds and ends. [Fr.]

brick, *brik, n.* (a block of) baked or 'burned' clay for building: (*slang*) one who stands up cheerfully to, or is helpful in, troubles.
brick′bat, *n.* a piece of brick, esp. as a missile.
brick′layer, *n.* one who builds with bricks.
to drop a brick, to make a tactless blunder.
[Fr. *brique*; conn. with **break.**]

bridal, *brīd′àl, n.* a wedding.—*adj.* of a bride or wedding.
bride, *n.* a woman about to be married, or newly married.
bride′groom, *n.* a man about to be married, or newly married.
brides′maid (*brīdz′*), *n.* unmarried woman attending bride at a wedding.
[O.E. *brȳd* (conn. Ger. *braut*); (*ale,* old word for a feast; *guma,* man).]

bridge[1], *brij, n.* a structure to carry traffic over a river, etc.: the narrow raised platform for the captain of a ship: the bony part of the nose: the support of the strings of a violin.—*v.t.* to be, or to build, a bridge over.
bridge′head, *n.* a fortification on the enemy side of a river: any advanced position seized in enemy territory.
[O.E. *brycg*; conn. with Ger. *brücke.*]

bridge[2], *brij, n.* a card game, played by two against two, the hand of the declarer's partner always being exposed.
[Origin uncertain.]

bridle, *brī′dl, n.* the harness about the head of a horse to which the reins are attached: any restraint.—*v.t.* to restrain.—*v.i.* to toss the head proudly like a restive horse (often with *up* and *at*; e.g. *She bridled up at this remark*).
bridle path, road, a path for horsemen.
[O.E. *brīdel.*]

brief, *brēf, adj.* short.—*n.* a short statement (esp. in a lawsuit, of a client's case).—*v.t.* to give detailed instructions to.
brief′ly, *adv.* **brief′ness, brev′ity,** *ns.*
in brief, in few words.
to hold a brief for, to speak in favour of.
[Fr. *bref*—L. *brevis,* short.]

brier. See **briar** (1) and (2).

brigade, *bri-gād′, n.* a body of troops consisting of two or more regiments, or battalions, etc.: a uniformed band organised for a purpose.
brigadier′ (*-dēr′*), the holder of a certain rank in the army. See Appendices.
[Fr.—Late Latin *briga,* strife.]

brigand, *brig′ànd, n.* a robber, esp. one of a band in unsettled country.
[Same root as **brigade.**]

bright, *brīt, adj.* shining: clear: cheerful: clever.
bright′en, *v.t., v.i.* to make, or become, bright or brighter.
bright′ly, *adv.* **bright′ness,** *n.*
[O.E. *byrht, beorht.*]

brilliant, *bril′yànt, adj.* sparkling: splendid: talented.—*n.* a fine diamond.
brill′iantly, *adv.*
brill′iance, brill′iancy, *ns.*
brilliantine, *bril′yàn-tēn, n.* a dressing to make the hair glossy.
[Fr.—Late Latin *bēryllus,* a beryl.]

brim, *brim, n.* the edge of a river, lake, cup, etc.: the rim of a hat.—*v.i.* to be full to the brim:—*pr.p.* **brimm′ing**; *pa.p.* **brimmed.**
brim′ful, *adj.* full to the brim.
to brim over, to overflow.
[M.E. *brymme.*]

brimstone, *brim′stōn, n.* sulphur.
[O.E. *byrnan,* to burn, and **stone.**]

brindle(d), *brin′dl(d), adj.* brownish or grey, marked with streaks.
[Prob. connected with **brand.**]

brine, *brīn, n.* very salt water: the sea.
brin′y, *adj.* very salt:—*comp.* **brin′ier**; *superl.* **brin′iest.**
brin′iness, *n.*
[O.E. *brȳne.*]

bring, *bring, v.t.* to fetch, to lead or carry (to a place): to cause to come (e.g. rain, relief), to result in: to put before a court of law, etc. (e.g. *to bring an action against someone*):—*pa.t., pa.p.* **brought** (*brōt*).
to bring about, to cause.
to bring forth, to give birth to, produce.
to bring home to, to prove to, to show clearly to.
to bring in, to introduce: to produce as profit: to pronounce (a verdict).
to bring off, to achieve (something attempted).
to bring oneself, to persuade oneself (to).
to bring out, to make clear, reveal: to publish.
to bring round, to restore from unconsciousness: to win over.
to bring to, to restore to consciousness: to bring (a ship, boat) to a standstill.
to bring up, to rear or educate: to introduce to notice (e.g. *Bring up the matter at the meeting*).
to bring up the rear, to come last.
[O.E. *bringan,* to carry, to bring.]

brink, *bringk, n.* the edge or border of a steep place or of a river.
[Prob. Dan. *brink,* precipice.]

briquette, *bri-ket′, n.* a brick-shaped block of fuel made of coal dust. [Fr.]

brisk, *brisk, adj.* lively: active.
brisk′ly, *adv.* **brisk′ness,** *n.*
[Perh. Celt; perh. Fr. *brusque.*]

brisket, *brisk′it, n.* the part of the breast of an animal next to the ribs.
[Perh. Fr. *brechet.*]

bristle, *bris'l*, *n.* a short, stiff hair.—*v.i.* to stand erect or stiffly as bristles do: to show anger:—*pr.p.* **brist'ling**; *pa.p.* **brist'led** (*bris'ld*).
brist'ly, *adj.* **brist'liness,** *n.*
to bristle with, to be full of.
[Conn. with O.E. *byrst*, a bristle.]

Britannia, *bri-tan'yȧ*, *n.* Britain: female figure personifying it. [L.]

British, *brit'ish*, *adj.* of Britain or the Commonwealth.
[O.E. *Bryttisc*; from Celtic.]

Briton, *brit'ȯn*, *n.* one of the early inhabitants of Britain: a native of Great Britain.
[L. *Britto*.]

brittle, *brit'l*, *ad.* easily broken: frail.
britt'leness, *n.*
[O.E. *brēotan*, to break.]

broach, *brōch*, *n.* a boring tool.—*v.t.* to pierce (a cask): to open up (a subject).
[Fr. *broche*—L. *brocc(h)us*, sticking out.]

broad, *brö̈d*, *adj.* wide: large: coarse (e.g. *a broad story*): of, in, a strong dialect: full (*broad daylight*): clear (*a broad hint*): general, without going into detail (e.g. *a broad outline*).—*n.* (in Norfolk) a lake-like expansion of a river.
broad'ly, *adv.*
broad'ness, breadth (*bredth*), *ns.*
broad'en, *v.t.* and *v.i.* to make, or become, broad or broader.
broad arrow, a mark (↑) stamped on British government property, including clothing worn by convicts.
broad'cast, *v.t.* to scatter (seed) by hand: to make widely known: to send out by wireless (entertainment programmes, news, messages, etc):—*pa.t.* and *pa.p.* **broad'cast.**—Also *n.* and *adj.*
broad'caster, *n.* **broad'casting,** *n.*
broad'cloth, *n.* a fine woollen cloth for men's clothes.
broad jump, (*U.S.*) long jump.
broad'-mind'ed, *adj.* ready to allow others to think or act as they choose without criticising them: tolerant, not prejudiced.
broad'side, *n.* the side of a ship: firing of all the guns on one side of a ship of war.
broad'sword, *n.* a cutting sword with a broad blade.
[O.E. *brād*.]

brocade, *brȯ-kād'*, *n.* a silk stuff having a design on it that appears raised.
[It. *broccato*.]

broccoli, *brok'ȯ-li*, *n.* a hardy variety of cauliflower.
[It.; pl. of *broccolo*, a sprout.]

brochure, *brō'shoor*, *brȯ-sho͞or'*, *n.* a pamphlet.
[Fr., small stitched book—*brocher*, stitch.]

brock, *brok*, *n.* a badger.
[O.E. *brocc*, from Celt.]

brogue, *brōg*, *n.* a stout shoe: a way of pronunciation, esp. Irish.
[Ir. *brόg*, Gael. *brȯg*, a shoe.]

broil[1], *broil*, *n.* a noisy quarrel.
[Fr. *brouiller*, to mix up.]

broil[2], *broil*, *v.t.* to grill.—*v.i.* to be very hot. [Origin uncertain.]

broke. See **break.**

broken, *brō'kn*. See **break.**—*adj.* incomplete: interrupted: irregular: imperfect (e.g. *He speaks broken English*): ruined.
brok'enly, *adv.* with voice unsteady.
brok'en-down', *adj.* not in working order, or good condition, or health.
brok'en-heart'ed, *adj.* crushed with grief.
brok'en-wind'ed, *adj.* (of a horse) having difficulty in breathing.

broker, *brō'kėr*, *n.* one employed to buy and sell for others.
brok'erage, *n.* the business of a broker: commission charged by a broker.
[M.E. *brocour*.]

bromide, *brō'mīd*, *n.* a compound of bromine, esp. one used as a sedative.
bromine, *brō'mēn*, *-min*, *n.* a liquid giving off strong fumes.
[Gk. *bromos*, a stink.]

broncho, bronco, *brong'kō*, *n.* (*U.S.*) a half-tamed horse.
[Sp. *bronco*, rough, sturdy.]

bronchus, *brongk'ůs*, *n.* either of the main forks of the windpipe:—*pl.* **bronch'i** (*brongk'ī*).
bronch'ial, *adj.*
bronchitis, *brong-kī'tis*, *n.* inflammation of the lining of bronchial tubes.
[Gk. *bronchos*, windpipe.]

brontosaurus, *bron-tȯ-sö̈'růs*, *n.* a dinosaur, found fossil in U.S.A.
[Gk. *brontē*, thunder, *sauros*, lizard.]

bronze, *bronz*, *n.* an alloy of copper and tin: its colour.—Also *adj.*
bronzed, *adj.* coated with bronze: sunburned.
Bronze Age, the period between the Stone and Iron Ages, in which tools and weapons were made from bronze.
[Fr.—It. *bronzo*—L. name of Brindisi.]

brooch, *brōch*, *n.* an ornamental clasp with an attached pin fitting into a hook.
[Fr. *broche*, a spit; same root as **broach.**]

brood, *bro͞od*, *v.i.* to sit as a hen on eggs: to hang or hover (over): to think anxiously for some time.—*n.* offspring: the number hatched at once.—*adj.* for breeding, as in *brood* mare, etc.
brood'y, *adj.* (of hen bird) ready to brood: deep in anxious thought.
[O.E. *brōd*; same root as **breed.**]

brook[1], *brook*, *n.* a small stream.
[O.E. *brōc*, water breaking forth.]

brook[2], *brook*, *v.t.* to bear, endure.
[O.E. *brūcan*, to use, enjoy.]

broom, *bro͞om*, *n.* a shrub of the pea family with yellow flowers: a long-handled sweeping brush.
broom'stick, *n.* the handle of a broom.
[O.E. *brōm*.]

broth, *broth, n.* a soup, esp. one containing vegetables and barley or rice.
[O.E.; same root as **brew.**]

brother, *bruTH'ėr, n.* the name given to a male child by the other children of his parents: a close friend: a fellow member of any group:—*pl.* **broth'ers, breth'ren** (the latter esp. used of fellow members of religious bodies, etc.).
broth'erly, *adj.* like a brother: kind.
broth'erliness, *n.*
broth'erhood, *n.* the state of being a brother: an association of men for any purpose.
broth'er-in-law, *n.* the brother of a husband or wife: a sister's husband:—*pl.* **broth'ers-in-law.**
[O.E. *brōthor*; conn. with Ger. *bruder.*]

brought. See **bring.**

brow, *brow, n.* the eyebrow: the forehead: the edge (of a hill).
brow'beat, *v.t.* to bully.
[O.E. *brū.*]

brown, *brown, adj.* of dark colour, between red and yellow: sunburnt.—Also *n.*—*v.t.* to roast brown.
brownie, *brown'i, n.* a friendly goblin: (*cap.*) a junior Girl Guide.
brown bread, bread made of unsifted wheat flour, or of other darkish material.
brown coal, lignite.
a brown study, deep thought.
[O.E. *brūn*; conn. Ger. *braun*, Du. *bruin.*]

browse, *browz, v.i.* to feed (on shoots or leaves of plants): to read here and there. —*v.t.* to feed on.
[O.Fr. *brouster—broust*, a sprout.]

bruin, *brōō'in, n.* a bear.
[Du. *bruin*, brown (see **brown**).]

bruise, *brōōz, v.t.* to injure by striking.—*n.* an injury with discoloration of the skin made by anything heavy and blunt.
bruis'er, *n.* a boxer: a tough.
[O.E. *brȳsan*, to crush.]

brunette, *brōō-net', n.* a woman with brown or dark hair and complexion.
[Fr.—*brun*, brown.]

brunt, *brunt, n.* the shock or force of a blow: the chief strain (*to bear the brunt of*).
[Origin uncertain.]

brush, *brush, n.* an instrument with bristles, wire, hair, for cleaning, scrubbing, painting: a bushy tail: a light passing touch: a skirmish: thicket: (*Austr.*) forest and undergrowth: backwoods.—*v.t.* to pass a brush over: to remove by sweeping.—*v.i.* to pass with light contact.
brush'wood, *n.* loppings and broken branches: thicket.
to brush up, to brighten: to revive in the memory.
[O.Fr. *brosse*, brushwood.]

brusque, *broosk, brusk, adj.* blunt and abrupt in manner.
brusque'ly, *adv.* **brusque'ness,** *n.*
[Fr.]

Brussels sprouts, *brus'lz sprowts, n.pl.* a variety of cabbage with sprouts on the stem like tiny cabbages: (in *sing.*) one of the sprouts.
[*Brussels*, in Belgium.]

brute, *brōōt, adj.* of the lower animals: soulless: stupid: cruel.—*n.* one of the lower animals: a brutal man.
brut'al, *adj.* like a brute: very cruel.
brut'alise, to make brutal.
brutal'ity (*pl.* **-ies**), *n.* **brut'ally,** *adv.*
brut'ish, *adj.* brutal: stupid.
brut'ishly, *adv.* **brut'ishness,** *n.*
[Fr. *brut*—L. *brūtus*, dull.]

bubble, *bub'l, n.* a bladder of liquid, etc., blown out with gas: anything empty.—*v.i.* to rise in bubbles:—*pr.p.* **bubb'ling**; *pa.p.* **bubb'led.**
bubb'ly, *adj.* **bubb'liness,** *n.*
[Prob. imit.]

buccaneer, *buk-ȧ-nēr', n.* a 17th-century pirate in the West Indies: an adventurer.
[Fr. *boucaner*, to smoke meat; from W. Indian word for wooden gridiron.]

buck, *buk, n.* the male of deer, goat, hare, rabbit: a dashing fellow: a counter, marker, in poker: (*U.S.*) a dollar.—*v.i.* (of a horse or mule—a **buck'jumper**) to attempt to throw the rider by rapid jumps into the air: (*coll.*) to resist.
bucked, *adj.* (*slang*), cheered.
buck'skin, *n.* a soft leather made of deerskin or sheepskin.
buck tooth, a projecting tooth.
to buck up (*slang*), to hurry: to cheer up.
[O.E. *buc, bucca.*]

bucket, *buk'it, n.* a vessel for drawing or holding water.
[Prob. O.E. *būc*, a pitcher.]

buckle, *buk'l, n.* a fastening for a strap or band, consisting of a rim and a movable tongue: a curled or warped state.—*v.t.* to fasten with a buckle: to prepare (oneself) for action.—*v.i.* to apply oneself (to).—*v.t.* and *v.i.* to warp: to bend or crumple (of a metal object—e.g. a wheel, a girder).
buck'ler, *n.* a small shield.
[Fr. *boucle*, boss of shield.]

buckram *buk'rȧm, n.* coarse cotton, etc., stiffened with size.
[O.Fr. *boquerant.*]

bud, *bud, n.* a shoot of a tree or plant, containing undeveloped leaves, or flower(s), or both.—*v.i.* to put forth buds: to begin to grow:—*pr.p.* **budd'ing**; *pa.p.* **budd'ed.**
to nip in the bud, to destroy at its very beginning.
[M.E. *budde.*]

Buddha, *bood'ȧ, n.* the Wise, a title applied to the founder of the Buddhist religion or **Buddh'ism.**
Buddh'ist, *n.* a believer in Buddhism.
[Sanskrit.]

budge, *buj, v.i.* and *v.t.* to move or stir.
[Fr. *bouger*—L. *bullīre*, to boil.]

budgerigar, *buj'ėr-i-gär, n.* an Australian small parrot or lovebird.—Also (*coll.*) **budg'ie.**
[Austr. native name.]

budget, *buj'it, n.* any plan showing how money is to be spent, esp. a statement and programme put before parliament by the Chancellor of the Exchequer.—*v.i.* to prepare a plan of expenditure: to allow (for) in a budget.—Also *v.t.*
[Fr. *bougette*, a small pouch.]

buff, *buf, n.* white leather from which the grain surface has been removed: a light yellow.
[Fr. *buffle*, a buffalo.]

buffalo, *buf'ȧ-lō, n.* a large kind of ox, esp. one used in Asia to draw loads, etc.: a fierce African ox: (*U.S.*) the American bison:—*pl.* **buff'aloes.**
[It. *buffalo*, from Gk. *boubalos.*]

buffer, *buf'ėr, n.* a device (e.g. one using padding or springs) for deadening the force with which a moving body strikes something.
[Prob. from old word *buff*, to strike.]

buffet[1], *buf'it, n.* a blow with the hand or fist, a slap.—*v.t.* to strike with the fist: to battle against: to knock about (e.g. *He was buffeted by the waves*; *buffeted by Fate*).
[O.Fr. *buffet—buffe*, blow, esp. on cheek.]

buffet[2], *bŭf'ā, n.* a refreshment bar.
[Fr.; origin unknown.]

buffoon, *bu̇-fōōn', n.* a clown: a fool.
buffoon'ery, *n.*
[It. *buffone*; conn. *buffare*, to jest.]

bug, *bug, n.* an insect, esp. one that infests houses and beds: a disease germ: (*U.S.*) a crazy idea. [Origin unknown.]

bugbear, *bug'bār, n.* something one fears or hates.
[M.E. *bugge*, a bogy, and **bear** (2).]

buggy, *bug'i, n.* a light one-horse vehicle: (*slang*) a motor vehicle. [Origin unknown.]

bugle, *bū'gl, n.* a hunting-horn, orig. a buffalo horn: a wind instrument, used chiefly for military signals.
bu'gler, *n.*
[L. *būculus—bōs, bovis*, an ox.]

build, *bild, v.t.* to form or construct.—*v.i.* to rely (on, upon):—*pa.p.* **built.**—*n.* form, make (e.g. *a man of heavy build*).
build'er, *n.*
build'ing, *n.* the art of erecting houses, etc.: anything built.
building society, a society that advances money for building houses.
built in, forming a permanent part of the building, etc.
built up, covered with houses, etc.
to build up, to form, strengthen, gradually (as a business, reputation).
[O.E. *gebyld.*]

bulb, *bulb, n.* an underground bud, with roots on the under side, as in onions, narcissi, etc.: the globe of an electric light.
bul'bous, *adj.* having, growing from, a bulb: like a bulb, e.g. in shape.
bul'bousness, *n.*
[L. *bulbus*—Gk. *bolbos*, an onion.]

bulge, *bulj, n.* the widest part of a cask: a swelling.—*v.i.* to swell out.
[Prob. L. *bulga*, leather knapsack.]

bulk, *bulk, n.* size: great size: large quantity: the greater part.—*v.i.* to be in bulk: to be of importance.
bulk'y, *adj.*:—*comp.* **bulk'ier**; *superl.* **bulk'iest.**
bulk'iness, *n.*
in bulk, (of cargo) loose in the hold, not packaged: in large quantities.
[Prob. Scand.]

bulkhead, *bulk'hed, n.* a partition between one part of a ship's interior and another.
[Origin uncertain.]

bull[1], *bool, n.* the male of the ox family and of whale, walrus, elephant, moose.—*adj.* male.
bull'ock, *n.* a young bull, or a male animal being reared solely to produce beef.
bull'dog, *n.* a dog of great courage, formerly used to bait bulls.
bull'fight, *n.* a spectacle in which a bull is goaded to fury by mounted men with lances, and finally killed by a swordsman on foot.
bull'finch, *n.* a red-breasted finch.
bull'frog, *n.* a large N. American frog.
bull ring, the enclosure in which a bullfight takes place.
bull's-eye, *n.* the centre of a target: a striped sweetmeat: a small circular opening or window.
bull terrier, a cross between bulldog and terrier.
to take the bull by the horns, to tackle a difficulty.
[M.E. *bole*; prob. conn. **bellow.**]

bull[2], *bool, n.* a formal letter, with seal attached, from the Pope.
[L. *bulla*, knob, seal.]

bulldog. See **bull** (1).

bulldoze, *bool'dōz, v.t.* to force by threats, etc. (into doing something): to force (one's way): to use a bulldozer on.
bull'dozer, *n.* a tractor for clearing obstacles and levelling ground.
[Origin uncertain.]

bullet, *bool'it, n.* a metal ball fired from a small firearm (rifle, pistol, etc.).
bull'et-proof, *adj.* through which a bullet cannot force its way.
[Fr. *boulette*—L. *bulla*, a ball.]

bulletin, *bool'i-tin, n.* an official report of news, or of a patient's progress. [Fr.]

bullfight, etc. See **bull** (1).

bullion, *bool'yȯn, n.* gold and silver in the mass not made into coins.
[M.E. *bullioun*; conn. L. *bullīre*, to boil.]

bullock. See **bull** (1).

bully[1], *bool'i, n.* a cruel and boastful tormentor of the weak.—*adj.* (*U.S.*)

excellent.—*v.t.* to torment, domineer over: to force (into doing something):—*pr.p.* **bull'ying**; *pa.p.* **bull'ied.**
[Orig. a term of affection.]

bully², *bool'i*, **bully-beef**, *bool'i-bēf*, *ns.* canned or pickled beef.
[Prob. Fr. *bouilli*, boiled beef.]

bulrush, *bool'rush*, *n.* a tall strong rush.
[Perh. **bull** (1) used to mean 'large'.]

bulwark, *bool'wȧrk*, *n.* a rampart: the side of a ship above the deck: any means of defence.
[M.E. *bulwerk*; prob. **'bole work'.**]

bumblebee, *bum'bl-bē*, *n.* a large loud-humming wild bee, a humble bee. [Imit.]

bump, *bump*, *v.i.* to knock: to jolt.—*v.t.* to strike against or on.—*n.* a dull, heavy blow: a lump or swelling.
bump'er, *n.* a bar on a motor car to lessen the shock of collision: a glass filled to the brim: anything large.—Also *adj.* [Imit.]

bumpkin, *bump'kin*, *n.* an awkward, clumsy rustic.
[Prob. Du. *boomken*, a log.]

bumptious, *bump'shŭs*, *adj.* full of one's own importance.
bump'tiously, *adv.*
bump'tiousness, *n.* [Prob. **bump.**]

bun¹, *bun*, *n.* a kind of sweet cake: a rounded mass of hair.
[Prob. from O.Fr. *bugne*, a swelling.]

bun², *bun*, *n.* a rabbit or squirrel.
bunn'y, *n.* a rabbit:—*pl.* **-ies.**
[Origin unknown.]

bunch, *bunch* or *-sh*, *n.* a number of things fastened or growing together: a cluster: a group.—*v.i.* to cluster.—*v.t.* to make a bunch of. [Origin uncertain.]

bundle, *bun'dl*, *n.* a number of things bound together.—*v.t.* to make into bundles: to put, push, hastily.—*v.i.* to go hurriedly or in confusion (away, off, out).
[Conn. with **bind.**]

bung, *bung*, *n.* the stopper of the hole in a barrel. [Origin uncertain.]

bungalow, *bung'gȧ-lō*, *n.* a lightly-built house of one storey in India: any similar house of one storey.
[Hindustani *banglā*, (adj.) of Bengal.]

bungle, *bung'gl*, *n.* anything clumsily done: a task or job badly carried out.—Also *v.t.* and *v.i.*
bung'ler, *n.* [Origin uncertain.]

bunion, *bun'yȯn*, *n.* a swelling on the first joint of the great toe. [Origin unknown.]

bunk¹, *bungk*, *n.* a sleeping-berth in a ship's cabin: a bed.
bunk'er, *n.* a large box esp. for stowing coals: a hollow containing sand on a golf course.—*v.t.* to put fuel into.—*v.i.* to take in fuel.
bunk'ered, *adj.* in a bunker: in difficulties.
bunk'ering, *n.* fuelling. [Prob. Scand.]

bunk². See **bunkum.**

bunkum, *bung'kŭm*, *n.* nonsense—also (*slang*) **bunk.**
[From *Buncombe*, U.S.A., whose member in Congress often spoke simply to please Buncombe.]

bunnies, bunny. See **bun** (2).

bunsen, *bōōn'sėn*, *bun'sėn*, *adj.* applied to some of the inventions of the chemist R. W. *Bunsen.*
bunsen burner, a gas burner in which air mingles with the gas and produces a smokeless flame of great heating power.

bunting, *bunt'ing*, *n.* a thin cloth for flags: flags, esp. a ship's. [Origin uncertain.]

buoy, *boi*, *n.* a floating anchored mark, acting as a guide, as a warning, or as a mooring point for boats.—*v.t.* (usu. with *up*) to keep afloat, or to raise the spirits of.
buoy'ancy, *n.* ability to float lightly on water or in the air: cheerfulness, ability to recover good spirits quickly.
buoy'ant, *adj.* tending to float: cheerful.
[Du. *boei.*]

bur¹, **burr**, *bûr*, *n.* the prickly case round seed(s) of certain plants, sticking readily to things it touches.
[Conn. with Dan. *borre.*]

bur², **burr**, *bûr*, *n.* rough sound of *r* pronounced in throat, as it is in Northumberland. [Prob. imit.]

burble, *bûr'bl*, *v.i.* to talk much, saying little, esp. from excitement. [Imit.]

burden¹, *bûr'dn*, *n.* a load: cargo: something difficult to bear: responsibility.—*v.t.* to load: to oppress.
bur'densome, *adj.* heavy: causing weariness or discomfort.
[O.E. *byrthen—beran*, to bear.]

burden², *bûr'dn*, *n.* a refrain or chorus of a song: the chief idea expressed in (e.g. *The burden of his complaint was that he was always given the most unpleasant jobs*).
[O.Fr. *bourdon*, drone of bagpipe.]

bureau, *bū'rō*, *bū-rō'*, *n.* a combined writing table and chest of drawers: an office for collecting and supplying information:—*pl.* **bureaux, -reaus** (*-rōz*).
bureaucracy, *bū-rok'rȧ-si*, *n.* government by officials, responsible only to their chiefs.
bur'eaucrat, *n.* one who practises or favours bureaucracy.
bureaucrat'ic, *adj.*
[Fr. *bureau* (Gk. *krateein*, to govern).]

burgess, *bûr'jės*, *n.* a citizen, esp. a freeman, of a borough.
[O.Fr. *burgeis.*]

burgh, *bur'ȯ*, *n.* a spelling of **borough** (in Scotland).
burgher, *bûr'gėr*, *n.* an inhabitant of a borough.

burglar, *bûrg'lȧr*, *n.* one who breaks into a house, etc. by night to steal.
burg'lary, *n.* **bur'gle**, *v.t.*
[Origin uncertain.]

burial. See **bury.**

burlesque, *bûr-lesk'*, *n.* a comic and exag-

gerated imitation in writing or acting.—Also *v.t.*
[It. *burlesco.*]

burly, *bûr'li, adj.* big and sturdy.
[M.E. *borlich.*]

Burmese, *bûr-mēz', adj.* of *Burma* or its language.—*n.* a native, or the language, of Burma.

burn[1], *bûrn, n.* a small stream.
[O.E. *burna*; conn. Du., Ger. *born.*]

burn[2], *bûrn, v.t.* to destroy or injure by fire: to expose to great heat.—*v.i.* to be on fire: to feel great heat or passion:—*pa.t.* and *pa.p.* **burned, burnt.**—*n.* a hurt or mark caused by fire.
burn'ing, *n.* and *adj.*
burn'er, *n.* the part of a lamp or gas jet from which the flame arises, or the whole fixture.
burnt offering, something burned on an altar as a sacrifice.
to burn one's boats, to destroy one's means of retreat, stake everything on success.
[O.E. *bærnan.*]

burnish, *bûr'nish, v.t.* to make bright by rubbing.
[Fr. *burnir.*]

burnt. See **burn** (2).

burr. Same as **bur** (1) and (2).

burrow, *bûr'ō, n.* a hole dug by certain animals for shelter.—*v.i.* to make, live in, holes underground.
[Same root as **borough.**]

bursar, *bûr'sȧr, n.* one who keeps the purse: in Scotland, a student helped by the funds of an endowment.
bur'sary, *n.* in Scotland, the grant paid to a bursar.
[Late L. *bursa*, a purse.]

burst, *bûrst, v.t.* to break open or in pieces suddenly.—*v.i.* to fly open or break in pieces: to come, go, suddenly or violently (into, out of): to break (into; e.g. *to burst into tears, song,* etc.).—*n.* a sudden outbreak: a spurt.
[O.E. *berstan*; conn. with Ger. *bersten.*]

bury, *ber'i, v.t.* to hide in the ground: to place (e.g. a dead body) in a grave, the sea, etc.: to cover, hide: to put (something) out of one's mind:—*pr.p.* **bur'ying**; *pa.p.* **bur'ied.**
bur'ial, *n.*
to bury the hatchet, to stop quarrelling.
[O.E. *byrgan*; conn. Ger. *bergen*, to hide.]

bus. Short for **omnibus**:—*pl.* **bus'es.**

bush, *boosh, n.* a shrub thick with branches: wild uncultivated country.
bush'y, *adj.* thick and spreading.
bush'iness, *n.*
bush'man, *n.* a settler in uncleared land: one of an aboriginal race in S. Africa.
bush'ranger (*-rānj-*), *n.* in Australia, one who leads a lawless life in the bush.
to beat about the bush, to talk without coming to the point.
[M.E. *busk, busch*; conn. Ger. *busch.*]

bushel, *boosh'l, n.* a dry measure of 8 gallons.
[O.Fr. *boissiel*, from the root of **box.**]

busier, busiest. See **busy.**

business, *biz'nis, n.* trade, profession, or work: one's concern or affair: one's duty: a matter or affair.
bus'inesslike, *adj.* practical, methodical, alert and prompt. [**busy.**]

bust, *bust, n.* a sculpture of the head and breast of a person: the upper part of the human body, esp. a woman's.
[Fr. *buste*; conn. It., Sp. *busto.*]

bustle[1], *bus'l, v.i.* to busy oneself noisily or fussily.—Also *n.* [Orig. uncertain.]

bustle[2], *bus'l, n.* a frame or pad making a skirt hang back from the hips.
[Origin unknown.]

busy, *biz'i, adj.* fully employed: active: diligent:—*comp.* **bus'ier**; *superl.* **bus'iest.**—*v.t.* to occupy (oneself):—*pr.p.* **bus'ying**; *pa.p.* **busied** (*biz'id*).
bus'ily, *adv.*
bus'yness, *n.* state of being busy. See also **business.**
bus'ybody, *n.* a meddling person.
[O.E. *bysig.*]

but, *but, prep.* only: except.—*conj.* on the other hand: nevertheless: except that.—*adv.* only (e.g. *There is but one objection*).
[O.E. *būtan—by*, by, *ūtan*, out.]

butcher, *booch'ėr, n.* one whose business is to kill cattle, etc., for food, or who deals in their flesh.—*v.t.* to kill for food: to kill cruelly.
butch'ery, *n.* great slaughter.
[O.Fr. *bo(u)chier*, one who kills he-goats.]

butler, *but'lėr, n.* a servant who has charge of the liquors, plate, etc.
[Same root as **bottle.**]

butt[1], *but, v.i.* and *v.t.* to strike with the head, as a goat does.—Also *n.*
to butt in, to interrupt, interfere.
[O.Fr. *boter*, to push, strike.]

butt[2], *but, n.* a large cask.
[Late L. *butta.*]

butt[3], *but, n.* a mark for archery practice: a victim of ridicule, target for the wit of others: (in *pl.*) a shooting range.
[Fr. *but*, goal.]

butt[4], *but, n.* the thick and heavy end: the stump. [Origin uncertain.]

butter, *but'ėr, n.* an oily substance made from cream by churning.—*v.t.* to put butter on.
butt'ery, *adj.* **butt'eriness,** *n.*
butt'ercup, *n.* a cup-like golden yellow flower.
butt'er-fing'ers, *n.* one who lets a ball, etc., he ought to catch slip through his fingers.
butt'erfly, *n.* an insect with large, beautiful wings: a gay, flighty person:—*pl.* **butt'erflies.**
butt'ermilk, *n.* the milk left after the butter has been separated from the cream by churning.
[Through L.—Gk. *bous*, ox, *tyros*, cheese.]

buttery[1]. See **butter.**
buttery[2], *but'ėr-i*, *n.* a storeroom for provisions, esp. liquors.
[Fr. *bouteillerie*, 'place for bottles'.]
buttock, *but'ȯk*, *n.* either half of the rump of the body behind.
[Dim. of **butt** (4).]
button, *but'n*, *n.* a knob or disk of metal, bone, etc., used as a fastening, ornament, or badge: a small knob pressed to operate something.—*v.t.* to fasten by means of buttons: to close (up) tightly.
butt'onhole, *n.* the hole or slit into which a button is passed: a flower or flowers worn in it.—*v.t.* to detain in talk (orig. *buttonhold*).
butt'ons, *n.* a boy servant in livery, a page.
[Fr. *bouter*, to push.]
buttress, *but'rės*, *n.* a support built on to the outside of a wall: any prop.—*v.t.* to prop or support.
[Fr. *bouter*, to push, bear against.]
buxom, *buk'sȯm*, *adj.* plump and attractive.
[M.E. *buhsum*, pliable—O.E. *būgan*, to bend.]
buy, *bī*, *v.t.* to purchase for money: to bribe: to get in exchange for something: —*pr.p.* **buy'ing**; *pa.p.* **bought** (*böt*).
buy'er, *n.*
[O.E. *bycgan.*]
buzz, *buz*, *v.i.* to make a noise like that of insects' wings: to hover (about).—*v.t.* to fly very low over or very close to.—Also *n.*
buzz'er, *n.* an electrical or other apparatus producing a buzzing sound. [Imit.]
buzzard, *buz'ȧrd*, *n.* a large bird of prey.
[Fr. *busard.*]

by, *bī*, *prep.* at the side of: via: denoting the agent, means, etc. (*done by me*; *broken by the wind*, etc.): measured in terms of (e.g. *by the yard*): (of time) at or before: during (*by day*).—*adv.* near: past: in reserve.—Also *adj.* and *pfx.*
by'-and-by', *adv.* in a little while.
by'-election, *n.* an election during the sitting of parliament to fill one seat.
by'gone, *adj.* past.—*n.* (in *pl.*) past causes of ill-will.
by'pass, *n.* a side track to avoid an obstruction or a busy area.—*v.t.* to avoid by taking such a route.
by'path, *n.* a secluded or indirect path.
by'-pro'duct, *n.* a product formed during the making of something else.
by'road, *n.* a side road.
by'stander, *n.* one who stands near, hence a spectator.
by'way, *n.* a way taken by few people.
by'word, *n.* a common saying: an object of general scorn.
by and large, on the whole.
[O.E. *bī*, *big*; conn. with Ger. *bei*, L. *ambi-*.]
bye, by, *bī*, *n.* (state of) one who has not drawn an opponent and passes without playing to the next round: in golf, the holes played after the match is won: in cricket, a run made when the batsman has not hit the bowled ball. [**by.**]
bylaw, bye-law, *bī'-lö*, *n.* a law of a local authority.
[Old Norse *byjar-lög*, town law.]
byre, *bīr*, *n.* a cowhouse.
[O.E. *bȳre.*]

C

cab, *kab*, *n.* a carriage for hire, horse-drawn or **(taxi-cab)** motor-driven: a driver's shelter on a vehicle.
[Short for earlier *cabriolet*—Fr.]
cabaret, *kab'ȧ-rā*, *n.* a restaurant with variety turns: an entertainment given in such a restaurant. [Fr.]
cabbage, *kab'ij*, *n.* a vegetable with leaves forming a head.
[L. *caput*, the head.]
caber, *kāb'ėr*, *kâb'ėr*, *n.* a long, heavy pole tossed by Highland athletes.
[Gael. *cabar.*]
cabin, *kab'in*, *n.* a hut or cottage: a small room, esp. in a ship.
cabin boy, a boy who waits on occupants of a ship's cabin.
[Fr. *cabane*—Late L. *capanna.*]
cabinet, *kab'in-it*, *n.* a case, or piece of furniture, for holding articles of value.
the cabinet, a selected number of the chief ministers who govern a country.
[Dim. of **cabin.**]
cable, *kā'bl*, *n.* a strong rope or chain for hauling or tying anything, esp. a ship's anchor: a wire for carrying electric current: a cablegram.—*v.t.* and *v.i.* to telegraph by cable.
cā'blegram, *n.* a telegram sent by cable.
[Late L. *caplum*, a halter.]
caboose, *ka-bōōs'*, *n.* a ship's kitchen: (*U.S.*) the van on a freight train for the train crew.
[Du. *kombuis*; conn. with Ger. *kabuse.*]
cacao, *kȧ-kā'ō*, or *kȧ-kä'ō*, *n.* the tropical tree from whose seeds cocoa and chocolate are made.
[Mexican *cacauatl.*]
cache, *kash*, *n.* a hiding-place for treasure, stores, etc.: treasure, stores, hidden.
[Fr. *cacher*, to hide.]

cachou, *kash'ōō, n.* a sweetmeat, used to perfume the breath. [Fr.]

cackle, *kak'l, n.* the sound made by a hen or goose: talk or laughter like this.—Also *v.i.*
[M.E. *cakelen.*]

cactus, *kak'tŭs, n.* a prickly plant whose stem stores water and does the work of leaves:—*pl.* **cac'ti, cac'tuses.**
[Gk. *kaktos.*]

cad, *kad, n.* a mean, low fellow.
cadd'ish, *adj.*
[Short for **cadet.**]

cadaverous, *kȧ-dav'ėr-ŭs, adj.* thin, haggard.
[L. *cadāver*, a dead body.]

caddie, *kad'i, n.* one who carries clubs for a golfer.
cadd'ie-car, -cart, *n.* a little two-wheeled cart for carrying golf clubs upright.
[Scot., from **cadet.**]

caddis, caddice, *kad'is, n.* the larva of the **caddis-fly,** which lives in water in a silken sheath or **caddis-case.**
[Orig. uncertain.]

caddy, *kad'i, n.* a small box for tea.
[Malay *kati*, weight of small packet of tea.]

cadence, *kā'dėns, n.* rise and fall of sound: rhythm.
[L. *cadĕre*, to fall.]

cadet, *kȧ-det', n.* a younger son: a student in a military or naval school. [Fr.]

cadge, *kaj, v.t.* and *v.i.* to beg.
cadg'er, *n.* a hawker.
[Prob. conn. with **catch.**]

cadmium, *kad'mi-ŭm, n.* a white metal resembling tin.
[Gk. *kadmeia*, calamine.]

caesium, *sēz'i-ŭm, n.* a soft metal used in electron tubes, etc.
[L. *caesius*, bluish grey.]

café, *caf'ā, n.* a restaurant.
café au lait (*ō lā*), **café noir** (*nwär*), white, black, coffee. [Fr.]

cafeteria, *ka-fi-tēr'i-ȧ, n.* a self-service restaurant with a counter.
[Amer. Spanish.]

caffeine, *kaf'e-in, -īn, -ēn, n.* a stimulating substance present in coffee and tea.
[Turkish *qahveh*, coffee.]

cage, *kāj, n.* a box of wire and wood, etc. for holding birds or animals: a lift in a mine, etc.—*v.t.* to imprison in a cage.
cage bird, a bird suitable for keeping in a cage.
[L. *cavea*, a hollow place.]

cairn, *kārn, n.* a heap of stones: a small Scottish terrier.
cairngorm (stone), *n.* brown or yellow quartz found in Cairngorm Mts.
[Celt. *carn.*]

caisson, *kās'ŏn, kȧ-soon', n.* an ammunition chest or wagon: a structure for keeping out the water while the foundations of a bridge are being built.
caisson disease, disease caused by sudden change from higher air pressure to lower, as in coming up out of a caisson.
[Fr.; from *caisse*, a case or chest.]

cajole, *kȧ-jōl', v.t.* to coax: to cheat by flattery. [Origin uncertain.]

cake, *kāk, n.* a small loaf of rich bread, flavoured: a flattened hard mass.—*v.t.* and *v.i.* to form into a cake.
[Old Norse *kaka*; conn. Ger. *kuche.*]

calabash, *kal'ȧ-bash, n.* a tree of tropical America with melon-like fruit: its dried shell used for holding liquids.
[Pers. *kharbuz*, melon.]

calamine, *kal'ȧ-mīn, -min, n.* a zinc salt: a pink powder containing a zinc salt, used in lotions.
[Late L. *calamīna.*]

calamity, *kȧl-am'i-ti, n.* a great misfortune:—*pl.* **calam'ities.**
calam'itous, *adj.*
[L. *calamitās.*]

calcium, *kal'si-ŭm, n.* a metal of which one compound (*calcium carbonate*) forms marble, limestone, chalk, and coral.
calcif'erous (*-sif'*), *adj.* containing lime.
cal'cify, *v.t., v.i.* make, become, limy.
[L. *calx*, a stone, lime.]

calculate, *kal'kū-lāt, v.t.* to count or reckon: to think out: (*U.S.*) to plan: (*U.S.*) to think.
cal'culated, *adj.* deliberate.
cal'culating, *adj.* selfish, scheming.
calculā'tion, *n.* **cal'culātor,** *n.*
calculated to, likely to.
to calculate on, to base one's plans or forecasts on.
[L. *calculāre*, to reckon by help of stones.]

calculus, *kal'kū-lus, n.* a stonelike mass which may form in certain parts of the body (*pl.* **cal'culī**): a mathematical system of calculation, as one that studies the changes in a constantly varying quantity (*pl.* **cal'culuses**). [L.]

Caledonian, *kal-i-dō'ni-ȧn, adj.* of the Highlands, or of Scotland.—Also *n.*
[L. *Calēdonia*, part of N. Britain.]

calendar, *kal'in-dȧr, n.* a table showing the months and days: a list or record.
[L. *calendārium*, an account book.]

calender, *kal'in-dėr, n.* a press with rollers for finishing the surface of cloth, paper, etc.—Also *v.t.*
[Gk. *kylindros*, roller; root as **cylinder.**]

calf[1], *käf, n.* the young of the cow, elephant, whale, etc.: calfskin leather:—*pl.* **calves** (*kävz*).
calve, *käv, v.t., v.i.* to bring forth (a calf).
calf'skin, *n.* hide or leather of calf.
[O.E. *cealf*; conn. with Ger. *kalb.*]

calf[2], *käf, n.* the thick fleshy part of the leg behind.
[Old Norse *kālfi.*]

calibre, caliber, *kal'i-bėr, n.* the size of the bore of a tube or gun: (of a person) degree of excellence or importance.

cal′ibrāte, *v.t.* to mark the scale on (a measuring instrument.)
[Fr. *calibre*, the bore of a gun.]

calico, *kal′i-kō, n.* a cotton cloth first brought from *Calicut* in India.

calif. Same as **caliph.**

caliph, *kal′if*, or *kā′lif, n.* the name taken by successors of Mohammed.
cal′iphate, *n.* the office, rank, or government of a caliph.
[Arabic *khalīfah*, a successor.]

calk. See **caulk.**

call, *köl, v.i.* to cry loudly: to make a short visit.—*v.t.* to name: to summon: to describe as (e.g. *to call someone an ass*).—*n.* a summons or invitation: a demand: a short visit: a telephone connexion or conversation, or a request for one: a cry, esp. of a bird: need (e.g. *You have no call to be offended by this*).
call′er, *n.*
call′ing, *n.* crying: naming: summoning: trade, profession.
call′-boy, *n.* a boy who calls the actors when they are wanted on the stage.
to call in question, to challenge, dispute.
to call out, to instruct (workers) to come on strike.
to call (someone) to account, to demand an explanation from him.
to call up, to summon, esp. to the armed forces: to bring into memory.
[O.E. *ceallian*; conn. Du. *kallen*.]

calligraphy, *kal-ig′rȧ-fi, n.* (fine) penmanship.
[Gk. *kallos*, beauty, *graphein*, to write.]

callipers, calipers, *kal′i-pėrz, n. pl.* compasses suitable for measuring the inside or outside diameter of bodies.
cal(l)iper (splint), support for a leg, consisting of two metal rods.
[**calibre.**]

callous, *kal′ŭs, adj.* hardened: unfeeling.
call′ously, *adv.* **call′ousness,** *n.*
callos′ity (*pl.* **callos′ities**), **call′us** (*pl.* **call′uses**), *ns.* hard thickening of the skin.
[L. *callus*, hard skin.]

callow, *kal′ō, adj.* unfledged: inexperienced.
[L. *calvus*, bald.]

calm, *käm, adj.* still or quiet.—*n.* absence of wind: tranquillity.—*v.t.* to make calm: to quiet.
calm′ly, *adj.* **calm′ness,** *n.*
[Gk. *kauma*, noonday heat.]

calomel, *kal′ō-mel, n.* popular name of one of the compounds of mercury and chlorine, used in medicine. [Fr.]

calorie, *kal′ȯr-i, n.* a measure of heat.
large, great, calorie, used in measuring the heat- or energy-producing value of food.
[L. *calor*, heat.]

calumny, *kal′ŭm-ni, n.* false accusation: slander:—*pl.* **cal′umnies.**
calum′niāte, *v.t.*
[L. *calumnia*.]

Calvary, *kal′vȧ-ri, n.* the name of the place where Christ was crucified: a representation of Christ's crucifixion.
[L. *calvāria*, a skull.]

calve, calves. See **calf** (1).

Calvinism, *kal′vin-izm, n.* the teaching of the religious reformer, John *Calvin.*
Cal′vinist, *n.* **Calvinist′ic,** *adj.*

calypso, *kȧ-lip′sō, n.* a West Indian folk song, telling of current event(s) and made up as the singer goes along.

calyx, *kal′iks*, or *kā′liks, n.* the outer covering or cup of a flower:—*pl.* **calyxes,** or **calyces** (*-sēz*).
[Gk. *kalyx*, a covering.]

camaraderie, *kâm-ȧ-râd′ėr-ē, n.* the spirit of comradeship. [Fr.]

camber, *kam′bėr, n.* a slight curve on an upper surface (e.g. of a deck, bridge, aeroplane wing, road).
[L. *camerāre*, to vault.]

Cambrian, *kam′bri-ȧn, adj.* Welsh.
[*Cymru*, Wales.]

cambric, *kām′brik, n.* a fine white linen, orig. manufactured at *Cambrai.*

came. See **come.**

camel, *kam′ėl, n.* an animal with one, or two, humps on its back, used as a beast of burden and for riding.
camel('s) hair, hair of the camel: hair of squirrel's tail used for paint brushes.
[Heb. *gāmāl*.]

camellia, *kȧ-mēl′yȧ*, or *-mel′*, or *i-ȧ, n.* an evergreen shrub, native of eastern Asia, grown for its beautiful waxy flowers.
[*Camellus*, a botanist.]

cameo, *kam′i-ō, n.* an engraved gem in which the design is in relief:—*pl.* **cam′eos.**
[It. *cammeo*—Late L. *cammaeus*.]

camera, *kam′ėr-ȧ, n.* the apparatus in which a photographer exposes a sensitive plate or film: (*television*) the apparatus that receives the picture and turns it into electrical impulses for sending out.
in camera, (of a law case) tried in secret.
[L., arch, vault.]

camomile, *kam′o-mīl, n.* a plant or its dried flowers, used in medicine.
[Gk. *chamaimēlon*.]

camouflage, *ka′moo-fläzh, n.* any device for deceiving an enemy who is looking from a distance for information about military equipment, factories, roads, etc.: disguise.—Also *v.t.*
[Fr. *camouflet*, a blown whiff of smoke.]

camp, *kamp, n.* the ground on which tents are pitched: a military station: temporary quarters for travellers, etc.: a party or side.—*v.i.* to encamp.
camp bed, camp chair, camp stool, a bed, chair, stool that can be folded up when not in use.
camp follower, one not a soldier who follows in the rear of an army.
[Fr.—L. *campus*, a plain.]

campaign, *kam-pān′, n.* the operations of

an army while in the field in one area or for one purpose (e.g. *the Burma campaign in the Second World War*): organised action in support of a cause.—*v.i.* to serve in a campaign.

campaign'er, *n.*

[L. *campania*; same root as **camp.**]

campanile, *kam-pan-ē'lā, n.* a bell-tower, esp. one apart from the church:—*pl.* **campaniles,** *-ē'lēz,* or sometimes It. **campanili,** *-ē'lē.*

[It., from *campana*, a bell.]

campanula, *kam-pan'ū-lȧ, n.* a plant with bell-shaped flowers.

[It. *campana*, a bell.]

camphor, *kam'fȯr, n.* a strongly scented solid oil, obtainable from the camphor laurel of India, China, and Japan, or manufactured.

cam'phorated, *adj.* treated, saturated, with camphor.

[Late L. *camphora.*]

campus, *kam'pu̇s, n.* (*U.S.*) college or school grounds: college.

[L., a field.]

can[1], *kan, kȧn,* used with other verbs, meaning to be able to, to know how to (e.g. *I can swim*):—*pa.t.* **could** (*kood*).

[O.E. *cunnan*, to know (how to do).]

can[2], *kan, n.* a vessel for holding liquids: a vessel of tin-plate in which food is preserved.—*v.t.* to preserve in cans.

cann'ery, *n.* a factory where goods are canned:— *pl.* **-ies.**

[O.E. *canne.*]

Canadian, *ka-nā'di-ȧn, adj.* of *Canada.*—*n.* a native of Canada.

canal, *kȧn-al', n.* an artificial watercourse, esp. for ships: a passage in the body carrying fluids, etc. (e.g. *the alimentary canal*).

can'alise, *v.t.* to direct into a channel, or towards an end, or to give an outlet to (e.g. *to canalise one's energies*).

[L. *canālis*, a water pipe.]

canard, *ka-när(d)', n.* a false rumour.

[Fr., 'duck'.]

canary, *kȧ-nā'ri, n.* a yellow domesticated variety of a kind of singing finch found in the Canary Islands.

can-can, *kan-kan, n.* a wild, high-kicking dance of French origin.

[Origin uncertain.]

cancel, *kan'sėl, v.t.* to strike out by crossing with lines: to mark with a postmark: to withdraw (e.g. an order, a subscription): to put off (something planned):—*pr.p.* **can'celling**; *pa.p.* **can'celled.**

cancellā'tion, *n.*

[L. *cancellī*, railings, lattice work.]

cancer, *kan'sėr, n.* a malignant growth: any evil that gradually destroys. [L.]

candelabrum, *kan-di-lā'brum, n.* a branched and ornamented candlestick:—*pl.* **candela'bra**—also used as *sing.* with *pl.* **candela'bras.** [L.]

candid, *kan'did, adj.* frank, open, sincere.

can'didly, *adv.*

can'didness, can'dour (*kan'dȯr*), *ns.*

[L. *candidus*, white.]

candidate, *kan'di-dit, -dāt, n.* one who offers himself for an office or honour.

candidature, *kan'di-di-chu̇r, n.*

[L. *candidātus*—root as **candid**: in ancient Rome, an applicant wore white.]

candied. See **candy.**

candle, *kan'dl, n.* a cylinder of wax, tallow, etc., surrounding a wick: a light.—*v.t.* to hold (an egg) up to a light to see if it is fresh.

can'dlestick, *n.* a holder for a candle.

to burn the candle at both ends, to exhaust one's strength (e.g. by working early and late).

not fit to hold a candle to, very much less good, etc., than.

Candlemas, *kan'dl-mȧs, n.* the R.C. festival of the purification of the Virgin Mary, on 2nd February, when candles are blessed: a quarter day in Scotland.

[L. *candēla*—*candēre*, to shine.]

candour. See **candid.**

candy, *kan'di* (also **sugar-candy,** *shoog'ȧr-kan'di*), *n.* a sweetmeat made of sugar.—*v.t.* and *v.i.* to crystallise as sugar:—*pr.p.* **can'dying**; *pa.p.* **can'died.**

[Arabic *qandah*, candy.]

candytuft, *kan'di-tuft, n.* a plant with flowers growing in tufts.

[*Candia* (or Crete) and **tuft.**]

cane, *kān, n.* the stem of a small palm or large grass, etc.: a walking-stick.—*v.t.* to beat with a cane.

cane sugar, sugar obtained from the sugar cane.

[L. *canna*, a reed.]

canine, *kan'īn, kān', adj.* like or of a dog.

canine teeth, in man, four sharp-pointed teeth between the incisors and premolars.

[L. *canis*, a dog.]

canister, *kan'is-tėr, n.* a box or case usu. of metal, for holding tea, shot, etc.

[L. *canistrum*, a wicker basket.]

canker, *kang'kėr, n.* a sore in which pus forms: fungus disease in trees: inflammation in horses' feet: eczema of dogs' ears: anything that corrupts or destroys.—Also *v.t.* and *v.i.*

cank'erworm, *n.* a worm that eats into plants.

[Same root as **cancer.**]

cannibal, *kan'i-bȧl, n.* an eater (esp. a human being) of the flesh of his own species.

cann'ibalism, *n.*

[Sp. *Canibal, Caribal* a Carib (who lived in the Caribbean area).]

cannon, *kan'ȯn, n.* (now *gun*) a firearm discharged from a carriage or mount (*pl.* in certain cases **cann'on**): a stroke in billiards—an oblique hit from one ball to another.—*v.i.* to hit and rebound as a ball in a cannon at billiards.

cann'on-ball, *n.* a ball, usu. iron, formerly shot from a cannon.
cannon fodder, men regarded merely as material to be used in war.
[L. *canna*, a reed.]

cannot, *kan'ot*, am, is, or are, unable to.
[**can, not.**]

canny, *kân'i*, *adj.* (*Scot.*) shrewd: cautious, careful: gentle:—*comp.* **cann'ier**; *superl.* **cann'iest.**
cann'ily, *adv.* **cann'iness,** *n.*
[From **can** (1).]

canoe, *kȧ-nōō'*, *n.* a light narrow boat driven by means of a paddle.—*v.i.* to go in a canoe:—*pr.p.* **canoe'ing**; *pa.p.* **canoed'.**
canoe'ist, *n.*
[Sp. *canoa*—Haitian.]

canon, *kan'ȯn*, *n.* a law or rule of the church: the books of the Bible accepted by the Christian Church: a cleric belonging to a cathedral: a list of saints: a musical composition in which one part follows another in imitation: rule, standard.
canon'ical, *adj.*
canon'icals, *n. pl.* official dress of the clergy.
can'onise, *v.t.* to place in the canon or list of saints.
canonisā'tion, *n.*
[Gk. *kanōn*, a straight rod.]

canopy, *kan'ȯ-pi*, *n.* a covering hung over a throne, bed, etc.:—*pl.* **can'opies.**—*v.t.* to cover as with a canopy:—*pr.p.* **can'opying**; *pa.p.* **can'opied** (*kan'ȯ-pēd*).
[Gk. *kōnōpeion*, a mosquito curtain.]

cant[1], *kant*, *n.* hypocritical, insincere speech: the special language of a class (e.g. *thieves' cant*).—Also *v.i.*
[L. *cantāre*, to sing.]

cant[2], *kant*, *n.* an inclination, slope: a toss or jerk.—*v.t.* and *v.i.* to toss suddenly: to tilt.
[Prob. conn. with Du. *kant*, edge.]

can't, *känt*, abbrev. of **cannot.**

cantaloup(e), *kan'tȧ-loop*, *n.* a small, ribbed variety of musk melon.
[It. *Cantalupo*, a town near Rome.]

cantankerous, *kan-tang'kėr-ůs*, *adj.* quarrelsome: cross and unreasonable.
[M.E. *contek*, strife.]

cantata, *kan-tä'tä*, *n.* a musical dramatic work sung by a chorus as a concert performance.
[L. *cantāre*, to sing.]

canteen, *kan-tēn'*, *n.* a small container used by soldiers for holding water, etc.: a refreshment room in barracks, factory, etc.: a case for cutlery.
[It. *cantina*, a cellar.]

canter, *kan'tėr*, *n.* an easy gallop.—Also *v.t.*, *v.i.*
[Orig. *Canterbury gallop*, from the easy pace of pilgrims riding to Canterbury.]

Canterbury bell, *kan'tėr-bėr-i bel*, *n.* a variety of campanula.
[Supposed to resemble the bells on the horses of pilgrims to Canterbury.]

canticle, *kan'ti-kl*, *n.* a song: a hymn.
[L. *canticulum*—*cantus*, a song.]

cantilever, *kan'ti-lēv-ėr*, *n.* a large bracket for supporting balconies, stairs, etc.
cantilever bridge, one composed of projecting arms built out from the piers and meeting in the middle of the span.
[**cant,** angle, and **lever.**]

canto, *kan'tō*, *n.* a division of a long poem:—*pl.* **can'tos.**
[L. *cantus*—*canĕre*, to sing.]

canton, *kan'tȯn*, *kan-ton'*, *n.* a district: one of the Swiss federal states.
canton'ment, *n.* (pron. *can-tōōn'ment* in army) the temporary quarters of troops: a permanent military town. [O.Fr.]

Canuck, Kanuck, *kan-uk'*, *n.* a (French) Canadian.

canvas, *kan'vȧs*, *n.* a coarse cloth made of hemp or flax, etc., used for sails, tents, etc., and for painting on: the sails of a ship.
under canvas, with sails spread: in tents.
[Gk. *kannabis*, hemp.]

canvass, *kan'vȧs*, *v.t.* and *v.i.* to go round asking for (support, votes, custom, etc.).
can'vasser, *n.* [From **canvas.**]

canyon, *kan'yȯn*, *n.* a deep gorge or ravine between high steep banks, worn by rivers.
[Sp. *cañón*, a hollow.]

caoutchouc, *kow'chook*, *n.* raw rubber, the latex or juice of rubber trees.
[Fr.—West Indian *cahuchu.*]

cap, *kap*, *n.* an unbrimmed covering for the head: a cover: the top.—*v.t.* to cover with a cap: to confer a degree on: (sport) to admit to a team: to outdo (e.g. *K. capped R's performance with a better one*):—*pr.p.* **capp'ing**; *pa.p.* **capped.**
[O.E. *cæppe*—Late L. *cappa*, hooded cape.]

capable, *kāp'ȧ-bl*, *adj.* able, clever in practical ways: clever, etc. enough to (*e.g. He is capable of doing better than he does*): bad enough to (*e.g. He is capable of letting someone else take the blame*): made so as to be able to (e.g. *a car capable of doing 90 miles an hour*).
cap'ableness, capabil'ity (*pl.* **-ies**), *ns.*
[L. *capĕre*, to hold, take.]

capacious, *kȧ-pā'shůs*, *adj.* roomy, wide.
[Same root as **capacity.**]

capacitor, *kȧ-pas'i-tȯr*, *n.* an apparatus for collecting and storing electricity.
[Same root as **capacity.**]

capacity, *kȧ-pas'i-ti*, *n.* power of holding, containing: volume: mental ability: position (e.g. *in his capacity as a leader*): greatest possible extent (e.g. *filled to capacity*; *working to capacity*):—*pl.* **-ies.**
[L. *capācitās*—*capĕre*, to hold.]

cape[1], *kāp*, *n.* covering for the shoulders, sometimes attached to a coat or cloak.
[O.Fr.—Late L. *cappa.*]

cape[2], *kāp*, *n.* a head or point of land running into the sea.
[Fr. *cap*—L. *caput*, the head.]

caper[1], *kā'pėr*, *n.* the pickled flower-bud of the caper shrub, used in sauces.
[L. *capparis*—Gk. *kapparis.*]

caper[2], *kā'pėr*, *v.i.* to leap or skip: to frolic.—*n.* a leap: a prank.
[L., a he-goat.]

capercailzie, *ka-pėr-kāl'yi*, *n.* a large kind of grouse.
[Gael. *capull coille*, 'horse of the wood'.]

capillary, *kȧ-pil'ȧr-i*, *kap'il-ȧr-i*, *adj.* (of a tube) having a very small bore.—*n.* a tube with a fine bore: (in *pl.*) the tiny vessels that join veins to arteries:—*pl.* **-ies.**
[L. *capillus*, hair.]

capital[1], *kap'it-ȧl*, *adj.* of the head: involving the loss of the head or of life (*capital punishment*): chief, principal: excellent.—*n.* the chief town or seat of government: a large letter: the money for carrying on a business: possessions bringing in income.
cap'italism, *n.* control of money and business by capitalists.
cap'italist, *n.* one who has much money in business concerns.
capital goods, producers' goods.
capital levy, a tax on capital.
capital ship, a warship of the largest and strongest class.
to make capital out of, to turn to one's advantage.
[L. *capitālis*—*caput*, the head.]

capital[2], *kap'it-ȧl*, *n.* the top part of a column, etc.
[L. *capitellum*—*caput*, head.]

capitulate, *kap-it'ūl-āt*, *v.i.* to yield, surrender.
capitulā'tion, *n.*
[Late L. *capitulāre*, to arrange under heads.]

capon, *kā'pȯn*, *n.* a cock bred solely for use as food.
[O.E. *capun.*]

caprice, *kȧ-prēs'*, *n.* an unreasonable change of mind or mood: a whim: a fanciful and sprightly work in music, etc.
capri'cious (*-ri'shȧs*), *adj.* full of caprice: changeable.
capri'ciously, *adv.*
capri'ciousness, *n.*
[Conn. with **caper** (2).]

capsicum, *kap'si-kȧm*, *n.* a tropical shrub yielding cayenne pepper.
[Perh. L. *capsa*, a case.]

capsize, *kap-sīz'*, *v.t.* and *v.i.* to upset.
[Origin uncertain.]

capstan, *kap'stȧn*, *n.* a machine turned by bars used for winding e.g. a ship's cable.
[L. *capĕre*, to take, hold.]

capsule, *kap'sūl*, *n.* the dry seedbox of a plant: a covering, or container, of an organ within the body: a small gelatine case for a dose of medicine, etc.: a close metal container.
[L. *capsula*—*capsa*, a case.]

captain, *kap'tin*, *n.* the commander of a ship or aircraft (see also *Appendices*): the leader of a team or club.—*v.t.* to be captain of.
cap'taincy, *n.* the rank of captain.
[Fr. *capitaine*—L. *caput*, head.]

caption, *kap'sh(ȯ)n*, *n.* a newspaper heading, or a note accompanying an illustration, cinematograph picture, etc.
[L. *captiō*, a seizing (used for legal arrest, then for part of document stating time, place, etc., of this).]

captious, *cap'shȧs*, *adj.* ready to find fault.
cap'tiously, *adv.* **cap'tiousness**, *n.*
[L. *captiō*, a seizing; root as **captive.**]

captivate, *kap'tiv-āt*, *v.t.* to charm.
[Same root as **captive.**]

captive, *kap'tiv*, *n.* a prisoner.—*adj.* kept a prisoner: held by a rope (as a balloon).
captiv'ity, *n.* state of being a prisoner, caged, etc.
cap'tor, *n.* one who captures.
cap'ture, *v.t.* to take by force, skill, etc., to seize: to take possession of (e.g. attention, imagination).—Also *n.*
[L. *captīvus*—*capĕre*, to take.]

car, *kär*, *n.* a vehicle on wheels, esp. an automobile: the part of a balloon that carries passengers.
[Late L. *carra*; a Celtic word.]

carafe, *kȧ-râf'*, *n.* a glass water bottle.
[Prob. Arabic *gharafa*, to draw water.]

caramel, *kar'ȧ-mėl*, *n.* sugar melted and browned, used for colouring or flavouring: sweet made with sugar, butter, etc.
[Fr.—Sp. *caramelo.*]

carat, *kar'ȧt*, *n.* a measure of weight for gems: a unit in stating the fineness of gold (*18-carat gold means an alloy in which 18 out of 24 parts are pure gold*).
[Arabic *qīrāt.*]

caravan, *kar'ȧ-van*, *-van'*, *n.* a company travelling together for safety, esp. across desert: a house on wheels.
caravanserai, *kar-ȧ-van'sėr-ī*, *n.* an inn or enclosed court where caravans stop.—Also **caravansarai, -sary.**
[Pers. *kārwān*, caravan (*sarāī*, inn).]

caraway, *kar'ȧ-wā*, *n.* a plant with spicy-tasting seeds.
[Prob. Arabic *karwiyā.*]

carbide, *kär'bīd*, *n.* a compound of carbon with another element: calcium carbide, used to make acetylene.
carbohydrate, *kär-bō-hī'drāt*, *n.* a compound of carbon, hydrogen, and oxygen, e.g. sugars, starches.
carbolic acid, *kar-bol'ik as'id*, *n.* an acid from coal tar, used as a disinfectant.
carbon, *kär'bon*, *n.* element of which pure charcoal is an example, occurring also as diamond and graphite.
car'bonate, *n.* a salt containing carbon, hydrogen, oxygen, and a metal.

carbonif'erous, *adj.* producing coal.
carbon copy, a duplicate of writing or typescript made by means of **carbon paper,** a paper coated with lamp black, etc.
carbon dioxide, a gas present in the air, and breathed out by animals and given out by plants.
carbon monoxide, a colourless, odourless, very poisonous gas.
Carborundum, *kär-bòr-un'dùm, n.* a proprietary name for a compound of silicon and carbon used as an abrasive.
[L. *carbō, -ōnis,* charcoal, coal.]

carboy, *kär'boi, n.* large bottle with a frame of basketwork. [Pers. *qarābah.*]

carbuncle, *kär'bung-kl, n.* a red precious stone (a garnet): an inflamed ulcer.
[L. *carbunculus*; root as **carbide,** etc.]

carburettor, *kär'bū-ret-òr* (or *ret'-*), **carburetter,** *n.* a part of an internal-combustion engine in which air is mixed with fuel in vapour form.
[Same root as **carbide,** etc.]

carcass, carcase, *kär'kàs, n.* a dead body: (disrespectfully) a live human body: the framework of anything.
[O.Fr. *carquois.*]

card[1], *kärd, n.* a small piece of pasteboard with figures for playing a game, or with greeting, invitation, etc.: (in *pl.*) game(s) played with cards.
card'board, *n.* a stiff, finely finished pasteboard.
card'-sharp'er, *n.* one who makes a business of cheating at cards played for money.
on the cards, not improbable.
[Gk. *chartēs,* a leaf of papyrus.]

card[2], *kärd, n.* an instrument for combing wool, etc.—*v.t.* to comb (wool, etc.).
[L. *carduus,* a thistle.]

cardiac, *kär'di-ak, adj.* of the heart.
[Gk. *kardia,* the heart.]

cardigan, *kär'di-gan, n.* a knitted woollen jacket. [A 19th-cent. Lord *Cardigan.*]

cardinal, *kär'din-àl, adj.* principal: of chief importance.—*n.* one of the dignitaries next in rank to the Pope in the R.C. Church.
cardinal numbers, numbers expressing how many (1, 2, 3, etc.).
cardinal points, the four chief points of the compass—north, east, south, west.
cardinal virtues, justice, prudence, temperance, fortitude.
[L. *cardō,* a hinge.]

care, *kār, n.* worry: cause of worry: keeping (e.g. *in my care*): attention and pains (e.g. *Do it with care*).—*v.i.* to be anxious (for, about): to be willing (to): to have a fondness (for): to look after, provide (for).
care'free, *adj.* light-hearted.
care'ful, *adj.* taking care or pains: full of anxiety.
care'fully, *adv.* **care'fulness,** *n.*
care'less, *adj.* **care'lessness,** *n.*
care'taker, *n.* one put in charge of anything, esp. a building.
care'-worn, *adj.* worn with care.
to take care, to be cautious, watchful, painstaking, etc.
to take care of, to look after.
[O.E. *caru.*]

career, *kà-rēr', n.* a rush: progress through life, esp. advancement in business or profession.—*v.i.* to move rapidly.
[Fr. *carrière,* a racecourse.]

caress, *kà-res', v.t.* to touch gently, to fondle.—Also. *n.*
[Late L. *cāritia—cārus,* dear.]

caret, *kar'ėt, n.* a mark, ∧, to show where to insert something omitted.
[L., 'there is lacking'.]

cargo, *kär'gō, n.* a ship's load:—*pl.* **car'goes.**
[Sp.; from same root as **car.**]

caribou, *kar-i-bōō', n.* American reindeer.
[Canadian Fr.]

caricature, *kar'i-kà-tyùr, -chùr, n.* a likeness so exaggerated as to appear ridiculous.—Also *v.t.*
caricatur'ist, *n.*
[It. *caricare,* to load, exaggerate.]

caries, *kā'ri-ēz, n.* decay, esp. of teeth. [L.]

carillon, *ka'ril-yon,* or *-ril', n.* set of bells for playing tunes: a melody played on them. [Fr.]

carking, *kärk'ing, adj.* burdensome, harassing, in phrase *carking care.*
[Same root as **charge.**]

carmine, *kär'mīn, -min, n.* purplish red.
[Fr. *carmin,* through Sp. from Arabic.]

carnage, *kär'nij, n.* slaughter.
[L. *carō, carnis,* flesh.]

carnal, *kär'nàl, adj.* fleshly: not spiritual.
[Root as **carnage, Carnivora, etc.**]

carnation, *kär-nā'sh(ò)n, n.* garden flower, a variety of pink.
[L. *carnātiō,* fleshiness.]

carnelian. Same as **cornelian.**

carnival, *kär'ni-vàl, n.* an R.C. feast before Lent: a fair-like entertainment.
[It. *carnevale.*]

Carnivora, *kär-niv'ò-ra, n. pl.* flesh-eating animals.
carniv'orous, *adj.* flesh-eating.
car'nivore (*-vōr, -vör*), *n.* a carnivorous animal.
[L. *carō,* flesh, *vorāre,* to devour.]

carob, *kar'òb, n.* a pod-bearing Mediterranean tree, a 'locust tree'.
[Arabic *kharrūbah.*]

carol, *kar'òl, n.* a song of joy or praise.—*v.i.* to sing:—*pr.p.* **car'olling**; *pa.p.* **car'olled.**
[O.Fr. *carole.*]

carotid, *kà-rot'id, adj.* of the two great arteries of the neck.
[Gk. *karōtidēs* (*pl.*)—*karos,* sleep; it was once thought that sleep was caused by compression of them.]

carouse, *kȧr-owz′*, *n.* a drinking-bout: a noisy revel.—Also *v.i.*
carous′al, *n.* a carouse: a feast.
[O.Fr. *carous*—Ger. *gar aus*, quite out (i.e. empty).]

carp[1], *kärp*, *v.i.* to find fault with small errors or misdeeds (with *at*).
[From Scand.]

carp[2], *kärp*, *n* a freshwater fish common in ponds.
[Late L. *carpa*.]

carpal, *kär′pȧl*, *adj.* and *n.* (bone) of the wrist.
[Gk. *karpos*, wrist.]

carpenter, *kär′pin-tėr*, *n.* worker in wood, esp. as used in building houses, etc.—Also *v.i.*
car′pentry, *n.* work of carpenter.
[O.Fr. *carpentier*—Late L. *carpentārius*.]

carpet, *kär′pit*, *n.* the woven covering of floors, stairs, etc.: an expanse (e.g. of growing flowers).—*v.t.* to cover with, or as with, a carpet:—*pr.p.* **car′peting**; *pa.p.* **car′peted.**
on the carpet, under discussion: up before someone in authority for reprimand.
[Late L. *carpeta*, coarse fabric made of torn up rags—L. *carpĕre*, to pluck.]

carriage, *kar′ij*, *n.* act, or cost, of carrying: a vehicle for carrying: behaviour, bearing.
carr′iageway, *n.* (part of) a road used by vehicles.
carriage free, free of charge for transport.
carriage paid (or **carriage forward**), with the cost of conveying prepaid (or not prepaid).
[Same root as **carry.**]

carrier. See **carry.**

carrion, *kar′i-ȯn*, *n.* dead animal flesh: anything vile.—*adj.* of, feeding on, putrid flesh (e.g. *carrion crow*).
[L. *carō*, flesh.]

carrot, *kar′ȯt*, *n.* a vegetable with a sweet reddish or yellowish tapering root.
carr′oty, *adj.* carrot-coloured (of hair).
[Fr. *carotte*—L. *carōta*.]

carry, *kar′i*, *v.t.* to convey or transport: to bear: to support: to hold (oneself, one's head, etc.; e.g. *Carry yourself less stiffly*): to take by force.—*v.i.* (of gun shot, sound, etc.) to travel (a certain distance):—*pr.p.* **carr′ying**; *pa.p.* **carr′ied.**
See also **carriage.**
carr′ier, *n.* one who carries, esp. for payment: a container for carrying: one who passes on an infectious disease without himself having any symptoms.
carrier pigeon, *n.* a pigeon that carries messages, trained to return home.
to carry all before one, to overcome all resistance.
to carry on, to manage (e.g. a business): (*coll.*) to behave badly: to continue (with).
to carry one's point, to get one's plan or view accepted.
to carry out, through, to accomplish.
to carry the day, to gain the victory.
to be carried away, to be highly excited: to be misled.
[L. *carrus*, a car; conn. with **car.**]

cart, *kärt*, *n.* a two-wheeled vehicle for carrying loads.—*v.t.* to convey in a cart.
cart′age, *n.* act, or cost, of carting.
cart′er, *n.* one who drives a cart.
cart′wheel, *n.* wheel of cart: sideways somersault.
to put the cart before the horse, to reverse the natural order.
[Prob. from Old Norse.]

carte, *kärt*, *n.* a bill of fare.
à la carte, (of a meal) chosen dish by dish.
carte-blanche (*-blon*^{g}*sh*), *n.* freedom to act as one thinks best. [Fr.]

cartel, *kär-tel′*, *n.* a combination of business firms. [Fr.]

cartilage, *kär′ti-lij*, *n.* in animals, a firm elastic substance often becoming bone later: gristle.
[Fr.—L. *cartilāgō*.]

cartography, *kär-tog′rȧ-fi*, *n.* map-making.
cartog′rapher, *n.*
[Gk. *chartēs*, a leaf of papyrus, *graphein*, to write.]

carton, *kär′tȯn*, *n.* a box of thin pasteboard.
[Fr.—L. *c(h)arta*; root as **card** (1).]

cartoon, *kär-tōōn′*, *n.* a preparatory drawing on strong paper to be transferred to a fresco, tapestry, etc.: any large drawing: a drawing satirising, making fun of, something: a cinematograph film made by photographing drawings.
cartoon′ist, *n.*
[Fr. *carton*; same root as **carton.**]

cartridge, *kär′trij*, *n.* a case containing the charge for a gun.
[Fr. *cartouche*.]

carve, *kärv*, *v.t.* to cut into designs, shapes, or pieces: to cut up (meat).
car′ver, *n.* one who carves: a carving-knife.
to carve out, to hew out: to gain by one's exertions (e.g. *He carved out a kingdom, a career, for himself*).
[O.E. *ceorfan*, cut; conn. Ger. *kerben*, notch.]

cascade, *kas-kād′*, *n.* a waterfall: an arrangement of pieces of apparatus in which each feeds into the next.—*v.i.* to fall in cascades.
[L. *cadĕre*, to fall.]

cascara, *kȧs-kä′rȧ*, *n.* a Californian bark used as a laxative.
[Sp. *cáscara*, bark.]

case[1], *kās*, *n.* state or condition: an instance, example (e.g. *two cases of mumps in the town*): a person under medical treatment: a legal trial: a statement of facts or arguments: (*grammar*) a form of a noun, pronoun, or

adjective expressing its relation to other words in the sentence (in older English different cases had different endings; today, in nouns only the possessive is distinct (e.g. *man's*); adjectives show no change. But see pronouns **I, he,** etc.).
in any case, under any circumstances: whatever the other facts or circumstances.
in case, lest, for fear.
to make out a case, to argue convincingly.
[L. *cāsus*, from *cadĕre*, to fall.]

case[2], *kās*, *n.* a covering, box, or sheath: the boards and back of a book: the tray in which a compositor has his type.—Also *v.t.*
case'-hard'en, *v.t.* to harden on the surface.
case'-hard'ened, *adj.* unfeeling.
case'-knife, *n.* a knife kept in a sheath.
case'ment, *n.* a window frame: a window that opens on hinges.
[L. *capsa*, a box—*capĕre*, to take.]

cash, *kash*, *n.* coin or money: ready money. —*v.t.* to turn into or exchange for money.
cashier[1], *kash-ēr'*, *n.* one who has charge of the receiving and paying of money.
cash register, a till recording the amount put in.
hard cash, spot cash, ready money.
[O.Fr. *casse*, a box.]

cashier[2], *kash-ēr'*, *v.t.* to dismiss from a post in disgrace.
[Through Du.—L. *cassus*, empty.]

cashmere, *kash'mēr*, *n.* (a shawl, fabric, made from) fine *Kashmir* goats' hair.

casino, *kȧ-sē'nō*, *n.* a building with public dance halls, gaming tables, etc.
[It.—L. *casa*, a cottage.]

cask, *kâsk*, *n.* a hollow round vessel for holding liquor, made of staves bound with hoops.
[Fr. *casque*—Sp. *casco*, skull, helmet, cask.]

casket, *kâs'kit*, *n.* a small case for holding jewels, etc.: a coffin. [Orig. uncertain.]

cassava, *kȧ-sä'vȧ*, *n.* the West Indian name of the plant from which tapioca is obtained.

casserole, *kas'ė-rōl*, *n.* a vessel in which food is both cooked and served. [Fr.]

cassock, *kas'ȯk*, *n.* a long black robe worn by clergy and choristers: a shorter garment, worn under the pulpit gown by Scottish clergymen.
[Fr. *casaque*.]

cast, *kâst*, *v.t.* to throw: to shed, drop: to mould or shape:—*pa.t.* and *pa.p.* **cast.**—*n.* a throw: the distance thrown: a squint, as of the eye: matter ejected by an earthworm, or by a hawk, etc.: fly, hook, and gut: the company of actors taking the parts in a play.
cast'ing, *n.* act of casting or moulding: something that is cast.
cast'away, *n.* a shipwrecked person.
casting vote, the deciding vote of the president of a meeting when the other votes are equally divided.
cast iron, an iron-carbon alloy with impurities.—*adj.* (**cast'-i'ron**) rigid: unyielding: very strong.
cast'-off, *adj.* laid aside or rejected.
cast steel, steel that has been cast, not shaped by mechanical working.
to cast down, to discourage, depress.
to cast in the teeth of, to fling as a reproach against.
to cast off, to throw off, to set aside as useless: to unmoor: to finish (knitting) with an edge that will not run: to disown.
to cast on, to make stitches.
to cast up, to add up: to bring up as a reproach.
[Old Norse *kasta*, to throw.]

castanets, *kas'tȧ-nets*, *n. pl.* two hollow shells of ivory or hard wood struck together as accompaniment to dances and guitars.
[Sp. *castañeta*—L. *castanea*, a chestnut.]

caste, *kâst*, *n.* a social class esp. in India
to lose caste, to descend in social rank.
[L. *castus*, pure, unmixed.]

castellan, castellated. See **castle.**

caster. Same as **castor.**

castigate, *kas'tig-āt*, *v.t.* to punish: to criticise severely.
castigā'tion, *n.*
[L. *castigāre*, *-ātum*.]

castle, *kâs'l*, *n.* a fortified house or fortress: the residence of a prince or nobleman: a mansion: a piece in chess.
castellan, *kas'tel-ȧn*, *n.* governor of a castle.
cas'tellated, *adj.* having turrets and battlements like a castle.
castles in the air, or **in Spain,** day-dreams: schemes that cannot be carried out.
[L. *castellum*, dim. of *castrum*, fort.]

castor, *kâs'tȯr*, *n.* a small wheel on legs of furniture: a vessel with perforated top for pepper, sugar, etc.—Also **cas'ter.** **[cast.]**

castor oil, *kâs'tȯr-oil*, an oil from a tropical plant, used as medicine and for other purposes. [Origin uncertain.]

casual, *kaz(h)'ū-ȧl*, *adj.* chance: offhand: careless: unceremonious.—*n.* a workman employed occasionally, not regularly.
cas'ually, *adv.* **cas'ualness,** *n.*
cas'ualty, *n.* an accident: a person (or thing) lost by wounds, death, desertion (or breakage), etc.:—*pl.* **cas'ualties.**
[L. *cāsuālis*—same root as **case** (1).]

casuistry, *kaz'ū-is-tri*, *kazh'*, *n.* quibbling: reasoning (e.g. about one's duty) that is not straightforward.
cas'uist, *n.* **casuist'ic(al),** *adjs.*
[Same root as **case** (1).]

cat, *kat*, *n.* a small wild or pet animal: any large wild animal (as tiger, lion) related to it: a spiteful woman: short for

cat-o'-nine'-tails, a whip with nine knotted cords or lashes.
cat-and-dog, *adj.* quarrelsome.
cat'call, *n.* a squeaking instrument formerly used in theatres to express disapproval: a shrill whistle.
cat'gut, *n.* a kind of cord made from the intestines of sheep and other animals, used for violin strings, surgical ligatures, etc.
cat'kin, *n.* a spike or tuft of small flowers, as in the willow, hazel, etc.
cat's'-paw, *n.* a light breeze: a dupe or tool (from fable of monkey who used paws of cat to draw chestnuts out of fire.)
[Late L. *cattus*, prob. Celt.]

cata-, *kat-a-*, *pfx.* down.
[Gk. *kata-*.]

cataclysm, *kat'ȧ-klizm*, *n.* a flood of water: a violent upheaval.
[Gk. *kata*, down, *klyzein*, to wash.]

catacomb, *kat'ȧ-kōm, -ko͞om*, *n.* an underground burial-place.
[Prob. Gk. *kata*, down, *kymbē*, hollow.]

catafalque, *kat'ȧ-falk*, *n.* structure on which coffin rests during lying-in-state. [Fr.]

catalogue, *kat'ȧ-log*, *n.* a list of names, books, etc.—*v.t.* to put in a catalogue:—*pr.p.* **cat'aloguing**; *pa.p.* **cat'alogued.**
[Fr.—Gk. *kata*, down, *legein*, to choose.]

catalysis, *kȧ-tal'i-sis*, *n.* the hastening, or slowing down, of a chemical change by a substance which itself undergoes no permanent chemical change.
cat'alyst (or **catalyt'ic agent**), *n.*
[Gk. *kata*, down, *lyein*, to loosen.]

catamaran, *kat-ȧ-mȧ-ran'*, *n.* a raft of logs lashed together: a swift sailing-boat with two hulls side by side.
[S. Indian language, 'tied wood'.]

catapult, *kat'ȧ-pult*, *n.* an old war engine for throwing stones, etc.: a forked stick with an elastic string fixed to the prongs for throwing small missiles.
[L. *catapulta*; from Gk.]

cataract, *kat'ȧ-rakt*, *n.* a waterfall: cloudiness of lens of eye causing blindness.
[L. *cataracta*; from Gk. (*kata*, down).]

catarrh, *kat-är'*, *n.* a discharge of fluid caused by inflammation of a mucous membrane.
[Gk. *kata*, down, *rheein*, to flow.]

catastrophe, *kat-as'trȯ-fi*, *n.* a sudden disaster: a great misfortune:—*pl.* **catas'trophes.**
catastroph'ic, *adj.*
[Gk. *kata*, down, *strophē*, a turn.]

catcall. See **cat.**

catch, *kach*, *v.t.* to take hold of (a thing in motion): to trap: to entangle: to seize, attract (person's attention): to hit (e.g. *I saw the ball catch him on the ear*): to succeed in hearing: to be in time for: to surprise, detect (e.g. *to catch him stealing*): to take (disease) by infection:—*pa.t.*, *pa.p.* **caught** (*köt*).—*n.* anything that seizes or holds: a snare: a haul of fish: anything worth catching: a song in which the parts are caught up by different voices in turn.
catch'er, *n.*
catch'ing, *adj.* infectious: attractive.
catch'y, *adj.* attractive and readily remembered, as a tune, etc.:—*comp.* **catch'ier**; *superl.* **catch'iest.**
catchment area, basin, *n.* the area from which a river or a reservoir draws its water supply.
catch'penny, *n.* worthless thing, intended merely to gain money.—Also *adj.*
catch'word, *n.* among actors, the cue: first word of a page given at the bottom of the page before: any word or phrase taken up and repeated.
to catch it, to get a scolding.
to catch on, to understand: to become popular.
to catch out, to put out at cricket by catching the ball: to catch, detect, in error, or in the act.
to catch sight of, to get a glimpse of.
to catch the eye, to attract attention.
to catch up, to overtake: to snatch hastily.
[O.Fr. *cachier*—L. *capĕre*, to take.]

catechise, *kat'i-kīz*, *v.t.* to teach by question and answer: to question searchingly.
cat'echism, *n.* a book (esp. religious) of instruction by means of question and answer: a series of probing questions on any subject.
cat'echist, cat'echīser, *ns.*
[Gk. *katēchizein*, to din into the ears.]

category, *kat'ė-gȯr-i*, *n.* a class or division consisting of things (or people) of the same kind:—*pl.* **cat'egories.**
categor'ical, *adj.* absolute, definite, explicit (e.g. *a categorical refusal to help*).
categor'ically, *adv.*
[Gk. *katēgoria*.]

cater, *kā'tėr*, *v.i.* to provide food, entertainment, etc. (for).
cat'erer, *n.* **cat'ering,** *n.*
[O.Fr. *acatour*, buyer of food; conn. with Fr. *acheter*, to buy.]

caterpillar, *kat'ėr-pil-ȧr*, *n.* grub of butterfly or moth.—*adj.* moving on endless belts (as e.g. *a caterpillar tractor*).
[Prob. O.Fr. *chatepelose*, 'hairy cat'.]

caterwaul, *kat'ėr-wöl*, *n.* the shriek or cry of the cat.—Also *v.i.*
cat'erwauling, *n.*
[**cat** and *waul* (prob. imit.).]

catgut. See **cat.**

cathedral, *kȧth-ēd'rȧl*, *n.* the principal church of a diocese, with bishop's throne.
[Gk. *kathĕdra*, a seat.]

Catherine-wheel, *kath'ė-rin-hwēl*, *n.* an ornamented circular window: a firework which rotates in burning.
[St. *Catherine* of Alexandria, who escaped torture on a wheel.]

cathode, *kath'ōd, n.* the conductor through which an electric current leaves a battery, etc.: also that at which, in a high vacuum (i.e. in a tube with an extremely thin gas), electrons are formed.
cathode rays, streams of electrons.
cathode ray tube, a device in which a narrow beam of electrons strikes against a screen, as in a television set.
[Gk. *kata*, down, *hodos*, a way.]

catholic, *kath'ol-ik, adj.* universal: of the R.C. Church: including all or much (as, *catholic tastes*).—*n.* (*cap.*) an adherent of the R.C. Church.
cathol'icism, *n.* tenets of R.C. Church.
catholic'ity (*-is'-*), *n.* quality of affecting, or including, all, much: breadth of view.
[Gk. *kata*, throughout, *holos*, the whole.]

catkin. See **cat.**

cattle, *kat'l, n.pl.* grass-eating animals, esp. oxen, bulls, and cows.
cattle cake, concentrated feed in block shape for cattle.
[Late L. *captāle*, orig. capital, property.]

caught. See **catch.**

ca(u)ldron, *köl'drȯn, n.* a large kettle.
[L. *caldārium—calidus*, hot.]

cauliflower, *kol'i-flow(ė)r, n.* a variety of cabbage whose flower head is eaten.
[L. *caulis*, cabbage.]

caulk, calk, *kök, v.t.* to make (e.g. a ship) watertight by pressing oakum, etc. into the seams.
[O.Fr. *cauquer*, press—L. *calcāre*, tread.]

cause, *köz, n.* the action, happening, etc., that produced an effect: motive: reason: a legal action: an aim for which an individual or party works.—*v.t.* to produce: to bring about: to lead (a person to do something).
[Fr.—L. *causa.*]

causeway, *köz'wā*, **causey,** *köz'i, n.* a raised pathway.
[L. *calx*, heel; and **way.**]

caustic, *kös'-, kos'tik, adj.* burning: severe, cutting (e.g. *caustic comments*).—*n.* a substance that burns or wastes away the skin and flesh.
caus'tically, *adv.* **caus'ticness,** *n.*
[Gk. *kausein*, to burn.]

cauterise, *kö'tėr-īz, v.t.* to burn with a caustic or a hot iron.
cauterisā'tion, *n.*
[Gk. *kautēr*, hot iron; root as **caustic.**]

caution, *kö'sh(ȯ)n, n.* care, heedfulness: a warning.—*v.t.* to warn.
cau'tionary, *adj.* containing warning.
cau'tious, *adj.* careful: watchful: prudent.
cau'tiously, *adv.* **cau'tiousness,** *n.*
[L. *cautiō—cavēre*, to beware.]

cavalcade, *kav-ȧl-kād', n.* a train or procession of persons, esp. on horseback.
cavalier, *kav-ȧl-ēr', n.* a knight: a Royalist in the time of Charles I.—*adj.* haughty: off-hand (e.g. *cavalier treatment*).
cavalry, *kav'ȧl-ri, n.* horse-soldiers.
[L. *caballus*, horse (*caballārius*, horseman).]

cave, *kāv, n.* a hollow place in a rock.
cave'man, *n.* one, esp. of the Stone Age, who lives in a cave: one who behaves violently, esp. towards woman:—*pl.* **-men.**
to cave in, to give way, collapse.
[L. *cavus*, hollow.]

cavern, *kav'ėrn, n.* a deep hollow place in rocks.
cav'ernous, *adj.* hollow: full of caverns.
[L. *caverna*; same root as **cave.**]

caviar(e), *kâv-i-är', kâv'i-är, n.* salted roe of sturgeon, etc.: something too fine for the vulgar taste.
[Prob. 16th-cent. It. *caviale.*]

cavil, *kav'il,* v.i. to make trifling objections:—*pr.p.* **cav'illing**; *pa.p.* **cav'illed.**
[L. *cavilla*, jesting.]

cavity, *kav'it-i, n.* a hollow place, a hole:—*pl.* **cav'ities.**
[Same root as **cave.**]

cavort, *kav-ört', v.i.* (*U.S. slang*) to prance, bound.
[Perh. from *curvet*, leap of horse.]

caw, *kö, v.i.* to cry as a crow.—Also *n.*
[From the sound.]

cayenne, *kā-en', n.* a red pepper.
[Perh. *Cayenne* in French Guiana; perh. Brazilian word.]

cayman, *kā'mȧn, n.* an alligator, esp. of South American kind:—*pl.* **cay'mans.**
[Sp. *caimán.*]

cease, *sēs, v.t.* and *v.i.* to stop.
cease'less, *adj.* never ceasing.
cease'lessly, *adv.*
ceas'ing, cessā'tion (*ses-*), *ns.*
[L. *cessāre—cēdĕre*, to yield.]

cedar, *sē'dȧr, n.* a cone-bearing evergreen tree with hard, sweet-scented wood.
[L. *cedrus.*]

cede, *sēd, v.t.* to yield or give up to another.
ce'ding, cession, *se'sh(ȯ)n, ns.*
[L. *cēdĕre*, to yield, give up.]

cedilla, *sė-dil'ȧ, n.* a mark put under the letter *c* (ç) to show that it is to have the sound of *s.* [Sp.]

ceiling, *sēl'ing, n.* the inner roof of a room: the upper limit: the limiting height for a particular aircraft.
[Late L. *caelum*, a canopy.]

celandine, *sel'ȧn-dīn, n.* (*greater celandine*) a plant of poppy family: also (*lesser celandine*) a kind of buttercup.
[Gk. *chelidōn*, a swallow; plant once said to flower when swallows came and to die when they went.]

celebrate, *sel'i-brāt, v.t.* to perform (a rite, e.g. mass): to hold festivities in honour of (an event).
cel'ebrated, *adj.* famous.
celebrā'tion, *n.* act of celebrating.
celeb'rity, *n.* fame: a well-known person:—*pl.* **celeb'rities.**
[L. *celeber*, renowned.]

celery, *sel'ėr-i, n.* a vegetable with long juicy stalks. [Fr. *céleri.*]

celestial, *sėl-est'yȧl, adj.* heavenly. [L. *caelestis—caelum,* heaven.]

celibacy, *sel'i-bȧs-i, n.* unmarried state.
cel'ibate, *adj.* living single: bound by vow not to marry.—Also *n.*
[L. *caelebs,* single.]

cell, *sel, n.* a small room: a unit of living matter: the unit of an electrical battery in which chemical action takes place: a small group in a larger organisation.
cell'ular, *adj.* consisting of, or containing, cells, or tiny hollow spaces.
cell'ulose (*-ōs*), *n.* the chief substance in cell walls of plants.
[L. *cella,* conn. with *celāre,* to cover.]

cellar, *sel'ȧr, n.* an underground room, esp. one for stores, e.g. for wine: a stock of wines.
cell'arage, *n.* cellars: charge for storing in cellars.
cell'arer, *n.* the caretaker of a cellar.
[L. *cellārium*; same root as **cell.**]

cello, 'cello, *chel'ō, n.* for **violoncello.**—**cellist, 'cellist,** for **violoncellist.**

cellophane, *sel'o-fān, n.* transparent wrapping material. [Orig. trademark.]

celluloid, *sel'ū-loid, n.* a hard elastic substance made from gun-cotton and camphor, etc. [Same root as **cell.**]

cellulose. See **cell.**

Celt, *kelt, selt, n.* one of the group of peoples who speak, or once spoke, Celtic.
Celt'ic, *adj.* of the Celts.—*n.* a group of related languages incl. Welsh, Irish, Gaelic. [L. *Celtae.*]

cement, *si-ment', n.* anything that makes two bodies stick together: mortar.—*v.t.* to join firmly.
[L. *caementum,* chip of stone.]

cemetery, *sem'i-tri, n.* ground set apart for burial of the dead:—*pl.* **cem'eteries.**
[Gk. *koimētērion.*]

cenotaph, *sen'ō-tȃf, n.* a monument to one who is buried elsewhere.
[Gk. *kenos,* empty, *taphos,* a tomb.]

censer, *sens'ėr, n.* a pan in which incense is burned.
[L. *incendĕre, incensum,* to burn.]

censor, *sen'sȯr, n.* an official who examines written and printed matter with power to delete any of the contents: a stern critic.—Also *v.t.*
censō'rious, *adj.* fault-finding.
censo'riously, *adv.*
censo'riousness, *n.*
cen'sorship, *n.* office or action of a censor. [Same root as **censure.**]

censure, *sen'shůr, v.t.* to blame: to condemn as wrong.—Also *n.*
[L. *censēre,* to estimate or judge.]

census, *sen'sůs, n.* an official counting of a country's inhabitants.
[L. *census,* a register.]

cent, *sent,* a coin = the hundredth part of a dollar, rupee, rand, etc.
per cent (see **per**). [L. *centum,* hundred.]

cent(i)-, *sent-(i-),* (as part of word) a hundred: a hundredth part.
[L. *centum,* a hundred.]

centaur, *sen'tör, n.* a monster in Greek story, half man, half horse.
[L. *Centaurus*—Gk. *Kentauros.*]

centenary, *sen-tēn'ȧr-i,* or *-ten'-,* or *sen'tin-, n.* a hundredth anniversary.—Also *adj.*
centenā'rian, *n.* one who is a hundred years old. [L. *centenī,* a hundred each.]

centigrade, *sen'ti-grād, adj.* divided into a hundred degrees, as the *centigrade* (or *Celsius*; from name of Swed. astronomer) *thermometer,* in which freezing point is zero and boiling point is 100.
[L. *centum,* hundred, *gradus,* step.]

centigram(me), *sen'ti-gram*; **centilitre,** *sen'ti-lē-tėr,* **centimetre,** *sen'ti-mē-tėr, ns.* See Metric System in Appendices.

centipede, *sen'ti-pēd, n.* a crawling flattened animal with many joints, most of the joints bearing one pair of legs.
[L. *centum,* hundred *pēs, pedis,* foot.]

central, centralise, etc. See **centre.**

centre, *sen'tėr, n.* the middle point, or middle, of anything.—*v.t.* and *v.i.* to place, or to be, in the centre:—*pr.p.* **cen'tring** (*-tėr-*); *pa.p.* **cen'tred** (*-tėrd*).
cen'tral, *adj.* belonging to the centre: principal.
cen'tralise, *v.t.* to bring to, collect at, one place, esp. at the middle, or the most important, point: to bring under one control (e.g. *to centralise the government*).
centralisā'tion, *n.*
central heating, heating of a building by water, steam, or air, from one source.
centre in, round, etc., to be collected, concentrated in, round, etc. [L. *centrum.*]

centri-, *sen-tri-,* (as part of word) centre.
centrif'ugal, *adj.* tending away from a centre: using or produced by **centrifugal force** (by which objects revolving round a centre tend to move outwards, away from the centre).
centrip'etal, *adj.* tending towards centre.
[L. *centrum,* centre; *fugĕre,* to flee, *petĕre,* to seek.]

century, *sen'tū-ri, n.* a period of a hundred years: hundred runs in cricket:—*pl.* **-ies.**
[L. *centuria—centum,* a hundred.]

ceramic, *sėr-am'ik, adj.* of ceramics or a ceramic.—*n.* potter's clay or a modern substitute: (in *pl.*) the art of pottery or the articles made by a potter.
[Gr. *keramos,* potter's earth.]

cereal, *sē'ri-ȧl, n.* (usu. in *pl.*) grain used as food, as wheat, barley: a food prepared from such grain.
[L., prob. from *creāre,* to create.]

cerebellum. See **cerebrum.**

cerebrum, *ser'i-brům, n.* the front and larger part of the brain.
cerebell'um, *n.* the hinder and lower part of the brain.

cer′ebro-spin′al, *adj.* of the brain and spinal cord. [L., the brain.]

ceremony, *ser′i-mȯ-ni, n.* a sacred rite: a formal act: pomp or formality:—*pl.* **cer′emonies.**

ceremō′nial, *adj.* relating to ceremony. —*n.* a system of ceremonies.

ceremō′nially, *adv.*

ceremō′nious, *adj.* carefully formal or polite. [L. *caerimōnia*, sacred rite.]

cerise, *ser-ēz′, -ēs′, n.* and *adj.* a light and clear red colour. [Fr., 'cherry'.]

certain, *sėr′tin, -tn, adj.* sure, without doubt: never failing in action or result: some, or one, not definitely named, or not known to the listener(s) (e.g. *certain MPs*; *a certain Mrs. Smith*).

cer′tainly, *adv.*—*interj.* yes.

cer′tainty, *n.* something which cannot be doubted: something which is sure to happen: freedom from doubt:—*pl.* **-ties.** [L. *certus.*]

certificate, *sėr-tif′i-kit, n.* written declaration of some fact: a testimonial of character.—*v.t.* (*-kāt*) to give a certificate to.

cer′tify, *v.t.* to declare formally: to guarantee:—*pr.p.* **cer′tifying**; *pa.p.* **cer′tified.**

certificā′tion, *n.*

certifi′able, *adj.* that, who, can be certified (esp. as insane).

[L. *certus*, certain, *facĕre*, to make.]

cesium. Same as **caesium.**

cessation. See **cease.**

cession. See **cede.**

cesspool, *ses′pōōl, n.* a pool or pit for collecting filthy water. [Origin uncertain.]

chafe, *chāf, v.t.* to make hot by rubbing: to fret or wear by rubbing.—*v.i.* to fret or rage.

[Fr. *chauffer*—L. *calefacĕre*, make hot.]

chaff, *châf, n.* the husks of corn as threshed or winnowed: good-humoured teasing. —*v.t.* to tease good-naturedly.

[O.E. *ceaf*: conn. Du. *kaf.*]

chaffer, *chaf′ėr, v.i.* to bargain, haggle.

[O.E. *cēap*, price, *faru*, way.]

chaffinch, *chaf′inch, -sh, n.* a songbird of the finch family.

[Said to delight in corn *chaff.*]

chagrin, *shä-grēn′, -grin′, n.* vexation, annoyance.—*v.t.* (*shä-grēn′*) to vex, annoy.

[Fr., shagreen, rough skin, ill-humour.]

chain, *chān, n.* a series of links or rings passing through one another: a series: anything that binds: a measure 66 feet long: (in *pl.*) fetters.—*v.t.* to fasten: to fetter.

chain gang, a gang of convicts chained together.

chain mail, armour made of iron links.

chain store, one of a number of shops linked under the same ownership.

[Fr. *chaîne*—L. *catēna.*]

chair, *chār, n.* a movable seat for one, with a back to it: the seat of a person in authority: the office of a professor, of one who conducts a meeting, etc.—*v.t.* to carry in triumph.

chair′man, -woman, *ns.* one who presides at a meeting.

chair′manship, *n.* [Gk. *kathedra.*]

chalet, *shâl′ā, n.* a summer hut in mountains for herdsmen, etc.: a wooden house. [Fr.]

chalice, *chal′is, n.* a cup or bowl: a communion cup. [L. *calix.*]

chalk, *chök, n.* white rock, a soft limestone: a chalklike substance used for writing.

chalk′y, *adj.* **chalk′iness,** *n.*

[L. *calx*, limestone.]

challenge, *chal′inj, v.t.* to summon to a contest: to express objection to (a juryman or jury, a decision, etc.): to claim or arouse (e.g. attention).—*n.* a summons to a contest: an objection.

chall′enger, *n.*

[L. *calumnia*, a false accusation.]

chamber, *chām′bėr, n.* a room: the place where an assembly meets: a law-making body: the back end of bore of gun.

cham′bermaid, *n.* a female servant in charge of bedrooms.

chamber music, music suitable for a room as opp. to a large hall: music for strings, with or without piano or wind.

chamber of commerce, an association in a town or district to watch over business interests. [Fr. *chambre*—L. *camera.*]

chamberlain, *chām′bėr-lin, n.* an officer managing household of king or nobleman: treasurer of a corporation.

[L. *camera*, a chamber, and *-ling.*]

chameleon, *kȧ-mēl′yȯn,* or *-i-ȯn,* a small lizard able to change colour.

[Gk. *chamai*, on the ground, *leōn*, lion.]

chamfer, *cham′fėr, n.* a bevelled edge or corner.—Also *v.t.*

[O.Fr. *chanfraindre*, 'break-corner'.]

chamois, *sham′wä, n.* an Alpine antelope: (*pron. sham′i*) a soft leather orig. made from its skin (also **shamm′y**). [Fr.]

champ, *champ, v.i.* to make a snapping noise with the jaws in chewing.—*v.t.* to chew. [Prob. from Scand.]

champagne, *sham-pān′, n.* a white or red, sparkling or still, wine from *Champagne* in France, or elsewhere.

champion, *cham′pi-ȯn, n.* one who fights for himself or for another: one who defends a cause: in games, a competitor who has defeated all others.—*adj.* first-class.—*v.t.* to defend, to support.

cham′pionship, *n.*

[Fr.—L. *campus*, plain, place for games.]

chance, *châns, n.* something that happens for no known reason: something thought of as causing unplanned events (e.g. *Chance brought them to the spot at the same moment*): risk: opportunity: possibility.—*v.t.* to risk.—*v.i.* to happen. *adj.* happening accidentally.

chanc'y, *adj.* (*coll.*) risky, uncertain.
an even chance, equal probability for and against.
the chances are, the probability is.
[O.Fr. *cheance*—L. *cadĕre*, to fall.]

chancel, *chân'sl, n.* the eastern part of a church, orig. separated from the nave by a screen of lattice-work.
[L. *cancelli*, lattices.]

chancellor, *chân'sel-ŏr, n.* a chief minister: the head of a university.
chancellery, *chân'se-le-ri*, or *-sle-, n.* department of a chancellor: office attached to an embassy, etc.
Chancellor of the Exchequer, chief minister of finance in British government.
Lord (High) Chancellor, the speaker of the House of Lords, keeper of the great seal, and first lay person of the state after royal persons.
[Late L. *cancellārius*, orig. a law-court official who stood near the *cancelli* (L.), crossbars, between court and judges.]

chancery, *chân'sĕr-i, n.* a division of the High Court of Justice.
[Same root as **chancellor.**]

chandelier, *shan-dė-lēr', n.* a frame with branches for holding lights.
chandler, *chand'lėr*, a candle maker: a dealer in candles: a dealer generally.
[Fr.—L. *candēla, a candle.*]

change, *chānj, v.t.* to exchange (for): to put, take, another in place of: to give or get smaller coin for.—*v.t.* and *v.i.* to make, or to become, different: to alter (with *from, to, into*): to put different clothes on, or put on different clothes: to go from one train, etc., to another (e.g. *I have to change trains; I change at Crewe*).—*n.* alteration: something different: small coins: money given back when too much is handed over as payment: variation (see **ring,** 2).
change'able, *adj.* changing often: fickle.
change'ableness, changeabil'ity, *ns.*
change'ling, *n.* a child taken or left in place of another.
to change hands, to pass into different ownership.
[Fr. *changer*—L. *cambīre*, to barter.]

channel, *chan'l, n.* the bed of a stream: a passage of deeper water through which ships can sail: a strait or narrow sea (e.g. *English Channel*): means of sending information, etc.: (*radio, etc.*) a path for signals in one direction.—*v.t.* to furrow.
[L. *canālis*, a canal.]

chant, *chânt, v.t.* to recite in a singing manner.—*n.* a kind of sacred music in which a number of syllables are recited to one tone.
[L. *cantāre*—*canĕre*, to sing.]

chanty. Same as **shanty** (2).

chaos, *kā'os, n.* complete disorder or confusion.
chaot'ic, *adj.* **chaot'ically,** *adv.* [Gk.]

chap[1], *chap, v.i.* to crack, as soil in dry weather or skin in cold weather.
[M.E. *chappen.*]

chap[2], *chap, n.* a fellow.
[For *chapman*, a pedlar, a customer.]

chap[3], **chap-fallen.** See **chop** (2).

chapel, *chap'ĕl, n.* a place of Christian worship not belonging to the established church of the country: one attached to a house or institution: a part of a church with its own altar.
[Late L. *cappella.*]

chaperon, *shap'ė-rōn, n.* lady under whose care girl appears in society.—Also *v.t.*
[Late L. *cappa*, a cloak.]

chaplain, *chap'lin, n.* a clergyman attached to a ship, regiment, institution, or family.
chap'laincy, *n.* office of chaplain.
[Late L. *cappellānus*; root as **chapel.**]

chapter, *chap'tėr, n.* a main division of a book: an assembly of the canons of a cathedral: an organised branch of a society (e.g. of freemasons).
chapter house, a house or room where a chapter meets.
[L. *capitum*—*caput*, the head.]

char[1], *chär, v.t.* and *v.i.* to scorch:—*pr.p.* **charr'ing**; *pa.p.* **charred.**
[Origin unknown.]

char[2], *chär, v.i.* to do house cleaning.
char'woman, *n.* a woman employed for this purpose.
[O.E. *c(i)erran*, to turn.]

character, *kar'ak-tėr, n.* a letter or mark: nature, qualities: strength of mind and purpose (e.g. *He was a man of character*): an odd, eccentric person: a person in a play or novel.
char'acterise, *v.t.* to be characteristic of, to distinguish, mark (e.g. *Good taste characterises her*): to describe (as).
characterīsā'tion, *n.* creation of character(s) in a play or novel: description.
characteris'tic, *adj.* typical (of a person, etc.; e.g. *He showed characteristic unwillingness to say what he thought*).—*n.* a typical quality.
character actor, an actor who often plays the part of an eccentric person.
[Gk. *charaktēr* (*charassein*, to engrave).]

charade, *shȧ-räd', n.* a game in which the syllables of a word, and then the whole word, are acted. [Fr.]

charcoal, *chär'kōl, n.* black part of partly burned wood, etc.
[**char** (1), and **coal.**]

charge, *chärj, v.t.* to load: to fill (with): to fill with electricity: to command: to accuse: to ask as the price: to record as debt in, against (e.g. *Charge it to my account, to me*): to attack at a rush (also *v.i.*).—*v.i.* to ask payment (for).—*n.* load: cost: the powder, or powder and shot, e.g. for a gun: a quantity of electricity: care: something looked after (e.g. a child): control: command: accusation: attack.

charge'able, *adj.* liable to be charged (e.g. *If he does this, he is chargeable with fraud*): that should be charged (e.g. *This expense is chargeable to the firm's account*).
charg'er, *n.* a large flat dish: a war-horse.
to be in charge of, to control and be responsible for.
to give in charge, to hand (a person) over to the police.
[Fr. *charger*—Late L. *carricāre,* to load.]

chargé-d'affaires, *shär-zhā-dä-fer, n.* an ambassador's deputy. [Fr.]

charily, chariness. See **chary.**

chariot, *char'i-ot, n.* a car used in ancient warfare or racing.
charioteer', *n.* chariot driver.
[Fr.—*char,* a car.]

charity, *char'i-ti, n.* love: kindly feeling: almsgiving: a fund or institution whose purpose is to give help:—*pl.* **-ies.**
char'itable, *adj.* **char'itably,** *adv.*
[Fr. *charité*—L. *cārus,* dear.]

charlatan, *shär'lȧ-tȧn, n.* a quack (see this word).
[It. *ciarlatano*—*ciarlare,* to chatter.]

charlock, *chär'lok, n.* wild mustard.
[O.E. *cerlic.*]

charlotte, *shär'lot, n.* a kind of fruit tart.
[From the name *Charlotte.*]

charm, *chärm, n.* a spell: something thought to have magical power: attractiveness.—*v.t.* to influence by a charm: to delight.
charmed, *adj.* protected, as by a spell: delighted.
charm'ing, *adj.* very attractive.
charm'ingly, *adv.* **charm'er,** *n.*
[Fr. *charme*—L. *carmen,* a song.]

charnel (house), *chär'nl (hows),* a place in which bodies or bones are put.
[O.Fr. *charnel*—L. *carō, carnis,* flesh.]

chart, *chärt, n.* a map of part of the sea, with its coasts, shoals, depth, etc.: a table giving information.—*v.t.* to make a chart of: to plan.
[Same root as **card** (1).]

charter, *chärt'ėr, n.* a formal writing giving titles, rights, or privileges, esp. one granted by the sovereign or government.—*v.t.* to let or hire, as a ship or aircraft, on contract.
chartered accountant, one qualified under the regulations of the Institute of Accountants.
[Same root as **card** (1).]

charwoman. See **char** (2).

chary, *chār'i, adj.* unwilling to risk (with *of*; e.g. *Be chary of lending money to a slight acquaintance*): cautious:—*comp.* **char'ier**; *superl.* **char'iest.**
char'ily, *adv.* **char'iness,** *n.*
[O.E. *cearig*—*cearu,* care.]

chase, *chās, v.t.* to pursue: to hunt: to drive (away).—*n.* pursuit: hunting.
[Fr. *chasser*—L. *capĕre,* take.]

chasm, *kazm, n.* a deep opening, gulf.
[Gk. *chasma.*]

chassis, *shas'ē, n.* the frame, wheels, machinery (but not body) of a motor car, etc.: an aeroplane's landing-carriage:—*pl.* **chassis** (*shas'ēz*).
[Fr. *châssis,* frame.]

chaste, *chāst, adj.* virtuous sexually: pure in taste and style.
chaste'ly, *adv.*
chaste'ness, chas'tity (*chas'*), *ns.*
[L. *castus,* pure.]

chasten, *chās'n, v.t.* to make better by punishment, suffering, etc.: to keep from being too great (e.g. *This failure chastened his pride*).
[**chaste,** with suffx. *-en.*]

chastise, *chas-tīz', v.t.* to punish: to beat.
chas'tisement, (*-tiz-*) *n.*
[Conn. with **chasten.**]

chastity. See **chaste.**

chasuble, *chaz'-* or *chas'ū-bl, n.* sleeveless vestment worn by priest celebrating mass.
[Late L. *casubula*—*casa,* a hut.]

chat[1], *chat, v.i.* to talk in an easy, friendly way:—*pr.p.* **chatt'ing**; *pa.p.* **chatt'ed.**—Also *n.*
chatt'y, *adj.* **chatt'iness,** *n.*
[Short for **chatter.**]

chat[2], *chat, n.* a small bird of thrush family.
[Imit.]

château, *shä'tō, n.* a (French) castle:—*pl.* **châ'teaux** (*-tōz*).
chatelaine, *shat'ė-lān, n.* the mistress of a castle or house.
[L. *castellum*—*castrum,* a fort.]

chattel, *chat'ėl, n.* usu. in *pl.* as in **goods and chattels,** all movable property.
[O.Fr. *chatel*—L. *capitāle,* property.]

chatter, *chat'ėr, v.i.* to talk idly or quickly: (of birds) to utter rapid short notes: (of teeth) to knock together.—*n.* idle talk.
chatt'erbox, *n.* a talkative person.
[Imit.]

chauffeur, *shō'fėr, n.* one employed to drive a private motor car. [Fr.]

cheap, *chēp, adj.* low in price: of small value.
cheap'en, *v.t.* to lower price of: to make vulgar, worthy of contempt, etc.
cheap'ly, *adv.* **cheap'ness,** *n.*
cheap'-jack, *n.* a travelling hawker.
[O.E. *cēap,* price—*cēapian,* to buy; conn. Ger. *kaufen.*]

cheat, *chēt, v.t.* to deceive: to swindle.—Also *v.i.* and *n.*
[M.E. *cheten.*]

check[1], *chek, v.t.* to stop: to hinder: to find fault with (a person): to test (e.g. a calculation) to see that it is correct.—*n.* a sudden stop: something that hinders progress: (chess) a position in which the king is open to attack: a pattern of squares.
checked, *adj.*

check′mate, *n.* (*chess*) a position from which the king cannot escape.—*v.t.* to put (opponent's king) in this position: to put a final stop to.
[O.Fr. *eschec* (*mat*), 'the king (is dead)'; from Pers. *shah*, king.]

check[2], **checker**(**s**). See **cheque.**

cheek, *chēk*, *n.* the side of the face below the eye: the side of a door, etc.: (*coll.*) impudence.
cheek′y, *adj.* **cheek′iness,** *n.*
cheek′bone, *n.* bone ridge below eye.
[O.E. *cēce*, *cēace.*]

cheep, *chēp*, *v.i.* to chirp, as a young bird.—Also *n.* [Imit.]

cheer, *chēr*, *n.* a shout of approval or welcome: entertainment: food.—*v.t.* to encourage: to applaud.
cheer′ful, *adj.* in good spirits: lively: ungrudging.
cheer′fully, *adv.* **cheer′fulness,** *n.*
cheer′y, *adj.* lively, merry.
cheer′ily, *adv.* **cheer′iness,** *n.*
cheer′less, *adj.* gloomy: without comfort.
[O.Fr. *chiere*, the face—Late L. *cara.*]

cheese, *chēz*, *n.* the curd of milk pressed into a hard mass.
cheese′-par′ing, *n.* stinginess.—Also *adj.*
[L. *cāseus.*]

cheetah, *chē′tȧ*, *n.* an Eastern animal like the leopard, used in hunting.
[Hindustani *chītā.*]

chef, *shef*, *n.* a cook, esp. a head cook.
chef d'œuvre (*shā dėvr′*), *n.* masterpiece.
[Fr.; root as **chief.**]

chemical, chemist, etc. See **chemistry.**

chemistry, *kem′is-tri*, *n.* the science that deals with the properties of substances and the ways in which they act on, or combine with, each other.
chem′ical, *adj.* of chemistry or chemical(s).—*n.* a substance used in a chemical process, either in research or in industry.
chem′ist, *n.* a scientist who studies chemistry: a druggist (see this word).
chem′ō-, *pfx.* chemical.
[From **alchemy.**]

cheque (*U.S.* **check**), *chek*, *n.* a written order on a printed form telling a bank to pay money to a person named.
cheque book, a book of cheque forms.
chequ′er, check′er, *v.t.* to mark with squares: to make (a career) varied, with ups and downs.
chequ′ers, (more often) **check′ers,** *n. pl.* the game of draughts.
[Same as **check.**]

cherish, *cher′ish*, *v.t.* to protect and love: to have in the mind or heart (e.g. *to cherish a hope, an idea, a feeling*).
[Fr. *chérir*—*cher*, dear.]

cheroot, *shė-rōōt′*, *n.* a cigar not pointed at either end.
[S. Indian word *shuruttu*, roll.]

cherry, *cher′i*, *n.* tree, or its small, usu. red, stone fruit.
[Gk. *kerasos*, cherry tree.]

cherub, *cher′ŭb*, *n.* a winged creature with human face: a beautiful child:—*pl.* **cher′ubs, cher′ubim** (*-oo-*).
cheru′bic (*-ōō′bik*), *adj.*
[Heb. *k'rūb*, pl. *k'rūbīm.*]

chess, *ches*, *n.* a game for two played with 'men' (**chess′men**) on a chequered board (**chess′board**).
[Orig. Pers. *sháh*; root as **check** (1).]

chest, *chest*, *n.* a large strong box: the part of the body between the neck and the abdomen.
chest of drawers, a set of drawers fitted in a single piece of furniture.
[O.E. *cest*—L. *cista.*]

chesterfield, *chest′ėr-fēld*, *n.* a long overcoat: a heavily padded sofa.
[A 19th-cent. Lord *Chesterfield.*]

chestnut, *ches′nut*, *n.* an edible nut in a prickly husk (the *Spanish* or *sweet chestnut*): the tree that bears it: (*slang*) a stale joke.—*adj.* reddish-brown.
See also **horse chestnut.**
[O.Fr. *chastaigne*—L. *castanea.*]

chevron, *shev′rȯn*, *n.* the V-shaped band on the sleeve of a non-commissioned officer's coat.
[Fr. *chevron*, a rafter.]

chevy. Same as **chiv(v)y.**

chew, *chōō*, *v.t.* to grind with the teeth.—Also *n.*
chew′ing-gum, *n.* a preparation made from sweetened and flavoured gums.
to chew the cud, to chew a second time food already swallowed (as a cow does): to think deeply.
[O.E. *cēowan.*]

chic, *shēk*, *adj.* stylish.—Also *n.* [Fr.]

chick, *chik*, *n.* a baby bird: a child.
chick′en, *n.* a young hen, etc.: flesh of a fowl: a child.
chick′en-heart′ed, *adj.* cowardly.
chick′en-pox, *n.* a contagious disease with fever and blister-like spots.
chick′weed, *n.* a garden weed liked by fowls and cage birds.
[O.E. *cicen*; conn. Ger. *küchlein.*]

chicory, *chik′ȯ-ri*, *n.* a plant with blue flowers: its carrot-like root (ground to mix with coffee).
[Gk. *kichōrion.*]

chide, *chīd*, *v.t.* to scold, rebuke:—*pa.t.* **chīd′ed, chĭd**; *pa.p.* **chīd′ed, chĭdd′en, chĭd.**
chīd′ing, *n.* and *adj.* [O.E. *cīdan.*]

chief, *chēf*, *adj.* head: most important.—*n.* the head of a clan or tribe: the head of a department or business.
chief′ly, *adv.* mainly.
chief′tain (*-tin*), *n.* the head of a clan.
[Fr. *chef*—L. *caput*, the head.]

chiffon, *shif′on*, *shē-fong*, *n.* a thin gauzy material.
[Fr., rag, scrap—*chiffe*, rag.]

chilblain, *chil'blān, n.* a red swelling, esp. on hands and feet, in cold weather. [**chill** and **blain.**]

child, *chīld, n.* a very young person: a son or daughter:—*pl.* **chil'dren** (*chil'*).
child'hood, *n.* state or time of being a child.
child'ish, *adj.* like the ways or interests of a child: weak, silly.
child'ishness, *n.* **child'ishly,** *adv.*
child'like, *adj.* like a child, innocent.
child's play, an easy task.
[O.E. *cild.*]

chill, *chil, n.* coldness: a cold that causes shivering: anything that disheartens.—Also *adj.*—*v.t.* and *v.i.* to make, or to grow, cold: (*v.t.*) to discourage (e.g. *to chill one's enthusiasm.*)
chill'y, *adj.* chill.
chill'ness, chill'iness, *ns.*
[O.E. *cele, ciele,* cold.]

chilli, *chil'i, n.* the pod of capsicum, used in sauces, etc., or, dried and ground, as Cayenne pepper:—*pl.* **-ies.** [Mexican.]

chime, *chīm, n.* a set of bells tuned in a scale: the ringing of bells in succession. —Also *v.t.* and *v.i.*
[L. *cymbalum,* a cymbal.]

chimney, *chim'ni, n.* a passage for the escape of smoke, etc., from a fireplace or furnace.
chim'ney-pot, or **-can,** *ns.* a pipe at the top of a chimney to increase draught.
chimney corner, the fireside, esp. as a place of warmth and comfort.
chim'neypiece, *n.* a shelf over the fireplace.
chim'ney-stack, *n.* a group of chimneys carried up together.
chim'ney-stalk, *n.* a very tall chimney.
chimney sweep(er), one who cleans chimneys.
[Fr. *cheminée*; Gk. *kamīnos,* furnace.]

chimpanzee, *chim-pan-zē',* also *chim'-, n.* an African ape, the most manlike of the apes. [West African.]

chin, *chin, n.* the jutting part of the face below the mouth.
[O.E. *cin*; conn. with Ger. *kinn.*]

china, *chīn'ȧ, n.* fine kind of earthenware orig. made in *China,* porcelain.
china clay, a fine white clay used in making porcelain, kaolin.
Chinese'(*-ēz'*), *n.* a native of China (*pl.* **Chinese'**): the language of China.—Also *adj.*
Chinese lantern, a paper lantern.

chinchilla, *chin-chil'ȧ, n.* a small rodent of South America: its soft grey fur. [Sp.]

chine, *chīn, n.* the spine or backbone: a piece of the backbone with adjoining flesh for cooking.
[Prob. Old German *scina,* a thorn.]

chink[1], *chingk, n.* a narrow opening.
[M.E. *chine,* a crack.]

chink[2], *chingk, n.* clink, as of coins.—Also *v.i., v.t.* [Imit.]

chintz, *chints, n.* cotton printed in several colours.
[Indian word *chint,* spotted cotton cloth.

chip, *chip, v.t.* to strike small pieces off.—Also *v.i.*:—*pr.p.* **chipp'ing**; *pa.p.* **chipped.**—*n.* small piece chipped off, or (in e.g. china) place damaged thus: (in *pl.*) small pieces of potato fried: a counter used in games.
to chip in, to interrupt.
[M.E. *chippen,* to cut in pieces.]

chipmunk, *chip'mungk, n.* small striped North Amer. squirrel. [Orig. uncertain.]

chiropodist, *ki-rop'o-dist* (also *shi-, chi-*), *n.* one who treats corns, bunions, etc.
chirop'ody, *n.* treatment of corns, etc.
[Gk. *cheir,* hand, *pous, podos,* foot.]

chirp, *chėrp, n.* the sharp, thin sound of certain birds and insects.—Also *v.i.*
chirp'y, *adj.* lively: merry:—*comp.* **chirp'ier**; *superl.* **chirp'iest.** [Imit.]

chisel, *chiz'ėl, n.* tool with a cutting edge at the end.—*v.t.* to cut, carve, etc. with a chisel:—*pr.p.* **chis'elling**; *pa.p.* **chis'elled.**
[O.Fr. *cisel*—L. *caedĕre,* to cut.]

chit[1], *chit, n.* a brief note: an order or pass.
[Indian word *chitthī.*]

chit[2], *chit, n.* a child: (*slightingly*) a girl.
[Short for **kitten.**]

chivalry, *shiv'ȧl-ri, n.* the customs of feudal knights: bravery and courtesy.
chiv'alrous, *adj.* showing the qualities of an ideal knight, generous, courteous, etc.
chiv'alrously, *adv.*
[Fr. *chevalerie*; root as **cavalcade,** etc.]

chive, *chīv, n.* a herb like the leek and onion, used as flavouring.
[Fr. *cive*—L. *coepa,* an onion.]

chivy, chivvy, *chiv'i, v.t.* to chase: to keep urging on, harass, annoy:—*pr.p.* **chiv(v)'ying**; *pa.p.* **chiv(v)'ied.**
[Prob. ballad of *Chevy Chase* (place name), describing battle.]

chlorine, *klō', klō'rēn, n.* a yellowish-green gas with a suffocating smell—used in bleaching, disinfecting, etc.
chlo'ride, *n.* any of certain compounds of chlorine (e.g. common salt, *sodium chloride,* which consists of chlorine and the metal sodium).
chlo'rinate, *v.t.* to treat with chlorine or a compound (as in purifying water).
chloroform, *klor'ō-förm, n.* a colourless liquid used as an anaesthetic.
chlor'ophyll (*-ȯ-fil*), *n.* the colouring matter of the green parts of plants.
[Gk. *chlōros,* pale green.]

chock, *chok, v.t.* to fix with a wedge.—*n.* a wedge to keep e.g. a cask from rolling.
chock-a-block', chock'-full, *adjs.* quite full. [Origin unknown.]

chocolate, *chok'ȯ-lit, n.* a paste made from pounded seeds of the cacao tree: a beverage, or sweetmeat, made from this. —Also *adj.*
[Sp.—Mexican *chocolatl.*]

choice, *chois, n.* act or power of choosing: the thing chosen: alternative.—*adj.* worthy of being chosen.
[Same root as **choose.**]

choir, *kwīr, n.* a chorus or band of singers: the part of a church where the singers stand.
[Fr. *choeur*; same root as **chorus.**]

choke, *chōk, v.t.* to throttle: to interfere with the breathing of: to block.—*v.i.* to have the breathing checked by something in the throat.—*n.* the action or sound of choking: a device to prevent the passage of too much gas, etc.
chok'y, *adj.* inclined to choke (*v.i.*):—*comp.* **chok'ier**; *superl.* **chok'iest.**
chok'ily, *adv.* **chok'iness,** *n.*
choke'-damp, *n.* carbon dioxide or other suffocating gas in coal mines.
to choke off, to get rid of (a person).
[Origin unknown.]

cholera, *kol'ėr-a, n.* a highly infectious deadly disease with bilious vomiting, etc.
[Gk. *cholera—cholē*, bile.]

choose, *chōōz, v.t.* to take (one thing) rather than another: to select.—*v.i.* to will, decide (e.g. *If he chooses to resign, let him do so*):—*pa.t.* **chose** (*chōz*); *pa.p.* **chosen.**
See also **choice.**
[O.E. *cēosan*; conn. with Du. *kiesen.*]

chop[1], *chop, v.t.* to cut with a sudden blow: to cut into small pieces.—*n.* a slice of mutton or pork containing a rib.
chopp'er, *n.* one who, or something that, chops.
chopp'y, *adj.* (of sea) running in irregular waves.
chopp'iness, *n.* [**chap** (1).]

chop[2], *chop, n.* used in *pl.* **chops,** the jaws, mouth of an animal.—Also **chap(s).**
chop'- (or more usu. **chap'-)fallen,** *adj.* dejected. [Orig. unknown.]

chop[3], *chop, v.i.* shift, change direction.
to chop and change, to keep changing.
[Conn. in some way with **chop** (1).]

chopper, choppy. See **chop** (1).

chopsticks, *chop'stiks, n.pl.* two small sticks of wood, ivory, etc., used by Chinese instead of a fork.
[Pidgin Eng. *chop-chop*, quick, and **stick.**]

choral, chorale. See **chorus.**

chord[1], *körd, n.* (*music*) a number of notes played together. [**accord.**]

chord[2], *körd, n.* alternative spelling of cord (*spinal, vocal, chord*): a straight line joining any two points on a curve.
[Gk. *chordē*, a gut string.]

chore, *chōr, chör, n.* a piece of housework, or other hard or dull job.
[Same word as **char** (2).]

choreography, *kor-i-og'rà-fi, n.* the art of arranging dances: the arrangement of a ballet.
choreog'rapher, *n.*
[Gk. *choreia*, dancing, *graphein*, to write.]

chorister. See **chorus.**

chortle, *chört'l, v.i.* to give a low deep laugh.
[Coined by Lewis Carroll perh. from *chuckle* and *snort.*]

chorus, *kōr'ŭs, kör', n.* a band of singers or dancers: the refrain of a song.—*v.t.* to sing or say together.
chor'al, *adj.* to be sung by a choir.
chorale (*-äl'*), *n.* a simple, slow tune for a psalm or hymn.
chor'ister (*kor'*), *n.* a member of a choir.
[Gk. *choros*, dance.]

chose, chosen. See **choose.**

chough, *chuf, n.* the red-legged crow.
[From its cry.]

chow, *chow, n.* a dog of prob. Chinese breed.
[Origin uncertain.]

Christ, *krīst, n.* Jesus of Nazareth.
christen (*kris'n*), *v.t.* to baptise in the name of Christ: to give a name to.
Christendom (*kris'n-*), *n.* the part of the world in which Christianity is the recognised religion.
Christian, *kris'chȧn, n.* a follower of Christ.—Also *adj.*
Christian'ity, *n.* the religion of Christ: the spirit of this religion.
Christian name, the personal name given (as at christening), in addition to the surname.
Christian Science, a religion which includes belief in healing by faith without medicine.
[Gk. *Christos—chriein*, to anoint.]

Christmas, *kris'mȧs, n.* an annual festival in memory of the birth of Christ, held on 25th December.
Christmas box, a Christmas gift.
Christmas Eve, (evening of) Dec. 24.
Christmas tree, a tree hung with Christmas gifts. [**Christ** and **mass.**]

chromatic, *krō-mat'ik, adj.* of colours: (*music*) proceeding by semitones.
chrōme, chrō'mium, *ns.* a metal whose compounds have beautiful colours.
chrō'mosome, one of the rod-shaped bodies into which a cell nucleus divides, and in which the genes (see this) are located.
[Gk. *chrōma*, colour.]

chron(o)-, *kron(-ō)-*, (as part of word) time.
chron'ic, *adj.* (esp. of a disease) lasting a long time: constant, continual.
chron'ically, *adv.*
chronicle, *kron'i-kl, n.* a record of events in order of time.
chron'icler, *n.* a writer of a chronicle.
chronograph, *kron'ō-grâf, n.* an instrument for taking exact measurements of time (e.g. a stop watch).
chronology, *kron-ol'ō-ji, n.* order in time.
chronological order, the order in which events happened.
chronometer, *kron-om'ė-tėr, n.* a very accurate form of timekeeper.

[Gk. *chronos*, time (*graphein*, write; *logos*, discourse; *metron*, measure).]

chrysalis, *kris'ȧ-lis, n.* the golden-coloured resting stage in the life-history of many butterflies.
[Gk. *chrȳsos*, gold.]

chrysanthemum, *kris-an'thė-mum, n.* an autumn garden flower related to the daisy, corn marigold, etc.
[Gk. *chrȳsos*, gold, *anthemon*, flower.]

chub, *chub, n.* a small fat river fish.
chubb'y, *adj.* short and thick, plump.
chubb'iness, *n.* [Origin unknown.]

chuck[1], *chuk, n.* the call of a hen: a word of endearment.

chuck[2], *chuk, v.t.* to pat gently (under the chin): to throw.
chuck'er-out, *n.* one who puts out undesirable people.
[Fr. *choquer*, to jolt; conn. with **shock.**]

chuckle, *chuk'l, n.* a quiet laugh.—Also *v.i.*
[Conn. with **chuck** (1).]

chum, *chum, n.* a close companion.
chumm'y, *adj.* (*coll.*) friendly:—*comp.* **chumm'ier**; *superl.* **chumm'iest.**
chumm'ily, *adv.* **chumm'iness,** *n.*
[Orig. uncertain.]

chunk, *chungk, n.* a thick piece of anything, as wood, bread, etc. [Orig. uncertain.]

church, *chûrch, n.* a building for public worship: (*cap.*) the whole body of Christians.
churchwar'den, *n.* a layman who looks after the interests of a parish or church: a long clay pipe.
church'yard, *n.* the burial ground round a church.
to go into the church, to become a clergyman.
[O.E. *circe*—Gk. *Kȳrios*, the Lord.]

churl, *chûrl, n.* an ill-bred, surly person.
churl'ish, *adj.*
churl'ishly, *adv.* **churl'ishness,** *n.*
[O.E. *ceorl*, a countryman.]

churn, *chûrn, n.* a machine for making butter: a large milk can.—*v.t.* to make (butter): to shake violently.—Also *v.i.*
[Old Norse *kirna.*]

chute, *shōōt, n.* a sloping channel for sending down water, rubbish, etc.
[Fr. *chute*, a fall.]

chutney, *chut'ni, n.* an East Indian sauce of mangoes, chillies, etc.
[Hindustani *chatnī.*]

cicatrix, *sik'ȧ-triks, n.* a scar over a wound that is healed. [L.]

cider, *sī'dėr, n.* an alcoholic drink made from apples.
[Fr. *cidre*—Gk. *sikera*, strong drink.]

cigar, *si-gär', n.* a roll of tobacco leaves for smoking.
cigarette', *n.* finely cut tobacco rolled in thin paper.
[Sp. *cigarro.*]

cinch, *sinch, n.* a horse's belly-band or girth: (*slang*) a certainty.
[Sp. *cincha*—L. *cingula.*]

cinder, *sin'dėr, n.* partly burned coal: anything charred by fire.
[O.E. *sinder*, slag.]

cine-, *sin'i-,* (as part of word) moving picture.
cin'e-cam'era, *n.* a camera for taking moving pictures. [**cinematograph.**]

cinematograph, *sin-i-mat'ō-grâf, n.* an apparatus for projecting moving pictures.
cin'ema, *n.* a building in which they are shown: (**the cinema**) the art, or business, of making motion pictures.
[Gk. *kinēma*, motion, *graphein*, to write.]

Cingalese. See **Sinhalese.**

cinnamon, *sin'ȧ-mȯn, n.* the spicy bark of a tree of the laurel family in Ceylon.
[Heb. *kinnamon.*]

cipher, *sī'fėr, n.* (*arithmetic*) the character 0: a nonentity: a monogram: a secret way of writing.
(Arabic *cifr*, empty.]

circle, *sėr'kl, n.* a figure bounded by one line every point of which is equally distant from the centre: a ring: a company or group (of people).—*v.t.* to move round.—*v.i.* to move in circles.
cir'clet, *n.* a little circle, esp. as ornamental headband.
See also **circular, circulate.**
[L. *circulus*—*circus*, circle.]

circuit, *sėr'kit, n.* the path of an electric current: a round made, esp. by judges for holding courts of law.
circū'itous, *adj.* roundabout, not direct.
[L. *circum*, round, *īre*, to go.]

circular, *sėr'kū-lȧr, adj.* round.—*n.* a notice, etc. sent to a number of persons.
cir'cularise, *v.t.* to send circular(s) to.
circular saw, a steel disk with teeth for sawing wood, metal, etc., usu. power-driven.
[L. *circulāris*; same root as **circle.**]

circulate, *sėr'kū-lāt, v.t.* and *v.i.* (to make) to go round in a fixed path: to spread.
circulā'tion, *n.* the act of moving in a closed path (as the blood): the sale of a book or periodical.
cir'culatory, *adj.*
[L. *circulāre*; same root as **circle.**]

circum-, *sėr-kum-,* (as part of word) about, round.
circumference, *sėr-kum'fėr-ėns, n.* the boundary line, esp. of a circle.
circumflex, *sėr'kum-fleks, n.* an accent (^), orig. showing rising and falling of the voice, on a vowel or syllable.—Also *adj.*
circumlocution, *sėr-kum-lō-kū'sh(ȯ)n, n.* roundabout phrase or way of speaking.
circumnavigate, *sėr-kum-nav'i-gāt, v.t.* to sail round (esp. the world).
circumnavigā'tion, *n.*
circumnav'igator, *n.*
circumscribe, *sėr-kum-skrīb', sėr', v.t.* to draw a line round: to draw (one figure) so as to enclose another, the outer touching the inner at as many points as possible: to confine, restrict.

circumspect, *sėr'kum-spekt, adj.* looking round on all sides, cautious, prudent.
cir'cumspectly, *adv.*
circumspec'tion, -spectness, *ns.*
[L. *circum,* about (*ferre,* to bear; *flectĕre, flexum,* to bend; *loqui, locutus,* to speak; **navigate**; *scrībĕre,* to write; *spicĕre, spectum,* to look).]

circumstance, *sėr'kum-stans, n.* a fact or event: (in *pl.*) time, place, etc. of an act or event: the state of one's affairs (e.g. *in bad circumstances,* poor): ceremony (*pomp and circumstance*).—*v.t.* to place in particular circumstances.
circumstantial (*-stan'shal*), *adj.* giving details that make the story look like the truth.
circumstantial evidence, evidence that makes a conclusion seem likely though it does not give direct proof.
[L. *circum,* about, *stans,* standing.]

circumvent, *sėr-kum-vent', v.t.* to prevent (a person) from carrying out a plan, outwit (him).
[L. *circum,* about, *venīre,* to come.]

circus, *sėr'kus, n.* travelling show with performances by horsemen, acrobats, animals, etc.: a group of houses in a circle.
[L., ring, circular arena; root as **circle.**]

cistern, *sis'tėrn, n.* a tank, etc., for storing water or other liquid.
[L. *cisterna—cista,* a chest.]

citadel, *sit'a-dėl, n.* a fortress in or near a city.
[It. *cittadella*; same root as **city.**]

cite, *sīt, v.t.* to summon, esp. to appear in court: to quote.
citā'tion, (*sī-,* or *si-*), *n.*
[L. *citāre,* to call.]

citizen, *sit'i-zėn, n.* an inhabitant of a city, town: a member of a state.
cit'izenship, *n.* the status, and the rights and or duties, of a citizen.
See also **civic, civil, city.**
[Same root as **city.**]

citron, *sit'ron, n.* the fruit of the citron tree, resembling a lemon.
citric acid, the acid to which lemons and certain other fruits owe their sourness.
citrus fruit, a citron, lemon, orange, lime, etc.
[L. *citrus.*]

city, *sit'i, n.* a large town: a town with corporation or cathedral: business centre or orig. area of large town:—*pl.* **-ies.**
[L. *cīvitās,* the state—*cīvis,* a citizen.]

civet, *siv'it, n.* a perfume obtained from the **civet(-cat),** a small flesh-eating animal of Africa, India, etc.
[Arabic *zabād.*]

civic, *siv'ik, adj.* of a city or citizen.
civ'ics, *n.* the science of citizenship.
[Same root as **city, citizen.**]

civil, *siv'il, adj.* of the state or community (e.g. *civil affairs*): ordinary, as opposed to military or ecclesiastical (e.g. *in civil life*): (of law cases) concerned with rights and the remedy of injuries other than criminal: polite.
civ'illy, *adv.*
civil'ity, *n.* politeness.
civil'ian, *n.* one engaged in civil as distinguished from military pursuits.
civilise, *siv'il-īz, v.t.* to change the ways of (a primitive people) to those found in a more advanced type of society: to make more refined and polite.
civilisā'tion, *n.* state of being civilised: civilised peoples.
civil engineer (see **engineer**).
civil liberties, the rights of a citizen according to the law of the country.
civil list, the expenses of the sovereign's household.
civil service, the paid service of the state, not including navy, army, and air force.
civil war, a war between citizens of the same state.
[Same root as **city, citizen.**]

clad, *klad, adj.* clothed: covered (e.g. *an ivy-clad wall*; *an armour-clad warship*).—*v.t.* to cover, face (one material) with another:—*pr.p.* **cladd'ing;** *pa.p.* **clad.**
cladd'ing, *n.*
See **clothe.**
[Conn. with **clothe.**]

claim, *klām, v.t.* to demand as a right: to assert (often with *that*).—*n.* a demand for something supposed due: a demand for payment of compensation, etc.: an assertion (that something is a fact): a piece of land allotted e.g. to a miner.
claim'ant, *n.* one who makes a claim.
[O.Fr. *claimer*—L. *clamāre,* to call out.]

clairvoyance, *klār-voi'ans, n.* the power of seeing things not present to the senses.
clairvoy'ant, *n.* and *adj.*
[L. *clārus,* clear, *vidēre,* to see.]

clam, *klam, n.* a shellfish with two shells hinged together: a silent or secretive person.
[O.E. *clam,* fetter.]

clamber, *clam'bėr, v.i.* to climb by grasping with hands and feet.—Also *n.*
[From root of **climb.**]

clammy, *klam'i, adj.* moist and sticky (and usu. cold).
clamm'iness, *n.*
[O.E. *clǣman,* to anoint.]

clamour, *klam'or, n.* a loud demand: uproar.—Also *v.i.*
clam'orous, *adj.* noisy: making loud demands.
clam'orously, *adv.*
[L. *clāmor.*]

clamp, *klamp, n.* a piece of timber, iron, etc. used to fasten things together or to strengthen framework.—*v.t.* to bind with a clamp.
to clamp down on, (*coll.*) to stop the activity of, suppress.
[Conn. with O.E. *clam,* fetter.]

clan, *klan, n.* a tribe or group of families under a single chieftain, commonly having the same surname.
clann'ish, *adj.* closely united and showing little interest in people not of the clan or group.
clans'man, *n.* a member of a clan.
[Gael. *clann*, offspring, tribe.]

clandestine, *klan-des'tin, -tīn, adj.* secret, hidden.
[L. *clandestinus—clam*, secretly.]

clang, *klang, v.i.* to produce a loud, deep, ringing sound.—Also *v.t.* and *n.*
clangour (*klang'gȯr*), *n.* a loud, ringing noise.
[L. *clangĕre*, to sound.]

clank, *klangk, n.* a sound such as is made by a chain.—Also *v.i.* and *v.t.*
[Prob. from **clink** and **clang.**]

clannish, etc. See **clan.**

clap, *klap, n.* a sudden blow: the noise made by two things striking together: a burst of sound.—*v.t.* to strike, thrust, together: (*Scot.*) to pat with the hand: to applaud with the hands: to put suddenly (e.g. *to clap a person in prison*; *to clap eyes on*).—Also *v.i.*:—*pr.p.* **clapp'ing**; *pa.p.* **clapped.**
clapp'er, *n.* the tongue of a bell.
clap'trap, *n.* insincere, empty words.
[Old Norse *klappa.*]

claret, *klar'it, n.* a red wine of Bordeaux.
[Fr. *clairet*; same root as **clear.**]

clarify, *klar'i-fī, v.t.* and *v.i.* to make, or become, clear:—*pr.p.* **clar'ifying**; *pa.p.* **clar'ified.**
clarificā'tion, *n.*
[L. *clārus* (see **clear**), *facĕre*, to make.]

clarinet, *klar-in-et'*, or *klar'-, n.* a wind instrument, usu. of wood.
[L. *clārus*, clear.]

clarion, *klar'i-ȯn, n.* a thrilling note.—Also *adj.*
[Fr. *clairon*—L. *clārus*, clear.]

clarity. See **clear.**

clash, *klash, n.* a loud noise as of weapons striking together: opposition.—*v.i.* to dash noisily (against, into): to disagree.—*v.t.* to strike noisily together. [Imit.]

clasp, *klâsp, n.* a hinged fastening: a bar on a medal ribbon: an embrace.—*v.t.* o fasten with a clasp: to grasp: to embrace.
clasp knife, *n.* a knife whose blade folds into the handle.
[M.E. *claspe, clapse.*]

class, *klâs, n.* a group of persons or things like in some way: a division according to quality, etc. (e.g. *first class*): the system of dividing people into social classes, as upper, middle, lower: a number of students or scholars taught together.—*v.t.* to place in a class.
classify, *klas'i-fī, v.t.* to arrange in classes: to put into a class (e.g. *to classify as*; see also **classified,** *adj.*):—*pr.p.* **class'ifying**; *pa.p.* **class'ified.**
classificā'tion, *n.*
class'ified, *adj.* (of information) on the secret list: (of a road) entitled to receive a government grant.
class'-con'scious, *adj.* very much aware of belonging to a certain class in society.
class legislation, laws favouring one section of the community.
class'mate, *n.* a pupil in the same class.
class war, a struggle between different classes in the community.
[L. *classis*, a division of the people (*facĕre*, to make).]

classical, *klas'i-kl, adj.* (of literature) considered to be of the highest class: of ancient Greece or Rome, or both.
class'ic, *adj.* standard, stock (e.g. *the classic example*, the example usu. given).
the classics, classical literature, esp. that of Greece and Rome.
[Same root as **class.**]

classify, etc. See **class.**

clatter, *klat'ėr, n.* a rattling noise (e.g. *the clatter of pots and pans*): noisy talk.—Also *v.i.* and *v.t.* [Imit.]

clause, *klöz, n.* part of a sentence with subject and predicate: part of a contract, will, or act.
[L. *clausus—claudĕre*, to shut.]

claustrophobia, *klös-trō-fō'bi-ȧ, n.* dread of narrow or closed places.
[L. *claustrum*, a barrier, Gk. *phobos*, fear.]

clavicle, *klav'i-kl, n.* the collar-bone.
[L. *clāvicula—clāvis*, a key.]

claw, *klö, n.* the hooked nail of an animal or bird: the leg of a crab, insect, etc., or its pointed end or pincer.—*v.t.* to scratch or tear.
[O.E. *clawu.*]

clay, *klā, n.* a soft, sticky earthy material: earth in general: the human body.
clay'ey, *adj.*
[O.E. *clǣg.*]

claymore, *klā'mōr, -mör, n.* large sword formerly used by Scottish Highlanders.
[Gael. *claidheamh-mōr*, great sword.]

clean, *klēn, adj.* free from dirt: pure: guiltless: neat: complete (e.g. *a clean sweep*).—*adv.* quite: entirely.—*v.t.* and *v.i.* to make, or to become, clean.
cleanly[1], *klēn'li, adv.* **clean'ness,** *n.*
clean'er, *n.*
cleanly[2], *klen'li, adj.* clean, esp. as a habit:—*comp.* **clean'lier**; *superl.* **clean'liest.**
clean'liness (*klen'*), *n.*
cleanse, *klenz, v.t.* to make clean or pure.
cleans'er, *n.*
clean'-limbed', *adj.* well-proportioned, handsome.
a clean slate, a fresh start: a record without stain on it.
a clean sweep. See **sweep.**
to have clean hands, to be free from guilt.

to make a clean breast of, to own up to (something).
[O.E. *clǣne, clǣnsian.*]

clear, *klēr, adj.* bright, undimmed (e.g. *a clear light*): free from obstruction or difficulty: plain, distinct (e.g. *clear writing*): obvious (e.g. *It is clear that he will not help us*).—*adv.* plainly: wholly: away from (e.g. *Stand clear of the gates!*).—*v.t.* to make clear: to empty: to free from suspicion, acquit: to leap, or pass, by or over: to make a profit of (e.g. *He cleared £50 on the deal*): to set (a ship) free for sailing.—*v.i.* to become clear.
clear'ly, *adv.*
clear'ness, clarity (*klar'i-ti*), *ns.*
clear'ance, *n.* act of clearing: a certificate that a ship has satisfied all demands of the custom house and has permission to sail: the distance between two objects, or between a moving and a stationary part of a machine.
clear'ing, *n.* act of making clear: land cleared of wood, etc., for cultivation.
clear'-cut, *adj.* with clear outline: plain and definite.
clear'way, *n.* a stretch of road on which motorists are forbidden to stop.
to clear out, to get rid of: to empty: to go away.
to clear up, to make, or become, clear.
See also **clarify.**
[Fr. *clair*—L. *clārus.*]

cleat, *klēt, n.* a wedge: a piece of wood nailed across something to keep it firm: a projecting piece of wood or metal with two arms to which ropes are made fast.
[M.E. *clete.*]

cleave[1], *klēv, v.t.* to split: to make (a way through):—*pr.p.* **cleav'ing**; *pa.t.* **cleft, clōve**; *pa.p.* **cleft, cloven.**
cleav'age, *n.*
cleav'er, *n.* a butcher's chopper.
cleft, *n.* an opening made by splitting: a crack, chink.
cloven hoof, a hoof, like those of cows, sheep, etc., which is in divisions, not solid: a sign of the devil or of an evil nature.
[O.E. *clēofan.*]

cleave[2], *klēv, v.i.* to stick: to remain faithful (to):—*pa.p.* and *pa.t.* **cleaved.**
[O.E. *clifian.*]

clef, *klef, n.* (*music*) a sign on the stave fixing the pitch of the notes.
[Fr.—L. *clāvis,* a key.]

cleft. See **cleave** (1).

clematis, *klem'à-tis, n.* a creeping plant.
[Gk. *klēmatis,* a plant, prob. periwinkle.]

clement, *klem'ėnt, adj.* mild: merciful.
clem'ency, *n.*
[Fr.—L. *clēmens.*]

clench, *klench,* or *-sh, v.t.* to close tightly (e.g. fist, teeth): to grasp.
[M.E. *clenchen.*]

clergy, *klėr'ji, n.* the ministers of the Christian religion.
cler'gyman, *n.* one of the clergy, a regularly ordained minister.
clerical[1], *kler'ik-àl, adj.* of the clergy.
cler'ic, *n.* a clergyman.
[Gk. *klērikos.*]

clerical. See **clergy** and **clerk.**

clerk, *klärk* (*U.S. klėrk*), *n.* one who leads the responses in the English Church service: an official in charge of correspondence, records, transactions of a court or corporation: one who does letters, accounts, etc. in an office.
cler'ical[2] (*kler'*), *adj.* of a clerk or of one who copies (e.g. *a clerical error*).
clerk'ess, *n.* a female clerk.
clerk of works, one who superintends the erection of a building, etc.
[O.E. *clerc,* a priest; same root as **clergy.**]

clever, *klev'ėr, adj.* able: skilful.
clev'erly, *adv.* **clev'erness,** *n.*
[Origin uncertain.]

cliché, *klē-shā, n.* a phrase too often used.
[Fr.—*clicher,* to make printing plates.]

click, *klik, n.* a short, ticking sound.—Also *v.i.*
[Dim. of **clack.**]

client, *klī'ėnt, n.* one who employs a lawyer: a customer.
clientèle (Fr.; *klē-on^g-tel*), *n.* a group of clients.
[L. *cliens—cluēre,* to hear, obey.]

cliff, *klif, n.* a high steep rock: the steep side of a mountain.
[O.E. *clif*; conn. with Du. *clif.*]

climate, *klī'mit, n.* the weather conditions of a region (temperature, moisture, etc.).
climat'ic, *adj.* **climat'ically,** *adv.*
[Gk. *klima, klimatos,* slope.]

climax, *klī'maks, n.* the highest point: the most dramatic moment.
[Gk. *klimax,* a ladder.]

climb, *klīm, v.i.* or *v.t.* to go up, rise, ascend, esp. with difficulty: (of plants) to ascend by clinging to (an object).—*n.* ascent: a place to be climbed.
climb'er, *n.* **climb'ing,** *n.* and *adj.*
to climb down, to come down, esp. using hands and feet: to become more humble, take back what one has said.
[O.E. *climban*; conn. with **clamber.**]

clime, *klīm, n.* region: climate.
[Same root as **climate.**]

clinch, *klinch,* or *-sh, v.t.* to fasten (a nail) by bending down the point: to settle or confirm (an argument, a bargain).—*v.i.* to grapple (with).—*n.* the act of clinching: in boxing, a holding grapple.
[Same word as **clench.**]

cling, *kling, v.i.* to stick close: to be fond of and too dependent on a person (with *to*): to refuse to give up (e.g. *to cling to a belief*):—*pa.p.* **clung.**
[O.E. *clingan.*]

clinic, *klin'ik, n.* a private hospital: a place where out-patients are treated or advised.

clin'ical, *adj.* of, at, a sick-bed: having to do with observing in a cool, unemotional way.
[Gk. *klinikos—klīnē*, a bed.]

clink[1], *klingk, n.* a ringing sound made by striking metal, etc.—Also *v.i.* and *v.t.*
clink'er, *n.* hard cinder formed in furnaces.
[A form of **click** and **clank.**]

clink[2], *klingk, n.* (*coll.*) prison.
[A former prison in Southwark, London.]

clip[1], *klip, v.t.* to cut with shears: to trim: to shorten (words) in speaking indistinctly:—*pr.p.* **clipp'ing**; *pa.p.* **clipped.** —*n.* wool shorn off sheep: a smart blow.
clipper, *n.* a type of fast sailing-ship.
clipp'ing, *n.* the act of cutting: the thing clipped off.
to clip the wings of, to take away from (a person) power to reach his ambition.
[Prob. from Old Norse *klippa*, to cut.]

clip[2], *klip, v.t.* to fasten with a clip.—*n.* a fastener for holding (e.g. papers) together.
[O.E. *clyppan*, to embrace.]

clique, *klēk, n.* group of persons, usu. in a bad sense.
cliqu'ish, *adj.* [Fr.]

cloak, *klōk, n.* a loose outer garment: a disguise.—*v.t.* to put a cloak on: to cover: to hide.
cloak'room, *n.* a room for coats, hats, etc.: a lavatory.
[Late L. *cloca*, a horseman's cape.]

clock, *klok, n.* an instrument for measuring time.
clock'wise, *adv.* in the direction of the movement of the hands of a clock.
clock'work, *n.* machinery as steady and regular as that of a clock (**like clockwork,** very steadily without faults or hitches).
to clock in, out, on, off, to register the time of arrival at or leaving work.
[M.E. *clokke.*]

clod, *klod, n.* a thick lump, esp. of earth: a stupid fellow.
clod'hopper, *n.* a rustic: a lout.
[A later form of **clot.**]

clog, *klog, n.* a block of wood: something that hinders: a shoe with a wooden sole. —*v.t.* to choke and stop.
[Origin uncertain.]

cloister, *klois'tėr, n.* a covered arcade forming part of a monastery or college: a monastery or nunnery.
clois'tered, *adj.* living away from the busy world.
[L. *claustrum—claudĕre*, to shut.]

close[1], *klōs, adj.* shut up: with no opening: hot and airless: stingy (also **close'-fist'ed**): near, in time or place: intimate (*a close friend*): unwilling to tell much, secretive: (of argument, examination, etc.) careful, with no weak spots.—*n.* a narrow entry: the enclosed place round a cathedral.
close'(ly), *advs.* **close'ness,** *n.*
close season, the time of the year when it is illegal to kill certain game or fish.
close'-up, *n.* a photograph or film taken near at hand and thus big in scale.
close call, shave, a narrow escape.
close harmony, harmony in which the parts are close together.
See also **close** (2).
[L. *claudĕre, clausum*, to shut.]

close[2], *klōz, v.t.* to shut: to end: to conclude (e.g. a bargain).—*v.i.* to come together: to grapple (with): to agree (with): to come to an end.—*n.* a pause or stop.
closure, *klōzh'ůr, n.* the end: the stopping of a parliamentary debate by vote of the House.
closed circuit, an electrical circuit in which there is a complete path, with no break, for the current to flow along.—*adj.* (of television) transmitted and reproduced for a special audience, not sent out to the general public.
closed shop, a factory, etc. in which only members of (*a*) a trade union, or (*b*) a particular trade union, will be employed.
to close down, to shut up: to bring, or come, to an end.
[Same root as **close** (1).]

closet, *kloz'it, n.* a recess off a room: a small private room.—*v.t.* to shut up in or take into, a room for a conference:—*pr.p.* **clos'eting**; *pa.p.* **clos'eted.**
[Same root as **close** (1) and (2).]

clot, *klot, n.* a mass stuck together of soft or fluid matter, as blood.—*v.t.* and *v.i.* to form into clots:—*pr.p.* **clott'ing**; *pa.p.* **clott'ed.**
[O.E. *clott*, clod.]

cloth, *kloth, n.* woven material from which garments, coverings, etc., are made: a piece of this: a tablecloth:—*pl.* **cloths** (*kloths, klōTHz*).
clothe, *klōTH, v.t.* to cover with garments: to provide with clothes:—*pr.p.* **clōth'ing** (TH); *pa.t., pa.p.* **clōthed** (TH), **clad.**
clothes, *klōTHz, n.pl.* garments.
clothier, *klōTH'i-ėr, n.* one who makes or sells clothes.
clothing, *kloTH'ing, n.* clothes.
[O.E. *clāth*, cloth; conn. Ger. *kleid*, garment.]

cloud, *klowd, n.* a mass consisting of tiny particles of water, often in a frozen state, floating in the atmosphere: a great number: a great volume (of dust or smoke): something causing gloom.—*v.t.* to overspread with clouds: to darken: to stain.—*v.i.* to become clouded or darkened.
cloud'y, *adj.* darkened with clouds: gloomy: not clear or transparent.
cloud'ily, *adv.* **cloud'iness,** *n.*
cloud'burst, *n.* a sudden flood of rain over a small area.

under a cloud, in trouble or disgrace.
[O.E. *clūd*, a hill, a cloud.]

clout, *klowt, n.* a piece of cloth: a blow.
[O.E. *clūt.*]

clove[1], *klōv, n.* the flower bud of the *clove tree*, dried as a spice.
[Fr. *clou*, a nail, from its shape.]

clove[2], **cloven.** See **cleave** (1).

clover, *klōv'ėr, n.* a plant with leaves in three parts, used for fodder.
clov'erleaf, *n.* a traffic arrangement in which one road passes above another and the roads connecting the two are in the pattern of a four-leaved clover.
to live in clover, to live luxuriously.
[O.E. *clāfre*; conn. Du. *klaver.*]

clown, *klown, n.* a buffoon, jester, in a circus, etc.: one who behaves ridiculously and without dignity.
clown'ish, *adj.*
[Prob. conn. with **clod** and **clot.**]

cloy, *kloi, v.t.* to weary with too much (esp. of sweetness):—*pr.p.* **cloy'ing**; *pa.p.* **cloyed.**
[O.Fr. *encloyer*, to stop up.]

club, *klub, n.* a heavy stick: a bat or stick used in certain games (e.g. golf, hockey): a number of persons meeting for study, games, etc.: the place where these people meet: (in *pl.*) one of the four card suits (marks on Spanish cards are club-shaped).—*v.t.* to beat with a club.—*v.i.* to join together for some purpose.
[Old Norse and Swed. *klubba.*]

cluck, *kluk, n.* the call of a hen to her chickens: any sound like it.—Also *v.i.*
[Imit.]

clue, *kloo͞, n.* anything that helps to lead to the solution of a mystery.
[O.E. *cliwen.*]

clump, *klump, n.* a cluster (e.g. of trees or shrubs): a blow.—*v.i.* to walk heavily.—*v.t.* to beat. [Prob. Scand.]

clumsy, *klum'zi, adj.* awkward in shape or movement: tactless, not skilfully made or carried out (e.g. *a clumsy apology*).
clum'sily, *adv.* **clum'siness,** *n.*
[M.E. *clumsen*, to be stiff.]

clung. See **cling.**

cluster, *klus'tėr, n.* a bunch: a group.—Also *v.i.* and *v.t.*
[O.E. *clyster.*]

clutch[1], *kluch, v.t.* to grasp: to hold tightly.—*n.* control (usu. in *pl.*; e.g. *to fall into his clutches*): a device by which two moving parts of a machine may be connected or disconnected.
[O.E. *clyccan*, to clench.]

clutch[2], *kluch, n.* a brood of chickens: a number of eggs on which a bird sits at one time. [From Old Norse.]

clutter, *klut'ėr, n.* confusion: litter.—*v.t.* to litter, fill in an untidy way.
[Perh. from **clot.**]

co-, *kō-*, a prefix showing jointness (e.g. **co-editor,** joint editor), connexion.
[L. *cum, with.*]

coach, *kōch, n.* a large, four-wheeled carriage: a railway carriage: a motor omnibus for tourists: a private tutor: a trainer in athletics.—*v.t.* to prepare (a person) for examination, contest, etc.
coach'man, *n.* the driver of an old horse-drawn carriage.
[*Kocs*, a village in Hungary.]

coagulate, *kō-ag'ū-lāt, v.t.* and *v.i.* (to cause) to become a thickened mass.
[L. *co-*, together, *agĕre*, to drive.]

coal, *kōl, n.* a black mineral (formed from wood of very old trees) that will burn.—*v.t.* and *v.i.* to supply with, or take in, coal.
coal'-bunk'er, *n.* a box for holding coal.
coal face, the exposed surface of coal in a mine.
coal'field, *n.* a district where there is coal to be mined.
coal'-gas, *n.* the mixture of gases obtained from coal, used for lighting and heating.
coal heaver, one employed in carrying or shovelling coal.
coal mine, pit, a mine or pit from which coal is dug.
coal tar, a thick, black liquid formed e.g. when gas is made from coal.
coaling station, a port at which steamships take in coal.
to haul (or **call**) **over the coals,** to scold, reprimand.
See also **collier.**
[O.E. *col*, conn. with Ger. *kohle.*]

coalesce, *kō-ȧl-es', v.i.* to grow together, unite.
coalition, *kō-ȧl-ish'(ȯ)n, n.* an alliance, esp. of states or of political parties.
[L. *co-*, together, *alescĕre*, to grow up.]

coarse, *kōrs, körs, adj.* common: rough: rude.
coarse'ly, *adv.* **coarse'ness,** *n.*
coars'en, *v.t., v.i.* to make, or become, coarse.
coarse'-grained, *adj.* large in grain, as wood: lacking in fine feelings.
[From phrase 'in course', hence *ordinary.*]

coast, *kōst, n.* border of land next the sea.—*v.i.* to sail along or near a coast: to travel downhill in a vehicle without using an engine.
coast'al, *adj.* of the coast.
coast'er, *n.* a vessel that sails along the coast.
coast'guard, *n.* a man, or body of men, employed to watch the coast for smugglers, ships in distress, etc.
[L. *costa*, a rib, side.]

coat, *kōt, n.* an outer garment with sleeves: the hair or wool of an animal: any covering (e.g. one of paint).—*v.t.* to cover with a coat or layer.
coat'ing, *n.* a covering.
coat of arms, a family badge or crest.
coat of mail, a piece of armour for the

upper part of the body made of metal plates or of linked metal rings.
[Late L. *cottus*, *cotta*, a tunic.]

coax, *kōks*, *v.t.* to persuade by flattery, patient and gentle treatment, etc.
[M.E. *cokes*, a fool.]

cob, *kob*, *n.* a short-legged strong horse: a male swan: (also **cob'nut**) a large hazel nut.—See also **corncob.**
[Origin uncertain.]

cobalt, *kō'bölt*, *n.* a silver-white metal, with compounds that give a blue colouring matter.
[Ger. *kobalt—kobold*, demon.]

cobble[1], **cobblestone,** *kob'l (stōn)*, *n.* a rounded stone used in paving.
[Origin uncertain.]

cobble[2], *kob'l*, *v.t.* to patch or mend (shoes, etc.), esp. badly.
cobb'ler, *n.* one who mends shoes.
[Origin unknown.]

coble, cobble[3], *kōb'l*, *kob'l*, *n.* a small flat-bottomed fishing-boat.
[Conn. W. *ceubal*, hollow trunk, boat.]

cobra, *kō'brȧ*, *kob'rȧ*, *n.* a poisonous snake which swells out its neck so that it resembles a hood.
[Port., 'snake of the hood'.]

cobweb, *kob'web*, *n.* the spider's web: anything flimsy.
[Prob. O.E. *attercop-web—ātor*, poison, *coppa*, a head, and **web.**]

coca, *kō'kä*, *n.* a shrub whose leaves yield **cocaine** (*kō'kä-in*, *ko-kān'*), a local anaesthetic. [Sp.—Peruvian.]

cochineal, *koch'i-nēl*, *n.* a scarlet dye, from dried bodies of an insect found on a cactus in Mexico, etc.
[Sp. *cochinilla.*]

cock, *kok*, *n.* the male of birds, esp. of the domestic fowl: a weathercock: a tap for liquor: the hammer in the lock of a gun. —*v.t.* to set upright: to draw back the cock of (a gun): to tilt up (e.g. brim of hat).
cock'er, *n.* a small kind of spaniel.
cock'erel, *n.* a young cock.
cock-and-bull story, an absurd, unbelievable one.
cock'chafer, *n.* a large greyish-brown beetle.
cock'crow, -ing, *n.* early morning.
cock'fight, *n.* a fight between gamecocks.
cock'fighting, *n.*
cock'pit, *n.* a pit or enclosed space where gamecocks fought: a place where many battles have been fought: a compartment in aircraft for pilot, etc., in a small ship for the steersman, in a racing car for driver(s).
cock'sure, *adj.* very sure: too confident.
cock'tail, *n.* a mixture of drinks, used as an appetiser.
[O.E. *cocc.*]

cockade, *kok-ād'*, *n.* a rosette worn on the hat as a badge.
[Fr. *cocarde—coq*, cock.]

cockatoo, *kok-ȧ-tōō'*, *n.* a parrot with a large crest. [Malay *kakatúa.*]

cockchafer, cockfight, etc. See **cock.**

cockle, *kok'l*, *n.* a shellfish with hinged, heart-shaped shell.
cock'leshell, *n.* the shell of a cockle: a frail boat.
[Gk. *konchylion—konchē*, a cockle.]

cockney, *kok'ni*, *n.* a native of the City of London. [Origin uncertain.]

cockpit. See **cock.**

cockroach, *kok'rōch*, *n.* a household pest, a beetle-like insect.
[Sp. *cucaracha.*]

cocksure, cocktail. See **cock.**

coco, *kō'kō*, *n.* a palm tree producing the **co'conut,** a large nut containing a white solid lining and a clear liquid.
coconut matting, matting made from the husk of the coconut. [Port. and Sp.]

cocoa, *kō'kō*, *n.* the seed of the cacao tree: a powder and drink made from the seeds. [**cacao.**]

cocoon, *kȯ-kōōn'*, *n.* the silk sheath spun by many insect larvae e.g. silkworms, and by spiders for their eggs.
[L. *concha*, a shell.]

cod, *kod*, **codfish,** *kod'fish*, *ns.* a food fish of northern seas.
cod'ling *n.* a small cod.
codliver oil, an oil obtained from cod's liver. [Origin uncertain.]

coddle, *kod'l*, *v.t.* to pamper, treat as an invalid. [Origin uncertain.]

code, *kōd*, *n.* a collection of laws or of rules (e.g. *the Highway Code*): a standard of behaviour: a secret system of words, letters, or symbols.
[Fr.—L. *cōdex*, book.]

codicil, *kod'i-sil*, *n.* a short addition to a will or treaty.
[L. *cōdicillus—cōdex*, book.]

co-education, *kō-ed-ū-kā'sh(ȯ)n*, *n.* education of pupils or students of both sexes in the same school or college. [Pfx. **co-.**]

coerce, *kō-ėrs'*, *v.t.* to compel (a person, an action; e.g. *I coerced him into going*; *to coerce obedience*).
coer'cion, *kō-ėr'sh(ȯ)n*, *n.*
[L. *co-*, together, *arcēre*, to shut in.]

co-exist, *kō-egz-ist'*, *v.i.* to exist at the same time.
co-exist'ence, *n.*
peaceful co-existence, living peacefully beside people who hold different views from oneself. [Pfx. **co-.**]

coffee, *kof'i*, *n.* a drink made from the ground beans of the **coffee tree.**
coff'ee-house, -room, stall, *ns.* a place where coffee, etc. is served.
[Arabic *qahwah*, orig. wine.]

coffer, *kof'ėr*, *n.* a chest for holding money or treasure.
coff'er-dam, *n.* a watertight structure used for building the foundations of bridges, etc.; under water.
[Gk. *kophinos*, a basket.]

coffin, *kof'in, n.* a chest for a dead body. [Same root as **coffer.**]

cog, *kog, n.* a tooth on a wheel: a person or thing having a necessary but subordinate part in an organisation, etc.

cogged, *adj.*

cog'wheel, *n.* a toothed wheel.

[M.E. *cogge.*]

cogent, *cō'jent, adj.* convincing, to the point (e.g. *a cogent argument, reason*).

[L. *co-*, together, *agĕre*, drive.]

cogitate, *koj'i-tāt, v.i.* to turn a thing over in one's mind, ponder.—Also *v.t.*

cogitā'tion, *n.*

[L. *cōgitāre*, to think deeply.]

cognac, *kōn'yak, kon', n.* French brandy. [Town of *Cognac.*]

cognisance, *kog'niz-ėns,* or *kon'-, n.* in the phrase **to take cognisance of,** to notice, take into consideration.

[L. *cognoscĕre*, to come to know.]

cohabit, *kō-hab'it, v.i.* to dwell together as, or as if, husband and wife.

[L. *co-*, together, *habitāre*, to dwell.]

cohere, *kō-hēr', v.i.* to stick together.

coher'ent, *adj.*, clear and logical (e.g. *He was able to give a coherent account of what had happened*).

coher'ency, coher'ence, *ns.*

[L. *co-*, together, *haerēre*, to stick.]

coiffeur, *kwäf-ėr', n.* a hairdresser.

coiffure *kwäf-ür', n.* style of hairdressing.

[Fr.—Late L. *cofia*, a cap.]

coign of vantage, *koin ov vän'tij,* a good position from which to see or to act.

[Fr. *coin*, a wedge, corner.]

coil, *koil, v.t.* and *v.i.* to wind in rings.—*n.* a length (e.g. of rope) wound in rings: one of these rings.

[L. *col-*, together, *legĕre*, to gather.]

coin, *koin, n.* a piece of stamped metal used as money.—*v.t.* to make metal into (money): to gain (money) quickly in great quantity: to invent (a word, phrase).

coin'age, *n.* act of making (money, or new word, etc.): the money used in a country.

[Fr. *coin*, a wedge—L. *cuneus.*]

coincide, *kō-in-sīd', v.i.* to occupy the same space or time: to be identical: to agree (e.g. *This coincides with what he told us*).

coin'cidence (*-sid-*), *n.* accidental, but striking, happening of one event at the same time as, or following, another.

coincident'al, *adj.*

[L. *co-*, together, *in*, in, *cadĕre*, to fall.]

coir, *koir, n.* the strong fibre of the coconut. [S. Indian word *kāyar*, cord.]

coke, *kōk, n.* a fuel obtained by driving off gases from coal. [Origin uncertain.]

colander, cullender, *kul'ėnd-ėr,* or *kol'-, n.* a strainer for draining off liquids.

[L. *cōlāre*, to strain.]

cold, *kōld, adj.* the opposite of hot: chilly: unfriendly.—*n.* lack of heat: chilliness: cold weather: an illness with catarrh, coughing, etc.

cold'ly, *adv.* **cold'ness,** *n.*

cold'-blood'ed, *adj.* having blood (like that of a fish) which takes the same temperature as the surroundings of the body: cruel, unfeeling.

cold cream, a cream-like ointment used to cool, etc., the skin.

cold feet, lack of courage.

cold front, the surface of an advancing mass of cold air where it meets a mass of warmer air.

cold war. See **war.**

to (give the) cold shoulder, to show that one is unwilling to be friendly with (a person).

in cold blood, deliberately.

to throw cold water on, to discourage.

[O.E. *cald*; conn. with Ger. *kalt.*]

colic, *kol'ik, n.* severe pain in the abdomen.

[Gk. *kolikos*; root as **colon** (2).]

coliseum. Same as **colosseum.**

collaborate, *kol-ab'ŏr-āt, v.i.* to work together on the same piece of work: to work along (with) treacherously.

collaborā'tion, *n.* **collab'orator,** *n.*

[L. *col-*, with, *laborāre*, to work.]

collapse, *kol-aps', v.i.* tc fall down: to break down: to become unable to continue.—Also *n.*

collaps'ible, -able, *adj.* (of e.g. boat, chair) able to be folded up.

[L. *col-*, together, and *lābī, lapsus*, to fall.]

collar, *kol'ȧr, n.* something worn round the neck: the part of a garment at the neck.—*v.t.* (*slang*) to seize.

coll'ar-bone, *n.* either of two bones joining breast bone and shoulder-blade.

[L. *collum*, the neck.]

colleague, *kol'ēg, n.* a person with whom one is associated in a profession or occupation.

[L. *col-*, together, *legĕre*, to choose.]

collect, *kol-ekt', v.t.* to bring together: to gather (payments or contributions): to put (one's thoughts) in order: to go for and remove.—*v.i.* to gather together: to grow in quantity (e.g. *Water collects in the rain-barrel*).—*n.* (*kol'ekt*) a short prayer of one sentence.

collect'ed, *adj.* composed, cool.

collect'edness, *n.*

collec'tion, *n.* act of collecting: gathering of contributions: money collected: a set of objects, etc., collected.

collect'ive, *adj.* of a number of people, or states, etc., taken together as one group: combined.

collect'or, *n.* one who collects, e.g. tickets, money, specimens.

collective security, a policy according to which the security of each is guaranteed by all.

[L. *col-*, together, *legĕre, lectum*, gather

colleen, *kol'ēn, kò-lēn', n.* a girl.
[Irish *cailín.*]
college, *kol'ij, n.* a learned society (e.g. *the college of surgeons*) : a society that is part of a university : the premises of a college.
collegiate, *kò-lē'ji-it, adj.*
[Same root as **collect.**]
collide, *kol-īd', v.i.* to dash together : to clash.
colli'sion, (*-i'*) *n.* crash, violent meeting (of e.g. two vehicles) : a clash, conflict (between e.g. views, purposes, persons).
[L. *co-*, together, *laedĕre*, to strike.]
collie, *kol'i, n.* a breed of sheepdog originating in Scotland. [Orig. uncertain.]
collier, *kol'yėr, n.* one who works in a coal-mine : a ship that carries coal.
coll'iery, *n.* a coal mine:—*pl.*-**ies.**
[Same root as **coal.**]
collop, *kol'op, n.* a slice of meat.
[Origin unknown.]
colloquy, *kol'ò-kwi, n.* a conversation.
collō'quial, *adj.* of, used in, common conversation.
collo'quially, *adv.*
collō'quialism, *n.* an expression used in ordinary talk.
[L. *col-*, together, *loquī*, to speak.]
collusion, *kò-lōō'zh(ò)n,* or *-lū', n.* a secret agreement to deceive.
[L. *col-*, together, *ludĕre, lusum*, play.]
colon[1], *kō'lon, n.* a punctuation mark (:).
[Gk. *kōlon*, a limb or member.]
colon[2], *kō'lon, n.* the greater portion of the large intestine.
[Gk. *kolon*, the large intestine.]
colonel, *kûr'nėl, n.* an army officer (see *Appendices*).
[Fr. and Sp. *coronel.*]
colonnade, *kol-òn-ād', n.* a row of columns, or of trees, placed at regular intervals.
[Fr.—same root as **column.**]
colony, *kol'òn-i, n.* a group of people who settle together in another country : the settlement so formed : a collection of animals, birds, living together:—*pl.* **-ies.**
colon'ial, (*-ōn'*), *adj.*
col'onise, *v.t.* to establish a colony in (a place).
colonisā'tion, *n.* **col'onist,** *n.*
[L. *colĕre*, to till.]
colossus, *kol-os'ùs, n.* a gigantic statue : anything gigantic.
coloss'al, *adj.*
colossē'um, *n.* a large place of entertainment, esp. a large open-air theatre (now in ruins) in Rome.
[Gk. *kolossos.*]
colour, *kul'òr, n.* a quality which an object has only when light falls on it (e.g. redness or blueness, etc.) : paint : race or race-mixture other than European : an appearance of truth (e.g. *to give colour to a statement*) : vividness : (in *pl.*) a flag (*sing.*, see **troop**).—*v.t.* to put colour on, stain, paint : to exaggerate : to affect (e.g. *Fear of loss coloured his attitude to the problem*).—*v.i.* to blush.
col'ouring, *n.* **colo(u)rā'tion,** *n.*
col'oured, *adj.* having colour : belonging to a dark-complexioned race.
col'ourful, *adj.* full of colour : vivid.
col'ourless, *adj.* without colour : not vivid, lively, or interesting.
colour bar, refusal to treat coloured people in the same way as white.
col'our-blind, *adj.* unable to distinguish certain colours.
local colour. See **local.**
off colour, faded : not at one's best.
to come off with flying colours, to win triumphantly.
to come out in one's true colours, to appear in one's real character.
[L. *color* ; conn. with *cęlāre*, to cover.]
colt, *kōlt, n.* a young horse.
colt'ish, *adj.* like a colt : frisky.
colts'foot, *n.* a yellow-flowered plant of early spring. [O.E.]
columbine, *kol'ùm-bīn, n.* a plant of the buttercup family with flowers like a group of pigeons. [L. *columba*, a dove.]
column, *kol'ùm, n.* a stone or wooden pillar used to support or adorn a building : a body of troops with narrow front : an upright row of figures : a vertical section of a page of print. [L. *columna.*]
coma, *kō'ma, n.* a long-continuing unconscious state.
com'atose (*-tōs*), *adj.* drowsy.
[Gk. *kōma.*]
comb, *kōm, n.* a toothed instrument for separating and cleaning hair, wool, flax, etc. : the crest of some birds : cells for honey.—*v.t.* to arrange, or clean, with a comb : to search (a place) thoroughly (for something).
comb'er, *n.* a long foaming wave.
[O.E. *camb.*]
combat, *kom'bat,* or *kum', v.t.* to fight or struggle against, oppose.—*n.* a struggle.
com'batant, *adj.* and *n.* (one who is) fighting.
com'bative, *adj.* quarrelsome.
[L. *com-*, together, *bātuĕre*, to strike.]
combe. Same as **coomb.**
combine, *kòm-bīn', v.t.* to join together in one whole : to unite : to possess together (e.g. *He combines stupidity with cunning*). —*v.i.* to come into close union : (*chemistry*) to unite and form a compound.—*n.* (*kom'bīn*), an association of trading companies : a combine harvester.
combinā'tion, *n.* union : a motor bicycle with sidecar : the series of letters or numbers that must be set in order on the dials of a **combination lock** to open it.
combinā'tions, *n. pl.* an undergarment combining vest and drawers.
combine harvester, a machine that both harvests and threshes.
[L. *combināre*, to join.]
combustible, *kom-bust'ibl, adj.* liable to

take fire and burn: excitable.—*n.* anything that will take fire.
combustion, *com-bus'ch(o)n, n.* burning.
[L. *combūrĕre, combustum,* to burn up.]

come, *kum, v.i.* to move towards this place (opp. of *go*): to draw near: to reach, stretch (to): to arrive: to amount (to): to become (e.g. *to come loose*):—*pr.p.* **com'ing**; *pa.p.* **come**; *pa.t.* **came.**
com'er, *n.* one who comes (usu. with *adj.*; e.g. *newcomer, late-comer, all comers*).
to come about, to happen.
to come across, to meet: to find by chance.
to come back, to return to popularity, office, etc. (*n.* **come'-back,** a return).
to come by, to obtain.
to come down, to descend: to be reduced: to lose money and position (*to come down in the world*) (*n.* **come'-down,** loss of rank: a disappointment).
to come home to one, to touch (one's interests, feelings) closely.
to come in for, to receive (e.g. abuse).
to come into, to fall heir to.
to come of, to be the result of.
to come out, to become known: to be published: to enter society: to go on strike.
to come round, to recover from a faint, ill-humour, etc.
to come to, to recover consciousness or sanity: to amount to.
to come to pass, to happen.
to come, future (e.g. *in days to come*).
[O.E. *cuman*; conn. with Ger. *kommen.*]

comedy, *kom'i-di, n.* a play of a pleasant or amusing kind.
comē'dian *n.* an actor of comic parts:—*fem.* **comedienne** (*kom-ē-dē-en'*).
[Gk. *kōmos,* revel, *ōidē,* song.]

comely, *kum'li, adj.* pleasing: good-looking.
come'liness, *n.*
[O.E. *cȳme,* suitable, *līc,* like.]

comet, *kom'it, n.* a heavenly body usu. with a shining tail.
[Gk. *komētēs,* long-haired.]

comfit, *kum'fit, n.* a sweetmeat.
[Fr. *confit.*]

comfort, *kum'fort, v.t.* to help (someone in pain or distress): to cheer.—*n.* encouragement: quiet enjoyment: anything that makes one feel more at ease, or happier, or better able to bear misfortune.
com'fortable, *adj.* in comfort, at ease: giving comfort.
com'forter, *n.* one who comforts: (*cap.*) the Holy Spirit: a woollen scarf: a dummy teat for a baby to suck.
[O.Fr. *conforter*—L. *con-, fortis,* strong.]

comic, *kom'ik, adj.* of comedy: causing mirth.—*n.* (*coll.*) an amusing person: (*coll.*) a comic paper.
com'ical, *adj.* funny.
comic paper, one containing stories told mainly in pictures.
comic strip, a strip of small pictures showing stages in an adventure.
[Gk. *kōmikos.*]

comma, *kom'a, n.* in punctuation, the point (,).
inverted commas, marks of quotation ("—", '—').
[Gk. *komma,* a section of a sentence.]

command, *kom-ând', v.t.* to order: to have authority over: to have within sight.—*n.* an order: control: the thing commanded.
commandant', *n.* an officer who has the command of a place or of a body of troops.
commandeer' (orig. *Afrikaans*), *v.t.* to seize for military use: (*coll.*) to seize for any purpose.
command'er, *n.* one who commands: any of several officers in armed forces (see *Appendices*).
command'er-in-chief, *n.* the officer in supreme command of an army, or of the entire forces of the state.
command'ing, *adj.* impressive (e.g. *He has a commanding appearance*): with a wide view (e.g. *a commanding position on the hill*).
command'ment, *n.* a command, esp. of God.
command'o, *n.* a unit of specially trained troops for tasks requiring special courage, skill, and initiative: one serving in such a unit.
[L. *com-, mandāre,* to entrust.]

commemorate, *ko-mem'o-rāt, v.t.* to honour the memory of by a solemn celebration: to serve as a memorial of.
commemorā'tion, *n.*
[L. *commemorāre,* to remember.]

commence, *kom-ens', v.i., v.t.* to begin.
commence'ment, *n.*
[L. *com-, initiāre,* to begin.]

commend, *kom-end', v.t.* to entrust (e.g. *I commend him to your care*): to praise.
commend'able, *adj.* praiseworthy.
commendā'tion, *n.* praise.
commend me to, give me for preference.
[L. *com-, mandāre,* to trust.]

comment, *kom'ent, n.* a remark, observation, criticism.—Also *v.i.* (or *ko-ment'*).
comm'entary, *n.* a series of comments, esp. by a spectator at a ceremony, etc.
comm'entator, *n.*
[L. *com-,* and *mens,* the mind.]

commerce, *kom'ers, n.* interchange of goods between nations or people, trade on a large scale: intercourse.
commer'cial, *adj.*
commercial traveller, the travelling representative of a business firm.
[L. *com-,* with, *merx,* merchandise.]

commère, *kom-mer'*, *n.* used as *fem.* of **compère.**
[Fr., godmother.]

commingle, *kò-ming'gl*, *v.t.* and *v.i.* to mingle: to mix (with).
[L. *com-*, together, **mingle.**]

commiserate, *kò-miz'ėr-āt*, *v.t.* and *v.i.* to feel or express sympathy (with).
commiserā'tion, *n.*
[L. *com-*, with, *miser*, wretched.]

commissar, *kom-i-sär'*, *n.* in U.S.S.R. the head of a government department.
commissariat (*-sā'ri-àt*), *n.* the department in charge of provisions, e.g. for an army.
[Same root as **commission.**]

commission, *kò-mish'(ò)n*, *n.* the act of committing: a document conferring authority: something to be done by one person on behalf of another: an order esp. for a work of art: the fee paid to an agent for transacting business: a body of persons appointed to investigate something.—*v.t.* to give a commission to or for: to empower.
commissionaire', *n.* a doorkeeper in uniform.
commiss'ioner, *n.* a representative of the government in a district or department: a member of a commission.
commission agent, a bookmaker.
commissioned officer, an officer in army, navy, air force, respectively of or above the rank of second lieutenant, sub-lieutenant, pilot officer.
in, out of, commission, in, or not in, active use: ready, or not ready, for action.
commit, *kò-mit'*, *v.t.* to give as a trust: to put in (with *to*, e.g. the grave, the flames): to send (to prison): to become guilty of (a crime, etc.): to bind, pledge (oneself; e.g. *to commit oneself to help*, or *to the cause of peace*):—*pr.p.* **committ'ing**; *pa.p.* **committ'ed.**
commit'ment, *n.* act of committing: an obligation, promise.
committ'al, *n.* act of committing.
committ'ed, *adj.* pledged to do, or to support, something.
committ'ee, *n.* a number of persons, selected from a larger body, to see to some special business.
to commit to memory, to learn by heart.
to commit to writing, to set down in writing.
[L. *com-*, with, *mittĕre*, *missum*, to send.]

commodious, *kò-mō'di-ùs*, *adj.* spacious: comfortable.
commod'ity (*-mod'*), *n.* an article or product used in trade:—*pl.* **-ities.**
[L. *com-*, with, *modus*, measure.]

commodore, *kom'ò-dōr*, *-dör*, *n.* an officer in the navy (see *Appendices*): president of yacht club.
[Perh. Du. *kommandeur.*]

common, *kom'òn*, *adj.* belonging equally to more than one: belonging to any member of a class (e.g. *'Man' is a common noun*; *'Jim' is a proper noun*): public (e.g. *common crier*, *nuisance*): usual: often seen or occurring: of little value: vulgar: without rank.—*n.* land used in common by the inhabitants of a town, parish, etc.
comm'oner, *n.* one who is not a noble.
comm'ons, *n. pl.* the common people: (*cap.*) the House of Commons.
common gender, either masculine or feminine (e.g. *The gender of the noun 'baby' is common*).
common law, in England, unwritten law based on custom.
comm'onplace, *adj.* very ordinary and uninteresting.—*n.* a remark often made.
comm'on-room, *n.* in college, school, etc. a sittingroom for the use of a group of people.
common sense, practical good sense.
commonweal, *kom'on-wēl*, *n.* the good of the people in general.
House of Commons, the lower House of Parliament in Britain and Canada.
in common, in joint possession or use: shared (e.g. *They had nothing in common*, they had no shared interests).
in common with, in the same way as (other person or persons).
the common people, ordinary people without rank.
short commons, little food.
to make common cause with, to side with. [L. *communis.*]

commonweal. See **common.**

commonwealth, *kom'òn-welth*, *n.* the whole body of the people: a form of government in which the power rests with the people: an association of states as the Commonwealth of Australia, the (British) Commonwealth of Nations.
[**common, wealth.**]

commotion, *kò-mō'sh(ò)n*, *n.* excited action: a disturbance.
[L. *com-*, *movēre*, *mōtum*, to move.]

communal. See **commune** (1).

commune[1], *kom'ūn*, *n.* in France, etc., a small division of the country.
commū'nal (or *kom'-*), *adj.* of a community: shared.
[Same root as **common.**]

commune[2], *kò-mūn'*, *v.i.* to talk together confidentially.
[O.Fr. *comuner*, to share; root as **common.**]

communicate, *kò-mū'ni-kāt*, *v.t.* to give: to make known, tell.—*v.i.* to have a connecting door: to partake of Holy Communion.
commū'nicant, *n.* one who partakes of Holy Communion.
communicā'tion, *n.* act, or means, of conveying information: piece of information: a letter, etc.: (in *pl.*) means of

sending messages or of transporting e.g. troops and supplies.

commū'nicative, *adj.* inclined to give information, not reserved.

communion, *kò-mūn'yòn, n.* fellowship, esp. religious.

(**Holy**) **Communion,** the celebration of the Lord's Supper.

[L. *commūniō*—same root as **common.**]

communiqué, *kom-ū'ni-kā, n.* an official announcement. [Fr.]

communism, *kom'ū-nizm, n.* a system under which there is no private property and the state owns everything.

comm'unist, *n.* one who believes in communism.—Also *adj.*

[Same root as **common.**]

community, *kò-mūn'i-ti, n.* a group of people living in one place: the public in general:—*pl.* **-ies.**

[L. *commūnitās*; same root as **common.**]

commute, *kò-mūt', v.t.* to exchange (a punishment) for one less severe: to exchange or substitute (one thing for, into, another):—*v.i.* (orig. *U.S.*) to travel with a season ticket, esp. between home in the suburbs and work in the city.

commut'er, *n.*

[L. *com-*, with, *mūtāre,* to change.]

compact[1], *kòm-pakt', adj.* closely placed or fitted together: firm: brief.—*v.t.* to press closely together.

[L. *com-*, together, *pangĕre, pactum,* fix.]

compact[2], *kom'pakt, n.* a bargain or agreement: a treaty.

[L. *com-*, together, *pacisci, pactus,* to make a bargain.]

companion[1], *kòm-pan'yòn, n.* a friend or associate: one paid to accompany and help another.—*adj.* accompanying: matching.

compan'ionable, *adj.* pleasant to have as a companion.

compan'ionship, *n.* state of being companions, or of having companion(s): friendly feeling.

See also **company.**

[Late L. *compānium,* messmate—L. *pānis,* bread.]

companion[2], *kòm-pan'yòn, n.* (on a ship) a window frame through which light passes to a lower deck or cabin.

compan'ion-ladder, -way, *ns.* the ladder or stair from an upper to a lower deck or to a cabin.

[Du. *kompanje,* storeroom.]

companionable, -ship. See **companion** (1).

company, *kum'pà-ni, n.* a group of people, e.g. of guests: persons united for trade, etc.: part of a regiment: the crew of a ship: companionship:—*pl.* **-ies.**

[Same root as **companion** (1).]

comparable, -ative. See **compare.**

compare, *kòm-pār', v.t.* to set (things) together to see how far they agree or disagree: to set (one thing) beside another for this purpose (e.g. *Compare my drawing with yours*): to represent as similar to (e.g. *She compared him to a bull in a china shop*).—Also *v.i.*

comparable, *kom'pàr-à-bl, adj.* of the same kind or on the same scale (with *with*): worthy to be compared (to).

compar'ative, *adj.* judged by comparing with something else (e.g. *When the children tired of playing express trains, we had comparative quiet*): (*grammar*) the degree of adjective or adverb between positive and superlative (e.g. *blacker, taller, farther, better, more courageous, more carefully*).

compar'atively, *adv.*

compar'ison, *n.* act of comparing.

there is no comparison between A and B, A is not good (etc.) enough to be compared with B.

to compare notes, to discuss and compare views, impressions, etc.

[L. *com-*, together, *parāre,* make equal.]

compartment, *kòm-pärt'mènt, n.* a separate part or division, e.g. of a railway carriage.

[L. *com-*, with, *partīre,* to part.]

compass, *kum'pàs, n.* limits: range of pitch possible to a voice or instrument: an instrument consisting of a magnetised needle, used to find directions: (in *pl.*) an instrument with two movable legs, for drawing circles, etc.—*v.t.* to pass or go round: to achieve, bring about (e.g. *to compass his downfall*).

[L. *com-*, together, *passus,* a step.]

compassion, *kòm-pash'(ò)n, n.* sorrow for the sufferings of another.

compassionate, *kòm-pash'(ò)n-it, adj.*

compass'ionately, *adv.*

[L. *com-*, with, *patī, passus,* to suffer.]

compatible, *kòm-pat'ibl, adj.* able to live or associate happily together: not contradictory (e.g. *The two statements are compatible*): in keeping or agreement (with).

compatibil'ity, *n.* **compat'ibly,** *adv.*

[L. *com-*, with, *patī,* to suffer.]

compatriot, *kòm-pā'tri-òt,* or *-pat'-, n.* a fellow-countryman.

[L. *com-*, with, and **patriot.**]

compeer, *kòm-pēr', kom', n.* one who is equal e.g. in age, rank: a companion.

[L. *com-*, with, *par,* equal.]

compel, *kòm-pel', v.t.* to force (e.g. *to compel someone to go*):—*pr.p.* **compell'ing**; *pa.p.* **compelled'.**

compell'ing, *adj.* forcing action, consideration, attention, belief, etc.

See also **compulsion.**

[L. *com-*, *pellĕre, pulsum,* to drive.]

compensate, *kom'pèn-sāt, v.t.* to make up to (someone) for loss or wrong.—*v.i.* to make up (for).

compensā'tion, *n.* reward for service: payment, etc., to make up for loss or injury.

[L. *com-*, *pensāre,* to weigh.]

compère, *kom′per, n.* one who introduces items of an entertainment.—Also *v.t.* [Fr., godfather.]

compete, *kȯm-pēt′, v.i.* to strive for e.g. a prize.
competi′tion (*-pet-i′*), *n.* act of competing: a contest for a prize: rivalry.
compet′itive, *adj.* (of examination, sports, etc.) in which a reward goes to the one, or ones, who do best.
compet′itor, *n.* one who competes: a rival.
[L. *com-*, together, *petĕre,* to seek.]

competent, *kom′pi-tėnt, adj.* capable: legally qualified.
com′petence, com′petency, *ns.* capability: qualification as required by law: sufficiency (e.g. of money to live on).
[L. *com-*, with, *petĕre,* to seek.]

compile, *kȯm-pil′, v.t.* to make (a book, etc.) by collecting the materials from other books, etc.
compilā′tion, *n.* **compil′er,** *n.*
[L. *com-*, together, *pilāre,* to plunder.]

complacent, *kȯm-plā′sėnt, adj.* showing satisfaction: self-satisfied.
complā′cence, complā′cency, *ns.*
complā′cently, *adv.*
[L. *com-*, *placēre,* to please.]

complain, *kȯm-plān′, v.i.* to express pain, sense of injury (*of* or *about*): to state a grievance.
complain′ant, *n.* one who complains.
complaint′, *n.* a statement of one's sorrow or dissatisfaction: an ailment.
[Fr. *complaindre*—L. *plangĕre,* lament.]

complement, *kom′pli-mėnt, n.* full number or quantity (e.g. *a ship's complement,* the full number of officers and crew): the angle that must be added to a given angle to make up a right angle.
complement′ary, *adj.* together making up a whole, or a right angle.
[Same root as **complete.**]

complete, *kȯm-plēt′, adj.* whole: perfect (e.g. *a complete idiot*): thorough (e.g. *a complete overhaul*): finished.—*v.t.* to finish: to make perfect.
complete′ness, *n.* state of being whole, perfect, thorough.
comple′tion, *n.* act of finishing.
[L. *com-*, and *plēre,* to fill.]

complex, *kom′pleks, adj.* composed of many parts: complicated, difficult.
complex′ity, *n.* **com′plexly,** *adv.*
[Same root as **complicate.**]

complexion, *kȯm-plek′sh(ȯ)n, n.* colour or look of the skin, esp. of the face: general appearance.
[Fr.—L. *complexiō,* structure of body.]

compliance, compliant. See **comply.**

complicate, *kom′pli-kāt, v.t.* to make complex or difficult.
complicā′tion, *n.* an additional circumstance making a situation more difficult: an additional disease making recovery from the first disease more difficult.

complicity, *kom-plis′i-ti, n.* state of being an accomplice (e.g. *He denied complicity in his brother's crime*).
See also **complex.**
[L. *com-*, together, *plicāre,* to fold.]

compliment, *kom′pli-mėnt, n.* an expression of praise or flattery.—*v.t.* (*kom-pli-ment′*) to pay a compliment to: to congratulate (on).
compliment′ary, *adj.* flattering, praising: given free (e.g. *a complimentary ticket*).
[L. *complēmentum.*]

comply, *kom-plī′, v.i.* to act in the way that someone else has commanded or wished: —*pr.p.* **comply′ing**; *pa.p.* **complied′.**
compli′ance, *n.*
compli′ant, *adj.* yielding: obliging.
[L. *complēre,* to fill full, to fulfil.]

component, *kȯm-pō′nėnt, adj.* forming one of the parts of a whole.—Also *n.*
[Same root as **compose.**]

comport, *kȯm-pōrt′, -pört′, v.t.* to bear, behave (oneself).
[L. *com-*, together, *portāre,* to carry.]

compose, *kȯm-pōz′, v.t.* to form by putting parts together: to make up, be the parts of: to set in order or at rest (e.g. one's thoughts, face): to settle (e.g. a dispute): to create (esp. in literature or music).—Also *v.i.*
composed′, *adj.* quiet, calm.
compos′er, *n.* a writer, esp. of a piece of music.
com′posite, *adj.* made up of two or more distinct parts: (also **composite flower**) a flower, such as that of the daisy, which is made up of a central head of tiny flowers, or 'tube florets', surrounded by a ring of tiny white or coloured flowers, or 'ray florets'.
composi′tion (*kom-*), *n.* the act of composing: material, ingredients: a mixture, compound: a work in literature, music, or painting: manner in which parts of such a work are combined.
compos′itor, *n.* one who puts together types for printing.
com′post, *n.* a mixture, esp. for manure.
compō′sure (*-zhėr*), *n.* calmness, self-possession.
See also **component.**
[L. *com-*, together, *pōnĕre, positum,* place.]

compos mentis, *kom′pos ment′is, adj.* of sound mind. [L.]

compound[1], *kȯm-pownd′, v.t.* to mix or combine.—*adj.* (*kom′pownd*) composed of a number of parts: not simple.—*n.* a mass made up of a number of parts: (*chemistry*) a new substance formed from two or more elements.
compound interest (see **interest**).
[L. *com-*, together, *pōnĕre,* to place.]

compound[2], *kom′pownd, n.* an enclosure round a house or factory (in India, etc.), or for native labourers (S. Africa).
[Malay *kampong,* enclosure.]

comprehend, *kom-prė-hend′*, *v.t.* to understand: to include.
comprehen′sible, *adj.* capable of being understood.
comprehen′sion, *n.* act or power of understanding.
comprehen′sive, *adj.* taking in, including, much.
comprehen′sively, *adv.*
comprehen′siveness, *n.*
comprehensive school, a school consisting of a combination of the various types of secondary school.
[L. *com-*, together, *prehendĕre*, to seize.]

compress, *kȯm-pres′*, *v.t.* to press together: to force into a narrower space.—*n.* (*kom′pres*) a pad used in surgery to apply pressure to any part: a folded cloth applied to the skin.
compress′ible, *adj.* that may be compressed.
compress′ion, *kom-presh′(ȯ)n*, *n.* act of compressing: state of being compressed: the stroke that compresses the gases in an internal-combustion engine.
compress′ion-igni′tion, *n.* ignition by means of the heat of compressed air.
[L. *com-*, together, *pressāre*, to press.]

comprise, *kom-prīz′*, *v.t.* to contain, include: to consist of.
[Through Fr. from root of **comprehend.**]

compromise, *kom′prō-mīz*, *n.* a settlement of differences in which both sides yield something.—*v.t.* to involve in scandal, suspicion, etc.—*v.i.* to make a compromise.
com′promised, *adj.* brought under suspicion.
[L. *com-*, together, *prōmittĕre*, to promise.]

comptroller. Older form of **controller.**

compulsion, *kȯm-pul′sh(ȯ)n*, *n.* the act of compelling: coercion: an impulse (to do something unreasonable or not sensible).
compul′sive, *adj.* of, arising from, an irrational impulse.
compul′sory, *adj.* that must be done or carried out.
[Same root as **compel.**]

compunction, *kȯm-pungk′sh(ȯ)n*, *n.* uneasiness of conscience, scruple (e.g. *He had no compunction about keeping the money*): remorse.
[L. *com-*, *pungĕre*, *punctum*, to prick.]

compute, *kȯm-pūt′*, *v.t.* to calculate: to estimate.
computā′tion, *n.*
comput′er, *n.* a large machine carrying out many stages of calculations.
[L. *com-*, together, *putāre*, to reckon.]

comrade, *kom′rid*, *kum′rid*, *n.* a close companion: a fellow communist or socialist.
com′radeship, *n.*
[Sp. *camarada*, a roommate—L. *camera*, a room.]

con[1], *kon*, *v.t.* to study carefully:—*pr.p.* **conn′ing**; *pa.p.* **conned.**
[O.E. *cunnian*, to try to know.]

con[2], **conn,** *kon*, *v.t.* to direct the steering of (a ship).
conn′ing-tow′er, *n.* the pilot house of a warship or submarine.
[Older form *cond*—L. *condūcĕre*, to conduct.]

con[3]. See **contra.**

concave, *kon′kāv′*, *adj.* curved inwards (opposed to *convex*).—Also *n.*
concave′ness, concav′ity (*-kav′*), *ns.*
[L. *con-*, and root as **cave.**]

conceal, *kȯn-sēl′*, *v.t.* to hide: to keep secret.
conceal′ment, *n.*
[L. *con-*, and *cēlāre*, to hide.]

concede, *kȯn-sēd′*, *v.t.* to admit (e.g. a point in an argument): to grant (e.g. a right).—*v.i.* to admit (that).
See also **concession.**
[L. *con-*, wholly, *cēdĕre*, *cessum*, yield.]

conceit, *kȯn-sēt′*, *n.* too high an opinion of oneself: a favourable opinion.
conceit′ed, *adj.* having a high opinion of oneself.
[From **conceive** (as *deceit—deceive*).]

conceive, *kȯn-sēv′*, *v.t.* to become pregnant with: to form in the mind: to imagine.—Also *v.i.*
conceiv′able, *adj.* **conceiv′ably,** *adv.*
See also **conception.**
[L. *con-*, *capĕre*, *captum*, to take.]

concentrate, *kon′sen-trāt*, or *kȯn-sen′-*, *v.t.* to bring to one place (e.g. *He concentrated his forces at the point where he hoped to break through*): to give (all one's energies, etc.) to one purpose (with *on*): to make stronger (e.g. a liquid by removing some of the water).—*v.i.* to give all one's attention to one thing.—*n.* concentrated animal feed.
concentrā′tion, *n.*
[Same root as **concentric.**]

concentric, *kȯn-sent′rik*, *adj.* having a common centre.
[L. *con-*, together, *centrum*, a point.]

conception, *kȯn-sep′sh(ȯ)n*, *n.* act of conceiving: the formation in the mind (of an idea): an idea (also **con′cept**).
[Same root as **conceive.**]

concern, *kȯn-sėrn′*, *v.t.* to have to do with: to make uneasy or worried: to interest, trouble (oneself; e.g. *Do not concern yourself about his future*).—*n.* something that concerns or belongs to one: anxiety: a business.
concerned′, *adj.* anxious.
concern′ing, *prep.* about.
[L. *con-*, together, *cernĕre*, to perceive.]

concert, *kon′sėrt*, *n.* a musical entertainment.—*v.t.* (*kȯn-sėrt′*) to arrange, plan.
concert′ed, *adj.* arranged beforehand: carried out by people acting together (e.g. *a concerted attack*).
concertina, *kon-sėr-tē′na*, *n.* a musical wind instrument with bellows and keys.

in concert, together.
[It. *concertare*, to sing together.]

concession, *kòn-sesh'*(*ò*)*n*, *n.* the act of conceding or granting: a grant, esp. of land: something yielded or allowed.
[Same root as **concede.**]

conciliate, *kòn-sil'i-āt*, *v.t.* to win over (someone previously unfriendly or angry).
conciliā'tion, *n.*
concil'iatory, *adj.* intended, showing desire, to conciliate (e.g. *a conciliatory manner*).
[L. *concilium*, council.]

concise, *kòn-sīs'*, *adj.* , brief: in few words.
concise'ly, *adv.* **concise'ness,** *n.*
[L. *con-*, and *caedĕre*, *caesum*, to cut.]

conclude, *kòn-kloo͞d'*, *v.t.* to end: to decide: to arrange (a treaty).—*v.i.* to end: to form a final judgment.
conclusion, *kòn-kloo͞'zh*(*ò*)*n*, *n.* the end: judgment.
conclusive (*-kloo͞'siv*), *adj.* final: convincing.
conclus'ively, *adv.*
conclus'iveness, *n.*
in conclusion, finally.
[L. *con-*, together, *claudĕre*, to shut.]

concoct, *kòn-kokt'*, *v.t.* to make up (as a dish in cookery, or an untrue story).
concoc'tion, *n.* a mixture (esp. a dish of food): a made-up story.
[L. *con-*, together, *coquĕre*, to cook.]

concord, *kon'körd*, or *kong'-*, *n.* agreement: a combination of pleasant sounds.
concord'ance, *n.* an index or dictionary of the words or passages of a book or author.
[L. *con-*, together, *cor*, *cordis*, heart.]

concourse, *kon'-*, *kong'kōrs*, *-körs*, *n.* a crowd: act of thronging together.
[L. *con-*, together, *currĕre*, to run.]

concrete, *kon'krēt*, or *-krēt'*, *adj.* (the opposite of *abstract*) denoting a thing, not a quality or state: made of (building) concrete.—*n.* a mixture of lime, sand, pebbles, etc., used in building.
concrete'ness, *n.*
concre'tion, *n.* a solid mass formed from a collection of material.
[L. *con-*, together, *crescĕre*, *crētum*, grow.]

concur, *kòn-kûr'*, *v.i.* to agree (e.g. *I cannot concur with you in this opinion*):—*pr.p.* **concurr'ing**; *pa.p.* **concurred'**.
concurr'ent, *adj.* agreeing: meeting in the same point: coming or existing together.
concurr'ence, *n.*
concurr'ently, *adv.* at the same time (e.g. *three sentences of six months, to run concurrently*).
[L. *con-*, together, *currĕre*, to run.]

concussion, *kòn-kush'òn*, *n.* violent shaking: a condition caused by a heavy blow, esp. on the head.
[L. *con-*, together, *quatĕre*, to shake.]

condemn, *kòn-dem'*, *v.t.* to blame: to sentence to punishment: to declare to be unfit to use.
condemned cell, a cell for a prisoner under sentence of death.
[L. *con-*, and *damnāre*, to condemn.]

condense, *kòn-dens'*, *v.t.* to make smaller in volume, size.—*v.i.* to be reduced to smaller size, etc.: (of vapour) to turn to liquid.
condensā'tion, *n.* act of condensing: liquid formed from vapour.
condens'er, *n.* a capacitor (see this).
condensed milk, milk made thicker, and smaller in quantity, by evaporation, and sugared.
[L. *con-*, and *densus*, dense.]

condescend, *kòn-di-send'*, *v.i.* to act patronisingly, treat person(s) as if one is better than he is (they are): to stoop, forget one's dignity.
condescend'ing, *adj.* patronising.
condescend'ingly, *adv.*
condescen'sion, *n.*
[L. *con-* and *descendĕre*, to descend.]

condiment, *kon'di-mėnt*, *n.* a seasoning used at table to give flavour to food.
[L. *condire*, to preserve, to pickle.]

condition, *kòn-dish'*(*ò*)*n*, *n.* (in *sing.* or *pl.*) state in which a person or thing is (e.g. *in a liquid condition*; *good housing conditions*): something that must exist or happen or be done before something else can or will: a term in an agreement.—*v.t.* to put into the required state, e.g. to clean, warm, etc. (the air admitted to a building).
condi'tional, *adj.* depending on certain conditions (e.g. *a conditional sale* of e.g. a house, one that will be completed only if certain things happen, or are done).
condi'tionally, *adv.*
on condition that, if, and only if (something is done).
[L. *condiciō*, an agreement.]

condole, *kòn-dōl'*, *v.i.* to express sympathy (with someone).
condol'ence (or *kon'*), *n.*
[L. *con-*, with, *dolēre*, to grieve.]

condone, *kòn-dōn'*, *v.t.* to excuse, forgive (an offence, wrong).
[L. *con-*, *donāre*, to give.]

condor, *kon'dòr*, *n.* a large vulture found among the Andes of S. America.
[Sp.—Peruvian *cuntur*.]

conducive, *kòn-dūs'iv*, *adj.* tending, helping, towards (e.g. *Late nights are not conducive to good health*).
[Same root as **conduct.**]

conduct, *kòn-dukt'*, *v.t.* to lead: to convey (water, etc.): to direct (e.g. an orchestra): to manage (e.g. a business): to behave (oneself): (*electricity, heat*) to transmit.—*n.* (*kon'dukt*) management: behaviour.
conduc'tion, *n.* transmission (e.g. of heat) by a conductor.
conduct'or, *n.* the person or thing that conducts: a director of orchestra or

choir: one in charge of a bus, etc. (*fem.* **conduct'ress**): a substance that transmits electricity, heat, etc.
[L. *con-*, *dūcĕre*, to lead.]

conduit, *kon'dit*, or *kun'*, *n.* a channel or pipe to convey water.
[Fr.—same root as **conduct.**]

cone, *kōn*, *n.*, a solid figure with a vertex, and a base that is a circle or an ellipse (see this word): the fruit of the pine, fir, etc.: anything cone-shaped.
con'ical (*kon'*), *adj.* cone-shaped.
[Gk. *kōnos.*]

coney. Same as **cony.**

confection, *kon-fek'sh(ȯ)n*, *n.* a sweetmeat: a ready-made article of women's dress.
confec'tioner, *n.* one who makes or sells sweets or cakes.
confec'tionery, *n.* the shop or business of a confectioner: sweetmeats:—*pl.* **-ies.**
[L. *con-*, together, *facĕre*, to make.]

confederacy. See **confederate.**

confederate, *kȯn-fed'ėr-it*, *n.* an ally: an accomplice.—Also *adj.*
confed'eracy, *n.* a league, alliance: conspiracy:—*pl.* **-ies.**
confederā'tion, *n.* a league, esp. of princes, states, etc.
[L. *con-*, together, *foedus*, a league; root as **federal.**]

confer, *kȯn-fėr'*, *v.t.* to give, esp. formally (e.g. an honour).—*v.i.* to consult each other: to carry on a discussion:—*pr.p.* **conferr'ing**; *pa.p.* **conferred'.**
con'ference, *n.* a meeting for discussion.
[L. *con-*, together, *ferre*, to bring.]

confess, *kȯn-fes'*, *v.t.* to acknowledge, admit: to make known (sins to a priest).—*v.i.* to make a confession.
confessed', *adj.* admitted.
confess'ion, *n.* acknowledgment of a crime or fault.
confess'ional, *n.* the seat or recess where a priest hears confessions.
confess'or, *n.* a priest who hears confessions and grants absolution.
confession of faith, the creed of a church or sect.
[L. *con-*, *fatēri*, to confess.]

confetti, *kȯn-fet'ē*, *n. pl.* bits of coloured paper thrown e.g. at weddings. [It.]

confidant(e). See **confide.**

confide, *kȯn-fīd'*, *v.i.* to tell secrets or private thoughts (e.g. *He confided in his brother*): to trust (in e.g. one's own strength).—*v.t.* to tell (secrets, plans, thoughts, etc. to someone): to entrust (something, to someone's care).
confid'ing, *adj.* trustful, unsuspicious.
confidant' (*-fid-*), *n.* one to whom secrets are told:—*fem.* **confidante'** (*-ant'*).
con'fidence, *n.* trust or belief: a piece of information given in the belief that it will not be passed on: self-reliance: boldness.
con'fident, *adj.* trusting firmly: bold.
confiden'tial, *adj.* secret, not to be told to others: entrusted with secrets (e.g. *confidential secretary*): secret-service (*confidential agent*).
confiden'tially, *adv.*
confidence trick (*U.S.* **game**), the trick of a swindler who first gains a person's trust and then persuades him to hand over money.
[L. *con-*, and *fidĕre*, to trust.]

confine, *kon-fīn'*, *v.t.* to limit, keep within limits (e.g. *They succeeded in confining the fire to a small area*): to shut up, imprison.
confine'ment, *n.* state of being shut up or imprisoned: being in bed at the birth of a child.
[L. *confīnis*, bordering—*fīnis*, end.]

confirm, *kȯn-fėrm'*, *v.t.* to strengthen (e.g. *This confirmed his resolve*): to make (a person) more firm (e.g. in a belief): to show (a statement) to be true: to admit to full communion.
confirmā'tion, *n.*
confirmed', *adj.* settled in a habit or way of life (e.g. *a confirmed drunkard, bachelor*): shown to be true.
[L. *con-*, and *firmus*, firm.]

confiscate, *kon'fis-kāt*, *v.t.* to seize (having authority to do so), esp. as a penalty.
confiscā'tion, *n.*
[L. *con-*, together, *fiscus*, state treasury.]

conflagration, *kon-flȧ-grāsh'(ȯ)n*, *n.* a great fire.
[L. *con-*, and *flagrāre*, to burn.]

conflict, *kon'flikt*, *n.* a struggle, contest.—*v.i.* (*kȯn-flikt'*) to contradict each other (e.g. *The two accounts of what had happened conflicted*).
conflict'ing, *adj.* clashing: contradictory.
[L. *con-*, together, *flīgĕre*, to strike.]

confluence, *kon'floo-ėns*, *n.* a flowing together, or the place of meeting, of rivers.
[L. *con-*, together, *fluĕre*, to flow.]

conform, *kȯn-fōrm'*, *v.i.* to behave, dress, worship, etc. in the way that most other people do: to be similar (to), have the same shape as (e.g. *to conform to a pattern*).
conformā'tion, *n.* form, shape, or structure.
conform'er, conform'ist, *ns.* one who conforms, esp. with the worship of the established church.
conform'ity, *n.* likeness: agreement (to, with): obedience, compliance (e.g. *in conformity with her wishes*).
[L. *con-*, with, *forma*, form.]

confound, *kȯn-fownd'*, *v.t.* to mix completely, confuse: to throw into disorder: to puzzle and surprise greatly.
confound'ed, *adj.* (*coll.*) horrible, very annoying.
See also **confuse.**
[L. *con-*, together, *fundĕre*, *fusum*, to pour.]

confront, *kȯn-frunt′, v.t.* to face in a hostile manner (e.g. *Enemies, difficulties, etc. confront me*): to bring (a person) face to face (with e.g. accusers, evidence, anything unpleasant to him).
[L. *con-*, together, *frons, frontis*, forehead.]

confuse, *kȯn-fūz′, v.t.* to throw into disorder: to perplex, bewilder: to embarrass: to fail to realise the difference between, mix up.
confused′, *adj.*
confū′sion, *n.* disorder: mixing up: bewilderment: embarrassment.
[Same root as **confound.**]

confute, *kȯn-fūt′, v.t.* to prove to be false or wrong.
[L. *confutāre.*]

congeal, *kȯn-jēl′, v.t.* and *v.i.* to freeze: to solidify, as by cold.
[L. *con-*, and *gelu*, frost.]

congenial, *kȯn-jēn′i-ȧl, adj.* (of people) having the same tastes and interests, in sympathy: pleasant, suited to one (*a congenial task*).
[Same root as **genial.**]

congenital, *kȯn-jen′ı-tȧl, adj.* born with a person (said of diseases or deformities).
congen′itally, *adv.*
[L. *con-*, together, *gignĕre, genitum*, beget.]

conger, *kong′gėr, n.* a large sea eel.
[L.—Gk. *gongros.*]

congested, *kȯn-jest′id, adj.* (of a part of the body) having too much blood: overcrowded.
congestion, *kȯn-jest′sh(ȯ)n, n.* an accumulation of blood in part of the body, or of traffic in one place: overcrowding.
[L. *con-*, together, *gerĕre, gestum*, bring.]

conglomeration, *kon-glom-ėr-ā′sh(ȯ)n, n.* a collection (of things of mixed kind).
[L. *con-*, *glomus, glomeris*, a ball of yarn.]

congratulate, *kȯn-grat′ū-lāt, -grach′, v.t.* to express joy to (a person) because of a success he has had: to think (oneself) lucky (e.g. *He congratulated himself on his escape*).
congratulā′tion, *n.*
[L. *con-*, *grātus*, pleasing.]

congregate, *kong′grė-gāt, v.t.* and *v.i.* to gather together.
congregā′tion, *n.* a gathering: a body of people in a church for a service, or belonging to a church.
Congregā′tionalism, *n.* a form of church government in which each congregation manages all its own affairs.
[L. *con-*, together, *grex, gregis*, a flock.]

congress, *kong′gres, n.* an assembly of diplomats or delegates: (*cap.*) the legislature or parliament of the United States, etc.
congressional, *kon-gresh′ȯn-al, adj.*
[L. *con-*, together, *gradī, gressus*, to go.]

congruent, *kong′groo-ėnt, adj.* of two geometrical figures, coinciding at all points when one is fitted on top of the other.
con′gruous, *adj.* suitable, appropriate.
congru′ity (*-groo͞′*), *n.*
[L. *congruĕre*, to run together.]

conical. See **cone.**

conifer, *kon′i-fėr, n.* a cone-bearing tree, as the fir, etc.
conif′erous, *adj.* cone-bearing.
[**cone,** and L. *ferre*, to bear.]

conjecture, *kȯn-jek′chůr, n.* an opinion formed on slight evidence: a guess.—*v.t.* to infer on slight evidence: to guess.
conjec′tural, *adj.*
[L. *con-*, together, *jacĕre*, to throw.]

conjugal, *kon′joo-gȧl, adj.* of marriage.
[L. *conju(n)x*, a spouse.]

conjugate, *kon′joo-gāt, v.t.* to give the different parts of (a verb).
[L. *conjugāre*, to yoke together.]

conjunction, *kȯn-jungk′sh(ȯ)n, n.* union, combination: a word that connects sentences, clauses, or words (e.g. *and, but*).
conjuncture, *kȯn-jungk′chůr, n.* combination of circumstances: a crisis.
in conjunction with, (acting) together with.
[L. *con-*, together; root as **junction.**]

conjure, *kun′jėr, v.i.* by swiftness of hand, etc., to perform tricks that seem magical. —*v.t.* to command (a devil or spirit): to produce as if by magic: (*kon-joo͞r′*) to tell solemnly, implore (e.g. *She conjured him not to say anything*).
con′juror, con′jurer, *n.*
a name to conjure with, the name of an important, very influential, person.
to conjure up, to bring up in the mind (a picture, etc.)
[L. *con-*, together, *jurāre*, to swear.]

conn. See **con** (2).

connect, *kȯn-ekt′, v.t.* to tie or fasten together, join, link: to establish a communication link between (e.g. *I am trying to connect you with FYL 4682*): to associate in the mind, think of together.—Also *v.i.*
connect′ed, *adj.* joined: (of statement) logically arranged, easy to follow.
connex′ion, connec′tion, *n.* something that connects: state of being connected: a circle of people associated with one, esp. in business: opportunity to change trains, buses, etc. on a journey without much delay: a relative.
connec′tive, *adj.* joining.
in this connexion, when we are considering this.
[L. *con-*, *nectĕre, nexum*, to tie.]

conning-tower. See **con** (2).

connive, *kȯn-īv′, v.i.* to wink (at a crime, etc.), make no attempt to hinder it.
conniv′ance, *n.*
[L. *connivēre*, to wink.]

connoisseur, *kon-es-ėr′*, or *kon-is-ūr′, n.* an expert critic of art, music, etc.: one who knows all about something (e.g. *a connoisseur of wine*).
[Through Fr.—L. *cognoscĕre*, to know.]

connotation, *kon-ōt-ā'sh(ȯ)n, n.* what is suggested by a word in addition to its simple meaning.
[L. *con-*, with, *notāre*, to mark.]

connubial, *ko-nū'bi-ȧl, adj.* of marriage.
[L. *con-*, with, *nubĕre*, to marry.]

conquer, *kong'kėr, v.t.* to gain by force: to overcome.—Also *v.i.*
con'queror, *n.*
con'quest, *kong'kwest, n.* act of conquering: something won by force or effort.
[L. *con-*, *quaerĕre*, to seek.]

consanguinity, *kon-sang-gwin'it-i, n.* relationship by blood.
[L. *con-*, with, *sanguis*, blood.]

conscience, *kon'shėns, n.* the knowledge or sense of right and wrong: conscientiousness: scruple (e.g. *He had no conscience about dismissing the men*).
conscientious, *kon-shi-en'shùs, adj.* guided by conscience: careful and earnest.
conscien'tiously, *adv.*
conscien'tiousness, *n.*
conscientious objector, one who objects on grounds of conscience, esp. to military service.
in all conscience, certainly.
[L. *conscientia*; root as **conscious.**]

conscious, *kon'shùs, adj.* aware of oneself and surroundings (e.g. *The patient was conscious*): aware or having knowledge (of; e.g. *He was conscious of their disapproval*): aware (that; e.g. *conscious that they disapproved*): deliberate, intentional (e.g. *He made a conscious effort to please*).
con'sciously, *adv.*
con'sciousness, *n.* feelings, thoughts, mind in its widest sense: awareness: the waking state of the mind.
[L. *conscius*—*conscīre*, to know well, to be conscious of (wrong).]

conscript, *kon'skript, n.* one enrolled by the state to serve in the armed forces, etc. —*v.t.* (*kȯn-skript'*) to compel to enlist.
conscrip'tion, *n.*
[L. *conscrībĕre*, to enrol—*scrībĕre*, *scriptum*, write.]

consecrate, *kon'si-krāt, v.t.* to set apart for a holy use: to make (e.g. a custom) be regarded as sacred: to devote (e.g. *He consecrated himself to the cause of peace*).
consecrā'tion, *n.*
[L. *consecrāre*, *-ātum*, to make wholly sacred—*sacer*, sacred.]

consecutive, *kȯn-sek'ū-tiv, adj.* following one after the other in regular order (e.g. *on two consecutive days*).
consec'utively, *adv.*
[L. *con-*, *sequī*, *secūtus*, to follow.]

consensus, *kȯn-sen'sùs, n.* general trend (e.g. *The consensus of opinion is that we should do this*): agreement.
[Same root as **consent.**]

consent, *kȯn-sent', v.i.* to agree (to).—*n.* agreement: permission.
[L. *con-*, with, *sentīre*, to feel, think.]

consequence, *kon'si-kwėns, n.* a result: importance (e.g. *The small error is of no consequence*): social standing.
con'sequent, *adj.* following, esp. as a natural result.
con'sequently, *adv.*
consequential, *kon-si-kwen'sh(ȧ)l, adj.* following as a result: self-important (e.g. *He has a consequential manner*).
[Same root as **consecutive.**]

conserve, *kȯn-sėrv', v.t.* to keep from damage, decay, or loss.—*n.* something preserved, as fruits in sugar.
conserv'ancy, *n.* a board with authority to control a port, river, or to protect trees, wild-life, etc.
conservā'tion, *n.*
conser'vatism, *n.* the opinions and principles of a Conservative: dislike of change, esp. sudden or extreme change.
conser'vative, *adj.* (*loosely*) moderate, understated (e.g. *a conservative estimate*). —*n.* (*politics*—*cap.*) one of the party that desires to preserve the institutions of the country against change: one who dislikes change.
conser'vatory, *n.* a greenhouse (usu. heated):—*pl.* **-ies.**
[L. *con-*, *servāre*, to keep.]

consider, *kȯn-sid'ėr, v.t.* to think: to think about carefully: to take into account: to regard as (e.g. *I consider you very foolish*): to pay attention to the comfort, wishes, etc., of (someone).—Also *v.i.*
consid'erable, *adj.* fairly large, great, or important.
consid'erably, *adv.*
consid'erate, *adj.* thoughtful about others.
considerā'tion, *n.* act of thinking about something: a fact to be taken into account in making a decision, etc. (e.g. *The size of the train fare is a consideration*): compensation or reward: thoughtfulness for others.
consid'ering, *prep.* taking into account (e.g. *Considering his deafness, he manages to understand very well*).
in consideration of, in return for.
to take into consideration, to make allowance for in considering a situation or problem.
[L. *considerāre*, to examine closely.]

consign, *kȯn-sīn', v.t.* to entrust (to e.g. a person's care): to put in, commit (to e.g. the grave, the flames): to send by rail, etc.
consignee', *n.* one to whom anything is consigned or sent by a **consign'or.**
consign'ment, *n.* the act of consigning: a load (of goods).
[L. *consignāre*, to mark with a seal.]

consist, *kȯn-sist', v.i.* to be composed (of).
consist'ence, consist'ency, *ns.* degree

of thickness (e.g. *the consistency of treacle*): state of being consistent.

consist'ent, *adj.* not contradictory (e.g. *The two statements are consistent; the second statement is consistent with the first*): always (acting, thinking) according to the same principles (e.g. *He was consistent in his opposition to war, never admitting that events made it necessary*).

consis'tently, *adv.* always in the same way: invariably.

[L. *con-*, together, *sistĕre*, to stand.]

console[1], *kon-sōl'*, *v.t.* to give comfort to: to lessen the grief or disappointment of.

consolā'tion, *n.*

consolation match, prize, race, etc., a match, prize, race, etc., in, or for, which only those who have been previously unsuccessful may compete.

[L. *con-*, *sōlāri*, to comfort.]

console[2], *kon'sōl*, *n.* the part of an organ containing keyboards, pedals, etc.: a panel with dials, switches, etc.: a radio, etc., set standing on the floor. [Fr.]

consolidate, *kon-sol'i-dāt*, *v.t.* to strengthen: to unite, combine.—*v.i.* to grow solid: to unite.

consolidā'tion, *n.*

[L. *con-*, and *solidus*, solid.]

consonant, *kon'son-ant*, *n.* a speech sound made by using lips, tongue, etc. to stop the breath stream wholly or partly: any letter of the alphabet except *a, e, i, o, u.* [L. *con-*, with *sonāre*, to sound. A consonant cannot form a syllable unless a vowel is sounded with it.]

consort, *kon'sört*, *n.* a wife or husband: an accompanying ship.—*v.i.* (*kon-sört'*), to keep company (with).

consortium, *kon-sört'yum, -i-um*, *n.* an association, union, esp. (for a special purpose) of international bankers or business men.

[L. *con-*, with, *sors*, lot, fate.]

conspicuous, *kon-spik'ū-us*, *adj.* catching the eye, very noticeable.

[L. *con-*, *specĕre*, to look.]

conspire, *kon-spīr'*, *v.i.* to plot or scheme together: (of e.g. events) to work together (to bring about a result).

conspiracy, *kon-spir'a-si*, *n.*

conspĭr'ator, *n.*

[L. *con-*, together, *spīrāre*, to breathe.]

constable, *kun'sta-bl*, or *kon'*, *n.* a policeman.

constab'ulary, *n.* a police force.

[O.Fr. *conestable*, name of a high officer of state—L. *comes stabulī*, count of the stable.]

constant, *kon'stant*, *adj.* unchanging: never stopping: faithful.

con'stancy, *n.*

con'stantly, *adv.* very often: always.

[L. *constāre*, to stand firm.]

constellation, *kon-stel-ā'sh(o)n*, *n.* a group of stars.

[L. *con-*, with, *stella*, a star.]

consternation, *kon-stėr-nā'sh(o)n*, *n.* astonishment, dismay.

[L. *con-*, wholly, *sternĕre*, to strew.]

constipate, *kon'stip-āt*, *v.t.* to stop up (esp. the bowels).

constipā'tion, *n.*

[L. *con-*, together, *stīpāre*, to pack.]

constitute, *kon'stit-ūt*, *v.t.* to appoint: to form, make up.

constit'uency, *n.* the voters, or place or area, represented by a member of parliament:—*pl.* **-ies.**

constit'uent, *adj.* helping to form: able to make laws (e.g. *a constituent assembly*).—*n.* a necessary part: one of those who elect a representative to parliament.

constitū'tion, *n.* the natural condition of body or mind (e.g. *He had a strong constitution and survived much hardship*): a set of rules governing a society: the principles and laws according to which a country is governed.

constitū'tional, *adj.* born in one (e.g. *a constitutional weakness*): legal: reigning, but controlled by the law of the land (*a constitutional monarch*).—*n.* a walk for the sake of one's health.

[L. *con-*, together, *statuĕre*, to set up.]

constrain, *kon-strān'*, *v.t.* to force (a person to do something).

constrained', *adj.* forced, embarrassed (e.g. *a constrained smile*).

constraint', *n.* compulsion: loss of freedom of action: a reserved or embarrassed manner.

[Fr. *constraindre*; root as **constrict.**]

constrict, *kon-strikt'*, *v.t.* to press together tightly (e.g. *His collar constricted his neck*).

constrict'or, *n.*

[L. *constringĕre, constrictum.*]

construct, *kon-strukt'*, *v.t.* to build, make: to draw (e.g. *to construct a triangle*).

construc'tion, *n.*

construc'tional, *adj.*

construc'tive, *adj.* having to do with making, not with destroying (opp. of *destructive*): pointing out something that should be done (e.g. *a constructive suggestion*).

construc'tor, *n.*

to put a (wrong) construction on, to take a (wrong) meaning out of.

[L. *con-*, *struĕre*, *structum*, to build.]

construe, *kon-strōō'*, *v.t.* to translate: to interpret, explain (e.g. *Do not construe my silence as meaning approval*).

[Same root as **construct.**]

consul, *kon'sul*, *n.* one of two chief magistrates in ancient Rome: an agent who looks after his country's affairs in a foreign country.

con'sular, *adj.*

con'sulate, *n.* the office or residence of a consul. [L.]

consult, *kon-sult'*, *v.t.* to ask advice or information from: to act in accordance with (e.g. *You should have consulted your*

father's wishes).—*v.i.* (of a doctor or lawyer) to give professional advice.
consult'ant, *n.* one who asks advice: one who gives professional advice.
consultā'tion, *n.*
consult'ing, *adj.* (of doctor or lawyer) who gives advice.
[L. *consultāre.*]

consume, *kȯn-sūm'*, *v.t.* to destroy, e.g. by fire: to eat: to waste or spend.—*v.i.* to waste away.
consum'er, *n.*
consumption, *kȯn-sum(p)'sh(ȯ)n*, *n.* act of consuming: the amount consumed: tuberculosis of the lungs.
consump'tive, *adj.* and *n.*
consumer(s') goods, goods to be used, without further manufacturing process, to satisfy human needs.
[L. *consūmĕre, -sumptum,* to destroy.]

consummate, *kon'sum-āt*, *v.t.* to complete.—*adj.* (*kon-sum'it*) complete, perfect (e.g. *He was a consummate actor*).
[L. *con,* with, *summa,* the sum.]

consumption, etc. See **consume.**

contact, *kon'takt*, *n.* touch: meeting: nearness, allowing passage of electric current or passing on of disease: a place where electric current may be allowed to pass: a person who has been in the company of someone with an infectious disease: a go-between.—*v.t.* and *v.i.* to bring, come, into touch, connexion, with.
[L. *con-*, wholly, *tangĕre, tactum,* touch.]

contagious, *kȯn-tā'jus*, *adj.* spreading from one person to another (e.g. *a contagious disease*; *excitement is contagious*).
[Same root as **contact.**]

contain, *kȯn-tān'*, *v.t.* to enclose: to include: to keep (an enemy force) from moving: to restrain (e.g. *He could not contain his anger*).
contain'er, *n.* a receptacle.
See also **contents.**
[L. *con-*, together, *tenēre,* to hold.]

contaminate, *kȯn-tam'i-nāt*, *v.t.* to make impure by touching or mixing (with something).
contaminā'tion, *n.*
[L. *contāminare.*]

contemplate, *kon'tem-plāt*, *kȯn-tem'plāt*, *v.t.* to look at attentively: to intend (e.g. *I contemplate going to France*).—*v.i.* to think seriously, meditate.
contemplā'tion, *n.*
con'templātive, *adj.* (or *-tem'plȧ-*).
[L. *contemplārī,* to survey (a place).]

contemporary, *kȯn-tem'pȯ-rȧr-i*, *adj.* living, happening at, belonging to, the same period: of the same age: (*loosely*) present day.—Also *n.* (*pl.* **-ies).**
[L. *con-*, together, *tempus,* time.]

contempt, *kȯn-tempt'*, *n.* scorn, very low opinion (with *for*).
contempt'ible, *adj.* despicable, deserving scorn: mean.
contempt'uous, *adj.* haughty, scornful.
contempt'uously, *adv.*
contempt of court, disobedience or lack of respect shown to or in a law court.
[L. *contemnĕre, -temptum,* to value little.]

contend, *kȯn-tend'*, *v.i.* to struggle (against).—*v.t.* to say, maintain (that).
contention, *kȯn-ten'sh(ȯ)n*, *n.* strife: debate: an opinion supported in debate.
conten'tious (*-shŭs*), *adj.* quarrelsome.
[L. *con-*, with, *tendĕre,* to stretch.]

content, *kȯn-tent'*, *adj.* satisfied: quietly happy.—*n.* satisfaction—often 'heart's content'.—*v.t.* to satisfy, please.
content'ed, *adj.* content.
content'edly, *adv.* **content'ment,** *n.*
[L. *contentus,* contained, satisfied.]

contents, *kon'tents*, *n. pl.* things contained: the list of subjects treated in a book.
[Same root as **contain.**]

contention. See **contend.**

contest, *kȯn-test'*, *v.t.* to argue against: to fight for.—*n.* (*kon'*) a struggle for superiority or victory: strife: debate.
contest'ant, *n.* one who contests.
[L. *contestārī,* to call to witness.]

context, *kon'tekst*, *n.* the parts of something written or spoken that go before and follow a passage under consideration and may fix its meaning (e.g. *This statement, taken out of its context, gives a wrong impression of the speaker's opinions*).
in this context, in this particular connexion.
[L. *con-*, together, *texĕre,* to weave.]

contiguous, *kȯn-tig'ū-ŭs*, *adj.* touching, very near.
contigū'ity, *n.*
[L. *contingĕre,* to touch on all sides.]

continent[1], *kon'ti-nėnt*, *n.* one of the great divisions of the land surface of the globe: (**the continent**) the mainland of Europe.
continent'al, *adj.* characteristic of the continent of Europe, European: characteristic of a great land area (e.g. *a continental climate*).
[L. *continēre,* to contain.]

continent[2], *kon'ti-nėnt*, *adj.* not indulging desire or passion.
con'tinence, *n.*
[Same root as **continent** (1).]

contingent, *kȯn-tin'jėnt*, *adj.* (of a happening) dependent (on some other happening or circumstance).—*n.* a quota or group, esp. of soldiers.
contin'gency, *n.* a chance happening:—*pl.* **contin'gencies.**
[Same root as **contact.**]

continue, *kȯn-tin'ū*, *v.t.* to go on with: to resume, begin again.—*v.i.* to last or endure: to go on, esp. after a break.
contin'ual, *adj.* unceasing: frequent.
contin'ually, *adv.*
contin'uance, *n.* going on without interruption (e.g. *The continuance of the drought may cause a water shortage*).
continuā'tion, *n.* going on: beginning again: something that increases or

carries on: a further instalment of a story, etc.

contin′ued, *adj.* uninterrupted: unceasing: in instalments.

continū′ity, *n.* state of being continuous: a complete scenario of a motion picture.

contin′uous, *adj.* joined together, or going on, without interruption.

[L. *continuāre—continuus,* joined.]

contort, *kon-tört′,* *v.t.* to twist or turn violently.

contor′tion, *n.* a violent twisting.

contor′tionist, *n.* one who practises contorted positions.

[L. *con,* and *torquēre, tortum,* to twist.]

contour, *kon′tōōr,* *n.* outline.

contour line, a line drawn on a map through all points at the same height above sea level.

contour map, a map in which the shape of land is shown by contour lines.

[L. *tornus,* lathe; same root as **turn.**]

contra, *kon′tra, prep.* against.—*n.* an argument against (usu. **con**).

[L. *contrā.*]

contraband, *kon′trȧ-band, adj.* excluded by law, prohibited.—*n.* smuggled or prohibited goods.

[L. *contrā,* against, Late L. *bandum,* ban.]

contract, *kȯn-trakt′,* *v.t.* to draw together, make smaller: to promise in writing (to do something): to become liable to pay (a debt): to take (a disease): to form (a habit).—*v.i* to shrink, become less: to bargain (for).—*n.* (*kon′trakt*) an agreement in writing, a bond.

contrac′tion, *n.* act of contracting: a word shortened in speech or spelling.

contract′or, *n.* one who promises to do work or furnish supplies at a fixed rate.

[L. *con-,* together, *trahĕre, tractum,* draw.]

contradict, *kon-trȧ-dikt′,* *v.t.* to deny, declare to be untrue: to accuse (a person) of a misstatement: to be contrary to (e.g. *His second statement contradicts his first*).

contradic′tion, *n.* a denial: a statement contradicting, not in keeping with, another.

contradict′ory, *adj.*

contradict′oriness, *n.*

[L. *contrādīcĕre.*]

contrail, *kon′trāl,* short for **condensation trail,** a trail of condensed vapours left by a high-flying aircraft.

contralto, *kȯn-tral′tō, n.* the lowest musical voice in women.

[It. *contra,* against, *alto,* high.]

contraption, *kȯn-trap′sh(ȯ)n, n.* a contrivance, makeshift machine.

[Perh. from **contrive.**]

contrary, *kon′trȧ-ri, adj.* opposite: unfavourable (e.g. *contrary winds*): contradictory: (*kon-trā′ri*) perverse, self-willed. *n.* the opposite (*pl.* **-ies).**

con′trariness, contrarī′ety, *ns.*

on the contrary, no, the very opposite is true.

to the contrary, supporting an opposite statement, view, or contradictory fact, etc. (e.g. *It may be true*; *there is no evidence to the contrary*).

[L. *contrā,* against.]

contrast, *kon-trâst′,* *v.i.* to show marked difference from (e.g. *His words contrast with his deeds*).—*v.t.* to compare so as to show differences.—*n.* (*kon′trâst*) unlikeness in things compared: thing showing marked unlikeness (to another).

[L. *contrā,* opposite to, *stāre,* to stand.]

contravene, *kon-trȧ-vēn′,* *v.t.* to disregard, break (a law).

contraven′tion, *n.*

[L. *contrā,* against, *venīre,* to come.]

contretemps, *kon^g-tre-ton^g,* *n.* something that happens at an awkward moment: a hitch.

[Fr.—L. *contrā,* against, *tempus,* time.]

contribute, *kȯn-trib′ūt, v.t.* to give along with others: to write (an article published in a magazine, etc.).—*v.i.* to give something: to help to bring about (e.g. *His gaiety contributed to his popularity*).

contribū′tion, *n.* something contributed.

contrib′utor, *n.*

contrib′utory, *adj.* contributing (e.g. *a contributory cause*; *a cause contributory to his downfall*).

[L. *con-,* with, *tribuĕre,* to give, pay.]

contrite, *kon′trīt, adj.* penitent, deeply sorry for something one has done.

con′triteness, contri′tion (*-tri′*), *ns.*

[L. *con,* wholly, *terĕre,* to rub, bruise.]

contrive, *kȯn-trīv′,* *v.t.* to plan: to invent: to manage (to do something).

contriv′ance, *n.* act of contriving: the thing contrived (esp. something mechanical): a plan or scheme.

[O.Fr. *con-,* and *trover,* to find.]

control, *kȯn-trōl′,* *n.* restraint, check (e.g. *Please keep the dog under control*): authority, command: a lever or wheel for controlling movements: an experiment done for use as a standard of comparison for other experiments.—*v.t.* to keep in check, restrain: to govern:—*pr.p.* **controll′ing;** *pa.p.* **contrōlled′.**

controll′er, *n.* one who, or something that, controls, esp. one who checks the accounts of others.

control tower, a building at an aerodrome from which take-off and landing instructions are given.

[Fr. *contre rôle,* a duplicate register—L. *contrā,* against, *rotulus,* a roll.]

controversy, *kon′trȯ-vėr-si, kȯn-trov′, n.* a discussion of opposing views: strife in words:—*pl.* **-ies.**

controver′sial (*-shȧl*), *adj.* of controversy: not unquestionably true, open to dispute (e.g. a statement).

controvert′ible, *adj.* able to be denied or disproved.
[L. *contrā*, against, *vertĕre*, to turn.]

conundrum, *kòn-un′drùm, n.* a riddle: a puzzling question. [Origin uncertain.]

conurbation, *kon-ûr-bā′sh(ò)n, n.* a group of towns forming a single built-up area.
[L. *con*, together, *urbs*, city.]

convalesce, *kon-vàl-es′, v.i.* to regain strength after illness.
convales′cent, *adj.* and *n.*
convales′cence, *n.*
convalescent hospital, one for convalescents.
[L. *con-*, *valescĕre—valēre*, to be strong.]

convection, *kòn-vek′sh(ò)n, n.* conveyance of heat through liquids by means of currents due to the movement of the heated parts.
[L. *convectiō*, a bringing together.]

convene, *kòn-vēn′, v.i.* and *v.t.* to come, or call, together.
convēn′er, *n.* one who convenes a meeting.
See also **convent, convention.**
[L. *con-*, together, *venīre*, *ventum*, come.]

convenient, *kòn-vēn′yènt, adj.* suitable: handy: easy to use or to reach.
conven′ience, *n.* suitableness, handiness: any means of giving ease or comfort.
conven′iently, *adv.*
at your convenience, when it suits you, gives you little trouble.
marriage of convenience, a marriage made for the sake of practical advantages, usu. money.
[L. *convenīre*, to come together, fit.]

convent, *kon′vènt, n.* a house for nuns (or monks), a nunnery (or monastery).
[L. *convenīre*; same root as **convene.**]

conventicle, *kon-vent′i-kl, n.* (17th century) an illegal gathering, esp. religious.
[L. *conventiculum*; root as **convene.**]

convention, *kòn-ven′sh(ò)n, n.* an assembly, esp. of representatives for some common purpose: a temporary treaty: an agreement: established usage.
conven′tional, *adj.* customary: bound by the accepted standards of conduct, manners, or taste: formal: not natural, impulsive, or original.
[Same root as **convene.**]

converge, *kòn-vèrj′, v.i.* to move towards, or meet in, one point or value.
conver′gence, *n.* **conver′gent,** *adj.*
[L. *con-*, together, *vergĕre*, to incline.]

converse[1]**.** See **convert.**

converse[2], *kòn-vèrs′, v.i.* to talk easily not formally.
conversā′tion, *n.* talk.
conversā′tional, *adj.*
conversa′tionalist, *n.* one who excels in conversation.
[L. *conversārī*, to live with.]

convert, *kòn-vèrt′, v.t.* to change from one thing into another: to change from one religion to another, or from a sinful to a holy life: to alter (into): to turn (to another purpose; e.g. *to convert to one's own use*).—*n.* (*kon′vèrt*) a converted person.
con′verse, *adj.* opposite.—Also *n.*
convert′er, *n.* one who converts: an apparatus for making a change in an electric current (also **convertor**).
convert′ible, *adj.* that may be converted: exchangeable at a fixed price for gold or other currency.—*n.* a car with folding top.
convertibil′ity, *n.*
[L. *con-*, and *vertĕre*, to turn.]

convex, *kon′veks′, adj.* curved on the outside, the reverse of *concave.*
convex′ity, *n.*
[L. *convexus—convehĕre*, to carry together.]

convey, *kòn-vā′, v.t.* to carry: to transmit: to communicate: to make over (property) legally.
convey′er, -or, *n.* (also *adj.*).
convey′ance, *n.* act of conveying: a vehicle of any kind: (*law*) the act of transferring property: the writing which transfers it.
convey′ancer, *n.* a lawyer who carries out transference of property.
convey′ancing, *n.* branch of law dealing with transfer of property.
conveyor belt, an endless, moving belt of rubber, metal, etc., carrying articles, e.g. from one part of a building to another.
[L. *con-*, and *via*, a way.]

convict, *kòn-vikt′, v.t.* to prove, pronounce, guilty.—*n.* (*kon′vikt*) one found guilty of crime, esp. one condemned to penal servitude.
convic′tion, *n.* act of convicting: strong belief.
[Same root as **convince.**]

convince, *kòn-vins′, v.t.* to persuade (a person) that something he has been uncertain about is true.
convic′tion, *n.* See **convict.**
[L. *con-*, *vincĕre*, *victum*, to conquer.]

convivial, *kòn-viv′i-àl, adj.* social, jovial.
convivial′ity. *n.* **conviv′ially,** *adv.*
[L. *con-*, together, *vīvĕre*, to live.]

convoke, *kòn-vōk′, v.t.* to call together.
convocā′tion, *n.* act of convoking: an ecclesiastical or university assembly.
[L. *con-*, together, *vocāre*, to call.]

convolvulus, *kòn-vol′vū-lùs, n.* a twining or trailing plant with trumpet-shaped flowers.
[L. *con*, together, *volvĕre*, to roll.]

convoy, *kòn-voi′, v.t.* to accompany for protection.—*n.* (*kon′voi*) a fleet of merchantmen escorted by ships of war: a column of military supplies.
[Fr. *convoyer*; same root as **convey.**]

convulse, *kòn-vuls′, v.t.* to shake violently (e.g. *to convulse with laughter, pain*): to

cause violent laughter in (e.g. *The thought convulsed him*).
convul′sion, *n.* any involuntary contraction of the muscles causing violent spasms: any violent disturbance.
convuls′ive, *adj.* **convuls′ively,** *adv.*
[L. *con-*, *vellĕre*, *vulsum*, to pull.]

cony, coney, *kō′ni*, *kun′i*, *n.* a rabbit.
[L. *cuniculus*.]

coo, *ko͞o*, *v.i.* to make a sound as a dove: to talk caressingly :—*pr.p.* **co͞o′ing**; *pa.p.* **co͞oed** (*ko͞od*).—Also *n.*

cooee, *ko͞o′ē*, **cooey,** *ko͞o′i*, *n.* the signal-call of Australian aborigines in the bush.

cook, *kook*, *v.t.* to prepare (food): to alter, make false (accounts, etc.).—*n.* one who cooks.
cook′er, *n.* a stove for cooking.
cook′ery, *n.* art or practice of cooking.
[L. *coquus*.]

cookie, *kook′i*, *n.* a kind of bun: (*U.S.*) a biscuit. [Du. *koekje*, a cake.]

cool, *ko͞ol*, *adj.* slightly cold: calm: indifferent: impudent.—*v.t.* and *v.i.* to make, or grow, cool or cooler.
cool′er, *n.* anything that cools: a vessel for cooling.
cool′-head′ed, *adj.* not easily excited, able to act calmly.
cool′ly, *adv.* **cool′ness,** *n.* [O.E. *cōl*.]

coolie, cooly, *ko͞ol′i*, *n.* an Indian or Chinese hired labourer.
[Prob. *Kuli*, a tribe of Bombay.]

coomb, combe, *ko͞om*, *n.* a deep little wooded valley: a hollow in a hillside.
[O.E. *cumb*.]

coon, *ko͞on*, *n.* the raccoon: a sly fellow: (*derogatory*) a Negro. [Abbrev. of **raccoon.**]

coop, *ko͞op*, *n.* a wicker basket: a box for fowls or small animals.—*v.t.* to shut in a coop or elsewhere.—Also **coop up.**
[M.E. *cupe*, *coupe*, basket.]

cooper, *ko͞op′ėr*, *n.* one who makes tubs, casks, etc.
coop′erage, *n.* the work or workshop of a cooper: the sum paid for a cooper's work.
[Late Latin *cūpa*, cask.]

co-operate, *kō-op′ėr-āt*, *v.i.* to work together for a purpose.
co-operā′tion, *n.* **co-op′erative,** *adj.*
co-operative society, a profit-sharing association of consumers for the cheaper purchase of goods or for other trading purposes.
[**co-**, and **operate.**]

co-opt, *kō-opt′*, *v.t.* to elect into a body by the votes of its members.
[L. *co-*, together, *optāre*, to choose.]

co-ordinate, *kō-ör′di-nāt*, *v.t.* to adjust (a movement, an action) so that it works in smoothly (with other movements or actions): to make (e.g. movements, efforts) work smoothly together.
co-ordinā′tion, *n.*
[L. *co-*, *ordō*, *ordinis*, order.]

coot, *ko͞ot*, *n.* a waterfowl with a white spot on the forehead.
[M.E. *cote*; conn. with Du. *koet*.]

cop, *kop*, *v.t.* (*slang*) to catch.
cop, copp′er, *ns.* policeman.
[Origin uncertain.]

copal, *kō′pal*, *n.* a hard resin got from many tropical trees.
[Sp.—Mexican *copalli*, resin.]

cope[1], *kōp*, *v.i.* to struggle (with) successfully.
[Gk. *kolaphos*, a blow.]

cope[2], *kōp*, *n.* a long cloak, orig. with a hood, worn by clergy.
cope′-, cop′ing-stone, *ns.* the stone that tops a wall: the finishing touch.
cop′ing, *n.* the topmost course (see **this**) of masonry of a wall.
[From root of **cap.**]

copious, *kō′pi-us*, *adj.* plentiful, overflowing.
cō′piously, *adv.* **cō′piousness,** *n.*
[L. *cōpia*, plenty.]

copper[1], *kop′ėr*, *n.* a metal of a red colour: money made of copper or a substitute: a vessel made of copper, as a clothes-boiler.
copp′erplate, *n.* a plate of polished copper on which something has been engraved: faultless handwriting.
[Late Latin *cuper*—L. *cuprum*.]

copper[2]. See **cop.**

coppice, *kop′is*, **copse,** *kops*, *n.* a wood of small growth for cutting from time to time.
[Late Latin *colpāre*, to cut.]

copra, *kop′ra*, *n.* the dried kernel of the coconut, yielding coconut oil.
[Port., from Malay.]

copse. See **coppice.**

copy, *kop′i*, *n.* an imitation: a reproduction: an individual specimen of a book: a model for imitation: matter for printing: material for a newspaper writer (e.g. *This is good copy*) :—*pl.* **cop′ies.** —*v.t.* to make a copy of: to imitate.—*v.i.* to crib work of e.g. a schoolfellow :—*pr.p.* **cop′ying**; *pa.p.* **cop′ied.**
cop′ybook, *n.* a writing or drawing book with models for imitation.
cop′yright, *n.* the sole right to reproduce a literary, dramatic, musical, or artistic work—also to perform, translate, film, or record such a work.—*adj.* protected by copyright.
cop′ywriter, *n.* a writer of copy (esp. advertisements) for the press.
[L. *cōpia*, plenty.]

coquet, coquette, *kȯ-ket′*, *v.i.* to flirt :—*pr.p.* **coquett′ing**; *pa.p.* **coquett′ed.**—*n.* (**coquette**) a woman who likes to flirt.
coquett′ish, *adj.* [Fr.]

coral, *kör′ȧl*, *n.* a hard substance of various colours, made up of skeletons of a kind of tiny animal, gradually built up from the bottom of the sea to form **coral reef, island.**
[Gk. *korallion*.]

cord, *körd, n.* thin rope or thick string: something resembling this: anything that binds.
cord'age, *n.* a quantity of ropes.
cord'ite, *n.* a smokeless explosive, so called from its cord-like appearance.
[L. *chorda.*]

cordial, *kör'di-àl, adj.* hearty, sincere: warm, affectionate.—*n.* anything which revives or comforts: an invigorating drink.
cordial'ity, *n.* warmth of feeling or the expression of it.
cord'ially, *adv.*
[L. *cor, cordis,* the heart.]

cordon, *kör'don, -dôn, n.* a cord or ribbon given as a badge of honour: a line of sentries or policemen to prevent access to an area.—*v.t.* (or **cordon off**) to enclose with a cordon. [Fr.]

corduroy, *kör-dù-roi', n.* a thick ribbed cotton fabric: (in *pl.*) trousers of this.
corduroy road, a track laid with tree trunks.
[Perh. Fr. *corde du roi,* king's cord.]

core, *kōr, kör, n.* inner part of anything, esp. fruit.—*v.t.* to take out the core of.
[Perh. conn. with L. *cor,* heart.]

co-respondent, *kō-rē-spond'ėnt, n.* (*law*) a person charged with adultery, along with the petitioner's wife or husband, who is the *respondent.*

cork, *körk, n.* the outer bark of the cork tree (an oak of S. Europe, N. Africa, etc.): a stopper, esp. of cork.—*adj.* made of cork.—*v.t.* to stop with a cork, to plug.
cork'screw, *n.* a screw for drawing corks from bottles.—*adj.* like a corkscrew in shape.
[Through Sp.—L. *cortex,* bark, rind.]

corm, *körm, n.* the short, bulb-like underground stem of the crocus, etc.
[Gk. *kormos,* the lopped trunk of a tree.]

cormorant, *kör'mò-rànt, n.* a web-footed sea bird, known for its large appetite.
[L. *corvus marinus,* sea crow.]

corn[1], *körn, n.* a grain, hard particle: seeds of cereal plants or the plants themselves: (in England) wheat, (in Scotland, Ireland) oats, (in North America) maize. —*v.t.* to sprinkle with grains of salt.
corned, *adj.* salted—e.g. **corned beef** (now also cooked and canned).
corn'cob, *n.* the long woody centre of the ear of maize.
corn'crake, *n.* bird with harsh croaking cry, living in cornfields.
corn exchange, *n.* a market where grain is sold.
corn'flour, *n.* finely ground flour esp. of maize.
corn'flower, *n.* a blue-flowered plant of cornfields.
[O.E.; conn. Ger. *korn,* L. *grānum.*]

corn[2], *körn, n.* a small hard growth chiefly on the foot.
to tread on one's corns, to hurt one's feelings.
[L. *cornū,* a horn.]

cornea, *kör'ni-a, n.* the transparent horny membrane that forms the front covering of the eye.
cor'neal, *adj.*
[L. *cornea (tela),* horny (tissue).]

cornelian, *kör-nēl'yàn, n.* a red stone used in jewellery.
[Prob. L. *cornus,* name of a red berry.]

corner, *kör'nėr, n.* the point where two lines or surfaces meet: a secret place: an awkward position, difficulty: in association football, a free kick from the corner flag: a business operation by which a few gain control of the whole available supply of something.—*v.t.* to put in a corner: to put in an embarrassing position from which escape is difficult: to gain control of the supplies of (something).
cor'nerstone, *n.* stone that joins the two walls of a building at a corner, esp. one built into the corner of the foundation: something of very great importance.
to turn the corner, to get past a difficulty or danger.
[L. *cornū,* a horn, corner.]

cornet[1], *kör'nit, n.* an instrument of brass, with three valves, more tapering than the trumpet: any funnel-shaped object.
[L. *cornū,* a horn.]

cornet[2], *kör'nit, n.* till 1871 a cavalry officer who carried the colours.
[Same root as **cornet** (1).]

cornice, *kör'nis, n.* plaster moulding round a ceiling.
[Perh. Gk. *korōnis,* a curved line.]

Cornish, *kör'nish, adj.* of *Cornwall.*—*n.* the people or former language of Cornwall.

corny, *kör'ni, adj.* (*U.S. slang*) old-fashioned, out-of-date, dull, foolish.

corolla, *kor-ol'a, n.* the inner covering of a flower, composed of petals.
[L. dim. of *corōna,* a crown.]

coronation, *kor-òn-ā'sh(ò)n, n.* the act of crowning a sovereign.
[L. *corōna,* a crown.]

coronach, *kor'o-nâH, n.* a funeral dirge or song of mourning.
[Gael. *corranach.*]

coroner, *kor'ò-nėr, n.* an officer of the Crown who enquires into the causes of accidental or suspicious deaths.
[L. *corōna.*]

coronet, *kor'o-net,* a *n.* small crown: an ornamental headdress.
[L. *corōna,* a crown.]

corporal[1], *kör'pò-ràl, n.* a non-commissioned officer (see *Appendices*).
[Fr. *caporal*—L. *caput,* the head.]

corporal[2], *kör'pò-ràl, adj.* of, relating to, the body: not spiritual.
cor'porate, *adj.* legally joined to form a body or corporation: united (e.g. *The success was due not to one man but to corporate effort.*)

corporā'tion, *n.* a body, such as a town council, with power given to it by law to act as one individual: (*coll.*) a large paunch.
corporal punishment, punishment by caning, birching, etc.
corporate spirit, willingness to work with others for the good of all.
[Same root as **corps, corpse.**]

corps, *kōr, kör, n.* a division of an army: an organised group:—*pl.* **corps** (*kōrz, körz*).
corpse, *körps,* or *körs, n.* a dead body, esp. of a human being.
corpulence, *kör'pū-lėns,* **corpulency,** *-lėn-si, ns.* fleshiness, fatness.
cor'pulent, *adj.*
corpuscle, *kör'pus-l,* or *-pus'l, n.* a cell lying in a fluid such as the blood plasma.
[L. *corpus, corporis,* body (Fr. *corps*).]

corral, *kȯr-al', n.* an enclosure for cattle etc.: in an encampment, an enclosure made by placing wagons in a circle.—*v.t.* to form (wagons) into a corral: to put in a corral:—*pr.p.* **corrall'ing;** *pa.p.* **corralled'.** [Sp.]

correct, *kȯr-ekt', v.t.* to remove faults from: to mark errors in: to set (a person) right: to punish.—*adj.* free from faults: true.
correc'tion, *n.* **correct'ly,** *adv.*
correct'ive, *adj.* intended to, having the power to, set right.—Also *n.*
[L. *corrigĕre, correctum.*]

correspond, *kor-is-pond', v.i.* to be in agreement (with; e.g. *His promises do not correspond with his actions*): to be similar in some way (e.g. *The American Congress corresponds to the British Parliament*): to communicate by letter (with).
correspond'ence, *n.* agreement: similarity, likeness: communication by letters: letters, etc.
correspond'ent, *n.* one with whom another exchanges letters: one who contributes letters or news to a newspaper, etc.
[L. *con-,* with, *respondēre,* to answer.]

corridor, *kor'i-dȯr, n.* a passageway, esp. one off which rooms open: a narrow strip of land serving as a passageway.
corridor carriage, train, a carriage, train, with a corridor from end to end.
[It. *corridore*—L. *currĕre,* to run.]

corrie, *kor'i, n.* a rounded hollow in a mountain.
[Gael. *coire,* a cauldron.]

corrigendum, *kor-i-jen'dum, n.* a mistake requiring correction:—*pl.* **corrigen'da.**
[L. *corrigĕre,* to correct.]

corroborate, *kȯ-rob'o-rāt, v.t.* to support, confirm (e.g. *She corroborated her sister's story; the witness's statement was corroborated by other evidence*).
corrob'orative, *adj.* tending to confirm or support (e.g. *corroborative evidence*).
corroborā'tion, *n.*
[L. pfx. *cor-, rōborāre,* to make strong.]

corroboree, *kȯ-rob'ȯ-rē, n.* a dance of Australian aborigines: a song for this: a festive gathering. [Native word.]

corrode, *kȯ-rōd', v.t.* to eat away (as rust, chemicals, etc. do.)—*v.i.* to be eaten away.
corrosion, *kȯ-rō'zh(ȯ)n, n.*
corro'sive (*-iv, -ziv*), *adj.* eating away as an acid does.—Also *n.*
[L. pfx. *cor-, rōdĕre,* to gnaw.]

corrugate, *kor'oo-gāt, v.t.* to wrinkle or draw into folds.
corrugā'tion, *n.*
corrugated iron, sheet iron rolled into a wavy surface for the sake of strength.
[L. pfx. *cor-, rūgāre,* to wrinkle.]

corrupt, *kȯr-upt', v.t.* to cause (fruit, flesh, etc.) to go bad: to make morally rotten: to bribe.—*v.i.* to rot.—*adj.* putrid, bad: wicked: dishonest.
corrup'tion, *n.* rottenness: evilness: bribery: a bad (or orig. bad) form of a word (e.g. *Caterpillar is probably a corruption of Old French chatepelose, a 'hairy cat'*).
corrupt'ible, *adj.* that may be corrupted: capable of being bribed.
[L. pfx. *cor-, rumpĕre, ruptum,* to break.]

corsage, *kör-säzh', kör', n.* the bodice or waist of a woman's dress: a small bouquet for pinning on to a dress.
[Same root as **corset.**]

corsair, *kör'sār, n.* a pirate, or pirate ship.
[Fr. *corsaire*—L. *cursus,* a running.]

corselet. Same as **corslet.**

corset, *kör'set, n.* a close-fitting stiff inner bodice, stays.
corslet, corselet, *körs'let, n.* armour for the body: a form of corset.
[O.Fr. *cors* (L. *corpus*), body.]

cortège, *kör-tezh', n.* a procession, esp. a funeral procession. [Fr.]

corundum *kȯ-run'dum, n.* a very hard mineral, forms of which include sapphire, ruby, emery.
[From Indian word meaning ruby.]

coruscate, *kor'us-kāt, v.i.* to sparkle.
coruscā'tion, *n.*
[L. *coruscāre.*]

corvette, *kör-vet', n.* an escort vessel, specially designed for protecting convoys against submarine attack. [Fr.]

cos, *kos, n.* long-leafed type of lettuce.
[From the Aegean island of *Cos.*]

cosmetic, *koz-met'ik, adj.* designed to increase the beauty of the face.—*n.* a preparation for this purpose.
[Gk. *kosmētikos*—*kosmos,* order, adornment.]

cosmic, cosmopolitan. See **cosmos.**

cosmos, *koz'mos, n.* the universe.
cos'mic, *adj.*
cosmic rays, streams of particles, very fast moving, coming from outer space.
cosmopolitan, *koz-mȯ-pol'i-tȧn, n.* a citizen of the world: a person who is free from national prejudices.—*adj.* at

home in all places: belonging to all parts of the world: containing people from all parts of the world (e.g. *New York is a cosmopolitan city*).
[Gk. *kosmos*, world (*politēs*, citizen—*polis*, city).]

cossack, *kos'ak, n.* one of a people in south-eastern Russia, famous as horsemen. [Turk.]

cosset, *kos'it, n.* a lamb reared by hand.—*v.t.* to pamper. [Origin unknown.]

cost, *kost, v.t.* to bring (a certain price): to be valued at (a certain price): to take, require, as if in payment (e.g. *The victory cost many lives*): to estimate the cost of producing (something):—*pa.t.* and *pa.p.* **cost.**—*n.* what is paid or suffered to obtain anything: (in *pl.*) expenses of a lawsuit.
cost'ly, *adj.* expensive, of great cost: valuable.
cost'liness, *n.*
[O.Fr. *couster*—L. *constāre*, to stand at.]

costermonger, *kos'tėr-mung-gėr*, **coster,** a seller of apples and other fruit, etc., from a barrow.
[From *costard*, a ribbed apple; perh. L. *costa*, rib.]

costliness, costly. See **cost.**

costive, *kos'tiv, adj.* having the motion of the bowels too slow, constipated.
[O.Fr. *costivé*—L. *constipātus*.]

costume, *kos'tūm, n.* dress: a woman's outer dress.
costum'er, costum'ier, *ns.* one who makes or deals in costumes.
costume jewellery, jewellery of inexpensive materials effective as part of an ensemble.
costume play, etc., one in which actors wear dress of earlier period.
[Fr.—L. *consuētūdō*, custom.]

cosy, cozy, *kō'zi, adj.* snug: comfortable.—*n.* a covering for a teapot.
co'sily, *adv.* **cos'iness,** *n.*
[Orig. Scot.; history unknown.]

cot[1], *kot, n.* a small dwelling, a cottage.
[O.E. *cot(e)*.]

cot[2], *kot, n.* a small bed or crib
[From Indian word *khāt*.]

cottage, *kot'ij, n.* a small house: a country residence.
cott'ager, *n.* one who lives in a cottage, esp. a labourer.
[Late Latin *cottagium*; conn. with **cot** (1).]

cotton, *kot'n, n.* soft substance like fine wool, the hairs covering the seeds of cotton plants: yarn or cloth made of cotton.—Also *adj.*
cotton gin, a machine for separating the seeds from the fibre of cotton.
cotton grass, a sedge with long, silky hairs.
cott'ontail, *n.* the ordinary American rabbit.
cotton wool, cotton in its raw or woolly state: loose cotton pressed in a sheet used to absorb fluid or to protect an injury: too great protection from the discomforts of life.
[Fr. *coton*—Arabic *qutun*.]

couch[1], *kowch, v.t.* to lay down on a bed: to express (in words).—*n.* a bed: a padded piece of furniture for resting on.
[Fr. *coucher*—L. *collocāre*.]

couch[2]**(-grass),** *kowch, kōōch, n.* a grass related to wheat, a troublesome weed.
[O.E. *cwice*; prob. *cwic*, living.]

cough, *kof, v.i.* to expel air with a harsh sound.—Also *n.* [M.E. *coughen*.]

could. See **can** (1).

council, *kown'sil, n.* a body of people meeting to talk over questions and to make decisions or laws.
coun'cillor, *n.* a member of a council.
council house, a house primarily for renting built by a local authority, e.g. a county council. [L. *concilium*.]

counsel, *kown'sil, n.* advice: a barrister or advocate.—*v.t.* to advise, recommend:—*pr.p.* **coun'selling**; *pa.p.* **coun'selled.**
coun'sellor, *n.* one who counsels.
to keep one's own counsel, to keep one's intentions secret.
to take counsel with, to discuss problem(s) with.
[L. *consilium*, advice.]

count[1], *kownt, n.* a foreign noble equal in rank to an English earl:—*fem.* **count'ess,** lady of rank of, or wife of, count, earl.
coun'ty, *n.* division of country:—*pl.* **-ies.**
county borough (see **borough**).
county council, a council for managing the affairs of a county.
county town, the town in which the public business of a county is done.
[O.Fr. *conte*—L. *comes*, a companion.]

count[2], *kownt, v.t.* to name the numbers up to (e.g. *to count twenty*): to find the total number of: to consider (e.g. *I count you as one of my friends*).—*v.i.* to name the numbers: to be considered: to be important (e.g. *Every effort will count*).—*n.* act of numbering: the number counted: a particular charge brought against prisoner, etc.
count'er, *n.* he who, or something that, counts: a token used in reckoning: a table on which money is counted or goods laid.
count'less, *adj.* very many.
count'down, *n.* a counting backwards to check progress twards the beginning of an event, regarded as zero.
count'ing-house, *n.* a room where accounts are kept.
to count for much, little, etc. to be important, unimportant, etc.: to have much, little, etc., effect on the result.
to count on, to rely on (a person): to expect, depend on (a happening).
to count out, not to include: to say that (a boxer) is the loser because he cannot get up within a count of ten seconds.

out for the count, unconscious, exhausted.
[O.Fr. *cònter*—L. *computāre.*]

countenance, *kown'tin-àns, n.* the face: good will, support.—*v.t.* to favour, encourage.
out of countenance, embarrassed, abashed.
[O.Fr. *contenance.*]

counter[1]. See **count** (2).

counter[2], *kown'tėr, adv.* in the opposite direction.—*adj.* contrary; opposite.—*v.t.* to meet or answer (a stroke or move) by another.
counteract', *v.t.* to act against, hinder, undo the effect of.
counterac'tion, *n.*
coun'ter-attack, *n.* an attack in reply to an attack.
coun'ter-attrac'tion, *n.* a rival attraction.
counterbal'ance, *v.t.* to balance by weight on the opposite side.
coun'tercharge, *n.* an accusation made in opposition to another.
coun'ter-claim, *n.* a claim made in opposition to another.
coun'ter-clock'wise, *adv.* in a direction opposite to that in which the hands of a clock move.
coun'terfoil, *n.* a coupon detached from a bank cheque, etc., and kept by the giver.
coun'ter-march, *v.i.* to march back or in an opposite direction.—Also *n.*
coun'ter-measure, *n.* an action taken to prevent, or to try to undo the effect of, another action.
coun'ter-mō'tion, *n.* a proposal in opposition to a motion already made.
coun'terpart, *n.* a duplicate of a legal document: a person or thing very like another.
coun'terplot, *n.* a plot intended to frustrate another plot.
coun'terpoise, *v.t.* to weigh against: to act in opposition to with equal effect.—*n.* an equally heavy weight in the other scale.
coun'ter-revolū'tion, *n.* a revolution undoing a previous revolution.
countersign', *v.t.* to sign on the opposite side: to sign in addition to another, so as to certify that a document is genuine.
coun'tersign, *n.* a military password.
[L. *contrā,* against.]

counterfeit, *kown'tėr-fit, -fēt, v.t.* to imitate: to copy unlawfully (e.g. money): to forge.—Also *n.* and *adj.*
[L. *contrā,* against, *facĕre,* to do.]

counterfoil. See **counter** (2).

countermand, *kown-tėr-mând', v.t.* to recall or to stop (e.g. order for goods) by a command contradicting one already given: to cancel (a command).
[L. *contrā,* against, *mandāre,* to order.]

counter-march, etc. See **counter** (2).

counterpane, *kown'tėr-pān, n.* a cover for a bed.
[L. *culcita puncta,* stitched pillow, cover.]

counterpart, etc. See **counter** (2).

counter-tenor, *kown'tėr-ten'ȯr, n.* a male voice higher than a tenor.
[Fr. *contreteneur.*]

country, *kun'tri, n.* districts where there are fields, moors, etc., as opposed to towns and built-up areas: the land in which one was born or in which one lives: a nation:—*pl.* **coun'tries.**
coun'trified, coun'tryfied, *adj.* looking, sounding, acting, like (that of) someone who lives in the country.
country dance, a dance in which partners are arranged in opposite lines.
coun'try-folk, *n.pl.* the people who live in the country.
coun'try-house, -seat, *ns.* a landowner's large house in the country.
coun'tryman, *n.* one who lives in the country: one born in the same country with another:—*fem.* **coun'trywoman.**
coun'tryside, *n.* a district or part of the country.
country cousin, a relative from the country, unaccustomed to town.
to go to the country, to hold a general election.
[O.Fr. *contrée.*]

county. See **count** (1).

coup, *kōō, n.* a sudden successful stroke, trick, or move: a coup d'état.
coup d'état (*dā-tä'*), a sudden and violent change in government.
[Fr., through L.—Gk. *kolaphos,* a blow.]

coupé, *kōō-pā, n.* a covered motor car seated for two.
[Fr. *couper,* to cut.]

couple, *kup'l, n.* something that joins two things together: two of a kind together: a pair.—*v.t.* to join: associate in thought.
coup'let, *n.* two lines of verse, one following the other, that rhyme with each other.
coup'ling, *n.* a link for joining together, e.g. railway carriages: an appliance for transmitting motion in machinery.
[L. *copula.*]

coupon, *kōō'pon, n.* a part of a ticket, etc. that can be torn off: a piece cut from an advertisement, etc., entitling one to something, e.g. to a gift: a betting form (*a football coupon,* one in which to enter one's forecast of the results of matches).
[Fr.—*couper,* to cut.]

courage, *kur'ij, n.* the quality that makes man able to meet dangers without giving way to fear, bravery.
courā'geous (*-jùs*), *adj.* brave, fearless.
courā'geously, *adv.*
courā'geousness, *n.*
[O.Fr. *corage*—L. *cor,* heart.]

courier, *kōō'ri-ėr, n.* a messenger: a state messenger: a travelling attendant, e.g. of people on a tour.
[Same root as **course.**]

course, *kōrs, körs, n.* path in which anything moves: a channel for water: the direction to be followed (e.g. *to fly on course*): the ground over which a race is run, golf is played, etc.: usual progress or development (e.g. *The disease has followed its normal course*): line of action (e.g. *Your best course would be to go to the police*): a series, as of lectures, etc.: a division of a meal: a row of bricks or stones in a wall.—*v.t.* to run through or over: to hunt (game) with greyhounds.—*v.i.* to move with speed.
cours′ing, *n.*
a matter of course, something that will, would, naturally, certainly, happen.
in due course, when the natural time for it comes.
in the course of, during.
of course, naturally, needless to say.
[L. *currĕre, cursum,* to run.]

court, *kōrt, kört, n.* a space enclosed in some way: one surrounded by house(s): persons who form a sovereign's suite or council: attentions with the aim of winning favour, affection, etc. (e.g. *to pay court to someone*): (*law*) the hall of justice: the judges and officials who preside there.—*v.t.* to pay attentions to: to woo: to try to gain (e.g. attention, applause).
court′ier, *n.* a member of a sovereign's court: a flatterer.
court′ly, *adj.* having fine manners.
court′ship, *m.* wooing.
court′house, *n.* a building where the law courts are held.
court′-mar′tial (*-shȧl*), *n.* a court held by officers of the armed forces to try offences against service discipline:—*pl.* **courts′-mar′tial.**
court′yard, *n.* a court or enclosed ground beside or within a house.
[L. *cors, cohors,* an enclosure.]

courteous, *kûrt′yus, adj.* polite, considerate and respectful.
court′eously, *adv.* **court′eousness,** *n.*
courtesy (*kûrt′i-si*), *n.* courteous behaviour: a courteous act:—*pl.* **-ies.**
[Same root as **court.**]

cousin, *kuz′n, n.* the son or daughter of one's uncle or aunt (**full cousin, first cousin**), or any descendant of either: also various other relations not in the same direct line as oneself.
[L. *consōbrīnus.*]

cove, *kōv, n.* a small inlet of the sea, a bay: a cavern or rocky recess.
[O.E. *cofa,* a room.]

covenant, *kuv′ė-nȧnt, n.* an agreement between two people or two parties to do, or to refrain from doing, something.—*v.t.* to agree by covenant (to do something).
Covenant′er, *n.* (*Scot.*) one who signed or was loyal to an agreement for the defence of Presbyterianism.
[L. *con-,* together, *venīre,* to come.]

Coventry, *kov′-, kuv′ėnt-ri, n.* in **to send to Coventry,** to shut out from one's company, refuse to speak to, etc.

cover, *kuv′ėr, v.t.* to put or spread something on, over, or about: to clothe: to hide: to protect: to include: to be sufficient for: to travel over (e.g. *to cover 40 miles in a day*): to point a weapon directly at.—*n.* something that covers, hides, protects: undergrowth, thicket concealing game, etc.
cov′erage, *n.* the area covered: the items included by an insurance policy, news reporting, etc.
cov′ert, *adj.* secret, concealed.—*n.* a place that gives concealment: a thicket.
cov′ertly, *adv.* secretly.
covering letter, a letter to explain documents enclosed with it.
cov′er-point (*cricket*), *n.* the player who supports point and stands to his right.
[Fr. *couvrir.*]

coverlet, *kuv′ėr-lit, n.* a bedcover.
[Fr. *couvrir,* to cover, *lit,* a bed.]

covert. See **cover.**

covet, *kuv′it, v.t.* to desire or wish for eagerly (esp. something belonging to someone else):—*pr.p.* **cov′eting**; *pa.p.* **cov′eted.**
cov′etous, *adj.* very desirous: greedy, grasping.
cov′etousness, *n.*
[O.Fr. *coveiter*—L. root as **cupidity.**]

covey, *kuv′i, n.* a brood or hatch (of partridges): a small flock of game birds.
[O.Fr. *covée*—L. *cubāre,* to lie down.]

cow[1], *kow, n.* the female of bovine and certain other animals, as the elk, elephant, whale, etc.
cow′boy (*U.S.*), *n.* a man who has charge of cattle on a ranch.
cow′catch′er (*U.S.*), *n.* an apparatus on the front of railway engines to throw off obstacles.
cow′herd, *n.* one who herds cows.
cow′hide, *n.* the hide of a cow made into leather: a whip made of cowhide.
cow′pox, *n.* a disease which appears in pimples on the teats of the cow, the matter from the pimples being used for vaccination against smallpox.
[O.E. *cū.*]

cow[2], *kow, v.t.* to subdue, frighten with threats.
[Perh. Old Norse *kūga.*]

coward, *kow′ȧrd, n.* one who turns tail, one without courage: often applied to one who brutally takes advantage of the weak.
cow′ard, cow′ardly, *adjs.*
cow′ardice, cow′ardliness, *ns.*
[O.Fr. *couard*—L. *cauda,* a tail.]

cower, *kow′ėr, v.i.* to sink down through fear, etc.: to crouch timidly.
[Conn. Old Norse *kūra,* to lie quiet.]

cowl, *kowl, n.* a cap or hood: a monk's hood: a cover for a chimney, etc.: an engine bonnet: a cowling.

cowl′ing, *n.* the casing of an aeroplane engine.
[O.E. *cugele*; conn. L. *cucullus,* hood.]

cowpox. See **cow** (1).

cowrie, cowry, *kow′ri, n.* a seashell used among primitive peoples as money and magical object :—*pl.* **cow′ries.**
[From an Indian word.]

cowslip, *kow′slip, n.* a kind of primrose, common in English pastures.
[O.E. *cū,* cow, *slyppe,* slime.]

coxcomb, *koks′kōm, n.* a strip of red cloth notched like a cock's comb, which jesters used to wear : a fop, conceited dandy.
[**cock's comb.**]

coxswain, *kok′sn,* or *kok′swān, n.* one who steers a boat : a petty officer in charge of a boat and crew.—Often **cox.**
[M.E. *cogge,* ship and **swain.**]

coy, *koy, adj.* coquettishly bashful.
coy′ly, *adv.* **coy′ness,** *n.*
[L. *quiētus,* quiet.]

coyote, *kō-yō′tā,* (*Amer.*) *kī-ōt′e, kī′ōt, n.* a small wolf (*prairie wolf*) of N. America.
[Mexican *coyotl.*]

coypu, *koi′pōō, n.* a large S. American furred water animal which has established itself in East Anglia.

cozy. Same as **cosy.**

crab[1], *krab, n.* a sea animal with shell and five pairs of legs, the first pair bearing claws.
to catch a crab, in rowing, to fail to dip the oar correctly and thus lose balance.
[O.E. *crabba*; conn. Ger. *krebs.*]

crab[2], *krab, n.* wild bitter apple : a sour-tempered person.—Also **crab apple.**
[Origin uncertain.]

crabbed, *krab′id, adj.* ill-natured : (of handwriting) badly-formed, cramped.
[**grab** (1); also partly **crab** (2).]

crack, *krak, v.i.* and *v.t.* to make, or cause to make, a sudden sharp sound : to break open (e.g. a nut) : to break partly, but not into pieces : (*v.t.*) to break a compound (e.g. petroleum) into simpler compounds : to make (a joke).—*n.* a sudden sharp splitting sound : a chink : a flaw : a blow : (*U.S.*) a biting comment : an expert.—*adj.* (coll.) very good (e.g. *a crack shot*).
cracked, *adj.* damaged : crazy.
crack′er, *n.* a thin crisp biscuit : a small firework, esp. one exploding when pulled apart.
to crack up, to praise : to fail suddenly, to go to pieces.
[O.E. *cracian.*]

crackle, *krak′l, v.i.* to give out slight but frequent cracks.—Also *n.*
crack′ling, *n.* the rind of roast pork.
crack′ly, *adj.* brittle. [**crack.**]

cradle, *krā′dl, n.* a bed in which a child is rocked : infancy : a frame of various kinds, e.g. one under a ship that is being built or repaired.—*v.t.* to lay as if in a cradle.
[O.E. *cradol.*]

craft, *krâft, n.* cunning : skill : an art, skilled trade : (as *pl.*) boats, ships : a (small) ship.
craft′y, *adj.* cunning.
craft′ily, *adv.* cunningly, secretly.
craft′iness, *n.*
crafts′man, *n.* one skilled at making something.
crafts′manship, *n.* skill in making.
[O.E. *cræft.*]

crag, *krag, n.* a rough steep rock.
cragg′ed, cragg′y, *adjs.* [Celt.]

cram, *kram, v.t.* to stuff, fill very full.—*v.i.* to eat greedily : to stuff the memory with facts for an examination (also *v.t.*).
[O.E. *crammian.*]

cramp, *kramp, n.* a painful contraction of the muscles : a tool with a movable part which can be screwed tight so as to press things together.—*v.t.* to put where there is not enough space : to restrict, hamper (e.g. *Lack of money cramped our efforts*) : to fasten with a cramp-iron.

cramp′(-ī′ron), *n.* a piece of metal bent at both ends for binding things together.
cramp′on, *n.* a grappling-iron : an iron plate with spikes, fot the foot, for hill-climbing, pole-climbing, etc.
[O.Fr. *crampe*; conn. with Ger. *krampf.*]

cran, *kran, n.* a measure of quantity of herrings just landed, containing about 1000 on an average.
[Prob. Gael. *crann,* a measure.]

cranberry, *kran′bėr-i, n.* the red acid berry of a small evergreen shrub : the shrub.
[By way of U.S.—Ger. for 'crane berry'.]

crane, *krān, n.* a large wading bird, with long legs, neck, and bill : machine for raising heavy weights.—*v.t.* or *v.i.* to stretch out (the neck).

crane′-fly, *n.* a fly with very long legs, the daddy-longlegs.
cranes′bill, crane's′-bill, *n.* a wild geranium.
[O.E. *cran.*]

cranium, *krā′ni-ŭm, n.* the skull : the bones enclosing the brain.
crā′nial, *adj.* of the cranium.
[Late Latin *crānium.*]

crank, *krangk,* a device for passing on motion, esp. for changing motion to and fro into motion round and round : an odd notion : a person with odd notions : an ill-tempered person.—*v.t.* to set going by turning a crank.
crank′y, *adj.* shaky : full of odd notions : cross.
crank′iness, *n.*
[O.E. *cranc.*]

cranny, *kran′i, n.* a chink, small narrow opening (e.g. in a wall) : hole :—*pl.* **-ies.**
[Fr. *cran,* a notch.]

crape, *krāp, n.* a thin silk fabric with wrinkled surface, usu. dyed black. [Same root as **crêpe.**]

crash[1], *krash, n.* a noise as of things breaking or falling on something hard: a collision: a serious business or other failure.—*v.i.* to fall to pieces with a loud noise: to be violently driven (against, into): to land in such a way as to be damaged or destroyed.—Also *v.t.*
crash′-dive′, *v.i.* of a submarine, to dive very fast.—Also *v.t.*
crash helmet, a cushioned safety head-dress worn by racing-motorists, motor cyclists, and airmen.
crash′-land′, *v.i.* of an aircraft, to make a landing with the undercarriage up.—Also *v.t.* [From the sound.]

crash[2], *krash, n.* a coarse strong linen. [Perh. from Russ.]

crass, *kras, adj.* thick: coarse: stupid. [L. *crassus,* fat.]

crate, *krāt, n.* an openwork container, now usu. made of wooden slats, for packing crockery, carrying fruit, etc. [L. *crātis,* a hurdle.]

crater, *krā′tėr, n.* the bowl-shaped mouth of a volcano: a hole made in the ground by the explosion of a shell, bomb, etc. [Gk. *kratēr,* a bowl for mixing wine.]

cravat, *krȧ-vat′, n.* a kind of scarf or necktie worn by men. [From the *Cravates* or Croat(ian)s.]

crave, *krāv, v.t.* to beg earnestly for: to long for: to require.
crav′ing, *n.* desire, longing. [O.E. *crafian.*]

craven, *krāv′n, n.* a coward.—*adj.* cowardly, spiritless. [Origin uncertain.]

craw, *krö, n.* the crop or first stomach of fowls. [M.E. *crawe*; conn. Du. *kraag,* neck.]

crawfish. See **crayfish.**

crawl, *kröl, v.i.* to move as a worm does: to behave in a much too humble manner: to move very slowly: to be covered with crawling things.—*n.* a slow pace: an alternate overhand swimming stroke. [From Scand.]

crayfish, *krā′fish,* **crawfish,** *krö′fish, n.* a freshwater shellfish: the small spiny lobster. [M.E. *crevice*; conn. with **crab.**]

crayon, *krā′on, n.* a coloured pencil of chalk or pipeclay, for drawing: a drawing in crayons. [Fr. from L. *crēta,* chalk.]

craze, *krāz, v.t.* to make (a person) mad.—*n.* a foolish enthusiasm, fashion, hobby.
craz′y, *adj.* frail: mad: made of irregular pieces (as a quilt or pavement).
craz′ily, *adv.* **craz′iness,** *n.* [From Scand.]

creak, *krēk, v.i.* to make a sharp, grating sound, as of a hinge.—Also *n.*
creak′y, *adj.* **creak′iness,** *n.* [Imit.]

cream, *krēm, n.* the oily substance that forms on milk: the best part of anything: any cream-like preparation or refreshment (e.g. *cold cream, ice cream*).—*v.t.* to take the cream off: to make cream-like.—*v.i.* to form cream.
cream′ery, *n.* a place where butter and cheese are made:—*pl.* **-ies.**
cream′y, *adj.* full of or like cream.
cream′iness, *n.*
cream of tartar, purified tartar from wines, an ingredient in baking powders. [L. *chrisma.*]

crease, *krēs, n.* a mark made by folding or doubling anything: (*cricket*) a line showing the position of batsman or bowler.—*v.t.* to make creases in.—*v.i.* to become creased. [Origin uncertain.]

create, *krē-āt′, v.t.* to bring into being: to give rise to: to give a rank, etc. to (e.g. *to create a man a peer*).
creā′tion, *n.* the act of creating: something created: the universe.
creā′tive, *adj.* able to create.
creā′tor, *n.*
creature, *krē′chur, n.* something that has been created, esp. an animal: a human being: a person ruled by the will of another.
the Creator, God. [L. *creāre, -ātum.*]

crèche, *kresh, n.* a public nursery for children. [Fr.]

credence, *krē′dėns, n.* belief.
credentials, *krė-den′shlz, n. pl.* evidence, esp. written evidence, of trustworthiness or authority.
credible (*kred′-*), *adj.* that may be believed.
credibil′ity, cred′ibleness, *ns.*
cred′ibly, *adv.*
cred′it, *n.* belief: good reputation: sale on trust: time allowed for payment: the side of an account on which payments received are entered.—*v.t.* to believe: to enter on the credit side of an account: to think (a person) has (e.g. *I do not credit him with much sense*).
cred′itable, *adj.* bringing honour.
cred′itor, *n.* one to whom a debt is owed.
cred′ulous, *adj.* believing too easily.
cred′ulousness, credu′lity, *ns.*
to be a credit to, to bring honour to.
to give credit to, to believe (a story): to admit that (a person) has earned praise (for some action). [L. *crēdĕre,* to believe.]

creed, *krēd, n.* a summary of one's religious, or other, beliefs. [L. *crēdo,* I believe; root as **credence.**]

creek, *krēk, n.* a small inlet or bay, or the tidal estuary of a river: in America and Australia, a small river. [Prob. Scand.; conn. Du. *kreek,* bay.]

creel, *krēl, n.* a basket, esp. for fish. [Prob. Celt.]

creep, *krēp, v.i.* to move on or near the

ground: to move slowly or stealthily: to grow along the ground or on supports, as a vine: to fawn or cringe: to shudder: —*pa.t.* and *pa.p.* **crept.**—*n.* a crawl: (in *pl.*) horrible shrinking.
creep'er, *n.* a creeping plant.
creep'y, *adj.* causing creeps, weird.
creep'ily, *adv.* **creep'iness,** *n.*
[O.E. *crēopan*; conn. Du. *kruipen.*]

cremation, *krem-ā'sh(o)n, n.* act of burning, esp. of the dead.
cremate', *v.t.*
crematōr'ium, *n.* a place where cremation is done.
[L. *cremāre*, to burn.]

creosote, *krē'ō-sōt,* **creasote,** *krē'ā-sōt, n.* an oily liquid obtained from wood tar.—*v.t.* to treat with creosote as preservative.
[Gk. *kreas*, flesh, *sōtēr*, saviour.]

crêpe, *krāp, n.* a crape-like fabric: rubber rolled in thin crinkly sheets.
crêpe-de-chine (*dė shēn*), *n.* a crape-like fabric, originally of silk.
[Fr.—L. *crispus*, crisp.]

crepitation, *krep-i-tā'sh(o)n, n.* a sound that can be heard in the lungs in certain diseases.
[L. *crepitāre*, to creak, rustle.]

crept. See **creep.**

crescendo, *kresh-en'dō, adv.* gradually increasing in force or loudness.—Also *n.*
[It.]

crescent, *kres'ėnt, adj.* shaped like the new or old moon.—*n.* something of this shape, e.g. a curved row of houses.
[L. *crescĕre*, to grow.]

cress, *kres, n.* a plant with sharp-tasting leaves used in salads.
(O.E. *cresse, cerse.*]

crest, *krest, n.* the comb or tuft on the head of a cock or other bird: the summit, highest part (e.g. of a hill, a wave): a plume of feathers on top of a helmet: a badge or emblem.
crest'fallen, *adj.* dejected, very much disappointed.
[O.Fr. *creste*—L. *crista.*]

cretin, *kre'tin,* or *krē', n.* a person suffering from cretinism.
cre'tinism, *n.* a disease caused by the fact that the thyroid gland does not work properly, one symptom being mental deficiency.
[Fr. *crétin*—L. *christianus*, Christian.]

cretonne, *kret-on',* or *kret', n.* a strong printed cotton fabric used for curtains or for covering furniture. [Fr.]

crevasse, *krė-vas', n.* a crack or split, esp. a cleft in a glacier.
crevice (*krev'is*), *n.* a crack: a narrow opening.
[L. *crepāre*, to crack.]

crew[1], *krōō, n.* a company, a gang, mob: a ship's company: the group of people in charge of an aeroplane in flight or a travelling bus, train, etc.
[O.Fr. *creue*, increase—*croistre*, to grow.]

crew[2]. See **crow.**

crib, *krib, n.* a manger: a stall for oxen; a child's bed: (*coll.*) a key or literal translation used by schoolboys.—*v.t.* to steal or copy (another's work):—*pr.p.* **cribb'ing**; *pa.p.* **cribbed.** [O.E.]

crick, *krik, n.* a cramp of the muscles, esp. of the neck. [Prob. imit.]

cricket[1], *krik'it, n.* an insect related to the grasshopper, the male of which makes a chirping noise with his wing-covers.
[O.Fr. *criquet*; conn. Ger. *kreckel.*]

cricket[2], *krik'it, n.* an outdoor game played with bats, a ball, and wickets, between two sides of eleven each: (*coll.*) fair play.
crick'eter, *n.*
[Fr. *criquet.*]

cried, crier. See **cry.**

crime, *krīm, n.* act(s) punishable by law: an offence, sin.
criminal (*krim'-*), *adj.* concerned with crime (e.g. *criminal law, a criminal lawyer*): guilty of crime: of the nature of crime.—*n.* one guilty of crime.
criminal'ity, *n.* **crim'inally,** *adv.*
criminol'ogy, *n.* the study of crime and criminals.
criminol'ogist, *n.*
[L. *crīmen, -inis.*]

crimp, *krimp, v.t.* to press into folds or pleats: to give a corrugated appearance to: to make crisp.
[O.E. *gecrympan*, to curl.]

crimson, *krim'zn, n.* a deep red colour, tinged with blue.—Also *adj.*
[Arabic *qirmiz*, kermes, the insect from which the dye was first made.]

cringe, *krinj, v.i.* to crouch with fear: to behave too humbly.
[Conn. with O.E. *cringan*, to shrink.]

crinkle, *kring'kl, v.t.* to wrinkle, crimp.—*v.i.* to wrinkle up.—*n.* a wrinkle.
crink'ly *adj.* wrinkly.
[Same root as **cringe.**]

crinoline, *krin'o-lin, n.* a stiff fabric of horsehair and flax, used to make skirts stick out: a petticoat or skirt on hoops of steel wire.
[L. *crīnis*, hair, *līnum*, flax.]

cripple *krip'l, n.* a lame or disabled person. —Also *adj.*—*v.t.* to lame: to deprive of power or strength.
[O.E. *crypel*; conn. with **creep.**]

crisis, *krī'sis, n.* the time of greatest importance or danger: the turning-point (of a disease):—*pl.* **crises** (*krī'sēz*), or (*coll.*) **cri'sises.**
See also **critical.**
[Gk. *krīsis;* same root as **criterion.**]

crisp, *krisp, adj.* (of hair) curling: having a wavy surface: dry and brittle: (of air) bracing: (of e.g. style) firm, decided.—*v.t.* to make crisp.
crisp'ly, *adv.* **crisp'ness,** *n.*
crisp'y, *adj.* **crisp'iness,** *n.*
[L. *crispus.*]

crisscross, *kris'kros, n.* a mark formed by

two lines in the form of a cross: a network of crossing lines.—Also *adj.*, *adv.*, *v.t.* and *v.i.*
[**Christ('s) cross.**]

criterion, *krī-tē'ri-on, n.* standard used, referred to, in judging:—*pl.* **critē'ria.**
critic, *krit'ik, n.* one who judges literary or artistic work: a fault-finder.
crit'ical, *adj.* of criticism: judging good and bad points: fault-finding: of a crisis: of great(est) importance (e.g. *Help arrived at the critical moment*): dangerous (e.g. *a critical shortage of food*).
crit'ically, *adv.*
crit'icise, *v.t.* to give an opinion of, or judgment on (something): to find fault with.
crit'icism, *n.*
[Gk. *kritērion*, *kritikos*—*krīnein*, to judge.]

croak, *krōk, v.i.* to utter a low hoarse sound, as a frog or raven: to grumble: to foretell evil: (*slang*) to die—Also *n.*
croak'er, *n.* [From the sound.]

crochet, *krō'shā, n.* fancy knitting done with a small hook.—Also *v.i.* and *v.t.*
[Fr. *croc*, a hook.]

crock[1], *krok, n.* a pot or jar.
crock'ery, *n.* earthenware and china vessels.
[O.E. *croc.*]

crock[2], *krok, n.* an old horse: a broken-down or useless person.
to crock up, (*coll.*) to break down in health. [Perh. **crack.**]

crocodile, *krok'o-dīl, n.* a large reptile found in the rivers of Asia, Africa, South America, and northern Australia: a double file of schoolgirls.
crocodile tears, sham tears, hypocritical grief.
[Gk. *krokodeilos*, lizard.]

crocus, *krō'kus, n.* a plant with brilliant yellow, purple, or white flowers, growing from a corm.
[L. *crocus*—Gk. *krokos.*]

croft, *kroft, n.* a small piece of enclosed land esp. for growing crops: a small farm.
croft'er, *n.* [O.E.]

cromlech, *krom'lek, n.* a circle of upright stones.
[W. *crom*, curved, *llech*, a stone.]

crone, *krōn, n.* a withered old woman.
[Origin uncertain.]

crony, *krōn'i, n.* a close companion:—*pl.* **crōn'ies.** [Origin unknown.]

crook, *krook, n.* a bend: a staff bent at the end, as a shepherd's or bishop's: a swindler.—*v.t.* and *v.i.* to bend into a hook.
crook'ed (*-id*), *adj.* not straight: dishonest: (*krookt*) bent like a crook.
crook'edly, *adv.* **crook'edness,** *n.*
[From Scand.]

croon, *kroon, v.t.* and *v.i.* to sing or hum in an undertone: to sing quietly in a very sentimental manner.—Also *n.*
croon'er, *n.* [Orig. chiefly Scot.]

crop, *krop, n.* the top of anything: a hunting whip: mode of cutting hair short: total growth or quantity harvested: the craw of a bird.—*v.t.* to cut off the top or ends: to cut short: to raise crops on:—*pr.p.* **cropp'ing**; *pa.p.* **cropped.**
crop'-eared, *adj.* having ears cropped, or hair cropped to show the ears.
to crop out, to appear above the surface.
to crop up, to come up unexpectedly.
[O.E., top shoot of plant, crop of bird.]

cropper, *krop'ėr, n.* a fall: a failure.
to come a cropper, to have a fall.
[Perh. from *neck and crop* (see **neck**).]

croquet, *krō'kā, n.* game in which wooden balls are driven by mallets through series of arches set in the ground.
[Fr.; same root as **crochet.**]

croquette, *krok-et', n.* a fried ball or cake of minced meat or fish.
[Fr. *croquer*, to crunch.]

crosier, crozier, *krō'zhyėr, n.* the staff of a bishop or abbot.
[Late Latin *crocia*, a crook.]

cross, *kros, n.* a gibbet, consisting of two beams, one placed across the other: (the symbol of) the Christian religion: the sufferings of Christ: any lasting cause of suffering or unhappiness: a hybrid (e.g. *a cross between a bulldog and a terrier*): a monument in a street, often a cross, where proclamations are made, etc.—*v.t.* to make the sign of the cross over: (to cause) to pass from one side to the other of: to thwart, oppose the wishes of (a person): to breed from (two different species of an animal or plant).—*v.i.* to lie or pass across: to meet and pass.—*adj.* lying across: ill-tempered: hybrid.
cross'ing, *n.* act of going across, or of opposing the wishes of another, etc.: the place where a roadway, etc., may be crossed.
cross'ly, *adv.* in an ill-tempered way.
cross'-benches, *n.pl.* seats in Parliament for members who do not wish to vote either on the Government side or on the Opposition.
cross'bones, *n.pl.* two thigh bones laid across each other—forming, with the skull, an emblem of death or piracy.
cross'bow, *n.* a bow placed crosswise on a *stock* or wooden bar, with devices for pulling back the string and shooting the arrow.
cross'breed, *n.* a breed produced by the crossing of different breeds.
cross'bred, *adj.*
cross'-coun'try, *adj.* across a country: across fields, etc., not on roads.
cross'-exam'ine, *v.t.* to test the evidence of (a witness on the other side) by questioning him: to question searchingly.
cross'-examinā'tion, *n.*
cross'-eyed, *adj.* having a squint.

cross'-fire', *n.* lines of gunfire from two, or more, points crossing each other.
cross'-grained', *adj.* (of wood) with irregular grain: ill-natured and unwilling to do what other people want.
cross'patch, *n.* an ill-natured person.
cross'piece, *n.* a piece lying across something else.
cross'-pur'pose, *n.* an opposing purpose or plan (**to be at cross-purposes,** to misunderstand each other, to be unconsciously talking of different things, working on different plans, etc.)
cross'-ques'tion, *v.t.* to cross-examine.
cross'-ref'erence, *n.* a reference from one part of a book to another (e.g. *crawfish. See crayfish*).
cross'road, *n.* a road crossing the principal road: (in *pl.*) the place of crossing of two roads: a point where an important choice of action has to be made.
cross'-sec'tion, *n.* a section made by cutting across (e.g. across a pipe at right angles to the length): a sample showing all the important parts (e.g. *A cross-section of British opinion on a subject would show what people of different social classes, doing different kinds of work, thought about it*).
cross'wise, *adv.* across.
crossword (puzzle), a word-puzzle in which a square is to be filled with words reading across and down found from clues.
crossed cheque, a cheque with two lines drawn across it to show that it may be paid only to a bank account.
to cross out, to draw a line through.
on the cross, diagonally.
[O.E. *cros*; through O. Norse—L. *crux.*]

crotchet, *kroch'it, n.* a note in music, equal to half a minim, ♩: a queer notion or opinion, an odd habit.
crotch'ety, *adj.* having crotchets, cranky: ill-tempered.
[Fr. *crochet,* a small hook.]

crouch, *krowch, v.i.* to bend down or lie close to the ground: to cringe.
[M.E. *cr(o)uchen.*]

croup, *kro͞op, n.* the rump of a horse.
[Fr. *croupe.*]

croupier, *kro͞o'pi-ėr, n.* one who sits at the lower end of the table as assistant chairman at a public dinner: one who collects the money at the gaming-table.
[Fr., 'one who rides on the *croup*'.]

crow, *krō, n.* name given to a number of large birds, generally black, including raven, rook, hooded crow, and carrion crow: the cry of a cock: an infant's cry of joy.—*v.i.* to croak: to cry as a cock or happy baby: to boast:—*pa.t.* **crew** (*kro͞o*) or **crowed**; *pa.p.* **crowed.**
crow'bar, *n.* a large iron lever bent at the end like the beak of a crow.
crow's'-foot, *n.* a wrinkle at the outer corner of the eye.
crow's'-nest, *n.* a shelter at the masthead of ship for lookout man: any high lookout.
as the crow flies, in a straight line.
to have a crow to pluck, pick, with, to have a dispute to settle with.
[O.E. *crāwe.*]

crowd, *krowd, n.* a number of persons or things closely pressed together, without order: people in general: (*coll.*) a set of people.—*v.t.* to fill by pressing together: to fill too full: to give too little space to.—*v.i.* to press on: to swarm, throng.
crowd'ed, *adj.*
[O.E. *crūdan,* to press.]

crown, *krown, n.* a circular head-ornament, esp. as a mark of royalty or honour: the sovereign: governing power in a monarchy: the top, e.g. of head, hat, hill: a 5s. piece.—*v.t.* to set a crown on: to reward, finish happily (e.g. *Success crowned her efforts.*)
crown colony, a colony without representative government, governed directly by the home government.
crown land, land belonging to the sovereign.
crown prince, in some countries, the heir to the throne.
[L. *corōna.*]

crozier. Same as **crosier.**

crucial, *kroo'shȧl, adj.* testing: of the greatest importance, decisive (e.g. *This was the crucial test*; *he came at the crucial moment.*)
See also **crux.**
[L. *crux, crucis,* a cross.]

crucible, *kro͞o'si-bl, n.* pot for melting metals, etc.: severe trial.
[Late Latin *crucibulum.*]

crucify, *kro͞o'si-fī, v.t.* to put to death on a cross: to torture:—*pr.p.* **cru'cifying**; *pa.p.* **cru'cified.**
cru'cifix, *n.* a figure or picture of Christ on the cross.
crucifix'ion, *n.* death on the cross, esp. that of Christ.
[L. *crux,* cross, *figĕre,* to fix.]

crude, *kro͞od, adj.* not prepared, unrefined (e.g. *crude oil*): blunt, tactless (e.g. *a crude statement, crude behaviour*).
crude'ness, crud'ity (*pl.* **-ies**), *ns.*
[L. *crūdus,* raw.]

cruel, *kro͞o'ėl, adj.* pleased at causing pain: merciless: very painful (e.g. *cruel sufferings*).
cru'elly, *adv.* **cru'elty** (*pl.* **-ies**), *n.*
[L. *crūdēlis.*]

cruet, *kro͞o'it, n.* a small jar or bottle for sauces, salt, pepper, etc.
cru'et(-stand), *n.* a frame for holding cruets.
[Dim. of O.Fr. *cruye,* a jar.]

cruise, *kro͞oz, v.i.* to sail, fly, or wander to and fro: to go at cruising speed.—*n.* a voyage from place to place for pleasure or in search of enemy ships, etc.
cruis'er, *n.*

cruising speed, (*aircraft*) the speed at which the engine works most efficiently and economically: (*motor car*) the best speed for a long drive.
[Du. *kruisen,* to cross.]

crumb, *krum, n.* a fragment or morsel, esp. of bread.
crumb′y, crumm′y, *adj.*
[O.E. *cruma.*]

crumble, *krum′bl, v.t.* to break into crumbs.—*v.i.* to fall into small pieces: to decay.
crum′bly, *adj.* apt to crumble, brittle.
[Orig. dim. of **crumb.**]

crumpet, *krump′it, n.* a soft cake or muffin.
[M.E. *crompid çake*; orig. uncertain.]

crumple *krump′l, v.t.* to crush into folds or wrinkles: to crease.—*v.i.* to become wrinkled: (usu. **crumple up**) to collapse.
[From *crump,* old word for 'to curl up'.]

crunch, *krunch,* or *-sh, v.t.* to crush with the teeth or underfoot: to chew (anything hard) and so make a noise.—*n.* (*coll.*) the testing moment, real trial of strength. [From the sound.]

crupper, *krup′ėr, n.* a strap of leather fastened to the saddle and passing under the horse's tail to keep the saddle in its place: the hind part of a horse.
[O.Fr. *cropiere—crope,* the croup.]

crusade, *kroo-sād′, n.* (*history*) a military expedition of Christians to win back the Holy Land from the Turks: a continued vigorous effort to help forward a (good) cause.—*v.i.* to take part in a crusade.
crusad′er, *n.*
[Fr. *croisade*—L. *crux,* a cross.]

crush, *krush, v.t.* to break, or crumple: to squeeze together: to overwhelm, subdue (e.g. *to crush one's enemies*).—*v.i.* to push one's way.—*n.* a tightly packed crowd: a drink made of juice of crushed fruit.
crush′-barr′ier, *n.* a barrier put up to keep back a crowd.
[O.Fr. *croissir.*]

crust, *krust, n.* the hard rind or outside coating e.g. of bread, pie: the outer part of the earth, the only part we have so far been able to study closely.—*v.t.* to form a crust on.—*v.i.* to form a crust.
crust′y, *adj.* having a crust: surly, irritable.
crust′ily, *adv.* **crust′iness,** *n.*
[L. *crusta,* rind.]

crutch, *kruch, n.* a staff with a crosspiece at the head to support a lame person: any support or prop.
[O.E. *crycc.*]

crux, *kruks, n.* a difficult point: the essential point (e.g. *That is the crux of the matter, of the problem*).
[Same root as **crucial.**]

cry, *krī, v.i.* to utter a shrill loud sound: to shed tears.—*v.t.* to utter loudly: to announce in public: to offer for sale by crying:—*pa.t., pa.p.* **cried.**—Also *n.*:—*pl.* **cries.**
cri′er, *n.*
cry′ing, *adj.* that cries: demanding to be put right (e.g. *a crying evil*).
a far cry, a great distance.
in full cry, in full pursuit, used of dogs in hunt.
to cry down, to speak slightingly of.
to cry off, to cancel an engagement or agreement.
to cry up, to praise.
[Fr. *crier*—L. *quiritāre,* to scream.]

crypt, *kript, n.* underground cell or chapel.
cryp′tic, *adj.* secret: very difficult to understand (e.g. *a cryptic saying*).
cryp′to-, (as part of word) hidden.
cry′pto, *n.* a secret member of a party.
[Gk. *kryptein,* to conceal.]

crystal, *kris′tl, n.* a clear quartz: (a piece of) a solid material (e.g. salt or ice) whose atoms are arranged in a regular pattern: anything bright or clear: cut glass: a vessel of cut glass: glassware.
crys′tal, crys′talline, *adjs.* consisting of crystal, or like crystal in clearness.
crys′tallīse, *v.t.* and *v.i.* to form into crystals: to cover with a coating of sugar crystals: to make or become definite or clear (e.g. *His thoughts about the matter had not had time to crystallise*).
crystallisā′tion, *n.*
crystal set, a simple wireless receiving apparatus with crystal rectifier.
[Gk. *krystallos,* ice—*kryos,* frost.]

cub, *kub, n.* the young of certain animals, as foxes, etc.: a young boy or girl.—*v.i.* to bring forth young:—*pr.p.* **cubb′ing**; *pa.p.* **cubbed.**
cubb′ing, *n.* hunting young foxes.

cube, *kūb, n.* a solid body having six equal square faces, a solid square: the third power of a quantity (e.g. $8=2\times2\times2=$ the cube of 2).—*v.t.* to raise to the third power.
cū′bic, -al, *adjs.* of a cube: of the third power or degree: solid (e.g. *a cubic inch*).
cub′ism, *n.* an attempt in painting to express the artist's emotions by putting different views of an object into the same picture and using geometrical shapes.
cube root, the number of which a given number is the cube (e.g. 2 is the cube root of 8).
[L. *cubus*—Gk. *kybos,* a die (see **die,** 2).]

cubicle, *kū′bi-kl, n.* a small place partitioned off from a larger room.
[L. *cubāre,* to lie down.]

cubit, *kū′bit, n.* a measure used long ago, equal to the length of the arm from the elbow to the tip of the middle finger (18 to 22 inches).
[L. *cubitum,* elbow.]

cuckoo, *kook′o͞o, n.* a bird that cries 'cuckoo', and that puts its eggs in the nests of other birds.

cucumber, *kū′kum-bėr, n.* a creeping plant, with long fruit used as a salad and pickle.
[L. *cucumis.*]

cud, *kud, n.* food brought from the first stomach of a ruminating animal (e.g. a cow) back into the mouth and chewed again.
[O.E. *cwidu.*]

cuddle, *kud'l, v.t.* to hug, to fondle.—Also *v.i.* and *n.* [Origin unknown.]

cudgel, *kuj'l, n.* a heavy staff, a club.—*v.t.* to beat with a cudgel:—*pr.p.* **cudg'elling**; *pa.p.* **cudg'elled.**
to take up the cudgels for (someone), to defend (him) vigorously.
[O.E. *cycgel.*]

cue[1], *kū, n.* the last words of another actor's speech, or a noise or movement, etc., serving as a sign to an actor to speak, etc.: a hint about how to act or behave (e.g. *In condemning the action the Press took their cue from the Government spokesman*).
[At one time written Q, for L. *quando*, 'when', i.e. when to begin.]

cue[2], *kū, n.* a pigtail: a tapering rod used in playing billiards.
[Another spelling of **queue.**]

cuff[1], *kuf, n.* a blow with the open hand.—Also *v.t.* [Origin unknown.]

cuff[2], *kuf, n.* the end of the sleeve near the wrist: a covering for the wrist.
[Origin uncertain.]

cuirass, *kwi-ras',* or *kū-, n.* a covering, orig. of leather, to defend breast and back.
[Fr. *cuirasse—cuir*, leather.]

cuisine, *kwi-zēn', n.* a kitchen: style of cookery.
[Fr.—L. *coquĕre*, to cook.]

cul-de-sac, *kul'-dė-sak, n.* a street closed at one end.
[Fr. *cul*, bottom, *de*, of, *sac*, sack.]

culinary, *ku'lin-ȧr-i, kū', adj.* of, used in, the kitchen or in cookery.
[L. *culina*, a kitchen.]

cull, *kul, v.t.* to select: to pick, gather.
[Fr. *cueillir*, gather; root as **collect.**]

cullender. Same as **colander.**

culminate, *kul'mi-nāt, v.i.* to reach the highest point: to reach the greatest development (e.g. *The disturbances culminated in a battle with knives*).
culminā'tion, *n.*
[L. *culmen*, a summit.]

culpable, *kul'pȧ-bl, adj.* deserving blame.
culpabil'ity, cul'pableness, *ns.*
cul'pably, *adv.*
[L. *culpa*, a fault.]

culprit, *kul'prit, n.* one who is in fault: a criminal: (*Eng. law*) a prisoner accused but not yet tried.
[*cul* (for *culpable*), *prit* (O.Fr. *prest*), ready (to prove it).]

cult, *kult, n.* a system of religious belief: great devotion to (e.g. *the cult of physical fitness*).
[Same root as **cultivate.**]

cultivate, *kul'ti-vāt, v.t.* to till or prepare (ground) for crops: to grow (a crop): to develop, or improve, by care or study (e.g. *to cultivate good manners*): to encourage (e.g. science, friendship): to seek the company of (a person).
cultivā'tion, *n.* the art or practice of cultivating: cultivated state.
cul'tivator, *n.* an implement for breaking up ground, esp. among crops.
culture, *kul'chůr, n.* cultivation: educated refinement: a type of civilisation (e.g. *Bronze Age culture*).
cul'tural, *adj.*
cul'tured, *adj.* cultivated: well educated, refined.
[L. *colĕre, cultum*, to till, worship.]

culvert, *kul'vėrt, n.* an arched watercourse under a road, etc.
[Perh. from Fr. *couler*, to flow.]

cumber, *kum'bėr, v.t.* to get in the way of: to burden uselessly.
cum'bersome, cum'brous, *adjs.* heavy, unwieldy: burdensome.
[O.Fr. *combrer*—L. *cumulus*, a heap.]

cumulative, *kūm'ū-lāt-iv, adj.* becoming greater by additions (e.g. *Frequent small doses have a cumulative effect*; *cumulative evidence*).
[L. *cumulus*, a heap; root as **cumber.**]

cunning, *kun'ing, adj.* skilful, clever (e.g. *a cunning device for opening the high window*): crafty, sly.—*n.* skill: craftiness, slyness.
[O.E. *cunnan*, to know.]

cup, *kup, n.* a drinking-vessel: the liquid contained in a cup: an ornamental vessel used as a prize.
cupboard, *kub'ȯrd, n.* a place for keeping food, dishes, etc.
cup'ful, as much as fills a cup:—*pl.* **cup'fuls.**
cup'-tie, *n.* one of a series of games in a competition in which the prize is a cup.
[O.E. *cuppe*—L. *cūpa*, a tub.]

Cupid, *kū'pid, n.* the Roman god of love.
cupid'ity, *n.* desire for wealth, greed.
[L. *Cupīdō, -inis—cupĕre*, to desire.]

cupola, *kū'po-la, n.* a rounded vault on the top of a building: a dome, esp. a small one.
[L. *cūpola*, dim. of *cūpa*, a cask.]

cupri-, *kūp-ri-,* **cupro-,** (as part of word) of or containing copper.
cup'ro-nick'el, an alloy of copper and nickel.—Also *adj.*
[L. *cuprum*, copper.]

cur, *kûr, n.* a mongrel dog: a surly, rude, or cowardly person.
[M.E. *curre.*]

curate, *kūr'it, n.* a clergyman in the Church of England assisting a rector or vicar.
[Same root as **cure.**]

curative. See **cure.**

curator, *kū-rā'tȯr, n.* one in charge of something, e.g. (esp. formerly) of a place where things are shown, such as a museum.
[L. *cūrātor.*]

curb, *kûrb, n.* a chain or strap attached to

the bit for holding back a horse: a check or restraint (e.g. *to put a curb on his wild enthusiasm*): a hearth fender (also **kerb**): the edge of a pavement (also **kerb**).—*v.t.* to restrain or check.
curb'stone, *n.* a stone edging a pavement.
[Same root as **curve.**]

curd, *kûrd, n.* milk thickened by acid: the cheese part of milk, as distinguished from the whey.
curd'le, *v.t.* and *v.i.* to turn into curd.
to curdle one's blood, to horrify one.
[Prob. Celt.]

cure, *kūr, n.* action of healing: something that heals or makes well.—*v.t.* to heal: to rid (one of e.g. a bad habit): to preserve, as by drying, salting etc.:—*pr.p.* **cur'ing**; *pa.p.* **cured.**
cur'able, *adj.*
cur'ative, *adj.* intended to, likely to, cure.—*n.* a remedy.
[L. *cūra*, care.]

curfew, *kûr'fū, n.* long ago, the ringing of a bell as a signal to put out fires and lights: an order forbidding people to be in the streets after a certain hour.
[O.Fr. *covre-feu—couvre* (*imper.*) cover, *feu*, fire.]

curio, *kū'ri-ō, n.* a rare and curious article:—*pl.* **cū'rios.** [For **curiosity.**]

curious, *kū'ri-ŭs, adj.* anxious (to find out): inquisitive: strange, odd.
curios'ity, *n.* inquisitiveness: eagerness to find out: something strange and rare:—*pl.* **curios'ities.**
[Fr. *curieux.*]

curl, *kûrl, v.t.* to twist into ringlets, to coil.—*v.i.* to move in curves: to play at the game of curling.—*n.* a ringlet of hair, etc.: a wave, bend, or twist.
curl'ing, *n.* a Scottish game played by hurling heavy smooth stones (**curling-stones**) over ice towards a mark.
curl'y, *adj.*:—*comp.* **curl'ier**; *superl.* **curl'iest.**
curl'iness, *n.*
[M.E. *crull.*]

curlew, *kûr'lū,* or *-lōō*, a moorland bird with long curved bill, long legs, and a plaintive cry.
[O.Fr. *corlieu.*]

currant, *kur'ânt, n.* a small black raisin or dried seedless grape: the fruit of several shrubs. [From *Corinth.*]

currency. See **current.**

current, *kur'ênt, adj.* passing from person to person (e.g. *This story is current*): present (e.g. *the current month*).—*n.* stream of water or air: a flow of electricity: course (*the current of events*).
curr'ently, *adv.*
curr'ency, *n.* fact, time, of being current: money of a country (*pl.* **-ies**).
[L. *currĕre*, to run.]

curriculum, *kur-ik'ū-lŭm, n.* a course, esp. of study at school or university.
[Same root as **current.**]

curry[1], *kur'i, n.* a seasoning of turmeric and mixed spices: a stew flavoured with it.—*v.t.* to cook with curry:—*pr.p.* **curr'ying**; *pa.p.* **curr'ied.**
[From Indian word *kari*, sauce.]

curry[2], *kur'i, v.t.* to dress (leather): to rub down and dress (a horse):—*pr.p.* **curr'ying**; *pa.p.* **curr'ied.**
curr'ier, *n.*
to curry favour, to seek favour by flattery.
[O.Fr. *correier.*]

curse, *kûrs, v.t.* to wish that evil may fall upon (someone): to vex or torment.—*v.i.* to swear.—Also *n.*
cursed, *kûrst, adj.* under a curse: (*kûr'-sid*) hateful.
[O.E. *cursian.*]

cursive, *kûr'siv, adj.* (of handwriting) flowing, with letters joined.
cursory, *kûr'sôr-i, adj.* running quickly over, hasty (e.g. *He gave it a cursory glance.*)
cur'sorily, *adv.*
[L. *currĕre, cursum*, to run.]

curt, *kûrt, adj.* rudely brief (e.g. *a curt refusal*).
curt'ly, *adv.* **curt'ness,** *n.*
[L. *curtus*, shortened.]

curtail, *kûr-tāl', v.t.* to cut short: to make less (e.g. powers, privileges):—*pr.p.* **curtail'ing**; *pa.p.* **curtailed'.**
curtail'ment, *n.*
[Old spelling *curtal*—L. *curtus*, short.]

curtain, *kûr't(i)n, n.* the hanging drapery at a window, around a bed, etc.—*v.t.* to enclose, or furnish, with curtains.
[Late Latin *cortina.*]

curtsy, curtsey, *kûrt'si, n.* a bow made by women by bending the knees.—*v.i.* to make a curtsy. [**courtesy.**]

curve, *kûrv, n.* a bend: a line that (is not straight yet) includes no angles.—*v.t.* to bend into a curve.—*v.i.* to bend or move in a curve.
cur'vature (*-vȧ-chûr*), *n.* curving (e.g. *curvature of the spine*).
[L. *curvus*, crooked, bent.]

cushion, *koosh'ôn, n.* a case filled with soft stuff, for resting on.
[L. *coxinum—coxa*, hip.]

cushy, *koosh'i, adj.* easy and comfortable (e.g. *a cushy job*).
[Indian word *khushi*, pleasure.]

cuspidor, *kus'pi-dör, n.* (*U.S.*) spittoon.
[L. *conspuĕre*, to spit upon.]

cuss, *kus, n.* (*slang*) a curse: a fellow.
cuss'ed, *adj.* cursed: obstinate.
cuss'edness, *n.* determination not to do what one wants to be done (e.g. *the cussedness of Fate*). [**curse.**]

custard, *kus'tȧrd, n.* milk, eggs, etc. cooked together.
[Earlier *crustade*, a kind of pie.]

custody, *kus'tô-di, n.* care, keeping (e.g. *in the custody of her mother*): imprisonment (e.g. *The accused is in custody*).

custō'dian, *n.* one who keeps, guards, takes care of, something.
[L. *custōs, custōdis,* a keeper.]

custom, *kus'tȯm, n.* what one is in the habit of doing: common usage: regular trade or business: (in *pl.*) duties on imports and exports.
cus'tomary, *adj.* usual, habitual.
cus'tomarily, *adv.*
cus'tomer, *n.* a person who buys from one: (*slang*) a person.
cus'tom-built', -made', *adjs.* made to order.
custom house, the place where duties on exports and imports are collected.
customs union, states united as a single area for purposes of customs duties.
to go through the customs, to have one's luggage passed by the customs authorities.
[O.Fr. *custume*—L. *consuētūdō,* custom.]

cut, *kut, v.t.* to make a slit in: to cleave or pass through: to fell, hew, mow, trim: to make by cutting: to wound or hurt: to shorten (e.g. a writing): to divide (a pack of cards), or to draw (a card) from the pack: to refuse to recognise (an acquaintance): to reduce (e.g. a price): to intersect (a line): to stay away from (e.g. *to cut a class*): to strike (a ball) obliquely to the off side by a sharp movement: to make (a ball) spin.—*v.i.* to make a cut: to intersect: to move quickly (through): (*slang*) to run away: (in motion pictures) to cease photographing:—*pr.p.* **cutt'ing**; *pa.t.* and *pa.p.* **cut.**—Also *n.*
cutt'er, *n.* the person or thing that cuts: a small swift vessel.
cutt'ing, *n.* a piece cut off a plant for planting to grow a new plant: a passage cut from a newspaper: a passage cut (e.g. through rock, for a road or railway).
cut'-and-dried', *adj.* (e.g. of opinions) ready made: arranged very exactly beforehand (e.g. *His plans were cut-and-dried*).
cut'-back, *n.* a return in the course of a story to something that happened earlier.
cut glass. See **glass.**
cut'throat, *n.* an assassin.
short cut, a short way.
to be cut out, up. See **to cut out, up.**
to cut corners, to round corners in the quickest (but dangerous) way: to do a job in the quickest way.
to cut dead, to ignore the presence of (someone).
to cut down, to take down by cutting: to reduce (e.g. *to cut down expenses*).
to cut in, to say, interrupting a speaker: to intrude: having left a line of traffic, to break into it again farther forward.
to cut off, to destroy: to get between (a person, etc.) and a point he wishes. to reach: to stop (e.g. *to cut off supplies*).
to cut off with a shilling, to disinherit
to cut out, to shape by cutting: to get rid of (e.g. *to cut out waste*): to take the place of, supplant (a rival): to disconnect from the source of power: (*v.i.* of an engine) to fail, stop: (**to be cut out**) to be suited to be (with *for, to be*—e.g. *He was not cut out for a parson*).
to cut the teeth, (of a baby) to have the teeth grow through the gums.
to cut up, to carve: to criticise severely: (**to be cut up**) to be distressed.
to cut up rough, to make a fuss, show annoyance. [Origin unknown.]

cute, *kūt, adj.* knowing, shrewd, cunning: (*U.S.*) quaintly pleasing. [**acute.**]

cuticle, *kū'ti-kl, n.* the outermost or thin skin.
[L. *cutis,* the skin.]

cutlass, *kut'lȧs, n.* a short, broad sword, with one cutting edge.
cutler, *kut'lėr, n.* one who makes or sells knives.
cut'lery, *n.* knives, forks, spoons.
[L. *culter,* knife.]

cutlet, *kut'lit, n.* a small slice of meat (mutton, veal, pork) with rib or other bone attached, fried or broiled: other food made up in similar shape.
[Fr. *côtelette*—L. *costa,* a rib.]

cuttle(fish), *kut'l, n.* a ten-armed sea creature able to give out a black, inky liquid when attacked.
[O.E. *cudele.*]

cyanogen, *sī-an'ȯ-jen, n.* a gas, compound of carbon and nitrogen.
cy'anide, *n.* a compound of cyanogen with a metal or metals (the cyanides are poisonous).
[Gk. *kyanos,* blue.]

cyclamen, *sik'lȧ-mėn, n.* a plant of the primrose family, with nodding flowers and petals bent back.
[Gk. *kyklaminos.*]

cycle, *sī'kl, n.* a period of time in which events happen in a certain order, and which constantly repeats itself (e.g. *the cycle of the seasons*): any series of events that repeats itself constantly: a series of poems, songs, etc. centring round a person or event: a bicycle.—*v.i.* to ride a bicycle.
cy'clic, *adj.* contained in a circle (e.g. *a cyclic quadrilateral*): of, in, cycles.
cy'clist, *n.* a person who rides a bicycle.
cycles (per second), (radio, etc.) a measure of wave frequency, the number of complete series of variations that occur in one second.
[Gk. *kyklos,* a circle.]

cyclone, *sī'klōn, n.* a system of winds blowing round a centre of low pressure: (*loosely*) a wind storm.
[Same root as **cycle.**]

cyclop(a)edia. Same as **encyclopaedia.**

cyclostyle, *sī'klō-stīl, n.* an apparatus for making copies of a writing.
[Gk. *kyklos,* circle, and **style.**]

cygnet, *sig'nit*, *n.* a young swan.
[Dim. of L. *cygnus*, a swan.]

cylinder, *sil'in-dėr*, *n.* a roller-shaped object: applied to many parts of machinery of this shape, solid or hollow.
cylin'drical, *adj.* cylinder-shaped.
cylinder head, the closed end of the cylinder of an internal-combustion engine.
[Gk. *kylindein*, to roll.]

cymbal, *sim'bȧl*, *n.* a hollow brass, plate-like, musical instrument, beaten together with another.
[Gk. *kymbalon—kymbē*, a cup.]

cynical, *sin'ik-ȧl*, *adj.* unwilling to recognise goodness.
cyn'ically, *adv.*

cyn'ic, *n.* one who takes a low view of human nature.
cynicism, *sin'i-sizm*, *n.* a cynical attitude: a cynical remark.
[Gk. *kynikos*, dog-like (surly, snarling).]

cypress, *sī'pres*, *n.* an evergreen tree whose branches used to be carried at funerals.
[L. *cupressus*—Gk. *kyparissos*.]

cyst, *sist*, *n.* a bladder or bag-like structure formed in the body.
[Gk. *kystis*, a bladder.]

czar, czarina. Same as **tsar, tsarina.**

Czech, *chek*, *n.* a member of a westerly branch of the Slavs: the language of the Czechs.
Czecho-Slovak, *n.* a native or citizen of Czechoslovakia.—Also *adj.*

D

dab[1], *dab*, *v.t.* to strike gently with something soft or moist: to peck:—*pr.p.* **dabb'ing**; *pa.p.* **dabbed.**—*n.* a gentle blow: a small lump of anything soft or moist: a small flounder (fish).
[Origin uncertain.]

dab[2], *dab*, *n.* an expert person.
[Prob. from **adept.**]

dabble, *dab'l*, *v.i.* to play in water with hands or feet: to do anything in a trifling way.
dabb'ler, *n.* [**dab** (1).]

dachshund, *daks'hoond*, *däks'hoont*, *n.* a type of small dog with very short legs.
[Ger. *dachs*, badger, *hund*, dog.]

dacoit, dakoit, *dȧ-koit'*, *n.* in India and Burma, one of a band of robbers.
[Hindustani.]

dad, *dad*, **daddy,** *dad'i*, *n.* father:—*pls.* **dads, dadd'ies.**
daddy-long'legs, *n.* the crane-fly.
[Origin uncertain.]

dado, *dā'dō*, *n.* the lower part of a room wall when decorated in a different way from the rest:—*pl.* **da'do(e)s.** [It.]

daffodil, *daf'ō-dil*, *n.* a yellow-flowered narcissus.
[Gk. *asphodelos*.]

daft, *dâft*, *adj.* silly: reckless.
[Same root as **deft.**]

dagger, *dag'ėr*, *n.* a short sword for stabbing: a mark of reference (†).
at daggers drawn, ready to fly at each other and fight. [M.E.]

dago, *dā'gō*, *n.* (not polite) a man of Spanish, Portuguese, or Italian origin.
[Prob. Sp. *Diego*, James.]

daguerreotype, *dä-ger'ō-tīp*, *n.* an early photograph taken on a silver, or silvered copper, plate.
[Louis *Daguerre*, the inventor.]

dahlia, *dāl'yä*, (*U.S.*) *däl'yä*, *n.* a garden plant with large flowers.
[From *Dahl*, a Swedish botanist.]

Dail, *doil*, *n.* the lower house of the legislature of the Republic of Ireland.
[Irish, assembly.]

dailies, daily. See **day.**

dainty, *dān'ti*, *adj.* pleasant to the taste: small or fragile and pretty or charming.—*n.* something choice to eat:—*pl.* **-ties.**
dain'tily, *adv.* **dain'tiness,** *n.*
[From L. *dignitās*, worthiness.]

dairy, *dā'ri*, *n.* the place where milk is kept, and butter and cheese are made: a shop supplying milk:—*pl.* **dai'ries.**
dai'ry-farm, *n.*
dai'rymaid, *n.* **dai'ryman,** *n.*
[O.E. *dǣge*, dairymaid.]

dais, *dā'is*, *dās*, *n.* a raised floor at the end of a hall.
[Through O.Fr.—Gk. *diskos*, a disk.]

daisy, *dā'zi*, *n.* a plant having heads with white or pink rays and a yellow disk (see **composite**):—*pl.* **dai'sies.**
[O.E. *dæges ēage*, day's eye.]

dakoit. See **dacoit.**

dale, *dāl*, *n.* low ground between hills.
dales'man, *n.* a man of the dales of the Lake District. [O.E. *dæl*.]

dally, *dal'i*, *v.i.* to idle: to play (with):—*pr.p.* **dall'ying**; *pa.p.* **dall'ied** (*dal'id*).
dall'iance, *n.*
[O.Fr. *dalier*, to chat.]

Dalmatian, *dal-mā'sh(ȧ)n*, *n.* a spotted dog.
[Conn., prob. wrongly, with *Dalmatia*.]

dam[1], *dam*, *n.* an embankment to hold back water: the body of water thus held in check.—*v.t.* to hold back by means of a dam: (with *up* or *back*) to control (emotion, tears):—*pr.p.* **damm'ing**; *pa.p.* **dammed.**
[M.E.; of Germanic origin.]

dam², *dam, n.* a mother, usu. of animals. [A form of *dame.*]

damage, *dam'ij, n.* injury: loss: the value of what is lost: (*coll.*) cost: (in *pl.*) payment due to one person for loss or injury suffered through fault of another.—*v.t.* to harm.—*v.i.* to suffer injury.
[L. *damnum,* loss.]

damask, *dam'àsk, n.* a material, now usu. of linen, with a woven design.
damask rose, a pink rose.
[*Damascus.*]

dame, *dām, n.* title of a lady of the same rank as a knight: (*slang*) a woman: the comic, vulgar old woman of pantomime (played by a man).
[Fr.—L. *domina,* lady.]

damn, *dam, v.t.* to condemn: to sentence to eternal punishment.—*n.* an oath, a curse.
dam'nable, *adj.* hateful: (*coll.*) annoying.
damnā'tion, *n.* eternal punishment.
damned, *damd, adj.* sentenced to everlasting punishment: hateful.
damning, *dam'ing, adj.* leading to conviction or to ruin (e.g. *damning evidence*).
[L. *damnāre,* to condemn.]

damp, *damp, n.* moist air: in mines, any gas other than air.—*v.t.* to wet slightly: to discourage.—*adj.* moist, moderately wet.
damp'en, *v.t.* and *v.i.* to make or become damp.
damp'er, *n.* a movable plate for controlling the draught, e.g. in a stove: a depressing person, thing, or happening: bread in a flat cake, esp. when baked over a camp fire.
damp'ness, *n.*
[15th cent.; conn. Ger. *dampf,* steam.]

damsel, *dam'zėl, n.* a young woman.
[O.Fr. *dameisele*—same root as **dame.**]

damson, *dam'z(ȯ)n, -son, n.* a small dark-coloured plum.
[*Damascus.*]

dance, *dâns, v.i.* to move in time, usu. to music: to move lightly and gaily: (of eyes) to sparkle.—Also *v.t.*—*n.* a series of steps in time to music: a social gathering at which people dance: a tune to accompany dancing.
dan'cer, *n.* **dan'cing,** *n.* and *adj.*
to dance attendance on (someone), to hang about (someone) ready to carry out his wishes.
to lead one a dance, to cause one needless trouble and difficulty.
[O.Fr. *danser*; prob. Germanic.]

dandelion, *dan'di-li-ȯn, n.* a common plant with leaves with jagged tooth-like edges, and yellow flower.
[Fr. *dent de lion,* lion tooth.]

dander, *dan'dėr, n.* anger (in the phrase, **to get one's dander up**).
[Prob. a form of **dandruff.**]

dandle, *dan'dl, v.t.* to fondle (a baby) in the arms. [Origin unknown.]

dandruff, *dand'rȧf, n.* a scaly scurf on the skin under the hair. [Origin unknown.]

dandy, *dan'di, n.* a person who pays much attention to dress. [Origin unknown.]

Dane, *dān, n.* a native of Denmark.
Danish, *dān'ish, adj.* belonging to Denmark.—*n.* the language of the Danes.
[Dan. *Daner* (pl.).]

danger, *dān'jėr, n.* circumstance(s) that may result in harm or injury: peril: risk.
dan'gerous, *adj.* very unsafe: (of a person) not to be trusted.
[O.Fr. *dangier,* absolute power.]

dangle, *dang'gl, v.i.* to hang loosely: to follow (after someone), to hang (about, around someone).—*v.t.* to hold swaying loosely: to keep before a person's mind (a hope, prize, temptation, etc.). [Scand.]

dank, *dangk, adj.* moist, wet.
[Origin uncertain.]

danseuse, *dong-sėz', n.* a female dancer, esp. a ballet dancer. [Fr.]

dapper, *dap'ėr, adj.* neat, smart: little and active. [Du., brave.]

dapple, *dap'l, adj.* marked with spots.
dapp'le-grey, *adj.* (of horse) of grey colour with darker spots.
[Origin unknown.]

dare, *dār, v.t.* to be bold enough to (e.g. *I dare not go*):—*3rd pers. sing.* **dare(s)**; *pa.t.* **durst, dared.**—*v.t.* to be bold enough (to; e.g. *I dare to contradict*): to take the risk of boldly (e.g. *I dare the steep ascent, your anger*): to challenge (e.g. *I dare you to do it*):—*3rd pers. sing.* **dares**; *pa.t.* **dared.**—*n.* a challenge.
dar'ing, *adj.* bold: courageous.—*n.* boldness.
dare'-dev'il, *n.* a rash, venturesome fellow.—*adj.* reckless.
I dare say, I suppose.
[O.E. *durran.*]

dark, *därk, adj.* without light: gloomy: blackish: difficult to understand: secret (e.g. *to keep something dark*): evil (e.g. *dark deeds*).—Also *n.*
dark'en, *v.t.* and *v.i.* to make, or become dark or darker.
a dark horse, a race horse, or a person, about whom little is known.
the Dark Ages, the period between the late 5th century and the 15th.
to be in the dark about, to know nothing about.
[O.E. *deorc.*]

darling, *där'ling, n.* one dearly loved: a favourite.—Also *adj.*
[O.E. *dēorling*—*dēore,* dear.]

darn, *därn, v.t.* to mend (clothes, etc.) with crossing rows of stitches.—*n.* the place so mended. [Origin unknown.]

dart, *därt, n.* a pointed weapon or toy for throwing with the hand: anything that pierces: (in *pl.*) a game in which darts are thrown at a board (**dart'-board**).—*v.t.* and *v.i.* to send, or to move, with speed. [O.Fr.]

dash, *dash, v.t.* to throw, thrust, violently, esp. so as to break: to ruin (e.g. *This dashed his hopes*): depress (e.g. *Nothing could dash his spirits*).—*v.i.* to rush.—*n.* a rush: a short race: a small quantity (e.g. *whisky and a dash of soda*): a mark (—) at a break in a sentence: liveliness, spirit.
dash'ing, *adj.* spirited: showy.
dash'board, *n.* a board in the front part of a vehicle to keep off splashes of mud, etc.: a board with dials in front of the driver's seat in a car.
[M.E. *daschen*; from Scand.]

dastard, *das'tȧrd, n.* a mean coward.—Also *adj.*
das'tardly, *adj.* (of conduct, person) cowardly and treacherous.
das'tardliness, *n.* [M.E.]

data, *dā'ta, n.pl.* facts given:—*sing.* **dā'tum.** [L.—*dăre*, to give.]

date[1], *dāt, n.* a statement of time (or time and place) of writing, sending, etc., noted on a letter, book, document: the time of an event: (*coll.*) an appointment or engagement.—*v.t.* to give a date to.—*v.i.* to have beginning (e.g. *This practice dates from the first century A.D.*): to become old-fashioned-looking.
date line, the line east and west of which the date differs by one day—the 180th meridian.
out of date, out-of-date, old-fashioned: (of a ticket, etc.) no longer valid.
up-to-date. See **up.**
[L. *datum* (*Romae, Neāpoli*), given, i.e. written (at Rome, Naples).]

date[2], *dāt, n.* the fruit of the **date palm,** a tall tree with leaves at the top, growing in the tropics.
[Through Fr.—Gk. *daktylos*, finger.]

datum. See **data.**

daub, *döb, v.t.* to smear: to paint without skill.—Also *n.*
[O.Fr. *dauber*, to plaster.]

daughter, *dö'tėr, n.* a female child.
daugh'ter-in-law, *n.* a son's wife:—*pl.* **daughters-in-law.**
[O.E. *dohtor.*]

daunt, *dönt, v.t.* to frighten: to discourage.
daunt'less, *adj.* not to be daunted.
daunt'lessly, *adv.* **daunt'lessness,** *n.*
[O.Fr. *danter*—L. *domāre*, to tame.]

dauphin, *dö'fin, n.* formerly, the eldest son of the King of France.
[From name of noble French family.]

davit, *dav'it, n.* one of a pair of pieces of timber or iron to raise a boat over a ship's side or stern.
[Prob. *David.*]

Davy(-lamp), *dā'vi(-lamp), n.* the safety-lamp for miners invented by Sir Humphry *Davy* (1778-1829).
Davy Jones's locker, *dā'vi Jōn'ziz lok'ėr,* the sea, as the grave of drowned men.

daw, *dö, n.* a jackdaw.
[M.E. *dawe.*]

dawdle, *dö'dl, v.i.* to waste time: to move slowly.
dawd'ler, *n.* **dawd'ling,** *n.* and *adj.*
[Perh. (dial.) *daddle*, to totter as a baby.]

dawn, *dön, v.i.* to become day: to begin to appear.—*n.* daybreak: beginning.—Also **dawn'ing.**
to dawn (up)on one, to become suddenly clear to one.
[O.E. *dagian*—*dæg*, day.]

day, *dā, n.* from sunrise to sunset: from midnight to midnight: the hours spent at work (*working day*): lifetime (e.g. *in my great-grandfather's day*): time of influence, activity, etc.
daily, *dā'li, adj., adv.* (of) every day.—*n.* a paper published every day: a servant who does not sleep in the house:—*pl.* **dai'lies.**
day'-book, *n.* a book in which money transactions are entered at once.
day'break, *n.* dawn, first appearance of light.
day'-dream, *n.* a fanciful plan, or imaginary pleasant event(s).—*v.i.* to make the former, or to experience the latter, in one's mind.
day'light, *n.* light of day.—Also *adj.*
day school, a school held during the weekday, as opposed to a night school, a boarding school, or a Sunday school.
day by day, every day.
day in, day out, on and on for an indefinite time.
the other day, not long ago.
to lose, or **win, the day,** to lose, or win, the fight.
[O.E. *dæg.*]

daze, *dāz, v.t.* to stun, stupefy.—*n.* a bewildered state.
dazed, *dāzd, adj.*
[Old Norse *dasask*, to be breathless.]

dazzle, *daz'l, v.t.* to daze or overpower with a strong light: to amaze by beauty or cleverness. [**daze.**]

de-, *dē-, di-, pfx.* down: away from: completely:—e.g. **depose, derail, denude** (see these words). Also used (as living prefix) to form words undoing an action:—e.g. **decentralise, decompress.** [L.]

deacon, *dē'kȯn, n.* in episcopal churches, a member of the clergy under priests: a church officer: in Scotland, the master of an incorporated company.
dea'coness, *n.* a woman who helps the clergy in social work.
[Gk. *diākonos*, a servant.]

dead, *ded, adj.* without life: without the appearance or feeling of life: (of a ball) out of play: complete (e.g. *a dead loss*): completely accurate.—*adv.* completely.
dead'en, *v.t.* to lessen, weaken (e.g. *to deaden pain*).
dead'ly, *adj.* causing death: very great (e.g. *deadly earnestness*).—*adv.* extremely.
dead'liness, *n.*
dead'(-and)-alive', *adj.* dull, not active.

dead'beat', *adj.* completely exhausted.
dead'-end', *n.* a pipe, road, etc., closed at one end.
dead heat, a race in which two or more competitors are equal.
dead language, one no longer spoken by ordinary people.
dead letter, one undelivered and unclaimed at the post office : a law which has been made but is not enforced.
dead'(-)line, *n.* the very latest time for finishing something.
dead'lock, *n.* a standstill resulting from a failure to agree.
in dead(ly) earnest. See **earnest.**
the dead, dead person(s).
to be dead set against, to be utterly opposed to.
See also **death, die.**
[O.E. *dēad.*]

deaf, *def, adj.* unable to hear : refusing to listen (e.g. *deaf to his plea for mercy*).
deaf'ness, *n.*
deaf'en, *v.t.* to make deaf : to daze with noise : to make (e.g. walls) soundproof.
deaf-mute, *def'-mūt', n.* one who is deaf and dumb.
[O.E. *dēaf.*]

deal[1], *dēl, n.* a portion, amount (e.g. *a great, good, deal*) : the act of dividing cards : a bargain, arrangement.—*v.t.* to divide, to distribute : to deliver (e.g. a blow).—*v.i.* to do business (with) : to trade (in) : (with *with*) to act towards (e.g. *You have dealt unfairly with me*) : to distribute cards :—*pa.t.* and *pa.p.* **dealt** (*delt*).
deal'er, *n.*
deal'ings, *n.pl.* transactions, often business (e.g. *I have no dealings with him*).
to deal with, to tackle and settle (e.g. task, problem, or the person causing it).
[O.E. *dǣl,* a part.]

deal[2], *dēl, n.* a fir or pine board of a standard size : softwood.—*adj.* of deal.
[Of Germanic origin.]

dean[1], **dene,** *dēn, n.* a small valley.
[O.E. *denu.*]

dean[2], *dēn, n.* a cathedral clergyman who presides over the canons : also the title of people holding other important offices in the church, universities, colleges, etc.
[Late Latin *decānus,* a chief of ten.]

dear, *dēr, adj.* high in price : beloved.—*n.* one who is beloved.—*adv.* at a high price.
dear'ly, *adv.* **dear'ness,** *n.*
dearth, *dėrth, n.* scarcity.
[O.E. *dēore.*]

death *deth, n.* dying, end of life.
death'ly, *adj.* like death.
death'less, *adj.* living for ever.
death'bed, *adj.* last minute (e.g. *a deathbed repentance*).
death'-blow, *n.* a blow that causes death or the end.
death duties, part of the value of possessions left by a dead person paid to the government.
death rate, the proportion of deaths to the population.
death roll, *n.* a list of the dead, or the number of dead (e.g. in an accident).
death's'-door, *n.* the point of death.
death's'-head, *n.* the skull of a human skeleton.
death'-trap, *n.* an unsafe structure or a dangerous place.
death warrant, an order for the execution of a criminal : something that causes an end to e.g. a plan, hope.
death'watch *n.* a watch by a dying person : an insect that makes a ticking noise.
to be in at the death, in hunting, to be up on the animal before the dogs have killed it.
See also **dead, die.**
[O.E. *dēath.*]

deb. Short for **débutante.**

débâcle, debacle, *dā-bäk'l, di-bak'l, n.* a complete break-up, collapse, or failure.
[Fr.]

debar, *di-bär', v.t.* to shut out, prevent (from ; e.g. *People under 21 are debarred from voting*) :—*pr.p.* **debarr'ing** ; *pa.p.* **debarred'.**
[Fr. *débarrer,* from root of **bar.**]

debase, *di-bās', v.t.* to make of less value, or less high quality : to make (oneself) less highly thought of by others.
debased', *adj.* lowered in quality : degraded, wicked.
[Pfx. *de-,* and **abase.**]

debate, *di-bāt', n.* a discussion, esp. a formal one before an audience : argument.—Also *v.t.* and *v.i.*
debat'able, *adj.* requiring discussion because perhaps not correct (e.g. *a debatable point, debatable statements*).
[L. *dē,* and *bātuĕre,* to beat.]

debauch, *di-böch', v.t.* to make morally bad.—*n.* a fit of drunkenness or debauchery.
debauched', *adj.*
debauch'ery, *n.* great indulgence in sensual pleasures.
[O.Fr. *desbaucher,* to corrupt.]

debenture, *di-ben'chŭr, n.* a written acknowledgment of a debt, issued by a company.
[L. *dēbentur,* there are due.]

debilitate, *di-bil'i-tāt, v.t.* to make weak.
debil'ity, *n.* bodily weakness.
[L. *dēbilis,* weak.]

debit, *deb'it, n.* an entry on the debtor side of an account.—*v.t.* to enter on the debtor side of an account.
[L. *dēbitum,* what is due—*dēbēre,* to owe.]

debonair, *deb-o-nār', adj.* gay and with pleasant manners.
[O.Fr. *de,* of, *bon,* good, *aire,* manner.]

debouch, *di-bo͞osh', v.i.* to come out from a narrow pass or confined place.
[Fr. *de,* from, *bouche,* mouth.]

débris, *dāb′rē,* **debris,** *deb-rē′* (or *deb′-*), *n.* ruins, rubbish: rocky fragments.
[Fr., from *briser,* to break.]

debt, *det, n.* what one owes to another: state of owing or being under an obligation (e.g. *I am in your debt for this help*).
debt′or, *n.* one who owes a debt.
debt of honour, a gambling debt.
[O.Fr. *det*—same root as **debit.**]

debunk, *dē-bungk′, v.t.* (*slang*) to take away an undeserved good reputation from (a person or thing).
[Pfx. *de-,* and **bunk** (2).]

début, debut, *dā′bū,* or *-bōō′, n.* a first public appearance on the stage, in society, etc.
débutante, debutante, *deb′ū-tȧnt, n.* a girl making her first appearance in society.
[Fr. *début,* a first stroke—*but,* aim.]

deca-, *dek′a-, pfx.* ten, ten times, as in the following:
decade, *dek′ād, n.* a series of ten years.
decagram, decametre, etc. See Appendices.
decalogue, *dek′ȧ-log, n.* the ten commandments (Gk. *logos,* discourse).
[Gk. *deka,* ten.]

decadence, *dek′ȧ-dėns,* or *di-kā′, n.* falling away from high standards in morals or in the arts.
dec′adent, *adj.*
[L. *dē,* down, *cadĕre,* to fall.]

decagram, decalogue, etc. See **deca-.**

decamp, *di-kamp′, v.i.* to make off, esp. secretly.
[Fr. *décamper.*]

decant, *di-kant′, v.t.* to pour off, leaving sediment: to pour from one vessel to another.
decant′er, *n.* an ornamental bottle for holding decanted liquor.
[L. *dē,* from, *canthus,* beak of a vessel.]

decapitate, *di-kap′i-tāt, v.t.* to behead.
decapitā′tion, *n.*
[L. *dē,* from, *caput,* the head.]

decarbonise, *dē-kär′bon-īz, v.t.* to remove carbon or carbon dioxide from.
[Pfx. **de-.**]

decathlon, *dek-ath′lȯn, n.* a two-day contest of ten events held at the modern Olympic Games since 1912.
[**deca-,** and Gk. *athlon,* a contest.]

decay, *di-kā′, v.i.* to fall in ruins: to rot: to fall into a worse state.—Also *n.*
decayed′, *adj.* rotted: having lost position, power or money.
[L. *dē,* from, *cadĕre,* to fall.]

decease, *di-sēs′, n.* death.
deceased′, *adj.* dead.—*n.* the dead person referred to.
[L. *dē,* away, *cēdĕre, cessum,* to go.]

deceit, *di-sēt′, n.* act of deceiving: fraud.
deceit′ful, *adj.* deceiving: insincere.
deceit′fully, *adv.* **deceit′fulness,** *n.*
deceive, *di-sēv′, v.t.* to mislead: to cheat.
deceiv′er, *n.*
See also **deception.**
[L. *dē,* from, *capĕre, captum,* take, catch.]

decelerate, *dē-sel′ėr-āt, v.t.* and *v.i.* to slow down.
[L. *dē,* down, *celer,* swift.]

December, *di-sem′bėr, n.* the twelfth (Roman tenth) month.
[L. *decem,* ten.]

decent, *dē′sėnt, adj.* proper: fairly good: (*coll.*) kindly, not severe.
dē′cency (*-sen-si*), *n.* **dē′cently,** *adv.*
[L. *decēre,* to be fitting, suitable.]

decentralise, *dē-sen′trȧl-īz, v.t.* to transfer from a central body (e.g. the central government) or position to local centres.
decentralisā′tion, *n.* [Pfx. **de-.**]

deception, *di-sep′sh(ȯ)n, n.* act of deceiving: something that deceives.
decep′tive, *adj.* misleading (e.g. *Appearances may be deceptive*).
decep′tively, *adv.* **decep′tiveness,** *n.*
[Same root as **deceit.**]

deci-, *des′i-, pfx.* one-tenth, as in the following:
decigram, -metre, etc. See Appendices.
decimate, *des′i-māt, v.t.* (of disease or slaughter) to reduce greatly in number (in Roman times, to slay every tenth man).
[L. *decimus,* tenth—*decem,* ten.]

decide, *di-sīd′, v.t.* to end, to settle.—*v.t., v.i.* to (cause one to) make up one's mind.
decid′ed, *adj.* settled: clear, definite (e.g. *a decided advantage*): resolute.
See also **decision.**
[L. *dē,* away, *caedĕre, caesum,* to cut.]

deciduous, *di-sid′ū-ùs, adj.* shedding leaves, or antlers, etc.
[L. *dē,* from, *cadĕre,* to fall.]

decimal, *des′i-m(ȧ)l, adj.* numbered by tens.—*n.* a decimal fraction.
decimal fraction, a fraction expressed as so many tenths, hundredths, thousandths, etc., and written as shown:— $0{\cdot}1 = \frac{1}{10}$, $2{\cdot}33 = 2\frac{33}{100}$, etc.
[L. *decem,* ten.]

decipher, *di-sī′fėr, v.t.* to read (secret writing), or make out (something that is not clear). [Pfx. **de-.**]

decision, *di-sizh′(ȯ)n, n.* the act of deciding: a judgment: firmness (e.g. *to act with decision*).
decī′sive, *adj.* deciding, putting an end to a contest, dispute, etc. (e.g. *a decisive battle, a decisive fact*): showing decision and firmness (e.g. *a decisive manner*).
decī′sively, *adv.* **decī′siveness,** *n.*
[Same root as **decide.**]

deck, *dek, v.t.* to adorn.—*n.* a platform extending from one side of a vessel to the other: a floor in a bus, bridge, mine-cage: (*U.S.*) a pack of cards.
deck′-chair′, *n.* a light collapsible chair of spars and canvas.
[Du. *dekken,* to cover.]

declaim, *di-klām′, v.i.* to make a speech in a very formal, or in a passionate, manner:

to speak violently (against someone).—Also *v.t.*

declamation, *dek-lȧ-mā'sh(ȯ)n, n.*

declamatory, *di-klam'ȧ-tȯr-i, adj.*

[L. *dē, clāmāre,* to cry out.]

declare, *di-klār', v.t.* to announce formally (e.g. *to declare war*): to say firmly, assert: to name (goods in one's possession) at a custom house: (*bridge*) to name (trump suit) or call (no trump).—*v.i.* (*cricket*) to end an innings before ten wickets have fallen.

declaration, *dek-lȧ-rā'sh(ȯ)n, n.* firm statement: formal announcement.

declared, *di-klārd', adj.* clearly and firmly stated (e.g. *his declared intention*).

declār'er, *n.*

to declare oneself, to say which side one is on, or what one is going to do.

to declare for (or **against**), to say that one supports (or opposes).

[L. pfx. *dē-, clārus,* clear.]

declassify, *dē'klas'i-fī, v.t.* to take off the secret list. [Pfx. **de-**.]

declension. See **decline.**

decline, *di-klīn', v.i.* to bend, or slope, down: to become less strong, or good, etc.: to refuse.—*v.t.* to refuse: to give the various cases of (a noun or adjective; *n.* in this sense **declen'sion**).—*n.* a down slope: a gradual loss of strength, etc.

[L. *dē,* down, *clīnāre,* to bend.]

declivity, *di-kliv'i-ti, n.* a down slope.

[L. *dē,* downward, *clīvus,* sloping.]

declutch, *dē-kluch', v.i.* to release the clutch. [Pfx. **de-**.]

decode, *dē-kōd', v.t.* to turn (a coded message) into ordinary language.

[Pfx. **de-**.]

decompose, *dē-kȯm-pōz', v.t.* to separate into parts or elements.—*v.i.* to decay, rot.

decomposi'tion, *n.*

[Fr. *décomposer.*]

decompress, *dē-kȯm-pres', v.t.* to decrease the pressure on, esp. gradually.

decompression (*-presh'(ȯ)n*), *n.*

[Pfx. **de-**.]

decontaminate, *dē-kon-tam'in-āt, v.t.* to free (a place, clothing, a person) from poisonous chemicals, dangerous radiation, etc.

decontaminā'tion, *n.* [Pfx. **dē-**.]

decontrol, *dē-kon-trōl', v.t.* to remove (esp. official) control from.—Also *n.*

[Pfx. **de-**.]

décor, *dā-kör, n.* decoration and arrangement of a stage or room. [Fr.]

decorate, *dek'ō-rāt, v.t.* to make look beautiful, striking, or gay: to give a medal or badge to, as a mark of honour.

decorā'tion, *n.*

dec'orative, *adj.* ornamental, beautiful.

dec'orator, *n.* a house-painter.

[L. *decȯrāre, -ātum.*]

decorous, *dek'ō-rus, di-kō'rus, adj.* behaving in a proper way: quiet and dignified.

decō'rum, *n.* polite and dignified behaviour: good taste.

[L. *decōrus,* suitable, seemly.]

decoy, *di-koi', v.t.* to lure into a trap.—*n.* anything intended to lead into a snare.

[Through Du.—L. *cavea,* a cage.]

decrease, *di-krēs', v.i.* to become less.—*v.t.* to make less.—Also *n.* (*dē'krēs*).

[L. *dē,* from, *crescĕre,* to grow.]

decree, *di-krē', n.* an order, edict or law: a judgment, decision.—*v.t.* to order, command (something): to give a decision or order (that).—Also *v.i.*:—*pr.p.* **decree'ing**; *pa.p.* **decreed'.**

decree nisi (*nī'sī*—L. *nisi,* unless), a divorce decree that becomes absolute unless cause is shown that it should not.

[L. *dēcrētum*—*dēcernĕre,* to decide.]

decrepit, *di-krep'it, adj.* infirm through old age: broken-down, or almost in ruins.

decrep'itness, decrep'itude, *ns.*

[L. *dēcrepitus,* noiseless, very old.]

decry, *di-crī', v.t.* to belittle: to express disapproval of:—*pa.p.* **decried'.**

[Fr. *de'-,* and *crier,* to cry.]

dedicate, *ded'i-kāt, v.t.* to consecrate (to some sacred purpose): to devote wholly or chiefly (e.g. *He dedicated his life to this good work*): to inscribe (esp. a book, to someone).

dedicā'tion, *n.*

[L. *dē,* down, *dicāre,* to declare.]

deduce, *di-dūs', v.t.* to conclude from facts one knows or assumes (e.g. *From the height of the sun I deduced that it was about ten o'clock and that we had travelled perhaps 90 miles*).

deduc'tion[1], *n.*

[L. *dē,* from, *dūcĕre, dūctum,* to lead.]

deduct, *di-dukt', v.t.* to substract (from).

deduc'tion[2], *n.* amount subtracted.

[Same root as **deduce.**]

deed, *dēd, n.* an act: an exploit: a legal document.

See also **do.**

[O.E. *dǣd*; conn. with Ger. *tat.*]

deem, *dēm, v.t., v.i.* to judge, think.

[O.E. *dēman.*]

deep, *dēp, adj.* going, or placed, far down or far in: plunged (in, e.g. difficulties): engrossed (in, e.g. study): intense, strong (e.g. learning, sleep, grief, colour): low in pitch: secretive, cunning.—*adv.* far in, into (e.g. *deep in the forest*).—*n.* (with *the*) the sea.

deep'ly, *adv.*

deep'ness, depth (see this), *ns.*

deep'en, *v.t.* to make deeper: to increase.—*v.i.* to become deeper.

deep'-dyed, *adj.* very great—in a bad sense.

deep'-laid', *adj.* (of e.g. a plan) carefully made.

deep'-seat'ed, *adj.* firmly rooted (e.g. *a deep-seated prejudice*).

in deep water, in difficulties.
[O.E. *dēop.*]

deer, *dēr, n.* a cud-chewing animal with antlers (usu. in the male only) :—*pl.* **deer.**
deer forest, a wild tract (not necessarily woodland) reserved for deer.
[O.E. *dēor.*]

deface, *di-fās', v.t.* to disfigure, spoil the appearance of.
deface'ment, *n.*
[Through O.Fr.—L. *dis-, faciēs,* face.]

defalcate, *dē'fal-kāt,* or *-fal', v.i.* to embezzle.
defalcā'tion, *n.*
[Late Latin *dēfalcāre,* to cut away.]

defame, *di-fām', v.t.* to speak evil of.
defamation, *def-à-mā'sh(ò)n, n.*
defam'atory, *adj.* slanderous.
[L. *dis-,* away, *fāma,* report.]

default, *di-fölt', v.i.* to fail to do something one ought to do, as, e.g. to appear in court, to pay money.—Also *n.*
default'er, *n.*
[Through O.Fr.—L. *dē-, fallĕre,* deceive.]

defeat, *di-fēt', v.t.* to win a victory over.—*n.* overthrow in battle : loss of a game, race, etc.
defeat'ism, *n.* frame of mind in which one expects and accepts defeat.
defeat'ist, *adj.*
[O.Fr. *defeit,* pa.p.—*desfaire,* to undo.]

defect, *di-fekt',* or *dē', n.* a fault, flaw.
defec'tion, *n.* desertion : failure in duty.
defec'tive, *adj.* faulty : incomplete.—*n.* a person not having normal mental or physical powers.
See also **deficient, deficiency.**
[L. *dēficĕre, dēfectum,* to fail.]

defence. See **defend.**

defend, *di-fend', v.t.* to guard, protect, against attack : to argue in favour of.
defend'ant, *n.* (*law*) a person accused or sued.
defend'er, *n.*
defence (*U.S.* **defense**), *di-fens', n.* a defending . means of protection : an accused person's plea, or (*law*) his party.
defence 'less, *adj.*
defens'ible, *adj.* possible to defend (e.g. *a defensible position* ; *a course of action that is defensible*).
defens'ive, *adj.* protective : resisting attack.
on the defensive, in a defensive position or state.
[L. *dēfendĕre, dēfensum,* to ward off.]

defer[1], *di-fėr', v.t.* to put off to another time :—*pr.p.* **deferr'ing** ; *pa.p.* **deferred.'**
defer'ment, *n.*
[L. *dis-,* asunder, *ferre,* to bear, carry.]

defer[2], *di-fėr', v.i.* to yield (to the wishes or opinions of another, or to authority) :—*pr.p.* **deferr'ing** ; *pa.p.* **deferred'.**
deference, *def'ėr-ėns, n.* yielding to the judgment or opinion of another, others : courteous willingness to do this.
deferen'tial (*-en'shål*), *adj.* showing deference or respect.
deferen'tially, *adv.*
[L. *dē,* down, *ferre,* to bear.]

defiance, defiant. See **defy.**

deficient, *di-fish'ėnt, adj.* wanting, lacking.
defic'iency, *n.* lack : amount lacking :—*pl.* **defic'iencies.**
def'icit (or *-fis'*), *n.* amount by which sum of money is less than sum required.
deficiency disease, one due to lack of an essential (as a vitamin) in diet—e.g. rickets, scurvy.
[Same root as **defect.**]

defile[1], *di-fīl', v.i.* to march off in file.—*n.* (*dē'fīl, di-fīl'*) a narrow pass, in which troops can march only in file.
[Through Fr.—L. *dis-, fīlum,* thread.]

defile[2], *di-fīl', v.t.* to make unclean : to corrupt.
defile'ment, *n.*
[L. *dē-,* O.E. *fȳlan—fūl,* foul.]

define, *di-fīn', v.t.* to fix the bounds or limits of : to outline clearly : to fix, or to state, the meaning of.
defin'able (*-fīn'*), *adj.*
def'inite (*-in-it*), *adj.* fixed : exact : clear.
def'initely, *adv.* **def'initeness,** *n.*
defini'tion, *n.* an explanation of the exact meaning of a word or phrase : sharpness of outline.
defin'itive, *adj.* decisive, settling once for all.
definite article. See **the.**
[L. *dē,* and *fīnis,* an end.]

deflate, *dē-flāt', v.t.* to let gas out of (e.g. a tyre) : to reduce in importance, self-confidence, etc.
deflā'tion, *n.*
[L. *dē,* down, *flāre, flātum,* to blow.]

deflect, *di-flekt', v.t.* to turn aside (from).
deflex'ion, deflec'tion, *n.*
[L. *dē,* from, *flectĕre,* to bend.]

deforest, *dē-for'ist, v.t.* to make bare of forests or trees.
deforestā'tion, *n.*
[O.Fr. *desforester.*]

deform, *di-förm', v.t.* to spoil the shape of : to make ugly.
deformā'tion (*dē-*), *n.* change of shape.
deform'ity, *n.* a part abnormal in shape : state of being badly shaped :—*pl.* **-ies.**
[L. *dē,* from, *forma,* beauty.]

defraud, *di-fröd', v.t.* to cheat : to deprive (of) by dishonest means.
[L. *dē,* from, *fraus, fraudis,* fraud.]

deft, *deft, adj.* skilful, quick and neat.
deft'ly, *adv.* **deft'ness,** *n.*
[O.E. (*ge*)*dæftan,* prepare, make fit.]

defunct, *di-fungkt', adj.* dead.—*n.* a dead person.
[L. *dēfungī, dēfunctus,* to finish.]

defy, *di-fī', v.t.* to chalenge : to resist boldly :—*pr.p.* **defy'ingl** ; *pa.p.* **defied'.**
defy'ing, defi'ance (*-fī'*), *ns.*
defī'er, *n.*

defi′ant, *adj.* **defi′antly,** *adv.*
[Through O.Fr.—L. *dis-, fīdere*, trust.]

degenerate, *di-jen′ėr-it, adj.* having lost high moral and/or physical qualities.—*n.* a person, plant, etc. that is degenerate.—*v.i.* (*-āt*) to become much less good or admirable.
degen′eracy (*-ȧs-i*), **degenerā′tion,** *ns.*
[L. *dē*, from, *genus, genĕris*, race, kind.]

degrade, *di-grād′, v.t.* to lower in rank: to punish by depriving of office: to make low, contemptible.
degradation, *deg-rȧ-dā′sh(ȯ)n, n.*
[L. *dē*, down, *gradus*, a step.]

degree, *di-grē′, n.* rank: a title given by a university (gained by examination or as an honour): a unit of temperature: one 360th part of a complete revolution (e.g. *There are 90 degrees in a right angle*): amount (e.g. *with some degree of certainty*).
by degrees, gradually.
in a high degree (small degree), to a great (small) extent.
third degree, an American police method of extorting a confession by bullying, etc.
to a degree, to a great extent.
[Root as **degrade.**]

dehydrate, *dē-hī′drāt, v.t.* to dry (foodstuffs).
dehydrā′tion, *n.*
[L. *dē*, from, Gk. *hydōr*, water.]

de-ice, *dē-īs′, v.t.* to prevent formation of, or to remove, ice.
de-ic′er, *n.* [Pfx. **de-.**]

deify, *dē′i-fī, v.t.* to treat, or worship, as a god:—*pr.p.* **dē′ifying**; *pa.p.* **dē′ified.**
deificā′tion, *n.*
dē′ity, *n.* a god or goddess: (*cap.*; with *the*) God:—*pl.* **dē′ities.**
[L. *deus*, a god (*facĕre*, to make).]

deign, *dān, v.i.* to condescend (to), do, or (*v.t.*) give, as a favour (e.g. *to deign to reply; to deign a reply*).
[L. *dignārī*, to think worthy.]

deities, deity. See **deify.**

deject, *di-jekt′, v.t.* to cast down in spirits, make gloomy.
dejec′ted, *adj.* **dejec′tedly,** *adv.*
dejec′tedness, dejec′tion, *ns.*
[L. *dē*, down, *jacĕre*, to cast.]

delay, *di-lā′, v.t.* to put off to another time: to hinder.—*v.i.* to put off time:—*pr.p.* **delay′ing**; *pa.p.* **delayed′.**—Also *n.*
[O.Fr. *delaier.*]

delectable, *di-lekt′ȧ-bl, adj.* delightful, pleasing.
delect′ableness, *n.* **delect′ably,** *adv.*
delectā′tion, *n.* delight.
[L. *dēlectāre*, to delight.]

delegate, *del′i-gāt, v.t.* to send as a representative: to entrust (e.g. *to delegate power to a person or assembly*).—*n.* (*-git, -gāt*) an elected representative.
delegā′tion, *n.* a body of delegates.
[L. *dē, lēgāre*, to send as ambassador.]

delete, *di-lēt′, v.t.* to blot out, erase.
delē′tion, *n.*
[L. *dēlēre, dēlētum*, to blot out.]

deleterious, *del-i-tē′ri-ůs, adj.* hurtful or destructive.
[Gk. *dēlētērios*, hurtful.]

delf, delft, *delf(t)*, **delft′-ware,** *n.* a kind of earthenware orig. made at *Delft*, Holland.

deliberate, *di-lib′ėr-āt, v.t.* to weigh well in one's mind.—*v.i.* to consider the reasons for and against: to reflect.—*adj.* (*-it*) intentional: cautious, unflurried (e.g. *his deliberate way of working*).
delib′erately, *adv.* **delib′erateness,** *n.*
deliberā′tion, *n.* careful thought: calmness, coolness (e.g. *moving with deliberation*): (in *pl.*) formal discussions.
[L. *dē-, librāre*, to weigh.]

delicate, *del′i-kit, adj.* pleasing to the senses, esp. the taste: dainty: of very fine texture: frail: requiring careful handling (e.g. a problem): deft: very finely made for very careful work (e.g. *a delicate instrument*).
del′icately, *adv.* **del′icateness,** *n.*
del′icacy, *n.* fineness: sensitiveness: great tactfulness: great skill: the quality of requiring great care: frailness: something delightful to eat (*pl.* **-ies**).
[L. *dēlicātus*, prob.—*dēliciae*, pleasures.]

delicatessen, *del-i-kȧ-tes′n, n.* prepared foods, esp. meat: a shop selling these.
[Ger. pl. of Fr. *délicatesse*, delicacy.]

delicious, *di-lish′ůs, adj.* highly pleasing to taste: giving exquisite pleasure.
deli′ciously, *adv.* **deli′ciousness,** *n.*
[L. *dēliciōsus*—root as **delicate.**]

delight, *di-līt′, v.t.* to please highly.—*v.i.* to have or take great pleasure (in).—*n.* great pleasure.
delight′ful, *adj.* **delight′fully,** *adv.*
[Through O.Fr. from L. *dēlicĕre.*]

delimit, *dē-lim′it,* or *di-, v.t.* to fix the limits of.
[L. *dēlimitāre.*]

delineate, *di-lin′i-āt, v.t.* to sketch, show by drawing: to describe.
delineā′tion, *n.*
[L. *dē*, down, *linea*, a line.]

delinquent, *di-ling′kwėnt, adj.* not carrying out one's obligations: guilty of misdeeds.—Also *n.*
delin′quency, *n.* failure in duty: minor law-breaking: a misdeed (*pl.* **-ies**).
[L. *dē-*, and *linquĕre*, to leave.]

delirious, *di-lir′i-ůs, adj.* wandering in mind, light-headed: wild with excitement.
delir′iousness, delir′ium, *ns.* state of being delirious: wild excitement.
[L. *dēlirus*, crazy—*dē*, out of, *līra*, a (straight) furrow.]

deliver, *di-liv′ėr,* to set free (from): to rescue: to bring and hand to another (e.g. *to deliver parcels*): to deal (a blow), send (e.g. a ball): to pronounce, speak (a judgment, a sermon): to help (a

woman) in giving birth to a child: to assist at the birth of (a child).
deliv'erance, *n.* rescue, freeing.
deliv'ery, *n.* act or manner of delivering:—*pl.*-**ies.**
[L. *dē*, from, *liberāre*, to set free.]

dell, *del*, *n.* a hollow, usu. with trees.
[Same root as **dale.**]

delphinium, *del-fin'i-ùm*, *n.* kinds of branching plants with irregular flowers, usu. blue.
[Gk. *delphinion*, larkspur.]

delta, *del'tȧ*, the fourth letter of the Greek alphabet: a tract of land formed at the mouth of a river, in shape like the Greek capital delta, Δ.
[Gk.—Heb. *daleth*, a tent door.]

delude, *di-lōōd'*, *-lūd'*, *v.t.* to deceive.
delusion, *di-lōō'zh(ò)n*, or *-lū'*, *n.* a false belief, esp. as a symptom of mental illness.
[L. *dēlūdĕre*, *dēlūsum*, to play false.]

deluge, *del'ūj*, *n.* a flood: a great quantity. —*v.t.* to fill, overwhelm, with a great quantity.
[Fr.—L. *dis-*, away, *luĕre*, to wash.]

delusion. See **delude.**

de luxe, *di looks'*, very luxurious or elegant.
[Fr., of luxury.]

delve, *delv*, *v.t.*, *v.i.* to dig.—*v.i.* to seek patiently and carefully (for e.g. information).
[O.E. *delfan*, to dig.]

demagogue, *dem'ȧ-gog*, *n.* a political orator who appeals to the passions and prejudices of the people.
[Gk. *dēmos*, people, *agōgos*, leading.]

demand, *di-mând'*, *v.t.* to ask, or ask for, firmly or sharply: to require (e.g. *This problem demands careful thought*).—Also *v.i.*—*n.* urgent request: question: urgent claim (e.g. *demands on one's time*): desire shown by consumers (for goods).
on demand, when asked for.
[Fr. *demander*; from Late L.]

demarcation, demarkation, *dē-märk-ā'-sh(ò)n*, *n.* the marking or describing of boundaries or limits: the strict marking off of work to be done by one kind of craftsmen from that to be done by craftsmen of other trades.
[Sp. *de*, from, *marcar*, to mark.]

demean, *di-mēn'*, *v.t.* to lower in dignity (usu. *to demean oneself*).
[Pfx. **de-,** and **mean** (1).]

demeanour, *di-mēn'ėr*, *n.* manner, bearing.
[O.Fr. *de-*, *mener*, to lead.]

dement, *di-ment'*, *v.t.* to make insane.
dement'ed, *adj.* out of one's mind.
[L. *dē*, from *mens*, *mentis*, mind.]

demerit, *dē-mer'it*, *n.* fault, shortcoming.
[L. *dēmerērī*, to deserve fully.]

demesne, *di-mān'*, or *-mēn'*, *n.* land which is one's property and in one's own use.
[Form of **domain.**]

demi-, *dem'i*, *pfx.* half, as in **demigod,** *dem'i-god*, *n.* one whose nature is partly divine: a man regarded with worshipful admiration.
[Fr.—L. *dimidius.*]

demise, *di-mīz'*, *n.* death.
[O.Fr.—L. *dis-*, *mittĕre*, *missum*, send.]

demob(bed). Short for **demobilise(d).**

demobilise, *dē-* or *di-mōb'il-īz*, or *-mob'-*, *v.t.* to disband (e.g. an army): (*coll.*) to discharge (a person) from an armed service.
demobilisā'tion, *n.* [Pfx. **de-.**]

democracy, *di-mok'rȧ-si*, *n.* (a country having) a form of government in which the people have power freely to elect representatives to carry on the government:—*pl.* **-ies.**
dem'ocrat, *n.* one who believes in democracy as a principle: a member of the **Democratic party** (one of the two great political parties in United States).
democrat'ic, *adj.* of democracy: believing in equal rights and privileges for all.
democrat'ically, *adv.*
[Gk. *dēmos*, the people, *krateein*, to rule.]

demolish, *di-mol'ish*, *v.t.* to lay in ruins: to destroy, put an end to.
demoli'tion (*dem-*), *n.*
[L. *de*, down, and *mōlīrī*, to build.]

demon, *dē'mon*, *n.* an evil spirit, a devil.
demoniac, *di-mō'ni-ak*, *adj.* possessed by evil spirit: frantic.—Also *n.*
demoniacal, *dē-mò-nī'ȧ-kl*, *adj.*
[Gk. *daimōn*, a spirit.]

demonstrate, *dem'òn-strāt*, *v.t.* to show or point out clearly: to prove.—*v.i.* to make a public expression of opinion (e.g. *A crowd collected to demonstrate against the new taxes*).
demonstrā'tion, *n.* proof beyond doubt: a practical display or exhibition: a display of emotion: a public expression of opinion, as by a mass-meeting, a procession, etc.
demon'strative, *adj.* pointing out: proving with certainty: in the habit of showing one's feelings.
dem'onstrator, *n.* a teacher or assistant who helps students with practical work: one who takes part in a public demonstration.
[L. *dēmonstrāre*—*monstrāre*, to show.]

demoralise, *di-mor'ȧl-īz*, *v.t.* to take away confidence and courage, to throw into confusion.
demoralisā'tion, *n.*
[Fr. *dé-*, un-, and *moraliser.*]

demote, *dē-mōt'*, *v.t.* to reduce in rank.
[L. *dē-*, down, and **promote.**]

demur, *di-mûr'*, *v.i.* to object (with *at*):—*pr.p.* **demurr'ing**; *pa.p.* **demurred'.**
[L. *dēmorārī*, to loiter, linger.]

demure, *di-mūr'*, *adj.* quiet, modest, shy (sometimes affectedly so).
[L. *maturus*, ripe; pfx. unexplained.]

demurred, demurring. See **demur.**

demy, *di-mī′, n.* a size of paper 22½ by 17½ in. for printing—for writing, 20 by 15½ in. [**demi-.**]

den, *den, n.* the lair of a wild beast: a haunt (of vice or of great poverty): a private room or retreat.
[O.E. *denn*, a cave.]

denationalise, *dē-nash′ȯn-ȧl-īz, v.t.* to return from State to private ownership.
[Pfx. **de-.**]

denial. See **deny.** **dene.** See **dean** (1).

denier, *den′i-ėr, n.* a unit of silk, rayon, and nylon yarn weight.
[Fr.—L. *dēnārius*, a Roman silver coin.]

denizen, *den′i-zn, n.* an inhabitant (human or animal).
[O.Fr. *deinzein—deinz* (Fr. *dans*), within.]

denominate, *di-nom′in-āt, v.t.* to give a name to: to call, name.
denominā′tion, *n.* a name or title: a class of units in money, weights, measures (e.g. *First reduce 7 tons and 5 cwt. to the same denomination*): a religious sect.
denom′inator, *n.* in a vulgar fraction, the number below the line.
[L. *dē-, nōmināre*, to name.]

denote, *di-nōt′, v.t.* to be the sign of: to mean.
[L. *dē-, notāre*, to mark.]

dénouement, denouement, *dā-nōō′mong, n.* the unravelling of a plot or story: the outcome.
[Fr.—L. *dis-*, apart, *nodāre*, to tie.]

denounce, *di-nowns′, v.t.* to inform against or accuse publicly: to notify formally termination of (a treaty, etc.).
See also **denunciate, denunciation.**
[L. *dē-, nuntiāre*, to announce.]

dense, *dens, adj.* thick, close, compact: very stupid.
dense′ly, *adv.* **dense′ness,** *n.*
dens′ity, *n.* the quality of being dense: the mass of unit volume of a substance.
[L. *densus*, thick.]

dent, *dent, n.* a small hollow made by pressure or a blow.—Also *v.t.* [**dint.**]

dental, *den′tȧl, adj.* of, or for, the teeth: (of a sound) produced with the aid of the teeth.
dentate, *den′tāt, adj.* toothed: notched.
dentifrice, *den′ti-fris, n.* a substance for cleaning the teeth.
dentine, dentin, *den′tin, n.* the substance of which teeth are mainly composed.
dentist, *den′tist, n.* one who takes out, etc., or cares for, teeth.
den′tistry, *n.* a dentist's work.
denture, *den′chůr, n.* a set of teeth, esp. artificial.
[L. *dens, dentis*, tooth (*fricāre*, to rub).]

denude, *di-nūd′, v.t.* to make bare: to strip (of; e.g. *land denuded of vegetation*).
denudā′tion, *n.* the wearing away of rocks by water, etc.
[L. *dē-, nūdāre*, to make naked.]

denunciate, *di-nun′s(h)i-āt, v.t.* to denounce.
denunciation, *(-s(h)i-ā′-), n.* act of denouncing or accusing.
denun′ciator, *n.* one who denounces.
[Same root as **denounce.**]

deny, *di-nī′, v.t.* to declare not to be true: to reject: to refuse (*e.g. He denied me food*): —*pr.p.* **deny′ing**; *pa.p.* **denied′.**
denī′al, *n.*
to deny oneself, to do without (things that one desires or needs).
[Fr. *dénier*—L. *dē-, negāre*, to say no.]

deodorise, *dē-ō′dȯ-rīz, v.t.* to take the smell from.
deō′dorant, deō′doriser, *ns.* a substance that destroys or conceals smells.
[L. *dē*, from, *odor*, smell.]

depart, *di-pärt′, v.i.* to go away: to die: (with *from*) to cease to follow (e.g. *to depart from one's original plan*).
depar′ture (*-chůr*), *n.*
a new departure, (the beginning of) a new course of action.
[L. *dis-*, apart, *partīrī*, to divide.]

department, *di-pärt′mėnt, n.* a part: a section of an administration (e.g. *the Department of Justice*), university, office, shop.
department′al, *adj.*
[Same root as **depart.**]

depend, *di-pend′, v.i.* to hang down (from): to rely (on): to receive necessary support from (with *on*): (of a future happening, etc.) to be decided by (e.g. *Its success depends on your efforts*).
depend′able, *adj.* trustworthy.
depend′ent (also **-ant**), *adj.*
depend′ant (also **-ent**), *n.* one who is kept, supported, by another.
depend′ence, *n.* state of being dependent: reliance, trust.
depend′ency, *n.* a colony without self-government:—*pl.* **-ies.**
[L. *dē*, from *pendēre*, to hang.]

depict, *di-pikt′, v.t.* to paint: to describe.
[L. *dē-, pingĕre, pictum*, to paint.]

depilatory, *di-pil′ȧ-tȯr-i, adj.* taking hair off.—Also *n.*
[L. *dē*, from, *pilus*, hair.]

deplete, *di-plēt′, v.t.* to empty (of): to reduce in number or amount.
deplē′tion, *n.*
[L. *dēplēre, dēplētum*, to empty.]

deplore, *di-plōr′, -plör′, v.t.* to express disapproval and regret about (something).
deplor′able, *adj.* sad: very bad.
deplor′ableness, *n.* **deplor′ably,** *adv.*
[L. *dē-, plōrāre*, to weep.]

deploy, *di-ploi′, v.t.* to spread out (troops) so as to form a longer front.—Also *v.i.*
deploy′ment, *n.*
[L. *dis-*, apart, *plicāre*, to fold.]

depopulate, *di-pop′ū-lāt* (or *dē-*), *v.t.* to reduce greatly the population of (a region).
depopulā′tion, *n.*
[L. *dēpopulārī*, to lay waste, destroy—*populus*, people.]

deport[1], *di-, dē-pōrt′, -pört′, v.t.* to send (an alien, criminal) out of the country.
deportā′tion, *n.*
[L. *dē-*, away, *portāre, -ātum*, to carry.]

deport[2], *di-pōrt′, -pört′, v.t.* to behave (one-self).
deport′ment, *n.* bearing, behaviour.
[L. *dē-*, *portāre*, to carry.]

depose, *di-pōz′, v.t.* to remove from a high position (e.g. from that of king): to testify on oath.
See also **deposition.**
[L. *dē*, from, *pausāre*, to pause, place.]

deposit, *di-poz′it, v.t.* to put or set down: to entrust for safe keeping (e.g. *to deposit money in a bank*).—*n.* solid matter that has settled down in a liquid: money put in a bank.
depos′itory, *n.* a place where anything is deposited—sometimes **depos′itary.**
[L. *dē*, down, *pōnĕre*, to place.]

deposition, *dep-ō-zish′(ō)n, n.* a written testimony used as evidence in court: removal (from office): act of depositing.
[**deposit**; blended with root of **depose.**]

depot, *dep′ō, dē′pō, n.* a storehouse: a military station or headquarters: (*U.S.*) a railway station.
[Fr. *dépôt*—same L. root as **deposit.**]

deprave, *di-prāv′, v.t.* to make bad or worse, to corrupt.
depraved′, *adj.* evil, corrupt.
depraved′ness, deprav′ity (*-prav′*), *ns.* great wickedness.
[L. *dē-*, *prāvus*, bad.]

deprecate, *dep′ri-kāt, v.t.* to express disapproval of (an action or a condition, state).
[L. *dē*, away, *precārī*, to pray.]

depreciate, *di-prē′shi-āt, v.t.* to lower the value of: to speak slightingly of.—*v.i.* to fall in value.
depreciā′tion, *n.* **depre′ciatory,** *adj.*
[L. *dē*, down, *pretium*, price.]

depredation, *dep-rė-dā′sh(ō)n, n.* act of robbing, robbery: destructive action suggesting robbery (e.g. *the sea's depredations on the land*).
[L. *dē-*, *praedārī*, to plunder.]

depress, *di-pres′, v.t.* to press down: to lower: to lessen the activity of (e.g. trade): to cast a gloom over.
depressed′, *adj.* **depress′ing,** *adj.*
depression, *di-presh′(ō)n, n.* a lowering: a hollow: low spirits: lack of activity in trade: a region of low pressure (e.g. *a depression over the Atlantic*).
[L. *dē*, down, *premĕre*, *pressum*, press.]

deprive, *di-prīv′, v.t.* (with *of*) to take something away from (e.g. *This move deprived the fugitive of his means of escape*).
depriv′al, *n.*
deprivation, *dep-riv-ā′sh(ō)n, n.* depriving: loss: hardship.
deprived′ (*-prīvd*). *adj.* underprivileged (see this word).
[Late L. *dēprīvāre*—*prīvus*, one's own.]

depth, *depth, n.* deepness: a deep place: intensity, strength (e.g. *the depth of her feelings*).
depth′-charge, *n.* a bomb that explodes under water.
out of one's depth, in water where one cannot touch bottom: in a situation with which one cannot deal.
See also **deep, deepness.**
[Late M.E.; perh.—**deep.**]

depute, *di-pūt′, v.t.* to appoint (a person) as one's substitute: to make over (one's authority to a person as deputy).
deputā′tion, *n.* persons appointed to represent and speak on behalf of others.
dep′utise, *v.i.* to act as deputy.
dep′uty, *n.* one appointed to act for another: a delegate:—*pl.* **-ies.**
[L. *dēputāre*, to prune, (later) to select.]

derail, *dē-rāl′, v.t.* to cause to leave the rails. [Pfx. **de-**.]

derange, *di-rānj′, v.t.* to put out of place, or out of working order: to make insane.
deranged′, *adj.* **derange′ment,** *n.*
[Fr. *déranger*.]

derate, *dē-rāt′, v.t.* to relieve, wholly or partly, from payment of local rates.
derāt′ing, *n.* and *adj.* [Pfx. **de-**.]

Derby, *där′bi, n.* an annual horse race held on Epsom Downs: a race or contest attracting much local interest.
[Earl of *Derby*.]

derelict, *der′ė-likt, adj.* abandoned, left to decay.—Also *n.*
derelic′tion, *n.* abandoning: neglect (of duty).
[L. *dē-*, *re-*, behind, *linquĕre*, to leave.]

deride, *di-rīd′, v.t.* to laugh at, mock.
derision, *di-rizh′(ō)n, n.* mockery: a laughing-stock.
derī′sive (*-siv*), **-sory,** *adjs.* mocking.
[L. *dē-*, *rīdēre*, *rīsum*, to laugh.]

derive, *di-rīv′, v.t.* to draw, take (from a source or origin): to trace (a word) to its root.—*v.i.* to come, arise (from).
derivation, *der-i-vā′sh(ō)n, n.* the tracing of a word to its root: source: descent.
deriv′ative, *adj.* derived from something else, not original.—*n.* a word, substance, formed from another word, substance.
[L. *dē*, from, *rīvus*, a river.]

dermatitis, *dėr-mȧ-tī′tis, n.* inflammation of the skin.
dermatol′ogy, *n.* science that is concerned with the skin and its diseases.
[Gk. *derma*, the skin.]

derogate, *der′ō-gāt, v.i.* to take away (from authority, dignity, merit, etc.).
derog′atory, *adj.* lowering to one's dignity, etc.: scornful, disparaging.
derog′atorily, *adv.* **derog′atoriness,** *n.*
[L. *dērogāre*, to repeal part of a law.]

derrick, *der′ik, n.* an apparatus like a crane for lifting weights.
[*Derrick*, a 17th-cent. hangman.]

dervish, *dėr′vish, n.* a member of a Mohammedan order vowed to poverty,

some practising howling, others violent dancing.
[Pers. *darvīsh*, a poor man.]

descant, *des'kant*, *n.* an accompaniment above the air.—*v.i.* (*des-kant'*) to talk at length about (with *on*).
[L. *dis*, apart, *cantus*, a song.]

descend, *di-send'*, *v.i.* to climb down: to pass to a lower place or condition: (with *on, upon*) to invade: to be derived.—*v.t.* to go down.
descend'ant, *n.* an offspring, near or distant.
descent', *n.* act of descending: slope: an attack: lineage.
[L. *dē*, down, *scandĕre*, to climb.]

describe, *di-skrīb'*, *v.t.* to trace out, draw (e.g. *to describe a circle*): to give an account of.
description, *di-skrip'sh(ȯ)n*, *n.* act of describing: an account of anything in words: sort or kind.
descrip'tive, *adj.*
[L. *dē*, down, *scrībĕre*, *scriptum*, to write.]

descry, *di-skrī'*, *v.t.* to espy, notice, see:—*pr.p.* **descry'ing**; *pa.p.* **descried'.**
[From two words: (1) L. *dēscrībĕre*, describe: (2) O.Fr. *descrier*, announce.]

desecrate, *des'i-krāt*, *v.t.* to treat without reverence: to profane.
desecrā'tion, *n.*
[Coined to correspond with **consecrate.**]

desert[1], *di-zėrt'*, *n.* something that is deserved (good or bad)—often in *pl.*
[Same root as **deserve.**]

desert[2], *di-zėrt'*, *v.t.* to leave, forsake.—*v.i.* to run away, esp. from the army.
desert'er, *n.* **deser'tion,** *n.*
[L. *dē*-, meaning opp. of, *serĕre*, join.]

desert[3], *dez'ėrt*, *n.* a place where there is too little water, and little or no plant life: a desolate place.—Also *adj.*
[L. *dēserĕre*, forsake; root as **desert** (2).]

deserve, *di-zėrv'*, *v.t.* to earn by one's actions, to merit.
deserv'ing, *adj.* worthy.
deserv'edly (*-id-li*), *adv.* justly.
See also **desert** (1).
[L. *dē*-, *servīre*, to serve.]

deshabille. Same as **dishabille.**

desiccate, *des'i-kāt*, *v.t.* to dry up: to preserve by drying.
desiccā'tion, *n.*
[L. *dēsiccāre*, to dry up.]

design, *di-zīn'*, *v.t.* to prepare a plan of: to intend.—*n.* a preliminary sketch, plan in outline: a plan formed in the mind: intention: arrangement of forms and colours.
design'edly (*-id-li*), *adv.* intentionally.
design'er, *n.* one who makes designs or patterns: a plotter.
design'ing, *adj.* artful, scheming.—*n.* the art of making designs or patterns.
des'ignate (*-ig-nāt*), *v.t.* to point out: to name: to be a name for: to appoint.—*adj.* (*-nit*, *-nāt*) appointed to office but not yet installed (placed after noun, e.g. *ambassador designate*).
designā'tion, *n.* a pointing out: name: title.
[L. *dē*-, off, *signum*, a mark.]

desire, *di-zīr'*, *v.t.* to long for: to ask.—*n.* an earnest longing or wish: a request.
desir'able, *adj.* worthy of desire: pleasing.
desir'ableness, desirabil'ity, *ns.*
desir'ous, *adj.* wishful.
[L. *dēsiderāre*, to long for.]

desist, *di-zist'*, *-sist'*, *v.i.* to stop (often with *from*; e.g. *Make him desist from trying to open it*).
[L. *dē*-, away, *sistĕre*, to cause to stand.]

desk, *desk*, *n.* a piece of furniture for use when writing or reading.
[Root as **disk** (in mediaeval L. *discus* = table).]

desolate, *des'o-lāt*, *v.t.* to lay waste, empty of people, make ruinous: to make wretched.—*adj.* (*des'o-lit*) very lonely or barren: joyless.
desolā'tion, *n.*
[L. *dē*-, pfx., *sōlāre*, to make alone.]

despair, *di-spār'*, *v.i.* to lose hope (of).—*n.* hopelessness: something that causes one to despair.
despair'ing, *adj.* **despair'ingly,** *adv.*
See also **desperate.**
[L. *dē*-, meaning 'not', *spērāre*, to hope.]

despatch. Same as **dispatch.**

desperado, *des-pėr-ä'dō*, *-ā'dō*, *n.* a reckless fellow: a ruffian:—*pl.* **despera'do(e)s.**
[Old Sp.—L. *dēspērātus*, despaired of.]

desperate, *des'pėr-it*, *adj.* despairingly reckless: hopeless: (*coll.*) extremely bad.
des'perately, *adv.* **des'perateness,** *n.*
desperā'tion, *n.* state of despair: recklessness.
[Same root as **despair.**]

despicable, *des'pik-ȧ-bl*, or *-pik'*, *adj.* contemptible, worthless.
despicably, *adv.* **despicableness,** *n.*
despise, *di-spīz'*, *v.t.* to look upon with contempt: to scorn.
[L. *dē*-, down, *specĕre*, to look.]

despite, *di-spīt'*, *prep.* in spite of.
[Same root as **despise.**]

despoil, *di-spoil'*, *v.t.* to strip completely (of possessions): to rob.
[L. *dē*-, *spolium*, spoil.]

despond, *di-spond'*, *v.i.* to be without hope, dejected.
despond'ence, despond'ency, *ns.*
despond'ent, *adj.*
despond'ently, dispond'ingly, *advs.*
[L. *dē*, away, *spondēre*, to promise.]

despot, *des'pot*, *n.* a ruler with absolute power: a tyrant.
despot'ic, -al, *adjs.* **despot'ically,** *adv.*
des'potism, *n.* absolute power: tyranny.
[Gk. *despotēs*, a master.]

dessert, *di-zėrt'*, *n.* fruits, confections, etc., served at the end of dinner.

dessert'spoon, *n.* a spoon between a tablespoon and a teaspoon in size.
[Through O.Fr.—L. *dis-*, *servire*, serve.]

destine, *des'tin, v.t.* to set apart for a certain use, state, etc. (e.g. *He destined this money to pay for a bicycle*; *a son who was destined for the Church*).
des'tined, *adj.* bound (for a place): intended: having as one's fate (e.g. *destined to succeed, destined to be hanged*).
destinā'tion, *n.* the place to which one, anything, is going.
des'tiny, *n.* unavoidable fate:—*pl.* **-ies.**
[L. *dēstināre.*]

destitute, *des'ti-tūt, adj.* in utter want: entirely lacking in (e.g. *destitute of common sense*).
des'tituteness, destitū'tion, *ns.*
[L. *dē*, away, *statuěre*, to place.]

destroy, *di-stroi', v.i.* to ruin, to do away with, to kill:—*pr.p.* **destroy'ing**; *pa.p.* **destroyed'.**
destroy'er, *n.* a person or thing that destroys: small fast warship armed with torpedoes, etc.
destruction, *di-struk'sh(ȯ)n, n.* act of destroying: ruin.
destruc'tible, *adj.* able to be destroyed.
destructibil'ity, *n.*
destruc'tive, *adj.* causing destruction: ruinous, deadly (e.g. *destructive to animals, destructive of happiness*): merely negative (e.g. *destructive criticism*).
destruc'tively, *adv.* **-tiveness,** *n.*
destruc'tor, *n.* a furnace for burning up refuse.
[L. *dē*, down, *struěre*, *structum*, to build.]

desultory, *des'ul-tȯr-i, adj.* jumping from one thing to another (e.g. *desultory reading*): rambling (e.g. *desultory remarks*).
des'ultorily, *adv.* **des'ultoriness,** *n.*
[L. *dē*, from, *salire*, to jump.]

detach, *di-tach', v.t.* to unfasten: to separate (from): to send off (e.g. troops) on special service.—Also *v.i.*
detach'able, *adj.*
detached', *adj.* unconnected: free from emotion, unprejudiced (e.g. *a detached attitude to the problem*).
detach'ment, *n.* act of detaching: state of not being influenced by emotion or prejudice: a body (e.g. of troops).
[O.Fr. *des-*, apart, and root of **attach.**]

detail, *dē'tāl, di-tāl', v.t.* to tell fully, give all the facts of: to choose, set (a person, to do a particular job).—*n.* a small part: an item.
detailed, *adj.* giving many details.
in detail, point by point, item by item.
[Fr. pfx. *dē-*, *tailler*, to cut.]

detain, *di-tān', v.t.* to delay, stop: to keep in custody.
detainee' (*-ē'*), *n.* one held in custody.
detention, *di-ten'sh(ȯ)n, n.* act of detaining: being detained: imprisonment: keeping in school as punishment.
[L. *dē*, from, *tenēre*, *tentum*, to hold.]

detect, *di-tekt', v.t.* to find (someone in the act of): to discover the presence or fact of (e.g. *to detect a smell of gas*).
detec'table, -ible, *adj.* **detec'tion,** *n.*
detec'tive, *n.* a person who tracks criminals or watches suspected persons.—Also *adj.*
detec'tor, *n.* an apparatus that detects (e.g. electric waves).
[L. *dē-*, opp. of, *tegěre*, *tectum*, to cover.]

detention. See **detain.**

deter, *di-tėr', v.t.* to frighten or prevent (from doing something):—*pr.p.* **deterr'ing**; *pa.p.* **deterred'.**
deterrent, *di-ter'ėnt, adj.* having the effect of deterring.—Also *n.* (term now often applied to a nuclear weapon, as a hydrogen bomb).
[L. *dē*, from, *terrēre*, to frighten.]

detergent, *di-tėr'jėnt, n.* a material that cleanses (usu. not including soap).—*adj.* cleansing.
[L. *dē*, off, *tergēre*, to wipe.]

deteriorate, *di-tē'ri-ȯ-rāt, v.t.* to make worse.—*v.i.* to grow worse.
deteriorā'tion, *n.*
[L. *dēteriōrāre.*]

determine, *di-tėr'min, v.t.* to fix or settle (e.g. *The committee were to determine the course to be taken*): to cause (a person) to decide (to): to find out exactly (*He tried to determine what had gone wrong*).
determinā'tion, *n.* act of determining: fixed purpose: firmness of character.
deter'mined, *adj.* fixed or settled: firm in purpose.
[L. *dē-*, *terminus*, a boundary.]

detest, *di-test', v.t.* to hate intensely.
detestā'tion (*dē-*), *n.*
detest'able (*di-*), *adj.* extremely hateful.
detest'ableness, *n.* **detest'ably,** *adv.*
[L. *dētestārī*, to curse while calling on a god as witness—*testis*, a witness.]

dethrone, *di-thrōn', v.t.* to remove from a throne: depose.
dethrone'ment, *n.* [Pfx. **de-.**]

detonate, *det'ȯ-nāt, dē'tȯ-nāt, v.i., v.t.* to explode, cause to explode, violently.
detonā'tion, *n.*
det'onator (*-ā-tȯr*), *n.* a substance or device that sets off an explosion.
[L. *dē*, down, *tonāre*, to thunder.]

detour, *dā'tōōr, di-tōōr', n.* a winding (e.g. of a river): a roundabout way.
to make a detour, to go by a roundabout way.
[Fr. *détourner*, to turn aside.]

detract, *di-trakt', v.i.* to take away (from), lessen, esp. reputation or worth.
detract'or, *n.* **detrac'tion,** *n.*
[L. *dē*, away, *trahěre*, *tractum*, to draw.]

detriment, *det'ri-mėnt, n.* harm, damage, disadvantage (in phrases, *without detriment to, to the detriment of*).
detrimen'tal, *adj.* and *n.* (something) disadvantageous or damaging.
[L. *dē*, off, *terěre*, *tritum*, to rub.]

de trop, *di trō, adj.* (of a person) in the way, unwelcome. [Fr.]

deuce[1], *dūs, n.* a card or die with two spots: (*lawn tennis*) a situation in which one side must gain *two* successive points to win the game, or two successive games to win the set—i.e. at three points each ('forty all'), at four, etc., points each, or at an equal number of games each.
[Fr. *deux*, two.]

deuce[2], *dūs, n.* the devil.
[Prob. **deuce** (1).]

(Deutsche) Mark, *(doich) märk, n.* German coin.
[Ger. *Deutsch*, German.]

devalue, *dē-val'ū, v.t.* to reduce the value of.
devaluā'tion, *n.* [Pfx. **de-**.]

devastate, *dev'às-tāt, v.t.* to lay waste: to overwhelm (a person) with grief.
dev'astating, *adj.* overwhelming.
devastā'tion, *n.*
[L. *dē-, vastāre*, to lay waste.]

develop, *di-vel'òp, v.t.* to bring to a more advanced state: to show gradually (e.g. a disease, a habit): to open (an attack): to make (a photograph) visible by treating film or plate, with chemicals or electrically.—*v.i.* to grow to a more advanced state: to come gradually into being.
devel'oper, *n.* **devel'opment,** *n.*
[Fr. *développer*; origin uncertain.]

deviate, *dē'vi-āt, v.i.* to turn aside (from).
deviā'tion, *n.*
devious, *dē'vi-ùs, adj.* roundabout (e.g. *devious paths*): rather dishonest (e.g. *by devious methods*).
de'viously, *adv.* **de'viousness,** *n.*
[L. *dē*, from, *via*, the way.]

device. See **devise.**

devil, *dev'l, n.* (*cap.*) spirit of evil, Satan: any evil spirit: a wicked person: a drudge.—*v.t.* to season highly and broil.—*v.i.* to drudge for another:—*pr.p.* **dev'illing**; *pa.p.* **dev'illed.**
dev'ilish, *adj.* very wicked: (*coll.*) very great (also *adv.*).
dev'ilry, *n.* conduct, or an action, worthy of a devil:—*pl.* **dev'ilries.**
dev'il-may-care, *adj.* reckless.
[O.E. *dēofol*—L. *diabolus*; from Gk.]

devious. See **deviate.**

devise, *di-vīz', v.t.* to invent, contrive: to plan, scheme.
devi'ser, *n.*
device, *di-vīs', n.* a contrivance, invention: a plan: an emblem: a motto: (in *pl.*) inclinations (e.g. *Leave him to his own devices*).
[O.Fr. *deviser*, divide, regulate; same root as **divide.**]

devoid, *di-void', adj.* (with *of*) free from (e.g. *devoid of fear, of meaning*).
[O.Fr. *desvoidier*, to empty out.]

devolve, *di-volv', v.i.* to fall as a duty (e.g. *This task will devolve upon you*).
[L. *dē*, down, *volvěre*, to roll.]

devote, *di-vōt', v.t.* to give up wholly (e.g. *to devote one's life, one's energies, to the cause of peace*).
devot'ed, *adj.* warmly loyal (e.g. *a devoted friend*).
devotee' (*-tē'*), *n.* an enthusiast for, supporter (of; e.g. *a devotee of racing*).
devō'tion, *n.* strong loyalty or affection: (in *pl.*) prayers.
[L. *dē*, away, *vovēre, vōtum*, to vow.]

devour, *di-vowr', v.t.* to eat up greedily: to take in eagerly by eye and mind.
[L. *dē-, vorāre*, to swallow.]

devout, *di-vowt', adj.* pious: earnest.
devout'ly, *adv.* **devout'ness,** *n.*
[Through O.Fr.; same root as **devote.**]

dew, *dū, n.* tiny drops of moisture deposited from the air on cooling, esp. at night.
dew'y, *adj.* **dew'iness,** *n.*
[O.E. *dēaw.*]

dexterity, *deks-ter'i-ti, n.* skill, esp. with the hands: mental skill.
dex'terous, dex'trous, *adj.* skilful.
[L. *dexter*, right, on the right side.]

dhow, *dow, n.* an Arab sailing ship.

diabetes, *dī-à-bē'tēz, -tiz, n,* a disease in which too much sugar is found in the urine.
diabetic (*-bet'ik, -bē'tik*), *adj.* of diabetes. —*n.* a sufferer from diabetes.
[Gk. *dia*, through, *bainein*, to go.]

diabolic(al), *dī-à-bol'ik(l), adjs.* devilish.
[L. *diabolus*, devil—Gk. *diabolos.*]

diadem, *dī'à-dem, n.* a band worn round the head as a badge of royalty.
[Gk. *dia*, round, *deein*, to bind.]

diaeresis, dieresis, *dī-ēr'i-sis, n.* a mark (¨) placed over the second of two vowels to show that each is to be pronounced separately, as *naïve.*
[Gk.—*dia*, apart, *haireein*, to take.]

diagnosis, *dī-àg-nō'sis, n.* conclusion as to what is wrong reached by examining a patient, a situation, etc.
diagnose (*-nōz', -nōs'*), *v.t.* to recognise (a disease, etc.) from symptoms.
diagnos'tic (*-nos'*), *adj.*
[Gk. *dia*, thoroughly, *gnōnai*, to know.]

diagonal, *dī-ag'ò-nàl, adj.* stretching from one corner to an opposite corner.—*n.* a straight line so drawn.
diag'onally, *adv.*
[Gk. *dia*, through, *gōnia*, a corner.]

diagram, *dī'à-gram, n.* a figure or plan showing briefly the facts of a statement that is difficult to follow or remember.
diagrammat'ic, *adj.*
[Gk. *dia*, round, *graphein*, to write.]

dial, *dī'àl, n.* the face of a watch or clock: a plate with a movable index used for various purposes (e.g. on a gas, electric, meter).—*v.t.* to turn a telephone or other dial in such a way as e.g. to connect with (another number).
[Late L. *diālis*, daily—L. *diēs*, day.]

dialect, *dī'à-lekt, n.* a form of a language used by a particular district or class.
[Gk. *dialektos*, speech.]

dialogue, *dī'ȧ-log, n.* conversation, esp. in a play or novel.
[Gk. *dialogos.*]

diameter, *dī-am'ė-tėr, n.* a straight line drawn from side to side of, and passing through the centre of, a circle.
diamet'ric, -al, *adjs.* complete (e.g. *The two are diametrical opposites*).
diamet'rically, *adv.*
[Gk. *dia,* through, *metron,* measure.]

diamond, *dī'ȧ-mȯnd, n.* a crystal form of pure carbon, extremely hard: a four-sided figure with all sides equal but angles not right angles: a playing card with red mark(s) of this shape: a diamond-shaped area.—Also *adj.*
diamond wedding, the sixtieth anniversary of a wedding.
rough diamond, an uncut diamond: a worthy but unpolished person.
[Same root as **adamant.**]

diaper, *dī'ȧ-pėr, n.* a baby's napkin: a design of small diamond shapes.
[Gk. *dia,* through, *aspros,* white.]

diaphanous, *dī-af'ȧ-nủs, adj.* transparent—now usu. because fine, delicate.
[Gk. *dia,* through, *phainein,* to show.]

diaphragm, *dī'ȧ-fram, n.* a thin dividing membrane: the midriff, the part separating chest from abdomen.
[Gk. *dia,* across, *phragma,* a fence.]

diarist. See **diary.**

diarrhoea, diarrhea, *dī-ȧ-rē'ȧ n.* looseness of the bowels.
[Gk. *dia,* through, *rheein,* to flow.]

diary, *dī'ȧ-ri, n.* a daily record of events:—*pl.* **di'aries.**
dī'arist, *n.* one who keeps a diary.
[L. *diārium—diēs,* a day.]

diatribe, *dī'ȧ-trīb, n.* an angry harangue (against someone or something).
[Gk. *dia,* through, *trībein,* to rub.]

dibble, *dib'l, n.* a pointed tool used for making holes to put seed or plants in.
[Prob. conn. with **dab.**]

dice. See **die** (2).

dickey[1], **dicky**[1], *dik'i, n.* a seat at the back of carriage, motor car: false shirt-front.
[Perh. dial. *dick,* a leather apron.]

dicky[2], **dickey**[2], *dik'i, adj.* (*coll.*) shaky.
[Origin unknown.]

dicky-bird, *dik'i-bėrd, n.* a small bird.
[From *Dick,* Richard.]

Dictaphone, *dik'tȧ-fōn. n.* a machine for recording, and later dictating, letters, etc.
[Trademark; L. *dictāre,* to dictate, Gk. *phōnē,* sound.]

dictate, *dik-tāt', v.t.* to say or read for another to write: to lay down with authority (e.g. *to dictate terms to a defeated enemy*): to make necessary (e.g. *Circumstances dictated this course of action*).—*v.i.* to give orders (to).—*n.* (*dik'tāt*) an order.
dictā'tion, *n.* act of dictating: something read for another to write down.
dictā'tor, *n.* an all-powerful ruler.
dictā'torship, *n.*
dictato'rial (*-tȧ-*), *adj.* like a dictator: overbearing (e.g. *his dictatorial manner*).
dictato'rially, *adv.*
[L. *dictāre—dīcĕre,* to say.]

diction, *dik'sh(ȯ)n, n.* manner of speaking: choice of words.
[L. *dicĕre, dictum,* to say.]

dictionary, *dik'sh(ȯ)n-ȧ-ri, n.* a book containing the words of a language alphabetically arranged, with their meanings, etc.: a work containing other information alphabetically arranged.
[Late L. *dictiōnārium.*]

dictum, *dik'tủm, n.* a saying, esp. a considered opinion:—*pl.* **dic'ta.** [L.]

did. See **do** (1).

didactic, -al, *di-dak'tik, -ȧl,* or *dī-, adjs.* intended to teach: pompous: moralising.
[Gk. *didaktikos—didaskein,* to teach.]

diddle, *did'l, v.t.* to swindle.
[Origin uncertain.]

die[1], *dī, v.i.* to lose life: to wither:—*pr.p.* **dy'ing**; *pa.t., pa.p.* **died** (*dīd*).
die'hard, *n.* one who keeps up a vain resistance: an extreme conservative.
to die away, to fade from sight or hearing.
to die out, to become extinct.
to be dying to, to be very keen to.
[Prob. from a lost O.E. *dēgan.*]

die[2], *dī, n.* a small cube with numbered faces used in gaming: a device for stamping coin, etc., or for cutting metal:—*pl.* (gaming) **dice** (*dīs*); (stamping) **dies** (*dīz*).
dice, *v.i.* to play with dice.—*v.t.* to mark with squares:—*pr.p.* **dic'ing**; *pa.p.* **diced** (*dīst*).
the die is cast, an irrevocable step has been taken.
[O.Fr. *de,* pl. *dez.*]

diesel (engine), *dēz'l,* an internal-combustion engine in which heavy oil is ignited by heat produced by compression.
dies'el-elec'tric, *adj.* using power obtained from a diesel-operated electric generator.
dies'el-hydraul'ic, *adj.* using power transmitted by means of one or more mechanisms filled with oil.
[Rudolf *Diesel,* inventor.]

diet[1], *dī'ėt, n.* food: food planned or prescribed.—*v.i.* to take food according to rule because of illness, in order to slim, etc.—*v.t.* to put on a diet:—*pr.p.* **di'eting**; *pa.p.* **di'eted.**
dietet'ic, *adj.*
dietet'ics, *n.* the science of regulating diet.
[Gk. *diaita,* mode of living, diet.]

diet[2], *dī'ėt, n.* an assembly, council, or parliament.
[Prob. Gk. *diaita,* as **diet** (1).]

differ, *dif'ėr, v.i.* (with *from*) to be unlike:

(often with *with, from*) to disagree (with): —*pr.p.* **diff'ering**; *pa.p.* **diff'ered.**

diff'erence, *n.* what makes one thing unlike another: a quarrel: amount by which one quantity or number is greater than another.

diff'erent, *adj.* not the same (with *from*).

differential, *dif-ėr-en'shl, n.* a price or wage difference.

differentiate, *dif-ėr-en'shi-āt, v.t.* and *v.i.* (1) to mark, be, or (2) see, tell, a difference, used in the following ways:

(1) *This slight difference in colour differentiates A from B*; or, *This differentiates A and B.*

(2) *Look at the specimens and try to differentiate A and B*; or (more usually) *between A and B* ('to differentiate between two people, etc.', sometimes means to treat one with more generosity than the other).

differentiā'tion, *n.*

[L. *dif-* (=*dis-*), apart, *ferre*, to bear.]

difficult, *dif'i-kŭlt, adj.* not easy: requiring hard work: hard to please, or to persuade (e.g. *She is a difficult person*).

diff'iculty, *n.* hardness, laboriousness: an obstacle, objection (e.g. *He is suitable otherwise but his age is a difficulty*): something that cannot be easily understood: (in *pl.*) troubles, esp. money troubles:—*pl.* **diff'iculties.**

[L. *dif-* (=*dis-*), not, *facilis*, easy.]

diffident, *dif'i-dėnt, adj.* lacking self-confidence, shy.

diff'idence, *n.* **diff'idently,** *adv.*

[L. *dif-* (=*dis-*), not, *fīdĕre*, to trust.]

diffraction, *di-frak'sh(ȯ)n, n.* the spreading of light and other rays passing through a narrow opening, or by the edge of an object.

[L. *dif-* (=*dis-*), apart, *frangĕre, fractum*, to break.]

diffuse, *di-fūz', v.t.* and *v.i.* to spread in all directions.—*adj.* (*di-fūs'*) widely spread: using many words.

diffused' (*-fūzd'*), *adj.*

diffu'sion (*-fū'zh(ȯ)n*), *n.*

[L. *dif* (=*dis-*), apart, *fundĕre, fūsum*, to to pour.]

dig, *dig, v.t.* to turn up (e.g. earth) with a spade, etc.: to make (a hole) thus: to poke or thrust:—*pr.p.* **digg'ing**; *pa.t.* and *pa.p.* **dug.**—Also *v.i.*—*n.* a thrust, a poke: an archaeological excavation.

digg'er, *n.*

digg'ings, *n.pl.* a place where digging or mining is carried on.

dug'out, *n.* a boat made by hollowing out the trunk of a tree: a rough dwelling or shelter, *dug out* of a slope or bank or in a trench.

[Prob. O.Fr. *diguer.*]

digest, *di-* or *dī-jest', v.t.* (of an animal or plant body) to break down food in the mouth, stomach, etc.: to endure patiently (e.g. an insult): to think over (e.g. unpleasant news).—*v.i.* to undergo digestion.—*n.* (*dī'jest*) an orderly summary of any written matter: a magazine consisting of extracts from other sources.

digest'ible, *adj.* that may be digested.

digestion, *di-jes'ch(ȯ)n*, or *dī-*, *n.* act of digesting: ability to digest.

digest'ive, *adj.*

[L. *dīgerĕre, dīgestum*, to separate.]

digger, digging(s). See **dig.**

digit, *dij'it, n.* a finger or toe: any of the figures 0 to 9.

dig'ital, *adj.*

digital computer, an electronic calculating machine using arithmetical digits.

[L. *digitus*, a finger or toe.]

digitalis, *dij-i-tā'lis, n.* a powerful heart stimulant obtained from dried leaves of the common foxglove.

[Same root as **digit.**]

dignify, *dig'ni-fī, v.t.* to confer honour on—sometimes undeserved honour (e.g. *a cottage dignified by the name of 'Four Winds House'*):—*pr.p.* **dig'nifying**; *pa.p.* **dig'nified.**

dig'nified, *adj.* showing dignity.

dig'nitary, *n.* a person holding high office, esp. in the church:—*pl.* **-ies.**

dig'nity, *n.* stateliness of manner: manner showing a sense of one's own worth or of the solemnity of the occasion: high rank:—*pl.* **-ies.**

to be on one's dignity, to be ready to take offence at any slight.

[L. *dignitās*, worthiness, *facĕre*, make.]

digress, *di-* or *dī-gres', v.i.* to wander from the point, or from the main subject.

digression (*-gresh'ȯn*), *n.*

[L. *dīgredī, dīgressus*, to step aside.]

dike, dyke, *dīk, n.* a trench, or the earth dug out and thrown up: a ditch: a mound raised to prevent flooding: (*Scot.*) a wall.

[O.E. *dīc.*]

dilapidated, *di-lap'i-dāt-id, adj.* in a state of disrepair, neglected, very shabby.

dilapidā'tion, *n.*

[L. *dī*, apart, *lapis, lapidis*, a stone.]

dilate, *di-*, or *dī-lāt', v.t.* and *v.i.* to make, or become, larger, swell out: (*v.i.* with *on, upon*) to comment at length upon.

dilā'tion, dilātā'tion, *ns.* enlargement.

[L. *dī-* (=*dis-*), *latus*, broad.]

dilatory, *dil'ȧ-tȯr-i, adj.* inclined to delay: delaying, putting off.

dil'atoriness, *n.*

[L. *dīlātōrius*, putting off (time).]

dilemma, *di-*, or *dī-lem'ȧ*, a position in which each of two (or more) courses is equally undesirable. [Gk.]

dilettante, *dil-ė-tan'ti, n.* one who dabbles in an art or science: a lover of the arts, connoisseur.

[It.; pr.p. of *dilettare*, to delight in.]

diligent, *dil'i-jėnt, adj.* earnestly working hard, industrious.

dil′igence, *n.* **dil′igently,** *adv.*
[Fr.—L. *dīligens*, pr.p. *dīligěre*, choose.]

dilly-dally, *dil′i-dal′i, v.i.* to loiter, trifle.
[Formed from **dally.**]

dilute, *di-*, or *dī-lūt′*, or *-lo͞ot′*, *v.t.* to lessen the strength, etc., of, by mixing, esp. with water: to increase the proportion of unskilled to skilled among (workers in an industry—*to dilute labour*). —*adj.* reduced in strength, weak.
dilu′tion, *n.*
[L. *dī-*, away, *luěre*, to wash.]

dim, *dim, adj.* not bright or distinct: not seeing, or understanding, etc., clearly.—*v.t.* and *v.i.* to make, or become, dark:—*pr.p.* **dimm′ing**; *pa.p.* **dimmed.**
dim′ly, *adv.* **dim′ness,** *n.*
[O.E. *dimm.*]

dime, *dīm, n.* 10 cents.
[L. *decima* (*pars*), a tenth (part).]

dimension, *di-*, *dī-men′sh(ȯ)n, n.* measure in length, breadth, or thickness.
[L. *dīmensiō*—*mētīrī*, to measure.]

diminish, *di-min′ish, v.t.* and *v.i.* to make, or become, less.
See also **diminution.**
[Indirectly same root as **diminution.**]

diminuendo, *di-min-ū-en′dō, adj.* and *adv.* (*music*) gradually letting the sound die away.—Also *n.*
[It.—L. *dīminuěre*, to lessen.]

diminution, *dim-in-ū′sh(ȯ)n, n.* lessening.
dimin′utive, *adj.* very small.—*n.* a word formed from another to express a little one of the kind (e.g. *codling* from *cod*).
See also **diminish.**
[L. *dīminuěre*, *dīminūtum*, to lessen.]

dimple, *dim′pl, n.* a small hollow, esp. on the surface of the body.—*v.i.* to form dimples.—*v.t.* to mark with dimples.
[Prob. conn. with Ger. *tümpel*, pool.]

din, *din, n.* a loud continued noise.—*v.t.* to repeat loudly and persistently:—*pr.p.* **dinn′ing**; *pa.p.* **dinned.**
[O.E. *dyn*, *dyne*; conn. Dan. *dön*, noise.]

dine, *dīn, v.i.* to take dinner.—*v.t.* to give dinner to.
din′er, *n.* one who dines: a restaurant car on a train.
dinner, *din′ėr, n.* chief meal of the day.
din′ingroom, *n.* room used for meals.
[Perh. O.Fr. *disner* (Fr. *dîner*).]

ding-dong, *ding′-dong, n.* the sound of bells. —*adj.* (e.g. of an argument, fight, etc.) stubbornly contested with alternate success and failure. [Imit.]

dinghy, *ding′gi, n.* a small rowing-boat or ship's tender.
[Indian *dīngī*, a small boat.]

dingo, *ding′gō, n.* the native dog of Australia:—*pl.* **dingoes,** *ding′gōz.*
[Native name.]

dingy, *din′ji, adj.* shabby, dirty-looking: not bright.
din′gily, *adv.* **din′giness,** *n.*
[Origin uncertain.]

dinner. See **dine.**

dinosaur, *dī′no-sör, n.* a large extinct reptile.
[Gk. *deinos*, terrible, *sauros*, lizard.]

dint, *dint, n.* the mark of a blow: force (e.g. *He managed to do it by dint of perseverance*).—*v.t.* to make a dint in.
[O.E. *dynt*, blow, conn. O. Norse *dyntr.*]

diocese, *dī′ō-sēs*, *-sis, n.* a bishop's district.
diocesan, *dī-os′ėsn*, *-ėzn, adj.* of a diocese.
[Gk. *dioikēsis*—*dioikeein*, to keep house.]

dip, *dip, v.t.* to plunge for a moment: to lower and raise again (as a flag).—*v.i.* (with *into*) to take a casual glance at, or brief interest in: to slope downwards:—*pr.p.* **dipp′ing**; *pa.p.* **dipped.**—*n.* a down slope: a bath(e): a candle made by dipping a wick in tallow.
dipp′er, *n.* a ladle: a bird that dives for food: (*cap.*) the Plough.
[O.E. *dyppan.*]

diphtheria, *dif-thē′ri-ȧ, n.* an infectious throat disease in which the air passages become covered with a leathery membrane.
[Gk. *diphthera*, leather.]

diphthong, *dif′thong, n.* (*loosely*) two letters expressing one sound, as *ph* in *photograph*, *ea* in *dead*, *eo* in *people*: two vowel sounds (represented by one letter or by two) pronounced as one syllable, as in *my* (*ma′i*), *roam* (*rō′ủm*): the symbols æ, œ.
[Gk. *di*, twice, *phthongos*, sound.]

diploma, *di-plō′mȧ, n.* a writing conferring an honour or a privilege.
diplomacy, *di-plō′mȧ-si, n.* the art of negotiating with foreign countries: skill in carrying out any negotiations.
diplomat′ic, *adj.* **diplomat′ically,** *adv.*
dip′lomat, diplo′matist, *ns.* one skilled in diplomacy.
[Gk. *diplōma*, a letter folded double.]

dipper, dipping. See **dip.**

dipsomania, *dip-sō-mā′ni-ȧ, n.* an irresistible craving for strong drink.
dipsomā′niac, *n.*
[Gk. *dipsa*, thirst, *mania*, madness.]

dire, *dīr, adj.* dreadful.
[L. *dīrus.*]

direct, *di-rekt′*, *dī′rekt, adj.* straight, not roundabout: (of manner) straightforward, frank: in an unbroken line of descent.—*v.t.* to turn in a particular direction (e.g. *to direct one's steps towards, one's attention towards, one's remarks to a person*): to show (a person) the way (to): to mark (an envelope, etc.) with a name and address: to instruct, order: to control, regulate (e.g. *to direct operations.*)
direc′tion, *n.* the act of aiming, or turning, towards something: the region in which something lies: the line or course in which anything moves: guidance: command: (in *pl.*) instructions (e.g. *directions for use*).

direc′tive, *n.* a general instruction as to procedure issued by a higher authority.
direct′ly, *adv.* in a direct manner: almost at once.
direct′ness, *n.*
direct′or, *n.* a person or thing that directs: one of a group of persons who manage the affairs of a business.
direct′ory, *n.* a book giving names and addresses, and sometimes telephone numbers:—*pl.* **-ies.**
direct current, an electric current flowing in one direction only.
direct speech, speech reported in exact words of the speaker (see **indirect**).
direct tax, income tax (also property tax, if any) as opp. to indirect tax (see this).
[L. *dīrigĕre, dīrectum,* to set in a straight line.]

dirge, *dėrj. n.* a funeral song or hymn.
[From *dirige,* the first word of part of service in Latin for the dead.]

dirigible, *dir′i-ji-bl, n.* a balloon or airship that can be steered.
[From root of **direct.**]

dirk, *dėrk, n.* a Highland dagger.
[Origin unknown.]

dirt, *dėrt, n.* mud, dust, dung, etc.
dirt′y, *adj.* not clean: soiled: unclean morally: stormy (e.g. *dirty weather*):—*comp.* **dirt′ier**; *superl.* **dirt′iest.**—*v.t., v.i.* to soil with dirt:—*pr.p.* **dirt′ying**; *pa.p.* **dirt′ied.**
dirt′ily, *adv.* **dirt′iness,** *n.*
dirt track, a motor-cycle racing track with earthy or cindery surface.
dirty money, extra pay for unloading unpleasant cargoes.
[M.E. *drit*; prob. from Old Norse.]

dis-, *dis-, pfx.* usu. reversing the meaning of the rest of the word (e.g. **disbelieve, discontent**). [L.]

disable, *dis-ā′bl, v.t.* to take away the ability or strength of: to cripple.
disabil′ity, *n.* the thing that prevents one from doing something: lack of power, esp. legal, to act:—*pl.* **-ies.**
disa′blement, *n.* the act of disabling or state of being disabled. [Pfx. **dis-.**]

disabuse, *dis-à-būz′, v.t.* to undeceive or set right (e.g. *Disabuse him of this idea*). [Pfx. **dis-.**]

disadvantage, *dis-ad-vân′tij, n.* a drawback, unfavourable circumstance.
disadvantā′geous (*-jŭs*), *adj.*
at a disadvantage, in an unfavourable position. [Pfx. **dis-.**]

disaffect, *dis-à-fekt′, v.t.* to make discontented or unfriendly.
disaffect′ed, *pa.p., adj.* discontented, disloyal.
disaffect′edness, disaffec′tion, *ns.*
[Pfx. **dis-.**]

disagree, *dis-à-grē′, v.i.* to differ: to quarrel: (of food) to cause indigestion (e.g. *Onions disagree with me*).
disagree′able, *adj.* unpleasant.
disagree′ably, *adv.*
disagree′ment, *n.* [Pfx. **dis-.**]

disallow, *dis-à-low′, v.t.* to refuse to allow or admit (e.g. a claim).
[O.Fr. *desalouer.*]

disappear, *dis-à-pēr′, v.i.* to vanish from sight: to fade out of existence.
disappear′ance, *n.* [Pfx. **dis-.**]

disappoint, *dis-à-point′, v.t.* to fall short of the hopes of (e.g. *This disappointed Mary*): to fail to fulfil (e.g. *This disappointed her hopes*).
disappoint′ment, *n.*
[O.Fr. *desapointer.*]

disapprobation. See **disapprove.**

disapprove, *dis-à-proo͞v′, v.i.* to have an unfavourable opinion (of).—Also *v.t.*
disapprov′al, disapprobā′tion, *ns.*
disapprov′ing, *adj.*
disapprov′ingly, *adv.* [Pfx. **dis-.**]

disarm, *dis-ärm′, v.t.* to take away weapons from: to make (an unfriendly person) feel friendly.—*v.i.* to reduce national armaments.
disarm′ament, *n.* reduction of fighting forces or equipment.
disarm′ing, *adj.* gaining goodwill or friendliness (e.g. *a disarming smile*).
disarm′ingly, *adv.* [Pfx. **dis-.**]

disarrange, *dis-à-rānj′, v.t.* to disturb the arrangement of, put in disorder.
[Pfx. **dis-.**]

disarray, *dis-à-rā′, n.* disorder: state of being incompletely dressed. [Pfx. **dis-.**]

disassociate, *dis-à-sō′shi-āt, v.t.* dissociate.
[Pfx. **dis-.**]

disaster, *diz-âs′tėr, n.* an unfortunate event: great misfortune.
disas′trous, *adj.* very unfortunate, ruinous.
disas′trously, *adv.*
disas′trousness, *n.*
[O.Fr. *desastre*—*des-* (with evil sense), *astre,* a star, destiny.]

disavow, *dis-à-vow′, v.t.* to deny that one has (e.g. *He disavowed knowledge of the affair*): to refuse to admit responsibility for.
disavow′al, *n.*
[O.Fr. *desavouer.*]

disband, *dis-band′, v.t.* to disperse, break up (esp. an army).—Also *v.i.*
disband′ment, *n.*
[O.Fr. *desbander,* to unbind.]

disbelieve, *dis-bi-lēv′, v.t.* not to believe.—Also *v.i.* (with *in*).
disbelief′, *n.* [Pfx. **dis-.**]

disburden, *dis-bûr′dn, v.t.* to remove a burden from: to unload. [Pfx. **dis-.**]

disburse, *dis-bûrs′, v.t.* to pay out.
disburs′al, disburse′ment, *ns.*
[O.Fr. *des-,* apart, *bourse,* a purse.]

disc. Same as **disk.**

discard, *dis-kärd′, v.t.* and *v.i.* to throw away (a card) as useless: to get rid of.
[L. *dis-,* away, and **card.**]

discern, *di-sėrn′, di-zėrn′, v.t.* to distinguish clearly by the eye or understanding.
discern′ible, *adj.* **discern′ibly,** *adv.*
discern′ing, *adj.* having insight and understanding.
discern′ment, *n.*
[L. *dis-*, thoroughly, *cernĕre*, perceive.]

discharge, *dis-chärj′, v.t.* to unload (cargo): to set free: to acquit: to dismiss: to fire (a gun): to let out (e.g. smoke): to perform (duties): to pay (a debt).—*n.* unloading: acquittal: dismissal: firing: giving out: performance: payment.
[O.Fr. *descharger.*]

disciple, *dis-ī′pl, n.* one who believes in the teaching of another.
[L. *discipulus*, from *discĕre*, to learn.]

discipline, *dis′i-plin, n.* training in an orderly mode of life: order kept by means of control: penance.—*v.t.* to bring under control: to punish, chastise.
disciplinā′rian, *n.* one who enforces strict discipline.
dis′ciplinary, *adj.* of discipline: punishing, intended to enforce control (e.g. *to take disciplinary action*).
[L. *disciplina*; same root as **disciple.**]

disclaim, *dis-klām′, v.t.* to deny, refuse to acknowledge.
disclaim′er, *n.* a denial.
[L. *dis-*, apart, *clāmāre*, to cry out.]

disclose, *dis-klōz′, v.t.* to lay open, reveal.
disclō′sure, *n.* act of disclosing: something that is disclosed.
[L. *dis-*, *claudĕre*, *clausum*, to shut.]

discolour, *dis-kul′ȯr, v.t.* to spoil the colour of: to stain.—Also *v.i.*
discolo(u)rā′tion, *n.*
[L. *dis-*, *colōrāre*, to colour.]

discomfit, *dis-kum′fit, v.t.* to abash, embarrass: to defeat:—*pr.p.* **discom′fiting**; *pa.p.* **discom′fited.**
discom′fiture, *n.*
[L. *dis-*, not, *conficĕre*, to prepare.]

discomfort, *dis-kum′fȯrt, n.* want of comfort, uneasiness.
[O.Fr. *des-*, *conforter*, to comfort.]

discommode, *dis-kȯ-mōd′, v.t.* to inconvenience.
[L. *dis-*, *commodāre*, to make fit.]

discompose, *dis-kom-pōz′, v.t.* to agitate, fluster. [Pfx. **dis-.**]

disconcert, *dis-kȯn-sėrt′, v.t.* to embarrass, take aback.
[O.Fr. *des-*, *concerter*, to arrange.]

disconnect, *dis-kȯ-nekt′, v.t.* to separate: to detach, disjoin.
disconnect′ed, *adj.* separated: (of speech, writing) rambling. [Pfx. **dis-.**]

disconsolate, *dis-kon′sȯ-lit, adj.* forlorn, dejected.
discon′solately, *adv.*
discon′solateness, *n.*
[L. *dis-*, not, *consōlari*, to console.]

discontent, *dis-kȯn-tent′, n.* dissatisfaction: ill-humour.
discontent′ed, *adj.* dissatisfied: fretful.
discontent′edly, *adv.*
discontent′edness, -content′ment, *ns.*
[Pfx. **dis-.**]

discontinue, *dis-kȯn-tin′ū, v.t.* to leave off, stop: to put an end to.—Also *v.i.*
discontin′uance, discontinuā′tion, *ns.*
discontinu′ity, *n.* lack of continuity.
discontin′uous, *adj.* not continuous, interrupted.
[L. *dis-*, not, *continuāre*, to continue.]

discord, *dis′körd, n.* disagreement, quarrelling: loud and/or inharmonious sound.
discord′ant, *adj.* disagreeing: harsh.
discord′ance, discord′ancy, *ns.*
[L. *discordia—dis-*, and *cor, cordis*, heart.]

discothèque, -theque, *dis-kō-tek, n.* club for dancing to gramophone records. [Fr.]

discount, *dis′kownt, n.* a sum taken off an account, benefiting the payer.—*v.t.* (*dis-kownt′*) to leave out of consideration: to allow for exaggeration in (e.g. a story): to buy or sell (e.g. a bill of exchange not yet due) deducting from the price the value of interest for the time it has still to run.
at a discount, below par: not in demand.
[O.Fr. *des-*, away, *compter*, to count.]

discountenance, *dis-kown′tėn-ȧns, v.t.* to show disapproval of.
[O.Fr. *des-*, not, *contenance*, countenance.]

discourage, *dis-kûr′ij, v.t.* to dishearten: to persuade against (with *from*; e.g. *The rain discouraged him from going camping*): to hinder: to oppose.
[O.Fr. *descourager.*]

discourse, *dis-kōrs′, -körs′, dis′-, n.* a speech, a sermon.—*v.i.* to talk: to hold forth (upon).
[L. *discursus—dis-*, away, *currĕre*, to run.]

discourteous, *dis-kûr′tyȯs, adj.* not polite, rude.
discour′teousness, discour′tesy, *ns.*
[Pfx. **dis-.**]

discover, *dis-kuv′ėr, v.t.* to find by chance: to find out.
discov′erer, *n.*
discov′ery, *n.* finding out: exploration: a thing discovered:—*pl.* **-eries.**
[O.Fr. *des-*, away, *couvrir*, to cover.]

discredit, *dis-kred′it, n.* loss of good reputation (e.g. *I know something to his discredit*): doubt: disbelief.—*v.t.* to disbelieve: to make unbelievable: to disgrace.
discred′itable, *adj.* disgraceful.
discred′itably, *adv.* [Pfx. **dis-.**]

discreet, *dis-krēt′, adj.* prudent, wise: not saying anything to cause trouble.
discreet′ness, discre′tion (*dis-kresh′(ȯ)n*), *ns.*
at the discretion of, left to the judgment or will of (someone).
[L. *discrētus—discernĕre*, to perceive.]

discrepancy, *dis-krep′ȧn-si, n.* disagreement, inconsistency (e.g. *There is some discrepancy between the two accounts of what happened*):—*pl.* **discrep′ancies.**
[L. *discrepans*, different.]

discrete, *dis-krēt′, adj.* separate.
[Same root as **discreet.**]
discretion. See **discreet.**
discriminate, *dis-krim′i-nāt, v.t.* to be the difference between (often with *from*; e.g. *These markings discriminate the one bird from the other*).—*v.i.* to observe a difference (between): (with *in favour of, against*) to treat favourably or unfavourably.
discrim′inating, *adj.* making distinctions: showing good judgment.
discriminā′tion, *n.* act of discriminating: ability to recognise small differences: good judgment.
[L. *discrīmināre*; conn. with **discern.**]
discursive, *dis-kûr′siv, adj.* wandering from the point.
[Same root as **discourse.**]
discus, *dis′kus, n.* a heavy disk thrown in competition in ancient and modern Olympic games.
[L.—Gk. *diskos.*]
discuss, *dis-kus′, v.t.* to talk about.
discussion, *dis-kush′(ò)n, n.*
[L. *dis-*, apart, *quatĕre*, to shake.]
disdain, *dis-dān′, v.t.* to think it unworthy of oneself (e.g. *I disdain to take the money*): to scorn, reject.—*n.* scorn: haughtiness.
disdain′ful, *adj.* **disdain′fully,** *adv.*
[O.Fr. *desdaigner*—L. *dis-*, *dignus*, worthy.]
disease, *diz-ēz′, n.* (an) illness of mind or body.
diseased′, *adj.*
[O.Fr. *desaise*—*des-*, not, *aise*, ease.]
disembark, *dis-ėm-bärk′, v.t.* to set ashore. —*v.i.* to land.
disembarkā′tion, *n.*
[O.Fr. *desembarquer.*]
disembody, *dis-ėm-bod′i, v.t.* to take (the spirit) away from the body:—*pr.p.* **disembod′ying**; *pa.p.* **disembod′ied.**
[Pfx. **dis-,** and **embody.**]
disembowel, *dis-ėm-bow′ėl, v.t.* to take the inside out of.
[Pfx. **dis-,** *embowel*, take inside out of.]
disenchant, *dis-ėn-chânt′, v.t.* to free from enchantment or from a pleasant false belief.
disenchant′ment, *n.* [Pfx. **dis-.**]
disencumber, *dis-ėn-kum′bėr, v.t.* to free from something that hampers or burdens.
[Pfx. **dis-.**]
disengage, *dis-ėn-gāj′, v.t.* to separate, disjoin: to free.—*v.i.* (of opponents) to withdraw from hostile positions.
disengaged′, *adj.* separated: freed: not occupied or engaged: not in a job.
disengage′ment, *n.*
[O.Fr. *desengager.*]
disentangle, *dis-ėn-tang′gl, v.t.* to free from entanglement: to unravel.
disentang′lement, *n.* [Pfx. **dis-.**]
disestablish, *dis-es-tab′lish, v.t.* to deprive (a church) of state support.
disestab′lishment, *n.* [Pfx. **dis-.**]
disfavour, *dis-fāv′ǒr, n.* displeasure, disapproval: state of being out of favour (e.g. *He was in disfavour because he had stayed out late*). [Pfx. **dis-.**]
disfigure, *dis-fig′ūr, v.t.* to spoil the beauty of, to deface.
disfig′urement, disfigūrā′tion, *ns.*
[O.Fr. *desfigurer.*]
disfranchise, *dis-fran′chīz, v.t.* to take the right to vote away from. [Pfx. **dis-.**]
disgorge, *dis-görj′, v.t.* to vomit: to throw out with violence: to give up (what one has wrongfully seized).
[O.Fr. *desgorger.*]
disgrace, *dis-grās′, n.* state of being out of favour: cause of shame: dishonour.—*v.t.* to dismiss from favour or office: to bring shame upon.
disgrace′ful, *adj.* very bad, shameful.
disgrace′fully, *adv.*
disgrace′fulness, *n.*
[L. *dis-*, not, *gratia*, favour.]
disgruntle, *dis-grun′tl, v.t.* to make dissatisfied and sulky.
[Pfx. *dis-*, and *gruntle*—**grunt.**]
disguise, *dis-gīz′, v.t.* to conceal by a change of dress, etc.: to hide (e.g. one's intentions).—*n.* dress and/or make-up intended to conceal who the wearer is.
[O.Fr. *des-*, not, *guise*, manner.]
disgust, *dis-gust′, n.* loathing: feeling of sickness.—*v.t.* to arouse these feelings in (someone).
disgust′ing, *adj.* **disgust′ingly,** *adv.*
[O.Fr. *desgouster*—*gouster*, to taste.]
dish, *dish, n.* a vessel in which food is served: the food in a dish.—*v.t.* to put in a dish, for table: (*coll.*) to defeat.
to dish up, to serve: to present (something presented before; e.g. *to dish up old arguments*).
[O.E. *disc*—L. *discus*, disk.]
dishabille, *dis-a-bēl′, n.* carelessness of dress: undress.—Also **deshabille′.**
[Fr. *déshabiller*, to undress.]
dishearten, *dis-här′tn, v.t.* to take courage or hope away from, depress.
[Pfx. **dis-.**]
dishevel, *di-shev′el, v.t.* to disorder, make untidy, as hair:—*pr.p.* **dishev′elling**; *pa.p.* **dishev′elled.**
[L. *dis-*, in different directions, *capillus*, hair.]
dishonest, *dis-on′ist, adj.* not honest: cheating: insincere.
dishon′estly, *adv.* **dishon′esty,** *n.*
[O.Fr. *deshoneste.*]
dishonour, *dis-on′ǒr, n.* disgrace: shame. —*v.t.* to deprive of honour: to disgrace: to refuse payment of (e.g. a cheque).
dishon′ourable, *adj.*
dishon′ourably, *adv.*
[O.Fr. *deshonneur.*]
disillusion, *dis-i-lōō′zh(ò)n*, or *-lū′, n.* setting free from false pleasant belief or view.—*v.t.* to do this, to undeceive.

disillu′sioned, *adj.* free from illusions, esp. taking a cynical view of life.
disillu′sionment, *n.* [Pfx. **dis-**.]

disincentive, *dis-in-sen′tiv, n.* something that discourages one from trying, or that stands in the way of progress. [Pfx. **dis-**.]

disinclination, *dis-in-kli-nā′sh(ȯ)n, n.* unwillingness.
disincline′, *v.t.* to make unwilling (to do, for).
disinclined′, *adj.* unwilling (to do, for). [Pfx. **dis-**.]

disinfect, *dis-in-fekt′, v.t.* to destroy disease germs in.
disinfect′ant, *n.* anything that destroys the causes of infection.
disinfec′tion, *n.* [Pfx. **dis-**.]

disingenuous, *dis-in-jen′ū-ŭs, adj.* not frank or open, crafty.
disingen′uousness, *n.* [Pfx. **dis-**.]

disinherit, *dis-in-her′it, v.t.* to take away from (a person) the right to inherit. [Pfx. **dis-**.]

disintegrate, *dis-in′ti-grāt, v.i.* to come to pieces: to crumble.—Also *v.t.*
disintegrā′tion, *n.* [Pfx. **dis-**.]

disinter, *dis-in-ter′, v.t.* to take out of a grave: to bring (e.g. something hidden, forgotten) to view.
disinter′ment, *n.* [Pfx. **dis-**.]

disinterested, *dis-in′tris-tid, adj.* not influenced by private feelings or selfish motives: (*wrongly*) uninterested. [Pfx. **dis-**.]

disjoin, *dis-join′, v.t.* to separate what has been joined.
disjoint′, *v.t.* to put out of joint: to separate united parts.
disjoint′ed, *adj.* not properly connected (e.g. *some disjointed remarks*).
disjoint′edly, *adv.* **disjoint′edness,** *n.*
[L. *dis-*, and *jungĕre*, to join.]

disk, disc, *disk, n.* a flat thin circular body: a gramophone record.
disk jockey, someone who gives a recital of gramophone records.
[Root as **discus.**]

dislike, *dis-līk′, v.t.* to be displeased with, to disapprove of.—Also *n.* [Pfx. **dis-**.]

dislocate, *dis′lō-kāt, v.t.* to put out of joint: to throw out of order (e.g. traffic, plans).
dislocā′tion, *n.*
[L. *dis-*, apart, *locāre*, to place.]

dislodge, *dis-loj′, v.t.* to drive from a place of rest, hiding, or defence: to knock accidentally out of place.
[O.Fr. *des-*, apart, *loger*, to lodge.]

disloyal, *dis-loi′ȧl, adj.* false, faithless.
disloy′ally, *adv.* **disloy′alty,** *n.*
[O.Fr. *des-*, not, *loial*, loyal.]

dismal, *diz′mȧl, adj.* gloomy, cheerless.
dis′mally, *adv.* **dis′malness,** *n.*
[L. *dies malī*, evil, unlucky days.]

dismantle, *dis-man′tl, v.t.* to strip of furniture, fittings, etc.: to pull down, or take to pieces.
[O.Fr. *des-*, away, *mantel*, a mantle.]

dismay, *dis-mā′, v.t.* to daunt, discourage or upset (a person).—Also *n.*
[L. *dis-*, away, and root of **may** (1).]

dismember, *dis-mem′bėr, v.t.* to tear limb from limb: to tear to pieces.
dismem′berment, *n.*
[O.Fr. *desmembrer—membre*, a member.]

dismiss, *dis-mis′, v.t.* to send away: to put away (from one's thoughts): to remove from office or employment: (*law*) to put out of court, to discharge.
dismiss′al, *n.*
[L. *dis-*, away, *mittĕre, missum*, to send.]

dismount, *dis-mownt′, v.i.* to come off a horse, etc.—*v.t.* to remove from a support, etc.: to unhorse.
[O.Fr. *des-*, opp. of, *monter*, to mount.]

disobedient. See **disobey.**

disobey, *dis-ȯ-bā′, v.t.* to neglect, or refuse, to do what is commanded.
disobedient, *dis-ȯ-bēd′yėnt, adj.* neglecting, or refusing, to obey.
disobēd′ience, *n.* **disobēd′iently,** *adv.*
[O.Fr. *des-*, opp. of, *obeir*, to obey.]

disoblige, *dis-ȯ-blīj′, v.t.* to show disregard for claims or wishes of (a person).
disoblig′ing, *adj.* unwilling to consider or to act according to the wishes of others.
disoblig′ingly, *adv.* [Pfx. **dis-**.]

disorder, *dis-ör′dėr, n.* want of order, confusion: disturbance, breach of the peace: a disease.—*v.t.* to disarrange: to upset health (physical or mental) of.
disor′dered, *adj.* (e.g. *a disordered mind*).
disor′derly, *adj.* out of order, in confusion: irregular, lawless.
disor′derliness, *n.*
[O.Fr. *des-*, opp. of, *ordre*, order.]

disorganise, *dis-ör′gȧn-īz, v.t.* to destroy the arrangement of: to throw into disorder.
disorganisā′tion, *n.* [Pfx. **dis-**.]

disown, *dis-ōn′, v.t.* to refuse to acknowledge as belonging to oneself. [Pfx. **dis-**.]

disparage, *dis-par′ij, v.t.* to talk slightingly of.
dispar′agement, *n.*
dispar′agingly, *adv.*
[O.Fr. *desparager*—L. *par*, equal.]

disparity, *dis-par′i-ti, n.* inequality, difference (in age, amount, etc.)
[L. *dispar*, unequal.]

dispassionate, *dis-pash′(ȯ)n-it, adj.* free from passion, cool, unbiassed (e.g. *a dispassionate observer*; *a dispassionate statement of the difficulties*).
dispass′ionately, *adv.* [Pfx. **dis-**.]

dispatch, despatch, *dis-pach′, v.t.* to send (e.g. a messenger): to put to death: to deal with (e.g. business) quickly.—*n.* a sending away (e.g. of mails): haste: a message: (in *pl.*) state papers (military, diplomatic, etc.).
dispatch box, a box for holding dispatches or valuable papers.

dispatch rider, a carrier of dispatches on motor bicycle, etc.
[It. *dispacciare* or Sp. *despachar*, hasten.]

dispel, *dis-pel′*, *v.t.* to drive away, make disappear (e.g. fears, darkness):—*pr.p.* **dispell′ing**; *pa.p.* **dispelled′**.
[L. *dis-*, away, *pellĕre*, to drive.]

dispensable, etc. See **dispense.**

dispense, *dis-pens′*, *v.t.* to give out, distribute, in portions (e.g. alms, favours): to deal out, administer (e.g. *He sat under a palm tree dispensing justice to the tribe*): (also *v.i.*) to make up (prescriptions).
dispens′er, *n.*
dispens′able, *adj.* that may be done without.
dispensary, *dis-pens′ȧr-i*, *n.*a place where medicines are given out:—*pl.* **-ies.**
dispensation, *dis-pen-sā′sh(ȯ)n*, *n.* the act of dealing out: an act of divine Providence: permission to neglect a rule.
to dispense with, to get rid of, or do without (e.g. *to economise by dispensing with two assistants*).
[L. *dis-*, apart, *pensāre*, to weigh.]

disperse, *dis-pėrs′*, *v.t.* to scatter in all directions: to spread (e.g. news): to cause to vanish.—*v.i.* to separate: to spread: to vanish.
dispers′al, disper′sion, *ns.*
[L. *dī-*, *spargĕre*, *sparsum*, scatter.]

dispirit, *dis-pir′it*, *v.t.* to discourage.
dispir′ited, *adj.* dejected. [Pfx. **dis-**.]

displace, *dis-plās′*, *v.t.* to disarrange: to remove from office: to take the place of.
displace′ment, *n.* a putting or being out of place: the quantity of water displaced by a floating body.
displaced person, one taken from his country as slave labour: a refugee.
[O.Fr. *des-*, not, *place*, place.]

display, *dis-plā′*, *v.t.* to show.—*n.* exhibition: a show intended to attract notice.
[O.Fr. *des-*, opp. of, *plier*, *ploier*, to fold.]

displease, *dis-plēz′*, *v.t.* to anger slightly: to be disagreeable, e.g. artistically, to.
displeased′, *adj.*
displeasure,′ *dis-plezh′ůr*, anger: disapproval.
[O.Fr. *des-*, not, *plaisir*, to please.]

disport, *dis-pōrt′*, *-pört′*, *v.t.* to amuse (oneself).—*v.i.* to frolic.
[O.Fr. *desporter*—*porter*, to carry.]

dispose, *dis-pōz′*, *v.t.* to arrange: to make inclined (e.g. *This disposed him to make light of what had happened*).
dispos′al, *n.* arrangement: getting rid (of): right of using, etc. (e.g. *I put a car at his disposal*).
disposed′, *adj.* inclined: having a certain feeling (towards; e.g. *well*, *ill*, *disposed towards his neighbours*).
to dispose of, to arrange what is to be done about: to get rid of.
See also **disposition** (from a different root).
[O.Fr. *dis-*, *poser*, to place.]

disposition, *dis-pȯ-zish′(ȯ)n*, *n.* arrangement: bestowal by will (of one's property etc.): natural tendency, temper (e.g. *The child has a placid disposition*).
[Fr.—L. *dis-*, apart, *pōnĕre*, to place.]

dispossess, *dis-pȯz-es′*, *v.t.* to put out of possession (of), deprive (of). [Pfx. **dis-**.]

disproof, *dis-proo͞f′*, *n.* act of disproving: proof that something is not true.
[Pfx. **dis-**.]

disproportion, *dis-prȯ-pōr′sh(ȯ)n*, *-pör′*, *n.* lack of proportion (in size, importance, etc.).
dispropor′tionate, *adj.* too large or too small in relation to something else.
dispropor′tionately, *adv.* [Pfx. **dis-**.]

disprove, *dis-proo͞v′*, *v.t.* to prove to be not true, false, wrong.
See also **disproof.**
[O.Fr. *desprover*.]

dispute, *dis-pūt′*, *v.t.* to argue about: to argue against: to resist, contest.—Also *v.i.*—*n.* a contest in words: a quarrel.
disput′able (also *dis′*), *adj.* that may be disputed: not certain.
disput′ant (or *dis′*), **disput′er,** *ns.*
disputā′tion, *n.* an argument.
disputa′tious (*-ā′shůs*), *adj.* inclined to argue.
[O.Fr. *desputer*.]

disqualify, *dis-kwol′i-fī*, *v.t.* to take away a qualification or right from: to make unfit for some purpose.
disqualificā′tion, *n.* [Pfx. **dis-**.]

disquiet, *dis-kwī′it*, *n.* unrest: uneasiness: anxiety.—*v.t.* to make uneasy, worry.
disqui′etude, *n.* [Pfx. **dis-**.]

disquisition, *dis-kwi-zish′(ȯ)n*, *n.* a long discourse.
[L. *dis-*, *quaerĕre*, *quaesītum*, to seek.]

disregard, *dis-ri-gärd′*, *v.t.* to pay no attention to.—*n.* want of attention: neglect (of—also with *for*). [Pfx. **dis-**.]

disrepair, *dis-ri-pār′*, *n.* state of being out of repair. [Pfx. **dis-**.]

disrepute, *dis-ri-pūt′*, *n.* bad repute.
disrep′utable, *adj.* disgraceful: of low character: not respectable.
disrep′utably, *adv.* [Pfx. **dis-**.]

disrespect, *dis-ri-spekt′*, *n.* want of respect: discourtesy: rudeness.
disrespect′ful, *adj.*
disrespect′fully, *adv.* [Pfx. **dis-**.]

disrobe, *dis-rōb′*, *v.t.* to undress.
[Pfx. **dis-**.]

disrupt, *dis-rupt′*, *v.t.* and *v.i.* to break up, throw into disorder (e.g. a meeting, traffic, friendly relations).
disrup′tion, *n.*
disrup′tive, *adj.* causing break-up, separation, disorder.
[L. *dis-*, apart, *rumpĕre*, to break.]

dissatisfy, *dis-sat′is-fī*, *v.t.* to fail to satisfy: to make discontented.
dissatisfac′tion, *n.* [Pfx. **dis-**.]

dissect, *di-sekt′*, *v.t.* to cut into parts for examination: to study and criticise (e.g. a man's character or motives).

dissec′tion, *n.* the act or the art of cutting in pieces for careful study.
[L. *dis-*, apart, *secāre*, to cut.]

dissemble, *di-sem′bl, v.t.* to disguise, mask (e.g. *He dissembled his true motives*).—Also *v.i.*
dissem′bler, *n.*
[L. *dis-*, not, *similis*, like.

disseminate, *di-sem′in-āt, v.t.* to spread abroad (e.g. news, information).
disseminā′tion, *n.*
[L. *dis-*, apart, *sēmināre*, to sow.]

dissent, *di-sent′, v.i.* to refuse to agree: to hold opinions different (from e.g. those of the church established by law).—Also *n.*
dissen′sion, *n.* disagreement: strife.
dissent′er, *n.* a member of a sect which has broken away from an established church.
dissen′tient (*-shėnt*), *n.* one who disagrees.—Also *adj.*
[L. *dis-*, apart, *sentīre*, to think.]

dissertation, *dis-ėr-tā′sh(ȯ)n, n.* a long formal piece of writing or talk.
[L. pfx. *dis-*, *serĕre*, to put together.]

disservice, *dis-sėr′vis, n.* injury, an ill turn.
[L. *dis-*, not, *servīre*, to serve.]

dissever, *di(s)-sev′ėr, v.t.* to sever: separate.
[L. *dis-*, apart, *sēparāre*, to separate.]

dissident, *dis′i-dėnt, n.* one who disagrees.—Also *adj.*
[L. *dis-*, apart, *sedēre*, to sit.]

dissimilar, *di(s)-sim′i-lȧr, adj.* unlike.
dissimilar′ity, *n.*
[L. *dis-*, not, *similis*, like.]

dissimulate, *di-sim′ū-lāt, v.t.* to conceal or disguise (e.g. one's feelings).—Also *v.i.*
dissimulā′tion, *n.*
[L. *dis-*, not, *similis*, like.]

dissipate, *dis′i-pāt, v.t.* to dispel, make disappear (e.g. fog, fears): to squander, waste.—Also *v.i.*
diss′ipated, *adj.* indulging too much in drinking and other pleasures.
dissipā′tion, *n.* scattering: wasteful spending (e.g. of money, energy): intemperance: frivolous amusement.
[L. *dissipāre*, to scatter abroad.]

dissociate, *di-sō′shi-āt, v.t.* to separate: to separate in thought (from): (with *oneself from*) to refuse to give one's support to.—Also *v.i.*
[L. *dis-*, apart, *sociāre*, to associate.]

dissolute, *dis′ȯl-ōōt, -ūt, adj.* loose in morals.
diss′olutely, *adv.* **diss′oluteness,** *n.*
[Same root as **dissolve.**]

dissolution. See **dissolve.**

dissolve, *di-zolv′, v.t.* to melt: to break up: to put an end to (e.g. a parliament, a marriage).—Also *v.i.*
dissolution, *dis-ȯl-ōō′sh(ȯ)n, -ū′-, n.*
[L. *dis-*, apart, *solvĕre*, *solūtum*, loose.]

dissonance, *dis′ō-nȧns, n.* a discord, esp. one deliberately used in music: disagreement.
diss′onant, *adj.*
[L. *dis-*, apart, *sonāre*, to sound.]

dissuade, *di-swād′, v.t.* to prevent (from) by advice or persuasion.
dissuā′sion, *n.*
[L. *dis-*, apart, *suādēre*, to advise.]

distaff, *dis′tâf, n.* the stick that holds the bunch of flax or wool in spinning.
distaff side, the female part of a family.
[O.E. *distæf*.]

distance, *dis′tȧns, n.* space (between): a far-off place or point (e.g. *in the distance*): reserve of manner.
dis′tant, *adj.* far off, or far apart, in place or time: not close (e.g. *a distant relation*): reserved, not friendly (e.g. *Her manner was distant*).
[L. *dis-*, apart, *stans*, standing.]

distaste, *dis-tāst′, n.* dislike.
distaste′ful, *adj.* disagreeable.
distaste′fully, *adv.*
distaste′fulness, *n.* [Pfx. **dis-.**]

distemper[1], *dis-tem′pėr, n.* a method of painting using e.g. size instead of oil: paint of this kind.—*v.t.* to paint in distemper.
[L. *dis-*, *temperāre*, to mix in proportion.]

distemper[2], *dis-tem′pėr, n.* a disordered state of body or mind: a disease, esp. of young dogs.
[Same root as **distemper** (1).]

distend, *dis-tend′, v.t.* to stretch outwards.—*v.i.* to swell.
disten′sion, *n.*
[L. *dis-*, apart, *tendĕre*, to stretch.]

distil, *dis-til′, v.i.* to fall in drops.—*v.t.* to let, or cause to, fall in drops: to turn a liquid into vapour by heat, and then the vapour back to liquid again, as a means of purifying, etc.: to extract the spirit from anything by this method:—*pr.p.* **distill′ing**; *pa.p.* **distilled′.**
distillā′tion, *n.* **distill′er,** *n.*
distill′ery, *n.* a place where distilling, esp. of whisky, is carried on:—*pl.* **-ies.**
[L. *dē*, down, *stillāre*, to drop.]

distinct, *dis-tingt′, adj.* separate: different: clear: easily seen, heard, etc.
distinct′ly, *adv.* **distinct′ness,** *n.*
distinc′tive, *adj.* marking difference: characteristic (e.g. *I recognised her from the back; she has a distinctive walk*).
distinction, *dis-tingk′sh(ȯ)n, n.* difference: outstanding merit: a mark of honour.
[Same root as **distinguish.**]

distinguish, *dis-ting′gwish, v.t.* to mark off as different (often with *from*): to make out, recognise: to give distinction to.—*v.i.* to recognise a difference (between).
disting′uishable, *adj.*
disting′uished, *adj.* marked out (by): eminent, famous.
[L. *distinguĕre*, *distinctum*.]

distort, *dis-tört′, v.t.* to twist out of shape: to misrepresent (e.g. *to distort the truth*): to make (sound) indistinct and harsh.

distor′tion, *n.*
[L. *dis-*, *torquēre, tortum,* to twist.]

distract, *dis-trakt′*, *v.t.* to draw away, esp. the mind or attention: to trouble, perplex: to make crazy.
distract′ed, *adj.*
distrac′tion, *n.* perplexity: agitation: madness: something that takes the mind off other, esp. more serious, affairs. See also **distraught.**
[L. *dis-*, apart, *trahĕre, tractum,* to draw.]

distrait, *dis-trā′*, *adj.* absent-minded, inattentive because worried. [Fr.]

distraught, *dis-tröt′*, *adj.* deeply agitated or worried: crazy.
[Same root as **distract.**]

distress, *dis-tres′*, *n.* extreme pain: a cause of suffering: misfortune or difficulty.—*v.t.* to cause pain or suffering to.
distress′ing, *adj.* **distress′ingly,** *adv.*
[O.Fr. *destresse.*]

distribute, *dis-trib′ūt, v.t.* to divide among several: to scatter (about a space).
distribu′tion, *n.*
[L. *dis-*, apart, *tribuĕre, tribūtum,* allot.]

district, *dis′trikt*, *n.* territory marked off for administrative or other purpose: a region.
[Fr.—Late Latin *dīstrictus.*]

distrust, *dis-trust′*, *n.* lack of trust or faith, suspicion.—*v.t.* to have no trust in.
distrust′ful, *adj.* **distrust′fully,** *adv.*
distrust′fulness, *n.* [Pfx. **dis-.**]

disturb, *dis-tûrb′*, *v.t.* to throw into confusion: to agitate, disquiet: to interrupt.
disturb′ance, *n.* tumult, disorder: interruption: confusion (of arrangement, etc.): act of disturbing.
disturb′er, *n.*
[L. *dis-*, *turbāre,* agitate—*turba,* crowd.]

disunite, *dis-ū-nīt′*, *v.t.* to separate, esp. in opinions or aims.—Also *v.i.*
disu′nity (*-ū′ni-*), *n.* [Pfx. **dis-.**]

disuse, *dis-ūs′*, or *dis′ūs′*, *n.* state of not being used.—*v.t.* (*dis-ūz′*) to cease to use. [Pfx. **dis-.**]

ditch, *dich*, *n.* a trench dug in the ground, esp. for water.—*v.i.* and *v.t.* to dig, or to drain by, ditches: to drive, throw, into a ditch: to crash-land (plane) in the sea: (*coll.*) to get rid of (a person).
ditch′er, *n.* a man or machine that makes, cleans, or repairs ditches.
[O.E. *dīc.*]

ditto, *dit′ō*, shortened to **do,** *n.* the same thing.—*adv.* in the same manner.
[It.—L. *dictum,* said.]

ditty, *dit′i*, *n.* a little poem to be sung:—*pl.* **ditt′ies.**
[O.Fr. *ditie*; same root as **dictate.**]

ditty-bag, *dit′i-bag*, *n.* a sailor's bag for needles, thread, etc.—Also **ditt′y-box.**
[Origin unknown.]

diurnal, *dī-ûr′nȧl*, *adj.* of, performed in, or lasting, a day.
[L. *diurnālis*—*diēs,* a day.]

divan, *di-van′*, or *dī′*, *n.* a couch of Eastern type.
[Arabic and Pers. *dīwān,* a long seat.]

dive, *dīv*, *v.i.* to plunge into water or down through the air: to go deeply (into).—*n.* a plunge: a swoop.
div′er, *n.*
[O.E. *dȳfan, dūfan.*]

diverge, *dī-* or *di-vėrj′*, *v.i.* to separate and go in different directions: to differ (from a standard).
diverg′ence, *n.* **diverg′ent,** *adj.*
[L. *dis-*, apart, *vergĕre,* to incline.]

divers, *dīv′ėrz*, *adj.* several.
[Same root as **divert.**]

diverse, *dī-vėrs′*, or *dī′-*, *adj.* different, unlike: of various kinds.
diverse′ly, *adv.* **diverse′ness,** *n.*
diver′sity, *n.* diverseness: point of difference (*pl.* **diver′sities).**

diversify, *dī-vėr′si-fī*, *v.t.* to give variety to:—*pr.p.* **diver′sifying**; *pa.p.* **diver′sified.**
[Same root as **divert.**]

diversion. See **divert.**

divert, *dī-*, *di-vėrt′*, *v.t.* to change direction, or route, of: to turn (to another purpose): to distract (the attention): to amuse.
divert′ing, *adj.* amusing.
diversion, *di-vėr′sh(ȯ)n*, *n.* a place where traffic is diverted: turning aside: amusement, recreation: a movement to mislead an opponent.
[L. *dī-*, aside, *vertĕre, versum,* to turn.]

divest, *dī-* or *di-vest′*, *v.t.* to strip or deprive (of anything).
[L. *dē,* away from, *vestīre,* to clothe.]

divide, *di-vīd′*, *v.t.* to break up, or mark off, into parts: to share (among): to keep apart: to cause (an assembly) to vote on a motion: to find out how many times one number contains another.—Also *v.i.*—*n.* a watershed.
divid′er, *n.* **divid′ing,** *adj., n.*
div′idend (*-i-dend*), *n.* the number that is to be divided: interest on shares, etc.
division, *di-vizh′(ȯ)n*, *n.* act of dividing: a partition, barrier: a section: an army unit: separation: difference in opinion, etc.: the finding how many times one number is contained in another.
divis′ible, *adj.* able to be divided.
divisional, *di-vizh′ȯn-ȧl*, *adj.* of, or marking, a division.
divis′or (*-vīz*), *n.* the number that divides the dividend.
[L. *dīvidĕre, dīvīsum.*]

divine, *di-vīn′*, *adj.* of, belonging to a god: holy: excellent.—*n.* a clergyman.—*v.t.* to perceive through keenness of understanding or insight.
divinā′tion (*di-vi-*), *n.* foretelling the future: insight, intuition.
divi′ner (*-vī′*), *n.* one who has, or claims, skill in finding hidden water or metals.
divi′ning-rod, *n.* a rod, usu. of hazel, used by a diviner.

divin'ity (*di-vin'*), *n.* the nature of God: a god or goddess (*pl.* **divin'ities).**
[L. *divīnus—dīvus, deus*, a god.]

divisible, division etc. See **divide.**

divorce, *di-vōrs', -vörs', n.* the legal ending of a marriage: a complete separation.—*v.t.* to dissolve the marriage of, or one's marriage with: to separate.
divor'cee (*-sē*), *n.* a divorced person.
[L. *divortĕre*, or *-vert-*; see **divert.]**

divulge, *di-vulj'*, or *di-*, *v.t.* to let out (a secret): to reveal (that).
[L. *di-*, abroad, *vulgāre*, to publish—*vulgus*, the people.]

dizzy, *diz'i, adj.* giddy: confused: causing giddiness.
dizz'ily, *adv.* **dizz'iness,** *n.*
[O.E. *dysig*, foolish.]

do[1], *dōō, v.t.* to carry out, perform (e.g. one's duty, a piece of work, justice): to perform some action on, as to clean (a room), cook (a steak), arrange (hair): (*slang*) to swindle: to make the round of (e.g. *to do all the picture galleries*)—*v.i.* to act (e.g. *Do as I do*): to get along, fare (e.g. *He is doing well*): to be sufficient (e.g. *Sixpence will do*):—*2nd sing.* (thou) **dost** (*dust*), *3rd* (he, etc.) **does** (*duz*), (formerly) **doth** (*duth*); *pa.t.* **did**; *pr.p.* **do'ing** (*dōō'*); *pa.p.* **done** (*dun*). Do is often used in place of other verbs, esp. to avoid repeating them (e.g. *I may not manage to go, but if I do, I hope to see John*). It is also used along with a more important verb (1) in questions (e.g. *Do you know where he is?*), (2) to give emphasis (e.g. *I do hope we win*), and (3) in sentences with 'not' (e.g. *I did not go*).—*n.* a swindle: a festivity.
doer, *dōō'ėr, n.*
do'ing, *n.* (*coll.*) a scolding: (in *pl.*) actions, behaviour: (in *pl.*; *slang*) things necessary.
done, *adj.* finished: exhausted.
See also **deed.**
[O.E. *dōn.*]

do[2], **doh,** *dō, n.* (*music*) the first tone or keynote of the scale.

do[3]. See **ditto.**

docile, *dō'sīl*, or *dos'il, adj.* (of person, animal) easy to manage.
docilely, *adv.* **docil'ity,** *n.*
[L. *docilis—docēre*, to teach.]

dock[1], *dok, n.* a weed with large leaves and a long root.
[O.E. *docce.*]

dock[2], *dok, v.t.* to cut short: to take something off (e.g. wages).—*n.* the part of a tail left after clipping.
[M.E. *dok.*]

dock[3], *dok, n.* an artificial basin for ships: (in *pl.*) group of basins, wharfs, etc.: box, etc., in court where the accused is placed. —*v.t., v.i.* to put in, or enter, a dock. .
dock'er, *n.* one who works at the docks.
dock'yard, *n.* an enclosure, esp. naval, with docks, slipways, stores, etc.
dry dock, graving dock, a dock that can be emptied of water so as to lay bare the hull of a ship for cleaning and repairs.
floating dock, a floating form of dry dock. [Origin uncertain.]

docket, *dok'it, n.* a note on a document naming its contents: a label: a list of cases in court: a permit or certificate.—*v.t.* to make a summary of, or a note of (contents):—*pr.p.* **dock'eting**; *pa.p.* **dock'eted.** [Perh. **dock** (2).]

doctor, *dok'tȯr, n.* a man or woman trained to treat the sick: one who has received from a university the highest degree in arts or science.—*v.t.* to treat as a doctor does: to patch up: to tamper with (e.g. *The drink was doctored*—i.e. something had been put into it).
doc'torate, *n.* the degree of doctor.
[L., a teacher—*docēre*, to teach.]

doctrine, *dok'trin, n.* a belief or teaching: a set of beliefs on one subject.
doc'trinal (or *-trī'nȧl*), *adj.*
[L. *doctrina—docēre*; root as **doctor.]**

document, *dok'ū-mėnt, n.* a paper containing information or proof or evidence.—*v.t.* (*dok'ū-mėnt*, or *-ment'*), to supply with documents: to prove by documents.
document'ary, *adj.* of, or found in, documents.—*n.* a motion picture showing facts of a particular human activity (e.g. *a documentary about pottery-making*).
[L. *documentum—docēre*; root as **doctor.]**

dodder, *dod'ėr, v.i.* to shake, to totter.
[Origin uncertain.]

dodge, *doj, v.t.* to avoid by a sudden movement (e.g. *She dodged the snowball*): to avoid having to carry out (a duty), or to answer (a question), etc.—Also *v.i.* —*n.* an act of dodging: a trick.
dodg'er, *n.* [Origin unknown.]

dodo, *dō'dō, n.* a large extinct bird.
[Port. *doudo*, silly.]

doe, *dō, n.* the female of the fallow deer, antelope, rabbit, and hare.
doe'skin, *n.* the skin of a doe (deer): a smooth, close-woven, woollen cloth.
[O.E. *dā.*]

doer, does. See **do** (1).

doff, *dof, v.t.* to take off (e.g. a hat).
[do, off.]

dog, *dog, n.* a domesticated, or wild, flesh-eating animal, esp. the male: a mean scoundrel: a man (e.g. *a gay dog*): a gripping, or holding, device.—*adj.* male (e.g. a *dog fox*): bad, pretended (e.g. *dog French*).—*v.t.* to follow closely as a dog does:—*pr.p.* **dogg'ing**; *pa.p.* **dogged.**
dogg'ed (*-id*), *adj.* keeping on at what one is doing, determined, persistent.
dogg'edly, *adv.* **dogg'edness,** *n.*
dog collar, a collar for a dog: a close-fitting collar worn by a clergyman.
dog days, a supposedly hot part of July

and August, the period when the Dogstar rises with the sun.

dog'fight, *n.* a fight between dogs: a single combat (esp. of aeroplanes).

dog'fish, *n.* a small shark.

dog'rose, *n.* a wild rose.

dog('s)'-ear, the corner of a leaf of a book turned down like a dog's ear.—*v.t.* to turn down the corners of pages of.

Dog'star, *n.* Sirius, the brightest star in the heavens.

dog'-tir'ed, *adj.* utterly exhausted.

dog violet, the common scentless wild violet.

dog'-watches, *n.pl.* on shipboard, the watch 4-6 p.m. or 6-8 p.m., consisting of two hours only instead of four.

dog in the manger, one who will not let others enjoy what he himself cannot use.

to go to the dogs, to go to ruin.

in the doghouse, in disgrace.

the dogs, greyhound racing.

[Late O.E. *docga.*]

doge, *dōj,* or *dō'jā, n.* (*history*) the chief magistrate in Venice and Genoa.

[L. *dux,* a leader.]

dogged, doggedly. See **dog.**

doggerel, *dog'ėr-ėl, n.* worthless verses in irregular rhythm. [Origin unknown.]

dogma, *dog'mȧ, n.* a doctrine laid down with authority, e.g. by the Church: a settled opinion.

dogmăt'ic, -al, *adjs.* asserting positively in an overbearing manner.

dogmat'ically, *adv.*

dog'matise, *v.i.* to state one's opinion dogmatically or arrogantly.

dog'matism, *n.* dogmatic manner, attitude.

[Gk., an opinion—*dokeein,* to think.]

doh. See **do** (2).

doily, *doi'li, n.* small ornamented mat.

[*Doily* or *Doyley,* a haberdasher.]

doings. See **do** (1).

doldrums, *dol'drŭmz, n.pl.* parts of the ocean about the equator where calms are frequent: low spirits.

[Prob. old word *dold,* stupid.]

dole, *dōl, n.* a share: state payment to an unemployed person.

[O.E. *dāl.*]

doleful, *dōl'f(oo)l, adj.* sorrowful, gloomy.

dole'fully, *adv.* **dole'fulness,** *n.*

[O.Fr. *doel,* grief—L. *dolēre,* feel pain.]

doll, *dol, n.* a toy in human form.

doll'y, *n.* a little doll: an instrument for turning or pounding, used in washing clothes, mining, etc.:—*pl.* **doll'ies.**

[Prob. *Dolly,* dim. of *Dorothy.*]

dollar, *dol'ȧr, n.* a silver coin (=100 cents) of U.S.A., Canada, etc.

[Ger. *t(h)aler*—the former *Joachimsthaler* silver mines, Bohemia.]

dolmen, *dol'men, n.* a prehistoric table-like stone structure.

[Breton *taol,* table, *men,* stone.]

dolphin, *dol'fin, n.* a porpoise-like animal about 8 or 10 feet long: a fish about 5 feet in length, noted for the brilliance of its colours when dying.

[Gk. *delphis, delphīnos.*]

dolt, *dōlt, n.* a dull or stupid fellow.

dolt'ish, *adj.* dull, stupid.

[Origin uncertain.]

Dom, *dom, n.* a title given to certain Roman Catholic dignitaries.

[Port. *Dom*—L. *dominus,* lord.]

domain, *dō-mān', n.* lands: one's sphere of influence or of knowledge.

[Fr.—L. *dominus,* a master.]

dome, *dōm, n.* a structure like a half sphere forming the roof of a building: anything so shaped.

domed, *adj.*

[L. *domus,* a house.]

domestic, *dō-mes'tik, adj.* belonging to the house: private: (of animals) tame, sharing man's life: not foreign (e.g. *the Government's domestic policies*).—*n.* a servant in the house.

domes'ticāte, *v.t.* to make domestic: to tame.

domestic'ity (*-tis'-*), *n.* home life.

domestic science, the household arts (such as catering, cookery, laundry-work) studied scientifically.

domicile, *dom'i-sil, -sīl, n.* a man's legal place of residence.—*v.t.* to establish in a fixed residence.

domicil'iary (*-sil'i-ȧr-i*), *adj.*

[L. *domus,* a house.]

dominant, *dom'in-ȧnt, adj.* ruling, most important, most influential.

dom'inate, *v.t.* to be lord over, have a very strong influence over (e.g. *The stronger man dominates the weaker*): to tower above (e.g. *The castle dominates the landscape*).—Also *v.i.* (sometimes *to dominate over*).

dominā'tion, *n.*

domineer', *v.i.* to be tyrannical, overbearing.

dominion, *dō-min'yȯn, n.* sovereignty: rule: a self-governing country of British Commonwealth: (*cap.*) official title of Canada and New Zealand.

[L. *domināri* (vb.)—*dominus,* master.]

domino, *dom'in-ō, n.* a hooded cape: an oblong piece divided by a line into two parts, each blank or marked with from one to six spots, with which the game of **dom'inoes** (*-ōz*) is played. [Fr.]

don[1], *don, n.* a Spanish title, corresponding to English Sir, Mr.: a fellow of a college.

donn'ish, *adj.* like a university don.

[Sp.—L. *dominus,* master.]

don[2], *don, v.t.* to put on (e.g. a coat):—*pr.p.* **donn'ing**; *pa.p.* **donned.**

[do, on.]

donation, *dō-nā'sh(ȯ)n, n.* a gift of money or goods to a fund or collection.

donāte', *v.t.* to give to a fund, etc.

dō'nor, *n.* a giver.

[Fr.—L. *dōnum,* a gift—*dăre,* to give.]

done. See **do** (1).
donkey, *dong'ki, n.* an ass :—*pl.*-**keys.**
donkey engine, a small auxiliary engine.
[Orig. slang ; perh. **dun** (1).]
donnish. See **don** (1).
don't, *dōnt,* abbrev. of **do not.**
doom, *dōōm, n.* judgment : destiny : ruin.—*v.t.* to condemn, destine (often in *pass.*, e.g. *The attempt was doomed to failure*).
dooms'day, *n.* the day of judgment.
[O.E. *dōm,* judgment.]
door, *dōr, dör, n.* the entrance into a building or room : a means of approach (e.g. *the door to success*).
door'keeper, *n.* one in charge of a door.
door'post, *n.* the jamb or side piece of a door.
door'step, *n.* a raised step leading to a door.
door'way, *n.* opening where there is or might be a door.
[O.E. *duru.*]
dope, *dōp, n.* a drug : anything that dulls the mind or senses.—Also *v.t.*
[Du. *doop,* a dipping, sauce.]
Doric, *dor'ik, adj.* of a style of Greek architecture.—*n.* a broad dialect, esp. broad Scots.
[Gk. *Dōrikos,* of Doris, part of ancient Greece.]
dormant, *dör'mȧnt, adj.* sleeping : not active (e.g. *a dormant volcano*).
dormer (window), *dör'mėr (win'dō),* a small window with a gable-shaped top jutting out from a sloping roof.
dormitory, *dör'mi-tȯr-i, n.* a large sleeping-room with many beds :—*pl.* **-ies.**
[Fr. *dormir*—L. *dormīre,* to sleep.]
dormouse, *dör'mows, n.* a squirrel-like gnawing animal related to mice :—*pl.* **dor'mice.**
[Perh. conn. with L. *dormīre,* to sleep (from their hibernation).]
dormy, dormie, *dör'mi, adj.* (*golf*) said of a player when he is as many holes 'up' as there are holes still to play.
[Perh. conn. with L. *dormīre,* to sleep.]
dorsal, *dör'sȧl, adj.* of the back.
[L. *dorsum,* the back.]
dose, *dōs, n.* the quantity of medicine, etc., to be taken at one time : anything disagreeable forced on one.—*v.t.* to give medicine in doses to.
dōs'age, *n.* a method or rate of dosing.
[Gk. *dosis,* a giving.]
doss, *dos, n.* (*slang*) a bed.—*v.i.* to (lie down to) sleep.
doss'-house, *n.* a cheap lodging-house.
[L. *dorsum,* back.]
dossier *dos'i-ā, n.* a bundle of documents relating to one person or subject. [Fr.]
dost. See **do** (1).
dot[1], *dot, n.* a small round spot : the shorter of the two signal elements in Morse.—*v.t.* to mark with dots : to set (objects) here and there :—*pr.p.* **dott'ing** ; *pa.p.* **dott'ed.**
dott'y, *adj.* feeble, crazy.
[Du. *dot,* knot, tuft.]
dot[2], *dot, n.* a dowry. [Fr.]
dotage, dotard. See **dote.**
dote, *dōt, v.i.* to show weak, or too great, affection for (with *on*) : to be weak-minded from old age.
dot'age, *n.* childishness of old age.
dot'ard, *n.* one who dotes.
[Conn. with Old Du. *doten,* to be silly.]
doth. See **do** (1).
double, *dub'l, adj.* twice as much (*e.g. double pay*) : consisting of two : having two similar parts : folded over : deceitful, insincere.—*n.* a person (or thing) so like another as to be mistaken for him (or it).—*v.t.* to multiply by two : to fold in two : to pass, esp. to sail, round.
doub'le-barr'elled, *adj.* (of a gun) having two barrels : with two possible meanings : (of a surname) made up of two names.
double bass, a stringed instrument, largest and deepest of violin kind.
doub'le-cross, doub'lecross, *v.t.* to swindle (one's companion in a swindle).
doub'le-deal'er, *n.* a deceitful person.
doub'le-deal'ing, *n.* deceit.
doub'le-deck'er, *n.* a ship, vehicle, with two decks.
doub'le-dyed, *adj.* deeply stained (with guilt).
doub'le-edged, *adj.* with two cutting edges.
doub'le-faced, *adj.* two-faced, insincere.
doub'le-quick, *adj.* and *adv.* very quick(ly).
doub'le-talk, *n.* talk that sounds to the purpose but really tells nothing.
at the double, running.
to double back, to turn sharply back in running.
[O.Fr. *doble*—L. *duplus*—*duo,* two.]
doublet, *dub'lit, n.* a close-fitting jacket formerly worn by men. [O.Fr.]
doubloon, *dub-loon', n.* an old Spanish gold coin.
[Sp. *doblon.*]
doubt, *dowt, v.i.* to be undecided in opinion. —*v.t.* to distrust, suspect : to be uncertain about (e.g. *I doubt the wisdom of your plan*).—*n.* uncertainty : suspicion.
doubt'er, *n.*
doubt'ful, *adj.* (1) feeling doubt, uncertain what to think, expect, etc. : (2) able to be doubted, not clear (e.g. *The meaning is doubtful*), questionable (e.g. *The wisdom of this action is doubtful*), suspicious (e.g. *a doubtful character loitering outside*) : (of future, result, etc.) uncertain, but probably not good.
doubt'fully, *adv.* **doubt'fulness,** *n.*
doubt'less, *adv.* probably.
[L. *dubitāre,* conn. with *dubius,* doubtful, moving in two (*duo*) directions.]

douche, *dōōsh, n.* a jet of water directed on the body (inside or outside) from a pipe.
[It. *doccia*, water-pipe—L. *dūcĕre*, lead.]

dough, *dō, n.* a mass of flour or meal moistened and kneaded, but not baked.
dough'nut, *n.* a ring-shaped cake fried in fat: a device of this shape.
[O.E. *dāh.*]

doughty, *dow'ti, adj.* strong: brave.
dough'tily, *adv.* **dough'tiness,** *n.*
[O.E. *dyhtig*, valiant.]

dour, *dōōr, adj.* (all meanings chiefly *Scot.*) sullen: harsh, grim: obstinate.
[Prob. L. *dūrus*, hard.]

douse, dowse, *dows, v.t.* to plunge into water: to lower (a sail): to put out.
[Conn. with Old Du. *dossen*, to beat.]

dove, *duv, n.* a pigeon: an emblem of innocence, or gentleness.
dove'cot, -cote, *n.* a building in which pigeons breed.
dove'tail, *n.* a mode of joining by fitting wedge-shaped pieces (*tenons*) into like cavities (*mortises*).—*v.t.* to fit (one thing exactly into another).
[Supposed O.E. *dūfe*; Ger. *taube.*]

dowager, *dow'à-jėr, n.* a title given to a widow to distinguish her from the wife of her husband's heir (e.g. *the dowager duchess*).
[O.Fr. *douagere*—L. *dōtāre*, to endow.]

dowdy, *dow'di, adj.* not smart: badly dressed. [Origin unknown.]

dower, *dow'ėr, n.* the part of a husband's property that goes to his widow: a dowry: natural gift(s).
dow'ered, *adj.*
dowry, *dow'ri, n.* the property a woman brings to her husband at marriage.
[O.Fr. *douaire*—same L. root as **endow.**]

down[1], *down, n.* soft feathers: a soft covering of fluffy hairs.
down'y, *adj.*
[Old Norse *dūnn.*]

down[2], *down, adv.* to, or in, a lower position or state: away from a centre (capital, university, etc.): in writing, type, etc. (e.g. *Put down what I dictate*): on the spot, in cash (e.g. *£1 down and £3 later*). —*adj.* moving in the direction indicated by *adv.* **down** (e.g. *the down train*): descending (e.g. *on the down grade*).—*prep.* in a descent along, through, or by: to or in a lower position on.—*v.t.* to knock or lay down.—*n.* (in phrase **ups and downs**) see **up.**
down'-and-out, *adj.* and *n.* (a person) at the end of his resources, without money or hope.
down'-at-heel, *adj.* having the back of the shoe trodden down: shabby.
down'cast, *adj.* (of eyes) looking downwards: depressed, dejected.
down'fall, *n.* fall, failure, ruin: a fall of rain, snow, etc.
down'heart'ed, *adj.* discouraged.
down'hill', *adv., adj.* down the hill.
down'pour, *n.* a heavy fall of rain, etc.
down'right, *adv.* in plain terms: thoroughly.—*adj.* plain spoken: absolute (e.g. *a downright nuisance*).
down'stage', *adv.* towards the footlights.
down'stairs', *adv.* in, or to, lower storey.
down'trodden, *adj.* trampled on, oppressed.
down'ward(s), *adv.* from higher to lower: from source to outlet.
down'ward, *adj.*
[O.E. *of dūne*, from the hill (see **downs**).]

downs, *downz, n.pl.* an upland tract of pasture land.
[O.E. *dūn*, a hill—Celt. *dun.*]

dowry. See **dower.**

dowse[1]. See **douse.**

dowse[2], *dowz, v.i.* to use a divining-rod.
[Orig. uncertain.]

doze, *dōz, v.i.* to sleep lightly or for short spells.—Also *n.*
[Conn. with Old Norse *dūsa.*]

dozen, *duz'n, n.* a set of twelve.
[O.Fr. *dozeine*—L. *duodecim.*]

drab, *drab, n.* thick grey cloth: a grey or dull-brown colour.—*adj.* dull, uninteresting.
drab'ly, *adv.* **drab'ness,** *n.*
[Fr. *drap*, cloth—Late L. *drappus.*]

draft, *drâft, n.* anything drawn: a smaller body (of men, animals, things) selected from a larger: (esp. *U.S.*) conscription: an order for the payment of money: a preliminary sketch.—*v.t.* to draw an outline of: to draw up in preliminary form: to draw off (for a special purpose).
drafts'man, *n.* one who draws up documents, plans, designs, etc.
[Same word as **draught.**]

drag, *drag, v.t.* to draw by force or roughly: to draw slowly: to explore (a river bed) with a drag-net or hook.—*v.i.* to move slowly and heavily:—*pr.p.* **dragg'ing**; *pa.p.* **dragged.**—*n.* a net (**drag'-net**) or hook for dragging along to catch things under water: anything that slows down, or interferes with progress: the force on an aeroplane, etc., that tends to reduce forward motion: (*U.S.*) influence.
[O.E. *dragan*, or Old Norse *draga.*]

draggle, *drag'l, v.t.* or *v.i.* to make or become wet and dirty. [**drag.**]

dragon, *drag'ȯn, n.* a winged reptile in old stories: a fierce person: a lizard of the E. Indies.
drag'onfly, *n.* insect with long body and brilliant colours:—*pl.* **drag'onflies.**
[Gk. *drakon.*]

dragoon, *drà-gōōn', n.* a horse-soldier. —*v.t.* to force by bullying.
[Fr. *dragon*, dragon, dragoon.]

drain, *drān, v.t.* to draw (off, away, e.g. water): to make dry: to exhaust.—*v.i.* to flow off, or become dry, gradually.—*n.* watercourse: ditch: sewer: a heavy outflow (e.g. of money).

drain′er, *n.* a utensil on which articles are placed to drain.
drain′age, *n.* process, method, or system of draining.
drainage basin, the area of land which drains into one river.
[O.E. *drēahnian.*]

drake, *drāk, n.* the male of the duck.
[Origin uncertain.]

dram, *dram, n.* $\frac{1}{16}$ of an ounce: a small drink, esp. of whisky.
[Gk. *drachmē,* a silver coin.]

drama, *drâm′ȧ, n.* a story or play for acting on the stage: dramatic literature: a series of deeply interesting events.
dramatic, *drȧ-mat′ik, adj.* of, or in the form of, a drama: vivid, striking.
dramat′ically, *adv.*
dram′atise, *v.t.* to turn into the form of a play: to make vivid and striking.
dram′ạtist, *n.* a writer of plays.
dram′atis perso′nae (*-sō′nē*), the characters of a play or dramatic event.
[Gk. *drāma—drāein,* to do, act.]

drank. See **drink.**

drape, *drāp, v.t.* to hang cloth in folds about.—*n.* (in *pl.*) curtains.
drāp′er, *n.* dealer in cloth, clothing, etc.
drāp′ery, *n.* cloth goods: hangings: a draper's business:—*pl.* **drap′eries.**
[O.Fr. *drap,* cloth.]

drastic, *drâs′tik, adj.* powerful in action (e.g. of a purgative): violent (e.g. of measures).
[Gk. *drastikos*—same root as **drama.**]

draught, *drâft, n.* act of drawing or pulling: a deep drink: a quantity (of fish) taken in a net: a current of air: the depth of water a ship requires to float freely: a thick disk used in the game of **draughts,** played on a chequered board.
Also a spelling for **draft.**
draugh′ty, *adj.* full of currents of air:—*comp.* **draugh′tier**; *superl.* **draugh′tiest.**
draugh′tily, *adv.* **draught′iness,** *n.*
draught animal, *n.* one used for drawing heavy loads.
[O.E. *draht*—same root as **draw.**]

draw, *drö, v.t.* to pull: to bring or take out: to deduce, form (e.g. *to draw conclusions*): to make a picture of: to describe: to require (a depth of water) for floating: (*sport*) to play (a game) in which neither person, side, wins.—*v.i.* to move (towards, or away from; *to draw near, back*): to play a game with indecisive result: to practise sketching: to cast lots (e.g. *Draw for partners*):—*pa.t.* **drew** (*drōō*); *pa.p.* **drawn.**—*n.* the act of drawing: an attraction: a drawn game: the selection of winning tickets in a lottery.
See also **draft, draught.**
draw′er, *n.* one who draws: a sliding box drawn out of a chest of drawers or other piece of furniture: (in *pl.*) an undergarment for the lower limbs.
draw′ing, *n.* representing objects by lines, shading, etc.: a picture so made.
draw′back, *n.* a disadvantage.
draw′bridge, *n.* a bridge that can be drawn up and let down.
draw′ing-pin, *n.* pin with large flat head, for fastening paper on a board.
to draw a blank, to get a lottery ticket that wins no prize: to obtain no result.
to draw on, to pull on (e.g. gloves): to make a demand upon (e.g. one's money resources, one's imagination, a person—for something).
to draw out, to prolong: to make (someone) speak freely.
to draw the line (at something), to refuse to do it, approve of it, etc.
to draw up, to draft (a document): to stop (as in driving a car): to move closer.
[O.E. *dragan.*]

drawingroom, *drö′ing-room, n.* (orig. *withdrawing-room*) a room to which to withdraw after dinner: a room for entertaining guests formally.

drawl, *dröl, v.t.* and *v.i.* to speak, or utter, in a slow, lengthened tone.—Also *n.*
[Connected with **draw.**]

dray, *drā, n.* a low strong cart.
[O.E. *dragan,* to draw.]

dread, *dred, n.* great fear.—*v.t.* to fear greatly.
dread′ful, *adj.* producing great fear: (*coll.*) very bad, annoying.
dread′fully, *adv.* **dread′fulness,** *n.*
dreadnought, *dred′nöt, n.* type of battleship with heavy guns.
[M.E. *dreden*; O.E. *ondrǣdan,* to fear.]

dream, *drēm, n.* thoughts, fancies, or a vision during sleep: a daydream: something very beautiful: an unrealised ambition.—*v.i.* to fancy events during sleep: to think idly.—Also *v.t.*:—*pa.t.* and *pa.p.* **dreamed** or **dreamt** (*dremt*).
dream′er, *n.*
dream′y, *adj.* full of dreams: fond of dreaming: vague, dim, idle:—*comp.* **dream′ier**; *superl.* **dream′iest.**
dream′ily, *adv.* **dream′iness,** *n.*
[M.E. *dream, dreme.*]

dreary, *drēr′i, adj.* gloomy: very dull:—*comp.* **drear′ier**; *superl.* **drear′iest.**
drear′ily, *adv.* **drear′iness,** *n.*
[O.E. *drēorig,* mournful, gory, cruel.]

dredge[1], *drej, n.* an apparatus for bringing up material from the bottom of a river or sea.—*v.t.* to deepen (e.g. a river) by bringing up mud.
dredg′er, *n.* a vessel fitted with dredging apparatus.
[Conn. with O.E. *dragan,* to draw, pull.]

dredge[2], *drej, v.t.* to sprinkle.
[O.Fr. *dragie,* sugarplum.]

dregs, *dregz, n.pl.* the grounds (of liquor): anything worthless.
[Prob. Old Norse *dreggjar.*]

drench, *drench* or *-sh, v.t.* to give medicine to (an animal) by force: to soak.—*n.* a

dose of medicine forced down the throat.
drench'ing, *n.* a soaking.
[O.E. *drencan—drincan,* to drink.]

dress, *dres, v.t.* to straighten (e.g. a line of soldiers): to prepare (food): to treat, bandage (wound): to clothe.—*v.i.* to come into line: to put on clothes.—*n.* covering for the body: a gown.
dress'y, *adj.* showy: fond of dress.
dress'ily, *adv.* **dress'iness,** *n.*
dress'er, *n.* one who dresses: a kitchen sideboard.
dress'ing, *n.* anything applied (as manure to land, sauce or stuffing to food): the bandage, etc., applied to a wound.
dress circle, *n.* first gallery in a theatre intended for people in evening dress.
dress'ing-gown, *n.* a loose garment worn when not fully dressed.
fancy dress, clothes of another country, historical period, etc., worn e.g. at a **fancy dress ball.**
morning dress, evening dress, full dress, dress for formal occasions.
[O.Fr. *dresser,* to prepare.]

dressage, *dres-äzh, n.* training of a horse in deportment and response to controls. [Fr.]

drew. See **draw.**

dribble, *drib'l, v.i.* to fall in small drops: to allow saliva to trickle from the mouth. —*v.t.* to spend in small amounts: (*football*) to kick (the ball) along little by little.
drib'let, dribb'let, *n.* a drop, trickle, small quantity.
[Old verb *drib*; conn. with **drip.**]

dried, drier. See **dry.**

drift, *drift, n.* a heap of matter driven together, as snow: the direction in which a thing is driven: state of drifting: the general meaning (of what is said).—*v.t.* to carry by drift.—*v.i.* to be floated or blown along: to be driven into heaps.
drift'er, *n.* a fisherman or a fishing-boat that uses a drift-net.
drift'-net, *n.* a net which is allowed to drift with the tide.
drift'wood, *n.* wood drifted by water.
[Same root as **drive.**]

drill[1], *dril, v.t.* to bore, pierce: to exercise (soldiers, pupils, etc.): to sow in rows.—*n.* an instrument that bores: exercise, esp. of soldiers: practice: a furrow with seeds or growing plants.
[Prob. Du. *drillen,* to bore.]

drill[2], *dril, n.* stout twilled linen or cotton cloth.
[Ger. *drillich*—L. *trilix,* three-threaded.]

drily. See **dry.**

drink, *dringk, v.t.* to swallow (a liquid): to take (in) through the senses.—*v.i.* to swallow a liquid: to make a habit of taking too much intoxicating liquor:—*pr.p.* **drink'ing**; *pa.t.* **drank**; *pa.p.* **drunk.**—*n.* something to be drunk: intoxicating liquor.
drink'er, *n.*
drunk, *adj.* intoxicated.—*n.* a drunk person.
drunk'ard, *n.* one who drinks too much.
drunk'en, *adj.* drunk: in the habit of drinking too much: caused by intoxication (e.g. *a drunken brawl*).
drunk'enly, *adv.* **drunk'enness,** *n.*
[O.E. *drincan.*]

drip, *drip, v.i.* to fall in drops: to let fall drops:—*pr.p.* **dripp'ing**; *pa.p.* **dripped.** —*n.* liquid that drips.
dripp'ing, *n.* something that falls in drops, as fat from meat in roasting.
drip'stone, *n.* a moulding over doorways, etc. throwing off rain.
[O.E. *dryppan*—same root as **drop.**]

drive, *drīv, v.t.* to urge, hurry, along: to control or guide (e.g. a car): to hit with force (e.g. a golfball from a tee, a nail, etc.): to impel (a person to; e.g. *Despair may drive a man to drink*): to carry on (a brisk trade): to conclude (a hard bargain).—*v.i.* to press (forward): to go in a vehicle: to work hard (at):—*pr.p.* **driv'ing**; *pa.t.* **drove**; *pa.p.* **driv'en.**—*n.* an excursion in a vehicle: a private road to a house: a road with houses: energy, push: a campaign for some purpose: a driving shot: a driving mechanism.
driv'er, *n.*
drive'-in, *n.* a store, cinema, etc., where people are catered for while remaining in their motor cars.—Also *adj.*
drove, *drōv, n.* a number of cattle, or other animals, driven.
drov'er, *n.* one whose job is to drive cattle.
to be driving at, to be trying to say or suggest.
[O.E. *drīfan.*]

drivel, *driv'l, v.i.* to speak like an idiot:—*pr.p.* **driv'elling**; *pa.p.* **driv'elled.**—*n.* nonsense.
driv'eller, *n.*
[M.E. *drevelen*—O.E. *dreflian.*]

drizzle, *driz'l, v.i.* to rain in small drops.—*n.* a small, light rain.
drizz'ly, *adj.*
[O.E. *drēosan,* to fall.]

droll, *drōl, adj.* odd: amusing.
droll'ness, droll'ery (pl. **-eries**), *ns.*
[Fr. *drôle.*]

dromedary, *drom'i-dàr-i,* or *drum'-, n.* a one-humped Arabian camel.
[Gk. *dromas, -ados,* runner.]

drone, *drōn, n.* the male of the honey bee: one who lives on the labour of others, as the drone bee does: a deep humming sound: a bass pipe of a bagpipe: a monotonous tiresome speaker.—*v.i.* to make a low humming sound: to speak in a dull, boring voice.—Also *v.t.*
[O.E. *drān,* bee; conn. Ger. *drohne.*]

drool, *drōōl, v.i.* to slaver: drivel. [**drivel.**]

droop, *drōōp, v.i.* to sink or hang down: to grow weak or faint.
[Old Norse *drupe*; conn. with **drop.**]

drop, *drop, n.* a small blob of liquid: a small quantity: a fall: a steep descent: a disappointment.—*v.i.* to fall in drops: to fall suddenly, or steeply.—*v.t.* to let fall: to give up (e.g. a friend, a habit): to utter or write in a casual manner (as *to drop a remark, a note*):—*pr.p.* **dropp′ing**; *pa.p.* **dropped.**
dropp′ing, *n.* dung.
drop kick (*Rugby*), a kick made as the ball, dropped from the hand, rebounds from the ground.
drop′-scene, drop′-curtain, *ns.* painted curtain lowered to hide all or part of the stage.
to drop off, to fall asleep.
to drop out, to withdraw.
[O.E. *dropa.*]

dropsy, *drop′si, n.* an unnatural collection of water in any part of the body.
drop′sical, *adj.*
[L. *hydropisis*—Gk. *hydōr*, water.]

dross, *dros, n.* small or waste coal: refuse.
[O.E. *drōs.*]

drought, *drowt,* also **drouth,** *drowth, ns.* want of rain or of water: thirst.
drought′y, drouth′y, *adjs.*
[O.E. *drūgath*, dryness; root as **dry.**]

drove. See **drive.**

drown, *drown, v.i.* to die of suffocation in liquid.—*v.t.* to kill thus: to flood: to overwhelm.
[M.E. *drounen*; origin unknown.]

drowse, *drowz, v.i.* to be heavy with sleep.
drow′sy, *drow′zi, adj.* sleepy:—*comp.* **drow′sier**; *superl.* **drow′siest.**
drow′sily, *adv.* **drow′siness,** *n.*
[Conn. O.E. *drūsian*, sink, grow sluggish.]

drub, *drub, v.t.* to beat or thrash:—*pr.p.* **drubb′ing**; *pa.p.* **drubbed.**
drubb′ing, *n.* a cudgelling.
[Perh. Arabic *daraba*, to beat.]

drudge, *druj, v.i.* to do dull, very hard, or mean work.—*n.* one who does such work.
drudg′ery, *n.* hard or humble work.
[Perh. conn. O.E. *drēogan*, undergo.]

drug, *drug, n.* any substance used in medicine: a substance used to dull pain or give pleasant sensations.—*v.t.* and *v.i.* to dose with a drug or drugs:—*pr.p.* **drugg′ing**; *pa.p.* **drugged.**
drugg′ist, *n.* one who sells medicines.
drug′-add′ict, *n.* one who has formed the habit of taking drugs.
[O.Fr. *drogue*, of uncertain origin.]

druid, *drōō′id, n.* a priest among ancient Celts of Britain and Gaul.
[Conn. with Gael. *draoi*, magician.]

drum, *drum, n.* a percussion instrument, a membrane stretched on a round frame (cylinder or half sphere): anything shaped like a drum, as a container for liquids: (**ear′drum**) the membrane in the middle ear.—*v.i.* to beat or tap in rhythm.—*v.t.* to force (an idea, a lesson, into someone) by much repetition:—*pr.p.* **drumm′ing**; *pa.p.* **drummed.**
drumm′er, *n.* **drumm′ing,** *n., adj.*
drum′-ma′jor, *n.* the marching leader of a military band.
drum′stick, *n.* the knobbed stick with which a drum is beaten: the lower joint of the leg of a cooked fowl. [Prob. imit.]

drunk. See **drink.**

dry, *drī, adj.* without, or with too little, moisture, sap, rain, etc.: thirsty: uninteresting: (of humour, manner) unemotional, cold: (of wine) not sweet:—*comp.* **drī′er**; *superl.* **drī′est.**—*v.t.* to free from water or moisture.—*v.i.* to become dry (also **dry up**):—*pr.p.* **dry′ing**; *pa.p.* **dried.**
drier, dryer, *drī′ėr, n* an apparatus, or substance, that dries or hastens drying.
dri′ly, dry′ly, *adv.* **dry′ness,** *n.*
dry battery, -cell, (*electricity*) one containing paste, not liquid.
dry′-clean, *v.t.* to clean with chemicals, without water.
dry dock (see **dock**).
dry′er, dry′ly (see above).
dry goods, drapery, etc. as opp. to hardware or groceries.
dry ice, solid carbon dioxide.
dry rot, decay of timber caused by fungi which make it dry and brittle.
dry′salter, *n.* a dealer in gums, dyes, etc.
dry′saltery, *n.*
[O.E. *drȳge* (adj.), *drūgian* (vb.).]

dryad, *drī′ad, -ad, n.* a wood nymph.
[Gk. *dryas, -ados*—*drys*, oak, tree.]

dual, *dū′al, adj.* consisting of two separate parts (e.g. *dual carriageway*): in the hands of two (e.g. *dual ownership*; *dual controls*).
du′al-pur′pose, *adj.* serving two purposes.
dual personality, a condition in which an individual shows at different times two very different characters.
[L. *duālis*—*duo*, two.]

dub[1], *dub, v.t.* to give knighthood to, by touching each shoulder with a sword: to nickname:—*pr.p.* **dubb′ing**; *pa.p.* **dubbed.**
dubb′ing, *n.* (or **dubb′in**) a grease for softening leather.
[O.E. *dubbian.*]

dub[2], *dub, v.t.* to give (a film) a new soundtrack (e.g. in a different language): to add sound effects or music to (a film, etc.).
dubb′ing, *n.* **[double.]**

dubious, *dū′bi-us, adj.* doubtful (e.g. *I am dubious about the wisdom of this action*): probably not honest (e.g. *dubious dealings*).
dū′biousness, dūbī′ety, *ns.*
[L. *dubius.*]

ducal. See **duke.**

ducat, *duk′at, n.* an old gold coin. [O.Fr.]

duchess, *duch′es, n.* the wife or widow of a

duke: a woman of the same rank as a duke in her own right.
duch'y, *n.* territory of a duke.
[O.Fr. *duchesse, duché—duc,* duke.]

duck[1], *duk, n.* coarse cloth for small sails, sacking, etc.: (in *pl.*) trousers, etc., of this.
[Du. *doeck,* linen cloth.]

duck[2], *duk, v.t.* to dip for a moment in water.—*v.i.* to dip or dive: to lower the head suddenly.—Also *n.*
[M.E. *douken.*]

duck[3], *duk, n.* a water bird, wild or domesticated, with short legs and broad flat bill: a female duck (the male being a **drake**): (cricket; orig. *duck's egg*) a score by a batsman of no runs.
duck'bill, *n.* a platypus.
duck'ling, *n.* a young duck.
[O.E. *duce*; conn. with **duck** (2).]

duck[4], *duk, n.* a transport vehicle for land and water.
[DUKW, initials used officially for it.]

duct, *dukt, n.* a tube or pipe for fluids, electric cable, etc.
[Same root as **ductile.**]

ductile, *duk'tīl, -til, adj.* capable of being drawn out into wire or threads.
[L. *dūcĕre, ductum,* to lead.]

dudgeon, *duj'ȯn, n.* resentment, anger.
[Origin unknown.]

due, *dū, adj.* owed: expected according to timetable, promise, etc. (e.g. *The bus is due now, in three minutes*): proper (e.g. *Take due care*).—*adv.* directly (e.g. *sailing due east*).—*n.* what is owed: what one has a right to: (in *pl.*) charge, fee, toll.
dū'ly, *adv.* properly: at the proper time.
due to, brought about by (e.g. *His success was due to hard work*). The use of *due to* (in place of *because of, owing to*) in sentences such as the following is wrong:—*The game was postponed because of (or owing to) frost.*
See also **duty.**
[O.Fr. *deü,* pa.p. of *devoir,* to owe.]

duel, *dū'ėl, n.* a combat, under fixed conditions, between two people over a matter of honour, etc.: any contest (a physical struggle or a battle of wits) between two people or two sides.—Also *v.i.*:—*pr.p.* **dū'elling**; *pa.p.* **dū'elled.**
dū'ellist, *n.*
[It. *duello*—L. *duellum,* war—*duo,* two.]

duenna, *dū-en'ȧ, n.* an elderly lady who acts as guardian to a younger.
[Sp. *dueña,* a form of *donña,* mistress.]

duet, *dū-et', n.* a musical composition for two performers.
duett'ist, *n.*
[It. *duetto*—L. *duo,* two.]

duffel, *duf'l, n.* a thick, coarse woollen cloth, with a thick nap.
[Du., from *Duffel,* a town near Antwerp.]

duffer, *duf'ėr, n.* a stupid person.
[Origin unknown.]

dug[1], *dug, n.* a nipple or udder of a cow etc.
[Conn. with Sw. *dægga,* to suckle.]

dug[2]. See **dig.**

duke, *dūk, n.* a nobleman of the highest rank.
ducal, *dū'kȧl, adj.* of a duke.
duke'dom, *n.* the title, rank, or territories of a duke.
See also **duchess, duchy.**
[O.Fr. *duc*—L. *dux,* a leader.]

dulcet, *dul'sit, adj.* sweet.
[L. *dulcis.*]

dull, *dul, adj.* slow of hearing, of learning, or of understanding: not bright or clear: blunt: not exciting or interesting.—*v.t.* or *v.i.* to make or to become dull.
dully, *dul'li, adv.* **dull'ness,** *n.*
[Conn. O.E. *dol,* foolish, *dwellan,* err.]

dumb[1], *dum, adj.* (*orig. U.S.*) very stupid.
[Ger. *dumm*; conn. with **dumb** (2).]

dumb[2], *dum, adj.* without the power of speech: silent.
dumb'ly, *adv.* **dumb'ness,** *n.*
dumb'bell, *n.* a double-headed weight swung in the hands to develop the muscles.
dumb show, gesture without words.
dumb'-wait'er, *n.* a movable table for food, dishes, etc. at meals.
dum(b)found', *v.t.,* **dum(b)found'er,** *v.t.* to make speechless with amazement.
dumm'y, *n.* one who is dumb: a sham article in a shop: a lay-figure: an exposed hand of cards:—*pl.* **-ies.**
[O.E.; conn. Ger. *dumm,* stupid.]

dump, *dump, v.t.* to set (down) heavily: to discard, as on a rubbish heap: to put quantities of (goods) at a low price on the market, esp. of another country.—*n.* a thud or dull blow: a place for rubbish.
[Conn. with Scand. words.]

dumpling, *dump'ling, n.* a thick pudding or mass of soft paste.
[Origin uncertain.]

dumps, *dumps, n.pl.* (usu. with *the*) gloom, ill-humour.
[Conn. with Ger. *dumpf,* gloomy.]

dumpy, *dump'i, adj.* short and thick.
dump'ily, *adv.* **dump'iness,** *n.*
[Origin unknown.]

dun[1], *dun,* adj. of a dark, brownish colour.
[O.E.]

dun[2], *dun, v.t.* to demand payment from:—*pr.p.* **dunn'ing**; *pa.p.* **dunned.**
[Perh. conn. with **din.**]

dunce, *duns, n.* a person slow at learning.
[From the *Dunses* (followers of the scholar *Duns* Scotus; died 1308) who in the 16th century opposed the study of Greek, etc.]

dunderhead, *dun'dėr-hed, n.* a stupid person. [Origin unknown.]

dune, *dūn, n.* a low hill of sand.
[Old Du. *dūna.*]

dung, *dung, n.* manure.
dung'hill, *n.* a heap of dung. [O.E.]

dungaree, *dung-gȧ-rē′*, or *dung′-*, *n.* a coarse cotton cloth: (in *pl.*) overalls made of this cloth.
[Hindustani *dungrī.*]

dungeon, *dun′jȯn*, *n.* (*orig.*) the principal tower of a castle: a dark prison, esp. a cell under ground.
[O.Fr. *donjon*—L. *dominus*, master.]

duo, *dū′ō*, *n.* a duet.
[It.; same root as **duet.**]

duodecimal, *dū-ō-des′i-ml*, *adj.* counting by twelves.
[L. *duodecim*, twelve.]

duodenum, *dū-o-dē′num*, *n.* the first part of the small intestine, so called because about twelve finger-breadths long.
duodē′nal, *adj.*
[L. *duodēnī*, twelve each.]

duologue, *dū′ō-log*, *n.* a conversation between two.
[L. *duo*, two, Gk. *logos*, discourse.]

dupe, *dūp*, *n.* one who is cheated.—*v.t.* to deceive: to trick. [Fr.]

duple, *dū′pl*, *adj.* double: having two beats to the bar.
duplex, *dū′pleks*, *adj.* twofold, double.
duplicate, *dū′pli-kit*, *adj.* exactly like.—*n.* another thing of the same kind: a copy. —*v.t.* (*dū′pli-kāt*) to double: to make an exact copy or copies of.
duplicā′tion, *n.*
dū′plicātor, *n.* a copying apparatus.
duplicity, *dū-plis′i-ti*, *n.* deceit, double-dealing.
in duplicate, in two copies.
[Same L. root as **double.**]

durable, *dūr′ȧ-bl*, *adj.* able to last: resisting wear.
dur′ableness, durabil′ity, *ns.*
durā′tion, *n.* the length of time anything continues.
[L. *dūrāre*, to harden, endure.]

durbar, *dûr′bär*, *n.* in India, an official reception: a court.
[Pers. *dar-bār*, a prince's court.]

duress, *dū-res′*, or *dū′*, *n.* illegal force used to make a person do something.
[O.Fr. *duresse*—L. *dūrus*, hard.]

during, *dū′ring*, *prep.* throughout the time of: in the course of.
[From old vb. *dure*, to last.]

durra, *doo′ra*, *n.* Indian millet.
[Arabic *dhurah.*]

durst. See **dare.**

dusk, *dusk*, *n.* twilight, partial darkness.
dusk′y, *adj.* dark-coloured: gloomy.
dusk′ily, *adv.* **dusk′iness,** *n.*
[Conn. with O.E. *dox*, dark.]

dust, *dust*, *n.* fine particles of solid matter: powdery matter carried in the air.—*v.t.* to free from dust: to sprinkle with a powdery substance.
dust′er, *n.* cloth for removing dust.
dust′y, *adj.* covered with, containing, or like, dust:—*comp.* **dust′ier**; *superl.* **dust′iest.**
dust′ily, *adv.* **dust′iness,** *n.*
dust′bin, *n.* bin for household rubbish.
dust′-cover, *n.* a book jacket.
dust′man, *n.* one who clears away household refuse.
Red Duster, *n.* the Red Ensign (see **Ensign**).
to raise a dust, to cause a commotion by complaining.
to throw dust in the eyes of, to deceive.
[O.E. *dūst.*]

Dutch, *duch*, *adj.* of Holland (the Netherlands), its people, or language.
double Dutch, any language unknown or not understood.
[Middle Du. *dutsch*, German, Dutch.]

duty, *dū′ti*, *n.* what one ought, morally or legally, to do: action(s) required (e.g. *The duties of this post are few*): a tax on goods:—pl. **du′ties.**
du′tiable, *adj.* liable to be taxed.
du′tiful, *adj.* attentive to duty.
du′tifully, *adv.*
du′ty-free, *adj.* free from tax.
on, off, duty, actually at, not at, work.
[Same root as **due.**]

dux, *duks*, *n.* (*Scot.*) the head boy or girl in school or class:—*pl.* **dux′es.**
[L., a leader.]

dwarf, *dwörf*, *n.* an animal, plant, or person much below the ordinary height.—*v.t.* to hinder from growing: to make to appear small.
[O.E. *dweorg*; conn. Ger. *zwerg.*]

dwell, *dwel*, *v.i.* to live (in a place): (with *on*) to fix the attention on, to talk at length about:—*pr.p.* **dwell′ing**; *pa.t.* and *pa.p.* **dwelt** (or **dwelled**).
dwell′er, *n.*
dwell′ing, *n.* the house, hut, etc. where one lives.
[O.E. *dwellan*, to delay.]

dwindle, *dwin′dl*, *v.i.* to grow less in size, waste away (e.g. *His fortune, his hopes, dwindled*).
[O.E. *dwīnan*, to fade.]

dye, *dī*, *v.t.* to stain: to give a new colour to:—*pr.p.* **dye′ing**; *pa.p.* **dyed.**—*n.* colour: a colouring material for garments, etc.
dy′er, *n.* one who dyes cloth, etc.
dye′(-)stuff, *n.* material used in dyeing.
dye-work(s), *n.* a factory where things are dyed.
dyed in the wool, dyed in the raw state: of firmly fixed opinions.
[O.E. *dēagian.*]

dying. See **die** (1).

dyke. Same as **dike.**

dynamic(al), *dī-nam′ik(ȧl)*, *adjs.* concerned with force: (of a person—**dynamic**) forceful, very energetic.
dynam′ically, *adv.*
dynam′ics, *n.* (*pl.* as *sing.*) the science that deals with forces acting on bodies to produce or alter motion.
dy′namite, *n.* a powerful explosive.

dy'namo, *n.* (short for **dynamo-electric machine**) a machine which generates electric currents by means of the relative movement of conductors and magnets :—*pl.* **dy'namos.**
[Gk. *dynamis*, power.]
dynasty, *din'ȧs-ti*, or *dīn'*, *n.* a succession of rulers of the same family.
dynas'tic, *adj.*
[Gk. *dynastēs*, a lord.]
dysentery, *dis'ėn-tri*, *n.* an infectious disease with severe diarrhoea.
[Gk. *dys-*, ill, *enteron*, intestine.]
dyspepsia, *dis-pep'si-ȧ*, *n.* indigestion.
dyspep'tic, *n.* and *adj.*
[Gk. *dys-*, ill, *peptein*, to digest.]

E

each, *ēch*, *adj.* every one of two or more.
[O.E. *ǣlc*.]
eager, *ē'gėr*, *adj.* anxious (to do, for) : keen.
ea'gerly, *adv.* **ea'gerness,** *n.*
[O.Fr. *aigre*—L. *ācer*, sharp.]
eagle, *ē'gl*, *n.* a large bird of prey noted for its keen sight.
ea'glet, *n.* a young eagle.
[O.Fr. *aigle*—L. *aquila*.]
ear[1], *ēr*, *n.* the part of the head by means of which we hear : the sense of hearing.
ear'ache, *n.* a pain in the ear.
ear'drum, *n.* (see **drum**).
ear'mark, *n.* an owner's mark on the ears of sheep : a distinctive mark.—*v.t.* to put an earmark on : to set aside (for a particular purpose).
ear'ring, *n.* an ornament attached to the lobe of the ear.
ear'shot, *n.* the distance at which a sound can be heard.
ear'wig, *n.* an insect once supposed to creep into the ear.
to set (people) by the ears, to make (people) quarrel.
[O.E. *ēare*.]
ear[2], *ēr*, *n.* a spike, e.g. of corn.
[O.E. *ēar*.]
earl, *ėrl*, *n.* a British nobleman ranking between a marquis and a viscount :—*fem.* **count'ess** (see **count,** 1).
earl'dom, *n.* the title, rank, or territories of an earl.
[O.E. *eorl*, a warrior, hero.]
early, *ėr'li*, *adv.* in the first part of a period of time, course, series (e.g. *early in his life*) : in good time.—*adj.* belonging to, happening, (1) near the beginning, or (2) in the distant past, or (3) in the near future :—*comp.* **ear'lier** ; *superl.* **ear'liest.**
ear'liness, *n.*
early bird, an early riser : one who gains by acting more promptly than his rivals.
[O.E. *ǣrlice*—*ǣr*, before.]
earmark. See **ear** (1).
earn, *ėrn*, *v.t.* to gain by work : to deserve.
earn'ings, *n.pl.* wages.
[O.E. *earnian*.]
earnest[1], *ėr'nist*, *adj.* serious.—*n.* seriousness.
ear'nestly, *adv.* **ear'nestness,** *n.*
in earnest, serious, not jesting (e.g. *I am in earnest when I say this*) : seriously, with energy, determination (e.g. *He set to work in earnest*).
in dead(ly) earnest (stronger, more emphatic, forms of the above).
[O.E. *eornost*, seriousness.]
earnest[2], *ėr'nist*, *n.* money given in token of a bargain made : a pledge.
[Origin uncertain.]
earring, earshot. See **ear** (1).
earth, *ėrth*, *n.* the third planet in order from the sun : the world : the inhabitants of the world : soil : dry land : a burrow : an electrical connexion with the earth.—*v.t.* to connect to earth electrically.
earth'en, *adj.* made of earth, or of baked clay.
ear'thy, *adj.* of, like, earth : coarse.
earth'iness, *n.*
earth'ly, *adj.* passed, happening, etc. on earth : worldly : possible on earth (e.g. *no earthly chance, use*).
earth'liness, *n.*
earth'enware, *n.* pottery coarser than china.
earth'quake, *n.* a shaking of the earth's crust.
earth'work, *n.* a fortification of earth.
earth'worm, *n.* an animal with a ringed body and no backbone, living in damp earth.
[O.E. *eorthe*.]
earwig. See **ear** (1).
ease, *ēs*, *n.* freedom from pain, or from worry : rest from work : freedom from difficulty (e.g. *to do it with ease*) : naturalness (*ease of manner*).—*v.t.* to free from pain, trouble or anxiety : to lessen (e.g. pressure) : to manoeuvre very gradually (into, out of, a position).—*v.i.* to become less (also **ease off**).
eas'y, *adj.* free from pain, trouble, anxiety, difficulty : (of manner) not stiff : not tight : not strict :—*comp.* **eas'ier** ; *superl.* **eas'iest.**
eas'ily, *adv.* **eas'iness,** *n.*
eas'y-gō'ing, *adj.* not inclined to worry.

ill at ease, uncomfortable, embarrassed.
[O.Fr. *aise.*]

easel, *ēz'l, n.* the frame on which painters support their pictures while painting.
[Du. *ezel,* or Ger. *esel,* an ass.]

east, *ēst, n.* the part of the heavens where the sun rises: a territory in this direction.—Also *adj.* and *adv.*
east'ern, *adj.* of, or towards, the east.
east'erly, *adj.* coming from the east: looking towards the east.—Also *adv.*
east'ward, *adv.* towards the east.
east wind, wind from the east.
the East, the countries east of Europe.
[O.E. *ēast.*]

Easter, *ēst'ėr, n.* a Christian festival commemorating the resurrection of Christ.
Eas'tertide, *n.* the time of Easter.
[O.E. *ēastre.*]

eat, *ēt, v.t.* and *v.i.* to (chew and) swallow:—*pr.p.* **eat'ing**; *pa.t.* **ate** (*et* or *āt*); *pa.p.* **eaten** (*ētn*).
eat'able, *adj.* fit to be eaten.—*n.* (in *pl.*) food.
to eat into, to waste away, corrode (e.g. *Acids eat into metal.*)
[O.E. *etan.*]

Eau de Cologne, *ō dė kȯ-lōn',* a perfumed spirit first made at Cologne.
eau de vie, *ō dė vē,* brandy.
[Fr. *eau,* water, *de,* of (*vie,* life).]

eaves, *ēvz, n.pl.* edge of roof sticking out beyond wall: anything similarly projecting.
eaves'drop, *v.i.* to listen in order to overhear private conversation.
eaves'dropper, *n.*
[O.E. *efes,* the clipped edge of thatch.]

ebb, *eb, n.* the going back of the tide: a decline.—Also *v.i.*
ebb'-tide, *n.* the ebbing tide.
[O.E. *ebba.*]

ebony, *eb'ȯn-i, n.* a black wood almost as heavy and hard as stone.—*adj.* made of, black as, ebony.
[Gk. *ebenos.*]

ebullient, *ė-bul'yėnt, adj.* high-spirited, very enthusiastic.
ebull'iently, *adv.* **ebull'ience,** *n.*
[L. *ē,* out, *bullīre,* to boil.]

eccentric, -al, *ek-sen'trik, -ȧl, adjs.* with axis or support not in the centre: odd, not normal (e.g. *His behaviour is eccentric; an eccentric old man*).—Also *n.*
eccen'trically, *adv.*
eccentric'ity (*-tris'-*), *n.* state of being eccentric: oddness of behaviour:—*pl.* **eccentric'ities.**
[Gk. *ek,* out of, *kentron,* centre.]

ecclesiastic, *i-klē-zi-as'tik, n.* a priest, clergyman.
ecclesias'tic(al), *adjs.* of the church or clergy.
[Gk. *ekklēsia,* assembly, church.]

echelon, *esh'ė-lon, āsh'ė-long, n.* a stepwise arrangement of troops, ships, etc. in parallel lines, each line being a little to the right or left of that in front of it: a group of people in a particular grade in an organisation.
[Fr. *échelle,* a ladder.]

echo, *ek'ō, n.* repetition of sound caused by the throwing back of sound waves from a surface which they strike: an imitator:—*pl.* **echoes** (*ek'ōz*).—*v.i.* to sound loudly with an echo.—*v.t.* to repeat (sound, a statement): to imitate:—*pr.p.* **ech'oing**; *pa.p.* **ech'oed** (*-ōd*).
[Gk. *ēchō,* sound.]

éclair, *ā-klār', n.* a long iced (usu. chocolate-iced) cake with cream filling.
[Fr., lightning.]

eclipse, *i-klips', n.* the disappearance of the whole or part of a heavenly body, e.g. of the sun when the moon comes between it and the earth: loss of brilliancy, decline, downfall.—*v.t.* to hide: to darken: to surpass (e.g. *His successes eclipsed those of his brother.*)
eclip'tic, *n.* the apparent path of the sun among the fixed stars.
[Gk. *ekleipsis.*]

economy, *i-kon'ȯ-mi,* or *ē-, n.* the thrifty management of money, etc: a saving (*pl.* **-ies**): organisation of money and resources (e.g. *the country's economy*).
econom'ic (*ē-,* or *e-*), *adj.* of, concerned with, economics.
econom'ical, *adj.* thrifty, not extravagant.
econom'ically, *adv.*
econom'ics, *n. pl.* the study of production and distribution of money and goods.
econ'omise (*i-,* or *ē-*), *v.i.* to spend money or goods carefully: to save.—*v.t.* to use, or spend, carefully.
econ'omist, *n.* one who studies economics.
[Gk. *oikos,* a house, *nomos,* a law.]

ecstasy, *ek'stȧ-si, n.* very great joy: overpowering emotion or feeling.
ecstat'ic, *adj.* rapturous.
ecstat'ically, *adv.* **ecstat'icness,** *n.*
[Gk. *ekstasis.*]

ecumenical, *ēk-* or *ek-ū-men'ik-ȧl, adj.* belonging to the whole Christian church.
[Gk. *oikoumenē* (*gē*), inhabited (world).]

eczema, *ek'si-mȧ, n.* a disease of the skin, often caused by irritants.
[Gk. *ek,* out of, *zeein,* to boil.]

eddy, *ed'i, n.* a current of water or air running back against the main stream:—*pl.* **edd'ies.**—*v.i.* to move round and round:—*pr.p.* **edd'ying**; *pa.p.* **edd'ied.**
[Prob. O.E. pfx. *ed-,* back.]

edelweiss, *ā'dėl-vīs, n.* a small white flower of the Alps, with woolly heads.
[Ger. *edel,* noble, *weiss,* white.]

edge, *ej, n.* the border of anything: the brink: the cutting side of an instrument: sharpness (e.g. of mind, appetite).—*v.t.* to border: to move by little and little.—*v.i.* to move sideways.

edg'y, *adj.* irritable.
edg'ily, *adv.* **edg'iness,** *n.*
edg'ing, *n.* a border or fringe round a garment, etc.
edge'ways, edge'wise, *advs.* sideways.
on edge, uneasy, nervous, irritable.
[O.E. *ecg.*]

edible, *ed'i-bl, adj.* suitable as food.
ed'ibleness, edibil'ity, *ns.*
[L. *edibilis—edĕre,* to eat.]

edict, *ē'dikt, n.* a decree, order, command, of someone in authority.
[L. *ē,* out of, *dicĕre,* to say.]

edification. See **edify.**

edifice, *ed'i-fis, n.* a large building.
[L. *aedificium*; same root as **edify.**]

edify, *ed'i-fī, v.t.* to increase the faith of: to improve the mind or morals of:—*pr.p.* **ed'ifying**; *pa.p.* **ed'ified.**
edificā'tion, *n.* instruction: progress in knowledge or in goodness.
ed'ifying, *adj.* instructive, improving.
[Fr. *édifier*—L. *aedificāre,* to build.]

edit, *ed'it, v.t.* to prepare for publication, or for broadcasting or telecasting.
edi'tion, *n.* number of copies of a book, etc., printed at a time.
ed'itor, *n.* one who edits books, etc.: one who conducts a newspaper, periodical, etc.:—*fem.* (*sometimes*) **ed'itress.**
editō'rial, *adj.* of or belonging to an editor.—*n.* an article in a newspaper written by an editor or leader writer.
[L. *ē,* from, *dăre,* to give.]

educate, *ed'ū-kāt, v.t.* to train and teach.
ed'ucator, *n.* **educā'tion,** *n.*
educā'tional, *adj.* of education: increasing knowledge and wisdom.
educā'tion(al)ist, *ns.* a person who knows much about methods of educating.
ed'ucative, *adj.* tending to educate.
[L. *ēducāre,* to bring up, to rear.]

eel, *ēl, n.* a fish with long smooth cylinder-shaped or ribbon-shaped body.
[O.E. *ǣl.*]

eerie, *ē'ri, adj.* weird, causing fear.
ee'rily, *adv.* **ee'riness,** *n.*
[M.E. *eri,* perh.—O.E. *earg,* cowardly.]

efface, *i-fās', v.t.* to rub out: to make seem unimportant: (with *oneself*) to shun notice.
[L. *ex,* out, *faciēs,* face.]

effect, *i-fekt', n.* result, consequence: impression produced (e.g. *The effect of yellow flowers in a dark room is good*): general meaning (e.g. *What he said was to this effect*): reality (*in effect*): (in *pl.*) goods, property: (in *pl.*; *theatre*) sound and lighting devices.—*v.t.* to bring about.
effec'tive, *adj.* having power to produce, or producing, a desired result: striking, pleasing.
effec'tively, *adv.*
effec'tual (*-tū-àl*), *adj.* successful in producing the desired result (e.g. *We took effectual measures to stop the thefts*).
to give effect to, to put into effect, to act in accordance with (a decision), put into operation (a law).
to take effect, to come into force (e.g. *This regulation does not take effect until 9th June*).
effective, effectual, efficient (see this), **efficacious** (see this) are used in slightly different ways. 'Efficient' (which suggests good results obtained by good methods) is the adjective most commonly applied to a *person,* and it can also be applied to a *tool* (e.g. *A knife does not make an efficient corkscrew*), and to *actions* (e.g. *efficient work*). 'Efficacious' is never used of a person, and 'effectual' rarely. 'Effectual' and '**effective**' are used of *actions,* effective **being** the stronger word, and when **effective** is used of a person it is with a particular action in mind (e.g. *an effective speaker,* not *an effective man*).
[L. *ex,* out, *facĕre, factum,* to make.]

effeminate, *i-fem'in-it, adj.* unmanly, weak.
effem'inateness, effem'inacy, *ns.*
[L. *ex,* out, *fēmina,* a woman.]

effervesce, *ef-ėr-ves', v.i.* to froth up, give off bubbles of gas: to be excited or very lively.
efferves'cence, *n.* **efferves'cent,** *adj.*
[L. pfx. *ex,* and *fervēre,* to boil.]

effete, *i-fēt', adj.* exhausted, worn out.
[L. *effētus.*]

efficacious, *ef-i-kā'shùs, adj.* (esp. of a medicine, remedy) producing the result intended.
effica'ciousness, eff'icacy (*-kà-si*), *ns.*
[L. *efficax*—same root as **effect.**]

efficient, *i-fish'ėnt, adj.* (of a person) capable, skilful: satisfactory in use: very practical (e.g. *an efficient method*).
efficiency, *i-fish'ėn-si, n.*
efficiently, *i-fish'ėnt-li, adv.*
[L. *efficiens*—same root as **effect.**]

effigy, *ef'i-ji, n.* a likeness of a person (esp. sculptured): the head on a coin:—*pl.* **eff'igies.**
[L. *effigiēs—ex-, fingĕre,* to form.]

effluent, *ef'loo-ėnt, n.* a stream that flows out of another stream or of a lake.
[L. *ex,* out, *fluĕre,* to flow.]

effluvium, *i-flōō'vi-ùm, n.* disagreeable vapours, e.g. from decaying matter:—*pl.* **efflu'via.**
[Late Latin—same L. root as **effluent.**]

effort, *ef'ȯrt, n.* a putting forth of strength: attempt: struggle.
eff'ortless, *adj.* without effort, or seeming to be so.
[Fr.—L. *ex,* out, *fortis,* strong.]

effrontery, *e-frunt'ėr-i, n.* impudence.
[L. *ex,* out, *frons, frontis,* the forehead.]

effusion, *i-fū'zhėn, n.* pouring out: shedding (of blood): passing (of a gas) through extremely small holes: a wordy and emotional letter, speech, etc.
effu'sive (*-siv*), *adj.* gushing, emotional.
[L. *ex,* out, *fundĕre, fusum,* to pour.]

eft, *eft, n.* a newt (see this word).
[O.E. *efeta*; origin uncertain.]

egg[1], *eg, n.* an oval body laid by a bird, etc. from which a young one is hatched: something resembling an egg.
[Old Norse.]

egg[2], *eg, v.t.* (followed by **on**) to urge, encourage (a person to do something).
[Old Norse *eggja—egg*, an edge.]

ego, *e'gō, ē'gō, n.* the 'I,' or self—the part of a person that is conscious and thinks.
egocen'tric, *adj.* self-centred.
e'goism (*-gō-izm*), *n.* self-interest: selfishness.
e'goist, *n.* one who thinks and speaks too much about himself.
egoist'ic, -al, *adjs.*
e'gotism, *n.* a frequent use of the pronoun I, speaking much of oneself.
e'gotist, *n.* an egoist, boastful person.
egotist'ic, -al, *adjs.* [L.]

egregious, *i-grē'jyus, adj.* outrageous, shocking (e.g. *an egregious lie*).
[L. *ē*, out of, *grex, gregis*, flock.]

egress, *ē'gres, n.* act of going out: the right to depart: the way out.
[L. *ēgredi, ēgressus*, to go out.]

Egyptian, *i-jip'sh(a)n, adj.* belonging to Egypt.—*n.* a native of Egypt.
Egyptol'ogy, *n.* the science of Egyptian antiquities.

eider (duck), *ī'dėr (duk), n.* a northern sea duck with fine down on its breast.
ei'derdown, *n.* the down or soft feathers of the eider duck: a quilt filled with this or other material.
[Prob. Old Norse *æthr*.]

eight, *āt, adj.* and *n.* the number next above seven (8 or VIII): (*n.*) the crew of an eight-oared racing boat.
eighth, *adj.* last of eight.—*n.* one of eight equal parts.
eighteen, *ā'tēn, ā-tēn', adj.* and *n.* eight and ten (18 or XVIII).
eighteenth, *adj.* last of eighteen.—*n.* one of eighteen equal parts.
eighty, *ā'ti, adj.* and *n.* eight times ten (80 or LXXX):—*pl.* **eigh'ties.**
eigh'tieth, *adj.* last of eighty.—*n.* one of eighty equal parts.
[O.E. *eahta*; *eahtatēne*; *eahtatig*.]

Eisteddfod, *ī-steTH'vod, n.* a congress or great meeting of Welsh bards and musicians.
[W. *eistedd*, to sit.]

either, *ī'THėr,* or *ē'THėr, adj.* or *pron.* the one or the other: (*adj.*) the one and the other (e.g. *There are trees on either side of the house*).
either . . . or, *conjs.* introducing alternatives (e.g. *You must either go to see him or send an excuse*).
[O.E. *ǣgther*.]

ejaculate, *i-jak'ū-lāt, v.t.* to utter, exclaim, suddenly.
ejaculā'tion, *n.* word(s) said thus.
[L. *ē*, from, *jaculāre*; root as **eject.**]

eject, *i-jekt', v.t.* to throw out: to expel, dismiss.
ejec'tion, *n.* act of ejecting.
eject'or-seat, *n.* an aeroplane seat that can be shot clear with its occupant in emergency.
[L. *ē*, from, *jacĕre, jactum*, to throw.]

eke, *ēk, v.t.* (followed by **out**) to make (something) seem sufficient by adding (e.g. *You could eke out the scanty supply of meat with plenty of potatoes*): to manage to make (a scanty living).
[O.E. *ēcan*, to increase.]

elaborate, *i-lab'ȯr-āt, v.t.* to work out in detail (e.g. *I expected John to elaborate our plan of escape*): to develop.—*v.i.* (with *upon*) to discuss with (usu.) unnecessary fullness.—*adj.* (*-it*) very detailed or complicated: (of style of dress, etc.) very formal or fashionable.
elab'orately, *adv.* **elaborā'tion,** *n.*
[L. *ē*, from, *labor*, labour.]

elapse, *i-laps', v.i.* (of time) to pass.
[L. *ē*, from, *lābī, lapsus*, to slip.]

elastic, *i-las'tik, adj.* (of material) able to take again its orig. form when forces that changed the form are removed: springy.—*n.* a string or ribbon with rubber strands.
elasticity, *e-las-tis'i-ti,* or *ē-, n.* ability to return to orig. shape: power to recover quickly from depression.
[Late Gk. *elastikos*.]

elate, *i-lāt', v.t.* to make glad or proud.
elat'ed, *adj.* **elat'edly,** *adv.*
elā'tion, *n.* high spirits caused by success.
[L. *ē*, from, *lātus*, carried.]

elbow, *el'bō, n.* the joint where the arm bends: any sharp bend.—*v.t.* to push with the elbow: to jostle.
el'bow-room, *n.* space enough for moving or acting.
[O.E. *elnboga*—roots of **ell** and **bow** (2).]

elder[1], *el'dėr, n.* a shrub or tree with purple-black fruit from which is made **elder-berry wine,** etc.: a related shrub with red berries.
[O.E. *ellærn*.]

elder[2], *el'dėr, adj.* older: senior.—*n.* a person who is older: an older, more experienced member of a tribe, etc.: an office-bearer in presbyterian churches.
el'derly, *adj.* getting old.
el'dest, *adj.* oldest.
elder statesman, an important senior member of a group.
[O.E. *eldra*, comp. of *eald*, old.]

elect, *i-lekt', v.t.* to choose by vote: to choose (to do something).—*adj.* chosen: chosen for office but not yet in it (e.g. *president elect*).
elec'tion, *n.* the public choosing, or choice, of person(s) for office.
electioneer', *v.t.* to work to bring about the election of a candidate.
elec'tor, *n.* a person who has a vote at an election.
elec'toral, *adj.* of elections or electors.

elec′torate, *n.* all the electors taken together.
[L. *ē*, from, *legĕre*, *lectum*, to choose.]

electric(al), *i-lek′trik(ȧl), adjs.* of, produced by, or worked by, electricity: (of atmosphere) full of excitement.
elec′trically, *adv.*
electrician, *ė-lek-trish′ȧn, n.* an engineer specialising in electrical appliances and installations.
electric′ity (*-tris′-*), *n.* the power to attract shown by amber (in which it was first noticed) and other substances when rubbed: a form of energy producing, in addition to attraction and repulsion, lighting and heating effects, decomposition of chemical substances, etc.
elec′trify, *v.t.* to give electricity to: to adapt to electricity as the moving power (e.g. *to electrify railways*): to excite suddenly: to astonish:—*pr.p.* **elec′trifying**; *pa.p.* **elec′trified.**
electrificā′tion, *n.*
electric chair, a chair used in electrocuting condemned criminals.
See also **electro-.**
[Gk. *ēlektron*, amber.]

electro-, *i-lek-trō-, pfx.* of, caused by, electricity.
elec′trocute (*-kūt*), *v.t.* to put to death, or to kill accidentally, by electricity.
electrocū′tion, *n.*
elec′trode, *n.* a conductor through which a current of electricity enters or leaves a battery, an arc lamp, etc.
electrol′ysis (*-is-is*), *n.* the breaking-up of a chemical compound by electricity.
elec′tro(-)mag′net, *n.* a piece of soft iron made magnetic by a current of electricity passing through a coil of wire wound round it.
electromagnetic waves, a travelling disturbance in space, of which light waves and the waves used in radio are examples.
elec′tron, *n.* a very light particle within the atom having the smallest possible charge of electricity.
electron′ic, *adj.* having to do with electrons or electronics.
electron′ics, *n.* the science of the conduction of electricity in a vacuum, a gas, etc., and the practical art of making devices such as cathode ray tube (see this).
electronic brain, an electronic computer.
elec′troplate, *v.t.* to cover with silver or other metal by means of electrolysis.
elec′troplating, *n.*
elec′trotype, *n.* a printing plate made by coating a mould with copper by means of electrolysis.
[Same root as **electric.**]

elegant, *el′i-gȧnt, adj.* (e.g. of clothes) expensive and in good taste: dressed in this way: graceful: refined.
el′egance, el′egancy (*pl.* **-cies**), *ns.*
[L. *ēlegans*—*legĕre*, to choose.]

elegy, *el′i-ji, n.* song of mourning:—*pl.* **-ies.**
[Gk. *elegos*, a lament.]

element, *el′i-mėnt, n.* an essential part of anything: a substance that cannot be split *by chemical means* into simpler substances (e.g. *Hydrogen, chlorine, iron, and uranium are elements*): (in *pl.*) the first things to be learned in any subject: (in *pl.*) the bread and wine used in the Eucharist: (in *pl.*) the forces of nature, as wind and rain: (*radio*) an electrode: a resistance wire in an electric heater.
elemen′tal, *adj.* of, like, the forces of nature.
elemen′tary, *adj.* very simple.
[L. *elementum.*]

elephant, *el′i-fȧnt, n.* an animal with very thick skin, a trunk, and two ivory tusks.
elephan′tine (*-tīn*), *adj.* very large: clumsy.
white elephant, a pale-coloured elephant: a useless possession, or a possession that causes one expense.
[Gk. *elephas.*]

elevate, *el′i-vāt, v.t.* to raise to a higher position: to raise in mind or morals: to cheer.
elevā′tion, *n.* the act of raising: rising ground: height: dignity: grandeur: ability of a dancer to remain in the air.
el′evator, *n.* a lift or machine for raising persons, goods, grain, etc., to a higher floor: a high storehouse for grain.
[L. *ē*, from, *levāre*, to raise—*levis*, light.]

eleven, *i-lev′n, adj.* and *n.* the number next above ten (11 or XI).
elev′enth, *adj.* last of eleven.—*n.* one of eleven equal parts.
at the eleventh hour, at the last moment, in the nick of time.
[O.E. *en(d)le(o)fan.*]

elf, *elf, n.* a tiny, mischievous fairy:—*pl.* **el′ves.**
elf′ish, *adj.* **elf′ishly,** *adv.*
[O.E. *ælf.*]

elicit, *i-lis′it, e-, v.t.* to draw out from a person (information, an admission).
[L. *ēlicĕre, ēlicitum.*]

eligible, *el′i-ji-bl, adj.* qualified, esp. legally, to be chosen: worthy to be chosen. Also *n.*
el′igibleness, eligibil′ity, *ns.*
[Fr.—same L. root as **elect.**]

eliminate, *i-lim′i-nāt, e-, v.t.* to get rid of: to omit, ignore.
eliminā′tion, *n.*
[L. *ē*, from, *līmen*, a threshold.]

élite, *ā-lēt,* **elite,** *i-lēt′, n.* the best or most important (of a class of people).
[Fr. *élite*—L. *electa (pars)*, chosen (part).]

elixir, *ė-lik′sėr, n.* a supposed liquid that would make people able to go on living for ever, or a substance that would turn base metals into gold.
[Arabic *el iksīr.*]

Elizabethan, *i-liz-à-bē'thàn, adj.* of Queen Elizabeth (reigned 1558–1603) or her time: also of Elizabeth II.

elk, *elk, n.* the largest of all deer, found in the north of Europe and Asia.
[Old Norse *elgr,* L. *alcēs,* Gk. *alkē.*]

ell, *el, n.* a measure of length orig. taken from the arm.
[O.E. *eln.*]

ellipse, *i-lips', n.* a regular oval (i.e. one which can be divided in two ways into two parts of the same size and shape).
ellip'tical, *adj.*
[Gk. *elleipsis.*]

elm, *elm, n.* a tall tree with tough wood and corrugated bark. [O.E.]

elocution, *el-ò-kū'sh(ò)n, n.* the art of speaking clearly and effectively: a stilted, unnatural way of speaking.
[L. *ē,* from, *loquī, locūtus,* to speak.]

elongate, *ē'long-gāt, v.t.* to make longer.
e'longāted, *adj.* long and (usu.) narrow.
elongā'tion, *n.*
[L. *ē,* from, *longus,* long.]

elope, *i-lōp', v.i.* to run away secretly, esp. with a lover.
elope'ment, *n.*
[From O.Fr.; conn. O.E. *hleapan,* leap, run.]

eloquence, *el'o-kwėns, n.* the power of expressing emotion or thought in words that impress or move other people: moving words.
el'oquent, *adj.* **el'oquently,** *adv.*
[L. *ēloquens*—same root as **elocution.**]

else, *els, adv.* otherwise: except the person or thing mentioned.
else'where', *adv.* in, or to, another place.
[O.E. *elles,* otherwise.]

elucidate, *i-lōōs'i-dāt, -lūs', v.t.* to make clear, explain (e.g. something difficult or mysterious).
elucidā'tion, *n.*
[L. pfx. *ē, lūcidus,* bright—*lux,* light.]

elude, *i-lōōd', -lūd', v.t.* to escape or avoid by trick or nimbleness: to escape the memory of (a person), or to prove too difficult for (a person) to understand.
elu'sive (*-siv*), *adj.* escaping often or cleverly: hard to grasp or to express.
[L. *ē,* from, *lūdĕre,* to play.]

elves. See **elf.**

em-. See **en-.**

emaciate, *i-mā'shi-āt, v.t.* and *v.i.* to make, or become, very thin by loss of flesh.
emā'ciated, *adj.* **emaciā'tion,** *n.*
[L. *maciēs,* leanness.]

emanate, *em'à-nāt, v.i.* to flow, come, out (from some source; e.g. *This information emanates from his family.*)
emanā'tion, *n.* something given out by a substance, e.g. scent, rays.
[L. *ē,* out, *mānāre,* to flow.]

emancipate, *i-man'si-pāt, v.t.* to set free from slavery or other restraint or control.
emancipā'tion, *n.* **eman'cipator,** *n.*
[L. *ē,* from *manus,* the hand, *capĕre,* take.]

embalm, *em-bäm', v.t.* to preserve (a dead body) from decay by treatment with spices or drugs.
[Fr. *embaumer.*]

embankment, *em-bangk'mėnt, n.* a bank or ridge made e.g. to keep back water or to carry a railway. [Pfx. **em-.**]

embargo, *em-bär'gō, n.* stoppage by authority of movement of ships in and out of a port, or of certain trade: a ban (on something):—*pl.* **embar'goes.**—Also *v.t.*:—*pr.p.* **embar'going**; *pa.p.* **embar'goed.**
[Sp.—*embargar,* to hinder, restrain.]

embark, *em-bärk', v.t.* to put on board ship.—*v.i.* to go on board ship: to engage (in, on, upon any action; e.g. *to embark on a war against the French*).
embarkā'tion, *n.*
[Fr. *em-,* in, *barque,* ship.]

embarrass, *em-bar'às, v.t.* to hinder, hamper (e.g. *Three suitcases embarrassed his progress*): to involve in difficulty, esp. money difficulty: to confuse, make selfconscious.
embarr'assment, *n.*
[Fr. *em-,* in, *barre,* bar.]

embassy, *em'bàs-i, n.* an ambassador and his staff: an ambassador's official residence: a deputation.
[O.Fr. *ambassé.*]

embattle, *em-bat'l, v.t.* to arrange in order for, or prepare for, battle.
embatt'led, *adj.*
[O.Fr. *em-,* in, *bataille,* battle.]

embed, *em-bed', v.t.* to fix deeply (in something).
[Pfx. **em-,** and **bed.**]

embellish, *em-bel'ish, v.t.* to make beautiful with ornaments: to increase the interest of (a story) by adding fictitious details.
embell'ishment, *n.*
[Fr. *em-,* in, *bel* (*beau*), beautiful.]

ember, *em'bėr, n.* a piece of live coal or wood: (in *pl.*) smouldering remains of a fire.
[O.E. *æmerge.*]

Ember(-)days, *em'bėr-dāz, n.pl.* in R.C. and English Church the three fast days in each quarter.
[O.E. *ymb,* round, *ryne,* a running.]

embezzle, *em-bez'l, v.t.* to take fraudulently (money that has been entrusted to one).
embezz'lement, *n.* **embezz'ler,** *n.*
[M.E. *embesilen,* to make away with.]

embitter, *em-bit'ėr, v.t.* to make bitter: to make hostile (with *against*).
embitt'ered, *adj.* soured. [Pfx. **em-.**]

emblazon, *em-blā'zòn, v.t.* to adorn with heraldic devices, etc. [Pfx. **em-.**]

emblem, *em'blėm, n.* an object chosen to represent a quality, state, etc. (e.g. *The dove is the emblem of peace*).
emblemat'ic, *adj.* (e.g. *The dove is emblematic of peace*).
[Gk. *emblēma.*]

embody, *em-bod'i, v.t.* to express in words, actions, etc. (e.g. *He embodied his views on justice in a long essay*): to include: to represent in living form (e.g. *Parker embodied my idea of fearless honesty*).
embod'iment, *n.* [Pfx. **em-**.]

embolden, *em-bōld'n, v.t.* to make bold: to give (one) courage (to do something).
[Pfx. **em-, bold,** and suffx. *-en.*]

emboss, *em-bos', v.t.* to ornament with raised design.
embossed', *adj.*
[Pfx. **em-,** and **boss** (1).]

embrace, *em-brās', v.t.* to take in the arms with affection: to take eagerly (e.g. an opportunity): to adopt (e.g. Christianity): to include (e.g. *The term man often embraces men, women, and children*). —Also *v.i.* and *n.*
[O.Fr. *embracer*—L. *in, brācchium,* arm.]

embrasure, *em-brā'zhür, n.* an opening in a wall (e.g. for cannon), widening from within.
[O.Fr. *embraser,* to slope sides of a window.]

embrocation, *em-brō-kā'sh(ò)n, n.* a lotion for moistening and rubbing part of the body.
[Gk. *embrochē.*]

embroider, *em-broid'ėr, v.t.* to ornament with designs in needlework: to add fictitious detail to (a story).
embroid'ery, *n.*:—*pl.* **-eries.**
[O.Fr. *embroder.*]

embroil, *em-broil', v.t.* to involve (a person) in a quarrel (with another or others): to throw into confusion.
embroil'ment, *n.*
[Pfx. **em-,** and **broil** (1).]

embryo, *em'bri-ō, n.* a young animal or plant in its earliest stages in seed, protective tissue, egg, or womb: the beginning stage of anything.—Also *adj.*
embryol'ogy, *n.* the science of the formation and development of the embryo.
embryol'ogist, *n.*
embryon'ic, *adj.* in an early stage of development.
[Gk. *embryon—bryein,* to swell.]

emend, *i-mend', v.t.* to correct errors in (esp. a book).
emendā'tion, *n.*
[L. *ē,* from, *menda,* a fault.]

emerald, *em'ėr-àld, n.* a green gemstone.
[O.Fr. *esmeralde.*]

emerge, *i-mėrj', v.i.*: to rise out (from water, etc): to come out.
emer'gence, *n.* act of coming out.
emer'gency, *n.* an unexpected happening or situation requiring immediate action:—*pl.* **-ies.**
emer'gent, *adj.* coming out.
[L. *ē,* out of, *mergĕre,* to plunge.]

emeritus, *i-mėr'i-tùs, adj.* retired (esp. of a professor); often after noun.
[L. *ēmeritus,* having served one's time.]

emery, *em'ėr-i, n.* a very hard mineral, used as powder, etc. for polishing.
[O.Fr. *esmeril*; orig. from Gk.]

emetic, *i-met'ik, adj.* causing vomiting.—*n.* a medicine that causes vomiting.
[Gk. *emetikos—emeein,* to vomit.]

emigrate, *em'i-grāt, v.i.* and *v.t.* to leave one's country and settle in another.
em'igrant, *adj.* emigrating or having emigrated.—Also *n.*
emigrā'tion, *n.*
[L. *ē,* from, *migrāre,* to remove.]

eminent, *em'i-nėnt, adj.* rising above others: distinguished.
em'inently, *adv.* very, obviously (e.g. *eminently suitable*).
em'inence, em'inency, *ns.* a rising ground, hill: distinction: a title of honour.
[L. *ē,* from, *minēre,* to stick out.]

emir, *ė-mēr',* or *e'-, n.* a chieftain in Arabia or north Africa.
[Arabic *amīr,* ruler.]

emissary, emission. See **emit.**

emit, *i-mit', v.t.* to give out (e.g. light, heat):—*pr.p.* **emitt'ing**; *pa.p.* **emitt'ed.**
emission, *i-mish'òn, n.*
em'issary (*em'*), *n.* one sent on a mission (often secret or underhand):—*pl.* **-ies.**
[L. *ē,* out of, *mittĕre, missum,* to send.]

emollient, *i-mol'yėnt, adj.* softening.—*n.* a softening application such as a poultice.
[L. pfx. *ē-, mollīre,* to soften.]

emolument, *i-mol'ū-mėnt, n.* (often in *pl.*) profit from employment, salary, fees.
[L. *ēmolumentum—ēmolĕre,* grind out.]

emotion, *i-mō'sh(ò)n, n.* moving of the feelings: agitation of mind.
emo'tional, *adj.* of the emotions: easily affected by joy, love, fear, etc.
emo'tionally, *adv.*
emo'tive, *adj.* arousing emotion.
[L. *ēmovēre, ēmotum,* to stir up.]

empanel, *em-pan'ėl, v.t.* to enter (the names of a jury) on a list. [Pfx. **em-**.]

emperor, *em'pėr-òr, n.* royal title of a head of an empire:—*fem.* **em'press.**
empire, *em'pīr, n.* a widespreading group of states, etc., under the same ruling power, not always an emperor.
[L. *imperātor,* ruler, *imperium,* rule.]

emphasis, *em'fȧ-sis, n.* stress put on words: importance given to something (e.g. *The emphasis of the talk was on the need to work hard*).
em'phasise (*-sīz*), *v.t.* to lay stress on.
emphat'ic, *adj.* expressed with emphasis: firm and definite.
emphat'ically, *adv.* **emphat'icness,** *n.*
[Gk.—*en,* in, *phainein,* to show.]

empire. See **emperor.**

empiric, empirical, *em-pir'ik, -àl, adjs.* depending on, known by, experiment or experience.
[Gk. *en,* in, *peira,* a trial.]

emplacement, *em-plās'mėnt, n.* a gun platform. [Fr.]

employ, *em-ploi′, v.t.* to occupy the time or attention of: to use: to give work to.—*n.* employment, service (e.g. *He was in my employ*).
employed′, *adj.* having a job: working.
employ′ee (or *-ē′*), *n.* one who works for an **employ′er.**
employ′ment, *n.* act of employing: state of being employed: occupation, esp. regular trade, etc.
[Fr. *employer*—L. *in*, in, *plicāre*, to fold.]

emporium, *em-pō′ri-um, -pö′, n.* a central place to which goods are brought for sale: a large shop.
[Gk. *empŏros*, a trader.]

empower, *em-pow′ėr, v.t.* to authorise (e.g. *I empowered him to draw the necessary money*): to enable. [Pfx. **em-.**]

empty, *emp′ti, adj,* having nothing inside: unoccupied: completely without (e.g. *empty of meaning*): having no practical result (used e.g. of dreams, threats, boasts).—*v.t.* and *v.i.* to make, or become, empty:—*pr.p.* **emp′tying**; *pa.p.* **emp′tied.**—*n.* an empty bottle, etc.:—*pl.* **emp′ties.**
emp′tiness, *n.*
[O.E. *ǣmettig.*]

emu, *ē′mū, n.* an Australian running bird, related to the ostrich.
[Port. *ema*, an ostrich.]

emulate, *em′ū-lāt, v.t.* to strive to equal or be better than: to imitate.
emulā′tion, *n.*
[L. *aemulārī.*]

emulsion, *i-mul′sh(ȯ)n, n.* a milky liquid prepared by mixing e.g. oil and water.
[L. *ēmulgēre, ēmulsum*, to milk, drain.]

en-, *en-.* pfx. used to form verbs from nouns and adjectives, meaning:—(1) to put into, e.g. **encase**; (2) to bring into the condition of, e.g. **enslave**; (3) to make, e.g. **endear.** Before *b, p,* and sometimes *m, en-* becomes *em-*, e.g. **embed, empower.**

enable, *en-ā′bl, v.t.* to make able.
[Pfx. **en-.**]

enact, *en-akt′, v.t.* to act the part of: to decree by law (that).
enact′ment, *n.* the passing of a bill into law: a law. [Pfx. **en-.**]

enamel, *i-nam′ėl, n.* a variety of glass applied as coating to a metal or other surface and fired: the coating of the teeth: a glossy paint: a complexion cosmetic.—Also *v.t.*:—*pr.p.* **enam′elling**; *pa.p.* **enam′elled.**
[O.Fr. *en*, in, *esmail*, enamel.]

enamour, *en-am′ȯr, v.t.* used in the phrase **to be enamoured of, with,** to be in love with, or delighted with.
[Through Fr.—L. *amor*, love.]

encamp, *en-kamp′, v.i.* to settle in a camp.—Also *v.t.*.
encamp′ment, *n.* a place where troops, etc., are encamped. [Pfx. **en-].**

encase, *en-kās′, v.t.* to enclose in a case: to surround, cover (with *in*). [Pfx. **en-.**]

enchain, *en-chān′, v.t.* to put in chains.
[Fr. *en*, in, *chaîne*, a chain—L. *catēna.*]

enchant, *en-chânt′, v.t.* to put a spell or charm on: to delight.
enchant′ed, *adj.*
enchant′er, *n.*:—fem. **enchant′ress.**
enchant′ment, *n.*
[L. *incantāre*, sing magic formula over.]

encircle, *en-sėrk′l, v.t.* to surround (with): to go or pass round. [Pfx. **en-.**]

enclave, *en′klāv, n.* a piece of territory entirely enclosed within foreign territory.
[L. *in*, and *clāvis*, a key.]

enclose, *en-klōz′, v.t.* to shut in: to surround: to put inside a letter or its envelope.
enclosure, *en-klō′zhėr, n.* enclosing: land surrounded by fence or wall: something put in along with a letter.
[Pfx. **en-.**]

encomium, *en-kō′mi-um, n.* an expression of very high praise.
[Gk. *enkōmion*, a song of praise.]

encompass, *en-kum′pȧs, v.t.* to surround.
[Pfx. **en-,** and **compass.**]

encore, *ong-kōr′, -kör′,* or *ong′-, n.* call for repetition of a performance, or for a further performance.—Also *v.t.* and *interj.*
[Fr. *encore*, again.]

encounter, *en-kown′tėr, v.t.* to meet, esp. unexpectedly: to meet (difficulties, an enemy).—*n.* a meeting: a fight.
[L. *in*, in, *contra*, against.]

encourage, *en-kur′ij, v.t.* to give courage or hope to (someone): to urge (a person to do something).
encour′agement, *n.*
encour′aging, *adj.*
encour′agingly, *adv.*
[O.Fr. pfx, *en-*, *corage*, courage.]

encroach, *en-krōch′, v.i.* (with *on*) to advance into (e.g. someone else's land; *In making his cabbage-patch larger, he encroached on Brown's wood*): to seize a part of (a right belonging to someone else; *Is the Government slowly encroaching on the liberty of the individual?*).
encroach′ment, *n.*
[O.Fr. *encrochier*, seize—*croc*, a hook.]

encrust, *en-krust′,* **incrust,** *in-, v.t.* to cover with a crust or hard coating e.g. of precious materials.
en-, incrustā′tion, *n.*
[L. *in*, on, *crusta*, crust.]

encumber, *en-kum′bėr, v.t.* to hamper the movement of, to burden: to load (e.g. an estate) with debt.
encum′brance, *n.* something that burdens.
[O.Fr. *encombrer*—*combre*, a barrier.]

encyclopaedia, *en-sī-klo-pē′di-ȧ, n.* a reference work containing information on every branch of knowledge, or on one particular branch (e.g. *an encyclopaedia of jazz*).

encyclopae′dic, *adj.* having a large amount of information on a great variety of subjects.

[Gk. *enkyklios*, circular, *paideia*, instruction.]

end, *end, n.* the last point or part: the finish: death: the result: the aim: a fragment, an odd piece.—*v.t.* to bring to an end: to destroy.—*v.i.* to come to an end: to result (in).

end′ing, *n.*

end′less, *adj.* continuous, because having the two ends joined (e.g. *an endless chain*): going on for ever or for a very long time.

end′ways, end′wise, *advs.* with the end forward.

at (a) loose end(s), with nothing to do.

to make both ends meet, to live within one's income, not overspend.

[O.E. *ende.*]

endanger, *en-dān′jėr, v.t.* to put in danger. [Pfx. **en-**.]

endear, *en-dēr′, v.t.* to make dear or more dear.

endear′ing, *adj.* arousing feelings of affection.

endear′ment, *n.* act of endearing: a caress or word of love. [Pfx. **en-**.]

endeavour, *en-dev′ȯr, v.i.* to strive (to): to attempt (to).—*n.* a strenuous attempt.

[Fr. *en*, in, *devoir*, duty.]

endemic, *en-dem′ik, adj.* (e.g. of a disease) regularly found in a people or a district owing to local conditions.

[Gk. *en*, in, *dēmos*, a people.]

endive, *en′div, n.* a salad plant related to chicory. [Fr.]

endorse, *en-dörs′, v.t.* to write e.g. one's signature, or a note of contents, on the back of (a cheque, a document): to give one's approval to (e.g. *I endorse your decision to build a factory*): to support (a statement).

[M.E. *endosse*; L. *in*, on, *dorsum*, back.]

endow, *en-dow′, v.t.* to give a permanent income to (usu. an institution or part of one): to give a talent, quality, etc. to (e.g. *Nature had endowed him with practical ability*).

endow′ment, *n.*

[Fr. *en, douer*—L. *dōs*, a dowry.]

endue, *en-dū′, v.t.* to endow, provide (with quality, e.g. courage, beauty; often in *pass.*):—*pr.p.* **endu′ing**; *pa.p.* **endued′**.

[Fr. *enduire.*]

endure, *en-dūr′, v.t.* to bear with patience: to undergo: to tolerate.—*v.i.* to remain firm: to last.

endur′able, *adj.* able to be borne.

endur′ance, *n.* the power of bearing, or of lasting: the time through which something lasts.

[Fr. *endurer*—L. *in*, in, *dūrus*, hard.]

endways, endwise. See **end.**

enema, *en′ė-mȧ, i-nē′mȧ, n.* a liquid medicine injected into the rectum: an instrument for doing this.

[Gk.—*enienai*, to send in.]

enemy, *en′i-mi, n.* a person who wishes to injure one: a person, force, ship, aeroplane, etc. armed to fight against one: an opponent (of; e.g. *an enemy of change, of gambling*):—*pl.* **en′emies.**

[O.Fr. *enemi*—L. *in-*, not, *amicus*, friend.]

energy, *en′ėr-ji, n.* the power of doing work: ability to act, or habit of acting, vigorously (e.g. *He has great energy and will quickly move the stones*): force:—*pl.* **en′ergies.**

energet′ic, *adj.* very active, vigorous.

energet′ically, *adv.*

en′ergise, *v.t.* to rouse to activity.

[Gk. *en*, in, *ergon*, work.]

enervate, *en′ėr-vāt, v.t.* to take strength or vigour from.

[L. *ē*, out of, *nervus*, a nerve.]

enfeeble, *en-fē′bl, v.t.* to weaken.

enfee′blement, *n.*

[O.Fr. *enfeblir*—*feible*, feeble.]

enfold, *en-fōld′, v.t.* to wrap up (in, with, something): to embrace. [Pfx. **en-**.]

enforce, *en-fōrs′, -förs′, v.t.* to compel obedience to (e.g. *to enforce a law, a command*): to force (an action or way of acting; e.g. *He will now try to enforce payment of the money*): to express more strongly (an argument).

[O.Fr. *enforcier*—L. *in-*, *fortis*, strong.]

enfranchise, *en-fran′chīz, -shīz, v.t.* to set free; to give voting rights to.

enfran′chisement (*-chiz-*), *n.*

[O.Fr. *en*, and *franc*, free.]

engage, *in-gāj′, v.t.* to bind by a promise: to hire (e.g. *to engage a workman*): to reserve (e.g. *to engage a table for four*): to take hold of, hold fast (e.g. attention, sympathy): to join battle with: (of part of a machine) to interlock with (another part): to cause to interlock.—*v.i.* to promise (to): to take part (in; e.g. *to engage in smuggling*).

engaged′, *adj.* bound by promise (esp. to marry): employed (in): busy: hired: reserved: occupied: in battle (with): interlocked.

engage′ment, *n.*

engag′ing (*-gāj′*), *adj.* attractive.

[Fr. *en*, in, *gage*, pledge.]

engender, *en-jen′dėr, v.t.* to cause (e.g. hatred, strife).

[O.Fr. *engendrer*—L. *generāre*, generate.]

engine, *en′jin, n.* a machine in which heat or other energy is used to produce motion: a locomotive.

engine driver, one who drives a locomotive.

engineer′, *n.* a person who designs or makes machinery: one who designs, constructs, or manages, public works such as roads, railways, bridges, sewers, etc. (**civil engineer**) or who does similar work in the army: an officer who manages a ship's engines: (*U.S.*) an engine driver.—*v.t.* to arrange, bring about, by skill or cunning.

engineer'ing, *n.* the art or profession of an engineer.

[O.Fr. *engin*—L. *ingenium*, skill.]

English, *ing'glish*, *adj.* belonging to *England* or its inhabitants or language.—*n.* the language of Britain, a great part of the British Commonwealth, and the U.S.A. (**Old English,** the English language as spoken down to about A.D. 1100; **Middle English,** from then till about 1500; **Modern English,** from about 1500 onwards).

[O.E. *Englisc*—*Engle*, Angles.]

engraft, *en-gräft'*, *v.t.* to graft, insert, introduce (into). [Pfx. **en-**.]

engrain(ed). Same as **ingrain(ed).**

engrave, *en-grāv'*, *v.t.* to cut (letters, etc.) on stone, wood, or metal, or to etch (them) with acid: to ornament (a hard surface) thus: to impress deeply (e.g. on the mind).

engrav'er, *n.* one who engraves.

engrav'ing, *n.* the art or act of an engraver: a picture taken from an engraved plate, a print.

[Pfx. **en-**, and **grave,** vb.]

engross, *en-grōs'*, *v.t.* to take up the interest or attention of wholly: to write in legal form.

engross'ment, *n.*

[Conn. with **gross.**]

engulf, *en-gulf'*, *v.t.* to swallow up wholly. [Pfx. **en-**.]

enhance, *en-hâns'*, *v.t.*to heighten, increase (e.g. *The fine clothes enhanced her beauty*): to raise the value of.

[O.Fr. *enhaucer*—*haucer*, raise.]

enigma, *i-nig'mȧ*, *n.* a puzzling statement, person, or thing.

enigmat'ic (*en-ig-*), *adj.* puzzling.

[Gk. *ainigma.*]

enjoin, *en- oin'*, *v.t.* to order (a person to do something).

See also **injunction.**

[L. *in*, *jungĕre*, *junctum*, to join.]

enjoy, *in-joi'*, *v.t.* to find pleasure in (e.g. *I enjoy skating*): (with *oneself*) to experience pleasure (*to enjoy oneself*): to experience (esp. a benefit—e.g. a long life, good health, a steady income).

enjoy'able, *adj.* **enjoy'ment,** *n.*

[O.Fr. *en*, *joie*, joy—L. *gaudēre*, rejoice.]

enlarge, *in-lärj'*, *v.t.* to make larger: to reproduce on a larger scale (e.g. a photograph).—*v.i.* to grow larger: to say, write, more about (with (*up*)*on*; e.g. *He enlarged upon his holiday plans*).

enlarge'ment, *n.*

[O.Fr. *en*, *large*, broad.]

enlighten, *en-līt'n*, *v.t.* to give information to (a person).

enlight'ened, *adj.* wise through knowledge, free from prejudice.

enlight'enment, *n.*

[O.E. *in*, in, *līhtan*, to light.]

enlist, *en-list'*, *v.t.* to engage as a soldier, etc.: to obtain, make use of in a cause (e.g. *May I enlist your help in this effort to raise money?*).—*v.i.* to register for service, esp. as a soldier: to enter heartily (in a cause, service).

enlist'ment, *n.*

[Pfx. **en-**, and **list** (2).]

enliven, *en-līv'n*, *v.t.* to make active: to make sprightly or cheerful.

[Pfx. **en-**, **life,** and suffx. **-*en*.**]

en masse, *on^g mas*, *adv.* all together in a body. [Fr.]

enmity, *en'mi-ti*, *n.* unfriendliness, ill-will.

[O.Fr. *enemistié*—L. *inimīcus*, enemy.]

ennoble, *i-nō'bl*, *v.t.* to make noble in character: to raise to the nobility.

enno'blement (*-nō'bėl-*), *n.*

[Fr. *ennoblir*—*en*, *noble*, noble.]

enormous, *i-nör'mủs*, *adj.* very large.

enor'mity, *n.* a great crime: great wickedness: outrageous or shocking nature (e.g. *the enormity of this remark*).

[L. *ē*, out of, *norma*, rule.]

enough, *i-nuf'*, *adj.* and *n.* (in the) quantity, number, degree, required.—Also *adv.*

well (good) enough, quite well (good).

[O.E. *genōh*, *genōg*.]

en pension, *on^g pon^g-syon^g*, at a fixed rate covering board and lodging. [Fr.]

enquire. See **inquire.**

enrage, *in-rāj'*, *v.t.* to make angry.

[O.Fr. *en*, *rage*, rage.]

enrapture, *in-rap'chủr*, *v.t.* to give great pleasure or delight to. [Pfx. **en-**.]

enrich, *in-rich'*, *v.t.* to make rich: to add something valuable to: to fertilise (soil).

[Fr. *en-*, *riche*, rich.]

enrol(l), *en-rōl'*, *in-*, *v.t.* to enter in roll, list, register, e.g. as pupil, member.—*v.i.* to register:—*pr.p.* **enrōll'ing**; *pa.p.* **enrōlled'.**

enrol'ment, *n.*

[O.Fr. *en*, *rolle*, roll.]

en route, *on^g ro͞ot*, on the way (for, to). [Fr.]

ensconce, *en-skons'*, *v.t.* to settle (oneself, etc.) comfortably (in).

[Pfx. **en-**, *sconce*, a small fort, shelter.]

ensemble, *on^g-son^g'bl'*, *n.* all the parts of a thing taken together: a woman's complete costume: (a performance of) all the singers, musicians, etc. together.

[Fr., together.]

enshrine, *in-shrīn'*, *v.t.* to enclose in, or as if in, a shrine: to cherish (e.g. in the memory). [Pfx. **en-**.]

enshroud, *en-shrowd'*, *v.t.* to cover completely. [Pfx. **en-**.]

ensign, *en'sīn*, *en'sin*, *n.* the flag of a nation, regiment, etc.

Blue, Red, White Ensign, flags of the naval reserve, merchant navy, and Royal Navy respectively.

[O.Fr. *enseigne*—L. *in*, *signum*, mark.]

ensilage, *en'sil-ij, n.* the storing in pits of green vegetable matter for use as fodder. [Fr. *ensiler* (vb.)—root of **silo.**]

enslave, *in-slāv', v.t.* to make (a person) a slave, or to obtain great power over (him).
enslave'ment, *n.* [Pfx. **en-.**]

ensnare, *in-snār', v.t.* to catch in a snare. [Pfx. **en-.**]

ensue, *in-sū', v.i.* to come after: to result (from):—*pr.p.* **ensū'ing**; *pa.p.* **ensūed'.** [O.Fr. *ensuir*—L. *sequī*, to follow.]

ensure, *in-shōōr', v.t.* to make sure, certain. [O.Fr. *en*, and *seur*, sure.]

entail, *in-tāl', v.t.* to bring as a result, require (e.g. *These alterations will entail great expense*).
[Pfx. **en-,** Fr. *taille*, cut, notch, tax.]

entangle, *in-tang'gl, v.t.* to make tangled: to involve (in difficulties): to ensnare.
entang'lement, *n.* a tangled obstacle: a difficult position. [Pfx. **en-.**]

entente, *ong-tongt, n.* an agreement between states. [Fr.]

enter, *en'tėr, v.i.* to go or come in: to put down one's name (for).—*v.t.* to come or go into (a place): to join or take part in: to begin: to enrol or record in a book.
en'try, *n.* act of entering: entrance: something written in a record:—*pl.* **-ies.**
to enter into, to become a party to (e.g. *to enter into an agreement with someone*): to take part heartily in: to sympathise with (another's feelings): to begin to discuss (a question): to be a part, or an ingredient, of.
to enter on, to begin.
[Fr. *entrer*—L. *intrāre.*]

enteric, *en-ter'ik, n.* typhoid fever.
enterī'tis, *n.* inflammation of the intestines.
[Gk. *enteron*, intestine.]

enterprise, *en'tėr-prīz, n.* something that is attempted (esp. if it requires boldness): willingness to try new lines of action.
enterpris'ing, *adj.*
[O.Fr.—*entre*, between, *prendre*, to take.]

entertain, *en-tėr-tān', v.t.* to receive as a guest: to amuse: to hold in the mind or feelings (e.g. *to entertain a belief*; *to entertain a great dislike*).
entertain'ing, *adj.* and *n.*
entertain'ment, *n.* act of entertaining: something that entertains, as a party, a theatrical show: amusement.
[L. *inter*, among, *tenēre*, to hold.]

enthral(l), *in-thröl', v.t.* to hold as by a spell: to delight:—*pr.p.* **enthrall'ing**; *pa.p.* **enthralled'.**
enthral'ment, *n.*
[Pfx. **en-,** and **thrall.**]

enthrone, *in-thrōn', v.t.* to place on a throne, as king or bishop.
enthrone'ment, *n.* [Pfx. **en-.**]

enthusiasm, *en-thū'zi-àzm, n.* intense interest in, or desire to help forward (e.g. *enthusiasm for the cause of peace*).
enthu'siast, *n.* a person filled with enthusiasm.
enthusias'tic, *adj.*
enthusias'tically, *adv.*
enthuse', *v.t.* and *v.i.* (*coll.*) to make, be, become, enthusiastic.
[Gk. *enthousiasmos*, god-inspired zeal.]

entice, *in-tīs', v.t.* to tempt (into doing something) by arousing hope or desire: to lead astray.
entice'ment, *n.* **entic'ing,** *adj.*
[O.Fr. *enticier*, set on fire, entice.]

entire, *in-tīr', adj.* whole: complete.
entire'ly, *adv.* **entire'ness,** *n.*
entire'ty (or *-tīr'ė-ti*), *n.* completeness: the whole.
[O.Fr. *entier*—L. *integer*, whole.]

entitle, *en-tī'tl, v.t.* to give as a name to (e.g. a book): to give (a person) a right (to).
[L. *in*, in, *titulus*, title.]

entity, *en'ti-ti, n.* a thing that exists.
[L. *ens*, *entis*, being.]

entomb, *en-tōōm', v.t.* to bury.
[Fr. *en*, in, *tombe*, tomb.]

entomology, *en-tò-mol'ò-ji, n.* the science of insects.
entomolog'ical (*-loj'*), *adj.*
entomol'ogist, *n.*
[Gk. *entoma*, insects, *logos*, discourse.]

entourage, *ong-tōō-räzh, n.* followers.
[Fr.—*entourer*, to surround.]

entr'acte, *ong-trakt, n.* the interval between acts in a play: music played then.
[Fr. *entre*, between, *acte*, an act.]

entrails, *en'trālz, n.pl.* the internal parts of an animal's body, the bowels.
[Late L. *intrālia*—*inter*, within.]

entrain, *en-trān', v.t.* and *v.i.* to put, or go, into a railway train (esp. of troops).
[Pfx. **en-.**]

entrance[1], *en'tràns, n.* act of entering: right to enter: a place of entering: a door: the beginning.
en'trant, *n.* one who enters (esp. a competition, a profession, etc.).
[L. *intrāre*, to enter.]

entrance[2], *in-trâns', v.t.* to put into a trance: to fill with rapturous delight.
entrance'ment, *n.* [Pfx. **en-.**]

entrap, *en-trap', v.t.* to catch as in a trap.
[Fr. *en*, in, *trappe*, a trap.]

entreat, *en-trēt', v.t.* to ask earnestly.
entreat'y, *n*:—*pl.* **-ies.**
[O.Fr. *entraiter*—*en*, and *traiter*, to treat.]

entrée, *ong'trā, n.* the right of admission: a dish served at dinner between chief courses. [Fr.]

entrench, *en-trench', -sh', v.t.* to dig trenches round (a place) for defence: to establish (e.g. oneself) in a strong position.
entrench'ment, *n.* [Pfx. **en-.**]

entrust, *en-trust', v.t.* to give into the care of another (e.g. *I entrusted my jewellery, this secret, to her*): to trust (with; e.g.

I entrusted her with the duty of locking up). [Pfx. **en-**.]

entry. See **enter.**

entwine, *en-twīn′*, *v.t.* to twine (with, about, round). [Pfx. **en-**.]

enumerate, *i-nū′mėr-āt*, *v.t.* to count the number of: to name over (e.g. *He enumerated my faults—laziness, vanity, etc.*)

enumerā′tion, *n.*

[L. *ē*, from, *numerāre*, to number.]

enunciate, *i-nun′s(h)i-āt*, *v.t.* to state formally: to pronounce distinctly.

enunciā′tion, *n.*

[L. *ē*, from, *nuntiāre*, to tell.]

envelop, *en-vel′ŏp*, *v.t.* to cover by wrapping: to surround entirely: to hide:—*pr.p.* **envel′oping**; *pa.p.* **envel′oped.**

envelope (*en′vėl-ōp, on′-*), *n.* a wrapper or cover, esp. for a letter.

envel′opment, *n.* act of enveloping.

[O.Fr. *enveloper*; origin uncertain.]

envenom, *en-ven′ŏm*, *v.t.* to arouse bitterness or hatred in.

[O.Fr. *en*, *venim*, venom, poison.]

environ, *en-vī′rŏn*, *v.t.* to surround.

envi′ronment, *n.* surrounding conditions, esp. as influencing development or growth.

envi′rons, *n.pl.* outskirts (of a place).

[Fr. *environ*, around.]

envisage, *en-viz′ij*, *v.t.* to picture in one's mind and consider: to think of, intend (e.g. *This was the plan envisaged*).

[Fr. *en*, *visage*, the face.]

envoy, *en′voi*, *n.* a messenger, esp. one sent to deal with a foreign government:—*pl.* **envoys.**

[Fr. *envoyer*, to send.]

envy, *en′vi*, *n.* a feeling of discontent at another's well-being or success: a good thing looked upon with grudging feeling (e.g. *Her mink coat was the envy of her friends*).—*v.t.* to feel envy towards: to grudge:—*pr.p.* **en′vying**; *pa.p.* **en′vied.**

en′viable, *adj.* that is to be envied.

en′vious, *adj.* feeling, or showing, envy.

[Fr. *envie*—L. *in*, on, *vidēre*, to look.]

enzyme, *en′zīm*, *n.* a substance produced by living cells which hastens or slows chemical changes without itself undergoing any marked alteration.

[Gk. *en*, in, *zȳmē*, leaven.]

epaulet(te), *ep′ŏ-let*, *n.* a shoulder ornament on a uniform.

[Fr. *épaulette*—*épaule*, shoulder.]

ephemeral, *i-fem′ėr-ȧl*, *adj.* lasting only for a day: short-lived.

[Gk. *ephēmeros*—*hēmera*, a day.]

epic, *ep′ik*, *n.* a long poem telling a story of great deeds: any story of great deeds.—*adj.* great, heroic.

[Gk. *epikos* (adj.)—*epos*, a word.]

epicure, *ep′i-kyūr*, *n.* a person of refined taste, esp. in food and drink.

epicure′an (*-rē′*), *adj.*

[Gk. *Epikouros*, philosopher who taught that pleasure is the highest good.]

epidemic, *ep-i-dem′ik*, *n.* an outbreak of a disease that attacks large numbers at one time.—Also *adj.*

[Gk. *epi*, among, *dēmos*, the people.]

epidermis, *ep-i-dėr′mis*, *n.* top skin, cuticle, covering the true skin.

[Gk. *epi*, upon, *derma*, skin.]

epigram, *ep′i-gram*, *n.* a short, neat saying in prose or verse.

epigrammat′ic, *adj.*

[Gk. *epi*, upon, *gramma*, a writing.]

epilepsy, *ep′i-lep-si*, *n.* a disease of the nervous system with attacks of unconsciousness with or without convulsions.

epilep′tic, *adj.* and *n.*

[Gk. *epilēpsia.*]

epilogue, *ep′i-log*, *n.* a speech at the end of a play: the concluding section of a book, programme, etc.

[Gk. *epilogos*, conclusion.]

Epiphany, *i-pif′ȧn-i*, *n.* a church festival (January 6) commemorating the showing of Christ to the Wise Men.

[Gk. *epi*, to, *phainein*, to show.]

episcopacy, *i-pis′kŏ-pȧs-i*, *n.* the government of the church by bishops.

epis′copal, *adj.* governed by bishops: belonging to bishops.

episcopā′lian, *adj.* of (government by) bishops.—*n.* a member of an episcopal church.

[Gk. *episkopos*, an overseer.]

episode, *ep′i-sōd*, *n.* an incident, or series of events, occurring in a longer story.

[Gk. *epi*, upon, *eisodos*, a coming in.]

epistle, *i-pis′l*, *n.* a letter, esp. one from an apostle.

epistolary, *i-pis′tŏ-lȧr-i*, *adj.* of, or in, a letter (e.g. *His epistolary style was dull*).

[Gk. *epistolē*, message, letter.]

epitaph, *ep′i-tâf*, *n.* a tombstone inscription.

[Gk. *epi*, upon, *taphos*, a tomb.]

epithet, *ep′i-thet*, *n.* an adjective describing a familiar or important quality of its noun (e.g. the *blue* sky; Richard *Lionheart*): an abusive name (e.g. *The other boys hurled epithets at him*).

[Gk. *epi*, on, *tithenai*, to place.]

epitome, *i-pit′ŏ-mi*, *n.* a short summary: something that represents another on a small scale.

epit′omise, *v.t.* to condense: to represent on a small scale.

[Gk.—*epi*, *tomē*, a cut.]

epoch, *ēp′ok*, or *ep′*, *n.* an age in history.

ep′och-mā′king, *adj.* great enough to affect the course of history and begin a new epoch.

[Gk. *epi*, upon, *echein*, to hold.]

equable, *ek′wȧ-bl*, or *ēk′-*, *adj.* not extreme (e.g. *In an equable climate the temperature does not vary widely*): not easily annoyed or agitated.

[L. *aequābilis*—same root as **equal.**]

equal, *ē′kwȧl*, *adj.* of the same size: the same in quantity: of the same value.—*n.*

one of the same age, rank, etc.—*v.t.* to be, or to make, equal to :—*pr.p.* **ē'qualling** ; *pa.p.* **ē'qualled.**
e'qualise, *v.t.* to make equal.
equality, *ē-kwol'i-ti, n.* **e'qually,** *adv.*
equal to, fit or able for (e.g. *Is he equal to this heavy task? I do not feel equal to telling him the truth.*)
equate, *i-quāt'*, or *ē-*, *v.t.* to state as equal (to) : to regard as in some way the same.
equā'tion, *n.* a statement that two things are equal or the same.
[L. *aequālis—aequus*, equal.]

equanimity, *ē-kwȧ-nim'i-ti, e-, n.* evenness of temper, calmness.
[L. *aequus*, equal, *animus*, mind.]

equator, *i-kwā'tȯr, n.* an imaginary circle passing round the globe, at an equal distance from N. and S. poles.
equato'rial, *adj.* (*-tō'*).
equatorial regions, the hot parts of the earth near the equator.
[Late L. *aequātor*—L. *aequus*, equal.]

equerry, *ek'wė-ri, i-kwe', n.* one in charge of horses : an official attending a prince or personage.
[Fr. *écurie*—Late L. *scūria*, a stable.]

equestrian, *i-kwes'tri-ȧn, adj.* of horsemanship : on horseback.—*n.* one who rides on horseback :—*fem.* (sham Fr.) **equestrienne'.**
[L. *eques*, horseman ; root as **equine.**]

equi-, *ē-kwi-, pfx.* equal, e.g. : *adjs.* **equian'gular,** having equal angles ; **equidis'tant,** equally distant (from) ; **equilat'eral,** having all sides equal.
[L. *aequus*, equal.]

equilibrium, *ē-kwi-lib'ri-ȯm, n.* a state of equal balance between weights or forces, or between opposing powers or influences, etc.
[L. *aequus*, equal, *lībra*, balance.]

equine, *ē'kwīn*, or *e'-*, *adj.* of, of the nature of, a horse.
[L. *equus*, a horse.]

equinox, *ē'kwi-noks*, or *e'-*, *n.* the time when the sun crosses the equator, making night and day equal in length, about March 21 and September 23.
equinoc'tial (*-shȧl*), *adj.* of the equinoxes, or the time of these.
equinoctial gales, high gales popularly supposed to be common about the times of the equinoxes.
[L. *aequus*, equal, *nox*, night.]

equip, *i-kwip', v.t.* to fit out with everything needed :—*pr.p.* **equipp'ing** ; *pa.p.* **equipped'.**
e'quipage (*e'kwi-*), *n.* carriage and attendants.
equip'ment, *n.* the act of equipping : outfit : the machines, tools, etc., necessary (for a particular kind of work).
[Fr. *équiper*, prob.—Old Norse *skipa*, to set in order—*skip*, a ship.]

equity, *ek'wi-ti, n.* fairness : justice : (in *pl.*, **eq'uities**) ordinary shares.
eq'uitable, *adj.* fair.
[L. *aequitās*—same root as **equal.**]

equivalent, *i-kwiv'ȧ-lėnt, adj.* equal in value, power, meaning, etc.—Also *n.*
[L. *aequus*, equal, *valēre*, to be worth.]

equivocal, *i-kwiv'ȯ-kȧl, adj.* capable of meaning two or more things : of uncertain nature.
equiv'ocate, *v.i.* to use words of uncertain meaning in order to mislead.
equivocā'tion, *n.*
[L. *aequus*, equal, *vox*, voice.]

era, *ē'rȧ, n.* a series of years alike in some way (e.g. *an era of reform*).
[Late L. *aera*, a number ; conn. *aes*, money.]

eradicate, *i-rad'i-kāt, n.* to root out, get rid of completely.
erad'icable, *adj.* **eradicā'tion,** *n.*
[L. *ērādīcāre—radix*, a root.]

erase, *i-rāz', v.t.* to rub out.
eraser, *i-rā'zėr, n.*
erasure, *i-rā'zhėr, n.* rubbing out.
[L. *ē*, from, *rādĕre*, *rāsum*, to scrape.]

ere, *ār, ėr, prep., conj.*, before. [O.E. *ǣr.*]

erect, *i-rekt', adj.* upright.—*v.t.* to set upright : to build : to construct.
erec'tion, *n.* act of erecting : a building or structure.
erect'ly, *adv.* **erect'ness,** *n.*
[L. *ērectus—ērigĕre*, to set upright.]

ermine, *ėr'min, n.* the stoat : its white winter fur, used with the black tail-tip attached for robes of judges, etc. [O.Fr.]

erode, *i-rōd', v.t.* (of acids, etc.) to eat away : (of water, ice, wind, etc) to wear away.
ero'sion, *i-rō'zh(ȯ)n, n.*
ero'sive (*-siv*), *adj.*
[L. *ē*, from, *rōdĕre*, *rōsum*, to gnaw.]

erotic, *i-rot'ik, adj.* of love.
[Gk. *Erōs*, god of love.]

err, *ėr, v.i.* to go astray : to make a mistake, be wrong : to sin.
errat'ic, *adj.* wandering : not dependable in conduct, etc.
erra'tum (*-rā'*, or *-rä'*), *n.* an error in writing or printing :—*pl.* **erra'ta.**
erro'neous (*-rō'*), *adj.* wrong : mistaken.
erro'neously, *adv.*
erro'neousness, *n.*
err'or, *n.* a blunder, mistake : wrongdoing.
[Fr. *errer*—L. *errāre*, to stray.]

errand, *er'ȧnd, n.* a short journey on which one is sent to say or do something for someone else : the object of a journey.
[O.E. *ǣrende.*]

errant, *er'ȧnt, adj.* wandering in search of adventure (as in *knight-errant*) : straying : erring.
err'antry, *n.* (only in *knight-errantry*).
[Same root as **err.**]

erratic, erratum, etc. See **err.**

ersatz, *er-zäts', adj.* substitute (e.g. *ersatz coffee*). [Ger.]

eruct, *i-rukt'*, **eructate,** *-āt, v.t.* to belch out.—Also *v.i.*

eructā'tion, *n.*
[L. *ē*, from, *ructāre*, to belch forth.]

erudite, *er'ōō-dīt*, or *er'ū-*, having learned much from books.
erudition (*-di'*), *n.*
[L. *ērudīre*, to free from roughness.]

erupt, *i-rupt'*, *v.i.* (of a volcano) to throw out lava, etc.: to break out, esp. violently.
erup'tion, *n.* a bursting forth (e.g. of lava, of feeling, of spots on the skin).
erup'tive, *adj.*
[L. *ē*, from, *rumpěre*, *ruptum*, to break.]

erysipelas, *er-i-sip'i-làs*, *n.* an infectious disease, usu. in the face, marked by a bright redness of the skin.
[Gk. *erythros*, red, *pella*, skin.]

escalator, *es'kà-lā-tòr*, *n.* a moving staircase.
[Through Fr. and Sp.—L. *scāla*, ladder.]

escape, *is-kāp'*, *v.t.* to get clear away from (e.g. custody): to manage to avoid (e.g. punishment): to slip from (the memory; e.g. *His name escapes my memory*, or *escapes me*).—*v.i.* to gain freedom: to flee: (of e.g. gas) to leak.—Also *n.*
es'capade, (*-kà-*), *n.* a mischievous adventure.
escap'ism (*-kāp'*), *n.* tendency to escape from reality into daydreams, etc.
escap'ist (*-kāp'*), *n.*
escape'ment, *n.* a device controlling movement, e.g. in a watch.
[O.Fr. *escaper*—Late L. *ex cappā*, 'out of one's cloak.']

escarpment, *is-kärp'mėnt*, *n.* the steep side of a hill or rock.
[Fr. *escarper*, to cut down steep.]

escheat, *is-chēt'*, *n.* property that falls to the state for want of an heir.—Also *v.i.*
[O.Fr. *eschete*—L. *ex*, *caděre*, to fall.]

eschew, *is-chōō'*, *v.t.* to shun, avoid, abstain from (e.g. evil, violence).
[O.Fr. *eschever*.]

escort, *es'kört*, *n.* person(s), ship(s), etc., accompanying for protection, guidance, custody, or courtesy.
escort', *v.t.* to attend as escort.
[Fr. *escorte*—L. *ex*, *corrigěre*, set right.]

escutcheon, *is-kuch'òn*, *n.* a shield on which a coat of arms is shown.
a blot on the escutcheon, a stain on one's good name.
[O.Fr. *escuchon*—L. *scūtum*, a shield.]

Eskimo, *es'ki-mō*, *n.* one of a people inhabiting the far north:—*pl.* **Es'kimo(s).** —Also *adj.*
[From Indian word meaning 'eaters of raw flesh'.]

espalier, *es-pal'yėr*, *n.* a lattice on which to train fruit trees: a fruit tree trained on stakes or lattice.
[It. *spalliera*, a support for the shoulders.]

esparto, *es-pär'tō*, *n.* a strong grass grown in Spain, N. Africa, etc., and used for making paper, etc.
[Sp.—Gk. *sparton*, a kind of rope.]

especial, *es-pesh'(à)l*, *adj.* beyond the ordinary (e.g. *with especial care*): particular (e.g. *his especial merit*).
espec'ially, *adv.* particularly, notably.
especially as, for the important reason that.
[O.Fr.; same L. root as **special.**]

Esperanto, *es-pėr-ân'tō*, *n.* an artificial international language.
[*Esperanza*, name assumed by inventor.]

espionage, *es-pyòn-äzh'*, or *es'-*, *n.* spying: use of spies.
[Fr. *espionnage—espion*, a spy.]

esplanade, *es-plà-nād'*, *n.* a level space for walking or driving, esp. at the seaside.
[Fr.—L. *ex*, out, *plānus*, flat.]

espouse, *is-powz'*, *v.t.* to give or take in marriage: to support (a cause).
espous'al, *n.* support (of a cause).
[O.Fr. *espouser*—L. root as **response.**]

espresso, *es-pres'ō*, *n.* a type of coffee-making machine in which pressure of steam is used to get as much flavour as possible out of the coffee beans. [It.]

esprit de corps, *es-prē dė kör*, loyalty to the society to which one belongs: public spirit.
[Fr. *esprit*, spirit, *corps*, body.]

espy, *is-pī'*, *v.t.* to catch sight of.
[O.Fr. *espier*.]

Esquimau(x). Spelling of **Eskimo(s).**

esquire, *es-kwīr'*, also *es'*, *n.* (*orig.*) a squire, an attendant on a knight: (*cap.*) a title of respect in addressing letters.—*Abbrev.* **Esq.**
[L. *scūtārius*, shield-bearer.]

essay, *es'ā*, *n.* an attempt: a written composition.—*v.t.* (*e-sā'*) to test (e.g. one's powers): to attempt:—*pr.p.* **essay'ing**; *pa.p.* **essayed'.**
ess'ayist, *n.* a writer of essays.
[O.Fr. *essai*.]

essence, *es'ėns*, *n.* the inner nature of anything, its most important quality: a substance obtained from a plant, drug, etc. in concentrated form (e.g. *essence of peppermint*).
essential, *i-sen'sh(à)l*, *adj.* absolutely necessary: of, being, or containing, an essence.
essen'tially, *adv.* in inner nature (e.g. *She is an essentially selfish person*).
[Fr.—L. *essentia—esse*, to be.]

establish, *is-tab'lish*, *v.t.* to settle firmly in a position: to settle in business: to found (e.g. a university, a business): to cause people to adopt (e.g. *to establish a custom*): to get people to accept as true, just, etc. (e.g. *to establish a fact, a claim*): to make (a church) the recognised state church.
estab'lishment, *n.* act of establishing: a permanent civil or military force or commercial staff: one's residence, household, and style of living: the church established by law.

the Establishment, the people holding important positions in a community.
[L. *stabilis*, firm—*stāre*, to stand.]

estate, *is-tāt'*, *n.* condition or rank: total possessions: property in land.
the estates of the realm, Lords Spiritual (i.e. bishops and archbishops in House of Lords), Lords Temporal (i.e. the peers), and Commons.
[O.Fr. *estat*—L. *status*, condition.]

esteem, *is-tēm'*, *v.t.* to value: to regard with respect: to consider to be (e.g. *I should esteem it a favour if you would go*).—*n.* favourable opinion: respect.
estimable, *es'tim-à-bl*, *adj.* deserving our good opinion.
es'timāte, *v.t.* to judge the worth of: to calculate.—Also *n.*
estimā'tion, *n.* a reckoning: judgment, opinion.
[Fr. *estimer*—L. *aestimāre.*]

estrange, *is-trānj'*, *v.t.* to make unfriendly (e.g. *The former friends were estranged by these events*).
estrange'ment, *n.*
[O.Fr. *estranger*; same root as **strange.**]

estuary, *es'tū-àr-i*, *n.* wide lower part of river up which the tide flows:—*pl.* **-ies.**
[L. *aestus*, burning, commotion, tide.]

et cetera, *et set'(ė-)rà*, usu. written **etc.** or **&c.,** Latin phrase meaning 'and the rest', 'and so on'.
etcet'eras, *n.pl.* things in addition, of the kind shown by the context.

etch, *ech*, *v.t.* or *v.i.* to make (designs) on metal, glass, etc., by eating out the lines with an acid: to treat (metal, etc.) thus.
etch'ing, *n.* the picture from an etched plate.
[Ger. *ätzen*; same root as Ger. *essen*, eat.]

eternal, *i-tėr'nàl*, *adj.* without beginning or end: unchanging: (*coll.*) never ceasing (e.g. *your eternal chattering*).
eter'nally, *adv.*
eter'nity, *n.* an endless, or seemingly endless, time: the state or time after death:—*pl.* **eter'nities.**
[Fr. *éternel*—L. *aeternus.*]

ether, *ē'thėr*, *n.* the clear, upper air: the non-material medium formerly supposed to fill all space: a colourless liquid used as a solvent of fats, etc., and as an anaesthetic.
ethe'real (*ē-*, or *i-thē'*), **ethē'rial,** *adj.* delicate: airy: spirit-like.
[Gk. *aithēr*—*aithein*, to burn, shine.]

ethical, *eth'ik-àl*, *adj.* of morals: morally right, or in keeping with high standards.
eth'ically, *adv.* **eth'icalness,** *n.*
eth'ics, *n.* the science of morals: moral principles.
[Gk. *ēthikos*—*ēthos*, custom.]

ethnology, *eth-nol'ò-ji*, *n.* the science that studies the varieties of the human race.
ethnolog'ical, *adj.*
[Gk. *ethnos*, a nation, *logos*, discourse.]

etiquette, *et'i-ket*, or *-ket'*, *n.* forms of ceremony in society or at court: the unwritten laws observed by members of a profession (e.g. *medical, legal, etiquette*).
[Fr. *étiquette*; same root as **ticket.**]

etymology, *et-i-mol'ȯj-i*, *n.* the study of the derivation and original meaning of words: the history (of a word).
etymolog'ical (*-loj'-*), *adj.*
[Gk. *etymos*, true, *logos*, a discourse.]

eu-, *ū-*, *pfx.* well. [Gk.]

eucalyptus, *ū-kà-lip'tùs*, *n.* a large Australian evergreen tree, yielding timber, oils, gum:—*pl.* **eucalyptuses, -lyptī.**
[Gk. *eu*, well, *kalyptos*, covered.]

Eucharist, *ū'kà-rist*, *n.* the sacrament of the Lord's Supper: the elements of the sacrament.
[Gk. *eucharistia*, thanksgiving.]

eugenic, *ū-jen'ik*, *adj.* of, or bringing about, race improvement.
eugen'ics, *n.pl.* the science of this.
[Gk. *eugenēs*, of good stock.]

eulogy, *ū'lo-ji*, *n.* high praise, written or spoken (with *on*):—*pl.* **eu'logies.**
eu'logise, *v.t.* to praise.
eulogis'tic, *adj.* full of praise.
[Gk. *eu*, well, *logos*, a speaking.]

euphemism, *ū'fim-izm*, *n.* a mild expression for something that is disagreeable (e.g. *to fall asleep* for 'to die').
euphemis'tic, *adj.*
[Gk. *eu*, well, *phēmē*, speaking.]

euphony, *ū'fò-ni*, *n.* pleasing sound.
euphō'nious, *adj.*
[Gk. *eu*, well, *phōnē*, sound.]

Eurasian, *ū-rā'zh(y)àn*, *-shàn*, *adj.* of mixed European and Asiatic descent: of Europe and Asia.—Also *n.*

eurhythmics, *ū-rith'miks*, *n.pl.* the art of rhythmic movement.
[Gk. *eu*, well, *rhythmos*, rhythm.]

European, *ū-rò-pē'àn*, *adj.* belonging to Europe.—*n.* a native of Europe.

euthanasia, *ū-thà-nāz'yà*, *n.* putting to death painlessly, esp. to end suffering.
[Gk. *eu*, well, *thanatos*, death.]

evacuate, *i-vak'ū-āt*, *v.t.* to throw out the contents of: to withdraw from (a fortified place, etc.): to clear out (troops, inhabitants, etc.) from a town, etc.
evacuā'tion, *n.*
evac'uee (or *ū-ē'*), *n.* a person removed in an evacuation.
[L. *ē*, from, *vacuāre*, *-ātum*, to empty.]

evade, *i-*, *ē-vād'*, *v.t.* to escape or avoid by trickery or skill: to avoid answering (a question).
evasion, *i-vā'zh(ȯ)n*, *n.* act of evading: a trick or excuse used to evade.
evasive, *i-vā'siv*, *adj.* having the purpose of evading (e.g. *to take evasive action*): shifty (e.g. *evasive eyes*): not frank and direct (e.g. *evasive answers*).
eva'sively, *adv.* **eva'siveness,** *n.*
[Fr. *évader*—L. *ē*, from, *vādĕre*, to go.]

evaluate, *i-*, or *ē-val'ū-āt*, *v.t.* to find the value of.

evaluā′tion, *n.*
[Fr. *evaluer*; root as **value.**]

evanescent, *ē-, ė-vȧn-es′ėnt, adj.* vanishing: passing quickly away.
evanes′cence *(-es′ens), n.*
[L. *ēvānescens—ē*, from, *vānus*, empty.]

evangelic(al), *ē-, ė-van-jel′ik(-ȧl), adjs.* of, in keeping with, the teachings of the gospel: seeking the conversion of sinners.
evan′gelist, *n.* one who preaches the gospel: a writer of a gospel (Matthew, Mark, Luke, or John).
evangelis′tic, *adj.*
[Gk. *eu*, well, *angellein*, to bring news.]

evaporate, *i-vap′ȯr-āt, v.i.* to pass off in vapour: to vanish.—*v.t.* to turn into, drive off as, vapour.
evaporā′tion, *n.*
[L. *ē*, from, *vapor*, vapour.]

evasion, evasive. See **evade.**

eve, *ēv, n.* the day (night) before a festival (e.g. *Christmas Eve*) or the time just before an event (e.g. *the eve of the battle*).
[Same word as **even** (2).]

even¹, *ē′vn, adj.* level: smooth: regular: divisible by 2 without a remainder: having no debt on either side: (of temper) not easily ruffled, calm.—*v.t.* to make even or smooth.—*adv.* still (e.g. *even better*). Used also to emphasise something unexpected about an action, etc. (e.g. *He swam daily in winter, and even enjoyed it*; *even Mary would not be so silly*; *he suspects even his friends*).
e′venly, *adv.* **e′venness,** *n.*
to be even with, to be revenged on.
[O.E. *efen.*]

even², *ē′vn, n.* evening.
evening, *ēv′ning, n.* the close of the day: the end of life.
evening star, a planet, esp. Venus, seen in the west after sunset.
e′vensong, *n.* prayer said or sung at evening.
e′ventide, *n.* evening: declining years.
[O.E. *ǣfen, ǣfnung.*]

event, *i-vent′, n.* something that happens, an incident or occurrence: an item in a programme of sports.
event′ful, *adj.* full of events: exciting.
event′ual *(-ū-ȧl), adj.* happening as a result: final.
event′ually, *adv.* finally, at length.
eventual′ity, *n.* a possible happening:—*pl.* **eventual′ities.**
at all events, in any case.
[L. *ē*, from, *venīre*, to come.]

ever, *ev′ėr, adv.* at all times (e.g. *He was ever ready to talk about his success*): at any time. Used also to give emphasis (e.g. *as politely as ever I can*; *ever so quietly*; *what ever did she say?*).
ev′ergreen, *adj.* always green.—*n.* a plant that remains green all the year.
everlast′ing, *adj.* endless: eternal.—*n.* eternity: a flower that when dried may be kept for years unchanged.
everlast′ingly, *adv.*
everlast′ingness, *n.*
evermore′, *adv.* for ever.
for ever, forever, always: continually: for all time.
[O.E. *ǣfre*, always.]

every, *ev′ri, adj.* each of a number without exception.
ev′eryone, ev′erybody *(ev′ri-), prons.* every person.
ev′eryday, *adj.* daily: common, usual: of weekdays, not Sunday.
ev′erything, *pron.* all things: all.
ev′erywhere, *ev′ri-hwār, adv.* in every place.
every other, every second (e.g. *every other day*).
[O.E. *ǣfre*, ever, and *ǣlc*, each.]

evict, *i-, ē-vikt′, v.t.* to turn out, expel (esp. by legal process, from house or land).
evic′tion, *n.*
[L. *ēvincĕre, ēvictus*, to overcome.]

evident, *ev′i-dėnt, adj.* clearly to be seen: clear to the mind: obvious.
ev′idently, *adv.*
ev′idence, *n.* indication, sign: proof: clearness: information in a law case.—*v.t.* to indicate, show, prove.
to turn King's (Queen's) evidence, (of an accomplice in a crime) to give evidence against his partner(s).
[L. *ē*, from, *vidēre*, to see.]

evil, *ē′vl, ē′vil, adj.* bad: wicked.—*n.* harm: wickedness: sin.
e′villy, *adv.* **e′vilness,** *n.*
e′vil-do′er, *n.* one who does evil.
e′vil-eye, *n.* a supposed power to cause harm by a look.
Also forming part of *adjs.*, as:—
e′vil-mind′ed, e′vil-smell′ing.
[O.E. *yfel.*]

evince, *i-vins′, v.t.* to show to the mind (a quality, etc.; e.g. *The child evinced remarkable powers of reasoning*).
[L. pfx. *ē-*, *vincĕre*, to overcome.]

eviscerate, *ē*, or *i-vis′ėr-āt, v.t.* to tear out the bowels of.
[L. *ē*, from, *viscera*, bowels.]

evoke, *i-vōk′, v.t.* to draw forth (e.g. *to evoke a reply, a storm of abuse*): to call up in the mind (e.g. a memory, a picture).
evocā′tion, *n.* **evoc′ative** *(-vok′), adj.*
[L. *ē*, from, *vocāre*, to call.]

evolution, evolutionary. See **evolve.**

evolve, *i-, ē-volv′, v.t.* to develop, show, work out, gradually.—Also *v.i.*
evolution, *ėv-, ēv-ȯl-ū′sh(ȯ)n* or *-ōō′, n.* gradual working out or development: the teaching that higher forms of life have gradually arisen out of lower: the giving off (e.g. of gas, heat): (usu. in *pl.*) orderly movements of a body of troops, flock of birds, etc.
evolu′tionary, *adj.*
[L. *ē*, from, *volvĕre, volūtum*, to roll.]

ewe, *ū, n.* a female sheep.
[O.E. *ēowu.*]

ewer, *ū'ėr, n.* a large water jug with a wide spout.
[Through Fr.—L. root as **aquarium.**]

ex-, *eks-, pfx.* meaning former or late (e.g. *ex-president*).
[L. *ex,* out of, from.]

exacerbate, *eks-as'ėr-bāt, v.t.* to make (ill-feeling, or a disease) worse: to irritate, enrage (a person).
exacerbā'tion, *n.*
[L. pfx. *ex-, acerbus,* bitter.]

exact, *ig-, eg-zakt', v.t.* to compel payment of (e.g. *to exact a fine from the culprit*): to extort: to insist upon having (e.g. *to exact obedience*).—*adj.* completely accurate.
exact'ly, *adv.* **exact'ness,** *n.*
exact'ing, *adj.* severe, demanding much from a person (e.g. *His boss is very exacting; the work is exacting*).
exac'tion, *n.* act of exacting: too much money, work, etc. forced from a person.
exac'titude (*-ti-tūd*), *n.* correctness.
[L. *ex,* from, *agĕre, actum,* to drive.]

exaggerate, *ig-, eg-zaj'ėr-āt, v.t.* to make (something) seem larger, greater, etc. than it is: to describe (something) so as to do this.—Also *v.i.*
exaggerā'tion, *n.*
[L. *ex-, aggerāre,* heap up—*agger,* a heap.]

exalt, *ig-, eg-zölt', v.t.* to raise in rank, etc.: to praise: to fill with the joy of success.
exaltā'tion, *n.*
exal'ted, *adj.* of high rank: noble.
[L. *exaltāre*—pfx. *ex-, altus,* high.]

exam. See **examine.**

examine, *ig-, eg-zam'in, v.t.* to test: to question: to look closely into.
examinā'tion, *n.* close inspection: test of knowledge (also **exam'**): formal questioning.
examinee' (*-ē'*), *n.* one who is examined.
exam'iner, *n.*
[L. *exāmen,* the tongue of a balance.]

example, *ig-, eg-zâm'pl, n.* a specimen, or illustration: a copy of a book: a person or thing that is either a pattern or a warning: a problem or exercise in mathematics.
exemplary, *eg-zem'plȧr-i, adj.* worthy of imitation (e.g. *exemplary behaviour*): serving as a model or warning.
exem'plify, *v.t.* to be an example of:—*pr.p.* **exem'plifying**; *pa.p.* **exem'plified** (*-fīd*).
exemplificā'tion (*-fi-kā'*), *n.*
to make an example of, to punish as a warning to others.
[L. *exemplum*—*ex,* out of, *emĕre, emptum,* take, buy.]

exasperate, *ig-, eg-zas'pėr-āt, v.t.* to irritate very much indeed: to make worse.
exasperā'tion, *n.*
[L. pfx. *ex-, asperāre,* to make rough.]

excavate, *eks'kȧ-vāt, v.t.* to scoop out (a hole): to dig out (soil): to lay bare (buried ruins) by digging.
excavā'tion, *n.*
ex'cavātor, *n.* one who excavates: a machine used for excavating.
[L. *ex-,* out, *cavus,* hollow.]

exceed, *ek-sēd', v.t.* to go beyond (e.g. *to exceed the speed limit*): to be greater than: to be too great for: to be better than.
exceed'ingly, *adv.*
See also **excess.**
[L. *ex-,* beyond, *cēdĕre, cessum,* to go.]

excel, *ik-, ek-sel', v.t.* to be better than.—*v.i.* to be very good (at, in):—*pr.p.* **excell'ing**; *pa.p.* **excelled'.**
excellence, *ek'sė-lėns,* **excellency** (*-lėn-si*), *ns.* great merit: any very high quality: (usu. *cap.*) a title of high honour.
excellent (*ek'-*), *adj.* unusually good: of great virtue, worth, etc.
excellently (*ek'-*), *adv.*
[L. *ex-,* out, up, *celsus,* high.]

except, *ik-, ek-sept', v.t.* to leave out.—*prep.* leaving out (e.g. *All approved except me*).—*conj.* with the exception (e.g. *The story is correct, except that it was John, not Jim, who fell in*).
excep'tion, *n.* act of excepting: something not included: something not according to the rule.
excep'tional, *adj.* **excep'tionally,** *adv.*
to take exception to, against, at, to object to: to take offence at.
[L. *ex,* from, *capĕre,* to take.]

excerpt, *ek'sėrpt,* or *ek-sėrpt', n.* a passage taken from a book, etc., an extract.
[L. *ex,* from, *carpĕre,* to pick.]

excess, *ik-, ek-ses', n.* a going beyond what is usual: an extreme amount (e.g. *an excess of generosity*): the amount by which one thing is greater than another.
excess'ive, *adj.* beyond what is right and proper, immoderate.
excess'ively, *adv.* **excess'iveness,** *n.*
[Same root as **exceed.**]

exchange, *iks-, eks-chānj', v.t.* to give or give up in return for something else: to give and receive (e.g. *to exchange blows, news*):—*pr.p.* **exchang'ing**; *pa.p.* **exchanged'.**—*n.* the giving and taking of one thing for another: the building where merchants, etc., meet for business: a central office where telephone lines are connected.
exchange'able, *adj.*
[O.Fr. *eschangier*—L. *ex, cambīre,* barter.]

exchequer, *iks-, eks-chek'ėr, n.* a national treasury: (*cap.*) the government department in charge of the nation's finances: one's funds, finances.
[O.Fr. *eschequier,* chessboard; from chequered cloth orig. on the table of the Exchequer.]

excise[1], *ek-sīz', n.* a tax on certain goods and on licences: the department concerned with such taxes.

excis'able (*-sīz'*), *adj.* on which excise duty has to be paid.
excise'man, *n.* an officer collecting excise.
[Old Du. *excijs*—O.Fr. *acceis,* tax.]

excise[2], *ek-sīz'*, *v.t.* to cut out or off.
excision, *ek-sizh'(ȯ)n, n.*
[L. *excīdĕre, excīsum,* to cut out.]

excite, *ik-sīt', v.t.* to rouse (e.g. feelings): to rouse emotion in, agitate (a person): to stir up (e.g. rebellion): to produce electric or magnetic activity in.
excit'able (*-sīt'*), *adj.* easily excited.
excitabil'ity (*-sīt-*), *n.*
excite'ment, *n.* excited state, or something that causes it.
[L. *ex,* out, *ciēre,* to set in motion.]

exclaim, *iks-klām', eks-, v.i.* to say suddenly and loudly.—Also *v.t.*
exclamā'tion (*eks-klam-*), *n.* an uttered expression of surprise, strong protest, etc.
exclamation mark, the mark following and showing an exclamation (!).
exclam'atory (*-klam'*), *adj.*
[L. *ex-,* out, *clāmāre,* to shout.]

exclude, *iks-kloo͞d', v.t.* to shut out: to thrust out: to except.
exclu'sion, *n.*
exclusive, *iks-kloo͞'siv, adj.* shutting or leaving out: limited to one individual or group (e.g. *an exclusive right*): limited to a high social group (e.g. *an exclusive club*): fashionable and expensive: single, sole (e.g. *Fishing was his exclusive interest*).
exclusive of, not including, not taking into account.
[L. *ex,* out, *claudĕre, clausum,* to shut.]

excommunicate, *eks-kom-ūn'i-kāt, v.t.* to expel from communion of the church.
excommunicā'tion, *n.*
[Late L. *excommunicāre,* to put out of the community—*communis,* common.]

excrement. See **excrete.**

excrescence, *iks-kres'ėns, n.* an abnormal outgrowth, e.g. a wart.
excres'cent, *adj.* growing out.
[L. *ex,* out, *crescĕre,* to grow.]

excrete, *iks-krēt', v.t.* to separate and discharge (waste matter).
excrē'ta, *n.pl.* poisonous or waste substances expelled from a cell, a tissue, or an animal body.
excre'tion (*-krē'*), *n.* **excre'tory,** *adj.*
excrement, *eks'krė-mėnt, n.* useless matter, esp. solid, discharged from the body, dung.
[L. *ex,* from, *cernĕre, crētum,* to separate.]

excruciate, *iks-kroo͞'shi-āt, v.t.* to torture.
excru'ciāting, *adj.* extremely painful.
excru'ciātingly, *adv.*
[L. *ex-, cruciāre, -ātum—crux,* cross.]

exculpate, *eks'kul-pāt, -kul'-, v.t.* to clear from the charge of a fault or crime.
exculpā'tion, *n.*
[L. *ex,* from, *culpa,* a fault.]

excursion, *iks-kûr'sh(ȯ)n, n.* a pleasure trip, or one for a special purpose: a trip at a reduced rate.
[L. *ex-,* out, *currĕre, cursum,* to run.]

excuse, *iks-kūz', v.t.* to free (a person) from blame or guilt: to overlook (a fault): to free from a duty or obligation (e.g. *I excused him from coming to the meeting*).
—*n.* (*iks-kūs'*) a reason for excusing, esp. one given by the offender.
excus'able, *adj.*
[L. *ex,* from, *causa,* cause, accusation.]

execrate, *eks'i-krāt, v.t.* to curse: to detest.
ex'ecrable, *adj.* abominable, very bad.
ex'ecrably, *adv.*
execrā'tion, *n.* a cursing.
[L. *exsecrārī,* to curse—*sacer,* sacred.]

execute, *eks'i-kūt, v.t.* to perform, carry out (e.g. *to execute his lord's commands*): to put to death by law.
execu'tion(*-kū'*), *n.*
execu'tioner, *n.*
exec'utant (*-ek'ū-*), *n.* one who carries out, performs: a technically skilful performer of music.
exec'utive, *adj.* concerned with management, or with putting laws or regulations into effect.—*n.* the branch of the government that puts the laws into effect: a person, or body of persons, that directs and manages.
exec'utor, *n.* the person appointed to see a will carried into effect:—*fem.* **exec'utrix.**
exec'utory, *adj.*
[L. *ex,* out, *sequī, secūtus,* to follow.]

exemplary, exemplify. See **example.**

exempt, *ig-zem(p)t', v.t.* to free from a duty which other people have to carry out (e.g. from military service, payment of taxes).—Also *adj.*
exemp'tion, *n.*
[L. *ex,* from, *emĕre, emptum,* to buy.]

exercise, *eks'ėr-sīz, n.* training by exertion or use of the body or mind: a written school task: (in *pl.*) military drill: an act of worship.—*v.t.* to train by use: to give exercise to: to use (e.g. *to exercise care, common sense*; *to exercise one's right to vote*): to worry (e.g. *He was exercised about the loss of time*).
[Through O.Fr.—L. *ex, arcēre,* restrain.]

exert, *igz-ėrt', v.t.* to bring into action (e.g. strength, influence).
exer'tion, *n.* a bringing into active use: striving, effort.
[L. *exserĕre, exsertum,* to thrust out.]

exhale, *eks-hāl', egz-āl', v.t.* and *v.i.* to breathe out: to give off, or to rise as, vapour, smell, etc.
exhalation, *eks-(h)ȧ-lā'sh(ȯ)n, egz-ȧ-, n.*
[L. *ex,* from, *hālāre,* to breathe.]

exhaust, *ig-zöst', v.t.* to empty (a vessel, e.g. a cask): to use up completely (e.g. air, one's supplies, one's strength): to tire out: to say all that can be said about (a subject of discussion).—*n.* the part of

an engine through which used working fluid from the cylinder escapes: the fluid so escaping.
exhaus′ted, *adj.* used up: empty: extremely tired.
exhaus′tion, *n.*
exhaus′tive, *adj.* very thorough.
[L. *ex*, from, *haurīre*, *haustum*, to draw.]

exhibit, *igz-ib′it*, *v.t.* to show: to show to the public.—*n.* (*law*) a document or an article produced in court to be used as evidence: an article at an exhibition.
exhib′itor, *n.*
exhibi′tion (*eks-i-*), *n.* display: a public show, esp. of works of art, manufactures, etc.: an allowance towards support given to a student (usu. competed for).
exhibi′tionism, *n.* purposely behaving in such a way as to attract attention to oneself.
exhibi′tionist, *n.*
[L. *exhibēre*, *exhibitum*.]

exhilarate, *igz-il′ȧ-rāt*, *v.t.* to make merry or very lively.
exhilarā′tion, *n.*
[Same root as **hilarious.**]

exhort, *ig-zört′*, *v.t.* to urge strongly and earnestly.
exhortā′tion (*eg-zör-*), *n.*
[L. pfx. *ex-*, *hortārī*, to urge.]

exhume, *eks-hūm′*, *v.t.* to take out of the ground: to unearth, discover.
exhumā′tion, *n.*
[L. *ex*, out of, *humus*, the ground.]

exigency, *ek′si-jen-si*, *eg-zij′*, *n.* pressing necessity, urgent requirement (often in *pl.*; e.g. *He was forced by the exigencies of the situation to take a risky step*).
[Same root as **exact.**]

exile, *eks′īl*, or *egz′īl*, *n.* (one who experiences) long absence from country or home: banishment.—*v.t.* to expel, send away, from one's country.
[L. *ex(s)ilium*, banishment.]

exist, *ig-zist′*, *v.i.* to be: to live: to continue to live.
exist′ence, *n.*
exist′ent, *adj.* existing, esp. now.
[L. *ex(s)istĕre*, to stand forth.]

exit, *eks′it*, *egz′-*, *n.* departure, esp. of a player from the stage: death: a way out:—*pl.* **ex′its.**—*v.i.* to go out.
[L. *exit*, he goes out, *exīre*, to go out.]

exodus, *eks′ō-dus*, *n.* a going out, esp. (*cap.*) that of the Israelites from Egypt.
[L.—Gk. *ex*, out, *hodos*, way.]

exonerate, *ig-zon′ėr-āt*, *v.t.* to free from blame, acquit.
exonerā′tion, *n.*
[L. *ex*, from, *onus*, *oneris*, burden.]

exorbitant, *ig-zör′bi-tȧnt*, *adj.* going beyond what is usual or reasonable (e.g. *an exorbitant price, exorbitant demands*).
exor′bitance, exor′bitancy, *ns.*
[L. *ex*, out of, *orbita*, a track.]

exorcise, *eks′ör-sīz*, *v.t.* to drive away (an evil spirit).
ex′orcist (*-sist*), *n.*
[Gk. *ex*, out, *horkos*, an oath.]

exotic, *ig-zot′ik*, *adj.* introduced from a foreign country (e.g. *an exotic plant*): (*coll.*) very unusual, colourful.—Also *n.*
[Gk. *exōtikos*—*exō*, outside.]

expand, *iks-pand′*, *v.t.* and *v.i.* to spread out: to make, or grow, larger: to tell, or speak, in greater detail.
expanse′, *n.* a wide area or extent (e.g *He saw only an expanse of ocean*).
expan′sion, *n.* expanding: increase in size or bulk.
expan′sive, *adj.* able to expand: wide: (of a person) expressing feelings freely, telling much.
[L. *ex*, out, *pandĕre*, *pansum*, to spread.]

expatiate, *iks-pā′shi-āt*, *v.i.* to talk, write, at length (on a subject).
[L. *ex*, out of, *spatiārī*, to roam.]

expatriate, *eks-pā′tri-āt*, *v.t.* to send out of one's country: to exile.—*adj.* and *n.* expatriated (person).
expatriā′tion, *n.*
[L. *ex*, out of; same root as **patriot.**]

expect, *iks-pekt′*, *v.t.* to look forward to as likely to happen: to look for as one's due (e.g. *I expect gratitude for my help*): (*coll.*) to suppose.
expec′tant, *adj.* looking or waiting for something to happen.
expec′tancy, *n.* state of expecting: hopefulness.
expectā′tion (*eks-*), *n.* state of expecting: something expected: (in *pl.*) prospect of good fortune, esp. through a will.
[L. *ex*, out, *spectāre*, to look.]

expectorate, *eks-pek′tō-rāt*, *v.t.* and *v.i.* to expel (phlegm) by coughing, etc.: (*coll.*) to spit.
expectorā′tion, *n.*
[L. *ex*, out, *pectus*, *pectoris*, breast.]

expedient, *iks-pē′di-ėnt*, *adj.* suitable, advisable, advantageous (sometimes used of actions that are not very just or upright).—*n.* a contrivance, emergency measure.
expe′dience (*-pē′*), **expe′diency,** *ns.* advisability: a regard for what is advantageous to oneself.
[L. *expediens*; same root as **expedite.**]

expedite, *eks′pi-dīt*, *v.t.* hasten, speed up.
expedi′tion (*-di′*), *n.* speed, promptness: an organised journey with a purpose: those making such a journey.
expedi′tionary, *adj.* of an expedition.
expedi′tious (*-di′*), *adj.* speedy.
[L. *expedīre*—*ex*, from, *pēs*, *pedis*, foot.]

expel, *iks-pel′*, *v.i.* to drive out: to banish:—*pr.p.* **expell′ing**; *pa.p.* **expelled′.**
expulsion, *iks-pul′sh(ȯ)n*, *n.*
[L. *ex*, from, *pellĕre*, *pulsum*, to drive.]

expend, *iks-pend′*, *v.t.* to spend (e.g. money, time, energy, on something).
expend′able, *adj.* that may be sacrificed, esp. in war to gain e.g. time.
expen′diture (*-chŭr*), *n.* act of expending: money spent.

expense′, *n.* cost: a cause of spending (e.g. *A house is a continual expense*).
expen′sive, *adj.* costly, dear.
[L. *ex*, out, *pendĕre, pensum,* to weigh.]

experience, *iks-pē′ri-ėns, n.* practical knowledge gained by trial or observation: an event by which one is affected, from which one learns.—*v.t.* to meet with, undergo: to feel.
expe′rienced (*-pē′*), *adj.* taught by experience—skilful, wise.
[L. pfx. *ex-*, and old verb. *periri*, try.]

experiment, *iks-per′i-mėnt, n.* something done in the hope of making a discovery, or as a test.—*v.i.* to search for knowledge by trial: to do experiments (on, with).
experiment′al, *adj.* based on experiment (e.g. *experimental proof*): used for experiment: done as an experiment (e.g. *an experimental flight*).
[Same root as **experience.**]

expert, *eks′pėrt, -pėrt′, adj.* skilful (at, in): showing special knowledge or skill.—*n.* (*eks′pėrt*), one who is expert.
expertly, *adv.* **expertness,** *n.*
expertise, *eks-pėr-tēz′*, expertness.
[Fr.—same root as **experience.**]

expiate, *eks′pi-āt, v.t.* to pay the penalty of: to make up for (wrong one has done).
expiā′tion, *n.*
[L. pfx. *ex-*, *piāre*, to atone for.]

expire, *iks-pīr′, v.i.* to breathe out (also *v.t.*): to die: to end: (of e.g. a ticket) to become out of date or void.
expirā′tion, *n.* act of expiring.
expi′ry (*-pī′*), *n.* the end (of a period of time, or of an agreement—e.g. a truce—with a time limit).
[L. *ex*, from, *spīrāre*, to breathe.]

explain, *iks-plān′, v.t.* to make clear, easy to understand: to be, give, a reason for (e.g. *That explains his silence*).
explanation, *eks-plȧ-nā′sh(ȯ)n, n.* act of explaining: a statement, fact, etc., that explains.
explan′atory (*-plan′*), *adj.* giving an explanation.
See also **explicable.**
[L. *ex*, out, *plānus*, plain.]

expletive, *eks-plē′tiv, n.* a meaningless oath or exclamation.
[L. *ex*, out, *plēre*, to fill.]

explicable, *eks′plik-ȧ-bl,* or *-plik′, adj.* capable of being explained.
[L. *ex*, out, *plicāre*, to fold.]

explicit, *iks-plis′it, adj.* distinctly stated (e.g. *I gave you explicit instructions*): outspoken.
explic′itly, *adv.* **explic′itness,** *n.*
[Same root as **explicable.**]

explode, *iks-plōd′, v.t.* to cause to blow up: to show to be wrong, and reject (e.g. a theory).—*v.i.* to burst with a loud report: to burst out (e.g. into laughter).
explosion, *iks-plō′zh(ȯ)n, n.* act of exploding: a sudden burst with a loud noise: an outburst of feelings, etc.
explo′sive (*-plō′siv, -ziv*), *adj.* liable to or causing explosion: bursting out with violence and noise.—*n.* something that will explode.
high explosive, a material with very violent explosive effect.
[L. *ex*, from, *plaudĕre*, to clap the hands.]

exploit, *eks′ploit, iks-ploit′, n.* a heroic deed: a remarkable, but foolish or unworthy deed.—*v.t.* (*iks-ploit′*) to work, use (e.g. natural resources): to make selfish gain out of (e.g. a person).
exploitā′tion (*eks-*), *n.* act of exploiting.
[O.Fr.—same root as **explicable.**]

explore, *eks-, iks-plōr′, -plör′, v.t.* to travel or search through for the purpose of discovery: to examine thoroughly.—Also *v.i.*
explorā′tion (*-plȯr-ā′*), *n.* **explor′er,** *n.*
explor′atory (*-plor′ȧ-*), *adj.* exploring, esp. investigating.
[L. *explōrāre*, to search out.]

explosion, explosive. See **explode.**

exponent, *eks-pōn′ėnt, n.* one who explains, is supporter (of a theory, belief): one who shows the meaning and value of works of others (e.g. who interprets music by playing it).
See also **exposition.**
[L. *ex*, out, *pōnĕre, positum*, to place.]

export, *eks-pōrt′, -pört′, v.t.* to carry or send (goods) out of a country.—*n.* (*eks′pōrt, -pört*) act of exporting: something that is exported.
exportā′tion, *n.* **export′er,** *n.*
[L. *ex*, out of, *portāre*, to carry.]

expose, *iks-pōz′, v.t.* to lay out (e.g. *to expose for sale*): to leave unprotected, lay open (to e.g. attack, the weather, observation): to make publicly known (crime, folly, criminal, impostor): to subject (to) the action of e.g. light.
exposure, *iks-pō′zhůr, n.* act of exposing: exposing photographic film or plate to light, or the length of time this is done.
[Fr. *exposer*—Late L. *pausāre*, to rest.]

exposition, *eks-pȯ-zish′(ȯ)n, n.* a public exhibition: detailed explanation or account (of a subject).
[Same root as **exponent.**]

expostulate, *iks-post′ū-lāt, v.i.* to protest, object: to argue, showing disapproval (e.g. *Jack expostulated with Jim about,* or *on,* or *for, his unfriendly manner to strangers*).
expostulā′tion, *n.*
[L. pfx. *ex-*, *postulāre*, to demand.]

expound, *iks-pownd′, v.t.* to present in detail (e.g. a theory): to explain fully.
[O.Fr. *espondre*—root as **exponent.**]

express, *iks-pres′, v.t.* to press or force out: to put into words (e.g. *Try to express the idea more simply*): (**express oneself**) to put one's thought, feeling, into words: (of e.g. look) to show (e.g. an emotion).—*adj.* clearly stated (e.g. *my express wish*): for a particular purpose (*an express messen-*

ger): by special messenger: travelling at high speed.—*adv.* with haste: by express train or messenger.—*n.* a messenger on a special errand: a very fast train, etc.
express'ly, *adv.* in clear words, definitely (e.g. *I told you expressly to put it away*): for a definite purpose (e.g. *I went expressly to tell her this*).
express'ive, *adj.* expressing (e.g. *a look expressive of annoyance*): expressing meaning or feeling clearly.
express'ively, *adv.* **express'iveness,** *n.*
express'ion, *-presh'(ò)n, n.* forcing out by pressure: showing meaning, feeling, by means of language, art, one's face, etc.: the look on one's face: show of feeling in performance of music: word, phrase (e.g. *You use too many slang expressions*).
[L. *ex*, from, *pressāre*, to press.]

expropriate, *eks-prō'pri-āt, v.t.* to take (property) from its owner.
expropriā'tion, *n.*
[L. *ex*, from, *proprium*, property.]

expulsion. See **expel.**

expunge, *iks-punj', v.t.* to erase, take out (e.g. from a list).
[L. *expungĕre*, to prick a mark.]

expurgate, *eks'pùr-gāt, v.t.* to purify (esp. a book) from anything supposed to be offensive or harmful.
expurgā'tion, *n.*
[L. *ex*, out, *purgāre*, to purge.]

exquisite, *eks'kwi-zit*, or *-kwiz'it, adj.* (of e.g. workmanship) of great excellence: very beautiful: (of pain or pleasure) extreme.
ex'quisitely (or *-kwiz'*), *adv.*
[L. *ex*, out, *quaerĕre*, *quaesitum*, to seek.]

ex-serviceman, -woman, *eks-sėr'vis-man, -woom-ån, n.* one formerly in one of the fighting services. [Pfx. **ex-.**]

extant, *iks-, eks-tånt', adj.* still existing.
[L. *ex*, out, *stans*, standing.]

extempore, *eks-tem'pò-ri, adv.* on the spur of the moment, without preparation.—*adj.* composed and delivered or performed in this way.
extem'porise, *v.i.* to speak, or compose and play, extempore.
extemporisā'tion, *n.*
[L. *ex tempore*, out of time.]

extend, *iks-tend', v.t.* to stretch out: to make longer (e.g. *to extend the time*): to make cover a larger area or greater number of things (*to extend one's power, the meaning of a term*): to hold out (e.g. the hand): to offer (e.g. sympathy).—*v.i.* to stretch, reach.
extended play, (of a gramophone record) giving longer playing time because the grooves are closer together.
exten'sion, *n.* act of extending: an added part.
exten'sive, *adj.* wide (e.g. *an extensive area, search*): large in amount (e.g. *extensive purchases, knowledge*).
extent', *n.* length, area, or volume: large space: scope, range (e.g. *to the full extent of his power*).
to a certain, some, extent, within certain limits (e.g. *This is to some extent true*).
[L. *ex*, out, *tendĕre*, *tensum*, to stretch.]

extenuate, *eks-ten'ū-āt, v.t.* to make (a crime, etc.) seem less serious by showing that there was some excuse for it.
extenuā'tion, *n.*
[L. *extenuāre*, to make thin, weaken.]

exterior, *eks-tē'ri-òr, adj.* outer: outside.—*n.* the outside (of something). [L.]

exterminate, *eks-tėr'mi-nāt, v.t.* to destroy utterly (e.g. vermin in a place, area).
exterminā'tion, *n.* **exter'minātor,** *n.*
[L. *ex*, out of, *terminus*, boundary.]

external, *eks-tėr'nål*, also *eks', adj.* outside: on the outside (e.g. *a lotion for external application*): outside oneself (*the external world*): (of trade) foreign.—*n.* (in *pl.*) the outward parts, circumstances, etc.
[L. *externus*.]

extinct, *iks-tingkt', adj.* (of fire, life) out, gone, dead: (of a volcano) no longer erupting: (of a kind of animal, etc.) no longer existing.
extinc'tion, *n.*
[Same root as **extinguish.**]

extinguish, *ik-sting'gwish, v.t.* to put out: to destroy, put an end to (e.g. hope).
exting'uisher, *n.* a spraying device for putting out fire.
See also **extinct.**
[L. *ex*, out, *stinguĕre*, *stinctum*, to quench.]

cxtirpate, *eks'tėr-pāt, v.t.* to destroy totally, root out, cxterminate.
extirpā'tion, *n.*
[L. *ex*, out, *stirps*, a root.]

extol, *iks-, eks-tol', v.t.* to praise highly:—*pr.p.* **extoll'ing**, *pa.p.* **extolled'.**
[L. *ex*, up, *tollĕre*, to lift or raise.]

extort, *iks-, eks-tört', v.t.* to obtain (from a person) by threats or violence (e.g. *to extort a promise, a confession, money*).
extor'tion, *n.* the crime or practice of extorting: a much too great charge.
extor'tionate, *adj.* (of a price) much too high.
extor'tioner, *n.*
[L. *ex*, out, *torquēre*, *tortum*, to twist.]

extra, *eks'trå, adj.* more than the usual or the necessary: additional.—*adv.* unusually.—*n.* what is extra: a film actor temporarily engaged to be one of a crowd.
[L. *extrā*, outside.]

extra-, *pfx.* outside: beyond. [L.]

extract, *iks-, eks-trakt', v.t.* to draw out, esp. by force (e.g. a tooth, money, a confession): to select (passages from a book, etc.): to take out (a substance forming part of a mixture or compound) by chemical or physical means.—*n.* (*eks'trakt*) anything drawn from a substance by heat, distillation, etc., as an essence: passage taken from book, etc.

extrac′tion, *n.* act of extracting: descent (e.g. *He is of Greek extraction*).
[L. *ex*, from, *trahĕre, tractum*, draw, pull.]

extradition, *eks-trȧ-dish′(ȯ)n, n.* delivering up by one government to another of fugitives from justice.
ex′tradite (*-trȧ-dit*), *v.t.*
[L. *ex*, from, *trādĕre, -itum*, deliver up.]

extramural, *eks-trȧ-mūr′ȧl, adj.* (of teachers, teaching) connected with a university but not under its direct control.
[L. *extrā*, outside, *mūrus*, a wall.]

extraneous, *eks-trān′yus, adj.* coming from outside and not belonging (e.g. *extraneous matter in the soup*).
[L. *extrāneus*, external—*extrā*, outside.]

extraordinary, *iks-trörd′nȧr-i*, or *-di-nȧr-*, *adj.* not usual or regular: wonderful, surprising: additional (e.g. *envoy extraordinary;* always after noun).
extraor′dinarily, *adv.*
extraor′dinariness, *n.*
[L. *extrā*, outside, *ordō, ordinis*, order.]

extraterritorial, *eks-trȧ-ter-i-tō′ri-ȧl, -tö′*, *adj.* outside a territory, or not subject to its laws.
[L. *extrā*, outside, *territōrium*, territory.]

extravagant, *iks-trav′ȧ-gȧnt, adj.* spending too freely: wasteful: (of e.g. grief, praise) too great.
extrav′agance, *n.*
[L. *extrā*, beyond, *vagans*, wandering.]

extravert, extrovert, *eks′trȧ-vėrt*, or *-trō-*, *n.* one whose interests are in matters outside of himself—opp. to *introvert*.
[L. *extrā*, outside, *vertĕre*, to turn.]

extreme, *iks-trēm′, adj.* far from the centre: far from the ordinary or normal: very great (e.g. *extreme pain*).—*n.* the farthest point: the highest degree (e.g. *foolish in the extreme*).
extreme′ly, *adv.* **extreme′ness,** *n.*
extremity (*-trem′i-ti*), *n.* the utmost limit: the highest degree: greatest necessity or distress: (in *pl.*) hands or feet:—*pl.* **extrem′ities.**
extre′mist (*-trē′*), *n.* a person who holds extreme views or is ready to use extreme measures.
the extreme penalty, death, execution.
extreme unction. See **unction.**
[L. *extrēmus*, superl. of *exter*, outside.]

extricate, *eks′tri-kāt, v.t.* to free (from difficulties): to disentangle.
extricā′tion, *n.*
[L. *ex*, from, *tricae*, hindrances.]

extrovert. See **extravert.**

extrude, *eks-trōōd′, v.t.* to force or thrust out.
extrusion, *eks-trōō′zh(ȯ)n, n.*
[L. *ex*, out, *trūdĕre*, to thrust.]

exuberant, *igz-ū′bėr-ȧnt*, or *-ōō′*, *adj.* luxuriant: overflowing: showing, or in, high spirits.
exu′berance, exu′berancy, *ns.*
[L. pfx. *ex-*, *ūber*, rich.]

exude, *igz-, egz-ūd′, v.t.* to give off by, or as if by, sweating.
[L. *ex*, from, *sūdāre*, to sweat.]

exult, *igz-ult′, egz-, v.i.* to rejoice greatly (at a happening): to triumph (over e.g. a defeated rival).
exul′tant, *adj.* **exultā′tion,** *n.*
[L. *ex*, out or up, *salīre, saltum*, leap.]

eye, *ī, n.* the bodily organ by which we see: anything like an eye, as the hole of a needle, loop or ring for a hook, etc.: a bud on a potato tuber:—*pl.* **eyes** (*īz*).—*v.t.* to look at: to observe closely:—*pr.p.* **eye′ing** or **ey′ing**; *pa.p.* **eyed** (*īd*).
eye′ball, *n.* the globe of the eye.
eye′brow, *n.* hairy arch above the eye.
eye′glasses, *n.pl.* pair of lenses to correct faulty sight, esp. ones held in position by spring gripping nose.
eye′lash, *n.* one of the hairs that edge the eyelid.
eyelet, *ī′lit, n.* a small hole for thread, lace, or cord.
eye′lid, *n.* the cover of the eye.
eye′-ō′pener, *n.* something astonishing.
eye′piece, *n.* the lens or lenses of a telescope, etc. to which the eye is applied.
eye′sight, *n.* power of seeing.
eye′sore, *n.* something unpleasant to look at.
eye′witness, *n.* one who sees a thing happen.
to see eye to eye with (someone), to think as he does.
with an eye to (an object), with that end in view.
[O.E. *ēage*.]

eyrie, eyry. Same as **aerie.**

F

fable, *fā′bl, n.* a short story, often with animal characters, intended to teach a moral lesson: an untrue story.
fā′bled (*-bld*), *adj.* mentioned in fable: fictitious, imaginary.
fabulous, *fab′ū-lus, adj.* told of in fable: very large, amazing.
[Fr.—L. *fābula*—*fārī*, to speak.]

fabric, *fab′rik, n.* cloth: framework, structure (of a building, etc.).
fab′ricate, *v.t.* to manufacture, make: to make up (a false story, lie).
fabricā′tion, *n.* **fab′ricator,** *n.*
[L. *fabrica*—*faber*, a worker.]

fabulous. See **fable.**

façade, *fa-säd′, n.* the front of a building:

a deceptive appearance shown to the world (e.g. *He trembled behind a brave facade*).—Also **facade.**
[Fr. *façade*—*face*, face.]

face, *fās*, *n.* the front part of the head from forehead to chin: any surface (e.g. *the rock face*; *the face of the earth*): appearance: impudence: a grimace (e.g. *He made a face at me*).—*v.t.* to be opposite to: to turn towards: to stand up to, resist: to be forced to tackle (a difficulty): to put a surface on.—*v.i.* to turn the face: to take, have, a direction (e.g. *to face east*).
facial, *fā'shȧl*, *adj.* of the face.
fac'ing, *n.* a coating or decoration of different material.
face value, the value as stated on the face of a coin, etc.: apparent value (of e.g. a promise, a result).
in (the) face of, in spite of: when forced to meet, deal with (e.g. opposition).
to save one's face, to avoid openly appearing foolish or wrong (*n.* and *adj.* **face'-saving**).
to lose face, to suffer loss of dignity.
to set one's face against, to oppose strongly.
[Fr.—L. *faciēs*.]

facet, *fas'it*, *n.* a side of a many-sided object, as a crystal: an aspect of a subject.
fac'eted, *adj.*
[Fr. *facette*, dim. of *face*, face.]

facial. See **face.**

facile, *fas'īl*, *-il*, *adj.* easy (e.g. *a facile victory*): usu. too easy, not deep, thorough, or well thought out (e.g. (*facile emotions, conclusions*): fluent (e.g. *a facile tongue*).
facility, *fas-il'i-ti*, *n.* ease and quickness: something that makes an action possible or easier (usu. in *pl.*, **facil'ities**; e.g. *facilities for cooking, transport facilities*).
facil'itate, *v.t.* to make easier.
[Fr.—L. *facilis*, easy—*facĕre*, to do.]

facing. See **face.**

facsimile, *fak-sim'i-li*, *n.* an exact copy.
[L. *facĕre*, to make, *similis*, like.]

fact, *fakt*, *n.* anything known to have happened or to be true: (*loosely*) anything supposed to be true and used in argument: reality.
fac'tual, *adj.* of, or containing, facts.
as a matter of fact, in fact, in reality.
the fact of the matter, the plain truth.
[L. *facĕre*, *factum*, to make, do.]

faction, *fak'sh(ȯ)n*, *n.* a group of people (part of a larger group) acting together (mostly used in a bad sense): strife between parties, e.g. in the state.
fac'tious, *fak'shus*, *adj.* disloyal, rebellious.
[L. *facĕre*, *factum*, to do.]

factor, *fak'tȯr*, *n.* one who does business for another: one of two or more quantities, which, when multiplied together, produce a given quantity (e.g. *2, 3, and 5 are factors of 30*): any circumstance that influences the course of events.
fac'tory, *n.* a building where goods are manufactured:—*pl.* **fac'tories.**
[L.—*facĕre*, *factum*, to make, do.]

factotum, *fak-tō'tum*, *n.* a person employed to do all kinds of work.
[L. *facĕre* (see **factor**), *tōtum*, all.]

faculty, *fak'ul-ti*, *n.* a power of the mind (e.g. reason): a natural power of the body (e.g. hearing): ability, knack: a department of study in a university (e.g. *the faculty of medicine*): the members of a profession:—*pl.* **fac'ulties.**
[L. *facultās*—*facilis*, easy.]

fad, *fad*, *n.* a whim, craze.
fadd'ish, fadd'y, *adjs.*
fadd'iness, *n.* [Origin uncertain.]

fade, *fād*, *v.i.* to lose freshness, colour, or strength of body: to die away.—*v.t.* to cause (an image or a sound) to become gradually less distinct or loud (also **fade out**).
[O.Fr. *fader*—L. *vapidus*, flat (of wine).]

faeces, feces, *fē'sēz*, *n.pl.* solid excrement.
faecal, *fē'kȧl*, *adj.*
[L., pl. of *faex*, grounds.]

fag, *fag*, *v.i.* to become weary: to work hard: to be a schoolboy fag.—*v.t.* to weary:—*pr.p.* **fagg'ing**; *pa.p.* **fagged.** —*n.* a schoolboy forced to do jobs for an older boy: hard work unwillingly done: (*slang*) a cigarette.
fag'-end, *n.* the last, least good part.
[Origin uncertain.]

fag(g)ot, *fag'ȯt*, *n.* a bundle of sticks.
[Fr. *fagot*.]

Fahrenheit, *far'ėn-hīt*, *fär'*, *adj.* (of a thermometer) having the freezing point of water marked at 32° and the boiling point at 212°.
[G.D. *Fahrenheit*, German scientist.]

fail, *fāl*, *v.i.* to become less strong: (of heart) to stop (see **heart**): to become less, or too little, in quantity (e.g. *The stream failed*): to be unsuccessful (e.g. *The attack failed*; *he failed in his test*): to neglect (to do something): to become bankrupt.—*v.t.* to be lacking to (e.g. *Words fail me*): to disappoint or desert (a person): to reject (an examination candidate) as not good enough.
fail'ing, *n.* a fault, weakness.—*prep.* if the thing mentioned is lacking (e.g. *Failing help from outside, the fort must surrender*).—*adj.* that fails.
fail'ure, *n.* lack of success: an unsuccessful person: insufficient amount: stoppage: neglect to carry out an action (e.g. *failure to reply*): bankruptcy.
[O.Fr. *faillir*—L. *fallĕre*, to deceive.]

fain, *fān*, *adj.* compelled (to).—*adv.* gladly (only in *would fain do*, etc.)
[O.E. *fægen*, joyful.]

faint, *fānt*, *adj.* lacking in strength: dim: lacking courage (e.g. *a faint heart*).—*v.i.* to lose courage: to swoon.

faint'ly, *adv.* **faint'ness,** *n.*
faint'-hearted, *adj.* lacking in spirit, cowardly.
[O.Fr. *feint*—same root as **feign.**]

fair[1], *fār, adj.* bright: clear: beautiful: of a light hue: free from clouds and rain: (of promises, etc.) seeming good, but not sincere: just (*a fair division of work*): pretty good.—*v.i.* (of weather) to become clear.—Also *adv.* (e.g. *fair and square*).
fair'ly, *adv.* **fair'ness,** *n.*
fair and square, honestly: straight (e.g. *He hit him fair and square*).
fair'-spoken, *adj.* pleasant, courteous: pleasant, but insincere or deceitful.
fair'way, *n.* channel by which vessels enter or leave a harbour: any clear course.
a fair copy, a clean copy after correction.
the fair (sex), the female sex.
to play fair. See **play.**
[O.E. *fæger.*]

fair[2], *fār, n.* a market of importance held at fixed times: an exhibition of goods from different firms, countries, etc.: a bazaar for charity, etc., often with amusements.
[L. *fēria,* holiday.]

fairy, *fār'i, n.* an imaginary small being in human form:—*pl.* **fair'ies.**—*adj.* like a fairy, fanciful, delicate.
fair'yland, *n.* the country of fairies.
fairy ring, circle, a circle in a pasture due to fungi.
fairy tale, *n.* a story about fairies: an untrue, unbelievable tale.
[O.Fr. *faerie,* enchantment.]

faith, *fāth, n.* trust, confidence: trust in God: a belief in religion: a religion: loyalty to one's promise (*to keep,* or *break, faith with someone*).
faith'ful, *adj.* believing: keeping one's promises: loyal: true, accurate.
faith'fully, *adv.* **faith'fulness,** *n.* See also **fidelity.**
faith'-heal'ing, or **-cure,** *n.* belief in, or a system or instance of, curing sickness through prayer and faith alone, without medicine, etc.
faith'less, *adj.* not believing, esp. in God: false: disloyal.
bad faith, treachery.
in good faith, with sincerity, not intending to deceive.
the faithful, believers.
[O.Fr. *feid*—L. *fides,* faith.]

fake, *fāk, v.t.* to make (something that pretends to be more valuable than it is; e.g. *to fake a picture, a piece of old jewellery*): to produce a false appearance of (e.g. *to fake a burglary*).—*n.* something faked: a person who fakes: impostor.—Also *adj.*
[Origin uncertain.]

fakir, *fa-kēr', fā'kir, n.* a (esp. Mohammedan) religious beggar in India, etc.
[Arabic *faqīr,* a poor man.]

falcon, *föl'kȯn, fö'kn, n.* hawk trained to hunt game: a long-winged hawk that usu. strikes its prey from above.
fal'coner, *n.* one who hunts with falcons.
fal'conry, *n.* hunting with falcons.
[O.Fr. *faucon*—Late L. *falco.*]

fall, *föl, v.i.* to drop from a height: to collapse: to die in battle: to be overthrown: (of a besieged place) to be captured: (of wind, water) to go down, sink: to become less high (e.g. *Prices fell*): (of the face) to show disappointment: (of eyes) to be lowered: (of eye, glance) to come by chance (on): to flow, or slope, downwards: to hang down: to yield to temptation: to pass into any state (e.g. *to fall asleep*): to become (e.g. *to fall due*): to occur: to come (to one) as one's share, duty, etc.: to begin energetically (e.g. *to fall to work, to complaining*; see below):—*pr.p.* **fall'ing**; *pa.t.* **fell**; *pa.p.* **fall'en.**—*n.* the act of falling: overthrow: drop from a higher to a lower, or a better to a worse, position or state: something that falls (e.g. *a fall of snow*): (usu. in *pl.*) water descending: autumn.
fall'-out, *n.* radioactive dust from a nuclear explosion or an atomic power plant.
to fall back, to retreat.
to fall back (up)on, to retreat (to): to use, etc. (something) for want of something better.
to fall behind, to make too little progress: to get in arrears (with e.g. payments).
to fall in, to take places in ranks.
to fall in with, to meet by chance: to act in agreement with (e.g. *to fall in with his wishes*).
to fall off, to become less good: to die away: to desert (from e.g. an allegiance).
to fall on, to begin eagerly: to begin to eat: to attack.
to fall on one's feet, to be lucky.
to fall out, to quarrel: to happen: to leave ranks.
to fall through, to come to nothing.
to fall to, to begin e.g. a task hastily and eagerly: to begin to eat (e.g. *Bring in breakfast and fall to*).
[O.E. *fallan.*]

fallacy, *fal'ȧ-si, n.* an unsound argument: a false idea or belief:—*pl.* **fall'acies.**
fallacious, *fȧ-lā'shùs, adj.* misleading, false: not showing sound reasoning.
[L. *fallĕre,* deceive; same root as **false.**]

fallen. See **fall.**

fallible, *fal'i-bl, adj.* liable to make mistakes, or to be mistaken.
fallibil'ity, *n.*
[Same root as **fallacy, false.**]

fallow[1], *fal'ō, adj.* left uncultivated or unsowed for a time.—*n.* land left thus for a year or more.—*v.t.* to plough (land) without seeding it.
[O.E. *fealh,* fallow land.]

fallow[2], *fal'ō, adj.* yellowish-brown.
fallow deer, *n.* a yellowish-brown deer smaller than the red deer.
[O.E. *falu.*]

false, *fōls, fols, adj.* wrong: purposely untrue (as *to bear false witness*): deceiving: untruthful: unfaithful: not genuine or real: (of teeth, etc.) artificial.
false′ly, *adv.* **false′ness, fal′sity,** *ns.*
false′hood, *n.* lying: deceitfulness: a lie.
falsify, *fōls′i-fī, fols′, v.t.* to alter (a document) so as to deceive: to represent incorrectly or falsely: to disappoint (one's hopes):—*pr.p.* **fal′sifying**; *pa.p.* **fal′sified.**
falsificā′tion, *n.*
to play false. See **play.**
[L. *fallĕre, falsum,* to deceive.]

falsetto, *fōl-set′ō, fol-, n.* a forced voice of range or register above the natural, esp. in a man.—Also *adj.*
[It. *falsetto,* dim. of *falso,* false.]

falsification, falsify, falsity. See **false.**

falter, *fōl′tėr,* or *fol′, v.i.* to stumble: to speak with hesitation (also *v.t.*): to waver.
fal′tering, *adj.* **fal′teringly,** *adv.*
[Origin uncertain.]

fame, *fām, n.* reputation, esp. if good: renown.
famed, fam′ous, *adjs.* well-known, renowned.
fam′ously, *adv.* (*coll.*) very well.
[L. *fāma—fārī,* to speak.]

familiar, *fȧ-mil′yȧr, adj.* well-known (e.g. *a familiar sight*): well-acquainted (e.g. *He was familiar with their customs*): close, intimate (*a familiar friend*): informal: too free or intimate.—*n.* a close friend: an attendant spirit.
famil′iarly, *adv.* **familiar′ity,** *n.*
famil′iarise, *v.t.* to make (a person) well-acquainted (with something).
[Same root as **family.**]

family, *fam′i-li, n.* parents and their children: the children alone: the descendants of one common ancestor: a group of animals, plants, languages, etc. having some likeness:—*pl.* **-ies.**
[L. *familia,* household, family.]

famine, *fam′in, n.* extreme scarcity esp. of food: hunger.
fam′ish, *v.t.* and *v.i.* to starve.
fam′ished, *adj.* very hungry.
[Fr.—L. *fames,* hunger; conn. Fr. *faim.*]

famous, famously. See **fame.**

fan[1], *fan, n.* a moving device for causing a current of air: a small hand device, usu. shaped like part of a circle, for cooling the face.—*v.t.* to cool with a fan: to increase the strength of (e.g. *This remark fanned the flames of his anger*): to clean (grain) with a fan:—*pr.p.* **fann′ing**; *pa.p.* **fanned.**
fan′light, *n.* a window above a door, esp. one shaped like a half circle.
fan′tail, *n.* a pigeon with tail feathers spread out like a fan.
to fan out, to spread out in the shape of a fan.
[O.E. *fann*—L. *vannus.*]

fan[2], *fan, n.* short for **fanatic,** an enthusiastic follower of some sport, or hobby, or public favourite.
fanatic, *fȧ-nat′ik, n.* a person filled with unreasonably great enthusiasm for something.
fanat′ic(al), *adjs.* **fanat′ically,** *adv.*
fanat′icism (*-is-izm*), *n.* excessive enthusiasm.
[L. *fānāticus,* inspired by a god.]

fancy, *fan′si, n.* power of the mind to imagine things, esp. things unlike reality: an image in the mind: an idea with little reality behind it: a liking, inclination (for):—*pl.* **-ies.**—*adj.* ornamental: not plain:—*comp.* **fan′cier**; *superl.* **fan′ciest.**—*v.t.* to picture, imagine: to think without being sure: to take a liking or inclination for: to breed (animals, e.g. birds, or plants) so as to develop certain qualities:—*pr.p.* **fan′cying**; *pa.p.* **fan′cied.**
fan′cier, *n.*
fan′ciful, *adj.* inclined to have fancies: created by fancy.
fan′cifully, *adv.*
fancy dress, dress chosen according to fancy, e.g. to represent a character in history or fiction.
[Shortened from **fantasy.**]

fanfare, *fan′fār, n.* a flourish or call on trumpets or bugles.
[Fr., perh. from the sound.]

fang, *fang, n.* a long pointed tooth: a poison-bearing tooth of a snake: the root of a tooth.
fanged, *adj.* having fangs.
[O.E.; from root of O.E. *fōn,* to seize.]

fanlight, fantail. See **fan** (1).

fantasia, *fan-tā′zi-ȧ, fan-tȧ-zē′ȧ, n.* a musical composition in irregular form.
[It.: same root as **fantasy.**]

fantasy, *fan′tȧ-zi, -si, n.* fancy: forming of mental pictures, esp. when unreal: an idea not based on reality:—*pl.* **fan′tasies.**
fantas′tic, *adj.* unreal: odd, unnatural: unbelievable.—Also **fantas′tical.**
fantas′tically, *adv.*
[Gk. *phantasia,* image; see **phantasy.**]

far, *fär, adj.* distant: more distant of two.—*adv.* to, at, over, a great distance: to, at, an advanced stage: very much (e.g. *a far harder task*):—*comp.* **far′ther** (also, with additional meaning, **fur′ther**—see this word); *superl.* **far′thest** (also **fur′thest**), **far′thermost** (also **fur′thermost**).
far′away′, *adj.* distant: absent-minded, dreamy (e.g. *a faraway expression*).
Far East, China, Japan, and other countries of E. and S.E. Asia.
far′-east′ern, *adj.*
far′-fetched′ (*-fecht′*), *adj.* (of an argument, comparison, etc.) not natural, reasonable, or obvious.
far′-flung′, *adj.* extending over a great distance.
far′-sight′ed, *adj.* foreseeing what is likely to happen and preparing for it.

far and away, by far, by a great deal.
a far cry, a long distance.
[O.E. *feor(r)*.]

farce, *färs*, *n.* a (style of) comedy depending on ridiculous situations: something absurd: a silly sham.
far'cical (*-si-kȧl*), *adj.* absurd.
[L. *farcīre*, to stuff.]

fare, *fār*, *v.i.* to travel: to get on (well, ill): to be fed.—*n.* the price paid for travelling in a vehicle, ship, etc.: a passenger in a public conveyance: food.
farewell', *interj.* may you fare well!—*n.* well-wishing at parting: departure.—*adj.* parting: final.
to fare with, to turn out for (e.g. *I wonder how it fares with the travellers.*)
[O.E. *faran*.]

farinaceous, *far-i-nā'shu̇s*, *adj.* containing flour, meal, or starch.
[L. *farina*, meal, flour—*far*, kind of grain.]

farm, *färm*, *n.* a tract of land used for cultivation or pasturage: land or water used for breeding animals (as *fox farm*, *oyster farm*).—*v.t.* to cultivate (land): to give, or to receive, a fixed payment in return for the right to collect (taxes): to let or lease.—*v.i.* to run a farm.
farm'er, *n.* **farm'ing,** *n.* and *adj.*
farm'stead, *n.* a farm with buildings belonging to it.
farm'yard, *n.* the yard surrounded by farm buildings.
[M.E. *ferme* (orig. leased land)—Late L. *firma*, fixed payment.]

farrago, *fa-rā'gō*, or *-rä'-*, *n.* a confused mixture (e.g. *a farrago of lies*):—*pl.* **farra'goes.**
[L. *farrāgō*, mixed fodder—*far*, grain.]

farrier, *far'i-ėr*, *n.* one who shoes horses: one who treats horses' diseases.
farr'iery, *n.* the farrier's art.
[O.Fr. *ferrier*—L. *ferrum*, iron.]

farrow, *far'ō*, *n.* a litter of pigs.—*v.i.* or *v.t.* to bring forth (pigs).
[O.E. *fearh*, a pig.]

farther, etc. See **far** and **further.**

farthing, *fär'*THing, *n.* an old coin, the fourth of a penny.
[O.E. *fēorthing*, a fourth part.]

fascinate, *fas'in-āt*, *v.t.* to control by the eye as a snake does: to charm, attract irresistibly.
fas'cinating, *adj.* **fascinā'tion,** *n.*
[L. *fascināre*, to bewitch, charm.]

Fascism, *fash'izm*, *n.* a system of government similar to that in Italy from 1922-1944, controlling everything and suppressing all criticism or opposition.
Fasc'ist, *n.* and *adj.*
[It. *fascismo*.]

fashion, *fash'(ȯ)n*, *n.* the make or cut of a thing: the exact shape in dress that is in favour at the time: the custom of the time: manner (e.g. *He replied in an irritable fashion*).—*v.t.* to make: to shape, form (into, to).
fash'ionable, *adj.* according to fashion or use at the time: following fashion in dress or living: moving in high society.
after, in, a fashion, in a way: to a certain extent.
[O.Fr. *fachon*—L. *facĕre*, to make.]

fast[1], *fâst*, *adj.* firm: fixed: steadfast (e.g. *a fast friend*): (of a colour) unfading.—*adv.* firmly: sound (*fast asleep*).
fast'ness, *n.* fixedness: a stronghold, castle.
fasten, *fâs'n*, *v.t.* to make fast: to fix securely: to attach.—Also *v.i.*
fastener (*fâsn'ėr*), *n.* a clip, catch, or other means of fastening.
fas'tening, *n.*
to fasten (up)on, to direct (e.g. one's eyes) on: to seize on (e.g. a fact, a statement); to fix (something disagreeable—e.g. blame) on (someone).
to make fast, to lock, bar: to fasten up.
to play fast and loose, to act unscrupulously (from name of cheating game).
[O.E. *fæst* (n.), *fæstnian* (vb.).]

fast[2], *fâst*, *adj.* quick: rapid: (of a clock, etc.) before time: dissipated.—Also *adv.*
[Same word as **fast** (1).]

fast[3], *fâst*, *v.i.* to go hungry: to eat no food, esp. as religious duty.—Also *n.*
fast'ing, *n.* and *adj.*
[O.E. *fæstan*.]

fasten. See **fast** (1).

fastidious, *fas-tid'i-u̇s*, *adj.* very critical, difficult to please (in e.g. one's taste in books, art, music): very careful because easily disgusted (e.g. *fastidious about cleanliness*).
fastid'iously, *adv.* **fastid'iousness,** *n.*
[L. *fastidium*, loathing.]

fat, *fat*, *adj.* plump: too plump: fruitful, profitable.—*n.* an oily substance under the skin: solid animal oil: the richest part of anything:—*comp.* **fatt'er**; *superl.* **fatt'est.**
fatt'ed, *adj.* made fat. **fat'ness,** *n.*
fatt'y, *adj.* containing, or like, fat.
fatt'iness, *n.*
fatt'en, *v.t.*, *v.i.*, to make, or grow, fat.
fat'head, *n.* a stupid person.
[O.E. *fætt*, fattened.]

fatal, etc. See **fate.**

fate, *fāt*, *n.* what is bound to happen, destiny, fortune: ruin, death: (*cap.*) any of the three goddesses controlling birth, life, and death of man.
fat'al (*fāt'*) *adj.* causing death: disastrous (e.g. *a fatal mistake*): fateful.
fat'alism, *n.* belief that everything that is to happen has been prearranged, and that there is no good trying to influence events.
fat'alist, *n.* **fatalist'ic,** *adj.*
fatality, *fȧ-tal'i-ti*, *n.* state of being unavoidable: a death caused by accident:—*pl.* **fatal'ities.**
fated, *fāt'id*, *adj.* doomed: destined (to; e.g. *He seemed fated to miss chances*).

fate′ful, *adj.* important because deciding something (e.g. *The fateful day arrived*).
[L. *fātum*, a thing foretold—*fāri*, speak.]

father, *fä′*THėr, *n.* a male parent: an ancestor or forefather: a protector: a monk, priest, religious teacher: the oldest member of any company: one of the leading men in a city, etc.: the person who begins, founds, or first makes something (e.g. *J. L. Baird was the father of television*).—*v.t.* to be the father of: to be considered as the author or originator of.
fath′erly, *adj.* of, like, or suitable in, a father.
fath′erliness, *n.*
fath′erhood, *n.* state of being a father.
fath′er-in-law, *n.* the father of one's husband or wife.
fath′erland, *n.* native country.
[O.E. *fæder*; conn. Ger. *vater*, L. *pater*.]

fathom, *fa*TH′*ȯm*, *n.* a unit used in measuring depth = 6 feet.—*v.t.* to measure depth of: to understand, get to the bottom of.
[O.E. *fæthm*.]

fatigue, *fȧ-tēg′*, *n.* weariness caused by hard work: a soldier's task (not military) given to him as a punishment: weakness (esp. of metals) caused by use.—*v.t.* and *v.i.* to exhaust or become exhausted: to weaken:—*pr.p.* **fatigu′ing**; *pa.p.* **fatigued′.**
[Fr.—L. *fatigāre*, to weary.]

fatuous, *fat′ū-ŭs*, *adj.* silly, idiotic.
fat′uousness, fatu′ity, *ns.*
[L. *fatuus*.]

faucet, *fö′sit*, *n.* a tap.
[Fr. *fausset*.]

fault, *fölt, folt*, *n.* an error: a blemish: a slight offence: (*geol.*) a fracture in the earth's crust.
fault′y, *adj.* **fault′iness,** *n.*
fault′less, *adj.* without fault, perfect.
fault′finder, *n.* **fault′finding,** *n.* and *adj.*
at fault, puzzled, at a loss: in fault.
in fault, to blame, guilty.
to find fault with, to criticise, complain of (for *ns.* and *adj.*, see above).
[O.Fr. *faute*—same L. root as **false.**]

faun, *fön*, *n.* a Roman country god with horns and a tail.
faun′a, *n.* the animals (collectively) of a region or a period.
[L. *Faunus, Fauna*, a god and goddess.]

faux pas, *fō pä*, *n.* a blunder, esp. something said that is indiscreet.
[Fr., false step.]

favour, *fā′vȯr*, *n.* goodwill: approval: a kind deed: state of being approved (*in favour, out of favour*): a knot of ribbons worn at a wedding or an election.—*v.t.* to regard with goodwill: to be on the side of: to prefer: to be an advantage to, help towards (e.g. *The dark night favoured his escape*): to oblige (with): (*coll.*) to resemble.
fā′vourable, *adj.* showing goodwill or approval: helpful, advantageous (to): promising.
fā′vourably, *adv.*
fā′voured, *adj.* preferred: enjoying special advantages: having a certain appearance (as in *ill-, well-, favoured*).
fā′vourite, *n.* a well, or best, liked person, thing, etc.: a person treated with too much friendliness: one (esp. a horse) expected to win.
fā′vouritism, *n.* unfair generosity to one rather than to another.
in favour of, in support of: for the benefit of: for the account of (e.g. *He drew a cheque in favour of John Smith*).
[L. *favor*.]

fawn[1], *fön*, *n.* a young deer in its baby coat: light yellowish-brown.—Also *adj.*
[O.Fr. *faon*.]

fawn[2], *fön*, *v.i.* to show affection as a dog does: to flatter in a too humble way (with *upon*).
[O.E. *fagnian*, rejoice; root as **fain.**]

fay[1], *fā*, *n.* a fairy.
[Fr. *fae*; same root as **fate.**]

fay[2]. See **fey.**

fealty, *fē′ȧl-ti*, *n.* loyalty of a vassal to his lord.
[O.Fr. *fealte*—L. *fidēlis*, faithful.]

fear, *fēr*, *n.* painful emotion roused by danger or thought of danger.—*v.t.* to expect with alarm: to be regretfully inclined to think (e.g. *I fear you will not find him at home*).—*v.i.* to be afraid.
fear′ful, *adj.* full of fears, timid: afraid (of something happening): terrible: (*coll.*) very bad.
fear′fully, *adv.* **fear′fulness,** *n.*
fear′less, *adj.* daring, brave.
for fear of, in order not to (e.g. *for fear of losing it*).
[O.E. *fǣr*.]

feasible, *fēz′i-bl*, *adj.* practicable, possible.
feas′ibleness, feasibil′ity, *ns.*
[Fr. *faisable*, that can be done.]

feast, *fēst*, *n.* an anniversary, esp of a religious event, celebrated with solemnity or joy: a large and rich meal: rich enjoyment (e.g. *The scene was a feast for the eyes*).—Also *v.t.* and *v.i.*
festal, *fes′tȧl*, *adj.* of, for, a feast: gay. See also **festival, festive,** etc.
[O.Fr. *feste*—L. *festum*, a holiday.]

feat, *fēt*, *n.* a deed of great strength, skill, or courage.
[Fr. *fait*—L. *facĕre*, to do.]

feather, *fe*TH′*ėr*, *n.* one of the growths that form the covering of a bird: anything like a feather in appearance.—*v.t.* to furnish or adorn with feathers: to turn (an oar, etc.) edgewise to lessen air resistance: to rotate (aircraft propeller blades, etc.) so as to reduce drag.
feath′ery, *adj.* like feathers.
feath′eriness, *n.*
feath′er-bed, *n.* a mattress filled with feathers.

feath′er-brain, *n.* a frivolous person.
feath′erweight, *n.* a boxer of not more than 9 st.
a feather in one's cap, an honour, cause for pride and pleasure.
to feather one's nest, to pile up wealth while holding a position of trust.
to show the white feather, to show cowardice.
[O.E. *fether.*]

feature, *fē′chůr, n.* a characteristic, quality: a part of the face: (in *pl.*) the face: the main picture in a programme: a special newspaper article.—*v.t.* and *v.i.* to give, or to have, an important part.
fea′tureless, *adj.* with no points of interest.
[O.Fr. *faiture*—L. *facěre*, to make.]

February, *feb′roo-ăr-i, n.* the second month of the year.
[L. *Februārius.*]

feces. See **faeces.**

feckless, *fek′lis, adj.* shiftless, inefficient.
[Scot. *feck*, value, result; perh. **effect.**]

fed. See **feed¹.**

federal, *fed′ėr-ăl,* (of a union or government) in which several states, while independent in home affairs, combine for national or general purposes.
fed′eralist, *n.* a supporter of a federal constitution or union.
fed′erate, *v.t.* and *v.i.* to join in a league or federation.
federā′tion, *n.* a federal union, or the act of uniting in one.
[L. *foedus, foederis*, a treaty.]

fee, *fē, n.* price paid for professional services: sum paid for a privilege (e.g. *entrance fee*).—*v.t.* to hire:—*pr.p.* **fee′-ing**; *pa.p.* **feed.**
[O.E. *feoh*, cattle, property.]

feeble, *fē′bl, adj.* very weak.
fee′bleness, *n.* **fee′bly,** *adv.*
fee′ble-mind′ed, *adj.* weak-minded.
[Through O.Fr.—L. *flēbilis*, tearful.]

feed¹, *fēd, v.t.* to give food to: to supply necessary material to (e.g. *to feed a fire*): to satisfy or encourage (e.g. *to feed his vanity*): to give cues to (a comedian):—*pa.t.* and *pa.p.* **fed.**—Also *v.i.*—*n.* food, esp. for cattle: one who, something that, feeds or supplies.
feed′er, *n.* and *adj.*
fed up, (*slang*) tired and disgusted.
[O.E. *fēdan.*]

feed², feeing. See **fee.**

feel, *fēl, v.t.* to become aware of by touch: to examine by touch: to grope (one's way): to be conscious of: to experience (e.g. an emotion):—*pr.p.* **feel′ing**; *pa.t.* and *pa.p.* **felt.**—Also *v.i.* and *n.*
feel′er, *n.* in animals, an organ with which to feel: a remark or action to find out the opinions of others.
feel′ing, *n.* sense of touch: a sensation: an impression: consciousness of pleasure or pain: emotion: affection.—*adj.* experiencing, or showing, emotion.
[O.E. *fēlan.*]

feet. See **foot.**

feign, *fān, v.t* to pretend to feel (e.g. sickness, grief): to sham.
feigned, *adj.*
feint, *fānt, n.* a pretence: a movement intended to deceive.
[Fr. pr.p. *feignant*—L. root as **fiction.**]

felicity, *fė-lis′i-ti, n.* happiness: skill or appropriateness (of phrase, expression).
felic′itate, *v.t.* to congratulate.
felic′itous, *adj.* happy: appropriate.
[L. *fēlīcitās.*]

feline, *fē′lin, adj.* of, like, a cat.
[L. *fēles*, a cat.]

fell¹. See **fall.**

fell², *fel, v.t.* to strike to the ground: to cut down.
[O.E. *fellan*, to cause to fall.]

fell³, *fel, n.* a hill: moorland.
[Old Norse *fjall.*]

fell⁴, *fel, n.* a skin.
[O.E. *fel*; conn. Ger. *fell*, L. *pellis.*]

fell⁵, *fel, adj.* cruel, fierce, deadly.
[O.Fr. *fel*, cruel; same root as **felon.**]

felloe, *fel′i, fel′ō,* **felly,** *n.* the circular rim of a wheel, or part of it.
[O.E. *felg.*]

fellow, *fel′ō, n.* a man: a worthless person: a companion and equal: one of a pair: one who holds a fellowship: one who belongs to a (usu. learned) society.—*adj.* belonging to the same group or class (e.g. *fellow citizen, fellow-countryman*).
fell′owship, *n.* friendliness: an association: money left to a college for the support of graduates called fellows.
fell′ow-feel′ing, *n*, sympathy.
fellow traveller, one who travels in the same vehicle: a communist sympathiser.
[M.E. *felawe*—Old Norse *fēlagi*, partner.]

felly. See **felloe.**

felo de se, *fel′ō di sē′, n.* (a) suicide.
[English-Latin, a felon towards himself.]

felon, *fel′ŏn, n.* one guilty of a serious crime.
felo′nious (*-lō′*), *adj.* criminal: wicked.
fel′ony, *n.* a crime punishable by penal servitude or death:—*pl.* **fel′onies.**
[Late L. *fellō, -ōnis*, a traitor.]

felt¹. See **feel.**

felt², *felt, n.* a woollen fabric made by pressure not weaving.—*v.i.* to become like felt.—*v.t.* to make into, or make like, felt. [O.E.]

female, *fē′māl, adj.* and *n.* (one) of the sex that produces young: (one) of the kind of flower that has a pistil and thus bears seeds: (a plant) with such flowers only.
[L. *femella*, girl—root as **feminine.**]

feminine, *fem′i-nin, adj.* of women: like a woman.
fem′inism, *n.* support of women's rights.
fem′inist, *n.* supporter of women's rights.
[L. *fēmina*, a woman.]

femur, *fē'mur*, *n.* the thigh bone.
fem'oral (*fem'*), *adj.* of the thigh. [L.]

fen, *fen*, *n.* low marshy land often covered with water.
fenn'y, *adj.* **fen'land,** *n.*
[O.E. *fenn.*]

fence, *fens*, *n.* a barrier for enclosing land: a receiver of stolen goods.—*v.t.* to enclose with a fence.—*v.i.* to practise fencing with sword or foil: to give answers that tell nothing or promise nothing.
fenc'er, *n.* a maker of fences: one who practises fencing with sword or foil.
fenc'ing, *n.* the act of, or material for, putting up a fence: the art of attack and defence with a sword, etc., practised with blunted weapons and protective clothing: turning aside questions or arguments.
[**defence.** See also **fend.**]

fend, *fend*, *v.t.* to ward (off), turn aside (e.g. *to fend off a blow*).—*v.i.* to look after (with *for*; e.g. *to fend for oneself*).
fend'er, *n.* anything used as a guard against touching or collision: a low metal guard round a hearth: a mudguard.
[**defend.** See also **fence.**]

fennel, *fen'ėl*, *n.* a plant with yellow flowers in parasol-shaped clusters.
[O.E. *finol.*]

ferment, *fėr'mėnt*, *n.* a substance that causes fermentation: internal motion among the parts of a fluid: agitation, tumult.—*v.t.* (*fėr-ment'*) to excite fermentation in: to stir up.—*v.i.* to undergo fermentation: to seethe with excitement.
fermentā'tion, *n.* a slow change in an organic substance, usu. giving off heat and gas, e.g. the change of grape sugar to alcohol: excitement.
[L. *fermentum—fervēre*, to boil.]

fern, *fėrn*, *n.* a plant with no flowers and beautiful feather-like leaves.
[O.E. *fearn.*]

ferocious, *fė-rō'shus*, *adj.* savage, fierce.
fero'ciously, *adv.*
fero'ciousness, feroc'ity (*-ros'*), *ns.*
[L. *ferox*, fierce.]

ferret, *fer'it*, *n.* a half-tamed variety of polecat used to hunt out rabbits and rats.—*v.t.* to search (out) cunningly:—*pr.p.* **ferr'eting**; *pa.p.* **ferr'eted.**
[O.Fr. *furet*—L. *fūr*, a thief.]

ferri-, ferro-, (ferr-), *pfxs.* of, containing, iron.
ferr'o-con'crete, *n.* reinforced concrete.
[L. *ferrum*, iron.]

ferrule, *fer'ūl*, *fer'ul*, *n.* a metal ring or cap to strengthen the tip of a stick, umbrella.
[L. *viriola*, a little bracelet.]

ferry, *fer'i*, *v.t.* to carry over water (or land) esp. along a regular route, by boat, ship, or aircraft:—*pr.p.* **ferr'ying**; *pa.p.* **ferr'ied.**—*n.* a place of carriage across water: a ferry boat.
[O.E. *ferian*, to convey, *faran*, to go.]

fertile, *fėr'til*, *-til*, *adj.* able to produce in great quantity: inventive (e.g. *a fertile imagination*).
fer'tileness, fertil'ity (*-til'*), *ns.*
fer'tilise (*-til-iz*), *v.t.* to make fertile: to make capable of development.
fertilisā'tion, *n.* act of fertilising.
fer'tiliser (*-iz-ėr*), *n.* a material used to make the soil more fertile.
[L. *fertilis—ferre*, to bear.]

ferule, *fer'ūl*, *n.* a rod for punishment.
[L. *ferula*, a cane.]

fervent, *fėr'vėnt*, *adj.* warm in feeling: enthusiastic.
fer'vency, *n.* eagerness: emotional warmth.
fer'vid, *adj.* very hot: having burning desire or enthusiasm.
fer'vour, *n.* warmth and earnestness.
[L. *fervēre*, to boil; root as **ferment.**]

festal. See **feast.**

fester, *fes'tėr*, *v.i.* to suppurate: to rot: to rankle (e.g. *The injustice festered in his mind*).
[O.Fr. *festre*—L. *fistula*, an ulcer.]

festival, *fes'ti-vål*, *n.* a joyful celebration: a season of performances of music, etc.
fes'tive, *adj.* of a feast: gay.
festiv'ity, *n.* merrymaking, celebration: gaiety:—*pl.* **festiv'ities.**
[L. *festivus*; same root as **feast.**]

festoon, *fes-tōōn'*, *n.* a garland hung between two points.—*v.t.* to adorn, hang (with festoons, etc.)
[Same root as **feast.**]

fetch, *fech*, *v.t.* to go and get: to bring: to be sold for (a stated price): to heave (a sigh): to draw (a breath): to deal (a blow).
fetch'ing, *adj.* charming.
[O.E. *feccan.*]

fête, *fāt* (Fr. *fet*), *n.* a festive entertainment, esp. out of doors, usu. held to raise money.—*v.t.* to entertain lavishly, make much of (a person):—*pr.p.* **fêt'ing**; *pa.p.* **fêt'ed.** [Fr.]

fetid, *fē'tid*, or *fet'*, *adj.* stinking.
[L. *foetidus.*]

fetish, *fet'ish*, *n.* an object worshipped because a spirit is supposed to lodge in it, or for other reason: something regarded with undue reverence.
[Port. *feitico*, magic, (orig.) artificial.]

fetlock, *fet'lok*, *n.* a tuft of hair that grows above a horse's hoof: the part where this hair grows.
[**foot, lock** (of hair).]

fetter, *fet'ėr*, *n.* a chain for the feet—used chiefly in *pl.*: anything that restrains.—*v.t.* to put fetters on: to restrain.
[O.E. *feter—fōt*, foot.]

fettle, *fet'l*, *n.* used in phrase *in fine* (or *good*) *fettle*, in good condition or spirits.
[M.E. *fettle*, make ready.]

fetus. See **foetus.**

feu, *fū*, *n.* (*Scot.*) a right to the use of land for an annual payment (**feu'-du'ty**; *-dū'ti*).
[O.Fr.; same as **fee.**]

feud, *fūd, n.* a deadly quarrel between families or clans: a lasting quarrel.
[O.Fr. *faide*—a Germanic word.]

feudal, *fū'dȧl, adj.* of or connected with the **feudal system,** the system in the Middle Ages by which 'vassals' held lands from more important lords, being bound in return to fight for these lords in war.
[Late L. *feudum*—a Germanic word.]

fever, *fē'vėr, n.* (disease, esp. infectious, marked by) great bodily heat and quickening of pulse: extreme excitement, agitation, anxiety.
fe'vered, *adj.*
fe'verish, *adj.* having a slight fever: restlessly excited.
fe'verishly, *adv.* **fe'verishness,** *n.*
[O.E. *fēfor*—L. *febris.*]

few, *fū, adj.* a small number of, not many.
a few, a small number (of).
[O.E. *fēawe.*]

fey, fay, *fā, adj.* fated soon to die—a state said to be marked by high spirits.
[O.E. *fǣge,* doomed.]

fez, *fez, n.* a, usu. red, brimless cap with black tassel:—pl. **fezz'es.**
[From *Fez* in Morocco.]

fiancé (*fem.* **fiancée**), *fē-ong'sā, n.* a person engaged to be married (with *my, your, his, her*). [Fr.]

fiasco, *fi-as'kō, n.* a failure, orig. in a musical performance.
[It. *fiasco,* bottle.]

fiat, *fī'at, n.* a formal command: a decree.
[L., 'let it be done'.]

fib, *fib, n.* a trivial lie.—Also *v.i.*
[Perh. **fable.**]

fibre, *fī'bėr, n.* fine thread, or thread-like substance: a material composed of fibres: texture: character (e.g. *moral fibre*).
fī'brous, *adj.*
[L. *fibra,* a thread.]

fibula, *fib'ū-lȧ, n.* the outer of the two bones from the knee to the ankle. [L.]

fickle, *fik'l, adj.* inconstant: changeable.
fick'leness, *n.*
[O.E. *ficol*; conn. with *gefic,* fraud.]

fiction, *fik'sh(ȯ)n, n.* a made-up story: a falsehood: novels and stories in prose.
fic'tional, *adj.* of fiction, not fact.
fictitious, *fik-tish'ūs, adj.* imaginary.
[Fr.—L. *fingĕre, fictum,* to form.]

fiddle, *fid'l, n.* a stringed instrument, esp. a violin.—*v.i.* to play on a fiddle: to make aimless movements (with): to tinker (with): to tamper with: to cheat.
fidd'ler, *n.*
to play second fiddle, to take a less important part than someone else.
[O.E. *fithele,* prob.—L. *vitula,* and thus conn. with **violin.**]

fidelity, *fi-del'i-ti,* or *fī-, n.* loyalty: faithfulness: exactness in reproducing (e.g. *fidelity to the text, to the score*).
[L. *fidēlis,* faithful; same root as **faith.**]

fidget, *fij'it, v.i.* to move uneasily, be restless:—*pr.p.* **fidg'eting**; *pa.p.* **fidg'eted.**—*n.* one who fidgets: (in *pl.*) nervous restlessness.
[Perh. Old Norse *fikja.*]

field, *fēld, n.* a piece of ground enclosed for tillage, pasture, or sport: the scene (of a battle): an expanse (e.g. *icefield*): land yielding a natural product (e.g. gold, coal): an area enclosed or marked off in some way: sphere of interest, knowledge, etc.: those taking part in a hunt or a horse race: players or competitors.—*v.t.* to catch or stop (a ball) and return to the fixed place: to put (a team) into the field to play.—*v.i.* to stand ready to stop the ball in cricket or baseball.
field'er, fields'man, *ns.*
field day, a day when troops are given exercises in the field: any day of unusual bustle or importance.
field'fare, *n.* a type of thrush.
field'-glasses, *n.pl.* a small telescope with two eyepieces.
field hospital, a temporary hospital near the scene of a battle.
field marshal, an army officer of highest rank. See *Appendices.*
field mouse. See **mouse.**
field work, work done out of doors, e.g. surveying, or collecting facts or information.
[O.E. *feld.*]

fiend, *fēnd, n.* (*cap.*) Satan: a devil: (*coll.*) an enthusiast.
fiend'ish, *adj.* **fiend'ishness,** *n.*
[O.E. *fēond,* enemy.]

fierce, *fērs, adj.* angry, savage: violent: intense, eager (e.g. *fierce rivalry*).
fierce'ly, *adv.* **fierce'ness,** *n.*
[O.Fr. *fers*—L. *ferus,* wild.]

fiery, *fīr'i, adj.* like, or of, fire: blazing: very red: full of passion: irritable:—*comp.* **fier'ier**; *superl.* **fier'iest.**
fier'ily, *adv.* **fier'iness,** *n.*
fiery cross, two sticks, charred and dipped in blood, sent round to summon clansmen to arms. [**fire.**]

fiesta, *fē-es'tä, n.* a saint's day: holiday: festivity. [Sp.]

fife, *fīf, n.* a small flute.
[Through Ger. or Fr.—L. *pīpāre,* cheep.]

fifteen, *fif'tēn, fif-tēn', adj.* and *n.* five and ten (15 or XV): (*n.*) a rugby team.
fifteenth, *adj.* last of fifteen.—*n.* one of fifteen equal parts.
fifth, *adj.* last of five.—*n.* one of five equal parts.
fifty, *fif'ti, adj.* and *n.* five times ten (50 or L):—*pl.* **fif'ties.**
fif'tieth, *adj.* last of fifty.—*n.* one of fifty equal parts.
fif'ty-fif'ty, half-and-half: (of chances) equal.
[O.E. *fiftēne*; *fifta*; *fīftig*; see also **five.**]

fig, *fig, n.* a small tree bearing a pear-shaped fruit: the fruit: the smallest bit.
[L. *ficus.*]

fight, *fīt, v.i.* to strive (for): to contend in war or single combat.—*v.t.* to engage in conflict with: to win (one's way) by a struggle:—*pr.p.* **fight'ing**; *pa.p.* **fought** (*föt*).—*n.* a struggle: a battle: the will or strength to fight (e.g. *There was no fight left in him*).
fight'er, *n.* **fight'ing,** *adj.* and *n.*
to fight shy of, to avoid.
[O.E. *fehtan.*]

figment, *fig'mėnt, n.* an invention (of the imagination).
[L. *figmentum*—root as **fiction.**]

figurative. See **figure.**

figure, *fig'ůr, n.* the form in outline: a geometrical form: a representation in drawing, etc.: appearance: a person noticed by the public (e.g. *a political figure*): a number, or the mark representing it: price (e.g. *a high figure*): a set of steps in a dance, or of movements in skating.—*v.t.* to mark with a design (*adj.* **fig'ured**): to imagine: (*coll.*) to conclude, assume.—*v.i.* to play a part (in):—*pr.p.* **fig'uring**; *pa.p.* **fig'ured.**
fig'urative (*fig'yůr-*), *adj.* of, or using, figures of speech.
fig'uratively, *adv.*
fig'urehead (*fig'ůr-*), *n.* a figure under a ship's bowsprit: a leader who does not have the real power.
fig'urine (*fig'yur-*), *n.* a small statuette.
figure of speech, an expression in which words are used in an unusual way for the purpose of making a striking effect (see **metaphor**).
to cut a figure, to make an impressive appearance.
[L. *figūra*; conn. root of **fiction**].

filament, *fil'ȧ-mėnt, n.* a thread-like object, e.g. the conductor in an electric light bulb (made to glow by the passage of current).
[Same root as **file** (1).]

filch, *filch, v.t.* to steal (something small).
[Origin unknown.]

file[1], *fīl, n.* a wire, etc., on which papers are strung: a folder, cabinet, etc., in which papers are kept: a list: a line of soldiers ranged behind one another.—*v.t.* to put on, or in, a file: to bring (a suit) before a law court.—*v.i.* to march, walk, in a file.
(in) single file, Indian file, (moving forward) singly, one behind another.
[L. *filum*, a thread.]

file[2], *fīl, n.* a steel instrument with rough surface for smoothing or rasping metals, etc.—*v.t.* to cut or smooth with a file.
fil'ing, *n.* a particle rubbed off with a file.
[O.E. *fīl.*]

filial, *fil'yȧl, -i-ȧl, adj.* of, suitable to, a son or daughter.
fil'ially, *adv.*
[L. *filius*, a son, *filia*, a daughter.]

filibuster, *fil'i-bus-tėr, n.* a pirate, or a military adventurer: (one who makes) a very long speech intended to hinder the passage of a law in a parliament, etc.—Also *v.i.*
[Sp. *filibustero*; root as **freebooter.**]

filigree, *fil'i-grē, n.* ornamental work in which threads of precious metal are interlaced: anything delicate.
[L. *filum*, thread, *granum*, a grain.]

Filipino, *fil-i-pē'nō, n.* a native of the *Philippine Islands*:—*fem.* **Filipi'na.**

fill, *fil, v.t.* to make full: to put (something) by degrees (into a container): to satisfy (a requirement): to supply (a vacant post): to occupy (time).—*v.i.* to become full.—*n.* as much as fills or satisfies.
fill'er, *n.*
fill'ing, *n.* anything used to fill up a hole, cavity, etc.
to fill in, to occupy (time): to complete (e.g. a form).
[O.E. *fyllan*; same root as **full.**]

fillet, *fil'it, n.* a band worn round the head: a thin narrow strip: a boneless slice of fish or meat.—*v.t.* to bone:—*pr.p.* **fill'eting**; *pa.p.* **fill'eted.**
[Fr. dim. *filet*; same root as **file** (1).]

fillip *fil'ip, n.* a jerk with a finger nail forced on and off the ball of the thumb: encouragement, a stimulus.
[A form of **flip.**]

filly, *fil'i, n.* a young mare:—*pl.* **-ies.**
[Dim. of *foal.*]

film, *film, n.* a thin skin or membrane: the sensitive coating of a photographic plate: a ribbon of celluloid with such a coating for ordinary photographs or for photographs for projecting by cinematograph: a motion picture: a slight haziness.—*v.t.* to cover with a film: to make a motion picture of.
fil'my, *adj.* very light and thin: misty:—*comp.* **fil'mier**; *superl.* **fil'miest.**
film star, a favourite cinematograph actor or actress.
[O.E. *filmen*; conn. with *fell*, a skin.]

filter, *fil'tėr, n.* a device or apparatus for freeing a liquid from solid matter: in photography, a device used to change the tone of certain colours.—*v.t.* to purify by means of a filter.—*v.i.* to pass through a filter, etc.: (of news) to leak out.
fil'ter-bed, *n.* a bed of sand, gravel, etc. used for filtering water or sewage.
See also **filtrate.**
[O.Fr. *filtre*—Late L. *filtrum*, felt.]

filth, *filth, n.* anything very dirty.
fil'thy, *adj.* **fil'thiness,** *n.*
[O.E. *fȳlth*; from root of **foul.**]

filtrate, *fil'trāt, v.t.* to filter.—*n.* a liquid that has been filtered. [**filter.**]

fin, *fin, n.* an organ by which fish, etc. balance and swim: a part of a mechanism like a fish's fin in shape or purpose.
finned, finn'y, *adjs.* [O.E. *finn.*]

final, *fī'nȧl, adj.* very last, with no repetition to follow: (of e.g. a decision) not to be questioned or altered.—*n.* last contest in knock-out competition: (in *pl.*) last

examination for a university degree, etc.
fin'ally, *adv.*
final'ity, *n.* quality of being final and decisive.
[L. *fīnālis—finis*, end.]

finale, *fi-nä'lā, n.* the end: the last movement in a musical composition: the last item in a concert.
[It.; from same L. root as **final.**]

finance, *fi-nans', fī-, n.* money affairs, esp. of a state or public body: (in *pl.*) money resources.—*v.t.* to provide money for.
finan'cial (*-shål*), *adj.* **finan'cially,** *adv.*
finan'cier (*-si-*), *n.* one skilled in finance.
[Late L. *fīnāre*, to pay a fine.]

finch, *finch, -sh, n.* any of a number of birds of the same family as the sparrows.
[O.E. *finc.*]

find, *fīnd, v.t.* to come upon or meet with: to discover: to succeed in obtaining (e.g. time, courage, to do something, or money for something): to declare after trial (e.g. *to find the prisoner guilty*):—*pr.p.* **find'ing**; *pa.t.* and *pa.p.* **found.**—*n.* something found, esp. of value or interest.
find'er, *n.* **find'ing,** *n.*
to find one's feet, to become able to cope readily with new conditions.
to find oneself, to come to full mastery of one's natural powers.
to find out, to discover by investigation or calculation: to detect (a person) in crime or fault, or to discover his true character.
[O.E. *findan.*]

fine[1], *fīn, adj.* excellent: not coarse: thin: delicate: slight, subtle (e.g. *a fine distinction,* a difference not easily seen or understood): (ironically) of high quality (e.g. *A fine mess you have made!*): containing a high proportion of precious metal (e.g. *fine gold*): sharp, keen.—*v.t.* to make fine.—*adv.* finely (usu. *coll.*): with little time, space, to spare.
fine'ly, *adv.* **fine'ness,** *n.*
fin'ery, *n.* fine or showy things.
fine arts, painting, sculpture, etc.
[L. *fīnītus*, finished; L. root as **finish.**]

fine[2], *fīn, n.* money to be paid as a punishment.—*v.t.* to impose a fine on.
in fine, in conclusion, in short.
[Late L. *fīnis*, a fine—L. *fīnis*, end.]

finesse, *fi-nes', n.* subtlety: cunning strategy.—Also *v.i.* [Fr.]

finger, *fing'gėr, n.* one of the five end parts of the hand: anything finger-shaped: a fingerbreadth.—*v.t.* to toy or meddle with: (music) to mark choice of fingers in playing.
fing'ering, *n.* touching: choice of fingers in playing music.
fing'er-board, *n.* the part of a musical instrument on which the fingers are placed.
fin'gerbreadth, *n.* a distance, height, measured by breadth of a finger.
fin'gernail, *n.* nail on finger.
fing'erpost, *n.* a signpost.
fing'erprint, *n.* an ink or other impression of the ridges of the finger tip used as a means of identification.
fing'erstall, *n.* a sheath for a finger.
a finger in (the pie), a share in (something being done).
to have (a subject) **at one's finger ends,** to be perfect master of it.
to put one's finger on, to point out exactly (e.g. *to put one's finger on the cause of the trouble*). [O.E.]

finical, *fin'i-kål, adj.* fussy, too particular about small details: (of things) with too much small detail.
fin'icking, fin'icky, *adjs.* finical.
[Prob. from **fine** (1).]

finish, *fin'ish, v.t.* to end: to complete the making of: to make perfect: to use up, etc., whole, or remainder, of: (*coll.*) to overcome or destroy: to complete the education of (a girl) before introduction to society.—*v.i.* to leave off: to end (in, by).—*n.* the end: the last touch: polish.
fin'ished, *adj.* not able for further effort, or capable of achieving further success: (of e.g. a performance, performer) polished, excellent.
[Fr. *finir, finissant*—L. root as **final.**]

finite, *fī'nīt, adj.* having an end or limit: applied to a part of a verb that has a subject (e.g. *He speaks,* but not *to speak,* or *speaking*).
[L. *fīnītus*; root as **finish, fine** (1), (2).]

Finn, *fin, n.* a native of Finland.
Finn'ish, *adj.*
[O.E. *Finnas,* Finns.]

finny. See **fin.**

fiord, fjord, *fyörd, n.* a long, narrow, rock-bound inlet. [Norw.]

fir, *fėr, n.* a cone-bearing tree valuable for its timber.
[O.E. *fyrh*; conn. with Ger. *föhre,* pine.]

fire, *fīr, n.* heat and light caused by burning: burning fuel in a grate, etc.: destructive burning (e.g. of house, forest): brightness of a gem: enthusiasm: discharge of firearms.—*v.t.* to set on fire: to bake, dry, etc., by heat: to fill with enthusiasm or inspiration (e.g. *The story fired his imagination*): to discharge (a gun, a missile): (*coll.*) to dismiss from a post.—*v.i.* to discharge firearms.
fir'ing, *n.* and *adj.*
See also **fiery.**
fire alarm, an apparatus for giving an alarm when fire breaks out.
fire'arm, *n.* (usu. in *pl.*) a weapon discharged by an explosion.
fire'brand, *n.* a piece of wood on fire: one who stirs up strife.
fire'brick, *n.* a brick made to resist high temperatures.
fire brigade, a company of men employed to put out fires.
fire'clay, *n.* a clay used in making firebricks.

fire′-damp, *n.* a gas that may catch fire in coal mines.
fire engine, a motor vehicle with equipment for fire fighting.
fire′-escape′, *n.* an iron stairway or other special means of exit from a building for use in case of fire.
fire extinguisher, an apparatus for putting out fires (usu. containing chemicals) that can be carried by one person.
fire′fly, *n.* insect, usu. a beetle, that gives off light by night.
fire′-i′ron (*-ėrn*), *n.* a fireside implement —e.g. a poker—not necessarily of iron.
fire′man, *n.* a man whose business it is to help in putting out fires: a man who tends the fires, e.g. of a steam engine.
fire′place, *n.* the place in a room where a fire is burned.
fire′-plug, *n.* a hydrant for use in case of fire.
fire′proof, *adj.* that will not burn easily: not easily cracked by strong heat.—*v.t.* to make fireproof.
fire′-rais′ing, *n.* the crime of arson.
fire′wood, *n.* wood for fuel.
fire′works, *n.pl.* a display of lights produced by exploding devices, usu. as entertainment: the materials for this (*sing.* used for one article): a display of temper, wit, etc.
firing line, area or troops within range of the enemy.
firing party, squad, a detachment told off to fire over the grave of one buried with military honours, or to shoot one sentenced to death.
[O.E. *fȳr.*]

firm[1], *fėrm, adj.* fixed: strong and steady: resolute.
firm′ly, *adv.* **firm′ness,** *n.*
[L. *firmus.*]

firm[2], *fėrm, n.* a business partnership or association.
[Same root as **farm.**]

firmament, *fėr′mȧ-mėnt, n.* the vault of the sky.
[L. *firmāmentum—firmus,* firm.]

first, *fėrst, adj.* before all others in place, time, or degree: most eminent: chief.—*adv.* before anything else, in time, space, rank, etc.
first′ly, *adv.* in the first place (e.g. *I can give three reasons for not going:—firstly, it is cold; secondly, it is wet; thirdly, I don't want to*).
first aid, treatment of a wounded or sick person before the doctor's arrival.
first′-born, *n.* the eldest child.—Also *adj.*
first′-class′, *adj.* of the best quality.
first fruits, the fruits first gathered in a season: the first profits or effects of anything.
first′-hand′, *adj.* obtained directly (e.g. *a first-hand account of the event,* account from someone who was present).
first′-rate, *adj.* of the highest excellence.
first water, the first or highest quality—used of diamonds and pearls.
[O.E. *fyrst,* superl. of *fore,* before.]

firth, *fėrth, n.* an arm of the sea, esp. a river mouth.
[Old Norse *fiörthr*; same root as **fiord.**]

fiscal, *fis′kȧl, adj.* of, concerning, the public revenue: of financial matters.—*n.* (*Scot.*) an officer who prosecutes in criminal cases in local and inferior courts—in full, *procurator-fiscal.*
[L. *fiscus,* a purse.]

fish, *fish, n.* a back-boned animal that lives in water, and breathes through gills: its flesh: (*coll.*) a person:—*pl.* **fish,** or **fish′es.**—*v.i.* to catch, or try to catch, fish: to search (for) under water, etc.: to try artfully to obtain (e.g. *to fish for information, for an invitation*).—*v.t.* to draw (out, up): to fish in (a stream).
fish′ing, *n.* and *adj.*
fish′er, fish′erman, *ns.*
fish′y, *adj.* of fish: like a fish: (*coll.*) suspicious, or improbable.
fish′iness, *n.*
fish′ery, *n.* the business of catching fish: a place for catching fish: the legal right to take fish:—*pl.* **fish′eries.**
fish′-hook, *n.* hook for catching fish.
fish′ing-line, *n.* a fibre cord used, with hook(s), etc., for catching fish.
fish′ing-rod, *n.* a long, tapering, easily bent, rod, usu. in sections, used along with fishing-line, etc.
fish′monger, *n.* one who sells fish.
fish′-slice, *n.* a broad-bladed implement for turning, or serving, fish.
to have other fish to fry, to have more important matters to attend to.
[O.E. *fisc.*]

fishplate, *fish′plāt, n.* an iron plate, one of a pair used to join railway rails.
[Prob. Fr. *fiche,* peg.]

fissile, *fis′il, adj.* that may be split.
fission, *fish′ȯn, n.* splitting.
fiss′ionable, *adj.* (of nuclei) fissile: (of material) having such nuclei.
fissure, *fish′ůr, n.* a narrow opening or split.
fission bomb, the atomic bomb, whose energy comes from splitting of nuclei of atoms.
[L. *findĕre, fissum,* to cleave.]

fist, *fist, n.* the closed or clenched hand.
fist′icuffs, *n.* boxing: blows.
[O.E. *fȳst.*]

fit[1], *fit, adj.* able (for): suitable (for): suitable or proper (e.g. *That is not a fit way to behave*): in good health:—*comp.* **fitt′er**; *superl.* **fitt′est.**—*v.t.* to be the right size or shape for (someone or something): to be suitable for (e.g. an occasion): to make (something) suitable.—Also *v.i.*:—*pr.p.* **fitt′ing**; *pa.p.* **fitt′ed.**—*n.* a thing that fits (e.g. *Your*

jacket is a good fit) : way in which a thing fits (e.g. *The fit of it is good*).
fit′ly, *adv.* suitably. **fit′ness,** *n.*
fitt′er, *n.* one who fits clothes : one who puts parts of machinery together.
fitt′ing, *adj.* that fits : suitable.—*n.* (usu. in *pl.*) a furnishing, fixture.
fitt′ingly, *adv.* suitably.
fit′ment, *n.* a furnishing, esp. if built-in.
to be fit to, to be in a state to (e.g. *to be fit to scream with rage*).
to fit out, to provide with all necessary clothes, or equipment, etc.
[Origin uncertain.]

fit[2], *fit, n.* an attack of illness, esp. epilepsy : an attack (of laughter, etc.) : a passing mood (e.g. *a fit of gloom*).
fit′ful, *adj.* coming in short spells.
fit′fully, *adv.* **fit′fulness,** *n.*
by fits and starts, in bursts with intervals between.
[O.E. *fitt*, a struggle.]

five, *fīv, adj.* and *n.* the number next above four (5 or V).
See **fifteen,** etc.
fiv′er, *n.* (*coll.*) a five-pound note.
[O.E. *fīf.*]

fives, *fīvz, n.pl.* any of several games played in a walled court with a ball struck by the hand in padded glove.
[Origin uncertain.]

fix, *fiks, v.t.* to place firmly, attach firmly : to direct steadily (e.g. *He fixed his eyes on the door*) : to settle definitely (e.g. *to fix the price*) : to make (a photograph) permanent by means of chemicals : (*coll.*) to put right, repair : (*coll.*) to arrange (a matter) dishonestly, or to bribe or silence (a person or persons).—*n.* (*coll.*) a difficulty.
fixed, *adj.* **fix′edly** (*-id-li*), *adv.*
fixā′tion, *n.* act of fixing : emotional development that stops too early in life : an obsession (see this).
fix′ative, *n.* something that sets colours.
fix′ture (*-chùr*), *n.* a furnishing or article of furniture that is fixed in position : an event arranged for a fixed time.
fixed stars, stars which appear always to occupy the same position in the sky—opp. to *planets.*
[L. *figĕre, fīxum*, to fix.]

fizz, *fiz, v.i.* to make a hissing sound.—*n.* any frothy drink.
fizz′y, *adj.* **fizz′iness,** *n.*
fizz′le, *v.i.* to hiss or splutter.
to fizzle out, to splutter and go out : to come to nothing. [Imit.]

fjord. See **fiord.**

flabbergast, *flab′ėr-gâst, v.t.* (*coll.*) to stun with surprise or disapproval.
[Perh. conn. with **flabby,** and **aghast.**]

flabby, *flab′i, adj.* soft, yielding : hanging loose.
flabb′ily, *adv.* **flabb′iness,** *n.* **[flap.]**

flag[1], *flag, v.i.* to grow tired or spiritless :—*pr.p.* **flagg′ing** ; *pa.p.* **flagged.**
[Perh. L. *flaccus*, flabby.]

flag[2], *flag, n.* a plant with sword-shaped leaves—an iris, or a reed.
[Origin uncertain.]

flag[3], *flag, n.* a piece of bunting, usu. with a design, used to show nationality, party, etc., or to mark a position, or to send information.—*v.t.* to signal, or signal to, by flag or hand.
flag′ship, *n.* the ship in which an admiral sails, and which carries the flag.
flag′staff, *n.* a pole on which a flag is hung. [Origin unknown.]

flag[4], *flag, n.* a flat paving-stone.
[Old Norse *flaga*, a slab.]

flagellation, *flaj-ėl-ā′sh(ȯ)n, n.* whipping or scourging.
[L. *flagellum*, a whip.]

flagon, *flag′ȯn, n.* a vessel with a narrow neck, handle, and lid, for liquids.
[Fr. *flacon.*]

flagrant, *flā′grȧnt, adj.* glaring, scandalous (e.g. *a flagrant error, fault, crime*).
fla′grancy, *n.* **fla′grantly,** *adv.*
[L. *flagrans, -antis*, burning.]

flail, *flāl, n.* an implement for threshing corn.—Also *v.t.*
[O.E. *fligel* ; L. root as **flagellation.**]

flair, *flār, n.* a talent, aptitude.
[Fr., 'scent'.]

flake, *flāk, n.* a small layer or film : a very small loose piece (e.g. of snow).—*v.t.* to form into flakes.—Also *v.i.*
flak′y, *adj.* **flak′iness,** *n.*
[Prob. Scand.]

flamboyant, *flam-boi′ȧnt, adj.* gorgeously coloured : too showy : intended to attract notice.
[Fr. *flamboyer*, to blaze.]

flame, *flām, n.* the gleam or blaze of fire : heat of rage, etc. : love.—*v.i.* to break out in flame.
flam′ing, *adj.* brilliant : violent.
flamm′able, *adj.* (*U.S.*, etc.) inflammable, easily set on fire.
[L. *flamma.*]

flamingo, *flȧ-ming′gō, n.* a water bird, pink or bright red, with long legs and neck :—*pl.* **flaming′o(e)s.**
[Sp. *flamenco*—L. *flamma*, a flame.]

flammable. See **flame.**

flan, *flan, n.* an open tart with custard, fruit, or other filling. [Fr.]

flange, *flanj, n.* an edge or rim, raised or sticking out.
[Prob. conn. with **flank.**]

flank, *flangk, n.* the side of an animal from ribs to thigh : the side or wing of an army, fleet, etc.—*v.t.* to pass round the side of : to be situated at the side of.
[Fr. *flanc.*]

flannel, *flan′(ė)l, n.* a warm soft cloth of wool or wool and other material : (in *pl.*) garments, esp. trousers, of this.

flannelette′, *n.* a cotton imitation of flannel.
[Perh. O.Fr. *flaine*, blanket.]

flap, *flap*, *n.* the blow, or the movement, of a broad loose object: anything broad and hanging loose.—*v.t.* and *v.i.* to move with a flap: to beat (wings):—*pr.p.* **flapp′ing**; *pa.p.* **flapped.** [Imit.]

flare, *flār*, *v.i.* to burn with a glaring, unsteady light: to widen out in a bell shape.—*n.* an unsteady glare: a flash: a sudden bright light used as a signal, etc.: a gradual widening, esp. of skirt.
to flare up, to blaze suddenly: suddenly to show anger.
flare′-up, *n.*
[Perh. Norw. *flara*, to blaze.]

flash, *flash*, *n.* a very brief gleam of light: a sudden short burst (e.g. of merriment): an instant of time: a distinctive mark on a uniform: a brief news dispatch by telegraph: in a film, a scene shown briefly as explanation or comment, esp. (**flash′-back**) a scene of the past.—*v.i.* to shine out suddenly: to burst out into violence.—*v.t.* to cause to flash.
flash′y, *adj.* showy, trying to be smart:—comp. **flash′ier**; *superl.* **flash′iest.**
flash′ily, *adv.* **flash′iness,** *n.*
flash′light, *n.* a sudden light used to take photographs: an electric torch.
[Imit.]

flask, *flâsk*, *n.* a narrow-necked vessel for liquid or powder, of metal, glass, etc.
[O.E. *flasce*.]

flat, *flat*, *adj.* smooth: level: stretched out: (of e.g. lemonade) no longer sparkling: tasteless: no longer blown up (*a flat tyre*): uninteresting: dull: (*music*) lower than the pitch intended or mentioned: downright (e.g. *a flat lie*):—*comp.* **flatt′er**; *superl.* **flatt′est.**—*n.* a level part: a plain: a tract covered by shallow water: a storey or floor of a house, esp. one, or part of one, as a separate residence: (*music*) a character (♭) which lowers a note a semitone.
flat′ly, *adv.* **flat′ness,** *n.*
flatt′en, *v.t.* and *v.i.* to make, or become, flat.
flat′fish, *n.* a fish (e.g. a sole) with flat body.
flat′-iron, *n.* an iron for smoothing cloth.
flat race, a race over level ground.
flat rate, a rate the same in all cases.
to flatten out, to bring an aeroplane into a horizontal course after a climb or dive.
[Old Norse *flatr*.]

flatter[1], **flattest.** See **flat.**

flatter[2], *flat′ėr*, *v.t.* to praise insincerely: to represent (a person, thing, etc.) as better, etc., than he, it, etc., really is (e.g. *The photograph flatters him*): to please (with false hopes).
flatt′erer, *n.* **flatt′ering,** *adj.*
flatt′ery, *n.* false praise:—*pl.* **-ies.**
[O.Fr. *flater*.]

flatulence, *flat′ū-lėns*, *n.* gas in the intestines.
[L. *flāre*, *flātum*, to blow.]

flaunt, *flönt*, *v.t.* and *v.i.* to show off.
[Prob. Scand.]

flautist, *flöt′ist*, *n.* a flute-player.
[It. *flautista*.]

flavour, *flā′vo̊r*, *n.* taste: interest: special quality.—*v.t.* to give flavour to.
flā′vouring, *n.* any substance used to give a flavour.
[O.Fr. *flaur*.]

flaw, *flö*, *n.* a break, crack: a defect.
flaw′less, *adj.* perfect.
[Old Norse *flaga*, a slab.]

flax, *flaks*, *n.* the fibres of a plant which are woven into linen cloth: this plant.
flax′en, *adj.* of, like, flax: light yellow. [O.E. *flæx*.]

flay, *flā*, *v.t.* to strip the skin off:—*pr.p.* **flay′ing**; *pa.p.* **flayed.**
[O.E. *flēan*.]

flea, *flē*, *n.* a blood-sucking insect that leaps.
[O.E. *flēah*; conn. **flee** and Ger. *floh*.]

fleck, *flek*, *n.* a spot or speckle.
[Old Norse *flekkr*.]

fled. See **flee.**

fledge, *flej*, *v.t.* to bring up (a bird) until it is ready to fly.
fledg(e)′ling, *n.* a bird just fledged.
[O.E. *flycge*, fledged—*flēogan*, to fly.]

flee, *flē*, *v.i.* to run away, esp. from danger.—*v.t.* to keep at a distance from:—*pr.p.* **flee′ing**; *pa.t.* and *pa.p.* **fled.**
See also **flight** (2).
[O.E. *flēon*.]

fleece, *flēs*, *n.* a sheep's coat of wool.—*v.t.* to clip wool from: to plunder, strip of possessions.
fleec′y, *adj.* woolly. **fleec′iness,** *n.*
[O.E. *flēos*.]

fleet[1], *flēt*, *n.* a number of ships, or aircraft, or motor cars, etc., in company: a division of the navy, commanded by an admiral: the navy.
[O.E. *flēot*, a ship—*flēotan*, to float.]

fleet[2], *flēt*, *adj.* swift, nimble.
fleet′ly, *adv.* **fleet′ness,** *n.*
[Prob. Old Norse *fliōtr*.]

fleeting, *flēt′ing*, *adj.* passing swiftly.
[O.E. *flēotan*, to float; conn. **fleet** (1).]

Fleet Street, *flēt strēt*, the press (from the street of that name which has many newspaper offices.)

Flemish, *flem′ish*, *adj.* of Flanders (west Belgium and part of France), its people, or its language.
[Du. *Vlaamsch*.]

flesh, *flesh*, *n.* the soft substance (muscle, etc.) that covers the bones of animals: animal food: the body: the soft substance of fruit.
flesh′ly, *adj.* of the body, not spiritual.
flesh′y, *adj.* fat. **flesh′iness,** *n.*
flesh and blood, human nature: kindred, relations.

in the flesh, alive: in person.
[O.E. *flǣsc.*]

fleur-de-lis, *flėr′-de-lē,* or *-lēs, n.* an ornament and heraldic device of the kings of France. [Fr.]

flew. See **fly.**

flex, *fleks, v.t.* and *v.i.* to bend.—*n.* a bending: a cord, esp. of insulated wire.
flexible, *fleks′i-bl, adj.* easily bent: easy to adapt: willing to change one's mind.
flex′ibleness, flexibil′ity, *ns.*
[L. *flectĕre, flexum,* to bend.]

flick, *flik, v.t.* to strike lightly.—*n.* a flip.
[Imit.]

flicker, *flik′ėr, v.i.* to flutter: to burn unsteadily.
[O.E. *flicorian*; imit.]

flier. See **fly.**

flight[1], *flīt, n.* act of passing through the air: distance travelled thus: a series (of steps): a flock (of birds) flying together: a volley (e.g. of arrows): passage (of time): soaring (of fancy): unit in Air Force, equivalent of platoon in army.
flight′less, *adj.* unable to fly.
flight′y, *adj.* changeable, acting according to the whim of the moment.
flight′iness, *n.*
flight′-lieuten′ant, *n.* rank in air force. See *Appendices.*
in the first flight, in the highest class.
See also **fly.**
[O.E. *flyht—flēogan,* to fly.]

flight[2], *flīt, n.* act of fleeing.
[M.E.; conn. **flee,** and Ger. *flucht.*]

flimsy, *flim′zi, adj.* thin: easily torn: weak (e.g. *a flimsy excuse*).—*n.* thin paper.
flim′sily, *adv.* **flim′siness,** *n.*
[Prob. suggested by **film.**]

flinch, *flinch, -sh, v.i.* to shrink back (from): to wince.
[Prob. conn. with L. *flectĕre,* to bend.]

fling, *fling, v.t.* to cast, toss, throw: to put suddenly.—*v.i.* to rush, dash:—*pr.p.* **fling′ing**; *pa.t.* and *pa.p.* **flung.**—*n.* a throw: a rather careless attempt: a spell of dissipation or pleasure: a lively dance.
[Old Norse *flengja.*]

flint, *flint, n.* a hard mineral from which fire is easily struck with steel: anything very hard or difficult to make an impression on. [O.E.]

flip, *flip, v.t.* and *v.i.* to flick: to flap.—*n.* a flick: a short flight.
flipp′er, *n.* a limb for swimming, as in seals, etc. [Imit.]

flippant, *flip′ȧnt, adj.* quick and pert in speech: frivolous.
flipp′ancy, flipp′antness, *ns.*
flipp′antly, *adv.* [Origin uncertain.]

flirt, *flėrt, v.t.* to move (a light article) jerkily.—*v.i.* to play at courtship: to trifle (with).—*n.* a man, or esp. woman, who is in the habit of flirting.
flirtā′tion, *n.* **flirtā′tious** (*-shu̇s*), *adj.*
[Imit.]

flit, *flit, v.i.* to flutter on the wing: to fly silently or quickly: to depart: (*Scot.*) to change one's house:—*pr.p.* **flitt′ing**; *pa.p.* **flitt′ed.**—Also *v.t.*
flitt′ing, *n.*
[Old Norse *flytja.*]

flitch, *flich, n.* the side of a hog salted and cured.
[O.E. *flicce.*]

flitter, *flit′ėr, v.i.* to flutter.
flitt′ermouse, *n.* a bat. [**flit.**]

float, *flōt, v.i., v.t.* to be, or cause to be, supported in or on a liquid: to drift: (*v.t.*) to launch (e.g. a scheme).—*n.* a raft: the cork on a fishing-line: a low cart: a platform on wheels.
flo(a)tā′tion, *n.* **float′ing,** *adj.* and *n.*
floating dock. See **dock.**
floating vote, voters not attached permanently to any one party.
[O.E. *flotian,* to float.]

flock[1], *flok, n.* a company, esp. of animals: a Christian congregation.—*v.i.* to come in crowds. [O.E. *flocc.*]

flock[2], *flok, n.* a lock of wool: woollen or cotton refuse.
[O.Fr. *floc*—L. *floccus.*]

floe, *flō, n.* a field of floating ice.
[Prob. Norw. *flo,* layer.]

flog, *flog, v.t.* to beat, strike, lash:—*pr.p.* **flogg′ing**; *pa.p.* **flogged.**
[Prob abbrev. of *flagellate,* to whip.]

flood, *flud, n.* a great flow of water: a deluge: the rise of the tide: any great quantity.—*v.t.* to overflow: to cover, or fill, as if with a flood.
flood′gate, *n.* a sluice.
flood′lighting, *n.* strong lighting from many points (*v.t.* **flood′light**).
flood′-tide, *n.* the rising tide.
[O.E. *flōd.*]

floor, *flōr, flör, n.* the part of a room on which we stand: platform: storey: any levelled area.—*v.t.* to make a floor in: to throw on the floor: (*coll.*) to defeat: to stump (e.g. *This question floored him*).
floor′ing, *n.* material for floors.
[O.E. *flōr.*]

flop, *flop, v.i.* to fall down suddenly.—*n.* a fall: a collapse: (*slang*) a failure. [**flap.**]

flora, *flō′rȧ, flö′rȧ, n.* the plants of a region or of a period: a list of these.
flo′ral, *adj.* of flowers.
floret, *flo′rit, n.* one of the closely packed small flowers that make up the head of a flower such as the daisy.
flo′rid (*flo′*), *adj.* flowery: too bright in colour: too richly ornamental.
flo′rist (*flo′*), *n.* a cultivator or seller of flowers.
See also **flour, flower.**
[L. *flōs, flōris,* a flower.]

florin, *flo′rin, n.* a cupro-nickel coin (orig. silver) worth 2 shillings (10 new pence).
[It. *fiorino.*]

floss, *flos, n.* a loose downy or silky substance from plant, or from outer part of silkworm cocoon: fine embroidery silk. [Prob. O.Fr. *flosche*, down.]

flotation. See **float.**

flotilla, *flō-til'ȧ*, *n.* a fleet of small ships. [Sp., dim. of *flota*, a fleet.]

flotsam, *flot'sȧm*, *n.* goods lost by shipwreck, and found floating on the sea. [O.Fr. *floter*, to float.]

flounce[1], *flowns*, *v.i.* to move suddenly or impatiently.—Also *n.* [Prob. conn. with Norw. *flunsa*, to hurry.]

flounce[2], *flowns*, *n.* a hanging strip gathered and sewed to the skirt of a dress. [O.Fr. *froncir*, to wrinkle.]

flounder[1], *flown'dėr*, *v.i.* to struggle awkwardly: to stumble helplessly in thinking or speaking. [Prob. **founder** and **blunder.**]

flounder[2], *flown'dėr*, *n.* a small flat fish. [From O.Fr.]

flour, *flowr*, *n.* finely ground meal of wheat or other grain: any fine soft powder.—*v.t.* to sprinkle with flour.

flour'y, *adj.* **flour'iness,** *n.* [Same word as **flower.**]

flourish, *flur'ish*, *v.i.* to grow luxuriantly: to prosper: to make ornamental strokes with the pen: to show off.—*v.t.* to brandish in show or triumph.—*n.* showy splendour: a mark made by a bold stroke of the pen: the waving of a weapon, etc.: a showy passage of music.

flour'ishing, *adj.* thriving: prospering. [Through O.Fr.—same root as **flora.**]

flout, *flowt*, *v.t.* to jeer at, treat with contempt. [Poss. M.E. *floute*, form of **flute.**]

flow, *flō*, *v.i.* to run, as water: to circulate, as blood: to move smoothly: to rise, as the tide: to be in great quantity: (of hair) to hang loose and waving.—Also *n.*

flow'ing, *adj.* [O.E. *flōwan.*]

flower, *flow'ėr*, *flowr*, *n.* the blossom of a plant, the part in which seed is formed: the best of anything: the prime of life.—*v.i.* to blossom: to flourish.

flow'ery, *adj.* full of, or adorned with, flowers: using, or containing, many fine-sounding words, figures of speech, etc.

flow'eriness, *n.* [L. *flōs, flōris*; same root as **flora.**]

flown. See **fly.**

flu, *flōō*, *n.* (*coll.*) abbrev. of **influenza.**

fluctuate, *fluk'tū-āt*, *v.i.* to move up and down or to and fro: to vary.

fluctuā'tion, *n.* [L. *fluctuāre*—*fluctus*, a wave.]

flue, *flōō*, *n.* a pipe for hot air, smoke, etc.: a small chimney. [Origin uncertain.]

fluent, *flōō'ėnt*, *adj.* able to express oneself quickly and easily (e.g. *He is a fluent speaker*): coming quickly and easily (e.g. *He spoke to her in fluent French*).

flu'ency, *n.* **flu'ently,** *adv.* [L. *fluens*—same root as **fluid.**]

fluid, *flōō'id*, *adj.* flowing: not solid, rigid, or stable: shifting: changing.—*n.* a substance whose particles can move about with freedom—a liquid or gas.

flu'idness, fluid'ity, *ns.* [L. *fluidus*—*fluĕre*, to flow.]

fluke[1], *flōōk*, *n.* a flounder: a worm causing a liver disease, esp. in sheep. [O.E. *flōc*, a plaice.]

fluke[2], *flōōk*, *n.* the part of an anchor that fastens in the ground. [Prob. from **fluke** (1).]

fluke[3], *flōōk*, *n.* an accidental success. [Origin unknown.]

flung. See **fling.**

flunkey, *flung'ki*, *n.* a footman: a cringing fellow. [Perh. *flanker*, one who runs alongside.]

fluor, *flōō'ȯr*, *n.* a mineral containing fluorine—also **flu'orspar.**

fluores'cence, *n.* the quality possessed by some varieties of fluor, etc., of giving out light under certain conditions.

fluores'cent, *adj.*

flu'oridate, *v.t.* to treat (drinking water) with a **flu'oride** (*-id*; a compound of fluorine and another element).

fluoridā'tion, *n.*

flu'orine, *n.* a pale greenish-yellow gas.

fluorescent lighting, brighter lighting obtained, for the same amount of electricity used, by having fluorescent material in the lamp. [L., flow (fluor is used as a flux); **fluid.**]

flurry, *flur'i*, *n.* a blast or gust: agitation: bustle.—*v.t.* to agitate, confuse:—*pr.p.* **flurr'ying**; *pa.p.* **flurr'ied.** [Imit.]

flush[1], *flush*, *n.* a flow of blood to the face: freshness, vigour (e.g. *in the first flush of youth*).—*v.i.* to become red in the face: to flow swiftly.—*v.t.* to make red in the face: to excite with joy (e.g. *flushed with victory*): to cleanse by a rush of water.—*adj.* well supplied with money. [Origin uncertain.]

flush[2], *flush*, *adj.* having the surface level (with another surface). [Prob. conn. with **flush** (1).]

flush[3], *flush*, *v.i.* (of birds) to start up and fly away.—*v.t.* to rouse (game birds).—*n.* a number of birds roused at one time. [M.E. *fluschen.*]

flush[4], *flush*, *n.* a run of cards all of the same suit. [Same root as **flux.**]

fluster, *flus'tėr*, *n.* flurry, agitation.—*v.t.* to make hot and confused. [Old Norse, *flaustr*, hurry.]

flute, *flōōt*, *n.* a musical wind instrument, a pipe with finger-holes and keys, blown through a hole in the side: a curved vertical furrow, e.g. on a pillar (called also **flut'ing**).—*v.i.* to play the flute.—*v.t.* to form grooves in.

flut'ist, *n.* See also **flautist.** [O.Fr. *fleüte.*]

flutter, *flut'ėr*, *v.i.* to flap the wings: to move in a quick irregular way: to be in

agitation or in uncertainty.—Also *v.t.*—*n.* a quick irregular motion: agitation: a gamble.
[O.E. *flotorian*, to float about.]

flux, *fluks, n.* act of flowing: act or state of changing: a flow of matter: a substance added to another to make it melt more readily.
[O.Fr.—same L. root as **fluid.**]

fly, *flī, v.i.* to move through the air, esp. on wings or in aircraft: to move swiftly: to pass away: to flee: to burst (e.g. *The glass flew into pieces*).—*v.t.* to avoid, flee from: to cause to fly: to cross by flying:—*pr.p.* **fly'ing**; *pa.t.* **flew** (*flōō*); *pa.p.* **flown** (*flōn*).—*n.* an insect with two transparent wings, esp. the common housefly: a fish-hook dressed to suggest a fly: a flap of material with buttonholes: a flap at the entrance to a tent: a light double-seated carriage: a flywheel: (in *pl.*) in a theatre, the part above the stage from which the scenes are controlled:—*pl.* **flies.**—*adj.* (*slang*) smart, knowing.
fly'er, flī'er, *n.*
fly'blow, *n.* the egg of a fly.
fly'blown, *adj.* tainted with these.
fly'ing-fish, *n.* a fish that can leap from water and stay in air for a short time.
fly'ing-fox, *n.* a large bat.
flying start, in a race, a start in which the signal is given after the competitors are in motion: a favourable beginning leading to an advantage over others or to rapid progress.
fly'leaf, *n.* a blank leaf at the beginning or end of a book.
fly'-over, *n.* a road or railway crossing above another.
fly'-pā'per, *n.* a sticky or poisonous paper for destroying flies.
fly'-past, *n.* a ceremonial flight of aircraft.
fly'-under, *n.* a road or railway crossing below another.
fly'weight, *n.* a boxer not heavier than 8 st.
fly'wheel, a large heavy wheel applied to machinery to keep the speed even.
flying doctor, a doctor, esp. orig. in remote parts of Australia, who can be called by radio and who flies to visit patients.
flying officer, rank in air force. See *Appendices.*
to fly in the face of, to defy, treat with contempt (person, custom, etc.)
to fly out, to break out in a rage.
to let fly, to hurl, shoot: (with *at*) to attack with missiles or words.
See also **flight** (1).
[O.E. *flēogan.*]

foal, *fōl, n.* the young of the horse, ass, etc. —*v.i., v.t.* to bring forth (a foal).
[O.E. *fola.*]

foam, *fōm, n.* froth: bubbles on the surface of liquor: (in poetry) the sea.—*v.i.* to gather foam: to run foaming (over, etc.): to be in a rage.
[O.E. *fām.*]

fob[1], *fob, v.t.* to foist (off upon): to put (off with).
[Akin to Ger. *foppen*, to jeer.]

fob[2], *fob, n.* a small pocket for a watch: a chain hanging from it.
[Perh. conn. with a Ger. word for pocket.]

fo'c'sle. Contr. form of **forecastle.**

focus, *fō'kus, n.* a point in which rays of light, etc., come together (e.g. light rays after passing through a lens): any central point:—*pl.* **fō'cuses, foci** (*fō'sī*). —*v.t.* to adjust (e.g. field-glasses) so as to get a clear picture: to bring (a picture) up clearly in this way: to direct to one point or subject (e.g. *The accident focused public attention on the necessity for a new road*):—*pr.p.* **fō'cus(s)ing**; *pa.p.* **fō'cus(s)ed.**
fō'cal, *adj.* having to do with a focus.
in (out of) focus, placed so as to give (or not to give) a clear picture.
[L. *focus*, a hearth.]

fodder, *fod'ėr, n.* food for cattle.
[O.E. *fodor*; conn. with **food, feed.**]

foe, *fō, n.* an enemy.
foe'man, *n.* an enemy in war:—*pl.* **foe'men.**
[M.E. *foo*—O.E. *fāh* (adj.).]

foetid, *fētid, adj.* Same as **fetid.**

foetus, fetus, *fē'tus, n.* the young animal in the egg or in the womb.
foe'tal, fē'tal, *adjs.*
[L. *fētus*, offspring.]

fog, *fog, n.* a thick mist: confusion or bewilderment.—*v.t.* to shroud in fog: to make indistinct, or difficult to understand:—*pr.p.* **fogg'ing**; *pa.p.* **fogged.**
fogg'y, *adj.* **fogg'iness,** *n.*
fog'-bank, *n.* a dense mass of fog.
fog'horn, *n.* a horn sounded as a warning signal in foggy weather: a deep, loud voice. [Origin uncertain.]

fogy, fogey, *fō'gi, n.* a dull, or old-fashioned, old fellow:—*pl.* **fogies, fogeys.** [Origin uncertain.]

foible, *foi'bl, n.* a failing, weakness.
[O.Fr. (*adj.*), weak; same root as **feeble.**]

foil[1], *foil, v.t.* to defeat, baffle (a person, an attempt):—*pr.p.* **foil'ing**; *pa.p.* **foiled.** —*n.* a light, blunt-edged sword with a button at the point, used in fencing.
[O.Fr. *fuler*, to stamp or crush.]

foil[2], *foil, n.* a leaf or thin plate of metal: a thin leaf of metal put under a precious stone to show it to advantage: any thing or person that serves as contrast for something or someone else.
[O.Fr.—L. *folium*, a leaf.]

foist, *foist, v.t.* to palm off (something undesirable on someone).
[Orig. of palming false dice; prob. Du. *vuisten*, to take in the hand.]

fold[1], *fōld, n.* a doubling of anything upon itself: a layer: a crease.—*v.t.* to lay in folds: to bring (wings) close to the body, (arms) together and close to the body: to clasp (one's hands): to wrap up: to embrace: (*cookery*) to mix lightly.

fold'er, *n.* a folding case for loose papers.

fold'ing, *adj.* that can be folded.

[O.E. *fealdan.*]

fold[2], *fōld, n.* an enclosure esp. for sheep: a flock of sheep in a fold: the Church, or a particular church.—*v.t.* to put into a fold.

[O.E. *falod, fald.*]

foliage, *fō'li-ij, n.* leaves.

folio, *fō'li-ō, n.* a leaf (two pages) of a book: a page number: a sheet of paper folded once: a book having pages of the largest size: a page in an account book, or two opposite pages numbered as one: *pl.* **fō'lios.**

[L. *folium*, a leaf.]

folk, *fōk, n.* people: one's own family:—*pl.* **folk, folks.**

folk'lore, *n.* the ancient beliefs, customs and traditions of the people.

folk song, tale, a song or story originating among the people and handed down by them.

[O.E. *folc.*]

follow, *fol'ō, v.t.* to go or come behind: to pursue: to come after: to result from: to go along (a road): to practise (a profession): to imitate: to obey (the rules): to act on (advice): to keep the eye or mind fixed on: to grasp or understand (e.g. *I do not follow your argument*).

foll'ower, *n.*

foll'owing, *n.* supporters.—*adj.* coming after or behind: about to be mentioned (e.g. *Pack the following articles:—3 cups, a spoon, sugar . . .*).

to follow up, to follow (an action) with others intended to increase e.g. an advantage.

[O.E. *folgian.*]

folly, *fol'i, n.* silliness or weakness of mind: a foolish action or thing:—*pl.* **foll'ies.**

[O.Fr. *folie.*]

foment, *fō-ment', v.t.* to apply a (usu.) warm liquid or damp cloth to: to stir up (e.g. strife).

fomentā'tion, *n.* act of fomenting, or the material used.

[L. *fōmentāre—fovēre*, to warm.]

fond, *fond, adj.* foolish (*fond hopes*): foolishly tender and loving: very affectionate: (with *of*) liking (e.g. *fond of animals, of sport, of boasting*).

fond'ly, *adv.* **fond'ness,** *n.*

fon'dle, *v.t.* to caress.

[M.E. *fonnen*, to act foolishly—*fon*, fool.]

fondant, *fon'dȧnt, n.* a soft sweetmeat that melts in the mouth.

[Fr. *fondre*, to melt.]

font, *font, n.* the, usu. stone, receptacle for holding baptismal water.

[O.E.—L. *fons, fontis*, fountain.]

food, *fōōd, n.* what one feeds on: nourishment: material for mental or spiritual activity (e.g. *This happening gave him food for thought*).

food'stuff, *n.* a material used as food.

[O.E. *fōda.*]

fool[1], *fōōl, n.* a person showing lack of ordinary sense: a person of weak mind: a jester.—*v.t.* to deceive.—*v.i.* to play the fool: to trifle.

fool'ish, *adj.* lacking common sense: weak in intellect: ridiculous.

fool'ishly, *adv.* **fool'ishness,** *n.*

fool'ery, *n.* foolish behaviour.

fool'hardy, *adj.* foolishly bold, rash.

fool'hardily, *adv.* **fool'hardiness,** *n.*

fool'proof, *adj.* that even a fool could understand: not likely to go wrong even if clumsily handled.

foolscap, *fōōlz'kap, n.* writing or printing paper, $17 \times 13\frac{1}{2}$ in., orig. bearing the watermark of a fool's cap and bells.

a fool's errand, a silly errand or one without result.

a fool's paradise, a state of happiness based on false beliefs or hopes.

[O.Fr. *fol*—L. *follis*, bellows.]

fool[2], *fōōl, n.* crushed fruit stewed, mixed with cream and sugar.

[Prob. **fool** (1).]

foolhardy, foolscap, etc. See **fool** (1).

foot, *foot, n.* the part of its body on which an animal stands or walks: the lower part: a measure, 12 inches (orig. the length of a man's foot): a division of a line of poetry:—*pl.* **feet** (**foot** in phrases such as *a ten-foot wall*).—*v.i.* (with *it*) to dance, to walk.—*v.t.* to attach a foot to (e.g. a sock): to pay (a bill):—*pr.p.* **foot'ing**; *pa.p.* **foot'ed.**

foot'ing, *n.* a foothold: foundation: position, conditions (e.g. *to be on a friendly footing with one's neighbours*).

foot'ball, *n.* (a game with) a large ball for kicking.

foot'board, *n.* board for getting in and out of vehicle, or one for driver's feet.

foot'fall, *n.* (the sound of) a footstep.

foot'hills, *n. pl.* lesser heights below high mountains.

foot'hold, *n.* a place on which to stand: a position from which to advance.

foot'light, *n.* one of a row of lights in front of and on a level with the stage in a theatre, etc.

foot'man, *n.* a servant in livery:—*pl.* **foot'men.**

foot'mark, foot'print, *ns.* the mark of a foot.

foot'note, *n.* note at foot of page referring to something in text above.

foot'pad, *n.* a highwayman on foot.

foot'-pass'enger, *n.* one who travels on foot.

foot'path, *n.* a path or way for pedestrians only.

foot'plate, *n.* the platform on which the driver of a locomotive engine stands.

foot'race, *n.* a race on foot.

foot'rule, *n.* a rule or measure marked in feet and inches.
foot'-soldier, *n.* one who marches and fights on foot.
foot'sore, *adj.* having painful feet because of much walking.
foot'step *n.* the mark, or sound, of a foot.
foot'wear, *n.* boots and shoes.
foot-and-mouth disease, a very serious, rapidly spreading, disease of cloven-footed animals (e.g. cows).
on foot, walking or running: in progress, happening.
to put one's foot down, to take a firm stand, to oppose or support something strongly.
to put one's foot in it, to blunder.
to set on foot, to set in motion (e.g. a plan).
[O.E. *fōt*, pl. *fēt*.]

fop, *fop, n.* an affected dandy.
fopp'ish, *adj.* **fopp'ishness,** *n.*
[Perh. conn. with Ger. *foppen*, to hoax.]

for, *för, fȯr, prep.* because of (e.g. *He wept for shame*): in payment of, or return for (e.g. £2.50 *for a book*; *a reward for his services*): on behalf of (e.g. *Please do it for me*): with a purpose as indicated (e.g. *He went for the milk*; *a case for holding books*): through the space or time of (e.g. *For seven miles he met no one*; *he walked for two hours*).—*conj.* because.
for all that, in spite of that. [O.E.]

forage, *for'ij, n.* food for horses and cattle: provisions.—*v.i.* to carry off fodder forcibly: to rummage about (for what one wants).
[O.Fr. *feurre*, fodder; orig. Germanic.]

foray, *for'ā, n.* a raid.
[Conn. in some way with **forage.**]

forbade. See **forbid.**

forbear[1], *fȯr-bār', v.i.* to be patient: to refrain (from: e.g. *We must forbear from making any comment*; also with infinitive; e.g. *He forbore to comment*):—*pa.t.* **forbore'**; *pa.p.* **forborne'.**
forbear'ance, *n.* patience, control of temper, long-suffering.
forbear'ing, *adj.*
[O.E. *forberan*.]

forbear[2]. Same as **forebear.**

forbid, *fȯr-bid', v.t.* to command not (to do): to prevent, make impossible:—*pa.t.* **forbade'** (*-bad'*); *pa.p.* **forbidd'en.**
forbidd'en, *adj.* prohibited: unlawful.
forbidd'ing, *adj.* raising dislike, unpleasant (e.g. *a forbidding appearance*).
[O.E. *forbēodan*.]

force[1], *fōrs, förs, n.* strength, power, energy: violence: power (of an argument) to convince: purpose, value: operation (e.g. *The rule has never been put into force*): a body of men prepared for action (e.g. *the police force*).—*v.t.* to push, draw, thrust, etc. by force: to gain by force (e.g. *to force an entry*): to compel (a person, an action; e.g. *forced him to go, forced a confession from him*): to cause (a plant) to grow or ripen rapidly.
forced, *adj.* accomplished by great effort (e.g. *a forced march*): unnatural (e.g. *His cheerfulness was rather forced*).
force'ful, *adj.* powerful, vigorous.
force'fully, *adv.* **force'fulness,** *n.*
forc'ible, *adj.* having force: done, carried out, by force.
forc'ibly, *adv.* **forc'ibleness,** *n.*
[L. *fortis*, strong.]

force[2], *fōrs, förs, v.t.* to stuff (e.g. a fowl).
force'meat, *n.* meat chopped fine and highly seasoned, esp. for stuffing.
[Fr. *farcir*; same root as **farce.**]

forceps, *för'seps, n.* a pincer-like instrument for holding or lifting.
[L. *formus*, hot, *capĕre*, to hold.]

ford, *fōrd, förd, n.* a place where water may be crossed on foot, on horseback, etc., or in vehicle.—Also *v.t.*
[O.E.; conn. with *faran*, to go.]

fore, *fōr, för, adj.* front (as in *fore wing*, or *forewing*, etc.).—*n.* the front (in phrase **to the fore,** in the front or an obvious place: ready: alive).—*adv.* at or towards the front of a ship.—*interj.* (*golf*) a warning cry to anybody in the way of the ball.
fore and aft, lengthwise of a ship.
[O.E.; conn. with **for.**]

fore-, *fōr-, för-, pfx.* before. [**before.**]

forearm[1], *fōr'ärm, för', n.* the part of the arm between elbow and wrist.
[Pfx. **fore-,** front part of, **arm** (1).]

forearm[2], *fōr-ärm', för-, v.t.* to arm or prepare beforehand. [Pfx. **fore-.**]

forebear, *fōr'bār, n.* (orig. *Scot.*) ancestor.
[Pfx. **fore-,** before, **be,** suffx. *-ar, -er.*]

forebode, *fōr-bōd', för-, v.t.* to be an omen of (e.g. *These early mishaps seemed to forebode a disastrous end to the expedition*).
forebod'ing, *n.* a feeling that something bad will happen. [Pfx. **fore-.**]

forecast, *fōr'kâst, för',* also *-kâst', v.t.* and *v.i.* to tell beforehand, predict (e.g. *He forecast good weather for the next three days*):—*pa.t.* and *pa.p.* **forecast.**—Also *n.*
[Pfx. **fore-,** and **cast,** to reckon.]

forecastle, fo'c'sle, *fōk'sl, n.* the forepart of a ship under the maindeck, the quarters of the crew. [Pfx. **fore-.**]

foreclose, *fōr-klōs', för-, v.t.* to take away from a person who has mortgaged property the right to redeem (the mortgage) and get his property back.
foreclos'ure (*-klōzh'ėr*), *n.*
[O.Fr. *forclos*, shut out.]

foredeck, *fōr'dek, för' n.* the forepart of a deck or ship. [Pfx. **fore-.**]

foredoom, *fōr-do͞om', för-, v.t.* to doom beforehand. [Pfx. **fore-.**]

forefather, *fōr'fä-THėr, för',* an ancestor. [Pfx. **fore-.**]

forefinger, *fōr'fing-gėr, för', n.* the finger next the thumb. [**fore, finger.**]

forefoot, *fōr'foot, fōr'*, *n.* one of the front feet of four-footed animal. [**fore, foot.**]

forefront, *fōr'frunt, fōr'*, *n.* the very front. [**fore, front.**]

forego[1], *fōr-gō', fōr-*, *v.t., v.i.* to go before—chiefly used in its *pr.p.* **forego'ing** and *pa.p.* **foregone'.**

foregone conclusion, a conclusion come to before study of the evidence: an inevitable result. [Pfx. **fore-.**]

forego[2], better **forgo** (see this word).

foreground, *fōr'grownd, fōr'*, *n.* the part of a picture or view nearest the observer's eye. [**fore, ground** (2).]

forehand, *fōr'hand, fōr'*, *adj.* made with the palm of the hand in front.—Also *n.* [**fore, hand.**]

forehead, *for'id, -ed,* or *-hed*, *n.* the part of the head above the eyes, the brow. [O.E. *forhēafod—hēafod*, head.]

foreign, *for'in, adj.* belonging to another country: concerned with dealings with countries other than one's own (e.g. *the Foreign Office, foreign exchange*): coming from an outside source (e.g. *a speck of dust or other foreign body in his eye*): not in keeping with (with *to*; e.g. *Deceit was foreign to her nature*).

for'eigner, *n.* a native of another country.

Foreign Office, the government department dealing with foreign affairs. [O.Fr. *forain*—L. *forās*, out of doors.]

forejudge, *fōr-juj', fōr-*, *v.t.* to judge before hearing the facts and proof. [Pfx. **fore-.**]

foreknowledge, *for-nol'ij, fōr-*, *n.* knowledge of a thing before it happens. [Pfx. **fore-.**]

foreland, *fōr'lȧnd, fōr'*, *n.* a headland. [**fore, land.**]

foreleg, *fōr'leg, fōr'*, *n.* a front leg. [**fore, leg.**]

forelock, *fōr'lok, fōr'*, *n.* the lock of hair on the forehead. [**fore, lock** (2).]

foreman, *fōr'mȧn, fōr'*, *n.* an overseer:—*pl.* **fore'men**:—*fem.* **fore'woman** (*pl.* **fore'women,** *-wim-in*). [**fore, man, woman.**]

foremast, *fōr'mâst, -mȧst, fōr'*, *n.* the mast that is next a ship's bow. [**fore, mast.**]

foremost, *fōr'mōst, fōr'*, *adj.* first in place, rank, or dignity.—Also *adv.* [O.E. *formest—forma*, first.]

forenoon, *fōr'nōōn, fōr-nōōn', fōr-*, *n*, the part of the day before midday. [Pfx. **fore-**].

forensic, *fō-ren'sik, adj.* belonging to courts of law. [L. *forensis—forum*, market place.]

forepart, *fōr'pärt, fōr'*, *n.* the front, or the early, part. [**fore, part.**]

forerunner, *fōr-run'ėr, fōr-*, *n.* a person or thing that goes, or happens, before. [Pfx. **fore-.**]

foresee, *fōr-sē', fōr-*, *v.t.* or *v.i.* to see or know beforehand:—*pa.t.* **foresaw'**; *pa.p.* **foreseen'.** [Pfx. **fore-.**]

foreshadow, *fōr-shad'ō, fōr-*, *v.t.* to indicate (a coming event), as a shadow in front shows an approaching object. [Pfx. **fore-.**]

foreshore, *fōr'shōr, fōr'*, *n.* the space between the high and low water marks. [Pfx. **fore-**, front part, **shore** (2).]

foreshorten, *fōr-shört'n, fōr-*, *v.t.* to cause (an object that sticks out towards the spectator) to appear as if shortened in the direction towards the spectator: to draw, etc. (an object) so as to show this apparent shortening. [**fore, shorten.**]

foresight, *fōr'sit, fōr'*, *n.* act of foreseeing: ability to see what is likely to happen: care for the future: a sight on the muzzle of a gun. [Pfx. **fore-.**]

forest, *for'ist, n.* a large tract of land covered with trees: a preserve for large game (*deer forest*).

for'ester, *n.* one who has charge of, or works in, a forest.

for'estry, *n.* the art of cultivating forests. [Late L. *forestis* (*silva*), outside (wood); i.e. not a park or walled-in wood.]

forestall, *fōr-stöl', fōr-*, *v.t.* to act before (someone), and so hinder his plans: to act before (something that is going to happen). [O.E. *foresteall*, an ambush.]

foretaste, *fōr'tāst, fōr'*, *n.* a slight experience beforehand (of something pleasant or unpleasant). [Pfx. **fore-.**]

foretell, *fōr-tel', fōr-*, *v.t.* to tell before, to predict:—*pa.t.* and *pa.p.* **foretold'.** [Pfx. **fore-.**]

forethought, *fōr'thöt, fōr'*, *n.* thought or care for the future. [Pfx. **fore-.**]

foretold. See **foretell.**

forever. See **ever.**

forewarn, *fōr-wörn', fōr-*, *v.t.* to warn beforehand. [Pfx. **fore-.**]

forewing. See **fore.**

forewoman. See **foreman.**

foreword, *fōr'wûrd, fōr'*, *n.* a preface. [**fore, word**; conn. Ger. *vorwort.*]

forfeit, *för'fit, v.t.* to lose the right to by some fault or crime: (*loosely*) to give up voluntarily (a right).—*n.* a penalty for a fault: a fine.

for'feiture, *n.* act of forfeiting: the thing forfeited. [O.Fr. *forfait*—Late L. *forisfacĕre*, to transgress.]

forgave. See **forgive.**

forge[1], *förj, n.* a furnace, esp. one in which iron is heated: a smithy: a place where anything is shaped or made.—*v.t.* to form by heating and hammering: to form: to counterfeit (e.g. a signature).—*v.i.* to commit forgery.

forg'er, *n.*

forg'ery, *n.* making or altering writing, or a picture, with the intention of deceiving:—*pl.* **forg'eries.** [O.Fr.—L. *fabrica*—same root as **fabric.**]

forge[2], *förj, fōrj, v.t.* to move steadily on (*to forge ahead*). [Origin uncertain.]

forget, *fór-get′, v.t.* to put away from the memory : to fail to remember, to neglect, omit :—*pr.p.* **forgett′ing**; *pa.t.* **forgot′**; *pa.p.* **forgott′en.**
forget′ful, *adj.* apt to forget : not thinking (of e.g. duty, other people).
forget′fully, *adv.* **forget′fulness,** *n.*
forget′-me-not, *n.* a small plant with blue flowers, regarded as the emblem of remembrance.
to forget oneself, to lose one's self-control or dignity.
[O.E. *forgietan.*]

forgive, *fór-giv′, v.t.* to pardon, or cease to feel resentment against (a person) : to pardon, overlook (a fault).—Also *v.i.* :—*pa.t.* **forgave′**; *pa.p.* **forgiv′en.**
forgive′ness, *n.* pardon.
forgiv′ing, *adj.* ready to pardon, merciful.
[O.E. *forgiefan.*]

forgo, *fór-gō′,* less correctly **forego,** *fōr-gō′, fòr-, v.t.* to give up, do without.
[Pfx. *for-*, not, and **go.**]

forgot, forgotten. See **forget.**

fork, *förk, n.* a pronged instrument : anything that divides into prongs or branches : one of the branches into which a road or river divides, also the point of separation.—*v.i.* to divide into two branches.
forked, fork′y, *adjs.* shaped like a fork.
[O.E. *forca*—L. *furca.*]

forlorn, *fór-lörn′, adj.* forsaken : wretched.
forlorn′ly, *adv.* **forlorn′ness,** *n.*
[O.E. *forloren,* pa.p. of *forlēosan,* to lose.]

forlorn hope, *fór-lörn′ hōp,* soldiers selected for service of uncommon danger : a desperate enterprise : a vain or faint hope.
[Du. *verloren hoop,* the lost troop.]

form, *förm, n.* shape : mode of arrangement : condition (e.g. *water in the form of ice*) : system (e.g. of government) : fixed procedure (e.g. *forms and ceremonies*) : a mere formality : a partly blank statement to be filled with details : a mould : a bench : a class in school : the bed of a hare.—*v.t.* to give shape to : to make : to conceive (an idea, opinion) in the mind : to develop (a habit).—*v.i.* to develop : to take up position in (a particular arrangement.)
for′mal, *adj.* according to the fixed procedure : marked by ceremony : stiff, coldly correct.
formal′ity, *n.* formal quality : a formal act :—*pl.* **formal′ities.**
for′mally, *adv.*
formā′tion, *n.* act of making : something that is formed : structure : prearranged order (e.g. *to fly in formation*).
form′ative, *adj.* giving form or shape.
See also **formula, formulate.**
[O.Fr. *forme*—L. *forma,* shape.]

format, *för′mat, n.* of books, etc., the size, shape, in which they are issued. [Fr.]

former, *för′mėr, adj.* before in time : past : first mentioned (of two).
form′erly, in former, past, times.
[Formed from O.E. *forma,* first.]

formidable, *för′mi-dȧ-bl, adj.* difficult to deal with.
for′midableness, *n.* **for′midably,** *adv.*
[Fr.—L. *formīdābilis*—*formīdō,* fear.]

formula, *förm′ū-lȧ, n.* a set form of words : a rule expressed in algebraic symbols : the composition of a substance expressed in chemical symbols :—*pl.* **form′ulas, form′ulae** (*-ē*).
form′ulate, *v.t.* to express in definite form : to make in detail (a plan).
[L. dim. of *forma*; same root as **form.**]

forsake, *fór-sāk′, v.t.* to desert : to give up :—*pr.p.* **forsāk′ing**; *pa.t.* **forsook′** : *pa.p.* **forsāk′en.**
[O.E. *forsacan*—*for-*, away, *sacan,* strive.]

forsooth, *fór-sōōth′, adv.* indeed (used mockingly ; e.g. *a wise plan, forsooth!*).
[**for,** and O.E. *sōth,* true.]

forswear, *fór-swār′, v.t.* to renounce, esp. upon oath.—*v.i.* (also, as *v.t.*, **forswear oneself**) to swear falsely :—*pa.t.* **forswore′**; *pa.p.* **forswōrn′** (*-ō-, -ö-*).
[Pfx. *for-*, not, **swear.**]

fort, *fōrt, fört, n.* a small fortress : an outlying trading-station.
fortify, *för′ti-fī, v.t.* to strengthen, esp. against attack or in readiness for an effort or ordeal :—*pr.p.* **for′tifying**; *pa.p.* **-fied.**
fortificā′tion, *n.* the art of strengthening a military position against attack : walls, etc. built to strengthen a position.
fortitude, *för′ti-tūd, n.* courage in enduring misfortune, pain, etc.
fortress, *för′tris, n.* a fortified place.
[L. *fortis,* strong.]

forte[1], *fōrt, fört, n.* something in which one excels.
[Fr. *fort,* strong.]

forte[2], *för′ti, adj., adv.* (*music*) loud :—*superl.* **fortis′simo,** very loud. [It.]

forth, *fōrth, förth, adv.* forward : onward : out : into the open.
forth′coming, *adj.* approaching in time : ready when required : (of a person) frank and sociable.
forth′right, *adj.* honest : downright.
forthwith′, *adv.* immediately. [O.E.]

fortieth. See **forty.**

fortification, fortified, fortify. See **fort.**

fortissimo. See **forte** (2).

fortitude. See **fort.**

fortnight, *fört′nīt, n.* two weeks.
[O.E. *fēowertēne niht,* fourteen nights.]

fortress. See **fort.**

fortune, *för′chùn, n.* whatever comes by chance, luck : prosperity, success : a large sum of money.
for′tunate (*-it*), *adj.* lucky.
for′tune-tell′er, *n.* one who pretends to foretell one's fortune.
for′tune-tell′ing, *n.*
[Fr.—L. *fortūna.*]

forty, *för'ti, adj.* and *n.* four times ten (40 or XL) :—*pl.* **for'ties.**
for'tieth (*-ti-ėth*), *adj.* last of forty.—*n.* one of forty equal parts.
forty winks, a short nap.
See also **four.**
[O.E. *fēowertig—fēower*, four, *tig*, ten.]

forum, *fōr'ům, för', n.* a market place, esp. that in ancient Rome where business was done and law cases were settled : a place, or opportunity, for discussion. [L.]

forward, *för'wȧrd, adv.* near, or to, the front (also **forwards**) : ahead : into view : into consideration (*to bring forward a suggestion*).—*adj.* near, or at the front : in an onward direction (e.g. *a forward movement*) : pert, bold.—*n.* a player in a forward position.—*v.t.* to send on (e.g. a letter) : to help on (e.g. a plan). [O.E. *foreweard.*]

fossil, *fos'il, n.* the remains of an animal or vegetable turned to stony substance : an old-fashioned person or thing.
foss'ilise, *v.t.* and *v.i.* to change into a fossil.
[L. *fossilis—foděre, fossum*, to dig.]

foster, *fos'tėr, v.t.* to bring up : to help to grow or develop, encourage.
fos'ter-broth'er, -child, -daugh'ter, etc., *ns.* child brought up with a family of different parentage.
fos'ter-fa'ther, -moth'er, -pa'rent, *ns.* one who brings up a child in place of its father, mother.
[O.E. *fōstrian*, to nourish.]

fought. See **fight.**

foul, *fowl, adj.* filthy : impure : obscene : stormy (*foul weather*) : against the rules (e.g. *a foul stroke*).—*v.t.* to make foul : to collide with : to become entangled with.—*n.* a breach of the rules in a game.
foully, *fowl'li, adv.* **foul'ness,** *n.*
foul play, unfair action in a game : dishonesty : murder.
to fall foul of, to come against : to quarrel with : to assault.
See also **filth.**
[O.E. *fūl.*]

found[1]. See **find.**

found[2], *fownd, v.t.* to build or base (e.g. *a house founded on a rock* ; *a story founded on fact*) : to start, establish, set up (e.g. *He left money to found a college*).
found'er, *n.*
foundā'tion, *n.* the act of founding : the base of a building : the basis (e.g. *The foundation of this rumour was a remark someone had misunderstood*) : a permanent fund for some special object.
foundation stone, one of the stones forming the foundation of a building.
well founded, reasonable : based on fact.
[L. *fundāre—fundus*, the bottom.]

found[3], *fownd, v.t.* to form by melting and pouring into a mould, to cast.
found'er, *n.*
found'ry, *n.* the place where founding is carried on :—*pl.* **-ries.**
[L. *funděre*, to pour ; root as **fuse.**]

founder[1], *fownd'ėr, v.i.* to collapse : to fill with water and sink.
[L. *fundus*, bottom.]

founder[2,3]. See **found** (2), (3).

foundling, *fownd'ling, n.* a small child found deserted.
[From **found,** *pa.p.* of **find.**]

foundry. See **found** (3).

fount, *fownt, n.* a spring of water : a source.
fount'ain (*-in*), *n.* a structure for producing a jet or jets of water : water spouting e.g. from this : a spring or source.
fount'ain-head, *n.* the source, the beginning.
fountain pen, a pen having a reservoir for holding ink.
[L. *fons, fontis*, a spring.]

four, *fōr, fôr, adj.* and *n.* the number next above three (4 or IV).
fourth, *adj.* last of four.—*n.* one of four equal parts.
four'teen (also *-tēn'*), *adj.* and *n.* four and ten (14 or XIV).
four'teenth (also *-tēnth'*), *adj.* last of fourteen.—*n.* one of fourteen equal parts.
See also **forty.**
four'-foot'ed, *adj.* having four feet.
four'-hand'ed, *adj.* of a game, played by four people.
four'-post'er, *n.* a large bed with four posts on which to hang curtains.
four'score, *adj.* four times a score—80.
four'some, *adj.* in which four act together (also *n.*).
four'square', *adj.* square : presenting a firm, bold front to all.
on all fours, on hands and knees : exactly like, strictly able to be compared (with).
[O.E. *fēower, fēowertēne.*]

fowl, *fowl, n.* a bird : a bird of the poultry kind, a cock or hen : the flesh of a fowl : —*pl.* **fowls, fowl.**—*v.i.* to kill, or try to kill, wild fowl (wild duck, etc.).
fowl'er, *n.* one who shoots or snares wild fowl.
[O.E. *fugol.*]

fox, *foks, n.* an animal akin to the dog (*fem.* **vix'en**) : a cunning person.
fox'y, *adj.* **fox'iness,** *n.*
fox'glove, *n.* a plant (*Digitalis*) with flowers like glove fingers.
fox'hole, *n.* a small hole in which one, or two, men can hide.
fox'hound, *n.* a hound for hunting foxes.
fox terrier, a terrier sometimes trained to unearth foxes.
fox'trot, *n.* a dance to syncopated music.
[O.E. *fox* ; fem. *fyxen.*]

foyer, *fwä'yā, n.* (in theatres) a lobby, an anteroom for waiting, etc.
[Fr.—L. *focus*, hearth.]

fracas, *frak'ä, n.* uproar : a noisy quarrel. [Fr.]

fraction, *frak'sh(ȯ)n, n.* a fragment, a small part : any part of a unit. e.g. $\frac{2}{3}$, $\frac{5}{8}$.
frac'tional, *adj.*
[Same root as **fracture.**]

fractious, *frak'shủs, adj.* ready to quarrel, peevish : difficult to manage.
frac'tiously, *adv.* **frac'tiousness,** *n.*
[**fraction** in old sense of quarrelling.]

fracture, *frak'chủr, v.t.* to break or crack.—*n.* the breaking of any hard body, esp. a bone : the part broken.
[L. *frangĕre, fractum,* to break.]

fragile, *fraj'il, adj.* easily broken : frail : delicate.
fragil'ity, *n.*
See also **frail.**
[L. *fragilis* ; same root as **fracture.**]

fragment, *frag'mėnt, n.* a piece broken off : a very small part.
frag'mentary (or *-men'*), *adj.* consisting of fragments.
[L. *fragmentum* ; same root as **fracture.**]

fragrant, *frā'grȧnt, adj.* sweet-scented.
frā'grance, frā'grancy, *ns.*
[L. *frāgrāre,* to smell.]

frail, *frāl, adj.* very easily shattered : weak in health : morally weak.
frail'ness, frail'ty (*pl.* **frail'ties**), *ns.*
[O.Fr. *fraile* ; same L. root as **fragile.**]

frame, *frām, v.t.* to form : to put together : to plan : to articulate (e.g. *He could scarcely frame the words*) : to enclose in a frame : to serve as a frame for.—*n.* a structure made to enclose or support anything : the skeleton : state (of mind).
fram'ing, *n.*
frame'work, *n.* the skeleton or outline of anything.
[O.E. *framian,* to be helpful.]

franc, *frangk, n.* the standard coin of France : also standard coins of Belgium and Switzerland.
[O.Fr. ; from words *Francorum Rex* (King of the Franks) on first coins.]

Franco-, (as part of word) French.

franchise, *fran'chīz, -shīz, n.* a right granted, esp. that of voting for a member of Parliament.
[O.Fr.—*franc,* free.]

frank, *frangk, adj.* open, candid, outspoken.—*v.t.* to mark by means of a **franking machine** to show that postage has been paid.
frank'ly, *adv.* **frank'ness,** *n.*
[O.Fr. *franc*—Late L. *francus,* free—the people called *Franks.*]

frankincense, *frangk'in-sens, n.* a sweet-smelling resin from Arabia.
[O.Fr. *franc encens,* pure incense.]

frantic, *fran'tik, adj.* mad : furious : desperate.
fran'tically, *adv.* **fran'ticness,** *n.*
See also **frenzy.**
[Gk. *phrenētikos,* mad—*phrēn,* mind.]

fraternal, *frȧ-tėr'nȧl, adj.* brotherly.
frat'ernise, *v.i.* to associate as brothers or friends.
frater'nity, *n.* a society of people having common interests :—*pl.* **-ies.**
fratricide, *frat'ri-sīd, n.* one who kills his brother : murder of a brother.
[L. *frāter,* brother (*caedĕre,* to kill).]

fraud, *fröd, n.* deceit : imposture : dishonesty : (*coll.*) a cheat, impostor : something that is not what it pretends to be.
fraud'ulent (*-ū-lėnt*), *adj.*
fraud'ulently, *adv.*
fraud'ulence, fraud'ulency, *ns.*
[L. *fraus, fraudis,* fraud.]

fraught, *fröt, adj.* laden, filled.
[Prob. Old Du. *vracht* ; conn. **freight.**]

fray[1], *frā, n.* a conflict : a brawl. [**affray.**]

fray[2], *frā, v.t.* to ravel out the edge of.—Also *v.i.*
[Fr. *frayer*—L. *fricāre,* to rub.]

freak, *frēk, n.* a sudden caprice or fancy : a prank : an abnormal natural object or occurrence.—*adj.* abnormal (e.g. *a freak storm, result*).
freak'ish, *adj.* apt to change the mind suddenly : very odd, like a freak.
[Origin uncertain.]

freckle, *frek'l, v.t.* to spot : to colour with spots.—*n.* a brownish-yellow spot on the skin : any small spot.
freck'ly, freck'led, *adjs.*
[Old Norse *freknur* (pl.).]

free, *frē, adj.* not bound : at liberty : not under a tyrannical government : unrestrained : frank : ready (e.g. *free to confess*) : lavish : not attached : exempt (from) : without payment : (of e.g. a translation) not word for word.—*v.t.* to set at liberty : to release from anything that restrains : to rid (with *from, of*) :—*pr.p.* **free'ing** ; *pa.p.* **freed.**
free'ly, *adv.* **free'ness,** *n.*
free'dom, *n.* liberty : absence of control or interference by other person or persons : absence of restraint on one's movements : exemption from (e.g. *freedom from taxation*) : privileges connected with a city : frankness, outspokenness.
free and easy, informal.
free fight, a mixed up fight in which a number of people take part.
free'-for-all', *n.* (*U.S.*) a race or contest open to anyone, or a free fight.
free'-hand, *adj.* (of drawing) done by hand alone, without help of instruments.
free'-hand'ed, *adj.* open-handed, liberal.
free'-heart'ed, *adj.* open-hearted : generous.
free'hold, *adj.* (of an estate) belonging to the holder or his heirs for all time, not just for a given number of years.
free'-lance', *adj.* and *n.* (a person who is) active in public affairs but not attached to any party, or (a journalist who is) not regularly employed by one newspaper.
free'man, *n.* one who is free, not a slave :

one who has received the freedom of a city, etc. :—*pl.* **free′men.**

free′māson, *n.* a member of a secret order whose aims are to encourage friendly feeling and mutual help.

free′māsonry, *n.* the system and practices of the freemasons: the sense of fellowship between or among people having the same interests.

free on board (F.O.B.), delivered to the vessel or other conveyance without charge.

free′thinker, *n.* a person who wants to form his own opinions, esp. in matters of religion.

free trade, foreign trade without customs duties or other restrictions.

free verse, verse in lines of irregular length.

free′-wheel′, *n.* the mechanism of a bicycle by which the back wheel can be disconnected and set free from the driving gear.—*v.i.* to use this mechanism, to coast.

free′will′, *n.* liberty of choice: power of acting freely.

a free hand, liberty to choose for oneself, or to act as one thinks best.

to make free with, to take liberties with (a person, possessions of another).

[O.E. *frēo*; conn. Ger. *frei.*]

freebooter, *frē′boot-ėr, n.* a pirate.

[Du. *vrij*, free, *buit*, booty.]

freeze, *frēz, v.i.* to become ice: to become solid from cold: to be very cold: to become motionless, stiff (e.g. *to freeze with terror*): to become fixed (to) by cold.—Also *v.t.* :—*pr.p.* **freez′ing**; *pa.t.* **froze**; *pa.p.* **froz′en.**

freezing point, the temperature at which a liquid becomes solid—that of water being 32° Fahrenheit, 0° centigrade.

[O.E. *frēosan.*]

freight, *frāt, n.* the load, cargo, of a ship, etc.: the charge for transporting goods by water, land, or air.—*v.t.* to load.

freight′er, *n.* a ship or aircraft used to carry freight.

[Prob. O.Du. *vrecht*; conn. **fraught.**]

French (in names of things sometimes spelt **french**), *french, -sh, adj.* of France or its people.—*n.* the people or language of France.

French′man, *n.* a native of France :—fem. **French′woman.**

French chalk, a soft mineral (soapstone) used in dry-cleaning, etc.

French polish, a varnish for furniture.

French window, a long window opening like a door.

to take French leave, to depart secretly without warning.

frenzy, *fren′zi, n.* a violent excitement: a fit of madness.

fren′zied, *adj.* **fren′ziedly,** *adv.*

[Gk. *phrenītis*, inflammation of brain—*phrēn*, mind; conn. with **frantic.**]

frequent, *frē′kwėnt, adj.* coming or occurring often.—*v.i.* (*frė-kwent′*) to visit often.

fre′quently, *adv.* **frequent′er,** *n.*

fre′quency, *n.* repeated occurrence: commonness of occurrence: the number per second of vibrations, waves, etc. :—*pl.* **fre′quencies.**

[L. *frequens*, crowded.]

fresco, *fres′kō, n.* a painting done on walls covered with damp plaster.

[It. *fresco*, fresh.]

fresh, *fresh, adj.* untired: blooming, healthy: new: another (e.g. *a fresh chapter*): (of wind) strong: (*slang*) making unwanted advances: without salt: (of food) not preserved: (*Scot.*) not frosty.

fresh′ly, *adv.* **fresh′ness,** *n.*

fresh′en, *v.t.* and *v.i.* to make, or become, fresh.

fresh′er, (1) *comp.* of **fresh,** (2) see **freshman.**

fresh′et, *n.* a pool or stream of fresh water: the sudden overflow of a river from rain or melted snow.

fresh′man, *n.* a university student in his first year (also **fresh′er**).

fresh′water, *adj.* living in water that is not salt.

[O.E. *fersc*; conn. Ger. *frisch.*]

fret[1], *fret, v.t.* to eat into: to wear away by rubbing: to ripple (water): to vex.—*v.i.* to wear, fray: to be discontented or unhappy :—*pr.p.* **frett′ing**; *pa.p.* **frett′ed.**

fret′ful, *adj.* peevish.

fret′fully, *adv.* **fret′fulness,** *n.*

[O.E. *fretan*, to gnaw—*etan*, to eat.]

fret[2], *fret, v.t.* to carve or make a network of straight lines on :—*pr.p.* **frett′ing**; *pa.p.* **frett′ed.**

fret′-saw, *n.* a saw with narrow blade and fine teeth, used for fretwork, etc.

fret′work, *n.* ornamental carved work: perforated woodwork.

[O.Fr. *frete*, trellis-work.]

fret[3], *fret, n.* a short ridge on the fingerboard of a guitar or other instrument.

[Prob. same as **fret** (2).]

friable, *frī′ȧ-bl, adj.* apt to crumble, easily reduced to powder.

frī′ableness, friabil′ity, *ns.*

[L. *friāre*, to crumble.]

friar, *frī′ȧr, n.* a member of a mendicant (see this word) monastic order.

frī′ary, *n.* a convent of friars.

[O.Fr. *frere*—L. *frāter*, brother.]

fricassee, *frik-a-sē′, n.* a dish of fowl, rabbit etc., cut up and served in sauce.

[Fr. *fricassée*; origin unknown.]

friction, *frik′sh(ȯ)n, n.* rubbing: resistance of a moving body to sliding, rolling, etc. caused by its surface and the surface of the body along which it moves: disagreement, strife.

[L. *fricāre*, *frictum*, to rub.]

Friday, *frī'di, n.* sixth day of the week.
[O.E. *Frīgedæg,* day of (goddess) *Frigg.*]
fridge, *frij, n.* a refrigerator.
fried. See **fry** (1).
friend, *frend, n.* an intimate acquaintance, a well-wisher, helper, supporter.
friend'less, *adj.* without friends.
friend'ly, *adj.* like a friend: kind, showing friendship: favourable.
friend'liness, *n.*
friend'ship, *n.* attachment from mutual liking: friendly assistance.
[O.E. *frēond*; conn. with *frēon,* to love.]
frieze[1], *frēz, n.* a heavy woollen cloth.
[Fr. *frise.*]
frieze[2], *frēz, n.* a decorative band along the top of the wall of a room.
[O.Fr. *frize.*
frigate, *frig'it, n.* orig. a light vessel driven by oars or sails: at different periods, name applied to different types of warship.
[O.Fr. *fregate*—It. *fregata.*]
fright, *frīt, n.* sudden fear: terror: (*coll.*) a person of ridiculous appearance.
fright'en, *v.t.* to make afraid, alarm: to scare (away, off).
fright'ful, *adj.* terrible, shocking: (*coll.*) very great.
fright'fully, *adv.* **fright'fulness,** *n.*
[O.E. *fyrhto*; conn. Ger. *furcht.*]
frigid, *frij'id, adj.* frozen: cold.
frigid'ity, frig'idness, *ns.*
frigid zones, the parts of the earth's surface within the Arctic and Antarctic circles.
[L. *frīgidus*—*frīgus,* cold.]
frill, *fril, n.* a trimming made from a strip of cloth gathered along one side: (in *pl.*) unnecessary adornment, or affectation.
[Origin unknown.]
fringe, *frinj, n.* a border of loose threads: hair cut falling over the brow: border outer edge, of area or group.—*v.t.* to border.
[O.Fr. *frenge*—L. *fimbriae,* threads.]
frisk, *frisk, v.i.* to gambol, leap playfully.—*v.t.* (*slang*) to search the pockets, etc., of (a person).
frisk'y, *adj.* lively, frolicsome.
frisk'ily, *adv.* **frisk'iness,** *n.*
[O.Fr. *frisque.*]
fritter[1], *frit'ėr, n.* a piece of fruit, etc. fried in batter.
[O.Fr. *friture*—*frire,* to fry.]
fritter[2], *frit'ėr, v.t.* (often **fritter away**) to squander, waste little by little.
[Prob. old *fitters,* rags, fragments.]
frivolous, *friv'ō-lŭs, adj.* trifling, silly, not serious: fond of gaiety.
friv'olously, *adv.* **friv'olousness,** *n.*
frivol'ity, *n.* silly, trifling nature (e.g. *the frivolity of this objection*): something that is frivolous or gay:—*pl.* **frivol'ities.**
[L. *frivolus.*]
frizz, friz, *friz, v.t.* and *v.i.* to form into, or become, small short crisp curls.—*n.* curl: a mass of curls.
frizzle[1], *friz'l, v.t., v.i., n.* curl.
[O.Fr. *friser,* to curl.]
frizzle[2], *friz'l, v.t.* to fry: to scorch.
[Perh. from **fry** (1), imitating sound.]
fro, *frō, adv.* away, back, in phrase **to and fro,** to a place and back again: first in one direction, then in the other.
[Old Norse *frā.*]
frock, *frok, n.* a monk's wide-sleeved garment: a woman's or child's dress.
frock coat, a double-breasted knee-length coat for men.
[O.Fr. *froc*—Late L. *frocus.*]
frog, *frog, n.* a tailless webfooted animal living part of life in water, part on land.
frog'man, *n.* a diver with devices like a frog's webbed feet attached to his own feet to help him in swimming under water.
[O.E. *frogga*; conn. Ger. *frosch.*]
frolic, *frol'ik, n.* a prank: a merrymaking.—*v.i.* to play pranks: to be merry, have fun:—*pr.p.* **frol'icking**; *pa.p.* **-icked.**
frol'icsome, *adj.* gay, playful.
[Du. *vrolijk,* merry.]
from, *from, prep.* meanings include:—out of: springing out of: beginning at.
[O.E. *fram, from.*]
frond, *frond, n.* a leaf of a palm or fern.
[L. *frons, frondis,* a leaf.]
front, *frunt, n.* the face, or forepart, of anything: the foremost line or position: the scene of actual fighting: the forces struggling for a political or other object: something worn on the chest: demeanour, bearing (e.g. *to present a bold front to the enemy*): land along the edge of sea, river, etc.: the bounding surface between two masses of air of different temperature, etc.—Also *adj.*—*v.t.* to stand in front of or opposite: to oppose face to face: to add a front to.—*v.i.* to face.
front'age, *n.* the front part of a building, or the length of this: the ground in front.
front'al, *adj.* of, belonging to, or in, the front (e.g. *to make a frontal attack*).
L. *frons, frontis,* the forehead.]
frontier, *frun'tyėr* (or *fron'*), *n.* the boundary of a country: (chiefly *U.S.*) the border of settled country.—Also *adj.*
fron'tiersman, *n.* a dweller on a frontier.
[O.Fr. *frontier*; same root as **front.**]
frontispiece, *frun'tis-pēs* (or *fron'*-), *n.* a picture in front of a book before the text.
[L. *frons, frontis,* forehead, *specĕre,* see.]
frost, *frost, n.* temperature at or below freezing point of water: minute particles of ice on a surface.—*v.t.* to cover with frost or something that looks like frost.
fros'ty, *adj.*:—*comp.* **fros'tier**; *superl.* **fros'tiest.**
fros'tily, *adv.* **fros'tiness,** *n.*
fros'ted, *adj.* frostlike in appearance (as glass that has been roughened).

frost′bite, *n.* injury to part of the body by severe cold.
frost′bitten, *adj.*
[O.E. *frost, forst.*]

froth, *froth, n.* foam.—*v.t.* to cause froth on.—*v.i.* to throw up froth.
froth′y, *adj.* full of froth: like froth: (of e.g. talk) empty, meaning little:—*comp.* **froth′ier**; *superl.* **froth′iest.**
froth′ily, *adv.* **froth′iness,** *n.*
[Old Norse *frotha.*]

frown, *frown, v.i.* to wrinkle the brow in anger, disapproval, or deep thought.—Also *n.*
frown′ing, *adj.* disapproving: gloomy.
to frown upon, to disapprove of.
[O.Fr. *froignier.*]

frowsty, *frow′sti, adj.* fusty.
frowzy, frowsy, *frow′zi, adj.* fusty: dingy: untidy, neglected.
[Origin unknown.]

froze, frozen. See **freeze.**

frugal, *froo͞′gȧl, adj.* economical: costing little, scanty (e.g. *They lived on frugal fare*).
fru′galness, frugal′ity, *ns.*
fru′gally, *adv.*
[L. *frūgālis—frux, frūgis,* fruit.]

fruit, *froo͞t, n.* the produce of the earth that is suitable for food: the part of a plant that contains the seed(s): product, result (e.g. *the fruit of his hard work*).—*v.i.* to produce fruit.
fruit′erer, *n.* one who sells fruit.
fruit′ful, *adj.* producing much fruit: producing good results.
fruit′less, *adj.* useless, without result.
fruit′fully, *adv.* **fruit′lessly,** *adv.*
fruit′y, *adj.* like fruit, esp. in taste — *comp.* **fruit′ier**; *superl.* **fruit′iest.**
[O.Fr.—L. *fructus—fruī,* to enjoy.]

fruition, *froo͞-ish′(ȯ)n, n. orig.* pleasurable use or possession: realisation, attainment (e.g. *the fruition of our hopes*).
[O.Fr.—L. *fruī,* to enjoy.]

frump, *frump, n.* a plain, dowdy woman.
[Origin uncertain.]

frustrate, *frus-trāt′,* or *frus′, v.t.* to thwart, to defeat, bring to nothing (e.g. *to frustrate one's efforts*).
frustrat′ed (or *frus′*), *adj.* thwarted: filled with a sense of disappointment and discouragement.
frustrā′tion, *n.*
[L. *frustrā,* in vain.]

fry[1], *frī, v.t.* and *v.i.* to cook in oil or fat: to burn, scorch:—*pr.p.* **fry′ing**; *pa.p.* **fried.**—*n.* a dish of something fried.
[Fr. *frire*—L. *frīgĕre.*]

fry[2], *frī, n.* a swarm of fishes just spawned: young of salmon in their second year.
small fry, persons or things of little importance.
[Old Norse *friō.*]

fuchsia, *fū′shi-ȧ, n.* a shrub with long hanging flowers, native to South America.
[Leonard *Fuchs,* German botanist.]

fuddle, *fudl, v.t.* to stupefy with drink.—*v.i.* to drink far too much.
[Origin uncertain.]

fudge, *fuj, n.* nonsense: a soft sweetmeat.—*v.t.* to patch up: to fake.
[Origin uncertain.]

fuel, *fū′ėl, n.* anything that feeds a fire, supplies energy, etc.—*v.t.* and *v.i.* to supply with, or to take in, fuel.
[O.Fr. *feuile*—L. *focus,* fireplace.]

fugitive, *fūj′i-tiv, adj.* running away: passing swiftly.—*n.* one who is running away (e.g. *a fugitive from justice*).
[L. *fugitīvus—fugĕre,* to flee.]

fugue, *fūg, n.* a musical composition in which a theme or melody is taken up by a number of different parts or voices in turn.
[Fr.—It. *fuga*—L. *fuga,* flight.]

fulcrum, *ful′krum, n.* the prop or fixed point on which a lever moves:—*pl.* **ful′crums, ful′cra.** [L.]

fulfil, *fool-fil′, v.t.* to carry out (e.g. a command, a promise): to satisfy (e.g. a requirement): to realise completely (e.g. *This fulfilled his hopes*):—*pr.p.* **fulfill′ing**; *pa.p.* **fulfilled′.**
fulfil′ment, *n.*
[O.E. *full,* full, *fylan,* to fill.]

full[1], *fool, adj.* holding as much as can be contained: with plenty (of; e.g. *a purse full of money*): complete (e.g. *a full year*): swelling: plump: (of clothes) with ample material.—*adv.* fully: exactly, directly (e.g. *It hit him full in the face*).—Also *n.* (e.g. *in full*; see below).
full′y, *adv.* completely. **ful(l)′ness,** *n.*
full-blood′ed, *adj.* vigorous, hearty: of unmixed blood.
full-blown′, *adj.* (of a flower) fully opened out: fully developed.
full dress, the dress worn on occasions of ceremony.
full′-dress′, *adj.* important, formal: with attention to every detail (e.g. *a full-dress investigation*).
full′-face′, *adj.* showing the front of the face completely.—Also *adv.* and *n.*
full′(y)-fash′ioned (*-ȯnd*), *adj.* (of knitted garments) made so as to fit the curves of the body exactly.
full′-length, *adj.* of the usual length: (of e.g. a portrait) showing the whole length.
full moon, (the time when) the whole moon (is) lit up.
full′-scale, *adj.* carried out with all forces, equipment, etc.: covering everything.
full stop, a point marking the end of a sentence.
full of (a subject), eager to talk about it.
in full, without reduction (e.g. *paid in full*): without abbreviation.
in the fullness of time, at the proper or destined time.
[O.E.; conn. Old Norse *fullr,* Ger. *voll.*]

full[2], *fool*, *v.t.* to scour and thicken (cloth). **full'er,** *n.* [L. *fullō*, a cloth fuller.]

fulminate, *ful'min-āt*, *v.i.* to speak violently (against; e.g. *He fulminated against these laws*).
[L. *fulmen*, lightning.]

fulsome, *ful'sŭm*, *fool'*, *adj.* overdone (e.g. *fulsome praise*): disgusting.
[**full** (1), and suffx. *-some.*]

fumble, *fum'bl*, *v.i.* to grope about awkwardly: to use the hands awkwardly.—*v.t.* to handle awkwardly: (games) to drop, fail to catch (the ball)
fum'bler, *n.* **fum'bling,** *n.* and *adj.*
[Du. *fommelen.*]

fume, *fūm*, *n.* smoke or vapour (often in *pl.*), esp. if strong smelling.—*v.i.* to give off fumes: to be in a rage.
fum'igate, *v.t.* to expose to fumes, esp. in order to disinfect.
fumigā'tion, *n.* **fum'igator,** *n.*
[L. *fūmus*, smoke.]

fun, *fun*, *n.* merriment: joking.
funny, *fun'i*, *adj.* full of fun, laughable: perplexing, odd:—*comp.* **funn'ier**; *superl.* **funn'iest.**
funn'ily, *adv.* **funn'iness,** *n.*
funny bone, a nerve in the elbow (because of the tingling sensation produced by a blow on it).
for fun, in fun, as a joke.
to make fun of, to laugh at, ridicule.
[Prob. old verb *fon*, make a fool of.]

function, *fungk'sh(ȯ)n*, *n.* a formal social gathering (e.g. a public dinner): proper or expected activity (e.g. *The function of the heart is to keep the blood circulating*), or duty (e.g. *One function of the Speaker of the House of Commons is to see that rules are observed*).—*v.i.* to perform a function: to operate.
func'tional, *adj.* of, or concerned with, a function (e.g. *A functional disease is one that affects the activity of an organ of the body*): capable of acting: (of e.g. a building) designed with a view to practical usefulness rather than attractive appearance.
func'tionary, *n.* an official:—*pl.* **-ies.**
[L. *fungī*, *functus*, to perform.]

fund, *fund*, *n.* a sum of money for a special purpose: a store laid up (e.g. *a fund of stories, of common sense*): (in *pl.*) money available for spending.
[L. *fundus*, bottom, estate.]

fundamental, *fun-dȧ-ment'ȧl*, *adj.* underlying, essential (e.g. *fundamental principles*): complete, affecting everything (e.g. *a fundamental change in his views*).—*n.* something that serves as a groundwork, an essential part.
fundament'ally, *adv.* at bottom, essentially (e.g. *The men were fundamentally different: one fundamentally honest, the other thinking first of what would be most profitable*).
[L. *fundamentum*; root as **found** (2).]

funeral, *fū'nėr-ȧl*, *n.* (the ceremony of) burial or cremation.
funereal, *fū-nē'ri-ȧl*, *adj.* of, or suiting, a funeral: dismal, mournful.
[L. *fūnus*, *fūněris*, a funeral procession.]

fungus, *fung'gŭs*, *n.* a plant that has no green colouring matter and has to live on dead or living plants or animals—e.g. mushrooms, moulds:—*pl.* **fungi** (*fun'jī*), **fun'guses.**
fungicide, *fun'ji-sīd*, *n.* a substance that kills fungi.
fungicid'al, *adj.*
fun'goid, *adj.* fungus-like.
[L. *fungus*, a mushroom.]

funicular (railway), *fū-nik'ū-lȧr*, a cable railway esp. one going up a hill.
[L. *fūniculus*, dim. of *fūnis*, rope.]

funk, *fungk*, *n.* (*coll.*) a state of terror: a coward.—*v.t.* and *v.i.* to shirk through fear. [Origin uncertain.]

funnel, *fun'l*, *n.* a passage for escape of smoke, etc.: a vessel, usu. a cone ending in a tube, for pouring fluids into bottles, etc.
funn'elled, *adj.* having funnel(s).
[Prob. through Fr.—L. *fundĕre*, to pour.]

funnily, funny, etc. See **fun.**

fur, *fûr*, *n.* the thick, soft, fine hair of certain animals: their skins with the hair attached: a garment, esp. a shoulder wrap, of fur: a fur-like coating.
furred, *adj.* having fur, or fur-like coating.
furr'y, *adj.* covered with fur: like fur.
furr'iness, *n.*
furr'ier, *n.* a dealer in furs.
[O.Fr. *forre*, *fuerre*, sheath.]

furbelow, *fûr'bė-lō*, *n.* a plaited border or flounce: a showy ornament.
[Fr. (in *pl.*), It., and Sp. *falbala.*]

furbish, *fûr'bish*, *v.t.* to rub until bright.
to furbish up, to restore, renovate (something old).
[O.Fr. *fourbir*; a Germanic word.]

furious, -ly, -ness. See **fury.**

furl, *fûrl*, *v.t.* to roll up. [Orig. uncertain.]

furlong, *fûr'long*, *n.* one-eighth of a mile.
[O.E. *furh*, furrow, *lang*, long.]

furlough, *fûr'lō*, *n.* leave of absence.
[Du. *verlof.*]

furnace, *fûr'nis*, *n.* an enclosed structure in which great heat is produced.
[L. *fornex*—*fornus*, an oven.]

furnish, *fûr'nish*, *v.t.* to fit up (e.g. a room): to supply (a person with something): to provide (e.g. food, reasons, an excuse).
fur'nishings, *n.pl.* fittings, esp. furniture.
furniture, *fûr'ni-chŭr*, *n.* movables, in e.g. a house, such as chairs, tables.
[O.Fr. *furnir*, *furnissant.*]

furore, *fū-rōr'ā*, *-rōr'*, *fū'rōr*, *-rōr*, *n.* a craze: wild general excitement, enthusiasm, or anger. [It.]

furrow, *fûr'ō*, *n.* the trench made by a plough: a groove: a wrinkle.—*v.t.* to form furrows in: to wrinkle.—Also *v.i.* [O.E. *furh.*]

further, *fûr'*THė*r*, *adv.* (*comp.* of **far**—see this word) at or to a greater distance or degree: (also) in addition.—*adj.* more distant: (also) additional.—*v.t.* to help on (e.g. a plan).

fur'therance, *n.* a helping forward.

fur'thermore, *adv.* moreover, besides.

fur'thest, fur'thermost. See **far.**

[O.E. *furthra* (adj.), *fyrthan* (vb.).]

furtive, *fûr'tiv, adj.* stealthy: secret.

fur'tively, *adv.* **fur'tiveness,** *n.*

[L. *furtīvus*—*fūr*, a thief.]

fury, *fū'ri, n.* rage: violent passion: madness: a fierce, violent woman:—*pl.* **-ies.**

fu'rious, *adj.* very angry: violent.

fu'riously, *adv.* **fu'riousness,** *n.*

[L. *furia.*]

furze, *fûrz, n.* gorse, whin.

[O.E. *fyrs.*]

fuse[1], *fūz, v.t.* to join by melting together: to unite into a whole.—*v.i.* to be reduced to a liquid: to blend: (of electric light) to go out by melting of a fuse.—*n.* a bit of fusible metal inserted as a safeguard in an electric circuit.

fus'ible, *adj.* that can be fused or melted.

fusion, *fū'zh(ȯ)n, n.* act of melting: a close union of things, as if melted together.

fusion bomb, the hydrogen bomb, whose energy comes from fusion of hydrogen nuclei to become helium nuclei.

[L. *fundĕre, fūsum*, to melt.]

fuse[2], *fūz, n.* any device for causing an explosion to take place at a certain time chosen beforehand, esp. a train of explosive material enclosed in a waterproof cord: see **fuze.**

[It. *fuso*—L. *fūsus*, a spindle.]

fuselage, *fūz'ėl-àzh*, or *-ij, n.* the body of an aeroplane.

[Fr.—L. *fūsus*, a spindle.]

fusilier, fusileer, *fū-zi-lēr', n.* an old word used in the names of certain regiments.

fusillade (*-lād'*), *n.* a discharge of numbers of firearms together or continuously: a volley (of missiles): an outburst (e.g. of questions).

[O.Fr. *fuisil*, a type of musket.]

fusion. See **fuse** (1).

fuss, *fus, n.* unnecessary bustle or agitation: complaints or protests.—*v.i.* to be agitated about unimportant things.—*v.t.* to agitate (a person).

fuss'y, *adj.* making a fuss: in the habit of doing so: too particular: (of clothes, etc.) with too much trimming, etc.:—*comp.* **fuss'ier**; *superl.* **fuss'iest.**

fuss'ily, *adv.* **fuss'iness,** *n.*

[Origin unknown.]

fusty, *fus'ti, adj.* having a mouldy, musty smell:—*comp.* **fus'tier**; *superl.* **fus'tiest.**

fus'tily, *adv.* **fus'tiness,** *n.*

[O.Fr. *fust*, cask.]

futile, *fū'tīl, -til, adj.* useless, producing no result.

fu'tilely, *adv.*

fu'tileness, futil'ity (*-til'*) *ns.*

[Fr.—L. *fūtilis*—*fundĕre*, to pour.]

future, *fū'chùr, adj.* about to be: that is to come.—*n.* time to come.

futurity, *fū-tū'ri-ti, n.* time to come: event(s) yet to come.

[L. *futūrus*, used as part of *esse*, to be.]

fuze. Spelling of **fuse** (2), esp. for a mechanical or electronic device to explode a shell, bomb, rocket, etc.

fuzz, *fuz, n.* fine light particles, as dust: fluff.—*v.t., v.i.* to cover, or become covered, with fine particles.

fuzz'y, *adj.* fluffy: blurred:—*comp.* **fuzz'ier**; *superl.* **fuzz'iest.**

fuzz'ily, *adv.* **fuzz'iness,** *n.*

[Origin uncertain.]

G

gab, *gab, n.* (*coll.*) idle chatter.—Also *v.i.*

[Origin uncertain.]

gabble, *gab'l, v.i.* to talk very quickly.—Also *n.*

gabb'ler, *n.* **gabb'ling,** *n.*

[Perh. **gab.**]

gaberdine, *gab'ėr-dēn*, **gabardine,** *n.* (long ago) a loose cloak: a twill fabric, esp. of cotton and wool.

[O.Fr. *gauvardine.*]

gable, *gā'bl, n.* the triangular part of an outside wall of a building between the top of the side wall and the slopes on the roof.

[Prob. Old Norse *gafl.*]

gad, *gad, v.i.* to rove restlessly or idly (often with *about*):—*pr.p.* **gadd'ing**; *pa.p.* **gadd'ed.**

gad'about, *n.* a person who gads.

[Origin uncertain.]

gadfly, *gad'flī, n.* a blood-sucking fly that distresses cattle:—*pl.* **gad'flies.**

[Old Norse *gaddr*, spike, and **fly.**]

gadget, *gaj'it, n.* a small (usu. clever) device or object. [Origin uncertain.]

Gael, *gāl, n.* a Scottish Highlander.

Gaelic, *gāl'ik, gal'ik, adj.* of the Gaels.—*n.* an ancient Celtic language, that of the Scottish Highlands: also that of Ireland (**Irish Gaelic**).

[Gael. *Gaidheal.*]

gaff, *gaf, n.* a hook for landing large fish.
[Fr. *gaffe.*]
gaffer, *gaf'ėr, n.* orig. a word of respect for an old man : the foreman of a squad of workmen.
[**godfather** or **grandfather.**]
gag, *gag, v.t.* to stop the mouth of (a person) forcibly : to compel to keep silence.—*v.i.* to introduce *gag* into a play :—*pr.p.* **gagg'ing** ; *pa.p.* **gagged.**—*n.* something thrust into a person's mouth to force him to be silent : (*slang*) words put into a part by an actor : a joke, hoax.
[Prob. imit. of sound of choking.]
gage[1], *gāj, n.* something thrown down as a challenge to fight : a pledge.
[O.Fr. *guage*, pledge ; conn. with **wage.**]
gage[2]. See **gauge.**
gaieties, gaiety, gaily. See **gay.**
gain, *gān, v.t.* to earn : to win : to obtain : to reach (e.g. *He managed at length to gain the shore*).—*v.i.* to profit : to improve, or appear better.—*n.* something gained : profit.
gain'er, *n.*
gain'ful, *adj.* profitable. **gain'fully,** *adv.*
to gain (up)on, to overtake by degrees.
[O.Fr.]
gainsay, *gān-sā', gān'sā, v.t.* to contradict : to deny :—*pa.t.* and *pa.p.* **gainsaid** (*-sād', -sed'*).
[O.E. *gegn*, against, and **say.**]
gait, *gāt, n.* way of walking.
[Old Norse *gata*, a way.]
gaiter, *gā'tėr, n.* a covering for the ankle, fitting down upon the shoe.
[Fr. *guêtre.*]
gala, *gä'la, gā'la, n.* a festivity, fête.
[Fr.—It. *gala*, finery.]
galantine, *gal'ȧn-tēn, -tin, n.* poultry, veal, etc., served cold in jelly.
[Fr. ; same root as **gelatine.**]
galaxy, *gal'ȧk-si, n.* (usu. *cap.*) the Milky Way, a band of stars stretching across the heavens : any similar system of stars : a splendid gathering of people :—*pl.* **gal'axies.**
[Gk. *galaxias—gala, galaktos*, milk.]
gale, *gāl, n.* a strong wind.
[Origin uncertain.]
Galilean, *gal-i-lē'ȧn, adj.* of *Galilee.*
gall[1], *göl, n.* bile : bitterness of feeling.
gall bladder, a cavity in the body containing bile.
gall'stone, *n.* a hard body formed in the gall bladder or bile ducts.
[O.E. *galla, gealla.*]
gall[2], *göl, n.* a growth produced by an insect, esp. on oaks.
[Fr. *galle*—L. *galla* (a type of oak gall).]
gall[3], *göl, n.* a sore due to rubbing.—*v.t.* to roughen, chafe, hurt by rubbing : to irritate.
gall'ing, *adj.* very annoying. [**gall** (1).]
gallant, *gal'ȧnt, adj.* brave : noble : splendid (e.g. *a gallant ship*) : attentive to ladies (also *gȧ-lant'*).—*n.* a man of fashion : suitor.
gall'antly, *adv.* **gall'antness,** *n.*
gall'antry, *n.* bravery : attention to ladies (often in bad sense) :—*pl.* **-ies.**
[Fr. *galant.*]
galleon, *gal'i-ȯn, gal'yȯn, n.* (*history*) a large Spanish sailing ship.
[Sp. *galeón.*]
gallery, *gal'ėr-i, n.* a long passage, or long narrow room : an upper floor of seats, esp. (in a theatre) the highest : the occupants of the gallery : any body of spectators (e.g. at a golf match) : a room or building for exhibition of works of art : a horizontal underground passage : —*pl.* **gall'eries.**
to play to the gallery, to play for the applause of the least cultured.
[O.Fr. *galerie*—It. *galleria.*]
galley, *gal'i, n.* a long, low ship with one deck, moved by oars (and often sails) : a ship's kitchen : (*printing*) an oblong tray holding type that has been arranged for printing :—*pl.* **gall'eys.**
galley slave, (long ago) a person forced to row in a galley : an overworked person.
[O.Fr. *galie*—Late L. *galea.*]
galling. See **gall** (3).
gallivant, *gal-i-vant', v.i.* to gad about.
[Perh. **gallant.**]
gallon, *gal'ȯn, n.* a measure of quantity of liquid. See *Appendices.*
[O.Fr. *jalon.*]
gallop, *gal'ȯp, n.* a horse's swiftest pace.—*v.i.* and *v.t.* to go, or cause to go, at a gallop :—*pr.p.* **gall'oping** ; *pa.p.* **gall'oped.**
[O.Fr. *galop.*]
gallows, *gal'ōz, n.* a wooden frame on which criminals are hanged.
gall'ows-bird, *n.* one who deserves hanging.
[M.E. *galwes* (pl.).]
gallstone. See **gall** (1).
Gallup poll, *gal'ŭp pōl*, a method of testing public feeling or opinion used by an American, George *Gallup.*
galop, *gal'ȯp, n.* a lively dance or dance tune. [Fr.]
galore, *gȧ-lōr', -lör', adv.* in abundance.
[Ir. *go, leōr.*]
galosh, *gȧ-losh',* **golosh,** *n.* an overshoe, now usu. of rubber.
[Fr. *galoche* ; origin uncertain.]
galvanise, *gal'vȧn-īz, v.t.* to stimulate by an electric current : to rouse suddenly to action : to coat (e.g. iron) with zinc.
[Luigi *Galvani*, Italian scientist.]
gambit, *gam'bit, n.* a chess opening in which a player sacrifices a pawn or piece in order to gain an advantage : an opening move, esp. of this type, in conversation, in a transaction, etc.
[It. *gambetto*, a tripping up—*gamba*, leg.]
gamble, *gam'bl, v.i.* to play for money : to

risk money, etc. on a result that depends on chance.—Also *n.*
to gamble away, to lose by gambling.
to gamble on (a happening), to take risks in the expectation that it will occur.
[Conn. **game** (1).]

gambol, *gam'bȯl, n., v.i.* leap, skip :—*pr.p.* **gam'bolling** ; *pa.p.* **gam'bolled.**
[Earlier *gambold*—Late L. *gamba*, a leg.]

game[1], *gām, n.* an amusement or sport : (in *pl.*) athletic sports : a contest in sport, or a division of it, or the number of points required for a win : animals, etc. hunted for sport : the flesh of some of these.—*adj.* of game animals : plucky.—*v.t.* and *v.i.* to gamble.
gam'ing, *n.* gambling.
game'ster, *n.* a gambler.
gam'y, *adj.* having the flavour of game, esp. game kept till tainted :—*comp.* **gam'ier** ; *superl.* **gam'iest.**
game'cock, *n.* cock trained to fight.
game'keeper, *n.* one who has care of game.
game preserve, reserve. See **preserve, reserve.**
the game is not worth the candle, the result is not worth the effort, expense, etc.
the game is up, the scheme has failed.
to make game of, to make fun of.
[M.E. *gamen* ; conn. with Old Norse.]

game[2], *gām, n.* lame. [Origin uncertain.]

gamin, *gam'in, n.* a street urchin : a small roguish boy :—*fem.* **gamine** (*gam-ēn', gam'*).—Also *adjs.* (the *fem. adj.* sometimes means 'small, pert, with elfish charm'). [Fr.]

gamma, *gam'a, n.* the third letter of the Greek alphabet.
gamma rays, powerful radiation given off by radium and other radioactive substances. [Gk.]

gammon, *gam'ȯn, n.* smoked or cured ham : the lower end of a cured leg of bacon.
[M.E. *gambon*—O.Fr. *gambe, jambe*, leg.]

gamut, *gam'ut, n.* the whole range of a voice or instrument : the full range of anything (e.g. of emotions).
[Mediaeval Latin.]

gamy. See **game** (1).

gander, *gan'dėr, n.* the male goose.
[O.E. *ganra, gandra.*]

gang, *gang, n.* a number of labourers, etc. working together : a band of people (usu. formed for a bad purpose).
gang'ster, *n.* a member of a gang of criminals or roughs.
[O.E. *gangan*, to go.]

ganglion, *gang'gli-ȯn, n.* a small lump on the sheath of a tendon, esp. on wrist or ankle. [Gk.]

gangrene, *gang'grēn, n.* death of a part of the body.
[Gk. *gangraina*, perh. *grainein*, to gnaw.]

gangway, *gang'wā, n.* a passage into, out of, or through, a place : a movable bridge from ship to shore.
[O.E. *gangweg* ; same root as **gang.**]

gannet, *gan'it, n.* a large web-footed bird of northern seas, a solan goose.
[O.E. *ganot.*]

gantry, *gan'tri, n.* a stand for barrels : a platform for a travelling crane, etc. : a structure supporting railway signals :—*pl.* **gan'tries.**
[Old word *gaun* (=gallon), **tree.**]

gaol, gaoler. Spellings of **jail, jailer.**

gap, *gap, n.* a break, opening, vacant space.
[Old Norse.]

gape, *gāp, v.i.* to open the mouth wide : to yawn : to stare with open mouth : to be wide open.
[Old Norse *gapa.*]

garage, *gar'äzh, gar'ij, gä-räzh', n.* a building where motor vehicles are kept or repaired.
[Fr.—*garer*, to make safe—Germanic.]

garb, *gärb, n.* dress : covering : (false) appearance.—*v.t.* to clothe.
[It. *garbo*, grace.]

garbage, *gär'bij, n.* refuse, rubbish.
[Origin uncertain.]

garble, *gär'bl, v.t.* to select dishonestly from (a book, etc.) giving a false idea of what it says : to muddle (e.g. *a garbled story of what had happened*).
[It. *garbellare*—Arabic *ghirbál*, sieve.]

garden, *gär'dn, n.* a piece of ground on which flowers, etc., are grown : a pleasant spot : a fertile region.—*v.i.* to work in a garden.
gardener, *gard'nėr, n.*
gard'ening, *n., adj.*
garden city, a model town with much ground between houses.
[O.Fr. *gardin.*]

gardenia, *gär-dē'ni-ȧ, n.* a tropical shrub, with beautiful, fragrant flowers.
[Dr. Alex. *Garden*, American botanist.]

gargle, *gär'gl, v.t., v.i.* to wash (the throat), preventing the liquid from going down by forcing out air against it.—Also *n.*
[O.Fr. *gargouille*, throat—L. *gurgulio.*]

gargoyle, *gär'goil, n.* a spout, ending in a grotesque head, jutting out from a roof gutter.
[Through O.Fr.—L. root as **gargle.**]

garish, *gār'ish, adj.* showy, gaudy.
gar'ishly, *adv.* **gar'ishness,** *n.*
[Earlier *gaurish*—*gaure*, to stare.]

garland, *gär'lȧnd, n.* a wreath of flowers or leaves.
[O.Fr. *garlande.*]

garlic, *gär'lik, n.* a plant with a bulb having a strong taste and smell.
[O.E. *gārlēac*—*gār*, spear, *lēac*, leek.]

garment, *gär'mėnt, n.* any article of clothing.
[O.Fr. *garniment*—*garnir*, to equip.]

garner, *gär'nėr, v.t.* to store : to collect.
[O.Fr. *gernier*, a granary.]

garnet, *gär'nit, n.* a precious stone, usu.

red, resembling the seeds of the pomegranate.
[Late L. *grānātum*, pomegranate.]

garnish, *gär'nish, v.t.* to adorn: to decorate (a dish of food).—Also *n.*
gar'nishing, gar'nishment, *ns.*
[O.Fr. *garnir, -issant*; root as **garment.**]

garotte. See **garrotte.**

garret, *gar'ėt, n.* a room just under the roof of a house.
[O.Fr. *garite*, watchtower—*garir*, defend.]

garrison, *gar'i-s(ȯ)n, n.* soldiers for guarding a fortress: a fortified place.—*v.t.* to supply (town, etc.) with troops.
[O.Fr. *garison*—same root as **garret.**]

garrotte, garotte, *gȧ-rot', n.* a mode of putting criminals to death—orig. a string round the throat tightened by twisting a stick, later a brass collar tightened by a screw.—*v.t.* to execute in this way: to half strangle, in order to rob:—*pr.p.* **gar(r)ott'ing**; *pa.p.* **gar(r)ott'ed.**
[Sp. *garrote.*]

garrulous, *gar'ū-lus, -ū-, adj.* talkative.
garru'lity (*-ōō', -ū'*), **garr'ulousness,** *ns.*
garr'ulously, *adv.*
[L. *garrīre*, to chatter.]

garter, *gär'tėr, n.* a band to support a stocking: (*cap.*) badge of the highest order of knighthood in Britain.
[O.Fr. *gartier*; prob. Celtic.]

gas, *gas, n.* a substance in a condition in which it has no definite boundaries but will fill any space: coal gas, or other gas for lighting and heating: gasolene (i.e. petrol): (*coll.*) empty talk:—*pl.* **gas'es.**—*v.t.* to treat, poison, etc. with gas.—*v.i.* to talk *gas*:—*pr.p.* **gass'ing**; *pa.p.* **gassed.**
gas'ify, *v.t.* and *v.i.* to turn into gas.
gasificā'tion, *n.*
gaseous, *gāz'i-us, gas', adj.* of, like, gas.
gass'y, *adj.* containing gas.
gass'iness, *n.*
gas engine, an engine worked by explosion of gas.
gas'-fitter, *n.* one who fits buildings with apparatus for using gas.
gas mask, a device covering nose, mouth, and eyes as a protection against poisonous gases.
gas meter, an instrument for measuring amount of gas.
gas'olene, gas'oline, *n.* petrol for vehicles, etc.
gasom'eter (better **gas holder**), *n.* a storage tank for gas.
gas'works, *n.* a place where gas is made.
[Word invented by 17th cent. scientist.]

gash, *gash, v.t.* to cut deeply into.—*n.* a deep, open cut.
[Earlier *garse*—L. *garsa.*]

gasify, gasolene, etc. See **gas.**

gasp, *gâsp, v.i.* to struggle for breath: to catch the breath: (with *for*) to desire eagerly.—*v.t.* (also **gasp out**) to utter with gasps.—Also *n.*
at the last gasp, at the point of death or of giving up.
[Old Norse *geispa*, to yawn.]

gastric, *gas'trik, adj.* of the stomach.
gastrī'tis, *n.* inflammation of the stomach.
gas'tro-enterī'tis, *n.* inflammation of the mucous membrane of the stomach and the intestines.
gastronomy, *gas-tron'ȯ-mi, n.* the art or science of good eating.
gas'tronome, *n.* one who studies gastronomy.
[Gk. *gastēr*, the belly.]

gate, *gāt, n.* a passage into a city, enclosure, large building: a frame for closing an entrance: the number of people who pay to get in to a football match, etc.: the total money paid for entrance.
gate'crasher, *n.* a person who comes uninvited (e.g. to a party).
gate'crash, *v.t.* and *v.i.*
gate'house, *n.* a house over, or near, the entrance to a city, college, etc.
gate'keeper, *n.* one in charge of a gate.
gate'way, *n.* the opening or structure for containing a gate: an entrance.
[O.E. *geat*, a way.]

gâteau, *gat'ō, n.* a fancy cake. [Fr.]

gather, *gaTH'ėr, v.t.* to collect, bring together: to draw together: to pick (e.g. flowers): in sewing, to draw up in puckers: to learn, conclude (e.g. *I gather from that remark that you have been to Italy*).—*v.i.* to come together: to increase: to suppurate.—*n.* a fold in cloth.
gath'erer, *n.* **gath'ering,** *n.*
to gather oneself together, to collect all one's powers as if about to leap.
[O.E. *gæderian*; same root as **together.**]

gauche, *gōsh, adj.* clumsy: tactless.
gaucherie (*gōsh'ė-rē, -rē'*), *n.* clumsiness: tactlessness.
[Fr. *gauche*, left.]

gaucho, *gow'chō, n.* a cowboy of the pampas of South America. [Sp.]

gaudy, *göd'i, adj.* showy: vulgarly bright:—*comp.* **gaud'ier**; *superl.* **gaud'iest.**
gaud'ily, *adv.* **gaud'iness,** *n.*
[L. *gaudēre*, to be glad.]

gauge, *gāj, n.* a measuring device: a standard of measure: an instrument recording rainfall, or force of wind: the distance between the rails of a railway line.—*v.t.* to measure: to estimate, judge.—Also **gage.** [O.Fr.]

gaunt, *gönt, adj.* thin: haggard: grim, desolate looking. [Origin uncertain.]

gauntlet[1], *gönt'lit, n.* the iron glove of armour, formerly thrown down in challenge: a long glove covering the wrist, or the part of it that does this.
to throw down the gauntlet, to give a challenge, be aggressive.
[O.Fr. *gantelet*, dim. of *gant*, glove.]

gauntlet[2], *gönt'lit, n.* the punishment of having to run through a lane of e.g. soldiers who strike as one passes.

to run the gauntlet, to undergo this punishment: to have to endure unpleasant remarks or treatment.
[Swed. *gatlopp—gata,* lane, *lopp,* course.]

gauze, *gōz, n.* a thin transparent fabric.
gauz′y, *adj.* :—*comp.* **gauz′ier**; *superl.* **gauz′iest.**
[Fr. *gaze*; origin uncertain.]

gave. See **give.**

gavel, *gav′l, n.* a chairman's hammer.
[Origin uncertain.]

gavotte, *gȧ-vot′, n.* a lively dance.
[*Gavots,* people of French Alps.]

gawk, *gök, n.* an awkward, shy or stupid person.—*v.i.* to stare stupidly.
gawk′y, *adj.* **gawk′ily,** *adv.*
gawk′iness, *n.* [Orig. uncertain.]

gay, *gā, adj.* lively: merry: bright:—*comp.* **gay′er**; *superl.* **gay′est.**
gay′ness, gai′ety (*pl.* **gai′eties**), *ns.*
gai′ly, *adv.*
[Fr. *gai.*]

gaze, *gāz, v.i.* to look steadily or fixedly.—*n.* a steady look of wonder, etc.
[Prob. conn. with old *gaw,* to stare.]

gazelle, *gȧ-zel′, n.* a small antelope with beautiful dark eyes.
[Fr.—Arabic *ghazāl,* a wild goat.]

gazette, *gȧ-zet′, n.* a newspaper, esp. an official one publishing government appointments, legal notices, etc.
gazetteer′, *n.* a geographical dictionary.
[Fr.—It. *gazzetta.*]

gear, *gēr, n.* equipment: tools: harness: tackle: clothes: (*dial.*) possessions: any moving part or system of parts for transmitting (passing on) motion.
gear′ing, *n.* means of transmission of motion, esp. a group of toothed wheels.
gear′-wheel, *n.* a wheel with teeth that transmit motion by acting on those of a similar wheel or on a chain.
high gear, low gear, a gear which gives a high, or a low, number of revolutions of the driven part relatively to the driving part.
in, out of, gear, connected, or not connected, with the motor.
[M.E. *gere*; prob. Old Norse *gervi.*]

geese. See **goose.**

Geiger counter, *gī′gėr kown′tėr,* an instrument used to detect the presence of radioactive substances.

geisha, *gā′sha, n.* a Japanese girl trained to entertain by her conversation, playing, dancing, etc. [Jap.]

gelatine, *jel′ȧ-tin, n.* a colourless, odourless, and tasteless substance, prepared from bones, hides, etc.
gelatinous, *jel-at′in-ŭs, adj.*
[Fr.—It. *gelatina,* jelly—L. *gelāre,* freeze.]

gelignite, *jel′ig-nīt, n.* an explosive.
[Perh. **gelatine** and L. *ignis,* fire.]

gem, *jem, n.* a precious stone, esp. when cut: anything admirable, or flawless.
gem′stone, *n.* a precious, or semi-precious, stone, esp. when uncut.
[O.E. *gim*; conn. with L. *gemma,* a bud.]

gendarme, *zhon^g-därm, n.* in France, a military policeman:—*pl.* **gendarmes** (pron. as *sing.*).
[Fr. *gens,* people, *de,* of, *armes,* arms.]

gender, *jen′dėr, n.* in grammar, any of (usu.) three classes (masculine, feminine, or neuter) into which nouns and pronouns are divided (e.g. the noun *drake* is masculine; the noun *vixen* is feminine; the pronoun *it* is neuter). See also **common.**
[L. *genus, generis,* a kind.]

gene, *jēn, n.* any of the material units passed on from parent to offspring that decide the characteristics of the offspring. See also **genetic, genetics.**
genealogy, *jēn-i-al′o-ji,* or *jen-, n.* history of relationship and descent of families: the pedigree of a person or family:—*pl.* **geneal′ogies.**
genealog′ical, *adj.*
genealogical tree, a table in the form of a tree with branches showing several generations of a family.
[Gk. *genea* (also *genos*), race (*logos,* discourse).]

genera. See **genus.**

general, *jen′ėr-ȧl, adj.* including, or affecting, every, or nearly every, person, thing, class, or place, etc. (e.g. *A general election is one affecting every constituency*): expressing a fact true of a number of examples (e.g. *He made the general statement that cuckoos leave their eggs in other birds' nests*): including, or dealing with, a number of different things (e.g. *a general cargo, a general servant, general science*): common, widespread (e.g. *It is the general opinion that this move was a mistake*): not going into detail (e.g. *Dick gave him general instructions about how to get there*): (after an official title) chief (e.g. *a governor-general*).—*n.* an army officer of high rank (see *Appendices*): (*R.C. Church*) the head of a religious order, responsible only to the Pope.
gen′erally, *adv.* usually: on the whole (e.g. *a generally good report*): in general (e.g. *disliked by people generally*).
gen′eralise, *v.i.* to make a general statement (e.g. *Do not generalise from one example*): to form an idea supposed to cover all cases.
generalisā′tion, *n.*
general′ity, *n.* quality of being general: a general statement: the majority of people:—*pl.* **general′ities.**
general post office, the head post office of a town or district.
general practitioner, a doctor who deals with all types of cases.
in general, considering most cases though not necessarily all.
[O.Fr.—L. *generālis—genus,* kind.]

generate, *jen′ėr-āt, v.t.* to produce, bring into being (e.g. heat, electricity, hatred).
generā′tion, *n.* production or formation:

a single stage in natural descent: the people of the same age or period.

gen′erator, *n.* producer: a machine for producing gas, or (dynamo) one for making electricity.

generating station, a building where electricity is made on a large scale.

[L. *generāre, -ātum—genus,* kind.]

generous, *jen′ėr-ůs, adj.* free in giving: very ready to admit the worth of others: large, not small or mean (e.g. *a generous gift*).

generos′ity (*pl.* **-ies**), **-ousness,** *ns.*

gen′erously, *adv.*

[L. *generōsus,* of noble birth.]

genesis, *jen′es-is, n.* origin: (*cap.*) the first book of the Bible.

genet′ic, *adj.* of, concerned with, origin or heredity.

genet′ics, *n.* science of heredity. [Gk.]

genial, *jē′ni-ål, adj.* cheering: kindly.

genial′ity, ge′nialness, *ns.*

ge′nially, *adv.*

[L. *geniālis*—same root as **genius.**]

genius, *jēn′yůs, jē′ni-ůs, n.* outstanding powers of mind: a person having such powers: a natural ability (e.g. *a genius for saying the right thing*): good or evil spirit, supposed to preside over each person, place, and thing (*pl.* in this sense, **genii,** *jēn′i-ī*): a demon, spirit (*pl.* **genii**):—*pl.* in first senses, **gen′iuses.**

[L., a guardian spirit.]

genocide, *jen′ō-sīd, n.* deliberate extermination of a race or people.

[Gk. *genos,* race, L. *caedĕre,* to kill.]

gent, *jent, n.* vulg. abbrev. of **gentleman.**

genteel, *jen-tēl′, adj.* (orig.) well-bred: too refined in manners.

genteelly, *jen-tēl′li, adv.*

See also **gentility.**

[Same root as **gentle**; later borrowing.]

gentian, *jen′shån, n.* an alpine plant, usu. blue-flowered.

[L. *gentiāna.*]

gentile, *jen′tīl, n.* anyone not a Jew.

[L. *gentīlis—gens,* a nation.]

gentle, *jen′tl, adj.* well-born: mild in manners, disposition, or action: soft: low: gradual (e.g. *a gentle slope*).

gent′ly, *adv.* **gent′leness,** *n.*

gentil′ity, *n.* good birth: refinement, real or affected.

gentry, *jen′tri, n.* class of people next below rank of nobility: (*coll.*) people of a particular type (e.g. *the bookmaking gentry*).

gent′leman, *n.* a man of good birth: a man of good feeling and instincts, courteous and honourable: (*politely*) a man:—*pl.* **gent′lemen**:—*fem.* **gent′lewoman.**

gent′lemanly, *adj.*

gent′lemanliness, *n.*

gent′leman-at-arms, *n.* a member of the royal bodyguard.

gentleman's (-men's) agreement, one resting on honour, not on law.

See also **genteel.**

[Fr. *gentil*—L. *gentīlis,* of the same clan, well-bred.]

genuflect, *jen′ū-flekt, v.i.* to bend the knee in worship or respect.

genūflex′ion (also **genūflec′tion**), *n.*

[L. *genū,* knee, *flectĕre,* to bend.]

genuine, *jen′ū-in, adj.* really what it pretends to be, not artificial or fake: sincere (e.g. *a genuine person*).

gen′uinely, *adv.* **gen′uineness,** *n.*

[L. *genuīnus,* native, natural, genuine.]

genus, *jē′nůs, n.* a group of related animals or plants:—*pl.* **genera** (*jen′*).

gener′ic (*jen-*), *adj.* having to do with a genus: (of name, term) general.

[L. *genus, generis,* birth.]

geo-, *jē-ō-, ji-o-* (as part of word) the earth.

geography, *ji-og′rå-fi, n.* the science that describes the surface of the earth and its inhabitants: a book containing such a description.

geog′rapher, *n.*

geographic(al) (*-raf′*), *adjs.*

geograph′ically, *adv.*

geographical mile. See **mile.**

geology, *ji-ol′ō-ji, n.* the science of the history and development of the earth's crust.

geol′ogist, *n.* **geolog′ic(al),** *adjs.*

geolog′ically, *adv.*

geometry, *ji-om′ė-tri, n.* a branch of mathematics dealing with lines, angles, figures: a textbook on this.

geomet′ric(al), *adjs.*

geomet′rically, *adv.*

[Gk. *gē,* earth (*graphē,* writing; *logos,* discourse: *metron,* measure).]

georgette, *jör-jet′, n.* a thin silk stuff.

[Named after a milliner.]

geranium, *jė-rān′yům, -i-ům, n.* plant with seed-vessels like in shape to a crane's bill.

[Gk. *geranion—geranos,* a crane.]

geriatrics, *jer-i-at′riks, n.* the branch of medicine concerned with the diseases of old age.

[Gk. *gēras,* old age.]

germ, *jėrm, n.* a very tiny form of animal or plant life that causes disease: the tiny beginning of anything (e.g. *the germ of an idea*).

germ′icide, *n.* a substance that destroys disease germs.

germ′ināte, *v.i.* to begin to grow (esp. of a seed).—*v.t.* to cause to sprout.

germinā′tion, *n.*

[L. *germen, germinis,* a bud, germ.]

german, *jėr′mån, adj.* (following the noun) full (e.g. *cousin german*).

germane, *jėr-mān′, adj.* closely related (e.g. *That fact is not germane to the present argument.*).

[O.Fr. *germain*—L. *germānus.*]

German, *jėr'mȧn, adj.* of *Germany* or its people.—*n.* a native or inhabitant, or the language, of Germany :—*pl.* **Ger'mans.**
German'ic, *adj.* of Germany, the Germans, or the German language : also of the language group called Germanic.—*n.* an old group of related languages, to one branch of which Old English and Old German belonged.
[L. *Germāni.*]

Gestapo, *ge-stä'pō, n.* the secret police in Germany under the Nazis.
[*ge*heime *sta*ats *po*lizei, secret state police.]

gesticulate, *jes-tik'ū-lāt, v.i.* to make vigorous gestures, esp. when speaking.
gesticulā'tion, *n.*
gesture, *jes'chůr, n.* a movement of the body expressing emotion : an act of courtesy or tact (esp. in the hope of achieving some end ; e.g. *He made a gesture of friendship towards his rival*).—Also *v.i.*
[L. *gestus.*]

get, *get, v.t.* to obtain, gain, capture : to fetch : to receive : to take (a disease) : to succeed in coming into touch with (e.g. a radio station) : to cause to be in any condition or position (e.g. *to get the fire lit, to get oneself untidy, to get the nails out of the box*) : to persuade (a person to do something) : to make ready (e.g. dinner).—*v.i.* to arrive at (e.g. *When does the train get to London?*) : to become (e.g. *to get old, thirsty*) : (*coll.*) to manage, or to be allowed (e.g. *Did he get to go?*) :—*pr.p.* **gett'ing** ; *pa.t.* **got** ; *pa.p.* **got,** (*U.S.*) **gott'en.**
get-at'-able, *adj.* easy, possible, to reach.
to get at, to reach : to find out : to hint at : to bribe.
to get it across to (someone), to make (someone) understand.
to get away with, to escape with : to do (something) without being reproved or punished.
to get off, to be let off punishment.
to get on with, to agree, be friendly, with : to make progress with.
to get over, to recover from.
to get round, to avoid (a difficulty) : to persuade, coax (a person).
to get there, to succeed.
to get up, to rise : to ascend : to prepare : to learn up : to dress.
[Old Norse *geta.*]

gewgaw, *gū'gö, n.* something showy and without value. [Origin unknown.]

geyser, *gē'-, gā'-, gī'zėr, n.* a spring that shoots out hot water and steam : a heater for bath water.
[*Geysir*, a geyser in Iceland.]

ghastly, *gâst'li, adj.* death-like : terrible : (*coll.*) very bad :—*comp.* **ghast'lier** ; *superl.* **ghast'liest.**
ghast'liness, *n.*
[M.E. *gastlich* ; same root as **ghost.**]

ghat, *göt, n.* in India, a mountain pass : a riverside landing-stair : a place of cremation (*burning ghat*).
[Hindustani *ghāt*, descent.]

ghee, *gē, n.* an Indian clarified butter.
[Hindustani *ghī.*]

gherkin, *gėr'kin, n.* a small cucumber.
[From Du.]

ghetto, *get'ō, n.* the Jews' quarter in some cities : a (usu. poor) area inhabited by any racial group :—*pl.* **ghett'os.** [It.]

ghost, *gōst, n.* a spirit, esp. of a dead person : a faint suggestion (e.g. *a ghost of an idea, of a chance*) : one who does another's work for him (e.g. writing books, speeches).
ghost'ly, *adj.* :—*comp.* **ghost'lier** ; *superl.* **ghost'liest.**
ghost'liness, *n.*
to give up the ghost, to die.
[O.E. *gāst* ; conn. Ger. *geist.*]

ghoul, *gōōl, gowl, n.* an Eastern demon said to prey on the dead : a person excessively interested in gruesome things.
ghoul'ish, *adj.* [Arabic *ghūl.*]

giant, *jī'ȧnt, n.* a huge being in old stories : an unusually big person or thing : a person of great ability :—*fem.* **gi'antess.**
gigantic, *jī-gan'tik, adj.* huge.
gigan'tically, *adv.*
[O.Fr. *geant*—Gk. *gigās, gigantos.*]

gibber, *jib'ėr, v.i.* to utter senseless sounds.
gibberish, *gib'ėr-ish, jib'-, n.* rapid, gabbling talk : nonsense. [Imit.]

gibbet, *jib'it, n.* a gallows with projecting arm from which to dangle corpses.
[O.Fr. *gibet*, a stick.]

gibbon, *gib'ȯn, n.* an ape with very long arms. [Fr.]

gibe. See **jibe.**

giblets, *jib'lets, n. pl.* the internal eatable parts of a fowl, etc.
[O.Fr. *gibelet.*]

giddy, *gid'i, adj.* unsteady, light-headed, dizzy : that causes giddiness (e.g. *a giddy height*) : flighty, impulsive :—*comp.* **gidd'ier** ; *superl.* **gidd'iest.**
gidd'ily, *adv.* **gidd'iness,** *n.*
[O.E. *gydig*, possessed by a god, insane.]

gift, *gift, n.* a thing given : a bribe : a good quality or ability given by nature.—*v.t.* to present, give : to endow (a person, with a talent).
gift'ed, *adj.* very talented.
to look a gift horse in the mouth, to criticise a gift. [Root of **give.**]

gig, *gig, n.* a light, two-wheeled carriage : a long, light boat.
[M.E. *gigge*, a whirling thing.]

gigantic(ally). See **giant.**

giggle, *gig'l, v.i.* to laugh with short catches of the breath, or in a silly manner.—Also *n.*
gigg'ler, *n.* **gigg'ly,** *adj.* **-liness,** *n.*
gigg'ling, *n.* and *adj.* [Imit.]

gild, *gild, v.t.* to cover with gold or gold-like substance : to give a false appearance to :—*pa.t., pa.p.* **gild'ed, gilt.**

gild'er, *n.* **gild'ing,** *n.*
gilt'-edged, *adj.* having edges gilt: of the highest quality (e.g. *gilt-edged securities—i.e.* stocks whose interest is considered perfectly safe).
to gild the pill, to make a disagreeable thing seem less so.
[O.E. *gyldan*; same root as **gold.**]

gill[1], *gil, n.* in fish, an organ for breathing: flap below the bill of a fowl.
[Prob. a Scand. word.]

gill[2], *jil, n.* a measure, ¼ pint.
[O.Fr. *gille, gelle.*]

gillie, *gil'i, n.* an attendant, esp. on a sportsman:—*pl.* **gill'ies.**
[Gael. *gille,* a lad, Ir. *giolla.*]

gillyflower, *jil'i-flow-(ė)r, n.* a name for various flowers that smell like cloves.
[Gk. *karyophyllon,* the clove tree.]

gilt. See **gild.**

gimbals, *jim'bȧlz, n.pl.* a two-ring contrivance for supporting an object, such as a ship's compass, so that it remains horizontal.
[L. *gemelli,* twins.]

gimcrack, *jim'krak, adj.* showy but ill-made, frail. [Origin uncertain.]

gimlet, *gim'lit, n.* a tool for boring holes, with screw point and crosspiece handle.
gim'let-eyed, *adj.* very sharp-sighted and observant.
[O.Fr. *guimbelet*—a Germanic word.]

gimmick, *gim'ik, n.* an addition intended to make an article for sale seem more attractive: a clever mechanical device: a device or trick adopted to attract notice. [Origin uncertain.]

gin[1], *jin, n.* shortened form of *geneva,* a spirit distilled from grain and flavoured with juniper berries, etc.
[Du. *genever*—L. *jūniperus,* juniper.]

gin[2], *jin, n.* a trap or snare: a machine for separating cotton from its seeds.—*v.t.* to catch in a gin: to free (cotton) from seeds:—*pr.p.* **ginn'ing**; *pa.p.* **ginned.**
[O.Fr. *engin,* engine.]

ginger, *jin'jėr, n.* the underground stem of a plant in the E. and W. Indies, with a hot taste.
ginger ale, ginger beer, non-alcoholic effervescent drinks flavoured with ginger.
gingerbread, *jin'jėr-bred, n.* a cake flavoured with treacle and usu. ginger.
to take the gilt off the gingerbread, to show that something is not really as attractive as it appeared to be.
[Gk. *zingiberis.*]

gingerly, *jin'jėr-li, adv.* with soft steps: with extreme care, gentleness.—Also *adj.*
gin'gerliness, *n.*
[Perh. L. *gentilis,* gentle.]

gingham, *ging'ȧm, n.* cotton cloth with stripes or checks.
[Malay *ginggang,* stripped.]

gipsy, gypsy, *jip'si, n.* a member of a wandering people of Indian origin, a Romany: dark-skinned person:—*pl.* **-ies.**
[**Egyptian,** because the people were once thought to have come from Egypt.]

giraffe, *ji-räf', n.* an African animal with very long neck and forelegs.
[Arabic *zarāfah.*]

gird[1], *gėrd, v.t.* to encircle with, or as if with, a belt: to fasten (on a sword) with a belt: to prepare (oneself) for action:—*pa.t.* and *pa.p.* **gird'ed** or **girt.**
gird'er, *n.* a great beam of wood, iron, steel, e.g. to support a floor, wall, roadway of a bridge.
girdle, *gėrd'l, n.* a waist belt or cord: anything that encloses like a belt.
[O.E. *gyrdan.*]

gird[2], *gėrd, v.i.* to gibe, jeer (at).
[Same as **gird** (1).]

girdle[1]. See **gird** (1).

girdle[2]. Same as **griddle.**

girl, *gėrl, n.* a female child: a young woman.
girl'hood, *n.* the state or time of being a girl.
girl'ish, *adj.* of, like, a girl.
Girl Guide, a member of an organisation for girls, like the Scouts.
[Origin uncertain.]

girt. See **gird** (1).

girth, *gėrth, n.* a belly-band of a saddle: measure round about.
[Old Norse *gjörth.*]

gist, *jist, n.* the main point or points (e.g. *Give me the gist of his argument*).
[O.Fr.—*gesir,* to lie, rest—L. *jacēre.*]

give, *giv, v.t.* to hand out or over: to pay: to yield as product or result: to do suddenly (e.g. a jump, a cry): to provide (e.g. *to give help*): to render (e.g. thanks): to pronounce (e.g. a decision): to apply (oneself to something).—*v.i.* to yield to pressure, etc.: to open, or lead, into (with *upon, on, into*):—*pr.p.* **giv'ing**; *pa.t.* **gave**; *pa.p.* **given** (*giv'n*).
giv'en, *adj.* stated (e.g. *under the given conditions*): in the habit of (e.g. *given to repeating himself*).
See also **gift.**
to give away, to hand out as a present: to give (the bride) to the bridegroom at a wedding ceremony: to allow (something) to become known.
to give chase, to run after someone.
to give in, to yield.
to give oneself away, to betray one's secret unawares.
to give out, to send out (e.g. a flash, a smell): to announce: to run short, be used up: (of e.g. engine) to fail.
to give over, to cease.
to give place to, to make room for: to be succeeded by.
to give up, to abandon.
to give way, to yield: to collapse under strain.
[O.E. *gefan, giefan*; conn. Ger. *geben.*]

gizzard, *giz'ȧrd, n.* a stomach, esp. the second stomach of a bird.
[M.E. *giser*—O.Fr. *guiser.*]

glacé, *glä'sā, adj.* iced: glossy. [Fr.]

glacial, *glā'shȧl, -si-ȧl, adj.* icy, very cold: produced by glacier: of an ice age.
glaciā'tion, *n.* freezing: formation of glaciers, or a time of this.
glacier, *glas'yėr, -i-ėr,* also *glās',* a mass of ice, fed by snow on a mountain, slowly creeping downhill.
[L. *glaciēs,* ice.]

glad, *glad, adj.* pleased: giving pleasure:—*comp.* **gladd'er**; *superl.* **gladd'est.**
glad'ly, *adv.* **glad'ness,** *n.*
gladd'en, *v.t.* to make glad, cheer.
glad'some, *adj.* (*poetic*) joyful.
[O.E. *glæd.*]

glade, *glād, n.* open space in a wood.
[Origin unknown.]

gladiator, *glad'i-ā-tȯr, n.* in ancient Rome, a man who was trained to fight with other men or with animals for the amusement of spectators.
[L.—*gladius,* a sword.]

gladiolus, *glad-i-ō'lus, n.* a plant with sword-shaped leaves and spikes of flowers, of different colours:—*pl.* **gladiō'luses, gladiō'li** (*ī*).
[Same root as **gladiator.**]

gladsome. See **glad.**

glamour, *glam'ȯr, n.* fascination or charm, esp. with little reality behind it.
glam'orous, *adj.* **glam'orously,** *adv.*
[M.E. *gramery,* skill in grammar, magic.]

glance, *glâns, v.i.* to fly obliquely (off; e.g. *The ball glanced off the edge of his bat*): to give a very brief look (at): to gleam, flash.—Also *n.* [Origin uncertain.]

gland, *gland, n.* a cell or group of cells that takes substances from the blood and stores them for use, or in order that the body may get rid of them (e.g. *sweat gland*).
glandular, *glan'dū-lȧr, adj.*
[L. *glans, glandis,* acorn.]

glare, *glār, v.i.* to give a dazzling light: to stare fiercely.—Also *n.*
glar'ing, *adj.* fiercely bright: very obvious (e.g. *a glaring error*).
glar'ingly, *adv.*
[M.E. *glāren,* to shine.]

glass, *glâs, n.* a hard, usu. breakable, material through which light can pass, made by fusing sand or similar substance with soda and lime or other chemicals: an article made of glass, esp. a drinking vessel or a mirror: (in *pl.*) spectacles.
glass'y, *adj.*:—*comp.* **glass'ier**; *superl.* **glass'iest.**
glass'ily, *adv.* **glass'iness,** *n.*
glass'ful:—*pl.* **glassfuls.**
glaze, *glāz, v.t.* to fit (e.g. frame) with glass: to put windows in (building): to cover with a thin surface of glass or something glassy: to make shiny.—*v.i.* to become glassy.—*n.* a glassy coating put on pottery: any shining appearance.
glass'house, *n.* greenhouse.
glāz'er, *n.* a workman who glazes pottery, paper, etc.
glāz'ier (*-yėr*), *n.* one who sets glass in window frames, etc.
cut glass, fine glass shaped or ornamented by cutting or grinding.
plate glass, glass in thick plates made by casting, rolling, grinding, and polishing.
[O.E. *glæs.*]

gleam, *glēm, v.i.* to shine faintly or very briefly.—Also *n.*
[O.E. *glǣm.*]

glean, *glēn, v.t.* to gather (grain) after the reapers: to collect (what is thinly scattered, e.g. news, facts).—Also *v.i.*
[O.Fr. *glener*; origin uncertain.]

glebe, *glēb n.* a field: the land attached to a parish church.
[L. *glēba,* a clod.]

glee, *glē, n.* gaiety: delight: (*music*) a song in parts.
glee'ful, *adj.* merry: triumphant.
gleefully, *adv.* **glee'fulness,** *n.*
[O.E. *glēo.*]

glen, *glen, n.* a narrow valley with a stream: a depression among hills.
[Gael. *gleann.*]

glib, *glib, adj.* ready, fluent, and insincere (e.g. *a glib tongue*):—*comp.* **glibb'er**; *superl.* **glibb'est.**
glib'ly, *adv.* **glib'ness,** *n.*
[Conn. with Du. *glibberig,* slippery.]

glide, *glīd, v.i.* to move smoothly and easily: to flow gently: to travel by glider.—*n.* act of gliding.
glīd'er, *n.* an aircraft without engine.
[O.E. *glīdan,* to slip.]

glimmer, *glim'ėr, v.i.* to burn or appear faintly.—*n.* a faint ray (of e.g. light, hope, understanding).
glimm'ering, *n.* glimmer.
[M.E. *glemern*; from root of **gleam.**]

glimpse, *glimps, n.* a very brief view.—*v.t.* to get a brief view of.
[M.E. *glymsen* (vb.).]

glint, *glint, v.i.* to gleam, sparkle.—Also *n.*
[Earlier *glent*; prob. Scand.]

glissade, *glēs-äd', v.i.* to slide, glide down.—*n.* act of sliding down a slope: a gliding movement in ballet.
[Fr.—*glisser,* to slip.]

glisten, *glis'n, v.i.* to shine faintly: to sparkle.
[O.E. *glisnian,* to shine.]

glitter, *glit'ėr, v.i.* to sparkle: to be splendid or showy.—Also *n.*
glitt'ering, *adj.*
[M.E. *gliteren.*]

gloaming, *glōm'ing, n.* twilight.
[O.E. *glōmung.*]

gloat, *glōt, v.i.* to gaze, or think, with wicked or malicious joy (e.g. *He gloated over John's defeat*).
[Perh. Old Norse *glotta,* to grin.]

globe, *glōb, n.* a ball: a sphere: the earth: a sphere representing the earth: a lamp glass.
glōb'al, *adj.* spherical: affecting the whole world.

globular, *glob'ū-lȧr, adj.* globe-shaped.
globule, *glob'ūl, n.* a drop.
globe'-trott'er, *n.* one who goes sight-seeing about the world.
[L. *globus.*]

gloom, *gloōm, n.* partial darkness, dimness: dismalness: lowness of spirits.
gloom'y, *adj.*:—*comp.* **gloom'ier**; *superl.* **gloom'iest.**
gloom'ily, *adv.* **gloom'iness,** *n.*
[Partly—root of **glum.**]

glorify, *glō'ri-fī, glö', v.t.* to make glorious: to praise highly or too highly:—*pr.p.* **glo'rifying**; *pa.p.* **glo'rified.**
glorificā'tion, *n.*
glo'ry, *n.* honour: an object of great pride: splendour: rays round the head of a saint: heaven:—*pl.* **glo'ries.**—*v.i.* to boast about (with *in*):—*pr.p.* **glo'rying**; *pa.p.* **glo'ried.**
glo'rious, *adj.* noble, splendid: (*coll.*) delightful.
glo'riously, *adv.*
[L. *glōria*, glory.]

gloss[1], *glos, n.* an explanation of a hard word, etc.—*v.t.* to make remarks in explanation of (something).
gloss'ary, *n.* a list of words with their meanings:—*pl.* **-ies.**
[Gk. *glōssa, glōtta*, tongue.]

gloss[2], *glos, n.* brightness as of a polished surface.—*v.t.* to give a shining, or a false, appearance to.
gloss'y, *adj.* smooth and shining:—*comp.* **gloss'ier**; *superl.* **gloss'iest.**
gloss'ily, *adv.* **gloss'iness,** *n.*
to gloss over, to make light of, explain away (e.g. a mistake).
[Conn. with **glass.**]

glossary. See **gloss** (1).

glottis, *glot'is, n.* the opening between the vocal cords.
glott'al, *adj.*
glottal stop, a speech sound made by closing the glottis (e.g. sound made by some speakers instead of *t* in word such as *water*).
[Gk. *glōttis—glōtta*, tongue.]

glove, *gluv, n.* a covering for the hand, esp. with a sheath for each finger.
[O.E. *glōf.*]

glow, *glō, v.i.* to burn without flame: to give out a steady light: to tingle with warmth or emotion.—Also *n.*
glow'ing, *adj.* that glows: very enthusiastic.
glow'worm, *n.* a beetle whose larvae and wingless females give out light.
[O.E. *glōwan.*]

glower, *glow'ėr, v.i.* to stare angrily, scowl.
[Origin unknown.]

glowing, glowworm. See **glow.**

glucose, *gloō'kōs, -kōz, n.* a kind of sugar obtained from fruit juices, etc.
[Gk. *glykys*, sweet.]

glue, *gloō, n.* an impure gelatine got by boiling animal refuse, used as an adhesive.—*v.t.* to join with, or as if with, glue:—*pr.p.* **glu'ing**; *pa.p.* **glued.**
glu'ey, *adj.*:—*comp.* **glu'ier**; *superl.* **glu'iest.**
See also **glutinous.**
[Late L. *glus, glūtis.*]

glum, *glum, adj.* sullen: gloomy.
[M.E. *glombe, glome*, to frown.]

glut, *glut, v.t.* to overfeed, cram: to overstock (the market):—*pr.p.* **glutt'ing**; *pa.p.* **glutt'ed.**—*n.* a too great supply.
glutton, *glut'(ȯ)n, n.* one who eats too much: an animal related to the weasel.
glutt'onous, *adj.* very greedy.
glutt'onously, *adv.*
glutt'onousness, glutt'ony, *ns.*
glutt'onise, *v.i.* to eat too much.
[L. *gluttīre*, to swallow.]

glutinous, *gloō'tin-ůs, adj.* gluey, sticky.
[L. *gluten*, glue; conn. *glus*, glue.]

glutton, etc. See **glut.**

glycerin(e), *glis'ėr-ēn, -in,* or *-ēn', n.* a sweet, sticky, colourless liquid.
[Gk. *glykeros*, sweet; conn. **glucose.**]

G-man, *jē'man, n.* an agent of the U.S. Federal Bureau of Investigation.
[*G*overnment *man.*]

gnarled, *närld, adj.* knotty, twisted.
[Form of **knurled,** used by Shakespeare.]

gnash, *nash, v.t., v.i.* to grind (the teeth) in rage, etc.: (of teeth) to strike together.
[M.E. *gnasten*; prob. from Old Norse.]

gnat, *nat, n.* a small fly of which the females are usu. blood-suckers.
[O.E. *gnæt.*]

gnaw, *nö, v.t., v.i.* to bite with a scraping or mumbling movement, or in agony or rage: to wear (away): to torment (e.g. *gnawed by a sense of guilt*).
[O.E. *gnagan.*]

gnome, *nōm, n.* a dwarf, goblin.
[Mediaeval L. *gnomus.*]

gnu, *noō, nū, n.* a large antelope in S. and E. Africa. [From Hottentot.]

go, *gō, v.i.* to move: (of mechanism) to act, work: to turn out, happen: to be spent, lost, etc. (e.g. *That's how the money goes*): to give way, break: to be in a stated condition (e.g. *to go barefoot, hungry*): to become (e.g. *to go mad, free*): to be guided (by): to stretch, extend: to be given (to one) as one's portion:—*pr.p.* **go'ing**; *pa.t.* **went** (orig. *pa.t.* of **wend**); *pa.p.* **gone** (*gon*); *pr.t. 3rd sing.* **goes** (*gōz*).—*n.* (all meanings *coll.*) an attempt, turn (at): a success: energy:—*pl.* **goes.**
go'ing, *n.* the act of moving: departure: conditions of travel or action (e.g. *It was heavy going*).
go'-ahead, *adj.* energetic, enterprising.
go'-between, *n.* one who carries messages between, or helps to make arrangements affecting, two people or parties.
goings'-on, *n.* behaviour (esp. bad).
to be going to, to be about (to), to intend (to).

to go back on, to fail to act up to (a promise).
to go in for (something), to make (something) one's study or occupation.
to go off, to leave: to become less good: to explode.
to go on, to continue: to make a fuss.
to go through, to search, or to examine in order: to experience (e.g. troubles): to spend or use up (e.g. a fortune): to rehearse, or to act or carry out, from beginning to end.
to go through with, to carry on with and finish.
to go under, to fail, be ruined.
to go with, to be often in the company of: to be a usual accompaniment of: to be suitable, pleasing, with (e.g. *Do the red gloves go with your red hat?*).
[O.E. *gan.*]

goad, *gōd, n.* a sharp-pointed stick for driving cattle: something that drives a person to action.—*v.t.* to drive with a goad: to urge on to action: to torment, annoy.
[O.E. *gād.*]

goal, *gōl, n.* the winning-post: the two upright posts between which the ball is sent in some games: end, aim (e.g. *the goal of his ambition*). [Origin uncertain.]

goat, *gōt, n.* a very agile, hairy, animal related to sheep.
goatee′, *n.* a beard on the chin only.
goat′-herd, *n.* one who looks after goats.
[O.E. *gōt.*]

gobble, *gob′l, v.t.* to swallow quickly.—*v.i.* to make a noise in the throat, as a turkey does.
[O.Fr. *gober,* to devour.]

goblet, *gob′lit, n.* a large drinking-cup without a handle.
[O.Fr. *gobelet.*]

goblin, *gob′lin, n.* a bogy or bogle: a mischievous sprite.
[O.Fr. *gobelin*—Late L. *gobelinus.*]

go-cart, *gō′-kärt, n.* a kind of wheeled chair in which a small child is pushed along.
go-kart, *n.* a low racing vehicle consisting of a frame with wheels, engine and steering gear.—Also **kart.**
[go, cart.]

god, *god, n.* a superhuman being with power over the lives of men: (*cap.*) in religions such as the Jewish faith and Christianity, the creator and ruler of the world: a person or thing considered of very great importance (e.g. *Money was his god*): (in *pl.*) (the occupants of) the gallery of a theatre:—*fem.* **godd′ess.**
god′less, *adj.* not acknowledging God: wicked.
god′ly, *adj.* keeping God's laws, pious:—*comp.* **god′lier**; *superl.* **god′liest.**
god′liness, *n.*
god′father, god′mother, *ns.* one who, at a child's baptism, guarantees that the child will receive religious education.
god′child, god′daughter, god′son, *ns.*
god′send, *n.* a very welcome piece of good fortune.
god′speed′ (also with *cap*), *n.* used in the phrase 'to wish one godspeed', to wish that God may speed one on a safe journey, or to success. [O.E.]

goes. See **go.**

goffer, *gof′ėr, v.t.* to pleat or crimp.
[O.Fr. *goffre,* a wafer.]

goggle, *gog′l, v.i.* to stare, roll the eyes: (of eyes) to bulge.—*adj.* rolling: staring with surprise.—*n.* a goggling look: (in *pl.*) spectacles worn to protect the eyes.
[M.E. *gogelen*; origin uncertain.]

going. See **go.**

goitre, *goi′tėr, n.* enlargement of the thyroid gland in the throat.
[L. *guttur,* the throat.]

go-kart. See **go-cart.**

gold, *gōld, n.* a precious metal, used as money: anything precious: a yellow colour.
gold′en, *adj.* of gold: of the colour of gold: happy (e.g. *golden hours*): very favourable (e.g. *a golden opportunity*).
gold′-digg′er, *n.* one who mines gold: (*slang*) a woman who attaches herself to a man for the sake of the presents he gives her.
gold dust, gold in fine particles.
gold′-field, *n.* a region where gold is found.
gold′finch, *n.* a finch, the male of which has black, red, yellow, and white plumage.
gold′fish, *n.* a Chinese and Japanese freshwater fish, golden-yellow in its domesticated state, brownish when wild.
gold leaf, gold beaten very thin.
gold mine, a mine from which gold is dug: a source of great profit.
gold plate, vessels and utensils of gold.
gold rush, a rush to a new gold-field.
gold′smith, *n.* a worker in gold and silver.
golden mean, a wise and moderate, not extreme, course of action.
golden eagle, the common eagle, which has a slight golden gleam about its head and neck.
golden wedding, the fiftieth anniversary of a wedding.
gold standard, a standard consisting of gold (or of a weight in gold) in relation to which money values are reckoned (**on, off, the gold standard,** using, or not using, gold as standard). [O.E.]

golf, *golf, gof, n.* a game with a ball and a set of clubs, in which the ball is played along a course and into a series of small holes set in the ground at intervals.—Also *v.i.*
golf′er, *n.* **golf′ing,** *n.* and *adj.*
golf club, a club formed of people whose purpose is to play golf: its premises: (also **golf-club**) the implement with which the golf ball is struck.

golf course, golf links, the ground on which golf is played. [Origin uncertain.]

gollywog, *gol'i-wog, n.* a doll with black face and bristling hair.
[*Golliwogg*, doll in story (1895).]

golosh. Same as **galosh.**

gondola, *gon'dò-là, n.* a long, narrow boat used on the canals of Venice.
gondolier (*-lēr'*), *n.* one who propels a gondola.
[It.; origin uncertain.]

gone. See **go.**

gong, *gong, n.* a metal disk, usu. rimmed, that sounds when struck or rubbed with a drumstick. [Malay.]

good, *good, adj.* virtuous (e.g. *a good man*): well-behaved: kind, generous (e.g. *She was good to me*): of satisfactory quality (e.g. *good food, a good reason*): pleasant (e.g. *a good time*): ample (e.g. *a good supply*): fairly large in amount (e.g. *A good deal of nonsense was talked*):—*comp.* **bett'er**; *superl.* **best.**—*n.* (opp. to **evil**) righteousness: virtuous actions: something that increases happiness or success: welfare (e.g. *for your good*): (in *pl.*) movable possessions: (in *pl.*) merchandise: (in *pl.*) articles sent by train.
good'ness, *n.*
goodbye', good-bye', *interj.* or *n.* contr. of 'God be with you', farewell:—*pl.* **goodbyes', good-byes'.**
good-day, good day, good evening, good morning, goodnight, good night, *interjs.* or *ns.* contr. of 'I wish you a good day', etc.
good'-for-nothing, *adj.* worthless.—*n.* an idle, worthless person.
Good Friday, the Friday of Passion Week.
good humour, a cheerful, amiable mood.
good-hu'moured, *adj.* being in, or showing, good humour.
good'-look'ing, *adj.* handsome.
good nature, kindness and readiness to be pleased.
good'-nā'tured, *adj.* showing good nature.
good Samaritan, a person who helps one in time of trouble (St. Luke's gospel, X, 30-37).
goods train, a train carrying only goods, freight train.
goodwill, good will, a friendly attitude: readiness, cheerful consent: the good reputation that a business has built up.
as good as, practically, all but (e.g. *He as good as told me to leave*).
for good (and all), permanently, for always.
no good, useless.
through the good offices of, through the kind help of (someone).
to be as good as one's word, to fulfil one's promise.
to make good, to carry out (a promise, a boast): to make up for (a loss): to prove (an accusation): to get on in the world: to do well after a bad start.
[O.E. *gōd*.]

googly, *gōōg'li, n.* (*cricket*) a ball that breaks in a different way from the way suggested by the bowler's action. [Orig. unknown.]

goose, *gōōs, n.* a web-footed animal like a duck, but larger: a silly person:—*pl.* **geese** (*gēs*).
goose'-flesh, *n.* a puckering of the skin through cold, horror, etc.
goose'(-)step, *n.* a method of marching with knees stiff and soles brought flat on the ground.
See also **gander, gosling.**
[O.E. *gōs* (pl. *gēs*).]

gooseberry, *gōōz'bėr-i,* or *gōōs', n.* a prickly shrub with globe-shaped fruit: the fruit itself: an unwanted third person:—*pl.* **goose'berries.**
[Perh. **goose, berry.**]

gopher, *gō'fėr, n.* a name in America applied to various burrowing animals.
[Perh. Fr. *gaufre*, honeycomb.]

gore[1], *gōr, gör, n.* blood, esp, when clotted.
gor'y, *adj.* **gor'ily,** *adv.* **gor'iness,** *n.*
[O.E. *gor*, filth.]

gore[2], *gōr, gör, v.t.* to pierce with horns, tusks, spear, etc.
[Conn. with O.E. *gār*, a spear.]

gore[3], *gōr, gör, n.* a triangular piece let into a garment to widen it.
[O.E. *gāra*, a triangular piece of land.]

gorge, *görj, n.* the throat: a ravine.—*v.t.* and *v.i.* to swallow, or feed, greedily.
[O.Fr.]

gorgeous, *gör'jùs, adj.* showy, splendid.
gor'geously, *adv.* **gor'geousness,** *n.*
[O.Fr. *gorgias*, gaudy.]

gorgon, *gör'gòn, n.* any of three monsters in old story whose look turned people to stone: an ugly woman: a terrifying woman.
[Gk. *Gorgō—gorgos*, grim.]

gorilla, *gor-il'à, n.* the largest of the apes.
[Gk. *gorillai* (pl.).]

gormandise, *gör'màn-diz, v.i.* to eat too quickly and too much.
[Same root as **gourmand.**]

gorse, *görs, n.* furze or whin, a prickly shrub with yellow flowers.
[O.E. *gorst*.]

gosling, *goz'ling, n.* a young goose.
[O.E. *gōs*, goose, dim. *-ling*.]

gospel, *gos'pėl, n.* the teaching of Christ: a narrative of the life of Christ, esp. one of those in the New Testament: absolute truth.
[O.E. *godspel—gōd*, good, *spell*, story.]

gossamer, *gos'à-mėr, n.* fine threads made by a spider which float in the air or form webs on bushes: any very thin material.
[M.E. *gossomer*; perh. *goose summer*, i.e. late mild autumn.]

gossip, *gos'ip, n.* one who goes about telling and hearing news or idle scandal: idle talk about others.

goss'iping, *n.* and *adj.* **goss'ipy,** *adj.*
[O.E. *godsib*, godfather.]

got. See **get.**

Goth, *goth*, *n.* one of a Germanic nation who invaded the Roman Empire.
Goth'ic, *adj.* of the Goths or their language: of a style of architecture with pointed arches: telling of horrors.
[L. *Gothī.*]

gotten. See **get.**

gouge, *gowj*, also *gōōj*, *n.* a chisel with hollow blade, for cutting grooves or holes.—*v.t.* to scoop out, as with a gouge: to force out, as the eye with the thumb.
[Late L. *gubia*, a kind of chisel.]

goulash, *gōō'lâsh*, *n.* a seasoned stew of meat and vegetables, etc. [Hungarian.]

gourd, *gōōrd*, *n.* a large fleshy fruit: its rind used as bottle, cup, etc.
[O.Fr. *gourde*—L. *cucurbita.*]

gourmand, *gōōr'månd, -mong*, *n.* a glutton. See also **gormandise.** [Fr.]

gourmet, *gōōr-mā*, *n.* a person with a delicate taste in food, orig. in wines.
[Fr., a wine-merchant's assistant.]

gout, *gowt*, *n.* acute inflammation of smaller joints, esp. of the big toe.
gout'y, *adj.* **gout'iness,** *n.*
[L. *gutta*, a drop.]

govern, *guv'ėrn*, *v.t.* and *v.i.* to rule: to control (e.g. one's temper): to guide, direct (e.g. a decision, a choice).
gov'erness, *n.* a woman in charge of teaching children in their home.
government, *guv'ėr(n)-mėnt*, *n.* ruling or managing: control: system of governing: (often *cap.*) the persons appointed to administer the laws (e.g. *steps taken by the government then in power*).—Also *adj.* (chiefly referring to government in last sense above; e.g. *government bonds, stores, responsibility*).
government'al, *adj.*
gov'ernor, *n.* a ruler: one with supreme authority: (*machinery*) a regulator, contrivance for keeping speed uniform.
gov'ernorship, *n.*
Gov'ernor-Gen'eral, *n.* the King's, Queen's, representative in a British dominion:—*pl.* **Gov'ernors-Gen'eral.**
[L. *gubernāre*—Gk. *kybernaein*, to steer.]

gown, *gown*, *n.* a woman's dress: an academic, a clergyman's, or an official, robe.
[O.Fr. *goune*—Late L. *gunna.*]

grab, *grab*, *v.t.* (*coll.*) to seize or grasp suddenly: to take possession of illegally:—*pr.p.* **grabb'ing**; *pa.p.* **grabbed.**—*n.* a sudden grasp or clutch: a device for gripping an object, or material, in order to lift or haul it.
[Conn. with Swed. *grabba*, to grasp.]

grace, *grās*, *n.* ease and elegance in the shape or the movement of a living creature: a pleasing quality: mercy: delay granted as a favour: a short prayer before or after a meal: a title used in addressing or speaking of a duke, a duchess, or an archbishop (e.g. *Your, His, Grace*): (usu. *cap.*) in Greek story, any of three beautiful sister goddesses.—*v.t.* to adorn: to honour (an occasion) by being present.
grace'ful, *adj.* **grace'fully,** *adv.*
grace'fulness, *n.*
grace'less, *adj.* without grace: having no sense of decency or of what is right.
gracious, *grā'shus*, *adj.* courteous: kind: merciful.
gra'ciously, *adv.* **gra'ciousness,** *n.*
grace note, *n.* a note not required for melody or harmony, added for effect.
days of grace, (three) days allowed for the payment of a bill of exchange, after it falls due.
to be in someone's good (bad) graces, to be in (not in) favour with him.
with (a) good (bad) grace, in an amiable (or an ungracious) way.
year of grace, year of Christian era, A.D.
[L. *grātia*, favour—*grātus*, agreeable.]

gradation. See **grade.**

grade, *grād*, *n.* a step in a scale e.g. of quality or of rank: (*U.S.*) a class in a school: slope (e.g. of a railway).—*v.t.* to arrange according to grade, e.g. according to size or quality.—*v.i.* to form a slope or an increasing, or decreasing, series.
gradation, *grȧ-dā'sh(ȯ)n*, *n.* a scale or series of steps: arrangement according to grade: passing from one colour, etc., to another by degrees.
gradient, *grā'di-ėnt*, *n.* the degree of slope (e.g. of a railway): a slope.
gradual, *grad'ū-ȧl*, *adj.* advancing or happening gently and slowly.
grad'ually, *adv.*
grad'uate, *v.t.* to arrange in grades: to mark (e.g. a thermometer scale) with divisions.—*v.i.* to change gradually: to receive a university degree, etc.—*n.* a person who has a university degree, etc.
graduā'tion, *n.*
grade crossing (*U.S.*), crossing **at grade** i.e. on the level.
the down (or **up**) **grade,** the descending (or ascending) part of a road, or of a life, career, etc.
[L. *gradus*, a step.]

graft[1], *grâft*, *v.t.* to transfer a shoot or part of one plant to another so that it unites with it and grows: to put skin from one part of the body on another part.—Also *n.*
[O.Fr. *grafe*—L. *graphium*, style, pencil.]

graft[2], *grâft*, *n.* (*slang*) profit by dishonest means, esp. in public life.—Also *v.i.*
[Origin uncertain.]

grail, *grāl*, *n.* the platter used by Christ at the last Supper.
[O.Fr. *graal* or *grael.*]

grain, *grān*, *n.* a single small hard seed: corn in general: a hard particle: a very small quantity: the smallest British, etc., weight: the arrangement and size of the fibres in wood, etc.: the side of leather from which the hair has been removed: its natural pattern or an imitation of it.—*v.t.* to paint (wood) in imitation of natural grain.

grained, *adj.* rough: furrowed.

grain'ing, *n.*

against the grain, against the fibre of the wood: against one's natural inclination.

to take with a grain of salt, to listen to (e.g. a statement) without really believing it.

See also **granary.**

[L. *grānum*, seed.]

gram(me), *gram*, *n.* a thousandth part of a kilogram(me).

[Gk. *gramma*, a letter, a small weight.]

grammar, *gram'ȧr*, *n.* (the study of the correct) use of words in speaking or writing: a book that teaches this.

grammat'ical, *adj.* according to the rules of grammar.

grammat'ically, *adv.*

grammar school, (*orig.*) a school in which Latin grammar was taught: a school giving an education specially suitable for pupils who go afterwards to a university.

[Gk. *gramma*, a letter.]

gramophone, *gram'o-fōn*, *n.* an instrument for reproducing sounds by means of a needle on a revolving grooved disk.

gramophone pick-up (see **pick-up**).

[Gk. *gramma*, letter, *phōnē*, sound.]

grampus, *gram'pŭs*, *n.* a whale, esp. the killer whale.

[L. *crassus*, fat, *piscis*, fish.]

granary, *gran'ȧr-i*, *n.* a storehouse for grain or threshed corn.

[L. *grānārium*—same root as **grain.**]

grand, *grand*, *adj.* of highest rank or importance: noble, dignified: magnificent, splendid: imposing: complete (e.g. *the grand total*): (*coll.*) very good, very fine: of the second degree of parentage or descent, as **grand'father,** a father's or mother's father, **grand'child,** a son's or daughter's child; so **grand'mother, grand'son, grand'daughter,** etc.—*n.* (*U.S. slang*) 1000 dollars: a grand piano.

grand'ly, *adv.* **grand'ness,** *n.*

grandeur, *grand'yŭr*, *n.* splendour of appearance: (of an idea, or of expression in words) loftiness.

grandfather clock, a clock with a long case standing on the ground.

grandmother clock, a smaller clock of the same kind as a grandfather.

grandil'oquent, *adj.* speaking grandly: pompous.

grandil'oquence, *n.*

grandil'oquently, *adv.*

gran'diose (*-ōs*, or *ōz*), *adj.* grand or imposing: pompous.

grand'-mas'ter, *n.* the head of a religious order of knighthood or of the Freemasons, etc.

grand opera, opera without spoken dialogue.

grand piano, a large harp-shaped piano, with horizontal strings.

grand'sire, *n.* a grandfather: any ancestor.

grand slam, the winning of all the tricks at bridge, etc.

grand'stand, *n.* an erection with raised rows of seats giving a good view (e.g. of a racecourse).

[Fr. *grand*—L. *grandis*, great.]

grange, *grānj*, *n.* a country house with farm buildings attached.

[O.Fr., barn—same root as **grain.**]

granite, *gran'it*, *n.* a hard rock composed of quartz and other minerals.

[It. *granito*, grained, granite.]

granny, *gran'i*, *n.* grandmother:—*pl.* **grann'ies.**

grant, *grânt*, *v.t.* to give (e.g. *to grant a right*): to agree to (e.g. a request): to admit as true (e.g. *I grant that I was stupid*).—*n.* a giving or bestowing: an allowance.

to take for granted, to assume, esp. without thinking about it.

[O.Fr. *graanter*—L. *crēdĕre*, to believe.]

granule, *gran'ūl*, *n.* a little grain.

gran'ūlar, *adj.*

gran'ūlāte, *v.t.* to break into small grains: to make rough on the surface.

granulā'tion, *n.* forming into grains: tissue formed in a wound in early stage of healing.

[Same root as **grain.**]

grape, *grāp*, *n.* a smooth-skinned berry or fruit from which wine is made.

grape'fruit, *n.* a large yellow-skinned fruit related to the orange and lemon.

grape'shot, *n.* shot that scatters on being fired.

grape'vine, *n.* vine on which grapes grow: rumour.

sour grapes, something that one pretends is not worth having because one cannot obtain it.

[O.Fr. *crape*, cluster, e.g. of grapes.]

graph, *grâf*, *n.* diagram in which a line shows the changes in a variable quantity (e.g. rising and falling temperature).

graph'ic, *adj.* of writing, or describing, or picturing: vivid (e.g. *a graphic account of an accident*).

graph'ically, *adv.*

graph'ite, *n.* a mineral, a form of carbon, known as 'black-lead', used in pencils.

graphic arts, drawing, painting, engraving, etc.

[Gk. *graphē*, a writing.]

grapnel, *grap'nĕl*, *n.* a small anchor with several claws: a grappling-iron.

grapp'le, *n.* a grappling-iron.—*v.t.* to seize, hold, with a grapple.—*v.i.* to

struggle (with): to try to deal (with, e.g. a problem).
grappling iron, an instrument for seizing and holding.
[O.Fr. *grape*, a hook.]

grasp, *grâsp, v.t.* to seize and hold: to understand.—*v.i.* (with *at*) to try to seize: (with *at*) to accept eagerly.—*n.* grip: power of seizing: power of understanding.
grasp'ing, *adj.* that grasps: greedy.
[M.E. *graspen, grapsen.*]

grass, *grâs, n.* plants with long, narrow leaves and tubular stem, including wheat and other cereals, and the plants (hay when dried) on which cattle, sheep, etc. graze.
grass'y, *adj.* covered with grass:—*comp.* **grass'ier**; *superl.* **grass'iest.**
grass'iness, *n.*
grass'hopper, *n.* a hopping insect that feeds on plants, chirping by rubbing its wings.
grass'land, *n.* land on which the chief natural vegetation is grass not trees.
grass snake, a harmless snake.
grass widow, a wife temporarily separated from her husband.
to let the grass grow under one's feet, to loiter, delay.
[O.E. *gærs, græs.*]

grate[1], *grāt, n.* a framework of iron bars for holding a fire.
grat'ing, *n.* a frame crossed by bars, used for covering or separating.
[Late L. *grāta*; same root as **crate.**]

grate[2], *grāt, v.t.* to rub, wear away, with anything rough: to irritate, jar on.—*v.i.* to make a harsh sound: to jar (on).
grat'er, *n.* an instrument with a rough surface for grating down a substance.
grat'ing, *adj.* jarring on the feelings, harsh, irritating.
[O.Fr. *grater*; a Germanic word.]

grateful, *grāt'fool, -fl, adj.* thankful, appreciative of kindness: agreeable, pleasing.
grate'fully, *adv.* **grate'fulness,** *n.*
gratitude, *grat'i-tūd, n.* thankfulness.
gratify, *grat'i-fī, v.t.* to please: to satisfy:—*pa.p.* **grat'ified.**
grat'ifying, *adj.* **gratificā'tion,** *n.*
[L. *grātus*, pleasing, thankful.]

grating. See **grate** (1), **grate** (2).

gratis, *grā'tis, grat'is, adv.* for nothing, without payment.
[Same root as **grateful.**]

gratitude. See **grateful.**

gratuity, *grȧ-tū'i-ti, n.* a money gift in return for service, a tip: a lump sum given, esp. to a soldier, when discharged, etc.:—*pl.* **gratu'ities.**
gratū'itous, *adj.* done or given for nothing: uncalled for, without excuse (e.g. *a gratuitous insult*).
gratū'itously, *adv.* **gratū'itousness,** *n.*
[Same root as **grateful.**]

grave[1], *grāv, v.t.* and *v.i.* to engrave:—*pa.p.* **graved** (or **grav'en**).—*n.* a pit dug out, esp. one in which to bury the dead.
grave'digger, *n.* one whose job is digging graves.
grave'stone, *n.* a stone placed as a memorial at a grave.
grave'yard, *n.* a burial ground.
[O.E. *grafan*, to dig; conn. Ger. *graben.*]

grave[2], *grāv, adj.* important, serious (e.g. *a grave responsibility*): threatening, critical: not gay, solemn.
grave'ly, *adv.* **grave'ness,** *n.*
gravity, *grav'i-ti, n.* graveness—importance, seriousness, or solemnity: gravitation, esp. the force by which bodies are attracted towards the earth.
grav'itate, *v.i.* to be strongly attracted, hence to move (towards).
gravitā'tion, *n.* act of gravitating: the tendency of matter to attract and be attracted.
[Fr.—L. *gravis*, heavy.]

grave accent, *gräv ak'sent*, a mark (`) over a vowel.
[Fr. *grave*; same as **grave** (2).]

gravel, *grav'l, n.* small stones:—*v.t.* to cover with gravel: to puzzle completely:—*pr.p.* **grav'elling**; *pa.p.* **grav'elled.**
grav'elly, *adj.*
[O.Fr. *gravele*; prob. Celt.]

graving dock, *grāv'ing dok*, a dry dock.
[Perh. O.Fr. *grave*, beach.]

gravity, gravitate. See **grave** (2).

gravy, *grāv'i, n.* the juices from meat that is cooking. [Origin uncertain.]

gray. Same as **grey.**

graze[1], *grāz, v.t.* to feed on (growing grass): to put to feed: (of land) to supply food for (animals).—*v.i.* to eat grass.
grazier, *grā'zyėr, n.* one who grazes cattle for the market.
graz'ing, *n.* act of feeding on grass: pasture.
[O.E. *grasian*—same root as **grass.**]

graze[2], *grāz, v.t.* to pass lightly along the surface of: to scrape skin from.
[Origin uncertain.]

grease, *grēs, n.* soft thick animal fat: oily matter of any kind.—*v.t.* (*grēz, grēs*) to smear with grease, lubricate.
greas'y, *grēz'i, grēs'i, adj.*:—*comp.* **greas'ier**; *superl.* **greas'iest.**
greas'ily, *adv.* **greas'iness,** *n.*
grease paint, a mixture of paint and e.g. tallow used by actors in making up.
[O.Fr. *gresse*, fatness—L. *crassus*, fat.]

great, *grāt, adj.* very large: very powerful, of high rank, etc: very important: highly gifted: noble, to be admired: in a high degree (e.g. *great pain, great friendship*): indicating one degree more remote in line of descent (used with uncle, aunt, and relations beginning with "grand"), e.g. **great'-un'cle** (one's father's or mother's uncle), **great'-grand'father, great'-grand'son.**
great'ly, *adv.* **great'ness,** *n.*

greater, *adj., comp.* of *great,* used in geographical names, as *Greater London* (the city and the area round it under the control of the Metropolitan Police).
Great Bear, a northern group of stars in which the seven brightest are known as the Plough.
great'coat, *n.* an overcoat.
[O.E. *grēat.*]

grebe, *grēb, n.* a short-winged almost tailless freshwater diving bird.
[Fr. *grebe.*]

Grecian. See Greek.

greed, *grēd, n.* a too great appetite or desire, esp. for food or money.
greed'y, *adj.* :—*comp.* **greed'ier** ; *superl.* **greed'iest.**
greed'ily, *adv.* **greed'iness,** *n.*
[O.E. *grǣdig,* greedy.]

Greek, *grēk, adj.* of Greece, its people, or its language.—Also *n.*
Grecian, *grē'shȧn, adj.* (used of architecture, straight nose, etc.).
Greek Orthodox Church, the form of Christianity prevailing in Greece, Russia, Turkey, etc.
[Gk. *Graikos* (*adj.*), Greek.]

green, *grēn, adj.* of the colour of growing plants : covered with grass, etc. : unripe : young : inexperienced : easy to deceive : not dried or cured, etc.—*n.* the colour of growing plants : a small grassy patch of ground : (in *pl.*) green vegetables.
green'ness, *n.*
green'ery, *n.* green plants : foliage.
green belt, a strip of open land surrounding a town.
green'fly, *n.* an aphis, plant louse :—*pl.* (*usu.*) **green'fly.**
green'grocer, *n.* a dealer in vegetables.
green'horn, *n.* an inexperienced youth, easily cheated (prob. orig. an ox with young horns).
green'house, *n.* a building with much glass, for plants.
green'room, *n.* a retiring-room for actors in a theatre, which orig. had walls coloured green.
the green'-eyed monster, jealousy.
the green light, permission to go ahead.
[O.E. *grēne.*]

greengage, *grēn'gāj', n.* a greenish yellow variety of plum.
[Said to be named from Sir W. *Gage.*]

greengrocer, greenhorn, etc. See **green.**

Greenwich (mean) time, *grin'ij* (*mēn*) *tīm,* a reckoning of time in which the sun's crossing of the meridian 0° is taken as 12 noon. (0° passes through the former observatory at Greenwich.)

greet, *grēt, v.t.* to salute with good wishes : to welcome : to meet (eye, ear, etc.).
greet'ing, *n.* act or words on meeting : (in *pl.*) a friendly message.
[O.E. *grētan* ; conn. Ger. *grüssen.*]

gregarious, *gri-gā'ri-ŭs, adj.* living in flocks : fond of company.
gregā'riously, *adv.*
gregā'riousness, *n.*
[L. *grex, gregis,* a flock.]

gremlin, *grem'lin, n.* a goblin accused of causing engine trouble, etc., for airmen.
[Origin uncertain.]

grenade, *gri-nād', n.* a small bomb thrown by hand or shot from a rifle : a glass projectile containing chemicals for putting out fires, etc.
grenadier, *gren-ȧ-dēr', n.* (*orig.*) a soldier who threw grenades : now title of first regiment of Foot Guards.
[Fr.—Sp. *granada,* pomegranate.]

grew. See **grow.**

grey, gray, *grā, adj.* of a mixture of black and white : ash-coloured : dull, dismal. —*n.* a grey colour : a grey horse.
grey'ly, *adv.* **grey'ness,** *n.*
grey'beard, *n.* an old man : a stoneware jar for liquor.
grey'lag, *n.* the common wild goose.
grey matter, *n.* the ashen-grey part of brain and spinal cord : (*coll.*) brains.
[O.E. *grǣg.*]

greyhound, *grā'hownd, n.* a tall, slender dog, with great speed and keen sight.
[O.E. *grīghund.*]

grid. See **gridiron.**

griddle, *grid'l, n.* a flat iron plate for baking. —Also (*Scot.,* etc.) **girdle** (*gėrd'l*).
[From a dim. of L. *crātis,* a hurdle.]

gridiron, *grid'ī-ėrn, n.* a frame of iron bars for cooking over a fire.
grid, *n.* a grating : a gridiron : a network of power-transmission lines.
[M.E. *gredire,* a griddle.]

grief. See **grieve.**

grieve, *grēv, v.t.* to cause sorrow to.—*v.i.* to feel sorrow : to mourn.
grief, *n.* deep sorrow, regret.
grief'-stricken, *adj.* overwhelmed with grief.
griev'ance, *n.* a real or fancied ground for complaint.
griev'ous, *adj.* painful : causing sorrow.
griev'ously, *adv.* **griev'ousness,** *n.*
to come to grief, to meet disaster.
[O.Fr. *grever*—L. *gravis,* heavy.]

griffin, *grif'in,* **griffon, gryphon,** *-ȯn, n.* an imaginary animal, with lion's body and eagle's beak and wings.
[L. *grȳphus*—Gk. *gryps,* name of a bird.]

grill, *gril, v.t.* to cook on a gridiron : to torment : to cross-examine severely.—*n.* a grating : a gridiron.
[O.Fr. *griller* ; same root as **griddle.**]

grille, *gril, n.* a lattice : a grating in a convent or jail door.
[Fr. ; same root as **grill.**]

grilse, *grils, n.* a young salmon on its first return from salt water. [Orig. unknown.]

grim, *grim, adj.* cruel, unrelenting (e.g. *a grim master, grim necessity*) : terrible, horrible (e.g. *grim sights in the disaster area, a grim task*) : (less strongly ; *coll.*) very unpleasant : resolute, unyielding (e.g. *grim determination*): (of joke, smile) causing, expressing, horror not amusement:—*comp.* **grimm'er**; *superl.* **grimm'est.**

grim'ly, *adv.* **grim'ness,** *n.*

[O.E. *grim(m).*]

grimace, *gri-mās'*, *n.* a twisting of the face, in jest, etc.—Also *v.i.* [Fr.]

grime, *grīm*, *n.* sooty dirt: ingrained dirt. —*v.t.* to make very dirty.

grim'y, *adj.* **grim'iness,** *n.*

[Conn. with Flemish *grijm.*]

grin, *grin*, *v.i.* to smile broadly: to show the teeth (as a snarling dog does) in expressing pain, etc.:—*pr.p.* **grinn'ing**; *pa.p.* **grinned.**

[O.E. *grennian.*]

grind, *grīnd*, *v.t.* to crush to powder: to wear down, sharpen, etc. by rubbing: to grate together, grit (the teeth): to oppress (often **grind down**).—*v.i.* to be rubbed together: to jar or grate: to drudge at any tiresome task: to study hard.—*pr.p.* **grind'ing**; *pa.t.* and *pa.p.* **ground** (*grownd*).—*n.* act, or sound, of grinding; hard dull work.

grind'er, *n.* one who, or something that, grinds: a tooth that grinds food.

grind'stone, *n.* a circular revolving stone for sharpening tools.

to keep one's nose to the grindstone, to toil, or force to toil, without ceasing.

[O.E. *grindan.*]

grip, *grip*, *n.* firm hold with hand or mind: power, control (e.g. *in the grip of circumstances*): the handle or part by which anything is grasped: way of grasping: (*coll. U.S.*) a travelling bag or small case. —*v.t.* to take fast hold of: to hold the attention or interest of:—*pr.p.* **gripp'ing**; *pa.p.* **gripped.**

to come to grips (with), to get into a close struggle (with): to tackle (with *with*; e.g. a problem).

[O.E. *gripe*, grasp; conn. *gripan*, seize.]

gripe, *grīp*, *n.* (esp. in *pl.*) severe pain in the intestines.

[O.E. *grīpan*, to seize; root as **grip.**]

grisly, *griz'li*, *adj.* frightful: hideous:—*comp.* **gris'lier**; *superl.* **gris'liest.**

gris'liness, *n.*

[O.E. *grislic.*]

grist, *grist*, *n.* corn for grinding.

to bring grist to the mill, to be a source of profit.

[O.E. *grist*; same root as **grind.**]

gristle, *gris'l*, *n.* a soft elastic substance in animal bodies, cartilage.

grist'ly, *adj.* **grist'liness,** *n.*

[O.E. *gristle.*]

grit, *grit*, *n.* hard particles: a coarse sandstone: courage, spirit.

gritt'y, *adj.* having hard particles: sandy: determined, plucky:—*comp.* **gritt'ier**; *superl.* **gritt'iest.**

gritt'ily, *adv.* **gritt'iness,** *n.*

[O.E. *grēot*; conn. Ger. *griess.*]

grizzle, *griz'l*, *v.i.* to grumble, fret. [Origin unknown.]

grizzled, *griz'ld*, *adj.* grey, or mixed with grey.

grizz'ly, *adj.* of a grey colour.—*n.* the grizzly bear:—*comp.* **grizz'lier**; *superl.* **grizz'liest.**

grizzly bear, a large, fierce bear of N. America.

[M.E. *grisel*—Fr. *gris*, grey.]

groan, *grōn*, *v.i.* to utter a deep sound of distress or disapproval: to be afflicted by (with *under*): (of a table, etc.) to be loaded with food.—*n.* a deep moan.

[O.E. *grānian.*]

groat, *grōt*, *n.* an old English silver coin.

[Middle Du. *groot*, great, thick (coin).]

grocer, *grōs'ėr*, *n.* a dealer in tea, sugar, etc.

groc'ery, *n.* shop, or business, of a grocer: (in *pl.*) goods sold by grocers:—*pl.* **groc'eries.**

[From *grosser*, wholesale dealer—**gross.**]

grog, *grog*, *n.* a mixture of spirits and cold water, without sugar.

grogg'y, *adj.* slightly drunk: weak from blows or illness.

[From 'Old Grog', nickname of Admiral Vernon, who ordered that rum for sailors should be mixed with water.]

groin, *groin*, *n.* the fold between the belly and the thigh: the angular curve formed by the crossing of two arches.

[Perh. O.E. *grynde*, abyss.]

groom, *groom*, *grōōm*, *n.* one who has charge of horses: an officer of the royal household: a bridegroom.—*v.t.* to clean, etc. (a horse's coat): to make smart and neat (e.g. *a well-groomed appearance*): to prepare (for political office, or stardom).

grooms'man, *n.* the attendant on a bridegroom at his marriage.

[M.E. *grom(e)*, boy, man.]

groove, *grōōv*, *n.* a furrow, or long hollow, such as is cut with a tool: fixed routine, rut.—*v.t.* to cut a groove in.

[Prob. Du. *groef* (earlier *groeve*).]

grope, *grōp*, *v.i.* to search (for something) as if blind or in the dark.—*v.t.* to search for by feeling (*to grope one's way*).

[O.E. *grāpian*; conn. with **grab.**]

gross, *grōs*, *adj.* coarse: very fat: glaring (e.g. *a gross error*): total, including everything.—*n.* the whole taken together: twelve dozen:—*pl.* **gross.**

gross'ly, *adv.* coarsely: very much (e.g. *grossly exaggerated*).

gross'ness, *n.*

in gross, in bulk, wholesale.

[Fr. *gros*—Late L. *grossus*, thick.]

grotesque, *grō-tesk'*, *adj.* fantastic, very odd and ugly.—Also *n.*

grotesque'ly, *adv.* **grotesque'ness,** *n.*

[Fr.—It. *grottesca.*]

grotto, *grot'ō*, *n.* a cave: an imitation cave. —Also **grot**:—*pl.* **grott'o(e)s.**

[It. *grotta*—Gk. *kryptē*, a crypt.]

grouch. See **grouse** (2).

ground[1], See **grind.**

ground[2], *grownd, n.* the solid surface of the earth: land: (in *pl.*) land attached to a house: soil: (in *pl.*) dregs, sediment: foundation: (often in *pl.*) sufficient reason, justification (e.g. *What are the grounds for this accusation?*): surface forming background of picture, etc.—*v.t.* to cause (a boat) to run aground: to bring to the ground: to attach (a flying man) to the ground staff: to issue an order that (an aeroplane) must not fly: to fix, base: to teach (someone) the first, most important, parts of a subject (e.g. *I tried to ground him in Latin*).—*v.i.* to come to the ground: to strike the bottom and remain fixed.

ground'ed, *adj.* not allowed to fly.

ground'less, *adj.* without foundation or reason.

ground floor, storey, floor on or near a level with the ground.

ground'nut, *n.* the peanut, a plant with pods that push down into the earth and ripen there.

ground plan, plan of the lowest storey of a building: first or outline plan.

ground rent, rent paid to a landlord for the use of the ground.

ground'sheet, *n.* a waterproof sheet spread on the ground by campers, etc.

grounds'man, *n.* man who takes care of sports field: an aerodrome mechanic.

ground staff, aircraft mechanics, etc., whose work is on the ground.

ground swell, a broad, deep rolling of the ocean due to past storm, etc.

ground'work, *n.* the foundation, first stages of, first work on, anything.

to fall to the ground, to come to nothing.

to gain ground, to advance: to make progress: to become more widely held (e.g. *The idea that rebellion was necessary was now gaining ground*).

to lose ground, to fall back, decline.

to stand, hold, one's ground, to stand firm.

[O.E. *grund.*]

groundsel, *grown(d)'sĕl, n.* a common yellow-flowered weed of waste ground.

[O.E. *gundeswelgė.*]

groundsheet, groundwork. See **ground.**

group, *grōōp, n.* a number of persons or things together: a school or party—*v.t.* and *v.i.* to form into a group or groups.

group captain, an air force officer (see *Appendices*).

[Fr. *groupe*—It. *groppo,* a bunch, knot.]

grouse[1], *grows, n.* any of a number of moorland game birds, esp. the **red grouse,** a plump bird with a short curved bill, short legs, and feathered feet:—*pl.* **grouse.** [Origin unknown.]

grouse[2], *grows* (also **grouch,** *growch*), *v.i.* to grumble.—*n.* a grumble.

[O.Fr. *groucher, grocher.*]

grove, *grōv, n.* a small wood.

[O.E. *grāf.*]

grovel, *grov'l* or *gruv'l, v.i.* to crawl on the earth: to make oneself too humble: to cower:—*pr.p.* **grov'elling**; *pa.p.* **grov'elled.**

[M.E. *groveling,* prone; from Old Norse.]

grow, *grō, v.i.* to have life: to develop: to become larger, etc.: to become (e.g. *He grew angry*).—*v.t.* to cause (e.g. plants) to grow:—*pa.t.* **grew** (*grōō*); *pa.p.* **grown** (*grōn*).

grow'er, *n.*

grown, *adj.* developed: adult (e.g. *a grown man*).

grown'-up, *adj.* grown, adult.—Also *n.*

growth, *n.* growing: development: tissue that grows in the body where it ought not to.

to grow upon, to gain a greater hold on (a person; e.g. of a habit, esp. bad): to begin to seem attractive to (a person).

to grow up, to become adult: (of e.g. a custom) to become common.

[O.E. *grōwan.*]

growl, *growl, v.i.* to utter a deep, rough sound as a dog does: to grumble in a surly way.—Also *n.* [Prob. imit.]

growth. See **grow.**

groyne, *groin, n.* a breakwater to check drifting of sand, etc.

[Prob. **groin.**]

grub, *grub, v.i.* to dig in the dirt: to work at a mean or laborious job: (*slang*) to eat.—*v.t.* (with *up*) to root out of the ground:—*pr.p.* **grubb'ing**; *pa.p.* **grubbed.**—*n.* the larva of a beetle, moth, etc.: (*slang*) food.

grubb'y, *adj.* dirty:—*comp.* **grubb'ier**; *superl.* **grubb'iest.**

grubb'ily, *adv.* **grubb'iness,** *n.*

[M.E. *grobe*; origin uncertain.]

grudge, *gruj, v.t.* to give, or allow, suffer, unwillingly (e.g. *I grudge the money*; *I grudge him his success*): to be unwilling (to).—*n.* a feeling of resentment (against someone) for a particular reason.

grudg'ing, *adj.* unwilling (e.g. *a grudging admission, grudging admiration*).

grudg'ingly, *adv.*

[Same root as **grouse** (2).]

gruel, *grōō'ĕl, n.* a thin food made by boiling oatmeal in water or milk: severe punishment.

gru'elling, *adj.* exhausting.

[O.Fr., hulled grain.]

gruesome, *grōō'sŭm, adj.* horrible.

[Conn. Ger. *grausam.*]

gruff, *gruf, adj.* rough or abrupt in manner or sound.

gruff'ly, *adv.* **gruff'ness,** *n.*

[Du. *grof.*]

grumble, *grum'bl, v.i.* to murmur with discontent: to growl: to rumble.

grum'bly, *adj.* **grum'bliness,** *n.*

[Conn. Ger. *grummeln.*]

grumpy, *grum'pi, adj.* surly, cross:—*comp.*

grum'pier; *superl.* **grum'piest.**
grum'pily, *adv.* **grum'piness,** *n.*
[Old word *grump*, a snub, sulkiness.]

grunt, *grunt, v.i.* to make a sound like a pig.—Also *n.*
[O.E. *grunnettan*, conn. Ger. *grunzen.*]

g-suit, *n.* a close-fitting suit with cells that can be inflated to prevent flow of blood away from the head, worn by airmen against blackout during high acceleration.
[*g* for acceleration of gravity.]

guanaco, *gwä-nä'kō, n.* a S. American wild animal related to the llama.
[American Sp.]

guano, *gwä'nō, n.* the dung of sea birds, used for manure. [Sp.]

guarantee, *gar-ȧn-tē', v.t.* to undertake as surety for another (e.g. *I guarantee his fulfilment of the contract*): to be responsible for (the truth of a statement): to answer for (the good qualities of an article): to promise (that): to secure (a person *against* e.g. loss):—*pr.p.* **guarantee'ing**; *pa.p.* **guaranteed'.**—*n.* a pledge or formal assurance.
guaranty, *gar'ȧn-ti, n.* (*law*) guarantee.
[O.Fr. *garant, n.*; same root as **warrant.**]

guard, *gärd, v.t.* to protect from danger or attack: to prevent from escaping: to keep under restraint (e.g. *to guard one's tongue*).—*v.i.* to take precautions (against).—*n.* a man or men stationed to watch and prevent from escaping, etc., or to protect: one who has charge of a railway train: state of watching: posture of defence: something that protects against injury, etc.: a cricketer's pad: (in *pl.*; *cap.*; Foot, Horse, Life Guards) household troops (see **house**).
guard'ed, *adj.* cautious (e.g. *guarded replies to searching questions*).
guard'ian, *n.* one who guards or takes care: (*law*) one who has the care of the person, property, and rights of another.—*adj.* protecting.
guard'ianship, *n.* protection, care.
guard'house, -room, *ns.* a house or room for accommodation of guards.
guards'man, *n.* a soldier of the guards.
on (or **off**) **one's guard,** on the watch, prepared (or the opposite).
to mount guard, to go on guard duty.
[O.Fr. *garder*; same root as **ward.**]

guava, *gwä'vä, n.* a tropical American tree with yellow, pear-shaped fruit.
[Sp. *guayaba*; from S. American name.]

gudgeon[1], *guj'ȯn, n.* a pivot: an iron pin.
[O.Fr. *goujon.*]

gudgeon[2], *guj'ȯn, n.* a small freshwater fish: a person easily cheated.
[O.Fr. *goujon.*]

guelder rose, *gel'dėr rōz,* the snowball tree, which has white balls of flowers.
[*Gelders, Gelderland* (Netherlands).]

guerrilla, *gė-ril'ȧ, n.* a member of a small band acting independently and harassing an enemy army by raids, etc.—*adj.* of this kind of soldier or method of fighting.
[Sp., dim. of *guerra*, war,]

guess, *ges, v.t.* to judge, form an opinion, when one has little or no evidence: to hit on the correct answer, etc., in this way: (*U.S.*) to think, suppose.—Also *n.*
guess'work, *n.* process or result of guessing.
[M.E. *gessen.*]

guest, *gest, n.* a visitor received and entertained.
[O.E. *g(i)est*; conn. L. *hostis*, stranger.]

guffaw, *gŭ-fö', v.i.* to laugh loudly.—*n.* a loud laugh. [Imit.]

guide, *gīd, v.t.* to lead or direct: to influence (e.g. *This guided me in my choice*).—*n.* one who conducts travellers, tourists, etc.: one who directs another in any way: a device to keep something moving along a particular line: a guide book: a Girl Guide.
guid'ance, *n.* direction: leadership.
guide book, a book of information for tourists.
[O.Fr. *guider.*]

guild, *gild, n.* in the Middle Ages, an association or union of merchants or of craftsmen of a particular trade: an association for mutual aid.
guild'hall, *n.* hall of a guild: town hall.
[O.E. *gield.*]

guile, *gīl, n.* cunning, deceit.
guile'ful, *adj.* crafty, deceitful.
guile'fully, *adv.* **guile'fulness,** *n.*
guile'less, *adj.* artless, frank.
guile'lessly, *adv.* **guile'lessness,** *n.*
[Norman Fr.; prob. same root as **wile.**]

guillemot, *gil'i-mot, n.* a diving bird with pointed bill and short tail.
[Fr., dim. of *Guillaume*, William.]

guillotine, *gil'o-tēn, -tēn', n.* an instrument for beheading: a machine for cutting paper, etc.: (in parliament) fixing of times for voting in order to cut short discussion.—Also *v.t.*
[J. I. *Guillotin*, a doctor, who proposed its use during the French Revolution.]

guilt, *gilt, n.* the state of having done wrong or of having broken a law.
guilt'y, *adj.* having done a wrong thing (e.g. *guilty of murder*): involving, or conscious of, wrongdoing (e.g. *a guilty act, a guilty conscience*):—*comp.* **guilt'ier**; *superl.* **guilt'iest.**
guilt'ily, *adv.* **guilt'iness,** *n.*
[O.E. *gylt.*]

guinea, *gin'i, n.* an old English gold coin, first made of gold brought from *Guinea*, in Africa: its value finally 21s.
guin'ea-fowl, *n.* an African bird of the pheasant family, grey with white spots.
guin'ea-pig, *n.* a small South American rodent (gnawing animal): a human being used as subject of experiment.

guise, *gīz, n.* appearance, esp. an assumed

or false appearance (e.g. *The fox in the story came in the guise of a priest*).
[O.Fr.]

guitar, *gi-tär'*, *n.* a musical nstrument with usu. six strings, plucked or twanged.
[Fr. *guitare*—L. *cithara.*]

gulch, *gulch, gulsh, n.* (*U.S.*) a narrow rocky valley, gully. [Origin uncertain.]

gulf, *gulf, n.* a large inlet of the sea: a very deep place: a deep, usu. impassable, division (between e.g. persons).
[O.Fr. *golfe*—Gk. *kolpos*, bosom.]

gull[1], *gul, n.* a web-footed sea bird with long wings.
[Perh. W. *gwylan*, to wail.]

gull[2], *gul, v.t.* to deceive, dupe.
gullible, *gul'i-bl, adj.* easily deceived.
gullibil'ity, gull'ibleness, *ns.*
[Origin uncertain.]

gullet, *gul'it, n.* the tube by which food passes to the stomach.
[O.Fr. *goulet*—L. *gula*, throat.]

gullible, etc. See **gull** (2).

gully, *gul'i, n.* a channel worn by running water, e.g. on a mountain side: (*cricket*) position between slips and point:—*pl.* **gull'ies.**
[Prob **gullet.**]

gulp, *gulp, v.t.* and *v.i.* to swallow eagerly, or with difficulty: to gasp, choke, as if swallowing in this way.—Also *n.*
[Conn. with Du. *gulpen.*]

gum[1], *gum, n.* the firm fleshy tissue that surrounds the bases of the teeth.
gum'boil, *n.* an abscess on the gum.
[O.E. *goma*, palate.]

gum[2], *gum, n.* a substance that is given out from certain plants, and hardens on the surface: a plant gum or similar substance used as an adhesive, etc.: a transparent sweetmeat: chewing-gum.—*v.t.* to coat, or to join, with gum:—*pr.p.* **gumm'ing**; *pa.p.* **gummed.**
gumm'y, *adj.* **gumm'iness,** *n.*
gum'boot, gum'shoe, *ns.* a rubber boot, a canvas shoe with a rubber sole.
gum'-tree, *n.* a tree yielding gum, etc., e.g. a eucalyptus tree.
[O.Fr. *gomme*—L. *gummi.*]

gumption, *gum(p)'sh(ö)n, n.* shrewdness: common sense.
[Orig. Scot.; origin unknown.]

gun, *gun, n.* a tube-shaped weapon from which projectiles are discharged, usu. by explosion: a cannon, rifle, or (*U.S.*) revolver.
gunn'er, *n.* one who works a gun: a private in the artillery: a branch officer in charge of naval guns, etc.
gunn'ery, *n.* the art of using guns, or the science of artillery.
gun'boat, *n.* a small vessel fitted to carry one or more guns.
gun'-carriage, *n.* the support on which an artillery weapon is mounted.
gun'-cotton, *n.* an explosive, cotton [illegible]ed with acids.
gun dog, a dog trained to help sportsmen shooting game.
gun'fire, *n.* firing of gun(s).
gun'man, *n.* a man who carries a gun, esp. a ruffian with a revolver.
gun'-met'al, *n.* an alloy of copper and tin: the dark grey colour of this alloy.
gun'powder, *n.* an explosive mixture of saltpetre, sulphur, and charcoal.
gun'-running, *n.* smuggling guns into a country.
gun'shot, *n.* the range of a gun.
gun'smith, *n.* one who makes or repairs guns.
great gun (*coll.*), a person of great importance.
to stick to one's guns, to hold to one's position in argument, etc.
[M.E. *gonne* prob.—*Gunhild*, woman's name.]

gunnel. See **gunwale.**

gunny, *gun'i, n.* a coarse jute fabric.
[Hindustani *gōn, gōnī*, sacking.]

gunpowder, etc. See **gun.**

Gunter's chain, *gun'tėrz chān*, a chain of 100 links, 66 feet long, used for land measurement.
[Edmund *Gunter*, astronomer.]

gunwale, gunnel, *gun'l, n.* the upper edge of the hull of a small boat.
[**gun** and *wale*, plank; guns were orig. set on it.]

gurgle, *gûr'gl, v.i.* to flow with, or make, a bubbling sound.—Also *v.t.* and *n.*
[Imit.; conn. Ger. *gurgeln*, **gargle,** etc.]

Gurkha, Goorkha, *goor'ka, n.* one of the chief race of Nepal.

gush, *gush, v.i.* to flow out suddenly or violently: to speak too enthusiastically, or to be too friendly and agreeable.—Also *n.*
gush'er, *n.* one who gushes: an oil well that flows without pumping.
gush'ing, *adj.* **gush'ingly,** *adv.*
[M.E. *gosche, gusche.*]

gusset, *gus'it, n.* a piece, usu. triangular or diamond-shaped, sewn into a garment to strengthen it or make some part of it larger.
[O.Fr. *gousset*—*gousse*, a pod, husk.]

gust, *gust, n.* a sudden blast of wind: a violent burst (e.g. of passion).
gust'y, *adj.*:—*comp.* **gust'ier**; *superl.* **gust'iest.**
gust'ily, *adv.* **gust'iness,** *n.*
[Old Norse *gustr.*]

gusto, *gus'tō, n.* enthusiasm, enjoyment.
[It.—L. *gustus*, taste.]

gusty. See **gust.**

gut, *gut, n.* the alimentary canal (see this term): (in *pl.*) bowels, entrails: intestines prepared for violin strings, etc.: (in *pl.*; *coll.*) toughness of character.—*v.t.* to take out the guts of: to reduce to a shell (by burning, plundering, etc.):—*pr.p.* **gutt'ing**; *pa.p.* **gutt'ed.**

gutt'er, *n.* one who guts fish, etc.
[O.E. *guttas* (*pl.*).]

gutter[1], *gut'ėr, n.* a channel for carrying away water, esp. at a roadside or at the eaves of a roof.—*adj.* low, disreputable (e.g. *the gutter press*, the cheap sensational newspapers).—*v.i.* (of a candle) to run down in drops: (of flame) to be blown downwards, threaten to go out.
the gutter, the places where the lowest kind of people live.
[O.Fr. *goutiere*—L. *gutta*, a drop.]

gutter[2]. See **gut.**

guttural, *gut'ůr-ȧl, adj.* (of sounds) formed in the throat: using such sounds, harsh. —Also *n.*
gutt'urally, *adv.*
[Fr.—L. *guttur*, throat.]

guy[1], *gī, n.* a rope, rod, etc., to steady anything.
[O.Fr. *guis, guie*, a guide.]

guy[2], *gī, n.* an image of *Guy* Fawkes, made on the anniversary of the Gunpowder Plot (5th November): a person of odd appearance: (*slang*) a man.—*v.t.* (*coll.*) to make fun of:—*pr.p.* **guy'ing**; *pa.p.* **guyed.**

guzzle, *guz'l, v.t., v.i.* to swallow greedily.
[Perh. conn. with Fr. *gosier* ,throat.]

gymkhana, *jim-kä'nȧ, n.* a meeting for athletic contests, etc.
[Hindustani *gend-khāna*, 'ball-house'.]

gymnasium, *jim-nā'zi-ům, n.* a hall, building, or school, for gymnastics:—*pl.* **gymnas'iums, gymnas'ia.**
gym'nast, *n.* one skilled in gymnastics.
gymnas'tics, *n.pl.* (used as *sing.*) exercises to strengthen the body: feats of agility.
gymnas'tic, *adj.*
[Gk. *gymnasion*—*gymnos*, naked.]

gynaecology, *gīn-, jīn-i-kol'ȯ-ji, n.* the branch of medicine which treats of the diseases of women.
gynaecol'ogist, *n.*
[Gk. *gynē*, a woman, *logos*, discourse.]

gypsum, *jip'sům, n.* a soft mineral, used to make plaster of Paris, etc.
[L.—Gk. *gypsos*, chalk.]

gypsy. See **gipsy.**

gyrate, *jī-rāt', v.i.* to spin, whirl.
gyrā'tion, *n.*
gyroscope, *jī'rō-skōp, n.* an apparatus in which a rapidly turning wheel is used e.g. to help to keep a compass needle always pointing to north whatever the motion of ship or aircraft.
[Gk. *gȳros*, a ring.]

H

habeas-corpus, *hā'bi-ȧs-kör'pus, n.* a writ requiring a jailer to produce a prisoner in person, and to state the reasons for his being in prison.
[L. *habēre*, to have, *corpus*, body.]

haberdashery, *hab'ėr-dash-ėr-i, n.* ribbons, needles, thread, buttons and other similar small articles. [Origin uncertain.]

habit, *hab'it, n.* one's ordinary behaviour, practice, custom: a tendency to act in a particular way because one has done so often before: dress (e.g. *a monk's habit*): a woman's dress for riding.
habit'ual, *adj.* constant: customary: by habit, confirmed (e.g. *a habitual drunkard*).
habit'ually, *adv.*
habit'uate, *v.t.* to accustom (a person to something).
habitué, *hȧ-bit'ū-ā, n.* a constant visitor, frequenter (e.g. *a habitué of the local inn*).
hab'it-forming, *adj.* (of a drug) which a taker will find it difficult or impossible to give up using.
[L. *habitus*, appearance, state, dress.]

habitable, *hab'it-ȧ-bl, adj.* fit to be lived in (chiefly of dwellings; see also **inhabitable**).
hab'itat, *n.* the natural home of an animal or plant.
habitā'tion, *n.* dwelling, residence.
[L. *habitāre, -ātum*, to inhabit.]

habitual, habituate, etc. See **habit.**

hack[1], *hak, v.t.* to cut, chop, clumsily: to notch: to kick.—*n.* a gash: a chap, crack, in the skin: a kick on the shin.
hack'saw, *n.* a saw for cutting metal.
hacking cough, a rough, dry cough.
[O.E. (*tō-*)*haccian*; conn. Ger. *hacken.*]

hack[2], *hak, n.* a horse kept for hire (also **hack'ney**; *pl.* **-neys**): a writer ready to do any kind of literary work for money. —Also *adj.*
hack'ney, *adj.* let out for hire.
hack'neyed, *adj.* used too much (e.g. *a hackneyed phrase*).
hack work, work done by a hack writer.
[M.E. *hakeney*; origin uncertain.]

hackle, *hak'l, n.* a comb for flax or hemp: a cock's neck-feather: (in *pl.*) the hair of a dog's neck, which rises in anger.
[Conn. with **heckle.**]

hackney. See **hack** (2).

had. See **have.**

haddock, *had'ȯk, n.* a sea fish of the cod family:—*pl.* **hadd'ock(s).**
[M.E. *haddok*; origin unknown.]

haem(o)-, hem(o)-, *hēm(o)-*, (as part of word) blood.
haemoglobin, hem-, *hē-mō-glō'bin, n.* the red oxygen-carrying pigment in red blood cells.
haemorrhage, hem-, *hem'ȯr-ij, n.* a dis-

charge of blood from damaged blood-vessels.

haemorrhoids, hem-, *hem'ór-oidz, n.pl.* swollen veins about the anus, liable to discharge blood, piles.

[Gk. *haima*, blood (L. *globus*, ball; Gk. *rhēgnynai*, to burst; Gk. *rheein*, to flow).]

haft, *hâft, n.* a handle (e.g. of a knife).

[O.E. *hæft.*]

hag, *hag, n.* an ugly old woman.

hagg'ish, *adj,* hag-like.

hag'ridden, *adj.* tormented, worried.

[O.E. *hægtesse*, a witch.]

haggard, *hag'ård, adj.* wild-looking from suffering, overwork, etc., very thin, hollow-eyed.

[O.Fr. *hagard*, an untamed hawk.]

haggish. See **hag.**

haggle, *hag'l, v.t.* to cut unskilfully.—*v.i.* to argue over a price, etc.

[Dial. *hag*, hack; of Scand. origin.]

hagridden. See **hag.**

hail[1], *hāl, n.* a call from a distance: greeting: earshot (e.g. *Keep within hail*).—*v.t.* to call out to: to welcome (as; e.g. *to hail as a hero, as saviour of the situation*).

hail'-fell'ow (-well'-met'), *adj.* very ready to be friendly and familiar.

to hail from, to come from, belong to (a place).

[Old Norse *heill*, health.]

hail[2], *hāl, n.* particles of ice falling from the clouds.—*v.i.* to shower hail, or as if hail.—Also *v.t.*

hail'stone, *n.* a single ball of hail.

[O.E. *hægl*, *hagol*; conn. Ger. *hagel.*]

hair, *hār, n.* a filament (i.e. thread-like object) growing from the skin: a mass of these, e.g. on the human head.

hair'y, *adj.*:—*comp.* **hair'ier**; *superl.* **hair'iest.**

hair'iness, *n.*

hair'breadth, *n.* a very tiny distance.—*adj.* (of e.g. an escape) very narrow.

hair'brush, *n.* a brush for the hair.

hair'cloth, *n.* cloth made partly or wholly of hair.

hair'cut, *n.* act, or style, of cutting hair.

hair'dresser, *n.* one who cuts, washes, etc., hair.

haired, *adj.* having hair of a stated kind (e.g. *fair-haired*).

hair'pin, *n.* a bent wire for fastening hair.—*adj.* (of a bend on a road) U-shaped.

hair'-raising, *adj.* terrifying.

hair shirt, a penitent's shirt of haircloth.

hair spring, a very fine spring coiled up within the balance-wheel of a watch.

not to turn a hair, to remain calm.

to make the hair stand on end, to terrify, or horrify.

to split hairs, to make small, unnecessary distinctions.

[O.E. *hǣr.*]

halcyon, *hal'si-ón, n.* the kingfisher.—*adj.* calm, happy.

[Gk. *alkyōn.*]

hale[1], *hāl, adj.* healthy, robust.

[O.E. *hāl*; conn. with **hail** (1).]

hale[2], *hāl, v.t.* to drag.

[Through O.Fr., but conn. Ger. *holen*, fetch.]

half, *häf, n.* one of two equal parts of a whole:—*pl.* **halves** (*hävz*).—Also *adj.*—*adv.* partly, to some extent (e.g. *I half hope he will not come*).

halve, *häv, v.t.* to divide into halves: in golf, to draw.

half'-and-half', *adv.* half one thing, half the other, in equal parts.

half'-back, *n.* in football, (a player in) a position directly behind the forwards.

half'-breed, *n.* a person descended from different races.

half'-bred, *adj.* mongrel.

half'-broth'er, half'-sis'ter, *ns.* a brother or sister by one parent only.

half'-caste, a half-breed.

half'(-)crown', *n.* a coin, of silver, then later cupro-nickel, worth 2s. 6d.

half'-heart'ed, *adj.* lacking in enthusiasm or spirit.

half mast, the position of a flag partly lowered in respect for the dead or in signal of distress.

half measures, a weak line of action: insufficient effort.

halfpenny, *hāp'ni, hā'pen-i, n.* a bronze coin worth half a penny:—*pl.* **halfpence** (*hā'pėns*), **-pennies** (*hāp'niz, hā'penēz*).

half'way', *adv.* to, or at, half the distance.—*adj.* equally distant from two points.

half'-wit, *n.* an idiot.

half'-witt'ed, *adj.*

to go halves, to share equally with another.

[O.E. *half*, *healf*, side, half.]

halibut, *hal'i-bút, n.* the largest of the flatfishes.

[M.E. *hali*, holy (because eaten on holy days), *butte*, flounder, plaice.]

halitosis, *hal-i-tō'sis, n.* bad breath.

[L. *hālitus*, breath, *-osis*, (diseased) state.]

hall, *höl, n.* the main room in a great house: a space just inside an entrance door: a large room for public gatherings: a manor-house.

hall'mark, *n.* the stamp, indicating purity, impressed on gold or silver articles at Goldsmiths' *Hall*: any mark of high quality.—*v.t.* to stamp with a hallmark.

[O.E. *hall*, *heall.*]

hallelujah, halleluiah, *hal-ė-lōō'yȧ, interj.* and *n.* 'Praise Jehovah': a song of praise to God. [From Heb.]

hallo(a). See **hello.**

halloo, *hȧ-lōō', n.* a cry to urge on a chase or to draw attention.—Also *v.i.* and *v.t.*

hallow, *hal'ō, v.t.* to make holy: to honour as holy.

hall'owed, *adj.* made, or honoured as, sacred (in church use, *hal'ō-id*).

hall'owe'en', *n.* the evening before All-hallows or All Saints' Day.
[O.E. *hālgian—hālig*, holy.]

hallucination, *hal-ōō-sin-ā'sh(ȯ)n*, or *-ū-*, *n.* a vision, sensation, etc., of something that does not really exist.
[L. *(h)a(l)lūcinārī*, to wander in mind.]

halo, *hā'lō*, *n.* a ring of light, esp. one round the sun or moon, or round the head of a saint in a painting :—*pl.* **halo(e)s** (*hā'lōz*).
[Gk. *halōs*, disk, halo.]

halt[1], *hölt*, *v.i.* and *v.t.* to make, or cause, a stop for a time.—*n.* a standstill : a stopping place.
[Ger. *halt*, stoppage.]

halt[2], *hölt*, *v.i.* to be lame, to limp.—*adj.* lame.—*n.* a limp. [O.E.]

halter, *hölt'ėr*, *n.* a rope for holding and leading a horse, etc. · a rope for hanging criminals.
[O.E. *hælftre* ; conn. Ger. *halfter.*]

halve, halves. See **half.**

halyard, *hal'yȧrd*, *n.* a rope for hoisting or lowering a sail, yard, or flag.
[From **hale** (2).]

ham, *ham*, *n.* the back of the thigh : the thigh of an animal, esp. of a hog : an actor who overacts : overacting : an amateur (esp. *a radio ham*).
[O.E. *hamm.*]

hamburger, *ham'bûrg-ėr*, *n.* a roll containing **hamburg steak,** chopped beef seasoned.
[*Hamburg*, Germany.]

hamlet, *ham'lit*, *n.* a small village.
[O.Fr. *hamelet* ; from Germanic.]

hammer, *ham'ėr*, *n.* a tool for beating or breaking hard substances, or driving nails : a striking-piece in a clock, piano, etc. : the apparatus that causes explosion of the charge in a firearm : an auctioneer's mallet : (*athletics*) a heavy metal ball with long handle of steel wire. —*v.t.* to drive, beat, or shape with a hammer : to beat severely.—Also *v.i.*
[O.E. *hamor.*]

hammock, *ham'ȯk*, *n.* strong cloth or netting hung by the ends, and used for lying on.
[Sp. *hamaca.*]

hamper[1], *ham'pėr*, *v.t.* to hinder, obstruct.
[Perh. conn. Old Norse *hemja*, restrain.]

hamper[2], *ham'pėr*, *n.* a large basket with a lid.
[O.Fr. *hanapier*, case for a drinking cup.]

hamster, *ham'stėr*, *n.* gnawing animal with large cheek pouches. [Ger.]

hamstring, *ham'string. n.* in man, a tendon behind the knee : in horses, etc., the great tendon at the back of the hock.—*v.t.* to lame by cutting the hamstring : to make powerless (person, efforts). :—*pa.p.* **ham'strung. [ham, string.]**

hand, *hand*, *n.* the part of the arm below the wrist : a pointer (e.g. on a watch) : a workman : a worker, helper : a share (in some action) : assistance (e.g. *to give a hand with the housework*) : pledge : style of handwriting : the cards held by a player at one deal : side (e.g. *on the one hand*) : direction (e.g. *on all hands, on every hand*).—*v.t.* to pass with the hand : to give, deliver (with *over, out*).

hand'ed, *adj.* used with another adj. to show a person's way of acting ; see **high-handed, left-handed,** etc.

hand'ful, *n.* enough to fill the hand : a small number or quantity : (*coll.*) a person or thing difficult to manage :—*pl.* **hand'-fuls.**

hand'less, *adj.* without hands : not skilful with the hands.

See also **handy, handle.**

hand-, (1) by hand (as **hand'-made, -sewn**) ; (2) worked by hand (as **hand'-or'gan**) ; (3) for the hand (as **hand'rail**) ; (4) held in the hand (as **hand'bag,** a bag for small articles).

hand'book, *n.* a small book of information and directions.

hand'craft, *n.* handicraft.

hand'cuff, *n.* (usu. in *pl.*) one of a pair of rings joined by a chain for putting on a prisoner's wrists.—*v.t.* to put handcuffs on.

hand'made. See above.

hand'-out, *n.* an official news item given to the press for publication.

hand'rail. See above.

hand'spring, *n.* a cartwheel or similar somersault.

hand's'-turn, *n.* a single small act of work.

hand'writing, *n.* (style of) writing.

hand and (or **in**) **glove (with)**, very friendly, or working closely (with).

hands down, with great ease.

hands up ! a call to surrender.

hand to hand, (of e.g. fight) carried on at close quarters.

at first hand, directly from the person concerned.

at hand, near in place or time.

in hand, actually in one's possession (e.g. *cash in hand*) : in preparation : under control.

on one's hands, (of something troublesome) under one's care.

out of hand, at once : out of control.

to live from hand to mouth, to supply present wants without thought for future needs.

to take in hand, to undertake.

to wash one's hands of (something), to refuse to take any responsibility in (the matter). [O.E.]

handicap, *hand'i-kap*, *v.t.* in a race or competition, to make (a good competitor or competitors) start at a disadvantage, so as to make chances of winning more equal : to make something more difficult for (a person) :—*pr.p.* **hand'icapping** ; *pa.p.* **hand'icapped.**—Also *n.* (e.g. *a*

golf handicap of 10 *strokes*; *his lameness is a handicap*).
[Prob. *hand i' cap* from drawing from a cap in an old lottery game.]

handicraft, *hand'i-krâft, n.* occupation or hobby in which things are made by hand.
[O.E. *handcraft*; infl. by **handiwork.**]

handiwork, *hand'i-wûrk, n.* thing(s) made by hand: work done by, or a result of the action of, a particular person, etc. (e.g. *This destruction is the handiwork of a madman*).
[O.E. *handgeweorc.*]

handkerchief, *hang'kėr-chif, n.* a piece of material for wiping the nose.
[**hand,** *kerchief*, cloth worn on head.]

handle, *hand'l, v.t.* to touch, hold, with the hand: to use: to manage (a person, or an affair): to deal in (goods).—*n.* part of an object intended to be held in the hand: something that may be used in achieving a purpose.
hand'ling, *n.*
[O.E. *handlian—hand*, hand.]

handmade, handrail, etc. See **hand.**

handsel, *han'sėl, n.* a gift at New Year or at the beginning of something: the first use of anything.—*v.t.* to give a handsel to: to use or experience (something) for the first time.
[O.E. *handselen*, hand gift.]

handsome, *han'sòm, adj.* good-looking: ample: generous.
hand'somely, *adv.* **hand'someness,** *n.*
[**hand** and suffx. *-some.*]

handspring, etc. See **hand.**

handy, *han'di, adj.* skilful in using one's hands: easy to handle or use: ready to use, in a convenient place:—*comp.* **hand'ier**; *superl.* **hand'iest.**
hand'yman, *n.* a man for doing odd jobs. [**hand.**]

hang, *hang, v.t.* to support from above, suspend: to put to death by suspending by the neck.—*v.i.* to be suspended: to be put to death by suspending by the ne ck:—*pa.t* and *pa.p.* **hanged** (by the neck), or **hung** (in other uses).—*n.* the way in which anything hangs.
hang'er, *n.* an object on which something is to be hung.
hang'ing, *n.* death by suspension by the neck: (usu. in *pl.*) curtain(s), etc.
hang'-dog, *adj.* mean, guilty-looking.
hang'er-on', *n.* a follower, one who hangs around hoping for benefits:—*pl.* **hang'ers-on'.**
hang'over, *n.* (*coll.*) uncomfortable after-effects of being drunk: something remaining (from).
to hang about, to loiter.
to hang around, to stay near (a person or place) for some purpose: to hang about.
to hang back, to hesitate.
to hang fire, to be long in exploding or going off: to delay or be delayed.
to hang on, to cling (to): to give close admiring attention to (*to hang on his words*): to linger: to depend upon.
to hang together, to keep united: to be consistent, agree (e.g. *His statements did not hang together*).
[O.E. *hangian* and two Old Norse verbs.]

hangar, *hang'ȧr, hang'gär, n.* a shed for aircraft. [Fr.]

hank, *hangk, n.* a skein, coil, loop.
[Old Norse *hanki.*]

hanker, *hangk'ėr, v.i.* to yearn, have a longing (with *after, for*).
hank'ering, *n.*
[Perh. conn. with **hang.**]

hanky, *hang'ki, n.* (*coll.*) handkerchief.

Hansard, *han'särd, n.* the printed reports of debates in parliament, first published by Luke *Hansard* (1752-1828).

hap, *hap, n.* chance.
hap'less, *adj.* unlucky.
happ'en, *v.i.* to take place, occur: to occur by chance: to chance (to do).
happ'ening, *n.* an event.
happ'y, *adj.* lucky: glad, enjoying oneself: pleased: well-chosen (e.g. *a happy phrase*):—*comp.* **happ'ier**; *superl.* **-iest.**
happ'ily, *adv.* **happ'iness,** *n.*
happ'y-go-luck'y, *adj.* trusting to luck.
hap'hazard (or *-haz'*), *adj.* chance: without planning or system (e.g. *a haphazard arrangement*).
hap'hazardly (or *-haz'*), *adv.*
hap'hazardness (or *haz'*), *n.*
to happen upon, to find by chance.
[Old Norse *happ*, good luck.]

hara-kiri, *hä'rȧ-ki'ri, n.* ceremonious suicide formerly common in Japan.
[Jap. *hara*, belly, *kiri*, cut.]

harangue, *hȧ-rang', n.* a loud pompous or wordy speech.—*v.i.* and *v.t.* to deliver, or to address by, a harangue:—*pr.p.* **haranguing** (*-rang'ing*); *pa.p.* **harangued** (*-rangd'*).
[Germanic *hring*, a ring of listeners.]

harass, *har'ȧs, v.t.* to worry by making repeated attacks on: to annoy, pester:—*pr.p.* **har'assing**; *pa.p.* **har'assed.**
[O.Fr. *harasser*, prob.—*harer*, set dog on.]

harbinger, *här'bin-jėr, n.* a forerunner.
[M.E. *herbergeour*, one who goes ahead to provide lodging; conn. with **harbour.**]

harbour, *här'bòr, n.* any refuge or shelter: a port for ships.—*v.t.* to lodge, shelter: to have (usu. evil, thoughts or feelings; e.g. *to harbour a grudge*).
har'bour-mas'ter, *n.* the public officer who has charge of a harbour.
[Prob. O.E. *here*, army, *beorg*, protection.]

hard, *härd, adj.* firm, solid: stiff: difficult: painful: severe: unfeeling: ungenerous: (of sound) harsh: (of colour) glaring: (of drink) alcoholic: (of *c* or *g*) pronounced as in *cat, good.*—*adv.* with vigour: earnestly.
hard'ly, *adv.* scarcely (see this word): with difficulty: harshly, severely.

hard′ness, *n.*
hard′en, *v.t.* and *v.i.* to make, or become, hard or harder: to make hardy.
hard′ened, *adj.* unfeeling.
hard′ship, *n.* thing(s) hard to bear (e.g. toil, poverty, etc.).
hard′-and-fast′, *adj.* rigid, not to be set aside (e.g. *a hard-and-fast rule*).
hard cash, ready money.
hard coal, anthracite.
hard′-earned′, *adj.* earned with difficulty.
hard′-head′ed, *adj.* shrewd, practical.
hard′-heart′ed, *adj.* unfeeling, pitiless.
hard′ware, *n.* articles of iron, copper, etc.: computer equipment for processing information.
hard′-wear′ing, *adj.* not quickly showing signs of damage through use.
hard′wood, *n.* hard timber obtained from the slow-growing trees (those that shed their leaves).
hard by, near.
hard lines, bad luck.
hard of hearing, pretty deaf.
hard up, short of money.
to be hard put to it, to be in, or have, great difficulty.
[O.E. *heard*; conn. Ger. *hart.*]

hardy, *här′di, adj.* daring, brave: able to bear cold or fatigue: (of plants) able to grow in the open air throughout the year: —*comp.* **har′dier**; *superl.* **har′diest.**
har′dily, *adv.* **har′diness,** *n.*
har′dihood, *n.* boldness: impudence.
[O.Fr. *hardi,* pa.p. of *hardir,* to harden.]

hare, *hār, n.* a timid, swift rodent (gnawing animal) with divided upper lip and long hindlegs.
hare′bell, *n.* a plant with blue bell-shaped flowers.
hare′-brained, *adj.* giddy, very rash.
hare′-lip′, *n.* a cleft upper human lip like that of a hare. [O.E. *hara.*]

harem, *hār′ėm, hä-rēm′, n.* the part of a Muslim house occupied by the women: the women themselves.
[Arabic *harīm,* anything forbidden.]

haricot, *har′i-kō, n.* kidney bean. [Fr.]

hark, *härk, v.i.* to listen (usu. with *to*).
to hark back, to return (to a previous subject—e.g. to a grievance).
[Same root as **hearken.**]

Harlequin, *här′lė-kwin, n.* a pantomime character in parti-coloured dress.
[Fr. (H)arlequin.]

harm, *härm, n.* injury: wrong.—*v.t.* to injure.
harm′ful, *adj.* doing harm.
harm′fully, *adv.* **harm′fulness,** *n.*
harm′less, *adj.* **harm′lessly,** *adv.*
[O.E. *hearm.*]

harmonic, etc. See **harmony.**

harmony, *här′mȯ-ni, n.* a (usu. pleasing) combination of musical notes, or of colours: happy, friendly, state without disagreements:—*pl.* **har′monies.**
harmon′ic (*-mon′*), *adj.* of, or concerned with, harmony.—*n.* an overtone.
harmon′ious (*-mōn′*), *adj.* pleasant sounding: pleasant to the eye: without disagreement or bad feeling.
harmon′iously, *adv.*
harmon′ica (*-mon′*), *n.* a mouth-organ.
har′monise, *v.i.* to be in harmony: to agree.—*v.t.* to bring into harmony: (*music*) to add parts to (a melody).
harmon′ium (*-mōn′*), *n.* a small organ.
[Gk. *harmonia—harmos,* joint, fitting.]

harness, *här′nis, n.* the equipment (straps, bands, etc.) of a horse.—*v.t.* to put the harness on: to make use of (natural power, as waterfall, etc.).
in harness, doing one's daily work, not retired.
[O.Fr. *harneis,* armour.]

harp, *härp, n.* a musical instrument played by plucking strings stretched from a curved neck to a soundboard.—*v.i.* to play on the harp: to dwell (on a subject) to a boring extent.
harp′er, harp′ist (name now used), *ns.*
[O.Fr. *hearpe*; conn. Ger. *harfe.*]

harpoon, *här-pōōn′, n.* a barbed dart, esp. one for killing whales.—*v.t.* to strike with the harpoon.
harpoon′er, *n.*
[Fr. *harpon*; a Germanic word.]

harpsichord, *härp′si-körd, n.* an old keyed musical instrument, now brought into use again.
[O.Fr. *harpechorde.*]

harpy, *här′pi, n.* (usu. *cap.*) in old story, a monster, half woman, half bird of prey: a grasping, shrewish, woman of low class:—*pl.* **har′pies.**
[Gk. pl. *Harpyiai,* snatchers, Harpies.]

harridan, *har′i-dȧn, n.* an ill-tempered old woman.
[Prob. O.Fr. *haridelle,* a lean horse.]

harrier[1], *har′i-ėr, n.* a small dog for hunting hares: a cross-country runner.
[**hare** or **harry.**]

harrier[2]. See **harry.**

harrow, *har′ō, n.* a spiked frame for smoothing and breaking up ploughed land, and for covering seeds.—*v.t.* to use a harrow on: to distress deeply.
harr′owing, *adj.* extremely distressing (e.g. *a harrowing story*).
[M.E. *harwe.*]

harry, *har′i, v.t.* to plunder: to harass, torment:—*pr.p.* **harr′ying**; *pa.p.* **-ied.**
harr′ier, *n.* a kind of hawk.
[O.E. *hergian—here,* an army.]

harsh, *härsh, adj.* rough: jarring on hearing, or sight, etc.: very strict or stern: cruel.
harsh′ness, *n.* **harsh′ly,** *adv.*
[M.E. *harsk*; of Scand. origin.]

hart, *härt, n.* a male deer (esp. red deer) from the age of six years:—*fem.* **hind**:—*pl.* **hart(s).**
[O.E. *heort.*]

hartebeest, *här'tė-bēst, n.* a South African antelope.
[S. Afr. Du., 'hart beast'; now *hartbees.*]

harum-scarum, *hā'rum-skā'rum, adj.* reckless, rash.—*n.* a giddy, rash person.
[Prob. old *hare*, harass, and **scare.**]

harvest, *här'vist, n.* time of gathering in ripened crops: the crops gathered in: fruits: the product or result of any action.—*v.t., v.i.* to gather (a crop).
har'vester, *n.* a reaper: a machine for gathering crops.
harvest home, the feast held at the bringing home of the harvest.
harvest moon, the full moon nearest September 23rd.
harvest mouse, a very small mouse that builds its nest on stalks of growing corn.
[O.E. *harfæst*; conn. with Ger. *herbst*, autumn.]

has. See **have.**

hash, *hash, v.t.* to mince, chop small.—*n.* a mixed dish of meat and vegetables in small pieces.
to make a hash of, to spoil completely.
[Fr. *hacher—hache,* hatchet.]

hashish, *hash'ish, -ēsh, n.* leaves, etc., of hemp, intoxicating when smoked, chewed, etc. [Arabic.]

hasn't, *haz'nt,* has not.

hasp, *hâsp, n.* hinged piece of metal used in fastening of a door, lid, etc.
[O.E. *hæpse.*]

hassock, *has'ok, n.* a tuft of grass: a stuffed stool for feet or knees.
[O.E. *hassuc.*]

hast. See **have.**

haste, *hāst, n.* hurry: rash speed.—Also (*poetic*) *v.i.*
hasten, *hās'ėn, v.i.* to move with speed: to do without delay (e.g. *He hastened to add an explanation*).
has'ty, *adj.* quick: hurried: too quick, rash (e.g. *a hasty temper, hasty words*):—*comp.* **has'tier**; *superl.* **has'tiest.**
has'tily, *adv.* **has'tiness,** *n.*
to make haste, to hasten, hurry.
[O.Fr.; same root as O.E. *hǣst,* violence.].

hat, *hat, n.* a covering for the head, usu. with crown and brim.
hatt'ed, *adj.*
hatt'er, *n.* a maker or seller of hats.
hat trick, (*cricket*) the taking of three wickets by three balls one after another.
[O.E. *hæt.*]

hatch[1], *hach, n.* the covering of an opening in a floor, wall, etc.: the opening itself.
hatch'way, *n.* the opening in a ship's deck into the hold, or from one deck to another.
[O.E. *hæcc, hæc,* a grating.]

hatch[2], *hach, v.t.* to produce from the egg: to develop or plan secretly (e.g. a plot).—*v.i.* to come from the egg.—*n.* act of hatching: brood hatched.
hatch'ery, *n.* a place for artificial hatching of eggs, esp. those of fish.
[M.E. *hacchen.*]

hatch[3], *hach, v.t.* to shade by fine lines, in drawing and engraving.
hatch'ing, *n.*
[O.Fr. *hacher,* to chop.]

hatchet, *hach'it, n.* a small axe.
hatch'et-faced, *adj.* having a narrow, sharp-featured face.
[Fr. *hachette*—same root as **hatch** (3).]

hate, *hāt, v.t.* to dislike very much.—*n.* hatred.
hate'ful, *adj.* arousing hate, detestable.
hate'fully, *adv.* **hate'fulness,** *n.*
hat'er, *n.*
hat'red (*hāt'*), *n.* extreme dislike, often with longing to injure.
[O.E. *hete,* hate, *hatian,* to hate.]

hath. See **have.**

haughty, *hö'ti, adj.* proud, arrogant.
haugh'tily, *adv.* **haugh'tiness,** *n.*
[O.Fr. *halt, haut,* high—L. *altus,* high.]

haul, *höl, v.t.* to drag: to pull with violence.—Also *v.i.*—*n.* a pull: quantity obtained at one time, e.g. of fish, stolen goods, or plunder.
haul'age, *n.* act of hauling: charge for hauling: transport, esp. heavy road transport.
haulier, *höl'yėr,* or *-i-ėr,* one who takes part in the road haulage business: one who hauls coal to the shaft.—Also **haul'er.**
[Same word as **hale** (2).]

haunch, *hönch, -sh, n.* the hip with buttock: leg and loin of venison, etc.
[O.Fr. *hanche*; prob. Germanic.]

haunt, *hönt, v.t.* to visit (a place or person) very often: to live in, or visit, as a ghost: to keep coming back to the memory of (e.g. *Her look of misery haunts me*).—*n.* a place one visits often.
haun'ted, *adj.* visited by ghost(s).
[O.Fr. *hanter*; prob. Germanic.]

have, *hav, v.t.* to own, possess: to enjoy or suffer (e.g. *to have good, bad, weather on holiday*): to hold in the mind (e.g. *to have a good idea*): to give birth to (a baby): to cause to be (e.g. *Have this picture framed*): to be compelled to (e.g. *I have to go now*).—Also used to form tenses of other verbs (e.g. *I have come, I had forgotten*):—*pr.p.* **hav'ing**; *pa.t.* and *pa.p.* **had**; *pr.t. 3rd sing.* **has** (*haz*).
hast, hath, old forms in the present tense (*thou hast, he hath*).
have'-not, *n.* a person, or group, lacking money or possessions.
had better, best. See **better, best.**
the ayes (noes) have it, the larger number of votes is in favour of (against) the motion.
to have had it, (*slang*) to be done for: not to be going to get it.
to have it out, to discuss thoroughly a subject of disagreement or ill-feeling.
to have up, to call before a court of justice, etc.
[O.E. *habben*; conn. Ger. *haben.*]

haven, *hā′vn, n.* a harbour or anchorage: any place of safety.
[O.E. *hæfen*; conn. Ger. *hafen.*]

haven't, *hav′nt,* have not.

haversack, *hav′ėr-sak, n.* a bag for a soldier's or traveller's food, etc.
[Fr. *havresac*—Ger. *habersack.*]

havoc, *hav′ȯk, n.* very great destruction.
[O.Fr. *havot,* plunder.]

haw, *hö, n.* the fruit of the hawthorn.
haw′thorn, *n.* a small tree of the rose family with white or pink blossom.
[O.E. *haga.*]

hawk[1]. See **hawker.**

hawk[2], *hök, n.* a bird of prey of the eagle family.—*v.i.* to hunt birds with trained hawks.
hawk′-eyed, *adj.* with very keen sight: very observant.
[O.E. *hafoc*; conn. Ger. *habicht.*]

hawker, *hök′ėr, n.* one who goes about offering goods for sale.
hawk, *v.t.* to carry round for sale.
[From Middle Ger.; conn. Ger. *höker.*]

hawser, *hö′zėr, n.* a small cable: a large rope for towing, etc.
[O.Fr. *haucier,* to raise—L. *altus,* high.]

hawthorn. See **haw.**

hay, *hā, n.* grass cut down and dried for fodder.
hay′cock, *n.* a cone-shaped pile of hay.
hay fever, irritation of nose, throat, etc. by pollen.
hay′maker, *n.* one who cuts and dries grass for hay: (in *pl.*) a country dance.
hay′rick, hay′stack, *ns.* a pile of stacked hay.
[O.E. *hīeg, hēg*; conn. Ger. *heu.*]

hazard, *haz′ȧrd, n.* chance, risk: a difficulty on a golf course (e.g. a bunker).
—*v.t.* to risk: to offer with some doubts (e.g. a suggestion).
haz′ardous, *adj.* dangerous, perilous.
haz′ardously, *adv.* **haz′ardousness,** *n.*
[O.Fr. *hasard.*]

haze, *hāz, n.* vapour or mist.
hāz′y, *adj.* misty: dim: confused in mind.
haz′ily, *adv.* **haz′iness,** *n.*
[Origin uncertain.]

hazel, *hā′zl, n.* a small tree with a nut (**hazel-nut**) that can be eaten—*adj.* of a light-brown colour, like a hazel-nut.
[O.E. *hæsel.*]

H-bomb, *n.* hydrogen bomb.

he, *hē, pron.* (*masc.*) refers to the male (or thing spoken of as male) already named (e.g. *John must go because he can run fastest*):—*objective* **him**; *possessive* **his** (*hiz*; sometimes described as a *possessive adj.*).—*adj.* male (e.g. *a he-goat*).
himself′, *pron.* (1) emphatic or (2) reflexive form of *he, him* (e.g. (1) *He himself said so*; (2) *He has hurt himself*).
[O.E. *hē.*]

head, *hed, n.* the uppermost or foremost part of an animal's body: the brain: the understanding: a chief or leader: the front or top of anything: a cape, promontory: a froth on beer, etc.: point of suppuration: an individual animal or person (e.g. *fifty head of cattle*): a chief point of a talk, sermon, etc.: the source or spring: a body of water: strength (as *to gather head*).—*v.t.* to lead: to get ahead of and turn (e.g. cattle; often with *off*): to strike (a ball) with the head.—*v.i.* to make straight (for a place).—*adj.* at the head: in the head: chief (e.g. **headmas′ter, head waiter**).
head′y, *adj.* intoxicating: rash, wilful: —*comp.* **head′ier**; *superl.* **head′iest.**
head′ily, *adv.* **head′iness,** *n.*
head′er, *n.* a fall, dive, head foremost.
head′ing, *n.* something that is at the head or top.
head′ship, *n.* the position of the person who has chief authority.
head′ache, *n.* pain in the head.
head′band, *n.* band worn round head.
head′dress, *n.* a covering for the head, esp. an ornamental one.
head′-hunt′ing, *n.* collecting human heads as trophies.
head′land, *n.* a point of land running out into the sea, a cape.
head′light, *n.* a light in front of a ship or vehicle.
head′line, *n.* a line (title, caption, etc.) at the top of a page, or at the beginning of a newspaper article: (in *pl.*) the chief points of (the news).
head′long, *adv.* head first: hastily: without thought, rashly.—*adj.* hasty: rash.
head′most, *adj.* most advanced, farthest forward.
head′phones, *n. pl.* telephone receivers that fix on the head, one on each ear, for listening to wireless messages, etc.
head′piece, *n.* a helmet: a hat: head, intelligence: the top part.
head′quarters(or *-kwör′*), *n.pl.* residence of a commander-in-chief or general: a central or chief office, etc.
head′stone, *n.* the principal stone of a building: a gravestone.
head′strong, *adj.* self-willed.
head′way, *n.* motion forward, esp. of a ship.
head wind, a wind blowing in the opposite direction from that in which e.g. a ship is moving, thus slowing it down.
heads or tails, a phrase used when tossing a coin to see whether the side with the sovereign's head will fall uppermost or the reverse.
head over heels, in a somersault: deeply, thoroughly.
off one's head, crazy.
over one's head, too difficult for one to understand.
to come to a head, to reach a climax, time of urgent need for action.

to have a head on one's shoulders, to have brains, ability.
to keep (lose) one's head, to keep (lose) one's presence of mind.
to make head against, to advance, make progress, against.
to make neither head nor tail of, to be unable to understand.
[O.E. *hēafod*; conn. Ger. *haupt*.]

heal, *hēl, v.t.* and *v.i.* to restore, or be restored, to health or normal condition: to mend (e.g. *to heal a quarrel*):—*pr.p.* **heal'ing**; *pa.p.* **healed.**
heal'er, *n.* **heal'ing,** *n.* and *adj.*
health, *helth, n.* wholeness or soundness, esp. of the body: state of the body (e.g. *in poor health*): a toast, as 'to drink one's health'.
health'y, *adj.* in good health: suggesting health: encouraging good health.
health'ily, *adv.* **health'iness,** *n.*
[O.E. *hǣlan*—*hāl*, whole.]

heap, *hēp, n.* a mass of things resting one above another: a mound: a great quantity (often in *pl.*).—*v.t.* to throw in a heap: to pile (up).
[O.E. *hēap*.]

hear, *hēr, v.t.* to perceive by the ear: to be told (e.g. *I hear, hear that, he is ill*): to listen to: to try (a case in a court of law).—*v.i.* to have the sense of hearing: to listen:—*pr.p.* **hear'ing**; *pa.t.* and *pa.p.* **heard** (*hėrd*).
hear'er, *n.* **hear'ing,** *n.* and *adj.*
hear'say, *n.* rumour, report.
hear, hear! exclamation of approval.
to give someone a hearing, to give him an opportunity to say what he wants to say.
within hearing, within earshot.
[O.E. *hȳran*.]

hearken, *härk'n, v.i.* to listen (to), esp. attentively.
[O.E. *he(o)rcnian*.]

hearsay. See **hear.**

hearse, *hėrs, n.* a carriage in which a corpse is conveyed to the grave.
[O.Fr. *herse*.]

heart, *härt, n.* the organ of the body that makes the blood circulate: a core: the most important part: the seat of the affections, etc., esp. love: courage (e.g. *His heart failed him*; *his heart failed*—the latter may also mean 'his heart stopped'): vigour: (in *pl.*) a card suit bearing heart-shaped pips.
hear'ted, *adj.* having a heart (usu. of a stated kind, e.g. *hard-hearted*).
hear'ten, *v.t.* to encourage: to cheer.
hear'ty, *adj.* warm, genuine: strong: healthy: (of a meal) large.
hear'tily, *adv.* **hear'tiness,** *n.*
heart'less, *adj.* pitiless: cruel.
heart'lessly, *adv.* **heart'lessness,** *n.*
heart'break, *n.* a deep sorrow.
heart'breaking, *adj.* crushing one with grief.
heart'broken, *adj.* deeply saddened.
heart'burn, *n.* a bitter, burning feeling caused by indigestion.
heart'burning, *n.* discontent, from envy.
heart'felt, *adj.* deep, sincere.
heart'-rending, *adj.* causing great pain or sadness.
heart'sick, *adj.* very depressed or unhappy.
heart'-whole', *adj.* not in love: whole-hearted, sincere.
at heart, inwardly, in real character.
by heart, in, from, memory.
heart to heart, frank: frankly.
to break one's heart, to cause one great grief: to feel great grief.
to take heart, to feel more hope, greater resolve.
to take to heart, to be upset by.
[O.E. *heorte*.]

hearth, *härth, n.* the floor of the fireplace: the fireside: the house itself.
[O.E. *heorth*.]

heartily, etc. See **heart.**

heat, *hēt, n.* the condition of a substance that gives one the sensation of warmth: sensation of warmth, esp. great warmth: a high temperature: the hottest period (e.g. *the heat of the day*): passion: violent or excited stage (e.g. *in the heat of the debate*): a preliminary race to eliminate some of the competitors.—*v.t.* to make hot: to agitate.—*v.i.* to become hot.
heat'er, *n.* **heat'ing,** *n.* and *adj.*
heat barrier, difficulty caused by heating of surrounding air and aircraft at very high speeds.
heat unit, amount of heat required to raise the temperature of a pound of water one degree Fahrenheit (*British Thermal Unit*).
heat wave, *n.* (*coll.*) a spell of very hot weather.
See also **hot.**
[O.E. *hǣto*; conn. with *hāt*, hot.]

heath, *hēth, n.* barren open country, esp. covered with low shrubs: a hardy evergreen low shrub.
[O.E. *hǣth*.]

heathen, *hē'*THn, *n.* one who believes in a lower form of religion, esp. with many gods: (*coll.*) an uncivilised person:—*pl.* **heath'en** (*the heathen*), **heathens.**—Also *adj.*
[O.E. *hæthen*; conn. Ger. *heide*.]

heather, *he*TH*'ėr, n.* kinds of heath.
heath'ery, *adj.* **heath'eriness,** *n.*
[Old Scots *hadder*; origin unknown.]

heave, *hēv, v.t.* to lift up with great effort: to throw: to haul: to force out (a sigh).—*v.i.* to rise and fall like waves: to retch:—*pa.t.* and *pa.p.* **heaved** or (among sailors) **hōve.**—Also *n.*
to heave in sight, to come into view.
to heave to, to bring a vessel to a standstill.
[O.E. *hebban*, pa.p. *hōf*.]

heaven, *hev'n, n.* the sky, upper regions of the air (usu. in *pl.*): the dwelling-place of God: (a place or state of) supreme happiness.
heav'enly, *adj.* of heaven: in the heavens: divine: beautiful: (*coll.*) very good, delightful.
heav'enliness, *n.*
heav'en-sent, *adj.* sent from heaven: very fortunate or suitable.
[O.E. *heofon.*]

heavily, etc. See **heavy.**

heavy, *hev'i, adj.* difficult to lift or carry: not easy to bear: oppressive: laden (with): clumsy: dull: deep-toned: dark, gloomy (e.g. *a heavy sky*): very sad: not easily digested:—*comp.* **heav'ier**; *superl.* **heav'iest.**—*n.* the villain in a play.
heav'ily, *adv.* **heav'iness,** *n.*
heav'y-han'ded, *adj.* clumsy: inclined to oppress, or to punish too much.
heav'y-hear'ted, *adj.* sorrowful.
heavy water, a kind of water heavier than ordinary water, used in nuclear reactors.
heav'yweight, *n.* a boxer not less than 12½ stone (or, amateur, not less than 12 stone 10 pounds).
[O.E. *hefig—hebban,* to heave.]

Hebrew, *hē'broo, n.* a Jew: the language of the Hebrews.—Also *adj.*
Hebraic(al), *hē-brā'ik(ȧl), adjs.*
[Gk. *Hebraios.*]

heckle, *hek'l, v.t.* to ask awkward questions, esp. at an election.
heck'ler, *n.* **heck'ling,** *n.* and *adj.*
[M.E. *hekelen,* to comb.]

hectare, *hek'tār* (Metric System). See *Appendices.*

hectic, *hek'tik, adj.* flushed with fever: excited, intense (e.g. *a hectic rush*).
hec'tically, *adv.* **hec'ticness,** *n.*
[Gk. *hektikos,* habitual.]

hecto-, *hek-tō-,* (as part of word) used to show multiplication by 100.
hectogram, etc. (Metric System). See *Appendices.*
[Gk. *hekaton,* hundred.]

hector, *hek'tȯr, v.t.* to bully, annoy.
[Gk. *Hector,* Trojan hero.]

he'd, *hēd,* he had: he would.

hedge, *hej, n.* a close row of bushes or small trees: a barrier.—*v.t.* to enclose with a hedge: to surround: to hem (in).—*v.i.* to make hedges: to avoid giving a straight answer.
hedg'er, *n.* one who plants or trims hedges.
hedg'ing, *n.* and *adj.*
hedge'hog, *n.* a prickly-backed animal with a snout like a pig.
hedge'hop, *v.i.* and *v.t.* to fly (an aeroplane) very close to the ground.
hedge'row, *n.* a line of hedge, often with trees.
hedge sparrow, warbler, a warbler, like a sparrow in appearance, seen in hedges.
[O.E. *hecg, hegg.*]

heed, *hēd, v.t.* to be attentive to: to concern oneself about.—*n.* notice, attention.
heed'ful, *adj.* **heed'less,** *adj.*
heed'lessly, *adv.* **heed'lessness,** *n.*
[O.E. *hēdan.*]

heel[1], *hēl, n.* the part of the foot sticking out behind: the covering or support of the heel in footwear: a thing like a heel in shape.—*v.t.* to strike, or pass back (a ball) with the heel: to put heels on.
heel'less, *adj.*
down at heel, shabby: slovenly.
on a person's heels, close behind him.
to come to heel, to obey as a dog does.
to take to one's heels, to flee.
[O.E. *hēla.*]

heel[2], *hēl, v.i.* (of e.g. a ship) to lean to one side.
to heel over, to heel too far to be able to right itself, oneself.
[O.E. *h(i)eldan,* to slope.]

heft, *heft, v.t.* to lift: to estimate a weight by hand.
hefty, *hef'ti, adj.* rather heavy: muscular: vigorous.—*comp.* **hef'tier**; *superl.* **hef'tiest.**
[Same root as **heave.**]

heifer, *hef'ėr, n.* a young cow.
[O.E. *hēahfore.*]

height, *hīt, n.* the state of being high: distance upwards: a hill: utmost degree (e.g. *the height of nonsense*).
height'en, *v.t.* to make higher: to make greater: to make brighter or more obvious.
[O.E. *hiehtho*; same root as **high.**]

heinous, *hā'nŭs, adj.* very wicked (e.g. *a heinous crime*).
[O.Fr. *hainos—haïr,* to hate.]

heir, *ār, n.* one who inherits anything after the death of the owner: a child, esp. a first-born son:—*fem.* **heiress** (*ār'es*; used esp. of a woman who has inherited, or will inherit, wealth).
heir apparent, the person acknowledged by law to be heir.
heir'loom, *n.* a valued inherited possession.
heir presumptive, one who will be heir if no nearer relative should be born.
to fall heir to, to inherit or receive (something that has belonged to another).
See also **heredity, heritable.**
[O.Fr. *heir*—L. *hērēs,* an heir.]

held. See **hold.**

helical. See **helix.**

helicopter, *hel'i-kop-tėr, n.* a flying-machine kept in the air by a power-driven screw or screws turning on a vertical axis.
[Gk. *helix,* screw, *pteron,* wing.]

heliotrope, *hel'i-ō-trōp, hēl', n.* a plant

whose flowers, according to story, always turn towards the sun: a shade of purple. [Gk. *hēlios*, sun, *tropos*, turning.]

helium, *hēl'i-ŭm, n.* a very light gas, not inflammable, present in the sun's atmosphere.
[Gk. *hēlios*, sun.]

helix, *hē'liks, n.* a line, thread, or wire curved as if wound regularly round and round along a cylinder:—*pl.* **hē'lixes** or **helices** (*hel'i-sēz*).
helical, *hel'i-kȧl, adj.*
[Gk. *helix*—*helissein*, to turn round.]

hell, *hel, n.* the place or state of punishment of the wicked after death: any place or state of wickedness or misery.
hell'ish, *adj.* **hell'ishly,** *adv.*
[O.E. *hel.*]

he'll, *hēl,* he will.

Hellene, *hel'ēn, n.* a Greek.
Hellen'ic (*-ēn'* or *-en'*), *adj.* Greek.
[Gk. *Hellēn.*]

hello, hullo, hallo, halloa, *hė-lō', interj.* expressing surprise, etc.: used also in calling attention or as a greeting.

helm, *helm, n.* the apparatus by which a ship is steered.
helms'man, *n.* one who steers.
[O.E. *helma.*]

helmet, *hel'mit, n.* a protective covering (orig. of armour) for the head.
hel'meted, *adj.* [O.E.]

help, *help, v.t.* to do something necessary or useful for (a person): to aid, to assist: to play a part in the success of (e.g. *Henry's good sense helped the negotiations*): to remedy, make less bad (e.g. *A hot drink will help your cold*): to prevent oneself from (e.g. *I could not help crying out*): to serve (food) at table.—Also *v.i.* —*n.* aid: assistance: relief, remedy: one who assists: (*U.S.*) a hired servant, esp. domestic.
help'ing, *adj.*—*n.* a portion served at a meal.
help'er, *n.* **help'ful,** *adj.*
help'fully, *adv.* **help'fulness,** *n.*
help'less, *adj.* unable (e.g. from weakness) to help oneself.
help'lessly, *adv.* **help'lessness,** *n.*
helpmate, -meet, *ns.* a husband or wife.
to help oneself, to get out of a difficulty or difficulties by one's own efforts: to take what one wants: to steal.
[O.E. *helpan.*]

helter-skelter, *hel'tėr-skel'tėr, adv.* in haste and confusion.—*adj.* disorderly.—*n.* a spiral slide in an amusement park.
[Imit.]

hem, *hem, n.* the border of a garment doubled up and sewed.—*v.t.* to form a hem on: to sew with the stitch usu. used in making a hem:—*pr.p.* **hemm'ing**; *pa.p.* **hemmed.**
to hem in, to shut in, prevent from moving.
[O.E. *hemm*, a border.]

hemi-, *hem-i-,* (as part of word) half.
hemisphere, *hem'i-sfēr, n.* a half sphere: half of the globe or a map of it.
hemispher'ical (*-sfer'*), *adj.*
[Gk. *hēmi-*, half (*sphaira*, sphere).]

hemlock, *hem'lok, n.* a poisonous plant with spotted stem: a poisonous drink made from it: (also **hemlock spruce**) a cone-bearing N. American tree.
[O.E. *hymlice.*]

hemorrhage, hemorrhoid. Same as **haemorrhage, haemorrhoid.**

hemp, *hemp, n.* a plant from different kinds of which are obtained a coarse fibre, a drug, and an oil: the fibre: the drug (known as hashish, marijuana, etc.).
hemp'en, *adj.*
[O.E. *henep*; conn. Gk. *kannabis.*]

hen, *hen, n.* the female of any bird, esp. the domestic fowl.—Also *adj.*
hen'pecked, *adj.* (of a man) ruled by his wife.
[O.E. *henn*, fem. of *hana*, a cock.]

hence, *hens, adv.* from this place: from this time (e.g. *a year hence*): from this reason, therefore.—*interj.* away! begone!
hence'forth, -for'ward, *advs.* from this time forth or forward.
[M.E. *hennes.*]

henchman, *hench'man, -sh'-, n.* a servant: an active supporter, often political:—*pl.* **-men.**
[O.E. *hengest*, a horse, and **man.**]

henna, *hen'ȧ, n.* a small Eastern shrub: a dye made from its leaves for nails and hair.
[Arabic *hennā'.*]

henpecked. See **hen.**

hept(a)-, *pfx.* seven. [Gk.]

her, hers, herself. See **she.**

herald, *her'ȧld, n.* in the past, an officer who made public proclamations, arranged ceremonies, and later kept a register of noble families and their coats of arms, etc.: a person, or thing, that goes before, or announces, something else.—*v.t.* to announce or be a sign of (something about to happen).
heral'dic, *adj.* of heralds or heraldry.
her'aldry, *n.* the science dealing with coats of arms and the persons who have a right to bear them, etc.: the pomp and ceremony in which heralds took part.
[O.Fr. *herault*; of Germanic origin.]

herb, *hėrb, n.* a plant with no woody stem above ground, i.e. not a tree or shrub: a plant used in medicine: a scented plant used in cookery (e.g. sage).
herbaceous, *hėr-bā'shŭs, adj.* herb-like: containing herbs, esp. tall plants that die down in winter (e.g. *a herbaceous border or flower bed*).
her'bage, *n.* grass for pasture.
her'bal, *adj.* of herbs, esp. herbs used for medicine.
her'balist, *n.* a person who deals in herbs.

herbiv′orous, *adj.* feeding on plants. [Fr. *herbe*—L. *herba*, grass, herb.]

herculean, *hėr-kū-lē′ȧn*, or *-kū′*, *adj.* having, or requiring, very great strength. [*Hercules*, old hero of great strength.]

herd[1], *hėrd*, *n.* a company of animals of one kind that keep, or are kept, together. —*v.i.* and *v.t.* to come, or drive, together.
the (common) herd, the mass of ordinary people who accept the same views and act alike.
[O.E. *heord*.]

herd[2], *hėrd*, *n.* one who looks after a herd of animals.—Also **herds′man.**
[O.E. *hirde*; conn. *herd* (1).]

here, *hēr*, *adv.* in, or to, this place: in this matter: in the present life or state.
here′about(s), *adv.* near this place.
hereaf′ter, *adv.* after this, in some future time or state.—*n.* a future state.
here′by′, *adv.* by means of (e.g. a document; *I hereby declare that I will not be responsible for any debts incurred by her*).
here′upon, *adv.* immediately after this.
herewith′ (or *hēr′*), *adv.* with this (e.g. with this letter).
here and there, in, or to, some scattered places.
here's to, I drink the health of.
neither here nor there, not important.
[O.E. *hēr*; conn. Ger. *hier*.]

heredity, *hi-red′i-ti*, *n.* the passing on of physical and mental characteristics from ancestors to their descendants.
hered′itary, *adj.* handed down from ancestors.
See also **heritable, inheritance.**
[L. *hērēs, hērēdis*, heir; root as **heir.**]

heresy, *her′i-si*, *n.* belief or opinion different from that held by the group of people to which one belongs:—*pl.* **her′esies.**
her′etic, *n.* one who upholds a heresy.
heret′ical, *adj.* **heret′ically,** *adv.*
[Gk. *hairesis*.]

heritable, *her′i-tȧ-bl*, *adj.* that may be inherited.
her′itage (*-tij*), *n.* something that is inherited.
[O.Fr. *heriter*, inherit; root as **heir.**]

hermetically sealed, *hėr-met′ik-ȧl-i sēld*, closed completely.
[Gk. *Hermēs Trismegistos*, Egyptian god of science.]

hermit, *hėr′mit*, *n.* a person, esp. an early Christian, who went to live by himself in a lonely place: a person who shuns the company of others.
her′mitage (*-ij*), *n.* the dwelling of a hermit.
[Gk. *erēmitēs*—*erēmos*, lonely.]

hernia, *hėr′ni-ȧ*, *n.* the thrusting out of (part of) a bodily organ through an opening or weak spot in its surrounding walls. [L.]

hero, *hē′rō*, *n.* a very brave man or boy: one greatly admired for noble qualities, real or imaginary: the principal male character in a book or play:—*pl.* **hē′roes**: —*fem.* **heroine** (*her′ō-in*).
heroic, *hė-rō′ik*, *adj.* very brave.
hero′ically, *adv.*
her′oism (*her′*), *n.* great bravery.
he′ro-wor′ship, *n.* very great admiration for, and devotion to, a person regarded as a hero (or heroine).
[Gk. *hērōs*.]

heroin, *her′ō-in*, *n.* a habit-forming drug, obtained from opium.
[Gk. *hērōs*, hero.]

heroine, heroism. See **hero.**

heron, *her′ȯn*, *n.* a large wading bird, with long legs and neck.
her′onry, *n.* a place where herons breed.
[O.Fr. *hairon*; a Germanic word.]

herring, *her′ing*, *n.* a common small sea fish used as food, found moving in great shoals:—*pl.* **herr′ing(s).**
herr′ingbone, *adj.* applied to masonry in which the stones make a pattern like numbers of herring spines laid side by side, to a stitch of spine-like appearance in sewing, etc.
red herring. See **red.**
[O.E. *hǣring*; conn. with Ger. *hering*.]

hers, herself. See **she.**

he's, *hēz*, he is.

hesitate, *hez′i-tāt*, *v.i.* to pause unwilling (to; e.g. *I hesitate to say he lied, but he certainly misled me*): to stammer.
hes′itancy, hesitā′tion, *ns.*
hes′itant, *adj.*
[L. *haesitāre*—*haesēre*, to stick.]

hessian, *hes′i-ȧn*, *hes′yȧn*, *n.* a coarse cloth made of jute.
[*Hesse* (Ger. *Hessen*) in Germany.]

hetero-, *het-ėr-ō-*, (as part of word) other, different.
heteroge′neous (*-jē′ni-ŭs*), *adj.* made up of parts or individuals of very different kinds (e.g. *a heterogeneous mixture, crowd*, etc.).
[Gk. *heteros*, other (*genos*, kind).]

hew, *hū*, *v.t.* to cut (away, down, in pieces, etc.) with blows: to shape: to cut (a path; e.g. to *hew one's way*):—*pa.p.* **hewed,** or **hewn.**
hew′er, *n.*
[O.E. *hēawan*; conn. with Ger. *hauen*.]

hex(a)-, *heks(a)-*, (as part of word) six.
hex′agon, *n.* a figure with six sides and six angles.
hexag′onal, *adj.*
[Gk. *hex*, six (*gōnia*, angle).]

hey, *hā*, *interj.* expressing joy, or a question, or calling attention.
hey′day, *n.* period of fullest vigour or greatest activity. [Imit.]

hiatus, *hī-ā′tŭs*, *n.* a break, gap: a place in a manuscript, etc., where something is missing:—*pl.* **hia′tuses.**
[L.—*hiāre, hiātum*, to gape.]

hibernate, *hī′bėr-nāt*, *v.i.* to pass the winter in sleep, as some animals do: to remain in an inactive state.

hibernā′tion, *n.*
[L. *hībernāre—hiems*, winter.]
Hibernian, *hī-bėr′ni-ȧn, adj.* of Ireland.
[L. *Hibernia*, Ireland.]
hiccough. A spelling of **hiccup.**
hiccup, *hik′up, n.* a sudden spasm of the diaphragm followed immediately by closing of the top of the windpipe: the sound caused by this.—Also *v.i.—v.t.* to say with a hiccup :—*pr.p.* **hicc′uping**; *pa.p.* **hicc′uped.** [Imit.]
hickory, *hik′ȯr-i, n.* a number of N. American trees of the walnut family, some having strong wood :—*pl.* **hick′ories.**
[Of American Indian origin.]
hid, hidden. See **hide** (1).
hide[1], *hīd, v.t.* to put out of sight: to conceal: to keep secret.—*v.i.* to go into, or stay in, place where one cannot be seen, or easily found :—*pa.t.* **hid**; *pa.p.* **hidd′en.**
hidd′en, *adj.* concealed: unknown.
hid′ing, *n.* the act or state of concealing: a place of concealment.
hide′-out, *n.* a place of hiding.
[O.E. *hȳdan*, to hide.]
hide[2], *hīd, n.* the skin of an animal: (*slang*) a human skin.
hid′ing, *n.* a thrashing.
hide′-bound, *adj.* (of an animal) with hide clinging too closely to the body: narrow-minded, not ready to accept new ideas or opinions.
[O.E. *hȳd.*]
hideous, *hid′i-ůs, -yůs, adj.* frightful, horrible: extremely ugly.
hid′eously, *adv.* **hid′eousness,** *n.*
[O.Fr. *hideus*; origin unknown.]
hiding. See **hide** (1) and (2).
hie, *hī, v.i.* to hasten :—*pr.p.* **hie′ing**; *pa.p.* **hied** (*hīd*).
[O.E. *hīgian.*]
hier-, *hī-ėr-*, (as part of word) sacred.
hierarchy, *hī′ėr-är-ki, n.* an arrangement in grades according to importance (orig. of angels, now of people in power): a controlling group of people.
hieroglyphic, *hī-ėr-ō-glif′ik, n.* one of the pictures used in picture-writing, esp. in that of ancient Egypt: a letter or symbol hard to read.
[Gk. *hieros*, sacred (*archein*, to rule; *glyphein*, to carve).]
hi-fi. See **high fidelity.**
higgle. Same as **haggle,** *v.i.*
higgledy-piggledy, *hig′l-di-pig′l-di, adv.* and *adj.* in any order, in confusion.
[Origin uncertain.]
high, *hī, adj.* tall, lofty: far up from e.g. the ground, sea level, low tide, zero on a scale: great (e.g. *high speed, price, hopes*): of important rank (e.g. *a high official*): chief (e.g. *High Court, the high altar*): noble (e.g. *high aims*): (of sound) acute in pitch, shrill: (of meat, etc.) beginning to go bad.
high′ly, *adv.* in high place or rank: very (e.g. *highly dangerous*): at a high rate (e.g. *highly paid*): with approval (e.g. *to think highly of someone*).
high′ness, *n.* quality of being high: (*cap.*) title of various princes.
See also **height.**
high′ball, *n.* (*U.S.*), liquor and an effervescent drink (e.g. whisky and soda) with ice in a tall glass.
high′-born, *adj.* of noble birth.
high′brow, *n.* a person with intellectual tastes.—Also *adj.*
High Church, a party within the Church of England which attaches importance to ritual and to the authority of the clergy.
high′ly-col′oured, *adj.* exaggerated.
High Commissioner, the chief representative in a British Commonwealth country of another country that is also a member of the Commonwealth. See also **Governor-General.**
highfalu′tin(g) (*-lōō′*), *adj.* pompous, lofty and affected (e.g. *a highfalutin style*).
high fidelity, good in reproduction of sound (*abbrev.* **hi-fi**).
high′flown, *adj.* (of style) using words that sound grand, bombastic.
high′-hand′ed, *adj.* taking power or authority to oneself: done without considering the views of others (e.g. *a high-handed action*).
high jinks, boisterous play.
high′lands, *n. pl.* a mountainous district, esp. (*cap.*) the north-west of Scotland.
high′land, High′land, *adj.*
high′lander, High′lander, *n.*
Highland dress, kilt, etc., as worn on formal occasions.
high latitudes, those far from the equator.
high life, life of fashionable society.
high′light, *n.* a bright spot in a picture or photograph: a striking or memorable part of an experience.—*v.t.* to draw the attention towards, emphasise.
high living, rich, luxurious feeding.
high′-mind′ed, *adj.* having, or showing, high principles.
high′-oc′tane, *adj.* (of petrol) of high octane number and so of high efficiency.
high′-press′ure, *adj.* having or using a pressure above normal: very active.
high′road, *n.* a highway: an easy way.
high seas, the open sea beyond territorial waters.
high′-sound′ing, *adj.* sounding, seeming, grand or important.
high′spir′ited, *adj.* bold, daring.
high′(ly)-strung′, *adj.* sensitive and nervous.
high summer, summer well advanced.
high tea, tea with meat, or fish, etc.
high time, quite time (that something was done).
high treason. See **treason.**
high water, the time at which the tide is highest.
high′way, *n.* a public, esp. main, road.

high′wayman, *n.* a robber who attacked travellers on the road.
high words, angry words.
[O.E. *hēah.*]

hike, *hīk, v.i.* to travel on foot with equipment on back.—Also *n.*
[Perh. **hitch.**]

hilarious, *hi-lā′ri-ŭs, adj.* very merry.
hila′riously, *adv.*
hila′riousness, hilarity (*hi-lar′-*), *ns.*
[Gk. *hilaros,* cheerful.]

hill, *hil, n.* a high mass of land, less than a mountain: an incline on a road: a heap.
hill′ock, *n.* a small hill.
hill′y, *adj.* **hill′iness,** *n.*
hill′top, *n.* top of hill.
[O.E. *hyll*; conn. with L. *collis,* hill.]

hilt, *hilt, n.* the handle, esp. of a sword.
up to the hilt, completely. [O.E.]

him, himself. See **he.**

hind[1], *hīnd, n.* a female deer, esp. of the red deer. [O.E.]

hind[2], *hīnd, n.* a farm servant.
[O.E. *hīna.*]

hind[3], *hīnd,* **hinder,** *hīnd′ėr, adjs.* situated at the back:—*superl.* **hind′most, hind′ermost,** farthest behind.
hind′leg, *n.* a back leg of a four-footed animal.
hind′quarters, *n.pl.* the rear parts of an animal.
[O.E. *hinder.*]

hinder[1], *hin′dėr, v.t.* to keep back, to stop, prevent progress of.
hin′drance, *n.*
[O.E. *hindrian.*]

hinder[2], **hind(er)most.** See **hind** (3).

Hindi, *hin′dē, n.* a very important literary language of India.
Hindustani, *hin-dōō-stän′i, n.* a form of this (from which many English words are borrowed), spoken by very large numbers of Indians.
Hindu, *hin′dōō, -dōō′, n.* an Indian who believes and lives according to the religion of **Hin′duism.**
[Hindi *Hind,* India.]

hindmost, hindquarters. See **hind** (3).

hinge, *hinj, n.* the hook or joint on which a door or lid turns.—*v.t.* to add hinges to.—*v.i.* to hang or turn as on a hinge: to depend (on; e.g. *Success hinges on what he does next*):—*pr.p.* **hing′ing** (*hinj′*); *pa.p.* **hinged.**
[Conn. with **hang.**]

hint, *hint, n.* a statement that passes on information without giving it openly or directly: a helpful suggestion (about, on, how to do something): a very small amount.—Also *v.t.* and *v.i.*
[O.E. *hentan,* to seize.]

hinterland, *hint′ėr-land, n.* a region lying inland from a port. [Ger.]

hip[1], *hip, n.* the projecting part formed by the side of the pelvis and the upper part of the thigh bone.
[O.E. *hype.*]

hip[2], *hip, n.* the fruit of the wild rose.
[O.E. *hēope.*]

hippopotamus, *hip-ō-pot′ȧ-mŭs, n.* a large African animal with very thick skin, living in or near water:—*pl.* **hippopot′amuses, hippopot′ami** (*-mī*).
[Gk. *hippos,* horse, *potamos,* river.]

hire, *hīr, v.t.* to obtain the use of at a price: (also **hire out**) to give someone the use of (something) for payment: to engage for wages.—Also *n.*
hire′ling, *n.* a hired servant, esp. one who will do anything for money.
hire purchase, a system by which a hired article becomes the property of the hirer after a certain number of payments.
[O.E. *hȳr,* wages.]

hirsute, *hėr-sūt′, adj.* hairy: shaggy.
[L. *hirsūtus.*]

his. See **he.**

hiss, *his, v.i.* to make a sound like that of the letter *s,* as the goose, serpent, etc. do: to express disapproval, etc., by hissing.—Also *v.t.* and *n.* [Imit.]

historian, etc. See **history.**

history, *his′tŏ-ri, n.* an account of events, e.g. of those that form the story of a nation: a past of more than common interest:—*pl.* **his′tories.**
histo′rian (*-tō′, -tö′*), *n.* a writer of history: one who is learned in history.
histor′ic (*-tor′*), *adj.* famous in history: memorable.
histor′ical (*-tor′*), *adj.* of history: accurate, not fiction or legend.
histor′ically, *adv.*
[Gk. *historia—histōr,* knowing.]

histrionic, *his-tri-on′ik, adj.* relating to acting, the stage, or actors.
[L. *histriō,* an actor.]

hit, *hit, v.t.* to strike: to reach with a blow or missile: to affect painfully (e.g. *The loss hit me hard*): to find or attain by chance.—*v.i.* to come in contact: (with *out*) to strike:—*pr.p.* **hitt′ing**; *pa.t.* and *pa.p.* **hit.**—*n.* a lucky chance: a success: a stroke.
hit′-and-run′, *adj.* of a driver of a vehicle who does not stop after he has caused an accident, or of his action: of any similar action.
to hit below the belt, to deal an unfair blow, make an unfair remark about (a person), etc.
to hit it off, to agree, get on together.
to hit off, to imitate, or to describe, very well.
to hit (up)on, to find by chance.
[O.E. *hyttan*; a Scand. word.]

hitch, *hich, v.i.* to move jerkily.—*v.t.* to move jerkily: to hook: to fasten.—*n.* a jerk: a halt caused by a small difficulty: a knot or noose.
hitch′-hike, *v.i.* to hike with the help of lifts in vehicles. [Origin uncertain.]

hither, *hiTH′ėr, adv.* to this place.
hith′erto, *adv.* up to this time.

hither and thither, in various directions.
[O.E. *hider*; a Scand. word.]

hive, *hīv, n.* a box or basket in which bees live and store up honey: a place in which people work very busily.
[O.E. *hȳf.*]

hoar, *hōr, hör, adj.* white or greyish-white, esp. with age or frost.
hoar′y, *adj.* white or grey with age: old:—*comp.* **hoar′ier**; *superl.* **hoar′iest.**
hoar′iness, *n.*
hoar′-frost, *n.* the white particles formed by the freezing of dew.
[O.E. *hār.*]

hoard, *hōrd, hörd, n.* a store: a hidden stock.—*v.t.* to store, esp. in great quantity or secretly.—Also *v.i.*
hoard′er, *n.* **hoard′ing,** *n.*
[O.E. *hord.*]

hoarding[1], *hōrd′ing, hörd′, n.* a screen of boards round a place where builders are at work, or one used for display of bills.
[Conn. with O.Fr. *hurdis.*]

hoarding[2]. See **hoard.**

hoarier, etc. See **hoar.**

hoarse, *hōrs, hörs, adj.* having a rough, husky voice: harsh.
hoarse′ly, *adv.* **hoarse′ness,** *n.*
[M.E. *hoors*; a Scand. word.]

hoary. See **hoar.**

hoax, *hōks, n.* a trick, a practical joke.—*v.t.* to trick for fun.
[Prob. **hocus-(pocus).**]

hob, *hob, n.* a surface beside a fireplace, on which anything may be kept hot.
hob′nail, *n.* a nail with a thick head.
hob′nailed, *adj.* [Origin uncertain.]

hobble, *hob′l, v.i.* to walk with difficulty, limp.—*v.t.* to fasten the legs of (horse, etc.) loosely together.—Also *n.*
[M.E. *hobelen.*]

hobby, *hob′i, n.* a favourite occupation:—*pl.* **hobb′ies.**
hobb′y-horse, *n.* a stick with a horse's head: a horse on a merry-go-round.
[M.E. *hobyn,* small horse; prob. *Robin.*]

hobgoblin, *hob′gob-lin, n.* a mischievous fairy.
[Form of *Rob* (Robert) and **goblin.**]

hobnail(ed). See **hob.**

hobnob, *hob′nob, v.i.* to drink together: to be friendly (with):—*pr.p.* **hob′nobbing**; *pa.p.* **hob′nobbed.**
[Prob. *hab, nab,* have, have not.]

hobo, *hō′bō, n.* (*U.S.*) a wandering workman: a tramp. [Origin unknown.]

Hobson's choice, the choice of taking what one is offered or doing without.
[*Hobson,* a Cambridge horse hirer.]

hock[1], *hok, n.* the joint on the hindleg of an animal corresponding to the heel in man.—Also **hough** (*hok*; Scot. *hoH*).
[O.E. *hōh,* heel.]

hock[2], *hok, n.* white Rhine wine.
[From *Hochheim* in Germany.]

hockey, *hok′i, n.* a game played with a club curved at one end and a ball or (in **ice hockey,** game played on ice) a puck.
hockey stick, club used in hockey.
[Perh. conn. with **hook.**]

hocus-pocus, *hō′kus-pō′kus, n.* nonsense intended to deceive (orig. the patter of conjurers etc. at fairs): trickery.
hoc′us, *v.t.* to cheat:—*pr.p.* **hoc′us(s)ing**; *pa.p.* **hoc′us(s)ed.**
[Sham Latin.]

hod, *hod, n.* a small trough on a pole for carrying bricks or mortar on the shoulder.
[Conn. with Middle Du. *hodde,* basket.]

hodgepodge. Same as **hotchpotch.**

hoe, *hō, n.* a tool for scraping up weeds and loosening the earth.—*v.t.* and *v.i.* to scrape or weed with a hoe:—*pr.p.* **hoe′ing**; *pa.p.* **hoed** (*hōd*).
[O.Fr. *houe*; a Germanic word.]

hog, *hog, n.* a pig, sow or boar: a greedy person: a coarse person.—*v.t.* and *v.i.* to eat, or seize, greedily:—*pr.p.* **hogg′ing**; *pa.p.* **hogged.**
hogg′ish, *adj.* **hogg′ishness,** *n.*
hog′skin, *n.* leather made from the skin of swine.
hog′wash, *n.* refuse of a kitchen, brewery, etc. used as pig food.
road hog, a selfish motorist who, by speeding and by cutting in, forces others to give way to him.
to go the whole hog, to do a thing thoroughly or completely.
[O.E. *hogg.*]

hogmanay, *hog-mȧ-nā′, n.* (*Scot.*) the last day of the year. [Origin unknown.]

hogshead, *hogz′hed, n.* 52½ imperial (see this) gallons, or other large measure.
[**hog's** and **head**; reason unknown.]

hoi polloi, *hoi po-loi′,* the many, the masses.
[Gk.]

hoist, *hoist, v.t.* to raise with tackle: to heave up: to raise (as a flag).—*n.* a lift for heavy goods.
hoist with one's own petard, caught in one's own trap (a petard being an old explosive device).
[Older *hoise*; prob. a Germanic word.]

hoity-toity, *hoi′ti-toi′ti, adj.* huffy: haughty.
[From old verb *hoit,* to romp.]

hokum, *hō′kum, n.* nonsense: insincere sentimental matter in a play, etc.
[Conn. with **hocus-pocus.**]

hold[1], *hōld, v.t.* to keep, or to grasp, in the hand: to have, possess: to keep (in readiness, in reserve): to have (a position): to defend successfully (e.g. *He held the castle against all attacks*): to keep in check (e.g. an enemy): to compel to carry out (e.g. *We hold him to his promise*): to (be able to) contain (e.g. *The glass holds half a pint*): to think strongly (that; e.g. *I hold that this was right*): to regard as (e.g. *I hold you responsible for his safety*).—*n.* act or manner of grasping: grip: something to grasp in order to carry, or for support:

means of controlling (e.g. *to have a hold on a person*).

hol′der, *n.* a person, thing, that holds.

hol′ding, *n.* land held from a larger landowner: (often in *pl.*) property, esp. shares, etc.

hold′all, *n.* a canvas bag, or other container, for clothes.

hold′-up, *n.* an attack for the purpose of robbery: a forced halt or stoppage.

to hold forth, to talk loud and long.

to hold oneself, to have one's body in a good, bad, etc. position (e.g. *He holds himself too stiffly*).

to hold one's own, to stand up successfully against attack.

to hold one's tongue, to be silent.

to hold over, to postpone.

to hold water, (of e.g. an explanation) to be reasonable and convincing.

to hold with, to approve of.

[O.E. *haldan, healdan.*]

hold[2]**,** *hōld, n.* the space below decks in a ship where cargo is stored.

[**hole** with added *d.*]

hole, *hōl, n.* an opening through something: a hollow place (e.g. in the ground): an animal's burrow: a difficulty (e.g. *I am in a hole and need your help*): (*slang*) an unattractive place.—*v.t.* to make a hole or holes in: to send into a hole.—Also *v.i.*

hole′-and-cor′ner, *adj.* secret, underhand.

to pick holes in, to find faults in.

[O.E. *hol,* a hollow place, cave.]

holiday, *hol′i-dā, n.* a time of freedom from work.

[**holy, day**; *orig.* a religious festival.]

holily, holiness. See **holy.**

hollow, *hol′ō, n.* a place where the surface is lower than it is round about: an empty space inside something.—*adj.* having a space inside, not solid: sunken: (of sound) dull, deep: worth little (e.g. *a hollow victory*): insincere.

holl′owness, *n.*

to hollow out, to make a hollow in: to form by taking out inner material.

[O.E. *holh*; same root as **hole.**]

holly, *hol′i, n.* an evergreen shrub with prickly leaves and scarlet berries:—*pl.* **holl′ies.**

[O.E. *hole(g)n.*]

hollyhock, *hol′i-hok, n.* a plant with spikes of large flowers, brought from the Holy Land.

[M.E. *holihoc—holi,* holy.]

holocaust, *hol′ō-köst, n.* a great destruction of life.

[Gk. *holos,* whole, *kaustos,* burnt.]

holograph, *hol′ō-gräf, n.* a will, etc., wholly in the writing of the person making it.

[Gk. *holos,* whole, *graphein,* to write.]

holster, *hōl′stėr, n.* a pistol case, on saddle or belt.

[Conn. with Du. *holster.*]

holus-bolus, *hōl′ůs-bōl′ůs, adv.* all together (e.g. *He thrust the things holus-bolus into the bag*). [Sham Latin.]

holy, *hō′li, adj.* pure in heart: religious: set apart for a sacred use.

hō′liness, *n.* state of being holy: religious goodness: (*cap.*) a title of the pope.

holy orders, grades in the Christian ministry (*to take holy orders,* to be ordained a priest).

Holy Week, the week before Easter.

Holy Writ, the Bible.

[O.E. *hālig,* whole, perfect, healthy.]

homage, *hom′ij, n.* great respect, esp. as shown by outward action (e.g. *to pay homage to a great man, to his high courage*).

[O.Fr.—L. *homō,* man; orig. vassal's (acknowledgment of) service due to feudal lord.]

home, *hōm, n.* the place where one usu. lives, or where one's family lives: native country: an institution for e.g. homeless children: a private hospital.—Also *adj.*—*adv.* to home: to the place where it belongs: to the point aimed at (e.g. *The blow went home*)—*v.i.* to return home.

hom′er, *n.* a pigeon trained to fly home.

hom′ing, *n.* returning home.—*adj.* showing a tendency to return home (e.g. *homing pigeons, the homing instinct*).

home′less, *adj.* without a home.

home′ly, *adj.* like a home: plain: simple: (*U.S.*; of person) ugly.

home′liness, *n.*

home′-bred, *adj.* bred at home: native: unpolished.

Home Counties, the counties over and into which London has spread.

home′land, *n.* native land.

home′made, *adj.* made at home: not very skilfully made.

home′sick, *adj.* pining for home.

home′stead, *n.* a house with outhouses.

home truth, (a statement of) an unpleasant or an undoubted truth.

home′ward, *adj.* and *adv.* in the direction of home (*adv.* also **home′wards**).

at home, familiar and at ease (with a person, a subject, etc.; in a subject, etc.).

to bring home to, to prove to (a person): (of an experience) to make (a person) realise or understand.

[O.E. *hām.*]

homicide, *hom′i-sīd, n.* manslaughter: one who kills another.

homici′dal, *adj.*

[L. *homō,* man, *caedĕre,* to kill.]

homily, *hom′i-li, n.* a sermon, a moral lecture:—*pl.* **hom′ilies.**

[Gk. *homīlia,* assembly, sermon.]

hom(o)-, *hom(-ō)-, hōm(-ō)-,* (as part of a word) the same.

homogeneous, *hom-ō-jē′ni-ůs, adj.* of the same kind: made up of parts that are all the same.

homogenē′ity, homogē′neousness, *ns.*
homogenise (*-oj′*, or *hom′*), *v.t.* to break up fat globules, etc. in (milk).
homonym, *hom′ō-nim, n.* a word having the same sound as another, but a different meaning (e.g. *sea, see*).
[Gk. *homos*, same (*genos*, kind; *onoma*, name).]

hone, *hōn, n.* a smooth stone used for sharpening, e.g. razors.—*v.t.* to sharpen.
[O.E. *hān*.]

honest, *on′ist, adj.* the opposite of thieving or fraudulent: dealing fairly, upright: sincere, truthful: gained fairly (e.g. *an honest living*).
hon′estly, *adv.* **hon′esty,** *n.*
[L. *honestus*—same root as **honour.**]

honey, *hun′i, n.* a sweet thick fluid made by bees from the nectar of flowers.
honeyed, *hun′id, adj.* sweet.
hon′eycomb, *n.* a mass consisting of rows of waxy cells formed by bees, in which they store their honey: anything like a honeycomb in shape.—*v.t.* to make many holes in (e.g. *a rock honeycombed by the work of underground water*): to spread into all parts of.
hon′eydew, *n.* a sweet sticky substance left on leaves by plant lice.
hon′eymoon, *n.* (a holiday spent in) the first few weeks after marriage.
hon′eysuckle, *n.* a climbing shrub with sweet-scented flowers.
[O.E. *hunig*.]

honk, *hongk, n.* the cry of the wild goose: the noise of a motor horn.—Also *v.t.* and *v.i.* [Imit.]

honorarium, *on-or-ā′ri-ŭm, n.* a fee paid, esp. to a professional man, for services for which no fixed price is asked.
[L. *honōrārium* (*dōnum*), honorary (gift).]

honorary. See **honour.**

honour, *on′ŏr, n.* fame, glory: the esteem due, or paid, to fine qualities: high principles (e.g. *a man of honour*): rank, title, or other distinction given: a source of credit: (in a card suit) one of the five highest cards.—*v.t.* to think very highly of: to give a title, etc. to: to accept (e.g. a bill of exchange) and pay when due: to carry out, live up to (e.g. *to honour one's obligations*).
hon′ourable, *adj.* worthy of honour: upright and honest: conferring honour: (*cap.*) prefixed as a title to names of certain persons.
hon′ourably, *adv.*
hon′ourableness, *n.*
honorary, *on′ŏr-ăr-i, adj.* given as a honour: (of a title or office) either without duties, or without payment (e.g. *Honorary President*).
maid of honour, a lady, usu. noble, attending a queen or princess.
[L. *honor*, or *honos*.]

hood, *hood, n.* a limp covering for the head and neck: a collapsible cover, part of a motor car, etc.: an ornamental fold worn hanging at the back of an academic gown.—*v.t.* to cover, esp. with a hood.
hood′ed, *adj.* (of a bird, etc.) having a hoodlike part on the head.
hoodwink, *hood′wingk, v.t.* to deceive, make believe something false.
[O.E. *hōd*.]

hoof, *hōōf, n.* horny substance on the feet of certain animals, as horses, etc.:—*pl.* **hoofs, hooves.**
[O.E. *hōf*.]

hook, *hook, n.* a bent object, such as would catch or hold anything: a boxer's blow with bent elbow.—*v.t.* to catch, fasten, hold, as with a hook: (*golf* and *cricket*) to pull sharply: (*Rugby*) to obtain possession of the ball in the scrum (**hook′er,** *n.* one whose part it is to do so.)
by hook or by crook, one way if not another, by some means.
on one's own hook, on one's own responsibility or account.
[O.E. *hōc*.]

hookah, *hook′ă, n.* the tobacco pipe of Arabs, Turks, etc., in which the smoke is passed through water.
[Arabic *huqqah*, bowl, casket.]

hooligan, *hōōl′i-găn, n.* a street rough, esp. if he is destructive.
hool′iganism, *n.*
[Said to be name of leader of a gang.]

hoop[1], *hōōp, n.* a band holding together the staves of casks, etc.: a large ring used as a toy, for expanding a skirt, etc: a ring.—*v.t.* to bind with hoops: to encircle.
[O.E. *hōp*.]

hoop[2], **hooping-cough.** See **whoop.**

hoot, *hōōt, v.i.* to shout in contempt: to cry like an owl: (of a motor horn, siren, etc.) to sound.—Also *v.t.* and *n.*
hoot′er, *n.* a siren, steam whistle. [Imit.]

hop[1], *hop, v.i.* to leap on one leg: to move in jumps, as some birds: to fly in an aircraft:—*pr.p.* **hopp′ing**; *pa.t.* and *pa.p.* **hopped.**—*n.* a leap on one leg: a jump: (*coll.*) a dance.
hopp′er, *n.* one who hops: a funnel, bin, etc. in which something is placed to be passed out later through a hole in the bottom: a barge with an opening in its bottom for discharging refuse.
[O.E. *hoppian*, to dance.]

hop[2], *hop, n.* a climbing plant: (in *pl.*) its fruit clusters used to flavour beer. [Du.]

hope, *hōp, v.t.* to desire and more or less expect (e.g. *He is late, but we hope he will still come*).—Also *v.i.* (with *for*; e.g. *We hope for peace*).—*n.* desire with expectation, or an instance of it: confidence in the future.
hope′ful, *adj.*
hope′fully, *adv.* **hope′fulness,** *n.*
hope′less, *adj.* giving no ground to expect good or success (e.g. *a hopeless attempt*): despairing: incurable (e.g. *a hopeless liar*).

to hope against hope, to go on hoping in spite of every discouragement.
[O.E. *hopian.*]

horde, *hōrd, hörd, n.* a wandering tribe: a very large number.
[Turk. *ordū,* camp.]

horizon, *hò-rī'z(ò)n, n.* the circle in which earth and sky seem to meet: the limit of one's experience, interests, etc.
horizontal, *hor-i-zon'tàl, adj.* of, near, or parallel to, the horizon: at right angles to vertical: flat, level.
horizon'tally, *adv.*
[Gk. *horizōn* (*kyklos*), bounding (circle).]

hormone, *hör'mōn, n.* any of a number of substances produced by certain glands of the body, each of which makes some organ of the body active.
[Gk. *hormaein,* to set in motion.]

horn, *hörn, n.* a hard outgrowth on the head of an animal, e.g. cow, sheep: the material of which this is made; a snail's tentacle: something made of horn, or resembling a horn in shape: a wind instrument orig. made from a horn, now of brass, etc.: a hooter, siren.
hor'ny, *adj.* **hor'niness,** *n.*
horn'beam, *n.* a tree like a beech with hard tough wood.
horn'bill, *n.* a bird with a horny growth on its bill.
to pull, draw, in one's horns, to restrain oneself, be more cautious. [O.E.]

hornet, *hör'nit, n.* a large kind of wasp.
[O.E. *hyrnet.*]

hornpipe, *hörn'pīp, n.* a lively dance, usu. by one person, associated with sailors: a tune for it.
[Name of old Welsh musical instrument.]

horoscope, *hor'ò-skōp, n.* an observation of the sky at the hour of a person's birth, from which the events of his life were foretold.
[Gk. *hōra,* hour, *skopeein,* to look at.]

horrible, horrid, etc. See **horror.**

horror, *hor'òr, n.* very great fear or loathing: a cause of such feeling: (*coll.*) a disagreeable person or thing.
horrible, *hor'i-bl, adj.* arousing horror: dreadful: (*coll.*) unpleasant.
horr'ibleness, *n.* **horr'ibly,** *adv.*
horrid, *hor'id, adj.* horrible, shocking: (*coll.*) unpleasant.
horr'idly, *adv.* **horr'idness,** *n.*
horrify, *hor'i-fī, v.t.* to fill with horror:—*pr.p.* **horr'ifying**; *pa.p.* **horr'ified.**
horrif'ic, *adj.* frightful.
[L.—*horrēre,* to bristle, shudder.]

hors de combat, *ör dė köm-bä,* no longer in a state to fight, or to take part. [Fr.]

hors-d'oeuvre, *ör-dėvr, n.* a whet for the appetite (olives, sardines, etc.) served before a meal or after soup. [Fr.]

horse, *hörs, n.* a solid-hoofed animal used to draw, e.g. vehicles, or carry goods or persons, esp. the male (*fem.* **mare**): cavalry: (as *pl.*) horsemen (e.g. *a regiment of horse*): a horse-like piece of apparatus for gymnastics: a support on which clothes are dried.
hor'sy, *adj.* horse-like: devoted to horse racing or breeding.
hor'siness, *n.*
horse'back, *n.* in phrase *on horseback,* on the back of a horse.
horse'-break'er, *n.* one who tames and trains horses.
horse chestnut, a tree with cone-shaped clusters of white or pink flowers: its bitter, shiny, brown seeds (not related to the **sweet chestnut**; see **chestnut**).
horse'flesh, *n.* meat from a horse: horses for riding, racing, etc.
horse'fly, *n.* any fly that bites horses:—*pl.* **horse'flies.**
horse'hair, *n.* hair from a horse's mane or tail: strong, shiny material woven from it.
horse'man, *n.* a rider: a skilled rider:—*fem.* **horse'woman.**
horse'manship, *n.* the art of riding and of training and managing horses.
horse'play, *n.* rough, boisterous, play.
horse'power, *n.* the power a horse can exert—a standard for estimating the power of engines.
horse'-rad'ish, *n.* a plant with a sharp-tasting root, used as a condiment.
horse sense, plain good sense.
horse'shoe, *n.* a curved iron shoe for a horse: anything shaped like a horseshoe.
horse'-soldier, *n.* a soldier of a mounted (see this) regiment.
horse'woman. See above.
to get on, mount, one's high horse, to put on a very superior air: to become huffy or resentful.
[O.E. *hors.*]

horticulture, *hör'ti-kul-chůr, n.* the art of cultivating gardens.
horticul'tural, *adj.*
horticul'turist, *n.*
[L. *hortus,* garden, *colĕre,* to cultivate.]

hosanna, *hō-zan'à, n.* an exclamation of praise to God.
[Gk. *hōsanna*; from Hebrew.]

hose, *hōz, n.* a close-fitting covering for the legs: stockings: socks (*half-hose*):—*pl.* **hose.**—*n.* (also **hose'pipe**) a flexible pipe for conveying water:—*pl.* **hos'es.**
hosier, *hōz'yėr, hozh', n.* a dealer in **hōs'iery,** i.e. knitted goods.
[O.E. *hosa.*]

hospice, *hos'pis, n.* a house for travellers esp. one kept by monks.
[Fr.; same root as **hospitable.**]

hospitable, *hos'pit-à-bl,* or *-pit', adj.* giving a generous welcome to guests.
hos'pitableness (or *-pit'*), *n.*
hos'pitably (or *-pit'*) *adv.*
hospital'ity, *n.* welcome to and entertainment of guests.

hospital, *hos′pit-àl, n.* a building for housing and treating sick and injured.
[L. *hospes, -itis,* stranger, guest, host.]

host[1], *hōst, n.* a person who entertains someone else in his house or elsewhere (*fem.* **hos′tess**): an innkeeper (*fem.* **hos′tess**): an animal or plant on which another lives as a parasite.
[O.Fr. *hoste*; same root as **hospitable.**]

host[2], *hōst, n.* an army: a very large number.
[O.Fr. *host*—L. *hostis,* an enemy.]

host[3], *hōst, n.* (R.C. Church) the consecrated wafer of the Eucharist—a thin round wafer of unleavened bread.
[L. *hostia,* a victim.]

hostage, *hos′tij, n.* one held by an enemy as a guarantee that demands, or the conditions of an agreement, will be carried out.
[O.Fr.—L. *obses, obsidis,* a hostage.]

hostel, *hos′tėl, n.* an inn: a residence for students or others: temporary accommodation for hikers, etc.
hos′telry, *n.* an inn.
[O.Fr.; same root as **hospital.**]

hostile, *hos′tīl, adj.* of an enemy: warlike: unfriendly.
hostil′ity (*-til′*), *n.* unfriendliness, ill-will: (in *pl.*, **hostil′ities**) acts of warfare.
[L. *hostīlis*—*hostis,* enemy.]

hot, *hot, adj.* having a high temperature: very warm: sharp in taste (e.g. pepper): fiery (e.g. *a hot temper*): passionate: (*slang*) excitingly good: (*music*; *slang*) with additions to the melody that suggest excitement: radioactive: (*slang*) recently stolen: unsafe or uncomfortable:—*comp.* **hott′er**; *superl.* **hott′est.**
hot′ly, *adv.* **hot′ness,** *n.*
See also **heat.**
hot′bed, *n.* a bed (usu. glass-covered) heated, e.g. by rotting manure, for making plants grow quickly: a place of rapid growth (of disease or vice).
hot′-blood′ed, *adj.* excitable: easily made angry.
hot′foot, *adv.* in great haste.
hot′head, *n.* a hotheaded person.
hot′headed, *adj.* easily made angry: inclined to act suddenly and rashly.
hot′house, *n.* a glass house kept hot for rearing tender plants.
hot′-plate, *n.* a portable heated metal plate, for keeping things hot.
in hot water, in trouble, in a scrape.
[O.E. *hāt.*]

hotchpotch, *hoch′poch,* **hotchpot,** *hoch′pot,* **hodge-podge,** *hoj′poj, ns.* confused mass of cooking ingredients, or of other things, mixed together.
[Fr. *hocher,* to shake, *pot,* a pot.]

hotfoot, etc. See **hot.**

hotel, *hō-tel′, n.* a, usu. large, house run for the purpose of giving travellers food, lodging, etc.
[O.Fr. *hostel*; same root as **hostel.**]

Hottentot. *hot′ėn-tot, n.* one of a native race of southern Africa: language of the Hottentots. [Du.]

hough. See **hock** (1).

hound, *hownd, n.* a dog used in hunting: a mean scoundrel.—*v.t.* to pursue or drive (e.g. *They hounded the man from place to place*).
[O.E. *hund*; conn. Gk. *kyōn,* L. *canis.*]

hour, *owr, n.* 60 minutes, the 24th part of a day: a time or occasion: (in *pl.*) set times of prayer: services for these.
hour′ly, *adj.* happening or done every hour.—Also *adv.*
hour′-glass, *n.* an instrument for measuring the hours by the running of sand through a narrow neck.
after hours, after the end of a working day, time of remaining open, etc.
at the eleventh hour, at the last possible moment.
in an evil hour, unluckily.
the small hours, the hours from 1 to 3 or 4 A.M.
[O.Fr. *hore*—L. *hōra*—Gk. *hōra.*]

house, *hows, n.* a building for living in: an inn: a household: a family: a business firm: a legislative body, or its meeting place: a theatre, etc.: an audience: a section of a school:—*pl.* **houses** (*how′ziz*).—*v.t.* (*howz*) to shelter: to store: to provide houses for.
housing, *howz′ing, n.* houses, or accommodation, or the act of providing these.
house agent, one who arranges the sale or letting of houses.
house′boat, *n.* a barge furnished for living in.
house′hold, *n.* those who are living together in the same house.—*adj.* of the household: of the house, domestic.
house′holder, *n.* the occupier of a house.
house′keeper, *n.* one who has the chief care of a house.
house′keeping, *n.* the management of a house or of domestic affairs.
house′master, *n.* the head of a boarding-house at a public school.
house surgeon, a resident surgeon in a hospital.
house′-warming, *n.* an entertainment given after moving into a new house.
housewife, *hows′wif, n.* the mistress of a house: (*huz′if*) a pocket sewing outfit:—*pl.* **house′wives.**
housewifery, *hows-wif′ė-ri, n.* housekeeping.
house′work, *n.* the work of keeping a house clean and tidy.
household troops, Guards regiments who attend the king or queen.
a household word, a familiar saying or name.
[O.E. *hūs.*]

hovel, *hov′ėl, huv′ėl, n.* a small or wretched dwelling. [Origin uncertain.]

hover, *hov′ėr, huv′ėr, v.i.* to remain in the

air without forward motion: to remain in an uncertain state, e.g. between two actions: to linger about.
hov'ercraft, *n.* a craft able to move a short distance above the surface of water or land by means of a down-driven blast of air.
[Origin uncertain.]

how, *how, adv.* in what manner: to what extent: by what means: in what condition.
howev'er, *adv.* and *conj.* in whatever manner or degree: nevertheless.
howsoev'er, *adv.* in whatever way.
[O.E. *hū, æfre.*]

howdah, *how'da, n.* a seat with canopy fixed on an elephant's back.
[Arabic *houdaj.*]

however. See **how.**

howitzer, *how'it-sėr, n.* a short cannon, used for shelling at a steep angle.
[Ger. *haubitze.*]

howl, *howl, v.i.* to utter or make a long, loud, whining sound.—*v.t.* to utter (words) in this way.—*n.* a loud cry: a loud sound made by the wind.
how'ler, *n.* (*slang*) a bad mistake.
[L. *ululāre—ulula*, an owl.]

howsoever. See **how.**

hub, *hub, n.* the centre, e.g. of a wheel.
[Prob. **hob.**]

hubbub, *hub'ub, n.* a confused sound of many voices, uproar.
[Prob. of Irish origin.]

huckster, *huk'stėr, n.* a hawker or pedlar: a mean fellow: (*U.S.*) an advertising man. [Origin uncertain.]

huddle, *hud'l, v.t.* to throw or crowd together in disorder: to put (on) hastily: to crouch, to draw (oneself) together (usu. with *up*): to do hastily and carelessly.—*v.i.* to crowd in confusion.—*n.* a confused mass. [Origin uncertain.]

hue[1], *hū, n.* colour: tint. [O.E. *hīw.*]

hue[2], *hū, n.* a shouting, used in the phrase **hue and cry,** a loud call to join in chasing a criminal: an outcry.
[Fr. *huer*; imit.]

huff, *huf, n.* a fit of anger or sulks.—*v.t.* and *v.i.* to swell: to give or take offence.
huff'y, *adj.* inclined to take offence, touchy: in a huff:—*comp.* **huff'ier**; *superl.* **huff'iest.**
huff'ily, *adv.* **huff'iness,** *n.* [Imit.]

hug, *hug, v.t.* to clasp close with the arms: to delight in, cling to (e.g. a thought, an opinion): to keep close to (e.g. *to hug the shore*):—*pr.p.* **hugg'ing**; *pa.p.* **hugged.**—Also *n.*
to hug oneself, to be very pleased.
[Origin uncertain.]

huge, *hūj, n.* very large.
huge'ly, *adv.* very greatly.
huge'ness, *n.* [O.Fr. *ahuge.*]

hulk, *hulk, n.* an old ship stripped of its equipment: anything large and difficult to handle.
hulk'ing, *adj.* large and clumsy.
[O.E. *hulc*, perh.—Gk. *helkein*, to draw.]

hull[1], *hul, n.* a husk or outer covering.—*v.t.* to separate from the hull.
[O.E. *hulu*; conn. *helan*, to cover, hide.]

hull[2], *hul, n.* the frame or body of a ship.—*v.t.* to pierce the hull of.
[Perh. same as **hull** (1).]

hullo. See **hello.**

hullabaloo, *hul'à-bà-lōō', n.* an uproar.
[Perh. from **hullo.**]

hum, *hum, v.i.* to make a sound like bees: to sing with closed lips: to pause in speaking and utter an indistinct sound: to be busily active.—*v.t.* to render by humming (e.g. *to hum a tune*):—*pr.p.* **humm'ing**; *pa.p.* **hummed.**—*n.* the noise of bees: a murmur.
humm'ing, *n.* a low, murmuring sound.
humm'ing-bird, *n.* a brilliant tropical bird with rapid flight, so called from the humming sound of its wings.
to make things hum, to cause brisk activity. [Imit.]

human, *hū'màn, adj.* of, belonging to, mankind: having the qualities of man.
hū'manly, *adv.* by man: in keeping with human nature: within human power (*If it is humanly possible, he will do it*).
hū'mankind, *n.* the human race.
human nature, the qualities, or conduct, that are common to all mankind (esp. the less admirable).
humane, *hū-mān', adj.* kind, sympathetic, merciful, not cruel.
humane'ly, *adv.* **humane'ness,** *n.*
humanise, *hū'màn-īz, v.t.* to make *human* or *humane*: to make gentler.
hūmanism, *n.* seeking, without religion, the best in, and for, human beings.
hūmanist, *n.* and *adj.*
humanitā'rian, *n.* a person who is anxious to increase the welfare of mankind by reforms, etc.—Also *adj.*
human'ity, *n.* the nature of human beings: kindness, generosity: mankind.
[L. *hūmānus—homō*, human being, man.]

humble, *hum'bl, adj.* low: lowly: modest, meek.—*v.t.* to bring down, defeat completely (e.g. *to humble one's enemies*): to make humble or meek:—*pr.p.* **hum'bling**; *pa.p.* **hum'bled.**
hum'bly, *adv.* **hum'bleness,** *n.*
See also **humility.**
[L. *humilis*, low—*humus*, the ground.]

humblebee, *hum'bl-bē, n.* a bumblebee.

humble pie, *hum'bl pī*, used in the phrase **to eat humble pie,** to be forced to apologise humbly: to suffer humiliation.
[Formerly a pie made from poorer parts of a deer; O.Fr. *nombles.*]

humbug, *hum'bug, n.* a trick, fraud: a person who pretends to be something he is not: nonsense: a peppermint sweet.—*v.t.* to deceive, hoax:—*pr.p.* **hum'bugging**; *pa.p.* **hum'bugged.**
[Origin unknown.]

humdrum, *hum'drum, adj.* dull, without variety (e.g. *a humdrum life*). [**hum.**]

humerus, *hū′mėr-ůs,* *n.* the bone of the upper arm.
[L. (*h*)*umerus,* the shoulder.]

humid, *hū′mid, adj.* moist, damp.
hu′midness, humid′ity, *ns.*
[L. *hūmidus*—*hūmēre,* to be moist.]

humiliate, *hū-mil′i-āt, v.t.* to humble: to wound the dignity of.
humiliā′tion, *n.*
humil′ity, *n.* modesty, humbleness.
[L. *humilis,* low; root as **humble.**]

humming. See **hum.**

hummock, *hum′ȯk, n.* a small hillock.
[Origin unknown.]

humorous, etc. See **humour.**

humour, *hū′mȯr,* or *ū′mȯr, n.* (also **sense of humour**) ability to see things as amusing or ridiculous (e.g. *He had a quiet humour and enjoyed the funny side of this misfortune*): the quality of being funny: temper, mood: fancy, whim.—*v.t.* to please (someone) by agreeing with him or doing as he wishes (e.g. *Try to humour the old man*).
hū′morist, *n.* one who amuses by pointing out the funny side of life.
hū′morous, *adj.* **hū′mourless,** *adj.*
hūmorously, *adv.* **hū′morousness,** *n.*
out of humour, irritable, cross.
[L. *hūmor,* liquid; from the belief that bodily fluids influenced one's nature.]

hump, *hump, n.* a lump on the back: a knoll: (*coll.*—**the hump**) a fit of depression.—*v.t.* (*Austr.*) to shoulder, to carry on the back.
hump′back(ed), *adjs.* having a hump on the back: (of a road, etc.) rising and falling so as to form a hump shape.
[Origin uncertain.]

humus, *hūm′ůs, n.* decomposed animal or vegetable matter in the soil.
[L. *humus,* the ground.]

hunch, *hunch, -sh, n.* a hump: a lump: (*coll.*) a strong feeling (that something will turn out in a certain way).—*v.t.* to hump, bend.
hunch′back, *n.* one with a hump on his back.
hunch′backed, *adj.* [Origin uncertain.]

hundred, *hun′drėd, n.* the number next above ninety-nine, ten times ten (100 or C): a division of a county in England:—*pl.* **hun′dreds,** or (after another number) **hun′dred** (e.g. *two hundred of them*).—Also *adj.*
hun′dredth, *adj.* last of a hundred.—*n.* one of a hundred equal parts.
hun′dredweight, *n.* 112 (orig. 100) pounds—*abbrev.* **cwt.** (c = 100).
[O.E. *hund* or *hundred.*]

hung. See **hang.**

hunger, *hung′gėr, n.* desire for, or lack of, food: any strong desire.—*v.i.* to desire food: to long (for).
hungry, *hung′gri, adj.* having, or showing eager desire (for food, etc.):—*comp.* **hung′rier**; *superl.* **hung′riest.**
hung′rily, *adv.* **hung′riness,** *n.*
hunger strike, refusal by a prisoner to eat, as a form of protest.
[O.E. *hungor.*]

hunt, *hunt, v.t.* to chase (animals) for prey or sport: to search for: to hound, drive (e.g. *The fugitives were hunted from place to place*).—*v.i.* to go in pursuit of game: to search.—*n.* a chase of wild animals: a search: a body of huntsmen.
hunt′er, *n.* one who hunts (*fem.* **hunt′ress**): a horse used in hunting.
hunts′man, *n.* a hunter: a man who manages the hounds during the hunt.
to hunt down, to search for until found: to persecute mercilessly.
[O.E. *huntian.*]

hurdle, *hûr′dl, n.* a movable frame of interlaced twigs, etc.: a barrier to be jumped in a race: an obstacle, difficulty.—*v.i.* to run in a race in which hurdles are used.
hur′dler, *n.* **hur′dling,** *n.*
[O.E. *hyrdel.*]

hurl, *hûrl, v.t.* to throw violently: to utter in uncontrolled anger (e.g. *to hurl abuse or threats at someone*).
[M.E. *hurlen*; perh. *hurr,* imit. of sound.]

hurly-burly, *hûr′li-bûr′li, n.* tumult: confusion. [Perh. **hurl.**]

hurrah, *hůr-ä′, interj.* a shout of enthusiasm or joy.—Also **hurray′**, *hů-rā′.*

hurricane, *hûr′i-kån, -kān, n.* a violent tropical storm: anything violent.
[Sp. *huracán*—Caribbean word.]

hurried, etc. See **hurry.**

hurry, *hûr′i, v.i.* to move or act quickly, often too quickly and in a confused way.—*v.t.* to cause to move or act with speed:—*pr.p.* **hurr′ying**; *pa.p.* **hurr′ied.**—*n.* (need for) acting with speed.
hurr′ied, *adj.* done, carried out, or working, quickly, or too quickly.
hurr′iedly, *adv.* **hurr′iedness,** *n.*
hurr′y-scurr′y, *n.* bustle and confusion.—Also *adv.*
in a hurry, in a short time: at a fast rate: eager (e.g. *She was in a hurry to open her presents*). [Prob. imit.]

hurt, *hûrt, v.t.* to cause pain to: to wound the feelings of: to damage.—Also *v.i.*:—*pa.t.* and *pa.p.* **hurt.**—*n.* pain: injury.
hurt′ful, *adj.* causing hurt or loss.
hurt′fully, *adv.* **hurt′fulness,** *n.*
[O.Fr. *hurter,* knock against or together.]

hurtle, *hûrt′l, v.t.* to dash, hurl.—*v.i.* to move rapidly with a whirl or clatter.
[Same root as **hurt.**]

husband, *huz′bånd, n.* the man to whom a woman is married—opp. of *fem.* **wife.**—*v.t.* to manage with care, spend carefully (e.g. *to husband one's resources,* or *one's strength*).
hus′bandman, *n.* a working farmer.
hus′bandry, *n.* business of a farmer.
[O.E. *hūsbōnda,* householder—*hūs,* house.]

hush, *hush, interj.* silence!—*v.t., v.i.* to quieten.—*n.* a silence, esp. after noise.

hush money, a bribe to say nothing.
to hush up, to keep (something) secret by preventing talk about it. [Imit.]
husk, *husk, n.* the dry, thin covering of certain fruits and seeds: (in *pl.*) refuse.—*v.t.* to remove the husk from.
[M.E. *huske.*]
husky[1], *hus'ki, adj.* (of a voice) rough in sound: (*U.S.*) big and strong:—*comp.* **hus'kier**; *superl.* **hus'kiest.**
hus'kily, *adv.* **hus'kiness,** *n.*
[From **husk.**]
husky[2], *hus'ki, n.* a Canadian sledge-dog:—*pl.* **hus'kies.** [Eskimo.]
hussar, *hoo-zär', n.* a light-armed cavalry soldier (orig. Hungarian): a member of a modern regiment with 'Hussars' in its name.
[Hungarian *huszar*—It. *corsaro.*]
hussy, *hus'i, huz'i, n.* a badly behaved or mischievous girl: a woman of low character:—*pl.* **huss'ies.**
[From **housewife.**]
hustings, *hus'tingz, n. sing.* electioneering platform: election proceedings.
[O.E. *hūsting,* council; from Old Norse.]
hustle, *hus'l, v.t.* to push (together): to push roughly (into).—*v.i.* to hurry.—*n.* great activity.
hus'tler (*-lėr*), *n.* an energetic person.
[Du. *huts(el)en,* to shake to and fro.]
hut, *hut, n.* a small or mean house: a small temporary building.
hut'ment, *n.* a (collection of) hut(s).
[Fr. *hutte*; a Germanic word.]
hutch, *huch, n.*: a coop for rabbits, etc.: a low wagon in which coal is drawn up out of the pit.
[O.Fr. *huche,* a chest.]
hyacinth, *hī'a-sinth, n.* a plant with a bulb, of the lily family: a red, brown, or orange precious stone.
[Gk. *Hyakinthos,* name of a beautiful young man in Gk. myth.]
hyaena. See **hyena.**
hybrid, *hī'brid, n.* the offspring of animals, or of plants, of two different breeds, etc.: a word formed of parts from different languages (e.g. *television*; see this word).
[L. *hibrida,* a mongrel.]
hydra, *hī'dra, n.* a water monster in Greek story with many heads each of which, when cut off, grew again as two: any evil difficult to root out.
[Gk.—*hydōr,* water.]
hydrangea, *hī-drān'j(y)a, n.* a shrubby plant with large heads of flowers.
[Gk. *hydōr,* water, *angeion,* vessel.]
hydr(o)-, *hī-dr(ō)-,* (as part of word) water.
hydrant, *hī'drant, n.* connexion for attaching hose to water main, a fire-plug.
hydraulic, *hī-drōl'ik, adj.* worked by water or other liquid: (of e.g. cement) hardening under water: relating to hydraulics.
hydraul'ics, *n.* study of behaviour of fluids in motion (e.g. of water in pipes) and of how to deal with them.
hydrocarbon, *hī-drō-kär'bon, n.* a chemical compound containing only hydrogen and carbon.
hydrochloric acid, *hī-drō-klor'ik as'id,* or *-klōr',* a strong acid, compound of hydrogen and chlorine.
hydroelectricity, *hī-drō-el-ek-tris'i-ti, n.* electricity produced by means of water-driven turbines.
hydroelec'tric, *adj.*
hydrogen, *hī'drō-jėn, n.* a gas which when combined with oxygen produces water, the lightest of all known substances, and very inflammable.
hydrogen bomb, one in which the explosion is caused by turning hydrogen into helium at very high temperature.
hydrophobia, *hī-drō-fō'bi-a, n.* horror of water: inability to swallow water (a symptom of rabies): rabies.
hydroplane, *hī'drō-plān, n.* an aeroplane with floats or a boat-like underpart.
[Gk. *hudōr,* water (Gk. *aulos,* pipe; *gennaein,* to produce; *pathos,* suffering; *phobos,* fear.]
hyena, hyaena, *hī-ē'na, n.* a bristly-maned animal, feeding on carrion, with a howl like hysterical laughter.
[Gk. *hyaina*—*hys,* a pig.]
hygiene, *hī'jēn,* or *-ji-ēn, n.* (rules of) cleanliness whose aim is to preserve health and prevent spread of disease.
hygien'ic (*-jēn',* or *-ji-en'*), *adj.*
hygien'ically, *adv.*
[Gk. *hygieia,* health.]
hymn, *him, n.* a song of praise.—*v.t.* to celebrate, worship in hymns.
hym'nal, *n.* a book of hymns.—Also **hym'nary** (*pl.* **-ies**).
[Gk. *hymnos.*]
hyper-, *hī'pėr-, pfx.* beyond: over.
hyperbole, *hī-pėr'bol-ė, n.* exaggeration for sake of effect in speech or writing.
hyperbol'ical, *adj.*
hyperbol'ically, *adv.*
hypercrit'ical, *adj.* too critical.
hypercrit'ically, *adv.*
hypersen'sitive, *adj.* too sensitive.
hyperten'sion, *n.* high blood pressure.
[Gk. *hyper,* beyond (*ballein,* to throw).]
hyphen, *hī'fėn, n.* a short stroke (-) joining two syllables or words (e.g. that in *co-exist, sleeping-bag*).
hy'phenate, *v.t.* to put a hyphen in.
[Gk.—*hypo,* under, *hen,* one.]
hypnosis, *hip-nō'sis, n.* a sleeplike state brought on by the action of another person, or operator, who can then influence the sleeper to do many things that he, the operator, wishes.
hypnotic, *hip-not'ik, adj.* of hypnosis: of hypnotism: causing sleepiness (e.g. *the hypnotic effect of slow regular sound or movement*): causing hypnosis (e.g. *a hypnotic stare*).

hyp′notise, *v.t.* to put in a state of hypnosis: to fascinate.
hyp′notism, *n.* the science of hypnosis: the art of producing hypnosis.
[Gk. *hypnos*, sleep.]

hypo-, *hī′pō-*, **hyp-,** pfx. under. [Gk.]

hypochondria, *hip-*, *hip-ō-kon′dri-à*, *n.* nervous anxiety about one's health.
hypochon′driac, *adj.—n.* a person who suffers from hypochondria. [Gk.]

hypocrisy, *hi-pok′ri-si*, *n.* pretending to be better than one is, or to have feelings one does not experience.
hypocrite, *hip′o-krit*, *n.* one who practises hypocrisy.
hypocrit′ical, *adj.*
hypocrit′ically, *adv.*
[From Gk. *hypokritēs*, an actor.]

hypodermic, *hīp-ō-dėr′mik*, *adj.* under the skin, esp. of a method of injecting a drug.—*n.* an injection under the skin or the syringe for giving this.
[Gk. *hypo*, under, *derma*, skin.]

hypotenuse, *hī-pot′ėn-ūz*, or *-ūs*, *n.* the side of a right-angled triangle opposite to the right angle.
[Gk. *hypo*, under, *teinein*, to stretch.]

hypothesis, *hī-poth′i-sis*, *n.* a supposition: something assumed for the sake of argument:—*pl.* **hypoth′eses.**
hypothet′ical, *adj.* supposed, assumed.
[Gk. *hypo*, under, *thesis*, placing.]

hysteria, *his-tē′ri-à*, *n.* mental illness causing loss of memory, sleepwalking, etc.: wild excitement.
hyster′ics (*-ter′*), *n.pl.* fits of hysteria: fits of laughing and crying.
hyster′ical, *adj.* **hyster′ically,** *adv.*
[Gk. *hysterā*, womb.]

I

I, *ī*, *pron.* the word used by a speaker or writer in mentioning himself or herself:—*objective* **me**; *possessive* **my** (*mī*; sometimes described as possessive *adj.*), **mine** (e.g. *I hope you will help me by giving me sweets for my stall at the sale*; *the stall next the door will be mine.*)
myself′, *pron.* (1) emphatic, or (2) reflexive, form of *I*, *me*; e.g. (1) *The majority decided, but I myself disapprove*; (2) *I blame myself.*
[M.E. *ich*, O.E. *ic*: conn. Ger. *ich*, L. *ego*.]

Iberian, *ī-bē′ri-àn*, *adj.* of Spain and Portugal.
[L. and Gk *Ibēria*.]

ibex, *ī′beks*, *n.* a large-horned wild mountain goat. [L.]

ibis, *ī′bis*, *n.* a wading bird with curved bill.
[L. *ibis*; prob.—Egyptian.]

ice, *īs*, *n.* water made solid by freezing: sugar coating on a cake: ice cream.—*v.t.* to cover with ice or icing:—*pr.p.* **ic′ing**; *pa.p.* **iced.**
ic′y, *adj.* very cold: slippery with ice:—*comp.* **ic′ier**; *superl.* **ic′iest.**
ic′ily, *adv.* **ic′iness,** *n.*
ic′ing, *n.* (act of producing) a covering of ice or of sugar.
ic′icle, *n.* a long hanging piece of ice formed by freezing of dropping water.
ice age, a time when a great part of the earth's surface was covered with ice.
ice′berg, *n.* a huge mass of floating ice (*berg* meaning 'mountain').
ice′breaker, *n.* a ship for breaking a channel through ice.
ice cream, cream, or other material, flavoured and artificially frozen.
ice field, a large area covered with ice, esp. floating ice.
ice floe, a mass of floating ice smaller than an ice field.
to cut no ice, to have no influence.
[O.E. *īs*; conn. with Ger. *eis*.]

Icelander, *īs′làn-dėr*, *n.* a native of Iceland.
Icelan′dic, *adj.* of Iceland, its people, or its language.—*n.* the language of Iceland: (also **Old Icelandic**) Icelandic from 9th to 16th centuries.

ichneumon, *ik-nū′mòn*, *n.* a small Egyptian animal once believed to destroy crocodiles' eggs: an insect whose larvae are parasites on other insects.
[Gk. *ichneuein*, to hunt after.]

ichthyology, *ik-thi-ol′ò-ji*, *n.* the study of fishes.
ichthyol′ogist, *n.* one who studies fishes.
ichthyosaurus, *ik-thi-ō-sör′ùs*, *n.* a giant fossil fishlike sea reptile.
[Gk. *ichthȳs*, fish (L. *logos*, discourse; Gk. *sauros*, lizard).]

icicle, icing, etc. See **ice.**

icon, *ī′kon*, *n.* an image: in the Greek Church, a figure in painting, etc. (not sculpture) of Christ or a saint.
icon′oclast, *n.* a breaker of images: one who attacks old cherished beliefs.
iconoclas′tic, *adj.* **icon′oclasm,** *n.*
[Gk. *eikōn*, an image (*klaein*, to break).]

icy, See **ice.**

idea, *ī-dē′à*, *n.* an image in the mind: a project, plan: an impression or opinion.
idē′al, *adj.* existing in the imagination only: highest and best.—*n.* standard of what is highest and best: a person who seems to reach this standard: one's highest aim.
idē′ally, *adv.* perfectly (e.g. *ideally suited to the job.*)
idē′alise, *v.t.* to regard (a person, thing) as very good, fine, etc.: to describe (him, her, it) as if he, etc., were this.

idē'alist, *n.* a person who has very high standards and aims: an unpractical person.
idealis'tic, *adj.* of, or suited to, an idealist.
[L.—Gk.—Gk. *idein,* to see.]

identify, *ī-den'ti-fī, v.t.* to recognise, or claim to recognise (as; e.g. *He identified the coat as his brother's*): to make, or prove to be, the same:—*pr.p.* **inden'tifying**; *pa.p.* **iden'tified.**
identificā'tion, *n.*
to identify oneself with, to give one's full support or interest to (e.g. a party, a policy, aims).
iden'tity, *n.* state of being the same (e.g. *The identity of 'Cyril Jones' and 'Ted Park' was proved by the handwriting on the two letters*): who or what a person is:—*pl.* **iden'tities.**
iden'tical, *adj.* the same in every detail.
iden'tically, *adv.* **iden'ticalness,** *n.*
[L. *idem,* same (*facĕre,* to make).]

ideology, *ī-di-ol'ŏ-ji,* or *id-i-, n.* beliefs, way of thinking of a large group, esp. of a political party (e.g. *communist ideology*):—*pl.* **ideol'ogies.**
[Gk. *idea,* idea, *logos,* discourse.]

idiocy. See **idiot.**

idiom, *id'i-ŏm, n.* an expression belonging to a particular language or dialect (e.g. '*You suit blue*', *for 'blue suits you', is a Scottish idiom*): an expression that has become fixed in form (e.g. *He contented himself with saying . . .,* not *. . . by saying . . .*), often with a meaning that cannot be guessed from the actual words (e.g. *to carry out,* to accomplish, complete): expressions generally (e.g. *English idiom*): individual style in music or painting.
idiosyncrasy, *id-i-o-sing'krȧ-si, n.* a characteristic of a person, esp. an eccentricity:—*pl.* **idiosyn'crasies.**
[Gk. *idios,* own, private (*idiōma,* peculiarity; *synkrāsis,* mixing together).]

idiot, *id'i-ŏt, id'yŏt, n.* a very feeble-minded person: a foolish or unwise person.
id'iocy (*-si*), *n.* state of being an idiot: folly, foolish act (*pl.* **id'iocies**).
idiot'ic, *adj.* **idiot'ically,** *adv.*
[Gk. *idiōtes,* a private person holding no public office; same root as **idiom.**]

idle, *ī'dl, adj.* doing nothing: not working: not in use: useless, having no effect or result (e.g. *idle threats*): groundless (e.g. *idle fears*).—*v.t.* to spend in idleness.—*v.i.* to be doing nothing.
id'ler, *n.* **id'leness,** *n.* **id'ly,** *adv.*
[O.E. *īdel*; conn. Ger. *eitel,* vain, empty.]

idol, *ī'dŏl, n.* an image worshipped as representing a god: a person or thing too much loved or honoured.
i'dolīse, *v.t.* to worship: to love excessively.
idolater, *ī-dol'ȧ-tėr, n.* a worshipper of idols: a great admirer:—*fem.* **idol'atress.**
idol'atry, *n.* the worship of idols: excessive love.
idol'atrous, *adj.* **idol'atrously,** *adv.*
[Gk. *eidōlon,* idol (*latreiā,* worship).]

idyll, *id'il, īd'il, n.* a short poem describing a simple scene: a story of happy innocence: a narrative poem.
idyll'ic, *adj.* simple and delightful.
idyll'ically, *adv.*
[L. *īdyllium.*]

if, *if, conj.* on condition that: in the case that: supposing that: whether.
[O.E. *gif*; conn. with Du. *of.*]

igloo, *ig'lōō, n.* a snow hut. [Eskimo.]

igneous, *ig'ni-ŭs, adj.* of, or like, fire: (of rock) produced by action of great heat within the earth.
ignite, *ig-nīt', v.t.* to set on fire.—*v.i.* to take fire.
igni'tion (*-ni'*), *n.* act of igniting: firing of an explosive mixture of gases, etc., e.g. by means of an electric spark: a device for doing this (e.g. in an internal-combustion engine).
[L. *ignis,* fire.]

ignoble, *ig-nō'bl, adj.* of low birth: of poor quality: dishonourable.
igno'bleness, *n.* **igno'bly,** *adv.*
[L. *in-,* not, (*g*)*nōbilis,* noble.]

ignominy, *ig'nŏ-min-i, n.* the loss of one's good name, public disgrace: base conduct or quality.
ignomin'ious, *adj.* (now usu.) humiliating (e.g. *an ignominious retreat*): discreditable, contemptible.
ignomin'iously, *adv.*
ignomin'iousness, *n.*
[L. *in-,* not, (*g*)*nomen,* (*g*)*nominis,* name.]

ignoramus, *ig-nŏ-rā'mŭs, n.* an ignorant person:—*pl.* **ignora'muses.**
ignorant, *ig'nŏr-ȧnt, adj.* without knowledge or information: resulting from, showing, lack of knowledge (e.g. *an ignorant statement*): unaware (of).
ig'norance, *n.* **ig'norantly,** *adv.*
ignore, *ig-nōr', -nör', v.t.* to take no notice of.
[L. *ignōrāre,* not to know.]

iguana, *i-gwä'nȧ, n.* a large tree-lizard of tropical America. [Sp.]

il-, *il-, pfx.* the form taken by **in-** (1) and (2) (see these) before *l* in Latin and in English words from Latin.

ill, *il, adj.* not well, sick: evil: bad: unlucky: unfriendly (e.g. *ill feeling*):—*comp.* **worse,** *wûrs*; *superl.* **worst,** *wûrst.*—*adv.* badly.—*n.* harm: misfortune: an ailment.
ill'ness, *n.* a bad condition of body or mind.
ill'-advised', *adj.* not wisely cautious, foolish.
ill at ease. See **ease.**
ill'-blood', ill'-feel'ing, *ns.* resentment.
ill'-bred', *adj.* rude, ill-mannered.
ill'-breeding, *n.*
ill'-disposed', *adj.* unfriendly (towards).

ill′-fat′ed, *adj.* doomed to end in, or bringing, disaster.
ill′-fā′voured, *adj.* ugly.
ill′-gott′en, *adj.* obtained by bad means (e.g. *ill-gotten gains*).
ill health, poor or bad health.
ill humour, bad temper.
ill′-hu′moured, *adj.*
ill′-mann′ered, *adj.* having, or showing, bad manners.
ill′-nā′tured, *adj.* peevish, cross.
ill′-starred′, *adj.* unlucky.
ill′-tem′pered, *adj.* having a bad temper: showing bad temper.
ill′-timed′, *adj.* done, etc. at an unsuitable time (of e.g. a remark, 'tactless').
ill′-use′ (*-ūz′*), *v.t.* to treat badly (often cruelly).—Also *n.* (*-ūs′*).
ill′-will′, *n.* unkind feeling (towards someone).
to take it ill, to be offended.
[Old Norse *illr*; not conn. with O.E. *yfel*, evil, but confused with it.]

I'll, *il*, I shall, or I will.

illegal, *i-lē′gȧl*, *adj.* against the law.
illeg′ally, *adv.* **illeg′alness,** *n.*
illegal′ity, *n.* illegalness: an illegal act:—*pl.* **illegal′ities.** [Pfx. **il-** (2).]

illegible, *i-lej′i-bl*, *adj.* (almost) impossible to read, not legible.
illegibil′ity, illeg′ibleness, *ns.*
illeg′ibly, *adv.* [Pfx. **il-** (2).]

illegitimate, *i-li-jit′i-mit*, *adj.* not according to law: born of parents not married to each other: not according to sound reasoning (e.g. *That is an illegitimate conclusion from the facts given*).
illegit′imacy, *n.* **illegit′imately,** *adv.* [Pfx. **il-** (2).]

illiberal, *i-lib′ėr-ȧl*, *adj.* mean, not generous: narrow-minded.
illiberal′ity, illib′eralness, *ns.*
illib′erally, *adv.* [Pfx. **il-** (2).]

illicit, *i-lis′it*, *adj.* unlawful: not permitted.
illic′itly, *adv.* **illic′itness,** *n.*
[L. *il-* (**il-**, 2), *licēre*, to be allowed.]

illiterate, *i-lit′ėr-it*, *adj.* unable to read and write: uneducated.
illit′eracy, illit′erateness, *ns.*
illit′erately, *adv.* [Pfx. **il-** (2).]

illness. See **ill.**

illogical, *i-loj′i-kl*, *adj.* not logical, not showing sound reasoning.
illog′icalness, illogical′ity, *ns.*
illog′ically, *adv.* [Pfx. **il-** (2).]

illuminate, *i-lū′mi-nāt*, or *-lōō′*, *v.t.* to light up: to throw light on (a subject): to decorate (an old manuscript) with ornamental lettering or illustrations.
illuminā′tion, *n.* **illu′minātor,** *n.*
illu′mine (*rather poetical*), *v.t.* to illuminate: to enlighten spiritually.
[L. *in* (**il-**, 1), on, *lūmināre*, cast light.]

illusion, *i-lōō′zh(ȯ)n*, or *-lū′*, *n*, a false impression, idea, or belief: something that produces a false impression.
illu′sory, *adj.* deceptive: unreal.
illu′soriness, *n.*
illu′sionist, *n.* a conjurer.
[L. *illūdĕre*, trick—*lūdĕre*, *lūsum*, play.]

illustrate, *il′ŭs-trāt*, *v.t.* to adorn (e.g. a book) or accompany (e.g. a lecture) with pictures: to make (e.g. a statement) clearer by giving examples.
ill′ustrated, *adj.* **ill′ustrator,** *n.*
illustrā′tion, *n.* a picture: an example: act of adding pictures or giving examples.
ill′ustrative, *adj.* illustrating (with *of*).
[L. *illūstrāre*, to light up.]

illustrious, *i-lus′tri-ŭs*, *adj.* very distinguished, famous.
illus′triously, *adv.* **illus′triousness,** *n.*
[Same root as **illustrate.**]

im-, *im-*, *pfx.* the form taken by **in-** (1) and (2) (see these) before *b*, *m*, or *p* in Latin and in English words from Latin.

I'm, *im*, I am.

image, *im′ij*, *n.* a likeness: a copy: a statue: an idol: something pictured in the mind: the picture in the minds of most people of the character, nature, of e.g. a politician, a country: a metaphor or simile.
im′agery, *n.* (making of) mental pictures: (use of) metaphors and similes.
[O.Fr.—L. *imāgō.*]

imagine, *i-maj′in*, *v.t.* to form a picture of in the mind: to think, believe (something that has no reality): to suppose (e.g. *I imagine you will not want to be out late*).—Also *v.i.*
imag′inable, *adj.* able to be imagined thought of (e.g. *for no imaginable reason*).
imag′inary, *adj.* existing only in the mind or imagination, not real.
imaginā′tion, *n.* power of imagining: the part of the mind that exercises this power: creative ability of a writer, etc.
imag′inative, *adj.* full of imagination.
imag′inativeness, *n.*
[Fr. *imaginer*—same L. root as **image.**]

imbecile, *im′bi-sēl*, *-sil*, *n.* a feeble-minded person not capable of managing his own affairs.—Also *adj.*
imbecility, *im-bi-sil′i-ti*, *n.* feebleness of mind: silliness: an instance of either:—*pl.* **imbecil′ities.**
[L. *imbēcillus*, weak, feeble.]

imbibe, *im-bīb′*, *v.t.* to drink, drink in: to receive into the mind.—Also *v.i.*
[L. *in*, in, *bibĕre*, to drink.]

imbue, *im-bū′*, *v.t.* to saturate (with): to fill, inspire (with feelings, ideas):—*pr.p.* **imbu′ing**; *pa.p.* **imbued′.**
[L. *imbuĕre*—same root as **imbibe.**]

imitate, *im′i-tāt*, *v.t.* (to try) to be like (something or someone).
im′itable, *adj.*
im′itātive, *adj.* inclined to imitate: used, chosen, to suggest a sound, etc.
im′itativeness, *n.* **im′itator,** *n.*
imitā′tion, *n.* act, or result, of imitating: something sham, not genuine.—Also *adj.*
[L. *imitārī*, *imitātus.*]

immaculate, *i-mak'ū-lit, adj.* spotless: pure: without flaw: very clean and neat.
immac'ulately, *adv.*
immac'ulacy, immac'ulateness, *ns.*
[L. *in*, not, *maculāre*, to spot.]

immaterial, *im-ȧ-tēr'i-ȧl, adj.* not material or consisting of matter: spiritual: not important (e.g. *It is immaterial what you do*).
immater'ially, *adv.* [Pfx. **im-** (2).]

immature, *im-ȧ-tūr', adj.* not ripe, fully grown, or fully developed.
immatur'ity, immature'ness, *ns.*
immature'ly, *adv.* [Pfx. **im-** (2).]

immeasurable, *i-mezh'ūr-ȧ-bl, adj.* very great.
immeas'urably, *adv.* [Pfx. **im-** (2).]

immediate, *i-mē'di-it, adj.* with nothing, no one, coming between (e.g. *his immediate successor*): with no time between, or without delay (e.g. *an immediate response*).
immed'iately, *adv.*
[Pfx. **im-** (2) and same root as **mediate.**]

immemorial, *i-mė-mōr'i-ȧl, -mör', adj.* going back beyond memory (e.g. *from time immemorial.*)
[Pfx. **im-** (2) and same root as **memory.**]

immense, *i-mens', adj.* vast: very great.
immense'ly, *adv.*
immense'ness, immen'sity, *ns.*
[Pfx. **im-** (2), L. *metīrī, mensus*, measure.]

immerse, *i-mėrs', v.t.* to plunge wholly into a liquid: to baptise by dipping the whole body: (with *oneself*) to give one's whole attention to (with *in*; e.g. *He immersed himself in his work*): (of e.g. thought, difficulties) to take up the attention of (a person).
immer'sion, *-sh(ȯ)n, n.*
[L. *in*, into, *mergĕre, mersum*, to plunge.]

immigrate, *im'i-grāt, v.i.* to come into a country to settle.
imm'igrant, *n.* one who immigrates.—Also *adj.*
immigrā'tion, *n.*
[L. *in*, into, and root as **migrate.**]

imminent, *im'i-nėnt, adj.* (esp. of something unpleasant) likely to happen very soon.
imm'inence, *n.*
[L. *in*, upon, *minēre*, to project.]

immobile, *i-mō'bil, -bil, adj.* not able to move, or to be moved: motionless.
immobil'ity, *n.*
immo'bilise (*-bil-īz*), *v.t.* to make immobile. [Pfx. **im-** (2).]

immoderate, *i-mod'ėr-it, adj.* going much beyond normal, excessive.
immod'erately, *adv.* [Pfx. **im-** (2).]

immodest, *i-mod'ist, adj.* not modest, shameless.
immod'estness, immod'esty, *ns.*
immod'estly, *adv.* [Pfx. **im-** (2).]

immoral, *i-mor'ȧl, adj.* not moral.
immoral'ity (*pl.* **-ies**), **-alness,** *ns.*
immor'ally, *adv.* [Pfx. **im-** (2).]

immortal, *i-mör'tȧl, adj.* never dying or ceasing: (of e.g. a name) never to be forgotten.—*n.* one (as a god) who lives for ever: a person who will always be remembered.
immortal'ity, *n.* (usu. of the spirit) state of living for ever: lasting fame.
immor'talise, *v.t.* to make famous for ever. [Pfx. **im-** (2).]

immovable, *i-mōō'vȧ-bl, adj.* impossible to move, change, or arouse emotion in.
immovabil'ity, immo'vableness, *ns.*
immo'vably, *adv.* [Pfx. **im-** (2).]

immune, *i-mūn', adj.* exempt: protected naturally or by some action against infection, persuasion, a feeling, etc. (e.g. *immune against typhoid*; *immune to all arguments*; *immune from doubts of himself.*)
immun'ity, *n.*
imm'unise, *v.t.* to make immune (esp. against disease by inoculation).
[L. *in*, not, *mūnus*, duty, service.]

immure, *i-mūr', v.t.* to shut up, imprison.
[L. *in*, in, *mūrus*, a wall.]

immutable, *i-mū'tȧ-bl, adj.* unchangeable, unalterable.
immutabil'ity, immu'tableness, *ns.*
immu'tably, *adv.* [Pfx. **im-** (2).]

imp, *imp, n.* a mischievous child: a little wicked spirit.
imp'ish, *adj.* **imp'ishly,** *adv.*
[O.E. *impa*, a shoot, graft.]

impact, *im-pakt', v.t.* to press firmly (in, into).—*n.* (*im'pakt*) the blow of one body in motion striking another: collision: forceful effect, influence.
[L. *impactus*—same root as **impinge.**]

impair, *im-pār', v.t.* to make less good, injure, weaken.
impair'ment, *n.*
[O.Fr. *empeirer*—L. *in*, *pējor*, worse.]

impale, *im-pāl', v.t.* to fix on a long pointed object such as a stake.
[L. *in*, in, *pālus*, a stake.]

impalpable, *im-pal'pȧ-bl, adj.* not able to be perceived by touch: not easily grasped by the mind.
impalpabil'ity, impal'pableness, *ns.*
impal'pably, *adv.* [Pfx. **im-** (2).]

impart, *im-pärt', v.t.* to give: to make known (e.g. a secret) to someone.
[L. *in*, on, *pars, partis*, part.]

impartial, *im-pär'sh(ȧ)l, adj.* not favouring one more than another, just.
impartial'ity, impar'tialness, *ns.*
impar'tially, *adv.* [Pfx. **im-** (2).]

impassable, *im-pâs'ȧ-bl, adj.* (of e.g. a thicket, a road) that cannot be passed through or over.
impassabil'ity, impass'ableness, *ns.*
impass'ably, *adv.* [Pfx. **im-** (2).]

impasse, *im-pâs', an^gpäs, n.* a position from which there is no escape or outlet. [Fr.]

impassioned, *im-pash'ȯnd, adj.* moved by, or showing, very strong feeling.
[Pfx. **im-** (1).]

impassive, *im-pas'iv*, *adj.* not feeling, or not showing, emotion.
impass'iveness, impassiv'ity, *ns.*
impass'ively, *adv.*
[Pfx. **im-** (2), **passive** (in sense of 'acted upon').]

impatient, *im-pā'shėnt*, *adj.* not patient: irritable: intolerant (of): restlessly eager (for, to do).
impa'tience, *n.* **impa'tiently,** *adv.*
[Pfx. **im-** (2).]

impeach, *im-pēch'*, *v.t.* to accuse, charge with treason, etc. (a person in public office): to find fault with (e.g. *to impeach a person's motives*): to question the truthfulness of (a witness).
impeach'able, *adj.* **impeach'ment,** *n.*
[O.Fr. *empe(s)ch(i)er*, to hinder.]

impeccable, *im-pek'ȧ-bl*, *adj.* faultless.
impeccabil'ity, *n.* **impecc'ably,** *adv.*
[Pfx. **im-** (2), L. *peccāre*, to sin.]

impecunious, *im-pi-kū'ni-ůs*, *adj.* poor (often through one's own actions).
[Pfx. **im-** (2), L. *pecūnia*, money.]

impede, *im-pēd'*, *v.t.* to hinder, obstruct.
imped'iment (*-ped'*), *n.* a hindrance: a small defect in speech, esp. a stutter.
impedimen'ta, *n.pl.* baggage, esp. military.
[L. *impedīre*, to hamper the feet—*pēs, pedis*, a foot.]

impel, *im-pel'*, *v.t.* to push forward, propel: to drive to action:—*pr.p.* **impell'ing**; *pa.p.* **impelled'.**
See also **impulse.**
[L. *in*, on, *pellěre*, *pulsum*, to drive.]

impend, *im-pend'*, *v.i.* to be about to happen, to threaten.
impen'ding, *adj.*
[L. *impendēre*, to hang over.]

impenetrable, *im-pen'i-trȧ-bl*, *adj.* that cannot be entered or passed through (e.g. *an impenetrable jungle*): impossible to understand (e.g. *an impenetrable mystery*): that cannot be reached (e.g. *a mind impenetrable to*, or *by*, *new ideas*).
[Pfx. **im-** (2).]

impenitent, *im-pen'i-tėnt*, *adj.* not repenting or sorry.
impen'itence, *n.* **impen'itently,** *adv.*
[Pfx. **im-** (2).]

imperative, *im-per'ȧ-tiv*, *adj.* expressing a command: urgent, or not to be avoided (e.g. *an imperative need to send help*).
imper'atively, *adv.* **-ativeness,** *n.*
[L. *imperāre*, to command.]

imperceptible, *im-pėr-sep'ti-bl*, *adj.* too small to be seen, heard, noticed, etc.
imperceptibil'ity, -tibleness, *ns.*
impercep'tibly, *adv.* [Pfx. **im-** (2).]

imperfect, *im-pėr'fekt*, *adj.* having a fault or defect, not perfect.
imper'fectly, *adv.* **imper'fectness,** *n.*
imperfec'tion, *n.* a defect, faulty detail: imperfectness. [Pfx. **im-** (2).]

imperial, *im-pē'ri-ȧl*, *adj.* of, or connected with, empire, emperor, or empress: commanding, domineering: (of weights and measures) according to the standard legal in Britain.
impe'rialism, *n.* (belief in) the policy of having, or extending, an empire or (*loosely*) control over other peoples.
impe'rialist, *n.*, *adj.*
imperialis'tic, *adj.*
impe'rious, *adj.* haughty, commanding: urgent, imperative.
impe'riously, *adv.* **impe'riousness,** *n.*
[L. *imperium*, command, supreme power.]

imperil, *im-per'il*, *v.t.* to put in danger:—*pr.p.* **imper'illing**; *pa.p.* **imper'illed.**
[Pfx. **im-** (1).]

imperious. See **imperial.**

imperishable, *im-per'ish-ȧ-bl*, *adj.* not perishable: lasting for ever.
imperishabil'ity, -ableness, *ns.*
imper'ishably, *adv.* [Pfx. **im-** (2).]

impermanent, *im-pėr'mȧ-nėnt*, *adj.* not permanent.
imper'manence, imper'manency, *n*
[Pfx. **im-** (2).]

impermeable, *im-pėr'mi-ȧ-bl*, *adj.* not allowing fluids to pass through.
impermeabil'ity, -meableness, *ns.*
imper'meably, *adv.* [Pfx. **im-** (2).]

impersonal, *im-pėr'sȯn-ȧl*, *adj.* not involving or referring to a person (a verb is impersonal when its subject is 'it'; e.g. *It rained for four days*): not showing or arising from personal feeling (e.g. *He took an impersonal interest in what happened.*)
impersonal'ity, imper'sonalness, *ns.*
imper'sonally, *adv.* [Pfx. **im-** (2).]

impersonate, *im-pėr'sȯn-āt*, *v.t.* to act the part of, or pretend to be (another person).
impersonā'tion, *n.* **imper'sonator,** *n.*
[Pfx. **im-** (1), **person,** vb. suffix *-ate.*]

impertinent, *im-pėr'ti-nėnt*, *adj.* impudent, rude: meddling, presumptuous.
imper'tinence, *n.*
imper'tinently, *adv.*
[Fr.—L. *impertinens*, not belonging.]

imperturbable, *im-pėr-tûr'bȧ-bl*, *adj.* not easily agitated, always calm.
imperturbabil'ity, -bableness, *ns.*
impertur'bably, *adv.* [Pfx. **im-** (2).]

impervious, *im-pėr'vi-ůs*, *adj.* not allowing entry or passage (to; *impervious to water*): not affected by (with *to*; e.g. *impervious to argument*).
[Pfx. **im-** (2), L. *per*, through, *via*, way.]

impetuous, *im-pet'ū-ůs*, *adj.* impulsive, acting with, or showing, suddenness and rashness.
impet'uously, *adv.* **-uousness,** *n.*
[Same root as **impetus.**]

impetus, *im'pi-tůs*, *n.* moving force, or energy with which a body moves: stimulus, encouragement (e.g. *This discovery gave a fresh impetus to the development of the industry*).
[L., attack.]

impiety, *im-pī'ė-ti*, *n.* want of piety.

impious, *im'pi-ůs*, *adj.* not pious, show-

ing lack of reverence for God or for what is sacred.
im′piously, *adv.* **im′piousness,** *n.*
[Pfx. **im-** (2).]

impinge, *im-pinj′*, *v.i.* (of e.g. light, sound; with *on, upon, against*) to strike or fall on: to encroach (on, e.g. another person's rights).
impinge′ment, *n.*
See also **impact.**
[L. *impingĕre, impactum,* to drive into.]

impious, etc. See **impiety.**

impish. See **imp.**

implacable, *im-plak′ȧ-bl, -plāk′, adj.* not to be appeased, soothed, or satisfied.
implacabil′ity, implac′ableness, *ns.*
implac′ably, *adv.*
[Pfx. **im-** (2), L. *plācāre,* to appease.]

implant, *im-plânt′*, *v.t.* to insert, esp. into living tissue: to fix in the mind, e.g. by teaching (an idea, etc.). [Pfx. **im-** (1).]

implement, *im′pli-mėnt, n.* a tool or instrument.—*v.t.* (*im-pli-ment′*) to fulfil, carry out (e.g. a promise).
[L. *implēre,* to fill.]

implicate, *im′pli-kāt, v.t.* to involve, or show to have taken part (in a crime or fault).
implicā′tion, *n.* state of being involved: something that is implied.
[Pfx. **im-** (1), L. *plicāre, plicātum,* or *plicitum,* to fold, twist, twine.]

implicit, *im-plis′it, adj.* meant but not put into actual words (e.g. *implicit agreement*) —opp. of **explicit**: (of trust, etc.) unquestioning, complete.
implic′itly, *adv.* **implic′itness,** *n.*
[Same root as **implicate.**]

implied, etc. See **imply.**

implore, *im-plōr′, -plör′, v.t.* to entreat (someone to do something): to ask earnestly for (e.g. help).
[Pfx. **im-** (1), L. *plōrāre,* to weep.]

imply, *im-plī′, v.t.* to involve, point to, as a necessary circumstance, result, etc. (e.g. *A quarrel implies disagreement about something*): to hint at or suggest: (of words) to mean:—*pr.p.* **imply′ing**; *pa.p.* **implied′.**
implied′, *adj.* suggested but not actually put into words.
implication, *n.* (See **implicate**).
[O.Fr. *emplier*—same root as **implicate.**]

impolite, *im-pȯ-līt′, adj.* not polite, rude.
impolite′ly, *adv.* **impolite′ness,** *n.*
[Pfx. **im-** (2).]

impolitic, *im-pol′i-tik, adj.* (of an action) not politic or wise. [Pfx. **im-** (2).]

imponderable, *im-pon′dėr-ȧ-bl, adj.* not able to be measured, estimated, etc. because too small, vague, or uncertain.—*n.* an imponderable influence, etc.
[Pfx. **im-** (2), L. *ponderāre,* to weigh.]

import, *im-pōrt′, -pört′, v.t.* to bring in (goods, for sale, etc.) from abroad: to imply, mean.—*n.* (*im′-*) something imported from abroad: meaning (of words, statements, etc.): importance.
importā′tion, *n.* **impor′ter,** *n.*
[Pfx. **im-** (1), L. *portāre,* to carry.]

important, *im-pōr′tȧnt, -pör′, adj.* having, or likely to have, results that matter: memorable because of this: having influence or power: pompous.
impor′tance, *n.* **impor′tantly,** *adv.*
[Same root as **import.**]

importune, *im-por-tūn′, v.t.* to urge, beseech, with troublesome persistence.
[L. *importūnus,* inconvenient.]

impose, *im-pōz′, v.t.* to make (a duty or burden) compulsory (e.g. *to impose a tax, an obligation,* or *a condition, on a person or persons*): to force, inflict: to thrust (oneself) into company of (with *on*).—*v.i.* (with *on, upon*) to take unfair advantage of (a person, his good nature, etc.), or to deceive, cheat (a person).
impos′ing, *adj.* impressive, stately, large.
See also **imposition.**
See also **impostor, imposture.**
[Fr. *im* (in), on, *poser,* to place.]

imposition, *im-pȯ-zish′(ȯ)n, n.* act of imposing: a burdensome, unjustified demand: a punishment task.
[Pfx. **im-** (1), L. *pōnĕre, positum,* place.]

impossible, *im-pos′i-bl, adj.* that cannot exist, be true, or be done.
impossibil′ity, *n.*:—*pl.* **impossibil′ities.**
imposs′ibly, *adv.* [Pfx. **im-** (2).]

impostor, *im-pos′tȯr, n.* one who pretends to be someone else, or to be something he is not, in order to deceive.
impos′ture (*-chůr*), *n.* fraud of this kind.
[Same root as **impose.**]

impotent, *im′pȯ-tėnt, adj.* without power, strength, or effectiveness.
im′potence, *n.* **im′potently,** *adv.*
[Pfx. **im-** (2).]

impound, *im-pownd′, v.t.* to shut in (e.g. a stray animal in a pound): to confine (e.g. water within a reservoir): to take, esp. legal, possession of. [Pfx. **im-** (1).]

impoverish, *im-pov′ėr-ish, v.t.* to make (e.g. a person, a country) poor: to make (e.g. soil) poor in quality.
impov′erished, *adj.*
impov′erishment, *n.*
[O.Fr. *empoverir*—*povre,* poor.]

impracticable, *im-prak′ti-kȧ-bl, adj.* (of e.g. a plan) not able to be put into practice or used: (of roads) impassable.
impracticabil′ity, -ticableness, *ns.*
imprac′ticably, *adv.* [Pfx. **im-** (2).]

impractical, *im-prak′ti-kl, adj.* not practical, not able to be done without undue trouble. [Pfx. **im-** (2).]

imprecation, *im-prė-kā′sh(ȯ)n, n.* a curse.
[Pfx. **im-** (1), L. *precārī, precātus,* pray.]

impregnable, *im-preg′nȧ-bl, adj.* that cannot be taken by, or overthrown by, attack.
[Pfx. **im-** (2), L. *pre(he)ndĕre,* seize.]

impregnate, *im-preg′nāt, v.t.* to saturate (with).
[Late L. *impraegnāre*; conn. **pregnant.**]

impresario, *im-prė-sä′ri-ō, -zä′, n.* manager of an opera company, etc.: one who puts on an entertainment. [It.].

impress, *im-pres′, v.t.* to press (something on something else): to fix (e.g. a fact) deeply on the mind: to stress, urge (e.g. *Impress the need for hurry*): to arouse feeling, e.g. admiration, interest, in (person, persons).—Also *v.i.*—*n.* (*im′pres*) a mark made by, or as if by, pressure.
impression, *im-presh′(ȯ)n, n.* act or result of impressing: mark: a single printing of a book: the idea or emotion left in the mind by any experience: a strong effect on the mind: a vague, uncertain memory (that).
impress′ionable (*-presh′*), *adj.* easily impressed or influenced.
impress′ive, *adj.* making a deep impression on the mind: solemn, arousing awe.
impress′ively, *adv.* **-iveness,** *n.*
[Pfx. **im-** (1), **press** (1).]

imprint, *im-print′, v.t.* to print, stamp: to fix in the mind: to place (a kiss).—*n.* (*im′-*) a mark made by pressure: a permanent effect produced on a person by someone else or by an experience: a printer's name and address on a book, etc.
[Pfx. **im-** (1).]

imprison, *im-priz′n, v.t.* to put in prison: to shut up.
impris′onment, *n.* [Pfx. **im-** (1).]

improbable, *im-prob′ȧ-bl, adj.* unlikely.
improb′ably, *adv.* **-ableness,** *n.*
improbabil′ity (*pl.* **-ities**), *n.* improbableness: something unlikely.
[Pfx. **im-** (2).]

impromptu, *im-promp′tū, -to͞o, adj.* made or done without preparation beforehand. —Also *adv.* or *n.*
[L. *in promptū*, in readiness.]

improper, *im-prop′ėr, adj.* not suitable: not correct: indecent.
improp′erly, *adv.* **improp′erness,** *n.*
impropriety, *-prȯ-prī′ė-ti, n.* improperness: something improper.:—*pl.* **-ies.**
improper fraction, one in which the numerator is larger than the denominator, e.g. $\frac{33}{7}$. [Pfx. **im-** (2).]

improve, *im-pro͞ov′, v.t.* and *v.i.* to make, or become, better.
improve′ment, *n.*
improv′ing, *adj.* intended to improve morals or mind.
to improve on, to produce something more useful, or striking, etc., than.
[O.Fr. *en prou*, into profit.]

improvident, *im-prov′i-dėnt, adj.* not thrifty, not taking thought for the future.
improv′idence, *n.*
improv′idently, *adv.* [Pfx. **im-** (2).]

improvise, *im′prȯ-vīz, v.t.* to compose and perform without preparation: to make a substitute for from materials at hand (e.g. *to improvise a bed*).—Also *v.i.*
improvisā′tion, *n.* **im′proviser,** *n.*
[L. *in*, not, *prōvīsus*, foreseen.]

imprudent, *im-pro͞o′dėnt, adj.* not showing caution or foresight, unwise.
impru′dence, *n.* **impru′dently,** *adv.*
[Pfx. **im-** (2).]

impudent, *im′pū-dėnt, adj.* insolent: shamelessly bold.
im′pudence, *n.* **im′pudently,** *adv.*
[Pfx. **im-** (2), L. *pudēre*, to be ashamed.]

impugn, *im-pūn′, v.t.* to attack in words or by arguments (e.g. *to impugn the truthfulness of an informant*).
[L. *in*, against, *pugnāre*, to fight.]

impulse, *im′puls, n.* a driving or impelling force, or its effect: a drive to action caused by a feeling, etc.: a sudden desire (to do something).
impul′sive, *adj.* inclined to act suddenly without careful thought: (of action) caused by impulse.
impul′sively, *adv.* **impul′siveness,** *n.*
[Same root as **impel.**]

impunity, *im-pū′ni-ti, n.* freedom from punishment, injury, or loss (e.g. *He had so far ignored the regulation with impunity*).
[L. *in*, not, *poena*, punishment.]

impure, *im-pūr′, adj.* mixed with something else: not morally pure.
impure′ness, impur′ity (*pl.* **-ities**), *ns.*
impure′ly, *adv.* [Pfx. **im-** (2).]

impute, *im-pūt′, v.t.* to consider (a happening, action, etc., usu. bad) to be caused, done, etc., by (with *to*; e.g. *I impute our failure to lack of preparation, to our leader*; *do not impute the theft*, or *impute laziness, to me*).
imputā′tion, *n.* act of imputing: suggestion of fault.
[L. *in*, in, *putāre*, to think, reckon.]

in, *in, prep.* expressing the relation of a thing to what surrounds or includes it (place, time, or circumstances; e.g. *in the garden, in his youth, in daylight*).—*adv.* inside, not out: towards the inside: (*cricket*) at the bat: short for various phrases, e.g. for *in office, in fashion.*—*adj.* that is in, inside, or coming in:—*comp.* **inn′er**; *superls.* **inn′ermost, in′most.**
inn′er (see above), farther in: more closely associated, more in the know (e.g. *in the inner circle of his helpers*): (of meaning) hidden: of the mind or spirit (e.g. *the inner life*).—*n.* (a hit on) the part of the target next the bull's eye.
ins and outs, windings: details of something complicated (e.g. of long negotiations).
to be in for, to be trying to get: to be about to receive (something unpleasant).
[O.E.; conn. Ger. *in*, L. *in*, Gk. *en.*]

in-, *in-, pfx.* in Engl. and L. words, means (1) in (e.g. *include*), into (e.g. *invade*); (2) not (e.g. *insincere*).

In- meaning 'not' is connected with *un-* and in a few cases either *un-* or *in-* may be used (e.g. *unsanitary, insanitary*). In some cases a noun has *in-* and the *adj.* has *un-* (e.g. *ingratitude, ungrateful*). The endings of advs. and nouns connected with adjs. in *in-* are the same as those of the advs. and nouns without the prefix, e.g. *(in)elegant, (in)elegance, (in)elegantly.* [L.; in sense (1), also O.E.]

inability, *in-ȧ-bil'i-ti, n.* lack of power, means, etc. (to do something). See also **unable.** [Pfx. **in-** (2).]

inaccessible, *in-ȧk-ses'i-bl, adj.* not to be approached, reached, or obtained.
inaccessibil'ity, -ibleness, *ns.*
inaccess'ibly, *adv.* [Pfx. **in-** (2).]

inaccurate, *in-ak'ū-rit, adj.* not accurate.
inacc'urately, *adv.* **-urateness,** *n.*
inacc'uracy, *n.* inaccurateness: a mistake:—*pl.* **-ies.** [Pfx. **in-** (2).]

inactive, *in-ak'tiv, adj.* not active: making no effort: out of use.
inactiv'ity, *n.* [Pfx. **in-** (2).]

inadequate, *in-ad'i-kwit, adj.* not suitable or sufficient: (of person) not able to deal with the situation.
inad'equately, *adv.* **-equateness,** *n.*
inad'equacy, *n.* inadequateness: defect, shortcoming:—*pl.* **-ies.** [Pfx. **in-** (2).]

inadmissible, *in-ȧd-mis'i-bl, adj.* not allowable.
inadmissibil'ity, -miss'ibleness, *ns.*
inadmiss'ibly, *adv.* [Pfx. **in-** (2).]

inadvertent, *in-ȧd-vėr'tent, adj.* not intentional or deliberate.
inadver'tence, inadver'tency, *ns.*
inadver'tently, *adv.*
[L. *in*, not, *ad*, to, *vertĕre*, to turn.]

inadvisable, *in-ȧd-vīz'ȧ-bl, adj.* unwise.
inadvisabil'ity, *n.* [Pfx. **in-** (2).]

inalienable, *in-āl'yen-ȧ-bl, adj.* (of rights) that cannot be tâken or given away. [Pfx. **in-** (2), and root of **alien.**]

inane, *in-ān', adj.* silly: meaningless.
inan'ity (*-an'*), *n.* silliness: a silly remark:—*pl.* **inan'ities.**
[L. *inānis*, empty.]

inanimate, *in-an'i-mit, adj.* lifeless, dead: dull, spiritless. [Pfx. **in-** (2).]

inapplicable, *in-ap'lik-ȧ-bl, -ȧ-plik', adj.* not suitable, not applying (to a situation, case under consideration).
[Pfx. **in-** (2).]

inappropriate, *in-ȧ-prō'pri-it, adj.* not appropriate or suitable.
inappro'priately, *adv.*
inappro'priateness, *n.* [Pfx. **in-** (2).]

inarticulate, *in-är-tik'ū-lit, adj.* uttered indistinctly: unable to express oneself clearly and fluently.
inartic'ulately, *adv.*
inartic'ulateness, *n.* [Pfx. **in-** (2).]

inartistic, *in-är-tis'tik, adj.* not artistic.
inartis'tically, *adv.* [Pfx. **in-** (2).]

inattentive, *in-ȧ-ten'tiv, adj.* not paying attention.
inatten'tion, inatten'tiveness, *ns.*
inatten'tively, *adv.* [Pfx. **in-** (2).]

inaudible, *in-ö'di-bl, adj.* not able to be heard.
inaudibil'ity, inau'dibleness, *ns.*
inau'dibly, *adv.* [Pfx. **in-** (2).]

inaugurate, *in-ö'gū-rāt, v.t.* to make a formal beginning of (something): to open formally to the public: to install (someone) formally in office.
inau'gural, *adj.* **inaugurā'tion,** *n.*
[L. *inaugurāre*; same root as **augur.**]

inauspicious, *in-ö-spish'ůs, adj.* not auspicious, unlucky.
inauspic'iously, *adv.*
inauspic'iousness, *n.* [Pfx. **in-** (2).]

inborn, *in'börn', adj.* born in one, natural.

inbred, *in'bred', adj.* natural: resulting from **in'breeding,** i.e. breeding animals by mating repeatedly within the same family.

incalculable, *in-kal'kū-lȧ-bl, adj.* that cannot be calculated, very great: that cannot be forecast.
incal'culableness, -abil'ity, *ns.*
incal'culably, *adv.* [Pfx. **in-** (2).]

incandescent, *in-kȧn-des'ėnt, adj.* glowing or white with heat.
[L. *in*, in, *candescĕre*, to glow.]

incantation, *in-kan-tā'sh(ȯ)n, n.* words said or sung as a spell.
[L. *in*, *cantāre*, *cantātum*, to sing.]

incapable, *in-kā'pȧ-bl, adj.* not capable (of): unfit, incompetent.
incapabil'ity, incap'ableness, *ns.*
incap'ably, *adv.* [Pfx. **in-** (2).]

incapacitate, *in-kȧ-pas'i-tāt, v.t.* to make incapable or unfit (for something).
incapac'ity, *n.* inability (for, to do): lack of physical or mental power: legal disqualification.
[Root as **(in)capable, capacity.**]

incarcerate, *in-kär'sėr-āt, v.t.* to imprison.
incarcerā'tion, *n.*
[L *in*, in, *carcer*, prison.]

incarnate, *in-kär'nit, -nāt, adj.* in bodily human form (e.g. *a devil incarnate*).
incarnā'tion, *n.* taking of human form by a divine being: a person representing a quality, etc., in a very marked way (e.g. *He is the incarnation of selfishness, of reasonableness*).
[L. *in*, in, *carō*, *carnis*, flesh.]

incautious, *in-kö'shůs, adj.* not cautious.
incau'tiously,' *adv.*
incau'tiousness, *n.* [Pfx. **in-** (2).]

incendiary, *in-sen'di-ȧ-ri, adj.* used for setting on fire (e.g. *incendiary bomb*): likely to cause strife (e.g. *an incendiary speech*).—*n.* one who sets fire to a building, etc. maliciously: one who stirs up strife: an incendiary bomb:—*pl.* **-ies.**
incen'diarism, *n.* act or practice of an incendiary.
[L. *incendĕre*, *incensum*, to kindle.]

incense[1], *in-sens', v.t.* to make angry.
[Same root as **incendiary.**]

incense[2], *in'sens, n.* material burned to give fragrant fumes, esp. in religious services. [Same root as **incendiary.**]

incentive, *in-sen'tiv, n.* something that moves to an action (e.g. *Hope of promotion was an incentive to hard work*).
[L. *incentivus,* striking up a tune.]

inception, *in-sep'sh(ȯ)n, n.* a beginning.
[Same root as **incipient.**]

incessant, *in-ses'ȧnt, adj.* going on without stopping, continual.
incess'antly, *adv.* **incess'antness,** *n.*
[L. *in,* not, *cessāre,* to cease.]

inch, *inch, n.* a measure of length, 1/12 of a foot (equal to 2·54 centimetres): (in *pl.*) height.
every inch, entirely, thoroughly.
[O.E. *ynce*—L. *uncia,* twelfth part.]

incidence, *in'sid-ėns, n.* the falling (of e.g. a ray of light on a surface): the range, or amount, of occurrence (of e.g. a disease).
in'cident, *adj.* (of e.g. a ray) falling or striking (on something): belonging naturally (e.g. *dangers incident to the life of an explorer*).—*n.* an event: one episode in a story.
inciden'tal, *adj.* occurring, etc., by chance in connexion with something else (*incidental benefits, an incidental remark*): additional, but less important (e.g. *money for fare, hotel bill, and incidental expenses*): liable to happen in (e.g. *dangers incidental to motor racing*).
inciden'tally, *adv.* by chance: (as *interj.*) by the way.
[L. *in,* on, *cadĕre,* to fall.]

incinerate, *in-sin'i-rāt, v.t.* to burn to ashes.
incinerā'tion, *n.*
incin'erator, *n.* a furnace, etc., for incinerating. [L. *in,* in, *cinis, cineris,* ashes.]

incipient, *in-sip'i-ėnt, adj.* beginning to exist (e.g. *an incipient cold*).
incip'ience, *n.* **incip'iently,** *adv.*
See also **inception.**
[L. *incipĕre, inceptum,* to begin.]

incise, *in-sīz', v.t.* to cut into: to make (marks, designs) by cutting.
incision, *in-sizh'ȯn, n.* act of cutting into (esp. by surgeon): a cut made for surgical or other purpose.
incisive, *in-sīs'iv, adj.* cutting: (of mind) clear and sharp: (of manner, etc.) clear, firm, or sharp, biting.
incis'or, *n.* a front, cutting tooth.
[L. *in,* into, *caedĕre, caesum,* to cut.]

incite, *in-sīt', v.t.* to urge on, move (to do something).
incite'ment, *n.*
[L. *in,* in, *citāre,* to rouse.]

incivility, *in-siv-il'i-ti, n.* impoliteness: an impolite act:—*pl.* **incivil'ities.**
See also **uncivil.** [Pfx. **in-** (2).]

inclement, *in-klem'ėnt, adj.* (of weather) stormy, very cold.
inclem'ency, *n.* [Pfx. **in-** (2).]

incline, *in-klīn', v.i.* to lean (towards): to slant, slope: to bow (the head): to have a tendency (e.g. *He is inclined to write too small*): to have a slight desire (e.g. *I am inclined to accept the invitation*).—Also *v.t.*—*n.* (*-klīn',* or *in'*) a slope.
inclination, *in-kli-nā'sh(ȯ)n, n.* a slope: a liking: a slight desire.
[L. *in,* into, *clīnāre,* to lean.]

include, *in-klōōd', v.t.* to take in, count.
inclusion, *in-klōō'zh(ȯ)n, n.*
inclusive, *in-klōō'siv, adj.* including everything mentioned or understood (e.g. *an inclusive charge; 7th to 9th May inclusive*—i.e. three days, 7th, 8th, 9th).
[L. *in,* in, *claudĕre, clausum,* to shut.]

incognito, *in-kog'ni-tō, adv.* with identity concealed, e.g. under a false name.
[It.—L. *in,* not, *cognitus,* known.]

incoherent, *in-kō-hēr'ėnt, adj.* (of a statement, etc.) loose, rambling, without logical connexion: (of a person) expressing himself in statements of this kind.
incoher'ence, incoher'ency, *ns.*
incoher'ently, *adv.* [Pfx. **in-** (2).]

income, *in(g)'kum, n.* money that comes in regularly, including salary, **etc.**
in'coming, *adj.* coming in.
income tax, a tax paid on income over a certain amount. **[in, come.]**

incommode, *in-kȯ-mōd', v.t.* to cause inconvenience or discomfort to.
[Fr.—L. *in,* not, *commodus,* convenient.]

incommunicable, *in-kȯ-mū'ni-kȧ-bl, adj.* that cannot be told or described to others.
[Pfx. **in-** (2).]

incommunicado, *in-kȯ-mū-ni-kä'dō, adj.* (of e.g. a prisoner) having no means of communicating with others.
[Sp. *incomunicado.*]

incomparable, *in-kom'pȧ-rȧ-bl,* without equal, matchless.
incom'parably, *adv.* beyond comparison (e.g. *incomparably more able than his successor*). [Pfx. **in-** (2).]

incompatible, *in-kȯm-pat'i-bl, adj.* incapable of existing, being used, etc., together: (of statements) contradictory: (of persons) sure, because of their natures, to disagree.
incompatibil'ity, -ibleness, *ns.*
incompat'ibly, *adv.* [Pfx. **in-** (2).]

incompetent, *in-kom'pė-tėnt, adj.* not legally qualified: (of evidence) not admissible: lacking ability, esp. in one's work.
incom'petence, incom'petency, *ns.*
incom'petently, *adv.* [Pfx. **in-** (2).]

incomplete, *in-kȯm-plēt', adj.* not complete.
incomplete'ly, *adv.*
incomplete'ness, *n.* [Pfx. **in-** (2).]

incomprehensible, *in-kom-pri-hen'si-bl, adj.* impossible to understand.
[Pfx. **in-** (2).]

inconceivable, *in-kon-sēv'ȧ-bl, adj.* that cannot be imagined or believed.
inconceiv'ably, *adv.* [Pfx. **in-** (2).]

inconclusive, *in-kon-klōō'siv, adj.* not settling a point that is debated or investigated (e.g. *inconclusive evidence*): with no definite result.
inconclu'sively, *adv.* [Pfx. **in-** (2).]
incongruous, *in-kong'groo-ŭs, adv.* out of keeping, out of place (e.g. *Heavy shoes look incongruous with evening dress*): not suitable or harmonious (e.g. *an incongruous mixture*): inconsistent (with).
incon'gruously, *adv.* **-gruousness,** *n.*
incongrū'ity, *n.* incongruousness: some thing incongruous:—*pl.* **-ies.**
[L. *in*, not, *congruĕre*, to run together.]
inconsequent, *in-kon'sė-kwėnt, adj.* not following logically from what goes before: showing lack of connexion in thought, etc. (e.g. *inconsequent statements, actions, an inconsequent person*).
incon'sequence, *n.* **-sequently,** *adv.*
inconsequen'tial (*-kwen'shål*), *adj.* of no consequence or importance: inconsequent.
[Pfx. **in-** (2), L. *con-*, *sequī*, to follow.]
inconsiderable, *in-kȯn-sid'ėr-å-bl, adj.* not important: small in amount, etc.
[Pfx. **in-** (2).]
inconsiderate, *in-kȯn-sid'ėr-it, adj.* not showing thought for the feelings or rights of others: thoughtless, foolish.
inconsid'erately, *adv.*
inconsid'erateness, *n.* [Pfx. **in-** (2).]
inconsistent, *in-kȯn-sis'tėnt, adj.* (of statements, etc.) contradictory in some way: not showing the same outlook or point of view (e.g. *His conduct on the two occasions was inconsistent; his method of trapping rabbits was inconsistent with his teaching about kindness to animals*): (of a person) not always speaking or acting according to the same principles or beliefs: not in keeping or agreement (with).
inconsis'tency, *n.*:—*pl.* **-ies.**
inconsis'tently, *adv.* [Pfx. **in-** (2).]
inconsolable, *in-kȯn-sōl'å-bl, adj.* not to be comforted.
inconsolabil'ity, -ableness, *ns.*
inconsol'ably, *adv.* [Pfx. **in-** (2).]
inconspicuous, *in-kȯn-spik'ū-ŭs, adj.* not noticeable.
inconspic'uously, *adv.*
inconspic'uousness, *n.* [Pfx. **in-** (2).]
inconstant, *in-kon'stånt, adj.* not constant: changeable, fickle.
incon'stancy *n.* [Pfx. **in-** (2).]
incontestable, *in-kȯn-tes'tå-bl, adj.* not to be disputed, undeniable. [Pfx. **in-** (2).]
incontinent, *in-kon'ti-nėnt, adj.* lacking control or restraint.
incon'tinence, *n.*
[Pfx. **in-** (2), L. *continēre*, to contain.]
incontrovertible, *in-kon-trȯ-vėr'ti-bl, adj.* (of e.g. truth, evidence) too clear and certain to be questioned or disputed.
incontrover'tibly, *adv.* [Pfx. **in-** (2).]
inconvenient, *in-kȯn-vēn'yėnt, adj.* causing trouble or difficulty: awkward.
inconven'ience, *n.*—Also *v.t.* to cause trouble or difficulty to (someone).
inconven'iently, *adv.* [Pfx. **in-** (2).]
incorporate, *in-kör'pȯ-rāt, v.t.* to contain as part of the whole (e.g. *The new statement incorporates all your suggestions*): to add, put in, so that it forms part of the whole: to merge, blend (with).
incor'porated, *adj.* formed into a corporation (*abbrev.* **Inc.**).
[L. *in*, into, *corpus*, *corporis*, body.]
incorrect, *in-kȯ-rekt', adj.* not accurate, wrong: (of e.g. behaviour) not according to best, or accepted, standards.
incorrect'ly, *adv.* [Pfx. **in-** (2).]
incorrigible, *in-kor'i-ji-bl, adj.* too bad for correction or reform: uncontrollable.
incorrigibil'ity, -ibleness, *ns.*
incorr'igibly, *adv.*
[Pfx. **in-** (2), same root as **correct.**]
incorruptible, *in-kȯ-rup'ti-bl, adj.* not capable of decay: always upright and just: that cannot be bribed.
[Pfx. **in-** (2).]
increase, *in-krēs', v.i., v.t.* to grow, or to make greater, in size or numbers.—*n.* (*in'krēs*) growth: amount added by growth, etc.
increas'ingly, *adv.* to an ever greater degree (e.g. *It became increasingly difficult to find helpers*).
in'crement (*-krė-*), *n.* increase: amount of increase: something added.
[L. *in*, in, *crescĕre*, grow.]
incredible, *in-kred'i-bl, adj.* impossible to believe, or seeming so.
incredibil'ity, incred'ibleness, *ns.*
incred'ibly, *adv.*
incredulous, *in-kred'ū-lŭs, adj.* not believing: showing disbelief.
incredū'lity, incred'ulousness, *ns.*
incred'ulously, *adv.* [Pfx. **in-** (2).]
increment. See **increase.**
incriminate, *in-krim'i-nāt, v.t.* to show (someone) to have committed, or taken part in, a crime.
incriminā'tion, *n.* **incrim'inating,** *adj.*
[Pfx. **in-** (1), and same root as **crime.**]
incrust. Same as **encrust.**
incubate, *in'kū-bāt, v.t.* to sit on (eggs) in order to hatch them: to hatch.—Also *v.i.*
incubā'tion, *n.*
in'cubātor, *n.* apparatus for hatching eggs, one to house premature babies, etc.
incubation period, period between infection and appearance of signs of disease.
[L. *in*, on, *cubāre*, *-atum* (*-itum*), to lie.]
incubus, *in'kū-bŭs, n.* something that oppresses as a nightmare does.
[Late L., nightmare—root as **incubate.**]
inculcate, *in'kul-kāt, in-kul', v.t.* to impress or teach by frequent repetitions (e.g. *to inculcate good principles in his son*): to teach (a person) thus (e.g. *to inculcate his pupil with love of wisdom*).
inculcā'tion, *n.*
[L. *in*, *calcāre*, tread—*calx*, heel.]

incumbent, *in-kum'bent, adj.* resting as a duty (on someone; e.g. *It is incumbent on us to support our leader now*).—*n.* one who holds an ecclesiastical benefice, etc.
[L. *incumbĕre,* to lie upon—*cubāre,* to lie.]

incur, *in-kûr', v.t.* to become liable to pay (a debt): to bring upon oneself by one's actions (e.g. *to incur someone's displeasure*): —*pr.p.* **incurr'ing;** *pa.p.* **incurred'.**
[L. *in,* into, *currĕre,* to run.]

incurable, *in-kūr'a-bl, adj.* not able to be cured or corrected.—*n.* a person who is incurable.
incur'ably, *adv.* [Pfx. **in-** (2).]

incursion, *in-kûr'sh(o)n, n.* a hostile entry, raid: a running in (of water).
[Same root as **incur.**]

indebted, *in-det'id, adj.* being in debt (to): obliged (to) for help or kindness.
indebt'edness, *n.*
[O.Fr. *en,* in, *dette,* debt.]

indecent, *in-dē'sent, adj.* offending against accepted standards of conduct—immodest, improper: (in weakened sense) not in good taste (e.g. *indecent haste*).
inde'cency, *n.*:—*pl.* **-ies.**
[Pfx. **in-** (2).]

indecipherable, *in-di-sī'fer-a-bl, adj.* impossible to read. [Pfx. **in-** (2).]

indecision, *in-di-sizh'(o)n, n.* inability to decide, hesitation.
indecisive, *in-di-sī'siv, adj.* not producing a clear decision or having a definite result: (of person) wavering, not arriving at firm decisions.
indeci'sively, *adv.*
See also **undecided.** [Pfx. **in-** (2).]

indeed, *in-dēd', adv.* in fact, in truth.—Also used for emphasis.—*interj.* expression of surprise, etc. [**in, deed.**]

indefatigable, *in-di-fat'i-ga-bl, adj.* untiring in effort.
indefat'igably, *adv.*
[L. *in,* not, *dē,* from, *fatigāre,* to tire.]

indefensible, *in-di-fen'si-bl, adj.* that cannot be defended: that cannot be justified or excused. [Pfx. **in-** (2).]

indefinable, *in-di-fīn'a-bl, adj.* that cannot be clearly described or put into words.
[Pfx. **in-** (2).]

indefinite, *in-def'in-it, adj.* without clearly marked outlines or limits (e.g. *an indefinite area, an indefinite time*): not fixed or exact, uncertain.
indef'initely, *adv.* **indef'initeness,** *n.*
indefinite article. See **a.**
[Pfx. **in-** (2).]

indelible, *in-del'i-bl, adj.* (of mark, or impression on mind) that cannot be rubbed out: (of pencil) making marks that cannot be erased.
indel'ibly, *adv.*
[Pfx. **in-** (2), L. *dēlēre,* to destroy.]

indelicate, *in-del'i-kit, adj.* coarse, immodest: lacking in good feeling or tact.
indel'icacy, *n.*:—*pl.* **-ies.**
indel'icately, *adv.* [Pfx. **in-** (2).]

indemnify, *in-dem'ni-fī, v.t.* to give (person) security (against loss or hurt): to compensate (person for).
indem'nity, *n.* security against, or compensation for, loss, etc.
[L. *in,* not, *damnum,* loss.]

indent, *in-dent', v.t.* to separate (copies of a document) by cutting along a zigzag line: to make notches, or recesses, in: to begin farther in from the margin.—*v.i.* to make out a written order with counterfoil (for).—Also *n.* (*in',* or *-dent'*).
indentā'tion, *n.* a notch: a recess (e.g. in a coastline).
inden'ture (*-chur*), *n.* a written agreement: a contract by which e.g. an apprentice is bound to work for a master for a given period.
[L. *in, dens, dentis,* a tooth.]

independent, *in-di-pen'dent, adj.* free from control by others: (of e.g. a country) self-governing: thinking or acting for oneself: not willing to accept help: self-confident (e.g. *an independent air*): not influenced by, or showing influence of, anyone or anything else (e.g. *an independent observer; he arrived at an independent conclusion*).
indepen'dence, *n.* **-pen'dently,** *adv.*
independent means, an income not dependent on employment by others.
independent of, not depending on.
[Pfx. **in-** (2).]

indescribable, *in-di-skrī'ba-bl, adj.* that cannot be described, either because vague or because too great (e.g. *indescribable horrors*).
indescri'bably, *adv.* [Pfx. **in-** (2).]

indestructible, *in-di-struk'ti-bl, adj.* that cannot be destroyed. [Pfx. **in-** (2).]

indeterminate, *in-di-tėr'mi-nit, adj.* not fixed in amount, etc.: vague, uncertain.
indeter'minatelv, *adv.* **-ateness,** *n.*
[Pfx. **in-** (2), and root of **determine.**]

index, *in'deks, n.* the forefinger: a pointer on a dial or scale: indication, pointer (to), sign (of): an alphabetical list of subjects e.g. dealt with in a book: a raised figure showing how many times a number is multiplied by itself (e.g. the 3 in the statement $5^3 = 5 \times 5 \times 5$):—*pl.* **in'dexes,** (*mathematics*) **in'dices** (*-di-sēz*).—*v.t.* to supply with, or enter in, an index.
[L.—same root as **indicate.**]

Indian, *in'di-an, ind'yan, adj.* belonging to India, or to the peoples (**Red Indians**), excluding Eskimos, found in America by the early European invaders.—Also *n.*
East Indian, West Indian, of the East, or West, Indies.
Indian corn, maize.
Indian file, ink. See **file, ink.**
Indian summer (orig. in America), a period of warm, dry, calm weather in late autumn.
India paper, a thin paper made in the Far East: a thin paper for Bibles, etc.

in′dia-rubb′er, *n.* rubber, esp. a piece for rubbing out pencil marks, etc.
[Gk. *Indos,* Indus river.]

indicate, *in′di-kāt, v.t.* to point out: to show: to be a sign of: to give some idea of: to point to as the best treatment or remedy.
indicā′tion, *n.*
indic′ative (*-ȧ-tiv*), *adj.* showing or suggesting the existence (of; e.g. *The change in her manner was indicative of a new attitude to us*): of the parts of the verb that make statements or ask questions (e.g. *am speaking*; *ran*; *will fly*).
in′dicator, *n.* a pointer: a pointer on a measuring instrument, or the instrument itself.
See also **index.**
[L. *indicāre,* to make known.]

indict, *in-dīt′, v.t.* to charge with a crime (formally or in writing): to accuse.
indict′able, *adj.* (of an offence) for which one can be charged in court.
indict′ment, *n.*
[Through Fr.—L. *in, dictāre,* declare.]

indifferent, *in-dif′ėr-ėnt, adj.* without interest, not caring: without feeling (towards, to): not making distinction or showing favour: unimportant (e.g. *It is indifferent to me what you do*): rather poor (in quality).
indiff′erently, *adv.* **indiff′erence,** *n.*
[L. *indifferens*; root as **different.**]

indigence. See **indigent.**

indigenous, *in-dij′i-nus, adj.* produced naturally in a country or soil (e.g. *plants indigenous to northern Europe*).
[L. *indigena,* a native; conn. with *gignĕre,* to produce.]

indigent, *in′di-jent, adj.* poor, in need.
in′digence, *n.* **in′digently,** *adv.*
[Late L. *indigēre* (—L. *egēre*), be in need.]

indigestion, *in-di-jes′ch(ȯ)n, n.* discomfort caused by imperfectly digested food.
indiges′tible, *adj.* not easily digested.
indigestibil′ity, -ibleness, *ns.*
indiges′tibly, *adv.* [Pfx. **in-** (2).]

indignant, *in-dig′nȧnt, adj.* angry and with a sense of injustice to oneself or other(s).
indig′nantly, *adv.* **indignā′tion,** *n.*
indig′nity, *n.* a hurt to dignity, affront, insult:—*pl.* **indig′nities.**
[L. *in,* not, *dignus,* worthy.]

indigo, *in′di-gō, n.* a violet-blue dye: the colour in the rainbow between blue and violet.
[Gk. *indikon,* Indian (dye).]

indirect, *in-di-rekt′, -dī-, adj.* not direct: not in a straight line: roundabout: not going straight to the point or subject: not the one directly aimed at or following directly (e.g. *an indirect result*).
indirect′ly, *adv.* **indirect′ness,** *n.*
indirect speech, speech reported not in the actual words of the speaker (e.g. *He said he had no time*—the speaker's words were probably, '*I have no time*').
indirect tax, a customs and excise duty, etc., which is collected indirectly from the customer, who has to pay higher prices for taxed goods. [Pfx. **in-** (2).]

indiscreet, *in-dis-krēt′, adj.* not prudent or cautious: giving too much information away: showing poor judgment (e.g. *giving indiscreet praise and blame*).
indiscretion, *in-dis-kre′sh(ȯ)n, n.* want of prudence, etc.: an indiscreet act.
indiscreet′ly, *adv.* [Pfx. **in-** (2).]

indiscriminate, *in-dis-krim′in-it, adj.* not making any distinction or difference because of differences in merit or worth or the opposite (e.g. *indiscriminate praise, blame, generosity, slaughter*).
indiscrim′inately, *adv.*
indiscrim′ināting, *adj.* not making, or able to make, distinctions.
[Pfx. **in-** (2); root as **discriminate.**]

indispensable, *in-dis-pen′sȧ-bl, adj.* that cannot be done without or neglected.
indispensabil′ity, -ableness, *ns.*
[Pfx. **in-** (2), and root as **dispense.**]

indisposed, *in-dis-pōzd′, adj.* (in predicate; not used before noun) unwilling (to): slightly ill.
indisposi′tion, *-pȯ-zish′(ȯ)n, n.*
indispose′, *v.t.* [Pfx. **in-** (2).]

indisputable, *in-dis-pū′tȧ-bl, -dis′pū-, adj.* certainly true.
indisputably (*-pū′,* or *-dis′*), *adv.*
[Pfx. **in-** (2).]

indissoluble, *in-di-sol′ū-bl,* or *-dis′ȯl-, adj.* that cannot be dissolved, undone, or broken: binding for ever.
indissolubil′ity, -ubleness, *ns.*
indissol′ubly (or *-dis′*) *adv.*
[Pfx. **in-** (2), and root as **dissolve.**]

indistinct, *in-dis-tingkt′, adj.* not clear to eye, ear, or mind: dim.
indistinct′ly, *adv.* **indistinct′ness,** *n.*
[Pfx. **in-** (2).]

indistinguishable, *in-dis-ting′gwish-ȧ-bl, adj.* that cannot be distinguished, i.e. seen, or seen as different or separate.
indistin′guishably, *adv.* [Pfx. **in-** (2).]

individual, *in-di-vid′ū-ȧl,* or *-vij′oo-, adj.* belonging to one only, or to each one separately, of a group: single, separate: having marked special qualities (e.g. *He had a very individual style*).—*n.* a single person or animal.
individ′ualist, *n.* one who shows great, or too great, independence in thought and action.
individual′ity, *n.* the qualities that distinguish one person from others.
individ′ually, *adv.* each separately: personally (e.g. *This rule affects me individually*).
[Pfx. **in-** (2), L. *dividĕre,* to divide.]

indivisible, *in-di-viz′i-bl, adj.* not able to be divided, or separated.
indivisibil′ity, -ibleness, *ns.*
indivis′ibly, *adv.* [Pfx. **in-** (2).]

indoctrinate, *in-dok′trin-āt, v.t.* to fill,

inspire (a person, with a doctrine, set of beliefs, etc.)
indoctrinā′tion, *n.*
[Pfx. **in-** (1), and root as **doctrine.**]

indolent, *in′dō-lėnt, adj.* lazy, avoiding exertion.
in′dolence, *n.* **in′dolently,** *adv.*
[L. *in*, not, *dolēre*, to suffer pain.]

indomitable, *in-dom′i-tȧ-bl, adj.* that cannot be overcome (used e.g. of courage, pride, a very resolute person).
indom′itably, *adv.*
[Pfx. **in-** (2), Late L. *domitāre*, to tame.]

indoor, *in′dōr, -dör, adj.* used, carried on, etc., inside a building (e.g. *indoor games*).
in′doors′, *adv.* [**in, door.**]

indubitable, *in-dū′bi-tȧ-bl, adj.* that cannot be doubted, certain.
indu′bitably, *adv.*
[Pfx. **in-** (2), L. *dubitāre*, to doubt.]

induce, *in-dūs′, v.t.* to lead, persuade (a person; e.g. *I could not induce her to come*): to bring on or bring about (e.g. *The heat induced sleepiness*).
induce′ment, *n.* something that persuades, an incentive.
[L. *in*, in, *dūcĕre, ductum*, to lead.]

induct, *in-dukt′, v.t.* to introduce formally (to, into, a new office, esp. a clergyman).
induc′tion, *n.* act of inducting: production by one body of an opposite electrical state in another.
[Same root as **induce.**]

indulge, *in-dulj′, v.t.* to yield to the wishes of (a person, oneself): not to restrain (a desire, etc.; e.g. *indulging his love of practical jokes*).
indul′gence, *n.* act of gratifying: too great leniency: a privilege granted: a pardon to a repentant sinner.
indul′gent, *adj.* **indul′gently,** *adv.*
[L. *indulgēre.*]

industry, *in′dus-tri, n.* steady attention to work: (any branch of) production or trade: ownership and management (e.g. *dispeace between industry and labour*).
indus′trial, *adj.* **indus′trially,** *adv.*
indus′trialise, *v.t.* to give (e.g. a country) industries on a large scale.
indus′trialist, *n.* one who takes part in running a large industrial organisation.
indus′trious, *adj.* diligent, hard working.
indus′triously, *adj.*
heavy (light) industry, industry making large (small) products.
[L. *industria*, diligence.]

inebriate, *in-ē′bri-āt, v.t.* to make drunk.—*n.* (*-it*, or *āt*) a drunk person.
inebriā′tion, *n.* **ine′briated,** *adj.*
[L. *in-*, *ēbrius*, drunk.]

inedible, *in-ed′i-bl, adj.* not fit to be eaten: not suitable as food. [Pfx. **in-** (2).]

ineducable, *in-ed′ū-kȧ-bl, adj.* impossible to educate. [Pfx. **in-** (2).]

ineffable, *in-ef′ȧ-bl, adj.* impossible to describe in words: not to be uttered.
[L. *in*, not, *fārī*, to speak.]

ineffective, *in-ė-fek′tiv, adj.* not producing the effect desired: not efficient.
ineffec′tively, *adv.* **-tiveness,** *n.*
ineffec′tual (*-fek′tū-ȧl*, or *-fek′chŭ-ȧl*), *adj.* without effect, useless: powerless.
ineffectual′ity, -tualness, *ns.*
ineffec′tually, *adv.*
ineffica′cious (*-kā′shus*), *adj.* not able to produce the desired effect.
ineff′icacy (*-i-kȧ-si*), *n.* lack of power to produce the desired effect.
inefficient, *in-i-fish′ėnt, adj.* not efficient: not accomplishing, or able to carry out, in the best way.
ineffic′iency, *n.* **ineffic′iently,** *adv.*
For slight differences in use of **ineffective,** etc., see **effective.** [Pfx. **in-** (2).]

inelegant, *in-el′i-gȧnt, adj.* not graceful: not in good taste.
inel′egance, -egancy, -egantness, *ns.*
inel′egantly, *adv.* [Pfx. **in-** (2).]

ineligible, *in-el′i-ji-bl, adj.* not eligible.
ineligibil′ity, *n.* [Pfx. **in-** (2).]

inept, *in-ept′, adj.* not suitable, out of place: (of a remark) foolish.
inep′titude, inept′ness, *ns.*
inept′ly, *adv.*
[Pfx. **in-** (2), L. *aptus*, apt.]

inequality, *in-i-kwol′i-ti, n.* want of equality, or an instance of it: unevenness:—*pl.* **inequal′ities.**
See also **unequal.** [Pfx. **in-** (2).]

inequitable, *in-ek′wi-tȧ-bl, adj.* unfair, unjust.
ineq′uitably, *adv.* **ineq′uity,** *n.*
[Pfx. **in-** (2).]

ineradicable, *in-i-rad′i-kȧ-bl, adj.* that cannot be rooted out or removed completely. [Pfx. **in-** (2).]

inert, *in-ėrt′, adj.* unable to move of itself: chemically inactive: unwilling to move or act.
inert′ly, *adv.* **inert′ness,** *n.*
inertia, *in-ėr′shi-ȧ, n.* inertness.
[L. *iners, inertis*, unskilled, idle.]

inescapable, *in-es-kā′pȧ-bl, adj.* that cannot be escaped or avoided.
[Pfx. **in-** (2).]

inessential, *in-i-sen′sh(ȧ)l, adj.* not necessary.—Also *n.* [Pfx. **in-** (2).]

inestimable, *in-es′ti-mȧ-bl, adj.* too great, of too great value, to be estimated.
ines′timably, *adv.* [Pfx. **in-** (2).]

inevitable, *in-ev′i-tȧ-bl, adj.* that cannot be avoided: certain, necessary.
inevitabil′ity, inev′itableness, *ns.*
inev′itably, *adv.*
[L. *in-*, not, *ē*, from, *vitāre*, to avoid.]

inexact, *in-ig-zakt′, adj.* not exactly correct or true.
inexac′titude, inexact′ness, *ns.*
inexact′ly, *adv.* [Pfx. **in-** (2).]

inexcusable, *in-iks-kūz′ȧ-bl, adj.* that cannot be excused or justified.
inexcus′ably, *adv.* [Pfx. **in-** (2).]

inexhaustible, *in-ig-zös′ti-bl, adj.* that cannot be tired: that cannot be used up.

inexhaustibil'ity, -tibleness, *ns.*
inexhaus'tibly, *adv.* [Pfx. **in-** (2).]

inexorable, *in-eks'ȯr-à-bl, adj.* impossible to move by entreaty: unalterable.
inexorabil'ity, -ableness, *ns.*
inex'orably, *adv.* relentlessly.
[L. *in-*, not, *ex*, out of, *ōrāre*, entreat.]

inexpedient, *in-iks-pē'di-ėnt, adj.* not advisable, or suitable, in the circumstances.
inexpe'dience, -pe'diency, *ns.*
[Pfx. **in-** (2).]

inexpensive, *in-ik-spen'siv, adj.* not costly.
inexpen'sively, *adv.* [Pfx. **in-** (2).]

inexperience, *in-iks-pē'ri-ėns, n.* lack of experience: lack of knowledge or skill. [Pfx. **in-** (2).]

inexpert, *in-iks-pėrt', adj.* unskilled: clumsy. [Pfx. **in-** (2).]

inexplicable, *in-eks'pli-kà-bl,* or *-plik'à-, adj.* impossible to explain or understand.
inex'plicably (or *-plik'*), *adv.*
[Pfx. **in-** (2).]

inexplicit, *in-iks-plis'it, adj.* not clearly stated and exact. [Pfx. **in-** (2).]

inexpressible, *in-iks-pres'i-bl, adj.* that cannot be expressed, indescribable.
inexpress'ibly, *adv.*
inexpress'ive, *adj.* without expression: not expressive. [Pfx. **in-** (2).]

inextinguishable, *in-iks-ting'gwish-à-bl, adj.* (of e.g. enthusiasm, hope) that cannot be put out or suppressed.
[Pfx. **in-** (2).]

inextricable, *in-eks'tri-kà-bl,* or *-trik', adj.* that cannot be disentangled: from which it is impossible to get free.
inex'tricably (or *-trik'*), *adv.*
[Pfx. **in-** (2), and root as **extricate.**]

infallible, *in-fal'i-bl, adj.* (of person or judgment) never making a mistake: always successful (e.g. *an infallible remedy*).
infallibil'ity, *n.* **infall'ibly,** *adv.*
[Pfx. **in-** (2).]

infamous, *in'fà-mus, adj.* having an evil reputation: disgraceful.
in'famy, *n.* evil reputation: public disgrace: evil act:—*pl.* **in'famies.**
[Late L. *infāmōsus*; root as **fame.**]

infant, *in'fant, n.* a baby: (*law*) a person under 21 years.—Also *adj.*
in'fancy, *n.* state or time of being a baby or (*law*) under 21: earliest stage:—*pl.* **in'fancies.**
infantile, *in'fàn-til, adj.* (of e.g. conduct) babyish: of babies (e.g. *infantile diseases*).
infan'ticide (*-sīd*), *n.* child murder: child murderer.
[L. *infans, -antis—in,* not, *fāri,* to speak (*caedĕre,* to kill).]

infantry, *in'fàn-tri, n.* foot-soldiers.
[Through Fr.—It. *infante,* youth, foot-soldier; same root as **infant.**]

infatuate, *in-fat'ū-āt, v.t.* to fill with blind foolish love.
infat'uated, *adj.* **infatuā'tion,** *n.*
[L. *in,* in, *fatuus,* foolish.]

infect, *in-fekt', v.t.* to fill with germs that cause disease: to pass on disease to: to give, pass on, a quality, feeling, to (e.g. *to infect with discontent, enthusiasm*).
infec'tion, *n.* **infec'tious** (*-shus*), *adj.*
[L. *in,* into, *facĕre,* to make.]

infer, *in-fėr', v.t.* to judge, conclude, from facts or evidence: (of facts, etc.) to imply, point to as a conclusion to be drawn: —*pr.p.* **inferr'ing**; *pa.p.* **inferred'.**
in'ference, *n.* something that is deduced or concluded: act of inferring.
[L. *in,* into, *ferre,* to bring.]

inferior, *in-fē'ri-ȯr, adj.* lower in place: lower in rank: less important: of poor quality.—Also *n.*
inferior'ity, *n.*
[L.; comp. of *inferus,* low.]

infernal, *in-fėr'nal, adj.* belonging to the lower regions, to hell: devilish: (*coll.*) annoying.
infer'nally, *adv.*
infer'no (from It.), *n.* hell: any place of horror or fire.
[L. *inferus,* low; see also **inferior.**]

infertile, *in-fėr'til, adj.* (of e.g. soil) not fertile, unproductive.
infertil'ity (*-til'*), *n.* [Pfx. **in-** (2).]

infest, *in-fest', v.t.* to swarm in or over (e.g. *Robbers infest the hills*; *a dog infested with fleas*).
[L. *infestus,* hostile.]

infidel, *in'fi-dėl, n.* one who does not hold the faith (esp. Christianity or Mohammedanism) of the speaker.—Also *adj.*
infidel'ity (*-fi-,* or *-fī-*), *n.* lack of religious faith: unfaithfulness: adultery: —*pl.* **infidel'ities.**
[L. *in-,* not, *fidēlis,* faithful.]

infield, *in'fēld, n.* land near the farm buildings: (*cricket*) the field near the wicket, or the fielders there. [**in, field.**]

infiltrate, *in'fil-trāt, -fil', v.t.* to filter into or through: (of soldiers) to get through the enemy lines a few at a time: (of members of e.g. a political party) to enter (an organisation) gradually with the purpose of influencing its decisions.
infiltrā'tion, *n.* [Pfx. **in-** (1).]

infinite, *in'fin-it, adj.* without end, limit, or bounds: very great.
in'finitely, *adv.* **in'finiteness,** *n.*
infin'ity, *n.* infinite space, time, or quantity: an infinitely distant place.
infinites'imal, *adj.* infinitely, or (*usu.*) extremely, small.
infinites'imally, *adv.* [Pfx. **in-** (2).]

infinitive, *in-fin'i-tiv, n.* part of the verb that expresses the action but has no subject (e.g. *to err, to lose, stay* in the sentences *To err is human*; *I hated to lose*; *you need not stay*).
[Same root as **infinite.**]

infinity. See **infinite.**

infirm, *in-fėrm′*, *adj.* feeble, sickly: weak, not resolute.
infir′mity, *n.* weakness: a bodily ailment:—*pl.* **infir′mities.**
infir′mary, *n.* a hospital:—*pl.* **-ies.**
[Pfx. **in-** (2); same root as **firm.**]

inflame, *in-flām′*, *v.t.* to cause to flame: to make hot or red: to excite anger, love, etc., in (someone).
inflamm′able (*-flam′*), *adj.* easily set on fire (see also **flammable**): easily excited to anger, etc.
inflammabil′ity, -ableness, *ns.*
inflammā′tion, *n.* heat in a part of the body with pain, redness, and swelling: kindling (of passion).
inflamm′atory, *adj.* tending to inflame angry passions (e.g. *inflammatory speeches*).
[L. *in*, into, *flamma*, a flame.]

inflate, *in-flāt′*, *v.t.* to swell with air or gas: to puff up (with e.g. pride): to increase unduly (e.g. prices, amount of money in circulation, a person's reputation).
inflated, *in-flā′tid*, *adj.*
inflation, *in-flā′sh(ȯ)n*, *n.* (esp. undue increase of money in circulation).
inflā′tionary, *adj.* of or causing inflation.
[L. *in*, into, *flāre*, to blow.]

inflect, *in-flekt′*, *v.t.* to vary the pitch of (e.g. the voice).
inflexion, -flection, *-flek′sh(ȯ)n*, *n.*
[Same root as **flex, flexible.**]

inflexible, *in-fleks′i-bl*, *adj.* rigid, unbending: unyielding (e.g. *inflexible determination*): unalterable.
inflexibil′ity, inflex′ibleness, *ns.*
inflex′ibly, *adv.* [Pfx. **in-** (2).]

inflict, *in-flikt′*, *v.t.* to give (e.g. a wound): to impose (punishment, or anything unpleasant).
inflic′tion, *n.*
[L. *in*, *flīgĕre*, *flictum*, to strike.]

inflorescence, *in-flor-es′ėns*, *n.* a group of flowers forming one head on a plant.
[L. *inflōrescĕre*, to begin to blossom.]

influence, *in′floo-ėns*, *n.* power to affect other people or events, esp. by means that are not obvious: a person who has this power: help given by friends in important positions (e.g. *He gained the job through influence*).—*v.t.* to have and use power to move or sway (e.g. *He influenced his son to refuse the firm's offer*).
influential, *in-floo-en′shȧl*, *adj.* having much influence: playing an important part (in; e.g. *influential in getting the plan adopted*).
influen′tially, *adv.*
[L. *in*, into, *fluĕre*, *fluctum*, to flow.]

influenza, *in-floo-en′zȧ*, *n.* a severe epidemic disease with varying symptoms, usu. including catarrh. [It.].

influx, *in′fluks*, *n.* a flowing in: (of people, goods, etc.) a coming into a place in large numbers or quantities.
[Same root as **influence.**]

inform, *in-förm′*, *v.t.* to tell, impart knowledge (of; e.g. *Inform him of our intention to buy*): to obtain knowledge for (oneself; e.g. *I took care to inform myself of all that happened*).—*v.i.* to carry tales to people in authority (e.g. *Jones informed against his fellow thieves*).
infor′mant, *n.* one who informs.
informā′tion, *n.* facts told to others: knowledge (about something).
infor′mative, *adj.* giving information.
infor′mer, *n.* one who gives information, esp. one who carries tales.
[L. *in*, into, *formāre*, to form.]

informal, *in-för′mȧl*, *adj.* not formal.
informal′ity, *n.*:—*pl.* **informal′ities.**
infor′mally, *adv.* [Pfx. **in-** (2).]

infra-, *pfx.* below, beneath.
infra-red, *in′frȧ-red′*, *adj.* beyond the red end of the visible spectrum (**infra-red rays** have heating and other useful effects).
[L. *infra*, below.]

infrequent, *in-frē′kwėnt*, *adj.* not frequent.
infrē′quency, *n.* [Pfx. **in-** (2).]

infringe, *in-frinj′*, *v.t.* to break (e.g. a law): to trespass on (another's right; e.g. *to infringe a copyright*).—Also *v.i.* (e.g. *to infringe on our liberties*).
infringe′ment, *n.*
[L. *in*, in, *frangĕre*, *fractum*, to break.]

infuriate, *in-fūr′i-āt*, *v.t.* to make very angry.
[L. *in*, in, and root of **fury.**]

infuse, *in-fūz′*, *v.t.* to introduce as if by pouring (into; e.g. *to infuse some enthusiasm into the players*): to fill, inspire (with): to extract properties from (a substance) by steeping.
infusion, *in-fū′zh(ȯ)n*, *n.* act of infusing: something infused.
[L. *in*, into, *fundĕre*, *fūsum*, to pour.]

ingenious, *in-jē′ni-ůs*, *adj.* (of person) skilful in inventing: (of thing) skilfully designed and made: skilfully planned.
ingē′niously, *adv.* **ingē′niousness,** *n.*
ingenuity, *in-jen-ū′i-ti*, *n.* ingeniousness. (The meaning arose by confusion; this was orig. a noun from *ingenuous.*)
[L. *ingenium*, natural ability.]

ingenuous, *in-jen′ū-ůs*, *adj.* frank, artless, free from deception.
ingen′uously, *adv.* **ingen′uousness,** *n.*
ingénue, *ang-zhā-nū* (from Fr.) *n.* an ingenuous girl, esp. on the stage.
[L. *ingenuus*, free-born, noble, frank.]

ingle, *ing′gl*, *n*, (*Scot.*) a fireplace.
ing′le-nook, *n.* a fireside corner.

inglorious, *in-glō′ri-ůs*, *-glö′*, *adj.* not glorious, shameful.
inglo′riously, *adv.* [Pfx. **in-** (2).]

ingot, *ing′got*, *n.* a mass of metal (e.g. of gold or silver) cast in a mould.
[Conn. O.E. *in*, in, *gēotan*, to pour.]

ingrained, *in-grānd′*, also *in′*, *adj.* fixed firmly in one's nature (e.g. *ingrained selfishness*).

[*ingrain*, to dye in the yarn; orig. to dye with 'grain', i.e. dried insects.]

ingratiate, *in-grā'shi-āt, v.t.* to get (oneself) into favour (with a person).
[L. *in*, into, *grātia*, favour.]

ingratitude, *in-grat'i-tūd, n.* lack of gratitude or thankfulness.
See also **ungrateful.** [Pfx. **in-** (2).]

ingredient, *in-grē'di-ėnt, n.* one of the things that goes into a mixture.
[L. *ingrediens*, entering—*gradī*, to walk.]

ingress, *in'gres, n.* entrance: right or means of entrance.
[L. *in*, into, *gradī, gressus*, to walk.]

ingrowing, *in'grō-ing, adj.* growing into the flesh. [**in, growing.**]

inhabit, *in-hab'it, v.t.* (of people, animals) to live in (a region).
inhab'itable, *adj.* fit to be lived in (see also **habitable**).
inhab'itant, *n.* one who lives permanently in a place.
[L. *in*, in, *habitāre*, to dwell.]

inhale, *in-hāl', v.t.* and *v.i.* to breathe in.
inhalation, *in-hȧ-lā'sh(ȯ)n, n.*
inhā'lant, *n.* a drug to be inhaled.
[L. *in*, in, *hālāre*, to breath.]

inharmonious, *in-har-mō'ni-ŭs, adj.* not harmonious. [Pfx. **in-** (2).]

inhere, *in-hēr', v.i.* to belong as a permanent quality, or as a right (with *in*).
inher'ent, *adj.* **inher'ently,** *adv.*
inher'ence, inher'ency, *ns.*
[L. *in*, in, *haerēre*, to stick.]

inherit, *in-her'it, v.t.* to receive (property, etc.) as heir: to possess (qualities) as handed down from previous generations. —Also *v.i.*
inher'itance, *n.* act of inheriting: anything inherited.
inher'itor, *n.*
[L. *in*, in, and same root as **heir.**]

inhibit, *in-hib'it, v.t.* to hold back, check, restrain: to forbid.
inhibi'tion, *n.* act of restraining: check to, or stoppage of, an action or function in the body: restraint (good or bad) on natural impulses.
inhib'ited, *adj.* suffering from restraint.
[L. *inhibēre*—*in, habēre, habitum*, have.]

inhospitable, *in-hos'pi-tȧ-bl*, or *-pit', adj.* not hospitable. [Pfx. **in-** (2).]

inhuman, *in-hū'mȧn, adj.* barbarous, cruel: not human.
inhuman'ity, *n.* **inhu'manly,** *adv.*
inhumane, *in-hū-mān', adj.* not humane.
inhumane'ly, *adv.* [Pfx. **in-** (2).]

inimical, *in-im'i-kȧl, adj.* unfriendly, hostile: unfavourable (to; e.g. *conditions inimical to healthy growth*).
inim'ically, *adv.*
[L. *inimīcus*, enemy—*in, amīcus*, friend.]

inimitable, *in-im'i-tȧ-bl, adj.* that cannot be imitated: extraordinarily good.
inim'itably, *adv.* [Pfx. **in-** (2).]

iniquity, *in-ik'wi-ti, n.* injustice: wickedness: a sin:—*pl.* **iniq'uities.**
iniq'uitous, *adj.* **iniq'uitously,** *adv.*
[L. *in*, not, *aequus*, equal.]

initial, *in-ish'ȧl, adj.* of, at, the beginning.—*n.* the letter beginning a word, esp. a name.—*v.t.* to put the initials of one's name on:—*pr.p.* **init'ialling** (*-ish'ȧl-*); *pa.p.* **init'ialled.**
init'ially (*-ish'ȧl-*), *adv.* at the beginning: at first.
initiate, *in-ish'i-āt, v.t.* to start, make a beginning in (e.g. *to initiate changes, legislation*): to introduce to knowledge (e.g. *to initiate him in business methods*): to admit, with ceremonies (into e.g. a secret society).—*n.* (also *-it*) one who has been initiated.
initiā'tion, *n.*
initiative, *in-ish'i-ȧ-tiv, n.* the first step, the lead (e.g. *Brown took the initiative, the others then joined in*): the right to make the first move: enterprise, ability to take first steps (e.g. *He failed because he had no initiative*).
[L. *initium*, beginning—*īre, itum*, go.]

inject, *in-jekt', v.t.* to force (a fluid, etc.) into e.g. a vein: to introduce (e.g. *This injected some life into the dull play*).
injec'tion, *n.*
[L. *in*, into, *jacĕre, jactum*, to throw.]

injudicious, *in-jōō-dish'ŭs, adj.* not wise or prudent, ill-judged.
injudic'iously, *adv.* [Pfx. **in-** (2).]

injunction, *in-jung(k)'sh(ȯ)n, n.* a command earnestly expressed: (*law*) an order requiring a person or persons not to do, or to do, something.
[L. *in*, in, and same root as **enjoin.**]

injure, *in'jŭr, v.t.* to wrong: to harm, damage.
in'jured, *adj.* hurt: offended.
in'jury, *n.*:—*pl.* **-ies.**
inju'rious (*-joo'*), *adj.* harmful.
injur'iously, *adv.* **inju'riousness,** *n.*
[L. *in-*, not, *jūs, jūris*, law.]

injustice, *in-jus'tis, n.* quality of being unjust: a wrong. [Pfx. **in-** (2).]

ink, *ingk, n.* a black, or coloured, liquid used in writing: a sticky substance used in printing: a dark liquid thrown out by cuttlefish, etc.
ink'y, *adj.* **ink'ily,** *adv.* **ink'iness,** *n.*
India(n) ink, a mixture of lamp black and something sticky: a liquid made with this.—Also called **China ink.**
[O.Fr. *enque*—Late L. *encaustum.*]

inkling, *ingk'ling, n.* a hint: a suspicion (with *of*).
[M.E. *inclen*, to hint.]

inky. See **ink.** **inlaid.** See **inlay.**

inland, *in'lȧnd, adj.* not beside the sea: carried on, etc., within a country (e.g. *inland trade*).—*adv.* (*in'land'*) in, or towards, parts away from the sea.
inland revenue, money collected within the country from taxes, excise, etc.
[O.E.]

inlay, *in-lā', v.t.* to ornament by inserting

pieces of fine material e.g. ivory:—*pr.p.* **inlay'ing**; *pa.p.* **inlaid'**.—Also *n.* (*in'lā*). [**in, lay** (2).]

inlet, *in'let, n.* an entrance: a small bay, usu. narrow: a piece inserted.
[**in, let** (1).]

inmate, *in'māt, n.* one of those who live in an institution. [**in, mate.**]

inmost. See **in.**

inn, *in, n.* a house providing food, lodging, for travellers, a small hotel.
inn'keeper, *n.* keeper of an inn. [O.E.]

innate, *i-nāt',* or *in', adj.* inborn, natural (e.g. *his innate gentleness*).
innate'ly, *adv.* **innate'ness,** *n.*
[L. *in,* in, *nascī, nātus,* to be born.]

inner, innermost. See **in.**

innings, *in'ingz, n.* (*cricket*) a team's turn to bat: a spell of power or opportunity to act. [**in.**]

innocent, *in'ō-sėnt, adj.* free from, or ignorant of, evil (e.g. *an innocent child*): not guilty (of a crime or fault): not having a bad or malicious intention (e.g. *an innocent remark*): harmless.
inn'ocence, *n.* **inn'ocently,** *adv.*
innocent of, lacking, without.
[L. *in,* not, *nocēre,* to hurt.]

innocuous, *i-nok'ū-ůs, adj.* harmless.
[Same root as **innocent.**]

innovate, *in'ō-vāt, v.i.* to introduce something new, make changes.—Also *v.t.*
innovā'tion, *n.* **inn'ovator,** *n.*
[L. *in,* in, *novus,* new.]

innuendo, *in-ū-en'dō, n.* a remark containing an underlying accusation or insult: insinuation (see this):—*pl.* **-does.**
[L. *in,* to, *nuĕre,* to nod, make a sign.]

innumerable, *i-nū'mėr-å-bl, adj.* that cannot be numbered, countless.
[L. *in,* not, and root as **numeral.**]

inoculate, *in-ok'ū-lāt, v.t.* to introduce a disease in mild form into the body of (a person, animal) through a puncture, so as to safeguard against later infection.
inoculā'tion, *n.*
[L. *in,* into, *oculus,* eye, eye-like spot.]

inoffensive, *in-ō-fen'siv adj.* not objectionable: harmless. [Pfx. **in-** (2).]

inoperable, *in-op'ėr-å-bl, adj.* not suitable for surgical operation.
[Pfx. **in-** (2); root as **operate.**]

inoperative, *in-op'ėr-å-tiv, adj.* not working or taking effect. [Pfx. **in-** (2).]

inopportune, *in-op'ŏr-tūn,* or *-tūn', adj.* ill-timed, inconvenient. [Pfx. **in-** (2).]

inordinate, *in-ör'di-nit, adj.* unreasonably great (e.g. *inordinate demands*).
inor'dinately, *adv.*
[L. *in,* not, *ordinātus,* in order.]

inorganic, *in-ör-gan'ik, adj.* not having the special characteristics of living bodies: (*chemistry*) dealing with elements and their compounds excluding many of the carbon compounds. [Pfx. **in-** (2).]

in-patient, *in'pā-shėnt, n.* a patient living, as well as treated, in a hospital.

inquest, *in'kwest, n.* a legal enquiry into a case of sudden death.
[O.Fr. *enqueste*; root as **inquire.**]

inquire, *in-kwīr', v.i.* to seek information: to make an investigation (into): to ask (after e.g. a person).—*v.t.* to ask.
inquir'er, *n.* **inquir'ing,** *adj.*
inquir'y (or *in'kwi-ri*), *n.* seeking for information: an investigation: a question:—*pl.* **inquir'ies** (or *in'kwi-*).
Also spelt **enquire, enquirer,** etc.
inquisition, *in-kwi-zish'ȯn, n.* searching examination, careful questioning: (*cap.*; *history*) a tribunal in the R.C. church for various purposes including questioning of heretics.
inquisitive, *in-kwiz'i-tiv, adj.* eager to know: prying into other people's affairs.
inquis'itively, *adv.* **-itiveness,** *n.*
[L. *in,* in, and root as **question.**]

inroad, *in'rōd, n.* a raid: an advance (into).
to make inroads on, to take away from (e.g. savings, liberty, one's time) to a serious extent. [**in, road.**]

insane, *in-sān', adj.* mad: very unwise.
insan'ity (*-san'*), *n.* [Pfx. **in-** (2).]

insanitary, *in-san'i-tår-i, adj.* not sanitary, dangerous to health.
insan'itariness, *n.* [Pfx. **in-** (2).]

insatiable, *in-sā'shå-bl, adj.* (of e.g. greed, curiosity) that cannot be satisfied.
insatiabil'ity, -ableness, *ns.*
insa'tiably, *adv.*
[L. *in,* not, and root as **satiate.**]

inscribe, *in-skrīb', v.t.* to engrave or write (something): to engrave or write on (something): to dedicate (e.g. a book).
inscrip'tion, *n.* act of inscribing: something inscribed: a record inscribed, or otherwise made, on stone, metal, etc.
[L. *in,* upon, *scrībĕre, scriptum,* write.]

inscrutable, *in-skrōōt'å-bl, adj.* that cannot be searched into and understood: (of e.g. person, smile) mysterious.
inscrutabil'ity, -ableness, *ns.*
inscrut'ably, *adv.*
[L. *in-,* not, and root as **scrutiny.**]

insect, *in'sekt, n.* a small animal with body in three parts—head, middle section (thorax), and abdomen—three pairs of legs, and often two pairs of wings (e.g. bee, beetle); in ordinary use including other small animals such as spiders (see this word).
insec'ticide (*-sīd*), *n.* a substance for killing insects.
insectiv'orous, *adj.* living on insects.
[L. *in,* into, *secāre, sectum,* to cut (*caedĕre,* **to** kill; *vorāre,* to devour).]

insecure, *in-si-kūr', adj.* not safe: not firmly fixed, likely to give way, etc.
insecur'ity, insecure'ness, *ns.*
insecure'ly, *adv.* [Pfx. **in-** (2).]

insensible, *in-sen'si-bl, adj.* unconscious: unaware, without understanding (e.g. *He was insensible of his brother's sacrifice*): not feeling (e.g. *insensible to fear*): so

small or gradual as not to be seen, etc. (e.g. *It moved, her feelings changed, by insensible degrees*).
insensibil'ity, *n.* **insen'sibly,** *adv.*
[Pfx. **in-** (2), **sensible** = conscious.]

insensitive, *in-sen'si-tiv, adj.* not sensitive. [Pfx. **in-** (2).]

inseparable, *in-sep'à-rà-bl, adj.* not to be separated or parted. [Pfx. **in-** (2).]

insert, *in-sėrt', v.t.* to put in.—*n.* (*in'sėrt*) something additional put in (e.g. extra leaf, leaves, in a magazine, etc.).
inser'tion, *n.* act of inserting: something inserted.
[L. *in*, in, *serěre, sertum*, to join.]

inset, *in'set, n.* an insert: a small picture, etc., within a larger one.—*v.t.* (*in-set'*) to set in:—*pr.p.* **insett'ing**; *pa.p.* **insett'ed.** [**in, set.**]

inshore, *in'shōr', -shör', adj.* (of e.g. fishing) carried on near the shore: operating near the shore.—*adv.* near, or towards, the shore. [**in, shore.**]

inside, *in-sīd', in', n.* the side, space, or part within: the entrails: inner nature.—*adj.* (*in'sīd'*), being on, or in, the inside: indoor: (of e.g. a spy, information) within, or coming from within, an organisation, building, etc.—Also *adv.* and *prep.* [**in, side.**]

insidious, *in-sid'i-ùs, adj.* watching an opportunity to trap (e.g. *an insidious enemy*): intended to ensnare (e.g. *insidious plans*): (of e.g. a disease, a vice) advancing unnoticed or secretly.
insid'iously, *adv.* **insid'iousness,** *n.*
[L. *insidiae*, an ambush—*sedēre*, sit.]

insight, *in'sīt, n.* power of seeing into and understanding e.g. truths, persons: an imaginative view (into). [**in, sight.**]

insignia, *in-sig'ni-à, n.pl.* badges of office or honour, authority, etc.
[L.—*insignis*, remarkable—*signum*, mark.]

insignificant, *in-sig-nif'i-kànt, adj.* unimportant, petty.
insignif'icance, *n.* [Pfx. **in-** (2).]

insincere, *in-sin-sēr', adj.* not sincere.
insincer'ity (*-ser'*), *n.*:—*pl.* **-ities.**
insincere'ly, *adv.* [Pfx. **in-** (2).]

insinuate, *in-sin'ū-āt, v.t.* to introduce slyly (e.g. *to insinuate doubts into one's mind*): to hint (that): to work (oneself or another) stealthily (e.g. *He insinuated himself into his master's favour by flattery and tale-bearing*): to move cautiously and on a winding or difficult course (in, through).
insin'uating, *adj.* hinting slyly: seeking favour (e.g. *an insinuating manner*).
insinuā'tion, *n.* act of insinuating: artful suggestion: a sly hint.
[L. *in*, in, *sinus*, a curve.]

insipid, *in-sip'id, adj.* tasteless: dull.
insipid'ity, insip'idness, *ns.*
[L. *in-*, not, *sapěre*, to taste.]

insist, *in-sist', v.i.* to put emphasis (on a point in a speech, etc.): to hold firmly to an intention (e.g. *He insisted on going by bus*), or to something desired (e.g. *He insisted on prompt action by the club*).—*v.t.* to go on saying or demanding (that; e.g. *He insists that he saw a ghost, that I should be dismissed*).
insis'tent, *adj.* insisting: compelling attention (e.g. *an insistent noise*).
insis'tence, *n.* **insis'tently,** *adv.*
[L. *in*, upon, *sistěre*, stand (—*stāre*).]

insolent, *in'sò-lėnt, adj.* (of person, remark, etc.) too bold, impertinent, insulting.
in'solence, *n.* **in'solently,** *adv.*
[L. *in-*, not, *solēre*, to be accustomed.]

insoluble, *in-sol'ū-bl, adj.* (of substance) impossible to dissolve: (of problem, difficulty) impossible to solve.
insolubil'ity, -ubleness, *ns.*
[Pfx. **in-** (2).]

insolvent, *in-sol'vėnt, adj.* not able to pay one's debts.
insol'vency, *n.* [Pfx. **in-** (2).]

insomnia, *in-som'ni-à*, sleeplessness.
[L. *in-*, not, and root as **somnolent.**]

insouciant, *in-sōō'si-ànt, -sōōs'yànt*, carefree, unconcerned.
insou'ciance (*-si-àns, -sōōs'yàns*), *n.*
[Fr.—L. *in-*, not, *sollicitāre*, agitate.]

inspect, *in-spekt', v.t.* to look at, examine carefully: to look at (e.g. troops) ceremonially.
inspec'tion, *n.*
inspec'tor, *n.* one who is appointed to inspect: a police officer below a superintendent and above a sergeant.
[L. *in*, into, *specěre, spectum*, to look.]

inspire, *in-spīr', v.t.* (of a divine or supernatural power) to teach (a person), or to influence (what he says or writes): (of a person or circumstance) to affect, influence, rouse, impel (e.g. *The leader inspired his followers with confidence*, or *inspired confidence in his followers*; *this small success inspired him to fresh efforts*): to inhale (also *v.i.*).
inspiration, *in-spir-ā'sh(ò)n, n.* something or someone that inspires: the influence that moves those who create great works of literature or art: an idea, plan, that has fortunate results: an act of taking in breath.
inspired' (*-spīrd'*), *adj.* moved by divine or other influence: brilliantly good: (of e.g. a newspaper article) secretly suggested by someone in authority.
[L. *in*, into, *spīrāre*, to breathe.]

inspirit, *in-spir'it, v.t.* to encourage, put new energy into. [**in, spirit.**]

instability, *in-stà-bil'i-ti, n.* lack of stability or steadiness.
See also **unstable.** [Pfx. **in-** (2).]

install, *in-stöl', v.t.* to introduce formally into an office (e.g. *to install a new bishop*): to place (e.g. *He installed himself in the best chair*): to fix in position and put in use (e.g. *to install a new heating system*).
installā'tion (*-stà-*), *n.* act of installing

(also **instalment**): something installed. [Pfx. **in-** (1), root as (church) **stall.**]

instalment[1], *in-stöl'mėnt, n.* one payment out of a number of payments into which a sum owed is divided: one part of a serial story.

[O.Fr. *estaler*, place, fix; conn. **install.**]

instalment[2]. See **install.**

instance, *in'stȧns, n.* an example: a case: urgent suggestion (e.g. *He did it at the instance of his companions*).—*v.t.* to mention as an example.

in the first instance, as the first step in an action.

[Same root as **instant.**]

instant, *in'stȧnt, adj.* immediate.—*n.* an extremely small space of time: a moment or point of time.

in'stantly, *adv.*

instantaneous, *in-stȧn-tān'yůs, -i-us, adj.* done, happening, or acting, in an instant.

[L. *instāre*, to stand on, be near, urge.]

instead, *in-sted', adv.* in place (of something or someone), as a substitute.

[**in, stead.**]

instep, *in'step, n.* the arched upper part of the foot. [Origin uncertain.]

instigate, *in'sti-gāt, v.t.* to urge, spur on (a person): to bring about by spurring person(s) on (e.g. *to instigate a plot, a crime*).

instigā'tion, *n.* **in'stigātor,** *n.*

[L. *instigāre, instigātum.*]

instil, *in-stil', v.t.* to put slowly into the mind or feelings (e.g. *to instil ideas, good principles, hatred*):—*pr.p.* **instill'ing**; *pa.p.* **instilled'.**

[L. *in*, in, *stillāre*, to drop, drip.]

instinct, *in'stingt, n.* esp. in animals, a natural tendency to certain actions and responses not taught by experience or reasoning: an ability to see truth or facts without conscious reasoning: a natural ability (for).

instinc'tive, *adj.* arising from instinct or natural impulse.

instinc'tively, *adv.* **-tiveness,** *n.*

[L. *instinguěre, instinctus*, to **instigate** (conn. with this word).]

institute, *in'sti-tūt, v.t.* to set up, establish: to set on foot, begin (e.g. an enquiry, a lawsuit).—*n.* a society, or the building used by it.

in'stitūtor, *n.*

institū'tion, *n.* a society set up for a particular purpose: the building it occupies: a home for e.g. old people, a mental hospital, a prison, etc.: an established law: a custom: act of establishing.

institū'tional, *adj.*

[L. *in*, and root as **statute.**]

instruct, *in-strukt', v.t.* to teach: to direct, order, command.

instruc'tion, *n.*

instruc'tive, *adj.* giving knowledge or information.

instruc'tively, *adv.* **-tiveness,** *n.*

instruc'tor, *n.*:—*fem.* **instruc'tress.**

[L. *instruěre, -structum*, to equip.]

instrument, *in'stroo-mėnt, n.* a tool, implement: something for producing musical sounds, e.g. piano, violin: a person or thing that is used as a means (e.g. *He did not himself kill the prisoner; the gaoler was his instrument in the murder*): a formal legal document.

instrumen'tal, *adj.* performed on, or written for, musical instrument(s): due to a faulty instrument or reading (e.g. *an instrumental error*): playing the important part (e.g. *He was instrumental in getting the law repealed*).

instrumen'talist, *n.* one who plays a musical instrument.

instrumental'ity, *n.* agency, means.

[L. *instrūmentum*; root as **instruct.**]

insubordinate, *in-sub-ör'di-nit, adj.* disobedient, rebellious.

insubordinā'tion, *n.* [Pfx. **in-** (2).]

insufferable, *in-suf'ėr-ȧ-bl, adj.* not to be endured, detestable.

[Pfx. **in-** (2), and root as **suffer.**]

insufficient, *in-sů-fish'ėnt, adj.* not enough: not of necessary quality, power, etc.

insuffic'iency, (*-fish'ėn-*), *n.*

insuffic'iently, *adv.* [Pfx. **in-** (2).]

insular, *in'sū-lȧr, adj.* of, belonging to, an island or islands: (of e.g. a person's views) narrow, prejudiced.

insular'ity, in'sularness, *ns.*

in'sulate, *v.t.* to cut off, isolate: to cover (e.g. wire) with a material that does not conduct electricity, or heat, sound.

insulā'tion, *n.* **in'sulator,** *n.*

[L. *insula*, island.]

insulin, *in'sū-lin, n.* an extract from a digestive gland in animals, used in treatment of diabetes, etc.

[Root as **insular**; small groups of cells in the gland are known as 'islets'.]

insult, *in-sult', v.t.* to treat with contempt or rudeness.—Also *n.* (*in'sult*).

insult'ing, *adj.* **insult'ingly,** *adv.*

[L. *insultāre*, to spring at, insult.]

insuperable, *in-sūp'ėr-ȧ-bl, adj.* that cannot be overcome or got over (e.g. *an insuperable difficulty, barrier*).

[L. *in-*, not, *superāre*, to pass over.]

insupportable, *in-sů-pōr'tȧ-bl,* or *-pör', adj.* unbearable (e.g. *The pain, such insolence, is insupportable*): impossible to justify or support by reasoning.

[Pfx. **in-** (2), and root as **support.**]

insure, *in-shōōr', v.t.* to arrange for payment of a sum of money on (something) if it should be damaged or lost: (sometimes) ensure.—Also *v.i.* (with *against*).

insur'ance, *n.* [**ensure.**]

insurgent, *in-sûr'jėnt, adj.* rising in revolt.—*n.* a rebel.

insur'gence, insur'gency, *ns.*

insurrec'tion, *n.* (a) revolt.

[L. *in*, upon, *surgěre, surrectum*, rise.]

insurmountable, *in-sùr-mown'tȧ-bl, adj.* that cannot be overcome or got over, insuperable. [Pfx. **in-** (2).]

insurrection. See **insurgent.**

intact, *in-takt', adj.* undamaged, whole. [L. *in-*, not, *tangĕre, tactum,* to touch.]

intake, *in'tāk, n.* a place at which e.g. water is taken into a channel, etc.: act of taking in: the thing or quantity taken in: a decrease in width made by taking stitches together. [**in, take.**]

intangible, *in-tan'ji-bl, adj.* not able to be felt by touch: not clear and definite to the mind: not possible to define exactly.
intan'gibleness, intangibil'ity, *ns.*
intan'gibly, *adv.* [Pfx. **in-** (2).]

integer, *in'ti-jėr, n.* a whole number.
in'tegral, *adj.* word most often used in **an integral part,** a part essential to the completeness of the whole.
in'tegrate, *v.t.* to bring, fit, together to form a whole: to fit (into a larger group): to bring (a racial group) into equal citizenship (with another group).
integrā'tion, *n.*
[L. whole, untouched; root as **intact.**]

integrity, *in-teg'ri-ti, n.* state of being whole and not made less in any way: uprightness, honesty.
[Same root as **integer.**]

intellect, *in'ti-lekt, n.* the thinking power of the mind: mental ability of a high order: a person having this.
intellec'tual (*-tū-ȧl,* or *-choo-ȧl*), *adj.* of, possessing, showing, appealing to, intellect (e.g. *intellectual ability, person, face, interests*).—*n.* a person of great mental ability: one whose interests are in literature, art, thinking about life, etc.
intelligent, *in-tel'i-jėnt, adj.* clever, alert, quick in mind: showing these qualities (e.g. *an intelligent question*).
intell'igently, *adv.*
intell'igence, *n.* mental brightness: information given, news: department of state or armed service(s) dealing with secret information.
intelligence test, questions and tasks arranged to test a person's ability, not his knowledge.
[L. *intelligĕre, intellectum,* understand.]

intelligible, *in-tel'i-ji-bl, adj.* able to be understood (e.g. *an intelligible statement*).
intell'igibleness, intelligibil'ity, *ns.*
intell'igibly, *adv.*
[Same root as **intellect.**]

intemperate, *in-tem'pėr-it, adj.* showing lack of restraint or moderation (e.g. *intemperate in his feelings; intemperate language*): in the habit of drinking too much.
intem'perance, intem'perateness, *ns.*
intem'perately, *adv.* [Pfx. **in-** (2).]

intend, *in-tend', v.t.* to plan, resolve (e.g. *I intend to sell it*): to mark mentally for a particular use (e.g. *I intend the silver teapot for you*).
inten'ded, *adj.*—*n.* (*coll.*) a fiancée.
intent', *n.* purpose (e.g. *criminal intent, with intent to steal*).—*adj.* bent, determined (on some action): with all one's mind (on; e.g. *intent on the job he was doing*): very attentive, earnest (e.g. *an intent expression*).
intent'ly, *adv.* **intent'ness,** *n.*
inten'tion, *n.* plan, purpose, aim: (in *pl.*) plans with regard to (proposal of) marriage.
inten'tional, *adj.* done, etc., on purpose (e.g. *an intentional snub*).
inten'tionally, *adv.*
well'- (ill'-) inten'tioned, *adj.* meaning well (ill): done, etc., with a good (bad) motive.
to all intents and purposes, practically, really.
[L. *in,* towards, *tendĕre, tentum,* or *tensum,* to stretch.]

intense, *in-tens', adj.* very great (e.g. *intense heat, bitterness*): having, or showing, very strong feeling or great earnestness.
intense'ness, inten'sity, *ns.*
intense'ly, *adv.* to a great degree.
inten'sify (*-si-fi*), *v.t.* and *v.i.* to make, or to become, more intense, greater (e.g. *to intensify one's efforts*):—*pr.p.* **inten'sifying**; *pa.p.* **inten'sified.**
inten'sive (*-siv*), *adj.* very great, very thorough (e.g. *intensive efforts, search*): (of land cultivation) using methods intended to get the most out of the soil of a limited area.
inten'sively, *adv.* **-siveness,** *n.*
[Same root as **intent** (see **intend**).]

intent, intention, etc. See **intend.**

inter, *in-tėr', v.t.* to bury:—*pr.p.* **interr'ing**; *pa.p.* **interred'** (*-tėrd'*).
inter'ment, *n.*
[L. *in,* into, *terra,* the earth.]

inter-, *in-tėr-, pfx.* in Eng. and L. words, between, among, together. [L.]

interact, *in-tėr-akt', v.i.* to act on one another. [Pfx. **inter-.**]

intercede, *in-tėr-sēd', v.i.* to try to act as peacemaker (between): to plead for (e.g. *to intercede with the king for the rebel knight*).
intercess'ion (*-sesh'*), *n.*
intercēd'er, intercess'or (*-ses'*), *ns.*
[L. *inter,* between, *cēdĕre, cessum,* go.]

intercept, *in-tėr-sept', v.t.* to stop or seize on the way from one place to another: to cut off, interrupt (e.g. a view, light).
intercep'tion, *n.*
intercep'tor, -ter, *n.*
[L. *inter,* between, *capĕre, captum,* seize.]

intercession, etc. See **intercede.**

interchange, *in-tėr-chānj', v.t.* to put each in the place of the other (e.g. *Interchange the two pictures*).—*v.t.* and *v.i.* to (cause to) occur in succession (e.g. *to interchange work with play*).—Also *n.*
interchange'able, *adj.* sufficiently alike

to be interchanged without altering the effect, etc. [Pfx. **inter-**.]

intercom, *in-tėr-kom′*, *n.* a telephone system within an aeroplane, tank, etc. [*Inter*nal *com*munication.]

intercourse, *in′tėr-kōrs, -körs*, *n.* dealings, communication (between people, etc.).
[L. *inter*, between, *currĕre, cursum*, run.]

interdependent, *in-tėr-di-pen′dėnt*, *adj.* dependent on each other.
interdepen′dence, *n.* [Pfx. **inter-**.]

interdict, *in-tėr-dikt′*, *v.t.* to forbid, prohibit, esp. by decree.—Also *n.* (*in′-*).
[L. *inter*, between, *dīcĕre, dictum*, say.]

interest, *in′trist, -tėr-ist*, *n.* curiosity and attention (e.g. *to attract one's interest*): something that arouses these feelings: power to arouse these feelings (e.g. *book of great interest*): concern, importance (e.g. *business deals of interest to me*): a share in ownership (e.g. *bought an interest in the business*): advantage (e.g. *It would be to your interest to keep in touch with him*): a group of people who support changes, e.g. new laws, that will be to their advantage and try to block those that will not (e.g. *the steel interest*, the makers of steel as a body acting together): sum paid on money lent.—*v.t.* to hold the attention of: to be of importance to.
in′terested, *adj.* ready to give one's attention: anxious to apply for a job, offer to buy something, etc.: in a position to gain or lose by some transaction (e.g. *the interested parties*): influenced by selfish motives.
in′teresting, *adj.* arousing or holding one's curiosity and attention.
compound interest, interest paid on sum lent plus previous interest.
in the interest(s) **of,** for the benefit of (e.g. a person): to encourage (e.g. *in the interest of safety, truth, good government*).
[L. *interest*, it concerns—*esse*, to be.]

interfere, *in-tėr-fēr′*, *v.i.* to come in the way of (e.g. *He let nothing interfere with his golf*): to meddle (e.g. *to interfere with the arrangements, in the affairs of others*).
interfēr′ence, *n.*
[L. *inter*, between, *ferīre*, to strike.]

interim, *in′tėr-im*, *n.* time between: the meantime.—*adj.* temporary. [L.]

interior, *in-tē′ri-ȯr*, *adj.* inner: inside a building: inland.—*n.* the inside: the part away from coast or frontier: a picture of a scene within a house: (*cap.*) a department dealing with the home affairs of a country. [L.]

interject, *in-tėr-jekt′*, *v.t.* to exclaim, interrupting another speaker or a sentence of one's own.
interjec′tion, *n.*
[L. *inter*, between, *jacĕre, jactum*, throw.]

interlace, *in-tėr-lās′*, *v.t., v.i.*, to lace or weave together. [Pfx. **inter-**.]

interlard, *in-tėr-lärd′*, *v.t.* to mix (with).
[Pfx. **inter-** and **lard** (vb).]

interleave, *in-tėr-lēv′*, *v.t.* to put blank pages between the pages of (a book), or between (pages).
[Pfx. **inter-**, and **leaf.**]

interlock, *in-tėr-lok′*, *v.t.* and *v.i.* to entangle firmly together: to fit into each other so as to work together.
[Pfx. **inter-**, and **lock** (1).]

interlope, *in-tėr-lōp′*, *v.i.* to intrude.
in′terloper, *n.*
[Pfx. **inter-**, and **lope.**]

interlude, *in′tėr-lōōd, -lūd*, *n.* a short piece of music played between the parts of a play, etc.: an interval, or what happens in it.
[L. *inter*, between, *lūdus*, play.]

intermarry, *in-tėr-mar′i*, *v.i.* (of race or group) to form marriages (with another race, group): to marry within a group of like or related persons.
intermarr′iage, *n.*
[Pfx. **inter-**.]

intermediate, *in-tėr-mē′di-it*, *adj.* placed or occurring between.
intermē′diary, *n.* a go-between, one who acts between persons or parties in a negotiation.
[L. *inter*, between, *medius*, middle.]

interment. See **inter.**

interminable, *in-tėr′mi-nȧ-bl*, *adj.* never ending: wearisomely long.
[Pfx. **in-** (2); root as **terminate.**]

intermission, *in-tėr-mish′ȯn*, *n.* interval, pause.
intermitt′ent, *adj.* stopping at intervals and beginning again.
intermitt′ently, *adv.* **-mitt′ence,** *n.*
[L. *intermittĕre, -missum*, place apart.]

intern, *in-tėrn′*, *v.t.* to compel (an enemy alien) to live within a certain area: to hold until the end of the war (a ship, plane) of a country that is fighting.—*n.* (*U.S.*) a resident doctor in a hospital.
internee′ (*-nē′*), *n.* one who is interned.
intern′ment, *n.*
[Fr. *interne*, internal—L. *internus.*]

internal, *in-tėr′nȧl*, *adj.* in the interior of the body: in one's mind or soul: within a country or organisation (e.g. *internal affairs*).
inter′nally, *adv.*
internal-combustion engine, an engine in which the fuel, such as petrol vapour, is burned within the working cylinder.
[L. *internus—inter*, within.]

international, *in-tėr-nash′ȯn-ȧl*, *adj.* of, between or among, different nations.—*n.* a game or contest between players of different nations: a player who takes part in this.
internat′ionally, *adv.* [Pfx. **inter-**.]

internationale, *in-tėr-nä-syō-näl′*, *n.* an international communist song. [Fr.]

internecine, *in-tėr-nē′sīn*, *adj.* deadly: (of e.g. war) destructive to both sides: within a group (e.g. *internecine feuds*).
[L. *inter* (emphatic), *necāre*, to kill.]

internee, internment. See **intern.**
interplanetary, *in-tėr-plan'ė-tȧ-ri, adj.* among the planets. [Pfx. **inter-.**]
interplay, *in'tėr-plā, n.* action of two things on each other. [Pfx. **inter-.**]
interpolate, *in-tėr'pȯ-lāt, v.t.* to put in, interject: to alter e.g. a book unfairly by putting in (word passage).
interpolā'tion, *n.*
[L. *inter,* between, *polīre,* to polish.]
interpose, *in-tėr-pōz', v.t.* to place between: to put in (a remark) interrupting speaker(s).—*v.i.* to come into e.g. a dispute to try to settle it, or to support one party.
[Pfx. **inter-,** and **pose** (1).]
interpret, *in-tėr'prit, v.t.* to explain the meaning of: to suppose the meaning of (a speech, action) to be (e.g. *I interpret your remark as a threat*): to bring out the meaning of (music, a play) by playing, acting: to translate orally.
interpretā'tion, *n.* **inter'preter,** *n.*
[L. *interpretārī,* to explain.]
interregnum, *in-tėr-reg'nu̇m, n.* the period between two reigns, or between the end of one government and the beginning of another.
[L. *inter,* between, *regnum,* rule.]
interrogate, *in-tėr'ȯ-gāt, v.t.* to question thoroughly, esp. formally.
interrogā'tion, *n.* **interr'ogator,** *n.*
interrog'ative (*-og'ȧ-tiv*), *adj.* asking a question.—*n.* an interrogative word (e.g. *why? who? where?*)
[L. *inter,* between, *rogāre, -ātum,* to ask.]
interrupt, *in-tė-rupt', v.t.* to make a break in (e.g. a speech, work): to stop (a person) in the course of something he is saying or doing: to block, cut off (e.g. a view).
interrup'tion, *n.*
[L. *inter, rumpĕre, ruptum,* break.]
intersect, *in-tėr-sekt', v.t.* to divide by cutting or crossing.—*v.i.* to cross.
intersec'tion, *n.* act or place of intersecting: a crossroads.
[Pfx. **inter-**; same root as **section.**]
intersperse, *in-tėr-spėrs', v.t.* to scatter (between, among, in; e.g. *He interspersed a few jokes among his serious remarks*): to scatter here and there (with; e.g. *farmland interspersed with trees*).
intersper'sion, *-spėr'sh(ȯ)n, n.*
[L. *inter,* among, *spargĕre,* scatter.]
interstellar, *in-tėr-stel'ȧr, adj.* among the stars (e.g. *interstellar space*).
[L. *inter,* between, *stella,* a star.]
interstice, *in-tėr'stis, n.* a small space between things, or parts, close together.
[L. *inter,* between, *sistĕre,* stand, place.]
intertwine, *in-tėr-twīn', v.t., v.i.* to twine or twist together. [Pfx. **inter-.**]
interval, *in'tėr-vȧl, n.* time or space between (e.g. *an interval of ten minutes, fifty years, of twenty feet*): the difference of pitch between two notes in music.
at intervals, at times, or places, with time, space, between.
[L. *intervallum,* space between ramparts (vallum) of camp and soldiers' tents.]
intervene, *in-tėr-vēn', v.t.* to be between two places: to occur between two points of time: to happen and so alter the course of events (e.g. *He planned to travel but death intervened*): to join in a dispute between others in the hope of settling it: to interfere.
interven'ing (*-vēn'*), *adj.*
interven'tion (*-ven'*), *n.*
[L. *inter,* between, *venīre,* to come.]
interview, *in'tėr-vū, n.* a formal meeting between a candidate for a position and representative(s) of those who are trying to fill it: a conversation with someone important or interesting that is telecast, broadcast, or is intended to be reported in e.g. a newspaper.—*v.t.* to see and question (a candidate, etc.).
in'terviewer, *n.* one who interviews.
[Fr. *entre,* between, *voir,* to see.]
intestate, *in-tes'tāt, -tit, adj.* without having made a will (e.g. *He died intestate.*)
[L. *in,* not, *testārī,* to make a will.]
intestine, *in-tes'tin, n.* the lower part of the food passage in men and animals: the upper section of this (**small intestine**), or the lower (**large intestine**).
intes'tinal (or *-tīn'*), *adj.*
[L. *intestīnus—intus,* within.]
intimate, *in'tim-it, adj.* close (e.g. *intimate friend, friendship, an intimate connexion*): closely acquainted (e.g. *an intimate gathering*): private, personal (e.g. *intimate thoughts, affairs*): deep, detailed (e.g. *an intimate knowledge of the subject*).—*n.* a familiar friend.—*v.t.* (*-māt*) to hint, indicate: to announce.
in'timacy (*-mȧ-si*), *n.* close familiarity.
in'timately, *adv.*
intimā'tion, *n.* hint: announcement.
[L. *intimus,* innermost—*intus,* within.]
intimidate, *in-tim'i-dāt, v.t.* to strike fear into (a person) so that he does what one wants him to do.
intimidā'tion, *n.*
[L. *in,* into, and root as **timid.**]
into, *in'too, prep.* expressing movement or direction inwards, change from one state to another (e.g. *ice into water*), etc.
intolerable, *in-tol'ėr-ȧ-bl, adj.* that cannot be endured or borne.
intol'erant, *adj.* not able or willing to endure (with *of*): not willing to consider opinions, etc. different from one's own.
intol'erance, *n.* [Pfx. **in-** (2).]
intonation, *in-tō-nā'sh(ȯ)n, n.* rise and fall of the voice in speech.
intone', *v.t. v.i.* to chant, utter in musical tones.
inton'ing, (*-tōn'*), *n.*
[L. *in tonum,* according to tone.]
intoxicate, *in-toks'i-kāt, v.t.* to make drunk: to excite with strong feelings.

intoxicā'tion, *n.*
intox'icating, *adj.* **-icatingly,** *adv.*
intox'icant, *n.* something that intoxicates.
[Gk. *toxikon*, arrow-poison—*toxon*, bow.]

intra-, *in-tra-*, *pfx.* within.
[L. *intrā* (adv.).]

intractable, *in-trak'tȧ-bl*, *adj.* (of person, etc.) stubborn: (of thing) hard to deal with. [Pfx. **in-** (2).]

intransigent, *in-tran'zi-jent*, or *-si-*, *adj.* refusing to compromise or come to an agreement.
intran'sigence, -sigency, *ns.*
[L. *in*, not, and root as **transact.**

intransitive, *in-tran'si-tiv*, *adj.* (of verb) that does not have an object (e.g. *The verbs to go, lie, faint, are intransitive*). [Pfx. **in-** (2).]

intrepid, *in-tre'pid*, *adj.* very bold, fearless (e.g. *an intrepid explorer*; *intrepid support of the cause*).
intrepid'ity, *n.* **intrep'idly,** *adv.*
[L. *in-*, not; root as **trepidation.**]

intricate, *in'tri-kit*, or *-trik'*, *adj.* tangled, complicated, having many details, difficult to understand or to deal with (e.g. *intricate paths, pattern, machinery, arrangements*).
In the following also *-trik'*:—
in'tricately, *adv.* **in'tricateness,** *n.*
in'tricacy (*-kȧ-si*), *n.* intricateness: something intricate:—*pl.* **in'tricacies.**
[L. *in*, in, *trīcae*, hindrances.]

intrigue, *in-trēg'*, *n.* underhand scheming: a plot: an illicit love affair.—*v.i.* to plot, etc.—*v.t.* to puzzle, fascinate:—*pr.p.* **intrig'uing**; *pa.p.* **intrigued** (*-trēgd'*).
intrig'uingly, *adv.*
[Fr.—same root as **intricate.**]

intrinsic, *in-trin'sik*, or *-zik*, *adj.* belonging to a thing as part of its nature (e.g. *The ring had intrinsic as well as sentimental value—its stones were fine*).
intrin'sically, *adv.*
[L. *intrinsecus*, (following into) inside.]

intro-, *in-trō-*, *pfx.* within.
[L. (adv.) *intrō.*]

introduce, *in-trȯ-dūs'*, *v.t.* to bring in: to put (into a place): to bring to notice: to bring forward (e.g. a subject, bill, suggestion): to provide a passage of explanation for the beginning of (e.g. a book): to make (a person) acquainted with (with *to*; e.g. *At the party I introduced A to B*).
introduc'tion, *n.*
introduc'tory, *adj.*
[L. *intrō*, inwards, *dūcĕre*, to lead.]

introspection, *in-trȯ-spek'sh(ȯ)n*, *n.* studying one's own mind and thoughts.
introspec'tive, *adj.*
[L. *intrō*, within; root as **inspect.**]

introvert, *in'trō-vėrt*, *n.* a person much interested in his own thoughts—opp. to *extravert.*
[L. *intrō*, inwards, *vertĕre*, to turn.]

intrude *in-trōōd'*, *v.t.* to force, thrust in: to thrust (oneself) uninvited or unwelcome (also *v.i.*).
intrud'er, *n.*
intru'sion, *in-trōō'zh(ȯ)n*, *n.*
intru'sive (*-siv*), *adj.* **intru'siveness,** *n.*
[L. *in*, in, *trūdĕre*, *trūsum*, thrust.]

intuition, *in-tū-ish'(ȯ)n*, *n.* the power of seeing the truth directly without reasoning: a truth so perceived.
intū'itive, *adj.*
[L. *in*, into, *tuērī*, *tuitus*, to look.]

inundate, *in'un-dāt*, *v.t.* to flood, overflow: to overwhelm (a person) with something in very great quantity (e.g. *to inundate him with circulars, questions*).
[L. *in*, in, *unda*, a wave.]

inure, *in-ūr'*, *v.t.* to make (a person) accustomed, hardened (to).
[Pfx. **in-** (1), old word *ure*, use, practice.]

invade, *in-vād'*, *v.t.* to enter as, or as if as, an enemy: to encroach on (someone else's right).
invād'er, *n.* **invā'sion,** *-zh(ȯ)n*, *n.*
[L. *in*, in, *vādĕre*, *vāsum*, to go.]

invalid[1], *in-val'id*, *adj.* (of reasoning, an argument) not sound: (of a contract, etc.) without legal force.
invalid'ity, *n.*
inval'idate, *v.t.* to make invalid.
[L. *in*, not, *validus*, strong.]

invalid[2], *in'vȧ-lēd*, *-lid*, *n.* a person who is ill or disabled.—Also *adj.*—*v.t.* to make an invalid: to discharge as an invalid (e.g. *He was invalided out of the army*).
[Same root as **invalid** (1).]

invaluable, *in-val'ū-ȧ-bl*, *adj.* of value too great to be estimated (e.g. *invaluable assistance*; *this information was invaluable to him*). [Pfx. **in-** (2).]

invariable, *in-vār'i-ȧ-bl*, *adj.* not changing, always the same.
invar'iably, *adv.* always. [Pfx. **in-** (2).]

invasion. See **invade.**

invective, *in-vek'tiv*, *n.* violent attack in words, violent abuse.
inveigh, *in-vā'*, *v.i.* to make an attack in words (against).
[L. *invehĕre*, *invectum*, to attack.]

inveigle, *in-vē'gl*, *-vā'*, *v.t.* to draw, entice, wheedle (into).
invei'glement, *n.*
[From *enveugle*—Fr. *aveugler*, to blind.]

invent, *in-vent'*, *v.t.* to make, or use, for the first time (e.g. a machine, a method): to make up (e.g. a story, an excuse).
inven'tion, *n.* **inven'tor,** *n.*
inven'tive, *adj.* quick to invent, ingenious (e.g. *an inventive mind*).
[L. *invenīre*, to come upon, find.]

inventory, *in'ven-tȯr-i*, *-tri*, *n.* a formal detailed list of goods (e.g. of house furniture, business stock):—*pl.* **-ies.**
[Same root as **invent.**]

inverse. See **invert.**

invert, *in-vėrt'*, *v.t.* to turn upside down: to reverse the order of.
inversion, *in-vėr'sh(ȯ)n*, *n.*

inverse, *in-vėrs′, in′, adj.* (of e.g. order) opposite, reverse.—*n.* the opposite.
inversely (*-vers′*, or *in′*) *adv.*
inverted commas. See **comma.**
[L. *in*, in, *vertĕre, versum*, to turn.]

invertebrate, *in-vėr′ti-brit, -brāt, adj.* (of an animal, e.g. a worm) not having a backbone.—Also *n.* [Pfx. **in-** (2).]

invest[1], *in-vest′, v.t.* to clothe: to clothe, surround, endow (a person, place, etc. with a quality; e.g. *to invest with virtue, interest, mystery*): to place formally in office or authority: to lay siege to.
inves′titure (*-ti-chůr*; now chiefly placing in office), **invest′ment,** *ns.*
[L. *in*, in, *vestīre*, to clothe.]

invest[2], *in-vest′, v.t.* to lay out (money) for profit, e.g. by buying shares: to spend (money, time, energy; usu. with *in*).
invest′ment, *n.* placing of money to gain profit: something in which money is invested.
inves′tor, *n.*
[Same root as **invest** (1).]

investigate, *in-ves′ti-gāt, v.t.* to inquire into with care.
investigā′tion, *n.* **inves′tigator,** *n.*
[L. *in*, *vestigāre*, track; conn. *vestigium*, footprint, and **vestige.**]

investment. See **invest** (1) and (2).

inveterate, *in-vet′ėr-it, adj.* firmly fixed in a habit by long practice (e.g. *an inveterate liar*): (of a habit, quality, etc.) firmly established.
invet′eracy (*-ȧ-si*), **-ateness,** *ns.*
invet′erately, *adv.*
[L. *in*, in, *vetus, veteris*, old.]

invidious, *in-vid′i-ůs, adj.* likely to cause ill-will or sense of injustice.
invid′iously, *adv.* **invid′iousness,** *n.*
[L. *invidia*, envy.]

invigilate, *in-vij′i-lāt, v.t.* and *v.i.* to supervise (examination).
invigilā′tion, *n.* **invig′ilātor,** *n.*
[L. *in*, on; same root as **vigil.**]

invigorate, *in-vig′ȯr-āt, v.t.* to give vigour, strength, energy, to.
invig′orating, *adj.* **invigorā′tion,** *n.*
[L. *in*, and root as **vigour.**]

invincible, *in-vin′si-bl, adj.* that cannot be overcome, defeated, or surmounted.
invincibil′ity, invin′cibleness, *ns.*
invin′cibly, *adv.*
[L. *in-*, not, *vincĕre, victum*, overcome.]

inviolable, *in-vī′ō-lȧ-bl, adj.* (of e.g. an oath, a right, a person) that must be treated as sacred, not to be broken, infringed, harmed.
inviolabil′ity, invī′olableness, *ns.*
invī′olably, *adv.*
invī′olate, *adj.* not violated, disturbed, broken, or infringed.
[L. *in-*, not, and root as **violate.**]

invisible, *in-viz′i-bl, adj.* not able to be seen, not visible.
invisibil′ity, invis′ibleness, *ns.*
invis′ibly, *adv.* [Pfx. **in-** (2).]

invite, *in-vīt′, v.t.* to ask to come (e.g. to a meeting, to stay): to ask for (e.g. *to invite suggestions*): to act in such a way, or be of such a kind, as to encourage (e.g. *to invite danger, criticism*).
invitā′tion, *n.*
invīt′ing, *adj.* attractive, tempting.
[L. *invītāre, -ātum.*]

invocation. See **invoke.**

invoice, *in′vois, n.* a list sent with goods giving details of price and quantity.—*v.t.* to make such a list of (goods).
[Fr. *envoy*, thing sent; root as **envoy.**]

invoke, *in-vōk′, v.t.* to address (God, etc.) in prayer, asking for help: to ask for (e.g. help): to quote as giving support to what one has said (e.g. *to invoke the Bible, the authority of one's party leader*): to call forth (a spirit).
invocā′tion, *n.*
[L. *in*, on, *vocāre, -ātum*, to call.]

involuntary, *in-vol′ůn-tȧr-i, adj.* not under control of the will: not done from choice: unintentional.
invol′untarily, *adv.* [Pfx. **in-** (2).]

involve, *in-volv′, v.t.* to wrap up (in): to cause to be associated with or concerned in (e.g. *A tried to involve B in the plot*): to include: to require, or bring as a result (e.g. *Automation involves reducing the number of workmen*): to make complicated: to lead into difficulty or disagreement (with another).
involved′, *adj.* (of e.g. a story) complicated: (of affairs) in confusion.
involve′ment, *n.*
[L. *in*, in, *volvĕre*, to roll.]

invulnerable, *in-vul′nėr-ȧ-bl, adj.* that cannot be wounded, damaged, successfully attacked. [Pfx. **in-** (2).]

inward, *in′wȧrd, adj.* being or placed within: in the mind or soul.—*adv.* (also **in′wards**) towards the inside: into the mind or soul.
in′wardly, *adv.* within: privately, in the thoughts (e.g. *He was inwardly pleased*; *inwardly laughing*).
[O.E. *inneweard* (*adv.*).]

iodine, *ī′ō-dēn, -dīn, n.* an element that is not a metal which gives a violet-coloured vapour.
ī′odise, *v.t.* to treat with iodine.
[Gk. *ion*, a violet, *eidos*, form.]

ion, *ī′ȯn, n.* an electrically charged atom or group of atoms that has become so by losing or gaining electrons.
ī′onise, *v.t., v.i.* to convert, or be converted, into ion(s).
īon′osphere, *n.* the regions of the upper atmosphere of the earth that contain ions and reflect radio waves.
[Gk. *ienai*, to go.]

iota, *ī-ō′tȧ, n.* a very small quantity.
[Gk. *iōta*, ι, i, smallest Gk. letter.]

I O U, *ī ō ū, n.* a signed acknowledgment of a debt.
[*I owe you.*]

ir-, *ir-*, *pfx.* the form taken by **in-** (1) and (2) (see these) before a following *r* in Latin and in English words from Latin.

irascible, *i-ras'i-bl, adj.* easily angered, irritable.
irascibil'ity, *n.* **iras'cibly,** *adv.*
ire, *īr, n.* anger.
irate, *ī-rāt', īr'āt, adj.* angry.
[L. *īrāscī*, to be angry—*īra*, anger.]

iridescence, -ent. See **iris.**

iris, *ī'ris, n.* the coloured part of the eye: a brightly-coloured flower with sword-shaped leaves :—*pl.* **ī'rises.**
iridescence, *ir-i-des'ens, n.* display of rainbow colours e.g. on a bubble.
irides'cent. *adj.*
[Gk. *īris, iridos*, rainbow.]

Irish, *ī'rish, adj.* of, or produced in, *Ireland.* —*n.* the Celtic language of Ireland: **(the Irish)** the natives of Ireland.
I'rishman, I'rishwoman, *ns.* :—*pls.* **-men, -women.**

irk, *ėrk, v.t.* to weary, annoy (e.g. *Letter-writing irks me*, or *It irks me to have to write letters*).
irk'some, *adj.*
[M.E. *irken.*]

iron, *ī'ėrn, n.* a common metal from which steel is made: a weapon or instrument made of iron, e.g. a branding implement, a flat-iron, a golf club: (in *pl.*) fetters: (*slang*) a pistol: strength, firmness (e.g. *a will of iron*).—Also *adj.*—*v.t.* to smooth with a flat-iron.—Also *v.i.*
Iron Age, an early period of history in which cutting tools and weapons were made of iron.
i'ronclad, *adj.* covered with iron plates.—*n.* a ship so protected.
iron curtain, the difficulties barring the way of people who want to find out what is happening in Communist countries.
i'ron-foun'der, *n.* one whose business is to make (articles of) cast iron.
iron lung, an apparatus in which changes of pressure are used to force a patient to breathe in and out.
i'ronmaster, *n.* owner of an ironworks.
i'ronmonger, *n.* a dealer in **i'ronmongery,** articles of metal, e.g. tools, locks, etc., and other goods.
i'ronworks, *n.pl.* works where iron is smelted or made into heavy goods.
to iron out, to smooth out (difficulties).
too many irons in the fire, too many jobs, etc., on hand at once.
[OE. *iren*; conn. Ger. *eisen.*]

ironical. See **irony.**

irony, *ī'rō-ni, n.* a way of ridiculing one's hearers by using words whose meaning is the exact opposite of the meaning intended (e.g. when someone has blundered—'*That was a clever thing you did!*'): a result that seems to mock previous thoughts or efforts (e.g. *By the irony of fate, he got what he had struggled for when it was no longer of use to him*): (in tragedy) words which, unknown to the speaker himself, have reference to unhappy past or future events about which the audience has been told :—*pl.* **i'ronies.**
ironic(al), *ī-ron'ik(al), adjs.*
iron'ically, *adv.*
[L. *īrōnia*—Gk. *eirōneia*, pretence.]

irradiate, *i-rā'di-āt, v.t.* to shed light or other rays on: to light up (esp. the face with joy). [Pfx. **ir-** (1).]

irrational, *i-rash'ȯn-ȧl, adj.* not reasonable (e.g. *irrational fears*).
irrational'ity, -alness, *ns.*
irra'tionally, *adv.* [Pfx. **ir-** (2).]

irreconcilable, *i-rek-ȯn-sīl'ȧ-bl, adj.* (of people) who cannot be reconciled or brought (back) to friendship or agreement: (of e.g. statements) that cannot both be true.
irreconcil'ably, *adv.* [Pfx. **ir-** (2).]

irrecoverable, *ir-i-kuv'ėr-ȧ-bl, adj.* that cannot be recovered or regained.
[Pfx. **ir-** (2).]

irredeemable, *ir-i-dē'mȧ-bl, adj.* that cannot be redeemed.
irredeem'ably, *adv.* hopelessly (bad, lost, etc.) [Pfx. **ir-** (2).]

irreducible, *ir-i-dū'si-bl, adj.* that cannot be reduced or made less. [Pfx. **ir-** (2).]

irrefutable, *i-ref'ū-tȧ-bl, -ri-fūt', adj.* (of e.g. an argument) that cannot be refuted or proved false. [Pfx. **ir-** (2).]

irregular, *i-reg'ū-lȧr, adj.* not regular: uneven, variable: not according to rule or regulation: (of troops) not forming part of the forces trained by the state.
irregular'ity (*pl.* **-ies.**), **-ularness,** *ns.*
irreg'ularly, *adv.* [Pfx. **ir-** (2).]

irrelevant, *i-rel'ė-vȧnt, adj.* not relevant, not having anything to do with the subject under discussion.
irrel'evance, -cy, irrel'evantness, *ns.*
irrel'evantly, *adv.* [Pfx. **ir-** (2).]

irreligious, *ir-i-lij'ȧs, adj.* not religious, impious. [Pfx. **ir-** (2).]

irremediable, *ir-i-mē'di-ȧ-bl, adj.* that cannot be remedied. [Pfx. **ir-** (2).]

irremovable, *ir-i-mōō'vȧ-bl, adj.* that cannot be removed.
irremo'vably, *adv.* [Pfx. **ir-** (2).]

irreparable, *i-rep'ȧ-rȧ-bl, adj.* (of injury, loss, etc.) not reparable, that cannot be undone, remedied, made good.
irrep'arably, *adv.* in a way that makes remedy, etc. impossible.
[Pfx. **ir-** (2).]

irreplaceable, *ir-i-plā'sȧ-bl, adj.* not replaceable, because too good, rare, etc.
[Pfx. **ir-** (2).]

irrepressible, *ir-i-pres'i-bl, adj.* (of e.g. person, high spirits) not to be repressed or kept under control.
irrepress'ibly, *adv.* [Pfx. **ir-** (2).]

irreproachable, *ir-i-prō'chȧ-bl, adj.* that cannot be reproached, free from blame: faultless. [Pfx. **ir-** (2).]

irresistible, *ir-i-zis'ti-bl, adj.* that cannot be resisted or withstood: extremely charming.
irresistibil'ity, irresis'tibleness, *ns.*
irresis'tibly, *adv.* [Pfx. **ir-** (2).]

irresolute, *i-rez'ȯ-loot, -lūt, adj.* not firm in purpose: hesitating.
irres'oluteness, irresolu'tion, *ns.*
irres'olutely, *adv.* [Pfx. **ir-** (2).]

irrespective, *ir-i-spek'tiv,* used in the phrase **irrespective of,** not taking into account, without regard to (e.g. *He chose his staff for their ability irrespective of their race*). [Pfx. **ir-** (2).]

irresponsible, *i-ri-spon'si-bl, adj.* not responsible—not capable of, or showing, reliability or a sense of duty (e.g. *an irresponsible person*; *irresponsible conduct*).
irresponsibil'ity, -sibleness, *ns.*
irrespon'sibly, *adv.* [Pfx. **ir-** (2).]

irretraceable, *ir-i-trā'sȧ-bl, adj.* (of a step) that cannot be retraced. [Pfx. **ir-** (2).]

irretrievable, *ir-i-trē'vȧ-bl, adj.* (of e.g. something lost, a mistake, ruin) that cannot be retrieved, recovered, undone, made up for.
irretrie'vably, *adv.* [Pfx. **ir-** (2).]

irreverent, *i-rev'ėr-ėnt, adj.* not reverent: showing lack of respect.
irrev'erence, *n.*
irrev'erently, *adv.* [Pfx. **ir-** (2).]

irrevocable, *i-rev'ȯ-kȧ-bl, adj.* that cannot be revoked or taken back (e.g. *an irrevocable decision*).
irrevocabil'ity, -ableness, *ns.*
irrev'ocably, *adv.* [Pfx. **ir-** (2).]

irrigate, *ir'i-gāt, v.t.* (of rivers) to supply (land) with water: to water (land) by means of canals, etc.
irrigā'tion, *n.*
[L. *in*, upon, *rigāre*, to wet.]

irritate, *ir'i-tāt, v.t.* to make angry or impatient: to make (the skin, etc.) red e.g. by rubbing.
irrita'tion, *n.* **irr'itating,** *adj.*
irr'itable, *adj.* easily annoyed.
irritabil'ity, irr'itableness, *ns.*
irr'itably, *adv.*
irr'itant, *n.* something that causes irritation.—Also *adj.*
[L. *irritāre, -ātum*, to snarl.]

irruption, *i-rup'sh(ȯ)n, n.* a breaking in, sudden invasion.
[L. *in*, in, *rumpěre, ruptum*, to break.]

is. See **be.**

Islam, *iz'lam, -läm', n.* the Mohammedan religion: the Mohammedan world.
Islam'ic, *adj.*
[Arabic *islām*, surrender (to God).]

island, *ī'lȧnd, n.* land surrounded by water: something resembling this.
islander, *ī'lȧnd-ėr, n.*
[O.E. *ea*, water, *land*, land (*s* from **isle**).]

isle, *īl, n.* an island.
isles'man (*īlz'*), *n.* an islander.
islet, *ī'lit, n.* a little isle.
[L. *nsula*, island.]

iso-, *ī-sō-, pfx.* equal.
i'sobar, *n.* a line on a map passing through places where atmospheric pressure is equal.
i'sotherm, *n.* a line passing through places that have the same temperature.
[Gk. *isos*, equal (*baros*, weight; *thermē*, heat).]

isolate, *ī'sȯ-lāt, v.t.* to set apart, place alone: to separate (something from something else): to keep (an infected person) away from others to whom he might give the disease.
i'solated, *adj.* lonely, remote: solitary, alone: single (e.g. *an isolated case*).
isolā'tion, *n.*
isolā'tionist, *n.* a person who objects to his country's playing a part in international affairs.
[Same root as **isle.**]

isosceles, *ī-sos'ė-lēz, adj.* (of a triangle) having two sides equal.
[Gk. *isos*, equal, *skelos*, a leg.]

isotherm. See **iso-.**

isotope, *ī'sȯ-top, n.* one of two or more kinds of atom of the same element, some being heavier than others (e.g. the atoms of 'heavy hydrogen') and some radioactive (e.g. the atoms of the kind of iodine occurring in fall-out from a nuclear explosion).
[Gk. *isos*, equal, *topos*, place.]

Israeli, *iz-rā'li, adj.* of modern Israel.—*n.* a native of Israel.

issue, *is'ū, ish'ōō, n.* a flowing out, or the place of it: act of sending out: distribution: publication: something that comes out: quantity distributed or published at one time: result, outcome: children (e.g. *died without issue*): a point, esp. important, under discussion or causing dispute.—*v.i.* to flow or come out: to spring (from any source): to result (from).—*v.t.* to send out: to publish.
at issue, being disputed.
to join issue (with), to enter a dispute, argument (with).
to take issue, to disagree (on a point).
[L. *ex*, out, *īre*, to go.]

isthmus, *is(th)'mus, n.* a narrow neck of land joining two larger pieces.
[Gk. *isthmos*.]

it, *it, pron.* the thing spoken of (e.g. *It is my hat*), or sometimes the person or animal (e.g. *Put the baby down if it is heavy*); used in certain sentences where there is no real subject (e.g. *It rains continually*): —objective **it**; possessive **its** (sometimes described as possessive *adj.*).
itself', *pron.* (1) emphatic, or (2) reflexive, form of *it*; e.g. (1) *The vase looks well there, but it itself is of no value*; (2 *The cow hurt itself by swallowing a piece of wire.*
[O.E. *hit*.]

Italian, *i-tal'yȧn, adj.* of Italy or its people.

—*n.* a native of Italy: the language of Italy.
ital′ic, *adj.* of a sloping type, used esp. for emphasis (e.g. *very*).—*n.* (in *pl.*) this type.
ital′icise (-*i-sīz*) *v.t.* to put in italics.

itch, *ich, v.i.* to have an irritating sensation in the skin: to have a restless desire (to do something).—Also *n.*
itch′y, *adj.* **itch′iness,** *n.*
[O.E. *giccan.*]

item, *ī′tėm, n.* a separate article, esp. one of a number named in a list: a separate piece of information or news.
[L. (adv.), in the same way, also.]

itinerant, *i-tin′ėr-ȧnt, ī-tin′, adj.* making journeys from place to place on business, etc.—*n.* a person who does so, esp. judge, preacher, pedlar.
itin′erancy, -eracy, *ns.*
itin′erary, *n.* a route: plan or record of a journey:—*pl.* **itin′eraries.**
[L. *iter, itineris,* a journey.]

its. See **it.** **it's,** it is.

itself. See **it.**

ivory, *ī′vȯ-ri, n.* the hard white substance forming most of the tusk of an elephant, walrus, etc.:—*pl.* **i′vories.**—*adj.* made of, or like, ivory.
[L. *ebur, eboris*; conn. with **elephant.**]

ivy, *ī′vi, n.* a creeping evergreen plant on trees and walls.
i′vied, *adj.* covered with ivy.
[O.E. *ifig.*]

J

jab, *jab, v.t.* and *v.i.* to poke, stab:—*pr.p.* **jabb′ing**; *pa.p.* **jabbed.**—*n.* a sudden thrust or stab. [Perh. imitative.]

jabber, *jab′ėr, v.i.* to chatter, talk rapidly.—Also *v.t.*—*n.* rapid confused speaking.
jabb′erer, *n.* **jabb′eringly,** *adv.* [Imit.]

jabot, *zha′bō, n.* a frill of lace, etc., formerly worn in front of a woman's dress or on a man's shirt front: a similar one worn with Highland full dress. [Fr.]

jack, *jak, n.* (*cap.*) a form of **John**: a worthless fellow: a sailor: any instrument that does the work of a boy or helper, as a *bootjack* for taking off boots, a machine for turning a spit in roasting meat, an instrument for lifting heavy weights: the male of some animals: the knave in a pack of cards: the small white ball which is the mark aimed at in bowls: a small ship's flag, esp. one showing nationality.
jack′-a-lan′tern, jack′-o-lan′tern, *n.* will-o'-the-wisp: (*U.S.*) a lantern carved out of a pumpkin.
jack′boot, *n.* a large boot reaching to the knee, formerly worn by cavalry: brutal military rule.
Jack Frost, frost personified (see this word).
jack′-in-the-box′, *n.* a box with a figure in it which springs up when the lid is opened.
jack′-knife, *n.* a large clasp knife: a type of fancy dive.
jack′-of-all′-trades, *n.* one who can turn his hand to any job.
jack′pot, *n.* a prize-money fund.
to hit the jackpot, to win a jackpot: to have a big success.
jack′-rabbit, *n.* a long-eared American hare.
jack′-tar′, *n.* a sailor.
every man jack, one and all.
yellow jack, yellow fever, a dangerous disease of hot countries.
to jack up, to lift (e.g. a car) by means of a jack.
[*Jacques,* James, most common French man's name.]

jackal, *jak′ȯl, n.* a wild animal, similar to dog and wolf, that eats carrion: a contemptible person—either one who does the dirty work for others, or one who claims a share of profit without facing the danger of obtaining it.
[Persian *shaghāl.*]

jackanapes, *jak′ȧ-nāps, n.* an impudent fellow. [Origin uncertain.]

jackaroo, *jak-ȧ-ro͞o′, n.* (*Austr.*) a newcomer from England, etc. gaining experience in the bush (see this word).
[**Jack** with the ending of kang*aroo.*]

jackass, *jak′ȧs, n.* a male ass: blockhead.
laughing jackass, an Australian kingfisher that laughs. [**Jack, ass.**]

jackboot. See **jack.**

jackdaw, *jak′dö, n.* a kind of small crow.
[**Jack, daw.**]

jacket, *jak′it, n.* a short coat: a cover, casing: a loose paper cover for a book.
jack′eted, *adj.* wearing, in, a jacket.
[O.Fr. *jaquet*; same root as **jack.**]

jackpot. See **jack.**

Jacobite, *jak′ō-bīt, n.* a supporter of James II or his descendants.
[L. *Jacōbus,* James.]

Jacob's ladder, *jā′kobz lad′ėr, n.* a ladder of ropes with wooden steps, used on a ship: a plant with ladder-like leaves.
[From the *ladder Jacob* saw in his dream, Gen. xxviii. 12.]

jade[1], *jād, n.* a gemstone, usu. green.
[Fr.—Sp. *ijada,* loin; stone once thought to cure pain there.]

jade[2], *jād, n.* a worn-out horse: a worthless woman.

ja′ded, *adj.* worn-out, tired: often used of appetite (for food or pleasure) that has been indulged too much.
[Prob. conn. Old Norse *jalda*, mare.]

jag, *jag, n.* a notch: a splinter: a prick: a sharp point of rock.—*v.t.* to prick: to notch: to tear (cloth, etc.) unevenly.

jagged, *jag′id, adj.* notched, rough-edged.
jagg′edly, *adv.* **jagg′edness,** *n.*
[Origin unknown.]

jaguar, *jag′ū-ar, jag′wär, n.* a South American beast of prey, one of the cat family, resembling the leopard.
[South American Indian *jaguāra*.]

jail, gaol, *jāl, n.* a prison.
jail′-bird, gaol′-bird, *ns.* a person who is or has been in jail.
jail′er, jail′or, gaol′er, *ns.* one who has charge of a jail or of prisoner(s).
[Norman Fr. *gaiole*—L. *cavea*, a cage.]

jalousie, *zhal′oo-zē*, or *-zē′, n.* an outside shutter with slats.
[Fr. *jalousie*, jealousy.]

jam[1], *jam, n.* a preserve of fruit boiled with sugar: something pleasant or easy.
[Perhaps from **jam** (2).]

jam[2], *jam, v.t.* to press or squeeze tight: to crowd full: to wedge: to bring (machinery) to a standstill by causing the parts to stick (e.g. *He jammed the wheel*): to interfere with (a wireless signal) by sending out other signals.—*v.i.* to become fixed, immovable (e.g. *The door often jams*): in jazz, to play enthusiastically with no set pattern:—*pr.p.* **jamm′ing**; *pa.p.* **jammed.**—Also *n.*
[Perh. imit.]

jamb, *jam, v.t.* the side post of a door or fireplace, etc.
[Fr. *jambe*, leg.]

jamboree, *jam-bō-rē′, n.* (*slang*) a noisy frolic: a large (international or national) gathering of Scouts. [Orig. uncertain.]

jangle, *jang′gl, v.t.* to sound (bells, etc.) harshly: to cause a feeling of irritation in (one's nerves).—*v.i.* to sound harshly: to quarrel.—*n.* a harsh, discordant sound: a quarrel.
jang′ler, *n.* **jang′ling,** *n.*
[O.Fr. *jangler*.]

janitor, *jan′i-tòr, n.* a doorkeeper: a caretaker:—*fem.* **jan′itress.**
[L. *jānitor*—*jānua*, a door.]

January, *jan′ū-àr-i, n.* the first month of the year.
[L. *Jānuārius*—*Jānus*, god of doors.]

japan, *jà-pan′, v.t.* to cover with a coat of hard black varnish like that on Japanese lacquered ware.
Japanese, *ja-pàn-ēz′, n.* a native of Japan (*pl.* **Japanese**): the language of Japan.—Also *adj.*

jar[1], *jär, v.i.* to make a harsh or unpleasant sound or vibration: to grate (on; e.g. *Her insincere praise jarred on me*).—*v.t.* to cause to vibrate unpleasantly:—*pr.p.* **jarr′ing**; *pa.p.* **jarred.**—*n.* harsh sudden vibration: a shock to body, nerves, feelings. [Imit.]

jar[2], *jär, n.* an earthen or glass bottle with a wide mouth.
[Fr. *jarre*, or Sp. *jarra*—Arabic *jarrah*.]

jargon, *jär′gòn, n.* confused talk difficult to understand: the special vocabulary of a trade, science, art, etc. [Fr.]

jasmine, *jas′min, n.* a climbing shrub with, in most kinds, fragrant flowers.
[Fr. *jasmin*—Arabic *yāsmīn*—Pers.]

jasper, *jas′pėr, n.* a precious stone, a type of quartz of various colours.
[O.Fr. *jaspe*—Gk. *iaspis*; Eastern word.]

jaundice, *jön′dis*, or *jän′, n.* diseased state which causes yellowness of eyes and skin.
jaun′diced, *adj.* suffering from jaundice: (of a person or his judgment) affected by envy, disappointment, etc. (e.g. *He took a jaundiced view of life.*)
[Fr. *jaune*, yellow—L. *galbus*, yellow.]

jaunt, *jönt, jänt, v.i.* to go from place to place, journey for pleasure.—*n.* an excursion or trip for pleasure.
jaun′ting, *adj.* and *n.* [Orig. uncertain.]

jaunty, *jön′ti, adj.* having a lively, carefree manner:—*comp.* **jaun′tier**; *superl.* **jaun′tiest.**
jaun′tily, *adv.* **jaun′tiness,** *n.*
[Fr. *gentil*.]

Javanese, *jä-và-nēz′, n.* a native of Java (*pl.* **Javanese**): language of central Java.—Also *adj.*

javelin, *jav′(ė)-lin, n.* a light spear thrown by the hand.
[Fr. *javeline*; prob. Celt.]

jaw, *jö, n.* the bones of the mouth in which the teeth are set: the side of the face: (in *pl.*) a narrow entrance, e.g. of a valley.
jaw′bone, *n.* [Orig. uncertain.]

jay, *jā, n.* a noisy bird of the crow family with bright feathers.
jay′walker, *n.* (*coll.*) a careless pedestrian who does not obey traffic regulations.
[O.Fr.]

jazz, *jaz, n.* music developed from the rhythms of the U.S. Negro, having special features of melody, syncopation, etc., and allowing freedom to improvise.—*v.i.* to dance to such music.
jazz′y, *adj.* loud in colour: suggesting jazz music:—*comp.* **jazz′ier**; *superl.* **jazz′iest.**
jazz band, *n.* combinations of instruments, such as drums, banjo, trumpet, saxophone, clarinet, and piano, suitable for playing jazz.
[U.S. Negro word.]

jealous, *jel′ùs, adj.* desiring to have what belongs to another, envious: fearing rivalry: guarding anxiously (with *of*; e.g. *jealous of his rights*).
jeal′ously, *adv.* **jeal′ousy** (*pl.* **-ies.**), *n.*
[O.Fr. *jalous*—Gk. *zēlos*, rivalry.]

jean, *jēn, jān, n.* type of cotton cloth: (in *pl.*) clothes of this, esp. trousers of blue jean.
[O.Fr. *Janne*—L. *Genua*, Genoa.]

jeep, *jēp, n.* a small motor vehicle used by U.S. and other armed forces.
[G.P. = General Purpose.]

jeer, *jēr, v.t.* to make fun of.—*v.i.* to scoff (at).—*n.* a taunting remark.
jeer'ingly, *adv.* [Orig. unknown.]

Jehovah, *ji-hō'vä, n.* the Hebrew God, a name used by Christians since 16th cent.

jelly, *jel'i, n.* the juice of a fruit boiled in sugar: anything in a half-solid state.
jell'ied, *adj.* in the state of jelly: covered with or in jelly.
jell'yfish, *n.* sea animal with a jelly-like body:—*pl.* **jell'yfish(es).**
[Fr. *gelée*—L. *gelāre,* to freeze.]

jemmy, *jem'i, n.* a burglar's short crowbar.
[A form of the name *James.*]

jenny, *jen'i, n.* the female of some birds and animals (e.g. *jenny wren, ass*): a spinning-jenny.
[From the name *Jenny.*]

jeopardy, *jep'ard-i, n.* danger, peril.
jeop'ardise, *v.t.* to put in danger.
[Fr. *jeu parti,* divided game, even chance.]

jerboa, *jėr-bō'a, n.* a small desert animal that has long hindlegs and jumps like a kangaroo.
[Arabic *yarbū.*]

jerk, *jėrk, n.* a short sudden movement.—*v.t.* to move with a jerk.—Also *v.i.*
jer'ky, *adj.*:—*comp.* **jer'kier**; *superl.* **jer'kiest.**
jer'kiness, *n.* [Imit.]

jerked meat, *jėrkt mēt, n.* meat cut into thin pieces and dried in the sun.
[Amer. Sp. *charqui*—Amer. Indian.]

jerkin, *jėr'kin, n.* short coat or waistcoat.
[Origin unknown.]

jerry-built, *jer'i-bilt, adj.* flimsy, built hastily and cheaply.
[Prob. the name *Jerry.*]

jersey, *jėr'zi, n.* combed wool: a close-fitting upper garment or jacket: a cow of Jersey breed.
[From the Channel Island *Jersey.*]

Jerusalem artichoke. See **artichoke.**

jest, *jest, n.* a joke: something said in fun: something to be laughed at.—*v.i.* to make a jest: to laugh (at).
jes'ter, one who jests: (in olden times) a king's or nobleman's fool, whose job it was to amuse his master.
jes'ting, *n.* and *adj.* **jes'tingly,** *adv.*
[O.Fr. *geste,* deed, story—L. *gerĕre,* do.]

Jesuit, *jez'ū-it, n.* one of the Society of Jesus, an order of monks founded in 1534.

jet[1], *jet, n.* a hard black mineral substance, used for ornaments.
jet'-black', *adj.* very black.
[From *Gagas,* town in Asia Minor, where it was obtained long ago.]

jet[2], *jet, n.* a gush of liquid or gas through a narrow opening or nozzle (e.g. *He directed a jet of water on the flames*): a jet aeroplane.—*v.t.* and *v.i.* to spout:—*pr.p.* **jett'ing**; *pa.p.* **jett'ed.**
jet aeroplane, one driven by air which is sucked in, heated, and forced out backwards.
jet propulsion, a method of producing forward motion by expelling air or liquid (which has been sucked in) at high speed from behind.
[O.Fr. *jetter*—L. *jacĕre,* to throw.]

jetsam, *jet'sam, n.* goods thrown overboard and washed up on the shore: goods from a wreck that (unlike *flotsam*) remain under water.
jett'ison, *n.* the act of throwing goods overboard to lighten a ship.—*v.t.* to throw overboard in times of danger: to abandon.
[Earlier *jetteson*—L. *jacĕre,* to throw.]

jetty, *jet'i, n.* a small pier:—*pl.* **-ies.**
[O.Fr. *jettee*; same root as **jet** (2).]

Jew, *jōō, n.* a person of Hebrew descent and religion:—*fem.* **Jew'ess** (not now polite).
Jew'ish, *adj.* **Jew'ishness,** *n.*
Jew's-harp, a small musical instrument played by holding between the teeth and striking a metal tongue with the finger.
[From the Hebrew *Yehūdāh,* Judah.]

jewel, *jōō'ėl, n.* a precious stone: anything or anyone highly valued.—*v.t.* to adorn or dress with jewels:—*pr.p.* **jew'elling**; *pa.p.* **jew'elled.**
jew'eller, *n.* one who makes or deals in ornaments of precious stones, etc.
jew'ellery, jew'elry, *jōō'ėl-ri, n.* articles made by jeweller.
[O.Fr. *jouel*; origin uncertain.]

jib, *jib, n.* a three-cornered sail in front of a ship's foremast: the jutting-out arm of a crane.—*v.i.* (of a sail) to shift from one side to the other: (of a horse) to shy or balk: (with *at*) to refuse to do (an action):—*pr.p.* **jibb'ing**; *pa.p.* **jibbed.**
[Orig. unknown.]

jibe, *jīb, v.i.* to scoff, jeer (at).—Also *v.t.*—*n.* a jeer, a taunt.—Also **gibe.**
[Origin uncertain.]

jig, *jig, n.* a lively dance: a pattern used in a machine shop.—*v.t.* and *v.i.* to dance (a jig): to move rapidly and jerkily:—*pr.p.* **jigg'ing**; *pa.p.* **jigged.**
jigg'er, *n.* anything that jigs: a warehouse crane: the rest for the cue in billiards: one of the 'iron' golf clubs: (*coll.*) a device, gadget.
jig'saw, *n.* a narrow saw (usu. power-driven) used for cutting curved lines.
jigsaw puzzle, *n.* a picture cut into pieces to be fitted together.
[Origin unknown.]

jilt, *jilt, v.t.* to discard (a lover) after encouragement. [Orig. unknown.]

jingle, *jing'gl, n.* a clinking sound, such as that of coins shaken together: verse in short lines with quick rhythm and repeated sounds. [Imit.]

jinn, *jin, n.pl.* (*sing.* **jinn'ee,** etc.) spirits in Mohammedan stories, often appearing as large and ugly men.—Also **djinn.**—*Pl.* forms often used as *sing.* [Arabic.]

jinricksha(w), *jin-rik′shä ,-shö.* See **rick-shaw.**

jinx, *jingks, n.* (*slang*) a bringer of bad luck: an evil spell or influence.

jitter, *jit′ėr, v.i.* (*slang*) to be nervous.
jitt′ery, *adj.* **jitt′eriness,** *n.*
(the) jitt′ers, *n.* jumps, alarm.
[Perh. *chitter,* to shiver.]

job, *job, n.* a person's daily work, employment: a definite piece of work: any work done for a fixed price: a state of affairs (e.g. *This is a bad job*).—*v.i.* to work at jobs.—*v.t.* to buy and sell, as a broker.
jobb′ing, *adj.* doing odd jobs for payment (e.g. *a jobbing gardener*).
jobb′ery, *n.* dishonest means used for private gain.
a job lot, *n.* a mixed collection (e.g. of goods), esp. if of poor quality.
[Origin unknown.]

jockey, *jok′i, n.* a man (orig. a boy) who rides in a horse race.—*v.t.* to jostle by riding against; to cheat: to trick (into doing something).—*v.i.* to cheat.
[From *Jock,* northern Eng. for **Jack.**]

jocose, *jō-kōs′, adj.* full of jokes: merry.
jocose′ly, *adv.* **jocose′ness,** *n.*
jocular, *jok′ū-lȧr, adj.* full of jokes: intended to be humorous (e.g. *a jocular remark*).
jocular′ity, *n.* **joc′ularly,** *adv.*
[L. *jocus,* a joke.]

jodhpurs, *jod′poorz, n.pl.* riding breeches that fit tightly from the knee to the ankle: short riding boots.
[From *Jodhpur,* in India.]

jog, *jog, v.t.* to shake: to nudge: to push with hand or elbow: to stir (e.g. *to jog one's memory*).—*v.i.* to move up and down with unsteady motion: to travel slowly: trudge (on, along):—*pr.p.* **jogg′ing**; *pa.p.* **jogged.**
jog′-trot′, *n.* a slow pace. [Imit.]

joggle, *jog′l, v.t.* to shake slightly: to jostle.—*v.i.* to shake. [Orig. uncertain.]

John, *jon, n.* the commonest English man's name.
John Bull, a name for the traditional, typical Englishman.

join, *join, v.t.* to connect, fasten (one thing to another): to put together: (*geometry*) to connect by a line: to unite (e.g. in marriage): to become a member of (e.g. a team): to go to and remain with (e.g. *He joined the group at the fire*).—*v.i.* to come (together): to unite (with): to take part (with).
join′er, *n.* one who joins or unites: a skilled worker in wood who finishes buildings (puts in doors, stairs, etc.).
joint, *n.* the place where two or more things join: a part of the body where two bones meet but are able to move in the manner of a hinge: a piece of meat for cooking containing a bone: (*U.S. slang*) a meeting place, usu. low-class.—*adj.* united: shared by two or more.—*v.t.* to cut (an animal) into joints.
join′ted, *adj.*
joint′ly, *adv.* together.
joint stock, stock or capital held by several people together.—*adj.* **joint′-stock′.**
out of joint, dislocated: in disorder, in a bad state: (see also **nose**).
to join battle, to begin a fight.
to join up, to enlist, e.g. in the armed forces.
See also **junction.**
[O.Fr. *joindre*—L. *jungĕre, junctum.*]

joist, *joist, n.* a beam to which the boards of a floor or the laths of a ceiling are fastened.—*v.t.* to fit with joists.
[O.Fr. *giste*—L. *jacēre,* to lie.]

joke, *jōk, n.* a jest, anything said or done to raise a laugh: something unintentionally amusing: something trifling, not serious.—*v.i.* to make jokes: to speak playfully.
jok′er, *n.* one who jokes: an extra card in a pack used in certain games.
See also **jocose, jocular.**
[L. *jocus.*]

jolly, *jol′i, adj.* merry, gay:—*comp.* **joll′ier**; *superl.* **joll′iest.**—*adv.* (*coll.*) very (e.g. *jolly good*).
joll′iness, *n.*
jollificā′tion, *n.* feasting and merriment.
joll′ity, *n.* merrymaking.
[O.Fr. *jolif, joli.*]

jollyboat, *jol′i-bōt, n.* a small boat belonging to a ship. [Orig. unknown.]

jolt, *jōlt, v.i.* to go forward with jerks, as a car on rough ground.—*v.t.* to shake suddenly.—Also *n.* [Orig. uncertain.]

jonquil, *jon′kwil, n.* a flower with rush-like leaves, a kind of narcissus.
[Fr. *jonquille*—L. *juncus,* a rush.]

jostle, *jos′l, v.t.* to shake or jar by knocking against: to elbow.—Also *n.*
[From **joust.**]

jot, *jot, n.* a very small part or amount.—*v.t.* to write briefly or quickly (usu. **jot down**):—*pr.p.* **jott′ing**; *pa.p.* **jott′ed.**
jott′er, *n.* one who jots: a book for notes.
jott′ing, *n.* a note to help the memory.
[L. *jota*—same root as **iota.**]

journal, *jûr′n(ȧ)l, n.* a diary; in book-keeping, a book containing an account of each day's business: a newspaper published every day (or less often): a magazine: the accounts kept by a society.
jour′nalese, *n.* the kind of writing found in the poorer newspapers.
jour′nalism, *n.* the business of running, or writing for, papers or magazines.
jour′nalist, *n.* an editor, manager, of, or writer for, paper(s), magazine(s).
journalis′tic, *adj.*
[Fr.—L. *diurnālis,* daily—*diēs,* day.]

journey, *jûr'ni, n.* a distance travelled: a tour:—*pl.* **jour'neys.**—*v.i.* to travel:—*pr.p.* **jour'neying**; *pa.p.* **jour'neyed.**
jour'neyman, *n.* a hired workman: one whose apprenticeship is finished.
[Fr. *journée—jour,* day; conn. **journal.**]

joust, *jowst, just, n.* in olden times at a tournament, a combat between two knights on horseback.—*v.i.* to fight on horseback in this way.
[O.Fr. *juste*—L. *juxtā,* near.]

jovial, *jō'vi-àl, adj.* joyous: full of good humour.
joviality (*-al'i-ti*), **jo'vialness,** *ns.*
jo'vially, *adv.*
[From L. *Jovis,* the god Jove, Jupiter.]

jowl, *jowl, n.* the jaw or cheek.
[From several Germanic words.]

joy, *joi, n.* gladness: a cause of gladness.—*v.i.* to rejoice or to be glad.
joy'ful, *adj.* feeling, showing, or giving joy.
joy'fully, *adv.* **joy'fulness,** *n.*
joy'less, *adj.* without joy, dismal.
joy'ous, *adj.* poetical form of joyful.
[Fr. *joie*—L. *gaudium,* gladness.]

jubilant, *jōō'bi-lànt, adj.* shouting for joy: rejoicing.
ju'bilance, -ancy, *ns.* **ju'bilantly,** *adv.*
ju'bilate, *v.i.* to rejoice.
jubilā'tion, *n.* jubilance: a celebration.
[L. *jūbilāre,* to shout for joy.]

jubilee, *jōō'bi-lē, n.* any season of great joy and feasting: celebration in memory of an event (e.g. a wedding) that happened 50 (also 25, 60 or 75) years before.
[Fr. *jubilé*—Hebrew, *yōbēl,* trumpet.]

judder, *jud'ėr, n.* aircraft vibration: shaking.—Also *v.i.*

judge, *juj, v.t.* to try and to decide (questions esp. of law or of guilt): to try (a person): to conclude (e.g. *I judge that to be true.*)—Also *v.i.*—*n.* one who judges: one who has been appointed to try accused persons: one who has the knowledge to decide on the worth of anything (e.g. *a judge of good food*).
judg'ment, judge'ment, *n.* act of judging: opinion or decision given: the working of the mind when it compares facts, weighs evidence, etc., in order to make a decision: doom.
judgment day, day of God's final judgment on mankind.
judicature, *jōō'di-kà-chùr, n.* all the judges of a country considered together.
judicial, *jōō-dish'àl, adj.* of, belonging to, a judge or a court: ordered by law: critical (e.g. *He looked at the picture with a judicial air*).
judic'ially, *adv.*
judicial separation, a court act which allows a man and wife to be separated legally but does not allow either to marry again.
judiciary, *jōō-dish'(y)àr-i, n.* the judicature, esp. when thought of as one of the three branches of government (*legislature, judiciary, and executive*).—Also *adj.*
judicious, *jōō-dish'ùs, adj.* wise—showing, or using, sound judgment (e.g. *a judicious man, choice*).
See also **jurisdiction,** etc.
[L. *jūs, jūris,* law (*dicĕre,* to say).]

judo, *jōō'dō, n.* a form of wrestling popular in Japan.
[Jap. *jū,* weakness, *dō,* way of life, art.]

jug, *jug, n.* a dish with a handle and spout for pouring liquids—*v.t.* to boil or stew (e.g. a hare) in a jar:—*pr.p.* **jugg'ing**; *pa.p.* **jugged.** [Orig. unknown.]

juggle, *jug'l, v.i.* to entertain by showing great skill of hands and body in keeping a number of objects in the air at once: to use trickery.—*v.t.* to perform feats of skill with (something): to give a false idea of (e.g. *to juggle the facts*; more usu. *to juggle with the facts*).—*n.* a piece of deception for purpose of cheating.
jugg'ler, *n.*
[O.Fr. *jogler*—L. *jocus,* a jest.]

jugular, *jug'ū-làr, n.* one of the large veins on either side of the neck bringing the blood back from the head.
[L. *jugulum,* collar-bone—*jungĕre,* join.]

juice, *jōōs, n.* the liquid part of fruits, vegetables, or of animal bodies: (*coll.*) electricity: (*coll.*) petrol.
juic'y, *adj.*—*comp.* **juic'ier**; *superl.* **juic'iest.**
juic'iness, *n.*
[Fr. *jus*—L. *jūs,* broth, mixture.]

ju-jitsu, *jōō-jit'sōō, n.* earlier form of judo.
[Japanese *jū-jutsu.*]

jujube, *jōō'jōōb, n.* the fruit of a shrub, which is dried as a sweet: a jellied sweet.
[Fr. *jujube*—Gk. *zizyphon.*]

juke box, *jook boks,* an instrument that plays gramophone records automatically —usu. run by inserting a coin in a slot.
[U.S. *juke joint,* place for dancing, etc.]

July, *jōō-lī', jōō'li, n.* the seventh month.
[From *Julius* Caesar, born in it.]

jumble, *jum'bl, v.t.* (often used with *up*) to mix together without order: to muddle.—Also *v.i.*—*n.* a confused mixture.
jumble sale, *n.* a sale of odds and ends.
[Origin unknown.]

jump, *jump, v.i.* to move by leaps, to spring or bound: to move suddenly: to rise suddenly (e.g. *News of this scarcity made the price jump*).—*v.t.* to help to leap: to leap over (e.g. *to jump a ditch*): to get on board (a train) by jumping.—*n.* act of jumping: a sudden movement or rise.
the jumps, nervousness.
to jump at, to take eagerly (e.g. *He jumped at the chance*).
to jump one's bail, to run away, losing the bail that has been paid.
to jump the gun, to start before the proper time, take an unfair advantage.
to jump to conclusions, to arrive at a

conclusion or judgment without waiting to make sure of the facts.
[Prob. imit. of the sound of jumping.]

jumper, *jump'ėr,* *n.* a loose-fitting blouse or jersey slipped over the head.
[Perh. Fr. *juppe* (now *jupe*), skirt.]

junction, *jungk'sh(ȯ)n,* *n.* a joining or union: place or point of joining, as a place where railway lines meet.
juncture, *jungk'chůr,* *n.* a joining, connexion: an important point of time (e.g. *At this juncture, she began to cry*).
[Same root as **join.**]

June, *jōōn,* *n.* the sixth month.
[L. *Jūnius.*]

jungle, *jung'gl,* *n.* a dense growth of trees and plants in tropical areas.
[Hindi *jangal.*]

junior, *jōōn'yȯr,* *adj.* younger: in a lower class or rank.—Also *n.*
[L.—*juvenis,* young.]

juniper, *jōō'ni-pėr,* *n.* an evergreen shrub.
[L. *jūniperus.*]

junk[1], *jungk,* *n.* a Chinese sailing boat with a high stern and flat bottom.
[Javanese *djong.*]

junk[2], *jungk,* *n.* pieces of old rope: rubbish in general: worthless articles: salt meat: narcotic drugs.—*v.t.* to throw away, discard as worthless.
junk'er, junk'ie, *ns.* a narcotics addict.
[Origin uncertain.]

junket, *jung'kit,* *n.* milk thickened by rennet, sweetened and flavoured: a feast or merrymaking: (*U.S.*) an outing at public expense.—*v.i.* to feast: (*U.S.*) to go on an outing at public cost.
junk'eting, *n.*
[Prob. from cheese orig. made in rush basket—L. *juncus,* a rush.]

junkie. See **junk** (2).

junto, *jun'tō,* *n.* a number of men joining together for a purpose, a clique, usu. political.
[Sp. *junta.*]

Jupiter, *jōō'pi-tėr,* *n.* the chief god of the Romans: the largest, and second brightest, planet.
[L. *Jūpiter* (*Jovis Pater*), Father Jove.]

jurisdiction, *jōō-ris-dik'sh(ȯ)n,* *n.* legal authority or power: the district over which a judge, court, etc., has power.
jurisprudence, *jōō-ris-prōō'dėns,* *n.* the science of law: a branch of law.
jurist, *jōō'rist,* *n.* one who has a skilled knowledge of law.
[L. *jūs, jūris,* law (*dīcĕre,* to say; *prūdentia,* knowledge, good sense.).]

jury, *jōō'ri,* *n.* a group of men or women legally selected to hear a case and to decide what are the facts (e.g. whether or not a prisoner accused of crime is guilty): a committee for judging the worth of plays, etc., or for deciding the winner of a competition.
ju'ror, *n.* person who serves on a jury.
[Through Fr.—L. *jūrāre,* to swear.]

just, *just,* *adj.* fair, without prejudice, not favouring one more than another: based on rights or on good grounds (e.g. *a just claim*): deserved (e.g. *his just reward*): exact, accurate.—*adv.* exactly, precisely (e.g. *It lay just there*): very lately, not long since: barely, by a small time (e.g. *He just managed to reach safety*).
just'ly, *adv.* **just'ness,** *n.*
just'ice (*-is*), *n.* fairness in making judgments: rightness: the awarding of punishments, or of rewards, that are deserved: a judge: a magistrate.
justifiable, etc. See below.
justify, *jus'ti-fī,* *v.t.* to prove or show to be just, right, or desirable (e.g. *Can you justify the spending of such a large sum?*) to clear from blame:—*pr.p.* **jus'tifying** *pa.p.* **jus'tified.**
jus'tifiable (*or-fī'*), *adj.* that can be justified or defended.
justificā'tion, *n.* **jus'tifier,** *n.*
Justice of the Peace (or **J.P.**), a citizen appointed to keep peace in his district, who can act as a judge in some matters.
justifiable homicide, the killing of a person in self-defence.
High Court of Justice, a part of the English Supreme Court.
High Court of Justiciary, the most important criminal court in Scotland.
[L. *jūstus,* just—*jūs, jūris,* law (*jūstitia,* justice; *facĕre,* to make).]

jut, *jut,* *v.i.* to stick out, to project:—*pr.p.* **jutt'ing**; *pa.p.* **jutt'ed.**
[A form of **jet** (2).]

jute, *jōōt,* *n.* the fibre of plants found in Pakistan and India, used for making coarse sacks, etc.
[From Indian word.]

juvenile, *jōō'vi-nil,* *adj.* young, youthful: suited to young people.—*n.* a young person.
juvenile delinquency, law-breaking by young person **(juvenile delinquent).**
[L. *juvenīlis*—*juvenis,* young.]

juxtaposition, *juks-tȧ-pȯ-zish'(ȯ)n,* *n.* a placing, or being placed, close together.
juxtapose', *v.t.* to place (things) side by side.
[L. *juxtā,* near, and **position.**]

K

kail. See **kale.**
kaiser, *kī'zėr,* ***n.*** an emperor, esp. a German emperor.
[Ger.; from Julius *Caesar.*]
kale, kail, *kāl,* ***n.*** a cabbage with open curled leaves.
[O.E. *cāl*—L. *caulis,* stalk, cabbage.]
kaleidoscope, *kȧ-lī'dō-skōp,* ***n.*** a toy in which loose pieces of coloured glass form changing patterns.
kaleidoscop'ic, *adj.* with changing colours: changing quickly (e.g. *a kaleidoscopic career*).
[Gk. *kalos,* beautiful, *eidos,* form, *skopeein,* to look at.]
kangaroo, *kang-gȧ-rōō',* ***n.*** a large Australian animal with very long hindlegs and great power of leaping (the female carries her young in a pouch on the front of her body). [Prob. native name.]
kaolin, *kā'ō-lin,* ***n.*** China clay.
[From a mountain in China.]
kapok, *kāp'ok, kap',* ***n.*** very light waterproof oily fibre covering seeds of a tropical tree, used to stuff pillows, lifebelts, etc.
[Malay *kāpoq.*]
karate, *ka-rä'tā,* ***n.*** a Japanese sport and method of defence and attack using blows and kicks. [Jap.]
kart. See **go-cart.**
kauri (pine), *kow'ri (pīn),* ***n.*** a forest tree of New Zealand. [Maori.]
kayak, *kī'ak,* ***n.*** an Eskimo sealskin canoe.
[Eskimo.]
kedge, *kej',* ***n.*** a small anchor.
[Origin unknown.]
kedgeree, *kej'(ė-)rē,* ***n.*** a mixture of rice with butter, spices, etc., or with fish.
[Hindustani *khichrī.*]
keel, *kēl,* ***n.*** the part of a ship stretching along the middle of the bottom and supporting the whole frame: anything suggesting this.—*v.i.* (often **keel over**) to turn keel upwards.
[Old Norse *kjölr.*]
keen, *kēn,* *adj.* sharp (e.g. *a keen blade*): very cold, biting (e.g. *a keen wind*): eager, enthusiastic (e.g. *a keen golfer*).
keen'ly, *adv.* **keen'ness,** ***n.***
keen about, (*coll.*) **keen on,** very enthusiastic about, much interested in.
keen prices, very low prices.
[O.E. *cēne,* bold, fierce, keen.]
keep, *kēp,* *v.t.* to feed, clothe, and house: to look after (e.g. a garden): to hold, not give or throw away: to have usu. in stock: to hold (*to keep, keep prisoner, keep a prisoner*): to detain, delay (e.g. *Sorry to keep you, keep you waiting*): to cause to continue in a certain state (e.g. *to keep peace, the peace*; *to keep the fire burning*): to act in the way laid down by (e.g. *to keep the law, a promise*): to note happenings in (e.g. a diary): to celebrate (e.g. Christmas).—*v.i.* to remain in good condition: to continue (e.g. *He kept saying so*):—*pr.p.* **keep'ing**; *pa.t.* and *pa.p.* **kept.**—***n.*** food and other necessaries: the strongest part of a castle.
keep'er, ***n.*** one who, or something that, keeps: a gamekeeper.
keep'ing, ***n.*** care, custody.
keep'sake, ***n.*** something given to be kept for the sake of the giver.
in (out of) keeping, suitable (or not suitable) in the circumstances or place.
to keep at it, to work on and on at anything.
to keep from, to refrain from: to prevent from.
to keep in with, to keep in favour with.
to keep one's hand in, to retain one's skill by practice.
to keep up, to keep (e.g. prices) from falling: to retain one's strength or spirit: to keep in repair (e.g. property: to carry on (e.g. a conversation).
to keep up with, to keep as far forward (in the race, etc.) as.
to keep up with the Joneses, to have everything one's neighbours have.
[O.E. *cēpan.*]
keg, *keg,* ***n.*** a small cask.
[Old Norse *kaggi.*]
kelp, *kelp,* ***n.*** large brown seaweed.
[Origin unknown.]
kennel, *ken'ėl,* ***n.*** a house for a dog.
[Norman Fr. *kenil,* from L. *canis,* dog.]
kept. See **keep.**
kerb, *kėrb,* ***n.*** the edging of a pavement: a fender at a fireside.
kerb'stone, ***n.***
[Same word as **curb.**]
kerchief, *kėr'chif,* ***n.*** a square piece of cloth to cover the head, neck, etc.
[O.Fr. *covrir,* to cover, *chief,* head.]
kernel, *kėr'nėl,* ***n.*** the softer substance within the shell of a nut and inside the stone of a pulpy fruit: the important part of anything.
[O.E. *cyrnel.*]
kerosene, -sine, *ker'ō-sēn,* ***n.*** paraffin oil.
[Gk. *kēros,* wax.]
kestrel, *kes'trėl,* ***n.*** a small kind of falcon.
[O.Fr. *quercerelle.*]
kettle, *ket'l,* ***n.*** a metal pot for heating liquids, with (usu.) spout, (usu.) lid, and handle.
kett'ledrum, ***n.*** a drum made of a half

globe of brass or copper with stretched parchment covering the open end.
[O.E. *cetel*; conn. with Ger. *kessel*.]

key, *kē*, *n.* a device by which something (e.g. a nut, a lock) is screwed or turned: in musical instruments, one of the small parts pressed to sound the notes: a similar part, e.g. in a typewriter: the chief note of a piece of music: pitch, tone of voice, etc.: something that explains a mystery: a book containing answers to exercises, etc.:—*pl.* **keys.**—*adj.* most important, controlling (e.g. *key industries, a key man*).
key'board, *n.* the keys in a piano, organ, etc. arranged along a flat board.
key'hole, *n.* the hole in which a key of a door, etc. is placed.
key'note, *n.* the chief note of a piece of music: the chief point (e.g. *The keynote of his speech was* 'Let us prepare!').
key'stone, *n.* the stone at the highest point of an arch holding the rest in position.
keyed up, tightened up: excited.
[O.E. *cæg*.]

khaki, *kä'ki*, *adj.* dull brownish or greenish yellow.—*n.* cloth of such colour used for soldiers' uniforms.
[Hindustani *khākī*, dusty.]

khan, *kän*, *n.* a prince, chief, or governor.
[Pers.]

kick, *kik*, *v.t.* to hit, put, or drive, with the foot.—*v.i.* to thrust out the foot with violence: to resist, object: (of a gun) to spring back violently when fired.—*n.* a blow with the foot: the spring back of a gun: (*slang*) a pleasant thrill.
to kick against the pricks, to resist when one can only hurt oneself by doing so (Acts ix. 5, where prick means 'goad').
to kick over the traces, to throw off control—see **trace** (2).
[M.E. *kiken*: origin unknown.]

kid[1], *kid*, *n.* a young goat: leather from the skin of a kid: (*slang*) a child.—*v.i.* (of a goat) to give birth to young.
[Old Norse *kith*.]

kid[2], *kid*, *v.t.* (*coll.*) to deceive, hoax (esp. for amusement):—*pr.p.* **kidd'ing**; *pa.p.* **kidd'ed.**
[Perh. **kid** (1).]

kidnap, *kid'nap*, or *-nap'*, *v.t.* to carry off (a human being) by force:—*pr.p.* **kid'napping** (or *-nap'*); *pa.t.* and *pa.p.* **kid'napped** (or *-napd'*).
kid'napper, *n.* one who kidnaps.
[**kid,** a child, *nap*, to steal.]

kidney, *kid'ni*, *n.* either of a pair of glands in the lower part of the back, one on each side (*pl.* **kid'neys**): sort, kind, character (e.g. *His brother was of a different kidney*).
kidney bean, a common kidney-shaped bean, or the plant that bears it.
[M.E. *kidenei*.]

kill, *kil*, *v.t.* to put to death: to destroy: to cause the death of: to put an end to: to stop (e.g. an engine, a ball in play).—*n.* act of killing by a hunter: animal(s) so killed: an enemy aeroplane, etc., destroyed.
kill'er, *n.*
kill'ing, *adj.* causing death: exhausting: (*coll.*) very funny.—Also *n.*
kill-joy, *kil'joi*, *n.* someone who keeps other people from enjoying themselves.
to be in at the kill, to be there at the most exciting moment.
to kill off, to destroy completely.
to kill time, to use up spare time, such as a time of waiting.
[M.E. *killen* or *cullen*.]

kiln, *kil*, *kiln*, *n.* a large oven in which bricks, hops, etc., are dried.
[O.E. *cyln*, from L. *culina*, a kitchen.]

kilo-, *kil-ō-*, *pfx.* used to show multiplication by 1,000, as in, e.g.:—
kilocycle, *kil'ō-sīkl*, *n.* (radio, etc.) a measure of wave frequency—1,000 cycles per second (see cycle).
kilogram (also **kilogramme**), **kilometre,** etc. See tables in *Appendices.*
kilowatt, *kil'ō-wŏt*, *n.* a measure of power, esp. electrical—1000 watts.
[Gk. *chilioi*, a thousand.]

kilt, *kilt*, *n.* a pleated tartan skirt reaching to the knees, part of Highland dress.
[Scand.; conn. Dan. *kilte*, tuck up.]

kimono, *ki-mō'nō*, *n.* a loose robe, fastened with a sash. [Jap.]

kin, *kin*, *n.* persons of the same family, relatives.
kin'dred, *n.* kin.—*adj.* related: of same or similar nature (**kindred spirits,** people having the same nature and tastes).
kins'man, kins'woman, kins'folk, a man, a woman, people, related to one.
next of kin, nearest relative(s) of a person who has died.
[O.E. *cynn*; conn. with Old Norse *kyn*.]

kind, *kīnd*, *n.* sort (e.g. *What kind of car is it?*): variety, race (e.g. *The tiger is an animal of the cat kind*).—*adj.* ready or anxious to do good to others: friendly, gentle.
kind'ness, kind'liness, *ns.*
kind'ly, *adv.* in a kind manner: please (e.g. *Would you kindly sit down*).
kind'ly, kind'hearted, *adjs.* kind.
in kind, (of payment) in goods, not money: in the same way, with the same treatment (e.g. *He spoke rudely to her and she replied in kind*).
of a kind, of the same sort (e.g. *They are two of a kind—both unreliable*): scarcely deserving the name (e.g. *hospitality of a kind*).
[O.E. (*ge*)*cynde*—same root as **kin.**]

kindergarten, *kin'dėr-gär-t(ė)n*, *n.* a school for very young children, who learn through games, toys, handcrafts.
[Ger. *kinder*, children, *garten*, garden.]

kindle, *kin'dl*, *v.t.* to set fire to: to stir up

(feelings; e.g. *This kindled the anger of the crowd.*)—*v.i.* to catch fire.
kind′ling, *n.* material for starting fire.
[M.E. *kindlen*; conn. O. Norse *kyndill*, torch.]

kindliness, kindly. See **kind.**

kindred. See **kin.**

kine, *kīn, n.pl.* (old word) cows.
[M.E., *kyen*, cows.]

kinema, kinematograph. Same as **cinema, cinematograph.**

king, *king, n.* male who succeeds by right of birth as head of nation: playing card having the picture of a king: the most important piece in chess:—*fem.* **queen.**
king′ly, *adj.* of royal rank: suitable for a king: very dignified.
king′liness, *n.*
king′cup, *n.* buttercup: marsh marigold.
king′dom, *n.* a state having a king (or queen) as its head: any of the three great divisions of natural objects—animal, vegetable, or mineral.
king′fisher, *n.* a bird with brilliant feathers, feeding on fish.
King′-of-Arms′ (sometimes **-at-Arms′**), a principal herald.
King's (or **Queen's) Counsel,** an honorary rank of barristers and advocates.
king's (queen's) English, correct standard speech.
to turn king's (queen's) evidence, to become a witness against an accomplice.
[O.E. *cyning*—same root as **kin.**]

kink, *kingk, n.* a twist in a string, rope, etc.: a mental twist or oddness.
[Prob. Du.; same in Ger., Swed., Norw.]

kinsfolk, -man, -woman. See **kin.**

kiosk, *ki-osk′, kē′, n.* a small out-of-doors roofed stall for the sale of papers, sweets, etc.: a public telephone box.
[Turk. *kiöshk*, summerhouse—Pers.]

kipper, *kip′ėr, n.* a herring split down the back and smoked.
[Earlier 'a spawning salmon'.]

kirk, *kėrk, n.* (*Scot.*) church.
kirk session, the lowest court (consisting of minister(s) and elders) in a Presbyterian church.
[A Northern Eng. form of **church.**]

kismet, *kis′met, kiz′, n.* fate, destiny.
[Turk. *qismet.*]

kiss, *kis, v.t.* to caress or touch with the lips esp. as a sign of affection: to touch gently.—Also *n.*
to kiss hands, (of e.g. a new prime minister) to kiss the sovereign's hand on accepting office.
to kiss the book, in England, to kiss a copy of the New Testament after taking a legal oath.
to kiss the dust, to be slain or defeated.
[O.E. *cyssan*, to kiss; conn. Ger. *küssen.*]

kit, *kit, n.* complete outfit.
kit′bag, *n.* a strong bag for holding one's kit.
[Middle Du. *kitte*, wooden jug or tub.]

kitchen, *kich′ėn, n.* a place where food is cooked.
kitchenette′, *n.* a tiny kitchen.
kitchen garden, a garden where vegetables for the kitchen are grown.
[O.E. *cycene*—L. *coquina*—*coquĕre*, cook.]

kite, *kīt, n.* a bird of prey of the hawk family: a light frame covered with paper or cloth, and with string attached, for flying in the air.
to fly a kite, to give out a hint to test public opinion (as a kite shows direction and force of wind).
[O.E. *cȳta.*]

kith, *kith, n.* in phrase **kith and kin,** friends and relatives.
[O.E. *cȳth*—*cunnan*, to know.]

kitten, *kit′n, n.* the young of a cat.—*v.t.* and *v.i.* (of a cat) to give birth to young.
kitt′enish, *adj.* playful (used slightingly of a woman).
[O.Fr. *kitoun*—*chat*, cat.]

kittiwake, *kit′i-wāk, n.* a kind of long-winged gull. [Imit. of its cry.]

kitty, *kit′i, n.* money put aside for a purpose, or the box, etc. containing it.
[Orig. unknown.]

kiwi, *kē′wi, n.* a wingless bird of New Zealand.
[Maori; from its cry.]

Klaxon, *klaks′ȯn, n.* electric motor-horn.
[Registered trademark.]

kleptomania, *klep-tō-mā′nyȧ, -ni-ȧ, n.* a violent urge to steal.
kleptomā′niac, *n.* one who suffers from kleptomania.
[Gk. *kleptein*, to steal, *mania*, madness.]

knack, *nak, n.*, the ability to do a particular thing skilfully.
[Orig. imit.; conn. Ger. *knacken*, crack.]

knacker, *nak′ėr, n.* a horse-slaughterer: a worn-out horse: one who buys and breaks up old houses, ships, etc.
[Origin unknown.]

knapsack, *nap′sak, n.* a bag carried on the back when e.g. hiking.
[From Ger. or Du. in 16th cent.]

knave, *nāv, n.* a dishonest man, rogue: a playing-card having the picture of a servant or soldier.
knav′ery, *n.* dishonesty:—*pl.* **-ies.**
knav′ish, *adj.* dishonest, rascally.
knav′ishly, *adv.* **knav′ishness,** *n.*
[O.E. *cnafa*, a boy; conn. Ger. *knabe.*]

knead, *nēd, v.t.* to press together into a mass, as damped flour into dough: to massage with a movement like this.
[O.E. *cnedan*; conn. with Ger. *kneten.*]

knee, *nē, n.* in man, the joint between the thigh and shin bones: a joint in an animal (e.g. a horse) regarded as corresponding to the human knee.
kneel, *nēl, v.i.* to rest or fall on bent knee(s):—*pa.t.* and *pa.p.* **kneeled, knelt.**
knee breeches, breeches coming to just below the knee, as in court dress.

knee′cap, *n.* the patella, a flat, round bone on the front of the knee joint: a warm covering for the knee.
knee′-jerk, *n.* a quick raising of the leg caused by a tap below the kneecap.
knee′pan, *n.* the kneecap.
[O.E. *cnēo(w)*; conn. Ger. *knie*, L. *genu*.]

knell, *nel, n.* the sound of a bell, esp. at a death or a funeral: a warning of the end or failure of something.
[O.E. *cnyllan*, to beat noisily.]

knew. See **know.**

knickerbockers, *nik′ėr-bok-ėrz, n.pl.* loose breeches gathered in at the knee.
knick′ers, *n.pl.* knickerbockers: woman's undergarment gathered in at the knee.
[Diedrich *Knickerbocker*, pretended by Washington Irving to be Dutch author of his own 'History of New York'.]

knickknack, *nik′nak, n.* a small trifling ornamental article. **[knack.]**

knife, *nīf, n.* an instrument for cutting: a surgeon's instrument: a weapon with a blade:—*pl.* **knives** (*nīvz*).—*v.t.* to stab with a knife.
[O.E. *cnīf*; conn. Ger. *kneifen*, to pinch.]

knight, *nīt, n.* (*history*) a man-at-arms of gentle birth: a man of rank (next below a baronet) with the title 'Sir' (not hereditary): a piece used in chess.—*v.t.* to make (a person) a knight.
knight′ly, *adj.* of a knight: (of conduct) suited to a knight: made up of knights.
knight′liness, *n.*
knight′hood, *n.* the rank or title of knight.
knight′-err′ant, *n.* a knight who travelled in search of adventure: a very chivalrous (see this word) man.
knight′-err′antry, *n.* the character or conduct of a knight-errant.
[O.E. *cniht*, youth, servant, warrior.]

knit, *nit, v.t.* to form (material, a garment) from yarn (of wool, etc.) by making and connecting loops, using knitting needles: to cause (e.g. broken bones) to grow together: (of common interests, etc.) to draw (persons) together: to wrinkle (the brows).—Also *v.i.*:—*pr.p.* **knitt′ing**; *pa.t.* and *pa.p.* **knitt′ed,** or **knit.**
knitt′er, *n.*
knitt′ing, *n.* the work of a knitter: material made by knitting: joining.
knitting needle, a thin rod, e.g. of steel, used in knitting.
[O.E. *cnyttan*—*cnotta*, a knot.]

knives. See **knife.**

knob, *nob, n.* a hard swelling or lump: a more or less round handle (e.g. on a door).
knobbed, *adj.* **knobb′y,** *adj.*
knobb′iness, *n.*
[M.E.; a Germanic word.]

knock, *nok, v.i.* to rap (on e.g. a door) for admittance: to be driven (against): (of machinery) to make a rattling or clanking noise.—*v.t.* to strike: to send by a blow: to drive (against, on, something): to make by a blow (e.g. *He knocked his opponent senseless*).—*n.* a sudden stroke: a rap.
knock′er, *n.* a device, e.g. of brass, fixed to a door for knocking.
knock′about, *adj.* rough: for rough use.
knock′-kneed, *adj.* having knees that touch in walking.
to knock down, to cause to fall by a blow: to give (an article) to the highest bidder with a tap of the auctioneer's hammer.
to knock off, to stop e.g. work: to make or carry out hastily.
to knock on the head, to bring (e.g. a plan) to a sudden stop.
to knock out, to strike insensible.
to knock up, to rouse by knocking: to exhaust: to make hastily: to score (a certain number of runs) in cricket.
[O.E. *cnocian*; perh. imit.]

knoll, *nōl, n.* a round hillock.
[O.E. *cnol*; conn. Ger. *knollen*, lump.]

knot, *not, n.* a lump or join made in string, rope, etc., by twisting ends together and drawing tight the loops thus formed: a lump or joint in something growing: a cluster: a tangle: a difficulty: a nautical mile per hour.—*v.t.* to form a knot or knots in.—*v.i.* to form a knot or knots:—*pr.p.* **knott′ing**; *pa.p.* **knott′ed.**
knott′y, *adj.* containing knots: (of e.g. a problem) difficult:—*comp.* **knott′ier**; *superl.* **knott′iest.**
knott′iness, *n.*
[O.E. *cnotta*; conn. Ger. *knoten*.]

know, *nō, v.t.* to be aware of, or have been informed of (a fact): to have learned and remember: to have experience of (e.g. *He had known sorrow*): to have as a friend or acquaintance: to recognise (e.g. *I know a good car when I see it*):—*pr.p.* **know′ing**; *pa.t.* **knew** (*nū*); *pa.p.* **known** (*nōn*).
know′ing, *adj.* shrewd, cunning: expressing secret understanding (e.g. *a knowing look*).
know′ingly, *adv.* in a knowing manner: intentionally.
knowledge, *nol′ij, n.* familiarity with the facts, etc.: information: learning.
know′ledgeable, *adj.* having, or showing, knowledge (e.g. *He is knowledgeable about plants*; *a knowledgeable essay*).
know′-how, *n.* the practical knowledge and skill to deal with something.
to be in the know, to have information possessed by a small group of people and not by those outside it.
to know better than, to be too wise (to do something).
to know on which side one's bread is buttered, to know which action will be more profitable to one.
to know the ropes, to know the detail

and methods of something as a sailor knows the rigging on a sailing ship.
[O.E. *cnāwan*; conn. with L. (*g*)*noscĕre*.]

knowledge, -able. See **know.**

knuckle, *nuk'l*, *n.* a joint of a finger, esp. one where the finger joins the hand: a knee-joint of calf or pig.
knuck'le-duster, *n.* a metal covering for the knuckles, for attack or defence.
to knuckle down, to yield (to someone).
[M.E. *knokel*; conn. Ger. *knöchel*.]

koala, *kō-ä'là*, *n.* an Australian pouched animal, like a small bear; also called 'native bear'.
[Austr. native name *kūlā*.]

kookaburra, *kook'à-bur-à*, or *-bur'*, the laughing jackass. [Austr. native name.]

kopje, *kop'i*, *n.* a low hill.
[Afrikaans—*kop*, head.]

Koran, *kō-rän'*, *n.* the Mohammedan Scriptures.
[Arabic *qurān*, reading.]

kosher, *kō'shėr*, *adj.* pure, clean, according to Jewish law (e.g. of meat killed and prepared by Jews).
[Heb. *kāshēr*, right, lawful.]

kowtow, *kow'tow'*, *n.* the Chinese ceremony of touching the ground with the forehead.—*v.i.* to perform that ceremony: to show too much respect for wishes and views of (with *to*; *I hate the way Tom kowtows to the head boy*).—Also **kotow** (*kō'tow'*).
[Chinese *k'o*, knock, *t'ou*, head.]

kraal, *kräl*, *n.* a S. African native village: an enclosure for cattle: also, a native hut with bush stockade round it. [Du.]

kremlin, *krem'lin*, *n.* a citadel, a fortress, esp. that of Moscow: (*cap.*) the Soviet government.
[Russ. *kreml*.]

krona, *kroo'nà*, a coin of Sweden:—*pl.* **kro'nor.**
krone, *krōn'ė*, *n.* a coin of Denmark: a coin of Norway.—*pl.* **kron'er.**
[Conn. with, and meaning, **crown.**]

kudos, *kū'dos*, *n.* credit, fame, renown.
[Gk. *kȳdos*, glory.]

kultur, *kool-toor'*, *n.* culture: civilisation: a type of civilisation (often used mockingly). [Ger.]

L

laager, lager, *lä'gėr*, *n.* a camp made by a ring of ox-wagons set close together for defence: an encampment. [Afrikaans.]

label, *lā'b(ė)l*, *n.* a small slip placed on or near anything to state its nature, ownership, etc.—*v.t.* to attach a label to: to mark, describe (sometimes with *as*):—*pr.p.* **lā'belling**; *pa.t.*, *pa.p.* **lā'belled.**
[O.Fr. *label*.]

labial, *lā'bi-àl*, *n.* a sound formed by the lips.
lā'biate, *adj.* having a lipped corolla.
[L. *labium*, a lip.]

laboratory, *là-bor'à-tòr-i*, or *lab'*, *n.* a place where scientific experiments are carried on: a place where drugs, etc., are prepared.
[L. *labōr*, work; same root as **labour.**]

labour, *lā'bòr*, *n.* hard work: labourers, artisans, etc.: the pains of childbirth.—*v.i.* to work hard: to take pains: to be oppressed by, suffer through (with *under*; e.g. *to labour under a disadvantage, a false belief*): to move slowly: (*naut.*) to pitch and roll heavily.
labō'rious, *adj.* requiring hard work: wearisome.
labō'riously, *adv.* **labō'riousness,** *n.*
lā'boured, *adj.* showing signs of effort.
lā'bourer, *n.* one who does heavy work requiring little skill: one who works hard.
lā'bour-sav'ing, *adj.* intended to lessen work.
Labour Bureau, Exchange, office for finding work for workers and workers for employers.
Labour Party, a party aiming at giving workers a fair share of wealth and opportunity through public ownership of industries and resources, and by other means: its representatives in parliament.
[L. *labor*.]

laburnum, *là-bûr'nùm*, *n.* a small tree of the pea family with hanging yellow flowers. [L.]

labyrinth, *lab'i-rinth*, *n.* a place full of puzzling windings, a maze.
[Gk. *labyrinthos*.]

lace, *lās*, *n.* a string for fastening: an ornamental fabric woven of fine thread.—*v.t.* to fasten with a lace: to add a dash of spirits to (e.g. coffee).
lac'ing, *n.* and *adj.*
[L. *laqueus*, a noose.]

lacerate, *las'ėr-āt*, *v.t.* to tear, wound: to cause great pain to (feelings, etc.).
lacerā'tion, *n.*
[L. *lacerāre*, *-ātum*, to tear.]

lachrymose, *lak'ri-mōs*, *adj.* shedding tears: given to weeping.
[L. *lacrima*, a tear.]

lacing. See **lace.**

lack, *lak*, *n.* absence or insufficiency (of something).—*v.t.* to have too little of: to have none of.—Also *v.i.* to be absent or too little (usu. in tenses with *pr.p.*;

e.g. *Funds were lacking*; *he is lacking in common sense*.)
lack'-lus'tre, *adj.* without brightness.
[M.E. *lak*, defect.]
lackadaisical, *lak-à-dā'zi-kàl, adj.* sentimental in an affected way: listless.
[From old interj. *lackadaisy*!]
lackey, lacquey, *lak'i, n.* a footman, manservant: a servile, mean-spirited person.
[O.Fr. *laquay*.]
laconic, *là-kon'ik, adj.* expressing, or expressed, in few words.
lacon'ically, *adv.*
[Gk. *Lakōnikos*, a Spartan.]
lacquer, *lak'ėr, n.* a varnish.—*v.t.* to cover with lacquer.
[Fr. *lacre*.]
lacquey. See **lackey.**
lacrosse, *là-kros', n.* a game played with a crosse, a long stick with a shallow net at one end. [Fr.]
lad, *lad, n.* a boy: a youth:—*fem.* **lass.**
[M.E. *ladde*, youth, servant.]
ladder, *lad'ėr, n.* a set of rungs between two supports, for climbing up (or down): a run, e.g. in a stocking, caused by breaking of a thread, the damaged part having the appearance of rungs.—*v.t.* and *v.i.* to cause, or to develop, a ladder, run.
[O.E. *hlæder*.]
lade, *lād, v.t.* to load.
la'den, *adj.* loaded: burdened (with).
la'ding, *n.* loading: cargo: freight.
[O.E. *hladan*, pa.t. *hlōd*, to load.]
ladle, *lād'l, n.* a large spoon for lifting out liquid, etc., from a container: container used for conveying molten metal.—*v.t.* to lift and carry, or deal (out), with, or as if with, a ladle.
[O.E. *hlædel*—same root as **lade.**]
lady, *lā'di, n.* the mistress of a house: used as the feminine of **lord**: (*cap.*) title given to the wife of a lord, a baronet, or a knight and used with Christian name of daughter of duke, marquis or earl, etc.: a woman of refined manners and instincts: —*pl.* **ladies** (*lā'diz*).
lā'dylike, *adj.* like a lady in manners.
lā'dyship, *n.* word used in speaking to, or about, a woman with the title 'Lady' (e.g. *Your Ladyship*; *Her Ladyship*).
lā'dybird, *n.* a little round beetle, often brightly spotted—also **lā'dybug.**
Lady Day, March 25, the day of the Annunciation of the Virgin.
[O.E. *hlǣfdige*, bread-kneader—*hlāf*, loaf.]
lag[1], *lag, n.* act of falling behind, or amount of that fall.—*v.i.* to move too slowly:—*pr.p.* **lagg'ing**; *pa.p.* **lagged.**
lagg'ard, *adj.* slow: backward.
lagg'ard, lagg'er, *ns.*
[Orig. unknown.]
lag[2], *lag, n.* a non-conducting covering for a boiler.—*v.t.* to cover with this.
lagg'ing, *n.*
[Prob. Old Norse *lögg*, barrel rim.

lager[1]. See **laager.**
lager[2]**(-beer),** *lä'gėr, n.* a light beer.
[Ger. *lager*, a storehouse, *bier*, beer.]
lagoon, *là-gōōn', n.* a shallow pond into which the sea flows.
[It. *laguna*—L. *lacūna*.]
laid, *lād.* See **lay** (2).
lain. See **lie** (2).
lair, *lār, n.* the den of a wild beast.
[O.E. *leger*, a bed.]
laird, *lārd, n.* (*Scot.*) a landed proprietor.
[Northern form of **lord.**]
laissez-faire, *lā'sā-fār', -fėr', n.* not interfering with the free action of the individual: the let-alone principle in government, business, etc.—Also **laiss'er-faire'.**
[Fr. *laisser*, to allow, *faire*, to do.]
laity. See **lay** (4).
lake[1], *lāk, n.* a large body of water within land.
[M.E. *lac*—L. *lacus*.]
lake[2], *lāk, n.* a reddish colouring matter.
[Fr. *laque*; from Hindustani.]
Lallan, *lal'àn,* **Lallans,** *n.* broad Scots.
[Scot. form of *Lowland*.]
lama, *lä'mä, n.* a Buddhist priest in Tibet.
la'masery (or *mä'*), *n.* a Tibetan monastery.
[Tibetan *blama* (the *b* silent).]
lamb, *lam, n.* the young of a sheep: its flesh: one gentle as a lamb.
lamb'like, *adj.* gentle. [O.E.]
lame, *lām, adj.* disabled in a leg: unsatisfactory (e.g. *a lame excuse*).—*v.t.* to cripple.
lame'ly, *adv.* **lame'ness,** *n.*
lame duck, a disabled, helpless, or inefficient person: a bankrupt.
[O.E. *lama*.]
lament, *là-ment', v.i.* to wail, mourn.—*v.t.* to mourn for: to regret.—*n.* a show of grief: a sorrowful song or poem.
lamentā'tion, *n.*
lamentable, *lam'ėn-tà-bl, adj.* sad: regrettable.
lam'entably, *adv.* **lam'entableness,** *n.*
[Fr. *lamenter*—L. *lāmentārī*.]
laminated, *lam'in-āt-id, adj.* in thin layers.
laminated plastics, sheets of paper, linen, etc. soaked in a resin and dried.
[L. *lāmina*, a thin plate.]
Lammas, *lam'às, n.* harvest feast, August 1.
[O.E. *hlāf*, loaf, *mæsse*, feast.]
lamp, *lamp, n.* a glass-covered light.
lamp'black, *n.* soot from the burning of oil, gas, tar, etc.: colouring matter made from this.
[Gk. *lampein*, to shine.]
lampoon, *lam-pōōn', n.* a low, abusive satire against a person.—Also *v.t.*
[O.Fr. *lampon*, orig. a drinking-song.]
lamprey, *lam'pri, n.* a water creature that fixes itself to its prey, etc., by its mouth.
[Perh. L. *lambĕre*, to lick, *petra*, rock.]
lance, *lâns, n.* a weapon with a long shaft a spearhead and often a small flag: the

bearer of a lance.—*v.t.* to open (e.g. an abscess) with a surgical instrument.
lan′cer, *n.* formerly, a soldier armed with a lance: a soldier of a regiment (formerly cavalry) called Lancers: (in *pl.*) a square dance of a certain arrangement.
lance corporal, an acting corporal.
[Fr.—L. *lancea.*]

lancet, *lân′set, n.* a surgical instrument used (esp. formerly) for opening abscesses, etc.
[O.Fr. *lancette*; conn. with **lance.**]

land, *land, n.* the solid portion of the surface of the globe: a country: an estate.—*v.t.* to set on land (or water): to bring onto land (e.g. a fish): to succeed in obtaining (e.g. *to land a prize, a job*): (*coll.*) to deal (a person e.g. a blow).—*v.i.* to come ashore: to come down on land (or water): to fall: to come by chance (on).
land′ed, *adj.* possessing land or estates: (*coll.*) in a difficult situation.
land′ing, *n.* a coming to shore or to ground: a place for doing so: level part of a staircase between flights of steps.
land breeze, a breeze blowing from the land towards the sea.
land′fall, *n.* an approach to land after a journey by sea or air: the land so approached.
land′ing-gear, *n.* the parts of an aircraft that carry the load when it alights.
land′ing-stage, *n.* a platform, fixed or floating, on which to land passengers or goods.
land′lady, *n.* a woman who has tenants or lodgers, or keeps an inn.
land′locked, *adj.* enclosed by land.
land′lord, *n.* one who has tenants or lodgers: the master of an inn.
land′lubber, *n.* a landsman.
land′mark, *n.* an object on land that serves as a guide to seamen or others: an event of great importance.
land mine, a mine laid on or near the surface of the ground to be exploded by something passing over it.
land′owner, *n.* one who owns land.
land′slide, *n.* a portion of land that falls down from the side of a hill: in an election, a great majority of votes for one side.
lands′man, *n.* one who lives or serves on land, inexperienced in seafaring.
land′ward, -s, *advs.* toward the land.
land′ward, *adj.* lying toward the land.
to land with (something), (*coll.*) to give, to be given (something considered unpleasant).
[O.E.; conn. Ger. *land.*]

landau, *lan′dö, n.* a carriage with a top that may be opened in the middle and thrown back.
[*Landau* in Germany.]

landscape, *land′skāp, n.* portion of land that the eye can take in in a single view: inland scenery: picture showing this.
[Du. *landschap.*]

lane, *lān, n.* narrow road, street, or passage: a regular course for ships: a division of a road for one line of traffic.
[O.E. *lane, lone.*]

language, *lang′gwij, n.* human speech: a distinct variety of speech (as *English, French, Latin,* etc.): any manner of expressing thought (e.g. *sign language*).
bad language, profane oaths, etc.
[Fr. *langage*—L. *lingua,* the tongue.]

languid, *lang′gwid, adj.* feeble, sluggish, spiritless.
lang′uidly, *adv.* **lang′uidness,** *n.*
languish, *lang′gwish, v.i.* to lose strength: to pine (for): to wear an expression of melancholy tenderness.
lang′uishing, *adj.*
languor, *lang′gòr, n.* state of being languid: listlessness: soft, tender mood.
lang′uorous (*-gòr-ùs*), *adj.*
[L. *languēre,* to be faint, weak.]

lank, *langk, adj.* tall and lean: long and limp: straight and limp.
lank′y, *adj.* lean, tall, and ungainly.
lank′iness, *n.*
[O.E. *hlanc.*]

lanolin(e), *lan′ō-lēn, -lin, n.* fat from wool.
[L. *lāna,* wool, *oleum,* oil.]

lantern, *lan′tėrn, n.* a case for holding or carrying a light.
lan′tern-jawed, *adj.* with long thin jaws, hollow-faced.
Chinese lantern, a collapsible paper lantern.
magic lantern, an instrument by means of which small pictures are thrown in larger form on a screen.
[Gk. *lampein,* to give light.]

lanyard, laniard, *lan′yàrd, n.* a short rope used on board ship for fastening, etc.: a cord for hanging a whistle, etc. round the neck.
[Fr. *lanière.*]

lap[1], *lap, v.t.* to lick up with the tongue: to wash or flow against: to drink (up) greedily.—Also *v.i.*:—*pr.p.* **lapp′ing**; *pa.p.* **lapped.**
[O.E. *lapian.*]

lap[2], *lap, n.* a fold: the part from waist to knees of a person sitting: a round of a racecourse, etc.—*v.t.* to wrap, surround: to make (something) lie partly (over): in a race, to get a lap ahead of (another competitor).
lap dog, a small dog fondled in the lap.
lap of honour, a round of the field run, etc. by a team, person, etc. that has won a notable victory.
[O.E. *læppa,* a loosely hanging part.]

lapel, *la-pel′, n.* part of a coat folded back, continuing the collar.
[Dim. of **lap** (2).]

lapis lazuli, *la-pis-laz′ū-li,* a deep blue stone.
[L. *lapis,* stone, and root as **azure.**]

Lapp, Laplander, *ns.* a native of *Lapland.*
Lap′landish, Lapp′ish, *adjs.*

lapse, *laps, v.i.* to slip, esp. by degrees: to fall away because of lack of effort: to pass into disuse.—*n.* a slip: passage (of time): a failure (in virtue, memory, etc.).
lapsed, *adj.* having fallen into disuse, or into sin or error.
[L. *lapsāre,* to slip.]

lapwing, *lap'wing, n.* a crested kind of plover, the peewit.
[M.E. *lappewinke*—O.E. *hlǣpewince.*]

larboard, *lär'bōrd,-bȯrd, lâb'ȯrd, n., adj.* formerly, port or left (side of a ship).
[M.E. *laddeborde*; origin unknown.]

larceny, *lär'sni, -sėn-i, n.* the legal term in England and Ireland for stealing: theft:—*pl.* **lar'cenies.**
[O.Fr. *larrecin*—L. *latrō,* a robber.]

larch, *lärch, n.* a cone-bearing tree related to the pines and firs.
[Gk. *larix.*]

lard, *lärd, n.* the melted fat of the pig.—*v.t.* to smear with lard: to stuff with bacon or pork: to mix freely (e.g. *He larded his conversation with Latin tags*).
[O.Fr.—L. *lāridum, lārdum.*]

larder, *lär'dėr, n.* a place where food is kept.
[O.Fr. *lardier,* bacon tub; root as **lard.**]

large, *lärj, adj.* great in size or in quantity: pompous.
large'ly, *adv.* mainly, chiefly: to a great extent: pompously.
large'ness, *n.*
a large order, a difficult task.
at large, at liberty: in general (e.g. *the country at large,* the people of the country as a whole): at considerable length.
[L. *largus,* copious.]

largess(e), *lär'jes, n.* money liberally given.
[Same root as **large.**]

largo, *lär'gō, adj.* (*music*) slow and dignified.—Also *n.* and *adv.*
[It.—L. *largus*; same root as **large.**]

lariat, *lar'i-ȧt, n.* a rope for picketing animals: a lasso.
[Sp. *la,* the, *reata,* rope.]

lark[1], *lärk, n.* a family of singing-birds which includes the skylark.
lark'spur, *n.* a flower with calyx suggesting a spur.
[O.E. *laewerce*; conn. Ger. *lerche.*]

lark[2], *lärk, n.* a frolic.—*v.i.* to frolic.
[Perh. from **lark** (1).]

larrikin, *lar'i-kin, n.* (*Austr.*) a hooligan.
[Origin uncertain.]

larva, *lär'va, n.* a developing animal in a state very different from the adult, e.g. the caterpillar of a butterfly:—*pl.* **larvae** (*lär'vē*).
lar'val, *adj.*
[L. *lārva,* a spectre, a mask.]

larynx, *lar'ingks, n.* the upper end of the windpipe.
laryngitis, *lar-in-jī'tis, n.* inflammation of the larynx.
[Gk. *larynx, laryngos.*]

lascar, *las'kȧr, n.* an East Indian sailor, etc.
[Perh. Hindustani, Pers. *lashkar,* army.]

lascivious, *lȧ-siv'i-ŭs, adj.* lustful.
lasciv'iously, *adv.* **lasciv'iousness,** *n.*
[Late L. *lascivus,* playful.]

laser, *lā'zėr, n.* a device for producing a narrow and very intense beam of light.
[*L*ight m*aser.*]

lash, *lash, n.* a thong or cord, esp. of a whip: an eyelash: a stroke with a whip, etc.—*v.t.* to strike with a lash: to fasten with a rope: to attack (e.g. *He lashed him with his tongue,* he said many harsh and painful things to him): to drive, urge (e.g. *He lashed himself into a rage*): to make a sudden or restless movement with (a tail).
lash'ing, *n.* and *adj.*
to lash out, to kick out: to hit out recklessly. [Origin uncertain.]

lass, *las, n.* a girl: a sweetheart.
[Origin uncertain.]

lassitude, *las'i-tūd, n.* weariness, listlessness.
[L. *lassitūdō*—*lassus,* faint.]

lasso, *las'ō, lȧ-sōō', n.* a long rope with a running noose for catching wild horses, etc.:—*pl.* **lasso(e)s.**—*v.t.* to catch with a lasso:—*pr.p.* **lass'ōing** (or *-ōō'-*); *pa.p.* **lass'oed** (or *-ōōd'*).
[Sp. *lazo*—L. *laqueus,* a noose.]

last[1], *lâst, n.* shoemaker's model of a foot.
[O.E. *lāst,* footprint.]

last[2], *lâst, v.i.* to continue in existence: to remain in good state.
last'ing, *adj.*
[O.E. *lǣstan,* to follow a track, keep on.]

last[3], *lâst, adj.* coming at the end of a series: next before the present: coming or remaining after all the others.
last, last'ly, *advs.*
on one's last legs, on the verge of utter failure or exhaustion.
the last post, the second of two bugle calls at the hour of retiring for the night: a farewell bugle call at military funerals.
to be the last person to do a thing, to be the least likely, suitable, willing, etc., to do it.
to die in the last ditch, to fight to the bitter end.
[O.E. *latost,* superl. of *læt*; see **late.**]

latch, *lach, n.* a small catch of wood or metal to fasten a door.—*v.t.* to fasten with a latch.
latch'key, *n.* a small front-door key.
[O.E. *læccan,* to catch.]

late, *lāt, adj.* after the expected or usual time: far on in day or night: recently past: deceased: out of office:—*comp.* **lat'er**; *superl.* **lat'est.**
late, *adv.* **late'ness,** *n.*
late'ly (*adv.*), **of late,** recently.
[O.E. *læt,* slow; conn. Ger. *lass,* weary. *Lætra, latost,* the orig. comp. and superl., developed into **latter, last**; **later, latest** are more modern formations.]

latent, *lā′tėnt, adj.* hidden (as, *a latent talent, latent hostility*): undeveloped, but capable of development.
[L. *latēre*, to lie hid.]

later. See **late.**

lateral, *lat′ėr-ȧl, adj.* of, at, to, from, the side.
lat′erally, *adv.*
[L. *latus, latėris*, a side.]

latex, *lā′teks, n.* milky juice of plants. [L.]

lath, *läth, n.* a thin slip of wood :—*pl.* **laths.** —*v.t.* to cover with laths.
[O.E. *lætt.*]

lathe, *lāTH, n.* a machine for turning and shaping articles of wood, metal, etc.
[Origin uncertain.]

lather, *lâTH′ėr, n.* a foam made with water and soap: froth from sweat.—*v.t.* to spread over with lather.—*v.i.* to form a lather.
[O.E. *lēathor.*]

Latin, *lat′in, adj.* and *n.* (of) ancient Latium, the district round Rome, or its inhabitants, or its language: also (of) languages descended from Latin or (of) peoples speaking them.
Lat′in-Amer′ican, *adj.* and *n.* (a person) of a country of Central or South America where a language derived from Latin (Spanish, Portuguese, French) is the official language.
Late Latin, Latin written after 200 A.D.

latitude, *lat′i-tūd, n.* freedom from restraint or control: angular distance from the equator (e.g. *The latitude of London is between 51 and 52 degrees north of the equator*): (in *pl.*) regions (e.g. *In these latitudes summer is short*).
[L. *lātitūdō,-inis—lātus*, broad.]

latrine, *la-trēn′, n.* a privy, in barracks, etc.
[L. *lātrina—lavāre*, to wash.]

latter, *lat′ėr, adj.* second-mentioned of two: modern, recent.
latt′erly, *adv.* of late: in the last part of a period of time.
Latter-day Saint, a Mormon.
[O.E. *lætra*, comp. of *læt*; see **late.**]

lattice, *lat′is, n.* a network of crossed laths or bars (also **latt′ice-work**): a window with small diamond-shaped panes.
[Fr. *lattis—latte*, a lath; conn. **lath.**]

laud, *löd, v.t.* to praise highly.
laud′able, *adj.* praiseworthy.
laud′ably, *adv.* **laud′ableness,** *n.*
laud′atory, *adj.* expressing praise.
[L. *laus, laudis*, praise.]

laudanum, *löd′(ȧ)-nŭm, n.* tincture of opium.
[Word coined 16th cent.]

laugh, *läf, v.i.* to make sounds with the voice expressing amusement, scorn, etc. —*n.* an act or sound of laughing.
laugh′able, *adj.* amusing, ridiculous.
laugh′ably, *adv.* **laugh′ing,** *n.* and *adj.*
laugh′ingly, *adv.* with a laugh: jestingly.
laugh′ter, *n.* the act or sound of laughing.
laughing jackass. See **jackass.**
laugh′ing-stock, *n.* an object of ridicule.
to laugh in, up, one's sleeve, to laugh secretly.
[O.E. *hlæhhan*; conn. Ger. *lachen.*]

launch[1], **lanch,** *lönch, länch*, or *-sh, v.t.* to throw or hurl: to start (a person, an enterprise) on a course: to cause (a boat, ship) to slide into the water.—*n.* the act or occasion of launching.
launching pad, a platform from which a rocket can be launched.
to launch (out), to throw oneself freely into some activity (e.g. spending money).
[O.Fr. *lanchier*; conn. with **lance.**]

launch[2], *lönch, länch*, or *-sh, n.* the largest boat carried by a warship: a power-driven boat for pleasure.
[Sp. *lancha*; perh. Malay *lanchār*, swift.]

launder, *lön′der, län′-, v.t.* and *v.i.* to wash and iron.
launderette′, *n.* a shop where customers may wash clothes in washing machines.
laun′dress, *n.* a woman who launders.
laun′dry, *n.* a place where clothes are washed: clothes to be washed :—*pl.* **-ies.**
[M.E. *lavander*—L. *lavāre*, to wash.]

laurel, *lö′rėl, n.* the bay tree once used for making honorary wreaths: any closely related tree: (in *pl.*) honours gained.
laureate, *lö′ri-āt, adj.* crowned with laurel: given special honour.
[Fr. *laurier*—L. *laurus.*]

lava, *lä′va, n.* matter thrown out in a molten stream from a volcano.
[It.—L. *lavāre*, to wash.]

lavatory, *lav′ȧ-tȯr-i, n.* a place for washing: now usu. a water-closet.
[L. *lavāre*, to wash.]

lavender, *lav′ėn-dėr, n.* a plant, with pale lilac flowers, yielding sweet-scented oil.
lavender water, a perfume containing oil of lavender.
[M.E. *lavendre*; conn. Fr. *lavande.*]

lavish, *lav′ish, v.t.* to expend, give, very freely.—*adj.* extravagant, unrestrained, very abundant.
lav′ishly, *adv.* **lav′ishness,** *n.*
[O.Fr. *lavasse*, heavy rain.]

law, *lö, n.* the rules of a community or state: a statute: a general statement about facts observed (e.g. *The second law of heat is that heat can never pass spontaneously from a colder to a hotter body*).
law′ful, *adj.* allowed by law: rightful.
law′fully, *adv.* **law′fulness,** *n.*
law′less, *adj.* not controlled by law, unruly, disorderly.
law′lessly, *adv.* **law′lessness,** *n.*
law′yer, *n.* one who practises law.
law′-abid′ing, *adj.* obedient to the law.
law′breaker, *n.* **law′breaking,** *n.*
law court, court of law, place in which persons accused of crimes or other offences are tried: those who try accused persons.

law'suit, *n.* a taking of a claim or dispute to a court of law for judgment.
common law, the unwritten law (esp. of England) arising from ancient usage.
international law, the rules accepted by civilised nations as governing their conduct towards each other.
statute law, law depending on Acts of Parliament (opp. to *common law*).
to lay down the law, to speak in a very positive rather bullying way.
[M.E. *lawe*; from root of **lie** (2), **lay** (2).]

lawn[1], *lön, n.* a sort of fine linen.
[Prob. from *Laon* in France.]

lawn[2], *lön, n.* a space of ground covered with well-kept short grass.
lawn tennis (see **tennis**).
[Earlier *laund*; from O. Fr.; prob. Celt.]

lax, *laks, adj.* slack: not strict in discipline or morals: careless.
lax'ity, lax'ness, *ns.* **lax'ly,** *adv.*
lax'ative, *n.* a medicine having the power of loosening the bowels.
[L. *laxus*, loose.]

lay[1]. See **lie** (2).

lay[2], *lā, v.t.* to cause to lie: to flatten (e.g. crops): to place: to cause (a ghost) to cease haunting: to wager, bet: to put forward (e.g. a claim): (also *v.i.*) to produce (eggs): to set (a trap):—*pr.p.* **lay'ing**; *pa.t.* and *pa.p.* **laid.**
lay'er, *n.* a thickness, covering, or stratum: a shoot bent down to earth in order to take root.
lay'-by, *n.* a place at the side of a road where motor vehicles may stand for a time.
laid up, ill in bed.
to lay about one, to deal blows on all sides.
to lay down, to set, put, down: to surrender, give up (arms, office): to arrange, establish (e.g. plan, rules): to store (supply of wine): to decree (that). See also **law.**
to lay hold of, to seize.
to lay in, to get in a supply of.
to lay off, to take off: to talk volubly: to dismiss temporarily.
to lay oneself out to, to put forth one's best efforts in order to.
to lay out, to display: to spend: to dress in grave-clothes: to fell.
to lay up, to put away, to store, for future use: to prepare future (trouble) for oneself.
to lay wait for, to lie in wait for.
to lay waste, to devastate, destroy.
[O.E. *lecgan*, to lay.]

lay[3], *lā, n.* a short poem telling a story: a song.
[O.Fr. *lai*.]

lay[4], *lā, adj.* of the people: not of the clergy.
lā'ity, *n.* lay persons.
lay brother, sister, one under religious vows, who serves a religious house, but does not have to take part in studies and certain religious services.
lay'man, *n.* one who is not of the clergy: one who does not belong to the profession mentioned e.g. (*Consult a trained lawyer, not a layman, about this*).
lay reader, in the Anglican Church, a layman who reads part of the service.
[Gk. *lāos*, the people.]

layette, *lā-et', n.* a complete outfit for a new-born child. [Fr.]

lay figure, *lā' fig'ūr*, a jointed model of the human body used as a support for drapery: a person lacking character or importance.
[Du. *led* (now *lid*), joint, **figure.**]

lazy, *lā'zi, adj.* disinclined for work or exertion: idle:—*comp.* **lā'zier**; *superl.* **lā'ziest.**
lā'zily, *adv.* **lā'ziness,** *n.*
la'zy-bones, *n.* a lazy person.
[Origin unknown.]

lea, *lē, n.* open country, esp. meadow.
[O.E. *lēah*.]

lead[1], *lēd, v.t.* to show the way by going first: to guide by the hand: to take the principal part in (e.g. *to lead an orchestra*): to convey (e.g. *to lead water to the fields*): to guide (e.g. *This leads me to think*): to live (e.g. *He leads an idle life*).—*v.i.* to be first: to be guide: to form a way (e.g. *This path leads to the pond*):—*pa.t.* and *pa.p.* **led.**—*n.* first place: direction, guidance: an electric wire or cable: a leash for a dog, etc.: a chief part in a play (e.g. *juvenile lead*).
lead'er, *n.* one who leads: a chief: editorial article in a newspaper (also **leading article**).
lead'ership, *n.* office of leader or conductor: ability to lead.
leading edge, the foremost edge of an aeroplane wing or propeller blade (opp. to **trailing edge**).
leading question, a question so put as to suggest the desired answer.
lead'ing-strings, *n.pl.* strings used to lead children beginning to walk.
[O.E. *lǣdan*, to lead, *lād*, a way.]

lead[2], *led, n.* a soft heavy bluish-grey metal: a plummet for sounding: a thin plate of lead separating lines of type: (in *pl.*) a flat roof covered with sheets of lead.—*v.t.* to cover or fit with lead: to separate lines of (type) with leads.
lead'en, *adj.* made of lead: heavy: dull.
lead pencil, a blacklead (see this word) pencil for writing or drawing.
[O.E. *lēad*.]

leaf, *lēf, n.* one of the, usu. green, structures of a plant growing from stem, branch, or root: a petal (as, *a rose leaf*): anything thin like a leaf: a part or division, as of folding doors, table tops, etc.:—*pl.* **leaves** (*lēvz*).
leaf'y, *adj.* **leaf'iness,** *n.*
leaf'less, *adj.* without leaves.

leaf′let, *n.* a little leaf: a short printed instruction, appeal, etc.
[O.E. *lēaf*; conn. Ger. *laub.*]

league[1], *lēg, n.* an old measure of length, varying, but usu. about 3 miles.
[Late L. *leuga,* mile of 1500 Roman paces (Roman pace = space between two positions of the same foot).]

league[2], *lēg, n.* a union for advantage of all who belong to it.—*v.t.* and *v.i.* to join in league:—*pr.p.* **leag′uing**; *pa.p.* **leagued.**
[Through Fr.—L. *ligāre,* to bind.]

leak, *lēk, n.* a crack or hole through which liquid may pass: an escape of gas, electric current, secret information, etc.—*v.i.* to have a leak: to pass through a leak.—*v.t.* to cause to leak or to leak out.
leak′y, *adj.* **leak′iness,** *n.*
leak′age, *n.* a leaking: something that enters or escapes by leaking.
to leak out, to come to be known in spite of efforts at concealment.
[Prob. O.E. *hlec,* leaky.]

lean[1], *lēn, v.i.* to be not quite vertical or upright: to rest (against): to bend (over): to rely (on): to have an inclination, preference (e.g. *I lean to this view*).—*v.t.* to support, rest:—*pa.p.* **leaned** or **leant** (*lent*).
lean′ing, *adj.*—*n.* inclination, preference: state of being not quite vertical.
lean′-to, *n.* a shed whose supports lean upon another building or wall.
[O.E. *hleonian.*]

lean[2], *lēn, adj.* thin, not fat: lacking in quality or contents (e.g. *a lean harvest, purse*).—*n.* flesh without fat.
lean′ness, *n.*
[O.E. *hlǣne.*]

leap, *lēp, v.i.* to jump: to rush eagerly.—*v.t.* to jump over:—*pr.p.* **leap′ing**; *pa.p.* **leaped** or **leapt** (*lept*).—*n.* act of leaping: space passed by leaping.
leap′-frog, *n.* a sport in which one player vaults over another.
leap year, every fourth year (excluding years divisible by 100 but not exactly divisible by 400, e.g. excluding 1900, including 2000), consisting of 366 days, adding one day in February.
[O.E. *hlēapan*; conn. Ger. *laufen,* run.]

learn, *lėrn, v.t.* to get to know: to gain knowledge or skill in: to commit to memory.—*v.i.* to gain knowledge:—*pa.p.* **learned** (*lėrnd*) or **learnt.**
learned, *lėr′nid, adj.* having learning: not in ordinary popular use (as, *learned words*).
lear′ner, *n.* one who learns or is in process of learning.
lear′ning, *n.* knowledge: scholarship.
[O.E. *leornian*; conn. with Ger. *lernen.*]

lease, *lēs, n.* a contract letting a house, etc., for a period: the period for which the contract is made.—*v.t.* to grant or take under lease:—*pr.p.* **leas′ing**; *pa.p.* **leased.**
lessee, *les-ē′, n.* one to whom a lease is granted.
less′or, *n.* one who grants a lease.
[Fr. *laisser,* to leave.]

leash, *lēsh, n.* a line by which a hawk or hound is held.—Also *v.t.*
[O.Fr. *lesse,* thong to hold a dog.]

least. See **little.**

leather, *leᴛʜ′ėr, n.* the prepared skin of an animal: a cricket ball, football.—*v.t.* to thrash.
leath′ery, *adj.* **leath′eriness,** *n.*
leath′er-jack′et, *n.* grub of a cranefly.
patent leather, leather with a finely varnished surface.
[O.E. *lether*; conn. with Ger. *leder.*]

leave[1], *lēv, n.* permission: permission to be absent: period covered by this: formal parting.
leave′-taking, *n.* saying goodbye.
to take leave of, to say goodbye to.
[O.E. *lēaf,* permission.]

leave[2], *lēv, v.t.* to allow to remain: to abandon: to depart from: to bequeath: to refer for decision or action (e.g. *Leave it to me*): to allow (to do; e.g. *Leave me to finish this*).—*v.i.* to depart:—*pr.p.* **leav′ing**; *pa.p.* **left.**
leav′ings, *n.pl.* things left: refuse.
to leave alone, not to interfere with.
to leave off, to stop (doing, etc).
[O.E. *lǣfan.*]

leaven, *lev′n, n.* the ferment that makes dough rise: anything that brings about a change.—*v.t.* to raise with leaven: to transform.
[L. *levāre,* to raise—*levis,* light.]

leaves. See **leaf.**

lecherous, *lech′ėr-ŭs, adj.* lustful.
lech′ery, *n.*
[O.Fr. *lecheor*—*lechier,* to lick.]

lectern, *lek′tėrn, n.* a church reading-desk.
[Late L. *lectrum,* pulpit.]

lecture, *lek′chŭr, n.* a formal talk intended to give information: a tiresome speech, warning or scolding.—Also *v.t.* and *v.i.*
lec′turer, *n.*
lec′tureship, *n.* the position of one whose job is lecturing in a college or university.
[L. *lectūra*—*legĕre, lectum,* to read.]

led. See **lead** (1).

ledge, *lej, n.* a shelf or shelf-like projection.
[M.E. *legge,* prob. from root of **lay** (2).]

ledger, *lej′ėr, n.* the chief account book in which entries from other books are recorded.
ledger line, (*music*) a short line added above or below the stave when required (often **leger line**).
[O.E. *licgan,* to lie, *lecgan,* to lay.]

lee, *lē, n.* the sheltered side.
lee shore, a shore on the lee side of a ship.
lee′ward (*lē′wėrd*; by sailors, *lōō′ėrd*), *adj.* in the direction towards which the wind blows.

lee'way, *n.* the distance a ship, aircraft, etc., is driven to leeward of her true course.
to make up leeway, to make up for lost time, ground, etc.
[O.E. *hlēo(w)*, shelter.]

leech, *lēch*, *n.* a blood-sucking worm: a person who sucks profit out of another: a physician.
[O.E. *lǣce.*]

leek, *lēk*, *n.* a vegetable closely related to the onion—national emblem of Wales.
[O.E. *lēac*, a leek plant.]

leer, *lēr*, *n.* a sly, sidelong, or lecherous look.—Also *v.i.*
leer'y, *adj.* wary, suspicious: knowing.
[O.E. *hlēor*, face, cheek.]

lees, *lēz*, *n.pl.* sediment, dregs, of liquor.
[Fr. *lie.*]

leet, *lēt*, *n.* (*Scot.*) a selected list of candidates.
[Perh. **élite**; but perh. O.E. *hlēt*, lot.]

left[1]. See **leave.**

left[2], *left*, *adj.* on, for, or belonging to, the side that in most people has the less skilful hand (opp. to *right*): (*cap.*) belonging to the political Left.—*n.* the left side: (*cap.*) those members of certain legislative assemblies who sit to the left of the presiding officer—by custom, the most democratic party.
left'-hand'ed, *adj.* having the left hand more skilful than the right: awkward: having a double or an unflattering meaning (*a left-handed compliment*).
left-hand drive, a driving mechanism on the left-hand side of a vehicle.
left-hand side, the left side.
[O.E. *left* for *lyft*, weak.]

leg, *leg*, *n.* a walking limb: a long, slender support e.g. of a table: (*cricket*) the part of the field behind and to the right of the batsman: a distinct stage of a course, e.g. of a flight: one event or part in a contest consisting of more than one event or part.
legg'ing, *n.* an outer covering for the lower leg.
legg'y, *adj.* having long and lank legs.
leg before wicket (abbrev. **l.b.w.**) having the leg in front of the wicket and thus saving the wicket.
a leg up, help.
[Old Norse *leggr*, a leg.]

legacy, *leg'à-si*, *n.* something left by will: anything handed down by a predecessor.
legatee', *n.* one to whom a legacy is left.
[L. *lēgāre*, *-ātum*, to appoint by law, leave by will, etc.; same root as **legal.**]

legal, *lē'gàl*, *adj.* of law: lawful.
lēgal'ity, *n.* **lē'gally,** *adv.*
lē'galise, *v.t.* to make legal or lawful.
[L. *lex*, *lēgis*, law.]

legate, *leg'it*, *-āt*, *n.* an ambassador, esp. from the Pope.
legā'tion, *n.* person(s) sent as legate(s) or ambassador(s): the official residence of a legation.
[L. *lēgāre*, *lēgātum*; same root as **legacy.**]

legato, *lā-gä'tō*, *adj.* and *adv.* (*music*) smooth(ly).
[It.—L. *ligāre*, *-ātum*, to tie together.]

legend, *lej'ènd*, *n.* a story handed down from one generation to another but not historically accurate: words accompanying an illustration or picture.
leg'endary, *adj.*
[Late L. *legenda*, to be read; root as **legible.**]

legerdemain, *lej'èr-dē-mān'*, *n.* sleight of hand.
[Fr. *leger*, light, *de*, of, *main*, hand.]

leger line. Same as **ledger line.**

legible, *lej'i-bl*, *adj.* clear enough to be read.
leg'ibleness, -ibil'ity, *ns.* **leg'ibly,** *adv.*
[L. *legĕre*, *lectum*, to read.]

legion, *lē'jòn*, *n.* in ancient Rome, a body of soldiers of from three to six thousand: a military force: a great number: a national association of those who have served in war.
lē'gionary, *n.* a soldier of a legion.
[L. *legiō*, *-ōnis—legĕre*, to levy.]

legislate, *lej'is-lāt*, *v.i.* to make laws.
legislā'tion, *n.*
leg'islātive, *adj.* law-making.
leg'islātor, *n.* a lawgiver: a member of a legislative body.
leg'islāture, *n.* the body of those in a state who have the power of making laws.
[L. *lex*, *lēgis*, law; same root as **legal.**]

legitimate, *li-jit'i-mit*, *adj.* lawful: born to parents who are married to each other: (of e.g. argument, deduction) reasonable, logical.
legit'imacy, *n.* **legit'imately,** *adv.*
legitimā'tion, *n.* act of making legitimate.
[Late L. *lēgitimāre*; same root as **legal.**]

leguminous, *le-gū'min-ùs*, *adj.* having a pod splitting along both sides: of peas, beans, etc.
[Fr. *légume*, a vegetable.]

leisure, *lezh'ùr*, *n.* time at one's own disposal: freedom from occupation.
leis'ured, *adj.* having leisure.
leis'urely, *adj.* and *adv.* not hasty or hastily.
[L. *licēre*, to be permitted.]

lemming, *lem'ing*, *n.* a small northern gnawing animal, closely related to the voles. [Norw.]

lemon, *lem'òn*, *n.* an oval citrus fruit (see **citrus**) with an acid pulp: the tree bearing it.
lemonade', *n.* a drink made with lemon juice.
lemon sole, a small kind of sole.
[O.Fr. *limon* (now the sour lime).]

lemur, *lē'mùr*, *n.* an animal related to monkeys.
[L. *lĕmŭrēs*, ghosts.]

lend, *lend*, *v.t.* to give the use of for a time:

to give, add (e.g. interest, beauty, courage) to something or someone:—*pr.p.* **lend'ing**; *pa.p.* **lent.**
lend'er, *n.*
to lend itself to, to be suitable for, adapt easily to.
to lend oneself to, to give one's support or approval to (e.g, a deception).
[O.E. *lǣnan—lǣn, lān,* a loan.]
length, *length, n.* quality of being long: extent from end to end: the longest measure of anything: a piece (e.g. of cloth).
length'en, *v.t.* and *v.i.* to increase in length.
length'ways, length'wise, *advs.* in the direction of the length.
length'y, *adj.* of great or wearisome length.
length'ily, *adv.* **length'iness,** *n.*
at length, in detail: at last.
[O.E. *lengthu—lang,* long.]
lenient, *lēn'yėnt, lē'ni-ėnt, adj.* (of punishment, person) mild, merciful.
lē'nience, lē'niency, *ns.*
lē'niently, *adv.*
[L. *lēnīre,* to soften—*lēnis,* soft.]
lens, *lenz, n.* a piece of transparent substance (e.g. glass) so shaped as to bring light rays together at a point, or to make them spread out from one:—*pl.* **lens'es.**
[(From its shape) L. *lens, lentis,* lentil.]
Lent, *lent, n.* an annual fast of forty days from Ash Wednesday to Easter, in commemoration of Christ's fast in the wilderness.
Lent'en, *adj.*
[O.E. *lencten,* the spring.]
lentil, *len'til, n.* an annual plant, common near the Mediterranean: its seed used for food.
[L. *lens, lentis.*]
lento, *len'tō, adj., adv.* slow(ly).
[It.—L. *lentus,* slow.]
leonine, *lē'ō-nīn, adj.* lionlike.
[L. *leō, leōnis,* lion.]
leopard, *lep'ȧrd, n.* a large spotted animal of the cat kind.
[L. *leopardus.*]
leotard, *lē'ō-tärd, n.* a skin-tight garment worn by dancers and acrobats.
[Julius *Leotard,* trapeze artist.]
leper, *lep'ėr, n.* one who has leprosy: an outcast.
leprosy, *lep'rȯ-si, n.* a name applied to several contagious skin diseases.
lep'rous, *adj.*
[Gk. *lepros,* scaly.]
leprechaun, *lep'rė-HHön, n.* a small Irish brownie.
[Perh. O.Ir. *lu,* small, *corp(an),* a body.]
leprosy, leprous. See **leper.**
lese-majesty, *lēz'-maj'is-ti, n.* treason.
[L. *laesa mājestās,* injured majesty.]
lesion, *lē'zhȯn, n.* a wound: a change due to disease.
[L. *laedĕre, laesum,* to hurt.]
less, *les, adj.* not so much: smaller.—Also *adv.*
less'er, *adj.* smaller: less important.
less'en, *v.t., v.i.* to make, become, less.
[See **little.**]
lessee. See **lease.**
lesson, *les'(ȯ)n, n.* a portion of Scripture read in divine service: a thing (to be) learned by a pupil at one time: something of moral importance (to be) learned from a story, experience, etc.
[Fr. *leçon*—L. *legĕre,* to read.]
lessor. See **lease.**
lest, *lest, conj.* for fear that.
[O.E. *thȳ lǣs the,* the less that.]
let[1], *let, v.t.* to allow, permit: to grant to a tenant or hirer: to cause (with infinitive without to; e.g. *He will let you know*): used in the imper. without to (e.g. *Let the people sing*):—*pr.p.* **lett'ing**; *pa.p.* **let.**
let alone, not to mention (e.g. *let alone the expense*).
to let alone, not to interfere with.
to let down, to lower: to disappoint, desert.
to let in for, to involve in (e.g. *The trip let me in for more expense than I intended*).
to let off, to discharge (a gun): to excuse.
to let out, to release: to hire: to give away (a secret).
to let, for letting (e.g. *house to let*).
[O.E. *lǣtan,* to permit.]
let[2], *let, n.* hindrance, obstruction (as in tennis): delay.
[O.E. *lettan,* to hinder—*læt,* slow.]
lethal, *lē'thȧl, adj.* causing death.
[L. *lēt(h)ālis—lēt(h)um,* death.]
lethargy, *leth'ȧr-ji, n.* heavy unnatural sleep: lack of interest or energy.
lethar'gic, -al (*-är'-*), *adjs.*
[L. and Gk. *lēthē,* forgetfulness.]
letter, *let'ėr, n.* a mark expressing a sound: a written or printed message: a printing type: (in *pl.*) learning, literature.
lett'ering, *n.* the act of forming letters: the letters formed.
lett'er-card, *n.* piece of paper gummed round the edges for use as paper and envelope combined.
letter of credit, a letter authorising a certain sum to be paid to the bearer.
lett'erpress, *n.* the printed matter in an illustrated book.
the letter, the strict verbal meaning (e.g. *the letter of the law*—often opp. to *the spirit,* the intention of framer of law).
[L. *lītera, littera.*]
lettuce, *let'is, n.* a green plant with large leaves used as a salad.
[L. *lactūca.*]
Levant, *li-vant', n.* the Eastern Mediterranean and its shores.
Levan'tine, *adj.*
[Fr. *levant,* rising (of the sun).]
levee[1], *lev'ā, lev'ē, le-vē', n.* a reception of

men only by a king, etc.—orig. on his rising from bed.
[Fr. *levée*—L. *levāre*, to raise.]

levee², *lev'e, le-vē'*, *n.* an embankment, esp. on the lower Mississippi.
[Fr. *levée*, raised.]

level, *lev'l*, *n.* an instrument for testing that a line or surface is horizontal: a flat stretch of country: height, position, strength, etc., in comparison with some standard (e.g. *The level o the river rose*; *a conference at summit level*; *a high level of intelligence*): appropriate position or rank.—*adj.* horizontal: even, smooth: in the same line or plane: equal in position or dignity.—*v.t.* to make horizontal: to make flat or smooth: to lay flat (e.g. *to level to, with, the ground*): to make equal: to aim (gun, etc. at):—*pr.p.* **lev'elling**; *pa.p.* **lev'elled.**
lev'eller, *n.* **lev'elling,** *n., adj.*
lev'elness, *n.* **lev'elly,** *adv.*
level crossing, a place at which a road crosses a railway at the same level.
lev'el-head'ed, *adj.* having sound common sense.
(**to find**) **one's level,** (to find) the place or rank to which one naturally belongs.
on the level, (*slang*) honest(ly), playing fair.
[L. *lībella*, a plummet—*lībra*, a balance.]

lever, *lē'vėr*, *n.* a bar, turning on a support called the prop or fulcrum, for prizing up an object: anything that exerts influence. —*v.t.* to move as with a lever.
lē'verage, *n.* the power gained by the use of the lever: power, advantage, that can be used to achieve a purpose.
[L. *levāre*, to raise.]

leveret, *lev'ėr-it*, *n.* a hare in its first year.
[L. *lepus*, *lepŏris*, a hare.]

leviathan, *li-vī'ȧ-thȧn*, *n.* a huge water animal: anything of huge size.
[Heb. *livyāthān.*]

levitation, *lev-i-tā'sh(ȯ)n*, *n.* the (illusion of) raising a heavy body in the air without support.
lev'itate, *v.t.* to cause to float in the air.
[L. *levis*, light; same root as **levity.**]

levity, *lev'iti*, *n.* thoughtlessness, frivolity.
[L. *levitās*—*levis*, light; root as **lever.**]

levy, *lev'i*, *v.t.* to raise, collect, esp. an army or a tax: to make (war):—*pr.p.* **lev'ying**; *pa.p.* **lev'ied** (*lev'id*).—*n.* troops or money collected by authority.
[L. *levāre*, to raise; same root as **lever.**]

lewd, *lōōd, lūd*, *adj.* lustful: indecent.
lewd'ness, *n.*
[O.E. *lǣwede*, ignorant, of the laity.]

lexicon, *leks'i-kȯn*, *n.* a dictionary.
lexicog'rapher, *n.* one who makes a dictionary.
lexicog'raphy, *n.*
[Gk. *lexicon*, a dictionary—*lexis*, a word.]

liable, *lī'ȧ-bl*, *adj.* legally responsible (for; e.g. *He is liable for this debt*): under an obligation (to do something): apt (to do, to happen).
liabil'ity, *n.* state of being liable: an obligation, debt, etc.: something disadvantageous:—*pl.* **liabil'ities.**
[Fr. *lier*—L. *ligāre*, to bind.]

liaison, *lē-ā-zon^g*, *li-āz'(ȯ)n*, *n.* (esp. *military*) contact, communication: illicit union between a man and a woman: in French, the linking of a final consonant to the initial vowel or *h* mute of the next word.
[Fr.—L. *ligāre*, bind; conn. **ligament.**]

liana, *li-ä'nȧ*, *n.* a general name for climbing plants in tropical forests.
[L. *ligāre*, to bind; same root as **liaison.**]

liar. See **lie** (1).

libel, *lī'bėl*, *n.* a publication or (loosely) statement damaging to a person's reputation: an unflattering portrait.—*v.t.* to damage the reputation of by a libel: to satirise unfairly:—*pr.p.* **lī'belling**; *pa.p.* **lī'belled.**
lī'beller, *n.*
lī'bellous, *adj.* **lī'bellously,** *adv.*
[L. *libellus*, dim. of *liber*, a book.]

liberal, *lib'ėr-ȧl*, *adj.* generous: ample: broadminded, unprejudiced: (of an education) not specialised or technical, aiming at general culture.—*n.* (*cap.*) a member of the Liberal Party.
liberal'ity, lib'eralness, *ns.*
lib'erally, *adv.*
Liberal Party, a political party founded in 1830 with democratic and liberal aims.
[L. *līberālis*, of a freeman; same root as **liberate.**]

liberate, *lib'ėr-āt*, *v.t.* to set free, release.
liberā'tion, *n.* **lib'erator,** *n.*
liberty, *lib'ėr-ti*, *n.* freedom from captivity or from slavery: freedom to do as one pleases: power of free choice: (in *pl.*) privileges, rights, etc. (as, *civil liberties*): too great freedom of speech or action:—*pl.* **-ies.**—*adj.* of, or having, leave to go ashore (e.g. *liberty man, boat*).
lib'ertine, *n.* one who leads a dissolute life, a rake.
[L. *liber*, free.]

library, *lī'brȧ-ri*, *n.* a building or room containing a collection of books: a collection of books—also of gramophone records.
librā'rian, *n.* the keeper of a library.
librā'rianship, *n.*
[L. *librārium*—*liber*, a book.]

libretto, *li-bret'ō*, *n.* a book of the words of an opera, oratorio, etc.: the text itself: —*pl.* **librett'i, librett'os.**
[It.—L. *liber*, book; root as **library.**]

lice. See **louse.**

licence, *lī'sėns*, *n.* permission: the document by which permission is legally given to drive or run car, keep dog, etc.: legal permission to sell alcoholic liquors, for consumption on the premises (**on'-licence**), or for taking away (**off licence**): too great freedom of action.

li′cense, *v.t.* to grant a licence to: to authorise or permit.
licensee′, *n.* one to whom a licence is granted.
li′censer, *n.* one who grants a licence.
licen′tious, *adj.* given to indulgence of the animal passions, dissolute.
licen′tiousness, *n.*
[Fr. *licence*—L. *licēre,* to be allowed.]

lichen, *lī′kėn, lich′ėn, n.* any of a large group of plants consisting of an alga and a fungus together, growing on stones, trees, etc.
[L. *līchēn*—Gk. *leichein,* to lick.]

lichgate, *lich′gāt, n.* a churchyard gate with a porch under which to rest a bier.
[O.E. *līc,* a corpse; conn. Ger. *leiche.*]

lick, *lik, v.t.* to pass the tongue over: to pass lightly over (e.g. *Flames licked the walls*): (*coll.*) to beat: (*coll.*) to overcome.—*n.* a passing of the tongue over: a slight smear: a blow.
lick′ing, *n.* a thrashing.
to lick into shape, to put into more perfect form, or make more efficient.
to lick the dust, to be utterly defeated.
[O.E. *liccian.*]

lid, *lid, n.* a cover of a container: the cover of the eye.
[O.E. *hlid*—*hlīdan,* to cover.]

lie[1], *lī, v.i.* to make a false statement with the intention of deceiving: to give a false impression:—*pr.p.* **ly′ing**; *pa.p.* **lied.**—Also *n.*
ly′ing, *n.* and *adj.*
liar, *lī′ȧr, n.* one who tells lies, esp. as a habit.
to give the lie to, to charge with falsehood: to show (e.g. a statement) to be false.
white lie, a lie told from good motives.
[O.E. *lēogan* (*vb.*), *lyge* (*n.*); conn. Ger. *lügen.*]

lie[2], *lī, v.i.* to be in, or take, a more or less horizontal position: to be situated: to extend, stretch: to remain in a certain place (e.g. *The book lies on the table*): to remain in a certain state (e.g. *to lie hidden, idle*): to consist (in; e.g. *His charm lies in his high spirits*):—*pr.p.* **ly′ing**; *pa.t.* **lay,** *pa.p.* **lain.**—*n.* slope and direction (e.g. *the lie of the land*).
to lie at one's door, (of a crime, error, blame) obviously to have been committed by, or to belong to, one, not another.
to lie in wait for, to be waiting ready to trap or attack; see also **wait.**
to lie low, to keep quiet or hidden.
to lie to, (of a ship) to lie almost at a stop with head to windward.
to lie up, (of a ship) to be in dock or beached for the winter.
to lie with, to rest with, to belong to as a privilege or as an obligation (e.g. *The decision lies with you*).
to take it lying down, to endure tamely.
[O.E. *licgan*; conn. with Ger. *liegen.*]

lied, *lēt, n.* a German song of ballad, not operatic, type:—*pl.* **lieder** (*lē′der*).
[Ger.]

liege, *lēj, n.* a vassal: a loyal vassal: a lord or superior.
[O.Fr. *lige*; prob. Germanic.]

lieu, *lū, lōō, n.* used in phrase **in lieu of,** in place of, instead of.
[Fr.—L. *locus,* place.]

lieutenant, *lėf-ten′ȧnt, n.* one representing, or performing the work of, another: a commissioned officer in the army or (pronounced *lė-ten′ȧnt*) navy (see *Appendices*): one next in rank to a superior named, as **lieuten′ant-comman′der, lieuten′ant-gen′eral,** officer next in rank below commander, general.
lieuten′ancy, *n.* office or commission of a lieutenant.
lord lieutenant, a magistrate appointed by the sovereign as the chief executive authority in a county.
[Fr. *lieu,* place, *tenant,* holding.]

life, *līf, n.* the sum of the activities of plants and animals that distinguish them from dead matter: the period between birth and death: a series of experiences: manner of living: liveliness: living things: the story of a life:—*pl.* **lives** (*līvz*).—*adj.* lasting for life: of life: (*art*) from a living model.
life′less, *adj.* dead: without vigour: uninteresting because of this.
life′like, *adj.* like a living person: vivid.
life assurance, insurance, any form of insurance payable at a person's death or at a certain age.
life′belt, *n.* a belt either blown up with air, or with cork attached, for holding a person up in water.
life′-blood, *n.* the blood necessary to life: any influence that gives strength and energy.
life′boat, *n.* a boat for saving shipwrecked persons.
life′buoy, *n.* buoy intended to support a person in the water till he can be rescued.
life history, life cycle, the various stages through which a living thing passes up to full development.
life jacket, a sleeveless jacket, of material that will float, for holding a person up in water.
life line, a rope for support in dangerous operations: a line thrown to rescue a drowning person: an essential line of communication.
life′long, *adj.* during the length of a life.
life preserver, a cane with a loaded head used as a bludgeon.
life sentence, a sentence of imprisonment for life (in practice only for a number of years): a lifetime of enduring something.
life′time, *n.* duration of life.
life-and-death struggle, a desperate struggle.

to the life, exactly like the original.
See also **live** (1).
[O.E. *lif*; conn. Ger. *leib*, body.]

lift, *lift, v.t.* to bring to a higher position: to make higher in rank or condition or the opinion of others: to make (one's spirits) joyful: to make (the voice) audible or loud: to take and carry away.—*v.i.* to rise: (of fog, cloud, etc.) to disappear.—*n.* act of lifting: upward movement: conveyance in one's car, etc.: an elevator: the force on an aircraft acting upwards at right angles to the *drag*.
to lift the face, to perform an operation for smoothing out wrinkles.
[Old Norse *lypta*—*lopt*, the air.]

ligament, *lig'a-mėnt, n.* the bundle of fibrous tissue joining the movable bones.
lig'ature, *n.* something that binds.
[L. *ligāre*, to bind; conn. **liaison.**]

light[1], *līt, n.* the agency (electromagnetic radiation) by which objects are made visible: a source of light, as the sun or a lamp: means of kindling: a bright appearance: mental or spiritual illumination (*by the light of nature*): a distinguished person: way of viewing, regarding (e.g. *to look at his action in a favourable, in a different, light*).—*adj.* not dark: bright.—*v.t.* to give light to: to set fire to:—*pa.t.* and *pa.p.* **light'ed,** or **lit.**
light'ness, *n.*
lighten, *līt'(ė)n, v.t.* to make brighter.—*v.i.* to become brighter: to flash.
light'er, *n.* a device for producing a light: one who lights.
light'house, *n.* a building with a light to guide or warn ships or aircraft.
light'ship, *n.* a stationary ship carrying a light, serving as a lighthouse.
light wave, one of the electromagnetic waves on which our seeing depends.
light'-year, *n.* the distance light travels in a year (nearly 6 billion miles)—a unit used to express distances of the stars.
light'ning, *n.* the flash (a very large spark) that marks the discharge of an electrified cloud either to earth or to another cloud.
lightning conductor, a metal rod for protecting buildings from lightning.
to light up, to put on lights (**lighting-up time,** the time when street lights, motor-car lights, etc., must be put on).
according to one's lights, in accordance with one's own standards.
in the light of, taking into consideration (facts learned, etc.).
to bring, come, to light, to discover, reveal, or be revealed.
to see the light, to be born: to come to an understanding of a situation, explanation, problem: to be converted.
to shed light on, to make (e.g. a reason, motive, situation) more clear.
[O.E. *leht*, *lēoht*; conn. with Ger. *licht*.]

light[2], *līt, adj.* not heavy: not as heavy as it should be: not massive in appearance: easy to endure, to do, or to digest: not heavily armed or burdened (e.g. *light infantry, truck*): (of mist, rain, frost) little in quantity, not intense: nimble: gay, lively; (of soil) sandy.—*adv.* in phrases such as *to travel light*, i.e. without much luggage.
lights, *n.pl.* the lungs of an animal.
light'ly, *adv.* in a light way: slightly.
light'ness, *n.*
lighten, *līt'(ė)n, v.t.* and *v.i.* to make, or become, less heavy.
light'er, *n.* a large open boat used in unloading and loading ships.
light'erage, price paid for unloading ships by lighters.
light'-armed', *adj.* with light weapons and equipment.
light engine, a locomotive without a train.
light'-fing'ered, *adj.* light or active with one's fingers: thievish.
light'-head'ed, *adj.* giddy, delirious: thoughtless, unsteady.
light'-heart'ed, *adj.* merry of heart: free from anxiety, cheerful.
light industry. See **industry.**
light'-mind'ed, *adj.* frivolous.
light'weight, *n.* (*boxing*) a man not more than 9 st. 9 lb. (amateur 7 lb.) or less than 9 st.: a person of little importance.
[O.E. *līht*, *lēoht*; conn. Ger. *leicht*.]

light[3], *līt, v.i.* to come by chance (on):—*pa.t.* and *pa.p.* **light'ed** or **lit.**
[O.E. *līhtan*, to dismount.]

lighten, lighter (1), (2). See **light** (1), (2).

lignite, *lig'nīt, n.* brown coal, coal retaining the texture of wood.
[L. *lignum*, wood.]

like[1], *līk, adj.* identical: similar.—*n.* one of the same kind: the same thing (e.g. *to do the like*).
lik'en, *v.t.* represent as like, similar (to).
like'ness, *n.* resemblance: one who, or something that, has a resemblance: a portrait.
like'ly, *adj.* probable: promising:—*comp.* **like'lier**; *superl.* **like'liest**:—*adv.* probably.
like'liness, -lihood, *ns.*
like'-mind'ed, *adj.* having a similar opinion or purpose.
like'wise, *adv.* in like manner: also.
to feel like, to be inclined for (any action or thing).
to look like, to suggest the effects, symptoms, or likelihood of (e.g. *It looks like rain*): to appear similar to.
[O.E. *gelīc*; conn. Old Norse *likr*.]

like[2], *līk, v.t.* to be pleased with: to enjoy.—*n.* a liking, in phrase 'likes and dislikes'.
lik(e)'able, *adj.* lovable, attractive.
lik'ing, *n.* a taste (for): satisfaction or taste (e.g. *to my liking*).
[O.E. *lician*; same root as **like** (1).]

lilac, *lī'lȧk, n.* a shrub with roughly

pyramid-shaped clusters of light-purple or white flowers.—*adj.* having purplish colour of lilac flower.
[Sp.—Pers. *lilak*, bluish.]

lilt, *lilt, v.i.* or *v.t.* to sing or play merrily.—*n.* a cheerful song: a springy movement.
[M.E. *lulte.*]

lily, *lil'i, n.* the white madonna lily, the tiger lily, or similar plant with bulb: extended to include other flowers of the same family, as narcissi.—*adj.* resembling a lily: white: pure.
lil'y-liv'ered, *adj.* cowardly (**liver,** 2).
lily of the valley, a small plant with white bell-shaped flowers.
[O.E. *lilie*—L. *lilium.*]

limb, *lim, n.* an arm, leg, or wing: a projecting part: a branch.
out on a limb, alone in a dangerous position.
[O.E. *lim*; conn. Old Norse *limr.*]

limber, *lim'bėr, adj.* supple.
to limber up, to exercise so as to become supple. [Origin unknown.]

limbo, *lim'bō, n.* the borderland of Hell: a place or condition of neglect.
[L. *in limbo—in*, in, *limbus*, border.]

lime[1], *līm, n.* quicklime, the white substance, prepared from limestone, used for cement.—*v.t.* to cover with, or manure with, lime.
lim'y, *adj.* **lim'iness,** *n.*
lime'kiln, *n.* a furnace in which limestone is burned to lime.
lime'light, *n.* a light produced by making quicklime very hot by means of a strong flame.
in the limelight, (on a stage) picked out by a strong light: (in life) conspicuous, attracting public attention.
lime'stone, *n.* a rock composed chiefly of calcium carbonate.
[O.E. *līm*; conn. with L. *līmus*, slime.]

lime[2], *līm, n.* a tree closely related to the lemon: its small greenish-yellow fruit.
([Fr.—Sp. *lima.*]

lime[3], *līm, n.* the linden tree.
[Unexplained form of *lind*, **linden.**]

limerick, *lim'ėr-ik, n.* humorous verse in a five-line stanza, the third and fourth lines being shorter than the others.
[Said to be from *Limerick* in Ireland.]

limit, *lim'it, n.* boundary: largest (or smallest) extent, degree, etc.: restriction.—*v.t.* to fix, or to keep to, a limit for (e.g. *to limit money spent*).
limitā'tion, *n.* the act of limiting: the state of being limited: restriction: shortcoming (e.g. *We all have our limitations*).
lim'itless, *adj.*
limited liability, limitation of the liability or responsibility of individual shareholders of a company by the value of stock each holds in it (abbrev. **Ltd.**).
limited monarchy, one in which the monarch shares power with others.
[L. *līmes*, boundary.]

limousine, *lim'oo-zēn, n.* a large closed motor car with a separate compartment for the driver. [Fr.]

limp[1], *limp, adj.* lacking stiffness: drooping. [Origin unknown.]

limp[2], *limp, v.i.* to walk lamely: (of damaged ship, aircraft, etc.) to move along with difficulty.—*n.* act of limping: a limping walk.
[O.E. *lemp-healt*, lame.]

limpet, *lim'pit, n.* a shellfish, with shell open beneath, that clings to rocks: a person difficult to dislodge, get rid of.
[O.E. *lempedu*, lamprey.]

limpid, *lim'pid, adj.* (of a stream, the air, eyes, etc.) clear.
limpid'ity, lim'pidness, *ns.*
[L. *limpidus*, liquid.]

linchpin, *linch'pin*, or *linsh'-, n.* a pin used to keep a wheel on its axle-tree.
[O.E. *lynis*, axle, and **pin.**]

linden, *lin'den, n.* a tree with heart-shaped leaves with notched edges, the lime.
[O.E. *linden* (adj.)—*lind*; Ger. *linde.*]

line[1], *līn, v.t.* to cover on the inside.
lin'ing, *n.*
[O.E. *līn*, flax.]

line[2], *līn, n.* a thread, cord, rope: a long narrow mark or band: (in *pl.*) outline (e.g. of a ship): a wrinkle: a row (e.g. of trees, people, printed words): lineage: a route, system: a railroad: a service of ships or aircraft: a telegraph or telephone wire or section of wires: a system (of pipes) for conveying e.g. oil: a trench: a series or succession: direction (e.g. *in the line of fire*): method (e.g. *on the lines of*): course of conduct (e.g. *to take the line of least resistance*): sphere of activity or interest (e.g. *in his own line*): class of goods: the equator: one row in the pattern of a poem as written, a division of the rhythm pattern: short letter: the regular army: (in *pl.*) a marriage certificate: (in *pl.*) a certificate of church membership: (in *pl.*) arrangement of troops for defence or attack: (in *pl.*) written punishment task.—*v.t.* to mark with lines: to form lines along (a street): to put in line.
lineage, *lin'i-ij, n.* ancestry, race, family.
lineal, *lin'i-al, adj.* (of ancestry) in a direct line (e.g. *a lineal descendant of the poet*).
lineament, *lin'i-a-mėnt, n.* feature, esp. of the face.
lin'ear (*lin'*), *adj.* involving measurement in one dimension only (measurement of length, or breadth, or height).
lin'er (*līn'*), *n.* a vessel or aircraft of a regular line or company.
line fish, fish caught with the line.
line(s)'man, *n.* one who attends to lines of railway, telegraph, telephone.

lines'man, *n.* in football, one who marks the spot at which the ball passes the boundary line: in tennis, one who decides on which side of a line the ball has fallen.
hard lines, bad luck.
one's line of country, one's field of study or interest.
to shoot a line, (*slang*) to boast, exaggerate.
[O.E. *līne*, cord; conn. L. *līnea*, thread.]

linen, *lin'ėn*, *n.* cloth made of flax: underclothing: sheets and tablecloths, etc.
[O.E. *līnen* (adj.)—*līn*, flax—L. *līnum.*]

ling[1], *ling*, *n.* a fish resembling the cod.
[Prob. conn. with O.E. *lang*, long.]

ling[2], *ling*, *n.* heather.
[Old Norse *lyng.*]

linger, *ling'gėr*, *v.i.* to loiter: to delay: to remain, last, continue, for a long time, or after the expected time.
ling'ering, *adj.*
[O.E. *lengan—lang*, long.]

lingerie, *lang-zhė-rē*, *n.* women's underclothing.
[Fr.—*linge*, linen—L. *līnum*, flax.]

lingo, *ling'gō*, *n.* (*in contempt*) language.
[L. *lingua*, tongue, language.]

lingua franca, *ling'gwȧ frangk'ȧ*, *n.* any language simplified in use by people of different nationalities, esp. traders.
[Ital., Frankish language.]

lingual, *ling'gwȧl*, *adj.* of the tongue.
ling'uist, *n.* one skilled in languages.
linguist'ic, -al, *adjs.* of languages.
linguist'ics, *n.pl.* the general science of languages.
[L. *lingua*, tongue, language.]

liniment, *lin'i-mėnt*, *n.* a kind of thin, usu. oily, ointment for rubbing the skin.
[L. *linĕre*, to besmear.]

link, *lingk*, *n.* a ring of a chain: a single part of a series: anything connecting.—*v.t.* to connect as by a link.—*v.i.* to be connected.
link'age, (*-ij*), *n.* act of linking or state of being linked.
missing link, something needed to complete a series: a supposed creature between man and his ape-like ancestors.
[O.E. *hlence*; conn. Ger. *gelenk*, joint.]

links, *lingks*, *n.pl.* a stretch of more or less flat ground along a seashore: a golf course.
[O.E. *hlinc*, a ridge of land, a bank.]

linnet, *lin'it*, *n.* a common finch (so called because it likes flax seed).
[O. Fr. *linot—lin*, flax.]

linocut, *lī'nō-kut*, *n.* a linoleum block cut in relief, or a print from it.
[*lino*leum and **cut**.]

linoleum, *li-nō'li-ům*, *-nōl'yům*, *n.* a material for covering floors, in making which linseed oil is used.
[L. *līnum*, flax, *oleum*, oil.]

Linotype, *līn'ō-tīp*, *n.* a machine producing castings of complete lines of words, etc.
[**line o' type.** Registered trademark.]

linseed, *lin'sēd*, *n.* flax seed.
linseed oil, oil from flax seed.
[O.E. *līn*, flax, *sǣd*, seed.]

lint, *lint*, *n.* linen scraped into a soft woolly substance for dressing wounds: fine pieces of fluff.
[M.E. *lynt*; conn. with O.E. *līn*, flax.]

lintel, *lint'(ė)l*, *n.* a timber or stone over a doorway or window.
[O.Fr. *lintel*—L. *līmes*, *-itis*, border.]

lion, *lī'ȯn*, *n.* a large, tawny flesh-eating animal of the cat family (*fem.* **lī'oness**): a very brave man: a famous person.
lī'onise, *v.t.* to treat (a person) as a celebrity.
lī'on-hear'ted, *adj.* of great courage.
lion's share, the largest share.
See also **leonine.**
[L. *leō*, *-ōnis.*]

lip, *lip*, *n.* either of the flaps of flesh in front of the teeth by which things are taken into the mouth: the edge of anything.
lipped, *adj.* having lips, or edges like lips.
lip reading, reading what a person says by watching the movement of his lips.
lip service, insincere expressions of approval or devotion (e.g. *Most of us pay at least lip service to democracy*).
lip'stick, *n.* rouge in stick form for the lips.
[O.E. *lippa*; conn. with L. *labium.*]

liquefy. See **liquid.**

liqueur, *li-kūr'*, or *lē-kėr*, *n.* a strong alcoholic drink, strongly flavoured.
[Fr.—L. *liquor*, liquid.]

liquid, *lik'wid*, *adj.* able to flow—fluid, but not in gas form: clear in appearance (e.g. *liquid eyes*): clear in sound: in cash, or convertible into it (*liquid assets*).—*n.* a liquid substance: a flowing consonant sound, as *l*, *r*.
liquefy, *lik'wi-fī*, *v.t.*, *v.i.* to make, or to become, liquid:—*pa.t.*, *pa.p.* **liq'uefied** (*fīd*).
liquefac'tion, *n.*
liq'uidate, *v.t.* to clear or pay off (a debt): to arrange or wind up (the affairs of a bankrupt): (*coll.*) to do away with, or to kill.
liquidā'tion, *n.* **liq'uidātor,** *n.*
liquid oxygen, helium, etc. these gases reduced to liquid condition at very low temperatures.
[L. *liquēre*, be liquid (*facĕre*, make).]

liquor, *lik'ȯr*, *n.* strong drink: a strong solution of a substance.
[L., liquid; root as **liquid.**]

liquorice, *lik'ȯr-is*, *n.* a plant with a sweet root used in medicine.
[Gk. *glykys*, sweet, *rhīza*, root.]

lira, *lē'rȧ*, *n.* an Italian coin:—*pl.* **lire** (*lē'rā*), **lir'as.**
[It.—L. *lībra*, a pound.]

lisp, *lisp*, *v.i.* to speak with the tongue against the upper teeth or gums, as in saying *th* for *s*: to speak as a small child

does.—Also *v.t.*—*n.* the act or habit of lisping.
[O.E. *wlisp*; conn. Ger. *lispeln.*]

list[1], *list, n.* a series, roll (e.g. of names, articles).—*v.t.* to place in a list.
[O.Fr. *liste*, of Germanic origin.]

list[2], *list, v.i.* to heel, lean, over to one side. —*n.* such a heeling over.
[Perh. **list** (3).]

list[3], *list, v.i.* (old verb) to choose, wish.
list′less, *adj.* without energy or interest, weary.
list′lessly, *adv.* **list′lessness,** *n.*
[O.E. *lystan* (impers.)—*lust*, pleasure.]

listen, *lis′n, v.i.* to give attention so as to hear: to follow advice.
list′ener, *n.*
list′en-in, *v.i.* to listen to a wireless broadcast.
[O.E. *hlysnan.*]

lists, *lists, n.pl.* a ground for jousting (see this), scene of fighting.
to enter the lists, to take part in a contest.
[O.E. (*sing.*) *liste.*]

lit. See **light** (1) and (3).

litany, *lit′à-ni, n.* an appointed form of prayer with responses, in public worship.
[Gk. *litesthai*, to pray.]

literal, *lit′ėr-àl, adj.* according to the plain, strict meaning with no exaggeration and nothing added by the imagination: following the meaning word for word (*a literal translation*): (of a person) unimaginative.
lit′erally, *adv.* **lit′eralness,** *n.*
[L. *litera, littera*, a letter.]

literary, *lit′ėr-àr-i, adj.* of literature or learning: concerned with the writing of books.
lit′eracy, *n.* state of being literate.
lit′erate (*-it*), *adj.* able to read and write.
literature, *lit′(ė)rà-chùr, n.* compositions in verse or prose, esp. those of fine quality: the whole body of literary compositions in a language: the whole body of writings on a given subject: writer's profession.
[Same root as **literal.**]

lithe, *lī*TH, *adj.* bending easily, supple.
lithe′ness, *n.*
[O.E. *lithe*, soft, mild.]

lithium, *lith′i-ùm, n.* the lightest metal.
[Gk. *lithos*, stone.]

lithograph, *lith′ō-grâf, v.t.* to print from stone, or a substitute, with greasy ink.—*n.* a print so made (*abbrev.* **lī′tho**).
lithog′rapher, *n.* **lithog′raphy,** *n.*
lithograph′ic, -al, *adjs.* **-ically,** *adv.*
[Gk. *lithos*, stone, *graphein*, to write.]

litigate, *lit′i-gāt, v.i.* to go to law.—*v.t.* to contest at law.
litigā′tion, *n.*
lit′igant, *n.* person engaged in lawsuit.
[L. *lis, lītis*, a dispute, *agĕre*, to do.]

litmus, *lit′mùs, n.* a substance, orig. obtained from certain lichens, turned red by acids, blue by bases.
[Old Norse *litr*, dye, *mosi*, moss.]

litre, *lē′tėr, n.* metric unit of capacity (see *Appendices*). [Fr.]

litter, *lit′ėr, n.* a heap of straw for animals to lie on: objects, esp. of little value, lying scattered about: a couch carried by men or animals: a number of animals born at one birth.—*v.t.* to cover (e.g. the ground) with scattered objects.—*v.i.* of animals, to produce a litter of young.
[L. *lectus*, a bed.]

little, *lit′l, adj.* small in size: small in amount or importance: not much:—*comp.* **less**; *superl.* **least** (*lēst*).—*n.* a small amount: a short time or distance. —*adv.* not much: to a small degree: not at all (e.g. *He little knows what is going to happen*, i.e. he does not know or suspect).
litt′leness, *n.*
See also **less, lesser, lessen.**
Little Bear, the northern group of stars that contains the pole star.
the little man, the underdog.
to make, think, little of (see **make, think**).
[O.E. *lȳtel*; *lǣssa, lǣst.*]

littoral, *lit′ōr-àl, adj.* belonging to the seashore.—*n.* the strip of land along it.
[L. *lītus, littus, -oris*, shore.]

liturgy, *lit′ùr-ji, n.* the regular form of service of a church.
litur′gic(al), *adjs.* **litur′gically,** *adv.*
[Gk. *leitourgiā.*]

live[1], *liv, v.i.* to have life: to continue to be alive: to dwell: to keep oneself alive (on; e.g. *to live on fish*): to be supported by (with *on*): to get a livelihood (by): to pass one's life (e.g. *to live in luxury*): to be lifelike or vivid.—*v.t.* to spend (e.g. *to live a life of ease*):—*pr.p.* **liv′ing**; *pa.p.* **lived.**
liv′er, *n.*
liv′ing, *adj.* having life: now alive: active, lively: (of a likeness) exact.—*n.* means of keeping oneself alive: the benefice (office to which property or revenue is attached) of a clergyman.
See also **life.**
living wage, a wage on which it is possible for a man and his family to live decently.
living language, one still spoken and still developing.
living prefix, one that can still be used to form new compound words (e.g. *re-*, again, *un-*, as opposed to *ad-*, *for-*).
to live down, to undo the effect of (a misdeed, scandal, etc.) by good conduct.
[O.E. *lifian.*]

live[2], *līv, adj.* having life, not dead (used before noun; e.g. *a live mouse*; but *the mouse was alive*): full of life, energy, activity: burning (e.g. *a live coal*): capable of exploding (e.g. *a live shell*):

(of a broadcast, telecast, or performance in the theatre) heard, seen, as the event takes place, not recorded.—Also *adv.*
lively, *liv'li, adj.* vigorous, active: sprightly:—*comp.* **live'lier**; *superl.* **live'liest.**
līve'liness, *n.*
live rail, a rail carrying an electric current.
live'stock, *n.* domestic animals, esp. horses, cattle, sheep, and pigs.
live wire, a wire carrying an electric current: a person of energy and forcefulness.
[From **alive.**]

livelihood, *līv'li-hood, n.* means of living.
[O.E. *līf*, life, *lād*, course.]

livelong, *liv'long, adj.* whole (*the livelong day*).
[Old word *lief*, dear, and **long.**]

lively, liveliness. See **live** (2).

liver[1]. See **live** (1).

liver[2], *liv'ėr, n.* a large gland carrying out several important functions in the life of the body, formerly thought to be the seat of courage.
liv'erish, liv'ery, *adjs.* suffering from disordered liver: irritable.
[O.E. *lifer*; conn. with Ger. *leber.*]

livery[1], *liv'ėr-i, n.* (*orig.*) the distinctive dress provided for his household by a king or nobleman: uniform worn by menservants.
liv'eried, *adj.* clothed in livery.
livery stable, a stable where horses and vehicles are kept for hire.
[Fr. *livrer*, to deliver, hand out.]

livery[2]. See **liver** (2). **lives.** See **life.**

livid, *liv'id, adj.* black and blue: very pale, esp. with emotion, e.g. anger.
liv'idly, *adv.* **liv'idness,** *n.*
[L. *līvēre*, to be of a lead colour.]

living. See **live** (1).

lizard, *liz'ȧrd, n.* a four-footed scaly reptile.
[Fr. *lézard*—L. *lacerta.*]

llama, *lä'mä, n.* a S. American cud-chewing animal of the camel family.
[Sp.; from native name.]

llano, *lyä'no, lä'nō, n.* one of the vast plains in northern South America:—*pl.* **llan'os.**
[Sp.—L. *plānus*, plain.]

Lloyd's Register, *loidz rej'is-tėr,* a list of ships classified (as A1, etc.) according to type, size, seaworthiness, etc.
[*Lloyd's* coffee-house, where a society carrying out insurance and acting as centre for shipping information, formerly connected with the register, orig. met.]

load, *lōd, n.* a freight or cargo: a burden: a heavy weight or task: the output of an electrical machine, generating station, etc.: the power carried by a circuit.—*v.t.* to put a load on, in: to burden: to give in abundance (*to load him with gifts, honours*): to increase weight of by adding something heavy (e.g. *to load a stick*): to weight (as, *to load dice*) for the purpose of cheating: to charge (a gun, a camera).
load'ing, *n.*
load'line, *n.* line along the ship's side to mark the depth to which her proper cargo causes her to sink.
load'-shedding, *n.* temporarily reducing the amount of electricity sent out by a power station.
[O.E. *lād*, course, journey, conveyance; confused with **lade,** not same root.]

loadstar. Same as **lodestar.**

loadstone. Same as **lodestone.**

loaf[1], *lōf, n.* a regularly shaped mass of bread:—*pl.* **loaves** (*lōvz*).
loaf'-sug'ar, *n.* sugar in the form of a cone, often later formed into cubes.
[O.E. *hlāf*, bread.]

loaf[2], *lōf, v.i.* to loiter, pass time idly.
loaf'er, *n.* [Origin uncertain.]

loam, *lōm, n.* a fertile soil containing vegetable matter.
[O.E. *lām*; conn. with Ger. *lehm.*]

loan, *lōn, n.* anything lent: the act of lending.—*v.t.* (chiefly *U.S.*) to lend.
[Old Norse *lān.*]

loath, loth, *lōth, adj.* unwilling (to).
nothing lo(a)th, willing, willingly.
[O.E. *lāth*, hateful.]

loathe, *lōTH, v.t.* to dislike greatly.
loath'ing, *n.*
loath'some (*th* or TH), *adj.* arousing loathing, horrible.
[O.E. *lāthian*—*lāth*; root as **loath.**]

loaves. See **loaf** (1).

lob, *lob, n.* in cricket, a slow high underhand ball: in tennis, a ball high overhead dropping near the back of the court.—*v.t.* to bowl or strike (a ball) as a lob:—*pr.p.* **lobb'ing**; *pa.p.* **lobbed.** [Prob. Du.]

lobate. See **lobe.**

lobby, *lob'i, n.* a hall or passage serving as an entrance usu. to several rooms.—*v.i.* to frequent the lobby of a legislative chamber (e.g. House of Commons) with the intention of influencing members' votes:—*pr.p.* **lobb'ying**; *pa.p.* **lobb'ied.**
[Late L. *lobia*; conn. Ger. *laub*, leaf.]

lobe, *lōb, n.* the soft lower part of the ear: a division of the lungs, brain, etc.: a division of a leaf.
lob'āte, lobed, *adjs.* having or consisting of lobes.
[Gk. *lobos.*]

lobster, *lob'stėr, n.* a shellfish with large claws, used for food.
[O.E. *loppestre*—L. *locusta.*]

lobworm, *lob'wûrm, n.* a lugworm.
[Old word, *lob*, something thick.]

local, *lō'kȧl, adj.* of a place: confined to a spot or district.—*n.* (*coll.*) the local inn or public house.
lō'cally, *adv.* near the place mentioned: in (a) certain place(s).
local'ity, *n.* position: a district: *pl.* **-ies.**
locale (*-käl'*), *n.* the scene (of an event).

lō'calise, *v.t.* to confine or restrict to a place or area.
locāte, *v.t.* to set in a particular position: to situate: to find the place of.
locā'tion, *n.* act of locating: situation.
local colour, details characteristic of the time or place spoken of.
local government, administration of local affairs of towns, counties, etc., opp. to national or central government.
on location, (*cinema*) in natural surroundings outside the studio.
[L. *locālis—locus*, a place.]

loch, *loH*, *n.* a lake: an arm of the sea. [Gael.]

lock[1], *lok*, *n.* a device for fastening doors, etc.: an enclosure in a canal for raising or lowering boats: the part of a firearm by which the charge is exploded: a grapple in wrestling.—*v.t.* to fasten with a lock: to close fast: to make immovable: to embrace closely.—Also *v.i.*
lock'er, *n.* a small cupboard, esp. for sports gear.
lock'et, *n.* a little ornamental case hung from the neck.
lock'jaw, *n.* a form of tetanus affecting the muscles of the jaw.
lock'out, *n.* the act of locking out, esp. used of the closing of works by employers during a trade dispute.
lock'smith, *n.* a smith who makes and mends locks.
lock'up, *n.* a place for locking up prisoners, motor cars, etc.
lock, stock, and barrel, completely.
[O.E. *loc.*]

lock[2], *lok*, *n.* a tuft or ringlet of hair.
[O.E. *locc*; conn. with Ger. *locke.*]

locomotive, *lō-ko-mōt'iv*, *adj.* capable of, or assisting in, movement from place to place: moving, travelling.—*n.* a railway engine.
locomō'tion, *n.*
[L. *locus*, place, *movēre*, to move.]

locum (-tenens), *lō'kum (-tēn'enz,-ten')*, *n.* substitute for absent doctor, clergyman.
[L. *locus*, a place (*tenēre*, to hold).]

locus, *lō'kus*, *n.* the line (or the surface) formed by taking all positions of a point (or of a line) that satisfy a given condition:—*pl.* **loci** (*lō'si*).
[L. *locus*, place.]

locust, *lō'kust*, *n.* an insect related to grasshoppers, very destructive to crops: a tree whose pods resemble insects.
[L. *locusta*, lobster, locust.]

locution, *lō-kū'sh(o)n*, *n.* word or phrase.
[L. *locūtiō—loquī*, to speak.]

lode, *lōd*, *n.* a vein in rock containing metal.
lode'star, *n.* the star that guides, the pole star: something that guides.
lode'stone, *n.* magnetic iron ore in the form in which it not only is attracted but also attracts.
[O.E. *lād*, a course.]

lodge, *loj*, *n.* a dwelling at a gate to the grounds of a large house: a house occupied during shooting or hunting season: a room at a college gate, etc., for the porter: the meeting-place of a branch of some societies: the branch itself.—*v.t.* to provide (person) with place to stay: to deposit: to fix (in): to make formally (e.g. *to lodge a complaint*).—*v.i.* to reside, on payment for room(s) and attendance, in someone else's house: to become fixed (in).
lodg'er, *n.*
lodg'ing, *n.* a room or rooms hired in the house of another (often in *pl.*).
lodging turn, a turn of railway work that makes it necessary to sleep away from home.
[O.Fr. *loge.*]

loess, *lės, lō'es*, *n.* a deposit of loam in certain river valleys.
[Ger. *löss.*]

loft, *loft*, *n.* a room or space under a roof: a gallery in a hall or church: slope on the face of a golf club.—*v.t.* to cause to rise into the air.
lof'ty, *adj.* very high: high in position, character, etc.: high-flown: haughty:—*comp.* **lof'tier**; *superl.* **lof'tiest.**
lof'tily, *adv.* **lof'tiness,** *n.*
[Late O.E. *loft*; same root as **lift.**]

log[1], *log*, *n.* a thick piece of unshaped wood: an apparatus, orig. a block of wood, for finding a ship's speed: a logbook.—*v.t.* to enter in a logbook.
log'book, *n.* an official record of a ship's or aeroplane's progress: a similar record kept by the headmaster of a school, etc.
logg'erhead, *n.* a blockhead, a dunce.
log'-line, *n.* the line fastened to the log and marked for finding the speed of a vessel.
log'rolling, *n.* causing log(s) to roll to a desired place: (in bad sense) mutual aid among politicians.
at loggerheads, quarrelling.
[Origin uncertain.]

log[2], *log*, abbrev. for **logarithm.**

loganberry, *lō'gan-ber-i*, *n.* a fruit usu. considered to be a cross between raspberry and blackberry, obtained by Judge *Logan.*

logarithm, *log'å-rithm, -riTHm*, *n.* the power to which a base (10 in **common logarithms**) must be raised to produce a given number (e.g. 3 is the logarithm of 1000 to the base 10 because 10^3 or $10 \times 10 \times 10 = 1000$).
logarith'mic(al), *adjs.*
[Gk. *logos*, ratio, *arithmos*, number.]

loggia, *loj'(y)å*, *n.* an open arcade, gallery, or balcony. [It.]

logic, *loj'ik*, *n.* the science and art of reasoning correctly: correctness of reasoning.
log'ical, *adj.* according to the rules of logic.

log′ically, *adv.*
[Gk. *logos*, word, reason.]

logistics, *lo-jis′tiks, n.* the art of transporting, housing, and supplying troops.
[Fr. *loger*, to lodge.]

loin, *loin, n.* the back of a beast cut for food: (in *pl.*) the lower part of the back.
loin′cloth, *n.* a piece of cloth worn round the hips, esp. in India and south-east Asia.
to gird up the loins, to prepare for energetic action.
[O.Fr. *loigne*—L. *lumbus*, loin.]

loiter, *loi′tėr, v.i.* to proceed, work, slowly.
loi′terer, *n.*
[Du. *leuteren.*]

loll, *lol, v.i.* to lie, etc., lazily about, to lounge: (of the tongue) to hang down or out. [Perh. imit.]

lollipop, *lol′i-pop, n.* a large sweetmeat on a stick: any sweetmeat.
lolly, *n.* (*slang*) a sweetmeat (*pl.* **loll′ies**): (*slang*) money.
[Perh. Northern dial. *lolly*, tongue.]

lone, *lōn, adj.* (used before noun) solitary, companionless (e.g. *a lone figure on the deserted beach*; but *he was alone on the beach*).
lōne′ly, *adj.* lacking, or feeling the lack of, companionship: (of place) isolated, with few people:—*comp.* **lone′lier**; *superl.* **lone′liest.**
lone′liness, *n.*
lone′some, *adj.* dismal or depressed because of solitariness.
lone′someness, *n.*
lone wolf, one who prefers to be by himself without companions.
[From **alone.**]

long, *long, adj.* not short—such that there is a considerable distance from one end to the other: (of time) such that there is a considerable interval from the first moment to the last: slow (in coming): tedious: far-reaching:—*comp.* **longer,** *long′gėr*; *superl.* **longest,** *long′gėst.*—*adv.* to a great extent of time: through the whole time (as, *all day long*).—*v.i.* to desire earnestly.
See also **length.**
long′ing, *n.* an eager desire, craving.—*adj.* yearning.
long′ingly, *adv.*
long ago, in the far past.
long′boat, *n.* the largest and strongest boat of a ship.
long′bow, *n.* a great bow drawn by hand (see **crossbow**).
long-dis′tance, *adj.* covering, travelling, etc. a long distance or time.
long′-drawn (out), *adj.* taking an unnecessarily long time.
long′hand, *n.* writing of the ordinary kind, as opposed to *shorthand.*
long′-head′ed, *adj.* far-seeing, shrewd: having a long head.
long leg, (*cricket*) a position in leg distant from the wicket.
long′-lived′, *adj.* living, or lasting, a long time.
long′-play′ing, *adj.* (of record) giving long reproduction because of very fine groove.
long′-range′, *adj.* able to reach a long distance: taking into consideration a long period of time.
long′shoreman, *n.* a stevedore: a man employed along the shore.
long′-sight′ed, *adj.* able to see far but not close at hand: having foresight.
long-sight′edness, *n.*
long stop, (*cricket*) one who stands behind the wicket-keeper and tries to stop balls missed by him.
long′-suff′ering, *adj.* enduring much and patiently.—*n.* long endurance or patience.
long′-term′, *adj.* (of a policy) concerned with the future not just with the present.
long′-tongued′, *adj.* talkative.
long′-wind′ed, *adj.* having ability to run far without rest: (of speaker or of speech) tiresomely long.
long home, the grave.
before long, ere long, soon.
in the long run, in the end.
the long and the short of it, the matter, story, etc. summed up briefly.
to draw the longbow, long bow, to exaggerate, tell tall stories.
[O.E. *lang.*]

longevity, *long-jev′i-ti, n.* great length of life.
[L. *longus*, long, *aevum*, age.]

longitude, *lon′ji-tūd, n.* arc of the equator between the meridian of a place and a standard meridian (usu. that of Greenwich) expressed in degrees E. or W.
longitud′inal, *adj.*
longitud′inally, *adv.*
[L. *longitūdō*, length—*longus*, long.]

look, *look, v.i.* to direct the eyes with attention: to seem: to face (e.g. *The house looks west*).—*v.t.* to express by a look (e.g. *She looked daggers at him*).—*n.* the act of looking or seeing: glance (e.g. *a look of scorn*): appearance.—*imper.* or *interj.* see, behold!
look′er-on, *n.* a mere spectator.
look-in′, *n.* (*coll.*) a chance of success: a share in an activity.
look′ing-glass, *n.* a piece of glass, to which a reflecting back has been added, in which one can see oneself.
look′out, *n.* a careful watch: a place from which to observe: a person employed in watching: prospect: concern (e.g. *That's your lookout*); in last two examples pronounced *look-owt′*.
to look after, to attend to, take care of.
to look at, to consider (e.g. *He would not look at the proposal*).
to look down on, to despise.

to look for, to search for: to expect.
to look in, to watch television.
to look into, to inspect closely, to investigate.
to look on, to be a spectator: to regard, view (e.g. *I look on this as a grave mistake*).
to look out, to watch (**look out!** *interj.* of warning, beware! take care!): to search for or select.
to look over, to examine, but not with great care.
to look sharp (see **sharp**).
to look up, to improve, become better: to pay a visit to (a person): to search for in a book of reference.
to look up to, to respect the conduct, opinions, etc., of.
[Old Norse *lōcian*.]

loom[1], *lo͞om*, *n.* a machine in which yarn or thread is woven into a fabric.
[O.E. *gelōma*, a tool.]

loom[2], *lo͞om*, *v.i.* to appear indistinctly, often threateningly. [Origin uncertain.]

loon, *lo͞on*, *n.* the diver, a fish-eating diving-bird.
[Old Norse *lōmr*.]

loop, *lo͞op*, *n.* a doubling of a cord, chain, etc., through which another cord, etc., may pass: a U-shaped bend (e.g. in a river).—*v.t.* to fasten with, or form into, a loop or loops.
to loop the loop, to move in a complete vertical loop or circle. [Orig. uncertain.]

loophole, *lo͞op'hōl*, *n.* a slit in a wall, etc.: means of escape or of getting round, avoiding obeying, e.g. law. [Orig. uncertain.]

loose, *lo͞os*, *adj.* slack, not tight: not tied: free: not compact: not strict in form or logic (e.g. *a loose statement, argument*): licentious (e.g. *loose living*).—*v.t.* to unfasten, untie.
loose'ly, *adv.* **loose'ness,** *n.*
loos'en, *v.t.* to make loose: to relax (e.g. a hold): to open, as the bowels.—*v.i.* to become loose, or less tight.
loose box, a part of a stable where a horse is kept untied.
at (a) loose end(s). See **end.**
on the loose, on holiday, esp. having a spree.
to break (to let) loose, to escape (to set free) from restraint or control.
[Old Norse *lauss*.]

loot, *lo͞ot*, *n.* plunder.—*v.t.* and *v.i.* to plunder, ransack.
[Hindi *lūt*.]

lop[1], *lop*, *v.i.* to hang down loosely.
lop'-eared, *adj.* having drooping ears.
lop'-sīd'ed, *adj.* leaning to one side, not having the two sides the same.
[Perh. conn. with **lob.**]

lop[2], *lop*, *v.t.* to cut off the top or ends of (esp. a tree): to cut (off unnecessary parts):—*pr.p.* **lopp'ing**; *pa.p.* **lopped.**
[O.E. *loppian*.]

lope, *lōp*, *v.i.* to run with a long stride.
[Old Norse *hlaupa*; conn. with **leap.**]

loquacious, *lō-kwā'shus*, *adj.* talkative.
loqua'ciousness, -quac'ity (*-kwas'*), *ns.*
[L. *loquax*—*loqui*, to speak.]

lord, *lörd*, *n.* a master: a superior: a husband: a ruler: a peer of the realm: the son of a duke or marquis, or the eldest son of an earl: (*cap.*) used as a part of various official titles, as **Lord Mayor, Lord Provost:** (*cap.*) God, Christ.—*v.i.* to act the lord, tyrannise—often **to lord it over** (someone).
lord'ly, *adj.* dignified: haughty: tyrannical: grand.
lord'liness, *n.*
lord'ship, *n.* a word used in speaking to, or about, a man with the title 'Lord' and also certain judges not having this title (e.g. *Your Lordship, His Lordship*): the territory belonging to a lord: rule, authority.
lords spiritual, the archbishops and bishops in the House of Lords—opp. to **lords temporal,** the peers proper.
Lord's Supper, the sacrament commemorating the last supper taken by Christ with His disciples before His crucifixion.
House of Lords, the upper house in the British parliament.
[O.E. *hlāf*, bread, *weard*, guardian.]

lore, *lōr*, *lör*, *n.* the whole body of knowledge (esp. knowledge handed down by word of mouth) on a subject.
[O.E. *lār*.]

lorgnette, *lör-nyet'*, *n.* eyeglasses with a handle.
[Fr. *lorgner*, to squint.]

lorry, *lor'i*, *n.* a road wagon without sides, or with low sides. [Origin uncertain.]

lose, *lo͞oz*, *v.t.* to have taken away from one (e.g. by death or accident): to cease to have: to mislay: to waste (time): to miss (e.g. *to lose one's way*): to cause to perish (usu. in passive; e.g. *The ship was lost in the storm*): to fail to gain—opp. of *win* (a game, prize).—*v.i.* to be unsuccessful: to be worse off as the result of some happening:—*pr.p.* **los'ing**; *pa.p.* **lost.**
los'ing, *adj.* and *n.*
loss, *los*, *n.* the act, or fact, of losing: destruction: defeat: something that is lost: the amount taken away or by which something is made less (e.g. *It is difficult to estimate the loss*).
lost, *lost*, *löst*, *adj.* parted with (e.g. *a long lost friend*): no longer possessed: missing: not won: thrown away (e.g. *a lost opportunity*): squandered: ruined: with attention wholly taken up (e.g. *lost in thought*).
lost to, no longer, or not, feeling, etc. (e.g. *lost to all sense of shame*): no longer belonging, or (of e.g. opportunity) open, to (person).
a losing fight, game, etc., one in which defeat is certain.

a lost cause, an aim, object, that cannot be achieved.

at a loss uncertain what to do.

to lose oneself, to lose one's way: to have all one's attention taken up by (with *in*; e.g. *to lose oneself in a book*).

to be lost (up)on, to be wasted, or have no effect, on (a person).

[O.E. *losian,* to be a loss.]

lot, *lot, n.* an object drawn from among a number so as to reach a decision by chance: one's fortune in life: a separate portion: a large quantity or number (*coll.,* usu. in *pl.,* e.g. *lots of people*).

[O.E. *hlot—hlēotan,* to cast lots.]

loth, *lōth, adj.* Same as **loath.**

lotion, *lō'sh(ȯ)n, n.* a wash (medicine or cosmetic).

[L. *lotiō—lavāre,* to wash.]

lottery, *lot'ėr-i, n.* a distribution of prizes by lot: anything of which the result is a matter of chance.

[It. *lotteria*; of Germanic origin.]

lotus, *lō'tůs, n.* either of two African water-lilies: in Greek legend, a tree of North Africa whose fruit made strangers forget their home.

[L.—Gk. *lōtos.*]

loud, *lowd, adj.* making a great sound: noisy: showy and in bad taste.

loud, loud'ly, *advs.* **loud'ness,** *n.*

loud'-hail'er, (*-hāl'*), *n.* a simple type of loudspeaker.

loud'-speak'er, *n.* an instrument for increasing the loudness of sounds so that they can be heard at a distance.

[O.E. *hlūd*; conn. with Ger. *laut.*]

lough, *loн, n.* the Irish form of **loch.**

lounge, *lownj, v.i.* to loll: to move about without energy or purpose.—*n.* a room where one may lounge.

loung'er, *n.* one who makes a habit of lounging, an idler.

lounge suit, a man's suit, less formal than morning or evening dress.

[Origin uncertain.]

lour, *lowr,* **lower**[1], *low'ėr, v.i.* to look sullen or threatening: to scowl.

lour'ing, low'ering, *adj.*

[M.E. *louren*; conn. Ger. *lauern,* lurk.]

louse, *lows, n.* a wingless insect, a parasite on men and animals: any of various other small parasites on animals or plants: —*pl.* **lice** (*līs*).

lousy, *low'zi, adj.* swarming with lice: (*slang*) of very poor quality, worthy of contempt.

lou'siness, *n.*

[O.E. *lūs,* pl. *lȳs*; conn. Ger. *laus.*]

lout, *lowt, n.* an awkward fellow.

lout'ish, *adj.*

[O.E. *lūtan,* to stoop.]

love, *luv, n.* great fondness, feeling roused by person or thing that gives one delight: strong attachment with sexual feeling: the object of affection: (*cap.*) the god of love, Cupid: a score of nothing in tennis, etc.—*v.t.* to be fond of: to delight in.—*v.i.* to have the feeling of love.

lov'er, *n.*

lov'ing, *adj., n.* **lov'ingly,** *adv.*

lov'able, *adj.* worthy of love.

lov'ably, *adv.* **lov'ableness,** *n.*

love'less, *adj.* without love.

love'ly, *adj.* rousing love or admiration: beautiful: (*coll.*) delightful in any way, including 'amusing'.

love'liness, *n.*

love affair, love and love-making not ending in marriage.

love'bird, *n.* a small parrot, strongly attached to its mate.

love'-letter, *n.* a letter expressing love.

love'lock, *n.* a lock of hair hanging at the ear.

love'lorn, *adj.* forsaken by one's love (O.E. *loren* 'lost'; conn. with **lose.**)

love'sick, *adj.* yearning, melancholy with love.

lov'ing-kind'ness, *n.* kindness full of love, tenderness, mercy.

a lover of, one who has a strong liking for (e.g. *He is a lover of art*).

for love or money, in any way whatever.

in love (with), feeling love, passion (for).

to make love to, to try to gain the affections of: to caress.

[O.E. *lufu*; conn. with Ger. *liebe.*]

low[1], *lō, adj.* not high: not lying or reaching far up: not loud: not high in pitch: small (e.g. *a low price*): feeble, weak: depressed, dejected: vulgar, coarse, indecent: (of latitude) near the equator: —*comp.* **low'er**[2]; *superl.* **low'est.**—*adv.* in, or to, a low position or state: not loudly: cheaply.

low'er[3], *v.t.* to make less high: to let down: to lessen.—*v.i.* to become less high or less.

low'ermost, *adj.* lowest.

low'ly, *adj.* humble in rank: modest in character or conduct.

low'liness, *n.*

low'brow, *n.* and *adj.* (one whose tastes are) not intellectual.

Low Church, (of) a party within the Church of England setting little value on sacraments and ceremonies or the authority of the priesthood.

low'-class, *adj.* of lower class: vulgar.

low comedy, comedy in which actions and happenings, rather than dialogue, are funny.

low'-down', *adj.* low in position: mean, worthy of contempt.

lower case, of small letters as opp. to capitals.

lower class, least skilled and educated, usu. poorest, section of community.—*adj.* **low'er-class.**

lower deck, the (quarters of) petty officers and men.

Lower House, the larger and more

representative branch of a legislature that has two chambers.
low gear. See **gear.**
low′lands, *n. pl.* land low in comparison with higher land, esp. (*cap*). south and east Scotland.
low′land, Low′land, *adj.*
low′lander, Low′lander, *n.*
low′-press′ure, *adj.* employing or exerting little pressure (of steam, steam-engine): at low atmospheric pressure.
low′-spir′ited, *adj.* not lively, sad.
Low Sunday, first Sunday after Easter.
low tide, water, the lowest point of the tide at ebb.
in low water, short of money, etc.
the low-down on, (*U.S. slang*) information, esp. damaging, about (a person, organisation, activity).
[Old Norse, *lagr*; conn. Du. *laag.*]

low[2], *lō, v.i.* to make the noise of cattle, moo.
[O.E. *hlōwan*; conn. with Du. *loeien.*]

lower[1]. See **lour.**

lower[2], **lower**[3]. See **low** (1).

loyal, *loi′ȧl, adj.* faithful.
loy′ally, *adv.* **loy′alty** (*pl.* **-ies**), *n.*
loy′alist, *n.* one who is loyal to his sovereign.
[Fr.—L. *lex, lēgis,* law.]

lozenge, *loz′inj, n.* a diamond-shaped parallelogram: a small sweetmeat.
[Fr. *losange.*]

lubber, *lub′ėr, n.* a clumsy, or lazy, fellow.
[Origin uncertain.]

lubricate, *lōō′bri-kāt, lū′-, v.t.* to oil.
lū′bricant, *n.* **lubricā′tion,** *n.*
lū′bricator, *n.*
[L. *lūbricāre—lūbricus,* slippery.]

lucerne, *lōō-sėrn′, lū-, n.* a valuable plant for feeding horses and cattle, alfalfa.
[Fr. *luzerne.*]

lucid, *lōō′sid, lū′-, adj.* easily understood: clear in mind: sane.
lucid′ity, lu′cidness, *ns.* **lu′cidly,** *adv.*
[L. *lux, lūcis,* light.]

luck, *luk, n.* fortune, good or bad: chance: good fortune.
luck′less, *adj.* unfortunate.
luck′y, *adj.* having good luck: bringing good fortune:—*comp.* **luck′ier**; *superl.* **luck′iest.**
luck′ily, *adv.* **luck′iness,** *n.*
to be down on one's luck, to be experiencing misfortune: to be depressed.
[M.E. *lucke,* from Ger. or Du.; conn. Ger. *glück,* good luck.]

lucre, *lōō′kėr, lū′-, n.* sordid gain: riches.
lu′crative, *adj.* profitable.
lu′cratively, *adv.* **lu′crativeness,** *n.*
[L. *lucrum,* gain.]

ludicrous, *lōō′di-krŭs, lū′-, adj.* absurd.
lu′dicrously, *adv.* **lu′dicrousness,** *n.*
[L. *lūdicrus—lūdĕre,* to play.]

ludo, *lōō′dō, n.* a game played with counters on a board.
[L., I play.]

luff, *luf, v.i.* to turn a ship towards the wind.
[M.E. *lof*(*e*), *loof.*]

lug, *lug, v.t.* to pull along, drag heavily:—*pr.p.* **lugg′ing**; *pa.p.* **lugged.**
lugg′age, *n.* baggage of a traveller.
[Conn. Swed. *lugga,* to pull by the hair.]

lug(sail), *lug′*(*sāl*), *lug′*(*sl*), *n.* square sail on a yard that crosses the mast obliquely.
lugg′er, *n.* a small vessel with lugsails.
[Origin uncertain.]

lugubrious, *lōō-gōō′bri-ŭs, lū′-,adj.* mournful.
lugū′briously, *adv.* **-briousness,** *n.*
[L. *lūgubris—lūgēre,* to mourn.]

lugworm, *lug′wûrm, n.* a worm found in sea sand, used for bait.
[Origin uncertain.]

lukewarm, *lōōk′wörm, adj.* slightly warm: (of e.g. interest, supporters) indifferent, not enthusiastic.
luke′warmly, *adv.* **luke′warmness,** *n.*
[M.E. *leuk, luke,* tepid.]

lull, *lul, v.t.* to soothe, to quiet.—*n.* an interval of calm.
lull′aby, (*-bī*), *n.* a song to lull children to sleep:—*pl.* **-ies.**
[Conn. Swed. *lulla,* Ger. *lullen.*]

lumbago, *lum-bā′gō, n.* a rheumatic pain in the lower part of the back.
lum′bar, *adj.* of lower part of back.
[L.—*lumbus,* loin.]

lumber[1], *lum′bėr, n.* anything no longer of use, esp. if bulky: timber sawed or split.
lum′berer, lum′berjack, lum′berman, *ns.* one employed in **lum′bering,** the felling, sawing, and removal of timber.
[Perh. from **lumber** (2).]

lumber[2], *lum′bėr, v.i.* to move heavily and clumsily.
[M.E. *lomeren.*]

luminary, *lōō′min-ȧr-i, lū′-, n.* a source of light, esp. one of the heavenly bodies: a very eminent person.
lumines′cence (*-es′ėns*), *n.* light (e.g. phosphorescence) that is not the result of high temperature.
lumines′cent, *adj.*
lu′minous, *adj.* giving light: shining: clear.
lu′minously, *adv.*
lu′minousness, luminos′ity, *ns.*
[L. *lūmen,* light—*lūcēre,* to shine.]

lump, *lump, n.* a small shapeless mass: a swelling: the whole together (e.g. *considered in the lump*): a heavy, spiritless person.—*v.t.* to treat as all alike (usu. **lump together**): (*coll.*) to put up with (e.g. *to lump it*).—*v.i.* to form into lumps.
lump′ish, *adj.* like a lump: heavy: dull.
lump′y, *adj.* **lump′iness,** *n.*
[Origin uncertain.]

lunacy, *lōō′nȧ-si, lū′-, n.* a kind of madness once believed to come with changes of the moon: insanity.
lu′natic, *adj.* and *n.*
lunatic fringe, the more extreme in

views or behaviour among the members of a group.
[L. *lūna*, moon; same root as **lunar.**]

lunar, *lōō'nȧr, lū'-, adj.* of the moon.—Also **lu'nary.**
[L. *lūna*, moon—*lūcēre*, to shine.]

lunch, *lunch,* or *-sh, n.* a meal between breakfast and dinner.—*v.i.* to take lunch.
luncheon (*lunch'ȯn, lunsh'*), *n.* lunch.
[Perh. altered from **lump.**]

lung, *lung, n.* one of the organs of breathing, either of two sacs in the body filled with constantly renewed air.
[O.E. *lungen.*]

lunge, *lunj, n.* a sudden thrust, as in fencing.—*v.i.* to make such a thrust.
[Fr. *allonger*, to lengthen.]

lupin, *lōō'pin, n.* a plant of the pea family, with flowers on long spikes.
[L. *lupīnus.*]

lurch[1], *lûrch, n.* in old card games, a state when the winner is far ahead of the loser.
to leave in the lurch, to desert (a person) when he has got into difficulties.
[O.Fr. *lourche.*]

lurch[2], *lûrch, v.i.* to pitch suddenly forward, or roll to one side.—Also *n.*
[Origin uncertain.]

lurcher, *lûr'chėr, n.* a crossbred dog with greyhound characteristics.
[From *lurch*, an old form of **lurk.**]

lure, *lūr, lōōr, n.* something used to entice, a bait.—*v.t.* to entice, tempt away.
[O.Fr. *loerre*; from German.]

lurid, *lū'rid, lōō'-, adj.* ghastly pale: gloomily threatening: sensational.
lu'ridly, *adv.* **lu'ridness,** *n.*
[L. *lūridus.*]

lurk, *lûrk, v.i.* to lie in wait: to be concealed.
[Perh. from **lour.**]

luscious, *lush'ůs, adj.* sweet in a great degree, esp. juicy and delicious.
lus'ciously, *adv.* **lus'ciousness,** *n.*
[Origin unknown.]

lush, *lush, adj.* green and luxuriant.
[M.E. *lasche*, slack.]

lust, *lust, n.* depraved desire: longing desire (for; e.g. *a lust for power*).—*v.i.* to desire eagerly (with *after, for*): to have depraved desires.
lust'ful, *adj.* **lust'fully,** *adv.*
lust'fulness, *n.*
lus'ty, *adj.* vigorous: healthy:—*comp.* **lus'tier**; *superl.* **lus'tiest.**
lus'tiness, *n.* **lus'tily,** *adv.*
[O.E. *lust*, pleasure.]

lustre, *lus'tėr, n.* gloss, brightness: splendour: renown.
lus'trous, *adj.* bright, shining.
[Fr.—L. *lustrāre*, to shine.]

lusty. See **lust.**

lute, *lōōt, lūt, n.* an old stringed instrument shaped like a half pear.
[Arabic *al*, the, *'ūd*, wood, lute.]

luxury, *luk'shů-ri, n.* free indulgence in costly pleasures: anything rare and delightful: something pleasant but not necessary:—*pl.* **-ies.**
luxū'riant (*lug-zūr'*), *adj.* very free in growth: over rich in ornament.
luxū'riance, luxū'riancy, *ns.*
luxū'riantly, *adv.*
luxū'riate, *v.i.* to be luxuriant: to live luxuriously: to revel (in).
luxū'rious, *adj.* supplied with luxuries.
luxū'riously, *adv.* **luxū'riousness,** *n.*
[O.Fr. *luxurie*—L. *luxus*, excess.]

lychgate. Same as **lichgate.**

lying. See **lie** (1); also **lie** (2).

lykewake, *līk'wāk, n.* (*Scot.* and *N. Engl.*) watch by the dead.
[O.E. *līc*, body, **wake.**]

lymph, *limf, n.* a colourless or yellowish fluid in animal bodies: a vaccine.
lymphat'ic, *adj.* of lymph: sluggish.—*n.* a vessel which conveys the lymph.
[L. *lympha*, water.]

lynch, *linch, -sh, v.t.* to condemn and put to death without the usual forms of law.
[William *Lynch* of Virginia (18th cent.).]

lynx, *lingks, n.* a catlike animal noted for its sharp sight.
lynx'-eyed, *adj.* sharp-sighted. [Gk.]

lyre, *līr, n.* musical instrument like harp.
lyre'bird, *n.* an Australian bird having the tail-feathers of the male arranged in a form like that of a lyre.
lyric, -al (*lir'-*), *adjs.* (of poetry) expressing individual emotions of the poet: expressing great enthusiasm.
lyric (*lir'*), *n.* lyric poem: words for song.
[Fr.—L. *lyra*—Gk.]

M

macabre, *ma-kä'br', -bėr, adj.* gruesome, horrible.
[Fr.; perh. Heb. *meqabēr*, gravedigger.]

macadamise, *mȧ-kad'ȧm-īz, v.t.* to cover with small broken stones, so as to form a smooth, hard surface.
[John *McAdam*, road surveyor.]

macaroni, *mak-ȧ-rō'ni, n.* a paste of hard wheat flour, pressed out through small holes to form long tubes, and dried.
[It. *maccaroni* (now *maccheroni*).]

macaroon, *mak-ȧ-rōōn', n.* a sweet cake or biscuit made of almonds, etc.
[Fr. *macaron.*]

macaw, *mȧ-kö', n.* a large long-tailed tropical American parrot.
[Port. *macao.*]

mace[1], *mās, n.* a metal or metal-headed war club, often spiked: a staff used as a mark of authority.
mac'er, *n.* a mace-bearer: in Scotland, an usher in a law court.

mace′-bearer, *n.* an official who carries a mace in a procession in front of a person in authority.
[O.Fr. *mace* (Fr. *masse*, sledge-hammer).]

mace[2], *mās, n.* spice obtained from the same fruit as nutmeg.
[O.Fr. *macis.*]

macerate, *mas′ėr-āt, v.t.* and *v.i.* to soften by steeping.
macerā′tion, *n.*
mac′erator, *n.* an apparatus for pulping paper.
[L. *mācerāre*, to steep.]

Mach number, *mäн num′bėr*, the ratio of the speed of an aircraft to the velocity of sound (e.g. Mach 5 means 5 times the speed of sound).
[*Mach*, German scientist.]

machination, *mak-i-nā′sh(ȯ)n, n.* a crafty scheme, plot.
[L. *māchinārī*; same root as **machine.**]

machine, *mȧ-shēn′, n.* a working arrangement of wheels, levers, or other parts (e.g. a *sewing-machine, printing-machine*): a bicycle or motor bicycle: one who can do only what he is told.—*v.t.* to shape, or finish, with a machine tool: to sew with a sewing-machine: to print.
machin′ery, *n.* machines in general: the working parts of a machine.
machin′ist, *n.* one who makes or repairs machinery: one skilled in the use of machine tools.
machine gun, a gun firing rapidly and automatically for relatively long periods.—Also (with hyphen) *v.t.*
machine shop, a workshop where metal, etc., is shaped by machine tools.
machine tool, a machine driven by power that shapes metal, wood, or plastics by cutting, pressing, or drilling.
See also **mechanic.**
[Fr.—L. *māchina*—Gk. *mēchanē.*]

mackerel, *mak′(ė-)rėl, n.* a food fish, bluish green with wavy markings.
[O.Fr. *makerel* (Fr. *maquereau*).]

mackintosh, *mak′in-tosh, n.* a waterproof overcoat, orig. of rubber-coated material.
[Charles *Macintosh*, the patentee.]

macro-, *mak-rō-*, (as part of word) large: long: too large, over-developed.
[Gk. *makros*, large.]

mad, *mad, adj.* insane: (of a dog) suffering from rabies: rash, foolish: furious (e.g. *a mad bull*): (*coll.*) very angry: frantic (with pain, etc.):—*comp.* **madd′er;** *superl.* **madd′est.**
mad′ly, *adv.* **mad′ness,** *n.*
madd′en, *v.t.* to make mad, esp. furiously angry.
madd′ening, *adj.* **madd′eningly,** *adv.*
mad′cap, *adj.* impulsive, rash.—Also *n.*
mad′house, *n.* a lunatic asylum: a place of confusion and noise.
mad′man, *n.*
like mad, frantically: very energetically.
[O.E. *gemǣd(e)d*, made mad (*pa.p.*).]

madam, *mad′ȧm, n.* a polite form of address to a lady:—*pl.* **mad′ams** or, in letters, **Mesdames** (*mā-dam′*).
[Fr. *madame*, i.e. *ma*, my, *dame*, lady.]

madcap, madden, etc. See **mad.**

madder[1], *mad′ėr, n.* a plant whose root gives a red dye.
[O.E. *mæd(d)re.*]

madder[2], **maddest.** See **mad.**

made. See **make.**

mademoiselle, *mad-mwä-zel, mad-(ė-)mȯ-zel′, n.* a form of address to a young lady.
[Fr. *ma*, my, *demoiselle*, young lady.]

madhouse. See **mad.**

Madonna, *mȧ-don′ȧ, n.* the Virgin Mary, esp. as seen in works of art.
[It., 'my lady'—L. *mea domina.*]

madrigal, *mad′ri-gȧl, n.* a song in several parts sung without accompaniment.
[It. *madrigale.*]

maelstrom, *māl′strȯm, n.* a whirlpool, or more correctly current, off the coast of Norway: any whirlpool: any place or state of confusion and struggle.
[Du. (now *maalstroom*), a whirlpool.]

maestro, *mīs′trō, mä-es′trō, n.* a master, esp. a musical composer or conductor.
[It.]

Mae West, *mā west,* (*slang*) an inflatable life-saving jacket.
[Name of a large-bosomed film actress.]

magazine, *mag-ȧ-zēn′*, also *mag′-, n.* a place for military stores: the gunpowder room in a ship: a compartment in a rifle for holding extra cartridges: a publication issued at intervals, containing articles, stories, etc., by various writers.
[Arabic *makhzan*, storehouse.]

magenta, *mȧ-jen′tȧ, n.* a reddish-purple colour.
[From battle of *Magenta* in Italy, 1859.]

maggot, *mag′ȯt, n.* a legless grub, esp. of a fly: a fad.
magg′oty, *adj.*
[Same root as **mawkish.**]

Magi. See **Magus.**

magic, *maj′ik, n.* any influence that produces results which cannot be explained, or are marvellous or surprising.—*adj.* used in magic (e.g. *magic wand*): using magic: magical.
mag′ical, *adj.* produced by, or as if by, magic: mysterious and beautiful.
mag′ically, *adv.*
magician, *mȧ-jish′ȧn, n.* one skilled in magic.
black magic, magic done with the help of evil spirits.
[Gk. *magikē* (*technē*), magic (art)—Pers.]

magisterial, *maj-is-tē′ri-ȧl, adj.* in the manner of a teacher or a magistrate.
magistē′rially, *adv.*
mag′istracy, *n.* the office or dignity of a magistrate.
mag′istrāte, *n.* one who has power to put the laws into force, esp. a justice of

the peace, or one who sits in a police court.
[L. *magister*, master.]

Magna Carta (Charta), *mag'na kär'ta, n.* the 'Great Charter' obtained from King John, 1215: any charter guaranteeing liberty. [L.]

magnanimity, *mag-nȧ-nim'i-ti, n.* nobleness of nature: generosity.
magnan'imous, *adj.*
magnan'imously, *adv.*
[L. *magnus*, great, *animus*, mind.]

magnate, *mag'nāt, n.* a man of rank or wealth, or of power.
[L. *magnus*, great.]

magnesia, *mag-nē'zhi-ȧ*, or *-zi-*, or *-s(h)i-, n.* a white magnesium salt used as a medicine.
magnē'sium, *n.* a silver-white metal, burning with a dazzling white light.
[Prob. *Magnesia*. See **magnet.**]

magnet, *mag'nit, n.* a piece of iron, or of certain other materials, that attracts or repels other pieces of iron, etc.: any thing, person, having strong attraction.
magnet'ic, *adj.* having the powers of a magnet: strongly attractive.
mag'netise, *v.t.* to make magnetic: to attract or to influence strongly.
mag'netism, *n.* the magnet's power to attract: the science that deals with magnets: attraction, charm.
magnē'to, *n.* a device producing electric sparks, esp. one for lighting the fuel in a motor car engine.
magnetic needle, any slender bar of magnetised steel, esp. that in mariner's compass which always points to the
magnetic north, a direction usu. either east or west of the geographical pole (the true north).
magnetic tape, material on which sound, pictures, or material for a computer, can be recorded.
[Gk. *magnētis* (*lithos*), Magnesian (stone), from one of the towns named *Magnesia*.]

magnificent, *mag-nif'i-sėnt, adj.* splendid in appearance: great in deeds: noble.
magnif'icence, *n.* **-icently,** *adv.*
magnify, *mag'ni-fi, v.t.* to make to appear greater: to exaggerate: (*Bible*) to praise highly:—*pr.p.* **mag'nifying;** *pa.p.* **mag'nified.**
magnificā'tion, *n.*
mag'nitude (*-tūd*), *n.* size: greatness: importance.
magnifying glass, a glass with curved surfaces which makes an object looked at through it appear larger.
[L. *magnus*, great, *facĕre*, to make.]

magnolia, *mag-nō'li-ȧ, -nōl'yȧ, n.* an American and Asiatic tree with large, usu. scented, flowers.
[From P. *Magnol*, French botanist.]

magnum, *mag'nŭm, n.* a two-quart bottle.
[L. *magnus, -a, -um*, large.]

magpie, *mag'pī, n.* a black-and-white chattering bird of the crow family, known also for its habit of collecting objects: a chattering person.
[*Mag*, for *Margaret*, and **pie** (1).]

Magus, *mā'gŭs, n.* a Wise Man of the East:—*pl.* **Ma'gi** (*-ji*).
[L.—Gk. *magos*—Pers. root as **magic.**]

Magyar, *mag'yär, n.* a Hungarian: the Hungarian language.

Maharaja(h), *mä-hä-rä'jä, n.* title given to a great Indian prince:—*fem.* **Maharani, Maharanee** (*-rä'nē*).
[Hindustani, 'great king' ('great queen').]

mahogany, *mȧ-hog'ȧ-ni, n.* a tropical American tree: its wood, valued for furniture making: the colour of this, a dark reddish-brown. [Origin unknown.]

Mahomedan. Same as **Mohammedan.**

mahout, *mä-howt', n.* the keeper and driver of an elephant.
[Hindustani *mahāut, mahāwat.*]

maid, *mād, n.* an unmarried woman, esp. a young one (also **maid'en**): a female servant.
maid'en, *adj.* unmated: first (as, *maiden battle, speech, voyage*).
maiden castle, a castle never captured.
[O.E. *mægden.*]

mail[1], *māl, n.* armour for the body made of steel rings: armour generally.
mailed fist, physical force.
[Fr. *maille*—L. *macula*, a spot, a mesh.]

mail[2], *māl, n.* letters, parcels, etc., by post. —*v.t.* (esp. *U.S.*) to post, send by post.
mail'-bag, *n.* a bag for letters, etc.
mail order, an order by post.
[O.Fr. *male*, a trunk.]

maim, *mām, v.t.* to cripple, disfigure, damage.
[O.Fr. *mahaing.*]

main, *mān, adj.* chief, principal, most important: sheer (e.g. *by main force*).—*n.* the chief pipe in a branching system of pipes: the high sea.
main'ly, *adv.* chiefly, more (of) the thing mentioned than anything else (e.g. *mainly dark grey*; *a crowd mainly of children*).
main'deck, main'mast, main'sail, etc., *ns.* the principal deck, mast, sail, etc. of a ship.
main'land, *n.* a large piece of land as opposed to neighbouring islands.
main'spring, *n.* the chief spring, esp. the spring that causes the wheels to move in a watch or clock: the chief motive or cause.
main'stay, *n.* a rope (usu. wire) stretching forward from the mainmast: chief support.
with might and main, with all one's strength (see derivation).
[O.E. *mægen*, strength.]

maintain, *mėn-tān'*, or *mān-, v.t.* to keep: to continue: to keep up: to keep in good condition: to pay the expenses of:—e.g. *to maintain silence*; *to maintain an attack,*

or *a correspondence*; *to maintain a road*; *to maintain a family*.
to maintain that, to continue to assert that, to argue that.
maintenance, *mān'tėn-ȧns, n.* support: upkeep: means of support.
[Fr. *maintenir*—L. *manū tenēre,* to hold in the hand.]

maize, *māz, n.* an important cereal in America, etc., with large ears—called also **(Indian) corn.**
[Sp. *maíz*—Haitian.]

majesty, *maj'is-ti, n.* greatness and glory (of God): impressive dignity: a title of monarchs:—*pl.* **maj'esties.**
majes'tic(al), *adjs.*
[Fr. *majesté*—L. *mājestās.*]

major, *mā'jȯr, adj.* greater, or great, in size, or importance, etc.—*n.* a person of full legal age (18 years): an army officer (see *Appendices*).
majority, *mȧ-jor'i-ti, n.* (the party having) the greater number—opp. to *minority*: the difference between the greater and the smaller number (e.g. *Black had* 17 *votes, White had* 11; *Black had, therefore, a majority of* 6.)
major scale, one in which the third note is a major third above the first.
major third, an interval of four semitones (e.g. C to E).
[L. *mājor,* comp. of *magnus,* great.]

make, *māk, v.t.* to construct, form (e.g. *to make a chair*): to bring about (a change): to perform (e.g. a journey): to carry out (e.g. an attempt): to compel: to cause (e.g. trouble): to prepare (e.g. tea): to earn (e.g. a living): to approach, reach (e.g. the shore): to amount to:—*pa.t., pa.p.* **made.**—*n.* form or shape: texture: brand.
mak'er, *n.* **mak'ing,** *n.*
made'-up', *adj.* wearing make-up: (of a garment) fully manufactured: (of e.g. a story) invented, not telling of facts.
make'shift, *n.* something, usu. not very satisfactory, used for a time because the proper thing cannot be had.—Also *adj.*
make'-up, *n.* powder, lipstick, etc. for a woman's face: actor's cosmetics, etc.
to be made, a made man, to be sure (because of something that has happened) to succeed in life.
to be the making of (someone), to result in his becoming a self-reliant person, or in his having a successful career.
to make away with. See **away.**
to make believe, to pretend (*n.* **make'-believe**).
to make good. See **good.**
to make light of, to treat as unimportant.
to make little of, to treat as easy, or as unimportant: to understand hardly at all.
to make much of, to make a fuss about, treat as important: to treat (a person) with honour: to understand much of.
to make nothing of, to be unable to understand, to solve, or to do: to consider of no difficulty or importance.
to make off, to run away.
to make off with, to steal.
to make out, to see, but not very clearly: to say, (try to) prove (e.g. *He made out that he had told them he would be late*): to draw up in writing.
to make up for, to atone for.
[O.E. *macian*; conn. with Ger. *machen.*]

mal-, *mal-, pfx.* bad(ly).
maladjusted, *mal-ȧ-jus'tid, adj.* unable to be happy and successful in one's home life, work, etc.
maladjust'ment, *n.*
maladministration, *mal-ȧd-min-is-trā'-sh(ȯ)n, n.* bad management, esp. of public affairs.
See also **male-.**
[Fr.—L. *malus,* bad.]

malady, *mal'ȧ-di, n.* an illness, disease.
[Fr. *maladie.*]

malaria, *mȧ-lā'ri-ȧ, n.* a fever caused by exceedingly small parasites carried from man to man by certain mosquitos.
[It.—*mala,* bad, *aria,* air.]

Malay, *mȧ-lā', adj.* a member of a race living in the Malay Peninsula, etc.: their language.—Also *adj.*—Also **Malay'an.**

malcontent, *mal'kon-tent, n.* a person who is dissatisfied and inclined to rebel.
[O.Fr.]

male, *māl,* of the sex that begets, not bears, young: (*bot.*) having stamens.—Also *n.*
[O.Fr.—L. *mās,* a male.]

male-, *mal-i-,* (as part of word in L. and Eng.) ill, evil.
malediction, *-dik'sh(ȯ)n, n.* a curse.
mal'efactor, (*-fak-tȯr*) *n.* an evil-doer.
malevolent, *mal-ev'ȯ-lėnt, adj.* wishing evil to others.
malev'olence, *n.* **malev'olently,** *adv.*
See also **mal-.**
[L. *male,* ill (*dicĕre,* to say; *facĕre,* to do; *velle* (pr.p. *volens*), to wish.]

malformation, *mal-fӧr-mā'sh(ȯ)n, n.* faulty or bad shape. [Pfx. **mal-.**]

malice, *mal'is, n.* ill-will, spite.
malicious, *mȧ-lish'ùs, adj.*
malic'iously, *adv.*
with malice aforethought, with deliberate intention to commit the evil act.
[Fr.—L. *malus,* bad (see **aforesaid**).]

malign, *mȧ-līn', v.t.* to speak evil of, esp. falsely.
maligner (*-līn'*), *n.*
malignly (*-līn'*), *adv.*
malignity, *mȧ-lig'ni-ti, n.* great ill-will, malevolence: deadliness.
malignant, *mȧ-lig'nȧnt, adj.* anxious to do harm: (of disease) causing death, or going from bad to worse.
malig'nance, -ancy, *ns.*
malig'nantly, *adv.*

[L. *malignāre*, to act maliciously (**malign** borrowed through Fr.).]

malinger, *mȧ-ling′gėr, v.i.* to pretend to be sick in order to avoid work.
[Fr. *malingre*, sickly.]

mallard, *mal′ȧrd, n.* the male of the common wild duck.
[O.Fr. *mallart, malart.*]

malleable, *mal′i-ȧ-bl, adj.* (esp. of metal) able to be beaten, rolled, etc., into shape: (of person) impressionable, easy to influence.
[L. *malleus*, a hammer.]

mallet, *mal′it, n.* a small wooden hammer: a long-handled hammer for playing croquet or polo.
[Fr. *maillet.*]

malnutrition, *mal-nū-trish′(ȯ)n, n.* faulty nutrition: underfeeding. [Pfx. **mal-**.]

malodorous, *mal-ō′dôr-ùs, adj.* evil-smelling. [Pfx. **mal-**.]

malpractice, *mal-prak′tis, n.* evil practice: wrongdoing. [Pfx. **mal-**.]

malt, *mölt, n.* barley or other grain soaked in water, allowed to sprout, and dried in a kiln.—*v.t.* to make into malt.
mal′ted, *adj.*
malt′ster, *n.* one whose job is making malt.
malted milk, powder made from dried milk and malted cereals.
malt liquor, a liquor (e.g. beer) made with malt.
[O.E. *m(e)alt*; conn. with Ger. *malz.*]

maltreat, *mal-trēt′, v.t.* to use roughly, or treat unkindly.
maltreat′ment, *n.* [Pfx. **mal-**.]

mama. See **mamma.**

mamba, *mam′bȧ, n.* a large deadly snake of S. Africa. [African word.]

mamma, mama, *mȧ-mä′, n.* mother.
mamm′y, *n.* a Negro nurse.
[Baby's sound *ma.*]

mammal, *mam′ȧl, n.* any member of the class of animals in which the females feed the young with their own milk.
[L. *mamma*, breast.]

mammoth, *mam′ȯth, n.* a large elephant of a kind no longer found living.—*adj.* very large.
[Russ. *mammot* (now *mamont*).]

mammy. See **mamma.**

man, *man, n.* a human being: human beings in general: a grown-up human male: a valet: a member of a team: a husband: a piece used in playing chess or draughts:—*pl.* **men.**—*v.t.* to supply (e.g. a ship, a gun) with men for service or defence:—*pr.p.* **mann′ing**; *pa.p.* **manned.**
man′ful, *adj.* manly: courageous.
man′fully, *adv.* **man′fulness,** *n.*
man′ly, *adj.* having qualities suitable to a man: brave and frank.
man′liness, *n.*
mann′ish, *adj.* (of a woman) like a man in manner.
man′hood, *n.* state of being a man: manly quality.
mankind′, *n.* the human race.
man′-at-arms′, *n.* a soldier.
man′-eater, *n.* an animal, esp. a tiger, who will eat human beings.
man′handle, *v.t.* to move by man-power: to handle roughly.
man′hole, *n.* a hole large enough for a man to enter e.g. a sewer by it.
man′-of-war′, *n.* a warship.
man′-power, *n.* power supplied by the physical effort of man: number of men available for service in armed forces, etc.
man′servant, *n.* a male servant with domestic duties.
man′slaughter, *n.* unintentional, but blameworthy, killing of a man.
man′trap, *n.* a trap to catch trespassers: a source of danger to human being(s).
man about town, a fashionable idler.
man in the street, the ordinary man
man of letters, a scholar: a writer.
man of the world, one who knows all about, and does not condemn, the more or less sinful conduct of men and women.
to a man, every one, without exception.
[O.E. *mann*; conn. Ger. *mann*, Du. *man.*]

manacle, *man′ȧ-kl, n.* a handcuff.—*v.t.* to handcuff.
[O.Fr. *manicle*—L. *manus*, hand.]

manage, *man′ij, v.t.* to control, to be in charge of: to deal with tactfully: to succeed (*to manage to do something*, to succeed in doing it).
man′ageable, *adj.* that can be done: that can be controlled.
man′agement, *n.* the act, or the art, of managing: the managers of a firm, etc. as a group.
man′ager, *n.*:—*fem.* **man′ageress.**
[L. *manus*, the hand.]

mandarin, *man′dȧ-rin, n.* an official of high rank (orig. in the days of the Chinese Empire): a person with position and influence, e.g. in literary circles: the standard national Chinese language: a small orange.
[Port. *mandarim.*]

mandate, *man′dāt,* (also *-dit*), *n.* a command, esp. one from a higher authority: power given to a nation or person to act in the name of another.—*v.t.* to give (a territory, etc.) into the charge of a nation, etc.
[L. *manus*, hand, *dăre*, to give.]

mandible, *man′di-bl, n.* a jaw or jawbone, esp. the lower: part of the beak of a bird, esp. the lower.
[L. *mandibula*—*mandĕre*, chew.]

mandoline, mandolin, *man′do-lin, n.* a round-backed instrument like a guitar.
[It. *mandolino.*]

mandrill, *man′dril, n.* a large West African baboon.
[Prob. **man,** and *drill* (baboon).]

mane, *mān, n.* long hair on the back of the

neck and neighbouring parts, as in the horse and the lion.
[O.E. *manu*; conn. with Ger. *mähne*.]

manful, etc. See **man.**

manganese, *mang'gȧ-nēz, n.* a hard brittle greyish-white metal.
[Same root as **magnesia.**]

mange, *mānj. n.* inflammation of the skin of animals caused by mites.
man'gy, *adj.* suffering from mange: (of outer clothing) having bare spots, very shabby: squalid, mean:—*comp.* **man'gier**; *superl.* **man'giest.**
man'gily, *adv.* **man'giness,** *n.*
[Fr. *mangé*, eaten.]

mangel-wurzel, *mang'gl-wûr'zl, n.* a variety of beet grown as cattle food.
[Ger. *mangold*, beet, *wurzel*, root.]

manger, *mān'jėr, n.* a trough in which food is laid for horses and cattle.
dog in the manger. See **dog**
[L. *mandūcāre*, to chew, eat.]

mangily, -iness. See **mange.**

mangle[1], *mang'gl, v.t.* to hack, or crush, to pieces: to spoil (e.g. a piece of music) by bad mistakes.
[Same root as **maim.**]

mangle[2], *mang'gl, n.* a machine with rollers for smoothing linen.—*v.t.* to smooth by this means.
[Du. *mangel*—Gk. word meaning 'pulley'.]

mango, *mang'gō, n.* a tree of India, etc., or its oblong fruit:—*pl.* **mang'oes.**
[Port. *manga*; from Malay, from Indian word.]

mangrove, *mang'grōv, n.* a tree that grows on swampy shores, coasts, or river banks in very hot countries. [Orig. unknown.]

mangy. See **mange.**

manhandle, -hole, -hood. See **man.**

mania, *mā'ni-ȧ, n.* madness: very great or unreasonable desire or enthusiasm (e.g. *He has a mania for sports cars*).
mā niac, *n.* a madman: a very rash or too enthusiastic person.—Also *adj.*
ma'nic, *mā'*, or *ma'*, *adj.* [L.—Gk.]

manicure, *man'i-kūr, n.* the care of hands and nails.—Also *v.t.*
man'icurist, *n*
[L. *manus*, hand, *cūra*, care.]

manifest, *man'i-fėst, adj.* easily seen by the eye, or understood by the mind.—*v.t.* to show plainly.
manifestā'tion, *n.* act of showing plainly: revelation, display, expression (e.g. *this manifestation of his ignorance*).
man'ifestly, *adv.* obviously.
[L. *manifestus*.]

manifesto, *man-i-fes'tō, n.* a public written declaration of the intentions of a ruler or of a party.
[It.—same root as **manifest.**]

manifold, *man'i-fōld, adj.* many and varied. —*v.t.* to make several copies of.
[**many,** and suffx. *-fold*.]

manikin, *man'i-kin, n.* dwarf: a little fellow.
[Du. *manneken*, dim. of *man*, man.]

Manila, Manilla, *mȧ-nil'ȧ, n.* Manila hemp, a fibre used in making ropes: paper formerly made from Manila hemp.

manipulate, *mȧ-nip'ū-lāt, v.t.* to handle with skill (e.g. an object, a question): to manage, influence, by unfair means or with cunning (e.g. a person, a committee): to give a false appearance to (e.g. accounts).
manipulā'tion, *n.* **manip'ulator,** *n.*
manip'ulative, *adj.* of, using, manipulation (e.g. *manipulative skill, practices*).
[Late L. *manipulāre*—*manus*, hand.]

manna, *man'ȧ, n.* food of the Israelites in the wilderness (Exodus 16): delicious food.
[Heb. *mān*, a gift.]

mannequin, *man'i-kin, n.* a person, usu. a woman, employed to wear and display clothes to possible buyers.
[Fr.—same root as **manikin.**]

manner, *man'ėr, n.* way (in which anything is done): personal style of speaking or behaving:—*pl.* **mann'ers,** social customs (of a particular time or place): social conduct towards others judged as pleasant and tactful, or the reverse: polite social conduct.
mann'erly, *adj.* showing good manners.
mann'erliness, *n.*
mann'erism, *n.* a noticeable habit in speaking, writing, or behaving—often wearisome to others.
all manner of, all kinds of.
[Fr. *manière*—L. *manus*, hand.]

manoeuvre, *mȧ-nōō'vėr*, or *-nū'-, n.* a clever movement (of troops, ships, or aircraft): a cunning plan: a trick.—*v.i.* to carry out a manoeuvre: to scheme.—*v.t.* to move skilfully, or to manage cunningly.
manoeu'vrable, *adj.* able to be moved in small space, etc.
[L. *manū*, by hand, *opera*, work.]

manor, *man'ȯr, n.* under the feudal system, the land belonging to a nobleman, or as much of it as he kept for his own use: an estate that originated in this way.
manor'ial (*-nōr'*, *-nör'*), *adj.*
man'or-house, *n.* the house of a lord of the manor.
[O.Fr. *manoir*—L. *manēre*, to stay.]

manse, *mans, n.* (in Scotland) the house of a clergyman.
mansion, *man'sh(ȯ)n, n.* a large house.
Mansion House, the official residence of the Lord Mayor of London.
[L. *manēre*, *mansum*, to stay; **manor.**]

mantel, *man'tl, n.* the chimneypiece.—Also **man'telpiece, man'telshelf.**
[Same word as **mantle.**]

mantilla, *man-til'ȧ, n.* a kind of veil covering the head and falling down on the shoulders.
[Sp.; dim. of *manta*, a cloak.]

mantis, *man'tis, n.* an insect rather like a locust, which bends its front legs as if in prayer. [Gk.]

mantle, *man'tl, n.* a cloak or loose outer garment: a covering: a network round a gas burner to give a white light.
[O.E. *mentel,* O.Fr. *mantel*; from L.]

manu-, *man-ū-,* (as part of word) hand.
manual, *man'ū-ȧl, adj.* of the hand: done, worked, or used by the hand: using the hands (*e.g. a manual worker*).—*n.* a handbook: keyboard of organ, etc.
man'ually, *adv.*
manufacture, *man-ū-fak'chủr, v.t.* to make, orig. by hand, now usu. by machinery and on a large scale.—*n.* the process of manufacturing: anything manufactured.
manufac'tory, *n.* a place where goods are made.
manufac'turer, *n.* one who owns a factory (in whole or in part).
manumit, *man-ū-mit', v.t.* to set free (a slave):—*pr.p.* **manumitt'ing**; *pa.p.* **manumitt'ed.**
manumiss'ion (*-mish'*), *n.*
[L. *manus,* hand, *manū,* by, from, hand (*facĕre,* make; *mittĕre, missum,* send).]

manure, *mȧ-nūr', v.t.* to add something, e.g. animal excrement, dung, to (land) so as to make it more fertile.—*n.* something that makes the land give better crops.
[Same root as **manoeuvre.**]

manuscript, *man'ū-skript, adj.* written by hand.—*n.* a book or document written by hand; an author's copy of a work in writing or typescript.
[**manū-,** L. *scrībĕre, scriptum,* to write.]

Manx, *mangks, n.* the Celtic language of the Isle of *Man*.—*adj.* of the Isle of Man or its inhabitants.
Manx cat, a breed of cat with a tail that has never developed.

many, *men'i, adj.* a great number of:—*comp.* **more** (*mōr, mör*); *superl.* **most** (*mōst*).
ma'ny-si'ded, *adj.* having many sides or aspects: having wide interests or varied talents.
ma'ny-si'dedness, *n.*
many a (with *sing.* noun), a large number of (e.g. *many a man*; *for many a day*).
one too many for one, too difficult for one to deal with or overcome.
more, *adj.* a larger number of (see also **much**).—*adv.* to a greater degree (e.g. *more foolish, more widespread*).—Also *n.* (e.g. *It costs a little more*).
most, *adj., adv.,* and *n.*
most'ly, *adv.* for the most part: chiefly.
[O.E. *manig* (*māra, mǣst,* used as comp. and superl.).]

Maori, *mow'ri, mä'ō-ri, n.* member of the brown race of New Zealand: language of this race:—*pl.* **Maoris.** [Maori.]

map, *map, n.* a drawing in outline of the surface features of the earth, the moon, etc., or of part of it, usu. on a flat surface: a similar plan of the stars in the sky.—*v.t.* to make a map of:—*pr.p.* **mapp'ing**; *pa.p.* **mapped.**
to map out, to plan in detail (a route, a course of action).
[L. *mappa,* a napkin, a painted cloth.]

maple, *mā'pl, n.* a tree of several kinds, some of which yield sugar.
[O.E. *mapul,* maple.]

mar, *mär, v.t.* to spoil, impair (e.g. enjoyment, beauty):—*pr.p.* **marr'ing**; *pa.p.* **marred.**
[O.E. *merran.*]

marathon, *mar'ȧ-thȯn, n.* a long-distance footrace (now usu. about 26 miles): any contest that requires great endurance.
[*Marathon,* a little over 20 miles from Athens. A soldier ran this distance without stopping, bringing news of Greek victory over the Persians, 490 B.C.]

maraud, *mȧ-röd', v.i.* to roam about in search of plunder.—Also *v.t.*
maraud'er, *n.*
[Fr. *maraud,* rogue.]

marble, *mär'bl, n.* any kind of limestone taking a high polish: a slab, work of art, or other object made of marble: a little hard ball (orig. of marble) used by boys in play.—*adj.* composed of marble: hard and cold.
[O.Fr. *marbre*; conn. Gk. *marmairein,* sparkle.]

marcasite, *mär'kȧ-sīt, n.* a compound of iron in crystal form used in ornaments.
[Late L. *marcasīta.*]

March, *märch, n.* third month of year.
[*Mars,* Roman god of war.]

march[1], *märch, n.* a boundary: a border district:—used chiefly in *pl.* **march'es.**—*v.i.* to have a common frontier (with).
[Fr. *marche.*]

march[2], *märch, v.i.* to walk in time with regular step: to go on steadily.—*v.t.* to make (someone) march or go.—*n.* a marching movement: distance covered by marching: regular forward movement (e.g. *the march of events*): a piece of music fitted for marching to.
[Fr. *marcher,* walk—L. *marcus,* hammer.]

marchioness. See **marquis.**

mare, *mār, n.* the female of the horse.
mare's'-nest, *n.* a supposed discovery that turns out to be imaginary: a hoax.
mare's'-tail, *n.* a tall, erect marsh plant.
[O.E. *mere,* fem. of *mearh,* a horse.]

margarine, *mär'gȧ-rēn, -jȧ-, -rēn', n.* a butter-like substance made chiefly of vegetable fats.
[Gk. *margaritēs,* a pearl.]

margin, *mär'jin, n.* an edge, border: the blank edge on the page of a book: something extra, beyond what appears to be necessary, to provide for unexpected happenings.
mar'ginal, *adj.*
marginal constituency, a constituency that does not provide a safe seat for any of the political parties.
marginal land, less fertile land which

will be cultivated only in times when there is special need for farm produce.
[Fr.—L. *margō, -inis*, edge, limit.]

marguerite, *mär′gė-rēt*, *n.* the oxeye daisy.
[Fr. *marguerite*—Gk. *margarītēs*, pearl.]

marigold, *mar′i-gōld*, *n.* a plant of the daisy type, or its yellow flower.
[From the Virgin *Mary* and **gold.**]

marijuana, marihuana, *ma-ri-*(H)*wä′nä*, *n.* dried flowers and leaves of hemp smoked in cigarettes for their temporarily exciting effect. [Amer. Sp.]

marine, *mȧ-rēn′*, *adj.* having to do with the sea : done, or used, at sea : living in, found in, the sea.—*n.* a soldier serving on board a ship : shipping as a whole (e.g. *the mercantile marine*).
mariner, *mar′in-ėr*, *n.* a sailor.
mariner's compass, form of compass suitable for use on board ship.
tell that to the marines, only the marines would believe that—I don't (from the sailor's contempt for the marine's ignorance of seamanship).
[Fr.—L. *marīnus*—*mare*, sea.]

marionette, *mar-i-ō-net′*, *n.* a puppet moved by strings.
[Fr., dim. of the name *Marion.*]

marital, *mȧ-rī′tȧl*, *mar′i-tȧl*, *adj.* having to do with a husband or with marriage.
[L. *maritālis*—root as **marry.**]

maritime, *mar′i-tīm*, *adj.* connected with the sea : relating to seagoing or sea trade : having a navy and sea trade.
[L. *maritimus*—root as **marine.**]

marjoram, *mär′jō-rȧm*, *n.* a scented plant used as a seasoning.
[O.Fr. *majorane.*]

mark[1], *märk*, *n.* a sign that can be seen : a stain : a scar : an object aimed at : a sign used as a guide to position : a cross used instead of a signature : a point given as a reward for good work, etc. : a distinguishing sign.—*v.t.* to make a mark on : to value (e.g. an examination paper) by giving marks : to show : to note : to watch closely, give attention to : to keep close to (an opponent) so as to hinder him if he receives the ball (in football, etc.) : to be a feature of (e.g. *Ancient villages marked the lonely valley*) : to be a sign of (e.g. *A movement in the crowd marked his approach*).
marked, *adj.* having marks : striking, noticeable (e.g. *marked signs of improvement*) : watched and suspected (e.g. *a marked man*).
mark′edly, (*-id-*), *adv.* noticeably.
mark′er, *n.* one who marks the score at games : a counter, etc., for scoring.
marks′man, *n.* one who shoots well.
marks′manship, *n.* ability to shoot.
beside the mark, not connected with what is being spoken about.
man of mark, one who has become known for his ability.
to make one's mark, to sign (e.g. a document) by making e.g. a cross : to gain great influence.
to mark time, to move the feet up and down as if marching but without going forward : to keep things going without making progress.
up to the mark, perfect according to a certain standard : in good health.
[O.E. *mearc*, a boundary.]

mark[2]. See **Deutsche Mark.**

market, *mär′kit*, *n.* a public place where people meet to buy and sell : sale (e.g. *to put on the market*) : demand (for ; e.g. *There is a market for cotton goods in hot countries*) : place where there is a chance of selling (e.g. *Countries that are developing their industries are a market for machinery*).—*v.t.* to put on sale : to sell.
mar′ketable, *adj.* fit to be sold : in demand.
market cross, a cross set up long ago where a market was held.
mar′ket-garden, *n.* a garden where fruit and vegetables are grown for sale.
market place, open space where market is held.
market price, the price at which a thing is being sold at the time.
market town, a town holding a public market, with fixed market days.
[L. *mercātus*, trade, a market.]

marl, *märl*, *n.* lime and clay soil used as fertiliser.
[O.Fr. *marle.*]

marline, *mär′lin*, *n.* a small rope for winding round a larger one to keep it from wearing.
mar′linespike, *n.* a spike for separating the strands of a rope in splicing.
[Du. *marling*—*marren*, bind, *lijn*, rope.]

marmalade, *mär′mȧ-lād*, *n.* a jam usu. made from oranges—orig. from quinces.
[Fr. *marmelade*—Gk. *melimēlon*, sweet apple.]

marmoset, *mär′mō-zet*, *n.* a very small American monkey.
[Fr. *marmouset*, grotesque figure.]

marmot, *mär′mȯt*, *n.* a burrowing rodent, also called woodchuck, ground hog.
[L. *mūs, mūris*, mouse, *mons*, mountain.]

maroon[1], *mȧ-rōōn′*, *n.* a dark brownish-red : a loud warning firework.
[Fr. *marron*, a chestnut.]

maroon[2], *mȧ-rōōn′*, *v.t.* (as a punishment) to put on shore on a lonely island : to leave in a lonely, helpless, or uncomfortable, position.
[Fr. *marron*, runaway slave.]

marquee, *mär-kē′*, *n.* a large tent.
[From Fr. *marquise*, as if this were *pl.*]

marquess. See **marquis.**

marquetry, marqueterie, *mär′ki-tri*, *n.* inlaid work, esp. in furniture.
[Fr. *marqueterie*—*marque*, a mark.]

marquis, marquess, *mär′kwis*, *n.* a title

next below that of duke :—*fem.* **mar'chioness** (*mär'shȯn-is*).
[O.Fr. *marchis*, lord of the marches.]

marriage. See **marry.**

marrow[1], *mar'ō, n.* the soft substance in the hollow parts of bones: a vegetable marrow (see **vegetable**): the best part of anything.
[O.E. *mearg*; conn. with Ger. *mark.*]

marrow[2], *mar'ō, n.* in phrase **the (very) marrow of**, something exactly like (another thing).
[M.E., companion, spouse, pair.]

marry, *mar'i, v.t.* to take (a person) as one's husband or wife: to give as husband or wife (e.g. *He married his son to an heiress*): (of clergyman, etc.) to perform the ceremony of marriage between (two people).—Also *v.i.* :—*pr.p.* **marr'ying**; *pa.p.* **marr'ied.**
marriage, *mar'ij, n.* the ceremony by which a man and woman become husband and wife: state of being married: a close union.
marr'iageable, *adj.* suitable, or at a proper age, for marrying.
marriage licence, written permission from the Church to be married (in a church), or from a registrar.
[Fr. *marier*—L. *maritus*, husband—*mās*, male.]

Mars, *märz, n.* the Roman god of war: the planet next after the earth in the order of distance from the sun.
See also **martial, Martian.**
[L. *Mars, Martis.*]

marsh, *märsh, n.* a piece of low, wet land.—*adj.* found in marshes.
marsh'y, *adj.* **marsh'iness,** *n.*
marsh gas, fire-damp (see this).
marsh mallow, a marsh plant with pink flowers: (**marsh'mall'ow**) a sweetmeat orig. made from its root.
marsh marigold, a marsh plant with golden flowers.
[O.E. *mer(i)sc*—*mere*, pool; Ger. *marsch.*]

Marseillaise, *mär-se-lāz', -sā-āz', -sā-yāz', n.* French national anthem first sung in Paris by men from *Marseilles* during the Revolution.

marshal, *mär'shȧl, n.* a high-ranking officer in the army or air force: an officer arranging ceremonies, etc.: (*U.S.*) a civil officer with certain legal duties.—*v.t.* to arrange in order (e.g. troops, or facts, arguments): to usher :—*pr.p.* **mar'shalling**; *pa.p.* **mar'shalled.**
marshalling yard, a place where railway wagons are sorted out and made up into trains.
[O.Fr. *mareschal*—Germanic root.]

marsupial, *mär-sū'pi-ȧl, -sōō', n.* an animal that carries its young in a pouch (e.g. a kangaroo).
[Gk. *marsypion*, a pouch.]

mart, *märt, n.* a place of trade, market.
[Du. *markt*—L. root as **market.**]

martello, *mär-tel'ō, n.* a round fort for coast defence.
[From Cape *Mortella* in Corsica.]

marten, *mär'tėn, n.* an animal related to the weasel, valued for its fur.
[Fr. *martre*; conn. O.E. *mearth*, marten.]

martial, *mär'shȧl, adj.* warlike: belonging to, suitable for, war (e.g. *martial music*).
martial law, military rule in time of war, or in great national emergency, when ordinary law is suspended.
[Fr. *martial*—L. *Mars*, god of war.]

Martian, *mär'shȧn, -shi-ȧn, adj.* of Mars (god or planet).—*n.* an imagined inhabitant of Mars.
[L. *Martius*—same root as **martial.**]

martin, *mär'tin, n.* a type of swallow.
[The name *Martin* (as **robin,** etc.)]

martinet, *mär-ti-net'*, or *mär'-, n.* one whose discipline is very strict.
[*Martinet*, a strict French officer.]

Martinmas, *mär'tin-mȧs, n.* the mass or feast of St *Martin*, Nov. 11.

martyr, *mär'tėr, n.* one who suffers death or hardship for what he believes: one who continually suffers from a disease (with *to*; e.g. *She is a martyr to rheumatism*).—*v.t.* to put (person) to death for his belief: to cause to suffer greatly.
mar'tyrdom, *n.* the sufferings or death of a martyr.
[O.E.—L.—Gk., a witness.]

marvel, *mär'vėl, n.* anything astonishing or wonderful.—*v.i.* to wonder (how, why): to feel astonishment (at; e.g. *I marvel at his rashness*) :—*pr.p.* **mar'velling**; *pa.p.* **mar'velled.**
mar'vellous, *adj.* very wonderful: beyond belief.
[Fr. *merveille*—L. *mīrārī*, to wonder.]

Marxist, *märks'ist, adj.* of the socialist Karl Marx or his theories.—*n.* a follower of Marx.

marzipan, *mär-zi-pan', n.* a sweetmeat of crushed almonds and sugar.
[From Arabic; older form *marchpane.*]

mascara, *mas-kä'rä, n.* colouring for the eyelashes.
[Sp. *máscara*, a mask; see **mask.**]

mascot, *mas'kȯt, n.* a person, animal, or thing supposed to bring good luck.
[Fr. *mascotte.*]

masculine, *mâs'kū-lin, adj.* having to do with, or belonging to, the male sex or a man: mannish.
mas'culineness, masculin'ity, *ns.*
[L. *masculus*, male—*mās*, a male.]

maser, *māz'ėr, n.* a device used to make stronger radar and radio astronomy signals very small when not amplified.
[*M*icrowave *a*mplification by *s*timulated *e*mission of *r*adiation.]

mash, *mash, n.* crushed malt and hot water: a mixture, e.g. of bran with meal or turnips, used as food for animals.—*v.t.* to make into a mash: to crush.
[O.E. *masc-* (found in compounds only).]

mask, *mâsk, n.* something for disguising, hiding, or protecting, esp. the face: a face that expresses nothing: a likeness of a face in clay, etc.: (usu. **masque**) a kind of dramatic entertainment popular in 16th and 17th centuries: a fox's head.—*v.t.* to hide: to disguise.
[Fr. *masque*—Sp. *máscara* or It. *maschera*.]

mason, *mā'sn, n.* a skilled worker or builder in stone: a freemason.
masonic, *mà-son'ik, adj.* of, connected with, freemasonry.
mā'sonry, *n.* work done in stone by a mason: freemasonry.
[O.Fr. *masson* (Fr. *maçon*).]

masque. See **mask.**

masquerade, *mâs-kė-rād', n.* a social gathering, usu. a ball, of people wearing masks: acting or living under false pretences.—*v.i.* to join in a masquerade: to pretend to be (*to masquerade as*).
[Fr. *mascarade*; same root as **mask.**]

mass[1], *mâs, n.* a lump of matter: a large quantity or number: the bulk, principal part or main body: measure of quantity of matter in any object:—*pl.* **mass'es.** —*v.t.* to bring together in large number or quantity (e.g. *to mass troops for an attack*).—Also *v.i.*
massive, *mas'iv, adj.* bulky and heavy: large and impressive: (of the features) large and bold: very great in number, quantity, or power.
mass'ively, *adv.* **mass'iveness,** *n.*
mass meeting, a large meeting for a public discussion.
mass production, production on a huge scale of articles all exactly the same.
mass'-produce', *v.t.*
mass'-produced', *adj.*
the masses, the common people, esp. working class.
[Fr. *masse*—L. *massa*, a lump.]

mass[2], *mâs, n.* the celebration of the Lord's Supper in the Roman Catholic church: music to go with this.
High Mass, mass celebrated with music and incense; **Low Mass,** mass celebrated without.
[O.E. *mæsse*—L. *mittĕre*, to send away.]

massacre, *mas'à-kėr, n.* the killing of a large number of people, esp. with great cruelty.—*v.t.* to kill with violence, slaughter:—*pr.p.* **mass'acring**; *pa.p.* **mass'acred.** [Fr.]

massage, *mas'äzh, mà-säzh', n.* rubbing, kneading, etc., of parts of the body to remove pain or stiffness.—*v.t.* to treat by massage.
masseur' (*-ėr*), *n.* a man who gives massage:—*fem.* **masseuse'** (*ėz'*).
[Fr.—Gk. *massein*, knead (barley cakes).]

massif, *mas'if, mâ-sēf', n.* a central mountain mass. [Fr.]

mast[1], *mâst, n.* a long upright pole, esp. one for carrying the sails of a ship.
mast'ed, *adj.* having a mast or masts.
mast'head, *n.* the top of a mast.
lower mast, topmast, topgallant mast, royal mast, names of the lengths (reckoning from the deck upwards) of which a built-up mast on a large sailing vessel is formed.
[O.E. *mæst*; conn. with Ger. *mast.*]

mast[2], *mâst, n.* the fruit of the oak, beech, chestnut, etc., on which swine feed.
[O.E. *mæst*; conn. with Ger. *mast.*]

master, *mâs'tėr, n.* one who commands or controls: an owner (e.g. of a slave, a dog): a male teacher: an employer: the commander of a merchant ship: one very skilled in an art, science, etc.: a painting by a great artist: a degree given by universities (e.g. *Master of Arts*).—*adj.* chief: controlling, directing: showing the ability of a master.—*v.t.* to overcome: to become skilful in (e.g. *Can he ever master mathematics?*).
mas'terful, *adj.* showing power, or determination to be in control.
mas'terfully *adv.* **master'fulness,** *n.*
mas'terly, *adj.* showing the skill of a master.
mas'terliness, *n.*
mas'tery, *n.* the power or authority of a master: victory (over): control (of): great skill in or knowledge (of).
master builder, etc., a builder, etc., who employs others.
master key, a key that opens a number of locks.
master mind, a person who shows great mental power: the person planning and controlling an undertaking or scheme.
mas'terpiece, *n.* a piece of work or art worthy of a master: one's greatest achievement.
master stroke, a very skilful move.
master switch, a switch for controlling a number of other switches.
past(-)master, one who has held the office of master, esp. among freemasons—hence anyone who has great experience or skill (e.g. *a past master in the art of giving nothing away*).
[L. *magister*, from root of *magnus*, great.]

masticate, *mas'ti-kāt, v.t.* to chew.
masticā'tion, *n.*
[L. *masticāre*; conn. Gk. *mastax*, jaw.]

mastiff, *mâs'tif, n,* a thick-set, powerful dog, formerly used in hunting.
[O.Fr. *mastin*—L. *mansuētus*, tame.]

mastoid, *mas'toid, n.* (*loosely*) an inflammation of the **mastoid process,** a bone projection behind the ear.
[Gk. *mastos*, a breast, *eidos*, form.]

mat[1], *mat, n.* a piece of material (plaited rushes, rubber, wire, carpet, etc.) for wiping shoes on, or for covering a floor, or for sleeping on, or for other purpose: a piece, e.g. of linen, put under dishes at table, etc.—*v.t.* and *v.i.* to make, become, thickly tangled:—*pr.p.* **matt'ing**; *pa.p.* **matt'ed.**

matt′ed, *adj.* thickly tangled.
matt′ing, *n.* material used as mats.
[O.E. *meatt(e)*—L. *matta.*]

mat[2], **matt,** *mat, adj.* having a dull surface, without gloss or shine.
[Fr. *mat*; conn. with Ger. *matt,* dull.]

matador, matadore, *mat′à-dör, n.* the man who kills the bull in a bullfight.
[Sp. *matador—matar,* to kill.]

match[1], *mach, n.* a short stick of wood or other material tipped with a material that catches fire when rubbed: a cord, etc., made to burn at a definite speed.
match′wood, *n.* splinters.
[O.Fr. *mesche* (Fr. *mèche*), wick, cord, etc.]

match[2], *mach, n.* a person or thing the same as another in some respect(s): an equal: a person able to cope with another (e.g. *In argument Jack is no match for Jim*): a marriage, or a person to be gained in marriage: a contest or game.—*v.i.* to be exactly or nearly alike (e.g. *Those earrings match*): to fit in, be suitable (with).—*v.t.* to be equal or similar to (something) in e.g. size, colour, or to (a person) in e.g. skill, courage: to set to compete (against; e.g. *to match Roland against Oliver*; *to match his skill against my better tools*): to hold one's own against: to pair: to join in marriage.
match′less, *adj.* having no equal.
[O.E. *gemæcca,* mate, spouse.]

mate[1], *māt, n.* a companion: a fellow workman: an equal: a husband or wife: an animal with which another is paired for breeding purposes: a merchant-ship's officer under the master.—*v.t.* and *v.i.* to marry: to pair.
[Prob. from Ger. or Du.]

mate[2], *māt, v.t., n.,* and *interj.* checkmate.

mater, *mā′tėr, n.* (*coll.*) mother.
maternal, *mà-tėr′nàl, adj.* of a mother: suitable to a mother, motherly.
mater′nally, *adv.*
mater′nity, *n.* state of being a mother.—*adj.* for expectant mother(s).
See also **matriarchy, matricide.**
[L. *māter,* mother.]

material, *mà-tē′ri-àl, adj.* consisting of matter: bodily, not spiritual: lacking spirituality (e.g. *His outlook and aims were material*): essential or important.—*n.* something out of which anything is, or may be, made: cloth.
mate′rially, *adv.* to a considerable or important extent (e.g. *Circumstances have altered materially since then*).
mate′rialise, *v.i.* to take bodily form: to become actual fact: (of e.g. something promised) to turn up as expected.
mate′rialism, *n.* the belief that nothing exists but matter, and that there are no spiritual forces: a tendency to attach too great importance to material things (e.g. to bodily comfort, money, success).
mate′rialist, *n.*
raw material. See **raw.**
[L. *māteria,* matter.]

maternal. See **mater.**

mathematics, *math-ė-mat′iks, n.* the science or branch of knowledge dealing with measurements, numbers, quantities, and the relationships between these or operations done on them.
mathemat′ical, *adj.* of, done by, mathematics: very exact or accurate.
mathematic′ian (*-ish′àn*), *n.* one who knows and can work with mathematics.
[Gk. *mathēmatikē* (*epistēmē*), mathematical (knowledge).]

matin, *mat′in, n.* (used in *pl.* **mat′ins,** often **mattins**) morning prayers or service: morning song of birds.
matinee, *mat′i-nā, n.* a public entertainment held in the daytime, usu. in the afternoon.
[L. *mātūtīnus,* belonging to morning.]

matriarchy, *mā′tri-är-ki, n.* government by a mother or by mothers.
mā′triarch, *n.* a woman who is head and ruler of her family and descendants.
mātriar′chal, (*-kàl*), *adj.*
matricide, *mat′ri-sīd, n.* the killing of one's own mother: one who kills his, or her, mother.
[L. *māter,* mother (*archē,* rule; *caedĕre,* to kill).]

matriculate, *mà-trik′ū-lāt, v.t.* to admit (a student) to membership of a college, etc., by entering his name in a register.—*v.i.* to become a member of a university, etc., by being enrolled.
matriculā′tion, *n.*
[Late L. *mātrīcula,* a register.]

matrimony, *mat′ri-mon-i, n.* state of being married: act of marrying.
matrimonial (*-mō′ni-àl*), *adj.*
[L. *mātrimōnium—māter,* mother.]

matrix, *mā′triks,* or *mat′riks, n.* something in which something else is embedded (e.g. rock in which a gem, metal, lies): a mould, esp. in which metals, etc., are shaped:—*pls.* **matrices** (*-sēz*), **-ixes.**
[L. *matrix,* womb—*māter,* mother.]

matron, *mā′tròn, n.* a married woman: an elderly lady: a woman in charge of nursing and domestic arrangements in a hospital, school, etc.
mā′tronly, *adj.* elderly and sedate.
[Fr. *matrone*—L. *māter,* mother.]

matt. See **mat** (2).

matted, etc. See **mat** (1).

matter, *mat′ėr, n.* something that takes up space, and which we can see, feel, etc.: physical substance, not spirit or mind: material (e.g. *dead, colouring, matter*): the subject being written, spoken, or thought, about: the trouble, difficulty, thing wrong (e.g. *What is the matter now?*): (in *pl.*) affairs (e.g. *He is clever in money matters*): pus.—*v.i.* to be of importance (e.g. *That matters a great deal to him*): to form or give out pus:—

pr.p. **matt'ering**; *pa.p.* **matt'ered.**
a matter of, used in giving quantity, time, etc. roughly (e.g. *It will take a matter of minutes,* i.e. a very short time).
a matter of course, a thing to be expected (e.g. *His promotion came as a matter of course*).
matt'er-of-fact', *adj.* keeping to the actual fact, not fanciful or imaginative: rather dull.
no matter, it makes no difference.
[O.Fr. *matiere*—L. root as **material.**]

mattins. See **matin.**

mattock, *mat'ȯk, n.* a kind of pickaxe with broad end for breaking the soil.
[O.E. *mattuc.*]

mattress, *mat'rės, n.* part of a bed consisting usu. of a large flat bag stuffed with horsehair or other material.
[Arabic *matrah,* place where anything is thrown, mat, cushion.]

mature, *mȧ-tūr', adj.* fully grown or developed: ripe: (of a plan) completely worked out: (of e.g. a bill of exchange) due.—*v.t., v.i.* to cause to be, or to become, ripe, grown, mature.
mature'ness, matur'ity, *ns.*
[L. *mātūrus,* ripe.]

maudlin, *möd'lin, adj.* sickly sentimental: half drunk.
[Gk. *Magdalēnē,* (woman) of Magdala, from the idea that Mary Magdalene was the penitent woman of Luke vii. 37 ff.]

maul, *möl, n.* a heavy wooden hammer.—*v.t.* to hurt badly by rough treatment.
[O.Fr. *mail*—L. *malleus.*]

maunder, *mön'dėr, v.i.* to talk in a rambling manner: to move or act without energy.
[Origin unknown.]

mausoleum, *mö-sö-lē'ům, n.* a very fine tomb or monument.
[Gk.; from the magnificent tomb of a man named *Mausōlus.*]

mauve, *mōv, n.* a delicate purple colour.
[Fr.—L. *malva,* mallow.]

mavis, *mā'vis, n.* the thrush.
[Middle Fr. *mauvis.*]

mawkish, *mö'kish, adj.* sickening: (of e.g. a story) weak and sentimental.
maw'kishness, *n.*
[Old Norse *mathkr,* maggot.]

maxim, *maks'im, n.* an expression of a truth or rule, esp. one serving as a guide to conduct.
[L. *maxima (sententia),* greatest (opinion).]

maximum, *maks'i-mům, adj.* greatest.—*n.* the greatest number or quantity: the highest point or degree:—*pl.* **max'ima.**
[L. *maximus* (superl. of *magnus*), greatest.]

may[1], *mā, v.i.* generally used with another verb to express permission, possibility, etc. (e.g. *That is all—you may go now*; *I may go, if the weather is good*): also to express a wish (e.g. *May you be successful!*):—*pa.t.* **might** (*mīt*). The forms 'may', 'might' are the same with all persons (I, you, etc.).
[O.E. *magan,* to be able, have power; *pa.t. mihte*; conn. Ger. *mögen.*]

may[2]. See **May.**

May, *mā, n.* the fifth month of the year: (without *cap.*) may blossom.—*v.i.* to gather may on May Day.
may (blossom), the hawthorn flower.
May Day, the first day of May.
may'fly, *n.* a type of small fly which lives only a short time, appearing in May.
may'pole, *n.* a pole for dancing round on May Day.
May Queen, *n.* a girl crowned with flowers as queen on May Day.
[Fr. *Mai*—L. *Māia,* mother of Mercury.]

maybe, *mā'bē, adv.* perhaps.
[For *it may be.*]

mayday, *mā'dā, n.* international distress signal sent out by ships and aircraft.
[Fr. *m'aidez* (*mā-dā*), help me.]

mayonnaise, *mā-ȯn-āz', mā'-, n.* a thick sauce made of yolk of egg, oil, vinegar or lemon, and seasoning. [Fr.]

mayor, *mā'ȯr, mār, n.* the chief public official (man or woman) of city, town, or borough.
may'orship, *n.* office of a mayor.
may'oress, *n.* a mayor's wife, or other lady who carries out the social duties of the position.
[Fr. *maire*—same L. root as **major.**]

maze, *māz, n.* a place full of windings: a state of not knowing what to think or do.—*v.t.* to puzzle, confuse.
[Conn. with **amaze.**]

mazurka, *mȧ-zûr'kȧ,* or *-zōōr', n.* a lively Polish dance: music for it. [Polish.]

me. See **I.**

mead[1], *mēd, n.* an alcoholic drink made from honey and water.
[O.E. *meodu*; conn. Gk. *methy,* wine.]

mead[2], *mēd,* **meadow,** *med'ō, ns.* a field of grass to be mown: a rich pasture-ground, esp. beside stream.
[O.E. *mǣd* (as object, *mǣdwe*)—*māwan,* mow.]

meagre, *mē'gėr, adj.* lean: poor in quality: scanty, not enough.
[Fr. *maigre*—L. *macer,* lean.]

meal[1], *mēl, n.* the food taken at one time.
[O.E. *mǣl,* time; conn. Ger. *mahl,* meal.]

meal[2], *mēl, n.* grain, or seeds such as peas, ground to powder.
meal'y, *adj.*:—*comp.* **meal'ier**; *superl.* **meal'iest.**
meal'iness, *n.*
meal'y-mouthed', *adj.* unwilling to use plain terms, not frank and sincere.
[O.E *melu*; conn. Ger. *mehl.*]

mean[1], *mēn, adj.* low in rank or birth: of little worth: (of e.g. a house) humble, shabby: (of a motive) not noble: selfish, petty: stingy, not generous with money.
mean'ly, *adv.* **mean'ness,** *n.*
no mean, (before noun) important, good (e.g. *This is no mean city*; *he is no mean actor*).
[O.E. *gemæne*; **common**; Ger. *gemein.*]

mean[2], *mēn, adj.* having the middle position : average.—*n.* something that is midway between two opposite ends or extremes.
means, *n.* (*sing.* or *pl.* verb) instrument, method, etc., by which a thing is, or may be, done or brought about (e.g. *It was, these were, the means by which we were saved*) : (*pl.* verb) money necessary e.g. for a living (e.g. *Our means are small*).
mean time, time based on the average interval between two appearances of the sun above the meridian (the interval varies a little).
mean'time, mean'while, *advs.* in the time between.
a man of means, a wealthy man.
golden mean, a wise middle course.
[O.Fr. *meien*—L. *medius*, middle.]

mean[3], *mēn, v.t.* to intend, have in mind as a purpose (e.g. *I mean to mend the leak*; *He means mischief*) : to have in mind for a special use (e.g. *I mean the box for him*) : to express, convey, indicate (e.g. '*Vacation*' *means* '*holiday*'; *what does his silence mean?*) : to intend to express (e.g. *By* '*difficult*' *I mean* '*stubborn*').—*v.i.* to have importance (e.g. *Her gift means much to her grandmother*) :—*pr.p.* **mean'ing**; *pa.p.* **meant** (*ment*).
mean'ing, *n.* what one intended to express : sense in which a statement, etc., is to be understood : purpose (e.g. *I now saw the meaning of his action*).—*adj.* showing feelings or conveying a message (e.g. *a meaning look*).
to mean well (ill), to have good (bad) intentions.
[O.E. *mǣnan*; conn. Ger. *meinen*, think.]

meander, *mē-an'dėr, n.* loop of a river : (in *pl.*) winding course.—*v.i.* to flow in a winding course : to wander about aimlessly.
[Gk. *Maiandros*, winding river in Asia.]

meant. See **mean.**

measles, *mē'zlz, n.* an infectious fever with red spots on the skin.
mea'sly, *adj.* ill with measles : (coll.) poor, mean, deserving contempt :—*comp.* **mea'slier**; *superl.* **mea'sliest.**
[M.E. *maseles*; conn. with Ger. *masern.*]

measure, *mezh'ůr, n.* the dimensions, size, or amount of a thing as discovered by measuring : an instrument for measuring (e.g. *a tape measure*) : a system of measuring (e.g. *dry, liquid, square measure*) : a certain amount (e.g. *I feel a measure of sympathy for her*) : musical time : a dance, esp. a slow and stately one : (often in *pl.*) plan of action, steps towards an end (e.g. *to take measures to stop vandalism*) : a bill brought before parliament : (*pl.*) rock strata (e.g. *the coal measures*).—*v.t.* to find the size or amount of : (with *off, out*) to mark off, weight out, etc. in portions : to judge in comparison with (e.g. *She measured her skill in cooking against her friend's*).—*v.i.* to be of (a certain size) : to take measurements.
meas'urement, *n.* act of measuring : dimension found by measuring.
meas'urable, *adj.* that can be measured.
meas'urably, *adv.*
meas'ured, *adj.* in rhythm, slow and steady (e.g. *with measured steps*) : slow, carefully considered (e.g. *measured speech*).
meas'ureless, *adj.* having no limits.
beyond measure, very great.
in a, some, measure, to some extent.
to take one's measure, to judge one's character, ability, etc.
[O.Fr. *mesure*—L. *mensūra.*]

meat, *mēt, n.* the flesh of animals used as food : anything eaten as food.
meat'y, *adj.* full of meat : full of matter for thought (e.g. *a meaty lecture*) :—*comp.* **meat'ier**; *superl.* **meat'iest.**
[O.E. *mete.*]

mechanic, *mė-kan'ik, n.* a skilled worker with tools or machines.
mechan'ical, *adj.* having to do with machines : worked or done by machinery : done, etc., without thinking, from force of habit : having a talent and liking for machinery.
mechan'ically, *adv.*
mechan'ics, *n.* (*sing.*) the science of the action of forces on objects : the art of machine building.
mech'anise, *v.t.* to make machine-like : to introduce machinery into (an industry) : to equip (troops) with armed armoured motor vehicles.
mechanisā'tion, *n.*
mech'anism, *n.* the parts of a machine taken as a whole : mechanical working : action by which a result is produced.
[Gk. *mēchanē* (*n.*); root as **machine.**]

medal, *med'ål, n.* a piece of metal in the form of a coin with a figure or inscription stamped on it ; a reward of merit.
medallion, *mė-dal'yȯn, n.* a large medal.
med'allist, *n.* one who has gained a medal.
[Fr. *médaille*; from L. *metallum*, metal.]

meddle, *med'l, v.i.* to interfere, try to play a part (in another's affairs ; e.g. *She was always trying to meddle in her neighbours' lives*; *to meddle with things she knew nothing about*) ; to tamper (with).
medd'ling, *n.* and *adj.*
medd'ler, *n.* one who meddles.
medd'lesome, *adj.* inclined to meddle.
[O.Fr. *medler* (Fr. *mêler*)—L. *miscēre*, mix.]

media. See **medium.**

mediaeval, *me-di-ē'vål, mē-, adj.* of, having to do with, the Middle Ages.
[L. *medius*, middle, *aevum*, age.]

medial, *mē'di-ål, adj.* middle : average.
[L. *medius*, middle.]

mediate, *mē'di-āt, v.i.* to come between two people who are disagreeing and, as the friend of each, try to settle their dispute.—*v.t.* to bring about (a settlement of a dispute, an agreement) by helping the two sides to arrange it.

mediā'tion, *n.* **me'diator,** *n.*

[Late L. *mĕdiāre*, to be in the middle.]

medical, *med'i-kȧl, adj.* of, having to do with, healing, medicine, or doctors.

medicate, *med'i-kāt, v.t.* to put a medicine into (something).

med'icated, *adj.* **medicā'tion,** *n.*

medicine, *med'sin, n.* any substance (esp. one taken by the mouth) used to treat or keep away disease: the science of curing people who are ill, or making their suffering less (esp. by means other than surgery).

medicinal, *me-dis'in-ȧl, adj.* having power to heal: used in medicine.

medic'inally, *adv.* for the purpose of (or with the effect of) curing an ailment (e.g. *alcohol taken medicinally*).

medicine man, among savage tribes, a witch doctor.

[L. *medicāre, -ātum*, heal, *medicīna* (n.)].

medieval. Same as **mediaeval.**

mediocre, *mē'di-ō-kėr*, or *-ō', adj.* (of e.g. person, performance, quality) middling, ordinary, not very good or great.

mediocrity, (*-ok'-*) *n.* mediocre quality: a person of little ability, etc.:—*pl.* **-ies.**

[Fr. *médiocre*—L. *medius*, middle.]

meditate, *med'i-tāt, v.i.* to think deeply (with *on, upon*; e.g. *meditating on his troubles*).—*v.t.* to think about: to consider, to plan (e.g. *I am meditating a campaign to encourage politeness*).

meditā'tion, *n.*

med'itative, *adj.* thoughtful.

med'itatively, *adv.* **-itativeness,** *n.*

[L. *meditārī.*]

Mediterranean, *me-di-tė-rā'nyȧn; -ni-ȧn, adj.* of, having to do with, the *Mediterranean Sea* or its shores (e.g. *Mediterranean fruits*).

Mediterranean climate, a climate like that round the Mediterranean Sea—mild, moderately wet, winters and warm dry summers.

[L. *medius*, middle, *terra*, land, earth.]

medium, *mē'di-ŭm, n.* a middle condition, way (e.g. *There is a medium between extravagance and meanness*): something through which an effect is produced (e.g. *Air is the medium through which sound is carried to a distance*): means (e.g. *TV is a powerful advertising medium*): a person through whom spirits are said to speak: a substance in which specimens are preserved, or in which bacteria are grown:—*pl.* **mē'dia** (not of persons), **mē'diums.** —*adj.* middle in size, quality, etc.

[L. *medium*—*medius*, middle.]

medlar, *med'lȧr, n.* a small tree with sour fruit something like a crab apple.

[O.Fr. *medler*—Gk. *mespilon.*]

medley, *med'li, n.* a mixture, jumble: a piece of music put together from a number of other pieces:—*pl.* **med'leys.** —Also *adj.*

[Same root as **meddle.**]

meek, *mēk, adj.* gentle, humble, patient.

meek'ness, *n.* **meek'ly,** *adv.*

[Old Norse *mjūkr.*]

meet[1], *mēt, v.t.* to come face to face with: to come into the company of for discussion, combat, etc.: to be introduced to: to join (e.g. *This road soon meets another*): to experience (e.g. *to meet disapproval*): to come up to (e.g. hopes): to satisfy (e.g. requirements): to answer, oppose (e.g. *to meet force with greater force*): to pay fully (e.g. debts).—*v.i.* to come together: to assemble:—*pa.t.* and *pa.p.* **met.**—*n.* a meeting, esp. of huntsmen.

meet'ing, *n.* a coming together: an assembly or gathering: a joining (e.g. of rivers).

[O.E. *mētan*, meet—(*ge*)*mōt*, meeting.]

meet[2], *mēt, adj.* fitting, proper (e.g. *It is meet that bravery should be rewarded.*)

[O.E. *gemǣte*, suitable.]

mega-, *meg-ȧ-*, **meg-,** *meg-*, (as part of a word) great, powerful: also a million:— e.g. **meg'aton,** *adj.* (of a bomb) giving an explosion as great as that of a million tons of T.N.T.

megalomania, *meg-ȧ-lō-mā'ni-ȧ, n.* the idea, usu. false, that one is great or powerful.

megaphone, *meg'ȧ-fōn, n.* a funnel-shaped device for causing sounds to be heard better and at a greater distance.

[Gk. *megas, megal-*, great (*mania*, madness; *phōnē*, voice).]

melancholy, *mel'ȧn-kȯl-i, n.* lowness of spirits, sadness.—*adj.* sad, low-spirited: dismal, depressing.

[Gk. *melās, -anos*, black, *cholē*, bile.]

mélange, *mā-lan*ᵍ*zh, n.* a mixture. [Fr.]

mêlée, *me'lā, n.* a confused fight between two groups of people.

[Fr.—*mêler*, to mix.]

meliorate, *mē'li-ō-rāt, v.t.* to make better. —*v.i.* to grow better.

meliorā'tion, *n.*

[L. *melior*, better.]

mellifluous, *mė-lif'loo-ŭs, adj.* (of e.g. voice, words) sweet as honey.—Also **mellif'luent.**

mellif'luence, *n.* **mellif'luently,** *adv.*

[L. *mel, mellis*, honey, *fluĕre*, to flow.]

mellow, *mel'ō, adj.* (of fruit) ripe, juicy, sweet: (of wine) kept till flavour is fine: (of sound, colour, light) soft, not harsh: (of character) softened by age or experience.— *v.t., v.i.* to soften by ripeness or age.

[Prob. O.E. *melu*, meal, and *mearu*, soft.]

melodic, melodious. See **melody.**

melodrama, *mel'ō-drä-mȧ, n.* sensational drama in which emotions are exaggerated.

melodramatic (*-drȧ-mat'ik*), *adj.* sensational: expressing more feeling than is suitable in the circumstances.

[Gk. *melos*, a song, *drāma*, action.]

melody, *mel'ȯ-di, n.* an air or tune: sweet music:—*pl.* **mel'odies.**
melod'ic, *adj.* having to do with melody.
melō'dious, *adj.* pleasing to the ear, tuneful.
melo'diously, *adv.* **-diousness,** *n.*
[Gk. *melos*, a song, and root as **ode.**]

melon, *mel'ȯn, n.* a large sweet fruit with much juice.
[Fr.—L. *mēlō*—Gk. *mēlon*, an apple.]

melt, *melt, v.i.* to become liquid, usu. by heat: to dissolve: to feel very hot: (often with *away*) to disappear almost unnoticed (e.g. *The crowd, his money, melted away*): to shade, change (into) gradually without distinct border line: to soften in feeling, relent, feel sudden affection, etc.—Also *v.t.*
melt'ing, *n.* and *adj.* **melt'ingly,** *adv.*
mōlt'en, *adj.* (of metal) melted.
in the melting-pot, in the process of changing and forming something new.
[O.E. *meltan* (*pa.p. molten*).]

member, *mem'bėr, n.* a limb of the body: one who belongs to a group of persons, e.g. to a society: one who belongs to a law-making body, e.g. the House of Commons: a part of a structure.
mem'bership, *n.* the state of being a member: body of members (e.g. *a society with a large membership*).
[Fr. *membre*—L. *membrum*, limb, part.]

membrane, *mem'brān, n.* a thin pliable layer of animal or vegetable tissue that lines parts of the body, forms the outside of cells, etc.
[L. *membrāna*, skin: root as **member.**]

memento, *mė-men'tō, n.* something kept as a reminder, souvenir, keepsake:—*pl.* **memen'to(e)s.**
[L. imper. of *meminisse*, to remember.]

memo. Abbrev. of **memorandum.**

memoir, *mem'wär, -wör, n.* (in *pl.*) a written account of events set down from personal knowledge: (in *pl.*) an autobiography: a biography (e.g. *He wrote a memoir of the Duke*).
[Fr. *mémoire*; root as **memorandum.**]

memorandum, *mem-ȯ-ran'dum, n.* a note to help one to remember: a written statement or summary of a matter being discussed:—*pl.* **memoran'dums, -da.**
memory, *mem'ȯ-ri, n.* power to remember: an imagined part of the mind where facts and experiences are stored (e.g. *a memory filled with stories about interesting people*): something remembered (e.g. *I have an early memory of seeing a comet*): what is remembered about a person, his reputation:—*pl.* **mem'ories.**
mem'orable, *adj.* worthy of being remembered: remarkable.
memo'rial (*-mō'*), *adj.* honouring the memory of a person or persons.—*n.* something (e.g. a monument) which honours persons, events of the past: a written statement of facts.
mem'orise, *v.t.* to learn (e.g. *to memorise a poem*): to store in the memory.
in memory of, as a remembrance of or memorial to.
[L. *memorāre*, remember, *memoria* (n.)]

menace, *men'ȧs, n.* a threat (e.g. *to utter menaces*): something likely to cause injury or destruction (to).—*v.t.* (of person, circumstance, etc.) to threaten to harm.
men'acing, *adj.* **men'acingly,** *adv.*
[Fr.—L. *mināciae*, threats.]

ménage, *mā-näzh, n.* household. [Fr.]

menagerie, *mė-naj'ėr-i, n.* a place for keeping wild animals for exhibition: a collection of such animals.
[Fr. *ménagerie*; root as **ménage.**]

mend, *mend, v.t.* to repair, put in good shape again: to correct, improve (e.g. one's ways, manners).—*v.i.* to grow better, esp. in health.
mend'ing, *n.* act of repairing: things requiring to be mended.
to mend matters, to make the situation better. [**amend.**]

mendacious, *men-dā'shus, adj.* untruthful.
menda'ciously, *adv.*
mendac'ity (*-das'*), *n.*
[L. *mendax, -ācis*; conn. *mentīri*, to lie.]

mendicant, *men'di-kȧnt, n.* a beggar.—Also *adj.*
[L. *mendīcāre*, to beg—*mendīcus*, beggar.]

menial, *mē'ni-ȧl, adj.* (of work) mean, humble.—*n.* (*orig.*) a household servant: one doing humble jobs.
[M.E. *meinie*, household—L. *mansiō*, dwelling.]

meningitis, *men-in-ji'tis,* inflammation of the membranes round the brain or spinal cord.
[Gk. *mēninx, -ingos*, a membrane.]

menses, *men'sēz, n.pl.* the monthly flow from the uterus.
men'struate, *v.i.* to discharge the menses.
[L. *mensis*, month, *menstruus*, monthly.]

mensurable, *men'shur-ȧ-bl, adj.* measurable.
mensurā'tion, *n.* the act or art of finding the length, area, volume, etc., of objects.
[L. *mensūrāre*, to measure.]

mental, *men'tȧl, adj.* of, having to do with, the mind: done, made, happening, in the mind (e.g. *mental arithmetic*; *a mental picture*): suffering from an illness of the mind (e.g. *a mental patient*): for those who are ill in mind (e.g. *a mental hospital*).
men'tally, *adv.* in the mind.
mentality (*-tal'i-ti*), *n.* mental power: way of thinking, outlook.
[Fr.—L. *mens, mentis*, the mind.]

menthol, *men'thol, n.* a sharp-smelling substance got from peppermint oil, etc., which gives relief in colds, etc.
[L. *mentha*, mint.]

mention, *men'sh(ȯ)n, v.t.* to speak of, refer to, briefly (e.g. *He mentioned the* *plan, but gave no details*): to remark (that): to name because of bravery, etc. (e.g. *a soldier mentioned in dispatches*). —*n.* a passing or brief reference (with *of*): an honourable reference.

men'tionable, *adj.* fit to be mentioned.
[L. *mentio, -ōnis* (n.).]

mentor, *men'tor, n.* a wise giver of advice.
[Gk. *Mentor*, wise tutor in Greek story.]

menu, *men'ū, n.* a card with a list of dishes to be served, or available to be ordered, at a meal.
[Fr.—L. *minūtus*, small.]

mercantile, *mėr'kȧn-tīl, adj.* having to do with merchants or trade.
mercantile marine, the ships and crews of a country that are employed in trading.
[Fr.—It.—same L. root as **merchant.**]

mercenary, *mėr'sėn-ȧr-i, adj.* hired for money: too strongly influenced by desire for money.—*n.* a soldier hired into a foreign service:—*pl.* **mer'cenaries.**
[L. *mercēnārius—mercēs*, pay, reward.]

merchant, *mėr'chȧnt, n.* a trader, esp. wholesale or in a large business: (*U.S.* and *Scot.*) a shopkeeper.—*adj.* having to do with trade: used in trade.
mer'chandise (*-dīz*), *n.* goods bought and sold for gain.
mer'chantman, *n.* a trading ship:—*pl.* **-men.**
merchant navy, service, the mercantile marine (see this).
merchant ship, a merchantman.
[O.Fr. *march(e)ant*—L. *mercārī*, trade.]

merciful, -fully, etc. See **mercy.**

mercury, *mėr'kū-ri, n.* a silvery liquid metal, quicksilver.
mercu'rial (*-kū'*), *adj.* (of person, temperament) lively, sprightly, showing quick changes of mood.
[L. *Mercurius*, messenger god Mercury.]

mercy, *mėr'si, n.* willingness not to harm a person, e.g. an enemy, who is in one's power: (esp. of God) an act of kindness or pity: (*coll.*) a piece of good luck:—*pl.* **mer'cies.**
mer'ciful, *adj.* willing to forgive or to punish only lightly: (of an event, when something bad is happening or expected) fortunate.
mer'cifully, *adv.* **mer'cifulness,** *n.*
mer'ciless, *adj.* without mercy: cruel.
at the mercy of, wholly in the power of: liable to be harmed by (e.g. *A camper is at the mercy of the weather*).
[Fr. *merci*—L. *mercēs*, pay, reward.]

mere[1], *mēr, n.* a pool or lake.
[O.E., sea, lake, pool; Ger. *meer*, sea.]

mere[2], *mēr, adj.* no more or better than (e.g. *a mere child*, a *mere nothing*):—*comp.* (none); *superl.* **mer'est** (e.g. *The merest child could do it*).
mere'ly, *adv.* simply, only.
[L. *merus*, unmixed.]

meretricious, *mer-ė-trish'ůs, adj.* flashy, showily attractive but false, insincere.
[L. *meretrix*, prostitute—*merēre*, earn.]

merge, *mėrj, v.i., v.t.* to be, or cause to be, swallowed up (in something greater): to combine or join.
mer'ger, *n.* a joining together of business firms.
[L. *mergěre, mersum*, immerse, engulf.]

meridian, *mė-rid'i-ȧn, adj. n.* the highest point (of the sun's course, of success): an imaginary circle or half circle on the earth's surface passing through the poles and any given place.
prime meridian, the meridian (0°) passing through Greenwich, from which longitudes are measured east or west.
[L. *meridiēs*, midday.]

meringue, *mė-rang', n.* a crisp cooked mixture of sugar and white of eggs, or a substitute.
[Fr., origin unknown.]

merino, *mė-rē'nō, n.* a sheep of Spanish origin that has very fine wool: a cloth made from the wool.—Also *adj.* [Sp.]

merit, *mer'it, n.* excellence that deserves honour or reward: worth, value: (in *pl.*) rights or wrongs (of a case).—*v.t.* to deserve as reward or punishment.
meritō'rious, *adj.* deserving (usu. moderate) reward or praise.
[O.Fr. *merite*—L. *merēre*, earn, deserve.]

mermaid, *mėr'mād, n.* an imaginary sea creature, woman to the waist with a fish's tail:—*masc.* **mer'man.**
[**mere** (1), **maid.**]

merry, *mer'i, adj.* cheerful, noisily or laughingly gay: slightly drunk:—*comp.* **merr'ier**; *superl.* **merr'iest.**
merr'ily, *adv.* **merr'iness,** *n.*
merr'iment, *n.* fun, gaiety, with laughter and noise.
merr'y-an'drew, *n.* a clown, fool.
merr'ymaking, *n.* a merry entertainment: act of making merry.
merr'ymaker, *n.*
merr'ythought, *n.* the forked breast bone of a fowl.
Merry England, orig. pleasant England.
to make merry, to be gay: to hold, take part in, a gay entertainment.
See also **mirth.**
[O.E. *myr(i)ge*, pleasant, delightful.]

mesdames. See **madam.**

mesembryanthemum, *mė-zem-bri-an'thi-mům, n.* any of a number of sun-loving plants most of which are S. African.
[Gk. *mesēmbriā*, midday, *anthemon*, flower.]

mesh, *mesh, n.* the opening between the threads of a net: (in *pl.*) the threads around the opening: network, net: means of catching.—*v.t.* to catch in a net.—*v.i.* (of teeth on geared wheels) to become engaged with each other.
[Middle Du. *maesche*; Ger. *masche.*]

mesmerise, *mez'mėr-īz, v.t.* to hypnotise (see this word): (*loosely*) to control the will, or fix the attention, of (a person).
mes'merism, *n.*
[From F. *Mesmer*, a German physician.]

mess, *mes, n.* a number of persons who take their meals together, esp. in the armed services: the place where they eat together: a dish of soft, pulpy or liquid stuff: the result of spilling e.g. this: a mixture disagreeable to the sight or taste: disorder, confusion.—*v.t.* (often with *up*) to make a mess of.—*v.i.* to belong to a mess (with), eat one's meals (with): to potter (about).
mess'y, *adj.*
mess'ily, *adv.* **mess'iness,** *n.*
mess'mate, *n.* a member of the same (usu. ship's) mess.
to make a mess of, to make dirty, untidy, or muddled: to do badly: to spoil, ruin (e.g. one's life).
[O.Fr. *mes*, dish—Late L. *mittĕre*, place.]

message, *mes'ij, n.* any information, spoken or written, passed from one person to another: an official notice from a president, etc., to a law-making body, etc.: the teaching of a poet, prophet, or wise man.
mess'enger, *n.* one who carries message(s).
[Fr.—L. *mittĕre*, *missum*, to send.]

Messiah, *mė-sī'a, n.* Christ: an expected deliverer.
[Heb. *māshīah*, anointed.]

messily, etc. See **mess.**

messrs, *mes'ėrz, n.pl.* English form of **messieurs** (see **monsieur**).

messy. See **mess.** **met.** See **meet.**

metabolism, *mė-tab'ol-izm, n.* the chemical changes in the cells of a living body which provide energy for living processes and activities.
[Gk. *metabolē*, change.]

metal, *met'l, n.* a substance (such as gold, silver, iron) which has a lustre or shine, conducts heat and electricity, can be hammered into shape, or drawn out in threads, etc.: broken stones used for making roads, etc.—Also *adj.*—*v.t.* to cover with metal:—*pr.p.* **met'alling**; *pa.p.* **met'alled.**
metallic, *mė-tal'ik, adj.* made of metal: like a metal (e.g. in look, sound.)
metallurgy, *me-tal'ûr-ji, met'ål-, n.* study of metals, or the art of getting metals from ores and preparing them for use.
metall'urgist (or *met'*), *n.*
metallur'gic (-al) (or *met'*), *adjs.*
[Gk. *metallon*, a mine (*ergon*, work).]

metamorphosis, *met-å-mör'fō-sis, n.* change of form, substance, appearance, character, condition, etc., by natural development, or by, or as if by, magic: the marked change that some living beings undergo during their growth, as caterpillar to butterfly, tadpole to frog, etc.:—*pl.* **metamorphoses** (*-sēz*).
metamor'phic, *adj.*
[Gk. *meta*, expressing change, *morphē*, form.]

metaphor, *met'å-fôr, n.* a way of showing vividly a quality or characteristic of a person or thing by giving the person, thing, the name of something which has that quality in a marked degree (e.g. *He is a tiger when angry*, i.e. he has the fierceness of a tiger . . .). Similar comparisons can be made by using an adjective, verb, or adverb (e.g. *a violent red colour*; *she sailed into the room*; *the story ended lamely*). 'Like' and 'as' are not used (see **simile**).
metaphor'ical, *adj.* expressing, in, metaphor(s), not literal fact.
metaphor'ically, *adv.*
mixed metaphor, a metaphor that is a confusion of two or more metaphors (e.g. *We are sailing fast towards bankruptcy, we must put the brake on.*)
[Gk. *meta*, over, *pherein*, to carry.]

metaphysics, *met-å-fiz'iks, n. sing.* philosophy, esp. the more difficult parts which discuss the reality behind physical and natural facts and the nature of knowledge and thought.
metaphys'ical, *adj.*
[Gk. *meta*, after, *physika*, physics.]

mete, *mēt, v.t.* to give out (punishment, reward)—usu. **mete out.**
[O.E. *metan*, measure; Ger. *messen.*]

meteor, *mē'tyȯr, n.* any of numberless small bodies travelling through space, seen when they enter the earth's atmosphere as fiery streaks in the sky—'falling', or 'shooting', 'stars': anything brilliant which does not last long.
meteoric, *mē-tė-or'ik, adj.* of, like, consisting of, a meteor or meteors: rapid: bright and successful for a short time (*a meteoric career*).
mē'teorite, *n.* a meteor (of stone or metal) which has fallen to earth.
meteorol'ogy, *n.* study of weather and climate.
meteorol'ogist, *n.*
meteorolog'ical, *adj.*
[Gk. *ta meteōra*, things on high.]

meter, *mē'tėr, n.* an instrument for measuring, esp. the quantity of electricity, gas, water, etc., used.
[Same root as **mete.**]

method, *meth'ȯd, n.* the way in which one does something: an orderly or fixed series of actions for doing something: arrangement according to a plan.
method'ical, *adj.* arranged, done, or in the habit of acting, in an orderly manner according to a plan (e.g. *a methodical filing system, search, person*).
method'ically, *adv.*

Meth'odist, *n.* one of a sect of Christians founded by John Wesley.
method acting, acting by living a part, not just using stage technique.
[Gk. *meta*, after, *hodos*, a way.]

methylated spirit(s), *meth'i-lā-tid spir'it(s).* an alcohol made unsuitable for drinking by adding certain substances.
[Gk. *meta*, after, with, *hȳlē*, wood.]

meticulous, *mė-tik'ū-lůs, adj.* very careful about small details : too careful.
[L. *meticulōsus*, frightened—*metus*, fear.]

métier, *mā-tyā, n.* one's trade, profession : something in which one is skilled.
[Fr.—L. *ministērium.*]

metre[1], *mē'tėr, n.* (in English verse) the regular arrangement of syllables that are stressed : the pattern seen in poetry of other kinds : rhythm.
met'rical, *adj.* with syllables arranged in regular order : made up of verses.
[O.E. *mēter*—Gk. *metron*, measure.]

metre[2], *mē'tėr, n.* the chief unit of length in the metric system (39·37 inches).
metric system, a system of weights and measures based on tens (e.g. 1 metre = 10 decimetres = 100 centimetres etc.).
[Fr. *mètre*—same root as **metre** (1).]

metronome, *met'rò-nōm, n.* an instrument that beats to mark musical time.
[Gk. *metron*, measure, *nomos*, law.]

metropolis, *mė-trop'ò-lis, n.* the chief city of a country : the chief cathedral city (as Canterbury in England) : a chief centre.
metropol'itan, *adj.*
[Gk. *mētēr*, mother, *polis*, a city.]

mettle, *met'l, n.* spirit, courage, pluck.
mett'led, mett'lesome, *adjs.* high-spirited.
to put a person on his mettle, to rouse him to put forth his best efforts.
[From the **metal** of a blade.]

mew[1], *mū, n.* a seagull.
[O.E. *mǣw* ; conn. Ger. *möwe* ; imit.]

mew[2], *mū, v.i.* to cry as a cat. [Imit.]

mew[3], *mū, v.t.* (usu. **mew up**) to shut up, confine (e.g. *They were mewed up in the house by heavy rain.*)
mews, *n.* a street or yard with, or orig. with, stables.
[O.Fr. *muer*, moult (L. *mutāre*, change) ; moulting hawks were kept in a cage. Royal stables once stood where king's hawks had earlier been mewed.]

mezzo-soprano, *med'zō-so-prä'nō, met'. n.* quality of voice between soprano and alto : low soprano. [It.]

miaow, *mi-ow', n.* cry of a cat.—Also *v.i.* [Imit.]

miasma, *mi-az'mȧ, mī-, n.* a poisonous atmosphere or influence.
[Gk. *miasma*, pollution.]

mica, *mī'kȧ, n.* a glittering mineral that divides easily into thin plates or layers and can usu. be seen through.
[L. *mīca*, a crumb.]

mice. See **mouse.**

Michaelmas, *mik'ȧl-mȧs, n.* the festival of St. *Michael*, Sept. 29.
Michaelmas daisy, an aster.

micro-, *mī-krō-*, (as part of word) very small: one millionth part (**micromicro-,** a millionth part of a millionth part).
microbe, *mī'krōb, n.* a very tiny living thing, a germ (esp. causing disease).
microfilm, *mī'krō-film, n.* a very small film on which documents, books, etc. are recorded.—Also *v.t.*
microgroove, *mī'krō-grōōv, n.* fine groove of long-playing record.
micrometer, *mī-krom'ė-tėr, n.* an instrument for measuring very small distances or angles.
micro-organism, *mī'krō-ör'gan-izm, n.* a very small organism (animal or plant).
microphone, *mī'krō-fōn, n.* an instrument for making sounds louder : an instrument for picking up sound waves to be broadcast (e.g. in radio or telephone) and turning them into electrical waves.—Also (*coll.*) **mike** (*mīk*).
microscope, *mī'krō-skōp, n.* an instrument which makes very small objects able to be seen by means of lenses, or reflecting mirrors, or other methods.
microscop'ic, *adj.* having to do with a microscope : seen only by the aid of a microscope : very tiny.
[Gk. *mīkros*, little (*bīos*, life ; *metron*, measure ; *phōnē*, voice ; *skopeein*, view.]

mid, *mid, adj.* (of a time, position, etc.) at, in, the middle of (e.g. *at mid term, in mid ocean*) :—*superl.* **mid'most.**—*prep.* amid.
mid'day, *n.* the middle of the day, noon.—Also *adj.*
mid'land, *adj.* in the middle of land, distant from the coast : of the Midlands.
Midlands, *n.pl.* counties in the centre of England.
mid'night, *n.* the middle of the night, twelve o'clock at night.—*adj.* being at midnight : dark as midnight.
mid'ship, *adj.* in the middle of a ship.
mid'shipman, *n.* a former rank of a young officer on a ship in the navy (orig. serving amidships), now shore ranking during training.
midst, *midst, n.* middle—used in phrase 'in the midst of' (e.g. *in the midst of these troubles*) ; also in phrases 'in our, your, their midst' (e.g. *foreigners living in our midst*, i.e. among us, in the same town, etc.).—*prep.* amid.
mid'summer, *n.* the middle of summer, the period about June 21.—Also *adj.*
mid'way, *adj.* and *adv.* in the middle of the distance, half way.
mid'-wick'et, *n.* fielder near bowler **(mid-off'** or **mid-on'),** or his place.
mid'winter, *n.* the middle of winter, the period about Dec. 21 or 22.
in mid air, in the air and well above the ground.
[O.E. *midd* ; conn. Ger. *mitte*, L. *medius*.]

midden, *mid'ėn, n.* dunghill: refuse heap.
[From Scand.]

middle, *mid'l, adj.* (used only before noun) equally distant from both ends: coming between.—*n.* the middle point or part: midst: central portion, waist.
midd'ling, *adj.* of middle size, quality, rate, state: second-rate, moderate.
midd'lemost, *adj.* nearest the middle.
midd'le-aged, *adj.* between youth and old age.
Middle Ages, the time between the downfall of the Roman empire and the Renaissance (renewed interest in art and learning).
middle class, the people (including professional people, bankers, shop-owners, etc.) who come between the working class and the aristocratic or the very wealthy.
Middle East, the countries of Asia west of India.
Middle English. See **English.**
midd'leman, *n.* a dealer who comes between the person who makes or grows a product and one who buys it: a go-between or agent.
[O.E. *middel*; Ger. *mittel.*]

midge, *mij, n.* any small gnat or fly: a very small person.
midg'et, *n.* a person not grown to ordinary size: anything very small of its kind.—Also *adj.*
[O.E. *mycge*; conn. with Ger. *mücke.*]

midland, midnight, etc. See **mid.**

midriff, *mid'rif, n.* the diaphragm or middle of the body, just above the stomach.
[O.E. *midd*, middle, *hrif*, the belly.]

midship, midst, midway, etc. See **mid.**

midwife, *mid'wīf, n.* a woman who helps at the birth of children.
mid'wifery (*-wif-ė-ri*), *n.* art or practice of a midwife.
[O.E. *mid*, with, *wīf*, woman.]

mien, *mēn, n.* expression of face, manner (e.g. *a man of proud mien*).
[Perh. same root as **demeanour.**]

might[1]. See **may** (1).

might[2], *mīt, n.* power, strength.
might'y, *adj.* having great power: very large: (*coll.*) very great.—*adv.* very.
might'ily, *adv.* **might'iness,** *n.*
[O.E. *miht, mecht*; root as **may** (1).]

mignonette, *min-yo-net', n.* a sweet-smelling plant with greyish-green flowers.
[Fr. from *mignon*, daintily small.]

migraine, *mē-grān', n.* a type of headache, usu. on one side of the head only.
[Gk. *hemi*, half, *kranion*, skull.]

migrate, *mī'grāt, v.i.* to pass regularly from one region to another, as certain birds and animals do: to change one's home to another country.
mī'gratory, *adj.* migrating: wandering.
mī'grant, *adj.* and *n.* **migrā'tion,** *n.*
[L. *migrāre, -ātum.*]

mikado, *mi-kä'dō, n.* a title of the Emperor of Japan.
[Jap., 'exalted gate'.]

mike. See **microphone.**

milch. See **milk.**

mild, *mīld, adj.* gentle in temper or behaviour: not sharp or bitter: (of punishment, etc.) not severe: (of weather) neither cold nor very hot.
mild'ly, *adv.* **mild'ness,** *n.*
[O.E. *milde*; conn. with Ger. *mild.*]

mildew, *mil'dū, n.* a disease on plants, cloth, etc. caused by the growth and spread of very tiny fungi.
[O.E. *mildēaw*, honeydew.]

mile, *mīl, n.* a length of 1760 yards (1·61 kilometres): in Roman times, 1000 paces.
mile'age, *n.* length in miles: expense of travel reckoned by the mile.
mile'stone, *n.* a stone set up to mark the distance of a mile: something which marks an important step or point (e.g. *Magna Carta was a milestone in British history*).
geographical, or **nautical, mile,** any of several units used for measurement at sea, in Britain 6080 ft. (1·85 km.).
[O.E. *mīl*—L. *mīlia* (pl.)—*mille* (passuum), 1000 (paces; see **league,** 1).]

milieu, *mēl-yė, n.* setting in place and time: social surroundings. [Fr.]

militant, *mil'i-tȧnt, adj.* fighting: warlike.
mil'itancy, *n.* **mil'itantly,** *adv.*
mil'itary, *adj.* having to do with soldiers or with warfare.—*n.* the army.
mil'itate, *v.i.* to work, exert force or influence (against: e.g. *These unforeseen events militated against his success*).
militia, *mi-lish'ȧ, n.* a body of men trained to fight as soldiers, but liable only for home service.
milit'iaman, *n.* a militia soldier.
[L. *miles, mīlitis*, soldier.]

milk, *milk, v.t.* to squeeze or draw milk, etc., from: to force, take, money, information, etc. from (a person) in order to use it for one's own profit.—*n.* a white liquid produced by female animals as food for their young.
milk'y, *adj.* **milk'iness,** *n.*
milk'er, *n.* a machine for milking cows: a cow that gives milk.
milk'ing, *n.* the act of drawing milk from cows, etc.: the amount of milk drawn at one time.
milch, *milch, milsh, adj.* giving milk.
milk bar, a place where milk drinks, etc., are sold.
milk'man, *n.* a man who sells, or delivers, milk.
milk'sop, *n.* an unmanly man or boy.
Milky Way, *n.* the Galaxy (see this).
[O.E. *milc*; conn. with Ger. *milch.*]

mill, *mil, n.* a machine for grinding (e.g. corn, coffee) by crushing between hard, rough surfaces: a building where grain is ground: one where manufacture of some kind is carried on (e.g. *a steel mill*). —*v.t.* to grind, press, or stamp, in a mill: to put ridges and grooves on the rim of (coins).—*v.i.* (*slang*) to box, fight: (of e.g. cattle) to move round and round in a group.

mill′er, *n.* one who works a grain mill.

mill′ing, *n.* the act of passing anything through a mill: ridges and grooves on the rim of a coin.

mill′-race, *n.* (the channel in which runs) the current of water that turns a mill-wheel.

mill′stone, *n.* one of the two stones used in a mill for grinding grain: a burden that crushes one's spirit.

mill′-wheel, *n.* a wheel, esp. a water-wheel, used for driving a mill.

[O.E. *myln*—L. *mola*—*molĕre*, to grind.]

millennium, *mi-len′i-ŭm, n.* a thousand years: the period during which, it was prophesied (Revelation xx), Christ will live again on earth: a coming golden age.—*pl.* **millenn′ia.**

[L. *mille*, 1000, *annus*, a year.]

millepede. See **millipede** (at **milli-**).

millet, *mil′it, n.* a grain used for food.

[Fr. *millet*—L. *milium.*]

milli-, *mil-i-*, (as part of word) thousand: thousandth part, e.g. **milligram, -litre, -metre** (see Appendices).

millipede, millepede, *mil′i-pēd, n.* a small many-legged creature with a long round body.

[L. *mille*, thousand (*pēs, pedis*, foot).]

milliner, *mil′in-ėr, n.* one who makes and sells hats for women.

mill′inery, *n.* articles made or sold by milliners: the hat industry.

[*Milaner*, trader in Milan silk, etc.]

million, *mil′yȯn, n.* a thousand thousands (1,000,000): a very great number.

millionaire′, *n.* a man having a million pounds, dollars, etc., or more.

[Fr.—L. *mille*, a thousand.]

millipede. See **milli-.**

mill-race, millstone. See **mill.**

mime, *mīm, n.* a play in which no words are spoken and the actions tell the story: an actor in such a play.

mimic, *mim′ik, n.* one who imitates or copies, esp. in a mocking way.—*v.t.* to imitate, esp. in a mocking way:—*pr.p.* **mim′icking**; *pa.p.* **mim′icked.**—*adj.* mock, sham (e.g. *a mimic battle*).

mim′icry (*-kri*), *n.* act of mimicking: (in an animal) likeness to another or to some object in its surroundings.

[Gk. *mimos*, mimic, mime.]

mimosa, *mi-mō′zȧ, n.* a tree with bunches of yellow, scented flowers.

[Same root as **mime.**]

minaret, *min′ȧ-rėt, n.* a slender tower on a mosque, from which the call to prayer is sounded.

[Arabic *manārat*, (orig.) lighthouse.]

mince, *mins, v.t.* to cut into small pieces, to chop fine.—*v.i.* to walk in an affected way with prim steps:—*pr.p.* **min′cing;** *pa.p.* **minced.**—*n.* meat chopped up.

min′cing, *adj.* **min′cingly,** *adv.*

min′cer, *n.* a machine for mincing.

mince′meat, *n.* anything cut to pieces: a mixture of raisins, other fruits, etc., usu. with suet (used in pastry to form a **mince′-pie′**).

to mince matters, words, to soften a statement, make it less frank, so as to be polite.

[O.Fr. *mincier*—root as **minute** (1).]

mind, *mīnd, n.* the power by which we think, etc.: intelligence, understanding: a person who has great powers of reasoning, etc.: intention (e.g. *to change one's mind*): inclination, desire (e.g. *I have a mind*, or *a good mind*, or *a great mind, to tell your father*): frank opinion (e.g. *to speak one's mind*).—*v.t.* to look after: to pay attention to, obey (e.g. *You should mind your parents*): to watch out for (e.g. *Mind the step!*): to be upset by, or to object to (e.g. *I mind your going very much*).

mind′ed, *adj.* (combined with other words) having a mind (e.g. *strong-minded, narrow-minded*): determined (to).

mind′ful, *adj.* bearing in mind (with *of*; e.g. *mindful of the danger*).

mind′less, *adj.* without mind: stupid.

mind's eye, part of imagination that forms pictures.

in two minds, undecided.

never mind, do not consider, trouble about, be upset by.

of one mind, in agreement.

on one's mind, troubling one.

presence of mind, a state of calmness and readiness for any action required.

to bear, keep, in mind, to remember, take into consideration.

to be out of one's mind, to be insane.

to lose one's mind, to become insane.

to make up one's mind, to decide.

to put in mind, to remind.

[O.E. *gemynd*; conn. L. *mens.*]

mine[1]. See **I.**

mine[2], *mīn, n.* a place from which metals, coal, etc., are dug: a rich source (of e.g. information): a heavy charge of explosive material for blowing up (e.g. a ship). —*v.t.* to make passages in or under: to lay mines in: to blow up with mines.—*v.i.* to dig or work a mine.

mī′ner, *n.* one who works in a mine.

mine′-field, *n.* an area covered with explosive mines.

mine′-layer, -sweeper, *ns.* ships used for placing, removing, mines in the sea.

[Fr.; of Celtic origin.]

mineral, *min′ėr-ȧl, n.* a substance found naturally in the earth and mined—metal, rock, coal, asphalt.—*adj.* of, having to do with, minerals.

mineral′ogy, *n.* study of minerals.

mineralog′ical, *adj.*
mineral′ogist, *n.*
mineral oil, an oil, esp. petroleum, obtained from minerals.
mineral water, a spring water containing minerals: a non-alcoholic drink.
[Fr.—same root as **mine** (2).]

mingle, *ming′gl, v.t.* to mix.—*v.i.* to mix: to go about among (with *with*; e.g. *The thief mingled with the guests*).
ming′ling, *n.* **mingled,** *ming′gld, adj.*
[O.E. *mengan*; conn. with Ger. *mengen.*]

mini-, *mi-ni,* (as part of word) small, e.g. **min′ibus,** a small bus, **min′iskirt,** a very short skirt. [Abbrev. of **miniature.**]

miniature, *min′yȧ-chůr, min′i-(ȧ-), n.* a painting on a very small scale: a small copy of anything.—*adj.* on a small scale.
min′iaturise (*-īz*), *v.t.* to reduce the size of (esp. electronic equipment) very greatly.
miniaturisā′tion, *n.*
[It. *miniatura*—Late L. word meaning to illuminate (a manuscript).]

minim, *min′im, n.* (*music*) a note equal to two crotchets.
[Same root as **minimum** (at one time a minim was the shortest note).]

minimum, *min′i-mům, adj.* smallest.—*n.* the smallest number or quantity: the lowest point or degree:—*pl.* **min′ima.**
min′imal, *adj.* the least possible: very small indeed.
min′imise, *v.t.* to make as little as possible (e.g. *He took steps to minimise the dangers*): (to try) to make seem little (e.g. *He spoke as if he had done it all, minimising help he had received*).
[L. *minimus* (superl. of *parvus*), smallest.]

minion, *min′yȯn, n.* a favourite, esp. of a prince: a follower who will do anything he is told to do.
[Fr. *mignon,* a darling.]

minister, *min′is-tėr, n.* a clergyman: the head of one of the divisions or departments of the government: the representative of a government at a foreign court.—*v.i.* to give help (to), supply necessary things (to).
ministē′rial, *adj.*
ministrā′tion, *n.* (often in *pl.*) the act of giving help, care, etc.
min′istry, *n.* the profession, duties, or period of service, of a minister of religion: the ministers of state as a group: a department of government, or the building where it works:—*pl.* **min′istries.**
[L., servant—*minor,* less.]

mink, *mingk, n.* a small weasel-like animal: its fur.
[Perhaps from Swed. *mänk.*]

minnow, *min′ō, n.* a very small freshwater fish.
[M.E. *men(a)we*—O.E. *myne.*]

minor, *mī′nor, adj.* less in importance, size, etc.: of little importance.—*n.* a person under age (under 18 years).
minor′ity, *n.* the state of being under age: (the party having) the smaller number.
minor interval, one that is a semitone less than the major, e.g. **minor third,** e.g. C to E flat (major, C to E).
minor scale, one in which the third note is a minor third above the first, and which contains other minor intervals.
[L., used as comp. of *parvus,* little.]

minster, *min′stėr, n.* the church of a monastery: a large church.
[O.E. *mynster*—L. *monastērium,* monastery.]

minstrel, *min′strėl, n.* a harper who went about the country in olden days reciting or singing poems: an entertainer, esp. one who sings Negro songs.
min′strelsy, *n.* a collection of songs: a group of minstrels: music.
[O.Fr. *menestrel*; root as **minister.**]

mint[1], *mint, n.* (*cap.*) place where money is coined by government: a large sum (of money).—*v.t.* to coin: to invent.
in mint condition, unused: undamaged.
[O.E. *mynet,* money; root as **money.**]

mint[2], *mint, n.* a plant, used for flavouring, with sweet-smelling leaves.
[O.Fr. *minte*—L. *mentha*—Gk. *minthē.*]

minuet, *min-ū-et′, n.* a slow, graceful dance with short steps: music for it.
[Fr. *menuet*—L. *minūtus,* small.]

minus, *mī′nůs, prep.* used to show subtraction (e.g. *Ten minus two equals eight,* $10-2=8$): (*coll.*) without.—*n.* and *adj.* (a quantity) less than zero or naught: (the sign) showing subtraction (−).
[L.; same root as **minor.**]

minute[1], *mī-nūt′, mi-, adj.* extremely small: paying attention to the smallest details (e.g. *minute care, a minute examination*).
minute′ly, *adv.* **minute′ness,** *n.*
[L. *minuěre, minūtus,* to make less.]

minute[2], *min′it, n.* the sixtieth part of an hour: (in measuring an angle) the sixtieth part of a degree: a very short time: (in *pl.*) the notes taken at a meeting recording what was said.
[Same word as **minute** (1).]

minutiae, *mi-nū′shi-ē, mī-, n. pl.* very small details.
[L. *pl.* of *minūtia,* smallness.]

minx, *mingks, n.* a pert young girl.
[Perh. from **minikin,** a darling.]

miracle, *mir′ȧ-kl, n.* an act beyond the power of man, or a fortunate happening that has no natural cause or explanation: a wonder, marvel.
miraculous, *mi-rak′ū-lůs, adj.*
a miracle of, a wonderful example of.
[L. *mirăculum*—*mirārī,* to wonder at.]

mirage, *mi′räzh, -räzh′, n.* something not really there that one imagines one sees, esp. the appearance of an expanse of water seen by travellers in a desert.
[Fr.; same root as **miracle.**]

mire, *mīr, n.* deep mud.—*v.t.* to cause to stick fast in mire: to stain with mud.
mir′y, *adj.*:—*comp.* **mir′ier**; *superl.* **mir′iest.**
mir′ily, *adv.* **mir′iness,** *n.*
[Old Norse *mȳrr*, bog.]

mirror, *mir′ȯr, n.* a looking-glass: a surface that reflects: something that gives a true picture or likeness.—*v.t.* to reflect as a mirror does.
[O.Fr. *mireor*; same root as **miracle.**]

mirth, *mėrth, n.* merriness: laughter or amusement caused by something funny.
mirth′ful, *adj.* merry: funny.
mirth′less, *adj.* joyless, cheerless.
[O.E. *myrgth*; same root as **merry.**]

mis-, *mis-, pfx.* wrong(ly): bad(ly).
[O.E.; also O.Fr. *mes-*—L. as **minus.**]

misadventure, *mis-ȧd-ven′chůr, n.* an unlucky happening: accident. [**mis-.**]

misadvise, *mis-ȧd-vīz′, v.t.* to give bad advice to. [Pfx. **mis-.**]

misalliance, *mis-ȧ-lī′ȧns, n.* an unsuitable alliance (esp. marriage with one of a lower rank) or combination.
misally, *mis-ȧ-lī′, v.t.*:—*pr.p.* **misally′ing**; *pa.p.* **misallied′.**
[Translation of Fr. *mésalliance.*]

misanthrope, *mis′ȧn-thrōp, miz′, n.* a hater of mankind.—Also **misan′thropist.**
misanthrop′ic, *adj.*
misan′thropy, *n.* hatred, distrust, of man.
[Gk. *mīseein*, to hate, *anthrōpos*, a man.]

misapply, *mis-ȧ-plī′, v.t.* to use for a wrong purpose: to apply to a wrong person or thing:—*pr.p.* **misapply′ing**; *pa.p.* **misapplied′.**
misapplicā′tion, *n.* [Pfx. **mis-.**]

misapprehend, *mis-ap-ri-hend′, v.t.* to misunderstand (meaning, person in what he says): to take a wrong meaning from. —Also *v.i.*
misapprehen′sion, *n.* misunderstanding of meaning, or false belief as to fact (*to be under a misapprehension*). [Pfx. **mis-.**]

misappropriate, *mis-ȧ-prō′pri-āt, v.t.* to put to a wrong use, esp. to use (another's money) for oneself.
misappropriā′tion, *n.* [Pfx. **mis-.**]

misbehave, *mis-bi-hāv′, v.i.* behave badly.
misbehav′iour (*-yėr*), *n.* [Pfx. **mis-.**]

miscalculate, *mis-kal′kū-lāt, v.t., v.i.* to calculate, estimate, or judge, wrongly. [Pfx. **mis-.**]

miscarriage, *mis-kar′ij, n.* failure (of a plan): failure to gain the right result (e.g. *By a miscarriage of justice the wrong man was condemned*): the act of bringing forth young too early for survival and development.
miscarr′y, *v.i.* to be unsuccessful: to have the wrong result: (of e.g. a letter) to go astray: (of a female) to have a miscarriage:—*pr.p.* **miscarr′ying**; *pa.p.* **miscarr′ied** (*-id*). [Pfx. **mis-.**]

miscegenation, *mis-i-jė-nā′sh(ȯ)n, n.* mixture of races resulting from marriage between people of different races.
[L. *miscēre*, to mix, *genus*, race.]

miscellaneous, *mis-ėl-ān′yůs, adj.* mixed, made up of several kinds.
miscell′any, *n.* a mixture of different kinds: a collection of writings on different subjects or by different authors.
[L. *miscellāneus*—*miscēre*, to mix.]

mischance, *mis-châns′, n.* bad luck: mishap, accident.
[O.Fr. *mescheance.*]

mischief, *mis′chif, n.* evil, trouble, harm, damage: action or behaviour that causes small troubles or annoyance to others.
mischievous, *mis′chi-vůs, adj.* harmful: tending, or inclined, to cause trouble or to annoy: (fond of) teasing, etc., in a playful manner.
mis′chief-maker, *n.* one who causes bad feeling or trouble, e.g. by carrying tales.
[O.Fr. *meschef.*]

misconceive, *mis-kȯn-sēv′, v.t.* to form a wrong idea of.—Also *v.i.*
misconcep′tion, *n.* [Pfx. **mis-.**]

misconduct, *mis-kon′dukt, n.* bad conduct. —*v.t.* (*-kȯn-dukt′*) to misbehave (oneself): to mismanage. [Pfx. **mis-.**]

misconstrue, *mis-kȯn-strōō′, -kon′, v.t.* to misunderstand, take a wrong meaning from (e.g. *He misconstrues the men's action; they are not out for gain, they really want to help*).
misconstruc′tion, *n.* [Pfx. **mis-.**]

miscount, *mis-kownt′, v.t.* to count wrongly.—*n.* a wrong count. [**mis-.**]

miscreant, *mis′kri-ȧnt, n.* a very wicked person, scoundrel, rascal.
[O.Fr. *mescreant* (orig. 'unbeliever'); L. root as **credit.**]

misdeal, *mis-dēl′, n.* a wrong deal, as at cards.—*v.t., v.i.* deal wrongly. [**mis-.**]

misdeed, *mis-dēd′, n.* an evil deed: (often) an instance of bad behaviour. [**mis-.**]

misdemeanour, *mis-di-mē′nȯr, n.* bad behaviour: a petty crime. [Pfx. **mis-.**]

misdirect, *mis-di-rekt′, -dī-, v.t.* to direct wrongly. [Pfx. **mis-.**]

miser, *mī′zėr, n.* a mean, ungenerous person who lives very poorly in order to store up wealth.
mi′serly, *adj.* **mi′serliness,** *n.*
[Same root as **miserable.**]

miserable, *miz′ėr-ȧ-bl, adj.* very unhappy: very poor in quantity or quality (e.g. *miserable payment, a miserable hovel*): shameful (e.g. *his miserable cowardice*).
mis′erableness, *n.* **mis′erably,** *adv.*
misery, *miz′ėr-i, n.* great unhappiness.
[L. *miser*, wretched, unfortunate, sad.]

misfire, *mis-fīr′, v.i.* to fail to explode or catch fire: to produce no effect, have no success.—Also *n.* [Pfx. **mis-.**]

misfit, *mis′fit, -fit′, n.* a bad fit: a thing that fits badly: a person not able to live or work happily in the society in which he finds himself. [Pfx. **mis-.**]

misfortune, *mis-för'chůn, n.* bad luck: a mishap or calamity. [Pfx. **mis-.**]

misgiving, *mis-giv'ing, n.* a feeling of fear or doubt e.g. about the result of an action.
[*misgive*, to give doubt to (e.g. 'My mind misgives me'); pfx. **mis-.**]

misgovern, *mis-guv'ėrn, v.t.* to govern or rule badly or unjustly. [Pfx. **mis-.**]

misguide, *mis-gīd', v.t.* to lead astray: to lead into thinking wrongly.
misguid'ed, *adj.* acting from, or showing, mistaken beliefs or motives (e.g. *misguided attempts to help*). [Pfx. **mis-.**]

mishandle, *mis-han'dl, v.t.* to handle without skill: to treat roughly. [**mis-.**]

mishap, *mis'hap, -hap', n.* an unlucky accident (often not serious). [**mis-.**]

misinform, *mis-in-förm', v.t.* to give wrong information to. [Pfx. **mis-.**]

misinterpret, *mis-in-tėr'prit, v.t.* to take a wrong meaning from: to explain wrongly. [Pfx. **mis-.**]

misjudge, *mis-juj', v.t., v.i.* to judge wrongly: to have an unjust opinion of (a person). [Pfx. **mis-.**]

mislay, *mis-lā', v.t.* to lay in a place and forget where it is:—*pa.p.* **mislaid'** (*-lād'*). [Pfx. **mis-.**]

mislead, *mis-lēd', v.t.* (of e.g. a remark) to give a wrong idea to (a person): to cause to make mistakes:—*pa.t., pa.p.* **misled'.** —Also *v.i.*
mislead'ing, *adj.* [Pfx. **mis-.**]

mismanage, *mis-man'ij, v.t.* to manage badly, without skill. [Pfx. **mis-.**]

misnomer, *mis-nō'mėr, n.* a wrong name: an unsuitable name (e.g. *'Road' was a misnomer; the way was a rutted track*).
[Pfx. **mis-**, and L. *nōmināre*, to name.]

misogynist, *mis-oj'i-nist, n.* a hater of women.
[Gr. *mīseein*, to hate, *gynē*, a woman.]

misplace, *mis-plās', v.t.* to put in the wrong place: to give (e.g. trust, affection) to an unworthy object. [Pfx. **mis-.**]

misprint, *mis'print, -print', n.* a mistake in printing.—Also *v.t.* [Pfx. **mis-.**]

mispronounce, *mis-prȯ-nowns', v.t.* to pronounce wrongly.
mispronunciā'tion (*-nun-*), *n.*
[Pfx. **mis-.**]

misquote, *mis-kwōt', v.t.* to make a mistake in repeating what someone has written or said. [Pfx. **mis-.**]

misread, *mis-rēd', v.t.* to read wrongly: to take a wrong meaning from reading.
misread'ing, *n.* [Pfx. **mis-.**]

misreport, *mis-ri-pōrt', -pört', v.t.* to report incorrectly. [Pfx. **mis-.**]

misrepresent, *mis-rep-ri-zent', v.t.* to give a false idea of (a person, what he does or says). [Pfx. **mis-.**]

misrule, *mis-rōōl', n.* unjust rule: disorder.—*v.t.* to rule badly. [Pfx. **mis-.**]

miss[1], *mis, n.* (*cap.*, with Christian name or surname) used in addressing formally an unmarried female (e.g. *You are Miss Smith, I believe*): a young woman or girl:—*pl.* **miss'es.** (On letters put *The Misses Smith*; *the Miss Smiths* is less formal).
[Shortened form of **mistress.**]

miss[2], *mis, v.t.* to fail to hit, reach, get, find, see, hear, understand: to fail to have, keep (e.g. *She missed her French lesson, her appointment*): to avoid (e.g. *He just missed being caught*): to fail to take advantage of (an opportunity): to discover the absence of (e.g. *He missed his umbrella when he reached home*): to feel the want of (e.g. *He misses his friends*). —*v.i.* to fail to hit: to be unsuccessful.— *n.* a failure to hit the mark: a loss.
miss'ing, *adj.* not in its place: not found: lacking.
[O.E. *missan*; conn. with Du. *missen.*]

missal, *mis'ȧl, n.* the book that contains the year's mass services for the Roman Catholic Church.
[Late L. *missāle—missa*, mass.]

missel thrush, *mis'l thrush*, a large thrush fond of mistletoe berries.
[O.E. *mistel*, mistletoe.]

misshapen, *mis-shāp'ėn, adj.* badly shaped. [Pfx. **mis-**, and **shape.**]

missile, *mis'il, -il, n.* a weapon or object for throwing or shooting.
guided missile, a jet- or rocket-propelled missile directed to its target by a built-in device, or by radio waves, etc.
[Same root as **mission.**]

missing. See **miss** (2).

mission, *mish'(ȯ)n, n.* a purpose for which a messenger, delegate, etc. is sent (e.g. *His mission was to seek help*): a group of delegates sent to carry out negotiations: persons sent to spread a religion: a station or post where these live: one's chosen purpose or duty (e.g. *He regarded it as his mission to get rid of the tyrant*).
miss'ionary, *n.* one sent on a missio esp. to spread religion:—*pl.* **-ies.**
[L. *mittěre, missum*, to send.]

missive, *mis'iv, adj. n,* something sent, esp. a letter.
[Same root as **mission.**]

misspell, *mis-spel', v.t.* to spell wrongly:— *pa.p.* **misspelt, misspelled.**
[Pfx. **mis-.**]

misspend, *mis-spend', v.t.* to waste, squander on wrong things (money, one's life).
misspent', *pa.p* and *adj.* [Pfx. **mis-.**]

misstate, *mis-stāt', v.t.* to state wrongly.
misstate'ment, *n.* [Pfx. **mis-.**]

mist, *mist, n.* a cloud of moisture in the air, very thin fog, or drizzle: anything that clouds the sight or the judgment.—*v.t.* and *v.i.* to blur, cloud over, as with mist.
mis'ty, *adj.—comp.* **mis'tier;** *superl.* **mis'tiest.**
mis'tily, *adv.* **mis'tiness,** *n.*
[O.E. *mist*, darkness; Du. *mist*, fog.]

mistake, *mis-tāk′*, *v.t.* to make an error about: to take (one person or thing for another): to understand wrongly (e.g. *You mistake my meaning, my intention*).—Also *v.i.*—*n.* act of understanding wrongly: an error, wrong action or statement: error arising from bad judgment (e.g. *It was a mistake to trust him*):—*pa.t.* **mistook′**; *pa.p.* **mistak′en.**
mistak′en, *adj.* in error (e.g. *You are mistaken about what happened*): showing bad judgment (e.g. *a mistaken attempt to help*).
mistak′enly, *adv.*
[Old Norse *mis-*, wrongly, *taka*, take.]

mister, *mis′tėr*, *n.* used formally before the name of a man (written **Mr**):—for the *pl.* **Messrs** (see this word) is used. [**master.**]

mistime, *mis-tīm′*, *v.t.* to time badly: to do or say at an unsuitable time. [**mis-.**]

mistiness, etc. See **mist.**

mistletoe, *mis′l-tō, miz′-*, *n.* a plant with white berries, growing on trees, used in Christmas decorations.
[O.E. *mistel*, mistletoe, *tān*, twig.]

mistress, *mis′tris*, *n.* (*fem.* of **master**) a woman who commands or controls: a state, etc. that controls: a female owner (of e.g. a dog) or employer: a woman teacher: a woman very skilled in an art: a woman who lives with a man without being his legal wife: used formally before the name of a married woman (written **Mrs**, pronounced *mis′iz*):—*pl.* **mis′tresses.**
[O.Fr. *maistresse*—L. *magister*, master.]

mistrial, *mis-trī′ȧl*, *n.* a trial declared to have no legal force because of error or fault in the proceedings. [Pfx. **mis-.**]

mistrust, *mis-trust′*, *n.* lack of trust.—*v.t.* to suspect, distrust. [Pfx. **mis-.**]

misty. See **mist.**

misunderstand, *mis-un-dėr-stand′*, *v.t.* to take a wrong meaning from (e.g. a statement, or a person or his words or actions):—*pa.t.*, *pa.p.* **misunderstood′.**
misunderstand′ing, *n.* a mistake as to meaning: a slight disagreement.
misunderstood′, *adj.* (of a person) not understood or appreciated. [Pfx. **mis-.**]

misuse, *mis-ūs′*, *n.* wrong use: use for a bad purpose.—*v.t.* (*mis-ūz′*) to use wrongly: to treat badly. [Pfx. **mis-.**]

mite[1], *mīt*, *n.* a very small insect living on other insects, animals, or plants, or in food (such as cheese).
mit′y, *adj.* full of mites.
[O.E. *mīte.*]

mite[2], *mīt*, *n.* anything very small: a tiny person.
[Middle Du. *mīte*; conn. **mite** (1).]

mitigate, *mit′i-gāt*, *v.t.* to make (e.g. pain, anger) less great: to make (e.g. punishment) less severe: to excuse (a wrong action) to some extent (e.g. *The circumstances mitigated his offence*).
mit′igating, *adj.* **mitigā′tion,** *n.*
[L. *mītigāre*—*mītis*, mild.]

mitre[1], *mī′tėr*, *n.* a headdress worn by archbishops and bishops.
[Fr.—Gk. *mitrā*, fillet (head band).]

mitre[2], *mī′tėr*, *n.* a joint made between two pieces that form an angle, usu. a right angle, the end of each piece being cut on a slant.—Also **mi′tre-joint.**
[Prob. **mitre** (1).]

mitten, *mit′n*, **mitt,** *mit*, *n.* kind of glove, having one cover for all the four fingers: a glove for the hand and wrist, but not the fingers.
[O.Fr. *mitaine*; origin uncertain.]

mity. See **mite** (1).

mix, *miks*, *v.t.* to unite or blend several things into one mass (e.g. by stirring): to form by doing this (e.g. *to mix cement*): to muddle, confuse (often **mix up**):—*v.i.* to blend (e.g. *Oil and water do not mix*): to associate as friends or in society (e.g. *He did not mix with his neighbours*).—*n.* mixture.
mixed, *adj.* jumbled together: confused: including people of both sexes.
mix′er, *n.* one who, or a machine which, mixes: (with *good* or *bad*) one who gets on well, or not well, with other people.
mix′ture (*-chůr*), *n.* act of mixing or state of being mixed: a mass or blend formed by mixing.
mixed′-up′, *adj.* confused: bewildered, not fitting into the life around one.
[O.E. *miscian*; conn. L. *miscēre*, *mixtum.*]

mizzen-mast, *miz′n-mâst*, *n.* the mast nearest the stern of a two- or three-masted ship.
[Fr. *misaine*—L. *medius*, the middle.]

mnemonic, *nē-mon′ik, ni-*, *n.* something (often a jingle) that helps the memory (e.g. the spelling rule '*i* before *e* except after *c*'.)
[Gk. *mnēmōn*, mindful—*mnēmē*, memory.]

moan, *mōn*, *n.* a low sound of grief or pain. —*v.i.* to utter a moan.
[O.E. *mǣnan*, to moan.]

moat, *mōt*, *n.* a deep trench round a castle, etc., usu. filled with water.
[O.Fr. *mote*, mound.]

mob, *mob*, *n.* the mass of the people: a (noisy or disorderly) crowd of people or animals.—*v.t.* to crowd round, or attack, in a disorderly way:—*pr.p.* **mobb′ing,** *pa.p.* **mobbed.**
[L. *mōbile* (*vulgus*), fickle (multitude).]

mobile, *mō′bīl, -bil, -bēl*, *adj.* able to move: easily or quickly moved: (of mind) quick: (of face) changing easily in expression.—*n.* an artistic object hung so that it moves slightly in the air.
mo′bileness, mobil′ity, *ns.*
mō′bilise, *v.t.* to put in readiness for service: to call (e.g. troops) into active service.
[Fr.—L. *mōbilis*—same root as **move.**]

moccasin, mocassin, *mok′ȧ-sin*, *n.* a shoe

of soft leather, worn by American Indians: a bedroom slipper something like this. [Native word.]

mocha, *mō'kȧ, n.* a fine coffee, brought from *Mocha* on the Red Sea.

mock, *mok, v.t.* to laugh at: to mimic in scorn: to disappoint or to bring no success to (e.g. hopes, efforts).—*adj.* sham, not real (e.g. *a mock battle*).

mock'ery, *n.* act of making fun of something: false show: something very far from what it should be (e.g. *a mockery of a reward*):—*pl.* **mock'eries.**

mock'ing, *adj.* and *n.*

mock'ingly, *adv.*

mock'ing-bird, *n.* an American bird of the same family as the thrushes, which copies the notes of other birds.

[O.Fr. *mocquer*; origin uncertain.]

mode, *mōd, n.* manner of acting, doing, etc.: fashion.

mo'dish, *adj.* fashionable, smart.

modiste (*-dēst'*), *n.* dressmaker: milliner

[Fr.—L. *modus*, measure.]

model, *mod'l, n.* something to be copied: something worth copying (e.g. *She is a model of kindness*): a copy of something made in a smaller size: a person who poses for an artist: one who wears clothes to show them off to possible buyers.—*adj.* acting as a model: fit to be copied, perfect (e.g. *model behaviour*).—*v.t.* to make a model or copy of: to shape: to form after a pattern (e.g. *He models his conduct on that of his brother*): to wear (clothes) to show them off:—*pr.p.* **mod'elling,** *pa.p.* **mod'elled.**

mod'elling, *n.* the art of making models, a branch of sculpture.

[O.Fr. *modelle*—same L. root as **mode.**]

moderate, *mod'ėr-āt, v.t.* and *v.i.* to make, or to become, less great or severe (e.g. *He was forced to moderate his demands*; *the pain moderated*).—*adj.* (*-it*) not unreasonably great (e.g. *The prices were moderate*): of medium quality: rather poor (e.g. *a man of only moderate ability*).—*n.* a person whose views, aims, are not extreme.

mod'erately, *adv.* **mod'erateness,** *n.*

moderā'tion, *n.* lessening of severity, etc.: moderateness.

mod'erator, *n.* a chairman of a meeting, esp. of clergymen.

[L. *moderāri*—*modus*, measure.]

modern, *mod'ėrn, adj.* belonging to the present or to time not long past: not ancient.—*n.* one living in modern times: one whose views or tastes are modern.

mod'ernness, moder'nity, *ns.*

mod'ernise, *v.t.* to bring up to date, adapt to suit present ideas or taste.

modernisā'tion, *n.*

[L. *modernus*—*modo*, just now.]

modest, *mod'ist, adj.* not vain, boastful, or pushing: shy: decent, showing good taste, not shocking: not very large, showy, etc. (e.g. *a modest income, house*).

mod'estly, *adv.* **mod'esty, -ness,** *ns.*

[L. *modestus*; same root as **moderate.**]

modicum, *mod'i-kŭm, n.* small quantity.

[L. *modicus* (*adj.*); root as **moderate.**]

modify, *mod'i-fī, v.t.* to change the form or quality of, alter, usu. slightly (e.g. *to modify a design, a plan, one's views*):—*pr.p.* **mod'ifying**; *pa.p.* **mod'ified.**

modificā'tion, *n.*

[L. *modus* (see **moderate**), *facĕre*, make.]

modish, modiste. See **mode.**

modulate, *mod'ū-lāt, v.t.* to vary the tone, pitch, etc. of (e.g. the voice): to soften, tone down: to vary some characteristic of (a radio wave).—*v.i.* to pass from one state to another: (*music*) to pass from one key to another.

modulā'tion, *n.* **mod'ulator,** *n.*

mod'ule, *n.* a unit of size for measuring or for regulating proportions: a self-contained unit forming part of a spacecraft.

[L. *modulārī*, *-ātus*; root as **moderate.**]

mohair, *mō'hār, n.* long silken hair of an Angora goat: cloth made of it.

[Arabic *mukhayyar*, and **hair.**]

Mohammedan, *mō-ham'i-dȧn, adj.* having to do with Mohammed or his religion.—*n.* a follower of Mohammed.

Mohamm'edanism, *n.* the religion founded by Mohammed, Islam.

[*Muhammad*, great prophet of Arabia; his name means 'praised'.]

moiety, *moi'ė-ti, n.* half: a small part:—*pl.* **moi'eties.**

[O.Fr. *moite*—L. *medius*, middle.]

moil, *moil, v.i.* to toil, drudge.

[O.Fr. *moillier*, to wet—L. *mollis*, soft.]

moist, *moist, adj.* damp: rainy: humid.

moisten, *mois'n, v.t.* to wet slightly.

mois'ture (*-chůr*), *n.* something that makes slightly wet. [O.Fr. *moiste.*]

molar, *mō'lȧr, adj.* used for grinding.—*n.* a back tooth which grinds food.

[Same L. root as **mill.**]

molasses, *mȯ-las'iz, n. sing.* treacle (see this word).

[Port. *melaço*—L. *mel*, *mellis*, honey.]

mole[1], *mōl, n.* a small, usu. dark, spot on the skin. [O.E. *māl.*]

mole[2], *mōl, n.* a small burrowing animal with very small eyes and soft fur.

mole'hill, *n.* a little heap of earth cast up by a mole. [M.E. *molhe.*]

mole[3], *mōl, n.* a breakwater, or a stone pier.

[Fr.—L. *mōles*, mass.]

molecule, *mol'ė-kūl, mōl', n.* the smallest part of a substance that has the properties or qualities of that substance.

molec'ular, *adj.*

[Fr. *molécule*—L. *mōles*, a mass.]

molehill. See **mole** (2).

molest, *mō-lest', mȯ-lest', v.t.* to meddle with, annoy, torment.

molestā'tion, *n.*

[Fr. *molester*—L. *molestus*, troublesome.]

mollify, *mol'i-fī, v.t.* to soften, calm (e.g.

a person): to make less (e.g. anger):—*pr.p.* **moll'ifying**; *pa.p.* **moll'ified.**
mollificā'tion, *n.*
[L. *mollis*, soft, *facĕre*, to make.]

mollusc, mollusk, *mol'usk*, *n.* a soft animal without backbone and usu. with a hard shell (e.g. a shellfish, snail):—*pl.* **moll'uscs, moll'usks, mollus'ca.**
[L. *molluscus*, softish—*mollis*, soft.]

mollycoddle, *mol'i-kod-l*, *n.* a milksop.—*v.t.* to pamper, coddle.
[Form of *Mary*, and **coddle.**]

molten. See **melt.**

moment, *mō'mėnt*, *n.* a very short space of time, instant: importance (e.g. *Nothing of moment happened*).
mō'mentary, *adj.* lasting for a moment, short-lived.
mo'mentarily, *adv.*
mo'mentariness, *n.*
momen'tous, *adj.* of great importance (e.g. *momentous events*).
momen'tously, *adv.* **-tousness,** *n.*
momen'tum, *n.* the quantity of motion in a body: force of motion gained by movement (e.g. *He tried to stop, but his momentum carried him over the cliff edge*).
[L. *mōmentum*—same root as **move.**]

mon-. See **mono-.**

monarch, *mon'ȧrk*, *n.* a king, queen, emperor, or empress.
monarchic(al) (*-ärk'*), *adjs.*
mon'archy, *n.* government by a monarch: a kingdom.
[Gk. *monos*, alone, *archein*, to rule.]

monastery, *mon'ȧs-tėr-i*, *n.* a house for monks: those living in it:—*pl.* **-ies.**
monas'tic(al), *adjs.* having to do with monks, monasteries, nuns (e.g. *monastic orders, vows*).
monas'ticism (*-izm*), *n.* the way of life in a monastery: the system of monks and monasteries.
[Gk. *monastēs*, a monk—*monos*, alone.]

monaural, *mon-ō'rȧl*, *adj.* (of a gramophone record) giving the effect of sound from a single direction.
[Pfx. **mon(-o)-,** L. *auris*, ear.]

Monday, *mun'di*, *n.* second day of week.
[O.E. *mōna*, moon, *dæg*, day.]

monetary, See **money.**

money, *mun'i*, *n.* coin (pieces of stamped metal) or notes, used in trading: wealth.—*pl.* **mon'eys, mon'ies.**
mon'eyed, *mun'id*, *adj.* rich.
monetary, *mun'i-tȧr-i*, *mon'-*, *adj.* having to do with money: consisting of money (e.g. *a monetary reward*).
mon'eylender, *n.* one whose business is lending money.
money order, an order for payment of money to a named person at a named post office (the sum concerned being paid in at another post office).
[O.Fr. *moneie*—L. *monēta*, mint, money.]

monger, *mung'gėr*, *n.* a trader, dealer (usu. as part of word, e.g. *fishmonger*).
[O.E. *mangere*—L. *mangō*.]

Mongol, *mong'gol*, *n.* and *adj.* (one) of the people living in *Mongolia*: (a person) with a mentally deficient condition called **mongolism.**

mongoose, *mong'gōōs*, *n.* a small weasel-like animal of India that kills snakes:—*pl.* **mon'gooses.**
[Indian word *mangūs*.]

mongrel, *mung'grėl*, *n.* an animal, esp. a dog, of a mixed breed.—*adj.* mixed in breed: of no special class or type.
[Prob. root as O.E. *mengan*, to mix.]

monition, *mon-ish'(ȯ)n*, *n.* a warning.
mon'itor, *n.* one who warns or scolds: a senior pupil who helps to see that school rules are kept (*fem.* also **mon'itress**): a screen in a television studio showing the picture being transmitted: an arrangement or instrument of different kinds for checking such things as quality of electrical communication, level of radioactivity: a large lizard.—*v.i.* to be, or to use, a monitor: to listen to foreign broadcasts in order to obtain news, code messages, etc.—Also *v.t.*
[L. *monēre*, *monitum*, to remind.]

monk, *mungk*, *n.* one of a religious group living apart from world in monastery.
monk'ish, *adj.* like a monk.
[O.E. *munuc*—L. *monachus*.]

monkey, *mungk'i*, *n.* any member of the highest group of animals, except man: used specially for those members of the group that are smaller and have long tails (i.e. leaving out the apes): a mischievous child:—*pl.* **monk'eys.**—*v.i.* to meddle (with something).
monkey nut, a peanut, groundnut.
monkey wrench, a wrench with a movable jaw. [Origin uncertain.]

mono-, *mon-ō-*, **mon-,** (as part of word) one, single.
monochromatic, *mon-ȯ-krō-mat'ik*, *adj.* of one colour only.
mon'ochrome, *n.* a painting, etc., in a single colour.
monocle, *mon'ȯ-kl*, *n.* a single eyeglass.
monogamy, *mȯ-nog'ȧ-mi*, *n.* marriage to one wife or husband only.
monog'amous, *adj.* **monog'amist,** *n.*
monogram, *mon'ȯ-gram*, *n.* a single design made up of several intertwined letters.
monolith'ic, *adj.* (of e.g. a state, business organisation) very large and very much the same throughout.
[Gk. *monos*, alone, single (Gk. *chrōma*, colour; L. *oculus*, eye; Gk. *lithos*, stone).]

mono- (*continued*).
monologue, *mon'ȯ-log*, *n.* a long speech by one person.
monomania, *mon-ō-mā'ni-ȧ*, *n.* madness limited to one subject: a too great interest in, or enthusiasm for, one thing.

monoma′niac, *n.*
monoplane, *mon′ō-plān, n.* an aeroplane with one set of wings.
monopoly, *mo-nop′ò-li, n.* sole right of making or selling something: something thus controlled: sole possession (of; e.g. *No race has a monopoly of courage*).
monop′olise, *v.t.* to have a monopoly of: to keep complete possession, control, etc. of: to take up completely (e.g. *She monopolised their time, attention*).
monorail, *mon′ō-rāl, n.* a railway with carriages suspended from, or running astride of, one rail.
monosyllable, *mon-ō-sil′à-bl, n.* a word of one syllable.
monosyllab′ic, *adj.* having one syllable: (speaking) in one-syllabled words only.
monotheism, *mon′ō-thē-izm, n.* the belief in only one God.
monotone, *mon′ō-tōn, n.* a single, unchanging tone of voice.
monot′onous, *adj.* in one unchanging tone: lacking in variety, dull.
monot′ony, *n.* lack of change: dullness.
[Gk. *monos,* alone, single (*logos,* speech; *pōleein,* to sell; *theos,* god; *tonos,* tone).]

Monotype, *mon′o-tīp, n.* a machine that casts and sets type for printing letter by letter.
[Pfx. **mono-**. Registered trademark.]

monseigneur, *mon^g-sen-yėr, n.* a title in France given to a person of high rank, a bishop, etc. (written **Mgr**).
monsieur, *mės-yė,* sir: a title (often written *M.*) in France equal to *Mr* in English:—*pl.* **messieurs,** *mes-yė.*
[Fr. *mon seigneur, mon sieur,* my lord.]

monsoon, *mon-so͞on′, n.* a wind that blows in the Indian Ocean, from the S.W. in summer, from the N.E. in winter: the rainy season caused by S.W. monsoon.
[Port. *monção*—Arabic *mausim,* season.]

monster, *mon′stėr, n.* a plant or animal of unusual form or appearance: a huge creature, causing fear: a horribly wicked person.—*adj.* huge.
mon′strous, *adj.* huge: horrible.
monstros′ity, *n.* something not natural: state of being monstrous:—*pl.* **-ities.**
[L. *monstrum,* omen, monster.]

month, *munth, n.* the time from new moon to new moon, called a *lunar* month: one of twelve divisions of the year (January, etc.), a calendar month.
month′ly, *adj.* completed in a month: happening once a month.—*n.* a paper published once in a month:—*pl.* **month′lies.**—*adv.* once a month: in every month.
[O.E. *mōnath*—*mōna,* moon.]

monument, *mon′ū-mėnt, n.* something put up in memory of a person or event, e.g. a building, tomb, etc.: a notable example (of): lasting evidence of (with *to*; e.g. *The work, result, is a monument to your industry*).
monument′al, *adj.* acting as a monument: of great size or lasting qualities.
[L. *monumentum*—*monēre,* to remind.]

moo, *mo͞o, v.i.* to low like a cow. [Imit.]

mood[1], *mo͞od, n.* any of four forms of the verb, expressing fact (*indicative mood*), possibility, etc. (*subjunctive*), command (*imperative*), and an idea without a subject (*infinitive*). [**mode.**]

mood[2], *mo͞od, n.* the state of a person's feelings, temper, mind, at the time in question.
mood′y, *adj.* often changing one's mood: gloomy, ill-humoured.
mood′ily, *adv.* **mood′iness,** *n.*
[O.E. *mōd,* mind; Ger. *mut,* courage.]

moon, *mo͞on, n.* the heavenly body that moves round the earth: a satellite of any other planet: a month.—*v.i.* to wander about or gaze absently.
moon′beam, *n.* a beam of light from the moon.
moon′light, *n.* the light of the moon.—*adj.* lighted by the moon: happening in moonlight or at night.
moon′lit, *adj.* lit by the moon.
moon′shine, *n.* the shining of the moon: false show, nonsense.
moon′stone, *n.* a gemstone with a pearly shine.
moon′struck, *adj.* crazed, lunatic.
[O.E. *mōna*; conn. Ger. *mond.*]

moor[1], *mo͞or, n.* a large stretch of open land with poor soil often covered with heath.
moor′cock, moor′fowl, *n.* a red grouse.
moor′hen, *n.* coot: female moorfowl.
moor′land, *n.* a stretch of moor.
[O.E. *mōr.*]

moor[2], *mo͞or, v.t.* to fasten, secure (a ship, etc.) by cable or anchor.—Also *v.i.*
moor′ing, *n.* act or means of fastening a ship: (in *pl.*) the place where a ship is fastened.
[Prob. O.E.; conn. Middle Du. *mâren.*]

Moor, *mo͞or, n.* a member of a dark-skinned race living in North Africa.
Moor′ish, *adj.*
[Fr. *More, Maure*—L. *Maurus.*]

moorcock. See **moor** (1).

mooring. See **moor** (2).

moose, *mo͞os, n.* the largest deer of America, rather like the European elk.
[N. Amer. Indian, *mus, moos.*]

moot, *mo͞ot, adj.* used chiefly in **moot point,** an undecided point, one to be argued about.
[O.E. (*ge*)*mōt,* assembly—*mētan,* to meet.]

mop, *mop, n.* a bunch of rags or coarse yarn fixed on a handle, for washing floors, dishes, etc: a thick mass of hair like a mop.—*v.t.* to rub or wipe with a mop: to wipe away tears, sweat, etc. from:—*pr.p.* **mopp′ing**; *pa.p.* **mopped.**
to mop up, to clean up or clear away: to kill or capture remnants of defeated enemy force in an area.
[O.Fr. *mappe*; same root as **map.**]

mope, *mōp, v.i.* to give way to low spirits, or sadness.
mop'ish, *adj.* [Origin unknown.]
moped, *mō'ped, n.* a *mo*tor-assisted *ped*al bicycle.
moraine, *mȯ-rān', n.* a line of rocks and gravel carried by, left by, glacier. [Fr.]
moral, *mor'ȧl, adj.* having to do with character or behaviour, esp. with right behaviour (e.g. *to lead a moral life*): virtuous in matters of sex: capable of knowing right and wrong (e.g. *Man is a moral being*).—*n.* (in *pl.*) one's principles and conduct: (in *sing.*) the lesson to be learned from something that happens, or from a story.
mor'ally, *adv.* in a moral manner: from the point of view of morals: practically (e.g. *morally certain*).
mor'alise, *v.t.* to make (more) moral.—*v.i.* to talk or write about morals or about lessons to be learned from events.
mor'alist, *n.* one who studies or teaches moral behaviour.
moral'ity, *n.* quality of being morally right or wrong: virtuous conduct: a mediaeval drama in which vices and virtues are characters:—*pl.* **-ities.**
a moral certainty, a probability of which one is convinced.
moral courage, courage to face disapproval and ridicule in support of what one believes right.
moral obligation, responsibility, one arising from sense of duty.
moral sense, (ability to have) feeling that some actions are right, others wrong.
moral support, encouragement, approval, but not physical help.
moral victory, a defeat whose effect on morale, etc., is good, not bad.
[L. *mōrālis—mōs, mōris*, custom, morals.]
morale, *mȯr-äl', n.* mood as regards courage and confidence or the reverse in e.g. an army (e.g. *In spite of reverses, morale was still high*).
[Fr. *moral*; same root as **moral.**]
morass, *mȯ-ras', n.* a stretch of soft, wet ground: a marsh.
[Du. *moeras.*]
morbid, *mör'bid, adj.* diseased (mentally or physically): (of mind, thoughts, person) not healthy, dwelling too much on gruesome and gloomy things.
mor'bidly, *adv.* **morbid'ity, -ness,** *ns.*
[L. *morbus*, disease.]
mordant, *mör'dȧnt, adj.* (of wit) biting, sarcastic: fixing colours.—*n.* a substance used in dyeing to fix colour: acid, etc., used in etching.
mor'dancy, *n.* **mor'dantly,** *adv.*
[L. *mordēre*, to bite.]
more. See **many** and **much.**
moreover, *mōr-ō'vėr, mör-, adv.* besides, also. [**more, over.**]
morgue, *mörg, n.* a place where dead bodies are laid for identification. [Fr.]
moribund, *mor'i-bund, adj.* about to die: in a dying state.
[L. *moribundus—mori*, to die.]
Mormon, *mör'mon, n.* one of a religious group with headquarters in Utah, U.S., founded in 1830 by Joseph Smith.
morn, *mörn, n.* morning.
morning, *mörn'ing, n.* the first part of the day: the early part of anything.—Also *adj.*
morning star, a planet, esp. Venus, when it rises before the sun.
[O.E. *morgen*; conn. Ger. *morgen.*]
morocco, *mȯ-rok'ō, n.* fine goat- or sheep-skin leather, first brought from *Morocco.*
moron, *mōr'on, mör', n.* a person of low mental ability: (*coll.*) a foolish person.
moron'ic, *adj.*
[Gk. *mōros*, stupid.]
morose, *mȯ-rōs', adj.* sullen, gloomy.
morose'ly, *adv.* **morose'ness,** *n.*
[L. *mōrōsus*, peevish—*mōs* (see **moral**).]
morphia, *mör'fi-ȧ, n.* a habit-forming drug that causes sleep or deadens pain.—Also **mor'phine.**
[Gk. *Morpheus*, god of dreams.]
morrow, *mor'ō, n.* the day following the present: the time just after any event.
[M.E. *morwe*; same root as **morning.**]
Morse, *mörs, n.* a code for signalling and telegraphy in which each letter is made up of dots and dashes (short and long sounds or movements), invented by Samuel F. B. *Morse.*
morsel, *mör'sėl, n.* a small piece of food: a small piece of anything.
[O.Fr.—L. *mordēre, morsum*, to bite.]
mortal, *mör't(ȧ)l, adj.* liable to death: human: causing death: punishable by death: (of enemy, fight) bitter, deadly: very great (e.g. *mortal fear*).—*n.* a human being.
mor'tally, *adv.*
mortal'ity, *n.* state of being mortal: number of deaths: deaths in proportion to the population, death rate.
mortal sin, one leading to death of the soul.
[Fr.—L. *mori, mortuus*, to die.]
mortar, *mör'tȧr, n.* a basin in which substances are ground with a pestle: a short gun for throwing shells: a mixture of lime, sand, water, etc., used in building.
mor'tar-board, *n.* a cap with a square flat top, worn on formal occasions at universities.
[O.E. *mortere*—L. *mortārium.*]
mortgage, *mör'gij, n.* (a document containing) a legal agreement by which a sum of money is lent on the security of buildings, land, etc. (the borrower promises to give up the buildings to the lender if he fails to repay the loan according to the conditions).—*v.t.* to pledge (buildings, etc.) as security for a debt: to pledge, and so risk losing control over.
mortgagor (*mör-gȧ-jör'*), *n.* one who

borrows money on mortgage from a **mortgagee** (*mör-gȧ-jē'*) or lender.
[O.Fr. *mort*, dead, *gage*, pledge.]

mortify, *mör'ti-fī, v.t.* to make one feel ashamed or hurt by wounding one's pride: to bring (one's desires, the body) under control by fasting, inflicting pain on oneself, etc.: to destroy the life in (a part of the body).—*v.i.* (of a part of the body) to die:—*pr.p.* **mor'tifying**; *pa.p.* **mor'tified.**
mortificā'tion, *n.*
[L. *mors, mortis*, death, *facĕre*, to make.]

mortise, *mör'tis, n.* a hole cut into a piece of wood to receive a *tenon*, a part shaped to fit the hole, on another piece.—Also **mor'tice.**
[Fr. *mortaise*; origin unknown.]

mortuary, *mör'tū-ȧ-ri, n.* a place where bodies are kept before burial:—*pl.* **mor'tuaries.**
[L, *mortuārius*; same root as **mortal.**]

mosaic, *mō-zā'ik, n.* a design formed by arranging small pieces of coloured marble, glass, etc.: anything made by piecing different things together.
[Fr. *mosaïque*—Gk. *mousa*, a Muse (hence an art).]

Moslem, *moz'lem, n.* a Mohammedan.—*adj.* of or belonging to the Mohammedans.
[Arabic *muslim*—*salama*, to submit (to God).]

mosque, *mosk, n.* a Mohammedan place of worship.
[Arabic *masjid*—*sajada*, pray.]

mosquito, *mos-kē'tō, n.* any of numbers of insects, the females of which pierce the skin of animals and suck blood:—*pl.* **mosqui'to(e)s.**
[Sp. dim. of *mosca*, a fly—L. *musca*.]

moss, *mos, n.* a small flowerless plant, found in moist places, on tree trunks, etc.: a clump of these plants: a bog.
moss'y, *adj.* **moss'iness,** *n.*
moss'-grown, *adj.* covered with moss.
[O.E. *mōs*, bog; conn. Ger. *moos*, moss.]

most, mostly. See **many** and **much.**

mote, *mōt, n.* a speck, e.g. of dust.
[O.E. *mot*.]

motel, *mō-tel', n.* a *motor hotel*, orig. one made up of units, each unit for a car and occupants.

moth, *moth, n.* any of a large number of insects, rather like butterflies, seen mostly at night and attracted by light: the larva of the **clothes moth,** which eats cloth.
moth'ball, *n.* a ball of a chemical used to protect clothes from moths.
moth'-eaten, *adj.* eaten or cut by moths: old and worn: (of an idea, person, etc.) behind the times and dull.
[O.E. *moththe*; conn. with Ger. *motte*.]

mother, *muTH'ėr, n.* a female parent, esp. a human one: the female head of a religious group, e.g. a convent: something that was the origin or the first example (e.g. *The English parliament is sometimes called the mother of parliaments*).—*adj.* acting the part of, or belonging to, a mother.—*v.t.* to care for as a mother does.
moth'erless, *adj.* without a mother.
moth'erly, *adj.* like a mother: suitable to a mother (e.g. *motherly love*).
moth'erliness, *n.*
moth'erhood, *n.* state of being a mother.
moth'er-coun'try, -land, *n.* country of one's birth: the country that has founded a colony.
moth'er-in-law, *n.* the mother of one's husband or wife:—*pl.* **mothers-in-law.**
moth'er-of-pearl, *n.* shining, hard, smooth substance on inside of certain shells, esp. that of the pearl oyster.
mother tongue, a person's native language.
[O.E. *mōdor*; Ger. *mutter*, L. *māter*.]

motif, *mō-tēf', n.* theme or important feature in a play or musical work.
[Fr.; same root as **motion, motive.**]

motion, *mō'sh(ȯ)n, n.* act, state, power, or manner, of moving: a single movement: a piece of mechanism: a proposal put before a meeting.—*v.t., v.i.* to make a movement or sign which tells (a person to do something; e.g. *Motion him*, or *motion to him, to come here*).
mō'tionless, *adj.* without motion.
motion (or **moving**) **picture,** picture showing action and movement, produced by running a series of photographs very rapidly across a screen.
in motion, moving.
motive, *mō'tiv, adj.* causing motion.—*n.* something that makes a person choose to act in a particular way (e.g. *His motive for asking me was not clear*).
mo'tivate, *v.t.* to be the thing that causes (a person) to act in a certain way (e.g. *Jealousy motivated him*): to be a motive, reason, for (an action).
[Fr.—L. *mōtiō*; same root as **move.**]

motley, *mot'li, adj.* of many different colours: made up of many different kinds (e.g. *a motley crowd*).—*n.* the dress of a jester. [Origin uncertain.]

motor, *mō'tȯr, n.* a machine (usu. a petrol engine) which gives motion or does work: a motor car.—*adj.* giving or transmitting (passing on) motion: driven by a motor.—*v.t.* and *v.i.* to carry (something), or to travel, by motor vehicle.
mo'torise, *v.t.* to supply (e.g. troops) with motor vehicles (e.g. *a motorised unit*)
mō'torist, *n* one who drives, and travels by, a motor car
motor bicycle, car, etc., bicycle, car, etc. moved by a motor.
mō'torway, *n.* a road for motor traffic, esp. one for fast traffic with no crossings on the same level.
[Same root as **motion.**]

mottled, *mot'ld, adj.* marked with spots of many colours or shades.
[Prob. from **motley.**]

motto, *mot'ō, n.* a short sentence or phrase which expresses a guiding principle (e.g. '*Honesty is the best policy' is my motto*) :—*pl.* **mottoes,** *mot'ōz.*
[It.—same root as **mutter.**]

mould[1], *mōld, n.* loose or crumbling earth : soil rich in rotted leaves, etc.
moul'der, *v.i., v.t.* to crumble to dust : to waste away gradually.
[O.E. *molde.*]

mould[2], *mōld, n.* a woolly or fluffy growth on bread, cheese, etc.—*v.i.* to become mouldy (e.g. *Bread moulds quickly*).
moul'dy, *adj.* overgrown or covered with mould : like mould : (*slang*) old and stale, or depressing.
moul'diness, *n.*
[M.E. *mowle* ; conn. Old Norse *mygla.*]

mould[3], *mōld, n.* a shape into which a substance in liquid form is poured so that it may take on that shape when it cools : a thing formed in a mould.—*v.t.* to form in a mould : to work into a shape : to give particular qualities to (e.g. character, opinions).
moul'der, *n.*
moul'ding, *n.* a decorated border, e.g. on a picture frame, wall, etc.
[L. *modulus*, a measure.]

moulder. See **mould** (1) and (3).

mouldiness, mouldy. See **mould** (2).

moult, *mōlt, v.i.* to cast feathers, shed a skin.—Also *v.t.*
[L. *mutāre*, to change.]

mound, *mownd, n.* a bank of earth or stones raised as a protection : a hill : a heap.
[Origin uncertain.]

mount[1], *mownt, v.i.* to go up, climb : to rise in level or in amount.—*v.t.* to go up : to get up upon : to place on horseback : to fix (e.g. a jewel) in a holder that shows it off, or (e.g. a photograph) on a backing : to put, have (guns) in position for use. —*n.* a riding animal or bicycle : a support or backing on which anything is placed for display.
moun'ted, *adj.* on horseback : provided with horses or other means of transport : set in position for use, or on support, background.
Mount'ies, *n.pl.* Canadian mounted police.
to mount an attack, offensive, etc., to prepare and carry it out.
to mount guard. See **guard.**
[Fr. *monter*, go up ; root as **mount** (2).]

mount[2], *mownt, n.* a mountain.
mountain, *mown'tin, n.* a high hill : anything very large.—*adj.* of a mountain : growing or living on a mountain.
mountaineer', *n.* a climber of mountains.
moun'tainous, *adj.* full of mountains : large as a mountain, huge.
mountain ash, rowan (not an ash).
[O.E. *munt*, O.Fr. *montaine*—L. *mons, montis.*]

mountebank, *mown'ti-bangk, n.* a quack, seller of sham remedies, who draws a crowd by means of jokes, etc. : a buffoon.
[It. *monta*, mount, *in*, on, *banco*, bench.]

mourn, *mōrn, mörn, v.i.* to grieve, be sorrowful.—*v.t.* to grieve for (a person, a loss).
mourn'er, *n.*
mourn'ful, *adj.* causing, feeling, or showing, sorrow.
mourn'ing, *n.* the act of showing grief : formal dress of mourners.—Also *adj.*
[O.E. *murnan, meornan.*]

mouse, *mows, n.* small gnawing animal of several kinds found in houses (**house mouse**) and in fields (**field mouse ;** see also **harvest mouse**) :—*pl.* **mice,** *mīs.*
mous'y, *adj.* like a mouse, esp. in colour.
mous'iness, *n.*
mouse'hole, *n.* a hole made or used by mice.
[O.E. *mūs*, pl. *mȳs* ; Ger. *maus*, L. *mūs.*]

mousse, *mo͞os, n.* a whipped-up mixture of cream, etc. sometimes frozen. [Fr.]

moustache, mustache, *mus-tâsh', n.* hair on the upper lip of a man.
[Fr.—Gk. *mystax*, upper lip.]

mouth, *mowth, n.* the opening in the head of an animal by which it eats and utters sounds : opening or entrance, e.g. of a bottle, river, etc. :—*pl.* **mouths** (-THz).—*v.t.* and *v.i.* (*mowTH*) to say in a pompous way, or with exaggerated mouth movements.
mouth'ful, *n.* as much as fills the mouth : a small quantity :—*pl.* **mouth'fuls.**
mouth'-organ, *n.* a small musical instrument played by the mouth.
mouth'piece, *n.* the piece of a musical instrument, or tobacco-pipe, held in the mouth : one who speaks for others.
down in the mouth, out of spirits, sad.
[O.E. *mūth* ; Ger. *mund*, Du. *mond.*]

move, *mo͞ov, v.t.* to cause to change place or position : to set in motion : to excite or stir (to action or to emotion ; e.g. *The scene moved him to take up the cause of the refugees, moved him to tears*) : to touch the feelings of (e.g. *The book moved him deeply*) : to propose (e.g. *I move the adoption of the minutes, that the meeting should now adjourn*).—*v.i.* to go from one place to another : to change homes : to carry oneself in walking, etc. : to change position.—*n.* the act of moving : a movement, esp. at chess : a step taken (e.g. *He now made his first move towards gaining control*).
movable, *mo͞ov'ȧ-bl, adj.* that may be moved, not fixed.—*n.* movable furnishing.—Also **move'able.**
move'ment, *n.* act or manner of moving : change of position : the moving part of a

mechanism: a main division of a long piece of music: actions intended to bring about a change or improvement (e.g. *a movement to reform the law*): change.
mov'ies, *n. pl.* (*coll.* esp. *U.S.*) motion pictures.
mov'ing, *adj.* causing motion: causing emotion, esp. pity.
moving picture. See **motion.**
See also **motion, mobile.**
[O.Fr. *movoir*—L. *movēre, mōtum.*]

mow, *mō, v.t.* to cut (grass), or to cut grass on (e.g. a lawn), with a scythe or machine: to cut (down) in great numbers (e.g. *Tanks mowed down the enemy*):—*pr.p.* **mow'ing**; *pa.t.* **mowed**; *pa.p.* **mowed** or **mown.**
mow'er, *n.* one who mows: machine with turning blades for cutting grass.
[O.E. *māwan*; conn. with Ger. *mähen.*]

much, *much, adj.* a great quantity of:—*comp.* **more** (*mōr, mör*); *superl.* **most** (*mōst*).—*adv.* to a great degree (e.g. *much brighter, much loved, much to be pitied*): often (e.g. *He spoke much of his childhood*): nearly (e.g. *much the same*).—*n.* a great deal: something important.
more, *adj.* a larger quantity of (see also **many**).
as much as to say, as if to say, the same as saying.
to be too much (for one), to be more than one can bear, believe etc.,
to make much of. See **make.**
[O.E. *micel* (*māra, mǣst* used as comp. and superl.).]

mucilage. See **mucus.**

muck, *muk, n.* dung: anything filthy.
muck'y, *adj.* **muck'iness,** *n.*
[Prob. conn. Old Norse *myki*, dung.]

mucus, *mū'kus, n.* the slimy fluid from the nose, etc. (produced by cells in the mucous membrane).
mu'cous, *adj.* like mucus: slimy.
mucilage, *mū'sil-ij, n.* a gluey substance found in some plants: gum.
mucous membrane, a membrane (thin layer of tissue) lining those passages of the body (e.g. of the nose) that communicate with the outside.
[L. *mūcus.*]

mud, *mud, n.* wet soft earth.
mudd'y, *adj.* covered with, or containing, mud: not clear or pure:—*comp.* **mudd'ier**; *superl.* **mudd'iest.**—*v.t., v.i.* to make, or become, muddy:—*pr.p.* **mudd'ying**; *pa.p.* **mudd'ied.**
mud'guard, *n.* a screen to catch mud splashes from wheels.
[Old Ger. *mudde*; conn. Du. *modder.*]

muddle, *mud'l, v.t.* to make (water) muddy: to bungle, make a mess of: to confuse, make stupid.—*n.* confusion, mess: bewilderment. **[mud.]**

muff[1], *muf, n.* a tube-shaped cover e.g. of fur for keeping the hands warm.
[Prob. Du. *mof.*]

muff[2], *muf, n.* a stupid fellow.—*v.t.* to fail to hold (a catch, ball): to do badly.—Also *v.i.* [Origin unknown.]

muffin, *muf'in, n.* a soft cake, eaten hot with butter. [Origin unknown.]

muffle, *muf'l, v.t.* to wrap up for warmth or in order to hide the face: to deaden the sound of (e.g. *to muffle his cries*).
muff'ler, *n.* a scarf for the throat.
[Fr. *mouffle*, mitten.]

mufti, *muf'ti, n.* clothes worn when he is off duty by someone who is usu. in uniform. [Arabic.]

mug, *mug, n.* a cup with more or less straight sides: its contents.
[Origin unknown.]

muggy, *mug'i, adj.* (of weather) close and damp.
[Perh. Old Norse *mugga*, mist.]

mulatto, *mū-lat'ō, n.* the child of a black and a white parent:—*pl.* **mulatt'oes.**
[Sp. *mulato*—*mulo*, mule.]

mulberry, *mul'bėr-i, n.* a type of tree on whose leaves silkworms feed: the fruit of this tree, usu. purple.
[O.E. *mōrberi*—L. *morum.*]

mulch, *mulch, -sh, n.* loose straw, etc., laid down to protect the roots of plants.—*v.t.* to cover with mulch.
[Conn. with M.E. *molsh*, soft.]

mulct, *mulkt, n.* a fine.—*v.t.* to fine (e.g. *to mulct a person* £500): to deprive, swindle (of).
[L. *mulcta*, a fine.]

mule[1], *mūl, n.* a kind of slipper usu. without a heel. [Fr.]

mule[2], *mūl, n.* an animal whose parents are a horse and an ass: an instrument for cotton spinning: a stubborn person.
mul'ish, *adj.* like a mule: stubborn.
muleteer', *n.* one who drives mules.
[O.E. *mūl*—L. *mūlus.*]

mull[1], *mul, v.t.* (with *over*) to think or ponder over. [Origin uncertain.]

mull[2], *mul, v.t.* to warm, spice, and sweeten (wine, ale, etc.).
mulled, *adj.* [Origin unknown.]

mullet, *mul'it, n.* a type of small sea-fish.
[O.Fr. *mulet*—L. *mullus.*]

mulligatawny, *mul-i-gȧ-tö'ni, n.* an E. Indian soup containing curry.
[From Indian word, 'pepper-water'.]

mullion, *mul'yȯn, n,* an upright division between the lights of windows, etc.
[O.Fr. *monial.*]

multi-, *mul-ti-*, (as part of word) many, much.
multifarious, *mul-ti-fā'ri-ùs, adj.* of many kinds (e.g. *multifarious activities*).
multilateral, *mul-ti-lat'ėr-ȧl, adj.* many-sided: involving several parties, states, etc. (e.g. *a multilateral treaty, multilateral disarmament*).
multilingual, *mul-ti-ling'gwȧl, adj.* in many languages: speaking many languages.

multimillionaire′, *n.* one having property worth several millions of pounds.
multiracial, *mul-ti-rā′sh(i-ȧ)l*, *adj.* of many races: including (people of) many races (e.g. *a multiracial population*).
[L. *multus*, many (perh. L. *fāri*, to speak; *latus*, *-eris*, side; *lingua*, tongue).]

multiple, *mul′ti-pl*, *adj.* having many parts, esp. of the same kind: repeated many times.—*n.* a number that contains another an exact number of times (e.g. 65 *is a multiple of* 5.)
[L. *multus*, many, *plēre*, to fill.]

multiply, *mul′ti-plī*, *v.t.* to increase the number, quantity, of: to take a number a given number of times and find the total (e.g. 4 taken 3 times, or 4+4+4, or 4 *multiplied by* 3, or 4×3, =12).—*v.i.* to become greater in number:—*pr.p.* **mul′tiplying**; *pa.p.* **mul′tiplied.**
multiplicā′tion, *n.*
multiplic′ity, *n.* a great number: state of being many and varied.
mul′tiplier, *n.* the number by which another is to be multiplied.
[L. *multus*, many, *plicāre*, to fold.]

multitude, *mul′ti-tūd*, *n.* a great number: a crowd: the mob: the state of being many (e.g. *the multitude of his difficulties*).
multitud′inous, *adj.* very many: looking like a multitude.
[L. *multitūdō—multus*, many.]

mum, *mum*, *adj.* silent, not speaking.—*v.i.* to act in dumb-show: to wear a mask, etc. at a festival:—*pr.p.* **mumm′ing.**
mumm′er, *n.*
mumm′ery, *n.* mumming: meaningless ceremonial:—*pl.* **mumm′eries.**
[Conn. with O.Fr. *momer*, mask oneself.]

mumble, *mum′bl*, *v.t.* and *v.i.* to utter, or speak, indistinctly.—Also *n.* [**mum.**]

mummer, etc. See **mum.**

mummie. See **mummy** (2).

mummy[1], *mum′i*, *n.* a human body preserved by the Egyptians, etc., in past times, using wrappings, spice, wax, etc.
mumm′ify, *v.t.* to make into a mummy:—*pr.p.* **mumm′ifying**; *pa.p.* **mumm′ified.**
mummificā′tion, *n.*
[O.Fr. *mumie*—Pers. and Arabic *mūmiyā.*]

mummy[2], **mummie**, *mum′i*, *n.* an affectionate name for mother.
[A form of **mammy.**]

mump, *mump*, *v.i.* to be sulky.
mumps, *n.* a disease of the glands of the neck, causing swelling.
[Orig. *n.* meaning 'grimace'.]

munch, *munch*, *-sh*, *v.t.*, *v.i.* to chew with a crunching sound. [Prob. imit.]

mundane, *mun′dān*, *adj.* belonging to the world: everyday, dull.
[L. *mundānus—mundus*, the world.]

municipal, *mū-nis′i-pȧl*, *adj.* having to do with the government of a city or town: carried on by a city or town.
munic′ipally, *adv.*
municipal′ity, *n.* a self-governing city or town:—*pl.* **-ities.**
[L. *mūnicipium*, a free town.]

munificence, *mū-nif′i-sėns*, *n.* fondness for giving gifts: generous quality.
munif′icent, *adj.* **munif′icently**, *adv.*
[L. *mūnus*, a present, *facěre*, to make.]

munition, *mū-nish′(ȯ)n*, *n.* (usu. in *pl.*) weapons and ammunition used in war: necessary equipment for any campaign.
[L. *mūnīre*, *mūnītum*, to fortify.]

mural, *mū′rȧl*, *adj.* having to do with a wall.—*n.* a painting on a wall.
[L. *mūrus*, a wall.]

murder, *mûr′dėr*, *n.* act of putting a person to death on purpose and unlawfully.—*v.t.* to kill on purpose and unlawfully: to ruin by saying, etc., very badly (e.g. *to murder a poem*).
mur′derer, *n.* **mur′deress**, *fem. n.*
mur′derous, *adj.* deadly: capable of, or guilty of, murder: very cruel (e.g. *a murderous light in his eye*).
mur′derously, *adv.*
[O.E. *morthor—morth*, death.]

murky, *mûr′ki*, *adj.* dark, gloomy: (of darkness) thick:—*comp.* **mur′kier**; *superl.* **mur′kiest.**
mur′kily, *adv.* **mur′kiness**, *n.*
[O.E. *mirce*; conn. Old Norse *myrkr.*]

murmur, *mûr′mür*, *n.* a low, confused sound, e.g. that of running water: a complaint, uttered in a low voice.—*v.i.* to grumble: to make a murmur.
[Fr.—L.; imit.]

muscle, *mus′l*, *n.* a bundle of fibres in the body which, by drawing together or stretching out, causes movements of the body.
muscular, *mus′kū-lȧr*, *adj.* having to do with muscle(s): strong.
muscular′ity, *n.* state of being strong.
[Fr.—L. *musculus.*]

muse[1], *mūz*, *v.i.* to think over a matter quietly: to be absent-minded.
[O.Fr. *muser*, to muse (Fr., to loiter).]

muse[2], *mūz*, *n.* (usu. *cap.*) one of the nine goddesses of poetry, music, and arts.
[Fr.—Gk. *mousa.*]

museum, *mū-zē′ům*, *n.* a place where collections of things of artistic, scientific, or historic interest are set out for show.
[L. *mūsēum*—Gk. root as **muse** (2).]

mush[1], *mush*, *n.* meal boiled in water, esp. Indian meal: anything pulpy. [**mash.**]

mush[2], *mush*, *v.i.* to travel on foot with dogs over snow.
[Prob. Fr. *marcher*, to walk.]

mushroom, *mush′room*, *n.* a type of fungus usually umbrella-shaped, esp. one that can be eaten: anything springing up very quickly and usu. dying rapidly (e.g. *a mushroom town, firm*).
[O.Fr. *mousseron*, perh.—*mousse*, moss.]

music, *mū′zik*, *n.* an arrangement of, or the art of combining or putting together,

sounds that please the ear: the score of a musical composition: any pleasant sound.
mū'sical, *adj.* **mū'sically,** *adv.*
musi'cian (*-shȧn*), *n.* one skilled in music: a performer of music.
music hall, (*orig.*) a hall for concerts: (a theatre for) variety entertainment.
[L. *mūsica*—same Gk. root as **muse** (2).]

musk, *musk, n.* a substance with a strong scent, obtained from the male musk deer: the musk deer.
mus'ky, *adj.* **mus'kiness,** *n.*
musk deer, a small hornless deer, found in mountains of Central Asia.
musk melon, the common melon.
musk rat, a musky-scented N. American water animal with valuable fur.
musk rose, a fragrant type of rose.
[Fr. *musc*—L. *muscus*; from Pers.]

musket, *mus'kit, n.* a gun once carried by foot soldiers.
musketeer', *n.* a soldier armed with a musket.
mus'ketry, *n.* the art of firing on the enemy with rifles.
[O.Fr. *mousquet*—It. *moschetto.*]

Muslim (*mus', muz'*). Same as **Moslem.**

muslin, *muz'lin, n.* fine soft cotton cloth looking like gauze.—Also *adj.*
[Fr. *mousseline*—city of *Mosul.*]

musquash, *mus'kwosh, n.* the musk rat: its fur. [Amer. Indian.]

mussel, *mus'l, n.* a shellfish enclosed within a shell in two parts, used for food.
[O.E. *mūs(c)le*—same L. root as **muscle.**]

must[1], *must, v.i.* generally used with another verb to express a necessity or requirement (e.g. *I must have more time if I am to finish it*). The form is the same with all persons (I, you, etc.), and the time is usu. present, sometimes past.—*n.* an essential, a necessity: a thing that should not be missed or neglected.
[O.E. *mōste, pa.t.* of *mōt*, may.]

must[2], *must, n.* grape juice not fully fermented.
[L. *mustus*, new, fresh.]

mustache. Same as **moustache.**

mustang, *mus'tang, n.* the wild horse of the American prairies. [Sp.]

mustard, *mus'tȧrd, n.* a hot seasoning made from the seeds of the mustard plant.
[O.Fr. *mostarde*—L. *mustum* (**must,** 2).]

muster, *mus'tėr, v.t.* to gather together (esp. troops for duty or inspection): to gather: (also *muster up*) to summon up and show (e.g. courage).—Also *v.i.*—*n.* gathering of troops, etc : an assembly.
muster roll, *n.* a register of those present at a muster.
to pass muster, to be accepted as satisfactory.
[O.Fr. *mostre*—L. *monēre*, to warn.]

musty, *must'i, adj.* mouldy, spoiled by damp: stale in smell or taste.
[Origin uncertain.]

mutation, *mū-tā'sh(ȯ)n, n.* act or process of changing: (a plant or animal showing) a characteristic not found in its parents which can yet be passed on to later generations.
[L. *mutāre*, to change—*movēre*, to move.]

mute, *mūt, adj.* dumb: silent: not sounded.—*n.* a dumb person: a silent person.—*v.t.* to deaden the sound of.
mut'ed, *pa.p.* and *adj.* **mute'ly,** *adv.*
[L. *mūtus.*]

mutilate, *mū'ti-lāt, v.t.* to cut off a limb, etc. from: to remove an important part of, damage badly.
mutilā'tion, *n.* **mu'tilator,** *n.*
[L. *mutilāre, -ātum.*]

mutiny, *mū'ti-ni, v.i.* to rise against those in authority in the army, navy, or air force: to refuse to obey any rightful authority:—*pr.p.* **mu'tinying;** *pa.p.* **mu'tinied.**—*n.* refusal to obey: a revolt.
mutineer', *n.* one who mutinies.
mū'tinous, *adj.* rebellious, unruly.
[Fr. *mutin*, riotous—L. root as **move.**]

mutter, *mut'ėr, v.i.* to utter words in a low voice: to murmur, grumble: to make a low, rumbling noise.—Also *v.t.* and *n.*
mutt'ering, *n.* and *adj.*
[Prob. imit; as L. *muttīre.*]

mutton, *mut'n, n.* flesh of sheep as food.
mutt'onhead, *n.* a heavy, stupid person.
[O.Fr. *moton*, a sheep.]

mutual, *mū'tū-ȧl, adj.* given, etc., by each to the other(s) (e.g. *mutual help, mutual dislike*): common to two or more, shared (e.g. *a mutual friend*).
mu'tually, *adv.*
[Fr. *mutuel*—L. *mūtāre*, to change.]

muzzle, *muz'l, n.* the jaws and nose of an animal such as a dog: an arrangement e.g. of straps round the muzzle of an animal to prevent it from biting: the open end of a gun, etc.—*v.t.* to put a muzzle on: to gag or silence.
[O.Fr. *musel.*]

muzzy, *muz'i, adj.* dazed, muddled.
muzz'iness, *n.* [Origin unknown.]

my. See **I.**

myopia, *mī-ō'pi-ȧ, n.* shortness of sight.
myop'ic (*-op'*), *adj.*
[Gk. *myōps*, short-sighted—*ōps*, eye.]

myriad, *mir'i-ȧd, n.* any very great number.—*adj.* numberless.
[Gk. *myrias, -ados*, ten thousand.]

myrrh, *mėr, n.* a gum with a bitter taste, used in medicines, perfumes, etc.
[O.E. *myrra*—L. and Gk. *myrrha.*]

myrtle, *mėr'tl, n.* an evergreen shrub with beautiful sweet-smelling leaves.
[L. *myrtus*—Gk. *myrtos.*]

myself. See **I.**

mystery, *mis'tėr-i, n.* something that cannot be, or has not been, explained: a deep secret: a puzzle or riddle: a puzzling quality:—*pl.* **mys'teries.**
mystē'rious, *adj.* difficult to understand:

secret: hidden: suggesting mystery.

mystic(al), *mis'tik(ål) adjs.* mysterious and holy: having a sacred or secret meaning which can usu. be understood only by a mind that is spiritually in touch with God.

mys'tic, *n.* one who seeks God in high religious feeling and spiritual joy.

mys'ticism, *(-sizm), n.* the beliefs of the mystics: the belief that one can gain direct knowledge of truth by spiritual means higher than that of the intellect.

mys'tically, *adv.*

mys'tify, *v.t.* to puzzle greatly: to bewilder, confuse purposely.

[Gk. *mystērion—myein*, close the eyes.]

myth, *mith, n.* an old story, long handed down, about gods or heroes, giving an explanation of some fact of nature: a fable: a person or thing imagined.

myth'ical, *adj.* having to do with myths: told of in a myth: imaginary.

mythol'ogy, *n.* a collection of myths: the study of myths.

mythol'ogist, *n.* **mytholog'ical,** *adj.*

[Gk. *mythos*, story.]

N

nacelle, *nå-sel', n.* an enclosed part of an aircraft, esp. one for housing the engine.

[Fr.—L. *nāvis*, ship.]

nag[1], *nag, n.* a horse, esp. a small one.

[M.E. *nagge*; origin unknown.]

nag[2], *nag, v.t.* to find fault with constantly: to distress, worry (e.g. *a pain that nags all the time*):—*pr.p.* **nagg'ing**; *pa.p,* **nagged.**

[Conn. Norw., Swed. *nagga*, to gnaw.]

nail, *nāl, n.* a horny plate at the end of a finger or toe: the claw of a bird or other animal: a thin pointed piece of metal for fastening wood.—*v.t.* to fasten with nail(s): to fasten (something up) in this way (in e.g. a box).

[O.E. *nægel.*]

naïve, naive, *nä-ēv', nāv. adj.* simple in thought, speech or manners.

naïveté, *nä-ēv'tā, n.*

[Fr.—L. *nātīvus*, natural.]

naked, *nā'kid, adj.* without clothes: (of e.g. trees) without the natural or usual covering.

na'kedly, *adv.* **na'kedness,** *n.*

[O.E. *nacod.*]

namby-pamby, *nam'bi-pam'bi, adj.* childish, not manly.

[Nickname of *Ambrose* Phillips, who wrote very simple poems.]

name, *nām, n.* word or words by which a person, place, thing, etc., is known or called: character (e.g. *to have a name for honesty*): a celebrity: authority (e.g. *I arrest you in the name of the Queen*).—*v.t.* to give a name to: to speak of by name, mention.

name'less, *adj.* without a name: not named.

name'ly, *adv.* that is to say.

name'plate, *n.* a piece of metal having on it a person's name.

name'sake, *n.* one having the same name as another.

[O.E. *nama.*]

nanny, *nan'i, n.* a children's nurse: (also **nann'y-goat)** a female goat:—*pl.* **nann'ies.**

[From *Nan—Ann(e).*]

nap[1], *nap, v.i.* to take a short sleep.—Also *n.*

to catch napping, to catch when one is unprepared or inattentive.

[O.E. *knappian.*]

nap[2], *nap, n.* a woolly surface on cloth (see **pile,** 3.)

[M.E. *noppe.*]

nap[3], *nap, n.* a game of cards. [*Nap*oleon.]

nape, *nāp, n.* the back of the neck.

[Origin uncertain.]

napalm, *nā'palm, n.* a jelly that catches fire very readily, used in bombs.

naphtha, *naf'thå, nap'thå, n.* liquids that catch fire readily, obtained from coal tar, wood, etc. [Gk.]

napkin, *nap'kin, n.* a small square of linen, paper, etc., used at table or for other purposes.

[Dim. of Fr. *nappe*—L. root as **map.]**

narcissus, *när-sis'ůs, n.* daffodil: other bulbed plants like it:—*pl.* **narciss'uses, -ciss'i** *(-ī).*

[*Narcissus*, a beautiful young man in Greek story.]

narcotic, *när-kot'ik, n.* a drug that eases pain or makes one sleep.

[Gk. *narkē*, numbness.]

narrate, *nå-rāt', v.t.* to tell the story of (e.g. *He narrated his adventures*).—Also *v.i.*

narrā'tion, *n.* **narrā'tor,** *n.*

narrative, *nar'å-tiv, n.* a story.—*adj.* telling a story.

[L. *narrāre, -ātum.*]

narrow, *nar'ō, adj.* having little breadth, not wide: only just successful, with little to spare (e.g. *a narrow escape, a narrow majority*): narrow-minded (see below).—Also *v.t.* and *v.i.*

narr'ows, *n.pl.* a sea passage of little width.

narr'ow-gauge', *adj.* (of a railway) with distance between the rails less than 4 ft. 8 in.

narr'ow-mind'ed, having opinions already formed and being unsympathetic towards other people's ideas.

[O.E. *nearu.*]

nasal, *nā'zȧl, adj.* of the nose: sounded through the nose.
[L. *nāsus,* the nose.]

nascent, *nas'ėnt, adj.* coming into existence, beginning to develop.
[L. *nasci,* to be born.]

nasturtium, *nȧ-stûr'shụm, n.* a climbing plant with broad flat leaves and brightly-coloured flowers.
[L. *nāsus,* nose, *torquēre,* to twist.]

nasty, *nâs'ti, adj.* dirty: very disagreeable: difficult to deal with (e.g. *a nasty problem*):—*comp.* **nas'tier;** *superl.* **nas'tiest.**
nas'tily, *adv.* **nas'tiness,** *n.*
[Origin uncertain.]

natal, *nā'tȧl, adj.* having to do with birth.
[L. *nasci, nātus,* to be born.]

nation, *nā'sh(ȯ)n, n.* people with a common history living in the same country, usu. under the same government: a race of people (e.g. *the Jewish nation*).
national, *nash'ȯn-ȧl, adj.* belonging to a nation: having to do with all the people of a country.—*n.* a person belonging to a particular nation (e.g. *The missing man was a British national*).
na'tionally, *adv.* by, to, etc., the nation as a whole.
na'tionalise, *v.t.* to make (something) the property of the nation (e.g. *Coal-mining is a nationalised industry*).
na'tionalism, *n.* desire to unite people of a nation under their own independent government.
na'tionalist, *n.*
national'ity, *n.* membership of a particular nation: a people or nation.
National Anthem, the special song or hymn of a country, e.g. in Britain 'God Save the Queen'.
National Debt, money borrowed by the Government and not yet paid back.
National Park, land, usually in the country, owned by or for the nation.
National Trust, a society which looks after interesting old buildings.
na'tion-wide, *adj.* taking place, acting, etc. throughout the nation.
[L. *natiō*; same root as **natal.**]

native, *nā'tiv, adj.* born in a person (e.g. *native intelligence*): being, having to do with, place of birth or origin (e.g. *my native land*).—*n.* a person born in a place named (e.g. *a native of Switzerland, of Leeds*): one of the inhabitants of a country at the time it was discovered.
the Nativ'ity (*na-*), the birth of Christ.
nativity play, a play telling the Christmas story.
[L. *nātīvus*; same root as **natal.**]

natty, *nat'i, adj.* trim, tidy, smart:—*comp.* **natt'ier**; *superl.* **natt'iest.**
natt'ily, *adv.* **natt'iness,** *n.*
[Same root as **neat.**]

nature, *nā'chụr, n.* the world around us (animals, plants, streams, mountains, etc.): human nature (see this): the quality, or qualities, that make a person or thing, what he, or it, is (e.g. *His nature is gentle*; *the nature of the ground is hilly*).
natural, *nach'ụr-ȧl, adj.* produced by nature, not made or worked on by men: having to do with nature: (of a quality) born in a person: (of manner) simple, unaffected: (of e.g. result) normal, expected: (*music*) not sharp or flat.—*n.* an idiot: one having a natural ability: something certain of success: a sign (♮) in music to show that a note is not sharp or flat.
na'turally, *adv.* by nature: simply: of course.
na'turalise, *v.t.* to give the rights of a native to (one born in another country).
na'turalist, *n.* one who studies animal and plant life.
naturalis'tic, *adj.* (of e.g. a picture) very like the natural thing, etc.
na'tured (*nā'*), *adj.* having a certain temper (e.g. *good-natured*).
na'turism, *n.* nudism.
natural gas, gas suitable for burning found in the earth.
natural history, the study of plants, animals and (formerly) rocks.
natural resources, forests, mines, water for power, etc.
nature study, learning to observe animals, plants, weather, etc.
in, of, the nature of, having the qualities of (e.g. *That remark was in the nature of a threat*).
[L. *nātūra*; same root as **natal.**]

naught, *nöt, n.* nothing. The name of the figure o is usu. spelt **nought.**
[O.E. *nāht*—*nā,* never, *wiht,* whit.]

naughty, *nö'ti, adj.* bad, ill-behaved.
naugh'tily, *adv.* **naugh'tiness,** *n.*
[Same root as **naught.**]

nausea, *nö'si-ȧ, n.* feeling of sickness.
nau'seate, *v.t.* to fill with disgust, to make sick.
nau'seating, nauseous (*nö'shụs*), *adjs.* sickening.
[Gk. *nautiā,* seasickness—*naus,* a ship.]

nautical, *nö'ti-kȧl, adj.* having to do with ships or sailors.
nautical mile. See **mile.**
[Gk. *nautēs,* sailor—*naus,* a ship.]

nautilus, *nö'ti-lụs, n.* a small sea-creature related to the octopus: (**pearly nautilus**) a shellfish of the Indian ocean, etc.
[Gk. *nautilos,* sailor—*naus,* ship.]

naval. See **navy** (under **navigate**).

nave[1], *nāv, n.* the main part of a church.
[L. *navis,* a ship.]

nave[2], *nāv, n.* the hub or central part of a wheel, through which the axle passes.
[O.E. *nafu.*]

navel, *nā'vėl, n.* the small hollow in the centre of the front of the body.
[O.E. *nafela.*]

navigate, *nav'i-gāt, v.t.* to manage, direct

on its course (a ship, aircraft, etc.).—*v.i.* to find one's way and keep one's course.
nav'igable, *adj.* able to be used by ships.
navigā'tion, *n.* art of directing ships, etc.
nav'igator, *n.* one who sails or steers a ship, etc.
navvy (short for **navigator**), *nav'i, n.* a labourer working on roads, etc.: a digging machine.
navy, *nā'vi, n.* a nation's fighting ships: the men who belong to these.
nāv'al, *adj.* having to do with the navy.
navy blue, *adj.* dark blue.
[L. *navigāre, -ātum—navis,* a ship.]

nawab, *nȧ-wäb', -wöb', n.* a Mohammedan prince or noble.
[Hindustani *nawwāb.*]

nay, *nā, adv.* no.
[M.E. *nai*; from Scand.]

Nazi, *nä'tsē, n.* and *adj.* for *Nationalsozialist,* National Socialist, (member) of a party headed by Hitler. [Ger.]

neap, *nēp, adj.* (of a tide) of smallest range (less high, and also less low, than a *spring tide*).
[O.E. *nēp.*]

Neapolitan, *nē-ȧ-pol'i-tȧn, adj.* belonging to the city of *Naples* or its inhabitants.
[L. *Neāpolitānus*—Gk. *Neāpolis,* Naples.]

near, *nēr, adv.* to or at a little distance.—*prep.* close to.—*adj.* not far away in place or time: close in relationship, friendship, etc.: barely avoiding, or almost reaching, something: stingy: (of horses, vehicles, etc.) left, left-hand (e.g. *the near foreleg, the near wheel of the cart*).—*v.t.* and *v.i.* to approach, come nearer.
near'ly, *adv.* closely: almost: stingily.
near'ness, *n.*
Near East, the countries of S.E. Europe.
near'-sight'ed, *adj.* short-sighted.
near'-sight'edness, *n.*
a near miss, a miss that is almost a hit.
[O.E. *nēar,* closer, more **nigh.**]

neat, *nēt, adj.* trim, tidy: skilful: skilfully made or done: well put (e.g. *a neat sentence*): (of liquor) not weakened by adding e.g. water.
neat'ly, *adv.* **neat'ness,** *n.*
[Fr. *net*—L. *nitidus,* shining.]

nebula, *neb'ū-la, n.* a faintly shining appearance in the night sky, in most cases produced by a great mass of gas and dust:—*pl.* **neb'ulae** (*-lē*).
neb'ulous, *adj.* misty, vague.
[L. *nebula,* mist.]

necessary, *nes'i-sȧr-i, adj.* not able to be done without, or to be escaped.—*n.* something that cannot be done without: (in *pl.*) food, clothing:—*pl.* **-ies.**
nec'essarily, *adv.*
necessity, *ni-ses'i-ti, n.* something that cannot be done without: state of things by which one is compelled to do something: great need: poverty:—*pl.* **-ities.**
necess'itate, *v.t.* to make necessary (e.g. *Icy roads necessitate great care*).
necess'itous, *adj.* very poor, in want.
of necessity, necessarily, unavoidably.
[L. *necessārius* (*adj.*), *necessitās* (*n.*).]

neck, *nek, n.* the part between head and body: any narrow connecting part (e.g. *a neck of land*).
neck'lace, *n.* a string of precious stones or beads worn round the neck.
neck'tie, *n.* a scarf or tie for the neck.
neck and neck, side by side: exactly equal.
neck or nothing, risking everything.
[O.E. *hnecca.*]

necr(o)-, *nek-r(ō)-,* (as part of word) dead (body).
necromancer, *nek'rō-man-sėr, n.* one who practises magic (e.g. by communicating with the dead).
nec'romancy, *n.*
necropolis, *nė-krop'ŏl-is, n.* a cemetery.
[Gk. *nekros* (*manteia,* foretelling the future; *polis,* city).]

nectar, *nek'tȧr, n.* the drink of the ancient Greek gods: a delicious drink: a sweet liquid from flowers, used by bees to make honey.
nectarine, *nek'tȧr-in,* or *-ēn, n.* a kind of peach.
[Gk. *nektar.*]

née, *nā, adj.* born, used chiefly of married women (e.g. *Mrs White, née Black,* means that Mrs White was Miss Black before marriage).
[Fr. *née,* from L. *nātus,* born.]

need, *nēd, n.* necessity: difficulty, want, poverty.—*v.t.* to be in want of.
need'ful, *adj.* necessary, required.
need'less, unnecessary.
need'y, *adj.* poor. **need'iness,** *n.*
needs, *adv.* compelled by necessity (e.g. *He must needs go*).
needs must, it has, had, to be.
[O.E. *nēd.*]

needle, *nēd'l, n.* a small, sharp piece, e.g. of steel, with an eye, used in sewing: a similar object (without an eye) used in knitting, art, medicine and music (e.g. *gramophone needle*): a pointer (e.g. in a compass): the long, pointed leaf of a pine, fir, etc.—*adj.* very important and keenly played (e.g. *a needle match*).—*v.t.* to irritate: to goad.
need'lewoman, *n.* one good at sewing.
need'lework, *n.* work done with a needle.
a needle in a haystack, something very difficult, or impossible, to find.
[O.E. *nǣdl*; conn. with Ger. *nadel.*]

ne'er, *nār, adv.* never.
ne'er-do-well' (weel'), *n.* a good-for-nothing person.

nefarious, *ni-fā'ri-ůs, adj.* extremely wicked.
nefa'riously, *adv.* **nefa'riousness,** *n.*
[L. *nefārius,* from *nefas,* crime.]

negative, *neg'ȧ-tiv, adj.* meaning or saying

'no' (e.g. *a negative answer*): less than zero (e.g. −4 *is a negative or minus value*): of the kind of electricity developed on resin when rubbed with flannel: having more electrons than normal (the **negative terminal** is the one from which electrons flow).—*n.* a word or words by which something is denied (e.g. *The answer is in the negative*): (*photography*) an image in which the lights and shades are the opposite of those in nature.—*v.t.* to prove the opposite: to refuse to adopt (e.g. *The Committee negatived the proposal*).
[L. *negāre, -ātum*, to deny.]

neglect, *ni-glekt′, v.t.* to treat carelessly: to fail to give proper attention to: to fail (to do something).—*n.* want of care or attention.
neglect′ful, *adj.* **neglect′fully,** *adv.*
See also **negligence.**
[L. *nec*, not, *legĕre, lectum*, gather.]

négligé, *neg′li-zhā, n.* easy informal dress: a dressing-gown or similar wrap.
[Fr. *négligé*, neglected.]

negligence, *neg′li-jėns, n.* carelessness.
neg′ligent, *adj.* **neg′ligently,** *adv.*
neg′ligible, *adj.* not worth considering, very small.
[Same root as **neglect.**]

negotiate, *ni-gō′shi-āt, v.i.* to bargain (with), discuss a subject (with), in order to reach agreement.—*v.t.* to arrange (e.g. a treaty or a loan): to get past (an obstacle or difficulty).
nego′tiable, *adj.* that can be negotiated: (of a paper concerned with payment of money) that can be transferred from one person to another.
negotiation, *ni-gō-shi-ā′sh(ö)n, n.* discussion aimed at reaching an agreement (e.g. *The dispute was settled by negotiation*).
nego′tiator, *n.*
[L. *negōtiāre, -ātum*, to trade.]

Negro, *nē′grō, n.* a member of an African race (esp. of the Congo and Sudan) with woolly hair and dark skin.—*pl.* **Ne′groes** (*-ōz*).—Also *adj.*
Ne′gress, *n.* (*not now polite*) a Negro girl or woman.
ne′groid, *adj.* like a Negro.
[Sp. *negro*—L. *niger*, black.]

neigh, *nā, v.i.* to whinny, utter the cry of a horse.—*n.* the cry of a horse.
[O.E. *hnǣgan.*]

neighbour, *nā′bŏr, n.* one who lives near another.
neigh′bourhood, *n.* district near a place (*in the neighbourhood of Paris*): district (e.g. *a poor neighbourhood*).
neigh′bouring, *adj.* near in place (e.g. *France and Belgium are neighbouring countries*).
neigh′bourly, *adj.* friendly.
neigh′bourliness, *n.*
[O.E. *nēah*, near, *(ge)būr*, farmer.]

neither, *nī′THer*, or *nē′, adj., pron., conj.,* not either.
neither . . . nor, not . . . and not (e.g. *Neither George nor Mary is at home*).
[O.E. *nāhwæther.*]

nemesis, *nem′i-sis, n.* punishment that is bound to follow wrongdoing. [Gk.]

neo-, *nē-ō-*, (as part of word) new. [Gk.]

neon, *nē′on, n.* a colourless gas, used with other gases very like it, in **neon lighting.** When an electric current is passed through a very small quantity of any of these gases in a tube a coloured light appears.
[Gk. *neos*, young, new.]

nephew, *nev′ū*, or *nef′ū, n.* the son of a brother or sister.
[Fr. *neveu*—L. *nepōs*, grandson.]

Neptune, *nep′tūn, n.* Roman god of the sea: a distant planet. [L. *Neptūnus.*]

nerve, *nėrv, n.* a bundle of fibres that carries messages between the brain or spinal cord and other parts of the body: a sinew (*to strain every nerve*, to do one's utmost): courage, coolness (e.g. *Don't lose your nerve*): (*coll.*) impudence: (in *pl.*) condition of being too easily excited and upset (e.g. *She suffers from nerves*).—*v.t.* to give courage to (e.g. *This nerved him, he nerved himself, to face the danger*).
nerve′less, *adj.* without strength.
ner′vous, *adj.* connected with the nerves (e.g. *nervous energy*): easily excited: timid.
ner′vously, *adv.* **ner′vousness,** *n.*
ner′vy, *adj.* suffering from, or causing, nervousness:—*comp.* **ner′vier**; *superl.* **ner′viest.**
nerve centre, the most important part of a system or organisation from which everything is controlled.
nervous system, the brain, spinal cord, nerves, of an animal or human being.
to get on one's nerves, to irritate one.
[L. *nervus*, sinew.]

nest, *nest, n.* a place or structure in which birds, certain animals (e.g. mice), certain insects (e.g. wasps) live and bring up their young: the occupants of a nest (e.g. *a nest of robins*): a set of things fitting one inside another (e.g. *a nest of tables*).—*v.i.* to build or occupy a nest.
nestle, *nes′l, v.i.* to lie close as in a nest: to settle comfortably.
nestling, *nes′ling, n.* a young bird in the nest.
nest′-egg, *n.* an egg put in a nest to encourage laying: something (usu. money) saved or stored.
nest′ing-box, *n.* a box made for birds to nest in.
[O.E. *nest* (n.), *nestlian* (vb.).]

net[1], *net, n.* cord knotted so as to form a loose arrangement of crossing lines and spaces, used for catching birds, fish, etc.: finer material with meshes (e.g. *curtain-net, hair-net*).—*v.t.* to catch as in a net:—*pr.p.* **nett′ing**; *pa.p.* **nett′ed.**

nett'ing, *n.* a net material (e.g. *wire-netting*).
net'ball, *n.* a game in which a ball is thrown into a net.
net'work, *n.* anything showing many lines crossing one another (e.g. *A network of roads covered the countryside*): a widespread organisation (e.g. *a network of radio stations*).
[O.E. *net(t)*.]

net[2], **nett,** *net, adj.* remaining after expenses or other charges have been paid (e.g. *The net profit from the sale was £100*).—*v.t.* to gain as profit:—*pr.p.* **nett'ing**; *pa.p.* **nett'ed.**
[Same root as **neat.**]

netball. See **net** (1).

nether, *neTH'ėr, adj.* lower.
neth'ermost, *adj.* lowest.
Neth'erlands, *n.* the Low Countries, i.e. Holland (Belgium is not now included).
[O.E. *neothera*.]

netting. See **net** (1) and (2).

nettle, *net'l, n.* a wild plant with stinging hairs.—*v.t.* to sting: to annoy.
nett'le-rash, *n.* a skin rash that looks like the effect of nettle stings.
[O.E. *netele*; conn. Ger. *nessel.*]

neur-(o-), *nūr-(ō-)*, (as part of a word) nerve(s).
neuralgia, *nū-ral'jȧ, n.* pain in the nerves usu. in the head or face.
neuritis, *nū-rī'tis, n.* inflammation of a nerve.
neurosis, *nū-rō'sis, n.* an emotional and mental illness with symptoms such as unreasonable anxiety.
neurotic, *nū-rot'ik, adj.* in a bad nervous state, having a neurosis.—*n.* a person with a neurosis.
[Gk. *neuron*, sinew, nerve (*algos*, pain; *-itis*, inflammation; *-osis*, condition).]

neuter, *nū'tėr, adj.* (in grammar) neither masculine nor feminine: without sex (as e.g. worker bees): deprived of power to reproduce —Also *n.*
neutral, *nū'trȧl, adj.* not taking sides (e.g. *Sweden was neutral in the war*): (of kind, colour, etc.) not definite (e.g. *Grey is a neutral colour*): (*chemistry*) being neither acid nor base.—*n.* a person or country not taking part in a war or quarrel: a position of gear (e.g. in a car) where no power passes.
neutral'ity, *n,* state of being neutral.
neu'tralise, *v.t.* to make neutral: to make (something) useless or harmless by having an opposite effect (e.g. *His failure to gain votes in the country neutralised his successes in the small towns*): to put out of action (e.g. an enemy force).
neu'tralism, *n.* neutrality as a policy.
neu'tralist, *n.*
[L. *neuter*, neither.]

neutron, *nū'tron, n.* one of the particles (without electrical charge) which, with protons, make up the nucleus of the atom.
[Same root as **neuter.**]

never, *nev'ėr, adv.* not ever: at no time.
nev'ermore', *adv.* never again.
nevertheless', *adv.* in spite of that.
[O.E. *næfre.*]

new, *nū, adj.* recent: not before seen or known: changed (e.g. *a new man*): fresh (e.g. *new milk*): just arrived (e.g. *a new pupil*).—*adv.* recently (e.g. *new-laid*).
new'ly, *adv.* **new'ness,** *n.*
new'comer, *n.* one who has lately come.
new look, a greatly changed appearance.
New World, North and South America.
New Year, a fresh year (beginning on January 1st, except for Jews and Moslems).
[O.E. *nīwe*; conn. Ger. *neu*, Gk. *neos.*]

newfangled, *nū-fang'gld, adj.* very fond of new things: (of things, ideas) new but not very good.
[**new** and M.E. *fangel*, ready to catch.]

news, *nūz, n.sing.* a report of a recent event: new information (e.g. *Have you any news of your friend?*).
new'sy, *adj.* full of news.
news'agent, *n.* one who sells newspapers.
news'boy, *n.* a boy who sells or delivers newspapers.
news'cast, *n.* broadcast of news in a radio or television programme.—Also *v.i.*
news'caster, *n.*
news'paper, *n.* a paper printed each day, or week, and containing news.
news'print, *n.* cheap paper on which newspapers are printed.
news'reel, *n.* a cinema or television film showing, or a radio programme telling about, recent events.
[M.E. *newes* (*pl.* of *adj.* **new**).]

newt, *nūt, n.* a small animal, rather like a lizard, living on land and in water.
[O.E. *an efeta* (see **eft**), which became *an ewt*, then *a newt*. See **nickname.**]

next, *nekst, adj.* nearest, closest, in place, time, etc. (e.g. *the next chapter*).—*adv.* after or alongside and in the nearest place, at the nearest time, etc. (e.g. *Alice led, Jane came next*; *do that sum next.*)
[O.E. *nehst*; same root as **nigh.**]

nib, *nib, n.* something small and pointed, esp. a writing point for a pen that is not a ball-point: (in *pl.*) cocoa or coffee beans broken into small pieces.
nibbed, *adj.*
[O.E. *nebb*, nose.]

nibble, *nib'l, v.t.* to take very small bites of (something).—*v.i.* (often with *at*) to begin to take, show, interest (e.g. *The purchaser nibbled at the bargain*).—*n.* act of nibbling.
[Origin unknown.]

nice, *nīs, adj.* agreeable, pleasant: careful, exact (e.g. *a nice sense of timing*).

nice'ly, *adv* pleasantly: very well (e.g. *It will do nicely*).
nice'ness, *n.* exactness: agreeableness.
nicety, *nīs'i-ti, n.* a delicate or exact detail:—*pl.* **nic'eties.**
to a nicety, with great exactness.
[O.Fr., foolish—L. *nescius,* ignorant.]

niche, *nich, n.* a hollow in a wall for a statue or ornament: a suitable place in life (e.g. *He found his niche in engineering*).
[O.Fr. *nicher,* to make a nest.]

nick, *nik, n.* a notch: the right, or the last possible, moment (*in the nick of time*).—*v.t.* to cut notches in. [Orig. uncertain.]

nickel, *nik'ėl, n.* a greyish-white metal used esp. for mixing with other metals, and for plating (e.g. *nickel-plating*): (*U.S.*) a 5-cent coin.
nick'el-sil'ver, *n.* a mixture of copper, zinc and nickel.
See also **cupro-nickel.**
[Ger. *kupfernickel,* the ore from which nickel is obtained.]

nickname, *nik'nām, n.* an added name, given in fun, or contempt, or admiration (e.g. *Wellington's nickname was 'the Iron Duke'*).—*v.t.* to give a nickname to.
[O.E. *ēcan,* to add, *nama,* name (*an ekename* became *a nekename.* See **newt.**)]

nicotine, *nik'ȯ-tēn, n.* a poisonous substance present in tobacco.
[Jean *Nicot,* who introduced tobacco into France in 1560.]

niece, *nēs, n.* the daughter of a brother or sister.
[O.Fr. *nece*—L. *neptis,* granddaughter.]

niggard, *nig'ȧrd, n.* one who dislikes spending or giving.
nigg'ardly, *adj.* mean (e.g. *a niggardly man*): of little value (e.g. *a niggardly gift*).
nigg'ardliness, *n.* [Origin uncertain.]

nigger, *nig'ėr, n.* (*impolitely*) a Negro.

niggle, *nig'l, v.i.* to spend time on small details.
nigg'ling, *adj.* unimportant, fussy.
[Prob. Scandinavian.]

nigh, *nī, adj.* and *prep.* near.
[O.E. *nēah* (*comp.* is *nehst*; see **next**).]

night, *nīt, n.* the time between sunset and sunrise: darkness.—*adj.* of, for, night: happening, active (e.g. *a night bird*), used, at night.
nightly', *adj.* and *adv.* by night: every night.
night club, a club open during the night for dancing or other entertainment.
night'dress, night'gown, night'shirt, *ns.* garments worn in bed.
night'fall, *n.* the beginning of the night.
night'long, *adj.* and *adv.* (lasting) all night.
night'mare, *n.* a frightening dream.
night'shade, *n.* a plant with poisonous berries.
night shift, a turn of duty during the night.
night'-watch'man, *n.* one who looks after a building during the night.
[O.E. *niht*; conn. with Ger. *nacht.*]

nightingale, *nīt'ing-gāl, n.* a small bird with a beautiful song, which it sings at night as well as by day.
[O.E. *niht,* night, *galan,* to sing.]

nightmare, nightshade. See **night.**

nil, *nil, n.* nothing.
[L. *nil,* short for *nihil,* nothing.]

nimble, *nim'bl, adj.* quick in movement: clever (e.g. *a nimble wit*).
nim'bleness, *n.* **nim'bly,** *adv.*
[Prob. O.E. *næmel,* from *niman,* to take.]

nimbus, *nim'bŭs, n.* a bright disk, or other figure, representing light round a person's head in a picture. [L.]

nine, *nīn, adj.* and *n.* the number next above eight (9 or IX).
ninth, *nīnth, adj.* last of nine.—*n.* one of nine equal parts.
nine'teen (also *-tēn'*), *adj.* and *n.* nine and ten (19 or XIX).
nine'teenth (also *-tēnth'*), *adj.* last of nineteen.—*n.* one of nineteen equal parts.
nine'pins, *n.* a game in which nine bottle-shaped pins have to be knocked down by a ball.
nine days' wonder, something that attracts attention for a short time and is then forgotten.
[O.E. *nigon*; *nigontȳne*; *nigontig.*]

ninny, *nin'i, n.* foolish person:—*pl.* **-ies.**
[Perhaps from **innocent.**]

nip, *nip, v.t.* to pinch: to cut, bite, etc. (off): to check growth of, damage (e.g. *The frost nips the dahlias*): (of cold) to pain (e.g. fingers):—*pr.p.* **nipp'ing**; *pa.p.* **nipped.**—*n.* a pinch: a small quantity: sharp coldness (e.g. *a nip in the air*).
nipp'er, *n.* something that nips, such as a crab's claw: (*slang*) a boy: (in *pl.*) pincers or pliers.
[Prob. from Middle Du.]

nipple, *nip'l, n.* the part of the breast through which a baby draws milk: a teat of a baby's bottle: anything like this, e.g. a small projection through which oil or grease is put into machinery.
[Perh. same root as **nib.**]

Nippon, *ni-pon', nip', n.* Japan. [Jap.]

nisi, *nī'sī,* unless, used in phrases such as **decree nisi** (see **decree**), etc. [L.]

nit, *nit, n.* the egg or young of a louse or other small insect.
nit'wit, *n.* (*slang*) a very foolish person.
[O.E. *hnitu.*]

nitre, etc. See **nitrogen.**

nitrogen, *nī'trȯ-jėn, n.* a colourless gas with no taste or smell, forming nearly four-fifths of the air.
nitrogenous, *nī-troj'ėn-ŭs, adj.* containing nitrogen (e.g. *a nitrogenous fertiliser*).
ni'tric, ni'trous, *adjs.* (*chemistry*) containing nitrogen in fixed proportions.
nitric acid, a strong acid in which nitrogen is an element.

ni′trate, *n.* any of a number of salts formed from nitric acid esp. one used as a fertiliser.

nitre. See **saltpetre.**

ni′tro-glyc′erine, *n.* powerful explosive.

[Fr. *nitrogène*; from Gk. words.]

no, *nō, adj.* not any (e.g. *We have no coal*): not a (e.g. *He is no singer, no beauty*).—*adv.* not at all (e.g. *The patient is no better*).—*n.* a refusal: a vote against:—*pl.* **noes** (*nōz*; e.g. *The noes have won*).

no one, not any person, nobody.

[O.E. *nā.*]

nobility. See **noble.**

noble, *nō′bl, adj.* great in character or of fine moral quality (e.g. *a noble mind, deed*): of high birth or rank.—*n.* a gold coin, no longer used: a man of high rank (also **no′bleman**).

no′bly, *adv.* **no′bleness,** *n.*

nobility, *nō-bil′i-ti, n.* nobleness: nobles (dukes, earls, etc.) considered together.

[Fr.—L. *nōbilis*, famous, high-born.]

nobody, *nō′bȯd-i, n.* no one: a person of no importance (*pl.* **-ies**). [**no, body.**]

nocturnal, *nok-tûr′nȧl, adj.* happening at night (e.g. *a nocturnal alarm*): active at night (e.g. *Though sometimes seen by day, the hedgehog is really a nocturnal animal*).

nocturne, *nok′tûrn, n.* a piece of music describing a night scene: a painting of a night scene.

[L. *nox, noctis*, night.]

nod, *nod, v.i.* and *v.t.* to give a quick forward shake of (the head), often showing agreement: to let the head droop in weariness: to make a careless mistake:—*pr.p.* **nodd′ing;** *pa.p.* **nodd′ed.**—*n.* a quick forward movement of the head.

[M.E. *nodde.*]

noddle, *nod′l, n.* head. [Orig. unknown.]

node, *nōd, n.* a knob, joint, e.g. where a leaf stalk joins a branch.

nodule, *nod′ūl, n.* a little rounded lump.

[L. *nōdus.*]

Noël, also **Nowel(l),** *nō-el′, n.* Christmas.

[Fr. *Noël*—same L. root as **natal.**]

noggin, *nog′in, n.* a small mug or cup.

[Origin unknown.]

noise, *noiz, n.* sound of any kind: a loud or disturbing sound.—*v.t* to spread by talk (e.g. *The story was noised abroad*).

noise′less, *adj.* silent, without sound.

noise′lessly, *adv.* **noise′lessness,** *n.*

nois′y, *adj.* making a loud sound:—*comp.* **nois′ier;** *superl.* **nois′iest.**

nois′ily, *adv.* **nois′iness,** *n.*

[Fr. *noise*, quarrel.]

noisome, *noi′sȯm, adj.* harmful to health: disgusting.

[*noy*, a form of **annoy.**]

nomad, *nō′mad, nom′, n.* one of a group of people without fixed home who wander with flocks searching for pasture: a wanderer.

nomadic, *nō-mad′ik, nȯ-, adj.*

nomad′ically, *adv.*

[Gk. *nomas*, pasture.]

no-man's-land, *nō′manz-land, n.* waste land which no one owns, especially between two armies.

nom de plume, *nom′dė-plōōm, n.* a name taken by a writer who wishes to conceal his own name.

[Formed in Engl. from Fr. *nom*, name, *de*, of, *plume*, pen.]

nomenclature, *no-men′klȧ-chȯr, nō′, n.* a set of names for things of one kind, e.g. the set of Latin names given to flowers in the science of botany.

[L. *nōmen*, a name, *calāre*, to call.]

nominal, *nom′in-ȧl, adj.* in name only, not real: trifling, not important (e.g. *a nominal fine*).

nom′inally, *adv.*

nominate, *nom′in-āt, v.t.* to name: to appoint (e.g. *They nominated Mary as Form Captain*): to propose for election or for approval (e.g. *They nominated four candidates for the post*).

nominā′tion, *n.*

nominative, *nom′in-ȧ-tiv, adj.* and *n.* (in grammar) (the case) showing the subject of the verb.

nominee, *nom-in-ē′, n.* one who is proposed for a position or duty.

[L. *nomen, nominis*, name.]

non-, *non-*, Latin *adv.* put before a word to change the meaning of that word to its opposite, e.g.:—

non-appear′ance, *n.* failure to appear.

non-attend′ance, *n.* absence.

non-com′batant, *n.* someone connected with the armed forces who does not fight, e.g. a doctor.—Also *adj.*

non-commiss′ioned, *adj.* (of officer in army) below rank of second-lieutenant.

non-committ′al, *adj.* unwilling to express, or not expressing, an opinion (e.g. *When questioned, he was non-committal; a non-committal answer*).

non-conduct′ing, *adj.* not readily transmitting heat, electricity, etc.

non-conduct′or, *n.*

non-conform′ist, *n.* one who does not agree with those in authority, especially in Church matters.—Also *adj.*

non-conform′ity, *n.* state of being a non-conformist.

non-exist′ent, *adj.* not existing, not real (e.g. *Some people think the Loch Ness monster is non-existent*).

non-exist′ence, *n.*

non-ferr′ous, *adj.* containing no iron (e.g. *non-ferrous metals*, all the metals except iron).

non-interven′tion, *n.* not interfering in the affairs, esp. quarrels, of e.g. another country.

non-pay′ment, *n.*

non-res′ident, *adj.* not living in the place mentioned (e.g. *In this boarding*

school, some of the teachers were non-resident).—Also *n*.
non'-stop', *adj*. going on without a stop.
[L. *nōn*, not.]
nonagenarian, *non-ȧ-jė-nā'ri-ȧn*, *n*. someone who is ninety years old.
[L. *nōnāginta*, ninety.]
nonchalance, *non'shȧ-lȧns*, *n*. coolness, lack of worry or excitement.
non'chalant, *adj*. **non'chalantly,** *adv*.
[L. *non*, not, *calēre*, to be warm, roused.]
nondescript, *non'di-skript*, *adj*. not easy to describe, neither one thing nor another (e.g. *a nondescript appearance*).—Also *n*.
[L. *nōn*, not, *dēscrībĕre*, to describe.]
none, *nun*, *pron*. (*plur*. or *sing*.) not one: not any (of).—*adv*. not at all (e.g. *none the worse*).
none the less, nevertheless, in spite of this.
[O.E. *nān*—*ne*, not, *ān*, one.]
nonentity, *non-en'ti-ti*, *n*. a person of no importance :—*pl*. **nonen'tities.**
[L. *nōn*, not, *entitās*, being.]
nonplus, *non'plus'*, *v.t*. to puzzle completely, bewilder (e.g. *The boy was nonplussed by the unexpected question*).
[L. *nōn*, not, *plūs*, more.]
nonsense, *non'sėns*, *n*. words that have no sense, or no meaning : foolishness.
[L. *nōn*, not, and **sense.**]
noodle[1], *nōōd'l*, *n*. a foolish person.
[Origin unknown.]
noodle[2], *nōōd'l*, *n*. a little piece of dried dough sometimes put in soup.
[Ger. *nudel*.]
nook, *nook*, *n*. corner, recess (e.g. *Some modern kitchens have a dining nook*).
[M.E. *nok*; prob. Scand.]
noon, *nōōn*, *n*. twelve o'clock, midday.
noon'day, noon'tide, *ns*. and *adjs*. midday.
[L. *nōna*, ninth (hour), 3 p.m.; name later transferred to midday.]
noose, *nōōs*, *n*. a loop in rope or cord which tightens when pulled : a snare.—*v.t*. to tie or catch in a noose.
[O.Fr. *nous*—L. *nōdus*, knot.]
nor, *nör*, *conj*. and not (with order of subject and verb reversed; e.g. *He did not know why then, nor did he ever find out*). See also **neither.**
[From *nother*, a form of **neither.**]
norm, *nörm*, *n*. a pattern : a standard to judge by.
nor'mal, *adj*. ordinary, usual.
nor'mally, *adv*. in an ordinary way : usually, as a rule.
normal'ity, nor'malness, *ns*.
[L. *norma*, a rule.]
Norman, *nör'man*, *n*. native of Normandy, the part of France conquered by Norsemen in 10th century.—Also *adj*.
[O.Fr. *Normanz*, Northmen (Norsemen).]
Norse, *nörs*, *adj*. and *n*. Norwegian (language or people), esp. ancient.
Norse'man, *n*. a Scandinavian of long ago, one of those who made settlements in Britain, etc.
Old Norse, Norwegian and Icelandic as spoken and written before the mid 14th century.
[Prob. Old Du. *noorsch*—*noord*, north.]
north, *nörth*, *adj*. the direction to the left of a person facing the rising sun : a territory in this direction.—Also *adj*., *adv*.
nor'therly (-TH-), *adj*. of, from, or looking towards, the north.—Also *adv*.
nor'thern (-TH-), *adj*. of, or towards the north.
nor'therner (-TH-), *n*. native of the north.
nor'thernmost (-TH-), *adj*. farthest north.
north'ward, *adj*. and (also **north'wards**) *adv*. towards the north.
north'-bound, *adj*. travelling northwards (e.g. *The north-bound train leaves at 8 a.m.*).
north-east' (or **-west'**), *n*. midway between north and east (or west) : in or from that direction.—Also *adj*.
north-eas'ter (or **-wes'ter**), *n*. wind blowing from north-east (or north-west).
north pole, *n*. the end of the earth's axis in the ice-covered Arctic Ocean : the highest point of the heavens as seen from there.
North Star, *n*. the Pole Star, a star which is very near the north pole of the heavens.
northern lights, *n*. greenish lights sometimes seen in the sky at night.
[O.E.]
Norwegian, *nör-wē'jȧn*, *adj*. belonging to Norway.—*n*. a native of Norway : the language of Norway.
[Old Norse *northr*, north, *vegr*, way.]
nose, *nōz*, *n*. the part of the face through which we breathe and smell : the jutting-forward part (e.g. *the nose of an aeroplane, car*).—*v.t*. to smell : to track by smelling : to make a way by feeling or pushing (e.g. *The ice-breaker nosed its way through the ice*).
nos'y (sometimes **nos'ey**), *adj*. having a large nose : fond of prying.
nos'ily, *adv*. **nos'iness,** *n*.
nose'bag, *n*. a bag for food, hung on a horse's head.
nose'-dive, *n*. a fall head first (e.g. *The aeroplane did a nose-dive into the sea*).—Also *v.i*.
to follow your nose, to go straight forward.
to pay through the nose, to pay heavily or too much for something.
to put one's nose out of joint, to make one feel disappointed and annoyed by taking one's place, or spoiling one's plans.
to poke one's nose into, to meddle in (someone else's business).
to turn up one's nose at, to refuse with contempt : to treat with contempt.
[O.E. *nosu*; conn. Ger. *nase*, L. *nāsus*.]

nosegay, *nōz′gā*, *n.* a bunch of sweet-smelling flowers. [**nose, gay.**]
nostalgia, *nos-tal′ji-ȧ, -jȧ*, *n.* homesickness: longing for past times.
nostal′gic, *adj.* feeling or expressing homesickness, etc. (e.g. *'Home, Sweet Home' is a nostalgic song*).
[Gk. *nostos*, a return, *algos*, pain.]
nostril, *nos′tril*, *n.* one of the openings of the nose.
[O.E. *nosu*, nose, *thyrel*, opening.]
nostrum, *nos′trum*, *n.* person's favourite medicine, remedy, scheme for reform.
[L. *nostrum* (neuter), our own—*nos*, we.]
not, *not*, *adv.* expressing refusal or denial.
[Same as **nought, naught.**]
notable. See **note.**
notary, *nō′tȧ-ri*, *n.* an official whose duties are concerned with formal documents and statements, e.g. who gives a certificate of the making of a contract.—Also **no′tary pub′lic** :—*pl.* **no′taries (pub′lic).**
[L. *notārius*—same root as **note.**]
notation, *nō-tā′sh(ȯ)n*, *n.* a system of signs with definite meaning (e.g. *Sol-fa notation is a way of writing music*).
[Same root as **note.**]
notch, *noch*, *n.* a nick, a small v-shaped cut.—*v.t.* to make a nick in.
[Prob. O.Fr. *oche* (*an oche* became *a noche*). See **newt, nickname.**]
note, *nōt*, *n.* a sign or piece of writing to draw attention to, or to remind of, something: (in *pl.*) ideas set down in short form (for e.g. a speech): a short explanation (e.g. *There is a note in your textbook about that difficult word*): a short letter: a letter from the head of one government to the head of another (e.g. *A note has been sent by the Prime Minister to the President*): a piece of paper used as money (e.g. *a five-pound note*): a mark standing for a sound in music: the sound itself (e.g. *The song ended on a high note*): the song or cry of a bird or animal (e.g. *The blackbird's note is sweeter than the crow's*).—*v.t.* to make a note of: to notice.
notable, *nō′tȧ-bl*, *adj.* worthy of being noted, memorable: important.—*n.* an important person (e.g. *The Prime Minister and other notables were present*).
no′tableness, *n.*
notabil′ity, *n.* notableness: a notable person:—*pl.* **-ies.**
no′tably, *adv.* in a notable way: noticeably: particularly (e.g. *Some of them looked alarmed, notably Mr Brown*).
no′ted, *adj.* well-known.
note′worthy, *adj.* notable, remarkable (e.g. *Nothing noteworthy happened*).
note′book, *n.* a small book in which to make notes.
note′case, *n.* a wallet for banknotes.
of note, distinguished.
to take note of, to notice and remember.
worthy of note, noteworthy.
[L. *nota*, a mark, *notāre, -ātum* (vb.)]
nothing, *nuth′ing*, *n.* no thing: not anything: (*arithmetic*) a nought: (in *pl.*) trivial remarks.—Also *adv.* not at all (e.g. *It was nothing like what I had said*).
noth′ingness, *n.* state of being nothing.
to come to nothing, to fail, have no result.
to make nothing of. See **make.**
[**no, thing.**]
notice, *nō′tis*, *n.* an announcement made, or shown, publicly: a warning (e.g. *I give notice that the next person who does it will be punished*): warning that an agreement is ending, e.g. that employment is ceasing (e.g. *His employer gave the boy a week's notice*): attention (e.g. *His gay hat, his skill, attracted notice*).—*v.t.* to see, observe, take note of.
no′ticeable, *adj.* likely to be, easily, seen, heard, felt, etc. (e.g. *a noticeable difference*).
no′ticeably, *adv.* **no′ticeableness,** *n.*
to give notice of, to give information, warning, about.
to take notice, to observe, pay attention (often with *of*).
See also **notify.**
[Fr.—L. *nōscĕre, nōtum*, to know.]
notify, *nō′ti-fī*, *v.t.* to inform (e.g. *He notified the milkman that he would be away for three days*): to give notice of:—*pr.p.* **no′tifying**; *pa.p.* **nō′tified.**
no′tifiable, *adj.* (of diseases) that must be reported to public-health authorities.
notificā′tion, *n.*
[Root of **notice,** and *facĕre*, to make.]
notion, *nō′sh(ȯ)n*, *n.* an idea: a fancy or vague belief.
[Fr.—L. *nōtiō*; same root as **notice.**]
notoriety. See **notorious.**
notorious, *nō-tō′ri-us, -tö′*, *adj.* well known in a bad way (e.g. *He is a notorious thief*).
notori′ety (*-rī′*), **noto′riousness,** *ns.*
noto′riously, *adv.* in a way, to a degree, that is very well known (e.g. *It is notoriously difficult to find a needle in a haystack*).
[Late L. *nōtōrius*; same root as **notice.**]
notwithstanding, *not-with-stand′ing*, *prep.* in spite of (e.g. *Notwithstanding the bad weather, all the children reached school*).—*adv.* nevertheless.
[**not, withstanding.**]
nougat, *nōō′gä*, *n.* a sticky sweet containing chopped nuts.
[Fr.—L. *nux, nucis*, a nut.]
nought. Same as **naught.**
noun, *nown*, *n.* (*grammar*) a word used as a name of a person, thing, etc. (e.g. *The words 'boy', 'James', and 'book' are all nouns*).
[L. *nōmen*, name.]
nourish, *nûr′ish*, *v.t.* to feed: to encourage growth of: to have, cherish (e.g. *He nourished feelings of envy towards his rival*).
nour′ishing, *adj.* (of food) giving the

body what is necessary for health and growth.

nour'ishment, *n.* something that nourishes (e.g. *Plants draw nourishment from the earth*).

See also **nutriment,** etc.

[L. *nūtrire, nūtrītum,* to feed.]

novel, *nov'l, adj.* new and strange (e.g. *Space travel was a novel idea to most people in* 1957).—*n.* a long story in prose.

nov'elist, *n.* the writer of a novel.

nov'elty, *n.* newness : something new or strange :—*pl.* **nov'elties.**

[O.Fr. *novelle*—L. *novus,* new.]

November, *nō-vem'bėr, n.* the eleventh month (ninth of the Roman year).

[L. *novem,* nine.]

novice, *nov'is, n.* a beginner : a nun or monk who has not yet taken all the vows : a show animal not yet a prize-winner.

[Fr.—same L. root as **novel.**]

now, *now, adv.* at the present time : as things are (e.g. *You see why I cannot now go*).—*conj.* (often **now that**) since, because (e.g. *I can go now* [*that*] *you have come*).

nowadays, *now'ȧ-dāz, adv.* at the present day.

now and then, now and again, sometimes, from time to time.

[O.E. *nū* (*dæg,* day).]

Nowel(l). See **Noël.**

nowhere, *nō'(h)wār, adv.* in or to no place.

[**no, where.**]

noxious, *nok'shus, adj.* harmful to man or other living things (e.g. *noxious fumes*) : harmful to morals or mind (e.g. *a noxious book*).

[L. *noxius—nocēre,* to hurt.]

nozzle, *noz'l, n.* a spout fitted to the end of a pipe, etc., through which liquid or gas can come out. [**nose.**]

nucleus, *nū'kli-us, n.* a central point or mass around which something collects, or from which something grows (e.g. *The three prize books formed the nucleus of his library*) : the part of a plant or animal cell that controls its development : the central part of an atom, consisting of two kinds of particle known as protons and neutrons (except in case of hydrogen where nucleus is one proton) :—*pl.***nuclei** (*nū'kli-ī*).

nu'clear (*-kli-ȧr*), *adj.* having to do with a nucleus, esp. of the atom.

nuclear energy, the energy released by splitting nuclei of atoms.

nuclear fission, splitting of nuclei of atoms.

nuclear reactor, apparatus for splitting nuclei of atoms.

[L.—*nux, nucis,* a nut.]

nude, *nūd, adj.* naked, without clothes.—*n.* an unclothed human figure or statue.

nū'dist, *n.* one who approves of going without clothes.

nu'dity, *n.* the state of being nude.

in the nude, naked.

[L. *nūdus,* naked.]

nudge, *nuj, n.* a gentle poke, e.g. with the elbow.—*v.t.* to poke gently.

[Origin uncertain.]

nugget, *nug'it, n.* a lump, esp. of gold.

[Origin unknown.]

nuisance, *nū'sȧns, n.* person or thing that is annoying, troublesome, or (*law*) that harms, inconveniences, or is offensive.

[Fr.—L. *nocēre,* to hurt.]

null, *nul, adj.* of no value or effect.

null'ity, *n.* the state of being null.

nullify, *nul'i-fī, v.t.* to undo the effect of : to make (e.g. a contract)) without legal force, or to declare it to be so.

decree of nullity, an order which says that a marriage has never been legal.

null and void, having no legal force, no longer binding or controlling.

[L. *nūllus,* none (*facĕre,* to make).]

numb, *num, adj.* having lost the power to feel or move.—*v.t.* to make numb, to deaden.

numb'ly, *adv.* **numb'ness,** *n.*

[O.E. *numen, pa.p.* of *niman,* take, seize.]

number, *num'bėr, n.* a numeral : a thing named by its place in a series (e.g. *He lives at Number* 7) : a collection of things, persons, etc. (e.g. *You may have a number of hobbies*) : one issue of a newspaper or magazine (e.g. *Most magazines publish a Christmas number*) : a song or piece of music, esp. one that is part of a musical play (e.g. *His latest musical play includes many popular numbers*).—*v.t.* to count : to give numbers to : to amount to in number (e.g. *His party numbers ten*).

num'berless, *adj.* more than can be counted.

his days are numbered, he has not long to live.

times without number, very often, too often to count.

[Fr. *nombre*; same root as **numeral.**]

numeral, *nū'mėr-ȧl, n.* a figure (e.g. 1, 2, etc.) used to express a number.

nū'merātor, *n.* (in fractions) the number above the line.

numerical, *nū-mer'ik-ȧl, adj.* using or consisting of numbers (e.g. *The secret messages were written in a numerical code*) : in numbers (e.g. *the great numerical strength of the enemy*).

numer'ically, *adv.*

nū'merous, *adj,* very many.

numerical order, the order in which we normally count (e.g. 1, 2, 3, 4; or 20, 21, 22, 23, etc.).

[L. *numerus,* number.]

numskull, *num'skul, n.* a blockhead.

[**numb, skull.**]

nun, *nun, n.* a woman who has taken vows to live in a convent and devote herself to religion.

nunn'ery, *n.* a house for nuns :—*pl.* **-ies.**

[O.E. *nunne*—Late L. *nunna, nonna.*]

nuptial, *nup'shȧl, adj.* having to do with marriage.
nup'tials, *n.pl.* a wedding ceremony.
[L. *nubĕre, nuptum,* to marry.]

nurse, *nûrs, n.* a woman (or man) who looks after sick or injured people, or after small children.—*v.t.* to look after (invalids) esp. in hospital: to suckle (see this word): to hold in the arms with care: to take care of (e.g. *This plant is delicate and must be nursed*): to manage with care (e.g. *You must nurse your resources*): to encourage oneself to feel (anger, hatred, etc.).
nur'sery, *n.* a room for children: a piece of ground where young plants and trees are grown: a place where people are encouraged in a habit or feeling (e.g. *Fagin's house was a nursery of, for, thieves*):—*pl.* **nur'series.**
nurs'ling, nurse'ling, *n.* something that is nursed: an infant.
nur'sery-man, *n.* a man who works in a place where plants and trees are grown for sale.
nursery school, a school for children under five.
nursing home, a private hospital.
[Fr. *nourrice*—L. root as **nourish.**]

nurture, *nûr'chu̇r, v.t.* to bring up: to cause to develop: to feed.—*n.* upbringing, training: food.
[Fr. *nourriture*—L. root as **nourish.**]

nut, *nut, n.* a fruit with one seed (kernel) in a hard shell: a small block, usu. of metal, for screwing on the end of a bolt: a small lump, e.g. of coal.
nutt'ing, *n.* gathering nuts.
nutt'y, *adj.* containing nuts: having the flavour of nuts:—*comp.* **nutt'ier**; *superl.* **nutt'iest.**
nut'-brown, *adj.* brown like a ripe nut.
nut'cracker, *n.* a bird of the crow family: (in *pl.*) a pair of hinged metal arms used for cracking nuts.
nut'hatch, *n.* a small climbing bird that lives on nuts and insects.
a hard nut to crack, someone or something difficult to deal with.
in a nutshell, expressed very briefly.
[O.E. *hnutu*;. conn. with Ger. *nuss.*]

nutmeg, *nut'meg, n.* the hard kernel or seed of the fruit of an East Indian tree, used as a spice in food.
[M.E. *notemuge*—**nut,** L. *muscus,* musk.]

nutrient, *nū'tri-ėnt, adj.* and *n.* (substance) giving nourishment.
nutriment, *nū'tri-mėnt, n.* nourishment, food.
nutrition, *nū-tri'sh(o̤)n, n.* act or process of nourishing.
nūtri'tious (*-shu̇s*), *adj.* nourishing.
nu'tritive, *adj.* serving as food: having to do with nutrition (e.g. *a substance of great nutritive value*).
[Same L. root as **nourish.**]

nuzzle, *nuz'l, v.t.* and *v.i.* to press, rub, or caress with the nose (e.g. *The dog nuzzled my hand*). [From **nose.**]

nylon, *nī'lon, n.* a fibre, or a material, made from chemicals, used for clothes, ropes, bristles, etc.: (in *pl.*; *coll.*) stockings made of this material.
[Name made up.]

nymph, *nimf, n.* a Greek goddess of lower rank living in sea, river, tree, or hill, etc.: a beautiful girl: a young insect that is of the same form as the adult.
[L. *nympha*—Gk. *nymphē.*]

O

O, oh, *ō, interj.* an exclamation expressing surprise, admiration, pain, longing, etc.

oaf, *ōf, n.* a stupid fellow: a lout, awkward person:—*pl.* **oafs.**
oaf'ish, *adj.*
[Old Norse *ālfr,* elf.]

oak, *ōk, n.* a tree related to the beech, having acorns as fruit: its hard wood.
oak'en, *adj.*
[O.E. *āc*; conn. with Ger. *eiche.*]

oakum, *ō'ku̇m, n.* tarry ropes untwisted, used for stopping up the seams of wooden parts of ships.
[O.E. *ācumba*—*cemban,* to comb.]

oar, *ōr, ör, n.* light pole with flat end (the blade) for rowing a boat: an oarsman.—*v.t., v.i.* to row.
oars'man, *n.* one who rows with an oar.
to put in one's oar, to interfere, meddle.
[O.E. *ār.*]

oasis, *ō-ā'sis, ō'ȧ-sis, n.* a fertile green spot in a sandy desert:—*pl.* **oases** (*-sēz*).
[Gk. *oasis* (an Egyptian word).]

oast, *ōst, n.* a large oven to dry hops.
[O.E. *āst.*]

oat. Sing. (seldom used) of **oats.**

oatmeal. See **oats.**

oath, *ōth, n.* a solemn promise (calling on God or something holy as witness) to speak the truth, to keep one's word, to be loyal, etc.: a swear word.—*pl.* **oaths,** ōTHz, *ōths.*
[O.E. *āth*; conn. with Ger. *eid.*]

oats, *ōts, n.pl.* a cereal, a type of grass whose seeds are used as food: the seeds.
oat'cake', *n.* a thin hard cake of oatmeal.
oat'meal, meal made by grinding oat grains.
[O.E. *āte* (sing.; O.E. pl, *ātan*).]

obdurate, *ob'dū-rit,* or *-rāt,* or *-dū', adj.* hardened, unyielding—impossible to turn

from a (bad) way of life (e.g. *an obdurate sinner*), to persuade, make feel pity, etc.
obduracy, obdurateness, *ns.*
[L. *ob*, against, and root as **durable.**]

obedience, obedient. See **obey.**

obeisance, *ō-bā'sȧns, n.* a bow or curtsy showing respect.
[Fr. *obéissance*—same root as **obey.**]

obelisk, *ob'i-lisk, n.* a tall, four-sided pillar with a pointed top.
[Gk. *obelos*, a spit.]

obese, *ō-bēs', adj.* very fat, fleshy.
obes'ity (*-bēs'*), **obese'ness,** *ns.*
[L. *ob-*, completely, *edĕre, ēsum*, to eat.]

obey, *ō-bā', ȯ-, v.i.* to do what one is told to do.—*v.t.* to do as one is told by (a person: e.g. *to obey one's father*), or in (a command; e.g. *to obey the order to lay down arms*): to follow the guidance of (e.g. one's conscience, an impulse).
obedience, *ō-bē'dyėns, -di-ėns, n.*
obe'dient, *adj.* **obe'diently,** *adv.*
[Fr. *obeir*—L. *ob-*, towards, *audīre*, hear.]

obituary, *ȯ-bit'ū-ȧr-i, n.* a notice (e.g. in a newspaper) of a person's death, with or without an account of his career:—*pl.* **obit'uaries.**
[L. *obīre*, to go to meet, to die.]

object, *ob'jekt, n.* a thing able to be seen or felt, a material thing (e.g. *Name all the objects in the shop window*): something to which attention is given (e.g. *The life of Nelson was the object of his study*): aim, purpose (e.g. *His object was to make money so that he could travel abroad*): a person or thing whose appearance causes scorn, amusement, or pity (e.g. *In the hut sat an object dressed in filthy rags*): (*grammar*) the word(s) in a sentence standing for the person or thing on which the action of the verb is done (e.g. *In 'He hit me', 'me' is the object of the verb 'hit'*); also the word(s) following a preposition (e.g. *In 'under the table', '(the) table' is the object of 'under'*).—*v.i.* (*ob-jekt'*) to feel, or express, disapproval of something (with *to*; e.g. *I object to smoking in theatres*).—*v.t.* to protest (e.g. *He objected that the instructions were not clear*).
objec'tor, *n.*
objec'tion, *n.* act of objecting: feeling of disapproval: reason for disapproving.
objec'tionable, *adj.* disagreeable, nasty.
objec'tive, *adj.* having to do with an object: outside the mind: not prejudiced, fair (e.g. *He tried to forget his own feelings and to take an objective view of the problem*).—*n.* aim, goal (e.g. *The enemy objective was a fort on the other side of the valley*).
objec'tively, *adv.* without prejudice.
objec'tiveness, objectiv'ity, *ns.*
object lesson, an example that should act as a warning.
[L. *ob*, in the way of, *jacĕre*, to throw.]

oblige, *ȯ-blij', v.t.* to force, compel (e.g. *The police obliged him to leave*): to do a favour or service for.
obligā'tion (*-gā'*), *n.* promise, or duty, by which one is bound (e.g. *I am under an obligation to care for him*): debt of gratitude for a favour received.
obligatory, *ȯ-blig'ȧ-tȯ-ri,* or *ob', adj.* required, commanded, not a matter of choice (e.g. *Evening dress is obligatory at this dance*): required as a duty (with *on*; e.g. *It is obligatory on us to help*).
oblig'ing (*j*), *adj.* ready to do good turn.
[L. *ob-*, down, *ligāre*, to bind.]

oblique, *ȯ-blēk', adj.* slanting, not straight up and down: not parallel: not straight or direct (e.g. *He steered an oblique course*): not straightforward (e.g. *oblique references, hints, sneers*).
oblique'ly, *adv.*
oblique'ness, obli'quity (*-bli'*), *ns.* (the latter is most often used of actions or outlook that are not straight morally or mentally).
[L. *oblīquus*—*līquis*, slanting.]

obliterate, *ȯ-blit'ėr-āt, v.t.* to blot out: to destroy completely.
obliterā'tion, *n.*
[L. *ob*, over, *litera*, a letter.]

oblivion, *ȯ-bliv'i-ȯn, n.* forgetfulness: state of being forgotten.
obliv'ious, *adj.* forgetful: not conscious, unaware (with *of* or *to*; e.g. *Deep in thought, he was oblivious of the crowds; he was so full of his plan that he was oblivious to our warnings.*)
[Fr.—L. *oblīviscī*, to forget.]

oblong, *ob'long, adj.* long in one direction, longer than broad.—*n.* a figure longer than broad.
[L. *oblongus*—*ob-*, *longus*, long.]

obnoxious, *ob-nok'shus, adj.* objectionable, causing dislike or offence.
obnox'iously, *adv.* **obnox'iousness,** *n.*
[Orig. 'liable to be hurt'—L. *noxa*, hurt.]

oboe, *ō'bō, n.* a high-pitched wooden wind instrument.
[It.—Fr. *haut*, high, *bois*, wood.]

obscene, *ob-sēn', adj.* indecent, very coarse.
obscene'ly, *adv.* **obscene'ness,** *n.*
obscen'ity (*-sen'i-ti*), *n.* obsceneness: an obscene remark, etc.:—*pl.* **-ies.**
[L. *obscēnus.*]

obscure, *ob-skūr', adj.* dark: not distinct: not clear or easily understood: unknown to fame, humble (e.g. *an obscure painter*).—*v.t.* to darken: to make (e.g. meaning) uncertain, not clear.
obscure'ly, *adv.* **obscure'ness,** *n.*
obscur'ity, *n.* obscureness: an instance of uncertain meaning:—*pl.* **-ies.**
[L. *obscūrus.*]

obsequies, *ob'sė-kwiz n.pl.* funeral rites.
[L. *exsequiae* (wrong, form is Late L.).]

obsequious, *ob-sē'kwi-us, adj.* trying to win favour by being too humble and ready to agree.

obsē′quiously, *adv.* **-quiousness,** *n.* [L. *ob-*, *sequī*, to follow.]

observe, *ob-zerv′*, *v.t.* to notice: to watch with attention: to obey (e.g. *to observe the rules*): to continue in (a way of behaving; e.g. *to observe silence*): to keep, in a way regarded as suitable (e.g. *to observe Sunday*): to say in passing (that).—*v.i.* to take notice: to remark (on).

obser′vance, *n.* the keeping of (a law, a special day, etc.): a usual ceremony, practice, etc. (e.g. *Fasting is an observance required by several religions*).

obser′vant, *adj.* quick to notice (e.g. *A scientist must be observant*): careful to keep (e.g. *always observant of the law*).

observā′tion, *n.* act of noticing: something observed: a remark.

observā′tional, *adj.* found by, based on, observation.

obser′vatory, *n.* a place for making observations of the stars, weather, etc.: —*pl.* **obser′vatories.**

obser′ver, *n.* one who observes: one who is sent to listen to, but not take part in, discussions.

obser′ving, *adj.* always taking notice.

[L. *ob*, before, *servāre*, to keep.]

obsess, *ob-ses′*, *v.t.* to fill the mind of, worry continually (e.g. *The thought of starving millions obsesses him*).

obsession (*-sesh′-*), *n.* an idea or emotion from which one cannot free oneself: state of being obsessed.

[L. *obsidēre*, *obsessum*, to besiege.]

obsolescent, *ob-so-les′ent*, *adj.* going out of use.

obsoles′cence, *n.*

ob′solete (*-lēt*), *adj.* gone out of use.

[L. *obsolescĕre*, *obsolētum*, to decay.]

obstacle, *ob′stȧ-kl*, *n.* anything that stands in one's path or hinders progress.

obstacle race, a race in which obstacles are laid in the course.

[L. *ob*, in the way of, *stāre*, to stand.]

obstetrics, *ob-stet′riks*, *n.* midwifery, the science of helping women before, in, and after the birth of children.

obstetric′ian (*-trish′ȧn*), *n.* one skilled in obstetrics.

[L. *obstetrix*, a midwife.]

obstinate, *ob′sti-nit*, *adj.* stubborn and unreasonable: stubborn, unyielding (e.g. *obstinate resistance*).

ob′stinately, *adv.* **ob′stinacy,** *n.*

[Same root as **obstacle.**]

obstreperous, *ob-strep′ėr-ŭs*, *adj.* noisy: uncontrolled, unruly.

[L. *ob-*, before, *strepĕre*, make a noise.]

obstruct, *ob-strukt′*, *v.t.* to block, close (e.g. a road): to keep from passing, hold back (e.g. a person): to shut off (e.g. a light, view).

obstruc′tion, *n.* act of obstructing: something that hinders progress or action.

[L. *ob*, in the way of, *struĕre*, build.]

obtain, *ob-tān′*, *v.t.* to get, gain possession of by effort.—*v.i.* to be in general use, to exist (e.g. *The custom of having several wives no longer obtains in Turkey*).

obtain′able, *adj.* **obtain′ment,** *n.*

[L. *ob*, against, *tenēre*, to hold.]

obtrude, *ob-trōōd′*, *v.t.* to thrust (something unwanted on someone): to push out:—*v.i.* to push oneself forward when not welcome.

obtrud′ing, obtru′sion, *ns.*

obtrusive, *ob-trōō′siv*, *adj.* pushing, impudent: very noticeable.

[L. *ob*, before, *trūdĕre*, *trūsum*, thrust.]

obtuse, *ob-tūs′*, *adj.* blunt, not pointed: stupid: not very sensitive.

obtuse′ly, *adv.* **obtuse′ness,** *n.*

obtuse angle, an angle greater than a right angle.

[L. *ob*, against, *tundĕre*, *tūsum*, to beat.]

obverse, *ob′vėrs*, *n.* side of coin bearing head or chief design: the front.

[L. *ob*, towards, *vertĕre*, *versum*, to turn.]

obviate, *ob′vi-āt*, *v.t.* to prevent, or get round, or remove (e.g. a necessity, a difficulty, a danger).

[L. *ob*, before, and *via*, a way.]

obvious, *ob′vi-ŭs*, *adj.* easily seen or understood, plain, evident.

ob′viously, *adv.* **ob′viousness,** *n.*

[Same root as **obviate.**]

occasion, *o-kā′zh(o)n*, *n.* a particular time (e.g. *on this occasion*): a special event, function (e.g. *a great occasion*): an opportunity: something that finally brings action, result, though not the main cause.—*v.t.* to cause (e.g. *Heavy snow occasioned the late arrival of the train*).

occā′sional, *ad*. happening now and then: for use when needed (e.g. *an occasional table*).

occā′sionally, *adv.* now and then, not often.

[L. *occāsiō*, a happening—*cadĕre*, fall.]

occident, *ok′si-dent*, *n.* (often *cap.*) the West.

occiden′tal, *adj.*

[L. *occidĕre*, (of sun, etc.) to set.]

occult, *o-kult′*, *adj.* mysterious, magical, supernatural.

[L. *occulĕre*, *occultum*, to hide.]

occupy, *ok′ū-pī*, *v.t.* to take, seize (e.g. *an enemy town*): to live in (e.g. a house): to hold, fill (e.g. a position; e.g. *to occupy the post of mayor*): to take up (time or space): to employ, use the energies of (e.g. *to occupy oneself in gardening*; *to occupy one's mind with money problems*):—*pr.p.* **occ′upying;** *pa.p.* **occ′ūpied.**

occ′upancy, *n.* act, or fact, or period, of occupying.

occ′upier, occ′upant, *ns.*

occupā′tion, *n.* state of being occupied possession (of a place): work that takes up one's attentions for a time: one's trade or job.

occupā'tional, *adj.* used e.g. in :—
occupational disease, a disease common among workers in a particular trade (e.g. *Lung ailments caused by dust are occupational diseases of miners*).
occupational therapy, treatment of a disease or injury by work that helps recovery.
[L. *ob*, to, on, *capĕre, captum*, to take.]

occur, *ŏ-kûr'*, *v.i.* to happen : to appear, be found (e.g. *Gold occurs in these rocks*) : to come into the mind (with *to*; e.g. *It occurs to me that I told you before*; *an idea occurs to me*) :—*pr.p.* **occurr'ing**; *pa.p.* **occurred'.**
occurr'ence, *n.* a happening, incident : the act or fact of happening or being found (e.g. *the occurrence of wild animals in the desert*).
[L. *ob*, in the way of, *currĕre*, to run.]

ocean, *ō'shȧn*, *n.* the large stretch of salt water covering the greater part of the surface of the earth : any of its five divisions (Atlantic, Pacific, Indian, Arctic, Antarctic) : a huge expanse or large quantity.
oceanic, *ō-shi-an'ik*, *adj.* having to do with the ocean : found in the ocean.
[Gk. *ōkeanos*, outer sea, i.e. not the Mediterranean.]

ochre, *ō'kėr*, *n.* fine clay, yellow, red, etc.
[Gk. *ōchros*, pale yellow.]

octa-, *ok-tȧ-*, **octo-, oct-,** (as part of word) eight.
oc'tagon, *n.* a figure with eight sides and eight angles.
octag'onal, *adj.*
oc'tane, *n.* a chemical put in measured quantities into numbered mixtures ; with these motor fuel is compared in order to give it an **octane number** (high numbers showing that the fuel is of high quality).
octave, *ok'tiv*, *n.* (*music*) a series of eight notes in a major or minor scale (e.g. middle C to the C next above) : the note of the same name next above, or below, a given note.
octavo, *ok-tā'vō*, *n.* the page size of (a book printed on) sheets folded into eight leaves :—*abbrev.* **8vo.**
octet, octette, *ok-tet'*, *n.* a group of eight (lines of poetry, singers, etc.).
October, *ok-tō'bėr*, *n.* the eighth month of the Roman year (which began in March), tenth in our calendar.
octogenarian, *ok-tō-ji-nā'ri-ȧn*, *n.* one who is eighty years old.
octopus, *ok'tȯ-pus*, *n.* a sea creature with eight arms.—*pl.* **oc'topuses.**
[Gk. *oktō*, eight (*gōnia*, angle; *pous*, foot).]

ocular, *ok'ū-lȧr*, *adj.* having to do with the eye.
oc'ulist, *n.* a doctor skilled in diseases of the eye.
[L. *oculus*, the eye.]

odd, *od*, *adj.* (of a number) leaving a remainder of one when divided by two : unpaired (e.g. *an odd glove*) : not one of a set or group : left over, or extra : unusual, queer, strange.—*n.* in *pl.* **odds,** *odz*, difference (e.g. *It makes no odds*) : difference in favour of one side (e.g. *to fight against heavy odds*) : the amount or proportion by which the bet of one exceeds that of another : chances, probability (e.g. *The odds are he will succeed*).
odd'ly, *adv.* **odd'ness,** *n.*
odd'ity, *n.* oddness, strangeness : a queer person or thing :—*pl.* **-ies.**
odd'ments, *n.* scraps, remnants.
odds and ends, objects, scraps, etc., of different kinds.
odd jobs, jobs of different kinds, not part of regular work or employment.
at odds, quarrelling.
[Old Norse *oddi*, point, odd number.]

ode, *ōd*, *n.* a poem written to a person or thing.
[Fr.—Gk. *ōidē*—*aeidein*, to sing.]

odium, *ō'di-ȧm*, *n.* hatred : dislike aroused by a bad, or an unpopular, action (*He suffered the odium of having betrayed his leader*; *the odium of having told the truth*).
o'dious, *adj.* hateful, disgusting.
o'diously, *adv.* **o'diousness,** *n.* [L.]

odour, *ō'dȯr*, *n.* smell.
o'dorous, *adj.* (sweet-) smelling.
o'dourless, *adj.* without odour.
in bad, ill (or **good**) **odour,** having a bad (or good) reputation (with a person or persons) : out of (or in) favour.
[L. *odor*.]

Odyssey, *od'is-i*, *n.* a Greek poem by Homer telling of the ten years' wanderings of *Odysseus* (*Ulysses*) : (usu. without *cap.*) wanderings, long journey.

oesophagus, *ē-sof'ȧ-gus*, *n.* the gullet.
[Gk. *oisophagos*—*phagein*, to eat.]

of, *ov*, *ȯv*, *adv.* orig. meant 'from' (see **off**); still has rather the same meaning in certain phrases, as in (1) below :—e.g. (1) from (e.g. *wide of the mark*; *within a week of his death*) : showing group from which a thing is chosen (*one of my hats, of my friends*) : showing material from which a thing is made (e.g. *a house of bricks*) : showing cause (e.g. *to die of hunger*) : showing some kind of losing or lack (e.g. *to get rid of*; *a land bare of trees*); (2) showing possession (e.g. *The cup is the property of British Rail*) : showing quality possessed (e.g. *a man of courage*); (3) about, concerning (e.g. *to talk of many things*), etc. [O.E.]

off, *of*, *adv.* away from a place or position of which one is thinking (e.g. *He went off without saying Goodbye*; *he took off his coat*) : away from a usual state (e.g. *His profits fell off*) : away from the usual working condition (e.g. *He shut the engine off*; *he took a day off*) : (in speaking of time) away (e.g. *The picnic is only a week off*).—*adj.* not to take place or continue (e.g. *The engagement is off*): more distant: (in speaking of side of horse, vehicle) right: remote, slight (e.g. *an off chance*): not given to usual business (e.g. *an off day*): not up to usual standard.—*prep.* not on, away from.—*n.* (*cricket*) the off side of the wicket.

off'ing, *n.* the part of the sea some distance from the shore, but still in sight of it: a place, or time, a short way off (e.g. *A policeman, a new job, is in the offing*).

off'-and-on', *adv.* occasionally.

off'-beat, *adj.* out of the ordinary.

off'-col'our, *adj.* out of condition: not feeling very well.

off'hand, *adv.* without preparing beforehand.—*adj.* free and easy, casual, often lacking in politeness (e.g. *an offhand manner*).

off'-li'cence, *n.* a licence to sell alcoholic liquors for drinking away from, not on, the premises.

off'-load, *v.t.* to unload.

off'set, *v.t.* to counterbalance, make up for (e.g. *This gain offset some of his losses*).

off'shoot, *n.* a shoot that goes off from the main stem: anything of smaller importance growing out of, or starting or arising from, something else.

off side, (*cricket*) the side of the field opposite to that on which the batsman stands: (*football*, etc.) in a position on the field in which it is not allowable to play the ball.

off'spring, *n.* child(ren), descendant(s).

badly, ill, off, poor: (with *for*) not well supplied with.

to be off, to go away quickly.

to finish off, to finish completely.

well off, rich: (with *for*) well supplied with. [**of.**]

offal, *of'ȧl, n.* parts of an animal unfit to use as food: entrails eaten as food (e.g. heart, liver): anything worthless. [**off, fall.**]

offend, *ȯ-fend', v.t.* to displease, make angry: to hurt the feelings of: to be disagreeable to (e.g. *The stuffiness offends me*).—*v.i.* to sin: to act wrongly in face of a law, usual custom, etc. (e.g. *to offend against good manners*).

offence', *n.* (any cause of) anger, displeasure, or hurt feelings: a crime: a sin.

offen'der, *n.* one who offends.

offen'sive, *adj.* causing displeasure or hurt: insulting: disgusting: used in attack (e.g. *an offensive weapon*).—*n.* act of attacking: position of attack.

on the offensive, attacking, or ready to attack.

to give offence, to cause displeasure.

to take offence at, to be made angry, or hurt, by.

to take the offensive, to attack first.

[L. *ob*, against, *fendĕre, fensum*, to strike.]

offer, *of'ėr, v.t.* to hold out, or put forward, for acceptance or refusal (e.g. a gift, goods for sale, payment, a suggestion): to say that one is willing (to do something; e.g. *to offer to help*): to give, put before one (e.g. *a choice, a chance*): to attempt (resistance).—*v.i.* to present itself, occur (e.g. *If the opportunity offers . . .*).—*n.* act of offering: a bid: something proposed.

off'ering, *n.* a gift: a church collection.

off'ertory, *n.* the verses or anthem said or sung while the offerings of the congregation are being collected: the money collected at a religious service.

[L. *ob*, towards, *ferre*, to bring.]

offhand. See **off.**

office, *of'is, n.* a place where business is carried on: the staff of such a place: (in *pl.*) rooms of a house apart from public rooms and bedrooms: a duty, job: a position of authority, esp. in the government: (in *pl.*) act(s) of help or service (e.g. *We found a flat through the kind offices of a friend*).

off'icer, *n.* a person who carries out a public duty (e.g. *an officer of the law*): a person holding a commission in the army, navy, or air force.

official, *ȯ-fish'ȧl, adj.* having to do with a position of authority (e.g. *official powers*): holding a public position: done by, or given out by, those in power (e.g. *an official action, announcement*).—*n.* one who holds an office: a public officer in a not very important position.

offic'ially, *adv.* as, because of being, an official (e.g. *He attended the ceremony officially*): formally (e.g. *The key was officially handed over*): according to what is said or professed (e.g. *Officially he is helping Smith; actually he is helping Lee*).

offic'iate, *v.i.* to carry out the duties of an office on a particular occasion (e.g. *The Rev. John White will officiate at the funeral*).

off'ice-bear'er, *n.* one who has a special duty to perform in a society, church, etc.

to hold office, to have, or continue in, a position in the government, etc. (*n.* **office holder**).

[Fr.—L. *officium*, a duty, service.]

officious, *ȯ-fish'ůs, adj.* offering help, etc., where it is not wanted, interfering.

[Same root as **office**.]

offing, offspring, etc. See **off.**

oft, *ŏft, oft,* **often,** *ŏf'n, of'n,* also *-tėn, adv.* many times, frequently. [O.E.]

ogle, *ō'gl, v.t.* to look at fondly (esp. too familiarly) with side glances.—Also *v.i.* [Conn. with Ger. *äugeln*.]

ogre, *ō'gėr, n.* a man-eating giant or monster of fairy tales. [Fr.]

oil, *oil, n.* the juice from the fruit of the olive tree: a greasy liquid (of animal, vegetable, or mineral origin) which will dissolve in ether or alcohol but not in water: (in *pl.*) oil paint.—*v.t.* to smear, or supply, with oil.

oil'y, *adj.* like oil: greasy: (of person, manner) too polite and agreeable:—*comp.* **oil'ier**; *superl.* **oil'iest.**

oil'ily, *adv.* **oil'iness,** *n.*

oil'cake, *n.* cattle food made of linseed, etc., when most of the oil has been pressed out.

oil'cloth, *n.* canvas made waterproof with linseed-oil paint, used as a covering.

oil colour, a colouring substance mixed with oil.

oil field, a district where mineral oil is found underground.

oil paint, oil colour.

oil painting, a picture painted in oil colours.

oil'skin, *n.* cloth made waterproof by means of oil: a garment of this.

oil well, a hole drilled to obtain petroleum.

[L. *oleum*—Gk. *elaiā*, olive.]

ointment, *oint'mėnt*, *n.* a greasy substance put on the skin to heal injuries, etc.

[Through O.Fr.—L. *ungĕre*, *unctum*, anoint.]

O.K., okay, *ō-kā'*, *v.t.* to mark or pass as all right.—Also *n.*, *adj.*, and *adv.*

[Prob. (*O*ld) *K*inderhook, used as slogan in U.S. presidency campaign of candidate born in that place.]

old, *ōld*, *adj.* advanced in age: having a certain age (e.g. *He is ten years old*): not new—having been long in existence, worn or worn out, out-of-date, old-fashioned: belonging to far-off times: long practised (e.g. *an old hand*, a person with much experience).

old-fash'ioned, *adj.* in a style common in the past: out-of-date.

old'-hat', *adj.* out-of-date.

old age, the later part of life.

Old English. See **English.**

old maid, an oldish woman unlikely ever to marry.

Old Norse, Old Testament, Old World. See **Norse, Testament, World.**

of old, long ago.

[O.E. (*e*)*ald*; conn. with Ger. *alt.*]

oleaginous, *ō-lė-aj'in-ŭs*, *adj.* oily.

[Same L. root as **oil.**]

olfactory, *ol-fak'tŏr-i*, *adj.* having to do with, or used in, smelling.

[L. *olfacĕre*, to smell—*olēre*, to smell.]

oligarchy, *ol'i-gär-ki*, *n.* government by a few people in power.

[Gk. *oligos*, few, *archē*, rule.]

olive, *ol'iv*, *n.* a tree grown round the Mediterranean for its oily fruit: its fruit: a brownish-green colour like the unripe olive.

olive oil, oil pressed from the fruit of the olive tree.

olive branch, a symbol of peace.

[Fr.—L. *oliva.*]

Olympus, *ō-lim'pŭs*, *n.* a mountain in Greece where the gods were thought to live.

Olym'pic, *adj.*

Olym'pian, *adj.* god-like.

Olym'piad (*-pi-ad*), *n.* a celebration of the modern Olympic games.

Olympic games, athletic contests held every four years at different centres since 1896, named after games held every four years in ancient Greece.

[Gk. *Olympos.*]

ombudsman, *om'boodz-man*, *n.* a 'grievance man' appointed to look into complaints against the government (in Britain, officially "Parliamentary Commissioner for Administration"). [Swed.]

omega, *ō'mi-gȧ*, *n.* the last letter of the Greek alphabet: the end.

omelet(te), *om'(i-)lit*, *n.* eggs, etc., beaten up, cooked and folded in a frying pan.

[Through Fr.; prob. L. *lāmella*, thin plate.]

omen, *ō'mėn*, *n.* a sign of a future event.

om'inous (*om'*), *adj.* having to do with an omen: suggesting future trouble.

om'inously, *adv.* **om'inousness,** *n.*

ill'-o'mened, *adj.* unlucky.

of good (ill) omen, telling beforehand of good (or bad) luck.

[L. *ōmen*, *ōminis.*]

omit, *ō-mit'*, *v.t.* to leave out: to fail to do, leave undone, etc.:—*pr.p.* **omitt'ing**; *pa.p.* **omitt'ed.**

omiss'ion, *n.* act of omitting: a thing omitted.

[L. *omittĕre*, *-missum*—*mittĕre*, send.]

omni-, *om-ni-*, (as part of a word) all.

omnibus, *om'ni-bŭs*, *n.* a large public road vehicle for many passengers (now usu. **bus**):—*pl.* **om'nibuses.**—*adj.* containing, or dealing with, many things (e.g. *an omnibus parliamentary bill*).

omnipotent, *om-nip'ŏ-tėnt*, *adj.* having unlimited, complete, power or authority.

omnip'otence, *n.* **omnip'otently,** *adv.*

omnipresent, *om-ni-prez'ėnt*, *adj.* present everywhere.

omnipres'ence, *n.*

omniscient, *om-nish'ėnt*, *adj.* knowing everything.

omnis'cience, *n.* **omnis'ciently,** *adv.*

omnivorous, *om-niv'ŏr-ŭs*, *adj.* feeding on both plant and animal food.

[L. *omnis*, all (*potens*, powerful; *praesens*, present; *sciens*, knowing—*scīre*, to know; *vorāre*, to devour.]

on, *on*, *prep.* touching the upper surface of (e.g. *on the table*): showing position more generally (e.g. *on the far side*; *on the Continent*): showing position in time (e.g. *on the last day*); the *prep.* is also used in many other ways, including the following:—

to show movement towards (e.g. *to advance on the town*): to show object (e.g. *money spent on clothes*; *to have pity on a person*): to show matter dealt with (e.g.

a book on astronomy): to show state, position (e.g. *on sale*; *on show*; *on guard*).—*adv*. in, or into, a position on a person or thing (e.g. *Put on your gloves*): forward (e.g. *I moved on*): in progress, action (e.g. *The play, the battle, is on*): not off.—*n*. (*cricket*) the on side.

onward, *on'wȧrd*, *adj*. going forward (e.g. *onward march, path*).—*adv*. (also **on'wards**) towards a point ahead, forward.

on'-li'cence, *n*. a licence to sell alcoholic drinks for drinking in the building where they are sold.

on side, (*cricket*) the side of the field on which the batsman stands.

on to, to a position on (also **onto**).

[O.E. *on*; conn. with Du. *aan*, Ger. *an*.]

once, *wuns*, *adv*. a single time: at a time in the past: at any one time (e.g. *If this were once to happen, he would resign*).

once for all, once only and finally.

once in a while, occasionally, rarely.

at once, without delay.

[O.E. *ānes*—*ān*, one.]

oncoming, *on'kum-ing*, *n*. approach.—*adj*. advancing, approaching.

[**on,** and *pr.p.* of **come.**]

one, *wun*, *adj*. a single: united, having the same opinions, qualities, etc.—*n*. the number showing unity (I or I): a single person or thing.—*pron*. a person (e.g. *One may say it without believing it*).

one another, each other.

oneself, one's self, *pron*.

one'-sid'ed, *adj*. larger, etc., on one side than on the other: unfair, unjust (e.g. *a one-sided view of the subject*).

all one, just the same, making no difference.

at one, in agreement.

[O.E. *ān*; conn. with Ger. *ein*, L. *unus*.]

onerous. See **onus.**

ongoings, *on'gō-ingz*, *n. pl*. same as **goings-on.**

onion, *un'yȯn*, *n*. (a bulb that can be eaten of) a plant of the lily family.

[Fr. *oignon*—L. *ūniō*, pearl, onion.]

onlooker, *on'look-ėr*, *n*. a spectator, esp. by chance. [**on, look.**]

only, *ōn'li*, *adj*. without others of the kind (e.g. *an only son*): without others worthy to be counted.—*adv*. not more than (e.g. *only two cups*; *only six yards*): alone, solely (e.g. *I tell it to you only*): no farther off than (e.g. *only yesterday*): showing the sole or most important result (e.g. *You will only annoy him*).—*conj*. except that (e.g. *He would come, only he is being sent abroad*).

only too, very (e.g. *only too glad*).

[O.E. *ān*, one, *-lic*, like.]

onrush, *on'rush*, *n*. rush forward.

onset, *on'set*, *n*. fierce attack: beginning (e.g. *the onset of a cold*). [**on, set.**]

onslaught, *on'slöt*, *n*. an attack, onset.

[Du. *aanslag*, an 'on-blow'.]

onto. See **on.**

onus, *ō'nus*, *n*. responsibility: blame.

on'erous, (*on'*, *ōn'*), *adj*. requiring much work or effort (e.g. *an onerous task*).

[L. *onus*, *oneris*, a burden.]

onward(s). See **on.**

onyx, *on'iks*, *n*. a precious stone with layers of different colours.

[Gk *onyx*, a fingernail]

ooze, *ōōz*, *n*. slimy mud: a gentle flow.—*v.i.* to flow gently: to leak out very slowly.—Also *v.t.*

oo'zy, *adj*. **oo'ziness,** *n*.

[O.E. *wāse*, mud, and *wōs*, juice.]

opacity. See **opaque.**

opal, *ō'pȧl*, *n*. a precious stone, milky white with changing rainbow colours.

opales'cent, *adj*. opal-coloured.

opales'cence, *n*.

[L. *opalus*.]

opaque, *ō-pāk'*, *adj*. not allowing light to pass through: not able to be seen through: dark, not shining.

opacity (*ō-pas'i-ti*), **opaque'ness,** *ns*.

[L. *opacus*.]

open, *ō'p(ė)n*, *adj*. not shut: not closed or covered: free to be entered, etc. (e.g. *open to the public*): not fenced: free from trees: free from obstruction: widely spaced: free from ice or frost (e.g. *open water, an open winter*): not kept secret or concealed: frank, candid.—*v.t.* to make open: to begin (e.g. *He opened the meeting*).—Also *v.i.*—*n*. clear space.

o'penly, *adv*. **o'penness,** *n*.

o'pening, *n*. an open place, gap, break: beginning: chance or opportunity (for).

o'pener, *n*. something that opens.

open air, the air out of doors (*adj*. **o'pen-air**).

open city, a city officially declared to be undefended and of no military importance.

o'pen-hand'ed, *adj*. giving freely, generous.

o'pen-heart'ed, *adj*. frank and kindly.

o'pen-mind'ed, *adj*. willing to consider new ideas.

open question, a matter not decided, still unsettled.

open verdict, verdict saying that a crime has been committed but not naming a criminal.

o'penwork, *n*. ornamental work, in any material, having openings through it.—Also *adj*.

open to, likely to receive or undergo (e.g. *open to attack, criticism*): ready to be influenced by (e.g. *open to suggestions*).

to lay open, to make open: to uncover, show.

to open up, to lay open: to accelerate.

[O.E.; conn. with Ger. *offen*.]

opera[1], *op'ėr-ȧ*, *n*. a dramatic work in which music by voices and orchestra is of the greatest importance.

operat'ic, *adj*. **operat'ically,** *adv*.

operett'a, *n.* a short, light musical drama.
opera glasses, binoculars for use in the theatre.
[It.—same L. root as **opus, operate.**]

opera². See **opus.**

operate, *op'ėr-āt, v.i.* to act, work: to bring about an effect: to exert influence (on, upon): to carry out military acts: (*surgery*) to cut a part of the body in order to undo the effect of disease, injury, deformity.—*v.t.* to work (e.g. a machine): to bring about (e.g. a change).
op'erator, *n.*
op'erable, *adj.* (*surgery*) that can be operated on.
operā'tion, *n.* action: method or way of working: military, etc. campaign: cutting of a part of the body in order to restore health or normal condition.
operā'tional, *adj.* having to do with operations: working in, or forming part of, an operation of war: ready for action.
op'erative, *adj.* working, in action: (of rule, law) in force, having effect.—*n.* a workman in a factory.
[L. *operārī, -ātus—opus, operis,* work.]

operetta. See **opera** (1).

ophthalmia, *of-thal'mi-ȧ, n.* painful redness of the eyes.
ophthal'mic, *adj.* having to do with the eye.
[Gk.—*ophthalmos,* eye.]

opiate. See **opium.**

opine, *ō-pīn', v.t.* and *v.i.* to suppose, think: to state as one's opinion.
[Same root as **opinion.**]

opinion, *ȯ-pin'yȯn, n.* what is generally thought about a matter (e.g. *public opinion*): what seems to one to be true: (in *pl.*) views, beliefs: a judgment, view, given formally by a lawyer or doctor: what one thinks of the value (of someone or something; e.g. *I have a high,* or *low, opinion of Jack*).
opin'ionated, opin'ionative, *adjs.* having strong opinions and refusing to give them up.
a matter of opinion, a question on which different views are held.
to be of the opinion that, to think that.
to have no opinion of, to have a very low opinion of, think very little of.
[L. *opīnio, opīniōnis.*]

opium, *ō'pi-ùm, n.* the dried juice of a type of poppy, containing materials used as drugs.
opiate, *ō'pi-it, -āt, n.* a medicine containing opium used to make one sleep: anything that dulls mind or feelings.
[L.—Gk. *opos,* sap, juice.]

opossum, *ȯ-pos'ùm, n.* a small American animal that carries its young in a pouch.
[West Indian.]

opponent. See **opposition.**

opportune, *op'ȯr-tūn, -tūn', adj.* coming at the right moment (e.g. *Without this opportune help, we should have had to give up*): convenient (e.g. *an opportune moment*).
opportunely, *adv.* **opportuneness,** *n.*
opportunist (*op',* or *-tūn'*) *n.* a person, esp. a politician, who forms his opinions and policy to suit the circumstances of the moment.
opportunism (*op',* or *-tūn'*), *n.* the conduct of an opportunist.
opportun'ity, *n.* a chance (to do something) :—*pl.* **opportun'ities.**
[Fr.—L. *ob,* before, *portus,* harbour.]

oppose, *ȯ-pōz', v.t.* to resist, fight against, by force or argument: to set (one force) against another (e.g. *He opposed his strength to the jammed door*).—*v.i.* to be, or act, on the opposing side.
oppos'er, *n.*
as opposed to, as distinct, separate, different, from.
See also **opposition, opponent.**
[L. *ob,* against, Fr. *poser,* to place.]

opposite, *op'ȯ-zit, adj.* in a position face to face, or a position in some way like this—not side by side: opposed (e.g. *the opposite side in a fight*): as different as possible (e.g. *in opposite directions*; *the opposite effect*).—*n.* something that is as different as possible (e.g. *Hate is the opposite of love*).
opposition, *op-ȯ-zish'(ȯ)n, n.* act of opposing: contrast: those who resist or oppose: (*cap.*) the political party opposed to the party in power.
opponent, *ȯ-pō'nėnt, n.* one who fights or strives against a person or course of action.
See also **oppose.**
[L. *ob,* against, *ponĕre, positum,* place.]

oppress, *ȯ-pres', v.t.* to lie heavy upon, depress (e.g. *This worry, the thought, oppresses me*): (of e.g. weariness) to overcome: to treat cruelly, govern harshly.
oppress'or, *n.*
oppress'ive, *adj.* harsh, heavy, unjust: (of weather) heavy, tiring.
oppress'ively, *adv.* **-iveness,** *n.*
oppress'ion, *-presh'(ȯ)n, n.* act of oppressing: state of being oppressed: oppressiveness.
[L. *ob,* against, *premĕre, pressum,* press.]

opprobrium, *ȯ-prō'bri-ùm, n.* the disgrace following shameful behaviour: contempt or odium aroused by some action.
oppro'brious, *adj.* disgraceful: expressing scorn (e.g. *called him opprobrious names*).
[L.—*ob,* against, *probrum,* reproach.]

opt. See **option.**

optic, -al, *op'tik, -ȧl, adjs.* having to do with sight or with optics.
optician, *op-tish'ȧn, n.* one who makes or sells spectacles, etc.
op'tics (*sing.*), *n.* the science of light.
[Gk. *optikos*; conn. with *ōps,* eye.]

optimism, *op'ti-mizm, n.* the habit of taking a hopeful view of things: hopefulness. Opp. of **pessimism.**
optimis'tic, *adj.* **optimis'tically,** *adv.*
op'timist, *n.* one who is always hopeful.
op'timum, *adj.* best (e.g. *optimum conditions for growth*).—Also **op'timal.**
[L. *optimus,* best.]

option, *op'sh(ȯ)n, n.* act of choosing: power of choosing: choice.
op'tional, *adj.* **op'tionally,** *adv.*
opt, *v.i.* to choose, decide (to do, for).
[L. *optāre,* to choose.]

opulent, *op'ū-lėnt, adj.* wealthy: luxurious, costly looking: luxuriant.
op'ulently, *adv.* **op'ulence,** *n.*
[L. *opulentus—ops,* power, possessions.]

opus, *ō'pŭs, op', n.* a work, esp. a musical composition:—*pl.* **op'era.** [L.]

or, *ör, conj.* showing an alternative or choice (e.g. *a cake or a bun*; *you may stay or leave*).
[M.E. *other,* either, or.]

oracle, *or'ȧ-kl, n.* in ancient times, an answer (usu. puzzling), supposed to come from a god, given by a priest or priestess in response to a question about the future: a special place where such answers were given: a person of great wisdom: a wise saying.
oracular, *o-rak'ū-lȧr, adj.*
[Same root as **orator.**]

oral, *ō'rȧl, ö', adj.* having to do with the mouth: spoken, not written.
o'rally, *adv.*
[L. *ōs, ōris,* mouth; root as **orator.**

orange, *or'inj, n.* a juicy gold-coloured fruit: the tree on which it grows: a reddish-yellow colour.—Also *adj.*
[Fr.—Arabic *naranj.*]

orang-utan, *o-rang'-ōō-tan', ö'rang-ōō'tan, n.* a large man-like ape, reddish brown in colour, living in trees in Sumatra and Borneo.
[Malay, 'man of the woods'.]

oration. See **orator.**

orator, *or'ȧ-tȯr, n.* a public speaker, esp. one with power to touch the feelings and persuade.
or'atory, *n.* art of public speaking: powerful and moving public speaking.
orator'ical, *adj.* **orator'ically,** *adv.*
oration, *ö-rā'sh(ȯ)n, n.* a formal speech, esp. one in fine language.
orate', *v.i.* to make such a speech.
[L. *ōrāre,* speak, pray—*ōs, ōris,* mouth.]

oratorio, *or-ȧ-tō'ri-ō, -tö', n.* a sacred, usu. Bible, story set to music.
[It.—same L. root as **orator.**]

orb, *örb, n.* a heavenly body (e.g. moon, star): the eye.
[L. *orbis,* a circle.]

orbit, *ör'bit, n.* the path in which a heavenly body moves round another (e.g. the path of the earth round the sun): the path in which a spacecraft, etc., goes round the earth, etc.—*v.t.* and *v.i.* to go round in orbit: to circle.
[L. *orbita,* wheel; same root as **orb.**]

orchard, *ör'chȧrd, n.* a garden of fruit trees,
[O.E. *ort-geard*; *ort* prob.—L. *hortus.* garden, and root as **yard.**]

orchestra, *ör'kės-trȧ, n.* the part of a theatre in which the musicians are placed: a company or group of musicians playing together under a conductor.
orches'tral, *adj.* (*music*) for, or given by, an orchestra.
or'chestrate, *v.t.* to arrange (piece of music) for performance by an orchestra.
[Gk. *orchēstra,* space in theatre in which chorus danced.]

orchid, *ör'kid, n.* a plant with a rich, showy flower.
[Gk. *orchis.*]

ordain, *ör-dān', v.t.* to make a law, rule, or decision (that): (of God, fate) to destine: to appoint (a person) by means of a church ceremony to be priest, minister, or elder.
or'dinance, *n.* something ordered by person(s) in authority: a law.
ordinā'tion, *n.* receiving into the Christian ministry or eldership.
[O.Fr. *ordener*—L. *ordināre*; same root as **order.**]

ordeal, *ör'dēl, ör-dēl', n.* a hard trial or test, painful experience.
[O.E. *ordēl—dǣl,* share.]

order, *ör'dėr, n.* (1) arrangement in space or time (e.g. *Put them down in any order*; *the order of events*): normal, fixed, or good arrangement or condition (e.g. *in working order,* in a condition in which it will work properly): system, method: peaceful condition (e.g. *The police keep law and order*); (2) a rule: a command: direction to make or supply goods, or the goods supplied; (3) a group, grade, class, or kind (e.g. *the lower orders of the community*; *courage of a high order*): a body of persons of the same profession, etc.: a monastic society (e.g. *the Franciscan order of monks*): (in *pl.*) the office and dignity of a priest or clergyman: an honour given by a monarch, etc. (e.g. *the Order of the Garter*).—*v.t.* to arrange: to give an order for: to command.
or'derly, *adj.* in good order: well behaved, quiet (e.g. *an orderly crowd*).—*n.* a soldier who carries official messages and orders for his superior officer: an attendant (e.g. in a hospital).
or'derliness, *n.*
order-of-the-day, *n.* business set down for the day: proclamation by commanding officer.
holy orders. See **holy.**
in order, correct according to what is regularly done (e.g. *It is in order to end the meeting now*).
out of order, not correct procedure: not working or working properly.

in order to, for the purpose of.
to take orders, to be ordained as a priest or minister.
[Fr. *ordre*—L. *ordō, ordinis.*]

ordinal, *ör'din-àl, adj.* showing order in a series.—*n.* an ordinal number (e.g. first, second, third, etc.).
[Same L. root as **order.**]

ordinance, ordination. See **ordain.**

ordinary, *ör'di-nà-ri, adj.* usual, common, normal, not specially good.—*n.* the common run of things.
in ordinary, (of e.g. a king's doctor) in regular and usual service.
[Same L. root as **order.**]

ordnance, *örd'nàns, n.* military supplies—weapons, ammunition, etc.
ordnance map, survey, official map, survey, of Great Britain and N. Ireland (at one time survey directed by the head of the board dealing with military supplies). [**ordinance.**]

ore, *ōr, ör, n.* naturally occurring rock or mineral from which metal(s), etc. can be obtained.
[O.E. *ār*, brass; L. *aes, aeris,* bronze.]

organ, *ör'gàn, n.* (in an animal or plant) a part that does a special job (e.g. heart, lung, leaf): a means of spreading information or opinions (e.g. newspaper): musical instrument, esp. a large wind instrument with pipes, played by means of keys.
or'ganist, *n.* one who plays an organ.
organ'ic, *adj.* having to do with organ(s) of animal or plant: originating from living creatures (e.g. *organic remains from past ages*): made up of parts all having their own work to do: (*chemistry*) containing carbon.
or'ganīse, *v.t.* to form into a whole where each part has its own job: to form a trade union, party, etc. among (a group of people): to arrange (e.g. *to organise a sale of work*).
or'ganised, *adj.*
organisā'tion, *n.* act of organising: a body of people working together for a purpose (e.g. *a business organisation*).
or'ganism, *n.* a living animal or plant.
organ grinder, a street musician who plays an organ by turning a crank.
organic chemistry, chemistry of compounds containing carbon.
[Gk. *organon,* tool, organ—*ergon,* work.]

organdie, -dy, *ör'gàn-di, n.* a fine thin stiff muslin:—pl. **-ies.**
[Fr. *organdi.*]

organic, organism, etc. See **organ.**

orgy, *ör'ji, n.* noisy or drunken feast: great indulgence in (with *of*; e.g. *an orgy of buying*):—*pl.* **-ies.**
[L. *orgia* (pl.)—Gk.]

oriel, *ō'ri-èl, ör',* a window in a recess built out from a wall.—Also *adj.* [O.Fr.]

orient, *ō'ri-ènt, ör', n.* (*cap.*) (the countries of) the East.—*v.t.* to set (e.g. oneself, a building) facing (to, or towards, the east or other direction): (with *oneself*) to find the direction in which one is facing, one's position: (with *oneself*) to come to understand new, at first bewildering, surroundings and way of life.
orien'tal, *adj.* (often *cap.*) in or from the East.—*n.* (*cap.*) a native of the East (usu. the Far East).
or'ientate, *v.t.* to orient.
orientā'tion, *n.* position with regard to the points of the compass; act or process of finding one's position in a place, or in a society.
orienteer'ing, *n.* sport of making one's way quickly across country with the help of map and compass.
[L. *oriens,* east, sunrise—*orīri,* rise.]

orifice, *or'i-fis, n.* a mouth-like opening.
[L. *ōs, ōris,* mouth, *facĕre,* to make.]

origin, *or'i-jin, n.* beginning: source from which anything first comes: parentage.
orig'inal, *adj.* existing from, or at, the beginning (e.g. *This part is the original building*): able to have new ideas (e.g. *an original mind*): new and different.—*n.* the actual painting, etc., made by an artist, etc., not a copy: the real person, place, etc., on whom, which, a picture, description, is based: a person with original mind: an odd person.
orig'inally, *adv.*
original'ity, *n.* ability to think, or to do things, without copying others: newness, freshness.
orig'ināte, *v.t.* to bring into being: to begin.—*v.i.* to begin.
original sin. See **sin.**
[Fr. *origine*—L. *orīri,* to rise.]

oriole, *ō'ri-ōl, ör', n.* a golden-yellow bird.
[O.Fr. *oriol*—L. *aureus,* golden.]

ornament, *ör'nà-mènt, n.* anything that adds, or is supposed to add, beauty: a person who brings honour or credit (to the time or surroundings in which he lives).—*v.t.* (*-ment'*) to adorn, decorate.
ornament'al, *adj.* used for ornament: beautiful.
ornamentā'tion, *n.*

ornate, *ör-nāt', adj.* much decorated or ornamented.
[L. *ornāre, -ātum*; same root as **adorn.**]

ornithology, *or-ni-thol'ò-ji, n.* the science and study of birds.
ornitholog'ical, *adj.*
ornithol'ogist, *n.* one who makes a special study of birds.
[Gk. *ornis, ornīthos,* bird, *logos,* talk.]

orographical, *or-ō-graf'i-kl, adj.* dealing with, showing the position of, mountains.
[Gk. *oros,* mountain, *graphein,* to write.]

orphan, *ör'fàn, n.* a child (or young animal) that has lost mother and father (or sometimes one parent only).—Also *adj.*
or'phanage, *n.* a home for orphans.
[Gk. *orphanos.*]

orth(o)-, *ör-th(ō)-*, (as part of word) right, straight, correct.
orthodox, *ör'thȯ-doks, adj.* holding views and beliefs (esp. in religion) that are the same as those generally held in one's country, etc.: (of views) usual, accepted: (of behaviour) conventional, proper.
or'thodoxy, *n.* holding of the commonly accepted opinions, esp. in religion.
orthography, *ör-thog'rȧ-fi, n.* the art or practice of spelling words correctly.
orthopaedics, -pedics, *ör-thō-pē'diks, n.* correction or prevention of bodily deformities, esp. in children.
orthopae'dic, -pe'dic, *adj.*
[Gk. *orthos,* straight (*doxa,* opinion; *graphein,* to write; *pais, paidos,* child.]

oscillate, *os'i-lāt, v.i.* to swing to and fro, as the pendulum of a clock does: to go back and forth between two limits (e.g. *He oscillated between two political parties, opinions,* etc.): (of a radio) to make a howling noise.
oscillā'tion, *n.*
[L. *ōscillāre, -ātum,* to swing.]

osculation, *os-kū-lā'sh(ȯ)n, n.* kissing.
[L. *osculum,* little mouth—*ōs,* mouth.]

osier, *ōzh'(y)ėr, ōz'i-ėr, ōz'yėr, n.* willow twigs used in making baskets. [Fr.]

osprey, *os'prā, n.* hawk that feeds on fish.
[L. *ossifraga* (adj. fem.), 'bone-breaking'.]

ossify, *os'i-fī, v.t.* to make into bone or harden into bone-like substance.—Also *v.i.*:—*pr.p.* **oss'ifying**; *pa.p.* **oss'ified.**
ossificā'tion, *n.*
[L. *os, ossis,* bone, *facĕre,* to make.]

ostensible, *os-ten'si-bl, adj.* (of e.g. a reason) pretended, claimed (e.g. *Illness was the ostensible reason for his absence, laziness the real one*).
osten'sibly, *adv.* according to the impression deliberately given, but not really.
ostentatious, *os-tėn-tā'shus, adj.* making a great show intended to impress (e.g. *his ostentatious spending and style of living*): fond of show: (of an action) done in such a way as to attract notice (e.g. *His ostentatious refusal of the money was intended to suggest that he was too generous to take any reward*).
ostentā'tion, ostentā'tiousness, *ns.*
ostentā'tiously, *adv.*
[L. *ostendĕre, ostensum,* or *-tum,* show.]

osteo-, *os-ti-ō-,* (as part of word) bone.
os'teopath, *n.* a person who practises
osteop'athy, method of treating disease by making sure that all bones and parts of the body are in correct position.
[Gk. *osteon,* bone; L. *os* is conn.]

ostracise, *os'trȧ-sīz, v.t.* to banish from society or one's company (e.g. *Why are his former friends ostracising Jack?*).
os'tracism (*-sizm*), *n.*
[Gk. *ostrakon,* a fragment of pottery used in ancient times to record a vote for banishment of a citizen.]

ostrich, *os'trich, n.* a large, swift-running bird, whose feathers are valuable.
[L. *avis,* bird, *strūthio,* ostrich.]

other, *uTH'ėr, adj.* the second of two (e.g. *Give me my other glove*): the remaining (e.g. *I'll take the baby; you take the other children*): different (e.g. *He was not ill; he stayed away for some other reason*): additional, more.—*pron.* other one: another.
oth'erwise, *adv.* in another way: under other conditions: in other respects.
other than, additional to (e.g. *I know of no reason for his failure other than bad luck*).
every other, each alternate or second.
no, none, other than (a person, thing), the very (person, thing) mentioned.
the other day, etc., a day, etc., or two ago: not long ago.
[O.E. *ōther*; conn. Ger. *ander,* L. *alter.*]

otter, *ot'ėr, n.* a water animal living on fish, of the weasel family.
[O.E. *otor*; conn. with **water.**]

ottoman, *n.* a low stuffed seat, or couch, usu. without a back.
[Fr.—Turk.—*Ottoman,* Turk—*Othman,* founder of Turkish Empire.]

ought, *öt,* used with other verbs: (1) meaning have it as a duty (e.g. *We ought to visit him*); (2) telling of something desirable or necessary to be done to the subject (e.g. *Your hair ought to be cut*).
[Old pa.t. of **owe.**]

ounce[1], *owns, n.* a weight—one-sixteenth of a pound: small quantity.
[L. *uncia,* twelfth part; conn. **inch.**]

ounce[2], *owns, n.* a spotted flesh-eating animal like the leopard. [Fr. *once.*]

our, ours, ourselves. See **we.**

oust, *owst, v.t.* to drive out (from position or possessions): to take the place of.
[O.Fr. *oster* (Fr. *ôter*), to remove.]

out, *owt, adv.* not within or inside: not at home: in or into the open air: away from one's home, etc. (e.g. *to set out for the office*): no longer in office, in the game, etc.: no longer in fashion: no longer hidden (e.g. *The secret is out*): as fully as possible, completely (e.g. *They talked the matter out*): to, or at, an end (*The candle burns out*): loudly and clearly (e.g. *to shout out*): on strike.—*adj.* (usu. joined to noun; see **out-**):—*comp.* **out'er**; *superl.* **out'ermost, out'most.**
out'ing, *n.* a trip, walk, etc., out of doors.
out'ward, *owt'wȧrd, adj.* on the outside or surface.—*adv.* (also **outwards**) toward the outside.
out'wardly, *adv.* on the outside: in appearance (e.g. *He is sad at heart, but outwardly he is cheerful*).
out and out, thoroughly, completely.
out-and-out, *adj.* thorough, complete.
out of, from something that contains, from a larger quantity, etc. (e.g. *Take it*

out of the box; *four out of five*): not in: completely lacking in (e.g. *We are out of coal*): foaled by.

out(-)of(-)date. See **date.**

out of doors, outside the house: in the open air.—*adj.* **out'-of-door(s)'.**

out-of-the-way', *adj.* uncommon.

out-patient, *owt'pā-shėnt, n.* a hospital patient who is not living in the hospital.

outward(s), outwardly. See above.

out'ward-bound, *adj.* sailing outwards or to a foreign port.

[O.E. *ūt*; conn. with Ger. *aus.*]

out-, *owt-, pfx.* (1*a*) before nouns and adjectives, meaning away from, not inside, the place, thing, mentioned or understood (e.g. **outhouse, outboard, outlying**); (1*b*) showing some kind of outward movement (e.g. **outburst, outlet**); (2) before some verbs showing that the action goes beyond a previous or a normal action (e.g. **outbid, outshine**). [**out.**]

outback, *owt'bak, n.* in Australia, country or settlements far away from the towns on the coast. [Pfx. **out-** (1*a*).]

outbalance, *owt-bal'ȧns, v.t.* to outweigh (see this). [Pfx. **out-** (2).]

outbid, *owt-bid', v.t.* to offer a higher price than. [Pfx. **out-** (2).]

outboard, *owt'bōrd, -bȯrd, adj.* outside of a ship or boat (e.g. *a boat with an outboard motor*). [Pfx. **out-** (1*a*).]

outbreak, *owt'brāk, n.* the breaking out or beginning (of e.g. anger, disease, war). [Pfx. **out-** (1*b*).]

outbuilding, *owt'bil'ding, n.* a building separate from, but used in connexion with, a main building. [Pfx. **out-** (1*a*).]

outburst, *owt'bûrst, n.* a bursting out (of e.g. cheering, anger): an explosion. [Pfx. **out-** (1*b*).]

outcast, *owt'kâst, n.* one who is driven away from society or home. [Pfx. **out-** (1*b*).]

outclass, *owt-klâs', v.t.* to be so much better than (someone, something) as to seem in a different class. [Pfx. **out-** (2).]

outcome, *owt'kum, n.* the result (of e.g. efforts, discussion). [Pfx. **out-** (1*b*).]

outcrop, *owt'krop, n.* part of a rock that can be seen at the surface of the ground: an outbreak. [Pfx. **out-** (1*b*).]

outcry, *owt'krī, n,* a loud cry of anger, distress, etc.: noise. [Pfx. **out-** (1*b*).]

outdated, *owt-dā'tid, adj.* out-of-date.

outdistance, *owt-dis'tȧns, v.t.* to leave far behind (e.g. in race). [Pfx. **out-** (2).]

outdo, *owt-dōō', v.t.* to do better than. [Pfx. **out-** (2).]

outdoor, *owt'dōr, -dȯr, adj.* outside the door or the house: in the open air.

out'doors, *adv.* [Pfx. **out-** (1*a*).]

outer, outermost. See **out.**

outfall, *owt'fȯl, n.* the place where water from a river, sewer, etc., comes out. [Pfx. **out-** (1*b*).]

outfield, *owt'fēld, n.* any open field at a distance from the farm buildings: in cricket or baseball, the outer part of the field. [Pfx. **out-** (1*a*).]

outfit, *owt'fit, n.* complete equipment or necessary articles (e.g. tools for a car, clothes for a trip).

out'fitter, *n.* one who sells outfits, esp. clothing. [Pfx. **out-** (1*b*).]

outflank, *owt-flangk', v.t.* to pass round the side of and get behind or beyond (an enemy force, etc.). [Pfx. **out-** (2).]

outgoing, *owt'gō-ing, n.* act or state of going out.—*adj.* (of e.g. train, tenant) leaving—opp. to *incoming.* [Pfx. **out-** (1*b*).]

outgrow, *owt-grō', v.t.* to grow larger than: to grow too big for (e.g. one's clothes): to lose (e.g. a habit) as one grows older.

out'growth, *n.* something that grows out: a natural result. [**out-** (2), (1*b*).]

outhouse, *owt'hows, n.* an outbuilding (see this). [Pfx. **out-** (1*a*).]

outing. See **out.**

outlandish, *owt-land'ish, adj.* foreign-looking: strange: odd, fantastic. [Pfx. **out-** (1*a*).]

outlast, *owt-lâst', v.t.* to last longer than. [Pfx. **out-** (2).]

outlaw, *owt'lö, n.* someone put outside the protection of the law: a lawless person, bandit.—*v.t.* to place (someone) beyond the protection of the law: to ban, prohibit.

out'lawry, *n.* act of outlawing: state of being outlawed.

[Old Norse *ūt*, out, *lög*, law.]

outlay, *owt'lā, n.* money paid out. [Pfx. **out-** (1*b*).]

outlet, *owt'let, n.* a way, passage, outwards: means of letting something out (e.g. *Sports are an outlet for energy*). [Pfx. **out-** (1*b*).]

outline, *owt'līn, n.* the line round a figure drawn, etc.: a sketch showing only the main lines: a short re-telling (of e.g. the main ideas of e.g. a plan, book, talk). —*v.t.* to draw the outer line of: to sketch roughly: to tell the main points of. [Pfx. **out-** (1*a*).]

outlive, *owt-liv', v.t.* to live longer than: to live or last through (e.g. a time of danger): to live down (see this). [Pfx. **out-** (2).]

outlook, *owt'look, n.* a view (e.g. *the outlook from my window*): mental view (e.g. *He has a gloomy outlook on life*): what is likely to happen in the future (e.g. *The weather outlook is good*). [Pfx. **out-** (1*a*).]

outlying, *owt'lī-ing, adj.* lying away from the centre, distant (e.g. *outlying villages*). [Pfx. **out-** (1*a*).]

outmanoeuvre, *owt-mȧ-nōō'vėr, -nū', v.t.* to defeat by greater skill in manoeuvring: to be able to manoeuvre more skilfully than. [Pfx. **out-** (2).]

outmoded, *owt-mō'did, adj.* no longer in

fashion: no longer accepted (e.g. *outmoded beliefs*). [Pfx. **out-** (1*a*).]

outnumber, *owt-num′bėr, v.t.* to be greater in number than. [Pfx. **out-** (2).]

out(-)of(-)date. See **date.**

outpost, *owt′pōst, n.* a post or station in front of the main body of an army, etc., or in the wilds. [Pfx. **out-** (1*a*).]

outpour, *owt-pōr′, -pör′, v.t.* to pour out.

out′pouring, *n.* a pouring out (e.g. of emotion). [Pfx. **out-** (1*b*).]

output, *owt′poot, n.* quantity of goods produced by a machine, factory, etc. [Pfx. **out-** (1*b*).]

outrage, *owt′rāj, -rij, n.* a wicked and violent act: an act that hurts feelings (with *to*), or that offends (e.g. *an outrage against decency*), etc.—*v.t.* (*-rāj*) to hurt by violence: to hurt, insult, shock.

outrā′geous, *adj.* violent: very wrong: not reasonable or moderate.

outrā′geously, *adv.* **-geousness,** *n.*

[O.Fr. *oultrage*—L. *ultrā*, beyond.]

outright, *owt′rīt, adj.* out-and-out, downright, direct.—*adv.* (*owt-rīt′*) completely (e.g. *to sell outright*): at once. [**out, right.**]

outrun, *owt-run′, v.t.* to run fasten than: to go beyond, become greater than, etc. [Pfx. **out-** (2).]

outset, *owt′set, n.* beginning. [Pfx. **out-** (1*b*).]

outshine, *owt-shīn′, v.t.* to shine brighter than, be cleverer than, more successful than, etc. [Pfx. **out-** (2).]

outside, *owt′sīd′, n.* the outer side: the surface: the farthest limit (e.g. *He will pay £1 at the outside*).—*adj.* on the outside: remote (e.g. *an outside chance*).—*adv.* on or to the outside: not within.—*prep.* not in: beyond.

out′sid′er, *n.* one not included in a social group, profession, etc.: a person not thought fit to be in one's society: a horse unlikely to win a race. [**out, side.**]

outsize, *owt′sīz, adj.* over normal size.—*n.* a very large size. [Pfx. **out-** (2).]

outskirts, *owt′skėrtz, n.* the outer border (e.g. *on the outskirts of the town*). [**out, skirt** (meaning 'border').]

outspan, *owt-span′, v.t.* and *v.i.* to unyoke (e.g. oxen from a wagon).—*n.* a stopping-place. [Du. *uitspannen.*]

outspoken, *owt-spō′kėn, adj.* (of person, thing said) expressing thoughts frankly or boldly. [Pfx. **out-** (1*b*).]

outstanding, *owt-stand′ing, adj.* striking, great, excellent: (of e.g. debts) unpaid: still to be done. [Pfx. **out-** (1*a*).]

outstretch, *owt-strech′, owt′, v.t.* to stretch out: to stretch beyond. [Pfx. **out-** (1*b*), (2).]

outstrip, *owt-strip′, v.t.* to leave behind in running, etc. [Pfx. **out-** (2), late M.E. *strip*, move fast.]

outvote, *owt-vōt′, v.t.* to defeat by casting more votes (e.g. *The supporters of the plan outvoted those who opposed it.*) [Pfx. **out-** (2).]

outward(s). See **out.**

outweigh, *owt-wā′, v.t.* to be heavier, or more important, than. [Pfx. **out-** (2).]

outwit, *owt-wit′, v.t.* to be too clever for, defeat by greater cunning:—*pr.p.* **outwitt′ing;** *pa.p.* **outwitt′ed.** [Pfx. **out-** (2), **wit** (*n.*).]

outwork, *owt′wûrk, n.* a fortified position outside main defences. [Pfx. **out-** (1*a*).]

outworn, *owt-wōrn′, -wörn′, owt′, adj.* worn out: out of date, no longer in use. [Pfx. **out-** (1*b*).]

ova, oval, ovary. See **ovum.**

ovation, *ō-vā′sh(ŏ)n, n.* an outburst of cheering and applause. [L. *ovāre, -ātum*, to rejoice.]

oven, *uv′n, n.* a closed space for baking, heating, or drying: a small furnace. [O.E. *ofen*; conn. with Ger. *ofen.*]

over, *ō′vėr, prep.* higher than, above—in place, rank, value, number, etc.; across, with or without touching (e.g. *to jump over the hole*; *to walk over the bridge*); on the far side of (e.g. *the town over the river*): on, here and there on, or on all parts of (e.g. *threw his coat over a chair*; *little towns dotted over the plain*; *stuck paper over the stain*): about, concerning (e.g. *talked over the problem*): about, on account of (e.g. *quarrelled over the money*): while working, etc., at (e.g. *fell asleep over his homework*).—*adv.* meanings like most of those of the *prep.* (e.g. *prep.*: *came over the bridge*; *adv.*: *came over to see me*): outward, downward (e.g. *spilling over*): so that it is no longer upright (e.g. *to knock over the vase*): above in number, quantity, etc. (e.g. *nine and over*): in addition, as remainder (e.g. *three left over*): again.—*adj.* often written as *pfx.* to another word—see **over-** (2) and (3): finished, at an end (e.g. *The war is over*).—*n.* (*cricket*) fixed number of balls bowled at one end before change to the other end.

over again, once more, afresh.

over and above, in addition to.

over and over, again and again.

all over, completely: at an end.

[O.E. *ofer*; conn. Ger. *über*, L. *super.*]

over-, *ō-vėr-, pfx.* occurs with certain meanings of the separate word **over** (*prep.*, *adv.* or *adj.*), e.g.:—

(1) above (e.g. *overhead*); across (e.g. *overlook*, to look across from a higher position); across the surface (e.g. *overrun, overflow*); beyond (e.g. *overseas*); away from the upright position (e.g. *overthrow*).

(2) upper (e.g. *overcoat*); higher in authority (e.g. *overlord*).

(3) beyond the usual (e.g. *overtime*), too great (e.g. *overweight*); also too much (e.g. *overeat*).

(4) completely (e.g. *overawe, overwhelm*).

overact, *ō′vėr-akt′*, *v.t.*, *v.i.*, to overdo, exaggerate (a part).
overac′ting, *n.* [Pfx. **over-** (3).]
overactive, *ō′vėr-ak′tiv*, *adj.* acting, working, too quickly or too hard.
o′veractiv′ity, *n.* [Pfx. **over-** (3).]
overall, *ō′vėr-öl*, *n.* a garment worn over ordinary clothes to keep them clean.—*adj.* including the whole or everything: considering everything. [Pfx. **over-** (1).]
over-anxious, *ō′vėr-angk′shus*, *adj.* too anxious or worried. [Pfx. **over-** (3).]
overarm, *ō′vėr-ärm′*, *adj.* with the arm raised above the shoulder.
[Pfx. **over-** (1).]
overawe, *ō-vėr-ö′*, *v.t.* to make silent by fear or wonder. [Pfx. **over-** (4).]
overbalance, *ō-vėr-bal′ans*, *v.t.* to cause to lose balance.—*v.i.* to lose balance and fall. [Pfx. **over-** (1).]
overbear, *ō-vėr-bār′*, *v.t.* to overcome, overrule (e.g. objections):—*pa.t.* **overbore′**; *pa.p.* **overborne′**.
overbear′ing, *adj.* haughty, domineering, too certain that one is right.
[**over, bear** (1).]
overboard, *ō′vėr-bōrd*, *-börd*, *adv.* over the side of a ship. [Pfx. **over-** (1).]
overburden, *ō-vėr-bûr′dn*, *v.t.* to load with too much weight, work, etc.
[**over-** (3).]
overcast, *ō-vėr-kâst′*, *v.t.* to cloud, cover with gloom: to sew over the edges of (a piece of cloth) slightly.—*adj.* (of the sky) cloudy.
[**over, cast** (meaning 'throw, fling'.]
overcharge, *ō′vėr-chärj′*, *v.t.* to charge (a person) too great a price: to charge (an amount) beyond the fair price: to load too heavily, fill too full.—Also *n.* (*ō′vėr-chärj*). [Pfx. **over-** (3).]
overcoat, *ō′vėr-kōt*, *n.* an outdoor coat worn over all other clothes. [**over-** (2).]
overcome, *ō-vėr-kum′*, *v.t.* to get the better of, defeat (as *pa.p.*, means 'helpless because of exhaustion or emotion').
[Pfx. **over-** (1).]
over-confident, *ō′vėr-kon′fi-dent*, *adj.* too sure of oneself, or too hopeful.
[**over-** (3).]
overdo, *ō-vėr-do͞o′*, *v.t.* to do, use, too much (e.g. *to overdo physical exercise, exclamation marks*): to overact: to cook too long.
overdone′ (*-dun′*), *adj.* [Pfx. **over-** (3).]
overdose, *ō′vėr-dōs*, *n.* too great a dose or amount (of medicine, etc.).—Also *v.t.* (*ō′vėr-dōs′*). [Pfx. **over-** (3).]
overdraw, *ō-vėr-drö′*, *v.t.* to draw more money from (one's account at the bank) than one has in it: to exaggerate in drawing or describing.
o′verdraft, *n.* money drawn from the bank beyond the sum that one has put in.
[Pfx. **over-** (3).]
overdress, *ō′vėr-dres′*, *v.t.*, *v.i.* to dress too showily, or more formally than is suitable for the occasion. [Pfx. **over-** (3).]
overdue, *ō′vėr-dū′*, *adj.* not paid, not done, etc., although the time for paying, doing, is past (e.g. *an overdue bill*; *the train is overdue*). [Pfx. **over-** (3).]
overeat, *ō′vėr-ēt′*, *v.i.* to eat too much (also **overeat oneself**). [Pfx. **over-** (3).]
overestimate, *ō′vėr-es′ti-māt*, *v.t.* to estimate, judge (the number, quantity, value, worth) to be greater than it really is: to think too highly of (a person).—Also *n.* (*-mit*). [Pfx. **over-** (3).]
overexpose, *ō-vėr-eks-pōz′*, *v.t.* to expose too much, esp. to light. [Pfx. **over-** (3).]
overflow, *ō-vėr-flō′*, *v.t.* to flow over: to flood.—*v.i.* to be running over: (of one's heart) to be filled (with emotion): (of a crowd) to seem to flood out (from a place that is too full).—*n.* (*ō′vėr-*) a flowing over: flood: a pipe or channel for spare water, etc. [**over-** (1).]
overgrow, *ō-vėr-grō′*, *v.t.* to grow across: to grow too great for.—*v.i.* to grow beyond the proper size.
overgrown′, *adj.* grown too large: covered or choked with spreading plants.
o′vergrowth, *n.* [Pfx. **over-** (1), (3).]
overhand, *ō′vėr-hand*, *adj.* overarm: (of stroke in tennis) made with the palm of the hand turned downwards (also *n.*).
[Pfx. **over-** (1).]
overhang, *ō-vėr-hang′*, *v.t.*, *v.i.* to hang over: to jut out over. [Pfx. **over-** (1).]
overhaul, *ō-vėr-höl′*, *v.t.* to turn over for examination, as for repair: to examine, or to repair, thoroughly: (esp. of ship) to catch up with, overtake (another).—*n.* (*ō′vėr-*). [Pfx. **over-** (1).]
overhead, *ō′vėr-hed′*, *adv.* above one's head.—Also *adj.*
overheads, overhead costs, the general expenses of a business (e.g. lighting, heating, rent, etc.). [Pfx. **over-** (1).]
overhear, *ō-vėr-hēr′*, *v.t.* to hear, by accident or intention, what was not meant to be heard. [Pfx. **over-** (1).]
overjoy, *ō-vėr-joi′*, *v.t.* to fill with great joy, make very glad.
overjoyed′, *adj.* [Pfx. **over-** (3).]
overlaid. See **overlay.**
overland, *ō′vėr-land*, *adj.* entirely across land (e.g. *an overland journey*).—Also *adv.* (*-land′*).—*v.i.* to drive flocks or herds across country. [Pfx. **over-** (1).]
overlap, *ō-vėr-lap′*, *v.t.* to go over and beyond the edge of. [Pfx. **over-** (1).]
overlay, *ō-vėr-lā′*, *v.t.* to cover by spreading something over:—*pa.p.* **overlaid′**.
[Pfx. **over-** (1).]
overleaf, *ō′vėr-lēf′*, *adv.* on the other side of the page. [Pfx. **over-** (1).]
overload, *ō-vėr-lōd′*, *v.t.* to load or fill too much. [Pfx. **over-** (3).]
overlook, *ō-vėr-look′*, *v.t.* to look across, or down upon, from a higher position: to fail to notice: to pass by without punishment (e.g. *We'll overlook your lateness this time*). [Pfx. **over-** (1).]

overlord, *ō′vėr-lörd, n.* (under feudal system) a lord who was over another lord: one who has power or control. [Pfx. **over-** (2).]

overmaster, *ō-vėr-mâs′tėr, v.t.* to overcome, overpower.
overmas′tering, *adj.* [Pfx. **over-** (4).]

overmuch, *ō′vėr-much′, adj.* and *adv.* too much. [Pfx. **over-** (3).]

overnice, over-nice, *ō′vėr-nīs′, adj.* too fussy, particular (e.g. *He is not overnice in his choice of friends*). [Pfx. **over-** (3).]

overnight, *ō′vėr-nīt′, adv.* during, or throughout, the night (e.g. *He travelled overnight*).—*adj.* done, made, during the night (e.g. *an overnight journey*; *an overnight decision*): lasting, staying, etc. for one night. [Pfx. **over-** (1).]

overpass, *ō′vėr-pâs, n.* a road going over above another road, railway, canal, etc. [Pfx. **over-** (1).]

overpower, *ō-vėr-pow′ėr, v.t.* to overcome by greater strength: (of strong emotion or bodily feeling—e.g. sleepiness) to make helpless. [Pfx. **over-** (4).]

overrate, *ō′vėr-rāt′, v.t.* to rate or value too highly. [Pfx. **over-** (3).]

overreach, *ō-vėr-rēch′, v.t.* to reach beyond: to miss by going beyond: (with *oneself*) to fail by being too cunning, too eager, or too greedy: to cheat (another person). [Pfx. **over-** (1).]

override, *ō-vėr-rīd′, v.t.* to trample down (opposition, advisers), firmly doing as one wishes: to set aside (a decision, law). [Pfx. **over-** (1).]

overrule, *ō-vėr-rōōl′, v.t.* to rule against, set aside, the arguments of (a person): to declare (a law) is not valid, (a decision) is not to stand. [Pfx. **over-** (1).]

overrun, *ō-vėr-run′, v.t.* to run beyond: to swarm, or to grow, over: to spread over (country) and take possession of it. [Pfx. **over-** (1).]

oversea, *ō′vėr-sē, adj.* beyond the sea.—Also **o′verseas** *adj., n.*—Also *adv.* [Pfx. **over-** (1).]

oversee, *ō-vėr-sē′, v.t.* to see or look over, to be in charge of.
o′verseer (*-sē-ėr*), *n.* [Pfx. **over-** (1).]

overshadow, *ō-vėr-shad′ō, v.t.* to throw a shadow over: to make seem less important by being better, greater, than. [Pfx. **over-** (1).]

overshoe, *ō′vėr-shōō, n.* a shoe, esp. waterproof, worn over another. [Pfx. **over-** (2).]

overshoot, *ō-vėr-shōōt′, v.t.* to shoot over or beyond (a mark). [Pfx. **over-** (1).]

oversight, *ō′vėr-sīt, n.* failure to notice: a mistake due to overlooking, or leaving out, something. [Pfx. **over-** (1).]

oversleep, *ō-vėr-slēp′, v.i.* to sleep beyond one's usual time. [Pfx. **over-** (3).]

overspend, *ō′vėr-spend′, v.t.* to spend more than (one's income, money allowed). [Pfx. **over-** (3).]

overstate, *ō′vėr-stāt′, v.t.* to state too strongly, exaggerate.
o′verstate′ment, *n.* [Pfx. **over-** (3).]

overstep, *ō′vėr-step′, v.t.* to go further than (the proper limit). [Pfx. **over-** (1).]

overstrung, *ō′vėr-strung′, adj.* in an overstrained state: nervy. [Pfx. **over-** (3), **string,** to make tense.]

overt, *ō′vėrt, ō-vėrt′, adj.* openly done: not hidden or secret. [Fr. *ouvert—ouvrir,* to open.]

overtake, *ō-vėr-tāk′, v.t.* to come up with, to catch: to come upon unexpectedly (e.g. *A storm overtook him*). [Pfx. **over-** (1).]

overtax, *ō′vėr-taks′, v.t.* to tax too highly: to put too great a strain on (e.g. *to overtax one's strength*). [Pfx. **over-** (3).]

overthrow, *ō-vėr-thrō′, v.t.* to throw down or upset: to defeat completely.—Also *n.* (*ō′vėr-*). [Pfx. **over-** (1).]

overtime, *ō′vėr-tīm, n.* time spent in working beyond usual hours: payment, usu. at special rate, for this: extra time allowed in match when result at full normal time is a draw. [Pfx. **over-** (3).]

overtone, *ō′vėr-tōn, n.* a tone heard with and above the main tone of a note played on a musical instrument: (in *pl.*) additional meaning, in something said or written, understood by people who know the speaker, circumstances, etc. [Pfx. **over-** (2).]

overture, *ō′vėr-chůr, n.* an act or proposal intended to open discussions (e.g. *Seeing that the struggle was likely to go on for a long time, he made an overture*—or *overtures—of peace*): a piece of music played as introduction to opera, etc. [Fr., an opening.]

overturn, *ō-vėr-tûrn′, v.t.* to throw down or over, upset (also *v.i.*): to destroy the power of. [Pfx. **over-** (1).]

overweening, *ō-vėr-wē′ning, adj.* very conceited, impertinently bold. [Old verb *overween,* think too much of oneself—**over-** (3), *ween,* think.]

overweight, *ō-vėr-wāt′, v.t.* to overload.—*n.* (*ō′vėr-*) weight beyond what is allowed, required, normal.—Also *adj.* (*ō′vėr-wāt′*). [Pfx. **over-**(3).]

overwhelm, *ō-vėr-(h)welm′, v.t.* (of e.g. the sea) to cover completely and crush: to defeat utterly: (of emotion) to overcome, make helpless.
overwhelm′ing, *adj.* very great. [Pfx. **over-** (4), *whelm* (*v.*), to engulf.]

overwork, *ō′vėr-wûrk′, v.t., v.i.* to work too much.—*v.t.* to use (e.g. an excuse) too often.—Also *n.* [Pfx. **over-** (3).]

overwrought, *ō-vėr-röt′, adj.* wearied by having worked too hard: excited, nervous: decorated all over. [Old pa.p. of **overwork.**]

oviparous, ovoid, ovule. See **ovum.**

ovum, *ō′vům, n.* a cell produced in an ovary: an egg:—*pl.* **o′va.**

o′val, o′void, *adjs.* egg-shaped (*oval* usu. of outline, not solid).—Also *ns.*

o′vary, *n.* the gland in a female that produces egg cells: the part of a plant that produces ovules :—*pl.* **o′varies.**

ovule, *ōv′ūl, n.* (in flowering plants) the part that becomes the seed. [L.]

owe, *ō, v.t.* to be in debt to, or under an obligation to (e.g. *I owe you sixpence*; *I owe you for my lunch*): to be in debt (to someone) for (e.g. *I owe my success to you*).

owing, *ō′ing, adj.* due, to be paid.

owing to, because of.

to owe someone a grudge, to feel a grudge against him.

See also **ought.**

[Same root as **own.**]

owl, *owl, n.* a bird of prey, with a loud cry, which comes out at night.

owl′et, *n.* a young owl.

owl′ish, *adj.*

[O.E. *ūle*; conn. with Ger. *eule.*]

own, *ōn, v.t.* to possess, have: to admit that (something) is one's own: to admit, confess.—*v.i.* to confess (to).—*adj.* belonging to oneself (used in phrases *my own, his own,* etc.).

own′er, *n.* a legal possessor.

own′ership, *n.* legal possession.

on one's own, by one's own efforts: without control or help, independent(ly).

to get one's own back, to get even, revenge oneself.

to hold one's own. See **hold.**

[O.E. *āgan,* to possess.]

ox, *oks, n.* the male of the cow used for drawing loads :—*pl.* **ox′en** (used for both male and female).

oxeye daisy, a large wild chrysanthemum.

[O.E. *oxa,* pl. *oxan*; conn. Ger. *ochse.*]

Oxbridge, *oks′brij, n. O*xford and Cam*bridge.*

oxide, *oks′īd, n.* a compound of oxygen and another element.

[Older Fr. *oxide—oxygène,* oxygen.]

Oxonian, *oks-ō′ni-ăn, adj.* having to do with Oxford University, or Oxford.—Also *n.*

[Mediaeval L. *Oxōnia,* Oxford.]

oxygen, *oks′i-jĕn, n.* a gas without taste, colour, or smell, forming part of the air, water, etc. and necessary for life and burning.

oxygen mask, a mask-like breathing device through which oxygen is supplied to people in places where air is very thin, as in high-flying aircraft.

oxygen tent, an oxygen-filled tent put round a patient to aid breathing.

[Fr. *oxygène*; made from Gk. words.]

oyster, *ois′tėr, n.* a shellfish with shell in two parts, used as food.

[O.Fr. *oistre*—Gk. *ostreon.*]

P

pace, *pās, n.* a step: rate of motion (of a man or a beast).—*v.t.* to measure by steps: to walk backwards and forwards: to set the rate of movement for (a fellow competitor in a race) by one's example.—*v.i.* to walk slowly.

pace′maker, *n.* one who sets the pace in a race, or acts as an example in some other activity.

[L. *passus,* a step—*pandĕre,* to stretch.]

pachyderm, *pak′i-dėrm, n.* a thick-skinned animal, such as an elephant.

[Gk. *pachys,* thick, *derma,* skin.]

pacify, *pas′i-fī, v.t.* to calm, soothe (e.g. *to pacify the angry victim of the trick*).

pacif′ic, *adj.* peace-making: peaceful: peaceable (e.g. *He has a pacific disposition*).

pacificā′tion, *n.*

pac′ifist, *n.* one who is against war, or believes all war to be wrong.

pac′ifism, *n.*

Pacific (Ocean), ocean so named because Magellan, the first European to sail on it, found it in calm weather.

[L. *pāx, pācis,* peace, *facĕre,* to make.]

pack, *pak, n.* a bundle to be carried on the back, as a pedlar's or soldier's: act or method of packing (e.g. *vacuum pack*): a complete set of cards: a number of animals of the same kind kept, or keeping, together (e.g. *a pack of hounds* for hunting, *a pack of wolves*): the forwards in a rugby football team: a mass of large pieces of floating ice (**pack′-ice**).—*v.t.* to put (clothes, etc.) into a bag or other luggage, or (goods) into a container: to press together closely: to crowd, to cram.—*v.i.* to gather into packs or crowd together: to form a scrum: to leave quickly (usu. *pack up*).—*adj.* used for carrying goods (e.g. *a pack horse*).

pack′age, *n.* a bundle, packet, parcel.—*v.t.* to make up in a parcel.

pack′et, *n.* a small package: a ship that carries letters, passengers, etc., on a regular run between two ports (also **pack′et-boat, -ship**): (*coll.*) a large amount of money.

pack′ing, *n.* the act of putting into packs: material for wrapping goods to pack: anything used to fill an empty space, or to make a joint close.

pack′man, *n.* a pedlar.

pack′saddle, *n.* saddle for pack horse etc.

to pack a jury, meeting, etc., to fill it with people who will be sure to give the verdict or decision one wants.

to send one packing, to send one away roughly.

[M.E. *packe*; a Germanic word.]

pact, *pakt, n.* an agreement or compact: a treaty.

[L. *paciscĕre, pactum,* to agree.]

pad[1], *pad, v.i.* to trudge (along): to walk making a dull, soft noise:—*pr.p.* **padd'ing**; *pa.p.* **padd'ed.**

[Du. *pad,* a path.]

pad[2], *pad, n.* a soft cushion-like mass to prevent jarring or rubbing: a firm cushion-shaped mass: sheets of paper fastened together in a block: a rocket launching platform: the paw of the fox, hare, etc.: (*slang*) a bed, room, or home, esp. one's own.—*v.t.* to stuff with anything soft: to fill out (a book or paper) to greater length with material that really adds nothing to the meaning:—*pr.p.* **padd'ing;** *pa.p.* **padd'ed.**

padd'ing, *n.* stuffing: useless matter put into a book to make it longer.

[Origin unknown; perh. conn. with **pod.**]

paddle[1], *pad'l, v.i.* to wade about in shallow water: to walk unsteadily, toddle: to dabble, play with the fingers (with *in, on, about*). [Origin uncertain.]

paddle[2], *pad'l, n.* a short oar with broad blade, used for moving canoes: the blade of an oar: one of the boards of a paddle-wheel.—*v.i.* to move forward by the use of paddles: to row gently.—*v.t.* to push (a canoe), or to convey (something), by paddling.

paddle steamer, a boat run by means of a paddle-wheel.

padd'le-wheel', *n.* a wheel with boards on its outer edge which, as the wheel turns, act as paddles. [Orig. unknown.]

paddock, *pad'ȯk, n.* a small closed-in field, usu. near a house or stable and used for pasture: an area enclosed by a fence at a racecourse for saddling the horses.

[Possibly from O.E. *pearroc,* park.]

paddy, *pad'i, n.* growing rice; rice in the husk.

paddy field, a muddy field in which rice is grown.

[Malay, *pādi.*]

padlock, *pad'lok, n.* a removable lock which has a metal link to pass through a staple or chain and then fasten firmly.—*v.t.* to fasten with a padlock. [Late M.E.]

padre, *pä'drā, n.* father, a title given to priests: a chaplain.

[L. *pater,* a father.]

paean, *pē'ȧn, n.* a song of triumph or joy.

[Gk. *Paiān,* name for god Apollo.]

pagan, *pā'gȧn, n.* a civilised heathen: later one who was not Christian, Jew, or Mohammedan: now often used to describe someone who does not believe in any religion.

pa'ganism, *n.*

[L. *pāgānus,* civilian; early Christians regarded themselves as 'soldiers' of Christ.]

page[1], *pāj, n.* a young boy waiting on a person of high degree: (also **page-boy**) a boy who does errands and carries messages.—*v.t.* to seek (a person) by calling out his name.

[Fr.; origin uncertain.]

page[2], *pāj, n.* one side of the blank, printed or written leaf of a book, letter, etc.—*v.t.* to number the pages of.

[Fr.—L. *pāgĭna.*]

pageant, *paj'ėnt, n.* a spectacle or display, esp. one on a moving vehicle in a parade: a series of dramatic scenes to show the history e.g. of a place.

page'antry, *n.* splendid show or display: a show of magnificence.

[M.E. *pagyn, pagent*; orig. uncertain.]

pagoda, *pa-gō'da, n.* a temple of China, India, etc. esp. in the form of a tower of many storeys narrowing upwards.

[Perh.—Pers. *but-kadah,* idol-house.]

paid. See **pay.**

pail, *pāl, n.* a deep rounded container with an arched handle, used for carrying liquids, a bucket.

[O.E. *pægel,* small wine measure.]

paillasse, palliasse, *pal-yas', pal'i-as, n.* a straw mattress.

[Fr. *paillasse*—L. *palea,* chaff.]

pain, *pān, n.* suffering, hurt to body or mind: threat of punishment (e.g. *under pain of death*): (in *pl.*) care (e.g. *He takes pains with his work*).—*v.t.* to cause suffering to, to distress (someone).

pained, *adj.* showing pain (e.g. *He had a pained expression*).

pain'ful, *adj.* causing pain: full of pain: requiring much work.

pain'less, *adj.* without pain.

pains'taking, *adj.* taking great care: done with careful attention.

[Gk. *poinē,* penalty.]

paint, *pānt, v.t.* to put colour on: to make (a picture) with colours: to describe in words.—*v.i.* to practise the art of painting: to colour the face.—*n.* a colouring substance.

paint'er, *n.* an artist in paint: a house-decorator.

paint'ing, *n.* the act of covering with colour or making a picture: a painted picture: a clear description in words.

paint'brush, *n.* brush for putting on paint.

[O.Fr. *peint*—L. *pingĕre,* to paint.]

painter[1]. See **paint.**

painter[2], *pānt'ėr, n.* a rope used to fasten a boat. [Origin uncertain.]

pair, *pār, n.* two of a kind (*a pair of shoes*): a set of two similar things which form one article (e.g. *a pair of scissors*): a husband and wife: two together, couple.—*v.t.* to join to form a pair: to sort out in pairs.—*v.i.* to mate: to go two and two

to pair off, to go off in pairs.
[Fr. *paire,* a couple—L. *pār,* equal.]

Pakistani, *pä-ki-stän'ē, adj.* of or having to do with Pakistan.—*n.* a native or citizen of Pakistan.

pal, *pal, n.* a partner, mate: chum.
[Gipsy.]

palace, *pal'ȧs, n.* a royal house: any splendid house: the official home of a bishop.
palatial, *pa-lā'sh(ȧ)l, adj.* like a palace, large, spacious.
palace revolution, a revolution within the government itself.
[Fr. *palais*—L. *Palātium,* the emperor's home.]

palae(o)-, pale(o)-, *pal-i-ō-,* or *pāl-i-ō-,* (as part of a word) old.
palaeolithic (*-lith'ik*), *adj.* belonging to the early Stone Age (i.e. when man used primitive stone tools).
[Gk. *palaios,* old (*lithos,* stone).]

palais de danse, *pa-lā dė dän*[g]*s, n.* a public dance hall.
[Fr. *palais,* palace, *de,* of, *danse,* dance.]

palate, *pal'ȧt, n.* the roof of the mouth, consisting of the *hard palate* in front and the *soft palate* behind: taste: liking (e.g. *had no palate for sermons*).
palatable, *pal'ȧt-ȧ-bl, adj.* pleasant to the taste: (of advice, truth, etc.) pleasing, acceptable (e.g. *He did not find this advice palatable.*)
pal'atal, *adj.* having to do with the palate.
[L. *palātum.*]

palatial. See **palace.**

palaver, *pa-läv'ėr, n.* a conference, esp. (19th cent.) with African tribesmen: idle talk: talk intended to deceive or flatter.
[Port. *palavra*; Gk. root as **parable.**]

pale[1], *pāl, n.* a piece of wood, a stake, driven into the ground for a fence: a fence: an enclosed space: limits.
pal'ing, *n.* wood or stakes for fencing: a fence.
beyond the pale, (of a person) given to behaving in a way of which the person speaking strongly disapproves: (of conduct) socially or morally very bad.
[Fr. *pal*—L. *pālus,* a stake.]

pale[2], *pāl, adj.* whitish in colour: wan: dim, not bright.—*v.t.* to make pale.—*v.i.* to turn pale, to lose colour:—*pr.p.* **pal'ing**; *pa.p.* **paled.**
[O.Fr. *palle*—L. *pallidus.*]

palette, *pal'it, n.* a little board on which a painter mixes his colours.
[Fr.—It. *paletta*—L. *pāla,* a spade.]

paling. See **pale** (1), or **pale** (2).

palisade, *pal-i-sād', n.* a fence of stakes.
[Fr. *palissade*; same root as **pale** (1).]

pall[1], *pöl, n.* a cloth which covers the coffin at a funeral: a cloak: a curtain or haze, e.g. of smoke, darkness.
pall'-bear'er, *n.* one of those mourners at a funeral who used to hold the corners of the pall but now attend the coffin.
[O.E. *pæll,* a rich robe—L. *pallium.*]

pall[2], *pöl, v.i.* to become uninteresting or boring—often *pall upon* (e.g. *Too much soft music palls upon one*).
[Probably from **appal.**]

pallet[1], *pal'it, n.* a flat wooden tool with a handle, as that used in making pottery: a board for carrying newly made bricks: a platform or tray used for lifting and stacking goods, used with a fork-lift truck. [**palette.**]

pallet[2], *pal'it, n.* a mattress or couch.
[Fr. *paille,* straw; root as **paillasse.**]

palliasse. Same as **paillasse.**

palliate, *pal'i-āt, v.t.* to make seem less grave (e.g. *to palliate one's faults*): to lessen, ease, without curing (e.g. *to palliate a disease*).
palliā'tion, *n.*
pall'iative, *adj.* making less severe or harsh.—*n.* something that lessens pain, as a drug or treatment.
[L. *palliāre,* to cover with a cloak—*pallium,* cloak.]

pallid, *pal'id, adj.* pale: wan, sickly.
pallor, *pal'ȯr, n.* unnatural paleness.
[L. root as **pale** (2).]

palm[1], *päm, n.* the surface of the inside of the hand, between the wrist and the fingers.—*v.t.* to conceal in the hand, as in a magician's act.
to palm off (*on,* or *upon*), to pass off, give with intention of cheating (e.g. *He palmed off a faulty set on me*).
palmist, *päm'ist, n.* a person who tells fortunes by reading the lines of the palm.
palm'istry, *n.* the telling of fortunes in this way.
[L. *palma*].

palm[2], *päm, n.* a tall tree with large fan-shaped leaves at the top, growing mainly in hot countries: a leaf of the palm tree carried as a sign of victory or rejoicing: a token of success.
palm'er, *n.* (*history*) pilgrim returned from the Holy Land, carrying palm leaf.
palm oil, an oil or fat obtained from the pulp of the fruit of palm trees.
palm sugar, sugar obtained from certain palms.
Palm Sunday, the Sunday before Easter, celebrated in memory of the strewing of palm branches when Christ entered Jerusalem.
[O.E.—L. *palma*; root as **palm** (1).]

palmist, palmistry. See **palm** (1).

palpable, *pal'pȧ-bl, adj.* able to be touched or felt: easily noticed by the senses (e.g. easily seen, heard, etc.): easily noticed by the mind, obvious (e.g. *palpable errors, lies*).
palpabil'ity, pal'pableness, *ns.*
[L. *palpāre,* to touch softly, stroke.]

palpitate, *pal'pi-tāt, v.t.* (of the heart) to throb, beat rapidly: to tremble.

palpitā′tion, *n.* rapid beating of the heart due to disease.
[L. *palpitāre*; same root as **palpable.**]

palsy, *pöl′zi, n.* paralysis.—*v.t.* to affect with palsy: to destroy power of action or energy in (someone).
[Same root as **paralysis.**]

paltry, *pöl′tri, adj.* trashy, worthless: mean: not worth considering:—*comp.* **pal′trier**; *superl.* **pal′triest.**
pal′trily, *adv.* **pal′triness,** *n.*
[Conn. Dan. *pialter*, rags.]

pampas, *pam′pȧz, n.pl.* a name for the vast treeless plains of South America.—Also *adj.* (*pam′pȧs*).
[South Amer. Indian, *pampa*, plain.]

pamper, *pam′pėr, v.t.* to indulge too much, spoil (e.g. a child, oneself, a taste, etc.): to feed to the full.
[Conn. with Ger. dial. *pampen*, to cram.]

pamphlet, *pam′flit, n.* a small book, stitched together but not bound: a tract or a small treatise, on some subject being discussed at the time.
pamphleteer′, *n.* a writer of pamphlets.—Also *v.i.*
[Possibly from a Latin poem *Pamphilus.*]

pan[1], *pan, n.* a broad, shallow container used e.g. in cooking: a container of larger size used in industry: anything of a similar shape, as the upper part of the skull (*brainpan*): part of the lock of old guns that holds priming.—*v.t.* to wash (gold-containing sand, etc.) with water in a pan.—*v.i.* to yield gold:—*pr.p.* **pann′ing**; *pa.p.* **panned.**
pan′cake, *n.* a thin cake of batter fried in a pan: a landing in which an aircraft with stalled engine drops almost straight to the ground.
to pan out, to turn out (well, badly).
[O.E. *panne.*]

pan[2], *pan, v.i.* to move a cinema or television camera so as to follow an object or produce a wide view (also *v.t.*):—*pr.p.* **pann′ing**; *pa.p.* **panned.**
[**pan(orama).**]

Pan- (placed before a word), **pan-** (as part of a word), all, every.
See **panacea, panorama.**
Pan-American, including all of America, North and South.
Pan′hellen′ic, including all Greece.
[Gk. *pān*, neuter of *pās*, all.]

panacea, *pan-ȧ-sē′ȧ, n.* a cure for all things.
[Gk. *pās, pān*, all, *akos*, cure.]

panama, *pan-ȧ-mä′, n.* a hat made of braided leaves of a South American plant, or an imitation of it.
[Sp. *Panamá.*]

pancake. See **pan** (1).

panchromatic, *pan-krō-mat′ik, adj.* sensitive to light of all colours, as in *panchromatic film* used in photography.
[Gk. *pās, pān*, all, *chrōma*, colour.]

pancreas, *pan(g)′krė-as, n.* a large gland of the body under and behind the stomach that gives off a fluid which aids digestion in the intestines.
[Gk. *pās, pān*, all, *kreas*, flesh.]

panda, *pan′dȧ, n.* a flesh-eating animal of the Himalayas, or (**giant panda**) a larger animal of Tibet. [Orig. uncertain.]

pandemonium, *pan-dė-mō′ni-ụm, n.* a noisy meeting: an uproar.
[*Pandaemonium*, capital of Hell in Milton's *Paradise Lost*—Gk. *pās, pān*, all, *daimōn* a spirit.]

pander, *pan′dėr, v.i.* deliberately to provide something that is pleasing to low morals or taste (e.g. *Some newspapers pander to the public's taste for scandal*).
[*Pandarus*, in story of Troilus and Cressida.]

pane, *pān, n.* a plate or sheet of glass.
[(O.)Fr. *pan* (L. *pannus*), a cloth, rag.]

panegyric, *pan-ė-jir′ik, n.* (with *upon*) a speech praising highly some person or event.
[Gk. *panēgyrikos*, (speech) for a festival.]

panel, *pan′(ė)l, n.* a rectangular area bordered by a frame of some sort, e.g. a part of a door lower than the general surface: a list of names, esp. of a jury: a group of persons chosen for a purpose, e.g. to judge a contest, be the guessers in radio or television games, etc.—*v.t.* to put panels on or in:—*pr.p.* **pan′elling**; *pa.p.* **pan′elled.**
pan′elling, *n.* (material for) panels.
[Same root as **pane.**]

pang, *pang, n.* a sudden, brief, sharp pain in body or emotions.
[Perh. a form of **prong.**]

panic, *pan′ik, n.* sudden or frantic fright: fear that spreads from person to person.—Also *adj.*—*v.i.* to lose through fear one's power to act sensibly:—*pr.p.* **pan′icking**; *pa.p.* **pan′icked.**
pan′icky (*coll.*), *adj.* inclined to panic: moved by panic: caused by panic.
pan′ic-strick′en, *adj.* overcome by fear.
[Gk. *pānikos*, of the god Pan, who was supposed to cause groundless fear.]

pannier, *pan′i-ėr, -yėr, n.* a basket, usu. one of a pair thrown over the back of a pack animal.
[L. *pānārium*, bread-basket; *pānis*, bread.]

panoply, *pan′ō-pli, n.* a full suit of armour: full dress or brilliant covering:—*pl.* **-ies.**
[Gk. *pās, pān*, all, *hopla*, arms.]

panorama, *pan-ō-rä′ma, n.* a wide or complete view: a picture seen a part at a time as it is unrolled.
panoramic (*-ram′ik*), *adj.*
[Gk. *pās, pān*, all, *horāma*, a view.]

pansy, *pan′zi, n.* a type of flower like the violet, usu. larger:—*pl.* **pan′sies.**
[Fr. *penser*, think—L. *pensāre*, weigh.]

pant, *pant, v.i.* to gasp for breath, be out of breath: to move (along), breathing with difficulty: to wish eagerly (*for* or *after* something).—*v.t.* to utter with gasps.
[Conn. with O.Fr. *pantoisier*, to pant.]

pantaloon, *pan-ta-lōōn'*, *n.* (in pantomime) a foolish old man: (in *pl.*) a kind of trousers.
[It. *pantalone*, from a saint of Venice.]

pantechnicon, *pan-tek'ni-kon*, *n.* a furniture-store: a furniture-van.
[Gk. *pās*, *pān*, all, *technē*, art.]

pantheon, *pan'thē-on*, *n.* a temple of all the gods, esp. (*cap.*) a round temple in Rome: a building containing the tombs of many of a country's famous men.
[Gk. *pās*, *pān*, all, *theos*, a god.]

panther, *pan'thėr*, *n.* a large leopard.
[Gk. *panthēr*.]

pantile, *pan'til*, *n.* a curving roof-tile.
[**pan** and **tile.**]

pantomime, *pan'tō-mīm*, *n.* dumb show: a dramatic show, usu. about Christmas, in which a fairy story is acted with songs, dancing, topical jokes, etc.
[Gk. *pantomīmos*, imitator of all.]

pantry, *pan'tri*, *n.* a room for storing food, or for dishes and silver:—*pl.* **-ies.**
[Fr. *panaterie*—L. *pānis*, bread.]

pants, *pants*, *n.* men's drawers: (*coll.*) trousers. [Short for **pantaloons.**]

papa, *pȧ-pä'*, *n.* (old-fashioned) father.
papacy, *pā'pȧ-si*, *n.* the office of pope: a pope's term of office: papal system of government.
papal, *pā'pȧl*, *adj.* having to do with the pope or the papacy.
papist, *pā'pist*, a follower of the pope: a Roman Catholic (name implying disapproval).
pa'pistry, *n.* popery (see this).
[Through Late L.—Gk. *papās*, father.]

papaw *pä-pö'*, *pö'pö*, *n.* (small S. American tree with) yellow fruit which contains a substance that aids digestion: also a N. American tree.—Also **paw'paw, papaya** (*pä-pä'yä*).
[Sp. *papayo*; from Amer. Indian word.]

paper, *pā'pėr*, *n.* the material on which we commonly write and print, made from wood pulp, esparto grass, or rags, etc.: similar material for wrapping, etc.: a document or official writing: a newspaper: an essay written to be read to e.g. a society: a material used to cover walls: (in *pl.*) documents proving identity, rights, etc.: a set of examination questions.—*adj.* consisting, or made, of paper.—*v.t.* to cover with paper.
pa'per-back, *n.* a book with a limp paper cover.
pa'per-hanger, *n.* one who papers walls.
pa'per-knife, *n.* a thin, flat blade for cutting the leaves of books.
paper money, pieces of paper stamped by a bank or government as having a certain value in money.
on paper, in theory, though perhaps not in practice (e.g. *The scheme seemed all right on paper.*)
[Fr. *papier*—Gk. *papȳros*, papyrus.]

papier-mâché, *pap'yā-mä'shā*, *n.* a substance made of paper pulp, or of sheets of paper pasted together, that can be moulded into shapes.
[Fr. *papier*, paper, *mâché*, chewed.]

papist, papistry. See **papa.**

papoose, *pȧ-pōōs'*, *n.* a North American Indian child.
[Amer. Indian, *papoos*, suckling.]

papyrus, *pȧ-pī'rus*, *n.* a reed from the pith of which people (esp. of Egypt) in olden times made material for writing on: material thus prepared: a manuscript on papyrus:—*pl.* **papy'ri** (*-rī*), **-ruses.**
[L.—Gk. *papȳros*; prob. from Egyptian.]

par, *pär*, *n.* the normal level, the standard: equal in value: (in golf) the number of strokes allowed for each hole if the play is perfect.
on a par with, equal to in kind (e.g. *Throwing up his job was on a par with his other follies*).
at par, at the exact face value (used in speaking of stocks and shares).
above par, higher than face value or normal level.
below par, less than face value: (*coll.*) not up to normal, esp. in health (e.g. *He felt below par that morning*).
[L. *pār*, equal.]

par(**a**)**-,** (as part of a word) beside, alongside of: beyond: abnormal: out of order.
para-mil'itary, *adj.* used as an addition to the regular military.
[Gk. *para*, beside, beyond.]

parable, *par'ȧ-bl*, *n.* a fable or story told to teach a lesson about one's duty.
parabola, *par-ab'ȯ-lȧ*, *n.* a type of regular curve—cables of suspension bridge, and path of ball thrown, both form arc of parabola.
parabolic, *par-ȧ-bol'ik*, *adj.*
[Gk. *parabolē*, placing alongside, comparison, parable.]

parachute, *par'ȧ-shōōt*, *n.* a contrivance opening like an umbrella for helping a person or object to come down to earth safely from an aeroplane, etc.—*v.i.* to descend by parachute.—*v.t.* to drop (something) by means of a parachute:—*pr.p.* **par'achuting**; *pa.p.* **par'achuted.**
par'achutist, *n.*
[It. *parāre*, to defend against (L. *parāre*, to prepare), and Fr. *chute*, fall.]

parade, *pȧ-rād'*, *n.* show, display: an orderly arrangement of troops for inspection or exercise: the ground on which troops assemble for this: a procession: public promenade, esp. at the seaside.—*v.t.* to show off.—*v.i.* to march up and down as if for show: to march in a procession.
[Fr.—Sp. *parada*—L. *parāre*, to prepare.]

paradise, *par'ȧ-dīs*, *n.* the garden of Eden: Heaven: any place of great happiness.
[Gk. *paradeisos*—O.Pers. word for park.]

paradox, *par'ȧ-doks*, *n.* a statement which

seems absurd and self-contradictory, but may actually be true (e.g. *The summary of the book takes ten times longer to read than the full version*): a statement that really contradicts itself and is, in fact, false.
paradox'ical, *adj.* **paradox'ically,** *adv.*
[Gk. *paradoxos*, contrary to opinion.]

paraffin (wax), *par'ȧ-fin (waks), n.* a white substance obtained from shale oil, etc.
paraffin (oil), oil used for burning, etc., obtained from shale, etc.
[L. *parum*, little, *affinis*, having affinity, related (paraffin does not readily unite with other chemicals).]

paragon, *par'ȧ-gon, n.* a model of perfection or excellence (e.g. *He was a paragon of good manners*).
[O.Fr.—O.It. *paragone*, touchstone.]

paragraph, *par'ȧ-grâf, n.* a division of a piece of writing in which the sentences are concerned with one general thought: a short news item or comment in a newspaper: a sign (usu. ¶) marking off a section of a book.—Also *v.t.*
[Gk. *para*, beside, *graphein*, to write.]

parakeet, *par'ȧ-kēt, n.* a small type of parrot.
[O.Fr. *paroquet.*]

parallel, *par'ȧ-lel, adj.* (of lines) going in the same direction and never meeting, remaining the same distance apart: alike in an important respect, similar (e.g. *There are parallel passages in the two books*).—*n.* a parallel line: a line of latitude: a similarity in the main points (e.g. *Is there a parallel between the Roman Empire and the British Empire?*): a person or thing similar in important points to another.—*v.t.* to mention (something) as similar to (with *with*): to match (often in passive; e.g. *His folly cannot be paralleled*): to correspond to:—*pr.p.* **par'alleling**; *pa.p.* **par'alleled.**
parallelogram, *par-ȧ-lel'ō-gram, n.* a four-sided figure in which the opposite sides are equal and parallel.
[Gk. *parallēlos*, beside each other; *grammē*, a line.]

paralysis, *pȧ-ral'i-sis, n.* palsy, a loss of power of motion or feeling in any part of the body.
par'alyse (*-līz*), *v.t.* to strike with paralysis: to make unable to move or act (e.g. *to paralyse with fear*).
paralytic, *par-ȧ-lit'ik, adj.* and *n.* (a person) afflicted with paralysis.
[Gk. *paralysis*, secret undoing, paralysis.]

paramount, *par'ȧ-mownt, adj.* above all others in rank or power: the very greatest (e.g. *It was of paramount importance.*)
[O.Fr. *paramont*; same root as **amount.**]

paramour, *par'ȧ-mōōr, n.* a lover, esp. of a married person.
[Fr. *par amour*, by or with love.]

parapet, *par'ȧ-pet, n.* a bank or wall to protect soldiers from the fire of an enemy in front: a low wall along the side of a bridge, etc.
[It. *parapetto* (*petto*—L. *pectus*, breast).]

paraphernalia, *par-ȧ-fėr-nāl'i-ȧ, -yȧ, n. pl.* formerly all the belongings of a woman who married other than the dowry (which went to her husband): belongings: equipment.
[Gk. *para*, beyond, *phernē*, a dowry.]

paraphrase, *par'ȧ-frāz, n.* expression of the same thing in other words: a rhymed version of a biblical passage.—*v.t.* to put into other words.—*v.i.* to make a paraphrase.
[Gk. *para*, beside, *phrasis*, a speaking.]

parasite, *par'ȧ-sīt, n.* an animal or plant that lives on another without giving it any benefit in return, as the flea, mistletoe, etc.: one who lives at the expense of someone else or of society.
parasitic (*-sit'ik*), *adj.*
[Gk. *para*, beside, *sītos*, food.]

parasol, *par'ȧ-sol, n.* a sunshade.
[Fr.—It. *parāre*, defend against, *sole*, sun.]

paratroops, *par'ȧ-troops, n.pl.* troops carried by air to be dropped by parachute.
par'atrooper, *n.* a member of a group trained for this purpose.
[**parachute** and **troops.**]

par avion, *pär av-yon^g^*, by air mail. [Fr.]

parboil, *pär'boil, v.t.* to boil slightly.
[Late L. *perbullīre*, to boil thoroughly; in English taken to mean '*part* boil'.]

parcel, *pär'sl, n.* a package, esp. one wrapped in paper: a part: a set, pack (e.g. *a parcel of fools*).—*v.t.* to divide (out) into portions: to make into a parcel:—*pr.p.* **par'celling**; *pa.p.* **par'celled.**
part and parcel, emphatic way of saying 'an essential part'.
[O.Fr. *parcelle*, a part—L. *pars, partis.*]

parch, *pärch, v.t.* (of the sun, fever, etc.) to make hot and very dry: to make thirsty.
parched, *adj.* [Origin unknown.]

parchment, *pärch'mėnt, n.* the skin of a goat, sheep or other animal cleaned, scraped, etc. for writing on: paper resembling this: a document on parchment.
[O.Fr. *parchemin—Pergamum* (now Bergama) in Asia Minor.]

pardon, *pär'd(ȯ)n, v.t.* to forgive (a person, or a sin, etc.): to free from punishment: to excuse.—*n.* forgiveness: a freeing from punishment, or the document declaring it.
par'donable, *adj.* excusable: able to be forgiven.
par'doner, *n.* in olden days, one who sold pardons from the Pope.
[L. *per*, through, away, *donāre*, to give.]

pare, *pār, v.t.* to cut off the outer surface or edge: to peel (e.g. an apple): to make smaller little by little.
par'ing, *n.* the act of shaving off or peeling: what is removed thus.
[Fr. *parer*—L. *parāre*, to prepare.]

parent, *pär'ėnt, n.* a father or mother: a forefather: a plant or animal which produces others: author, source (e.g. *He was the parent of the new philosophy.*)
par'entage, *n.* origin, lineage, family (e.g. *He was of noble parentage*).
parental, *pȧ-ren'tȧl, adj.*
par'enthood, *n.* state of being a parent.
[Fr., kinsman—L. *parěre,* to bring forth.]

parenthesis, *pȧ-ren'thė-sis, n.* a word or group of words that interrupts a sentence giving an explanation, comment, etc. (e.g. *I have asked Smith—John Smith, I mean—to come to tea*; the words between dashes are the parenthesis): (usu. in *pl.*) a round bracket ( ), one of the means used to mark off a parenthesis:—*pl.* **paren'theses.**
parenthetic, *par-ėn-thet'ik, adj.*
[Gk. *para,* beside, *en,* in, *thesis,* placing.]

par excellence, *pär ek-se-lon^g^s,* above all others (e.g. *Shakespeare is the writer of tragedy par excellence*). [Fr.]

pariah, *pâr'i-ȧ, pȧ-rī'ȧ, n.* a social outcast: a wandering dog (**pariah dog**).
[Tamil (a S. Indian language) *paraiyar.*]

paring. See **pare.**

parish, *par'ish, n.* a district having its own church and clergyman: a division of a county for local government purposes (not in Scotland): the people of a parish.—*adj.* belonging to a parish.
parishioner, *pȧ-rish'ȯn-ėr, n.* one who belongs to a church parish.
parish pump, (often used as *adj.*) (concerned with) small local affairs (e.g. *parish pump politics*).
parish register, a book in which the births, marriages, and deaths of a parish are recorded.
See also **parochial.**
[Through Fr. and L.—Gk. *paroikiā.*]

Parisian, *pä-riz'yȧn, -rizh(y)ȧn, adj.* having to do with Paris.—*n.* a person born or living in Paris.
[Fr. *Parisien*—L. *Parīsii* (*pl.*).]

parity, *par'i-ti, n.* the state of being equal.
[Fr. *parité*—L. *pāritās*—*pār,* equal.]

park, *pärk, n.* a piece of land surrounding a mansion: a piece of ground for public recreation: a piece of country kept in its natural condition, as a nature reserve: a piece of ground where motor cars or other vehicles may be left for a time.—*v.t.* to put in a parking place: (*coll.*) to place and leave.
parking meter, a coin-operated meter which charges for car parking time.
[O.Fr. *parc*; a Germanic word.]

parky, *pär'ki, adj.* (*slang*) chilly.

parlance, *pär'lȧns, n.* a way of speaking, language (e.g. *in legal parlance*).
par'ley, *v.i.* to discuss, hold a conference, esp. with an enemy.—*n.* a conference, esp. with an enemy.
[Fr. *parler*—Gk. *parabolē,* parable.]

parliament, *pär'li-mėnt, n.* (often with *cap.*) a law-making body, esp. the legislature of Great Britain (consisting of House of Commons and House of Lords) and of certain other countries in the Commonwealth.
parliamentā'rian, *n.* one skilled in the ways and rules of the parliament.
parliament'ary, *adj.* connected with parliament: done by parliament: according to the rules of law-making bodies.
[Fr. *parlement*—*parler,* to speak; same root as **parable, parlance.**]

parlour, *pär'lȯr, n.* a room used for entertaining guests: (*U.S.*) business rooms of a firm providing services (e.g. *beauty parlour*).
par'lour-maid, *n.* a female servant who waits at table.
[Fr. *parler,* speak; root as **parlance.**]

parlous, *pär'lus, adj.* (*coll.*) used in the same way as *awful* and *terrible* are: full of danger. [Form of **perilous.**]

Parmesan, *pär-mė-zan',* or *pär'-, adj.* of Parma.
Parmesan cheese, a skim-milk cheese.

parochial, *pär-ō'ki-ȧl, adj.* of or relating to a parish: interested only in local affairs: not broad-minded, narrow.
parō'chialism, *n.* narrowness of interests.
[L. *parochiālis*; same root as **parish.**]

parody, *par'ȯ-di, n.* a writing in which words and style of a serious author are imitated so as to produce an amusing effect.—*v.t.* to make a parody of:—*pr.p.* **par'odying**; *pa.p.* **par'odied.**
par'odist, *n.* one who writes a parody.
[Gk. *para,* beside, *ōidē,* an ode.]

parole, *pȧ-rōl', n.* word of honour (esp. given by a prisoner of war that he will not escape): release of a prisoner, etc. with the condition that he will have to return if his conduct is bad.—*v.t.* to release on parole.
[Fr. *parole,* word; same root as **parable.**]

paroxysm, *par'oks-izm, n.* a fit of acute pain: a fit of laughter, rage, etc.
[Gk. *para,* beyond, *oxys,* sharp.]

parquet, *pär'kā, -kit, n.* a floor covering of wood blocks set in a pattern.
par'quetry, *pär'kit-ri, n.*
[Fr. *parquet*—same root as **park.**]

parr, *pär, n.* a young salmon before it descends to the sea. [Origin uncertain.]

parricide, *par'i-sīd, n.* murder of a parent or near relative: a person who commits this crime. (See **patricide**).
parricid'al, *adj.*
[L. *parri-* (orig. uncertain; not *pater,* father), and *caeděre,* to slay.]

parrot, *par'ȯt, n.* a bird of warm regions, with bright feathers and hooked bill, a good imitator of human speech: a person who repeats words or ideas without understanding them.
[Perh. Fr. *Perrot, Pierrot*—*Pierre,* Peter.]

parry, *par'i, v.t.* to keep off, turn aside (blow, question, etc.) :—*pr.p.* **parry'ing**; *pa.p.* **parried.**
[Perh. through Fr. from same root as *para-* in **parachute, parasol.**]

parse, *pärz, v.t.* to name the parts of speech of (words in a sentence) and say how the words are connected with each other.
pars'ing, *n.*
[L. *pars* (*ōrātiōnis*), a part (of speech).]

parsimony, *pär'si-mȯn-i, n.* great care in spending money, etc. : stinginess.
parsimo'nious (*-mō'ni-ŭs*), *adj.*
[L. *parsimonia—parcĕre, parsum,* spare.]

parsley, *pärs'li, n.* a bright-green leafy herb, used in cookery.
[From Gk. *petros,* rock, *selinon,* parsley.]

parsnip, *pärs'nip, n.* a plant with a yellowish root used as a vegetable.
[L. *pastināca—pastinum,* a dibble.]

parson, *pär's(ȯ)n, n.* the clergyman of a parish : (*coll.*) any minister of religion.
par'sonage, *n.* the home set aside for the parson.
[O.Fr. *persone*; same root as **person.**]

part, *pärt, n.* something less than the whole—a portion (of a thing), some (of a number of things) : a section : a separate piece or member (e.g. of a body, of a machine) : an equal division of a whole (e.g. *a fourth part,* i.e. a quarter) : a character in a play : his words and actions : a copy of the actor's words : a melody given to one instrument or voice performing with others.—*v.t.* and *v.i.* to divide into parts, break apart : to separate, send or go different ways.
part'ing, *n.* act of separating, etc. : a place of separation (e.g. *the parting of the ways*) : a leave-taking.
part of speech, one of the classes (e.g. noun, verb) into which words are divided in grammar.
a man of parts, a talented man.
for my part, as far as concerns me.
for the most part, in most cases.
in good part, without taking offence (e.g. *He took my refusal in good part*).
to part with, to give up.
to do one's part, to do one's share.
to take part, to have an active part or share (in e.g. a play, a battle).
to take someone's part, to side with him, support him.
See also **partial.**
[O.E. and Fr. *part*—L. *pars, partis.*]

partake, *pär-tāk', v.i.* (with *of*) to eat or take some (food, drink) : (with *in*) to take part (in ; e.g. *He will partake in the festivities*) :—*pr.p.* **partak'ing**; *pa.t.* **partook'**; *pa.p.* **partak'en.**
Verb from *n.* **partak'er,** i.e. **part, taker.**

partial, *pär'sh(ȧ)l, adj.* in part only, not total or complete (e.g. *The attempt was a partial failure*) : tending to favour one person or side, biassed, unfair : (with *to*) fond of (e.g. *He was partial to tripe, to long walks*).
partiality (*-shi-al'i-ti*), *n.*
[Late L. *partiālis*; same root as **part.**]

participate, *pär-tis'i-pāt, v.i.* to take a share or part (in e.g. a discussion, sports) ; often used as **partake,** but not of material things such as food.
participā'tion, *n.*
partic'ipant, partic'ipator, *ns.*
[L. *pars,* part, *capĕre,* to take.]

participle, *pär'ti-si-pl, n.* an adjective formed from a verb, ending in *-ing* or *-ed* (e.g. The verb *to act* forms the adjectives *acting* and *acted,* as in *acting manager, an acted story*).
particip'ial, *adj.*
[L. *participium—pars,* part, *capĕre,* take.]

particle, *pär'ti-kl, n.* a tiny piece (of matter, e.g. of dust) : any of the parts of an atom : a tiny amount (e.g. *a particle of truth*).
particular, *pȧr-tik'ū-lȧr, adj.* pointing out specially a single person or thing (e.g. *this particular waiter, in this particular race*) : personal (e.g. *my particular dislikes*) : special (e.g. *to take particular care*) : very careful, exact (e.g. *particular in her dress*).—*n.* a single point, a detail.
partic'ularise, *v.i.* to mention the details.—Also *v.t.*
partic'ularly, *adv.* in a very high degree (e.g. *He was particularly glad*).
in particular, especially.
[L. *particula—pars, partis,* a part.]

parti-coloured, *pär'ti-kul-ėrd, adj.* with different colours in different parts.
[**party, coloured.**]

parting. See **part.**

partisan, *pär-ti-zan', pär', n.* a devoted follower, or member of a party or side : a light soldier who scours the country and raids the enemy, a guerilla.
par'tisanship (or *-zan'*), *n.*
[Fr. *partisan*; same root as **part.**]

partition, *pȧr-tish'(ȯ)n, n.* act of dividing : state of being divided : something that divides, as a wall between rooms.
[L. *partitio—partire,* to divide.]

partner, *pärt'nėr, n.* one who shares with another the ownership of a business : one who plays or works on the same side with another : one who dances with another : a husband or wife.—*v.t.* to act as a partner to.
part'nership, *n.* state of working together for some end : an association of persons as partners.
[Through Fr. and L. ; root as **part.**]

partridge, *pär'trij, n.* a bird of the pheasant family, shot for sport.
[Fr. *perdrix*—L. *perdix*—Gk.]

party, *pär'ti, n.* a large group of persons united for political or other action (e.g. *Conservative* or *Labour party*) : a smaller group formed for a purpose (e.g. *a raiding party*) : a meeting, esp. of guests :

an entertainment, celebration a person taking part in, or approving of, an affair (e.g. *He was a party to the crime*): either of the persons or groups concerned in a contract, or in a lawsuit.—*adj.* having to do with a party.

party line, a telephone line used by several subscribers: a boundary between properties: a policy strictly laid down for a political party by its leaders.

[Fr. *parti(e)*—L. *partīre*, to divide.]

parvenu, *pär′vė-nū*, *n.* a person who has risen in society, an upstart.

[Fr.—L. *pervenīre*, arrive—*venīre*, come.]

pass, *pâs*, *v.t.* to go alongside, over, through, and then beyond (e.g. *to pass another car, to pass a large stream*): to go, be, beyond (e.g. *This passes my comprehension*): to cause to go (e.g. *Pass the rope through the ring*): to send from person to person, place to place, etc.: to be successful in (an examination): to approve (e.g. an examination candidate, a resolution): to make (a law): to pronounce (judgment): to spend (time).—*v.i.* to go past or by, and away: to go (through, over, etc.): to go (from one place, person, state, etc. to another; e.g. *to pass from Athens to Rome, from mother to daughter, from joy to despair*): (with *as, for*) to be regarded, accepted as (e.g. *dyed rabbit passing as an expensive fur*; *rudeness passing for wit*):—*pa.t.* and *pa.p.* **passed** (see also **past**).—*n.* a narrow way through mountains: a ticket for free travel or admission: giving of the ball from one member of a team to another: a thrust, threatening move or (*slang*) unwanted amorous approach: success in an examination, without honours.

pass′able, *adj.* that may be travelled over or through: moderately good.

passage, *pas′ij*, *n.* act of passing: crossing: a voyage: a sum paid for a voyage: making (of a law): a long narrow way, as a corridor, or a channel: a portion of a book, etc. or piece of music: an incident between two people, etc., esp. (**passage of arms**) a quarrel.

pass′er, pass′er-by, *ns.* one who passes near:—*pl.* **pass′ers(-by)**.

passing, *pâs′ing*, *adj.* going by: not lasting long: made in passing, casual (e.g. *a passing remark*).—*adv.* (old-fashioned) very (e.g. *She was passing fair*).—*n.* act of one who, that, passes: death.

pass′book, *n.* a bankbook.

pass′key, *n.* a latchkey: a key for opening several locks.

pass′word, *n.* (*military*) a secret word by which a friend can be recognised and allowed to pass or to enter camp, etc.

in passing, in the course of doing or saying something else.

to pass off, (of e.g. sickness) to go away gradually: to be carried through successfully: to palm off.

to pass over, to overlook, ignore: to say nothing about.

to pass the buck, (*slang*) to shift the responsibility or blame (to someone else).

to bring to pass, to cause to happen.

[Fr. *pas*, step (L. *passus*), *passer*, to pass.]

passé, *pas′ā*, *pas-ā′*, *adj.* past one's best: out of date (e.g. *Last year's styles are now passé*). [Fr.]

passenger, *pas′ėn-jėr*, *n.* one who travels, esp. one who travels by public transport (train, bus, ship, etc.) or another's car.

[O.Fr. *passagier*, with an *n* put in.]

passe-partout, *pas-pär-too̅′*, *n.* a gummed paper used in a simple method of framing pictures, etc.

[Fr. *passer*, to pass, *par*, over, *tout*, all.]

passing. See **pass**.

passion, *pash′(o̊)n*, *n.* strong feeling, esp. anger: strong love: great liking: (with *cap.*) the sufferings and death of Christ.

pass′ionate, *adj.* easily moved to anger or other strong feeling: intense, very great (e.g. *a passionate loyalty*).

pass′ionless, *adj.* unemotional, calm.

passion play, a religious drama showing the sufferings and death of Christ.

Passion Week, the week before Easter.

[L. *passiō, -ōnis*—*pati*, to suffer.]

passive, *pas′iv*, *adj.* not resisting: not showing energy or movement: not active, but acted upon: of a form of the verb used when the subject is acted upon (e.g. *The boy was bitten by a dog*).

pass′iveness, passiv′ity, *ns.*

passive resistance, refusing to obey the law when it goes against one's conscience and submitting to punishment rather than have any violence.

[L. *passīvus*; same root as **passion.**]

passover, *pâs′ō-vėr*, *n.* annual feast of the Jews in memory of the time when the angel *passed over* their doors though he killed the first-born sons of the Egyptians, and of their deliverance from Egypt (Exodus XII).

passport, *pâs′pōrt*, *-pört*, *n.* document giving permission to travel abroad.

[Fr. *passeport*—*passer*, pass, *port*, port.]

past, *pâst*, *adj.* having happened in a time gone by (e.g. *He thanked me for past kindness*): ended.—*prep.* beyond, farther than (e.g. *He ran past the house*).—*n.* something that has passed, esp. time: a past history, career, esp. a scandalous one.

[Form of *pa.p.* of verb **pass.**]

paste, *pāst*, *n.* a soft damp mixture: dough for pies, etc.: a smooth food mixture made by grinding (e.g. *almond paste*): a mixture used for sticking paper, etc. together: a clay mixture for making china: glass for making artificial jewels.—*v.t.* to fasten with paste.

pās′ty[1], *ad*. like paste. **pas′tiness,** *n.*

pasty[2], *pâs′ti*, *n.* a meat-pie baked without a dish.

pastry, *pās'tri,* *n.* articles of food made of paste or dough : crust of pies, etc.:—*pl.* **pas'tries.**
paste'board, *n.* a stiff board made of sheets of paper pasted together.
[O.Fr.—Gk. *pasta,* porridge.]

pastel, *pas'tėl,* *n.* chalk mixed with other materials, used for crayons : a drawing made with these crayons.
pastel shades, quiet colours.
[Fr. ; same root as **paste.**]

pasteurise, *pas'tėr-iz,* *v.t.* to make (milk, etc.) free from certain germs, and less apt to sour, by heating to a given temperature for a given time.
pasteurisā'tion, *n.*
[Louis *Pasteur,* French chemist.]

pastiche, *pas-tēsh',* *n.* a musical or literary composition made up of parts from, or imitations of, other compositions.
[Fr. ; same root as **paste.**]

pastille, *pas-tēl',* *n.* a small sweet, often medicated for coughs, etc.
[L. *pastillus.*]

pastime, *pâs'tim,* *n.* something that serves to pass the time, a recreation.
[**pass, time.**]

pastiness. See **paste.**

pastor, *pâs'tȯr,* *n.* a clergyman (orig. a shepherd).
pas'toral, *adj.* having to do with shepherds, or their life, or country life in general : having to do with a pastor.—*n.* a poem, etc. that claims to show shepherd or country life.
pas'torate, pas'torship, *ns.* the office of a pastor.
pasture, *pâs'chůr, -tyůr,* *n.* growing grass for grazing animals.—*v.t.* to graze (cattle).—Also *v.i.*
pas'turage, *n.* grazing land.
[L. *pascĕre, pastum,* to feed.]

pastry, pasty (1) and (2). See **paste.**

pasture. See **pastor.**

pat, *pat,* *n.* a gentle tap, as with the palm of the hand : a small lump of butter : a light sound.—*v.t.* to strike gently : to tap :—*pr.p.* **patt'ing** ; *pa.p.* **patt'ed.**—*adj.* hitting the point exactly : thoroughly memorised : ready to be given easily (e.g. *He had his answer pat*).
a pat on the back, a mark of approval.
[Prob. imit.]

patch, *pach,* *n.* a piece put on to mend or cover a hole, etc. : a scrap of material : a small piece of ground.—*v.t.* to mend with a patch : (usu. *patch up*) to mend clumsily or in a hurry (e.g. building, quarrel).
patch'y, *adj.* uneven, mixed in quality :—*comp.* **patch'ier** ; *superl.* **patch'iest.**
patch'ily, *adv.* **patch'iness,** *n.*
patch'work, *n.* work formed of pieces sewed or put together : work clumsily done.
not a patch on, not fit to be compared with.
[Perh. M.E. *pacche* ; conn. with **piece.**]

pate, *pāt,* *n.* (the top of) the head.
[Origin unknown.]

pâté, *pä-tā,* *n.* pie : patty.
pâté de fois gras (*dė fwa grä*), paste, etc. of fat goose liver. [Fr.]

patella, *pȧ-tel'ȧ,* *n.* the kneecap, kneepan.
[L.—*patina,* a pan.]

patent, *pā'tėnt, pat',* *adj.* (*pā'tėnt*) lying open, obvious : (usu. *pat'ėnt*) protected by patent.—*n.* (*pat'*) official document, open, and having the Great Seal of the government attached, giving a right or privilege, such as a title of nobility, or the right to all the profits from an invention for a number of years.—*v.t.* to obtain a patent for.
patentee', *n.* one who holds a patent.
pā'tently, *adv.* openly, clearly.
[L. *patens, -entis*—*patēre,* to lie open.]

pater, *pā'tėr,* *n.* father (with *my, his,* etc.).
paternal, *pa-tėr'nȧl,* *adj.* fatherly : on father's side of family (e.g. *paternal grandmother,* one's father's mother).
pater'nally, *adv.*
pater'nity, *n.* state of being a father.
paternoster, *pat'ėr-nos'tėr,* or *pāt',* *n.* the Lord's Prayer.
patricide, *pat'ri-sid,* *n.* the murder of a father by his son or daughter : a person who commits this crime.
[L. *pater* (Gk. *patēr*), father (*noster,* our ; *caedĕre,* to kill).]

path, *pâth,* *n.* a way for foot-passengers : a track : course of action or conduct.
path'finder, *n.* one who explores the route, a pioneer.
path'less, *adj.* without paths, untrodden.
path'way, *n.* a path.
[O.E. *pæth.*]

pathetic, *pȧ-thet'ik,* *adj.* touching, causing pity or sorrow.
pathet'ically, *adv.*
pathos, *pā'thos,* *n.* the quality that arouses pity (e.g. *He told the story with pathos, and tears filled my eyes*).
[Gk. *pathētikos* (adj.) ; *pathos,* feeling.]

pathology, *pȧ-thol'ȯ-ji,* *n.* science of diseases.
pathol'ogist, *n.* a specialist in the cause and effects of disease : one who makes post-mortem examinations.
[Gk. *pathos,* suffering, *logos,* discourse.]

pathos. See **pathetic.**

patience, *pā'shėns,* *n.* ability to wait quietly : ability to suffer annoyance, pain, etc. calmly : perseverance : a card game, usu. for one person.
pā'tient (*-shėnt*), *adj.* enduring delay, etc. without complaining : not easily angered.—*n.* a person under medical treatment.
pā'tiently, *adv.*
[Fr.—L. *patientia* ; root as **passion.**]

patio, *pat'i-ō,* *n.* a courtyard conn. with a house, esp. inner court open to the sky.
[Sp.—L. *spatium,* space.]

patois, *pât'wä, n.* a dialect of a language spoken by the common people. [Fr.]

patriarch, *pā'tri-ärk, n.* one who governs his family by right as father, or as head of the tribe: the head of the **Greek Orthodox Church,** etc.
patriarch'al, *adj.*
[Gk. *patēr*, father, *archē*, rule.]

patrician, *pa-trish'an, n., adj.* aristocrat(ic).
patrimony, *pat'ri-mon-i, n.* property handed down from father or ancestors.
[L. *pater*, father; *patrimōnium*, estate.]

patricide. See **pater.**

patrimony. See **patrician.**

patriot, *pā'tri-ot, pat', n.* one who truly loves and serves his country.
patriotic, *pat-ri-ot'ik, pāt-, adj.* like a patriot: inspired by love of, or duty towards, one's country.
patriot'ically, *adv.*
pa'triotism, *n.* love of one's country.
[Gk. *patriōtēs*, fellow-countryman.]

patrol, *pa-trōl', v.t.* to go the rounds of (camp, town), walk through (streets), sail (an area of sea, etc.), in order to watch or protect.:—*pr.p.* **patroll'ing**; *pa.p.* **patrolled'.**—*n.* the act of keeping watch in this way: a body of men who do so: a small group of scouts or of girl guides.
[Fr. *patrouiller*; orig. to paddle in mud.]

patron, *pā'tron, n.* a protector: one who encourages, supports, another: one who has the right to appoint to an office.
patronage (*pat', pāt'*), *n.* support given by a patron: the right of giving offices or church appointments.
pat'ronise (*pat'*), *v.t.* to act as a patron towards (someone): to encourage: to treat (person) as if one is better than he is.
patron saint, a saint chosen as a protector.
[Fr.—L. *patrōnus*—*pater*, father.]

patter[1], *pat'ėr, v.i.* to strike against something with quick taps.—*n.* the sound so made (e.g. *a patter of rain on the roof*).
[From **pat.**]

patter[2], *pat'ėr, v.i.* and *v.t.* to mumble: to talk, or say, rapidly.—*n.* chatter: many words sung or spoken very rapidly.
[**paternoster.**]

pattern, *pat'ėrn, n.* a person or thing suitable to copy: an example of excellence: a model or guide for making something: a decorative design (e.g. on cloth, wallpaper): a sample (e.g. *a book of tweed patterns*).
patt'ern-maker, *n.* one who makes patterns, esp. in wood or metal, for use in a foundry.
[Fr. *patron*, patron, pattern; **patron.**]

patty, *pat'i, n.* a little pie:—*pl.* **patt'ies.**
[Fr. *pâté*; same root as **pasty** (2).]

paucity, *pö'sit-i, n.* smallness of number or quantity (e.g. *a paucity of supporters, paucity of evidence*).
[L. *paucitās*—*paucus*, few.]

paunch, *pönch, pönsh, n.* the belly: a potbelly.
[O.Fr. *panche*—L. *pantex.*]

pauper, *pö'pėr, n.* a very poor person: one who lives on charity, esp. public.
pau'perise, *v.t.* to make a pauper of. [L.]

pause, *pöz, n.* a stop for a time: hesitation caused by doubt: (*music*) (mark showing) holding of a note or rest.—Also *v.i.*
[L. *pausa*—Gk. *pauein*, cause to stop.]

pavan(e), *pav'an,* or *-an', n.* a slow stately dance: the music for it.
[Fr. *pavane*, peacock, from It. or Sp.]

pave, *pāv, v.t.* to cover with flat stones, etc. so as to form a level surface for walking on.
pave'ment, *n.* a paved surface.
pav'ing-stone, *n.* piece of stone prepared for paving.
to pave the way for, to, to make an easy way for (something to happen).
[Fr. *paver*—L. *pavīre*, to beat hard.]

pavilion, *pa-vil'yon, n.* a large tent: an ornamental building: a clubhouse for changing on a games field.
[Fr. *pavillon*—L. *pāpiliō*, butterfly, tent.]

paw, *pö, n.* a foot with claws: the hand (used scornfully).—*v.i.* to draw the forefoot along the ground.—*v.t.* to scrape with the forefoot: to handle roughly or clumsily: to strike wildly with the hands (e.g. *to paw the air.*)
[O.Fr. *poe, powe*; prob. Germanic word.]

pawky, *pök'i, adj.* (*Scot.*) sly, shrewd, cunning:—*comp.* **pawk'ier**; *superl.* **pawk'iest.**
[*pawk*, a trick; origin uncertain.]

pawl, *pöl, n.* a short bar falling between teeth of a notched wheel to prevent it from running back. [Orig. uncertain.]

pawn[1], *pön, v.t.* to give over (an article of value) in return for a loan of money on the understanding that when the money is returned, with interest, the article will be given back.—*n.* state of being pawned (e.g. *His watch is in pawn*).
pawn'broker, *n.* one who lends money on pawns or pledges.
[O.Fr. *pan.*]

pawn[2], *pön, n.* a small piece of lowest rank in chess: a person who is considered unimportant and is used for a purpose by someone else.
[O.Fr. *paon*, a foot-soldier—L. *pēs*, foot.]

pawpaw. See **papaw.**

pay, *pā, v.t.* to rid oneself of (a debt), esp. by returning money owed: to give (money), or to give money to (a person), for goods or services: to reward, or punish: to give (attention, homage.)—*v.i.* to hand over money: to be profitable, worth the effort (e.g. *It pays to be careful*): to be punished (for; e.g. *He will pay for his crime*).—*n.* money given for service, wages, salary:—*pr.p.* **pay'ing**; *pa.p.* **paid.**
pay'able, *adj.* that should be paid: due.

pay′ment, *n.* act of paying: money paid: reward: punishment.
pay-as-you-earn′, a method of income-tax collection in which the taxes are taken out of the pay before it is given to the worker (often **P.A.Y.E.**).
payee′, *n.* one to whom money is paid.
pay′(-)load, *n.* the part of an aeroplane's load for which money is obtained: the part of a rocket used as warhead, or for obtaining information.
payol′a, *n.* graft, or blackmail money.
pay′roll, *n.* list of employees to be paid, with amounts due them: the money for paying wages.
to pay off, to pay in full and discharge from work: to give good results.
to pay out, to cause to run out, as rope: to punish.
[Fr. *payer*—L. *pācāre,* quiet—*pax,* peace.]

pea, *pē, n.* a climbing plant bearing in pods round seeds used as food.—Older sing. **pease** (pl. *peasen*).
[O.E. *pise*—L. *pĭsum*—Gk. *pĭson.*]

peace, *pēs, n.* a state of quiet: freedom from war or disturbance: a treaty that ends a war: ease (of mind, conscience).
peace′able, *adj.* inclined to peace (e.g *She has a peaceable nature*): peaceful.
peace′ful, *adj.* quiet: not intended or likely to cause war or disturbance.
peace′maker, *n.* one who makes peace: one who helps to make enemies friendly.
to hold one's peace, to be silent.
[O.Fr. *pais*—L. *pax, pācis,* peace.]

peach, *pēch, n.* a juicy, velvety-skinned fruit with a stone in the centre.
[O.Fr. *pesche*—L. *persicum,* Persian (apple).]

peacock, *pē′kok, n.* a large bird noted for gay coloured feathers, esp. in the tail:—*fem.* **pea′hen.**
[O.E. *pēa (pawa)*—L. *pāvō,* peacock.]

pea-jacket, *pē′-jak′it, n.* a coarse thick jacket worn by seamen.
[Older Du. *pie,* a coarse coat, **jacket.**]

peak[1], *pēk, n.* a point: the top of a mountain: the highest point (e.g. *at the peak of his career*): the brim of a hat that juts out.
peaked, *adj.* pointed.
peak load, the greatest load on an electricity distribution system.
[Prob. conn. with **pike.**]

peak[2], *pēk, v.i.* to look thin and sickly.
peak′y, *adj.* having a sickly look.
[Origin unknown.]

peal, *pēl, n.* a loud sound: a set of bells tuned to each other: the changes rung on such bells.—*v.i.* to sound loudly.
[Prob. short for **appeal.**]

peanut, *pē′nut, n.* a groundnut (see this word), monkey nut.
[**pea, nut.**]

pear, *pār, n.* a fruit narrowing towards the stem and bulging at the end: the tree which bears this, of the apple family.
[O.E. *pere, peru*—L. *pirum,* pear.]

pearl, *pėrl, n.* a growth found in the shells of oysters and other shellfish which is used as a gem: something resembling a pearl in shape, size, colour, or value.—*adj.* of, or like, a pearl: (of barley, tapioca, etc.) having grains of medium size.—*v.i.* to fish or dive for pearls.
pear′ly, *adj.* like pearl: rich in pearls:—*comp.* **pear′lier**; *superl.* **pear′liest.**
pearl′-diver, -fisher, *ns.*
[O.Fr. *perle.*]

peasant, *pez′ȧnt, n.* one who works and lives on the land.—Also *adj.*
peas′antry, *n.* the body of peasants.
[O.Fr. *paisant*—*pays,* country; from L.]

pease. See **pea.**

peat, *pēt, n.* a piece of material cut from a bog, dried for fuel: the decayed vegetable matter from which this is cut.
peat′y, *adj.* **peat′iness,** *n.*
[M.E. *pete*—*peta*; prob. orig. Celtic.]

pebble, *peb′l, n.* a small roundish stone, usu. worn by water: colourless quartz.
pebb′ly, *adj.* **pebb′liness,** *n.*
[O.E. *papol.*]

pecan, *pi-kan′, n.* a North American hickory: its thin-shelled nut.
[Amer. Indian name.]

peck[1], *pek, n.* a measure for dry goods, one-fourth of a bushel.
[O.Fr. *pek,* horse's feed of oats.]

peck[2], *pek, v.t.* to strike, or to pick up, with the beak: to strike repeatedly with anything pointed: to kiss with a dabbing movement: to eat little.
peck′ish, *adj.* rather hungry.
[Prob. a form of **pick.**]

peculate, *pek′ū-lāt, v.t.* and *v.i.* embezzle, pilfer.
peculā′tion, *n.*
[Same root as **peculiar.**]

peculiar, *pi-kūl′yȧr, adj.* belonging to, characteristic of, only one (country, person, etc.; e.g. *a custom peculiar to England*): odd, strange.
peculiarity, *pi-kū-li-ar′i-ti, n.* something that is found in one only: an odd trait: oddity:—*pl.* **peculiar′ities.**
[L. *pecūlium,* private property; conn. with *pecūnia,* money, and *pecus,* cattle.]

pecuniary, *pi-kūn′yȧr-i, -i-ȧr-i, adj.* consisting of money (e.g. *a pecuniary reward*): having to do with money.
[L. *pecūnia,* money.]

pedagogue, *ped′ȧ-gog, n.* a teacher.
pedagogy (*-goj′i*), *n.* science of teaching.
[Gk. *paidagōgos,* a slave who led a boy to school—*pais, paidos,* boy, *agein,* lead.]

pedal, *ped′ȧl, adj.* having to do with the foot.—*n.* a lever pressed by the foot (e.g. in cycle, piano).—*v.t.* to work the pedals of:—*pr.p.* **ped′alling**; *pa.p.* **ped′alled.**
[L. *pedālis*; same root as **pedestal,** etc.]

pedant, *ped′ȧnt, n.* one who makes a great display of learning: one who attaches great importance to tiny details.

pedant'ic, *adj.*
ped'antry, *n.* display of knowledge: too great concern with tiny details.
[It. *pedante*; conn. with **pedagogue.**]

peddle, *ped'l, v.i.* to travel from door to door selling small objects: to trifle.—*v.t.* to sell as a pedlar (e.g. *to peddle brushes*).
pedd'ler, *n.* pedlar.
pedd'ling, *adj.* unimportant.—*n.* the trade of a pedlar.
[Perh. from **pedlar.**]

pedestal, *ped'ės-tål, n.* the foot or support of a column, statue, vase, etc.
pedestrian, *pi-des'tri-ån, adj.* going on foot: dull, common.—*n.* a foot-passenger.
pedicure, *ped'i-kūr n.* the treatment of corns, bunions, etc.: a chiropodist.
[L. *pēs, pedis,* foot (It. *piedistallo*; L. *pedester*; *cūra,* care).]

pedigree, *ped'i-grē, n.* a list of the ancestors from whom one has descended: old or distinguished lineage.
ped'igree(d), *adjs.* having known ancestry: pure-bred.
[Prob. Fr. *pied de grue,* crane's foot, from mark on old genealogical tables.]

pedlar, *ped'lår, n.* one who goes about with a pack of goods for sale.
ped'lary, *n.* wares or trade of a pedlar.
[Uncertain; earlier than **peddle.**]

peel[1], *pēl, v.t.* to strip off skin or bark from: to strip off (skin etc.).—*v.i.* to come off, as skin, rind.—*n.* rind, esp. that of oranges, lemons, etc.
[L. *pilāre,* to take off hair.]

peel[2] **(tower),** *pēl (tow'ėr), n.* a fortified tower.
[L. *pālus,* a stake.]

peep[1], *pēp, v.i.* to cheep as baby bird.
[Imit.]

peep[2], *pēp, v.i.* to look through a narrow opening: to look slyly or carefully: (to begin) to appear (e.g. *violets peeping through the grass*).—*n.* a sly look: a glimpse: a first appearance.
peep'er, *n.* one that peeps: a prying person.
peep'-show, *n.* a show looked at through a small hole.
Peeping Tom, a prying fellow, esp. one who peeps in at windows.
[Origin uncertain.]

peer[1], *pēr, n.* an equal in rank or merit: a nobleman of the rank of baron upwards: a member of the House of Lords.
peer'age, *n.* a peer's title: all the peers taken together.
peer'less, *ad.* unequalled, matchless.
[O.Fr.—L. *pār, paris,* equal.]

peer[2], *pēr, v.i.* to look closely, searchingly (e.g. to *peer into the dark*).
[Origin unknown.]

peevish, *pēv'ish, adj.* ill-natured, cross, fretful.
peev'ishly *adv.* **peev'ishness,** *n.*
[Origin unknown.]

peewit, *pē'wit, pū'it, n.* the lapwing, so named from its cry. [Imit.]

peg, *peg, n.* a pin (esp. of wood) for hanging up, fastening, tightening, or for marking a position or point.—*v.t.* to fasten or mark with a peg.—*v.i.* (with *away*) to work very hard (e.g. *He pegged away at his chores*):—*pr.p.* **pegg'ing**; *pa.p.* **pegged.**
to take down a peg, to humble.
[Conn. Germanic words, as Dan. *pig.*]

Pekin(g)ese, *pē-kin(g)-ēz', n.* a small pug-nosed dog of Chinese breed.—Also **Peke.**
[*Peking,* China.]

pelf, *pelf, n.* money, riches (in bad sense).
[O.Fr. *pelfre,* booty; root as **pilfer.**]

pelican, *pel'i-kån, n.* a type of water bird with an enormous pouched bill.
[Gk. *pelekan.*]

pellet, *pel'it, n.* a little ball: a small pill: a ball of shot.
[O.Fr. *pelote*—L. *pila,* a ball.]

pell-mell, *pel'-mel', adv.* in great disorder: helter-skelter (e.g. *The children rushed pell-mell into the room*).
[O.Fr. *pesle-mesle*—*mesler,* to mix.]

pellucid, *pe-lū'sid, -lōō', adj.* perfectly clear.
[L. *per,* through, *lūcēre,* to shine.]

pelt[1], *pelt, n.* a raw skin or hide.
pelt'ry, *n.* pelts: furs.
[**peltry** occurs first—L. *pellis,* skin.]

pelt[2], *pelt, v.t.* to strike repeatedly with blows or objects, e.g. stones; to throw (things, at):—*v.i.* (of rain, etc.) to fall heavily. [Origin unknown.]

pelvis, *pel'vis, n.* the bony cavity forming the lower part of the abdomen.
pel'vic, *adj.*
[L. *pelvis,* a basin.]

pen[1], *pen, n.* a small enclosure, esp. for animals.—*v.t.* to put or keep in a pen:—*pr.p.* **penn'ing**; *pa.p.* **penned.**
[O.E. *penn.*]

pen[2], *pen, n.* an instrument used for writing in ink.—*v.t.* to write:—*pr.p.* **penn'ing**; *pa.p.* **penned.**
pen'knife, *n.* small pocket knife, orig. for mending pens made from quills.
pen'manship, *n.* (art of) handwriting.
pen'-name, *n.* name assumed by author.
[O.Fr. *penne*—L. *penna,* a feather.]

penal, *pē'nål, adj.* having to do with punishment.
pe'nalise, *v.t.* to punish: to attach a penalty or disadvantage to (e.g. breaking of rule in a game).
penalty, *pen'ål-ti, n.* punishment: a fine: a loss that must be suffered for breaking the rules:—*pl.* **pen'alties.**
penal servitude, hard labour in prison as punishment for a crime.
penalty kick, goal, a free kick awarded because a player on the opposite side has broken a rule, a goal scored by it.
[L. *poena*—Gk. *poinē,* punishment.]

penance, *pen'åns n.* punishment a person

undergoes willingly because he is sorry for wrongdoing.
[Same root as **penitence.**]

pence. See **penny.**

pencil, *pen'sl, n.* an instrument containing graphite or coloured chalk for writing, drawing, etc.: any stick of similar shape (e.g. *an eyebrow pencil*): a number of rays coming to a point.—*v.t.* to write or draw with a pencil.
[O.Fr.—L. *pēnicillum*, a painter's brush.]

pendant, *pen'dȧnt,* **pendent,** *n.* anything that hangs, esp. an ornament on a chain.
pen'dent, *adj.* hanging: not yet decided.
pen'ding, *adj.* awaiting a decision.—*prep.* awaiting, until (e.g. *They held him in prison pending trial*).
pendulum, *pen'dū-lum, n.* a weight hung from a fixed point and swinging freely to and fro, as in a clock.
pen'dulous, *adj.* hanging loosely: swinging freely.
[L. *pendēre*, hang.]

penetrate, *pen'i-trāt, v.t.* to force a way into: to pierce: to reach the mind or feelings of: to see into, understand.
pen'etrable, *adj.* able to be penetrated.
pen'etrating, *adj.* piercing: keen, understanding (e.g. *a penetrating look, a penetrating mind*).
penetrā'tion, *n.* the act of entering into: cleverness in understanding.
[L. *penetrāre—penitus*, inward.]

penguin, *peng'gwin,* or *pen'-, n.* a large sea-bird of Antarctic regions.
[Origin uncertain.]

penicillin, *pen-i-sil'in, n.* a substance, obtained from mould, which stops the growth of many disease bacteria.
[Same root as **pencil.**]

peninsula, *pen-in'sū-lȧ, n.* a piece of land that is almost surrounded by water.
penin'sular, *adj.* in the form of a peninsula: living on a peninsula.
[L. *paene*, almost, *insula*, an island.]

penitent, *pen'i-tėnt, adj.* sorry for sin, repentant.—*n.* one who is sorry for his sins.
pen'itence, *n.* state of being sorry.
penitentiary, *pen-i-ten'shȧr-i, n.* (*U.S.*) a state or federal prison.
[L. *paenitēre*, to cause to repent.]

penknife, penmanship. See **pen** (2).

pennant, *pen'ȧnt, n.* a long narrow flag at the masthead of a warship.
[Combination of **pendant** and **pennon.**]

pennon, *pen'ȯn, n.* a flag of various shapes.
[L. *penna*, feather.]

penny, *pen'i, n.* a coin (orig. silver, later copper, then bronze) orig. equal to 1/12 of a shilling, now (**new penny**) equal to one hundredth of a pound:—*pl.* **pennies,** *pen'iz* (used in giving number of coins; e.g. *I have six pennies*), or **pence,** *pens* (used in giving a value; e.g. *The chocolate costs five pence*); abbrev. used is *p.*
penn'iless, *adj.* without money: poor.
penny-wise but pound-foolish, saving small sums but not caring about large.
penn'yworth, *n.* a penny's worth: a bargain (*a good, bad, pennyworth*).
a pretty penny, a large sum of money.
[O.E. *penig*; conn. with Ger. *pfennig.*]

pension, *pen'shȯn, n.* a sum of money given regularly to a person because of past services or old age: a boarding school or boarding house on the Continent.—*v.t.* to grant a pension to (someone).
pen'sionable, *adj.* (of a person) entitled to, (of service) entitling to, a pension.
pen'sioner, *n.* one who receives a pension: a dependent, hireling.
to pension off, to dismiss, or allow to retire, with a pension.
[L. *pensiō—pendĕre*, to weigh, pay.]

pensive, *pen'siv, adj.* dreamily thoughtful: suggesting sad thought.
[Fr. *penser*, think—L. *pensāre*, weigh.]

pent, *pent, adj.* shut in or up.
[Conn. with **pen** (1).]

pent(a)-, *pent(a)-*, (as part of a word) five.
pentagon, *pen'tȧ-gon, n.* (*geometry*) a figure with five sides and five angles: (*cap.*) headquarters of U.S. armed forces in Washington (from shape of building).
pentameter, *pen-tam'ė-tėr, n.* a line in poetry with five stresses.
pentathlon, *pen-tath'lon, n.* in ancient Greek games, a contest in five events: a five-event Olympic games contest for women: (**modern pentathlon**) an Olympic games contest in swimming, cross-country riding and running, fencing and revolver-shooting.
[Gk. *pente*, five (*gōniā*, angle; *metron*, measure; *athlon*, contest).]

penthouse, *pent'hows, n.* a shed or lean-to joined to a main building: an apartment or dwelling built on a roof.
[L. *appendicium*, an appendage.]

penultimate, *pė-nult'i-mit, adj.* last but one.
[L. *paene*, almost, *ultimus*, last.]

penury, *pen'ū-ri, n.* great poverty, want.
penū'rious, *adj.* scanty: stingy, mean.
[L. *pēnūria*, want.]

peon, *pē'on, n.* in Spanish-speaking America, member of labouring class.
[Sp. *peón*—L. *pēs, pedis*, foot.]

peony, *pē'ȯ-ni, n.* a garden plant with large red, pink, or white flowers.
[O.Fr. *pione*—L. *paeōnia*, healing.]

people, *pē'pl, n.* a nation, a community, or a race (in these senses treated as *sing.*, with *pl.* **peoples**; e.g. *the peoples of the world*): the mass of the nation: human beings: persons generally (e.g. *So people say*): near relatives (e.g. *His people came from France*): followers: servants.—*v.t.* to fill with inhabitants, people, animals: (of persons, etc.) to inhabit, fill.
See also **populace, popular.**
[O.Fr. *poeple*—L. *populus.*]

pep, *pep, n.* (*coll.*) energy, vigour. [**pepper.**]
pepper, *pep'ėr, n.* a seasoning made from the dried berries of a **pepper plant.**—*v.t.* to sprinkle with pepper: to hit or pelt, e.g. with shot.
pepp'ery, *adj.* like pepper: hot-tempered: fiery (e.g. *peppery words*).
pepp'eriness, *n.*
pepp'er-and-salt', *adj.* mixed black and white.
pepp'ercorn, *n.* the berry of the pepper plant: something of little value.
pepp'ermint, *n.* a type of mint: a sweet with a sharp taste.
[O.E. *pipor*—Gk. *peperi.*]
per, *pėr, prep.* for each (e.g. *sixpence per dozen*): by (e.g. *per parcel post*).
per annum, for each year.
per cent, *pėr sent', adv.* in the hundred, for every hundred pounds, etc. Symbol %.
percent'age, *n.* rate or amount in a hundred: a proportion.
[L. *per*, for each, by (*centum*, hundred; *annus*, year).]
per-, *per-, pfx.* through, thoroughly, very. [L.]
perambulate, *pėr-am'bū-lāt, v.t.* to walk about, through, over.—*v.i.* to stroll.
peram'bulātor, *n.* one who walks: light carriage for a child (abbrev. **pram**).
[L. *perambulāre*, to walk through.]
perceive, *pėr-sēv', v.t.* to become aware of (something) through the senses: to see: to understand.
percep'tible, *adj.* able to be seen, heard, etc.: enough to be noticed (e.g. *a perceptible delay*).
percep'tibly, *adv.*
percep'tion, *n.* the act of perceiving: awareness of objects: ability to recognise objects or feelings.
percep'tive, *adj.* able, or quick, to perceive or understand.
[L. *percipěre*, *-ceptum*—*capěre*, to take.]
per cent, percentage. See **per.**
perceptible, etc. See **perceive.**
perch[1], *pėrch, n.* a type of freshwater fish. [Fr. *perche*—Gk. *perkē.*]
perch[2], *pėrch, n.* a rod on which birds sit or roost: any high seat.—*v.i.* and *v.t.* to alight or rest on a perch or high place, or to cause to do so.
[Fr. *perche*—L. *pertica*, a rod.]
perchance, *pėr-châns', adv.* by chance: perhaps.
[O.Fr. as spoken in England *par chance.*]
percolate, *per'kō-lāt, v.t., v.i.* to pass through holes, filter.
per'colator, *n.* a device for percolating, esp. for making coffee.
[L. *percōlāre*, to strain through.]
percussion, *pėr-kush'(ō)n, n.* striking of one body against another, impact: in medicine, tapping the body to find by the sound the condition of the organ underneath: musical instruments played by striking, as drums, cymbals, etc.
[L. *per-*, thoroughly, *quatěre*, to shake.]
perdition, *pėr-dish'(ō)n, n.* utter ruin: damnation, lasting punishment.
[L. *perděre*—*per-*, entirely, *dăre*, give up.]
peregrinate, *per'ė-gri-nāt, v.i.* to travel about.
peregrinā'tion, *n.*
[L. *peregre*, abroad—*per*, *ager*, field.]
peremptory, *per-ėm(p)'tȯr-i, adj.* (of a command, etc.) to be obeyed at once: (of manner) commanding, dictatorial.
peremp'torily, *adv.* **-toriness,** *n.*
[L. *peremptōrius*, decisive—*emĕre*, to buy.]
perennial, *pėr-en'yȧl, adj.* (of plants) coming up again year after year: (of e.g. stream) never drying up: continual.
[L. *perennis*—*per*, through, *annus*, year.]
perfect, *pėr'fekt, adj.* complete, accurate exact: faultless: completely skilled.—*v.t.* (or *pėr-fekt'*), to make perfect: to finish: to improve.
perfect'ible, *adj.* capable of being made perfect.
perfectibil'ity, *n.*
perfec'tion, *n.* state of being perfect: the highest state or degree.
perfec'tionist, *n.* one who believes that perfection is possible: one who is not content with less than perfection.
[L. *per-*, thoroughly, *facěre*, do.]
perfidious, *pėr-fid'i-ŭs, adj.* treacherous, untrustworthy, false.
perfid'iousness, per'fidy (*pl.* **-ies**), *ns.*
[L. *perfidia*, faithlessness—*fidēs*, faith.]
perforate, *pėr'fō-rāt, v.t.* to make a hole or holes through: to pierce.
perforā'tion, *n.* act of perforating: a hole, or row of holes, made by boring.
[L. *perforāre*, to bore through.]
perform, *pėr-förm', v.t.* to do: to carry out (duties, etc.): to carry out, fulfil (e.g a promise, a command): to act.—*v.i.* to act a part on stage: to play e.g. on a musical instrument.
perform'ance, *n.* carrying out (of a task, etc.): success in working (e.g. *good performance of the car's engine*): an entertainment on stage: an act or action.
perform'er, *n.*
[O.Fr. *parfournir*—*fournir*, to furnish.]
perfume, *pėr'fūm, n.* a sweet scent, fragrance: a liquid containing fragrant oil, scent.—*v.t.* (also *pėr-fūm'*), to scent.
[Fr. *parfum*—L. *per*, through, *fūmus*, smoke.]
perfunctory, *pėr-fungk'tō-ri, adj.* done merely as a duty: done hurriedly, mechanically: acting without interest.
[L. *perfungī*, *perfunctus*, to perform.]
perhaps, *pėr-haps', adv.* it may be, possibly.
[M.E. *per*, by, and pl. of *hap*, chance.]
peri-, *per-i-*, (as part of word) around. [Gk.]
peril, *per'il, n.* great danger.
per'ilous, *adj.* very dangerous.

per′ilously, *adv.* **per′ilousness,** *n.*
[Fr. *péril*—L. *perīculum.*]

perimeter, *pėr-im′i-tėr, n.* (*geometry*) the outside boundary of a figure: the sum of the sides of a figure.
[Gk. *peri*, around, *metron*, measure.]

period, *pē′ri-ŏd, n.* a division of time: a stage of history: the time a planet, etc. takes to move round its orbit: the time taken for one complete movement of something (e.g. a pendulum) that goes on repeating the same movement: a sentence: a full stop, the mark (.) to end a sentence: a conclusion, end.
periodic, *pē-ri-od′ik, adj.* happening again and again at regular intervals, or (loosely) from time to time.
period′ical, *n.* a magazine that appears at regular intervals.—*adj.* issued, done, etc. at intervals.
period′ically, *adv.*
[Gk. *peri*, around, *hodos*, a way.]

peripatetic, *per-i-pà-tet′ik, adj.* walking about: going from place to place.
[Gk. *peri*, around, *pateein*, to walk.]

periphery, *pėr-if′ėr-i, n.* the bounding line or surface.
periph′eral, *adj.*
[Gk. *peri*, around, *pherein*, to carry.]

periscope, *per′i-skōp, n.* a tube with mirrors by which an observer in a trench, submarine, etc. can see what is going on above.
[Gk. *peri*, around, *skopeein*, look at.]

perish, *per′ish, v.i.* to decay, rot: to die: to be destroyed: to be uncomfortable because of (e.g. *They were perished with cold*).
per′ishable, *adj.* that may perish: liable to go bad quickly, as food.
per′ishing, *adj.* extremely cold.
[L. *per-*, to the bad, *īre*, to go.]

periwinkle[1], *per′i-wingk-l, n.* a creeping evergreen plant usu. with blue flowers.
[O.E. *peruince*—L. *pervinca.*]

periwinkle[2], *per′i-wingk-l, n.* a small shell-fish, a sea snail, eaten as food.
[O.E. (pl.) *pinewinclan.*]

perjure, *pėr′jŭr, v.t.* (with *oneself*) to tell a lie when one has sworn to tell the truth.
per′jury, *n.* false swearing: (*law*) the crime of knowingly giving false evidence on oath:—*pl.* **per′juries.**
[L. *perjūrāre*, to swear falsely.]

perk[1], *pėrk, v.i.* to recover energy, become lively (usu. *perk up*).
perk′y, *adj.* lively, spry, jaunty.
perk′ily, *adv.* **perk′iness,** *n.*
[Origin unknown.]

perk[2], (*coll.*) short for **perquisite.**

perm, *pėrm, n.* (*coll.*) abbrev. for **permanent wave.**

permanent, *pėr′mà-nėnt, adj.* lasting indefinitely: not temporary.
per′manence, per′manency, *ns.* fact or state of being permanent: **(permanency)** a person, thing, or position that is permanent:—*pl.* **per′manencies.**
permanent wave, an artificial wave in the hair, usu. lasting some months.
permanent way, the finished track of a railway.
[L. *permanēre*, last; root as **remain.**]

permeate, *pėr′mi-āt, v.t.* to pass through the pores of: to soak into, pervade.
per′meable, *adj.* **permeabil′ity,** *n.*
[L. *permeāre*, to pass through.]

permit, *pėr-mit′, v.t.* to allow: to give consent to: to make possible.—*n.* (*pėr′mit*) permission, esp. in writing.
permiss′ible, *adj.* allowable.
permiss′ion (*-mish′ŏn*), *n.* act of permitting: freedom given to do something.
permiss′ive, *adj.* allowing freedom (of e.g. choice), permitting much.
[L. *permittěre, -missum*, let pass through.]

permutable, *pėr-mūt′à-bl, adj.* capable of being changed or interchanged.
permutā′tion, *n.*
[L. *per-*, *mutāre*, to change.]

pernicious, *pėr-nish′ŭs, adj.* very harmful or bad.
perniciously (*-nish′*), *adv.*
perniciousness (*-nish′*), *n.*
[L. *perniciōsus*—*nex, necis*, violent death.]

pernickety, *pėr-nik′ė-ti, adj.* fussy, hard to please: requiring great care.
[Scots; origin unknown.]

peroration, *per-ŏ-rā′sh(ŏ)n, n.* closing part of a speech, summing up of argument.
[L. *perōrāre*, end speech—*ōrāre*, speak.]

peroxide, *pėr-oks′īd, n.* an oxide with a large amount of oxygen: (*coll.*) hydrogen peroxide, a colourless oily liquid.
[*per-*, meaning excess, and **oxygen.**]

perpendicular, *pėr-pėn-dik′ū-lår, adj.* standing upright: vertical: (*geometry*) at right angles (to a line or surface).—*n.* a line at right angles to another.
perpendicular′ity, *n.*
perpendic′ularly, *adv.*
[L. *perpendiculum*, a plumb line—*per-*, completely, *pendēre*, cause to hang.]

perpetrate, *pėr′pė-trāt, v.t.* to commit (e.g. an offence, sin, error).
perpetrā′tion, *n.* **per′petrator,** *n.*
[L. *per-*, thoroughly, *patrāre*, to perform.]

perpetual, *pėr-pet′ū-ål, adj.* never ceasing: lasting for ever: very frequent.
perpet′ually, *adv.*
perpetuate, *pėr-pet′ū-āt, v.t.* to cause to last, go on existing, for a long time.
perpetuā′tion, *n.* continuation or preservation for a very long time.
perpetū′ity, *n.* endless time or duration.
in perpetuity, for ever.
[L. *perpetuus.*]

perplex, *pėr-pleks′, v.t.* to puzzle, bewilder: to make complicated (e.g. a problem, situation).
perplex′ity, *n.* state of being perplexed: something that perplexes:—*pl.* **-ities.**
[L. *perplexus*, entangled.]

perquisite, *pėr′kwi-zit, n.* something of

value that one is allowed by employers over and above salary or wages.
[L. *perquīrĕre*, to seek diligently.]

persecute, *pėr'sė-kūt, v.t.* to cause to suffer or die, esp. for religious beliefs or political opinions : to harass, worry, continually.
per'secutor, *n.* **persecū'tion,** *n.*
[L. *per-*, *sequī*, *secūtus*, to follow.]

persevere, *pėr-sė-vēr', v.i.* to continue steadily to try to do a thing, even though difficulties arise.
persevēr'ance, *n.* **persevēr'ing,** *adj.*
[L. *per-*, very, *sevērus*, strict.]

Persian, *pėr'sh(y)ȧn, -zh(y)ȧn, adj.* of, from, or relating to Persia.—*n.* a native of Persia : the language of Persia.

persist, *pėr-sist', v.i.* to continue to try in spite of opposition or difficulty, to persevere : to be insistent in repeating e.g. a question : to continue to exist (e.g. *The belief persists that killing spiders brings rain*).
persis'tence, *n.* doggedness, perseverence : continued existence.
persis'tent, *adj.* constantly coming again (e.g. rumours) or long-continued (e.g. efforts) : obstinate.
[L. *persistĕre—per-*, *stāre*, to stand.]

person, *pėr'sȯn, n.* an individual human being : one's outward body : a living soul.
personable, *pėr'sȯn-ȧ-bl, adj.* of good appearance.
per'sonage, *n.* a person, esp. of rank, importance, or character.
per'sonal, *adj.* relating, belonging, to an individual (e.g. *his personal luggage*) : private (e.g. *for personal reasons*) : for one particular person (e.g. *a personal favour*) : carried out, done, in person (e.g. interview, service) : having to do with the body (e.g. *personal charms, injury*) : aimed in an unkind manner at a particular person (e.g. *personal remarks*).
per'sonally, *adv.* in person : as a person : as far as I (etc.) am concerned (e.g. *Personally I prefer the black one*).
personal'ity, *n.* all of an individual's characteristics (emotional, physical, intellectual, etc.) as they appear to other people : notable character : a person of distinctive character : (in *pl.*) remarks (esp. nasty ones) made about other people :—*pl.* **personal'ities.**
per'sonāte, *v.t.* to pretend to be (someone else), esp. for the purpose of fraud : to play the part of.
personify, *pėr-son'i-fī, v.t.* to speak of (something not material) as if it were a person (e.g. *We personify Justice as a blind woman holding scales*) : to be typical, a perfect example, of (e.g. *Mary is pride personified*) :—*pr.p.* **person'ifying**; *pa.p.* **person'ified.**
personificā'tion, *n.*
personnel' (Fr.), *n.* the persons employed in any service.
first person, the person speaking (I, etc.).
second person, the person spoken to (you).
third person, the person spoken about (he, etc.).
in person, by one's own act, not through someone else : in bodily presence (e.g. *He was there in person*).
to be(come) personal, to make personal (usu. offensive) remarks.
[L. *persōna*, person (*facĕre*, to make).]

persona grata, *pėr-sō'nȧ grā'ta*, a person welcomed with pleasure. [L.]

perspective, *per-spek'tiv, n.* the art of drawing or otherwise showing solid objects, a scene, etc., on a flat surface so as to give the correct appearance of solidity, shape and distance.
in (or **out of**) **perspective,** having (or not having) the appearance of correct size, position, etc. (e.g. *In this photograph his feet are out of perspective*) : (of an event, subject) in (or not in) its true importance when other things are considered with it.
[L. *per*, through, *specĕre*, to look.]

perspicacious, *pėr-spi-kā'shus, adj.* having a keen mind that notices and understands much.
perspicacity (*-kas'i-ti*), *n.*
[Same root as **perspective.**]

perspire, *pėr-spīr', v.i.* to give off fluid through the pores of the skin, to sweat.
perspiration *pėr-spir-ā'sh(ȯ)n, n.*
[L. *per*, through, *spīrāre*, to breathe.]

persuade, *pėr-swād', v.t.* to cause (someone to do something) by arguing or advising : to convince (e.g. *We persuaded him that it was best to go by air*).
persuasion, *pėr-swā'zh(ȯ)n, n.* act of persuading : settled opinion (e.g. *It is my persuasion that any change would be for the better*) : a group of people with the same religious creed (e.g. *of the Catholic persuasion*).
persuas'ive (*-swās'* or *-swāz'*), *adj.* having power to win over or influence (e.g. *He is a persuasive speaker*).
[L. *per-*, *suādēre*, *suāsum*, to advise.]

pert, *pėrt, adj.* saucy, free in speech, cheeky.
pert'ly, *adv.* **pert'ness,** *n.*
[Short for *apert*—L. *aperīre*, to open.]

pertain, *pėr-tān', v.i.* to belong (to) as a necessary or characteristic part (e.g. *all the duties pertaining to nursing*) : to have to do with, have reference (to ; e.g. *the documents pertaining to the case*).
per'tinent, *adj.* having close connexion with the subject spoken about, to the point, relevant.
per'tinence, per'tinency, *ns.*
[O.Fr. *partenir*—L. *per-*, *tenēre*, to hold.]

pertinacious, *pėr-ti-nā'shus, adj.* (often as a bad quality) holding firmly to an opinion or purpose : persistent.
pertinacity (*-nas'i-ti*), *n.*
[L. *pertināx*; same root as **pertain.**]

perturb, *pėr-tûrb′*, *v.t.* to disturb greatly: to trouble, make anxious.
perturb′able, *adj.*
perturbā′tion, *n.* uneasiness of mind.
[L. *per-*, *turbāre*, disturb—*turba*, crowd.]

peruke, perruque, *pėr-ōōk′*, *n.* a wig.
[Fr. *perruque*—It. *parrucca.*]

peruse, *pėr-ōōz′*, *v.t.* to read, esp. carefully.
perus′al, *n.*
[L. *per-*, thoroughly, *ūtī*, to use.]

Peruvian, *pėr-ōō′vi-ȧn*, *adj.* having to do with *Peru*, in South America.—*n.* a native of *Peru*.

pervade, *pėr-vād′*, *v.t.* to pass or spread through the whole of (e.g. *A smell of burning pervaded the house*).
[L. *per*, through, *vādĕre*, to go.]

perverse, *pėr-vėrs′*, *adj.* turned aside from right or truth: obstinate in doing the wrong thing: wilful, unreasonable.
perversion, *pėr-vėr′sh(ȯ)n*, *n.* a turning away from what is normal: a wrong or corrupted form of anything (e.g. *This statement is a perversion of the truth*).
pervers′ity (*pl.* **-ies**), **perverse′ness,** *ns.*
pervert′, *v.t.* to turn away from what is normal or right (e.g. *to pervert the course of justice*): to distort, give a wrong meaning to (e.g. *You have perverted my statement*): to lead (a person) astray, into sin, error, or abnormality.
per′vert, *n.* one who has been perverted, who is abnormal, unnatural.
[L. *per-*, wrongly, *vertĕre*, to turn.]

pessimism, *pes′i-mizm*, *n.* the belief that the world is bad rather than good: a state of mind that thinks everything will turn out badly, hopelessness. Opp. of **optimism.**
pess′imist, *n.* one who looks too much on the dark side of things.
pessimis′tic, *adj.*
[L. *pessimus*, worst.]

pest, *pest*, *n.* anything (e.g. an insect, animal) destructive to food or material: a troublesome person.
pest′icide, *n.* a pest killer.
pest′ilence, *n.* any deadly disease that spreads from person to person.
pes′tilent, *adj.* very unhealthy: endangering morals, peace, etc.: annoying.—Also **pestilen′tial,** *-sh(ȧ)l.*
[Fr. *peste*—L. *pestis.*]

pester, *pes′tėr*, *v.t.* to annoy (someone) continually (e.g. *pestering him for help*).
[Prob. O.Fr. *empestrer*, entangle, hobble.]

pesticide, pestilence, etc. See **pest.**

pestle, *pes′l*, *pest′l*, *n.* a chemist's tool for grinding things to powder.
[O.Fr. *pestel*—L. *pinsĕre*, *pistum*, pound.]

pet[1], *pet*, *n.* a much loved tame animal: a favourite person esp. one who is given too much.—*adj.* kept as a pet: favourite.—*v.t.* to treat as a pet: to fondle.
pet aversion, chief obect of dislike.
pet name, a name used in affection.
[Origin unknown.]

pet[2], *pet*, *n.* a fit of sulks.
pett′ish, *adj.* peevish, sulky.
[Origin unknown.]

petal, *pet′ȧl*, *n.* one of the leaves forming a flower.
[Gk. *petalon*, a leaf.]

peter, *pē′tėr*, *v.i.* (*coll.*; with *out*) to dwindle away to nothing.
[U.S. mining slang; origin unknown.]

petite, *pė-tēt′*, *adj.* (*fem.*) small and neat in figure. [Fr.]

petition, *pė-tish′(ȯ)n*, *n.* a formal request to an authority (parliament, court of law) asking for a favour of some sort: a written request signed by several persons: a prayer.—*v.t.* to send a petition to: to ask (someone for something, or to do something).
[L. *petītiō*—*petĕre*, to ask.]

petrel, *pet′rėl*, *n.* a dark-coloured, small, long-winged sea bird.
[L. *Petrus*, Peter.]

petrify, *pet′ri-fī*, *v.t.* to turn into stone: to make stiff with fear or horror.—*v.i.* to become stone or hard like stone:—*pr.p.* **pet′rifying**; *pa.p.* **pet′rified.**
petrifac′tion, *n.* turning to stone: turning stiff: a petrified object.
[L. *petra*, rock, *facĕre*, to make.]

petro-, *pet-rō-*, (as part of a word) stone.
petrochemical, *pet-rō-kem′i-kȧl*, *n.* any chemical obtained from petroleum.
petrol, *pet′rol*, *-rȯl*, *n.* purified petroleum for motor cars, aeroplanes, etc.
petroleum, *pė-trō′li-ŭm*, *-trōl′yŭm*, *n.* a mixture of fuel oils got from oil wells.
[L. *petra* (Gk. *petrā*), rock (*oleum*, oil).]

petticoat, *pet′i-kōt*, *n.* an underskirt or skirt: a woman. **[petty, coat.]**

pettifogger, *pet′i-fog-ėr*, *n.* a lawyer who practises only in trifling cases, esp. one who uses mean and crooked methods.
pett′ifogging, *adj.*
[**petty**; origin of second part uncertain.]

petty, *pet′i*, *adj.* of small importance: trivial: small-minded, narrow: mean:—*comp.* **pett′ier**; *superl.* **pett′iest.**
pett′ily, *adv.* **pett′iness,** *n.*
petty cash, small sums of money paid or received.
petty larceny, theft of money or articles of little value.
petty officer, a naval officer ranking with an army non-commissioned officer.
[Fr. *petit*, little.]

petulant, *pet′ū-lȧnt*, *adj.* showing peevish impatience or irritation.
pet′ulance, *n.* **pet′ulantly,** *adv.*
[L. *petulāns*—*petĕre*, to seek.]

petunia, *pė-tū′ni-ȧ*, *n.* a type of tropical S. American plant with funnel-shaped flowers, related to tobacco.
[South American Indian, *petun*, tobacco.]

pew, *pū*, *n.* an enclosed compartment or fixed bench with back in a church.
[O.Fr. *puie*, balcony—L. *podium.*]

pewter, *pū′tėr*, *n.* an alloy or mixture of

tin with e.g. lead: utensils or dishes made of pewter.—Also *adj.*
[O.Fr. *peutre*; conn. It. and Ger. words.]

phalanges. See **phalanx.**

phalanx, *fal'angks, fāl'*, *n.* a body of troops etc. in close formation: a solid body of supporters (in first two senses, *pl.* **phal'anxes**): a bone of a finger or toe (*pl.* **phalanges,** *fa-lan'jēz*).
[Gk. *phalanx, phalangos.*]

phantasy, *fan'tà-si, -zi,* fantasy :—*pl.* **-ies.**
phan'tom, *n.* a ghost, apparition: a vision: appearance without reality.
[Gk. *phantasma,* appearance—*phainein,* to show ('phantom' through O.Fr.).]

Pharaoh, *fā'rō, n.* title of the king in ancient Egypt.

Pharisee, *far'i-sē, n.* one of a religious group among the Jews who held strictly to the old laws: anyone who is more concerned with the forms of religion than with the spirit.
pharisā'ical, *adj.*
[Gk. *pharisaios*—Heb. *pārūsh,* separated.]

pharmaceutical, *fär-mà-sū'tik-àl, adj.* having to do with the knowledge or art of preparing medicines or drugs.—*n.* a chemical used in medicine.
pharmaceu'tics, *n.* the science of making medicines.
pharmacy, *fär'mà-si, n.* the art of preparing medicines: a chemist's shop.
phar'macist, *n.* a druggist, chemist.
[Gk. *pharmakon,* a drug.]

pharyngitis, *far-in-jī'tis, n.* inflammation of the **pharynx** (*far'ingks*), the tube that connects the mouth with the tube leading to the stomach.
[Gk. *pharynx, pharyngos.*]

phase, *fāz, n.* any of the appearances or stages of a thing that goes through a series of changes again and again (e.g. *the phases of the moon*—full, half, etc.): a stage in development (e.g. *a phase of a man's career, a new phase in the war*): side, aspect, of a situation or question.
[Gk. *phasis—phaein,* to shine.]

pheasant, *fez'(à)nt, n.* a type of long-tailed richly coloured half-wild game bird in Britain: the bird as food.
[Gk. *Phāsiānos (ornis),* (bird) from river Phasis (in Asia).]

phenomenon, *fė-nom'ė-nòn, n.* anything (fact, occurrence) observed by the senses or by one of them (e.g. *the phenomenon of rust eating away iron*): anything (occurrence, person, thing, appearance) remarkable :—*pl.* **phenom'ena.**
phenom'enal, *adj.* very unusual or remarkable: known by the senses.
[Gk. *phainein,* to show.]

phew, *fū, interj.* an exclamation of disgust.

phial, *fī'àl, n.* a small glass bottle, esp. for holding medicines.
[Gk. *phialē,* a broad shallow bowl.]

phil(o)-, *fil(-ō)-,* (as part of a word) loving, friend.
philharmonic, *fil-här-mon'ik, adj.* loving music (used in names of societies, etc.).
philander, *fil-an'dėr, v.i.* to make love, esp. in a trifling manner.
philan'derer, *n.*
philanthropy, *fil-an'thrò-pi, n.* love of mankind, esp. as shown by work done, or money given, for the welfare of large numbers of people.
philan'thropist, *n.* one who tries to do good to his fellow men.
philanthrop'ic, *adj.* **-ically,** *adv.*
philately, *fil-at'ė-li, n.* the study and collection of postage stamps.
-phile, *-fīl, suffix* lover—e.g. **Anglophile.**
-philia, *-fil-i-à, suffix* love.
See also **philology, philosopher.**
[Gk. *philos,* loving, *phileein,* to love (*harmoniā,* harmony; *anēr, andros,* man; *anthrōpos,* man; *atelēs,* tax-free).]

Philistine, *fil'is-tīn, n.* an individual of one of the ancient peoples of Palestine: a person who cares nothing for literature, art, etc., whose interests are in material things, and whose ideas are ordinary.
[Gk. *Philistinos*—Heb. *P'lishtīm.*]

phil(o)- (continued).
philology, *fil-ol'ò-ji, n.* the science which deals with words and their history.
philol'ogist, *n.* one who is skilled in philology.
philosopher, *fil-os'ò-fėr, n.* a lover of wisdom: one who studies philosophy: one who practises the principles of philosophy by acting calmly and reasonably in the affairs of life.
philosoph'ic, *-sof',* or *-zof', adj.* having to do with philosophy: calm, not easily upset or disturbed.
philos'ophise, *v.i.* to form theories about the reason and nature of things: to moralise.
philos'ophy, *n.* study of the world of nature, esp. of the laws of physics (*natural philosophy*), or of the principles of human behaviour (*moral philosophy*), and reasoning about what we really know of ourselves and the universe, as opp. to what we seem to know (see **metaphysics**): a person's view of life and principles of conduct: calmness of temper.
[Gk. *philos,* loving (*logos,* word; *sophiā,* wisdom).]

phlegm, *flem, n.* the thick slimy matter brought up from the throat by coughing: coolness of temper, calmness.
phlegmatic, *fleg-mat'ik, adj.* not easily excited: calm.
[Gk. *phlegma,* flame, inflammation.]

phlox, *floks, n.* a garden plant with flat-shaped flowers, often bluish-red.
[Gk. *phlox,* flame, wallflower.]

phobia, *fō'bi-à, n.* a fear, dislike, or hatred, esp. without reason (orig. used as a suffix only—e.g. **Anglophobia**).
[Gk. *phobos,* fear.]

phoenix, *fē'niks, n.* in old stories, a miraculous bird, the only one of its kind, which burned itself every 500 or 600 years and then rose again from its ashes as a young bird—hence an emblem of everlasting life.

[L. *phoenix*—Gk. *phoinix*.]

phone, *fōn, n., v.i., v.t.* (*coll.*) (to) telephone.

phonetic, *fō-net'ik, adj.* having to do with the sounds of language: spelled according to sound (e.g. *'sivik' is a phonetic spelling of 'civic'*).

phonet'ics, *n.* the science that deals with pronunciation and the spelling of sounds of speech.

[Gk. *phōnētikos*; same root as **phonic.**]

phon(e)y, *fōn'i, adj.* (*slang*) fake, not genuine, of no value. [Origin unknown.]

phon(o)-, *fōn(o)-*, (as part of word) sound.

phonic, *fōn'ik, fon', adj.* of speech sounds.

phon'ics, *n.* a method of teaching reading by means of the sounds of the letters.

phonograph, *fō'nō-grâf, n.* a gramophone. See also **phonetic.**

[Gk. *phōnē*, sound (*graphein*, write).]

phosphorus, *fos'fȯr-ūs, n.* a waxy, poisonous, inflammable substance which gives out light in the dark.

phosphor'ic, phos'phorous, *adjs.* having to do with or containing phosphorus.

phosphate, *fos'fāt, n.* a salt or salts containing phosphorus used as fertilizer.

phosphoresce' (*-es'*), *v.i.* to shine in the dark, as phosphorus does.

phosphores'cence, *n.*

phosphores'cent, *adj.*

[Gk. *phōs*, light, *phoros*, bearing.]

phot(o)-[1], *fōt(-o)-*, (as part of a word) light. (See also next article.)

photo-electric'ity, *n.* electricity produced by the action of light.

photo-elec'tric, *adj.*

photo-sen'sitive, *adj.* affected by light, either visible or invisible.

[Gk. *phōs*, *phōtos*, light.]

photo, *fō'tō, n., v.t., adj.* an abbreviation of **photograph.** Also, as part of word, **photo-**[2].

(See also article above.)

photochrome, *fō'tō-krōm, n.* a photograph in colour.

pho'to-fin'ish, *n.* finish of a race so close that a special type of photography is used to show the winner.

photogenic, *fō-tō-jen'ik, adj.* photographing well, making a good subject for a picture.

photography, *fō-tog'rȧ-fi, n.* the art of taking pictures by means of a camera, making use of the action of light on chemically prepared films and plates.

pho'tograph, *n.* an image so produced.

photog'rapher, *n.* **photograph'ic,** *adj.*

photoplay, *fō'tō-plā, n.* a drama shown in moving pictures.

Photostat, *fō'tō-stat, n.* trademark for a device for making drawings, maps, etc. directly on prepared paper, without a reversed image.

[**photo-** (1) (Gk. *chrōma*, colour; *gen-* root of *gignesthai*, to be produced; *graphein*, write, draw; *statos*, placed).]

photosynthesis, *fō-tō-sin'thi-sis, n.* (in plants) the process of building up food which takes place in the presence of light.

[**photo-** (1), Gk. *syn*, with, *thesis*, placing.]

phrase, *frāz, n.* a group of words expressing a single idea (e.g. *after dinner*, *on the water*): a short saying: (*music*) a short group of notes.—*v.t.* to express in words.

phraseol'ogy (*frāz-i-ol'*), *n.* manner of putting phrases together, style.

phras'ing, *n.* the wording of a speech or written passage: (*music*) the grouping of notes to form musical phrases.

[Gk. *phrasis*—*phrazein*, to speak.]

phrenology, *fren-ol'ȯ-ji, n.* the study of the shape of the skull, supposed to show a person's mental powers.

[Gk. *phrēn*, midriff, heart, mind; each supposed a seat of human qualities.]

phut, *fut, adj.* (*slang*) burst, finished, unable to be used.

[Hindustani *phatnā*, to split.]

physi(o)-, *fiz-i(ō)-*, (as part of a word) nature, natural: having to do with the body.

physic, *fiz'ik, n.* medicine.—*v.t.* to give medicine to:—*pr.p.* **phys'icking**; *pa.p.* **phys'icked.**

phys'ical, *adj.* having to do with the body (e.g. *physical strength*, *physical exercises*): having to do with physics.

phys'ically, *adv.*

physician, *fi-zish'ȧn, n.* a doctor, one who decides on treatment and medicine but does not perform operations: a healer or healing influence.

phys'icist (*-i-sist*), *n.* a specialist in physics.

phys'ics, *n.* a branch of science studying facts and laws of mechanics, heat, sound, light, magnetism, electricity, and the structure of the atom (but not concerned with purely chemical changes or living processes).

physical geography, the study of the earth's natural features (e.g. mountains, rivers, etc.).

physiognomy, *fiz-i-on'ȯ-mi, -og'nȯ-mi, n.* the face, esp. with its characteristic expression: the art of judging character from the face.

physiography, *fiz-i-og'rȧ-fi, n.* description and history of the earth's surface: physical geography.

physiology, *fiz-i-ol'ȯ-ji, n.* the science dealing with living processes in animals and plants (e.g. blood circulation, photosynthesis in plants, etc.).

physiolog'ical (*-log'*), *adj.*

physiolog'ically, *adv.*

physiotherapy, *fiz-i-ō-ther'ȧ-pi, n.* treatment of disease without drugs, using fresh air, massage, etc.

physique, *fiz-ēk', n.* the build or structure of one's body (e.g. *He has a poor, a powerful, physique*).

[Gk. *physikos,* natural, *physis,* nature (*gnōmōn,* interpreter; *graphein,* to write; *logos,* discourse; *therapeuein,* to heal; Fr. *physique,* from Gk.).]

pi, *pī, n.* the Greek letter π which is used to stand for the number by which the diameter of a circle must be multiplied in order to find the circumference (approximately 3.14). [Gk.]

pianoforte, *pyâ'nō-fŏr-tā* or *pē-â', usu.* shortened to **piano,** *pyâ'nō,* or *pē-â', n.* a musical instrument played by touching keys and so causing hammers to strike wires stretched across a soundboard:—*pls.* **pia'nofortes, pia'nos.**

pianissimo, *pyâ-nis'si-mō, adj.* and *adv.* very soft(ly).

pianist (*pya', pē'a-*), *n.* one who plays the piano, esp. with skill.

[It.—*piano,* soft, *forte,* loud.]

piazza, *pē-ät'sä, -äd'za, -az'ė, n.* a market-place or square in a town: (*U.S.*) a veranda.

[It.—Gk. *plateia,* a street.]

pibroch, *pē'broH, n.* a type of bagpipe music, variations on a theme.

[Gael. *piobaireachd,* pipe music.]

picador, *pik'ȧ-dŏr, n.* a mounted bull-fighter, with a lance.

[Sp.—*pica,* a pike.]

piccaninny, pickaninny, *pik'a-nin-i, n.* a Negro child.

[Port. *pequenino,* little; or Sp.]

piccolo, *pik'ö-lō, n.* small flute, pitched an octave higher than an ordinary flute.

[It., little.]

pick, *pik, n.* a tool for breaking ground, rock, etc., with head pointed at one end or both ends and fixed to a handle in the middle: any instrument for picking (as in *toothpick*): act of choosing: a portion or amount picked: the best, best part (of something).—*v.t.* to pull apart: to gather (flowers): to peck, bite, or nibble: to remove something from (something) with a pointed instrument: to open (e.g. a lock) with a sharp instrument: to rob (e.g. *to pick pockets*): to choose: to seek (e.g. *to pick a quarrel*).

pick'ing, *n.* act of one that picks: something picked or picked up.

pick'-up, *n.* a thing or person picked up: a device for picking up an electric current: a device holding the needle which follows the track on a disk gramophone record: a device enabling gramophone records to be reproduced through a radio loud-speaker: accelerating power (of vehicle).

to pick holes in, to point out faults in.

to pick at, to find fault with.

to pick off, to kill or wound one by one.

to pick one's way, to choose carefully where to put one's feet.

to pick to pieces, to take apart: to criticise, tell the faults of, in detail.

to pick up, to lift from the ground: to take into a vehicle (e.g. *On the way there in my car I picked up Jack*): to make the acquaintance of informally: to get by chance: to get, esp. little by little (e.g. *to pick up a language, a habit*): to come upon, make out (e.g. *to pick up signals, the track over the hill*): to improve, gain strength (e.g. *He picked up slowly after his illness; business is picking up*): to accelerate.

[Conn. with **pike.**]

pickax(e), *pik'aks, n.* a tool used in digging, a pick.

[M.E. *pikois*—O.Fr. *pic,* a pick.]

picket, *pik'it, n.* a pointed stake driven into the ground, used for fences, tethering a horse, surveying, etc.: a small patrol or group of men for guarding or special duty: a group of men on strike stationed at place of employment to keep others from going to work.—*v.t.* to tether or tie to a stake: to set a guard of soldiers, strikers, at (a place).

[Fr. *picquet*—*pic,* a pick.]

pickle, *pik'l, n.* a liquid in which food is preserved: vegetables preserved in vinegar: an unpleasant situation.—*v.t.* to preserve in salt liquid or vinegar.

[M.E. *pikkyll*; conn. with Du. *pekel.*]

picnic, *pik'nik, n.* an informal outing on which food is eaten in the open air: a very informal meal: an easy or pleasant experience.—Also *adj.* (e.g. *a picnic lunch*).—*v.i.* to have a picnic:—*pr.p.* **pic'nicking**; *pa.p.* **pic'nicked.**

[Fr. *pique-nique.*]

pictorial, *pik-tō'ri-ȧl, -tö', adj.* having to do with painting or drawing: filled with pictures (e.g. *a pictorial magazine*): expressed in pictures: calling up pictures in the mind.

picture, *pik'chůr, n.* image, representation, of an object or scene by painting, drawing, or photography: a portrait: a symbol or type (e.g. *a picture of health*): a description so clear as to form in the mind an image of the thing described: a film show: (in *pl.*) the cinema, moving pictures.—*v.t.* to represent in a picture: to form a likeness of in the mind: to describe clearly.

picturesque, *pik-chůr-esk', adj.* such as would make a good or striking picture, usu. suggesting beauty or quaintness: (of language) colourful rather than matter-of-fact.

picture gallery, a hall or gallery where pictures are shown to the public.

in the picture, having a share of attention: being informed and therefore able to understand the situation.

[L. *pictor*, painter, *pictūra*, painting (It. *pittoresco*, from L.).]

piddle, *pid'l, v.i.* to deal in trifles.
[Origin uncertain.]

pidgin (English), *pij'in (ing'glish)*, a language with mainly English words but its own grammar and constructions, esp. one used to talk to Chinese.
[Chinese way of saying **business.**]

pie[1], *pī, n.* a magpie: a chatterer. [Fr.]

pie[2], *pī, n.* meat or fruit baked within a crust of prepared paste.
[Origin unknown.]

piebald, pyebald, *pī'böld, adj.* black and white (or, loosely, other colours) in patches. [**pie** (1), **bald.**]

piece, *pēs, n.* a part or portion: a single article: a definite length, as of cloth or paper: a composition in writing, music, drama, painting: a coin: a man in chess, draughts, etc.—*v.t.* to make larger by adding a piece: to patch: to put (together).
piece goods, textile fabrics made in definite lengths.
piece'meal, *adv.* in pieces: bit by bit.—*adj.* done bit by bit: in pieces.
piece'work, *n.* work paid for by number of pieces or quantity done, not by time.
a piece of one's mind, a frank outspoken scolding or opinion.
of a piece, of the same kind (e.g. *This deceit was of a piece with his usual conduct*).
to go to pieces, to break into parts: to break down nervously or physically.
[O.Fr.—Late L. *pecia*, piece of land.]

pièce de résistance, *pyes dė rā-zēs-tong̃s*, the main dish of a meal: the most important article, incident, event. [Fr.]

pied, *pīd, adj.* with two or more colours in patches. [**pie** (1).]

pier, *pēr, n.* a pillar, the support of an arch, bridge, etc.: a stone, wooden, etc. platform stretching from the shore into the sea or other water for use as a landing place, etc.
pier'-head, the seaward end of a pier.
[M.E. *pēr*, Late L. *pēra.*]

pierce, *pērs, v.t.* to thrust a hole through: to force a way into: to touch the emotions of, move deeply: to see right through (e.g. a mystery).
pierc'ing. *adj.* loud and shrill: sharp, biting (e.g. cold): seeing very clearly.
[O.Fr. *percer*; of uncertain origin.]

pierrot, *pē'ėr-ō, n.* a comic entertainer with white face and loose white clothes. [Fr.]

piety, *pī'ė-ti, n.* devoutness, reverence for God: dutiful carrying out of one's religious duties: a religious act (*pl.* **pi'eties**).
pious, *pī'ŭs, ad.* showing piety, real or sham: sacred: done with a good motive (e.g. *a pious deception*).
[O.Fr. *piete*—L. *pietās*; L. *pius* (adj.).]

piffle, *pif'l, n.* nonsense, worthless talk.
[Origin uncertain.]

pig, *pig, n.* a swine, a farm animal from which we get bacon, pork, etc.: (an oblong piece of) metal run while molten into a mould (e.g. *pig-iron*):—*v.i.* to live in dirt or muddle: to feed like a pig:—*pr.p.* **pigg'ing**; *pa.p.* **pigged.**
pigg'ish, *adj.* greedy: dirty.
pig'head'ed, *adj.* stubborn.
pig'skin, *n.* pig's leather: a saddle.
pig'sty, *n.* a pen for keeping pigs.
pig'tail, *n.* the hair of the head plaited behind in one braid.
[M.E. *pigge.*]

pigeon[1], *pij'in, n.* a bird, esp. domesticated, of the dove family.
pig'eon-heart'ed, *adj.* timid, meek.
pig'eon-hole, *n.* a compartment, e.g. in a desk, for storing papers, etc.—*v.t.* to arrange, classify: to file: to put aside to be dealt with later, if ever.
clay pigeon, *n.* a disk, etc., thrown from a trap and shot at for shooting practice.
[O.Fr. *pijon*—L. *pīpiō*, a cheep.]

pigeon[2], *pij'in, n.* spelling of 'pidgin' (see derivation of this).
that's (not) my pigeon, that is (not) my affair.

pigment, *pig'mėnt, n.* paint: any substance used for colouring: a substance in plants or animals that gives colour to skin.
pigmentā'tion, *n.* coloration by pigments in the tissues.
[L. *pīgmentum—pingĕre*, to paint.]

pigmy, pygmy, *pig'mi, n.* one of a race of very small human beings: a dwarf.—Also *adj.* very small.
[Gk. *pygmē*, 13½ inches.]

pike, *pīk, n.* a weapon with long shaft and sharp head like a spear: a sharp-pointed hill: a very greedy freshwater fish with a pointed snout.
[O.E. *pīc*, pick, spike.]

pilchard, *pil'chȧrd, n.* a small sea-fish like the herring, often called *sardine*.
[Origin unknown; perh. Scand.]

pile[1], *pīl, n.* a number of things lying one on top of another: a tall or large building: (*slang*) a large amount of money, fortune (e.g. *He has made his pile*).—*v.t.* to heap (often *up* or *on*): to cover with something in piles (e.g. *to pile a table with books*).—*v.i.* to become piled up: to gather: to crowd (e.g. *to pile into a bus*).
atomic pile, a device using uranium rods embedded in graphite to obtain a slow regular amount of nuclear energy.
[Fr.—L. *pīla*, a pillar.]

pile[2], *pīl, n.* a large stake or pillar driven into the ground as a foundation for a building, etc.
pile'-driver, *n.* a machine for driving in piles.
[O.E. *pīl*—L. *pīlum*, a javelin.]

pile[3], *pīl, n.* a raised surface on certain cloths, e.g. velvet (produced in different way from *nap*).
[L. *pĭlus*, a hair.]

pile[4], *pīl, n.* (usu. in *pl.*) haemorrhoid (see this word).
[L. *pĭla,* a ball.]

pilfer, *pil′fėr, v.i.* and *v.t.* to steal, esp. in small quantities.
[Connected with **pelf.**]

pilgrim, *pil′grim, n.* one who travels a distance to visit a holy place.
pil′grimage, *n.* a journey to a shrine or holy place: any long journey.
Pilgrim Fathers, the Puritans who sailed in the *Mayflower* and founded Plymouth, Massachusetts, in 1620.
[L. *peregrīnus,* stranger; same root as **peregrinate.**]

pill, *pil, n.* a little ball of medicine: anything unpleasant which must be accepted or endured.
[L. *pila,* a ball.]

pillage, *pil′ij, n.* the act of plundering: booty.—*v.t.* to plunder, loot, take money and goods from.—Also *v.i.*
[L. *pilāre,* to take the hair off.]

pillar, *pil′ȧr, n.* an upright support for a roof, arch, etc., a column: a shaft like this as a monument: anything that supports (e.g. *He is a pillar of the church*).
pill′ar-box, a short hollow pillar in which to post letters.
from pillar to post, from one place to another: from one difficulty to another.
[O.Fr. *piler*—L. *pīla,* a pillar.]

pillion, *pil′yȯn, n.* a light saddle for a woman, usu. behind the man's: a seat for baggage or passenger on a motor bicycle.
[Prob. Ir. *pillīn,* Gael. *pillean,* a pad.]

pillory, *pil′ȯr-i, n.* a wooden frame on a post, with holes to hold firmly the head and hands of prisoners:—*pl.* **pill′ories.** —*v.t.* to mock, laugh at publicly:—*pa.t.* and *pa.p.* **pill′oried.**
[O.Fr. *pilori.*]

pillow, *pil′ō, n.* a cushion for a sleeper's head: any support used for a similar purpose.—*v.t.* to rest on, or as on, a pillow.
pillowcase, -slip, *ns.* a cover for a pillow.
[O.E. *pyle*—L. *pulvīnus.*]

pilot, *pī′lȯt, n.* one who steers ships in and out of a harbour, along a dangerous coast, etc.: one who actually operates the flying controls of an aircraft: a mechanism that regulates another: (**automatic pilot**) a device for directing an aeroplane, ship: a guide, leader.—*v.t.* to act as pilot or guide to.
pi′lot-balloon′, *n.* a small balloon sent up to find how the wind blows.
pi′lot-boat, *n.* a boat used by pilots for meeting and leaving ships.
pi′lot-light, *n.* a small electric light used to show e.g. that power is switched on: a small gas light kept burning to light a larger jet.
pilot officer, an Air Force officer. See *Appendices.*
pilot plant, trial machinery set up to test a new process before it becomes full-scale.
[O.Fr. *pillotte*—It. *pilota.*]

pimento, *pi-men′tō, n.* allspice or Jamaica pepper: the tree producing it.
[Port. *pimenta*—L. *pīgmentum,* paint.]

pimpernel, *pim′pėr-nel, n.* a plant with small, often scarlet, flowers that close when bad weather is coming.
[(O.)Fr. *pimprenelle.*]

pimple, *pim′pl, n.* a small pointed swelling on the skin.
pim′pled, pim′ply, *adjs.* having pimples.
[Origin unknown.]

pin, *pin, n.* a pointed instrument of wood or metal used to fasten things together: a peg: anything of little value: a leg (e.g. *to knock him off his pins*).—*v.t.* to fasten with a pin: to hold fast, pressed against something (e.g. *The heavy log pinned him to the ground*):—*pr.p.* **pinn′ing**; *pa.p.* **pinned.**
pin money, money given to a wife for private expenses.
pin′point, *n.* anything very sharp and tiny.—*v.t.* to place, or show the place of, very exactly.—*adj.* very accurate.
pin′prick, *n.* a very small irritation, worry, or pain.
pin′-stripe, *n.* a very narrow stripe in cloth.
to pin it on to (someone), to prove, or make it seem, that he did it.
to pin one's faith, hopes, etc. on, or **to,** to put entire trust in: to rely on.
to pin someone (down) to, to make him keep strictly to (e.g. truth, facts, promise).
[O.E. *pinn*—L. *pinna,* a feather.]

pinafore, *pin′ȧ-fōr, -fȯr, n.* an apron covering the whole front.
[**pin,** O.E. *on foran,* in front.]

pince-nez, *pan^g s′-nā, n.* a pair of eyeglasses with a spring for catching the nose.
[Fr., pinch nose.]

pincers, *pin′sėrz, n.* a gripping tool, used for drawing out nails, etc.
[O.Fr. *pincer,* to pinch.]

pinch, *pinch* or *-sh, v.t.* to squeeze between the thumb and finger or between any two surfaces, as the jaws of a tool: to nip: to hurt by tightness: (of hunger or cold) to give pain: to limit too much, stint (e.g. *to pinch oneself for food*): to make (a face) look thin and haggard: (*slang*) to steal: (*slang*) to catch or arrest.—Also *v.i.*—*n.* an act of pinching: a very small amount (e.g. *a pinch of salt*): pressure, distress (e.g. *the pinch of poverty*): emergency.
pinched, *adj.*
at a pinch, in a case of emergency.
[O.Fr. *pincier.*]

pine[1], *pīn, n.* a cone-bearing evergreen tree with needle-shaped leaves.
pī′ny, *adj.* like, of, or covered with, pine trees.

pine'apple, *n.* a fruit growing in hot countries shaped like a large pine-cone.
pine'-needle, *n.* the needle-shaped leaf of the pine tree. [O.E. *pīn*—L. *pīnus.*]

pine[2], *pīn*, *v.i.* to waste away, esp. with pain, grief: to long (for, to do).
[O.E. *pīn*, torture—root as **penal.**]

ping, *ping*, *n.* a whistling sound such as that of a bullet.
ping'-pong', *n.* (should have *cap.*) a trademark for table tennis. [Imit.]

pinion[1], *pin'yȯn*, *n.* a bird's wing: a feather.—*v.t.* to cut the wings of (a bird) so that it is unable to fly: to pin back (the arms).
[O.Fr. *pignon*—L. *pinna*, wing.]

pinion[2], *pin'yȯn*, *n.* a small toothed wheel fitting into notches e.g. on another wheel.
[Fr. *pignon*—O.Fr. *penon*, a battlement.]

pink[1], *pingk*, *v.t.* to wound, esp. slightly, e.g. with rapier: to decorate (cloth, etc.) by cutting small holes or scallops.
[A Germanic word.]

pink[2], *pingk*, *n.* a scented garden flower (when double, known as 'carnation'): a light red colour: a scarlet hunting-coat: the person wearing it: perfect condition (e.g. *in the pink of health*). [Uncertain.]

pink[3], *pink*, *v.i.* to make a tinkling or pinging noise. [Imit.]

pinnace, *pin'is*, *n.* a light sailing ship: a warship's small boat.
[Older Fr. *pinasse.*]

pinnacle, *pin'ȧ-kl*, *n.* a slender turret: a high pointed rock or mountain: the highest point.
[Fr. *pinacle*—L. *pinna*, feather.]

pint, *pīnt*, *n.* a measure of capacity, one-eighth of a gallon (0·57 litre).
[Fr. *pinte*; origin unknown.]

pioneer, *pī-ȯn-ēr'*, *n.* a soldier who builds roads, etc.: one who goes before to clear the way for others: one of the first to do, study, etc., something (e.g. *pioneers in the field of science*).—*v.i.* to act as a pioneer.—*v.t.* to take the first steps in (a new development).
[O.Fr. *pion*, foot-soldier—L. *pēs*, foot.]

pious. See **piety.**

pip[1], *pip*, *n.* a seed of fruit.
[From **pippin.**]

pip[2], *pip*, *n.* a spot on dice, cards, etc.: a star as a mark of rank.
[Origin unknown.]

pip[3], *pip*, *n.* a short note given on the radio and by telephone as a time signal. [Imit.]

pipe, *pīp*, *n.* a musical instrument in which the sound is made by blowing in a tube: any tube, esp. one of earthenware, metal, etc. for carrying water, gas, etc.: a tube with a bowl at the end for smoking: a voice, esp. a high voice: the note of a bird.—*v.i.* to play a pipe.—*v.t.* to play (tune) on a pipe: to utter shrilly: to convey by pipe.
pip'er, *n.* a player on a (bag)pipe.
pip'ing, *adj.* playing a pipe: thin and high-pitched.—*n.* singing (of birds): a system of pipes: small cord used as a trimming for clothes, or sugar trimming a cake.
pipe'line, *n.* a long line of pipes to carry oil from an oil field, etc.: a direct course along which information, etc., is passed.
pipe organ, an organ with pipes.
piping hot, very hot.
in the pipeline, soon to become available, in preparation.
to pipe down, to become quiet, stop talking.
[O.E. *pīpe*—L. *pīpāre*, to cheep.]

pipette, *pip-et'*, *n.* a small glass tube for measuring liquid and conveying it from one vessel to another.
[Fr., from *pipe*, pipe.]

pipit, *pip'it*, *n.* a small bird, rather like a lark. [Imit.]

pippin, *pip'in*, *n.* a kind of apple.
[O.Fr. *pepin.*]

piquant, *pē'kȧnt*, *adj.* sharp: arousing the interest (e.g. *a piquant face, situation*).
pi'quancy, *n.* **pi'quantly,** *adv.*
[Fr., pr.p. of *piquer*, to prick.]

pique, *pēk*, *n.* anger caused by wounded pride, resentment.—*v.t.* to wound the pride of: to arouse (curiosity): to pride (*oneself on* or *upon*):—*pr.p.* **pi'quing**; *pa.p.* **piqued.**
[Fr. *pique*, a pike; same root as **piquant.**]

pirate, *pī'rit*, *n.* one who robs ships at sea: his vessel: one who seizes rights of another (e.g. one who publishes for his own benefit the work of another).—*v.t.* to take without permission.
piracy, *pī'rȧ-si*, *n.* **pīra'tical,** *adj.*
[L. *pīrāta*—Gk. *peiraein*, to attempt.]

pirouette, *pir-ōō-et'*, *n.* a spinning round on tiptoe in dancing.—Also *v.i.* [Fr.]

pistachio, *pis-tâ'shi-ō*, *n.* a greenish seed or nut, used as flavouring.
[It. *pistacchio*—Gk. *pistākion.*]

pistil, *pis'til, -tl*, *n.* the seed-bearing part of a flower.
[L. *pistillum*, a pestle.]

pistol, *pis'tl*, *n.* a small hand-gun.
[O.Fr. *pistole.*]

piston, *pis'tȯn*, *n.* a sliding piece, usu. of metal, which moves up and down a hollow cylinder in engines, pumps, etc.
[Fr.—It. *pistone*—L. root as **pestle.**]

pit, *pit*, *n.* a hole in the earth: a mine shaft: a covered heap (of potatoes, etc.): a hole used as a trap for wild beasts: a hole in ground or floor made to allow underparts of cars to be repaired easily: place beside the course for refuelling and repairing racing cars: the hole or scar left by smallpox: the ground floor of a theatre behind the stalls.—*v.t.* to lay or store in a pit: to set (against) in a contest (e.g. *to pit John against James*):—*pr.p.* **pitt'ing**; *pa.p.* **pitt'ed.**
pit'fall, *n.* a trap for beasts: a danger, usu. hidden.

pit′-prop, *n.* a timber or metal upright support used to hold up the roof in a coal mine.

pit of the stomach, the depression on the body below the breastbone.

[O.E. *pytt*—L. *puteus*, a well.]

pitch[1], *pich, n.* a black shining substance obtained by distilling coal tar or wood.—*v.t.* to cover with pitch.

pitch′-black, *adj.* black as pitch.

pitch′-dark, *adj.* completely dark.

pitch′-pine, *n.* a North American tree from which pitch is obtained.

[O.E. *pic*—L. *pix, picis.*]

pitch[2], *pich, v.t.* to set up, fix firmly in position (e.g. camp, a tent): to throw, toss, or hurl: (*music*) to set at a particular level, set the keynote (e.g. *to pitch one's voice too high*): (*baseball*) to deliver (the ball) to the batsman.—*v.i.* to fall forward: (of a ship) to rise and fall with the waves so that the bow and stern lurch up and down: to slope down: to let one's choice fall (*upon*).—*n.* a throw: the field for certain games: (cricket) the ground between the wickets: place at which e.g. a street trader is stationed: the height or depth of a note: slope or the amount of slope (e.g. *the pitch of the roof*): distance between similar points, e.g. on the thread of a screw: a point, peak, extreme.

pitcher[1], *n.*

pitch′fork, *n.* a fork for pitching hay, etc.: a tuning-fork.—*v.t.* to throw with a pitchfork: to thrust suddenly (into; e.g. *This accident pitchforked him into the position of leader*).

pitch pipe, the small pipe used to set the pitch for singers.

pitched battle, a battle on chosen ground between sides which have been arranged in position beforehand: a fierce battle.

to pitch into, to attack violently.

[Connected with **pick, pike.**]

pitcher[2], *pich′ėr, n.* a large jug for holding or pouring liquids.

[O.Fr. *picher*—Gk. *bīkos*, wine vessel.]

piteous. See **pity.**

pitfall. See **pit.**

pith, *pith, n.* a soft spongy substance inside something, e.g. that in the centre of the stems of plants: the important part (e.g. *the pith of the matter under discussion*).

pith′y, *adj.* full of pith: full of meaning (e.g. *a pithy saying*).

[O.E. *pitha*; conn. Du. *pit.*]

pitiable, pitiful, etc. See **pity.**

piton, *pē-ton*[g], *n.* a steel peg to be driven into rock or ice, used in climbing. [Fr.]

pittance, *pit′ȧns, n.* a very small allowance, a dole: a very small income.

[O.Fr. *pitance*—L. *pietās*, pity.]

pity, *pit′i, n.* feeling for the sufferings of others, sympathy, compassion: a cause of grief: a regrettable fact.—*v.t.* to feel pity for:—*pr.p.* **pit′ying**; *pa.p.* **pit′ied.**

pit′iable, *adj.* to be pitied: contemptible.

pit′iful, *adj.* sad: contemptible.

piteous, *pit′ė-ůs, adj.* arousing pity.

pit′iless, *adj.* without pity: cruel.

[O.Fr. *pite*; same root as **piety.**]

pivot, *piv′ȯt, n.* the pin or centre on which anything turns: that on which anything depends (e.g. a key person, most important fact, etc.).—*v.i.* and *v.t.* (to cause) to turn on, or as if on, a pivot.

piv′otal, *adj.* [Fr.]

pixy, pixie, *pik′si, n.* a small fairy.

[Origin unknown.]

pizza, *pēt′sa, n.* a large flat tart of bread dough spread with tomato, etc., and baked in a hot oven. [It.]

pizzicato, *pit-si-kä′tō, adj.* (*music*) played, not with the bow, but by plucking the strings. [It.]

placable, *plak′-* or *plāk′ȧ-bl, adj.* willing to forgive.

placate, *plȧk-āt′, plāk-, v.t.* to pacify, soothe, appease (an angry person).

[L. *plācāre*, appease, *placēre*, please.]

placard, *plak′ärd, n.* a written or printed paper or poster placed on a wall, etc. (e.g. as an advertisement).—*v.t.* to stick placards on.

[O.Fr. *plackart*—*plaquier*, to lay flat.]

place, *plās, n.* an open space in a town: a village, town, or city (e.g. *in my native place*): a dwelling or home: a building or room with a special purpose (e.g. *one's place of business*): a seat or accommodation in a theatre, train, at table, etc.: position: a particular spot: proper position or dignity: rank: office or employment, esp. in the government: a position won in a competition: (*racing*) a position in the first three: the position of a number in a row or series (e.g. *in the first decimal place*).—*v.t.* to put in any place: to find a place for: to remember who (a person) is.

placed, *adj.* having a place: among the first three in a race or contest.

in place, in proper position: suitable in the circumstances.

in place of, instead of.

out of place, not in position: not suitable in the circumstances.

to be one's place, to be one's duty.

to give, take, place. See **give, take.**

[O.E. *plæce*, Fr. *place*—L. *platēa.*].

placid, *plas′id, adj.* calm, not easily disturbed: peaceful.

[L. *placidus*—*placēre*, to please.]

plagiarise, *plā′jėr-īz, v.t.* to steal from (the writings or ideas of someone else).

pla′giarism, *n.* an act, or the practice, of plagiarising.

[L. *plăgiārius*, a kidnapper.]

plague, *plāg, n.* a deadly epidemic or spreading disease, esp. a fever carried by rat fleas: a great and troublesome quantity (e.g. *a plague of flies*): a

nuisance.—*v.t.* to pester or annoy:—*pr.p.* **plag'uing**; *pa.p.* **plagued.**
[O.Fr.—L. *plāga*, a blow.]

plaice, *plās*, *n.* a yellow-spotted broad flatfish like the flounder.
[O.Fr. *plaïs*—Late L. *platessa*, flatfish.]

plaid, *plād*, *plad*, *n.* a long piece of cloth worn over the shoulder, usu. in tartan (as part of Highland dress).
[Perh. Gael. *plaide*, blanket (but Gael. word may be from Scots).]

plain, *plān*, *adj.* flat, level: clear (e.g. view): clear to the mind, obvious: easily understood (e.g. *plain words*)—often unkindly frank: outspoken: simple, without ornament, not luxurious (e.g. *plain living*): not coloured: not highly born or gifted: without beauty.—*n.* a level stretch of land.
plain'-clothes', *adj.* wearing ordinary clothes, not uniform, as a policeman on detective work.
plain sailing, plane sailing: sailing on an easy course: easy progress.
plains'man, *n.* one who lives in a plain.
plain'-spok'en, *adj.* speaking one's thoughts openly and honestly, or bluntly.
[Fr.—L. *plānus*, level, flat.]

plaint, *plānt*, *n.* a complaint: a mournful song.
plaint'iff, *n.* (*Eng. law*) one who begins a suit against another.
plaint'ive, *adj.* mournful, sorrowful.
plaint'ively, *adv.* **plaint'iveness,** *n.*
[O.Fr. *pleinte*—L. *plangĕre*, to lament.]

plait, *plat*, *plāt*, *n.* a fold made by doubling cloth back on itself (now usu. **pleat**): twined hair, etc.: pigtail or braid:—*v.t.* to braid (hair).
[O.Fr. *pleit*—L. *plicāre*, to fold.]

plan, *plan*, *n.* a drawing of a building showing the shape it makes on the ground or parallel to the ground: a scheme, arrangement to do something: way of doing it.—*v.t.* to make a plan of: to decide on (a course of action):—*pr.p.* **plann'ing**; *pa.p.* **planned.**
[Fr.—L. *plānus*, flat.]

plane[1], *plān*, *n.* any flat or level surface: one of the surfaces such as wings and tail which support an aeroplane in flight: short for aeroplane: any grade or level of life, development, or thought (e.g. *Man is on a higher plane than the apes*).—*adj.* perfectly level: lying within a plane.—*v.t.* to make smooth.—*v.i.* (of a boat) to lift out of the water while in motion, soar.
plane figure, a figure all of whose points lie in one plane or surface.
plane sailing, calculating a ship's position as if the earth were flat.
[L. *plānum*; conn. **plain, plane** (2).]

plane[2], *plān*, *n.* a carpenter's tool for making a smooth surface.—*v.t.* to make (a surface) level by using a plane.
Fr.—Late L. *plānāre*, to smooth.]

plane[3], **plane tree,** *plān' trē*, *n.* a tree with broad leaves.
[Fr.—L. *platanus*—Gk. *platys*, broad.]

planet, *plan'it*, *n.* any body (except a comet or meteor) that revolves about the sun or other fixed star.
plan'etary, *adj.*
plan'etoid, *n.* a minor planet.
[Fr. *planète*—Gk. *planētēs*, wanderer.]

plank, *plangk*, *n.* a long piece of timber, thicker than a board: one of the aims that forms the 'platform' or programme of a political party.—*v.t.* to cover with planks: (*slang*) to lay (down, e.g. money).
plank'ing, *n.* planks.
[L. *planca*, a board.]

plankton, *plangk'tȯn*, *n.* the floating organisms in seas, lakes, etc.
[Gk. *planktos*, wandering.]

plant, *plânt*, *n.* any member of the vegetable kingdom, having stem, root, and leaves: machinery used in a factory: a factory: (*slang*) a swindle, a put-up job.—*v.t.* to put into the ground for growth: to set down firmly: to implant, to cause (e.g. an idea) to take hold: to found, settle (e.g. a colony): (*slang*) to deliver (a blow in a particular place): (*slang*) to place (something) as false evidence or a false clue, or to place (a spy).
plantā'tion, *n.* a place planted, esp. with trees: a large estate used for growing cotton, rubber, tea, etc. in southern U.S. or other warm countries: a colony.
plant'er, *n.* one who plants: the owner of a plantation.
plant house, a building in which to grow plants of warmer climates.
[O.E. *plante*—L. *planta*, cutting.]

plantain[1], *plan'tān*, *n.* a coarse banana.
[Origin uncertain.]

plantain[2], *plan'tān*, *n.* a plant with leaves pressed flat on the ground.
[L. *planta*, the sole of the foot.]

plaque, *plâk*, *n.* a thin piece or tablet of metal, etc. used for ornament (e.g. on a wall), or, with an inscription, to commemorate something. [Fr.]

plasma, *plaz'ma*, *n.* the liquid part of blood, lymph, and milk: a very hot gas.
[Gk. *plasma*, a thing moulded.]

plaster, *plâs'tėr*, *n.* a sticky substance sprea on a cloth, applied to the body to cure an ailment (e.g. *a mustard plaster*): a sticky material, often in strips, used e.g. to hold in place dressings on wounds: a mixture of lime, water, and sand which sets hard and is used to coat walls, ceilings, etc.—*adj.* made of plaster.—*v.t.* to apply plaster to: to smear: to cover too thickly (with).
plas'terer, *n.* one who plasters.
plaster cast, a copy got by pouring a mixture of plaster of Paris and water into a mould of the object.

plaster of Paris, a quick-hardening plaster.
[O.E. *plaster*, O.Fr. *plastre*; from Gk.]

plastic, *plas'tik, adj.* easily moulded or shaped, as clay or wax: concerned with modelling objects: easily influenced.—*n.* a substance that can be moulded: a chemical compound made artificially (not found in nature) that can be used to form materials of many kinds.
plasticity (*-tis'i-ti*), *n.* state, quality, of being plastic or easily moulded.
plastic arts, sculpture, pottery, etc.
plastic operation, or **surgery,** an operation which repairs damaged parts of the body.
[Gk. *plastikos—plassein*, to mould.]

plate, *plāt, n.* a flat sheet of metal: an engraved piece of metal, often one used for printing: a whole page illustration on different paper inserted in a book: a sheet, usu. of glass, coated with a substance sensitive to light and used in photography: the part of false teeth that fits to the mouth: gold and silver articles: a shallow dish for holding food: a helping (of food), a plateful: a platelike dish used for a church collection.—*v.t.* to cover (a metal) with a thin coating of nickel, silver, gold, etc.
plate'ful, *n.*:—*pl.* **plate'fuls.**
plate armour, armour of metal plates.
plate'-glass, *n.* a fine kind of glass cast in thick sheets, used for windows, etc.
plate'layer, *n.* one who lays and fixes the rails of a railway.
[O.Fr. *plate*—Gk. *platys*, broad.]

plateau, *pla'tō, pla-tō', n.* a broad level stretch of high land, a tableland:—*pl.* **plateaux, plateaus** (*-ōz*). [Fr.]

platen, *plat'n, n.* in printing, a plate or roller that presses paper against inked type: the roller of a typewriter.
[Fr. *platine—plat*, flat.]

platform, *plat'förm, n.* a raised level surface, as that in a railway station: a raised floor for speakers, entertainers, etc.: a position for mounting a gun: a piece of flooring at the entrance to a bus, etc.: the plan or policy made public by a political party.
[Fr. *plateforme*, platform of bus, etc.—*plat*, flat, *forme*, form.]

platinum, *plat'in-ům, n.* a valuable heavy steel-grey metal used in electrical and electronic apparatus, jewellery, etc.
[Sp. *platina—plata*, silver.]

platitude, *plat'i-tūd, n.* a dull, ordinary remark made as if it were important.
platitud'inous, *adj.*
[Fr.—*plat*, flat.]

Platonic, *plȧ-ton'ik, adj.* having to do with the old Greek philosopher Plato or his teaching: (of love) on a spiritual level, without physical passion.
platon'ically, *adv.*
[Gk. *platōnikos—Platōn*, Plato.]

platoon, *plȧ-to͞on', n.* a part, subdivision, of a company of soldiers.
[Fr. *peloton*, group of men—L. *pĭla*, ball.]

platter, *plat'ėr, n.* a large flat plate.
[O.Fr. *plat*, a plate.]

platypus, *plat'i-pus, n.* a small water animal of Australia and Tasmania, with webbed feet, that lays eggs.
[Gk. *platys*, flat, *pous*, foot.]

plaudit, *plöd'it, n.* (usu. in *pl.* **plaudits**) a round of applause: praise.
[L. *plaudite* (Roman actor's call for applause); same root as **plausible.**]

plausible, *plöz'i-bl, adj.* seeming to be worthy of (orig.) praise, (now) belief: (of e.g. an explanation) reasonable.
[L. *plaudĕre, plausum*, to clap the hands.]

play, *plā, v.i.* to gambol, frisk, as a young animal does: to take part in games or amusements: to amuse oneself (with): to trifle (with; e.g. *The child plays with his food*): to gamble: to act on a stage: to perform on an instrument: to move to and fro, to flicker: to move freely as part of a mechanism.—*v.t.* to act (a part): to take part in (a game): to compete against in a game: to perform music on: to carry out (a trick): to bring about (e.g. *to play havoc*): to direct on (e.g. *They played hoses on the fire*): to give a certain freedom of action to (e.g. *to play a fish*).—*n.* recreation: amusement: the playing of a game: gambling: a drama, acted story: manner of dealing (e.g. *fair play*): freedom of movement (e.g. *to give full play to*).
play'er, *n.*
play'ful, *adj.* (of e.g. kitten) full of desire to play: joking, not serious.
played out, exhausted: used up.
play'fellow, play'mate, *ns.* a friend with whom one plays.
play'house, *n.* a theatre.
play'thing, *n.* a toy: someone, etc. treated as if a toy.
play'wright, *n.* a dramatist.
play upon words, a pun, etc.
to hold in play, to keep (a person) busy, esp. in order to gain time.
to play ball (with), to work for the same end, co-operate (with).
to play fair (false), to act, or act towards, in a fair and honest (dishonest) way.
to play for time, to act so as to gain time and better opportunity.
to play into a person's hands, to act so as to give him the advantage.
to play off, to pass (a thing) off (as something else): to set (one person) against (another): to decide (a tie) by playing again.
to play on, to work upon and make use of (e.g. *to play on a person's fears*).
to play out, to play to the end, finish.
to play the game, act fairly and honestly.
to play up to, (*coll.*) to flatter.
in (out of) play, in (out of) a position in

which the rules allow it to be played (of a ball in a game).
[O.E. *pleg(i)an*, vb., *plega*, n.]

plea, *plē*, *n.* an excuse: a prisoner's answer to a charge: urgent request.
plead, *plēd*, *v.i.* to carry on a lawsuit: to argue in favour of a cause in court, or to give an answer in defence: to beg earnestly (with *with*; e.g. *You must plead with Mary not to go*).—*v.t.* to support (a cause) by argument: to give as an excuse (e.g. *to plead ignorance*):—*pa.t.* and *pa.p.* **plead'ed,** or **pled.**
plead'ings, *n.* the statements of the two sides in a lawsuit.
to plead guilty, or **not guilty,** to admit, or deny, guilt.
special pleading, unfair argument aiming at winning rather than at truth.
[O.Fr. *plai*, lawsuit, *plaidier*, plead.]

please, *plēz*, *v.t.* to give pleasure to: to delight: to satisfy.—*v.i.* to give pleasure: to choose (e.g. *He does as he pleases*).
pleas'ant, *plez'ȧnt*, *adj.* agreeable: cheerful.
pleas'antly, *adv.* **pleas'antness,** *n.*
pleas'antry, *n.* good-humoured joking.
pleas'ing, *adj.* attractive, charming.
pleasure, *plezh'ůr*, *n.* state of enjoyment or joy: delight: frivolous enjoyment as one's chief aim (e.g. *to live a life of pleasure*): what one wishes (e.g. *What is your pleasure?*).
pleas'urable (*plezh'*), *adj.* delightful.
pleas'ure-boat, *n.* a boat used for amusement.
at pleasure, when or if one pleases.
(if you) please, if you are willing (added for politeness to a command or request).
[O.Fr. *plaisir*, to please—L. *placēre*.]

pleat, *plēt*. See **plait.**

plebeian, *plė-bē'ȧn*, *adj.* of the common people: common, vulgar.—Also *n.*
plebiscite *pleb'i-sit*, *-sīt*, *n.* a direct vote of the whole nation or region on a special point.
[L. *plēbs*, the people (*scīscĕre*, vote for).]

pledge, *plej*, *n.* something handed over by a person who borrows money, etc., which will not be returned to him if he does not repay, etc.: a solemn promise.—*v.t.* to give as security, to pawn: to promise: to drink to the health of.
[O.Fr. *plege*.]

plenary, *plē'nȧr-i*, *adj.* full, complete: fully attended (e.g. an assembly).
plenary powers, full powers to carry out some business.
plenipotentiary, *plen-i-pō-ten'shȧr-i*, *adj.* having full powers.—*n.* a person with full powers, as an ambassador.
plenitude, *plen'i-tūd*, *n.* fullness: abundance.
[L. root as **plenty** (*potentia*, power).]

plenty *plen'ti*, *n.* a full supply: abundance (of food, money, etc.).
plenteous (*poetic*), *plen'tyůs*, **plen'tiful,** *adjs.* generously sufficient, abundant.
[O.Fr. *plente*—L. *plēnus*, full.]

plethora, *pleth'ȯr-a*, *n.* state of having too much e.g. blood: a too large quantity (of).
plethoric (*-thor'ik*), *adj.*
[Gk. *plēthōra*, fullness.]

pleurisy, *ploo͞'ri-si*, *n.* inflammation of membrane covering the lung.
[Gk. *pleurā*, rib, side.]

pliable, plied, pliers. See **ply** (1).

plight[1], *plīt*, *v.t.* to pledge (e.g. one's word, troth—see this):—*pa.p.* **plight'ed.**
[O.E. *pliht*, risk, *plēon*, to risk.]

plight[2], *plīt*, *n.* state, situation (usu. bad; e.g. *a hopeless plight*, *sad plight*).
[O.Fr. *plite*—L. *plicāre*, to fold.]

plimsoll, *plim'sȯl*, *-sol*, *n.* a rubber-soled canvas shoe. [Perh. from next entry.]

Plimsoll('s) line or **mark,** a ship's load-line (see this word). [Samuel *Plimsoll*].

plod, *plod*, *v.i.* to walk heavily and slowly: to work or study steadily, toil:—*pr.p.* **plodd'ing**; *pa.p.* **plodd'ed.**
plodd'er, *n.* a dull or slow but hard-working person. [Prob. imit.]

plop, *plop*, *n.* the sound of a small object falling into water.—*v.i.* to make the sound of a plop. [Imit.]

plot, *plot*, *n.* a small piece of ground: the main story told in a play, novel, etc.: a secret plan or scheme, esp. for doing evil.—*v.t.* to make a plan of, show by a graph: to mark (points) on a graph: to work out secret plans for (something evil), plan (to do).—*v.i.* to form a plot:—*pr.p.* **plott'ing**; *pa.p.* **plott'ed.**
plott'er, *n.*
[O.E.; conn. Fr. *complot*, conspiracy.]

plough, *plow*, *n.* a tool for turning up the soil: (*coll.*) failure in an examination.—*v.t.* to turn up (the ground) in furrows: (of ship) to make a way through (e.g. the sea).—*v.i.* to tear or force a way (through; e.g. *The car ploughed through the crowd*).—*v.t.* and *v.i.* to fail in (an examination).
ploughshare, *plow'shār*, *n.* the blade of the plough, which cuts the slice of earth.
the Plough, a group of stars forming a shape like a plough, containing the Pointers (two stars in line with the North Star).
to plough back, to put (profits of a business) back into the business.
to put one's hand to the plough, to begin a project or business.
[Late O.E. *plōh*, land suitable for crops (*scear*, ploughshare—*scieran*, to cut).]

plover, *pluv'ėr*, *n.* the lapwing or related bird.
[Fr. *pluvier*—L. *pluvia*, rain.]

plow (chiefly *U.S.*). Same as **plough.**

pluck, *pluk*, *v.t.* to pull off or out: to strip the feathers off (a fowl): to pull (a string of a musical instrument): (*coll.*) to fail (a candidate) in an examination.—

v.i. to tug (at).—*n.* the heart, liver, and lungs of an animal—whence used for courage, spirit: an act of plucking.
pluck'y, *adj.* brave, resolute:—*comp.* **pluck'ier**; *superl.* **pluck'iest.**
pluck'ily, *adv.* **pluck'iness,** *n.*
to pluck up, to pull out by the roots: to rouse up in oneself (e.g. courage).
[O.E. *pluccian*; conn. with Du. *plukken.*]

plug, *plug,* *n.* a block, peg, or wad of material, used to stop a hole: a fitting put into a socket to get electric current: a connexion in a water main for a hose; device releasing flow of water: a cake of tobacco: a sparking plug.—*v.t.* to stop with a plug: (*slang*) to shoot, or to hit with the fist: (*coll.*) to advertise or publicise by repeating or mentioning often. —*v.i.* (*coll.*) to plod, keep working (at a dull or difficult task):—*pr.p.* **plugg'ing**; *pa.p.* **plugged.**
[Prob. Du.]

plum, *plum,* *n.* a fruit of blue-red colour with a stone in the centre: the tree bearing it: a raisin when used in cake or pudding: a good thing (e.g. *a plum of a job*).
plum'-pudding, *n.* a pudding of flour, suet, raisins, currants, etc.
[O.E. *plūme*—L. *prūnum*; from Gk.]

plumage. See **plume.**

plumb, *plum,* *n.* a lead weight hung on a string (or **plumb line**), used to tell a straight up and down position by builders, etc., a plummet.—*adj.* straight up and down, vertical.—*adv.* vertically: exactly: (*coll.* esp. *U.S.*) downright (e.g. *That is plumb stupid*).—*v.t.* to test by a plumb line (e.g. *to plumb a wall*): to test the depth of (the sea, etc.): to reach the bottom of (e.g. *to plumb the depths of misery*).
plumber, *plum'ėr,* *n.* a person who fits and mends pipes (water, gas, and sewage fittings).
plumbing, *plum'ing,* *n.* the craft of a plumber: the pipes fitted by a plumber.
plumb bob, the weight at the end of a plumb line.
[Fr. *plomb,* lead—L. *plumbum.*]

plume, *ploōm,* *n.* a feather, esp. a large showy one: a bird's crest: something looking like a feather (e.g. *a plume of smoke*): a tuft of feathers used as an ornament, as on a helmet.—*v.t.* to pride (oneself: e.g. *He plumed himself on his success*).
plumage, *ploōm'ij,* *n.* feathers.
borrowed plumes, finery, or honour, that does not really belong to one.
[O.Fr.—L. *plūma,* a small feather.]

plummet, *plum'it,* *n.* a plumb bob for measuring depths.—*v.i.* to plunge.
[O.Fr. *plomet*; same root as **plumb.**]

plump[1], *plump,* *v.i.* to drop or fall suddenly (into a liquid): to give all one's votes to one candidate (*to plump for Jones*).—*v.t.* to fling down or let fall flat or heavily. —*n.* the sound or act of plumping.—*adv.* with a plump: in plain language, bluntly: directly, without a pause.—*adj.* blunt, direct.
[Conn. Du. *plompen.*]

plump[2], *plump,* *adj.* pleasantly fat and rounded, well filled out.—Also *v.t.*, *v.i.*
plump'ness, *n.*
[Middle Du. *plomp,* blunt, Ger. *plump.*]

plunder, *plun'dėr,* *v.t.* to carry off the goods of (another) by force: to loot, rob (a place).—Also *v.i.*—*n.* booty.
[Ger. *plündern,* to pillage.]

plunge, *plunj,* *v.t.* to thrust suddenly (into water, other liquid, a hole): to push deep into (e.g. *to plunge a person in gloom, a nation into war*).—*v.i.* to throw oneself (e.g. into water): to rush (e.g. into danger): to pitch forward suddenly, as a ship or horse: to gamble recklessly.—*n.* act of plunging: a dive.
plung'er, *n.* one who plunges: a piston used as a forcer in pumps, etc.
[O.Fr. *plonger*; same root as **plumb.**]

plural, *ploōr'ȧl,* *adj.* expressing more than one.—*n.* (*grammar*) the form of a word showing more than one (e.g. *boxes* is the plural of *box*).
[L. *plurālis*—*plūs, plūris,* more.]

plus, *plus,* *prep.* with the addition of.—*adj.* positive: positively electrified.—*adv.* (*coll.*) and a little more.—*n.* the sign (+) before positive quantities or between numbers to be added.
[L. *plūs,* more; same root as **plural.**]

plush, *plush,* *n.* a cloth of cotton, silk, etc. with long pile.—*adj.* luxurious (e.g. *plush apartments*).
plush'y, *adj.* **plush'iness,** *n.*
[Fr. *peluche*—L. root as **pile** (3).]

plutocracy, *ploō-tok'rȧ-si,* *n.* government by the rich: a ruling body of rich men.
plutocrat, *ploō'tō-krat,* *n.* one who is powerful because of his money.
[Gk. *ploutos,* wealth, *krateein,* to rule.]

ply[1], *plī,* *n.* a fold, layer: a strand of rope, etc.—*v.t.* and *v.i.* to bend, fold:—*pr.p.* **ply'ing**; *pa.p.* **plied.**
pliable, *plī'ȧ-bl,* *adj.* easily bent or folded, flexible: easily persuaded.—Also **plī'ant.**
pliabil'ity, pli'ancy, *ns.*
pli'er, *n.* one who plies: (in *pl.*) small pincers for bending or cutting wire, etc.
ply'wood, boarding made of thin layers of wood glued together.
[O.Fr. *pli,* a fold—L. *plicāre,* to fold.]

ply[2], *plī,* *v.t.* to work at steadily: to use with vigour (e.g. *to ply an axe*): to keep supplying (e.g. *to ply the guests with food*): to address continually (e.g. *to ply someone with questions*).—*v.i.* to make regular journeys over a route (e.g. *The ship plies between London and Glasgow*):—*pr.p.* **ply'ing**; *pa.p.* **plied.** [**apply.**]

pneumatic, *nū-mat'ik,* *adj.* filled with air: moved by air.
pneumat'ically, *adv.*

pneumonia, *nū-mō′ni-ȧ, n.* a disease in which the lungs become inflamed.
[Gk. *pneuma*, breath, *pneumōn*, lung—*pneein*, to breathe.]

poach[1], *pōch, v.t.* to cook (eggs, etc.) in very hot liquid, e.g. water.
[O.F. *pochier*, to pocket (the egg white being a 'pocket' round the yolk).]

poach[2], *pōch, v.i.* to intrude on another's ground in order to hunt game or catch fish illegally: to try to play a ball one's partner should play.—Also *v.t.*
poach′er, *n.*
[Prob. **poke** (2).]

pock, *pok, n.* a small blister on the skin, as in smallpox.
pock′mark, *n.* the pit or scar left by a pock.—Also *v.t.*
See also **pox.**
[O.E. *poc*; conn. Ger. *pocke*.]

pocket, *pok′it, n.* a little pouch or bag, esp. in a garment or a billiard table: (one's) money or resources: (**air pocket**) an area of different pressure: a small isolated area or patch (e.g. *a pocket of unemployment*).—*v.t.* to put in the pocket: to steal.
pock′et-book, *n.* a wallet for papers or money carried in the pocket.
pocket money, money for personal expenses: an allowance, esp. to a child.
in, out of, pocket, with, or without, money: richer, or poorer, after a deal.
[M.E. *poket*; conn. Fr. *poche*.]

pod, *pod, n.* the long seed-case or shell in peas, beans, etc.—*v.i.* to form pods.
[Origin unknown.]

podgy, *poj′i, adj.* short and fat.
[Origin uncertain.]

poem, *pō′im, n.* a piece of writing in lines which usu. have a regular beat and often rhyme: a piece of writing in striking language or showing imagination or beauty of thought, which may or may not be in metre.
poet, *pō′it, n.* the author of a poem: one with a great imagination and the ability to express this in striking language:—*fem.* **po′et, po′etess** (the latter unflattering).
poetic, *pō-et′ik, adj.* having to do with poetry, like poetry: in the language of poetry: imaginative.
po′etry, *n.* the art of the poet: the special quality of poems: poems as a whole.
poetic justice, ideal justice, giving out of rewards and punishments as deserved.
poet laureate, an official poet attached to the royal household.
[Fr. *poème, poète*—Gk. *poieein*, to make.]

poignant, *poin′ȧnt, -yȧnt, adj.* sharp, very painful (e.g. *poignant regret*): very sad (e.g. *a poignant scene*): (of interest) very keen.
[O.Fr. *poignant*—L. *pungĕre*, to sting.]

point, *point, n.* a dot: a mark of punctuation, esp. the full stop: the dot used in writing decimals (e.g. 4·2, *four point two*): an exact place, spot: a moment in time (e.g. *at the point of death*): a place in a scale (e.g. *boiling point*): a division on a compass: a mark in scoring a competition, game, or test: a sharp end of anything: a cape or headland: a movable rail for passing (e.g. a locomotive) from one track to another: a detail to be taken into account: the main question in an argument or discussion: the meaning or force of a story or joke: an aim (e.g. *He gained his point*): a trait, quality (e.g. *I do not like him, but he has his good points*): in various games, (the position of) a certain player, e.g. in cricket (that of) a fielder near the batsman on the off side.—*v.t.* to give a point to: to aim or direct (at): to draw attention to (*to point out*): to fill the joints of (stone- or brickwork) with mortar: to give force or special meaning to (a remark).—*v.i.* to direct the finger or eye towards an object: to show game by looking, as a dog does.
point′ed, *adj.* having a sharp point: sharp: having force or meaning: (of a remark) obviously aimed at someone.
point′er, *n.* a rod for pointing: a dog trained to look for game: a hint, suggestion.
point′less, *adj.* having no meaning: senseless.
point duty, the duty e.g. of a policeman stationed at a particular point to regulate traffic.
point of order, a question raised in a meeting as to whether the business is being done according to the rules.
point of view, the way in which one looks at things.
a case in point, an example illustrating the matter being discussed.
in point of fact, in fact.
on the point of (doing something), just going to (do it).
to make a point of, to treat as important: to insist upon (doing something, or having something done).
to the point, connected with the matter being discussed.
[Fr. *point*, dot, *pointe*, sharp point.]

point-blank, *point′-blangk′, adj.* (of a shot) fired levelly, from close range: direct, plain (e.g. *a point-blank question*).
[**point** (vb.) and **blank** (of the target).]

poise, *poiz, v.t.* to balance evenly: to hold ready to throw or drop.—Also *v.i.*—*n.* state of balance: dignity and self-confidence: carriage (of body, head).
[O.Fr. *poiser* (vb.)—L. *pensum*, weight.]

poison, *poi′zn, n.* any substance which, when taken into the body, kills, or harms health: anything harmful.—*v.t.* to injure or kill, or to make harmful, with poison: to corrupt, or cause to think evil (e.g. a person, his mind).

pois'oner, *n.* **pois'onous,** *adj.*
[O.Fr. *puison*—same L. root as **potion.**]

poke[1], *pōk, n.* a bag, sack. [M.E.]

poke[2], *pōk, v.t.* to push (something into something): to thrust at: to stir (up).—*v.i.* to grope or feel (about): to go prying or searching (into): to stick out.—*n.* a prod, nudge: a look, search.
po'ker, *n.* a rod for stirring a fire.
pō'ky, *adj.* small, cramped, and shabby: (of e.g. a job) pottering, dull:—*comp.* **pok'ier**; *superl.* **pok'iest.**
to poke one's nose into, to pry into (other people's concerns).
[M.E. *pōken*; of Germanic origin.]

poker[1]. See **poke** (2).

poker[2], *pō'kėr, n.* a gambling card game.
poker face, *n.* a blank face or expression telling nothing of the emotions behind it, useful to a poker player.
[Origin uncertain.]

polar. See **pole** (1).

polder, *pōl'dėr, pol', n.* land below sea level reclaimed for use. [Du.]

pole[1], *pōl, n.* the north or the south end of the earth's axis: either of the two points in the heavens (north and south) to which the earth's axis points and around which the stars appear to turn: opposite points of a magnet: an electrical terminal.
pol'ar, *adj.* having to do with a pole: near, or living near, a pole (e.g. *polar regions, polar bear*).
[L. *polus*—Gk. *polos,* axis.]

pole[2], *pōl, n.* a long rounded rod or post, usu. of wood: a measure of length, or of area.—*v.t.* to push (e.g. a boat) with a pole.
[O.E. *pāl*—L. *pālus,* a stake.]

Pole, *pōl, n.* a native or citizen of *Poland.*
Pol'ish, *adj.* of Poland or its people.—*n.* the language of Poland.

pole-ax(e), *pōl'-aks, n.* a battleaxe having a long handle.
[Orig. *pollax*—**poll,** head, and **axe.**]

polecat, *pōl'kat, n.* an animal like a weasel which gives off a strong smell: (*U.S.*) a skunk.
[M.E. *polcat.*]

polemic(al), *po-lem'ik(-ȧl), adjs.* having to do with controversy or dispute.
[Gk. *polemikos*—*polemos,* war.]

police, *pol-ēs', n.* the body of men employed to keep order, enforce laws, etc. in a country.—*v.t.* to control by means of police.
police court, a court that tries people guilty of small offences.
police'man,-woman, *ns.*
police office, station, the headquarters of the police in a district.
police state, a country in which secret police keep down all opposition to the government.
[Fr.—Gk. *politeiā*—*polis,* a city.]

policy[1], *pol'i-si, n.* a course of action decided on by a government, political party, person, etc.: wisdom in managing affairs.
See also **politic.**
[O.Fr. *policie*—same root as **police.**]

policy[2], *pol'i-si, n.* a writing containing an agreement with an insurance company.
[Fr. *police*—Gk. *apodeixis,* proof.]

polio, *pōl'i-ō, n.* short for **poliomyelitis,** *pōl-i-ō-mī-e-lī'tis, n.* inflammation of the grey matter of the spinal cord, a disease also called 'infantile paralysis'.
[Gk. *polios,* grey, *myelos,* marrow.]

Polish. See **Pole.**

polish, *pol'ish, v.t.* to make smooth and shiny by rubbing: to improve, make polite and refined (manners, literary style, etc.).—*v.i.* to take a polish.—*n.* gloss: a substance used to produce a smooth surface: refinement.
[O.Fr. *polir, polissant*—L. *polīre.*]

polite, *po-līt', adj.* having or showing good manners, courteous.
[L. *polītus*—same root as **polish.**]

politic, *pol'i-tik, adj.* (of actions) wise, following a good policy, leading to one's advantage: (of persons) shrewd.
polit'ical, *adj.* having to do with government: having to do with parties that have different views of government.
polit'ically, *adv.*
politician, *-tish'ȧn, n.* one whose business is politics: one skilled in the ways of party politics (often used in a bad sense).
pol'itics, *n.* political affairs, or methods, or principles: the art or science of government.
political economy, economics.
See also **policy** (1).
[Gk. *polītikos*—*polītēs,* citizen, *polis,* city.

polka, *pol'ka, pōl', n.* a dance in 2-4 time.
[Prob. Polish *polka,* a Polish woman.]

poll, *pōl, n.* the head: an individual: a counting of voters: (usu. in *pl.*) a place of voting: a total number of votes: the taking of public opinion by means of questioning.—*v.t.* to cut the hair or horns from, or to cut the top off: to receive (a number of votes).
polled, *adj.* hornless.
polling booth, place where people vote.
[A Germanic word.]

pollard, *pol'ȧrd, n.* a tree having the top cut off: an animal which has had its horns taken off. [**poll.**]

pollen, *pol'ėn, n.* the fertilising powder in flowers.
pollinā'tion, *n.* the carrying of pollen to the stigma of a flower by insects, etc.
[L. *pollen,* fine flour.]

pollute, *pol-ōōt', -ūt', v.t.* to make filthy, contaminate: to use (something sacred) without respect.
pollū'tion, *n.*
[L. *polluěre*—*per-, luěre,* to wash.]

polo, *pō'lō, n.* a game like hockey played on horseback.

polo neck, on a garment, a close-fitting neck with a part turned over at the top.
[From a Tibetan word meaning 'ball'.]

poltergeist, *pol′tėr-gist,* *n.* a noisy ghost, said to move furniture.
[Ger. *poltern,* make noise, *geist,* spirit.]

poltroon, *pol-trōōn′,* *n.* a mean coward.
poltroon′ery, *n.* mean cowardice.
[Fr. *poltron*—It. *poltrone,* sluggard.]

poly-, *pol-i-,* (as part of word) much, many.
polygamy, *pol-ig′à-mi,* *n.* the custom of having more than one husband or wife at the same time.
polyg′amist, *n.* **polyg′amous,** *adj.*
polyglot, *pol′i-glot,* *adj.* using many languages.—*n.* one who speaks or writes many languages.
polygon, *pol′i-gon,* *n.* a figure of many angles and sides.
polymerisation, *pol-i-mėr-i-zā′sh(ȯ)n,* *n.* a process by which many of the plastics are obtained (the combining of several molecules of a substance to form one large molecule of a new substance).
polyp, *pol′ip,* *n.* an animal with many arms or tentacles (either an animal more or less fixed to the place where it lives or one joined to others).
polysyllable, *pol′i-sil-à-bl,* *n.* a word of three or more syllables.
polytechnic, *-tek′nik,* *n.* a school in which various technical subjects are taught.
polytheism, *-thē-izm,* *n.* belief in many gods.
pol′ythene, polyeth′ylene, *ns.* name for several types of plastics which can be moulded when hot.
[Gk. *polys,* many (*gamos,* marriage; *glōtta,* tongue; *gōniā,* corner; *meros,* part; *pous,* foot; *technē,* art; *theos,* god).]

pomade, *po-mäd′, -mād′,* *n.* ointment for the hair. [Fr. *pommade.*]

pomegranate, *pom′gran-it,* *n.* a large fruit with a thick rind and many seeds.
[L. *pōmum,* apple, *grānātum,* seeded.]

pommel, *pum′ėl,* *n.* the knob on a sword-hilt: the high part in front of a saddle.—*v.t.* to pummel. [O.Fr. *pomel.*]

pomp, *pomp,* *n.* splendid display, great ceremony.
pomp′ous, *adj.* grand and self-important in manner.
pomp′ousness, pompos′ity, *ns.*
[Fr. *pompe*—Gk. *pompē*—*pempein,* send.]

poncho, *pon′chō,* *n.* a South American cloak, a blanket with a hole in the middle for the head:—*pl.* **pon′chos.**
[Sp.—South American Indian word.]

pond, *pond,* *n.* a small lake, usu. artificial.
[M.E. *ponde*; from **pound,** enclosure.]

ponder, *pon′dėr,* *v.t.* to think over, consider.—*v.i.* to think (about, over).
pon′derous, *adj.* weighty, clumsy, difficult to handle: (of manner, style) solemn and dull.
pon′derously, *adv.* **pon′derousness,** *n.*
[L. *ponderāre,* to weigh, ponder.]

poniard, *pon′yȧrd,* *n.* a small dagger.
[Fr. *poignard*—*poing,* fist—L. *pugnus.*]

pontiff, *pon′tif,* *n.* (*Roman Catholic*) a bishop, esp. the pope.
pontif′ical, *adj.* belonging to a pontiff: speaking, or spoken, pompously, as if with authority.
pontif′icals, *n.pl.* the dress or robes of a bishop or pope.
pontif′icate, *n.* the office and dignity or reign of a pope.—*v.i.* to speak in a pompous manner.
[L. *pontifex,* a high priest.]

pontoon, *pon-tōōn′,* *n.* a flat-bottomed boat: a float: such a boat or float used to support a bridge.
[Fr. *ponton*—L. *pons,* bridge.]

pony, *pō′ni,* *n.* a small horse.
po′ny-trekking, *n.* the pastime of riding cross-country in small parties.
[Scots *powny*; prob. L. *pullus,* young animal.]

poodle, *pōō′dl,* *n.* a curly-haired dog, fond of water, often clipped in a fancy manner.
[Ger. *pudel* (*hund*), splash (dog); conn. with **puddle.**]

pooh, *pōō,* *interj.* sound of scorn.—*v.t.* **pooh-pooh′,** to make light of. [Imit.]

pool[1], *pōōl,* *n.* a small body of still water: a deep part of a stream.
[O.E. *pōl*; conn. with Ger. *pfuhl.*]

pool[2], *pōōl,* *n.* the stakes or amount of money played for in certain games and contests: a game in which the winner takes the pool or part of it: a variety of billiards: a common or joint stock or fund: a combination, e.g. of firms to gain control of the market.—*v.t.* to put into a joint fund or stock.
football pool, a gamble in which players predict the results of certain games, the ones who are right winning a part of the money paid to enter the gamble.
[Fr. *poule,* a hen, stakes.]

poop, *pōōp,* *n.* the back part or stern of a ship: a high deck in the stern.
[Fr. *poupe*—L. *puppis.*]

poor, *pōōr, pör,* *adj.* having little money or few possessions: not good, inferior, unsatisfactory (e.g. *goods of poor quality*): lacking (in): to be pitied (e.g. *Poor Tom has had many troubles*).—*n.* **(the poor)** those with little money.
poor′ly, *adv.* **poor′ness,** *n.*
poor′ly, *adj.* not in good health.
poverty, *pov′ėr-ti,* *n.* poorness, state of lacking money, etc., or good qualities: lack, scarcity (of e.g. ideas).
pov′erty-stricken, suffering from poverty.
poor′house, *n.* house paid for by public money for sheltering the very poor.
[O.Fr. *povre, poure*—L. *pauper,* poor.]

pop[1], *pop,* *n.* a sharp, quick sound, as of drawing a cork: a shot.—*v.i.* to make a pop: to shoot: to come or go suddenly (*to pop in, out,* etc.).—*v.t.* to cause to make a pop: (*slang*) to pawn:—*pr.p.*

popp′ing; *pa.p.* **popped.**
pop′corn, *n.* kind of maize which bursts open when heated.
pop′gun, *n.* a tube and rammer for shooting pellets by compressed air.
to pop off, (*slang*) to die.
[Imit.]
pop[2]. Short for **popular.**
pop[3], *pop, n.* (*slang*) father. [*poppa*—**papa.**]
pope, *pōp, n.* (often with *cap.*) the bishop of Rome, head of the Roman Catholic Church.
pope′dom, *n.* office, dignity, or authority of the pope.
pop′ery, *n.* a hostile term for Roman Catholicism.
[O.E. *pāpa*—L.—Gk. *pappas*, a father.]
popinjay, *pop′in-jā, n.* a parrot: a target shaped like one: a fop or dandy.
[O.Fr. *papegai*; from Late L. and Gk.]
poplar, *pop′lȧr, n.* a spire-shaped tree, tall and quick-growing.
[O.Fr. *poplier*—L. *pōpulus*, poplar tree.]
poplin, *pop′lin, n.* a strong dress material ribbed crosswise.
[Fr. *popeline*—It. *papalina*, papal; it was made at the papal town of Avignon.]
poppy, *pop′i, n.* a cornfield flower of showy colours, usu. red: a related plant from which opium is obtained:—*pl.* **popp′ies.**
[O.E. *popig*—L. *papāver*.]
populace, *pop′ū-lȧs, n.* the common people.
pop′ulāte, *v.t.* to fill with people.
populā′tion, *n.* the people, or number of people, living in any place.
pop′ulous, *adj.* (of country, region) full of people.
[Fr.—same L. root as **popular, people.**]
popular, *pop′ū-lȧr, adj.* pleasing to most people: widely held (e.g. *a popular belief*): easily understood by ordinary people (e.g. *a popular account of modern science*): of the people (e.g. *chosen by popular vote*).
popular′ity, *n.* **pop′ularly,** *adv.*
pop′ularise, *v.t.* to make generally known or widely liked: to simplify so as to make easily understood by ordinary people.
popular front, an alliance of those parties in a country that want to make the greatest changes (e.g. of Communists with Labour).
[L. *populus*, the people.]
porcelain, *pōrs′lin, pōrs′-, n.* a fine thin white china.
[It. *porcellana*, orig. a kind of shell.]
porch, *pōrch, pörch, n.* a building forming an enclosure or covering for a doorway: (*U.S.*) a veranda.
[O.Fr. *porche*—L. *porta*, a gate.]
porcupine, *pör′kū-pīn, n.* a gnawing animal with bristling quills or spines in its hair.
[O.Fr. *porc espin*, spine pig—L. *procus*, pig.]
pore[1], *pōr, pör, n.* a tiny opening esp. that of a sweat gland.
por′ous, *adj.* having pores: (of a material) through which fluid will pass.
[Fr.—L. *porus*—Gk. *poros*, a passage.]
pore[2], *pōr, pör, v.i.* to look with great attention (e.g. *He pores over his books*).
[Origin uncertain.]
pork, *pörk, pōrk, n.* the flesh of the pig.
pork′er, *n.* a young pig.
pork chop, a slice from a pig's rib.
pork-pie hat, a soft felt hat with a round flat crown and turned-up brim.
[Fr. *porc*—L. *porcus*, a pig.]
pornography, *pör-nog′rȧ-fi, n.* indecent literature or art.
pornograph′ic, *adj.* **pornog′rapher,** *n.*
[Gk. *pornē*, a whore, *graphein*, to write.]
porous. See **pore** (1).
porpoise, *pör′pu̇s, n.* a blunt-nosed sea animal like the dolphin.
[L. *porcus*, pig, *piscis*, fish.]
porridge, *por′ij, n.* a food made from oatmeal in boiling water or milk. [**pottage.**]
port[1], *pōrt, pört, n.* the left side of a ship.—*v.i.* and *v.t.* to turn left.
[Origin uncertain.]
port[2], *pōrt, pört, v.t.* to hold (a rifle) in a slanting position across the body.
port′able, *adj.* easily carried or moved.
port′age, *n.* act, or cost, of carrying: route over which boats, goods, have to be carried overland between waterways.
[Fr. *porter*, to carry—L. *portāre*.]
port[3], *pōrt, pört, n.* a harbour: a town with a harbour.
port of call, a port where vessels can call for stores or repairs.
port of entry, a port where goods are allowed by law to enter.
[O.E.—L. *portus*; conn. L. *porta*, gate.]
port[4], *pōrt, pört, n.* a town gate or its former position (chiefly Scot.).
[Fr. *porte*—L. *porta*, gate.]
port[5], *pōrt, pört, n.* a dark-red wine.
[From *Oporto*, in Portugal.]
portal, *pōr′tȧl, pör′-, n.* doorway or entrance, esp. a magnificent one.
[O.Fr.—L. *porta*; root as **port** (3), (4),]
portcullis, *pōrt-kul′is, pört-, n.* a grating that can be let down to close a gateway.
[O.Fr. *porte coleice*, sliding gate.]
portend, *pör-tend′, pōr-, v.t.* (of an omen) to give warning of, foretell.
portent, *pōr′tent, pör′, n.* a forewarning, sign of what is to come.
portent′ous, *adj.* like a warning: very great: dreadful: impressive (e.g. *She had a portentous manner*).
[L. *portendĕre*—*tendĕre, tentum*, stretch.]
porter[1], *pōrt′ėr, pört′, n.* a doorkeeper or gatekeeper.
[O.Fr. *portier*—L. *porta*, gate.]
porter[2], *pōrt′ėr, pört′, n.* one who carries luggage, etc. for hire: a dark brown beer.
[O.Fr. *porteour*—L. *portāre*, to carry.]
portfolio, *pōrt-fō′li-ō, pört-, n.* a portable

case for loose papers, drawings, etc.: a collection of such papers: a list of investments held: the post of a minister of state.—*pl.* **portfo'lios.**
[L. *portāre*, to carry, *folium*, a leaf.]

porthole, *pōrt'hōl, pört'-, n.* an opening in a ship's side for light and air.
[**port** (4), **hole.**]

portico, *pōr'ti-kō, pör', n.* (*architecture*) a porch, or a covered walk, consisting of a row of columns supporting a roof:—*pl.* **por'ticos, -coes.**
[It.—L. *porticus*, a porch.]

portion, *pōr'sh(ȯ)n, pör', n.* a part: a helping: a share (of an estate) inherited: a dowry: one's destiny or fate.—*v.t.* to divide (out) in portions.
por'tionless, *adj.* having no dowry or property.
[O.Fr.—L. *portiō, -ōnis.*]

portly, *pōrt'li, pört'li, adj.* dignified in manner, stately: bulky, stout:—*comp.* **port'lier**; *superl.* **port'liest.**
port'liness, *n.* [**port** (2).]

portmanteau, *pōrt-man'tō, pört-, n.* a large leather travelling-bag.
[Fr.—*porter*, carry, *manteau*, cloak.]

portrait, *pōr'trit, pör', n.* the likeness of a real person drawn, painted, or photographed: a description in words of a person or place.
por'traiture (*-chùr, -tūr*), *n.* the art or act of making portraits.
portray', *-trā', v.t.* to paint or draw the likeness of: to describe in words:—*pr.p.* **portray'ing**; *pa.p.* **portrayed'** (*-trād*).
portray'al, *n.* the act of portraying.
[Fr.—L. *prōtrahĕre*, draw forth.]

Portuguese, *pōr-tū-gēz', pör-, adj.* having to do with *Portugal.*—*n.* a native of (*pl.* **Portuguese**), or the language of, Portugal.

pose[1], *pōz, n.* a position or attitude: a character, attitude, or manner, put on to impress others, a pretence (e.g. *His dislike of praise was only a pose*).—*v.i.* to take a position, esp. for effect (e.g. *to pose for a picture*): to claim to be what one is not (e.g. *He posed as a doctor*).—*v.t.* to put forward (a problem or question): to arrange (e.g. a model) in a pose.
pos'er, *n.* one who poses.
[Fr. *poser*, to place—L. *pausa*, a pause.]

pose[2], *pōz, v.t.* (of a question, problem, or questioner) to puzzle (a person), put (him) in a difficulty.
pos'er, *n.* a difficult question or problem.
[Shortened from **oppose.**]

poser (1), (2). See **pose** (1), (2).

position, *poz-ish'(ȯ)n, n.* situation (*the position of the house*): place (e.g. *a fortified position*): posture (e.g. *with head bent, in a cramped position*): one's way of looking at a subject, one's side in an argument or dispute (e.g. *to explain one's position about disarmament*): place in society: official employment, job.
[Fr.—L. *positiō*—*pōnĕre*, to place.]

positive, *poz'i-tiv, adj.* definite (e.g. *a positive statement*): that cannot be doubted (e.g. *positive proof*): certain, convinced (e.g. *I am positive she did it*): confident in one's opinion (e.g. *Don't be so positive; you don't really know*): meaning or saying 'yes' (e.g. *a positive answer*): (*coll.*) downright, out-and-out (e.g. *The state of the garden was a positive disgrace*): greater than zero (e.g. +4 *is a positive or plus value*): having fewer electrons than normal (the **positive terminal** is the one to which electrons flow through a circuit): (*grammar*) of the first degree of comparison of adjectives or adverbs (e.g. *positive 'tall', comparative 'taller', superlative 'tallest'; he worked fast, faster, fastest*).—*n.* something that is positive: (*photography*) a print from a negative, having the lights and shades as in the original.
positive pole, of a magnet, the end (or pole) which turns to the north when the magnet swings freely.
[L. *positīvus*, fixed by agreement.]

posse, *pos'ė, n.* a force or group (e.g. of police).
[L. *posse*, to be able.]

possess, *poz-es', v.t.* to have, to own: to have (a quality, e.g. *He possesses courage*): to have control of one's mind (e.g. *Fear, anger, possessed me*).
possessed', *adj.* in the power of an evil spirit: self-possessed, calm.
possession, *poz-esh'(ȯ)n, n.* state of possessing or being possessed: a thing owned: a territory governed or controlled (e.g. *foreign possessions*).
possess'ive, *adj.* showing possession (esp. in grammar; e.g. *John's* book, *badgers'* habits, *my, mine, his, her,* etc.): showing origin, measure, etc. (e.g. the *sun's* light, a two *days'* rest): tending to treat person(s) or thing(s) as a possession, esp. to try to control person(s) emotionally (e.g. *They were children of a possessive mother*).
possess'iveness, *n.*
[O.Fr. *possesser*—L. *possidēre.*]

possible, *pos'i-bl, adj.* not unlikely: able to happen or to be done, etc.: able, as far as one knows, to be true or correct (e.g. *a possible explanation*).
possibil'ity, *n.* state of being possible: something that may happen or be done:—*pl.* **possibil'ities.**
poss'ibly, *adv.*
[L. *possibilis*—*posse*, to be able.]

post[1], *pōst, n.* a stake or pole of wood or other material, usu. fixed upright.—*v.t.* to fix (e.g. a notice) on a post, board, etc.: to give information about to the public by naming in a list, etc. (e.g. *to post a soldier, a ship, as missing*).
post'er, *n.* a large bill or placard.
[L. *postis*, a doorpost—*pōnĕre*, to place.]

post[2], *pōst, n.* a fixed place or position, esp.

one where a soldier is stationed: any place of duty: an office, job, or appointment: a store, settlement, or camp in thinly inhabited country (e.g. *a trading post, military post*): a public letter-carrier: a system of carrying mail.—*v.t.* to station: to give over (a letter, etc.) to the post office for carrying: (*bookkeeping*) to transfer (an entry) to the ledger: (*coll.*) to supply with necessary information (often **post up**).—*v.i.* to travel with speed.

post'age, *n.* money paid for sending a letter by public post.

post'al, *adj.* having to do with the mail service.

postage stamp, a small printed label or design to show that postage has been paid.

postal order, an order bought at a post office to serve as a cheque for the amount printed on it.

postcard (or **post card**) *n.* a card on which a message may be sent by post.

post'-free', *adj.* without charge for postage: postage prepaid.

post haste, post'-haste', *adv.* with great speed.

post'man, *n.* a letter carrier.

post'mark, *n.* a mark put on a letter at the post office cancelling the stamp and showing the date of sending.

post'master, *n.* the manager of a post office.

Postmaster General, the minister at the head of the post-office department.

post(-)office, an office for receiving and sending off letters by post, etc.: (*cap.*) the government department concerned with sending mails, etc.

post-office savings bank, a branch of the post office in which money may be deposited at a certain rate of interest.

[Fr. *poste*—same L. root as **post** (1).]

post-, *pōst-,* (placed before word) after, behind.

post'date', *v.t.* to date after the real time: mark with a date later than the time of signing.

post'-grad'uate, *adj.* (of studies) continued after graduation. [L.]

postage, etc. See **post** (2).

postdate. See **post-**.

poster. See **post** (1).

poste restante, *pōst res-tän^g t, n.* (used in addressing letters) department of a post office where letters are kept till called for. [Fr., remaining post.]

posterior, *pos-tē'ri-ȯr, adj.* coming after: situated behind.—*n.* (often in *pl.*) hinder part of the body, buttocks.

posterity, *-ter'i-ti, n,* descendants, following generations.

[L. *posterior,* comp. of *posterus—post,* after.]

posthumous, *post'ū-mu̇s, adj.* born after the father's death: published after the author's or composer's death.

post'humously, *adv.*

[L. *posthumus—postumus,* last (*h* by confusion with *humus,* ground); root as **post-**.]

postilion, *pos-til'yȯn, n.* one who guides the horses of a carriage and rides one of them.—Also **postill'ion.**

[Fr. *postillon*—It. *posta,* post.]

postman, etc. See **post** (2).

post-mortem, *pōst-mör'tėm, adj.* after death.—*n.* (often without hyphen) an examination of a dead body to find out the cause of death.

[L. *post,* after, *mors, mortis,* death.]

postpone, *pōs(t)-pōn', v.t.* to put off to a future time, to delay.

postpone'ment, *n.*

[L. *post,* after, *pōnĕre,* to put.]

postscript, *pōs(t)'skript, n.* a part added to a letter or a book after it is signed or finished.

[L. *post,* after, *scriptum,* written.]

postulate, *pos'tū-lāt, v.t.* to assume or take for granted: to assume as true (that).

[L. *postulāre,* to demand.]

posture, *pos'chu̇r, -tūr, n.* the position and carriage of the body as a whole: pose.—*v.i.* to pose.

[L. *positūra—pōnĕre,* to place.]

posy, *pō'zi, n.* a bunch of flowers: a motto, as on a ring.

[From *poesy,* old word for **poetry.**]

pot, *pot, n.* a deep bowl or jar, esp. one used for cooking: a drinking vessel: a vessel for plants: a hole filled with water: a large sum (of money): an important person (usu. *big pot*).—*v.t.* to plant in a pot: to put in a pot in order to preserve: to kill by a pot-shot: to pocket (as a billiard ball): to make a short version of (e.g. a book).—*v.i.* to shoot (usu. *pot at*):—*pr.p.* **pott'ing**; *pa.p.* **pott'ed.**

pot'belly, *n.* a large round belly.

pot'bellied, *adj.*

pot'boiler, *n.* a work of art or writing produced only for the money it brings in.

pot'hole, *n.* a hole made in rock by swirling water: a round hole in a road surface.

pot'holing, *n.* exploring rock (limestone) potholes.

pot'house, *n.* an alehouse.

pot'-luck', *n.* what may happen to be in the pot for a meal without special preparation for guests.

pot'-shot, *n.* a shot for the sake of food rather than sport: a shot within easy range: a random shot.

[Late O.E. *pott*; origin unknown.]

potash, *pot'ash, n.* potassium carbonate, a substance orig. got from the ashes of wood, used in making glass, soap, etc.: other potassium salts used as fertilisers.

potass'ium, *n.* a silvery white metal.

[**pot, ash** (2), or older Du. *potasschen.*]

potation, *pō-tā'sh(ȯ)n, n.* drinking: a drink.

[L. *pōtātiō*—same root as **potion.**]

potato, *pȯ-tā'tō, n.* a plant, orig. South

American, whose tubers (see this word) are used as food:—*pl.* **pota'toes.**
[Sp. *patata*—Haitian *batata*, sweet potato (see **sweet**).]

potbelly, etc. See **pot.**

potent, *pō'tėnt, adj.* powerful, strong (used of people, drugs, motives, reasons, influence, etc.).
po'tency, *n.* power: strength.
po'tentate, *n.* one with power, a prince.
potential, *-ten'shl, adj.* possible, in the making (e.g. *a potential danger*).—*n.* power to produce, develop, act: possible resources.
potential'ity, *n.* possibility: something that may develop:—*pl.* **potential'ities.**
poten'tially, *adv.*
[L. *potēns, -entis*—*posse*, to be able.]

pothole, etc. See **pot.**

potion, *pō'sh(ȯ)n, n.* a drink: a dose of medicine or poison.
[Fr.—L. *pōtiō*—*pōtāre*, to drink.]

pot-luck. See **pot.**

pot-pourri, *pō-pōō'rē, n.* a mixed dish: a mixture of dried petals, of tunes, etc.
[Fr. *pot*, pot, *pourri*, rotten.]

potsherd, *pot'shėrd, n.* (*archaeology, etc.*) a piece of broken pottery. **[pot, shard.]**

pot-shot. See **pot.**

pottage, *pot'ij, n.* a thick soup of meat and vegetables.
[Fr. *potage*—*pot*, jug, pot.]

potter[1], *pot'ėr, n.* one who makes articles of baked clay.
pott'ery, *n.* vessels of baked clay: a place where these are made:—*pl.* **-ies.**
[pot.]

potter[2], *pot'ėr, v.t.* to busy oneself with small jobs: to dawdle.
[Old verb *pote*, to push.]

pouch, *powch, n.* a pocket or bag: anything like a pocket, as a kangaroo's sac for carrying its young.—*v.t.* to pocket.—*v.i.* to form a pouch.
[Old Norman Fr. *pouche*.]

pouf(f), pouffe, *pōōf, n.* a large hassock or cushioned seat.
[Fr. *pouf*.]

poulterer, *pōl'tėr-ėr, n.* one who sells poultry and game for food.
poult'ry, *n.* domestic or farmyard fowls as a whole.
[Fr. *poulet*, chicken—Late L. *pulla*, hen.]

poultice, *pōl'tis, n.* a soft mixture spread on a cloth and put on sores, etc.—*v.t.* to put a poultice on.
[L. *pultēs*—Gk. *poltos*, porridge.]

pounce, *powns, n.* the claw of a bird (e.g. hawk): a sudden spring or swoop.—*v.i.* to sweep down suddenly, attack: to spring, dash: to seize (upon, e.g. an idea, statement).
[L. *pungěre, punctum*, to prick.]

pound[1], *pownd, n.* a unit of weight = 16 ounces or approx. 0·454 kilograms (abbrev. *lb.*): a unit of money, orig. the value of a pound weight of silver: since 1971, 100 new pence (the *pound sterling*, written £ for *libra*), orig. 20 shillings: also a note of this value.
pound'age, *n.* a charge or tax, of so much per pound, on a money transaction.
pound'er, (as part of a word) one who has, or thing that weighs, a certain number of pounds (e.g. *a 12-pounder*).
[O.E. *pund*—L. *penděre*, to weigh.]

pound[2], *pownd, n.* a pen in which stray animals are put.—*v.t.* to put in a pound. [O.E. *pund*, enclosure.]

pound[3], *pownd, v.t.* to beat into small pieces: to beat or bruise.—*v.i.* to walk with heavy steps.
[O.E. *pūnian*, to beat.]

pour, *pōr, pör, v.t.* to make flow in a stream: to send forth like a stream (e.g. *He poured forth his troubles*).—*v.i.* to stream: to rain heavily.
[M.E. *pouren*; origin uncertain.]

pout, *powt, v.i.* to push out the lips crossly in displeasure: (of lips) to stick out.—*n.* a pushing out of the lips.
pout'er, *n.* a type of pigeon that puffs out its crop.
[M.E. *powte*, of uncertain origin.]

poverty. See **poor.**

powder, *pow'dėr, n.* dust: any substance in fine particles: gunpowder: face-powder.—*v.t.* to make into powder: to sprinkle with powder: to salt by sprinkling.—*v.i.* to crumble into powder: to use powder on the face, etc.
pow'dery, *adj.* like powder: covered with powder.
pow'dered, *adj.* in the form of fine dust: sprinkled with powder: salted.
powder magazine, a place where gunpowder is stored.
powder puff, a soft pad for dusting powder on the skin.
[Fr. *poudre*—L. *pulvis*, dust.]

power, *pow'ėr, n.* strength, might: force: ability to do anything—physical or mental: authority: someone who has authority or strong influence: a nation with much influence in international affairs (e.g. *the big powers*): legal right: legal permission to act: (*coll.*) a great deal or great many: the product obtained by multiplying a number by itself a given number of times (e.g. $2 \times 2 \times 2$, or 2^3, is the third power of 2): (*physics*) the rate of doing work.—*adj.* concerned with power: worked by steam or oil, or electricity, etc.—*v.t.* to cause to move or work (by fuel, engine, etc.).
pow'erful, *adj.* **pow'erfully,** *adv.*
pow'erfulness, *n.*
pow'erless, *adj.* without power or ability.
pow'er-driven, *adj.* worked by electricity, etc., not by hand.
pow'er-house, -station, *n.* a place where electricity is generated or produced.
power politics, international politics where the actions of nations are based

on the amount of armed strength they can use to back their opinions.
in one's power, at one's mercy: within the limits of what one can do.
the powers that be, the ruling authorities at the moment.
in power, (esp. of political party) in office, control.
[O.Fr. *poer*—L. *posse,* to be able.]

powwow, *pow'wow, n.* a meeting for discussion held by, or with, American Indians: any conference.
[Amer. Indian *powwaw, powah.*]

pox, *poks, n.* (*pl.* of **pock**) a disease with eruptions or pimples on the skin (e.g. *smallpox, chicken-pox*).

practicable, etc. See **practice.**

practice, *prak'tis, n.* actual doing (e.g. *In practice, the longer method is better*): habit, usual action: repeated performance to gain skill (e.g. *practice for a race, practice on the piano*): a professional man's business (e.g. *a doctor's practice*).
prac'ticable, *adj.* capable of being used or done.
prac'ticableness, practicabil'ity, *ns.*
prac'tical, *adj.* having to do with practice or action: efficient when put to use: taught by practice (e.g. *a practical knowledge of carpentry*): inclined by nature to act and to act capably.
prac'tically, *adv.* in a practical way: in effect or reality (e.g. *He said nothing but practically his silence was an admission of guilt*): (*coll.*) almost.
practise, *prak'tis, v.t.* to put, make a habit of putting, into practice or action: to do exercises in, train in, so as to get and keep a skill (e.g. *to practise judo*): to follow (a profession; e.g. *to practise law*).—Also *v.i.*
practitioner (*-tish'ȯn-ėr*), *n.* one who is in practice, or who practises.
general practitioner, one who practises general medicine, not specialising in one branch of it.
practical joke, a joke consisting of action, not words, usu. an annoying trick.
practical politics, ideas or measures that may be carried out at once or in the near future.
[O.Fr. *practique*—Gk. *prăssein,* to do.]

pragmatical, *prag-mat'i-kl, adj.* practical: matter-of-fact: too busy in the affairs of others, meddlesome.
[Gk. *prăgma,* deed—*prăssein,* to do.]

prairie, *prā'ri, n.* a treeless plain, covered naturally with grass.
prairie dog, a burrowing, gnawing, and barking North American animal.
[Fr.—L. *prātum,* a meadow.]

praise, *prāz, v.t.* to speak highly of (a person or thing): to extol (God) with gratitude and reverence.—*n.* expression of approval or honour: singing part of church service.
praise'worthy, *adj.* worthy of praise.
[O.Fr. *preisier*—L. *pretium,* price.]

praline, *prâ'lēn, n.* a sweet with nutty centre and a brown coating of sugar.
[Fr. *praline*; from proper name Praslin.]

pram, *pram, n.* short for **perambulator.**

prance, *prâns, v.i.* (of a horse) to spring from the hind legs: to go with a dancing movement: to swagger, strut.
[M.E. *praunce*; origin unknown.]

prank, *prangk, n.* a mischievous trick.
[Origin unknown.]

prate, *prāt, v.i.* to talk foolishly: to talk too much.—Also *v.t.*
prat'ing, *n.* and *adj.*
prattle, *prat'l, v.i.* to talk much and idly, or as a child does.—*n.* empty talk.
[Conn. with Ger., Du., and Dan. words.]

prawn, *prön, n.* a small shellfish like the shrimp.—*v.i.* to fish for prawns.
[M.E. *prayne, prane*; origin unknown.]

pray, *prā, v.i.* to ask earnestly (*to pray to someone, for something*): to speak and tell one's desires to God.—*v.t.* to beg earnestly or reverently:—*pr.p.* **pray'ing**; *pa.p.* **prayed.**
pray'er, *n.* act of praying: a request: solemn request and giving of thanks to God: (in *pl.*) divine service, worship.
prayer book, a book containing prayers or forms of devotion.
[O.Fr. *preier*—L. *precārī*—*prex,* a prayer.]

pre-, *prē-, pfx.* before (e.g. *predecease, prearrangement*): happening before (e.g. *pre-war*). [L. *prae-.*]

preach, *prēch, v.t.* to give (a sermon): to teach, talk in favour of (e.g. *to preach patience*).—*v.i.* to give a public speech on sacred subjects: to give advice in an offensive manner.
preach'er, *n.*
[Fr. *prêcher*—L. *praedicāre,* to proclaim.]

preamble, *prē-am'bl, n.* preface, introduction (e.g. to an Act of Parliament).
[L. *prae,* before, *ambulāre,* to go, walk.]

prearrange, *prē-ȧ-rānj', v.t.* to arrange beforehand.
prearrange'ment, *n.* [Pfx. **pre-.**]

precarious, *pri-kā'ri-ŭs, adj.* depending on chance, or on the will of another: uncertain, risky: insecure (e.g. *a precarious situation*).
preca'riously, *adv.*
preca'riousness, *n.*
[L. *precārius*—*precārī,* to pray.]

precaution, *pri-kö'sh(ȯ)n, n.* care, or an action taken beforehand, to prevent or avoid disease, accident, etc.
precau'tionary, *adj.* using precaution (e.g. *to take precautionary measures*): (of speech, words) advising precaution.
[L. *prae,* before, *cautiō,* caution.]

precede, *prē-sēd', v.t.* to go before in time, rank, or importance.—Also *v.i.*
precedent, *pres'i-dėnt, prēs'-, n.* a past happening which may serve as an example to be followed in the future.

prec'edented, *adj.* having been done before: justified by an example.
precē'ding, *adj.* going before: previous.
[Fr. *précéder*—L. *prae*, before, *cēdĕre*, go.]

precentor, *pri-, prē-sen'tȯr, n.* the person in charge of, or leader of, the singing in a church.
[L. *prae*, before, *canĕre*, to sing.]

precept, *prē'sept, n.* a rule to guide one's action: a commandment.
precep'tor, *n.* a teacher.
[L. *praecipĕre, -ceptum*, to give rules to.]

precinct, *prē'singkt, n.* (in *pl.*) the parts immediately round any place: a space, esp. an enclosure, round a building (e.g. a church): a district, or subdivision of one (e.g. *a police precinct*).
[L. *prae*, before, *cingĕre*, to gird.]

precious, *presh'ŭs, adj.* of great price or worth: highly valued by (with *to*).—*adv.* (*coll.*) very, extremely (e.g. *precious little*).
[O.Fr. *precios*—L. *pretium*, price.]

precipice, *pres'i-pis, n.* a steep cliff.
precip'itāte, *v.t.* to throw headlong: to force (into hasty action): to bring on suddenly (e.g. *to precipitate a quarrel*): (*chemistry*) to bring (a substance) in solid form out of a state of solution.—*v.i.* (of vapour) to turn into, fall as, rain, hail, etc.—*adj.* (*-tit*) headlong: hasty.—*n.* a substance separated from solution.
precip'itately, *adv.*
precipitā'tion, *n.* act of precipitating: great hurry: rash haste: rain, etc., or amount of it.
precip'itance, precip'itancy, *ns.* headlong haste, rashness.
precip'itous, *adj.* like a precipice, steep.
[L. *prae*, before, *caput*, head.]

précis, *prā'sē, n.* a summary of a writing:—*pl.* **précis,** *-sēz.*
[Fr.—L. root as **precise.**]

precise, *pri-sīs', adj.* very definite (e.g. *precise instructions*): exact (e.g. *his precise words*): very accurate: particular, prim in manner.
precise'ly, *adv.* **precise'ness,** *n.*
preci'sion (*-si'*), *n.* preciseness: exactness.—*adj.* used to produce very accurate results (e.g. *precision instruments*).
[Fr. *précis*—L. *prae*, *caedĕre*, to cut.]

preclude, *pri-kloo͞d', v.t.* to prevent (a person from): to make impossible by some action (e.g. *to preclude mistakes, doubt*).
preclusion, *pri-kloo͞'zh(ȯ)n, n.*
[L. *prae*, before, *claudĕre*, to shut.]

precocious, *pri-kō'shŭs, adj.* early in reaching a stage of development, esp mental.
preco'ciousness, precoc'ity (*-kos'*), *ns.*
[L. *prae*, before, *coquĕre*, to cook, ripen.]

preconceive, *prē-kon-sēv', v.t.* to form (a notion or idea about something) before having actual knowledge.
preconcep'tion, *n.* opinion formed without actual knowledge.
[L. *prae*, before, *concipĕre*, conceive.]

precursor, *prē-kûr'sȯr, n.* a forerunner: a predecessor: a person or thing that is a sign of a coming event (e.g. *A too dry summer is a precursor of a poor harvest*).
[L. *prae*, before, *currĕre*, to run.]

predate, *prē-dāt', v.t.* to date before the true date: to be earlier than. [Pfx. **pre-.**]

predator, *pred'ȧ-tȯr, n.* a bird or animal (e.g. hawk) living by prey: a creature that plunders (e.g. crops).
pred'atory, *adj.* plundering: living by plunder or prey (e.g. *a predatory bird*).
[L. *praeda*, booty.]

predecease, *prē-di-sēs', v.t.* to die before.—Also *n.* [Pfx. **pre-.**]

predecessor, *prē-di-ses'ȯr, n.* one who has held an office or position before another (e.g. *Jones was my predecessor as chairman*): an ancestor.
[L. *prae*, before, *dē*, away, *cēdĕre*, to go.]

predestine, *prē-, pri-des'tin, v.t.* (of fate, God) to decide, decree beforehand (e.g. *Fate predestined this loss*; *his success was predestined*): to appoint, choose (*Fate predestined him to suffer*).
predestinā'tion, *n.* (*theology*) God's decree fixing what is to happen for all eternity.
[L. *prae*, before, *destināre*, to destine.]

predetermine, *prē-di-tėr'min, v.t.* to determine or settle beforehand.
[L. *prae*, before, *dētermināre*, determine.]

predicament, *pri-dik'ȧ-mėnt, n.* an unfortunate or difficult position.
[Late L. *praedicāmentum*, something asserted; same root as **predicate.**]

predicate, *pred'i-kit, n.* (*grammar*) what is stated about the subject (e.g. Jack *is a foolish boy*; the chains *clanked*; the bullet *hit the roof*).
[L. *praedicāre*, to proclaim.]

predict, *pri-dikt', v.t.* to foretell (esp. after a study of the facts).
predic'table, *adj.*
predic'tion, *n.* act of predicting: something that is foretold.
predic'tor, *n.* one who predicts: a device used in anti-aircraft defence which tells the gun crew the exact position of an aircraft.
[L. *prae*, before, *dīcĕre*, to say.]

predilection, *prē-di-lek'sh(ȯ)n, n.* a preference or special liking (for).
[L. *prae*, before, *dīlectiō*, choice.]

predispose, *prē-dis-pōz', v.t.* to incline (a person) beforehand (e.g. *The stranger's friendly manner predisposed us to trust him*): to make liable (e.g. *Too little to eat predisposed him to take the disease*).
predisposi'tion, *n.* [Pfx. **pre-.**]

predominate, *pri-dom'in-āt, v.i.* to be the stronger, or have the greater authority: to have control (over): to exist in the greater or greatest quantity.
predom'inant, *adj.* ruling: superior in position: more, most, noticeable.
predom'inance, *n.* **-inantly,** *adv.*
[L. *prae*, before, *dominārī*, to be master.]

pre-eminent, *prē-em'in-ėnt, adj.* standing

above all others in good, or bad, qualities: outstanding.
pre-em′inence, *n.* **-inently,** *adv.*
[L. *prae*, before, *ēminēre*, to stand out.]

pre-emption, *prē-em(p)′sh(ȯ)n. n,* act or right of buying in preference to others.
[L. *prae*, before, *emĕre*, to buy.]

preen, *prēn, v.t.* to arrange (feathers), as birds do: to pride (oneself).
[Apparently from **prune** (1).]

pre-establish, *prē-ės-tab′lish, v.t.* to establish, decide, prove, beforehand.
[Pfx. **pre-.**]

pre-exist, *prē-ėg-zist′, v.i.* to exist beforehand or previously.
pre-exist′ence, *n.* [Pfx. **pre-.**]

prefabricated, *prē-fab′ri-kā-tid, adj.* made of parts manufactured beforehand and ready to be fitted together. [Pfx. **pre-.**]

preface, *pref′is, n.* something said, written, or done, by way of introduction in the beginning: foreword.—*v.t.* to introduce by a preface (e.g. *He prefaced his remarks with an appeal for silence*).
[Fr. *préface*—L. *prae*, before, *fārī*, speak.]

prefect, *prē′fekt, n.* one set in authority over others: in a school, a pupil with certain powers: in France, the governor of a department.
[Fr. *préfet*—L. *praeficĕre*, to set over.]

prefer, *pri-fėr′, v.t.* to regard with greater favour, like better (with *to*; e.g. *I prefer walking to cycling*):—*pr.p.* **preferr′ing**; *pa.p.* **preferred′.**
pref′erable, *pref′-, adj.* to be preferred, more desirable.
pref′erably, *adv.*
pref′erence, *n.* the act of choosing: greater liking: thing that is preferred.
preferential, *pref-ėr-en′shl, adj.* showing, having the benefits arising from, a preference (e.g. *preferential treatment*).
prefer′ment, *n.* promotion.
preference shares, or **stock,** shares on which the dividends must be paid before those on ordinary shares are paid.
[Fr. *préférer*—L. *praeferre*, to bear before.]

prefix, *prē-fiks′, v.t.* to put before or at the beginning.—*n.* (*prē′*) syllable or word put before another word to alter its meaning in some way (e.g. *dis*like, *un*tie, *re*write, *super*natural, *semi*circle).
[L. *praefīgĕre*, to fix before.]

pregnant, *preg′nȧnt, adj.* having a child or young in the womb: full of meaning (e.g. *a pregnant remark*).
[L. *praegnans*—*prae*, *gnāscī*, to be born.]

prehensile, *pri-hen′sil, adj.* able to grasp or hold on to something.
[L. *praehendĕre*, to seize.]

prehistoric, -al, *prē-his-tor′ik, -ȧl, adjs.* belonging to a time before written history. [Pfx. **pre-.**]

prejudge, *prē-juj′, v.t.* to judge before hearing the whole case, condemn before knowing the facts.
[L. *praejūdicāre*, to judge before.]

prejudice, *prej′oo-dis, n.* an opinion formed without careful thought: an unreasonable or unfair feeling (in favour of, or against, something): injury, harm (e.g. *to the prejudice of his own interests*).—*v.t.* to bias the mind of: to damage, spoil (e.g. *This rash act prejudiced his chances of success*).
prej′udiced, *adj.* having, or showing, prejudice.
prejudicial, *prej-oo-dish′l, adj.* damaging, disadvantageous (to).
[L. *prae*, *jūdicium*, judgment.]

prelate, *prel′it, n.* a churchman of high rank, as a bishop or archbishop.
prel′acy, *n.* the office of a prelate.
[Fr. *prélat*—L. *praelātus*, borne before.]

preliminary, *pri-lim′in-ȧr-i, adj.* introductory, preparing the way.—*n.* something that goes before or prepares the way:—*pl.* **prelim′inaries.**
[L. *prae*, before, *līmen*, a threshold.]

prelude, *prel′ūd, n.* an introductory event, often leading up to another of greater importance: (*music*) an introductory passage or movement: a short piece e.g. for piano.
[L. *prae*, before, *lūdĕre*, play.]

premature, *prem′ȧ-tūr, -tūr′,* or *prēm′-, adj.* coming, born, etc., before the right time.
prematurely, *adv.* **prematureness,** *n.*
[L. *praemātūrus*, ripe before.]

premeditate, *prē-med′i-tāt, v.t.* to think out beforehand: to plan, intend (e.g. *a premeditated murder*).
premeditā′tion, *n.*
[L. *praemeditārī*, to meditate before.]

premier, *prem′i-ėr, -yėr, adj.* first, chief, leading.—*n.* the prime minister.
première, *prem-yer′, n.* the first performance, e.g. of a play.
[Fr.—L. *prīmus*, first.]

premise, *prem′is, n.* something assumed from which a conclusion is drawn: (in a legal document, in *pl.*) the house, etc., mentioned above: (in *pl.*) a building and its grounds.
[Fr. *prémisse*—L. *prae*, *mittĕre*, to send.]

premium, *prē′mi-ŭm, n.* a reward, prize: money paid, usu. yearly, for insurance: the fee paid for training in a trade or profession: a sum above the original price or par, e.g. of stock.
at a premium, above par: in demand.
[L. *prae*, above, *emĕre*, to buy.]

premolar, *prē-mō′lȧr, n.* a tooth between canine and molars, a bicuspid. [**pre-.**]

premonition, *prē-mȯn-ish′(ȯ)n, n.* a forewarning: a feeling (that something is going to happen).
premon′itory, *adj.* giving warning.
[L. *prae*, before, *monēre*, to warn.]

preoccupy, *prē-ok′ū-pī, v.t.* to fill the mind of, take up the attention of:—*pr.p.* **preocc′upying**; *pa.p.* **preocc′upied.**
preocc′upied, *adj.* lost in thought.

preoccupā'tion, *n.*
[L. *prae,* before, root as **occupy.**]

prepaid. See **prepay.**

prepare, *pri-pār',* *v.t.* to make ready: to train, equip (for): to make (someone) ready, fit, to bear a shock.—Also *v.i.*
preparation, *prep-à-rā'sh(ò)n, n.* the act of preparing: study of work for lesson in class (abbrev. **prep**): state of being prepared: something which has been prepared (e.g. face cream).
prepar'atory, *adj.*
prepared', *adj.* ready: willing.
preparatory school, one which prepares pupils for a public school.
preparatory to, before (doing something).
[L. *prae,* before, *parāre,* make ready.]

prepay, *prē'pā',* *v.t.* to pay in advance:—*pa.t.* and *pa.p.* **pre'paid'.** [Pfx. **pre-.**]

preponderate, *pri-pon'dėr-āt, v.i.* to be greater in weight, number, power.
prepon'derant, *adj.*
[L. *prae,* before, *pondus,* a weight.]

preposition, *prep-ō-zish'(ò)n, n.* a word placed before a noun or pronoun to show its relation to another word (e.g. a sum *of* money; lost *by* Mary; dropped *under* the table; a prize *for* you).
preposi'tional, *adj.*
[L. *prae,* before, *pōnĕre,* to place.]

prepossess, *prē-poz-es',* *v.t.* to fill the mind beforehand with a feeling or opinion (e.g. *He was prepossessed with the idea that he must not yield on any point*): to prejudice, esp. favourably (e.g. *I was prepossessed by, with, her*).
prepossess'ing, *adj.* attractive.
[Pfx. **pre-.**]

preposterous, *pri-pos'tėr-ùs, adj.* against reason or common sense, utterly absurd.
[L. *prae,* before, *posterus,* after.]

prerequisite, *prē-rek'wi-zit, n.* something that must be done, a condition that must be fulfilled, before something else can happen.—Also *adj.*
[L. *prae,* before, *requīrĕre,* to need.]

prerogative, *pri-rog'à-tiv, n.* a special right or privilege belonging to a person because of his rank, etc.
[L. *praerogātivus,* asked first for his vote, as a richer Roman citizen was—*prae,* before, *rogāre,* to ask.]

presage, *pres'ij, n.* a sign of the future, omen: a feeling of what is going to happen.—*v.t.* (also *pri-sāj'*) to foretell.
[L. *praesāgium,* a foreboding.]

presbyter, *prez'bi-tėr, n.* one who managed the affairs of an early Christian church: a clergyman ranking below a bishop: a church elder.
Presbytē'rian, *adj.* having to do with a form of church government in which there is no higher office than the presbyter or elder (clergymen being considered as 'ruling and teaching elders').—*n.* a member of a church governed in this way.
Presbyte'rianism, *n.*
pres'bytery, *n.* a group of ministers and elders forming the church court of a district: *(R.C.)* a priest's house:—*pl.* **pres'byteries.**
[Gk. *presbyteros,* elder—*presbys,* old.]

prescribe, *pri-skrib',* *v.t.* to lay down as a rule to be followed: to order the use of (a medicine).
prescrip'tion, *n.* something prescribed: a written direction for preparing a medicine.
[L. *prae,* before, *scrībĕre,* to write.]

presence, *prez'ėns, n.* fact or state of being present (opp. of *absence*): personal appearance and manner (e.g. *He has a good presence*).
present[1], *prez'ėnt, adj.* in the place thought, etc. of—opp. of *absent*: belonging to the time in which we are, not past or future (e.g. *the present premier*): now being considered (e.g. *It has nothing to do with the present subject*): (*grammar*) showing time just now, or making a general statement (e.g. *I approve of this*; *she is coming towards us*; *she comes on Mondays*).—*n.* the time we are now at.
pres'ently, *adv.* soon.
presence chamber, the room in which great personages receive company.
presence of mind, coolness and readiness in any emergency or surprise.
in the presence of, while in the same place as and very near (e.g. *He said it in the presence of his family*).
See also **present** (2).
[O.Fr.—L. *praesentia* (n.), *praesens* (adj.).]

present[2], *pri-zent',* *v.t.* to introduce (a person) to another or others: to introduce at court: to show to the public: to put on the stage: to give, esp. formally (e.g. *He presented a rose to her*; *they presented her with a silver teapot*): to put something before the mind of (a person—e.g. *John's refusal to help presented her with a problem about what to do next*): to appoint to a church living: to point (a gun) before firing.—*n.* (*prez'ėnt*) a gift (object or money given). (Noun directly from *presence*—above).
present'able, *adj.* fit to be given or seen.
presentation, *prez-ėn-tā'sh(ò)n, n.* act of presenting: a showing (e.g. of a play: a setting forth (e.g. of ideas): a formal giving of a gift to mark an occasion such as retirement from office: the gift itself.
to present arms, to bring a rifle to the saluting position, held perpendicularly in front of the centre of the body.
to present itself, to appear, arise, turn up: to suggest itself (to one's mind).
to present oneself, to introduce oneself: to arrive, appear.
[O.Fr. *presenter*—same root as **presence.**]

presentiment, *pri-zent'i-mėnt,* or *-sent',*

n. a vague feeling that something unpleasant is about to happen, foreboding.
[L. *prae*, before, and **sentiment.**]

preserve, *pri-zėrv′*, *v.t.* to keep alive, or safe from harm: to keep in existence: to keep up, continue (e.g. *to preserve silence*): to keep from decay: to cook (fruit, etc.) with sugar.—*n.* something preserved, e.g. fruit: a place of protection for e.g. game (**game preserve**): sphere into which others, regarded as outsiders, are not allowed to enter (e.g. *Is the diplomatic service a preserve of boys who have been to public schools?*).
preservā′tion, *n.* act of preserving: state of being preserved.
preserv′ative, *n.* and *adj.* (something) that preserves.
[Fr. *préserver*—L. *prae*, *servāre*, to keep.]

preside, *pri-zīd′*, *v.i.* to sit in the chair or chief seat (e.g. at a meeting): to exercise authority or control (over).
pres′idency, *prez′i-dėn-si*, *n.* the office of a president: his term of office.
pres′ident, *n.* the head of a college, council, board, etc.: the head executive officer of a republic.
presidential, *pre-zi-den′sh(å)l*, *adj.* having to do with a president.
to preside at the piano, organ, to act as pianist, organist.
[Fr. *présider*—L. *prae*, *sedēre*, to sit.]

press[1], *pres*, *v.t.* to push against: to weigh down: to squeeze: to thrust: to urge strongly (to do): to offer urgently (with *on*): to harass with difficulties or dangers (e.g. *He was now hard pressed*): to insist on (e.g. *to press a point*): to smooth out, iron (e.g. clothes).—*v.i.* to push with force: to crowd: to make haste necessary (e.g. *Time presses*).—*n.* an act of pressing: a crowd: stress: a printing machine: newspapers and magazines as a whole: the journalistic profession.
press′ing, *adj.* requiring action at once: earnest (e.g. *a pressing invitation*).
pressure, *presh′ůr*, *n.* act of pressing: state of being pressed: force on a surface: strong persuasion: difficulties, trouble: urgency.
press′urise (*presh′*), *v.t.* to fit (aeroplane cabin, etc.) with a device that keeps the air pressure in it nearly normal.
press conference, a meeting of an important person with the press to make an announcement or answer questions.
pressure group, a group of people who put pressure on e.g. the government to gain a certain result.
in the press, about to be published.
[Fr. *presser*—L. *premĕre*, to squeeze.]

press[2], *pres*, *v.t.* (formerly) to carry off (a person) and force him into service, usu. in the navy: to take (into use, service) in an emergency for want of some thing, person, more suitable.
press′gang, *n.* a group of men hired to seize others for the navy.
[Old *prest*, engage by paying earnest.]

prestige, *pres-tēzh′*, *n.* influence of a person due to his rank or reputation.
[Fr.—L. *praestinguĕre*, to dazzle.]

presto, *pres′tō*, *adv.* quickly: at once.
[It.—L. *praestō*, at hand.]

presume, *pri-zūm′*, *v.t.* to take for granted: to take as true without proof.—*v.i.* to venture without right (to): to take too much liberty, act impertinently: to take advantage of (*You presume on his good-nature*).
presum′ably, *adv.* probably, it may be supposed.
presum′ing, *adj.* acting without permission, unsuitably bold.
presumption, *pri-zum(p)′sh(ȯ)n*, *n.* something supposed: strong likelihood: behaviour going beyond proper bounds.
presumptuous (*-zump′tū-ůs*) *adj.* presuming.
[L. *prae*, before, *sūmĕre*, *sumptum*, take.]

presuppose, *prē-sů-pōz′*, *v.t.* to take for granted: to require as necessity (e.g. *True kindness presupposes sympathy*).
[L. *prae*, before, and root of **suppose.**]

pretend, *pri-tend′*, *v.t.* to make a false show of, of being (e.g. *to pretend friendship, to be friendly*): to feign (that).—*v.i.* to make believe: to lay claim (to e.g. the crown): to claim to have (a quality; e.g. *He pretended to genius*).
pretence′, *n.* act of pretending: make-believe: a claim: a false reason given.
preten′sion, *n.* claim: too great show.
preten′tious (*-shůs*), *adj.* claiming more than is right: showy.
preten′tiousness, *n.*
[L. *prae*, *tendĕre*, to stretch.]

preternatural, *prē-tėr-na′chůr-ål*, *adj.* beyond what is natural, abnormal.
preterna′turally, *adv.*
[L. *praeter*, beyond, *nātūra*, nature.]

pretext, *prē′tekst*, *n.* a reason given to hide the real motive: an excuse.
[L. *prae*, before, *texĕre*, to weave.]

pretty, *prit′i*, *adj.* pleasing or attractive to eye, ear, or mind, but not grand or beautiful: (*coll.*) fairly large (e.g. *a pretty sum of money*): fine (usu. said of something bad; e.g. *a pretty mess*):—*comp.* **prett′ier**; *superl.* **prett′iest.**—*adv.* moderately: very.
prett′ily, *adv.* **prett′iness,** *n.*
pretty much, very nearly.
[O.E. *prættig*, tricky.]

prevail, *pri-vāl′*, *v.i.* to gain control or victory (with *over*, *against*): to succeed: to persuade (with *on*; e.g. *She prevailed on him to stay*): to be usual, common: to be in the largest number (e.g. *Chinese prevail in this area*).
prevail′ing, *adj.* controlling: most common.
prev′alent, *adj.* widespread, common.

prev′alence, *n.*
[L. *prae*, before, *valēre*, to be powerful.]

prevaricate, *pri-var′i-kāt, v.t.* to avoid telling the truth, to quibble.
[L. *praevāricāri*, to walk crookedly.]

prevent, *pri-vent′, v.t.* to hinder: to keep from happening, make impossible.
preven′tion, *n.* act of preventing.
preven′tive, *adj.* and *n.* (something) tending to hinder or keep away (e.g. disease).—Also **preven′tative.**
[L. *prae*, before, *venīre*, to come.]

preview, *prē′vū, n.* a view of a performance, etc. before it is open to the public.—Also *v.t.* (*prē-vū′*). [Pfx. **pre-.**]

previous, *prē′vi-ŭs, adj.* before in time: former.
pre′viously, *adv.* **pre′viousness,** *n.*
[L. *prae*, before, *via*, a way.]

prey, *prā, n.* an animal that is, or may be, killed and eaten by another: a victim.—*v.i.* to make raids (on, upon): to seize and eat other animals: to live (on a victim): to waste or worry (with *on*; e.g. *Cares prey on his mind*).
bird, beast, of prey, one that lives on other animals.
[O.Fr. *preie*—L. *praeda*, booty.]

price, *prīs, n.* the amount, usu. in money, for which a thing is sold, cost: what one gives up or suffers in order to gain something (e.g. *The price of freedom is often great*).—*v.t.* to fix the price of: (*coll.*) to ask the price of.
price′less, *adj.* of very great value: (*coll.*) absurd, amusing.
a price on one's head, a reward offered for one's capture.
beyond, without, price, priceless.
one's price, the terms on which one will agree to do something, or the amount needed to bribe one.
[O.Fr. *pris*—L. *pretium*, price.]

prick, *prik, n.* act, or sensation, of piercing with a small sharp point e.g. of needle.—*v.t.* to pierce slightly with a sharp point: to pain sharply: to stick up (the ears): to mark with prick(s) or dot(s).
prickle, *prik′l, n.* a little prick: a sharp point growing on a plant or animal.
prick′ly, *adj.* **prick′liness,** *n.*
the prick(s) **of conscience,** painful awareness that one has done wrong.
to prick up one's ears, to begin to listen with interest.
to kick against the pricks. See **kick.**
[O.E. *prica*, point; conn. with Du. *prik.*]

pride, *prīd, n.* state of feeling proud: too great an opinion of oneself: proper self-respect: a feeling of pleasure in having done something: something of which one is proud (e.g. *His son was his pride and joy*).—*v.t.* (with *oneself*) to allow oneself to feel pride (e.g. with *on*; *He prides himself on his good French*).
proud, *prowd, adj.* thinking too highly of oneself: haughty: having proper self-respect: being highly pleased: giving reason for pride (e.g. *It was a proud moment for him*).
to give pride of place to, to give the most important place to.
[O.E. *prȳte* (n.)—*prūt* (adj.).]

priest, *prēst, n.* one who performs sacrifices or sacred rites (*fem.* **priest′ess**): a clergyman, minister.
priest′hood, *n.* the office of a priest: those who are priests.
[O.E. *prēost*—Gk. root as **presbytery.**]

prig, *prig, n.* a smug, self-righteous person.
prigg′ish, *adj.* [Origin unknown.]

prim, *prim, adj.* (of person, manner) exact and correct, prudishly proper, formal:—*comp.* **primm′er**; *superl.* **primm′est.**
[Late 17th-century slang.]

prima ballerina, *prē′mä bal-ė-rē′nä*, leading lady in a ballet company (It.).
prima donna, *prē′mä don′(n)ä*, leading lady in opera (It. 'first lady').
[Same L. root as **prime** (1).]

primacy, primary, etc. See **prime** (1).

prime[1], *prīm, adj.* first in order of time, rank, or importance: chief: of the highest quality (e.g. *prime meat*).—*n.* the time of full health and strength (e.g. *in the prime of life*).
pri′mal, *adj.* first: original.
primacy, *prī′mȧ-si, n.* the state of being first: the office of an archbishop.
primary, *prī′mȧr-i, adj.* first: original: chief: of the first stage, elementary (e.g. *primary schools*).—*n.* (*U.S.*) a preliminary election in which voters of each party nominate candidates.
primate, *prī′mit, -māt, n.* an archbishop: (*-māt*) a member of the highest order of mammals—men, monkeys, lemurs.
prime minister, the chief minister of state.
prime number, a number divisible only by itself and 1 (e.g. 3, 5, 7, 11, etc.).
primary colours, those from which all others can be made—red, blue, yellow: also the seven colours of the rainbow.
See also **primer,** etc.
[L. *prīmus*, first.]

prime[2], *prīm, v.t.* to supply (a firearm) with powder: to prepare for painting by laying on a first coat of paint or oil: to fill (a person) with liquor: to bring into working order by putting in water, gas, or oil (e.g. to prime a pump by putting in water to swell the sucker): to prepare with full information (e.g. *to prime someone with the facts*; *to prime oneself about something*).
[Origin uncertain.]

primer, *prī′mėr, prim′ėr, n.* a first reading-book: a simple introduction to any subject.
primeval, *prī-mē′vȧl, adj.* belonging to the first ages of the world.
primitive, *prim′i-tiv, adj.* belonging to the beginning, or to earliest times:

old-fashioned, out-of-date: crude, clumsy. See also **prime** (1), etc.
[L. *primus*, first (*aevum*, an age).]

primrose, *prim'rōz, n.* a pale yellow spring flower of woods and meadows.—*adj.* pale yellow: flowery, gay.
[O.Fr. *primerose*—L. *prima*, first.]

prince, *prins, n.* a son of a king, etc.: a noble ruler: one of the most important or greatest members of a group or class (e.g. *a merchant prince, a prince of poets*): —*fem.* **princess,** *prin-ses'* (with Christian name, *prin'ses*).
prince'ly, *adj.* suited to a prince: splendid.
prince'liness, *n.*
principal, *prin'si-pl, adj.* highest in rank, character, or importance: chief.—*n.* a chief person: the head of a school, college, or university: one who takes a leading part, esp. in a transaction: money on which interest is paid.
principal'ity, *n.* the territory of a prince.
prin'cipally, *adv.* chiefly, for the most part.
[L. *princeps* and *principālis*, first, chief, *principium*, beginning; all from *primus*, first, *capĕre*, take.]

principle, *prin'si-pl, n.* an important general truth or law: (in *pl.*) rules to guide one's actions: a sense of what is right in conduct: manner of working (e.g. *the principle of a jet engine*).
prin'cipled, *adj.* having, showing, good principles.
in principle, so far as the general idea is concerned, without taking details into account.
on principle, for the sake of obeying a principle. [Same as **prince, principal.**]

print, *print, n.* a mark made by pressure: printed lettering: an engraving: a printed cotton cloth: a photograph made from a negative: printed state (e.g. *The book is in print*).—*v.t.* to mark: to stamp a pattern on: to mark letters on paper with type: to publish: to make a finished photograph.—Also *v.i.*
print'er, *n.* one who prints, esp. books, newspapers, etc.
print'ing-press, *n.* a machine by which impressions are put on paper.
out of print, sold out and unable to be obtained from the publisher.
[O.Fr. *preindre*—L. root as **press** (1).]

prior, *prī'ọr, adj.* earlier: previous (to).—*n.* head of a priory:—*fem.* **pri'oress.**
prior'ity, *n.* state of being first (or earlier, higher) in time or position: the right to be first (e.g. *A fire engine has priority in traffic*): thing having, requiring, this:—*pl.* **-ies.**
pri'ory, *n.* a convent of monks or nuns, next in rank below an abbey:—*pl.* **-ies.**
[L. *prior*, former.]

prise. See **prize** (1).

prism, *prizm, n.* (*geometry*) a solid whose ends are two figures equal in all respects and parallel to each other, and whose sides are parallelograms: a prism-shaped piece of glass, etc., used to divide light into separate colours, or for other purposes in optical instruments.
[Gk. *prisma*, a piece sawn off.]

prison, *priz'n, n.* a building for the holding of criminals, etc., a jail: any place of confinement.
pris'oner, *n.* one under arrest or locked up in a prison: a captive.
[O.Fr. *prisun*—L. *praehensiō*, a seizing.]

privacy, *prīv'ȧ-si, priv'-, n.* state of being away from company: secrecy.
private, *prī'vit, adj.* having to do with a person or a group, not with the general public: personal (e.g. *my private views*): hidden from view: secret, not made generally known: (of a soldier) not an officer: (of a member of parliament) not in the cabinet: (of a person) not in public office.—*n.* a common soldier.
in private, privately, in secret.
See also **privilege, privy.**
[L. *prīvātus*, private—*prīvāre*, separate.]

privation, *prī-vā'sh(ọ)n, n.* state of being in want, poverty, hardship: act of taking away.
[L. *prīvātiō*—*prīvāre*, separate, deprive.]

privet, *priv'it, n.* a half-evergreen shrub used for hedges. [Origin unknown.]

privilege, *priv'i-lij, n.* an advantage or favour granted to, or enjoyed by, only one person or a few.—*v.t.* to grant a privilege to.
[L. *prīvus*, private, *lex, lēgis*, law.]

privy, *priv'i, adj.* private: belonging to a person, esp. to the king or queen.—*n.* (old-fashioned) a room or small building in which to get rid of waste matter from the body.
privy council, a body of persons appointed as advisers to the crown in affairs of state, their duties now being mainly formal.
privy to, knowing about (e.g. a secret plan).
[Fr. *privé*—same L. root as **private.**]

prize[1], prise, *prīz, v.t.* to force (esp. *up* or *open*) with a lever or tool.
[Fr. *prise*, hold, grip.]

prize[2], *prīz, n.* anything taken from an enemy in war, esp. a ship.
[Fr. *prise*, capture, thing captured.]

prize[3], *prīz, n.* a reward, or a symbol of success, won in competition or by chance: anything well worth working for: a valued possession.—*adj.* very fine, that has won a prize (e.g. *a prize pig*).—*v.t.* to value highly (e.g. *He prized my friendship*).
prize'(-)fight, *n.* a public boxing-match for money.
prize'fighter, *n.* **prize'fighting,** *n.*
[O Fr. *pris*—L. root as **price.**]

pro-, *prō-, pfx.* (as part of a word) before (e.g. *prologue*): (before a word) in place of (e.g. **pro-cathedral,** a church used for a time as a cathedral): in favour of (e.g. **pro-Chinese,** favouring the Chinese).

pro and con, for and against (L. *prō et contrā*).

pros and cons, arguments for and against an opinion, plan, etc.

[L. *prō* (prep.), before.]

probable, *prob′à-bl, adj.* that may be expected to happen: that is likely to be true.

probabil′ity, *n.* likeliness: appearance of truth: probable event, etc.:—*pl.* **-ies.**

prob′ably, *adv.*

[L. *probābilis*—same root as **probation.**]

probate, *prō′bāt, -bit, n.* the official copy of a will, or the proof before a court that it is a lawful one.

[L. *probātus,* tested; root as **probation.**]

probation, *prō-bā′sh(ò)n, n.* testing: a time of testing: the suspending of a sentence (depending on good behaviour) requiring the offender who is allowed free to report to a **probation officer** at certain times.

probā′tionary, *adj.* on probation.

probā′tioner, *n.* one who is undergoing a time of testing before e.g. becoming a full member of a profession: an offender on probation.

[L. *probātiō—probāre,* to test, prove.]

probe, *prōb, n.* a long thin instrument used to explore a wound, etc.: an investigation.—*v.t.* to examine with a probe: to examine searchingly.

[L. *proba,* proof; root as **probation.**]

probity, *prōb′i-ti, prob′-, n.* honesty: uprightness.

[L. *probitās—probus,* good.]

problem, *prob′lėm, n.* a matter in which it is difficult to decide the best course of action: a person difficult to deal with: a question to be solved.

problemat′ical, *adj.* doubtful, uncertain (e.g. *His future is problematical*).

[Gk. *problēma—pro, ballein,* to throw.]

proboscis, *prō-bos′is, n.* the snout or trunk of some animals, as the elephant.

[Gk. *proboskis—pro, boskein,* to feed.]

proceed, *prō-sēd′, v.i.* to go on: to go on (to do something): to continue (with): to come, arise (from): to take legal action (against).—*v.t.* to say in continuation of what one has said.

pro′ceeds, *n.pl.* money taken at a sale or made by some action.

procē′dure, *n.* method or order of conducting business, esp. in a law case or in a meeting: course of action: a step taken.

proceed′ing, *n.* an action: a going forward: (in *pl.*) steps in a legal action: (in *pl.*) a record of the business of a society.

process, *prō′ses, pros′-, n.* a continued series of actions, events, etc. causing change: course (e.g. *in the process of time*): an operation, method, used in manufacturing, preparing, etc.: a legal action: a projecting part in a body, esp. a bone.

procession, *prō-sesh′(ò)n, n.* a large company (people or vehicles) moving forward in order.

process′ional, *adj.* having to do with a procession.—*n.* a hymn sung during a procession.

[L. *prōcēdĕre, prōcessum,* to go forward.]

proclaim, *prō-klām′, v.t.* to make known, cry aloud: to announce or declare officially.

proclamation, *prok-là-mā′sh(ò)n, n.* official notice given to the public.

[Fr. *proclamer*—L. *prōclāmāre,* cry out.]

proclivity, *prō-kliv′i-ti, n.* a leaning, inclination (e.g. *a proclivity towards gambling*):—*pl.* **-ies.**

[L. *prō,* forward, *clīvus,* a slope.]

procrastinate, *prō-kras′ti-nāt, v.i.* to put off action, be very slow to act.

procrastinā′tion, *n.*

[L. *prō,* onward, *crās,* tomorrow.]

procreate, *prō′krē-āt, v.t.* to bring (offspring) into being: to produce.

[L. *prō,* forth, *creāre,* to produce.]

procure, *prō-kūr′, v.t.* to get, obtain: to bring about (e.g. *steps to procure his appointment*).

procure′ment, *n.*

procurator-fiscal. See **fiscal.**

[Fr. *procurer*—L. *prōcūrāre,* to manage.]

prod, *prod, v.t.* to poke, urge into action:—*pr.p.* **prodd′ing**; *pa.p.* **prodd′ed.**—*n.* an act of prodding: a sharp instrument.

[Origin unknown.]

prodigal, *prod′i-g(à)l, adj.* wastefully, recklessly, extravagant: giving very freely (e.g. *He was prodigal of promises*): very plentiful.—*n.* a waster: a spendthrift.

prodigal′ity, *n.* **prod′igally,** *adv.*

[Fr. —L. *prōdigĕre,* to squander.]

prodigy, *prod′i-ji, n.* a wonder: a person of unusual genius or cleverness (esp. a **child prodigy**): a monster.

prodig′ious (*-dij′ùs*), *adj.* astonishing: huge, enormous: monstrous.

prodig′iously, *adv.* **prodig′iousness,** *n.*

[Fr. *prodige*—L. *prōdigium,* a sign.]

produce, *prō-dūs′, v.t.* to bring forward or out: to bring into being, yield: to bring about, cause: to make, manufacture: to put on the stage: to make (a line) longer.—*n.* (*prod′ūs*) something that is produced, esp. crops, etc., from a farm.

produc′er, *n.* one who produces: a farmer or manufacturer: one who is in general charge of the preparation of a play or a motion picture.

product, *prod′ukt, n.* a thing produced: a result: a work: (*arithmetic*) the result of multiplication: (in *pl.*) the crops, manufactured goods, etc., that a country yields.

produc′tion, *n.* the act or process of producing: something that is produced: a work of art or literature.

produc'tive, *adj.* having the power to produce: fruitful: bringing results.
produc'tiveness, productiv'ity, *ns.*
producer(s') goods, goods, such as tools and raw materials, used in the making of *consumer(s') goods*.
[L. *prōdūcĕre*, to lead forward.]

profane, *prȯ-fān'*, *adj.* not sacred: showing contempt for holy things.—*v.t.* to violate, treat with no reverence: to put to an unworthy use.
profan'ity, *n.* want of respect for sacred things: bad language, swearing.
[L. *profānus*, outside the temple.]

profess, *prȯ-fes'*, *v.t.* to make open declaration of: to pretend (e.g. *He professes to be a friend*): to claim knowledge of or skill in.
professed', *adj.* declared: pretended.
profession, *prȯ-fesh'(ȯ)n*, *n.* the act of professing: declaration of religious belief: pretence: an employment not mechanical and requiring special knowledge: the people engaged in such an employment (e.g. *The medical profession believe this*).
profess'ional, *adj.* having to do with a profession: making one's living by an art, game, etc. (e.g. *a professional actor, golfer*): showing the skill, etc., of one who is trained.—Also *n.*
profess'ionally, *adv.*
profess'or, *n.* a teacher of the highest grade in a university.
professō'rial, *adj.* **profess'orship,** *n.*
[L. *prō*, publicly, *fitēri*, *fessus*, confess.]

proffer, *prof'ėr*, *v.t.* to offer for acceptance: —*pr.p.* **proff'ering**; *pa.p.* **proff'ered.**— Also *n.*
[L. *prō*, forward, and root of **offer.**]

proficient, *prȯ-fish'ėnt*, *adj.* skilled, expert: qualified (in, at).—*n.* an expert.
profi'ciency, *n.* **profic'iently,** *adv.*
[L. *prōficĕre*, to make progress.]

profile, *prō'fīl*, *n.* a head, face, etc., seen from the side: the outline of an object: (*orig. U.S.*) a short sketch of character and career.
[It. *profilo*—L. *prō*, *filum*, thread.]

profit, *prof'it*, *n.* gain: benefit.—*v.t.* to bring gain or advantage to.—*v.i.* to gain, or receive benefit (e.g. *to profit from mistakes*).
prof'itable, *adj.* bringing profit or gain.
profiteer', *n.* one who makes large profits unfairly.—Also *v.i.*
profit sharing, *n.* an agreement by which workers receive a fixed share of the profits of a business.
[Fr.—L. *prōfectus*, progress.]

profligate, *prof'li-git*, *adj.* living in an immoral, dissipated way: extravagant.— *n.* one leading a profligate life.
prof'ligacy (*-ȧs-i*) *n.*
[L. *prō*, forward, *flīgĕre*, to dash.]

profound, *prō-fownd'*, *adj.* very deep: deeply felt (e.g. *profound sympathy*): difficult to understand or solve (e.g. *a profound problem*): showing great knowledge and understanding (e.g. *a profound comment*; *a profound thinker*).
profound'ness, profund'ity (*-fund'*), *ns.* the state or quality of being profound: great depth (of e.g. ocean, knowledge).
[Fr. *profond*—L. *prō*, *fundus*, bottom.]

profuse, *prȯ-fūs'*, *adj.* abundant, excessive, extravagant (e.g. *profuse thanks*; *profuse in his apologies*).
profusion, *prȯ-fū'zh(ȯ)n*, *n.* great abundance: extravagance, wastefulness.
[L. *prō*, forth, *fundĕre*, to pour.]

progenitor, *prō-jen'i-tȯr*, *n.* a forefather, an ancestor.
prog'eny (*proj'*), *n.* descendants: children: offspring.
[L. *prō*, before, *gignĕre*, to beget.]

prognosticate, *prog-nos'ti-kāt*, *v.t.* to foretell, forecast.
prognos'ticator, *n.*
[Gk. *pro*, before, *gignōskein*, to know.]

programme, program, *prō'gram*, *n.* a sheet or booklet giving details of proceedings at a ceremony: the items of an entertainment, etc.: a scheme or plan: the actions to be carried out by an electronic computer in dealing with certain facts.—*v.t.* to prepare a programme for (a computer).
[Gk. *programma*, proclamation.]

progress, *prō'gres*, *prog'res*, *n.* forward movement: advance: improvement, a gradual becoming better, or becoming more skilful: course (of a story, an event).—*v.i.* (*prȯ-gres'*) to go forward: to continue: to advance: to improve.
progression, *prȯ-gresh'(ȯ)n*, *n.* motion onward: advance: connected series.
progress'ive, *adj.* moving forward, advancing by stages: favouring reforms, keen to adopt new methods.
progress'ively, *adv.* **-iveness,** *n.*
in progress, going on, taking place.
[O.Fr. *progresse*—L. *prō*, *gradi*, to step.]

prohibit, *prō-hib'it*, *v.t.* to forbid: to prevent.
prohibition, *prō-(h)i-bi'sh(ȯ)n*, *n.* act of forbidding: forbidding by law of making and selling of alcoholic drinks.
prohibitive (*-hib'*), **prohib'itory,** *adjs.* tending to prohibit (as high prices that make it nearly impossible to buy).
[L. *prō*, before, *habēre*, to have.]

project, *proj'ekt*, *n.* a scheme, plan: a task, or piece of research.—*v.t.* (*pro-jekt'*) to throw out, forward, or up: to propose, plan: to cast (e.g. a light, image) on a surface or into space:—*v.i.* to jut out.
projec'tile, *n.* a missile.
projec'tion, *n.* an act or method of projecting: something that is projected: a planning: something which juts out: a method of making maps showing the earth's surface on a plane.
projec'tor, *n.* a machine for projecting,

esp. a beam of light, or an image (as in motion pictures): one who plans business deals.
[L. *prō*, forth, *jacĕre*, to throw.]

proletarian, *prō-le-tā'ri-ȧn*, *adj.* and *n.* (a member) of the lower wage-earning class, having little or no property.
proletā'riat (*-ȧt*), *n.* the wage-earning class with little or no property.
[L. *prōlētārius*, citizen of lowest class.]

proliferate, *prō-lif'ėr-āt*, *v.i.* (of plant or animal tissue) to grow rapidly by producing new parts: to increase much and rapidly.—Also *v.t.*
proliferā'tion, *n.*
prolif'ic, *adj.* bringing forth many offspring, much fruit, much literary work, etc.: abounding (with *in* or *of*).
[L. *prōles*, offspring, *facĕre*, to make.]

prolix, *prō'liks*, *prō-liks'*, *adj.* long, wordy, and dull: speaking or writing thus.
prolixity, prolixness, *ns.*
[L. *prō*, forward, *liquī*, to flow.]

prologue, *prō'log*, *n.* an introduction to a poem, play, etc.: any introductory event or action.
[Fr.—Gk. *pro*, before, *logos*, speech.]

prolong, *prō-long'*, *v.t.* to make longer (e.g. *to prolong a discussion*).
prolongation, *prō-long-gā'sh(ȯ)n*, *n.* a lengthening, in time or space: a piece added.
[L. *prō*, forward, *longus*, long.]

promenade, *prom-ė-näd'*, *prom'*, *n.* a walk, etc., in a public place for pleasure or to be seen: an esplanade, public walk.—*v.i.* and *v.t.* to walk, etc. publicly in a leisurely way.
promenade concert, one in which some of the audience are not seated.
[Fr. from (*se*) *promener*, to walk.]

prominent, *prom'i-nėnt*, *adj.* standing out: easily seen: famous, distinguished (e.g. *a prominent citizen*).
prom'inence, *n.* **prom'inently,** *adv.*
[L. *prōminēre*, to jut out.]

promiscuous, *prȯ-mis'kū-ůs*, *adj.* mixed in kind: not making distinction between one thing, or person, and another (e.g. *promiscuous in his choice of friends*): (*coll.*) casual, random, without plan.
promiscu'ity, promis'cuousness, *ns.*
promis'cuously, *adv.*
[L. *prō-*, *miscēre*, to mix.]

promise, *prom'is*, *n.* a statement to another that one will do, or not do, something: a sign (of what may be expected in the future; e.g. *a promise of success, of storms*): indication of future excellence (e.g. *a writer who shows promise*, or *of promise*; *a child of promise*).—*v.t.* to give one's word (to do, not to do, something): to say that one will give (e.g. gift, help): to assure (e.g. *She will be there, I promise you*): to show signs of (something to come; e.g. *The sky promises a fine day*).—*v.i.* to make a promise.
prom'ising, *adj.* full of promise.
prom'isingly, *adv.* **prom'isingness,** *n.*
promissory note, a written promise to pay a sum of money to another at a certain date or on demand.
[L. *prō*, forward, *mittĕre*, *missum*, to send.]

promontory, *prom'ȯn-tȯr-i*, or *-tri*, *n.* a headland or high cape jutting into the sea:—*pl.* **prom'ontories.**
[L. *prō*, forward, *mons*, a mountain.]

promote, *prȯ-mōt'*, *v.t.* to raise to a higher rank or position: to help the growth of, encourage (e.g. *to promote the cause of peace*): to help to arrange (a business enterprise, the passing of a law, etc.).
promō'ter, *n.* **promō'tion,** *n.*
[L. *prō*, forward, *movēre*, to move.]

prompt, *prom(p)t*, *adj.* ready in action: done, sent, etc. without delay.—*v.t.* to move to action (e.g. *Mary prompted the other children to ask for more*): to inspire (e.g. *Fear prompted this reply*): to give forgotten words or cue to (e.g. an actor).
prompt'er, *n.* one who prompts, esp. actors.
prompt'ing, *n.* **prompt'ly,** *adv.*
prompt'ness, prompt'itude (*-tūd*), *ns.* quickness, readiness.
[L. *promptus*—*prōmĕre*, to bring forward.]

promulgate, *prom'ůl-gāt*, *v.t.* to proclaim, make widely known (a law, a doctrine).
promulgā'tion, *n.*
[L. *prōmulgāre*, *-ātum*.]

prone, *prōn*, *adj.* lying face downward, or flat: inclined (to; e.g. *prone to laziness*; *prone to accidents*, *accident-prone*).
[L. *prōnus*.]

prong, *prong*, *n.* the spike of a fork.
pronged, *adj.* having prongs.
[M.E. *prange*; origin unknown.]

pronoun, *prō'nown*, *n.* a word used instead of a noun to show without naming e.g.) *he*, *she*, *it*, *you*, *who*).
[L. *prō*, instead of, and **noun.**]

pronounce, *prȯ-nowns'*, *v.t.* to speak, utter (words, sounds): to give (judgment) officially or formally: to declare (e.g. *He pronounced the vase to be an imitation*).
pronounced', *adj.* noticeable, decided (e.g. *a pronounced squint*).
pronounce'ment, *n.* an announcement or statement.
pronunciation, *prȯ-nun-si-ā'sh(ȯ)n*, *n.* act, or way, of saying a word.
[L. *prō*, *nuntiāre*, announce.]

proof. See **prove.**

prop[1], *prop*, *n.* a support: a supporter on whom one depends.—*v.t.* to hold up by placing something under or against.
[M.E. *proppe*; from Du.]

prop[2], short for **propeller, property.**

propagate, *prop'ȧ-gāt*, *v.t.* to cause (plants or animals) to produce offspring: to spread from one to another (e.g. *to propagate a rumour, belief, knowledge*): to transmit, pass on (sound).—*v.i.* to breed, produce young.

propagan'da, *n.* action for the spread of particular ideas or opinions.

propagand'ist, *n.* one who works to spread political or other ideas.

propagā'tion, *n.* the spreading of anything: the producing of young.

[L. *propāgāre*; conn. *propāgō,* layer.]

propel, *prō-pel',* *v.t.* to drive forward:—*pr.p.* **propell'ing;** *pa.p.* **propelled'.**

propell'er, *n.* a shaft with blades for driving a ship, aeroplane, etc.

propulsion, *prō-pul'sh(ó)n,* *n.* act of driving forward.

[L. *prō,* forward, *pellĕre, pulsum,* drive.]

propensity, *pro-pens'i-ti,* *n.* a natural leaning, tendency, towards (e.g. *a propensity to contradict, for writing poetry*).

[L. *prō,* forward, *pendēre,* to hang.]

proper, *prop'ėr, adj.* fitting, right: correct: prim, well-behaved: suitable, belonging (to): strictly so-called (e.g. *London proper, not including Greater London*): (*coll.*) thorough.

prop'erly, *adv.* in the right way: (*coll.*) thoroughly.

proper noun, name, a noun, name, naming a particular person, thing, place (with *cap.*; e.g. *John*; *the Pole Star*; *the ship called the Revenge*; *New York*).

See also **propriety.**

[Fr. *propre*—L. *prōprius,* own.]

property, *prop'ėr-ti,* *n.* a quality of a thing (e.g. *Hardness is a property of the diamond*): something that is one's own: land or buildings: (in *pl.*) small articles or furniture used by actors in a play **(props)**:—*pl.* **prop'erties.**

[O.Fr. *properte*—same L. root as **proper.**]

prophecy, *prof'ė-si,* *n.* prediction, foretelling the future: thing foretold:—*pl.* **-ies.**

prophesy, *prof'ė-sī, v.i.* to foretell the future.—Also *v.t.* (e.g. *to prophesy disaster, to prophesy that . . .*):—*pr.p.* **proph'esying;** *pa.p.* **proph'esied.**

proph'et, *n.* one who tells beforehand of things to come: one who tells the will of God:—*fem.* **proph'etess.**

prophet'ic(al), *adjs.* foreseeing or foretelling events.

prophet'ically, *adv.*

[Gk. *prophēteia*—*prophētēs,* prophet.]

propinquity, *prō-ping'kwi-ti, n.* nearness in place, time, blood relationship.

[L. *propinquus,* near—*prope,* near.]

propitiate, *prō-pish'i-āt, v.t.* to calm the anger of: to gain the favour of.

propitiā'tion, *n.*

propi'tious, *adj.* favourable (e.g. *The time seemed propitious for the rebellion*; *the weather proved propitious to the attempt*).

[L. *propitiāre,* to make favourable.]

proportion *prō-pōr'sh(ó)n,* or *-pör', n.* the ratio or comparative size, number, quantity, of one thing considered alongside another (e.g. *The proportion of women to men at the concert was large; in the proportion of three ounces of butter to four of flour*): a part, esp. considered alongside the whole (e.g. *A small proportion of the class failed*): balance or suitability in size of different parts (e.g. *Her feet are out of proportion to her body*): balance in importance, strength, etc. (e.g. *His anger was out of proportion to the harm done*): (in *pl.*) dimensions (e.g. *a giant of vast proportions*).—*v.t.* to make in correct proportion (to).

propor'tional, propor'tionate, *adjs.* in proportion.

in (out of) proportion, correct (or not correct), suitable (or not suitable), in size, etc. when compared with something else.

[L. *prō,* in comparison with, *portiō,* part.]

propose, *prō-pōz', v.t.* to put forward for consideration, to suggest (e.g. a plan, a candidate): to intend (e.g. *He proposes to build a new house*).—*v.i.* to make an offer, especially of marriage.

propōs'al, *n.* act of proposing: anything proposed: an offer of marriage.

[Fr.—*prō-*, forward, *poser,* to place.]

proposition, *prop-ó-zish'(ó)n, n.* a proposal, suggestion: a statement: (*slang,* orig. *U.S.*) any situation, thing, or person considered as something to be coped with.

[L. *prōpositiō*—same root as **position.**]

propound, *prō-pownd', v.t.* to offer for consideration, state (e.g. a problem).

[L. *prō,* forth, *pōnĕre,* to place.]

proprietor, *prō-prī'ė-tor, n.* an owner:—*fem.* **proprī'etress, proprī'etrix.**

proprī'etary, *adj.* owning property: legally made by a firm having sole right to do so (e.g. *a proprietary drug*).

proprietary name, trademark.

[L. *proprius,* own.]

propriety, *prō-prī'ė-ti, n.* fitness, suitability, rightness: the standard of behaviour and morals accepted in society as correct: (in *pl.*, **propri'eties**) the details of this.

[Fr. *propriété*—L. *proprius,* own.]

props. See **property.**

propulsion. See **propel.**

prorogue, *prō-rōg', v.t.* to bring the meetings of (parliament) to an end for a time:—*pr.p.* **prorog'uing;** *pa.p.* **prorogued'.**

[L. *prō,* forward, *rogāre,* to ask.]

prosaic, *prō-zā'ik, adj.* dull, uninteresting: matter-of-fact.

prosa'ically, *adv.* [From **prose.**]

proscenium, *prō-sē'ni-ùm, n.* the front part of the stage.

[Gk. *pro,* before, *skēnē,* the stage.]

proscribe, *prō-skrīb', v.t.* to outlaw: to prohibit or refuse to tolerate.

[L. *prō,* before, *scrībĕre,* write (Romans posted up names of those condemned).]

prose, *prōz, n.* writing that is not in verse:

ordinary spoken and written language.—*adj.* of, in, prose: dull.
pros'y, *adj.* dull, tiresome.
pros'ily, *adv.* **pros'iness,** *n.*
See also **prosaic.**
[L. *prōsa—prorsus,* straightforward.]

prosecute, *pros'ė-kūt, v.t.* to bring a legal action against: to follow up (e.g. an enquiry): to carry on (e.g. *He prosecutes his studies*).
prosecū'tion, *n.* act of bringing a court case against another: the party bringing a court action: the carrying on, continuing (of e.g. an enquiry, a task).
pros'ecūtor, *n.* the law officer who leads a case against a prisoner.
[L. *prō,* onwards, *sequī,* to follow.]

prospect, *pros'pekt, n.* a wide view: a scene: outlook for the future, likely result (e.g. *faced with the prospect of defeat*): (in *pl.*) measure of success to be expected (e.g. *He has good prospects in his present job*).—*v.i.* (*pros-pekt'*) to make a search (for, e.g. gold).
prospec'tive, *adj.* expected, likely to be or happen, future.
prospec'tus, *n.* a small book giving information about a business, school, literary work, etc.
[L. *prō,* forward, *specĕre,* to look.]

prosper, *pros'pėr, v.i.* to succeed, turn out well.—*v.t.* to cause to thrive.
prosper'ity, *n.* success, good fortune.
pros'perous, *adj.* **pros'perously,** *adv.*
[L. *prosper,* or *prosperus,* successful.]

prostitute, *pros'ti-tūt, v.t.* to offer or sell for evil use.—*n.* a woman who offers herself to many men for money.
prostitū'tion, *n.*
[L. *prōstituĕre,* to set up for sale.]

prostrate, *pros'trāt, -trit, adj.* lying with face on the ground: reduced to helplessness: worn out, exhausted.—*v.t.* (*pros-trāt', pros'*) to throw forwards on the ground: to defeat utterly: to exhaust: to bow (oneself) in reverence (e.g. *He prostrated himself before the king*).
prostrātion, *n.*
[L. *prō, sternĕre, strātum,* spread.]

prosy. See **prose.**

protagonist, *prō-tag'on-ist, n.* chief actor or character: champion (of a cause).
[Gk. *prōtos,* first, *agōnistēs,* combatant.]

protect, *prō-tekt', v.t.* to guard, defend (*from, against, danger, injury, loss, change*): to put safety devices on: to aid (an industry) by putting a tax on goods of rival foreign firms.
protec'tion, *n.*
protec'tive, *adj.* giving protection, intended to protect.
protec'tor, *n.* a guardian: one who shields from harm or injury.
protec'torate, *n.* a country that is partly governed and defended by a stronger country.
[L. *prō,* in front, *tegĕre, tectum,* to cover.]

protégé, *prō-tā-zhā, prot-, n.* one having help from an important person in making his career, etc. (e.g. *He was a protégé of a cabinet minister*):—*pl.* **protégés;** *fem.* **protégée** (*pl.* **protégées**).
[Fr. *proteger,* protect; root as **protect.**]

protein, *prō'tēn, -tē-in, n.* any of a large number of substances (present in milk, eggs, meat, etc.) essential as part of the diet of human beings and animals.
[Gk. *prōteios,* primary—*prōtos,* first.]

pro tempore, *prō tem'pō-rē,* for the time being, temporarily.—Abbrev. **pro tem.** [L.]

protest, *prō-test', v.i.* to express an objection (*protest at, against*).—*v.t.* to make a solemn declaration of (e.g. *He protested his innocence*).—*n.* (*prō'test*) a strong statement of objection or disapproval.
Prot'estant (*prot'*), *n.* a member of one of the western Christian churches founded at the Reformation (by breaking away from the Roman Catholic Church) or later.
Prot'estantism, *n.* Protestant religion.
protestation, *prō-tes-tā'sh(ȯ)n, prot-, n.* solemn declaration (with *of*; e.g. *his protestation of loyalty*): a protest (against).
[L. *prōtestārī,* to bear witness in public.]

prot(o)-, *prō-t(ō)-,* (as part of a word) first in time, earliest.
[Gk. *prōtos,* first.]

protocol, *prō'tō-kol, n.* a draft of a treaty: a body of rules, etiquette, for diplomatic ceremonies.
[Gk. *prōtos,* first, *kolla,* glue; orig. leaf glued to manuscript giving contents.]

proton, *prō'ton, n.* a particle with positive charge forming the nucleus of the hydrogen atom and part of the nucleus of all other atoms.
[Gk. neuter of *prōtos,* first.]

protoplasm, *prō'tō-plazm, n.* the half-liquid substance which is the chief material found in all living cells.
[Gk. *prōtos,* first, *plasma,* form.]

prototype, *prō'tō-tīp, n.* the first model from which anything is copied.
[Gk. *prōtos,* first, *typos,* type.]

protract, *prō-trakt', v.t.* to draw out or lengthen in time (e.g. *Let us not protract the discussion*).
protrac'tor, *n.* an instrument for drawing angles on paper.
[L. *prō,* forth, *trahĕre, tractum,* to draw.]

protrude, *prō-trōōd', v.t.* and *v.i.* to stick, thrust, out or forward.
protrusion, *prō-trōō'zh(ȯ)n, n.* act of sticking out: something that sticks out.
[L. *prō,* forward, *trūdĕre,* to thrust.]

protuberance, *prō-tūb'ėr-ȧns, n.* a bulging out, a swelling.
protu'berant, *adj.* swelling.
[L. *prō,* forward, *tūber,* a swelling.]

proud. See **pride.**

prove, *prōōv, v.t.* to test: to show to be true: to show correctness of (a result)—

v.i. to turn out to be (e.g. *The report proves to be true*) :—*pa.p.* (*usu.*) **proved.**

proven, *prōōv'n* (Scots law, *prōv'n*), *pa.p.* (chiefly *U.S.*) and *adj.* proved.

proof, *prōōf*, *n.* evidence that convinces: a test making something clear beyond doubt: act of showing to be true: a copy taken from printing type for correction before printing: (*photography*) the first print from a negative: standard of strength of whisky, etc.—*adj.* firm (against), able to withstand (e.g. *proof against the arguments of the rebels*; often used as part of a word, e.g. in **bullet-proof, fireproof**).

proof'ing, *n.* the process of making waterproof, fireproof, etc.: material used for this.

[O.Fr. *prover*—L. *probāre*, to prove.]

provender, *prov'in-dėr*, *n.* food, esp. a dry meal for horses and cattle.

[Late L. *provenda*, daily allowance of food.]

proverb, *prov'ėrb*, *n.* a short familiar sentence expressing a moral lesson or something supposed to be true (e.g. 'A penny saved is a penny earned').

prover'bial, *adj.* like a proverb: widely known, or spoken of by everyone (e.g. *the cat's proverbial nine lives*).

[L. *prō*, before, publicly, *verbum*, word.]

provide, *prō-vīd'*, *v.t.* to make ready beforehand: to supply: to supply (a person with)—*v.i.* to get what is necessary ready for (e.g. *to provide for, against, a hard winter*).

provided (often **provided that**), *conj.* on condition (that), if.

provision, *prō-vizh'(ō)n*, *n.* act of providing (for, against): an agreement or arrangement made earlier: a clause in a law or a deed: a store or stock: (in *pl.*) (a store of) food.—*v.t.* to supply with food.

provisional (*-vizh'*), *adj.* temporary, not final, with the possibility of change (e.g. *a provisional government*).

proviso, *prō-vī'zō*, *n.* a condition made, esp. in a document (e.g. *He agreed to come, with the proviso that he must not be asked to sing*) :—*pl.* **provī'so(e)s.**

provī'sory, *adj.* provisional: having to do with a proviso.

[L. *prō*, before, *vidēre, vīsum*, to see.]

providence, *prov'i-dėns*, *n.* foresight: thrift: the care of God for all creatures: an event showing God's care.

prov'ident, *adj.* seeing beforehand, and providing for the future: thrifty.

providential, *prov-i-den'sh(ȧ)l*, *adj.* coming from divine will or God's care: fortunate (e.g. *the providential arrival of help*). [Same root as **provide.**]

province, *prov'ins*, *n.* a division of a country or part of an empire: the extent or limits of one's duty, knowledge, etc. (e.g. *Keeping the garden is outside my province*): (in *pl.*) all parts of the country outside the capital.

provincial, *prō-vin'sh(ȧ)l*, *adj.* having to do with a province: unpolished in manners, or narrow in interests.

provin'cialism, *n.* a manner, custom, or way of speaking found in the country: interest in area where one lives and not in one's country as whole.

[L. *prōvincia*, a province.]

provision, proviso, etc. See **provide.**

provocation, etc. See **provoke.**

provoke, *prō-vōk'*, *v.t.* to rouse to anger, annoy: to stir up (a person, etc. to action): to give rise to, result in (e.g. laughter, trouble).

provocā'tion, *n.* act of provoking: something that rouses anger.

provoc'ative, *adj.* tending to provoke or excite: encouraging one to think.

[L. *prō*, forth, *vocāre*, to call.]

provost, *prov'ost*, *n.* the head of a cathedral: the head of a college: (*Scotland*) the chief magistrate of a burgh.

Lord Provost, the chief magistrate of each of five large Scottish cities.

[O.E. *profast*—L. *prae*, over, *pōnĕre*, place.]

prow, *prow*, *n.* the front part of a ship.

[Fr. *proue*—L. *prōra*.]

prowess, *prow'es*, *n.* bravery, esp, in war: great skill, ability, etc.

[O.Fr. *prou*, valiant.]

prowl, *prowl*, *v.i.* to move about stealthily, or quietly, esp. seeking plunder.

[M.E. *prollen*; origin unknown.]

proximity, *proks-im'i-ti*, *n.* state of being very near in place, time, etc.

[L. *proximus*, next—*prope*, near.]

proxy, *prok'si*, *n.* one who acts or votes for another: the writing by which he is allowed to do so.

[Short for *procurator*, agent—**procure.**]

prude, *prōōd*, *n.* a woman who prides herself on modesty and correct behaviour.

prud'ish, *adj.*

pru'dery, *n.* state of being like a prude: prudish actions, speeches (*pl.* **-ies**).

[O.Fr. *prode*—*prou*, excellent.]

prudent, *prōō'dėnt*, *adj.* cautious and wise.

pru'dence, *n.* wisdom in managing practical affairs: caution.

pruden'tial, *adj.* using caution.

[L. *prūdens*—same root as **provide.**]

prudery, prudish. See **prude.**

prune[1], *prōōn*, *v.t.* to trim (a tree, etc.) by cutting off unnecessary parts: to cut off (e.g. twigs): to delete parts of (e.g. story): to take out (unnecessary details).

[O.Fr. *proignier*; origin uncertain.]

prune[2], *prōōn*, *n.* a dried plum.

[Fr.—L. *prūnum*.]

prurient, *prōō'ri-ėnt*, *adj.* finding pleasure in indecent thoughts.

[L. *prūrīre*, to itch.]

pry[1], *prī*, *v.i.* to peer or peep (into what is closed, or into what is not told): to try

to find out about other people's affairs :— *pr.p.* **pry'ing;** *pa.p.* **pried.**
pry'ing, *adj.* curious : peering.
[M.E. *prien*; origin unknown.]

pry[2]. Same as **prize (1).**

psalm, *säm, n.* a sacred song or hymn, esp. one from the Book of Psalms.
psalmist, *säm'ist, n.* a writer of psalms.
[Gk. *psalmos*, music of, to, stringed instrument—*psallein*, to pluck.]

psalter, *söl'tėr, n.* a book of psalms.
psal'tery, *n.* an ancient stringed instrument.
[O.E. *saltere*—Gk. *psaltērion*, psaltery.]

pseud(o)-, *sū-d(ō)-*, (as part of word) false, sham, fake :—e.g. **pseu'do-antique'** (e.g. *He bought a pseudo-antique vase*).
pseudo, *adj.* sham (e.g. *His foreign accent is pseudo*).
pseudonym, *sū'dō-nim, n.* a false name assumed by an author (e.g. *Mark Twain was the pseudonym of Samuel Clemens*).
pseudon'ymous, *adj.*
[Gk. *pseudo-*, false (*onoma*, name).]

psyche, *sī'kē, n.* soul, spirit, mind.
psy'chic, *adj.* having to do with soul or mind : sensitive to forces that have no physical cause : connected with such forces.—Also **psy'chical.**
psychī'atrist, *n.* one who treats diseases of the mind.
psychī'atry, *n.* the treatment of mental diseases.
psycho-anal'ysis, *n.* a method of treating nervous diseases by tracing forgotten events or thoughts in the patient's mind and bringing them to light.
psycho-an'alyse, *v.t.*
psycho-an'alyst, *n.*
psychol'ogy, *n.* the science that studies the human mind and mental life.
psycholog'ical, *adj.* **-ically,** *adv.*
psychol'ogist, *n.*
psy'chopath, *n.* a very ill-balanced person who is not morally responsible, e.g. for crimes he may commit.
psychō'sis, *n.* any grave illness of the mind.
psychosomat'ic, *adj.* having to do with the relationship of mind and body, as with physical diseases coming from a mental disturbance.
psychother'apy, *n.* the treatment of disease by hypnosis, psycho-analysis, etc.
psychological moment, the best moment.
psychological warfare, the use of propaganda to influence enemy opinion or state of mind.
[Gk. *psychē*, soul (*iatreia*, healing, *logos*, discourse, *pathos*, suffering, *soma*, body, *therapeia*, healing).]

ptomaine, *tō'mān*, or *-mān'*, *n.* a substance that forms in food that is going bad and causes serious illness.
[Gk. *ptōma*, a corpse—*piptein*, to fall.]

pub, *pub, n.* (*coll.*) short for **public house.**

puberty, *pū'bėr-ti, n.* the beginning of sexual maturity.
[Fr. *puberté*—L. *pūbēs*, grown up.]

public, *pub'lik, adj.* of, or concerning, the people in general : having to do with a community or nation : common, or shared in by all : generally known : not private.—*n.* the people in general : a certain section of people (e.g. *an author's public, the reading public*).
pub'licly, *adv.*
publicity, *pub-lis'i-ti, n.* the state of being public or open to the knowledge of all : advertising.
pub'lican, *n.* keeper of an inn or public house.
publicā'tion, *n.* the act of making public, or of putting a book, etc. on sale : something published, as a book.
publish, *pub'lish, v.t.* to make public : to announce formally : to put out for sale (e.g. a book).
pub'lisher, *n.*
public house, *n.* a house where alcoholic liquors are sold to the public, an inn or tavern.
public opinion poll, a testing of public opinion by questioning certain people (taken as samples) in a community.
public relations, the activities of a firm, government, person, to keep on good terms with its public.
public school, a school maintained by a local education authority : a fee-paying school run partly on money given to it in the past.
public servant. See **servant.**
public spirit, an unselfish desire, shown in one's actions, for welfare of fellow citizens.
pub'lic-spir'ited, *adj.*
in public, in open view, among people (e.g. *They quarrelled in public*).
[L. *pūblicus*—*populus*, the people; *publish* came through Fr.]

puce, *pūs, n.* a brownish-purple.
[Fr. *puce*—L. *pūlex*, a flea.]

pucker, *puk'ėr, v.t.* and *v.i.* to wrinkle.—*n.* a fold or wrinkle.
[Prob. from same root as **poke,** a bag.]

pudding, *pood'ing, n.* a type of sausage (e.g. *black pudding*) : a soft food made of sugar, milk, eggs, etc.
[M.E. *poding*; origin unknown.]

puddle, *pud'l, n.* a small muddy pool.—*v.t.* to cause (molten pig iron) to undergo the process of **puddling,** which turns it into wrought iron.—*v.i.* to dabble.
[From O.E. *pudd*, ditch.]

puerile, *pū'ėr-īl, adj.* childish, silly.
pu'erileness, pueril'ity, *ns.*
[L. *puerīlis*—*puer*, a boy.]

puff, *puf, v.i.* to blow out in small gusts : to breath heavily (as after running) : to swell (up, out).—*v.t.* to drive with a puff : to blow up, inflate : to praise, esp. as advertisement.—*n.* a sudden gust of wind: a piece of light pastry: a powder puff: praise, esp. as advertisement.

puff′y, *adj.* breathing heavily: puffed out with air: flabby:—*comp.* **puff′ier;** *superl.* **puff′iest.**

puff′iness, *n.*

puff′ball, *n.* a type of round fungus.

puffed up, swollen with pride.

[O.E. *pyffan*; conn. with Ger. *puffen.*]

puffin, *puf′in, n.* a type of sea-bird with a short thick beak.

[Origin uncertain.]

pug, *pug, n.* a monkey: a type of small dog.

pug′-nose, *n.* a short thick nose with the tip turned up.

pug′-nosed, *adj.* [Origin unknown.]

pugilism, *pū′jil-izm, n.* the art of boxing: prizefighting.

pu′gilist, *n.*

[L. *pugil*, a boxer; conn. **pugnacious.**]

pugnacious, *pug-nā′shus, adj.* fond of fighting, quarrelsome.

pugnac′ity, *n.* readiness to fight.

[L. *pugnāre*, to fight.]

puissant, *pū′is-ȧnt, pwis′, adj.* powerful. [Fr.]

pukka, *puk′ȧ, adj.* good: genuine, real.

[Hindustani *pakka*, ripe.]

puke, *pūk, v.i.* to vomit.

[Perh. conn. with Ger. *spucken.*]

pule, *pūl, v.i.* to whimper or whine.

[Imit.; conn. with Fr. *piauler.*]

pull, *pool, v.t.* to pluck (e.g. flowers): to move, or try to move, towards oneself, drag, draw, tug: to row (a boat): to draw out (e.g. *to pull a tooth*): to stretch, or strain: to hold back (esp. a horse in racing): (*U.S.*) to draw out (a knife, gun): to send (a ball) to the left (in case of left-handed players, to the right) of the direction intended.—*v.i.* to do an action of pulling.—*n.* the act of pulling: a pulling force: a draught of liquor: an advantage (in a contest—as in weight, quickness, etc.).

to pull off, to gain, or to succeed in, by effort.

to pull oneself together, to regain self-control.

to pull one's weight, to take one's full share in an undertaking.

to pull round, to bring, or come, back to good health.

to pull through, to get safely to the end of a difficult or dangerous experience.

to pull up, to stop, halt.

[O.E. *pullian*, to pluck, draw.]

pullet, *pool′it, n.* a young hen.

[Fr. *poulette—poule*, a hen.]

pulley, *pool′i, n.* a wheel with a grooved rim in which fits a cord, chain, etc., used for lifting weights, changing direction of pull, etc.:—*pl.* **pull′eys.**

[M.E. *poley, puly*—O.Fr. *polie.*]

Pullman (car), *pool′mȧn (kär), n.* a railway saloon or sleeping-car, first made by G. M. *Pullman* in America.

pulmonary, *pul′mȯn-ȧr-i, adj.* having to do with, or affecting, the lungs.

[L. *pulmo, pulmōnis*, a lung.]

pulp, *pulp, n.* the soft fleshy part of a fruit: any soft mass, as the tissue in the cavity of a tooth: the soft mass (made from e.g. wood) which is made into paper.—*v.t.* to reduce to pulp.

[L. *pulpa*, flesh, pulp.]

pulpit, *pool′pit, n.* a raised structure, esp. in a church, occupied by a preacher.

[L. *pulpitum*, a stage.]

pulsate, *pul′sāt, v.i.* to beat, throb.

pulsā′tion, *n.* a beating or throbbing.

pulse, *puls, n.* a regular beat or throb: the beating of heart and arteries.

[L. *pulsāre*, beat—*pellěre, pulsum*, drive.]

pulse[1]**.** See **pulsate.**

pulse[2]**,** *puls, n.* the edible seeds of beans, peas, etc.

[L. *puls*, porridge; conn. Gk. *poltos.*]

pulverise, *pul′vėr-īz, v.t.* to make or crush into dust or fine powder.

pulverisā′tion, *n.* **pul′veriser,** *n.*

[L. *pulvis, pulveris*, powder.]

puma, *pū′mȧ, n.* a wild cat-like animal found in America. [Peruvian.]

pumice (stone), *pu′mis (stōn), n.* a piece of light hardened glassy lava, used for smoothing or cleaning.

[L. *pūmex, pūmicis—spuma*, foam.]

pummel, *pum′l, n.* to beat with the fists:—*pr.p.* **pumm′elling**; *pa.p.* **pumm′elled.**

[Orig. 'strike with sword **pommel**'.]

pump[1]**,** *pump, n.* a machine for raising water, etc. or for compressing or moving gases.—*v.t.* to raise or force with a pump: to draw out information from (a person) by cunning questions.

[Origin uncertain.]

pump[2]**,** *pump, n.* a light dancing shoe.

[Origin unknown.]

pumpkin, *pum(p)′kin, n.* a large roundish thick-skinned yellow or orange fruit of the gourd family.

[O.Fr. *pompon*—Gk. *pepōn*, ripe.]

pun, *pun, v.i.* to play upon words alike in sound but different in meaning (e.g. *They went and told the sexton, and the sexton tolled the bell*):—*pr.p.* **punn′ing**; *pa.p.* **punned.**—*n.* a play upon words.

pun′ster, *n.* one who makes puns.

[Origin unknown.]

punch[1]**,** *punch* or *-sh, n.* a drink of spirits, water, sugar, juices and spice.

[Hindustani *pānch*, five (it had orig. five ingredients).]

punch[2]**,** *punch* or *-sh, v.t.* to strike, esp. with the fists: to stamp or pierce by a thrust of a tool or machine.—*n.* a thrust, blow: striking power, vigour: a tool for punching holes.

punch′-drunk′, *adj.* (of a boxer) dizzy, having a brain injury, through blows.

punch line, (*U.S.*) the last line of a story or joke which gives it meaning or an unexpected twist.
[**pounce;** or shortened from **puncheon.**]

puncheon, *pun'ch(ȯ)n,* *n.* a tool for piercing or stamping metal plates.
[O.Fr. *poinçon*—L. *pungĕre,* to prick.]

punctilious, *pungk-til'i-ůs,* *adj.* giving great care to small points, esp. in behaviour or ceremony.
[It. *puntiglio,* small point—L. *punctum,* point; same root as **punctuate.**]

punctual, *pungk'tū-ȧl, adj.* strict in keeping time of appointments: up to time, not late: prompt.
punc'tually, *adv.* **punctual'ity,** *n.*
[L. *punctum,* point; root as **punctuate.**]

punctuate, *pungk'tū-āt, v.t.* to divide into sentences, etc. by commas, full stops, etc.: to interrupt at intervals (e.g. *silence punctuated by,* or *with, bird cries*): to emphasise (e.g. *He punctuated the refusal by banging the table*).
punctuā'tion, *n.*
punctuation marks, the comma, semi-colon, colon, period, etc.
[L. *punctum,* point—*pungĕre, punctum,* prick.]

puncture, *punk'chůr,* *n.* act of pricking, piercing: a small hole made with a sharp point: a hole in a tyre.—*v.t.* to prick: to pierce with a sharp point.
[L. *punctūra*; same root as **punctuate.**]

pundit, *pun'dit,* *n.* a Hindu scholar: any learned man.
[Hindustani *pandit.*]

pungent, *pun'jėnt, adj.* sharp in taste or smell: painful: biting, sarcastic (e.g. *a pungent remark*).
[L. *pungens*; same root as **punctuate.**]

punish, *pun'ish, v.t.* to cause (a person) to suffer for a fault or crime: to make person(s) suffer for (an offence; e.g. *to punish carelessness*): (*coll.*) to handle roughly.
pun'ishable, *adj.* (of persons or crimes) that may be punished (e.g. *punishable by death*).
pun'ishment, *n.* act or method of punishing: penalty imposed for an offence.
punitive, *pū'ni-tiv, adj.* inflicting punishment: aiming at punishment.
[Fr. *punir*—L. *punīre.*]

punster. See **pun.**

punt[1], *punt, n.* a flat-bottomed boat with square ends.—*v.t.* to move (a punt, etc.) by pushing a pole against the bottom of a river, etc.
[O.E. *punt*—L. *pontō.*]

punt[2], *punt, n.* the act of kicking a dropped football before it touches the ground.—*v.t.* to kick in this manner.
[Origin uncertain.]

punt[3], *punt, v.i.* to bet on a horse.
punt'er, *n.* a habitual gambler.
[Fr. *ponter.*]

puny, *pū'ni, adj.* little and weak: feeble:—*comp.* **pu'nier**; *superl.* **pu'niest.**
[O.Fr. *puisné, puis né,* born afterwards.]

pup, *pup, n.* a young dog, seal, etc.
[Short for **puppy.**]

pupa, *pū'pȧ, n.* a stage (often passed in a cocoon) in the growth of an insect between the larva (e.g. caterpillar) and the perfect form (e.g. butterfly).
[L. *pupa,* a girl, a doll.]

pupil[1], *pū'pil, n.* one who is being taught by a teacher or tutor.
[Fr. *pupille*—L. *pūpus,* boy, *pūpa,* girl.]

pupil[2], *pū'pil, n.* the round opening in the middle of the eye through which the light passes.
[L. *pūpilla*; conn. with **pupil** (1).]

puppet, *pup'it, n.* a doll moved by wires or hands: one who acts just as another tells him.
pupp'etry, *n.* the art of producing puppet-shows.
pupp'et-show, *n.* a drama performed by puppets on a small stage.
[L. *pūpa,* girl, doll.]

puppy, *pup'i, n.* a young dog: a conceited young man:—*pl.* **pupp'ies.**
[Fr. *poupée,* a doll—L. *pūpa.*]

purchase, *pûr'chȧs, v.t.* to buy: to obtain by work, effort, etc.—*n.* anything that is bought: act of buying (e.g. *money for the purchase of books*): any extra power, or advantage, in raising or moving things, obtained by using e.g. a lever, a capstan: means of exerting force.
pur'chaser, *n.*
purchase tax, a tax on certain goods sold within the country.
[O.Fr. *porchacier,* to seek eagerly.]

pure, *pūr, adj.* clean, spotless: free from dirt or infection (e.g. *pure milk*): not mixed with anything less valuable (e.g. *pure gold*): free from faults (e.g. *Though a German, he spoke very pure Russian*): innocent: that and that only (e.g. *a pure accident*): utter (e.g. *That is pure nonsense*): (*music*) clear and smooth in tone: perfectly in tune.
pure'ly, *adv.* in a pure manner: wholly, entirely: solely, merely.
pure'ness, pur'ity, *ns.*
purify, *pū'ri-fī, v.t.* to make pure:—*pr.p.* **pu'rifying**; *pa.p.* **pu'rified.**
purificā'tion, *n.* act of purifying.
pure'-blood'ed, *adj.* whose ancestors are all of the same race.
pure'-bred', *adj.* (of animal) whose ancestors are all of the same breed.
pure mathematics, science, mathematics or science in theory, apart from practical uses.
[L. *pūrus* (*facĕre,* to make).]

purée, *pū'rā, n.* food material reduced to a pulp and passed through a sieve. [Fr.]

purgatory, etc. See **purge.**

purge, *pûrj, v.t.* to purify, clean: to clear (something) of unwanted things, or (e.g. a political party) of people who are thought not to be loyal to it: to empty (the bowels).—Also *v.i.*:—*pr.p.* **purg'ing.**—*n.* act of purging: a medicine that purges.

purgation, *pûr-gā'sh(ȯ)n, n.*

purgative, *pûr'gȧ-tiv, adj.* and *n.* (something) that purges.

pur'gatory (*-gȧ-*), *n.* (*R.C.*) a place or state in which the soul is made clean of sins before entering heaven: any state of suffering for a time:—*pl.* **pur'gatories.**

[L. *purgāre*—same root as **pure.**]

purification, purify. See **pure.**

Puritan, *pūr'i-tȧn, n.* one of a religious group which desired to keep religion pure in belief and simple in ceremony: (often without *cap.*) a person who believes in strict (often narrow) morals and self-restraint and seriousness.

puritan'ical, *adj.*

pur'itanism, *n.* the principles and ways of Puritans.

[Same root as **pure.**]

purity. See **pure.**

purl[1], *pûrl, v.i.* to flow with a murmuring or rippling sound.—Also *n.*

[Norwegian *purla*, to babble.]

purl[2], *pûrl, v.t.* to fringe with a wavy edging, as in lace: to knit in stitches made with the wool, etc., in front of the work. [Origin unknown.]

purlieus, *pûr'lūz, n. pl.* borders or outskirts: neighbourhood.

[*puralee*, land marked out by beating the bounds (—O.Fr. *allee*, a going), influenced by Fr. *lieu*, place.]

purloin, *pûr-loin', v.t.* to filch, steal.

[O.Fr. *porloigner*, put away—*loin*, far.]

purple, *pûr'pl, n.* a colour formed by mixture of blue and red: a purple dress or robe, orig. worn by royalty: royal rank or any high position.—Also *adj.*

[Gk. *porphyrā*, a shellfish yielding dye.]

purport, *pûr'pōrt, -pört, n.* meaning: substance, gist.—*v.t.* (*-port', -pört'*) to mean: to seem, be given appearance of (e.g. *It was a letter purporting to come from you*).

[O.Fr. *pur*, forward, *porter*, to carry.]

purpose, *pûr'pus, n.* the aim towards which an effort or action is directed: use, function (of e.g. tool): constancy of aim (e.g. *a man of purpose*).—*v.t.* to intend.

pur'poseful, *adj.* knowing what one wants to do: serving a purpose.

pur'posely, *adv.* intentionally.

on purpose, purposely.

to good purpose, with good results.

to the purpose, to the point, relevant.

[O.Fr. *propos*—same L. root as **propose.**]

purr, *pûr, v.i.* to utter a low, murmuring sound, as a cat when pleased. [Imit.]

purse, *pûrs, n.* a small bag for carrying money: a sum of money (often given as a prize).—*v.t.* to draw (esp. the lips) together as the mouth of a purse that is closed by strings: to wrinkle.

purs'er, *n.* the officer in charge of a ship's accounts, cabins, stewards, etc.

[Late L. *bursa*—Gk. *byrsa*, a hide.]

pursue, *pûr-sū', -sōō', v.t.* to follow, esp. in order to overtake and capture: to seek to gain (e.g. *to pursue pleasure*): to follow (a path): to carry on, continue: to be engaged in (e.g. enquiries, studies): to persecute, annoy.—*v.i.*to go in pursuit.

pursū'ance (or *-sōō'*), *n.* act of carrying out.

pursū'er, *n.* one who pursues: (*Scots law*) one who brings another to court.

pursuit, *-sūt, -sōōt', n.* act of pursuing: what one pursues or is engaged in—occupation, employment, hobby.

[O.Fr. *porsievre*—L. root as **prosecute.**]

purulent. See **pus.**

purvey, *pûr-vā', v.t.* to provide, supply.—*v.i.* to supply provisions or meals as one's business.

purvey'ance, *n.*

purvey'or, *n.* one whose business is to provide food.

[O.Fr. *porveoir*—L. root as **provide.**]

pus, *pus, n.* a thick yellowish fluid produced in wounds, abscesses, etc.

purulent, *pūr'yė-lėnt, adj.*

[L. *pūs, pūris*, matter.]

push, *poosh, v.t.* to press against with force: to drive, move thus: to thrust (out): to advance, carry to a further point: to urge (to; e.g. *They pushed him to accept the post*): to recommend vigorously (e.g. *to push a product by advertising on television*).—*v.i.* to make a thrust: to make an effort: to press (on, forward).—*n.* a thrust: effort: energy and forcefulness (e.g. *He has push and will get on in his profession*).

push'er, *n.* one who pushes: (*coll.*) an ambitious and forceful person.

push'ing, *adj.* pressing forward in business: too sure of oneself, presuming.

push button, a small knob pressed to close an electric circuit.

push-button war, one using guided missiles, released by push button.

[Fr. *pousser*—L. *pulsāre*, to beat.]

pusillanimous, *pū-si-lan'i-mus, adj.* lacking firmness of mind: cowardly.

[L. *pusillus*, little, *animus*, mind.]

pustule, *pus'tūl, n.* a small pimple containing pus.

[L. *pustula.*]

put, *poot, v.t.* to move or push (into): to lay, set (e.g. *to put books on a table*): to bring into a position or state (e.g. *to put oneself in the hands of a doctor*; *to put John in a temper*): to apply (to; e.g. *to put to a new use*): to give, attribute (e.g. *He put the wrong meaning on what I said*): to express (a question).—*v.i.* to make one's way at sea, etc. (e.g. *He put out for the island*):—*pr.p.* **putt'ing**; *pa.p.* **put.**

See also **putt.**
a put-up job, an underhand scheme.
(**hard**) **put to it,** hard pressed: having great difficulty in (e.g. *hard put to it to find any money*).
to put about, to change course, or course of, at sea: to publish (e.g. news): to upset.
to put in for, to make a claim or application for.
to put off, to take off: to delay, postpone: (*coll.*) to turn (a person) away from his purpose or inclination.
to put out, to extinguish, as a fire: to annoy or embarrass.
to put through, to bring to an end, accomplish.
to put two and two together, to draw a conclusion from certain circumstances.
to put (**a person**) **up to an action,** to suggest it and encourage (him) to carry it out.
to put up with, to endure, bear patiently.
[M.E. *puten.*]

putative, *pū′tȧ-tiv,* *adj.* supposed, commonly regarded as such.
[L. *putāre, -ātum,* think, suppose.]

putrefy, *pū′tri-fī,* *v.t.* and *v.i.* to rot:—*pr.p.* **pu′trefying**; *pa.p.* **pu′trified.**
putrefac′tion, *n.*
pu′trid, *adj.* rotten: stinking: (*slang*) wretchedly bad.
[L. *putrefacĕre,* to make rotten.]

putsch, *pooch,* *n.* a sudden revolutionary outbreak.
[Swiss Ger. dialect *putsch,* thrust.]

putt, also **put,** *put,* *v.t.* (*Scot.*) to hurl (as a weight): (*golf*) to send a ball forward lightly on the green:—*pr.p.* **putt′ing**; *pa.p.* **putt′ed.**—Also *n.*
putt′er, *n.* a club used in putting.
[A Scottish form of **put.**]

putty, *put′i,* *n.* a cement of whiting and oil: a powder for polishing glass, etc.—*v.t.* to fix or fill with putty:—*pr.p.* **putt′ying**; *pa.p.* **putt′ied.**
[Fr. *potée,* potful—*pot.*]

puzzle, *puz′l,* *v.t.* to be difficult for (one) to understand (e.g. *The girl, the situation, puzzles me*): to worry with a difficult question (e.g. *to puzzle one's brains about what to do*).—*v.i.* to be bewildered: to work long and carefully (over a problem).—*n.* a difficulty that causes much thought: a riddle or game which tests one's thinking.
puzz′ling, *adj.* baffling, difficult.
to puzzle out, to discover the solution of by hard mental effort (e.g. *to puzzle out a mystery*). [Origin uncertain.]

pygmy. Same as **pigmy.**

pyjamas, *pi-jä′mȧz,* *n. pl.* a sleeping-suit.
pyja′ma, *adj.* e.g. in **pyjama jacket, trousers.**
[Hindustani *pāe,* leg, *jāmah,* clothing.]

pylon, *pī′lon,* *n.* a guiding mark at an air field: a high structure supporting electric power-cables.
[Gk. *pylōn,* gateway—*pylē,* a gate.]

pyramid, *pir′ȧ-mid,* *n.* a solid shape with a base and triangle-shaped sides meeting in a point: a structure like this, esp. one of those used as tombs in ancient Egypt.
[Gk. *pȳramis, -idos.*]

pyre, *pīr,* *n.* a pile of wood, etc., for burning a dead body.
[L. *pyra*—Gk. *pȳr,* fire.]

Pyrex, *pī′reks,* *n.* a registered trademark applied to a type of glassware for cooking that will stand heat.
[Gk. *pȳr,* fire, and L. *rex,* king.]

pyro-, *pīr-o-,* (as part of word) fire. [Gk.]

pyrotechnics, *pī-rō-tek′niks,* *n.* the art of making fireworks: a showy display (e.g. in a speech, a musical performance).
[Gk. *pȳr,* fire, *technē,* art.]

python, *pī′thȯn,* *n.* a type of snake that crushes its victim.
[Gk. *pȳthōn.*]

pyx, *piks,* *n.* (*R.C.*) a vessel in which the host is kept, or carried to the sick: a box at the Mint with sample coins for testing.
[L. *pȳxis,* a box—Gk. *pȳxos,* box tree.]

Q

quack[1], *kwak,* *n.* the cry of a duck.—*v.i.* to make such a sound. [Imit.]

quack[2], *kwak,* *n.* one who pretends that he has skill and knowledge (esp. in medicine) that he does not really possess.—Also *adj.*
quack′ery, *n.* the pretences or methods of a quack:—*pl.* **-ies.**
[Earlier *quacksalver*; from Du.]

quadr(i)-, *kwod-r(i)-,* (as part of a word) four.
quadrangle, *kwod-rang′gl,* or *kwod′,* *n.* (*geometry*) a figure with four angles (and therefore four sides): a four-sided open space enclosed by buildings (e.g. in a college)—abbrev. **quad.**
quadrang′ular (*-rang′gū-*), *adj.*
quadrant, *kwod′rȧnt,* *n.* a quarter of the circumference of a circle: a street roughly of that shape: a fourth part of the area of a circle: an instrument used in navigation, astronomy, etc., for measuring the angular height above the horizon e.g. of the sun.
quadrennial, *kwod-ren′yȧl,* *adj.* every four years.
quadrilateral, *kwod-ri-lat′ėr-ȧl,* *n.* (*geometry*) a figure bounded by four straight lines: an area so bounded.—Also *adj.*
quadruped, *kwod′roo-ped,* *n.* a four-footed animal.
quadruple, *kwod-roo′pl,* *adj.* consisting of four parts: four times as much or many.—*v.t.* and *v.i.* to make, or to become, four times as great.
quadru′plet (also *kwod′*), *n.* a set of four

things: one of four born at a birth—abbrev. **quad.**
[L. *quattuor*, four (*angulus*, angle; *quadrans*, quarter; *annus*, year; *latus*, *-eris*, side; *pēs*, *pedis*, foot; *quadruplus*, fourfold).]

quadrille, *kwȯ-dril'*, *n.* square dance for four couples: music for such a dance.
[L. *quadra*, a square.]

quadruped, quadruple, etc. See **quadr(i)-.**

quaff, *kwâf*, or *kwof*, *v.t.* and *v.i.* to drink in large draughts. [Origin unknown.]

quagmire, *kwag'mīr*, *kwog'*, *n.* boggy ground into which one may sink.
[*quag*, a boggy place, and **mire.**]

quail[1], *kwāl*, *v.i.* to shrink with fear, flinch.
[M.E. *quayle.*]

quail[2], *kwāl*, *n.* a small bird of the partridge family.
[O.Fr. *quaille.*]

quaint, *kwānt*, *adj.* pleasantly odd or strange, esp. because old-fashioned.
quaint'ly, *adv.* **quaint'ness,** *n.*
[L. *cognitus*, known.]

quake, *kwāk*, *v.i.* to tremble, esp. with fear: to quiver:—*pr.p.* **quā'king;** *pa.p.* **quāked.**—*n.* a shudder: an earthquake.
[O.E. *cwacian.*]

Quaker, *kwā'kėr*, *n.* one of the Society of Friends, a religious sect founded by George Fox:—*fem.* **Qua'keress.**
[A nickname given because Fox bade a judge before whom he was summoned *quake* at the word of the Lord.]

qualify, *kwol'i-fī*, *v.i.* to prove oneself fit (also *v.t.*, to make fit) for a certain activity or position: to reach a certain standard of knowledge or ability.—*v.t.* to mention a quality of (e.g. *An adjective qualifies a noun*; *in the phrase 'the red book', 'red' qualifies 'book'*): to make (a statement) less strong (e.g. *He said he was never late, but when she looked surprised, he qualified the claim—'Well, almost never', he said*):—*pr.p.* **qual'ifying;** *pa.p.* **qual'ified.**
qualificā'tion, *n.* act of making fit for an activity or position: quality or attainment that makes one fit or suitable: making, or something that makes, a statement less strong.
qual'ified, *adj.* **qual'ifier,** *n.*
[L. *quālis*, of what kind (*facĕre*, make).]

quality, *kwol'i-ti*, *n.* nature: the degree of goodness or badness of something: characteristic (e.g. *She may be bad-tempered, but she has one good quality—fairness*):—*pl.* **qual'ities.**
[Fr. *qualité*—L. *quālis*, of what kind.]

qualm, *kwäm*, *kwöm*, *n.* a sensation of faintness or sickness: an uneasiness esp. of conscience. [Origin uncertain.]

quandary, *kwon'dȧ-ri*, *-dā'ri*, *n.* a state of perplexity about what to do: a plight, dilemma, difficult situation:—*pl.* **-ies.**
[Origin unknown.]

quantity, *kwon'ti-ti*, *n.* an amount, esp. a large amount:—*pl.* **quan'tities.**
quan'titative, *adj.* having to do with quantity, not quality.
[Fr. *quantité*—L. *quantus*, how much.]

quantum, *kwon'tŭm*, *n.* an amount: a unit of energy in atomic physics.
[L. *quantum*—*quantus*, how great.]

quarantine, *kwor'ȧn-tēn*, *n.* (a period of) compulsory isolation (orig. forty days for a ship) to prevent spread of disease: the place in which the period is spent.—*v.t.* to put in quarantine.
[It. *quarantina*—L. *quadrāgintā*, forty.]

quarrel, *kwör'ėl*, *n.* an angry dispute: a disagreement: a break in friendship.—*v.i.* to disagree, dispute angrily: to object to, find fault (with something):—*pr.p.* **quarr'elling;** *pa.p.* **quarr'elled.**
quarr'elsome, *adj.* inclined to quarrel.
quarr'elsomeness, *n.*
[O.Fr. *querele*—L. *querī*, to complain.]

quarry[1], *kwor'i*, *n.* an excavation from which stone is cut or blasted:—*pl.* **quarr'ies.**—*v.t.* to dig (stone) from a quarry.—*v.i.* to make, or dig in, a quarry:—*pr.p.* **quarr'ying;** *pa.p.* **quarr'ied.**
quarr'yman, *n.* a man who works in a quarry.
[L. *quadrāre*, to square.]

quarry[2], *kwor'i*, *n.* a hunted animal: a prey, victim:—*pl.* **-ies.**
[L. *corium*, hide.]

quart- *kwört-*, (as part of word) fourth.
quart, *n.* the fourth part of a gallon.
quarter, *kwor'tėr*, *n.* a fourth part: the fourth of a year, or of the moon's period: a direction: a district: (in *pl.*) lodgings for soldiers, staff, etc.: mercy granted to an enemy.—*v.t.* to divide in four equal parts: to lodge in quarters.
quar'terly, *adj.* of, having to do with, a quarter, esp. of a year: once a quarter.—*n.* a magazine, etc., published every three months.
quartet, quartette, *kwor-tet'*, *n.* a set of four: a piece of music for four voices or instruments: a set of performers for such pieces.
quarto, *kwör'tō*, *adj.* folded into four leaves, or eight pages (often written **4to**).—*n.* a book of sheets so folded, in any of three standard sizes.
quarter day, the first or last day of a quarter, on which e.g. rent is paid.
quar'ter-deck, *n.* the after part (i.e. that at the stern) of the upper deck.
quar'termaster (*army* and *navy*). See *Appendices.*
quarter sessions, a court held quarterly.
at close quarters, very near.
[L. *quartus*, fourth—*quattuor*, four.]

quartz, *kwörts*, *n.* the commonest rock-forming mineral, silica, occurring in many varieties.
[Ger. *quarz.*]

quash, *kwosh*, *v.t.* to annul (e.g. *He was*

convicted of theft, but the conviction was later quashed).
[L. *quassāre*, to shake.]

quasi-, *kwā′sī-*, *kwä′zi-*, (put before a word) in appearance only, not reality (e.g. *quasi-historical*). [L.]

quater-, *kwat-ėr-*, (as part of word) four times.
quatercentenary, *kwat-ėr-sin-tēn′ȧ-ri*, or *kwot-*, or *-ten′*, *n.* a 400th anniversary.
[L. *quater*, four times; root as **quart-.**]

quatrain, *kwot′rān*, *n.* a stanza of four lines of verse. [Fr.]

quaver, *kwā′vėr*, *v.i.* to tremble, quiver: to speak or sing in a shaky voice.—Also *v.t.*—*n.* a trembling, esp. of the voice: (*music*) half a crotchet.
[M.E. *cwavien*, shake; conn. **quake.**]

quay, *kē*, *n.* a landing place, wharf.
quay′side, *adj.* and *n.*
[O.Fr. *kay* (modern Fr. *quai*).]

queasy, *kwē′zi*, *adj.* sick: squeamish.
quea′siness, *n.* [Origin uncertain.]

queen, *kwēn*, *n.* the wife of a king: a female monarch: the egg-laying female of bees and other insects that live together in communities: a piece in chess. —*v.t.* (with *it*) to act as if a queen.
queen′ly, *adj.* of a queen: suitable to a queen (e.g. *queenly dignity*).
queen mother, the mother of the reigning king or queen.
For **Queen's Counsel,** etc. (so called during the reign of a queen), see **King's.**
[O.E. *cwēn.*]

queer, *kwēr*, *adj.* odd, strange: sick or faint.
queer′ly, *adv.* **queer′ness,** *n.*
Queer Street, trouble, esp. money difficulties.
to queer the pitch, to spoil the plans (of someone). [Origin uncertain.]

quell, *kwel*, *v.t.* to crush (e.g. a rebellion): to subdue (a person): to quiet (e.g. uproar, fears).
quell′er, *n*,
[O.E. *cwellan*, to kill.]

quench, *kwench*, or *-sh*, *v.t.* to put out (e.g. flame, enthusiasm): to slake (thirst).
[Conn. with O.E. *ācwencan*, quench.]

querulous, *kwer′oo-lůs*, or *-ū-*, *adj.* complaining, peevish.
quer′ulously, *adv.* **quer′ulousness,** *n.*
[L. *queri*, to complain; conn. **quarrel.**]

query, *kwē′ri*, *n.* a question: a question mark:—*pl.* **que′ries.**—*v.t.* to question, doubt (a statement): to mark with a query:—*pr.p.* **que′rying**; *pa.p.* **quē′ried.**
[L. *quaere*, ask!—same root as **question.**]

quest, *kwest*, *n.* search, pursuit.—*v.i.* to go searching (for).
[O.Fr. *queste*; same root as **question.**]

question, *kwes′ch(ȯ)n*, *n.* a sentence requiring an answer, an inquiry: a problem: a matter about which there is doubt: room for discussion, doubt, etc. (e.g. *There was no question of dismissing him, no question about his honesty*): a separate item in a test or examination, to be answered or discussed.—*v.t.* to put questions to (a person): to regard as doubtful (e.g. *I question if he can come*).
ques′tionable, *adj.* able to be doubted: prob. not true, honest, respectable, etc.
ques′tionably, *adv.* **-ableness,** *n.*
questionnaire, *kwes-ti-ȯ-nār′*, or *-tyȯn-*, also *kes-*, *n.* a set of written questions to obtain information on which to base a report (e.g. a report on industrial conditions).
in question, under consideration: being disputed.
out of the question, not to be considered as possible.
[L. *quaerĕre*, *quaesitum*, to seek, ask.]

queue, *kū*, *n.* a pigtail at the back of the head: a line of people waiting their turn (e.g. *a queue for the bus*).—*v.i.* to stand in a queue.
[Fr.—L. *cauda*, a tail.]

quibble, *kwib′l*, *v.i.* to avoid, shift from, the real point that is being discussed by bringing forward other points, arguments etc.: to object to (with *at*, *about*; e.g. *He quibbles at the price*):—*pr.p.* **quibb′ling**; *pa.p.* **quibbled.**—Also *n.*
[Origin uncertain.]

quick, *kwik*, *adj.* done or happening in a short time: speedy, rapid: acting or responding at once (e.g. *a quick brain*; *quick sympathy*): hasty (e.g. *a quick temper*).—*adv.* without delay: rapidly. —*n.* the living (*the quick and the dead*): the sensitive part, esp. under one's nails.
quick′ly, *adv.* **quick′ness,** *n.*
quick′en, *v.t.* to make alive: to excite, make more lively: to make faster.—*v.i.* to become lively or alive: to move faster.
quick′ening, *n.*
quick′lime, *n.* lime when recently burnt but not treated with water.
quick′sand, *n.* sand that sucks in anyone who stands on it.
quick′silver, *n.* mercury (so called because it is quick-moving and silvery in colour).
quick′-tem′pered, *adj.* easily made angry.
quick′-witt′ed, *adj.* alert, sharp, thinking quickly.
[O.E. *cwic*; Old Norse, *kvikr*, living.]

quid, *kwid*, *n.* (*slang*) a pound (20s.):—*pl.* **quid.** [Origin unknown.]

quiescent, *kwī-es′ėnt*, *adj.* resting: not in an active state.
quies′cence, *n.* **quies′cently,** *adv.*
[L. *quiescens*; same root as **quiet.**]

quiet, *kwī′ėt*, *adj.* at rest: calm: gentle: silent.—*n.* rest, peace.—*v.t.* and *v.i.* (also **quiet′en**) to make, or become, quiet.
qui′etly, *adv.*
qui′etness, qui′etude (*-tūd*), *ns.*
[L. *quiētus*—*quiescĕre*, to rest.]

quill, *kwil*, *n.* the hollow part at the foot of a large feather: a large feather: a spine of e.g. a porcupine.
[Origin unknown.]

quilt, *kwilt*, *n.* a bed cover filled with down, etc., stitched to keep the filling in place.
[O.Fr. *cuilte*—L. *culcita*, a cushion.]

quince, *kwins*, *n.* a fruit with an acid taste, used in making jam, etc.
[*Cydonia*, city of ancient Crete.]

quin-, quinqu(e)-, *kwin-kw(i)*, (as part of word) five. See also **quint-**.
quincentenary, *kwin-sin-tēn'ȧ-ri*, or *-ten'*, *n.* a 500th anniversary.—Also *adj.*
quinquereme, *kwin'kwi-rēm*, *n.* an ancient ship with five 'banks', or rows, of oars.
[L. *quinque*, five (L. *rēmus*, oar).]

quinine, *kwin-ēn'*, or *kwin'*, *n.* a bitter substance got from the bark of the cinchona (*sing-kō'nȧ*) tree, native of the Andes region, used in medicine.
[Sp. *quina*, bark—Peruvian *kinakina*.]

quinqu(e)-. See **quin-**.

quint-, *kwint-*, (as part of word) fifth. See also **quin-**.
quintet, quintette, *kwin-tet'*, *n.* a set of five: a piece of music for five voices or instruments: a set of performers for such pieces.
[L. *quintus*, fifth—*quinque*, five.]

quip, *kwip*, *n.* a quick, witty reply.
[Origin uncertain.]

quire, *kwīr*, *n.* a twentieth of a ream.
[L. *quattuor*, four.]

quirk, *kwėrk*, *n.* a twist, turn: a trick: an oddity (e.g. of character).
quirk'y, *adj.* inclined to trickery: tricky, difficult.
quirk'iness, *n.* [Origin unknown.]

quisling, *kwiz'ling*, *n.* a traitor who takes office in a government formed by an enemy occupying his country.
[A Norwegian, Vidkun *Quisling*, acted thus during Second World War.]

quit, *kwit*, *v.t.* to depart from, leave: (*U.S.*) to leave off, stop: (with *oneself*) to behave (e.g. *How did he quit himself in the difficult situation?*).—*v.i.* to leave, vacate, e.g. a house: (*coll.*) to desert one's job or task:—*pr.p.* **quitt'ing**; *pa.p.* **quitt'ed**.
quits, *adj.* even, neither owing nor owed.
quitt'ance, *n.* release.
quitt'er, *n.* one who gives up easily.
to be, get, quit of, to be, get, rid of.
[L. *quiētāre*, to make quiet.]

quite, *kwīt*, *adv.* completely: exactly: indeed: yes. [A form of **quit**.]

quiver[1], *kwiv'ėr*, *n.* a case for arrows.
[O.Fr. *cuivre*.]

quiver[2], *kwiv'ėr*, *v.i.* to tremble, shiver.—*n.* a trembling motion. [Orig. uncertain.]

qui vive, *kē vēv*, *n.* alert; used in the phrase **on the qui vive**.
[From French sentry's challenge, '(long) live who?' i.e. whose side are you on?]

quixotic, *kwiks-ot'ik*, *adj.* like Don Quixote the knight in the romance of that name by Cervantes—having noble ideals, generous aims, and no understanding of the realities of life or concern for one's own welfare.
quixot'ically, *adv.*

quiz, *kwiz*, *n.* a competition to test knowledge, mainly for the amusement of an audience:—*pl.* **quizz'es**.—*v.t.* to question:—*pr.p.* **quizz'ing**; *pa.p.* **quizzed**.
quizz'ical, *adj.* (of e.g. a look) humorously questioning or gently mocking.
[Origin unknown.]

quoit, *koit*, *n.* a heavy, flat ring for throwing on to, or as near as possible to, a small rod: (in *pl.*) the game played with these rings. [Origin unknown.]

quondam, *kwon'dam*, *adj.* former.
[L., formerly.]

quorum, *kwō'rum*, *kwö'*, *n.* the smallest number of members necessary at a meeting before business can proceed.
[L. *quorum*, of whom; first word of official document naming members of a body.]

quota, *kwō'tȧ*, *n.* share that one must receive or contribute.
[L. *quot*, how many.]

quote, *kwōt*, *v.t.* to refer to: to give the actual words of: to name (a price).
quōtā'tion, *n.* act of quoting: something quoted.
quotation marks, marks used at the beginning and end of a written or printed quotation (" ", or ' ').
[Late L. *quotāre*, to divide into verses.]

quoth, *kwōth*, *v.t.*, *pa.t.* (with subject I, he, she, usu. following verb) said.
[O.E. *cwethan*, to say.]

quotient, *kwō'shėnt*, *n.* the number of times one quantity is contained in another (e.g. *In* 12÷3=4, 4 *is the quotient*).
[L. *quotiens*, how often—*quot*, how many.]

R

rabbet, *rab'it*, *n.* a cut or groove, usu. rectangular, made in the edge or face of one piece of wood to receive the end of another piece.—*v.t.* and *v.i.* to make, or to join by, a rabbet:—*pr.p.* **rabb'eting**; *pa.p.* **rabb'eted**.
[O.Fr. *rabat*—*rabattre*, to beat back.]

rabbi, *rab'ī*, *n.* a Jewish priest or teacher of the Jewish law:—*pl.* **rabb'īs**.
[Heb.—*rabh*, master.]

rabbit, *rab'it*, *n.* a small burrowing animal with long ears and short tail: (*slang*) a timid person: (*slang*) someone not good at games or sport.

rabbit hutch, warren. See **hutch, warren.**
[M.E. *rabet*; origin uncertain.]

rabble, *rab'l, n.* a noisy crowd: the socially lowest class of people.
[Conn. with Old Du. *rabbelen*, to gabble.]

rabid, *rab'id, adj.* mad, suffering from rabies: violent, extreme (e.g. *a rabid supporter of the local team*; *a rabid nationalist*).
rabies, *rā'bēz,* or *-bi-ēz, n.* a disease that causes madness in dogs and other animals, also called hydrophobia (which is really one symptom of rabies).
[L. *rabidus*, mad, *rabiēs*, madness.]

raccoon, racoon, *rȧ-kōōn', n.* a small animal related to bears. [Amer. Indian.]

race[1], *rās, n.* living beings with the same ancestors and characteristics (e.g. *the human race*; *the white races*; *the race of fishes*).
racial, *rā'sh(ȧ)l, adj.* of, having to do with, race.
ra'cialism, *n.* belief that some races of men are better than others: policy based on this belief.—Also **ra'cism.**
race hatred, dislike of people of a different race.
[Fr.—It. *razza*; origin uncertain.]

race[2], *rās, n.* a competition between persons, animals or vehicles to see which can move most quickly (e.g. *a horse race*): a rush (e.g. *a race for a train*): a channel taking water to a mill-wheel (*a mill-race*). —*v.i.* to run swiftly: to take part in a race.—*v.t.* to run (e.g. car engine) wildly.
ra'cer, *n.* person, animal, or vehicle taking part in racing.
race card, a programme of races.
race'course, -track, *n.* a course over which races are run.
race'horse, *n.* a horse bred for racing.
race meeting, gathering for fixed series of horse, or dog, etc., races.
[Old Norse *rās*; conn. O.E. *rǣs*, rush.]

racial, racialism, racism. See **race.**

rack[1], *rak, n.* a framework on which things are arranged for keeping, etc.: a shelf for luggage in e.g. a railway carriage: a bar with teeth to fit into and move a toothed wheel, etc.: an instrument to torture people by stretching them.—*v.t.* to torture: to strain (e.g. *He racked his brains for the answer*).
[Same root as **reach.**]

rack[2], *rak, n.* Same as **wrack**; used in the phrase **rack and ruin,** a state of neglect and decay.

rack[3], *rak, n.* flying cloud or mist.
[Old Norse *rek*, drifting wreckage.]

racket[1], **racquet,** *rak'it, n.* a bat with a wooden or metal frame strung with catgut or nylon, etc., used in tennis and other games.
rackets, racquets, (*pl.* used as *sing.*) a game in which rackets are used, played against a wall.
[Fr. *raquette* perh.—Arabic *rāha*, the palm of the hand.]

racket[2], *rak'it, n.* din, a great noise: a dishonest way of making money.
racketeer', *n.* one who makes money by dishonest means. [Prob. imit.]

racoon. See **raccoon.**

racquet(s). See **racket(s).**

racy, *rā'si, adj.* having a distinctive flavour, as wine: lively, spirited (e.g. *He has a racy style of writing*):—*comp.* **rā'cier;** *superl.* **rā'ciest.**
rā'cily, *adv.* **rā'ciness,** *n.*
[From **race** (1).]

radar, *rā'dar, n.* a method of using radio waves to locate ships, aircraft etc. in darkness or fog. The waves are reflected by the ship or aircraft, and show its direction and distance by forming a picture on a radar screen.
[American code word, from initial letters of *ra*dio *d*etecting *a*nd *r*anging.]

radial, *rā'di-ȧl, adj.* arranged like the spokes of a wheel: having to do with the radius (see this word) of the forearm.
ra'dially, *adv.*
[Same root as **radiant, radius.**]

radiant, *rā'di-ȧnt,* or *-dyȧnt, adj.* sending out rays of light or heat: glowing: beaming with joy (e.g. *She has a radiant smile*).
rā'diance, -ancy, *ns.* **rā'diantly,** *adv.*
See also **radiate, radio.**
[L. *radiāre, -ātum*, radiate—*radius*, ray.]

radiate, *rā'di-āt, v.i.* to send out rays of e.g. heat or light: to spread out in many directions (e.g. *All the roads radiate from the town centre*).—*v.t.* to send out in rays, or as if in rays (e.g. *His face radiated kindness*).
rādiā'tion, *n.* act of sending out rays: something sent out in waves or rays, as in **radioactivity** (see this under **radio**).
rā'diātor, *n.* apparatus for heating a room by hot water, gas, electricity, etc.: apparatus in a car which cools the engine.
radiation sickness, illness caused by exposure to dangerous rays.
[Same root as **radiant.**]

radical, *rad'i-kȧl, adj.* belonging to the very root or basic character (e.g. *The machine has radical faults, and should be scrapped*): thorough (e.g. *The arrangements are not efficient and need a radical overhaul*): (*botany*) coming from near the root: (*politics*; usu. with *cap.*) bent on thorough reform.—*n.* a root: (often with *cap.*) one who wants great changes, esp. political.
rad'ically, *adv.* **rad'icalness,** *n.*
rad'icalism, *n.* the beliefs or spirit of a radical.
[L. *rādīx, -īcis*, a root.]

radicle, *rad'i-kl, n.* the part of a seed that becomes a root.
[L. *rādīcula*, little root; see **radical.**]

radio-, *rā-di-ō-,* (as part of word) rays,

radiation: radioactive: radium: radio (wireless).

radio, *n.* wireless communication: a wireless receiving or transmitting set: a wireless message or broadcast.—*v.t.* to send out (a message) by radio: to send a message to (a person, etc.) by radio:—*pr.p.* **rā'dioing**; *pa.p.* **rā'dioed.**

ra'dioac'tive, *adj.* giving off dangerous rays.

ra'dioactiv'ity, *n.*

ra'diogram, *n.* a radiograph: a message sent by wireless: (short for **radio-gramophone**) a combined wireless receiver and gramophone.

ra'diograph, *n.* an X-ray (or other radiation) photograph.

radiog'rapher, *n.* one who makes these.

radiog'raphy, *n.* making of radiographs.

radiol'ogy, *n.* the study of radia tion an. radioactivity: their use in medicine.

radiol'ogist, *n.* one who studies or practises radiology.

ra'diother'apy, *n.* treatment of disease by radiation, e.g. by X-rays.

[L. *radius*, ray; same root as **radiant.**]

radish, *rad'ish, n.* a plant with a red or white root eaten raw in salads.

[Fr. *radis*—L. *rādix*, a root.]

radium, *rā'di-ŭm, n.* a rare metal which sends out rays used in treating certain diseases; used also in making luminous paints, etc.

[L. *radius*, ray; same root as **radiant.**]

radius, *rā'di-ŭs, n.* (*geometry*) a straight line from the centre of a circle to its circumference: the outside bone of the forearm: the area within a given distance from a central point (e.g. *They searched within a radius of one mile from the school*):—*pl.* **rā'dii** (*-di-ī*).

[L. *radius*, ray; same root as **radiant.**]

raffia, *raf'i-ȧ, n.* strips of fibre from the raffia palm, used for making mats, etc.

[From its name in Madagascar.]

raffle, *raf'l, n.* a way of raising money by selling marked or numbered tickets, some of which win a prize.—*v.t.* to dispose of by using as prize in raffle.

[O.Fr. *rafle*, a game with dice.]

raft, *râft, n.* a platform of logs or planks made to float on water.

[Old Norse *raptr*, a rafter.]

rafter, *râf'tėr, n.* a sloping beam supporting the roof of a house.

[O.E. *ræfter*, a beam.]

rag[1], *rag, n.* a small piece of worn or torn cloth: (in *pl.*) shabby or torn clothes (e.g. *Cinderella was dressed in rags*).—*adj.* made of rags or cloth (e.g. *a rag doll, a rag book*).

ragg'ed, *adj.* in rags: torn: uneven (e.g. *The wind blew the ragged clouds across the sky*).

ragg'edly, *adv.* **ragg'edness,** *n.*

rag'man, *n.* a man who buys and sells rags.

ragtag and bobtail, the rabble (see this word.)

[O.E. *ragg—raggig*, shaggy.]

rag[2], *rag, v.t.* to tease, or play tricks on (someone).—*n.* (with *cap.*) (a period of) jokes and foolery to raise money for charity (e.g. *The students' Rag begins today*): a trick or practical joke.

[Perh. same as **rag** (1).]

ragamuffin, *rag'ȧ-muf-in, n.* a ragged, dirty person. [Perh. from **rag** (1).]

rage, *rāj, n.* a fit of violent anger: violence (e.g. *The rage of the sea died down when the wind dropped*): something very fashionable (e.g. *Fur hoods were all the rage*).—*v.i.* to be very angry: (of e.g. the wind) to be violent: (of e.g. battle, argument) to continue violently.

rag'ing, *adj.* and *n.*

[Fr.—L. root as **rabid, rabies.**]

raglan, *rag'lȧn, n.* an overcoat having the sleeve and shoulder in one.—Also *adj.*

[From a Lord *Raglan.*]

ragtag. See **rag** (1).

ragwort, *rag'wûrt, n.* a large coarse weed with a yellow flower.

[**rag** (1) and O.E. *wyrt*, a plant.]

raid, *rād, n.* a quick short, usu. surprise, attack in order to damage or to seize something (e.g. *The enemy made a raid on the docks*).—*v.t.* to make a raid on (e.g. *The police raided the gambling club*): to help oneself to things from (e.g. *to raid the larder*).—Also *v.i.*

rai'der, *n.* one who makes a raid: a raiding plane or ship.

[O.E. *rād*, a riding.]

rail[1], *rāl, n.* a bar between two supports, e.g. in a fence: a steel bar used as part of a track for trains, etc.: the railway (e.g. *Some goods are sent by rail*).—*v.t.* to enclose with rails (e.g. *The playground has been railed*).

rail'ing, *n.* a fence of posts and rails.

rail'head, *n.* the farthest point reached by a railway.

rail'road, *n.* (chiefly *U.S.*) a railway.

rail'way, *n.* a track laid with rails on which wagons, etc. run.

[O.Fr. *reille*—same L. root as **rule.**]

rail[2], *rāl, v.i.* to speak angrily and bitterly (with *at, against*; e.g. *The rivals railed at each other*).

raillery, *rā'lė-ri, n.* good-tempered mockery.

(Long ago the verb as well as the noun could have a pleasant meaning).

[Fr. *railler*; perh. conn. Late L. vbs meaning 'to bray', 'to neigh'.]

rail[3], *rāl, n.* any of a number of related birds including the corncrake.

[O.Fr. *rasle* (Fr. *râle*).]

raiment, *rā'mėnt, n.* (*old-fashioned*) clothing. [Conn. with **array.**]

rain, *rān, n.* water from the clouds in drops: anything falling like rain (e.g. *The wind brought down a rain of nuts from the tree*).

—*v.i.* and *v.t.*, to fall, or send down, like rain.

rain′y, *adj.* wet with rain : showery :—*comp.* **rain′ier ;** *superl.* **rain′iest.**

rain′iness, *n.*

rain′less, *adj.* having no rain.

rain′bow, *n.* the coloured bow or arch seen opposite the sun when the sun's rays strike raindrops : similar bow (called *lunar rainbow*) formed by moon.

rain′coat, *n.* a light coat to keep out rain.

rain′fall, *n.* the amount of rain that falls in a certain time (e.g. *Do you know the annual rainfall of this country?*).

rain gauge (*gāj*), an instrument for measuring rainfall.

rain′proof, *adj.* not allowing rain to pass through (e.g. *This material is rainproof*).

a rainy day, hard times (*to save up for a rainy day*).

to rain cats and dogs, to rain very hard.

[O.E. *regn* ; a Germanic word.]

raise, *rāz, v.t.* to cause to rise (e.g. *to raise prices*) : to lift up : to set up (e.g. *to raise a statue to someone*) : to make higher (e.g. *to raise the building by a storey*) : to grow or breed (e.g. *to raise crops, pigs*) : to bring up (e.g. *to raise a family*) : to cause, give rise to (e.g, *to raise a laugh*) : to put forward, suggest (e.g. *to raise an objection*).

to raise a siege, to bring it to an end.

to raise one's voice, to speak more loudly.

[M.E. *reisen* ; conn. with **rise.**]

raisin, *rā′z(i)n, n.* a dried grape.

[Fr., grape—L. *racēmus*, bunch of grapes.]

rajah, *rä′jȧ, n.* (*India*) a king or prince.

[Hindustani *rājā.*]

rake[1], *rāk, n.* a tool having a bar with teeth on the end of a long handle, used for smoothing, gathering together, etc.—*v.t.* to draw a rake over : to scrape (together) : to sweep with gunfire from end to end (e.g. *The destroyer raked the pirate ship with all her guns*) : to search closely.—*v.i.* to work with a rake : to make a search.

rake′-off, *n.* share of profits, generally illegal.

to rake up, to bring to light (an old story, generally unpleasant).

[O.E. *raca* ; conn. Ger. *rechen*, to rake.]

rake[2], *rāk, n.* a slope or slant in a ship or building (e.g. *The rake of the floor in a theatre enables everyone to see the stage*).

ra′kish, *adj.* slanting, jaunty (e.g. *She wore her hat at a rakish angle*).

ra′kishly, *adv.* **ra′kishness,** *n.*

[Origin uncertain.]

rake[3], *rāk, n.* a man who lives an immoral life.

[Earlier *rakehell*—**rake** (1), **hell.**]

rallentando, *ral-ėn-tan′dō, adj.* and *adv.* becoming slower.—*n.* a passage of music so played.

[It., from *rallentare*, to slacken.]

rally[1], *ral′i, v.t.* to gather together again (e.g. *The Colonel tried to rally his men*) : to make an effort to revive and use to the full (e.g. *You must rally your wits, all your powers, to deal with the difficult situation*).—*v.i.* to come together for joint action or effort (e.g. *All supporters of the football club must rally to save its existence*) : to recover in health (e.g. *She rallied from her severe illness*) :—*pr.p.* **rall′ying** ; *pa.p.* **rallied** (*ral′id*).—*n.* act of rallying : a gathering (e.g. *a Scouts' rally*) : recovery from illness, not always complete : a series of quick shots in tennis and similar games :—*pl.* **rall′ies.**

[Fr. *rallier*—same root as **ally.**]

rally[2], *ral′i, v.t.* to tease :—*pa.p.* **rall′ying ;** *pa.p.* **rall′ied.**

[Same root as **rail** (2).]

ram, *ram, n.* a male sheep : a battering ram (see this) : something heavy, or a part of a machine, for forcing by pressure.—*v.t.* to make (e.g. earth) firm by pounding : to drive by heavy blows : to thrust tightly (into) : to cram (with) : to drive against, crash hard into (a ship, a vehicle, etc.):—*pr.p.* **ramm′ing** ; *pa.p.* **rammed.**

ramm′er, *n.*

ram′rod, *n.* a rod for ramming down the charge in a gun loaded through the muzzle : person holding himself, herself, very stiffly, or who is very strict.

to ram down one's throat, to try to force one to believe, accept, etc. (a statement, idea).

to ram home, to force understanding and acceptance of (an idea). [O.E.]

ramble, *ram′bl, v.i.* to walk about for pleasure : to wander : to talk in an aimless or confused way (e.g. *The old lady rambled for a long time about her youth*).—*n.* a walk with no fixed aim.

ram′bler, *n.* one who rambles : a trailing climbing rose or other plant.

ram′bling, *adj.* wandering : confused.

[M.E. *romblen*, perh. conn. with **roam.**]

ramification, *ram-i-fi-kā′sh(ȯ)n, n.* division into branches : a branch : a branch or part of a subject, plot etc. (e.g. *The main plot was simple, but it had complicated ramifications*) : a consequence, esp. indirect and one of many.

[L. *rāmus*, a branch, *facĕre*, to make.]

rammer. See **ram.**

ramp, *ramp, v.i.* to climb : to grow thickly : to rage.—*n.* a slightly sloping surface or way : (*slang*) a swindle.

rampāge′, *v.i.* to rush about wildly or angrily.—*n.* excited, angry behaviour.

rampā′geous, *adj.* wild, out of control (e.g. *The puppy became rampageous when it first saw snow*).

ram′pant, *adj.* widespread and threatening (e.g. *Forest fires were rampant*) : (*heraldry*) standing on the left hindleg (e.g. *The Scottish standard has a lion rampant in red on a yellow ground*).

ram′pancy, *n.* **ram′pantly,** *adv.*
on the rampage, rampaging.
[Fr. *ramper*, to creep, to climb.]

rampart, *ram′pärt, n.* a flat-topped mound or wall for defence: a defence (e.g. *The sea has often been Britain's rampart against attack*).
[Fr. *rempart—remparer*, to defend.]

ramrod. See **ram.**

ramshackle, *ram′shakl, adj.* shaky, badly made. [Origin uncertain.]

ran. See **run.**

ranch, *rânch*, or *-sh, n.* a farm, esp. one consisting of grassland used for raising cattle or horses.—*v.i.* to manage or work on a ranch.
ran′cher, *n.* one employed in ranching.
[Sp. *rancho*, mess, camp, etc.]

rancid, *ran′sid, adj.* tasting or smelling stale (e.g. *In hot weather, butter soon becomes rancid*).
rancid′ity, ran′cidness, *ns.*
[L. *rancidus*.]

rancour, *rang′kür, n.* bitter feeling, hatred and ill-will.
ran′corous, *adj.* **ran′corously,** *adv.*
[L. *rancor*, an old grudge; same root as **rancid.**]

rand, *rând, rânt, n.* (*S. Africa*) a ridge overlooking a valley: (*S. Africa*) standard coin. (=100 cents).
[O.E. and Du. *rand*, border.]

random, *ran′dòm, adj.* chance, haphazard (e.g. *A random snowball hit the classroom window*).
at random, without plan or purpose.
[Fr. *randon—randir*, to gallop.]

ranee. Same as **rani.**

rang. See **ring** (2).

range, *rānj, v.t.* to set in a row: to place in order: to wander over (e.g. *The shepherd ranges the hills*).—*v.i.* to extend (e.g. *The U.S.S.R. ranges from the Arctic to the Black Sea*): to vary (e.g. *Your marks range from* 10 *to* 90).—*n.* a line (e.g. *a range of mountains*): variety (e.g. *the range of goods for sale*): distance covered by a shot, sound, or something thrown: a place where shooting is practised: a kitchen stove with broad flat top.
ran′ger, *n.* a keeper who looks after a forest or park.
range′-finder, *n.* an instrument for finding the range of a target: a similar fitting attached to a camera.
to range oneself with, to take sides with.
[Fr. *ranger*, to range—*rang*, a rank.]

rani, *rä′ni, n. fem.* of **rajah.**
[Hindustani *rānī*.]

rank[1], *rangk, n.* a line or row (e.g. *He stood in the front rank*): order or high position (e.g. *He rose to the rank of General*): (in *pl.*) private soldiers, or ordinary people.—*v.t.* to put in order of importance (e.g. *I rank horses higher than donkeys*).—*v.i.* to have a place in a scale of importance (e.g. *Certain animals rank above others in intelligence*).
rank′er, *n.* a private soldier.
rank and file, private soldiers: ordinary people.
[O.Fr. *renc*; conn. Germanic *hrinc*, ring.]

rank[2], *rangk, adj.* growing freely, coarsely (e.g. *The grass was rank*): unpleasantly strong in taste or smell (e.g. *The bacon was rank*): utter, extreme (e.g. *He showed rank stupidity*).
rank′ly, *adv.* **rank′ness,** *n.*
[O.E. *ranc*, proud, strong.]

rankle, *rangk′l, v.i.* to cause annoyance or bitterness (e.g. *The unkind remark rankled in Mary's mind for days*).
[O.Fr. *rancler*, fester, perh.—Late L. *dranculus*, ulcer—L. *draco*, dragon.]

ransack, *ran′sak, ran-sak′, v.t.* to search thoroughly: to plunder (e.g. *The army ransacked the conquered city*).
[Old Norse *rann*, house, *sækja*, to seek.]

ransom, *ran′sòm, n.* sum of money paid so that a captive may be set free.—*v.t.* to pay money to free (a captive).
held to ransom, kept prisoner until money is paid.
[Fr. *rançon*—same L. root as **redeem.**]

rant, *rant, v.i.* to talk long, angrily, and foolishly (about): (of an actor) to speak a part too loudly and dramatically.
rant′er, *n.* **rant′ing,** *n.* and *adj.*
[A Germanic word.]

rap, *rap, n.* a sharp blow: a sound made by knocking.—*v.t.* to hit sharply: (with *out*) to speak, utter, hastily (e.g. *The heckler rapped out his question*).—*v.i.* to knock or tap:—*pr.p.* **rapp′ing**; *pa.p.* **rapped.**
[Imit.]

rapacious, *rà-pā′shùs, adj.* greedy: eager to seize as much as possible (e.g. *rapacious invaders*).
rapā′ciously, *adv.*
rapā′ciousness, rapa′city (*-pa′si-ti*), *ns.*
[L. *rapāx, -ācis*; root as **rape** (1).]

rape[1], *rāp, v.t.* to seize and carry away: to take by force.—Also *n.*
[L. *rapĕre, raptum*.]

rape[2], *rāp, n.* a plant like the turnip, with seeds yielding oil.
[L. *rāpa*, a turnip.]

rapid, *rap′id, adj.* quick, fast.
rap′ids, *n.pl.* a part in a river where the current flows swiftly over sloping ground.
rapid′ity, rap′idness, *ns.*
rap′idly, *adv.*
[L. *rapidus*; same root as **rape** (1).]

rapier, *rā′pi-ėr, n.* a long thin sword for fencing.
[Fr. *rapière*.]

rapine, *rap′īn, n.* plunder: robbery by force.
[L. *rapīna*; same root as **rape** (1).]

rapt, *rapt, adj.* carried away: lost in thought or wonder (e.g. *Rapt in his book, the reader did not hear my question*).
rapture, *rap′chùr, n.* great delight.

rap'turous, *adj.* **rap'turously,** *adv.* [Same root as **rape** (1).]

rare[1], *rār, adj.* (of meat) undercooked. [M.E. *rere*—O.E. *hrere*, boiled lightly.]

rare[2], *rār, adj.* thin (e.g. *The air is rare at great heights*): uncommon: unusually good.
rare'ly, *adv.* **rare'ness,** *n.*
rarity, *rār'i-ti, rar', n.* rareness (esp. in the sense of uncommonness): a rare, uncommon object:—*pl.* **rar'ities.**
rarefy, *rār'i-fī, rar', v.t.* and *v.i.*, to make, or to become, rare or thin:—*pr.p.* **rar'efying** (*-i-fī-ing*); *pa.p.* **rar'efied.**
Welsh rāre'bit. See **Welsh.**
[Fr.—L. *rārus.*]

rascal, *ras'kȧl, n.* a rogue, scamp.
rascal'ity, *n.* character, conduct, or an act, of a rascal:—*pl.* **-ities.**
ras'cally, *adj.* mean, dishonest (e.g. *His rascally behaviour turned his supporters against him*).
[O.Fr. *rascaille*, badly behaved mob.]

rase, *rāz.* Same as **raze.**

rash[1], *rash, adj.* acting without thought: too hasty, reckless (e.g. *That rash move will lose you the game*).
rash'ness, *n.* **rash'ly,** *adv.*
[A Germanic word.]

rash[2], *rash, n.* a redness, or outbreak of spots, on the skin.
[Perh. O.Fr. *rasche.*]

rasher, *rash'ėr, n.* a thin slice (of bacon).
[Origin uncertain.]

rasp[1], *râsp, n.* a coarse file: a grating sound.—*v.t.* to rub with a rasp (e.g. *A horse's hoof must be rasped before the shoe is put on*): to say in a grating voice.—*v.i.* to have a grating effect (e.g. *His voice rasped unpleasantly*).
ras'ping, ras'py, *adjs.* **ras'piness,** *n.*
[O.Fr. *raspe.*]

rasp[2], *râsp, n.* raspberry.

raspberry, *râz'bėr-i, râs', n.* red or yellow fruit, rather like a blackberry:—*pl.* **-ies.**
raspberry vinegar, a drink of raspberry juice, vinegar and sugar.
[Earlier *rasp*(*is*), raspberry, and **berry.**]

rasping. See **rasp** (1).

rat, *rat, n.* a gnawing animal like the mouse, but larger.—*v.i.* to hunt or catch rats: to desert one's friends or fellow members of a group (e.g. *A good Union member will not rat during a strike*):—*pr.p.* **ratt'ing;** *pa.p.* **ratt'ed.**
ratt'er, *n.* killer of rats (e.g. *This terrier is a good ratter*).
ratt'y, *adj.* of a rat: like a rat: (*slang*) angry:—*comp.* **ratt'ier**; *superl.* **ratt'iest.**
ratt'iness, *n.*
rats'bane, *n.* poison for rats.
to smell a rat, to suspect something.
[O.E. *ræt.*]

ratable. See **rate.**

ratafia, *rat-ȧ-fē'ȧ, n.* a flavouring essence: a biscuit or cake with this (almond) flavour. [Fr.]

ratchet, *rach'it, n.* a pawl (see this) and/or a ratchet wheel: a toothed bar.
ratchet wheel, a toothed wheel used with a ratchet or catch which allows turning in one direction only.
[Origin uncertain.]

rate[1], *rāt, n.* standard of payment (e.g. *Some men are paid at a higher rate than others*): speed (e.g. *Your rate of work is too slow*): standard of quality (e.g. *This book is first rate*): (often used in *pl.*) a tax paid yearly by owners of property to provide money for local public services (e.g. *the water rate*).—*v.t.* to put a value on for purposes of taxation: to value (e.g. *I rate this book highly*).—*v.i.* to be classed (as): to rank (e.g. *How do you rate in your new office?*).
rat(e)'able, *adj.* on which rates are to be paid (*The rateable value of a house is a fixed sum supposed to equal the sum that could be obtained as rent*).
rāt'ing, *n.* fixing of rates: grade or position: a sailor below the rank of commissioned officer.
rāte'payer, *n.* one who pays rates.
at any rate, under any circumstances: at least.
at that rate, if that is so.
[L. *rērī, ratus*, to think, judge.]

rate[2], *rāt, v.t.* to scold.
rāt'ing, *n.* a scolding.
[M.E. *raten*; origin uncertain.]

rather, *rä'THer, adv.* more willingly (e.g. *I would rather walk than cycle*): (with *than*) in preference to: more correctly speaking (e.g. *He agreed, or rather he did not say 'No'.*): to some extent (e.g. *Today is a rather better day than yesterday*).—*interj.* certainly (e.g. *Would you like to go to the match? Rather!*).
[O.E. *hrathor.*]

ratify, *rat'i-fī, v.t.* to agree to, to approve (e.g. *Parliament ratified the treaty*):—*pr.p.* **rat'ifying;** *pa.p.* **rat'ified.**
ratificā'tion, *n.*
[Root as **rate** (1), and *facĕre*, make.]

rating. See **rate** (1) and (2).

ratio, *rā'shi-ō, n.* the proportion of one thing to another (e.g. *There is a ratio of* 10 *girls to* 11 *boys in the school*).
ration, *ra'sh(ȯ)n, n.* a fixed allowance or portion (e.g. *In wartime each person had a ration of butter*): (in *pl.*) food for the day, esp. of soldiers.—*v.t.* to share out in fair portions.
[Same root as **rational.**]

rational, *ra'shȯn-ȧl, adj.* having or using reason (e.g. *Man is a rational animal*): reasonable (e.g. *That is a rational idea, explanation*).
ra'tionally, *adv.*
ra'tionalness, -al'ity, *ns.*
ra'tionalise, *v.t.* to invent a reasonable and creditable explanation of (a feeling or action) so as not to feel guilty about it: to organise work in (e.g. a factory,

industry) so as to make it efficient and economical.

rationalisā′tion, *n.*

ra′tionalist, *n.* a person who thinks that human reason is the only guide to truth.

[L. *ratiō, -ōnis*, calculation, reason—same root as **rate** (1).]

ratlin(e), ratling, *rat′lin, n.* one of the small lines or ropes forming steps in the rigging of ships. [Origin uncertain.]

rattan, ratan, *ra-tan′, n.* a tall thin palm tree: a cane made from this.

[Malay *rōtan.*]

rat-tat, *rat′tat′, n.* a knocking sound.

[Imit.]

rattier, rattiest, etc. See **rat.**

rattle, *rat′l, v.i.* to clatter: to move quickly and noisily: to chatter.—*v.t.* to cause to rattle: (*slang*) to confuse, upset (e.g. *Don't let this news rattle you*).—*n.* short quick sounds (e.g. *the rattle of coins*): a sound in the throat of a dying person (the **death-rattle**): a child's toy: two wild flowers—*yellow rattle* and *red rattle*—whose seeds rattle in the seedbox: the rings of a rattlesnake's tail.

ratt′ling, *adj.* lively, vigorous: (*slang*) excellent (or as *adv.*; e.g. *a rattling good story*): that rattles.

ratt′ler, ratt′lesnake, *ns.* poisonous American snake with rattling bony rings on the tail.

ratt′lebrain, -pate, *n.* a noisy, empty-headed person.

[M.E. *ratelen*; a Germanic word.]

ratty. See **rat.**

raucous, *rö′kus, adj.* hoarse, harsh (e.g. *He spoke in a raucous voice*).

rau′cously, *adv.* **rau′cousness,** *n.*

[L. *raucus.*]

ravage, *rav′ij, v.t.* to lay waste, plunder (e.g. *The enemy ravaged the country*).—*n.* great harm: (in *pl.*) damaging effects (of e.g. war, time).

rav′ager, *n.* **rav′aging,** *n.* and *adj.*

[Fr. *ravager*; same root as **ravish.**]

rave, *rāv, v.i.* to rage: to talk as if mad or over-excited (e.g. *Some people rave about their favourite singers*).

rāv′ing, *n.* and *adj.*

[Perh. O.Fr. *raver*, to be delirious.]

ravel, *rav′l, v.t.* to tangle (e.g. *Try not to ravel the wools*): to make confused and difficult to understand: also (opp. meanings) to untwist (e.g. a rope), take to pieces (a knitted material): to fray: (with *out*) to make clear (meaning, etc.). —*v.i.* to become tangled: to fray, or to untwist:—*pr.p.* **rav′elling**; *pa.p.* **rav′elled.**—Also *n.*

[Prob. Du. *ravelen.*]

raven[1], *rā′vn, n.* a large black glossy bird related to the crows.—*adj.* (of hair) glossy black.

[O.E. *hræfn.*]

raven[2], *rav′n, v.i.* to seek for prey: to eat greedily: to be very hungry.

ravening (*rav′en-*), **rav′enous,** *adjs.*

rav′enously, *adv.* **rav′enousness,** *n.*

[O.Fr. *ravine*, plunder; root as **rape** (1).]

ravine, *ra-vēn′, n.* a deep, narrow valley.

[O.Fr., torrent—root as **raven** (2).]

raving. See **rave.**

ravioli, *râ-vi-ō′li, n.* small envelopes of paste containing minced meat. [It.]

ravish, *rav′ish, v.t.* to rape: to plunder (e.g. country): (of e.g. beauty) to fill (one) with delight (as if carrying one away in spirit to another world).

rav′isher, *n.* **rav′ishing,** *adj.* and *n.*

[Fr. *ravir*—same root as **rape** (1).]

raw, *rö, adj.* not cooked or prepared: in the natural state (e.g. *raw cotton*): having the skin rubbed and sore (e.g. *My heel is raw with too much walking*): untrained, inexperienced (e.g. *raw recruits*): chilly and damp (e.g. *What a raw day this is!*).

raw′ness, *n.*

raw′boned, *adj.* thin, gaunt.

raw′hide, *adj.* of untanned leather.

raw material, material from which something is manufactured or developed.

[A Germanic word.]

ray[1], *rā, n.* a narrow beam of light, heat, etc. or a stream of subatomic particles: a gleam (e.g. *There is a ray of hope for him*): one of a group of lines going outwards from a centre: fringed outer part of a flower cluster.

[O.Fr. *rais*—L. root as **radiant, radius.**]

ray[2], *rā, n.* a type of flat-bodied fish, often with whiplike stinging tail.

[Fr. *raie*—L. *raia.*]

rayon, *rā′on, n.* artificial silk. [**ray** (1).]

raze, *rāz, v.t.* to demolish, knock down, lay flat (e.g. *It is time the heaps of mine refuse were razed to the ground*): to blot out (e.g. *Try to raze this happening from your memory*).

[L. *rādĕre, rāsum*, to scrape.]

razor, *rā′zor*, a sharp-edged instrument for shaving esp. the face.

rā′zorbill, *n.* a bird, a kind of auk, with a sharp-edged bill.

razor blade, sharp blade for shaving.

[O.Fr. *rasour*—same root as **raze.**]

re, *rē, prep.* (*commercial*) in the matter of.

[L. *in rē* (—*rēs*, thing), in the matter.]

re-, *rē-, pfx.* again. [L.]

reach[1], *rēch, v.t.* to arrive at: to stretch or extend to: to go as far as (e.g. *The noise reached our ears*).—*v.i.* to stretch out the hand (for something): to stretch, extend: to have power of acting (e.g. *as far as the eye can reach*).—*n.* extent of stretch (e.g. *He has a long reach*): distance that can be covered easily (e.g. *within reach of home*): part of a stream between bends.

reach′-me-down, *adj.* ready-made.—*n.* a cheap ready-made garment.

[O.E. *rǣcan*, to reach.]

reach[2]. Same as **retch.**

react, *ri-akt′, v.i.* to act in response to something: to undergo chemical change by action with another substance (e.g. *Iron reacts with acid*): (*loosely*) to behave in, be affected by, given circumstances (e.g. *How do you react to his rudeness?*).
reac′tion, *n.* behaviour as the result of an action or a stimulus: return towards former state, esp. to less free political conditions: chemical change: a change within the nucleus of an atom.
reac′tionary, *adj.* favouring return to former state.—*n.* one who tries to revive former political conditions:—*pl.* **-ies.**
nuclear reactor. See **nucleus.**
[L. *reagĕre, -actum—agĕre,* to do.]

re-act, *rē′akt′, v.t.* to act again. [Pfx. **re-.**]

read, *rēd, v.t.* to look over and understand, or to say aloud (written or printed words): to look at and understand (signs, or signs on; e.g. *to read the clock*): to study.—*v.i.* to practise reading: to study:—*pa.t.* and *pa.p.* **read** (*red*).
read′able (*rēd′*), *adj.* distinct enough to be read: quite interesting.
readabil′ity, read′ableness, *ns.*
read′er, *n.* one who reads: one who reads lessons or prayers in church: a higher grade of university lecturer: a proof corrector: one who reads and reports on manuscripts for a publisher: a reading-book (usu. for schools).
read′ing, *adj.* interested in reading: used for reading (e.g. **reading-desk, -lamp**), or for learning to read (e.g. **reading-book**).—*n.* the action of the verb *read*: study: public recital e.g. of a bill before Parliament: interpretation, meaning, given to (e.g. *an actor's reading of a part*): the figure indicated on an instrument such as a thermometer.
to read between the lines, to see a hidden meaning.
to read up, to study.
[O.E. *rǣdan,* to discern, read.]

readdress, *rē-ȧ-dres′, v.t.* to change the address on. [Pfx. **re-.**]

readily, readiness. See **ready.**

reading. See **read.**

readjust, *rē-ȧ-just′, v.t.* to put in order again, or arrange in a new way.
readjust′ment, *n.* [Pfx. **re-.**]

readmit, *rē-ȧd-mit′, v.t.* to admit again.
readmiss′ion, -mitt′ance, *ns.* [**re-.**]

ready, *red′i, adj.* prepared: at hand: willing: quick to act:—*comp.* **read′ier**; *superl.* **read′iest.**
read′ily, *adv.* **read′iness,** *n.*
read′y-made′, *adj.* (of e.g. clothes) made for anyone who will buy, not made to order for a particular person: not original.
ready money, money at hand, cash: (**ready-money**) requiring payment on the spot (e.g. *a ready-money transaction*).
ready reckoner, a book of tables giving answers to calculations required in ordinary business.
in readiness, ready, prepared: as a preparation (for).
[O.E. (*ge*)*rǣde.*]

real, *rē′ȧl, adj.* actually existing: sincere (e.g. *a real love of beauty*): not imitation (e.g. *real leather*): consisting of land or houses (*real estate*).
re′ally, *adv.* in fact. **re′alness,** *n.*
reality, *rē-al′i-ti, n.* realness: something that is real (*pl.* **real′ities**): the actual state of things: what actually exists.
rē′alise, *v.t.* to come to understand (e.g. *I realise you did not mean it*): to make real (e.g. *His fears—*i.e. the things he feared *—were realised*): to achieve (e.g. *He realised his ambition*): to turn into actual money: to make, obtain (e.g. *He realised £6000 on the sale of his house*).
realisā′tion, *n.*
rē′alism, *n.* the habit of taking a practical view of life: (in art or literature) the giving of details of actual life.
rē′alist, *n.* one who believes in realism.
realis′tic, *adj.* showing, dealing with, actual life: taking a practical view.
realis′tically, *adv.*
[Late L. *rēālis*—L. *rēs,* thing.]

realm, *relm, n.* a kingdom: a part of human life or action (e.g. *the realm of sport*).
[O.Fr. *realme*—L. root as **regal.**]

ream, *rēm, n.* 20 quires (usu. 480 sheets; also 500 sheets, or 516 sheets): (in *pl.*; *coll.*) large quantities.
[Arabic *rizmah,* a bundle.]

reanimate, *rē-an′i-māt, v.t.* to restore to life: to put new life or spirit into.
reanimā′tion, *n.* [Pfx. **re-.**]

reap, *v.t.* to cut down (grain): to obtain (an advantage or reward).
reap′er, *n.* one who reaps: a reaping machine.
reaping machine, a machine for cutting grain.
[O.E. *rīpan,* or *ripan.*]

reappear, *rē-ȧ-pēr′, v.i.* to appear again.
reappear′ance, *n.* [Pfx. **re-.**]

rear[1], *rēr, n.* the back part or position: a position behind.
rear′most, *adj.* last.
rear′ward, *adj., adv.* towards, or in, the rear.
rear′wards, *adv.*
rear admiral. See Appendices.
rear′guard, *n.* troops protecting the rear of the main army. [**arrear.**]

rear[2], *rēr, v.t.* to raise: to set up: to bring up (e.g. a child).—*v.i.* to rise on hindlegs.
[O.E. *rǣran.*]

rearm, *rē′ärm′, v.t.* to arm again: to give better weapons to.—Also *v.i.*
rearm′ament, *n.* [Pfx. **re-.**]

reason, *rē′zn, n.* cause: excuse or explanation: the mind's power to form opinions

and judgments: common sense.—*v.i.* to use one's reason: to argue.—*v.t.* (usu. with *out*) to think out clearly.
rea'sonable, *adj.* sensible: fair.
rea'sonably, *adv.* **rea'sonableness,** *n.*
rea'soning, *n.* act of using the reason, of thinking things out: argument, line of thought.
by reason of, because of.
in reason, within limits of common sense.
to listen to reason, to allow oneself to be persuaded to take a sensible view.
[Fr. *raison*—L. root as **rational,** etc.]

reassemble, *rē-à-sem'bl, v.t.* and *v.i.* to put, or come, together again. [Pfx. **re-.**]

reassure, *rē-à-shōōr', v.t.* to take away doubts or fears from (a person).
reassur'ance, *n.* [Pfx. **re-.**]

rebate, *ri-bāt', n.* discount: money repaid to the payer (esp. of a tax).—Also *v.t.* [Pfx. **re-** and **abate.**]

rebel, *reb'(ė)l, n.* one who rebels.—*v.i.* (*ri-bel'*) to oppose someone in authority (esp. to oppose government with force): —*pr.p.* **rebell'ing;** *pa.p.* **rebelled'.**
rebell'ion (*-bel'yȯn*), *n.* revolt on a large scale, uprising against authority: refusal to obey.
rebell'ious (*-bel'yu̇s*), in rebellion: inclined to rebel: like that of a rebel (e.g. *in a rebellious mood*).
rebell'iously, *adv.* **rebell'iousness,** *n.*
[L. *re-*, against, *bellum*, war.]

rebind, *rē'bind', v.t.* to put new binding on:—*pa.t.* and *pa.p.* **rebound'.** [**re-.**]

rebound[1], *ri-bownd', v.i.* to bound or spring back.—*n.* act of rebounding (e.g. *John caught the ball on its rebound from the goal post*).
[Fr. *rebondir.*]

rebound[2]. See **rebind.**

rebuff, *ri-buf', n.* a refusal: a snub.—*v.t.* to snub: to refuse.
[O.Fr. *rebuffe*—It. *ri-*, back, *buffo*, puff.]

rebuke, *ri-būk', v.t.* to scold, reprove sternly.—*n.* a reproach, scolding.
[O.Fr. *re-*, *bucher*, to strike.]

rebut, *ri-but', v.t.* to produce evidence, or arguments, showing the falseness of (something said; e.g. *to rebut an accusation*):—*pr.p.* **rebutt'ing;** *pa.p.* **rebutt'ed.**
rebutt'al, *n.*
[O.Fr. *roboter*—same root as **butt.**]

ecalcitrant, *ri-kal'si-trȧnt, adj.* obstinate, disobedient.—*n.* a person resisting, disobedient to, authority.
recal'citrance, -ancy, *ns.*
[L. *recalcitrāre*, kick back—*calx*, heel.]

recall, *ri-köl', v.t.* to call back: to remember.—*n.* act of recalling. [**re-.**]

recant, *ri-kant', v.i.* to take back what one has said: to give up religious or political beliefs.—Also *v.t.*
recantā'tion, *n.* act of recanting.
[L. *recantāre*—*cantāre*, to sing.]

recap. Abbrev. of **recapitulate, -ation.**

recapitulate, *rē-kȧ-pit'ū-lāt, v.t.* to go over again the chief points of (e.g. a statement, an argument).
recapitula'tion, *n.*
[L. *re-*, again, *capitulum*, heading.]

recapture, *rē-kap'chu̇r, v.t.* to capture back, retake, regain.—*n.* act of retaking. [Pfx. **re-.**]

recast, *rē'kâst', v.t.* to cast or shape anew: —*pa.t.* and *pa.p.* **recast'.** [Pfx. **re-.**]

recede, *ri-sēd', v.i.* to go or move back (e.g. *When the rain stopped, the floods receded*).
reced'ing, *adj.* sloping backwards (e.g. *a receding chin*).
See also **recess, recession.**
[L. *re-*, back, *cēdere*, *cessum*, go, yield.]

receipt. See **receive.**

receive, *ri-sēv', v.t.* to have given to one (e.g. *to receive a present, thanks, praise*): to have brought to one: to meet or welcome (e.g. guests), or to give a formal audience to (e.g. *The Pope received the pilgrims*):—*pr.p.* **receiv'ing.**
received', *adj.* (of e.g. an opinion) generally accepted.
receiv'er, *n.* a person or thing that receives: one who accepts goods knowing them to be stolen: a radio or television set that receives broadcasts: the part of a telephone through which messages are received.
receipt, *ri-sēt', n.* act of receiving: a written acknowledgment of anything received: a recipe, esp. in cookery: (in *pl.*) amount of money received, esp. in business (e.g. *Our receipts are higher this year*).—*v.t.* to mark as paid (e.g. *to receipt a bill*).
See also **recipient, receptacle.**
[Through Fr.—L. *recipĕre*, *receptum.*]

recent, *rē'sėnt, adj.* happening, done, made, etc., a short time ago.
re'cently, *adv.*
re'centness, re'cency, *ns.*
[L. *recens, -entis*; conn. Gk. *kainos*, new.]

receptacle, *ri-sep'tȧ-kl, n.* an object in which anything may be received or contained (e.g. a dustbin).
reception, *ri-sep'sh(ȯ)n, n.* act of receiving or being received: a welcome (e.g. *a warm reception*): a party where guests are received formally (e.g. *a wedding reception*): (*radio*) quality of signals (e.g. *Reception is good tonight*).
recep'tionist, *n.* a woman employed, e.g. in an office, to receive callers.
recep'tive, *adj.* (of person, mind) quick to take in and accept ideas, etc.
recep'tiveness, receptiv'ity, *ns.*
[Same L. root as **receive.**]

recess, *ri-ses', n.* an alcove, or place set back in a wall: a short stop in work (e.g. of law court, school): a holiday (esp. of Parliament): (in *pl.*) inner parts.
recession, *ri-sesh'(ȯ)n, n.* act of receding

or going back: a decline for a time (e.g. *a trade recession*).
in recess, (of Parliament) on holiday.
[Same root as **recede.**]

recipe, *res'i-pi*, *n.* directions for making something, esp. something to be cooked. [L. *recipe* (imperative), take; **receive.**]

recipient, *ri-sip'i-ėnt*, *n.* one who receives. [Same L. root as **receive.**]

reciprocal, *ri-sip'rȯ-k(ȧ)l*, *adj.* given and received, shared, mutual (e.g. *reciprocal affection*): given, etc., in return (e.g. *Some countries have agreements for reciprocal aid*).
recip'rocally, *adv.*
reciprocity, *res-i-pros'i-ti*, *n.* state of being reciprocal or mutual: (*international trade*) giving and receiving advantages.
reciprocate, *ri-sip'rȯ-kāt*, *v.t.* to feel in return (e.g. *Jones reciprocates Lewis's dislike of him*): to repay in the same way (e.g. *A good turn deserves to be reciprocated*).—*v.i.* to make a return for something done, given, etc.: (of part of a machine) to move backwards and forwards in a straight line.
reciprocā'tion, *n.* act of reciprocating.
[L. *reciprocus—re-*, back, *pro-*, forward.]

recite, *ri-sīt'*, *v.t.* to repeat from memory: to make a detailed statement about (e.g. *He loved to recite his grievances*).
recīt'al, *n.* act of reciting: a public performance, e.g. of music.
recitation, *res-i-tā'sh(ȯ)n*, *n.* a poem or passage for repeating from memory: the act of repeating it.
recitative, *res-i-tȧ-tēv'*, *n.* a style of song resembling speech (It. *recitativo*).
[L. *recitāre—citāre*, to call.]

rĕckless, *rek'les*, *adj.* careless, very rash.
reck'lessly, *adv.* **reck'lessness,** *n.*
[O.E. *reccan*, to take care, heed.]

reckon, *rek'(ȯ)n*, *v.t.* to count: to consider: to think, believe.—*v.i.* to calculate.
reck'oner, *n.*
reck'oning, *n.* a calculation (e.g. *Your reckoning is wrong*): a bill: the working out of a ship's position at sea.
day of reckoning, day for settling accounts, or for paying for one's sins or mistakes.
to reckon on, to rely on, base one's plans on.
to reckon with, to settle accounts (with): to allow for, take into consideration (person, his actions, a possibility or probability, etc.).
[O.E. (*ge*)*recenian*, to explain.]

reclaim, *ri-klām'*, *v.t.* to win (someone) back from evil ways: to make (land) fit for use, or to recover (land) from under water: to obtain from waste material: (*rē-klām'*) to claim back.
reclaim'able, *adj.*
reclamation, *rek-lȧ-mā'sh(ȯ)n*, *n.* act of reclaiming: state of being reclaimed.
[Orig. to call back (esp. a hawk)—L. *re*, *clāmāre*, to call.]

recline, *ri-klīn'*, *v.i.* to lean or lie on back or side.
reclin'ing, *adj.* and *n.*
[L. *reclīnāre—clīnāre*, to bend.]

recluse, *ri-kloos'*, *n.* one who lives alone and shuns company: one who does this for religious reasons.
[L. *re-*, away, *claudĕre*, *clausum*, shut.]

recognise, *rek'ȯg-nīz*, *v.t.* to know again: to acknowledge, admit (e.g. *All recognised his skill*): to show appreciation of (e.g. *They recognised the boy's courage by a suitable gift*).
recognis'able, *adj.*
recognisance, *ri-kog'ni-zȧns*, or *-kon'i-*, *n.* a legal promise to do something, made before a magistrate, or the sum pledged as surety for this.
recognition, *rek-ȯg-nish'(ȯ)n*, *n.* act or sign of recognising: acknowledgment.
[L. *re-*, again, *cognoscĕre*, to know.]

recoil, *ri-koil'*, *v.i.* to shrink back: (of gun when fired) to jump back. —*n.* rebound, sudden jumping back.
[Fr. *reculer—cul*, bottom.]

recollect, *rek-ȯl-ekt'*, *v.t.* to remember: (with oneself) to recover composure, collect one's thoughts.
recollec'tion, *n.* act or power of recollecting: a thing remembered. [Pfx. **re-.**]

recommend, *rek-ȯ-mend'*, *v.t.* to advise: to speak well of (e.g. *I can recommend these cakes*).
recommend'able, *adj.*
recommendā'tion, *n.*
[L. *re-*, again, and root as **commend.**]

recommit, *rē-kom-it'*, *v.t.* commit again.
recommit'ment, recommitt'al, *ns.*
[Pfx. **re-.**]

recompense, *rek'ȯm-pens*, *v.t.* to repay or reward (a person), or to make up to (him) for loss.—*n.* reward: something to make up for injury or loss.
[L. *re-*, again; root as **compensate.**]

recompose, *rē-kom-pōz'*, *v.t.* to compose, form again: to arrange anew.
recomposi'tion, *n.* [Pfx. **re-.**]

reconcile, *rek'ȯn-sīl*, *v.t.* to bring or restore (enemies) to friendship: to bring to accept patiently (e.g. *This reconciled me, I reconciled myself, to the loss*): to bring (e.g. different aims, points of view) into agreement: to show that (e.g. two statements) are not contradictory: to settle (e.g. a quarrel).
reconciliā'tion, *n.*
[L. *re-*, *conciliāre*, to call together.]

recondition, *rē-kȯn-dish'(ȯ)n*, *v.t.* to restore to good condition. [Pfx. **re-.**]

reconnaissance, *ri-kon'i-sȧns*, *n.* a cautious exploring to obtain information before e.g. a battle. [Fr.]

reconnoitre, *rek-ȯ-noi'tėr*, *v.t.* and *v.i.* to explore or examine before a battle or similar action:—*pr.p.* **reconnoi'tring**

(*-tėr-*); *pa.p., pa.t.* **reconnoi'tred** (*-tėrd*). [Through Fr.—L. *recognoscĕre*, recognise.]

reconsider, *rē-kön-sid'ėr v.t.* to consider again with a view to altering(e.g. *Will you not reconsider your decision to go?*): to alter (a decision).

reconsiderā'tion, *n.* [Pfx. **re-.**]

reconstitute, *rē-kon'sti-tūt, v.t.* to restore to its original form (e.g. *The dried milk must be reconstituted before use*): to form, make up, in a different way.

reconstitu'tion, *n.* [Pfx. **re-.**]

reconstruct, *rē-kön-strukt', v.t.* to rebuild: to piece together in imagination (e.g. *Let us try to reconstruct the crime*).

reconstruc'tion, *n.* [Pfx. **re-.**]

record, *ri-körd', v.t.* to set down in writing for future use: (of instrument) to show as reading (e.g. *Yesterday the thermometer recorded* 30°*C.*, 86°*F.*): to register, show in required form (e.g. *Did you record your vote?*): to make by means of an instrument marks representing (sounds) from which the sounds can later be reproduced (e.g. *They recorded the song, the Premier's speech*).—*n. n.* (*rek'örd*) a written report of facts or events (e.g. *The records of a school society*): an event or performance that has never been equalled (e.g. *John holds the school record for the mile*): a plate, disk, etc. on which sounds are recorded (e.g. *a gramophone record*).

record'er, *n.* one who keeps records: a judge in certain courts: a musical instrument blown through a hole at one end.

record'ing, *n.* the process of making a record (esp. of sound on a gramophone record or magnetic tape): the sound record so made.

record office, a place where public records are kept.

rec'ord-player, *n.* a gramophone worked by electricity, not an earlier type, usu. portable.

off the record, (of information given) not to be published.

to beat, break, the record, to do better than any previous performance.

[L. *recordārī*, call to mind.]

recount[1], *rē'kownt', v.t.* to count over again.—*n.* a second count (e.g. *Sometimes in an election there has to be a recount of votes*). [Pfx. **re-.**]

recount[2], *ri-kownt', v.t.* to tell in detail (e.g. *He recounted his adventures*).

[O.Fr. *re-*, again, *conter*, to tell.]

recoup, *ri-ko͞op', v.t.* to make good (losses), recover (expenses).

[Fr. *recouper*, to cut again.]

recourse, *ri-kōrs', -körs', n.* in the phrase **to have recourse to,** to turn to for help in emergency.

[Fr. *recours.*]

recover[1], **re-cover,** *rē'kuv'ėr. v.t.* to cover again. [Pfx. **re-.**]

recover[2], *ri-kuv'ėr, v.t.* to get or find again: (with *oneself*) to come back to normal (e.g. *The actor forgot a line, but quickly recovered himself*): to obtain as compensation (e.g. *He recovered the cost of the repairs from the person who caused the damage*).—*v.i.* to regain health or position.

recov'erable, *adj.* able to be regained.

recov'ery, *n.* act of recovering: return to former state e.g. of health:—*pl.* **-ies.**

[O.Fr. *recovrer*—L. root as **recuperate.**]

recreant, *rek'ri-ȧnt, adj.* cowardly: false.—*n.* a cowardly person: a deserter.

[O.Fr. *pr.p.* of *recroire*, yield in battle.]

recreate, *rē'krė-āt', v.t.* to create again, esp. in the mind (e.g. *Try to recreate the scene*).

recreā'tion, *n.* [Pfx. **re-.**]

recreation[1], *rek-ri-ā'sh(ȯ)n, n.* rest from work: sport or amusement: time for this.

recreā'tional, *adj.*

[L. *recreātio, -ōnis*, recovery.]

recreation[2]. See **recreate.**

recriminate, *ri-krim'in-āt, v.i.* to accuse one's accuser.

recriminā'tion, *n.* accusation of an accuser (often in *pl.*).

recrim'inative, recrim'inatory, *adjs.*

[L. *re-*, *crīmināri*, accuse; conn. **crime.**]

recrudescence, *rėk-ro͞od-es'ns, n.* breaking out afresh into activity, etc. (e.g. *a recrudescence of violence*).

[L. *recrūdescĕre*, to become raw again, (of wound) to open; root as **crude.**]

recruit, *ri-kro͞ot', n.* a newly enlisted soldier or member.—*v.i.* to enlist new soldiers, etc.: to obtain fresh supplies: to get back health, etc. (e.g. *The invalid went to the seaside to recruit*).—*v.t.* to enlist or raise: to renew or restore.

recruit'er, *n.* **recruit'ment,** *n.*

[Through Fr.—L. *recrescĕre*, grow again.]

rect(i)-, *rek-t(i)-*, (as part of word) right, straight.

rectangle, *rek'tang-gl, -tang', n.* four-sided figure with opposite sides equal and all angles right angles.

rectang'ular, *adj.* of the form of a rectangle: having right angles.

rectify, *rek'ti-fī, v.t.* to put right: (*chemistry*) to purify (a liquid) by distilling: to change (an electric current) from alternating to direct:—*pr.p.* **rec'tifying**; *pa.p.* **rec'tified.**

rec'tifiable, *adj.* **rectificā'tion,** *n.*

rec'tifier, *n.* an apparatus that changes an alternating current into a direct current.

rectilinear, *rek-ti-lin'i-ȧr, adj.* made up of straight lines.

rectitude, *rek'ti-tūd, n.* honesty of character: uprightness.

[L. *rectus*, straight (*angulus*, angle; *facĕre*, to make; *līnea*, a line).]

rector, *rek'tȯr, n.* (Church of England, etc.) a clergyman in charge of a parish: (in Scotland) the headmaster of some secondary schools: the head of some colleges.
rector'ial (*-tōr', -tör'*), *adj.* of a rector.—*n.* election of a Lord Rector.
rec'tory, *n.* the house in which a Church of England, etc. rector lives:—*pl.* **-ies.**
Lord Rector, (in Scotland) elected honorary head of a University.
[L.—*regĕre, rectum,* to rule.]

rectum, *rek'tŭm, n.* the lower part of the alimentary canal, ending in the anus.
[L. neuter of *rectus,* straight.]

recumbent, *ri-kum'bėnt, adj.* lying down.
[L. *re-,* back, *cubāre,* to lie down.]

recuperate, *ri-kū'pėr-āt, v.t., v.i.* to recover.
recuperā'tion, *n.*
recu'perative, *adj.* helping recovery.
[L. *recuperāre*; conn. with **recover** (2).]

recur, *ri-kûr', v.i.* to come back (to the mind): to occur again:—*pr.p.* **recurr'ing**; *pa.p.* **recurred'.**
recurr'ence, *n.* act of happening again (e.g. *He had a recurrence of his illness*).
recurr'ent, *adj.* returning at intervals.
recurring decimal, decimal fraction in which a figure or a group of figures is repeated again and again indefinitely.
[L. *re-,* back, *currĕre,* to run.]

red, *red, adj.* of a colour like blood: revolutionary: communist: (*cap.*) connected with the U.S.S.R. (e.g. *the Red Army*):—*comp.* **redd'er**; *superl.* **redd'est.**—Also *n.*
redd'en, *v.t., v.i.* to make, or grow, red.
redd'ish, *adj.* like, or tinged with, red.
red'ness, *n.*
red admiral, a common butterfly with an orange-red band across each forewing.
red'breast, *n.* the robin.
redbrick', *adj.* applied to the more recent type of English university as opp. to Oxford and Cambridge.
red'cap, *n.* a goldfinch: (*slang*) a military policeman.
Red Cross, a world organisation for helping sick and wounded in time of war or disaster, so called from their flag, a red cross on a white ground.
red flag, a danger signal: (*caps.*) a communist and socialist song.
red'-hand'ed, *adv.* in the act of doing wrong (e.g. *The police caught the thief red-handed*).
red herring, a cured herring: in a discussion, something mentioned to take attention off the subject (as a herring would put hounds off the scent they were following): a false clue.
Red Indian, an American Indian.
red lead, an oxide of lead used in paint-making.
red'-letter, *adj.* happy, worthy to be remembered (e.g. *a red-letter day*), from the custom of marking holidays etc. in red in old calendars.
red light, a signal to stop: danger signal.
red'skin, *n.* a Red Indian.
red tape, the tape used in government offices: unnecessary rules about how things should be done.
red'wood, *n.* an American timber tree of great height.
to see red, to become very angry.
[O.E. *rēad.*]

redeem, *ri-dēm', v.t.* to buy back: to get or win back: to save from sin: to fulfil (a promise): to make up for (e.g. *He redeemed his lateness by hard work*).
redeem'able, *adj.* **redeem'er,** *n.*
redeem'ing, *adj.* making up for bad qualities (e.g. *The house is ugly, but its position on the hill is a redeeming feature*).
redemption, *ri-dem(p)'sh(ȯ)n, n.* act of redeeming: salvation: improvement: atonement.
[L. *re(d)-,* back, *emĕre, emptum,* buy.]

redeploy, *rē-di-ploi', v.t.* to move (forces—military, labour) to another area where they will be more effective.
redeploy'ment, *n.* [Pfx. **re-.**]

redirect, *rē-di-rekt', -dī-, v.t.* to direct again, esp. to put a new address on (a letter). [Pfx. **re-.**]

redolent, *red'ō-lėnt, adj.* fragrant: smelling (of; e.g. *The room was redolent of tobacco*).
red'olence, *n.*
[L. *re(d)-,* again, *olēre,* to smell.]

redouble, *ri-dub'l, v.t.* and *v.i.* to make twice as great, increase (e.g. *He redoubled his efforts*): (*bridge*; *rē'dub'l*) to double (a bid already doubled).
[Fr. *redoubler*; root as **re-, double.**]

redoubt, *ri-dowt', n.* in war, a separate fortified position, e.g. on a hill: an inner last retreat.
[Fr. *redoute*—Late L. *reductus,* secret place—L. *redūcĕre,* to lead back.]

redoubtable, *ri-dowt'ȧ-bl, adj.* (of person) bold, arousing fear, awe, or respect.—Also **redoubt'ed.**
[O.Fr. *redouter,* to fear greatly.]

redound, *ri-downd', v.i.* to have the result of adding (to; e.g. *This action redounds to his credit, advantage*).
[L. *re(d)-, undāre,* surge—*unda* wave.]

redraft, *rē'drâft', n.* a new draft or copy.—Also *v.t.* [Pfx. **re-.**]

redress, *ri-dres', v.t.* to set right, or make up for (e.g. a wrong).—*n.* relief, remedy: compensation (e.g. *Is there no redress for dismissal from the job?*)
to redress the balance, to make things more equal again.
[O.Fr. *redrecier*; root as **re-, dress.**]

re-dress, *rē'dres', v.t.* to dress again.
[Pfx. **re-.**]

redskin. See **red.**

reduce, *ri-dūs', v.t.* to make smaller: to

make less (e.g. *The train reduced speed*): to put, change, into other terms (e.g. *Reduce the pounds to shillings*), or another state (e.g. *to reduce the town to ruins*; *reduce your ideas to order*): to put into a place of less importance (e.g. *Sergeant Smith was reduced to the ranks*): to weaken: to subdue.—*v.i.* to slim.

reduced′, *adj.* made less: weakened: poor (e.g. *in reduced circumstances*).

reduc′ible, *adj.* able to be reduced.

reduction, *ri-duk′sh(ȯ)n*, *n.* act of reducing or state of being reduced: amount by which a thing is reduced (e.g. *Great reductions in price this week.*)

[*L. re-*, back, *dūcĕre*, *ductum*, to lead.]

redundant, *ri-dun′dȧnt*, *adj.* beyond what is necessary: expressing an idea conveyed by (an)other word(s) (e.g. *In 'the final end of the quarrel', 'final' is redundant*): (of worker) dismissed because no longer required.

redun′dance, -dancy (*pl.* **-ies**), *ns.*

[L. *redundans*, *-antis*; root as **redound.**]

reduplicate, *ri-dū′pli-kāt*, *v.t.* to repeat, copy (e.g. an action, an object, machine).

reduplicā′tion, *n.*

[L. *reduplicāre*, *-ātum*; root as **double.**]

redwood. See **red.**

re-echo, *rē-ek′ō*, *v.t.* to echo back: to repeat like an echo.—*v.i.* to resound (e.g. *The boys cheered until the hall re-echoed*). —Also *n.* [Pfx. **re-.**]

reed, *rēd*, *n.* a tall stiff grass growing near water: a vibrating part of a musical wind instrument: the part of a loom used to separate the threads.—Used as part of the names of birds usu. found among reeds, e.g. **reed warbler.**

reed′y, *adj.* full of reeds: like a reed: having the sound of a reed instrument (e.g. *The child's voice was high and reedy*): —*comp.* **reed′ier**; *superl.* **reed′iest.**

reed′iness, *n.*

[O.E. *hrēod*; conn. with Ger. *ried.*]

reef[1], *rēf*, *n.* a chain of rocks near the surface of water.

[Du. *rif*—Old Norse.]

reef[2], *rēf*, *n.* part of a ship's sail that may be rolled up to reduce the area acted on by the wind.—*v.t.* to gather up in this way: to reduce in size.

reef′er, *n.* one who reefs: a short jacket worn by sailors, or similar coat: (*slang*) a marijuana cigarette.

reef knot, a square, very secure knot.

[Same Old Norse root as **reef** (1).]

reek, *rēk*, *n.* smoke: fumes.—*v.i.* to give off smoke or fumes: to smell strongly of (e.g. *His clothes reek of mothball*).

[O.E. *rēc.*]

reel, *rēl*, *n.* a bobbin or cylinder of wood or metal on which thread, cable, fishing line, etc., may be wound: a lively dance, esp. Highland or Irish: a length of cinematograph film (1000 feet).—*v.t.* to wind on a reel: (with *in*) to draw in (fish) by winding the line on the reel.—*v.i.* to dance the reel: to sway, stagger.

(right) off the reel, without stop or hesitation.

to reel off, to repeat quickly and easily.

[Prob. O.E. *hrēol.*]

re-elect, *rē-ė-lekt′*, *v.t.* to elect again.

re-elec′tion, *n.* [Pfx. **re-.**]

re-embark, *rē-im-bärk′*, *v.t.* and *v.i.* to go, or put, on board again.

re-embarkā′tion (*-em-*), *n.* [Pfx. **re-.**]

re-enter, *rē-en′tėr*, *v.t.*, *v.i.* to enter again.

re-en′try, *n.* :—*pl.* **-ies.** [Pfx. **re-.**]

re-establish, *rē-is-tab′lish*, *v.t.* to establish again, to restore.

re-estab′lishment, *n.* [Pfx. **re-.**]

re-examine, *rē-eg-zam′in*, *v.t.* to examine again.

re-examinā′tion, *n.* [Pfx. **re-.**]

refectory, *ri-fek′tȯ-ri*, *n.* a dining hall, for monks, students, etc. :—*pl.* **-ies.**

[L. *reficĕre*, *refectum*—*facĕre*, make.]

refer, *ri-fėr′*, *v.t.* to hand over for consideration (e.g. *Refer this matter to your parents*): to direct for information (e.g. *For the historical facts, I refer you to the encyclopaedia*).—*v.i.* to turn (to) for information: to relate or apply (to; e.g. *This remark refers to something I told him in my letter*): (with *to*) to mention (e.g. *Do not refer to John's illness*):—*pr.p.* **referr′ing**; *pa.p.* **referred′.**

referee, *ref-ė-rē′*, *n.* one to whom anything is referred: an umpire or judge.

ref′erence, *n.* the act of referring: a mention: a note about a person's character, work: person giving this.

reference book, a book to be consulted sometimes for information, e.g. an encyclopaedia.

reference library, a library of books to be looked at but not taken away.

referen′dum, the practice of, or the action of, giving to all the people (of e.g. a country) an opportunity to vote on an important question (e.g. *Parliament passed the law, but would it have been approved by the people if a referendum had been carried out?*).

terms of reference, (a guiding statement laying down) the exact work or enquiries to be carried out by e.g. a committee.

without reference to, without taking into consideration.

with reference to, in connexion with, referring to (e.g. *With reference to your caravan holiday, I have some advice to give you*).

[L. *re-*, back, *ferre*, to carry.]

refill, *rē′fil*, or *-fil′*, *v.t.* to fill again.—*n.* a fresh fill. [Pfx. **re-.**]

refine, *ri-fīn′*, *v.t.* to purify: to free from coarseness: to improve, make more exact, delicate, or elegant.

refined′, *adj.* freed from impurities: polished, well-mannered.

refine'ment, *n.* good manners: good taste: an improvement: a refined, perfected, feature or method.
refin'ery, *n.* a place for refining sugar, oil, etc.:—*pl.* **refin'eries.**
refin'ing, *adj.*
to refine (up)on, to improve on.
[Pfx. **re-** and **fine** (1).]

refit, *rē'fit',* *v.t.*, *v.i.* to fit out, or be fitted out, again. [Pfx. **re-.**]

reflect, *ri-flekt',* *v.t.* to throw back (light, heat, etc.): to mirror, give an image of (e.g. *The still water reflects the swan*): to cast (e.g. *His refusal to yield reflects credit on him*): to realise while thinking (e.g. *He reflected that this was his last chance*).—*v.i.* to throw back: to mirror: to think carefully.
reflec'ted, *adj.* **reflec'ting,** *adj.*
reflection, reflexion, *ri-flek'sh(ò)n,* *n.* act of throwing back (e.g. a ray of light): an image: act of thinking carefully: a thought or remark: blame, unfavourable criticism (*He did the wrong thing, but I make no reflection on his motives for it*).
reflec'tive, *adj.* thoughtful.
reflec'tively, *adv.*
reflec'tor, *n.* a reflecting surface.
[L. *re-*, again, *flectĕre*, *flexum*, to bend.]

reflex, *rē'fleks,* *adj.* bent or turned back: happening without being intended (e.g. *The knee-jerk is a reflex action*).—*n.* a reflex action.
reflex'ive, *adj.* referring back, as in **reflexive pronoun,** a pronoun which shows that the object of an action is the same as the subject (or doer) of the action just mentioned (e.g. in *He cut himself badly*, 'himself' refers back to 'he' and is a reflexive pronoun).
reflexion. See **reflect.**
[Same root as **reflect.**]

reform[1], **re-form,** *rē'förm',* *v.t.* and *v.i.* to form again or anew.
re'(-)formā'tion, *n.* **re'(-)formed',** *adj.*
[Pfx. **re-.**]

reform[2], *ri-förm',* *v.t.* to improve, remove faults from (person, conduct, way of running an organisation, etc.): to put an end to (abuses, i.e. bad customs).—*v.i.* to give up evil ways.—*n.* improvement: change for the better.
reformā'tion (*ref-*), *n.*
refor'matory, *n.* a name (not used officially) for a school for reforming young wrongdoers.
reformed', *adj.* improved, esp. in conduct.
reform'er, *n.* one who wishes to bring about improvements: (with *cap.*) one of the leaders of the Reformation.
the Reformation, the 16th-century religious movement which led to the forming of the Protestant churches.
[L. *reformāre*, *-ātum*—*forma*, form.]

refract, *ri-frakt',* *v.t.* to change the direction of (a ray, e.g. of light)—as when a slanting ray is bent by passing from air into water.
refrac'tion, *n.*
[L. *rē-*, back, *frangĕre*, *fractum*, to break.]

refractory, *ri-frak'tò-ri,* *adj.* (of person, etc.) stubborn, unruly: (of a substance) difficult to work, melt, etc.—*n.* a substance, such as a brick for lining a furnace, able to stand great heat.
refrac'toriness, *n.*
[Same root as **refract.**]

refrain[1], *ri-frān',* *n.* a line of words or music repeated regularly in a song.
[O.Fr.—L. *refringĕre*; root as **refract.**]

refrain[2], *ri-frān',* *v.i.* to keep oneself (from some action; e.g. *You are asked to refrain from smoking*).
[O.Fr. *refrener*—L. *frēnum*, bridle.]

refresh, *ri-fresh',* *v.t.* to make fresh again: to give new strength and energy to: to make (memory) more clear by studying, etc., again: to cheer, give pleasure to.
refresh'ing, *adj.* **refresh'ingly,** *adv.*
refresh'er, *adj.* (of a course of study or training) intended to keep up the knowledge or skill one already has.
refresh'ment, *n.* act of refreshing: state of being refreshed: something that refreshes, e.g. food or drink.
[Pfx. **re-**, and **fresh.**]

refrigerate, *ri-frij'ėr-āt,* *v.t.* to make cold: to preserve (e.g. food) by exposing to great cold.
refrigerā'tion, *n.*
refrigerator, *ri-frij'ėr-ā-tòr,* *n.* a storage machine which preserves food by keeping it cold.
[L. *refrigerāre*—*frigus*, cold.]

refuel, *rē'fū'ėl,* *v.t.*, *v.i.* to supply with, or take in, fresh fuel:—*pr.p.* **refu'elling**; *pa.p.* **refu'elled.** [Pfx. **re-.**]

refuge, *ref'ūj,* *n.* a place of shelter (from danger or trouble): a street island for pedestrians.
refugee' (*-jē'*), *n.* one who seeks shelter in another country esp. from religious or political persecution.
[Fr.—L. *re-*, back, *fugĕre*, to flee.]

refund, *ri-* or *rē'fund',* *v.t.* to repay.—*n.* repayment.
[L. *re-*, back, *fundĕre*, *fūsum*, to pour.]

refuse[1], *ri-fūz',* *v.t.* to say that one will not, decline (to take, do, etc., something).—Also *v.i.*
refus'al, *n.*
[Fr. *refuser*—same L. root as **refund.**]

refuse[2], *ref'ūs,* *n.* rubbish.
[O.Fr. *refus*, refusal; root as **refuse** (1).]

refute, *ri-fūt',* *v.t.* to prove (something, a person) wrong (e.g. *You cannot refute that argument*).
[L. *refūtāre.*]

regain, *ri-gān',* or *rē',* *v.t.* to gain back: to get back to (e.g. *to regain the shore*).
[Fr. *regaigner* (now *regagner*).]

regal, *rē'gȧl,* *adj.* royal, kingly.
re'gally, *adv.*

re'galness, regal'ity, *ns.*
[L. *rēgālis*—*rex*, a king—*regĕre*, to rule.]
regale, *ri-gāl'*, *v.t.* to entertain with food, or with conversation.—*v.i.* to feast:—*pr.p.* **regal'ing;** *pa.p.* **regaled'.**
[Fr. *régaler*; perh. O.Fr. *gale*, pleasure.]
regalia, *ri-gā'li-à*, *n.pl.* marks or signs of royalty (e.g. crown and sceptre): any ornaments to show a person's position of authority.
[From L. *rēgālis*; same root as **regal.**]
regard, *ri-gärd'*, *v.t.* to look at carefully: to look on (e.g. *to regard with amusement*): to consider (as; e.g. *I regard you as a nuisance*): to think highly of: to pay heed to.—*n.* attentive look: concern (for): affection: respect: (in *pl.*) good wishes.
regard'ing, *prep.* concerning.
regard'less, *adj.* not considering or caring about (with *of*; e.g. *regardless of consequences, of cost*).
as regards, with regard to (something), as far as (it) is concerned.
[Fr. *regarder*—*re-*, *garder*, keep watch.]
regatta, *ri-gat'à*, *n.* a meeting for yacht or boat races.
[It. (Venetian) *regata*.]
regency. See **regent.**
regenerate, *ri-jen'ėr-āt*, *v.t.* to produce, or to make, anew: to bring (something used) back to its condition before use: to reform morally.—Also *v.i.*—*adj.* (*-it*) remade in better form, esp. spiritually.
regen'eracy, *n.* regenerate state.
regenerā'tion, *n.* act of regenerating: regeneracy.
[L. *re-*, again, *generāre*, to bring forth.]
regent, *rē'jėnt*, *n.* one who governs in place of a king or queen.
re'gency, *n.* position of a regent: (period of) rule by a regent.
[L. *regens*, ruling; root as **regal.**]
regicide, *rej'i-sīd*, *n.* the killing, or killer, of a king.
[L. *rex*, *regis*, king, *caedĕre*, to kill.]
régime, *rā-zhēm'*, *n.* system of rule, government (e.g. *under the Communist régime*). [Fr.]
regiment, *rej'(i-)mėnt*, *n.* a body of soldiers commanded by a colonel.—*v.t.* to organise, control, too strictly.
regimentā'tion, *n.* too severe control.
regiment'al, *adj.* of a regiment (e.g. *the regimental mascot*).—*n.* (in *pl.*) uniform of a regiment.
[Late L. *regimentum*—L. root as **regal.**]
region, *rē'jȯn*, *n.* a district: a part of the earth's surface or of the universe: a part, division, of the body (e.g. *I had a pain in the heart region*).
rē'gional, *adj.* **rē'gionally,** *adv.*
[L. *regiō*, *regiōnis*; root as **regal.**]
register, *rej'is-tėr*, *n.* a written record: a book containing such records (e.g. *attendance register, marriage register*): a range of a voice or musical instrument (e.g. *the upper register of the voice*).—*v.t.* to enter in a register: (of an instrument, e.g. a thermometer) to record, show: (*coll.*) to show in one's appearance (e.g. *to register amusement*): to pay a fee so that (a letter, etc.) may have special care.—*v.i.* to enter one's name (e.g. at a hotel).
reg'istered, *adj.* **registrā'tion,** *n.*
reg'istrar (or *-trär'*), *n.* one who keeps official records.
reg'istry, *n.* an office or place where registers are kept:—*pl.* **-ies.**
register office, registry office, an office where records of births, marriages, etc. are kept, and where marriages are performed.
[Late L. *regesta*—*regerĕre*, to record.]
Regius, *rē'ji-ùs*, *adj.* used in title **Regius professor,** the holder of a university chair founded by a king.
[L. *rex*, *regis*, king.]
regress, *ri-gres'*, *v.i.* to go back to a state lower or less perfect.
regression, *ri-gresh'(ȯ)n*, *n.*
[L. *re-*, back, *gradī*, *gressus*, to walk.]
regret, *ri-gret'*, *v.t.* to feel sorry about (something): to be sorry (to say):—*pr.p.* **regrett'ing;** *pa.p.* **regrett'ed.**—*n.* a sorrowful wish that something had happened differently.
regret'ful, *adj.* feeling regret.
regret'fully, *adv.*
regrett'able, *adj.* that should be regretted.
regrett'ably, *adv.*
[From O.Fr.; perh. conn. Scot. *greet*, cry.]
regular, *reg'ū-làr*, *adj.* according to rule, or to habit: usual: happening at fixed times or intervals: even (e.g. *regular teeth*): (of soldiers) belonging to the regular (i.e. permanent) army.—*n.* a soldier of the regular army: a member of a religious order: a frequent visitor, etc.
reg'ularise, *v.t.* to make regular, esp according to law, custom, rule.
regular'ity, *n.* **reg'ularly,** *adv.*
reg'ulāte, *v.t.* to control by rules: to keep in order.
regulā'tion, *n.* act of regulating: a rule or order.
reg'ulātor, *n.* a person, or a device, that regulates: a controlling lever esp. for the speed of a watch.
[L. *rēgula*, a rule—*regĕre*, to rule.]
regurgitate, *ri-gûr'ji-tāt*, *rē'*, *v.t.* to bring back into the mouth after swallowing.
[L. *re-*, back, *gurges*, whirlpool.]
rehabilitate, *rē-(h)à-bil'i-tāt*, *v.t.* to give back rights or powers that have been lost: to restore to health: to clear the character of.
rehabilitā'tion, *n.*
[Late L. *re-*, *habilitāre*, to make able.]
rehash, *rē'hash'*, *n.* something (esp. book,

speech etc.) made of materials previously used.—Also *v.t.* [Pfx. **re-**.]

rehearse, *ri-hėrs′*, *v.t.* to practise beforehand: to relate, tell, in order (e.g. *He rehearsed all the events of the day*).—*v.i.* to take part in a rehearsal or practice.
rehear′sal, *n.*
dress rehearsal, (*theatre*) final rehearsal with costumes, etc.
[O Fr. *re-*, again, *hercer*, harrow (land).]

rehouse, *rē′howz′*, *v.t.* to provide with a new or different house or houses.
rehous′ing, *n.* [Pfx. **re-**.]

reign, *rān*, *n.* rule of a king or queen: time of this: time during which something is very powerful (e.g. *a reign of terror*).—*v.i.* to be ruler.
[O.Fr. *regne*—L. root as **regal, regent.**]

reimburse, *rē-im-bûrs′*, *v.t.* to repay.
reimburse′ment, *n.*
[L. *re-*, *in*, and root as **disburse.**]

rein, *rān*, *n.* one of two straps for guiding a horse.—*v.t.* to control with reins: to check.
to draw rein, to stop.
to give rein to, to allow (e.g. one's imagination, passion) to act unchecked.
[O.Fr. *reine*—L. *retinēre*, hold back.]

reincarnation, *rē′in-kär-nā′sh(ȯ)n*, *n.* (belief in) rebirth of the soul in another body after death: an instance of this. **[re-.]**

reindeer, *rān′dēr*, *n.* a kind of deer found in the far North.
reindeer moss, a lichen, the winter food of the reindeer.
[Old Norse, *hreinndȳri.*]

reinforce, *rē-in-fōrs′*, *-förs′*, *v.t.* to strengthen with new forces or material (e.g. *We reinforce concrete by embedding steel bars or mesh in it*).
reinforce′ment, *n.* strengthening: (in *pl.*) extra troops or help.
[Pfx. **re-** and **enforce.**]

reinstate, *rē′in-stāt′*, *v.t.* to put back in a former position.
reinstate′ment, *n.*
[Pfx. **re-,** old verb *instate*, to install.]

reinvigorate, *rē′in-vig′ȯr-āt*, *v.t.* to put new vigour into. [Pfx. **re-**.]

reissue, *rē′is′ū*, *-ish′ū*, *v.t.* to issue again.—*n.* a second or later issue (e.g. of stamps.) [Pfx. **re-**.]

reiterate, *rē-it′ė-rāt*, *v.t.* to repeat, esp. again and again.
reiterā′tion, *n.* repetition.
[Pfx. **re-,** L. *iterāre*—*iterum*, again.]

reject, *ri-jėkt′*, *v.t.* to throw out or away: to refuse to take or to grant.—*n.* (*rē′jėkt*) a person or thing put aside as unsatisfactory (e.g. *export rejects*, manufactured articles too imperfect to export).
rejec′tion, *n.*
[L. *re-*, back, *jacĕre*, *jactum*, throw.]

rejoice, *ri-jois′*, *v.t.* to make joyful.—*v.i.* to feel joy.
rejoic′ing, *n.* act of feeling or expressing joy: (in *pl.*) celebrations.
to rejoice in, to be glad to have (something).
[Fr. *réjouir*—L. *re-*, *gaudēre*, rejoice.]

rejoin[1], *rē′join′*, *v.t.*, *v.i.* to join again. [Pfx. **re-**.]

rejoin[2], *ri-join′*, *v.t.* to say in answer.
rejoin′der, *n.* an answer, esp. to a reply.
[Fr. *rejoindre*—*re-*, *joindre*, join.]

rejuvenate, *ri-jōō′vi-nāt*, *v.t.* to make young again.
rejuvenā′tion, *n.*
[L. *re-*, again, *juvenis*, young.]

rekindle, *rē′kin′dl*, *v.t.* to set on fire, or to arouse, anew. [Pfx. **re-**.]

relapse, *ri-laps′*, *v.i.* to fall back into a former state or way of life.—Also *n.*
[L. *re-*, back; root as **lapse.**]

relate, *ri-lāt′*, *v.t.* to tell: to show a connexion between (e.g. two facts): to show the connexion of (one thing) with another (e.g. *to relate slum housing with*, or *to*, *petty crime*).—*v.i.* to have reference (to).
relā′ted, *adj.* connected, e.g. by common ancestry, origin, nature.
relā′tion, *n.* act of telling: way of being connected: a person connected with one by birth or marriage: (in *pl.*) behaviour or feeling between people (e.g. *to establish good relations with someone*).
relā′tionship, *n.* state, or way, of being related.
relative, *rel′ȧ-tiv*, *adj.* comparative (e.g. (e.g. *the relative speed of car and train*): related: referring (to).—*n.* a relation.
rel′atively, *adv.* in comparison with something else.
relativ′ity, *n.* the fact or state of being relative: a scientific theory about motion and position in space.
[L. *re-*, back, *fĕrre*, *lātum*, to bring.]

relax, *ri-laks′*, *v.t.* to loosen (e.g. one's hold): to make less strict or severe (e.g. *Rules were relaxed on Speech Day*).—*v.i.* to become less tense, rest completely: to take recreation: to become less strict.
relaxāt′ion (*rē-*), *n.*
relax′ing, *adj.* (of climate) making people less energetic than usual.
[L. *re-*, again, and root as **lax.**]

relay[1], *rē′lā′*, *v.t.* to lay again. [Pfx. **re-**.]

relay[2], *ri-lā′*, also *rē′lā*, *n.* a fresh set of men or animals to relieve others: the sending out of a broadcast received from another station.—*v.t.* to send on or out (esp. such a broadcast):—*pr.p.* **relay′ing**; *pa.p.* **relayed′.**
relay (*rē′lā*) **race,** a race in which members of a team take over from each other, each individual competitor running, etc., an arranged distance.
[O.Fr. *relais*, relay of dogs or horses.]

release, *ri-lēs′*, *v.t.* to let go: to set free: to permit to be made public (e.g. news or a film).—*n.* a setting free: permitting to make publicly known, or available.
[O.Fr. *relaissier*—L. root as **(re)lax.**]

relegate, *rel'i-gāt, v.t.* to put down (to a lower grade, position, etc.): to leave to someone else (e.g. a duty).
relegā'tion, *n.*
[L. *re-*, away, *lēgāre, -ātum*, to send.]

relent, *ri-lent', v.i.* to become less severe, more forgiving.
relent'less, *adj.* without pity: not turned aside from one's aim by anything.
relent'lessly, *adv.* **relent'lessness,** *n.*
[L. *re-*, back, *lentus*, yielding.]

relevant, *rel'ė-vȧnt,* having to do with the matter being spoken of or considered.
rel'evance, *n.*
[L. *relevans—relevāre*, raise up, help.]

reliable, reliance, etc. See **rely.**

relic, *rel'ik, n.* (in *pl.*) a dead body: something left from a past time or age, or connected with a dead person (e.g. *relics of a saint*).
reliquary, *rel'i-kwȧr-i, n.* a receptacle for relic(s):—*pl.* **-ies.**
[L. *relinquĕre, relictum*, leave behind.]

relief, *ri-lēf', n.* a lessening of pain or anxiety, or of boredom, etc.: release from a post or duty: the person(s) taking the duty over: help given to people in need (e.g. *famine relief*): state of standing out from the background (e.g. *a carving in relief*).
relief map, a map which shows, by colouring or other means, the highlands and lowlands of a country.
relieve, *ri-lēv', v.t.* to ease (pain, worry, etc.): to give help to (people in distress): to raise the siege of: to take over a duty from (someone).
reliev'ing, *adj.* and *n.*
[O.Fr. *relever*—L. *re-*, *levāre*, raise.]

religion, *ri-lij'ȯn, n.* belief in, or worship of, a God or gods.
relig'ionist, *n.* someone attached to a particular religion.
relig'ious, *adj.* concerned with religion: devoted to religion, pious: faithful, conscientious (e.g. *He was religious in his efforts*; *with religious care*).
relig'iously, *adv.* **relig'iousness,** *n.*
[L. *religiō, -ōnis.*]

relinquish, *ri-ling'kwish, v.t.* to give up: to let go.
relinquishment (*-ling'*), *n.*
[O.Fr. *relinquir*—L. root as **relic.**]

reliquary. See **relic.**

relish, *rel'ish, n.* a flavour: something to give a flavour: liking (for): enjoyment.—*v.t.* to like the taste of: to enjoy.
[O.Fr. *relaisser*, to leave behind.]

reluctance, *ri-luk'tȧns, n.* unwillingness.
reluc'tant, *adj.* **reluc'tantly,** *adv.*
[L. *reluctans, pr.p.—reluctārī*, struggle.]

rely, *ri-lī', v.i.* to trust confidently, depend (on e.g. person, person's help, a happening):—*pr.p.* **rely'ing;** *pa.p.* **relied'.**
reli'able, *adj.* trustworthy.
reli'ably, *adv.*
reliabil'ity, reli'ableness, *ns.*
reli'ance, *n.* trust, dependence.
reli'ant, *adj.* depending (on): self-reliant.
[O.Fr. *relier*—L. *religāre*, to bind back.]

remain, *ri-mān', v.i.* to stay or be left behind: to go on unchanged.
remains', *n. pl.* what is left, e.g. after a meal: a dead body.
remain'der, *n.* (e.g. *in arithmetic*) something that is left after the removal of the rest.—*v.t.* to sell off as surplus.
See also **remnant.**
[O.Fr. *remaindre*—L. *re-*, *manēre*, stay.]

remake, *rē'māk', v.t.* to make again. [Pfx. **re-.**]

remand, *ri-mȧnd', v.t.* to send back (esp. a prisoner to await further evidence).
remand home, a home to which a child or young person may be sent by a magistrate.
[L. *re-*, back, *mandāre*, to order.]

remark[1], *rē'märk', v.t.* to mark again. [Pfx. **re-.**]

remark[2], *ri-märk', v.t.* to notice: to comment, say.—*v.i.* to comment (on).—*n.* a comment, something said.
remark'able, *adj.* unusual: worth mentioning.
remark'ably, *adv.* **-ableness,** *n.*
[O.Fr. *remarquer—marquer*, to mark.]

remedy, *rem'i-di, n.* a cure for an illness or evil:—*pl.* **rem'edies.**—*v.t.* to cure: to put right:—*pr.p.* **rem'edying;** *pa.p.* **rem'edied** (*-did*).
remē'diable, *adj.* that may be cured.
remē'dial, *adj.* able, or intended, to cure.
[L. *re-*, *medērī*, cure; root as **medicine.**]

remember, *ri-mem'bėr, v.t.* to keep in the mind, or to bring back into the mind after forgetting for a time: to reward, make a present to, or tip.
remem'brance, *n.* memory: a keepsake: (in *pl.*) a friendly greeting.
reminiscence, *rem-in-is'ėns, n.* something remembered: (usu. in *pl.*) an account of remembered past events: a suggestion (of; e.g. *There is a reminiscence of her mother in her haughty manner*).
reminis'cent, *adj.* reminding one (of).
reminisce, *rem-in-is', v.i.* to talk about things remembered.
[L. *re-*, back, *memor*, mindful; *reminisci*, to remember; same root as **memory.**]

remind, *ri-mīnd', v.t.* to cause to remember (e.g. *Remind me to post the letter*; *she reminded me of my promise*): to make (one) think of (e.g. *The hat reminds me of a beehive*).
remin'der, *n.* something that reminds.
[Pfx. **re-** and **mind.**]

reminisce, etc. See **remember.**

remiss, *ri-mis', adj.* careless, slack, in carrying out duties.
remiss'ness, *n.*
[Same root as **remit.**]

remission. See **remit.**

remit, *ri-mit', v.t.* to relax, lessen (e.g. *to*

remit effort): to pardon (e.g. a sin): to cancel (e.g. a debt): to send (money): to hand over (e.g. *to remit a prisoner to a higher court*).—*v.i.* to grow less:—*pr.p.* **remitt′ing**; *pa.p.* **remitt′ed.**

remission, *ri-mish′(ȯ)n, n.* forgiveness: cancelling (e.g. *He earned remission of part of his sentence*).

remitt′ance, *n.* the sending of money, etc., to a distance: the thing sent.

[L. *re-*, back, *mittĕre, missum*, to send.]

remnant, *rem′nȧnt, n.* a small piece or number left over from a larger piece or number.

[Same root as **remain.**]

remodel, *rē′mod′l, v.t.* to model again, esp. so as to change the shape:—*pr.p.* **re′mod′elling**; *pa.p.* **re′mod′elled.** [Pfx. **re-.**]

remonstrance, *ri-mon′strȧns, n.* a strong protest.

remon′strāte (or *rem′*), *v.t.* to make a protest (e.g. *I remonstrated with him about his treatment of his friend*).

[L. *re-*, again, *monstrāre*, to point out.]

remorse, *ri-mörs′, n.* sorrow for a fault or sin.

remorse′ful, *adj.* **remorse′fully,** *adv.*

remorse′less, *adj.* cruel: relentless.

remorse′lessly, *adv.* **-lessness,** *n.*

[L. *re-*, back, *mordēre, morsum*, to bite.]

remote, *ri-mōt′, adj.* distant in time or place: out of the way (e.g. *a remote village*): slight (e.g. *a remote chance*).

remote′ly, *adv.* **remote′ness,** *n.*

remote control, control of apparatus by means of distant electric switches, or by radio waves.

[Same root as **remove.**]

remount, *rē′mount′, v.t.* and *v.i.*, to mount again.—*n.* fresh horse(s). [Pfx. **re-.**]

remove, *ri-mōōv′, v.t.* to take off: to take away: to dismiss, put out (e.g. a person from a post).—*v.i.* to change one's dwelling place.—*n.* a stage, step away (e.g. *This harsh treatment is only one remove from bullying*).

remov′able, *adj.* that can be removed.

remov′al, *n.* act of taking, or of going, away: change of home.

[L. *re-*, away, *movēre, mōtum*, to move.]

remunerate, *ri-mū′nė-rāt, v.t.* to pay (a person) for a service.

remunerā′tion, *n.* payment.

remun′erative, *adj.* profitable.

[L. *remūnerārī—mūnus, mūneris*, a gift.]

renaissance, *ri-nā′sȧns, n.* a new birth or revival: (*cap.*) revival of arts and literature in Europe in the 14th to 16th centuries.—Also *adj.* (with *cap.*).—Also **renascence** (*ri-nas′ns*).

renas′cent, *adj.* being reborn or revived.

[L. *re-*, again, *nascī*, to be born (the form *renaissance* came through Fr.).]

renal, *rē′n(ȧ)l, adj.* of the kidneys.

[L. *rēnēs*, the kidneys.]

renascence, etc. See **renaissance.**

rend, *rend, v.t., v.i.* to tear apart, split: to pull or tear roughly:—*pa.p.* **rent.**

rent, *n.* a tear, split.

[O.E. *rendan.*]

render, *ren′dėr, v.t.* to give (back): to give (e.g. aid, thanks): to present (e.g. a bill): to translate (e.g. *to render Latin into English*): to represent, e.g. in a painting: to perform (e.g. music): to cause to be (e.g. *This rendered me speechless*): to melt and purify (fat).

ren′dering, *n.*

rendi′tion, *n.* interpretation, manner of performance of a dramatic part or piece of music: translation.

[Fr. *rendre*—L. *re-*, again, *dăre*, to give.]

rendezvous, *ron′di-vōō, rāng- n.* a meeting place: a meeting by appointment.—*v.i.* to meet at an appointed place. [Fr.]

rendition. See **render.**

renegade, *ren′i-gād, n., adj.* (one) faithless to party or principles.

[Sp. *renegado*—L. *negāre*, deny.]

renew, *ri-nū′, v.t.* to begin again (e.g. an attempt): to make as if new: to put in a fresh store of (e.g. *to renew the water in the tank*): to recover (youth, energy, etc.): to continue for a longer period (e.g. membership, a licence).

renew′able, *adj.* able to be renewed.

renew′al, *n.* [Pfx. **re-.**]

rennet, *ren′it, n.* a substance used for curdling milk to make junket, etc.

[O.E. *rinnan*, to run.]

renounce, *ri-nowns′, v.t.* to give up, esp. formally (a title, claim, intention, etc.).—*v.i.* to play a card not of the suit led.

renounce′ment, *n.* act of giving up, esp. formally.

renunciation, *ri-nun-si-ā′sh(ȯ)n, n.* renouncement: self-denial.

[L. *re-*, away, *nuntiāre, -ātum*, announce.]

renovate, *ren′ō-vāt, v.t.* to make new, or as if new, again: to mend.

renovā′tion, *n.* **ren′ovātor,** *n.*

[L. *re-, novāre, -ātum—novus*, new.]

renown, *ri-nown′, n.* fame, high repute.

renowned′, *adj.* famous.

[Fr. *renom*—L. *re-*, again, *nōmen*, name.]

rent[1]. See **rend.**

rent[2], *rent, n.* payment for use of someone else's property, esp. houses and lands.—*v.t.* to hold or use by paying rent: to let or hire out for rent.

ren′tal, *n.* rent: income from rents.

rent restriction, limiting a landlord's right to raise rent.

[L. *reddita* (*pecūnia*), money paid.]

renunciation. See **renounce.**

rep[1], **repp,** *rep, n.* a corded cloth.

[Fr. *reps*, perh.—Eng. **ribs.**]

rep[2], *rep, n.* abbreviation for **repertory** (theatre), **repetition, reputation.**

repaid. See **repay.**

repair[1], *ri-pār′, v.i.* to go (e.g. *He repairde to his house*).

[L. *re-*, back, *patria*, native country.]

repair[2], *ri-pār′*, *v.t.* to mend: to put right: to make up for (a wrong).—*n.* (often in *pl.*) mending: sound condition.
repair′er, *n.* one who repairs.
reparable, *rep′ȧr-a-bl, adj.* able to be mended, or put right.
reparā′tion, *n.* putting right a wrong: compensation.
[L. *re-*, again, *parāre*, prepare.]

repartee, *rep-ȧr-tē′*, *n.* a quick, witty reply: speech of this kind: skill in it.
[O.Fr. *repartie.*]

repast, *ri-pâst′*, *n.* a meal.
[O.Fr.—L. *re-*, *pascĕre*, *pastum*, to feed.]

repatriate, *rē-pat′ri-āt*, or *-pā′tri-*, *v.t.* to send (someone) back to his own country.
repatriā′tion, *n.*
[L. *re-*, back, *patria*, one's country.]

repay, *rē-pā′*, *v.t.* to pay back: to make a return for:—*pr.p.* **repay′ing;** *pa.p.* **repaid′.**
repay′able, *adj.* to be repaid (e.g. *money repayable within ten years*).
repay′ment, *n.* [Pfx. **re-.**]

repeal, *ri-pēl′*, *v.t.* to cancel (e.g. a law).—Also *n.*
[O.Fr. *rapeler—re-*, root as **appeal.**]

repeat, *ri-pēt*, *v.t.* to say or do again: to say from memory: to tell (something heard) when one ought not to: to copy (e.g. the speech or actions of someone else).—*v.i.* to occur again: (of guns) to fire several shots without reloading.—*n.* (*music*) a passage to be repeated: a second, or later, performance.—Also *adj.*
repeat′able, *adj.* fit to be repeated: that can be repeated.
repeat′ed, *adj.* occurring many times.
repeat′edly, *adv.* many times.
repeat′er, *n.* **repeat′ing,** *n.* and *adj.*
repetition, *rep-i-tish′(ȯ)n*, *n.* act of repeating: recital from memory: a repeat performance or occurrence.
repetitive, *ri-pet′i-tiv*, *adj.* repeating something too often.
repeating decimal, recurring decimal.
to repeat oneself, to say the same thing more than once.
[Fr. *répéter*—L. *re-*, again, *petĕre*, seek.]

repel, *ri-pel′*, *v.t.* to drive back or away: to be distasteful to:—*pr.p.* **repell′ing;** *pa.p.* **repelled′.**
repell′ent, *adj.* disgusting.—*n.* something that drives away (e.g. insects).
See also **repulse.**
[L. *re-*, back, *pellĕre*, *pulsum*, drive.]

repent, *ri-pent′*, *v.i.* to be sorry for what one has done or left undone: to regret (with *of*; e.g. *He repented of his generosity to the ungrateful boy*).—*v.t.* to regret (e.g. *He repented his generosity*).
repent′ance, *n.* **repent′ant,** *adj.*
[O.Fr. *repentir*—L. root as **penitent.**]

repercussion, *rē-pėr-kush′(ȯ)n*, *n.* an echo: an after effect of an action or event (esp. if bad).
[L. *repercutĕre*, *-cussum—quatĕre*, strike.]

repertoire. See **repertory.**

repertory, *rep′ėr-tȯr-i*, *n.* a stock of pieces that a person or company can perform.—Also **repertoire,** *rep′ėr-twär* (from Fr. *répertoire*).
repertory theatre, a theatre with a more or less permanent company acting a series of plays.
[L. *reperīre*, *repertum*, to find again.]

repetition, repetitive. See **repeat.**

repine, *ri-pīn′*, *v.i.* to fret (with *at* or *against*): to feel discontent.
repīn′ing, *n.* and *adj.*
[Prob. from **pine** (2).]

replace, *ri-plās′*, *rē-*, *v.t.* to put back: to fill the place of (e.g. *to replace the old lock by a new*; *chosen to replace the retiring president*).
replace′able, *adj.* that can be replaced.
replace′ment, *n.* act of replacing: a substitute. [Pfx. **re-.**]

replenish, *ri-plen′ish*, *v.t.* to fill again: to stock up.
replen′ishment, *n.*
[O.Fr. *replenir*—L. root as **replete.**]

replete, *ri-plēt′*, *adj.* full: well stocked (with).
replete′ness, replē′tion, *ns.* fullness almost to excess.
[L. *re-*, again, *plēre*, *plētum*, to fill.]

replica, *rep′lik-ȧ*, *ri-plē′kȧ*, *n.* an exact copy, esp. of a work of art.
[It.—L. *replicāre*, to repeat.]

reply, *ri-plī′*, *v.i.*, *v.t.* to answer, respond, in words or by an action:—*pr.p.* **reply′ing;** *pa.p.* **replied′** (*-plīd′*).—Also *n.*
[O.Fr. *replier*—L. root as **replica.**]

report, *ri-pōrt′*, *-pört′*, *v.t.* to pass on news (that something has happened): to give news, or an account, of: to take notes of (e.g. a speech), esp. for a newspaper: to make a formal complaint against (a person): to present (oneself for duty).—*v.i.* to make a statement: to present oneself for duty.—*n.* a statement of facts: a newspaper account: a rumour: a written statement on e.g. a pupil's work: a loud noise.
report′er, *n.* one who reports, esp. for a newspaper.
report′ing, *n.* and *adj.*
[L. *re-*, back, *portāre*, to carry.]

repose[1], *ri-pōz′*, *v.t.*, *v.i.* to rest.—*n.* rest: calm.
[Fr. *reposer*—L. root as **pause.**]

repose[2], *ri-pōz′*, *v.t.* to place (trust, etc., in a person or thing).
repository, *ri-poz′i-tȯr-i*, *n.* a place where something is stored:—*pl.* **-ies.**
[L. *repōnĕre*, *-positum*, put back again.]

repossess, *rē′poz-es′*, *v.t.* to regain possession of.
repossession, *rē-poz-esh′(ȯ)n*, *n.*
[Pfx. **re-.**]

repp. See **rep** (1).

reprehend, *rep-ri-hend′*, *v.t.* to find fault with, reprove.

reprehens′ible, *adj.* blameworthy.
reprehens′ibly, *adv.* in a manner deserving blame.
[L. *re-*, *prehendĕre*, *prehensum*, seize.]

represent, *rep-ri-zent′*, *v.t.* to point out (e.g. *He represented the difficulties to the rest of the committee*): to claim to be (with *as*; e.g. *She represents herself as an expert*): to speak or act for someone or something else (e.g. *Will you represent the school at the Sports Meeting?*): to act the part of (a character in e.g. a play): (of e.g. a picture) to show: to correspond to or imply (e.g. *This rise represents an increase of* 5%).
representation, *rep-ri-zen-tā′sh(ò)n*, *n.* act of representing or being represented: an image or picture: a dramatic rendering: a strong statement or appeal.
representative, *rep-ri-zen′tà-tiv*, *adj.* typical: carried on by elected persons (e.g. *representative government*).—*n.* one who represents another, e.g. in business or government.
House of Representatives, lower house of U.S. Congress, etc.
[L. *re-*, again, *praesentāre*, place before.]

repress, *ri-pres′*, *v.t.* to put down by force, quell, suppress: to keep under control, check (e.g. a desire, action): to keep under too severe control.
repress′ible, *adj.* **repressed′,** *adj.*
repression, *ri-presh′(ò)n*, *n.*
repress′ive, *adj.* severe, harsh.
[L. *re-*, *premĕre*, *pressum*, to press.]

reprieve, *ri-prēv′*, *v.t.* to delay execution of (someone): to give an interval of ease or freedom to.—*n.* a delay of execution: an interval of rest or relief.
[M.E. *repreven.*]

reprimand, *rep′ri-mând*, *n.* a severe scolding.—*v.t.* to reprove severely.
[Fr. *réprimande*—L. root as **repress.**]

reprint, *rē′print′*, *v.t.* to print again: to print more copies of.—*n.* (*rē′print*) a new printing. [Pfx. **re-.**]

reprisal, *ri-prīz′àl*, *n.* an act of returning like for like (e.g. *The raid was a reprisal for an earlier attack by the other side*).
[Fr. *reprise*—L. root as **reprehend.**]

reproach, *ri-prōch′*, *v.t.* to scold, chide (e.g. *She reproached me for not telling her*): to blame for (with *with*; e.g. *She reproached me with the failure of her plan*).—*n.* blame: reproof: disgrace (e.g. *to bring reproach on one's family*).
reproach′ful, *adj.* full of, or expressing, disappointment and blame.
reproach′fully, *adv.* **-fulness,** *n.*
[Fr. *reprocher*; perh. L. *prope*, near.]

reprobate, *rep′rō-bāt*, *n.* a person of evil habits.—Also *adj.*—*v.t.* to disapprove of, condemn.
reprobā′tion, *n.*
[L. *reprobāre*, *-ātum*, to reprove.]

reproduce, *rē-prò-dūs′*, *v.t.* to produce a copy of: to produce (young).—Also *v.i.*
reproduction, *rē-prò-duk′sh(ò)n*, *n.* act of reproducing: a copy.
reproduc′tive, *adj.* [Pfx. **re-.**]

reproof[1], *rē′prōōf′*, *v.t.* to make waterproof again. [Pfx. **re-.**]

reproof[2], *ri-prōōf′*, *n.* scolding: a scolding, mild rebuke.
reproval, *ri-prōō′v(à)l*, *n.* reproof.
reprove′, *v.t.* to blame, rebuke, find fault with.
reprov′ing, *adj.* **reprov′ingly,** *adv.*
[O.Fr. *reprover*—L. root as **reprobate.**]

reptile, *rep′til*, *n.* a crawling or creeping animal, cold-blooded and scaly, e.g. a snake, crocodile.
reptilian, *rep-til′i-àn*, *adj.* belonging to, or resembling, these animals.
[L. *repĕre*, *reptum*, to creep.]

republic, *ri-pub′lik*, *n.* a form of government without a king or queen, the country being ruled by an elected representative of the people.
repub′lican, *adj.*
Republican, *n.* and *adj.* (a member) of one of the two great political parties in U.S.A.
[L. *rēspublica*, state—*rēs*, affair, *publica*, public.]

republish, *rē-pub′lish*, *v.t.* publish again.
republicā′tion, *n.* [Pfx. **re-.**]

repudiate, *ri-pū′di-āt*, *v.t.* to disown (e.g. a son): to refuse to recognise (e.g. authority), accept (an idea), acknowledge (e.g. a debt, obligation, or claim).
repudiā′tion, *n.*
[L. *repudiāre*, *-ātum*—*repudium*, divorce.]

repugnance, *ri-pug′nàns*, *n.* strong dislike, disgust: unpleasantness.
repug′nant, *adj.* unpleasant: distasteful (to).
[L. *re-*, against, *pugnāre*, to fight.]

repulse, *ri-puls′*, *v.t.* to drive back (an enemy): to snub.—*n.* a defeat: a snub.
repulsion, *ri-pul′sh(ò)n*, *n.* disgust: a driving back.
repul′sive, *adj.* that disgusts: that drives back or off.
repul′sively, *adv.* **repul′siveness,** *n.*
[Same root as **repel.**]

repute, *ri-pūt′*, *v.t.* to consider, believe (usu. in passive; e.g. *He is reputed to be wealthy*).—*n.* reputation.
reputable, *rep′ūt-à-bl*, *adj.* respectable, well thought of.
reputā′tion (*rep-*), *n.* opinion generally held of a person or thing: good opinion, respect: good name.
reputed, *ri-pūt′id*, *adj.* supposed (e.g. *the reputed author of the article*): believed (to be).
reput′edly, in common opinion.
of repute, reputation, well thought of by many people.
[L. *re-*, *putāre*, to think, consider.]

request, *ri-kwest′*, *n.* a favour asked for: the asking of a favour.—*v.t.* to ask, or ask for, politely or as a favour.

by, on, request, when asked (e.g. *Buses stop on request*).
in request, in demand, sought after.
[O.Fr. *requeste*—L. root as **require.**]

requiem, *rek'wi-ėm, n.* mass for the souls of the dead: music for this mass.
[L. *requiēs*, rest; first word of mass.]

require, *ri-kwīr', v.t.* to need: to demand.
require'ment, *n.* a need: something needed.
requisite, *rek'wi-zit, adj.* required: necessary.—*n.* something necessary (e.g. *toilet requisites*).
requisi'tion, *n.* a formal demand or request, e.g. for military or other supplies.—*v.t.* to demand or take in this way.
[L. *re-*, *quaerĕre*, *quaesītum*, to seek.]

requite, *ri-kwīt'*, to repay or avenge (one action) by another: to repay (a person).
requit'al, *n.*
[Pfx. **re-**, and **quit.**]

rescind, *ri-sind', v.t.* to annul, cancel (a decision, an order, a law).
[L. *re-*, back, *scindĕre*, to cut.]

rescue, *res'kū, v.t.* to free from danger, harm, or captivity.—*pr.p.* **res'cūing;** *pa.p.* **res'cued** (*-kūd*).—*n.* act of saving from danger, etc.
res'cuer, *n.* one who rescues.
[L. *re-*, away, *ex*, out, *quatĕre*, to shake.]

research, *ri-sėrch', n.* careful search or study to find out new facts (e.g. *cancer research*).—Also *v.i.*
research'er, *n.* one who does research.
[O.Fr. *recerche*—same root as **search.**]

resemble, *ri-zem'bl, v.t.* to be like.
resem'blance, *n.*
[Fr. *re-*, again, *sembler*, to seem.]

resent, *ri-zent', v.t.* to feel injured or insulted and annoyed by.
resent'ful, *adj.* **resent'fully,** *adv.*
resent'ment, *n.* state of feeling badly treated and annoyed.
[L. *re-*, in return, *sentīre*, feel.]

reserve, *ri-zėrv', v.t.* to keep back for later use, or for a special use: to book (e.g. *Have you reserved a seat?*).—*n.* something that is reserved: shyness, habit of not speaking thoughts freely: (esp. in *pl.*) extra troops kept until wanted, or other useful possessions kept back: a piece of public land kept e.g. for protection of wild animals (*game reserve*) or natural plant life.
reservā'tion (*rez-*), *n.* act of reserving: act of booking seats, rooms etc.: rooms, etc., so booked: an exception or condition made openly or mentally (*He agreed to the plan with one reservation*): a land reserve.
reserved', *adj.* not showing thoughts or feelings: booked in advance.
reserv'ist, *n.* a member of a reserve force, not in regular army, navy, or air force.
[L. *re-*, back, *servāre*, to save.]

reservoir, *rez'ėr-vwär, n.* a container: a store: a lake where water for drinking, etc., is stored. [Fr.]

reset, *rē'set', v.t.* to set again: (*printing*) to set up in type again:—*pr.p.* **re'sett'ing;** *pa.p.* **re'set'.** [Pfx. **re-.**]

reside, *ri-zīd', v.i.* to live (in, at, abroad): to be present in, be a part of (e.g. *Wisdom resides in his heart*): (of powers, rights; with *in*) to belong to.
residence, *rez'i-dens, n.* a grand house: act, or period, of dwelling in a place (e.g. *during his residence in Spain*).
res'ident, *n.* one who resides.—*adj.* dwelling (in a place): requiring one to live on the premises (e.g. *a resident post*).
residential, *rez-i-den'sh(ȧ)l, adj.* for (esp. good) houses: connected with residence.
in residence, staying in a place esp. to carry out duties there.
[L. *residēre*, remain behind—*sedēre*, sit.]

residue, *rez'i-dū, n.* what is left over: remainder.
[L. *residuum*—same root as **reside.**]

resign, *ri-zīn', v.t.* to give up (e.g. a position): to give (something) over (to someone): (with *oneself*) to submit quietly (e.g. *to resign oneself to one's fate*).—*v.i.* to give up office, etc.
resignation, *rez-ig-nā'sh(ȯ)n, n.* act of giving up: state of being resigned, quiet acceptance of the situation or events.
resigned, *ri-zīnd', adj.* not complaining.
[L. *resignāre*, *-ātum*, cancel, resign.]

resilient, *ri-zil'i-ėnt, adj.* springing back, elastic: coming back quickly from depression to good spirits, or illness to health.
resil'ience, resil'iency, *ns.*
[L. *re-*, back, *salīre*, to leap.]

resin, *rez'in, n.* a sticky substance that oozes out of certain trees and other plants.
res'inous, *adj.* like or containing resin.
[L. *rēsīna.*]

resist, *ri-zist', v.t.* to struggle against, esp. successfully: to refrain from (e.g. *I could not resist saying so*): to be little affected by (e.g. *a metal that resists rust*).
resis'tance, *n.* act or power of resisting: (in full, **resistance movement**) opposition in a country to forces of another country that has conquered and occupied it: the ability of a substance to oppose an electric current, turning its energy into heat.
resis'tant, *adj.* making resistance: (with *to*) not affected by.
resis'tible, *adj.* able to be resisted.
resis'tor, *n.* a piece of apparatus used to offer electrical resistance.
[L. *re-*, against, *sistĕre*, to make to stand.]

resolute, *rez'ȯl-ōōt, -ūt, adj.* firm, determined.
res'olutely, *adv.* **res'oluteness,** *n.*
resolution, *rez-ȯl-ōō'sh(ȯ)n, -ū', n.* resoluteness, firmness of mind or purpose: a proposal put before a public meeting:

a firm decision (e.g. *a New Year resolution*): solution (of a difficulty).

resolve, *ri-zolv′, v.t.* to decide: to pass as a resolution: to solve: to take away (doubt): to break up, or transform (into; e.g. *to resolve (something) into the parts of which it is made up*).—*n.* purpose, decision: firmness of purpose.

resolved′, *adj.* fixed in purpose, determined.

[L. *re-, solvĕre, solūtum,* to loose, free.]

resonance, *rez′ȯn-ȧns, n.* increase of intensity of sound, by echoing, etc.

res′onant, *adj.* echoing, resounding, ringing: (of a body) increasing the sound by vibrating.

res′onator, *n.* something that resonates.

[L. *re-,* back, *sonāre,* to sound.]

resort, *ri-zört′, v.i.* to go: to turn (to) in difficulty.—*n.* act of resorting, or something resorted to: popular place, e.g. for holidays.

in the last resort, when all else fails.

[O.Fr. *resortir—sortir,* to go out.]

resound, *ri-zownd′, v.i.* to sound loudly: to echo.—*v.t.* to utter loudly (the praises of someone).

resoun′ding, *adj.* loud, echoing: emphatic. [Pfx. **re-.**]

resource, *ri-sōrs′, -sörs′, n.* a source of help: (in *pl.*) money or other property, or means of raising money: (in *pl.*) means of helping or entertaining oneself.

resource′ful, *adj.* quick-witted, good at finding ways out of difficulties.

resource′fully, *adv.* **-fulness,** *n.*

[O.Fr. *ressource*—L. *resurgĕre,* rise again.]

respect, *ri-spekt′, v.t.* to show or feel esteem for, regard highly: to treat with care or consideration (e.g. *to respect other people's property*).—*n.* high opinion, esteem: (in *pl.*) a greeting: a detail, point (e.g. *in this respect*): reference (*with respect to*).

respec′table, *adj.* worthy of respect or notice: fairly good: fairly large: decent, proper.

respec′tably, *adv.*

respectabil′ity, respec′tableness, *ns.*

respect′ful, *adj.* showing or feeling respect.

respect′fully, *adv.* **respect′fulness,** *n.*

respec′ting, *prep.* concerning.

respec′tive, *adj.* belonging to each separately (e.g. *The boys went to their respective homes*).

respec′tively, *adv.* in the order given (e.g. *Give the large, medium, and small bed to the father, mother, and baby bear respectively*).

in respect of, as regards.

[L. *re-,* back, *specĕre, spectum,* to look.]

respire, *ri-spīr′, v.i.* to breathe.

respiration, *res-pir-ā′sh(ȯ)n, n.* breathing.

res′pirātor, *n.* a mask worn over mouth and nose to purify the air breathed in.

respiratory (*res′pir-,* or *ri-spīr′*), *adj.* connected with breathing.

artificial respiration, a method of forcing air into the lungs of an unconscious person.

[L. *re-,* again, *spīrāre,* to breathe.]

respite, *res′pīt, -pit, n.* a pause: a rest (from).—*v.t.* to grant a delay to.

[O.Fr. *respit*; same L. root as **respect.**]

resplendent, *ri-splen′dėnt, adj.* very splendid: brilliant.

resplen′dence, *n.* **-dently,** *adv.*

[L. *re-, splendēre,* to shine.]

respond, *ri-spond′, v.i.* to answer: to react (to something done; e.g. *The illness responded to treatment*).—*v.t.* to answer.

response′, *n.* an answer: the answer made by the people to the priest during a church service: action or feeling in reply to a request, speech, action, etc.

respon′sible, *adj.* trustworthy (e.g. *a responsible person*): involving care of people or affairs (e.g. *a responsible post*): obliged to give a satisfactory account of one's conduct, management, etc. (e.g. *I am responsible to my employer for the care of the petty cash*).

respon′sibleness, *n.*

responsibil′ity, *n.* responsibleness: something for which one is responsible: —*pl.* **responsibil′ities.**

respon′sibly, *adv.* in a trustworthy or serious way.

respon′sive, *adj.* quick to respond, e.g. by giving interest, sympathy: quick to react.

respon′sively, *adv.* **-siveness,** *n.*

[L. *re-, spondēre, sponsum,* to promise.]

rest[1], *rest, n.* state of being still, not working: peace: sleep: a support or prop (e.g. *a book rest*): (*music*) a pause, or the mark showing it.—*v.i.* to stop work: to be still, relax: to lean (on): to depend (on), be based (on; e.g. *The conclusion rests on good evidence*).—*v.t.* to give rest to (e.g. *Rest your back*): to place, lean (something; with *on, against*); to base (something; with *on*).

rest′ful, *adj.* **rest′fully,** *adv.*

rest′fulness, *n.*

rest′less, *adj.* unable to rest: uneasy, fidgeting.

rest′lessly, *adv.* **rest′lessness,** *n.*

rest cure, treatment by rest.

rest′ing-place, *n.* a place for rest, esp. the grave.

to rest with, to be the duty or right of (e.g. *The choice rests with you*; *it rests with you to decide*). [O.E.]

rest[2], *rest, n.* what is left, remainder: all the others.—*v.i.* to remain, be (e.g. *Rest assured that . . .,* you may be sure that . . .).

[Fr. *reste*—L. *re-,* back, *stāre,* stand.]

restaurant, *res′tė-ronᵍ, n.* a place where meals are served to customers.

restaurateur, *res-tȯr-ȧ-tėr′, n.* the keeper of a restaurant.

[Fr.—root as **restore.**]

restitution, *res-ti-tū'sh(ȯ)n, n.* act of giving back what was lost or taken away: compensation for harm done.
[L. *re-*, again, *statuĕre*, make to stand.]

restive, *res'tiv, adj.* impatient of delay, or control, etc.
[O.Fr. *restif*; same root as **rest** (2).]

restore, *ri-stōr', -stör', v.t.* to bring, put, or give back: to repair (e.g. a picture): to cure (a person).
restor'er, *n.*
restoration, *res-tō-rā'sh(ȯ)n, n.* act of restoring: repair: (with *cap.*) return of Charles II as King in 1660.
restorative, *ris-tōr'ȧ-tiv, -tör', adj.* restoring, able to restore.—*n.* a substance that restores.
[O.Fr. *restorer*—L. *restaurāre, -ātum.*]

restrain, *ri-strān', v.t.* to hold back (from): to check: to keep in prison, etc.
restrained', *adj.* kept under control: not showing excess (e.g. of emotion).
restraint', *n.* act of restraining: state of being restrained: want of liberty.
[O.Fr. *restraindre*—L. *re-*, back, *stringĕre, strictum*, to draw tightly.]

restrict, *ri-strikt', v.t.* to limit, keep within bounds of e.g. space, time, quantity.
restric'ted, *adj.*
restric'tive, *adj.* limiting.
restric'tion, *n.* act of restricting: something (e.g. a rule) which limits freedom.
restrictive practice, a practice in trade or industry that keeps up prices or limits output and so is against the good of the public.
[L. root as **restrain.**]

result, *ri-zult', v.i.* to end (in): to follow as a consequence.—*n.* outcome, effect, consequence: the number, etc. obtained by working out a sum, etc.
resul'tant, *adj.* resulting.
[L. *re-*, back, *saltāre*, to leap.]

resume, *ri-zūm', -zōōm', v.t.* to take up, begin, again (e.g. *to resume work*): to take again: to take back.—*v.i.* to begin again (e.g. *After tea the meeting resumed*).
resumption, *ri-zump'sh(ȯ)n, -zum', n.*
[L. *re-*, back, *sūmĕre, sūmptum*, to take.]

résumé, *rā-zü-mā, n.* a summary. [Fr.]

resurgent, *ri-sûr'jėnt, adj.* rising again.
resur'gence, *n.*
[Same root as **resurrect.**]

resurrect, *rez-ůr-ekt', v.t.* to restore to life: to bring back into use.
resurrec'tion, *n.* act of resurrecting: rising from the dead, esp. (*cap.*) of Christ.
[L. *re-*, *surgĕre, surrectum*, to rise.]

resuscitate, *ri-sus'i-tāt, v.t.* to revive, e.g. from unconsciousness.
resuscitā'tion, *n.*
[L. *re-*, *sub-*, *citāre*, put in motion.]

ret, *ret, v.t.* and *v.i.* to soften, rot (flax) by soaking:—*pr.p.* **rett'ing**; **rett'ed.**
[Conn. with **rot.**]

retail, *rē'tāl, n.* sale of goods to consumer, or in small quantities.—*adj.* concerned, connected, with such sale.—*v.t.* to sell in this way: to repeat in detail (e.g. a story).
retail'er, *n.* a shopkeeper.
[O.Fr. *retail*, piece cut off—*tailler*, cut.]

retain, *ri-tān', v.t.* to keep in one's possession: to continue to have: to hold back or in place: to reserve the services of (someone) by paying a fee.
retain'ing, reten'tion, *ns.*
retain'er, *n.* a person owing service to a family: a fee paid (e.g. to a lawyer) to retain his services.
reten'tive, *adj.* having the power of retaining, keeping (e.g. *a soil retentive of moisture*: *a retentive memory*).
retaining wall, a wall to prevent a ridge of earth from slipping down.
[L. *re-*, back, *tenēre, tentum*, to hold.]

retake, *rē'tāk', v.t.* to take again: to recapture: to film again:—*pa.t.* **re'took'**; *pa.p.* **re'tak'en.**—*n.* part of a motion picture filmed again. [Pfx. **re-.**]

retaliate, *ri-tal'i-āt, v.i.* to strike back when struck, to return like for like (esp. evil).
retaliā'tion *n.*
[L. *retāliāre, -ātum*—*tālis*, such.]

retard, *ri-tärd', v.t.* to hinder, delay.
retardā'tion, *n.*
retard'ed, *adj.* slow in development, mental or physical.
[L. *re-*, *tardāre, -ātum*—*tardus*, slow.]

retch, *rech, v.i.* to try to vomit.
[O.E. *hrǣcan.*]

retention, retentive. See **retain.**

reticent, *ret'i-sėnt, adj.* reserved, not saying much.
ret'icence, *n.*
[L. *re-*, *tacēre*, be silent.]

retina, *ret'i-nȧ, n.* the layer at the back of the eye that receives the picture of anything seen.
[Late L. *rētina*, perh.—L. *rēte*, net.]

retinue, *ret'i-nū, n.* those who attend on a person of high rank or importance.
[Fr. *retenue*; same root as **retain.**]

retire, *ri-tīr', v.i.* to withdraw (from): to go back: to go to bed: to give up work.
reti'ral, retire'ment, *ns.*
retired', *adj.* having given up work: (of a place) quiet, secluded.
reti'ring, *adj.* going back, withdrawing: giving up work: avoiding notice, shy.
[Fr. *re-*, back, *tirer*, to draw.]

retort[1], *ri-tört', v.i.* to make a quick, and sharp or witty, reply.—Also *v.t.*—Also *n.*
[L. *re-*, back, *torquēre, tortum*, to twist.]

retort[2], *ri-tört', n.* a glass flask, esp. one with its neck bent down, for distilling liquids: (*industrial use*) a closed oven, e.g. for heating coke.
[Same root as **retort** (1).]

retouch, *rē'tuch', v.t.* to touch up in order to improve. [Pfx. **re-.**]

retrace, *rē-trās', rē', v.t.* to trace, go over, again. [Pfx. **re-.**]

retract, *ri-trakt', v.t.* to take back (something said or given): to draw back (e.g. *A cat retracts its claws*).—Also *v.i.*

retrac'tion, *n.*

retract'able, *adj.* able to be drawn back or up.

[L. *re-*, back, *trahĕre*, *tractum*, to draw.]

retread[1], *rē'tred'*, *v.t.* to tread again:—*pa.t.* **re'trod'**; *pa.p.* **re'trodd'en.**

[Pfx. **re-.**]

retread[2], *rē'tred'*, *v.t.* to make a new tread on (worn tyre):—*pa.t. pa.p.* **re'tread'ed.** —*n.* new tread: retreaded tyre. [**re-.**]

retreat, *ri-trēt'*, *n.* a movement backward, e.g. from danger: a withdrawal: a quiet place: a refuge.—*v.i.* to draw back, retire: to go away.

[Through O.Fr.—L. root as **retract.**]

retrench, *rē-trench'*, *-sh*, *v.i.* and *v.t.* to cut down (expenses).

retrench'ment, *n.*

[O.Fr. *retrencher*—same root as **trench.**]

retribution, *ret-ri-bū'sh(ȯ)n*, *n.* deserved punishment.

[L. *retribuĕre*, *retribūtum*, give back.]

retrieve, *ri-trēv'*, *v.t.* to search for and fetch, as a dog does: to recover or rescue: to restore: to make amends for (e.g. *He retrieved his mistake*).

retriev'er, *n.* a dog trained to find and fetch game that has been shot.

[Fr. *re-*, again, *trouver*, to find.]

retro-, *ret-rō*, (as part of word) backwards.

retrograde, *ret'rō-grād*, *adj.* going backward: falling from better to worse.

retrogression, *ret-rō-gresh'(ȯ)n*, *n.*

retrospect, *ret'rō-spekt*, *rē'trō-*, *n.* a view of, or thought about, the past.

retrospec'tion, *n.* looking back on things past.

retrospec'tive, *adj.* looking back: going back to a date in the past: (of e.g. a law) applying to past as well as present and future.

[L. *retrō*, back (*gradī*, *gressus*, to go: *specĕre*, *spectum*, to look).]

retry, *rē'trī'*, *v.t.* to try again (in a court of justice):—*pr.p.* **re'try'ing**: *pa.p.* **re'tried'.**

rē'trī'al, *n.* a second trial. [Pfx. **re-.**]

return, *ri-tûrn'*, *v.i.* to come or go back.—*v.t.* to give, throw, send, pay, back: to retort, reply: to elect (to parliament).—*n.* act of returning: a repetition: something returned (often in *pl.*): proceeds, profit.

return'able, *adj.* that may be, or must be, returned.

returning officer, officer in charge at an election.

return match, a second match played by the same set of players.

return ticket, a ticket entitling a passenger to travel to a place and back again to the starting-point.

by return, by the next post back.

[Fr. *re-*, back, *tourner*, to turn.]

reunion, *rē-ūn'yȯn*, *n.* a meeting of people who have not met for some time.

reunite, *rē'ū-nīt'*, *v.t.*, *v.i.* to join after separation. [Pfx. **re-.**]

rev, *rev*, *v.t.* to increase the speed of revolution in (an engine; often with *up*). —Also *v.i.*:—*pr.p.* **revv'ing**; *pa.p.* **revved.**

revs, *n.pl.* revolutions.

[From **revolution.**]

reveal, *ri-vēl'*, *v.t.* to make known: to show.

revelation, *rev-ė-lā'sh(ȯ)n*, *n.* act of revealing: something, esp. unsuspected, that is made known or shown: (*cap.*) the last book of the New Testament.

[L. *re-*, reverse of, *velāre*, to veil.]

reveille, *ri-val'i*, *ri-vel'i*, *n.* a bugle call at daybreak to awaken soldiers.

[Fr. *réveillez*, awake—L. root as **vigil.**]

revel, *rev'l*, *v.i.* to make merry: to find great enjoyment (in):—*pr.p.* **rev'elling**; *pa.p.* **rev'elled.**—*n.* (usu. in *pl.*) merrymaking.

rev'eller, *n.* **rev'elry,** *n.* revelling.

[O.Fr. *reveler*—L. *rebellāre*, to rebel.]

revelation. See **reveal.**

revenge, *ri-venj'*, *v.t.* to seek satisfaction for (an injury done) by injuring in return (e.g. *to revenge his father's death by killing the assassin*): to avenge (oneself, e.g. on one's enemies).—*n.* an injury in return for an injury: desire for this.

revenge'ful, *adj.* anxious for revenge.

revenge'fully, *adv.* **reveng'er,** *n.*

[Fr. *re-*; root as **avenge, vengeance.**]

revenue, *rev'ėn-ū*, *n.* income, esp. income of a country from all sources: department of civil service dealing with this.

inland revenue, income from taxes and duties within the country: department dealing with this.

revenue officer, one whose duty is to check smuggling.

[L. *re-*, back, *venīre*, to come.]

reverberate, *ri-vėr'bėr-āt*, *v.i.* to echo and re-echo, resound.

reverberā'tion, *n.*

[L. *re-*, back, *verberāre*, to beat.]

revere, *ri-vēr'*, *v.t.* to respect greatly.

reverence, *rev'ėr-ėns*, *n.* deep respect: outward expression of this: a bow.

rev'erent, *adj.* **rev'erently,** *adv.*

rev'erend, *adj.* worthy of respect: (with *cap.*; usu. written **Rev.**) a title put before the names of a clergyman (e.g. *The Rev. John Brown*).

reverential, *rev-ėr-en'sh(á)l*, *adj.* showing great respect.

[O.Fr. *reverer*—L. *verērī*, to feel awe.]

reverie, *rev'ė-ri*, *n.* a state of dreamy thought: a day-dream.

[Fr. *reverie*—*rever*, to dream.]

reverse, *ri-vėrs'*, *v.t.* to turn the other way, e.g. upside down: to set moving backwards: to undo (e.g. *to reverse a decision*). *v.i.* to move backwards.—*n.* the opposite

(of): the back (of e.g. a coin): a defeat: in motor car, reversing gear.
rever'sal, *n.* act of reversing or being reversed.
rever'sible, *adj.* able to be reversed: (of clothes) able to be worn with either side out.
reversion, *ri-vėr'sh(ȯ)n, n.* (the right to) the future possession (of something in the hands of another).
revert, *ri-vėrt', v.i.* to return to a former state, subject, or owner.
[L. *re-*, back, *vertĕre, versum,* to turn.]

review, *ri-vū', n.* a second look at, or consideration of (e.g. *a review of the subject of parking in cities*): an inspection (of troops): a critical essay on a book, play, etc., or a magazine devoted to such essays.—*v.t.* to examine again: to go over the whole of (e.g. *to review the facts, the situation*): to write a review of: to inspect (usu. troops).
review'er, *n.* [Pfx. **re-**.]

revile, *ri-vīl', v.t.* to say harsh things about.
[O.Fr. *reviler*—L. *re-*, *vīlis*, worthless.]

revise, *ri-vīz', v.t.* to examine and correct: to change (e.g. *to revise one's opinion*).
revis'al, revision, *ri-vizh'(ȯ)n, ns.*
revis'er, *n.* **revis'ory,** *adj.*
[L. *re-*, *vidēre, vīsum,* to see.]

revive, *ri-vīv', v.t.* and *v.i.* to bring, or come, back to life, strength, active state, use, etc.
revīv'er, *n.*
revīv'al *n.* return to life or strength: bringing back to use, or (of a play) to the stage: (time of) new interest, in e.g. religion, learning.
revīv'alist, *n.* one who helps to produce a religious revival.
revivify, *rē-viv'i-fī, v.t.* give new life to.
[L. *revivĕre,* to live again.]

revoke, *ri-vōk', v.t.* to cancel (e.g. a decision).—*v.i.* (*at cards*) to fail to follow suit when one can do so.
rev'ocable, *adj.* **revocā'tion,** *n.*
[L. *re-*, back, *vocāre,* to call.]

revolt, *ri-vōlt', v.i.* to rebel: to rise up (against): to feel disgust (at).—*v.t.* to disgust.—*n.* rebellion.
revol'ting, *adj.* disgusting.
revol'tingly, *adv.* **revol'tingness,** *n.*
[Fr. *revolter*—L. root as **revolution.**]

revolution, *rev-ȯl-ōō'sh(ȯ)n,* or *-ū', n.* turning round a centre: a complete turn: a great change: the complete overthrowing of a government.
revolu'tionary, *adj.* (aimed at) bringing about great changes (or tending to do so): turning.—*n.* a revolutionist:—*pl.* **-ies.**
revolu'tionise, *v.t.* to cause great changes in.
revolu'tionist, *n.* one who approves of revolution.
revolve, *ri-volv', v.t.* and *v.i.* to roll or turn round: to turn over (in the mind).
revol'ver, *n.* a pistol with a revolving magazine.
[L. *re-*, *volvĕre, volūtum,* to turn.]

revue, *ri-vū', n.* a light theatre show, consisting usu. of sketches satirising recent events. [Fr.]

revulsion, *ri-vul'sh(ȯ)n, n.* disgust: a recoil (from): a sudden change (of feeling; e.g. from love to hate).
[L. *revellĕre, revulsum,* to pluck back.]

reward, *ri-wörd', n.* something given in return for good (or sometimes evil) behaviour or work or service.—*v.t.* to give a reward to: to repay (e.g. a service).
reward'ing, *adj.* giving pleasure or profit.
[O.Fr. *rewarder, -garder*; root as **regard.**]

reword, *rē'wûrd', v.t.* to put into different words. [Pfx. **re-**.]

rhapsody, *rap'sȯ-di, n.* emotional, excited music, poetry or speech.
rhap'sodise, *v.i.* to write or talk with great enthusiasm.
[Gk. *rhapsōidiā,* a long poem.]

rhea, *rē'ȧ, n.* a South American ostrich.
[Gk. *Rhĕā,* Mother of the gods.]

rhetoric, *ret'ȯr-ik, n.* the art of good speaking or writing: showy, insincere expressions.
rhetor'ical, *adj.* showy in style.
rhetorical question, one which the speaker answers himself, or which does not need an answer.
[Gk. *rhētōr,* a public speaker.]

rheumatism, *rōō'mȧ-tizm, n.* a disease causing pain and stiffness in the joints.
rheumat'ic, *adj.* caused by, connected with, having, rheumatism.—*n.* one who suffers from rheumatism: (in *pl.*) rheumatic pains.
rheu'matoid, *adj.* resembling rheumatism.
[Gk. *rheuma, -atos,* mucus—*rheein,* flow.]

rhinoceros, *rī-nos'ėr-ȯs, n.* a large thick-skinned animal with one, or two, horns on its nose:—*pl.* **rhinoc'eros(es).**
[Gk. *rhīs, rhīnos,* nose, *keras,* horn.]

rhododendron, *rō-dō-den'drȯn, rod-ō-, n.* a shrub with large showy flowers.
[Gk. *rhodon,* rose, *dendron,* tree.]

rhubarb, *rōō'bärb, n.* a plant whose stalks are used in cooking and roots in medicine.
[Gk. *rhā,* rhubarb, *barbaron,* foreign.]

rhyme, *rīm, n.* a word like another in its final sound or sounds (e.g. *beef* is a rhyme to *leaf* and *belief*; *sensible* and *reprehensible* are rhymes): likeness of this kind in sound of words: poetry: a short poem.—*v.i.* (of words) to be rhymes: to write verses.—Also **rime.**
rhy'mer, *n.* one who writes verses.
[Confusion of O.E. *rīm,* number, and **rhythm.**]

rhythm, *riTHm,* or *th, n.* a regular repeated pattern of stresses or long and short sounds in music or verse: a regularly repeated pattern of movements.

rhyth′mic(al), *adjs.* **-mically,** *adv.*
[Gk. *rhythmos—rheein*, to flow.]

rib, *rib, n.* one of the bones that curve round and forward from the backbone: one of the members of the frame of a ship, curving upwards from the keel: a support for the fabric of an aeroplane wing or an umbrella: a ridge.—*v.t.* to form ribs in, or provide with ribs:—*pr.p.* **ribb′ing**; *pa.p.* **ribbed.**
ribb′ing, *n.* an arrangement of ribs.
[O.E. *ribb.*]

ribbon, *rib′on, n.* a long narrow strip of material.—Also (in some cases) **rib′and.**
ribb′on-build′ing, *n.* growth of towns in long strips along the main roads.
[O.Fr. *riban.*]

rice, *rīs, n.* a grass grown in tropical countries, the seed of which is used for food.
rice paper, paper made from straw of rice, or from the pith of a tree.
[O.Fr. *ris*—Gk. *oryza*—an Eastern word.]

rich, *rich, adj.* wealthy: costly, valuable (e.g. *rich materials*; *a rich reward*): having plenty of (with *in*; e.g. *a district rich in coal*): deep in colour: (of food) containing much fat, egg, sugar, etc.
rich′ly, *adv.* **rich′ness,** *n.*
riches, *rich′iz, n.pl.* wealth.
[O.E. *rīce*, mighty; *riches* is from Fr. *richesse*—same Germanic root as *rich.*]

rick, *rik, n.* a stack (of hay, etc.).
[O.E. *hrēac*—Old Norse *hraukr.*]

rickets, *rik′its, n.sing.* a disease of children, causing softening and bending of the bones.
rick′ety, *adj.* affected by rickets: unsteady (e.g. *a rickety table*).
[Origin uncertain.]

rickshaw, ricksha, *rik′shaw, n.* abbrev. of **jinrick′sha(w),** a small two-wheeled carriage drawn by a man.
[Jap. (*jin*, man), *riki*, power, *sha*, carriage.]

ricochet, *rik′ō-shā*, or *-shet, n.* a glancing, rebound, e.g. of a bullet.—*v.i.* to glance (off):—*pr.p.* **ric′ochet(t)ing** (*-shā-ing, -shet-ing*); *pa.p.* **ric′ochet(t)ed** (*-shād, -shet-id*). [Fr.]

rid, *rid, v.t.* to free from, to clear (of):—*pr.p.* **ridd′ing**; *pa.t.* **rid** or **ridd′ed**; *pa.p.* **rid.**
ridd′ance, *n.* clearance: deliverance.
a good riddance, a welcome relief from something.
to get rid of, to free oneself from.
[Old Norse, *rythja*, to clear.]

ridden. See **ride.**

riddle[1], *rid′l, n.* a question intended to puzzle, conundrum: a person, happening, etc. difficult to understand.
[O.E. *rǣdelse—rǣdan*, to guess, read.]

riddle[2], *rid′l, n.* a large coarse sieve.—*v.t.* to sift with a riddle: to make full of holes (e.g. *to riddle with bullets*).
[O.E. *hriddel.*]

ride, *rīd, v.i.* to travel, be carried, on a horse, bicycle, etc. or in a car, etc.: to lie at anchor: (with *up*) to work up out of position.—*v.t.* to travel on (a horse, etc.): to take part in (a horse race): to control (a person) in a tyrannical way:—*pr.p.* **rid′ing**; *pa.t.* **rode** (*rōd*); *pa.p.* **ridd′en.**—*n.* a journey on horseback, in a vehicle, etc.: a road for riding on on horseback.
rid′er, *n.* one who rides: something, e.g. an extra clause, added to a document.
riding school, a place where one is taught to ride a horse.
to ride for a fall, to take too great risks.
to ride out a storm, to keep afloat in it.
to ride to hounds, to take part in fox hunting.
[O.E. *rīdan.*]

ridge, *rij, n.* a raised part between furrows: a long narrow top or crest, e.g. of hills.—*v.t.* and *v.i.* to form into ridges: to wrinkle.
ridg′y, *adj.* **ridg′iness,** *n.*
ridge of high pressure, a long narrow area of high pressure as shown on a weather map.
[O.E. *hrycg*, an animal's back.]

ridicule, *rid′i-kūl, n.* mockery.—*v.t.* to laugh at, to mock.
ridic′ūlous, *adj.* absurd, deserving to be laughed at.
ridic′ulously, *adv.* **ridic′ūlousness,** *n.*
[L. *rīdiculus—rīdēre*, to laugh].

riding. See **ride.**

rife, *rīf, adj.* very common (e.g. *Disease and hunger were rife in that country*).
rife with, very full of.
[O.E. *rȳfe.*]

riff-raff, *rif′-raf, n.* worthless things or people.
[M.E. *rif and raf*—O.Fr. *rif et raf.*]

rifle[1], *rī′fl, v.t.* to search thoroughly and rob (place, person): to steal.
[O.Fr. *rifler*, scrape, scratch, plunder.]

rifle[2], *rī′fl, n.* a gun fired from the shoulder with spiral grooves in its barrel.—*v.t.* to cut spiral grooves inside a gun barrel.
rī′fling, *n.* the spiral grooves in a gun barrel.
rifle range, a place for rifle practice.
[Conn. with **rifle** (1).]

rift, *rift, n.* a split or crack: a disagreement between friends.
rift valley, valley formed by the fall of part of the earth's crust between faults in the rock.
[Conn. with Dan., Norw. *rift*, a cleft.]

rig, *rig, v.t.* to fit (up; e.g. *to rig up a rough shelter*): to fit (out, e.g. with clothes):—*pr.p.* **rigg′ing**; *pa.p.* **rigged.**—*n.* the arrangement of sails etc. of a sailing ship: equipment e.g. for drilling an oil well: (*slang*) clothing.
rigg′ing, *n.* system of ropes, etc. which works a ship's masts and sails.

rig′-out, *n.* (*slang*) an outfit.
[Prob. from Scand.]

right, *rīt, adj.* opp. to *left*: correct: true: straight: just, good, proper.—*adv.* to or on the right side: correctly: straight.—*n.* the right side: truth: justice: the thing(s) one ought to do: legal or just claim (e.g. *to have a right to something*): (*cap.*) a party with conservative views.—*v.t.* to set right: (with *oneself, itself*) to recover upright position.
right′ful, *adj.* by right (e.g. *one's rightful king*).
right′fully, *adv.* according to right (e.g. *It rightfully belongs to me*).
right′ly, *adv.* correctly.
right′ness, *n.* correctness: justice.
right angle, an angle of 90 degrees, one quarter of a complete revolution.
right′-han′ded, *adj.* having the right hand more skilful than the left.
right-hand side, the right side.
Right Honourable, a courtesy title, given e.g. to Cabinet ministers.
right of entry, legal right to enter.
right off, at once.
right of way, the public right to use a path over private ground: a path to which this right applies: right to move first in traffic, e.g. at a crossroads.
right′-wing′, *adj.* of the more conservative section of a political party.
by rights, rightfully.
in one's own right, not through someone else (e.g. a *peeress in her own right*, i.e. not because wife of a peer).
one's right-hand man, one's most useful helper.
to put to rights, to put in good order, or satisfactory state.
See also **righteous.**
[O.E. *riht.*]

righteous, *rī′chŭs, adj.* living a good life: just: morally right.
right′eously, *adv.* **right′eousness,** *n.*
[O.E. *riht*, right, *wīs*, wise, or *wīse*, way.]

rigid, *rij′id, adj.* completely stiff: not bending: very strict.
rig′idly, *adv.* **rig′idness, rigid′ity,** *ns.*
[L. *rigidus*—*rigēre*, to be stiff.]

rigmarole, *rig′mă-rōl, n.* a long rambling speech.
[*ragman-roll*, a long list of names.]

rigour, *rig′ŏr, n.* strictness: harshness: (of weather, etc.) severity.
rig′orous, *adj.* very strict.
rig′orously, *adv.* **rig′orousness,** *n.*
[L. *rigor*, stiffness—root as **rigid.**]

rill, *ril, n.* a very small brook.
[Conn. Du. *ril*, Ger. *rille*, a channel.]

rim, *rim, n.* an edge, border, brim:—*v.t.* to form a rim to:—*pr.p.* **rimm′ing**: *pa.p.* **rimmed.**
rim′less, without rim or border.
[O.E. *rima* (found only in compounds).]

rime[1], *rīm, n.* ice formed from frozen fog.
rī′my, *adj.* covered with rime:—*comp.* **ri′mier**; *superl.* **ri′miest.**
[O.E. *hrīm.*]

rime[2]. Same as **rhyme.**

rind, *rīnd, n.* peel, skin, firm covering.
[O.E. *rinde.*]

ring[1], *ring, n.* a small hoop, esp. of metal, worn on the finger, in the ear, etc.: a hollow circle: anything resembling a circle (e.g. *the circus ring*): a group of people in control of a business or industry.—*v.t.* to encircle, go round: to mark by putting a ring on (e.g. a bird).
ringed, *adj.* marked with ring(s).
ring′let, *n.* a long curl of hair.
ring finger, the finger on which the wedding ring is worn (usu. third on left hand).
ring′leader, *n.* one who takes the lead in mischief, etc.
ring′master, *n.* one who is in charge of performances in a circus ring.
ring road, route, a road that circles a town or a town centre.
ring′side, *adj.* (of a view) very clear, as from the front row of seats at a boxing match.
ring′worm, *n.* a skin disease causing ring-shaped patches.
the ring, prize fighting, or the enclosed space for it.
[O.E. *hring.*]

ring[2], *ring, v.i.* to give a clear bell-like sound: to be filled (e.g. with sound): to sound, seem to be (e.g. *His words ring true*): to call (for) by means of a bell.—*v.t.* to cause (bell, etc.) to sound: to telephone (often with *up*):—*pa.t.* **rang**; *pa.p.* **rung.**—*n.* the sound of a bell: a clear sound.
ring′ing, *n.* and *adj.*
to ring down, or **up, the curtain,** to give the signal for lowering or raising the curtain in a theatre.
to ring off, to end a telephone conversation and connexion.
to ring the bell, to achieve something.
to ring the changes, go through all possible arrangements with a chime of bells: to use a small number of things in a variety of ways.
[O.E. *hringan.*]

rink, *ringk, n.* a sheet of ice, often artificial, for skating: an area of ice for curling: part of a bowling green used by one set of players: a team of bowlers.
[Orig. Scots; origin uncertain.]

rinse, *rins, v.t.* to wash lightly to remove soap, etc.: to pour, or take, liquid into and let it out of (e.g. *Rinse your cup, your mouth*).—*n.* act of, or liquid for, rinsing.
[Fr. *rincer.*]

riot, *rī′ŏt, n.* a noisy disturbance by a crowd: wild disorder: brilliance (of colour).—*v.i.* to take part in a riot: to grow, or to behave, in an uncontrolled way.
rī′oter, *n.* **rī′oting,** *n.* and *adj.*

rī′otous, *adj.* uncontrolled.
rī′otously, *adv.*
to run riot, to act, or (of plants) grow, without control.
[O.Fr. *riot, riotte.*]

rip, *rip, v.t.* to tear apart or off.—*v.i.* to come apart: (*coll.*) to move very fast:—*pr.p.* **ripp′ing;** *pa.p.* **ripped.**—*n.* a tear, rent.
rip′-cord, *n.* a cord for opening a parachute.
rip′saw, *n.* a saw for cutting along the grain of wood.
[Origin uncertain.]

ripe, *rīp, adj.* ready for harvest: fully developed: ready (for; e.g. *ripe for mischief*).
ripe′ness, *n.*
rī′pen, *v.t., v.i.* to make, grow, ripe or riper.
[O.E. *rīpe*, ripe, *rīpian*, to ripen.]

ripple, *rip′l, n.* a little wave or movement on water: a sound like rippling water.—Also *v.t.* and *v.i.* [Origin uncertain.]

rise, *rīz, v.i.* to get up from bed: to stand up: to go up higher (e.g. *The smoke is rising*): to swell: to become higher: to come into being in, come from (e.g. *The river rises in the hills*): to be promoted: to come (into view or notice): to respond to: to rebel:—*pa.t.* **rose** (*rōz*); *pa.p.* **risen** (*riz′n*).—*n.* progress upwards: a slope upwards: increase: beginning.
ris′er, *n.* one who rises, esp. from bed: front upright part of a step.
ris′ing, *n.* act of rising: a revolt.—*adj.* coming up: increasing.
[O.E. *rīsan.*]

risk, *risk, n.* chance of loss or injury.—*v.t.* to take a chance of losing, damaging, etc. (e.g. one's life, something breakable): to take a chance of experiencing (e.g. *to risk disaster*).
ris′ky, *adj.* that may result in loss or injury:—*comp.* **ris′kier;** *superl.* **ris′kiest.**
ris′kiness, *n.*
[Fr. *risque*—It. *risco.*]

risotto, *rē-sot′to, n.* a savoury rice dish. [It.]

rissole, *ris′ōl, n.* a fried cake or ball of minced food. [Fr.]

rite, *rīt, n.* a ceremony, esp. religious.
ritual, *rit′ū-àl, n.* a set way of carrying out religious worship, etc.—*adj.* concerned with rites (e.g. *ritual laws*): forming a rite or ceremony (e.g. *a ritual dance*).
[L. *rītus*; adj. *rītuālis.*]

rival, *rī′vàl, n.* one who tries to equal or beat another.—*v.t.* to equal (someone or something in a quality; e.g. *He rivals his brother in skill*):—*pr.p.* **rī′valling;** *pa.p.* **rī′valled.**
rī′valry, *n.*:—*pl.* **-ries.**
[L. *rivālis*, orig. one who draws water from the same river—*rivus*, river.]

rive, *rīv, v.t.* and *v.i.* to tear apart: to split.—*pa.t.* **rīved;** *pa.p.* **riven** (*riv′n*). [Old Norse *rīfa.*]

river, *riv′ėr, n.* a large stream of water flowing across country.
river horse, a hippopotamus.
[O.Fr. *rivere*—L. *rīpa*, bank.]

rivet, *riv′it, n.* a bolt for fastening plates of metal together.—*v.t.* to fasten with rivets: to fix firmly (e.g. *The sight rivets him to the spot*):—*pr.p.* **riv′eting;** *pa.p.* **riv′eted.**
riv′eter, *n.* one whose work is riveting.
[O.Fr.—*river*, to clinch.]

rivulet, *riv′ū-let, n.* a small stream.
[It. *rivoletto*—L. *rivus*, a stream.]

road, *rōd, n.* a way for vehicles and people: a highway: a path, course (e.g. *the road to ruin*): (in *pl.*) roadstead.
road hog, See **hog.**
road′house, *n.* an inn beside a main road offering refreshments, entertainment, and often lodging, to road users.
road′man, *n.* one who keeps roads in repair.
road metal, broken stones used for roads.
road sense, skill in knowing how to drive etc. on roads.
road′stead, *n.* a place near shore where ships may lie at anchor.
road′ster, *n.* something (e.g. car) suitable for use on roads: someone who travels by road.
road surveyor, one who takes charge of making and repairing roads.
road′way, *n.* the part of a road used by cars, etc.
road′worthy, *adj.* fit to be used on the road.
road′worthiness, *n.*
[O.E. *rād*, a riding, raid.]

roam, *rōm, v.i.* to walk without fixed purpose, wander about.—*v.t.* to wander over.
roam′er, *n.*
[M.E. *romen*; origin uncertain.]

roan, *rōn, adj.* and *n.* (a horse, etc.) with spots of grey or white on darker, esp. red-brown, background. [O.Fr.]

roar, *rōr, rör, v.i.* give a loud, deep sound: to laugh loudly: (of a horse) to breathe noisily.—*v.t.* to say very loudly.—Also *n.*
roar′ing, *n.* and *adj.* **roar′er,** *n.*
[O.E. *rārian.*]

roast, *rōst, v.t.* to cook before a fire, or (uncovered) in an oven: to heat strongly.—Also *v.i.*—*adj.* roasted (e.g. *roast beef*).—*n.* a joint for roasting.
[O.Fr. *rostir* (Fr. *rôtir*).]

rob, *rob, v.t.* to steal from (a person, place): to cheat, deprive (of):—*pr.p.* **robb′ing:** *pa.p.* **robbed.**
robb′er, *n.*
robb′ery, *n.* act of stealing:—*pl.* **-ies.**
[O.Fr. *rober*; of Germanic origin.]

robe, *rōb, n.* a long loose garment: (in *pl.*)

dress showing certain ranks or positions. —*v.t.*, *v.i.* to dress, esp. in official dress.
[Fr. *robe*, orig. booty; conn. with **rob.**]

robin, *rob'in, n.* the **robin redbreast,** a small bird known by its red breast.
[A form of *Robert.*]

robot, *rō'bôt, n.* a mechanical man: a person who behaves like a machine: an automatic traffic signal.
[Czech *robota* (from play by a Czech).]

robust, *rō-bust', rō', adj.* strong, healthy: rough, vigorous (e.g. *a robust style*).
robustly, *adv.* **robustness,** *n.*
[L. *rōbustus—rōbur*, strength, oak.]

rock[1], *rok, n.* a large lump or mass of stone: a hard sweetmeat made in sticks.
rock'y, *adj.* full of rocks: like rock:—*comp.* **rock'ier;** *superl.* **rock'iest.**
rock'iness, *n.*
rock bottom, lowest depths, esp. of poverty.
rock crystal, colourless quartz.
rockery, rock garden, *n.* collection of stones among which grow **rock plants** (plants naturally fitted to do so).
rock salt, salt as a mineral.
on the rocks, penniless: (of a drink) on ice.
[O.Fr. *roke*—Late L. *rocca.*]

rock[2], *rok, v.t.* and *v.i.* to sway backwards and forwards, or from side to side.
rock'er, *n.* one who rocks: curved support on which anything rocks.
rock'ing, *n.* and *adj.*
rock'y, *adj.* inclined to rock: shaky:—*comp.* **rock'ier;** *superl.* **rock'iest.**
rock'iness, *n.*
rock'ing-chair, *n.* a chair on rockers.
rock'ing-horse, *n.* a toy horse on rockers.
[O.E. *roccian.*]

rocket, *rok'it, n.* a metal cylinder shot through the air by means of an exhaust of hot gas (a rocket carries its own oxygen and does not suck in air as a jet plane does): a firework, signal light, etc., moved in a similar way: a **rocket engine** used to drive a missile or vehicle.—*v.i.* and *v.t.* to fly, or make fly, like a rocket.
rock'etry, *n.* skill in making and using rockets.
rocket propulsion, driving by means of a rocket engine.
[It. *rocchetta*; of Germanic origin.]

rockier, etc., **rocky.** See **rock** (1) and (2).

rod, *rod, n.* a long thin stick or bar: a fishing-rod: a measure of length (5½ yards): (U.S.) a gun.
[O.E. *rodd.*]

rode. See **ride.**

rodent, *rō'dėnt, n.* a gnawing animal, e.g. rabbit, mouse, squirrel.
[L. *rōdens*, gnawing—*rōdĕre*, to gnaw.]

rodeo, *rō-dā'ō, n.* a round-up of cattle: a show of skill in riding, etc. by cowboys.
[Sp. *rodear*, surround—L. *rota*, a wheel.]

roe[1], *rō, n.* the eggs or spawn of fishes.
[M.E. *rowe*; from Scand.]

roe[2], *rō, n.* (also **roe deer**) a small deer found in Europe and Asia: a female red deer.
roe'buck, *n.* the male roe deer.
[O.E. *rā, rāha*; a Germanic word.]

rogue, *rōg, n.* a rascal, dishonest person: one who is playfully mischievous: a plant, etc. different from the normal.
roguery, *rō'gėr-i, n.* dishonesty: innocent mischief: dishonest action (*pl.* **-ies**).
roguish, *rō'gish, adj.* **rō'guishly,** *adv.*
rogue elephant, a savage elephant cast out of the herd.
rogues' gallery, a police collection of photographs of criminals.
[Origin uncertain.]

rôle, role, *rōl, n.* a part played, esp. by an actor or actress. [Fr.]

roll, *rōl, n.* a sheet of paper or material wound round into tube, cylinder, form: a list, esp. of names: a small loaf: act of rolling: side to side rocking movement, e.g. of ship or aircraft: a long, rumbling sound.—*v.t.* and *v.i.* to move as if a ball: to turn like a wheel: to rock from side to side: to sound as if a drum.—*v.t.* to wrap round and round: to flatten with roller(s): to move (one's eyes) from side to side.—*v.i.* to move as a great river or the sea: to move on wheels, or (of person) in a vehicle: to wallow (in money).
roll'er, *n.* something cylinder-shaped for flattening, etc. (e.g. the rollers of a mangle): a long heavy wave.
roll'-call, *n.* the calling of names from a list.
roll'er-skate, *n.* a skate with wheels instead of a blade.
roll'er-towel, *n.* a towel with joined ends hung over a roller.
roll'ing-pin, *n.* a wooden, glass, etc., roller for flattening out dough.
rolling stock, the stock of engines, wagons etc. that run on a railway.
rolled gold, metal coated with gold and rolled very thin.
[O.Fr. *rolle*—L. *rotula*—*rota*, a wheel.]

rollicking, *rol'ik-ing, adj.* noisy and gay.
[Origin unknown.]

roly-poly, *rō'li-pō'li, n.* roll-shaped jam or fruit pudding: short plump person.
[Prob. **roll.**]

Roman, *rō'mȧn, adj.* connected with Rome or with Roman Catholic Church: (*of printing type*) ordinary upright kind: (*of numbers*) written in letters, e.g. I, II, III, IV, V (for 1, 2, 3, 4, 5).—*n.* a native of Rome.
Roman Catholic, recognising the Pope (the Bishop of Rome) as head of the Church.
Roman Catholicism, the beliefs, government, etc. of the Roman Catholic Church.
[L. *Rōmānus—Rōma*, Rome.]

romance, *rō-mans′*, *n.* a tale of events not likely to happen in real life at the present time: a love story.—*v.i.* to write or tell fanciful tales: to lie.—Also *adj.*
romanc′er, *n.*
romantic, *rō-man′tik*, *adj.* full of romance: fanciful: dealing with love.
Romance language, one (French, Italian, Spanish, etc.) developed from Latin.
[Late L. *rōmānicē*, in Roman language.]

Romany, *rom′à-ni*, *n.* a gipsy: the language of gipsies:—*pl.* **-ies.**—Also *adj.*
[Romany *rom*, man.]

romp, *romp*, *v.i.* to play in a boisterous way: to move (along, home, etc.) easily and quickly.—*n.* one who romps: a lively game: a quick, easy run.
rom′per, *n.* one who romps: (usu. in *pl.*) a child's overall with trousers.
[Same word as **ramp.**]

rood, *rōōd*, *n.* a crucifix esp. in a church: a measure of area, usu. ¼ acre.
rood loft, gallery over the rood screen.
rood screen, screen of stone or wooden pillars, separating the East end of a church from the rest of it (the rood screen used to carry a crucifix, and in some churches still does).
[O.E. *rōd*, gallows, cross.]

roof, *rōōf*, *n.* the top covering of a building, car, etc.: upper part of the mouth:—*pl.* **roofs.**—*v.t.* to cover with a roof.
roof′ing, *n.* a roof: materials for a roof. —*adj.* used for making a roof.
roof′less, *adj.* having no roof: having no house.
roof garden, garden made on flat roof.
roof′tree, *n.* the beam at the highest part of a roof.
[O.E. *hrōf.*]

rook¹, *rook*, *n.* a kind of crow: a cheat, swindler.—*v.t.* to take away all his money from (a person)
rook′ery, *n.* a nesting-place of rooks, other birds that nest together, or seals:—*pl.* **rook′eries.**
[O.E. *hrōc.*]

rook², *rook*, *n.* a castle in chess.
[O.Fr. *roc*—Pers. *rukh.*]

room, *rōōm, room*, *n.* space: opportunity or scope (e.g. *There is room for improvement*): a compartment in a house: (in *pl.*) lodgings.
room′y, *adj.* spacious, having plenty of room:—*comp.* **room′ier**; *superl.* **room′iest.**
room′iness, *n.*
[O.E. *rūm.*]

roost, *rōōst*, *n.* a perch on which a bird rests at night.—*v.i.* to settle or sleep on a perch.
roost′er, *n.* a domestic cock.
to come home to roost, to come back on oneself (e.g. *His unfriendliness to his neighbours has come home to roost*).
[O.E. *hrōst.*]

root¹, *rōōt*, *n.* the underground part of a plant, which draws up food from the soil, esp. a part that never bears leaves, etc.: the base of anything, e.g. a tooth: a source, cause (e.g. *Money is the root of evil*): a word from which other words have grown.—*v.i.* to form roots and begin to grow: to be fixed.—Also *v.t.*
root′ed, *adj.* firmly planted: firmly established, deep-seated (e.g. *I have a rooted dislike of crowds*).
root′let, *n.* a little root.
root and branch, leaving nothing behind, completely.
square root. See **square.**
to root up, out, to tear out by the roots: to get rid of completely.
to take root, to grow firmly.
[Late O.E. *rōt.*]

root², *rōōt*, *v.i.* (of e.g. pigs) to turn up soil with the snout: to poke, search about.—Also *v.t.*—Also **rout** (see **rout,** 2).
[O.E. *wrōtan*—*wrōt*, a snout.]

rope, *rōp*, *n.* a thick twisted cord: a string (of pearls, onions, etc.).—*v.t.* to fasten with a rope: to lasso: to enclose, mark off, with a rope.
ro′pery, *n.* works where ropes are made.
rō′py, *adj.* (of e.g. a liquid) forming sticky threads: of poor quality.
rō′piness, *n.*
rope trick, a disappearing trick with a rope.
ro′ping-down, *n.* letting oneself down a rock face using a double rope.
to rope in, to bring in (an unwilling helper).
to give a person rope, to give him freedom to ruin himself, etc.
to know the ropes. See **know.**
[O.E. *rāp.*]

rosary. See **rose** (2).

rose¹. See **rise.**

rose², *rōz*, *n.* a flower, often scented, growing on a usu. prickly bush: a deepish pink colour: a spray, nozzle with holes, e.g. on a watering-can.
ro′sy, *adj.* rose-coloured: bright, hopeful:—*comp.* **ro′sier**; *superl* **ro′siest.**
ro′sily, *adv.* **ro′siness,** *n.*
roseate, *rō′zi-it*, *adj.* rosy.
rosary, *rō′zà-ri*, *n.* a rose garden (also **rosery**): a series of prayers: a string of beads used in saying prayers:—pl. **ro′saries.**
rosette, *rō-zet′*, *n.* a rose-shaped arrangement of ribbon, etc.
rose′-coloured, *adj.* pink: showing things as better than they are (e.g. *She saw her job through rose-coloured spectacles*).
rose window, a circular window with delicate ornamentation.
rose′wood, *n.* a valuable dark wood from abroad, used for furniture.
[O.E. *rōse*—L. *rosa.*]

rosemary, *rōz'mȧ-ri, n.* a small sweet-scented evergreen shrub.
[L. *rōs marinus,* sea dew.]
rosery, rosette, etc. See **rose** (2).
rosily, etc. See **rose** (2).
rosin, *roz'in, n.* the sticky sap of some trees in a hard form.
[Formed from **resin.**]
rosiness. See **rose** (2).
roster, *rōs'tėr, ros'-, n.* a list showing order of rotation of duties.
[Du. *rooster,* orig. gridiron (from ruled lines).]
rostrum, *ros'trům, n.* a platform for public speaking. [L.]
rosy. See **rose** (2).
rot, *rot, v.i.* and *v.t.* to go bad, or cause to go bad, decay:—*pr.p.* **rott'ing**; *pa.p.* **rott'ed.**—*n.* decay: used of some diseases (e.g. *foot rot* of sheep, *dry rot* of timber): (*coll.*) nonsense.
rott'en, *adj.* decayed: going bad: very bad: deserving contempt.
rott'enness, *n.*
rott'er, *n.* a worthless person.
[O.E. *rotian*; *rotten* is from Old Norse.]
rota, *rō'tȧ, n.* a roster, list showing a repeating order of duties.
rotary, *rō'tȧ-ri, adj.* turning like a wheel: (with *cap.*) belonging to an international system of clubs with a wheel as badge.
ro'tate, *v.t., v.i.* to turn like a wheel: to go, or make go, through a series of changes repeated again and again.
rotā'tion, *n.* **rotā'tor,** *n.*
rotatory, *rō'tȧ-tȯ-ri,* or *-tā', adj.*
rotation of crops, a regular order in which one kind, etc., follows another on the same piece of land.
Rotarian, *rō-tā'ri-ȧn, n.* a member of a Rotary club.
Rotā'rianism, the system of Rotary clubs.
[L. *rota,* wheel; *rotāre, -ātum,* to turn.]
rote, *rōt, n.* in the phrase **by rote,** by heart, without thinking of the meaning.
[Origin unknown.]
rotor, *rō'tȯr, n.* a rotating part of a dynamo, motor etc., or a system of rotating aerofoils as in a helicopter.
[For **rotator.**]
rotten, rotter. See **rot.**
rotund, *rō-tund', adj.* round: plump.
rotun'dity, rotund'ness, *ns.*
[L. *rotundus*; same root as **round.**]
rouble, *rōō'bl, n.* a Russian coin.
[Russ. *rubl'.*]
rouge, *rōōzh, n.* a powder used for reddening the cheeks or lips: also one for polishing metal, etc.—*v.t.* and *v.i.* to colour with, or use, rouge. [Fr.]
rough, *ruf, adj.* not smooth: uneven: unpolished: coarse, harsh: not exact (e.g. *a rough guess*): stormy.—*n.* a noisy, violent person: waste or untended ground: a drawing, etc., in an unfinished state.
rough'ly, *adv.* **rough'ness,** *n.*
rough'en, *v.t., v.i.* to make, or become, rough.
rough'age, *n.* bran or fibre in food.
rough'-and-read'y, *adj.* not carefully done, but good enough for the purpose: vigorous but unpolished.
rough'-and-tum'ble, *n.* a scuffle, disorderly struggle.—Also *adj.*
rough'cast, *n.* plaster mixed with small stones, used on outside walls.—*v.t.* to cover with roughcast.
rough house, a free fight.
rough'-rider, *n.* a rider of untrained horses.
rough'-shod, *adj.* (of horses) shod with shoes with nails sticking out to prevent slipping.
to be rough on, to be hard luck for.
to ride rough-shod over, to treat (a person) with no regard for his feelings.
to rough it, to live without ordinary comforts.
to rough out, to sketch, shape, roughly.
to cut up rough. See **cut.**
[O.E. *rūh.*]
roulette, *rōō-let', n.* a gambling game in which a ball is spun on a wheel on a table. [Fr.]
round, *rownd, adj.* having a curved outline: shaped like a ring, circle, cylinder, or globe: plump: with movement in a circle (e.g. *a round trip*).—*adv.* about: on all sides, around: in a circle: from one to another.—*prep.* on all sides of: all over.—*n.* something round in shape: a burst (of firing, applause:) a single bullet or shell, or a number or these all fired at one time: things happening in order (e.g. *a round of duties*): usual route: a song in which different singers take up the tune in turn: each stage in a competition, or in a contest (e.g. boxing): (*golf*) play over the whole course.—*v.t.* to make round: to go round (e.g. *to round the Cape*).—*v.i.* to become round.
round'ly, *adv.* plainly, frankly.
round'ness, *n.*
round'ers, *n.* game with bat and ball.
round'about, *adj.* not direct.—*n.* a merry-go-round: an arrangement at a road junction where, to avoid the paths of traffic crossing one another, vehicles must go round all or part of a circle.
round game, game played by any number of players, each playing for himself.
round robin, a paper signed by many people, usu. with the names in a circle.
rounds'man, *n.* man who goes round for a shopkeeper, e.g. delivering milk.
round'-ta'ble, *adj.* (of a conference, etc.) taking place at a round table, at which all are of equal importance.
round'-up, *n.* act of rounding up.
to round off, to finish off neatly.
to round up, to drive together, gather (cattle, people e.g. helpers).

[O.Fr. *rund*—L. *rotundus*—*rota*, wheel.]

rouse, *rowz, v.t.* to awaken: to stir up: to excite.—*v.i.* to awake.
rous'ing, *adj.* stirring: exciting.
roust, *v.t.* to stir (up): to rout (out).
[Origin uncertain.]

rout[1], *rowt, n.* a noisy crowd: a complete defeat: disorderly flight.—*v.t.* to defeat completely.
[O.Fr. *route*—L. *rumpĕre, ruptum*, break.]

rout[2], *rowt, v.t., v.i.* Same as **root** (2).
to rout out, to get by searching: to force up or out.

route, *rōōt* (in army, also *rowt*), *n.* course to be followed, road.—*v.t.* to fix the route of: to send (by a chosen route).
route march, a long march of troops in training. [Fr.]

routine, *rōō-tēn', n.* a regular, fixed order of doing things.—*adj.* regular, ordinary. [Fr.]

rove, *rōv, v.t.* to wander over or through.—*v.i.* to wander about.
rō'ver, *n.* a wanderer: pirate: unsettled person.
rō'ving, *adj.* and *n.*
[Partly from Du. *rooven*, to rob.]

row[1], *rō, n.* a line of persons or things.
[O.E. *rāw.*]

row[2], *rō, v.t.* to drive (a boat) by oars.—Also *v.i.*—*n.* a trip in a rowing-boat.
row'er, *n.* one who rows.
row'boat, row'ing-boat, *ns.* a boat moved by oars.
[O.E. *rōwan*; conn. L. *rēmus*, oar, and **rudder.**]

row[3], *row, n.* a noisy quarrel: a noise.
[18th-century word; origin unknown.]

rowan, *row'ȧn, n.* a tree with clusters of small red fruit: the fruit.
[Conn. with Norw. *raun.*]

rowdy, *row'di, n.* a rough, quarrelsome, noisy person:—*pl.* **row'dies.**—*adj.* disorderly and noisy:—*comp.* **row'dier;** *superl.* **row'diest.**
row'dily, *adv.* **row'diness,** *n.*
row'dyism, *n.* behaviour of a rowdy.
[U.S.; origin unknown.]

rowlock, *rol'ok, rul', n.* rest for the oar on the side of a rowing-boat.
[Prob. for *oarlock*—O.E. *ārloc.*]

royal, *roi'ȧl, adj.* of, having to do with, given by, a king or queen (e.g. *royal family, royal charter*): magnificent, splendid.
roy'ally, *adv.* **roy'alness,** *n.*
roy'alty, *n.* state of being royal: royal person: money paid to the author of a book etc. for each copy sold, and to landowners for use of minerals found in their land:—*pl.* **-ies.**
roy'alist, *n.* one who supports a king.
royal blue, a bright deep blue.
Royal Commission, persons chosen by the government and formally appointed by the king or queen to make a report on an important matter.
[Fr.—same L. root as **regal.**]

rub, *rub, v.t.* to move (one thing on, against, the surface of another; e.g. *Don't rub your sleeve on the wet paint*): to wipe, clean, polish (something: also **rub up**): (with *away, out*) to remove (a mark).—Also *v.i.*:—*pr.p.* **rubb'ing;** *pa.p.* **rubbed.**—*n.* act of rubbing: a difficulty.
rubb'ing, *n.* and *adj.*
rubb'er, *n.* something with which to rub, or to rub out: an elastic material made from juice (latex) of certain plants, or an artificial substitute for it.
rubb'ery, *adj.* **rubb'eriness,** *n.*
rubber stamp, an instrument with rubber letters or figures for stamping e.g. names, dates, on books: a person who gives his approval e.g. to a plan without consideration.
to rub along, to get along fairly well.
to rub in, to work in by rubbing (e.g. *to rub in liniment*): to go on repeating to a person (something he finds unpleasant).
to rub the wrong way, to annoy, esp. by tactlessness.
to rub shoulders with, to meet, mix with.
to rub up, to refresh one's memory of (e.g. *to rub up one's French*).
[Origin uncertain.]

rubber[1]. See **rub.**

rubber[2], *rub'ėr, n.* (in cards, etc.) an odd number of games (three, five) the winner being the side that first takes two, three, games. [Origin uncertain.]

rubbish, *rub'ish, n.* waste material, litter: nonsense.
rubb'ishy, *adj.* **rubb'ishiness,** *n.*
[Origin uncertain; conn. with **rubble.**]

rubble, *rub'l, n.* broken stone from ruined buildings: small rough stones used in building. [Origin uncertain.]

rubicund, *rōō'bi-kùnd, adj.* reddish faced.
[L. *rubicundus*—*rubēre*, to be red.]

ruby, *rōō'bi, n.* red gem:—*pl.* **-ies.**—*adj.* red.
[O.Fr. *rubi*—L. *ruber*, red.]

ruck[1], *ruk, n.* a wrinkle or fold.—*v.t.* and *v.i.* to wrinkle.
[Old Norse *hrukka.*]

ruck[2], *ruk, n.* a crowd: ordinary people.
[From Scand.]

rucksack, *rook'sak,* or *ruk'-, n.* a bag carried on the back by tourists, etc.
[Ger.—*rücken*, back, *sack*, a bag.]

ruction, *ruk'sh(ȯ)n, n.* (often in *pl.*) a disturbance; a quarrel.
[Perh. for **insurrection.**]

rudder, *rud'ėr, n.* flat piece of wood or metal hinged at the stem of a boat for steering: similar arrangement for steering an aeroplane.
[O.E. *rōthor*, oar; conn. Ger. *ruder*, oar.]

ruddy, *rud'i, adj.* red: rosy, as in good health:—*comp.* **rudd'ier;** *superl.* **-iest.**
rudd'iness, *n.*
[O.E. *rudig.*]

rude, *rōōd, adj.* not polite, showing bad

manners: roughly made (e.g. *a rude shelter*): rough, not refined.
rude'ly, *adv.* **rude'ness,** *n.*
[L. *rudis*, rough, untilled, unpolished.]

rudiment, *rōō'di-mėnt, n.* (usu. in *pl.*) one of the first simple rules or facts of anything (e.g. *the rudiments of cookery*): anything in its earliest state.
rudimen'tary, *adj.* in an early stage of development.
rudimen'tariness, *n.*
[L. *rudīmentum*—same root as **rude.**]

rue[1], *rōō, n.* a strong-smelling shrub with bitter leaves.
[Fr. *rue*—L. *rūta*—Gk. *rhȳtē.*]

rue[2], *rōō, v.t.* to be sorry for, regret:—*pr.p.* **ru(e)'ing**; *pa.p.* **rued** (*rōōd*).
rue'ful, *adj.* sorrowful.
rue'fully, *adv.* **rue'fulness,** *n.*
[O.E. *hrēow*, n., *hrēowan*, vb.]

ruff[1], *ruf, n.* a frill, usu. starched and pleated, worn round the neck in the reigns of Elizabeth I and James I: frilled appearance on neck of bird or animal. [Perh. from **ruffle.**]

ruff[2], *ruf, v.t., v.i.* to trump in a card game. —Also *n.*
[Perh. conn. O.Fr. *roffle*, a card game.]

ruffian, *ruf'i-ȧn, -yȧn, n.* a brutal, violent person.
ruff'ianly, *adj.* **ruff'ianliness,** *n.*
[O.Fr. *ruffian*; origin uncertain.]

ruffle, *ruf'l, v.t.* to make (something) wrinkled, not smooth: (of a bird) to put up (its feathers) in anger: to annoy, agitate, disturb.—*v.i.* to become not smooth: to become agitated, annoyed.—*n.* a frill, esp. at neck or wrist.
[Origin uncertain.]

rug, *rug, n.* a mat for the floor: a thick covering, esp. for use when travelling.
[Conn. Norw. dial. *rugga*, coarse cover.]

Rugby, rugby, *rug'bi, n.* a form of football in which the ball may be carried.
[From *Rugby* school.]

rugged, *rug'id, adj.* rough: uneven: strong, stern (e.g. *a rugged character*).
rugg'edly, *adv.* **rugg'edness,** *n.*
[Prob. Scand. and conn. with **rug.**]

ruin, *rōō'in, n.* downfall: complete loss of money, etc.: wrecked or decayed state: cause of downfall (e.g. *Drink was his ruin*): (often in *pl.*) broken-down remains, e.g. of buildings.—*v.t.* to cause decay or ruin to: to spoil completely.
ruinā'tion, *n.* act of ruining: state of being ruined: something that ruins.
ru'inous, *adj.* ruined: leading to disaster or ruin.
[L. *ruīna*—*ruěre*, to tumble down.]

ruing. See **rue** (2).

rule, *rōōl, n.* a strip of wood or metal used for measuring: government (e.g. *a country under foreign rule*): a regulation, order: a principle on which one acts: what usually happens, is done, etc. (e.g. *Dick was an exception to the rule that fat people are good-natured*).—*v.t.* to draw (a line): to draw lines on: to govern: to decide (that).—*v.i.* to be in power.
ru'ler, *n.* one who rules: instrument for drawing straight lines.
ru'ling, *adj.* reigning: most important. —*n.* a decision.
as a rule, usually.
rule of the road, rules to be kept in traffic.
rule of thumb, a rough-and-ready method (also as *adj.* **rule-of-thumb'**).
to rule out, deliberately to leave out, not take into consideration.
[O.Fr. *reule*—same L. root as **regular.**]

rum[1], *rum, n.* a spirit made from sugar-cane. [Origin uncertain.]

rum[2], *rum, adj.* odd, queer.
[16th-century slang.]

rumba, *rum'bȧ, n.* S. American dance.
[Sp.]

rumble, *rum'bl, v.i.* to make a low grumbling or rolling sound.—Also *n.*
rum'bling, *n.* and *adj.*
[Prob. conn. Du. *rommelen.*]

ruminant, *rōō'mi-nȧnt, n.* an animal (e.g. cow) that chews the cud.—*adj.* ruminating.
ru'minate, *v.i.* to chew the cud: to be deep in thought.—Also *v.t.*
ruminā'tion, *n.* deep thought.
[L. *rūmināre, -ātum*—*rūmen*, gullet.]

rummage, *rum'ij, n.* a thorough search.—*v.i., v.t.* to search.
rummage sale, a jumble sale.
[Older Engl., packing cargo; from Fr.]

rummy, *rum'i, n.* a card game for two or more. [Origin unknown.]

rumour, *rōō'mȯr, n.* a story which may not be true: general talk.—*v.t.* to spread a rumour of (usu. in passive; e.g. *His death was rumoured*): to say widely (that).
[O.Fr.—L. *rūmor*, a noise.]

rump, *rump, n.* the hind part of an animal: meat from this part (e.g. *rump steak*).
[Scand.]

rumple, *rum'pl, n.* a fold or wrinkle.—*v.t.* to crease, make untidy.
[Old Du. *rompel.*]

rumpus, *rum'pus, n.* an uproar: a disturbance. [Origin uncertain.]

run, *run, v.i.* to move swiftly: to hurry: to race: (of trains, etc.) to travel: (of water, etc.) to flow: (of a machine) to work: to spread (e.g. *This colour runs*): to reach, stretch (to): to go on being repeated (e.g. *This play runs for two weeks*), to continue:—*v.t.* to cause to run: to keep and use (a motor car): to hunt: to organise, conduct (e.g. a business): to get through (a blockade): to smuggle (guns): to bring on oneself (e.g. *to run a risk*):—*pr.p.* **runn'ing**; *pa.t.* **ran**; *pa.p.* **run.**—*n.* act of running: a trip: distance or time of running: a spell or period (e.g. *a run of bad luck*):

a rush to obtain (with *on*; e.g. *a run on tickets for the show*): a rush to obtain something (e.g. money) from (e.g. *a run on the bank*): a ladder e.g. in a stocking: a single score (e.g. in cricket): the free use (of a place): a pen for fowls.

runn'er, *n.* one who runs: a messenger: a rooting stem of a plant: a blade of a skate or sledge.

runn'el, *n.* a little river or stream.

runn'ing, *n.* act of moving fast, flowing, etc.: management, control.—*adj.* kept for use when running (e.g. *running shoes*): giving out fluid (e.g. *a running ear*).—*adv.* one after another (e.g. *three days running*).

run'about, *n.* a small light car, etc.

run'away, *n.* a person or animal that runs away.—Also *adj.*

run'-down', *adj.* in poor health.

runn'er-up', *n.* one who is second in a race or competition.

runn'ing-board, *n.* a footboard by the side of a motor car or engine.

running commentary, a description (esp. broadcast) of a game or event while it is happening.

running knot, one that slips along the string to alter the size of the loop.

runn'ing-lights, *n.pl.* lights shown by ships after sunset.

run-of-the-mill', *adj.* ordinary.

run'way, *n.* path for aircraft to take off from or land on.

a run for one's money, a spell of fun or success in return for effort.

in (or **out of**) **the running,** having (or not having) a chance of success.

to run down, (of a vehicle or driver) to knock down: to speak ill of: to catch by chasing.

to run in, to arrest: to start (a new machine) working properly.

to run it fine, to leave it nearly too late.

to run out, to leak: to become short (of): to put a batsman out while he is running.

to run over, to overflow: to knock down or pass over with a car or other vehicle: to practise.

to run to seed, to decay, go to waste.

to run up, to make or build hastily.

[O.E. *rinnan*, to run.]

rung[1], *rung, n.* a step of a ladder. [O.E. *hrung*.]

rung[2]. See **ring**[2].

runnel, runner, running. See **run.**

runt, *runt, n.* a small stunted animal: a cabbage stalk. [Origin uncertain.]

rupee, *rōō-pē', n.* a coin of India, Pakistan, Ceylon. [Hindustani *rūpiyah*.]

rupture, *rup'chŭr, n.* a breaking (e.g. of friendship): hernia (see this word).—*v.t., v.i.* to break, burst.

[L. *rumpĕre, ruptum*, to break.]

rural, *rōō'răl, adj.* of or connected with the country.

[L. *rūs, rūris*, country; conn. **rustic.**]

ruse, *rōōz, n.* a trick: a cunning scheme.

[O.Fr.—*ruser*, to get out of the way.]

rush[1], *rush, v.i.* to move quickly, hurry.—*v.t.* to hurry (someone).—*n.* a quick movement forward: a hurry.

rush hour, hour or time when most people are travelling.

[O.Fr. *ruser*; same root as **ruse.**]

rush[2], *rush, n.* a tall grasslike plant growing in or near water.

rush'y, *adj.* **rush'iness,** *n.*

rush'-bottomed, *adj.* having a seat made with rushes.

[O.E. *risce*.]

rusk, *rusk, n.* a kind of biscuit like very hard toast.

[Sp. *rosca*, a roll.]

russet, *rus'it, n.* a reddish-brown colour: an apple of this colour.—Also *adj.*

[O.Fr. *rousset*.]

Russian, *rush'yăn, n.* a native of Russia: the language of Russia.—*adj.* of, or connected with, Russia.

Russian tea, tea with lemon instead of milk.

Russo-, *rus-ō*, (as part of word) Russian.

rust, *rust, n.* the reddish-brown coating formed on iron and steel by air and moisture: a plant disease causing a rusty appearance: the colour of rust.—*v.i., v.t.* to form rust, cause rust on.

rus'ty, *adj.* covered with rust: looking like rust: showing signs of wear: showing lack of recent practice (e.g. *My French is rusty*; *I haven't played for so long that I am rusty*):—*comp.* **rus'tier;** *superl.* **rus'tiest.**

rus'tiness, *n.*

rust'less, rust'proof, *adjs.* not rusting.

[O.E. *rūst*.]

rustic, *rus'tik, adj.* having to do with the country: simple, unpolished (e.g. *a rustic fence*).—*n.* a country dweller, usu. a simple, uneducated one.

rus'ticate, *v.i.* to live in the country.

[Same root as **rural.**]

rustiness. See **rust.**

rustle, *rus'l, v.i.* to make a soft, whispering sound: to act energetically.—*v.t.* to steal (esp. cattle).

rus'tler, *n,* a cattle thief.

rus'tling, *n.* and *adj.* [Imit.]

rustless, rusty, etc. See **rust.**

rut, *rut, n.* a deep track made by wheels: a fixed way of behaving, dull routine (e.g. *to get into a rut*).—*v.t.* to mark with ruts:—*pr.p.* **rutt'ing;** *pa.p.* **rutt'ed.**

[Origin unknown.]

ruthless, *rōōth'lis, adj.* cruel, without pity.

ruth'lessly, *adv.* **ruth'lessness,** *n.*

[M.E. *ruthe*, pity; from **rue** (2).]

rye, *rī, n.* a grasslike cultivated plant: its grain, used for making bread, etc.: whisky made from rye.

rye'-grass, *n.* a kind of grass grown for hay and as cattle feed.

[O.E. *ryge*.]

S

Sabbath, *sab'ȧth, n.* a day of the week regularly set aside for religious services and rest—e.g. among the Jews, Saturday, among most Christians, Sunday.
sabbat'ical, *adj.*
[Heb. *Shabbāth.*]

sable[1], *sā'bl, n.* a marten found in arctic regions, valued for its glossy fur: its fur.
[Fr.; prob. of Slav origin.]

sable[2], *sā'bl, adj.* black: dark.
[Fr.; perh. same as **sable** (1).]

sabot, *sab'ō, n.* a wooden shoe worn by the peasants of several countries.
sab'otage (*-täzh*), *n.* deliberate destruction of machinery, etc., during labour troubles, or in war: anything done to hinder effort, spoil a plan, etc.—*v.t.* to destroy, damage, cause to fail, by sabotage.—Also *v.i.*
sab'oteur (*-tėr*), *n.* one who sabotages.
[Fr. *sabot*; *saboter*, make noise with one's sabots, scamp work, sabotage.]

sabre, *sā'bėr, n.* a one-edged sword, slightly curved towards the point, used by cavalry. [Fr.]

sac, *sak, n.* (in plant or animal body) a bag, often containing a liquid.
[Fr.—L. *saccus*, a bag.]

saccharine, *sak'ȧ-rēn, -rīn, adj.* having to do with, or like, sugar: sickly-sweet (e.g. *a saccharine smile*).
sacch'arin(e) (*-rin, -rēn*), *n.* a very sweet substance, used as a substitute for sugar.
[Gk. *sakcharon*, sugar; Eastern origin.]

sachet, *sâ'shā, n.* small bag, usu. containing scented powder, etc. [Fr.]

sack[1], *sak, n.* a large bag of coarse material for holding grain, flour, etc.: the amount a sack will hold: a short, loose-fitting dress or coat.—*v.t.* to put into a sack: (*coll.*) to dismiss from one's job.
sack'ing, *n.* coarse cloth or canvas for sacks, etc.
sack'cloth, *n.* cloth for sacks: coarse cloth formerly worn as a sign of mourning or of sorrow for sin.
to get the sack, to be dismissed.
to give the sack, to sack, dismiss.
[O.E. *sacc*—L. *saccus*—Gk. *sakkos.*]

sack[2], *sak, n.* plundering (of a captured town).—*v.t.* to plunder: take everything valuable from.
[Fr. *sac*—L. root as **sack** (1).]

sacrament, *sak'rȧ-mėnt, n.* a religious ceremony such as the Lord's Supper and baptism.
sacramen'tal, *adj.* belonging to or being a sacrament.
[L. *sacrāmentum*, oath; root as **sacred.**]

sacred, *sā'krid, adj.* dedicated, esp. to God, holy: to be treated with reverence: connected with religion (e.g. *sacred music*).
sa'credly, *adv.* **sa'credness,** *n.*
See also following words.
[(Orig. pa.p.—O.Fr. *sacrer*, vb.)—L. *sacer.*]

sacrifice, *sak'ri-fīs, n.* the act of offering something, esp. a victim on an altar, to a god: the thing so offered: something given up in order to benefit another person, or to gain a more important end: the act of giving up in this way: loss of profit.—*v.t.* (*-fīs*; also *-fīz*) to make a sacrifice of: to give up for something better or thought to be more important (e.g. *He sacrificed his life to save the child, for the good cause*; *sacrificed his happiness to his ambition*).
sacrificial (*-fish'ȧl*), *adj.* having to do with sacrifice.
[L. root as **sacred**; *facĕre*, to make.]

sacrilege, *sak'ri-lij, n.* the using of a holy thing or place in an evil way.
sacrilegious, *sak-ri-lij'ụs, adj.*
[L. root as **sacred,** *legĕre*, gather, steal; orig. theft from a temple.]

sacristan, *sak'ris-tȧn, n.* an official with certain duties in a church.
[Same L. root as **sacred.**]

sacrosanct, *sak'rō-sang(k)t, adj.* holy and worthy of reverence: not to be harmed.
[L. roots as **sacred** and **sanctity.**]

sad, *sad, adj.* sorrowful, unhappy: showing grief: (often used playfully) terrible, shocking: (of e.g. colour) dull: (of e.g. bread) not properly risen, damp and heavy:—*comp.* **sadd'er**; *superl.* **sadd'est.**
sad'ly, *adv.* **sad'ness,** *n.*
sadd'en, *v.t.* and *v.i.* to make, or grow, sad.
[O.E. *sæd*, weary; conn. L. *sat(is)*, enough.]

saddle, *sad'l, n.* a seat for a rider used on a horse, etc. or on a bicycle, etc.: anything of a similar shape: a type of cut from the back of an animal used as food.—*v.t.* to put a saddle on: to put a burden, or a responsibility on (with *with*; e.g. *He saddled his parents with his debts, with the boring visitor, with the care of his children*).
sadd'ler, *n.* a maker of saddles and harness.
[O.E. *sadel*; conn. with Ger. *sattel.*]

sadism, *sad', sād'*, or *säd'izm, n.* pleasure in torturing, or in watching cruelty to, someone, esp. a loved one.
sad'ist, *n.* one who takes such pleasure.

sadis′tic, *adj.* **sadis′tically,** *adv.*
[Marquis de *Sade*, 1740-1814.]

safari, *sȧ-fä′ri*, *n.* an expedition, esp. for hunting: persons, animals, etc. forming this:—*pl.* **-ris.** [From Arabic.]

safe, *sāf*, *adj.* unharmed: free from danger: free, secure (from): not risky: reliable, trustworthy: cautious (e.g. *a safe driver*).—*n.* a steel or iron chest, etc., for money, valuables, etc.: a cupboard, cabinet, for meats, etc.
safe′ly, *adv.* **safe′ty, safe′ness,** *ns.*
safe′-con′duct, *n.* a document, passport, given to a person to enable him to travel without arrest, etc., esp. in time of war.
safe′guard, *n.* anything that prevents danger or gives security or protection.
safe keeping, protection: custody.
safe seat, a seat that the political party spoken, thought, of will certainly win.
safety belt, a belt fixed to a seat in a car or aircraft used to keep a passenger from being jolted out of the seat.
safety lamp, a lamp used in mines which does not set fire to the gases found there.
safety valve, a valve that opens when pressure becomes too great: a harmless outlet for emotion, etc.
safe and sound, unharmed.
(in order) to be on the safe side, so as not to run much risk (e.g. *Take a waterproof to be on the safe side*).
[O.Fr. *sauf*—L. root as **save.**]

saffron, *saf′rȯn*, *n.* a type of crocus with deep yellow flowers, or a colouring substance prepared from it.
[Fr. *safran*; from Arabic.]

sag, *sag*, *v.i.* to bend, sink, or droop, esp. in the middle:—*pr.p.* **sagg′ing;** *pa.p.* **sagged.**
[Conn. with Swed. *sacka*, to sink down.]

saga, *sä′ga*, *n.* a story of a hero, or a family, composed very long ago in Norway or Iceland: a novel about several generations of a family: a long detailed story.
[Old Norse.]

sagacious, *sȧ-gā′shŭs*, *adj.* having, or showing, good judgment, shrewd and practical: (of animals) intelligent.
saga′ciously, *adv.*
saga′ciousness, sagac′ity (*-gas′i-ti*), *ns.*
[L. *sagax*, *sagācis.*]

sage[1], *sāj*, *n.* a plant whose leaves are used for flavouring and stuffings: (also **sage green**) a greyish green.
sage′brush, *n.* a growth of shrubs, with scent like sage, on dry American plains.
[O.Fr. *sauge*—L. *salvia.*]

sage[2], *sāj*, *adj.* wise.—*n.* a man of great wisdom (esp. one of **the seven sages** of ancient Greece).
[Fr.—L. *sapĕre*, to be wise.]

sago, *sā′gō*, *n.* a starchy substance obtained from inside the trunk of E. Indian palms, used in e.g. puddings.
[Malay *sāgū.*]

sahib, *sä′ib*, *n.* a term of respect given in India to persons of rank or to Europeans.
[Arabic, friend.]

said, *sed*, *adj.* before-mentioned (e.g. *the said witness*). See **say.**

sail, *sāl*, *n.* a sheet of canvas, etc., spread to catch the wind, by which a ship is driven forward: a ship or ships (e.g. *a fleet of forty sail*): a journey in a ship: an arm of a windmill.—*v.i.* to be moved by sails: to go by water in a ship (with, or without, sails): to begin a voyage: to glide easily (along) on water or in air: (*coll.*) to go easily and successfully (e.g. *He sailed through his exams*).—*v.t.* to navigate or steer: to move upon in a ship (e.g. *to sail the sea*).
sail′ing, *n.* and *adj.*
sail′er, *n.* a sailing ship.
sail′or, *n.* one whose job is helping to sail a ship, esp. a common seaman.
sail′cloth, *n.* strong cloth for sails.
to set sail, to set out on a voyage.
[O.E. *segel*; conn. with Ger. *segel.*]

saint, *sānt*, (before a name) *s(i)nt*, *n.* a very good or holy person, esp. one canonised (formally recognised after death) by the R.C. or other Church.
saint′ly, *adj.*:—*comp.* **saint′lier;** *superl.* **saint′liest.**
saint′liness, *n.*
saint′ed, *adj.* holy, saintly: gone to heaven.
Saint's day, a day set apart for remembering a particular saint.
Latter-day saints, the Mormons' name for themselves.
[Fr.—L. *sanctus*; root as **sanctity.**]

sake[1], *sāk*, *n.* cause, purpose (e.g. *for the sake of peace*): benefit, advantage (e.g. *for my sake*).
[O.E. *sacu*, strife; same root as **seek.**]

sake[2], *sä′ki*, *n.* a kind of Japanese beer made from rice. [Jap.]

salaam, *sȧ-läm′*, *n.* an Eastern greeting: a deep bow with palm of right hand on forehead.—Also *v.i.* and *v.t.*
[Arabic *salām*, peace.]

salad, *sal′ȧd*, *n.* a mixture of raw vegetables, etc. cut up and seasoned.
salad dressing, sauce of olive oil, etc. put on salads.
[Fr. *salade*—L. *sal*, salt.]

salamander, *sal′ȧ-man-dėr*, or *-man′-*, *n.* a small lizard-like animal, once believed to be able to live in fire.
[Fr. *salamandre*; origin prob. Eastern.]

salami, *sȧ-lä′mi*, *n.* a highly seasoned Italian sausage. [It. pl. of *salame.*]

salary, *sal′ȧ-ri*, *n.* fixed wages regularly paid for services (usu. for professional, not mechanical, work):—*pl.* **-ies.**
sal′aried, *adj.* receiving a salary.
[L. *salārium*, money for salt (L. *sal*); this was part of Roman soldier's pay.]

sale, *sāl*, *n.* the exchange of anything for money: demand, market (e.g. *There is no sale for fur coats in the jungle*): a public

offer of goods to be sold, esp. at reduced prices or by auction.
sal(e)'able, *adj.* fit to be sold: easy to sell.
sale'room, *n.* an auction room.
sales'man, -woman, *ns.* a person who sells, or shows, goods to customers.
sales'manship, *n.* the art of persuading people to buy.
sale of work, a sale of needlework and other articles to raise money for charity, etc.
[Late O.E. *sala*; prob. —Old Norse.]

salient, *sā'li-ènt, adj.* (of e.g. an angle) pointing outwards: outstanding, chief (e.g. *the salient points of a speech*).—*n.* an outward pointing angle, esp. in a line of defences.
[L. *saliens, -ientis,* leaping, gushing.]

saline, *sā'līn, sa'līn, sà-līn', adj.* containing salt: salty.
salin'ity (*-lin'*), *n.* saltness.
[Fr.—L. *sal,* salt.]

saliva, *sà-lī'và, n.* spittle, the liquid from the glands of the mouth, a digestive fluid.
salivary, (*sa'li-,* or *sà-lī'-*), *adj.* having to do with saliva.
sal'ivāte, *v.t.* to produce saliva, esp. too much.
[L. *salīva.*]

sallow[1], *sal'ō, n.* a type of willow.
[O.E. *s(e)alh*; conn. with L. *salix.*]

sallow[2], *sal'ō, adj.* (of complexion) pale, yellowish, rather sickly-looking.
[O.E. *salo, salu.*]

sally, *sal'i, n.* a sudden rush forth (e.g. from fort) to attack attackers: an excursion, jaunt: outburst of e.g. wit, anger. —*v.i.* to rush out suddenly:—*pr.p.* **sall'ying**; *pa.p.* **sall'ied.**
to sally forth, to go out, e.g. for a walk.
[Fr. *saillie*—L. *salīre,* to leap.]

salmon, *sam'òn, n.* a large fish, with silvery sides and yellowish-pink flesh, that swims up rivers to spawn: the colour of its flesh.
salmon leap, a waterfall which salmon leap over in going upstream.
[Fr. *saumon*—L. *salmo*—*salīre,* to leap.]

salon, *sal'on*[g], *n.* a drawingroom: a gathering of notable people at the house of a well-known hostess: (a large hall, etc., used for) exhibition of pictures (or other purpose). [Fr.]

saloon, *sà-lōōn', n.* a large public room: a diningroom for ship's passengers: railway carriage not divided into compartments: a motor car with a closed-in body of one compartment: (*U.S.*) a drinking bar. [**salon.**]

salt, *sölt, solt, n.* common salt, a substance used for seasoning, either mined from the earth (**rock salt**) or obtained from brine, etc.: any other substance, formed, as common salt is, from a metal and an acid: (in *pl.*) a mixture of salts used as a medicine: (*coll.*) a sailor, esp. an old sailor: something that gives liveliness, interest, etc.—*adj.* containing salt: seasoned or cured with salt: growing in, or covered with, salt water: (*slang*) expensive.—*v.t.* to sprinkle, cure, with salt: to overcharge (a person for goods).
sal'ty, *adj.* **sal'tiness,** *n.*
salt(-)lick, a place where salt is found or is placed for animals.
salt marsh, a marsh flooded at times by the sea.
above (or **below**) **the salt,** among those of high (or low) social rank.
to take with a grain of salt, to hear, receive, with slight feeling of disbelief.
worth one's salt, worth at least the value of the salt one eats.
[O.E. *salt*; conn. with L. *sal,* Gk. *hals.*]

saltcellar, *sölt'sel-àr, solt', n.* a small table dish for holding salt.
[**salt,** and Fr. *salière* (root as **salary**).]

saltpetre, *sölt-pē'tèr, solt-, n.* nitre, a nitrogen salt used in gunpowder, etc.
[Late L. *sal petrae,* salt of the rock.]

salubrious, *sà-lōō'bri-ùs,* or *-lū'-, adj.* (of air, place, etc.) health-giving.
salu'briousness, salū'brity, *ns.*
salutary, *sal'ū-tàr-i, adj.* giving health or safety: wholesome: having good effect.
sal'utariness, *n.*
[L. *salūbris, salūtāris*—*salūs,* health.]

salute, *sà-lōōt', -lūt', v.t.* greet with words, a kiss, a gesture (e.g. of the hand), or show respect to by a formal gesture: to honour (person) by firing guns, striking the flag, etc.—*v.i.* to make a formal gesture of greeting or respect.—Also *n.*
salutā'tion, *n.* act, or words, of greeting: the introductory words of a letter.
[L. *salūtāre*—root as **salubrious**; see also **salvo.**]

salvage, *sal'vij, n.* act of saving a ship or cargo, or of saving goods from a fire, etc.: reward paid for this: goods saved from waste.—*v.t.* to save from loss or ruin.
salve, *v.t.* to salvage.
[Fr.—L. root as **salvation, save.**]

salvation, *sal-vā'sh(ò)n, n.* act of saving: means or cause of saving (e.g. *This deep sleep was the patient's salvation*): the saving of man from sin and its results.
[Late L. *salvāre, -ātum,* to save.]

salve[1]. See **salvage.**

salve[2], *säv,* also *salv, n.* an ointment to heal or sooth: anything to soothe the feelings or conscience.—*v.t.* to soothe.
[O.E. *sealf*; conn. with Ger. *salbe.*]

salver, *sal'vèr, n.* a tray for presenting things.
[Sp. *salva*—*salvar,* to save.]

salvo, *sal'vō, n.* a burst of gunfire, in salute, etc., or a discharge of bombs, etc.: a round of applause:—*pl.* **salvo(e)s.**
[It. *salva*—L. *salvē,* greeting!—root as **save.**]

Samaritan, *sȧ-mar'i-tȧn, n.* an inhabitant of *Samaria* (ancient Palestine). See **good.**

same, *sām, adj.* exactly alike, identical : not different : unchanged : mentioned before.—*pron.* the thing just mentioned.
same'ness, *n.* tiresome lack of variety.
all, just, the same, for all that.
at the same time, still, nevertheless.
[O.E. (*adv.*) ; conn. L. *similis*, like.]

samovar, *sam'ō-vär, -vär', n.* a Russian tea urn. [Russ.]

sampan, *sam'pan, n.* a small Chinese boat. [Chinese *san*, three, *pan*, board.]

sample, *sâm'pl, n.* a small portion to show the quality of the whole, a specimen, example.—Also *adj.*—*v.t.* to test a sample of.
sam'pler, *n.* one who samples : a piece of embroidery, etc. to show one's skill.
[M.E. *essample*—L. root as **example.**]

sanatorium, *san-ȧ-tō'ri-ŭm, -tö', n.* hospital, esp. for people with diseases of the lungs.
[L. *sānāre*, heal ; root as **sane, sanitary.**]

sanctity, *sang(k)'ti-ti, n.* purity, holiness : sacredness : (of an oath, custom, etc.) quality that should make it unbreakable or impossible to change.
sanc'tify (*-fi*), *v.t.* to make sacred or holy : to free from sin :—*pr.p.* **sanc'tifying** ; *pa.p.* **sanc'tified** (*-fīd*).
sanctificā'tion, *n.*
sanctimō'nious, *adj.* pretending, or making a show of, holiness.
sanctimō'niously, *adv.*
sanctimō'niousness, *n.*
sanc'tuary, *n.* a sacred place : (the most sacred part of) a temple or church : a place where one can be safe from arrest or violence : an animal or plant reserve :—*pl.* **-ies.**
sanc'tum, a private room.
[L. *sanctus*, sacred ; conn. with L. *sacer.*]

sanction, *sang(k)'sh(ŏ)n, n.* permission, approval, support (given e.g. by a person in authority, by custom ; e.g. *The headmistress, the tradition of the school, does not sanction the use of lipstick by the girls*) : (in *pl.*) a measure applied, e.g. to a nation, to force it to stop a course of action.—*v.t.* to permit, give sanction for.
[L. *sancīre*, make sacred, decree, ratify ; root as **sanctity.**]

sanctuary, etc. See **sanctity.**

sand, *sand, n.* a mass of fine particles of crushed or worn rock, esp. quartz : (often in *pl.*) land covered with sand, esp. the seashore.—*v.t.* to sprinkle with sand : to add sand to : to smooth with sand.
san'dy, *adj.* **san'diness,** *n.*
sand'bag, *n.* a bag filled with sand.—*v.t.* to protect with sandbags : to hit or stun with one.
sand'bank, *n.* a bank of sand formed by tides and currents.
sand dune. Same as **dune.**
sand'-glass, *n.* an hour-glass, or a similar device for measuring shorter periods of time.
sand martin, a martin that nests in sandy banks.
sand'paper, *n.* paper covered with sand for smoothing and polishing.—*v.t.* to use sandpaper on.
sand'piper, *n.* a type of wading bird.
sand'stone, *n.* a soft rock made of layers of sand pressed together.
[O.E. ; conn. with Ger. *sand*, Du. *zand.*]

sandal, *san'd(ȧ)l, n.* a sole bound to the foot with straps : a light, low shoe or slipper.
san'dalled, *adj.* wearing sandals.
[L. *sandalium*—Gk. *sandalion.*]

sandalwood, *san'd(ȧ)l-wood, n.* a wood from Asia noted for its fragrance.
[Late L. *santalum.*]

sandwich, *san(d)'wij, -wich, n.* two slices of bread with any kind of food between : anything like this in arrangement.—*v.t.* to place (something, between two layers or between two objects).
[Named from an Earl of *Sandwich.*]

sane, *sān, adj.* sound in mind, not mad : sensible (e.g. *It is the sane thing to do*).
sane'ly, *adv.*
sane'ness, san'ity (*san'*), *ns.*
[L. *sānus*, healthy, *sānitās*, health.]

sangfroid, sang-froid, *song-frwä', n.* coolness, self-possession, in danger, etc.
[Fr. *sang*, blood, *froid*, cold.]

sanguinary, *sang'gwin-ȧr-i, adj.* bloodthirsty : (of e.g. battle) with much bloodshed.
[L. *sanguis, sanguinis*, blood.]

sanguine, *sang'gwin, adj.* (of complexion) ruddy : cheerful, hopeful.
san'guinely, *adv.* **san'guineness,** *n.*
[L. root as **sanguinary.**]

sanitary, *san'i-tȧr-i, adj.* having to do with conditions or arrangements that encourage health, esp. good drainage, etc. : free from dirt, etc.
sanitā'tion, *n.* sanitary, healthy, condition, or arrangements for bringing this about.
sanitā'rium, (*U.S.*) a sanatorium.
[Fr. *sanitaire*—same L. root as **sane.**]

sanity. See **sane.** **sank.** See **sink.**

Sanskrit, *san'skrit, n.* the ancient literary language of India.

Santa Claus, *san'tȧ klöz, n.* in nursery story, Father Christmas, who brings children Christmas presents.
[U.S. form of Du. *Sante Klaas*, St Nicholas.]

sap[1], *sap, n.* juice, esp. the liquid that flows in plants : (*slang*) a weakling or fool.
sapp'y, *adj.* **sapp'iness,** *n.*
sap'ling, *n.* a young tree.
[O.E. *sæp* ; conn. Du. *sap*, Ger. saft.]

sap[2], *sap, n.* a trench or tunnel leading towards the enemy's position.—*v.t.* to approach, or weaken, destroy, by digging beneath : (partly from **sap**[1]) to weaken,

exhaust (e.g. *to sap one's strength*):—*pr.p.* **sapp'ing**; *pa.p.* **sapped.**—Also *v.i.*
sapp'er, *n.* one, esp. a soldier, who saps.
[It. *zappa*, spade, hoe.]

sapience, *sā'pi-ėns, n.* judgment, wisdom (often used in irony—see this word).
sa'pient, *adj.* wise.
[L. *sapientia—sapĕre*, to be wise.]

sapling. See **sap** (1).

sapper. See **sap** (2).

sapphire, *saf'īr, n.* (a precious stone of) a beautiful blue colour.—Also *adj.*
[L. *sapphīrus*—Gk. *sappheiros.*]

sarcasm, *sär'kaz-ėm, n.* a cutting or biting remark in scorn or contempt, esp. one in ironical (see *irony*) wording: the use of such remarks.
sarcas'tic, *adj.* containing sarcasm: often using sarcasm.
sarcas'tically, *adv.*
[Gk. *sarkazein*, tear flesh, bite the lips, speak bitterly—*sarx*, flesh.]

sarcophagus, *sär-kof'ȧ-gus, n.* a stone coffin: a tomb.
[Gk. *sarx*, flesh, *phagein*, to eat.]

sardine, *sär-dēn', sär', n.* a young pilchard or other fish tinned in oil.
[Fr.—It. *sardina*—L. *sardīna.*]

sardonic, *sär-don'ik, adj.* (of smile, person, etc.) bitterly scornful.
sardon'ically, *adv.*
[Late Gk. *sardonios*—Gk. *sardanios.*]

sargasso, *sär-gas'ō, n.* a type of seaweed.
[Port. *sargaço.*]

sari, *sä'rē, n.* Hindu woman's outer garment, wrapped round waist and passed over the shoulder:—*pl.* **sar'is.**

sarong, *sä-rong', n.* a type of skirt worn by women and men in Malaya.

sarsaparilla, *sär-sȧ-pȧ-ril'ȧ, n.* a trailing plant: a flavouring made from its root: a soft drink.
[Sp. *zarzaparrilla.*]

sartorial, *sär-tōr'i-ȧl, -tör', adj.* having to do with dress, or with tailor-made clothes (e.g. *The tramp cared nothing about sartorial elegance*).
[L. *sartor*, a mender, tailor.]

sash[1], *sash, n.* a band or scarf worn round the waist or over the shoulder.
[Arabic *shāsh.*]

sash[2], *sash, n.* a frame, esp. a sliding frame, for panes of glass.
[Fr. *châssis*—L. *capsa*, a case.]

sassafras, *sas'ȧ-fras, n.* a type of laurel tree of N. America: the dried bark, esp. of its root, used in medicine and for flavouring.
[Sp. *sasafrás.*]

Sassenach, *sas'ė-naн, n.* an Englishman: (wrongly; Scott, etc.) a Lowlander.
[Gael. *Sasunnach.*]

sat. See **sit.**

Satan, *sā'tȧn, n.* the Devil: the chief of the fallen angels.
Satan'ic (*sȧ-tan'*), *adj.*
[O.Fr.—Heb. *sātān*, enemy.]

satchel, *sach'ėl, n.* a small bag, esp. for schoolbooks.
[O.Fr. *sachel*—L. *saccellus*, a sack.]

sate, *sāt, v.t.* to make (a person) feel he has had more than enough (e.g. *to sate a person with food, advice*).
[O.E. *sadian*, to become satisfied; influenced by L. *satis* (see **satiate**).]

sateen, *sȧ-tēn', n.* a glossy-looking cotton or woollen cloth. [**satin.**]

satellite, *sat'ė-līt, n.* a follower who attaches himself to a more powerful person: a planet that revolves around a larger planet, or a man-made object launched into orbit round a planet: a town, nation, etc., controlled by a more powerful neighbour.
[Fr.—L. *satelles*, attendant, guard.]

satiate, *sā'shi-āt, v.t.* to give more than enough to, sate utterly, and so sicken.
satiā'tion, *n.* **sā'tiable,** *adj.*
satiety, *sȧ-tī'ė-ti, n.* satiation: an excessive amount.
[L. *satiāre—satis*, enough.]

satin, *sat'in, n.* a closely woven silk with a glossy surface.—Also *adj.*
sat'iny, *adj.* **sat'ininess,** *n.*
sat'inwood, *n.* a beautiful smooth wood from East Indies.
[Fr.; prob. from Arabic.]

satire, *sat'īr, n.* a piece of writing making fun of people esp. of their vices, foolish actions and beliefs, etc.: ridicule, cutting comment.
satir'ic(al) (*-ir'*), *adjs.* **satir'ically,** *adv.*
sat'irīse, *v.t.* to ridicule, compose a satire on (persons or their ways).
sat'irist, *n.* a writer of satire.
[L. *satira*, a poem that ridicules.]

satisfy, *sat'is-fī, v.t.* to give enough to (a person): to please, make content: to pay (a creditor): to give enough to quiet, get rid of (e.g. *to satisfy hunger, curiosity, a desire*): to fulfil (requirements, conditions laid down): to convince (e.g. *His explanation should satisfy them that he is innocent*): to lay one's doubts to rest by investigation (e.g. *I must go out and satisfy myself that the loafer has moved away*):—*pr.p.* **sat'isfying**; *pa.p.* **sat'isfied** (*-fīd*).—Also *v.i.*
satisfac'tion, *n.* act of satisfying: state of being satisfied: feeling of comfort and pleasure: something that satisfies: payment: amends, compensation.
satisfac'tory, *adj.* satisfying, meeting requirements (e.g. *a satisfactory report, response*): convincing (e.g. *a satisfactory explanation*).
satisfac'torily, *adv.* **-toriness,** *n.*
[L. *satis*, enough, *facĕre*, to make.]

saturate, *sat'ū-rāt, v.t.* to soak, or to fill, completely (with e.g. water, dirt, a smell, a crowd): to cover (a target) completely with bombs, etc.
sat'urated, *adj.*
saturā'tion, *n.* act of saturating: state of being saturated: (of colour) freedom

from white.

[L. *saturāre, -ātum*; conn. *satis*, enough.]

Saturday, *sat'ur-di, n.* seventh day of week.

[O.E. *Sæterdæg*, day of (planet) Saturn.]

saturnine, *sat'ur-nīn, adj.* gloomy, given to saying little, as those born under planet *Saturn* were supposed to be: sardonic (see this word).

satyr, *sat'ėr, n.* a god of the woods supposed to be half man, half goat, and very wanton.

[L. *satryus*—Gk. *satyros*.]

sauce, *sös, n.* a dressing poured over food to give flavour (e.g. *tomato sauce*): (*coll.*) impudence, cheek.

sauce'pan, *n.* a rather deep pan.

[Fr.—L. *salsa*, salted thing—*sal*, salt.]

saucer, *sö'sėr, n.* a shallow dish placed under a cup: anything of that shape.

[O.Fr. *saussier(e)*, dish for **sauce.**]

saucy, *sö'si, adj.* bold, forward, cheeky: smart and trim:—*comp.* **sau'cier;** *superl.* **sau'ciest.**

sau'cily, *adv.* **sau'ciness,** *n.* [**sauce.**]

sauerkraut, *sowr'krowt, n.* a German dish of cabbage cut fine and pickled in salt.

[Ger., 'sour cabbage'.]

saunter, *sön'tėr, v.t.* to wander about without hurry, stroll.—Also *n.*

[Origin uncertain.]

sausage, *sos'ij, sös', n.* chopped meat seasoned and stuffed into a tube of e.g. animal gut.

sau'sage-roll', *n.* minced meat cooked in a roll of pastry.

[Fr. *saucisse*—same root as **sauce.**]

sauté, *sō'tā, adj.* fried lightly and quickly. [Fr.]

sauterne(s), *sō-tėrn', n.* a white wine made at *Sauternes*, in France, etc.

savage, *sav'ij, adj.* in a state of nature: (of an animal) wild: fierce and cruel: very angry.—*n.* a human being in an uncivilised state: a cruel or fierce person.

sav'agely, *adv.* **sav'ageness,** *n.*

sav'agery, *n,* savageness: state of being savage: a savage deed:—*pl.* **-eries.**

[O.Fr. *salvage*—L. *silva*, a wood.]

savanna, savannah, *sȧ-van'ȧ, n.* a grassy plain with few trees.

[Sp. *zavana* (now *sabana*).]

savant, *sâ'vonᵍ, sa'vant, n.* a learned man.

[Fr., from *savoir*, to know.]

save, *sāv, v.t.* to rescue, bring out of danger: to prevent the loss of, or damage to: to keep or preserve (from): to keep from spending, using, wasting (e.g. money, time, energy): to rescue from evil or sin.—*v.i.* to put money aside for future use.—*prep.* except (e.g. *All, save one, were there*).

sa'ver, *n.* person or thing that keeps from spending, using, wasting.

saviour, *sā'vyȯr, n.* one who saves from evil or danger: (*cap.*) Jesus Christ.

sa'ving, *adj.* thrifty: making an exception (e.g. *a saving clause in an agreement*): making up for bad qualities (e.g. *She has the saving grace—or good quality—of honesty*).—*n.* (in *pl.*) money put aside for the future: a lessening (of expense, etc.).

savings bank, a bank which receives small deposits and gives interest.

to save up, gradually to put aside money for future use.

See also **safe, salvation.**

[Fr. *sauver*—L. *salvus*, safe.]

savoir faire, *sav'wär-fär',* ability to act in any social situation with self-confidence, skill and tact. [Fr.]

savour, *sā'vȯr, n.* taste: characteristic flavour or quality: quality that pleases or interests (e.g. *a book, an occupation, without savour*).—*v.i.* to have the taste, smell, or quality (of; e.g. *This action savours of rebellion*).—*v.t.* to recognise and appreciate the special quality of (e.g. *to savour delicious food, a witty book*): to taste, or to have experience of.

sā'voury, *adj.* having an attractive taste or smell (salt or sharp, not sweet): (of news, etc.) appealing to one's appetite for scandal, etc.—*n.* a small hot tasty course or dish, esp. at the end of a formal dinner:—*pl.* **-ies.**

sa'vouriness, *n.*

[Fr. *saveur*—L. *sapĕre*, to taste.]

savoy, *sȧ-voi', n.* type of winter cabbage.

[Fr. *Savoie*.]

saw[1]**.** See **see.**

saw[2]**,** *sö, n.* an instrument for cutting, having a blade, band, or disk of thin steel with a toothed edge.—*v.t.* to cut with a saw.—*v.i.* to use a saw:—*pa.t.* **sawed;** *pa.p.* **sawed** or **sawn.**

saw'dust, *n.* dust or small pieces of wood, etc., made in sawing.

saw'horse, *n.* a support for wood while it is being sawn.

saw'mill, *n.* a mill for sawing timber.

saw'yer, *n.* one whose job is to saw.

[O.E. *saga*; conn. with Ger. *säge*.]

saw[3]**,** *sö, n.* an old wise saying, proverb.

[O.E. *sagu*; conn. with **say** and **saga.**]

saxifrage, *sak'si-frij, n.* type of rock plant.

[L. *saxum*, stone, *frangĕre*, to break.]

Saxon, *sak'sȯn, n.* one of a North German people who conquered part of Britain in the 5th and 6th centuries.

[L. *Saxŏnes* (pl.): conn. Ger. *Sachse*.]

saxophone, *sak'sȯ-fōn, n.* a wind instrument with a curved, usu. metal, tube and finger keys.

[*Sax*, the inventor, Gk. *phōnē*, voice.]

say, *sā, v.t.* to utter (a word, etc.; e.g. *to say Yes*): to express, state, in words: to assert, declare (e.g. *I say it is so*): to repeat (prayers): to tell (e.g. *to say one's mind*):—*pr.p.* **say'ing;** *pa.t., pa.p.* **said** (*sed*); *pr.t.* 3rd person sing. **says** (*sez*).—*n.* what one wants to say (*to say one's say*): right to speak, or influence on what is decided (e.g. *I have no say in the matter*):

opportunity of speaking (*to have one's say*).
say'ing, *n.* something often said, esp. a proverb, etc.
I say! *interj.* expressing surprise or protest, or trying to attract someone's attention.
that is to say, in other words.
to have the say, to be the one in authority.
[O.E. *secgan*; Old Norse *segja.*]

scab, *skab, n.* a crust formed over a sore: any of several diseases of animals, or of plants (e.g. *potato scab*): a scoundrel: a blackleg.
scabbed, scabb'y, *adjs.*
scabb'iness, *n.*
[From Old Norse; conn. with **scabies.**]

scabbard, *skab'ȧrd, n.* a sheath, case in which the blade of a sword is kept.
[M.E. *scauberk*—Germanic.]

scabby, etc. See **scab.**

scabies, *skā'bi-ēz, n.* a skin disease, also called '*the itch*', caused by a mite.
[L. *scabĕre*, to scratch.]

scabious, *skā'bi-ůs, n.* a plant with heads of often blue flowers.
[From **scabies**; some were thought to cure this.]

scaffold, *skaf'ȯld, -ōld, n.* a system of platforms for men at work on a building: a raised platform, esp. for use when putting a criminal, etc., to death.
scaff'olding, *n.* scaffold(s) for workmen: materials for scaffolds: framework.
[O.Fr. *escadafault* (Fr. *échafaud*).]

scalable, scalar. See **scale.**

scald, *sköld, v.t.* to burn with hot liquid: to cook or heat just short of boiling.—Also *n.*
[O.Fr. *escalder*—L. *ex, calidus*, hot.]

scale[1], *skāl, n.* something with marks made at regular distances, for use as a measure (e.g. *the scale on a thermometer*): a system of numbers: a system of increasing values (e.g. *a wage scale*): (*music*) group of notes going up or down in order of pitch with a regular (not necessarily equal) space between them: dimensions of one thing as compared with another (e.g. of a map as compared with the actual country it shows; e.g. *a map drawn to a scale of one inch to the mile*): size of an activity, of production, etc. (e.g. *manufacture on a large*, or *small, scale*).—*v.t.* to climb up (e.g. a mountain): to change something (up, down) according to a fixed scale.
scā'lable, *adj.* that can be climbed.
sca'lar, *adj.* arranged like a ladder or measuring scale: (*mathematics*; of a quantity) having size but not direction.
[L. *scāla*, ladder—same root as **scan.**]

scale[2], *skāl, n.* a small thin plate or flake on the skin of a fish, snake, plant leaf bud, etc.—*v.t.* to clear of scales: to remove in thin layers.—*v.i.* to come (off) in flakes.
sca'ly, *adj.*:—*comp.* **sca'lier**; *superl.* **sca'liest.**
sca'liness, *n.*
[O.Fr. *escale*, husk; from Germanic.]

scale[3], *skāl, n.* the dish of a balance: (usu. in *pl.*) a weighing machine.—*v.t.* to show (a weight) in the scales.
[Old Norse *skāl*, bowl; conn. **shell.**]

scalene, *skā'lēn, -lēn', adj.* (of a triangle) having three unequal sides.
[Gk. *skalēnos*, uneven.]

scaliness, etc. See **scale** (2).

scallop, *skol'ȯp, skal', n.* a type of shellfish, with hinged, more or less fan-shaped, shells: a wave in the edge of anything.—*v.t.* to cut into curves: to cook (esp. oysters) by baking, e.g. in a scallop shell, with breadcrumbs.
[O.Fr. *escalope.*]

scallywag, *skal'i-wag, n.* a good-for-nothing, a scamp. [Origin uncertain.]

scalp, *skalp, n.* the outer covering of the skull: the skin and hair of the top of the head once cut off a defeated enemy by N. American Indians.—*v.t.* to cut the scalp from.
[Conn. with Old Norse *skālpr*, sheath.]

scalpel, *skal'pėl, n.* small knife with thin blade used in surgical operations.
[L. *scalprum*, knife; conn. **sculpture.**]

scaly. See **scale** (2).

scamp[1], *skamp, n.* a rascal: a lively tricky fellow.
scam'pish, *adj.*
scam'per, *v.i.* to run away in haste: to run about gaily.—*n.* a hurried flight: a romp.
[Old *scamp*, to go about idly.]

scamp[2], *skamp, v.t.* to do (work) carelessly and hastily.
[Perh. conn. with **skimp** or **scant.**]

scampi, *skam'pē, n.* Norway lobsters (small, slender lobsters of European seas) when considered as food.
[It., *pl.* of *scampo.*]

scan, *skan, v.t.* to examine the metre or rhythm of (a line of verse; in English verse, to find or mark accented syllables, etc.): to examine carefully: (*coll.*) to cast an eye quickly over (e.g. *to scan a newspaper*): (*television*, etc.) to pass a beam of light, electrons, radar, etc., over every part of.—*v.i.* (of English verse) to have accented syllables in correct places:—*pr.p.* **scann'ing**; *pa.p.* **scanned.**
scann'er, *n.* **scann'ing,** *n.*
scan'sion, *n.* scanning of verse.
[L. *scandĕre, scansum*, to climb.]

scandal, *skan'd(ȧ)l, n.* a disgraceful action, circumstance, or person, arousing the strong disapproval of people in general: the disapproval aroused: damage to reputation, disgrace: gossip about people's misdeeds, real or invented (e.g. *ladies talking scandal about their neighbours*).
scan'dalise, *v.t.* to shock, horrify: to slander.—*v.i.* to talk scandal.

scan'dalous, *adj.* shocking, disgraceful: slanderous (e.g. *C spread scandalous stories about B*): loving scandal.
[Gk. *skandalon,* a cause of stumbling.]

Scandinavian, *skan-di-nā'vi-ȧn, adj.* of *Scandinavia* (Norway, Sweden, Denmark, and Iceland).
[L. *Scandināvia,* earlier *Scandia.*]

scanning, scansion, etc. See **scan.**

scant, *skant, adj.* barely sufficient, cut down or reduced much (e.g. *a scant allowance, scant attention, scant justice*).—*v.t.* to give too little of.
scant'ly, *adv.* **scant'ness,** *n.*
scan'ty, *adj.* little or not enough in amount (e.g. *scanty clothing, vegetation*): —*comp.* **scan'tier**; *superl.* **scan'tiest.**
scan'tily, *adv.* **scan'tiness,** *n.*
scant of, having too small a supply of.
[Old Norse *skamt—skammr,* short.]

scapegoat, *skāp'gōt, n.* one who bears the blame for wrongdoing of others.
[**escape, goat**; once a year the Jewish high priest laid the sins of the people on a goat and allowed it to escape into the wilderness.]

scapegrace, *skāp'grās, n.* a good-for-nothing, a scamp.
[One who **escapes** the **grace** of God.]

scapula, *skap'ū-lȧ, n.* the shoulder-blade.
scap'ular, *adj.*
[L. *scapulae,* the shoulder-blades.]

scar[1], *skär, n.* the mark left by a wound or sore: any mark or blemish.—*v.t.* to mark with a scar:—*pr.p.* **scarr'ing,** *pa.p.* **scarred.**
[Gk. *escharā,* scar (e.g. from burn), hearth.]

scar[2], *skär, n.* a bare rocky place on the side of a hill: a steep rock.
[From Old Norse.]

scarab, *skar'ȧb, n.* a type of beetle: a gem cut in the form of a beetle.
[L. *scarabaeus*; conn. with Gk. *kārabos.*]

scarce, *skārs, adj.* not plentiful, not enough to meet the demand: rare, seldom found.
scarce'ly, *adv.* barely, not quite: probably, or definitely, not (e.g. *You could scarcely expect her to cross the swollen stream*).
scarce'ness, scar'city (*pl.* **-ies**), *ns.*
to make oneself scarce, go, run away.
[Through O.Fr.—L. *excerpĕre,* pick out.]

scare, *skār, v.t.* to startle, frighten: to drive (away, off) by frightening.—*n.* a sudden, usu. unnecessary, fright or alarm.
scare'crow, *n.* a figure set up to scare away birds: a cause of a needless fear: a person in rags, or very thin or odd-looking.
scare'monger, *n.* one who spreads alarming rumours.
[Old Norse *skirra,* to avoid.]

scarf[1], *skärf, n.* piece of material worn loosely on the shoulders or round neck or head.—*pl.* **scarves, scarfs.**
[Prob. conn. Fr. *écharpe,* sash.]

scarf[2], *skärf, v.t.* to join (two pieces of timber) by a **scarf joint,** part of each piece being cut away so that one fits over the other. [Perh. Scand.]

scarify, *skar'i-fī, v.t.* to make slight cuts or scratches in (e.g. the skin): to pain by criticising very severely:—*pr.p.* **scar'ifying**; *pa.p.* **scar'ified.**
scarificā'tion, *n.*
[Gk. *skarīphasthai,* scratch an outline.]

scarlatina, *skär-lȧ-tē'nȧ, n.* scarlet fever, esp. when mild.

scarlet, *skär'lit, n.* a bright red colour: red cloth or clothes.—Also *adj.*
scarlet fever, an infectious fever usu. with sore throat and rash.
[Perh. Pers. *saqalāt,* scarlet cloth.]

scarp, *skärp, n.* a steep slope.
[It. *scarpa*; conn. **escarpment.**]

scarves. See **scarf** (1).

scathe, *skāTH, n.* damage, injury.—*v.t.* to injure.
scā'thing, *adj.* damaging: (of e.g. remarks, criticism) bitter, cruel.
scathe'less, *adj.* unharmed.
[Old Norse *skathi,* to harm.]

scatter, *skat'ėr, v.t.* to spread widely, send in all directions: to throw loosely about, sprinkle.—*v.i.* to go away in all directions. —*n.* a sprinkling, scattering.
scatt'ered, *adj.* thrown, sent, or placed widely here and there.
scatt'ering, *n.* act of spreading, or being spread, widely: a small number here and there.
scatt'erbrain, *n.* a forgetful, unreliable person: one unable to keep his attention fixed.
scatt'erbrained, *adj.* [Orig. uncertain.]

scavenger, *skav'in-jėr, n.* one who cleans the streets or picks up refuse.
scav'enge, *v.i.* to act as a scavenger: to search (for food, etc.).
[Orig. *scavager,* inspector of goods for sale, streets, etc.]

scenario, *si-nä'ri-ō, n.* an outline of a film, play, etc. scene by scene.
[It.; same L. root as **scene.**]

scene, *sēn, n.* (*orig.*) a stage (this explains such phrases as *to come on the scene,* to appear and take part in some action): the place where something, real or imaginary, happens: a particular area of activity (e.g. *There have been changes on the business scene*): stage scenery (also in *pl.*): a landscape, view: an embarrassing show of strong feeling, esp. of bad temper.
sce'nery, *n.* painted background of hangings, movable structures, etc.,used on a stage: the general appearance of a stretch of country.
scenic, *sē'nik, sen', adj.* having to do with scenery, real or theatrical (e.g. *The stage was small but the scenic effect was good*).
[L. *scēna*—Gk. *skēnē,* a tent, stage.]

scent, *sent, v.t.* to discover by the sense of smell: to have some suspicion of (e.g. I

scent a mystery here): to cause to smell pleasantly (e.g. *Hawthorn scents the air*).—*n.* a perfume: odour: the trail of smell by which an animal or person may be tracked.
scen′ted, *adj.* **scent′less,** *adj.*
on the scent, on the trail that will lead to the hunted animal or to the information wanted.
off the scent, on the wrong track.
[Fr. *sentir*—L. *sentire*, to feel.]

sceptic, *skep′tik, n.* one who questions commonly held opinions, or doubts common beliefs: one who is always ready to doubt what he is told, etc.
scep′tical, *adj.* unwilling to believe without absolute evidence: showing, or feeling, doubt (e.g. *a sceptical glance*; *I am sceptical about his ability to keep his promise*).
scep′tically, *adv.* **scep′ticalness,** *n.*
scep′ticism, (*-ti-sizm*), *n.* an attitude of doubt.
[L. *scepticus*—Gk. *skeptikos*, thoughtful.]

sceptre, *sep′tėr, n.* a rod or staff carried on certain formal occasions by monarchs: royal power.
[Gk. *skēptron*, stick, sceptre.]

schedule, *shed′ūl*, (*U.S.*) *sked′ūl, n.* a list of articles: statement of details (added to document): a form for filling in information: (*U.S.*) a timetable, programme.—*v.t.* to form into a schedule or list: (*U.S.*) to plan, arrange (e.g. *to schedule a meeting*).
sched′uled, *adj.* planned, arranged (e.g. *scheduled for*, or *to happen at*, *7 p.m.*).
[L. *scheda*, strip of papyrus.]

scheme, *skēm, n.* a diagram: a system: an arrangement (e.g. *a colour scheme*): a plan for building operations of several kinds, or the buildings, etc., put up (e.g. *a housing scheme*): a plan of action: a crafty or dishonest plan.—*v.i.* to plan craftily, lay schemes (for).—Also *v.t.*
schē′mer, *n.* **schē′ming,** *n.* and *adj.*
[Gk. *schēma*, form.]

scherzo, *skėrt′sō, n.* (*music*) a lively movement e.g. in a sonata.
[It.; conn. Ger. *scherz*, jest.]

schism, *sizm, n.* breaking away, division: a group of persons breaking away from a main group (e.g. in a church).
[Gk. *schisma*, a cleft—*schizein*, to split.]

schist, *shist, n.* a type of rock easily split into layers.
[Fr. *schiste*—same Gk. root as **schism.**]

schizophrenia, *skit-sō-frē′ni-ȧ, skid-zō-, n.* a form of insanity: split personality.
[Gk. *schizein*, to split, *phrēn*, mind.]

scholar, *skol′ȧr, n.* a pupil, student: the holder of a scholarship: a person of great learning.
schol′arly, *adj.* having, showing, the knowledge and love of accuracy of a truly learned person.
schol′arliness, *n.*
schol′arship, *n.* scholarliness: learning: money awarded to a good student to enable him to go on with further studies.
scholastic, *skol-as′tik, adj.* having to do with schools or with education.
school, *skōōl, n.* a place for teaching, esp. children: the pupils of a school: a series of meetings for instruction (e.g. *a music summer school*): a group of people with the same opinions, ideas, or methods of working (*a philosopher of the school of Plato*; *an artist of the school of Raphael*): students and instructors in a branch of learning, in e.g. a university (e.g. *the mathematical school at Cambridge*).—*v.t.* to send to, or educate in, a school: to train by practice (e.g. *We must school ourselves in patience*, or *to be patient*).
school′ing, *n.* instruction in school: training.
school′book, *n.* a book for use in school.
school′boy, *n.* **school′girl,** *n.*
school′child, *n.*:—*pl.* **school′children.**
school′fellow, *n.* one taught at the same school, esp. in the same class.
school′marm, *n.* a schoolmistress, esp. one who is prim and too particular about trifles.
school′master, *n.* a master or teacher in a school:—*fem.* **school′mistress.**
school′mate, a schoolfellow, esp. a friend.
[O.E. *scōlere*—*scōl*, school; through L.—Gk. *scholē*, leisure, discussion, school.]

school[1]. See **scholar.**

school[2], *skōōl, n.* a number of fish, whales, or other water animals of one kind, swimming about together.
[Du. *school*; same root as **shoal** (1).]

schooner, *skōōn′ėr, n.* a swift-sailing ship, with two or more masts.
[Name given in New England (U.S.A.).]

schottische, *sho-tēsh′, shot′ish, n.* a dance or dance tune like the polka.
[Ger., (the) Scottish (dance).]

sciatic, *sī-at′ik, adj.* in region of hip.
sciat′ica, *n.* a severe pain in the upper part of the leg.
[Late L. *sciaticus*—Gk. *ischion*, hip.]

science, *sī′ėns, n.* knowledge gained by observation and experiment, carefully arranged so that it can be studied as a whole: a branch of such knowledge (e.g. the facts learned about heat, or light, electricity, chemistry, biology, etc.): trained skill (e.g. in games).
scientif′ic, *adj.* having to do with science: careful, thorough (e.g. *They made a scientific search for the document*).
scientif′ically, *adv.*
sci′entist, *n.* one who studies science.
science fiction, stories dealing with future times on earth or in space.
[L. *scientia*, knowledge—*scire*, to know.]

scimitar, *sim′i-tȧr, n.* a short, single-edged, curved sword, used by Turks.
[Pers. *shamsir.*]

scintillate, *sin'ti-lāt, v.i.* to sparkle, twinkle (also used of e.g. eyes, wit, a person).
scintillā'tion, *n.*
[L. *scintilla*, a spark.]

scion, *sī'ȯn, n.* a cutting or twig for grafting on another plant: a young member of a family (esp. noble or wealthy): a descendant.
[O.Fr. *sion, cion*; origin unknown.]

scissors, *siz'ȯrz, n.pl.* a cutting instrument with two blades: shears.
[O.Fr. *cisoires*—L. *caedĕre, caesum*, cut.]

sclerosis, *sklėr-ō'sis, n.* hardening, e.g. of arteries or nerve tissue.
[Gk. *sklēros*, hard.]

scoff, *skof, v.i.* to mock, jeer (at): to express scorn.—*n.* an expression of scorn: an object of scorn.
[Conn. old Dan. word *scoff*, jest.]

scold, *skōld, n.* a rude, bad-tempered person, esp. a woman.—*v.t.* to find fault with (someone) angrily or sternly.—Also *v.i.*
scold'ing, *n*, and *adj.*
[Old Norse *skāld*, reciter of poems.]

scone, *skon*, in England often *skōn, n.* (*Scot.*) a flat plain cake baked on a girdle (griddle) or in an oven.
[Perh. old Du. *schoon* (*brot*), fine (bread).]

scoop, *skōōp, n.* a ladle or deep shovel in which water or loose material can be taken up and carried: an unexpected gain, large haul of e.g. money: a piece of news which one newspaper prints before others have heard about it.—*v.t.* to lift (up) with a scoop: to dig (out, a hole): to get (news) before a rival.
[M.E. *scope*; from Du.]

scoot, *skōōt, v.i.* (*coll.*) to move or go swiftly, dart.
scoot'er, *n.* a two-wheeled vehicle driven by the foot or by an engine.
[Prob. conn. with **shoot.**]

scope, *skōp, n.* area (of e.g. a subject) covered, included (e.g. *The enquiry is concerned with large businesses; small firms are outside its scope*): room or opportunity (e.g. *His job, instructions, gave no scope for originality*).
[Gk. *skopeein*, to look at.]

scorch, *skörch, v.t.* to burn slightly, singe: to dry up with heat: to subject (e.g. a person) to burning criticism.—*v.i.* to be burned on the surface: to be dried up: to drive at very high speed.—Also *n.*
scorch'ing, *adj.* very hot: (of criticism) bitterly scornful.
scorched earth, complete destruction in a region to hinder the advance of an enemy. [Prob. Scandinavian.]

score, *skōr, skör, n.* a notch: a line: an arrangement of music on a number of staves (see this word): the total of points gained in a game or an examination: a point gained: amount owed: a set of twenty: (in *pl.*) a great many: reason (e.g. *He declined on the score of lack of practice*): account, matter (e.g. *Don't worry on that score*).—*v.t.* to mark with notches or lines: to gain or record (points) in a game.—*v.i.* to gain a point, or a success.
scor'er, *n.*
to settle old scores, to have revenge for an old wrong or grudge.
[From Scandinavian.]

scorn, *skörn, n.* extreme disapproval, contempt, angry disgust: the object of contempt.—*v.t.* to look down on, despise: to refuse, esp. proudly (e.g. *He scorns to ask for help*).
scorn'ful, *adj.* **scorn'fully,** *adv.*
[O.Fr. *escarn*, mockery.]

scorpion, *skör'pi-ȯn, n.* an animal of the same class as spiders, with a tail with a sting.
[L. *scorpio*—Gk. *skorpios*.]

scot, *skot, n.* a payment: a tax.
scot'-free, *adj.* without payment or loss: unhurt, unpunished. [From Scand.]

Scot, *skot, n.* a native of Scotland: one of a people who came to Scotland from Ireland about the 5th century.
Scotch, *skoch, adj.* form of **Scottish,** correctly applied to certain products (e.g. *Scotch whisky, Scotch terrier*).—*n.* Scotch whisky.
Scotch mist, *n.* a fine rain.
Scotch tape, a transparent strip with one sticky side.
Scots, *skots, adj.* Scottish (used of law, language).—*n.* a form of English spoken, esp. long ago, in the Lowlands of Scotland—as spoken in later times, called also **Broad Scots.**
Scott'icism, *n.* a Scottish word, phrase, or idiom.
Scott'ish, *adj.* of Scotland, its people, or its form of English.
Scots pine, the only native British pine.
[O.E. *Scottas* (n.pl.), M.E. *Scottis* (adj.).]

scotch, *skoch, v.t.* to cut or wound slightly: to stamp out (e.g. a rumour).
[Origin unknown.]

Scotch. See **Scot.**

scot-free. See **scot.**

Scotland Yard, *skot'lȧnd yärd, n.* the Criminal Investigation Department of the London Metropolitan Police.
[Name of street where once located.]

Scottish. See **Scot.**

scoundrel, *skown'drėl, n.* a low, mean, unscrupulous person, utter rascal.
scoun'drelly, *adj.* [Origin unknown.]

scour[1], *skowr, v.t.* to clean by hard rubbing, scrub: to clear out (e.g. a pipe) by a current of water.—Also *n.*
[L. *ex, cūrāre*, to take care of.]

scour[2], *skowr, v.i.* to rush along: to move (about, over) quickly, esp. in search of something.—*v.t.* to pass over or along in search (e.g. *They scoured the neighbourhood for the child*).
[Perh. Old Norse *skūr*, storm.]

scourge, *skûrj, n.* a whip made of leather

thongs: a means of punishment, or conqueror, etc. who punishes: a cause of calamity, esp. widespread.—*v.t.* to whip: to punish severely.
[O.Fr. *escorge*—L. *excoriāre*, to flog.]

scout[1], *scowt*, *n.* one sent out to bring in information, observe the enemy, etc.: a (Boy) Scout: a road patrolman to help motorists.—*v.i.* to act as a scout.
[O.Fr. *escoute*—L. *auscultāre*, to listen.]

scout[2], *skowt*, *v.t.* to reject (idea, suggestion) with scorn.
[Conn. with Old Norse *skūta*, a taunt.]

scowl, *skowl*, *v.i.* to wrinkle the brow in displeasure or anger: (of e.g. mountain) to look gloomy or threatening.—Also *n.*
[Conn. with Dan. *skule*, to scowl.]

scrabble, *skrab'l*, *v.t.* and *v.i.* to scratch, scrape: to scribble, scrawl.—*n.* (*cap.*) a word-building game.
[Du. *schrabben*, to scratch.]

scrag, *skrag*, *n.* anything thin, or lean, and rough: the bony part of the neck.
scragg'y, *adj.* lean, gaunt: rugged.
scragg'iness, *n.*
[Conn. Du. *kraag*, Ger. *kragen*, neck.]

scramble, *skram'bl*, *v.i.* to climb (up, along) on hands and knees or with difficulty: to dash or struggle (for something one wants).—*v.t.* to toss or mix together: to jumble up (a message) so that it has to be decoded before it can be understood, or the sound of (a telephone conversation) so that it becomes clear only in a special receiver.—*n.* act of scrambling: a struggle for what can be had: motor cycle trial over rough country.
scram'bler, *n.* **scram'bling,** *n.*
scrambled eggs, eggs beaten up with milk, butter, etc., heated until thick.
[Origin uncertain.]

scrap[1], *skrap*, *n.* a small piece, fragment (e.g. *a scrap of paper*): a piece left over: a picture to be kept in a scrapbook: parts or articles no longer required for orig. purpose (e.g. *metal scrap*).—*v.t.* to throw away as useless: abandon (e.g. plan).—*pr.p.* **scrapp'ing**; *pa.p.* **scrapped.**
scrapp'y, *adj.* in small pieces, portions (e.g. *a scrappy meal*): not connected so as to make a satisfactory whole (e.g. *a scrappy essay*):—*comp.* **scrapp'ier**; *superl.* **scrapp'iest.**
scrapp'ily, *adv.* **scrapp'iness,** *n.*
scrap'book, *n.* a blank book in which to stick pictures, etc.
scrap heap, a heap of e.g. old metal.
scrap iron, metal, iron, metal, for remelting and using again.
[Old Norse *skrap*, scraps.]

scrap[2], *skrap*, *n.* (*slang*) a fight.—Also *v.i.*:—*pr.p.* **scrapp'ing**; *pa.p.* **scrapped.**
[Origin unknown.]

scrape, *skrāp*, *v.t.* to rub, and (usu.) mark, with something sharp: to grate against with harsh noise: (with *off*) to remove by drawing a sharp edge over (e.g. *to scrape off skin*): to gain (e.g. a living), collect (e.g. money; often with *up*, *together*), with great effort or in small quantities.—Also *v.i.*—*n.* an act of scraping: a mark, or sound, made by scraping: a difficulty that may lead to disgrace or punishment.
scrap'er, *n.* **scrap'ing,** *n.* and *adj.*
to scrape through, only just to avoid failure.
[O.E. *scrapian*, or Old Norse *skrapa*.]

scrapping, etc. See **scrap** (1) or (2).

scratch, *skrach*, *v.t.* to draw a sharp point over the surface of: to mark by so doing: to tear or dig with nails or claws (e.g. *to scratch a hole*): to rub with the nails to relieve itching: to write in a hurry: to rub (out): to withdraw (e.g. a horse) from a race or competition.—Also *v.i.*—*n.* a mark, or sound, made by scratching: a slight wound.—*adj.* made up of people hurriedly got together (e.g. *a scratch team*): receiving no handicap.
scratch'y, *adj.* likely to scratch: harsh or grating: uneven in quality.
scratch'ily, *adv.* **scratch'iness,** *n.*
to start from scratch, to start from the line marked, or at the time chosen, for competitors who are given no handicap: to start from nothing (e.g. *He now has a large business but he started from scratch*).
to come up to scratch, (formerly, of a boxer) to come up to the starting line drawn across the ring: to be of satisfactory quality, or in satisfactory condition. [Blend of two M.E. verbs.]

scrawl, *skröl*, *v.t.*, *v.i.* to mark or write hastily or untidily.—*n.* untidy, hasty, or bad writing. [Origin uncertain.]

scrawny, *skrö'ni*, *adj.* thin and tough-looking.
scraw'niness, *n.*
[Conn. with Norw. *skran*, lean.]

scream, *skrēm*, *v.i.*, *v.t.* to cry out in a loud shrill voice, as in fear, pain, mirth.—*v.i.* (of colours) to have a startling unpleasant effect together.—Also *n.*
[Early M.E. *scræmen*.]

scree, *skrē*, *n.* loose stones lying on a rocky slope.
[Old Norse *skritha*, to slide.]

screech, *skrēch*, *v.i.* to utter a harsh, or shrill, cry.—Also *v.t.* and *n.*
screech owl, an owl with harsh cry, esp. the barn owl.
[M.E. *scrichen*.]

screed, *skrēd*, *n.* a piece torn off: a long tiresome speech, letter, etc.
[O.E. *scrēade*.]

screen, *skrēn*, *n.* something that shuts off from view, or that protects from danger, heat, wind, etc.: a decorated partition in a church: the sheet or surface on which motion pictures are shown: the motion picture business: the surface on which a television picture appears.—*v.t.* to shelter, or hide: to make a motion

picture of: to show on a screen: to put through a coarse sieve: to test (people) to find out which kind of work they can best do: to examine closely the record, esp. political, of (a person) to find out whether it is safe to employ him where loyalty matters.
[Conn. O.Fr. *escren* and Ger. *schirm.*]

screw, *skrōō, n.* a kind of nail with slotted head and a winding groove or ridge (called the thread) on its surface: a turn or twist e.g. of a screw: spin given to a ball: a **screw-propeller** (with spiral blades, used in steamships and aircraft): a twisted cone of paper: (*coll.*) wages, salary: (*coll.*) a worn-out horse: a stingy fellow.—*v.t.* to fasten, tighten, force, or force (out) by a screw or a screwing motion: to turn (round, e.g. one's head): to pucker (up, e.g. one's face).
screw′-driv′er, *n.* an instrument for putting in, or taking out, screws.
a screw loose, something not right, e.g. in a person's character or mind.
to screw up courage, etc. to manage to make oneself brave, etc., enough (to do something).
[Earlier *scrue*—O.Fr. *escroue.*]

scribble, *skrib′l, v.t.* to write badly or carelessly: to fill with worthless writing. —Also *v.i.*—*n.* careless writing: meaningless marks: a hastily written letter, etc. [Formed from **scribe.**]

scribe, *skrīb, n.* a public or official writer: a writer: (*history*) a teacher of the law among the Jews.
[L. *scrība*—*scrībĕre, scriptum,* write.]

scrimmage, *skrim′ij,* **scrummage,** *skrum′ij, n.* a tussle, rough struggle: (*rugby*) see **scrum.**—*v.i.* to take part in a scrimmage.
[Prob. from **skirmish.**]

scrimp, *skrimp, v.i.* to be sparing or stingy with money (e.g. *She scrimps and saves for her sons' education*).—*v.t.* to keep to a very small amount (e.g. *He scrimps his wife for money*; *to scrimp food*).
scrim′py, *adj.* too small or little:—*comp.* **scrim′pier**; *superl.* **scrim′piest.**
scrim′pily, *adv.* **scrim′piness,** *n.*
[O.E. *scrimman,* to shrink.]

scrip[1], *skrip, n.* a writing: a preliminary certificate for shares allotted: share certificate.
scrip issue, shares given to shareholders without payment as a bonus.
[**script** and perh. **scrap.**]

scrip[2], *skrip, n.* small bag or pouch.
[Conn. with Old Norse *skreppa,* a bag.]

script, *skript, n.* a manuscript: the text of a talk, play, etc.: handwriting like print, or print like handwriting.
[Same root as **scribe.**]

scripture, *skrip′chŭr, n.* sacred writings of a religion, esp. (**Scripture, -s**) the Bible.
scrip′tural, *adj.*
[Same root as **script, scribe.**]

scrivener, *skriv′nĕr, n.* a scribe: one who draws up contracts.
[O.Fr. *escrivain*—L. root as **scribe.**]

scroll, *skrōl, n.* a roll of paper: a schedule or list: an ornament shaped like a partly opened scroll.
[Earlier *scrowl(e)*—O.Fr. *escro(u)e.*]

scrub[1], *skrub, v.t.* and *v.i.* to rub hard in order to clean: to cancel, call off (e.g. an arrangement):—*pr.p.* **scrubb′ing,** *pa.p.* **scrubbed.**—Also *n.*
[Perh. Old Du. *schrubben.*]

scrub[2], *skrub, n.* a stunted tree or bush: (country covered with) low trees and bushes: an undersized animal: an unimportant person.
scrubb′y, *adj.* stunted: covered with scrub: mean, shabby.
scrubb′iness, *n.*
[A form of **shrub.**]

scruff, *skruf, n.* the back of the neck.
[Perh. Old Norse *skopt, scoft,* the hair.]

scrum, *skrum, n.* a scrimmage: (*rugby*) a struggle for the ball by the rival forwards bunched tightly round it.
[For **scrummage**; see **scrimmage.**]

scruple, *skrōō′pl, n.* a small weight: a difficulty or hesitation over what is right or wrong which keeps one from action (e.g. *I have scruples,* or *no scruples, about accepting the money*).—*v.t.* to hesitate (to do something) because of a scruple.
scrup′ūlous, *adj.* having scruples, very upright in conduct: careful, exact in the smallest details (e.g. *scrupulous honesty, cleanliness*).
scrup′ulously, *adv.*
scrup′ulousness, scrupulos′ity, *ns.*
[L. *scrūpus,* a sharp stone, anxiety.]

scrutiny, *skrōō′ti-ni, n.* a close or careful examination: a searching look.
scru′tinise, *v.t.* to examine carefully.
[L. *scrūtāri,* to search even to the rags, examine thoroughly—*scrūta,* rags.]

scud, *skud, v.i.* to move or run swiftly: to run before a gale:—*pr.p.* **scudd′ing**; *pa.p.* **scudd′ed.**—*n.* act of moving quickly: cloud, shower, spray, driven by wind. [Orig. uncertain.]

scuffle, *skuf′l, v.i.* to struggle, fight, confusedly: to shuffle along.—*n.* a confused fight at close quarters.
[Conn. Swed. *skuffa,* shove, and **shuffle.**]

scull, *skul, n.* a short, light oar.—*v.t., v.i.* to move (a boat) with a pair of these, or with an oar worked at the stern of the boat.
scull′er, *n.* a small boat rowed by one man. [Orig. unknown.]

scullery, *skul′ĕr-i, n.* a room for rough kitchen work, e.g. cleaning utensils.
[O.Fr. *escuelerie*—*scutella,* tray.]

sculptor, *skulp′tŏr, n.* an artist in carving or modelling figures or designs in marble, clay, etc.:—*fem.* **sculp′tress.**
sculp′ture (*-chŭr*), *n.* the art of, or the work done by, a sculptor.—*v.t.* to carve:

to give the appearance of sculpture to. [L. *sculpĕre*, *sculptum*, to carve.]

scum, *skum*, *n.* unclean foam or skin on the surface of a liquid: anything worthless (e.g. *the scum of the earth*, people of very low character).
[Conn. Dan. *skum*, Ger. *schaum*, foam.]

scupper, *skup′ĕr*, *n.* hole in ship's side to drain the deck. [Orig. uncertain.]

scurf, *skûrf*, *n.* a crust of flaky scales.
scur′fy, *adj.* **scur′finess,** *n.*
[O.E. *scurf*, *sceorf*; from Scand.]

scurrilous, *skur′i-lŭs*, *adj.* (of a joke, etc.) coarse, indecent: abusive, very insulting (e.g. *a scurrilous attack on his rival*).
scurr′ilously, *adv.* **scurr′ilousness,** *n.*
scurril′ity, *n.* scurrilousness: an instance of this (*pl.* **-ities**).
[L. *scurra*, a buffoon.]

scurry, *skur′i*, *v.i.* to hurry along, scamper. —Also *n.*
[From **hurry-scurry**; see **hurry.**]

scurvy, *skûr′vi*, *adj.* mean, low-down (e.g. *a scurvy fellow, trick*).—*n.* a disease due to lack of fresh fruit and vegetables.
scur′vily, *adv.* **scur′viness,** *n.*
[**scurf.**]

scut, *skut*, *n.* short tail of hare, etc.
[Orig. unknown.]

scuttle[1], *skut′l*, *n.* (also **coal′-scuttle**) a box for holding coal.
[O.E. *scutel*—L. *scutella*, a tray.]

scuttle[2], *skut′l*, *v.i.* to hurry, or hurry away. —Also *n.* [Orig. uncertain.]

scuttle[3], *skut′l*, *n.* an opening with a lid in a ship's deck or side.—*v.t.* to make a hole in (a ship) in order to sink it.
[O.Fr. *escoutille*, a hatchway.]

scythe, *sīTH*, *n.* a large curved blade, on a handle, for cutting grass, etc.—*v.t.* to cut with a scythe.—Also *v.i.*
[O.E. *sīthe*; conn. Old Norse *sigthr*.]

sea, *sē*, *n.* the mass of salt water covering the greater part of the earth's surface: a great stretch of water (salt or fresh) less than an ocean: a swell or wave (e.g. *The ship was lost in a heavy sea*, or *heavy seas*): the tide: a quantity or number felt to be like the sea in extent, etc. (e.g. *a sea of faces, of sand, of passion*).
sea′ward, *adj.* towards the sea.—Also *adv.* (also **seawards**).
sea anemone, a small plant-like animal found on rocks on the seashore.
sea′board, *n.* seacoast.—Also *adj.*
sea breeze, a breeze blowing from the sea towards the land.
sea′coast, *n.* the land next to the sea.
sea dog, the common seal: the dogfish: an old sailor: a pirate.
sea′farer (*-fār-*), *n.* a traveller by sea, usu. a sailor.
sea′faring, *n.* travelling by sea, esp. if working as a sailor.—Also *adj.*
sea fight, a battle between ships.
sea′front, *n.* a promenade with its buildings facing the sea.
sea′going, *adj.* (of a ship) sailing on the ocean, not a coast or river vessel.
sea′gull, *n.* a gull (see this word).
sea horse, a type of small fish looking a little like a horse: a walrus.
sea kale, a cabbage-like plant.
sea legs, ability to walk on a ship's deck when it is rolling.
sea level, the level of the surface of the sea.
sea lion, *n.* a large seal found in the Pacific Ocean (it roars and the male has a mane).
sea′man, *n.* a sailor: one of a ship's crew other than an officer.
sea′manship, *n.* the art of handling ships at sea.
sea mew, a seagull.
sea′plane, *n.* an aeroplane that can land on or take off from the sea.
sea′port, *n.* a port on the seashore.
sea power, a nation with a strong navy: naval power, control of the sea.
sea rover, a pirate: pirate ship.
sea′scape, *n.* a picture of a scene at sea.
sea serpent, an imaginary sea monster.
sea′shell, *n.* empty shell of a sea creature.
sea′shore, *n.* the land close to the sea.
sea′sick, *adj.* ill because of the motion of a ship at sea.
sea′sickness, *n.*
sea trout, any of a number of trout living in the sea but spawning in rivers.
sea urchin, a small creature with a shell that bears spines.
sea wall, a wall to keep out the sea.
sea′weed, *n.* plant(s) growing in the sea.
sea′worthy, *adj.* suitably built and in sufficiently good condition to sail at sea.
sea′worthiness, *n.*
sea wrack, (coarse) seaweed, esp. if cast up on the shore.
all at sea, at a loss, bewildered.
at sea, away from land: lost, puzzled.
heavy sea, a sea in which the waves have great force.
to go to sea, to become a sailor.
to ship a sea, (of a ship, boat) to have a wave wash over the side.
[O.E. *sǣ*; conn. with Ger. *see*, Du. *zee*.]

seal[1], *sēl*, *n.* a piece of wax or other material bearing a design, attached to a document to show that it is genuine and legal (e.g. *Four of the copies of Magna Carta have the Great Seal of King John attached*): (in *pl.*) a mark or sign (of office): a stamp, object with a raised design, for marking wax, etc.: a piece of wax used to keep closed (e.g. a letter): (something that makes) a tight join or complete closure: an adhesive piece of paper with a design (e.g. *Christmas seals for parcels*).—*v.t.* to mark or fasten with a seal: to close completely (e.g. *He must seal the windows to keep all air out*): to decide, make certain (e.g. *This mistake sealed his fate*):

to make legal and binding (e.g. *to seal a bargain*).

seal'ing-wax, *n.* wax for sealing letters.

to seal off, to cut off approach to, isolate completely.

to set one's seal on, to give recognition, one's approval, to.

to set one's seal to, to give one's authority or agreement to.

under seal of secrecy, silence, etc., under promise of keeping secret, etc.

[O.Fr. *seel*—L. *signum*, a mark.]

seal[2], *sēl, n.* any of various sea animals valuable for skin, oil.—*v.i.* to hunt seals.

seal'er, *n.* man or ship engaged in seal fishery.

seal'skin, *n.* the fur esp. of the 'fur seal': a garment made of this.

[O.E. *seolh*; conn. with Old Norse.]

seam, *sēm, n.* the line formed by the sewing together of two pieces of cloth, etc.: a line of meeting: a crack: a wrinkle: a thin layer in the earth of coal, etc.—*v.t.* to make a seam in: to sew.

sea'my (*sē'*), *adj.*:—*comp.* **sea'mier;** *superl.* **sea'miest**; used esp. in phrase **the seamy side,** the inner side of a garment: the more unpleasant or disreputable side (e.g. of life).

seamstress, *sem'strės, sēm', n.* one who sews, esp. for a living.

[O.E. *sēam*; conn. Ger. *saum.*]

séance, *sā'än^gs, n.* a meeting at which Spiritualists seek to obtain messages from the dead.

[Fr.—L. *sedēre*, to sit.]

sear, *sēr, v.t.* to burn the surface of: to dry up or wither: to injure or pain as if with fire.—Also *v.i.*—*adj.* usu. spelt **sere** (see this).

[O.E. *sēar*, dry, *sēarian*, to dry up.]

search, *sėrch, v.t.* to look over (a place) carefully in order to find something: to examine (a person, his pockets, etc.) closely.—Also *v.i.*—*n.* act of searching: careful examination: an attempt to find (with *for*).

search'ing, *adj.* (of eyes, look, etc.) very observant: (of e.g. enquiry, investigation) very thorough: (of a question) likely to get right at the truth: (of e.g. wind) piercing.

search'light, *n.* a strong beam of light for picking out objects by night.

search warrant, legal permission given to the police to search a house, etc., e.g. for stolen goods.

to search out, to find by searching.

[O.Fr. *cercher*—L. *circus*, a circle.]

seashore, seasick, etc. See **sea.**

season, *sē'z(ȯ)n, n.* one of the four divisions of the year: the usual, proper, or suitable, time (for anything): a short time.—*v.t.* to add, e.g. salt, in order to improve the flavour of (food): to make more enjoyable, add zest to: to dry (timber) until it is ready for use: to accustom (to; e.g. *troops seasoned to battle*; *seasoned troops*).

sea'sonable, *adj.* happening at the right time: (of weather) suited to the season.

sea'sonably, *adv.* **sea'sonableness,** *n.*

sea'sonal, *adj.* (of work, games) taking place at a particular season only.

sea'soning, *n.* something added to food to give it more taste.

season ticket, a ticket which can be used repeatedly during a certain period.

in season, fit and ready for eating, hunting, etc.: at a suitable time.

out of season, not in season.

[O.Fr. *seson*—L. *satiō, -ōnis*, a sowing.]

seat, *sēt, n.* a chair, bench, etc.: the part of a chair on which the body rests, or of the body or a garment on which one sits: the manner in which one sits (esp. on a horse): a place from, or in, which something is carried on or happens (e.g. *the seat of government, a seat of learning, the seat of the disease*): a (country) mansion: a right to sit and express one's opinion (e.g. *to have a seat in Parliament*).—*v.t.* to cause to sit down: to have seats for (a certain number): to put a seat on (a garment).

seat'ed, *adj.*

seat'ing, *n.* supply, or arrangement, of seats.

to take a seat, to sit down.

[O. Norse *sǣti*; conn. O.E. *sǣt*, ambush.]

secateurs, *sek'ȧ-tėrz, n.* pruning shears.

[Fr. *sécateur*—L. *secāre, -ātum*, to cut.]

secede, *si-sēd', v.i.* to withdraw, break away from, a group, society, etc.

secē'der, *n.* **secess'ion** (*-sesh'*), *n.*

[L. *sē-*, apart, *cēdĕre, cessum*, to go.]

seclude, *si-kloo͞d', v.i.* to shut off, keep away (from company of others, or from sight).

seclu'ded, *adj.*, private, remote (e.g. *a secluded spot*).

seclusion, *si-kloo͞'zh(ȯ)n, n.* privacy, solitude: a secluded place.

[L. *sē-*, apart, *claudĕre, clausum*, shut.]

second, *sek'ȯnd, adj.* next after, or following, the first in time, place, etc.: other, alternate (e.g. *every second day*): of the same kind as (e.g. *The admiral was not a second Nelson*).—*n.* a person, thing, that is second: a supporter: one who helps, backs, a person who is e.g. fighting: 60th part of a minute of time, or (in measuring angles) of a degree: (in *pl.*) articles not quite perfectly made.—*v.t.* to support, back up: to make the second speech in support of (a motion): (*si-kond'*) to transfer temporarily to a special job.

sec'ondary, *adj.* second in position or importance: (of education) between primary and university, etc.

sec'onder, *n.* one who seconds e.g. a motion.

sec'ondly, *adv.* in the second place (see **firstly**).

sec′ond-best′, *adj.* next to the best: not the best.
sec′ond-class′, *adj.* of class next to the highest: second-rate: (of a citizen) not having a citizen's full privileges.
sec′ond-hand′, *adj.* not new: that has been used by, or has come from, another: dealing in second-hand goods.
second lieutenant. See Appendices.
second nature, firmly fixed habit (e.g. *It was second nature to,* or *with, him to think carefully before spending*).
sec′ond-rate′, *adj.* inferior, not of the best quality.
sec′ond-rat′er, *n.*
at second-hand, through, from, another.
to come off second best, to get the worst in a contest, receive the least attention, etc.
[L. *secundus—sequī, secūtus,* follow.]

secret, *sē′krit, adj.* hidden from, not known to or told to, others: secretive (see below).—*n.* a fact, purpose, method, etc., that is not told, or not known: the explanation (e.g. *the secret of his success*): the best method of achieving (e.g. *the secret of good health*).
se′cretly, *adv.* **se′cretness,** *n.*
se′crecy, *n.* secretness: mystery (e.g. *an air of secrecy*).
secrete, *si-krēt′, v.t.* to hide in a secret place: (of a gland or similar organ of the body) to separate from the blood and store (e.g. *The liver secretes bile*).
secrē′tion, *n.* act of secreting: fluid secreted.
sē′cretive, *adj.* inclined to conceal one's activities, thoughts, etc.
Secret Service, government department dealing with spying, etc.
[L. *sē-*, apart, *cernĕre, crētum,* separate.]

secretary, *sek′ri-t(ȧ-)ri, n.* one employed to write letters and carry out business for another, or for a society:—*pl.* **-ies.**
secretā′rial, *adj.* having to do with a secretary, or with his, her, duties.
Secretary of State, a cabinet minister holding one of the more important positions.
[Late L. *sēcretārius*; root as **secret.**]

secrete, etc. See **secret.**

sect, *sekt, n.* a group of people united by holding certain views, esp. in religion—usu. not the views of the majority.
sectā′rian, *adj.* having to do with a sect: devoted, or loyal, to a sect: (esp. of views) narrow.—*n.* member of a sect.
[L. *secta—sequī, secūtus,* follow.]

section, *sek′sh(ȯ)n, n.* a part or division: a thin slice for examination under microscope: the view of the inside of anything when it is cut through from top to bottom: a small military unit: a district or a community having separate interests or characteristics.
sec′tional, *adj.* built up by sections: local, having to do with a part of the community (e.g. *It was to the general interest to bypass the town, but sectional interests were against it*).
sector, *sek′tȯr, n.* part of a circle bounded by an arc and two radii: a division of an army front: a section, e.g. of occupied territory.
[L. *secāre, sectum,* to cut.]

secular, *sek′ū-lȧr, adj.* having to do with the things of the world, not spiritual: not under church control (e.g. *secular courts*): not sacred (e.g. *secular music*): (of clergy) not belonging to a religious order.
sec′ularise, *v.t.* to turn (something) from sacred to common use.
sec′ularism, *n.* the belief that politics, morals, education, etc. should be independent of religion.
[L. *saeculum,* an age, generation.]

secure, *si-kūr′, adj.* free from danger, safe: firmly fixed, not likely to fall, etc.: without fears, confident (e.g. *secure in the knowledge that he had prepared most carefully*): sure, certain (e.g. a *secure victory*).—*v.t.* to make safe (from, against): to make firm: to fasten: to seize, take possession of: to obtain (e.g. *to secure a good job*): to ensure, make it certain (that such-and-such will happen): to guarantee (against).
secure′ly, *adv.* **secure′ness,** *n.*
secur′ity, *n.* secureness: a pledge, something given or promised as guarantee of payment, etc. (e.g. *He borrowed the money on the security of his house*): someone who gives a pledge on behalf of another: (in *pl.*) certificates or other evidence of ownership or of money lent:—*pl.* **secur′ities.**
security measures, measures to prevent spying or leakage of information.
security risk, a person considered unsafe for state service because likely to be disloyal.
[L. *sē-*, without, *cūra,* care.]

sedan, *si-dan′, n.* (also **sedan chair**) a covered chair for one carried on two poles. [Origin unknown.]

sedate, *si-dāt′, adj.* (of person, manner) calm, serious.
sedate′ly, *adv.* **sedate′ness,** *n.*
sed′ative, *adj.* tending to calm, soothe. —*n.* a soothing medicine.
sedā′tion, *n.* use of sedatives to calm a patient.
[L. *sēdāre, -ātum,* cause to sit, calm.]

sedentary, *sed′(ė)n-tȧ-ri, adj.* (of an occupation, e.g. in an office) requiring much sitting: taking little exercise.
sed′entariness, *n.*
[L. *sedēre, sessum,* to sit.]

sedge, *sej, n.* a coarse grass growing in swamps and rivers.
sedg′y, *adj.* overgrown with sedge.
sedg′iness, *n.*
[O.E. *secg.*]

sediment, *sed′i-mėnt, n.* what settles at the

bottom of a liquid, dregs: matter deposited on the land by water or ice.
sedimen'tary, *adj.*
sedimentary rocks, rocks formed from layers of sediment.
[Same root as **sedentary.**]

sedition, *si-dish'(ò)n, n.* stirring up of rebellion against the government: action or language intended to do this.
sedi'tious (*-shùs*), *adj.* (of speech, action, person) encouraging rebellion.
[L. *sēd-*, away, *īre*, to go.]

seduce, *si-dūs', v.t.* to lead astray from right conduct or belief, e.g. from loyalty, chastity, faith: to attract.
seduc'tion, *n.* act of tempting into wrongdoing: attraction.
seduc'tive, *adj.* attractive, tempting.
[L. *sē-*, apart, *dūcĕre*, to lead.]

sedulous, *sed'ū-lùs, adj.* working steadily and hard (e.g. *a sedulous student*; *sedulous in his efforts*): constant, persistent (e.g. *sedulous attempts*).
[Same root as **sedentary.**]

see[1], *sē, n.* the district over which a bishop or archbishop has authority.
[O.Fr. *se, sied*—L. root as **sedentary.**]

see[2], *sē, v.t.* to perceive, be aware of, by means of the eye: to have a picture of in the mind: to understand (e.g. *I see what you mean*): to find out (e.g. *I'll see what is happening*): to make sure (e.g. *See that he does what he promised*): to look at, visit (e.g. a play, sights): to accompany (e.g. *I'll see you home*): to meet: to consult (e.g. a lawyer): to experience (e.g. trouble).—*v.i.* to have power of vision: to look (into): to consider (e.g. *Let me see—what should we do next?*):—*pa.t.* **saw**; *pa.p.* **seen.**
seer, *sē'ėr, n.* one who sees: (*sēr*) one who sees into the future, a prophet.
see'ing, *n.* sight, vision.—*adj.* having sight, or power of noticing.—*conj.* (with *that*) since, because, considering.
to see fit, to think suitable (to do), decide (to do).
to see through, to take part in, or support, to the end: to see the reality behind (a pretence, etc.).
to see to it that, to make sure that (something is done).
See also **sight.**
[O.E. *sēon*; conn. Ger. *sehen*, Du. *zien.*]

seed, *sēd, n.* the part of a flowering plant from which a new plant may be grown: a seed-like part such as a grain of wheat: a quantity of seeds or of grains for sowing: children, descendants: the beginning from which anything grows (e.g. *a seed of doubt*; *seeds of rebellion*): a seeded player.—*v.i.* to produce seed.—*v.t.* to sow: to remove the seeds from: to arrange (the draw for a tournament) in such a way that the best players will not meet in the early rounds: to deal with (good competitors) in this way.
seed'y, *adj.* full of seeds: shabby, uncared-for: not very well:—*comp.* **seed'ier**; *superl.* **seed'iest.**
seed'iness, *n.* **seed'ily,** *adv.*
seed'ling, *n.* a young plant just sprung from a seed.
seed'bed, *n.* ground prepared for growing seeds.
seed'-coat, *n.* the outer covering of a seed.
seed'-vessel, *n.* the container of a plant seed or seeds, consisting of a single part (**seed'-case** or pod) or of two or more parts (**seed'box**).
[O.E. *sǣd*; conn. with *sāwan*, to sow.]

seeing. See **see** (2).

seek, *sēk, v.t.* to look for: to try to get (e.g. fame, advice): to try (to do): to go to (e.g. *to seek the shade*).—*v.i.* to search (for):—*pa.t.* and *pa.p.* **sought** (*sŏt*).
(much) sought after, (of person, thing) in great demand, much desired.
to seek after, to go in search of.
[O.E. *sēcan*; conn. with Ger. *suchen.*]

seem, *sēm, v.i.* to appear to be (e.g. *He seems kind*): to appear (to be, to do; e.g. *He seems to be reading*). Also used impersonally with *it*, meaning 'the evidence shows or suggests' (e.g. *It seems to me that you were very foolish*): it is said that (e.g. *It seems he had no money at all*).
seem'ing, *adj.* having the appearance, but usu. not the reality (e.g. *a seeming success*).
seem'ly, *adj.* fitting, suitable: (of behaviour) decent, proper: handsome: —*comp.* **seem'lier**; *superl.* **seem'liest.**
seem'liness, *n.*
[Prob.—Old Norse; conn. with **same.**]

seen. See **see** (2).

seep, *sēp, v.i.* to ooze gently, leak (away, through, out of, into).
seep'age, *n.* act of seeping: fluid that has seeped out.
[O.E. *sipian*, to soak.]

seer. See **see** (2).

seesaw, *sē'sö*, or *-sö', n.* a plank balanced so that its ends may move up and down: an up-and-down motion: a movement from success to failure and back again.—*v.i.*, *v.t.* to move, or make move, in a seesaw manner.
[Conn. with **saw** (2).]

seethe, *sēTH, v.t.* to boil: to soak.—*v.i.* to be very angry or excited:—*pa.p.* **seethed.**
sodd'en, *adj.* (old *pa.p.*) completely soaked: (of food) heavy, not well baked.
[O.E. *sēothan*; conn. with Ger. *sieden.*]

segment, *seg'mėnt, n.* a part cut off: part of a circle cut off by a straight line: any of the parts into which e.g. an insect body is naturally divided.—*v.t.*, *v.i.* to divide into segments.
[Same root as **section.**]

segregate, *seg'ri-gāt, v.t.* to separate from

others (e.g. *to segregate the infected sheep*): to keep in separate groups (e.g. *to segregate the sexes*; *to segregate one race of people from another*).
segregā'tion, *n.*
[L. *sē-*, apart, *grex, gregis*, a flock.]

seine, *sān, n.* large fishing net with floats on one edge, sinkers on the other.
[O.E. *segne*—Gk. *sagēnē*, a fishing net.]

seismograph, *sīs'mō-grâf, n.* an instrument that records earthquake shocks.
seis'mic, *adj.* having to do with an earthquake.
[Gk. *seismos*, an earthquake, *graphein*, to write.]

seize, *sēz, v.t.* to take suddenly, esp. by force: to snatch, grasp: to take prisoner: to overcome (e.g. *Faintness, fury, seized him*).—*v.i.* (of machinery) to become stuck, jam.
sei'zure, *n.* act of seizing: capture: grasp: sudden attack (e.g. of illness).
[O.Fr. *seisir*; from Germanic.]

seldom, *sel'dȯm, adv.* rarely, not often.
[O.E. *seldum, seldan*; conn. Ger. *selten.*]

select, *si-lekt', v.t.* to pick out from a number according to preference, choose. —*adj.* picked out: very good: (of a society) exclusive, admitting only certain people.
selec'tion, *n.* act of selecting: thing(s) chosen.
selec'tive, *adj.* using power of selection: (of a radio set) able to receive any station without interference from others.
selec'tiveness, selectiv'ity, *ns.*
select committee, a group from parliament chosen to report and advise on some matter.
[L. *sē-*, aside, *legĕre, lèctum*, choose.]

self, *self, n.* one's own person: one's personality, nature: personal advantage (e.g. *He always thinks first of self*):—*pl.* **selves** (*selvz*).
self'ish, *adj.* thinking of one's own pleasure or good, not caring much about others.
self'less, *adj.* utterly unselfish, thinking of others before oneself.
[O.E. *self*; conn. with Ger. *selbe.*]

self-, *self-,* (as part of word) (1) showing that the person or thing acting is acting upon himself or itself (e.g. *self-torture*): (2) showing that the thing is acting automatically, without outside aid (e.g. *a self-adjusting machine*; *self-closing doors*): (3) by oneself (e.g. *self-imposed, self-made* —see below): (4) in, within, etc., oneself or itself (e.g. *self-centred, self-contained*— see below).
Examples include the following:—
self'-advert'isement, *n.* calling public attention to oneself.
self'-assert'ing, self'-assert'ive, *adjs.* in the habit of putting forward oneself, one's claims, one's opinions.
self'-assur'ance, *n.* self-confidence.

self- (*continued*).
self'-cen'tred, *adj.* with one's thoughts centred in oneself and one's affairs.
self'-col'oured, *adj.* of one colour: of the natural colour.
self'-conceit', *n.* too high an opinion of one's abilities, etc., vanity.
self'-con'fidence, *n.* belief or trust in one's own powers.
self'-con'fident, *adj.*
self'-con'scious, *adj.* too conscious of oneself when in the presence of others, embarrassed by a sense of inferiority or awkwardness.
self'-con'sciousness, *n.*
self'-contained', *adj.* hiding one's feelings within oneself, reserved: complete in itself: (of a house) intended for use of one family and not sharing entry, etc., with others.
self'-control', *n.* control of oneself.
self'-defence', *n.* the act of defending one's own person, property, etc.
self'-denī'al, *n.* refusal to yield to natural desires: doing without something in order to give to others.
self'-determinā'tion, *n.* power of a community or country to decide its own form of government.
self'-ed'ucated, *adj.* educated by one's own efforts, without help in money from others: self-taught.
self'-effac'ing, *adj.* keeping oneself in the background, modest: not claiming rights or reward.
self'-efface'ment, *n.*
self'-esteem', *n.* self-respect: conceit.
self'-ev'ident, *adj.* clear enough to need no proof.
self'-explan'atory, *adj.* needing no explanation.
self'-express'ion, *n.* giving expression to one's personality, e.g. in art, poetry.
self'-gov'ernment, *n.* self-control: government by the people of the country without outside control.
self'-impor'tance, *n.* an absurdly high sense of one's own importance.
self'-impor'tant, *adj.*
self'-imposed', *adj.* (of e.g. a task) imposed on one, laid on one, by oneself.
self'-indul'gence, *n.* gratifying too much one's appetites or desires.
self'-indul'gent, *adj.*
self'-in'terest, *n.* selfish desire to work for one's private aims or advantage.
self'-made', *adj.* made by oneself owing wealth or important position to one's efforts, not to birth, education, etc.
self'-por'trait, *n.* an artist's (or other's) portrait (or description) of himself.
self'-possessed', *adj.* calm in manner.
self'-possess'ion, *n.* calmness, composure: ability to act calmly in an emergency.
self'-preservā'tion, *n.* (a natural ten-

self- (*continued*).
dency towards) trying to keep oneself safe from destruction or harm.
self′-protec′tion, *n.*
self′-propelled′, *adj.* moved by its own motor, etc., not pulled or pushed.
self′-relī′ance, *n.* healthy confidence in one's own abilities.
self′-relī′ant, *adj.*
self′-respect′, *n.* respect for oneself and concern for one's character and reputation.
self′-respec′ting, *adj.*
self′-righ′teous, *adj.* thinking highly of one's own goodness.
self′-righ′teousness, *n.*
self′-sac′rifice, *n.* the act of giving up one's own life, possessions or advantage, etc. in order to help others.
self′same, *adj.* the very same.
self′-seek′er, *n.* one who has only selfish aims.
self′-ser′vice, *adj.* (of a restaurant, shop) in which customers are not waited on but serve themselves.
self′-star′ter, *n.* a small electric motor or other device for starting an engine.
self′-suffi′cient, *adj.* needing no help from outside: not dependent on imports from other countries: having too great confidence in oneself.
self′-suffi′ciency, *n.*
self′-suppor′ting, *adj.* supporting oneself or itself (esp. providing enough for one's living).
self′-taught′, *adj.* taught by oneself without help from others.
self′-willed′, *adj.* determined to have one's own way.
self-raising flour, flour so prepared that it rises without addition of baking-powder or similar ingredient. **[self.]**

sell, *sel, v.t.* to give or hand over for money: to have, keep, for sale: to betray in return for e.g. money.—*v.i.* to make sales: to be sold (e.g. *It sells for tenpence a pound*):—*pa.t., pa.p.* **sold** (*sōld*).—*n.* a fraud or disappointment.
sell′er, *n.* **sell′ing,** *n.* and *adj.*
to sell off, to sell quickly and cheaply.
to sell out, to sell the whole stock: to betray (friends or companions) by secret agreement.
[O.E. *sellan*, to hand over.]

seltzer, *selt′zėr, n.* a mineral water.
[Nieder-*Selters*, in Germany.]

selvage, selvedge, *sel′vij, n.* the firm edge of a piece of cloth: a border.
[self, edge.]

selves. See **self.**

semaphore, *sem′ȧ-fōr, -fȯr, n.* an apparatus for signalling by means of movable arms: signalling by means of a flag held in each hand.
[Gk. *sēma*, a sign, *pherein*, to bear.]

semblance, *sem′blȧns, n.* appearance, often with little or no reality behind (**e.g.** *He gave the speaker a semblance of attention*).
[Fr.—*sembler*, seem—L. *similis*, like.]

semi-, *sem′i-,* (as part of word) half: (*loosely*) partly.
sem′i-ann′ual, *adj.* half-yearly.
sem′ibreve (*-brēv*), *n.* a half *breve* (old note in music), equal to four crotchets.
sem′icircle, *n.* a half circle.
sem′icōlon, *n.* the point (;) which marks a more distinct division of a sentence than a comma does.
sem′i-detached′, *adj.* partly separated: (of a house) joined to another house on one side but separate on the other.
sem′i-fīn′al, *adj.* and *n.* (a stage, match, etc.) immediately before the final.
sem′i-fin′alist, *n.*
sem′i-offic′ial, *adj.* partly official: having some official authority.
sem′i-pre′cious, *adj.* (of a gemstone) valuable, but not of the highest value.
sem′iquaver, *n.* a note half the length of a quaver.
sem′itone, *n.* half a tone in the musical scale.
[L. *sēmi-*, half; conn. with Gk. *hēmi-*.]

seminar, *sem′i-när, n.* a group of advanced students working under a teacher in a branch of study.
sem′inary, *n.* (formerly) a school: a college educating for priesthood or ministry:—*pl.* **-ies.**
[L. *sēminārium*, a seed plot.]

Semitic, *sė-mit′ik, adj.* having to do with Hebrew or Arabic languages: Jewish.
[Gk. *Sēm*, Shem (Genesis x).]

semolina, *sem-ō-lē′nȧ, n.* hard particles of wheat sifted from flour.
[It. *semolino*—L. *simila*, fine flour.]

senate, *sen′it, n.* a lawmaking body, esp. the upper house of the parliament in some countries (e.g. U.S., Australia, etc.): the governing council in some British universities.
sen′ator, *n.* a member of a senate.
[L. *senātus*—*senex*, old, an old man.]

send, *send, v.t.* to cause (a person) to go, or (something) to be carried (to a place): to cause (e.g. a ball) to go with speed or force: to give (out, e.g. a smell).—Also *v.i.*:—*pa.t., pa.p.* **sent.**
sen′der, *n.*
send′-off, *n.* a start: a farewell party, etc., to show good wishes for a person setting out on a journey, career, etc.
to send down, to expel, or to banish for a time, from a university.
to send for, to summon (a person), order (a thing) to be brought or posted to one.
[O.E. *sendan*; conn. with Ger. *senden.*]

senile, *sē′nīl, adj.* showing the feebleness or childishness of old age.
senility, *sė-nil′i-ti, n.*
[Same root as **senate.**]

senior, *sēn′yȯr, adj.* older in age: higher in rank or standing (e.g. *senior officials*):

more advanced (e.g. *senior pupils*).—Also *n.*

seniority, *sē-ni-or'i-ti, n.* state of being senior.

[L., comp. of *senex*; root as **senate.**]

senna, *sen'ȧ, n.* the dried leaves of certain plants, used as medicine.

[Arabic *sanā.*]

señor, *se-nyor', n.* a gentleman: the Spanish word for Mr.

señor'a, *n.* a lady: Mrs.

señori'ta (*-ē'ta*), *n.* a young lady: Miss.

sensation, *sen-sā'sh(ȯ)n, n.* feeling, knowledge of physical experience gained through the senses: a vague effect on the senses (e.g. *a sensation of faintness, of floating*): a state of excitement or interest (e.g. *The elopement created a sensation*), or something that causes this.

sensā'tional, *adj.* causing great excitement: aiming, or aimed, at doing this.

sensā'tionally, *adv.*

sensā'tionalism, *n.* sensational facts, language, etc.: attempt, tendency, to be sensational.

[Same root as **sense.**]

sense, *sens, n.* a power by which we notice or feel objects (sight, hearing, smell, taste, and touch): a sensation, feeling, vague impression (e.g. *a sense of chill, of strangeness*): a special ability to appreciate something (e.g. *a sense of humour*; *a musical sense*): a moral feeling (e.g. *a sense of duty, of shame*): (in *pl.*) one's right mind (e.g. *Is he out of his senses?*): practical wisdom (e.g. *She has no sense*): what is sensible or reasonable (e.g. *It would be sense to tell her so*; *it does not make sense*): meaning (e.g. *What is the sense of the word in this phrase?*): general opinion (e.g. *the sense of the meeting*).—*v.t.* to feel, realise (e.g. *I sensed his disapproval*, or *that he disapproved*).

sense'less, *adj.* stunned, unconscious: foolish, lacking good sense.

sense'lessly, *adv.* **sense'lessness,** *n.*

sen'sible, *adj.* wise, reasonable: able to be felt or noticed, esp. by one of the senses: aware (e.g. *I am sensible of the danger*, or *that there is danger*).

sen'sibleness, *n.* **sen'sibly,** *adv.*

sensibil'ity, *n.* ability to feel, or to appreciate: sensitiveness, tendency to feel esp. pain (*pl.* **-ies**; e.g. *We must not wound his sensibilities*).

sen'sitise (*-īz*), *v.t.* to make sensitive, esp. to rays of light.

sen'sitive, *adj.* feeling, esp. readily, strongly, or painfully: strongly affected by light, etc.: showing or measuring small amounts or changes.

sen'sitiveness, sensitiv'ity, *ns.*

sen'sory, *adj.* of the senses: (of a nerve) bringing impulses to the brain that result in a sensation.

sensual, *sen'sū-ȧl, sen'shoo-ȧl, adj.* having to do with the senses and not the mind: (of person) indulging too much in coarser pleasures of the senses: (of pleasures) bodily, fleshly.

sen'sually, *adv.*

sensual'ity, sen'sualness, *ns.*

sen'suous, *adj.* of, having a pleasant effect on, the senses: easily affected through the senses. (*Sensual* implies excess of which one disapproves; *sensuous* does not).

sensitive plant, a plant that closes leaves, etc., when touched.

[L. *sentire, sensum*, to feel, think.]

sent. See **send.**

sentence, *sen'tėns, n.* a judgment: a punishment decreed by a court or a judge: a number of words which together make a complete statement, command, or question (e.g. *I saw her on Monday*; *go away! what do you mean by that?*).—*v.t.* to condemn (a person, to a stated punishment; e.g. *sentenced him to four months*—usu. in prison).

senten'tious (*-shus*), *adj.* (of person, style) full, or too full, of wise sayings or moralising.

[Same root as **sense.**]

sentient, *sen'shėnt, adj.* that has feeling or consciousness (e.g. *a sentient being*).

[Same root as **sense.**]

sentiment, *sen'ti-mėnt, n.* (show of) the softer emotions, sometimes partly insincere: a feeling, emotion (e.g. *a sentiment of pity*; *patriotic sentiment*): feeling as opposed to reason: a thought, opinion.

sentimen'tal, *adj.* having, or expressing too much emotion or feeling (usu. worked up or partly insincere).

sentimen'tally, *adv.*

sentimental'ity, -men'talness, *ns.*

sentimen'talist, *n.* one who delights in sentiment or sentimentality.

sentimen'talise, *v.t.* to be sentimental about (person, event, etc.) overlooking what is unpleasant or cruel.—Also *v.i.* (with *over, about*).

[Same root as **sense.**]

sentinel, *sen'ti-nėl, n.* one posted on guard, a sentry.

to stand sentinel, to keep watch.

[Fr. *sentinelle*—It. *sentinella.*]

sentry, *sen'tri, n.* a soldier on guard to stop anyone who has not a right to pass:—*pl.* **sen'tries.**

sen'try-box, *n.* a small shelter for a sentry. [Orig. uncertain.]

sepal, *sep'ȧl, n.* one of the leaves forming the calyx outside the petals of a flower.

[Fr. *sépale.*]

separate, *sep'ȧ-rāt, v.t.* to disconnect: to take, set, force, apart: to keep apart, divide.—*v.i.* to come apart: to go different ways: (of a husband and wife) to live apart by choice.—*adj.* (*sep'ȧ-rit*) existing, placed, etc., apart: not connected (*two separate problems*): distinct, different (e.g. *on two separate occasions*).

separā'tion, *n.* **sep'arable,** *adj.*
sep'aratist, *n.* one who withdraws, or urges separation, from an established church, etc.
sep'arātor, *n.* a machine for dividing milk from cream.
[L. *sēparāre, -ātum,* to put aside.]

sepia, *sē'pi-ȧ, n.* the ink of a cuttlefish: a brown paint or colour.
[Gk. *sēpia,* cuttlefish.]

sepsis, *sep'sis, n.* a poisoned condition of the blood caused by bacteria in e.g. a wound.
sep'tic, *adj.* having to do with, or causing, sepsis: suppurating.
septicae'mia (*-sē'mi-ȧ*), *n.* serious general blood-poisoning.
septic tank, a tank in which sewage is partly made pure by action of bacteria.
[Gk.—*sēpein,* to rot.]

sept, *sept, n.* a division of a tribe, or of a clan. [Prob. **sect.**]

sept-, *sept-,* (as part of word) seven.
septuagenarian, *sep-tū-ȧ-ji-nā'ri-ȧn, n.* a person from seventy to seventy-nine years old.—Also *adj.*
[L. *septem,* seven(*septuāgintā,* seventy).]

September, *sep-tem'bėr, n.* the ninth (Roman seventh) month.
[L.—*septem,* seven.]

septic, septicaemia. See **sepsis.**

septuagenarian. See **sept-.**

sepulchre, *sep'ul-kėr, n.* a tomb.
sepulchral, *si-pul'krȧl, adj.* having to do with a tomb or with burials: dismal, gloomy: (of voice) deep, hollow in tone.
sepul'chrally, *adv.*
[L. *sepelīre, sepultum,* to bury.]

sequel, *sē'kwėl, n.* outcome: result, consequence: a story which is a continuation of an earlier story.
sequence, *sē'kwėns, n.* the order (of events) in time: a number (of things) following in order: a connected series: a part of a film showing one incident without breaks or change of scene.
[L. *sequī, secūtus,* to follow.]

sequester, *si-kwes'tėr, v.t.* to withdraw (e.g. *to sequester oneself from society*): (*law*) to take (property) from the owner until e.g. debts are paid.
seques'tered, *adj.* lonely, secluded.
[L., one who held property during dispute.]

sequin, *sē'kwin, n.* a small round shining ornament, one of a number sewn on e.g. a dress.
[It. *zecchino* (orig. name of old coin).]

sequoia, *si-kwoi'ȧ, n.* a giant tree growing in California, also called 'redwood'.
[From name of an American Indian.]

seraglio, *si-râl'yō, n.* a harem.
[It. *serraglio.*]

seraph, *ser'ȧf, n.* an angel of the highest rank:—*pl.* **ser'aphs, ser'aphim.**
seraph'ic, *adj.* like, befitting, an angel.
[Heb. *Serāphīm* (*pl.*).]

sere, *sēr, adj.* dry and withered. [**sear.**]

serenade, *ser-ė-nād', n.* music sung or played in open air at night (esp. by lover under lady's window), or suitable for this purpose.—*v.t.* to entertain (person) with a serenade.—Also *v.i.*
[It. *serenata*—L. root as **serene.**]

serene, *si-rēn', adj.* (of e.g. sea) calm: (of e.g. sky) clear, unclouded: not worried, quietly happy.
serene'ly, *adv.*
serene'ness, seren'ity, (*-ren'*), *ns.*
[L. *serēnus,* clear.]

serf, *sėrf, n.* a person who was bought and sold with the land on which he worked:—*pl.* **serfs.**
serf'dom, *n.* state of a serf.
[Fr.—L. *servus,* a slave.]

serge, *sėrj, n.* a strong cloth, now usu. made of wool.
[L. *sērica,* silk—*Sēres,* the Chinese.]

sergeant, *sär'jȧnt, n.* a non-commissioned officer (see *Appendices*): an officer of the police force.
Sergeant-at-arms, an officer of a lawmaking body, e.g. parliament, whose duty is to make arrests, etc. (also **Serjeant-**).
[Fr. *sergent*—L. *servīre,* to serve.]

serial. See **series.**

series, *sē'(i)rēz, n.* a set of things in line or following one another in some kind of order: a group of things with something in common (e.g. *It was published in the Peewit series of children's books*):—*pl.* **sē'ries.**
sē'rial (*-ri-ȧl*), *adj.* in a series: in a row: (of story, etc.) published, broadcast, etc., in instalments.—*n.* a serial story, etc.
se'rially, *adv.*
sē'rialise, *v.t.* to publish, etc., as a serial.
[L. *seriēs*—*serĕre,* to join.]

serious, *sē'(i)ri-us, adj.* grave, thoughtful: in earnest (e.g. *I am not joking; I am serious about this*): requiring deep thought, or causing anxiety (*a serious matter, injury, situation*).
sē'riously, *adv.* **sē'riousness,** *n.*
[L. *sērius.*]

Serjeant. See **sergeant.**

sermon, *sėr'mȯn, n.* a serious talk, esp. one given from the pulpit and based on a verse from the Bible: a lecture on one's behaviour or duty.
[L. *sermō, -ōnis.*]

serpent, *sėr'pėnt, n.* a snake.
ser'pentine, *adj.* like a serpent: winding, full of twists.
[L. *serpens*—*serpĕre,* to creep.]

serrated, *sė-rā'tid, ser'ȧ-tid, adj.* notched as a saw edge is.
serrā'tion, *n.* state of being notched: a notched edge: a tooth or notch.
[L. *serra,* a saw.]

serried, *ser'id, adj.* crowded, set close together (e.g. *serried ranks*).
[Fr. *serrer,* to crowd—L. *sera,* door bar.]

serum, *sē'rum, n.* a watery fluid from the

body, esp. the fluid that separates from blood when it clots: this fluid taken from an animal that has been made immune to a disease, or from a human being, and injected into a human being to help him to fight the disease.
[L. *serum*, whey.]

servant, *sėr′vȧnt, n.* one hired to work for another: a domestic: one in the service of the state, etc. (*a public servant*).
serve, *v.t.* to work for: to wait upon, help to food: to hand out (food) at table: to wait on (a customer): to be of use, suitable, adequate, to or for (e.g. *That will serve me, will serve my purpose*): to undergo (e.g. a prison sentence): to present formally (a writ): to strike (a ball) to begin a rally in tennis.—*v.i.* to act as a servant: to portion out food at table: to carry out duties (e.g. in the armed forces): to be used, be suitable to use (e.g. *The box serves as a chair*; *it will serve to hold the door shut*): (*tennis*) to put the ball in play.
ser′ver, *n.*
service, *sėr′vis, n.* act of serving: employment in one of the armed forces, etc.: duty required of an employee: (in *pl.*) the armed forces: a public department, or the people in it (e.g. *the civil service*): help (e.g. *This was a service to mankind*; often in *pl.*, e.g. *He gave his services to the society without charge*): use (e.g. *We must now bring the new brush into service*): supply of something provided according to a regular arrangement (e.g. *The bus service is poor*): a performance of public worship, or of a religious ceremony (e.g. *a marriage service*): a set of dishes (e.g. *a dinner service*).—*v.t.* to keep (a machine, e.g. a car) in good running order, by regular repairs, etc.: to send out supplies to regularly (e.g. *One firm services the entire area*).
ser′viceable, *adj.* useful: wearing well (e.g. *serviceable clothes*).
ser′vile (*-vil*), *adj.* having to do with slaves or servants: (of person or conduct) cringing, showing lack of spirit.
ser′vileness, servil′ity (*-vil′*), *ns.*
ser′vitor, *n.* a male servant.
servitude, *sėr′vi-tūd, n.* state of being a slave, or a servant, or other person very strictly controlled.
ser′viceman, *n.* a man in one of the armed services:—*fem.* **ser′vicewoman.**
active service, service in battle.
at one's service, (of helpful person or thing) ready if one wants to use him, it.
penal servitude. See **penal.**
to be of service to, to be useful to.
to have seen service, to have been in active military service: to have been put to hard use.
to serve one right, to be no worse than one deserves.
[L. *servire*, to serve, *servus*, a slave.]

serviette, *sėr-vi-et′, n.* a table napkin.
[Fr.]

servile, servitude, etc. See **servant.**

session, *sesh′(ȯ)n, n.* sitting of a court, council, parliament, etc., or time during which this takes place: a series of sittings: period of the year during which classes are held in a school, etc.
[Same root as **sedentary.**]

set, *set, v.t.* to place, put: to fix in proper place (e.g. broken bones): to put together (type for printing): to put into type (e.g. a book): to arrange (a table) for a meal: to put (a hen) on eggs, or (eggs) under a hen: to plant (seedlings): to mount (e.g. gems) in a frame of metal: to adorn, scatter (with gems, etc.): to put (a clock) to the correct time, or to fix (an instrument) so that it will give a desired signal, make a desired record, etc.: to cause (e.g. jelly, mortar) to become firm, solid: to fix (hair) in waves or curls: to prepare (the scene) for action, in theatre, etc.: to put in a certain state (e.g. *to set on fire*; *to set free*): to start (e.g. *to set people talking, complaining*): to pitch (e.g. *The song is set too high for me*): to compose music for (words; *to set, set to music*): to fix, arrange (date, limit, price, value, etc.): to put before one to be done, solved, followed, etc. (e.g. a task, examination, problem, or an example): to prepare (an examination).—*v.i.* to go out of sight below the horizon: to become firm or solid: (of bone) to knit: (of fruit) to begin to develop: to have or take a direction (e.g. *The stream sets to the north*): (of a dog) to point out game:—*pr.p.* **sett′ing**; *pa.p.* **set.**—*adj.* fixed, arranged beforehand: carefully composed beforehand (e.g. *a set speech*): deliberate (e.g. *with the set intention of doing so*): ready (e.g. *all set to leave home*): stiff (e.g. *with a set face*).—*n.* a group of persons in the habit of meeting or associating: a group of things used together: a series (e.g. of stamps): an apparatus, e.g. for receiving radio or television signals or programmes: scenery made ready for a scene in a play or motion picture: a fixing of hair waves, etc.: direction, e.g. of current: bent, inclination of mind: carriage, pose (e.g. *the set of his head*): a number of games in tennis: a street paving block (also **sett**): a badger's burrow (usu. **sett**).
sett′er, *n.* a dog of certain breeds that can be trained to point out game.
sett′ing, *n.* act of one who, thing that, sets: frame in which gems are set: arrangement of a piece of music: scene: background.
set′back, *n.* a movement in the wrong direction, check, reverse, relapse.
set fair, (of weather) steadily fair.
set piece, a carefully prepared performance: a picture in fireworks.

set square, a triangular drawing instrument with one right angle.

set'-to', *n.* a hot argument or fight.

to set about, to begin (doing something): to attack (a person).

to set against, to make (a person) feel unfriendly towards (someone else).

to set alight. See below.

to set apart, to put at some distance (from): to separate: to keep for special use or purpose.

to set fire, light, to, or **set on fire, set alight,** to cause to begin to burn.

to set forth, to put out on show: to express in words (e.g. *to set forth arguments*): to start (for a place, on a journey to a place).

to set in, to begin (e.g. *Winter set in*).

to set off, to cause to explode: to start (a person) off (doing something): to show to advantage: to begin a journey.

to set on, to attack: to urge (e.g. person, dog) to attack.

to set oneself, to try in a determined manner (to do something).

to set one's teeth, to clench one's teeth: to face resolutely something unpleasant to be done or suffered.

to set on fire. See above.

to set out, to begin a journey: to begin with an intention (e.g. *to set out to win*).

to set up, to put upright: to build: to raise (e.g. *to set up a howl*): to help to begin (e.g. *to set one's son up in business*): (*printing*) to put in type.

[O.E. *settan—sittan*, to sit.]

sett. See **set** (*n.*).

settee, *sė-tē'*, *n.* a long seat with a back.

[Prob. **settle.**]

setter, setting, etc. See **set.**

settle, *set'l*, *n.* a long high-backed bench.—*v.t.* to place at rest or in comfort (e.g. *to settle oneself in a chair*): to go in numbers, or cause others to go, to live in (empty country): to establish (someone, e.g. in a job): to quiet (e.g. nerves, stomach): to decide: to agree upon (e.g. price, date): to bring to an end (e.g. a dispute): to pay (a bill) completely.—*v.i.* to come to rest: to sink to the bottom: to make one's home in a place permanently: to grow calm or clear: to decide (on): to come to an agreement (with): to pay debts to (e.g. *to settle with one's creditors*).

settle'ment, *n.* act of settling: payment: arrangement: a small community: a colony newly established: money given to a woman on her marriage.

sett'ler, *n.*

[O.E. *setl*, seat, *setlan*, to place.]

seven, *sev'n*, *adj.* and *n.* the number next above six (7 or VII).

sev'enth, *adj.* last of seven.—*n.* one of seven equal parts.

seventeen (*sev'*, or *-tēn'*), *adj.* and *n.* seven and ten (17 or XVII).

seventeenth (*sev'*, or *-tēnth'*), *adj.* last of seventeen.—*n.* one of seventeen equal parts.

sev'enty, *adj.* and *n.* seven times ten (70 or LXX):—*pl.* **sev'enties.**

sev'entieth, *adj.* last of seventy.—*n.* one of seventy equal parts.

[O.E. *seofon*; *seofontēne*; *seofontig.*]

sever, *sev'ėr*, *v.t.* and *v.i.* to separate, part (e.g. *This severed him from his family*): to cut or to break, or to be broken, off (e.g. *He severed an arm with his sword*; *the branch severed from the tree*).—*v.t.* to cut in two: to break off (relations, ties).

sev'erance, *n.*

[Fr. *sevrer*, wean—L. root as **separate.**]

several, *sev'ėr-ȧl*, *adj.* more than one (usu. more than three) but not very many: various: separate, respective (e.g. *The boys went their several ways*).

sev'erally, *adv.* separately, singly.

[O.Fr.—L. root as **separate.**]

severe, *sė-vēr'*, *adj.* serious (e.g. *a severe illness*): very strict (e.g. *a severe master*): (of criticism, rebuke, etc.) harsh: (of weather) very cold: very plain (e.g. *a severe style*).

severe'ly, *adv.*

severe'ness, sever'ity (*-ver'*), *ns.*

[L. *sevērus.*]

sew, *sō*, *v.t.* to fasten together with a needle and thread: to make or mend in this way.—Also *v.i.*:—*pa.t.* **sewed**; *pa.p.* **sewn,** or **sewed.**

sew'er, *n.* **sew'ing,** *n.* and *adj.*

[O.E. *sīwian.*]

sewer[1]. See **sew.**

sewer[2], *sū'ėr*, *n.* a channel for receiving water and waste matter from drains of buildings and streets.

sew'age, *n.* matter carried off by sewers.

sew'erage, *n.* system of sewers in a town, etc.

[O.Fr. *seuwiere*, canal—L. *ex*, *aqua*, water.]

sex, *seks*, *n.* either of the two classes into which animals are divided according to the part they play in reproduction (*male sex, female sex*): characteristics, instincts, etc., connected with this division.

sex'ual, *adj.* having to do with sex.

sexed, *adj.* having sex or sexual feeling.

[Fr. *sexe*—L. *sexus.*]

sex-, *seks-*, (as part of word) six.

sexagenarian, *seks-ȧ-ji-nā'ri-ȧn*, *n.* a person from sixty to sixty-nine years old.—Also *adj.*

[L. *sex*, six (*sexāgintā*, sixty).]

sextant, *seks'tȧnt*, *n.* an instrument for finding distances (measured by angle), e.g. distance between two stars, or height of sun above horizon.

[L. *sextans*, sixth part (i.e. of circle).]

sexton, *seks'tȯn*, *n.* an officer who rings a church bell, attends the clergyman, sees to the digging of graves, etc.

[O.Fr. *secrestein*—L. root as **sacred.**]

shabby, *shab'i*, *adj.* (of clothes, etc.) worn-

looking: poorly dressed: (of action, person, etc.) mean, unfair, not generous: —*comp*. **shabb'ier**; *superl*. **shabb'iest.**
shabb'ily, *adv*. **shabb'iness,** *n*.
[O.E. *sceabb*, scab.]

shack, *shak*, *n*. a roughly built hut.
[Amer.; origin uncertain.]

shackle, *shak'l*, *n*. a ring or other device that clasps a prisoner's or slave's wrist or ankle and is fastened to another on the other arm or leg, or to something else: a hobble for a horse, etc.: anything that checks one's freedom.—*v.t.* to put shackles, or a check, on.
[O.E. *sceacel*.]

shade, *shād*, *n*. slight darkness caused by cutting off some light: a place not in full sunlight: (in *pl.*) darkness (e.g. *the shades of night*): darker parts in a picture, etc. (e.g. *a portrait with no light and shade*): a screen, etc., to shelter from light, heat, or dust: degree of colour (e.g. *a deep, dark, shade of green*): a very small amount (e.g. *a shade of difference*; *a shade too big*): a ghost.—*v.t.* to screen, shelter: to mark with different tones of colour or shadow: to darken.—*v.i.* to change gradually e.g. from one colour (into another).
In many cases either the noun *shade* or the noun *shadow* (see below) can be used, but there are some senses or phrases in which the one form only is possible. These include:—*a window shade*; *a shade of red*; *my shadow on the wall*; *Eric is Jim's shadow*.
shā'ding, *n*. the act of making a shade, or of marking shadows: the marking that shows darker places in a picture: gradual change.
shā'dy, *adj*. sheltered from light or heat: (*coll.*) dishonest, etc. (e.g. *a shady business*, or *person*):—*comp*. **shā'dier**; *superl*. **shā'diest.**
shā'diness, *n*.
shadow, *shad'ō*, *n*. shade caused by an object coming in the way of a light: the dark shape of that object on e.g. the ground: (in *pl.*) darkness: a dark part, in e.g. a picture: unhappiness, trouble, etc. (e.g. *A shadow fell on his life, friendship, reputation*): an appearance without reality: a very small amount (of e.g. doubt, suspicion, evidence): a very close companion.—*v.t.* to shade, darken: to hide: to follow (a person) about and watch him closely.—*adj*. unreal: ready to come into operation when required.
See **shade** above.
shad'owy, *adj*. full of shadows: faint, slight: not real, fanciful.
shad'owiness, *n*.
shadow cabinet, leaders of the opposition in parliament, each chosen to take a particular office when there is a change of government.
in the shade, in a place screened from light: in an unimportant position where no notice is taken of one.
to shade off, to lessen gradually to little or nothing.
[O.E. *sceadu* (when object, *sceadwe*).]

shaft, *shâft*, *n*. anything long and straight: the main upright part (of e.g. a pillar): the long rod on which the head of a spear, golf club, etc. is fixed: an arrow: something sharp thought of as like an arrow (e.g. *shafts of love, ridicule*): a pole e.g. of a carriage: a long revolving bar transmitting motion in an engine: a ray or beam (of light): a well-like space (e.g. *a lift shaft*): a passage in a mine.
[O.E. *sceaft*.]

shag, *shag*, *n*. a rough mass of hair or wool: a kind of tobacco cut into shreds: a diving bird, the cormorant.
shagg'y, *adj*. covered with rough hair, wool, or other growth: untidy.
shagg'ily, *adv*. **shagg'iness,** *n*.
[O.E. *sceaga*.]

shagreen, *shȧ-grēn'*, *n*. dyed leather with rough surface made of skin of horse, seal, shark, etc.
[Same root as **chagrin.**]

Shah, *shä*, *n*. the king of Persia. [Pers.]

shake, *shāk*, *v.t.* and *v.i.* to move, or be moved, esp. to and fro, with quick, short movements: to make, or to be made, unsteady: to (make to) tremble:—*pa.t.* **shook**; *pa.p.* **shā'ken.**—*n*. a shaking or trembling: a shock: a drink made by shaking the ingredients together.
sha'ky, *adj*. (of person, voice, etc.) trembling through age, illness, etc.: (of writing, etc.) produced by a shaky person: likely to collapse: not steady: not to be relied on (e.g. *a shaky supporter*): —*comp*. **shā'kier**; *superl*. **shā'kiest.**
shā'kily, *adv*. **shā'kiness,** *n*.
shake'-down, *n*. a makeshift bed, e.g. of straw, or mattress on the floor.
no great shakes, (*coll.*) not very important, or not very good.
to shake hands, to greet by clasping hands and moving them up and down.
[O.E. *sceacan*.]

Shakespearian, *shāk-spē'ri-ȧn*, *adj*. having to do with *Shakespeare* or his work.

shale, *shāl*, *n*. a clay rock that splits into layers, from which oil is sometimes obtained. [Conn. with **scale** (2).]

shall, *shal*, *sh(ė)l*, *v.t.* now used to form future tenses of other verbs when the subject is *I* or *we* (e.g. *I, we, shall never forget*); when the subject is *he, she, it, you*, or *they*, *shall* means 'must', or expresses a promise (e.g. *You shall go, whether you want to or not*; *he shall have it, if I can find it*):—*pr.t.* 2nd person sing. (thou) **shalt.** There is a conditional form **should** (*shood, shėd, shd*; e.g. *I, we, should go, if they would let me, us*). *Should* also means 'ought to' (e.g. *I, he, should have gone, but I, he, did not*).

See also **will** and **would**.
[O.E. *sceal*; conn. with Ger. *soll.*]

shallot, *shȧ-lot′*, *n.* a kind of onion.
[O.Fr. *eschalote.*]

shallow, *shal′ō*, *adj.* not deep: (of mind or nature) that does not think, or feel, deeply.—*n.* (often in *pl.*) a place where the water is not deep.
[M.E. *schalowe.*]

shalt. See **shall.**

sham, *sham*, *adj.* not real, pretended, imitation (e.g. *a sham fight, lord*; *sham jewellery*).—*n.* something which is not what it is supposed to be: pretence.—*v.t.* to pretend, or pretend to be (e.g. *to sham illness*; *to sham dead*).—Also *v.i.*:—*pr.p.* **shamm′ing**; *pa.p.* **shammed.**
[17th century slang word.]

shamble, *sham′bl*, *v.i.* to walk in a shuffling or awkward way.—Also *n.*
[Perh. from same root as **shambles.**]

shambles, *sham′blz*, *n. pl.*, *sing.* slaughter-house: (as if *sing.*) a scene of blood and slaughter, or of destruction (e.g. *After the raid the streets were a shambles*).
[O.E. *scamel*, stool (M.E., butcher's stall).]

shame, *shām*, *n.* a painful feeling caused by awareness of guilt, fault, or failure: dishonour, disgrace: a cause of disgrace: (*coll.*) hard luck, a pity.—*v.t.* to make feel shame: to do so by one's greater excellence: to drive by shame (into; e.g. *This shamed him into paying his share*).
shame′ful, *adj.* disgraceful.
shame′fully, *adv.* **shame′fulness,** *n.*
shame′less, *adj.* feeling, showing, no shame: impudent, unscrupulous.
shame′faced, *adj.* very bashful: (of e.g. confession) showing shame.
for shame! you should be ashamed.
to have no shame, to be shameless.
to put to shame, to make feel shame (e.g. by greater excellence).
to think shame to, to be ashamed to.
[O.E. *sc(e)amu*; conn. with Ger. *scham.*]

shamming, shammed. See **sham.**

shammy. See **chamois.**

shampoo, *sham-pōō′*, *v.t.* to wash (scalp and hair):—*pr.p.* **shampoo′ing**; *pa.p.* **shampooed′** (*-pōōd′*).—*n.* act of shampooing: soap, etc., used for this purpose.
[Hindustani *chāmpnā*, to squeeze.]

shamrock, *sham′rok*, *n.* a plant with leaves divided in three, a type of clover—the national plant of Ireland.
[Ir. *seamrōg.*]

shanghai, *shang-hī′*, *v.t.* to drug or make drunk and carry off as a sailor: to compel (into doing something):—*pr.p.* **shang-hai′ing**; *pa.p.* **shanghaied′** (*-hīd′*).
[*Shanghai* in China.]

shank, *shangk*, *n.* the part of the leg between the knee and the foot: a straight or long part, shaft.
[O.E. *sc(e)anca*, leg; conn. Du. *schonk.*]

shan't, *shänt*, abbrev. of **shall not.**

shanty[1], *shan′ti*, *n.* a roughly built hut, etc.:—*pl.* **shan′ties.**
[Fr. *chantier*, (timber) yard.]

shanty[2], *shan′ti*, *n.* a sailors' song with chorus.—Also **chan′ty**:—*pl.* **-ies.**
[Said to be—Fr. *chanter*, to sing.]

shape, *shāp*, *v.t.* to make (into a certain form; e.g. *to shape dough into little cakes*): to model, mould: to settle the nature or direction of (e.g. *This event shaped his life*).—*v.i.* to take shape, develop: to show promise of doing (e.g. *He shapes well at football*).—*n.* form or figure: condition (e.g. *in good shape*): a jelly, etc., turned out of a mould.
shape′less, *adj.* having no shape or regular form.
shape′ly, *adj.* well-proportioned, of attractive shape.
shape′liness, *n.*
to take shape, to take definite form (e.g. *The book, plan, is taking shape*).
[O.E. *scieppan*, create; Ger. *schaffen.*]

shard, *shärd*, *n.* a broken piece of earthen-ware.
[O.E. *sceard.*]

share[1], *shār*, *n.* one of the parts of something that is divided among several people, etc.: one of the parts into which the capital of a business firm is divided.—*v.t.* to divide among a number of people: to have in common (e.g. *They share a liking for sport*).—*v.i.* to receive, or take, a share (in).
share′holder, *n.* one who owns shares in a business company.
[O.E. *scearu*; same root as **shear.**]

share[2], *shār*, *n.* the iron blade of a plough which cuts the ground.
[O.E. *scear*; conn. **share** (1) and **shear.**]

shark, *shärk*, *n.* a large, fierce, flesh-eating fish: a swindler, or a greedy unscrupulous person. [Orig. uncertain.]

sharp, *shärp*, *adj.* cutting, piercing: having a thin edge or fine point: stinging, hurting (e.g. *a sharp wind*; *sharp words*): (of pain, etc.) keen, intense: alert (e.g. *a sharp lookout*): raised a semitone: too high in pitch: shrill: quick to see, hear, or understand: clear-cut (e.g. *a sharp outline*).—*adv.* with pitch too high: briskly: abruptly: punctually (e.g. *at* 10 *a.m. sharp*).—*n.* a sign (♯) in music to show that a note is to be raised a semitone: a cheat.
sharp′ly, *adv.* **sharp′ness,** *n.*
shar′pen, *v.t., v.i.* to make, grow, sharp.
shar′per, *n.* a cheat, esp. at cards.
sharp practice, cunning, barely honest, dealing: an instance of this.
sharp′-shoot′er, *n.* a good marksman, esp. a soldier given duties that need skilled shooting.
sharp′-sight′ed, *adj.* having keen sight.
sharp′-witt′ed, *adj.* having quick wit.
to look sharp, to be quick.
[O.E. *scearp*; conn. with Ger. *scharf.*]

shatter, *shat'ėr, v.t.* to break in pieces: to upset completely, ruin (e.g. health, nerves, hopes).
[Prob. conn. with **scatter.**]

shave, *shāv, v.t.* to scrape, cut off the surface of: to cut (off) closely (e.g. hair from the face): to graze, touch lightly, the surface of in passing.—*v.i.* to use a razor in removing hair.—*n.* the act of shaving: a narrow miss or escape.
shā'ven, *adj.* shaved.
shā'ving, *n.* the act of scraping off: a thin slice, esp. of wood planed off.
[O.E. *sc(e)afan*; conn. Ger. *schaben.*]

Shavian, *shā'vi-ȧn, adj.* having to do with the playwright George Bernard *Shaw.*

shawl, *shöl, n.* a wrap or loose covering for the shoulders.
[Pers. *shāl.*]

she, *shē, pron. (fem.)* refers to the female (or thing spoken of as female) already named (e.g. *When they noticed the girl, the ship, she was already near*):—*objective* **her**; *possessive* **her** (sometimes described as possessive *adj.*), **hers** (e.g. *Give Mary her book*; *you know it is hers*).—*adj.* female (e.g. *a she-devil*).
herself', *pron.* (1) emphatic or (2) reflexive form of *she, her* (e.g. (1) *She herself told me*; (2) *She has made herself look a fright*).
[O.E. *sēo (fem.* of definite article).]

sheaf, *shēf, n.* a bundle (of e.g. corn, papers) bound or tied together:—*pl.* **sheaves** (*shēvz*).
[O.E. *scēaf*; conn. with Ger. *schaub.*]

shear, *shēr, v.t.* to clip, cut the wool from (a sheep):—*pa.t.* **sheared**; *pa.p.* **sheared** or **shorn.**
shears, *n. pl.* scissors: now usu. large scissors or cutting implement.
[O.E. *sceran*; conn. with Ger. *scheren.*]

sheath, *shēth, n.* a case for a sword or blade: a long close-fitting covering:—*pl.* **sheaths** (*shēTHz*).
sheathe, *shēTH, v.t.* to put into, or cover with, a sheath or case.
[O.E. *scēath*; conn. with Ger. *scheide.*]

sheave, *shēv, n.* a grooved pulley over which a rope, belt, runs:—*pl.* **sheaves.**
[M.E. *shefe*; conn. Ger. *scheibe,* disk.]

sheaves. See **sheaf, sheave.**

shed[1], *shed, v.t.* to throw or cast off (e.g. clothing, skin, leaves): to pour out (e.g. tears): to send forth, throw (e.g. *to shed light on, a gloom over*):—*pr.p.* **shedd'ing**; *pa.p.* **shed.**
[O.E. *scēadan,* to separate.]

shed[2], *shed, n.* a building for storage or shelter: an outhouse. [**shade.**]

sheen, *shēn, n.* shine, brightness, gloss.
[O.E. *scēne,* beautiful; Ger. *schön.*]

sheep, *shēp, n.* an animal raised for its wool, flesh, etc.: a silly, helpless creature:—*pl.* **sheep.**
sheep'ish, *adj.* bashful, foolishly shy.
sheep'-cote, *n.* a shelter for sheep.
sheep dip, a liquid for disinfecting sheep.
sheep dog, a dog trained to watch sheep, or of a breed used for this work.
sheep run, a feeding ground for sheep.
sheep'shank, *n.* a knot for shortening a rope.
sheep'skin, *n.* the skin of a sheep: leather prepared from it.
[O.E. *scēap*; conn. with Ger. *schaf.*]

sheer[1], *shēr, adj.* pure (e.g. *sheer delight*): downright (e.g. *sheer foolishness*): very steep, vertical: (of a cloth) very thin.—*adv.* straight up or down, very steeply.
[M.E. *schēre*; orig. uncertain.]

sheer[2], *shēr, v.i., v.t.* to turn aside from a straight line, swerve.
to sheer off, to turn aside: to move away.
[**shear**; conn. Ger. *scheren,* depart.]

sheet[1], *shēt, n.* a large, thin piece (of ice, glass, metal, etc.): a broad piece of linen, etc. for a bed: a piece of paper: a sail.
sheet'ing, *n.* cloth for sheets: lining or covering of wood or metal.
sheet lightning, lightning, the reflection and spreading of flashes by the cloud, which appears to be in great sheets.
[O.E. *scēte.*]

sheet[2], *shēt, n.* a rope attached to the lower corner of a sail.
[O.E. *scēata,* corner; conn. **sheet** (1).]

sheet-anchor, *shēt-ang'kȯr, n.* a large anchor for use in emergency: a thing or person one counts on in danger, or when all else has failed.
[M.E. *shute anker*; orig. uncertain.]

sheik(h), *shāk, shēk, n.* a chief or head.
[Arabic *shaikh.*]

shekel, *shek'l, n.* Jewish weight and coin: (in *pl.*; *slang*) money.
[Heb. *sheqel.*]

shelf, *shelf, n.* a board for laying things on, fixed in a cupboard or on a wall: a flat layer of rock, a ledge: a flat bank of sand:—*pl.* **shelves.**
shelve, *v.t.* to put up shelves in (e.g. a library): to put (e.g. a problem) aside for consideration later: to dismiss, retire (a person).—*v.i.* to slope in a way that suggests a shelf (e.g. *The land shelves towards the sea*).
on the shelf, no longer in use, at work, or having prospects (esp. of marriage).
[Conn. with O.E. *scylf,* shelf, ledge.]

shell, *shel, n.* a hard outer covering of a shellfish, egg, nut, etc.: a husk or pod: any framework, as of a building not completed or burnt out: a frail boat: a metal case, filled with explosive material, fired from a gun.—*v.t.* to separate from the shell: to fire shells at.
shell'y, *adj.* covered with shells.
shell'iness, *n.*
shellac (*-lak',* or *she'*), *n.* a resin in thin

sheets, used for making varnish.—*v.t.* to coat with this varnish :—*pr.p.* **shellacking ;** *pa.p.* **shellacked.**

shell'fish, *n.* a sea animal covered with a shell (e.g. oyster, crab).

shell'proof, *adj.* able to resist shells or bombs.

[O.E. *sc*(*i*)*ell.*]

shelter, *shel'tėr, n.* a building or structure that protects against wind, rain, attack, etc. : protection from harm.—*v.t.* to give protection to : to hide.—*v.i.* to take shelter. [Orig. uncertain.]

shelve, shelves. See **shelf.**

shepherd, *shep'ėrd, n.* one who looks after sheep:—*fem.* **shep'herdess.**—*v.t.* to watch over carefully : to guide.

shepherd's pie, a dish of meat with potatoes on the top.

[O.E. *scēaphirde* (**sheep, herd**).]

sheriff, *sher'if, n.* the chief representative of the crown in a county, whose duties include keeping the peace, presiding at elections, etc. : (in Scotland) the chief judge of the county.

[O.E. *scīr*, shire, *gerēfa*, high official.]

sherry, *sher'i, n.* a fortified wine which gets its name from the town of *Jerez* in Spain :—*pl.* **sherr'ies.**

shied, shier, etc. See **shy.**

shield, *shēld, n.* a broad piece of metal, etc., carried for defence against weapons : anything that protects : a person who protects : a trophy shaped like a shield.—*v.t.* to protect by sheltering.

[O.E. *sceld* ; conn. with Ger. *schild.*]

shift, *shift, v.i.* to manage, get on, do as one can (e.g. *He must shift for himself*) : to change position or direction (e.g. *The huge mass, the wind, shifted*).—*v.t.* to change (e.g. the scene on stage): to change the position of : to transfer (to, upon ; e.g. *He tried to shift the burden, blame, to his brother*) : to dislodge, get rid of.—*n.* a change : a change of position, a transfer : a set of persons taking turns with another set (e.g. *The night shift now came on duty*) : time worked by such a set : a means used, measure taken, in an emergency : a dodge, trick.

shif'ter, *n.* one who shifts : a trickster.

shift'less, *adj.* inefficient, lazy, without steady purpose.

shif'ty, *adj.* tricky, not trustworthy : (of eyes, looks) not frank and honest.

shif'tily, *adv.* **shif'tiness,** *n.*

to make shift, to manage somehow.

[[O.E. *sciftan*, to divide.]

shilling, *shil'ing, n.* a coin, formerly silver, later cupro-nickel, worth orig. 12 pence, now 5 new pence.

[O.E. *scilling* ; conn. Ger. *schilling.*]

shilly-shally, *shil'i-shal'i, n.* hesitation, indecision.—*v.i.* to hesitate in making up one's mind, waver :—*pr.p.* **shill'y-shall'ying ;** *pa.p.* **shill'y-shall'ied.**

[shall I?]

shimmer, *shim'ėr, v.i.* to shine with a quivering light, glisten.—*n.* a trembling light, glimmer.

[O.E. *scimerian—scimian*, to shine.]

shin, *shin, n.* the front part of the leg below the knee.

shin'bone, *n.* the tibia (see this).

[O.E. *scinu* ; conn. Du. *scheen.*]

shindy, *shin'di, n.* (*slang*) an uproar :—*pl.* **-ies.**

shine, *shin, v.i.* to give out or reflect light : to be bright : to be very good (at ; e.g. *He shines at games*).—*v.t.* to cause to shine :—*pa.t., pa.p.* **shone** (*shon*).—*n.* brightness : an act of polishing.

shin'ing, *adj.* very bright and clear : greatly to be admired (e.g. *shining courage, a shining example*).

shī'ny, *adj.* glossy, polished :—*comp.* **shī'nier ;** *superl.* **shī'niest.**

shī'nily, *adv.* **shī'niness,** *n.*

[O.E. *scinan* ; conn. with Ger. *scheinen.*]

shingle[1], *shing'gl, n.* a slab of wood, etc. used in the same way as a roofing slate : a woman's haircut showing the shape of the head at the back.—*v.t.* to cover (e.g. a roof) with shingles : to cut in the manner of a shingle.

[L. *scindula—scindĕre*, to cut.]

shingle[2], *shing'gl, n.* coarse gravel consisting of rounded stones, esp. on the seashore. [Orig. uncertain.]

shingles, *shing'glz, n. pl.* a disease with firm blister-like swellings along nerves, sometimes spreading round the body.

[L. *cingulum*, belt—*cingĕre*, to gird.]

shinier, shiny, etc. See **shine.**

ship, *ship, n.* a large vessel for journeys on sea, lake, or river : an aircraft.—*v.t.* to take on to a ship : to send by ship : to engage for work on a ship.—*v.i.* to embark : to hire oneself for work on a ship :—*pr.p.* **shipp'ing ;** *pa.p.* **shipped.**

ship'ment, *n.* act of putting on board ship : goods sent by ship.

shipp'ing, *n.* ships as a whole : transport by ship.

ship'board, *n.* a ship's side : a ship.

ship'-brok'er, *n.* a person who carries through sales, or insurance, of ships.

ship canal, a canal deep enough for seagoing vessels.

ship chandler, one who deals in ships' stores.

ship'master, *n.* the captain of a ship.

ship'mate, *n.* a fellow sailor.

ship'shape, *adj.* in good order, neat, trim.

ship'wreck, *n.* the wreck (esp. by accident) of a ship : ruin, disaster.—*v.t.* to wreck.

ship'wright, *n.* one employed in building or repairing ships.

ship'yard, *n.* a yard where ships are built or repaired.

[O.E. *scip* ; conn. with Ger. *schiff.*]

shire, *shīr*, (as part of word, *-shėr*), *n.* a

county: also applied to some smaller districts.
[O.E. *scīr*, office, authority.]

shirk, *shėrk, v.t.* to slink out of facing or doing (something one ought to).—Also *v.i.*
shir'ker, *n.* [Orig. uncertain.]

shirt, *shėrt, n.* a man's garment with sleeves, worn on the upper part of the body: a woman's tailored blouse.
shirt'ing, *n.* cloth for shirts.
shirt'waist, *n.* (*U.S.*) a tailored blouse with ends for tucking under the skirt.
shirt'waister, *n.* a tailored dress with top like a shirtwaist.
[O.E. *scyrte*; conn. with **short.**]

shiver[1], *shiv'ėr, n.* a small chip, splinter.—*v.t., v.i.* to break into fragments.
[M.E. *scifre.*]

shiver[2], *shiv'ėr, v.i.* to quiver, tremble (with e.g. cold or fear).—Also *n.*
shiv'ery, *adj.* inclined to shiver.
shiv'eriness, *n.*
[M.E. *chievere*; orig. unknown.]

shoal[1], *shōl, n.* a great number, esp. of fishes together in one place.
[O.E. *scolu*, troop; conn. **school** (2).]

shoal[2], *shōl, n.* a shallow place, sandbank.
[O.E. *sceald*, shallow.]

shock[1], *shok, n.* a violent blow coming suddenly: a jarring or shaking as if by a blow: unexpected bad news or experience: an earthquake: the effect on the body of an electric current: state of exhaustion, depression, etc., caused by being injured, etc.: (*coll.*) a stroke of paralysis.—*v.t.* to give a shock to: to upset or horrify.—*v.i.* to be horrified.
shock'er (*coll.*), *n.* a person or thing that shocks.
shock'ing, *adj.* causing horror or dismay, disgusting.
shock'ingly, *adv.* (*coll.*) very (e.g. *shockingly untruthful*).
shock'-absorber, *n.* a device for reducing shock in an aeroplane or motor car.
shock action, tactics, action in which suddenness and force are used to achieve a purpose.
shock troops, soldiers specially trained for hard fighting.
[Perh. Fr. *choq* (n.), *choquer* (vb.).]

shock[2], *shok, n.* a number of sheaves of corn placed together on end.
[M.E. *schokke.*]

shock[3], *shok, n.* a bushy mass (of hair).
shock'headed, *adj.* having such hair.
[Perh. **shag.**]

shocking, etc. See **shock** (1).

shod. See **shoe.**

shoddy, *shod'i, n.* wool or cloth made from old wool and cloth pulled to pieces.—*adj.* made of shoddy: of poor material or quality but pretending to be good (e.g. *shoddy furniture, person, excuse*).
shodd'iness, *n.* [Orig. unknown.]

shoe, *shōō, n.* a stiff outer covering for the foot, not coming above the ankle: a rim of iron nailed to the hoof of an animal: a metal tip: a piece attached where there is friction, the touching part of a brake:—*pl.* **shoes.**—*v.t.* to put shoe(s) on:—*pr.p.* **shoe'ing**; *pa.p.* **shod.**
shoe'lace, shoe'string, *ns.* a string for fastening a shoe.
shoe'maker, *n.* one who makes, repairs, or sells, shoes.
in someone's shoes, in his place.
on a shoestring, with very little money.
[O.E. *scōh*; conn. with Ger. *schuh.*]

shone. See **shine.** **shook.** See **shake.**

shoot, *shōōt, v.t.* to send, fire (arrow, bullet, etc.) from bow, gun, etc.: to send, let fly (e.g. a ball) swiftly and with force: to throw out suddenly (e.g. rubbish): to slide (a bolt): to ask or say suddenly (e.g. *Don't shoot questions at me*): to hit or kill with arrow, bullet, etc.: to score (a goal): to pass swiftly over (rapids), under (a bridge): to pass over (country) shooting game: to put forth (buds, etc.): to photograph, esp. for motion pictures. —*v.i.* to fire a weapon: to kick a ball: to kill e.g. game birds for sport: to move suddenly or quickly: to grow, put out buds, etc.: to photograph or film:—*pa.t., pa.p.* **shot.**—*n.* act of shooting: a shooting party: a new growth, sprout: a chute.
shoot'ing, *n.* and *adj.*
shot, *adj.* hit or killed by shooting: (of silk) showing changing colours: streaked (with colour): mixed (with).
shooting star, a meteor (see this).
See also **shot** (1).
[O.E. *scēotan*; conn. with Ger. *schiessen.*]

shop, *shop, n.* a place where goods are sold: a workshop, or a place where any kind of industry is carried on: details of one's own work, or talk about these: (*slang*) an institution.—*v.i.* to visit shops for the purpose of buying:—*pr.p.* **shopp'ing**; *pa.p.* **shopped.**
shopp'er, *n.*
shop'keeper, *n.* one who keeps a shop of his own.
shop'lifter, *n.* one who steals goods from a shop.
shop'lifting, *n.*
shop steward, a representative of factory or workshop employees elected from their own number.
to talk shop, (*coll.*) to talk about one's work when one is off duty.
[O.E. *sceoppa*, a treasury.]

shore[1], *shōr, shör, n.* a prop, beam, to support a building or to keep a ship in dock steady.—*v.t.* to prop (up), support.
[Conn. with Du. *schoor.*]

shore[2], *shōr, shör, n.* land bordering on the sea or on any expanse of water.
[M.E. *schore*; conn. with Du. *schoor.*]

shorn. See **shear.**

short, *shört, adj.* not long: not tall: brief,

not lasting long: not as much as it should be, not enough (e.g. *My change is short, short rations*): having too little (of; e.g. *I am short of money*): (of manner of speaking) rude, sharp: (of e.g. pastry) crumbling easily. — *adv.* suddenly, abruptly (e.g. *He stopped shŏrt when he saw me*): in a place not as far as intended (e.g. *The shot fell short*).

shorts, *n. pl.* short trousers.

short'ly, *adv.* in a short time, soon: briefly: abruptly, curtly.

shor'ten, *v.t.* to make shorter.

shortening, *shört'ning, n.* act of making, or becoming, shorter: fat suitable for making pastry.

short'bread, *n.* a crisp, brittle cake of flour and butter.

short'-cir'cuit, *n.* a short cut in an electric circuit, usu. made accidentally and causing sparking and fire.—*v.t.* to make a short circuit in: to get over or round (a difficulty or hindrance).

short'coming, *n.* act of falling short: a fault or lack.

short cut. See **cut.**

short'hand, *n.* a method of swift writing using strokes, etc., for speech sounds and groups of sounds.

short'-hand'ed, *adj.* having fewer workers, helpers, than are necessary.

short'-lived' (*-livd'*), *adj.* living only for a short time: not lasting long.

short'-sight'ed, *adj.* seeing clearly only things that are near: (of person, action) foolishly ignoring what is likely to happen in the future.

short'-sight'edness, *n.*

short'-tem'pered, *adj.* easily made angry.

short'-term', *adj.* (of an arrangement, esp. money) lasting a short time: (of plan, policy) concerned only with the near future.

in short, in a few words.

short of, less than: without going so far as (e.g. *They will use any means short of war*).

to make short work of, to do, deal with, settle, very quickly.

[O.E. *sc(e)ort.*]

shot[1], *shot, n.* a single act or sound of shooting: something that is shot, e.g. bullet, projectile: a number of bullets together: a marksman: distance covered by a bullet, etc.: a throw, stroke, in a game: an attempt (at doing something, at guessing, etc.): a photograph, a scene in a motion picture: the act of making this: an injection (e.g. *a shot of cocaine*).

shot'gun, *n.* a smooth-bore gun for small shot.

a big shot, (*coll.*) an important person.

[O.E. *sc(e)ot*; same root as **shoot.**]

shot[2]. See **shoot.**

should. See **shall.**

shoulder, *shōl'dėr, n.* the part of the body between the neck and the upper arm: the upper joint of a foreleg of an animal cut for the table: something that sticks out or curves gently.—*v.t.* to push with the shoulder: to carry on the shoulder: to bear the full weight of.

shoul'der-blade, *n.* the broad flat bone of the shoulder.

to (give the) cold shoulder. See **cold.**

[O.E. *sculdor*; conn. with Ger. *schulter.*]

shout, *showt, n.* a loud call: a loud burst (of e.g. laughter, applause):—*v.i., v.t.* to utter, or utter with, a shout.

[Orig. unknown.]

shove, *shuv, v.t., v.i.* to thrust: to push along: to push aside rudely.—Also *n.*

[O.E. *scūfan*; conn. Ger. *schieben.*]

shovel, *shuv'l, n.* a broad spade-like tool, scoop: a machine for scooping up.—*v.t.* to move with, or as if with, a shovel:—*pr.p.* **shov'elling**; *pa.p.* **shov'elled.**

[O.E. *scofl*—same root as **shove.**]

show, *shō, v.t.* to allow, or cause, to be seen: to exhibit, display (e.g. an art collection): to point out (e.g. the way): to guide or conduct (e.g. *Show her to a seat*): to demonstrate or prove (e.g. *to show the truth of his story*).—*v.i.* to be able to be seen:—*pa.t.* **showed** (*shōd*); *pa.p.* **shōwn** or **shōwed.**—*n.* act of showing: display: an entertainment: (*coll.*) a theatrical performance: a false appearance (e.g. *a show of penitence*).

showy, *shō'i, adj.* making a striking show: gaudy, bright and cheap:—*comp.* **show'ier**; *superl.* **show'iest.**

show'ily, *adv.* **show'iness,** *n.*

show business, the branch of the theatrical profession concerned with variety entertainments.

show'down, *n.* a showing of one's cards, resources, plans: open struggle or argument after time of hidden conflict.

show'man, *n.* a person who owns a show: one who is skilled in displaying things (e.g. his own merits) so as to arouse public interest.

show'room, *n.* a room where goods are displayed for people to see.

a show of hands, a vote by raising hands.

to show off, to show, display, to advantage: to try to make an impression by one's possessions or talents.

to show up, to stand out clearly: to expose (e.g. faults): to come, turn up.

[O.E. *scēawian*; Ger. *schauen,* to see.]

shower, *show'ėr, showr, n.* a short fall, of e.g. rain, or of tears, bullets, etc.: a large quantity (of e.g. presents, questions): a shower-bath.—*v.t.* to pour down (e.g. *They showered confetti on the bride*): to give in great quantity (e.g. kindnesses, invitations).—Also *v.i.*

showery, *show'ėr-i, showr'i, adj.* raining now and then.

showeriness, *n.*

shower-bath, *n.* a bath in which water is sprayed from above.
[O.E. *scūr*; conn. with Ger. *schauer.*]

showing, shown, etc. See **show.**

shrank. See **shrink.**

shrapnel, *shrap'n(ė)l, n.* a shell holding e.g. bullets, which scatter after explosion: shell, bomb, or mine, fragments.
[Surname of inventor.]

shred, *shred, n.* a fragment, esp. strip, torn or cut off: a scrap (e.g. *not a shred of evidence*).—*v.t.* to cut or tear into shreds:—*pr.p.* **shredd'ing;** *pa.p.* **shredd'ed.**
[Same root as **screed.**]

shrew, *shrōō, n.* a small mouse-like animal with a sharp nose: a quarrelsome or scolding woman.
shrew'ish, *adj.* **shrew'ishness,** *n.*
shrewd, *adj.* showing keen judgment.
shrewd'ly, *adv.* **shrewd'ness,** *n.*
[O.E. *screawa.*]

shriek, *shrēk, v.i., v.t.* to utter, or utter with, a shrill scream or laugh.—Also *n.*
[Conn. with **screech.**]

shrift. See **shrive.**

shrill, *shril, adj.* high in tone and piercing: sharp sounding through impatience.
shrill'ness, *n.* **shril'ly,** *adv.*
[Same root as Ger. *schrill.*]

shrimp, *shrimp, n.* a small long-tailed shellfish: a small person.—*v.i.* to catch shrimps.
[Conn. with O.E. *scrimman*, shrink.]

shrine, *shrīn, n.* a case for holding holy objects: a holy or sacred place.
[O.E. *scrin*—L. *scrinium*, case for papers—*scribĕre*, to write.]

shrink, *shringk, v.i.* to grow smaller: to draw back in fear or disgust (from).—*v.t.* to cause to become smaller:—*pa.t.* **shrank;** *pa.p.* **shrunk.**
shrink'age, *n.* the amount by which a thing grows smaller.
shrunk'en, *adj.* grown smaller: shrivelled.—Also **shrunk.**
[O.E. *scrincan.*]

shrive, *shrīv, v.t.* to hear the confession of and give pardon to (a person):—*pa.t.* **shrōve** or **shrīved;** *pa.p.* **shriv'en** (*shriv'*) or **shrīved.**
shrift, *n.* act of shriving.
to give short shrift to, to waste little time or consideration on.
Shrove Sunday, Monday, Tuesday, days immediately before Ash Wednesday.
[O.E. *scrifan*, write—L. root as **scribe.**]

shrivel, *shriv'l, v.i., v.t.* to dry up, wrinkle, wither:—*pr.p.* **shriv'elling;** *pa.p.* **shriv'elled.** [Origin uncertain.]

shroud, *shrowd, n.* cloth around a dead body: anything that covers: (in *pl.*) ropes from the masthead to a ship's sides.—*v.t.* to cover with a shroud: to hide.
[O.E. *scrūd*; O. Norse *skrūth*, clothing.]

shrove. See **shrive.**

shrub, *shrub, n.* a low woody plant, bush.
shrubb'y, *adj.* **shrubb'iness,** *n.*
shrubb'ery, *n.* a growth of shrubs.
[O.E. *scrybb*; same word as **scrub (2).**]

shrug, *shrug, v.i.* to draw up the shoulders to show doubt, lack of interest, etc.:—*pr.p.* **shrugg'ing;** *pa.p.* **shrugged.**—Also *n.* [Origin unknown.]

shrunk, shrunken. See **shrink.**

shudder, *shud'ėr, v.i.* to shiver, tremble, from cold, fear, disgust.—Also *n.*
[Conn. with Ger. *schaudern.*]

shuffle, *shuf'l, v.t.* to mix (e.g. playing cards): to shove (the feet) along without lifting them: to move (something) quietly and hastily.—*v.i.* to mix cards: to move without lifting the feet: to avoid answering question(s) honestly and directly.—Also *n.*
shuff'ler, *n.* **shuff'ling** *n.* and *adj.*
[Conn. with **shove.**]

shun, *shun, v.t.* to avoid, keep clear of:—*pr.p.* **shunn'ing;** *pa.p.* **shunned.**
[O.E. *scunian.*]

shunt, *shunt, v.t., v.i.* to turn aside, on to a side track (e.g. an engine, train, electric current).—*n.* an act of moving out of the way: a switch.
[Perhaps connected with **shun.**]

shut, *shut, v.t.* to close the opening of: to lock, fasten: to confine (e.g. *Shut him in his kennel*).—*v.i.* to become closed:—*pr.p.* **shutt'ing;** *pa.t., pa.p.* **shut.**
shutt'er, *n.* a cover over a window or opening.
to shut down, to close (works), or (of works) to be closed, for a time or permanently.
to shut up, to close completely: (*coll.*) to stop speaking: (*coll.*) to silence.
[O.E. *scyttan*, to bar; conn. with **shoot.**]

shuttle, *shut'l, n.* (weaving) the device that carries the weft thread from side to side through the warp threads: a similar device in a sewing-machine.—*adj.* running backwards and forwards (e.g. *a shuttle bus service*).
shutt'lecock, *n.* a cork, etc., stuck with feathers, used in badminton, etc.
[O.E. *scytel*, arrow; conn. with **shoot.**]

shy[1], *shī, adj.* (of e.g. wild animal) easily frightened, timid: bashful, anxious not to attract attention to oneself: not very willing to (with *of*; e.g. *He is shy of giving his opinion*): suspicious (of):—*comp.* **shy'er, shī'er;** *superl.* **shy'est, shī'est.**—*v.i.* (of e.g. horse) to start aside from fear: to take alarm, hesitate (at; e.g. *I shy at the thought of tackling him*):—*pr.p.* **shy'ing;** *pa.p.* **shied** (*shīd*).
shy'ly, *adv.* **shy'ness,** *n.*
shy'ster, *n.* a person who is unscrupulous or dishonest in his professional conduct.
[O.E. *scēoh*; conn. Ger. *scheu.*]

shy[2], *shī, v.t.* to toss, throw.—*n.* a try, attempt:—*pl.* **shies.** [Orig. uncertain.]

sibilant, *sib'i-lȧnt, adj.* and *n.* hissing (sound).
[L. *sibilāre, -ātum*, to hiss.]

sic, *sik, adv.* so, thus. This word is put into a quotation after something that is, or seems to be, an error to show that the passage is given exactly as in the original (e.g. *Cockroaches were brought to this country by sea; the writer says: 'We were much troubled on the ship by what the Spaniards call cacarootches [sic]'.*) [L.]

sick, *sik, adj.* not well, ill: vomiting or inclined to vomit: thoroughly tired (of): disgusted: of, or for, the sick (e.g. **sick′-room,** room in which a sick person is living).

sick′ness, *n.*

sick′ly, *adj.* ailing, not healthy: causing sickness: suggesting sickness, pale, feeble (e.g. *a sickly complexion, smile*):—*comp.* **sick′lier;** *superl.* **sick′liest.**

sick′liness, *n.*

sick′en, *v.t., v.i.* to make, or become, sick.

sick′ening, *adj.* making sick, disgusted, or tired and bored.

sick′-leave, *n.* leave of absence because of sickness.

[O.E. *sēoc*; conn. with Ger. *siech.*]

sickle, *sik′l, n.* a tool with curved blade for cutting grain, etc.

[O.E. *sicol*—L. *secāre,* to cut.]

side, *sīd, n.* a bounding line, or a surface or surface part, esp. one that is not top, bottom, front, or back: either surface of paper, etc.: the right or left part of the body, esp. between armpit and hip: region, division (e.g. *the north side of the town*): a slope (of a hill): aspect (e.g. *We must look at all sides of the problem*): a party, team, etc., opposed to, fighting against, another: air of superiority (e.g. *After he became rich, he put on side*).—*adj.* at, towards, or from, one side: indirect, additional, but less important, etc. (see **side effect, issue**).

sid′ing, *n.* short line of rails on which wagons, etc., are shunted from the main line.

side′board, *n.* a piece of diningroom furniture for holding dishes, etc.

side′car, *n.* small car for passenger(s), attached to motor bicycle.

side effect, an effect (usu. bad) of a drug, etc., in addition to its good effect on the ailment for which it is given.

side issue, a matter that is not the main problem under consideration though to some extent connected with it.

side light, light coming from the side: a light carried on the side of a vehicle: (**side′light**) information that throws light (on a puzzling subject).

side line, a branch route or track: (**side′line**) a business carried on outside one's regular job or activity.

side′long, *adj.* from or to the side, not direct (e.g. *a sidelong glance*).—Also *adv.*

side show, a less important show, or a show that is part of a larger one.

side′slip, *v.i.* to skid, slide sideways.—Also *n.*

side′-splitting, *adj.* causing one to hurt one's sides with laughter.

side′step, *v.t.* to avoid by stepping to one side: to avoid having to tackle (e.g. a problem).

side′track, *v.t.* to turn into a siding: (*coll.*) to turn (a person) from his purpose: to turn (a subject) away from discussion.

side′walk (*U.S.*), pavement or footpath.

side′ways, side′wise, *adv.* with the side facing to the front (e.g. *to move sideways*).

on the side, (*slang*) by means, sometimes unworthy, other than one's regular job (e.g. *to earn money on the side*): in addition.

to side with, to give one's support to (one party in a disagreement, etc.).

to take sides, to choose to support a party, opinion, etc.

[O.E. *side*; conn. with Ger. *seite.*]

sidle, *sīd′l, v.i.* to go or move sideways: to edge along in a stealthy manner.

[From old adv. *sidling,* now **sidelong.**]

siege, *sēj, n.* an attempt to take a fort or town by keeping it surrounded by an armed force: a constant attempt to gain possession or control (of).

to lay siege to, to besiege.

[O.Fr. *sege,* seat—L. *sēdēs.*]

sienna, *si-en′ȧ, n.* a material used for colouring, brownish-yellow(**raw sienna**), or (when roasted) reddish-brown (**burnt sienna**).

[It. *terra di Sien(n)a,* Siena earth.]

sierra, *si-er′ȧ, n.* a range of mountains with jagged peaks.

[Sp.—L. *serra,* a saw.]

siesta, *si-es′tȧ, n.* a short sleep or rest, esp. one taken in the afternoon.

[Sp.—L. *sexta* (*hōra*), sixth (hour), i.e. noon.]

sieve, *siv, n.* a vessel with a bottom containing very small holes, used to separate liquids or fine grains from coarser solids.—*v.t.* to put through a sieve.

sift, *sift, v.t.* to separate by passing through a sieve: to examine closely (e.g. *to sift the evidence*).

[O.E. *sife*; conn. with Ger. *sieb.*]

sigh, *sī, v.i.* to take a long, deep-sounding breath showing tiredness, sadness, or longing: (of wind) to make a sound like this: to long (for): to grieve.—*v.t.* to express by sighs.—Also *n.*

[From *pa.t.* of M.E. verb—O.E. *sīcan.*]

sight, *sīt, n.* ability to see: act of seeing: a view, glimpse: something unusual that is seen (e.g. something worth seeing, ridiculous, terrible): a device in a gun or other instrument to guide the eye.—*v.t.* to get a view of, see suddenly: to look at through a sight.

sight′ed, *adj.* having sight, or a certain type of sight (e.g. *short-sighted*).

sight′ly, *adj.* pleasing to the eye.

sight′liness, *n.*
sight′-read′ing, *n.* reading or playing music at first sight of the notes.
sight′-see′ing, *n.* visiting scenes or objects of interest.
at sight, as soon as seen (e.g. *a bill payable at sight*): without previous study or practice.
at thirty (etc.) days' sight, (of bill of exchange) (payable) thirty (etc.) days after it is presented.
in (or **out of**) **sight**, where it, etc., can (or cannot) be seen.
[O.E. *siht*—*sēon*, see; conn. Ger. *sicht*.]

sign, *sīn, n.* a movement (e.g. wave of the hand, nod of the head) by which one can show one's meaning: a mark with a meaning: proof or evidence of something present (e.g. *signs of life*) or to come (e.g. *A red sunset is a sign of good weather*): (*mathematics*) a mark to show what is to be done (e.g. + *is a sign of addition*): a notice displayed publicly showing an inn, etc., or giving a shopkeeper's name or trade.—*v.t.* to show (one's meaning), or to give a message to (a person), by means of a sign (e.g. *He signed approval, signed the other to go ahead*): to write (one's name) on a document: to put one's signature on (a document).—Also *v.i.*
signal, *sig′n(ȧ)l, n.* a sign (e.g. gesture, light, sound) arranged beforehand giving command, warning, etc., or showing moment to begin some action: wave, sound, sent out by, or received by, a wireless set, etc.—*adj.* notable (e.g. *a signal success*).—*v.t.* to make signals to (a person): to send (information) by signals:—*pr.p.* **sig′nalling**; *pa.p.* **sig′nalled.**
sig′nally, *adv.* notably, extremely.
sig′nalman, *n.* one who sends signals: one who works railway signals.
signature, *sig′nȧ-chur, n.* a signing: a signed name: (*music*) flats and sharps, etc., that show the key, or a sign showing the time.
sig′natory, *n.* one who has signed an agreement to do something:—*pl.* **-ies.**
signet (*sig′*), *n.* small seal, e.g. on ring.
signify, *sig′ni-fī, v.t.* to be a sign of: to mean: to make known (e.g. *to signify one's approval*).—*v.i.* to have meaning or importance:—*pr.p.* **sig′nifying**; *pa.p.* **sig′nified** (*-fīd*).
signif′icant, *adj.* having meaning or importance, esp. much meaning (e.g. *significant facts, a significant glance*).
signif′icantly, *adv.* in a significant manner: to an important degree (e.g. *The sales were significantly smaller*).
signif′icance, *n.* meaning: importance.
significā′tion, *n.* act of signifying: significance.
sign′board, *n.* a board with a notice, etc.
sign′post, *n.* a post on which a sign (esp. one showing direction) is hung.
to sign away, to transfer (esp. property, rights) to another person by signing.
to sign on, to engage oneself for work by signing.
to sign off, to stop work: to stop broadcasting.
[L. *signum*, sign (*facĕre*, to make).]

signor, *sē′nyor, n.* (*cap.*) Italian word for Mr (**signore,** *-nyō′rā*, a gentleman).
signo′ra, *n.* a lady: Mrs.
signori′na, (*-ē′*) *n.* a young lady: Miss.

silage. See **silo.**

silence, *sī′lėns, n.* absence of sound or of speech, or a time of this: failure to mention or tell something.—*v.t.* to cause to be silent.—*interj.* be silent!
sī′lent, *adj.* **sī′lently,** *adv.*
sī′lencer, *n.* a device (e.g. on gun, in engine) for making noise less.
[L. *silēre*, to be silent.]

silhouette, *sil-oo-et′, n.* an outline drawing filled in with black: the profile of a person.—*v.t.* to show like a silhouette against a background.
[*Silhouette*, French finance minister, after whom anything cheap was named.]

silica, *sil′i-kȧ, n.* a very common whitish substance, found in the form of quartz, sandstone, flint, etc.
[L. *silex, silicis*, flint.]

silk, *silk, n.* the very fine, soft, fibres spun by silkworms to form cocoons: thread, cloth, made from the fibres.—Also *adj.*
sil′ken, *adj.* made of silk: silky.
sil′ky, *adj.* like silk, soft, smooth:—*comp.* **sil′kier**; *superl.* **sil′kiest.**
sil′kiness, *n.*
silk′worm, *n.* the caterpillar of certain moths which spins silk.
[O.E. *seolc*; prob. from Gk. word meaning 'Chinese'.]

sill, *sil, n.* the wood or stone at the foot of an opening, as the ledge under a door or window.—Also **cill.**
[O.E. *syl*.]

silly, *sil′i, adj.* foolish, not sensible:—*comp.* **sill′ier**; *superl.* **sill′iest.**—*n.* a silly person.
sill′iness, *n.*
[O.E. *sǣlig*, happy (conn. Ger. *selig*); later 'innocent', 'simple-minded'.]

silo, *sī′lō, n.* a tower-like building for storing grain: a pit or building for preparing silage.
si′lage, *sī′lij, n.* ensilage (see this).
[Sp.—Gk. *siros*, a pit.]

silt, *silt, n.* fine sand and mud carried and left behind by flowing water.—*v.t., v.i.* (with *up*) to fill, block, with mud.
[M.E. *sylt*; conn. Dan. *sylt*, salt marsh.]

silvan, sylvan, *sil′vȧn, adj.* wooded: living in woods: located in woods.
[Fr.—L. *silva*, a wood.]

silver, *sil′vėr, n.* a soft white metal able to take on a high polish: money made of silver or a substitute: anything looking like silver.—*adj.* made of, or looking like,

silver: (of sound) silvery.—*v.t.*, *v.i.* to cover with, or to become like, silver.
sil′vering, *n.* covering with silver: coating of (or like) silver on an object.
sil′very, *adj.* like silver: (of sound) clear and musical.
sil′veriness, *n.*
sil′verfish, *n.* a whitish goldfish: a wingless silvery insect sometimes found in houses.
silver paper, a wrapping material made of metal and having a silvery appearance.
sil′ver-plate′, *n.* dishes, spoons, etc. silver, or plated with silver.
sil′versmith, *n.* one who makes or sells articles of silver.
sil′ver-tongued, *adj.* eloquent, pleasing in speech.
silver wedding, the twenty-fifth anniversary of marriage.
[O.E. *silfer*, *seolfor*; conn. Ger. *silber*.]

similar, *sim′i-lȧr*, *adj.* like, alike, in most ways: having a resemblance (to).
similar′ity, sim′ilarness, *ns.*
sim′ilarly, *adv.* in the same, or a similar, way: likewise, also.
simile, *sim′i-li*, *n.* an expression, figure of speech, in which one thing is compared to another unlike it in all but one way, or certain ways (e.g. *a wind like a knife*; *a mind sharp as a needle*); a simile always uses 'like' or 'as' (see **metaphor**): —*pl.* **sim′iles.**
simil′itude, *n.* likeness.
[L. *similis*, like.]

simmer, *sim′ėr*, *v.i.* to be, remain, on the point of boiling, esp. if making a gentle hissing sound: (of e.g. anger, excitement, revolt) to be ready to burst out: (of person) to go on feeling annoyance without saying much.—Also *v.t.* [Imit.]

simper, *sim′pėr*, *v.i.* to smile in a silly manner.—Also *n.* [Orig. uncertain.]

simple, *sim′pl*, *adj.* easy (e.g. *a simple problem*): plain (e.g. *a simple dress*): mere, bare (e.g. *the simple facts*): ordinary: of humble rank: too trusting, easily cheated: foolish, silly.—*n.* a simple person: a healing plant.
simplic′ity (*-plis′*), **sim′pleness,** *ns.*
sim′ply, *adv.* in a simple manner: merely: absolutely (e.g. *simply lovely*).
sim′plify, *v.t.* to make simpler:—*pr.p.* **sim′plifying**; *pa.p.* **sim′plified.**
simplificā′tion, *n.* act of making simpler: a simpler form.
sim′pleton, *n.* a simple, foolish, person.
[L. *simplex*, simple (*facĕre*, to make).]

simulate, *sim′ū-lāt*, *v.t.* to make a pretence of (e.g. *to simulate illness*, *unwillingness*): to have the appearance of.
simulā′tion, *n.*
[L. *simulāre*, to make **similar** (see this).]

simultaneous, *sim-ul-tā′nyus*, *adj.* happening, done, at the same time (e.g. *He received a simultaneous protest from all his listeners*).
simultā′neously, *adv.*
simultaneous translation, translation of a speaker's words into other languages at the same time as he is speaking.
[Conn. L. *simul*, at the same time.]

sin, *sin*, *n.* a wicked act, esp. one that breaks a law of one's religion: wrongdoing: a shortcoming: (*coll.*) shame, pity (e.g. *It is a sin to spoil the beautiful old town*).—*v.i.* to do wrong, commit sin:—*pr.p.* **sinn′ing**; *pa.p.* **sinned.**
sin′ful, *adj.* **sinn′er,** *n.*
sin′fully, *adv.* **sin′fulness,** *n.*
original sin, the supposed sinfulness of all human beings, held to be due to the sin of Adam.
[O.E. *syn*, *sinn*; conn. with Ger. *sünde*.]

since, *sins*, *adv.* (often **ever since**) from then till now (e.g. *We fought, and I have avoided him ever since*): at a later time (e.g. *We fought, but we have since become friends*): ago (e.g. *It happened long since*). —*prep.* from the time of (e.g. *since his arrival*).—*conj.* after, or from, the time in the past when (e.g. *Since he agreed to come he has taken ill*; *I have been at home since I returned from Italy*): because (e.g. *Since you are going I will go too*).
[M.E. *sins*, *sithens*—O.E. *sīth*, late.]

sincere, *sin-sēr′*, *adj.* honest in word and deed: true, genuine (e.g. *a sincere desire*; *sincere friends*).
sincerity (*-ser′*), **sincere′ness,** *ns.*
sincere′ly, *adv.*
[L. *sincērus*, clean.]

sine, *sī′ni*, *prep.* without.
sine die (*dī′ē*), without fixed date for resumption, indefinitely (used in speaking of e.g. adjournment of a meeting).
sine qua non, a necessity. [L.]

sinecure, *sī′nė-kūr*, *sin′-*, *n.* a job with salary but little or no work.
[**sine,** and L. *cūra*, care.]

sinew, *sin′ū*, *n.* a tendon (see this word): strength: (in *pl.*) equipment, resources for (e.g. *lacking the sinews of war*).
sin′ewy, *adj.* having sinews, esp. well-developed ones: strong, tough, vigorous.
[O.E. *sinu*, *sinwe*.]

sinful, etc. See **sin.**

sing, *sing*, *v.i.* to make musical sounds with one's voice: to ring, hum, murmur, etc. —*v.t.* to utter musically: to utter with enthusiasm (e.g. *to sing her praises*):—*pa.t.* **sang**; *pa.p.* **sung.**
sing′ing, *n.* and *adj.* **sing′er,** *n.*
sing′song, *n.* boring up-and-down tone of voice: jingly verse: (*coll.*) a meeting where everyone should sing.
to sing another song, or **tune,** to change one's attitude, esp. behave more humbly.
to sing out, to shout, call out.
See also **song.**
[O.E. *singan*; conn. with Ger. *singen*.]

singe, *sinj*, *v.t.*, *v.i.* to burn on the surface,

scorch :—*pr.p.* **singe'ing ;** *pa.p.* **singed.** —Also *n.*
[O.E. *sen(c)gan.*]

Singhalese. Same as **Sinhalese.**

single, *sing'gl, adj.* one only : not double : unmarried : for one person : between two, man to man (e.g. *single combat*) : for one direction of a journey (e.g. *a single ticket*) : sincere.—*v.t.* to choose, pick (out).
sin'gly, *adv.* one by one : separately : single-handed.
sin'gleness, *n.* state of being single : sincerity : state of having one only (e.g. *singleness of aim, purpose*).
sin'gle-han'ded, *adj.* by oneself, with no help.
sin'gle-hear'ted, *adj.* sincere.
sin'gle-min'ded, *adj.* bent on one purpose only : sincere.
singular, *sin'gū-lȧr, adj.* (*grammar*) showing one person or thing : exceptional, unusual, strange.
singular'ity (*pl.* **-ies**), **sin'gularness,** *ns.*
sin'gularly, *adv.* unusually : strangely.
[L. *singulus*, only one.]

singsong. See **sing.**

Sinhalese, *sing-hȧ-lēz', sin-*, **Singhalese,** *sing-hȧ-, sing-gȧ-, adj.* of Ceylon, or of one (the most numerous) of the peoples of Ceylon or their language.—Also *n.*—Also **Cing'alese.**
[Sanskrit *Sinhala*, Ceylon.]

sinister, *sin'is-tėr, adj.* of, on, the left side : suggesting evil, present or to come (e.g. *sinister happenings, a sinister look*).
sin'isterly, *adv.* **sin'isterness,** *n.* [L.]

sink, *singk, v.i.* to go down, wholly or partly, below the surface of e.g. water : to pass slowly to a lower position or level, or a less active state (e.g. *The sun, a fire, a voice, hopes, sink*) : to slope downwards : (of dying person) to become weaker : to lower oneself (into e.g. a chair) : to pass (into e.g. silence, sleep).—*v.t.* to cause to go below the surface, or to a lower position, level or state : to make by digging (e.g. a well) : to drive (e.g. knife, teeth, into something) : to invest, usu. at a loss (e.g. *to sink money in a business*) : to avoid bringing (e.g. one's own desires, unpleasant facts) into consideration, etc. : —*pa.t.* **sank ;** *pa.p.* **sunk.**—*n.* a drain to carry off dirty water : a kitchen or scullery basin with a drain : a hollow in a land surface : a place where evil and vice live and thrive.
sink'er, *n.* anything that causes sinking, esp. a weight on a fishing-line.
sunk, *adj.* on a lower level than the surroundings : sunken : (*coll.*) done for, unable to carry on.
sunk'en, *adj.* hollowed (esp. of cheeks) : sunk.
Sunk and *sunken* are used in much the same way, except that *sunk* is the usu. *adj.* for something that has been made or placed at a lower level (e.g. *a sunk garden*).
sinking fund, money put aside every year for paying off debts.
[O.E. *sincan* ; conn. with Ger. *sinken.*]

sinner. See **sin.**

sinuous, *sin'ū-ùs, adj.* bending in and out : (of person) making strong, smooth movements (also used of movement, grace).
sin'uously, *adv.* **sin'uousness,** *n.*
sinuos'ity, *n.* sinuousness : a bend.
[L. *sinus*, a bend, fold, bay.]

sinus, *sī'nùs, n.* a cavity, hollow, as an air cavity in the head connected with the nose :—*pl.* **sī'nuses.**
sinusī'tis, *n.* inflammation of one of the sinuses of the nose.
[Same root as **sinuous.**]

sip, *sip, v.t., v.i.* to drink in very small quantities :—*pr.p.* **sipp'ing ;** *pa.p.* **sipped.**—Also *n.*
[Conn. with **sup.**]

siphon, *sī'fȯn, n.* a pipe or tube with a bend through which liquid can be drawn off from one container to another at a lower level : (also **siphon bottle**) a glass bottle with bent tube for soda water, etc.—*v.t.* to draw (off) by means of a siphon.
[Gk. *siphōn.*]

sir, *sėr, n.* a word of respect used in speaking or writing to a man : the title of a knight or baronet.
sire, *sīr, n.* formerly word of address to king : a male parent, esp. of a horse : (in *pl.*) ancestors, forefathers.—*v.t.* (of male animal) to beget.
[O.Fr. *sire*—L. *senior*, elder.]

siren, *sī'rėn, n.* a ship's foghorn : a factory hooter : a similar sound to give warning of an air raid : a dangerously attractive woman.
[Gk. *Seirēn*, one of certain sea-nymphs who lured sailors to danger by singing.]

sirloin, *sėr'loin, n.* the upper part of the loin of beef.
[Fr. *sur*, over, *loigne*, loin.]

sirocco, *si-rok'ō, n.* dry wind from Africa.
[It. *s(c)irocco*—Arabic *sharq*, the east.]

sisal, *sīs', sis'(ȧ)l, n.* fibre from a West Indian plant, used in making ropes.
[*Sisal*, a Yucatan port.]

sister, *sis'tėr, n.* the name given to a female by other children of the same parents : a member of a sisterhood : a nurse in a hospital, esp. one with authority : a female of the same kind or class.—*adj.* closely related : alike, e.g. in design (e.g. *sister ships*).
sis'terhood, *n.* state of being a sister : a group of women formed for purposes of religion, good works, etc.
sis'terly, *adj.* like a sister, kind, loving.
sis'terliness, *n.*
sis'ter-in-law, *n.* a husband's or wife's sister, or a brother's wife :—*pl.* **sis'ters-in-law.**
[Old Norse *systir* ; conn. O.E. *sweostor.*

sit, *sit, v.i.* to rest on the lower part of the body, be seated : (of birds) to perch : to rest on eggs in order to hatch them : to be an official member (e.g. *to sit in Parliament*) : (of Parliament, etc.) to be in session : to be located (e.g. *The wind sits in the west*) : to pose, be a model : to hang, fit (e.g. *The coat sits well*).—*v.t.* to seat : to have a seat on, ride : to take (an examination) :—*pr.p.* **sitt'ing** ; *pa.p.* **sat.**

sitt'er, *n.* one who poses : a sitting bird : an easy target : a baby-sitter.

sitt'ing, *n.* state of resting on a seat : a seat in a church pew : brooding on eggs : a meeting of a court, etc. : a time of posing for an artist or photographer.—*adj.* seated : brooding : meeting, in session : actually in office or possession (e.g. *the sitting member of parliament for Bath* ; *the sitting tenant*).

sit-down strike, a strike in which workers stay in the factory but refuse to work.

sitt'ingroom, *n.* a room chiefly for sitting in.

to sit back, to rest : to take no part in an activity.

to sit down, to take a seat.

to sit in, (*U.S.*) to be present (at a conference or meeting) without being an actual member.

to sit out, to remain seated during (a dance) : to sit to the end of.

to sit tight, to refuse to move or act.

to sit up, to sit with one's back straight : to keep watch during the night.

[O.E. *sittan* ; Ger. *sitzen*, L. *sedēre.*]

site, *sit, n.* the ground on which e.g. a building is, was, or is to be, put up or placed.—*v.t.* to locate, place (building, etc.).

situate, *sit'ū-āt, v.t.* to locate, place : to place with regard to problems, etc. (usu. in *pa.p.* ; e.g. *Having inherited money, he was now more happily situated*).

situā'tion, *n.* position : circumstances, state of affairs, esp. difficult (e.g. *In this situation help was necessary*) : employment, job (esp. unimportant).

[L. *situs.*]

six, *siks, adj.* and *n.* the number next above five (6 or VI).

sixth, *adj.* last of six.—*n.* one of six equal parts.

sixteen, *siks'tēn, siks-tēn', adj.* and *n.* six and ten (16 or XVI).

sixteenth, *adj.* last of sixteen.—*n.* one of sixteen equal parts.

sixty, *siks'ti, adj.* and *n.* six times ten (60 or LX) :—*pl.* **six'ties.**

six'tieth, *adj.* last of sixty.—*n.* one of sixty equal parts.

six'pence, *n.* coin formerly silver, later cupro-nickel, worth six pennies.

six'penny, *adj.* worth or costing sixpence : of little value.

sixty-four dollar question, the most difficult question (*orig.* in a quiz).

[O.E. *siex* ; *si(e)xtēne* ; *si(e)xtig.*]

size[1], *sīz, n.* space taken up by anything : measurements, dimensions : largeness : one of a number of classes in which shoes, dresses, etc. are grouped according to measurements (e.g. *I take size 5 in shoes*).

sī'zable, size'able, *adj.* fairly large.

sized, *adj.* having a certain kind of size (e.g. *middle-sized*).

to size up, to form an opinion about the worth, nature, etc. of (person, situation).

[From **assize** in sense of standard of quantity, etc., fixed by regulation.]

size[2], *sīz,* **sizing,** *sī'zing, n.* weak glue, or other material for glazing.—*v.t.* to cover with size.

[Perh. same as **size** (1).]

sizzle, *siz'l, v.i.* to make a hissing sound.—*v.t., v.i.* to fry or scorch. [Imit.]

sjambok, *sham'bok, n.* a heavy whip made of a strip of hide.—Also **jam'bok.**

[Afrikaans (now *sambok*)—Malay.]

skate[1], *skāt, n.* a steel blade or rollers which can be fixed to a shoe for gliding on ice, etc.—*v.i.* to move on skates.

skā'ter, *n.* **skā'ting,** *n.*

[Du. *schaats.*]

skate[2], *skāt, n.* large flatfish.

[From Scand.]

skean-dhu, *skēn'dōō, n.* a Highlander's dagger, worn in the stocking.

[Gael. *sgian*, knife, *dhu*, black.]

skein, *skān, n.* a length of thread or yarn, loosely coiled.

[O.Fr. *escaigne.*]

skeleton, *skel'i-t(ŏ)n, n.* the bony framework of an animal : any framework or outline : a very thin person.—*adj.* (of e.g. a staff, crew) reduced to very small number.

a skeleton in the cupboard, a closely kept secret, hidden shame.

skeleton key, a key with parts filed away that can open different locks.

[Gk. *skeleton* (*sōma*), a dried (body).]

sketch, *skech, n.* a rough plan, or drawing or painting : an outline or short account : a short slight play, dramatic scene, etc.—*v.t.* to draw, describe, or plan, roughly : to give the chief points of.—Also (in art sense) *v.i.*

sketch'y, *adj.* roughly done or carried out : slight, incomplete (e.g. *a sketchy knowledge*).

sketch'ily, *adv.* **sketch'iness,** *n.*

[Du. *schets*—It. *schizzo.*]

skew, *skū, adj. adv.* off the straight, slanting.—*v.t., v.i.* to set, be set, at a slant. [Same root as **eschew.**]

skewer, *skū'ėr, n.* a long pin of wood or metal for keeping meat together while roasting.—*v.t.* to fasten, fix, with a skewer, or with something sharp.

[Earlier *skiver* ; orig. unknown.]

ski, *skē, n.* one of a pair of long narrow strips of wood for gliding over snow :—

pl. **ski, skis.**—*v.i.* to travel on, use, skis :—*pr.p.* **ski'ing** ; *pa.p.* **skied** (*skēd*).
ski'ing, *n.* and *adj.* [Norw.]

skid, *skid, n.* a wedge, etc., put under a wheel to check it on a steep place : plank(s), log(s), etc., on which things can be moved by sliding : a slide sideways (e.g. *The road was wet and my car went into a skid*).—*v.t.* to cause to slide sideways.—*v.i.* (of wheels) to slide along without turning : to slip sideways.
[Scand. origin.]

skiff, *skif, n.* a small light boat.
[Conn. **ship.**]

skill, *skil, n.* cleverness at doing something —either from practice or from natural gift : an ability required for a craft (*a manual skill*).
skil'ful, *adj.* having, or showing, skill.
skil'fully, *adv.* **skil'fulness,** *n.*
skilled, *adj.* skilful : requiring skill, esp. skill gained by training (e.g. *a skilled job*).
[Old Norse *skil*, distinction.]

skillet, *skil'it, n.* a small metal dish with a long handle used in cooking.
[Orig. uncertain.]

skim, *skim, v.t.* to remove floating matter from the surface of (e.g. *to skim soup*) : to take (e.g. cream) from the surface of liquid : to glide lightly over : to read hurriedly, skipping parts.—*v.i.* to glide along near the surface, or lightly :—*pr.p.* **skimm'ing** ; *pa.p.* **skimmed.**
skim milk, milk from which the cream has been skimmed. [Conn. **scum.**]

skimp, *skimp, v.t.* to give (person) hardly enough : to do (job) imperfectly.—*v.i.* to spend too little.
skim'py, *adj.* (of quantity) too small : (of e.g. dress) not long, full, enough : stingy.
skim'pily, *adv.* **skim'piness,** *n.*
[Perh. **scamp** and **scrimp.**]

skin, *skin, n.* the natural outer covering of an animal : a thin outer layer, as on a fruit : a film on liquid : a container of animal skin, etc., for e.g. liquids.—*v.t.* to strip the skin from : (*slang*) to strip of money, to fleece :—*pr.p.* **skinn'ing ;** *pa.p.* **skinned.**
skinn'y, *adj.* very thin.
skinn'iness, *n.*
skin'-deep, *adj.* no deeper than the skin (e.g. *The cut, his sorrow, was skin-deep*).
skin'flint, *n.* mean, grasping person.
skin'-tight', *adj.* fitting as tightly as the skin.
by the skin of one's teeth, very narrowly, only just (e.g. *We escaped by the skin of our teeth*).
to get under one's skin, to annoy one greatly : to fill one's thoughts.
to save one's skin, to escape without injury, esp. in a cowardly way.
[O.E. *scinn* ; from Scand.]

skip, *skip, v.i.* to spring or hop over a turning rope : to leap, esp. lightly or joyfully : to leave out parts of e.g. a book.—Also *v.t.* and *n.*
skipp'ing-rope, *n.* rope used in skipping.
[M.E. *skippen* ; perh. Scand.]

skipper, *skip'ėr, n.* the captain of a merchant or small ship, aircraft (*coll.*), or team.—*v.t.* to act as skipper of.
[Du. *schipper—schip*, ship.]

skirmish, *skėr'mish, n.* a fight between small parties of soldiers : a short, sharp contest or disagreement.—Also *v.i.*
[From O.Fr., but of Germanic origin.]

skirt, *skėrt, n.* a garment that hangs from the waist : the lower part of a dress, etc. : (in *pl.*) the outer edge or border.—*v.t.* to lie on, or pass along, the edge of.
skirting (board), the narrow board next the floor round the walls of a room.
[Old Norse *skyrta*, shirt ; conn. **shirt.**]

skit, *skit, n.* a short piece of writing or dramatic scene making fun of person(s), etc. (e.g. *a skit on opera singers*).
[Orig. uncertain.]

skittish, *skit'ish, adj.* (of a horse) easily frightened : too frisky or lively.
[Perh. conn. with **skit.**]

skittle, *skit'l, n.* a pin for the game of **skittles,** a form of ninepins in which a cheese-shaped missile is used.
[Orig. uncertain.]

skulk, *skulk, v.i.* to lie hidden for a bad purpose : to move in a sneaking way : to avoid doing one's job.
[M.E. *skulken* ; of Scand. origin.]

skull, *skul, n.* the bony case that encloses the brain : the head.
skull'cap, *n.* a cap that fits closely to the head.
skull and cross-bones, a design on a pirate's flag, etc.
[M.E. *scolle* ; perh. Scand.]

skunk, *skungk, n.* a small American animal which defends itself by squirting out an evil-smelling liquid : a mean, low fellow.
[North Amer. Indian *segonku.*]

sky, *skī, n.* (often in *pl.*, **skies**) the upper atmosphere, the heavens : weather or climate (e.g. *stormy skies* ; *Arctic skies*).—*v.t.* to raise, or hit, high into the air : hang (e.g. picture) above line of sight :—*pr.p.* **sky'ing ;** *pa.p.* **skied** (*skīd*).
sky'-blue, *adj.* blue like the sky.
sky'-div'ing, -jump'ing, *ns.* the sport of jumping from aircraft with delayed opening of parachute.
sky'-high, *adj.* very high.
sky'lark, *n.* the common lark, which sings while hovering overhead.—*v.i.* to be merry in a rough, mischievous way.
sky'larking, *n.* and *adj.*
sky'light, *n.* window in a roof or ceiling.
sky'line, *n.* the horizon.
sky'scrāper, *n.* a high building of many storeys.
[Old Norse *skȳ*, a cloud.]

slab, *slab, n.* a thick plate or slice of e.g. stone, cake. [M.E.; orig. unknown.]

slabber. Same as **slobber.**

slack[1], *slak, n.* small coal and coal dust. [Conn. Ger. *schlacke.*]

slack[2], *slak, adj.* not firmly stretched: not firmly in position: not holding fast: not strict: lazy and careless: not busy (e.g. *the slack season*): (of tide, etc.) moving slowly.—*n.* the loose part of a rope: (in *pl.*) trousers.—*v.i.* to do less work than one should: to slacken.

slack'en, *v.t., v.i.* to make, or become, looser, or less active, less tense, etc.

slack'er, *n.* one who slacks.

slack water, turn of the tide.

[O.E. *sleac.*]

slag, *slag, n.* metal refuse from smelting works.

[Conn. with **slack** (1).]

slain. See **slay.**

slake, *slāk, v.t.* to quench, satisfy (e.g. thirst, anger): to put out (fire): to mix (lime) with water.

[Same root as **slack** (2).]

slalom, *slä'lòm, n.* a downhill or zigzag ski run among posts or trees: an obstacle race in canoes. [From Norw.]

slam[1], *slam, v.t., v.i.* to shut with noise, bang: to put, come, noisily, hurriedly (down, against, etc.):—*pr.p.* **slamm'ing**; *pa.p.* **slammed.** [Perh. from Scand.]

slam[2], *slam, n.* (in cards) the winning of every trick (also **grand slam**).

little slam, winning of every trick but one. [Orig. uncertain.]

slander, *slân'dėr, n.* false statement(s) made with desire to harm a person's reputation (in English law, term applies to spoken words only; see **libel**).—*v.t.* to speak slander against.

slan'derous, *adj.* **slan'derously,** *adv.*

[Through O.Fr.—L. root as **scandal.**]

slang, *slang, n.* words or phrases in everyday speech coined in attempt to be new, different, and striking, usu. lasting only a short time, but sometimes later accepted for dignified use (see **donkey**): special language of a group (see **argot, cant, jargon**).—*v.t.* to scold, abuse.

slang'y, *adj.* **slang'iness,** *n.*

[Orig. uncertain.]

slant, *slânt, v.t., v.i.* to slope: to place, lie, move, diagonally (e.g. *Cross straight; do not slant across the street*): to give (facts) in a way that makes them seem to mean what one wishes them to mean.—*n.* a turning away from a straight line: way of looking at (with *on*; e.g. *a new slant on the question*).

slan'ting, *adj.* and *n.*

[M.E. *slent*; conn. Norw. *slenta.*]

slap, *slap, n.* a blow with the hand or anything flat: a snub.—*v.t.* to give slap to:—*pr.p.* **slapp'ing**; *pa.p.* **slapped.**

slap'dash, *adv.* in a bold, careless way.—*adj.* off-hand, hasty.

slap'stick comedy, knockabout comedy or farce.

[Imit.; conn. Ger. *schlappe,* blow.]

slash, *slash, v.t.* to make long cuts in: to strike violently: to criticise harshly: (*U.S.* or *slang*) to reduce greatly.—Also *v.i.*—*n.* a long cut: a sweeping blow.

[Perh. O.Fr. *esclachier,* to break.]

slat, *slat, n.* a thin strip of wood.

slatt'ed, *adj.* having slats.

[O.Fr. *esclat* (masc.); root as **slate** (1).

slate[1], *slāt, n.* an easily split rock of dull blue, grey, etc., used for roofing, etc. or writing upon.—*adj.* made of slate: slate-coloured.—*v.t.* to cover with slate.

slā'ty, *adj.* **slā'tiness,** *n.*

[O.Fr. *esclate* (fem.); root as **slat.**]

slate[2], *slāt, v.t.* to say harsh things to or about.

slā'ting, *n.* a harsh scolding.

[From Old Norse.]

slatted. See **slat.**

slattern, *slat'ėrn, n.* a slut, dirty woman.

slatt'ernly, *adj.* **slatt'ernliness,** *n.*

[Conn. dial. *slatter,* to spill.]

slaughter, *slö'tėr, n.* killing of animals, esp. for food: brutal killing: killing of great numbers of people.—Also *v.t.*

slaugh'ter-house, *n.* a place where animals are killed for the market.

[Old Norse *slātr,* butcher's meat.]

Slav, *släv, n.* a person whose language is **Slav(onic)** (Russian, Polish, Czech, etc.).

[Late Gk. *Sklabos*; from Slavonic words.]

slave, *slāv, n.* one who is forced to work for a master to whom he belongs: one who is completely devoted (to another whom he serves): one who has lost power to resist (e.g. *He is a slave to drink*): one who works very hard.—*v.i.* to work like a slave.

slā'ver, *n.* a dealer in slaves: a ship used to carry slaves.

slā'very, *n.* the state of being a slave: the system of ownership of slaves.

slā'vish, *adj.* slave-like: (acting or thinking) exactly according to instructions or to rules: (of e.g. imitation) too close.

slā'vishly, *adv.* **slā'vishness,** *n.*

slave driver, an overseer of slaves: a hard master.

[O.Fr. *esclave,* orig. a **Slav.**]

slaver[1], *slav'ėr,* or *slāv'ėr, n.* saliva running from the mouth.—*v.i.* to let the saliva run out of the mouth.

[From Scand.; conn. with **slobber.**]

slaver[2]. See **slave.**

slay, *slā, v.t.* to kill:—*pr.p.* **slay'ing**; *pa.t.* **slew**; *pa.p.* **slain.**

[O.E. *slēan*; conn. Ger. *schlagen,* strike.]

sled, *sled, n.* a vehicle with runners made for sliding on snow.—*v.i.* to travel in a sled:—*pr.p.* **sledd'ing**; *pa.p.* **sledd'ed.**

[From Middle Du.]

sledge[1], *slej, n., v.i.* Same as **sled.**

sledge′-dog, *n.* a dog trained to pull a sledge.
[Middle Du. *sleedse.*]

sledge[2], *slej, n.* a large heavy hammer.—Also **sledge′-hammer.**
[O.E. *slecg—slēan,* to slay.]

sleek, *slēk, adj.* smooth and glossy: well fed and cared for: smoothly polite.—*v.t.* to make sleek.
sleek′ly, *adv.* **sleek′ness,** *n.* [**slick.**]

sleep, *slēp, v.t.* to take rest in a state of unconsciousness: to be motionless: to be dead: (of limbs) to be numb: (of a top) to spin so steadily that it looks as if it were standing still:—*pa.t.* and *pa.p.* **slept.**—Also *n.*
slee′per, *n.* one who sleeps: a wooden or steel beam supporting railway lines: sleeping-car, or -berth, on railway train.
sleep′less, *adj.* unable to sleep: always watchful, alert, active.
slee′py, *adj.* drowsy, inclined to sleep: not alert, or seeming not to be (e.g. *a sleepy manner*): very quiet (e.g. *a sleepy town*):—*comp.* **slee′pier**; *superl.* **slee′piest.**
slee′pily, *adv.* **slee′piness,** *n.*
slee′ping-bag, *n.* a bag for sleeping in, used by campers, etc.
slee′ping-car, *n.* railway coach with berths or beds.
sleeping partner, a partner who has money invested in a business but takes no part in its management.
sleep′walker, *n.* one who walks while asleep.
slee′pyhead, *n.* a lazy person.
[O.E. *slǣpan*; conn. Ger. *schlafen.*]

sleet, *slēt, n.* rain mixed with snow or hail.—*v.i.* to shower sleet.
[M.E.; prob. conn. Ger. *schlosse.*]

sleeve, *slēv, n.* the part of a garment that covers the arm: a container for a gramophone record: (in machinery) something that covers as a sleeve does.
sleeve′less, *adj.* without sleeves.
to have up one's sleeve, to keep hidden for use if the need arises.
[O.E. *slēfe.*]

sleigh, *slā, n.* a sledge, esp. a large horse-drawn one.—Also *v.i.*
[Du. *slee.*]

sleight, *slīt, n.* cunning; used in phrase **sleight-of-hand,** (skill in) tricks depending on quickness of hand.
[Old Norse *slǣgth.*]

slender, *slen′dėr, adj.* thin or narrow: slim: slight (e.g. *a slender chance*): small in amount (e.g. *a slender income*).
[Orig. unknown.]

slept. See **sleep.**

sleuth, *slōōth, n.* a tracker or detective.
sleuth′-hound, *n.* a bloodhound.
[Old Norse *slōth,* track.]

slew[1], *slōō, v.t.* and *v.i.* to turn, swing (ship, boat) round. [Orig. uncertain.]

slew[2]. See **slay.**

slice, *slīs, n.* a thin broad piece: a broad-bladed implement, esp. for serving fish: a slash: (*golf*) a sliced stroke.—*v.t.* to cut in slices: to cut through: to cut (off, from, etc.): to hit (a ball) in such a way that it curves away to the right (in the case of left-handed player, to the left).
slī′cing, *n.* and *adj.*
[Through O.Fr.—Old Ger. *slīzan,* split.]

slick, *slik, adj.* sleek, smooth: smooth in speech and manner: skilful, often in a sly way.—*v.t.* to polish: to tidy up.
slick′ly, *adv.* **slick′ness,** *n.*
[Conn. with **sleek.**]

slide, *slīd, v.i.* to slip or glide: to pass along smoothly: to pass quietly or secretly: to take its course (e.g. *Do nothing; just let the matter slide*).—*v.t.* to push smoothly along: to slip:—*pa.t.* and *pa.p.* **slid** (*slid*).—*n.* a slippery track: a chute: a groove or rail on which a thing slides: a sliding part, e.g. of a trombone: a piece of glass, etc., on which to place objects to be looked at through a microscope: a picture for showing on a screen.
slī′der, *n.* one who, or something that, slides.
slide′-rule, *n.* an instrument for multiplying, dividing, etc. made of rulers sliding against each other.
sliding scale, a scale of wages, charges, etc. which can be changed as conditions change.
[O.E. *slīdan,* to slide.]

slier, sliest. See **sly.**

slight, *slīt, adj.* small in amount (e.g. *a slight breeze, improvement*): (of person) slender in build: of little importance.—*v.t.* to treat as unimportant, insult by ignoring.—*n.* an insult by showing no interest in or respect for.
slight′ly, *adv.* in a small degree: slenderly.
slight′ing, *adj.* insulting or discourteous.
slight′ingly, *adv.*
[Conn. O.E. *eorthslihtes,* close to ground.]

slily. See **sly.**

slim, *slim, adj.* slender, slight: poor (e.g. *a slim chance*):—*comp.* **slimm′er**; *superl.* **slimm′est.**—*v.i.* to practise rules for making the figure more slender:—*pr.p.* **slimm′ing**; *pa.p.* **slimmed.**
slimm′ing, *n.* **slim′ness,** *n.*
[Conn. with Ger. *schlimm,* bad.]

slime, *slīm, n.* fine, thin, slippery mud: wet filth: a secretion (e.g. mucus).
slī′my, *adj.* covered with slime: disgustingly meek or flattering.
slī′miness, *n.*
[O.E. *slīm*; conn. with Ger. *schleim.*]

sling, *sling, n.* a strap with a string attached to each end for hurling e.g. a stone: a hanging bandage to support an injured limb: a band, rope net, etc., used in hoisting and lowering or carrying a weight.—*v.t.* to throw with a sling: to move or swing by means of a rope, rope net, etc.: (*coll.*) to throw:—*pa.t.*, *pa.p.* **slung.** [From Scand.]

slink, *slingk, v.i.* to sneak (away):—*pa.t.*, *pa.p.* **slunk.**
slink'y, *adj.* sneaky: close-fitting.
[O.E. *slincan*, creep; Ger. *schleichen.*]

slip[1], *slip, v.i.* to slide or glide: to move quietly or secretly: to move out of place, or out of one's grasp (e.g. *I let the hammer slip*): to lose one's footing: to make a mistake.—*v.t.* to cause to slide or pass, or to give, quietly or secretly (e.g. *to slip on a ring*; *to slip a letter into his hand*; *to slip him money*): to escape (e.g. one's memory, attention):—*pr.p.* **slipp'ing**; *pa.p.* **slipped.**—*n.* act of slipping: a slight error: a garment easily slipped on, esp. under a dress: a pillow cover: (*cricket*) fielder, or (often in *pl.*) position, on the offside, somewhat behind the batsman: an artificial slope leading down to water, on which ships are built or repaired (also **slip'way).**
slipp'er, *n.* a loose indoor shoe.
slipp'ery, *adj.* so smooth as to cause slipping: not to be trusted, shifty.
slipp'eriness, *n.*
slip'-knot, *n.* a knot that slips along rope or string.
slip road, a local bypass.
slip'shod, *adj.* having shoes worn away at the heel: (of work, etc.) careless.
slip'stream, *n.* the stream of air driven back by an aircraft propeller.
slip'-up, *n.* (*coll.*) mistake or failure.
slipway. See **slip** (*n.*) above.
to slip off, to take off: to move off noiselessly or hastily.
to slip on, to put on in a hurry.
to give the slip to, to escape from secretly.
[Du. *slippen*; or O.E. *slipor*, slippery.]

slip[2], *slip, n.* a cutting from a plant: a young shoot or person: a strip or narrow piece of e.g. paper.
[Middle Du. *slippen*, to cut.]

slit, *slit, v.t.* to make a long cut in: to cut into strips:—*pr.p.* **slitt'ing**; *pa.p.* **slit.**—*n.* a long cut, or narrow opening.
[O.E. *slītan*; conn. with Ger. *schlitzen.*]

slither, *sliTH'ėr, v.i.* to slide, slip about, as on mud: to walk, move, with gliding motion.
[O.E. *slidderian*, to slip.]

sliver, *sliv'ėr, slī', n.* a long thin piece cut off.—*v.t.*, *v.i.* to split.
[O.E. (*tō-*)*slīfan*, to split.]

slobber, *slob'ėr, v.i.* to slaver: to be sentimental.—Also *v.t.* and *n.*
slobb'ery, *adj.* unpleasantly moist.
[Prob. from Du.]

sloe, *slō, n.* a small sour plum, the fruit of the blackthorn: the blackthorn.
[O.E. *slā*; conn. with Du. *slee.*]

slog, *slog, v.i.* to hit, or work, hard: to walk on steadily.—*v.t.* to hit hard: to make (one's way) with difficulty:—*pr.p.* **slogg'ing**; *pa.p.* **slogged.**—*n.* a hard blow: a hard spell of work.
slogg'er, *n.* [Orig. uncertain.]

slogan, *slō'gȧn, n.* a war cry among ancient Highlanders: a catchword, or phrase expressing view, aim, etc., of e.g. a political party, or one used in advertising.
[Gael. *sluagh*, army, *gairm*, cry.]

slogging, etc. See **slog.**

sloop, *slo͞op, n.* a light boat: a one-masted sailing-vessel.
[Du. *sloep.*]

slop, *slop, n.* spilled liquid: (in *pl.*) dirty water: (in *pl.*) thin, tasteless food: gush, sentimentality.—*v.t.*, *v.i.* to spill: to gush.—*v.i.* to walk (through slush, water, etc.):—*pr.p.* **slopp'ing**; *pa.p.* **slopped.**
slopp'y, *adj.* wet: muddy: careless, slovenly: very sentimental.
slopp'ily, *adv.* **slopp'iness,** *n.*
[O.E. (*cū-*)*sloppe*, (cow-) droppings.]

slope, *slōp, n.* an upward or downward slant: a surface with one end higher than the other.—*v.t.* to make with a surface that is not level, not horizontal: to put in a sloping position or direction.
[O.E. *āslūpan*, to slip away.]

slopping, sloppy, etc. See **slop.**

slot, *slot, n.* a narrow opening to receive a coin, or to receive part of a machine, etc. —*v.t.* to cut a slot in.
slot machine, machine, e.g. one containing small articles for sale, worked by putting coin in slot.
[O.Fr. *esclot.*]

sloth, *slōth, sloth, n.* laziness, esp. as a habit: a slow-moving animal that lives in trees in South America.
sloth'ful, *adj.* **sloth'fully,** *adv.*
sloth'fulness, *n.*
[M.E. *slawthe*—O.E. *slāw*, slow.]

slouch, *slowch, n.* a hunched-up loose position of the body in walking.—*v.t.* to move or walk with a slouch.
slouch hat, a hat with a broad, soft brim turned down.
[Conn. O. Norse *slōkr*, slouching fellow.]

slough[1], *slow, n.* a bog, swamp, marsh.
[O.E. *slōh.*]

slough[2], *sluf, n.* cast-off skin of a snake.—*v.i.* to cast the skin: to come (off).—*v.t.* to cast off.
[M.E. *sloh*; orig. uncertain.]

sloven, *sluv'n, n.* a person carelessly or dirtily dressed, or slipshod in work.
slov'enly, *adj.* **slov'enliness,** *n.*
[Conn. with **slobber.**]

slow, *slō, adj.* not fast: leisurely: not hasty: (of e.g. clock) behind in time: not quick at learning: dull, not lively or interesting.—*adv.* slowly.—*v.t.*, *v.i.* to make, or become, slower.
slow'ly, *adv.* **slow'ness,** *n.*
slow'-mō'tion, *n.*, *adj.*, *adv.* (speed)

much slower than normal, or (*motion-picture*) actual, movement.
[O.E. *slāw*.]

sludge, *sluj*, *n.* soft mud : slimy sediment. [Conn. **slush.**]

slug[1], *slug*, *n.* a heavy, lazy fellow : an animal related to snails but with no shell.
slugg'ard, *n.* one who is slow and lazy in habits.
slugg'ish, *adj.* lazy, without energy : having little motion or power.
[Prob. Scand.]

slug[2], *slug*, *n.* a lump of metal, esp. one for firing from a gun : a heavy blow.
[Perh. **slug** (1).]

sluice, *sloōs*, *n.* an artificial channel for water, provided with a **sluice gate** (a sliding gate) or other device for controlling the flow : the gate : the water in the channel.—*v.t.* to flood, or clean out, with a flow of water.—*v.i.* to pour.
[Through Fr.—L. root as **exclude.**]

slum, *slum*, *n.* an overcrowded part of a town where living conditions are dirty and unhealthy. [Orig. slang.]

slumber, *slum'bėr*, *v.i.* to sleep, esp. lightly : to be careless or idle.—*n.* light sleep.
[M.E. *slūmeren*—O.E. *slūma* (*n.*).]

slump, *slump*, *v.i.* to fall or sink suddenly into water or mud : to drop limply and heavily : (of stocks, trade, etc.) to lose value suddenly.—*n.* a serious fall of prices, business, etc. [Prob. imit.]

slung. See **sling.** **slunk.** See **slink.**

slur, *slûr*, *v.t.* to run down, speak evil of : to pass over lightly so as not to attract attention to (e.g. *to slur*, or *slur over*, *one's mistakes, the help one has received*) : to sound indistinctly (e.g. *He slurs his words*) :—*pr.p.* **slurr'ing** ; *pa.p.* **slurred.** —*n.* a blot or stain (on one's reputation) : a remark suggesting that one has this : (*music*) a mark showing that notes are to be sung to the same syllable or played with a smooth gliding effect : a running together of sounds. [Orig. unknown.]

slush, *slush*, *n.* liquid mud : melting snow : (something said or written showing) weak sentimentality.—*v.t.* to wash by throwing water on.
slush'y, *adj.* **slush'iness,** *n.*
[Orig. uncertain.]

slut, *slut*, *n.* a dirty, untidy woman.
slutt'ish, *adj.* [Orig. uncertain.]

sly, *slī*, *adj.* (of person, action, manner, etc.) cunning, crafty, deceitful : playfully mischievous (e.g. *a sly reference to his friend's mistake*) :—*comp.* **sly'er, slī'er** ; *superl.* **sly'est, slī'est.**
sly'ly, *adv.* **sly'ness,** *n.*
on the sly, secretly.
[From Old Norse ; conn. with **sleight.**]

smack[1], *smak*, *n.* taste or flavour : a trace. —*v.i.* to have a taste, suggestion (of ; e.g. *This smacks of treason*).
[O.E. *smæc*.]

smack[2], *smak*, *n.* a small fishing vessel.
[Du. *smak* ; conn. with Ger. *schmacke.*]

smack[3], *smak*, *v.t.* to strike smartly, slap : to put, etc., with speed and noise : to kiss noisily : to make a noise with (the lips), expressing enjoyment.—Also *n.*—*adv.* with sudden violence (*e.g. to run smack into a door*). [Prob. imit.]

small, *smöl*, *adj.* little, not big or much : of little importance (*e.g. a small point in an argument*) : working, or doing business, etc., with little material, or with little success or influence (e.g. *a small tradesman, thief, poet*) : (of rain) in fine drops : (of voice) soft : mean, petty (e.g. *It was small of him to do that*). —*adv.* into small pieces.—*n.* the slenderest part, esp. of the back.
small arms, weapons, esp. firearms, that can be carried by a man.
small beer, a weak kind of beer : people of little importance.
small hours, the hours immediately after midnight.
small'-min'ded, *adj.* having, or showing, an ungenerous mind with narrow interests and sympathies.
small'pox, *n.* a serious disease causing *pocks* or blisters, usu. leaving marks on skin.
small talk, light conversation.
in a small way, to a small extent : with little money or stock.
to feel small, to feel that one has made a fool of oneself, or has appeared dishonourable.
[O.E. *smæl* ; conn. with Ger. *schmal.*]

smart, *smärt*, *n.* quick stinging pain.—*v.i.* to feel such a pain : to be punished.—*adj.* sharp and stinging : brisk (e.g. *a smart walk*) : quick in learning : quick and efficient : witty : trim : well-dressed, fashionable.
smart'ly, *adv.* **smart'ness,** *n.*
smar'ten, *v.t.* to make smart(er).
[O.E. *smeortan* (vb.) ; Ger. *schmerzen.*]

smash, *smash*, *v.t.* to shatter, break in pieces : to strike with great force : to ruin.—*v.i.* to fly into pieces : to be ruined : to dash violently (into, against, etc.)—Also *n.*, *adv.* [Imit.]

smattering, *smat'ėr-ing*, *n.* a very slight knowledge (of a subject).
[M.E. *smateren*, to chatter.]

smear, *smēr*, *v.t.* to spread (something sticky or oily) : to spread or smudge (a surface with) : to slander (a person or reputation).—*v.i.* to become smeared.—Also *n.*
smear'y, *adj.* **smear'iness,** *n.*
[O.E. *smeru*, grease ; conn. Ger. *schmer.*]

smell, *smel*, *n.* the sense, located in the nose, that makes us aware of vapours or fine particles arising from substances : an act of using this sense : odour, perfume, scent, fragrance, stink, stench, etc. : a suggestion, trace.—*v.t.* to notice

by using the sense of smell: to use this sense on (e.g. *Smell this egg*).—*v.i.* to have an odour:—*pa.t.*, *pa.p.* **smelled, smelt.**
smell'y, *adj.* having a bad smell.
smell'iness, *n.*
smell'ing-salts, *n.* chemicals in a bottle used to revive fainting persons.
to smell out, to find out by prying.
[M.E. *smel*; prob.—O.E. (not recorded).]

smelt[1]. See **smell.**

smelt[2], *smelt, n.* a fish of the salmon kind.
[O.E.]

smelt[3], *smelt, v.t.* to melt (ore) in order to separate metal from other material.
[Swed. *smälta.*]

smile, *smīl, v.i.* to express pleasure, amusement, etc., by drawing up the corners of the lips: to look happy: to be favourable (e.g. *Fortune smiled*).—*v.t.* to express (e.g. approval) by smiling: to give (a smile).—Also *n.*
smil'ing, *adj., n.* **smil'ingly,** *adv.*
[M.E. *smilen.*]

smirch, *smėrch, v.t.* to stain, soil.
[O.Fr. *esmorcher*, to hurt.]

smirk, *smėrk, v.i.* to put on a conceited or foolish smile.—Also *n.*
[O.E. *smercian.*]

smite, *smīt, v.t.* to strike, hit hard:—*pa.t.* **smōte;** *pa.p.* **smitt'en.**
[O.E. *smitan*, to smear.]

smith, *smith, n.* one who forges with the hammer: a worker in metals.
smith'y (-TH-, -*th*-), *n.* workshop of a smith.
[O.E.; conn. with Ger. *schmied.*]

smithereens, *smiTH-ėr-ēnz', n.pl.* (*coll.*) small fragments, pieces.
[Ir. *smidirin.*]

smitten. See **smite.**

smock, *smok, n.* a shirt-like garment worn over the clothes to protect them.
[O.E. *smoc.*]

smog, *smog, n. smo*ky f*og.*

smoke, *smōk, n.* the cloudlike gases and particles of soot that come off something burning: (*coll.*) a cigar or cigarette: an act of smoking.—*v.i.* to send up, give off, smoke or vapour: to draw in and puff out the smoke of tobacco, etc.—*v.t.* to dry, cure (e.g. ham), darken (e.g. glass), etc., by smoke: to draw in and puff out the smoke from.
smoke'less, *adj.* having no smoke.
smo'ky, *adj.* giving out smoke: like smoke, e.g. in colour: filled with smoke: —*comp.* **smo'kier;** *superl.* **smo'kiest.**
smo'kily, *adv.* **smo'kiness,** *n.*
smo'ker, *n.* one who smokes tobacco: a railway carriage, or a concert, etc., in which smoking is allowed.
smo'king, *adj.* and *n.*
smoke screen, a dense cloud of smoke to hide movements or objects from the enemy.
smoke'stack, *n.* a ship's funnel or a factory chimney.
to smoke out, to drive out by smoke: to force into the open.
[O.E. *smoca.*]

smolt, *smōlt, n.* young salmon at stage when goes to sea. [Orig. uncertain.]

smooth, *smōōTH, adj.* having an even surface: not rough: hairless: without lumps: (of movement—e.g. flow—speech, etc.) easy, even, without breaks or stops: (of person, machine, etc.) moving in such a way: deceiving by agreeable manner (also **smooth'-spoken, smooth'-tongued**).—*v.t.* to make smooth: to free from difficulty: to calm, soothe (person, feelings): to pass (over) quickly (e.g. *He smoothed over his own guilt*).—*v.i.* to become smooth.—*n.* smooth part.
smooth'-bore, *adj.* (of firearm) having bore or inner tube smooth, not rifled.
[O.E. *smōth*, usually *smēthe.*]

smote. See **smite.**

smother, *smuTH'ėr, v.t.* to kill by keeping the air from, esp. by means of a thick covering: to cause to die down or be hidden (e.g. rebellion, grief).—*n.* smoke: thick floating dust.
[M.E. *smorther*—O.E. *smorian.*]

smoulder, *smōl'dėr, v.i.* to burn slowly or without flame: to continue in a hidden state (e.g. *The rivalry between them smouldered*): to show suppressed anger, jealousy, etc. (e.g. *His eyes smouldered*).
[M.E. *smolderen*; origin unknown.]

smudge, *smuj, n.* a smear.—*v.t.* and *v.i.* to soil with spots or stains.
smudg'y, *adj.* **smudg'ily,** *adv.*
smudg'iness, *n.* [Orig. uncertain.]

smug, *smug, adj.* well satisfied, openly pleased, with oneself.
[Conn. with Ger. *schmuck*, fine.]

smuggle, *smug'l, v.t.* to bring into, or send out from, a country without paying duty: to send or take secretly.—Also *v.i.*
smugg'ler, *n.* a person who smuggles: a vessel used in smuggling.
smugg'ling, *n.* and *adj.*
[Conn. with Ger. *schmuggeln.*]

smut, *smut, n.* soot: a spot of dirt: a disease that blackens plants, esp. grasses: indecent language.—*v.t.* to soil, spot, or blacken with smut.
smutt'y, *adj.* **smutt'iness,** *n.*
[Conn. with Ger. *schmutz*, dirt.]

snack, *snak, n.* a light, hasty meal.
[Old noun *snack*, snap or bite.]

snag, *snag, n.* a sharp part left when a branch is broken off: a tree hidden in water, dangerous to boats: a difficulty or drawback.—*v.t., v.i.* to catch, or tear, on a snag:—*pr.p.* **snagg'ing;** *pa.p.* **snagged.**
[Conn. with Old Norse *snagi*, peg.]

snail, *snāl, n.* a soft-bodied small crawling animal with a coiled shell.

a snail's pace, a very slow speed.
[O.E. *snægl*; conn. with Ger. *schnecke.*]

snake, *snāk*, *n.* a legless reptile with a long body: anything snake-like in form or movement: a cunning, deceitful person.
[O.E. *snaca.*]

snap, *snap*, *v.t.* to bite suddenly: to seize (usu. with *up*; e.g. *He snapped up the purse*): to shut, break suddenly, etc., with a sharp sound: to cause (fingers) to make a sharp sound: to bark out, make angrily (a remark, answer): to take a photograph of, esp. with a hand camera.—*v.i.* to make a bite (often with *at*): to grasp (at): to shut, etc., with a sharp noise: to speak sharply.—*n.* act of snapping, or the noise made by it: a small catch or lock: a sudden spell of cold weather: liveliness, energy: a snapshot:—*pr.p.* **snapp'ing**; *pa.p.* **snapped.**
snapp'ish, *adj.* apt to snap or bite, or to speak sharply and irritably.
snapp'y, *adj.* snappish: quick or sudden: (*coll.*) smart.
snapp'ily, *adv.* **snapp'iness,** *n.*
snap'dragon, *n.* a garden plant whose flower when pinched open and then let go closes up again like a mouth.
snap'shot, *n.* a quickly taken photograph.
[Du. *snappen*; conn. Ger. *schnappen.*]

snare, *snār*, *n.* a running noose of string, etc., for catching an animal: a trap: a trick to catch: a danger or temptation.—*v.t.* to catch in a snare.
[Old Norse *snara.*]

snarl[1], *snärl*, *v.i.* to make an angry noise with show of teeth: to speak in a sharp quarrelsome manner.—Also *v.t.* [Imit.]

snarl[2], *snärl*, *v.t.*, *v.i.* to tangle.—*n.* a knot: a difficult state, condition. [**snare.**]

snatch, *snach*, *v.t.* to seize suddenly: to pull away quickly (from): to take as opportunity occurs (e.g. *He managed to snatch an hour's sleep*).—*v.i.* to try suddenly or eagerly to take (with *at*; e.g. *He snatched at the offered help*).—*n.* an attempt to seize: a small piece (e.g. of music), or small quantity.
[Perh. **snack.**]

sneak, *snēk*, *v.i.* to creep or steal (off, away, about, etc.) meanly: to behave meanly: to tell tales, inform.—*v.t.* (*slang*) to take secretly, or steal.—*n.* a deceitful, underhand person: a telltale.
sneak'y, *adj.* **sneak'iness,** *n.*
sneak'ing, *adj.* mean: underhand: not told openly (e.g. *I have a sneaking feeling, suspicion, hope, sympathy*, etc.).
sneak thief, thief who gets in through unlocked door, etc.
[Conn. with O.E. *snican*, to crawl.]

sneer, *snēr*, *v.i.* to show contempt by scornful expression of the face, jeering tone of voice, or harsh words.—Also *n.*
[M.E. *snere.*]

sneeze, *snēz*, *v.i.* to blow out air suddenly, involuntarily, and violently through the nose.—Also *n.*
not to be sneezed at, not to be treated as unimportant.
[O.E. *fnēosan.*]

snick, *snik*, *v.t.* to cut, snip, nick.—*n.* a small cut or nick. [Orig. uncertain.]

snicker. Same as **snigger.**

snide, *snīd*, *adj.* (*orig. U.S. slang*) cheap: not sincere: superior in attitude: sneering (e.g. *a snide remark*).

sniff, *snif*, *v.i.* to draw in air through the nose with a slight noise: to smell a scent: (with at) to treat with suspicion or scorn.—Also *v.t.* and *n.* [Imit.]

snigger, *snig'ėr*, *v.i.* to laugh in a half-hidden sly way, e.g. at someone's embarrassment or pain.—Also *n.* [Imit.]

snip, *snip*, *v.t.* to cut off sharply, esp. with a single cut of the scissors:—*pr.p.* **snipp'ing**; *pa.p.* **snipped.**—*n.* a cut with scissors: a small shred: a certainty.
snipp'et, *n.* a little piece.
[Conn. with Du. *snippen.*]

snipe, *snīp*, *n.* a bird with a long straight bill, found in marshy places.—*v.i.* to shoot from a place of hiding (at single enemies).
snip'er, *n.* **snip'ing,** *n.* [Prob. Scand.]

snippet, etc. See **snip.**

snivel, *sniv'l*, *v.i.* to run at the nose: to whine, complain, tearfully:—*pr.p.* **sniv'elling**; *pa.p.* **sniv'elled.**—*n.* cowardly, or pretended, weeping: a sniff: mucus of the nose.
[O.E. *snofl*, mucus.]

snob, *snob*, *n.* one who admires people of high rank, social class, etc. and looks down on those he considers inferior.
snobb'ish, *adj.* **snobb'ishly,** *adv.*
snobb'ishness, snobb'ery (*pl.* **-ies**), *ns.*
[Originally a slang word.]

snooker, *snōō'kėr*, *n.* game played on the billiard table, a variety of pool.

snoop, *snōōp*, *v.i.* to spy or pry in a sneaking manner.
[Du. *snoepen*, to enjoy on the sly.]

snooze, *snōōz*, *v.i.* to doze, sleep lightly.—*n.* a nap. [Orig. uncertain.]

snore, *snōr*, *snör*, *v.i.* to breathe roughly and hoarsely in sleep.—Also *n.* [Imit.]

snorkel, *snör'kėl*, *n.* tube(s) with end(s) above water for bringing air to underwater swimmer or submarine.—Also **snort.**
[Ger. *schnorchel.*]

snort[1], *snört*, *v.i.* to force air noisily through the nostrils, as horses do: to make a similar noise, esp. to show disapproval.—*v.t.* to utter with a snort.—Also *n.* [Imit.]

snort[2]. See **snorkel.**

snot, *snot*, *n.* mucus of the nose.
snott'y, *adj.* stand-offish, with nose in the air.
[M.E. *snotte*; conn. with **snout.**]

snout, *snowt, n.* the sticking-out nose part of an animal, esp. of a pig.
[Conn. Du. *snuit*, Ger. *schnauze.*]

snow, *snō, n.* frozen water vapour which falls in light, white crystals or flakes: a fall, or a layer, of these flakes.—*v.i., v.t.* to shower down in, or like, flakes of snow.
snow'y, *adj.* covered with snow: white like snow: pure:—*comp.* **snow'ier**; *superl.* **snow'iest.**
snow'iness, *n.*
snow'ball, *n.* a ball made of snow pressed hard together: something that grows rapidly as a snowball rolled in snow.—*v.t.* to pelt with snowballs.—*v.i.* to throw snowballs: to grow greater more and more quickly.
snow'bound, *adj.* kept in one place by heavy snow.
snow'-capped, *adj.* with tops covered in snow.
snow'drift, *n.* a bank of snow blown together by the wind.
snow'drop, *n.* a small white flower growing from a bulb in early spring.
snow'fall, *n.* a fall of snow.
snow'flake, *n.* a flake of snow.
snow'line, *n.* the line on a mountain above which there is always snow.
snow'man, *n.* a human figure made out of snow.
snow'-plough, *n.* a machine for clearing snow from roads and railways.
snow'shoe, *n.* a strung frame, one of a pair put on the feet to allow one to walk on snow without sinking.
snow'storm, *n.* a storm with falling snow.
snowed up, blocked by, or cut off by, snow.
to snow under, to cover, bury, as if with snow.
[O.E. *snāw*; conn. with Ger. *schnee.*]

snub, *snub, v.t.* to check or stop, esp. by a cutting remark: to insult, treat scornfully.—*pr.p.* **snubb'ing**; *pa.p.* **snubbed.**—*n.* an act of snubbing.—*adj.* (of nose) flat and broad, slightly turned up at the end. [Scand.]

snuff[1], *snuf, v.i.* to sniff: to use snuff.—*v.t.* to discover by smelling.—*n.* powdered tobacco to be taken up into the nose: a pinch of this: a sniff.
snuff'box, *n.* a box for holding snuff.
[Middle Du. *snuffen.*]

snuff[2], *snuf, n.* the burnt portion of a wick of candle or lamp.—*v.t.* to nip off the burnt portion of a wick.
to snuff out, to put, or go, out: to put a sudden end to, or come to a sudden end (e.g. *The rebellion snuffed out*).
[M.E. *snoffe*; perh. conn. **snuff** (1).]

snuffle, *snuf'l, v.i.* to breathe heavily, or to speak, through the nose.—*n.* an act or sound of snuffling: (in *pl.*) blocked-up state of the nose. [**snuff** (1).]

snug, *snug, adj.* lying close and warm: in hiding: (of house, room, etc.) cosy, comfortable; also neat and trim: comfortably large (e.g. *a snug income*):—*comp.* **snugg'er**; *superl.* **snugg'est.**
snug'ly, *adv.* **snug'ness,** *n.*
snugg'le, *v.i.* to nestle. [Orig. unknown.]

so, *sō, adv.* in this or that way (e.g. *You must do it so*): as stated (e.g. *Is it really so?*): as shown (e.g. *He held his hands about two feet apart, saying 'It is so big'*): to a great, or too great, extent or degree (e.g. *It is so heavy that I cannot lift it*).—*conj.* therefore (e.g. *He did not come back, so I left*).
so'-and-so, *n.* this or that person or thing: a person or thing one despises or is annoyed by:—*pl.* **so'-and-sos.**
so'-called, *adj.* named or described thus, usu. wrongly (e.g. *a so-called artist, bargain*).
so-so, *adj.* neither very good nor very bad.
so as, in order (to).
so far, to a certain degree, point, or time (e.g. *The result is so far satisfactory, satisfactory so far*).
so forth, more of the same.
so much for, that is the end of.
so that, with the purpose that: with the result that.
so to speak, if one may use that expression.
just so, in order (e.g. *He liked everything to be just so*).
or so, or about that number or amount (e.g. *six or so*).
[O.E. *swā*; conn. Ger. *so.*]

soak, *sōk, v.t.* to let stand in a liquid until wet through and through: to drench (with): to draw in through pores, suck (up): (*slang*) to beat: (*slang*) to overcharge.
soak'ing, *n.* and *adj.*—Also *adv.* (*soaking wet*).
[O.E. *socian*; conn. with *sūcan*, suck.]

so-and-so. See **so.**

soap, *sōp, n.* a mixture containing oils, fats, and salts, used in washing.—*v.t.* to rub with soap.
soap'y, *adj.* like soap: covered with soap: too fond of flattering:—*comp.* **soap'ier**; *superl.* **soap'iest.**
soap'iness, *n.*
soap'box, *n.* a box for packing soap: a makeshift platform for a man addressing a crowd out-of-doors.
soap'-suds, *n.pl.* soapy water, esp. when worked into a froth.
[O.E. *sāpe*; conn. Du. *zeep*, Ger. *seife.*]

soar, *sōr, sör, v.t.* to fly high into the air: to rise high (e.g. *Prices, hopes, soared*).
[O.Fr. *essorer*, expose to, raise into, air.]

sob, *sob, v.i.* to catch the breath in distress, weep noisily: (of e.g. wind) to make a noise like this.—*v.t.* to utter with sobs:—*pr.p.* **sobb'ing**; *pa.p.* **sobbed.**—Also *n.*
sob'stuff, *n.* a story, etc., intended to draw tears. [Imit.]

sober, *sō'bėr, adj.* not drunk: not overdone, excessive, or too emotional (e.g. *a sober description, estimate*): serious in mind: quiet in colour.—*v.t., v.i.* to make, or become, sober.
so'berness, sobrī'ety, *ns.*
[Fr. *sobre*—L. *sē-*, not, *ēbrius*, drunk.]

so-called. See **so.**

soccer. See **association.**

sociable, *sō'shȧ-bl, adj.* fond of, and friendly in, the company of others: (of action, etc.) showing this spirit.
sociabil'ity, so'ciableness, *ns.*
social, *sō'sh(ȧ)l, adj.* having to do with society in any sense: having to do with the rules, arrangements, and habits of a community or group (e.g. *the social life of a savage tribe, of bees*): having to do with the welfare of people in a community (e.g. *She did social work in the slums*): having to do with rank or class (e.g. *They were not social equals*): growing or living in societies (e.g. *social insects*): having to do with friendly companionship (e.g. *He spent a social evening with his family*): sociable.—*n.* a gathering of members of a group for entertainment, etc.
so'cially, *adv.*
so'cialism, *n.* the belief that a country's wealth (its land, mines, industries, railways, etc.) should belong to the people as a whole, not to private owners: a system in which the state runs the country's wealth.
so'cialist, *n.* a believer in socialism.
society, *sȯ-sī'i-ti, n.* system of living together as a group, not as separate individuals: a body of people who live in this way—mankind as a whole, or a smaller community: the class of people who have rank and/or wealth: a group of people joined for a purpose (e.g. *a dramatic society*): companionship (e.g. *I enjoy the society of young people*):—*pl.* **soci'eties.** *Adj.* is **social** (above).
sociology, *sō-si-ol'ȯ-ji, n.* the science which studies man as a member of human groups, the everyday life of people, and their culture.
sociol'ogist, *n.*
social insurance, insurance against unemployment, etc., in which the government plays a part.
social security, the principle or practice of providing social insurance.
social service, welfare work.
[L. *socius*, companion; same root as **associate** (*logos*, discourse).]

sock, *sok, n.* a short stocking.
[O.E. *socc*—L. *soccus.*]

socket, *sok'it, n.* a hollow into which something is fitted.
[O.Fr. *soket.*]

sod, *sod, n.* a piece of earth with grass growing on it, a turf.
[Conn. with Du. *zode.*]

soda, *sō'dȧ, n.* washing soda (**sodium carbonate,** a salt, in crystal form, of sodium): baking soda (**sodium bicarbonate**): soda water.
sodium, *sō'di-ům, n.* a soft silvery metal that forms compounds such as salt (*sodium chloride*), washing soda, and baking soda.
soda fountain, a counter where soda water and iced drinks are sold.
soda water, a fizzing liquid containing gas under pressure (formerly made with baking soda). [Mediaeval Latin.]

sodden. See **seethe.**

sodium. See **soda.**

sofa, *sō'fȧ, n.* a long seat with stuffed bottom, and with back and end(s).
[Arabic *suffah.*]

soft, *soft, adj.* not hard or firm: easily put out of shape when pressed: not strict enough: weak in mind: weak in muscle: pleasing to the touch: not loud (e.g. *a soft voice*): (of colour) not glaring: not hard in outline: (of drink) not alcoholic: (of water) free from certain salts: (of *c* or *g*) pronounced as in *city, gentle.*—*adv.* gently, quietly.
soft'ly, *adv.* **soft'ness,** *n.*
soften, *sof'n, v.t., v.i.* to make, or become, soft or softer, or less hardy or strong: (*v.t.*) to make less painful (e.g. *to soften the blow*).
soft'-heart'ed, *adj.* kind-hearted, generous, sympathetic.
soft'-spoken, *adj.* having, or in, a gentle voice or manner.
soft'ware, *n.* in computers, programmes, etc.
soft'wood, *n.* soft timber of a cone-bearing, quick-growing tree (e.g. fir).
soft soap, a half-liquid kind of soap: flattery.
a soft thing, an easy job or situation.
[O.E. *sōfte*, ; conn. with Ger. *sanft.*]

soggy, *sog'i, adj.* very wet: damp and heavy. [Orig. unknown.]

soigné, *swä-nyā*, **soignée** (*fem.*), *adj.* very well groomed, carefully dressed. [Fr.]

soil[1], *soil, n.* the upper layer of the earth in which plants grow: loose earth: earth of a country (e.g. *on Irish soil*).
[O.Fr. *soel*—L. *solum*, ground.]

soil[2], *soil, n.* dirt: sewage: a spot or stain. —*v.t., v.i.* to dirty: to stain.
[O.Fr. *soil*, pigsty—L. *sus*, pig.]

soirée, *swär-ā, swor'ā, n.* an evening social meeting with tea, etc. [Fr.—*soir*, evening.]

sojourn, *so'-, sō'-, su'jůrn, v.i.* to stay for a time.—*n.* a temporary stay.
[L. *sub* and root as **journal, journey.**]

solace, *sol'ȧs, n.* something that makes pain or sorrow easier to bear: comfort in distress.—*v.t.* to comfort: to amuse (oneself): to soothe (e.g. *to solace grief*).
[O.Fr. *solas*—L. *sōlāri*, to comfort.]

solan (goose), *sō'lȧn (gōōs), n.* the gannet.
[Old Norse *sūla.*]

solar, *sō′lȧr, adj.* having to do with the sun: influenced by the sun.
solar system, the sun with the planets (earth, etc.) moving round it.
[L. *sōlāris—sōl,* the sun.]
sold. See **sell.**
solder, *sol′dėr, sod′ėr, n.* melted metal or alloy used to join metal surfaces: something that unites.—*v.t.* to join (esp. two metals) with solder, etc.: to mend, patch (up).
[O.Fr. *souldure*—L. root as **solid.**]
soldier, *sōl′jėr, n.* a man in military service: a private, not an officer.—*v.i.* to serve as a soldier.
sol′dierly, *adj.* like a soldier.
sol′diery (*-jėr-i*), *n.* soldiers in general.
soldier of fortune, one ready to serve under any flag if there is a good chance of pay or advancement.
[L. *solidus,* a coin, pay of soldier.]
sole[1], *sōl, n.* the underside of the foot: the bottom of a boot or shoe: the bottom, under surface, of anything.
[O.E.—L. *solea,* a sandal, sole (fish).]
sole[2], *sōl, n.* a small flat fish with small twisted mouth.
[Fr.—L. *solea*; conn. with **sole** (1).]
sole[3], *sōl, adj.* only (e.g. *the sole heir*): acting without another (e.g. *the sole author of the plot*): not shared, belonging to one person or group only (e.g. *the sole right to decide*).
sole′ly, *adv.* only: merely.
[Fr.—L. *sōlus,* alone.]
solecism, *sol′ė-sizm, n.* a bad mistake (in writing, speaking, manners).
[Gk. *soloikismos*; from ancient city *Soloi,* where bad Greek was spoken.]
solely. See **sole** (3).
solemn, *sol′ėm, adj.* carried out with special (esp. religious) ceremonies: (of an oath) made with an appeal to God: serious and earnest: awed: awe-inspiring, wonderful: gloomy, sombre (e.g. *Black is a solemn colour*): stately.
sol′em(n)ness, *n.*
solem′nity, *n.* solemnness: solemn ceremony or rite:—*pl.* **-ies.**
sol′emnise, *v.t.* to perform with religious ceremonies (e.g. a marriage).
[L. *sol(l)emnis,* or *sol(l)ennis.*]
sol-fa, *sol′fä′, n.* (*music*) a system of syllables to be sung to the notes of the major scale (*do, re, me, fa, so(l), la, ti, do*).
[Named by Italian musician].
solicit, *sȯ-lis′it, v.t.* to ask earnestly for (something; e.g. *to solicit a favour*): to ask (a person for something).—Also *v.i.*
solicitā′tion, *n.*
solic′itor, *n.* one who asks earnestly: one who is legally qualified to act for another in a court of law—a lawyer who prepares deeds, manages cases, etc.
solic′itous, *adj.* asking earnestly: very anxious (about, for).
solic′itude, *n.* anxiety or uneasiness of mind esp. if more than necessary (e.g. *her solicitude about my health*).
[L. *sollicitāre,* to agitate—*sollus,* whole, *citus,* aroused.]
solid, *sol′id, adj.* not easily changing shape, not in form of liquid or gas: having length, breadth, and height: full of matter, not hollow: hard, firm, or strongly made: dense looking: completely of one substance (e.g. *solid silver*): real, genuine, good (e.g. *solid arguments*): sound in finances (e.g. *a solid business man*): (*coll.*) without a break in time (e.g. *five solid hours*).—*n.* a substance that is solid: a figure that has three dimensions.
solid′ity, sol′idness, *ns.*
solidar′ity, *n.* a firm union of interests, feelings, actions (of e.g. a group).
solid′ify, *v.t., v.i.* to make, or become, solid: to harden.
solidificā′tion, *n.*
[L. *solidus.*]
soliloquy, *so-, sȯ-lil′ȯ-kwi, n.* talking to oneself: a speech to oneself, esp. on the stage:—*pl.* **solil′oquies.**
solil′oquise, *v.i.* to speak to oneself.
[L. *sōlus,* alone, *loquī,* to speak.]
solitaire, *sol-i-tār′, n.* a gem, esp. a diamond, set by itself: a game one person can play. [Fr.]
solitary, *sol′i-tȧr-i, adj.* alone, without companions: living, or growing, alone: (of place) remote, lonely: single (e.g. *not a solitary example*).—*n.* one who lives alone: a hermit:—*pl.* **-ies.**
solitude, *sol′i-tūd, n.* state of being alone: want of company: a lonely place.
[L. *sōlitārius*—L. root as **sole** (3).]
solo, *sō′lō, n.* a musical piece for one voice or instrument: anything (e.g. song, aeroplane flight) in which only one takes part:—*pl.* **so′los.**—*adj.* performed as a solo: for one.—*v.i.* to fly alone.
so′loist, *n.* one who plays or sings a solo.
[It.—L. root as **sole** (3).]
solstice, *sol′stis, n.* the time of longest daylight (*summer solstice,* about June 21st) or longest dark (*winter solstice,* about December 21st).
[L. *sōl,* sun, *sistĕre,* make to stand.]
soluble, *sol′ū-bl, adj.* able to be dissolved or made liquid: (of problem, difficulty) solvable.
solu′tion, *-ōō′* or *-ū′, n.* act of dissolving: a liquid with something dissolved in it: an act of discovering an answer to a problem or difficulty: the answer found.
solve, *solv, v.t.* to discover the answer to: to clear up, explain (a mystery): to find a way round, out of (a difficulty).
sol′vable, *adj.* able to be solved.
sol′vency, *n.* state of being solvent or able to pay all debts.
sol′vent, *adj.* able to pay all debts.—*n.*

anything that dissolves another substance.
[L. *solvĕre*, *solūtum*, loosen, dissolve.]

solve, solvent, etc. See **soluble.**

sombre, *som'bėr*, *adj.* dark: gloomy, dismal.
som'brely (*-bėr-*), *adv.* **som'breness,** *n.*
[Fr.—L. *sub*, under, *umbra*, shade.]

sombrero, *som-brā'rō*, *n.* a broad-brimmed hat, usu. of felt.
[Sp.—*sombra*, shade—L. as **sombre.**]

some, *sum*, *sům*, *adj.* several: a few: a little: certain (e.g. *Some people are superstitious*).—*pron.* a number or part out of a larger number or quantity (e.g. *The sweets are*, or *the cake is*, *good*; *do take some*): certain people (e.g. *Some believed him*).
some'body, *n.* and *pron.* someone.
some'how, *adv.* in some way or other.
some'one, *n.* and *pron.* some person: a person of importance.
some'thing, *n.* a thing not known, or not stated (e.g. *He had left something behind*): a thing of importance: (referring to character or quality) a suggestion, small degree (of; e.g. *There is something of his father in him*; *he is something of a poet*).
some'time, *adv.* at a time not definitely known or stated (e.g. *He went*, or *will go*, *sometime in the spring*).
some'times, *adv.* at times, now and then.
some'what, *n.* something (e.g. *He is somewhat of a bore*).—*adv.* rather, a little (e.g. *He is somewhat sad*).
some'where, *adv.* in some place.
[O.E. *sum*.]

somersault, *sum'ėr-sölt*, *n.* a leap in which a person turns with his heels over his head: a complete turnover or change of opinion.—Also *v.i.*
[Through O.Fr.—L. *suprā*, over, *saltus*, leap.]

somnambulist, *som-nam'bū-list*, *n.* a sleepwalker.
somnolence, *som'nō-lens*, *n.* sleepiness.
som'nolent, *adj.* sleepy: drowsy.
[L. *somnus*, sleep (*ambulāre*, to walk).]

son, *sun*, *n.* a male child: a native or inhabitant (e.g. *a son of Italy*).
son'-in-law, *n.* one's daughter's husband:—*pl.* **sons'-in-law.**
[O.E. *sunu*; conn. with Ger. *sohn*.]

son et lumière, *son ā loom'yėr*, a dramatic show, with lighting effects, music, etc., given after dark with e.g. a famous building as scene. [Fr.]

sonata, *sō-nä'tȧ*, *n.* a piece of music with three or more movements, usu. for one instrument.
[It.—L. *sonāre*, to sound.]

song, *song*, *n.* something (to be) sung: singing: the notes of a bird: a poem or poetry in general: a mere trifle (e.g. *He bought the lamp for a song*).
song'bird, *n.* a bird that sings.
song'ster, *n.* a singer:—*fem.* **song'stress.**
[O.E. *sang*—same root as **sing.**]

sonic, *son'ik*, *adj.* having to do with, or using, sound waves.
sonic bang, boom (*flying*), shock wave or explosion that, at the speed of sound, travels far enough to be heard by people on the ground.
[L. *sonus*, sound, and suffix, *-ic*.]

sonnet, *son'it*, *n.* a poem of fourteen lines with rhymes arranged in a particular way (e.g. *abbaabba cdcdcd*).
[It. *sonetto*—L. *sonus*, a sound.]

sonorous, *sō-nō'rus*, *-nö'*, *adj.* giving out a deep sound when struck: (of sound, voice) deep, resonant: high-sounding (e.g. *sonorous phrases*).
[L. *sonāre*, to sound; root as **sonic.**]

soon, *sōōn*, *adv.* immediately or in a short time: early (e.g. *Can you come as soon as that?*): willingly (e.g. *I would as soon go as stay, sooner go than stay*).
[O.E. *sōna*.]

soot, *soot*, *n.* the black powder left by smoke from burning coal, etc.
soot'y, *adj.* **soot'iness,** *n.*
[O.E. *sōt*.]

soothe, *sōōTH*, *v.t.* to calm, comfort, quiet (a person, feelings): to ease (pain).
sooth'ing, *adj.* **sooth'ingly,** *adv.*
[O.E. (*ge*)*sothian*, show to be true.]

soothsayer, *sōōth'sā-ėr*, *n.* one who can, or pretends to, tell the future.
[O.E. *sōth*, true.]

sop, *sop*, *n.* bread or other food dipped in liquid: something given to quiet or bribe.—*v.t.* to dip in liquid: to suck or mop (up):—*pr.p.* **sopp'ing**; *pa.p.* **sopped.**
sopp'ing, *adj.* soaking wet.—Also *adv.*
sopp'y, *adj.* very wet: foolishly sentimental.
[O.E. *sopp*; prob. conn. *sūpan*, to sup.]

sophisticate, *sȯ-fis'ti-kāt*, *v.t.* to take away the simple and natural qualities of: to make worldly-wise by education or experience: to make (e.g. one's tastes) those of a person of worldly experience: to adulterate (e.g. wine): to make (e.g. a machine, machinery) more elaborate and efficient or (a car) more luxurious.
sophis'ticated, *adj.* **sophisticā'tion,** *n.*
[Gk. *sophos*, wise.]

soporific, *sō-pȯr-if'ik*, *sop-*, *adj.* causing sleep.—*n.* something that causes sleep.
[L. *sopor*, deep sleep, *facĕre*, to make.]

sopping, etc. See **sop.**

soprano, *sȯ-prä'nō*, *n.* a singing voice of highest pitch: a singer with such a voice: a part for such a voice.
[It.; from *sopra*—L. *suprā*, above.]

sorcery, *sör'sėr-i*, *n.* use of power gained from evil spirits: magic:—*pl.* **-ies.**
sor'cerer, *n.*:—*fem.* **sor'ceress.**
[O.Fr. *sorcerie*—L. *sors*, *sortis*, lot, fate.]

sordid, *sör'did, adj.* (of place, etc.) dirty, mean, poor: (of actions, etc.) showing low standards or ideals: (of e.g. motives) selfish, mercenary.
[L. *sordidus*, dirty.]

sore, *sōr, sör, n.* a painful injured or diseased spot: an ulcer or boil: a cause of pain or grief.—*adj.* painful: suffering pain: irritated or offended.
sore'ly, *adv.* painfully: very greatly (e.g. *sorely in need of new shoes*).
sore'ness, *n.*
[O.E. *sār*; conn. with Ger. *sehr*, very.]

sorrel[1], *sor'ėl, n.* a plant with sour-tasting leaves.
[O.Fr. *sorele—sur*, sour.]

sorrel[2], *sor'ėl, adj.* reddish-brown.—*n.* reddish-brown colour: a sorrel horse.
[O.Fr. *sorel*; perh. from Germanic.]

sorrow, *sor'ō, n.* pain of mind, grief: a trouble, misfortune.—*v.i.* to feel sorrow, grieve, mourn (for).
sorr'owful, *adj.* **sorr'owfully,** *adv.*
sorr'owfulness, *n.*
See **sorry** (not same origin).
[O.E. *sorg*; conn. with Ger. *sorge.*]

sorry, *sor'i, adj.* feeling sorrow (much or little) because of some action or happening (*sorry for my sins, that I mislaid the book*): feeling pity or sympathy (for; e.g. *sorry for her, for his loss*): poor, worthless (e.g. *proved to be a sorry friend*): miserable, unhappy (e.g. *a sorry state of affairs*):—*comp.* **sorr'ier**; *superl.* **sorr'iest.**
sorr'iness, *n.*
See **sorrow** (not same origin).
[O.E. *sārig*, wounded—*sār*, pain.]

sort, *sört, n.* a class or kind (e.g. *people of this sort*): something like but not exactly (e.g. *wearing a sort of a crown*).—*v.t.* to separate into classes or groups: to pick (out), choose.
sor'ter, *n.* one who separates and arranges, esp. letters.
in some sort, in a way: to some extent.
of a sort, of sorts, of a rather poor kind.
out of sorts, slightly unwell: not in good spirits or temper.
[L. *sors, sortis*, lot, fate, condition.]

sortie, *sör'tē, n.* a sudden attack by the defenders of a place against those who are trying to take it.
[Fr.—*sortir*, to go out.]

SOS, *es'ō'es'*, a code signal calling for help (in Morse . . . — — — . . .).
—*n.* any signal of distress or call for help.
—Also *v.t., v.i.*

so-so. See **so.**

sot, *sot, n.* a man continually drunk.
sott'ish, *adj.* foolish: stupid with drink.
[O.Fr.]

sotto voce, *sot'ō vō'chė, vō', adv.* in a low voice, so as not to be heard.
[It., 'below the voice'.]

soufflé, *sōō'flā, n.* a light dish, made with white of egg whisked into a froth.
[Fr. *souffler*, to blow, puff—L. *sufflāre.*]

sought. See **seek.**

soul, *sōl, n.* the innermost being of a person, the part which thinks, feels, desires, etc.: nobleness of mind: the moving spirit or leader: a person (e.g. *a wonderful old soul*): a perfect example (of; e.g. *He is the soul of honour*).
soul'ful, *adj.* full of feeling.
soul'less, *adj.* without fine feeling or nobleness: (of life, task) dull, petty.
[O.E. *sāwol*; conn. with Ger. *seele.*]

sound[1], *sownd, adj.* healthy: in good condition: (of sleep) deep: (of e.g. a thrashing) thorough: (of reasoning) free from mistake: trustworthy: good in quality: showing good sense (e.g. *sound advice*).—*adv.* soundly (only in *to sleep sound* and *sound asleep*).
sound'ly, *adv.* **sound'ness,** *n.*
[O.E. *gesund*; conn. with Ger. *gesund.*]

sound[2], *sownd, n.* a narrow passage of water connecting e.g. two seas.
[O.E. *sund*, swimming, sea, channel.]

sound[3], *sownd, n.* sensation of hearing: something that is heard, esp. a musical tone or an element of speech: mere noise: hearing distance (e.g. *within sound of Bow Bells*).—*v.i.* to give out a sound: to be able to be heard: to seem to be (e.g. *That sounds like a train; it sounds like an attempt at blackmail*).—*v.t.* to cause to make a sound: to make the sound of (e.g. *Sound the letter h*): to express loudly (e.g. *to sound his praises*): to examine by listening carefully (e.g. *to sound the patient's chest*).
sound'ing, *adj.* giving a sound, esp. a deep one: having a sound, or giving an impression, of a particular kind (see **high-sounding**).
sound'board, *n.* a thin plate of wood that increases sound in a musical instrument.
sound'proof, *adj.* not allowing sound to pass in, out, through.—*v.t.* to make soundproof.
sound'-track, *n.* the strip on which the sounds for a motion picture are recorded.
sound barrier, difficulty in increasing speed which an aeroplane meets when flying near the speed of sound.
[M.E. *soun*—L. *sonāre*, to sound.]

sound[4], *sownd, v.t.* to measure the depth of (water, etc.): to measure (the depth): to try to find out the thoughts and plans of (a person): to try to find out (views, opinions).—*v.i.* to take soundings: (of a whale) to dive deep.
sound'ing, *n.* act of measuring depth, finding out views, etc.: a measured depth.
sounding line, a line with a weight (lead, plummet) at the end for measuring depth.

to sound the depth of, to experience the greatest degree of (e.g. misery).
[Perh. L. *sub*, under, *unda*, wave.]

sounding (1), (2). See **sound** (3), (4).

soup, *sōōp*, *n.* a liquid food, made by boiling meat, vegetables, etc., together.
[O.Fr. *soupe*; conn. with **sop.**]

sour, *sowr*, *adj.* having an acid taste or smell, usu. as a stage in going bad: peevish, discontented, bitter: (of soil) cold and wet.—*v.t.*, *v.i.* to make, or become, sour.
[O.E. *sūr*; conn. with Ger. *sauer.*]

source, *sōrs*, *sörs*, *n.* a spring of water, esp. the beginning of a stream: place, circumstance, thing, etc., from which anything begins or comes (e.g. *the source of our meat supply*, *of the trouble*, *of the story*).
[O.Fr. *sorse*—L. *surgĕre*, to rise.]

souse, *sows*, *v.t.* to plunge into water or other liquid: to steep in pickle.
[O.Fr. *souse*, pickle; a Germanic word.]

south, *sowth*, *n.* the part of the heavens in which the sun is seen at noon in Britain, etc.: a territory in that direction.—Also *adj.* and *adv.*
southerly, *suTH'ėr-li*, *adj.* towards the south (e.g. *in a southerly direction*): (of wind) south.
south'ern (*suTH'*), *adj.* of, or towards, the south.
south'erner (*suTH'*), *n.* a person living in the south.
south'ward, *adv.* towards the south.
south-east (south-west), *n.* the direction halfway between south and east (south and west).—Also *adj.*
south-east'er (south'-wester), *n.* wind blowing from south-east (south-west).
sou'west'er, *n.* a south-wester: a waterproof hat with flap at the back of the neck.
south pole, the end of the earth's axis in Antarctica: the south-seeking pole of a magnet.
south wind, wind from the south.
[O.E. *sūth*; conn. with Ger. *süd.*]

souvenir, *sōō'vė-nēr*, *-nēr'*, *n.* an object kept to help in remembering a place, person, occasion.
[Fr.—L. *subvenīre*, to come to mind.]

sovereign, *sov'rin*, *suv'*, *adj.* supreme, absolute (e.g. *our sovereign lord, the King*; *sovereign power*): (of a state) self-governing: (of remedy) very effective: extreme (e.g. *sovereign contempt*).—*n.* a king or queen: a gold coin worth 20s.
sov'ereignty, *n.* highest power.
[O.Fr. *sovrain*—L. *super*, above.]

soviet, *sō'vi-et*, *-et'*, or *sov' n.* a council, esp. a governing one in Russia (Union of Soviet Socialist Republics).
[Russ. *sovet.*]

sow[1], *sow*, *n*, a female pig.
[O.E. *sū*; conn. Ger. *sau*; also L. *sūs.*]

sow[2], *sō*, *v.t.* to scatter over, or put in, the ground (seed): to plant seed over (land): to spread (e.g. trouble, dispeace).—Also *v.i.*:—*pa.t.* **sowed**; *pa.p.* **sown,** or **sowed.**
[O.E. *sāwan*; conn. with Ger. *säen.*]

soya bean, soybean, *soi'(ė) bēn*, *n.* a type of bean grown in Japan, China, etc.
[Jap. *shō-yu.*]

spa, *spä*, *n.* a place where there is a mineral spring.
[From *Spa* in Belgium.]

space, *spās*, *n.* the boundless region about the earth containing all heavenly bodies and all material objects: a part of this: room: an open or empty place: a distance between objects: a length of time (e.g. *in the space of a day*).—*v.t.* to set (things) apart from each other (also **space out**).
spa'cing, *n.*
spa'cious (*-shŭs*), *adj.* with plenty of room.
spa'ciously, *adv.* **spa'ciousness,** *n.*
spatial, *spā'sh(ȧ)l*, having to do with space.
space capsule, a capsule-shaped spacecraft.
space'craft, *n.* a device, manned or unmanned, for journeying in space.
space'man, *n.* a traveller in space.
space'ship, *n.* a manned spacecraft.
space station, a satellite to be used as a landing-stage in space travel.
space travel, travel in space far from the earth's surface.
[Fr. *espace*—L. *spatium.*]

spade[1], *spād*, *n.* a tool with a broad blade and handle, used for digging.
spade'work, *n.* hard work, esp. in getting a plan ready to be carried out.
to call a spade a spade, to speak plainly, not softening anything by using vague or inoffensive words.
[O.E. *spadu*; conn. with **spade** (2).]

spade[2], *spād*, *n.* a playing card of one of the four suits.
[Sp. *espada*, sword—L. *spatha*; marks on Sp. cards are sword-shaped.]

spaghetti, *spȧ-get'i*, *n.* an Italian food paste in long solid cords.
[It. pl. of *spaghetto*—*spago*, a cord.]

span[1], *span*, *n.* the space from the tip of the thumb to the tip of the little finger when the hand is spread out: nine inches: the distance from wing-tip to wing-tip in an aeroplane: an arch of a bridge between supports: the full time anything lasts.—*v.t.* to measure by spans, etc.: to stretch across (e.g. *A bridge spans the river*):—*pr.p.* **spann'ing**; *pa.p.* **spanned.**
[O.E. *spann*; conn. with Ger. *spanne.*]

span[2], *span*, *n.* a pair of horses or a team of oxen.—*v.t.* to yoke. [Du.]

spangle, *spang'gl*, *n.* a thin glittering piece of metal used as ornament on garment.—

v.i. to glitter.—*v.t.* to sprinkle with spangles, or with small bright objects.
[O.E. *spange*; conn. Ger. *spange*, clasp.]

Spaniard, *span'yård, n.* a native of *Spain.*
Span'ish, *adj.* having to do with Spain. —*n.* the people or language of Spain.

spaniel, *span'yėl, n.* a kind of dog of Spanish origin, with large hanging ears.
[O.Fr. *espaigneul*—Sp. *español*, Spanish.]

Spanish. See **Spaniard.**

spank[1], *spangk, v.i., v.t.* to move, walk, or drive, with speed. [Orig. uncertain.]

spank[2], *spangk, v.t.* to strike with the flat of the hand, to smack.—*n.* a loud slap, esp. on the buttocks.
spank'ing, *n.* a series of slaps. [Imit.]

spanner, *span'ėr, n.* the tool for tightening or loosening nuts, screws, etc. [Ger.]

spar[1], *spär, n.* a rafter: a pole: a ship's mast, yard, etc.
[M.E. *sparre*; conn. with Ger. *sparren.*]

spar[2], *spär, v.i.* to fight with the fists: to exchange insulting remarks:—*pr.p.* **sparr'ing**; *pa.p.* **sparred.**
[O.Fr. *esparer*, to kick out.]

spare, *spār, v.t.* to use in small amounts, or little (e.g. *Do not spare the sugar; spare the rod; in trying to reach this result, spare no effort, expense, etc.*): to do without (e.g. *I cannot spare her today*): to afford (e.g. *Try to spare time for it*): to treat with mercy: to refrain from putting to death, injuring, etc.: to avoid causing (trouble, etc.) to (a person).—*adj.* scanty (e.g. *a spare allowance of food*): thin (e.g. *a spare man*): extra, not actually being used.—*n.* a spare part: another of the same kind kept for emergencies.
spare'ly, *adv.* **spare'ness,** *n.*
spar'ing, *adj.* careful, economical (e.g. *Be sparing in your use of pepper, use of adjectives*).
spar'ingly, *adv.*
spare part, a duplicate part of a machine kept for emergencies.
to spare, over and above what is needed (e.g. *He has money and to spare*).
[O.E. *sparian.*]

spark, *spärk, n.* a small red-hot particle thrown off by something burning: an electric flash across a gap: a trace (e.g. of life, humour): a lively fellow.—*v.i.* to throw off sparks.
spark'ing-plug, *n.* a device in a motor-car engine that produces a spark to set on fire the explosive gases.
sparkle, *spärk'l, n.* a little spark: liveliness or brightness: bubbling, as in wines.—*v.i.* to shine, glitter: to bubble: to be lively or witty.
[O.E. *spearca*; conn. L. *spargĕre*, scatter.]

sparrow, *spar'ō, n.* a small dull-coloured bird, related to the finches.
sparr'owhawk, *n.* short-winged hawk.
[O.E. *spearwa.*]

sparse, *spärs, adj.* thinly scattered: scanty.
[L. *spargĕre, sparsum*, to scatter.]

Spartan, *spär'tån, adj.* (of person) enduring bravely: (of conditions of life) hard, without luxury.
[*Sparta*, in ancient Greece.]

spasm, *spazm, n.* a sudden jerk of the muscles which one cannot prevent: a strong short burst (of e.g. anger, work).
spasmod'ic, *adj.* that come(s) in bursts, stop(s) and start(s) again (e.g. *He made a spasmodic attempt, spasmodic efforts*).
spasmod'ically, *adv.*
spastic (*spas'*), *adj.* having to do with a spasm.—*n.* one suffering from spastic paralysis.
spastic paralysis, a form of paralysis resulting from an injury to the part of the brain that controls the muscles.
[Gk. *spasma, -atos*, convulsion.]

spat. See **spit.**

spate, *spāt, n.* (orig. *Scot.*) a flood.
[Origin uncertain.]

spatial. See **space.**

spatter, *spat'ėr, v.t.* to scatter, sprinkle (e.g. mud): to splash (something) with mud, liquid, etc.—*n.* act of spattering: what is spattered.
[Conn. with Du. *spatten.*]

spatula, *spat'ū-la, n.* an implement with broad blunt blade.
[L.—Gk. *spathē*, a broad blade.]

spawn, *spön, n.* a mass of eggs of fishes, frogs, etc.: brood, offspring: material from which mushrooms are grown.—*v.i.* to produce spawn.—*v.t.* to produce (something worthless) in large quantities: to give rise to.
[O.Fr. *espandre*, spill—L. root as **expand.**]

speak, *spēk, v.i.* to utter words: to talk: to hold a conversation (with): to make a speech: to be evidence (of; e.g. *His success speaks of careful planning*).—*v.t.* to be able to talk in (e.g. *He speaks Russian*): to tell, make known (e.g. *to speak one's thoughts, the truth*): to utter (e.g. *You speak sense*): (of ship) to hail (another):—*pa.t.* **spoke** (*spōk*); *pa.p.* **spo'ken.**
speak'er, *n.* one who speaks: (*cap.*) the person who presides over meetings of the House of Commons, etc.
speak'ing, *n.* and *adj.*
spokes'man, *n.* one who speaks for another or others.
to speak out, up, to speak clearly and sufficiently loudly: to say boldly what one thinks.
to speak to, to talk with: to scold.
to speak well for, to be a credit to (e.g. *The exhibition speaks well for the city*): to lead one to expect good from (the future).
See also **speech.**
[O.E. *sp(r)ecan*; conn. Ger. *sprechen.*]

spear, *spēr, n.* a long weapon used in war and hunting, with an iron or steel point on the end: a barbed implement for

catching fish: a shoot (e.g. of grass).—*v.t.* to pierce or kill with a spear.
spear'head, *n.* the foremost part of an attacking force.
[O.E. *spere*; conn. with Ger. *speer.*]

special, *spesh'(à)l, adj.* out of the ordinary, exceptional (e.g. *a special occasion*): greater than ordinary (*with special care*; *a special friend*): belonging to, or limited to, one person or thing (e.g. *The party needs his special talents*; *my own special chair*): appointed, put on, etc., for a particular purpose (e.g. *a special messenger, train*): additional to the ordinary (e.g. *a special edition of a newspaper*).
spec'ially, *adv.*
spec'ialise, *v.i.* to give one's attention to, work in, a single branch of study or business.
specialisā'tion, *n.*
spec'ialist, *n.* one who specialises.
spec'ialised, *adj.* (of knowledge) of the accurate, detailed kind obtained by specialising.
speciality, *spesh-i-al'i-ti,* **specialty,** *spesh'àl-ti, ns.* a special activity, or subject about which one has special knowledge: a special product (e.g. *Brown bread is this baker's speciality, specialty*):—*pls.* **-ies.**
Special is now more common than *especial*; for cases in which *especial* can still be used, see this word.
[L. *speciālis*—same root as **species.**]

specie, *spē'shi, n.* gold and silver coin.
[Same root as **species.**]

species, *spē'shēz, spē'shiz, n.* a group of plants, or of animals, alike in certain ways: a kind or sort.
[L. *speciēs*, appearance, kind—*specĕre*, to look at.]

specify, *spes'i-fī, v.t.* to make particular, definite, mention of: to name in an agreement as a necessary condition or a thing required:—*pr.p.* **spec'ifying**; *pa.p.* **spec'ified.**
specif'ic, *adj.* definite, explicit.
specif'ically, *adv.*
specificā'tion, *n.* act of specifying: thing specified: a statement containing all the details of e.g. a building plan or a contract.
[L. root as **species** (*facĕre*, make).]

specimen, *spes'i-mėn, n.* something used as a sample of a whole or group, esp. an object to be studied or to be put in a collection (e.g. *to look at specimens under the microscope*).
[L.—same root as **species.**]

specious, *spē'shùs, adj.* looking well at first sight or on the surface but really not good (e.g. *a specious claim, argument*): false.
[L. *speciōsus*, showy—root as **species.**]

speck, *spek, n.* a small spot: a tiny piece (e.g. of dust).
speckle, *spek'l, n.* a little spot.
speck'led, *adj.* marked with speckles.
[O.E. *specca.*]

spectacle, *spek'tà-kl, n.* a sight, esp. one that is very striking: a play, etc., with scenery, dressing, etc., on a grand scale: (in *pl.*) glasses worn to help eyesight.
spectacular (*-tak'ū-lȧr*), *adj.* making a great show: dramatic.
spectator (*-tā'tȯr*), *n.* one who looks on.
[L. *spectāre*, to look at—*specĕre.*]

spectre, *spek'tėr, n.* a ghost.
spec'tral, *adj.* ghostly, like a ghost.
[L. *spectrum*—*specĕre*, to look at.]

spectrum, *spek'trùm, n.* the band of colours as seen in the rainbow, produced when white light is split up by going through a prism (see this word), etc.:—*pls.* **spectra, -ums.**
spec'troscope, *n.* an instrument for forming and viewing spectra.
[L.—root as **spectacle, spectre.**]

speculate, *spek'ū-lāt, v.i.* to think about (with *on*): to make guesses (about): to buy and sell shares, etc., with hope of a profit and risk of a loss.
speculā'tion, *n.* act of speculating: a conclusion, guess: a risky investment of money for the sake of profits.
spec'ulative, *adj.* having to do with speculation: inclined to indulge in speculation.
spec'ulator, *n.*
[L. *specula*, lookout; root as **spectacle.**]

sped. See **speed.**

speech, *spēch, n.* the power of speaking: language: way of speaking: words spoken: formal talk given to a meeting, etc.
speech'less, *adj.* unable to speak, often because of surprise.
speech day, a day at the end of a school year when speeches are made and prizes are given out.
[O.E. *sp(r)æc*; conn. **speak.**]

speed, *spēd, n.* quickness of moving: rate of motion.—*v.i.* to move quickly, hurry: to drive at high, or too high, speed.—*v.t.* to cause to go with speed: to help the success of (an undertaking): to send (a person on his way) with good wishes:—*pa.p.* **sped,** (chiefly *v.i.*, 2) **speed'ed.**
speed'ing, *n.* driving at high, or dangerously or illegally high, speed.
speed'y, *adj.* swift: prompt:—*comp.* **speed'ier**; *superl.* **speed'iest.**
speed'ily, *adv.* **speed'iness,** *n.*
speedom'eter, *n.* an instrument for measuring speed.
speed'way, *n.* a road for fast traffic: a motor-cycle racing track.
speed'well, *n.* a small plant with blue flowers.
to speed up, to quicken the rate of (*pa.t.* **speeded up**; *n.* **speed'-up**).
[O.E. *spēd*; conn. with Du. *spoed.*]

spell[1], *spel, n.* a charm, words that are supposed to have magic power: the influence of magic (*under a spell*), or other strong influence.

spell′-bound, *adj.* fascinated, charmed, held in wonder.

[O.E. *spell*, story; from Old Norse.]

spell[2], *spel, v.t.* to name or give in order the letters of (a word): (of letters) to form (a word): to mean, amount to (e.g. *This spells disaster*): to read slowly, letter by letter.—*v.i.* to spell words, esp. correctly:—*pr.p.* **spell′ing**; *pa.p.* **spelled, spelt.**

[O.Fr. *espeller*; conn. with **spell** (1).]

spell[3], *spel, n.* a turn at work: a short time: a stretch of time.

[O.E. *spelian*, to act for another.]

spencer, *spens′ėr, n.* a short jacket reaching to the waist.

[After an Earl *Spencer*.]

spend, *spend, v.t.* to pay out (money): to give (e.g. energy, thought) to any purpose (with *on*): to use up, wear out (e.g. *The storm will spend itself, its force*): to pass (time; e.g. *He will spend a week in Spain*).—*v.i.* to use up or pay out money:—*pa.t.* and *pa.p.* **spent.**

spent, *adj.* exhausted: with power gone (e.g. *a spent bullet*).

spendthrift, *spend′thrift, n.* one who spends money freely and carelessly.

[O.E. *spendan*—same L. root as **expend.**]

spew, *spū, v.t., v.i.* to vomit.

[O.E. *spīwan*; Ger. *speien*, L. *spuěre*.]

sphere, *sfēr, n.* a solid body with a surface on which all points are an equal distance from the centre: a globe: a ball: a star or planet: (**celestial sphere**) what looks like the hollow sphere of the heavens in the inside of which the stars seem to be placed: a group in society (e.g. *He moves in the highest spheres*): range of activity or influence (e.g. *the western sphere of influence*).

spherical, *sfer′i-kȧl, adj.*

[Fr.—L. *sphaera*—Gk. *sphaira*.]

Sphinx, *sfingks, n.* a monster of old Egyptian and Greek story: (without *cap.*) a puzzling person whose thoughts one cannot guess.

[Gk.—*sphingein*, to bind tight.]

spice, *spīs, n.* a strong-smelling, sharp-tasting vegetable substance used to season food (e.g. pepper, nutmeg): anything that adds liveliness or interest: a smack, flavour (e.g. *a remark with a spice of malice*).—*v.t.* to season with spice: to give variety or liveliness to.

spicy, *spī′si, adj.* tasting or smelling of spices: lively, sometimes with a touch of indecency.

spi′ciness, *n.*

[O.Fr. *espice*—L. root as **species.**]

spick-and-span, *spik′and-span′, adj.* neat and trim and spotless.

[**spike** (2), nail, *span(-new)*, chip(-new).]

spicy. See **spice.**

spider, *spī′dėr, n.* a small creature with body in two sections, eight legs, and no wings, which spins a web to catch flies.

spi′dery, *adj.* spider-like: sprawling and thin (e.g. *spidery handwriting*).

spi′deriness, *n.*

[M.E. *spither*—O.E. *spinnan*, to spin.]

spiel, *spēl, n.* a long story, esp. to persuade e.g. to buy.

[Ger., play, game.]

spigot, *spig′ȯt, n.* a small pointed peg or plug, esp. for a cask: (*U.S.*) tap, faucet.

[Conn. with root of **spike** (2).]

spike[1], *spīk, n.* an ear of corn: a head of flowers.

[L. *spīca*.]

spike[2], *spīk, n.* a hard, thin, pointed object: a large nail: a pointed piece of metal on the sole of a shoe to prevent slipping.—*v.t.* to fasten, set, or pierce, with a spike or spikes: to make (a gun) useless, formerly by driving a spike into the opening through which fire was passed to the explosive.

spiked, *adj.* having spikes.

spik′y, *adj.* **spik′iness,** *n.*

[O.E. *spicing*; perh. conn. **spike** (1).]

spill[1], *spil, n.* a thin strip of wood or twisted paper for lighting a pipe, etc.

[Orig. uncertain.]

spill[2], *spil, v.t.* to allow (liquid, etc.) to run out or overflow: to shed (blood): to cause or allow to fall to the ground.—Also *v.i.*:—*pa.t.* and *pa.p.* **spilled, spilt.** —*n.* a fall, tumble.

to spill the beans, (*coll.*) to give information, esp. without meaning to.

[O.E. *spillan*.]

spin, *spin, v.t.* to draw out (wool, etc.) and twist into thread: to shape (e.g. glass) into threadlike form: to make by spinning: to draw out as a thread, as spiders do: to twirl rapidly: to hurl:—*v.i.* to work at the trade of, or perform the act of, spinning: to whirl: to go swiftly, esp. on wheels:—*pr.p.* **spinn′ing**; *pa.t., pa.p.* **spun.**—*n.* a whirling or turning motion: a cycle ride: a spurt at high speed: the movement of an aircraft in a steep turning dive.

spinn′er, *n.* **spinn′ing,** *n., adj.*

spinn′eret, *n.* an organ for producing thread, as in a spider.

spinn′ing-wheel, *n.* a machine for spinning yarn, a wheel moved by hand, or by a foot treadle, which drives spindle(s).

to spin a yarn, to tell a long story, esp. one that is not true.

to spin out, to make last a long time.

[O.E. *spinnan*; conn. with Ger. *spinnen*.]

spinach, *spin′ij, -ich, n.* a plant whose young leaves are boiled as a vegetable.

[O.Fr. *espinage*.]

spinal. See **spine.**

spindle, *spin′dl, n.* the pin by which thread is twisted in spinning: a pin on which anything turns: anything very slender.

spin'dly, *adj.* very long and slender, esp. if lacking strength.
spin'dliness, *n.*
[O.E. *spinel*—same root as **spin.**]

spindrift, *spin'drift, n.* the spray blown from the crests of waves.
[Scot. form of *spoon*, to scud, and **drift.**]

spine, *spīn, n.* a thorn : a thin, stiff, pointed part growing on an animal : the backbone of an animal : a ridge.
spin'al, *adj.* of the backbone.
spine'less, *adj.* having no spine : weak, not able to make a firm stand.
spī'ny, *adj.* full of spines : thorny.
spinal cord, a cord of nerve tissue running up through the backbone, and forming the most important part of the central nervous system.
[O.Fr. *espine*—L. *spina*, a thorn.]

spinet, *spin'et, n.* a small harpsichord.
[It. *spinetta.*]

spinner. See **spin.**

spinney, *spin'i, n.* a small clump of trees.
[O.Fr. *espinei*—L. *spina*, a thorn.]

spinning. See **spin.**

spinster, *spin'stėr, n.* an unmarried woman : an old maid. **[spin.]**

spiral, *spī'rȧl, adj.* winding round and round, getting always farther and farther away from a centre : helical (see this word), like the thread of a screw.—*n.* a spiral line or object : a spiral course : an increase or decrease, rise or fall, getting ever more and more rapid (e.g. in prices or in the value of money).—*v.i.* to go or move in a spiral.
spir'ally, *adv.*
[Gk. *speira*, a coil.]

spire, *spīr, n.* an object (e.g. treetop) which tapers to a point : a tapering structure on a roof or steeple, esp. of a church : a steeple.
[O.E. *spīr*, shoot, sprout.]

spirit, *spir'it, n.* the soul : a being without body : a ghost : a principle or emotion that makes a person act (e.g. *the spirit of reform, of rivalry*) : (usu. in *pl.*) mood (e.g. *in good, low, spirits*) : liveliness : courage, boldness (e.g. *He acted with spirit*) : a lively or courageous person : the real meaning (e.g. *the spirit of the law*) : a liquid obtained by distillation or cracking (e.g. *motor spirit*) : a strong distilled alcoholic drink (esp. whisky or brandy).—*v.t.* to carry secretly, as if by magic.
spir'ited, *adj.* full of courage or liveliness (e.g. *a spirited attack, description*).
spir'itless, *adj.* without liveliness, courage, etc.
spir'itual, *adj.* having to do with the spirit or soul : sacred : having to do with the church.—*n.* an American Negro hymn with a strong rhythm.
spir'itually, *adv.* **spiritual'ity,** *n.*
Spir'itualism, *n.* the belief that the spirits of the dead can talk to living people esp. through certain other people (mediums) who are specially sensitive.
Spir'itualist, *n.* one who believes in Spiritualism.
in (or **out of**) **spirits,** feeling cheerful (or the reverse).
[L. *spiritus*, breath—*spīrāre*, to breathe.]

spirt. Same as **spurt.**

spit[1], *spit, n.* an iron bar on which meat is roasted : a long narrow strip of land or sand jutting into the sea.—*v.t.* to stab with something sharp :—*pr.p.* **spitt'ing**; *pa.p.* **spitt'ed.**
[O.E. *spitu* ; conn. with Du. *spit.*]

spit[2], *spit, v.t.* to throw out from the mouth : to send out with force.—*v.i.* to throw out saliva from the mouth : to rain in scattered drops : to make a spitting sound, as an angry cat does :—*pr.p.* **spitt'ing** ; *pa.p.* **spat.**—*n.* spittle : a light fall of rain or snow : (*coll.*) exact likeness (e.g. *the very spit of him*).
spittle, *n.* spit, saliva, the liquid that forms in the mouth.
spit'fire, *n.* a hot-tempered person.
[O.E. *spittan.*]

spite, *spīt, n.* grudge, ill-will, desire to hurt.—*v.t.* to annoy, thwart, out of spite.
spite'ful, *adj.* showing spite or desire to hurt.
spite'fully, *adv.* **spite'fulness,** *n.*
in spite of, in defiance of (e.g. *He went in spite of his father's orders*) : although such-and-such had occurred, or is or was fact, etc. (e.g. *In spite of the rain that had fallen, the ground was still dry*). **[despite.]**

spitfire, spittle. See **spit** (2).

spitting. See **spit** (1) and (2).

splash, *splash, v.t.* to spatter with liquid or mud : to throw (about, e.g. liquid) : to display, or print, in a place, or in type, that will be noticed.—*v.i.* to dash liquid about : to fall, or move, with splash(es).—*n.* a scattering of liquid, or the noise of this : a wet or dirty mark : a bright patch (e.g. *a splash of colour*) : display, publicity : a sensation.
splash'y, wet and muddy.
[Earlier *plash* ; prob. imit.]

splatter. Same as **spatter.**

splay, *splā, v.t.* to turn out at an angle.—*n.* a slant of the side of a doorway or window. **[display.]**

spleen, *splēn, n.* a spongy organ of the body, close to the stomach : ill-humour, bad-temper.
splenet'ic (*spli-*), *adj.* irritable, sullen, spiteful.
[Gk. *splēn.*]

splendid, *splen'did, adj.* brilliant, magnificent, very rich and grand : (*coll.*) very good or fine.
splen'didly, *adv.*
splen'dour, splen'didness, *ns.*
[L. *splendēre*, to shine.]

splenetic. See **spleen.**

splice, *splīs, v.t.* to join (two ends of a rope)

by weaving the threads together: to join together (two pieces of timber) by overlapping.—Also *n.*
[Middle Du. *splissen.*]

splint, *splint, n.* a piece of wood, etc., used to keep a broken arm or leg in its proper position.
splint′er, *n.* a small sharp piece of wood, etc., broken off.—*v.t., v.i.* to split into splinters.
splinter group, a group formed by breaking away from a larger group.
[Middle Du. or Middle Ger. *splinte.*]

split, *split, v.t.* to cut or break lengthwise: to break in pieces: to divide into parts: (of disagreement) to divide, disunite (people).—*v.i.* to be broken apart, or in pieces: to be divided or separated: (*coll.*) to let out secret(s):—*pr.p.* **splitt′ing**; *pa.p.* **split.**—*n.* a crack, break, rent, division, separation: (usu. in *pl.*) the feat of going down to the floor with one leg forward and the other back.
splitt′ing, *adj.* cutting: very bad (e.g. *a splitting headache*).
split infinitive, an infinitive with an adverb between 'to' and the verb (e.g. *Be sure to carefully dry it*).
split personality, a mental disease in which the sufferer has two or more personalities, with different attitudes and types of conduct.
split second, a fraction of a second.
to split one's sides, to shake violently with laughter.
[Du. *splitten*; conn. Ger. *spleissen.*]

splutter. Same as **sputter.**

spoil, *spoil, v.t.* to take valuables away from by force, plunder: to damage or ruin: to give (esp. a child) too much of what he or she wants, or to make his, her, character, behaviour, worse by doing so.—*v.i.* to decay, become bad:—*pa.t., pa.p.* **spoiled, spoilt.**—*n.* plunder: (in *pl.*) profits.
spoliation, *spō-li-ā′sh(ȯ)n, n.* plundering.
spoiling for, eager for (e.g. *He was spoiling for a fight*).
[L. *spolium*, plunder; root as **despoil.**]

spoke[1], *spōk, n.* one of the ribs or bars from the centre to the rim of a wheel, etc.
spokeshave, *spōk′shāv, n.* a small plane with handles, for shaping curves in wood.
to put a spoke in one's wheel, to put a difficulty in one's way.
[O.E. *spāca*; conn. with Ger. *speiche.*]

spoke[2], **spoken.** See **speak.**

spokeshave. See **spoke** (1).

spokesman. See **speak.**

spoliation. See **spoil.**

sponge, *spunj, n.* a sea animal, or its soft skeleton which has many pores and is able to suck up and hold water: a piece of such a skeleton, or a substitute, used for washing, etc.: a sponge pudding or cake: one who lives at the expense of others, a parasite: a drunkard.—*v.t.* to wipe, soak (up), remove, with sponge.—*v.i.* to get a living, things one wants, from others (with *on*).
spong′er, *n.* one who lives on others.
spongy, *spun′ji, adj.* like a sponge: porous, with holes: wet and soft.
spon′giness, *n.*
sponge cake, pudding, a very light one of flour, eggs, and sugar, etc.
to throw up the sponge, to give up the fight, admit defeat.
[Gk. *spongiā.*]

sponsor, *spon′sȯr, n.* one who gives his word that another will do something, act in a certain way: a godfather or godmother: one who makes himself responsible for e.g. the introduction of a law: (*U.S.*) a business firm that pays for a radio or television programme and is allowed time to advertise.
[L.—*spondēre, sponsum*, to promise.]

spontaneous, *spon-tā′ni-ŭs, -tān′yŭs, adj.* said, done, etc., of one's freewill: natural, impulsive (e.g. *She has a spontaneous manner*): occurring naturally (e.g. *a spontaneous growth of trees*).
sponta′neously, *adv.*
sponta′neousness, *n.*
spontane′ity (*-nē′*), *n.*
[L. *sponte*, of one's own accord.]

spoof, *spōōf, n.* (*slang*) a trick, hoax.—Also *v.t., v.i.,* and *adj.*
[Game invented by a comedian.]

spook, *spōōk, n.* a ghost.
spook′y, *adj.* **spook′iness,** *n.*
[Conn. Ger. *spuk*, Du. *spook.*]

spool, *spōōl, n.* a bobbin, reel, holder, on which thread, photograph film, etc. is wound.
[M.E. *spole*; conn. with Ger. *spule.*]

spoon, *spōōn, n.* an instrument, with a shallow bowl and a handle, for lifting food to the mouth: a wooden-headed golf club.—*v.t.* to lift with a spoon: to scoop (up).—*v.i.* to make love in a sentimental way.
spoon′ful, *n.* as much as fills a spoon: a small amount:—*pl.* **spoon′fuls.**
spoon′-feed′, *v.t.* to feed with a spoon: to pamper: to teach (a person) in a way that does not allow him to think for himself.
spoon′-feed′ing, *n.* **spoon′-fed′,** *adj.*
[O.E. *spōn*, chip; conn. with Ger. *span.*]

spoonerism, *spōō′nė-riz-ėm, n.* a slip that changes the position of first sounds of words (e.g. 'shoving leopard' for 'loving shepherd').
[Rev. W. A. *Spooner.*]

spoor, *spōōr, n.* footprints or tracks, esp. of a hunted animal. [Afrikaans.]

sporadic, *spo-rad′ik, adj.* happening here and there, or now and again.
[Gk. *sporadikos*, scattered; as **spore.**]

spore, *spōr, spör, n.* the tiny seedlike body from which ferns, etc., grow.
[Gk. *speirein*, to sow (seed), scatter.]

sporran, *spor'ȧn, n.* a pouch worn in front of the kilt.
[Gael. *sporan.*]

sport, *spōrt, spört, v.i.* to play, gambol: to make merry: to trifle (with).—*v.t.* to wear in public (e.g. *to sport a new tie*).—*n.* a pastime, amusement: a game, or games, or a contest, in which the body is exercised (e.g. football, athletics): fishing, hunting, etc.: a person who has sportsmanlike qualities: jest (e.g. *I said it in sport*): one who is laughed at: one who is tossed about like a plaything (e.g. *the sport of the wind, of Fortune*): (of plant or animal) differing greatly from the normal.
sport'ing, *adj.* having to do with, or taking part in, sports, or in sports involving betting.
sport'ive, *adj.* playful, merry.
sports car, car for two designed to run at high speed on roads.
sports'man, *n.* one who hunts, fishes, etc.: (sometimes) one who takes part in athletic sports: one who shows a good spirit in sport: one ready to win or lose with good grace:—*fem.* **sports'-woman.**
sports'manlike, *adj.*
sports'manship, *n.*
sporting chance, an off, slight, chance.
[Shortened from **disport.**]

spot, *spot, n.* a mark made by a drop of grease, paint, etc.: a stain: a small, usu. round, part of a different colour: a pimple: a place, small area (e.g. *a shady spot*): the exact place (e.g. *the spot where the bomb fell*): a spotlight.—*v.t.* to mark with spots: to stain (a reputation): (*coll.*) to catch sight of, see, recognise.—*v.i.* to become marked with spots:—*pr.p.* **spott'ing**; *pa.p.* **spott'ed.**
spot'less, *adj.* without a spot: pure.
spott'ed, spott'y, *adj.* marked with spots.
spott'iness, *n.*
spott'er, *n.* one who keeps on the watch for something.
spot'light, *n.* a circle of light that is thrown on an actor or on a small part of the stage.—*v.t.* to show up with, or as if with, a spotlight.
in a spot, in trouble.
on the spot, at once: in the very place referred to or required: (*slang*) in a dangerous, difficult, or embarrassing, position: alert, ready to act.
[M.E. *spotte.*]

spouse, *spowz, n.* a husband or wife.
[Same root as **espouse.**]

spout, *spowt, v.i., v.t.* to throw out e.g. water in a jet: to blow, as a whale: to talk, or utter, a lot, or loudly and dramatically.—*n.* a mouth such as that of a kettle or teapot: a jet or strong flow of e.g. water: the blowhole of a whale.
[M.E. *spouten*; conn. with Du. *spuiten.*]

sprain, *sprān, v.t.* to wrench (a joint, e.g. ankle) tearing or stretching ligaments.—Also *n.* [Orig. uncertain.]

sprang. See **spring.**

sprat, *sprat, n.* a small fish somewhat like the herring.
[O.E. *sprot*; conn. with Ger. *sprotte.*]

sprawl, *spröl, v.i.* to stretch the body carelessly, when sitting or lying: (of e.g. writing, vines, buildings) to spread widely in an irregular way.—Also *v.t.* and *n.*
[O.E. *spreawlian.*]

spray[1], *sprā, n.* a cloud of small flying drops: such a cloud of e.g. insecticide: an instrument for sending it out.—*v.t.* to sprinkle with, or to squirt in, mist-like jets.
[Prob. Middle Du. *sprayen.*]

spray[2], *sprā, n.* a shoot or twig spreading out in branches or flowers. [M.E.]

spread, *spred, v.t.* to cause to go more widely or more thinly over a surface (e.g. *to spread jam*): to open out (e.g. one's arms, a map): to scatter, distribute over a region, time, etc. (e.g. *to spread the population*; *to spread the meetings over several days*): to send about, give to others (news, disease, etc.): to coat (a surface with something).—*v.i.* to run, scatter, be distributed, etc:—*pa.t., pa.p.* **spread** (*spred*).—*n.* act of spreading: space covered, extent of spreading: a meal (esp. large) laid out: a cover for a bed or a table: anything for spreading on bread.
spread'-ea'gled, *adj.* with arms and legs spread out.
[O.E. *sprǣdan.*]

spree, *sprē, n.* a reckless bout of merry-making, drinking, or spending.
[Orig. slang.]

sprig, *sprig, n.* a small shoot or twig: a young person.
sprigged, *adj.* with design of sprigs.
[Orig. unknown.]

sprightly, *sprit'li, adj.* lively, brisk, gay.
spright'liness, *n.* [**sprite.**]

spring, *spring, v.i.* to move, start up, suddenly: to leap, jump: to fly (back) as a piece of stretched elastic when let go: to appear, arise (e.g. *Water springs from the ground*; *industries spring up*): to come, result, from (e.g. *His energy springs from good health*).—*v.t.* to leap over: to cause (a mine, trap) to go off: to produce suddenly (with *on*; e.g. *to spring a surprise on someone*): to put springs in:—*pa.t.* **sprang**; *pa.p.* **sprung.**—*n.* a leap: a sudden movement: ability to stretch and fly back again: bounce, energy (e.g. *He has a spring in his step*): a coil of e.g. wire for setting in motion (e.g. *a watch spring*), or reducing shocks (e.g. *car springs*): a source, cause (of life or action): a small stream flowing out from the ground: (often *cap.*) the season when plants begin to grow.—*adj.* having, or run by,

spring(s): (often *cap.*) of, appearing in, or used in, the season of Spring.
spring'y, *adj.* having spring, elastic, bounding.
spring'iness, *n.*
sprung, *adj.* (of wood) split, cracked: (of e.g. sinew) strained.
spring'er, *n.* a type of gun dog.
spring'bok, *n.* a South African antelope: (*cap.*) a South African.
spring cleaning, a thorough house-cleaning, esp. in Spring.
spring'board, *n.* a board from which to take off in vaulting, etc., or in diving.
spring tide, the very high tide when the moon is full or new.
spring'time (or *cap.*), *n.* season of Spring.
to spring a leak, to begin to leak.
[O.E. *springan*; conn. Ger. *springen.*]

sprinkle, *spring'kl, v.t.* to scatter in small drops or pieces: to put here and there: to scatter (with).—Also *v.i.* and *n.*
sprink'ler, *n.*
sprink'ling, *n.* small quantity sprinkled: a small number (e.g. *a sprinkling of people*). [M.E.]

sprint, *sprint, n.* a short run, row, or race at full speed.—Also *v.i.*
sprin'ter, *n.* [Scand.]

sprite, *sprīt, n.* an elf, fairy, or impish person. [Same root as **spirit.**]

sprocket, *sprok'it, n.* one of a set of teeth on the rim of a wheel that fit into the links of a chain. [Orig. unknown.]

sprout, *sprowt, n.* a young shoot or bud.—*v.i.* to push out new shoots: to begin to grow.—Also *v.t.*
[O.E. *sprūtan*; conn. Du. *spruiten.*]

spruce[1], *sproōs, adj.* neat, smart.—*v.t., v.i.* (with *up*) to make, become, smarter.
[Prob. *Spruce,* Prussia; Prussian leather was fashionable in 16th century.]

spruce[2], *sproōs, n.* a kind of fir tree, an evergreen with hanging cones: the wood from the spruce fir.
[M.E. *Spruce,* Prussia.]

sprung. See **spring.**

spry, *sprī, adj.* lively, active, nimble:—*comp.* **spry'er**; *superl.* **spry'est.**
spry'ly, *adv.* **spry'ness,** *n.*
[Orig. uncertain.]

spume, *spūm, n.* foam, froth: scum.—*v.i.* to foam.
[L. *spūma*—same root as **spew.**]

spun. See **spin.**

spunk, *spungk, n.* (*coll.*) spirit, pluck.
[Conn. with Ir. *sponc,* tinder.]

spur, *spûr, n.* an instrument with sharp point(s) worn on a rider's heel and used to drive on his horse: anything that urges a person on to do something: a claw-like point at the back of a bird's (e.g. cock's) leg: a sticking out branch or root: a small range of mountains running off from a larger range.—*v.t.* to use spurs on: to urge on.—*v.i.* to press forward with the spur: to hasten:—*pr.p.* **spurr'ing**; *pa.p.* **spurred.**
on the spur of the moment, suddenly without planning beforehand.
[O.E. *spura*; conn. with Ger. *sporn.*]

spurious, *spūr'i-ůs, adj.* not genuine or real, false.
[L. *spurius,* false.]

spurn, *spûrn, v.t.* to refuse, cast aside, with scorn.
[O.E. *spurnan*; prob. conn. with **spur.**]

spurred, spurring. See **spur.**

spurt, *spûrt, v.t., v.i.* to spout, gush: (*v.i.*) to make a great effort suddenly and for a short time.—*n.* a sudden gush: a great but short effort. [Orig. unknown.]

sputter, *sput'ėr, v.i.* to make a noise as of spitting and throw out moisture in scattered drops: to speak in hurried confused way because of rage or excitement.—Also *v.t.*
[Imit.; conn. Du. *sputteren.*]

sputum, *spū'tům, n.* spittle with mucus from the nose, throat, etc.
[L. *spuěre, spūtum,* to spit.]

spy, *spī, n.* a secret agent employed to gather information, esp. military: one who watches others secretly: act of spying:—*pl.* **spies.**—*v.t., v.i.* to watch secretly: (*v.t.*) to find (out) by close search: (*v.t.*) to catch sight of:—*pr.p.* **spy'ing**; *pa.p.* **spied.**
spy'glass, *n.* a small telescope.
[O.Fr. *espie*; same root as **espy.**]

squabble, *skwob'l, v.i.* to quarrel noisily about very little.—Also *n.*
squabb'ling, *n.* and *adj.* [Scand.]

squad, *skwod, n.* a small group of soldiers drilled or working together: any working party: a group.
[Fr. *escouade.*]

squadron, *skwod'rǒn, n.* a division of a regiment, section of a fleet, or group of aeroplanes.
squad'ron-lead'er, *n.* R.A.F. officer. See *Appendices.*
[It. *squadra,* square—L. root as **square.**]

squalid, *skwol'id, adj.* dirty, uncared-for: poor, mean, miserable.
squal'idness, squal'or, *ns.*
[L. *squālidus,* stiff with dirt.]

squall, *skwöl, v.i., v.t.* to cry out loudly.—*n.* a loud cry: a strong and sudden gust of wind.
squall'y, *adj.* with many squalls or gusts of wind:—*comp.* **squall'ier**; *superl.* **squall'iest.**
squall'iness, *n.* [Imit.]

squander, *skwon'dėr, v.t.* to spend (e.g. money, strength) wastefully.
[Orig. unknown.]

square, *skwār, n.* a four-sided figure with all sides equal in length and all angles right angles: an open place in a town, with the buildings round it: the product when a number is multiplied by itself ($9=3\times3$, *or* 3^2, i.e. *is the square of* 3):

(*coll.*) a person who is not modern in ideas.—*adj.* shaped like a square or a right angle: (of a person's build) broad, thick-set: fair, honest (e.g. *a square deal*): (of account) settled: even, quits: equal in score: solid, satisfying (e.g. *a square meal*).—*v.t.* to make square: to straighten (the shoulders): to multiply (a number) by itself: to settle (e.g. a debt): (*coll.*) to bribe, or to arrange a matter with.—*v.i.* to fit, agree (e.g. *to square with requirements, with previous statements*): to settle, a debt, etc. (with someone).—*adv.* at right angles: solidly: fairly, honestly: directly.

square foot, inch, an area equal to a square in which each side is one foot, inch.

square root, the number which, multiplied by itself, gives the number being considered (3 is the square root of 9, or √9, because 3×3=9).

square sail, a four-sided sail.

on the square, honestly.

to square up, to settle accounts.

to square up to, to face up to, defy.

[O.Fr. *esquarre*—L. *ex*, *quadra*, square.]

squash[1]**,** *skwosh, v.t.* to press or crush into pulp: to crush flat: to put down (e.g. *to squash a revolt*): to snub.—*v.i.* to become crushed or pulpy: to crowd.—*n.* anything soft and easily crushed, or the sound of its fall: a mass of people crowded together: a drink containing the juice of crushed fruits.

squash'y, *adj.* pulpy: soft and wet.

squash (rackets), a game played in a walled court with a soft ball.

[O.Fr. *esquacer*—L. *quassāre*, to shake.]

squash[2]**,** *skwosh, n.* a gourd used as vegetable. [From Amer. Indian name.]

squat, *skwot, v.i.* to sit down on the heels or in a crouching position: to settle on land or in property without a right:—*pr.p.* **squatt'ing**; *pa.p.* **squatt'ed.**—*adj.* dumpy.

squatt'er, *n.*

[O.Fr. *esquatir*, crush; conn. **squash** (1).]

squaw, *skwö, n.* an American Indian woman, esp. wife. [From Amer. Indian.]

squawk, *skwök, n.* a harsh croaky call.—*v.i.* to give such a sound. [Imit.]

squeak, *skwēk, v.i.* to give a shrill cry or sound: (*slang*) to be an informer, or to confess.—*n.* a thin high sound: a narrow escape: a bare chance.

squeak'y, *adj.* **squeak'ily,** *adv.*

squeak'iness, *n.* [Imit.]

squeal, *skwēl, v.i.* to give a longish shrill cry: (*coll.*) to be an informer.—Also *n.* [Imit.]

squeamish, *skwē'mish, adj.* a little bit sick: easily shocked or disgusted: very scrupulous and particular in conduct.

[M.E. *scoymous.*]

squeeze, *skwēz, v.t.* to crush, press hard, press together tightly: to grasp tightly: to force (through, into) by pressing: to force out liquid from.—*v.i.* to press: to force a way.—*n.* act of squeezing: pressure: an embrace: a few drops got by squeezing.

[O.E. *cwīsan.*]

squelch, *skwelch, -sh, n.* sound made by walking through mud, or by a soft wet object falling: a pulpy mass.—*v.i.* to take heavy steps in water, etc. [Imit.]

squib, *skwib, n.* a firework. [Perh. imit.]

squid, *skwid, n.* sea creature with ten arms, esp. one of the smaller ones, which are used for bait.

[Orig. unknown.]

squint, *skwint, adj.* off the straight.—*v.i.* to look to the side: to have the eyes looking different ways: to screw up the eyes in looking at something.—*v.t.* to cause to squint.—Also *n.*

[Earlier **asquint**; orig. uncertain.]

squire, *skwīr, n.* in Middle Ages, a lad who served a knight in preparation for becoming one himself: one who escorts a lady: an English gentleman, esp. of an old family, who owns land. [**esquire.**]

squirm, *skwėrm, v.i.* to wriggle, twist the body: to feel ashamed. [Prob. imit.]

squirrel, *skwir'ėl, n.* a gnawing animal with a bushy tail, living in trees.

[Gk. *skia*, shade, *oura*, tail.]

squirt, *skwėrt, v.t.* to shoot out (liquid) in a jet: to wet (something) in this way.—Also *v.i.*—*n.* an instrument for squirting: (*coll.*) one who deserves to be despised.

[Orig. uncertain.]

stab, *stab, v.t.* to wound or pierce with a pointed weapon: to pain suddenly and deeply: to aim (at).—*n.* act of stabbing: wound made by sharp point: (*slang*) an attempt (at something):—*pr.p.* **stabb'ing**; *pa.p.* **stabbed.**

[Perh. old *stob*, stump, stake.]

stable[1]**,** *stā'bl, adj.* standing firm: likely to last (e.g. *a stable government*): (of person, character, etc.) steady in purpose, not likely to be changed by stress of circumstances: (*chemistry*) not easily decomposed or broken down.

stabil'ity (*stȧ-*), **sta'bleness,** *ns.*

stab'ilise (*stāb'*, *stab'*), *v.t.* to make steady: to fit (aeroplane, ship) with a device that keeps it steady; to fix the value of (a country's currency).

stab'iliser, *n.*

[L. *stabilis*—*stāre*, to stand.]

stable[2]**,** *stā'bl, n.* a building for keeping animals, usu. horses: horses under one ownership.—*v.t.* to put or keep in a stable.

[L. *stabulum*; root as **stable** (1).]

staccato, *stȧ-kä'tō, adj.* and *adv.* (*music*) with each note sounded separately and clearly: (of speech, speaking) jerky, in a jerky manner.

[It. *staccare*, for *distaccare*, to separate.]

stack, *stak, n.* a large pile of hay, wood, etc.: a group of things (e.g. chimneys, rifles) standing together: the funnel of a steamer, etc.: (*coll.*; often in *pl.*) a large quantity.—*v.t.* to pile into a stack.
[Old Norse *stakkr*, a stack of hay.

stadium, *stā'di-ŭm, n.* large sports-ground or racecourse.
[L.—Gk. *stadion.*]

staff, *stâf, n.* a stick carried in the hand: a pole: a stick or sign of authority: lines and spaces on which music is written or printed (see also **stave**): a group of officers helping a commanding officer: the people employed in a business, school, etc.:—*pl.* **staffs.**—*v.t.* to supply with a staff.
staff officer, officer serving as member of a staff.
the staff of life, bread.
[O.E. *stæf*; conn. with Ger. *stab.*]

stag, *stag, n.* a male deer, esp. a red deer.
stag party, a party without women.
[O.E. *stagga.*]

stage, *stāj, n.* (1) a shelf, floor, storey: a raised platform, esp. for acting on: the theatre, or the job of working in it: (2) a place of rest on a journey or road: the part of a journey between two such places: period, step, in development (e.g. *the first stage of the war*; *at that stage in her life*): stage coach.—*v.t.* to put (a play) on the stage: to organise: to carry out publicly (e.g. *to stage a demonstration*).
stage coach, a horse-drawn public coach that ran regularly from stage to stage.
stage direction, an order to an actor playing a part to do this or that.
stage fright, nervousness before an audience, esp. the first time.
stage hand, a workman employed about the stage.
stage manager, one who has general charge of scenery, properties, etc.
stage'-man'age, *v.t.* to act as stage manager of: to arrange (an event): to do so for a bad purpose.
old stager, one who has worked long in one job, profession, etc.
[O.Fr. *estage*—L. *stāre*, to stand.]

stagger, *stag'ėr, v.i.* to sway from side to side, reel, totter.—*v.t.* to cause to reel: to give a shock to: to arrange (hours of work, etc.) so that some are working while others are free.—Also *n.*
stagg'ering, *adj.* overpowering (e.g. *a staggering blow*).
[Old Norse *stakra*, to push.]

stagnant, *stag'nȧnt, adj.* (of water) standing still, not flowing and thus impure: not active, dull.
stagnā'tion, *n.* **stag'nantly,** *adv.*
stag'nate, *v.i.* to be, or become, stagnant: to pass time in a dull state without change or development.
[L. *stagnum*, a swamp.]

staid, *stād, adj.* serious in manner.
[Old *pa.p.* of **stay** (2).]

stain, *stān, v.t.* to give a different colour to: to spot, mark: to be a black mark on (character, reputation, etc.).—*v.i.* to take a stain.—*n.* a dye or colouring matter: a spot, mark: a cause of shame.
stain'less, *adj.* free from stain: not easily stained or rusted.
stained glass, glass painted with certain colours fixed into the surface.
stainless steel, an alloy, mixture of steel and chromium, which does not rust.
[For *distain*, take away colour; **tinge.**]

stair, *stār, n.* a number of steps from landing to landing (usu. in *pl.*): one of these steps.
stair'case, stair'way, *ns.* a stretch of stairs with rails on one or both sides.
[O.E. *stǣger*—*stīgan*, to go up.]

stake, *stāk, n.* (1) a strong stick pointed at one end: a post to which a person sentenced to be burned was tied: (**the stake**) death by burning: (2) money put down as a bet: something to gain or lose.—*v.t.* (1) to fasten with, support with, a stake: to pierce with a stake: to mark the bounds of with stakes (e.g. *to stake off, out, ground for a pitch*): (2) to put down (money) as a bet: to risk (e.g. *He staked everything on the success of this attack*).
at stake, to be won or lost: in danger (e.g. *His life is at stake*).
to stake a claim, to assert a right (to something).
[O.E. *staca.*]

stalactite, *stal'ȧk-tīt, stȧ-lak', n.* an icicle-shaped piece usu. of calcium carbonate (see this) hanging from the roof of a cave, formed by dripping water containing the carbonate.
stalagmite, *stal'ȧg-mīt, stȧ-lag', n.* a piece of the same substance and similar shape coming up from the floor of a cave.
[Gk. *stalassein*, to drip.]

stale, *stāl, adj.* not fresh: dry, flat, tasteless from keeping too long: no longer interesting because heard, done, etc., too often: not able to do one's best because of too much training, study, etc.
[Perh. from root *sta-*, as in **stand.**]

stalemate, *stāl'māt, n.* (*chess*) a position in which a player cannot move without putting his king into check: (in a contest) a position in which neither side can win, a deadlock, draw.
[O.Fr. *estal*, position, and check*mate.*]

stalk[1], *stök, n.* the main stem of a plant: a stem on which a flower, etc. grows: a tall chimney.
[M.E. dim. *stalke*—O.E. *stæla.*]

stalk[2], *stök, v.i., v.t.* to walk stiffly or proudly: to go after (game, etc.) keeping under cover.—*n.* act of stalking: a stalking walk.
[O.E. (*bi*)*stealcian*—root as **steal.**]

stall[1], *stöl*, *n*. (a division for one animal in) a stable, cowshed, etc.: a table, booth, or stand where articles are laid out for sale: a seat in church esp. for choir or clergy: a seat in a theatre, in the front section of the ground floor: loss of flying speed in aircraft: a standstill.—*v.t.* to put or keep in a stall: to bring to a standstill.—*v.i.* (of aircraft) to lose flying speed and so fall out of control for a time: (of car engine) to stop because of too great load or because of too sudden braking.

[O.E. *steall*; conn. Ger. *stall*.]

stall[2], *stöl*, *v.i.* (*slang*) to avoid for the time being action or decision.—*v.t.* (usu. with *off*) to put off, keep at a distance (e.g. *Stall off that question by changing the subject*).

[From old word *stale*, a decoy.]

stallion, *stal'yȯn*, *n*. a male horse, esp. one kept for breeding.

[O.Fr. *estalon*—Germanic *stal*, stall.]

stalwart, *stöl'wȧrt*, *adj*. strong, sturdy: brave, resolute.—*n*. a bold person.

[Scot. form of *stalworth*—O.E. *stǣl*, place, *wierthe*, worth.]

stamen, *stā'mėn*, *n*. a fine stalk in the middle of a flower together with the sac on the end of it that holds pollen:—*pl*. **sta'mens.**

stam'ina (*stam'*-), *n*. strength, power to endure fatigue, etc.

[L. *stamen*, upright thread in a loom.]

stammer, *stam'ėr*, *v.i.* to stumble in speaking: to stutter.—Also *v.t.* and *n*.

[O.E. *stamerian*; conn. Ger. *stammeln*.]

stamp, *stamp*, *v.t.* to bring (the foot) down heavily: to bring the foot, etc., down heavily on: to fix a mark on by pressing, or by cutting with a downward blow: to stick a postage stamp on: to fix or mark deeply (e.g. *His experiences had stamped certain ideas on his mind and a sad expression on his face*): to mark (as), prove to be (e.g. *By doing this he stamped himself as untrustworthy*).—*v.i.* to step, or to set down the foot, with force.—*n*. the act of stamping: a mark or design made by stamping: a postage stamp (see **post**): a clear mark (e.g. *His story had the stamp of truth*): kind, sort (e.g. *a man of a different stamp*): an instrument or machine for stamping.

stamp duty, *n*. a tax on e.g. legal papers, paid by using specially stamped paper or by putting on a stamp.

to stamp out, to put out by trampling or other force (e.g. fire, rebellion): to make by stamping from a sheet of e.g. metal with a cutter.

[M.E. *stampen*; conn. Ger. *stampfen*.]

stampede, *stam-pēd'*, *n*. a sudden wild rush of frightened animals, or of a large number of people.—*v.i.*, *v.t.* to rush, or send rushing, in a stampede.

[Sp. *estampida*; same root as **stamp.**]

stance, *stans*, *n*. manner of standing e.g. in playing golf, cricket.

[Fr. *stance* (now meaning 'stanza').]

stanch, *stän(t)sh*, **staunch,** *stön(t)sh*, *v.t.* to stop the flow of (e.g. blood).

[O.Fr. *estanchier*.]

stanchion, *stan'sh(ȯ)n*, *n*. an upright bar, post, etc., in a window, screen, or ship.

[O.Fr. *estançon*—L. *stāre*, to stand.]

stand, *stand*, *v.i.* to be in an upright position, not lying or sitting down: to rise to one's feet: to resist, fight (against): to hold a place (e.g. *The chest stands in the hall*): to be (e.g. *to stand firm, alone*): to be at the moment (e.g. *as the matter, the account, stands*): to remain in force (*This law still stands*): to act as (e.g. sponsor): to be a candidate.—*v.t.* to set upright or on end: to undergo (trial for crime): to bear (e.g. *Can you stand the cold?*): to bear the presence of (someone): to pay for (something) for someone (e.g. *Let me stand you tea*):—*pa.t.*, *pa.p.* **stood** (*stood*).—*n*. an act, or place, of standing: a post, station: a halt, standstill: a place for vehicles waiting to be hired: rows of raised seats for spectators: (*U.S.*) a witness box: something for putting things on: a piece of furniture for hanging things from: a great effort (*for* or *against*; e.g. *to make a stand for freedom*).

stan'ding, *adj*. upright on feet or on end: remaining in force, use, or readiness: not moving.—*n*. action of verb 'to stand' (e.g. *Standing is not allowed*): position, rank, among others: time of lasting (e.g. *an agreement of long standing*).

stand'-by, *n*. someone or something ready when he, it, is needed.

stand'-in', *n*. one who takes the place of another for a time.

stand'ing-room, *n*. room for standing, without a seat.

stand'-off(ish), *adj*. distant, not friendly, in manner.

stand'point, *n*. position from which one looks at something (e.g. *He thought only of his profits*; *from his standpoint the new law was bad*).

stand'still, *n*. a complete stop.

stand'-up, *adj*. done in a standing position: (of a fight) in earnest.

to stand by, to stand close to: to remain faithful to: to accept and act according to (a decision): to be waiting ready to act, help, etc.

to stand down, to leave the witness box: to withdraw from a contest.

to stand fast, to refuse to give in.

to stand for, to be a candidate for: to be a symbol of (e.g. *John Bull stands for England*): (*slang*) to approve of or allow to happen.

to stand in, to be a stand-in.

to stand off, to remain at a distance.

to stand one's ground, to refuse to move or to give in.
to stand out, to stick out: to be noticeable (e.g. *She stands out in a crowd*): to continue to fight or urge (*for, against*).
to stand to, to set to work: to be likely to (e.g. *She stands to win the contest*).
to stand to reason that, to be reasonable or likely that.
to stand up for, to support or try to defend.
to stand up to, to face boldly: to bear (e.g. pain), carry out (e.g. a task), bravely.
to stand well, to be in favour (with).
[O.E. *standan*; Ger. *stehen*, L. *stāre*.]

standard, *stan'dȧrd*, *n.* a flag or figure on a pole, esp. one carried, etc., by an armed force: a shrub or tree not trained against a support: a weight, measure, etc., used in expressing other weights, etc. (e.g. *The pound is the standard of weight*): a model by which things are judged: a level of excellence aimed at (e.g. *These people have high, low, standards of cleanliness and morals*): grade, level (e.g. *The standard of work done in this school is high, low*).—*adj.* accepted as a standard or model: usual: (of a type of goods) widely available.
stan'dardise, *v.t.* to make or keep of one size, shape, etc. (e.g. *to standardise each part of a machine so that it is easy to obtain a new part to replace it*).
standardisā'tion, *n.*
stan'dard-bear'er, *n.* one who carries a standard or banner.
[O.Fr. *estandard*.]

stand-by, etc. See **stand.**

stank. See **stink.**

stanza, *stan'zȧ*, *n.* a group of lines making up a part of a poem, usu. with a special rhyme scheme and length of line.
[It. *stanza*, a stop—L. *stāre*, stand.]

staple[1], *stā'pl*, *n.* chief product of trade or industry: main item (of diet, reading, etc.): a fibre of raw cotton, etc., or its length or fineness.—*adj.* leading, main.
[Middle Du. *stapel*, trading centre.]

staple[2], *stā'pl*, *n.* a bent rod or wire, both ends of which are driven through sheets of paper to fasten them together, or into a wall, etc.—*v.t.* to fasten with a staple.
[O.E. *stapol*, a prop.]

star, *stär*, *n.* any of the bright heavenly bodies, esp. those whose places appear to be fixed and which shine with their own light: an object or figure with pointed rays, usu. five: a very brilliant person: a leading actor or actress in films or plays.—Also *adj.*—*v.t.* to mark with a star: to have (a certain person) as a star performer.—*v.i.* to act a chief part:—*pr.p.* **starr'ing**; *pa.p.* **starred.**
starred, *adj.* covered with stars: marked with a star, to show excellence, etc.: playing a leading part.
starr'y, *adj.* full of stars: like, or shining like, stars.
starr'iness, *n.*
See also **stellar.**
star'dom, *n.* the state of being a leading performer.
star'fish, *n.* a small sea creature with five points or arms.
star'light, *n.* light from the stars.
Stars and Stripes, the flag of the United States of America.
[O.E. *steorra*: conn. Ger. *stern*, L. *stella*, Gk. *astēr*.]

starboard, *stär'bō(r)d*, *-bōrd*, *-bȯrd*, *n.* the right-hand side of a ship, when one is looking towards the bow.—Also *adj.*
[O.E. *stēor*, steering, *bord*, board.]

starch, *stärch*, *n.* a white food substance found esp. in flour, potatoes, etc.: a preparation of this used for stiffening clothes: stiffness, formal manner.—*v.t.* to stiffen with starch.
star'chy, *adj.* like, or containing, starch: stiff, formal, in manner.
star'chiness, *n.*
[Conn. with **stark.**]

stardom. See **star.**

stare, *stār*, *v.i.* to look in a fixed way through wonder, horror, rudeness, etc.—Also *n.*
to stare one in the face, to be obvious: (of something unpleasant) to be, seem to be, waiting for one in near future.
[O.E. *starian*; conn. with **stern** (1).]

starfish. See **star.**

stark[1], *stärk*, *adj.* stiff: sheer, out-and-out (e.g. *stark foolishness*): (of style) unadorned, simple.—*adv.* completely (e.g. *stark mad*).
[O.E. *stearc*, hard, strong.]

stark[2]**(-naked),** *stärk'(-nā'kid)*, *adj.* completely naked, quite bare.
[O.E. *steort*, tail, *nacod*, naked.]

starlight. See **star.**

starling, *stär'ling*, *n.* a small bird with glossy dark feathers.
[O.E *stærling*, dim. of *stær*, starling.]

start, *stärt*, *v.i.* (1) to dart or move suddenly out, forward, or up: to jump or jerk suddenly, e.g. in surprise: (2) to begin: to set forth on a journey, etc.—*v.t.* (1) to drive from a hiding place: (2) to begin: to set going: to set up (e.g. in business).—*n.* (1) a sudden movement of the body: a surprised or frightened feeling: (2) a beginning: a setting in motion: the advantage of beginning before, or farther forward than, rivals, or the amount of this.
star'ter, *n.* **star'ting,** *adj.*, *n.*
star'ting-point, *n.* the point from which motion or action begins.
to start up, to rise suddenly: to set in motion.
[M.E. *sterten*; conn. Du. *storten*, plunge.]

startle, *stär'tl*, *v.i.*, *v.t.* to feel, or cause, a sudden surprise or alarm.

start'ling, *adj.* **start'lingly,** *adv.*
[O.E. *steartlian,* to kick; or from **start.**]

starve, *stärv, v.i.* to die of, or suffer greatly from, hunger: to be in want of, feel a great longing (for; e.g. *I starve for company*).—*v.t.* to cause to starve.
starvā'tion, *n.*
starve'ling, *n., adj.* starved (creature).
[O.E. *steorfan,* die; conn. Ger. *sterben.*]

state, *stāt, n.* (1) condition (e.g. *The road is in a bad state*): ceremonial pomp (e.g. *The king drove there in state*): (2) a group of people under one government, or their territory, either a separate country, or (as in the United States) a division of a federation: the government. —*adj.* (1) ceremonial: (2) having to do with a state, or with the government.—*v.t.* to set out, tell, definitely and in detail, or formally: to assert: to say.
stat'ed, *adj.* fixed, regular (e.g. *at stated times*).
state'ly, *adj.* noble-looking, dignified, impressive.
state'liness, *n.*
state'ment, *n.* the act of stating: something that is stated.
state'-aid'ed, *adj.* receiving money from the state.
state'room, *n.* a large cabin in a ship.
states'man, *n.* one skilled in government esp. one who manages affairs with wisdom and foresight.
states'manship, *n.*
states'manlike, states'manly, *adjs.*
[Same L. root as **station.**]

static, *stat'ik, adj.* standing still: stable.—*n.* disturbances, noises, in wireless reception.
[Gk. *histanai,* to cause to stand.]

station, *stā'sh(ȯ)n, n.* a fixed stopping-place, esp. for a railway or bus line, with its buildings: a local office, headquarters (e.g. *a police station, wireless station*): a fixed place or post, esp. military: a position: position in life, or in the scale of nature (e.g. *a lowly station*).—Also *adj.*—*v.t.* to appoint to a post, or put in position (at, in, a particular place).
stā'tionary, *adj.* standing, not moving: not changing place.
stā'tioner, *n.* one who sells paper and other articles used in writing.
stā'tionery, *n.* goods sold by a stationer, paper, envelopes, etc.
[Fr.—L. *stāre, statum,* to stand.]

statistics, *stȧ-tis'tiks, n. pl.* figures and facts set out in order (e.g. *the statistics of road accidents*): (with *sing.* verb) the study of such facts.
statis'tical, *adj.* **statis'tically,** *adv.*
[Same L. root as **state, station.**]

statue, *stat'ū, n.* a likeness of a person or animal in wood, stone, etc.
stat'uary, *n.* statues.
statuesque, *stat-ū-esk', adj.* like a statue in dignity, etc.
stat'uette, *n.* a small statue.
[Same L. root as **station.**]

stature, *stach'ür, n.* height of body.
[Same L. root as **station.**]

status, *stā'tŭs, n.* social position, or rank in a group: position of affairs.
status (in) quo, the state of affairs before a certain event, date.
status symbol, a possession supposed to show high social position (e.g. a large car). [Same L. root as **station.**]

statute, *stat'ūt, n.* a written law of a country.
stat'utory, *adj.* required by statute: that may be punished by law (e.g. *a statutory offence*).
[L. *statuĕre,* lay down—*stāre,* stand.]

staunch[1], *stönch, -sh, adj.* firm, trusty, steadfast (e.g. *a staunch believer, supporter*).
staunch'ly, *adv.* **staunch'ness,** *n.*
[Same root as **stanch.**]

staunch[2]. See **stanch.**

stave, *stāv, n.* one of the side pieces of a cask or tub: a stick, rod: (*music*) a staff: a stanza, verse, of a poem, song.—*v.t.* (with *in*) to crush in, make hole in: (with *off*) to keep away (e.g. *to stave off a cold*), delay (e.g. *to stave off the evil day*):—*pa.t., pa.p.* **stāved** or **stōve.** [**staff.**]

stay[1], *stā, n.* a rope supporting a mast: a prop, support.—*v.t.* to support:—*pa.t., pa.p.* **stayed.**
[O.E. *stæg,* rope.]

stay[2], *stā, v.i.* to spend time in a place, etc.: to remain, continue to be (*to stay quiet*): to stop: to pause: to wait (for).—*v.t.* to stop: to hold back: to continue running for the whole of (*to stay the course*):—*pa.t., pa.p.* **stayed.**—*n.* a stop or halt: a living for a time.
stay'ing-power, *n.* ability to go on long without giving up.
stay-in strike, a strike in which workers are in their places but do no work.
to stay put, (*coll.*) to remain in the same place or position.
[From O.Fr.—L. root as **station.**]

stead, *sted, n.* place; used as part of word (e.g. **instead**), and in phrases, e.g.:—
in one's stead, in place of one (e.g. *I could not go, and she went in my stead*).
to stand one in good stead, to prove of service, help, to one in time of need.
[O.E. *stede*; conn. with Ger. *stadt,* town.]

steadfast. See **steady.**

steady, *sted'i, adj.* standing, or fixed, firmly: (of e.g. nerve) not easily upset: not changing in views, habits, etc. (e.g. *a steady supporter*): hard working and sensible: (of movement, activity) regular, constant (e.g. *a steady beat, flow; steady work*):—*comp.* **stead'ier**; *superl.* **stead'iest.**—*v.t., v.i.,* to make, or become, steady:—*pr.p.* **stead'ying** (*-i-ing*); *pa.p.* **stead'ied.**
stead'fast, *adj.* steady, fixed (e.g. *a*

steadfast look): firm, resolute: faithful.
stead'y-go'ing, *adj.* of steady habits or action. [**stead.**]

steak, *stāk, n.* a slice of meat (esp. hindquarters of beef) or fish.
[Old Norse *steikja*, to roast on a spit.]

steal, *stēl, v.t.* to take (what does not belong to one), esp. secretly: to take quickly and secretly (e.g. *to steal a look, a nap*).—*v.i.* to be a thief: to move, pass, quietly so as not to be seen, heard, noticed:—*pa.t.* **stōle**; *pa.p.* **stōl'en.**
steal'ing, *n.* and *adj.*
stealth, *stelth, n.* secret manner of acting.
steal'thy (*stel'*), *adj.* acting, or done, with stealth, in a secret manner.
steal'thily, *adv.* **steal'thiness,** *n.*
[O.E. *stelan*; conn. with Ger. *stehlen.*]

steam, *stēm, n.* the invisible gas or vapour that rises from boiling water: (*loosely*) the moist cloud seen when this vapour condenses as it touches cold air: any mist or film of liquid drops: steam power.—*v.i.* to give off steam: to become dimmed with steam, etc. (e.g. *the windows steamed*, or *steamed up*): to move, travel, by means of steam.—*v.t.* to cook by steam: to put into steam.—*adj.* using, or driven by, steam.
steam'y, *adj.* **steam'iness,** *n.*
steam'er, *n.* a steamboat, steamship: a container in which food, etc., is steamed.
steam'boat, steam'ship, *ns.* a ship driven by steam.
steam power, the force of steam used to work machinery.
steam roller, a locomotive engine driven by steam with large heavy roller(s), used, esp. formerly, to flatten material in making roads: any power that crushes or compels without mercy.—*v.t.* (**steam'-roller**) to crush or force as if with a steam roller.
full steam ahead, at the greatest speed possible: with the greatest amount of effort.
to let off steam, to let steam into the air: to work off energy or anger.
to steam open, to open by using steam to soften the sticky part.
under one's own steam, by one's own efforts without help.
[O.E. *stēam*; conn. with Du. *stoom.*]

steed, *stēd, n.* a horse for riding.
[O.E. *stēda*, stallion.]

steel, *stēl, n.* iron hardened by treatment, containing some carbon, etc.: a cutting tool or weapon: an object for some other use made of steel: a quality of steel, as strength, coldness (e.g. *a grip of steel*; *eyes of steel*).—*v.t.* to harden (e.g. *He steeled his heart*): to gather courage in oneself (e.g. *He steeled himself to meet the attack*).
steel'y, *adj.* **steel'iness,** *n.*
[O.E. *stēle*; conn. with Ger. *stahl.*]

steep[1], *stēp, adj.* (of hill, stairs, etc.) rising nearly straight, not sloping gradually: (*coll.*; of e.g. a price, something one is asked to do or believe) too great or much.
steep'ly, *adv.* **steep'ness,** *n.*
[O.E. *stēap*; conn. with **stoop.**]

steep[2], *stēp, v.t.* to wet thoroughly in liquid in order to take out dirt, soften, etc.: to give (oneself, a person) the fullest knowledge of a subject (e.g. *He steeped himself in Russian literature*).—Also *v.i.* and *n.*
[M.E. *stepe.*]

steeple, *stēp'l, n.* a high tower of a church, etc., usu. rising to a point: a spire.
steep'lechase, *n.* a race, on foot or horse, across country (perh. orig. with church steeple as goal): a race over a course on which obstacles have been made.—Also *v.i.*
steep'le-jack, *n.* one who climbs steeples, tall chimneys, etc., to make repairs.
[O.E. *stēpel*—same root as **steep.**]

steer[1], *stēr, n.* a young ox raised solely to produce beef.
[O.E. *stēor*; conn. with Ger. *stier*, bull.]

steer[2], *stēr, v.t.* to guide, control the course of (e.g. a ship, car, bill in parliament, discussion): follow (a course).—Also *v.i.*
steer'ing, *n.* act of one who steers: steering-gear.
steer'age, *n.* act of steering: part of a ship set aside for passengers who pay the lowest fares.
steer'ing-gear, *n.* the mechanism for steering a ship, car, etc.
steer'ing-wheel, *n.* wheel turned in steering a ship, etc.
steers'man, *n.* one who steers a ship.
to steer clear of, to avoid.
[O.E. *stēoran.*]

stellar, *stel'ȧr, adj.* having to do with the stars.
[L. *stella*, a star.]

stem[1], *stem, n.* a stalk—either the slender centre part of a plant which grows upward from the root, or a part on which leaf, flower, or fruit, grows: a tree trunk: anything stalk-like, e.g. the slender part of a wineglass: front part of ship.—*v.t.* to make way, progress, against (the tide, opposition, etc.).—*v.i.* to spring (from; e.g. *a feeling of hate that stems from envy*): —*pr.p.* **stemm'ing**; *pa.p.* **stemmed.**
stemmed, *adj.* having a stem.
from stem to stern, from one end of a vessel to the other: completely.
[O.E. *stemn*; conn. with Ger. *stamm.*]

stem[2], *stem, v.t.* stop flow of (e.g. blood):—*pr.p.* **stemm'ing,**; *pa.p.* **stemmed.**
[Old Norse *stemma.*]

stench, *stench, -sh, n.* a strong bad smell.
[O.E. *stenc*, scent, smell; conn. **stink.**]

stencil, *sten's(i)l, v.t.* to paint (design) by brushing over a plate or sheet on which a pattern is cut out: to decorate, stamp (material, object) thus: to cut a stencil

for making copies of (typewriting, writing) :—*pr.p.* **sten′cilling**; *pa.p.* **sten′cilled.**—*n.* a plate or card prepared for stencilling: stencilled lettering or design: a piece of waxed paper on which letters are cut by means of a typewriter or a pointed tool.
[L. *scintilla*, a spark.]

stenography, *sten-og′rȧ-fi, n.* the art, or any method, of writing in shorthand.
stenog′rapher, *n.*
[Gk. *stenos*, narrow, *graphein*, to write.]

stentorian, *sten-tō′ri-ȧn, -tö′, adj.* (of voice) very loud or powerful.
[*Stentor*, a herald in Homer's *Iliad*.]

step, *step, n.* one movement of the leg in walking, running, dancing: the distance passed over by this: the sound made: a footprint: (*dancing*) a pattern of movement that is repeated: a short journey: manner of walking (e.g. *with a proud step*): one of the parts of a stair or ladder on which one stands: a doorstep: (*in pl.*) a stepladder: a stage upward or downward (e.g. *His new job was a step up*): a move towards an end (e.g. *the first step in carrying out our plan*): a move, action.—*v.i.* to take a step: to walk.—*v.t.* to measure by taking steps:—*pr.p.* **stepp′ing**; *pa.p.* **stepped.**
stepp′ing-stone, *n.* a stone rising above water or mud, used to cross on: anything that helps one to advance or rise.
step′ladder, *n.* a ladder with a support on which it rests.
step′-rocket, *n.* a rocket with sections which work one after another.
in step, with the same feet going forward at the same time, as in marching: changing, acting, etc. in agreement (with).
out of step, not in step.
to step into, to come into without effort.
to step out, to go out a little way: to begin to walk more quickly.
to step up, to come forward: to increase (e.g. production).
to break step, to get out of step.
to keep step, to continue in step.
to take steps, to do something for a purpose (e.g. *I shall take steps to make sure that your father hears this.*)
[O.E. *stæpe*; conn. with Ger. *stapfe.*]

step-, *step-,* (as part of word) showing a relationship arising from a second (or later) marriage, not a blood relationship, e.g. :—
step′father, *n.* one's mother's husband, but not one's own father.
step′sister, *n.* a daughter of a step-parent by another marriage.
Also **step′mother, step′brother, step′-child, step′son, step′daughter,** etc.
[O.E. *stēop*, orig. meaning 'orphan'.]

steppe, *step, n.* a dry, grassy, esp. treeless, plain, as in the south-east of Europe and in Asia.
[Russ. *step.*]

stereo-, *stē-ri-ō-, ster-i-ō-,* (as part of word) having to do with the three dimensions of space.
ste′reo, *n.* short for various nouns beginning *stereo-.*
stereophonic, *stē-ri-ō-fon′ik, ster-, adj.* giving the effect of sound coming from different directions.
ste′reoscope, *n.* an instrument which gives the effect of solidity to a picture by showing two images (taken from slightly different points of view) of the same object or scene in such a way that they appear to be one.
stereoscop′ic, *adj.*
ste′reotype, *n.* a metal plate having on its surface matter for printing e.g. a page of a book.—*v.t.* to make a stereotype of: to make in one fixed, monotonous form.
ste′reotyped, *adj.* (of e.g. opinions, phrases) fixed, not changing.
[Gk. *stereos*, solid (*phōnē*, sound; *skopeein*, to look at; *typos*, blow, impression).]

sterile, *ster′il, adj.* not bringing forth, or unable to produce, offspring, fruit, seeds, results, ideas, etc.: free from germs.
ster′ileness, steril′ity (*-il′*), *ns.*
ster′ilise (*-il-iz*), *v.t.* to cause to be sterile: to kill germs in (e.g. milk) by boiling or other means.
sterilisā′tion, *n.*
ster′iliser, *n.* an apparatus for sterilising.
[L. *sterilis.*]

sterling, *stėr′ling, n.* British money of standard value (e.g. *payable in sterling*).—*adj.* of, in, etc., sterling (e.g. *sterling prices, payments*, but *the pound, £100, sterling*): (of silver) of standard quality: of very high worth (e.g. *a man of sterling character*).
sterling area, a group of countries whose currencies have close connexions with the pound sterling, not gold or dollars.
[Prob.—old coin with star (O.E. *steorra*).]

stern[1], *stėrn, adj.* (of look, manner, voice) grim, hard, showing displeasure: firm, strict: hard to endure.
stern′ly, *adv.* **stern′ness,** *n.*
[O.E. *styrne*; conn. with **stare.**]

stern[2], *stėrn, n.* the back part of a ship: the rump or tail.
[Conn. Old Norse *stjörn*, steering.]

stertorous, *stėr′tȯ-rŭs, adj.* with a snoring sound.
[L. *stertĕre*, to snore.]

stethoscope, *steth′ō-skōp, n.* an instrument by which a doctor can listen to the beats of the heart, etc.
[Gk. *stēthos*, chest, *skopeein*, to look at.]

stevedore, *stē′vė-dōr, -dör, n.* one who loads and unloads ships.
[Sp. *estibador*, packer—L. *stīpāre*, press.]

stew, *stū, n.* a dish of stewed food, esp. meat with vegetables: state of worry: (*slang*) one who studies hard, esp. unintelligently.—*v.t.* to simmer or boil slowly with some moisture: to steep (tea)

too much : to make (a person) very hot.—Also *v.i.*
[O.Fr. *estuve*, stove ; prob. conn. **stove.**]

steward, *stū'ård, n.* one who manages an estate or farm for someone else : one who helps to arrange, and is an official at, races, dance, entertainment, etc. : one who sees to stores and serving of meals in ship, etc. : passenger's attendant on ship or aeroplane : an overseer, foreman : —*fem.* **stew'ardess.**
[O.E. *stig*, hall, *weard*, ward, guard.]

stick[1], *stik, v.t.* to pierce with something sharp : to thrust (into, through, out, etc.) : to fix by means of a pointed end, or by gum, etc. : (*coll.*) to put (e.g. *Stick it there*) : to set, decorate (with) : (*coll.*) to puzzle, or to bring to a stop (e.g. *That problem will stick him*).—*v.i.* to be, become, or remain, fixed : to be caught, held back (e.g. *He will stick in the mud*) : (of e.g. door, lid) to jam : to fail to go on (in something one is doing) : to hold fast (to, by, e.g. a friend, a decision) : to keep working at (e.g. *Stick to your job*) :—*pa.p.* **stuck.**
stick'y, *adj.* (of e.g. treacle, fly-paper) able to adhere or cling closely : (*coll.*; of weather) hot and damp : apt to become jammed : difficult to deal with (e.g. *a sticky problem*) :—*comp.* **stick'ier** ; *superl.* **stick'iest.**
stick'ily, *adv.* **stick'iness,** *n.*
stick'-in-the-mud, *n.* a person who never makes any advance or does anything new.
to stick up for, to speak in defence of.
[O.E. *stician* ; conn. with **stick** (2).]

stick[2], *stik, n.* small shoot or branch from a tree or shrub : a piece of wood cut for burning, etc. : a piece of wood shaped for playing hockey, beating a drum, or other purpose : a holder for a candle : something in the form of a stick or rod (e.g. *a stick of sealing wax*).
[O.E. *sticca* ; conn. with **stick** (1).]

stickleback, *stik'l-bak, n.* a small river-fish with prickles or spines on its back.
[O.E. *sticel*, prick, thorn, and **back.**]

stickler, *stik'lėr, n.* one who is determined to be very exact, accurate, correct (e.g. *a stickler for the truth, for convention*).
[O.E. *stihtan*, arrange.]

sticky. See **stick** (1).

stiff, *stif, adj.* not easily bent : rigid : moving, or moved, with difficulty (e.g. *stiff fingers* ; *a stiff lock*) : thick, not tending to flow (e.g. *a stiff dough*) : firm : hard (e.g. *a stiff examination*) : strong (e.g. *a stiff breeze* ; *a stiff dose*) : (*coll.*) too high (e.g. *a stiff price*) : not natural and easy, cold in manner.—*n.* (*slang*) a corpse : (*slang*) a dull, formal person.
stiff'en, *v.t., v.i.* to make, or become, stiff : to make, or become, more stubborn (*to stiffen resistance* ; *resistance stiffened*).
[O.E. *stīf* ; conn. with Ger. *steif.*]

stifle, *stī'fl, v.t.* to stop the breath of completely : to make breathing difficult for : to put out (e.g. flames) : to hold back (e.g. a yawn, sobs).—*v.i.* to die, or to suffer, through lack of air.
sti'fling, *adj.* very hot and stuffy.
[Origin uncertain.]

stigma, *stig'må, n.* a mark of disgrace : (in a flower) the top of the pistil which receives the pollen.
stig'matise, *v.t.* to mark, describe (as, usu. something bad ; *to stigmatise a man as ignorant because he knows no Greek*).
[Gk., tattoo mark.]

stile, *stīl, n.* a step, or set of steps, for climbing over a wall or fence.
[O.E. *stigel* ; Ger. *steigen*, to mount.]

stiletto, *sti-let'ō, n.* a dagger, or a pointed instrument, with narrow but thick blade :—*pl.* **-os, -oes.**
[It. *stilo*, dagger—L. root as **style.**]

still[1], *stil, n.* an apparatus, or place, in which something (e.g. whisky) is distilled.
still'room, *n.* pantry where drinks and certain foods are kept. **[distil.]**

still[2], *stil, adj.* without movement : calm : silent : (of drink) not effervescing.—*v.t.* to silence : to calm.—*adv.* up to the present time, or to the time spoken of (e.g. *Hair was still worn long*) : for all that (*He saw the bus start but he still ran on*) : even (e.g. *still more, worse*).
still'ness, *n.*
still'born, *adj.* dead when born.
still life, a picture of something that is not living (e.g. a table with fruit, etc.).
[O.E. *stille* ; conn. with Ger. *still.*]

stilt, *stilt, n.* one of a pair of poles with foot rests on which a person may stand and thus walk raised off the ground.
stilt'ed, *adj.* stiff, not natural in manner, pompous.
[M.E. *stilte* ; Du. *stelt*, Ger. *stelze.*]

stimulant, *stim'ū-lånt, n.* something that makes a part of the body more active for a time (e.g. *a heart stimulant*) : a happening that makes one feel livelier : a stimulating drug : an alcoholic drink.—Also *adj.*
stim'ulāte, *v.t.* to act as a stimulant to, make more active : to incite, move (to do something).
stimulā'tion, *n.* **stim'ulative,** *adj.*
stim'ūlus, *n.* something that rouses (e.g. a person, the mind) to action or greater effort : any action or influence that causes a reaction in a living thing (e.g. *The stimulus of light causes the flower to open*) : —*pl.* **stim'uli** (*-lī*).
[L. *stimulāre, -ātum*, to goad.]

sting, *sting, n.* a part of some plants and animals (e.g. nettle, wasp) used to prick and to introduce an irritating or poisonous fluid into the wound : act of piercing with a sting : the wound or pain caused by a sting : any sharp pain (e.g. *the sting of a whip, the wind, a friend's unkindness*) :

the power to hurt: stimulus.—*v.t.* to wound or hurt by means of a sting, etc.: to goad, stir up (to action, feeling).—*v.i.* to have a sting: to give pain: to smart, feel painful:—*pa.p.* **stung.**
[O.E. *stingan.*]

stingy, *stin'ji, adj.* mean, not generous, in spending or giving: scanty.
stin'gily, *adv.* **stin'giness,** *n.* [**sting.**]

stink, *stingk, v.i., v.t.* to give out, or to fill with, a strong bad smell:—*pa.t.* **stank**; *pa.p.* **stunk.**
[O.E. *stincan.*]

stint, *stint, v.t.* to give (a person) a very small allowance (e.g. *to stint oneself in food*): to supply (something) in a stingy way.—Also *v.i.*—*n.* limit or restriction (e.g. *He praised him, gave to him, without stint*): set task, share of piece of work.
[O.E. *styntan*—root as **stunt** (1).]

stipend, *sti'pĕnd, n.* a salary paid for services (esp. to a clergyman in Scotland).
stipend'iary, *n.* a paid magistrate.
[L. *stips,* donation, *pendĕre,* to weigh.]

stipple, *stip'l, v.t.* to engrave, paint, draw, etc., in dots or separate touches: to produce an effect that suggests stippled work.—*n.* stippled work: an effect of stippling.
[Du. *stip(pel),* a dot, speck.]

stipulate, *stip'ū-lāt, v.t.* and *v.i.* to state as a necessary condition for an agreement (e.g. *I stipulated that, if I did the job, I must be paid immediately*; *I stipulated for immediate payment*).
stipulā'tion, *n.* something stipulated.
[L. *stipulārī*; conn. *stipāre,* press firm.]

stir, *stėr, v.t.* to set (liquid, etc.) in motion: to move slightly: to arouse emotion in (*The story of such courage stirred him*).—*v.i.* to move: to be active:—*pr.p.* **stirr'ing**; *pa.p.* **stirred.**—*n.* disturbance, bustle, excitement.
stirr'ing, *adj.* putting in motion: active: exciting.
to stir up, to mix by stirring: to rouse, cause (e.g. *to stir up trouble*): to move to action: to excite, make angry, etc.
[O.E. *styrian*; Ger. *stören,* disturb.]

stirrup, *stir'ŭp, n.* a metal ring or loop hung from the saddle, for a horseman's foot while mounting or riding.
stirrup cup, a drink given to a guest who is leaving (orig. on horseback).
[O.E. *stigan,* to mount, *rāp,* a rope.]

stitch, *stich, n.* a loop made by drawing a thread through cloth by means of a needle: a loop made in knitting: a sharp pain in one's side: a bit of clothing (e.g. *He had not on a stitch*).—*v.t.* to sew with a regular line of stitches.
[O.E. *stice,* a prick.]

stoat, *stōt, n.* a type of weasel, called the ermine when in winter fur.
[M.E. *stote*; origin unknown.]

stock[1], *stok, n.* a post, log, block of wood: the trunk or main stem of a plant: the handle of a whip, rifle, etc.: family, race (e.g. *He is of good stock*): a store or supply (of e.g. goods): the cattle, horses, etc. kept on a farm: the liquid obtained by boiling meat or bones to make soup: money lent to the government at fixed interest: corporation's or company's capital divided into shares: (in *pl.*) the frame holding a ship while it is building: (in *pl.*) a wooden frame, with holes for the ankles, and sometimes wrists, to which law-breakers were fastened as a punishment.—*v.t.* to store: to keep for sale (e.g. *He stocks lemons*): to fill (with): to supply with farm animals.—*adj.* kept in stock: usual, widely known and used (e.g. *He made the stock joke*).
stock'y, *adj.* having a strong stem: short and rather stout.
stock'ily, *adv.* **stock'iness,** *n.*
stock'breeder, *n.* one who raises livestock.
stock'broker, *n.* a person who buys and sells stock and shares for others.
stock exchange, *n.* place where stocks, etc., are bought and sold: brokers and dealers who work there.
stock'holder, *n.* one who holds stocks in a public fund, or in a company.
stock'-in-trade, *n.* the whole of the goods a shopkeeper keeps for sale: equipment for business, or for some enterprise (e.g. *His stock-in-trade as a political speaker included certain high-sounding phrases which he always used*).
stock market, a market for the sale of stocks, the stock exchange.
stock'pile, *n.* a store, reserve supply.—*v.i.* to build up a reserve supply.
stock'room, *n.* a room where goods are stored or kept in reserve.
stock'-still', *adj.* motionless.
stock'-taking, *n.* a regular check of the goods in a shop or warehouse.
stock'yard, *n.* a large yard with pens, stables, etc. where cattle are kept for market or slaughter.
on the stocks, (of a ship) being built: being prepared.
to take stock, to make a list of goods on hand: (with *of*) to look at carefully to try to decide worth, importance.
to take no stock in, not to have confidence in.
[O.E. *stocc,* stick; conn. Ger. *stock.*]

stock[2], *stok, n.* a scented garden flower on a shrubby plant.
[**stock** (1), stem.]

stockade, *sto-kād', n.* a fence of strong posts put up round an area for defence.—*v.t.* to fortify with such.
[Fr. *estacade*; conn. with **stake.**]

stockbreeder, etc. See **stock** (1).

stocking, *stok'ing, n.* a close covering for the foot and lower leg.
[Old *stock,* hose.]

stock-in-trade, etc. See **stock** (1).

stocky. See **stock** (1).

stodgy, *stoj'i, adj.* (of food) heavy and not easily digested: (of people, writing) heavy and dull.
stodg'ily, *adv.* **stodg'iness,** *n.*
stodge, *v.t., v.i.* to stuff, cram.
[Perh. imit.]

stoic, *stō'ik, n.* one who bears pain or misfortune without showing any sign of feeling it.
stō'ical, *adj.* **stō'ically,** *adv.*
stō'icism (*-is-izm*), **stō'icalness,** *ns.*
[Gk. *stoa*, porch, the Porch (place where Greek philosopher taught stoicism).]

stoke, *stōk, v.t.* to feed with fuel.
stoke'hole, *n.* the space where a ship's stokers work: a hole through which a furnace is stoked.
stok'er, *n.* one who, or something that, feeds a furnace with fuel.
[Du. *stoker*, stoker—*stoken*, to stoke.]

stole[1], *stōl, n.* a narrow strip of e.g. silk round the neck and hanging down in front worn by clergymen: a woman's garment of similar shape of e.g. fur.
[L. *stŏla*, married woman's long robe.]

stole[2], stolen. See **steal.**

stolid, *stol'id, adj.* (of person or manner) dull, heavy, not emotional.
stolid'ity, -idness, *ns.* **stol'idly,** *adv.*
[L. *stolidus.*]

stomach, *stum'ȧk, n.* the bag-like part of the body into which the food passes when swallowed, and where most of it is digested: (*loosely*) the belly: appetite or desire (e.g. *I have no stomach for the job*).—*v.t.* to bear, put up with (e.g. *He could not stomach them, their conduct*).
[Gk. *stomachos*, throat, (later) stomach.]

stone, *stōn, n.* a piece of loose rock: a piece of this shaped for a purpose (e.g. *grindstone, tombstone*): a precious stone or gem: the hard shell round the seed of some fruits (e.g. cherry): the seed of a grape: a standard weight of 14 lb. (in *pl.* often **stone**): a piece of hard material formed in the bladder.—*adj.* made of stone: made of stoneware.—*v.t.* to throw stones at: to rub, etc., with a stone: to take stones out of.
stō'ny, *adj.* made of, or like, stone: covered with stones: hard, cold (e.g. *a stony stare*):—*comp.* **stō'nier**; *superl.* **stō'niest.**
stō'nily, *adv.* in a cold, hard manner.
stō'niness, *n.*
Stone Age, early period in history when tools, weapons, were made of stone.
stone'-blind', -cold', -dead', -deaf', *adjs.* completely blind, cold, dead, deaf.
stone fruit, a fruit whose seeds are covered with a hard shell.
stone'wall', *v.i.* to bat in cricket so as to stay in rather than to score: to hold up business of e.g. parliament by talking, etc.
stone'ware, *n.* a hard kind of pottery.
stone'work, *n.* structure, or part of it, made of stone.
sto'ny(-broke), *adj.* penniless.
a rolling stone, a person who does not settle in any place or job.
a stone's-throw, a very short distance.
to leave no stone unturned, to try every means possible.
[O.E. *stān*; conn. with Ger. *stein.*]

stood. See **stand.**

stooge, *stōōj, n.* comedian's assistant: a person used by another (e.g. by a gangster) in carrying out his plans.—*v.i.* to act as a stooge. [Orig. uncertain.]

stool, *stōōl, n.* a low seat without a back: a low support for the feet, or knees, when sitting or kneeling: evacuation of the bowels, or matter evacuated: a piece of wood to which a pigeon is fastened as a decoy for wild birds.
stool'-pigeon, *n.* a decoy pigeon: decoy: informer or spy esp. for police.
[O.E. *stōl*; conn. with Ger. *stuhl.*]

stoop, *stōōp, v.i.* to bend the body forward and downward: to lower oneself from dignity (to do something; *He would not stoop to ask for help, stoop to cheating*).—*v.t.* to cause to stoop.—Also *n.*
stooped, *adj.* having a stoop.
[O.E. *stūpian.*]

stop, *stop, v.t.* (1) to stuff up and thus close (a hole; also **stop up**): to block: (*music*) to close (a hole), or press down (a string), so as to alter pitch: (2) to bring to a standstill, prevent from moving: to prevent (a person, etc.) from doing something: to put an end to (e.g. *Stop this nonsense!*): to keep back (e.g. *to stop payment of a cheque*).—*v.i.* to cease going forward, working, etc.: to come to an end: (*coll.*) to stay:—*pr.p.* **stopp'ing**; *pa.p.* **stopped.**—*n.* act of stopping: state of being stopped: a halt: a pause: a stopping-place: (*coll.*) a stay: a device for bringing motion to a standstill or limiting action: a means of altering musical pitch: a set of pipes in an organ, or a knob, etc. for bringing them into use: a mark of punctuation: a full stop (.).
stopp'age (*ij*), *n.* act of stopping, or state of being stopped: obstruction of a passage in the body: money kept back.
stopp'er, *n.* one who stops: something that closes a hole or the neck of a bottle.
stopp'ing, *n.* and *adj.*
stopp'ing-place, *n.* place where bus, etc., regularly stops.
stop'cock, *n.* a tap and valve for controlling flow of liquid.
stop'gap, *n.* a person or thing that fills a gap in an emergency.
stop press, a space in a newspaper for last-minute news.
stop'watch, *n.* a watch with a hand that can be stopped and started, used in timing a race, etc.
[O.E. *stoppian*, to stop up.]

storage. See **store.**

store, *stōr*, *stör*, *n.* large amount, number: (in *pl.*) supplies of food, ammunition, etc.: (in *pl.*) goods gathered for later use: a storehouse: a shop, esp. one with many branches.—*v.t.* to gather and put in a place for keeping: to furnish (a place, with supplies, etc.).

stor'age, (*-ij*), *n.* act of storing, or state of being stored: price charged for keeping goods.

store'house, store'room, *ns.* a place, room, in which things are stored.

in store, prepared or destined (for a person; e.g. *There was a scolding, a surprise, in store for me*).

to set (great) store by, to value highly (e.g. a person's approval, opinion).

[O.Fr. *estor*—L. *instaurāre*, to provide.]

storey, story, *stō'ri*, *stö'*, *n.* set of rooms on the same floor: a floor, or the distance between one floor and the next.

sto'reyed, sto'ried, *adj.* having storeys. [Same word as **story** (below).]

storied. See **storey** and **story.**

stork, *störk*, *n.* a wading bird with long bill, neck, and legs.

[O.E. *storc*; conn. with Ger. *storch.*]

storm, *störm*, *n.* a violent disturbance in the air producing wind, rain, etc.: a violent outbreak (of e.g. anger, applause): a heavy shower (of; e.g. *a storm of bullets*). —*v.i.* to blow, rain, etc. with violence: to show, express, great anger: to rage (at).—*v.t.* to attack and take by force.

stor'my, *adj.* having many storms: blowing furiously: violent: noisy.

stor'mily, *adv.* **stor'miness,** *n.*

storm'-beaten, *adj.* beaten or injured by storms.

storm'bound, *adj.* prevented by storm from getting in touch with the outside.

storm signal, a signal shown to warn of a coming storm.

storm'-tossed, *adj.* tossed about by storms.

storm troops, shock troops (see this).

[O.E. *storm*; same root as **stir.**]

story, *stō'ri*, *stö'*, *n.* an account of an event, a series of events, real or imaginary: a brief tale leading up to a conclusion that is amusing, or supposed to be so: an untruth: a storey (see this).

stō'ried, *adj.* having a history, having many stories told about it.

[L. *historia.*]

stoup, *stōōp*, *n.* a basin for holy water.

[Conn. with O.E. *stēap.*]

stout, *stowt*, *adj.* strong in body or material (e.g. *stout fellows*; *a stout stick*): brave, forceful, resolute (e.g. *They put up a stout resistance*): (of person) fat and solid.—*n.* a strong dark beer.

stout'-heart'ed, *adj.* having a brave heart.

[O.Fr. *estout*, bold; Ger. *stolz*, proud.]

stove[1], *stōv*, *n.* a closed device for heating a room or for cooking: a kiln.

[O.E. *stofa*, a hot air bath room.]

stove[2]. See **stave.**

stow, *stō*, *v.t.* to place or pack out of the way or in a suitable place: to fill, pack (e.g. *to stow the case with boxes*).

stow'age (*ij*), *n.* act of stowing, or state of being stowed: room for articles to be laid away.

stow'away, *n.* one who hides himself in a ship so that he may get a passage for nothing.

[M.E. *stowen*, to place—O.E. *stōw*, place.]

straddle, *strad'l*, *v.i.* to stand or walk with legs far apart: (of legs) to spread wide apart.—*v.t.* to stand or sit with legs on either side of (e.g. a chair, horse): to cover the area containing (a target) with bombs.—Also *n.*

[Same root as **stride.**]

straggle, *strag'l*, *v.i.* to stray from the course or line of march: (of e.g. trailing plant) to wander beyond proper limits: to scatter irregularly (e.g. *The crowd straggled over the park*).

stragg'ler, *n.* one who straggles, esp. who is left behind: a plant that straggles.

stragg'ly, *adj.* spread out thinly, untidily.

stragg'liness, *n.* [Orig. uncertain.]

straight, *strāt*, *adj.* not bent or curved: direct (e.g. *the straight way to the church*): direct, frank, to the point (e.g. *a straight answer*): honest, fair (e.g. *straight dealings*): placed levelly (e.g. *The pictures are not straight*): in order (e.g. *Try to get your accounts straight*): unmixed (e.g. *a straight whisky*).—*adv.* in the shortest way: honestly, fairly: plainly.

straight'ness, *n.*

straight'en, *v.t.* to make straight.

straightfor'ward, *adj.* going forward in a straight course: honest, frank.

straightfor'wardly, *adv.*

straightfor'wardness, *n.*

straight'way, *adv.* at once.

straight thinking, clear logical thinking, not affected by feelings, etc.

a straight fight, election contest involving two candidates only.

a straight talk, a frank talk, esp. one expressing disapproval.

in the straight, on the straight part esp. of a racecourse.

[O.E. *streccan*, *streht*, to stretch.]

strain[1], *strān*, *v.t.* to stretch, draw tightly: to work, exert, to the fullest (e.g. *to strain every nerve, one's ears, eyes*): to injure by overworking, or using wrongly: to stretch too far (the meaning, the law, one's patience, resources): to separate solid from liquid by passing through a sieve.—*v.i.* to make violent efforts.—*n.* act of straining: a great effort: an injury caused by straining, esp. to the muscles: (effect of) too much work, worry, etc. (e.g. *suffering from strain*; *the strain of* *nursing*): too great a demand (e.g. *a strain on my purse, patience*).

strain′er, *n.* something that strains, esp. a screen or sieve for separating solids from liquids.

strained, *adj.* showing effort, not easy and natural.

strained relations, a state of unfriendly feeling because of something that has happened.

to strain a point, to make a special effort, or go beyond the usual limit.

to strain at, to resist, balk at (e.g. *to strain at the lead*).

[O.Fr. *straindre*—L. *stringĕre*, stretch.]

strain², *strān, n.* race, stock, family: (of plants, animals) a variety with certain characteristics: a tendency, streak, in character (e.g. *a strain of recklessness*): (often in *pl.*) a passage of a song or poem: mood, tone, style (e.g. *He said he hated me—and more in the same strain*).

[O.E. (*ge*)*strēon*, gain, begetting.]

strait, *strāt, n.* (often in *pl.*) a narrow strip of sea between two pieces of land: (usu. in *pl.*) difficulties, need (e.g. *When this happened, he was in great straits*).

strait′ened, *adj.* used esp. in phrase **in straitened circumstances,** in need, having little money.

strait′-jack′et, *n.* a jacket with long sleeves tied behind to hold back the arms of someone who is being restrained.

strait′-laced, *adj.* (orig.) in tightly laced stays: strict and prudish in words and behaviour.

[O.Fr. *estreit*—L. root as **strain** (1).]

strand¹, *strand, n.* the shore or beach of a sea or lake.—*v.t., v.i.* to run aground on the shore: to put into, arrive in, a helpless, friendless, position.

strand′ed, *adj.*

[O.E. *strand*; conn. with Ger. *strand.*]

strand², *strand, n.* one of the threads that make up a rope: a long lock of hair.

[Orig. uncertain.]

strange, *strānj, adj.* not known, seen, or heard, before: not one's own (e.g. *a strange dog in our garden*): new, unfamiliar (e.g. *This method was strange to me*): foreign (e.g. *strange languages*): unusual, odd, queer.

strange′ly, *adv.* **strange′ness,** *n.*

stranger, *strān′jėr, n.* a person one does not know: a guest or visitor: one who has had no experience of (with *to*; e.g. *He was a stranger to fear*).

[O.Fr. *estrange*—L. *extrā*, beyond.]

strangle, *strang′gl, v.t.* to kill by tightening a cord round the throat, or by stopping the breath by any means: to stop the growth of: to suppress (e.g. *to strangle a sob*).—Also *v.i.*

strangle′hold, *n.* a choking hold in wrestling: any force that prevents freedom of action, expression, or growth.

strangulate, *strang′gū-lāt, v.t.* to compress, constrict (a passage in the body) so as to stop circulation, etc.

strangulā′tion, *n.* action of strangling or strangulating: state of being strangled or strangulated.

[L. *strangulāre*—Gk. *strangos*, twisted.]

strap, *strap, n.* a narrow strip of leather or cloth, esp. one with a buckle: a razor strop: a loop of e.g. leather for taking hold of.—*v.t.* to beat with a strap: to fasten or bind with a strap:—*pr.p.* **strapp′ing**; *pa.p.* **strapped.**

strapp′ing, *adj.* tall and strong. [**strop.**]

strata. See **stratum.**

stratagem, *strat′ȧ-jėm, n.* action planned to deceive and outwit an enemy: a cunning or careful plan.

strat′egy, *n.* the art of planning a campaign or large military operation: the art of carrying out a plan skilfully: a stratagem:—*pl.* **strat′egies.**

strategic, *strȧ-tē′jik, adj.* having to do with strategy: done as part of a strategy or plan (e.g. *a strategic retreat*): important to the success of a plan (e.g. *a strategic position*, one which gives the holder an advantage over his enemy).

stratē′gically, *adv.* **strat′egist,** *n.*

[Gk. *stratēgos*, a general.]

stratify, etc. See **stratum.**

stratum, *strā′tŭm, n.* a bed of earth or rock, made up usually of a series of layers: any layer: level (of society):—*pl.* **stra′ta.**

stratify, *strat′i-fī, v.t., v.i.* to form in layers:—*pr.p.* **strat′ifying**; *pa.p.* **-ified.**

stratificā′tion, *n.*

stratosphere, *strat′ō-sfēr, n.* a layer of the earth's atmosphere, some miles above the earth.

[L. *strātum*, covering for e.g. bed, a pavement (*facĕre*, to make; **sphere**).]

straw, *strö, n.* the stalk on which grain grows: a number of dried stalks of corn, etc.: a tube for sucking up a drink: a straw hat: a trifle, anything worthless.

straw′berry, *n.* the red fruit of a plant of the rose family, with long creeping shoots: the plant itself.

straw hat, a hat made of straw, etc.

straw vote, a vote taken unofficially to get some idea of the general opinion.

[O.E. *strēaw*; conn. with Ger. *stroh.*]

stray, *strā, v.i.* to wander: to wander (from e.g. the proper place or company): to turn away from duty or virtue.—*n.* a domestic animal, etc., that has strayed: a wandering or homeless person.—*adj.* wandering, lost: casual, isolated, single (e.g. *a stray remark*; *a stray example*).

[L. *extrā*, beyond, *vagārī*, wander.]

streak, *strēk, n.* a line or long mark different in colour from the surface that surrounds it: a stripe: a flash: a trace in one's character (of e.g. humour, meanness).—*v.t.* to mark with streaks.—*v.i.* (*coll.*) to run swiftly.

streak′y, *adj.* marked with streaks: (of

bacon) fat and lean in layers: varying good and bad (e.g. *a streaky performance*).
streak'ily, *adv.* **streak'iness,** *n.*
[O.E. *strica*, stroke, mark; Ger. *strich*.]

stream, *strēm*, *n.* a flow of (water, blood, air, light, etc.): a river, brook, etc.: anything flowing or moving without a break (e.g. *a stream of people, cars, tears, abuse*).—*v.t.*, *v.i.* to flow, or cause to flow: to stretch in a long line.
stream'er, *n.* a flag streaming in the wind: a long ribbon, etc., esp. for decoration.
stream'let, *n.* a little stream.
stream'lined, *adj.* shaped so as to go most easily through air or water: simplified so as to be as efficient as possible: very up to date.
[O.E. *strēam*; conn. with Ger. *strom*.]

street, *strēt*, *n.* a road lined with houses, etc., broader than a lane.
streets ahead of, very much better than.
not in the same street, of a completely different quality, usu. worse.
[O.E. *strǣt*—L. *strāta* (*via*), paved (way); conn. Ger. *strasse*, It. *strada*, **stratum.**]

strength. See **strong.**

strenuous, *stren'ū-us*, *adj.* vigorous, energetic (e.g. *a strenuous person, resistance*): (of e.g. task) requiring much effort.
[L. *strēnuus*; conn. Gk. *strēnēs*, strong.]

streptococcus, *strep-tō-kok'us*, *n.* any of a group of bacteria that cause diseases e.g. pneumonia.
[Gk. *streptos*, twisted, *kokkos*, grain.]

stress, *stres*, *n.* force, pressure, pull, etc. of one thing on another: influence or effect acting in a bad direction (e.g. *Under stress of circumstances he took to theft*): physical or nervous strain: emphasis, importance (e.g. *He laid stress on the fact that it was urgent to do something*): force given to one part of a word (e.g. *In 'widow' the stress is on wid'-*).—*v.t.* to put stress, pressure, emphasis, or a physical or nervous strain, on. [**distress.**]

stretch, *strech*, *v.t.* to draw out to greater length, or too far, or more tightly, or from one point to another (e.g. *to stretch a piece of elastic, a muscle, a violin string, a rope from post to post*): to lay (oneself) at full length: to straighten or extend (e.g. oneself, wings): to hold (out, etc. e.g. the hand): to make cover more than is right (e.g. *to stretch the truth, law, meaning*).—*v.i.* to be able to be drawn out to greater length, etc.: (usu. with *out*) to lay oneself at full length: to reach (out, for something): to extend (from one point to another, or for a stated distance).—*n.* act of stretching: state of being stretched: reach, utmost extent: an unbroken length of space or time (e.g. *a stretch of grass, of two years*): a straight part of a racecourse.
stretch'er, *n.* anything for stretching: a frame for carrying sick or wounded.
stretch'er-bear'er, *n.* one who carries a stretcher.
at a stretch, continuously (e.g. *to work four hours at a stretch*).
to stretch a point, to do more than one is bound, or entitled, to do.
[O.E. *streccan*.]

strew, *strōō*, *v.t.* to scatter loosely: to cover by scattering (with):—*pa.t.* **strewed**; *pa.p.* **strewed** or **strewn.**
[O.E. *streowian*.]

stricken, *strik'ėn*, *adj.* struck: wounded: deeply affected (by illness, etc.). See also **grief-, panic-stricken.** [**strike.**]

strict, *strikt*, *adj.* exact (e.g. *in the strict meaning of the term*): allowing no exception (e.g. *strict orders, honesty*): severe, harsh (e.g. *strict laws*): (of person) compelling exact obedience to rules (e.g. *Their father was very strict*).
strict'ly, *adv.* **strict'ness,** *n.*
stricture, *strik'chur*, *n.* an unfavourable remark, criticism (on).
[L. *stringĕre*, *strictum*, to draw tight.]

stride, *strīd*, *v.i.* to walk with long steps: to take a long step.—*v.t.* to walk along, step over, or straddle:—*pa.t.* **strōde**; *pa.p.* **stridd'en.**—*n.* a long step: the space stepped over: a step forward (e.g. *great strides toward independence*).
[O.E. *strīdan*, *strǣd*.]

strident, *strī'dėnt*, *adj.* (of e.g. voice) loud and grating or harsh-sounding.
strī'dently, *adv.* **strī'dency,** *n.*
[L. *strīdens*—*strīdēre*, to creak.]

strife, *strīf*, *n.* conflict, fighting, quarrelling. [**strive.**]

strike, *strīk*, *v.t.* to hit with force: to attack: to stab, pierce (e.g. to the heart): to dash (against, on; e.g. *to strike one's head on a beam*): to knock against, collide with: to give (a blow): to light (a match), or to produce (a light, sparks), by rubbing: to touch (a note, string), or to make (a musical note) sound: (of a clock) to sound (e.g. the hour, ten): to cancel, mark out (with *out, off, from*; e.g. *to strike from the record*): (of a tree) to thrust (roots) down in the earth: to lower, let down (flag, tent, sail): to come across suddenly or unexpectedly (e.g. *to strike oil*).—*v.i.* to give a quick blow: to attack: to knock (against): (of a clock) to sound a time: to fall (on, across; e.g. *The sunlight strikes across the treetops*): to take a course (e.g. *To get there, you strike across this field*): to stop work in support of a claim, or as a protest:—*pa.t.*, *pa.p.* **struck** (older *pa.p.* **strick'en**; see this word).
The above meanings are concerned with actions that can be seen or heard; other meanings depend more on pictures in the mind, e.g.:—
to come to (one) suddenly or with force, or to affect, impress (one; e.g. *A thought strikes me*; *I am struck by the resemblance*;

it strikes me with surprise; *how does it strike you?*): to catch (the eye): to make by, or as if by, a blow (*to strike dead, blind, deaf, dumb*, etc.): to make (a bargain, agreement). See also phrases below.—*n.* act of striking for higher wages, etc.: a find (e.g. oil).

strik'er, *n.*

strik'ing, *adj.* that strikes, or is intended to do so: very noticeable (e.g. *a striking likeness*): impressive.

strik'ingly, *adv.* **strik'ingness,** *n.*

striking distance, distance short enough for a blow, attack, etc. to be delivered, carried out, successfully.

to strike a balance, to find the difference between the debit and credit side of an account: to find a fair middle course.

to strike an attitude. See **attitude.**

to strike an average, to estimate, or to calculate, an average: to arrive at a statement expressing something between two contradictory or extreme statements.

to strike camp, to take down tents, etc., and move on.

to strike home, (of a blow, remark, etc.) to strike to the point aimed at, or to the point where it will be felt most.

to strike fear, terror, into, to frighten, terrify.

to strike up, to begin to play, sing (a tune): (*coll.*) to form suddenly (e.g. a friendship, acquaintance).

See also **stroke** (1).

[O.E. *strican*, stroke, move over lightly.]

string, *string*, *n.* a long narrow cord, made by twisting threads, used for tying, fastening, etc.: a nerve, tendon, fibre: a stretched piece of catgut, silk, wire, etc., in a musical instrument: (in *pl.*) the stringed instruments played by a bow in an orchestra: group of things threaded on a cord, e.g. beads, onions: number of things coming one after the other (e.g. *a string of cars, of curses*).—*v.t.* to put on a string: to tie with string: to remove the strings from (e.g. beans): to stretch out in a long line.—*v.i.* to move in a long line:—*pa.p.* **strung.**

stringed, *adj.* having strings.

string'y, *adj.* made up of small threads, strings, or fibres: long, thin, and wiry.

string'iness, *n.*

to have strings attached (*coll.*; of a gift, service, etc.) to be given, done, with the understanding that the person who receives it will act in a certain way.

to pull the strings, to control the actions of others, be the real mover in something that is done.

to pull strings, to use one's influence, or that of others, to gain an advantage.

[O.E. *streng*; conn. with Ger. *strang*.]

stringent, *strin'jėnt*, *adj.* binding strongly, strictly enforced (e.g. *stringent rules*): compelling (e.g. *stringent necessity*).

strin'gently, *adv.* **strin'gency,** *n.*

[L. *stringens—stringĕre*, to draw tight.]

stringy. See **string.**

strip, *strip*, *v.t.* to pull (off): to skin, peel, or remove fruit or leaves from: to make bare or empty: to undress: to deprive (person of something).—*v.i.* to undress:—*pr.p.* **stripp'ing**; *pa.p.* **stripped.**—*n.* a long narrow piece.

stripp'er, *n.*

comic strip. See **comic.**

[O.E. *strypan*; Ger. *streifen*, streak.]

stripe, *strīp*, *n.* a band of different colour, etc., from the background on which it lies: a blow with a whip or rod: a decoration on a uniform sleeve showing rank, etc.—*v.t.* to make stripes on: to form with lines of different colours, etc.

[Old Du. *strijpe*, a stripe in cloth.]

stripling, *strip'ling*, *n.* a lad who has not reached full growth. [**strip.**]

strive, *strīv*, *v.i.* to try or work hard (to do, or for, something): (*old-fashioned*) to struggle, fight (with, against):—*pa.t.* **strōve**; *pa.p.* **striv'en** (*striv'*).

striv'ing, *n.* (*usu.*) trying very hard.

See also **strife.**

[O.Fr. *estriver*.]

strode. See **stride.**

stroke[1], *strōk*, *n.* an act of striking: a blow: a sudden attack of apoplexy or paralysis: a sudden happening or experience (e.g. *a stroke of lightning, of good luck*): the sound of a clock: a dash in writing: the sweep of an oar in rowing: one complete movement, e.g. of the piston of a steam engine: a movement in one direction of a pen, pencil, or paintbrush: a method of striking in games, swimming, etc.: a single effort or action: an achievement, feat.—*v.t., v.i.* to row the stroke oar of (a boat).

stroke oar, the oar nearest the stern in a rowing boat, or its rower. [Conn. **strike.**]

stroke[2], *strōk*, *v.t.* to rub gently in one direction, esp. as a sign of affection.

[O.E. *strācian*; same root as **strike.**]

stroll, *strōl*, *v.i.* to wander, roam: to walk about idly.—Also *n.*

strolling player, actor, one who wandered round the country giving performances. [Orig. unknown.]

strong, *strong*, *adj.* able to withstand attack of any kind—firm, solid, hard-wearing, well-fortified, etc.: powerful in attack (e.g. *a strong wind*): (of person, etc.) having great physical power: healthy: (of e.g. person, character) forceful, able to command respect or obedience: having a quality in a great degree (e.g. *a strong smell, colour*; *strong dislike*): having much of the important ingredient (e.g. *strong tea, a strong whisky*): of the stated number of persons (e.g. *a force* 30,000 *strong*. 'Strong' always follows the number).

strong'ly, *adv.* **strength,** *streng(k)th*, *n.*

strength'en, *v.t.*, *v.i.* to make, or become, strong or stronger.
strong'hold, *n.* a place built to stand against attack, a fortress: a place where a belief or view is strongly held (e.g. *a stronghold of conservatism*).
strong language, forceful emphatic language: swearing.
strong'-mind'ed, *adj.* having strong powers of reasoning: determined to have one's views known and considered.
strong'-room, -box, *n.* a room or case of great strength for storing valuables.
on the strength, a permanent member of the unit, organisation, etc.
on the strength of, encouraged by or counting on (e.g. *On the strength of this offer of help he went ahead with the plan*).
[O.E. *strang* (adj.), *strengthu* (n.).]

strop, *strop*, *n.* a strip of e.g. leather on which a razor is sharpened.—*v.t.* to sharpen on a strop.
[O.E.; same as **strap.**]

strontium, *stron'shi-ŭm*, *n.* a metal occurring in radioactive form in fall-out (see this).
[*Strontian* (*stron-tē'ăn*) in Argyllshire.]

strove. See **strive. struck.** See **strike.**

structure, *struk'chŭr*, *n.* a building, esp. a large one: the way the parts of anything are arranged (e.g. *the structure of a flower, of a novel*): the manner in which something is organized (e.g. *the structure of society*).
struc'tural, *adj.* **struc'turally,** *adv.*
[L. *struěre*, *structum*, to build.]

struggle, *strug'l*, *v.i.* to make great effort by twisting about, etc. (e.g. *Joe struggled in Jim's grasp*): to fight (with, against, for): to try or work hard (to): to make one's way with difficulty (e.g. *to struggle through the mud, struggle along with little money*).—*n.* a hard effort: a fight.
[M.E. *strogelen.*]

strum, *strum*, *v.t.* to play on (a musical instrument), or to play (a tune) in an unskilful, noisy way.—Also *v.i.* [Imit.]

strut[1], *strut*, *v.i.* to walk about in a stiff, vain, self-important manner:—*pr.p.* **strutt'ing**; *pa.p.* **strutt'ed.**—Also *n.*
[O.E. *strūtian*; conn. with **strut** (2).]

strut[2], *strut*, *n.* a bar, column, taking pressure or supporting weight in the direction of its length. [Orig. uncertain.]

strychnine, *strik'nēn, -nin*, *n.* a poison used in small quantities as a medicine.
[Gk. *strychnos*, name of a plant.]

stub, *stub*, *n.* the stump left after a tree is cut down: a short end (e.g. of a pencil, cigarette).—*v.t.* to put (out, e.g. a cigarette) by pressure on the end: to strike (e.g. the toe) against anything hard: —*pr.p.* **stubb'ing**; *pa.p.* **stubbed.**
stubb'y, *adj.* short, thick, and strong.
[O.E. *stubb.*]

stubble, *stub'l*, *n.* the stubs, ends, of corn left in the ground when the stalks are cut: a short rough growth (e.g. of beard).
[O.Fr. *estuble*—L. *stīpes*, a stalk.]

stubborn, *stub'ŏrn*, *adj.* (of persons) unwilling to give way, obstinate: (of resistance, attempt, etc.) carried on with great determination: difficult to move, work or deal with, or manage.
[Perh. **stub.**]

stubby. See **stub.**

stucco, *stuk'ō*, *n.* a plaster of lime and fine sand, etc., used for covering, or decorating, walls, etc.: work done in stucco.—*v.t.* to cover with stucco. [It.]

stuck. See **stick** (1).
stuck'-up, *adj.* self-important, snobbish, haughty in manner.

stud[1], *stud*, *n.* a collection of horses and mares kept for breeding, or for racing or hunting.
[O.E. *stōd*; conn. with Ger. *gestüt.*]

stud[2], *stud*, *n.* a nail with a large head: a knob for ornament: a double-headed button used for fastening a collar.—*v.t.* to cover with studs: to sprinkle, or be sprinkled over, thickly (e.g. *a lake studded with islands*; *flowers studded the grass*).
[O.E. *studu*, a post.]

student, studied, etc. See **study.**

studio, *stū'di-ō*, *n.* the workshop of an artist, etc.: a building or place where motion pictures are made: a room from which radio or television programmes are broadcast:—*pl.* **stu'dios.** [It.]

studious. See **study.**

study, *stud'i*, *v.t.* to give time and attention to gaining knowledge of (e.g. *to study mathematics*): to memorise (a part in a play): to observe closely (e.g. *to study the habits of bees, the face of the accused*): to look at carefully so as to understand (e.g. a problem, situation): to consider, try to act so as to satisfy, etc. (e.g. *to study a person, his feelings, wishes, needs, convenience*).—Also *v.i.*:—*pr.p.* **stud'ying**; *pa.p.* **stud'ied.**—*n.* applying the mind to a subject so as to gain information or understanding: (object of) earnest effort (e.g. *He made it his study to please his employer*): a room where one studies: a piece of work in art, music, or literature that has an experimental quality or a partly educational purpose:—*pl.* **stud'ies.**
stud'ied, *adj.* planned, intentional (e.g. *a studied insult*): too careful, not natural (e.g. *studied politeness*).
student, *stū'dĕnt*, *n.* one who studies, esp. at a university, etc.: one who is fond of study.
studious, *stū'di-ŭs*, *adj.* fond of study: studying carefully and much: careful (to do, of): studied, careful (e.g. *studious avoidance of subjects about which they disagreed*).
stū'diously, *adv.* **stū'diousness,** *n.*
to make a study of, to study in detail.
[L. *studium*, zeal, eagerness, study.]

stuff, *stuf, n.* the material of which anything is made: fabrics, cloth, esp. woollen: worthless matter: possessions, esp. household goods: (*slang*) way of behaving or talking (e.g. *rough stuff*).—*v.t.* to fill by crowding: to cram (into): to fill with seasoning (e.g. *to stuff a turkey*): to fill the skin of (a dead animal) so that it may be kept.—*v.i.* to cram in food.
stuff'ing, *n.* material used to stuff.
stuffy, *stuf'i, adj.* (of a room, etc.) close, badly ventilated: (*coll.*) angry, sulky: (*coll.*) dull, old-fashioned and prim:—*comp.* **stuff'ier**; *superl.* **stuff'iest.**
stuff'ily, *adv.* **stuff'iness,** *n.*
that's the stuff! that's what is wanted!
[O.Fr. *estoffe.*]

stultify, *stul'ti-fī, v.t.* to make futile, of no value (e.g. *to stultify all he had done by one wrong step*):—*pr.p.* **stul'tifying**; *pa.p.* **stul'tified.**
[L. *stultus*, foolish, *facĕre*, to make.]

stumble, *stum'bl, v.i.* to strike the feet against something and trip or lose balance: to falter: to light (on), find by chance: to slide into wrongdoing or mistake.—Also *n.*
stum'bling-block, *n.* a difficulty in the way of a plan: a cause of error.
[M.E. *stomble*; conn. with **stammer.**]

stump, *stump, n.* the part of a tree left in the ground after the trunk is cut down: the piece of a limb, tooth, pencil, etc. remaining after a part is cut or worn away: (*cricket*) one of the three sticks forming a wicket.—*v.t.* to put out (a batsman who is not in his ground) by striking the stumps with the ball: to puzzle completely, or make helpless to act (e.g. *The problem stumped her*): (*slang*) to pay (up).—*v.i.* to walk along heavily.
stum'py, *adj.* short and thick.
stump orator, one who makes speeches on makeshift platforms, usu. to gain popular support.
[Late M.E. *stompe*; conn. Ger. *stumpf.*]

stun, *stun, v.t.* (of loud noise, blow, bad news, etc.) to daze, knock senseless, bewilder: to surprise greatly, amaze:—*pr.p.* **stunn'ing**; *pa.p.* **stunned.**
[Same root as **astonish.**]

stung. See **sting.** **stunk.** See **stink.**

stunt[1], *stunt, v.t.* to stop the growth of: to check (growth, etc.).
stunt'ed, *adj.*
[O.E., stupid; O. Norse *stuttr*, short.]

stunt[2], *stunt, n.* a daring feat: something done to attract notice. [U.S. slang.]

stupefy, *stū'pi-fī, v.t.* (of drink, sorrow, etc.) to make stupid, deaden the senses or feelings of: to arouse amazement (usu. disapproving) in (a person).—Also *v.i.*:—*pr.p.* **stup'efying**; *pa.p.* **-efied.**
stupefac'tion, *n.*
stupendous, *stū-pen'dus, adj.* amazing, wonderful, because of size or power.

stupid, *stū'pid, adj.* dull in understanding, slow at learning: foolish, not sensible (e.g. *It was a stupid thing to do*): stupified (e.g. *He is stupid with lack of sleep*).—*n.* a stupid person.
stu'pidly, *adv.* **stu'pidness,** *n.*
stupid'ity, *n.* stupidness: a stupid act:—*pl.* **stupid'ities.**
stu'por, *n.* a state (caused e.g. by drugs) in which one is not, or is not wholly, conscious: a dazed condition from amazement, etc.
[L. *stupēre*, to be struck senseless.]

sturdy, *stûr'di, adj.* strong, healthy: of strong material: firm, resolute (e.g. *sturdy resistance, defenders, independence*):—*comp.* **stur'dier**; *superl.* **stur'diest.**
stur'dily, *adv.* **stur'diness,** *n.*
[O.Fr. *estourdi*, stunned, dazed, violent.]

sturgeon, *stûr'jon, n.* a large fish which yields caviare.
[O.Fr. *esturgeon.*]

stutter, *stut'ėr, v.i.* to utter one's words in a jerky way, pausing and repeating parts of them.—Also *n.*
stutt'erer, *n.* one who stutters.
[Old word *stut*, to stutter.]

sty[1], *stī, n.* a pigsty, pen for pigs: any very dirty place:—*pl.* **sties.**
[O.E. *stī*; conn. with *stig*, hall.]

sty[2], *stī, n.* a small inflamed swelling on the eyelid:—*pl.* **sties.**—Also **stye.**
[O.E. *stīgend*, prob. *stīgan*, to rise.]

stye. See **sty** (2).

style, *stīl, n.* an ancient pointed tool for writing: the pin of a sundial: the middle part of the pistil of a flower: way of expressing thought in language, or ideas in music, art, etc. (e.g. *She has an easy, flowing style*): way of moving, etc., in doing something, e.g. in playing a game: skilful way or manner of doing something: fashion, manner (e.g. *in the style of* 1850): air of fashion or elegance: title or name.—*v.t.* to name, call (e.g. *He styled himself 'Lord John' and his house 'castle'*).
sty'lish, *adj.* smart, in fashion, showy.
styl'ishly, *adv.* **styl'ishness,** *n.*
sty'lus, *n.* a style (writing tool or sundial pin): a cutting tool used in making gramophone records: a gramophone needle.
in style, fashionably: with no expense or effort spared.
[L. *stilus*, stake, writing tool.]

styptic, *stip'tik, n.* something which stops bleeding.
[Gk. *styptikos*—*styphein*, to contract.]

suave, *swäv, adj.* (of person, manner) polite, agreeable (esp. on the surface).
suave'ness, suav'ity, (*swav'*), *ns.*
[Fr.—L. *suāvis*, sweet.]

sub-, *sub-, pfx.* under.
In Latin, and in English words from Latin, this appears before *c, f, g, m, p, r, s* as **suc-** (e.g. *succeed*), **suf-** (e.g.

*suf*fer), **sug-** (e.g. *sug*gest), **sum-** (e.g. *sum*mon), **sup-** (e.g. *sup*port), **sur-** (e.g. *sur*prise), and **sus-** (e.g. *sus*pend).
Shades of meaning in modern words include :—
(1) below (e.g. *subway*); (2) less in rank or importance, or under a superior (e.g. *sublibrarian*); (3) less than (e.g. *subnormal intelligence*), or slightly less than (e.g. *a subtropical climate*); (4) formed by dividing into smaller groups or sections (e.g. *a subdivision, subsection*). [L.]

sub, *sub, n.* (*coll.*) short for *subordinate, subaltern, subscription*, etc.

subacute, *sub-ȧ-kūt′, adj.* (of disease) moderately acute. [Pfx. **sub-** (3).]

subaltern, *sub′l-tėrn,* (*U.S.*) *sub-öl′tėrn, n.* an officer in the army under the rank of captain.
[L. *sub*, under, *alternus*, one after other.]

subatomic, *sub-ȧ-tom′ik, adj.* smaller than an atom : happening within an atom.
[**sub-** (3).]

subcommittee, *sub′kȯ-mit′i, n.* a committee having powers given to it by a larger committee. [**sub-** (2).]

subconscious, *sub-kon′shu̇s, adj.* having to do with workings of the mind of which a person himself is not aware (e.g. *His generosity really arose from a subconscious desire for praise*).
subcon′sciously, *adv.* [**sub-** (3).]

subcontractor, *sub′kȯn-trak′tȯr, n.* one who undertakes work for a contractor (i.e. is not directly employed by person who wants work done). [**sub-** (2).]

subdivide, *sub-di-vīd′, v.t., v.i.* to divide into smaller parts or divisions.
subdivi′sion, *n.* [**sub-** (4).]

subdue, *sub-dū′, v.t.* to conquer : to make tame, obedient : to overcome (e.g. a desire) : to soften, make less bright (e.g. colour, light), make quieter (e.g. sound, manner).
subdued′, *adj.* **subdū′al,** *n.*
[Confusion of three L. verbs.]

subeditor, subinspector. **sub-** (2).

subject, *sub′jekt, adj.* under the power of another, not independent (e.g. *a subject nation*) : apt to suffer from (with *to*; e.g. *subject to hay fever, to sand storms*) : depending on (a condition) for being carried out, etc. (e.g. *This plan is subject to your approval, to our obtaining funds*).—*n.* one under the power of another : one who is ruled over (in reality or in theory) by a king, etc. : a person or thing on which work is done (e.g. *the subject of the biography, of the experiment*), or about which something is said (e.g. *I see the subject of our talk making his way towards us*) : the idea, theme, topic of a work of literature, art, music, etc. : material, circumstances, etc., suitable for certain treatment (e.g. *The hydrogen bomb is not a subject for laughter*) : a branch of learning (e.g. *He studied two subjects—history and Italian*) : a person (in certain phrases only; e.g. *She is a nervous subject*) : (*grammar*) the word(s) in a sentence standing for the person or thing that does the action of the verb (e.g. *In 'He hit me', 'he' is the subject of the verb 'hit'*).—*v.t.* (*su̇b-jekt′*) to bring under, or under the power of (with *to*; e.g. *to subject to control*, or *to a conqueror*) : to make liable (to), cause to suffer from (e.g. *Such an action would subject you to much criticism*) : to cause to undergo (e.g. *to subject to heavy rain, pressure, questioning*).
subjec′tion, *n.* act of subjecting : state of being subjected.
subjec′tive, *adj.* having to do with the subject of a verb : arising from, influenced by, one's own mind and emotions (e.g. *He took a subjective, not an objective or impartial, view of the problem*).
subject to. See **subject,** *adj.*
[L. *sub*, under, *jacĕre, jactum*, throw.]

subjoin, *sub-join′, v.t.* to add at the end.
[L. *sub*, under, and root as **join.**]

subjugate, *sub′joo-gāt, v.t.* to conquer : to make unresisting, obedient.
[L. *sub*, under, *jugum*, a yoke.]

subjunctive, *sub-jungk′tiv, adj.* and *n.* (having to do with) a mood of the verb chiefly concerned with something that may happen or have happened, etc. It is now hardly ever used in English, but survivals include the following :—*If it be so* (indicative mood, *If it is so*); *if it were known that he has been in prison*; *I propose, insist, that he be dismissed*).
[L. *sub*, and root as **join.**]

sublease, sublet, *sub′lēs′, sub′let′, ns.* a lease, let, to another person by one who is himself a tenant of the property.—Also *vs.t.* [**sub-** (2).]

sublieutenant, *sub-lė(f)-ten′ȧnt, n.* (*navy*) a junior officer next below a lieutenant.
[**sub-** (2).]

sublimate, *sub′lim-āt, v.t.* to purify (a solid substance) by turning it into vapour by means of heat and then allowing the vapour to become solid again : to turn (an emotion, impulse) into one of higher or nobler quality.
sublime, *sub-līm′, adj.* lofty, noble, causing feelings of awe or deep respect (e.g. *a sublime scene*; *sublime truths*) : (of an unworthy feeling) very great (e.g. *sublime indifference*).—*v.t.* to sublimate.
sublime′ly, *adv.*
sublime′ness, sublim′ity (*-lim′*), *ns.*
[L. *sublīmāre, -ātum*, to lift up.]

subliminal, *sub-lim′i-nȧl, adj.* (producing sensations) so small as to be below the level of conscious thought or feeling.
[L. *sub*, under, *līmen*, the threshold.]

submarine, *sub-mȧ-rēn′, adj.* under, or in, the sea.—*n.* (*sub′*) a ship which can travel under water. [**sub-** (1).]

submerge, *sub-mėrj′,* **submerse,** *sub-mėrs′, v.t.* to plunge under water : to flood with water.—*v.i.* to sink under water.

submerg'ence, submer'sion, *ns.*

submer'sible, *adj.* that can be submerged.

[L. *sub*, under, *mergĕre, mersum*, plunge.]

submit, *sub-mit'*, *v.t.* to yield (e.g. oneself, one's will, to another, his will, his wishes): to yield, subject (to treatment, conditions, influence; e.g. *to submit oneself to the influence of one's elders, one's possessions to rough usage*): to offer to another for acceptance or an opinion (e.g. *I submitted my story to a magazine editor*): to offer (a thought) for consideration (e.g. *I submit that the other plan was a better one*).—*v.i.* to yield, give in:—*pr.p.* **submitt'ing**; *pa.p.* **submitt'ed.**

submission, *sub-mish'(ŏ)n*, *n.* act of submitting: something (e.g. an idea) that is submitted: humble behaviour, obedience.

submiss'ive, *adj.* willing or ready to submit: humble, obedient.

submiss'ively, *adv.* **-iveness,** *n.*

[L. *sub*, under, *mittĕre, missum*, to send.]

subnormal. See **sub-.**

subordinate, *sù-bör'd(i-)nit*, *adj.* lower in order, rank, nature, power, etc.: under the authority of, subject (to another person): of little or less importance (e.g. *The aim of actually bringing about improvements was subordinate; it was subordinate to a desire to have people think him a reformer*).—*n.* a person who is subordinate.—*v.t.* (*-āt*) to look upon or treat as of less importance than (with *to*).

subordinā'tion, *n.* state of being subordinate: act of subordinating.

[L. *sub*, under, *ordō, ordinis*, order.]

suborn, *sub-örn'*, *v.t.* to persuade (a person) to do an unlawful act, esp. by bribery.

[L. *sub*, under, secretly, *ornāre*, fit out.]

subpoena, *sub-pē'nȧ*, *n.* a writ commanding a person to appear in court under threat of penalty if he does not obey.—*v.t.* to summon (a person) by subpoena:—*pr.p.* **subpoe'naing**; *pa.p.* **subpoe'na'd, subpoe'naed** (*-nad*).

[L. *sub*, under, *poena*, punishment.]

subscribe, *sub-skrīb'*, *v.t.* to write (usu. one's name) at the end of e.g. a statement or document: to give consent or agreement to (something written) by signing one's name underneath: to give (money to; e.g. *to subscribe £1 to charity*).—*v.i.* to contribute (to, for): (with *for*) to promise to buy (a book, series of magazines, newspaper for a certain time): to show one's agreement with (with *to*; e.g. *I subscribe to that statement*).

subscrip'tion, *n.* act of subscribing: a name subscribed; money subscribed.

[L. *sub*, under, *scrībĕre, scriptum*, write.]

subsequent, *sub'sė-kwėnt*, *adj.* following or coming after (e.g. *his subsequent repentance*).

sub'sequently, *adv.*

[L. *sub*, under, after, *sequī*, to follow.]

subserve, *sub-sėrv'*, *v.t.* to help forward (e.g. *to subserve a plan, purpose*).

subser'vient, *adj.* serving as a means (to an end): too ready to do as one is told.

subser'vience, *n.*

[L. *sub*, under; root as **serve.**]

subside, *sub-sīd'*, *v.i.* (of e.g. flood water) to sink in level: to settle down into the ground: (*coll.*) to fall (into a chair): (of storm, fever, noise, etc.) to become less and less.

subsi'dence (or *sub'si-*), *n.*

[L. *sub*, down, *sīdĕre*, to settle.]

subsidy, *sub'si-di*, *n.* money given by one state to another in payment for help of some kind: money granted by the government to a service (e.g. a form of transport) which is important to the public, or to growers of an important crop (e.g. wheat) to help keep its price down:—*pl.* **sub'sidies.**

subsid'iary, *adj.* giving help or additional supplies: contributing, but of less importance (e.g. *a subsidiary stream*): (of a company, firm) controlled by another company.—Also *n.*:—*pl.* **-ies.**

sub'sidīse, *v.t.* to give a subsidy to.

[Same root as **subside.**]

subsist, *sub-sist'*, *v.i.* to have existence or reality: to keep oneself alive (on; *He subsists on eggs, milk, and bread*).

subsis'tence, *n.* state of existing: means of keeping alive, livelihood: (state of having) the barest necessities of life.

[L. *sub*, under, *sistĕre*, to stand.]

subsoil, *sub'soil*, *n.* the layer of earth beneath the surface soil. [**sub-** (1).]

substance, *sub'stȧns*, *n.* a material object that can be seen and felt (e.g. *a sticky substance*): (*chemistry*) an element, compound or mixture: material: solidity, worth (e.g. *This cloth has no substance*): property, wealth (e.g. *a man of substance*): general meaning, gist (e.g. *He spoke for an hour, but the substance of his talk could have been given in five minutes*).

substantial, *sub-stan'sh(ȧ)l*, *adj.* solid, strong (e.g. *a substantial building, table*): important in amount, size, etc. (e.g. a *substantial sum of money*): having property or wealth: in the main though not in all details (e.g. *This was the substantial truth; they were in substantial agreement*).

substan'tially, *adv.* in total effect (e.g. *This statement is substantially true*).

substantiate (*-stan'shi-āt*), *v.t.* to show the truth of, or grounds for (e.g. a statement, a charge).

sub'stantive, *n.* (*grammar*) a noun.

[L. *sub*, under, *stāre*, to stand.]

substitute, *sub'sti-tūt*, *v.t.* to put in place of another person or thing (with *for*).—*v.i.* to act as a substitute.—*n.* one who, or something that, is put in place of, or

used instead of or for want of, another: a deputy.—Also *adj*.
substitū'tion, *n*.
[L. *sub*, under, *statuĕre*, to set.]

subterfuge, *sub'tėr-fūj*, *n*. a trick or plan for avoiding a difficulty, etc.
[L. *subter*, under, *fugĕre*, to flee.]

subterranean, *sub-tė-rān'yȧn*, *-rā'ni-ȧn*, *adj*. under the ground: hidden, secret.
[L. *sub*, under, *terra*, the earth.]

subtitle, *sub'tī-tl*, *n*. a second or explanatory title to a book. [**sub-** (2).]

subtle, *sut'l*, *adj*. faint, delicate, difficult to describe (e.g. *a subtle perfume*; *a subtle feeling of horror*): not easily grasped by the mind, difficult to put into words (e.g. *a subtle difference*): (of mind) able to grasp difficult points, esp. small differences of e.g. meaning: sly, cunning.
subtly (*sut'li*), *adv*. (note this form).
subtleness (*sut'*), *n*.
subt'lety, *n*. subtleness: something subtle: power of seeing and understanding small differences in e.g. meaning:—*pl*. **subt'leties.**
[L. *subtīlis*—*sub*, under, *tēla*, a web.]

subtract, *sub-trakt'*, *v.t.* to take away (a part from): to take (one number or quantity from another) in order to find the difference.—Also *v.i.*
subtrac'tion, *n*.
[L. *sub*, *trahĕre*, *tractum*, draw away.]

subtropical. See **sub-.**

suburb, *sub'ȯrb*, *n*. an area of houses in the outskirts of a large town.
subur'ban, *adj*. having to do with the suburbs: narrow in outlook.
subur'bia, *n*. (the people who live in) suburbs as a whole.
[L. *sub*, under, near, *urbs*, a city.]

subvert, *sub-vėrt'*, *v.t.* to overthrow, ruin completely (e.g. a person's morals, loyalty, arguments, a government).
subver'sion, *n*.
subver'sive, *adj*. likely to destroy (e.g. government) or to corrupt (e.g. *subversive influence*; *subversive of morality*).
[L. *sub*, under, *vertĕre*, *versum*, to turn.]

subway, *sub'way*, *n*. an underground way for traffic, pedestrians, or electric trains. [**sub-** (1).]

succeed, *suk-sēd'*, *v.t.* to come after, follow in order (e.g. *Spring succeeds winter*): to follow, take the place of (e.g. *He succeeded his brother in office*).—*v.i.* to follow in order: to manage to do what one has aimed at (with *in*): to get on well.
success', *n*. favourable result (e.g. *the success of our efforts*): a person or thing that turns out well.
success'ful, *adj*. turning out as one had planned: having gained wealth or position.
success'fully, *adv*. **success'fulness,** *n*.
success'ion, *n*. act of following after: a number (of persons or things) following each other in time or place (e.g. *a succession of visitors, victories*): the right of becoming the next holder (*the succession to . . .*): order of succeeding.
success'ive, *adj*. following in order.
success'or, *n*. one who succeeds or comes after, or follows in office, etc.
in succession, one after another.
[L. *sub*, up, *cēdĕre*, *cessum*, to go.]

succinct, *suk-singkt'*, *adj*. short, in few words.
succinct'ly, *adv*. **succinct'ness,** *n*.
[L. *sub*, up, *cingĕre*, *cinctum*, to gird.]

succour, *suk'ȯr*, *v.t.* to help in time of need.—*n*. aid: one who gives help.
[L. *sub*, up, *currĕre*, to run.]

succulent, *suk'ū-lėnt*, *adj*. (of fruit, etc.) full of juice or moisture.
succ'ulence, *n*.
[L. *succus*, juice—*sūgĕre*, to suck.]

succumb, *su-kum'*, *v.i.* to yield (with *to*; e.g. *to succumb to temptation*): to die.
[L. *sub*, under, *-cumbĕre* (found only in compounds), to lie down.]

such, *such*, *adj*. of the kind mentioned or thought of (e.g. *Such people are not to be trusted*): similar (e.g. *silk, rayon, and such materials*): of the kind (that, as; e.g. *His anger was such that he lost control of himself*, or *such as to make him lose all control*): used to give importance or emphasis (e.g. *This is such a fine day*).—Also *pron*.
such and such, referring to a person or thing not named (e.g. *Such and such a person may say*).
such as, of the same kind, in the same class, as (e.g. *game birds such as grouse*): for example.
as such, considered as what one would expect from the name (e.g. *The music is of no worth as such*—i.e. as music—*but it provides a friendly background noise*).
[O.E. *swylc*—*swa*, so, *līc*, like.]

suck, *suk*, *v.t.* to draw into the mouth: to draw milk from with the mouth: to lick and roll about in the mouth: (often with *in*, *up*, etc.) to draw in, take up (e.g. *Plants suck*, or *suck up, water from the ground*).—*n*. a sucking movement, sound, or force.
suck'er, *n*. one who sucks: an organ on an animal by which it sticks to objects: something like this: a side shoot from the underground stem of a plant: a person who is easily fooled.
suckle, *suk'l*, *v.t.* (of woman, female animal) to nurse at the breast, give her milk to: to rear, bring up.
suck'ling, *n*. a child or animal still being fed on its mother's milk.
to suck dry, to drain all the liquid, or money or resources, or strength, etc., from.
[O.E. *sūcan*; conn. with Ger. *saugen*.]

suction, *suk'sh(ȯ)n*, *n*. act of sucking: act or process of reducing the air pressure on part of the surface of a substance (e.g.

a liquid) and thus causing it to be drawn up into e.g. a tube.
[L. *sūgĕre, sūctum*, suck; conn. **suck.**]

sudden, *sud'ėn, adj.* unexpected, unprepared for (e.g. *a sudden attack*): happening, etc., all at once (e.g. *a sudden departure, realisation*): sharp, abrupt (e.g. *a sudden turn in the road*).
sudd'enly, *adv.* **sudd'enness,** *n.*
all of a sudden, suddenly.
[O.Fr. *sodain*—L. *sub*, up, *īre*, to go.]

suds, *sudz, n.pl.* soap-suds.
[O.E. *soden*, pa.p. of *sēothan*, to seethe.]

sue, *sū* or *sōō, v.t.* to start a law case against. —*v.i.* to make a legal claim: to beg (for): —*pr.p.* **su'ing**; *pa.p.* **sued.**
See also **suit.**
[Through O.Fr.—L. *sequī*, to follow.]

suède, suede, *swād, swed, n.* leather made from sheep or lamb skins with a soft, dull surface.—Also *adj.*
[Fr. *Suède*, Sweden.]

suet, *sū'it, sōō', n.* a hard animal fat.
[O.Fr. *seu*—L. *sēbum*, fat.]

suffer, *suf'ėr, v.t.* to undergo (e.g. *to suffer a change*): to endure or bear (e.g. pain): to allow (person, thing, to do something): to put up with, tolerate (e.g. *He would not suffer any interference with his plan*). —*v.i.* to feel pain: to undergo loss or injury: to be punished (for).
suff'erable, *adj.* bearable: allowable.
suff'erance, *n.* usu. in phrase **on sufferance,** e.g. *He was there on sufferance*, i.e. he was suffered or allowed to be there but no one really wanted him, or he was there for so long as he behaved well.
suff'ering, *n.* and *adj.*
[L. *sub*, under, *ferre*, to bear.]

suffice, *su̇-fīs', v.i.* to be enough, sufficient, or good enough (e.g. *The meat we have will suffice for lunch*; *the netting will suffice to mend the fence*).—*v.t.* to be sufficient for (a person; e.g. *Will that suffice you?*).
sufficient, *su̇-fish'ėnt, adj.* enough in quantity: effective enough (to).
sufficiency, *su̇-fi'shėn-si,* **n.** a large enough quantity to meet one's needs: ability: self-confidence.
[L. *sub*, under, *facĕre*, to make.]

suffix, *suf'iks, n.* a small part placed after the root of a word (e.g. *-ly* in 'quickly'; *-ness* in 'kindness').
[L. *sub*, under, *figĕre, fixum*, to fix.]

suffocate, *suf'ō-kāt, v.t.* to kill by stopping the breath: to cause to feel unable to breathe freely: to destroy or take away conditions necessary for growth or expression (e.g. *to suffocate his poetic talent*).
suff'ocating, *adj.* **suffocā'tion,** *n.*
[L. *sub*, under, *fauces*, the throat.]

suffrage, *suf'rij, n.* a vote: the right to vote.
[L. *suffrāgium*, a vote.]

suffuse, *su-fūz', v.t.* to spread over or cover (with a liquid, colour, or light; e.g. *The story suffused her eyes with tears*).
suffū'sion, *n.*
[L. *sub*, under, *fundĕre, fūsum*, pour.]

sugar, *shoog'ȧr, n.* a sweet substance obtained from the sugar cane and the sugar beet, also from maple, palm trees, etc.: too much flattery or compliment.—*v.t.* to sprinkle or mix with sugar.
sug'ared, *adj.* sweetened with sugar: charming: too sweet.
sug'ary, *adj.* tasting of, or like, sugar: sickly sweet.
sug'ariness, *n.*
sugar beet, a type of beet (see this).
sugar cane, a tall grass that grows in hot countries from which sugar is obtained.
[Fr. *sucre*, through Sp., Arabic, Pers.—Sanskrit *carkarā*, grains of sand, sugar.]

suggest, *su̇-jest', v.t.* to propose (e.g. *to suggest a plan of action, a person to fill a post*): to put into one's mind.
suggestion, *su̇-jes'ch(ȯ)n, n.* act of suggesting: a proposal, idea brought forward: the process by which a person accepts without thought an idea put into his mind by someone else, e.g. under hypnotism: a slight trace (e.g. *a suggestion of a cold*).
sugges'tible, *adj.* easily influenced by suggestion.
sugges'tive, *adj.* that suggests: that suggests something rather improper: bringing to one's mind the idea or picture (of; e.g. *a hat suggestive of a bowl*).
[L. *sub*, under, *gerĕre, gestum*, carry.]

suicide, *sū'i-sīd, sōō'-, n.* one who kills himself: the taking of one's own life.
suicī'dal, *adj.* having to do with suicide: certain to ruin e.g. one's career (e.g. *This action was suicidal*; *he now had no chance of success*).
[L. *sui*, of himself, *caedĕre, caesum*, kill.]

suit, *sūt, n.* act of suing: an action at law: courtship of a particular woman: a set of cards of one kind (e.g. of hearts): a number of things made to be worn together, as e.g. pieces of clothing.—*v.t.* to fit, make suitable (to; e.g. *He suited his speech to his audience*): to look well on (e.g. *The hat suits her*): to please (e.g. *Suit yourself*): to be convenient to (e.g. *The time chosen did not suit him*): to agree with (e.g. *The heat did not suit me*). —*v.i.* to go well (with).
suit'ed, *adj.* fitted, suitable (to, for): dressed in a suit or clothes (e.g. *velvet-suited, sober-suited*).
suit'able, *adj.* fitting, meeting requirements (e.g. *a suitable place and time*): convenient, etc. (to a person).
suitabil'ity, suit'ableness, *ns.*
suit'ably, *adv.*
suit'or, *n.* one who tries to gain the love of a woman.

suit′case, *n.* a travelling-case for carrying clothes, etc.
to follow suit, to do as someone else has just done.
[Same root as **sue.**]

suite, *swēt, n.* a body of followers or attendants who go with an important person: a number of things in a set, as rooms, furniture, or pieces of music.
[Fr.—*suivre,* to follow; conn. **suit.**]

sulky, *sulk′i, adj.* silent and angry, sullen, because of something (usu. small) that one resents:—*comp.* **sulk′ier**; *superl.* **sulk′iest.**
sulk′ily, *adv.* **sulk′iness,** *n.*
sulk, *v.i.* to be sulky.
sulks, *n.pl.* a fit of sulkiness.
[O.E. *solcen,* slow—*seolcan,* to be slow.]

sullen, *sul′ėn, adj.* gloomily angry and silent: dark, dull (e.g. *a sullen sky*).
sull′enly, *adv.* **sull′enness,** *n.*
[O.Fr. *solain*—L. *sōlus,* alone.]

sully, *sul′i, v.t., v.i.* to dirty: to make, or become, less pure or bright:—*pr.p.* **sull′ying**; *pa.p.* **sull′ied.**
[Same root as **soil** (2).]

sulphur, *sul′fŭr, n.* a yellow substance found in the earth which burns with a blue flame giving off a choking smell, used in matches, gunpowder, etc.
sulphate, sulphide, *ns.* words used in naming different compounds of sulphur (e.g. *potassium sulphate*).
sulpha drugs, or **sulphon′amides,** a group of drugs with a powerful action against certain bacteria.
sulphuric (*sul-fūr′ik*) **acid,** a powerful acid much used in industry.
[L. *sulphur.*]

sultan, *sul′tȧn, n.* the king or ruler of some countries (e.g. long ago of Turkey).
sultana, *sul-tä′nȧ, fem.* the mother, wife, or daughter of a sultan: a small kind of raisin.
[Arabic *sultān,* victorious, a ruler.]

sultry, *sul′tri, adj.* hot and moist, close: hot with anger: passionate:—*comp.* **sul′trier**; *superl.* **sul′triest.**
sul′triness, *n.*
[Earlier *sweltry*; from **swelter.**]

sum, *sum, n.* the amount of two or more things taken together: total: a quantity of money: a problem in arithmetic or algebra: the general meaning, gist, of something said or written (also **sum and substance**).—*v.t.* to add together:—*pr.p.* **summ′ing**; *pa.p.* **summed.**
summation, *sum-ā′sh(ȯ)n, n.* act of forming a total or sum.
summ′ing-up′, *n.* act of one who sums up: a summary.
sum total, the sum of several smaller sums: the main point, total effect.
in sum, in short.
to sum up, to give the important points of (e.g. *The chairman will now sum up the discussion*).

summary, *sum′ȧ-ri, n.* a shortened form (of a statement, story, etc.) giving only the main points.—*adj.* short, brief: without waste of time or words (e.g. *a summary dismissal*): (of a method of trial) without formalities, speedy:—*pl.* **summ′aries.**
summ′arily, *adv.*
summ′arise, *v.t.* to state briefly, make a summary of: to be a summary of.
[L. *summa*—*summus*; see **superior.**]

summer, *sum′ėr, n.* the warmest season of the year—in cooler northern regions May or June to July or August.—Also *adj.*—*v.i.* to pass the summer.
summ′erhouse, *n.* a small building for sitting in in a garden.
summ′ertime, *n.* the summer season: (**summer time**) time one hour ahead of time as reckoned by the position of the sun, adopted in Britain in 1916 for summer months, for short period (1968-71) used in winter also.
[O.E. *sumer*; conn. Ger. *sommer.*]

summit, *sum′it, n.* the highest point.
summit conference, a meeting between heads of states, etc
[L. *summum*; see **superior.**]

summon, *sum′ȯn, v.t.* to order to appear, esp. in court: to call (to do something), expecting to be obeyed (e.g. *She summoned me to put coal on the fire*): (also **summon up**) to rouse, call into action (e.g. *to summon up courage, energy*).
summ′ons, *n.* a call to appear, esp. in court: a call (to surrender, etc.).—*v.t.* to give a summons to appear in court:—*pl.* **summ′onses.**
[O.Fr. *somoner*—L. *sub, monēre,* to warn.]

sump, *sump, n.* a small pit into which water drains and out of which it can be pumped: the oil container in a motor vehicle.
[Conn. with Ger. *sumpf.*]

sumptuous, *sump′tū-ŭs, adj.* costly, splendid (of e.g. clothes, furnishings, food).
[L. *sumptuōsus,* costly—*sumptus,* cost.]

sun, *sun, n.* the large sphere which gives light and heat to the earth and other planets revolving round it: sunshine: anything like the sun in position of importance or brightness.—*v.t.* to expose (oneself) to the sun's rays: to enjoy (oneself in a person's company, etc.) as if in warmth and brightness:—*pr.p.* **sunn′ing**; *pa.p.* **sunned.**
sun′less, *adj.* without sun: without happiness or cheerfulness.
sunn′y, *adj.* filled with sunshine: cheerful:—*comp.* **sunn′ier**; *superl.* **sunn′iest.**
sunn′iness, *n.*
sun′bathing, *n.* sunning oneself, esp with little clothing on.
sun′beam, *n.* a ray of the sun.
sun′burn, *n.* a burning or browning, esp of the skin, by the sun.
sun′burned, sun′burnt, *adjs.*
sun′dial (*-dī-ȧl*), *n.* an instrument foı

telling time from the shadow of a rod or plate on its surface cast by the sun.

sun′flower, *n.* a large yellow flower with petals like rays of the sun, from whose seeds we get oil.

sun′light, *n.* the light of the sun.

sun′lit, *adj.* lighted up by the sun.

sun′rise, *n.* the rising of the sun in the morning, or the time of this: the east.

sun′set, *n.* the setting of the sun, or the time of this: the west.

sun′shine, *n.* bright sunlight: warmth and brightness.

sun′stroke, *n.* a serious illness caused by being in blazing sunshine for too long.

under the sun, in the world, on earth.

[O.E. *sunne.*]

sundae, *sun′dā, n.* an ice cream with fruits in syrup, etc. [Perh. **Sunday.**]

Sunday, *sun′di, n.* the first day of the week, called this because in ancient times it was a day for worship of the sun: a Sunday paper (usu. in *pl.—the Sundays*).

Sunday school, a school for learning about religion held on Sunday.

[O.E. *sunnan dæg*; conn. Ger. *sonntag.*]

sunder, *sun′dėr, v.t., v.i.* to sever.

[O.E. *syndrian—sundor*, separate.]

sundry, *sun′dri, adj.* several, more than one or two: various.

sun′dries, *n.pl.* various small things, odds and ends.

all and sundry, everybody of all kinds.

[Same root as **sunder.**]

sung. See **sing.**

sunk, sunken. See **sink.**

sunlight, etc. See **sun.**

sup, *sup, v.t.* to take into the mouth in small amounts, esp. from a spoon.—*v.i.* to eat supper:—*pr.p.* **supp′ing**; *pa.p.* **supped.** —*n.* a small mouthful.

supp′er, *n.* a meal taken at the end of the day.

[O.E. *sūpan* and O.Fr. *soper*; conn. **sop.**]

super-, *sū′pėr-, so͞o′-, pfx.* has meanings such as the following:—

(1) above, on the top of (e.g. *superstructure*); (2) in addition (e.g. *supertax*); (3) beyond, beyond the normal (e.g. *supernatural*); (4) of higher quality than (e.g. *superman*); (5) excessively (e.g. *supersensitive*).

[L. *super*, above.]

super, *sū′pėr, so͞o′, n.* (1) short for *superintendent, supervisor*, etc.: (2) an extra actor employed to come on to stage or screen without speaking (for *supernumerary*; see this): an unimportant person.—*adj.* (*coll.*) extremely good.

superabundant, *sū′pėr-ȧ-bun′dȧnt, so͞o′-, adj.* very abundant or more than enough (e.g. *superabundant rainfall, enthusiasm*).

superabound′, *v.i.*

superabun′dantly, *adv.*

superabun′dance, *n.* [**super-** (5).]

superannuate, *sū-pėr-an′ū-āt, so͞o-, v.t.* to retire a person from employment because of old age, esp. on pension: to discard, put out of use.

superannuā′tion, *n.* putting out of employment or use: pension, retirement allowance.

[L. *super*, above, *annus*, a year.]

superb, *sū-pėrb′, so͞o-, adj.* grand, stately, magnificent: very fine (e.g. *a superb diamond, method*).

[L. *superbus*, proud—*super*, above.]

supercharger, *sū′pėr-chär-jėr, so͞o′, n.* a device for supplying more air to the cylinders of an internal-combustion engine so as to increase power.

[**super-** (2).]

supercilious, *sū-pėr-sil′i-ůs, so͞o-, adj.* tending to look down on others, haughty.

supercil′iously, *adv.* **-iousness,** *n.*

[L. *supercilium*, an eyebrow.]

supereminent, *sū-pėr-em′i-nėnt, so͞o-, adj.* very distinguished. [**super-** (3).]

superficial, *sū-pėr-fish′(ȧ)l, so͞o-, adj.* of, or near, the surface: (of e.g. a wound) not going deep: not thorough (e.g. *a superficial examination of the material*): outward, but not real or in detail (e.g. *The flower has a superficial likeness to a violet; his interest is superficial*): (of person) shallow in nature or in knowledge.

superficially (*-fish′ȧ-li*), *adv.* **-ness,** *n.*

superficial′ity, *n.* superficialness: (in *pl.* **-ities**) superficial qualities or characteristics.

[L. *super*, above, *faciēs*, face.]

superfine, *sū′pėr-fīn, so͞o′, adj.* unusually or excessively fine. [**super-** (3).]

superfluous, *sū-pėr′flo͞o-ůs, so͞o-, adj.* beyond what is enough or is needed: unnecessary.

super′fluously, *adv.* **-fluousness,** *n.*

superflū′ity, *n.* a quantity more than enough: unnecessary thing:—*pl.* **-ies.**

[L. *super*, above, *fluĕre*, to flow.]

superhuman, *sū-pėr-hū′mȧn, so͞o-, adj.* beyond what is human: divine: greater than would be expected of an ordinary man (e.g. *to make a superhuman effort*).

[**super-** (4).]

superimpose, *sū-pėr-im-pōz′, so͞o-, v.t.* to lay or impose (one thing on another thing, usu. unlike it; e.g. *to superimpose a modern roof on an ancient cottage; to superimpose new customs on old*).

[**super-** (1).]

superintend, *sū-pėr-in-tend′, so͞o-, v.t.* to have charge of, to control, manage.—Also *v.i.*

superinten′dent, *n.* one who has charge of a building, department of work, institution, etc.: a police officer above a chief inspector.

[L. *super*, above, *in*, on, *tendĕre*, stretch.]

superior, *sū-pē′ri-ȯr, so͞o-, adj.* higher in rank: higher in excellence: greater in number or power (e.g. *superior forces*): above the common in quality (e.g. *a*

superior article): showing that one has a feeling of greater knowledge or importance (e.g. *a superior smile, air*): too courageous or self-controlled to yield (to; e.g. *He was superior to temptation*).—*n.* a person who is better than, or higher in rank than, others.
superior'ity, *n.* :—*pl.* **superior'ities.**
[L. *superus*, high (comp. *superior*; superl. *suprēmus* or *summus*)—*super*, above.]

superlative, *sū-pėr'lȧ-tiv*, or *sōō-*, *adj.* of the highest degree or quality (e.g. *a superlative example*; *superlative skill*).—*n.* (*grammar*) the highest degree of adjectives or adverbs (e.g. *shortest, silliest, best, farthest*; *most beautiful, most clumsily*).
[L. *super*, above, *ferre*, *latum*, carry.]

superman, *sū'pėr-man*, *sōō'*, *n.* a man of amazing powers: an imagined man of the future who will be more powerful than men of today. [**super-** (4).]

supermarket, *sū'pėr-mär-kit*, *sōō'*, *n.* a large, usu. self-service, store selling food and other goods. [**super-** (3).]

supernatural, *sū-pėr-nach'ūr-ȧl*, *sōō-*, *adj.* not happening as in the course of nature, miraculous: spiritual. [**super-** (3).]

supernumerary, *sū-pėr-nūm'ėr-ȧr-i*, or *sōō-*, *adj.* over and above the number stated, usual, or necessary.—*n.* a person or thing beyond the stated, usual, or necessary number: an extra actor (usu. **super**).
[L. *super*, over, *nūmerus*, a number.]

superphosphate, *sū-pėr-fos'fāt*, *sōō-*, *n.* an acid phosphate, used as a fertiliser. [**super-** (3).]

superscribe, *sū-pėr-skrīb'*, *sōō-*, *v.t.* to write or engrave (an inscription) on the outside or top: to write the name on the outside or cover of (something).
superscrip'tion, *n.*
[L. *super*, above; root as **scribe, script.**]

supersede, *sū-pėr-sēd'*, *sōō-*, *v.t.* to take the place of (e.g. *A new leader superseded the old*; *transport by road is superseding transport by rail*): to replace (by; e.g. *We must supersede our present arrangements by more efficient ones*).
[L. *super*, above, *sedēre*, to sit.]

supersensitive, *sū-pėr-sen'si-tiv*, *sōō-*, *adj.* extremely sensitive, or too sensitive. [**super-** (5).]

supersonic, *sū-pėr-son'ik*, *sōō-*, *adj.* (of vibrations and waves) of a frequency higher than that of sound that can be heard by man: (*aircraft*) faster than sound in air. [**super-** (3).]

superstition, *sū-pėr-stish'(ȯ)n*, *sōō-*, *n.* belief in magic and things that cannot be explained by reason: an instance of this: worship, or fear, arising from this.
superstitious, *sū-pėr-stish'ūs*, *sōō-*, *adj.*
supersti'tiously, *adv.* **-tiousness,** *n.*
[L. *superstitiō*, amazement, dread.]

superstructure, *sū'pėr-struk-chūr*, *sōō'*, *n.* a structure above or on something else. [**super-** (1).]

supertax, *sū'pėr-taks*, *sōō'*, *n.* an extra tax on large incomes. [**super-** (2).]

supervise, *sū'pėr-vīz*, *sōō'-*, *-vīz'*, *v.t.* superintend, be in charge of (work, workers).
supervision (*-vizh'ȯn*), *n.* act of supervising: inspection, control.
su'pervīsor (or *-vīz'*) *n.*
[L. *super*, over, *vidēre*, *vīsum*, to see.]

supine, *sū'pīn*, *sōō'*, or *-pīn'*, *adj.* lying on the back: not acting because lazy or indifferent: lacking energy.
[L. *supīnus*—*sub*, under.]

supper. See **sup.**

supplant, *sù-plânt'*, *v.t.* to take the place of (someone), esp. by unfair or cunning means, or of (something).
supplan'ter, *n.*
[L. *supplantāre*, to trip up one's heels.]

supple, *sup'l*, *adj.* bending easily without breaking, etc.: (of body movement) easy, graceful, agile: (of person) moving, bending, etc., easily.—*v.t., v.i.* to make, become, supple.
supp'leness, *n.*
supp'ly, *adv.* (note this form).
[L. *supplex*, bending the knees.]

supplement, *sup'li-mėnt*, *n.* an addition made to supply something lacking, correct errors, etc.: a special part of a magazine or newspaper added to the ordinary part.—*v.t.* (*sup-li-ment'*, or *sup'*) to add to (with *with*; *We can supplement the meal provided with fruit and sweets*): to be an addition to.
supplement'ary, *adj.* added to supply what is lacking: additional.
[Same root as **supply, 2.**]

suppliant, *sup'li-ȧnt*, *adj.* asking earnestly, begging humbly.—*n.* one who asks humbly.
supplicā'tion, *n.* earnest prayer or entreaty.
[L. *supplicāre*, beseech—root as **supple.**]

supply[1]. See **supple.**

supply[2], *sù-plī'*, *v.t.* to provide (what is wanted; e.g. *to supply water to the town*): to meet (a need, lack): to fill (a vacant place): to provide (person, etc., with; e.g. *to supply me, a hotel, with vegetables*): —*pr.p.* **supply'ing**; *pa.p.* **supplied'.**—*n.* act of supplying: something supplied: something that fills a want (e.g. *Get me a supply of paper*): (usu. in *pl.*) amount of food, money, etc., available: (in *pl.*) stores for e.g. army: a grant by parliament for expenses of government: a person who fills another's place for a time:—*pl.* **supplies'.**
[L. *sub*, up, *plēre*, to fill.]

support, *sù-pōrt'*, *-pört'*, *v.t.* to hold up, bear part of the weight of: to bear, tolerate (e.g. *I cannot support his impudence*): to take the side of, back, or help (a person; e.g. *I support him against those*

who are finding fault with him, in his efforts to raise money): to give approval or aid to (a cause, course of action, etc.; e.g. *Do you support this campaign, plan?*): to speak in favour of (a theory, belief, motion): to say that (a statement) is true: to supply with means of living (e.g. *He supports his father and mother*): to play (a part, rôle): to act with (a more important actor).—*n.* act of supporting: something that supports.
support'er, *n.* **support'able,** *adj.*
[L. *sub*, up, *portāre*, to carry.]

suppose, *sù-pōs'*, *v.t.* to take as true for the sake of argument or discussion (e.g. *Let us suppose I win £100 in the competition. What shall I do with it?*): to think, believe, or to think probable: to presuppose, involve (e.g. *The second stage of the plan supposes success of the first*). The imperative followed by a clause is used to suggest or command in an indirect way (e.g. *Suppose we give the prize to Mary; suppose you go now*).
supposed', *adj.* believed on too slight evidence to exist or to be so (e.g. *the once supposed phoenix, impossibility of splitting the atom*): wrongly believed to be such (e.g. *his supposed wife*).
suppos'edly, (*-id-li*), *adv.* according to what is, was, supposed (e.g. *The supposedly safe bridge collapsed*).
supposi'tion, *n.* act of supposing: something that is supposed.
[L. *sub*, under, *pōněre*, *positum*, place.]

suppress, *sù-pres'*, *v.t.* to crush, put down (e.g. rebellion, rebels): to stop, abolish (e.g. parking in narrow streets, freedom of speech): to keep in (e.g. a sigh, an angry retort): to keep from being published or being known (e.g. a book, a name, evidence, the truth).
suppress'or, *n.*
[L. *sub*, under, *preměre*, *pressum*, press.]

suppurate, *sup'ū-rāt*, *v.t.* (of e.g. a wound) to gather pus or matter, fester.
[L. *sub*, under, and root as **pus.**]

supra-, *sū'pra-*, *sōō'*, *pfx.*, above (in e.g. *a supranational authority*, one having powers higher than those of any one nation). [L.]

supreme, *sū-prēm'*, *sōō-*, *adj.* highest, greatest, utmost (e.g. *the supreme ruler; supreme courage, contempt*).
supreme'ly, *adv.*
suprem'acy (*-prem'*), *n.* state of being supreme: highest authority or power (e.g. *Papal supremacy*): highest position through achievements (e.g. *his supremacy as a painter*).
[See **superior.**]

surcharge, *sûr-chärj'*, *v.t.* to overcharge: to charge in addition: to mark (a postage stamp) with a surcharge.—*n.* (*sûr'*) additional tax or charge: something printed on a postage stamp to alter its value.
[Fr. *sur*—L. *super*, over, and **charge.**]

sure, *shōōr*, *shör*, *adj.* firm, strong (e.g. *a sure foundation*): to be depended on, trustworthy (e.g. *a sure friend*): never missing (e.g. *a sure aim*), slipping (e.g. *a sure foot*), failing (e.g. *a sure method*): certain (to do, happen, etc.): having no doubt, or having good reason to believe (e.g. *He is quite sure, sure of this fact, sure that he can do it*); sometimes suggesting a little doubt (e.g. *I am sure you will do as I ask*).—Also *adv.*
sure'ly, *adv.* firmly: without missing, slipping, failing, etc.: certainly, without doubt; sometimes expressing a little doubt (e.g. *Surely you will try; surely you will not go*).
sure'ness, *n.*
sure'-foot'ed, *adj.* not likely to slip or stumble.
sure enough, in very fact (e.g. *Sure enough he was late as I said he would be*).
be sure, see to it that (e.g. *Be sure you do it*).
to make sure, to act so that something is sure, or to check to see that it has already been made so.
to be sure! certainly: I admit (e.g. *To be sure I could buy a new one*).
[Through O.Fr.—L. root as **secure.**]

surety, *shōōr'ti*, *shör'*, *n.* one who promises to take responsibility if another person fails to do something, e.g. to appear in court: pledge, guarantee.
[Through O.Fr.—L. root as **security.**]

surf, *sûrf*, *n.* the foam made by the dashing of waves.
surf'ing, surf'-riding, *ns.* sport of riding on a surfboard.
surf'board, *n.* a board on which a bather rides towards shore on the surf.
[Earlier *suffe*; origin unknown.]

surface, *sûr'fis*, *n.* the outside part or face (e.g. *the surface of the earth*).—*v.t.* to put a (usu. smooth) surface on.—*v.t.*, *v.i.* to bring, or come, to the surface of e.g. sea.—*adj.* being on the surface only: travelling on the surface.
sur'faceman, *n.* a workman employed in keeping railway tracks, or roads, in repair: a miner in open-air working.
[Fr. *sur*, above, *face*, face.]

surfboard. See **surf.**

surfeit, *sûr'fit*, *n.* too much of anything: too much eating and drinking: sickness or disgust caused by this.—*v.t.* to fill with, or give, too much of anything.
[O.Fr. *surfait*—L. *super*, above, *facěre.*]

surfing, etc. See **surf.**

surge, *sûrj*, *n.* the rising or swelling of a large wave: a movement like this of e.g. a crowd: a sudden rise or increase (of e.g. emotion, pain, sound).—*v.i.* to rise high: to move (forward) like a wave.
[L. *surgěre*, to rise.]

surgeon, *sûr'jȯn*, *n.* one who treats injuries or diseases by operations on the living body, e.g. by cutting out diseased parts: an army, navy, or ship's doctor.

sur'gery, *n.* act or art of treating diseases, injuries, by operation: doctor's or dentist's consulting room:—*pl.* **-ies.**

sur'gical, *adj.* **sur'gically,** *adv.*

[O.Fr. *serurgien*—Gk. *cheir*, hand, *ergon*, work.]

surly, *sûr'li, adj.* gruff, ill-natured, rude: (of dog) very unfriendly: (of sky) dark and threatening:—*comp.* **sur'lier**; *superl.* **sur'liest.**

sur'liness, *n.*

[Earlier *sirly*, for **sir, like.**]

surmise, *sûr'mīz, -mīz', n.* guessing, supposing, conjecturing: something that is supposed or guessed.—*v.t.* (*-mīz'*) to imagine to be, infer, from slight evidence (*I surmise a party from the blaze of lights in the house*): to guess, suppose (that).

[O.Fr.—*surmettre*, to accuse.]

surmount, *sûr-mownt', v.t.* to be the top, or on the top, of (e.g. *A spire surmounts the tower*): to climb, get, over: to get the better of, overcome (e.g. a difficulty).

surmount'able, *adj.*

[Fr. *sur*, above, and root as **mount** (1).]

surname, *sûr'nām, n.* a person's last name, the family name.

[Fr. *sur*, over, above, and Eng. **name.**]

surpass, *sùr-pâs', v.t.* to go beyond, exceed: to be better than: to be beyond the reach or powers of (e.g. *to surpass description, my understanding*).

surpass'ingly, *adv.* extremely.

[Fr. *sur*, beyond, *passer*, to pass.]

surplice, *sûr'plis, n.* a loose white garment worn by clergymen and members of a choir.

[L. *super*, over, *pellis*, skin.]

surplus, *sûr'plùs, n.* the amount left over when what is required is taken away: excess: amount by which assets are greater than liabilities.

[Fr. *sur*, over, *plus*, more.]

surprise, *sûr-prīz', n.* act of coming upon without warning (in the phrase *to take by surprise*): the emotion caused by an unexpected or sudden happening—a less strong word than *astonishment* or *amazement*: an unexpected happening, etc.—*v.t.* to come upon suddenly or unawares: to lead by means of surprise (into; e.g. *to surprise him into an admission of guilt*; *to surprise an admission from, out of, him*): to cause some wonder, surprise, to.

[Fr.—L. *super*, *prehendĕre*, catch.]

surrealism, *su-rē'âl-izm, n.* a modern form of art claiming to show the activities of the unconscious mind.

[Fr. *sur*, above, *realisme*, realism.]

surrender, *sù-ren'dėr, v.t.* to hand over, yield (to another): to give up (e.g. a right, a claim): to abandon (oneself to e.g. grief).—*v.i.* to give oneself up to another.—*n.* act of surrendering.

[O.Fr. *sur*, over, *rendre*, to render.]

surreptitious, *sûr-ėp-ti'shùs, adj.* done in a secret, underhand way: enjoyed secretly.

[L. *surripĕre, -reptum*, snatch secretly.]

surround, *sù-rownd', v.t.* to come round about, esp. so as to cut off ways of escape: to enclose (e.g. *to surround the town with a wall*): to lie, be, all round (e.g. *The sea surrounds Britain*; *mystery surrounds his death*).—*n.* a border.

surroun'ding, *adj.* lying round.—*n.* act of coming, or of putting, round about: (in *pl.*) region, type of country, round: (in *pl.*) people among whom, or conditions in which, one lives.

[Middle Fr. *suronder*, overflow—L. *unda*, wave; influenced by **round.**]

surtax, *sûr'taks, n.* an additional tax on certain goods.

[Fr. *sur*, over, and **tax.**]

surveillance, *sûr-vāl'âns, n.* a close watch or constant guard (e.g. *Keep the prisoner under surveillance*): supervision.

[Fr. *sur*, over, *veiller*, to watch.]

survey, *sûr-vā', v.t.* to look over (e.g. a scene before one): to get a general view of (e.g. a mass of information, one's prospects) by examining carefully: to measure and estimate the position, shape, etc. of (a piece of land): to supervise.—*n.* (*sûr'vā*) an examination in detail, in order to come to general conclusions, estimate value, etc.: a writing giving results of this: a measuring, etc., of land, or of a country: a map made using measurements, etc., obtained.

survey'or, *n.* one who surveys, esp. officially, examines and supervises road-making, building work, etc.

[L. *super*, over, *vidēre*, to see.]

survive, *sûr-vīv', v.t.* to live longer than, outlive: to come through alive (e.g. *He survived the accident*): to continue to exist after, in spite of.—*v.i.* to remain alive or in existence.

survī'val, *n.* the state of surviving: anything (e.g. a custom, belief) that survives from earlier times: a relic.

survī'vor, *n.*

[L. *super*, beyond, *vīvĕre*, to live.]

susceptible, *sù-sep'ti-bl, adj.* liable to be affected by (e.g. *susceptible to colds, flattery*): easily affected, impressionable (e.g. *They are susceptible children*): capable (of; e.g. *This theory is not susceptible of proof*).

susceptibil'ity, *n.* state of being susceptible: (in *pl.*) feelings:—*pl.* **-ities.**

[L. *sub*, up, *capĕre*, *captum*, to take.]

suspect, *sùs-pekt', v.t.* to have doubts about, distrust (e.g. *to suspect a person's motives*): to imagine (a person, etc.) to be guilty: to be inclined to think (that; e.g. *I suspect that we have lost the ball*).—*n.* (*sus'pekt*) a person, etc., thought to be guilty.—*adj.* suspected, arousing doubt.

suspicion, *sùs-pi'sh(ò)n, n.* act of suspecting: mistrust, feeling of doubt: an opinion formed on little evidence (e.g. *I have a suspicion that he took my book*): a very slight amount (e.g. *Add a suspicion of garlic*).

suspi′cious, *adj.* suspecting, or inclined to suspect (e.g. *I am suspicious of the tramp*; *I have a suspicious nature*): showing suspicion (e.g. *He gave a suspicious glance*): (of action, etc.) causing suspicion.

suspi′ciously, *adv.* **suspi′ciousness,** *n.*

[L. *suspicĕre, suspectum,* look at secretly.]

suspend, *sŭs-pend′, v.t.* (1) to hang (e.g. *to suspend a weight on a string*): to keep from falling or sinking (e.g. *dust suspended in the air*; *particles suspended in a liquid*): (2) to stop, or discontinue, usu. for a time (e.g. *to suspend business for a week*): to take away a privilege, etc., from, esp. for a time (e.g. *to suspend a student,* i.e. not to allow him to attend classes, etc.): to postpone (e.g. *to suspend sentence*).

suspen′der, *n.* something that suspends: one of a pair of straps to support socks, (*U.S.*) trousers, etc.

suspense′, *n.* state of being undecided (e.g. *The matter is in suspense*): a state of uncertainty and worry (e.g. *He was in suspense until the winner was announced*).

suspen′sion, *n.* act of suspending: state of being suspended: a taking away of an office or privilege for a time: the state of a solid which is mixed with a liquid or gas and does not sink or dissolve in it. (Compare **suspense** above).

suspension bridge, a bridge which has its roadway suspended from cables hanging from towers.

to suspend judgment, to wait for more information before making up one's mind.

to suspend payment, to stop payments owed to creditors and thus become bankrupt.

[L. *sub,* beneath, *pendĕre, pensum,* hang.]

suspicion, suspicious, etc. See **suspect.**

sustain, *sŭs-tān′, v.t.* to hold up, bear the weight of: to support, back up: to show to be true (a statement) or just, legal (a claim): to give strength to (e.g. *You have eaten too little to sustain you on the journey*; *this belief sustained him*): to bear (e.g. attack) without giving way: to suffer, undergo (defeat, injury, loss, etc.): to act (part, rôle, character): to keep up (e.g. *He sustained the conversation with difficulty*): to keep (a note) sounding on evenly.

sustained′, *adj.* (of musical note, effort, etc.) continued without break.

sustain′er, *n.* the main motor in a rocket, continuing with it throughout its flight.

sus′tenance (*-tin-ăns, -tnăns*), *n.* nourishment for the body (food or drink) or for the mind.

[L. *sub,* under, up, *tenēre,* to hold.]

svelte, *svelt, adj.* slender, graceful. [Fr.]

swab, *swob, n.* a mop for cleaning or drying decks or floors: a piece of cotton wool, etc., used by doctors for several purposes: a specimen of mucus, etc., to be examined for bacteria, taken with a swab.—*v.t.* to clean or wipe with a swab.

[Du. *zwabber.*]

swaddle, *swod′l, v.t.* to bind (a baby) tightly round with strips of cloth (as used to be done): to wrap up (usu. person) almost completely.

swaddling clothes, bands of cloth, or clothes, for a baby.

[O.E. *swethel,* bandage; conn. **swathe.**]

swag, *swag, v.i.* to travel about carrying a bundle.—*n.* a bundle of belongings: plunder, things stolen.

[*swag,* sway, lurch; prob. Scand.]

swagger, *swag′ĕr, v.i.* to swing the body proudly: to brag noisily.—*n.* a self-confident swinging manner of walking: boastfulness: a conceited attitude.

[swag.]

swain, *swān, n.* a young peasant: an admirer, suitor.

[Old Norse *sveinn,* boy, servant.]

swallow[1], *swol′ō, v.t.* to take (e.g. food) through the throat into the stomach: (of e.g. mud) to take in and hide completely: to use up quickly (e.g. money): to accept meekly (e.g. an insult): to accept as true (something untrue that one is told): to keep back (e.g. tears, a laugh, an angry reply).

to swallow up, to take in, use up, completely or quickly.

[O.E. *swelgan.*]

swallow[2], *swol′ō, n.* an insect-eating bird with long wings which goes to warmer climates in winter.

swall′owtail, *n.* a dress coat with tails: a type of butterfly.

[O.E. *swalewe*; conn. Ger. *schwalbe.*]

swam. See **swim.**

swamp, *swomp, n.* wet, spongy ground, esp. with growth of trees or shrubs.—*v.t.* to cause (e.g. a boat) to fill with water: to overwhelm through, because of, quantity (e.g. *They swamped me with work*; *the work swamped me*).

swam′py, *adj.*:—*comp.* **swam′pier**; *superl.* **swam′piest.**

swam′piness, *n.* [Orig. uncertain.]

swan, *swon, n.* a large, stately bird, usu. white, with a long graceful neck, of the duck family.

swan song, the last work, utterance, of a poet, musician, etc. (swans were once said to sing just before death).

[O.E. *swan*; conn. with Ger. *schwan.*]

swank, *swangk, n.* (*slang*) bragging, showing off.—Also *v.i.*

swan′ky, *adj.* boastful: stylish:—*comp.* **swan′kier**; *superl.* **swan′kiest.**

swan′kiness, *n.* [Orig. uncertain.]

swap, *swop.* Same as **swop.**

sward, *swörd, n.* the grassy surface of land: green turf.
[O.E. *sweard,* skin, rind.]

swarm[1], *swörm, n.* a large number of small animals in movement together, esp. a number of bees following a queen to form a new colony: a great number, crowd.—*v.i.* to gather as bees do: to appear in large numbers: to be crowded (with; e.g. *The street swarmed with umbrellas*).
[O.E. *swearm*; conn. with Ger. *schwarm.*]

swarm[2], *swörm, v.t., v.i.* to climb by clinging to with arms and legs and drawing oneself up (e.g. *They swarmed,* or *swarmed up, the wall; they swarmed up*).
[Orig. uncertain.]

swarthy, *swörTH'i, adj.* dark-skinned.
[O.E. *sweart,* black.]

swash, *swosh, v.t., v.i.* to dash or splash.
swash'buckler, *n.* a bragging, swaggering adventurer (*buckler* means 'a shield').
swash'buckling, *adj.* having to do with a swashbuckler. [Imit.]

swastika, *swas'ti-kȧ, swos', n.* a cross with the ends bent at right angles, adopted as the badge of the Nazi party in Germany before the Second World War.
[Sanskrit *svastika,* fortunate.]

swath, *swöth, n.* a line of grass or corn cut by the scythe: a strip.
[O.E. *swathu,* a track.]

swathe, *swāTH, v.t.* to bind, wrap round, with a band or with loose material.
[O.E. *swethian*; conn. with **swaddle.**]

sway, *swā, v.t., v.i.* to swing, move, to and fro (e.g. *Wind sways trees; trees sway in the wind*): (to cause) to bend or move to one side, or in a particular direction: to influence, or have influence (e.g. *The speaker knew how to sway his audience, their opinions; the thought of cost always swayed with him*): to govern.—*n.* motion of swaying: rule, control, or influence (e.g. *to hold, have, sway over*).
[M.E. *sweyen.*]

swear, *swār, v.i.* to make a solemn promise (e.g. to tell the truth) calling God to witness: to vow: to curse, or to utter the name of God or of sacred things irreverently.—*v.t.* to put on oath to act in a certain way (e.g. *Swear her to secrecy,* i.e. make her swear not to tell): to declare on oath (that): to take (an oath): —*pa.t.* **swore** (*ō* or *ö*); *pa.p.* **sworn** (*ō* or *ö*).
sworn, *adj.* keeping steadily, as if bound by oath, to a certain attitude or way of behaving (e.g. *a sworn opponent of higher taxes; sworn friends, enemies*).
to swear by, to put complete trust in, reliance on.
to swear in, to introduce into an office by making swear an oath.
to swear off, to promise to give up (e.g. *to swear off drinking, cigarettes*).
to swear to, to make a solemn statement on oath, or as if on oath, about (something; e.g. *I swear to the truth of this statement, to his having said this, to the identity of this man*).
[O.E. *swerian*; conn. with Ger. *schwören.*]

sweat, *swet, n.* the moisture from the skin, perspiration: moisture in drops on any surface: state of one who sweats: (*coll.*) hard work: a state of great nervousness and worry.—*v.i.* to give out sweat or other moisture: to toil, work hard: to suffer (for something one has done).—*v.t.* to cause to sweat: to get rid of by sweating (e.g. *to sweat away fat*): to make work hard for very little pay: to squeeze money from.
sweat'ed, *adj.* esp. in phrase *sweated labour,* work or workers paid at too low a rate.
sweat'er, *n.* a heavy jersey used e.g. by athletes.
sweat'y, *adj.* wet or stained with sweat: *comp.* **sweat'ier**; *superl.* **sweat'iest.**
sweat'iness, *n.*
[O.E. *swāt* (n.), *swǣtan* (v.).]

Swede, *swēd, n.* a native of Sweden: (without *cap.*) a large yellow turnip.
Swēd'ish, *adj.* having to do with Sweden.—*n.* the language of Sweden.

sweep, *swēp, v.t.* to clean by using a brush or broom: to gather (together) by sweeping: to move, carry (away, along, off, etc.) with a long brushing movement, or without caring what anyone else wants (e.g. *He sweeps the things off the table and into his case; he sweeps his guest away to another room*): to clear, to rid of (e.g. *He sweeps the seas, the seas of enemy ships*): to pass over lightly or rapidly (e.g. *His fingers sweep the strings; his eyes sweep the horizon*).—*v.i.* to use a broom on floor(s), etc.: to move quickly in a proud manner (e.g. *She sweeps from the room*), or with force (e.g. *The wind sweeps over the plain*): to curve widely or stretch far (e.g. *The hills sweep down to the sea*):—*pa.p.* **swept.**—*n.* act of sweeping: a sweeping movement: movement, or range, of something turning (e.g. *the sweep of the oars*): a curve: a stretch: a chimney sweeper: (*coll.*) a sweepstake.
sweep'er, *n.*
sweep'ing, *adj.* that sweeps: (of e.g. victory, changes) very great: not taking into account the exceptions (e.g. *All men are liars is a sweeping statement*), or all the factors or evidence (e.g. *Don't make sweeping charges against me,* i.e. don't make accusations against me without looking properly at the facts).—*n.* (in *pl.*) rubbish, dust, etc.
sweep'stake(s), *n. sing.* or *pl.* a prize for, or a gamble on, a race, etc., entrants staking money which goes to the winner(s).
at one sweep, by one action, at one time.

to sweep one off one's feet, to fill one with such emotion or enthusiasm that one no longer uses common sense.

to make a clean sweep, to get rid of everything that may be considered rubbish, e.g. to turn all those of a different party, or those who are inefficient, out of office.

[Conn. with O.E. *swāpan*, to sweep.]

sweet, *swēt*, *adj.* tasting like sugar: not sour or salt: pleasant to the taste: pleasing to smell or hearing—fragrant, melodious: (of person, one's nature, an action) agreeable, kindly.—*n.* a small piece of sweet substance, e.g. of chocolate, candy: something sweet served towards the end of a meal, a pudding: a term of endearment: (in *pl.*) enjoyable things (e.g. *the sweets of victory*).

sweet'ly, *adv.* in an agreeable manner: easily, without jarring (e.g. *The machinery moves sweetly*).

sweet'ness, *n.*

sweet'en, *v.t.*, *v.i.* to make, or become, sweet or sweeter.

sweet'ener, *n.* **sweet'ening,** *n.*

sweet'heart, *n.* a person loved and loving, darling.

sweet'meat, *n.* a confection, dainty, made wholly or chiefly of sugar.

sweet pea, a climbing annual garden plant with sweet-scented flowers.

sweet potato, a plant in tropical countries whose tuber-like roots (see **tuber**) are eaten as a vegetable.

[O.E. *swēte*; conn. Ger. *süss*, L. *suāvis*.]

swell, *swel*, *v.i.* to grow larger or greater: (of the sea) to rise into waves: to bulge out: to become as if puffed out with excitement, pride, or anger: to grow louder.—*v.t.* to increase the size of, or number of: to increase the sound of:—*pa.t.* **swelled**; *pa.p.* **swollen** (*swō'lėn*), (*rare*) **swelled.**—*n.* act of swelling: a bulge: increase in size: a gradual rise in the height of the ground: waves rolling in one direction as after a storm: (*slang*) a dandy, or one fashionably and showily dressed, or an important person.—*adj.* (*slang*) fashionable, showy: (*slang*) very fine, just what is wanted.

swell'ing, *n.* action of verb to swell: an enlarged part of the body.

swoll'en, *adj.* that has swelled: become too great.

[O.E. *swellan*; conn. Ger. *schwellen*.]

swelter, *swelt'ėr*, *v.i.* to be faint or limp from heat.—*n.* intense heat.

swelt'ering, *adj.* very hot.

[O.E. *sweltan*, to die.]

swept. See **sweep.**

swerve, *swėrv*, *v.i.* to turn (from a line or course), esp. quickly: to turn aside (from the right course of action).—*n.* act of swerving. [Orig. uncertain.]

swift, *swift*, *adj.* moving, or able to move, very fast: happening or done quickly (e.g. *a swift change*): quick, ready (to do something; e.g. *swift to take offence*).—*n.* a bird that flies very rapidly and is something like the swallow, though not related.

swift'ly, *adv.* **swift'ness,** *n.*

[O.E. *swift*; same root as **swoop.**]

swig, *swig*, *n.* (*coll.*) a large drink or mouthful.—*v.t.* to gulp down:—*pr.p.* **swigg'ing**; *pa.p.* **swigged.**

[Orig. unknown.]

swill, *swil*, *v.t.* or *v.i.* to drink in quantity or greedily: to wash out, rinse.—*n.* a large drink of liquor: (partly) liquid food or kitchen waste given to pigs.

[O.E. *swilian*, to wash.]

swim, *swim*, *v.i.* to move on or in water by using hands and feet, fins, etc.: to float, not to sink: to move with a gliding motion: to be dizzy: to be covered or filled with (e.g. *greasy food that swims in fat*).—*v.t.* to cross by swimming (e.g. *to swim the river*): to make (animals) swim (across water):—*pr.p.* **swimm'ing**; *pa.t.* **swam**; *pa.p.* **swum.**—*n.* act of swimming: any motion like swimming: dizziness.

swimm'er, *n.* **swimm'ing,** *n.*, *adj.*

swimm'ingly, *adv.* in a gliding manner: smoothly, easily, with success.

swimm'ing-bath, *n.* a bath large enough for swimming in.

in the swim, in the main stream of affairs, business, fashion, etc.

[O.E. *swimman*; conn. Ger. *schwimmen*.]

swindle, *swin'dl*, *v.t.* to cheat (a person): to get (money out of a person) by cheating.—*n.* a fraud: anything not what it appears to be.

swin'dler, *n.*

[Ger. *schwindler*, a cheat.]

swine, *swīn*, *n.* a pig: (*coll.*) a low person:—*pl.* **swine.**

swi'nish (*swī'*), *adj.* low, gross, beastly.

[O.E. *swīn*; conn. Ger. *schwein*, L. *sūs*.]

swing, *swing*, *v.i.* to sway or wave to and fro, as an object hanging in air: to be hanged: to move back and forward on a swinging seat: to hang (from): to turn round a fixed point, as a ship at anchor, a door on its hinges: to turn quickly: to turn (from one opinion, etc., to another): to move forward with a steady swaying movement (e.g. *soldiers swinging along*).—*v.t.* to cause to move or sway to and fro, or round (e.g. a golf club): to cause to turn about a point: to cause (people) to come round (to e.g. an opinion): to influence the result of (e.g. *to swing the election*):—*pa.p.* **swung.**—*n.* the act of swinging: motion to and fro, or the distance covered by it: steady, swaying or marked movement.

swing'ing, *n.* and *adj.*

in full swing, going on energetically (e.g. *Work, the party, was in full swing*).

[O.E. *swingan*; conn. Ger. *schwingen*.]

swinish. See **swine.**

swipe, *swīp, n.* a blow aimed wildly.—*v.t., v.i.* to hit hard and rather wildly. [**sweep.**]

swirl, *swėrl, v.t., v.i.* to sweep along with a whirling motion.—*n.* whirling motion, as of wind or water.
[Orig. Scot.; orig. uncertain.]

swish, *swish, v.t.* to strike (something), or to cut the air with (a thin rod), making a whistling or hissing sound: to flog.—*v.i.* to move with whistling or hissing sound.—Also *n.* [Imit.]

Swiss, *swis, adj.* having to do with *Switzerland* or its people.—*n.* a native of Switzerland: a type of German spoken there.

switch, *swich, n.* a small twig, etc., that bends easily used in whipping: a device (usu. movable rails) used to change trains from one track to another: a small lever or handle for turning an electric current on or off: an act of switching: a change (*a switch of attention, support, to another person*).—*v.t.* to strike with a switch: to change from one line of rails to another: to turn (off, on, e.g. current, light) by means of a switch: to change over (e.g. *to switch the men to more urgent work*): to turn (the conversation) quickly (from one matter to another).—*v.i.* to change over (from, to).
switch′back, *n.* (*orig.*) a zigzag railway, for climbing steep hills: a steeply up-and-down railway or road.
switch′board, *n.* a board with arrangements for switching electrical currents or making connexions between telephones, etc. [Earlier *swits.*]

swivel, *swiv′l, n.* a support or base for e.g. a gun which allows it to be turned round: a connecting part between e.g. two parts of a chain which allows each part to move round separately.—*v.i.* to turn as if on a swivel:—*pr.p.* **swiv′elling**; *pa.p.* **swiv′elled.**
[Conn. with O.E. *swīfan*, revolve.]

swollen. See **swell.**

swoon, *swōōn, v.t.* to faint.—Also *n.*
[O.E. *geswōgen*, fainted.]

swoop, *swōōp, v.t.* to sweep down upon and seize (usu. with *up*; e.g. *She swoops, swoops up, the child from the sea's edge*).—*v.i.* to come down with a sweep (as a hawk on its prey).—*n.* a sudden downward rush.
at one fell swoop, all at one time, at one stroke.
[O.E. *swāpan*, to sweep; conn. **sweep.**]

swop, *swop, v.t.* to give (one thing) for another, exchange:—*pr.p.* **swopp′ing**; *pa.p.* **swopped.**—*n.* an exchange.
[M.E. *swappe*, hit, strike hands in making a bargain.]

sword, *sörd, n.* a weapon with a long blade, sharp on one or both edges: this weapon taken as a symbol of authority or war: military power.
sword dance, a dance over and between swords crossed on the ground, or in which swords are drawn.
sword′fish, *n.* a large fish with a long pointed upper jaw like a sword.
sword′-play, *n.* fencing: skilful argument.
swords′man, *n.* a man skilled in the use of a sword.
the sword of justice, the power of the law to compel people.
to cross swords, to fight: to disagree, or argue, fiercely.
[O.E. *sweord*; conn. with Ger. *schwert.*]

swore, sworn. See **swear.**

swot, *swot, v.t., v.i.* (*coll.*) to study hard, esp. by memorising, for an examination.—*n.* one who does this. [**sweat.**]

swum. See **swim.**

swung. See **swing.**

sycamore, *sik′ȧ-mōr, -mör, n.* name given to several different trees—in England, a maple (in Scotland called a plane tree), in America, a plane tree.
[Gk. *sȳkomoros.*]

sycophant, *sik′ō-fȧnt, n.* a flatterer who seeks to gain by pleasing.
[Gk. *sȳkophantēs.*]

syl-. See **syn-.**

syllable, *sil′ȧ-bl, n.* a word or part of a word uttered by only one effort of the voice (e.g. *man, thirst*, or the parts of *kind-ness, faith-ful-ness, con-ser-va-tism*).
syllab′ic, *adj.*
[Gk. *syn*, with, *lambanein*, take.]

syllabus, *sil′ȧ-bŭs, n.* a programme, e.g. of a course of lectures, or courses of study:—*pl.* **-buses.** [L.]

sylph, *silf, n.* a spirit of the air: a slender, graceful woman.
[Fr. *sylphe;* of Celtic origin.]

sylvan. Same as **silvan.**

sym-. See **syn-.**

symbol, *sim′bŏl, n.* a thing accepted as standing for another because it suggests the most important quality of the other in some way (e.g. *The cross is the symbol of Christianity*; *white is the symbol of purity*; *the dove is the symbol of peace*): a sign used as a short way of stating something, esp. in algebra or chemistry (e.g. *x is a symbol used for an unknown quantity*; *O is the symbol for oxygen*).
symbol′ic(al), *adjs.* having to do with symbol(s): (of language, or of mathematical, etc., statement) using symbols: being a symbol (of).
sym′bolise, *v.t.* to be a symbol of (e.g. *A ring symbolises love that never ends*).
sym′bolism, *n.* the practice of expressing or representing by symbols.
[Gk. *syn*, together, *ballein*, to throw.]

symmetry, *sim′i-tri, n.* the state in which two parts, on either side of a dividing line, are equal in size, shape, and position (e.g. *A larger window to the left of the door spoiled the symmetry of the front of the building*).

symmet'ric(al), *adjs.* having symmetry, not lop-sided.
symmet'rically, *adv.*
[Gk. *syn*, together, *metron*, a measure.]

sympathetic, etc. See **sympathy.**

sympathy, *sim'pȧ-thi, n.* the state of having the same feelings or outlook (e.g. *In this family parents and children are not in sympathy*): ability to understand the feelings of others: pity, sorrow for another, or an expression of this.
sympathet'ic, *adj.* showing or feeling sympathy: inclined to be in favour of (with *to, towards*; e.g. *I am sympathetic to the scheme*).
sym'pathīse, *v.i.* to feel with or for another: to express sympathy (with): to understand and approve of (with *with*; e.g. *I sympathise with your aims*).
[Gk. *syn*, with, *pathos*, suffering.]

symphony, *sim'fȯ-ni, n.* a long serious piece of music for an orchestra of many instruments, usu. in four, or three, movements: something harmonious and pleasant to the eye (e.g. *The scene was a symphony in green and gold*).
symphon'ic, *adj.* of, or like, a symphony.
[Gk. *syn*, together, *phōnē*, a sound.]

symposium, *sim-pō'zi-ŭm, n.* a collection of essays on a single subject by different writers, or a conference where opinions on a subject are gathered.
[Gk. *syn*, together, *posis*, a drinking.]

symptom, *sim(p)'tȯm, n.* something that is a usual sign (of a disease; e.g. *Spots are one symptom of measles*): a sign (of a state, usu. bad; e.g. *Small outbreaks of violence were symptoms of general unrest*).
symptomat'ic, *adj.* often in phrase **symptomatic of,** a sign or symptom of.
[Gk. *syn*, with, together, *piptein*, fall.]

syn-, *sin-, pfx.* together, with.
Before *l*, **syn-** becomes **syl-**; before *b, m, p*, **sym-**; before *s*, **sy-**. [Gk.]

synagogue, *sin'ȧ-gog, n.* a Jewish place of worship: a group of Jews gathered to worship.
[Gk. *syn*, together, *agein*, to lead.]

synchronise, *sin'krȯ-nīz, v.i.* to take place at the same time (e.g. *B's arrival at the party synchronised with A's leaving it*): to agree in time (e.g. *In the film, the movements of the hero's lips did not synchronise with the sounds supposed to come from them*).—*v.t.* to cause to happen at the same time: to cause (clocks, watches) to agree in time.
[Gk. *syn*, together, *chronos*, time.]

syncopate, *sing'kȯ-pāt, v.t.* to change the rhythm of (music) by putting the accent on beats usu. not accented.
syn'copated, *adj.* **syncopā'tion,** *n.*
[Gk. *syn*, together, *koptein*, to cut off.]

syndicate, *sin'di-kit, n.* a council or number of persons who join together to manage an important piece of business: a group of newspapers under the same management: an agency that supplies articles, photographs, etc., for publication at the same time in newspapers, etc., in different places.—*v.t.* (*-kāt*) sell, use, for publication in a number of newspapers.
[Gk. *syn*, with, together, *dikē*, justice.]

synod, *sin'ȯd, n.* a council of clergymen: among Presbyterians, a church court made up of several presbyteries.
[Gk. *syn*, together, *hodos*, a way.]

synonym, *sin'ȯ-nim, n.* a word having the same, or very nearly the same, meaning as another.
A few pairs of synonyms have exactly the same meaning (e.g. *ass, donkey*; *brave, courageous*; *to hide, to conceal*), but in most cases there is a slight difference between them.
(1) They may differ in shade of meaning (e.g. *terror* is stronger than *fear*; *conceited* shows more disapproval than *proud*).
(2) They may be alike in one sense, or a few senses, only (e.g. *ask, inquire*; both mean 'to put a question', but *ask* also means 'to beg' or 'to invite,' while *inquire* does not).
(3) One of them may be usual in a certain phrase (e.g. *to set at liberty*, not *at freedom*).
synon'ymous, *adj.* having the same meaning as (with *with*).
[Gk. *syn*, with, *onoma*, a name.]

synopsis, *si-nop'sis, n.* a short statement giving the main points (of a book, etc.): a general view of a subject (e.g. *a synopsis of the political situation*).
[Gk. *syn*, with, together, *opsis*, view.]

syntax, *sin'taks, n.* correct arrangement of words in sentence: rules governing this.
[Gk. *syn*, *tassein*, put in order.]

synthesis, *sin'thė-sis, n.* the act of making a whole by putting together its separate parts, e.g. of forming new chemicals, words (by use of pfxs., suffxs.):—*pl.* **-sēs.**
synthet'ic, *adj.* formed by synthesis: made artificially by putting different substances together—usu. like, but not the same as, the natural product (e.g. *Buna is a trademark for certain synthetic rubbers*): not natural (e.g. *a synthetic fine accent*; *synthetic charm*).
syn'thesīse, *v.t.* to make by synthesis.
[Gk. *syn*, with, together, *thesis*, a placing.]

syringe, *sir'inj, -inj', n.* a tube with a piston or a rubber bulb, by which liquids are sucked up and squirted out: a tube used by surgeons for injecting, etc.—*v.t.* to inject, or to clean, with a syringe.
[Gk. *syrinx*, *syringos*, musical pipe.]

syrup, *sir'ŭp, n.* water or the juice of fruits boiled with sugar and made thick and sticky: treacle, molasses, esp. when made pure for table use.
syr'upy, *adj.*
[Fr. *sirop*—Arabic *sharāb*.]

system, *sis'tėm, n.* an arrangement of many

parts which work together (e.g. *a system of railways*; *the solar system*; *a spy system*); the body thought of as working as a whole: a set of organs in the body that work together for one purpose (e.g. *the digestive system*): a way of organising (e.g. *a system of government*; *the feudal system*): a method of working regularly followed: orderliness (e.g. *There is no system in his work*): a way of classifying (e.g. plants), of numbering (e.g. *the decimal system*), etc.
systemat'ic, *adj.* having to do with classification: showing system: methodical, thorough.
sys'tematise (*-tīz*), *v.t.* to make into a system: to make orderly and methodical.
[Gk. *syn*, together, *histannai*, to set.]

T

T, *tē*, letter of alphabet, used in phrase **to a T,** exactly, perfectly.

tab, *tab*, *n.* a small tag, flap, or strap.
[Origin unknown.]

tabard, *tab'ȧrd*, *n.* a short, sleeveless or short-sleeved, coat with coat-of-arms on it worn by heralds. [Fr.]

tabby, *tab'i*, *n.* a striped cat, esp. female:—*pl.* **tabb'ies.**—*adj.* striped, or of mixed colouring.
tabb'y-cat, *n.* a tabby.
[Fr. *tabis*—Arabic *'attābī*, kind of silk.]

tabernacle, *tab'ėr-nȧ-kl*, *n.* (Bible; *cap.*) a tent used by the Jews as a temple in the desert: a small church.
[L. *tabernāculum*—*taberna*, hut.]

table, *tā'bl*, *n.* a piece of furniture with a flat top standing on legs: food, supply of food on table (e.g. *the pleasures of the table*): board on which a game (e.g. billiards) is played: a set of facts or figures set out in columns (e.g. *timetable*).—*v.t.* to make into a list or table: to lay on the table: to put forward (a motion) for discussion: to put off discussion of (a motion in Parliament).
tā'blecloth, *n.* cloth for covering a table.
tā'bleland, *n.* stretch of high land with a level surface.
table linen, tablecloths, napkins, etc.
tā'blespoon, *n.* large size of spoon.
tā'blespoonful, *n.* as much as will fill a tablespoon:—*pl.* **ta'blespoonfuls.**
table tennis, a game played on a table with small bats and light balls.
to turn the tables on (someone), to put (someone) in the position or state in which you have just been.
See also **tabular.**
[Fr.—L. *tabula*, board, painting.]

tableau, *tab'lō*, *n.* a striking group or scene:—*pl.* **tableaux** (*tab'lōz*).
[Fr.—same L. root as **table.**]

table d'hôte, *täb'l dōt'*, *n.* a meal of several courses at a fixed price.
[Fr., the host's table.]

tablet, *tab'lit*, *n.* a small flat surface on which to write or cut words, or paint: a small flat cake or piece of e.g. a drug in solid form, soap, chocolate: a kind of toffee.
tabloid, *tab'loid*, *n.* proprietary name (see this) for a small tablet of medicine: (*U.S.*) a small-sized newspaper giving many pictures.—*adj.* small and compressed. [**table.**]

taboo, *tȧ-bōō'*, *n.* in the South Pacific, a religious system by which the use of certain things is forbidden: any ban or refusal to permit (e.g. *She placed a taboo on the wearing of earrings in school*).—*adj.* forbidden for religious reasons or not approved by social custom (e.g. *Wine drinking is taboo among Moslems*).—*v.t.* to forbid the use of: to ban:—*pr.p.* **tabōō'ing,** ; *pa.p.* **tabooed** (*tȧ-bōōd'*).
[Polynesian *tapu.*]

tabor, *tā'bȯr*, *n.* a small drum.
[O.Fr. *tabour*; an Oriental word.]

tabu. Same as **taboo.**

tabular, *tab'ū-lȧr*, *adj.* having a flat top like a table: arranged in a table or column (e.g. *He gave the results in tabular form*).
tab'ulāte, *v.t.* to arrange (information) in lists or columns.
tabulā'tion, *n.*
[Same root as **table.**]

tacit, *tas'it*, *adj.* understood but not spoken, silent (e.g. *tacit agreement*).
tac'itly, *adv.*
tac'iturn, *adj.* not inclined to talk.
tac'iturnness, taciturn'ity, *ns.*
tac'iturnly, *adv.* silently, as if unwilling to speak.
[L. *tacēre*, *tacitum*, to be silent.]

tack[1]**,** *tak*, *n.* a short pointed nail with a flat head: in sewing, a long stitch that will later be taken out again: the direction or course of a ship moving against the wind and at an angle to it: a change of this: the run on this temporary course: one of the parts of a zigzag course on land: a course, or change of course, of action: adhesiveness, sticky condition.—*v.t.* to fasten with tacks: to sew with tacks: to change (a ship) to the opposite tack: to sail (a ship) by a series of tacks.—Also *v.i.*
tack'y, *adj.* sticky. **tack'iness,** *n.*
[O.Fr. *taque*, a nail.]

tack[2]**,** *tak*, *n.* food (*hard tack*, ship's hard biscuit). [Origin unknown.]

tackle, *tak'l*, (by seamen often *tāk'l*), *n.* ropes, rigging, etc., of a ship: tools, gear (e.g. *fishing tackle*): ropes, etc., for raising weights: (in football) act of tackling.—*v.t.* (*Rugby football*) to seize (a

player with the ball) in order to bring him down: (*Association*) to obstruct (him) in order to take the ball from him: to grapple with, try to get the better of (e.g. heavier man, problem).—Also *v.i.*
[M.E. *takel*; conn. with Middle Du.]

tact, *takt, n.* skill and care in dealing with people, so as to avoid hurting or offending.
tact'ful, *adj.* **tact'less,** *adj.*
tact'fully, *adv.* **tact'lessly,** *adv.*
tact'fulness, *n.* **tact'lessness,** *n.*
[L. *tangĕre, tactum*, to touch.]

tactics, *tak'tiks, n. sing.* the art of moving troops, ships, etc. successfully for, or in, a battle: way of acting in order to gain advantage.
tac'tical, *adj.* concerned with tactics: connected with successful planning.
tac'tically, *adv.*
tactician, *tak-tish'ȧn, n.* one good at planning in difficult circumstances.
[Gk. *taktikē* (*technē*), (art of) arranging men in battle.]

tadpole, *tad'pōl, n.* a young frog or toad in its first state.
[**toad** and **poll,** head.]

taffeta, *taf'i-tȧ, n.* a thin, shiny silk cloth.
[Pers. *tāftah*, woven.]

taffrail, *taf'rāl, n.* the rail round the stern of a ship.
[Du. *tafereel*, panel, *tafel*, table.]

Taffy, *taf'i, n.* (*coll.*) a Welshman.
[Imitation of Welsh pron. of *Davy*.]

tag, *tag, n.* a metal point at the end of a shoelace: a label: a well-known quotation, e.g. a line of verse.—*v.t.* to put tag(s) or point(s) on.—*v.i.* to attach oneself to (a person; with *on to, after*):—*pr.p.* **tagg'ing**; *pa.p.* **tagged.**
tag'rag, *n., adj.* ragtag. [**tack** (1).]

tail, *tāl, n.* the part of an animal, bird or fish that sticks out behind the rest of the body: anything like a tail in shape or position (e.g. *the tail of a kite*; *a tail of hair*): the rear or end of anything (e.g. *the tail of the queue*): (in *pl.*) the side of a coin that does not bear the head: (in *pl.*) (swallow)tail coat.—*v.t.* (*slang*) to follow closely, shadow: to take the tails off (e.g. gooseberries).
tailed, *adj.* **tail'less,** *adj.*
tail coat, a swallowtail coat, part of full evening dress for a man.
tail light, light at the back of a car, etc.
tail spin, (of aeroplane) a steep, spinning dive downwards.
tail wind, wind from behind.
to tail off, to become fewer or worse towards the end.
to turn tail, to run away.
to twist someone's tail, deliberately to annoy him.
[O.E. *tægel*.]

tailor, *tā'lȯr, n.* one who cuts out and makes suits and overcoats:—*fem.* **tail'or-ess.**—*v.t.* to make (outer clothes): to fit with these.—Also *v.i.*
tail'ored, *adj.* tailor-made: well dressed in tailor-made garments.
tail'oring, *n.* the work of a tailor.
tail'or-made, *adj.* made by a tailor.
[Fr. *tailleur—tailler*, to cut.]

taint, *tānt, v.t.* to spoil by touching with something bad: to infect.—*n.* a trace of decay or infection: a touch of evil in character or nature.
[Through O.Fr.—same root as **tinge.**]

take, *tāk, v.t.* to lay hold of, grasp: to choose (e.g. *Take a card*): to accept (something offered): to endure (e.g. blows, criticism) without showing pain, anger, etc.: to assume (e.g. *to take responsibility, a liberty*): to have room for: to swallow (food, drink): to use, etc., regularly (e.g. *to take sugar, a morning paper*): to capture: to carry away: to subtract (e.g. *Take 2 from 4*): to steal: to succeed in getting (e.g. a prize): to lead, drive, or carry (e.g. *to take pigs to market, an umbrella to church*): to employ, use (e.g. *to take a knife, care, time, strong measures*): to require (e.g. *This takes courage*): to travel by: to experience, enjoy (e.g. a rest): to feel (e.g. pride, pleasure): to begin to feel, show (e.g. courage, comfort, pity; *to take pity on*): to go to a place of (shelter): to become infected with (e.g. mumps): to understand (meaning, person in what he says).—*v.i.* to root: (of e.g. an inoculation) to be effective: to please, win approval:—*pa.t.* **took** (*took*); *pa.p.* **tā'ken.**—*n.* quantity (of e.g. fish) taken at one time.
tā'ker, *n.*
tā'king, *adj.* pleasing, attractive.—*n.* action of the verb *take*: (in *pl.*) total money taken (e.g. at a concert).
taken up with. See **to take up.**
taken with, attracted by, pleased with.
to take account of. See **account.**
to take advantage of, to use the opportunity given by (a happening or condition): to use (a person) unfairly for one's own ends.
to take after, to be like in appearance or ways.
to take a joke, to be amused, not hurt, by a joke made about oneself.
to take care of. See **care.**
to take down, to write down: to bring down to a lower place or level: to humble (a person).
to take for, to believe to be: to mistake for.
to take heed, to pay attention: to be careful.
to take ill, to become ill.
to take in, to include: to receive: to understand (e.g. *I did not take in what he said*): to make smaller: to cheat.
to take into one's head, to have a sudden idea (that), a sudden resolve (to do something).

to take it, to endure calmly, to bear it: to understand from something said, etc. (that).
to take it out of, to treat (a person) harshly, esp. because of something he has done: (of work, heat, etc.) to exhaust.
to take leave of. See **leave.**
to take (one's) life, to kill (one).
to take off, to remove: to imitate unkindly: (*flying*) to leave the ground (*n.* **take'-off**).
to take on, to undertake (a task): to accept as an opponent: to take aboard: to assume, have (e.g. a new meaning).
to take orders, to become a priest or minister: to receive, accept, instructions (from).
to take over, to take control of (e.g. a business; *n.* and *adj.* **take'-over**).
to take part, to share, help (in).
to take place, to happen.
to take to, to go, turn, to (e.g. the hills, flight) in an emergency: to begin to do, use, regularly (e.g. *to take to playing the harp, to drink*): to be attracted by.
to take up, to lift, raise: to shorten (a garment): to receive for carrying (goods), admit (passengers): to occupy (space, time, energy): to begin to learn, practise, show interest in, support (**taken up with,** giving much of one's interest to).
to take (it) upon oneself to do something, to do it when one has no right, or no wise reason.
to take exception, offence, umbrage, etc. See **except, offend, umbrage,** etc.
[Old Norse *taka.*]

talc, *talk, n.* a soft mineral, soapy to the touch.
tal'cum (pow'der), *n.* a powder made from talc.
[Fr.—Sp. *talco*—Arabic *talq.*]

tale, *tāl, n.* a story: an untrue story, lie.
tale'-bear'er, *n.* someone who gives information about others that is likely to cause trouble.
tale'-bear'ing, *n.* and *adj.*
to tell tales (out of school), to give away information that should be secret.
[O.E. *talu*, a reckoning, a tale, speech.]

talent, *tal'ėnt, n.* special skill (e.g. *a talent for drawing*): (in ancient times) a measure of weight, or the value of this weight of gold or silver.
tal'ented, *adj.* skilled, gifted.
[Gk. *talanton*, a weight, e.g. of gold.]

talisman, *tal'iz-mȧn, -is-, n.* a charm, supposed to protect the wearer:—*pl.* **tal'ismans.**
[Fr.—Arabic *tilsam*; from Late Gk.]

talk, *tök, v.i.* to speak: to gossip: to give information.—*v.t.* to express (e.g. sense): to use in speech (e.g. *to talk French*).—*n.* conversation: a discussion: a lecture: the subject of conversation: gossip.
talk'ing, *adj.* and *n.* **talk'er,** *n.*
talk'ie, *n.* (*coll.*) a talking film.
talk'ative, *adj.* in the habit of talking too much.
talk'ativeness, *n.*
a talking to, a scolding.
to talk big, to boast.
to talk down, to silence (another) by talking much oneself.
to talk over, to discuss: to persuade.
to talk round, to discuss without coming to the point: to persuade.
to talk shop. See **shop.**
[**tale** or **tell.**]

tall, *töl, adj.* high, higher than usual: hard to believe (*a tall story*).
tall'ness, *n.*
tall'boy, *n.* a high chest of drawers.
a tall order, (instructions to do, etc.) something unreasonably difficult or much.
[Origin unknown.]

tallow, *tal'ō, n.* hard fat of animals, melted and used to make candles and soap.
[Old Du. *talgh, talch.*]

tally, *tal'i, n.* (old-fashioned) a stick with notches cut in it to keep a score or account: an account: a label:—*pl.* **tall'ies.**—*v.t.* to count (up).—*v.i.* to agree (with), match (e.g. *His story tallies with yours*):—*pr.p.* **tall'ying**; *pa.p.* **tall'ied.**
[Fr. *taille*—L. *talea*, a cutting.]

tally-ho, *tal'i-hō, interj.* a cry used by huntsmen.

talon, *tal'ȯn, n.* the claw of a bird of prey, e.g. hawk.
[Fr.—L. *tālus*, the heel.]

tamable. See **tame.**

tambourine, *tam-boo-rēn', n.* a small one-sided drum with bells or jingles, played with the hand.
[Fr. *tambourin*—*tambour*, drum.]

tame, *tām, adj.* not wild: used to living with human beings: dull, not exciting.—*v.t.* to make tame: to subdue, humble (spirit, pride).
tāme'ly, *adv.* **tāme'ness,** *n.*
tā'mer, *n.* one who tames.
tām'able, tame'able, *adj.*
[O.E. *tam*; conn. with Ger. *zahm.*]

Tamil, *tam'il n.* a language of south-east India and north, east, and central Ceylon.

tamper, *tam'pėr, v.i.* to meddle (with) so as to damage, alter, etc.: to influence secretly, unfairly (with *with*; e.g. *to tamper with a witness*). [**temper.**]

tan, *tan, v.t.* to turn (an animal's skin) into leather by treating it e.g. with bark containing tannin: to make brown, to sunburn: (*coll.*) to beat.—*v.i.* to become brown, tanned:—*pr.p.* **tann'ing**; *pa.p.* **tanned.**—*n.* yellowish-brown colour: sunburn.
tann'er, *n.* one whose work is tanning.
tann'ing, *n.* and *adj.*
tann'ery, *n.* place where leather is made.
tann'in, *n.* any of a number of related substances obtained from plants, used in

tanning, dyeing, etc.: one of these, present in tea.
[O.E. *tannian.*]

tandem, *tan′dem, adv.* (e.g. of horses) harnessed one behind the other.—*n.* a pair or team of horses harnessed one behind the other: a bicycle with two seats so arranged.
[Orig. joke; L. *tandem,* at length (time).]

tang, *tang, n.* a prong or tapering part of a knife or tool that fits into the handle: a strong taste, flavour, or smell (e.g. *a tang of the sea*).
tang′y, *adj.* **tang′iness,** *n.*
[Old Norse *tangi.*]

tangent, *tan′jėnt, n.* a line which touches a curve but does not cut it.
to go off at a tangent, to go off suddenly in another direction, or on a different line of thought. [Root as **tangible.**]

tangerine, *tan-jė-rēn′, tan′, n.* a small orange, orig. from *Tangier* (Morocco).

tangible, *tan′ji-bl, adj.* able to be felt by touch: real, definite (e.g. *tangible gains*).
[L. *tangĕre, tactum,* to touch.]

tangle¹, *tang′gl, n.* an untidy, confused knot or state.—*v.t., v.i.* to twist, knot, together: to make, or become, difficult.
[Origin uncertain.]

tangle², *tang′gl, n.* certain large seaweeds.
[Through Scot.—Scand.]

tango, *tang′gō, n.* a dance of S. American origin.—*v.i.* to perform this dance. [Sp.]

tank, *tangk, n.* a large container for liquids or gas: a large armoured car on caterpillar wheels, mounted with guns.
tank′er, *n.* ship, etc., for carrying liquids, esp. oil: aircraft used to transport fuel.
[L. *stagnum,* stagnant pool.]

tankard, *tangk′ård, n.* a large metal (or glass) drinking-mug.
[O.Fr. *tanquard.*]

tanner¹, *tan′ėr, n.* (*slang*) a sixpence.

tanner², tannin, etc. See **tan.**

tansy, *tan′zi, n.* a plant with small yellow flowers.
[Gk. *athanasia,* immortality.]

tantalise, *tan′tå-līz, v.t.* to tease, torment, by offering something and keeping it just out of reach.
tantalis′ing, *adj.*
[*Tantalus* in Gk. story, made to stand in water with fruit above his head, unable to reach either water or fruit.]

tantamount, *tan′tå-mount, adj.* (with *to*) the same as in effect, meaning, etc. (e.g. *This humbler speech was tantamount to an admission that he had been wrong*).
[O.Fr. *tant,* so much, *amonter,* amount.]

tantrum, *tan′trŭm, n.* a fit, outburst, of bad temper. [Orig. unknown.]

tap¹, *tap, n.* a light knock or touch.—*v.t.* to strike lightly.—*v.i.* to give a gentle knock:—*pr.p.* **tapp′ing**; *pa.p.* **tapped.**
tap dance, a dance done with special shoes that make a tapping noise.
[Fr. *taper*; a Germanic word.]

tap², *tap, n.* a stopper or screw to control the flow of liquid or gas.—*v.t.* to draw off (liquid) by opening a tap: to get liquid from (a container) by piercing it or by opening a tap: to draw from (any rich source, e.g. a region of the country): (*slang*) to get money from (a person) as a loan or gift: to take off a message secretly from (telephone wires):—*pr.p.* **tapp′ing**: *pa.p.* **tapped.**
tapp′ing, *n., adj.* **tap′ster,** *n.* barman.
tap′room, *n.* room where beer is served from the cask.
on tap, ready to be drawn off from the cask: ready for immediate use.
[O.E. *tæppe.*]

tape, *tap, n.* a narrow strip of cloth used for tying, binding, etc.: a piece of string stretched above the finishing line on a race track: a narrow strip of paper, plastic, or metal, as *ticker tape* (see this), *adhesive tape, video tape* (see this).
taped, *adj.* (*slang*) recorded on magnetic tape: (*slang*) sized up: (*slang*) arranged to one's liking.
tape measure, tape, marked with inches, etc., for measuring.—Also **tape′line.**
tape recorder, a machine which records sounds on magnetised tape, so that they can be played back later.
tape′worm, *n.* a worm, often very long, found in intestines of men and animals.
red tape. See **red.**
[O.E. *tæppe,* band; L. root as **tapestry.**]

taper, *tā′pėr, n.* a long, thin wax candle or light.—*v.t., v.i.* to make, or to become, thinner towards the end.
tā′pering, *adj.* growing gradually thinner.—Also *n.*
[O.E. *tapor.*]

tapestry, *tap′is-tri, n.* a cloth with a picture woven into it, hung on wall or used to cover furniture:—*pl.* **-ies.**
[Through O.Fr., L., Gk.—Pers.]

tapeworm. See **tape.**

tapioca, *tap-i-ō′kå, n.* a white starchy food obtained from the underground part of the cassava plant.
[Brazilian *tipioka.*]

tapir, *tā′pėr, n.* wild animal of S. America rather like a pig. [Brazilian.]

taproom, etc. See **tap** (2).

tar, *tär, n.* any of a number of thick, dark, sticky mixtures obtained from wood, coal, etc.: (*slang*) a sailor.—*v.t.* to smear with tar:—*pr.p.* **tarr′ing**; *pa.p.* **tarred.**
tarr′y, *adj.* **tarr′iness,** *n.*
to tar and feather, to punish by smearing with tar and covering with feathers.
to be tarred with the same brush, stick, to have the same faults (as someone else).
[O.E. *teoru, teru.*]

tarantula, *tå-ran′tū-lå, n.* a poisonous spider found in S. Italy.
[*Taranto,* town in S. Italy.]

tardy, *tär′di, adj.* slow: late:—*comp.*

tar′dier; *superl.* **tar′diest.**
tar′dily, *adv.* **tar′diness,** *n.*
[L. *tardus.*]

tare[1], *tăr, n.* (*Bible*) a weed growing among corn: a vetch. [Orig. uncertain.]

tare[2], *tăr, n.* weight of container (e.g. truck) when empty: deduction for this. [Fr.; through Sp. from Arabic.]

target, *tär′git, n.* orig. a small shield: a mark, or position, to be shot, or aimed, at: a result, etc., aimed at: a person, etc., made the object of unfriendly remarks or conduct (e.g. *She made him a target for her scorn, for practical jokes*).
[O.E. *targe.*]

tariff, *tar′if, n.* a list of charges or prices: a list of taxes to be paid on goods.
[Arabic *ta'rīf*, giving information.]

tarmac(adam), *tär′mak(ad′àm), n.* a macadamised surface bound with tar.

tarn, *tärn, n.* a small mountain lake.
[Old Norse *tjörn.*]

tarnish, *tär′nish, v.t.* to make (metal) dull or discoloured: to stain (e.g. one's reputation).—*v.i.* to become dull or stained.—*n.* film on metal: stain.
[Fr. *ternir.*]

tarpaulin, *tar-pö′lin, n.* a strong cloth made waterproof e.g. by coating with tar.
[**tar,** and dial. *pauling*, cart cover.]

tarry[1]. See **tar.**

tarry[2], *tar′i, v.i.* to be slow: to wait (for): to stay:—*pr.p.* **tarr′ying**; *pa.p.* **tarr′ied.**
[M.E. *targen*, to delay—L. as **tardy.**]

tart[1], *tärt, adj.* sharp or sour: sharp in spirit (e.g. *a tart reply*).
tart′ly, *adv.* **tart′ness,** *n.*
[O.E. *teart*—*teran*, to tear.]

tart[2], *tärt, n.* a pie containing fruit or jam.
tart′let, *n.* a small tart.
[O.Fr. *tarte*; orig. uncertain.]

tartan, *tär′tàn, n.* a woollen cloth with a pattern in different colours consisting of lines at right angles to each other, worn orig. in the Scottish Highlands: any cloth with such a pattern: any one of the patterns (e.g. *the Cameron tartan*).
[Middle Fr. *tiretaine*, kind of cloth.]

Tartar, *tär′tàr, n.* (more correctly **Tatar,** *tä′tàr*) in old times a native of *Ta(r)tary* in Central Asia, noted for fierceness: now, a difficult, fierce, irritable person.

tartar, *tär′tàr, n.* a substance that forms inside wine casks: a hard substance that gathers on the teeth.
tartar′ic, *adj.* obtained from tartar.
cream of tartar. See **cream.**
[Fr. *tartre.*]

task, *tâsk, n.* a set amount of work: a duty: any work, esp. hard.—*v.t.* to set a task for: to put a strain on (e.g. one's powers).
task′master, *n.* one who sets a task.
task force (*U.S.*), a combined land, sea and air force under one commander, with one special task to carry out.
to take to task, to find fault with.
[O.Fr. *tasque*; same L. root as **tax.**]

tassel, *tas′l, n.* an ornament made from a bunch of silk or other threads tied together at one end: flower group like this e.g. a larch, hazel, catkin.
tass′elled, *adj.* hung with tassels.
[O.Fr.]

taste, *tāst, v.t.* to try by eating or drinking a little: to recognise (a flavour; e.g. *I can taste ginger in this cake*): to eat or drink a little of: to experience (e.g. *He has tasted success*).—*v.i.* to have a flavour (of; e.g. *This tastes of onion*): to have a certain kind of flavour (e.g. *to taste sour*): to try a little (of): to distinguish flavours.—*n.* act or sense of tasting: a flavour: a small quantity: liking, preference (e.g. *a taste for music*): judgment, sense of what is beautiful, etc. (e.g. *good taste in dress*).
taste′ful, *adj.* showing good taste.
taste′fully, *adv.* **taste′fulness,** *n.*
taste′less, *adj.* without flavour: not in good taste.
taste′lessly, *adv.* **taste′lessness,** *n.*
tas′ter, *n.* one whose work is to taste and judge tea or wine.
tas′ty, *adj.* savoury, having a good taste:—*comp.* **tas′tier**; *superl.* **tas′tiest.**
tas′tiness, *n.*
to one's taste, to one's liking.
[O.Fr. *taster*, touch, taste.]

Tatar. See **Tartar.**

tatter, *tat′ėr, n.* a torn piece: a rag.
tatt′ered, *adj.* in tatters or rags.
[M.E., of Scand. origin.]

tatting, *tat′ing, n.* knotted thread work or lace: act of making this.
tat, *v.i.* to do tatting. [Orig. unknown.]

tattle, *tat′l, n.* idle chatter.—*v.i.* to gossip: to let out secrets.
tatt′ler, *n.* [Imit.]

tattoo[1], *tà-to͞o′, n.* a signal at night by drum and bugle to call soldiers to quarters: a soldiers' outdoor display with music:—*pl.* **tattoos′.**
the devil's tattoo, drumming the fingers e.g. on a table.
[Du. *taptoe*, the tap (room is) shut.]

tattoo[2], *tà-to͞o′, v.t.* to make a pattern on the skin of (e.g. person, arm) by pricking it and putting in colouring: to make (a pattern) in this way:—*pr.p.* **tattoo′ing**; *pa.p.* **tattooed′** (*-to͞od′*; also *adj.*).
[*tatū*, native word in Tahiti.]

taught. See **teach.**

taunt, *tönt, v.t.* to tease, jeer at, unkindly.—*n.* a jeering remark.
taun′ter, *n.* **taun′tingly,** *adv.*
[16th century; orig. uncertain.]

taut, *töt, adj.* drawn tight: (of e.g. nerves) in a state of strain.
taut′en, *v.t., v.i.* to make, or become, taut.
[Perh. O.E. *togen*, drawn, and **tight.**]

tavern, *tav′ėrn, n.* a place where wines and spirits are sold and drunk: an inn.
[Fr. *taverne*—L. *taberna.*]

tawdry, *tö'dri, adj.* showy, cheap, flashy :—*comp.* **taw'drier** ; *superl.* **taw'driest.**
taw'drily, *adv.* **taw'driness,** *n.*
[*St. Audrey* (*lace*), 16th century woman's neck tie.]

tawny, *tö'ni, adj.* yellowish-brown, as if tanned.
taw'niness, *n.*
[Fr. *tanner*, to tan.]

tax, *taks, n.* a government charge on certain things to provide money for the state : a strain, burden (e.g. *Delay is a tax on my patience*).—*v.t.* to lay a tax on : to put a strain on (e.g. *to tax one's strength*) : to accuse of (with *with* ; e.g. *Tax him with having spilt the ink*).
tax'able, *adj.* liable to be taxed.
taxā'tion, *n.* act or system of taxing.
tax'-free, *adj.* not taxed.
tax'-gath'erer, *n.* one who collects taxes.
tax'payer, *n.* one who pays taxes.
[O.Fr. *taxe*—L. *taxāre*, charge.]

taxi(cab), *tak'si(-kab), n.* a car which may be hired with driver.—*v.i.* **(taxi)** go by taxi : (of aircraft) to run along the ground :—*pr.p.* **tax'iing** ; *pa.p.* **tax'ied.**
[**taximeter.**]

taxidermy, *tak'si-dėr-mi, n.* act of preparing and stuffing skins of animals, etc.
tax'idermist, *n.* one who does this work.
[Gk. *taxis*, arrangement, *derma*, skin.]

taximeter, *tak'si-mē-tėr, tak-sim'ė-tėr, n.* an instrument fitted to some cars to show the fare due for the distance travelled.
[Fr. *taxe*, price, Gk. *metron*, measure.]

tea, *tē, n.* a shrub grown in parts of Asia, esp. India, Ceylon, and China : its dried and prepared leaves : a drink made by adding boiling water to the dried leaves : a drink like tea in appearance (e.g. *beef tea*) or made in the same way (e.g. *camomile tea*) : an afternoon meal at which tea is drunk.
tea caddy, caddy (see this).
tea cosy, cosy (see this).
tea'cup, *n.* a cup of moderate size from which tea is drunk.
tea'cupful, *n.* as much as fills a teacup :—*pl.* **tea'cupfuls.**
tea party, an afternoon party at which tea is served.
tea'pot, *n.* a pot with a spout, used for making and pouring out tea.
tea'room, *n.* restaurant where tea, etc., may be had.
tea rose, rose that smells like tea.
tea service, set, articles (teapot, cups, etc. ; not cutlery) used at tea.
tea'spoon, *n.* a small spoon used with a teacup.
tea'spoonful, *n.* as much as fills a teaspoon :—*pl.* **tea'spoonfuls.**
tea'-urn, *n.* urn for making tea.
(not) one's cup of tea, (*slang*) (not) to one's liking.
[From South Chinese *te* (pron. *tā*).]

teach, *tēch, v.t.* to give (a person) knowledge or skill : to give knowledge of (e.g. *to teach French*) : to explain, show (that, how to) : to train in (e.g. *Life teaches patience*).—*v.i.* to be a teacher :—*pa.p.* **taught** (*töt*).
teach'able, *adj.* able or willing to learn.
teach'er, *n.* one whose profession, or talent, is to give knowledge or skill.
teach'ing, *adj.*—*n.* the work of a teacher : act of giving knowledge or skill : (often in *pl.*) beliefs, rules of conduct, etc., preached or taught.
[O.E. *tǣcan.*]

teacup. See **tea.**

teak, *tēk, n.* an East Indian tree : its very hard wood : also an African tree.
[*tēkkȧ* (name in S. Indian language).]

team, *tēm, n.* a group of people acting together : a side in a game (e.g. *a football team*) : two or more animals working together (e.g. *a team of horses*).
team'ster, *n.* one who drives a team.
team spirit, willingness to work loyally as a team, or as a member of a team.
team'work, *n.* work for which a team is required : working together : quality of this (e.g. *good teamwork*).
to team with, to join forces with.
[O.E. *tēam*, children, a family.]

teapot. See **tea.**

tear[1], *tēr, n.* a drop of liquid coming from the eye : (in *pl.*) grief.
tear'ful, *adj.* inclined to weep, or to cause tears.
tear'fully, *adv.* **tear'fulness,** *n.*
tear'less, *adj.* shedding, or causing, no tears.
tear gas, a gas causing blinding tears, used against e.g. rioters.
tear'stained, marked with tears.
in tears, weeping.
[O.E. *tēar.*]

tear[2], *tār, v.t.* to pull with force (apart, away, down, etc.) : to make a rent in : to wound (e.g. *The story tears my heart*). —*v.i.* to have rent(s) made in it : (*coll.*) to move or act with great speed or force : —*pa.t.* **tore** (*tōr, tör*) ; *pa.p.* **torn** (*tōrn, törn*).—*n.* a rent : (*coll.*) a rush.
[O.E. *teran.*]

tearoom. See **tea.**

tease, *tēz, v.t.* to pull out (wool) with a comb : to sort out (a tangle) : to annoy, irritate on purpose : to pretend playfully to do so.—*n.* one who teases.
[O.E. *tǣsan*, to pluck.]

teasel, *tēz'l, n.* a plant with large prickly heads.
[O.E. *tǣs(e)l*—same root as **tease.**]

teaspoon, etc. See **tea.**

teat, *tēt, n.* the part of the breast through which the young suck milk : the rubber end of a baby's feeding-bottle.
[O.E. *tit.*]

teazle. Same as **teasel.**

technical, *tek'ni-kȧl, adj.* belonging to a particular art, skill, etc. (e.g. *the technical*

terms used by artists, by civil engineers): having special knowledge of a practical art (e.g. *a technical expert in electrical devices*): having to do with technique (e.g. *This technical advance*—i.e. advance in method or equipment—*made the work easier*): judged by strict laws or rules (e.g. *This was a technical assault, defeat*).
tech′nically, *adv.*
technical′ity, *n.* a technical detail, or term:—*pl.* **-ities.**
technician, *tek-nish′ȧn, n.* one having trained skill in the practical side of an art.
technique, *tek-nēk′, n.* the way in which a skilled process is carried out (e.g. *His technique as a pianist is faultless*).
technol′ogy, *n.* (study of) science applied to practical purposes.
technolog′ical, *adj.* **technol′ogist,** *n.*
[Gk. *technē*, art; conn. *tiktein*, produce.]

ted, *ted, v.t.* to spread or turn, as cut grass, for drying:—*pr.p.* **tedd′ing**; *pa.p.* **tedd′ed.**
tedd′er, *n.* a machine for spreading hay.
[Scand.]

teddy(-bear), *ted′i(-bār), n.* a stuffed toy bear.
[After U.S. President Theodore (*Teddy*) Roosevelt, who hunted big game.]

Te Deum, *tē dē′ŭm, n.* a hymn of praise and thanksgiving beginning *Te Deum laudamus*, 'We praise thee, O God.'

tedious, *tē′di-ŭs, adj.* tiresome, long-lasting and slow.
tē′diously, *adv.* **tē′diousness,** *n.*
tē′dium, *n.* tediousness.
[L. *taedium* (n.)—*taedet*, it wearies.]

tee, *tē, n.* (*golf*) the peg or heap of sand on which the ball is placed for the first stroke at each hole: the level ground where this is used.—*v.t.* to place (ball) on the tee.
[Prob. from letter *T*.]

teem[1], *tēm, v.i.* to be full of, swarm (with).
[O.E. *tēam*, offspring; as **team.**]

teem[2], *tēm, v.i.* (*dial.*) to rain heavily.
[Old Norse *tæma*—*tōmr*, empty.]

teens, *tēnz, n.pl.* the years of one's age from thir*teen* to nine*teen*.
teen′age, *adj.* suitable for, or characteristic of, persons between these ages.
teen′ager, *n.* a person in the teens.

teeth, teething. See **tooth.**

teetotal(l)er, *tē-tō′tȧl-ėr, n.* one who never takes an alcoholic drink.
teetō′tal, *adj.* never taking alcohol: complete, entire. [**total.**]

tele-, *tel-i-,* (as part of word) at a distance.
telecast, *tel′i-kâst, n.* a *tele*vision broad*cast*.—Also *v.t.*
telegram, *tel′i-gram, n.* message sent by telegraph.
telegraph, *tel′i-grâf, n.* an instrument or system for sending messages to a distance, esp. using wires and electricity. —*v.t.* to send (a message) by telegraph: to inform by telegraph (that).
telegraph′ic, *adj.*
teleg′raphist, *n.* one who works a telegraph.
teleg′raphy, *n.* art of making or using telegraphs.
telegraphic address, a shortened address (e.g. of a business firm) used in telegraphing.
telepathy, *ti-lep′ȧ-thi, n.* passage of thought from one person to another without the help of hearing, sight, or other physical sense.
telepath′ic, *adj.*
telephone, *tel′i-fōn, n.* instrument for speaking to a person at a distance by sending an electric current along a wire, or by sending out radio waves.—*v.i., v.t.,* to send (a message) by telephone.
telephon′ic (-*fon′***),** *adj.*
telephonist, *ti-lef′ȯn-ist, n.* one whose work is operating a telephone switchboard.
teleph′ony, *n.* the use of a telephone system for sending messages.
telephotography, *tel-i-fō-tog′rȧ-fi, n.* the taking of photographs at a distance (but within sight) using a special **tel′epho′to lens**: (sometimes) sending pictures, etc. by telegraph.
teleprinter, *tel′i-prin-tėr, n.* a telegraph system in which messages are sent out at one place, and received and printed at another, by instruments resembling typewriters.
telescope, *tel′i-skōp, n.* an instrument using a lens or a mirror to make distant things seem larger and nearer.—*v.t.* to push together so that one thing slides inside another as do parts of a small jointed telescope: to crush into each other with force (e.g. *The crash telescoped the coaches*): to run together in thought, etc. (e.g. *His memory telescoped events really separated by several years*).—*v.i.* to be pushed, crushed, or run, together.
telescop′ic (-*skop′***),** *adj.*
television, *tel-i-vizh′ȯn, n.* the sending from a distance, and reproduction as pictures on a screen, of view(s) of still or moving objects: this system: a television receiving set.
tel′evise, *v.t.* to send out a view of (e.g. a golf match) by television.
[Gk. *tēle*, at a distance (*gramma*, letter; *graphein*, to write; *pathos*, feeling; *phōnē*, voice; *skopeein*, to look at.]

tell, *tel, v.t.* to say in words (e.g. the truth, a lie): to give the facts of (a story): to make known (e.g. *to tell what has happened*): to inform (e.g. person): to order, command (e.g. person): to make out, distinguish (e.g. *I cannot tell what it is, tell one from the other*): to count (e.g. *to tell one's beads*).—*v.i.* to make known something one should not: to have a marked effect or result (e.g. *Perseverance tells*):—*pa.p.* **told** (*tōld*).
tell′er, *n.* one who tells: a bank clerk

who receives and pays out money: one who counts votes in an election.
tell'ing, *n.*—*adj.* having a marked effect.
tell'tale, *n.* one who gives away private information about others.—*adj.* giving information not intended to be given (e.g. *telltale jam on the child's face*).
all told, counting all (e.g. *an audience of nine persons all told*).
to tell off, to count off: to choose for duty (e.g. *She told off two of us to stoke the fires*): (*coll.*) to scold (*n.* **telling-off**).
to tell on, to have an effect on.
[O.E. *tellan.*]

temerity, *ti-mer'i-ti, n.* rashness.
[L. *temere,* by chance, rashly.]

temper, *tem'pėr, v.t.* to bring to the right degree of hardness, etc. by heating and cooling (e.g. *to temper steel*): to make less severe (e.g. *to temper the wind to the shorn lamb*).—*n.* the amount of hardness, etc., of a material such as metal, glass: disposition, usual state of mind: mood: anger: tendency to anger.
tem'pered, *adj.* having usu. a certain state of mind (e.g. *a good-tempered man*): brought to a certain temper, as steel.
in a temper, out of temper, angry, irritated.
to lose one's temper, to show anger.
[L. *temperāre,* to combine, mix, properly, to be moderate.]

temperament, *tem'pėr-ȧ-mėnt, n.* natural quality of mind and feeling, disposition (e.g. *The deer had a nervous temperament*): unusual nature not restrained by ordinary rules of behaviour.
temperament'al, *adj.* having to do with temperament: showing quick changes of mood: excitable, irritable.
temperament'ally, *adv.* by temperament (e.g. *She is excitable and therefore temperamentally unfit to be a nurse*).
[Same root as **temper.**]

temperance, *tem'pėr-ȧns, n.* moderation and self-control in action or speech (e.g. in eating, criticism): moderation in taking alcoholic drinks: also habit of never taking them.
temperate, *tem'pėr-it, adj.* moderate in passions or appetites: not extremely hot or cold (e.g. *Britain has a temperate climate*).
tem'perately, *adv.* **tem'perateness,** *n.*
tem'perature (*-pri-chůr*), *n.* degree of heat or cold: a body heat above normal.
temperate zones, the parts of the earth's surface between the Tropic of Cancer and the Arctic Circle and between the Tropic of Capricorn and the Antarctic Circle.
[Same root as **temper.**]

tempest, *tem'pest, n.* a violent storm with high wind.
tempes'tūous, *adj.* very stormy: like, or (of person) behaving like, a tempest.
tempes'tūously, *adv.*
tempes'tūousness, *n.*
[L. *tempestās,* time, weather, storm.]

template, *tem'plāt, n.* a pattern, usu. cut from a thin plate, by means of which the shape of something to be made can be marked out.—Also **templet** (*-plit*).
[L. *templum,* small timber.]

temple[1], *tem'pl, n.* a building in which people worship: a church.
[L. *templum.*]

temple[2], *tem'pl, n.* either of the flat parts of the head above the cheekbones.
[O.Fr.—L. *tempora,* the temples.]

templet. See **template.**

tempo, *tem'pō, n.* speed at which music should be played: speed of any activity.
[It.]

temporal, *tem'pȯ-rȧl, adj.* belonging to time: concerned with this life, not eternity: secular, not spiritual.
tem'porary, *adj.* lasting, used, only for a time.
tem'porarily, *adv.* for the time being (e.g. *The line is temporarily out of order*).
tem'porise (*-īz*), *v.i.* to speak or act vaguely, evasively, avoid deciding or promising anything: to yield for the time being.
[Fr.—L. *tempus, temporis,* time.]

tempt, *temt, v.t.* to try to persuade, or to entice, esp. to evil: to attract.
temptā'tion, *n.* act of tempting: state of being tempted: something that tempts: temptingness.
temp'ter, temp'tress (*fem.*), *ns.*
temp'ting, *adj.* attractive.
temp'tingly, *adv.* **temp'tingness,** *n.*
[O.Fr. *tempter*—L. *tentāre,* feel, test.]

ten, *ten, adj.* and *n.* the number next above nine (10 or X).
tenth, *adj.* last of ten.—*n.* one of ten equal parts.
ten'fold (*-fōld*), *adj., adv.* (so as to be) ten times as much or as many (e.g. *a tenfold increase; it increased tenfold*).
[O.E. *tēn*; conn. Ger. *zehn,* L. *decem.*]

tenable, *ten'ȧ-bl, tēn'-, adj.* (of position, theory) able to be held or defended.
[Fr.—L. *tenēre,* to hold.]

tenacious, *ten-ā'shůs, adj.* keeping a firm hold (often with *of*): sticky, adhesive: (of memory) holding facts for a long time: determined, persevering, obstinate.
tenā'ciously, *adv.*
tenā'ciousness, tenacity (*-as'-*), *ns.*
[Same L. root as **tenable.**]

tenant, *ten'ȧnt, n.* one who pays rent to another for the use of a house, building, land, etc.
ten'ancy, *n.* the holding of a house, etc., by a tenant: period of this.
ten'anted, *adj.* occupied.
ten'antless, *adj.* without a tenant.
ten'antry, *n.* all the tenants on an estate.
[Same root as **tenable.**]

tench, *tensh, -ch, n.* a freshwater fish.
[O.Fr. *tenche*—L. *tinca.*]

tend[1], *tend, v.t.* to take care of, look after.
ten′der, *n.* one who tends: small craft that carries stores, etc., for a larger one: truck with coal and water attached to steam railway engine.
[Shortened from **attend.**]

tend[2], *tend, v.i.* to move, lean, slope, in a certain direction (with *towards*): to be inclined, likely (to have a certain result, or to end in a certain way; e.g. *His actions tend to cause trouble*; *a course tending to disaster*): to have a leaning, natural readiness (to; e.g. *He tends to take a gloomy view*).
ten′dency, *n.* :—*pl.* **ten′dencies.**
[L. *tendĕre, tensum*, stretch, extend, go.]

tender[1]. See **tend** (1).

tender[2], *ten′dėr, v.t.* to offer: to present formally (e.g. one's resignation).—*v.i.* to make an offer (*for* work, a contract—e.g. to offer to do a piece of work at a certain price).—*n.* an offer.
legal tender, coins which must be accepted when offered in payment (e.g. *Farthings are no longer legal tender*; *small coins are legal tender for small sums only*).
[Same root as **tend** (2).]

tender[3], *ten′dėr, adj.* soft, not hard or tough: easily hurt or damaged: hurting when touched: very young: easily moved to feel pity, love, etc.: showing care, love, etc.: gentle.
ten′derly, *adv.* **ten′derness,** *n.*
ten′derfoot, *n.* a beginner.
ten′der-hear′ted, *adj.* full of kind feeling and sympathy.
[Fr. *tendre*—L. *tener*.]

tendon, *ten′dȯn, n.* a sinew, a tough cord or band joining a muscle to a bone or other part.
[Same root as **tend** (2).]

tendril, *ten′dril, n.* a thin curling part of a plant by which it holds to a support.
[Orig. uncertain.]

tenement, *ten′i-mėnt, n.* property (piece of land, house, flat): a high building divided into flats, each occupied by a different tenant.
[Same root as **tenant, tenable.**]

tenet, *tē′nėt, ten′, n.* political, religious, etc., belief held by person, group.
[Same root as **tenable.**]

tenfold. See **ten.**

tennis, *ten′is, n.* a game for two to four persons, using a ball and rackets, orig. one played in a building of special shape, now usu. one played outside on a lawn, etc. (in full, *lawn tennis*).
tennis court, a place prepared for tennis.
[Fr. *tenir*, hold—L. root as **tenable.**]

tenon, *ten′ȯn, n.* a projection at the end of a piece of wood shaped to fit a *mortise* (see this).
[Fr.—same root as **tenable.**]

tenor, *ten′ȯr, n.* the general course (e.g. *the even tenor of country life*): the general meaning (e.g. *the tenor of his remarks*): the highest normal man's voice; a musical part for such a voice: a man who sings this part.—Also *adj.*
[L., course—same root as **tenable.**]

tense[1], *tens, n.* the form of a verb that shows time of action (e.g. *'I am' is in the present tense, 'I was' is in the past*).
[O.Fr. *tens*—L. *tempus*, time.]

tense[2], *tens, adj.* (of e.g. rope) tightly stretched: nervous, strained (e.g. *tense with excitement*; *a tense moment*).
tense′ly, *adv.* **tense′ness,** *n.*
ten′sion, *n.* act of stretching: tenseness: mental strain.
[Same root as **tend** (2).]

tent, *tent, n.* a movable shelter made usu. of canvas supported by pole(s).
tent peg, pin, a strong peg of wood or iron fixed in the ground to which a tent rope is fastened.
[Fr. *tente*—L. root as **tend** (2).]

tentacle, *ten′tȧ-kl, n.* a long thin bendable part of an animal, used to feel, etc. (e.g. an arm of an octopus), or something that suggests it.
[Fr. *tentacule*—L. root as **tempt.**]

tentative, *ten′tȧ-tiv, adj.* made, etc., as a trial, as something that can be withdrawn if not approved of (e.g. *a tentative offer, suggestion*): uncertain, hesitating.
ten′tatively, *adv.* **ten′tativeness,** *n.*
[Same L. root as **tempt.**]

tenterhook, *ten′tėr-hook, n.* a sharp hooked nail used to hold cloth stretched.
to be on tenterhooks, to be in a state of great anxiety about what will happen.
[Root as **tend** (2), and **hook.**]

tenth. See **ten.**

tenuous, *ten′ū-ŭs, adj.* thin or weak (e.g. *the tenuous threads of the spider's web*; *a tenuous hold on life*).
[L. *tenuis*, drawn out, thin, slight.]

tenure, *ten′ūr, n.* the holding of property, or of an office or employment: the conditions, or the period, of this.
[Fr.—L. *tenēre*, hold; root as **tenable.**]

tepid, *tep′id, adj.* slightly warm, lukewarm: not enthusiastic (e.g. *a tepid welcome*).
tep′idly, *adv.*
tepid′ity, tep′idness, *ns.*
[L. *tepidus*.]

tercentenary, *tėr-sen-tē′nȧ-ri*, or *-ten′*, or *-sen′*, *n.* the 300th anniversary.—Also *adj.*
[L. *ter*, thrice, and **centenary.**]

term, *tėrm, n.* a length of time (e.g. *his term of office*; *a term of three years*): certain days on which rent is paid: a division of a school, etc., year: a word or expression (e.g. *a scientific term*): (usu. in *pl.*) a condition (e.g. *the terms of the agreement*): (in *pl.*) fixed charges: footing, nature of relationship between persons, etc. (e.g. *on friendly, good, bad, terms*; *equal terms*, neither party having an advantage).—*v.t.* to name, call.
terminol′ogy, *n.* the special words and

expressions used in a particular art, science, etc.
terms of reference. See **reference.**
in terms of, from the point of view of (e.g. *He judged everything in terms of money*—i.e. of money gained or lost—*not in terms of human happiness*).
to come to terms, make terms, to reach an agreement.
[Fr. *terme*—L. root as **terminate.**]

termagant, *tėr′mȧ-gȧnt, n.* a bad-tempered, violent woman.
[*Termagant, Tervagant,* a violent god supposed by Mediaeval Christians to be worshipped by Mohammedans.]

terminable, etc. See **terminate.**

terminate, *tėr′mi-nāt, v.t.* to put an end to (e.g. a discussion, treaty, life): to be, or be at, the end or limit of.—*v.i.* to come to an end either in space or in time.
terminā′tion, *n.* act of ending: end.
ter′minable, *adj.* (of agreement, etc.) that may come, be brought, to an end.
ter′minal, *adj.* having to do with, or growing at, the end.—*n.* an end: a point of connexion in an electric circuit: a terminus: an airport when considered as the end of a long-distance flight.
ter′minus, *n.* the end: one of the end places or points on a railway, etc.
[*L. terminus,* boundary.]

termite, *tėr′mīt, n.* a pale insect a little like an ant (hence called *white ant*) which eats wood, etc.
[Late L. *termites* (*pl.*)—*terĕre,* to bore.]

tern, *tėrn, n.* a sea bird, smaller than a gull, with forked tail.
[Conn. Dan. *terne.*]

terrace, *ter′ės, n.* a raised level bank of earth: any raised flat place: a row of houses.—*v.t.* to form into a terrace or terraces.
[Fr. *terrasse*—L. *terra,* the earth.]

terra-cotta, *ter′ȧ-cot′ȧ, n.* clay burned in a kiln, brownish red in colour, used for statues, tiles, etc.: a brownish-red colour.
[L. *terra,* earth, *coquĕre,* to cook.]

terra firma, *ter′ȧ fėr′mȧ, n.* land as opposed to water. [L.]

terrain, *ter′ān, n.* a stretch of land, esp. considered with reference to its physical features, or to its suitability for e.g. a battle: field of activity.
[Fr.—L. root as **territory.**]

terrestrial, *tė-res′tri-ȧl, adj.* having to do with, or existing on, the earth: living on the ground.
[L. root as **territory.**]

terrible. See **terror.**

terrier, *ter′i-ėr, n.* a name given to many kinds of small dog (orig. to one that hunted burrowing animals).
[L. *terra,* earth, ground.]

territory, *ter′i-tō-ri, n.* a stretch of land, region: the land under the control of a ruler or state: an area, as that given by a firm to a salesman to be worked by him: field of activity:—*pl.* **-ies.**
territō′rial, *adj.*
territorial waters, seas close to the shores of a country and considered as belonging to it.
[L. *terra,* the earth.]

terror, *ter′ȯr, n.* very great fear: anything that causes great fear.
terr′ible, *adj.* causing great fear: causing great hardship or distress (e.g. *a terrible disaster*).
terr′ibly, *adv.* frighteningly: (*coll.*) extremely, greatly, very.
terr′ify, *v.t.* to frighten greatly:—*pr.p.* **terr′ifying**; *pa.p.* **terr′ified.**
terrif′ic, *adj.* causing terror, dreadful: (*coll.*) huge, amazing.
terr′orise, *v.t.* to terrify: to compel to obey by making oneself greatly feared.
terrorisā′tion, *n.*
terr′orism, *n.* a state of terror: use of terrorist methods.
terr′orist, *n.* one who tries to frighten people into some action by e.g. bomb explosions, murders.—Also *adj.*
terr′or-strick′en, -struck, *adj.* seized by great fear.
[L. *terrēre,* to frighten.]

terse, *tėrs, adj.* (of e.g. statement) short and well put: (of style, person) using such statements.
terse′ly, *adv.* **terse′ness,** *n.*
[L. *tergēre, tersum,* rub clean, polish.]

tessera, *tes′ė-rȧ, n.* a small square or rectangular piece used in forming a **tessellated pavement,** a paved surface with a mosaic design.
[L. *tessera, tessella*; from Gk.]

test, *test, n.* something done to find out whether a thing is good, etc. (e.g. *Tests were carried out on the new plane*): a happening that shows up good or bad quality (e.g. *This was a test of his courage*): a means of finding the presence of (with *for*; e.g. *a test for radioactivity*): a set of questions or exercises.—*v.t.* to try, carry out test(s) on.
test match, in cricket, etc., one of a number of matches between two countries.
test pilot, *n.* one who tests new aircraft.
test tube, a glass tube closed at one end, used in chemistry tests.
to put to the test, to test, try.
[Orig. pot in which metals were tried or refined—L. *testa,* earthen pot.]

testament, *tes′tȧ-mėnt, n.* a solemn written statement, esp. of what one desires to be done with one's personal property after death: a covenant between God and man, as in the Bible—the **Old Testament** dealing with the covenant made by God with Moses, and the **New Testament,** dealing with the promises of God through Christ.

testā'tor, *n.* one who makes and leaves a will :—*fem.* **testā'trix.**
[Same root as **testify.**]

testify, *tes'ti-fī, v.i.* to give evidence, esp. in a law court: to give evidence (against person): to support the truth or reality of (with *to*; e.g. *He will testify to my presence in the house*): to show, be evidence of (with *to*).—*v.t.* to declare, esp. solemnly (e.g. *I testify my willingness*): to say in evidence (that) :—*pr.p.* **tes'tifying**; *pa.p.* **tes'tified.**
testimony, *tes'ti-mȯ-ni, n.* evidence, statement to prove a fact: open statement of belief :—*pl.* **tes'timonies.**
testimō'nial, *n.* a written statement telling what one knows of a person's character, abilities, etc.: something given to a person to show respect or thanks for services.
[L. *testārī, -ātus* (vb.), *testis* (n.), witness.]

testy, *tes'ti, adj.* easily made angry: peevish.
[O.Fr. *teste*, head; same root as **test.**]

tetanus, *tet'ȧ-nůs, n.* a serious disease caused by a bacillus, entering usu. through a wound, which makes muscles rigid, esp. lockjaw (see this).
[Gk. *tetanos—teinein*, to stretch.]

tête-à-tête, *tet'-ȧ-tet', n.* a private talk usu. between two people.—*adv.* together, in private conversation.
[Fr. *tête*, head—root as **testy, test.**]

tether, *teTH'ėr, n.* a rope or chain for tying an animal, allowing it to feed within a certain area only.—*v.t.* to tie with a tether: to keep from moving beyond certain limits.
at the end of one's tether, in a position where one has used up all strength, patience, resources, etc.
[M.E. *tethir*; from Old Norse.]

tetra-, *tet-rȧ-*, (as part of word) four.
tetram'eter, *n.* a line of verse with four stresses.
tetrarch, *tet'rärk, tē', n.* in Roman times, orig., ruler of fourth part of province: a subordinate ruler.
[Gk. *tetra*, four (*metron*, measure; *archein*, to rule).]

Teuton, *tū'ton, n.* one of a tall blonde race, including Germans.
Teuton'ic, *adj.* of Germans: (of language) Germanic (see this).
[L. *Teutōnes*; root as Ger. *Deutsch.*]

text, *tekst, n.* the main part of a book, not drawings, notes, etc.: the words of an author as opp. to e.g. comments by another: a passage from the Bible on which a sermon is preached: the theme of a writing or speech.
tex'tūal, *adj.* having to do with, or found in, the text.
text'book, *n.* a book giving the main facts of a subject.
[Same root as **textile.**]

textile, *teks'tīl, -til, adj.* having to do with weaving: woven.—*n.* a cloth or fabric formed by weaving.
[L. *texĕre, textum*, weave, compose.]

texture, *teks'chůr, n.* anything woven: the quality in a material produced by the manner in which threads are woven in it (e.g. *This tweed has a loose texture*): quality to touch, taste, of a substance resulting from the way particles are arranged (e.g. *the texture of wood, stone, an apple, a date*).
[Same root as **textile.**]

than, *THan, conj.* a word placed after the comparative of an adjective or adverb to introduce the second part of a comparison (e.g. *This is better than that*; *it is easier than I thought*; *more carefully than usual*).
For use with *other*, see this word.
[O.E. *thonne.*]

thane, *thān, n.* in England before the Norman Conquest, one, between earl and freeman in rank, who held land from the king or a higher noble.
[O.E. *thegn.*]

thank, *thangk, v.t.* to express gratitude to (someone) for a favour: to admit that one owes a result to (e.g. *He has to thank calm weather for his safe return*; *he has to thank himself for this disaster*).—*n.* (usu. in *pl.*) expression of gratitude.
thank'ful, *adj* grateful: relieved and glad.
thank'fully, *adv.* **thank'fulness,** *n.*
thank'less, *adj.* not winning thanks or achieving good results (e.g. *a thankless task*).
thank'lessly, *adv.* **thank'lessness,** *n.*
thanks'giving, *n.* act of giving thanks: a church service giving thanks to God: a day set apart for this, esp., in the United States, the last Thursday in November (with *cap.*).
thanks, thank you, I thank you.
thanks to, as a result of: because of the action of.
to give thanks, to express gratitude (to).
[O.E. *thanc*, will, thanks; conn. **think.**]

that, *THat, pron.* or *adj.* used to point out a person, thing, etc., esp. one more distant or mentioned earlier (opp. to *this*; e.g. *Don't take that, take this*; *on that occasion we were less well prepared than we are today*) :—*pl.* **those.**
Also used in subordinate clauses in place of *who(m), which* (e.g. *We hired the horses that we rode*).—*conj.* used to introduce a clause, either to make a simple connexion (e.g. *I said that I knew*), or with the following meanings :—(*old-fashioned*) for the purpose of achieving a result (e.g. *These things have I spoken unto you that in me ye might have peace*): with a certain result (*He whispered so loudly*, or *made such a noise, that I heard*): because (e.g. *It is not that I mind personally, but for your own sake don't go*).
[O.E. *thæt*; see **the**; see also **this.**]

thatch, *thach, v.t.* to cover with straw, reeds, etc.—*n.* straw, etc. used to cover e.g. roofs.
thatched, *adj.* **thatch'ing,** *n.*
[O.E. *thæc,* roof, thatch.]
thaw, *thö, v.i.* to melt or grow liquid, as ice: to become less stiff, more friendly, in manner.—*v.t.* to cause to melt.—*n.* the melting of ice or snow by heat: the change of weather that causes it.
[O.E. *thawian.*]
the, THė, THē, definite article (also called demonstrative *adj.*), used to point to a particular person, thing, etc. (e.g. *Find the thief*; *the dress I bought*; *the idea that came to me*); also used in reference to any or all of a kind or species (e.g. *The rich man usually has rich friends*; *the elephant is an animal with a trunk*).—*adv.* in phrases such as *to be the better for a rest* (i.e. 'by that much better'), or *a short sermon, the shorter the better.*
[O.E. *sē* (masc.), *sēo* (fem.), *thæt* (neut.); masc. and fem. later became *the.*]
theatre, *thē'ȧ-tėr, n.* a place where public performances, mainly drama, are seen: any place in which the seats rise by steps as in a theatre: a room for surgical operations: scene of action (e.g. *The theatre of war was in France*): the profession or life of actors: dramatic literature.
theat'rical, *adj.* having to do with a theatre or actors: (of person) behaving as if in a play: (of action, etc.) suited to stage not real life.
theat'rically, *adv.*
theatre-in-the-round, use of a stage which has audience all round it.
[Gk. *theātron—theaesthai,* to see.]
thee. See **thou.** **theft.** See **thief.**
their(s). See **they.**
theism, *thē'izm, n.* belief in the existence of God or a god.
thēoc'racy, *n.* a state which regards God or god(s) as its head, the laws as divine commands, and is governed by priests.
thēol'ogy, *n.* the science that deals with the study of God and of man's duty to Him:—*pl.* **-ies.**
theolog'ical, *adj.*
theolog'ian (*-lōj'*), **theol'ogist,** *ns.* one who makes a study of theology.
thēos'ophy (*-ȯ-fi*), *n.* any of various systems of belief which claim that one can obtain knowledge of God through direct inspiration.
thēos'ophist, *n.*
[Gk. *theos,* a god (*krateein,* to rule; *logos,* discourse; *sophos,* wisdom).]
them. See **they.**
theme, *thēm, n.* a subject for discussion, or on which a person speaks or writes: (*music*) subject, a short melody which may be repeated in different forms.
theme song, a melody that is repeated often in a musical drama, film, or radio or television series, and is connected with a certain character, idea, etc.
[Fr. *thème*—Gk. *thema—tithĕnai,* place.]
themselves. See **they.**
then, THen, *adv.* at that time: after that: in addition (e.g. *I have four pound notes, and then I have two pounds in silver*): in that case (e.g. *If you are not ill, then why will you not get up?*): as a result, therefore (e.g. *If the sides are equal, then the angles must be equal*). [**than.**]
thence, THens, *adv.* from that time or place: for that reason.
thence'forth, thencefor'ward, *advs.* from that time forward.
[M.E. *thennes.*]
theocracy. See **theism.**
theodolite, *thē-od'ȯ-līt, n.* an instrument for measuring angles used in surveying land. [Orig. uncertain.]
theologian, theology, etc. See **theism.**
theorem, *thē'ȯ-rėm, n.* something (to be) proved true by a series of steps in reasoning.
thē'ory, *n.* an explanation that one thinks is correct but which has not been tested: the principles or methods of a branch of knowledge (e.g. *He knew much about the theory of music but he was a poor performer*):—*pl.* **thē'ories.**
theoret'ic, -al, *adjs.* (opp. of *practical*) having to do with theory, or with theory only: not learned from experience (e.g. *theoretical knowledge*): (of a result) arrived at by calculation, not experiment.
theoret'ically, *adv.* in theory.
thē'orise, *v.i.* to form a theory or theories (about something) without experiment or experience.
[Gk. *thēorein,* to view; root as **theatre.**]
theosophy, etc. See **theism.**
therapeutic, *ther-ȧ-pū'tik, adj.* having to do with healing or curing.
therapeu'tics, *n. sing.* the branch of medicine concerned with the treatment and cure of diseases.
ther'apy, *n.* treatment of disease, or of a bad condition: power to heal.
ther'apist, *n.*
[Gk. *therapeuein,* to take care of, heal.]
there, THār, THėr, *adv.* (opp. to *here*) in that place: at that point (in e.g. a speech, events): to that place or point: in that matter (e.g. *You are wrong there*).—Also used as a subject when the real subject follows the verb (e.g. *There is no one at home*).—*n.* that place or point.—Also *interj.*
there'about(s), *advs.* about, near, that place: near that number or degree.
thereaft'er, *adv.* after that.
thereby', *adv.* by that means: as a result of that.
there'fore (*-fȯr*), *adv.* for that or this reason: as a result.
therein', *adv.* in that place: in that fact or circumstance (e.g. *Therein lies the difficulty*).

thereon′, *adv.* on that or it.
there′upon′, *adv.* following that: because of that: immediately.
therewith′, *adv.* with that: thereupon.
[O.E. *thǣr, thēr*; conn. with **the.**]

therm-, *thėrm-*, **thermo-,** *thėr-mō-*, (as part of word) heat.
therm, *n.* a measure of heat, used in the measurement of gas.
thėr′mal, *adj.* having to do with heat, or with hot springs.—*n.* a rising column of warm air.
thermion′ic, *adj.* having to do with
ther′mions, electrically charged particles given off from extremely hot substances.
thermometer, *thėr-mom′i-tėr*, *n.* an instrument for measuring temperature.
thermonū′clear, *adj.* having to do with the fusion of atomic nuclei at very high temperatures, as in the hydrogen bomb.
Thermos (flask), *thėr′mos (flâsk)*, *n.* (*orig. trademark*) a flask or bottle with a vacuum jacket, for keeping liquids hot or cold.
ther′mostat, *n.* an automatic device for controlling temperature.
[Gk. *thermos*, hot (*metron*, measure; *histanai*, cause to stand).]

thesaurus, *thē-sö′rus, thi-*, *n.* a storehouse esp. of knowledge, a dictionary, etc.
[Gk. *thēsauros*; same root as **treasure.**]

these. See **this.**

thesis, *thē′sis*, *n.* a view, assertion, esp. one put forward for discussion: a long essay on a subject set for study:—*pl.* **theses,** *thē′sēz.*
[L.—Gk. *tithenai*, to set, place.]

they, *thā*, *pron. pl.* the people referred to: some people, people in general (e.g. *They say bread is fattening*):—*objective* **them**; *possessive* **their** (sometimes described as possessive *adj.*), **theirs** (e.g. *They—the two boys—left their skates in the pile, and afterwards were not sure which were theirs*).
themselves′ (*-selvz′*), *pron. pl.* (1) emphatic, or (2) reflexive form of *they, them* (e.g. (1) *They themselves thought so*; (2) *they cut themselves with the razor.*)
[Old Norse *their* (nominative masc.).]

thick, *thik*, *adj.* not thin: having considerable distance through (e.g. *a thick slice, body*): (of e.g. paste, soup) fairly solid or firm: (of e.g. a wood, a crowd) dense, difficult to pass through: difficult to see through: (of speech) not clear: (of person, mind) stupid: (*coll.*) very friendly, or working closely together.—*n.* the thickest, most crowded or active part (e.g. *in the thick of the fight*).—*adv.* thickly (e.g. *Missiles came thick and fast*).
thick′ly, *adv.* **thick′ness,** *n.*
thick′en, *v.t., v.i.* to make, or become, thick or thicker.
thick′ening, *n.* making, or becoming, thick: something used to thicken.
thick′et, *n.* a group of trees or shrubs set close together.
thick′-head′ed, *adj.* stupid.
thick′-set′, *adj.* closely planted: having a short, thick body.
thick′-skinned′, *adj.* not sensitive or easily hurt (e.g. by insults).
a bit thick, (*coll.*) going too far, more than one can be expected to stand.
through thick and thin, in spite of all difficulties, without wavering.
[O.E. *thicce.*]

thief, *thēf*, *n.* one who steals or takes unlawfully what is not his own:—*pl.* **thieves.**
thieve, *v.i.* to be a thief.—*v.t.* to take (something) unlawfully.
thiev′ing, *n*, and *adj.*
thiev′ery, *n.* act, or practice, of a thief:—*pl.* **thiev′eries.**
thiev′ish, *adj.* inclined to thieve: of a thief (e.g. *thievish acts*).
theft, *theft*, *n.* thievery: an instance of stealing.
[O.E. *thēof* (n.), *thēofian* (vb.).]

thigh, *thī*, *n.* the thick fleshy part of the leg from the knee to the trunk.
[O.E. *thēoh.*]

thimble, *thim′bl*, *n.* a small cap to protect the finger and push the needle in sewing.
thim′bleful, *n.* a small quantity.
[O.E. *thȳmel—thūma*, thumb.]

thin, *thin*, *adj.* having little distance through (e.g. *a thin slice, rope*): slim, not fat: not set close or crowded together (e.g. *a thin crop*; *the crowd was thin in that corner*): (of e.g. soup) lacking strength, watery: not dense: not difficult to see through: poor in quality: (of e.g. voice) lacking in fullness or power: not convincing (e.g. *a thin excuse*):—*comp.* **thinn′er**; *superl.* **thinn′est.**—*adv.* not thickly: in a scattered state:—*v.t., v.i.* to make, or become, thin, thinner, or less close or crowded (with *away, out*, etc.):—*pr.p.* **thinn′ing**; *pa.p.* **thinned.**
thin′ly, *adv.* **thin′ness,** *n.*
thinn′ish, *adj.*
thin′-skinned′, *adj.* having a thin skin: sensitive, easily hurt.
a thin time, (*coll.*) a time of little enjoyment.
[O.E. *thynne.*]

thine. See **thy.**

thing, *thing*, *n.* an object that is not living: a living being (e.g. *She is a nice old thing*): (in *pl.*) belongings, esp. clothes: any individual object, fact, circumstance, action, quality, or idea of which one may think or to which one may refer.
the thing, the proper or right thing.
just one of those things, just something that has to be accepted, a happening that one can do nothing about.
to be a good (bad) thing, to be a wise (unwise) action, or fortunate (unfortunate) happening.
to make a good thing of, to profit by.
to make a thing of, to make a fuss about.
[O.E. *thing, thinc.*]

think, *thingk, v.i.* to turn over ideas, or to reason, in the mind: to form a picture, idea, in the mind (of; e.g. *to think of past happiness*): to intend (with *of*; e.g. *She is thinking of going*).—*v.t.* to form (a thought): to judge, believe or consider: to expect:—*pa.p.* **thought,** *thöt.*
think'er, *n.* one who thinks, esp. one who is capable of fruitful thought.
to think fit to, to choose to (do something).
to think little, nothing, of, to have a poor opinion of: not to regard as difficult.
to think out, to make in detail (a plan): to solve by careful thought.
See also **thought** (*n.*)
[O.E. *thencan,* pa.t. *thōhte.*]

third, *thėrd, adj.* last of three.—*n.* one of three equal parts.
third-par'ty, *adj.* having to do with a third person or party, as in *third-party risks* (where the first party is the insured person, e.g. the car owner, the second the insurance company, and the third, say, a passenger in the car).
third'ly, *adv.* in the third place (see **firstly**).
third'-rate', *adj.* of poor quality.
third degree. See **degree.**
[O.E. *thridda*—same root as **three.**]

thirst, *thėrst, n.* the dry feeling in the mouth and general discomfort caused by want of drink: an eager desire (for e.g. information, power).—*v.i.* to feel thirst: to have a great desire (for).
thirst'y, *adj.* suffering from thirst: (of earth) dry, parched: eager (for).
thirst'ily, *adv.* **thirst'iness,** *n.*
[O.E. *thurst, thyrst.*]

thirteen, *thėr'tēn, -tēn', adj.* and *n.* three and ten (13 or XIII).
thir'teenth (also *-tēnth'*), *adj.* last of thirteen.—*n.* one of thirteen equal parts.
thir'ty, *adj.* and *n.* three times ten (30 or XXX):—*pl.* **thir'ties.**
thir'tieth, (*-ti-ėth*) *adj.* last of thirty.—*n.* one of thirty equal parts.
See also **three.**
[Root as **three**; O.E. *tēn, -tig,* ten.]

this, THis, *pron.* or *adj.* used to point out a person, thing, etc., esp. one near or being spoken about at the time (opp. to *that*; e.g. *This is more suitable than that*; *I am glad to be present on this occasion*):—*pl.* **these.**
[O.E.; pl. *thās* gave **those,** later pl. *thǣs* gave **these.**]

thistle, *this'l, n.* a prickly plant with purple heads of flowers.
this'tledown, *n.* the light feathery bristles of the seeds of a thistle.
[O.E. *thistel.*]

thither, THiTH'*ėr, adv.* to that place: to that end or result.
[O.E. *thider.*]

tho', THō, short for **though.**

thole, *thōl, n.* a pin in the side of a boat to keep the oar in place.
[O.E. *thol.*]

thong, *thong, n.* a piece of leather to fasten anything: the lash of a whip.
[O.E. *thwang.*]

thorax, *thō'raks, thö', n.* the part of the body between the neck and the belly, the chest: the middle section of an insect's body. [L.—Gk.]

thorn, *thörn, n.* a sharp, woody part sticking out from the stem of a plant: a prickle (as on a rose): a shrub or small tree having thorns.
thor'ny, *adj.* full of thorns: prickly: difficult, causing argument (e.g. *a thorny problem, subject*).
thor'niness, *n.*
a thorn in the flesh, a cause of constant irritation. [O.E.]

thorough, *thûr'ȯ, adj.* complete (e.g. *a thorough rogue, master of his trade*): (of person, manner of working, something done) very careful, covering every detail.
thor'oughly, *adv.* **thor'oughness,** *n.*
thor'oughbred, *adj.* and *n.* (a horse, etc.) bred from a dam and sire of the best blood: (a person) well-bred and spirited.
thor'oughfare, *n.* a public road, street: a passage through, or right to use it (e.g. *a notice saying ' No Thoroughfare '*).
thor'oughgo'ing, *adj.* thorough, complete (e.g. *a thoroughgoing nuisance*).
[A longer form of **through.**]

those. See **that.**

thou, THow, *pron.* 2nd person *sing.*, now replaced by **you** except in solemn language as in church:—*objective* **thee**; *possessive* **thy** (sometimes described as possessive *adj.*), **thine.**
thyself', *pron.* (1) emphatic or (2) reflexive, form of *thou, thee.*
[O.E. *thū*; conn. with L. *tū,* Gk. *sy, ty.*]

though, THō, *conj.* although: however (e.g. *I wish I had not said it though*): if (*as though, even though*).
[M.E. *thoh*—Scand.; conn. O.E. *thēah.*]

thought[1]. See **think.**

thought[2], *thöt, n.* the act of thinking: something that one thinks, an idea: an opinion, or opinions as a whole (e.g. *the political thought on this subject*): consideration (e.g. *after much thought*): (often in *pl.*) intention (e.g. *I had no thought, thoughts, of going*): expectation (of; *I had no thought of failing*).
thought'ful, *adj.* deep in thought: showing thought: thinking of others, considerate.
thought'fully, *adv.*
thought'fulness, *n.*
thought'less, *adj.* not thinking what the results of one's actions may be: showing such lack of thought (e.g. *She was hurt, was warned, by the other's thoughtless words*).
thought'-reading, *n.* knowing what is

passing in another's mind by watching his expressions, or by telepathy.
on second thoughts, after thinking the question, etc., over more fully.
to take thought, to consider (how to): take care about (with *for*).
See also **think.**
[O.E. *gethōht*; same root as **think.**]

thousand, *thow'zȧnd, n.* ten times a hundred (1,000 or M): any great number:—*pl.* **thousands,** (after another number) **thousand.**—Also *adj.*
one in a thousand, rare and excellent.
[O.E. *thūsend*; conn. Ger. *tausend.*]

thrall, *thrōl, n.* a slave (to some power, influence, etc.).
thral'dom, *n.* slavery.
[Old Norse *thræll.*]

thrash, *thrash, v.t.* to beat out (grain) from the straw by e.g. flail, machinery (more often **thresh**): to beat soundly: (with *out*) to discuss thoroughly, so as to reach agreement.—*v.i.* to thresh grain: to move, toss, violently (about).
thrash'er, thresh'er, *n.*
thrash'ing, thresh'ing, *n., adj.*
[Northern form of O.E. *therscan.*]

thread, *thred, n.* a very thin line or cord of any substance, esp. one twisted and drawn out: the line, ridge, round a screw: a connected series of details in proper order, or an awareness of this (e.g. *I lost the thread of his story, argument*).—*v.t.* to pass a thread through the eye of (a needle): to put (e.g. beads) on a thread: to make (one's way) where the passage is narrow (e.g. *He threaded his way among the trees, through the crowd*).
thread'bare, *adj.* worn to the bare thread: (of e.g. excuse) used too often.
[O.E. *thrǣd—thrāwan,* to twist.]

threat, *thret, n.* a warning that one intends to punish or to hurt: a warning of something bad that may come (e.g. *a threat of rain*): something likely to cause harm etc. (e.g. *His presence is a threat to the success of our plot*).
threat'en, *v.t.* to utter threats to harm (someone, etc.): to be a threat to: to suggest the approach of (something unpleasant): to state one's intention (to do).—Also *v.i.*
threat'ening, *adj.*
[O.E. *thrēat—thrēotan,* annoy, weary.]

three, *thrē, adj.* and *n.* the number next above two (3 or III).
third, thirteen, thrice. See separate articles.
three'fold, *adj.* having three parts: three times as great or as much.—Also *adv.* (e.g. *It repaid him threefold*).
threepence, *thrip'ens, threp'ens, n.* three pennies:—*pl.* **threep'ences.**
threepenny piece, bit (*thrip'-, threp'-*), *n.* a coin of the value of three pence.
three'score', *n.* and *adj.* three times twenty, sixty.
three'some (*-sum*), *n.* a group of three.—Also *adj.*
[O.E. *threo* (fem., neut.), *thri* (masc.).]

thresh, *thresh.* See **thrash.**

threshold, *thresh'(h)ōld, n.* the piece of timber or stone under the door of a building: doorway, entrance: the place or point of entering or beginning (e.g. *at the threshold of his career*).
[O.E. *therscwald.*]

threw. See **throw.**

thrice, *thrīs, adv.* three times.
[Same root as **three.**]

thrift, *thrift, n.* careful management of money or goods in order to save.
thrif'ty, *adj.* showing thrift.
thrif'tily, *adv.* **thrif'tiness,** *n.*
thrift'less, *adj.* not thrifty, spending carelessly, extravagant.
[Same root as **thrive.**]

thrill, *thril, v.i., v.t.* to feel, or make feel, keen emotion or excitement.—*n.* an excited feeling: vibration, quivering.
thrill'ing, *adj.*
thrill'er, *n.* an exciting (usu. detective) novel or play.
[O.E. *thyrlian,* to bore a hole.]

thrive, *thrīv, v.i.* to prosper, gain wealth: to be successful: to grow strong, flourish:—*pa.t.* **thrōve, thrīved;** *pa.p.* **thriv'en** (*thriv'*), **thrīved.**
thrī'ving, *adj.* successful: growing well.
[Old Norse *thrīfa,* to grasp.]

throat, *thrōt, n.* front part of neck, where gullet and windpipe are.
[O.E. *throte.*]

throb, *throb, v.i.* (of e.g. heart) to beat with more than usual force: (of e.g. engine) to beat regularly:—*pr.p.* **throbb'ing**; *pa.p.* **throbbed.**—Also *n.* [Imit.]

throe, *thrō, n.* (usu. in *pl.*) suffering, pain, great effort or struggle.
in the throes of, engaged in, struggling with (e.g. revolution, moving house).
[Conn. with O.E. *thrēa,* suffering.]

thrombosis, *throm-bō'sis, n.* the forming of a clot in a blood-vessel.
[Gk. *thrombos,* a clot.]

throne, *thrōn, n.* the seat of a king or a bishop: the king or his power.—*v.t.* to place on a royal seat.
[Gk. *thronos,* seat.]

throng, *throng, n.* a crowd: a great number.—*v.t.* to fill (a place) with a crowd: (of a crowd) to fill very full.—*v.i.* to crowd (together).
[O.E. *gethrang*; Ger. *drang,* pressure.]

throttle, *throt'l, n.* throat or windpipe: (in engines) a device by which steam or petrol can be turned on or off.—*v.t.* to choke by gripping the throat: to shut off (e.g. steam) from an engine: to slow (engine) by reducing flow of fuel: to silence, suppress. [**throat.**]

through, *throō, prep.* from end to end, or from side to side, of: into and out of at the other end: from beginning to end of:

by means of (e.g. *He got the job through his uncle's influence*): as a result of (e.g. *through his own stupidity*).—Also *adv.*—*adj.* going from starting-point to destination without break or change (e.g. *a through train*): (*coll.*) finished.
through'-and-through', thoroughly.
throughout', *prep.* everywhere in: from one end to the other of.—Also *adv.*
through with, finished with: no longer willing to associate with.
[O.E. *thurh.*]

throve. See **thrive.**

throw, *thrō, v.t.* to hurl, fling, cast, propel: to cause to fall to the ground: to put in position in a way that suggests throwing (e.g. *to throw a bridge across a river*): (*coll.*) to hold, give (a party).—Also *v.i.*:—*pa.t.* **threw** (*thrōō*); *pa.p.* **thrown** (*thrōn*).—*n.* the act of throwing: the distance to which anything is or may be thrown (e.g. *a stone's-throw*).
to throw in, to add, give, as a free gift: to make (a comment) casually, in passing.
to throw off, to cast off hastily: to give off: to get rid of (e.g. a cold, depression).
to throw on, to put on (e.g. clothes) quickly or carelessly.
to throw oneself into, to play one's part in heartily, with energy.
[O.E. *thrāwan*, to turn, twist.]

thrush, *thrush, n.* a singing bird with brown back and spotted under parts.
[O.E. *thrysce.*]

thrust, *thrust, v.t.* to push or drive with force: to press (in): to stab, pierce: to force (oneself, one's company, on someone).—Also *v.i.*:—*pa.t., pa.p.* **thrust.**—*n.* a stab: pushing force or pressure: the forward force developed by a propeller, high speed jet, etc.
[Old Norse *thyrsta.*]

thud, *thud, n.* a dull, hollow sound of a blow or of a heavy body falling.—*v.i.* to move, fall, with such a sound:—*pr.p.* **thudd'ing**; *pa.p.* **thudd'ed.** [Imit.]

thug, *thug, n.* a ruffian, a man who lives by violence.
thugg'ery, *n.* conduct of thug(s).
[Hindustani, *thag, thug.*]

thumb, *thum, n.* the short, thick finger of the human hand: what corresponds to it in other animals.—*v.t.* to turn over, or to soil, with the thumb or fingers.
thumb'nail, *n.* nail on thumb.—*adj.* small but complete (e.g. *a thumbnail sketch*).
thumb'screw, *n.* old instrument of torture screwed tight on thumb(s).
rule of thumb, a rough-and-ready practical method, found by experience to work.
under one's thumb, completely under one's influence.
[O.E. *thūma.*]

thump, *thump, n.* a heavy blow.—*v.t., v.i.* to beat, fall, or move, with a dull, heavy blow or sound.
thump'ing, *adj.* (*coll.*) very big. [Imit.]

thunder, *thun'dėr, n.* the deep rumbling sound heard after a flash of lightning: any loud, rumbling noise.—*v.i.* to give forth thunder (often *it thunders*): to sound as thunder: to storm, threaten.—*v.t.* to say loudly and angrily.
thun'dery, *adj.* **thun'deriness,** *n.*
thun'dering, *adj.* very big or great.
thun'derous, *adj.* giving forth a sound like thunder: angry-looking.
thun'derbolt, *n.* a flash of lightning and peal of thunder: a very great and sudden surprise.
thun'derstruck, *adj.* overcome, made silent, by surprise.
to steal one's thunder, to take away one's chance of producing an effect by taking one's idea, information, etc. and using it first.
[O.E. *thunor*; conn. with Ger. *donner.*]

Thursday, *thûrz'di, n.* fifth day of week.
[O.E. *Thunres dæg*, day of Thunor (Thor, god of **thunder**).]

thus, THus, *adv.* in this or that manner: to this degree or extent (e.g. *thus far*): because of this.
[O.E. *thus*; prob.—*thes*, this.]

thwack, *thwak, v.t.* to strike with something flat.—Also *n.* [Imit.]

thwart, *thwört, v.t.* to hinder (a person) from carrying out a plan, or from doing what he wants: to frustrate (e.g. a purpose).
[Conn. Old Norse *thvert*, across.]

thy. See **thee.**

thyme, *tīm, n.* a sweet-smelling herb used for seasoning.
[Gk. *thyein*, to fill with sweet smells.]

thyroid, *thī'roid, adj.* having to do with a large gland in the neck which has great influence on growth of body.
[Gk. *thyreos*, shield, *eidos*, form.]

thyself. See **thee.**

tiara, *ti-ä'rȧ, n.* a kind of crown: a jewelled ornament for the head.
[Gk. *tiāra.*]

tibia, *tib'i-ȧ, n.* the larger of the two bones between knee and ankle. [L.]

tic, *tik, n.* a twitching motion of certain muscles, esp. of the face. [Fr.]

tick[1], *tik, n.* a blood-sucking mite-like animal.
[M.E. *teke*; conn. Ger. *zecke.*]

tick[2], *tik, n.* the case or cover in which feathers, etc. are put to make e.g. a mattress.
tick'ing, *n.* the cloth of which ticks are made.
[M.E. *tikke*; conn. Gk. *thēkē*, a case.]

tick[3], *tik, v.t.* (often with *off*) to mark off (e.g. items in a list).—*n.* a light mark used for this purpose.
[M.E. *teck*, a touch; conn. Du. *tik.*]

tick[4], *tik, v.t.* to make a small, quick noise, esp. regularly as a watch.—*n.* the sound of a watch or clock: a moment.
tick'ing, *n.* and *adj.*
ticker tape, paper ribbon used in an automatic machine (**tick'er**) which receives by telegraph and prints the latest stock exchange prices, etc. [Imit.]

ticket, *tik'it, n.* a marked card, esp. one giving the owner a right to travel, to be admitted, etc.: (*slang*) release from the armed forces.—*v.t.* to put a label on.
[O.Fr. *e(s)tiquet(te)*, label.]

ticking. See **tick** (2) and (4).

tickle, *tik'l, v.t.* to touch lightly and cause to laugh: to please, amuse (e.g. *This story tickled the old man*).
tick'lish, *adj.* easily tickled: (of e.g. person) easily upset, touchy: (of e.g. problem, situation) difficult to handle.
[Orig. uncertain.]

tide, *tīd, n.* the rise and fall of the sea which happens regularly twice each day: (in e.g. *Whitsuntide*) season.—*v.t.* to carry (a person over a difficulty, difficult time) as if by the tide: to get, pass (over a difficulty).
tī'dal, *adj.* having to do with tides: affected by tides (e.g. *a tidal river*).
tide'mark, *n.* high-water mark.
tide'wa'ter, *n.* the water of the part of a river affected by the tide: the seaboard.
tidal wave, a great wave caused by the tide or an earthquake.
[O.E. *tīd*, time, tide.]

tidier, etc. See **tidy.**

tidings, *tī'dingz, n. pl.* news (of something).
[From Old Norse—*tīth*, time.]

tidy, *tī'di, adj.* neat: in good order: (*coll.*) fairly big (e.g. *a tidy sum of money*):—*comp.* **tī'dier**; *superl.* **tī'diest.**—*v.t.* to make neat, put in good order:—*pr.p.* **tī'dying**; *pa.p.* **tī'died.**
tī'dily, *adv.* **tī'diness,** *n.*
[M.E. *tidy*, seasonable—root as **tide.**]

tie, *tī, v.t.* to fasten with a cord: to make a bow or knot in: to form (a knot): to join, unite: (also **tie down**) to bind or oblige (a person to take some action): to limit, restrict.—*v.i.* to score the same number of points:—*pr.p.* **ty'ing** (*tī'*); *pa.p.* **tied** (*tīd*).—*n.* a knot, bow, etc.: a necktie: a state of being equal in number of e.g. votes or points: one game or match in a series: (*music*) a curved line drawn over notes of the same pitch to show they are to be treated as one note the length of both, or all, together.
[O.E. *tēag*, rope.]

tier, *tēr, n.* a row, esp. when several rows are placed one above another.
[O. Fr. *tire*, order—*tirer*, to draw.]

tiff, *tif, n.* a slight quarrel.
[Orig. uncertain.]

tiger, *tī'gėr, n.* a large, striped, fierce, cat-like animal from Asia:—*fem.* **tī'gress.**
tiger lily, a lily with large spotted or streaked flowers.
[Gk. *tigris*; of Asiatic origin.]

tight, *tīt, adj.* (of e.g. rope) firmly stretched, not loose: packed or wedged closely: (of e.g. lid) fitting closely: (of e.g. clothes) fitting too closely: (of e.g. boat) not leaky: (*coll.*) tipsy, drunk: (of e.g. money) not easy to obtain: difficult to get through or out of (e.g. *a tight place*): (*coll.*) stingy.
tight'ly, *adv.* **tight'ness,** *n.*
tight'en, *v.t., v.i.,* to make, or become, tight or tighter.
tights, *n. pl.* a skin-tight garment (worn orig. by acrobats, dancers, etc.).
tight'rope, *n.* a tightly stretched rope on which acrobats perform.
[From Scand.]

tile, *tīl, n.* a piece of baked clay used in covering floors, roofs, etc.—*v.t.* to cover with tiles.
tī'ling, *n.* roof of tiles: tiles in general.
[O.E. *tigele*—L. *tegĕre*, to cover.]

till[1], *til, n.* a money box or drawer in, or on, a counter, etc.
[M.E. *tillen*, to draw out.]

till[2], *til, prep.* to the time of (e.g. *till death, till Sunday*).—*conj.* to the time when (e.g. *till I am forced to stop*).
[O.E. *til*—Scand.]

till[3], *til, v.t.* to prepare (land) and raise crops: to plough.
till'age, *n.* act of tilling: tilled land.
till'er, *n.*
[O.E. *tilian.*]

tiller[1], *til'ėr, n.* the handle or lever for turning a rudder from side to side.
[Late L. *tēlārium*, part of loom.]

tiller[2]. See **till** (3).

tilt, *tilt, v.i.* to joust (see this): to thrust (at), attack in words: to fall into a sloping position, or be raised at an angle.—*v.t.* to slant: to raise one end of.—*n.* a thrust (at): a dispute (with): state of sloping: dip, slant.
full tilt, with full speed and force.
[O.E. *tealt*, tottering.]

timber, *tim'bėr, n.* wood for building, etc.: trees suitable for this: woods: a wooden beam for the framework of a house or ship.
timber line, *n.* on a mountain or in cold regions, the line beyond which there are no trees. [O.E.]

timbre, *tan^g^br'*, or *tim'bėr, n.* quality of a musical sound or voice.
[O.Fr.—same L. root as **tympanum.**]

timbrel, *tim'brėl, n.* an ancient instrument like a tambourine.
[Same root as **timbre.**]

time, *tīm, n.* hour of the day (e.g. *What time is it?*): a point at which, or period during which, something happens: (often in *pl.*) a period marked off from others in some way (e.g. *in the time of King John; in modern, future, hard,* *times*): an interval, space (e.g. *There is no time between trains*): a suitable season or moment (e.g. *Now is the time to make a change*): one of a number of occasions or repetitions (e.g. *four guests at a time*; *he won four times*): (in *pl.*) used in stating a multiplication sum (e.g. *Four times twenty-one* $=4\times21=84$): (*music*) grouping of notes in bars of equal duration according to position of principal accents: also, rate of performance.—*adj.* having to do with time: arranged to go off, etc., at a particular time (e.g. *a time bomb*).—*v.t.* to measure the minutes, seconds, etc., taken, or to be taken, by (e.g. *I timed the race, work*): to choose the time for (well, badly, etc.; e.g. *He timed his intervention perfectly*).

time′less, *adj.* never ending: not belonging, etc., to any particular time.

time′ly, *adj.* in good time: coming at the right moment (e.g. *timely help*).

time′liness, *n.*

time′-hon′oured, *adj.* thought much of for a long time, or because it has lasted long (e.g. *a time-honoured custom*).

time′keeper, *n.* a timepiece: one who keeps the time of workmen, etc.

time limit, a fixed period within which a thing must be completed.

time′piece, *n.* a watch or clock.

time′server, *n.* one who meanly suits his opinions or actions to the circumstances or to the person in power.

time′serving, *adj.* and *n.*

time′table, *n.* a table or list showing the times of e.g. arrival and departure of trains.

time′worn, *adj.* worn by time: old.

at times, occasionally, now and then.

in time, early enough.

on time, up to time.

the time being, the present time.

time and (time) again, repeatedly, over and over.

time and motion study, an investigation of the motions performed and the time taken in industrial work with a view to cutting out unnecessary movement and so speeding up production.

to do time (*coll.*), to serve a prison sentence.

up to time, punctual(ly), (in a place) at the time fixed, stated.

[O.E. *tīma*.]

timid, *tim′id, adj.* shy: easily frightened: cautious.

tim′idly, *adv.* **timid′ity, -idness,** *ns.*

timorous, *tim′ȯr-ůs, adj.* very easily frightened, very timid: full of fears.

[L. *timēre*, to fear.]

timpani, *tim′pȧn-ē, n. pl.* kettledrums.

tim′panist, *n.* one who plays these.

See also **tympanum.** [It.]

tin, *tin, n.* a silvery-white metal: a box or can made of **tin-plate,** i.e. thin iron covered with tin, or other metal: a sealed metal can containing food.—Also *adj.*—*v.t.* to cover with tin: to pack in tins:—*pr.p.* **tinn′ing;** *pa.p.* **tinned.**

tinn′y, *adj.* like tin: (of sound) thin, like that of a tin being struck.

tin′smith, *n.* a manufacturer of tin cans: a worker in tin.

tin foil, tin or other metal in thin leaves for wrapping articles.

tin hat, a metal helmet or hat worn for protection. [O.E.]

tincture, *tingk′chůr, n.* a tinge (of colour): a slight taste: a medicine mixed in alcohol.—*v.t.* to tinge (with).

[Same root as **tinge.**]

tinder, *tin′dėr, n.* anything used for kindling, or easily lighting accidentally from a spark, esp. very dry material.

[O.E. *tynder*.]

tine, *tīn, n.* a spike of fork or antler.

[O.E. *tind*, a point.]

tinge, *tinj, v.t.* to tint, colour slightly: (with *with*) to add a slight amount of something to.—*n.* a slight amount (e.g. *a tinge of green*; *a tinge of sadness in his voice*):—*pr.p.* **ting(e)′ing.**

[L. *tingĕre, tinctum*, to wet, dye.]

tingle, *ting′gl, v.i.* to feel a sharp or thrilling sensation, as in hearing a shrill sound: to feel a prickling or stinging sensation.—*n.* a tingling feeling.

[M.E. *tinglen*; conn. with **tinkle.**]

tinker, *tingk′ėr, n.* a mender of kettles, pans, etc.—*v.i.* to do clumsy work: to meddle (with).

[M.E. *tinkere*—same root as **tinkle.**]

tinkle, *ting′kl, v.i., v.t.* to make, or cause to make, little light sounds (as of small bells): to clink, jingle.—Also *n.*

[M.E. *tinken, tinklen*; imit.]

tinning, etc. See **tin.**

tinsel, *tin′sėl, n.* a shiny, glittering substance or cloth, used for decoration: anything showy but of little value.

[L. *scintilla*, a spark.]

tint, *tint, n.* a variety of a colour, esp. one diluted and made lighter.—*v.t.* to give a slight colouring to.

[Same root as **tinge, tincture.**]

tiny, *tī′ni, adj.* very small:—*comp.* **tī′nier;** *superl.* **tī′niest.** [Orig. uncertain.]

tip[1], *tip, n.* the small top, point, end, esp. of anything long.—*v.t.* to form a point to: to cover the end of:—*pr.p.* **tipp′ing;** *pa.p.* **tipped.** [**top.**]

tip[2], *tip, v.t.* to strike lightly: to cause to slant: (with *over*) to overturn (e.g. *He tips over his chair*): to empty (out, into, etc.): to give a hint to, private information to (also **tip off**): to give a small gift of money to (e.g. a waiter).—*v.i.* to slant: to give tips.—*n.* a tap or light stroke: a dump for rubbish: private information, hint: small gift of money.

tip′ster, *n.* one whose business is to give private hints about racing, etc.

tip′-off, *n.* a warning, hint.

straight tip, a hint that can be depended upon in betting, etc.
to tip the scale, to make one side of the scale go down: to prove to be the important factor in a decision (e.g. *This fact tips the scale in his favour*).
[Prob. orig. rogues' word.]

tipple, *tip'l, v.i., v.t.* to drink (alcoholic drinks) in small quantities and often.
tipp'ler, *n.* a constant drinker.
tipsy, *tip'si, adj.* rather drunk.
tip'sily, *adv.* **tip'siness,** *n.*
[Conn. Norw. dial. *tipla.*]

tiptoe, *tip'tō, n.* used in phrase **on tiptoe,** walking on the ends of the toes in order to go quietly or through excitement.—*adv.* on tiptoe (e.g. *She went tiptoe to the door*).—*v.i.* to walk on tiptoe.
[**tip** (1), **toe.**]

tiptop, *tip'top', adj.* extremely good.
[**tip** (1), **top** (1).]

tirade, *ti-rād'*, or *ti-*, *n.* a long, bitter scolding speech.
[Fr.—It. *tirare,* to pull, shoot.]

tire[1]. Same as **tyre.**

tire[2], *tīr, v.t., v.i.* to make, or become, weary, without strength or without patience or interest to go on.
tired, *adj.* wearied: (with *of*) bored with.
tired'ness (*tīrd'*), *n.*
tire'less, *adj.* never becoming weary, never resting.
tire'some, *adj.* making tired: long and dull: annoying.
[O.E. *tēorian,* to be tired.]

tissue, *tis'ū*, or *tish'o͞o*, *n.* very finely woven cloth: substance of which organs of the body are made: a connected series (e.g. *a tissue of lies*).
tissue paper, a thin, soft almost transparent paper, used in wrapping, etc.
[Fr. *tissu,* woven—L. root as **textile.**]

tit[1], *tit, n.* any of several kinds of small bird.
[Old Norse *tittr,* a little bird.]

tit[2], *tit, n.* used in phrase **tit for tat** (*tip* for *tap*), blow for blow, repayment of injury with injury.

tit[3]. Same as **teat.**

Titan, *tī'tȧn, n.* one of the giants in old Greek tales: (without *cap.*) a person of great power, ability, or size.
titan'ic, *adj.* huge: very strong.
titanium, *ti-tā'ni-ŭm, n.* metal used in aircraft, steel industry, etc. [Gk.]

titbit, *tit'bit, n.* a choice little bit.
[Perh. earlier *tit,* something small, **bit.**]

tithe, *tīTH, n.* a tenth part: a small part: (usu. in *pl.*) money, land, or stock paid over for support of church and clergy.
[O.E. *tēotha,* tenth.]

title, *tī'tl, n.* a name or phrase placed over, or at the beginning of, a thing, by which that thing is known (e.g. *'Great Expectations' is the title of a book*): a name showing rank or honour, or office held, or used in ordinary formal address (e.g. *Lord* Chatham, *Cardinal* Wolsey, *Mrs* Pankhurst): legal right (to e.g. an estate): something that gives right or claim (e.g. *He had no title to interfere, to expect consideration from us*).
tī'tled, *adj.* having a title.
title deed, a document that proves a right to ownership.
title page, page of a book containing its title and usu. the author's name.
title rôle, the part in a play of the character named in the title (e.g. *He plays Macbeth, the title rôle in 'Macbeth'*).
[O.Fr.—L. *titulus.*]

titter, *tit'ėr, v.i.* to laugh with little noise, nervously or half secretly. [Imit.]

tittle, *tit'l, n.* a very small part.
[O.Fr. *title*—*titulus,* a title.]

tittle-tattle, *tit'l-tat'l, n.* idle gossip.
[**tattle.**]

to, *too, tȯ,* or *to͞o, prep.* in the direction of (e.g. *facing to the east*): as far as (e.g. *to town, to the end*): showing the purpose of an action (e.g. *I came to his assistance*): showing the result (e.g. *I tore it to shreds*): used as the sign of the infinitive (e.g. *He knew how to sing*): introducing the indirect object of a verb (e.g. *He gave the letter to her*): showing belonging (e.g. *the key to the door, problem*): compared with (e.g. *This selfish act is nothing to his selfish actions in the past*).—*adv.* into place or condition required (e.g. *Pull the door to*; *the fainting man came to*).
to and fro. See **fro.**
[O.E. *tō*; conn. with Ger. *zu.*]

toad, *tōd, n.* reptile like a large frog.
toad'y, *n.* a mean hanger-on and flatterer. —*v.i.* to give way to person's wishes and flatter him in order to gain his favour (e.g. *Do not toady to the rich man*):—*pr.p.* **toad'ying**; *pa.p.* **toad'ied.**
toad'stool, *n.* an umbrella-shaped fungus esp. the poisonous kinds of mushroom.
[O.E. *tādige, tādie.*]

toast, *tōst, v.t.* to brown by means of the heat of fire, gas flame, or electricity: to warm (e.g. feet): to drink to the health, success, of (a person, etc.).—*n.* bread toasted: the person, thing, to whom a toast is drunk: an act of drinking a toast, call to drink a toast.
toas'ter, *n.* one who, or something that, toasts, esp. now a machine.
toast'master, *n.* the announcer of toasts at a public dinner.
toast'-rack, *n.* a stand with partitions for slices of toast.
to drink a toast to, to toast.
[O.Fr. *toster*—L. root as **torrid.**]

tobacco, *to-bak'ō, n.* a plant, native to America, whose dried leaves are used for smoking, chewing, or as snuff.
tobacc'onist, *n.* one who sells tobacco.
[Through Sp. *tabaco,* from Haiti word.]

toboggan, *tȯ-bog'ȧn, n.* kind of sled turned up at the front for sliding down snow-

covered slopes, etc.—*v.i.* to slide over snow on such a sled.
tobogg'aning, *n.*
[From. Amer. Indian word.]

today, to-day, *too-dā'*, *tŏ-*, *n.* this day: the present time.—*adv.* on the present day: nowadays.
[O.E. *tō dæge.*]

toddle, *tod'l*, *v.i.* to walk with short, unsteady steps, as a child does.
todd'ler, *n.* a young child.
[Orig. uncertain.]

toddy, *tod'i*, *n.* a mixture of spirits, sugar, and hot water:—*pl.* **-ies.**
[Hindustani *tārī—tār*, palm tree.]

to-do, *too-dōō'*, *n.* bustle, stir, uproar.
[Infinitive of **do.**]

toe, *tō*, *n.* one of the five end parts of the foot: the front of an animal's hoof, of a shoe, a golf club, etc.—*v.t.* to touch or strike with the toe(s): to put toe(s) on.
toed, *tōd*, *adj.* having toes, usu. of a certain kind (e.g. *square-toed*).
toe'nail, *n.* nail on toe.
on one's toes, ready to act.
to toe the line, to have one's toes on e.g. the starting line: to act as one ought, esp. according to a rule laid down.
[O.E. *tā.*]

toffee, toffy, *tof'i*, *n.* a sweet made of sugar and butter.—Also **taff'y.**
[Orig. uncertain.]

tog, *tog*, *n.* (*slang*) a garment (usu. in *pl.*).
[Prob. **toga.**]

toga, *tō'gȧ*, *n.* the loose outer garment worn by a Roman citizen.
[L.—*tegĕre, tectum*, to cover.]

together, *too-geTH'ėr*, *tŏ-*, *adv.* in or into one place, time, company, mass, etc.: in or into union (e.g. *to nail the planks together*): by joint action (e.g. *Together we persuaded him*).
[O.E. *tōgædere.*]

toil, *toil*, *v.i.* to work hard and long: to move, travel, with effort.—*n.* work of a very tiring kind.
toil'-worn, *adj.* worn with hard work.
[O.Fr. *touiller*, to entangle.]

toilet, *toi'lit*, *n.* act of washing, dressing, making up (e.g. *to make a hasty toilet*): a particular costume: a lavatory.
toilette, *twä-let'*, *n.* a toilet performed with special care: a fashionable and showy costume.
[Fr. *toilette—toile*, cloth—L. *tela*, web.]

toils, *toilz*, *n. pl.* used in phrase **in the toils of,** snared by, under power, fascination, of.
[Root as **toilet.**]

token, *tō'kėn*, *n.* a visible sign, evidence (e.g. *Please accept this book as a token, in token, of my gratitude*): a keepsake: a piece of metal stamped for use as a coin or ticket.—*adj.* acting as a symbol or sign of one's opinion, feeling, intentions (e.g. *a token strike, payment*).
by the same token, as further supporting evidence. [O.E. *tācen.*]

told. See **tell.**

tolerable, *tol'ėr-ȧ-bl*, *adj.* able to be borne, endured: fairly good or pleasant.
tol'erably, *adv.* **tol'erableness,** *n.*
tol'erance, *n.* putting up with and being fair to people whose ways and opinions are different from one's own: ability to take (drug), endure (bad conditions) without effect, esp. bad effect.
tol'erant, *adj.* **tol'erantly,** *adv.*
tol'erāte, *v.t.* to bear, endure: to put up with: to allow by not hindering.
tolerā'tion, *n.* act of tolerating: permitting by a government of religious freedom.
[L. *tolerāre, -ātum—tollĕre*, lift up.]

toll[1], *tōl*, *v.t.* to sound (a large bell) slowly and regularly, as for a funeral.—*v.i.* to be sounded thus.
toll'ing, *n.* and *adj.*
[M.E. *tollen*, to pull, entice.]

toll[2], *tōl*, *n.* a tax paid on crossing a bridge, using a road, etc.: loss inflicted by disaster (*a heavy toll of human lives*).
[O.E. *tol(l)*; conn. with **tell,** to count.]

tomahawk, *tom'ȧ-hök*, *n.* a light axe—weapon and tool—of North American Indians. [Amer. Indian.]

tomato, *tŏ-mä'tō*, *n.* a juicy fruit, usu. red, sometimes yellow:—*pl.* **toma'toes.**
[Sp. *tomate*—Mexican Indian *tomatl.*]

tomb, *tōōm*, *n.* a hole in earth or rock, or a vault, etc., in which a dead body is placed.
tomb'stone, *n.* a stone put up over a tomb in memory of the dead.
the tomb, death.
[Fr. *tombe*—L. *tumba*—Gk. *tymbos.*]

tomboy, *tom'boi*, *n.* a girl who prefers boyish games to games usu. thought suitable for girls.
tom'cat, *n.* a full-grown male cat.
tomfool, *tom'fōōl'*, *n.* a great fool.—*adj.* foolish.
tomfool'ery, *n.* silly actions: nonsense.
tom'tit', *n.* a small bird, tit.
Tom, Dick, and Harry, any persons taken at random: everybody.
[Name *Tom.*]

tome, *tōm*, *n.* a book, esp. a large, heavy, or learned one.
[Gk. *tomos—temnein*, to cut.]

tomfool. See **tomboy.**

tomorrow, to-morrow, *too-mor'ō*, *tŏ-*, *n.* and *adv.* the day after today.
[O.E. *tō morgen.*]

tomtit. See **tomboy.**

tom-tom, *tom'tom*, *n.* drum used in India, beaten by the hands. [Imit.]

ton, *tun*, *n.* a varying measure of space available, or of volume, used in speaking of a ship's cargo or of amount of sea water displaced by ship: a measure of weight, usu. 2240 pounds.
tonn'age, *n.* the space available in a ship, measured in tons: total amount of

merchant shipping reckoned by its carrying capacity: total weight in tons.

[O.E. *tunne*, vat, tub.]

tone, *tōn*, *n.* a musical sound: quality of a sound (e.g. *a harsh tone*): rising or falling of the voice, or sharpness or softness of its sound, by which a speaker's meaning, feelings, mood, are shown (*a tone of command*; *a tender tone*): shade of colour (e.g. *a light tone of pink*): stylishness (e.g. *to give tone to the party*).—*v.t.* to give the proper tone to: to change the colour of.—*v.i.* to fit (in with), blend (with).

tonic, *ton'ik*, *adj.* having to do with tones or sounds: giving or increasing strength. —*n.* a medicine that gives one strength and energy: anything that does this: a keynote, first note of a scale.

to tone down, to make softer, less strong, less extreme (e.g. colour, sound, an exaggerated statement): to become softer, etc.

to tone up, to give strength to (e.g. muscles).

[Gk. *tonos*, a sound.]

tongs, *tongz*, *n. pl.* an instrument for lifting and grasping, made of two movable metal arms joined at one end.

[O.E. *tange.*]

tongue, *tung*, *n.* the fleshy organ in the mouth, used in tasting, swallowing, and speaking: a language (e.g. *speaking in strange tongues*): an animal's tongue served as food: something like a tongue in shape, e.g. a jet (of flame), a strip of leather under the laces in a shoe, a point of land.

tongu'ing (*tung'*), *n.* use of tongue in playing wind instrument.

tongue'-tied, *adj.* not able to speak freely, from shyness, etc.

tongue'-twister, *n.* a word, phrase, sentence, difficult to say clearly (e.g. *She sells sea shells*).

[O.E. *tunge.*]

tonic. See **tone.**

tonight, to-night, *too-nīt'*, *tŏ-*, *n.* and *adv.* the night of the present day.

[O.E. *tō niht.*]

tonnage. See **ton.**

tonsil, *ton'sil*, *n.* either of two masses of tissue at the back of the throat.

tonsillī'tis, *n.* reddening and painfulness of tonsil(s).

[L. *tonsilla*, a stake, (in *pl.*) tonsils.]

tonsure, *ton'shür*, *n.* the shaving of the head by priests and monks: the part of the head so shaven.

[L. *tondēre*, *tonsum*, clip, shave.]

too, *tōō*, *adv.* over, extremely (e.g. *too much*): also (e.g. *I want to come too*).

[A form of *to*, meaning ' added to '.]

took. See **take.**

tool, *tōōl*, *n.* an instrument for doing work, esp. by hand: an instrument for carrying out a purpose (e.g. *Advertising is a powerful tool in increasing sales*): a person used by another in gaining his own ends. —*v.t.* to mark with a tool, esp. to put designs on (e.g. a book cover).

[O.E. *tōl, tohl.*]

toot, *tōōt*, *v.i.* to make short unmusical sounds on a flute or horn: to sound a motor horn.—Also *v.t.* and *n.*

too'tle, *v.i.* to make weak sounds on flute, etc.—Also *v.t.*

[Prob. imit.]

tooth, *tōōth*, *n.* one of the hard bodies in two rows in the mouth, used for biting and chewing: anything tooth-like: one of the points on a saw, comb, cogwheel, etc.:—*pl.* **teeth.**

toothed, *adj.* having teeth.

tooth'less, *adj.* having no teeth.

teething, *tēTH'ing*, *n.* the process of growing first teeth.—Also *adj.*

tooth'ache, *n.* a pain in a tooth.

tooth'pick, *n.* an instrument for picking out anything in or between the teeth.

tooth and nail, with all one's strength.

a sweet tooth, a love of sweet things.

in the teeth of, straight against (e.g. *to walk in the teeth of the wind*): in defiant resistance to.

to show one's teeth, to show one's anger and power to injure.

[O.E. *tōth* (pl. *tēth*).]

tootle. See **toot.**

top[1], *top*, *n.* the highest part of anything: the upper surface: the highest place or rank: the part of a plant above ground: a circus tent.—*adj.* highest, chief.—*v.t.* to cover on the top: to rise above: to do better than: to reach the top of: to take off the top of:—*pr.p.* **topp'ing;** *pa.p.* **topped.**

top'most, *adj.* highest: uppermost.

top'-boots, *n. pl.* long-legged boots with a showy band of leather round the top.

top'coat, *n.* an overcoat.

top dog, the winner: the leader.

top'-dress'ing, *n.* a dressing of manure laid on the surface of the land.

top hat, a tall silk hat.

top'-heav'y, *adj.* having the upper part too heavy for the lower.

top'notch', *adj.* of highest quality.

top'-sec'ret, *adj.* (of information) very secret because of highest importance.

in the top flight, among those of the highest quality or position. [O.E.]

top[2], *top*, *n.* a child's toy set spinning by a string, whip, or spring. [Orig. uncertain.]

topaz, *tō'paz*, *n.* a precious stone of many different shades.

[Gk. *topazion.*]

topcoat, etc. See **top** (1).

tope, *tōp*, *v.i.* to drink heavily.

top'er, *n.* **top'ing,** *n.*, *adj.*

[Orig. uncertain.]

topee. Same as **topi.**

topi, *tō'pi*, *n.* helmet-like hat used in hot countries to protect from sun.
[Hindustani *tōpī*, hat.]

topic, *top'ik*, *n.* a subject spoken, written, or argued about.
top'ical, *adj.* having to do with a topic or subject: of interest at the moment, concerned with current events.
[Gk. (pl.) *ta topika—topos*, place.]

topmost, etc. See **top** (1).

topography, *tŏ-pog'rȧ-fi*, *n.* (the description of) the features of the land in a certain region.
topog'rapher, *n.* one skilled in topography.
[Gk. *topos*, place, *graphein*, write.]

topple, *top'l*, *v.i.* to fall forward, to tumble (down, over).—*v.t.* to cause to fall over. [**top** (vb.).]

topsyturvy, *top'si-tûr'vi*, *adv.* turned upside down: in confusion.—Also *adj.*
[Prob. **top, so,** old vb. *terve*, overturn.

tor, *tör*, *n.* a hill, rocky hilltop.
[O.E. *torr*.]

torch, *törch*, *n.* flaming twisted tow carried as a light: a small hand light with switch and electric battery.
[L. *torquēre*, *tortum*, to twist.]

tore. See **tear.**

toreador, *tor'i-ȧ-dör*, *n.* a bullfighter, esp. on horseback. [Sp.]

torment, *tör'ment*, *n.* very great suffering, distress, or worry: something that causes such pain.—*v.t.* (*tŏr-ment'*) to torture, put to very great pain, physical or mental: to worry: to tease.
tormen'tor, *n.* one who torments.
[L. *tormentum*, engine for hurling stones—same root as **torture.**]

torn. See **tear.**

tornado, *tör-nā'dō*, *n.* a whirling wind that causes great damage:—*pl.* **tornā'does.**
[16th cent.—Sp. *tronada*, thunderstorm.]

torpedo, *tör-pē'dō*, *n.* a type of fish with organs on the head that give an electric shock: a large cigar-shaped self-propelled missile, fired from ships or planes, which explodes when it hits its mark:—*pl.* **torpē'does.**—*v.t.* to attack with, damage or destroy by means of, torpedo(es).
torpe'do-boat, *n.* a small swift warship which attacks with torpedoes.
torpedo-boat destroyer, larger, swifter type of torpedo-boat.
[L.—*torpēre*, to be stiff.]

torpid, *tör'pid*, *adj.* slow, sluggish.
torpid'ity, tor'por, *ns.*
[L. *torpēre*, to be stiff.]

torrent, *tor'ĕnt*, *n.* a rushing stream (of water, lava, etc.): a violent flow (of e.g. rain, words, insults).
torren'tial (*-shȧl*), *adj.* like a torrent.
[L. *torrens*, *-entis*, burning, boiling, rushing—root as **torrid.**]

torrid, *tor'id*, *adj.* burning hot: parched by heat.
torrid zone, a broad band round the earth on either side of the equator, between the tropics of Cancer and Capricorn.
[L. *torrēre*, *tostum*, to burn.]

torsion, *tör'sh(ŏ)n*, *n.* act of twisting or turning an object.
[L. *torquēre*, *tortum*, to twist.]

torso, *tör'sō*, *n.* the trunk without head or limbs, esp. of statue:—*pl.* **tor'sos.** [It.]

tortoise, *tör'tŭs*, *n.* a slow-moving reptile covered with a hard shell (a turtle or, more usu., a land type of turtle).
tor'toise-shell, *tör'tĕ-shel*, *n.* the shell of a type of sea turtle.—*adj.* of the colour of this shell, mixed red, yellow, and black.
[O.Fr. *tortis*—L. *tortus*, twisted.]

tortuous, *tör'tū-ŭs*, *adj.* twisting, winding: (of e.g. methods) deceitful, crooked.
[Fr.—L. root as **torsion, torture.**]

torture, *tör'chŭr*, *n.* severe pain inflicted as a punishment or to force a confession: great suffering of body or mind.—*v.t.* to inflict torture on: to twist out of the natural shape, position, or meaning, etc.
[Same L. root as **torsion, tortuous.**]

Tory, *tō'ri*, *tö'*, *n.* a Conservative (see this word) in English politics:—*pl.* **-ies.**
[Ir. *toiridhe*, a pursuer; first applied to Irish highway robbers, then to hot-headed followers of James II, then to political party.]

toss, *tos*, *v.t.* to throw lightly or carelessly: to throw about lightly or restlessly: to throw up (a coin) to see which side is uppermost when it falls: to toss up with (e.g. *I'll toss you for the seat*): to throw up with force or with a jerk (e.g. *The bull tossed its master*; *she tossed her head in scorn*).—*v.i.* to throw oneself from side to side restlessly: (of e.g. ship) to be thrown about.—Also *n.*
toss'-up, *n.* the tossing of a coin to decide something: something not settled, an even chance (e.g. *It is a toss-up whether we can catch the train*).
to take a toss, to be thrown by a horse: to suffer defeat, etc.
to toss off, to drink off: to produce quickly and easily (e.g. rhymes).
to toss up, to stake e.g. money, or make a choice depend, on which side of a tossed coin falls uppermost.
to win, lose, the toss, to guess rightly, wrongly, which side of a coin will fall uppermost. [Orig. uncertain.]

tot[1], *tot*, *n.* a small child: a small amount of a liquor. [Orig. unknown.]

tot[2], *tot*, *v.t.* to add up (usu. **tot up**).—*n.* an addition of a long column. [**total.**]

total, *tō'tȧl*, *adj.* whole (e.g. *The total number, loss, was four cows*): complete (e.g. *The burned ship was a total loss*: *a total rejection of the offer*).—*n.* the sum: the entire amount.—*v.t.* to add up: to amount to (e.g. *The bill totalled*

fifty pounds):—*pr.p.* **tō′talling**; *pa.p.* **tō′talled.**
tō′tally, *adv.* completely.
total′ity, *n.* the whole sum, amount.
tō′talisātor, *n.* a machine recording number and nature of bets, so that winners may share total stakes.
totalitā′rian, *adj.* belonging to a system of government by one party that allows no rivals.
[Fr.—L. *tōtus.*]

totem, *tō′tem, n.* an animal, plant, or object taken as the badge or sign of a tribe, etc. among American Indians and other primitive groups: an image of this.
totem pole, a pole, set up in front of an American Indian house, on which totems were carved and painted.
[Amer. Indian.]

totter, *tot′ėr, v.i.* to walk unsteadily: to be unsteady, shake as if about to fall (e.g. *The house, his empire, totters*).
tott′ery, *adj.* shaky. **tott′eriness,** *n.*
[M.E.; perh. Scand.]

toucan, *to͞o′kan,* or *-kan′, n.* a South American bird with a huge beak.
[Fr.; from Brazilian.]

touch, *tuch, v.t.* to be, or to come, in contact with, to lay hand, etc., against: to reach as high as: to call at (port): to handle, move, etc., slightly: to mark slightly (with e.g. colour): to come up to (another) in goodness, skill, etc.: to play on (a musical instrument): to take, taste (e.g. *He won't touch fruit*): to speak of (a subject) in passing (e.g. *He touched that point briefly*): to concern, affect (a person): to move, make feel pity, etc.: (*coll.*) to persuade (someone) to give or lend money (e.g. *I touched him for £1*). Meanings found only with 'not' include those in the following sentences:—*I did not touch it* (steal it), *touch him* (strike, etc., him); *I will not touch it* (have anything to do with it).—*v.i.* to be in contact: to call (at a port): to speak of (with *on*).—*n.* act of touching: the sense by which one becomes aware of contact: communication (e.g. *I am in touch with the owner*): sympathy, understanding (e.g. *out of touch with present taste in art*): a slight quantity or degree (e.g. *a touch of salt, of imagination, of cold*): skill in, or style of, handling a musical instrument: (*football*) the part of the field outside lines (**touch′-lines**) marking sides of area of play.
touched, *adj.* stirred to gentle emotion: (*coll.*; of person) slightly crazy.
touch′ing, *adj.* moving, causing emotion.—*adv.* concerning.
touch′ingly, *adv.*
touch′y, *adj.* easily offended.
touch′iness, *n.*
touch′-and-go′, *adj.* very uncertain (e.g. *It was touch-and-go whether he would recover*).
touch′-down, *n.* the touching to the ground behind the goal line of a football by a player: alighting of aircraft on ground.—Also *v.i.* (**touch down**).
touch′stone, *n.* a stone used in testing purity of gold and silver: anything used as a test.
touch′wood, *n.* wood made into a substance that catches fire readily.
to touch off, to cause to explode, or to become active (e.g. *A spark touched off the gunpowder*; *his remark touched off an argument*).
to touch up, to improve (e.g. a drawing) by a number of small touches.
[O.Fr. *tochier* (Fr. *toucher*).]

tough, *tuf, adj.* not easily broken: not easily chewed: able to stand hardship or strain: hardened in wrongdoing: difficult: (*coll.*; of luck) hard.—*n.* a rough, bully.
tough′en, *v.t.* or *v.i.* to make, or become, tough. [O.E. *tōh.*]

toupee, *to͞o′pā, n.* a small wig or patch of false hair.
[Fr. *toupet.*]

tour, *to͞or, n.* a going round: a journey to various places, ending at starting point.—*v.t., v.i.* to travel from place to place (in).
tour′ism, *n.* touring for pleasure: tourists in general.
tour′ist, *n.* a sight-seeing traveller.
tourist class, a type of less expensive accommodation on ships and aircraft.
[Fr.—same L. root as **turn.**]

tour de force, *to͞or dė fōrs, n.* a feat of strength or skill. [Fr.]

tournament, *to͞or′nȧ-mėnt, n.* in the Middle Ages, a sport in which knights fought on horseback: any contest in skill consisting of a series of games in which a number of people take part (e.g. *a tennis, chess, tournament*).
[O.Fr. *tornoiement*—L. root as **turn.**]

tourniquet, *to͞or′ni-kā, -ket, n.* a bandage or other device for pressing tightly on the main artery of thigh or arm to prevent great loss of blood.
[Fr.—L. root as **turn.**]

tousle, *tow′zl, v.t.* to make untidy, tangle (esp. hair).—Also *n.*
[M.E. *tusen.*]

tout, *towt, v.i.* (*coll.*) to go about seeking custom, support, votes, etc.—*n.* one who does this: one who obtains secretly, or gives, information for betting.
[Conn. with O.E. *tōtian*, to look out.]

tow[1], *tō, n.* coarse part of flax or hemp.
tow′-headed, *adj.* flaxen-haired.
[O.E. *tow*(*cræft*), spinning.]

tow[2], *tō, v.t.* to pull (vessel) through water, or pull (e.g. vehicle), with a rope.—*n.* a rope for towing with: act of towing.
tow′line, *n.* rope, etc., used in towing.
to have, take, in tow, have, take, under one's guidance or protection.
[O.E. *togian*, to pull; conn. **tug.**]

toward(s), *tō-wörd(z)′*, *too-wörd(z)′*, *törd(z)*, *prep.* (moving, facing, etc.) in the direction of: as regards (e.g. *his attitude towards his son, towards the plan*): as part of, a help to (e.g. *towards the price of*): near, about (in e.g. time, number).
[O.E. *tō*, to, *ward*, showing direction.]

towel, *tow′ėl*, *n.* a cloth or paper for wiping e.g. the skin after washing.
tow′elling, *n.* cloth for towels.
[Fr. *toaille*—Germanic word, to wash.]

tower, *tow′ėr*, *n.* a high narrow building, standing alone or forming part of another: a fortress.—*v.i.* to rise above surrounding things or people (with *over, above*).
tow′ering, *adj.* very high: very violent (e.g. *a towering rage*).
[O.Fr. *tur*—L. *turris*.]

towline. See **tow** (2).

town, *town*, *n.* a place larger than a village: the people living in it.
town centre, *n.* the most important shopping area of a town.
town council, governing body in a town, elected by the ratepayers.
town councillor, a member of a town council.
town hall, a public hall for the official business of a town.
towns′folk, towns′people, *ns. pl.* the people of a town.
towns′man, *n.* an inhabitant of a town (esp. in *fellow townsman*, fellow citizen):—*fem.* **towns′woman.**
to go to town, to go to London or nearest large town: to let oneself go, act freely, spend freely.
[O.E. *tūn*, an enclosure, town.]

tox(o)-, *toks(-ō)-*, (as part of word) poison.
toxicology, *tok-si-kol′ŏ-ji*, *n.* the science of poisons.
tox′ic, *adj.* caused, or affected, by a poison: poisonous.
tox′in, *n.* naturally produced poison (e.g. that of a snake).
[Gk. *toxikon*, arrow poison—*toxon*, bow.]

toy, *toi*, *n.* a child's plaything: a thing for amusement only.—Also *adj.*—*v.i.* to trifle, play (e.g. *He toyed with his food, with the idea*).
toy dog, a dog of a very small kind—of various breeds.
[Orig. uncertain.]

trace[1], *trās*, *n.* a mark left: a line of footprints: a small amount: a line or outline lightly drawn or marked, or copied through thin paper: the line drawn by an instrument recording a changing quantity (e.g. temperature).—*v.t.* to follow the tracks of, or the course of (e.g. *He traced the deer*; *traced the river to the sea, to its source*; *traced the trouble to its source*; *traced the course of Roman history*): to copy (map, etc.) through thin paper (and transfer it to a new sheet): to make (e.g. letters) with care.
trace′able, *adj.* able to be traced (to), or shown to be due (to).
trā′cery, *n.* delicate work in interlacing lines, e.g. decorative stonework holding the glass in some church windows, or frost patterns:—*pl.* **-ies.**
trā′cing, *n.* copy made by tracing.
[Fr.—L. *trahĕre*, *tractum*, to drag.]

trace[2], *trās*, *n.* one of the straps by which a carriage or cart is drawn.
to kick over the traces. See **kick.**
[O.Fr. *trays*—L. root as **trace** (1).]

trachea, *trȧ-kē′ȧ*, *trā′ki-ȧ*, *n.* the windpipe.
[Gk. *tracheia* (*artēria*) rough (artery).]

tracing. See **trace** (1).

track, *trak*, *v.t.* to follow by marks, footsteps, evidence, etc.—*n.* a mark left: (in *pl.*) footprints: a beaten path: course laid out for races: a line of rails.
track′less, *adj.* without a path.
on the wrong side of the tracks, in a slum or bad part of town.
to keep (lose) track of, to keep (not to keep) oneself aware of the whereabouts or progress of.
to make tracks for, to go off towards, esp. hastily.
[Middle Fr. *trac*; prob. Germanic.]

tract, *trakt*, *n.* a region, stretch of land: parts forming a bodily system (e.g. *the digestive tract*): a short essay or pamphlet, esp. on a religious subject.
[L. root as **tractable, trace** (1), (2).]

tractable, *trak′tȧ-bl*, *adj.* easily worked: (of person) easily managed or led.
tractabil′ity, trac′tableness, *ns.*
trac′tion, *n.* act of dragging or pulling, or state of being pulled.—Also *adj.*
trac′tor, *n.* a motor vehicle used for pulling loads, working ploughs, etc.
[Same L. root as **trace** (1), (2).]

trade, *trād*, *n.* buying and selling: occupation, craft, job (e.g. *He is a mason by trade*): men engaged in the same kind of work.—*v.i.* to buy and sell: to carry goods (to a place): to have dealings (with a person): to deal (in).—*v.t.* (orig. U.S.) to exchange, barter.
trā′der, *n.* one who trades: a merchant ship.
trade′mark, trade′(-)mark, *n.* a registered mark or name belonging to a firm or person (and forbidden to be used by others) put on goods to show that they were made by him or it.
trades′man, *n.* a shopkeeper: a workman in a skilled trade:—pl. **-men.**
trades′people, *n. pl.* tradesmen.
trade union, workers of the same trade who join together so that they can bargain about wages, conditions, hours, etc.
trade unionism, the system of joining in trade unions: trade unions as a whole.
trade unionist, believer in trade unionism: member of trade union.
trade wind, a wind blowing steadily towards the equator.

to trade in, to give in part payment.
to trade on, to take advantage of unfairly (e.g. *He traded on the fact that the manager was his cousin*).
[M.E., trodden path ; conn. with **tread.**]

tradition, *trȧ-dish'(ȯ)n, n.* the handing down of stories, opinions, practices, from earlier to later generations : a belief or custom handed down in this way.
tradi'tional, *adj.* **tradi'tionally,** *adv.*
[L. *trans*, over, *dăre*, *datum*, to give.]

traduce, *trȧ-dūs', v.t.* to speak evil falsely about.
[L. *trādūcĕre* (*transdūcĕre*), to lead along in public to show disgrace.]

traffic, *traf'ik, n.* trade : dealings (esp. when dishonest) : passing to and fro : the vehicles, etc., using road(s), railway(s), waterway(s), airway(s).—*v.i.* to trade : to deal (in).—*v.t.* to exchange :—*pr.p.* **traff'icking ;** *pa.p.* **traff'icked.**
traffic lights, lights of changing colour for controlling traffic at street crossings.
[O.Fr. *trafique*.]

tragedy, *traj'i-di, n.* a play about unhappy event(s) and with a sad ending : a very sad happening, or one with very unfortunate results.
tragē'dian, tragēdienne', *ns.* an actor, actress, of tragic rôles.
trag'ic, *adj.* having to do with tragedy : sorrowful : terrible.
trag'icom'edy, *n.* a play, or events, both sad or serious and funny.
[Gk. *tragōidia*, ' goat-song '.]

trail, *trāl, v.t.* to draw along, in, through (e.g. *He trailed his foot along the sand, in, through the water*) : to hunt by tracking.—*v.i.* to hang down (from), or be dragged loosely (behind) : (of e.g. smoke) to stream, float (from and behind) : to walk slowly and wearily : (of plant) to run or climb.—*n.* the track followed by a hunter : a track or path through a wild region : something left stretching behind (e.g. *a trail of smoke, of debts, of misery*).
trail'er, *n.* one who trails : a climbing plant : a vehicle dragged behind another : a strip of film shown to advertise a coming motion picture.
trailing edge, the rearmost edge of an aeroplane wing or propeller blade (opp. to **leading edge**).
[Through O.Fr.—L. as **trace** (1), (2).]

train, *trān, v.t.* to educate (e.g. *to train a child in good habits*) : to tame and teach (animal) : to cause (plant) to grow in a particular way : to prepare (person) for a sport, a trade, war, etc., or (horse) for racing : to aim, point at (with *on* ; e.g. *They trained the gun on the hill*).—*v.i.* to make oneself ready (for something) by practice, etc.—*n.* a part of a dress that trails behind the wearer : the attendants who follow an important person : baggage animals, etc., in file : a line of linked carriages behind a railway engine : a series (e.g. of incidents), line (e.g. of thought).
trained, *adj.* skilled through training.
trainee', *n.* one who is being trained.
train'er, *n.* one who prepares men for sport or horses for a race.
train'ing, *n.* preparation for a sport : teaching in the practical side of a profession, craft, etc.—Also *adj.*
train'-bear'er, *n.* one who holds up the train of a robe or gown on a formal occasion.
train'-ferry, *n.* a ship that carries railway trains across water, e.g. across the Channel.
in train, in order, ready (for).
[Fr.—same L. root as **trace** (1), (2).]

trait, *trāt*, or *trā, n.* a noticeable feature of a person's character or mind (e.g. *Willingness to listen is one of his good traits*).
[Fr.—same L. root as **trace** (1), (2).]

traitor, *trā'tȯr, n.* one who betrays when he has been trusted : one who betrays his country, goes over to the enemy.
trai'torous, *adj.* **trai'torously,** *adv.*
See also **treason.**
[Fr. *traître*—L. *trādĕre*, to give up.]

trajectory, *trȧ-jek'tȯ-ri, n.* the curved path of a body (e.g. bullet) propelled through air.
[L. *trans*, across, *jacĕre*, to throw.]

tram(**car**), *tram*(*-kär*), *n.* a car running on rails and driven usu. by electricity, used to carry passengers along streets.
tram'way, -line, *n.* rails for tramcars.
[Dial. Eng. *tram*, a beam.]

trammel, *tram'l, n.* type of net : (often in *pl.*) anything that hinders movement.—*v.t.* to keep back, hinder.
[L. *tres*, three, *macula*, mesh.]

tramp, *tramp, v.t.* to travel over on foot : to walk with heavy footsteps.—*v.i.* to go on foot : to wander about as a tramp.—*n.* a journey on foot : a heavy tread or footstep : a cargo boat with no fixed trade route : a person who wanders with no fixed home, usu. begging, a vagrant.
trample, *tram'pl, v.t.* to tread under foot, stamp on : to treat roughly, unfeelingly.—*v.i.* to tread heavily : to walk (over, on) : to behave cruelly (with *on* ; e.g. *to trample on the losers, one's feelings*).
[M.E. *trampe* ; a Germanic word.]

trampolin(**e**), *tram'pō-lin, n.* an elastic mattress-like piece of apparatus for gymnasts, acrobats, etc.
[It. *trampolino*, springboard.]

tramway. See **tram.**

trance, *trâns, n.* a sleeplike or half-conscious state : a state in which one is not aware of surroundings because lost in thought.
[L. *transīre*, *transitum*, to go across.]

tranquil, *trang'kwil, adj.* quiet, peaceful.
tran'quilly, *adv.*
tranquill'ity, tran'quilness, *ns.*

tran'quillise, *v.t.* to make quiet.
tran'quilliser, *n.* a drug to calm nerves or cause sleep.
[Fr.—L. *tranquillus.*]

trans-, *trânz-, trâns-, pfx.* across, through, on the other side of. [L.]

transact, *trânz-akt', trâns-, v.t.* to carry through (business).—Also *v.i.*
transac'tion, *n.* (act of carrying through) a deal, piece of business.
[L. *trans,* through, root as **act.**]

transatlantic, *trânz-, trans-ât-lan'tik, adj.* crossing the Atlantic Ocean: beyond, on the other side of, it. [Pfx. **trans-.**]

transcend, *trân-send', v.t.* to rise, be, above or beyond: to do, be, better than.
transcen'dent, *adj.* supreme or very high in excellence, etc. (e.g. *transcendent goodness, importance*).
transcen'dence, -dency, *ns.*
[L. *trans,* beyond, *scandĕre,* to climb.]

transcontinental, *trânz-kon-ti-nen'tȧl, adj.* crossing a continent. [Pfx. **trans-.**]

transcribe, *trân-skrīb', v.t.* to write over from one book into another, or from one form into another (e.g. from shorthand into ordinary lettering): to make an arrangement (see this word) of (a musical composition): to record for future broadcasting, etc.
tran'script, *n.* something transcribed: a written copy.
transcrip'tion, *n.* act of transcribing: a transcript.
[L. *trans,* over, *scrībĕre, scriptum,* write.]

transept, *trân'sept, n.* part of a cruciform (cross-shaped) church at right angles to the main part or nave.
[L. *trans,* across, *saeptum,* enclosure.]

transfer, *trâns-fėr', v.t.* to carry, send, etc., from one place to another: to hand over to another person, esp. legally: to convey (e.g. a design) from one surface to another.—*v.i.* to move oneself from one place, conveyance, job (to another):—*pr.p.* **transferr'ing;** *pa.p.* **transferred'.** —*n.* (*trans'*) act of transferring: something transferred: a ticket that allows the holder to continue his journey in a second vehicle.
transfer'able (or *trans'*), *adj.* that may be transferred from one place or person to another.
trans'ference, *n.* the act of transferring from one person or place to another.
[L. *trans,* across, *fĕrre,* to carry.]

transfigure, *trâns-fig'ėr, v.t.* to transform in appearance to something finer, more beautiful, etc.
transfiguration, *-fig-ū-rā'sh(ȯ)n, n.*
the Transfiguration, the change in appearance of Christ described in Matthew xvii: festival (6th August) commemorating this.
[L. *trans,* across, root as **figure.**]

transfix, *trâns-fiks', v.t.* to pierce through: (of horror, surprise, etc.) to make unable to move, act, think.
[L. *trans,* through, root as **fix.**]

transform, *trâns-förm', v.t.* to change the appearance, nature, character of.—*v.i.* to be changed in appearance, etc.
transformā'tion, *n.*
transform'er, *n.* a device for changing electrical energy from one voltage to another.
[L. *trans,* across, root as **form.**]

transfuse, *trâns-fūz', v.t.* to pour from one thing into another: to transfer (blood of one person) to body of another.
transfū'sion, *n.* act of transfusing.
[L. *trans,* over, *fundĕre, fūsum,* pour.]

transgress, *trânz-gres', trâns-, v.t.* to go beyond (e.g. *This, he, transgresses the bounds of common sense*): to break (a law, command).—Also *v.i.* (with *against*).
transgress'ion (*-gresh'ȯn*), *n.* breaking of a law or command: a fault: a sin.
transgress'or, *n.* one who breaks a law: a sinner.
[L. *trans,* across, *gradī, gressus,* to step.]

tranship. Same as **trans-ship.**

transient, *trân'zi-ėnt, trân'si-, tran'shėnt, adj.* passing, not lasting (e.g. *a transient feeling of annoyance*): (of person) passing through place, not staying long.
tran'sience, tran'sientness, *ns.*
[Same root as **transit.**]

transistor, *tran-sis'tȯr, n.* an amplifier (see this) with a crystal and two cat's whiskers (fine wires): a later development of this which, though very small in size, is able to perform many of the functions of valves.

transit, *trân'sit, -zit, n.* a passing over: the carrying, etc., from one place to another (e.g. *The parcel was lost in transit*): the passing of a planet between the earth and the sun.—*v.t.* to pass across or through.
transi'tion, *n.* passage from one place, state, subject, etc. to another (e.g. *a quick transition from anger to amusement*).
transi'tional, *adj.* (e.g. *the transitional period, or time of transition*).
tran'sitive, *adj.* (of verb) that has an object (e.g. *to hit, to save,* in *to hit the ball, to save money*).
tran'sitory, *adj.* passing away: lasting only for a short time.
tran'sitorily, *adv.* **tran'sitoriness,** *n.*
[L. *trans,* across, *īre, itum,* to go.]

translate, *trâns-lāt', trânz-, v.t.* to remove to another place or state: to put into another language (e.g. *Translate this English book, the remark, into Russian*).
translā'tion, *n.* act of translating: a version in another language.
translā'tor, *n.*
[L. *trans,* over, *fĕrre, lātum,* to carry.]

translucent, *trâns-lōō'sėnt, -lū', trânz-, adj.* allowing light to pass, but not transparent (see this).

translu′cence, translu′cency, *ns.*
[L. *trans*, across, *lūcēre*, to shine.]

transmigrate, *trânz′mi-grāt, trâns-, -mī′*, *v.i.* to migrate: (of soul) to pass into another body after death.
transmigrā′tion, *n.*
[L. *trans*, across, root as **migrate.**]

transmission. See **transmit.**

transmit, *trânz-mit′, trâns-, v.t.* to pass on to another person or place: to be the means of passing on (e.g. heat, news, message).—*v.i.* to send out radio or other signals:—*pr.p.* **transmitt′ing;** *pa.p.* **transmitt′ed.**
transmiss′ion, *n.* the sending from one place or person to another: something transmitted: (sending out of) radio signals or programme.
transmitt′er, *n.* one who transmits: a set or station sending out radio waves for conversion into sound or pictures by a receiving set or station.
[L. *trans*, across, *mittĕre, missum*, send.]

transmute, *trânz-mūt′, trâns-, v.t.* to change, transform, esp. to another substance or nature (e.g. *Long before men could split the atom they tried to transmute common metals to gold*).
transmutā′tion, *n.*
[L. *trans*, over, *mūtāre*, to change.]

transom, *trân′sȯm, n.* a beam across a window or the top of a door.
[Conn. **traverse.**]

transparency, *trâns-pār′ėn-si, trânz-, -par′-, n.* quality of being transparent: something transparent: a picture on semi-transparent material seen by light shining through:—*pl.* **-ies.**
transpar′ent, *adj.* (of material, or of pretence, disguise, etc.) that can be seen through easily (e.g. *Ordinary glass is transparent; transparent lies*): clear, obvious (e.g. *her transparent honesty*).
[L. *trans*, through, root as **appear.**]

transpire, *trân-spīr′, v.t., v.i.* to pass out (moisture, etc.) through pores of the skin, or through surface of leaves.—*v.i.* (of e.g. secret) to become known: (*wrongly*) to happen.
transpirā′tion, *n.*
[L. *trans*, through, root as **expire,** etc.]

transplant, *trâns-plant′, v.t.* to remove and plant in another place: to remove and re-settle: to remove (skin) and graft it in another place, (an organ) and graft it in another individual.—*v.i.* to (be able to) survive transplantation—*n.* (*trans′*) a plant, organ, etc., transplanted.
transplantā′tion, *n.* [Pfx. **trans-.**]

transport, *trâns-pōrt′, -pört′, v.t.* to carry from one place to another: to send (e.g. a prisoner) to another land: (of strong emotion) to carry away (e.g. *Joy transported him; he was transported with grief*).—*n.* (*trans′*) carrying from one place to another: means of doing this: a ship, truck, etc. for carrying troops and their stores: strong attack of emotion (e.g. *a transport of rage; transports of joy*).
transportā′tion, *n.* act of transporting: sending of convict overseas: (*U.S.*) means of transport.
[L. *trans*, across, *portāre*, to carry.]

transpose, *trânz-pōz′, v.t.* to cause (two or more things) to change places: to alter the order of: (*music*) to change the key of.
transposi′tion, transpō′sal, *ns.*
[L. *trans*, across, *pōnĕre, positum*, place.]

trans-ship, *trans-ship′, trânz-, v.t., v.i.* to change from one ship, etc., to another.
[Pfx. **trans-.**]

transverse, *trânz-vėrs′, adj.* lying across.
transverse′ly, *adv.*
[L. *trans*, across, *vertĕre, versum*, turn.]

trap, *trap, n.* an instrument for catching animals: a plan or trick for catching a person unawares: a bend in a pipe always full of water, for preventing escape of air, gas: a light carriage with two wheels.—*v.t.* to catch in a trap, or by a trick:—*pr.p.* **trapp′ing;** *pa.p.* **trapped.**
trapp′er, *n.* one who traps animals for their fur.
trap′-door, *n.* a door in a floor.
[O.E. *træppe.*]

trapes, *trāps, v.i.* to gad about idly.
[Orig. uncertain.]

trapeze, *trȧ-pēz′, n.* a swing used in doing gymnastic exercises.
[Gk. *trapeza*, a table.]

traps, *traps, n. pl.* personal belongings, luggage.
trapp′ings, *n. pl.* gay or dignified clothes or ornaments proper to a person or an occasion: ornaments put on horses.
[Same root as **drape.**]

trash, *trash, n.* something of little worth or use, rubbish.
trash′y, *adj.* **trash′iness,** *n.*
[Probably Scand.]

trauma, *trö′mȧ, n.* a condition caused by violent injury: a shock, distressing experience, having a lasting effect.
[Gk., a wound.]

travail, *trav′āl, n.* very hard, esp. painful, work: pain suffered during childbirth.—Also *v.i.*
[O.Fr. *travailler* (vb.).]

travel, *trav′ėl, v.i.* to move: to go on a journey.—*v.t.* to journey along, through (e.g. *He will travel the roads of, travel, Germany*):—*pr.p.* **trav′elling;** *pa.p.* **trav′elled.**—*n.* act of passing from place to place: (often in *pl.*) journeys, esp. in foreign lands: written account of such journeys.
trav′elled, *adj.* having done much varied travelling.
trav′eller, *n.* one who travels: a travelling representative of business firm.
trav′elling-bag, *n.* a traveller's bag for clothes, etc. carried in the hand.
travelogue, *trav′ė-log, n.* a talk, article

or esp. motion picture with commentary, about travels. [**travail.**]

traverse, *trav′ėrs, n.* anything laid or built across: sideways course in rock climbing: zigzag track of ship.—*v.t.* to pass over, across, or through: to move sideways, or from side to side, over.
[Through O.Fr.—root as **transverse.**]

travesty, *trav′is-ti, n.* a grotesque, bad, imitation (e.g. *He sat proudly in a travesty of an armchair*; *the trial was a travesty of justice*).—*v.t.* to imitate badly.
[Fr. *travestir,* to disguise.]

trawl, *trōl, v.i.* to fish by dragging a trawl along the bottom of the sea.—*n.* an open-mouthed bag-shaped net.
traw′ler, *n.* one who trawls: a boat used in trawling.
[Perh. from Middle Du.]

tray, *trā, n.* a flat board or sheet of metal, wood, or plastic, with low edge, for carrying or holding articles.
[O.E. *trēg.*]

treachery, *trech′ėr-i, n.* (an act of) betraying the trust another has put in one, disloyalty, unfaithfulness :—pl. **-ies.**
treach′erous, *adj.* guilty of treachery, or liable to betray: (of memory) untrustworthy: (of e.g. ice, bog) dangerous.
treach′erously, *adv.* **-erousness,** *n.*
[O.Fr. *tricherie*; root as **trick.**]

treacle, *trē′kl, n.* a dark sticky liquid that drains from sugar at different stages in its manufacture, molasses.
[O.Fr. *triacle*—Gk. *thēriakē,* remedy against bites—*thērion,* wild beast.]

tread, *tred, v.i.* to set the foot down (on): to walk or go.—*v.t.* to walk on, along: to crush under foot, trample (e.g. *Passers-by will tread it into the ground*) :—*pa.t.* **trod**; *pa.p.* **trod** or **trodd′en.**—*n.* a step, way of stepping: the part of a shoe, wheel, or tyre, that touches the ground.
tread′le, *n.* a part of a machine moved by the foot.
tread′mill, *n.* device turned by the weight of e.g. person(s) made to walk on steps fixed round a large cylinder (used long ago in prisons): any unchanging, wearisome routine.
to tread in one's steps, to follow one's example.
to tread on one's toes, to offend one, hurt one's feelings. See also **corn** (2).
to tread water, to keep upright position in deep water.
[O.E. *tredan.*]

treason, *trē′zn, n.* disloyalty to ruler or government by trying to overthrow him, it, giving information to enemy, etc. (also called **high treason**): (*rarely*) treachery.
trea′sonable, *adj.* (of action) consisting of, or involving, treason.
[O.Fr. *traïson*—L. root as **betray.**]

treasure, *trezh′ůr, n.* wealth stored up: anything greatly valued.—*v.t.* to store, store (up), or keep in mind, because one values (e.g. *The old woman treasures her possessions, memories, your visits*).
treas′urer, *n.* one who has charge of collected funds (e.g. of a club).
treas′ury, *n.* a place where money is kept: (*cap.*) a department of a government which has charge of the finances :—*pl.* **treas′uries.**
treasure-trove, *trezh′ůr-trōv, n.* treasure or money found in the earth, the owner being unknown.
[Fr. *trésor*—Gk. *thēsauros* (*trove* from O.Fr. *trover,* to find).]

treat, *trēt, v.t.* to handle, use, deal with, act towards (in a certain manner; e.g. *to treat with care, kindly*): to try to cure or give relief to (e.g. *He treated her for rheumatism, treated her chilblains*): to write or speak about (e.g. *She treated this subject fully in her lecture*): to pay for a meal, drink, etc. for (another person).—*v.i.* to deal (with), try to arrange a settlement (with e.g. enemy): to speak or write about (with *of*; e.g. *The second book treats of insects*).—*n.* an entertainment: a cause of special enjoyment or pleasure (e.g. *It was a treat to see her so happy*).
treat′ise (*-is*), *n.* a long, formal, detailed, carefully arranged essay.
treat′ment, *n.* act, or manner, of treating: remedies (for disease): behaviour to (person; with *of*; e.g. *Her treatment of her mother was cruel*).
treat′y, *n.* a formal agreement between states (about e.g. alliance, terms of peace) :—*pl.* **treat′ies.**
to treat as, to consider to be, deal with as if (e.g. *Do not treat the matter, him, as unimportant*).
[O.Fr. *traitier*—L. *tractāre,* to handle.]

treble, *treb′l, adj.* triple, threefold (e.g. *walls of treble thickness*): high in pitch.—*n.* the highest part in singing (soprano), or for instrument: (a singer with) a high voice.—*v.t., v.i.,* to make, or become, three times as much.
treb′ly, *adv.*
[O.Fr.—same L. root as **triple.**]

tree, *trē, n.* a large plant with a single firm woody trunk, from which grow woody branches: anything like a tree: a piece of wood shaped for a special purpose.—*v.t.* to drive into or up a tree: to force into a hopeless situation.
tree′less, *adj.* **tree′lessness,** *n.*
tree′top, *n.*
genealogical (or **family**) **tree.** See **genealogy** (at **gene**).
[O.E. *trēo*(*w*).]

trefoil, *trē′foil, tre′, n.* any plant whose leaves are divided into three leaflets (e.g. the clovers): an ornament or shape (e.g. in stone tracery) suggesting a three-part leaf.
[L. *tres,* three, *folium,* a leaf.]

trek, *trek, v.i.* to journey by ox-drawn

wagon: to migrate (to a new home): (*coll.*) to make a long hard journey (to):—*pr.p.* **trekk′ing**; *pa.p.* **trekked.**—*n.* a journey, esp. by wagon: a long or wearisome journey.
[Du. *trekken*, to draw, travel.]

trellis, *trel′is, n.* a device consisting of crossed strips usu. of wood (**trell′is-work**), for holding up growing plants, etc.
[O.Fr. *treillis.*]

tremble, *trem′bl, v.i.* to shake, shiver, from fear, cold, or weakness: to fear greatly (e.g. *I tremble for Mary if she does this*; *tremble at the sight, to think what will happen*).—*n.* act of, or fit of, trembling.
trem′bling, *n.* and *adj.*
trem′ūlous, *adj.* trembling: shaking: showing fear, etc. (e.g. *a tremulous voice*).
tremor, *trem′ŏr, n.* a shaking, quivering, vibration: a thrill (of e.g. excitement).
earth tremor, a slight earthquake.
[O.Fr. *trembler*—L. *tremĕre*, to shake.]

tremendous, *trė-men′dŭs, adj.* very large, great, or powerful.
tremen′dously, *adv.* (*coll.*) very.
[L. *tremendus*, fit to be trembled at.]

tremor, tremulous. See **tremble.**

trench, *trench*, or *-sh, v.t.* to dig a ditch in: to dig (ground) deeply with the spade or plough.—*v.i.* to make trench(es).—*n.* a long narrow cut in the earth: one dug by soldiers as a shelter from enemy fire.
tren′cher, *n.* one who digs trenches.
trench coat, *n.* a lined, belted waterproof overcoat, esp. military.
[M.E.—O.Fr. *trenchier*, to cut.]

trenchant, *tren′chănt, -shănt, adj.* (orig. of weapon, now of e.g. remark, style of writing or speaking, policy) cutting straight to the point, vigorous, effective.
[Same root as **trench.**]

trencher[1]. See **trench.**

trencher[2], *tren′chėr, -shėr, n.* a wooden plate or tray used long ago for cutting meat on, or serving food, at meals: a mortar-board (see this).
a good, poor, etc., **trencherman, -woman,** one who eats much, little.
[Same root as **trench.**]

trend, *trend, v.i.* to run, bend, take a general direction (e.g. *Here the river trends round to the east*; *the discussion soon trended away from the coming concert towards the faults of last year's*).—*n.* the general direction, course (of e.g. a river, events, opinion, fashion).
[O.E. *trendan.*]

trepidation, *trep-i-dā′sh(ŏ)n, n.* nervousness, flurry, fear of what is coming.
[L. *trepidāre, -ātum*, hurry with alarm.]

trespass, *tres′păs, v.i.* to enter unlawfully (on another's land, etc.): to take or demand too much of (with *on*; e.g. *He trespasses on your time, kindness*): to sin.—*n.* act of trespassing on property, rights, generosity, etc.: a sin.
tres′passer, *n.*
[L. *trans*, across, *passus*, a step.]

tress, *tres, n.* a plait or lock of hair: (in *pl.*) hair, usu. long.
[Fr. *tresse*; orig. uncertain.]

trestle, *tres′l, n.* a wooden support, usu. a bar with legs, for a table, platform, etc.
[O.Fr. *trestel*; orig. uncertain.]

trews, *trōōz, n. pl.* trousers of tartan cloth.
[Ir. *trius*, Gael. *triubhas.*]

tri-, *trī, pfx.* three: thrice: in three parts.
[Gk. and L.]

trial. See **try.**

triangle, *trī′ang-gl, n.* a figure with three angles and three sides: a musical instrument of this shape, played by striking with a small rod: an emotional situation in which three people are involved with each other.
triang′ūlar, *adj.*
[L. *trēs*, three, *angulus*, angle.]

tribe, *trīb, n.* a race or family who all come from the same ancestor: a group of families, usu. of primitive or wandering people, under the government of a chief.
trīb′al, *adj.* **tribes′man** (*trībz′*), *n.*
trib′alism, *n.* state of existing as a separate tribe: tribal life or feeling.
[L. *tribus*, division (orig. three; L. *trēs, tria*) of people in ancient Rome.]

tribulation, *trib-ū-lā′sh(ŏ)n, n.* trouble, hardship, or an instance of it (e.g. *He is always in tribulation*; *many tribulations*).
[L. *trībulāre*, oppress, trouble—*tribulum*, board with sharp teeth for rubbing grain from its stalks.]

tribune, *trib′ūn, n.* a high official elected by the common people in ancient Rome to defend their rights.
tribunal, *trī-bū′năl, n.* a court of justice: a group of persons appointed to give judgment esp. on appeals against regulations made by the state.
[Same root as **tribe.**]

tribute, *trib′ūt, n.* money paid at intervals by one ruler or nation to another in return for peace or protection: an expression, in word or action, of thanks, respect, praise (e.g. *many and varied tributes to his great deeds—speeches, gifts, tears, rejoicing*).
trib′ūtary, *adj.* paying tribute: giving supplies of anything.—*n.* one who pays tribute: a stream that flows into another:—*pl.* **trib′utaries.**
to be a tribute to, (usu. of something good) to be a result of (e.g. *This success is a tribute to his careful planning*).
to pay tribute to, to express respect, etc., for.
[L. *tribuĕre, tribūtum*, to give, pay.]

trice, *trīs, n.* used in phrase **in a trice,** in an instant.
[Earlier *at a trice*, at one pull—Middle Du. *trīsen*, hoist, haul up.]

trick, *trik, n.* cunning action taken to cheat or deceive, or to surprise and annoy:

skilful action intended to puzzle or amuse (e.g. *a conjuring trick*): skill, knack (e.g. *He had not learned the trick of getting the old machine to work*): habit (e.g. *He has a trick of pulling his ear when thinking*): the cards falling to the winner at the end of a round.—*adj.* used to deceive e.g. the eye (e.g. *trick photography*).—*v.t.* to cheat: to deceive by skilful action: to dress, decorate (with *out*, *up*).

trick'ery, *n.* act or practice of trying to cheat by trick(s):—*pl.* **-eries.**

trick'y, *adj.* in the habit of playing tricks: requiring skill, not easy to do or to handle:—*comp.* **trick'ier**; *superl.* **trick'iest.**

trick'iness, *n.*

trick'ster, *n.* a cheat.

[O.Fr. *trichier*, to deceive.]

trickle, *trik'l*, *v.i.* to flow gently or in a small stream: to drip: to come, go, etc. slowly and in small numbers.—Also *n.* [M.E. *triklen*.]

tricolour, tricolor, *tri'kul-or*, *tri'-*, *n.* the flag of France, which has three upright stripes—red, white, and blue.

[L. *trēs*, three, *color*, colour.]

tricycle, *tri'si-kl*, *n.* a vehicle with three wheels and a seat.

[Gk. *tri-*, *treis*, three, *kyklos*, circle.]

trident, *tri'dent*, *n.* any three-pronged instrument, as spear or sceptre.

[L. *trēs*, three, *dens*, *dentis*, tooth.]

tried, trier. See **try.**

triennial, *tri-en'yal*, *-i-al*, *adj.* lasting three years: happening every third year.

[L. *trēs*, three, *annus*, year.]

tries. See **try.**

trifle, *tri'fl*, *v.i.* to amuse oneself in an idle way (with): to act towards without sufficient respect (e.g. *Don't trifle with the bull*; *I am in no mood to be trifled with*): to act, or to talk, idly, without seriousness. —*n.* anything of little value or importance: a small amount or sum: a pudding of sponge cake, wine, whipped cream, etc.

tri'fler, *n.* one who trifles.

tri'fling, *adj.* of small value or importance: acting or talking without seriousness.—Also *n.*

[O.Fr. *trufle*, mockery, deception.]

trigger, *trig'er*, *n.* a catch on a gun which when pulled causes the weapon to fire: something that starts a series of events.—*v.t.* (often **trigger off**; of small event) to start (a violent or important happening).

[Du. *trekker*—*trekken*, to pull.]

trigonometry, *trig-o-nom'e-tri*, *n.* the branch of mathematics which studies the relationship between the sides and angles of triangles.

trigonomet'ric, -al, *adjs.*

[Gk. *trigōnon*, triangle, *metron*, measure.]

trill, *tril*, *v.t.* and *v.i.* to sing or play with a quivering sound: to utter with vibration of e.g. the tip of the tongue against the gums of the upper teeth (e.g. *Only some people trill every r*).—*n.* a trilled sound or letter.

[It. *trillare*.]

trillion, *tril'yon*, *n.* a million multiplied twice by itself, written as 1 followed by 18 noughts: (*U.S.*) ten thousand multiplied twice by itself, 1 followed by 12 noughts.

[Pfx. **tri-, (m)illion.**]

trilogy, *tril'o-ji*, *n.* a group of three related plays, novels, etc., intended to be seen, read, as one whole.

[Gk. *tri-*, thrice, *logos*, discourse.]

trim, *trim*, *adj.* in good order, tidy, neat:—*comp.* **trimm'er**; *superl.* **trimm'est.**—*v.t.* to make trim: to clip (e.g. hair, hedge): to decorate: to arrange (sails, cargo) for sailing: to alter (one's opinions) to suit the circumstances (also *v.i.*):—*pr.p.* **trimm'ing**; *pa.p.* **trimmed.**—*n.* act of trimming: something trimmed off: dress (e.g. *in hunting trim*): state or degree of readiness or fitness (e.g. *in fine trim for the battle of wills*; *in poor trim after illness*).

trim'ly, *adv.* **trim'ness,** *n.*

trimm'er, *n.* one who trims.

trimm'ing, *n.* act of one who trims: something fancy used to trim e.g. clothes.

[O.E. *trymian*, strengthen, set in order.]

trinitrotoluene, *tri-ni-trō-tol'ū-ēn*, *n.* a powerful explosive (abbrev. T.N.T.)

[Named from chemicals forming it.]

trinity, *trin'i-ti*, *n.* a group of three: (*cap.*) (the union in one of) Father, Son, and Holy Ghost.

[L. *trinitās*.]

trinket, *tring'kit*, *n.* small ornament, esp. if of little value. [Orig. uncertain.]

trio, *trē'ō*, *n.* a set of three: (*music*) (a piece of music for) three performers:—*pl.* **tri'os.** [It.]

trip, *trip*, *v.i.* to move with short, light steps: to stumble and fall: to make a mistake.—*v.t.* (often with *up*) to cause (a person) to stumble and fall: (often with *up*) to cause to make, or to catch in, an error (e.g. *If I can trip him up over the details of the scene, I can prove he was not there*):—*pr.p.* **tripp'ing**; *pa.p.* **tripped.** —*n.* a light, short step: a false step, mistake: a short voyage or journey.

tripp'er, *n.* one who makes, goes on, a popular trip or outing.

tripp'ing, *n.* and *adj.*

[O.Fr. *treper*, *trip(p)er*.]

tripartite, *tri-pär'tit*, or *trip'är-tit*, *adj.* divided into three parts: having to do with, binding, three countries, etc. (e.g. *a tripartite agreement*).

[L. *ter*, thrice, *partitus*, divided.]

tripe, *trip*, *n.* parts of stomach, esp. of sheep or cattle, prepared as food: (*coll.*) rubbish, poor stuff. [Fr.]

triple, *trip'l*, *adj.* made up of three: three times as large.—*v.t.*, *v.i.* to make, become, three times as large, to treble.

trip′let, *n.* three of a kind: three lines rhyming together: a group of three notes played, etc., in the time of two: one of three children born at one birth.
in triplicate, in three copies exactly alike.
[L. *triplus,* threefold—*trēs,* three.]

tripod, *trī′pod, n.* anything on three feet or legs, e.g. stool, rest for camera.
[Gk. *tri-,* three, *pous, podos,* foot.]

tripos, *trī′pos, n.* an examination for honours at Cambridge University. [**tripod.**]

trite, *trīt, adj.* (of e.g. saying, remark) used so often that all interest is gone from it.
trite′ly, *adv.* **trite′ness,** *n.*
[L. *terĕre, trītum,* to rub, wear away.]

triumph, *trī′ŭmf, n.* in ancient Rome, a procession in honour of a victorious general: victory: success: a state of great joy for success.—*v.i.* to win a great victory or success: to rejoice for this: openly to show one's rejoicing (over person one has defeated).
trium′phal, *adj.* having to do with triumph: used in celebrating triumph.
trium′phant, *adj.* celebrating, showing joy for, success: victorious.
[Gk. *thriambos,* hymn to god Bacchus.]

triumvirate, *trī-um′vėr-it, n.* a group of three, esp. of men sharing power.
[L. *trēs,* three, *vir,* a man.]

trivet, *triv′it, n.* a small stand with three feet, or one for hooking on to a grate.
[O.Fr. *trepied*—same L. root as **tripod.**]

trivia, *triv′i-ȧ, n. pl.* trifles: unimportant matters.
trivial, *triv′i-ȧl, adj.* of little importance: trifling.
triv′ially, *adv.* **triv′ialness,** *n.*
trivial′ity, *n.* trivialness: something unimportant:—*pl.* **-ities.**
[L. *trivium,* a place where three ways meet, a town square or street.]

trod, trodden. See **tread.**

Trojan, *trō′jȧn, adj.* having to do with ancient *Troy.*—*n.* one who lived in ancient Troy: (*coll.*) one who shows pluck and endurance.

troll[1], *trōl, n.* (in story) a creature (giant or dwarf) who lives in a cave, hill, etc.
[Old Norse.]

troll[2], *trōl, v.t., v.i.* to sing loudly and light-heartedly: to fish with a moving line.
[O.Fr. *troller,* stroll.]

trolley, trolly, *trol′i, n.* a small cart or truck: a small table, or shelved stand, on wheels, used e.g. for serving tea, etc.: the wheel or other device, on e.g. an overhead pole, through which electricity passes from a live wire to an electric street-car, bus, etc.
troll′ey-bus, *n.* a bus that receives power from an overhead wire by a trolley.
[Same root as **troll** (2).]

trollop, *trol′ŏp, n.* a careless, untidy woman: a loose woman.
[Same root as **troll** (2).]

trombone, *trom-bōn′, trom′, n.* a musical wind instrument, a tube twice bent back in U shape and flaring out at one end.
[It.—*tromba,* trumpet.]

troop, *trōōp, n.* a crowd of people, etc.: a unit in cavalry, etc.: (in *pl.*) soldiers.—*v.i.* to collect in numbers: to go in a crowd, or in haste (e.g. *The children trooped after him through the house*).
troop′er, *n.* a horse-soldier.
troop′ship, *n.* a ship carrying soldiers.
trooping the colour, carrying the flag ceremonially along ranks of Guards.
[Fr. *troupe*; orig. uncertain.]

trophy, *trō′fi, n.* anything taken from enemy and kept as memorial of victory: anything won by skill:—*pl.* **-ies.**
[Fr. *trophée*—Gk. root as **tropic.**]

tropic, *trop′ik, n.* either of two imaginary circles about $23\frac{1}{2}°$ (about 1600 miles) north (*Tropic of Cancer*) and south (*Tropic of Capricorn*) of the equator above which the sun appears to turn at midsummer and midwinter: (in *pl.*) the hot lands in this region of the earth.
trop′ic, -al, *adjs.* having to do with the tropics: very hot: growing in hot countries.
[Gk. *tropē,* turning, rout of enemy.]

trot, *trot, v.i.* (of horse) to go forward, lifting the feet quicker and higher than in walking: to move fast with short steps.—*v.t.* to make (horse) trot:—*pr.p.* **trott′ing;** *pa.p.* **trott′ed.**—*n.* the pace of horse, or of person, when trotting.
to trot out, to bring forward (usu. something already well known) for admiration: to offer (e.g. old or not very good excuse). [Fr.]

troth, *trōth, troth, n.* one's word; used in phrase **to plight one's troth,** to pledge one's word to marry a certain person.
[Same root as **truth.**]

troubadour, *trōō′bȧ-dōōr, n.* a wandering poet or singer in France in the Middle Ages.
[Fr.—*trouver,* find, compose.]

trouble, *trub′l, v.t.* to disturb, stir up (e.g. water): to cause worry, uneasiness, sorrow, or inconvenience, to: (also *v.i.*) to make an effort, take pains (to).—*n.* worry, uneasiness: difficulty: disturbance, dispeace: something that causes worry or difficulty: a disease: care taken in, effort given to, doing something.
troub′lesome, *adj.* causing difficulty or inconvenience.
troub′le-shoot′er, *n.* one who detects and puts right any trouble, mechanical or other.
[O.Fr. *tourbler*—L. root as **disturb.**]

trough, *trof, trŏf, n.* a long, open container for water or other liquid, often used in feeding animals: a long hollow or narrow channel, e.g. the dip between two sea waves: an area of low pressure.
[O.E. *trog*; conn. with Ger. *trog.*]

trounce, *trowns, v.t.* to punish or beat severely: (*coll.*) to defeat. [Orig. unknown.]

troupe, *trōōp, n.* a company, esp. of dancers, actors, etc. [Fr.]

trousers, *trow'zėrz, n. pl.* outer garment for lower part of body and each leg separately.

Sing. used in **trouser button, leg,** etc. [O.Fr. *trousses,* page's breeches.]

trousseau, *trōō'sō, n.* a bride's outfit of clothes, etc.:—*pl.* **trou'sseaux** (*-sōz*). [Fr.—*trousse,* a bundle.]

trout, *trowt, n.* types of fish related to the salmon, most living wholly in fresh water. [O.E. *truht*—Gk. *trōktēs,* a sea fish.]

trowel, *trow'el, n.* a tool used in spreading plaster, paint, etc. and in gardening. [O.Fr. *truelle*—L. *trua,* a ladle.]

troy weight, *troi' wāt, n.* a system of weights, for gold, gems, etc. [From *Troyes,* in France.]

truant, *trōō'ȧnt, n.* a pupil who stays away from school without excuse or permission: anyone who stays away from work without good reason.—*adj.* wandering, esp. from duty.

tru'ancy, *n.*

to play truant, to be a truant. [O.Fr. *truand*; prob. from Celt.]

truce, *trōōs, n.* a rest from fighting agreed to by both sides in a war or argument: a temporary freedom (from e.g. pain). [O.E. *trēow,* truth, treaty; conn. **true.**]

truck[1], *truk, v.i.* to give goods instead of money for other goods.—*n.* exchange of goods: (*coll.*) odds and ends, rubbish: (*coll.*) business dealings. [O.Fr. *troquer.*]

truck[2], *truk, n.* an open railway wagon for goods: a wheeled barrow for luggage, used by porters: a transport motor vehicle. [Gk. *trochos,* wheel, or **truckle.**]

truckle, *truk'l, v.i.* to yield meanly to the will of another (with *to*).

truck'le-bed, *n.* a low bed that could be pushed under a larger one. [Gk. *trochlea,* a pulley.]

truculent, *truk'ū-lent,* or *trōōk'-, adj.* threatening, very aggressive, in manner.

truc'ulently, *adv.* **truc'ulence,** *n.* [L. *truculentus*—*trux,* wild, fierce.]

trudge, *truj, v.i.* and *v.t.* to travel on foot, esp. with labour or weariness.—*n.* a heavy, tired walk. [Orig. uncertain.]

true, *trōō, adj.* agreeing with fact (e.g. *a true story*): accurate, correct (e.g. *a true copy*; *a true idea of its importance*): properly so called (e.g. *The spider is not a true insect*): placed, fitted, etc., accurately: perfectly in tune: rightful (e.g. *the true heir*): sincere: loyal.

tru'ly, *adv.* faithfully: sincerely: truthfully: accurately: really, genuinely.

true'ness, *n.*

truism, *trōō'izm, n.* a truth so obvious or plain that it is not worth stating.

truth, *trōōth, n.* trueness (e.g. *the truth of this statement*): a true statement: the facts: an accepted principle (e.g. *the truths of religion*):—*pl.* **truths** (*trōōTHz, trōōths*).

truth'ful, *adj.* **truth'fully,** *adv.*

truth'fulness, *n.*

true'-hear'ted, *adj.* faithful, loyal.

true'-love, *n.* a sweetheart. [O.E. *trēowe*; conn. with Ger. *treu.*]

truffle, *truf'l, troof'l, n.* a round fungus (see this) found underground, used in cookery. [O.Fr.; conn. with L. root of **tuber.**]

truism. See **true.** **trump.**[1] See **trumpery.**

trump[2], *trump, n.* in some card games, (a card of) a suit (chosen by chance or deliberately) which has more value than (cards of) the other suits: (*coll.*) a good, trusty fellow.—*v.t.* to play a trump card on.—Also *v.i.*

trump card, a means of winning, esp. something held in reserve until the crucial moment. [**triumph.**]

trumpery, *trum'pėr-i, n.* something showy but worthless: nonsense:—*pl.* **-ies.**—Also *adj.*

to trump up, to make up falsely (e.g. evidence, a charge; *adj.* **trumped'-up**). [Fr. *tromper,* to deceive.]

trumpet, *trum'pit, n.* a brass musical instrument, a long tube, usu. bent once or twice in U-shape, and flaring out at the end: one who praises.—*v.t.* to proclaim loudly: to sound the praises of.—*v.i.* to sound a trumpet, or to make a sound that suggests one.

trum'peter, *n.*

to blow one's own trumpet, to sound one's own praises. [O.Fr. *trompette*—*trompe,* trumpet.]

truncate, *trung'kāt, v.t.* to cut the top or end off.

trun'cated, *adj.* [Same root as **trunk.**]

truncheon, *trun'ch(ȯ)n, -sh(ȯ)n, n.* a short heavy staff or baton such as that used by policemen. [O.Fr. *tronçon.*]

trundle, *trun'dl, v.t., v.i.* to roll along as a wheel, or on wheels. [O.E. *trendel,* a circle, wheel.]

trunk, *trungk, n.* the main stem of a tree: the body of a man or an animal apart from the limbs: the main body of anything: the long snout of an elephant: a box or chest for clothes, esp. on a journey: (in *pl.*) short, light pants, for e.g. running, swimming.

trunk call, a long-distance telephone message sent by a main or trunk line.

trunk line, a main line of a railway, canal, telephone system, etc.

trunk road, a main road.

[O.Fr. *tronc*—L. *truncus*, trunk without branches—*truncus*, maimed.]

truss, *trus*, *n.* a bundle (e.g. of hay): a combination of beams, etc., forming a rigid framework: a bandage or apparatus used in hernia.—*v.t.* to bind, tie tightly (up): to skewer (a bird) for cooking. [Through O.Fr.—L. as **torture,** etc.]

trust, *trust*, *n.* confidence, belief, in the reality, truth, or goodness of (with *in*; e.g. *trust in his friendship, promises, in one's leaders*): something (e.g. a duty) given one in the belief that one will carry it out, etc. faithfully: charge, keeping: an arrangement by which property is given to a person, in the confidence that he will use it for a stated purpose: in modern business, a number of firms worked together as if they were one.—*v.t.* to put one's faith or confidence in: to give (something to a person) so that he may take care of it: to hope confidently. —*v.i.* to feel trust (in).

trustee' (*-tē'*), *n.* one who holds property in trust for another or others.

trust'ful, trust'ing, *adjs.* ready to trust, not inclined to be suspicious.

trust'fully, *adv.* **trust'fulness,** *n.*

trus'ty, *adj.* honest: strong, firm.

trus'tily, *adv.* **trus'tiness,** *n.*

trust'worthy, *adj.* worthy of trust, able to be depended upon.

trust territory, a territory which does not govern itself but is ruled by a country chosen by the Trusteeship Council of the United Nations.

[M.E.; from Scand.]

truth. See **true.**

try, *trī*, *v.t.* to test the qualities of by experiment or use (e.g. *to try a new soap*): (of experience) to test the strength of (e.g. *disasters that try one's courage, faith*): to test too severely, strain (e.g. *I think the strong light will try my eyes*; *the children try her, her patience*): to attempt to use, open, etc. (e.g. *Try the other path, the door*): to put on trial in a court of law.—*v.i.* to make an attempt: to make an effort:—*pr.p.* **try'ing**; *pa.p.* **tried** (*trīd*). —*n.* an attempt, effort: (a score of three points for) a touch-down:—*pl.* **tries.**

trial, *trī'ȧl*, *n.* act of testing or trying (e.g. *the trial of a new method, of the strength of one's loyalty*): act of straining severely: a test: a strain: the judging of a prisoner in a court of law: an attempt, effort: an affliction, trouble.—Also *adj.*

tried, *adj.* tested, proved to be good.

tri'er, *n.* one who tries, keeps on trying.

try'ing, *adj.* testing: causing strains, discomfort, or irritation.

trial and error, a type of learning, esp. among animals, in which several methods are tried until one is found that gives the result desired; each time the action is repeated the number of unsuccessful attempts becomes smaller.

on trial, being tried, or tested.

to try on, to put on (e.g. clothes) to see the effect: (*slang*) to attempt (an action) in the hope that it will be permitted.

to try out, to test by using.

[O.Fr. *trier*, to pick out.]

tryst, *trīst*, *trist*, (chiefly *Scot.*) an appointment to meet at an arranged place (**tryst'ing-place**). [**trust.**]

tsar, tzar, czar, *tsär*, *n.* title of the former emperors of Russia.

tsarina (*-ē'nȧ*), *n.* Russian empress.

[Russ.—L. *Caesar.*]

tsetse (fly), *tset'si* (*flī*), *n.* any of a number of small flies found in Africa which by their bite pass on to men and animals developing parasites which cause fatal diseases (in man, sleeping sickness). [Native word.]

T-square, *tē'-skwār*, *n.* a T-shaped ruler.

tub, *tub*, *n.* an open wooden container for water: a fixed basin used for washing clothes: a bath: a small cask: a clumsy boat.

tubb'y, *adj.* like a tub, plump, round.

[M.E. *tubbe*; a Germanic word.]

tuba, *tū'bȧ*, *n.* large trumpet-shaped instrument with deep tone. [L.]

tube, *tūb*, *n.* a long hollow cylinder, used to contain, or allow flow of, liquid, etc.: an organ of this kind in animal or plant: a container from which a substance (e.g. paint, toothpaste) can be squeezed: a cathode ray tube: an underground railway in tube-shaped tunnel.

tū'bing, *n.* tubes as a whole: material for tubes.

tū'būlar, *adj.* tube-shaped.

[Fr.—L. *tubus*, a pipe.]

tuber, *tū'bėr*, *n.* a swelling in an underground stem of a plant where food is stored (e.g. *The potato is a tuber*).

tuberous root, a thickened root suggesting a tuber.

[L. *tūber*—root as **tumour.**]

tubercle, *tū'bėr-kl*, *n.* a small swelling.

tuber'cular, *adj.* like, or having, tubercles: tuberculous.

tuber'culous, *adj.* affected with, or caused by, tuberculosis.

tuberculō'sis, *n.* an infectious disease, esp. of the lungs, in which tubercles form.

tubercle bacillus, the organism that causes tuberculosis.

[Same root as **tuber.**]

tubing, tubular. See **tube.**

tuck, *tuk*, *v.t.* to press (in to a place): to fold (under): to gather (up): to press clothes closely round (e.g. a child in bed; with *in* or *up*): (*slang*; with *in*) to eat with enjoyment or greedily.—*n.* a fold stitched in a piece of cloth: (*slang*) sweets, etc.

[M.E. *tucke.*]

Tudor, *tū'dŏr*, *adj.* having to do with the royal line of the *Tudors* (1485-1603), or with their time, or with the style of building common then.

Tuesday, *tūz'di, n.* third day of week. [O.E. *tiwes dæg,* day of god *Tiw.*]

tuft, *tuft, n.* a small bunch of grass, hair, feathers, etc. [O.Fr. *tuffe.*]

tug, *tug, v.t.* to pull hard: to drag along.—*v.i.* to pull with great effort:—*pr.p.* **tugg'ing;** *pa.p.* **tugged.**—*n.* a strong pull: a tugboat.

tug'boat, *n.* a strongly-built powerful ship for towing larger ships.

tug'-of-war', *n.* a contest in strength between teams pulling at opposite ends of a rope: a hard struggle between opposing persons, etc.

[Conn. with **tow** (2).]

tuition, *tū-ish'(ȯ)n, n.* teaching: private coaching or instruction: fee for this. [Same root as **tutor.**]

tulip, *tū'lip, n.* a plant with bulb and bell-shaped flowers of various colours. [O.Fr. *tulipe*—same root as **turban.**]

tulle, *tūl, tōōl, n.* a material of thin silk or rayon net. [Fr., from town of *Tulle.*]

tumble, *tum'bl, v.i.* to fall, to come down suddenly and violently: to roll, toss (about): to act, move, in a hurried, clumsy way: to do acrobatic tricks.—*v.t.* to throw over or down: to throw carelessly: to throw into disorder.—*n.* a fall: a somersault: a confused state.

tum'bler, *n.* one who tumbles, does acrobatic tricks: a large drinking-glass: a kind of pigeon.

tum'ble-down, *adj.* (of e.g. a house) shabby, falling to pieces.

to tumble to, (*slang*) to understand suddenly without explanation.

[M.E. *tum(b)le*—O.E. *tumbian.*]

tumbrel, tumbril, *tum'bril, n.* in French Revolution, a cart with two wheels used to take victims to the guillotine. [O.Fr. *tomberel*—*tomber,* to fall.]

tumid, *tū'mid, adj.* swollen: (of language) pompous, high-flown. [Same root as **tumour.**]

tummy, *tum'i, n.* (*childish*) stomach.

tumour, *tū'mȯr, n.* a swelling, growth of abnormal tissue, in the body. [L. *tumēre,* to swell.]

tumult, *tū'mult, n.* uproar made by a crowd: confusion with loud sounds: high excitement or agitation.

tumultuous, *tū-mul'tū-ůs, adj.*

[Root as **tumour.**]

tumulus, *tū'mū-lůs, n.* an artificial mound of earth, esp. over a tomb. [L.]

tun, *tun, n.* a large cask, esp. for wine. [O.E. *tunne.*]

tuna, *tōō'nȧ, n.* a tunny, or fish like it. [Sp.]

tundra, *tun'-, tōōn'drȧ, n.* a level treeless plain in northern Russia, both in Europe and in Asia. [Lapp.]

tune, *tūn, n.* notes arranged in pleasing order, an air, melody: state of giving a sound or sounds of the correct pitch (e.g. *to be in tune*), or of giving correct vibrations: frame of mind, temper (e.g. *He was not in good tune*).—*v.t.* to put (a musical or other instrument) in tune.

tune'ful, *adj.* **tune'fully,** *adv.*

tune'fulness, *n.* **tune'less,** *adj.*

tū'ner, *n.* **tū'ning,** *n.* and *adj.*

tū'ning-fork, *n.* a steel instrument with two prongs which, when struck, gives a musical sound of a certain pitch.

to tune in, (*radio*) to adjust a radio receiving set so as to get the programme from a particular station.

to change one's tune, to change one's attitude, or way of talking.

to the tune of, to the amount of.

[Same root as **tone.**]

tungsten, *tung'sten, n.* a bright grey metal. [Swed.—*tung,* heavy, *sten,* stone.]

tunic, *tū'nik, n.* a garment reaching to knees worn in ancient Greece and Rome: a short, loose, usu. belted, often sleeveless or short-sleeved, garment: a close jacket worn by soldiers and policemen. [Fr. *tunique*—L. *tunica.*]

tuning. See **tune.**

tunnel, *tun'ėl, n.* an underground passage, esp. one by which a road or railway is carried under a hill, etc.—*v.i.* to make a tunnel: (of animal) to burrow.—*v.t.* to make tunnel, burrow, in (e.g. hill):—*pr.p.* **tunn'elling;** *pa.p.* **tunn'elled.** [O.Fr. *tonnel,* a cask.]

tunny, *tun'i, n.* a large sea fish. [L. *thunnus*—Gk. *thynein,* to dart along.]

turban, *tûr'bȧn, n.* a head-covering worn by Mohammedans, etc., a long sash wound round the head or round a cap. [Earlier *turbant*—Pers. *dulband.*]

turbid, *tûr'bid, adj.* (of liquid, etc.) muddy, clouded: (of thought, etc.) confused. [Same L. root as **turbulent.**]

turbine, *tûr'bin, -bīn, n.* an engine, usu. with curved blades, turned by the action of water, steam, or gas, etc.

turbo-, *tûr-bō-,* (as part of word) turbine: used in naming engines of which a turbine forms a part, or aeroplanes having such engines.

[Fr.—L. root as **disturb, turbulent.**]

turbot, *tûr'bȯt, n.* a large, flat fish used as food. [O.Fr.]

turbulent, *tûr'bū-lėnt, adj.* (of e.g. times, place, conditions) disturbed, tumultuous: (of person, conduct) inclined to cause disturbance or riot. [Fr.—L. root as **trouble, disturb.**]

tureen, *tů-rēn', tū-, n.* a large dish for holding soup at table. [Fr. *terrine*—L. *terra,* earth.]

turf, *tûrf, n.* earth on the surface of land matted with roots of grass, etc.: a cake of turf cut off, sod: in Ireland, peat:

(**the turf**) horse racing, the racecourse :—*pl.* **turfs.**—*v.t.* to cover with turf.
tur'fy, *adj.* **tur'finess,** *n.* [O.E.]

turgid, *tûr'jid, adj.* swollen : (of language, style) pompous, sounding grand but meaning very little.
tur'gidly, *adv.* **turgid'ity, -ness,** *ns.*
[L. *turgēre*, to swell.]

Turk, *tûrk, n.* a native of *Turkey.*
Turk'ish, *adj.* having to do with the Turks or Turkey.—*n.* the language of the Turks.
Turkish bath, a kind of hot-air bath, the patient being sweated, rubbed down, and then cooled.

turkey, *tûrk'i, n.* a large farmyard bird, native of America, so called through confusion with the guinea-fowl thought to have come from *Turkey.*

turmeric, *tûr'mėr-ik, n.* the underground part of a plant grown in India ; used in curry powder, etc.
[Prob.—an Eastern word.]

turmoil, *tûr'moil, n.* state of confusion, commotion, agitation (e.g. *turmoil of war* ; *the city was, his thoughts were, in a turmoil*). [Orig. unknown.]

turn, *tûrn, v.i.* to go round, revolve (e.g. *The wheel turns*) : to move round something as centre (with *on* ; e.g. *The door turns on its hinges*) : to move so as to face in, or to go in, the opposite direction : to take a different direction (e.g. *His thoughts turned to supper*) : to change (*to, into* ; e.g. *The ice turned to water*) : (of milk, etc.) to sour : (of head, brain) to become dizzy.—*v.t.* to cause to go round, revolve completely or partly : to reach and go round (e.g. *The ship turned the headland*) : to aim, point (e.g. *He turned the hose on the men*) : to direct, apply (e.g. *He turned his attention to painting*) : to change (into) : to make sour : to make giddy : to shape in a lathe.—*n.* act of turning : a new direction : a winding, bend : a turning-point : a walk to and fro : a spell (of e.g. work) : a short act in a programme of several : one's chance to do, have, something shared with others (e.g. *It is my turn to bat now, my turn of the armchair*) : requirement at the moment (e.g. *This will serve our turn*) : act of helpfulness or the opposite (e.g. *She did him a good turn*) : (*coll.*) a nervous shock.
tur'ner, *n.* one who uses a lathe.
turn'ing, *n.* act of going round, revolving, or of going in a different direction : a winding : a street corner : act of shaping.
turn'coat, *n.* one who deserts his party.
tur'ning-point, *n.* point at which a turn is made, or at which an important change takes place.
turn'key, *n.* one who keeps the keys in a prison.
turn -out, *n.* a crowd, gathering, for a special purpose : clothes, kind of dress : output (of e.g. a factory).
turn'over, *n.* act of turning over : rate of change or replacement : change (to e.g. different method of working) : the total amount of the sales in a business during a certain time.
turn'pike, *n.* a gate set across a road which is opened when the traveller has paid a toll or fee : (also **turn'pike-road**) a main road where a toll is collected.
turn'stile, *n.* a gate which turns round and allows one person only to pass at a time.
turn'table, *n.* a revolving platform for turning a railway engine round.
turn'-up, *n.* (*coll.*) a disturbance : (*coll.*) an unexpected happening : a piece of material folded up.
to turn (someone) (a)round one's finger, to make (him) do readily what one wishes.
to turn down, to say no to (e.g. an offer).
to turn in, (*coll.*) to go to bed : to hand over to person(s) in authority.
to turn off, to dismiss, get rid of : to shut off (e.g. water from a tap).
to turn on, to set running (e.g. water) : to put on (a light, charm) : to move round : to depend on (e.g. *What we do next turns on the success of the first step*) : to face angrily and unexpectedly.
to turn one's hand to, to apply oneself to : to work at with some skill.
to turn one's head, to make one dizzy : to fill one with pride or conceit.
to turn out, to drive out : to empty : to make for selling or for use : to get out of bed, or out of the house : to come or gather (e.g. *A crowd turned out for the match in spite of rain*) : to put out (e.g. a light) : to prove to be the fact (e.g. *It turned out that he had done it*).
to turn the scale, to be the fact, etc., that causes the decision or result.
to turn the scale at, to weigh (e.g. *to turn the scale at 17 stone*).
to turn the stomach, to disgust.
to turn to, to set to work : to change to : to go to for help, etc.
to turn up, to appear, arrive : to be found : to happen : to look up in e.g. a book.
to a turn, exactly, perfectly.
by turns, one after another.
in turn, in order, one after the other.
not to turn a hair, to be quite calm and undisturbed.
to have turned, be turned, to be beyond (e.g. *He has turned 30*).
to take one's turn, to follow an arrangement which allows others to have a fair chance : to take one's part, with others, e.g. in a task.
to take turns, to do (e.g. to work) one after the other.
[O.E. *tyrnan*—L. *tornāre*, turn in lathe.]

turnip, *tûr′nip*, *n.* a plant or its large round root used as vegetable and for feeding cattle.
[Perh. **turn,** O.E. *nǣp*, turnip.]

turnpike, turntable, etc. See **turn.**

turpentine, *tûr′pėn-tīn*, *n.* (also **oil of turpentine**) colourless inflammable oil obtained from resin of certain trees, used in paint and varnish, etc.
[Gk. *terebinthos*.]

turpitude, *tûr′pi-tūd*, *n.* wickedness.
[L. *turpitūdō—turpis*, base, low.]

turquoise, *tûr′kwäz, -k(w)oiz*, *n.* a greenish-blue precious stone.
[O.Fr., Turkish (stone).]

turret, *tûr′it*, *n.* a small tower on a building: a tower, often revolving, within which guns are mounted, as on a warship.
turr′eted, *adj.* having turrets.
[O.Fr. *touret—tour*, a tower.]

turtle[1], *tûr′tl*, **turtle-dove,** *tûr′tl-duv*, *n.* a beautiful, softly-cooing dove.
[O.E.; conn. with L. *turtur*.]

turtle[2], *tûr′tl*, *n.* a tortoise, esp. one found in water (esp. ocean): the flesh of certain turtles used for making soup.
to turn turtle, (of e.g. boat) to capsize, turn bottom up.
[Same root as **tortoise.**]

tusk, *tusk*, *n.* a large tooth sticking out of the mouth of certain animals (e.g. elephant, walrus), usu. one of a pair.
[O.E. *tusc*; conn. O. Norse *toskr*.]

tussle, *tus′l*, *n.* a struggle.—*v.i.* to struggle, wrestle.
[Same root as **tousle.**]

tussock, *tus′ok*, *n.* a tuft of grass.
[Orig. uncertain.]

tutelage, *tū′tė-lij*, *n.* state of being under a guardian.
[Same root as **tutor.**]

tutor, *tū′tor*, *n.* one who has charge of the education of another: one who teaches and examines students: a book of lessons in music.—*v.t.* to teach: to direct the studies of.
tutō′rial, *adj.* having to do with a tutor. —*n.* a meeting for study between a tutor and student(s).
See also **tuition.**
[L. *tūtor*, guardian—*tuērī*, *tuitus*, watch.]

tutu, *tōō′tōō*, *n.* a ballet dancer's short, stiff, spreading skirt. [Fr.]

twaddle, *twod′l*, *n.* silly talk or writing.
[Earlier form *twattle*—**tattle.**]

twain, *twān*, *n.* two people, things.
in twain, in two, asunder.
[O.E. *twēgen*; see **two.**]

twang, *twang*, *n.* a sound as of a tight string of a musical instrument pulled and let go: a sharp, nasal tone of voice.—*v.i.*, *v.t.* to have, make, or cause to make, one of these sounds. [Imit.]

tweak, *twēk*, *v.t.* to pull with sudden jerk, twitch.—*n.* a sudden sharp pull.
[Same root as **twitch.**]

tweed, *twēd*, *n.* a kind of woollen cloth with rough surface, in various patterns: (in *pl.*) garments of tweed.—Also *adj.*
[Misreading of Scot. *tweel*, twill.]

tweezers, *twēz′ėrz*, *n. sing.* small pincers for pulling out hairs, holding small things, etc.
[*tweeze*, surgeon's case—Fr. *étui*, case.]

twelve, *twelv*, *adj.* and *n.* the number next above eleven (12 or XII).
twelfth, *twelfth*, *adj.* last of twelve.—*n.* one of twelve equal parts.
Twelfth′-night, *n.* the eve of Jan. 6th, which is the twelfth day after Christmas.
twelve′month, *n.* a year.
[M.E.—O.E. *twelf*; conn. Ger. *zwölf*.]

twenty, *twen′ti*, *adj.* and *n.* two times ten (20 or XX):—*pl.* **twen′ties.**
twen′tieth (*-ti-ėth*), *adj.* last of twenty.—*n.* one of twenty equal parts.
[O.E. *twentig—twēgen*, two, *-tig*, ten.]

twi-, *twī-*, *pfx.* two: double: twice. [O.E.]

twice, *twīs*, *adv.* two times.
[O.E. *twiges*; conn. with **twi-, two.**]

twiddle, *twid′l*, *v.t.* to play with, twirl idly.
to twiddle one's thumbs, to turn thumbs round each other: to be idle.
[Orig. uncertain.]

twig, *twig*, *n.* a small shoot or branch.
[O.E. *twig*; conn. with **twi-.**]

twilight, *twī′līt*, *n.* the faint light after sunset, and before sunrise: a state or time before or esp. after full brightness or strength (e.g. *the twilight of this dictator's power*).
[**twi-, light** (1).]

twill, *twil*, *n.* (woven fabric with) a ridged appearance.—*v.t.* to weave in this way.
[Scot. and north Engl.; conn. **twi-.**]

twin, *twin*, *n.* one of two children or animals born at one birth: one very like another.—*adj.* being two, or one of two, born at a birth: very like another: double: consisting of two similar parts.
twin′-en′gined, *adj.* having two engines.
twin′-screw′, *adj.* having two parallel propellers, on separate shafts.
[O.E. *twinn*, double; conn. **twi-.**]

twine, *twīn*, *n.* a cord made of two or more threads twisted together: a coil, twist.—*v.t.* to twist together: to wind about (something).—*v.i.* to wind together, join closely: to wind itself (about, round).
[O.E. *twīn*, double thread; conn. **twi-.**]

twinge, *twinj*, *n.* a sudden, sharp pain.
[O.E. *twengan*, to pinch.]

twinkle, *twing′kl*, *v.i.* (of e.g. star) to shine with a slightly trembling light: (of eyes) to shine with amusement.
twink′le, twink′ling, *ns.* the act, style, of shining of star or laughing eye: an instant.
[O.E. *twinclian*.]

twirl, *twėrl*, *v.t.* to turn round rapidly, esp. with the fingers.—*v.i.* to be whirled round.—*n.* a whirl, motion in a circle.
[O.E. *thwirel*, whisk—*thweran*, to churn.]

twist, *twist*, *v.t.* to wind together (two or

more threads): to form (e.g. rope) in this way: to wind (about, round, something): to form into a coil: to bend out of shape (e.g. *The fire twisted the girders*): to wrench round painfully (e.g. arm): to make seem to have a meaning that they do, it does, not (e.g. *to twist the facts, what has been said*).—*v.i.* to move, turn, be bent, etc., round something, or this way and that (e.g. *The vine twists round the post*; *the road twists up the hill*).—*n.* act of twisting: a wrench, violent turn: something that is twisted: a roll of tobacco or of bread.

twis'ter, *n.* person or thing that twists: (*coll.*) a dishonest and unreliable person.

[M.E. a rope; conn. **twi-.**]

twit, *twit, v.t.* to remind (a person) laughingly of a fault, etc., to tease:—*pr.p.* **twitt'ing;** *pa.p.* **twitt'ed.**

[O.E. *æt*, against, *wītan*, to blame.]

twitch, *twich, v.t.* to pull with a sudden jerk, snatch.—*v.i.* to move jerkily.—*n.* a sudden, quick pull: a jerking of the muscles.

[O.E. *twiccian*, to pluck.]

twitter, *twit'ėr, n.* a chirp, of e.g. a bird: slight nervous excitement.—*v.i.* to chirp, make small noises: to be excited.

twitt'ering, *n.* [Imit.]

two, *tōō, adj.* and *n.* the number next above one (2 or II).

See **second, twice, twenty.**

two'-faced, *adj.* deceitful, insincere.

two'fold, *adj.* double (in senses of 'in two parts', 'two times as great or as much').—Also *adv.*

two'-hand'ed, *adj.* having, or used with, two hands: to be used, played, by two persons: using either hand equally well.

twopence, *tup'ėns, n.* the sum of two pennies.

twopenny (*tup'*), *adj.* costing twopence.

two'some (*-sům*), *n.* a group of two: a match between two.—Also *adj.*

in two, (broken) in two pieces.

[O.E. *twā* (fem. and neut.), *twēgen* (masc.); conn. with **twain, twi-.**]

tycoon, *tī-kōōn', n.* (*coll.*) a businessman of great wealth and power.

[Jap. *taikun*, a great prince.]

tympanum, *tim'pȧ-nům, n.* the eardrum: a drum:—*pl.*—**nums, -na.**

tym'pani, *n.* timpani.

tym'panist, *n.* timpanist.

[Gk. *tympanon*, a kettledrum.]

type, *tīp, n.* a sort, kind (e.g. *a new type of farming*): a pattern, example, showing the normal or standard characteristics: a rectangular block, usu. of metal, on one end of which is cast a letter, sign, etc. used in printing: a set of these.—*v.t.* to produce a copy of by means of a typewriter: (*coll.*) to make (e.g. an actor) always play the same sort of part.

typ'ical (*tip'*), *adj.* having to do with type: having, or showing, the usual characteristics (e.g. *a typical athlete*; *it was typical of him to take all the credit*).

typ'ically, *adv.* **typ'icalness,** *n.*

typ'ify (*tip'*), *v.t.* to serve as the type, or an example, of:—*pr.p.* **typ'ifying;** *pa.p.* **typ'ified.**

ty'pist (*tī'*), *n.* one who uses a typewriter.

typecast, *tīp'kâst, v.t.* to cast (an actor) in the part of a character very like himself.

type'script, *n.* a copy of a book, etc., made by a typewriter: typewriting.

type'write, *v.t., v.i.* to produce by means of, or to use, a typewriter.

type'writer, *n.* a machine which puts letters on a sheet of paper when its keys are struck.

type'writing, *n.* and *adj.*

typog'raphy (*tī-*), *n.* art of printing: the general appearance of printed matter.

[Gk. *typos*, impression, mark of seal.]

typhoid, *tī'foid, adj., n.* (having to do with) a fever caused by a bacillus in bad food or drinking water.

[Gk. *typhos* (see **typhus**), *eidos*, form.]

typhoon, *tī-fōōn', n.* a violent storm of wind in the Chinese seas.

[Partly Chinese *t'ai fung*, great wind.]

typhus, *tī'fůs, n.* a dangerous, quick spreading, fever, with dark rash, stupor, etc.

[Gk. *typhos*, smoke, stupor.]

typical, typify, typist, etc. See **type.**

tyrant, *tī'rȧnt, n.* one who uses his power harshly or cruelly.

tyrann'ical, tyrannous (*tir'ȧ-nůs*), *adjs.* cruel, unjustly severe.

tyr'annise (*tir'-*), *v.i.* to act as a tyrant: to rule (over) harshly.

tyr'anny (*tir'-*), *n.* the rule of a tyrant: complete power used unfairly, or cruelly: harshness.

[O.Fr. *tirant*—Gk. *tyrannos.*]

tyre, tire, *tīr, n.* a metal hoop that binds the rim of a wheel: a hoop of thick rubber, solid or filled with air, fitted round a wheel rim. [**attire.**]

tyro, tiro, *tī'rō, n.* one only learning an art or skill:—*pl.* **tyros, ti'ros.**

[L. *tīrō*, a young recruit.]

tzar. Same as **tsar.**

U

U-bend, -turn, *ns.* bend, turn, making shape of letter U.

ubiquitous, *ū-bi'kwi-tůs, adj.* present everywhere.

ubi'quity, ubi'quitousness, *ns.*

[L. *ubique,* everywhere.]

udder, *ud'ėr, n.* the milk bag of a cow, sheep, etc.

[O.E. *ūder*; conn. with Ger. *euter.*]

ugli, *ug'li, n.* a cross between the grapefruit and the tangerine.

[From the fruit's *ugly* appearance.]

ugly, *ug'li, adj.* unpleasant to look at: hateful (e.g. *an ugly deed*): dangerous (e.g. *an ugly situation*):—*comp.* **ug'lier**; *superl.* **ug'liest.**

ug'liness, *n.*

ugly duckling, despised member of a family who later proves the most successful.

[Old Norse *uggligr,* frightful.]

ukulele, ukelele, *ū-ků-lā'li, n.* a small, usually four-stringed guitar.

[Hawaiian=flea, from the movement of the fingers.]

ulcer, *ul'sėr, n.* an open sore, a break in skin or mucous membrane, often with pus.

ulcerā'tion, *n.* the formation of ulcers.

ul'cerous, *adj.*

[Fr. *ulcère*—L. *ulcus, ulcĕris.*]

ulna, *ul'nȧ, n.* inner and larger bone of the forearm. [L.]

ult. See **ultimo** (under **ultimate**).

ulterior, *ul-tē'ri-ȯr,* adj. beyond what is seen or admitted (e.g. *an ulterior motive,* a hidden, usu. bad, motive).

[L. *ulterior,* farther off; conn. **ultimate.**]

ultimate, *ul'ti-mit, adj.* farthest: final.

ul'timately, *adv.* in the end.

ultimatum, *ul-ti-mā'tům, n.* a final demand made by one party to another, containing a threat to break off peaceful discussion.

ul'timo (*-mō*), *n.* in the month just past (e.g. *on the 30th ultimo*):—*abbrev.* **ult.**

[L. *ultimus,* last; **ulterior, ultra-.**]

ultra-, *ul'tra-, pfx.* (1) beyond in place (e.g. **ultraviolet**): (2) beyond in degree (e.g. **ultramicroscopic**): (3) extreme(ly), excessive(ly) (e.g. *ultra-careful.*)

[L. *ultrā,* beyond.]

ultramarine, *ul-trȧ-mȧ-rēn', adj.* situated beyond the sea: of a deep sky-blue colour.—*n.* blue colouring matter.

[L. *ultrā,* beyond, and **marine.**]

ultramicrascopic, *ul'trȧ-mī-krō-skop'ik, adj.* smaller than microscopic, too small to be seen with an ordinary microscope. [**ultra-** (2).]

ultrasonic, *ul-trȧ-son'ik, adj.* beyond the range of human hearing.

[L. *ultrā,* beyond, *sonus,* sound.]

ultraviolet, *ul'trȧ-vī'ȯ-lit, adj.* (of rays) beyond the violet end of the visible spectrum. [**ultra-** (1).]

umbel, *um'bėl, n.* a flower head in which a number of stalks, each bearing flowers, branch out from one centre.

umbellif'erous, *adj.* bearing umbels.

[L. *umbella*; L. root as **umbrella.**]

umber, *um'bėr, n.* a brown pigment or colouring material.

[*Umbria,* in Italy.]

umbilical, *um-bil'i-kl, adj.* of the navel.

[L. *umbilīcus,* the navel.]

umbrage, *um'brij, n.* a sense of injury or offence (*to take, give, umbrage*).

[Fr.—same L. root as **umbrella.**]

umbrella, *um-brel'ȧ, n.* a folding shelter against rain, carried in the hand: a protective force of aircraft: general cover or protection (e.g. *This action was taken under the umbrella of the United Nations*).

[It. *ombrella*—L. *umbra,* a shadow.]

umpire, *um'pīr, n.* a judge called in to settle a dispute: (in cricket, etc.) a person who enforces the rules and decides doubtful points.—Also *v.i.* and *v.t.*

[M.E. *nompere,* not a *peer* (i.e. equal); hence odd man, arbitrator.]

un-[1], *un-, pfx.* (a) used to make verbs showing the reversal of an action (e.g. **unfasten**). (b) Sometimes the *pfx.* merely strengthens the meaning (e.g. **unloose**). [O.E. *un-, on-, an-.*]

un-[2], *un-, pfx.* not; used to indicate the opposite of the word to which it is attached (e.g. **unequal,** not equal; **unconsciousness,** lack of consciousness). [O.E.]

unable, *un-ā'bl, adj.* without sufficient strength, power, skill, or opportunity. See also **inability.** [**un-** (2).]

unaccountable, *un-ȧ-kown'tȧ-bl, adj.* not to be explained or accounted for: not to be held responsible.

unaccount'ably, *adv.* [**un-** (2).]

unadulterated, *un-ȧ-dul'tėr-āt-id, adj.* not adulterated: unmixed. [**un-** (2).]

unadvised, *un-ȧd-vīzd', adj.* not advised: not prudent, rash.

unadvīs'edly (*-id-li*), *adv.* [**un-** (2).]

unaffected, *un-ȧ-fek'tid, adj.* not acted on or changed: not influenced (by something): without artificiality of manner (e.g. *a frank, unaffected girl*): sincere.

unaffect'edly, *adv.*

[**un-** (2), and **affect** (2).]

For words in UN not found above, see **un-** (1) *or* (2).

unalloyed, *un-à-loid′, adj.* not alloyed or mixed, pure. [**un-** (2).]

unanimity. See **unanimous.**

unanimous, *ū-nan′i-mus, adj.* agreeing, one and all, in opinion or resolve: agreed to by all (e.g. *a unanimous decision*).

unanim′ity, unan′imousness, *ns.* **unan′imously,** *adv.*

[L. *ūnus*, one, *animus*, mind.]

unanswerable, *un-ân′sėr-à-bl, adj.* not able to be answered, or to be proved false (e.g. *an unanswerable argument*). [**un-** (2).]

unapproachable, *un-à-prōch′à-bl, adj.* impossible to reach: stiff and unfriendly: that cannot be equalled. [**un-** (2).]

unarmed, *un-ärmd′, adj.* without weapons, defenceless. [**un-** (2), and **arm** (2).]

unassuming, *un-à-sūm′ing,* or *sōōm′-, adj.* modest. [**un-** (2).]

unattached, *un-à-tacht′, adj.* not belonging to a particular regiment, etc.: not engaged to be married, or married. [**un-** (2).]

unattended, *un-à-ten′did, adj.* not accompanied: not in the care of an attendant. [**un-** (2).]

unauthorised, *un-öth′ör-īzd, adj.* not having the permission of the people in authority (e.g. *unauthorised use of the firm's equipment*). [**un-** (2).]

unavailing, *un-à-vāl′ing, adj.* achieving nothing, useless (e.g. *unavailing efforts*). [**un-** (2), and pr.p. of **avail.**]

unaware, *un-à-wār′, adj.* not aware, ignorant (usu. with *of*).—*adv.* (also **unawares′**) without warning: unconsciously, unintentionally. [**un-** (2).]

unbalanced, *un-bal′ànst, adj.* disordered in mind: not taking into account all the facts (*an unbalanced view*): (*book-keeping*) not made up to show balance of debtor and creditor. [**un-** (2).]

unbar, *un-bär′, v.t.* to remove a bar from: to open:—*pr.p.* **unbarr′ing**; *pa.p.* **unbarred′** (*-bärd′*). [**un-** (1, a).]

unbearable, *un-bār′à-bl, adj.* too painful to bear, or to tolerate (e.g. *unbearable toothache, injustice*). [**un-** (2).]

unbecoming, *un-bi-kum′ing, adj.* (of clothes) not suited to the wearer: (of behaviour) not what should be expected from the person or in the circumstances. [**un-** (2).]

unbelief, *un-bi-lēf′, n.* want of belief.

unbeliev′er, *n.* one who does not believe.

unbeliev′ing, *adj.* [**un-** (2).]

unbend, *un-bend′, v.t.* to straighten (something with bend in it): to slacken the string on (a bow): to relax (the mind) with light amusement.—*v.i.* to behave in a friendly, not formal, way:—*pa.p.* **unbent′.**

unben′ding, *n.* and *adj.* [**un-** (1).]

unbending[1]**.** See **unbend.**

unbending[2]**,** *un-ben′ding, adj.* not bending: not changing purpose or opinion: stiff and formal. [**un-** (2).]

unbias(s)ed, *un-bī′àst, adj.* free from bias, not showing prejudice or favouritism, etc. [**un-** (2).]

unbidden, *un-bid′n, adj.* without being told to: uninvited.

[**un-** (2), and **bidden** *pa.p.* of **bid.**]

unblushing, *un-blush′ing, adj.* without shame. [**un-** (2).]

unbolt, *un-bōlt′, v.t.* to open the bolt of (e.g. a door):—*pa.p.* and *adj.* **unbol′ted.** [**un-** (1, a).]

unbosom, *un-bōōz′òm, v.t.* (with *oneself*) or *v.i.* to tell freely one's troubles, etc.

[O.E. *un-*, removal from, **bosom.**]

unbound, *un-bownd′, adj.* not bound: loose. [**un-** (2).]

unbounded, *un-bown′did,* not limited: very great. [**un-** (2), and **bound** (2).]

unbridled, *un-brīd′ld, adj.* without a bridle: not held in check (e.g. *unbridled rage*). [**un-** (2).]

unbuckle, *un-buk′l, v.t.* to undo the buckle or buckles of. [**un-** (1, a).]

unburden, *un-bûr′dn, v.t.* to take a load off: (with *oneself*) to tell one's secrets freely (also *v.i.*). [**un-** (1, a).]

unbutton, *un-but′n, v.t.* to unfasten the buttons of. [**un-** (1, a).]

uncalled-for, *un-köld′-för, adj.* quite unnecessary: rude (e.g. *That criticism is uncalled-for*).

[**un-** (2), **called,** and **for.**]

uncanny, *un-kan′i, adj.* strange, full of mystery: more than human (e.g. *uncanny skill*).

uncann′ily, *adv.* **uncann′iness,** *n.*

[**un-** (2), **canny**; in sense of 'not safe to meddle with'.]

uncared-for, *un′kārd′-för, adj.* not taken care of, neglected. [**un-** (2).]

uncertain, *un-sėr′t(i)n, adj.* not knowing definitely (e.g. *I am uncertain of his whereabouts*): not definitely known (e.g. *His whereabouts are uncertain*): depending on chance: changeable (e.g. *uncertain weather*): vague: hesitating. [**un-** (2).]

unchain, *un-chān′, v.t.* to free from chain(s). [**un-** (1, a).]

uncharted, *un-chärt′id, adj.* not shown on a chart or map: of which a detailed map has never been made. [**un-** (2).]

uncivil, *un-siv′il, adj.* not courteous, rude.

unciv′illy, *adv.* **unciv′ilness,** *n.*

See also **incivility.** [**un-** (2).]

unclassified, *un-klas′i-fīd adj.* not on the security list; (of a road) not in a class entitled to a government grant. [**un-** (2).]

uncle, *ung′kl, n.* the brother of one's father or mother: an aunt's husband.

[O.Fr.—L. *avunculus.*]

unclean, *un-klēn′, adj.* dirty: vile. [**un-** (2).]

For words in UN not found above see, **un-** (1) *or* (2), *page* 570.

unclose, *un-klōz′*, *v.t.* to open. [**un-** (1, a).]
unclothe, *un-klōTH′*, *v.t.* to take the clothes off. [**un-** (1, a).]
uncoil, *un-koil′*, *v.t.*, *v.i.* to unwind. [**un-** (1, a).]
uncoloured, *un-kul′ȯrd*, *adj.* not coloured, undyed: truthful, not exaggerated. [**un-** (2).]
uncommitted, *un-kȯ-mit′id*, *adj.* not pledged to support any party or policy. [**un-** (2).]
uncommon, *un-kom′ȯn*, *adj.* rare: unusual.
uncommonly, *adv.* very. [**un-** (2).]
uncompromising, *un-kom′prȯ-mīz-ing*, *adj.* (of a person) not willing to compromise or give in: very emphatic (e.g. *an uncompromising refusal*). [**un-** (2), and *pr.p.* of **compromise.**]
unconcern, *un-kȯn-sėrn′*, *n.* lack of interest or anxiety. [O.E. *un-*, lack of, and **concern.**]
unconditional, *un-kȯn-dish′ȯn-ȧl*, *adj.* made without conditions or stipulations, complete (e.g. *unconditional surrender*, *an unconditional promise*).
uncondi′tionally, *adv.* [**un-** (2).]
unconfirmed, *un-kȯn-fėrmd′*, *adj.* not confirmed: (of e.g. rumour) not as yet shown to be true. [**un-** (2).]
unconscionable, *un-kon′sh(ȯ)n-ȧ-bl*, *adj.* without conscience (of e.g. a rascal): excessive (e.g. *unconscionable demands*). [**un-** (2), and **conscience.**]
unconscious, *un-kon′shus*, *adj.* not aware (of): insensible: not present to the conscious mind (e.g. *an unconscious prejudice*).—*n.* the deepest level of mind.
uncon′sciously, *adv.*
uncon′sciousness, *n.* [**un-** (2).]
uncouple, *un-kup′l*, *v.t.* to disconnect (e.g. railway wagons). [**un-** (1, a).]
uncouth, *un-ko͞oth′*, *adj.* clumsy, awkward: rude: odd in appearance. [O.E. *uncūth*, not known.]
uncover, *un-kuv′ėr*, *v.t.* to remove the cover of: to lay open.—*v.i.* to take off one's hat. [**un-** (1, a).]
uncrowned, *un-krownd′*, *adj.* (in *uncrowned king*) having power like a king's without the title. [**un-** (2).]
unction, *ungk′sh(ȯ)n*, *n.* an anointing: divine grace: too great warmth or earnestness of manner.
unctuous, *ungk′tū-us*, *adj.* oily: making a false, unpleasant show of holiness, earnestness, sympathy, etc.
extreme unction, praying over and anointing a person who is near death. [Same root as **unguent.**]
uncurl, *un-kûrl′*, *v.t.* to straighten out.—*v.i.* to relax, unwind. [**un-** (1, a).]
uncut, *un′kut′*, *adj.* not cut: (of gem) not shaped by cutting. [**un-** (2).]
undaunted, *un-dawn′tid*, *adj.* not discouraged: fearless. [**un-** (2).]
undeceive, *un-di-sēv′*, *v.t.* to free from a mistaken belief, tell the truth to (someone). [**un-** (1, a).]
undecided, *un-di-sī′did*, *adj.* not having the mind made up: not settled. [**un-** (2).]
undefiled, *un-di-fīld′*, *adj.* pure: not stained, or spoiled in any way. [O.E. *un-*, not, and **defile** (2).]
undeniable, *un-di-nī′ȧ-bl*, *adj.* not able to be denied: obviously true. [O.E. *un-*, not, and **deny.**]
under, *un′dėr*, *prep.* in a position lower than or beneath: less than: subject to the authority of (e.g. *working under a new boss*): beneath the weight of (e.g. *He sank under his burden*): going through, suffering (e.g. attack): having, using (a name, title): in accordance with (e.g. *under this agreement*).—*adv.* in, or to, a lower place or condition.—*adj.* lower in position, rank, amount, etc.
under age, still too young (for some legal or other purpose).
un′derarm, *adj.*, *adv.* (of action) with arm below shoulder.
under arms, ready for battle.
under canvas, in tents.
under fire, exposed to enemy attack: receiving severe criticism.
under one's (very) nose, right in front of one and in plain view (e.g. *He took my paper under my very nose*).
under the breath, in a low voice.
under way, (of ship, etc.) in motion. [O.E.]
under-, *un′dėr-*, *pfx.* (1) beneath (e.g. **underlie**): (2) too little (e.g. **underpay**): (3) lower in position (e.g. **undercurrent**): (4) less in rank (e.g. **Undersecretary**). [**under.**]
undercarriage, *un′dėr-kar-ij*, *n.* the supporting framework, of e.g. a wagon: the landing-gear of an aircraft. [**under-** (3).]
underclothes, *un′dėr-klōTHz*, *n.pl.* clothes worn under the outer garments.—Also **un′derclōthing.** [**under-** (3).]
undercover, *un′dėr-kuv′ėr*, *adj.* working or done in secret. [**under-** (1).]
undercurrent, *un′dėr-kur′ėnt*, *n.* flow or movement under surface. [**under-** (3).]
undercut, *un-dėr-kut′*, *v.t.* to strike a blow upward: to sell at a lower price than (a competitor).
un′dercut, *n.* a blow struck upward: under side of a sirloin. [**under-** (3).]
underdeveloped, *un′dėr-di-vel′ȯpd*, *adj.* not well grown: (*photography*) not sufficiently developed: (of country) not having efficient modern agriculture and industry or high standard of living.
underdo, *un-dėr-do͞o′*, *v.t.* to do less than is needed: to cook incompletely.
underdone′ (*-dun′*), *adj.* [**under-** (3).]

For words in UN not found above, see **un-** (1) *or* (2), *page* 570.

underdog, *un'dėr-dog, n.* the loser in a struggle (e.g. for existence).
[**under-** (3).]

underestimate, *un-dėr-es'ti-māt, v.t.* to estimate at less than the real value or amount: to think less strong, great, etc., than he, it, really is (e.g. *to underestimate an opponent*).—*n.* (*-mit*) an estimate that is too low. [**under-** (2).]

under-exposed, *un-dėr-eks-pōzd', adj.* (*photography*) not exposed long enough to light. [**under-** (2).]

underfed, *un-dėr-fed', adj.* not given enough to eat. [**under-** (2).]

underfoot, *un-dėr-foot', adv.* under the feet: on the ground. [**under-** (1).]

undergarment, *un'dėr-gär-mėnt, n.* any article of clothing habitually worn under others. [**under-** (3).]

undergo, *un-dėr-gō', v.t.* to endure: to experience: to go through (a process, e.g. repair):—*pr.p.* **undergo'ing**; *pa.t.* **underwent'**; *pa.p.* **undergone'.**
[M.E. *undergon—under*, under, *gon*, go.]

undergraduate, *un-dėr-grad'ū-it, n.* a student who has not taken his first degree.
[**under-** (4).]

underground, *un'dėr-grownd, adj.* below the surface of the ground: secret.—*n.* a railway operating beneath the streets: a secret movement against a ruling power.
[**under-** (3).]

undergrowth, *un'dėr-grōth, n.* low woody plants growing among trees.
[**under-** (3).]

underhand, *un'dėr-hand, adj.* with the hand on a lower level than the shoulder: sly, mean. [**under, hand.**]

underhung, *un-dėr-hung', adj.* (of e.g. sliding door) supported from below: (of lower jaw) sticking out beyond upper.
[**under, hung.**]

underlie, *un-dėr-lī', v.t.* to lie under: to be the hidden cause or source of.
underly'ing, *adj.* [**under-** (1).]

underline, *un-dėr-līn', v.t.* to draw a line under: to emphasise. [**under-** (1).]

underling, *un'dėr-ling, n.* a subordinate: an inferior in rank.
[**under,** and suffx. *-ling.*]

undermentioned, *un-dėr-men'sh(ȯ)nd, adj.* mentioned below or in the text following.
[**under-** (1).]

undermine, *un-dėr-mīn', v.t.* to make a passage under: to make insecure: to weaken (e.g. health, authority): to do so by underhand means. [**under-** (1).]

undermost, *un'dėr-mōst, adj.* lowest in place or condition.
[**under,** and suffx. *-most.*]

underneath, *un-dėr-nēth', adv.* beneath, in a lower place.—Also *prep.*
[**under,** and O.E. *neothan*, beneath.]

underpass, *un'dėr-pâs, n.* a road passing under another road, a railway, etc.
[**under-** (3).]

underpay, *un-dėr-pā', v.t.* to pay too little: —*pa.p.* and *adj.* **underpaid'.**
underpay'ment, *n.* [**under-** (2).]

underpin, *un-dėr-pin', v.t.* to put something under (e.g. a building) for support: —*pr.p.* **underpinn'ing**; *pa.p.* **underpinned'.** [**under-** (1).]

underprivileged, *un-dėr-priv'i-lijd, adj.* not enjoying normal social and economic rights. [**under-** (2).]

underrate, *un-dėr-rāt', v.t.* to think too little of. [**under-** (2).]

Undersecretary, *un-dėr-sek'ri-tȧ-ri, n.* an official next in rank below a Secretary of State. [**under-** (4).]

undersell, *un-dėr-sēl', v.t.* to sell at lower price than (competitor). [**under-** (1).]

underside, *un'dėr-sīd, n.* the side lying underneath, often hidden. [**under-** (1).]

undersign, *un-dėr-sīn', v.t.* to sign one's name at the foot of.
the un'dersigned, the person or persons whose names are signed below.
[**under-** (1).]

undersized, *un'dėr-sīzd, adj.* below the usual size. [**under-** (2).]

underskirt, *un'dėr-skėrt, n.* a skirt worn under another. [**under-** (1).]

understand, *un-dėr-stand', v.t.* to see the meaning of: to know thoroughly: to gather (that): to take for granted as part of an agreement: to take (something) as meant though not expressed:—*pa.t.* and *pa.p.* **understood'.**
understand'ing, *n.* the act or power of grasping meaning: intelligence: an informal agreement: appreciating another's feelings, point of view.—Also *adj.*
[O.E. *understandan*, to perceive, etc.]

understate, *un-dėr-stāt', v.t.* to state at too low an amount, etc.: to state less than the truth about (something).
understate'ment, *n.* [**under-** (2).]

understood. See **understand.**

understudy, *un'dėr-stud-i, v.t.* and *v.i.* to study (a dramatic part) so as to be able to take the place of another actor: to learn the part of (another actor) for this purpose:—*pr.p.* **un'derstudying**; *pa.p.* **un'derstudied.**—*n.* an actor who learns a part thus:—*pl.* **un'derstudies.**
[**under-** (3).]

undertake, *un-dėr-tāk', v.t.* to take upon oneself (a duty, task, etc.): to promise (to do something): —*pa.t., pa.p.* **undertook'.**
un'dertaker, *n.* a manager of funerals.
undertak'ing, *n.* a project, task taken on, business: a pledge, promise: (*un'der-*) conducting funerals.
[M.E. *undertaken—under, taken*, take.]

undertone, *un'dėr-tōn, n.* a low tone of voice: a partly hidden emotion, meaning, quality. [**under-** (3).]

undertook. See **undertake.**

For words in UN not found above, see **un-** (1) *or* (2), *page* 570.

undertow, *un′dėr-tō, n.* a current below the surface, in a different direction from the surface movement. [**under-** (3).]
undervalue, *un-dėr-val′ū, v.t.* to value below the real worth.
undervaluā′tion, *n.* [**under-** (2).]
underwear, *un′dėr-wār, n.* underclothes. [**under-** (3), **wear.**]
underwent. See **undergo.**
underworld, *un′dėr-wûrld, n.* the place of evil spirits, or of the dead: the habitual lawbreakers, esp. when banded together. [**under-** (3).]
underwrite, *un-dėr-rīt′, v.t.* to accept for insurance: to guarantee (money or shares): to accept liability for.
un′derwriter, *n.* one who insures, e.g. shipping. [**under-** (1), **write.**]
undesirable, *un-di-zīr′ȧ-bl, adj.* not to be wished for: objectionable. [**un-** (2).]
undid. See **undo.**
undistinguished, *un-dis-ting′gwisht, adj.* ordinary, commonplace. [**un-** (2).]
undo, *un-dōō′, v.t.* to reverse, wipe out the effect of (what has been done): to unfasten: to ruin:—*pr.p.* **undo′ing**; *pa.t.* **undid′**; *pa.p.* **undone′**.
undo′ing, *n.* ruin. **undone,′** *adj.* [**un-** (1, a).]
undoubted, *un-dowt′id, adj.* not doubted or denied (e.g. *the undoubted excellence of the work*). [**un-** (2).]
undress, *un′dres′, v.t.* and *v.i.* to take the clothes off.—*n.* plain dress (not uniform).
undressed′, *adj.* not dressed: not bandaged: not prepared (for use, display, etc.). [**un-** (1, a).]
undue, *un-dū′, adj.* too great, more than is necessary.
undu′ly, *adv.* [**un-** (2).]
undulate, *un′dū-lāt, v.i.* to move as waves do: to have a rolling appearance (e.g. *These low hills and valleys undulate*).
un′dulating, *adj.* **undulā′tion,** *n.* [L. *unda*, a wave.]
unduly. See **undue.**
unearned, *un-ėrnd′, adj.* not gained by work: not deserved.
unearned income, income from money invested. [**un-** (2).]
unearth, *un-ėrth′, v.t.* to bring out from the earth, or from a place of hiding: to bring to light (e.g. facts, a plot). [O.E. *un-* removal from, and **earth.**]
unearthly, *un-ėrth′li, adj.* supernatural. weird: (*coll.*) absurdly early, loud, etc. [**un-** (2).]
uneasy, *un-ē′zi, adj.* restless: anxious: not certain to last (e.g. *an uneasy peace*).
unea′sily, *adv.* **unea′siness,** *n.* [**un-** (2).]
unemployed, *un-em-ploid′, adj.* not put to use: out of work.
unemploy′ment, *n.* [**un-** (2).]
unequal, *un-ē′kwȧl, adj.* differing in quantity or quality (e.g. *an unequal division of the spoils*): unfair: varying: not having enough strength or ability for (with *to*; e.g. *unequal to the task*).
une′qualled, *adj.* without equal (e.g. *He was unequalled as a mimic*; *a landscape unequalled for beauty*).
une′qually, *adv.* **une′qualness,** *n.* See also **inequality.** [**un-** (2).]
unerring, *un-er′ing, adj.* never making a mistake, always right or accurate (e.g. *unerring skill at darts*).
unerr′ingly, *adv.* [**un-** (2).]
uneven, *un′ē′vn, adj.* not smooth or level: irregular, not uniform: not divisible by two without remainder.
une′venly, *adv.* **une′venness,** *n.* [**un-** (2).]
unexampled, *un-ėg-zâm′pld, adj.* not following any example, alone of its kind (e.g. *unexampled courage, stupidity*). [**un-** (2).]
unexceptionable, *un-ėk-sep′sh(ȯ)n-ȧ-bl, adj.* in which one can find nothing to criticise, without fault. [**un-** (2).]
unexpected, *un-ėk-spek′tid, adj.* not expected, sudden. [**un-** (2).]
unfailing, *un-fā′ling, adj.* never giving out (e.g. *unfailing supplies, courage*): sure, to be counted on. [**un-** (2).]
unfair, *un-fār′, adj.* not fair or just. [**un-** (2), and **fair** (1).]
unfaithful, *un-fāth′fool, -fl, adj.* disloyal. [**un-** (2).]
unfasten, *un-fâs′n, v.t.* to undo, unfix. [**un-** (1 a).]
unfathomable, *un-faᴛʜ′ȯm-ȧ-bl, adj.* too deep to be plumbed, or to be understood. [**un-** (2).]
unfeeling, *un-fē′ling, adj.* hard-hearted. [**un-** (2).]
unfeigned, *un-fānd′, adj.* sincere. [**un-** (2).]
unfettered, *un-fet′ėrd, adj.* free, not restrained or checked. [**un-** (1, a).]
unfilial, *un-fil′yȧl, -i-ȧl, adj.* (of child's behaviour to a parent) not what it should be, not dutiful. [**un-** (2).]
unfit, *un-fit′, adj.* not suitable: not good enough, or not in a suitable state (to, for; e.g. *unfit to travel*; *food unfit for humans*): not in full vigour of body or mind.—*v.t.* to make unfit or unsuitable:—*pr.p.* **unfitt′ing**; *pa.p.* **unfitt′ed.**
unfit′ness, *n.* [**un-** (2).]
unfix, *un-fiks′, v.t.* to undo the fixing of: to unsettle. [**un-** (1, a).]
unflagging, *un-flag′ing, adj.* not tiring or losing vigour. [**un-** (2).]
unflinching, *un-flinch′ing,* or *-sh′, adj.* not flinching or shrinking because of pain, danger, or opposition. [**un-** (2).]
unfold, *un-fōld′, v.t.* to spread out: to give details of (e.g. a plan). [**un-** (1, a), and **fold** (1).]
unforgettable, *un-fȯr-get′ȧ-bl, adj.* never

For words in UN not found above, see **un-** (1) *or* (2), *page* 570.

to be forgotten, because of beauty, or horror, etc.
[**un-** (2), **forget,** suffx *-able.*]

unfortunate, *un-fŏr'chŭ-nit, adj.* unlucky. [**un-** (2).]

unfounded, *un-fown'did, adj.* not based on facts or reality (e.g. *unfounded rumours, fears, hopes*).
[**un-** (2), and **found** (2).]

unfrequented, *un'fri-kwen'tid, adj.* not often visited, lonely. [**un-** (2).]

unfruitful, *un-frōōt'fool, -fl, adj.* not producing fruit, results, etc. [**un-** (2).]

unfurl, *un-fûrl', v.t.* and *v.i.* to unfold, shake out (a sail, a flag). [**un-** (1, a).]

ungainly, *un-gān'li, adj.* awkward, clumsy.
ungain'liness, *n.*
[O.E. *un-*, not, Old Norse *gegen*, ready.]

ungetatable, *un-get-at'ȧ-bl, adj.* in a place where it cannot be reached: hard to reach.
[**un-** (2), **get at,** suffx *-able.*]

ungodly, *un-god'li, adj.* not godly, sinful: (*coll.*) outrageous (e.g. *at the ungodly hour of 3 a.m.*).
ungod'liness, *n.* [**un-** (2).]

ungovernable, *un-guv'ėr-nȧ-bl*, uncontrollable. [**un-** (2).]

ungracious, *un-grā'shŭs, adj.* not showing appreciation: rude, surly. [**un-** (2).]

ungrammatical, *un-grȧ-mat'i'kȧl, adj.* not according to the rules of grammar.

ungrateful, *un-grāt'fool, -fl, adj.* not thankful. See **ingratitude.** [**un-** (2).]

ungrounded, *un-grown'did, adj.* unfounded, groundless. [**un-** (2).]

ungrudging, *un-gruj'ing, adj.* giving, or given, freely. [**un-** (2).]

unguarded, *un-gär'did, adj.* without protection: careless, not prudent (e.g. *an unguarded remark*; *in an unguarded moment*). [**un-** (2).]

unguent, *ung'gwėnt, n.* ointment.
[L. *unguĕre, unctum*, to anoint.]

unhallowed, *un-hal'ōd, adj.* unholy: very wicked. [**un-** (2).]

unhappy, *un-hap'i, adj.* not happy, miserable: not fortunate.
unhapp'ily, *adv.* **unhapp'iness,** *n.*
[**un-** (2).]

unharness, *un-här'nis, v.t.* to take the harness off. [**un-** (1, a).]

unhealthy, *un-hel'thi, adj.* not healthy: sickly: morally undesirable.
unheal'thily, *adv.* **unheal'thiness,** *n.*
[**un-** (2).]

unheard-of, *un-hėrd'-ŏv, adj.* not (yet) heard about: unexampled, esp. in a bad way. [**un-** (2).]

unhinge, *un-hinj', v.t.* to take from the hinges: to derange (the mind).
[**un-** (1, a).]

unholy, *un-hō'li, adj.* not sacred or hallowed: sinful: (*coll.*) excessive (esp. of noise). [**un-** (2).]

unhook, *un-hook', v.t.* to take down from a hook: to unfasten the hooks of (e.g. a dress). [**un-** (1, a).]

unhorse, *un-hörs', v.t.* to throw from a horse. [**un-** (1, a).]

uni-, *ū-ni-, pfx.* one, single. [L. *ūnus*, one.]

unicorn, *ū'ni-körn, n.* an animal in old story, like a horse, but with one straight horn on the forehead.
[L. *ūnus*, one, *cornū*, a horn.]

unification, unified. See **unify.**

uniform, *ū'ni-förm, adj.* not varying, the same always or in all parts (e.g. *a uniform flow of water*; *a uniform custom*).—*n.* the dress worn by soldiers, etc.
unifor'mity, u'niformness, *ns.*
[L. *ūnus*, one, and suffx. *-form.*]

unify, *ū'ni-fī, v.t.* to make into one:—*pr.p.* **u'nifying;** *pa.p.* **u'nified.**
unificā'tion, *n.*
[L. *ūnus*, one, *facĕre*, to make.]

unilateral, *ū-ni-lat'ė-rȧl, adj.* one-sided: on one side only: (of e.g. a legal or other act) carried out by, affecting or binding, one side only.
[L. *ūnus*, one, and **lateral.**]

unimpeachable, *un-im-pēch'ȧ-bl, adj.* not liable to be doubted (e.g. *an unimpeachable witness*): blameless. [**un-** (2).]

uninhibited, *un-in-hib'i-tid, adj.* not repressed, unrestrained. [**un-** (2).]

unintelligible, *un-in-tel'i-ji-bl, adj.* not able to be understood. [**un-** (2).]

uninterrupted, *un-in-tė-rup'tid, adj.* not interrupted: continuing without stoppage or break: (of view) not blocked in any way. [**un-** (2).]

uninvited, *un-in-vīt'id, adj.* without an invitation: not asked for or encouraged.
[**un-** (2).]

union, *ūn'yȯn, n.* a joining together: the state of being united: marriage: states joined together: an association of persons for common purposes: a trade union.
Un'ionist, *n.* orig. one opposed to 'Home Rule' (self-government) for Ireland: a Conservative.
Union Jack, the national flag of the United Kingdom.
[Fr.—L. *ūnus*, one.]

unique, *ū-nēk', adj.* without a like or equal.
[Fr.—L. *ūnicus—ūnus*, one.]

unison, *ū'ni-sȯn, n.* identity, exact sameness, of pitch (e.g. *singing not in harmony but in unison*): agreement.
[L. *ūnus*, one, *sonus*, sound.]

unit, *ū'nit, n.* a single thing or person: a fixed quantity by which other quantities of the same kind are measured: a group within a larger body (e.g. *an army unit*).
u'nitary, *adj.* existing as a unit, not divided: using unit(s).
See also **unity.**
[L. *ūnus*, one.]

Unitarian. See **unity.**

unite, *ū-nīt', v.t.* to join into one.—*v.i.* to become one: to act together.

For words in UN not found above, see **un-** (1) *or* (2), *page* 570.

unī'ted, *adj.* joined: acting together, or thinking, feeling, alike.
[L. *ūnire*, *ūnitum*; same root as **unit.**]

unity, *ū'ni-ti*, *n.* state of being one: state of being in complete agreement: the number one.
Unitā'rian, one who rejects the idea of the Trinity and believes that God the Father alone is divine.
[L. *ūnitas*; same root as **unit.**]

universal. See **universe.**

universe, *ū'ni-vėrs*, *n.* all created things together with the earth and the heavenly bodies: mankind: the world.
universal, *ū-ni-vėr'sȧl*, *adj.* affecting or including all mankind: in general use.
universal'ity, univer'salness, *ns.*
univer'sally, *adv.*
[L. *ūniversus*, whole, entire; as **unit.**]

university, *ū-ni-vėr'si-ti*, *n.* a centre of learning having power to grant degrees:—*pl.* **univer'sities.**
[L. *ūniversitās*; same root as **universe.**]

unjust, *un-just'*, *adj.* not just, unfair. [**un-** (2).]

unkempt, *un-kemt'*, *adj.* untidy.
[O.E. *un-*, not, *cemban*, to comb.]

unkind, *un-kind'*, *adj.* not kind: harsh. [**un-** (2).]

unknot, *un-not'*, *v.t.* to free from knots. [**un-** (1, a).]

unlace, *un-lās'*, *v.t.* to undo the lace in (a shoe, etc.). [**un-** (1, a).]

unladen, *un-lād'n*, *adj.* without a load. [**un-** (2).]

unlearned, *un-lėr'nid*, *adj.* ignorant, not scholarly: (*-lėrnd'*) never learned, or known without learning. [**un-** (2).]

unless, *un-les'*, *conj.* if not, supposing that not (e.g. *Do not speak unless he does*, i.e. if he does not speak).
[O.E. *on lesse that*, in a less case than.]

unlike, *un-līk'*, *adj.* not like, different: not characteristic of (e.g. *It was unlike Mary to say anything cruel*). [**un-** (2).]

unlikely, *un-līk'li*, *adj.* not probable. [**un-** (2).]

unload, *un-lōd'*, *v.t.* to take the load from. [**un-** (1, a).]

unlock, *un-lok'*, *v.t.* to open (something locked): to reveal (e.g. hidden fact, facts, or feeling). [**un-** (1, a).]

unlooked-for, *un-lookt'-fōr*, *adj.* not expected. [**un-** (2), and **look for.**]

unloose, *un-lōōs'*, *v.t.* to make loose.
unloo'sen, *v.t.* unloose. [**un-** (1, b).]

unlucky, *un-luk'i*, *adj.* not lucky.
unluck'ily, *adv.* [**un-** (2).]

unmanned, *un-mand'*, *adj.* not supplied with men: overcome by emotion. [**un-** (2).]

unmanly, *un-man'li*, *adj.* weak, cowardly. [**un-** (2).]

unmask, *un-mäsk'*, *v.t.* to take a mask off (someone): to show (someone) in his true character: to lay bare. [**un-** (1, a).]

unmatched, *un-machd'*, *adj.* without equal. [**un-** (2).]

unmeaning, *un-mē'ning*, *adj.* having no meaning: not intentional.
[O.E. *un-*, not, and **mean** (3).]

unmeasured, *un-mezh'ùrd*, *adj.* boundless, limitless: unrestrained. [**un-** (2).]

unmentionable, *un-men'sh(ȯ)n-ȧ-bl*, *adj.* scandalous, indecent. [**un-** (2).]

unmistakable, *un-mis-tā'kȧ-bl*, *adj.* very clear, very obvious. [**un-** (2).]

unmitigated, *un-mit'i-gā-tid*, *adj.* complete (e.g. *an unmitigated nuisance*).
[O.E. *un-*, not, L. *mītigāre*, to make mild.]

unmoved, *un-mōōvd'*, *adj.* firm: calm. [**un-** (2).]

unnatural, *un-nach'ù-rȧl*, *adj.* strange: artificial: cruel, wicked. [**un-** (2).]

unnecessary, *un-nes'i-sȧ-ri*, *adj.* not necessary: that might have been avoided. [**un-** (2).]

unnerve, *un-nėrv'*, *v.t.* to weaken, frighten, make irresolute. [**un-** (1, a).]

unnumbered, *un-num'bėrd*, *adj.* countless, in very great number. [**un-** (2).]

unobtrusive, *un-ob-trōō'siv*, *adj.* not obvious: modest, quiet. [**un-** (2).]

unoccupied, *un-ok'ū-pīd*, *adj.* not occupied, vacant: idle, not doing anything. [**un-** (2).]

unpack, *un-pak'*, *v.t.* to take out of packing: to open (luggage) and remove clothes, etc.—Also *v.i.* [**un-** (1, a).]

unparalleled, *un-par'ȧ-leld*, *adj.* having no equal: unexampled. [**un-** (2).]

unpick, *un-pik'*, *v.t.* to take out stitches of (knitting, sewing). [**un-** (1, b).]

unpleasant, *un-plez'ȧnt*, *adj.* disagreeable. [**un-** (2).]

unplumbed, *un-plumd'*, *adj.* of unknown depth: not tested or explored. [**un-** (2).]

unpopular, *un-pop'ū-lȧr*, *adj.* generally disliked.
unpopular'ity, *n.* [**un-** (2).]

unpractical, *un-prak'ti-kȧl*, *adj.* (of person, method) not practical. [**un-** (2).]

unprecedented, *un-pres'i-den-tid*, *prēs'-*, or *-den'-*, *adj.* never known before, unexampled, novel, unique. [**un-** (2).]

unpremeditated, *un-prē-med'i-tā-tid*, *adj.* not planned beforehand. [**un-** (2).]

unprepossessing, *un-prē-po-zes'ing*, *adj.* unattractive. [**un-** (2).]

unpretentious, *un-pri-ten'shùs*, *adj.* (of persons or things) modest, not showy, not affected. [**un-** (2).]

unprincipled, *un-prin'sip-ld*, *adj.* without moral principles. [**un-** (2).]

unprofessional, *un-prō-fesh'ȯn-ȧl*, *adj.* (of a person's conduct) not in keeping with standards of his profession. [**un-** (2).]

unpromising, *un-prom'is-ing*, *adj.* not likely to bring enjoyment, success, etc. [**un-** (2).]

unqualified, *un-kwol'i-fīd*, *adj.* not having

For words in UN not found above, see **un-** (1) *or* (2), *page* 570.

essential qualifications (e.g. for a post): complete (e.g. *unqualified praise*). [**un-** (2).]

unquestionable, *un-kwes'ch(ȯ)n-ȧ-bl, adj.* not doubtful, certain, beyond dispute. [**un-** (2).]

unquiet, *un-kwī'ėt, adj.* not at rest: anxious. [**un-** (2).]

unquote, *un-kwōt', v.i.* (*U.S.*) word used to show the end of a passage quoted. [**un-** (1, a).]

unravel, *un-rav'ėl, v.t.* to disentangle: to solve (problem, mystery):—*pr.p.* **unrav'elling**; *pa.p.* **unrav'elled.** [**un-** (1, a).]

unreadable, *un-rēd'ȧ-bl, adj.* illegible: too boring to read. [**un-** (2).]

unreal, *un-rē'ȧl, adj.* not real.
unreal'ity, *n.*:—*pl.* **-ies.**
unre'alised, *adj.* not realised (in any sense of verb).
unrealis'able, *adj.* [**un-** (2).]

unreasonable, *un-rē'zȯn-ȧ-bl, adj.* not guided by reason: not moderate or sensible.
unrea'soning, *adj.* not using reason. [**un-** (2).]

unregenerate, *un-ri-jen'ėr-it, adj.* not having repented: wicked. [**un-** (2).]

unremitting, *un-ri-mit'ing, adj.* never ceasing (e.g. *unremitting efforts*). [**un-** (2).]

unrequited, *un-ri-kwī'tid, adj.* not paid back): not given in return (e.g. *unrequited love*). [**un-** (2).]

unreserved, *un-ri-zėrvd', adj.* not reserved: complete (e.g. *unreserved approval*): frank.
unreser'vedly (*-vid-li-*) *adv.* completely. [**un-** (2).]

unrest, *un-rest', n.* uneasiness: rebellious feeling among a number of people (e.g. *political unrest*). [**un-** (2).]

unrivalled, *un-rī'vȧld, adj.* matchless. [**un-** (2).]

unroll, *un-rōl', v.t.* to open out (something rolled).—Also *v.i.* [**un-** (1, a).]

unruly, *un-ro͞o'li, adj.* not obeying law or rules: disorderly.
unru'liness, *n.*
[**un-** (2), and **rule.**]

unsaddle, *un-sad'l, v.t.* to take the saddle off. [**un-** (1, a).]

unsaid, *un-sed', adj.* not said. [**un-** (2).]

unsanitary. See **in-**

unsavoury, *un-sā'vȯ-ri, adj.* disgusting: immoral. [**un-** (2), and **savoury.**]

unscathed, *un-skāᴛʜd', adj.* not harmed. [**un-** (2).]

unscramble, *un-skram'bl, v.t.* to decode (a message), or make clear the words of (a telephone message). [**un-** (1, a).]

unscrew, *un-skro͞o', v.t.* to unfasten by loosening screws. [**un-** (1, a).]

unseal, *un-sēl', v.t.* to remove the seal of: to open. [**un-** (1, a).]

unseasonable, *un-sē'z(ȯ)n-ȧ-bl, adj.* (of weather) not suitable for the time of year: not well timed (e.g. *the unseasonable arrival of guests*): unsuitable (e.g. *at unseasonable hours*). [**un-** (2).]

unseat, *un-sēt', v.t.* to throw from a seat: to remove from an official position. [**un-** (1, a).]

unseen, *un-sēn', adj.* not seen.—*n.* an unfamiliar passage for translation. [**un-** (2).]

unsettle, *un-set'l, v.t.* to disturb, upset.
unsett'led, *adj.* (of weather) changeable: disturbed: not decided: (of e.g. a bill) unpaid. [**un-** (1, a).]

unsheathe, *un-shēᴛʜ', v.t.* to draw from the sheath or scabbard. [**un-** (1, a).]

unship, *un-ship', v.t.* to take out of a ship. [**un-** (1, a).]

unsightly, *un-sīt'li, adj.* ugly. [**un-** (2), *sightly*, pleasant to look at.]

unsophisticated, *un-sȯ-fis'ti-kā-tid, adj.* simple: not worldly-wise. [**un-** (2).]

unsound, *un-sownd', adj.* (of fruit, etc.) not in good condition: (of reasoning, etc.) not correct: (of mind) not sane. [**un-** (2).]

unsparing, *un-spār'ing, adj.* giving freely: never weakening (e.g. *unsparing efforts*): merciless (e.g. *criticism*). [**un-** (2).]

unspeakable, *un-spē'kȧ-bl, adj.* too good or too bad to be put into words. [O.E. *un-*, not, **speak,** suffx. *-able*.]

unstrung, *un-strung', adj.* with strings removed or slackened: unnerved. [**un-** (1, a).]

unstudied, *un-stud'id, adj.* not studied: natural, easy. [**un-** (2).]

unsuspected, *un-sus-pek'tid, adj.* not imagined or known to exist. [**un-** (2).]

unthinkable, *un-thingk'ȧ-bl, adj.* very unlikely indeed: too bad to be thought of.
unthink'ing, *adj.* showing lack of thought.
[O.E. *un-*, not, **think,** suffx. *-able*.]

untie, *un-tī', v.t.* to loosen, unfasten: *pr.p.* **unty'ing**; *pa.p.* **untied'**. [**un-** (1, a).]

until, *un-til', prep., conj.* same as **till** (2). [M.E. *untill*.]

untimely, *un-tīm'li, adj.* happening too soon: not suitable to the occasion (e.g. *untimely mirth*). [**un-** (2).]

untiring, *un-tīr'ing, adj.* not wearying: (of e.g. effort) not slackening.

untold, *un-tōld', adj.* not told: too great to be counted, measured. [**un-** (2).]

untoward, *un-tō'ȧrd, un-tȯ-wörd', adj.* unfortunate, inconvenient (e.g. *untoward circumstances*).
[**un-** (2), *toward*, coming, favourable.]

untried, *un-trīd', adj.* not attempted: not tested by experience. [**un-** (2).]

untrodden, *un-trod'n, adj.* seldom or never trodden (e.g. *untrodden paths*). [**un-** (2).]

untroubled, *un-trub'ld, adj.* not anxious: calm. [**un-** (2).]

untrue, *un-tro͞o', adj.* false: disloyal.

For words in UN not found above, see **un-** (1) *or* (2), *page* 570.

untruth′, *n.* falseness : a lie. [**un-** (2).]

untwist, *un-twist′, v.t.* to straighten out (something twisted). [**un-** (1, a).]

unutterable, *un-ut′ėr-ȧ-bl, adj.* too great to be expressed : very horrible.
[O.E. *un-*, not, **utter** (2), suffx. *-able.*]

unvarnished, *un-vär′nisht, adj.* not varnished : plain, straightforward (e.g. *the unvarnished truth*). [**un-** (2).]

unveil, *un-vāl′, v.t.* to remove a veil from : to uncover ceremonially (e.g. a new statue). [**un-** (1, a).]

unwary, *un-wā′ri, adj.* not cautious.
unwā′rily, *adv.* **unwa′riness,** *n.*
[**un-** (2).]

unwelcome, *un-wel′kȯm, adj.* received unwillingly or with disappointment.
[**un-** (2).]

unwell, *un-wel′, adj.* not in good health.
[**un-** (2).]

unwept, *un-wept′, adj.* not mourned.
[**un-** (2).]

unwieldy, *un-wēl′di, adj.* awkward to handle.
unwiel′diness, *n.*
[O.E. *un-*, not, and **wield.**]

unwilling, *un-wil′ing, adj.* not willing, reluctant. [**un-** (2).]

unwind, *un-wind′, v.t., v.i.* to wind down or off :—*pa.p.* **unwound′.** [**un-** (1, a).]

unwise, *un-wīz′, adj.* not wise : foolish. [**un-** (2).]

unwitting, *un-wit′ing, adj.* not aware : unintentional.
[**un-** (2), and old word *wit*, to know.]

unwonted, *un-wōn′tid, adj.* unaccustomed, not usual. [**un** (2), and **wont.**]

unworthy, *un-wûr′THi, adj.* not worthy : base, discreditable : not deserving (e.g. *unworthy of notice*) : less good than one would expect (of ; e.g. *This drawing is unworthy of you*).
unwor′thily, *adv.* **unwor′thiness,** *n.*
[**un-** (2).]

unwound. See **unwind.**

unwrap, *un-rap′, v.t.* to open (something wrapped or folded) :—*pr.p.* **unwrapp′ing** ; *pa.p.* **unwrapped′.** [**un-** (1, a).]

unwritten, *un-rit′n, adj.* not written : not recorded in writing. [**un-** (2).]

up, *up, adv.* towards a higher place : on high : from a lower to a higher position : towards a city, esp. London (with *to*) : at a college or university : to, as far as, the place where one is, the stopping-place, etc. (e.g. *The bus came up*) :—*superl.* **upp′ermost.**—*prep.* to a higher level on (e.g. a hill) : towards the source of (a river) : into a stretch of (e.g. *to go up country*).—*adj.* top (e.g. *the up side*): going up : risen : (of time) ended : wrong, amiss (e.g. *What's up?*) :—*comp.* **upp′er** ; *superls.* **upp′ermost, up′most.**
upp′er, *comp. adj.* higher in position, dignity, etc.—*n.* the part of a boot or shoe above the sole and welt.
upp′er-class, *adj.* of a high rank in society.
upp′ercut, *n.* a swinging blow aimed upwards.—Also *v.t.* and *v.i.*
the upp′erhand, superiority, control.
ups and downs, turns of good and bad fortune.
up to, (*coll.*) engaged in doing : able and ready for : a duty before (a person ; e.g. *It is up to me*).
up to date, to the present time : in touch with the latest ideas or practices (also **up′-to-date**). [O.E.]

up-, *pfx.* has *adj.*, *adv.*, or *prep.* sense, as shown in examples below.

upbraid, *up-brād′, v.t.* to reproach.
[O.E. *upbregdan.*]

upbringing, *up′bring-ing, n.* the rearing and training given to, received by, a child. [**up,** *adv.*]

up-country, *up-kun′tri, adv.* and *adj.* inland. [**up,** *prep.*]

up-grade, *up′grād, n.* a rising slope.—*v.t.* (also **upgrade**)to raise to position of greater importance in e.g. a business : to improve the quality of. [**up,** *adj.*]

upheaval, *up-hē′vȧl, n.* a violent shaking : a great disturbance. [**up,** *adv.*]

upheld. See **uphold.**

uphill, *up′hil′, adj.* rising : difficult.—*adv.* upwards. [**up,** *prep.*]

uphold, *up-hōld′, v.t.* to support (a person or something he does) : to maintain (e.g. a view, tradition) :—*pr.p.* **uphold′ing** ; *pa.p.* **upheld′.** [**up,** *adv.*]

upholster, *up-hōl′stėr, v.t.* to fit (seats) with springs, stuffing, covers, etc.
uphōl′sterer, *n.* one who makes, repairs or sells, upholstered furniture.
uphōl′stery, *n.* covers, cushions, etc.
[**up, hold,** and suffx. *-ster.*]

upkeep, *up′kēp, n.* keeping a house, car, etc. in repair, or cost of this. [**up,** *adv.*]

upland, *up′lȧnd, n.* high ground.—Also *adj.* [**up,** *adj.*]

uplift, *up-lift′, v.t.* to lift up, raise : to improve morally, etc. : to raise the spirits of.—*n.* (*up′lift*) (something that gives) strong mental or moral encouragement. [**up,** *adv.*]

upmost. See **up.**

upon, *ŭ-pon′, prep.* on the top of. [**up, on.**]

upper, uppermost. See **up.**

upright, *up′rīt, adj.* standing straight up : just and honest.—*n.* a vertical post.
up′rightly, *adv.* **up′rightness,** *n.*
[**up,** *adv.*]

uprising, *up-rīz′ing, n.* act of rising against government, etc. : a revolt. [**up,** *adv.*]

uproar, *up′rōr, -rör, n.* noise and shouting : a noisy disturbance.
uproar′ious, *adj.* very noisy.
uproar′iously, *adv.* **-iousness,** *n.*
[Du. *oproer*, revolt.]

uproot, *up-rōōt′, v.t.* to tear up by the roots. [**up,** *adv.*]

For words in UN not found above, see **un-** (1) *or* (2), *page* 570.

upset, *up-set′*, *v.t.* to turn upside-down: to overturn: to put out of order: to distress.—*adj.* worried, anxious: ill.—*n.* (*up′*) distress or its cause.
up′set price, the price at which the bidding starts at an auction sale.
[**up,** *adv.*]

upshot, *up′shot*, *n.* (*orig.*, at archery) the last shot: the result or end of a matter.
[**up,** *adj.*]

upside-down, *up′sīd-down*, *adv.* with the top part underneath: in confusion.
[**up,** *adj.*, **side,** and **down.**]

upstage, *up′staj′*, *adv.* away from the footlights. [**up,** *prep.*]

upstairs, *up′stärz′*, *adv.* in or to an upper storey.—Also *n.* and *adj.* [**up,** *prep.*]

upstanding, *up-stan′ding*, *adj.* standing up: robust: worthy, honest. [**up,** *adv.*]

upstart, *up′stärt*, *n.* one who has risen quickly to wealth or power, but seems to lack dignity or ability. [**up,** *adv.*]

upstream, *up′strēm′*, *adv.* towards the upper part of a stream. [**up,** *prep.*]

uptake, *up′tāk*, *n.* power of understanding.
[**up,** *adv.*]

up-to-date. See **up.**

upward, *up′ward*, *adj.* going up: directed up (e.g. *an upward glance*).
up′ward, up′wards, *advs.*
upward(s) of, more than.
[**up,** and suffx. *-ward.*]

uranium, *ū-rā′ni-ŭm*, *n.* a radioactive metal.
[Gk. *ouranos*, heaven.]

urban, *ûr′bȧn*, *adj.* of, consisting of, or living in, city or town.
urbane, *ûr-bān′*, *adj.* smoothly polite.
urban′ity, (*-ban′*), *n.* highly civilised politeness: (in *pl.*, **-ies**) polite actions.
[L. *urbs*, city.]

urchin, *ûr′chin*, *n.* a hedgehog: a small boy: a dirty or ragged boy.
[Through O.Fr.—L. *ēricius*, hedgehog.]

Urdu, *ōōr′dōō*, *n.* form of Hindustani with many Persian and Arabic words, the official language of Pakistan.
[Hindi *urdū*, camp (language); conn. **horde.**]

urge, *ûrj*, *v.t.* to drive (on): to try to persuade.—*n.* a strong impulse.
ur′gent, *adj.* requiring immediate attention: eagerly pressing for action.
ur′gency, *n.*
[L. *urgēre*, to press.]

urine, *ū′rin*, *n.* the fluid passed out of the body of animals.
[Fr.—L. *ūrīna.*]

urn, *ûrn*, *n.* a vessel used for keeping the ashes of the dead: a large metal can, with tap, for making tea, etc.
[L. *urna—urĕre*, to burn.]

us. See **we.**

usage. See **use** (1).

use[1], *ūz*, *v.t.* to employ as an instrument (e.g. *to use a fork*): to bring into action (e.g. *to use common sense*): (often with *up*) to spend, consume, all of: to treat (e.g. *to use him well*).—Also *v.i.*; now only in *pa.t.* **used,** *ūst* (e.g. *I used to go often*).—*n.* (*ūs*); see **use** (2).
us′able, *adj.*
usage, *ū′zij*, *n.* act or manner of using: custom, habit: treatment (e.g. *rough usage*).
used, *ūzd*, *adj.* employed, put to a purpose: not new: accustomed through experience (e.g. *used to hardship*).
See also **use** (2), **usual, utility.**
[L. *ūti*, *ūsus.*]

use[2], *ūs*, *n.* act of using or putting to a purpose: suitability for a purpose (e.g. *of no practical use*): practice, custom.—*v.t.* (*ūz*); see **use** (1).
use′ful, *adj.* helpful: serving a practical purpose.
use′fully, *adv.* **use′fulness,** *n.*
use′less, *adj.* having no use or effect.
use and wont, customary practice.
(of) no use, useless.
to have no use for, to have no need for: to disapprove of (e.g. a person).
to make use of, to employ: to treat (a person) as a means to one's own gain.
[L. *ūsus*; same root as **use** (1).]

used. See **use** (1) (*pa.t.* of *v.i.*; also *adj.*).

usher, *ush′ėr*, *n.* one who shows people to their seats in a theatre, etc.:—*fem.* **usherette′.**—*v.t.* to lead (in, into, to).
[Through O.Fr.—L. *ostium*, door.]

usual, *ū′zhū-ȧl*, *adj.* done, happening, etc., most often (e.g. *the usual routine*; *this result is usual*): customary (e.g. *his usual carelessness*).
u′sually, *adv.* on most occasions.
[Same root as **use** (1).]

usurp, *ū-zûrp′*, *v.t.* to seize (power or rights belonging to another).
usurpā′tion, *n.* **usur′per,** *n.*
[L. *ūsurpāre.*]

usurer. See **usury.**

usury, *ū′zhū-ri*, *n.* taking of interest on money, esp. if rate of interest is high.
u′surer, *n.* a grasping moneylender.
[L. *ūsūra*, interest; same root as **use.**]

utensil, *ū-ten′sil*, *n.* an instrument or vessel used in everyday life.
[L. *ūtensilia* (pl.); same root as **use.**]

utilise, *ū′ti-līz*, *v.t.* to make use of (something available, at hand).
utilisā′tion, *n.*
[Fr. *utiliser*—L. root as **use.**]

utility, *ū-til′i-ti*, *n.* usefulness: a useful service:—*pl.* **util′ities.**
utilitā′rian, *adj.* useful (often in contrast to ornamental).
[L. *utilitās*—same root as **use.**]

utmost, *ut′mōst*, or *-mȯst*, *adj.* most distant: greatest possible (e.g. *Take the utmost care*).
to do one's utmost, to make the greatest possible effort.
See also **utter** (1).
[O.E. *ūtemest—ūt*, out.]

Utopian, *ū-tō'pi-ȧn, adj.* ideally perfect.—*n.* one who tries to plan a perfect society. [*Utopia,* imaginary island described by Sir T. More—Gk. *ou,* not, *topos,* place.]

utter[1], *ut'ėr, adj.* extreme, complete.
utt'erly, *adv.* completely.
utt'ermost, *adj.* utmost.
[O.E. *ūtor,* outer—*ūt,* out.]

utter[2], *ut'ėr, v.t.* to give out (words, cries, etc.): to make public (a libel): to put into circulation (e.g. counterfeit money).
utt'erance, *n.* way of speaking: something said.
[O.E. *ūtian,* to put out—*ūt,* out.]

uttermost. See **utter** (1).

U-turn. See **U-bend.**

uvula, *ū'vū-lȧ, n.* the small 'tongue' which hangs down in the back of the throat.
[L. *ūva,* a bunch of grapes.]

uxorious, *uk-sōr'i-ůs, -sör', adj.* foolishly fond of one's wife. .
[L. *uxōrius.*]

V

vacant, *vā'kȧnt, adj.* empty: unoccupied: showing no intelligence or no interest (e.g. a *vacant stare*).
vā'cancy, *n.* emptiness: empty space: an unoccupied post (e.g. *a vacancy for a typist*):—*pl.* **vā'cancies.**
vacate, *vȧ-kāt', v.t.* to leave empty, cease to occupy or own.
vacā'tion, *n.* a holiday.
[L. *vacans, -antis,* empty.]

vaccinate, *vak'si-nāt, v.t.* to protect against smallpox by putting cowpox vaccine into the blood.
vaccinā'tion, *n.*
vaccine, *vak'sēn, n.* a preparation containing the virus (see this word) of cowpox: disease germ prepared for inoculation (see this word).
[L. *vaccīnus,* of a cow—*vacca,* cow.]

vacillate, *vas'i-lāt, v.i.* to sway to and fro: to waver, show indecision.
vacillā'tion, *n.*
[L. *vacillāre, -ātum.*]

vacuous, *vak'ū-ůs, adj.* empty, silly, stupid.
vacū'ity, *n.* emptiness: emptiness of mind.
vac'ūum, *n.* a space empty of all matter: (in practice) a space from which almost all air or other gas has been removed:—*pl.* **vac'ūa.**
vac'ūum-brake, *n.* a brake system which works quickly and strongly by withdrawal of air from brake cylinders.
vac'ūum-cleaner, *n.* an apparatus for removing dust by suction.
vac'ūum-flask, *n.* a vessel with double walls, which have a vacuum between them, to keep the contents from losing or gaining heat.
vac'ūum-packed, *adj.* packed in a container from which most of the air has been removed.
vac'ūum-tube, *n.* a sealed glass tube in which a vacuum has been made.
[L. *vacuus,* empty; conn. with **vacant.**]

vagabond, *vag'ȧ-bond, adj.* wandering: having no settled home.—*n.* one who has no settled home: a rascal (*rogues and vagabonds*).
[L. *vagus,* wandering; root as **vagrant.**]

vagary, *vāg'ȧ-ri, vȧ-gā'ri, n.* a queer fancy: odd or unexpected behaviour (often in *pl.,* **-ies.**)
[Prob. same L. root as **vagrant.**]

vagrant, *vā'grȧnt, adj.* unsettled, wandering (e.g. *a vagrant life*).—*n.* one who has no fixed home: a tramp.
vā'grancy, *n.* the state of being a tramp.
[Perh. a Germanic word, but influenced by L. *vagārī,* to stray.]

vague, *vāg, adj.* not definite (e.g. *a vague statement*): indistinct: not clear or forceful in thinking or character.
vāgue'ly, *adv.* **vāgue'ness,** *n.*
[Fr.—same L. root as **vagabond.**]

vain, *vān, adj.* unavailing, unsuccessful (e.g. *vain efforts, a vain attempt*): empty, worthless (e.g. *vain threats, boasts, promises*): conceited.
vain'ly, *adv.* **vain'ness,** *n.*
van'ity (*van'*), *n.* empty pride: worthlessness: something worthless, as empty pleasure:—*pl.* **van'ities.**
in vain, with no success (e.g. *He tried in vain*).
to take in vain, to use (one's name) in an irreverent way.
[Fr.—L. *vānus,* empty.]

vainglory, *vān-glō'ri, -glö', n.* boastful pride.
vainglō'rious, *adj.*
vainglō'riously, *adv.* [**vain, glory.**]

valance, *val'ȧns, n.* hanging drapery for a bed, etc. [Orig. uncertain.]

vale, *vāl, n.* a tract of low ground, esp. between hills, a valley.
[Fr. *val*—L. *vallis.*]

valediction, *val-i-dik'sh(ȯ)n, n.* a farewell.
valedic'tory, *adj.* saying farewell.
[L. *valē,* farewell, *dīcĕre,* to say.]

valency, *vā'lėn-si, n.* (*chemistry*) the combining power of an atom or group (e.g. *In water, H_2O, oxygen shows valency two*):—*pl.* **vā'lencies.**
[L. *valēre,* to be strong.]

valentine, *val'ėn-tīn, n.* a sweetheart chosen, or a love-letter, etc., sent, on *St Valentine's Day,* 14th February.
[Name of saint.]

valet, *val'it,* or *val'ā, n.* a manservant, one

who looks after his master's clothes, etc. —*v.t.* and *v.i.* to serve as a valet:—*pr.p.* **val'eting;** *pa.t.* **val'eted.**
[Fr.; conn. with **vassal, varlet.**]

valetudinarian, *val-i-tū-di-nā'ri-ȧn, n.* and *adj.* (a person) in poor health: (one) too much concerned about his health.
[L. *valētūdō,* state of health; conn. **valour.**]

valiant, *val'yȧnt, adj.* (of a deed, etc.) brave, heroic: bold in danger.
val'iancy, val'iantness, *ns.*
[Fr. *vaillant*—same L. root as **valour.**]

valid, *val'id, adj.* sound, reasonable, acceptable (e.g. *That is not a valid excuse, objection, proof*): legally in force (e.g. *He has a valid passport*).
valid'ity, val'idness, *ns.*
[L. *validus,* strong—root as **valour.**]

valley, *val'i, n.* low land between hills or mountains: a region drained by a river and its tributaries:—*pl.* **vall'eys.**
[O.Fr. *vallee*—same root as **vale.**]

valour, *val'ȯr, n.* courage, stoutness of heart: bravery in battle.
val'orous, *adj.* **val'orously,** *adv.*
[O.Fr.—L. *valēre,* to be strong.]

value, *val'ū, n.* worth: importance: usefulness: price: purchasing power (e.g. of a coin): a fair return (as in *value for one's money*): length of a musical note (e.g. *The value of a quaver is an eighth of the value of a semibreve*): a particular number, quantity, put as equal to an expression in algebra (e.g. *In this case the value of y is* 9).—*v.t.* to put a price on: to prize, regard as good or important:—*pr.p.* **val'uing;** *pa.p.* **val'ued.**
val'uable, *adj.* having considerable value.—*n.* (often in *pl.*) thing(s) of special value.
valuā'tion, *n.* act of valuing: estimated price.
val'uator, val'uer, *ns.* one who has been trained to estimate the value of property.
[Fr. *pa.p.*—same L. root as **valour.**]

valve, *valv, n.* a device for allowing a liquid or gas to pass through an opening in one direction only (e.g. the valve of a bicycle tyre): a structure with the same effect in an animal body (e.g. controlling flow of blood): a part of a wireless or television set: one of the separate parts of the shell of animal such as oyster.
valvular, *val'vū-lȧr, adj.* of valve(s).
[Fr.—L. *valva,* a folding door.]

vamp, *vamp, n.* front part of upper of boot or shoe: a patch: a simple musical accompaniment.—*v.t., v.i.* to patch: to play (a simple type of accompaniment.)
[Fr. *avant-pied,* front part of foot.]

vampire, *vam'pīr, n.* a dead person imagined to rise by night and suck the blood of sleeping people: one who extorts money from others.
vampire bat, a blood-sucking bat.
[Fr.; of Slavonic origin.]

van[1], *van, n.* the front (formerly of an army or fleet): the leaders in any movement.
[**vanguard.**]

van[2], *van, n.* a covered wagon for carrying goods on road or rail. [**caravan.**]

vandal, *van'dȧl, n.* a person who carelessly spoils natural beauty: one who damages a public building or other property.
van'dalism, *n.* behaviour of a vandal.
[From L. name of Germanic people who ravaged parts of Roman Empire.]

vane, *vān, n.* a weathercock: one of the blades of a windmill or propeller, etc.
[Older form *fane*—O.E. *fana.*]

vanguard, *van'gärd, n.* the part of an army going in front of the main body: the front line: leaders in any movement.
[Fr. *avant,* before, *garde,* guard.]

vanilla, *vȧ-nil'ȧ, n.* a flavouring obtained from a tropical orchid.
[Sp. *vainilla,* little pod.]

vanish, *van'ish, v.i.* to go out of sight: to fade away to nothing.
to reach vanishing point, to reach point at which disappears.
[Fr. *vanir*—L. *vānescĕre*—root as **vain.**]

vanity. See **vain.**

vanquish, *vangk'wish, v.t.* to defeat.
[Through Fr.—L. *vincĕre*; as **victor.**]

vantage ground, point, *vân'tij,* a position favourable for success in a contest, or from which one has a clear view.
[**advantage.**]

vapid, *vap'id, adj.* (of wine, talk, etc.) flat, uninteresting.
[L. *vapidus,* (of wine) flat.]

vapour, *vā'pȯr, n.* the gaseous (gas-like) state of a substance that is normally liquid or solid (e.g. *water vapour, mercury vapour*): mist or smoke in the air.—*v.i.* to talk wildly, to make empty boasts.
vā'porise (*-īz*), *v.t.* and *v.i.* to (cause to) change into vapour.
vā'porīser, *n.* an apparatus for sending liquid out in a fine spray.
to have a fit of the vapours, to make a great show of being in bad spirits. [Fr.]

variable, variation, etc. See **vary.**

varicose, *var'i-kōs, adj.* permanently enlarged, as in **varicose veins,** a condition in which veins, usu. of the leg, are swollen.
[L. *varicōsus,* full of swollen veins.]

variegate, *vā'ri-ė-gāt, v.t.* to mark with different colours: to give variety to.
variegā'tion, *n.*
[L. *varius,* various, *agĕre,* to make.]

variety, *vȧ-rī'ė-ti, n.* the quality of being of many kinds, or of being varied: a mixed collection (e.g. *a variety of toys for sale, of excuses*): sort, kind: mixed theatrical entertainment including dances, songs, short sketches, etc.:—*pl.* **-ies.**
various, *vā'ri-ůs, adj.* varied, different, unlike each other: several (e.g. *Various people have said it*).
vā'riously, *adv.*

variety show, a programme of variety.
variety theatre, one which presents variety shows.
See also **variegate, vary.**
[L. *varietās*; same root as **vary.**]

varlet, *vär′lit, n.* a rascal, low fellow.
[Same root as **vassal.**]

varnish, *vär′nish, n.* a sticky liquid which gives a glossy surface to wood, paper, etc. —*v.t.* to cover with varnish: to give a falsely good appearance to (e.g. *He tried to varnish his behaviour*).
[Fr. *vernis.*]

varsity, *vär′si-ti, n.* short for 'university'.
[This form of the word has *ä*, the 18th century pronunciation of *e* before *r*, and spelling to show the pronunciation.]

vary, *vā′ri, v.t.* to make different: to free from sameness or monotony.—*v.i.* to be, or become, different: to differ (from):—*pr.p.* **vā′rying**; *pa.p.* **vā′ried.**
vā′riable, *adj.* that may be varied: changeable.—*n.* something that varies, e.g. in value.
variabil′ity, va′riableness, *ns*
va′riance, *n.* a change of condition: a difference: state of disagreement.
va′riant, *n.* a different form or version.—Also *adj.*
variā′tion, *n.* the act, or process, of varying: an instance of this: extent to which a thing changes (e.g. *Farther from the sea the variation in temperature is greater*): one of a series of musical changes made on a basic theme or melody: (*ballet*) a solo dance.
at variance, in disagreement (e.g. *The two men, their views, were at variance*; *A was at variance with B about the plan*).
[L. *variāre*—*varius,* various.]

vasculum, *vas′kū-lum, n.* a botanist's box for specimens.
[Same root as **vase.**]

vase, *väz,* or *vāz, n.* a jar, used in ancient days for domestic purposes and in sacrifices, but now mainly as an ornament or for holding cut flowers.
[Fr.—L. *vās.*]

Vaseline, *vas′ė-lēn, n.* (orig. trademark) an ointment made from petroleum.
[Ger. *wasser,* water, and Gk. *elaion,* oil.]

vassal, *vas′ȧl, n.* under the feudal system, one who held land from, and paid homage to, a superior: a dependant, retainer.
vass′alage (*-ȧ-lij*), *n.* state of being a vassal.
[Fr.—Late L. *vasāllus*; of Celt. origin.]

vast, *väst, adj.* of very great size or amount.
vast′ly, *adv.* **vast′ness,** *n.*
[L. *vastus*; root as **waste.**]

vat, *vat, n.* a large vessel or tank, esp. one for holding liquors.
[O.E. *fæt*; conn. Ger. *fass,* cask]

Vatican, *vat′i-kȧn, n.* the palace of the Pope, standing on the Vatican Hill in Rome, in independent territory (**the Vatican City**): the government or authority of the Pope.
[L. *Mons Vāticānus,* Vatican Hill.]

vaudeville, *vō′dė-vil, n.* an entertainment with songs and dances, usu. comic.
[From the place of origin, the *vau* (*val*) *de Vire,* a valley in Normandy.]

vault[1]**,** *völt, n.* an arched roof: an underground room, a cellar.—*v.t.* to cover with an arched roof.
vaul′ted, *adj.* having an arched roof.
vaul′ting, *n.* arched ceiling(s), etc.
[O.Fr. *volte*—L. *volvĕre, volūtum,* roll.]

vault[2]**,** *völt, n.* a leap aided by the hands or by a pole.—*v.t.* to leap, leap (over).
[O.Fr. *volter,* turn (a horse), leap.]

vaunt, *vönt, v.i.* to boast, brag.—*v.t.* to boast about (e.g. one's success).
[Root as **vain, vanity.**]

veal, *vēl, n.* the flesh of a calf.
[Through O.Fr.—L. *vitellus,* little calf.]

vector, *vek′tȯr, n.* a straight line drawn from a given point to represent both the direction and the size of a quantity such as a velocity or a force.
[L. *vehĕre, vectum,* to carry, convey.]

veer, *vēr, v.i.* (of the wind) to change direction: to change course: to change in mood or outlook (e.g. *to veer away from opinions formerly held*).
[Fr. *virer,* to turn; conn. with **gyrate.**]

vegetable, *vej′i-tȧbl, n.* a plant: a plant grown for food.—*adj.* belonging to plants: obtained from, or consisting of, plants (e.g. *vegetable dyes, oils*; *a vegetable diet*).
vegetār′ian, *adj.* consisting of vegetables (e.g. *a vegetarian diet*).—*n.* a person who believes it right to eat no flesh, but vegetable food only.
vegetār′ianism, *n.*
veg′etāte, *v.i.* to grow by roots and leaves: to live an idle, aimless life.
vegetā′tion, *n.* plants in general: the plants of a particular region (e.g. *the dense vegetation of a jungle*).
vegetable marrow, the fruit of a kind of gourd.
the vegetable kingdom, all the plants of the world.
[O.Fr.—L. *vegetus,* active, lively.]

vehement, *vē′(h)i-mėnt, adj.* very eager, violent, passionate (e.g. *a vehement person*; *vehement arguments, denials*).
vē′hemence, *n.* **vē′hemently,** *adv.*
[L. *vehemens, -entis.*]

vehicle, *vē′i-kl, n.* any means of transport on wheels or runners: a means of conveying information, etc. (e.g. *The daily papers, TV, and radio are vehicles for the spread of news*): a substance not itself active used in making up medicine or paints.
vehicular (*vė-hik′ū-lȧr*), *adj.* (e.g. *Vehicular traffic on this bridge is forbidden*).
[L. *vehiculum*—root as **vector.**]

veil, *vāl, n.* anything that hides an object: a piece of cloth or netting worn to shade

or hide the face: a nun's headdress (hence **to take the veil,** to become a nun): a deceptive appearance, or something (e.g. mystery, silence) that hides facts.—*v.t.* to cover with a veil: to hide.
[L. *vēlum*, a sail, curtain.]

vein, *vān, n.* one of the tubes that carry the blood back to the heart: a small rib in a leaf: a thin seam of mineral (e.g. *a vein of gold in quartz*): a streak of different colour: a strain in character (e.g. *He has a vein of stubbornness*): manner, style: mood (e.g. *in the vein for joking*).
vein'ing, *n.* the arrangement of veins in a leaf: vein-like markings.
venous, *vē'nus, adj.* of vein(s): flowing in veins (e.g. *venous blood*).
[Fr. *veine*—L. *vēna*.]

veld, *felt, velt, n.* (South Africa) unforested, or thinly forested, grass country.
[Du. *veld*, field.]

vellum, *vel'um, n,* a fine parchment made from the skin of calves, kids, or lambs.
[O.Fr. *velin*—same root as **veal.**]

velocity, *vė-los'i-ti, n.* rate of movement (e.g. *wind velocity*): speed in a stated direction (e.g. that of a body falling vertically): swiftness:—*pl.* **-ies.**
[L. *vēlōcitās*, swiftness.]

velour(s), *vė-lōōr', n.* a velvet-like material: a hat made of such material. [Fr.]

velvet, *vel'vit, n.* a cloth made from silk, etc., with a soft, thick surface.—*adj.* made of velvet: soft like velvet.
velveteen', *n.* a material resembling, but cheaper than, velvet.
[L. *villus*, hair, shaggy hair.]

venal, *vē'nȧl, adj.* able to be bought (used of one who can be bribed): disreputable and done for a bribe (e.g. *a venal act*).
vēnal'ity, *n.* willingness to be bribed: quality of being done for a bribe.
[L. *vēnālis*, for sale.]

vend, *vend, v.t.* to sell.
ven'dor, *n.* one who sells (e.g. *a street vendor*, one who sells in the streets).—Also **ven'der.**
vending machine, a slot machine.
[L. *vendĕre*, to sell.]

vendetta, *ven-det'-ȧ, n.* a feud started by a murder: a quarrel long pursued. [It.]

veneer, *vi-nēr', v.t.* to cover wood with a thin piece of wood of finer quality: to give a good appearance to what is really not good.—*n.* a thin coating, as of wood: false show (e.g. *a veneer of good manners hiding brutality*).
[Formerly *fineer*; conn. with **furnish.**]

venerable, *ven'ėr-ȧ-bl, adj.* worthy of great respect because of age, or for special goodness.
ven'erāte, *v.t.* to honour greatly: to regard with religious awe.
venerā'tion, *n.* the act of venerating: reverence, great respect (e.g. *His pupils regarded him with veneration*).
(L. *venerārī*, *-ātus*.]

Venetian, *ve-nē'sh(ȧ)n, adj.* of or belonging to *Venice*.
Venetian blind, a window blind made of thin movable strips of wood, metal, or plastic.
[L. *Venetia*, Venice.]

vengeance, *ven'jȧns, n.* punishment for an injury carried out by the sufferer or his friends.
venge'ful, *adj.* eager for vengeance.
with a vengeance, in a very great or unexpected degree (e.g. *This was generosity with a vengeance*).
[Through O.Fr.—L. *vindicāre*, to claim.]

venial, *vē'ni-ȧl, adj.* pardonable (e.g. *a venial fault, not a deadly sin*).
[L. *venia*, pardon.]

venison, *ven'zn, ven'i-zn, ven'i-sn, n.* flesh of deer.
[Through O.Fr.—L. *vēnārī*, to hunt.]

venom, *ven'ȯm, n.* poison: spite, malice.
ven'omous, *adj.* poisonous: full of malice.
ven'omously, *adv.* **-ousness,** *n.*
[Fr. *venin*—L. *venēnum*, poison.]

venous. See **vein.**

vent[1], *vent, n.* a small opening: a hole to allow air, smoke, etc. to pass out: outlet, expression (e.g. *He gave vent to his rage*).—*v.t.* to let out (e.g. smoke): to give outlet or expression to (e.g. *He vented his rage in a sneer, on his son*).
ventilate, *ven'ti-lāt, v.t.* to allow fresh air to enter (e.g. a room): to expose (a subject) to discussion: to give utterance to (e.g. *to ventilate one's grievances*).
ventilā'tion, *n.*
ven'tilātor, *n.* a device for bringing in fresh air.
[L. *ventus*, wind.]

vent[2], *vent, n.* a slit in the back of a coat.
[Through Fr.—L. *findĕre*, to split.]

ventilate, etc. See **vent** (1).

ventral, *ven'trȧl, adj.* belonging to the belly.—*n.* a fin on the lower side of a fish's body.
ven'tricle, *n.* a small cavity, esp. in the brain or heart.
[L. *venter*, the belly.]

ventriloquist, *ven-tril'ō-kwist, n.* one who can speak so that his voice seems to come from some other person or place.
ventril'oquism, *n.*
[L. *venter*, the belly, *loquī*, to speak.]

venture, *ven'chủr, n.* an undertaking, scheme, that involves some risk.—*v.t.* to do or say (something when one is not sure what the effect will be; e.g. *I ventured a remark*, or *to remark*).
ven'turous, ven'turesome, *adjs.* daring.
at a venture, at random.
[**adventure.**]

venue, *ven'ū, n.* the scene of an action or event. [(O.)Fr. *pa.p.* of *venir*, to come.]

Venus, *vē'nus, n.* Roman goddess of beauty and love: a beautiful woman: brightest of the planets. [L.]

veracious, *vė-rā'shŭs, adj.* truthful (esp. habitually): true.
verā'ciously, *adv.*
veracity (*-ras'i-ti*), **vera'ciousness,** *ns.*
[L. *vērax, -acis*; root as **verity,** etc.]

veranda(h), *vė-ran'dȧ, n.* a kind of covered balcony, with a roof sloping beyond the main building, supported by light pillars. [Hindustani word.]

verb, *vėrb, n.* a word used to state what a person or thing does, experiences, etc. (e.g. He *ran*; I *have* a feeling; what *is* this?)
ver'bal, *adj.* connected with verbs (e.g. *verbal endings, such as '-fy', '-ise'*): having to do with words (e.g. *to make verbal changes in a document*): spoken, not written (e.g. *a verbal message*).
ver'bally, *adv.* in or by speech.
verbā'tim, word for word.
ver'biage, *n.* use of many unnecessary words, or an instance of this.
verbose' (*-bōs'*), *adj.* (of a person or a statement, etc.) using too many words.
verbos'ity (*-bos'*), *n.* wordiness: love of talking.
[L. *verbum*, a word.]

verdant, *vėr'dȧnt, adj.* green with grass and/or leaves.
ver'dūre, *n.* green vegetation.
[Fr.—L. *viridans, -antis*, growing green.]

verdict, *vėr'dikt, n.* the finding or decision of a jury at the end of a trial: decision, opinion given.
[L. *vērē*, truly, *dictum*, a saying.]

verdigris, *vėr'di-grēs, n.* the greenish rust of copper, brass, or bronze.
[O.Fr. *verd de Grece*, green of Greece.]

verdure. See **verdant.**

verge, *vėrj, n.* the brink, extreme edge: the grass edging of a garden bed or border.
ver'ger, *n.* an official in church who shows people to seats, etc.: an official who carries a symbol of office, e.g. a staff, before a bishop, etc.
on the verge of, on the point of.
[L. *virga*, a slender branch.]

veriest, *ver'i-ist, adj.* used in expressions such as *The veriest child would know this* (i.e. anyone, however young and ignorant, would know this). **[very.]**

verify, *ver'i-fī, v.t.* to confirm the truth or correctness of (something) by considering evidence, looking up facts, etc.:—*pr.p.* **ver'ifying**; *pa.p.* **ver'ified.**
ver'ifīable, *adj.* able to be verified.
verificā'tion (*-if-i-*), *n.*
verily, *ver'i-li, adv.* truly, certainly.
verisimilitude, *ver-i-sim-il'i-tūd, n.* appearance of truth: likeness to life.
ver'itable, *adj.* genuine, real (e.g. *a veritable triumph*).
ver'itably, *adv.*
verity, *ver'i-ti, n.* truth:—*pl.* **ver'ities.**
[L. *vērus*, true, *vēritās*, truth (*facĕre, factum*, to make; *similis*, like).]

vermicelli, *vėr-mi-sel'i*, or *-chel'i, n.* stiff paste of hard wheat-flour made into small worm-like rolls—smaller than spaghetti.
[It., 'little worms'—L. *vermis*, worm.]

vermicide, vermiform. See **vermin.**

vermilion, *vėr-mil'yȯn, n.* a bright red paint.—*adj.* of a beautiful red colour.
[O.Fr.—L. *vermiculus*, a little worm, an insect used as red dye.]

vermin, *vėr'min, n.* pests, such as fleas, rats, etc.: persons considered worthless and hateful.
ver'minous, *adj.* full of vermin (e.g. *verminous clothing*).
vermicide, *vėr'mi-sīd, n.* a killer of worms, esp. in the intestines.
ver'miform, *adj.* having the shape of a worm.
[Fr.—L. *vermis*, a worm.]

vermouth, *vėr'mėth, -mo͞oth, -mo͞ot', n.* a drink containing white wine flavoured with wormwood.
[Ger. *wermuth* (now *-mut*), wormwood.]

vernacular, *vėr-nak'ū-lȧr, n.* the native speech of a country: the native dialect of a region: spoken language as opposed to literary.—Also *adj.*
[L. *vernăculus*, a home-born slave.]

vernal, *vėr'nȧl, adj.* belonging to spring: appearing or occurring in spring.
[L. *vernālis*—*vēr*, spring.]

vernier, *vėr'ni-ėr, n.* a scale for measuring parts of the divisions of a larger scale.
[Name of inventor.]

verruca, *ve-ro͞o'kȧ, n.* a wart. [L.]

versatile, *vėr'sȧ-tīl*, or *-til, adj.* able to turn easily and successfully from one task or pursuit to another: (of a material) capable of being used for many purposes.
versatil'ity (*-til'*), *n.*
[L. *versāre*, turn often—*vertĕre*, turn.]

verse, *vėrs, n.* a line of poetry: also a stanza of several lines: a short section in a chapter of the Bible: poetry as distinct from prose.
ver'sify, *v.i.* to make verses.—*v.t.* to turn into verse:—*pr.p.* **ver'sifying**; *pa.p.* **ver'sified.**
versificā'tion, *n.* the writing of verses: the scheme of feet and lines followed in a poem.
ver'sion, *n.* a translation, as in the 1611 *Authorised Version* of the Bible: an account from one point of view (e.g. *The boy gave his version of what had occurred*).
[L. *versus*, turning, line, verse.]

versed, *vėrst, adj.* thoroughly acquainted, skilled (e.g. *versed in the affairs of the village*; *versed in carpentry*).
[Same L. root as **versatile.**]

versus, *vėr'sŭs, prep.* against; shortened to **v.** or **vs.** [L.]

vertebra, *vėr'tė-brȧ, n.* a bone of the spine:—*pl.* **vertebrae** (*vėr'tė-brē*).
ver'tebrate, *n.* an animal having a backbone.—Also *adj.*
[L.—*vertĕre*, to turn.]

vertex, *vėr'teks, n.* the top or summit: the point of a cone, pyramid, or angle:—*pl.* **vertices** (*vėr'ti-sēz*).
ver'tical, *adj.* standing upright: straight up and down.
ver'tically, *adv.*
[L., eddy, summit—*vertĕre,* to turn.]

vertigo, *vėr'ti-gō, vėr-tī'gō, n.* giddiness.
vertig'inous (*-tij'*), *adj.* causing giddiness (used of e.g. height, a high place).
[L.—root as **vertex, vertical.**]

verve, *vėrv, n.* lively spirit (e.g. *The musical performance lacked verve*). [Fr.]

very, *ver'i, adv.* to a great degree.—*adj.* exact (e.g. *the very person I want to see*). See also **verity, veriest.**
[L. *vērus,* true.]

Very light, *ver'i līt, n.* a flare for signalling, fired from a pistol. [Name of inventor.]

vesicle, *ves'i-kl, n.* a small bladder-like cavity in the body: a blister.
[L. *vēsīca,* bladder, blister.]

vesper, *ves'pėr, n.* the evening star: (in *pl.*) evening service. [L.]

vessel, *ves'ėl, n.* a container, usu. for liquid: a ship: a tube (as in *blood-vessel*).
[O.Fr.—L. dim. of *vās,* a vase.]

vest, *vest, n.* a waistcoat: an undergarment worn next the skin.—*v.t.* to clothe, cover: to grant (authority, power) to (e.g. *They vested all power in him*; *vested him with all power*).
vested interests, rights, rights held by certain bodies or groups of people, often for a long time, and difficult to take away: the people enjoying such rights and benefits.
[L. *vestis,* a garment.]

vestibule, *ves'ti-būl, n.* an entrance hall.
[L. *vestibulum.*]

vestige, *ves'tij, n.* a footprint: a trace.
vestig'ial, *adj.* surviving only as a trace.
[Fr.—L. *vestīgāre,* to track.]

vestment, *vest'ment, n.* a garment: (in *pl.*) articles of dress worn by the clergy during divine service.
vestry, *ves'tri, n.* a room in or near a church where vestments are kept: a number of persons, in an English parish, appointed to share in the management of church affairs:—*pl.* **-ies.**
ves'tryman, *n.* a member of a vestry.
vesture, *ves'chůr, n.* clothing: a covering. [Same root as **vest.**]

vet. See **veterinary.**

vetch, *vech, n.* a plant of the pea kind.
[Through O.Fr.—L. *vicia.*]

veteran, *vet'ė-rȧn, adj.* old, experienced.—*n.* one who has given long service: an old soldier: (*U.S.*) anyone who has served in the armed forces.
[L. *veterānus—vetus,* old.]

veterinarian. See **veterinary.**

veterinary, *vet'ė-ri-nȧ-ri, adj.* having to do with the curing of diseases in animals.
vet'erinary (surgeon), *n.* a doctor for animals—often shortened to **vet.** Also **veterinā'rian.**
vet, *v.t.* to check and pass as correct (e.g. *to vet a report*).
[L. *veterinae,* animals that carry or pull.]

veto, *vē'tō, n.* the power or right to forbid: an act of forbidding:—*pl.* **ve'toes.**—*v.* to forbid: to refuse to consent to:—*pr.p.* **vē'toing**; *pa.p.* **vē'toed** (*-tōd*).
[L. *veto,* I forbid—*vetāre.*]

vex, *veks, v.t.* to annoy: to grieve.
vexā'tion, *n.* state of being vexed: a cause of annoyance or trouble.
vexā'tious, *-shůs, adj.* causing annoyance: troublesome.
[L. *vexāre,* to shake, to trouble.]

via, *vī'ȧ* or *vē'ȧ, prep.* by way of (e.g. *to Exeter via London*). [L.]

viable, *vī'ȧbl, adj.* capable of living and developing: (of e.g. a scheme) workable.
[Fr.—L. *vīta,* life.]

viaduct, *vī'ȧ-dukt, n.* a long bridge carrying a road or railway.
[L. *via,* a way, *dūcĕre, ductum,* to lead.]

vial, *vī'ȧl, n.* a small bottle.
[Same as **phial.**]

viand, *vī'ȧnd, n.* (usu. in *pl.*) food.
[Fr. *viande,* meat.]

vibrate, *vī'brāt, v.i.* to shake, tremble: to swing to and fro.—*v.t.* to cause to shake.
vī'brant, *adj.* thrilling: full of energy.
vībrā'tion, *n.* a rapid to-and-fro motion, as of a plucked string.
vī'bratory, *adj.* having to do with vibration.
[L. *vibrāre,* to tremble.]

vicar, *vik'ȧr, n.* one who holds authority as delegate or substitute for another: a clergyman of the Church of England.
vic'arage, *n.* the house of a vicar.
vicā'rious (*vī-,* or *vi-*), *adj.* filling the place of another person: endured on another person's behalf, in his place (e.g. *vicarious suffering, punishment*).
[L. *vicārius,* a substitute.]

vice[1]**, vise,** *vīs, n.* an instrument for holding an object firmly, usu. between two metal jaws. [Fr. *vis,* screw.]

vice[2]**,** *vīs, n.* a serious moral fault: a bad habit.
vicious, *vish'ůs, adj.,* having bad faults: evil: full of malice (e.g. *vicious comments*): of a horse, etc., fierce.
vicious circle, a series, e.g. of causes and results, in which the last leads back to the first again (for instance, worry makes a person feel tired and tiredness makes him worry more.)
[Fr.—L. *vitium,* a fault.]

vice[3]**,** *vī'si, prep.* in place of.
vice versa, *vī'si vėr'sȧ,* the other way round (e.g. *John will take Jim's place, and vice versa,* i.e. and Jim will take John's; *I needed his help, and vice versa,* i.e. he needed mine). [L.]

vice-, *vīs-, pfx.* indicating a person second in rank or importance, who acts, when necessary, in place of his chief, as **vice-president,** etc. [**vice** (3).]

viceroy, *vīs'roi, n.* one who governs a large country in the name of his sovereign.
[**vice** (3), and Fr. *roi,* king.]

vicinity, *vi-sin'i-ti, n.* neighbourhood: nearness.
[L. *vīcīnus,* neighbouring.]

vicious. See **vice** (2).

vicissitude, *vi-sis'i-tūd, n.* change from one state to another: (in *pl.*) changes of fortune, ups and downs.
[L. *vicissitūdō,* change, alteration.]

victim, *vik'tim, n.* an animal offered as a sacrifice: a person who is killed or seriously harmed, intentionally or by accident.
vic'timise, *v.t.* to make (a person) suffer in some undeserved way: to swindle.
victimisā'tion, *n.*
[Fr.—L. *victima,* animal for sacrifice.]

victor, *vik'tȯr, n.* one who wins a battle or other contest.
victō'rious, *adj.* successful in a contest.
victo'riously, *adv.*
vic'tory, *n.* the defeat of an enemy or rival:—*pl.* **vic'tories.**
[L. *vincĕre, victum,* to conquer.]

Victorian, *vik-tō'ri-ȧn, adj.* having to do with the reign of Queen Victoria: (of outlook on morals, etc.) strict, conventional, prudish.

victorious, etc. See **victor.**

victual, *vit'l, n.* (usu. in *pl.*) food for human beings.—*v.t.* to supply with food.
victualler, *vit'lėr, n.* one who supplies provisions.
[L. *victus,* means of living.]

vicuna, *vi-kōōn'yȧ, -kūn'ȧ, n.* S. American animal, related to the llama, which yields a fine wool. [From Peruvian.]

video, *vid'ė-ō, n.* and *adj.* (having to do with) television.
video tape, magnetic tape carrying pictures and sound.
[L. *vidēre,* to see.]

vie, *vī, v.i.* to contend as rivals (e.g. *They vied with each other in attempts to help*):—*pr.p.* **vy'ing;** *pa.p.* **vied.**
[O.Fr. *envier,* challenge—L. *invītāre,* invite.]

Viennese, *vē-ė-nēz', adj.* of Vienna.—*n. sing.* and *pl.* inhabitant(s) of Vienna.

view, *vū, n.* sight: a scene, or a picture of one: opinion (e.g. *Give me your view, views, on the subject*).—*v.t.* to look at: to watch (television programmes; also *v.i.*): to see in the mind (e.g. *I view the problem in a different way*): to consider (as; e.g. *I view it as a joke*).
view'er, *n.*
view'point, *n.* point from which a scene is viewed: attitude to a subject.
in view, in sight: before one as an aim, or as something likely to happen.
in view of, taking into consideration.
on view, ready to be looked at and examined.
with a view to, with one's thoughts or aim directed towards (e.g. *with a view to cutting down expenses*).
[Fr. *vue* (*fem.*) *pa.p.* of *voir,* to see.]

vigil, *vij'il, n.* keeping awake, esp. on the night before a religious feast.
vig'ilance, *n.* watchfulness, alertness to danger.
vig'ilant, *adj.* **vig'ilantly,** *adv.*
vigilan'te (*-ti*), *n.* a member of a group carrying out rough justice in an unsettled country, or watching over the morals or welfare of a community.
[L. *vigil,* watchful, a watchman.]

vignette, *vin-yet', n.* a small design or portrait, not enclosed by a definite border: a character sketch.
[Orig. design of vine leaves—L. *vīnea,* vine.]

vigour, *vig'ȯr, n.* strength and energy.
vig'orous, *adj.* strong, forceful.
[L. *vigor,* strength.]

viking, *vī'king* (also *vik'ing*), *n.* a Norse invader of western Europe (8th-10th centuries).
[Old Norse *vīkingr.*]

vile, *vīl, adj.* wicked: very bad or objectionable.
vile'ly, *adv.* **vile'ness,** *n.*
vil'ify (*vil'*), *v.t.* to speak evil of:—*pr.p.* **vil'ifying;** *pa.p.* **vil'ified.**
[L. *vīlis,* cheap, worthless.]

villa, *vil'ȧ, n.* a house, esp. in suburbs (often used to distinguish any house with a garden from a flat or apartment).
vill'age, *vil'ij, n.* a group of houses, etc. smaller than a town.
vill'ager, *n.* one who lives in, and has most of his interests in, a village.
[L. *villa,* a country house.]

villain, *vil'ȧn, n.* a man of very bad character: (*playfully*) a rascal.
vill'ainous, *adj.* wicked: (*coll.*) ugly, or very bad.
vill'ainy, *n.* wickedness: a wicked action:—*pl.* **-ies.**
[Orig. one who worked on an estate—L. root as **villa.**]

villein, *vil'in, n.* a serf.
[Same word as **villain.**]

vindicate, *vin'di-kāt, v.t.* to defend successfully: to clear from blame.
vindicā'tion, *n.* **vin'dicator,** *n.*
vindic'tive, *adj.* revengeful: spiteful, anxious to hurt.
[L. *vindicāre, -ātum,* claim, free, avenge.]

vine, *vīn, n.* a plant bearing grapes: a climbing or trailing plant.
vine'-dresser, *n.* one who tends vines.
vī'nery, *n.* glasshouse for vines:—*pl.* **-ies.**
vineyard, *vin'yȧrd, n.* a plantation of grape vines.
vin'iculture, *n.* cultivation of grapes for wine.

vintage, *vin'tij, n.* the gathering of grapes: wine of a particular year or region: wine of good quality.—Also *adj.*
vint'ner (*vint'*), *n.* a wine seller.
vintage car, *n.* one of a very early model, still able to run.
[L. *vīnea,* vine, grapes—*vīnum,* wine (vintage—L. *vīndēmia—dēmĕre,* remove).]
vinegar, *vin'i-gȧr, n.* a sour liquid used in preparing food, made from e.g. wine.
[Fr. *vin,* wine, *aigre,* sour.]
vinery, vintage, etc. See **vine.**
viola[1], *vē-ō'lȧ,* or *vī', n.* kind of large violin.
[O.Fr. *viole.*]
viola[2], *vī'ō-lȧ,* or *-ō', n.* a member of the plant group which includes violets and pansies: a single-coloured pansy. [L.]
violate, *vī'ō-lāt, v.t.* to break (an oath, a law, etc.): to treat with disrespect (a sacred place, e.g. temple, or object): to disturb roughly (e.g. someone's privacy or peace).
violā'tion, *ns.* **vī'olātor,** *ns.*
[L. *violāre, -ātum,* injure—*vis,* force.]
violent, *vī'ō-lėnt, adj.* acting with great force (e.g. *a violent storm, blow,* etc.): caused by force (*a violent death*): powerful, uncontrollable (e.g. *violent behaviour, a violent temper*).
vī'olence, *n.* great roughness and force.
vī'olently, *adv.*
acts of violence, those in which force is used illegally.
[L. *violentus*—same root as **violate.**]
violet, *vī'ō-lit, n.* a plant of the kind to which pansies belong, esp. one of the smaller ones, such as the familiar **dog violet**: a colour, bluish or light purple, esp. that seen at the end of the spectrum (or display of rainbow colours) opposite to the red.
[Fr. *violette*—L. root as **viola** (2).]
violin, *vī-ō-lin'* (or *vī'-*), *n.* a musical instrument of four strings played with a bow.
vī'olinist (or *-lin'*), *n.* a violin player.
[It. *violino.*]
violoncello, *vī-ō-lŏn-chel'ō* or *vē-, n.* a large musical instrument of the violin class.—See also **cello.**
violoncell'ist, *n.* a violoncello player.
[It. *dim.* of *violone,* a bass violin.]
viper, *vī'pėr, n.* a kind of poisonous snake, esp. the common adder: a base, malicious person.
vī'perish, vī'perous, *adjs.* like a viper, venomous, treacherous.
[L. *vīpera,* adder, snake.]
virago, *vi-rā'gō, vi-rā'gō, n.* a bold, ill-tempered woman:—*pl.* **-gos.** [L.]
virgin, *vėr'jin, n.* one not yet mated.
vir'gin, vir'ginal, *adjs.* maidenly, pure: new or unused (e.g. *virgin soil*).
virgin'ity, *n.* the state of maidenhood.
the Virgin, Mary, the mother of Christ.
[L. *virgō, virginis.*]
virginal[1]. See **virgin.**
virginal[2], *vėr'jin-ȧl, n.* a keyboard instrument earlier than the piano.
[Same root as **virgin.**]
virile, *vir'īl* or *-il, adj.* manly: vigorous.
viril'ity, *n.* manhood: manliness.
[L. *vir,* man.]
virtual. See **virtue.**
virtue, *vėr'tū, n.* moral goodness: a particular merit, such as 'truthfulness': a good quality (e.g. *the virtues of nylon*).
vir'tual, *adj.* not actually but having the same effect, power, etc. (e.g. *the virtual end of the attempt; the virtual ruler of the country*).
vir'tually, *adv.* in effect though not strictly speaking (e.g. *He was virtually penniless*).
vir'tuous (*-tū-ůs*), *adj.* morally good.
vir'tuously, *adv.* **vir'tuousness,** *n.*
by (or **in**) **virtue of,** because of (e.g. *By virtue of the position he held, he was able to move about freely*).
[L. *virtūs,* courage, moral excellence.]
virtuoso, *vėr-tū-ōz'ō, -ōs'ō, n.* one who knows much about e.g. music, painting: a skilled performer:—*pl.* **virtuō'sos.**
virtuosity (*-os'i-ti*), *n.* unusual skill in one of the fine arts. [It.]
virtuous, etc. See **virtue.**
virulent, *vir'ū-lėnt, adj.* full of poison: bitter in dislike or hatred.
vir'ulently, *adv.* **vir'ulence,** *n.*
[L. *vīrulentus*; same root as **virus.**]
virus, *vī'rus, n.* poison: something which is smaller than known bacteria, can grow on body cells, and is a cause of disease. (*Different viruses cause influenza, mumps, smallpox, etc.*).
[L. *vīrus,* poison.]
visa, *vē'zȧ, n.* a mark or stamp put on a passport by the authorities of a country to show that the bearer may travel in that country.
[L. *vīsa, pa.p.* of *vidēre,* to see.]
visage, *viz'ij, n.* the face or look. [Fr.]
vis-à-vis, *vēz'-ȧ-vē, adj.* face to face, opposite.
[Fr.—O.Fr. *vis,* face (*a,* to, *vis,* face).]
viscera, *vis'ė-rȧ, n.pl.* the inner parts of the body. [L.]
viscid, *vis'id, adj.* sticky.
[L. *viscidus*; root as **viscous.**]
viscose, viscosity. See **viscous.**
viscount, *vī'kownt, n.* a title of nobility next below an earl.
viscountess, *vī'kownt-es, n. fem.*
[L. *vice,* in place of, *comes,* companion.]
viscous, *vis'kus, adj.* sticky, not flowing readily.
viscos'ity (*-kos'*), **vis'cousness,** *ns.*
vis'cose (*-kōs*), *n.* a syrupy liquid made from wood pulp, one stage in the manufacture of rayon.
[L. *viscōsus—viscum,* bird-lime.]
visible, *viz'i-bl, adj.* able to be seen.

visibil′ity, *n.* the clearness with which objects may be seen.
vis′ibly, *adv.*
vision, *vizh′(ȯ)n, n.* the act or sense of seeing: something seen in the imagination (in the 'mind's eye'): a supernatural appearance: the power of imagining, hence of foreseeing events, consequences, etc.
vis′ionary, *adj.* seen in imagination only, not real.—*n.* one who forms plans that are difficult or impossible to carry out:—*pl.* **-aries.**
See also **visual.**
[L. *vidēre, vīsum,* to see.]

visit, *viz′it, v.t.* to go to see: to inspect (an institution such as a school): to come upon, attack (e.g. *Epidemics visited the shattered city*): to inflict (on; e.g. *He visited his anger, grief, on them*).—*n.* a call at a person's house: a short stay.
vis′itor, *n.* one who makes a visit.—Also (*poetical*) **vis′itant.**
visitā′tion, *n.* a formal visit by a superior: a great calamity, viewed as a warning or punishment (e.g. *These visitations of disease seemed punishment for their sins*).]
[L. *vīsitāre,* go to see—*vidēre,* see.]

visor, *vīz′ȯr, n.* the part of a helmet covering the face: a mask: an eye-shade.
[Fr. *visière*—O.Fr. *vis,* face.]

vista, *vis′tȧ, n.* a view, esp. one seen along an avenue of trees: a picture in the mind (e.g. *a long vista of past events*).
[It.]

visual, *viz′ū-ȧl, adj.* belonging to sight.
vis′ualise (*-īz*), *v.t.* to form a clear picture of (something) in the mind.
vis′ually, *adv.* by sight.
visual aids (to learning), pictures, films, etc.
[Same root as **visible.**]

vital, *vī′tȧl, adj.* having to do with life: necessary to life: showing life and vigour: essential, of the greatest importance (e.g. *Speed is vital to the success of our plan*).
vī′talise (*-īz*), *v.t.* to give life or vigour to.
vītal′ity, *n.* life: liveliness: ability to go on living.
vī′tals, *n.pl.* the organs of the body essential to life.
vital statistics, tables of figures dealing with population and its changes from year to year: (*coll.*) chest, waist, and hip measurements.
[L. *vītālis*—*vīta,* life.]

vitamin, *vit′ȧ-min, vīt′, n.* any of a group of substances necessary for healthy life, different ones occurring in different natural foods such, e.g., as raw fruit.
[A coined word—L. *vīta,* life.]

vitiate, *vish′i-āt, v.t.* to spoil, to make impure or faulty.
vitiā′tion, *n.*
[L. *vitiāre*—root as vice.]

viticulture, *vit′i-kul-chůr, n.* cultivation of vine.—See also **viniculture (vine.)**
[L. *vītis,* vine, *colĕre,* to cultivate.]

vitreous, *vit′ri-ůs, adj.* glass-like.
vit′rify, *v.t., v.i.* to make, or become, glass-like:—*pr.p.* **vit′rifying;** *pa.p.* **vit′rified.**
vitrified fort, an ancient fort in which the stones have been made glassy by fire.
[L. *vitrum,* glass.]

vitriol, *vit′ri-ȯl, n.* sulphuric acid.
vitriol′ic, *adj.* biting, scathing (e.g. *vitriolic abuse*).
[(O.)Fr.—L. root as **vitreous.**]

vituperate, *vi-tū′pė-rāt,* or *vī-, v.t.* to abuse (e.g. *The two women were vituperating each other fiercely*).—Also *v.i.*
vitūperā′tion, *n.*
[L. *vitium,* a fault, *parāre,* to prepare.]

vivacious, *vi-vā′shůs,* or *vī-, adj.* lively sprightly.
vivac′ity (*vas′*), **viva′ciousness,** *ns.*
viva′ciously, *adv.*
[L. *vīvax, vīvācis*—*vīvĕre,* to live.]

vivarium, *vī-vā′ri-ům,* or *vi-, n.* an enclosure, tank, etc. for keeping living creatures.
[L. *vīvārium*—*vīvus,* alive.]

viva voce, *vī′vȧ vō′si, adv.* by word of mouth.—*n.* an oral examination.
[L., with living voice.]

vivi-, *viv-i-,* (as part of word) alive.
[L. *vīvus.*]

vivid, *viv′id, adj.* life-like: brilliant, striking.
viv′idly, *adv.* **viv′idness,** *n.*
viv′ify, *v.t.* to make vivid, give life to.
[L. *vīvidus*—*vīvĕre,* to live.]

viviparous, *vi-vip′ȧ-růs,* or *vī-, adj.* producing young alive (i.e. not in eggs).
[L. *vīvus,* alive, *parĕre,* to produce.]

vivisection, *viv-i-sek′sh(ȯ)n, n.* the performance of experiments on living animals.
[L. *vīvus,* living, *sectiō,* cutting.]

vixen, *vik′sn, n.* a female fox: an ill-tempered woman.
vix′enish, *adj.*
[O.E. *fyxen.*]

viz., *viz, adv.* meaning (and usu. read as) 'namely' (e.g. *three boys, viz. John, James, and Peter*).
[Abbrev. of L. *vidēlicet*—*vidēre,* to see, *licet,* it is permitted.]

vizier, *vi-zēr′, vi′zi-ėr, n.* an Eastern minister of state. [From Arabic.]

vocabulary, *vȯ-kab′ū-lȧ-ri,* or *vō- n.* a list of words in alphabetical order, with meanings: the stock of words which a person knows and can use:—*pl.* **-ies.**
[L. *vocāre,* to call; conn. *vox,* voice.]

vocal, *vō′kȧl, adj.* having to do with the voice: talkative, esp. about views, grievances, etc.
vō′calist, *n.* a singer.
vocal cords, folds of membrane in the

larynx which vibrate and produce sounds.
[L. *vōcālis*—*vox*, *vōcis*, voice.]

vocation, *vō-kā'sh(ȯ)n*, *n.* a calling (e.g. *He had a sense of vocation, of being called by God to do this work*): a profession or other way of living.
vocā'tional, *adj.* (of training, etc.) preparing for a trade or business.
[L. *vocāre*, *-ātum*, to call.]

vociferate, *vō-sif'ė-rāt*, *v.i.* to shout.—*v.t.* to utter with a loud voice.
vocif'erous, *adj.* loud of voice, noisy.
vocif'erously, *adv.*
vocif'erousness, *n.*
[L. *vox*, *vōcis*, voice, *ferre*, to carry.]

vodka, *vod'kȧ*, *n.* a spirit made from grain, sometimes from potatoes. [Russ.]

vogue, *vōg*, *n.* the current fashion: popularity.
[Fr.—*voguer*, to sail.]

voice, *vois*, *n.* sound from the mouth: (quality of) singing sound: expressed opinion, vote (e.g. *the voice of the people*): right to express an opinion (e.g. *I had no voice in the matter*).—*v.t.* to give expression to (an opinion, etc.).
[Fr. *voix*—L. *vox*, *vōcis*.]

void, *void*, *adj.* empty: not valid or binding (see **null**): lacking entirely (with *of*; e.g. *a statement void of meaning*).—*n.* empty space. [O.Fr.]

volatile, *vol'ȧ-tīl*, *adj.* (of a liquid) changing quickly to vapour: lively but changeable in feeling (e.g. *She is volatile, has a volatile nature*).
vol'atilise (or *-at'-*), *v.t.* to cause to evaporate.
[L. *volāre*, *-ātum*, to fly.]

volcano, *vol-kā'nō*, *n.* usu. a cone-shaped mountain, through which molten rock, hot ash and other material reaches the earth's surface:—*pl.* **volca'noes.**
volcan'ic (*-kan'*), *adj.* having to do with a volcano: caused or produced by the heat inside the earth.
[It.—L. *Volcānus*, *Vulcānus*, god of fire.]

vole, *vōl*, *n.* a small animal with gnawing teeth, e.g. the **water vole,** often called the 'water rat'. [Scandinavian origin.]

volition, *vō-lish'(ȯ)n*, *n.* will, act of willing (e.g. *No one told him to; he did it of his own volition*).
See also **voluntary.**
[L. *volo*, I wish, will, *velle*, to will.]

volley, *vol'i*, *n.* a flight of missiles: in tennis, the return of a ball before it touches the ground:—*pl.* **voll'eys.**—*v.t.* to shoot in a volley: to return (a ball) before it bounces.
[Fr. *volée*—L. *volāre*, to fly.]

volt, *vōlt*, *n.* the unit used in measuring the force driving electricity through a circuit.
vōl'tage, *n.* force measured in volts (e.g. *Low voltage reduces current, causing lights to burn dimly.*)
[*Volta*, name of Italian scientist.]

volte-face, *vōlt-fäs*, *n.* sudden and complete change of opinion. [Fr.]

voluble, *vol'ū-bl*, *adj.* (speaking) with too great a flow of words.
volubil'ity, *n.* **vol'ubly,** *adv.*
[L. *volūbilis*—*volvěre*, *volūtum*, to roll.]

volume, *vol'ūm*, *-yùm*, *n.* a book: one of a series of connected books: extent of space occupied (e.g. *the volume of a solid*): amount (e.g. *the volume of trade*): fullness (of sound).
volu'minous, *adj.* able to fill many volumes (e.g. *voluminous correspondence*): (of a writer) producing many books, etc.: large and full (e.g. *a voluminous dress*).
to speak volumes, to have much meaning (e.g. *Her frown spoke volumes*).
[L. *volvěre*, *volūtum*, to roll; orig. book in form of roll.]

voluntary, *vol'ùn-tȧ-ri*, *adj.* done by choice, not by accident or under compulsion —*n.* a piece of music played (at his own choice) by an organist.
vol'untarily, *adv.* **vol'untariness,** *n.*
volunteer, *vol-ùn-tēr'*, *v.i.* to offer oneself for a service or duty.—*v.t.* to offer (e.g. an opinion, information).—*n.* one who offers service of his own accord.
[L. *voluntās*, will; root as **volition.**]

voluptuous, *vȯ-lup'tū-ùs*, *adj.* causing, or filled with, pleasure: too much given to bodily pleasure.
[L. *voluptās*, pleasure.]

vomit, *vom'it*, *v.i.* to throw up the contents of the stomach.—*v.t.* to throw out (e.g. *The blaze vomited flame and smoke*).—*n.* matter ejected from the stomach.
[L. *vomère*, *-itum.*]

voodoo, *vōō'dōō*, *n.* one who practises witchcraft.
[Word in Fr. spoken in W. Indies, etc.]

voracious, *vȯ-rā'shùs*, *vō-*, *adj.* very greedy, difficult to satisfy (e.g. *a voracious animal, appetite*): very eager (e.g. *a voracious reader; voracious for pleasure*).
vora'city (*-ra'si-*), **vora'ciousness,** *ns.*
vora'ciously, *adv.*
[L. *vorax*, *-ācis*—*vorāre*, to devour.]

vortex, *vör'teks*, *n.* a whirlpool: a whirlwind:—*pl.* **vor'tices** (*-ti-sēz*), **vor'texes.**
[L.—*vortěre*, *vertěre*, to turn.]

votary, *vō'tȧ-ri*, *n.* a person bound by a vow, or devoted to a service: a believer in, supporter or admirer (of):—*pl.* **vo'taries.**
[Same L. root as **vow.**]

vote, *vōt*, *n.* a formal expression of a wish or opinion, esp. at an election or in a debate: a sum of money granted by Parliament for a certain purpose.—*v.i.* (with *for*) to support (a candidate, a proposal).
vō'ter, *n.* one who votes.
[Same L. root as **vow.**]

vouch, *vowch*, *v.i.* (with *for*) to say one is sure something is fact or truth (e.g. *I can vouch for his honesty, for the truth of the*

statement): (with *for*) to guarantee the honesty, etc. of (a person).
vouch'er, *n.* a paper which confirms that a sum of money has been, or will be, paid.
vouchsafe, *vowch-sāf'*, *v.t.* to be good enough to give (e.g. *He vouchsafed a reply, a nod, information*).
[Through O.Fr.—L. *vocāre*, to call, i.e. as witness.]

vow, *vow*, *n.* a solemn promise, esp. one made to God.—*v.t.* to make a solemn promise (that): to threaten (e.g. *to vow revenge*): to assert solemnly (that).
[O.Fr. *vou*—L. *vōtum*, a vow.]

vowel, *vow'ėl*, *n.* a simple sound made by the voice with no interruption by movement of tongue, teeth, or lips: a letter used to represent such a sound, as *a, e, i, o, u.*
[Fr. *voyelle*—L. *vox*, *vōcis*, voice.]

voyage, *voi'ij*, *n.* a journey, esp. one made by sea.—*v.i.* to make a journey.
voy'ager, *n.* a traveller making a journey (usu. a long one). [Fr.]

vulcanise, *vul'kȧ-nīz*, *v.t.* to combine (esp. rubber) with sulphur by heat.
[Same L. root as **volcano.**]

vulgar, *vul'gȧr*, *adj.* having to do with the common people (*The vulgar tongue is the language commonly spoken in a country*): ill-mannered: coarse.
vul'garise, *v.t.* to make common or ordinary: to make unrefined, coarse.
vul'garism, *n.* an expression not used in careful, educated speech.
vulgar'ity, *n.* coarseness:—*pl.* **-ies.**
Vul'gate, *n.* an ancient (4th century) Latin version of the Bible.
vulgar fractions, common (i.e. not decimal) fractions.
[L. *vulgāris*—*vulgus*, the people.]

vulnerable, *vul'nėr-ȧ-bl*, *adj.* exposed to attack (e.g. *The enemy's position was vulnerable*): liable to be hurt in body or feelings: open to temptation or influence: (in game of bridge) liable to double penalties.
vulnerabil'ity, vul'nerableness, *ns.*
[L. *vulnus*, *vulneris*, a wound.]

vulpine, *vul'pīn*, *adj.* of, or like, a fox: cunning.
[L. *vulpes*, a fox.]

vulture, *vul'chūr*, *n.* a large bird of prey, living chiefly on dead bodies.
[L. *vultur*.]

vying. See **vie.**

W

wad, *wod*, *n.* a pack of loose material stuffed in to aid packing: a bundle (esp. of bank notes).—*v.t.* to pad:—*pr.p.* **wadd'ing;** *pa.p.* **wadd'ed.**
wadd'ing, *n.* materials for wads: cotton wool. [Orig. unknown.]

waddle, *wod'l*, *v.i.* to take short steps and move from side to side in walking (as a duck does).—*n.* a clumsy, rocking way of walking. [Origin unknown.]

wade, *wād*, *v.i.* to walk through something that yields to the feet (e.g. water): to make one's way with difficulty (e.g. *to wade through a book*).—*v.t.* to cross by wading.
wā'der, *n.* one who wades: a bird that wades in search of food (also **wading bird**): (in *pl.*) high waterproof boots used by anglers.
[O.E. *wadan*, to move.]

wafer, *wā'fėr*, *n.* a thin biscuit: a thin disk of unleavened bread used at Holy Communion: a thin disk or slice.
[O.Fr. *waufre*.]

waffle[1], *wof'l*, *n.* a kind of batter cake cooked in a **waffle-iron,** a special metal utensil for this purpose. [Du. *wafel*.]

waffle[2], *wof'l*, *v.i.* to waver: to talk on and on foolishly.—Also *n.* [Orig. unknown.]

waft, *wâft*, *wŏft*, *v.t.* to bear lightly through e.g. air or water.—*v.i.* to float or drift lightly.—*n.* a breath, puff.
[From same root as **wave.**]

wag[1], *wag*, *v.t.* and *v.i.* to move (e.g. one's head) from side to side, or up and down:—*pr.p.* **wagg'ing;** *pa.p.* **wagged.**—*n.* a single wagging movement.
[O.E. *wagian*.]

wag[2], *wag*, *n.* an amusing person, one who is always joking: a wit.
wagg'ery, *n.* mischievous fun: a joke showing this:—*pl.* **wagg'eries.**
wagg'ish, *adj.* roguish.
wagg'ishly, *adv.* **wagg'ishness,** *n.*
[Origin unknown.]

wage, *wāj*, *v.t.* to carry on (e.g. war).—*n.* payment for work (also **wag'es,** *n.pl.*).
wa'ger, *n.* a bet.—*v.t.* and *v.i.* to bet on the result of anything.
[O.Fr. *guage* (n.), pledge; **gage** (1).]

waggery, etc. See **wag** (2).

waggle, *wag'l*, *v.t.* and *v.i.* to wag, esp. in an uncertain, irregular way.
wagg'ly, *adj.* **wagg'liness,** *n.*
[From **wag** (1).]

wagon, waggon, *wag'ȯn*, *n.* a four-wheeled vehicle for carrying heavy loads.
wag(g)'oner, *n.* driver of a wagon.
[Du. *wagen*.]

wagtail, *wag'tāl*, *n.* a small bird with a long tail which it flicks up and down.
[**wag** (1), **tail.**]

waif, *wāf*, *n.* an uncared-for child.
waifs and strays, persons without homes or possessions. [O.Fr.]

wail, *wāl*, *v.i.* to give sad or complaining

cries.—*v.t.* to mourn, grieve over.—*n.* a cry of woe: loud weeping.

wail'ing, *n.* and *adj.*

[Old Norse *væla.*]

wain, *wān, n.* a wagon.

[O.E. *wægen*; conn. with **wagon.**]

wainscot, *wān'skȯt, n.* a wooden lining applied to the walls of rooms.

wain'scoting, wain'scotting, *n.* materials for making a wainscot.

[M.E., imported fine oak wood.]

waist, *wāst, n.* the narrow part of the human body between ribs and hips.

waist'coat (*wās', wāst'*), *n.* a short, usu. sleeveless, jacket worn immediately under the outer jacket.

[Conn. with O.E. *wæstme,* growth.]

wait, *wāt, v.i.* to remain in the same place, or without acting (for, until; e.g. *to wait for a sign from the leader*): to act as a waiter at table.—*v.t.* to await, or be on the watch for (e.g. an opportunity): to serve as a waiter at (table).—*n.* a delay: (in *pl.*) singers who go from house to house at Christmas: ambush (in phrases *to lay wait, lie in wait, for*; see **lay,** (2), **lie,** (2).)

wait'er, *n.* one who waits: a man who serves at table (*fem.* **wait'ress**).

waiting room, a room in which people wait (e.g. at a station).

to wait (up)on, to pay a formal visit to: to serve (a person) at table: to serve as attendant to.

[O.Fr. *waitier*; conn. with **wake** (1).]

waive, *wāv, v.t.* to give up, not insist upon (e.g. a claim, a right).

[From same O.Fr. root as **waif.**]

wake[1], *wāk, v.i.* to cease from sleep, idleness, indifference, etc.: to be awake.—*v.t.* to arouse from sleep, etc.:—*pa.t.* **waked** (*wākt*) or **wōke**; *pa.p.* **wāked, wō'ken.**—*n.* watching all night, esp. beside a corpse: annual holiday (North of England).

wake'ful, *adj.* not asleep: not able to sleep: watchful.

wake'fully, *adv.* **wake'fulness,** *n.*

wa'ken, *v.t., v.i.* to wake, arouse or be aroused.

[O.E. *wacian* and (in compounds) *wacan.*]

wake[2], *wāk, n.* a streak of smooth-looking or foamy water left in the track of a ship.

in the wake of, immediately behind or after.

[Conn. with Old Norse *vök,* hole in ice.]

wale. Same as **weal** (1).

walk, *wök, v.i.* to move, or to travel, on foot.—*v.t.* to cause to walk: to move or travel along (the streets, the plank, etc.).—*n.* act of walking: way of walking: distance walked over: place for walking (e.g. a path): social position or the sphere in which one lives or works (*one's walk of life*).

walk'er, *n.* **walk'ing,** *n.* and *adj.*

walk'ie-talk'ie, *n.* a wireless set for sending and receiving messages, carried on the body.

walk'ing-stick, *n.* a stick used when walking.

walk'over, *n.* an easy victory.

to walk the plank, to walk along a plank placed across a ship's side and fall into the sea (old pirate method of putting to death).

[O.E. *wealcan,* to roll, turn.]

wall, *wöl, n.* an erection of brick, stone, etc. used to separate or to enclose: the side of a building.—*v.t.* to enclose with, or as if with, a wall.

wall'flower, *n.* a spring flower, sometimes growing on old walls.

wall'paper, *n.* paper used in house decorating.

with one's back to the wall, in a desperate situation, at bay.

[O.E. *weall*—L. *vallum,* a rampart.]

wallaby, *wol'ȧ-bi, n.* a small kind of kangaroo:—*pl.* **-bies, -by.**

[Austr. native name.]

wallet, *wöl'it, n.* a pocket book.

[M.E. *walet,* a bag.]

wallop, *wol'ȯp, v.t.* (*slang*) to beat, flog.—*n.* a blow. [Origin unknown.]

wallow, *wol'ō, v.i.* to roll about with enjoyment in mud etc. as an animal does: to live in filth or vice.

to wallow in money, to be very rich.

[O.E. *wealwian*; conn. L. *volvĕre,* roll.]

walnut, *wöl'nut, n.* a tree, the wood of which is used for making furniture etc.: its nut.

[O.E. *wealh,* foreign, *hnutu,* a nut.]

walrus, *wöl'rus,* or *wol', n.* a large sea animal related to seals. [Du.]

waltz, *wöl(t)s, n.* a dance with a whirling motion, performed by couples: music for this.—Also *v.i.*

[Ger. *walzer.*]

wampum, *wom'pŭm, n.* (N. Amer. Indian) shells or beads used as money.

wan, *won, adj.* pale and sickly looking.

wan'ly, *adv.* **wan'ness,** *n.*

[Origin unknown.]

wand, *wond, n.* a long slender rod e.g. as used by conjurors.

[Old Norse *vöndr,* a shoot of a tree.]

wander, *won'dėr, v.i.* to ramble, stroll, with no definite object: to go astray, move away (from the subject, the point, the present scene; e.g. *His mind wanders*).—*v.t.* to ramble over.

wan'derer, *n.*

[O.E. *wandrian*; **wend, wind** (2).]

wanderlust, *vän'der-loost, won'dėr-lust, n.* a thirst for travel. [Ger.]

wane, *wān, v.i.* to become smaller, esp. of the moon—opp. to **wax**: to lose power or importance.—*n.* decrease.

on the wane, becoming less.

[O.E. *wanian.*]

wangle, *wang'gl,* (*coll.*) *v.t.* to get or

achieve by trickery, etc.—Also *v.i.* and *n.* [Origin unknown.]

want, *wont, n.* poverty: scarcity: need.—*v.t.* to lack: to feel the need of: to wish for.—*v.i.* to be in need: to be without something desired or necessary.
wan'ted, *adj.* sought for (e.g. by the police or in order to speak to someone).
wan'ting, *adj.* absent: lacking (in; e.g. *wanting in taste*): not good, etc., enough (*found wanting*).—*prep.* without.
[Old Norse *vant*, lacking.]

wanton, *won'tȯn, adj.* playful, irresponsible: not chaste: motiveless (e.g. *wanton destruction*): unprovoked (e.g. *a wanton assault*).—*n.* a trifler: one who is wanton in morals.
wan'tonly, *adv.* **wan'tonness,** *n.*
[O.E. *wan*, without, not, *togen*, trained.]

war, *wör, n.* an open armed struggle esp. between nations.—*v.i.* to make war: to fight (against):—*pr.p.* **warr'ing;** *pa.p.* **warred.**
war'like, *adj.* fond of war: threatening war (e.g. *warlike preparations*): of war.
warr'ior, *n.* a fighting man (or woman) in any kind of conflict.
war cry, cry of encouragement, threat, etc., before or during battle: slogan.
war'fāre, *n.* armed contest.
war'head, *n.* the section of a torpedo or other missile containing the explosive.
war'monger, *wör'mung-gėr, n.* one who encourages war, esp. for personal gain.
war'ship, *n.* a vessel for war.
war'time, *n.* time of war.—Also *adj.*
war of nerves, attempts to lower morale by means of threats, rumours, etc
cold war, a struggle for the upperhand by all means short of actual fighting.
on the warpath, in fighting mood.
[O.E. *werre.*]

warble, *wör'bl, v.i.* to sing in a quavery manner: to sing sweetly as birds do.—Also *v.t.*—*n.* the act of warbling.
war'bler, *n.* a singer: a small singing bird.
[O.Fr. *guerbler.*]

ward, *wörd, v.t.* to guard or take care of: to keep away (with *off*; e.g. *to ward off danger, a blow, a cold*).—*n.* one who is under a guardian: a division of a city for local election purposes: a room with several beds, in a hospital, etc.
ward'en, *n.* a man who guards a game reserve: the head of certain colleges: one appointed to look after the civil population in case of e.g. air raids.
ward'er, *n.* one who guards, esp. (formerly) one in charge of prisoners:—*fem.* **ward'ress.**
ward'robe, *n.* a cupboard for clothes.
ward'room, *n.* a room used by officers of a warship for meals
ward'ship, *n.* the state of being, or of being under, a guardian.
[O.E. *weardian*; same root as **guard.**]

ware, *wār, n.* manufactured articles esp. pottery: often used as part of a word (e.g. *ironware*): (in *pl.*) goods for sale.
ware'house, *n.* a store for goods.—*v.t.* to put in a warehouse.
[O.E. *waru*; conn. with Ger. *ware.*]

warfare, warhead, etc. See **war.**

warily, wariness. See **wary.**

warm, *wörm, adj.* moderately hot: having, showing, strong emotions, sympathies, etc.: enthusiastic: angry.—*v.t.* and *v.i.* to make, or become, warm.—*n.* act of warming.
warm'ly, *adv.* **warm'er,** *n.*
warm'ness, warmth, *ns.*
warm'-blood'ed, *adj.* having a blood temperature greater than that of the surrounding atmosphere and changing little: passionate.
warm front, the surface of an advancing mass of warm air where it meets a mass of colder air.
warm'heart'ed, *adj.* kind, affectionate.
[O.E. *wearm.*]

warmonger. See **war.**

warn, *wörn, v.t.* to give (a person) notice of danger: to caution (against): to urge or advise (e.g. *I warned him not to be late*): to tell (a person) beforehand.
war'ning, *n.*
[O.E. *warnian*; conn. with **beware.**]

warp, *wörp, v.t.* to twist out of shape: to cause to think, reason, choose, etc., wrongly (e.g. *His experiences had warped his judgment, mind*).—*v.i.* to become twisted out of the straight.—*n.* the threads stretched lengthwise in a loom, to be crossed by a weft or woof.
warped, *adj.* twisted: embittered in outlook (e.g. *a warped nature*).
[O.E. *weorpan*, to cast; Ger. *werfen.*]

warrant, *wor'ȧnt, v.t.* to guarantee: to justify (e.g. *A slight cold does not warrant your staying off work*).—*n.* something that justifies, or that guarantees: something that gives authority, esp. a writ for arresting a person.
warr'antable, *adj.* justifiable.
warr'anter, warr'antor, *n.*
warrant officer, *n.* an officer holding a warrant (lower in rank than a commissioned officer).
[O.Fr. *warant*; a Germanic word.]

warren, *wor'ėn, n.* (also **rabbit-warren**) a place where many rabbits have their burrows, or where people live crowded together: a building with many passages.
[O.Fr. *warenne*; conn. **ward,** guard.]

warrior. See **war.**

wart, *wört, n.* small hard growth on the skin.
wart'y, *adj.*
[O.E. *wearte.*]

wary, *wā'ri, adj.* cautious, on one's guard:—*comp.* **wā'rier;** *superl.* **wā'riest.**
wā'rily, *adv.* **wā'riness,** *n.*
[O.E. *wær*, aware.]

was. See **be.**

wash, *wosh, v.t.* to wet with, or clean with, water or other liquid: to flow against: to sweep (away, along, etc.) by the action of water: to cover with a thin coat e.g. of paint.—*v.i.* to clean oneself, clothes, etc., with water: to flow (over, against, along): (*coll.*) to stand the test (e.g. *This statement will not wash*).—*n.* a washing: the breaking of waves e.g. on shore: the rough water left by a moving boat: a liquid with which anything is washed: a thin coat of paint, etc.

wash-, (as part of word) for washing in, with, etc. (e.g. **wash'bowl**).

wash'er, *n.* person, thing, that washes: a flat ring of rubber, metal etc., to keep nuts or joints tight, etc.

wash'ing, *n.* the act of cleaning by water: clothes washed or to be washed.

wash'erwoman, -man, *ns.* one who is paid to wash clothes.

washhand basin, *n.* a basin in which to wash face and hands.

washing machine, *n.* a machine, driven e.g. by electricity, for washing clothes.

washed'-up', (*slang*) exhausted, at the end of one's resources.

to wash up, to wash dishes, etc. after a meal.

[O.E. *wascan*; conn. with Ger. *waschen.*]

wasp, *wosp, n.* a stinging winged insect with slender waist.

was'pish, *adj.* like a wasp: spiteful.

was'pishly, *adv.* **was'pishness,** *n.*

[O.E. *wæsp*; conn. with L. *vespa.*]

wassail, *wos'ăl, v.i.* to hold a merry drinking meeting.—Also *n.*

wass'ailer, *n.* **wass'ailing,** *n.*

[Old Norse, *ves heill*, 'be in health', said in drinking a person's health.]

waste, *wāst, adj.* rejected as useless or worthless (e.g. *waste paper*; *waste materials from manufacture*): uncultivated (e.g. ground): desert, desolate.—*v.t.* to make ruined and desolate: to wear out gradually: to use with too little result or return (e.g. money, time, effort).—*v.i.* to decay gradually.—*n.* loss, destruction: extravagant use, bringing too poor a result: uncultivated country: an unbroken expanse (of e.g. water, snow).

wās'tage, *n.* loss by use, decay, etc.

waste'ful, *adj.* involving or causing waste: extravagant.

waste'fully, *adv.* **waste'fulness,** *n.*

wās'ter, wās'trel, *ns.* a ne'er-do-well.

waste'basket, waste'paper basket, one for paper being thrown away.

waste pipe, pipe to carry off water from e.g. sink.

[L. *vastus*, empty, waste, vast.]

watch, *woch, n.* close observation: guard: one who is, or those who are, on guard or lookout: a sailor's period of duty on deck (usu. four hours): a small timepiece, carried in the pocket, or worn on the wrist, etc.—*v.i.* to look with attention: to keep guard.—*v.t.* to observe closely: to wait for (e.g. one's opportunity).

watch'er, *n.*

watch'ful, *adj.* on the alert: cautious.

watch'fully, *adv.* **watch'fulness,** *n.*

watch'man, *n.* one who guards (esp. premises).

watch'word, *n.* a slogan, motto (e.g. *The watchword of the party was 'Opportunity for all'*).

to watch over, to keep guard over, care for and protect.

[O.E. *wacan*, wake; conn. **wake** (1).]

water, *wö'tėr, n.* a clear liquid without taste or smell, which falls as rain, etc.: any collection of it, as an ocean, lake, river, etc.: saliva: urine.—*v.t.* to supply with water: to weaken by adding water.—*v.i.* to gather saliva (e.g. *At the sight of food his mouth watered*): to take in water.

wa'tery, *adj.* like water: thin: threatening rain (e.g. *a watery sky*).

wa'teriness, *n.*

water buffalo, the common domestic buffalo of hot Eastern countries.

water butt, a large barrel for rainwater.

wa'ter-closet, *n.* a privy in which a rush of water is provided for carrying waste away through pipes.—Also **W.C.**

water colour, a colour thinned down with water instead of oil: a painting in such colours.

wa'tercourse, *n.* a channel for water, bed of stream, etc.

wa'terfall, *n.* a fall of water from a height.

wa'terfowl, *n.* birds, esp. game birds, that live on, or beside, water.

water ga(u)ge, *n.* an instrument for measuring the quantity or height of water.

wa'terglass, *n.* a chemical used to make a clear coating, on e.g. eggs, in order to preserve, etc.

wa'terhen, *n.* the moorhen, coot.

watering place, place where water may be obtained: holiday resort where people drink mineral water, bathe, etc.

water line, the line on a ship to which water rises.

wa'terlogged, *adj.* (of ship, etc.) unmanageable because flooded by water: (of ground) saturated.

water main, a large underground pipe carrying a public water supply.

wa'terman, *n.* a boatman, a ferryman.

wa'termark, *n.* a tide mark: a mark worked into paper to show its size or its manufacturer.

water melon, one of the two types of melon, the other being *musk melon.*

wa'termill, *n.* a mill driven by water.

water power, the power of water used to move machinery, etc.

wa′terproof, *adj.* not allowing water to soak through.—*n.* a garment made of a waterproof material.—*v.t.* to make proof against water.

water rat, the water vole (see **vole**).

wa′tershed, *n.* the line separating two river basins: a district from which several rivers rise.

wa′terspout, *n.* a pipe from which water spouts: a moving column of water, caused by storm wind, seen at sea.

water supply, obtaining of, and distribution of, water to a community: the amount of water so supplied.

wa′tertight, *adj.* so tightly made that water cannot pass through: in which no fault can be found (e.g. *a watertight excuse*).

wa′terway, *n.* a channel along which ships can sail.

wa′terwheel, *n.* a wheel moved by water.

wa′terworks, *n.pl.* the apparatus by which water is collected and supplied e.g. to a town: (*slang*) tears.

like water, very freely, in great quantity (e.g. *He spent money like water*).

[O.E. *wæter*; conn. with Ger. *wasser.*]

watt, *wot, n.* a unit of power.

watt′age, *n.* power in watts.

[After James *Watt* (1736-1819).]

wattle, *wot′l, n.* an Australian acacia: a structure made of twigs and branches: the fleshy part hanging from the throat of e.g. a turkey.

[O.E. *watel*, a hurdle.]

wave, *wāv, n.* a surge travelling on the surface of water: a vibrating disturbance travelling e.g. through the air: a succession of curves in the hair: a rise, increase for a time (of e.g. emotion, crime, prosperity): a gesture with e.g. one's hand.—*v.i.* to move backwards and forwards, flutter: to curve first one way then the other.—Also *v.t.*

wā′vy, *adj.* **wā′viness,** *n.*

wave′length, *n.* distance in the line of advance of a wave from one point to next similar point (e.g. in wave in water, from one highest point to the next).

wā′ver, *v.i.* to falter, be irresolute.

wā′verer, *n.*

[O.E. *wafian*, to wave.]

wax[1], *waks, n.* beeswax (see this word): any substance like it, as that in the ear: sealing-wax.—Also *adj.*—*v.t.* to smear or rub with wax.

wax′en, wax′y, *adjs.* resembling wax: pale, pasty.

wax′cloth, *n.* oilcloth for a floor.

wax′works, *n.pl.* an exhibition of figures (usu. of well-known people) made of wax.

[O.E. *weax.*]

wax[2], *waks, v.i.* to grow, increase (esp. of the moon)—opp. to **wane.**

[O.E. *weaxan*; conn. Ger. *wachsen.*]

way, *wā, n.* passage: road: room to go forward or to pass: direction: distance (e.g. *a long way*): condition (e.g. *He is in a bad way*): means (e.g. *Find a way to do this*): manner (e.g. *in a polite way*): habitual manner (e.g. *He thanked them warmly, as was his way*): the course of action one prefers (e.g. *to have one's way, own way*).

way′fārer, *n.* a traveller esp. on foot.

way′fāring, *adj.* and *n.*

waylay′, *v.t.* to lie in ambush for, or in wait for, and stop (a person):—*pr.p.* **waylay′ing**; *pa.p.* **waylaid′** (*-lād′*).

way′side, *n.* the side of a road, path, etc. —Also *adj.*

way′ward, *adj.* wilful, following one's own inclinations or whims: turning and changing in unexpected ways.

way′wardness, *n.*

ways and means, resources: methods (e.g. of raising money).

by the way, incidentally, in passing.

by way of, by the route passing, or through: for, or as if for, the purpose of (e.g. *He did it by way of helping me*).

to be under way, (esp. of a ship) to be in motion.

to give way. See **give.**

to have a way with one, to have an attractive manner.

to make one's way, to go (to): to get on in the world.

[O.E. *weg*; conn. Ger. *weg*, L. *via.*]

W.C. See **water-closet.**

we, *wē, pron. pl.* I and another or others:— *objective* **us**; *possessive* **our** (*owr*; sometimes described as possessive *adj.*), **ours** (e.g. *We—Mary and I—are glad you can meet us and give us a good map for our journey*; *ours is very old*).

ourselves′ (*-selvz′*), *pron. pl.* (1) emphatic, or (2) reflexive form of *we, us* (e.g. (1) *We ourselves are going*; (2) *we hid ourselves when we saw him*).

[O.E. *wē, ūs, ūre*; Ger. *wir, uns, unser.*]

weak, *wēk, adj.* lacking strength of body, mind, or character: easily led or influenced: (of e.g. resistance) easily overcome.

weak′ly, *adv.* **weak′ness,** *n.*

weak′ling, *n.* a weak person, animal, or plant.

weak′-kneed′ (*-knēd′*), *adj.* having weak knees: lacking firm will, too ready to give in.

weak′-min′ded, *adj.* having little intelligence: too easily persuaded.

[From Scand.; conn. O.E. *wac*, weak.]

weal[1], *wēl, n.* a raised mark on the skin caused by e.g. a blow with a whip.

[O.E. *walu*, the mark of a blow.]

weal[2], *wēl, n.* welfare, good fortune.

wealth, *welth, n.* riches: a great quantity (of).

weal′thy (*wel′*), *adj.*:—*comp.* **weal′thier**; *superl.* **weal′thiest.**

weal'thiness, *n.*
[O.E. *wela*, wealth, bliss.]

wean, *wēn, v.t.* to accustom (a child, young animal) to food other than the mother's milk: to turn away the interest or attachment of (e.g. *We must wean Mary from this bad habit*).
[O.E. *wenian.*]

weapon, *wep'ȯn, n.* any instrument or means of offence or defence.
[O.E. *wǣpn.*]

wear, *wār, v.t.* to be dressed in: to arrange (clothes, hair, in a particular way): to have on the face (e.g. a beard): to have, show (e.g. *She wears a pleased expression*): to damage, eat away, make gradually less, by use or exposure: to make (a hole) in this way: to exhaust, tire.—*v.i.* to be damaged or made less by use: to last when used (e.g. *This material wears well*): —*pa.t.* **wore** (*wōr, wör*); *pa.p.* **worn** (*wōrn, wörn*).—*n.* act of wearing: damage by use: durability: articles worn.
wear'able, *adj.* fit to be worn.
wear'er, *n.*
wear'ing, *adj.* made for wear: exhausting (e.g. *I find her chatter most wearing*).
to wear out, to become unfit for further use: to exhaust (**worn'-out',** *adj.*).
wear and tear, damage by ordinary use.
[O.E. *werian.*]

weary, *wē'ri, adj.* tired, with strength or patience exhausted: tiring, boring (e.g. *a weary job*):—*comp.* **wea'rier**; *superl.* **wea'riest.**—*v.t.* and *v.i.* to tire: to make, or become, bored or impatient:—*pr.p.* **wea'rying**; *pa.p.* **wea'ried.**
wea'rily, *adv.* **wea'riness,** *n.*
wea'risome, *adj.* causing weariness.
wea'risomely, *adv.* **-someness,** *n.*
[O.E. *wērig.*]

weasel, *wē'zl, n.* a small flesh-eating animal with long slender body: a cunning, treacherous person.
[O.E. *wesle*; conn. Ger. *wiesel.*]

weather, *weTH'ėr, n.* condition of the atmosphere (heat, coldness, cloudiness, etc.).—*v.t.* and *v.i.* to affect, or to be affected, by exposure to the air (to dry, discolour, wear away, etc.).—*v.t.* to come safely through (storm, difficulty).
weath'er-beaten, *adj.* showing effects of exposure to the weather.
weath'ercock, *n.* a flat piece of metal (often in the form of a cock) turning and showing the direction of the wind: one who changes his opinion often and easily.
weather glass, a barometer.
weather report, a statement about and forecast of the weather.
to keep one's weather eye open, to be alert, on one's guard.
under the weather, indisposed, ill.
[O.E. *weder.*]

weave[1], *wēv, v.t.* to interlace (threads, etc. as in a loom to form cloth): to make (something) in this way: to put details together to make (a story): (with *together*) to unite.—Also *v.i.*:—*pa.t.* **wōve**; *pa.p.* **wōven.**
wea'ver, *n.* **wea'ving,** *n.*
[O.E. *wefan.*]

weave[2], *wēv, v.i.* to move in and out, or to and fro, in a fight, in a dance, or through traffic.
[Prob. from Old Norse.]

web, *web, n.* something that is woven: the fine snare for flies, etc., spun by a spider, etc.: the skin between the toes of a waterfowl.
webbed, *adj.*
webb'ing, *n.* a rough woven fabric of hemp.
[O.E. *webb.*]

wed, *wed, v.t., v.i.* to marry:—*pr.p.* **wedd'ing**; *pa.p.* **wedd'ed.**
wedd'ing, *n.* marriage: marriage ceremony.
wedlock, *wed'lok, n.* matrimony: married state.
born in or **out of, wedlock,** legitimate, or illegitimate.
[O.E. *weddian—wedd*, pledge (*lāc*, gift).]

we'd, *wēd, abbrev.* we had, we should, or we would.

wedge, *wej, n.* a piece of wood or metal, thick at one end and sloping to a thin edge at the other, used in splitting, or in fixing tightly: anything shaped like a wedge.—*v.t.* to fix with a wedge or wedges: to press, thrust (in) tightly (e.g. *He wedged himself in among the crowd at the door*).—*v.i.* to become fixed or jammed by, or as if by, a wedge.
the thin edge of the wedge, a small beginning that will lead to greater developments.
[O.E. *wecg.*]

wedlock. See **wed.**

Wednesday, *wenz'di, wednz'di, n.* the fourth day of the week.
[O.E. *Wōdenes dæg*, day of god Woden.]

wee, *wē, adj.* small, tiny.
[M.E. *we*, a bit.]

weed[1], *wēd, n.* any useless troublesome plant: a worthless person.—*v.t.* to free from weeds: (with *out*) to remove (anything offensive or useless).—*v.i.* to remove weeds.
weed'er, *n.*
weed'y, *adj.* weed-like: full of weeds: lanky:—*comp.* **weed'ier**; *superl.* **-iest.**
weed'iness, *n.*
[O.E. *wēod*, a herb.]

weed[2], *wēd, n.* (in *pl.*) mourning garments.
[O.E. *wǣd(e)*, clothing.]

week, *wēk, n.* the space of seven days, esp. from Sunday to Saturday: the six days of the week leaving out Sunday.
week'ly, *adj.* happening, or done, once a week.—*adv.* once a week.—*n.* a publication coming out once a week:—*pl.* **-ies.**
week'day, *n.* any day except Sunday.

week′end, week′-end (or *-end′*), *n.* the period including the end of one week and the beginning of the next.
this day week, a week from today.
[O.E. *wice*; conn. Ger. *woche.*]

weep, *wēp, v.i.* to shed tears: to drip, ooze.—Also *v.t.*:—*pa.t., pa.p.* **wept.**
wee′ping, *adj.* shedding tears: (of trees) with drooping branches (e.g. *a weeping willow*).
[O.E. *wēpan.*]

weevil, *wē′vil, n.* any beetle that damages stored grain.
wee′viled, wee′villed, wee′vily, wee′villy, *adjs.* infested by weevils.
[O.E. *wifel*, beetle.]

weft, *weft, n.* in making cloth in a loom, the threads woven into, and crossing the warp.—Also **woof.**
[O.E.; same root as **weave.**]

weigh[1]**,** *wā, v.t.* to find the heaviness of (something): to be equal to in heaviness (e.g. *This parcel weighs* 1 *lb.*): to measure (out): to raise (ship's anchor): (of burden, cares, etc.) to press heavily (down): to ponder, consider (arguments, etc.).—*v.i.* to have heaviness: to be considered of importance: to press heavily (on).
weight, *wāt, n.* the amount which anything weighs: a piece of metal of a standard weight (e.g. *a ½ lb. weight, a 7 lb. weight*): pressure: importance (e.g. *a matter of some weight*).—*v.t.* to attach, or add, a weight or weights to: to hold down in this way.
weigh′ty, *adj.* heavy: important:—*comp.* **weigh′tier**; *superl.* **weigh′tiest.**
weigh′tily, *adv.* **weigh′tiness,** *n.*
to weigh in, to find one's weight before a fight, *after* a horse-race (**weigh out,** before): to join in a project.
[O.E. *wegan*, to carry, weigh.]

weigh[2]**,** *wā, n.* a very common misspelling of *way* in the phrase 'under way.'

weir, *wēr, n.* a dam across a river: a fence of stakes set in a stream for catching fish.
[O.E. *wer*, an enclosure.]

weird, *wērd, adj.* mysterious, supernatural: odd, very queer.
[O.E. *wyrd*, fate.]

welcome, *wel′kòm, adj.* received with gladness: causing gladness.—*n.* reception: kindly reception.—*v.t.* to receive with kindness or pleasure: to accept, or undergo, gladly.
welcome to, given permission and encouragement to take (something).
[O.E. *will*, wish, *cuma*, comer, guest.]

weld, *weld, v.t.* to join together (e.g. metal) by pressure with or without heat: to unite closely (e.g. different groups of people).—*n.* a welded joint.
[Conn. with root of **well** (1).]

welfare, *wel′fār, n.* the state of faring well: condition as regards health, etc.
welfare state, a country with a public health service, insurance against unemployment, pensions, etc.
welfare work, efforts to improve the living conditions of e.g. the needy, or employees or workers. [**well, fare.**]

well[1]**,** *wel, n.* a spring: a lined shaft made in the earth so as to obtain water, oil, etc.: any similar walled space, e.g. the space round which a staircase winds.—*v.i.* (of water from the earth, tears) to rise, gush (often *up, out,* or *forth*).
[O.E. *wella—weallan*, to boil.]

well[2]**,** *wel, adj.* in health: (used in predicate) fortunate (e.g. *It was well that you saw him coming*):—**bett′er** used as *comp.*—*adv.* properly: thoroughly: successfully: conveniently:—**bett′er** used as *comp.*—*interj.* expressing surprise, etc.
well′-advised′, *adj.* wise, prudent (e.g. *You would be well-advised to sell now*).
well′-being, *n.* welfare.
well′-bred′, *adj.* having good manners: of good parentage.
well′-conduc′ted, *adj.* properly managed: behaving properly.
well′-disposed′. See **dispose.**
well′-earned′, *adj.* thoroughly deserved.
well′-informed′, *n.* having, or based on, wide information.
well′-known′, *adj.* familiar: celebrated.
well′-mann′ered, *adj.* polite.
well′-mean′ing, *adj.* (of person, action) having good intentions.—Also (of action) **well′-meant′.**
well′-off′. See **off.**
well′-read′, *adj.* having read much and profitably.
well′-timed′, *adj.* done, said, etc., at a suitable time.
well′-to-do′, *adj.* having enough money to live comfortably.
well′-wisher, *n.* one who wishes success, etc., to person(s) or cause.
well′-worn′, *adj.* that has been worn or used often, or too often (e.g. *a well-worn excuse*).
as well, in addition.
as well as, 'both . . . and'.
[O.E. *wel*; conn. with Ger. *wohl.*]

wellingtons, *wel′ing-tonz, n.pl.* rubber boots loosely covering calves of legs.
[After Duke of *Wellington* (1769-1852).]

Welsh, *welsh, adj.* of Wales or its inhabitants.—*n.pl.* (**the Welsh**) the inhabitants of Wales: (in *sing.*) their Celtic language.
Welsh′man, *n.* a native of Wales:—*pl.* **Welsh′men.**
Welsh rarebit, *n.* melted cheese on toast.
[O.E. *welisc*, foreign.]

welsh, *welsh, v.i.* to cheat by dodging payment or not carrying out an obligation.
[Origin unknown.]

welt, *welt, n.* a band or strip fastened to an edge, for strength or for ornament: a narrow strip of leather used in one method of sewing the upper to the sole of a shoe.

[M.E. *welte*; origin uncertain.]

welter, *wel′tėr, v.i.* (of e.g. sea) to roll, heave: to roll about (in), or be drenched (in e.g. dirt, blood).—*n.* state of confusion: confused mass.
[M.E. *walten*, to roll over.]

welterweight, *wel′tėr-wāt, n.* (a boxer of) weight between *light* and *middle* (10 st. 7 lb.; amateur 10 st. 8 lb.).
[Origin unknown.]

wench, *wench, -sh, n.* a girl.
[O.E. *wencel*, a child.]

wend, *wend, v.i.* to go, wind:—*pa.t.* **wen′ded** (old *pa.t.* **went**; see **go**.)
to wend one's way, to follow the road in a leisurely fashion.
[O.E. *wendan*, to cause to wind.]

went. See **go.** **wept.** See **weep.**

were. See **be.**

we're, we are.

west, *west, n.* one of the four chief points of the compass: the region where the sun sets: the region in the west of any country: (*cap.*) Europe, or Europe and America, as opposed to Asia, the East.—*adj.* situated towards, or (of wind) coming from, the west.—*adv.* towards the west.
wes′tering, *adj.* going towards the west.
wes′terly, *adj.* lying or moving towards the west: (of wind) from the west.—*adv.* towards the west.
wes′tern, *adj.* situated in, or belonging to, the west.—*n.* a film or novel about the Wild West (see below).
wes′terner, *n.* a person belonging to the west.
west′(ern)most, *adj.* most westerly.
west′ward, *adj.* and (also **west′wards**) *adv.* towards the west.
West End, *n.* the fashionable district in the west of London, or of other large town.
to go west, to die: to become useless.
Wild West, the western United States, before the establishment of law and order.
[O.E. *west*; conn. Ger. *west*, Fr. *ouest*.]

wet, *wet, adj.* containing water: having water on the surface: rainy.—*v.t.* to make wet:—*pr.p.* **wett′ing**; *pa.p.* **wet, wett′ed.**
wet′ness, *n.* **wett′ish,** *adj.*
wet dock, a dock for floating ships at all states of the tide.
a wet blanket, a cause of discouragement: a depressing companion.
in the wet, in the rain, or other wet conditions.
[O.E. *wǣt*; same root as **water.**]

whack, *hwak, wak, v.t.* and *v.i.* to strike smartly, making a sound in doing so.—*n.* a blow: an attempt: a share.
whack′ing, *adj.* very large.—*n.* a beating.
(All meanings of **whack, whacking,** are *coll.*) [Imit.]

whale, *hwāl, wāl, n.* a large sea mammal (animal that suckles its young).—*v.i.* to catch whales.
whal′er, *n.* a ship, or a person, engaged in whale fishing.
whal′ing, *n.* and *adj.*
whale′bone, *n.* a light bendable substance got from the upper jaw of certain whales.
whale oil, oil obtained from the blubber of a whale.
bull, cow, or **calf, whale,** *n.* an adult male, female, or a young, whale.
[O.E. *hwæl*.]

wharf, *hwörf, wörf, n.* a landing-stage for loading, unloading, ships:—*pl.* **wharfs, wharves.**—*v.t.* to fasten up beside a wharf.
wharf′age, *n.* the dues paid for using a wharf.
wharfinger, *hwörf′in-jėr, n.* one who owns, or has the care of, a wharf.
[O.E. *hwerf*, a dam.]

what, *hwot, wot,* used as *pron.* or *adj.* in questions (e.g. *What are you hiding? What book is that?*) and also in dependent (i.e. not main) clauses (e.g. *Give me what you have*; *give me what money you have*).—*interj.* expressing astonishment (*What!*)
whatev′er, *pron.* anything that: no matter what (also *adj.*).
whatsoev′er, *adj.* of whatever kind.
what's what, the true state of affairs.
[O.E. *hwæt—hwā*, who; Ger. *was*.]

whatnot, *hwot′not, wot′, n.* a piece of furniture used for holding books, ornaments, china, etc. [**what, not.**]

whatso ver. See **what.**

wheat, *hwēt, wēt, n.* grain from which flour, much used in making bread, cakes, etc., is obtained.
wheat′en, *adj.* made of wheat: wholemeal (see this).
[O.E. *hwǣte—hwīt*, white.]

wheedle, *hwēd′l, wēd′l, v.t.* to entice by soft words, cajole (into doing something): to coax (something out of a person).
wheed′ler, *n.* **wheed′ling,** *n., adj.*
[Orig. unknown.]

wheel, *hwēl, wēl, n.* a circular frame turning on an axle: a steering-wheel.—*v.t.* to move or convey on wheels.—*v.i.* to turn about a centre: to turn: (of e.g. birds) to move in a curving course.
wheel(ed), *adjs.* having wheel(s).
wheel′barrow, *n.* a barrow with one wheel in front, and two handles and legs behind.
wheel′house, *n.* the shelter in which a ship's steering-wheel is placed.
wheel′wright, *n.* a craftsman who makes wheels and wheeled carriages.
wheels within wheels, a situation in which many different influences are at work.
[O.E. *hwēol*.]

wheeze, *hwēz, wēz, v.i.* to breathe with a

hissing sound and with difficulty: to make a noise of this kind.—Also *n*.
whee'zy, *adj*.
whee'zily, *adv*. **whee'ziness,** *n*.
[O.E. *hwēsan*.]

whelk, *hwelk, welk, n*. a small shellfish with a spiral shell, used as food.
[O.E. *weoluc*.]

whelp, *hwelp, welp, n*. the young of dogs, lions, etc.: (in contempt) a young man. —*v.i., v.t.* (of female dog, etc.) to give birth to young.
[O.E. *hwelp*.]

when, *hwen, wen, adv*. and *conj*. at what time (e.g. *When did he leave? I know when to say nothing*): at the time that (e.g. *when he came here*): while (e.g. *when I was abroad*): even though (e.g. *He bought it when he was told not to*): considering that (e.g. *Why walk when you have a car?*): and then (e.g. *He waited until dark, when he unwillingly went home*).—*pron*. at which (e.g. *at the moment when he arrived*).
whence (also **from whence**), *adv*. and *conj*. from what place, source, etc.
whenev'er, *conj*. at any, every, time.
[O.E. *hwænne*; root as **who.**]

where, *hwār, wār, adv*. and *conj*. at or in what place: at or in what place?: and in that place (e.g. *He went to London, where he set up in business*).—*pron*. in which (e.g. *He could not find the place where he had left it*): to which.
whereabout(s)', *advs*. and *conjs*. about where: near what?—*n*. (**where'abouts**) place (roughly indicated) where person, thing, is (e.g. *his whereabouts*; *the whereabouts of his new house*).
whereas', *conj*. when in fact: but, on the other hand.
whereby', *adv*. and *conj*. by which.
wherefore, *adv. conj*. (*old fashioned*) why? why: and for this reason.—*n*. the cause.
where'upon, *adv*. and *conj*. at or after which.
wherev'er, *adv*. and *conj*. in, at, or to, any place no matter what.
where'withal, *n*. the means (e.g. *He had not the wherewithal to buy food*).
[O.E. *hwǣr*; same root as **who.**]

wherry, *(h)wer'i, n*. a shallow, light boat:—*pl*. **wherr'ies.** [Orig. unknown.]

whet, *hwet, wet, v.t*. to sharpen (a tool) by rubbing: to make keen (e.g. *to whet the appetite*):—*pr.p*. **whett'ing;** *pa.p*. **whett'ed.**—*n*. act of sharpening: something that sharpens e.g. appetite, desire.
whet'stone, *n*. a stone for sharpening edged instruments.
[O.E. *hwettan—hwæt*, sharp.]

whether, *hweTH'ėr, weTH', conj*. introducing the first of two alternative words, phrases, or clauses, the second being introduced by *or*, or (in the case of clauses) sometimes by *or whether* (e.g. *whether I should go or whether I should stay*).—Also *adv*. (in questions; e.g. *Whether will you go or stay?*).
whether or no, whether or not: whatever the circumstances.
[O.E. *hwæther*; same root as **who.**]

whey, *hwā, wā, n*. the watery part of milk separated from the curd (the thick part), esp. in making cheese.
[O.E. *hwæg*.]

which, *hwich, wich*, used as a *pron*. or *adj*. in questions (e.g. *Which do you mean? Which cup shall I take?*), and also in dependent (i.e. not main) clauses (e.g. *Tell me which you prefer*; *say which road is prettier*; *the road which I took was rough*): —*objective* **which**; *possessive* **whose** (*hōōz*; often replaced by **of which**).
whichev'er, *pron*. and *adj*. any(one), no matter which.
which is which, which is the one and which is the other (e.g. *The twins are Mary and Anne, but I do not know which is which*).
[O.E. *hwilc*—root as **who, -līc**, like.]

whiff, *hwif, wif, n*. a sudden puff (of air, smoke, smell, shot, etc.). [Imit.]

Whig, *hwig, wig, n*. a member of one of the two English political parties in late 17th century, 18th, and early 19th; later known as Liberal.
[*whiggamore*; origin uncertain.]

while, *whīl, wīl, n*. space of time: time and trouble spent (only in **worth (one's) while**).—*conj*. during the time that: although.—*v.t*. (with *away*) to cause (time) to pass without weariness (e.g. *He read to while away the time*).
whilst, *conj*. while.
[O.E. *hwīl*; conn. Ger. *weile*.]

whim, *hwim, wim, n*. an odd, absurd fancy or sudden desire or change of mind.
whim'sical, *adj*. (of a person) full of whims: quaintly humorous: odd, fanciful (e.g. *The story was full of whimsical ideas*).
whim'sicalness, whimsical'ity, *ns*.
whim'sically, *adv*.
whim'sy, whim'sey, *n*. a whim: quaint, fanciful humour:—*pl*. **whim'sies, -seys.**

whimper, *hwim'pėr, wim', v.i*. to cry with low whining voice.—*n*. a peevish cry.
[Imit.; perh. from root of **whine.**]

whin, *hwin, win, n*. a prickly shrub, gorse, furze. [Orig. unknown.]

whine, *hwīn, wīn, v.i*. to utter a complaining cry: to complain in a feeble way or unnecessarily.—*n*. a plaintive cry.
whī'ner, *n*. **whī'ningly,** *adv*.
whinn'y (*hwin', win'*), *v.i*. to neigh:—*pr.p*. **whinn'ying**; *pa.p*. **whinn'ied.**—Also *n*.
[O.E. *hwinan*, to whizz, whine.]

whip, *hwip, wip, n*. a lash with a handle, for punishing or driving: a stroke given as by a whip: in parliament, a member chosen by his party to make sure that no one fails to vote in important divisions:

a notice sent out by a parliamentary whip.—*v.t.* to lash: to drive or punish with lashes: to beat into a froth (eggs, cream, etc.): to sew lightly (edges of material): to snatch (with *up*, *away*, *out*).—*v.i.* to move nimbly: to move in the manner of a whip lash: —*pr.p.* **whipp'ing**; *pa.p.* **whipped, whipt.**

whipp'ing, *n.* and *adj.*

whip hand, the hand that holds the whip in driving (**to have the whip hand over one,** to be in a position to compel one).

whipp'er-snapp'er, *n.* a boastful but unimportant person.

whipping boy, someone punished for the faults of another, a scapegoat.

[M.E. *whippen.*]

whippet, *hwip'it, wip', n.* a racing dog like a small greyhound. [Prob. **whip, it.**]

whir(r), *hwėr, wėr, n.* a sound from rapid whirling.—*v.t.* and *v.i.* to move with a whirring, buzzing, sound:—*pr.p.* **whirr'ing**; *pa.p.* **whirred.** [Imit.]

whirl, *hwėrl, wėrl, n.* a rapid turning: an excited confusion (of emotion, activity, etc.): commotion.—*v.i.* to go round rapidly.—*v.t.* to turn (round) rapidly: to carry (away) rapidly.

whirl'pool, *n.* a circular current in a river or sea, caused by opposing tides, winds, or currents.

whirl'wind, *n.* a violent current of wind with a whirling motion.

[Old Norse *hvirfla*, to turn round.]

whisk, *hwisk, wisk, v.t.* to move, sweep, or stir, rapidly.—*v.i.* to move nimbly and rapidly.—*n.* a rapid, sweeping motion: a kitchen tool for beating eggs, cream, etc.: implement for flapping flies away.

whis'ker, *n.* something that whisks: (usu. in *pl.*) hair on the side of a man's face (**side whiskers**): a long bristle on the upper lip of a cat, etc.

whis'kered, *adj.*

[Conn. Old Norse, *visk*, wisp of hay.]

whisky, (*Ir.* and *U.S.*) **whiskey,** *hwis'ki, wis', n.* an alcoholic drink made from grain:—*pl.* **whis'kies,** (*Ir.* and *U.S.*) **whis'keys.**

[Gael. *uisge*, water, *beatha*, life.]

whisper, *hwis'pėr, wis', v.i.* to speak very softly: (of trees, etc.) to make a soft sound: to spread rumours.—*v.t.* to say very softly: to spread (a rumour).—*n.* a sound made very softly; a secret hint: a rumour.

whis'perer, *n.*

whispering campaign, an attack made by secretly spreading rumours.

[O.E. *hwisprian*; conn. with Ger. *wispern* and with **whistle.**]

whist, *hwist, n.* a card game played by two against two.

[Orig. *whisk*; origin unknown.]

whistle, *hwis'l, wis', v.i.* to make a sound by forcing breath through lips or teeth: to make such a sound with an instrument: to sound shrill: to whizz (through the air).—*v.t.* to make, produce (a sound, tune, etc.) by whistling: to call by a whistle.—*n.* the sound made by whistling: an instrument for whistling.

whis'tler, *n.*

[O.E. *hwistlian.*]

whit, *hwit, wit, n.* a very small particle or amount.

[Same as **wight,** a creature.]

Whit. See **Whitsun.**

white, *hwīt, wīt, adj.* of the colour of pure snow: pure: bright: light-coloured (e.g. *white wine*): pale, wan: of light complexion (as Europeans).—*n.* the colour of snow: something white (e.g. a white man, the part of an egg surrounding the yolk).

whī'ten, *v.t., v.i.* to make, or become, white or whiter.

white'ness, *n.* **whī'tish,** *adj.*

whī'ting[1], *n.* a small sea fish related to the cod.

whī'ting,[2], white'ning, *n.* ground chalk free from stony matter.

white ant, a termite (see this).

white'bait, *n.* fry of herring and sprat.

white corpuscle, *n.* one of the colourless cells in blood plasma, etc.

white elephant, feather. See **elephant, feather.**

white flag, *n.* a sign of truce or of surrender.

white heat, the degree of heat at which bodies become white.

white'-hot, *adj.*

white horse, *n.* a white-topped wave.

White House, official residence of the President of U.S.A. at Washington.

white lead, carbonate of lead used in paint, putty, etc.

white light, light of the colour of sunlight at noon.

white meat, flesh of poultry, and rabbit, veal, pork.

white paper, a statement printed on white paper, issued by government for the information of parliament.

white'wash, *n.* a mixture of whiting or lime and water, used for whitening walls: anything that conceals a stain.—*v.t.* to cover with whitewash: to cover up faults, etc. in (e.g. conduct): to attempt to clear (a reputation).

[O.E. *hwīt*; conn. with Ger. *weiss.*]

whither, *hwiTH'ėr, wiTH', adv.* and *conj.* to what place?: to which place.

[O.E. *hwider*; same root as **who.**]

whitlow, *hwit'lō, wit',* inflammation, and usu. suppuration, of finger or toe, esp. near nail.

[M.E. *whitflawe*; **white, flaw.**]

Whitsun, *hwit'sŭn, wit',* **Whit,** *adjs.* of **Whitsuntide,** the week beginning with **Whit Sunday** (or **Whitsunday**), the seventh Sunday after Easter.

[**white, Sunday.**]

whittle, *hwit'l, wit',* *v.t.* to pare or cut off with a knife: to shape (e.g. a twig) with a knife: (with *away, down*) to make gradually less.
[O.E. *thwītan.*]

whiz(z), *hwiz, wiz,* *v.i.* to make a hissing sound like an arrow flying through the air: to move rapidly:—*pr.p.* **whizz'ing**; *pa.p.* **whizzed.** [Imit.]

who, *hōō, pron.* what person(s)?: also used in dependent (i.e. not main) clauses (e.g. *The man, men, who came, took it away*):—*objective* **whom** (*hōōm*; e.g. *The man whom I saw, and to whom I gave the note*); possessive **whose** (*hōōz*; e.g. *I saw someone whose face was familiar*).
whoev'er, (*old-fashioned*) **whosoev'er,** *prons.* whatever person.
[O.E. *hwā*; conn. Ger. *wer,* L. *quis.*]

whole, *hōl, adj.* consisting of all: complete: not broken: sound in health.—*n.* the entire thing.
whole'ness, *n.*
wholly (*hōl'li, hō'li*), *adv.* completely, altogether.
whole'hear'ted, *adj.* generous, sincere, enthusiastic (e.g. *His plan had my whole-hearted support*).
whole'meal, *n.* flour made from the entire wheat grain or seed.
whole'sale', *n.* the sale of goods in large quantity to a retailer.—*adj.* buying and selling thus: on a large scale (e.g. *wholesale slaughter*).
whole'some, *adj.* healthy, sound.
whole'somely, *adv.* **-someness,** *n.*
up(on) the whole, taking everything into consideration.
[O.E. *hāl,* healthy; Ger. *heil,* **hale** (2).]

who'll, who will. **whom.** See **who.**

whoop, hoop, *hwōōp, hōōp, n.* a loud eager shout: the noisy sound of breathing-in heard in whooping cough.—*v.i.* to give a loud cry of delight, triumph, scorn, etc.
whoop'er, *n.* a kind of swan.
whooping cough, hooping cough, an infectious disease with violent cough and whoop.
[O.Fr. *houper,* to shout.]

whore, *hōr, hör, n.* a prostitute.
[O.E. *hōre*; conn. Ger. *hure.*]

whorl, *hwörl, hwûrl, wörl, wûrl, n.* a number of leaves in a circle round the stem: a turn in a spiral shell.
whorl'ed, *adj.* having whorls. **[whirl.]**

whortleberry, *hwûr'tl-ber-i, hûr',* bilberry.
[Conn. O.E. *hortan,* whortleberries.]

whose. See **who** and **which.**

why, *hwī, wī, adv.* for what cause or reason (e.g. *Why did you go? Tell me why you went*).—*pron.* on account of which (*the reason why I came*).—*interj.* expressing surprise or protest.
the why and the wherefore, the whole reason.
[O.E. *hwī, hwȳ*; from root of **who.**]

wick, *wik, n.* the twisted threads of cotton, etc. in a candle, lamp, etc. which draw up the liquid that burns.
[O.E. *weoce.*]

wicked, *wik'id, adj.* evil in behaviour, sinful: mischievous and spiteful: roguish: (*coll.*) very bad.—*n.* (as *pl.*) wicked persons.
wick'edly, *adv.* **wick'edness,** *n.*
[M.E. *wick(e)*—O.E. *wicca,* wizard.]

wicker, *wik'ėr, n.* a small twig (e.g. a willow twig) that will bend easily.—*adj.* (of e.g. a table, basket) made of twigs.
wick'erwork, *n.* basketwork.
[From Scand.; conn. O.E. *wīcan,* bend.]

wicket, *wik'it, n.* a small door or gate, esp. one forming part of a larger one: (*cricket*) a set of three upright stumps at which the bowler aims the ball: one of these stumps: the ground between the bowler and the batsman: a batsman's innings.
wick'et-keeper, *n.* the fielder who stands immediately behind the wicket.
[(O.)Fr. *guichet.*]

wide, *wīd, adj.* broad, not narrow: stretching far (e.g. *wide estates*): opened as far as possible (e.g. *with wide eyes*; *the window is wide*): far apart: far from the point aimed at (with *of*; e.g. *wide of the mark*).—*n.* a ball bowled beyond the batsman's reach.
wide, wide'ly, *advs.*
wide'ness, width (*width*), *ns.*
wi'den, *v.t., v.i.* to make, or become, wide or wider.
wide'-awake', *adj.* fully awake: on the alert: not easily cheated or misled.—*n.* a kind of soft felt hat.
wide'spread, *adj.* spread over a large area or among many people.
[O.E. *wīd*; conn. with Ger. *weit.*]

widgeon, *wij'ọn, n.* a kind of wild duck.
[Origin uncertain.]

widow, *wid'ō, n.* a woman whose husband is dead.—Also *v.t.* to take a husband, or anything valued, away from (someone).
wid'ower, *n.* a man whose wife is dead.
[O.E. *widuwe*; Ger. *witwe,* L. *vidua.*]

wield, *wēld, v.t.* to exercise (authority, power): to manage, use (e.g. sword, pen).
wiel'der, *n.*
wiel'dy, *adj.* manageable.
[O.E. *wealdan.*]

wife, *wīf, n.* a married woman: the woman to whom one is married: a woman:—*pl.* **wives** (*wīvz*).
wife'ly, *adj.*
[O.E. *wīf*; conn. with Ger. *weib.*]

wig, *wig, n.* an artificial covering of hair for the head.
wigged, *adj.* wearing a wig.
[For *periwig*—Fr. *perruque.*]

wiggle, *wig'l, v.i.* and *v.t.* to move, or cause to move, irregularly from side to side.
wigg'ly, *adj.* **wigg'liness,** *n.*
[Conn. with **wag, waggle.**]

wigwam, *wig'wam, -wom, n.* Indian hut of skins, etc., usu. rounded in shape.
[From Amer. Indian word.]

wild, *wild, adj.* not tamed: not cultivated: uncivilised: lawless: violent: distracted (e.g. *wild with anxiety*): very stormy (e.g. *a wild night*): rash: wide of the mark (e.g. *a wild guess*).—*n.* (also in *pl.*) an uncultivated region.
wild'ly, *adv.* **wild'ness,** *n.*
wild'cat, *adj.* unreliable, rash (e.g. *a wildcat scheme*).
wil'derness (*wil'*), *n.* desert or wild country: an empty, unhappy place: a wild part of a garden: a large confused mass (e.g. *a wilderness of old car bodies*).
wild'fire, *n.* formerly, name of material burning strongly, used in war (still found in **to spread like wildfire**—of e.g. news): lightning without thunder.
wild'fowl, wild birds, esp. water birds shot as game.
wild-goose chase, an absurd attempt to catch or find something one cannot possibly obtain.
wild oats. See **oat.**
[O.E. *wilde*; conn. with Ger. *wild.*]

wile, *wīl, n.* a trick, deceitful move: (in *pl.*) persuasive manner (e.g. *She used her wiles to get her own way*).—*v.t.* to lure.
wily, *wī'li, adj.* crafty, artful, sly.
wī'lily, *adv.* **wī'liness,** *n.*
[O.E. *wīl*; prob. same root as **guile.**]

will, *wil, n.* the power to choose or decide: desire (e.g. *against one's will*): determination (e.g. *the will to succeed*): feeling towards someone or something (*good will, ill will*): (document containing) a formal statement about what is to be done with one's property after one's death.—*v.t.* to desire, intend, to (e.g. *I will speak out*), be willing to (e.g. *I will go if you ask me*): (to try) to influence by exerting the will (e.g. *She willed him to pick it up*): to bequeath, hand down, by will.—Also *v.i.*:—*pa.t.* **willed** (in sense, 1, **would,** *wood, wėd, wd*).—Also used to form future tenses of other verbs when the subject is *he, she, it, you,* or *they* (e.g. *He, you, they, will certainly arrive late*); also to form a *pr.t.* describing a habit (e.g. *Each morning he will go for a walk*):—*pr.t.* 2nd person (thou) **wilt**; *pa.t.* **would.** There is also a conditional form **would** (e.g. *He would be foolish if he did not go,* or *foolish not to go*).
See also **shall** and **should**
wil'ful, *adj.* obstinate, set on one's own way: intentional (e.g. *wilful damage*).
wil'fully, *adv.* **wil'fulness,** *n.*
will'ing, *adj,* ready to agree (to do something): eager.
will'ingly, *adv.* **will'ingness,** *n.*
at will, as, or when, one chooses.
with a will, eagerly: energetically.
[O.E. ***willa***; conn. L. ***velle,*** to wish.]

will-o'-the-wisp, *wil'-ō-thi-wisp', n.* a pale light seen over marshes at night, supposed to be due to burning marsh gas: an aim that one is always trying to achieve and that can never be accomplished (e.g. *Poor Jack was always chasing the will-o'-the-wisp of success*).
[**William, wisp** (of lighted hay).]

willow, *wil'ō, n.* a tree with slender, easily bent branches: the wood of the willow: a cricket bat.
will'owy, *adj.* easily bent: slender, graceful: with many willows.
willow pattern, a blue design of Chinese style used on china made in England.
[O.E. *welig.*]

willy-nilly, *wil'i-nil'i, adv.* whether one wishes it or not (e.g. *He must go, willy-nilly*).
[**will** (vb.) and old word *nill,* will not.]

wilt[1], *wilt, v.i.* (of flowers) to droop: to lose energy.
[Conn. with Ger. *welk,* withered.]

wilt[2]. See **will. wily.** See **wile.**

win, *win, v.t.* to gain, obtain, by contest (e.g. a victory), by luck (e.g. a prize in a lottery), by effort (e.g. love, consent, a wife): to succeed in making (one's way): to reach (a place).—Also *v.i.*:—*pr.p.* **winn'ing**; *pa.t., pa.p.* **won** (*wun*).—*n.* a victory, success.
winn'er, *n.*
winn'ing, *n.* the act of one who wins: (in *pl.*) something (esp. money) that is won.—*adj.* victorious, successful: attractive, charming (e.g. *She has winning ways*).
winn'ingly, *adv.* **winn'ingness,** *n.*
winn'ing-post, *n.* post marking place where a race finishes.
to win the day. See **day.**
[O.E. *winnan,* to work, fight, suffer.]

wince, *wins, v.i.* to shrink or start back quickly in pain: to be hurt (e.g. by an unkind remark).
[O.Fr. *guenc(h)ir*; conn. with **wink.**]

winch, *winch, -sh, n.* a crank or handle for turning a wheel: a hoisting machine, windlass.
[O.E. *wince.*]

wind[1], *wind, n.* air in motion: a current of air (gale, etc.): air bearing the scent e.g. of game: breath: flatulence: empty, unimportant words: the wind instruments in an orchestra: the players of these instruments.—*v.t.* to put out of breath.
win'ded, *adj.* out of breath.
win'dy, *adj.* exposed to the wind (e.g. *a windy corner*): tempestuous (e.g. *a windy day*): (*coll.*) nervous, scared:—*comp.* **win'dier**; *superl.* **win'diest.**
win'diness, *n.*
wind'ward, *n.* the point from which the wind blows.—Also *adj.* and *adv.*
wind'bag, *n.* a very talkative person.
wind'bound, *adj.* hindered from sailing by an unfavourable wind.

wind′break, *n.* something, e.g. a group of trees, sheltering from wind.

wind′fall, *n.* fruit blown from a tree: any unexpected gain or advantage.

wind instrument, a musical instrument sounded by wind, esp. by the breath.

wind′jammer (*-jam-*), *n.* a large sailing vessel: (*coll.*) wind-resisting golf blouse.

wind′mill, *n.* a machine for grinding grain or pumping water worked by wind.

wind′pipe, *n.* the passage for the breath between mouth and lungs, the trachea.

wind′screen, *n.* a transparent screen above the dashboard in a car.

wind′-swept, *adj.* exposed to wind and showing effects of it.

to get the wind up, to become nervous or anxious.

to get wind of, to get a hint of, hear indirectly about.

in the wind, afoot, about to happen.

close to, near, the wind, near the danger point: near the limit of what may be said with propriety.

second wind, natural breathing recovered after breathlessness.

[O.E. *wind*; conn. Ger. *wind*, L. *ventus*.]

wind[2], *wīnd*, *v.t.* to turn, twist, coil: to screw the mechanism of (e.g. a clock): to make (one's, its, way) by turning and twisting (also *v.i.*).—*v.i.* to turn completely or often: to turn (round something):—*pr.p.* **wīn′ding**; *pa.p.* **wound** (*wownd*).

wīn′der, *n.* one who winds: an instrument for winding.

wīn′ding, *adj.* curving: full of bends.—*n.* a turning: a twist.

to wind up, to coil completely: to wind the spring or mechanism of (e.g. a watch) completely: to excite very much (usu. in *pass.*; e.g. *He was wound up about something*): to bring or come to an end (e.g. a meeting, business).

[O.E. *windan*; conn. **wend, wander.**]

windlass, *wind′lȧs*, *n.* a machine for raising weights by winding a rope round a revolving cylinder.

[Old Norse *vinda*, to wind, *āss*, pole.]

windjammer. See **wind** (1).

window, *win′dō*, *n.* an opening in a wall of a building, etc. for air and light, fitted with a wooden or metal frame, and usu. glass.

window dressing, arranging goods in a shop window effectively: giving an unduly attractive or favourable appearance to something (e.g. a plan, cause, or situation).

[Old Norse *vindr*, wind, *auga*, eye.]

windpipe, etc. See **wind** (1).

wine, *wīn*, *n.* a drink made from the fermented juice of grapes or other fruit: a rich red colour.

wine′press, *n.* a machine in which grapes are pressed in making wine.

[O.E. *win*, Ger. *wein*—L. *vīnum*.]

wing, *wing*, *n.* the limb of a bird, bat, or insect, by which it flies: a limb in the same position of certain birds that do not fly: a side structure on a stage, aeroplane, building, etc.: a player at either end of the forward line in football, etc.: (in *pl.*) a badge worn by flying members of the R.A.F.—*v.t.* to give speed to: to wound in the wing, or in the arm or shoulder.—*v.i.* to soar.

winged, *wingd* or *wing′id*, *adj.* having wings: swift: (*wingd*) wounded in the wing, shoulder, or arm.

wing commander. See *Appendices*.

on, upon, the wing, flying, in motion: departing.

to take wing, to fly off, flee, depart.

under one's wing, under one's protection, guidance.

[Old Norse *vængr*.]

wink, *wingk*, *v.i.* to shut and open an eye quickly: to give a hint by winking: (of e.g. lights) to flicker, twinkle.—*v.t.* to close and open (eye) quickly.—*n.* act of winking: a hint given by winking.

forty winks, a short sleep.

to wink at, purposely to take no notice of (action that is e.g. against rules).

[O.E. *wincian*; conn. with Ger. *winken*.]

winkle, *wing′kl*, *n.* periwinkle (2).

to winkle out, to force out gradually and with difficulty (perh. not from *periwinkle* but from Ger. *winkel*, corner).

winning, winner. See **win.**

winnow, *win′ō*, *v.t.* to separate the chaff from (the grain) by wind: to separate, sift (e.g. *to winnow the truth from a mass of statements*).—Also *v.i.*

[O.E. *windwian*.]

winsome, *win′sȯm*, *adj.* charming.

win′somely, *adv.* **win′someness,** *n.*

[O.E. *wynsum*, pleasant.]

winter, *win′tėr*, *n.* the cold season of the year—in the northern temperate regions (Europe, etc.) from November or December to January or February: any cheerless time.—Also *adj.*—*v.i.* to pass the winter.—*v.t.* to keep, feed (cattle, etc.) during winter.

win′try, *adj.* like winter, cold, stormy: (of e.g. a smile) dreary, not warm or cheerful:—*comp.* **win′trier**; *superl.* **win′triest.**

win′triness, *n.*

winter quarters, lodging, place of stay (esp. of soldiers) during the winter.

winter sports, skiing, tobogganing, etc.

[O.E.; conn. Ger. *winter*.]

wipe, *wīp*, *v.t.* to clean or dry by rubbing: (with *away*, *off*, *out*, *up*) to clear away.—*n.* act of cleaning by rubbing.

wī′per, *n.* **wī′ping,** *n.*

[O.E. *wipian*.]

wire, *wīr*, *n.* a thread of metal: a metal string of a musical instrument: the metal thread used in telegraphy, etc.: a telegram.—*adj.* formed of wire.—*v.t.* to supply (e.g. a building) with wires necessary for carrying an electric current:

to send by, or to inform by, telegraph.—*v.i.* to telegraph.
wire′less, *adj.* without wires, esp. of telegraphy and telephony.—*n.* wireless telegraphy or telephony: a message sent by one of these: apparatus for wireless telegraphy: broadcasting generally.—*v.t.* and *v.i.* to communicate by wireless telegraphy.
wir′ing, *n.*
wīr′y, *adj.* made of, or like, wire: lean and strong (e.g. *his wiry body*):—*comp.* **wīr′ier**; *superl.* **wīr′iest.**
wīr′ily, *adv.* **wīr′iness,** *n.*
wire′-nett′ing, *n.* material with wide mesh woven of wire.
wire′puller, *n.* one who influences the actions of others by secret means (as if making puppets move), an intriguer.
wire′pulling, *n.*
[O.E. *wīr.*]

wisdom. See **wise** (1).

wise[1], *wiz, adj.* learned: able to use knowledge well, judging rightly (e.g. *He is wise—ask his advice*): prudent, sensible (e.g. *a wise decision*).
wise′ly, *adv.*
wise′ness, wis′dom (*wiz′*), *ns.*
wisdom tooth, one of four back teeth cut after childhood, usu. about the age of twenty.
[O.E. *wīs*; from root of **wit** (1) and (2).]

wise[2], *wiz, n.* way, manner; used as suffx. (e.g. *crosswise*).
in any (no) wise, in any (no) way.
[O.E. *wīse*; Ger. *weise,* **wit** (1), (2).]

wiseacre, *wiz′ā-kėr, n.* one who puts on an air of great wisdom: a simpleton, unconscious of being one.
[From Middle Du.]

wish, *wish, v.i.* to have a desire (for): to express a desire.—*v.t.* to desire or long for: to express a desire (that, to do, etc.): to hope for on behalf of (someone; e.g. *I wish you luck*).—*n.* desire, longing: thing desired: expression of desire.
wish′er, *n.* **wish′ing,** *n.* and *adj.*
wish′ful, *adj.* **wish′fully,** *adv.*
wishful thinking, belief that something will happen arising merely from a wish that it should: wishing for something that is unlikely to happen.
[O.E. *wȳscan—wūsc* (n.); Ger. *wunsch.*]

wishy-washy, *wish′i-wosh′i, adj.* (of liquid) thin and weak: feeble, of poor quality. [**wash.**]

wisp, *wisp, n.* a small tuft or thin strand (e.g. *a wisp of hair*). [M.E.]

wistful, *wist′fool, -fl, adj.* thoughtful and rather sad: yearning with little hope.
wist′fully, *adv.* **wist′fulness,** *n.*
[Prob. from *wistly,* intently.]

wit[1], *wit, v.t.* and *v.i.* to know—an old verb now used in:—
witt′ingly, *adv.* knowingly.
to wit, that is to say.
[O.E. *witan*; conn. with Ger. *wissen.*]

wit[2], *wit, n.* understanding: (in *pl.*) natural mental ability: common sense: expression of ideas in a lively amusing way: a person who expresses himself thus.
wit′less, *adj.* **wit′lessness,** *n.*
witt′ed, *adj.* having wit or understanding—usu. with another *adj.*, as *quick-witted.*
witt′y, *adj.* clever and amusing:—*comp.* **witt′ier**; *superl.* **witt′iest.**
witt′ily, *adv.* **witt′iness,** *n.*
witt′icism, *n.* a witty remark.
at one's wits' end, utterly perplexed and desperate.
to live by one's wits, to live by cunning rather than by hard work.
[O.E.; same root as **wit** (1).]

witch, *wich, n.* a woman supposed to have powers of magic through being in league with the devil: a hag: (*coll.*) a fascinating woman.
witch′ery, *n.* witchcraft: fascination.
witch′craft, *n.* the magic practised by a witch: power like that of a witch or magician: fascination.
witch doctor, in African tribes, one whose profession is to cure illness and keep away evil magical influences.
[O.E. *wicca,* wizard, *wicce,* witch.]

with, *wiTH, with, prep.* against (e.g. *to fight with a rival*): in the company of: on the side of: in the same direction as (e.g. *to drift with the stream*): by, by means of (e.g. *Cut it with a knife*): having (e.g. *a man with a ladder*): in the keeping of (e.g. *Leave the coat with me*).
to feel, to be, or **to think, with (someone),** to feel as, be of same opinion as, the other person concerned. [O.E.]

with-, *wiTH-,* or *-th, pfx.* against. [**with.**]

withdraw, *wiTH-draw′* (or *-th*), *v.t.* to draw back or away: to take away (e.g. *to withdraw one's support for a plan*): to take back (something one has said).—*v.i.* to retire, go away:—*pa.t.* **withdrew′**; *pa.p.* **withdrawn′.**
withdraw′al, *n.*
withdrawn′, *adj.* (of place) isolated, lonely: (of manner) not responsive or friendly. [Pfx. **with-.**]

withe, *wiTH,* **withy,** *wiTH′i, ns.* a bendable twig, esp. of willow: a band of twisted twigs.
[O.E. *withthe*; conn. Ger. *weide,* willow.]

wither, *wiTH′ėr, v.t., v.i.* to fade, dry up, decay: to feel, or to make to feel, embarrassed or very unimportant (e.g. *She withered him with a look*).
[O.E. *wedrian*; same root as **weather.**]

withers, *wiTH′ėrz, n.pl.* the ridge between the shoulder bones of a horse.
[O.E. *wither* (from *with*), against.]

withhold, *wiTH-hōld′* (or *with-*), *v.t.* to hold back: to refuse to give:—*pa.p.* **withheld′.** [Pfx. **with-.**]

within, *wiTH-in′, prep.* inside: in the limits of, not going beyond (e.g. *within* *sight, within one's rights*).—*adv.* in, or into, the inner part: inwardly.

without, *wiTH-owt',* *prep.* outside of: not having, free from.—*adv.* on, or to, the outside.

[O.E. **with-,** *innan,* in, *ūtan,* outside.]

withstand, *wiTH-stand'* (or *with-*), *v.t.* to oppose or resist successfully:—*pa.p.* **withstood'.** [Pfx. **with-.**]

withy. See **withe.**

witness, *wit'nis, n.* a person who sees or has direct knowledge of a thing: one who gives evidence: testimony, evidence.—*v.t.* to see, be present at: to sign one's name to show one knows (another's signature), on e.g. a will, is genuine: to bear witness (that): to be evidence or proof of.—*v.i.* to give evidence.

witness box, stand, the stand from which a witness gives evidence in a court of law.

to bear witness, (of person, fact, etc.) to give, or be evidence (with *to, that*; e.g. *to bear witness to his honesty, that he is honest*).

[O.E. *witnes,* testimony—*witan,* to know.]

witticism, witty, etc. See **wit** (2).

wives. See **wife.**

wizard, *wiz'ȧrd, n.* a man who practises magic: one who works wonders.

[M.E. *wysard*—*wys,* wise, suffx. *-ard.*]

wizened, *wiz'nd, adj.* dried up, shrivelled.

wiz'en, *v.i., v.t.* become, make, dry.

[O.E. *wisnian,* to wither.]

woad, *wōd, n.* plant yielding blue dye: dyestuff made from its leaves.

[O.E. *wād*; conn. Ger. *waid.*]

wobble, *wob'l, v.i.* to rock unsteadily from side to side: to waver.

wobb'ly, *adj.* **wobb'liness,** *n.*

[Germanic word; conn. with **waver.**]

woe, *wō, n.* grief, misery: an affliction, trouble.

woe'ful, *adj.* **woe'fully,** *adv.*

woe'fulness, *n.*

woe'begone (*-bi-gon*), *adj.* dismal looking.

[O.E. (interj.) *wā*; Ger. *weh*; L. *vae.*]

woke, woken. See **wake** (1).

wold, *wōld, n.* open uncultivated country.

[Northern O.E. *wald.*]

wolf, *woolf, n.* a beast of prey, of the dog family, that goes round with others in a pack: a greedy and cruel person:—*pl.* **wolves** (*wōlvz*).—*v.t.* to eat greedily.

wolf'ish, *adj.* like a wolf.

wolf'ishly, *adv.* **wolf'ishness,** *n.*

to cry wolf, to give a false alarm.

to keep the wolf from the door, to keep away hunger or want.

[O.E. *wulf*; conn. Ger. *wolf,* L. *lupus.*]

woman, *woom'ȧn, n.* an adult human female: human females considered together: a domestic help:—*pl.* **women** (*wim'in*).

wom'anhood, *n.* the state, or qualities, of a woman.

wom'ankind, wom'enkind, wom'enfolk, *ns.* women generally.

wom'anlike, *adj.* and *adv.*

wom'anly, *adj.* natural, suitable, to a woman: showing qualities of a woman.

wom'anliness, *n.*

[O.E. *wīfman*—*wīf,* woman, *man,* man.]

womb, *wōōm, n.* the organ in which the young of mammals are developed and kept until birth; any deep cavity.

[O.E. *wamb*; Ger. *wamme,* paunch.]

wombat, *wom'bat, n.* an Australian pouched animal. [Native name.]

won. See **win.**

wonder, *wun'dėr, n.* the state of mind produced by something unexpected or extraordinary: a strange thing: quality of being strange or unexpected (e.g. *the wonder of the discovery*).—*v.i.* to be surprised (at, that): to feel curiosity or doubt (about).—*v.t.* to feel curiosity about, or desire to know (e.g. *I wonder what the news is*).

won'derful, *adj.* arousing wonder, strange.

won'derfully, *adv.* **won'deringly,** *adv.*

won'derland, *n.* a land of wonders.

[O.E. *wundor*; conn. with Ger. *wunder.*]

wont, *wōnt, n.* habit, custom.

won'ted, *adj.* usual, accustomed.

[O.E. *gewunod,* pa.p. of *wunian,* dwell.]

won't, *wōnt,* will not.

[M.E. *wol not.*]

woo, *wōō, v.t.* to seek in marriage, court: to seek to win over (a person), or to gain (e.g. success):—*pr.p.* **woo'ing**; *pa.p.* **wooed** (*wōōd*).

woo'er, *n.* **woo'ing,** *n.*

[O.E. *wogian.*]

wood, *wood, n.* the hard part of a tree: trees cut or sawn, timber: a group of growing trees (also in *pl.*).

wood'ed, *adj.* covered with trees.

wood'en, *adj.* made of, or like, wood: (of e.g. face, manner) stiff, dull, without liveliness or charm.

wood'y, *adj.* having many woods: like wood.

wood'enness, *n.* **wood'iness,** *n.*

wood'craft, *n.* skill in everything to do with life in forests.

wood'cut, *n.* an engraving cut on wood, or an impression from it.

wood'cutter, *n.* one who cuts wood.

wood'land, *n.* land covered with woods.

wood'pecker, *n.* a bird that pecks holes in the bark of trees in search of insects.

wood pulp, wood fibre reduced to a pulp, used in making paper.

wood spirit, an alcohol obtained from wood, etc.

wood'wind, *n.* the section of an orchestra in which wind instruments of wood are played.

wood'work, *n.* the wooden part of any structure: carpentry.

wood'worm, *n.* a beetle larva that bores in wood. [O.E. *wudu.*]

wooer, wooing. See **woo.**

woof, *wōōf, n.* same as **weft.** [O.E. *ōwef—ōwebb*; root as **web.**]

wool, *wool, n.* the soft hair of sheep and other animals: yarn made of wool: fabric of wool: any light, fleecy or fibrous substance resembling wool.
wooll'en, *adj.* and *n.* (cloth or garment; usu. in *pl.*) made of wool.
wooll'y, *adj.* made of, or like, wool: vague, hazy.—*n.* a knitted garment:—*pl.* **wooll'ies.**
wooll'iness, *n.*
wool'-gathering, *n.* absentmindedness: inattentive state.
wool'sack, *n.* the seat of the Lord Chancellor in the House of Lords, a large square sack covered with scarlet.
[O.E. *wull*; conn. with Ger. *wolle.*]

word, *wûrd, n.* a spoken or written sign denoting a thing, an idea, etc.: (in *pl.*) speech, talk: a brief conversation (e.g. *to have a word with someone*): (in *pl.*) a quarrel: news (e.g. *word of his arrival*): a rumour: a promise: a password.—*v.t.* to express in words (e.g. *You must word the message more plainly*).
wor'dy, *adj.* containing too many words:—*comp.* **wor'dier**; *superl.* **wor'diest.**
wor'dily, *adv.* **wor'diness,** *n.*
wor'ding, *n.* the manner of expressing in words, choice of words.
word for word, in the exact words (e.g. *He repeated the message word for word*).
hard words, harsh, angry words.
in a word, in short: to sum up.
the last word, the limit, the worst: the very latest, most up-to-date.
to break one's word, to fail to keep one's promise.
to say, etc., **a good word for,** to defend, support: to recommend.
[O.E.; conn. with Ger. *wort,* L. *verbum.*]

wore. See **wear.**

work, *wûrk, n.* effort put out to make or to achieve something: toil, labour: employment: a task: anything made or done: a fortification: a building, etc.: needlework: a production of art (a book, painting, piece of music, etc.): manner of working, workmanship (e.g. *This is good work*): (in *pl.*) a factory, workshop: (in *pl.*) the mechanism e.g. of a watch: (in *pl.*) doings (e.g. *wild work*).—*v.i.* to make efforts (to achieve something): to toil, labour: to be employed: (of a machine) to act, or be in action: to produce results (e.g. *if the plan works*): to make one's, its, way, carefully or with effort: to ferment, boil, bubble: to move with, or as if with, emotion (e.g. *His face worked*).—*v.t.* to make by labour: to bring about by action: to solve (e.g. a problem): to manage, control: to keep going (e.g. a machine): to embroider: to excite gradually (into a feeling; e.g. *He worked himself into a rage*):—*pa.p.* **worked** (also **wrought;** see this word).
work'able, *adj.* which may be carried out, practical (e.g. *a workable plan*).
work'ing, *n.* action, operation: (in *pl.*) the parts of a mine, etc., where work is, or has been, carried on.
work'aday, *adj.* ordinary, unexciting.
working class(es), manual workers.
working day, a day on which work is done, as distinguished from a holiday: the period of actual work each day.
working man, member of working class.
work'man, *n.* one who works with hands.
work'man-like, *adj.* befitting a skilled workman: well performed.
work'manship, *n.* the skill of a workman: manner of making.
work'shy, *adj.* avoiding work: lazy.
work study, time and motion study (see **time**).
to work off, to get rid of.
to work one's passage, to earn one's passage by service.
to work out, to solve or study fully: to come out by degrees: to turn out in the end.
to work to rule, to keep all the regulations very carefully with the deliberate intention of slowing down work.
to work up, to excite, rouse: to make by degrees.
to have one's work cut out, to be faced with a difficult task.
[O.E. *weorc*; conn. Ger. *werk.*]

world, *wûrld, n.* the earth and its inhabitants: the universe: any planet or heavenly body: state of existence, present or to come (e.g. *the next world*): public life or society (e.g. *the ways of the world*): sphere of life or activity (e.g. *in my world*; *the insect world*), or of particular interests (e.g. *the literary world*): a great deal (e.g. *The holiday did him a world of good*).
world'ly, *adj.* belonging to this world: having a fondness for material good things, not spiritual.—Also *adv.*
world'liness, *n.*
world'ly-wise', *adj.* showing the wisdom of those experienced in ways of world.
world'-wide', *adj.* extending over, or found everywhere in, the world.
all the world, everybody: everything.
the New World, the western hemisphere, the Americas.
the Old World, the eastern hemisphere, Europe, Africa, Asia.
[O.E. *w(e)orold—wer,* man.]

worm, *wûrm, n.* an earthworm (see this word), or any backboneless creature resembling it: anything spiral e.g. the thread of a screw: a mean grovelling person: (in *pl.*) any disease caused by worms in the intestines.—*v.i.* to make one's way, or to work, slowly or secretly. —*v.t.* to treat for, rid of, worms: to work (oneself into a position) slowly or secretly: to work (one's way) thus: to obtain (information) by slow or indirect means (e.g. *to worm the facts out of someone*).

wor'my, *adj.* like a worm: having worms.

wor'miness, *n.*

worm'-eaten, *adj.* eaten into by wood-worms: old: worn-out.

[O.E. *wyrm*, dragon, snake, worm.]

worn, worn-out. See **wear.**

worry, *wur'i, v.t.* to shake, tear with the teeth, etc. as a dog does its prey: to annoy, pester: to cause anxiety to.—*v.i.* to be too anxious: to get (along) in spite of difficulties:—*pr.p.* **worr'ying;** *pa.p.* **worr'ied.**—*n.* anxiety, uneasiness, or a cause of this:—*pl.* **worr'ies.**

[O.E. *wyrgan*, to strangle, kill.]

worse. See **bad** and **ill.**

wor'sen (*wûr'*), *v.i., v.t.* to grow, or make, worse.

[O.E. *wyrsa.*]

worship, *wûr'ship, n.* religious service: deep reverence: adoration: a title of honour (*your, his,* etc., *Worship*) e.g. in addressing the mayor of certain English cities.—*v.t.* to pay honour to (*to worship God*): to adore or admire deeply.—*v.i.* to show deep reverence: to take part in religious service: —*pr.p.* **wor'shipping;** *pa.p.* **wor'shipped.**

wor'shipful, *adj.* worthy of honour, used as a term of respect: full of reverence.

wor'shipper, *n.*

[O.E. *weorth*, worth, *-scipe*, -ship.]

worst, *wûrst, adj.* and *adv.* See **bad** and **ill.**—*n.* the highest degree of badness: the least good part (esp. of news): one's utmost in evil or mischief (e.g. *to do one's worst*).—*v.t.* to defeat:—*pa.p.* **worst'ed.**

[O.E. *wyrst*; from same root as **worse.**]

worsted[1], *woost'id, woorst', n.* a firm woollen fabric: twisted yarn spun out of long, combed, wool.—Also *adj.*

[*Worstead*, village near Norwich.]

worsted[2]. See **worst.**

worth, *wûrth, n.* value: price: importance: excellence of character.—*adj.* equal in value to (e.g. *worth a penny*): good enough for (e.g. *worth considering*).

worth'less, *adj.* of no value or merit.

worth'lessly, *adv.* **-lessness,** *n.*

worthy (*wûr'*THi), *adj.* good, deserving (e.g. *a worthy cause*): deserving (of): suited to, in keeping with: of sufficient merit (to do):—*comp.* **worth'ier**; *superl.* **worth'iest.**—*n.* a notable person, esp. local:—*pl.* **wor'thies.**

worth'ily (TH), *adv.* **worth'iness,** *n.*

[O.E. *weorth, wurth*; conn. Ger. *wert.*]

would. See **will.**

would'-be, *adj.* trying, or merely pretending, to be.

[O.E. *wolde, pa.t.* of *willan*; as **will.**]

wound[1]. See **wind** (2).

wound[2], *wōōnd, n.* any cut or injury caused by force: a hurt to feelings.—*v.t.* to make a wound in; to injure in feelings.

[O.E. *wund*; conn. with Ger. *wunde.*]

wove, woven. See **weave** (1).

wrack, *rak, n.* seaweed cast up on the shore: destruction.

[Conn. with **wreck.**]

wraith, *rāth, n.* an apparition, esp. of a living person. [Orig. unknown.]

wrangle, *rang'gl, v.i.* to dispute noisily.—*n.* an angry argument.

wrang'ler, *n.*

[Conn. with old Ger. *wrangen*, to struggle, and with **wring.**]

wrap, *rap, v.t.* to roll or fold (round something): to cover by folding or winding something round (often with *up*):—*pr.p.* **wrapp'ing;** *pa.p.* **wrapped.** —*n.* a covering e.g. a shawl.

wrapp'er, *n.* a garment like a dressing-gown: a loose paper book-cover: a paper band, e.g. on newspaper for post.

wrapped up in, devoted to, giving all one's affection or attention to.

[M.E. *wrappen, wlappen*; conn. **lap** (2).]

wrath, *röth, roth, râth, n.* violent anger.

wrath'ful, *adj.* **wrath'fully,** *adv.*

[O.E. *wrāth.*]

wreak, *rēk, v.t.* to act as prompted by (e.g. *to wreak one's anger*): to carry out (e.g. vengeance).

[O.E. *wrecan*, to avenge.]

wreath, *rēth, n.* a garland of flowers or leaves: a drift or curl of smoke, mist, etc.:—*pl.* **wreaths** (*rē*THz).

wreathe, *rē*TH, *v.t., v.i.* to twine about.

[O.E. *writha*; conn. **writhe.**]

wreck, *rek, n.* a very badly damaged ship: the remains of anything ruined: a person ruined mentally or physically destruction (of something).—*v.t., v.i.* to destroy, or be destroyed.

wreck'age, *n.* remains of something wrecked.

wreck'er, *n.* a person who destroys, esp. who purposely wrecks a ship for plunder.

[M.E. *wrek*; conn. with **wreak, wrack.**]

wren, *ren, n.* a very small song bird.

[O.E. *wrenna.*]

wrench, *rench,* or *-sh, v.t.* to pull with a twist: to force by violence: to sprain.—*v.i.* to undergo a violent twist.—*n.* a violent twist: an instrument for turning nuts, bolts, etc.: pain at parting from someone or something.

[O.E. *wrencan*; conn. with **wring.**]

wrest, *rest, v.t.* to twist, or take away, by force (from): to get by toil (e.g. *to wrest a living from the soil*).

[O.E. *wræstan—wræst*, firm.]

wrestle, *res'l, v.i.* to struggle with someone,

trying to bring him down: to struggle (with; e.g. *to wrestle with a problem*).
wrest'ler, *n.* **wrest'ling,** *n.*
[O.E. *wræstlian*; conn. with **wrest.**]

wretch, *rech, n.* a miserable, unhappy creature: a worthless person.
wretch'ed, *adj.* very miserable: worthless.
wretch'edly, *adv.* **wretch'edness,** *n.*
[O.E. *wrecca*, an outcast.]

wrier, wriest. See **wry.**

wriggle, *rig'l, v.i.* to twist to and fro: to move forward by doing this (as a worm does): to escape by cunning (e.g. *to wriggle out of a difficulty*).
wrigg'ler, *n.* **wrigg'ling,** *n.* and *adj.*
[M.E. *wrikken*, to twist.]

wright, *rit, n.* a maker (used as part of words; e.g. *shipwright, wheelwright*).
[Same root as **work.**]

wring, *ring, v.t.* to twist: to force water from (material) by twisting or by pressure: to clasp and unclasp (one's hands) in an agitated manner, e.g. in grief: to force from, out of (e.g. *to wring a confession from someone*): to distress (*to wring one's heart*):—*pa.p.* **wrung.**
wring'er, *n.* a machine for forcing water from wet clothes.
[O.E. *wringan*; conn. **wreak, wry.**]

wrinkle, *ring'kl, n.* a small crease on a surface (e.g. on one's face).—*v.t.* to make wrinkles or creases in.—*v.i.* to shrink into ridges.
wrink'ly, *adj.* full of wrinkles.
[M.E. *wrinkel*; conn. with **wring.**]

wrist, *rist, n.* the joint which joins the hand to the arm.
wrist(let) watch, watch worn on wrist.
[Same root as **writhe.**]

writ, *rit, n.* (*law*) a document by which one is summoned, or required to do something.
Holy Writ, the Scriptures. [**write.**]

write, *rīt, v.t.* to form letters with a pen, pencil, etc.: to put into writing: to compose (e.g. a poem).—*v.i.* to send a letter (to someone):—*pa.p.* **wrī'ting;** *pa.t.* **wrote** (*rōt*); *pa.p.* **writt'en.**
wrī'ter, *n.*
wrī'ting, *n.* putting down in letters: something composed and written.
to write down, to record: to write slightingly about: to write so as to be understood or appreciated by (e.g. *He wrote down to readers he considered to have no intelligence and no taste*).
to write off, to cancel (esp. in book-keeping): to regard as lost for ever.
to write out, to copy.
to write up, to bring (a record) up to date: to write a description of, to write in praise of.
[O.E. *wrītan*; orig. 'to scratch'.]

writhe, *rīTH, v.i.* to twist violently this way and that: to squirm (under, at).
[O.E. *wrīthan*; conn. **wreath, wrist.**]

wrong, *rong, adj.* not right: evil: not correct: not what is intended or suitable: mistaken (e.g. *You are wrong in thinking he left*).—*n.* whatever is not right or just: an injury done to another.—*adv.* not correctly: astray (e.g. *to go wrong*).—*v.t.* to do wrong to, treat unfairly, harm.
wrong'ly, *adv.*
wrong'ful, *adj.* not lawful.
wrong'fully, *adv.* **wrong'fulness,** *n.*
wrong'doer, *n.* one who does wrong.
wrong'doing, *n.*
wrong'head'ed, *adj.* obstinately holding to wrong ideas or to an unwise course.
in the wrong, guilty of error or injustice.
to put in the wrong, to cause to seem to be in the wrong.
[O.E. *wrang*; prob. from Old Norse.]

wrote. See **write.**

wrought, *rōt, adj.* (an old *pa.t.* and *pa.p.* of **work**) made, manufactured.
wrought'-i'ron, *n.* iron containing only small amounts of other materials.
[O.E. *geworht.*]

wrung. See **wring.**

wry, *rī, adj.* twisted or turned to one side: (of e.g. smile, remark) slightly bitter or mocking: (of humour) having a clever twist:—*comp.* **wri'er, wry'er;** *superl.* **wri'est, wry'est.**
wry'ly, *adv.* **wry'ness,** *n.*
[O.E. *wrigian*, strive; conn. **writhe.**]

wynd, *wīnd, n.* a narrow lane in a town.
[**wind** (2).]

X

X-rays, *eks'rāz, n.pl.* powerful invisible rays which can go through matter that light rays cannot penetrate.

xeno-, *zen-ō-*, (as part of word) stranger, e.g.:—**xenophobia,** *zen-ō-fō'bi-ȧ, n.* hatred of strangers.
[Gk. *xenos*, stranger (*phobia*, hatred).]

xero-, *zer-ō-*, (as part of word) dry, e.g.:—**xerography,** *zer-og'rȧ-fi, n.* a photographic process in which the plate is sensitised electrically and developed by dusting with electrically charged fine powder.
[Gk. *xēros*, dry (*graphein*, to write).]

xylo-, *zī-lō-*, (as part of word) wood, e.g.:—**xylophone,** *zī'lō-fōn, n.* a musical instrument consisting of a series of bars which are struck by wooden hammers held in the hands.
[Gk. *xylon*, wood (*phōnē*, sound).]

Y

yacht, *yot, n.* a vessel fitted for racing, or for pleasure trips.—*v.i.* to sail in a yacht.
yacht'ing, *n.* **yachts'man,** *n.*
[Du. *jacht—jagen,* to hunt, race.]

yak, *yak, n.* a long-haired ox found in Tibet. [From Tibetan.]

yam, *n.* the potato-like tuber (see this word) of several tropical plants.
[From Port. or Sp.]

Yankee, *yang'ki, n.* a citizen of the New England states of U.S.A., or of the northern states (as opp. to the southern), or simply a citizen of U.S.A.—Also **Yank.**
[Perh. *Janke*—Du. *Jan,* John.]

yap, *yap, v.i.* to bark sharply. [Imit.]

yard[1], *yärd, n.* a measure of length, 3 feet (0·9144 of a metre): a long beam on a mast for spreading sails.
yard'arm, *n.* either end (right or left) of a ship's yard.
[O.E. *gyrd*; conn. Ger. *gerte,* twig, rod.]

yard[2], *yärd, n.* an enclosed place, esp. near a building: one used for special work (e.g. *dockyard, railway yard, wood yard*).
[O.E. *geard,* hedge, enclosure.]

yarn, *yärn, n.* spun thread: one of the threads of a rope: a story, esp. a sailor's.—*v.i.* to tell stories.
[O.E. *gearn,* thread; conn. Ger. *garn.*]

yarrow, *yar'ō, n.* a strongly scented plant with flat-topped clusters of small flowers.
[O.E. *gearwe*; conn. with Ger. *garbe.*]

yashmak, *yash'mak,* or *-mak', n.* veil worn by Mohammedan women, covering the face below the eyes.
[Arabic *yashmaq.*]

yawl, *yöl, n.* a ship's small boat: a small fishing or sailing boat. [Du. *jol.*]

yawn, *yön. v.i.* to open the mouth wide and take a deep breath, without meaning to do so, as a result of sleepiness or boredom: to gape (e.g. *A great hole yawned in his path*).—Also *n.*
yawn'ing, *n.* and *adj.*
[O.E. *geonian.*]

yaws, *yöz, n.* a skin disease of hot countries.
[Orig. unknown.]

ye. See **you.**

year, *yēr, n.* the time taken by the earth to go once round the sun: 1st January to 31st December: (in *pl.*) age (e.g. *wise for his years*).
year'ling, *n.* an animal a year old.
year'ly, *adj.* happening every year: lasting a year.—Also *adv.*
year'-book, *n.* a book published annually giving events of previous twelve months.
[O.E. *gēar*; conn. with Ger. *jahr.*]

yearn, *yėrn, v.i.* to feel great desire (for): to feel pity or tenderness.
yearn'ing, *n., adj.* **yearn'ingly,** *adv.*
[O.E. *giernan—georn,* eager.]

yeast, *yēst, n.* a substance which causes fermentation used in brewing and baking.
yeas'ty, *adj.* frothy. **yeas'tiness,** *n.*
[O.E. *gist.*]

yell, *yel, v.i., v.t.,* to howl or cry with a sharp noise.—Also *n.*
[O.E. *gellan*; conn. O.E. *galan,* sing.]

yellow, *yel'ō, adj.* of the colour of gold or of the primrose.—Also *n.*—*v.i.* to become yellow(ish), e.g. with age.
yell'ow-hamm'er, *n.* one of the finches.
[O.E. *geolu*; conn. with Ger. *gelb.*]

yelp, *yelp, v.i.* to utter a sharp bark or cry.—Also *n.*
[O.E. *gielpan,* to boast.]

yeoman, *yō'man, n.* a small farmer or landowner:—*pl.* **yeo'men.**
yeo'manry, *n.* yeomen: volunteer cavalry force.
yeoman of the guard, one of a company forming part of the king's or queen's bodyguard on certain occasions.
[M.E. *yoman.*]

yes, *yes, adv.* word showing agreement or consent.
yes'-man, *n.* an obedient follower who never disagrees with his chief.
[O.E. *gēa,* yes, *si,* let it be.]

yesterday, *yes'tėr-di, n.* the day just past.—Also *adv.*
[O.E. *geostran-* (as part of word only).]

yet, *yet, adv.* in addition, besides (e.g. *yet another mistake*): up to the present time (e.g. *Have you heard yet?*): before the matter is finished (e.g. *I will get even with him yet*): even (e.g. *a yet more terrible experience*):—*conj.* nevertheless: however.
as yet, up to the time referred to.
[O.E. *giet.*]

yew, *ū n.* an evergreen tree, once planted in graveyards: its wood, used for making bows.
[O.E. *ēow*; conn. with Ger. *eibe.*]

Yiddish, *yid'ish, n.* a language that grew

out of Hebrew and old German, spoken by Jews.
[Ger. *jüdisch*, Jewish.]

yield, *yēld, v.t.* to give up: to grant: to give out, produce (e.g. *The seeds yield oil*).—*v.i.* to submit, admit that one's opponent has won: to give way under pressure (e.g. *At last the door yielded*).—*n.* amount produced (e.g. *the yield of ground under wheat, of a mine*).
yiel'ding, *adj.* and *n.*
[O.E. *gieldan*, pay; conn. Ger. *gelten.*]

yodel, *yō'dėl, v.i., v.t.* to sing changing often from ordinary voice to falsetto and back again:—*pr.p.* **yo'del(l)ing;** *pa.p.* **yo'del(l)ed.**—Also *n.*
[Ger. *jodeln.*]

yoga, *yō'gȧ, n.* a Hindu philosophy.
yo'gi, *n.* one who practises the *yoga* system. [Hindustani.]

yog(h)urt, yoghourt, *yō'gŭrt, n.* a slightly acid curdled milk. [Turk. *yōghurt.*]

yoke, *yōk, n.* something that joins together: a frame of wood joining oxen pulling e.g. a cart, or one for carrying pails, etc.: a pair (e.g. of oxen): a mark of slavery: part of a garment that fits the shoulders.—*v.t.* to put a yoke on: to join together.
[O.E. *geoc*; conn. Ger. *joch*, L. *jugum.*]

yokel, *yō'kl, n.* a country man or boy.
[Orig. unknown.]

yolk, *yōk, n.* the yellow part of an egg.
[O.E. *geoloca*—*geolu*, yellow.]

yonder, *yon'dėr, adv.* in that place (at a distance but within sight).—Also *adj.*
[M.E.]

yore, *yōr, yör, n.* used in phrase **of yore,** in times past.
[O.E. *geāra*, formerly.]

yorker, *yör'kėr, n.* (*cricket*) a ball pitching just under the bat. [Orig. unknown.]

you, *ū, pron.* 2nd person *pl.* and *sing.*, the word used in referring to person(s) to whom one is speaking or writing:—*objective* **you**; *possessive* **your** (sometimes described as possessive *adj.*), **yours** (e.g. *Give me your book*; *this one is not yours*). **Ye** is an older form, no longer used, for *you* (as subject, not object).
You (orig. *pl.* only) is always used with *pl.* verb (e.g. *You were foolish to do that, Mary*).
[O.E. *ēow.*]

you'd, you would. **you'll,** you will.

young, *yung, adj.* in early life: in the first part of growth.—*n.* the offspring of animals.
young'ster, *n.* a young person, not yet grown-up.
youth, *yōōth, n.* state of being young: early part of life: a young man: young people as a group.
youth'ful, *adj.* young: fresh and vigorous.
youth'fulness, *n.*
youth hostel, a hostel for hikers, etc., provided by Youth Hostels Association.
[O.E. *geong*, *geogoth*: Ger. *jung*, *jugend.*]

you're, you are.

yowl, *yowl, v.i.* to cry mournfully.—Also *n.*
[M.E. *yowlen.*]

yule, *yūl, n.* the season, or feast, of Christmas.
yule'tide, the Christmas season.
[O.E. *geol.*]

Z

zeal, *zēl, n.* warm enthusiasm: eager, energetic support (for).
zealot, *zel'ot, n.* one full of zeal, an enthusiast.
zealous (*zel'*), *adj.* full of enthusiasm and energy in support of something.
zeal'ously, *adv.* **zeal'ousness,** *n.*
[O.Fr. *zele*—Gk. *zeein*, to boil.]

zebra, *zē'brȧ, n.* a striped African animal of the horse kind.
zebra crossing, a street pedestrian crossing marked with stripes. [African.]

zenana, *zi-nä'nȧ, n.* (India) women's apartments.
[Pers. zanana—zan, a woman.]

zenith, *zen'ith, n.* the point of the sky which is exactly overhead: highest point (of e.g. one's career).
[Arabic *samt-ar-ras*, direction of head.]

zephyr, *zef'ir, n.* west wind: soft wind.
[Gk. *zephyros.*]

zero, *zē'rō, n.* nothing, or the sign for it: the point from which a scale begins: the exact time fixed for an attack or other operation.
[Same root as **cipher.**]

zest, *zest, n.* enthusiasm and pleasure.
zest'ful, *adj.*
[Fr. *zeste*, skin of orange or lemon as flavouring.]

zigzag, *zig'zag, n.* a line, or road, with sharp angles.—*adj.* having sharp turns.—*v.i.* to have, or to go forward making, sharp turns:—*pr.p.* **zig'zagging**; *pa.p.* **zig'zagged.**—Also *adv.*
[Fr.—Ger. *zick-zack.*]

zinc, *zingk, n.* a bluish-white metal.
[Ger. *zink.*]

zinnia, *zin'i-ȧ, n.* a tropical American plant of the thistle family.
[From name of botanist.]

zip, *zip, n.* a whizzing sound: a zip-

fastener.—*v.i.*, *v.t.* to whizz: to fasten with a zip-fastener:—*pr.p.* **zipp′ing**; *pa.p.* **zipped.**
zip′-fastener, *n.* a device for fastening in which two sets of teeth are made to fit into each other by pulling a slide.
[Imit.]

zither, *zith′ėr*, *n.* a flat musical instrument with many strings. [Ger.]

zodiac, *zō′di-ak*, *n.* an imaginary belt in the heavens, divided into twelve equal parts, called the **signs of the zodiac,** each part named from a group of stars, some of the names being those of animals.
[Gk. *zōdiakos*—*zō(i)on*, animal.]

zone, *zōn*, *n.* one of the five great belts into which the surface of the earth is divided according to temperature: any belt-like area: a region in which all parts have the same characteristics.
[Gk. *zōnē*, a girdle.]

zoo-, *zō-o-*, (as part of word) animal.
zoo, *zōō*, *n.* a zoological garden.
zoology, *zō-ol′ò-ji*, *zōō-*, *n.* the science that studies animal life.
zoolog′ical, *adj.* having to do with animals, or with a zoo.
zoolog′ically, *adv.*
zool′ogist, *n.* one who studies animal life.
zoological garden, a place where wild animals are kept and shown.
[Gk. *zō(i)on*, an animal (*logos*, discourse).]

LIVING SUFFIXES

The following are some of the more difficult suffixes used to form new words.

-ana sayings of, anecdotes about, or (in recent use) objects connected with (e.g. *Shakespeareana*).

-asis disease (e.g. *elephantiasis*, greatly increased size of body tissues).

-dom rank (e.g. *earldom*): condition (e.g. *martyrdom*): region controlled or covered (e.g. *kingdom*, *Christendom*): persons of a certain kind collectively (e.g. *officialdom*, ‘officials, or their ways’).

-ectomy surgical removal (e.g. *tonsillectomy*, removal of tonsils).

-escent (often) in process of becoming (e.g. *obsolescent*, ‘becoming obsolete, going out of use’): giving off radiation, esp. light (e.g. *phosphorescent*).—*n.* **-escence.**

-ese used in making name of a native, or of the language, of an area (e.g. *Japanese*): style of language characteristic of a group (e.g *journalese*).

-esque in the style of (e.g. *Miltonesque*).

-ette little (e.g. *kitchenette*): female (e.g. *usherette*): imitation (e.g. *leatherette*).

-ism characteristic act, feature, behaviour (e.g. *Spoonerism*, *colloquialism*, *barbarism*): system of belief or principles (e.g. *Hinduism*, *socialism*): diseased state caused by too much (e.g. *alcoholism*).

-itis disease, usu. inflammation (e.g. *appendicitis*).

-oid (thing) resembling (e.g. *anthropoid*; an anthropoid, or anthropoid ape, resembles a man).

-osis state (e.g. *hypnosis*): diseased state (e.g. *silicosis*, ‘disease caused by breathing in silica dust’).

-tomy surgical cutting (e.g. *tracheotomy*, ‘cutting into the trachea or windpipe’).

SOME ABBREVIATIONS IN EVERYDAY USE

(For *Abbreviations Used in the Dictionary*, see beginning of Dictionary, page iv).

A1. See Dict.
A.A. Automobile Association.
A.A.A. Amateur Athletic Association.
A.B. able-bodied seaman.
A.C. (*elect.*) alternating current.
a/c account.
A.D. (L. *anno Domini*) in the year of our Lord (e.g. A.D. 1600, 1850 A.D.).
ad. advertisement.
A.D.C. aide-de-camp.
ad lib. (L. *ad libitum*) as long, or as much, as one pleases.
aet. (L. *aetatis*) of age, aged (so many years).
A.E.A. Atomic Energy Authority.
A.E.U. Amalgamated Engineering Union.
a.m. (L. *ante meridiem*) before noon.
amp. ampere(s).
anon. See **anon** (2) in Dict.
appro. approval, approbation.
approx. approximate(ly).

B.A. (L. *Baccalaureus Artium*) Bachelor of Arts: British Association.
Bart., Bt. Baronet.
B.B.C. British Broadcasting Corporation.
B.C. Before Christ: British Columbia.
B.E.A. British European Airways.
Beds Bedfordshire.
B.M.A. British Medical Association.
B.O.A.C. British Overseas Airways Corporation.
Bros. Brothers.
B.Sc. (L. *Baccalaureus Scientiae*) Bachelor of Science.
Bt. See **Bart.**
Bucks Buckinghamshire.

C (L. *centum*) a hundred.
C. Centigrade.
c., ca. (L. *circa*) about.
Cambs Cambridgeshire.
cap. (L. *caput*, head) capital.
Capt. Captain.
c.c. cubic centimetres.
cf. (L. *confer*) compare.
C.I.D. Criminal Investigation Department.
C.I.F., c.i.f. cost, insurance, freight.
C.-in-C. Commander-in-Chief.
circ. (L. *circa*) about.
cm. centimetre(s).
C.O. Commanding Officer.
Co. Company: County.
c/o. care of, at the address of.
c.o.d. cash (or collect) on delivery.
C. of E. Church of England.
Col. Colonel.
comp. compare.
con. (L. *contra*) against.
Coy. Company.
Cr. credit: creditor.
cwt. hundredweight(s)—*c* for *centum*, hundred, and *wt* for weight.

D Roman numeral, 500.
d. died: (L. *denarius* or *denarii*) penny or pence.
3D three-dimensional (having, or appearing to have, length, breadth, and height).
2d, 3d second, third.
D.C. (It. *da capo*) repeat from the beginning: District of Columbia (area covered by Washington, cap. of U.S.A.): (*elect.*) direct current.
dm. decimetre(s).
D.M. Deutsche Mark.
do. ditto (see Dict.).
doz. dozen.
D.P. Displaced Person.
Dr debtor: Doctor.
D.V. (L. *Deo volente*) if God is willing.

E. East.
E. & O.E. errors and omissions excepted.
E.C. East Central.
E.E.C. European Economic Community (Common Market).
E.F.T.A. (*ef'ta*) European Free Trade Association.
e.g. (L. *exempli gratia*) for example.
elect. electric(ity).
E.R. *Elizabeth Regina*, Queen Elizabeth.
Esq. See **Esquire** in Dict.
etc., &c. (L. *et ceteri* or *cetera*) and others of the same kind, and so on.
et seq. (L. *et sequens*) and the following:—*pl.* **et seq(q).**

f. forte (see **forte**, 2 in Dict.)
F.A. Football Association.
Fahr. Fahrenheit.
F.B.I. Federation of British Industries: Federal Bureau of Investigation (U.S.A.).
fcp., fcap. foolscap.
ff. fortissimo (see **forte,** 2 in Dict.): also 'and the following lines, pages'.
f.o.b. free on board.
F.P. fire-plug: former pupil.
ft. foot: feet.

g Symbol used for acceleration due to gravity, approx. 32 ft. per sec. per sec.
g. gram(s).
gal(s). gallon(s).
G.B. Great Britain.
G.C. George Cross.
Gen. General.
G.H.Q. General Headquarters.

G.I. general, government, issue: one of the rank and file in the U.S. army.
Glos. Gloucestershire.
gm. gram(s).
G.M. George Medal.
G man. See Dict.
G.M.T. Greenwich Mean Time.
G.O.C. General Officer Commanding.
G.P. general practitioner.
G.P.O. General Post-office.

H. Hydrant.
h. and c. hot and cold (water taps).
Hants Hampshire.
Herts Hertfordshire.
H.H. His (or Her) Highness.
hi-fi. See Dict.
H.M. His (or Her) Majesty.
H.M.S. His (or Her) Majesty's Ship (used for warships only).
Hon. Honourable: Honorary.
h.p. horsepower (see **horse** in Dict.).
H.P. hire purchase.
H.Q. headquarters.
H.R.H. His (or Her) Royal Highness.

I Roman numeral, 1.
ibid. (L. *ibidem*) in the same place.
i.e. (L. *id est*) that is: that means.
I.L.P. Independent Labour Party.
in. inch(es):— *pl.* also **ins.**
Inc. Incorporated (see Dict.).
incog. incognito (see Dict.).
inf. (L. *infra*) below.
infra dig. (L. *infra dignitatem*) beneath one's dignity.
inst. instant (meaning 'of the present month'; e.g. *the 20th inst.*): also institute.
I.O.M. Isle of Man.
IOU, I.O.U. See Dict.
I.O.W. Isle of Wight.
I.R.A. Irish Republican Army.
ITA, I.T.A. Independent Television Authority.
i.t.a. Initial Teaching Alphabet (*orig.* Augmented Roman Alphabet).
ital. italic.
ITV, I.T.V. Independent Television.
I.W. Isle of Wight.

J.P. Justice of the Peace.
Jr., Jun., Junr. Junior.

K.C. King's Counsel (see Dict.).
kg. kilogram(s).
km. kilometre(s).
Kt. Knight.

L Roman numeral, 50.
Lancs Lancashire.
lb. (L. *libra*) pound(s):— *pl.* also **lbs.**
l.b., l.b.w. See **leg** in Dict.
l.h.s. left-hand side.
Lieut. Lieutenant.
Lincs Lincolnshire.
L.P. long-playing.
L.S.D., £ s. d. (L. *librae, solidi, denarii*) pounds, shillings, and pence: money: also lysergic acid (a drug).
Lt. Lieutenant.
Ltd. Limited (see **limited liability** in Dict.).

m. metre(s): mile(s).
M (L. *mille*) a thousand.
M. Monsieur (see Dict.).
M.A. (L. *Magister Artium*) Master of Arts.
M.B. (L. *Medicinae Baccalaureus*) Bachelor of Medicine.
M.C. Master of Ceremonies: Military Cross.
M.C.C. Marylebone Cricket Club.
M.D. (L. *Medicinae Doctor*) Doctor of Medicine: mentally deficient.
memo. See Dict.
Messrs See Dict.
Mlle Mademoiselle (see Dict.).
mm. millimetre(s).
MM. Messieurs (see **Monsieur** in Dict.).
Mme Madame (see Dict.).
M.O. Medical Officer.
M.O.H. Medical Officer of Health.
M.P. Member of Parliament: Military Police.
m.p.h. miles per hour.
Mr Mister (see Dict.).
Mrs Mistress (see Dict.).
MS. manuscript:— *pl.* **MSS.**
Mt(s). mountain(s).

N. North.
N.A.A.F.I. (*naf'i*) Navy, Army, and Air Force Institute(s).
NALGO (*nal'gō*) National and Local Government Officers' Association.
NATO (*nā'tō*) North Atlantic Treaty Organisation.
N.B. North Britain, British.
N.B., n.b. (L. *nota bene*) note well.
N.C.B. National Coal Board.
N.C.O. non-commissioned officer.
2nd second.
N.E. or **NE.** North-east.
nem. con. (L. *nemine contradicente*) no one contradicting.
N.H.S. National Health Service.
No., no. (L. *numero*) (in) number: *pl.* **Nos., nos.**
non. com. non-commissioned.
Northants Northamptonshire.
Nos., nos. See **No.**
Notts Nottinghamshire.
N.S. Nova Scotia.
N.S.W. New South Wales.
N.T. New Testament.
N.T.P. normal temperature and pressure.
N.U.M. National Union of Mineworkers.
N.U.R. National Union of Railwaymen.
N.U.T. National Union of Teachers.
N.W. or **NW.** North-west.
N.Y. New York.
N.Z. New Zealand.

ob. (L. *obiit*) died.
O.C. Officer Commanding.
O.E.C.D. Organisation for Economic Co-operation and Development.
O.H.M.S. On His (or Her) Majesty's Service.
O.K. See Dict.
o.p. out of print.
op. (L. *opus*) work: also operation.
O.T. Old Testament.
oz. ounce(s).

p. page:—*pl.* **pp**: also *piano*, soft(ly): (new) penny, pence.
par., para. paragraph.
P.A.Y.E. pay-as-you-earn. (see **pay** in Dict.).
P.C. Police Constable: Privy Councillor: postcard.
pd. paid.
P.E. Physical Education.
P.G. paying guest.
pinx, pxt (L. *pinxit*) he (or she) painted it.
P.M. Prime Minister.

p.m. (L. *post meridiem*) after noon.
P.M.G. Postmaster General.
P.O. Post-office : postal order.
P.O.W. prisoner of war.
pp. pages : also *pianissimo* (see Dict.).
P.R.O. Public Relations Officer.
Pro. Professional.
Prof. Professor.
pro tem. (L. *pro tempore*) for the time being.
prox. (L. *proximo*) next.
P.S. (L. *post scriptum*) post-script.
P.T. Purchase Tax.
pt. pint(s).
P.T.O. Please turn over.
pty, Pty. proprietary (see Dict.).
P.W.D. Public Works Department.

Q queue.
Q.C. Queen's Counsel.
q.e.d. (L. *quod erat demonstrandum*) which was to be shown or proved.
qr. quarter.
qt. quart(s).
q.v. (L. *quod vide*) which see (i.e. 'Look this up').

R. (L. *rex, regina*) King, Queen ; also rand.
R.A.C. Royal Automobile Club.
R.A.F. Royal Air Force.
R.C. Roman Catholic.
R.D. refer (worthless cheque) to drawer.
ref. reference.
Rev., Revd. Reverend.
r.h.s. right-hand side.
R.I.P. (L. *requiescat in pace*) may he (or she) rest in peace.
R.N. Royal Navy.
R.S.V.P. (Fr. *Répondez s'il vous plaît*) Reply, if you please.
Rt. Hon. Right Honourable.

s. second : shilling(s).
S. South.
S.A. South Africa.
Salop (not an abbreviation but another name) Shropshire.
S.A.R.A.H. Search and rescue and homing.
sc. (L. *scilicet*), namely, that is to say : (L. *sculpsit*) engraved (it).
scil. (L. *scilicet*). See **sc.**
S.C.M. Student Christian Movement.
sculp., sculpt. (L. *sculpsit*) engraved (it) : sculpture : sculptor.
s.d. (L. *sine die*; see Dict.).
S.E. or **SE.** South-east.
SEATO (*sē'tō*) South-east Asia Treaty Organisation.
sec. second.
Sec., Secy. Secretary.
S.H.A.P.E. (*shāp*) Supreme Headquarters Allied Powers Europe.
SI Système International.
SOS See Dict.
sq. square.
Sr. Senior.
SS. Steamship.
St Saint : Strait : Street.
st. stone (weight).
1st first.
Staffs Staffordshire.
S.T.D. subscriber trunk dialling.
S.W. or **SW.** South-west.

T.B. tuberculosis.
T.T. teetotal: teetotaller : Tourist Trophy : tuberculin tested (tested for presence of tubercle bacillus).
T.U.C. Trades Union Congress.
TV television.

U.K. United Kingdom (of Great Britain and Northern Ireland).
ult. (L. *ultimo*) last (meaning 'of last month', e.g. *the 15th ult.*).
U.N.E.S.C.O., Unesco (*ū-nes'kō*) United Nations Educational Scientific and Cultural Organisation.
UNICEF (*ūn'i-sef*) United Nations Children's Fund ('International' and 'Emergency' orig. in title).
U.N.O. (*ū'nō*) United Nations Organisation.
U.S.(A.) United States (of America).
U.S.S.R. Union of Soviet Socialist Republics (i.e. Russia).

v. (L. *versus*) against : (L. *vide*) see.
V.C. Victoria Cross.
V.H.F. very high frequency.
V.I.P. Very Important Person.
viz. See Dict.
vol(s). volume(s).

W. West.
W.C. water-closet : West Central.
W.D. War Department.
W.E.A. Workers' Educational Association.
Wilts Wiltshire.
WHO World Health Organisation.

X Roman numeral, 10.
Xmas. Christmas.

yd. yard(s) :— *pl.* also **yds.**
Y.H.A. Youth Hostels Association.
Y.M.C.A. Young Men's Christian Association.
Yorks Yorkshire.
Y.W.C.A. Young Women's Christian Association.

& (L. *et*) and.
&c. See **etc.**

RANKS IN THE ROYAL NAVY, THE ARMY, AND THE ROYAL AIR FORCE

ROYAL NAVY	ARMY	AIR FORCE
1. Admiral of the Fleet	1. Field Marshal	1. Marshal of the Royal Air Force
2. Admiral	2. General	2. Air Chief Marshal
3. Vice Admiral	3. Lieutenant-General	3. Air Marshal
4. Rear Admiral	4. Major-General	4. Air Vice-Marshal
5. Commodore	5. Brigadier	5. Air Commodore
6. Captain	6. Colonel	6. Group Captain
7. Commander	7. Lieutenant-Colonel	7. Wing Commander
8. Lieutenant-Commander	8. Major	8. Squadron Leader
9. Lieutenant	9. Captain	9. Flight-Lieutenant
10. Sublieutenant	10. Lieutenant	10. Flying Officer
11. Acting Sublieutenant	11. Second Lieutenant	11. Pilot Officer
	Non-commissioned officers	
Chief Petty Officer	Staff Sergeant	Flight-sergeant
Petty Officer	Sergeant	Sergeant
	Corporal	Corporal

Note :—*quartermaster*: in the navy, a petty officer or rating in charge of steering, signals, etc.; in the army, an officer (assisted by a *quartermaster-sergeant*) who arrangés billeting, looks after rations, clothing, etc.

RANKS IN THE WOMEN'S SERVICES

WOMEN'S ROYAL NAVAL SERVICE	WOMEN'S ROYAL ARMY CORPS	WOMEN'S ROYAL AIR FORCE
5. Commandant	5. As army	5. Air Commandant
6. Superintendent	6. ,,	6. Group Officer
7. Chief Officer	7. ,,	7. Wing Officer
8. First Officer	8. ,,	8. Squadron Officer
9. Second Officer	9. ,,	9. Flight Officer
10. Third Officer	10. ,,	10. Flying Officer
		11. Pilot Officer

BRITISH WEIGHTS AND MEASURES

The term ‘ weight ’ is used in the following tables, because it is the term in everyday use, but what is measured is really ‘ mass ’.

LENGTH

Following an Act of Parliament which came into operation in 1964, the YARD is defined as equal to 0·9144 metre. The international Yard, equal to 0·9144 metre, is exactly the same length.

12 inches = 1 foot	10 chains = 1 furlong
3 feet = 1 yard	8 furlongs / 1,760 yards = 1 mile
22 yards = 1 chain	

AREA

1 acre = 4,840 square yards | 640 acres = 1 square mile

CAPACITY

The GALLON is the space occupied, under certain conditions, by 10 pounds weight of distilled water. (The U.S. pint, gallon, are a little smaller.)

Liquid	*Dry materials* (as grain)
4 gills = 1 pint	2 gallons = 1 peck
2 pints = 1 quart	4 pecks / 8 gallons = 1 bushel
4 quarts = 1 gallon	

WEIGHT

The POUND (and also the International Pound) is equal to 0·45359237 kilogram.

16 ounces = 1 pound	4 quarters / 112 pounds = 1 hundredweight
14 pounds = 1 stone	20 hundredweights / 2,240 pounds = 1 ton
2 stone / 28 pounds = 1 quarter	

Measures used in Britain for medicines became metric in March 1969. All the measures shown in the tables above will be replaced gradually by metric measures in the next few years.

THE METRIC SYSTEM

The Greek prefixes, **deca-, hecto-, kilo-,** show 10, 100, 1000, times the unit.

The Latin prefixes, **deci-, centi-, milli,** show $\frac{1}{10}$, $\frac{1}{100}$, $\frac{1}{1000}$, part of the unit.

The METRE, at one time the distance, at the melting point of ice, between two points on a metal bar kept at the International Bureau of Weights and Measures near Paris, is now (for scientific purposes) defined even more precisely in terms of wavelengths of a particular radiation, under exactly specified conditions.

1 decametre	= 10 metres	1 decimetre	= $\frac{1}{10}$ metre
1 hectometre	= 100 metres	1 centimetre	= $\frac{1}{100}$ metre
1 kilometre	= 1000 metres	1 millimetre	= $\frac{1}{1000}$ metre

SQUARE MEASURE

1 are = 100 square metres　　1 hectare = 100 ares, or 10,000 square metres

CAPACITY

The unit of capacity is the LITRE, the volume of a kilogram of pure air-free water at temperature of greatest density (approximately equal to 1 cubic decimetre).

1 hectolitre = 100 litres　　1 centilitre = $\frac{1}{100}$ litre

WEIGHT

The unit of weight, formerly the GRAM(ME), is now the KILOGRAM(ME), and this standard is represented by a metal cylinder kept at the International Bureau of Weights and Measures.

1 decagram	= 10 grams	1 decigram	= $\frac{1}{10}$ gram
1 hectogram	= 100 grams	1 centigram	= $\frac{1}{100}$ gram
1 kilogram	= 1000 grams	1 milligram	= $\frac{1}{1000}$ gram

1000 kilograms = 1 metric ton, or tonne (*tun*).

The SI system of units (Système International d'Unités), accepted by scientists all over the world, uses a small number of units and expresses other units in terms of these. Of the units in the tables above only the metre and the kilogram are SI units.

COMPARISON OF BRITISH AND METRIC SYSTEMS

Metric to British system		*British to metric system*	
LENGTH		**LENGTH**	
1 cm.	= 0·39 in. (less than $\frac{2}{5}$ in.)	1 in.	= 2·54 cm. exactly
1 metre	= 39·37 in. (about $1\frac{1}{12}$ yd.)	***1 yd.**	**= 0·9144** metre
1 km.	= 0·62 mile	1 chain	= 20·12 metres
		1 mile	= 1·61 km. (5 miles = about 8 km.)
AREA		**AREA**	
1 hectare	= 2·47 acres (nearly $2\frac{1}{2}$ acres)	1 acre	= 0·405 hectare = $40\frac{1}{2}$ ares
1 sq. km.	= 0·386 sq. mile (100 hectares = 247 acres)	1 sq. mile	= 2·59 sq. km. (100 sq. miles = roughly 260 sq. km.)
CAPACITY		**CAPACITY**	
1 litre	= 1·7598 pt. (about $1\frac{3}{4}$ pt.)	1 pt.	= 0·57 litre (more than $\frac{1}{2}$ litre)
1 hectolitre	= 21·9975 gal. (nearly 22 gal.)	1 gal.	= 4·55 litres (11 gal. = about 50 litres)
WEIGHT		**WEIGHT**	
1 kg.	= 2·205 lb.	***1 lb.**	**= 0·45359237 kg.**
1 metric ton (1000 kg.)	= 2204·62 lb. (1 ton = 2240 lb.)	1 cwt.	= 50·8 kg.
		1 ton	= 1016·05 kg.

* By Act of Parliament.

THERMOMETER SCALES

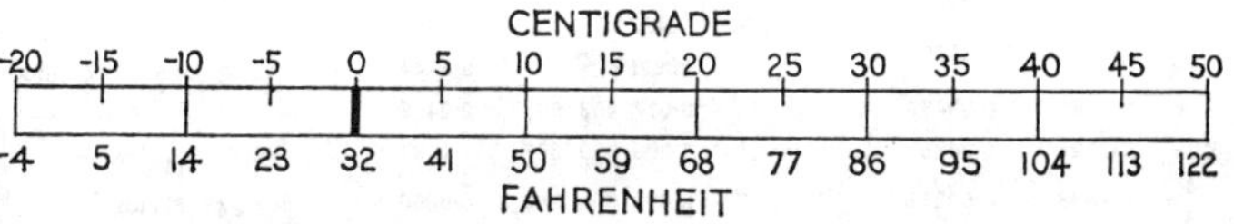

LOGARITHMS OF NUMBERS

x	0	1	2	3	4	5	6	7	8	9	Δ	ADD 1	2	3	4	5	6	7	8	9
1	·0000	0043	0086	0128	0170	0212					42	4	8	13	17	21	25	29	34	38
						0212	0253	0294	0334	0374	40	4	8	12	16	20	24	28	32	36
11	·0414	0453	0492	0531	0569	0607					39	4	8	12	16	19	23	27	31	35
						0607	0645	0682	0719	0755	37	4	7	11	15	18	22	26	30	33
12	·0792	0828	0864	0899	0934	0969					35	4	7	11	14	18	21	25	28	32
						0969	1004	1038	1072	1106	34	3	7	10	14	17	20	24	27	31
13	·1139	1173	1206	1239	1271	1303					33	3	7	10	13	16	20	23	26	30
						1303	1335	1367	1399	1430	32	3	6	10	13	16	19	22	26	29
14	·1461	1492	1523	1553	1584	1614	1644	1673	1703	1732	30	3	6	9	12	15	18	21	24	27
15	·1761	1790	1818	1847	1875	1903	1931	1959	1987	2014	28	3	6	8	11	14	17	20	22	25
16	·2041	2068	2095	2122	2148	2175	2201	2227	2253	2279	26	3	5	8	10	13	16	18	21	23
17	·2304	2330	2355	2380	2405	2430	2455	2480	2504	2529	25	2	5	7	10	12	15	17	20	22
18	·2553	2577	2601	2625	2648	2672	2695	2718	2742	2765	23	2	5	7	9	12	14	16	19	21
19	·2788	2810	2833	2856	2878	2900	2923	2945	2967	2989	22	2	4	7	9	11	13	15	18	20
20	·3010	3032	3054	3075	3096	3118	3139	3160	3181	3201	21	2	4	6	8	11	13	15	17	19
21	·3222	3243	3263	3284	3304	3324	3345	3365	3385	3404	20	2	4	6	8	10	12	14	16	18
22	·3424	3444	3464	3483	3502	3522	3541	3560	3579	3598	19	2	4	6	8	10	11	13	15	17
23	·3617	3636	3655	3674	3692	3711	3729	3747	3766	3784		2	4	6	7	9	11	13	15	17
24	·3802	3820	3838	3856	3874	3892	3909	3927	3945	3962	18	2	4	5	7	9	11	13	14	16
25	·3979	3997	4014	4031	4048	4065	4082	4099	4116	4133	17	2	3	5	7	9	10	12	14	15
26	·4150	4166	4183	4200	4216	4232	4249	4265	4281	4298		2	3	5	6	8	10	11	13	14
27	·4314	4330	4346	4362	4378	4393	4409	4425	4440	4456	16	2	3	5	6	8	9	11	13	14
28	·4472	4487	4502	4518	4533	4548	4564	4579	4594	4609	15	2	3	5	6	8	9	11	12	14
29	·4624	4639	4654	4669	4683	4698	4713	4728	4742	4757		1	3	4	6	7	9	10	12	13
30	·4771	4786	4800	4814	4829	4843	4857	4871	4886	4900	14	1	3	4	6	7	8	10	11	13
31	·4914	4928	4942	4955	4969	4983	4997	5011	5024	5038		1	3	4	5	7	8	10	11	12
32	·5051	5065	5079	5092	5105	5119	5132	5145	5159	5172		1	3	4	5	7	8	9	11	12
33	·5185	5198	5211	5224	5237	5250	5263	5276	5289	5302	13	1	3	4	5	7	8	9	10	12
34	·5315	5328	5340	5353	5366	5378	5391	5403	5416	5428		1	3	4	5	6	8	9	10	11
35	·5441	5453	5465	5478	5490	5502	5514	5527	5539	5551		1	2	4	5	6	7	8	10	11
36	·5563	5575	5587	5599	5611	5623	5635	5647	5658	5670	12	1	2	4	5	6	7	8	10	11
37	·5682	5694	5705	5717	5729	5740	5752	5763	5775	5786		1	2	3	5	6	7	8	9	10
38	·5798	5809	5821	5832	5843	5855	5866	5877	5888	5899		1	2	3	5	6	7	8	9	10
39	·5911	5922	5933	5944	5955	5966	5977	5988	5999	6010	11	1	2	3	4	6	7	8	9	10
40	·6021	6031	6042	6053	6064	6075	6085	6096	6107	6117		1	2	3	4	5	6	7	9	10
41	·6128	6138	6149	6160	6170	6180	6191	6201	6212	6222		1	2	3	4	5	6	7	8	9
42	·6232	6243	6253	6263	6274	6284	6294	6304	6314	6325		1	2	3	4	5	6	7	8	9
43	·6335	6345	6355	6365	6375	6385	6395	6405	6415	6425	10	1	2	3	4	5	6	7	8	9
44	·6435	6444	6454	6464	6474	6484	6493	6503	6513	6522		1	2	3	4	5	6	7	8	9
45	·6532	6542	6551	6561	6571	6580	6590	6599	6609	6618		1	2	3	4	5	6	7	8	9
46	·6628	6637	6646	6656	6665	6675	6684	6693	6702	6712		1	2	3	4	5	6	7	7	8
47	·6721	6730	6739	6749	6758	6767	6776	6785	6794	6803		1	2	3	4	5	5	6	7	8
48	·6812	6821	6830	6839	6848	6857	6866	6875	6884	6893	9	1	2	3	4	5	5	6	7	8
49	·6902	6911	6920	6928	6937	6946	6955	6964	6972	6981		1	2	3	4	4	5	6	7	8

USEFUL CONSTANTS WITH THEIR LOGARITHMS

	No.	Log.
π	3·14159	0·4971
$\frac{1}{\pi}$	0·3183	$\bar{1}$·5029
π^2	9·8696	0·9943
$\sqrt{\pi}$	1·7725	0·2486
$\frac{4}{3}\pi$	4·1888	0·6221

	No.	Log.
1 radian	57°·296	1·7581
	3437′·7	3·5363
	206265″	5·3144
arc 1°	0·017 453 293	$\bar{2}$·2419
arc 1′	0·000 290 888	$\bar{4}$·4637
arc 1″	0·000 004 848	$\bar{6}$·6856

	No.	Log.
e	2·71828	0·4343
M	0·4343	$\bar{1}$·6378
$\frac{1}{M}$	2·3026	0·3622

$$\log_e x = \frac{1}{M} . \log_{10} x$$

$$\log_{10} x = M . \log_e x$$

LOGARITHMS OF NUMBERS

x	0	1	2	3	4	5	6	7	8	9	Δ	ADD								
												1	2	3	4	5	6	7	8	9
50	·6990	6998	7007	7016	7024	7033	7042	7050	7059	7067		1	2	3	3	4	5	6	7	8
51	·7076	7084	7093	7101	7110	7118	7126	7135	7143	7152		1	2	3	3	4	5	6	7	8
52	·7160	7168	7177	7185	7193	7202	7210	7218	7226	7235		1	2	2	3	4	5	6	7	7
53	·7243	7251	7259	7267	7275	7284	7292	7300	7308	7316		1	2	2	3	4	5	6	6	7
54	·7324	7332	7340	7348	7356	7364	7372	7380	7388	7396	8	1	2	2	3	4	5	6	6	7
55	·7404	7412	7419	7427	7435	7443	7451	7459	7466	7474		1	2	2	3	4	5	5	6	7
56	·7482	7490	7497	7505	7513	7520	7528	7536	7543	7551		1	2	2	3	4	5	5	6	7
57	·7559	7566	7574	7582	7589	7597	7604	7612	7619	7627		1	2	2	3	4	5	5	6	7
58	·7634	7642	7649	7657	7664	7672	7679	7686	7694	7701		1	2	2	3	4	4	5	6	7
59	·7709	7716	7723	7731	7738	7745	7752	7760	7767	7774		1	1	2	3	4	4	5	6	7
60	·7782	7789	7796	7803	7810	7818	7825	7832	7839	7846	7	1	1	2	3	4	4	5	6	6
61	·7853	7860	7868	7875	7882	7889	7896	7903	7910	7917		1	1	2	3	4	4	5	6	6
62	·7924	7931	7938	7945	7952	7959	7966	7973	7980	7987		1	1	2	3	3	4	5	6	6
63	·7993	8000	8007	8014	8021	8028	8035	8041	8048	8055		1	1	2	3	3	4	5	6	6
64	·8062	8069	8075	8082	8089	8096	8102	8109	8116	8122		1	1	2	3	3	4	5	5	6
65	·8129	8136	8142	8149	8156	8162	8169	8176	8182	8189		1	1	2	3	3	4	5	5	6
66	·8195	8202	8209	8215	8222	8228	8235	8241	8248	8254		1	1	2	3	3	4	5	5	6
67	·8261	8267	8274	8280	8287	8293	8299	8306	8312	8319		1	1	2	3	3	4	4	5	6
68	·8325	8331	8338	8344	8351	8357	8363	8370	8376	8382		1	1	2	3	3	4	4	5	6
69	·8388	8395	8401	8407	8414	8420	8426	8432	8439	8445		1	1	2	3	3	4	4	5	6
70	·8451	8457	8463	8470	8476	8482	8488	8494	8500	8506		1	1	2	2	3	4	4	5	6
71	·8513	8519	8525	8531	8537	8543	8549	8555	8561	8567	6	1	1	2	2	3	4	4	5	5
72	·8573	8579	8585	8591	8597	8603	8609	8615	8621	8627		1	1	2	2	3	4	4	5	5
73	·8633	8639	8645	8651	8657	8663	8669	8675	8681	8686		1	1	2	2	3	4	4	5	5
74	·8692	8698	8704	8710	8716	8722	8727	8733	8739	8745		1	1	2	2	3	4	4	5	5
75	·8751	8756	8762	8768	8774	8779	8785	8791	8797	8802		1	1	2	2	3	3	4	5	5
76	·8808	8814	8820	8825	8831	8837	8842	8848	8854	8859		1	1	2	2	3	3	4	5	5
77	·8865	8871	8876	8882	8887	8893	8899	8904	8910	8915		1	1	2	2	3	3	4	4	5
78	·8921	8927	8932	8938	8943	8949	8954	8960	8965	8971		1	1	2	2	3	3	4	4	5
79	·8976	8982	8987	8993	8998	9004	9009	9015	9020	9025		1	1	2	2	3	3	4	4	5
80	·9031	9036	9042	9047	9053	9058	9063	9069	9074	9079		1	1	2	2	3	3	4	4	5
81	·9085	9090	9096	9101	9106	9112	9117	9122	9128	9133		1	1	2	2	3	3	4	4	5
82	·9138	9143	9149	9154	9159	9165	9170	9175	9180	9186		1	1	2	2	3	3	4	4	5
83	·9191	9196	9201	9206	9212	9217	9222	9227	9232	9238		1	1	2	2	3	3	4	4	5
84	·9243	9248	9253	9258	9263	9269	9274	9279	9284	9289		1	1	2	2	3	3	4	4	5
85	·9294	9299	9304	9309	9315	9320	9325	9330	9335	9340		1	1	2	2	3	3	4	4	5
86	·9345	9350	9355	9360	9365	9370	9375	9380	9385	9390	5	1	1	2	2	3	3	4	4	5
87	·9395	9400	9405	9410	9415	9420	9425	9430	9435	9440		0	1	1	2	2	3	3	4	4
88	·9445	9450	9455	9460	9465	9469	9474	9479	9484	9489		0	1	1	2	2	3	3	4	4
89	·9494	9499	9504	9509	9513	9518	9523	9528	9533	9538		0	1	1	2	2	3	3	4	4
90	·9542	9547	9552	9557	9562	9566	9571	9576	9581	9586		0	1	1	2	2	3	3	4	4
91	·9590	9595	9600	9605	9609	9614	9619	9624	9628	9633		0	1	1	2	2	3	3	4	4
92	·9638	9643	9647	9652	9657	9661	9666	9671	9675	9680		0	1	1	2	2	3	3	4	4
93	·9685	9689	9694	9699	9703	9708	9713	9717	9722	9727		0	1	1	2	2	3	3	4	4
94	·9731	9736	9741	9745	9750	9754	9759	9763	9768	9773		0	1	1	2	2	3	3	4	4
95	·9777	9782	9786	9791	9795	9800	9805	9809	9814	9818		0	1	1	2	2	3	3	4	4
96	·9823	9827	9832	9836	9841	9845	9850	9854	9859	9863		0	1	1	2	2	3	3	4	4
97	·9868	9872	9877	9881	9886	9890	9894	9899	9903	9908		0	1	1	2	2	3	3	4	4
98	·9912	9917	9921	9926	9930	9934	9939	9943	9948	9952		0	1	1	2	2	3	3	4	4
99	·9956	9961	9965	9969	9974	9978	9983	9987	9991	9996	4	0	1	1	2	2	2	3	3	4

Only the decimal portion (*mantissa*) of each logarithm is shown in this table. The integral portion (*characteristic*) must be determined independently.

ANTILOGARITHMS

x	0	1	2	3	4	5	6	7	8	9	Δ	ADD 1	2	3	4	5	6	7	8	9
·00	1000	1002	1005	1007	1009	1012	1014	1016	1019	1021	2	0	0	1	1	1	1	1	2	2
·01	1023	1026	1028	1030	1033	1035	1038	1040	1042	1045		0	0	1	1	1	1	2	2	2
·02	1047	1050	1052	1054	1057	1059	1062	1064	1067	1069		0	0	1	1	1	1	2	2	2
·03	1072	1074	1076	1079	1081	1084	1086	1089	1091	1094		0	0	1	1	1	1	2	2	2
·04	1096	1099	1102	1104	1107	1109	1112	1114	1117	1119		0	1	1	1	1	2	2	2	2
·05	1122	1125	1127	1130	1132	1135	1138	1140	1143	1146		0	1	1	1	1	2	2	2	2
·06	1148	1151	1153	1156	1159	1161	1164	1167	1169	1172		0	1	1	1	1	2	2	2	2
·07	1175	1178	1180	1183	1186	1189	1191	1194	1197	1199		0	1	1	1	1	2	2	2	2
·08	1202	1205	1208	1211	1213	1216	1219	1222	1225	1227		0	1	1	1	1	2	2	2	3
·09	1230	1233	1236	1239	1242	1245	1247	1250	1253	1256		0	1	1	1	1	2	2	2	3
·10	1259	1262	1265	1268	1271	1274	1276	1279	1282	1285		0	1	1	1	1	2	2	2	3
·11	1288	1291	1294	1297	1300	1303	1306	1309	1312	1315	3	0	1	1	1	2	2	2	2	3
·12	1318	1321	1324	1327	1330	1334	1337	1340	1343	1346		0	1	1	1	2	2	2	2	3
·13	1349	1352	1355	1358	1361	1365	1368	1371	1374	1377		0	1	1	1	2	2	2	3	3
·14	1380	1384	1387	1390	1393	1396	1400	1403	1406	1409		0	1	1	1	2	2	2	3	3
·15	1413	1416	1419	1422	1426	1429	1432	1435	1439	1442		0	1	1	1	2	2	2	3	3
·16	1445	1449	1452	1455	1459	1462	1466	1469	1472	1476		0	1	1	1	2	2	2	3	3
·17	1479	1483	1486	1489	1493	1496	1500	1503	1507	1510		0	1	1	1	2	2	2	3	3
·18	1514	1517	1521	1524	1528	1531	1535	1538	1542	1545		0	1	1	1	2	2	2	3	3
·19	1549	1552	1556	1560	1563	1567	1570	1574	1578	1581		0	1	1	1	2	2	3	3	3
·20	1585	1589	1592	1596	1600	1603	1607	1611	1614	1618		0	1	1	1	2	2	3	3	3
·21	1622	1626	1629	1633	1637	1641	1644	1648	1652	1656		0	1	1	2	2	2	3	3	3
·22	1660	1663	1667	1671	1675	1679	1683	1687	1690	1694		0	1	1	2	2	2	3	3	3
·23	1698	1702	1706	1710	1714	1718	1722	1726	1730	1734	4	0	1	1	2	2	2	3	3	4
·24	1738	1742	1746	1750	1754	1758	1762	1766	1770	1774		0	1	1	2	2	2	3	3	4
·25	1778	1782	1786	1791	1795	1799	1803	1807	1811	1816		0	1	1	2	2	2	3	3	4
·26	1820	1824	1828	1832	1837	1841	1845	1849	1854	1858		0	1	1	2	2	3	3	3	4
·27	1862	1866	1871	1875	1879	1884	1888	1892	1897	1901		0	1	1	2	2	3	3	3	4
·28	1905	1910	1914	1919	1923	1928	1932	1936	1941	1945		0	1	1	2	2	3	3	4	4
·29	1950	1954	1959	1963	1968	1972	1977	1982	1986	1991		0	1	1	2	2	3	3	4	4
·30	1995	2000	2004	2009	2014	2018	2023	2028	2032	2037		0	1	1	2	2	3	3	4	4
·31	2042	2046	2051	2056	2061	2065	2070	2075	2080	2084		0	1	1	2	2	3	3	4	4
·32	2089	2094	2099	2104	2109	2113	2118	2123	2128	2133		0	1	1	2	2	3	3	4	4
·33	2138	2143	2148	2153	2158	2163	2168	2173	2178	2183	5	1	1	2	2	3	3	4	4	5
·34	2188	2193	2198	2203	2208	2213	2218	2223	2228	2234		1	1	2	2	3	3	4	4	5
·35	2239	2244	2249	2254	2259	2265	2270	2275	2280	2286		1	1	2	2	3	3	4	4	5
·36	2291	2296	2301	2307	2312	2317	2323	2328	2333	2339		1	1	2	2	3	3	4	4	5
·37	2344	2350	2355	2360	2366	2371	2377	2382	2388	2393		1	1	2	2	3	3	4	4	5
·38	2399	2404	2410	2415	2421	2427	2432	2438	2443	2449		1	1	2	2	3	3	4	4	5
·39	2455	2460	2466	2472	2477	2483	2489	2495	2500	2506		1	1	2	2	3	3	4	5	5
·40	2512	2518	2523	2529	2535	2541	2547	2553	2559	2564		1	1	2	2	3	4	4	5	5
·41	2570	2576	2582	2588	2594	2600	2606	2612	2618	2624	6	1	1	2	2	3	4	4	5	5
·42	2630	2636	2642	2649	2655	2661	2667	2673	2679	2685		1	1	2	2	3	4	4	5	6
·43	2692	2698	2704	2710	2716	2723	2729	2735	2742	2748		1	1	2	3	3	4	4	5	6
·44	2754	2761	2767	2773	2780	2786	2793	2799	2805	2812		1	1	2	3	3	4	4	5	6
·45	2818	2825	2831	2838	2844	2851	2858	2864	2871	2877		1	1	2	3	3	4	5	5	6
·46	2884	2891	2897	2904	2911	2917	2924	2931	2938	2944		1	1	2	3	3	4	5	5	6
·47	2951	2958	2965	2972	2979	2985	2992	2999	3006	3013		1	1	2	3	3	4	5	5	6
·48	3020	3027	3034	3041	3048	3055	3062	3069	3076	3083	7	1	1	2	3	4	4	5	6	6
·49	3090	3097	3105	3112	3119	3126	3133	3141	3148	3155		1	1	2	3	4	4	5	6	6

ANTILOGARITHMS

x	0	1	2	3	4	5	6	7	8	9	Δ	ADD 1	2	3	4	5	6	7	8	9
·50	3162	3170	3177	3184	3192	3199	3206	3214	3221	3228		1	1	2	3	4	4	5	6	7
·51	3236	3243	3251	3258	3266	3273	3281	3289	3296	3304		1	2	2	3	4	5	5	6	7
·52	3311	3319	3327	3334	3342	3350	3357	3365	3373	3381		1	2	2	3	4	5	5	6	7
·53	3388	3396	3404	3412	3420	3428	3436	3443	3451	3459		1	2	2	3	4	5	6	6	7
·54	3467	3475	3483	3491	3499	3508	3516	3524	3532	3540	8	1	2	2	3	4	5	6	6	7
·55	3548	3556	3565	3573	3581	3589	3597	3606	3614	3622		1	2	2	3	4	5	6	7	7
·56	3631	3639	3648	3656	3664	3673	3681	3690	3698	3707		1	2	3	3	4	5	6	7	8
·57	3715	3724	3733	3741	3750	3758	3767	3776	3784	3793		1	2	3	3	4	5	6	7	8
·58	3802	3811	3819	3828	3837	3846	3855	3864	3873	3882		1	2	3	4	4	5	6	7	8
·59	3890	3899	3908	3917	3926	3936	3945	3954	3963	3972	9	1	2	3	4	5	5	6	7	8
·60	3981	3990	3999	4009	4018	4027	4036	4046	4055	4064		1	2	3	4	5	6	6	7	8
·61	4074	4083	4093	4102	4111	4121	4130	4140	4150	4159		1	2	3	4	5	6	7	8	9
·62	4169	4178	4188	4198	4207	4217	4227	4236	4246	4256		1	2	3	4	5	6	7	8	9
·63	4266	4276	4285	4295	4305	4315	4325	4335	4345	4355	10	1	2	3	4	5	6	7	8	9
·64	4365	4375	4385	4395	4406	4416	4426	4436	4446	4457		1	2	3	4	5	6	7	8	9
·65	4467	4477	4487	4498	4508	4519	4529	4539	4550	4560		1	2	3	4	5	6	7	8	9
·66	4571	4581	4592	4603	4613	4624	4634	4645	4656	4667		1	2	3	4	5	6	7	9	10
·67	4677	4688	4699	4710	4721	4732	4742	4753	4764	4775	11	1	2	3	4	6	7	8	9	10
·68	4786	4797	4808	4819	4831	4842	4853	4864	4875	4887		1	2	3	4	6	7	8	9	10
·69	4898	4909	4920	4932	4943	4955	4966	4977	4989	5000		1	2	3	5	6	7	8	9	10
·70	5012	5023	5035	5047	5058	5070	5082	5093	5105	5117		1	2	4	5	6	7	8	9	11
·71	5129	5140	5152	5164	5176	5188	5200	5212	5224	5236	12	1	2	4	5	6	7	8	10	11
·72	5248	5260	5272	5284	5297	5309	5321	5333	5346	5358		1	2	4	5	6	7	9	10	11
·73	5370	5383	5395	5408	5420	5433	5445	5458	5470	5483		1	3	4	5	6	8	9	10	11
·74	5495	5508	5521	5534	5546	5559	5572	5585	5598	5610		1	3	4	5	6	8	9	10	12
·75	5623	5636	5649	5662	5675	5689	5702	5715	5728	5741	13	1	3	4	5	7	8	9	10	12
·76	5754	5768	5781	5794	5808	5821	5834	5848	5861	5875		1	3	4	5	7	8	9	11	12
·77	5888	5902	5916	5929	5943	5957	5970	5984	5998	6012		1	3	4	5	7	8	10	11	12
·78	6026	6039	6053	6067	6081	6095	6109	6124	6138	6152	14	1	3	4	6	7	8	10	11	13
·79	6166	6180	6194	6209	6223	6237	6252	6266	6281	6295		1	3	4	6	7	9	10	11	13
·80	6310	6324	6339	6353	6368	6383	6397	6412	6427	6442		1	3	4	6	7	9	10	12	13
·81	6457	6471	6486	6501	6516	6531	6546	6561	6577	6592	15	2	3	5	6	8	9	11	12	14
·82	6607	6622	6637	6653	6668	6683	6699	6714	6730	6745		2	3	5	6	8	9	11	12	14
·83	6761	6776	6792	6808	6823	6839	6855	6871	6887	6902		2	3	5	6	8	9	11	13	14
·84	6918	6934	6950	6966	6982	6998	7015	7031	7047	7063	16	2	3	5	6	8	10	11	13	14
·85	7079	7096	7112	7129	7145	7161	7178	7194	7211	7228		2	3	5	7	8	10	12	13	15
·86	7244	7261	7278	7295	7311	7328	7345	7362	7379	7396	17	2	3	5	7	9	10	12	14	15
·87	7413	7430	7447	7464	7482	7499	7516	7534	7551	7568		2	3	5	7	9	10	12	14	16
·88	7586	7603	7621	7638	7656	7674	7691	7709	7727	7745		2	4	5	7	9	11	12	14	16
·89	7762	7780	7798	7816	7834	7852	7870	7889	7907	7925	18	2	4	5	7	9	11	13	14	16
·90	7943	7962	7980	7998	8017	8035	8054	8072	8091	8110		2	4	6	7	9	11	13	15	17
·91	8128	8147	8166	8185	8204	8222	8241	8260	8279	8299	19	2	4	6	8	10	11	13	15	17
·92	8318	8337	8356	8375	8395	8414	8433	8453	8472	8492		2	4	6	8	10	12	14	15	17
·93	8511	8531	8551	8570	8590	8610	8630	8650	8670	8690		2	4	6	8	10	12	14	16	18
·94	8710	8730	8750	8770	8790	8810	8831	8851	8872	8892	20	2	4	6	8	10	12	14	16	18
·95	8913	8933	8954	8974	8995	9016	9036	9057	9078	9099		2	4	6	8	10	12	15	17	19
·96	9120	9141	9162	9183	9204	9226	9247	9268	9290	9311	21	2	4	6	8	11	13	15	17	19
·97	9333	9354	9376	9397	9419	9441	9462	9484	9506	9528		2	4	7	9	11	13	15	17	20
·98	9550	9572	9594	9616	9638	9661	9683	9705	9727	9750	22	2	4	7	9	11	13	15	18	20
·99	9772	9795	9817	9840	9863	9886	9908	9931	9954	9977	23	2	5	7	9	11	14	16	18	21

32

FUNCTIONS OF THE INTEGERS 1-50

No.	Square	Cube	Square Roots		Cube Roots			Factorials		Reci-procals
x	x^2	x^3	$\sqrt{x}$ or $x^{\frac{1}{2}}$	$\frac{1}{\sqrt{x}}$	$\sqrt[3]{x}$	$\sqrt[3]{10x}$	$\sqrt[3]{100x}$	* $x!$	$\log x!$	$\frac{1}{x}$ or x^{-1}
1	1	1	1·0000	1·0000	1·000	2·154	4·642	1	0·0000	1·00000
2	4	8	1·4142	0·7071	1·260	2·714	5·848	2	0·3010	0·50000
3	9	27	1·7321	·5774	1·442	3·107	6·694	6	0·7782	·33333
4	16	64	2·0000	·5000	1·587	3·420	7·368	24	1·3802	·25000
5	25	125	2·2361	0·4472	1·710	3·684	7·937	120	2·0792	0·20000
6	36	216	2·4495	·4082	1·817	3·915	8·434	720	2·8573	·16667
7	49	343	2·6458	·3780	1·913	4·121	8·879	5040	3·7024	·14286
8	64	512	2·8284	·3536	2·000	4·309	9·283	40320	4·6055	·12500
9	81	729	3·0000	·3333	2·080	4·481	9·655	362880	5·5598	·11111
10	1 00	1 000	3·1623	0·3162	2·154	4·642	10·000	3·6288	6·5598	0·10000
11	1 21	1 331	3·3166	·3015	2·224	4·791	10·323	3·9917	7·6012	·09091
12	1 44	1 728	3·4641	·2887	2·289	4·932	10·627	4·7900	8·6803	·08333
13	1 69	2 197	3·6056	·2774	2·351	5·066	10·914	6·2270	9·7943	·07692
14	1 96	2 744	3·7417	·2673	2·410	5·192	11·187	8·7178	10·9404	·07143
15	2 25	3 375	3·8730	0·2582	2·466	5·313	11·447	1·3077	12·1165	0·06667
16	2 56	4 096	4·0000	·2500	2·520	5·429	11·696	2·0923	13·3206	·06250
17	2 89	4 913	4·1231	·2425	2·571	5·540	11·935	3·5569	14·5511	·05882
18	3 24	5 832	4·2426	·2357	2·621	5·646	12·164	6·4024	15·8063	·05556
19	3 61	6 859	4·3589	·2294	2·668	5·749	12·386	1·2165	17·0851	·05263
20	4 00	8 000	4·4721	0·2236	2·714	5·848	12·599	2·4329	18·3861	0·05000
21	4 41	9 261	4·5826	·2182	2·759	5·944	12·806	5·1091	19·7083	·04762
22	4 84	10 648	4·6904	·2132	2·802	6·037	13·006	1·1240	21·0508	·04545
23	5 29	12 167	4·7958	·2085	2·844	6·127	13·200	2·5852	22·4125	·04348
24	5 76	13 824	4·8990	·2041	2·884	6·214	13·389	6·2045	23·7927	·04167
25	6 25	15 625	5·0000	0·2000	2·924	6·300	13·572	1·5511	25·1906	0·04000
26	6 76	17 576	5·0990	·1961	2·962	6·383	13·751	4·0329	26·6056	·03846
27	7 29	19 683	5·1962	·1925	3·000	6·463	13·925	1·0889	28·0370	·03704
28	7 84	21 952	5·2915	·1890	3·037	6·542	14·095	3·0489	29·4841	·03571
29	8 41	24 389	5·3852	·1857	3·072	6·619	14·260	8·8418	30·9465	·03448
30	9 00	27 000	5·4772	0·1826	3·107	6·694	14·422	2·6525	32·4237	0·03333
31	9 61	29 791	5·5678	·1796	3·141	6·768	14·581	8·2228	33·9150	·03226
32	10 24	32 768	5·6569	·1768	3·175	6·840	14·736	2·6313	35·4202	·03125
33	10 89	35 937	5·7446	·1741	3·208	6·910	14·888	8·6833	36·9387	·03030
34	11 56	39 304	5·8310	·1715	3·240	6·980	15·037	2·9523	38·4702	·02941
35	12 25	42 875	5·9161	0·1690	3·271	7·047	15·183	1·0333	40·0142	0·02857
36	12 96	46 656	6·0000	·1667	3·302	7·114	15·326	3·7199	41·5705	·02778
37	13 69	50 653	6·0828	·1644	3·332	7·179	15·467	1·3764	43·1387	·02703
38	14 44	54 872	6·1644	·1622	3·362	7·243	15·605	5·2302	44·7185	·02632
39	15 21	59 319	6·2450	·1601	3·391	7·306	15·741	2·0398	46·3096	·02564
40	16 00	64 000	6·3246	0·1581	3·420	7·368	15·874	8·1592	47·9116	0·02500
41	16 81	68 921	6·4031	·1562	3·448	7·429	16·005	3·3453	49·5244	·02439
42	17 64	74 088	6 4807	·1543	3·476	7·489	16·134	1·4050	51·1477	·02381
43	18 49	79 507	6·5574	·1525	3·503	7·548	16·261	6·0415	52·7811	·02326
44	19 36	85 184	6·6332	·1508	3·530	7·606	16·386	2·6583	54·4246	·02273
45	20 25	91 125	6·7082	0·1491	3·557	7·663	16·510	1·1962	56·0778	0·02222
46	21 16	97 336	6·7823	·1474	3·583	7·719	16·631	5·5026	57·7406	·02174
47	22 09	103 823	6·8557	·1459	3·609	7·775	16·751	2·5862	59·4127	·02128
48	23 04	110 592	6·9282	·1443	3·634	7·830	16·869	1·2414	61·0939	·02083
49	24 01	117 649	7·0000	·1429	3·659	7·884	16·985	6·0828	62·7841	·02041
50	25 00	125 000	7·0711	0·1414	3·684	7·937	17·100	3·0414	64·4831	0·02000

* If x is greater than 9, multiply by 10^c where c is the characteristic of $\log x!$

FUNCTIONS OF THE INTEGERS 50-100

No.	Square	Cube	Square Roots		Cube Roots			Factorials		Reci-procals
x	x^2	x^3	$\sqrt{x}$ or $x^{\frac{1}{2}}$	$\frac{1}{\sqrt{x}}$	$\sqrt[3]{x}$	$\sqrt[3]{10x}$	$\sqrt[3]{100x}$	* $x!$	log $x!$	$\frac{1}{x}$ or x^{-1}
50	25.00	125 000	7·0711	0·1414	3·684	7·937	17·100	3·0414	64·4831	0·02000
51	26 01	132 651	7·1414	·1400	3·708	7·990	17·213	1·5511	66·1906	·01961
52	27 04	140 608	7·2111	·1387	3·733	8·041	17·325	8·0658	67·9066	·01923
53	28 09	148 877	7·2801	·1374	3·756	8·093	17·435	4·2749	69·6309	·01887
54	29 16	157 464	7·3485	·1361	3·780	8·143	17·544	2·3084	71·3633	·01852
55	30 25	166 375	7·4162	0·1348	3·803	8·193	17·652	1·2696	73·1037	0·01818
56	31 36	175 616	7·4833	·1336	3·826	8·243	17·758	7·1100	74·8519	·01786
57	32 49	185 193	7·5498	·1325	3·849	8·291	17·863	4·0527	76·6077	·01754
58	33 64	195 112	7·6158	·1313	3·871	8·340	17·967	2·3506	78·3712	·01724
59	34 81	205 379	7 6811	·1302	3·893	8·387	18·070	1·3868	80·1420	·01695
60	36 00	216 000	7·7460	0·1291	3·915	8·434	18·171	8·3210	81·9202	0·01667
61	37 21	226 981	7·8102	·1280	3·936	8·481	18·272	5·0758	83·7055	·01639
62	38 44	238 328	7·8740	·1270	3·958	8·527	18·371	3·1470	85·4979	·01613
63	39 69	250 047	7·9373	·1260	3·979	8·573	18·469	1·9826	87·2972	·01587
64	40 96	262 144	8·0000	·1250	4·000	8·618	18·566	1·2689	89·1034	·01562
65	42 25	274 625	8·0623	0·1240	4·021	8·662	18·663	8·2477	90·9163	0·01538
66	43 56	287 496	8·1240	·1231	4·041	8·707	18·758	5·4434	92·7359	·01515
67	44 89	300 763	8·1854	·1222	4·062	8·750	18·852	3·6471	94·5619	·01493
68	46 24	314 432	8·2462	·1213	4·082	8·794	18·945	2·4800	96·3945	·01471
69	47 61	328 509	8·3066	·1204	4·102	8·837	19·038	1·7112	98·2333	·01449
70	49 00	343 000	8·3666	0·1195	4·121	8·879	19·129	1·1979	100·0784	0·01429
71	50 41	357 911	8·4261	·1187	4·141	8·921	19·220	8·5048	101·9297	·01408
72	51 84	373 248	8·4853	·1179	4·160	8·963	19·310	6·1234	103·7870	·01389
73	53 29	389 017	8·5440	·1170	4·179	9·004	19·399	4·4701	105·6503	·01370
74	54 76	405 224	8·6023	·1162	4·198	9·045	19·487	3·3079	107·5196	·01351
75	56 25	421 875	8·6603	0·1155	4·217	9·086	19·574	2·4809	109·3946	0·01333
76	57 76	438 976	8·7178	·1147	4·236	9·126	19·661	1·8855	111·2754	·01316
77	59 29	456 533	8·7750	·1140	4·254	9·166	19·747	1·4518	113·1619	·01299
78	60 84	474 552	8·8318	·1132	4·273	9·205	19·832	1·1324	115·0540	·01282
79	62 41	493 039	8·8882	·1125	4·291	9·244	19·916	8·9462	116·9516	·01266
80	64 00	512 000	8·9443	0·1118	4·309	9·283	20·000	7·1569	118·8547	0·01250
81	65 61	531 441	9·0000	·1111	4·327	9·322	20·083	5·7971	120·7632	·01235
82	67 24	551 368	9·0554	·1104	4·344	9·360	20·165	4·7536	122·6770	·01220
83	68 89	571 787	9·1104	·1098	4·362	9·398	20·247	3·9455	124·5961	·01205
84	70 56	592 704	9·1652	·1091	4·380	9·435	20·328	3·3142	126·5204	·01190
85	72 25	614 125	9·2195	0·1085	4·397	9·473	20·408	2·8171	128·4498	0·01176
86	73 96	636 056	9·2736	·1078	4·414	9·510	20·488	2·4227	130·3843	·01163
87	75 69	658 503	9·3274	·1072	4·431	9·546	20·567	2·1078	132·3238	·01149
88	77 44	681 472	9·3808	·1066	4·448	9·583	20·646	1·8548	134·2683	·01136
89	79 21	704 969	9·4340	·1060	4·465	9·619	20·724	1·6508	136·2177	·01124
90	81 00	729 000	9·4868	0·1054	4·481	9·655	20·801	1·4857	138·1719	0·01111
91	82 81	753 571	9·5394	·1048	4·498	9·691	20·878	1·3520	140·1310	·01099
92	84 64	778 688	9·5917	·1043	4·514	9·726	20·954	1·2438	142·0948	·01087
93	86 49	804 357	9·6437	·1037	4·531	9·761	21·029	1·1568	144·0632	·01075
94	88 36	830 584	9·6954	·1031	4·547	9·796	21·105	1·0874	146·0364	·01064
95	90 25	857 375	9·7468	0·1026	4·563	9·830	21·179	1·0330	148·0141	0·01053
96	92 16	884 736	9·7980	·1021	4·579	9·865	21·253	9·9168	149·9964	·01042
97	94 09	912 673	9·8489	·1015	4·595	9·899	21·327	9·6193	151·9831	·01031
98	96 04	941 192	9·8995	·1010	4·610	9·933	21·400	9·4269	153·9744	·01020
99	98 01	970 299	9·9499	·1005	4·626	9·967	21·472	9·3326	155·9700	·01010
100	100 00	1000 000	10·0000	0·1000	4·642	10·000	21·544	9·3326	157·9700	0·01000

* Multiply by 10^c, where c is the characteristic of log $x!$

COUNTRIES OF THE WORLD

Country	Area in sq. miles	Population	Capital	Population of Capital
Afghanistan	250,000	13,800,000	Kabul	450,000
Albania	11,100	1,814,000	Tirana	152,500
Algeria	952,200	10,453,600	Algiers	820,000
Argentina	1,084,120	22,520,000	Buenos Aires	7,200,000
Australia	2,967,910	11,540,000	Canberra	93,300
Austria	32,366	7,073,800	Vienna	1,636,600
Bahamas (British)	5,386	138,100	Nassau	89,000
Barbados	166	246,400	Bridgetown	94,000
Belgium	11,778	9,500,000	Brussels	1,066,000
Bolivia	424,160	4,330,000	La Paz	461,000
Botswana	222,000	543,100	Gaberones	5,000
Brazil	3,286,000	87,200,000	Brasilia	300,000
Bulgaria	42,823	8,226,500	Sofia	801,000
Burma	261,789	25,246,000	Rangoon	1,530,500
Burundi	10,747	3,000,000	Bujumbura	70,000
Cambodia	71,000	5,749,000	Phnôm-Penh	600,000
Cameroun				
East	165,845	3,900,000	Yaoundé	90,000
West	16,500	1,000,000	Buea	3,000
Canada	3,851,809	19,919,000	Ottawa	290,700
Central African Republic	237,308	2,090,000	Bangui	238,000
Chad	493,846	3,400,000	Fort Lamy	45,000
Chile	286,397	8,515,000	Santiago	1,169,500
China	3,768,100	700,000,000	Peking	5,420,000
Colombia	456,535	17,484,500	Bogotá	1,697,300
Congo	131,545	880,000	Brazzaville	136,000
Costa Rica	19,653	1,463,000	San José	185,600
Cuba	44,206	7,800,000	Havana	787,800
Cyprus	3,572	594,000	Nicosia	103,700
Czechoslovakia	49,362	14,200,000	Prague	1,025,000
Dahomey	44,524	2,350,000	Porto Novo	65,000
Denmark	16,611	4,767,500	Copenhagen	874,400
Dominican Republic	18,700	3,572,700	Santo Domingo	529,400
Ecuador	104,500	5,000,000	Quito	348,100
El Salvador	8,236	3,008,000	San Salvador	255,750
Ethiopia	395,000	21,500,000	Addis Ababa	443,000
Finland	129,627	4,650,700	Helsinki	519,000
France	212,919	46,200,000	Paris	2,790,000
Gabon	102,692	470,000	Libreville	31,000
Gambia	4,000	315,500	Bathurst	28,000
Germany—				
Federal Republic	95,962	59,300,000	Bonn	140,800
Democratic Republic	41,722	17,000,000	East Berlin	1,000,000
Ghana	92,100	7,950,000	Accra	533,000
Great Britain	94,500	54,800,000	London, Greater	7,913,600
England & Wales	58,633	48,075,000	London (Cardiff)	—
Scotland	30,405	5,191,000	Edinburgh	468,800
Northern Ireland	5,462	1,484,700	Belfast	397,500
Greece	50,942	8,510,000	Athens	1,852,700
Guatemala	42,042	4,278,000	Guatemala City	577,100
Guiana (French)	23,000	33,700	Cayenne	18,700
Guinea	95,000	3,000,000	Conakry	112,500

Country	Area in sq. miles	Population	Capital	Population of Capital
Guyana	83,000	653,000	Georgetown	168,000
Haiti	10,700	4,700,000	Port-au-Prince	250,000
Honduras	43,227	2,360,000	Tegucigalpa	190,800
Honduras (British)	8,867	106,000	Belize City	32,800
Hungary	35,900	10,160,000	Budapest	1,875,000
Iceland	39,758	193,750	Reykjavik	78,400
India	1,262,275	500,000,000	Delhi	2,000,000
Indonesia	575,450	97,000,000	Djakarta	4,000,000
Iran	627,000	25,750,000	Téhran	2,800,000
Iraq	169,240	8,260,000	Baghdad	1,007,000
Irish Republic	26,600	2,880,000	Dublin	568,000
Israel	7,993	2,600,000	Jerusalem	192,000
Italy	116,280	53,600,000	Rome	2,500,000
Ivory Coast	124,024	3,850,000	Abidjan	257,500
Jamaica	4,411	1,811,000	Kingston	511,500
Japan	142,726	98,300,000	Tokyo	11,096,000
Jordan	37,730	2,016,000	Amman	341,600
Kenya	224,960	9,365,000	Nairobi	266,800
Korea (North)	46,814	11,040,000	Pyongyang	940,000
Korea (South)	38,452	28,647,100	Seoul	3,795,000
Laos	88,780	2,300,000	Vientiane	125,000
Lebanon	3,400	1,750,000	Beirut	500,000
Lesotho	11,720	976,000	Maseru	9,000
Liberia	43,000	1,016,000	Monrovia	80,000
Libya	679,358	1,559,400	Tripoli	231,950
Luxembourg	999	333,300	Luxembourg	78,700
Madagascar	229,233	6,335,800	Tananarive	321,650
Malaysia	128,338	9,388,800	Kuala Lumpur	500,000
Malaya	50,700	8,039,000	Kuala Lumpur	—
Sabah	29,388	518,100	Kota Kinabulu	21,500
Sarawak	48,250	831,700	Kuching	50,700
Malawi	48,779	4,042,400	Zomba	19,600
Mali	463,085	4,300,000	Bamako	120,000
Malta	122	316,500	Valetta	17,700
Mauritania	417,617	1,000,000	Nouakchott	5,500
Mauritius	720	681,600	Port Louis	131,400
Mexico	761,530	45,700,000	Mexico City	3,353,000
Mongolia	604,095	1,120,000	Ulan Bator	250,000
Morocco	111,370	13,320,000	Rabat	261,450
Nepal	54,600	9,500,000	Kathmandu	195,260
Netherlands	15,785	12,377,000	Amsterdam (*seat of govt.* The Hague)	862,500
New Zealand	103,736	2,676,900	Wellington	131,843
Nicaragua	57,143	1,616,100	Managua	275,000
Niger	457,227	3,350,000	Niamey	30,000
Nigeria	356,669	55,653,800	Lagos	450,000
Norway	125,249	3,708,000	Oslo	483,200
Pakistan	365,929	93,720,600	Rawalpindi	340,200
Panama	29,201	1,286,700	Panama City	343,700
Paraguay	156,443	2,094,000	Asuncion	305,100
Peru	496,093	11,400,000	Lima	1,716,000
Philippines	115,600	27,088,000	Quezon City	397,990
Poland	120,359	31,550,000	Warsaw	1,249,000
Portugal	34,831	8,889,000	Lisbon	802,230
Rumania	91,699	19,105,000	Bucharest	1,511,000
Rwanda	10,166	3,000,000	Kigali	7,000
Saudi Arabia	800,000	3,500,000	Riyadh	300,000
			Mecca	200,000
Senegal	75,847	3,400,000	Dakar	380,000

Country	Area in sq. miles	Population	Capital	Population of Capital
Sierra Leone	27,925	2,183,000	Freetown	128,000
Singapore	225	1,913,500	—	—
Somali	246,135	2,500,000	Mogadiscio	100,000
Somaliland (French)	8,500	108,000	Djibouti	70,000
South Africa	471,445	18,298,000	Pretoria	422,590
Spain	194,883	30,430,700	Madrid	2,558,600
Sri Lanka	25,332	14,270,000	Colombo	562,160
Sudan	967,500	13,000,000	Khartoum	135,000
Surinam	63,227	350,000	Paramaribo	123,000
Swaziland	6,700	389,500	Mbabane	14,000
Sweden	173,620	7,772,500	Stockholm	788,500
Switzerland	15,941	5,429,000	Bern	165,900
Syria	71,772	4,500,000	Damascus	530,000
Tanzania				
Tanganyika	361,800	10,175,000	Dar es Salaam	150,000
Zanzibar	640	299,100	Zanzibar Town	58,000
Thailand	198,250	30,591,000	Bangkok	1,800,000
Togo	21,539	1,650,000	Lomé	80,000
Trinidad & Tobago	1,980	828,000	Port of Spain	94,000
Tunisia	63,362	4,500,000	Tunis	642,400
Turkey	301,302	31,391,200	Ankara	650,000
Uganda	93,981	7,189,600	Kampala	12,000
Union of Soviet Socialist Republics	8,650,000	234,000,000	Moscow	6,464,000
United Arab Republic	386,198	29,600,000	Cairo	4,000,000
United States of America	3,553,890	196,842,000	Washington	764,000
Upper Volta	105,432	4,900,000	Ouagadougou	51,000
Uruguay	72,172	2,592,600	Montevideo City	1,203,700
Venezuela	352,143	9,030,000	Carácas	786,700
Vietnam (North)	63,344	18,200,000	Hanoi	643,500
Vietnam (South)	66,263	15,100,000	Saigon	1,400,000
Yemen	75,000	4,500,000	San'a	80,000
South Yemen	61,890	900,000	—	—
Yugoslavia	98,725	19,508,000	Belgrade	598,000
Zaïre	895,348	25,600,000	Kinshasa	1,900,000
Zambia	290,586	3,782,000	Lusaka	151,400
Zimbabwe-Rhodesia	150,820	6,500,000	Salisbury	566,000

FAMOUS MOUNTAINS

	Location	Height (feet)
Everest	Nepal/Tibet	29,028
K2	Kashmir	28,250
Kanchenjunga	Sikkim	28,208
Nanga Parbat	Kashmir	26,660
Anapurna	Nepal	26,504
Nanda Devi	India	25,645
Kamet	India/Tibet	25,447
Communism Peak	U.S.S.R.	24,590
Aconcagua	Argentina	22,834
McKinley	Alaska	20,320
Cotopaxi	Ecuador	19,612
Kilimanjaro	Tanzania	19,340
Elbruz	U.S.S.R.	18,526
Popocatapetl	Mexico	17,887
Kenya	Kenya	17,058
Ararat	Turkey	17,000
Ruwenzori	Uganda/Congolese Republic	16,763
Mont Blanc	France	15,771

FAMOUS VOLCANOES

	Location	Height (feet)
Cotopaxi	Ecuador	19,612
Mauna Loa	Hawaii	13,680
Erebus	Antarctica	12,450
Etna	Sicily	10,958
Ruapehu	New Zealand	9,175
Paricutin	Mexico	7,451
Hekla	Iceland	4,892
Vesuvius	Italy	4,190
Stromboli	Italy	3,038
Krakatau	Indonesia	2,667

FAMOUS LAKES

	Location	Area (sq. m.)
Caspian Sea	U.S.S.R.	143,550
Superior	Canada/U.S.A.	31,800
Victoria	Africa	26,800
Aral Sea	U.S.S.R.	25,300
Huron	Canada/U.S.A.	23,000
Michigan	U.S.A.	22,400
Tanganyika	Africa	12,700
Great Bear	Canada	12,275
Baikal	U.S.S.R.	11,780
Nyasa	Africa	11,430
Great Slave	Canada	10,980
Chad	Africa	10,000
Erie	Canada/U.S.A.	9,940
Ladoga	U.S.S.R.	7,000
Onega	U.S.S.R.	3,800
Titicaca	Bolivia/Peru	3,200

FAMOUS RIVERS

	LOCATION	LENGTH (miles)
Nile	Africa	4,160
Amazon	South America	3,900
Yangtze-Kiang	China	3,400
Congo	Africa	3,000
Mekong	S.E. Asia	2,800
Ob	U.S.S.R.	2,700
Lena	U.S.S.R.	2,680
Mackenzie	Canada	2,635
Hwang Ho	China	2,600
Niger	Africa	2,600
Amur	U.S.S.R.	2,500
Parana	South America	2,500
Yenisei	U.S.S.R.	2,500
Mississippi	U.S.A.	2,340
Volga	U.S.S.R.	2,300
Colorado	U.S.A.	2,000
St. Lawrence	Canada	2,000
Yukon	Canada	2,000
Brahmaputra	Tibet/India	1,800
Danube	Europe	1,720
Euphrates	Turkey/Syria/Iraq	1,700
Indus	Tibet/India/Pakistan	1,700
Zambesi	Africa	1,600
Ganges	India	1,560

FAMOUS BRIDGES

	LOCATION	WATERWAY (miles)
Zambesi	Africa	$2\frac{1}{8}$
Storström	Denmark	2
Tay (Rail)	Scotland	2
Upper Sone	India	$1\frac{7}{8}$
Godavari	India	$1\frac{3}{4}$
Forth (Rail)	Scotland	$1\frac{1}{2}$
Salazar, Lisbon	Portugal	$1\frac{1}{4}$
Tay (Road)	Scotland	$1\frac{1}{4}$
Forth (Road)	Scotland	$1\frac{1}{8}$
Golden Gate, San Francisco	U.S.A.	$1\frac{1}{8}$
Hardinge	India	1
Orinoco	Venezuela	1
Severn	England	1
Victoria Jubilee, Montreal	Canada	1
Sydney Harbour	Australia	$\frac{3}{4}$

LARGEST CITIES

Tokyo	Japan	11,096,000	**Djakarta**	Indonesia	4,000,000
Shanghai	China	10,000,000	**Rio de Janeiro**	Brazil	3,857,000
New York	U.S.A.	8,085,000	**Seoul**	Korea	3,795,000
London, Greater	England	7,913,600	**Leningrad**	U.S.S.R.	3,665,000
			Chicago	U.S.A.	3,575,000
Buenos Aires	Argentina	7,200,000	**Berlin (E & W)**	Germany	3,399,000
Moscow	U.S.S.R.	6,464,000	**Mexico City**	Mexico	3,353,000
Peking	China	5,420,000	**Tientsin**	China	3,220,000
Sao Paulo	Brazil	4,981,000	**Osaka**	Japan	3,133,000
Bombay	India	4,538,000	**Calcutta**	India	3,003,500
Cairo	U.A.R.	4,000,000	**Téhran**	Iran	2,800,000

ADDITIONAL WORDS IN CURRENT USE

ac′tivist, *n.* one who plays a specially active part in putting a plan into practice or in spreading political ideas.

ad′mass, *n.* the large numbers of people influenced by constant advertising on radio and television and in the press, etc., and by ideas spread in similar ways.

an′chorman, *n.* a person on whom the success of an activity depends, esp. the person on television responsible for the smooth running of a dialogue between, or discussion among, others.

après-ski, apres-, *a-pre-skē,* *n.* (evening period of) amusements after skiing.—Also *adj.*

autistic, *ö-tis′tik.* *adj.* (of a child) shut away in a fantasy world and having little or no interest in other people.

autocross′, *n.* a motor-car race round a grass field.

belt, *n.* in certain sports, an award for a particular success or excellence, as **Lonsdale belt.**

biathlon, *bī-ath′lon,* *n.* an international competition in skiing and shooting.

black box, a unit of electronic equipment in package form, used in an aircraft or spacecraft for automatic control or as a flight-recorder (see p. 619).

bonsai, *bon′sī, bōn′,* *n.* a dwarf tree grown in a pot by special methods of cultivation. [*Jap.*]

breath′alyser, *n.* any of several devices for measuring the amount of alcohol in a person's breath.

bug, *v.t.* to plant a concealed listening device in.

camp, *adj.* (*slang*) theatrical, affected, exaggerated: homosexual.—*n.* absurd exaggeration in manner.

cann′abis, *n.* a resin obtained from hemp: hashish: marijuana.

cardio-, (as part of a word) heart, as in **car′diograph,** an instrument for recording movements of the heart; **cardiol′ogy,** the science that deals with the structure, functions and diseases of the heart.

cassette′, *n.* a holder with reel of magnetic tape, esp. tape on which there is pre-recorded material: a holder for a film in a miniature camera, etc.

charisma, *kå-riz′må,* *n.* spiritual power given by God: (now usu.) gift or personal quality which makes a person able to impress many others: an impressive quality in a position or office such as makes one believe, without proof, that the holder has leadership ability.

cheong-sam, *chong′-sam′,* *n.* a Chinese dress, tight-fitting, high-necked, with slits at the sides.

cliff′-hanger, *n.* a very exciting adventure or contest: an ending that leaves one in suspense.—*n., adj.* **cliff′-hanging.**

collage, *kol-äzh,* *n.* (the art of making) a picture consisting of miscellaneous pieces of material pasted on to a background.

contain′erise, *v.t.* to put (freight) into large standard sealed containers. These are taken to a **container port, terminal,** and loaded by a bridge-type **container crane** into a **container ship** specially designed to store containers.

cosmesis, *kos-mē′sis,* *n.* surgery or treatment to correct defects of the face, etc.

coun′ter-intell′igence, *n.* (an organisation carrying out) measures aimed at preventing an enemy from obtaining information.

cryo-, *krī-ō-,* (as part of a word) frost, very low temperature, as in **cryosur′gery,** surgery with instruments at very low temperature.

cyclamate, *sīk′lå-māt, sik-,* *n.* a sweetening agent much stronger than sugar.

da′ta-pro′cessing, *n.* (of a computer) dealing in a prearranged way with (facts) fed into it: subjecting (information) to treatment by a computer.

debug′, *v.t.* to remove concealed listening devices from: to put right faults in (a mechanism esp. in an aeroplane or computer).

Decca, *dek′å,* *n.* a series of chains of radio transmitting stations which combine to guide aircraft or ships.

decibel, *des′i-bel,* *n.* a unit used in expressing intensity of sound.

defect′, *v.i.* to desert to another country, transfer loyalty to a rival cause.

desal′inate, *v.t.* to take the salt out of (esp. sea water).—*n.* **desalinā′tion.**

discotheque (p. 140).—**mobile discotheque,** records, a record-player, and an amplifier taken by a disk jockey to a place where music, esp. dance music, is required.

dolce vita, la, *dol′chā vē′tä, la,* the sweet life—a life of luxury.

drag′ster, *n.* a car used in **drag racing,** a contest in acceleration, with standing start and quarter-mile course.

dyslexia, *dis-leks′i-å,* *n.* word-blindness, inability to read, spell, etc., due to any of several causes, but not to lack of intelligence.

encephalogram, *en-sef′å-lō-gram, -kef′,* *n.* in full **electroencephalogram,** a record made of the small electrical impulses sent out by the brain.

es′calate, *v.t., v.i.* to increase rapidly in scale or intensity.

explosion, *n.* a great and rapid increase or expansion, as *population explosion.—adj.* (in industry, etc.) using an explosion to carry out work, as *explosion welding.—adj.* **explo′sive,** containing an explosive, as *explosive bolt, rivet.*

fix, *n.* (*slang*) a shot of heroin or other drug.

flann′elgraph, *n.* a board covered with flannel or felt, and letters, pictures, etc., backed with material which will stick when pressed against the board.

flight′-recorder, *n.* a device which records on tape or wire information about the working of an aircraft or its systems.

flip′side, *n.* the side of a gramophone record carrying the less important song, etc., the reverse of the side which is expected to make the record sell.

flow sheet, chart, a chart showing the successive stages of an industrial process.

fork-lift truck, a power-driven truck with an arrangement of steel prongs which can lift, carry, and stack where required, heavy packages.

freight′liner, *n., adj.* (a train) having specially designed containers and rolling-stock and used for rapid transport of goods.

gerrymander, *jer′i-man-dėr, v.t.* to re-arrange (e.g. voting districts) so as to give an unfair advantage to (e.g. one particular party): to reorganise for one's own advantage.—Also *n.*

giga-, *jī-ga-,* (as part of a word) a thousand million times the unit named.

Giro, *jī′rō, n.* a banking system by which money can be transferred direct from the account of a holder to that of any of his creditors.

golden handshake, a large sum of money given to an employee or member forced to leave a firm.

grade, *n.* a hundredth part of a right angle.

grass′-roots, *n.* (orig. *U.S.*) the rural areas of a country or the people living there, still having the true character of their race: foundation, origin, primary aim or meaning.

hallucinogen, *hal-(y)ōō′sin-ō-jen, n.* a drug causing hallucinations.

hard, *adj.* (of drug) habit-forming.—*n.* **hard′ware,** articles of metal or mechanical equipment used in war, in space flights, and mechanical or electronic equipment necessary for data-processing.

hijack, *hī′jak, v.t.* to stop and rob (vehicle): to force a pilot to fly (aeroplane) to a place not on his scheduled route.—*n.* **hi′jacker.**

hipp′y, *n.* one of a group of rebels against middle-class ways who live together in unconventional communities and wear colourful clothes.

homo-.—homosexual, *adj.* feeling sexual attraction towards members of one's own sex.—Also *adj.—n.* **homosexual′ity.**

hooked, *adj.* dependent on a hard drug.

hot line, a direct telephone line available for immediate use in emergency, orig. one between Washington and the Kremlin.

hov′ercraft, *n.* a craft able to move a short distance above the surface of water or land supported by a down-driven blast of air.—*ns.* **hover-barrow, -bus, -train.**

hydrofoil, *hī′drō-foil, n.* a device on a boat for raising it from the water as its speed increases: a craft with hydrofoils.

Iden′ti-kit, *n.* a device for building up a likeness of a person from a large number of different features on transparent slips.

imbal′ance, *n.* lack of balance or suitable proportion between e.g. debits and credits.

in, *adj.* fashionable: within a group, as **in-fighting,** struggle among members of an organisation for power or privilege.

inertia selling, sending a householder goods which he has not ordered and charging for them if they are not returned.

initial teaching alphabet, an alphabet with more than forty letters, used in the first stages of learning to read.

innum′erate, *adj.* not numerate.

investment trust, an organisation which invests its stockholders' money and distributes the net return among them.

jack′-knife, *v.i., v.t.* (of e.g. an articulated truck) through faulty control, to double up forming an angle of 90° or less.

kinet′ic, *adj.* having to do with motion.—**kinetic art,** art in which movement, produced by air currents, electricity, etc., plays an essential part.

kiss of life, a mouth-to-mouth method of restoring a person whose breathing has ceased by blowing one's own breath into his body.

Levis, *lē′vēz, n.* heavy, close-fitting trousers, with low waist and copper rivets at points of strain. [Trademark.]

lido, *lē′dō, n.* a bathing-beach: an open-air swimming-pool.

lim′bo, *n.* a West Indian dance in which the dancer bends backwards and passes under a bar lowered a little farther each time he passes.

Lonsdale belt, award for gaining the same boxing title three times running.

mainline, *v.i.* (*slang*) to inject e.g. heroin into a vein.

marina, *mȧ-rē′nȧ, n.* a yacht station with everything that may be wanted for a yachting holiday.

met′cast, *n.* a meteorological (i.e. weather) forecast.

met′ricate, *v.t., v.i.* to change over to the metric system.—*n.* **metricā′tion.**

microminiaturisā′tion, *n.* reduction to an extremely small size (of e.g. electronic equipment).

mod′ule, *n.* a unit of size used in standardised design of e.g. buildings: a self-contained unit forming part of a spacecraft.

Molotov cocktail, *mol′ȯ-tof,* a missile consisting of a bottle with inflammable liquid and a wick to be ignited just before throwing.

monocoque, *mon-o-kok′, -kōk′, n.* a motor-vehicle structure in which body and chassis are in one and share stresses.

motocross′, *n.* racing on motor bicycles round a short very rough circuit.

muscular dystrophy, *dis′trȯ-fi,* a hereditary disease in which muscles deteriorate.

nitrogen narcosis (*nar-kō′sis*), (also **the narks**) the intoxicating and anaesthetic effect of too much nitrogen in the brain, experienced by divers at considerable depths.

non-event, an event, planned to be important, that fails to attract notice and achieves no result.

num′erate, *adj.* having some understanding of mathematics and science.—*n.* **num′eracy.**

obsolescence, planned, going out of date (also deterioration) of a product, planned by the maker so that it will have to be replaced soon by something newer.

oceanaut, *ō′shėn-öt, n.* one who lives, observes, and explores under the sea.

open university (at one time called *university of the air*), a university, expected to enrol students in 1971, in which the courses will be carried out by correspondence, radio, television, etc.

oracy, *ō′rȧ-si, ö′, n.* ability to express oneself orally with fluency.

or′bital, *adj.* having to do with an orbit.

package deal, a deal or bargain consisting of a number of items which has to be accepted as a whole; **package tour,** a pre-arranged tour payment for which covers all expenses.

phase, *fāz, v.t.* to do by stages.—*adj.* **phased.**

pico-, *pē-kō-, pī-kō-,* (as part of a word) a millionth of a millionth of the unit named.

piped music, background music sent out from a central studio to other buildings.

pop art, art using commonplace subjects from modern town life.

prestressed-concrete, concrete with pre-stretched wires or bars embedded in it.

printed circuit, a circuit formed by printing the design of the wiring on copper foil fixed to a flat base and etching away the unprinted foil.

psychedelic, psychodelic, *sī-kė-del′ik, -dēl′, adj.* (of a drug) producing pleasant physical sensations and a feeling of exultation and self-confidence: (of art, colour patterns, shifting lights, etc.) causing sensations in some way like those produced by a psychedelic drug.

rapture of the deep, depth, nitrogen narcosis.

Russian roulette, an act of bravado, loading a revolver with one bullet, spinning the cylinder, and firing at one's own head: any risky action.

sacred cow, a person, institution, etc., treated as too sacred to be criticised.

sauna, *sow′nä, sö′, n.* a Finnish steam bath.

scientology, *sī-ėn-tol′ȯ-ji, n.* a system of training which claims to develop an individual's personal qualities to their highest point and to teach him to communicate fully with others.

selective weedkiller, one which, in suitable concentration, kills weeds without permanently damaging crops.

shish kebab, *shish′ ke-bäb,* small pieces of meat, etc., cooked on a skewer.

shopping precinct, a planned area with shops and traffic-free ways for the pedestrian.

shot-gun marriage, merger, one forced upon one or both of those entering it.

side′boards, side′burns, *ns. pl.* short side whiskers.

skid row, a squalid place where vagrants, chronic drunks, etc., live.

skin diver, a naked diver for pearls: a diver wearing simple equipment and not being connected with a boat.

soft′ware, *n.* (computers) written programmes, flow charts, etc.

spina bifida, *spīn′ȧ bī′fi-dȧ,* a congenital defect in which the two parts of the spinal column have not united along the middle vertical line.

sup′erconductor, *n.* a metal which offers little or no resistance to the passage of electricity; the phenomenon was discovered at very low temperatures.

suspension building, building from the top downwards round a central core.

sys′tem-built′, *adj.* built from prefabricated parts of standard size.—*n.* **sys′tem-build′ing.**

systems analyst, a specialist who plans how computers are to be used in an industry and how they should be fitted into the general scheme of work.

technocracy, *tek-nok′rȧ-si, n.* government by technical experts.

thalidomide, *thal-id′ȯ-mīd, n.* a tranquilliser whose use was discontinued when it was shown that pregnant women who took it gave birth to children whose limbs were not properly developed.

tribology, *trīb-ol′ȯ-ji, trib-, n.* a science dealing with friction, lubrication, etc.

trimaran, *trī′mȧ-ran, n.* a boat having three hulls (see **catamaran** in Dict.).

ufol′ogy, *n.* study of Unidentified Flying Objects.

unit trust, a type of investment trust in which given amounts of different securities form a unit and units are sold to the public.

Notes

Notes

Notes